Welfare Benefits and Tax Credits Handbook

22nd edition

Child Poverty Action Group

Child Poverty Action Group works on behalf of the more than one in four children in the UK growing up in poverty. It does not have to be like this. We use our understanding of what causes poverty and the impact it has on children's lives to campaign for policies that will prevent and solve poverty – for good. We provide training, advice and information to make sure hard-up families get the financial support they need. We also carry out high-profile legal work to establish and protect families' rights. If you are not already supporting us, please consider making a donation, or ask for details of our membership schemes, training courses and publications.

Published by Child Poverty Action Group
30 Micawber Street
London N1 7TB
Tel: 020 7837 7979
staff@cpag.org.uk
www.cpag.org.uk

A CIP record for this book is available from the British Library
ISBN: 978 1 910715 60 4

Child Poverty Action Group is a charity registered in England and Wales (registration number 294841) and in Scotland (registration number SC039339), and is a company limited by guarantee, registered in England (registration number 1993854). VAT number: 690 808117

Cover design by Colorido Studios
Internal design by Devious Designs
Typeset by DLxml, a division of RefineCatch Limited, Bungay, Suffolk
Content management system by Konnect Soft
Printed in the UK by CPI Group (UK) Ltd, Croydon CR0 4YY

The authors

Mark Brough is a freelance writer. He previously worked for many years as a welfare rights adviser for people with learning disabilities.

Barbara Donegan is a welfare rights worker at CPAG in Scotland.

Carolyn George is a freelance writer on welfare rights.

Alison Gillies is a welfare rights worker at CPAG in Scotland.

Will Hadwen is a freelance welfare rights worker for CPAG in Scotland and a freelance trainer.

Daphne Hall is an editor for *rightsnet*, and a freelance trainer and writer on welfare rights.

Gwyneth King was until recently a welfare rights worker at CPAG Scotland and is now director of Finchett King Law.

Henri Krishna is a welfare rights worker at CPAG in Scotland.

Susan Mitchell works in the advice sector and is a freelance writer on welfare rights.

Paul Moorhouse works part time for Dalkeith and District CAB and is a freelance author on welfare rights.

Simon Osborne is a welfare rights worker at CPAG, based at CPAG in Scotland.

Judith Paterson is Head of Advice and Rights at CPAG in Scotland.

Ed Pybus is a welfare rights worker at CPAG in Scotland.

Jon Shaw is a welfare rights worker at CPAG in Scotland.

Angela Toal is a welfare rights worker at CPAG in Scotland.

Paul Treloar is senior technical advice manager with Age UK.

Nick Turnill is a welfare rights worker at Oxfordshire Welfare Rights and a freelance welfare rights worker for CPAG.

Rebecca Walker is an advice worker at Maternity Action and Sheffield Citizens Advice and Law Centre and a freelance trainer and writer on welfare rights.

Martin Williams is a welfare rights worker at CPAG.

Mark Willis is a welfare rights worker at CPAG in Scotland.

Acknowledgements

The authors would like to thank Louise Cook at DWP Scotland, Lynsey Dalton, Barbara Gray, Arnie James, Alison Lord, David Malcolm, Daniel Norris, Kelly Smith, Jessica Strode, Ros White and Katie Wood at Maternity Action for their invaluable contribution.

Our thanks are also due to Simon Osborne, the book's content consultant.

We must acknowledge the efforts of the many authors of previous editions of the *National Welfare Benefits Handbook*, the *Rights Guide to Non-Means-Tested Benefits* and the *Jobseeker's Allowance Handbook*, on which this book is based.

Thanks are also due to Alison Key, Nicola Johnston and Pauline Phillips for editing and managing the production of the book, and to Kathleen Armstrong and Anne Ketley for proofreading the text. Particular thanks must go to Katherine Dawson and Anne Ketley for producing the index. Special thanks to Alison Key for her work editing this *Handbook* for over 20 year – we wish her all the best for the future.

The law covered in this book was correct on 2 March 2020 and includes regulations laid up to this date.

Foreword

Welcome to the 2020/21 edition of the *Welfare Benefits and Tax Credits Handbook*. As the *Handbook* approaches its fiftieth edition, we are proud that it is still an essential resource for anyone giving welfare rights advice and that it remains the most comprehensive guide to an increasingly complex social security system.

We are delighted to have recently launched AskCPAG.org.uk – which includes the new, improved digital version of this *Handbook*. Fully searchable and updated throughout the year, AskCPAG has decision-making tools and appeal letter generators that help you get fast and accurate results for your clients. You can sign up for a free trial at cpag.org.uk/shop/subscriptions.

As the *Handbook* goes to print, the UK is undergoing dramatic and sudden changes to social and working life as the coronavirus pandemic takes hold. In response, the government has made a series of significant changes to the social security system, including increases in universal credit and working tax credit rates. Other measures include the suspension of medical assessments, jobseeking conditions and most job centre appointments. CPAG welcomes these amendments and has called on the government to take further steps such as increases to the rates of child benefit and legacy benefits, and the removal of the two-child limit and benefit cap. CPAG is supporting the advice community by publishing a series of briefings detailing the changes to the benefit system made in response to coronavirus and other new resources on AskCPAG. Thanks to funding from the Money and Pensions Service, a digital version of CPAG's *Debt Advice Handbook* is also available on AskCPAG with free, open access for all.

As for universal credit, the last year has seen significant developments. Perhaps the biggest news was the start of the managed migration pilot (now termed 'Move to UC' and recently suspended due to coronavirus). After hard-fought campaigns telling the DWP that it must safely move people across to universal credit, the department declined to take on the responsibility of automatically drawing up people's claims but is instead piloting an approach called 'Who knows me'. The idea is to use existing relationships claimants have with the job centre, third parties (such as landlords) or HM Revenue and Customs to encourage people to voluntarily claim universal credit. During the pilot, no claimant's legacy benefits are to be terminated even if they do not claim universal credit.

While it is positive that the department is taking the managed migration slowly and carefully, and considering whether DWP can avoid terminating people's legacy benefits altogether, it is disappointing that there was so little willingness to put robust safeguards into the managed migration legislation (though campaigning by charities did lead to some improvements). CPAG will continue to press for such safeguards when managed migration is resumed.

Less positively, since May 2019 mixed-age couples, in which one member is above pension age and the other below, have been required to claim universal credit rather than having the option of claiming pension credit. This policy has left thousands worse off than they would have been under pension credit.

We were, however, pleased to see steps to improve the complicated system for reclaiming childcare costs under universal credit. Parents now have an extra month in which to report childcare costs and the Flexible Support Fund will be used to pay the first payment of childcare costs when someone moves into a job, with budgeting loans to be available for people struggling to meet later payments. It is encouraging that the huge difficulties caused by requiring upfront childcare fees has been recognised, but this approach seems at best a partial solution. The Flexible Support Fund is underfunded and poorly advertised, and the vast majority of working parents would not qualify for budgeting advances.

CPAG continues to engage with ministers and DWP officials about universal credit, raising issues such as childcare costs and problematic deductions, based on cases submitted to our Early Warning System. We also use the findings to generate media coverage and encourage questions in parliament. Recently, we have been focusing on difficulties claimants have had with mandatory reconsiderations and housing cost calculations. We have been pleased to see some improvements to universal credit payment statements to make calculations of deductions and housing costs more transparent; yet the wording about appeal rights remains woefully inadequate. Although securing change is slower than we would like, each small success that improves the experience of claimants shows the value of this work, and we continue to raise awareness of issues people are facing. Sign up to the Early Warning System's bulletin at cpag.org.uk/policy-campaigns/early-warning-system, and send us your cases so we can continue this vital work.

Meanwhile in Scotland, a new social security system is being built. By the end of 2020, the Scottish government hopes to introduce a new Scottish child payment – a key part of its child poverty strategy. There is an ambitious schedule to take over the administration and payment of other disability and carers' benefits in the coming years but, at the time of writing, this programme has been delayed by the coronavirus pandemic.

With families under unprecedented financial pressure, the welfare rights movement is more important than ever. CPAG will continue to advocate for changes that will improve the social security system, and for well-funded, expert advice services that people need.

Alison Garnham
Chief Executive

Contents

Abbreviations		xii
Universal credit rates		xiii
Means-tested benefit rates		xiv
Non-means-tested benefit rates		xviii
Tax credit rates		xxi

Part 1   Introduction

Provides an overview of the benefits and tax credits system and explains how to use this book to identify which benefits, tax credits or statutory payments you can get and the amount you should receive. Read this part to understand how the information in the book is organised and how to find answers to specific questions about your entitlement.

Chapter 1	How to use this book	3

Part 2   Universal credit

Covers the main rules for universal credit. Use this part if you are on a low income to check when you come under the universal credit system, whether you qualify for universal credit and to work out how much benefit you will get. It contains chapters on who can be included in your claim and on how your needs, housing costs, income and capital are calculated.

Chapter 2	The introduction of universal credit	19
Chapter 3	Universal credit	35
Chapter 4	People included in the claim	57
Chapter 5	The maximum amount	65
Chapter 6	The housing costs element	82
Chapter 7	Income	115
Chapter 8	Capital	137

Part 3   Other means-tested benefits and tax credits

Contains chapters on all the means-tested benefits and tax credits, other than universal credit. Use this part if you are on a low income to check the main qualifying conditions.

Chapter 9	Income-related employment and support allowance	157
Chapter 10	Housing benefit	172

Contents

· ·

Chapter 11	Income support	232
Chapter 12	Income-based jobseeker's allowance	250
Chapter 13	Pension credit	270
Chapter 14	Child tax credit	284
Chapter 15	Working tax credit	298

4

Part 4   **General rules for other means-tested benefits**

Explains the general rules for means-tested benefits, including who can be included in your claim, how your needs, income and capital are calculated, and the help you can get for certain housing costs. Use this part to check how much benefit you should get.

Chapter 16	People included in the claim	317
Chapter 17	Applicable amounts	332
Chapter 18	Help with ground rent, service charges and other housing costs	359
Chapter 19	Housing benefit rent restrictions	381
Chapter 20	Income: under pension age	419
Chapter 21	Income: over pension age	466
Chapter 22	Capital: under pension age	488
Chapter 23	Capital: over pension age	516

5

Part 5   **Other benefits**

Contains chapters on other benefits, statutory payments and additional help you may be able to get. Use this part to check whether you qualify for any of these benefits or payments, and for information on how to claim, the amount you may receive and how you are paid.

Chapter 24	Attendance allowance	531
Chapter 25	Bereavement benefits	545
Chapter 26	Carer's allowance	561
Chapter 27	Child benefit and guardian's allowance	578
Chapter 28	Disability living allowance	602
Chapter 29	Discretionary housing payments	641
Chapter 30	Contributory employment and support allowance	647
Chapter 31	Health benefits	666
Chapter 32	Industrial injuries benefits	681
Chapter 33	Contribution-based jobseeker's allowance	704
Chapter 34	Maternity allowance	725
Chapter 35	Personal independence payment	740
Chapter 36	Retirement pensions	778
Chapter 37	Social fund payments	793
Chapter 38	Statutory maternity, adoption, paternity and other parental pay	811
Chapter 39	Statutory sick pay	836
Chapter 40	Other payments	851

Part 6   **Special benefit rules**

Explains how particular circumstances, such as going into hospital, affect your entitlement to benefits and statutory payments. Use this part if any of the circumstances apply to you.

Chapter 41   Benefits for students   879
Chapter 42   Benefits in hospital, care homes, prison and in other
              special circumstances   919

Part 7   **National insurance, work and work-related rules**

Outlines the national insurance contribution conditions for contributory benefits and when you might qualify for national insurance credits, and explains the benefit rules on work and limited capability for work. Use this part to check whether you qualify for contributory benefits, to find out how work affects your benefit entitlement, what you may have do to prepare for and find work in order to get benefit, and what might happen if you do not do so.

Chapter 43   National insurance contributions   959
Chapter 44   Work and benefits   992
Chapter 45   Limited capability for work   1012
Chapter 46   Universal credit work-related requirements   1049
Chapter 47   Universal credit system sanctions   1080
Chapter 48   Claimant responsibilities: other benefits   1115
Chapter 49   Sanctions: other benefits   1146

Part 8   **Claiming benefits and getting paid**

Gives general information on how to claim benefits and how you are paid, including details on the benefit cap, overpayments and hardship payments. Use this to check how to claim, how to get your claim backdated, and for what to do if your circumstances change, if you have been overpaid or if you have been accused of fraud.

Chapter 50   Claims   1167
Chapter 51   Getting paid   1188
Chapter 52   Hardship payments   1221
Chapter 53   Overpayments   1235
Chapter 54   Fraud and penalties   1269

Contents

Part 9   **Getting a benefit decision changed**

Covers the different ways to challenge decisions, including appealing. Use this part if you are unhappy with a decision and want to know your rights and how to enforce them.

Chapter 55	Decisions	1287
Chapter 56	Revisions and supersessions	1302
Chapter 57	Appealing to the First-tier Tribunal	1339
Chapter 58	Appealing to the Upper Tribunal and the courts	1397
Chapter 59	Challenging decisions on statutory payments	1429
Chapter 60	Complaints	1440

Part 10   **General rules for tax credits**

Covers the general rules that apply to tax credits. Use this part to calculate the amount you should receive, and for information on claims and decisions.

Chapter 61	Tax credit amounts	1451
Chapter 62	Income: tax credits	1476
Chapter 63	Claims, decisions and getting paid: tax credits	1497
Chapter 64	Overpayments of tax credits	1522
Chapter 65	Investigations, penalties and fraud: tax credits	1535
Chapter 66	Getting a tax credit decision changed	1544

Part 11   **Immigration and residence rules for benefits and tax credits**

Explains how your immigration status affects your benefit and tax credit entitlement in the UK and what happens if you go abroad. Use this part if you have come from abroad or are considering going abroad.

Chapter 67	Coming from abroad: immigration status	1559
Chapter 68	Coming from abroad: residence rules	1581
Chapter 69	Going abroad	1647
Chapter 70	European Union co-ordination rules	1669

Part 12   **Scottish social security benefits**

Contains information on the benefits which are part of the Scottish social security system. Use this part to check whether you can get a Scottish benefit, how to claim and what to do if you are unhappy with a determination.

Chapter 71	The Scottish social security system	1687
Chapter 72	Best Start grants	1697

Chapter 73   Funeral support payment   1705
Chapter 74   Scottish child payment   1713
Chapter 75   Young carer grant   1719
Chapter 76   Claiming Scottish benefits and getting paid   1725
Chapter 77   Getting a determination changed   1732

Appendices
Appendix 1   Information and advice   1761
Appendix 2   Useful publications   1763
Appendix 3   Disability which puts a person at a disadvantage in
              getting a job   1768
Appendix 4   Prescribed degrees of disablement   1770
Appendix 5   Prescribed industrial diseases   1773
Appendix 6   Upper and lower earnings limits   1786
Appendix 7   Minimum working conditions   1787
Appendix 8   Statutory payments for a birth and maternity allowance   1788
Appendix 9   Pension age for women born between 6 April 1950 and
              5 December 1953   1791
Appendix 10   Abbreviations used in the notes   1793

              Index   1807

Abbreviations

AA	attendance allowance	IS	income support
CA	carer's allowance	ISA	individual savings account
CFCD	Counter Fraud, Compliance and Debt	JSA	jobseeker's allowance
	Directorate	MA	maternity allowance
CJEU	Court of Justice of the European Union	MS	Medical Service
CRU	Compensation Recovery Unit	NI	national insurance
CTB	council tax benefit	PAYE	pay as you earn
CTC	child tax credit	PC	pension credit
DLA	disability living allowance	PIP	personal independence payment
DWP	Department for Work and Pensions	REA	reduced earning allowance
EC	European Community	SAP	statutory adoption pay
ECtHR	European Court of Human Rights	SAYE	save as you earn
EEA	European Economic Area	SDA	severe disablement allowance
ESA	employment and support allowance	SMP	statutory maternity pay
EU	European Union	SPBP	statutory parental bereavement pay
EWC	expected week of childbirth	SPP	statutory paternity pay
HB	housing benefit	SSP	statutory sick pay
HMCTS	HM Courts and Tribunals Service	SSPP	statutory shared parental pay
HMRC	HM Revenue and Customs	SSS	Social Security Scotland
IB	incapacity benefit	UC	universal credit
ICE	Independent Case Examiner	UEST	Under Eighteens Support Team
IIDB	industrial injuries disablement benefit	WTC	working tax credit

Universal credit rates

Standard allowance

		£pm
Single	Under 25	342.72
	25 or over	409.89
Couple	Both under 25	488.59
	One or both 25 or over	594.04

Elements

First child (if born before 6 April 2017)		281.25
First child (if born on or after 6 April 2017), second child, and each subsequent child who qualifies		235.83
Disabled child addition	Lower rate	128.25
	Higher rate	400.29
Limited capability for work		128.25
Limited capability for work-related activity		341.92
Carer		162.92
Childcare costs	One child	up to 646.35
	Two or more children	up to 1,108.04
	Percentage covered	85%

Capital limits

	Lower	Upper
	6,000	16,000

Tariff income: £4.35 per £250 between lower and upper limits

Means-tested benefit rates

Income support/income-based jobseeker's allowance

Personal allowances		£pw
Single	Under 25	58.90
	25 or over	74.35
Lone parent	Under 18	58.90
	18 or over	74.35
Couple	Both under 18	58.90
	Both under 18, certain cases	89.00
	One under 18, one 18–24	58.90
	One under 18, one 25 or over	74.35
	One under 18, certain cases	116.80
	Both 18 or over	116.80

Premiums		
Carer		37.50
Disability	Single	34.95
	Couple	49.80
Enhanced disability	Single	17.10
	Couple	24.50
Severe disability	One qualifies	66.95
	Two qualify	133.90
Pensioner	Couple	148.40

Children
(Pre-6 April 2004 claims with no child tax credit)

Child under 20 personal allowance	68.27
Family premium	17.60
Disabled child premium	65.52
Enhanced disability premium (child)	26.60

Capital limits	Lower	Upper
Standard	6,000	16,000
Care homes	10,000	16,000

Tariff income: £1 per £250 between lower and upper limit

Income-related employment and support allowance

Personal allowances		Assessment phase	Main phase
Single	Under 25	58.90	74.35
	25 or over	74.35	74.35
Lone parent	Under 18	58.90	74.35
	18 or over	74.35	74.35
Couple	One or both under 18	58.90–116.80	74.35–116.80
	Both 18 or over	116.80	116.80

Components

Work-related activity		–	29.55
Support		–	39.20

Premiums

Carer		37.50	37.50
Severe disability (one qualifies)		66.95	66.95
Severe disability (two qualify)		133.90	133.90
Enhanced disability	Single	17.10	17.10
	Couple	24.50	24.50
Pensioner	Couple, no component	148.40	–
	Couple, work-related activity component	–	118.85
	Couple, support component	–	109.20

Capital limits
As for income support

Pension credit
Guarantee credit

Standard minimum guarantee	Single	173.75
	Couple	265.20
Severe disability addition	One qualifies	66.95
	Two qualify	133.90
Carer addition		37.50
Child addition	Standard amount	54.32
	Standard amount for eldest child born before 6 April 2017	64.82
	Disabled child increase	29.52
	Severely disabled child increase	92.12

Savings credit

Threshold	Single	150.47
	Couple	239.17
Maximum	Single	13.97
	Couple	15.62

Capital disregard

Standard/care homes	10,000

No upper limit
Deemed income: £1 per £500
above disregard

Housing benefit
Personal allowances

Single	Under 25	58.90
	Under 25 (on main phase ESA)	74.35
	25 or over	74.35
Lone parent	Under 18	58.90
	Under 18 (on main phase ESA)	74.35
	18 or over	74.35
Couple	Both under 18	89.00
	Both under 18 (claimant on main phase ESA)	116.80
	One or both 18 or over	116.80
Dependent children	Under 20	68.27
Pension age (and claimant/partner not on IS, income-based JSA, income-related ESA or UC)	Single	187.75
	Couple	280.85

Components

Work-related activity	–	29.55
Support	–	39.20

Premiums

Carer		37.50
Disability	Single	34.95
	Couple	49.80
Disabled child		65.52
Enhanced disability	Single	17.10
	Couple	24.50
	Child	26.60
Severe disability	One qualifies	66.95
	Two qualify	133.90
Family	Ordinary rate	17.60
	Some lone parents	22.20

Capital limits	Lower	Upper
Standard	6,000	16,000
Care home or over pension age	10,000	16,000

Tariff income: £1 per £250 between lower and upper limits;
£1 per £500 for those over pension age
No upper limit or tariff income for those on pension credit guarantee credit

Social fund payments

Maternity grant		500.00
Cold weather payment		25.00
Winter fuel payment	Under 80	200.00
(over pension age)	80 or over	300.00
	Care home (under 80)	100.00
	Care home (80 or over)	150.00

Best Start grant (Scotland only)
Pregnancy and baby payment

First child	600.00
Any subsequent child	300.00
Early learning payment	250.00
School-age payment	250.00

Non-means-tested benefit rates

	£pw
Attendance allowance	
Higher rate	89.15
Lower rate	59.70
Bereavement benefits	
Widowed parent's allowance/widowed mother's allowance	121.95
Bereavement support payment	
Higher rate	
Lump sum	3,500
Monthly amount	350.00
Standard rate	
Lump sum	2,500
Monthly amount	100.00
Carer's allowance	67.25
Carer's allowance supplement (Scotland only)	230.10 (June 2020)
	230.10 (December 2020)
Child benefit	
Only/eldest child	21.05
Other child(ren)	13.95
Increase for child	
(some existing claimants only)	
Only/eldest child	8.00
Other child(ren)	11.35
Partner's earnings limits	
Only/eldest child	230.00
Additional amount for each other child	30.00
Disability living allowance	
Care component	
Highest rate	89.15
Middle rate	59.70
Lowest rate	23.60

Mobility component
Higher rate	62.25
Lower rate	23.60

Contributory employment and support allowance
Assessment phase
Under 25	58.90
25 or over	74.35

Main phase
16 or over	74.35
Work-related activity component	29.55
Support component	39.20

Guardian's allowance
	17.90

Short-term incapacity benefit
Under pension age
Lower rate	86.10
Higher rate	101.90
Adult dependant	51.65

Over pension age
Lower rate	109.50
Higher rate	114.15
Adult dependant	63.80

Long-term incapacity benefit
	114.15
Age addition (under 35)	12.10
Age addition (35–44)	6.70
Adult dependant	66.30

Industrial injuries disablement benefit
20%: £36.40 to 100%: £182.00

Contribution-based jobseeker's allowance
Under 25	58.90
25 or over	74.35

Maternity allowance
Standard rate	151.20

Personal independence payment
Daily living component
Standard rate	59.70
Enhanced rate	89.15

Mobility component
Standard rate	23.60
Enhanced rate	62.25

Retirement pensions

State pension (full rate)	175.20
Category A	134.25
Category B (widow(er)/surviving civil partner)	134.25
Category B (spouse/civil partner)	80.45
Category D	80.45

Severe disablement allowance

	80.85
Age addition (under 40)	12.10
Age addition (40–49)	6.70
Age addition (50–59)	6.70
Adult dependant	39.75

Statutory maternity, adoption, paternity, shared parental pay and parental bereavement

Standard rate	151.20

Statutory sick pay

	95.85

National insurance contributions

Lower earnings limit	120.00
Primary threshold	183.00
Employee's class 1 rate	12% of £183 to £962
	2% above £962
Class 2 rate (self-employed)	3.05

Tax credit rates

	£ per day	£ per year
Child tax credit		
Family element (child born before 6 April 2017)	1.50	545
Child element	7.76	2,830
Disabled child element	9.36	3,415
Severely disabled child element	3.80	1,385
Working tax credit		
Basic element	8.33	3,040
Couple element	5.61	2,045
Lone parent element	5.61	2,045
30-hour element	2.27	825
Disabled worker element	8.83	3,220
Severe disability element	3.81	1,390
Childcare element		
70% of eligible weekly childcare costs:		
One child		weekly maximum 175
Two or more children		weekly maximum 300

Thresholds

Income threshold	
Working tax credit only or with child tax credit	6,530
Child tax credit only	16,385
Taper	41%
Income decrease disregard	2,500
Income increase disregard	2,500

Part 1

Introduction

Chapter 1

How to use this book

This chapter covers:
1. About this *Handbook* (below)
2. Using this *Handbook* (p4)
3. How this *Handbook* is organised (p6)
4. Finding out which benefits and tax credits you can get (p8)
5. Working out how much benefit you should receive (p16)
6. Finding information on challenging a decision (p17)

1. **About this** *Handbook*

This *Handbook* is the definitive guide to benefits, tax credits and statutory payments, condensing a huge and complex area of law into a comprehensive and user-friendly book. It contains everything you need to know in order to understand your entitlement to benefits, tax credits and statutory payments, and aims to answer any questions you may have about your entitlement. The book explains how you claim and how much money you should get, how decisions are made and how to get them changed. It provides examples to illustrate how the rules work in practice and tactics to help you deal with common problems.

The book also helps you find the specific legislation, caselaw or official guidance relevant to the information contained in the text, should you need it. If you are an adviser, this *Handbook* is an essential tool, containing all you need to provide practical, effective and accurate advice.

Updates and digital access

This *Handbook* is published annually. The information in it is updated throughout the year to reflect changes in legislation and new caselaw. These updates are published in CPAG's bi-monthly *Welfare Rights Bulletin* and at AskCPAG.org.uk, CPAG's online service. Subscribing to AskCPAG gives you digital access to this *Handbook*, as well as to other CPAG publications. It also has tools to help solve difficult benefit queries and help you draft mandatory reconsideration letters or appeal submissions on commonly disputed matters. For further information, see AskCPAG.org.uk.

Scope of this *Handbook*

The information in this *Handbook* applies to Great Britain.

Scotland

If you live in Scotland, some benefits and payments, and some limited aspects of universal credit, are different to those in England and Wales. This is because the responsibility for certain benefits, and for certain aspects of universal credit, has been devolved to the Scottish Parliament. Social Security Scotland administers and pays benefits that come under the Scottish social security system, known in this *Handbook* as 'Scottish benefits'. Some of the new Scottish benefits are already available, some will be brought in during the course of 2020 and others after that. If you are resident in Scotland, see Chapter 71 for further information.

Northern Ireland

Northern Ireland has its own benefits and tax credits legislation. Although many rules are very similar to those in Great Britain, the administration and adjudicating bodies are often different, and sometimes particular provisions in Northern Ireland are different – eg, because a particular rule does not apply there or because certain provisions have been put in place in Northern Ireland to mitigate some of the effects of recent welfare reform.

2. **Using this *Handbook***

There is a large amount of information in this *Handbook*, but you do not need to read it from cover to cover to find out about your benefit entitlement. If you are unfamiliar with the benefits system, a good place to start is the section in this chapter called 'Finding out which benefits and tax credits you can get' (see p8). This explains the best way to determine which benefits, tax credits or statutory payments you may qualify for and to establish how they interact with each other.

If you want to find the answer to a particular question, or to understand the rules for a specific benefit, it should be easy to locate the information you need by using the detailed index or by using the individual benefit, tax credit and statutory payment chapters as your starting point.

Using the index

A simple way to find specific information in this book is to use the index. The index is designed to be detailed and intuitive to ensure you can easily locate the information you need.
- Use the entries in bold type, arranged alphabetically, to help you to find general information on a subject.

- Use the sub-entries under these, also arranged alphabetically, to find more specific information relevant to the question you have.
- Use the list at the start of the index to understand the abbreviations used.

For example, if you want to find information on how to claim attendance allowance, you can locate this either by looking up 'claims' and finding the 'AA' sub-heading underneath, or by looking up 'attendance allowance' and finding the 'claims' sub-heading underneath.

Using the individual benefit chapters

Another good starting point for finding specific information in this book is the chapter on the particular benefit, tax credit or statutory payment to which your question relates. These chapters follow a common structure to help you find the information contained in them easily, and they refer you to other relevant information that is elsewhere in the book.

- Find the chapter about the particular benefit, tax credit or statutory payment by using the contents list on pvii. Find the relevant part of the book and then locate the appropriate chapter in that part. To assist with this, tabs on the left-hand page identify the number of the part you are in. The parts and chapters are also identified at the top of each page.
- Familiarise yourself with the standard way information is presented in these chapters (see p7). This will help you to locate information in the text easily. For example, if you want to know whether there are age limits for claiming a particular benefit, it is helpful to know that each chapter has a section called 'The rules about your age'.
- Alternatively, use the chapter contents at the start of each chapter to direct you to the likely section in the chapter to check. The sections within each chapter are identified at the top of the left-hand page.
- Follow any cross references in the text to find any other relevant information contained in the book.

Finding the law

To help you trace the source of the information given in the text, references to the law (both legislation and caselaw) and to guidance are given. It may be helpful to use these references, particularly if you are challenging a decision, as they provide the legal justification for the statements made in the text. For a useful introduction to legal sources, see pp1379–84.

- Find the information in the book relevant to the issue you want to check and find the note for that information.
- Check the relevant note at the end of the chapter for the legal reference.
- Check Appendix 10 for an explanation of the abbreviations used in the references.

Part 1: Introduction
Chapter 1: How to use this book
3. How this *Handbook* is organised

1

- See Appendices 1 and 2 for where to find the law and guidance online and for other useful sources of information.

The law referred to in this *Handbook* only applies in Great Britain. See p4 if you live in Northern Ireland.

3. **How this *Handbook* is organised**

The book is split into parts, and related chapters are grouped under these parts. A description of the information covered in each part, together with a list of chapters it contains, is included in the table of contents on pvii.

By developing a basic understanding of the purpose of each part, you can immediately identify where certain information will be in the book. For example, once you know that Part 11 covers the immigration and residence rules for benefits and tax credits, you know to use this part if you need to check whether your immigration status affects your right to a particular benefit.

Similarly, the common structure of many of the chapters is designed to make it easier to find information in them.

How the parts are organised

- **Part 1:** Introduction.
- **Part 2:** Universal credit. This contains chapters on the introduction of universal credit, the rules of entitlement, who is included in your claim and how your needs, income and capital affect your entitlement and the amount you receive. There is also a chapter that explains the help you can get within your universal credit for rent and certain other housing costs.
- **Part 3:** Other means-tested benefits and tax credits. This contains chapters on each of the other main means-tested benefits and tax credits.
- **Part 4:** General rules for other means-tested benefits. This contains chapters explaining who is included in a claim for a means-tested benefit and how your needs, income and capital affect your entitlement, and chapters on the help you can get with your rent and certain other housing costs and when the amount of such help is restricted.
- **Part 5:** Other benefits. This contains chapters on non-means-tested benefits, statutory payments and other help you may get, arranged in alphabetical order.
- **Part 6:** Special benefit rules. This contains chapters explaining the rules for particular groups of people: students, people in hospital or care homes, prisoners and people leaving care or without accommodation.
- **Part 7:** National insurance, work and work-related rules. This contains chapters covering the national insurance (NI) contribution conditions for contributory benefits and the qualifying conditions for NI credits, how work affects your

benefit entitlement, how limited capability for work is assessed, and the
conditions you may have to meet to prepare for or find work, and what
happens if you do not meet them.

- **Part 8:** Claiming benefits and getting paid. This contains chapters on claiming
and backdating benefit, how and when you should be paid, whether you are
entitled to hardship payments or affected by the benefit cap, and information
on overpayments and penalties.
- **Part 9:** Getting a benefit decision changed. This contains chapters on
challenging decisions and how to complain.
- **Part 10:** General rules for tax credits. This contains chapters on the general
rules for tax credits, including how your entitlement is worked out and how to
challenge decisions.
- **Part 11:** Immigration and residence rules for benefits and tax credits. This
contains chapters explaining your entitlement if you are a European Economic
Area national or a person subject to immigration control, or if you are going
to, or coming from, abroad.
- **Part 12:** Scottish social security benefits. This contains information on the
Scottish social security system and gives details of the benefits and payments
that are administered by Social Security Scotland, including how to claim
Scottish benefits, how claims are administered and paid, and how to challenge
determinations.
- **Appendices.** These contain further information, such as sources of information
and advice, tables of relevant dates and the legislation on particular
assessments.

How the chapters are organised

To help you locate information easily, many of the *Handbook* chapters have a
similar structure. Each chapter contains the following.
- **Chapter contents:** to help you find the section you need.
- **Key facts:** covering the key points about the information in the chapter. If the
chapter is about a specific benefit, tax credit or statutory payment, these
include certain standard information, such as how work affects your
entitlement, whether the benefit is means tested or non-means tested, whether
you must have paid NI contributions to qualify and who administers your
claim.
- **Endnotes:** to the numbered references in the text. These are at the end of each
chapter and, in most cases, cite the legal source of the information in the text.

The chapters on specific benefits, tax credits and statutory payments usually also
follow a similar structure, with the information organised under the following
headings.
- **Who can get the particular benefit, tax credit or statutory payment:**
explains the qualifying conditions.

Part 1: Introduction
Chapter 1: How to use this book
4. Finding out which benefits and tax credits you can get

- **The rules about your age:** any age limits that are relevant.
- **People included in the claim:** who you can claim for, or whether you have to make a joint claim with someone else.
- **The amount of benefit:** the rules about how much money you should receive, with cross references to rules that are common to more than one benefit or tax credit.
- **Special benefit rules:** to alert you to when there are additional rules that apply to people in particular circumstances – eg, people in hospital.
- **Claims and backdating:** how to claim, who should claim, the information you must provide, the date your claim is treated as having been made, whether your claim can be backdated, whether a claim for one benefit can be treated as a claim for another, and whether claims can be made in advance.
- **Getting paid:** how and when you are paid, and what to do if your circumstances change.
- **Tax, other benefits and the benefit cap:** whether the benefit, tax credit or statutory payment is taxable, how it interacts with other benefits or tax credits, and whether it is affected by rules on the benefit cap, plus information on other help you may get.

The text under these headings refers you to any other information in the book that is relevant. This is to ensure that, not only is information easy to find within each chapter, but also that you can answer almost any question you have on your entitlement by using the individual benefit, tax credit or statutory payment chapter as a starting point.

4. Finding out which benefits and tax credits you can get

To find out about all the help you can get, it is important to check your entitlement in the following order.
- First check whether you qualify for any non-means-tested benefits or statutory payments.
- Next, check your entitlement to means-tested benefits.
- Finally, check whether there is any other help available to you.

Step one: do you qualify for any non-means-tested benefits or statutory payments?

What are non-means-tested benefits and statutory payments?

A non-means-tested benefit is a benefit for which it is not necessary to carry out a detailed assessment of your income or capital to work out your entitlement. You may need to meet national insurance contribution conditions to qualify for some non-means-tested benefits ('contributory benefits') and you may qualify for others just because of your circumstances. Certain non-means-tested benefits ('earnings-replacement benefits') are intended to compensate you for loss of earnings. Your entitlement to non-means-tested benefits is not affected by any savings that you have and your income only affects your entitlement to some earnings-replacement benefits.

Statutory payments are payments an employer may be required to pay you if you are an employee and are unfit for work or off work on maternity, paternity, adoption, shared parental or parental bereavement leave. Your entitlement to statutory payments depends on the level of your past earnings (and, for statutory shared parental pay, the past earnings of your partner), but it is not affected by any other income or savings you have.

Both jobseeker's allowance (JSA) and employment and support allowance (ESA) have a non-means-tested, contributory element (contribution-based JSA and contributory ESA) and a means-tested element (income-based JSA and income-related ESA). Depending on your circumstances, it is possible to get either or both elements. However, income-based JSA and income-related ESA are being replaced by universal credit, so in most cases new claims can only be made for contribution-based JSA and contributory ESA. If you qualify for both elements, in effect, the means-tested element tops up the contributory element.

- Use the table on p10 to see which non-means-tested benefits or statutory payments you might get. Check the benefits under all the circumstances that apply to you.
- Check which of these are 'earnings-replacement benefits' (these are marked with an * in the table).
- Turn to the chapter on the benefits you are interested in, looking at any earnings-replacement benefits or statutory payments first. The chapters are arranged in alphabetical order in Part 5 and, for people living in Scotland, in Part 12.
- Check whether you meet the qualifying conditions for the benefit by looking at the section explaining who can get that benefit. Cross references take you to further details you may need to check.
- Look in the section 'Tax, other benefits and the benefits cap' for details of how the benefit might be affected by other benefits you already get or want to claim. Because of the 'overlapping benefit' rules, certain non-means-tested benefits cannot be paid in full at the same time.
- If you think you qualify, use the section 'How to claim' for further information on what to do next.

Part 1: Introduction
Chapter 1: How to use this book
4. Finding out which benefits and tax credits you can get

Your circumstances	Benefits you might get	Chapter
Bereaved	Bereavement support payment* or	Chapter 25
	Widowed parent's allowance*	Chapter 25
	Statutory parental bereavement pay	Chapter 38
Carer	Carer's allowance* and, if you live in	Chapter 26
	Scotland, carer's allowance	
	supplement	
Pregnant or have recently given birth	Statutory maternity pay	Chapter 38
	Maternity allowance*	Chapter 34
	Statutory paternity pay	Chapter 38
	Statutory shared parental pay	Chapter 38
	Child benefit	Chapter 27
Recently adopted a child	Statutory adoption pay	Chapter 38
	Statutory paternity pay	Chapter 38
	Statutory shared parental pay	Chapter 38
	Child benefit	Chapter 27
Father of a baby or partner of	Statutory paternity pay	Chapter 38
someone who has recently given	Statutory shared parental pay	Chapter 38
birth or adopted a child		
Responsible for a child	Child benefit	Chapter 27
	Guardian's allowance	Chapter 27
Disabled	Disability living allowance**	Chapter 28
	Personal independence payment**	Chapter 35
	Attendance allowance**	Chapter 24
	Industrial injuries benefits	
		Chapter 32
Unfit for work	Contributory employment and	Chapter 30
	support allowance*	Chapter 39
	Statutory sick pay	Chapter 32
	Industrial injuries benefits	
Pensioner	State pension*	Chapter 36
Unemployed and seeking work, or	Contribution-based jobseeker's	Chapter 33
working part time and seeking more	allowance*	
work		

* Earnings-replacement benefits
** From summer 2020, child disability payment is planned to replace disability living allowance for new claimants living in Scotland. During the course of 2021, disability assistance for working-age people and disability assistance for older people will replace personal independence payment and attendance allowance for new claimants living in Scotland (although the names of these two new benefits may change). See Chapter 71 for details.

Step two: do you qualify for any means-tested benefits and tax credits?

Universal credit (UC) is gradually replacing other means-tested benefits and tax credits for people of working age. Except in very limited circumstances, you cannot make a new claim for income support (IS), income-based JSA, income-related ESA, housing benefit (HB), child tax credit (CTC) or working tax credit (WTC). These are often known as 'legacy benefits'. If you are already getting IS, income-based JSA, income-related ESA, HB, CTC or WTC, provided you continue to satisfy the qualifying conditions, you can continue to receive it until you transfer to UC (see p27).

What are means-tested benefits and tax credits?

A means-tested benefit is one for which an assessment of your needs, income and capital is necessary to work out your entitlement. You only qualify for means-tested benefits if your (and your partner's) income and capital are not too high. Entitlement to tax credits, which are also means tested, depends on your assessed needs and the level of your (and your partner's) income. The assessment of the amount you need to live on for means-tested benefits and tax credits may increase if you get certain non-means-tested benefits. Depending on your circumstances and when you made your claim, you may be entitled to a combination of non-means-tested benefits, a statutory payment, means-tested benefits and/or tax credits. You may get more than one means-tested benefit or tax credit, but you cannot qualify for certain means-tested benefits at the same time.

- Use Chapter 2 to see whether you come under the UC system and how this affects the benefits you can get, then use the tables below to see which means-tested benefits and/or tax credits might be relevant to your circumstances.
- Turn to the chapter(s) on the relevant benefit(s).
- Follow the procedure explained for checking non-means-tested benefits, by looking at the sections on who can get the benefit, 'Tax, other benefits and the benefit cap' and 'How to claim' in any relevant chapters.

If you come under the UC system

Your circumstance	Benefit	Chapter
Come under the UC system	Universal credit	Chapter 3

If you do not come under the UC system

Your circumstances	Benefits and other help you might get	Chapter
Carer	Income support	Chapter 11
Pregnant or recently given birth	Income support	Chapter 11
	Income-related employment and support allowance	Chapter 9
	Child tax credit	Chapter 14
	Working tax credit (in limited circumstances)	Chapter 15

Part 1: Introduction
Chapter 1: How to use this book
4. Finding out which benefits and tax credits you can get

1

Recently adopted a child	Child tax credit	Chapter 14
	Working tax credit (in limited circumstances)	Chapter 15
	Income support (in some circumstances)	Chapter 11
Responsible for a child	Child tax credit	Chapter 14
	Pension credit	Chapter 13
	Income support (in some circumstances)	Chapter 11
Disabled or unfit for work	Income-related employment and support allowance	Chapter 9
	Income support (in limited circumstances)	Chapter 11
	Working tax credit (in limited circumstances)	Chapter 15
Pensioners	Pension credit	Chapter 13
Tenant	Housing benefit	Chapter 10
Working	Working tax credit	Chapter 15
Unemployed and seeking work, or working part time and seeking more work	Income-based jobseeker's allowance	Chapter 12

Step three: can you get any other help?

What further help is there?

If you are entitled to certain benefits or tax credits, you may qualify for other benefits on that basis. These are called 'passported benefits'. Some of these passported benefits can also be awarded on the basis of your circumstances or age, or if you have a low income.

Other assistance may be available to people in certain circumstances and may be means tested – eg, council tax reduction.

Some types of passported benefits or other assistance are different in England, Wales and Scotland.

Entitlement to some of these payments is discretionary.

- Use the tables on pp13–16 to see the other help you may be able to get in your circumstances and to see whether the benefits or tax credits you get help you qualify for any additional 'passported benefits'.
- Use the relevant chapters to check whether you qualify for such help and how to apply.
- Check whether you qualify for council tax reduction (see p851).
- Check Chapter 40 to see whether there are any other payments or other kinds of help you might be able to get.

Your circumstances	Benefits and other help you might get	Chapter
Bereaved	In England and Wales, funeral expenses payment or,	Chapter 37
	in England, children's funeral fund payment	Chapter 37
	In Scotland, funeral support payment	Chapter 73
Pregnant or recently given birth or adopted a child	In England and Wales, Sure Start maternity grant	Chapter 37
	In Scotland, Best Start grant pregnancy and baby payment	Chapter 72
	Health benefits	Chapter 31
	In England and Wales, Healthy Start food	Chapter 40
	In Scotland, Best Start foods	Chapter 40
	Healthy Start vitamins	Chapter 40
Responsible for a child	In England and Wales, Sure Start maternity grant (if child is no more than 12 months old)	Chapter 37
	In Scotland, Best Start grant pregnancy and baby payment	Chapter 72
	In Scotland, Best Start grant early learning payment	Chapter 72
	In Scotland, Best Start grant school-age payment	Chapter 72
	In Scotland, by December 2020 for children under 6, Scottish child payment	Chapter 74
	Free school lunches	Chapter 40
	Health benefits for child	Chapter 31
	In England and Wales, Healthy Start food	Chapter 40
	In Scotland, Best Start foods	Chapter 40
	Healthy Start vitamins	Chapter 40
	Cold weather payment (in some circumstances)	Chapter 37
Disabled or unfit for work*	Cold weather payment	Chapter 37
Carer	In Scotland, young carer grant	Chapter 75
Young person starting work	In Scotland, from spring 2020, job start payment	Chapter 40
Pensioners	Winter fuel payment	Chapter 37
	Cold weather payment	Chapter 37
	Health benefits	Chapter 31
Aged 60 or over	Some health benefits	Chapter 31

Part 1: Introduction
Chapter 1: How to use this book
4. Finding out which benefits and tax credits you can get

1

Own a home	Council tax reduction	Chapter 40
	In England and Wales, discretionary reduction in council tax	Chapter 40
Have a mortgage	Loan for mortgage interest	Chapter 40
Tenant	Council tax reduction	Chapter 40
	Discretionary housing payment	Chapter 29
	In England and Wales, discretionary reduction in council tax	Chapter 40
Not enough money to meet certain needs	Budgeting loan	Chapter 37
	Budgeting advance of universal credit	Chapter 3
	Health benefits	Chapter 31
	Council tax reduction	Chapter 40
	Other payments	Chapter 40

*Note: in Scotland, winter heating assistance is planned to be introduced by the end of 2020 for some people getting child disability payment.

Passported benefit	Passports
Free school lunches (p866)**	Some people on universal credit
	Income support
	Income-based jobseeker's allowance
	Income-related employment and support allowance
	Some people on child tax credit
	Guarantee credit of pension credit (England and Wales only)
Health benefits (Chapter 31)	Some people on universal credit
	Income support
	Income-based jobseeker's allowance
	Income-related employment and support allowance
	Some people on child tax credit
	Some people on working tax credit
	Guarantee credit of pension credit
	Note: some health benefits are free for everyone in Scotland and Wales.
Sure Start maternity grant, in England and Wales (p796)	Universal credit
	Income support
	Income-based jobseeker's allowance
	Income-related employment and support allowance
	Some people on child tax credit
	Some people on working tax credit
	Pension credit
Best Start grants, in Scotland (Chapter 72)	Universal credit
	Income support

	Income-based jobseeker's allowance
	Income-related employment and support allowance
	Housing benefit
	Child tax credit
	Working tax credit
	Pension credit
Social fund funeral expenses payment, in England and Wales (p798)	Universal credit
	Income support
	Income-based jobseeker's allowance
	Income-related employment and support allowance
	Housing benefit
	Some people on child tax credit
	Some people on working tax credit
	Pension credit
Funeral support payment, in Scotland (Chapter 73)	Universal credit
	Income support
	Income-based jobseeker's allowance
	Income-related employment and support allowance
	Housing benefit
	Child tax credit
	Some people on working tax credit
	Pension credit
Social fund cold weather payment (p805)	Some people on universal credit
	Some people on income support
	Some people on income-based jobseeker's allowance
	Some people on income-related employment and support allowance
	Pension credit
Social fund budgeting loan (p792)	Income support
	Income-based jobseeker's allowance
	Income-related employment and support allowance
	Pension credit
Scottish child payment (by Christmas 2020 for children under 6 – Chapter 74)	Universal credit
	Income support
	Income-based jobseekers allowance
	Income-related employment and support allowance
	Child tax credit
	Working tax credit
	Pension credit

** In England and Scotland, all children in certain year groups are entitled to free school lunches and, in Scotland, pre-school children of parents getting certain benefits may qualify. In Wales, children in local authority maintained primary schools are entitled to free school breakfasts. In England and Wales, children may continue to qualify for free school lunches after entitlement to the passporting benefit ends. See p866 for further information.

Part 1: Introduction
Chapter 1: How to use this book
6. Finding information on challenging a decision

5. **Working out how much benefit you should receive**

How much benefit will you get?

The amount you get depends on which benefit you are claiming. Some non-means-tested benefits are paid at different rates depending on your circumstances. The amount of some contributory benefits may depend on your national insurance contribution record (or that of your spouse or civil partner), and some (but not all) non-means-tested earnings-replacement benefits are affected by certain types of income. The amount of means-tested benefits you get always depends on your circumstances and involves a detailed assessment of your needs, your income and your capital. Your entitlement to tax credits also depends on an assessment of your needs and income. Tables of benefit and tax credit rates for 2020/21 are on ppxiii–xxi.

- Look at the chapters dealing with the benefit(s) you are interested in, checking the non-means-tested benefits and statutory payments chapters first. This is because any non-means-tested benefits you get may affect the amount of means-tested benefit to which you are entitled.
- If you are not already getting the benefit, check you meet the entitlement conditions and then look at the section 'The amount of benefit'. Follow any relevant cross references for more detailed information about different aspects of the calculation.
- Check the section 'Tax, other benefits and the benefit cap' for additional information on how the benefit or tax credit may be affected by other benefits or tax credits you receive.
- If in doubt, use Appendix 1 for details of where you can get further help.

6. **Finding information on challenging a decision**

Who makes decisions?

The Department for Work and Pensions (DWP) is responsible for administering most benefits. HM Revenue and Customs (HMRC) is responsible for administering tax credits, child benefit and guardian's allowance. HMRC also makes decisions on your national insurance (NI) contribution record and on your entitlement to statutory payments if you and your employer do not agree. Social Security Scotland administers Scottish benefits. Local authorities administer housing benefit, council tax reduction schemes, certain education benefits and welfare assistance schemes (for help with community care and when you are in a crisis). The Welsh government administers the Discretionary Assistance Fund for Wales.

. . . .

HM Courts and Tribunals Service, which is part of the Ministry of Justice, is responsible for administering benefit and tax credit appeals. The Scottish Courts and Tribunals Service administers appeals about Scottish benefits.

. . . .

If you are unhappy with a decision that has been made on your claim, you can try to get it changed. The ways you can challenge a decision, and the procedures and time limits for doing so, depend on the benefit concerned and on whether the decision you want to challenge is an initial decision on your claim or a decision that has been made following a revision, supersession or appeal. Use the following steps if you are considering challenging a decision.

*   First check whether the decision is correct. See p4 for how to find answers to specific questions.
*   If you think it is not correct, turn to the chapter on the benefit to which the decision relates and check the last bullet point in the key facts at the start of the chapter. This explains where to find information on challenging a decision relating to that benefit.
*   Check the chapters in Part 9, Chapter 66 for tax credits, or Chapter 77 for Scottish benefits, to find information on how you may be able to challenge the decision. For decisions relating to NI contributions, see p960. Check the information at the start of the chapter to be sure it is relevant to the benefit to which your challenge relates.
*   Alternatively, look up 'challenging a decision' in the index. The sub-entries under it may help you to find the page number for the type of decision you want to challenge.

Part 2

Universal credit

- income-based jobseeker's allowance (JSA);
- income-related employment and support allowance (ESA);

Chapter 2

The introduction of universal credit

This chapter covers:
1. The introduction of universal credit (below)
2. The universal credit system (p23)
3. Transferring to universal credit (p27)
4. Change of circumstances (p32)

Key facts
- Universal credit (UC) has now been introduced nationwide for most new claimants.
- When you come under the UC system, UC replaces most other means-tested benefits and tax credits.
- Current claimants of means-tested benefits and tax credits do not automatically come under the UC system, but can transfer to UC – eg, by claiming UC after a change of circumstances, or under the government's 'managed migration' transfer process.
- The managed migration transfer process is due to start in November 2020. It is currently being tested.

1. The introduction of universal credit

Universal credit (UC) combines means-tested support for adults under pension age and children into one benefit.

Because UC is being introduced gradually, this *Handbook* refers to you as coming 'under the UC system' when the UC rules apply to you.

When you come under the UC system (see p23), UC replaces the following means-tested benefits and tax credits (known as 'legacy benefits'):
- income support (IS);
- income-based jobseeker's allowance (JSA);
- income-related employment and support allowance (ESA);

Part 2: Universal credit
Chapter 2: The introduction of universal credit
1. The introduction of universal credit

- housing benefit (HB), except for 'specified' and 'temporary' accommodation (see p174);
- child tax credit (CTC);
- working tax credit (WTC).

UC does not replace pension credit (PC). However, if you or your partner are over pension age or are entitled to PC, you may come under the UC system in certain situations (see p25).

Even if you come under the UC system, you can still claim non-means-tested benefits. So, for example, you can still claim contribution-based JSA, contributory ESA, child benefit and carer's allowance, as well as UC.

Timetable

- UC has now been introduced across Great Britain for most new claimants.
- Initially, UC was only introduced for new claimants who satisfied certain 'gateway' conditions and lived in 'gateway' (or 'live service') areas of the country. These gateway areas began being converted to 'full service' areas from November 2014. By 12 December 2018, all gateway areas had been converted.
- Between 1 January 2018 and 11 December 2018, new claimants in gateway areas were unable to claim UC and could make a new claim for the legacy means-tested benefits and tax credits instead. From 12 December 2018, new claims for UC are possible in most cases (see p23 for when this is not possible) and new claims for the legacy means-tested benefits and tax credits are not possible (but see p24 for exceptions).
- Between 6 April 2017 and 31 January 2019, new claimants with three or more children were unable to claim UC and could make a new claim for the old means-tested benefits and tax credits instead. See Chapter 2 of the 2018/19 edition of this *Handbook* for details.
- Existing awards of the legacy means-tested benefits and tax credits continue for the time being (but see p27 if your circumstances change). Under the government's official 'managed migration' transfer process, existing awards will be closed and claimants invited to claim UC. The main part of this process is expected to take place between November 2020 and September 2024. Before then, the DWP is testing the process in up to 10,000 cases.

Note: the official plans for the introduction of UC are subject to change. See AskCPAG.org.uk and CPAG's *Welfare Rights Bulletin* for updates.

2. **The universal credit system**

When you come under the universal credit system

You come under the universal credit (UC) system when you make a claim for UC (if you are in a couple, you must usually claim UC jointly with your partner).[1] You are usually considered to have made a claim for UC at the point you submit your online UC claim form. See p44 for more details on claiming UC. Your entitlement to other means-tested benefits and tax credits stops if you claim UC. See p25 for how these benefits and tax credits are affected.

You also come under the UC system if you (or your partner) make a new claim for jobseeker's allowance (JSA) or employment and support allowance (ESA) of any kind. You cannot then get income-based JSA or income-related ESA, but if you are entitled to contribution-based JSA or contributory ESA, you come under the UC system for these benefits (see p26).

If you have a severe disability, in some circumstances until 27 January 2021, you are prevented from making a claim for UC and so cannot come under the UC system (even if you make a new claim for JSA or ESA) until you are affected by the official 'managed migration' process (see p30). You also do not come under the UC system in any other situation where you are prevented by law from claiming UC (see below).

Once you have claimed and are entitled to UC, you remain under the UC system.

People prevented from claiming universal credit

In some cases, you are prevented by law from making a claim for UC. If this applies, you can make a new claim for the legacy means-tested benefits and tax credits instead (see p24). You are prevented from claiming UC if:

- you (or, if you are in a couple, your partner) are severely disabled and satisfy certain other conditions, but only until 27 January 2021 (see below); or
- you (or, if you are in a couple, you and your partner) are a 'frontier worker' – ie, you work in Great Britain or Northern Ireland but live elsewhere;[2] or
- you come into another specified category of case from whom it has been decided not to accept claims, in order to safeguard or test the efficient administration of UC.[3] At the time of writing, no other category of case had been specified.

People who are severely disabled

From 16 January 2019 to 26 January 2021 inclusive, you are prevented by law from making a new claim for UC, and so cannot come under the UC system, if:[4]

- you (or your partner, if you are claiming as a couple) are entitled to income support (IS), income-based JSA, income-related ESA or housing benefit (HB) that includes a severe disability premium (see p346), or you (or your partner, if

Part 2: Universal credit
Chapter 2: The introduction of universal credit
2. The universal credit system

you are claiming as a couple) were entitled to IS, income-based JSA, income-related ESA or HB within the last month, your award included a severe disability premium and you have continued to satisfy the conditions for the premium during that past month; *and*

• neither you nor your partner (if you have one) have received official notice from the DWP that you are affected by the 'managed migration' process to UC (see p30).

Note: if you are now single, to be prevented from claiming UC under these rules, you must either currently be the claimant of a benefit that includes a severe disability premium, or have yourself been claiming such a benefit including the premium within the last month. For example, the fact that your former partner was claiming the benefit is not enough to mean that you are now prevented from claiming UC, even if you are severely disabled.

If you become a member of a couple and one of you is already getting UC, see p32.

If you should have been prevented from claiming UC under the above rule but are wrongly allowed to claim UC, you may be entitled to an additional 'transitional SDP amount' in your UC (see p27).[5] However, in February 2020, the DWP confirmed that where you were 'inadvertently' or 'incorrectly' allowed to claim UC where you should not have been, the policy is that the UC can be stopped and your legacy benefits reinstated. This can be done where the error is identified before UC has been paid, or otherwise where you should have been prevented from claiming UC and reinstating your legacy benefits is in your 'best interests'. In practice, some people have had difficulty getting their legacy benefits reinstated under these arrangements – seek advice. The DWP says that tax credits cannot be reinstated in this situation, and as a result would need to be reclaimed after your legacy benefits have been resinstated. The DWP says that in this situation it will consider complaints of financial loss from loss of tax credits, and whether it should award compensation.[6] See AskCPAG.org.uk and CPAG's *Welfare Rights Bulletin* for updates.

Who can make a new claim for means-tested benefits and tax credits

Even if you have not claimed UC, you cannot usually make a new claim for IS, income-based JSA, income-related ESA, HB (if you are under pension age), child tax credit (CTC) or working tax credit (WTC).[7]

However, you can make a new claim instead of claiming UC in the following circumstances.

• You can make a new claim for IS, income-based JSA, income-related ESA, HB, CTC or WTC until 27 January 2021 if you (or your partner, if you are in a couple) are severely disabled and are prevented by law from claiming UC (see p23).[8]

- You can make a new claim for CTC if you are already entitled to WTC, and a new claim for WTC if you are already entitled to CTC.[9]
- You can make a new claim for HB if you are in a couple and only one of you has reached pension age (ie, you are in a 'mixed-age couple') in certain circumstances (see p172 for details).
- You can make a new claim for HB if you live in 'specified' or 'temporary' accommodation (see p172). You may still need to claim UC for your other basic needs.
- You can make a new claim for IS, income-based JSA, income-related ESA, HB, CTC or WTC if you are prevented by law from claiming UC because you (or if you are in a couple, you and your partner) are a 'frontier worker', or because you are in a category of case from whom it has been decided not to accept claims for UC.[10]

Examples

Jules is getting income-based JSA and HB. She then has a baby (her first child). Jules cannot make a new claim for CTC. Instead, she claims and gets UC. Her entitlement to income-based JSA and HB comes to an end.

Sanjay is getting income-related ESA, which includes the severe disability premium. He is prevented from claiming UC until 27 January 2021. When Sanjay moves into rented accommodation in August 2020 and needs help with the rent, he can make a new claim for HB.

Steve is getting income-related ESA. Following a reassessment, he fails the work capability assessment. He decides to claim income-based JSA while he is challenging this decision. Steve was not entitled to the severe disability premium in his ESA, so he must now claim UC rather than income-based JSA. Because he has claimed UC, Steve cannot get income-related ESA from that point on. If his challenge to the work capability assessment decision is successful, this will be reflected in his UC award.

How your means-tested benefits and tax credits are affected

UC replaces means-tested benefits and tax credits, so the general rule is that if you claim UC you no longer qualify for:[11]

- IS. **Note:** if you claim UC on or after 22 July 2020, your IS continues to be paid for the first two weeks of your claim for UC;
- income-based JSA. This is 'abolished' (replaced by UC) in your case, if you come under the UC system and you (or, if you are in a couple, your partner) make a new claim for income-based or contribution-based JSA, income-related or contributory ESA or UC. **Note:** if you claim UC on or after 22 July 2020, your income-based JSA continues to be paid for for the first two weeks of your claim for UC;[12]

Part 2: Universal credit
Chapter 2: The introduction of universal credit
2. The universal credit system

• income-related ESA. This is 'abolished' (replaced by UC) in your case, if you come under the UC system and you (or, if you are in a couple, your partner) make a new claim for income-related or contributory ESA, income-based or contribution-based JSA or UC. **Note:** if you claim UC on or after 22 July 2020, your income-related ESA continues to be paid for the first two weeks of your claim for UC;[13]

• HB, except for 'specified' and 'temporary' accommodation (see p174). Your HB continues to be paid for the first two weeks of your claim for UC;

• CTC;

• WTC;

• PC. PC is not being replaced by UC, but you cannot get PC and UC at the same time. Single people must be under the qualifying age for PC (this is the same as the age at which you could get a state pension – see p779) to get UC. A couple with only one partner who has has reached pension age (a 'mixed-age couple') can choose to claim PC instead of UC only in certain circumstances (see p271). If you come under the UC system as a single person, but later become a member of a couple and your partner is entitled to PC, see p32.

If you are already getting IS, income-based JSA, income-related ESA, HB, CTC or WTC and make a claim for UC, your award stops. This should only happen if is clear that you meet all the basic conditions for UC on p36, apart from having accepted a claimant commitment.[14] The DWP is likely to decide that you meet these basic conditions automatically.

If you are already getting IS, income-based JSA, income-related ESA, HB, CTC or WTC and are prevented by law from claiming UC (see p23), your award should continue even if you try to claim UC. If you are prevented from claiming UC and you are a member of a mixed-age couple, your award of means-tested benefit can continue despite the rules about your age that apply to IS (see p238), income-based JSA (see p255), income-related ESA (see p162) and HB (see p187).

If you are are entitled to UC, you cannot also be entitled to IS, income-based JSA, income-related ESA, HB, CTC or WTC (or PC), even if you could make a new claim for them.[15]

Contribution-based jobseeker's allowance and contributory employment and support allowance

If you (or if you are in a couple, your partner) make a new claim for JSA or ESA, in most cases you come under the UC system. You cannot get income-based JSA or income-related ESA because they are replaced by UC (but see p24 for when this does not apply), but you can still get contribution-based JSA and contributory ESA.[16]

When paid under the UC system, the DWP refers to contribution-based JSA and contributory ESA as 'new-style' JSA and 'new-style' ESA. The rules about getting paid these benefits (eg, the rules on overpayments, claimant responsibilities and sanctions) are those that apply in the UC system.

If you come under the UC system and have a low income, usually you must claim UC if you need to 'top up' your new-style JSA or ESA. If you are prevented from making a claim from UC (see p23), you can instead top up your new-style JSA with income-based JSA and your new-style ESA with income-related ESA.[17]

If you do not come under the UC system, you can top up your your contribution-based JSA with income-based JSA and your contributory ESA with income-related ESA. You do not need to make a new claim; your current award is adjusted.[18]

Example

Robin gets contributory ESA. When he claimed, he did not come under the UC system, so this is not new-style ESA. Robin's income has now decreased. He can top up his contributory ESA with income-related ESA. He does not need to make a new claim – his current ESA award can be adjusted. However, the DWP tells Robin that he must claim UC as a top-up. Robin refuses to do so and points out that his ESA is not new-style ESA. The DWP checks this and adjusts his ESA award to include income-related ESA.

For some practical points about making a claim, see p715 for contribution-based JSA and p658 for contributory ESA.

3. Transferring to universal credit

Universal credit (UC) has been introduced for new claimants. If you are getting the old means-tested benefits and tax credits, at some point you may transfer to UC. The process of transferring to UC is known as 'migration'. You can transfer to UC:

- at any time, under 'natural migration' (see below);
- mainly from November 2020, under the government's 'managed migration' process (see p30).

Natural migration

You can transfer to UC at any time if you claim UC. Where you transfer to UC outside the 'managed migration' process, this is called 'natural migration'.

Natural migration can happen at any time, usually after there has been a change in your circumstances and you decide to claim UC. For example:

- you have your first child. You cannot usually make a new claim for child tax credit (but see p24 for when you can) and so may need to claim UC for means-tested support for your child;

Part 2: Universal credit
Chapter 2: The introduction of universal credit
3. Transferring to universal credit

- you move into a different local authority area and need help with your rent. Any previous housing benefit (HB) award will have stopped and you cannot usually make a new claim for HB (but see p24 for when you can), so you may need to claim UC. If you move within the same local authority area, your HB award continues;
- you fail the work capability assessment for employment and support allowance (ESA) and decide to claim another benefit while the DWP considers your request for this to be looked at again.

Note: between 16 January 2019 and 26 January 2021 inclusive, some severely disabled people are prevented from claiming UC and so cannot transfer to UC under natural migration (see p23). If you are severely disabled but *have* transferred to UC, see p29.

Example
Asha is getting working tax credit (WTC) and HB. She moves to a different flat. Because this is in the same local authority area, she does not need to make a new HB claim and both her HB and WTC continue. Asha moves again, this time to a property in a different local authority area. Her current HB claim comes to an end. Asha is not in 'specified' or 'temporary' accommodation, and is not prevented from claiming UC and so cannot make a new claim for HB. Instead, she claims UC. She has now transferred to UC via natural migration, and her entitlement to WTC also comes to an end.

Note:
- A change in your circumstances does not, in itself, mean you transfer to UC. You must make a claim for UC for this to happen. Some claimants have been wrongly told that they must claim UC, or had appointments arranged by their local job centre or local authority to arrange a transfer to UC following a change in their circumstances, even though the change does not require them to claim UC. If this happens to you, do not claim UC unless you are sure you want to.
- Depending on your circumstances, you can be worse off after you transfer to UC via natural migration. This because there is no transitional protection included in your UC maximum amount that ensures that the amount of your UC is not less than the amount you were getting on your old means-tested benefits and tax credits. You are particularly likely to be worse off if you or a member of your family have a disability, as UC does not include the same disability additions as the legacy benefits.
- Rules preventing severely disabled people from transferring to UC via natural migration (see p23) were introduced following a High Court decision (upheld by the Court of Appeal) which held that the lack of transitional protection for severely disabled claimants who moved house and then lost out after claiming

UC was unlawful.[19] Further court decisions about the lack of transitional protection in other situations may follow. See AskCPAG.org.uk and CPAG's *Welfare Rights Bulletin* for updates.

People who are severely disabled

Between 16 January 2019 and 26 January 2021 inclusive, you are prevented from transferring to UC via natural migration if you (or, if you are in a couple, your partner) are severely disabled and are prevented from claiming UC (see p23). If, however, you have transferred to UC via natural migration and you or your partner were entitled to the severe disability premium (see p346) in your previous award of income support (IS), income-based jobseeker's allowance (JSA) or income-related ESA, you may be entitled to an additional amount of UC. This is called a 'transitional SDP amount'. This could apply where, for example, you claimed UC before 16 January 2019. **Note:** in some cases where you should have been prevented from transferring to UC but were 'inadvertently' or 'incorrectly' allowed to claim it, the DWP may, instead of paying a transitional SDP amount, stop your UC and reinstate your old legacy benefits (see p23).

You are entitled to a transitional SDP amount if:[20]

- you (or your partner where you get UC as a couple) claimed UC and within the month before your UC entitlement started, you (or your partner where you get UC as a couple) were entitled to IS, income-based JSA or income-related ESA that included the severe disability premium. If your benefit stopped during the month, you must have continued to satisfy the conditions for the severe disability premium; *and*
- your award of UC has continued (and since claiming UC you have not become, or stopped being, a member of a couple); *and*
- you (or your partner) still get a 'qualifying benefit' for the severe disability premium (see p346); *and*
- no one has become your carer (or your partner's carer if the severe disability premium was paid to your partner), or a carer for both you and your partner if both of you were entitled to the severe disability premium).

Once you are entitled to a transitional SDP amount under the rules above, it continues to be included in your UC even if (for example) you stop getting a 'qualifying benefit' or someone becomes a carer for you. However, if your UC award ends (including if this is because you become or stop being a member of a couple), you cannot get a transitional SDP amount in any subsequent award.[21]

You cannot get a transitional SDP amount if you were only entitled to HB, even if this included a severe disability premium.

The DWP can decide to pay you either in a lump sum or in monthly payments. It is likely to pay any arrears as a lump sum and then ongoing payments monthly. If you get a lump sum, it is disregarded as capital for your UC while you remain entitled to UC, or for 12 months if that is longer.

Part 2: Universal credit
Chapter 2: The introduction of universal credit
3. Transferring to universal credit

The amount for each UC monthly assessment period is:[22]

- if you are a single claimant, £120 if the limited capability for work-related activity element (see p72) is included in your UC, or £285 if it is not;
- if you are in a joint claim, £405 if the severe disability premium was payable at the couple rate (see p347) and no one has since become entitled to carer's allowance (CA) or the UC carer element for you or your partner;
- if you are in a joint claim, £120 if a limited capability for work-related activity element is included in your UC and either the severe disability premium was *not* payable at the couple rate, or it was but someone has since become entitled to CA or the UC carer element for you or your partner;
- if you are in a joint claim, £285 if the £405 rate does not apply and there is no limited capability for work-related activity element included in your UC.

Note:
- If you start to get the limited capability for work-related activity element, the amount of the payment changes to £120 unless it is already £405.
- In the future, the DWP will 'convert' your transitional SDP amount so that, instead of being a separate additional payment of UC, it becomes part of your maximum amount of UC. When this happens, it will be treated as if it were a transitional element (see p77). This means that, from that point, the amount can be reduced – eg, by an increase in your income.[23] No date for this conversion has yet been set.

Managed migration

From November 2020, the DWP is expected to start transferring people who are still getting the legacy means-tested benefits and tax credits to UC. Before then, the DWP is testing this process in up to 10,000 cases. The DWP calls this process 'managed migration'. **Note:** in late March 2020, the testing of managed migration was suspended due to the coronavirus pandemic.

Note: if you are transferred to UC under the managed migration process and the amount of your UC is less than the amount you were getting on your means-tested benefits and tax credits, you are entitled to a 'transitional element' in your UC (see p77).

- The DWP begins the managed migration process by sending you (and your partner, if you are in a couple) a 'migration notice'.[24] This tells you that your means-tested benefit or tax credit award will end on your 'migration day', and invites you to make a claim for UC instead.
- When you are sent the migration notice, you become a 'notified person'.[25]
- You are given a date by when you must make your UC claim. This is your 'deadline day'. This day must be at least three months from the date of your migration notice. You can be given longer to make your claim if the DWP agrees that there is a good reason – eg, if you are unwell or need to arrange help in order to make your claim.[26]

- The DWP can cancel your migration notice – eg, if it was sent in error or if this is considered necessary to protect your interests.[27]
- If you have not claimed UC by your deadline day, but you do so within a month of that day (ie, by your 'final deadline'), you will still have claimed in time to get a transitional element in your UC.[28]

You have no choice about being affected by managed migration. You are affected when you are sent your 'migration notice'.

You have made your claim for UC when you submit it – ie, in most cases, when you have completed and submitted the online claim form. This establishes the date of your claim (see p47). After you claim, you are likely to be required to provide further information (eg, about your identity or income), usually at an interview (see p1174). If you do not provide the information within the time allowed (you should be given at least a month, but can be given longer), the DWP is likely to decide that you are not entitled to UC and say that your claim has been 'closed' (see p45). Although you can challenge this decision, unless it is changed you are not entitled to a transitional element as you have been refused UC. If you make another claim before your final deadline and are awarded UC, the rules say that you cannot get a transitional element included, although it is not clear whether this is the official intention.[29]

Your entitlement to your old means-tested benefits and tax credits ends when you claim UC or (except in the testing period – see the box below), if you do not claim, on the day before your deadline day.[30] Your HB continues for the first two weeks of your UC claim (see p220). If you transfer on or after 22 July 2020, your IS, income-based JSA and income-related ESA continue for the first two weeks of your UC claim (see p25). If you are transferred as part of the testing process before then, you may be entitled to a hardship payment instead (see p1219).

When you make your claim for UC, you are not automatically entitled – you must still satisfy the usual rules of entitlement (see Chapter 3). However, there are exceptions to this under the managed migration rules.[31]

- If you are a student when your old means-tested benefits and tax credits end, you can get UC even if you are in full-time education – you do not have to satisfy the usual rule about not 'receiving education' (see p880).
- If you are entitled to tax credits when you claim UC and have capital of over £16,000, the capital above £16,000 is ignored when calculating your entitlement to UC. This is called a 'transitional capital disregard' and can apply for up to 12 months beginning with your first month on UC.

Have you been sent a migration notice?

If you have been sent a migration notice by the DWP, you are affected by managed migration. Note the following.

1. There is no choice about being affected. However, in the testing period involving the first 10,000 cases the DWP has said that, in practice, your old means-tested benefits and tax credits will not end unless you decide to claim UC. Get advice if this affects you.

Part 2: Universal credit
Chapter 2: The introduction of universal credit
4. Change of circumstances

2. If you need more time to claim UC than you have been given (eg, because you are unwell or need help with the online claim), contact the DWP and explain this.

3. If you are vulnerable because of your health, or have complex needs (eg, because you are homeless), the DWP should consider extending the deadline for your claim.

4. If you would be worse off on UC, you should be protected by a transitional element in your UC, provided you claim UC within the time allowed and later supply any further information required. If you claim UC outside the time limit, you will not have transferred to UC under the managed migration rules and are not entitled to this element.

5. If you submit your claim in time but then fail to supply any further information that is required, the DWP is likely to regard this as a 'failed claim' and then say that your claim is 'closed'. This means that you have been refused UC. You can challenge the decision to 'close' your claim (see p45). You could try making another claim before your final deadline, but the DWP may still refuse to award you a transitional element.

6. If you are awarded UC but are in financial difficulty while waiting to be paid, you can apply for an advance of UC (see p1192).

4. **Change of circumstances**

Generally, once you have claimed and are entitled to universal credit (UC), you remain under the UC system. So, provided you continue to satisfy the general rules of entitlement (see p36), you continue to get UC, even if your circumstances change – eg, you have a child or you become ill.[32] There are different rules for couples (see below).

If you stop being entitled to UC, you cannot usually make a new claim for any of the old means-tested benefits and tax credits (see p24). If your UC ended but you may now be entitled again, unless the rules about couples apply, to get UC again you must reapply for it. If it is less then six months since your award ended, you can reclaim by logging back into your UC online account. This 'rapid reclaim' allows you to reclaim more quickly (see p44 for more details).

Couples

If you were getting UC as a single person but then become part of a couple, you should report this change. You continue to come under the UC system as a couple with your new partner without having to make a new claim, and you continue to get UC provided you still satisfy the basic rules.[33] If your new partner is getting pension credit (PC), see p33.

If your partner was not entitled to UC as a single person, any award s/he has of income support (IS), income-based jobseeker's allowance, income-related employment and support allowance, housing benefit (HB) (except for 'specified' or 'temporary' accommodation – see p174), child tax credit (CTC) or working tax credit stops and you are treated as claiming UC as a couple.[34] If your partner was entitled to UC as a single person, you are entitled to UC as a couple without having to make a claim.[35] **Note:** as you do not have to make a new claim for UC in these situations, the rules preventing a new claim for UC by a severely disabled person (see p23) do not apply.[36]

Example

Gareth has been entitled to UC as a single person since April 2018. He meets Jane and moves in with her in August 2020. Jane has a two-year-old son and has been getting IS as a lone parent, together with CTC and HB. She is severely disabled and is getting a severe disability premium in her benefit. Gareth and Jane now come under the UC system as a couple. They satisfy the basic rules of entitlement for UC as a couple, and are therefore entitled to UC without having to make a new claim. Jane's awards of IS, CTC and HB end.

If your new partner is getting PC, you are treated as having made a joint claim for UC and your partner's PC stops.[37] You do not need to make a new claim for UC. From 15 May 2019, if only one of you is under pension age, you cannot usually make a new claim for PC (see p271 for details).

If you were claiming UC as a couple but then separate from your partner, you should report the change. Both you and your ex-partner can stay on UC as single claimants without having to make new claims, and you both keep your existing UC assessment period (see p39 for what this is).[38]

Example

Rose and Nelson were entitled to UC as joint claimants. They separate and Nelson notifies the DWP of the fact that they are no longer a couple. Both Nelson and Rose can be entitled to UC as single people and do not need to make new claims. The date they are paid their UC remains as it was when they were a couple.

Notes

2. The universal credit system

1 Art 3(3) and Sch 5 WRA(No.9)O, as applied in UC areas by subsequent commencement orders
2 Art 4(11) WRA 2012(No.32)O
3 Reg 4 UC(TP) Regs
4 Reg 4A UC(TP) Regs
5 Explanatory Memorandum to the Universal Credit (Managed Migration Pilot and Miscellaneous Amendments) Regulations 2019, No.1152
6 HB Memo A1/19 para 7.51; freedom of information request and answer FOI2020/01998, 'Severe Disability Premium' (7 February 2020), DWP; Housing Benefit Adjudication Circular A3/2020, updated 28 February 2020
7 The basic rules are in Art 6 (11) WRA(No.21)O and Art 7 WRA(No.23)O, as applied in subsequent commencement orders
8 Art 5A WRA(No.9)O, Art 6(11) WRA(No.21)O and Art 7 (2) WRA(No.23)O, as applied in subsequent commencement orders
9 Art 6(4) WRA(No.21)O and Art 7(5) WRA(No.23)O, as applied in subsequent commencement orders
10 Art 5A WRA(No.9)O and Art 7 WRA(No.23)O, as applied in subsequent commencement orders
11 Regs 5, 6, 8, 46 and 47 UC(TP) Regs
12 Art 4 WRA(No.9)O; regs 46 and 47 UC(TP) Regs
13 Art 4 WRA(No.9)O; regs 46 and 47 UC(TP) Regs
14 Reg 8 UC(TP) Regs
15 Reg 5 UC(TP) Regs
16 These benefits are not abolished under the UC system and can be claimed under the JSA Regs 2013 and the ESA Regs 2013.
17 Art 6 WRA(No.9)O; Vol V8 para V8100 ADM
18 *LH v SSWP (ESA)* [2014] UKUT 480 (AAC), reported as [2015] AACR 14

3. Transferring to universal credit

19 *TP and AR v SSWP* [2018] EWHC 1474 (Admin), upheld in *R (TP, AR & SXC) v SSWP* [2020] ECA Civ 37
20 Reg 63 and Sch 2 UC(TP) Regs
21 Memo ADM 15/19, para 18
22 Sch 2 para 2 UC(TP) Regs
23 Reg 63(5)-(8) UC(TP) Regs
24 Reg 44 UC(TP) Regs
25 Reg 44(6) UC(TP) Regs
26 Regs 44(1)(b) and 45 UC(TP) Regs
27 Reg 44(5) UC(TP) Regs
28 Regs 46(4) and 48 UC(TP) Regs
29 Reg 57 UC(TP) Regs; The Universal Credit (Managed Migration) Regulations 2018 (draft); *Draft Universal Credit (Managed Migration) Regulations 2018: SSAC report and government statement*, November 2018, p14
30 Regs 46, 48 and 49 UC(TP) Regs
31 Regs 51 and 60 UC (TP) Regs

4. Change of circumstances

32 A change does not automatically bring UC entitlement to an end, and instead the award can be adjusted to reflect the new circumstances.
33 Reg 9(7) and (8) UC,PIP,JSA&ESA(C&P) Regs
34 Regs 5, 7 and 12A UC(TP) Regs; reg 9(8) UC,PIP,JSA&ESA(C&P) Regs
35 Reg 9(7) UC,PIP,JSA&ESA(C&P) Regs; paras M4051-60 ADM
36 Memo ADM 01/19
37 Reg 9(8) UC,PIP,JSA&ESA(C&P) Regs; reg 5 UC(TP) Regs
38 Reg 9(6) UC,PIP,JSA&ESA(C&P) Regs

Chapter 3

Universal credit

This chapter covers:
1. Who can get universal credit (p36)
2. The rules about your age (p37)
3. People included in the claim (p38)
4. The amount of benefit (p39)
5. Special benefit rules (p44)
6. Claims and backdating (p44)
7. Getting paid (p49)
8. Tax, other benefits and the benefit cap (p54)

Key facts
- Universal credit (UC) is a benefit for people on a low income who are in or out of work.
- UC replaces income support, income-based jobseeker's allowance, income-related employment and support allowance, housing benefit, child tax credit and working tax credit.
- UC has been introduced nationwide for most new claimants.
- UC is a means-tested benefit.
- You do not have to have paid national insurance contributions to qualify.
- UC can be paid in addition to non-means-tested benefits, but some of these are taken into account as income when calculating your UC.
- A benefit cap may be applied if the total amount of certain benefits you receive exceeds a specified amount, and your UC can be reduced.
- UC is administered and paid by the DWP.
- If you disagree with a UC decision, you can apply for a revision or supersession (see Chapter 56), or appeal against it (see Chapter 57). You must apply for a mandatory reconsideration before you can appeal.

1. **Who can get universal credit**

You qualify for universal credit (UC) if you (and your partner if you are in a couple):

- satisfy the **'basic conditions'** – ie:[1]
  - you are aged 18 or over and under pension age (see p779). **Note:** some 16/17-year-olds can get UC (see p37); *and*
  - you are not 'receiving education', although there are some exceptions (see p37); *and*
  - you satisfy the 'habitual residence' and the 'right to reside' tests (see Chapter 68), and you are in, or treated as in, Great Britain (see Chapters 68 and 69); *and*
  - you are not a 'person subject to immigration control' (see p1559); *and*
  - you have accepted a 'claimant commitment' (see p1047). This is an agreement that you will meet certain requirements.[2] In particular, the claimant commitment includes the work-related requirements you normally must meet, which may include attending work-focused interviews, work preparation, work search and work availability; *and*
- satisfy the **'financial conditions'** – ie:[3]
  - your income is not too high; *and*
  - your savings and other capital are £16,000 or less. If you transfer to UC from tax credits under the 'managed migration' process and have capital of over £16,000, that excess capital is ignored for UC for up to 12 months (see p27).

Note: you are prevented from claiming UC in certain circumstances, in particular until 27 January 2021 if you are entitled to a severe disability premium in your means-tested benefit and are not yet affected by the 'managed migration' process (see p23 for details).

Couples

If you are a member of a couple (see p57), you must usually make a joint claim. Both of you must satisfy the above conditions of entitlement (and your income and capital are assessed jointly).[4]

Both of you do *not* need to meet all the basic conditions if one of you is:[5]

- over pension age; *or*
- 'receiving education' (but see p37 if one of you is aged 16 or 17).

If you are a member of a couple and one of you does not satisfy the conditions for UC, you may be able to claim as a single person. If so, your UC amounts are for a single person, but your income and capital are still assessed jointly. You can claim as a single person if your partner is:[6]

- aged 16 or 17 and is not someone who can get UC as an under-18-year-old (see below for who can); *or*
- not in (or treated as in) Great Britain, including if s/he has failed the habitual residence or right to reside test (see Chapter 68); *or*
- a 'person subject to immigration control' (see Chapter 67); *or*
- a prisoner or serving a sentence while detained in hospital, or is a member of a religious order and is fully maintained by the order.

You can also claim as a single person if you are in a polygamous marriage and:[7]
- your spouse is still married to someone else from an earlier marriage; *and*
- the other person in the earlier marriage is still living in the same household as your spouse.

Receiving education

In general, you cannot claim UC if you are 'receiving education'. The basic rule is that if you are a qualifying young person (see p62) or undertaking full-time education, study or training, you are regarded as 'receiving education'.[8] There are exceptions – eg, if you have a child or a disability, are on a traineeship, or are without parental support. For full details, see Chapter 41. **Note:** if you are transferred from a means-tested benefit or tax credits to UC under the 'managed migration' process (see p30), you can claim UC, even though you do not satisfy the basic rules because you are in full-time education (see p30).

If you are a member of a couple making a joint claim and one of you is receiving education (and not eligible for UC) but the other is not, you may still be entitled to UC as a couple (see p36).

2. The rules about your age

In most cases, you (and your partner if you are making a joint claim) must be 18 or over to claim universal credit (UC). However, some 16/17-year-olds can claim UC (see below).[9]

You must be under pension age (see p779).[10] If you are in a couple, at least one of you must be under pension age. If one of you has reached pension age, this is sometimes called being in a 'mixed-age couple'.

16/17-year-olds

You must normally be at least 18 years old to qualify for UC. If you are aged 16 or 17, you can get UC if one of the following applies.[11]
- You have limited capability for work, or you have submitted and are covered by a medical certificate saying you are not fit for work and you are waiting for an assessment of your capability for work.

- You have 'regular and substantial caring responsibilities for a severely disabled person' – ie, you meet the conditions of entitlement to carer's allowance (CA) (see Chapter 26), or would do but for the fact that your earnings are too high.[12] This does not apply if you receive earnings from those caring responsiblities. You do not have to claim CA. **Note:** you do not qualify under this rule if you were previously being looked after by a local authority (see p948).
- You are responsible for a child aged under 16 (see p63).
- You are a member of a couple and your partner satisfies the basic rules of entitlement for UC and is responsible for a child.
- You are pregnant and there are 11 weeks or less before the week your baby is due. **Note:** you do not qualify under this rule if you were previously being looked after by a local authority (see p948).
- You had a baby (or your baby was stillborn) not more than 15 weeks ago. **Note:** you do not qualify under this rule if you were previously being looked after by a local authority (see p948).
- You are without parental support (including support from someone acting in place of your parent – eg, a foster parent). For these purposes, you are treated as without parental support if you are not being looked after by a local authority, and:[13]
  - you are an orphan – ie, you do not have any parents; *or*
  - you have to live away from your parents because you are estranged from them (see p886 for the meaning) or there is a serious risk to your physical or mental health or you would experience significant harm if you lived with them; *or*
  - you are living away from your parents and they are unable to support you financially because they have a 'physical or mental impairment', or they are in custody, or they are prohibited from entering Great Britain – eg, because of the Immigration Rules.

  Note: you do not qualify under this rule if you were previously being looked after by a local authority (see p948).

Note: if you are a member of a couple and one of you is either 18 or over or satisfies the rules above, but the other does not, the one who is 18 or over or who satisfies the above rules can claim UC as a single person, but the other partner's income and capital are taken into account.[14]

3. **People included in the claim**

If you are single, you claim universal credit (UC) for yourself. If you are a member of a couple, you and your partner must usually make a joint claim for UC (see p45).[15] See p57 for who counts as a couple.

Your maximum amount (see Chapter 5), which forms part of the calculation of your benefit, includes elements for a child(ren) for whom you are responsible. **Note:** the number of children included in your maximum amount may be limited to two (see p66).

There are some situations in which you must show that you are 'responsible' for a child – eg:

- in order to take advantage of the special rules to help you meet the claimant responsibilities (see p1050 and p1140);
- so you can benefit from a 'work allowance' when calculating your UC entitlement (see p41);
- for some of the rules for the housing costs element (see Chapter 6).

You can count as responsible for any child under 16 and for any 'qualifying young person' (see p62 for who counts as a child).[16] You do not have to be the child's parent. For when you count as responsible for a child, see p63.

4. The amount of benefit

Universal credit (UC) is a means-tested benefit. The amount of UC you get depends on your needs (your 'maximum amount') and how much income and capital you (and your partner) have. If you are severely disabled and transferred to UC from your old means-tested benefit, you may also get a transitional amount (known as 'transitional SDP amount') to ensure you are not worse off on UC.

The amount you get is calculated over a monthly 'assessment period' (see below). As your income increases, your UC award is reduced.

Assessment period

The '**assessment period**' is one calendar month, beginning with the first date of entitlement to UC.[17] Each subsequent assessment period (ie, a calendar month) usually begins on the same day of the month, except if:

– the first day of entitlement to UC falls on the 31st of the month, in which case each assessment period begins on the last day of the month;

– the first day of entitlement to UC falls on the 29th or 30th of the month, in which case each assessment period begins on the 29th or 30th. In February, it begins on the 27th (or in a leap year, on the 28th);

– your entitlement has started before the actual date of claim because of the backdating rules, in which case the first assessment period begins on the first day of entitlement and ends on the day before the date of claim;

– your first date of entitlement is changed, in which case the first assessment period is changed, but your other assessment periods still begin and end as they did originally.

Examples
Carmen claims UC on 31 July. She is making a new claim as a single person. Her first monthly assessment period is from 31 July until 30 August inclusive. Her next assessment period begins on 31 August, and the one after that begins on 30 September.

Kobe claims UC on 2 November. His first assessment period is set to begin on 2 November, but he requests that his claim be backdated to 26 October as his disability meant he could not claim earlier, and this is accepted. Kobe's first assessment period now begins on 26 October and ends on 1 November, his second assessment period begins on 2 November, with all subsequent assessment periods beginning on the second day of the month.

Working out your universal credit

Your UC is worked out in the following way.
- **Step one:** calculate your maximum amount. See Chapter 5 for details of this.
- **Step two:** work out your earnings and check whether any can be ignored.
- **Step three:** work out your other income and how much can be ignored.
- **Step four:** calculate your total income.
- **Step five:** calculate your UC entitlement.

Step one: calculate your maximum amount
Your maximum monthly UC is made up of the total of:[18]
- a standard allowance – for a single claimant or a couple (see p66);
- a child element for each child, with an increase for a disabled or severely disabled child (see p66). **Note:** the number of children for whom you can get a child element may be limited to two;
- a limited capability for work element, if you can still get it (see p70), or a limited capability for work-related activity element (p72) for an adult with ill health or disability. The limited capability for work element was abolished for new claims made on or after 3 April 2017 (see p70);
- a carer element for someone looking after a severely disabled person (see p73);
- a housing costs element for people paying rent or service charges (see Chapter 6). **Note:** you cannot get UC for help with your mortgage or loan for repairs and improvements. Instead, the DWP may offer you a loan to help meet your mortgage interest payments (see p855);
- a childcare costs element (see p74);
- a transitional element – if you transfer to UC from the old means-tested benefits and tax credits under the 'managed migration' process (see p30) and your UC is worth less than your old benefits (see p77).

Example

Gail and Joe are a couple both aged over 25. They claim UC in May 2020. They have two children born after 6 April 2017. Gail works; Joe is ill and has limited capability for work and work-related activity. They do not have housing or childcare costs.

Gail and Joe's maximum amount for UC is calculated as follows:

Standard allowance	£594.04
Child element (first child)	£235.83
Child element (second child)	£235.83
Limited capability for work-related activity element	£341.92
Total	**£1,407.62**

Step two: work out your earnings and how much can be ignored

See Chapter 7 for how to work out your earnings.

Once you have established your earnings, check whether any can be ignored when calculating your UC. This is done by comparing your earnings with a set amount, called a 'work allowance' (see below).

If your earnings do not exceed the work allowance, they are all ignored. If your earnings are more than your work allowance, 63 per cent of the excess is taken into account as income.[19] You are only entitled to a work allowance if certain circumstances apply. If no work allowance applies to you, 63 per cent of all your earnings are taken into account.

The way your earnings reduce the amount of your UC is sometimes called the **'taper'** – ie, the rate at which your UC tapers away as your earnings increase. As your earnings rise above any that are ignored, your UC reduces by 63 pence for every extra pound you earn.

The work allowance

A work allowance only applies if you (or your partner) are responsible for a child or have limited capability for work.[20]

The amount of the allowance depends on whether your UC includes a housing costs element. Only one work allowance can apply.

Note: if you are entitled to UC but also get housing benefit because you are in temporary accommodation, your UC is treated as if it includes a housing costs element.[21]

Amount of the work allowance

UC includes a housing costs element	£292
UC does not include a housing costs element	£512

Examples

Anne is a lone parent with a child aged six. She rents her home and is entitled to a housing costs element in her UC. She has a part-time job from which her earnings for UC over her assessment period are £350.

Because Anne has a child, a work allowance applies and so some of her earnings can be ignored. Anne's UC includes a housing costs element, so her work allowance is £292. Anne's earnings exceed her work allowance by £58 (£350 – £292). Sixty-three per cent of this excess is £36.54. Therefore, £36.54 of Anne's earnings is taken into account when calculating her UC.

Gail and Joe are a couple with two children. They are not entitled to a housing costs element in their UC. Gail has earnings from work. Joe is ill and has limited capability for work and work-related activity. Gail's earnings for UC over their assessment period are £1,200.

Because they have children and also because Joe has limited capability for work, a work allowance applies and some of Gail's earnings can be ignored. Their UC does not include a housing costs element, so the work allowance is £512. Gail's earnings exceed the work allowance by £688 (£1,200 – £512). Sixty-three per cent of this excess is £433.44. So £433.44 of Gail and Joe's earnings is taken into account when calculating their UC.

Step three: work out your other income and how much can be ignored

See Chapter 7 for how to work out your other income and how much can be ignored.

If you have other income (eg, other benefits), unless it is ignored, it affects your UC by reducing it pound for pound. This is in addition to any reductions from your earnings.

Income from capital

If you and your partner have more than £16,000 capital, you cannot get UC. An exception applies if you are transferred to UC from tax credits under the 'managed migration' process (see p27). If your capital is more than £6,000 but £16,000 or less, you count as having an income of £4.35 a month for every £250, or part of £250, over £6,000.[22] This assumed monthly income is sometimes referred to as 'tariff income'.

For how to calculate your capital, including assumed monthly income, see Chapter 8.

Step four: calculate your total income

Add together the income that is to be taken into account under Steps two and three.

Step five: calculate your universal credit entitlement

Deduct your total income to be taken into account (Step four) from your maximum UC (Step one).

Note: if you are not entitled to UC under these steps because your maximum UC does not yet include the limited capability for work-related activity element as you are still in the three-month waiting period (see p72), you are entitled to UC at the minimum amount of one pence.[23]

If you transferred from your old means-tested benefits and tax credits to UC under 'natural migration' and are entitled to a 'transitional SDP amount' (see p29), this is added to your overall entitlement, as an additional amount of UC.

Example

Gail and Joe are a couple both aged over 25, with two children. Gail works and earns £1,200 in their monthly assessment period. Joe is ill and has limited capability for work and work-related activity. He gets fortnightly payments of contributory employment and support allowance (ESA) of £227.10. For UC purposes, this is converted to a monthly figure of £492.05. They do not have housing costs or childcare costs included in their UC. They have savings of £5,000.

Their total income to be taken into account under Step four is £433.44 in earnings, plus £492.05 contributory ESA during their monthly assessment period = £925.49

Their maximum UC under Step one = £1,407.62

Their monthly UC entitlement = £1,407.62 – £925.49 = £395.46

Transitional protection

From some point, currently expected to be from November 2020 in most cases, claimants with existing awards of means-tested benefits and tax credits will begin to be transferred to UC under the DWP's 'managed migration' process (see p30). This process is currently being tested in up to 10,000 cases. If you are transferred to UC in this way and your UC maximum amount would be less than the amount you were getting on your previous benefit, a 'transitional element' is included in your UC maximum amount (see p77).

Transitional protection only applies if you transfer to UC under the 'managed migration' process. It does not apply if you claim UC after a change of circumstances and transfer under the 'natural migration' process. So you could find that if you claim UC, it is worth less than the means-tested benefits or tax credits you were getting previously.

5. **Special benefit rules**

Special rules may apply to:
- 16/17-year-olds (see p37);
- people subject to immigration control (see Chapter 67);
- people who have come from or are going abroad (see Chapters 68 and 69);
- people who are studying (see Chapter 41);
- people in prison or detention (see Chapter 42).

6. **Claims and backdating**

The general rules about claims and backdating are covered in Chapter 50. This section explains the specific rules that apply to universal credit (UC).

You can usually make a new claim for UC whenever you want. However, claims for UC are prevented in some circumstances. In particular, until 27 January 2021 some severely disabled people are prevented from making a new claim for UC until they are affected by the 'managed migration' process (see p23). Claiming UC brings you under the UC system (see p23).

Making a claim

Claims for UC must be made at gov.uk/apply-universal-credit. If you need help claiming online, you can call the UC helpline, free of charge, on 0800 328 5644 (textphone: 0800 328 1344, Welsh language: 0800 328 1744, or if you cannot speak or hear on the phone Relay UK 18001 then 0800 328 5644, Monday to Friday 8am to 6pm). The DWP adviser can complete an online form on your behalf or arrange for you to be helped at your local job centre. Alternatively, your local Citizens Advice office can help you make a claim.

A claim can be made by telephone if the DWP allows it.[24] In exceptional circumstances, if you are unable to use either a computer or a telephone, the DWP may make a home visit to help you claim, but you should not rely on this.

You can amend or withdraw your claim before a decision is made (see p1169). If you are in financial need while waiting to be paid, you may be able to get an advance payment of UC (see p1192).

> *Forms*
> There are no paper claim forms for UC. The claim form is only available online.

If you were previously getting UC and it is less than six months since your award ended, you can reclaim by logging onto your online UC account. This usually allows you to reclaim more quickly, and you have the same assessment payment as previously. If you are reclaiming after stopping work, you are only paid in full for the whole of the first assessment period if you reclaim within seven days of your job ending, although you can be allowed longer if you have a 'good reason' for not reclaiming within this time.[25]

Note: if you are transferring to UC from the old means-tested benefits and tax credits under the 'managed migration' process, some special rules about claiming UC apply (see p27).

When you do not need to make a claim

You do not need to make a new claim (and you keep the same assessment period as before) if you have previously claimed UC and:[26]

- you were entitled to UC as a single claimant and you are now part of a couple and your partner was also entitled to UC as a single claimant. Although you do not need to make a new joint claim, you must tell the DWP that you are now part of a couple; or
- you are now a member of a couple and either you or your partner (but not both of you) were entitled to UC as a single claimant and that award has now been terminated; or
- you were a member of a couple making a joint claim but have now ceased to be a couple (but you must tell the DWP that you are now single or are a member of a new couple).

Who should claim

If you are single, you claim on your own behalf as a single person. If you are a member of a couple, you must normally make a joint claim with your partner.[27] For when you count as a couple, see p38. If you are a member of a couple and one of you does not satisfy the conditions for UC, you can claim as a single person (although your income and capital are assessed jointly with your partner) in certain circumstances (see p36). The DWP treats your joint claim as one made by a single person.[28]

If you are unable to manage your own affairs, another person can claim UC for you as your 'appointee' (see p1170).[29]

Information to support your claim

For the general information requirements that apply to all benefits, see p1170.

The DWP asks you to have certain information to hand when making your online claim. This includes:

- your bank, building society or credit union account details;
- the type of accommodation you have (eg, whether you are a private tenant, council tenant, housing association tenant or home owner) and your landlord's details, if you have one;
- an email address;

- your national insurance (NI) number (if you do not have an NI number, you will satisfy the NI number requirement if you have applied for one – see p1171);
- information about your housing – eg, how much rent you pay;
- details of your income – eg, recent payslips and any other benefits you are getting;
- details of savings and any investments – eg, shares or a property that you rent to others;
- details of how much you pay for childcare if you want help with your childcare costs included in your UC;
- proof of your identity – eg, a driving licence, passport, or a debit or credit card.

It is important that you provide any information required when you claim. Until you do, you may not count as having made a valid claim (see p1172). Your claim is valid if you provide the information requested on the online claim form.[30] In practice, in most cases if you have completed the online form and submitted it you will have made a valid claim. You are then usually asked to provide further information or evidence (eg, about your identity, or payslips, your rent agreement and bank statements). During the coronavirus pandemic, this will usually be online by telephone rather than at your local job centre.

If you do not comply, the DWP is likely to say that you have made a 'failed claim' and that your claim has been 'closed'. You should comply if you can. If you cannot, tell the DWP in advance. If your claim is closed, you should be given a decision about this.

Has your claim been closed?

If you are told that your claim has been closed, do the following.

1. If you can still access your online journal, use it to challenge the decision to close your claim. Download any documents and take screenshots of the decision to close your claim and of your challenge to that decision, then make a new claim for UC as soon as possible. You will get a new online journal for your new claim, but may lose access to your old journal.

2. If you do not have access to your online journal, make a new claim for UC. You can then challenge the decision to close your claim on your new online journal.

3. There is nothing in the law about 'closing' a claim. What has actually happened is that the DWP has made a decision that you are not entitled to UC. Arguably, the law does not say that you cannot be entitled to UC merely because you have not attended the interview.[31] So you may be able to argue that there is no basis for deciding that you were not entitled to UC. In any case, you must have been given at least a month to attend, or longer if considered reasonable.[32] The most common reason for a decision that you are not entitled to UC having failed to attend the interview is because there is a doubt about your identity. If this is not in doubt (eg, if the DWP has accepted proof of your identity for your subsequent claim), you could argue that the decision to close your earlier claim

should now be changed. See AskCPAG.org.uk for a useful tool for challenging a decision to 'close' your claim.

If you are working for an employer, the DWP uses a 'real-time information system' to obtain information about your earnings. Your employer is required to send information to HM Revenue and Customs every time your wages are paid.

You may also be asked to provide information after you are awarded UC, and if you fail to do so, your UC could be suspended or even terminated (see p1200).

The date of your claim

The date of your claim is important as it determines when your entitlement to UC starts. This is not necessarily the date from when you are paid. For information about when payment of UC starts, see p49.

Your **'date of claim'** is usually the date on which your online claim is received by the DWP.[33] If you received help from the DWP (or someone providing services to the DWP) with making your claim before you claimed online, your date of claim is the date you notified the DWP that you needed help. **Note:** the DWP does not accept that this applies if you get help from a Citizens Advice office.

If you claim by telephone, your date of claim is the date on which the claim is 'properly completed', or earlier if you previously notified your intention to claim and the claim is made within a month of that. If you had to delay completing your online claim before submitting it (eg, in order to obtain some of the required information), you may be able to argue that your date of claim should be when you started completing the online form. See AskCPAG.org.uk for a useful tool for challenging a decision about this.

Note: if a claim is considered 'defective', you are given a short time to correct the defects (see p1173). If you do, your claim is treated as having been made when you initially claimed.[34] In practice, however, very few UC claims are actually defective because without the required information on the online form, it is not possible to complete the claim. Instead, your claim is valid if you have been able to submit the online claim form, although you are also usually asked to provide further information or evidence in order to be entitled to UC (see p1174).

In some cases, you can claim in advance (see p48) and in some cases your claim can be backdated (see below). If you want this to be done, make this clear when you claim or the DWP might not consider it.

Backdating your claim

A claim for UC can be backdated for a maximum of one month, but only in certain circumstances. If you are making a joint claim, both you and your partner must satisfy one (or more) of these circumstances. Your claim can be backdated if you could not reasonably be expected to have claimed earlier because:[35]

- you were previously getting income support, jobseeker's allowance, employment and support allowance, housing benefit, child tax credit or working tax credit, and you were not notified that your entitlement was going to end before it did; *or*
- you have a disability (the rules do not define this); *or*
- you were unwell and this meant you could not claim online or by telephone on time, and you have now supplied medical evidence showing that you were unwell; *or*
- you could not claim online because of a system failure or planned system maintenance, and you have now claimed on the first day that the system was working; *or*
- you made a joint claim for UC and this was either turned down or awarded but later terminated because your partner did not accept her/his claimant commitment, but you have now ceased to be a couple and you have reclaimed UC as a single person.

Note: if you are transferring to UC from the old means-tested benefits and tax credits under the 'managed migration' process (see p30), but you have missed the 'deadline day' allowed for making a claim for UC, you are treated as having claimed on that day if you claim by your 'final deadline'. You do not have to satisfy the bullet points above. See p30.

If you might have qualified for benefit earlier, but did not claim because you were given the wrong information by the DWP or because you were misled by it, you could ask for compensation (see p1439) or complain to the Ombudsman through your MP (see p1444).

If you claim the wrong benefit

There are no rules for when a claim for another benefit can be treated as a claim for UC. You should claim UC as soon as you can and, if necessary, ask for the claim to be backdated.

Claiming in advance

If you claim UC when you are not yet entitled, but the DWP thinks that you will be entitled within one month of the day you claimed, it can make an advance award. If this applies, your claim is treated as having been made on the first day on which you are entitled to UC.[36] However, the DWP only accepts advance claims in very limited circumstances: from prisoners who are to be released within a month and from care leavers who make their claim one month before their 18th birthday.[37]

7. **Getting paid**

The general rules on getting paid are covered in Chapter 51. This section explains the specific rules that apply to universal credit (UC).

When is universal credit paid?

You are normally paid within seven days of the end of an assessment period. UC is usually paid monthly, in arrears. If you live in Scotland, you can request that you be paid twice monthly.[38] Otherwise, if you find being paid monthly is difficult to budget for, you may be able to request more frequent payments under an 'alternative payment arrangement' (see p50).

Your award is assessed over an 'assessment period' of one calendar month, beginning from the date your entitlement starts (see p39).[39] UC should normally be paid directly into your account within seven days of the last day of the monthly assessment period or, if this is not possible, 'as soon as reasonably practicable' thereafter.[40]

Your online UC account should show when you will get your first payment of UC. In practice, you can expect to get your first payment about five weeks after claiming (although this may take longer in some cases). If you are in financial need in the meantime, or if there is a delay in subsequent payments, you may be able to get an advance payment of UC (see p1192). The advance must be repaid. Otherwise, you may be able to get help from your local authority (see p861).

Couples can decide which partner is paid. The DWP can decide that the other partner should be paid instead or can split the payments between you if it considers it to be in your interests, the interests of a child for whom you are responsible (see p63), or in the interests of a severely disabled person and your UC includes a carer element (see p73).[41] Couples with children making a new claim are guided to use the bank account of the main carer for their UC payments.

If you need a loan for an item you cannot afford, you can ask for a budgeting advance of UC (see p51).

Your UC can be paid in whole or in part to another person on your behalf, if the DWP considers this is necessary to protect your interests, or those of your partner, a child for whom you are responsible (see p63), or a severely disabled person and your UC includes a carer element (p73).[42]

The housing costs element to cover your rent is normally paid to you, rather than your landlord, unless paying your landlord would be in your interest. Official guidance says that your landlord can request that payment be made to her/him, and this will be granted automatically if your rent is over two months in arrears.[43] If you live in Scotland, you can request that payment be made directly to your landlord.[44] Otherwise, you may be able to request payment to your landlord under an 'alternative payment arrangement' (see below).

Note:

- Deductions can be made from your UC to pay third parties (see p1202).
- Your UC might be paid at a reduced rate if you have been sanctioned (see Chapter 47) or committed a benefit offence (see p1278).
- For information on missing payments, see p1189. If you cannot get your UC payments because you have lost your bank or post office card or you have forgotten your PIN, see p1188. If your payment service card is lost or stolen or if you have forgotten your memorable date, see p1189.
- If payment of your UC is delayed, see p1295. If you are waiting for a decision on your claim, or to be paid, you might be able to get an advance (p1192). If you wish to complain about how your claim has been dealt with, or claim compensation, see Chapter 60.
- If payment of your UC is suspended, see p1200.
- If you are overpaid UC, you might have to repay it (see Chapter 53) and, in some circumstances, you may have to pay a penalty (see p1268). If you have been accused of fraud, see Chapter 54.

Alternative payment arrangements

If you find monthly payments difficult to budget for, or if having your UC housing costs element paid to you rather than to your landlord is leading to serious rent arrears, or if you need the payment of your UC to be split between you and your partner, it may be possible to have an alternative payment arrangement. This is discretionary and there is no right of appeal. You must show that you cannot manage the usual payment arrangement and, as a result, there is a risk of financial harm to you or to someone in your family. According to government guidance, the following applies.[45]

- The DWP must be satisfied that alternative payment arrangements should apply, based on your inability to cope with usual payment and on your circumstances. For example, are you managing to pay your bills on time? Can you manage a monthly budget? Are you used to managing money with your partner?
- Alternative payment arrangements are considered in the following order of priority:
  - paying rent directly to your landlord to safeguard your home;
  - more frequent payment – ie, two payments a month, rather than just one. Exceptionally, more frequent payments can be considered;
  - splitting payment between the partners in a couple in specific situations – eg, if one partner is mismanaging the UC award or if there is domestic violence.

- The DWP splits claimants into those with circumstances with a 'high likely need' for alternative payment arrangements and those with 'less likely need'. **You are in high likely need if you:**
  - have drug, alcohol and other addiction problems;
  - have learning difficulties;
  - have severe debt problems;
  - are living in temporary or supported accommodation;
  - are homeless;
  - have experienced domestic violence or abuse;
  - have a mental health condition;
  - are currently in rent arrears or at threat of eviction or repossession;
  - are aged 16 or 17, or have left local authority care;
  - are a family with multiple and complex needs.

  You are in less likely need if you:
  - have third-party deductions in place – eg, for utility arrears;
  - are a refugee or asylum seeker;
  - have a history of rent arrears;
  - were previously homeless or living in supported accommodation;
  - have a physical disability;
  - have just left prison or hospital;
  - are recently beareaved;
  - have problems with language skills;
  - are an ex-servicewoman/man;
  - are not in education, employment or training.

Budgeting advances

Budgeting advances are extra amounts of UC that are intended to help you with expenses – eg, buying essential furniture or household equipment, or expenses related to maternity or getting and keeping a job. Budgeting advances must be repaid, usually by deductions from future payments of your UC and usually over 12 months, although this can be extended by up to six months.[46] They are discretionary. If you are refused a budgeting advance, you do not have a right to appeal against this decision.

If you are awarded a budgeting advance, the DWP must send you notice in writing that you will have it deducted from subsequent payments of your UC and that, if it is not deducted, you must otherwise repay it. The same rules apply to deductions from your UC that apply to the recovery of overpayments on p1248.

To get a budgeting advance:[47]

- you must apply for one; *and*
- you (or your partner if you are a couple) must be getting UC and (unless the expense is 'necessarily related' to employment) have been getting UC or income support (IS), income-based jobseeker's allowance (JSA), income-related

employment and support allowance (ESA) or pension credit (PC) for a continuous period of at least six months when the claim is made; *and*

- if you are not a member of a couple, your earnings from work must not exceed £2,600 in the period covered by the previous six complete monthly assessment periods. If you are a member of a couple, your joint earnings from work must not exceed £3,600 in this period. **Note:** if you are self-employed, your actual earned income is taken into account, not any assumed minimum income under the 'minimum income floor' (see p121); *and*
- there must be no outstanding budgeting advance (ie, which has not yet been recovered) paid to you (or your partner) and the DWP is satisfied that the budgeting advance can reasonably be expected to be recovered, taking into account all your debts and other liabilities.

The minimum amount of a budgeting advance is £100. The maximum payable is:
- if you are single and not responsible for a child, £348;
- if you are in a couple and not responsible for a child, £464;
- if you are responsible for a child and either single or in a couple, £812.

For when you are responsible for a child, see p323.

If your capital (or your joint capital if you are a couple) is over £1,000, the budgeting advance is reduced by the amount the capital exceeds £1,000. For how your capital is calculated, see Chapter 8.

Change of circumstances

You must report changes in your circumstances that you have been told you must report, as well as any that you might reasonably be expected to know might affect your right to, the amount of, or the payment of, your benefit. You should do this as soon as possible. You are usually expected to report a change on your online UC journal. Changes can be reported by telephoning the UC helpline on 0800 328 5644 (textphone: 0800 328 1344, Welsh language: 0800 328 1744, or if you cannot speak or hear on the phone Relay UK 18001 then 0800 328 5644, Monday to Friday 8am to 6pm). However, it is advisable also to report the change on your online journal. See p1199 for further information.

If you become a member of a couple with someone who is not entitled to UC, her/his entitlement to IS, income-based JSA, income-related ESA, HB (except for 'specified' or 'temporary' accommodation – see p174), child tax credit or working tax credit ends (see p32).

If you are working and being taxed through PAYE (pay as you earn), the DWP should get information about changes in your earnings automatically from HM Revenue and Customs through the 'real-time information system'. However, if your employer has not reported your earnings, you should report them yourself. The DWP may specifically require you to do this.[48] Check with your employer that your earnings are being reported as you are paid. If you are self-employed, you must report your earnings every month.

When you notify the DWP of a change of circumstances, the decision on your UC is changed by a supersession of your UC award. This usually takes effect from the first day of the monthly assessment period in which the change occurred, or is expected to occur.[49] So a change that occurs part way through a monthly assessment period can be treated as having occurred on the first day of the period. However, if the change is that you have reached (or will reach) pension age and you have claimed PC in advance (see p279), the supersession takes effect from the day you reach pension age. Other exceptions may apply (see p1320).

Note:

- If you are required by the DWP to report your earnings, you reported them when you were required to do so and your earnings decrease, the supersession takes effect from the first day of the assessment period in which the decrease occurred.[50]

- A change of circumstances which is advantageous to you is only backdated to the start of the assessment period in which it occurred if you report it before the end of that assessment period, unless the time allowed is extended. Otherwise, the change applies from the start of the assessment period in which you reported it. For full details, see p1322.

Examples

Terry, a lone parent with one child (born before 6 April 2017), is entitled to maximum UC of £691.14 a month – ie, a standard allowance of £409.89, plus a child element of £281.25. His assessment period begins on 5 October. Halfway through this assessment period, Terry stops being responsible for a child as his son goes to live with his mother, and so Terry is no longer entitled to the child element. His maximum UC entitlement reduces to £409.89 a month. This change is not advantageous to Terry, but is backdated to the start of the assessment period – ie, to 5 October. This includes a period before he lost entitlement to the child element.

However, Terry is not overpaid UC as he does not get paid until seven days after the end of the assessment period on 4 November. So Terry gets paid just £409.89 for the whole of the assessment period in which the change occurred.

Julie is entitled to maximum UC of £409.89 per month (a standard allowance). Towards the end of her monthly assessment period, she has a child and her maximum UC entitlement increases by £235.83 as it now includes a child element. The change is advantageous to Julie. She reports the change before the end of the assessment period and it is backdated to the start of the assessment period – ie, including a period before she had her child. When Julie gets paid (after the end of the assessment period in which the change occurred), she gets the additional £235.83 for the whole period. If Julie did not report the change until the start of her next assessment period, it may only have applied from the start of that period.

8. Tax, other benefits and the benefit cap

Tax

Universal credit (UC) is not taxable.

Means-tested benefits and tax credits

The general rule is that if you claim UC, you come under the UC system and can no longer get income support (IS), income-based jobseeker's allowance (JSA), income-related employment and support allowance (ESA), child tax credit (CTC) or working tax credit (WTC). You cannot qualify for housing benefit (HB), except if you are living in 'specified' or 'temporary' accommodation (see p174).

If you are in a couple and claim UC, your partner's IS, income-based JSA, income-related ESA, HB, WTC or CTC stops and you get UC as a couple instead (see p32). You cannot get pension credit (PC) at the same time as UC. If one (but not both) of you has reached pension age (ie, the qualifying age for PC) so that you are in a 'mixed-age couple', from 15 May 2019 you cannot usually make a new claim for PC and must claim UC instead. You may still be able to claim PC in certain circumstances (see p271).

Non-means-tested benefits

For the rules on entitlement to national insurance credits for people on UC, see p971.

When you come under the UC system (see p23):
- you can still claim contribution-based JSA or contributory ESA. These are taken into account in full as income for UC (and so reduce your UC entitlement);
- you can claim other non-means-tested benefits at the same time as UC – eg, carer's allowance (CA), child benefit, personal independence payment, statutory sick pay and statutory maternity, adoption, paternity and shared parental pay;
- it can be worth claiming non-means-tested benefits. For example, if you get CA, you may be entitled to a carer element in your UC (see p73). If your child gets disability living allowance, you may be entitled to a disabled child addition (see p66).

For how non-means-tested benefits are treated when working out your income for UC, see Chapter 7.

The benefit cap

In some cases, there is a limit on the total amount of specified benefits you can receive (a 'benefit cap'). UC is one of the specified benefits. The benefit cap only applies if you are getting UC or HB. See p1194 for further information.

Passports and other sources of help

If you are entitled to UC, you may also qualify for health benefits such as free prescriptions (see Chapter 31) and other payments such as free school lunches (see Chapter 40).[51] You may also qualify for social fund payments (see Chapter 37) or, in Scotland, a Best Start grant or funeral support payment (see Chapters 72 and 73), Healthy Start food and vitamins (see p862) or, in Scotland, Best Start foods (see p865), and help from your local welfare assistance scheme (see p861). You may be entitled to a council tax reduction (see p851).

Notes

1. Who can get universal credit
1 ss3 and 4 WRA 2012; reg 9 UC Regs
2 s14 WRA 2012
3 s5 WRA 2012
4 ss3 and 4 WRA 2012
5 Reg 3(2) UC Regs
6 Reg 3(3) UC Regs
7 Reg 3(4) UC Regs
8 Reg 12 UC Regs

2. The rules about your age
9 s4(3) WRA 2012; reg 8 UC Regs
10 s4(4) WRA 2012
11 Reg 8(1) and (2) UC Regs
12 Reg 30 UC Regs
13 Reg 8(3) and (4) UC Regs
14 Reg 3(3) UC Regs

3. People included in the claim
15 s2 WRA 2012
16 s10 WRA 2012

4. The amount of benefit
17 Regs 21 and 21A UC Regs
18 s8 WRA 2012
19 Reg 22 UC Regs
20 Reg 22 UC Regs
21 Reg 5A UC(TP) Regs
22 Regs 18 and 72 UC Regs
23 Reg 28(7) UC Regs

6. Claims and backdating
24 Reg 8 UC,PIP,JSA&ESA(C&P) Regs
25 Regs 21(3C) and 22A UC Regs

26 Reg 9(6)-(8) UC,PIP,JSA&ESA(C&P) Regs; reg 21(3) UC Regs
27 s2 WRA 2012
28 Reg 9 UC,PIP,JSA&ESA(C&P) Regs
29 Reg 51 UC,PIP,JSA&ESA(C&P) Regs
30 Reg 8 UC,PIP,JSA&ESA(C&P) Regs
31 The DWP usually relies on reg 37 UC,PIP,JSA&ESA(C&P) Regs. However, this does not say anything about 'closing' a claim or not being entitled merely for failing to provide the evidence or information.
32 Reg 37(3) UC,PIP,JSA&ESA(C&P) Regs
33 Reg 10 UC,PIP,JSA&ESA(C&P) Regs
34 Reg 10(2) UC,PIP,JSA&ESA(C&P) Regs
35 Reg 26 UC,PIP,JSA&ESA(C&P) Regs, as modified by reg 15 UC(TP) Regs
36 s98 WRA 2012; reg 32 UC,PIP,JSA&ESA(C&P) Regs
37 para A2048 ADM

7. Getting paid
38 Reg 47 UC,PIP,JSA&ESA(C&P) Regs; Universal Credit (Claims and Payments) (Scotland) Regulations 2017, No.227
39 s7 WRA 2012; reg 21 UC Regs
40 Reg 47(2) UC,PIP,JSA&ESA(C&P) Regs
41 Reg 47(6) UC,PIP,JSA&ESA(C&P) Regs
42 Reg 58 UC,PIP,JSA&ESA(C&P) Regs
43 HB Circular A13/2013
44 Universal Credit (Claims and Payments) (Scotland) Regulations 2017, No.227
45 DWP, *Alternative Payment Arrangements*, updated 25 June 2019, available at gov.uk

2

46 DWP, *Universal Credit: debt and
    deductions that can be taken from
    payments*, updated October 2019, at
    gov.uk
47 Regs 12-15 SS(PAB) Regs
48 Reg 61 UC Regs
49 Sch 1 para 20 UC,PIP,JSA&ESA(DA) Regs
50 Sch 1 para 22 UC,PIP,JSA&ESA(DA) Regs

8. Tax, other benefits and the benefit cap
51 Sch 2 para 39 WRA 2012

Chapter 4

People included in the claim

This chapter covers:
1. Couples (below)
2. Children (p62)

This chapter covers the rules for universal credit. For other means-tested benefits, see Chapter 16. For child tax credit, see Chapter 14 and for working tax credit, see Chapter 15.

Key facts

- Your partner and your children can be included in your universal credit (UC) claim.
- You count as a member of a couple if you are married or in a civil partnership and are living with your partner in the same household. You also count as a couple if you are not married or in a civil partnership, but are living with your partner as if you were living together as a married couple or civil partners.
- A child or 'qualifying young person' can be included as part of your family in your claim if you are responsible for her/him. S/he must normally live with you.
- You can continue to count as a couple, and children and young people can continue to be included in your UC, while you are living apart temporarily.

1. Couples

Your partner is included in your claim if you count as a 'couple'. You and your partner count as a couple if you are both aged 16 or over and you are:[1]
- married or civil partners and members of the same household; *or*
- not married or civil partners but 'living together as a married couple or civil partners'.

Spouse or civil partner

You can still be treated as part of a couple, even if you are married to someone else or in a civil partnership with someone else.[2]

There are special rules if you are polygamously married. If your spouse has another spouse from an earlier marriage and you all live in the same household, you can get universal credit (UC) as a single person.[3] You count as polygamously married if you are part of a marriage in which one of you is married to more than one person and your marriages took place in a country that permits polygamy (see also p551).[4]

You count as someone's **civil partner** if you have been registered as her/his civil partner.

Living together as a married couple or civil partners

You count as a couple if you are 'living together as a married couple or civil partners'. This is referred to as 'cohabiting' in this *Handbook*. This applies to both different and same-sex relationships.[5] The factors below are used as 'signposts' to determine whether or not you are cohabiting.[6] No one factor, in itself, is conclusive, as it is your overall relationship and your particular circumstances that are looked at.[7] The 'emotional aspect' of the relationship (your interdependence, devotion, love and affection) should also be considered.[8] This does not necessarily conflict with the factors below but, like your individual circumstances, should not be regarded as conclusive. For example, if your partner stays with you for three nights or more a week, you should not automatically be treated as living together as a couple.

Are you cohabiting?

1. Do you live in the same household? See below.
2. Do you have a sexual relationship? See below.
3. What are your financial arrangements? See p59.
4. Is your relationship stable? See p59.
5. Do you have children? See p59.
6. How do you appear in public? See p59.

Living in the same household

If you live in the same household, you may be treated as cohabiting. For what counts as a 'household', see p59.

Even if you *do* share a household, you may not be cohabiting. It is essential to look at *why* two people are in the same household.[9] For example, if you are living in the same household for 'care, companionship and mutual convenience', you can argue that you are not 'living together as husband and wife or civil partners'.[10]

Being in a sexual relationship

In practice, a decision maker may not ask you about the existence of a sexual relationship, in which case s/he only has the information if you volunteer it.

However, if you are appealing about whether you are a member of a couple, the First-tier Tribunal should consider this and may ask you about it.[11] If you do not have a sexual relationship, you should say so (and perhaps offer to show your separate sleeping arrangements).

Having a sexual relationship is not sufficient, by itself, to prove you are cohabiting. If you have never had a sexual relationship, there is a strong (but not necessarily conclusive) presumption that you are not cohabiting.[12] A couple who abstain from a sexual relationship before marriage should not be counted as cohabiting until they are formally married.[13]

Your financial arrangements

If one person is supported by the other or your household expenses are shared, this may be treated as evidence that you are cohabiting. However, it is important to consider how expenses are shared. There is a difference between, on the one hand, paying a fixed weekly contribution or rigidly sharing bills 50/50 (which does *not* suggest cohabitation) and, on the other hand, a common fund for income and expenditure (which might).

A stable relationship

Marriage and civil partnership are expected to be stable and lasting and so an occasional or brief association should not be regarded as cohabitation. However, the fact that your relationship is stable does not make it cohabitation – eg, you can have a stable relationship as a landlord and lodger, but not be cohabiting.

The way you spend your time together, the activities you undertake together and the things you do for each other are relevant, so questions about how you spend your holidays and how you organise the shopping, the laundry and cleaning may be important.

Children

If you have had a child together and live in the same household as the other parent, there is a strong (but not conclusive) presumption of cohabitation.

Your appearance in public

Decision makers may check the electoral roll and claims for other benefits to see whether you present yourselves as a couple. If you do not have a committed emotional loving relationship that is publicly acknowledged, you can argue that you are not living together as a married couple or civil partners.[14]

Households

The term **'household'** is not defined. Whether you and another person should be treated as members of the same household is decided on the particular facts of your case. In all cases, you must spend the major part of your time in the same household.

2

A house or flat can contain a number of separate households and if one person has exclusive occupation of separate accommodation from another, they are not considered to be living in the same household. Physical presence is not, in itself, conclusive. There must be a 'particular kind of tie' binding two people together in a domestic establishment. So, for example, a husband and wife may live in separate households in the same care or nursing home.[15] A household must also involve two or more people living together as a unit and having a reasonable level of independence and self-sufficiency. In one case, it was held that a married couple sharing a room in a residential home because they needed help organising their personal care and domestic activities were not self-sufficient and did not live in a domestic establishment, and therefore did not share a household.[16]

Is there a separate household?

If you think you should not be treated as a member of the same household as someone, check whether you can show that you maintain separate households. A separate household may exist if there are:

– independent arrangements for storing and cooking food or separate eating arrangements;
– independent financial arrangements or separate commitments for housing costs;
– no evidence of family life.

You cannot be a member of more than one household at the same time.[17] So if you are a member of one couple, you cannot also be treated as part of another. If two people maintain separate homes (ie, they each have a separate address where they usually live), they cannot share the same household.[18] Even if you have the right to occupy only part of a room, you may have your own household.[19]

If you are separated from your partner, but living under the same roof, you should not be treated as a couple if you are maintaining separate households. Any 'mere hope' of a reconciliation is not a 'reasonable expectation' if at least one partner has accepted that the relationship is at an end.[20]

Note: if you are still married or in a civil partnership, a shared attitude that the relationship is at an end may not be enough to show there is no shared household.[21]

Couples living apart

If you separate permanently (ie, you do not intend to resume living with your partner), you no longer count as a couple.[22] When deciding whether you intend to resume living together or not, your intention must be 'unqualified' – ie, it must not depend on something over which you have no control, such as the right of entry to the UK being granted by the Home Office[23] or the offer of a suitable job.[24]

If you and your partner are living apart temporarily, you continue to count as a couple because you are still treated as members of the same household. If you were not living together in the same household before your time apart, you should not be regarded as living apart temporarily.[25] Your former household need not have been in the UK.[26]

However, you no longer count as a couple if you have been separated (or expect to be separated) for more than six months.[27]

If either you or your partner go abroad, see p1664.

If your partner is in hospital, see p921. If s/he is in a care home, see p932. If your partner is a prisoner or serving a sentence while in hospital, see p940.

In any situation in which you must claim UC as a single person despite being a member of a couple, your income and capital is still assessed jointly (see p138).

Challenging a decision that you are a couple

Your UC may be stopped or adjusted if the decision maker decides you are a member of a couple.

If you disagree with a decision that you are a couple, you can apply for a revision or supersession (see Chapter 56), or appeal (see Chapter 57).

How do you show that you are not a couple?

1. Consider carefully what evidence to submit:
– if you are married or in a civil partnership, to show that you are not living in the same household with your spouse or civil partner;
– if you are not married or in a civil partnership, in relation to each of the six questions on p58, the emotional aspect of your relationship and any other matters you consider relevant.

2. Provide evidence if the other person has another address (eg, a rent book and other household bills), receipts for board and lodging, statements from friends and relatives, or evidence of a formal separation, divorce proceedings or a dissolution application or order.

You do not have to prove that you are not a couple when you first claim, but you must provide any information that is reasonably required to decide your claim.[28] A decision should then be made on all the available evidence.[29] However, if your UC award as a single person is stopped because it is alleged that you are part of a couple, the onus is on the decision maker to prove that you are.[30]

Although UC can continue to be paid to you as a couple, it will be affected – eg, because your alleged partner must also satisfy the basic conditions for UC and your income and capital are assessed jointly.

2. **Children**

A child (see below) may count as part of your family and be included in your universal credit (UC) claim if you or your partner are 'responsible' for her/him – ie, s/he 'normally lives' with you (see p63).[31] You do not have to be the child's parent.

A child stops being included in your UC if you no longer fulfil these conditions or if s/he no longer counts as a child.

If you are responsible for a child, you can get an additional amount (a child element) included in your UC. However, in most cases, you can only get child elements for a maximum of two children (see p66).

Who counts as a child

A person usually counts as a child if:[32]

- s/he is aged under 16; *or*
- s/he is aged 16 or over but under 20 and counts as a 'qualifying young person' under the UC rules. This includes most young people studying for GCSEs or A levels or who are doing approved training. Specifically, it means someone who:[33]
  - is aged 16 but who has not reached 1 September following her/his 16th birthday; *or*
  - is aged 16–19 but who has not yet reached 1 September following her/his 19th birthday, and has been accepted for (or has enrolled on) approved training or non-advanced education at school or college, or another institution approved by the Secretary of State (see below). During term time there must be more than 12 hours, on average, of tuition, practical work, supervised study and examinations a week. Meal breaks and unsupervised study are not included.

Note: a 19-year-old must have started (or been accepted for or enrolled on) the education or training before reaching 19 in order to count as a qualifying young person.

Approved training and non-advanced education for universal credit

'**Approved training**' is training that is approved by the DWP and provided under section 2(1) of the Employment and Training Act 1973 or section 2(3) of the Enterprise and New Towns (Scotland) Act 1990.

A course is '**non-advanced**' if it is below the level of 'advanced education'. Courses that count as advanced education include university degrees and other courses above GCSE, A level and Scottish National Qualifications above higher or advanced higher level.[34] See p580 for more examples of advanced and non-advanced courses.

Who does not count as a child

A person does not count as a child if s/he is getting UC, income support (IS), income-based jobseeker's allowance (JSA), income-related employment and support allowance (ESA), working tax credit, child tax credit, contribution-based JSA under the UC system or contributory ESA under the UC system in her/his own right and so does not count as a qualifying young person (see p579).[35]

Responsibility for a child

A child is included in your UC claim if you are 'responsible' for her/him. You are treated as responsible for a child if s/he 'normally lives' with you.[36] When deciding whether a child lives with you, the DWP should consider the amount of time s/he spends with you, as well as the nature of the support you provide. **Note:** in practice, when deciding whether you are responsible for a child, the DWP checks to see whether you are entitled to child benefit for her/him. However, this is not the legal test of responsibility. In particular, the fact that you do not get child benefit for the child does *not* show that s/he is not 'normally living' with you.

If the child normally lives with two (or more) people who are not a couple (eg, if s/he lives in the homes of her/his separated parents), you are responsible if you have the main responsibility. In this situation, you can agree with the other person who this should be. The DWP can, however, decide otherwise or, if you cannot agree, decide which person has the main responsibility. Both the amount of time the child spends with you and the nature of the support you provide should be taken into account.[37] You cannot be treated as responsible for a child during any period in which s/he is:[38]

- being looked after by a local authority, except during planned short breaks in local authority care to provide respite care for the person who normally looks after her/him and except if the child is living with you and you are her/his parent or (unless you are a foster parent) someone with parental responsibility for her/him; *or*
- a prisoner; *or*
- temporarily absent from your household (see p59) and s/he has been, or is expected to be, absent for more than six months, including if this is for medical treatment abroad; *or*
- temporarily absent from your household and s/he has been, or is expected to be, absent from Great Britain for more than one month, unless it is under the same circumstances (medical treatment or death of a close relative) as those that apply to when you can get UC while absent (see p1663).

If UC is paid for a child, it cannot be split between parents if a child spends her/his time equally between their two homes. The person who has main responsibility for the child has the child included in her/his UC.

Notes

1. Couples

1 s137(1) SSCBA 1992; CFC/7/1992; s39 WRA 2012
2 R(SB) 8/85
3 Reg 3(4) and (5) UC Regs
4 Reg 3(5) UC Regs
5 s39 WRA 2012
6 *Crake and Butterworth v SBC* [1982] 1 All ER 498; [1981] 2 FLR 264 (QBD)
7 R(SB) 17/81; R(G) 3/71; CIS/87/1993
8 *PP v Basildon District Council (HB)* [2013] UKUT 505 (AAC)
9 *Crake and Butterworth v SBC* [1982]; [1981] 2 FLR 264 (QBD), quoted in R(SB) 35/85
10 R(SB) 35/85
11 CIS/87/1993; CIS/2559/2002; CIS/2074/2008
12 CIS/87/1993
13 CSB/150/1985
14 *JP v SSWP (IS)* [2014] UKUT 17 (AAC)
15 *Santos v Santos* [1972] 2 All ER 246; CIS/671/1992; CIS/81/1993
16 CIS/4935/1997
17 R(SB) 8/85
18 R(SB) 4/83
19 CSB/463/1986
20 CIS/72/1994
21 CIS/2900/1998
22 Reg 3(6) UC Regs
23 CIS/508/1992; CIS/13805/1996
24 CIS/484/1993
25 Reg 3(6) UC Regs; *Broxtowe BC v CS (HB)* [2014] UKUT 186 (AAC)
26 CIS/508/1992
27 Reg 3(6) UC Regs
28 Reg 37 UC,PIP,JSA&ESA(C&P) Regs
29 CIS/317/1994
30 R(I) 1/71

2. Children

31 s10 WRA 2012; reg 4(2) UC Regs
32 s40 WRA 2012; regs 2 and 5 UC Regs
33 Reg 5 UC Regs
34 Reg 12(3) UC Regs
35 Reg 5(5) UC Regs
36 Reg 4 UC Regs
37 Reg 4 UC Regs; *MC v SSWP (UC)* [2018] UKUT 44 (AAC)
38 Reg 4(6) and (7) UC Regs

Chapter 5

The maximum amount

This chapter covers:
1. What is the maximum amount (below)
2. The standard allowance (p66)
3. Elements (p66)

Key facts
- Together with your income and capital, the maximum amount of universal credit (UC) is used to calculate the amount of UC to which you are entitled.
- The maximum amount is made up of a standard allowance plus, where applicable, one or more elements, depending on your circumstances.

1. What is the maximum amount

Your maximum universal credit (UC) is made up of the total of:
- a standard allowance, either for a single claimant or for a couple making a joint claim (see p66);
- a child element for each child, subject to a 'two-child limit' (exceptions may apply), with an increase for a disabled or severely disabled child (see p66);
- an element for an adult assessed as having limited capability for work and work-related activity (see p72). A separate element, abolished for new claimants, for someone assessed as just having limited capability for work can still be paid in some cases (see p70);
- a carer element for someone caring for a severely disabled person (see p73);
- a childcare costs element (see p74);
- a housing costs element for help with your rent or any service charges that you pay (see p76);
- a transitional element if you have transferred to UC under the 'managed migration' process and would otherwise be worse off than on your old benefits or tax credits (see p77).

After a death

If any of the following people dies, your maximum amount of UC continues to be calculated as if that person had not died for the remainder of the monthly assessment period (see p39) in which the death occurs, and for the next two assessment periods:[1]

- your partner, if you have a joint UC claim with her/him (see p45);
- a child for whom you (or your partner in a joint claim) are responsible (see below);
- a severely disabled person for whom you (or your partner in a joint claim) have regular and substantial caring responsibilities (see p73);
- someone who counts as a non-dependant for the purpose of the housing element (see p96).

For example, if you have a joint claim and your partner dies, your standard allowance (and any element paid in respect of your partner) continues at the couple rate for the remainder of the assessment period in which s/he died, and for the next two assessment periods.

2. The standard allowance

A standard allowance is always included in your universal credit (UC) maximum amount. The amount depends on your age and whether you are claiming as a single person or making a joint claim with your partner (see p45).[2] See p57 for who counts as a couple, including when one of you is temporarily absent.

If you are making a joint claim with your partner and your partner dies, see p65.

Note: if one member of a couple does not satisfy the rules of entitlement for UC, the other partner may be able to claim as a single person (see p45). In this case, the standard allowance for a single claimant applies.

Rates of standard allowance

Single claimant	*per month*
Under 25	£342.72
25 or over	£409.89
Joint claimants	
Both under 25	£488.59
One or both 25 or over	£594.04

3. Elements

Child element

If you are responsible for a child or young person, you can get a child element included in your universal credit (UC) maximum amount. You are 'responsible' for a child if s/he is normally living with you (see p63).[3] The child must be aged under 16, or 16–19 and a 'qualifying young person' for UC purposes (see p62).[4]

Before 6 April 2017, you got a child element for each child or young person you or your partner were responsible for. From 6 April 2017, a 'two-child limit' applies (see below).

There is a higher rate of the child element for the eldest or only child.[5] This was abolished from 6 April 2017, but continues to apply if your eldest or only child was born before that date.[6]

If a child is disabled, the child element is increased by a '**disabled child addition**'. You get the lower rate if the child is entitled to disability living allowance (DLA) or personal independence payment (PIP). You get the higher rate instead if s/he is entitled to the DLA care component at the highest rate, the daily living component of PIP at the enhanced rate, or if s/he is certified as severely sight impaired or blind by a consultant ophthalmologist.[7] The disabled child addition is still paid for a child, even if you cannot get a child element for her/him because of the two-child limit.[8]

If your child dies, see p65.

Rates of child element

	per month
First child born before 6 April 2017	£281.25
Second child/all children born on or after 6 April 2017	£235.83
Disabled child addition	
Lower rate	£128.25
Higher rate	£400.29

The two-child limit

You cannot get an element for a child born on or after 6 April 2017 if you already have two or more other children included in your award, unless an exception applies (see p68). This is known as the 'two-child limit'.[9] You can always get an element for a child born before 6 April 2017.

When establishing the number of children you have for this purpose, a child who is covered by the first two exceptions (ie, you have adopted her/him or s/he is living with you under a 'non-parental care arrangement') is ignored.

So you can get an element for:
- any child born before 6 April 2017; *and*
- a child born on or after 6 April 2017 who is not counted as your third or subsequent child; *and*
- a third or subsequent child born on or after 6 April 2017 to whom an exception applies.

Examples

Sam has three children. One was born before 6 April 2017, the others were born on 6 May 2017 and 4 November 2019. No exceptions apply to the children. Sam gets a child element for two children: the one born before 6 April 2017, and the one born on 6 May 2017.

Gina and Lesley have four children. Two were born before 6 April 2017, two (Kate and Raj) after that date. Kate has been adopted by Gina and Lesley. Gina and Lesley get child elements for three children: the two born before 6 April 2017, and one for Kate, as she is covered by an exception. Although Kate is not included when establishing how many children Gina and Lesley have, they still have three other children. One of these, Raj was born after 6 April 2017. He is not covered by any of the exceptions and so no child element is included for him.

The number and order of children (ie, whether a child is the first, second, third or subsequent child) is determined by allocating each child a date according to her/his date of birth, so that the eldest child is regarded as the first.[10]

Note: from 28 November 2018, a child who is covered by the first two exceptions below (ie, you have adopted her/him or s/he is living with you under a non-parental caring arrangement') is not counted.[11] Before this date, the High Court held that it was unlawful for you to be affected by the two-child limit because such a child was counted towards the number of your children.[12] If you were affected, you can argue that this was wrong and ask for the decision to be changed.

The child element can become payable for a third child to whom the two-child limit would apply when an older child leaves the household (as you are no longer responsible for her/him), or when a young person leaves education (as s/he no longer qualifies). In these situations, you should report the change as soon as possible to ensure you continue to receive the maximum two child elements.

Note: the two-child limit is currently the subject of a legal challenge. See cpag.org.uk/content/two-child-limit-challenge for details, and AskCPAG.org.uk and CPAG's *Welfare Rights Bulletin* for updates.

Exceptions

The two-child limit does not apply to the following children.[13]

- A child living with you under a 'non-parental caring arrangement'. This means either that s/he is a child whose parent is aged under 16 and you are responsible for the parent, *or* that the child is living with you on a long-term basis because s/he is unable to live with her/his parents and you are caring for her/him as a family member or friend. You or your partner must not be the child's parent or step-parent and you must:
  - be named in a child arrangements order under section 8 of the Children Act 1989 or a residence order under Article 8 of the Children (Northern Ireland) Order 1995 as a person with whom the child is to live; *or*

- be the appointed or special guardian, or be entitled to guardian's allowance, for the child; *or*
- have a kinship care order under section 72(1) of the Children and Young People (Scotland) Act 2014, or parental responsibilities or rights under section 80 of the Adoption and Children (Scotland) Act 2007 for the child; *or*
- continue to be responsible for the child if any of the above bullet points applied immediately before the child's 16th birthday; *or*
- be caring for the child because otherwise it is likely s/he would be taken into the care of the local authority.
- A child who is being adopted by you from local authority care or who has been placed with you for adoption. This exception does not apply if:
  - you or your partner were the child's step-parent immediately before the adoption;
  - you or your partner have been the child's parent (other than by adoption) at any other time;
  - the child is being adopted directly from abroad.
- A child born in a multiple birth, other than the first born if you already have two or more children. So, if you have:
  - no older children, you get the child element for all children in a multiple birth;
  - one older child, you get the child element for all children in a multiple birth;
  - two or more older children, you get the child element for all but one of the children in a multiple birth.
- A child who is likely to have been conceived as a result of rape, or in a controlling or coercive relationship (a 'non-consensual conception'). You must not be living at the same address as the alleged perpetrator for this exception to apply, even though you might have been living with that person at the time of conception. A 'controlling or coercive relationship' includes behaviour that causes you to fear, on at least two occasions, that violence will be used against you, or that causes you serious alarm or distress which has a substantial adverse effect on your day-to-day activities. You must provide evidence from an 'approved person' that you have had contact with her/him or another approved person about the rape or relationship. A list of 'approved persons' is in official guidance and includes healthcare professionals, social workers and approved organisations such as specialist rape charities (see gov.uk/government/publications/support-for-a-child-conceived-without-your-consent/approved-third-party-professionals-who-can-complete-these-forms). Third-party evidence is not required if there has been a conviction for rape or coercive, controlling behaviour in the UK, or for a similar offence abroad, or if you have been awarded criminal injuries compensation after a sexual offence, physical abuse or mental injury, and it is likely that the offence or injury resulted in the conception. You can be treated as having provided evidence if you have already provided it to HM Revenue and Customs (HMRC) for child tax credit (CTC).

If you are the step-parent of the child but are no longer part of a couple with the child's parent, the exception can continue to apply if you are still responsible for the child, and the only reason for any breaks in your claim is your becoming single or part of a couple again. Get advice.

Limited capability for work element

The limited capability for work element was abolished for new claims from 3 April 2017.[14] You can no longer get the element if you are making a new claim for UC, unless you are covered by one of the exceptions in the bullets below. If you are already on UC but then start to have limited capability for work, you cannot get the element unless you have been getting the limited capability for work-related activity element (see p72). If you (or your partner in a joint claim) are also entitled to the limited capability for work-related activity element (see p72), you receive that instead – you cannot get both elements.

You can get the limited capability for work element if you (or your partner) are entitled to UC and have limited capability for work (see Chapter 45) and:[15]

- you were getting the element in your current award of UC (or had limited capability for work and were waiting for the element to be included in your UC) immediately before 3 April 2017; *or*
- you were getting the limited capability for work-related activity element in your current award of UC immediately before 3 April 2017 and on a reassessment it is decided that you are entitled to the limited capability for work element instead; *or*
- the decision that you had limited capability for work before 3 April 2017 is not made until after this date and you have supplied a medical certificate, including if the decision is made following a revision or an appeal; *or*
- you were entitled to employment and support allowance (ESA) or to national insurance (NI) credits for limited capability for work (see p971) immediately before 3 April 2017, and you remained entitled after this date until you claimed UC; *or*
- you claimed ESA before 3 April 2017, but the initial decision on your claim was changed following a revision or an appeal, and on or after 3 April 2017 your UC award needs to be changed to take account of this; *or*
- you were entitled to incapacity benefit, severe disablement allowance, income support (IS) 'on the grounds of disability' or NI contribution credits for incapacity for work (see p971) immediately before 3 April 2017, and you remained entitled after this date until you claimed UC. Certain other conditions apply. If you are in this situation, get specialist advice.

There may be a three-month waiting period before the element can be included in your UC for the first time.[16] In practice, it will usually be included straight away, either under the same rules that allow the limited capability for work-related activity element to be included straight away (see p72) or because you are transferring to UC from ESA (see below).

Note: your entitlement to the element can continue if your UC stops and then starts again because you have become, or stopped being, a member of a couple, or if your UC stops because your income is too high but then starts again within six months. If you work and earn an amount at least equal to a certain earnings threshold, you may be treated as *not* having limited capability for work or you may be reassessed (see p1015).

If your partner was entitled to the element, but dies, see p65.

Rate of limited capability for work element

	per month
Limited capability for work	£128.25

Transfers to universal credit

If you transfer to UC from ESA (under either the 'managed migration' or 'natural migration' process) and were entitled to the work-related activity component in your ESA (see p653) on the date you claimed UC, you are treated as having limited capability for work and the limited capability for work element can be included in your UC straight away.[17] However, in practice, the DWP has not always applied this rule, so challenge the failure to do this if necessary. See AskCPAG.org.uk for a useful tool to help with such a challenge.

If you were still in the ESA 'assessment phase' (see p651) when you transferred, the time you spent in the assessment phase counts towards the three-month waiting period period that might otherwise apply before the element is included in your UC.[18]

Joint claims

If you are making a joint claim with your partner, only one limited capability for work element can be included, even if you both meet the conditions.[19]

If you were previously getting UC as a single person but then form a couple with someone who was not entitled to UC, but who was getting ESA that included the work-related activity component (see p653), the limited capability for work element is included in your joint UC award.[20]

If one of you satisfies the conditions for both the limited capability for work element and the carer element (see p73), usually the carer element is included in your maximum amount instead of the limited capability for work element. However, if you qualify for one of these elements and your partner qualifies for the other, both elements can be included.[21]

> *Example*
>
> Tom and Sharon have a joint claim for UC, made before 3 April 2017. They have a disabled son, George. Tom has limited capability for work. Sharon is George's carer and satisfies the conditions for the carer element. Both the limited capability for work element and the carer element were included in Tom and Sharon's UC award before 3 April 2017, and continue for as long as they remain entitled.
>
> If Tom were also a carer for George, they could nominate Sharon as the main carer for George so that both the limited capability for work and carer elements can continue to be paid.

Limited capability for work-related activity element

A limited capability for work-related activity element is included in your maximum amount if you (or your partner in a joint claim) have been assessed as having limited capability for work-related activity.[22] If this applies to you, you are also regarded as having limited capability for work. For the assessment of limited capability for work-related activity, see p1028 – the rules are very similar to those that apply for ESA.

If you are qualifying for the element for the first time, there is usually a three-month waiting period before it is included in your maximum amount. The three-month period begins on the day on which you provide a medical certificate. In practice, you may already have provided a medical certificate three months or more ago (ie, as evidence of having limited capablity for work), in which case you will already have served the waiting period.[23] The element is then included from the beginning of the assessment period (see p39) that follows the assessment period in which the three months ended. The element can be included straight away if you (or your partner in a joint claim):[24]

- are terminally ill; *or*
- were entitled to the element (or the limited capability for work element) immediately before your current UC award started and your previous UC award ended because you became a member of a couple or you stopped being a member of a couple; *or*
- were entitled to the element (or the limited capability for work element) and your previous UC award ended within the six months before your current award started, because your income was too high; *or*
- are entitled to the limited capability for work element in your UC, but are then assessed as entitled to the limited capability for work-related activity element; *or*
- are entitled to an award of ESA that includes the support component.

If your award of UC immediately follows an 'extended period of sickness' on jobseeker's allowance (JSA) (see p710), the element can be included after 13 weeks, beginning with the first day of that period.[25]

If you partner is entitled to the element but dies, see p65.

If you also satisfy the conditions for the carer element (see below), the limited capability for work-related activity element is paid instead. However, if you are in a couple, if one of you can qualify for the limited capability for work-related activity element and the other qualifies for the carer element, both elements can be included.[26]

Rate of limited capability for work-related activity element

	per month
Limited capability for work-related activity	£341.92

Transfers to universal credit

If you transfer from ESA to UC (under either the 'managed migration' or 'natural migration' process) and were entitled to the support component in your ESA (see p652) on the date you claim UC, you are treated as having limited capability for work-related activity and the element is included in your UC straight away. The same applies if you were not entitled to ESA but, on the date you claim UC, were entitled to credits for limited capability for work and were assessed as having limited capability for work-related activity (see p1027). If you were still in the 'assessment phase' for ESA (see p651), but had been in it for less than 13 weeks, the time you spent in the assessment phase counts towards the three-month period. If you had already been in the assessment phase for at least 13 weeks and it is decided that you have limited capability for work-related activity for UC, the element is awarded from the beginning of your first assessment period.[27] In practice, the DWP has not always applied this rule, so point it out if necessary. For more information on transferring to UC from ESA, see AskCPAG.org.uk.

Joint claims

If you are making a joint claim with your partner, only one limited capability for work-related activity element can be included, even if you both meet the conditions.[28]

If you were previously getting UC as a single person but then form a couple with someone who was not entitled to UC but was getting ESA that included the support component (see p652), the limited capability for work-related activity element is included in your joint UC award.[29]

Carer element

A carer element is included in your maximum amount if you have 'regular and substantial' caring responsibilities for a severely disabled person. This means that you satisfy, or would satisfy were it not for the level of your earnings, the conditions for carer's allowance (CA) (see p562). You do not need to have claimed

CA (however, if you live in Scotland and you do claim CA, it can be increased by a CA supplement – see p569). If you get the carer element, the severely disabled person cannot get a severe disability premium in her/his means-tested benefit (see p346). **Note:** you do not qualify for the carer element if you have any earnings from your caring responsibilities.[30]

If you are claiming as a single person, only one carer element can be included, even if you care for more than one disabled person. If you are making a joint claim, you can get two carer elements if both you and your partner satisfy the conditions, provided you are not caring for the same person. If you are both caring for the same person, you get one carer element. You can decide between you which partner should be entitled – eg, if it is necessary for your partner to be entitled to the carer element so that you can also get the limited capability for work or limited capability for work-related activity element. If you do not decide which one of you should be entitled to the carer element, the DWP decides for you.[31] Similarly, if someone other than your partner is caring for the same person, only one of you can get CA or the carer element of UC for that care. You can decide between you who should be entitled.[32]

If the person you care for dies, the element should continue to be paid for a time (see p65). If the DWP fails to do this, see AskCPAG.org.uk for a useful tool for challenging the decision.

Rate of carer element

	per month
Carer	£162.92

Childcare costs element

A childcare costs element is included in your maximum amount if you are working (or have an offer of work) and you have childcare costs for 'relevant childcare' (see p75 for what this covers).

The amount of the element is 85 per cent of your childcare costs, up to a maximum of £646.35 a month for one child and £1,108.04 a month for two or more children.[33]

Note:
- If you have upfront childcare costs (eg, a deposit, retainer or fees) in advance of the childcare starting and you have started work but not yet received your first wages, the government has said that your work coach can pay those costs direct to the childcare provider using the Flexible Support Fund (see p873). Once you have received your first wages, any further upfront childcare costs (eg, during the school holidays) can be met from a budgeting advance (see p51). If you get a budgeting advance, you can still get up to 85 per cent of the

childcare costs (subject to the overall limits) covered by the childcare costs element, once you have submitted a paid receipt.[34]
- If you are entitled to UC, you cannot also get tax-free childcare payments. In the future, if you register for the tax-free childcare scheme, all your UC could be terminated.[35] See p871 for more details.

To get the childcare costs element, you must be in paid work (there are no minimum hours) or have an offer of paid work that is due to start before the end of your next UC monthly assessment period (see p39).[36] If you are in a couple, your partner must also be in paid work, unless s/he cannot provide childcare her/himself because s/he has limited capability for work (see Chapter 45), or s/he is caring for a severely disabled person and gets (or would be entitled to) CA (see p561), or s/he is temporarily absent from your household. **Note:** you stop counting as a couple if your partner is (or is expected to be) absent from Great Britain for more than six months.[37] If your partner is temporarily absent abroad, see p1647.

You are treated as still in paid work if you are getting statutory sick pay, statutory maternity pay, statutory adoption pay, statutory paternity pay, statutory shared parental pay, statutory parental bereavement pay or maternity allowance. You are also treated as still in paid work if your work ended during your current assessment period or in the previous one – you can continue to get the childcare costs element for one month after your work ends.[38]

In addition, you must meet all the following conditions.[39]
- You pay charges for 'relevant childcare' (see below) for a child for whom you are responsible – ie, s/he normally lives with you.
- The child is aged under 16 or has not reached the 1 September following her/his 16th birthday.
- The childcare is to enable you to do paid work (or was to enable you to do paid work but that work has stopped).
- You report the charges to the DWP no later than the end of the monthly UC assessment period that follows the assesment period in which the charges were paid. (Before 16 October 2019, you had to report the charges by the end of the assessment period in which the charges were paid.) The DWP may allow you to report them later than this, under the same rules that apply to late notification of a change in circumstances (see p1324).

Relevant childcare

'**Relevant childcare**' means care for a child provided by the following.

In England:[40]

– a registered childcare provider – ie, someone registered with Ofsted under Part 3 of the Childcare Act 2006; *or*

– a school on school premises out of school hours (or at any time if the child has not reached compulsory school age); *or*

– an official domiciliary care provider – ie, one registered with the Care Quality Commission.

In Scotland:[41]

– a registered childminder or similar provider of daycare – ie, registered as such under the Public Services Reform (Scotland) Act 2010; *or*

– a childcare agency under the Public Services Reform (Scotland) Act 2010; *or*

– a local authority registered to provide childminding or daycare under the Public Services Reform (Scotland) Act 2010.

In Wales:[42]

– a registered childminder or daycare provider – ie, registered under Part 2 of the Children and Families (Wales) Measure 2010; *or*

– someone providing daycare that would count for registration, were it not for the fact that it is provided in a care home, hospital, children's home, residential family centre or school; *or*

– someone providing childcare under a Welsh Assembly scheme for tax credit purposes; *or*

– out of school hours, a school on school premises or a local authority; *or*

– an official domiciliary care worker – ie, under the Domiciliary Care Agencies (Wales) Regulations 2004; *or*

– a foster parent (but not for the child who s/he is fostering) if, were it not for the fact that the child is too old, the childcare would count as registered childcare or daycare – ie, under Part 2 of the Children and Families (Wales) Measure 2010.

The following *does not count* as relevant childcare:[43]

– care provided by a 'close relative' of the child (ie, parent, parent-in-law, son, daughter, son-in-law, daughter-in-law, stepson, stepdaughter, stepbrother, stepsister and a partner of any of these) wholly or mainly in the child's home;[44]

– care provided by a foster parent, foster carer or kinship carer for a child who the person is fostering or looking after as a kinship carer.

Rates of childcare costs element

	per month
Maximum for one child	£646.35
Maximum for two or more children	£1,108.04

Housing costs element

A housing costs element is included in your maximum amount for qualifying housing costs. Housing costs can be either rent or service charges. See Chapter 6 for when you are entitled and the amount of your housing costs element. **Note:**

you cannot get a housing costs element for your mortgage interest payments or for a loan for repairs and improvements. Instead, the DWP may offer you a loan (see p855).

Transitional element

If you transfer to UC under the 'managed migration' process (see p27) and the amount of your UC would be less than the total amount of your old means-tested benefits and tax credits, a transitional element is included in your UC. This is intended to ensure that you are not worse off at the point you transfer to UC.[45] If you disagree with a decision about the transitional element, see p79.

Note: at the time of writing, the rules described below were about the testing period of the managed migration process (see p30). See AskCPAG.org.uk and CPAG's *Welfare Rights Bulletin* for updates.

You *cannot* get a transitional element if:[46]

- you were claiming your old means-tested benefits or tax credits as a couple, you transfer to UC under the managed migration process, but you claim UC as a single person or as a member of a different couple;
- you were claiming your old means-tested benefits or tax credits as a member of a polygamous marriage, you transfer to UC under the managed migration process, but you claim UC as a single person or as a member of a couple;
- it is decided that you are not entitled to UC at all, but you then reclaim and are awarded UC. You cannot usually get a transitional element included in your later claim, unless the reason you were not entitled to UC was because your earnings (or in a joint claim, your and your partner's combined earnings) were too high.[47] In this case, if you reclaim UC and it starts within three months of the end of what would have been your first UC monthly assessment period, you can be entitled to a transitional element in your UC.

To get a transitional element, you must transfer to UC under the managed migration process. This means the DWP must have sent you a 'migration notice' informing you that you are affected by the process. You must then have made a 'qualifying claim' for UC – ie, you claim before the 'final deadline'.[48] The final deadline is one month from the date you were told you must claim UC by (known as your 'deadline day').[49]

Even if you make your claim in time, you are usually required to provide further information at an interview. If you do not do so, the DWP regards this as a 'failed claim' and 'closes' your claim. This is actually a decision that you are not entitled to any UC at all, so you cannot get a transitional element. The rules say you cannot get a transitional element if you reclaim, even if you do so before your final deadline, although it is not clear that this is the official intention.[50] If your claim is 'closed', you can challenge this decision (see p45).

To decide whether you are entitled to a transitional element, the DWP compares:[51]

- your 'total legacy amount'. This is the total amount of your old means-tested benefit and tax credit awards on the day before your first day of UC entitlement, converted to a monthly amount. If the benefit cap for UC would apply to you (see p1194) and your total legacy amount exceeds the level of the UC benefit cap, your total legacy amount is reduced by the level of the excess, minus your working tax credit (WTC) childcare costs; *and*

- your 'indicative UC amount'. This is the amount of UC you would get, based on your circumstances on the day before your first day of UC entitlement. The DWP assumes that if you get CTC for a child, you are responsible for that child, that if you get childcare costs in your WTC, these apply in the childcare costs element of your UC, and that your earnings are the same as those used to calculate your tax credits or (if you do not get tax credits) benefits. The DWP can use any further information and evidence if necessary. If the benefit cap for UC would apply to you (see p1194), your indicative UC amount is limited to the amount of the benefit cap.

The weekly rate of your old means-tested benefits is converted to a monthly amount by multiplying it by 52 and dividing by 12. The daily rate of your tax credit award is converted to a monthly amount by multiplying it by 365 and dividing by 12.

If the amount of UC to which you are entitled is less than your total means-tested benefit and tax credit awards, the difference between the two is the amount of your transitional element. If the amount of UC is the same as, or more than, your total means-tested benefit and tax credit awards, you do not get a transitional element.

The amount of your transitional element can reduce over time. This is because, after your first monthly UC assessment period, the amount is reduced by any increase in the other elements included your UC, except increases in the childcare element.[52]

Example

Tina is a lone parent getting IS, HB and CTC. Her four-year-old child is disabled and gets DLA. On the day before she makes her UC claim, she is entitled to CTC (including the disabled child element) at a daily rate of £18.62, IS at a weekly rate of £74.35 and HB at a weekly rate of £225.

Her CTC is converted to a monthly amount of £566.35 (£18.62 x 365, divided by 12).

Her IS is converted to a monthly amount of £322.18 (£74.35 x 52, divided by 12).

Her HB is converted to a monthly amount of £975 (£225 x 52, divided by 12).

So Tina's total benefits and tax credits (her 'total legacy amount') = £566.35 + £322.18 + £975 = £1,863.53

> Tina is entitled to UC:
> Standard allowance £323.22
> Child element £281.25
> Disabled child addition £128.25
> Housing costs element £975
> Tina's 'indicative UC amount' is £323.22 + £281.25 + £128.25 + £975 = £1,707.72
>
> The total amount of Tina's old benefits and tax credits is higher than the amount of UC she would get, so she gets the difference as a transitional element in her UC – ie, £1,863.53 – £1,707.72 = £155.81 per month. This will be reduced by future increases in her other elements. For example, if her housing costs element increases by £25 a month, the transitional element will be £155.81 – £25 = £130.81.

When the transitional element stops

Your entitlement to a transitional element ends if:[53]

- at the time of your UC claim, your earnings from work (or in a joint claim, your and your partner's combined earnings) were at least the level at which you are not subject to work-search requirements (see p1072), but they have now been below this amount for three consecutive UC monthly assessment periods; or
- you originally claimed UC as a couple, but you are now single, or you originally claimed UC as a single person, but you are now part of a couple; or
- your UC comes to an end. In this case, you cannot get a transitional element in any future award of UC, unless your previous UC award ended because your earnings (or in a joint claim, your and your partner's combined earnings) increased so that your income was too high and your new UC award starts within three months of the end of your last UC monthly assessment period. In these circumstances, your new UC award includes the same transitional element as in your previous award.

Changing a decision about the transitional element

The transitional element is part of the calculation of your UC. You can challenge the decision on your entitlement to the element by requesting a revision (see Chapter 56) or appealing against the decision on your UC entitlement – you must ask for a mandatory reconsideration first (see Chapter 57).

There are also some special rules about changing decisions involving the transitional element. These rules are to make it clear that the decision about your UC can be revised or superseded under the normal rules in certain circumstances which could affect your transitional element.

The decision about your UC can be revised or superseded if information used in the original calculation of your transitional element is now considered to be wrong because:[54]

- you (or your partner in a joint claim) misrepresented something; or

- you (or your partner in a joint claim) failed to report information you were required to report, and that failure was to your advantage; *or*
- there was an 'official error'. This means an error made by an officer of the DWP, HMRC, a local authority or a person employed by someone acting on behelf of these bodies. The rules on what counts as an official error are the same as what can count under the normal rules for revisions (see p1307).

If, since the date on which your UC entitlement started, a decision about your old means-tested benefit or tax credit award has been revised or superseded, or has been the subject of an appeal decision, the decision about your UC can still be revised or superseded – ie, to take account of the effect of any change in your old means-tested benefit or tax credit on your transitional element.[55]

Notes

1. What is the maximum amount
1 Reg 37 UC Regs

2. The standard allowance
2 Reg 36 UC Regs

3. Elements
3 Regs 4 UC Regs
4 Reg 24 UC Regs
5 Reg 36 UC Regs
6 *Welfare Reform,* House of Commons, *Hansard,* Written Statement, HCWS96, 20 July 2016
7 Reg 24 UC Regs
8 s10(2) WRA 2012; reg 36 UC Regs
9 s10(1A) WRA 2012; reg 24A UC Regs
10 Reg 24B(1) UC Regs
11 Reg 24B(2A) UC Regs
12 *SC and Others v SSWP* [2018] EWHC 864 (Admin)
13 Sch 12 UC Regs
14 s16 WRWA 2016
15 Sch 2 Part 2 ESAUC(MA) Regs
16 Reg 28 UC Regs, as applied by Sch 2 Part 2 ESAUC(MA) Regs
17 Reg 19 UC(TP) Regs; Vol M6, para M6192 ADM
18 Regs 20 and 21 UC(TP) Regs
19 Reg 27(4) UC Regs
20 Reg 19(3) UC(TP) Regs

21 Reg 29(4) UC Regs
22 Reg 27 UC Regs
23 See the official guidance and example in para F5046 ADM
24 Reg 28 UC Regs
25 Reg 20A UC(TP) Regs
26 Reg 19(4) UC Regs
27 Regs 19, 20 and 21 UC(TP) Regs
28 Reg 27(4) UC Regs
29 Reg 19(4) UC Regs
30 Regs 29 and 30 UC Regs
31 Reg 29(2) and (3) UC Regs
32 Reg 29(3) UC Regs; s70(7) SSCBA 1992
33 Regs 34 and 36 UC Regs
34 *Universal Credit,* House of Commons, *Hansard,* Written Question, 282562, answered 5 September 2019, available at parliament.uk
35 DWP, *Universal Credit: increasing the childcare offer,* December 2014
36 Reg 32 UC Regs
37 Reg 3(6) UC Regs
38 Reg 32(2) UC Regs
39 Reg 33 UC Regs
40 Reg 35(2) UC Regs
41 Reg 35(3) UC Regs
42 Reg 35(4) UC Regs
43 Reg 35(7) UC Regs

44 Reg 2, definition of 'close relative', UC
Regs
45 Regs 50 and 52 UC(TP) Regs
46 Regs 50(2) and 57 UC(TP) Regs
47 Reg 57(2)(a) UC(TP) Regs
48 Regs 48 and 50 UC(TP) Regs
49 Reg 46(4) UC(TP) Regs
50 Reg 57(1)(b) UC(TP) Regs; *Draft
Universal Credit (Managed Migration)
Regulations 2018: SSAC report and
government statement*, November 2018,
p14. You cannot get a transitional
element if you are not entitled to an
award of UC.
51 Regs 52-54 UC(TP) Regs
52 Reg 55 UC(TP) Regs
53 Regs 56 and 57 UC(TP) Regs
54 Reg 62(1)(a) UC(TP) Regs
55 Reg 62(1)(b) UC(TP) Regs

The housing costs element

This chapter covers:
1. Who can get a housing costs element (p83)
2. Liability for payments (p87)
3. Occupying accommodation as a home (p91)
4. How the housing costs element is calculated: general rules (p94)
5. The amount for private rented tenants (p103)
6. The amount for social rented sector tenants: the 'bedroom tax' (p107)
7. Service charge payments for owner-occupiers (p110)

Key facts
- Your universal credit (UC) can include a housing costs element to help with your rent and/or service charges.
- If you are a private tenant, the amount of rent used to calculate your housing costs element is based on a local housing allowance for a property with the number of bedrooms the rules allow. This may be lower than the rent you must pay.
- If you are a social rented sector tenant (eg, your landlord is a local authority or housing association) and your home has more bedrooms than the rules allow, your housing costs element is usually reduced by a percentage.
- If you are an owner-occupier (unless you have a shared ownership tenancy), you cannot get a housing costs element for your service charges if you (or your partner) have any earned income, however low your earnings are.
- If you are an owner-occupier (unless you have a shared ownership tenancy), you might not get a housing costs element during an initial 'waiting period'.
- If your housing costs element is for rent and you need extra financial assistance to meet your housing costs, you may be able to get discretionary housing payments from your local authority.

Future changes
In the future, the rules on UC housing costs may be different in Scotland.[1] See AskCPAG.org.uk and CPAG's *Welfare Rights Bulletin* for updates.

1. Who can get a housing costs element

Your universal credit (UC) maximum amount can include a housing costs element if:[2]

- your accommodation is in Great Britain; *and*
- your accommodation is residential – ie, not for a business. If your accommodation is partly for a business and partly residential, you can qualify for a housing costs element for the part that is residential; *and*
- you (or your partner, if you are a joint claimant) make payments for eligible rent (see p84) or eligible service charges (see p85); *and*
- you (or your partner, if you are a joint claimant) are liable for the eligible rent or service charge payments, or are treated as liable (see p87); *and*
- you normally occupy the accommodation for which you make the eligible rent or eligible service charge payments as your home, or you are treated as doing so (see p91).

The accommodation can comprise the whole of a building or part of a building – eg, a flat in a block, a bedsit in a house or a room in a shared house. You can get a housing costs element whether or not the accommodation comprises separate and self-contained premises.[3]

A housing costs element can include any of the eligible payments that you make. If you have a shared ownership tenancy (ie, you are buying part of your home and renting the rest), your housing costs element can include rent, as well as the service charge payments you make.[4]

Make sure you tell the DWP that you pay rent or service charges when you claim UC, so a housing costs element is included. If you are already getting UC and want to get help with your housing costs, apply via your online account.

Note:

- You cannot get a housing costs element for help with your mortgage interest payments (or alternative finance payments). The DWP may offer you a loan for mortgage interest instead. See p855 for information and get independent financial advice before accepting a loan.
- If a housing costs element is included in your UC maximum amount, you qualify for a lower work allowance and, therefore, more of your earnings are taken into account (see p41).
- Your housing costs element is normally paid to you, but see p49 for when it can be paid direct to your landlord.
- If you are getting housing benefit (HB) and make a new claim for UC, your HB entitlement continues for two weeks (called 'HB run-on' in this *Handbook* – see p220). You do not have to pay HB run-on back, even if you qualify for a UC housing costs element for your rent. If your HB is being paid direct to your landlord, your HB run-on payments are usually also paid to her/him. If this

Part 2: Universal credit
Chapter 6: The housing costs element
1. Who can get a housing costs element

happens, you should ask your landlord to pay you the HB run-on – eg, if you are up to date with your rent payments.

When you cannot get a housing costs element

Your UC maximum amount cannot include a housing costs element if you:

- rent your accommodation and you are 16 or 17 and are, or have been, looked after by a local authority;[5]
- are an owner-occupier (unless you have a shared ownership tenancy – ie, you are buying part of your home and renting the rest), during an assessment period in which you (or your partner) have any earned income (see p116), however much your earnings are.[6] This includes earnings from work you can do while claiming contributory employment and support allowance (see p1042) or from work of less than 16 hours a week you can do while claiming contribution-based jobseeker's allowance (JSA – see p991). The nature and duration of the work is not relevant – eg, it does not matter if your job is part time or temporary;
- live in 'specified' or 'temporary' accommodation (see p85), for the rent you pay for that accommodation. You *can* get HB for this.

Rent payments

Eligible rent payments include the rent you pay to your landlord, but can also include other types of payment, such as payments as a licensee and for bed and breakfast or hostel accommodation. The eligible payments are:[7]

- rent;
- payments for a licence or permission to occupy accommodation;
- mooring charges payable for a houseboat;
- site rent for a caravan or mobile home (but not for a tent); *and*
- contributions made by a resident of a charity's almshouse towards its maintenance and the essential services in it. The almshouse must be provided by a housing association.

Payments that are not eligible

The following types of payments are *not* eligible rent payments:[8]

- ground rent;
- payments for a tent or its pitch;
- payments for approved premises – eg, a bail or probation hostel;
- payments made for 'specified' or 'temporary' accommodation (see p85). You *can* get HB for these (see Chapter 10); *and*
- payments made for a care home (see p85).

Definitions

'Specified accommodation' is:[9]

– accommodation provided by a relevant body to meet your need for, and where you get, care, support or supervision; *or*

– temporary accommodation (eg, a refuge) provided by a local authority or a relevant body for people who have left home because of domestic violence; *or*

– a local authority hostel for homeless people where you get care, support or supervision to assist you to be rehabilitated or resettled within the community; *or*

– 'exempt accommodation', such as specified types of supported accommodation (see p403 – the meaning is the same as for HB).

For these purposes, a 'relevant body' is a county council (in England) or a housing association, registered charity or voluntary organisation.

Your accommodation is **'temporary accommodation'** if you live in a specified type of homeless accommodation that does not count as 'exempt accommodation' (see p403 – the meaning is the same as for HB) and your rent is payable to a local authority or a provider of social housing (see p92 for the meaning).[10]

'Care home' means a care home (in England), a care home service (in Wales and Scotland) or an independent hospital.[11]

Service charge payments

Eligible service charge payments are those which are:[12]

- for the costs of, or charges for, services or facilities for the use or benefit of people occupying the accommodation – eg, window cleaning or garden maintenance; *or*
- fairly attributable to the costs of, or charges for, services or facilities connected with the accommodation that are available for the use or benefit of people occupying the accommodation – eg, provision of laundry facilities.

The payments do not usually have to be separately identified – eg, in your tenancy agreement or lease. It does not matter if they are paid in addition to, or as part of, your rent, or if they are made under the same or a different agreement to that under which you occupy your home. However, if you live in social rented sector accommodation (eg, your landlord is a local authority or housing association) or you are an owner-occupier, there are extra conditions and the rules specify the only categories that are eligible (see p86).

Payments that are not eligible

Payments are not eligible and cannot be included in your housing costs element if:[13]

- the services or facilities to which the payments relate are for someone occupying a tent, approved premises (eg, a bail or probation hostel), a care

Part 2: Universal credit
Chapter 6: The housing costs element
1. Who can get a housing costs element

home (see p85) or 'exempt accommodation' (see p403 – you may instead qualify for HB); *or*
- you have taken out a loan to make the payments, which is secured on your home.

Extra conditions for social rented sector tenants and owner-occupiers

If you live in social rented sector accommodation or you are an owner-occupier, service charge payments are only eligible if you must make them as a condition of occupying your accommodation – eg, as part of your tenancy agreement or lease, not as an optional extra.[14] The costs and charges must be reasonable, must be for services and facilities that are reasonable to provide and must be in one of the following categories.[15]

- Payments to maintain the general standard of accommodation – ie, for:
  - cleaning the outside of windows on the upper floors of a multi-storey building; *or*
  - if you have a shared ownership tenancy (ie, you are buying part of your home and renting the rest) or are an owner-occupier, internal or external maintenance or repair of the accommodation. The payments must be separately identifiable.
- Payments for the general upkeep of communal areas – ie, for the ongoing maintenance of, and the supply of, water, fuel or any other commodity to internal or external areas – eg, communal gardens, tenant parking facilities, laundry rooms and children's play areas.
- Payments for basic communal services. They must be for the provision, ongoing maintenance, cleaning or repair of basic services generally available to everyone living in the accommodation – eg, refuse collection, communal lifts, secure building access, fire alarm systems or wireless or television aerials to receive a service free of charge. The DWP says it should also include payments for someone employed to provide an eligible service (eg, a concierge, groundskeeper or caretaker), as well as the costs of managing and administering eligible services.[16]
- Accommodation-specific charges. These must be for the use of essential items specific to the particular accommodation you occupy – eg, for furniture or domestic appliances.

However, payments are *not* eligible and cannot be included in your housing costs element if they are:[17]
- for services or facilities for which public funding is available, whether or not you are entitled to such funding; *or*
- connected to the use of an asset which will result in the transfer of that asset, or any interest in it – eg, payments for furniture and equipment that will eventually become yours; *or*

- for food, medical services or personal services (including laundry, cleaning or personal care).

Social rented sector accommodation

Your accommodation is social rented sector accommodation if your landord is a 'provider of social housing'. A provider of social housing is a local authority, a non-profit registered provider of social housing, a profit-making registered provider of social housing (if you have been housed in social housing) or a registered social landlord.[18]

2. Liability for payments

To qualify for a housing costs element, you (or your partner, if you are a joint claimant) must be liable to make eligible payments on a commercial basis (see below), or you (or s/he) must be treated as liable (see p88).[19] **Note:** you (or your partner) can be treated as not liable to make payments, even if you are (see p89).

In deciding whether your agreement is on a commercial basis, the DWP must look at the whole agreement and take all the circumstances into account. The DWP should consider, among other things, the following.[20]

- Whether your agreement includes terms that are not legally enforceable. This might arise, for example, if you do household chores. However, if you do chores in exchange for a lower rent, it could be considered commercial.
- The rent you have agreed to pay. However, the rent does not have to be a market rent. Your agreement can count as commercial even if your landlord is not collecting the full contractual rent from you – eg, if it is not being met in full because of the way your housing costs element is calculated.
- Your relationship to the person to whom you are liable. However, just because s/he is a relative or close friend, or s/he provides you with care and support, does not mean that your agreement is non-commercial.

Note: if you are jointly liable to make payments with someone, the way your housing costs element is calculated takes this into account (see p104 and p109).

Liability to pay rent

For you to be liable to pay rent, your agreement must be legally enforceable.[21] It is not enough if you only have a moral obligation, such as a promise to pay something whenever you can afford to do so. You can count as liable to pay rent even if someone else has been paying it on your behalf, or if your landlord has failed to provide notice of an address so rent is treated as not being due.[22] You can be liable to pay rent by yourself or you can be jointly liable to do so.

Part 2: Universal credit
Chapter 6: The housing costs element
2. Liability for payments

Does your agreement have to be in writing?

If you have a written agreement with your landlord, this should establish that you are liable to pay rent, provided the liability is a genuine part of the agreement.[23]

Your agreement can be legally enforceable, even if it is not in writing. The fact that you have made a firm promise to pay money to your landlord in return for occupying the property should be sufficient to show you are liable to pay rent and so allow you to qualify for a housing costs element.[24] If the DWP refuses to accept that you have a legal liability, apply for a revision or appeal.

Note: even if the DWP accepts that your agreement is legally enforceable, it may still treat you as not liable to pay rent (see p89).

People treated as liable to make payments

You (or your partner) are treated as liable to make payments:[25]

- if a child or qualifying young person for whom you (or your partner) are responsible (see p63) is liable to make the payments; *or*
- if you are a member of a couple but you are claiming universal credit (UC) as a single person (other than if you are in a polygamous marriage) and your partner is liable to make the payments. See p36 for when you can claim as a single person; *or*
- if someone else is liable to make the payments but is not doing so (see below); *or*
- if payments are waived by the person to whom you are liable (eg, your landlord) as reasonable compensation for your carrying out reasonable repairs or redecoration which s/he would otherwise have had to carry out; *or*
- during rent-free periods.

Another person is liable but is not paying

You (or your partner, if you are a joint claimant) are treated as liable to make payments if someone else is liable to make them but is not doing so, and you must make the payments yourself to continue to live in your home.[26] In addition, you must show that:

- it would be unreasonable to expect you to make other arrangements; *and*
- it is reasonable in all the circumstances to treat you as liable.[27]

This might apply, for example, if you have given up your home to live with and care for someone and s/he has now gone into a care home (you can be treated as liable for the payments on her/his home), or if you have separated from your partner (even if you have not lived in the home continuously since your partner left), or if the liable person ceases to qualify for a housing costs element because s/he has become a full-time student.[28]

It does not matter whether or not the landlord is prepared to transfer the tenancy to you or wants to evict you. If the DWP refuses to treat you as liable, point out that the eligibility rules for the housing costs element and the rules for transferring tenancies are separate. If you are refused the housing costs element, ask for a revision or appeal.

People treated as not liable to make payments

You (or your partner) can be treated as though you are *not* liable to make payments in the following situations.[29]

- You are liable to make the payments to someone who also lives in the accommodation, and who is:
    - your partner, or a child or qualifying young person for whom you (or your partner) are responsible (see p63); *or*
    - a close relative of yours or your partner, or of a child or qualifying young person for whom you (or your partner) are responsible.

    For example, this applies if you are living with, and pay rent to, your parents. If you are liable to pay service charge payments to the same person, you are also treated as not liable for those payments.

- You are liable to make the payments to a trustee of a trust or a company and the trustees or beneficiaries of the trust, or the owners or directors of the company, include you, your partner or a qualifying young person (or in the case of trusts, a child) for whom you (or your partner) are responsible (see p63), or a close relative of any of these. The close relative must live with you in the accommodation. If you are liable to pay service charge payments to a trustee of the same trust (or of another trust whose trustees or beneficiaries include any of these people), or to the same company (or a company whose owners or directors include any of these people), you are also treated as not liable for those payments.

- The payments are for any increase in what you would otherwise be required to pay for your accommodation that are to cover any outstanding arrears for that accommodation (or for any accommodation you previously occupied) or that are for any other unpaid payment or charge.

- The DWP considers your liability to be 'contrived' (see p90).

- You are treated as not liable to make service charge payments if you are liable to make them to someone who lives in your household (see p59 for the meaning), unless you also pay rent.[30]

Part 2: Universal credit
Chapter 6: The housing costs element
2. Liability for payments

Close relative

A '**close relative**' is a parent, parent-in-law (including a civil partner's parent), son, son-in-law (including a son's civil partner), daughter, daughter-in-law (including a daughter's civil partner), brother, sister, step-parent (including a parent's civil partner), stepson (including a civil partner's son), stepdaughter (including a civil partner's daughter), or the partners of any of these.[31] It also includes half-brothers and sisters.[32] Relations with in-laws or step-relatives are severed by divorce (or dissolution of a civil partnership) but arguably not by death – eg, a stepchild is still a stepchild after the death of her/his mother.

Contrived agreements

You can be treated as not liable to make payments if your liability was 'contrived' to get the housing costs element included in your UC, or to increase the amount of your housing costs element.[33] The DWP says this applies if either you or your landlord, or both of you, contrived the liability.[34] For your agreement to count as contrived, it must amount to an abuse of the UC scheme or take improper advantage of it – ie, that the main reason you entered into the agreement to make payments was to obtain or increase your UC housing costs element.[35] All the circumstances should be taken into account when deciding whether this is the case, including what the person you are liable to pay has to say.[36] An agreement can count as contrived even if it was created from the best of motives.[37]

Have you been told your agreement is contrived?

The DWP may say that your agreement is contrived if you are in any of the situations described on pp178–80 for housing benefit. If it does, get advice. 'Contrived' is not defined in the rules. You can argue the following.

1. Your agreement should not count as contrived just because the person you are liable to pay is your parent[38] or because you hope to be able to claim UC to help you with your rent – ie, if your main purpose is to get accommodation, not to obtain the UC housing costs element.[39]

2. You should not be regarded as having a contrived agreement just because you try to find out what payments can be covered by UC – eg, before moving in.

3. If you are a tenant of a landlord who deliberately charges high rents in order to have them paid by UC, you may be affected by this provision, even though you had no such intention yourself. Argue that a high rent, in itself, does not mean that the liability is contrived.[40]

4. If your landlord says s/he will evict you if you cannot get the UC housing costs element, or get it increased, this suggests that the agreement is *not* contrived.[41]

5. If the DWP says your agreement is contrived and does not include a housing costs element in your UC, you can appeal.

3. **Occupying accommodation as a home**

To qualify for the universal credit (UC) housing costs element, you must normally occupy the accommodation for which you make eligible payments as your home.[42] You cannot usually get a housing costs element for any other home. However, there are special rules if you:
- have just moved into your home (see below);
- are liable to make payments for more than one dwelling (see below);
- are temporarily absent from home (see p92);
- are in temporary accommodation while repairs are carried out on your home (see p93);
- have left your previous home because of a fear of domestic violence (see p93).

Moving home

If you have moved into new accommodation, you are treated as occupying it for up to one month before you moved in, provided you were liable (or treated as liable) for the eligible rent or service charges for the accommodation immediately before you moved in, and:[43]
- there was a delay in moving into your accommodation, this was reasonable and was necessary to enable the accommodation to be adapted to meet needs you, your partner (if you are a joint claimant) or a child or qualifying young person for whom you (or your partner, if you are a joint claimant) are responsible (see p63) have because of a disability. The adaptations do not need to involve a change to the fabric or structure of the dwelling, but must be reasonably required and be clearly connected to your disability needs.[44] The person with the disability must be getting the middle or highest rate of the disability living allowance care component, attendance allowance, armed forces independence payment or the daily living component of personal independence payment.
  Note: in these circumstances you may also qualify for a housing costs element for your former home (see below), or for housing benefit (HB) for your former home (if it was 'specified' or 'temporary' accommodation – see p85); *or*
- you became liable to make payments on your new accommodation while you were a hospital inpatient or while you were living in a care home (see p85 for the meaning), or if you make a joint claim, while both of you were.

More than one dwelling

You cannot usually be treated as occupying more than one dwelling.[45] If you do, to decide which dwelling you normally occupy as your home, the DWP must consider all the circumstances. **Note:** different rules apply if you are living away from your normal home because of a fear of domestic violence (see p93).

Part 2: Universal credit
Chapter 6: The housing costs element
3. Occupying accommodation as a home

You *can* get a housing costs element:

- for both your previous and your new accommodation for up to one month if there was a delay in moving into your new accommodation, this was reasonable and was necessary to enable it to be adapted to meet needs you, your partner (if you are a joint claimant) or a child or qualifying young person for whom you (or your partner, if you are a joint claimant) are responsible (see p63) have because of a disability.[46] The conditions are the same as those for moving home (see p91). This only applies if, immediately before you moved, you qualified for a housing costs element for your previous accommodation and were also liable for the eligible rent or service charges (see p84, p85 and p87) for your new accommodation. **Note:** if you are only liable to make payments for your new accommodation, you may qualify for a housing costs element for that accommodation (see p91).

- for two dwellings indefinitely if you have been housed in two dwellings by a 'provider of social housing' (see below) because of the number of children and qualifying young people who live with you.[47] You must normally occupy both dwellings with the children or qualifying young people for whom you (or your partner, if you are a joint claimant) are responsible (see p63). You must be liable for the eligible rent or service charges (see p84, p85 and p87) for both dwellings.

Provider of social housing

A '**provider of social housing**' is a local authority, a non-profit registered provider of social housing, a profit-making registered provider of social housing (if you have been housed in social housing) or a registered social landlord.[48]

Temporary absence from home

If you are only temporarily absent from your normal home, you continue to be treated as occupying it for up to six months, whatever the reason for your absence.[49] You can be treated as occupying your normal home for a longer period if you have to live in other accommodation while repairs are being carried out on your normal home (see p93) or you are living away from home because of a fear of domestic violence (see p93).

You can argue that you count as temporarily absent from accommodation even if you have not yet stayed there – eg, you move your furniture and belongings in but then have to go into hospital.[50] A new period of absence starts if you return home for even a short stay. A stay of at least 24 hours may be enough.[51]

If you are a prisoner or are on temporary release from prison, you can get a housing costs element under this rule while you are temporarily absent from home, provided you were entitled to UC as a single person immediately before you became a prisoner, your UC included a housing costs element and your prison sentence is not expected to last more than six months.[52] If you are a member of a couple, your partner may instead be able to claim UC with a housing costs element in your absence.

Note:

- You are no longer treated as occupying your normal home when your absence has lasted, or is expected to last, longer than six months. The decision whether or not your absence from home is expected to last longer than six months should initially be based on the circumstances on the date you leave your home.[53] If at any time after that date you no longer intend to return, or it becomes likely that you will be away from home for more than six months, your entitlement can be reconsidered.[54]
- If you are temporarily absent from Great Britain for longer than a set period (from one to six months depending on the circumstances), your entitlement to UC may be affected. See p1663 for further information.
- If your partner, child or non-dependant is temporarily absent from your home, this may affect how many bedrooms you are allowed when working out the amount of your housing costs element (see p100).

Temporary accommodation while repairs are carried out

If you are required to move into temporary accommodation because essential repairs are being carried out on your normal home, but you intend to return to that home, the following applies.[55]

- If you are liable to pay eligible rent or service charges for only one of the homes, you are treated as occupying that home and you get a housing costs element indefinitely for the payments you make in respect of it.
- If you are liable to pay eligible rent or service charges for both homes, you are treated as occupying only your normal home and you get a housing costs element indefinitely for the payments you make in respect of it.

'**Essential repairs**' means basic works rather than luxuries, but they need not be necessary to make the house habitable.[56]

Domestic violence

Special rules apply if you are living in accommodation other than your normal home, and it is unreasonable to expect you to return to your normal home because of a reasonable fear of violence. You must fear violence in the home, or violence from a former partner against you or any child or qualifying young person for whom you are responsible (see p63). You must intend to return to your normal home. If these rules apply:[57]

- you are treated as occupying both the accommodation you are living in and your normal home for up to 12 months if:
  - you are liable to pay eligible rent or service charges for both your current accommodation and your normal home; *and*

Part 2: Universal credit
Chapter 6: The housing costs element
4. How the housing costs element is calculated: general rules

  – it is reasonable to include an amount for the payments for both homes in your housing costs element; *or*
- if you are only liable to pay eligible rent or service charges for one of the homes, you are treated as occupying that home indefinitely (but see below). It must be reasonable to include an amount for the payments for that accommodation in your housing costs element. **Note:** if one of the homes is 'specified' or 'temporary' accommodation (eg, a refuge – see p85), you can qualify for HB for the accommodation and can get a housing costs element for your other home.

In both cases, you are no longer treated as occupying your normal home when your absence has lasted, or is expected to last, longer than 12 months.[58] The decision whether or not your absence from home is expected to last longer than 12 months should initially be based on the circumstances on the date you leave your home.[59] If, at any time after that date, you no longer intend to return, or it becomes likely that you will be away from home for more than 12 months, your entitlement can be reconsidered.[60]

4. How the housing costs element is calculated: general rules

How the amount of your housing costs element is calculated depends on whether you live in private rented accommodation (see p103) or in social rented sector accommodation (see p107). For service charge payments, it depends on whether you rent your accommodation or are an owner-occupier.

In all cases, to calculate your housing costs element you must first work out the monthly equivalent of your rent or service charge payments, if these are paid other than calendar monthly. You must then work out:
- who counts as a member of your 'extended benefit unit' (broadly, the people who live with you – see p96); *and*
- the number of bedrooms you are allowed (known as the 'size criteria' – see p97); *and*
- whether a deduction must be made for any non-dependant living with you (a 'housing costs contribution' – see p102).

How do you work out monthly equivalents?
If you pay your rent or service charges:[61]
– weekly, multiply by 52 and divide by 12;
– two-weekly, multiply by 26 and divide by 12;
– four-weekly, multiply by 13 and divide by 12;
– three-monthly, multiply by four and divide by 12;
– annually, divide by 12.

If you have a regular rent-free or service charge-free period, to work out the monthly equivalent divide the total payments you make over the year by 12 – eg, if you have four rent-free weeks each year and so only pay rent for 48 weeks, divide the total of the 48 weeks' payments by 12.

Note:

- If you are a joint tenant, the housing costs element calculation takes this into account (see p104 and p109).
- Special rules apply if you qualify for a housing costs element for more than one dwelling (see below).
- If a housing costs element is included in your universal credit (UC) maximum amount, you only get a lower work allowance and so more of your earnings are taken into account (see p41).
- If you have a shared ownership tenancy (ie, you are buying part of your home and renting the rest), your housing costs element can include amounts for the rent and service charge payments you make.[62] Your service charge payments are calculated as for rent payments.
- Your housing costs element is normally paid to you, but see p49 for when it can be paid direct to your landlord.

If you have more than one dwelling

Special rules apply if you qualify for a housing costs element for more than one dwelling.

If you have been **housed in two dwellings** by a provider of social housing (see p92) because of the number of your children, your housing costs element is worked out using a single calculation.[63] All the eligible payments for both dwellings are taken into account, and the number of bedrooms you are treated as having is the total number in both dwellings. Your housing costs element is calculated as for social rented sector tenancies (see p107) if you pay rent to a social sector landlord for both dwellings. Otherwise, your housing costs element is calculated as for private sector tenancies (see p103), in which case there is a special rule for working out your 'cap rent' (see p105).

If there was a **delay in moving** into your home because it was being adapted for a disabled person and you qualify for a housing costs element for both your old and your new accommodation (see p92), amounts are calculated for each home as for social rented sector or private sector tenancies (as appropriate) and your housing costs element is the total of these.[64] However, housing costs contributions for a non-dependant (see p102) are only deducted from the rent payments for your old home.

If you are living away from your normal home because of a **fear of domestic violence** and qualify for a housing costs element for both your current

Part 2: Universal credit
Chapter 6: The housing costs element
4. How the housing costs element is calculated: general rules

accommodation and your normal home (see p93), amounts are calculated for each home as for social rented sector or private sector tenancies (as appropriate) and your housing costs element is the total of these.[65] However, housing costs contributions from non-dependants (see p102) are only deducted from the rent payments for the accommodation you are occupying.

Extended benefit unit

The members of your 'extended benefit unit' are:[66]

- you; *and*
- your partner (if you are a joint claimant); *and*
- any child or qualifying young person for whom you (or your partner, if you are a joint claimant) are responsible (see p63); *and*
- any non-dependant (see below for who counts).

People can continue to count as members of your extended benefit unit while absent from home for a temporary period (see p92 and p100). You can continue to count as responsible for a child or qualifying young person while s/he is absent from your household for a period (see p63).

Who counts as a non-dependant

People who normally live in your accommodation with you (other than your partner and your children) are called 'non-dependants'.[67] Examples of non-dependants are adult sons or daughters (and their children), or friends or elderly relatives who share your home. If someone is only staying with you temporarily and has a home elsewhere, or is homeless and is only using your address as a postal address, s/he does not count as a non-dependant. If you think the DWP has wrongly assumed that a person is (or is not) your non-dependant, ask for a revision or appeal. **Note:** some people do not count as non-dependants even if they normally live with you (see p97).

A person is only 'living with you' if s/he has her/his home with you and shares some accommodation with you.[68] This includes sharing the kitchen (unless it is only used by someone else to prepare food for her/him[69]).

A person only counts as 'normally living with you' if s/he has been there long enough to regard your home as her/his normal home.[70] **Note:** for these purposes, someone can only have one normal home at a time.[71]

A number of factors should be taken into account to decide whether a person normally lives with you, including:

- the relationship between you;
- how much time s/he spends at your address;
- where her/his post is sent;
- where s/he keeps her/his clothes and personal belongings;
- whether her/his stay or absence from your address is temporary or permanent and, if s/he is absent temporarily, how long the absence has lasted (see p100);

- whether s/he has another place that could be regarded as home and if, for instance, s/he pays rent there or just travels around.

People who are not non-dependants

Even if they normally live with you, the following people do *not* count as non-dependants. When your housing costs element is calculated, you are not allowed bedrooms for any of them under the rules (see below). However, no deduction for a housing costs contribution (see p102) is made from your housing costs element for them.[72]

- A child or qualifying young person for whom no one in your extended benefit unit (see p96) is responsible (see p63).
- Your (or your partner's, if you are a joint claimant) foster child(ren).
- Someone to whom you (or your partner, if you are a joint claimant) are liable to pay rent or service charges, and any member of her/his household – eg, your resident landlord and her/his family.
- Someone who has already been treated as the non-dependant of another UC claimant, if the other claimant is also liable to pay rent or service charges for the accommodation you occupy. This means that you are not allowed a bedroom for her/him, but also that a deduction from your housing costs element for a housing costs contribution (see p102) is not made for her/him. It is only made from the housing costs element of the other claimant.
- Someone who is liable to pay rent or service charges on a commercial basis for the accommodation you occupy, whether this is to you (or your partner, if you are a joint claimant), or to another person – eg, s/he is your lodger or subtenant, or a joint tenant.

Note: your partner and any child or qualifying young person for whom you or your partner are responsible (see p63) do not count as non-dependants.[73] However, you are allowed bedrooms for them if they count as members of your extended benefit unit (see p96).

The number of bedrooms you are allowed

If you live in rented accommodation, to calculate your housing costs element you need to know how many bedrooms you are allowed under the rules (known as the 'size criteria'). You are only allowed a bedroom for someone if s/he is a member of your 'extended benefit unit' (see p96). If your home has more bedrooms than you are allowed, your full rent might not be included in your housing costs element.

You are allowed:[74]

- one bedroom for each of the following members of your 'extended benefit unit':
  - you (and your partner);

Part 2: Universal credit
Chapter 6: The housing costs element
4. How the housing costs element is calculated: general rules

- a qualifying young person for whom you (or your partner, if you are a joint claimant) are responsible (see p63);
- a non-dependant aged at least 16 (see p96 for who counts). **Note:** you are allowed one bedroom for every non-dependant, even if they are members of a couple;
- two children under 16 of the same gender;
- two children under 10;
- any other child under 16.

Note: if someone fits into more than one category, s/he is treated as being in the category that results in the lowest number of bedrooms; *and*

- one or more additional bedrooms in certain situations (see below).

If you are a private tenant, the maximum number of bedrooms you are allowed, including any additional bedrooms, is four.[75] If you are a social rented sector tenant, there is no maximum number of bedrooms.

Note:

- 'Bedroom' is not defined, but see p101 for what may count.
- A bedroom can be included for a person in your extended benefit unit during her/his temporary absence from home (see p100). In some cases, this only applies for a period.

What if a member of your extended benefit unit dies?

If your partner (if you are a joint claimant), a child or qualifying young person for whom you (or s/he) were responsible (see p63), a non-dependant or a severely disabled person for whom you were caring dies, your UC continues to be calculated as if s/he had not died for the assessment period in which the death occurred and the following two assessment periods. So if you are no longer allowed as many bedrooms under the rules, this does not affect your housing costs element until after the three assessment periods.[76]

Additional bedrooms

In certain situations, in addition to the number of bedrooms you are allowed under the rules above, you are allowed one or more additional bedrooms. If more than one situation applies, you are allowed the total number of additional bedrooms to which you are entitled.[77] 'Bedroom' is not defined, but see p101 for what may count.

- **Non-resident carers.** You are allowed one additional bedroom for a non-resident carer if you, any other person in your extended benefit unit (see p96), or a child or young person in respect of whom you meet the 'foster parent condition' (see p99) need someone to stay overnight to provide care regularly, and overnight care has been arranged and is provided.[78] The person must get attendance allowance (AA), the middle or highest rate of the disability living allowance (DLA) care component, the daily living component of personal independence payment (PIP) or armed forces independence payment. Even if more than one person requires overnight care, only one additional bedroom is allowed.

- **Member of a couple who cannot share a bedroom.** Unless you are a member of a couple claiming UC as a single person, you are allowed one additional bedroom if you and your partner are not reasonably able to share a bedroom because of your (or her/his) disability. The disabled partner must be getting the higher rate of AA, the middle or highest rate of the DLA care component, the daily living component of PIP or armed forces independence payment.
- **Disabled child who cannot share a bedroom.** You are allowed one additional bedroom if you or any other person in your extended benefit unit (see p96) are responsible for a child under 16 who would normally be expected to share a bedroom under the rules above, but cannot reasonably do so because of her/his disability. The child must be getting the middle or highest rate of the DLA care component. If more than one child qualifies, you are allowed as many additional bedrooms as you need to ensure that each has her/his own bedroom. **Note:** if, before 4 December 2013, you were not allowed an additional bedroom for a disabled child, when you should have been, apply for a revision on grounds of official error.[79]
- **Adoption, fostering and kinship carers.** You are allowed one additional bedroom if you (or your partner, if you are a joint claimant) meet the 'foster parent condition'.

You meet the **'foster parent condition'** if you have a child placed with you for adoption or you are a foster parent (in Scotland this includes kinship carers). If you are a foster parent, this applies even if you do not currently have a child placed with you, provided you have become an approved foster parent, or have fostered a child, within the last 12 months. You are only allowed one additional bedroom even if, for example, you have more than one foster child, or if both you and your partner are foster parents or adopters.

Examples

Michael and Barbara have two daughters, aged 10 and 13, and two sons, aged 15 and 22. The 10-year-old daughter is severely disabled and is unable to share a bedroom because of this. Michael's parents live with them. They claim UC. They are allowed one bedroom for Michael and Barbara, one bedroom for the daughters, one bedroom for each of their sons and one bedroom for each of Michael's parents. They are allowed an additional bedroom for their 10-year-old daughter. This is a total of seven bedrooms. They are private tenants, so the housing costs element calculation is based on a four-bedroom property – the maximum allowed. If they had been social rented sector tenants, their housing costs element would have been calculated based on a seven-bedroom property.

Kian is the foster parent of two sisters, aged 10 and 16. He has two sons, aged 10 and 12, one of whom is getting the middle rate of the DLA care component and cannot share a

Part 2: Universal credit
Chapter 6: The housing costs element
4. How the housing costs element is calculated: general rules

bedroom because of his disability. Kian is allowed one bedroom for himself, and would normally be allowed one bedroom for his two sons. However, he is allowed one additional bedroom for his disabled son, and one additional bedroom because he is a foster parent. He is, therefore, allowed a total of four bedrooms.

Note:

* The rules were amended from 1 April 2017 to allow an additional bedroom if you cannot share a bedroom because of a disability and if people living with you require overnight care. If you were already getting a UC housing costs element on that date and had not been allowed an additional bedroom, the DWP should reassess your UC and pay you any arrears due. If the DWP says that arrears can only be backdated to 1 April 2017, argue this is wrong and apply for a revision or appeal.[80]
* If you live in a dwelling adapted for you under a 'sanctuary scheme', and your rent is restricted because you have more bedrooms than the rules allow, you can argue that the rules discriminate against you.[81] It is not yet clear if the government will amend the rules. See AskCPAG.org.uk and CPAG's *Welfare Rights Bulletin* for updates.
* There are a number of other situations when you may need more bedrooms than shown above – eg, if you need an additional room to store equipment required because of a severe disability, or if you provide accommodation for a disabled person under an adult placement scheme, or if you share the care of your child but s/he counts as normally living with her/his other parent. You should appeal if you are affected, but your appeal may be held up while the courts are considering other cases.[82]

Temporary absence from home

When determining how many bedrooms you are allowed, a person can continue to be included in your extended benefit unit (see p96) while temporarily absent from your home.

You (or your partner) are included during:[83]

* the one- to six-month period in which you (or your partner) continue to qualify for UC while temporarily absent from Great Britain (see p1663); *or*
* the first six months you are a prisoner, provided immediately before becoming a prisoner you were entitled to UC as a single person, you were getting a housing costs element and your sentence is not expected to last longer than six months.

Note: you (and your partner) can be treated as occupying your home during other periods when you are temporarily away (see p92 and p93).

If, immediately before the start of the period of absence, s/he was included in your extended benefit unit and you were getting a housing costs element, **your child or qualifying young person is included:**[84]
- during the first six months of her/his absence if s/he is:
  - being looked after by a local authority; *or*
  - a prisoner, provided her/his sentence is not expected to last longer than six months;
- in any other case, for the period you continue to be treated as responsible for her/him while s/he is absent from your household (see p63).

If, immediately before the start of the period of absence, s/he was included in your extended benefit unit, **your non-dependant is included:**[85]
- indefinitely, if s/he is your (or your partner's) son, daughter, stepson or stepdaughter who is a member of the armed forces deployed on operations;
- during the one- (or two-) month period in which s/he continues (or would have continued) to qualify for UC while temporarily absent from Great Britain (see p1663);
- during the first six months of her/his absence if s/he is:
  - temporarily absent from Great Britain to receive medical treatment or convalescence or to take her/his partner, child or a qualifying young person for medical treatment or convalescence (see p1663);
  - a prisoner, provided her/his sentence is not expected to last longer than six months;
- in any other case, for up to six months. However, s/he is no longer included if the absence lasts (or is expected to last) longer than six months.

Note: unless your non-dependant is a member of the armed forces deployed on operations, you must also have been getting a housing costs element immediately before the start of the period of absence.

What counts as a bedroom

When working out the number of bedrooms you are allowed, you may need to consider what counts as a bedroom. For example, you may need to argue that a room is a bedroom; or it may be more advantageous for you to argue that a room is not a bedroom.

'Bedroom' is not defined in the rules. It is the ordinary meaning of the word that is relevant. It could be, for example, a lounge or living room, provided it contains a bed or is used for sleeping.[86]

The starting point is whether the room can be used as a bedroom – ie, a room is a bedroom if it is furnished and can be used for sleeping in. How a property is described by the landlord (eg, as a two- or three-bedroom house) or whether a room is designated as a bedroom may be relevant. However, the basis on which

Part 2: Universal credit
Chapter 6: The housing costs element
4. How the housing costs element is calculated: general rules

your rent is charged (eg, if your flat has two bedrooms but your landlord only charges the rent for a one-bedroom flat) is not relevant.[87]

You can try to argue that the DWP should not count a room in your home as a bedroom and, therefore, that your housing costs element should not be reduced (or reduced as much) under the rules on p103 or p107. In deciding whether a room is a bedroom, the DWP should, for example, take into account:[88]

- the size of the room (the dimensions and height) – eg, whether it can accommodate a single bed and somewhere to store clothes, whether it has a flat surface on which to place things safely, such as a glass of water, and whether there is space to dress and undress. If a room is too small, provide a measured plan and photographs if you can; *and*
- whether the room is safe to sleep in – eg, if it is contaminated with asbestos; *and*
- access to the room and whether it has adequate natural and electric lighting, heating, ventilation and privacy.

Suggest your personal use of the room should also be taken into account (eg, if you have a disability and you use the room to store your equipment), as well as whether your home has been converted or adapted – eg, if two small bedrooms have been converted into one big bedroom, or if a bedroom has been redesignated. However, the DWP is likely to say that in deciding how many bedrooms there are in your home:

- it is the classification and description of the property when it is empty that is relevant and that this can only be changed if the property has been structurally altered with the approval of your landlord;[89]
- even if your home could be occupied in more than one way (eg, as either one- or two-bedroom), it can use the way your landlord designates the property to determine how many bedrooms it has.[90]

Housing costs contributions

If your extended benefit unit includes a 'non-dependant' (see p96), a set deduction is usually made from your housing costs element.[91] This is because it is assumed that the non-dependant makes a contribution towards your outgoings, whether or not s/he does so. The DWP calls these deductions 'housing costs contributions'. They are also known as 'non-dependant deductions'. In some circumstances, no deductions are made. **Note:**

- If you are an owner-occupier, no deduction is made from your service charge payments unless you have a shared ownership tenancy.
- A non-dependant can only be a member of the extended benefit unit of one UC claimant (or pair of joint claimants),[92] so a deduction is only made from that UC claimant's (or pair of joint claimants') housing costs element.

When no deduction is made

No deduction is made for any of your non-dependants if you (or your partner, if you are a joint claimant):[93]

- are certified as severely sight impaired or blind by a consultant ophthalmologist; or
- get AA (or equivalent benefits paid because of an injury at work or a war injury), the middle or highest rate of the DLA care component, the daily living component of PIP or armed forces independence payment, or would receive one of these but for being in hospital.

If deductions must be made, no deduction is made for any non-dependant who is:[94]

- getting AA, the middle or highest rate of the DLA care component, the daily living component of PIP or armed forces independence payment, or who would receive it but for being in hospital; or
- getting carer's allowance; or
- getting pension credit; or
- a prisoner; or
- under 21 years old; or
- your (or your partner's, if you are a joint claimant) son, daughter, stepson or stepdaughter who is in the armed forces and is deployed on operations. **Note:** this only applies if s/he lived with you immediately before leaving, and intends to live with you at the end of the operations; or
- responsible for a child under five.

The amount of the deduction

If a deduction must be made, it is made for every non-dependant who is a member of your extended benefit unit (see p96).[95] The deduction is a fixed amount of £75.15 for the assessment period, whether or not s/he is a member of a couple, irrespective of her/his income and what s/he pays you.[96]

5. The amount for private rented tenants

If you are a private tenant, your housing costs element is calculated as follows.[97]

- **Step one:** work out the monthly equivalent of your 'core rent'. This is broadly the amount of rent and service charges you must pay (see p104).
- **Step two:** work out your 'cap rent'. This is the maximum amount of rent that can be included in your housing costs element (see p105). It may be lower than the rent you must pay.
- **Step three:** if your extended benefit unit (see p96) includes any non-dependants, deduct any housing costs contribution that applies (see p102) from the lowest of your core rent or your cap rent. This is the amount of your

Part 2: Universal credit
Chapter 6: The housing costs element
5. The amount for private rented tenants

housing costs element. It can never be lower than nil – ie, no further reduction can be made to your universal credit (UC) award.[98]

Note: if you qualify for a housing costs element for more than one dwelling, special rules apply (see p95).

Examples

Hannah is a joint tenant of a four-bedroom private flat with Carol, a friend. Her son, aged 27 lives with them. The rent for the flat is £1,000 a month, including eligible service charge payments. Hannah claims UC. Her extended benefit unit includes Hannah and her son, who counts as a non-dependant; Carol does not count as a non-dependant.

Step one: Hannah's core rent is £1,000 ÷ 2 x 1 = £500 a month.

Step two: Hannah's cap rent is the local housing allowance for two-bedroom accommodation. In her area this is £400 a month. Her cap rent is lower than her core rent.

Step three: Hannah's housing costs element is, therefore, £400 (the cap rent) – £75.15 (housing costs contribution) = £324.85

Note: if Carol also claims UC, her extended benefit unit does not include Hannah's son as a non-dependant, so Carol's cap rent is the local housing allowance for one-bedroom shared accommodation. However, no housing costs contribution is deducted.

Patrick and Isla rent a two-bedroom private flat. They pay £150 a week. Their rent includes eligible service charges for the communal lift. Patrick's uncle Gerald and Gerald's 24-year-old son live with them.

Step one: Patrick and Isla's core rent is £150 x 52 ÷ 12 = £650 a month.

Step two: their cap rent is the local housing allowance for three-bedroom accommodation (they are allowed one bedroom for themselves and one bedroom each for Gerald and his son). In their area, the local housing allowance rate for three-bedroom accommodation is £800 a month. Their core rent is lower than their cap rent.

Step three: Patrick and Isla's extended benefit unit includes two non-dependants. Housing costs contributions of £75.15 x 2 = £150.30 are, therefore, deducted. Their housing costs element is, therefore, £650 (the core rent) – £150.30 (housing costs contributions) = £499.70.

Core rent

If you are solely liable to make payments, your 'core rent' is the total amount of all the eligible rent and service charge payments (see p84 and p85) that you are liable (or treated as liable) to make – ie, the amounts you actually pay using the monthly equivalent.[99]

Jointly liable for payments

If you are jointly liable to make payments with someone, different rules apply. Your core rent is worked out using the following steps.[100]

- **Step one:** work out the sum of all of the eligible rent and eligible service charge payments for which you and your joint tenant(s) are liable, for the whole of the accommodation, using the monthly equivalents.
- **Step two:**
  - if the only people who are jointly liable are in the list of 'relevant family members' below (eg, only you and your partner are liable), your core rent is the amount in Step one; *or*
  - if one or more people in the list of relevant family members below are jointly liable with one or more others who are not relevant family members (eg, you, your partner and a friend are joint tenants), divide the amount in Step one by the total number of people who are liable and multiply by the number of relevant family members who are liable. This is your core rent. However, if the DWP is satisfied that it would be unreasonable to take this amount as your core rent, it must apportion the amount in a manner it considers appropriate, taking into account the number of people who are jointly liable and the amount of the rent and service charge payments for which each is liable.

Relevant family members

The '**relevant family members**' are you, your partner and any child or qualifying young person for whom you (or your partner, if you are a joint claimant) are responsible (see p63).[101]

Example

Jan and her partner Lois are joint tenants of a two-bedroom private flat with a friend.
Step one: the rent is £120 a week. The monthly equivalent is £120 x 52 ÷ 12 = £520
Step two: Jan and Lois are jointly liable with a person who is not a 'relevant family member'. Their core rent is, therefore, £520 ÷ 3 (the number of joint tenants) x 2 (the number of relevant family members) = £346.67 a month.

Cap rent

Your cap rent is the maximum amount of rent that can be included in your housing costs element. It is normally the local housing allowance for the category of dwelling that applies to you, in the area where you live.[102] This depends on how many bedrooms you are allowed under the rules (see p97), up to a maximum of four bedrooms. To work out which category of dwelling applies, see below. For information about the local housing allowance rates, see p107. **Note:** your cap rent may be lower than the amount of rent you must pay.

If you have been housed in two dwellings by a provider of social housing (see p92), but you only pay rent to a social sector landlord for one of them, your

Part 2: Universal credit
Chapter 6: The housing costs element
5. The amount for private rented tenants

housing costs element is calculated under the rules for private sector tenancies. In this case, if the cap rents for the two dwellings are different (eg, because they are in different areas), the lowest amount at the time your housing costs element is first calculated is used.[103] Your housing costs element continues to be calculated on the basis of the cap rent for that dwelling until you move to other accommodation.

Categories of dwelling

The category of dwelling that applies to you depends on how many bedrooms you are allowed under the rules (see p97) and whether or not the one-bedroom shared accommodation category applies.

One-bedroom shared accommodation

The one-bedroom shared accommodation category of dwelling applies if you are a single person (or a member of a couple claiming as a single person – see p36), you are under 35 and you do not have any children for whom you are responsible or non-dependants.[104] This applies even if you do not live in shared accommodation.

There are exceptions. This category of dwelling does *not* apply (even if you live in shared accommodation) if:[105]

- you are getting attendance allowance, the middle or highest rate of the disability living allowance care component, the daily living component of personal independence payment or armed forces independence payment; *or*
- you meet the 'foster parent condition' (see p99); *or*
- you are at least 18 but under 22 and were looked after by a local authority under specified provisions before you were 18 (see p948);[106] *or*
- you are a single claimant and are:
  - aged at least 25 and have been living in one or more hostels for homeless people for three months or more (this does not have to be continuous) and while living there you have accepted support services to assist you in being rehabilitated or resettled in the community; *or*
  - an offender subject to specific multi-agency public protection risk arrangements. It is understood that this applies if you are a level 2 or 3 offender.[107]

One-bedroom self-contained accommodation

The one-bedroom self-contained accommodation category of dwelling applies if you are only allowed one bedroom under the rules (see p97) and the one bedroom shared accommodation category (see above) does not apply.[108] It must be reasonable for you to occupy this category of accommodation.

Dwellings with two or more bedrooms

If you are allowed more than one bedroom under the rules, the category of dwelling that applies is that for a dwelling with the number of bedrooms you are allowed (see p97), up to a maximum of four.[109] So this category applies, for example, if you are a lone parent or a member of a couple with children, you have a non-dependant living with you, you are allowed an additional bedroom for a non-resident carer or because you are a foster parent or adopter or someone who lives with you is a 'member of a couple who cannot share a bedroom'. It must be reasonable for you to occupy this category of accommodation, taking into account the number of people in your 'extended benefit unit' (see p96 for who counts).[110]

Local housing allowance rates

Local housing allowances for each category of dwelling are normally set by the rent officer annually on the last working day of January, to take effect the following April. From April 2020, the local housing allowance is the lowest of two figures:[111]

- the amount of rent at the 30th percentile point of local market rents for assured tenancies in what is known as a 'broad rental market area'; *or*
- for the specified categories of dwelling below, the amount listed.

Category of dwelling	Maximum local housing allowance
One-bedroom shared accommodation	£1,283.96
One-bedroom self-contained accommodation	£1,283.96
Two-bedroom accommodation	£1,589.99
Three-bedroom accommodation	£1,920.00
Four-bedroom accommodation	£2,579.98

You can find the current local housing allowance rates in your area at lha-direct.voa.gov.uk.

6. The amount for social rented sector tenants: the 'bedroom tax'

If you are a social rented sector tenant, a deduction is usually made when your housing costs element is calculated if you have more bedrooms in your home than the number you are allowed under the rules (see p97).[112] This is commonly referred to as the 'bedroom tax' or, by the DWP, as the 'removal of the spare room subsidy' or the 'under-occupation charge'. 'Bedroom' is not defined. See p101 for what may count.

Part 2: Universal credit
Chapter 6: The housing costs element
6. The amount for social rented sector tenants: the 'bedroom tax'

Social rented sector accommodation

Your accommodation is social rented sector accommodation if your landlord is a 'provider of social housing'. A provider of social housing is a local authority, a non-profit registered provider of social housing, a profit-making registered provider of social housing (if you have been housed in social housing) or a registered social landlord.[113]

How your housing costs element is calculated depends on whether you are solely or jointly liable for your rent and service charges. **Note:**

- If you qualify for a housing costs element for more than one dwelling, special rules apply (see p95).
- Your housing costs element may be lower than as calculated below if the DWP thinks your rent or service charges are higher than is reasonable for a housing costs element to meet.[114] In this case, the DWP can apply to the rent officer. If the rent officer thinks that your landlord could reasonably have expected to get a lower amount of rent than what you pay, the lower amount is used to calculate your housing costs element, unless the DWP is satisfied that this is not appropriate.
- Your housing costs element can *never* be lower than nil – ie, no further reduction can be made to your universal credit (UC) award.[115]
- If your rent or service charge payments have been reduced by a provider of social housing under a government-approved tenant incentive scheme, your rent and service charges are worked out under Steps two and three as if no reduction had been made.[116]

Solely liable to make payments

If you are solely liable to make rent and service charge payments, your housing costs element is worked out as follows.[117]

- **Step one:** work out the number of bedrooms in your home and also the number of bedrooms you are allowed under the rules (see p97).
- **Step two:** work out the amount of your eligible rent payments (see p84), using the monthly equivalent (see p94).
- **Step three:** work out the amount of your eligible service charge payments (see p85) using the monthly equivalent (see p94).
- **Step four:** total the payments in Step two and Step three. Deduct any amount that relates to the supply of a 'commodity' to your accommodation – eg, for water or fuel. Unless Step five or Step six applies, this is your housing costs element.
- **Step five:** unless you have a shared ownership tenancy, if you have more bedrooms in your home than the number you are allowed (see Step one), reduce the amount in Step four by:[118]
  - 14 per cent, if you have one too many bedrooms; *or*
  - 25 per cent if you have two or more too many bedrooms.

Unless Step six applies, this is your housing costs element.
- **Step six:** if your 'extended benefit unit' includes any non-dependants, deduct any housing costs contribution that applies (see p102) from the amount in Step four or Step five as appropriate.[119] This is your housing costs element.

Example

Kirsty rents a four-bedroom house from the local authority. She lives there with her 14-year-old daughter. Her rent is £125 a week. She has four rent-free weeks every year. Her 'extended benefit unit' does not include any non-dependants.

Step one: she has four bedrooms in her home. She is allowed two bedrooms under the rules: one bedroom for her and one bedroom for her daughter.

Step two: the monthly equivalent of her rent payments is £125 x 48 ÷ 12 = £500

Step three: she does not have any service charge payments.

Step four: the total payment is £500 a month.

Step five: she has two bedrooms too many. The amount in Step four must be reduced by 25 per cent. 25% x £500 = £125. £500 – £125 = £375

Kirsty's housing costs element is, therefore, £375 a month.

Jointly liable to make payments

If you are jointly liable to make payments with someone (eg, you are a joint tenant), different rules apply.[120] Work out the total of the monthly equivalent of the eligible rent and service charge payments (see p84 and p85) for which you and your joint tenant(s) are liable, for the whole of the dwelling. Remember to deduct any amount that relates to the supply of a 'commodity' to your accommodation – eg, for water or fuel. Then, if:

- the only people who are jointly liable are in the list of 'relevant family members' on p105 (eg, you and your partner are the only joint tenants), a reduction is made as under Step five on p108 if you have more bedrooms in your home than you are allowed under the rules (see p97). However, if you have a shared ownership tenancy (ie, you are buying part of your home and renting the rest), no reduction is made; *or*
- one or more people in the list of 'relevant family members' on p105 are jointly liable with one or more others who are not relevant family members (eg, you and a friend are joint tenants), divide the total rent and service charge payments by the total number of people who are liable and multiply by the number of relevant family members who are liable to get the amount that can be included. However, if the DWP is satisfied that it would be unreasonable to take this amount as your rent, it must apportion the amount in a manner it considers appropriate, taking into account the number of jointly liable people and the amount of the rent and service charge payments for which each is liable. **Note:** no reduction is made as under Step five on p108.

Part 2: Universal credit
Chapter 6: The housing costs element
7. Service charge payments for owner-occupiers

In all cases, if your extended benefit unit includes any non-dependants, deduct any housing costs contribution that applies (see p102).[121]

Example

Len and his partner are joint tenants of a three-bedroom housing association flat with a friend. The rent is £180 a week.

The monthly equivalent of the rent payments is £180 x 52 ÷ 12 = £780 a month.

They do not have any service charge payments.

The total payment is £780 a month.

Len and his partner are relevant family members. The amount that can be included in the housing costs element is, therefore, £780 ÷ 3 (the number of joint tenants) x 2 (the number of relevant family members) = £520 a month. No reduction is made as under Step 5 on p108.

Their 'extended benefit unit' does not include any non-dependants. The housing costs element is, therefore, £520 a month.

---

7. Service charge payments for owner-occupiers

If you are an owner-occupier and you make payments for eligible service charges (see p85), an amount for these is included in your housing costs element.[122]

The amount is calculated as follows.[123]

- **Step one:** work out the amount of each eligible service charge payment.
- **Step two:** work out the period for which each payment is payable, and if payments are made other than calendar monthly, work out the monthly equivalent (see p94).
- **Step three:** add all the monthly amounts together. This is the amount that can be included in your housing costs element.

Note:
- If you have a shared ownership tenancy (ie, you are buying part of your home and renting the rest), your housing costs element can also include an amount for your rent. In this case, your service charge payments are are not calculated under these rules. They are calculated as for rented accommodation.[124] See p103 if you live in private rented accommodation and p107 if you live in social rented sector accommodation.
- You cannot get a housing costs element (other than for rent and service charges if you have a shared ownership tenancy) if you (or your partner) have *any* earned income, however much your earnings are.[125] This includes earnings from work you can do while claiming contributory employment and support allowance (ESA – see p1042) or from work of less than 16 hours a week you can do while claiming contribution-based jobseeker's allowance (JSA – see p991).

- You may only qualify for a housing costs element after a 'waiting period' (see below).
- If your partner (if you are a joint claimant) or a child or qualifying young person for whom you (or s/he) were responsible (see p63), or a severely disabled person for whom you were caring, dies, your universal credit (UC) continues to be calculated as if s/he had not died for the assessment period in which the death occurred and the following two assessment periods. This means, for example, that her/his absence from your home does not affect your housing costs element until after the three assessment periods.[126]

The waiting period

If you are an owner-occupier, a housing costs element for service charge payments cannot usually be included until the end of a 'waiting period'. The DWP may call this a 'qualifying period'. See below for exceptions.

If:[127]

- you have a new award of UC (ie, you claim for the first time or claim after a break in your entitlement to UC), a housing costs element for service charge payments cannot be included until there have been nine consecutive assessment periods in which you have been getting UC, provided you would qualify for a housing costs element were it not for the waiting period rule;
- a housing costs element for service charge payments ceases to be included in your UC award for any reason (eg, because you have earnings from a temporary job), but your entitlement to UC continues, that element cannot be included again until there have been nine consecutive assessment periods in which you would otherwise qualify for a housing costs element were it not for the waiting period rule.

If you cease to qualify for a housing costs element for service charge payments for any reason during a waiting period, the waiting period stops running.[128] A new waiting period starts again from the beginning under whichever of the above rules apply.

Example
Claire makes a claim for UC. She is unemployed at the time and has no income. She is an owner-occupier, pays eligible service charge payments for the cleaning of the common areas in her block of flats and for a concierge service and (but for having to serve a waiting period) she qualifies for a housing costs element. She waits nine consecutive assessment periods and a housing costs element for service charge payments is then included in her UC. Claire gets a part-time temporary job so she no longer qualifies for a housing costs element, although her entitlement to UC continues. When her job ends, a housing costs element will be included again once she has been getting UC for a further nine consecutive assessment periods.

Part 2: Universal credit
Chapter 6: The housing costs element
7. Service charge payments for owner-occupiers

2

Note: there are no waiting period rules for rent payments, so if you have a shared ownership tenancy (ie, you are buying part of your home and renting the rest), your housing costs element can include the rent and all service charge payments you make straight away, without a waiting period.

Exceptions

There are limited exceptions to the general waiting period rule.

- If you are entitled to contribution-based JSA or contributory ESA under the UC system immediately before your award of UC starts, any period when you were only getting one of those benefits may be treated as an assessment period (or part of an assessment period) that counts towards your waiting period.[129]

- If you (or your partner or a former partner) were entitled to income support (IS), income-based JSA or income-related ESA in the one month before the date you claimed (or are treated as claiming) UC (or you would have been entitled but for your entitlement ending because the benefit was abolished):[130]
  - if your (or your partner's or former partner's) IS/JSA/ESA included help with housing costs (see Chapter 18), you do not have to serve a waiting period, and your UC award can include a housing costs element for service charge payments straight away; *or*
  - if your (or your partner's or your former partner's) IS/JSA/ESA did not yet include help with housing costs because you were serving a waiting period (see p368), your UC waiting period is 273 days, minus the number of days you were entitled to IS/JSA/ESA (this includes time in which you were treated as entitled under the linking rules – see p375), as well as any time between the date the IS/JSA/ESA ended and the date you are awarded UC.

- If an award of UC made while you were a joint claimant ended because you (and your now former partner) ceased to be a couple, you were joint owner-occupiers, you occupy the same home you occupied with your former partner and you are awarded UC in your own right:[131]
  - if a housing costs element was not yet included in your joint award of UC, any assessment period (or part of an assessment period) in respect of which you had been getting UC counts towards the waiting period for your new award. For example, if you and your former partner had been getting UC for 45 days, a housing costs element can be included once you have been getting UC for nine assessment periods, minus 45 days;
  - if a housing costs element was included in your joint award of UC, you do not have to serve another waiting period; a housing costs element is included straight away.

  This can also apply to your former partner – ie, if s/he continues to occupy the same accommodation and also claims, and is awarded, UC.

Notes

1 s35 and Sch 9 SS(S)A 2018, not yet in force

1. Who can get a housing costs element
2 s11 WRA 2012; regs 25 and 26 UC Regs
3 s11(2)(c) WRA 2012
4 Reg 26(4)-(6) UC Regs
5 Reg 8(4) and Sch 4 para 4 UC Regs
6 Reg 26(5) and Sch 1 para 3(h) and (i) and Sch 5 para 4 UC Regs
7 Reg 25(2)(a) and Sch 1 para 2 UC Regs
8 Sch 1 paras 2 and 3 UC Regs
9 Sch 1 para 3A UC Regs
10 Sch 1 para 3B UC Regs
11 Sch 1 para 1 UC Regs
12 Reg 25(2)(c) and Sch 1 para 7(1), (2) and (4) UC Regs
13 Sch 1 para 7(1) and (3) UC Regs; reg 2 and Sch 1 para 5(2) LMI Regs
14 Sch 1 para 8(3) UC Regs
15 Sch 1 para 8(4) and (5) UC Regs
16 para F2074 ADM
17 Sch 1 para 8(6) UC Regs
18 Schs 3 para 4(3) and 4 para 2 UC Regs

2. Liability for payments
19 Reg 25(3) UC Regs
20 R v Poole BC ex parte Ross [1995] 28 HLR 351 (QBD); CH/1076/2002; CH/296/2004; CH/1097/2004
21 R v Rugby BC HBRB ex parte Harrison [1994] 28 HLR 36 (QBD); CH/2959/2006
22 s48 Landlord and Tenant Act 1987; CH/3579/2003; CH/257/2005
23 R(H) 3/03
24 R v Poole BC ex parte Ross [1995] 28 HLR 351 (QBD); R v Warrington BC ex parte Williams [1997] 29 HLR 872 (QBD)
25 Sch 2 paras 1-4 UC Regs
26 Sch 2 para 2 UC Regs
27 FK v Wandsworth BC (HB) [2016] UKUT 570 (AAC); Babergh DC v GW (HB) [2017] UKUT 40 (AAC)
28 Ewens v Secretary of State for Social Security, reported as R(IS) 8/01
29 Sch 2 paras 5-7, 9 and 10 UC Regs
30 Sch 2 para 8 UC Regs
31 Reg 2 UC Regs

32 R(SB) 27/87; Bristol CC v JKT [2016] UKUT 517 (AAC)
33 Sch 2 para 10 UC Regs
34 para F2142 ADM
35 R v Solihull MBC ex parte Simpson [1995] 1 FLR 140 (CA); CH/39/2007
36 R (Mackay) v Barking and Dagenham HBRB [2001] EWHC Admin 234
37 CH/2258/2004
38 R (Mackay) v Barking and Dagenham HBRB [2001] EWHC Admin 234
39 R v Sutton LBC HBRB ex parte Keegan [1992] 27 HLR 92 (QBD)
40 R v Manchester CC ex parte Baragrove Properties Ltd [1991] 23 HLR 337 (QBD); R v Gloucestershire CC ex parte Dadds [1997] 29 HLR 700 (QBD); CH/39/2007
41 R v Poole BC ex parte Ross [1995] 28 HLR 351 (QBD)

3. Occupying accommodation as a home
42 Reg 25(4) and Sch 3 paras 1(1) and 2 UC Regs
43 Sch 3 paras 7 and 8 UC Regs
44 Bury MBC v DC (HB) [2011] UKUT 43 (AAC); R (Mahmoudi) v LB Lewisham and Another [2014] EWCA Civ 284
45 Sch 3 para 1(2)-(4) UC Regs
46 Sch 3 para 5 UC Regs
47 Sch 3 para 4 UC Regs
48 Schs 3 para 4(3) and 4 para 2 UC Regs
49 Sch 3 para 9 UC Regs
50 R(H) 9/05
51 R v Penwith DC ex parte Burt [1988] 22 HLR 292 (QBD)
52 Regs 2 and 19(1)(b), (2) and (3) UC Regs
53 CH/1237/2004
54 CH/3893/2004
55 Sch 3 paras 3 and 9(2) UC Regs
56 R(SB) 10/81
57 Sch 3 paras 6 and 9(3) UC Regs
58 Sch 3 para 9(3) UC Regs
59 CH/1237/2004
60 CH/3893/2004

4. How the housing costs element is calculated: general rules
61 Sch 4 para 7 and Sch 5 para 13 UC Regs
62 Reg 26(4)-(6) UC Regs

63 Sch 4 para 17 UC Regs
64 Sch 4 para 18 UC Regs
65 Sch 4 para 19 UC Regs
66 Sch 4 paras 1, definitions of 'renters' and 'joint renters', and 9(1) UC Regs
67 Sch 4 para 9(2) UC Regs
68 *AM v SSWP (IS)* [2011] UKUT 387 (AAC)
69 CSIS/185/1995
70 CIS/14850/1996
71 *JP v Bournemouth BC (HB)* [2018] UKUT 75 (AAC)
72 Sch 4 para 9(2) UC Regs
73 Sch 4 para 9(2)(a), (b) and (g) UC Regs
74 Sch 4 paras 2, 8 and 10 UC Regs
75 Sch 4 para 26 UC Regs
76 Reg 37 UC Regs
77 Reg 2 and Sch 4 paras 2 and 12 UC Regs
78 Reg 2, definition of 'AA', and Sch 4 para 12(3) UC Regs
79 *Burnip v Birmingham CC and Others* [2012] EWCA Civ 629, reported as [2013] AACR 7
80 *R (Carmichael) v SSWP and R (Rutherford) v SSWP* [2016] UKSC 58; *RR v SSWP* [2019] UKSC 52
81 *JD and A v the United Kingdom* [2019] ECHR 753
82 *R (MA and Others) v SSWP* [2014] EWCA Civ 13; *R (Cotton and Others) v SSWP and New Forest DC and Others* [2014] EWHC 3437 (Admin); *SSWP v PE and Bolton MBC* [2017] UKUT 393 (AAC)
83 Sch 4 para 11(3) UC Regs
84 Sch 4 para 11(2) UC Regs
85 Sch 4 para 11(4)-(6) UC Regs
86 *Bolton MBC v BF (HB)* [2014] UKUT 48 (AAC)
87 *CB v Manchester City Council and SSWP (HB)* [2015] UKUT 556 (AAC)
88 *SSWP v Nelson and Nelson* [2014] UKUT 525 (AAC), reported as [2015] AACR 21; *Stevenage BC v ML (HB)* [2016] UKUT 164 (AAC); *M v SSWP* [2017] UKUT 443 (AAC); *E v Bristol City Council* [2018] UKUT 287 (AAC)
89 *SSWP v the City of Glasgow Council and IB* [2017] CSIH 35, 31 May 2017, reported as [2017] AACR 29
90 *SSWP v RR (HB)* [2018] UKUT 180 (AAC)
91 Sch 4 paras 13, 22 and 33 UC Regs
92 Sch 4 para 9(2)(f) UC Regs
93 Sch 4 para 15 UC Regs
94 Sch 4 para 16 UC Regs
95 Sch 4 para 13 UC Regs
96 Sch 4 para 14(1) UC Regs

5. The amount for private rented tenants
97 Reg 26(2) and Sch 4 para 22 UC Regs
98 Sch 4 para 14(3) UC Regs
99 Sch 4 paras 3(1), 6 and 23 UC Regs
100 Sch 4 paras 3(1), 6 and 24 UC Regs
101 Sch 4 para 2 UC Regs, definition of 'listed persons'
102 Sch 4 paras 25(1), (2) and (5) and 26 UC Regs
103 Sch 4 para 25(3) and (4) UC Regs
104 Sch 4 paras 27 and 28 UC Regs
105 Sch 4 para 29 UC Regs
106 Sch 4 para 29(2) UC Regs
107 www.justice.gov.uk/downloads/ offenders/mappa/mappa-guidance-2012-part1.pdf
108 Sch 4 paras 8 and 25(2) UC Regs
109 Sch 4 paras 8, 25(2) and 26 UC Regs
110 Sch 4 para 8(1) UC Regs
111 Sch 4 para 25(2) and (5) UC Regs; Arts 3 and 4 and Sch 1 RO(UCF)O

6. The amount for social rented sector tenants: the 'bedroom tax'
112 Sch 4 paras 2 and 30 UC Regs
113 Schs 3 para 4(3) and 4 para 2 UC Regs
114 Sch 4 para 32 UC Regs
115 Sch 4 para 14(3) UC Regs
116 Sch 4 para 32A UC Regs
117 Sch 4 paras 3, 6, 30-34 and 36 UC Regs
118 Sch 4 paras 34 and 36 UC Regs
119 Sch 4 para 33 UC Regs
120 Sch 4 paras 3, 6, 30-32, 35 and 36 UC Regs
121 Sch 4 para 33 UC Regs

7. Service charge payments for owner-occupiers
122 Reg 26(3) UC Regs
123 Sch 5 para 13 UC Regs
124 Reg 26(4)-(6) UC Regs
125 Sch 5 para 4 UC Regs
126 Reg 37 UC Regs
127 Sch 5 para 5(1) and (2) UC Regs
128 Sch 5 para 5(3) UC Regs
129 Reg 2, definitions of 'JSA' and 'ESA', and Sch 5 para 6 UC Regs
130 Reg 29 UC(TP) Regs
131 Sch 5 paras 1(2) and 7 UC Regs

Chapter 7

Income

This chapter covers:
1. Whose income counts (below)
2. What counts as income (p116)
3. Earnings (p116)
4. Other income (p126)
5. Notional income (p131)
6. Working out monthly income (p133)

Key facts
- Your entitlement to universal credit (UC) and how much you get depends on your income.
- Your own income counts and, if you are a member of a couple, your partner's income also counts.
- Your earnings from employment and self-employment are taken into account on a monthly basis over each 'assessment period'.
- If earnings from self-employment are low, your UC award may be worked out on more earnings than you get, based on the number of hours the DWP expects you to work.
- Certain other kinds of income are also taken into account.

1. Whose income counts

If you are single, only your own income counts when working out your universal credit (UC) award.[1]

Couples usually make a joint claim, and your UC award is worked out using both your income and your partner's income.[2]

There are some situations in which one member of a couple qualifies for UC but the other does not – eg, in certain circumstances if your partner is under age 18, does not meet residence tests, is out of the country or is in prison (see p36). In these cases, you make a single claim. You do not get any amount for your partner in your UC award, but your partner's income (and capital) is still added to yours when working out how much UC you get.[3]

Children's income is ignored.

2. What counts as income

The amount of universal credit (UC) you are entitled to depends on how much income you have.

'Income' for UC means:[4]

- earnings from employment (see p117) and self-employment (see p118);[5] *and*
- certain other income:[6]
  - certain benefits (see p126);
  - maintenance for you or your partner, but not for a child (see p127);
  - student loan and grants. See p882 for how much of the loan counts and which grants are ignored;
  - certain income from employment and training schemes (see p127);
  - occupational and personal pensions and annuities (see p128);
  - certain insurance payments (see p128);
  - income from a trust (see p128 for which types are ignored);
  - income you are assumed to have from savings and other capital (see p129);
  - sports awards from UK Sport (see p130);
  - miscellaneous income (see p130);
  - capital that is treated as income (see below).

In some situations, you may be treated as having income that you do not actually have. This is called 'notional income' (see p131). If a type of income is not specified in the rules as being included for UC, it is ignored and does not affect your award. See p130 for some examples of income that is ignored.

Income or capital?

Any amounts that are paid regularly and that refer to a specific period are treated as income and not as capital.[7] This is the case even if payments might otherwise be regarded as capital or as being part capital – eg, payments under an annuity are treated as income.

If you have a lump sum that is payable by instalments, each instalment is treated as income while your capital remains above the £16,000 upper limit for getting UC. Once the amount of any instalments outstanding, together with any other capital you have, is below this limit, each instalment is treated as capital.[8]

3. Earnings

How earnings are treated depends on whether you are employed (see p117) or self-employed (see p118).

Employed earnings

To work out the amount of earnings from employment to take into account in your universal credit (UC) assessment, do the following.
- Check whether the payment counts as earnings (see below).
- Work out your monthly earnings for the assessment period (see p133).
- Calculate your net earnings for the assessment period (see p118).

If you also have self-employed earnings, these are also worked out (see p118) and added to your monthly employed earnings to give your total earned income. To work out how your earnings affect your UC award, check if you have a work allowance (see p41). The work allowance is deducted from your earnings and 63 per cent of what is left is taken into account as income in your UC award. If you do not have a work allowance, 63 per cent of your total earnings is taken into account. See p41 for more about how your earnings affect your UC award.

What counts as earnings

'Earnings' means 'remuneration or profits derived from... employment'. This includes:[9]
- wages and overtime pay (including earnings under the coronavirus Job Retention Scheme);
- tips, bonuses and commission;
- fees;
- holiday pay;
- statutory sick pay or other sick pay from your employer;
- statutory maternity pay, statutory adoption pay, statutory paternity pay, statutory shared parental pay, statutory parental bereavement pay or other pay from your employer while you are on maternity, adoption, paternity or parental leave;
- any refund of income tax or national insurance (NI) contributions for a tax year when you were in paid work. This includes tax from unearned income but not from self-employment (see p119);
- an equal pay settlement – eg, through a 'single status' agreement.[10]

The DWP usually gets information on your earnings from the records your employer sends to HM Revenue and Customs (HMRC) each time you are paid (see p133). So what counts for earnings for UC is normally what is recorded on PAYE (pay as you earn) records and is defined in terms of what counts as taxable income. However, there are differences, and not all kinds of taxable income count for UC purposes.

What does not count as earnings

Types of income not taken into account as earnings for UC include the following (some of which are taxable):[11]
- expenses incurred 'wholly, exclusively and necessarily' in the course of your employment;[12]

- certain taxable and tax-exempt expenses and allowances – eg, mileage allowance or homeworkers' additional expenses (these are usually listed on HMRC Form P11D which your employer gives you);[13]
- expenses if you are a service user being consulted about provision of services by certain public bodies;[14]
- benefits in kind – eg, a salary sacrifice scheme, non-cash vouchers (eg, for childcare), living accommodation connected with work, cars and car fuel benefits, parking or meals;[15]
- allowances for special types of employment – eg, certain armed forces allowances, free coal to miners or allowances in lieu of coal, and offshore oil and gas workers' travel, subsistence and accommodation allowances.[16]

Payments when you stop work

Your final earnings when you stop work are taken into account in the assessment period in which they are paid.[17] This includes arrears of pay, pay in lieu of notice and accrued holiday pay.[18] The following lump-sum payments are taken into account as capital:[19]

- statutory and contractual redundancy pay;
- employment tribunal awards for unfair dismissal;
- pay in lieu of notice or damages for breach of contract.

Working out net earnings

From your monthly earnings for the assessment period, deduct the following payments you make in that period:[20]

- income tax; *and*
- class 1 NI contributions; *and*
- any contribution you make towards a personal or occupational pension scheme. If you pay contributions through your employer, your payslips should show your wages after the contributions have been deducted, so there is no further deduction to make.

Also deduct any charity payments made under a payroll giving scheme.

Self-employed earnings

To work out the amount of your self-employed earnings to take into account in the UC assessment, do the following.[21]

- Work out your actual receipts for the assessment period (see p119).
- Deduct any permitted expenses from your receipts (see p119).
- From the result (or your share of it, if you are in a business partnership), deduct any payment made in the assessment period for income tax and NI contributions. If the result is negative, there is a loss and the amount of your self-employed earnings is nil (but set minimum earnings may apply – see p121).

- Deduct any contributions made by you to a personal or occupational pension (but not if these have already been deducted from your employed earnings). If the result is negative, the amount of your self-employed earnings is nil (but set minimum earnings may apply – see p121).
- Deduct any unused losses carried forward from earlier assessment periods, starting from the earliest (see p120).
- Check whether the amount worked out as above (adding any earnings from employment) is above a set minimum level of earnings (see p121).

Receipts from self-employment

The starting point to work out how much self-employed earnings are taken into account is the actual amount of receipts into the business in the assessment period – eg, sales, takings and payment for work.[22] Include:[23]

- any refund of income tax, VAT or NI contributions for the self-employment;
- receipts in kind – ie, the value of the goods or service you provided for which you accepted payment in kind;[24]
- sale of business assets (if previously deducted from earnings for UC as an expense). If you stop using an asset for the business but do not sell it, the market value counts as a receipt.

Permitted expenses

Expenses must be reasonable and 'wholly and exclusively' incurred for purposes of your business.[25] Reasonable expenses may include:[26]

- regular costs – eg, rent, wages, utilities and insurance;
- stock purchase;
- stationery and advertising;
- repairs of business assets;
- transport (but see below for flat-rate deductions);
- equipment purchase and hire;
- up to £41 repayment of interest on a loan – eg, for an overdraft or credit card;
- VAT.

These are just examples. The deduction allowed is usually the actual amount of permitted expenses paid in the assessment period. However, there are flat-rate deductions for the use of a vehicle that you can choose to include instead of the actual expense of buying and using the vehicle:[27]

- for a motorcycle, 24 pence a mile;
- for a car, van or other vehicle, 45 pence a mile for the first 833 miles, then 25 pence a mile after that (for a car, you must use this rate rather than the actual expense).

If an expense has been incurred partly for business and partly for private purposes, it can be apportioned and the part that is identifiably for business deducted.[28] There are set deductions for the following.[29]

- If you use your own home for 'income-generating activities' for the business, instead of deducting actual expenses, there is a flat-rate deduction that depends on the number of hours completed in the assessment period. Income-generating activities include providing services to customers, business administration, sales and marketing, but do not include being on call.[30] The deduction is:
  - £10 for work of at least 25 hours, but no more than 50 hours in the month; *or*
  - £18 for work of more than 50 hours, but no more than 100 hours in the month; *or*
  - £26 for more than 100 hours' work in the month.
- If you live in premises that you use mainly for your business, deduct an amount from the expenses relating to the premises, depending on the number of people living there:
  - £350 if you live alone; *or*
  - £500 if you live with one other person; *or*
  - £650 if you live with two or more other people.

Example

Margo runs a guest house. She and her partner, Jerry, live in the guest house. Margo works out her expenses as £1,500 for the monthly assessment period for the whole house. She finds it difficult to say which expenses are for the business. Instead of apportioning expenses for business and personal use, she deducts £500 from the £1,500 for the whole house. The expenses allowed are £1,000.

Offsetting losses

If your receipts in an assessment period are less than your expenses, income tax and NI contributions (but not adding pension contributions), this amount is a loss. A loss from a previous assessment period is deducted from the next assessment period in which there is a profit. The loss is deducted from your self-employed earnings worked out as above after tax, NI contributions and pension contributions are deducted. If there is not enough profit to use up the whole loss, the amount left over (the 'unused loss') is carried forward.[31] If there are unused losses to apply from more than one assessment period, these are deducted in order starting with the earliest. Losses from a previous UC award are offset against profits in a new award if the break in your claims is no more than six months. However, losses from months between awards cannot be offset unless you have made a UC claim for those months.

Example

Nellie is a self-employed gardener. Business is slow in the winter. For the assessment periods ending:

– 28 February, she receives £300 cash from customers, pays £600 for new equipment, has travel expenses of £100, pays no tax or NI and pays £50 into her pension. Her self-employed earnings are nil and she has a loss of £400 (£300 – £600 – £100).

– 28 March, she receives £300 cash from customers, has travel expenses of £100, pays no tax or NI and pays £50 into her pension. Before offsetting her losses, her self-employed earnings are £150 (£300 – £100 – £50). She uses up £150 of her £400 loss from the previous month, giving self-employed earnings of nil and leaving £250 unused losses to carry forward.

– 28 April, she receives £1,700 cash from customers, has travel expenses of £200, pays no tax or NI and pays £50 into her pension. Before offsetting her losses, her self-employed earnings are £1,450 (£1,700 – £200 – £50). She uses up the remaining £250 unused losses, giving self-employed earnings of £1,200.

(In February and March, Nellie's earnings are below the set minimum, so are treated as being at the 'minimum income floor' – see below.)

Minimum level of earnings

Note: the DWP is not applying this rule during the coronavirus pandemic. If your main work is self-employment but your earnings are low, your UC may be worked out on higher earnings than you have. This is called the **'minimum income floor'** and is generally at the level of the national minimum wage for the number of hours the DWP expects you to work – usually 35 hours a week. This applies if:[32]

- you are in 'gainful self-employment' (see p123); *and*
- you are not in a 'start-up' period (see p123); *and*
- you would be subject to all work-related requirements were it not for having the minimum income floor applied. (Having the minimum income floor applied means no work-related requirements can be imposed on you.) If you are not subject to any work-related requirements (for a reason other than having the minimum income floor applied), or just subject to work-focused interviews or work preparation, your actual earnings from self-employment are taken into account, however low they are.

If you are single and the minimum income floor applies to you, your earnings are treated as being at the individual earnings threshold in any assessed income period in which your earned income from self-employment, together with any earnings from employment, is below this level.[33] The individual earnings threshold is the same threshold used to decide your work-related requirements (see p1065), with a notional amount for tax and NI contributions deducted.

> *Example*
> Jake has a window cleaning business. He is single. For the current assessment period, he declares earnings of £300. The DWP works out Jake's minimum income floor to be £1,202.66 a month (35 hours a week x £8.72 x 52 ÷ 12, less £119.87 for notional tax and NI contributions). Jake's UC award for the assessment period is worked out on earnings of £1,202.66.

If you are in a couple and the minimum income floor applies to you, your combined earnings for the UC assessment are usually your partner's earnings added to the minimum income floor for you. However, you cannot be treated as having combined earnings of more than a certain amount. This amount is the same as the joint earnings threshold for couples used to decide if there are any work-related requirements to fulfil (see p1065), but with a notional amount for tax and NI contributions deducted.[34]

- If your actual combined earnings are above the joint earnings threshold, your actual earnings count in the UC assessment, with no minimum income floor.
- If your actual combined earnings (ie, ignoring the minimum income floor) are below the joint earnings threshold in any assessed income period, your earnings are treated as being the individual earnings threshold (see p1065) less:
  - a notional amount for tax and NI contributions; *and*
  - an amount to ensure that, when added to your partner's earnings, you are not treated as having more than the joint earnings threshold.

If you are in a couple but claiming as a single person (eg, because your partner is a 'person subject to immigration control' – p36), the minimum income floor does not apply to your partner's self-employed earnings. Instead her/his actual earnings are combined with yours.

> *Example*
> Maja and Jan are a couple. Jan is a self-employed builder and Maja works part time in a shop. They have a two-year-old child and Maja is the 'responsible carer'. Jan declares earnings of £500 and Maja £700. The DWP works out Jan's minimum income floor to be £1,202.66 a month (35 hours a week x £8.72 x 52 ÷ 12, less £119.87 for tax and NI contributions).
> Jan and Maja's actual combined earnings are £1,200 (£500 + £700).
> This is below their joint earnings threshold of £1,807.25 (£1,202.66 for Jan plus £604.59 for Maja (16 hours a week x £8.72 x 52 ÷ 12 with no tax or NI contribution deduction at this earnings level)).
> Adding Jan's minimum income floor to Maja's actual earnings gives £1,902.66 (£1,202.66 + £700). This is £95.41 above their joint earnings threshold of £1,807.25, so Jan is treated as having earnings of £1,107.25 (£1,202.66 – £95.41).

Gainful self-employment

When you claim UC or when you tell the DWP that you are self-employed, you are asked to attend a 'gateway' interview if you are someone who must meet all the work-related requirements. You are asked to bring evidence that you are in 'gainful self-employment'. This means that:[35]

- the self-employment is your main employment – ie, it is your only employment or, if you also work for an employer, you normally spend more hours on, or have more earnings from, your self-employment; *and*
- your earnings count as self-employed earnings – ie, they are not employed earnings and are from carrying out a 'trade, profession or vocation'.[36] If it is not clear whether you are employed or self-employed, the DWP may look at a number of factors including whether you pay your own tax, whether your work is supervised and whether you can decide your own hours;[37] *and*
- your self-employment is 'organised, developed, regular and carried on in expectation of profit' – eg, whether you work for financial gain, how many hours you do, whether you have a business plan or have taken steps to get work, what work is arranged, whether you are registered as self-employed with HMRC, and whether you advertise your business.[38]

The DWP may decide that you are in gainful self-employment even though you are off sick and not able to do any work, or you currently have no income at all from your business. If you disagree with a decision to apply a minimum income floor, you can ask for a revision and then appeal. You may be able to argue, for example, that your self-employment is no longer organised or regular and you no longer have an expectation of profit. Bear in mind that business assets can only be disregarded for a limited time (see p497). If you are off sick and your weekly earnings are below 16 times the hourly rate of the minimum wage (see Appendix 7), send the DWP medical certificates so that it can assess whether you have limited capability for work. See p1015 for how your earnings affect this assessment. If so, only your actual earnings should be taken into account – because you should no longer be subject to all the work-related requirements (see p121).

If your business is new, but the DWP decides that it counts as gainful self-employment, you have a start-up period before the minimum income floor applies (see below).

If you are not in gainful self-employment, you must still report your earnings and these are taken into account in your UC award, but no minimum income floor is applied.

Start-up period

If you are self-employed, you may have 12 months, called the 'start-up period', in which the minimum income floor does not apply and your UC is worked out on your actual earnings, however low they are.[39]

Before 20 July 2020, the start-up period applies to a new business which begins (as your main employment) in the year before the beginning of the assessment period in which the DWP decides you are in gainful self-employment. From 20 July 2020 (or earlier if you are transferred to UC through 'managed migration'[40] (see p30)), the start-up period applies irrespective of when your self-employment began. However, if you have ever had the minimum income floor applied to that self-employment before, it applies again without another start-up period.

The start-up period runs from the beginning of the assessment period in which the DWP decides you are in gainful self-employment. You are expected to take active steps to increase your earnings to the level of your individual earnings threshold – ie, the level that means you no longer have to meet work-related requirements (see p1065). The DWP can end the start-up period if it decides you are not doing this, or are no longer in gainful self-employment.

The start-up period continues to run even if your UC stops and starts during the year.[41] Once you have had one start-up period, you cannot have another for the same self-employment. If you begin new self-employment, you can have a new start-up period provided more than five years have passed since the start of the earlier period.

Surplus earnings from employment and self-employment

If you earn above a certain threshold and your UC stops, an amount of 'surplus earnings' may be carried over to a new UC claim if you claim again within six months. This applies if:[42]

- your earnings (and your partner's earnings, if you are a couple) in the assessment period in which your UC ended were above the 'relevant threshold' (see below). Your actual self-employed earnings are included, not the minimum income floor; *and*
- you make a new claim within six months of your previous UC entitlement – ie, the start of the new assessment period is within six months of the end of the previous one; *and*
- you have not been entitled to UC since the end of your previous award, and neither has your partner in a joint claim; *and*
- you have not recently experienced domestic violence (either now or when your previous UC ended – see p1061).

The 'relevant threshold' is:
- £2,500; *plus*
- any work allowance to which you are entitled; *plus*
- maximum UC (see p65) less any income you have other than earnings, multiplied by 100 and divided by 63.

The amount above this threshold is your surplus earnings. **Note:** the £2,500 figure may decrease to £300 from April 2021.[43] See AskCPAG.org.uk and CPAG's *Welfare Rights Bulletin* for updates.

If you have surplus earnings included in a new claim for UC, the amount of your award may be reduced in the first month or you may get no UC. The amount of surplus earnings is recalculated each time you claim over the six months by adding your actual earnings to the surplus from the last claim. Any amount above the relevant threshold becomes the new surplus which is again added to your actual earnings the next time you claim. This means that if your actual earnings drop below the relevant threshold and you make a new claim, the surplus goes down. If the first reclaim is unsuccessful, you can claim again in the following month(s) until you become entitled. Once the six-month period is over, any remaining surplus is ignored.

To become entitled to UC again without delay, claim as soon as your earnings are below the relevant threshold because the surplus does not decrease until you actually claim. However, bear in mind that the surplus can also increase if you claim again when your earnings are still above the threshold. In this case, consider waiting until your earnings decrease before you make a new claim.

If you separate from your partner, any surplus earnings from a previous joint claim are normally shared equally in a new single claim, but if an equal share is not reasonable ask the DWP to change it.

Examples

Sonia and Marek claim UC jointly. Marek works part time and earns £600 a month. Their maximum UC is £507.37 a month. Sonia starts work in December and earns £3,400 that month. Their UC stops on 15 December at the end of the final assessment period. The relevant threshold is £3,305.35 (£2,500 (plus £507.37 maximum UC x 100 ÷ 63)). Their surplus earnings are therefore £694.65 (£4,000 actual earnings minus the relevant threshold of £3,305.35). Sonia's work ends and they reclaim UC in January. Their claim is turned down because their income is too high (£694.65 surplus earnings plus £600 Marek's earnings = £1,294.65 x 63 per cent = £815.63). However, because £1,294.65 is less than the £3,305.35 relevant threshold, there are no more surplus earnings to carry forward. They claim again in February and are awarded UC with just Marek's £600 earnings taken into account.

Asha's UC stops in December when she gets a bonus on top of her earnings. She has surplus earnings of £500. In January her earnings are back to normal. However, she does not claim again until February. The claim is turned down because her earnings are too high once the £500 surplus is added to February's earnings. She claims again in March and is awarded UC. If Asha had started claiming again in January, the £500 surplus would have been used up in January and she would have got UC again from her second claim in February instead of having to wait until March.

4. Other income

Only certain specified types of income, other than earnings, are taken into account for universal credit (UC). These are listed on p116 and explained in more detail below. This kind of income reduces your UC pound for pound. Any other income is ignored.

Benefits

Some benefits are taken into account as income; others are disregarded.

Benefits that are taken into account
The following benefits count in full:[44]
- carer's allowance (CA) – but not CA supplement in Scotland;
- employment and support allowance (ESA);
- incapacity benefit;
- industrial injuries benefit, except constant attendance allowance and exceptionally severe disablement allowance, which are disregarded;
- jobseeker's allowance (JSA);
- maternity allowance;
- retirement pensions;
- severe disablement allowance;
- widow's pension and widowed parent's allowance;
- foreign social security benefits and state retirement pensions that are similar to those listed above;
- an overpayment of income support (IS), income-based JSA (not joint-claim JSA), income-related ESA or housing benefit if you are not entitled to that benefit and the overpayment falls within a UC assessment period.[45]

Statutory sick pay, statutory maternity pay, statutory adoption pay, statutory paternity pay, statutory shared parental pay and statutory parental bereavement pay are treated as earnings and so may benefit from the work allowance.

Benefits that are not taken into account
All other benefits are ignored – eg:
- armed forces independence payment;
- attendance allowance;
- bereavement support payment;
- Best Start grant (in Scotland);
- child benefit;
- disability living allowance;
- funeral support payment (in Scotland);

- guaranteed income payment and surviving guaranteed income payment under the Armed Forces Compensation Scheme;
- guardian's allowance;
- two-week run-on of IS, income-based JSA and income-related ESA (see p246);
- industrial injuries constant attendance allowance and exceptionally severe disablement allowance;
- personal independence payment;
- social fund payments;
- war disablement pension;
- war widow's, widower's or surviving civil partner's pensions.

Maintenance payments

Maintenance for a child is ignored completely.

Any maintenance for you or your partner made by your or your partner's spouse/civil partner or former spouse/civil partner under a court order or under a maintenance agreement counts in full as income.

If a former partner makes payments direct to a third party (eg, your mortgage lender), this should not count as your income.[46] However, if there is income available to you which you choose not to access, you may be treated as having it under the 'notional income' rules (see p131).

If you *pay* maintenance to a former partner or a child not living with you, your payments are not disregarded when working out your income for UC.

Student loans and grants

For the special rules on the treatment of student loans, grants and other types of student support, see Chapter 41.

Employment and training schemes

The following payments from employment or training programmes under section 2 of the Employment and Training Act 1973 or section 2 of the Enterprise and New Towns (Scotland) Act 1990 are taken into account:[47]

- those made as a substitute for UC – eg, a training allowance;
- those intended for certain living costs. Payments for food, ordinary clothing or footwear, fuel, rent or other housing costs, including council tax, are all taken into account.

All other payments are disregarded – eg:

- travel expenses;
- training premium;
- childcare expenses;
- special needs payments.

Occupational and personal pensions and annuities

The following income is taken into account:[48]

- an occupational pension;
- income from a personal pension;
- income from a retirement annuity contract (including an annuity purchased for you or transferred to you on divorce);
- payments from a former employer for early retirement on the grounds of ill health or disability, unless this was under a court order or settlement of a claim;
- an overseas pension;
- a Civil List Act pension;
- payment under an equity release scheme. This provides regular payments from a loan secured on your home;
- payments from the Financial Assistance Scheme and periodic payments from the Pension Protection Fund (these help some people with underfunded occupational schemes whose employer has gone out of business).

See p132 if you are over pension age and have not drawn your pension.

Income from an annuity is taken into account, except income from an annuity bought from personal injury compensation, which is ignored.[49] An annuity is usually when you pay a lump sum to an insurance company, often on retirement, with the capital built up in your personal pension, which then pays you an income for the rest of your life. It may also be through a home income plan where the annuity is bought with a loan secured on the home.

Insurance payments

Payments under a policy to insure against the risk of losing income due to illness, accident or redundancy are taken into account in full.[50]

Trusts, personal injury payments and special compensation schemes

If you get an amount awarded to you because of a personal injury, it can be disregarded in certain circumstances.[51]

- If you receive the compensation in regular payments, they are disregarded as income.
- If the compensation is in a trust, both the capital value of the trust and any income from it are ignored. For more about how payments from personal injury trusts or other trusts are treated, see p140 and p146.
- If the compensation was used to buy an annuity, payments under the annuity are ignored.

- If the compensation is administered by the court on your behalf or can only be used by direction of the court, the capital is ignored and regular payments are disregarded as income.
- If the compensation is not used in one of the above ways, it is disregarded as capital for 12 months. This gives you a chance to spend some or all of it, or to put it in a trust or buy an annuity.

Payments from the Thalidomide Trust to someone disabled by thalidomide during her/his mother's pregnancy are disregarded.[52]

Income from a trust that is not set up from personal injury compensation is taken into account, whether it is a discretionary trust or other type of trust.

Special compensation schemes

Payments from certain special schemes approved or set up by government are ignored if they are:[53]

- to support people with a disability to live independently;
- for those with variant CJD (Creutzfeldt-Jacob disease) or infected from contaminated blood products;
- compensation for the London bombings in July 2005, London terrorist attacks in 2017 and Manchester bombing in 2017;
- World War Two compensation (rather than a war pension).

Income from capital

If you have capital over £16,000, you are not entitled to UC. If your capital is below this level, it can affect the amount of income that is taken into account. This is either because you have actual income from the capital, such as income from a trust, or because it is assumed that the capital gives you a certain amount of income.

Assumed monthly income from capital

If your capital is over £6,000 but not more than £16,000, you are treated as having some income from it. This 'assumed monthly income', often called 'tariff income', is set at the rate of £4.35 a month for every £250, or part of £250, between £6,000.01 and £16,000.[54]

Example
Nuala and Geraint have savings of £7,000. This is above the £6,000 limit, so they are treated as having an income of £17.40 a month from their savings (4 x £4.35).

When working out how much capital you have, some capital is disregarded (see p141). You are not treated as having an assumed monthly income from disregarded capital.[55]

Rental and other income from capital

If your capital is treated as giving you tariff income, any actual income you have from the same capital is treated as part of your capital from the day it is due to be paid to you.[56] For example, if you own a property, other than the home in which you live, rent is taken into account not as income but as capital and added to the capital value of the property itself (see also p131). However, if the value of the property can be disregarded (see p493), there is no tariff income, which means that the rental income is also ignored.[57] If you are running a property business, rental income counts as self-employed earnings (see p118).

Example

Sadiq owns a flat that he rents out for £1,000 a month which he uses to pay the mortgage. He does not live in the flat himself and is not running a property business, so the rent he gets does not count as income for UC but is added to his capital. The flat is valued at £100,000 but only £7,000 counts as capital once his outstanding mortgage is deducted. He has an assumed income of £34.80 (£7,000 + £1,000 = £8,000 (8 x £4.35 = £34.80).

Actual income from from an annuity and from a trust is taken into account, unless the income is disregarded because the annuity or trust is from personal injury compensation (see p128). In these two cases, the capital is not treated as giving you any assumed monthly income.[58] See p128 for more about how trusts are treated.

Sports awards

A sports award from UK Sport out of National Lottery funds for living expenses is taken into account. This covers food, ordinary clothing and footwear, fuel, rent, housing costs and council tax for you, your partner or dependent child.[59] Amounts for anything else are ignored – eg, sportswear.

Specified miscellaneous income

If a type of income is not listed in the rules as being taken into account (p116), it is ignored for UC. The category of 'miscellaneous income' only includes unearned income that is taxable under the HM Revenue and Customs 'sweep-up' provisions in Part 5 of the Income Tax (Trading and Other Income) Act 2005.[60] This includes copyright royalties if your writing does not amount to a trade or profession, and unusual tax situations – eg, tax avoidance schemes.

Other income

Only income specified in the rules and described above can affect your UC. Any other kind of income is ignored – eg:

- adoption allowances, fostering allowances, child arrangement order payments and kinship care payments;
- support from a charity;
- voluntary payments – eg, if a relative gives you regular money. However, if it is voluntary maintenance for you (rather than for a child, which is always ignored) from a separated or former spouse or civil partner, this is taken into account;
- payments to third parties – eg, if a relative pays your phone bill for you;
- mortgage protection policy payments;
- rental income from a room you let in your own home.[61] This is because actual income that comes from capital that is disregarded (the value of the home you live in is disregarded) is not in the list of income that is taken into account. However, if you rent out a property that you do not live in, the capital value of that property is taken into account and the rent is treated as capital, not as income. This is because actual income that comes from capital that is *not* disregarded is generally treated as capital (see p130);
- victims' payments to people injured in a 'Troubles-related incident'.[62]

5. Notional income

In some circumstances, you can be treated as having income that you do not actually have. This is called 'notional income'. You may be treated as having notional income if:

- you deliberately reduce your earnings in order to claim, or increase the amount of, universal credit (UC) (see below); *or*
- you work free of charge or for less than the going rate (see below); *or*
- you fail to apply for available income (see p132).

Deliberately getting rid of income

If you deliberately reduce your earnings from employment or self-employment in order to claim UC or increase the amount you get, you are treated as though you still have that income.[63] In particular, this applies if you got UC, or more UC, and the DWP believes this was a foreseeable result and was what you intended. Even if your employer has arranged for you to lose income, you may still be treated as though you had the income if you or your employer intended you to get UC, or more UC, by doing so.

Cheap or unpaid labour

If you are doing work free of charge or for less than the going rate (eg, you are working for a relative), you are treated as though you had earnings that would be reasonable for that work.[64] The comparison is with what the pay would be for similar work in the same location.

You are not treated as having more income than you receive for that work if:[65]

- the person cannot afford to pay you, or pay you more than s/he does; *or*
- you work for a charitable or voluntary organisation or as a volunteer and it is accepted that it is reasonable for you to give your services free of charge or at less than the going rate; *or*
- you are on a government-approved employment or training programme; *or*
- you are a service user who is being consulted about provision of services by certain public bodies.

Failing to apply for income

If you fail to apply for income that would be available to you if you applied for it, you are treated as having that income.[66]

However, you cannot be treated as having another benefit that you have not applied for, with the exception of retirement pension.

If you are over pension age, you may be treated as having pension income even though you have not applied for it. If you are under pension age, you can choose not to apply for pension income without your UC award being affected (see below).

This rule does not apply to earnings from employment or self-employment.

Deferring a state pension

If you are over pension age and you defer your state pension, retirement pension, graduated retirement benefit or any shared additional pension paid on divorce, you are treated as having that income for UC.

The amount that counts is the pension to which you would expect to be entitled, less any overlapping benefit you get – eg, carer's allowance. To take account of the time it can take to process claims, you are only treated as having this income from the date you could expect to get it were you to make a claim.

Leaving funds in an occupational or personal pension

Although you can usually choose to take some, or all, of your occupational or personal pension from age 55, your UC is not affected if you do not, unless you are over pension age.

If you are over pension age, the following applies.

- You are treated as having income from an occupational pension you have elected to defer beyond the scheme's retirement age,[67] as though you had claimed it. The time it might take to process it is taken into account and any overlapping benefit is deducted.
- If you have a defined contribution occupational or personal pension, you are generally expected to buy an annuity or take the equivalent income that would be payable through an annuity.[68] If you leave funds in your pension pot, you

are treated as having notional income based on the annuity those funds could yield. If you take one or more lump sums from your pension pot, these count as capital and notional income is worked out on what is left in your pension pot.

See p128 for how pension payments are treated.

6. Working out monthly income

Universal credit (UC) is paid in arrears for the previous monthly assessment period (see p39). Awards are worked out month by month. Your award is then adjusted as your earnings or other income increase or decrease, but always for a whole assessment period.[69] UC awards are not adjusted for income changes part way through the monthly assessment period. See p52 for reporting changes in your earnings and when this affects your award.

Earnings

When you first claim, the DWP can make a decision on whether you qualify for UC based on an estimate of your earnings.[70] At the end of the first assessment period, your award is based on your actual earnings instead.[71]

The amount of earnings used to work out your UC award for each assessment period is based on the actual amount you received in that assessment period.[72] There is no averaging from one month to the next.

Wage cycles

The frequency of your wages or salary payments may not correspond with your UC assessment period. For example, if you are paid monthly there may be some assessment periods in which you are paid twice, even though this is for work done in different assessment periods. If this happens, the DWP will calculate your UC as if you have a much higher income than usual in one month and much lower in the next month. A court has decided this is not correct but the DWP is appealing. You can ask for a mandatory reconsideration and appeal, and can argue that your UC should be calculated by applying the wages over two assessment periods, if it is clear that they were for different months.[73] However, a decision on your case may be postponed pending the outcome of the DWP's appeal. If you get no UC payment in one month, your UC will not restart automatically the following month. You should log into your UC account to restart your claim. See AskCPAG.org.uk and CPAG's *Welfare Rights Bulletin* for updates.

If you are employed, your employer is required to report your earnings to HM Revenue and Customs (HMRC) every time you are paid. This is called 'real-time information'. The employed earnings figure used in the UC assessment is taken from the amount in the report(s) received by the DWP in that assessment period.[74]

The DWP is not obliged to use the real-time information report – eg, if:[75]
- your employer fails to provide an accurate report on time (which can include reporting a payment after the date it was paid to you);[76]
- HMRC fails to pass on a report;
- the information in the report is wrong.

If you think the DWP has used the wrong earnings figure or the real-time information report is wrong, send any evidence you have of the correct amount and ask for a formal decision. You can then ask for a revision and appeal.[77] However, unless the DWP thinks it is a failure or mistake, if no real-time information report is received, you are simply treated as having no earnings for that assessment period.

If you are self-employed, you must report your earnings every month. Your UC award is based on the actual amount received in the assessment period and the actual amounts paid – eg, tax and expenses. The way you work out your earnings for the assessment period is explained on p118.

If you are asked to self-report, you must act quickly in order for your earnings to be taken into account in the same assessment period as you received them. If you report late, the DWP can treat your earnings as received in that later period. If you fail to provide information or evidence, payment of your UC may be suspended (see p1200).

Other income

Any other income you have that is not earnings is worked out as a monthly amount – eg:[78]
- multiply weekly payments by 52 and divide by 12;
- multiply fortnightly payments by 26 and divide by 12;
- multiply payments for four weeks by 13 and divide by 12;
- multiply payments for three months by four and divide by 12;
- a payment of income for a whole year is divided by 12.

If your income varies and there is a cycle that can be identified, take one cycle and convert this into a monthly amount. If there is no cycle to the income, it is worked out by taking three months of income, or another period if that would give a more accurate picture, and calculating an average monthly amount.

Note: there are different rules for working out student income (see p882).

Example
Dan gets contributory employment and support allowance (ESA) of £148.70 every two weeks. The amount of ESA taken into account in his UC award is £322.18 (£148.70 x 26 ÷ 12).

If you start or stop getting any unearned income, the amount taken into account is worked out over the number of days for which the income is paid in that assessment period. For example, if ESA of £148.70 a fortnight is awarded from 18 November (giving a monthly amount of £322.18) and your assessment period runs from 29 October to 28 November, the amount taken into account for that period is £116.51 (£322.18 x 12 ÷ 365 x 11 days).

Notes

1. Whose income counts
1 s8(4)(a) WRA 2012
2 s8(4)(b) and Sch 1 para 4(5) WRA 2012; reg 22(1) UC Regs
3 Regs 3(3) and (6) and 22(3) UC Regs

2. What counts as income
4 s8(3) WRA 2012
5 Reg 52 UC Regs
6 Reg 66 UC Regs
7 Reg 46(3) UC Regs
8 Reg 46(4) UC Regs; para H5102 ADM

3. Earnings
9 Reg 55(2), (4) and (4A) UC Regs; HMRC, *Employment Income Manual*, para 00520
10 *Minter v Kingston upon Hull City Council and Potter v SSWP* [2011] EWCA Civ 1155; HMRC, *Employment Income Manual*, para 02530
11 Reg 55(2) and (3)(a) UC Regs
12 Part 5 Ch 2 and s336 IT(EP)A 2003
13 Part 4 IT(EP)A 2003
14 Regs 53(2) and 55(3)(b) UC Regs
15 Part 3 Chs 2-11 and Part 4, Ch 6 IT(EP)A 2003
16 Part 4 Ch 8 IT(EP)A 2003
17 Reg 54(1) UC Regs
18 Reg 55(2) UC Regs. These are 'general earnings' under s7(3) IT(EP)A 2003 – see HMRC, *Employment Income Manual*, para 12850.
19 Reg 55(2) UC Regs. These come under s401 IT(EP)A 2003 and are, therefore, not 'general earnings' under s7(3) – see HMRC, *Employment Income Manual*, paras 12960 and 13005.
20 Reg 55(5) UC Regs

21 Reg 57 UC Regs
22 Regs 54 and 57(3) UC Regs
23 Reg 57(4) and (5) UC Regs
24 para H4184 ADM
25 Reg 58(1) UC Regs
26 Reg 58(2) and (3) UC Regs; para H4214 ADM
27 Reg 59(2) UC Regs
28 Reg 58(1)(b) UC Regs
29 Reg 59(3) and (4) UC Regs
30 para H4241 ADM
31 Reg 57A UC Regs; reg 4 Universal Credit (Surpluses and Self-employed Losses) (Digital Service) Amendment Regulations 2015, No.345
32 Reg 62(1) and (5) UC Regs
33 Reg 62(2) and (4) UC Regs
34 Reg 62(3) and (4) UC Regs
35 Reg 64 UC Regs
36 Reg 57(1) UC Regs
37 para H4016 ADM
38 para H4050 ADM
39 Reg 63 UC Regs
40 Reg 59 UC(TP) Regs
41 para H4102 (Example 2) ADM
42 Reg 54A UC Regs
43 Secretary of State determination under reg 5 Universal Credit (Surpluses and Self-employed Losses) (Digital Service) Amendment Regulations 2015, No.345

4. Other income
44 Reg 66(1)(a) and (b) UC Regs; reg 28(1) UC(TP) Regs
45 Reg 10 UC(TP) Regs
46 Because there is no rule to treat payments to a third party as yours: DWP email to CPAG, 7 February 2013

47 Reg 66(1)(f) UC Regs
48 Regs 66(1)(la) and 67 UC Regs; reg 16
    SPC Regs
49 Reg 66(1)(i) UC Regs
50 Reg 66(1)(h) UC Regs
51 Reg 75 UC Regs
52 Memo ADM 24/17
53 Reg 76 UC Regs
54 Reg 72(1) UC Regs
55 Reg 72(2) UC Regs
56 Reg 72(3) UC Regs
57 Regs 66 and 72 UC Regs
58 Reg 72(2) UC Regs
59 Reg 66(1)(g) UC Regs
60 Reg 66(1)(m) UC Regs; Part 5 IT(TOI)A
    2005
61 para H5112 ADM
62 Reg 26 VP Regs

5. Notional income
63 Reg 60(1) and (2) UC Regs
64 Reg 60(3) UC Regs
65 Reg 60(4) UC Regs
66 Reg 74 UC Regs
67 para H5170 ADM; *BRG v SSWP (SPC)*
    [2014] UKUT 246 (AAC)
68 para H5172 ADM

6. Working out monthly income
69 Sch 1 paras 20-30 UC,PIP,JSA&ESA(DA)
    Regs
70 Reg 54(2)(a) UC Regs
71 para H3011 ADM
72 Reg 54 UC Regs
73 *R (Johnson and Others) v SSWP* [2019]
    EWHC 23 (Admin)
74 Reg 61(2)(a) UC Regs
75 Reg 61 UC Regs
76 *SSWP v RW (rule 17) (UC)* [2017] UKUT
    347 (AAC)
77 Reg 41 UC,PIP,JSA&ESA(DA) Regs
78 Reg 73 UC Regs

Chapter 8

Capital

This chapter covers:
1. The capital limits (below)
2. Whose capital counts (p138)
3. What counts as capital (p138)
4. Disregarded capital (p141)
5. Notional capital (p148)
6. How capital is valued (p151)

This chapter explains how capital affects your entitlement to universal credit. Chapter 22 explains the rules for income support, income-based jobseeker's allowance, income-related employment and support allowance and working-age housing benefit (HB) if you and your partner are under pension age. Chapter 23 explains the rules for pension credit and for pension-age HB if you and your partner are over pension age. If you are in a couple and one of you is over pension age but not the other, see p188 for whether the working-age or pension-age HB rules apply. For the capital limits for health benefits, see Chapter 31. There are no capital rules for non-means-tested benefits.

Key facts
- Capital includes savings, investments, property and lump-sum payments.
- Some kinds of capital are ignored when working out your universal credit (UC) – eg, the value of the home in which you live.
- If you have more than £16,000 capital, you are not entitled to UC.
- If you have capital above a certain amount, your UC is affected, because this is assumed to give you a certain monthly income.
- If you deliberately get rid of capital in order to get more UC, you are treated as still having it. This is called 'notional capital'.

1. The capital limits

There is a lower and upper capital limit.[1]
- The lower limit is £6,000.
- The upper limit is £16,000.

If you have over £16,000 of capital, you are not entitled to universal credit (UC). The first £6,000 is ignored and does not affect your benefit. If you have between £6,000.01 and £16,000, you may be entitled to benefit, but it is assumed that you have some income from your capital.

This assumed monthly income, often called 'tariff income' (see p129), is £4.35 a month for every £250, or part of £250, of your capital between £6,000.01 and £16,000.

When working out the value of your capital, some capital is disregarded (see p141). You may also be treated as having capital which you do not actually have (see p148).

Example
Fatima has £7,100 savings. She is assumed to have £21.75 a month income from her savings (5 x £4.35).

Any amount of capital above £16,000 is ignored for up to 12 monthly assessment periods if you were entitled to tax credits and had over £16,000 immediately before becoming entitled to UC on a claim made through the 'managed migration' process (see p30). This is referred to as the **'transitional capital disregard'**. The disregard ends if your capital drops below £16,000 and also in any of the circumstances in which someone loses a UC transitional element (see p79).[2]

2. **Whose capital counts**

Your partner's capital

If you are a member of a couple (see p319), you must usually make a joint claim for universal credit (UC) and your partner's capital is added to yours when working out your entitlement (see p36).[3]

In the limited circumstances when you must make a single claim for UC despite being a member of a couple, your partner's capital (and income) is still added to yours.[4]

Your child's capital is not taken into account and does not affect your benefit.

3. **What counts as capital**

All your capital is taken into account, unless it is disregarded (see p141) or is treated as income (see p116).

The term 'capital' is not defined. In general, it means lump-sum or one-off payments, rather than a series of payments – eg, it includes savings, property and statutory redundancy payments.[5]

Capital payments can normally be distinguished from income because they are not payable for any specified period and are not part of a regular series of payments (although capital can be paid by instalments).[6]

Note: some capital is treated as income (see p116) and some income is treated as capital (see p141).

Savings

Your savings generally count as capital – eg, cash you have at home, premium bonds, shares, unit trusts and money in a bank or building society account.

If you have put aside money to pay bills, this is still counted as your capital.[7] If your savings are just below the capital limit, you could pay bills by monthly direct debit or use a budget account to keep your capital below the limit.

Income not spent by the end of the assessment period after the one in which you received it is treated as your capital.[8]

Fixed-term investments

Fixed-term investments count as capital. However, if an investment is currently unobtainable, it may have little or no value. If you can convert the investment into a form that lets you access it or sell your interest, or raise a loan through a reputable bank using the asset as security, the amount you can get for it counts.

Property and land

Any property or land you own counts as capital. However, many types of property are disregarded (see p141). If there is doubt about who owns the property, see below.

Loans and ownership of capital

Usually it is clear when capital belongs to you and should be taken into account. However, it may be less clear if you are holding money for someone else or if you have been given a loan which you are expected to repay.

A loan to you usually counts as money you possess and therefore counts as capital. However, you can argue that a loan, money or other assets you hold for someone else should be disregarded if it is:

- a loan granted on condition that you only use the interest, but do not touch the capital because the capital element has never been at your disposal;[9] or
- money you have been given to be used for a particular purpose on condition that it must be returned if not used in that way;[10] or

- property you have bought on behalf of someone else who is paying the mortgage;[11] *or*
- money held in your bank account on behalf of another person, which is to be returned to her/him at a future date;[12] *or*
- savings from someone else's benefit paid to you as an 'appointee' – eg, your child's disability living allowance;[13] *or*
- a loan, which you are under an immediate obligation to repay;[14] *or*
- your asset but you have expressed a clear intention that it is for someone else's benefit and renounced its use for yourself;[15] *or*
- some property and you lead someone to believe that you are transferring your interest in it to her/him but fail to do so (eg, it is never properly conveyed) and that person acts on the belief that s/he owns it (eg, spends money on repairs). You can argue the asset has been transferred and you are like a trustee.[16] This is called '**proprietary estoppel**'.

If you lend money to someone, it could still count as your 'notional capital' (see p148), depending on your reasons for lending it. You usually have a legal right to be repaid and this, in itself, could have a capital value (although the value would normally be less than the amount loaned, and could be nil if you have no expectation of getting the money back).[17]

Trusts

Capital in a non-discretionary trust is taken into acount because you can obtain the capital from the trustee at any time. If this takes you over the £16,000 capital limit, you are not entitled to UC. However, if your capital is between £6,000.01 and £16,000, you are not treated as having an assumed monthly income from the capital.[18] Capital in a discretionary trust does not normally count as your capital because payments are at the discretion of the trustee and you cannot demand payment.[19]

There is no difference between a discretionary and non-discretionary trust in the way that payments to you from the trust are treated. In either case, they are taken into account. Generally, regular payments for a particular period are treated as income, and a lump sum is treated as capital.[20] If trustees of a discretionary trust choose to pay your bills direct or buy you something that is disregarded (eg, because it is a personal possession), this should not affect your benefit.

If the trust is from money for a personal injury to you or your partner, the rules are more generous (see p146).

Note: putting money in a discretionary trust has the advantage of the value of the trust itself being disregarded. However, if you transfer money into a trust in order to get more benefit, it can still count as yours under the notional capital rules (see p148).

Money held by your solicitor

Money held by your solicitor normally counts as your capital. This includes compensation payments (but see p146 for when payments for personal injury are disregarded).[21] If you have had legal aid and your solicitor is holding money back while working out the statutory charge to be deducted for legal costs, it does not count as your capital.[22]

Income treated as capital

Unless the capital is disregarded (see below) or does not give you an assumed monthly income, actual income from capital (eg, interest on your savings, share dividends or rent from a property that is not your home) is treated as capital from the day it is due to be paid.[23] This avoids any double counting of income from capital that is also treated as giving you an assumed monthly income (see p129).

Example
Gordon has £6,800 savings, which gives him interest of £8 a month. His UC assessment takes into account an assumed monthly income from his savings of £17.40 (£4.35 a month for each £250, or part of £250, above the £6,000 lower capital limit). The actual £8 interest is added to his capital.

4. Disregarded capital

Your home

If you own the home in which you live, its value is ignored.[24] This disregard can continue to apply if you are temporarily away from home.[25]

If you own more than one property, only the one you occupy is disregarded under this rule.[26]

Exceptionally, two separate properties can be regarded as a single home, as though one were an annexe of the other, if you personally (rather than a member of your family) normally occupy both properties.[27] This is more likely if you have a large family, but you could argue that it should apply if neither property on its own meets your family's needs – eg, if you are a carer living between two properties.[28]

Your home can include croft land and smallholdings if they cannot be sold separately.[29]

When the value of the property is disregarded

The value of the property can be disregarded, even if you do not normally live in it, in the following circumstances.

- If you have left your former home following a relationship breakdown, the value of the property is ignored for six months from the date you left. It may also be disregarded for longer if any of the steps listed below are taken. If it is occupied by your former partner and s/he is a lone parent, its value is ignored for as long as s/he lives there.[30]

- If you have sought legal advice or have started legal proceedings in order to occupy property as your home, its value is ignored for six months from the date you first took either of these steps.[31] The six months can be extended if it is reasonable to do so, if you need longer to move in.

- If you are taking reasonable steps to dispose of a property, its value is ignored for six months from the date you first took such steps (which may be before you claim benefit).[32] The steps you take must be 'reasonable'. Advertising at an unrealistic sale price does not count, but placing the property with an estate agent or contacting a possible buyer should,[33] as might taking ancillary proceedings to resolve financial issues in a divorce.[34] The disregard can continue beyond six months, even for years if it is reasonable – eg, if a court orders that a former matrimonial home should not be sold until the children are grown up.[35] Taking a property off the market and putting it on again does not necessarily begin a new six-month period, but it may do if the second attempt to sell is quite separate.[36]

- If you are carrying out essential repairs or alterations which are needed so that you can occupy a property as your home, the value of the property is ignored for six months from the date you began the repairs.[37] 'Steps' may include applying for planning permission or a grant or loan to make the property habitable, employing an architect or finding someone to do the work.[38] If you cannot move into the property within that period because the work is not finished, its value can be disregarded for as long as is necessary to allow the work to be carried out.

- If you have acquired a property and intend to live in it as your home but have not yet moved in, its value is ignored for six months from the date you acquired it, or for longer if that is reasonable.[39]

- If you sell your home and intend to use the money from the sale to buy another home, the capital is ignored for six months from the date you received the money.[40] This also applies even if you do not own your home but, for a price, you surrender your tenancy rights to a landlord.[41] If you need longer to complete a purchase, your capital can continue to be ignored if it is reasonable to do so. You do not need to have decided within the six months to buy a particular property. It is sufficient if you intend to use the proceeds to buy some other home within the six- month (or extended) period,[42] although your 'intention' must involve more than a mere 'hope' or 'aspiration'.[43] There must be an element of 'certainty' which you may be able to show by evidence of a practical commitment to another purchase, although this need not involve any binding obligation.[44] If you intend to use only part of the proceeds of sale to buy another home, only that part is disregarded even if, for example, you have put the rest of the money aside to renovate your new home.[45]

- **If your home is damaged or you lose it altogether**, an insurance policy payment is ignored for six months from the date it is received, or longer if it is reasonable to do so.[46]
- **If you have taken out a loan or been given money for the express purpose of essential repairs or alterations to your home**, it is ignored for six months, or longer if it is reasonable to do so.[47] If it is a condition of the loan that it must be returned if the improvements are not carried out, you could argue that it should be ignored altogether.[48]
- **If you have deposited money with a housing association as a condition of occupying your home**, this is ignored indefinitely.[49] If money which was deposited for this purpose is now to be used to buy another home, this is ignored for six months, or longer if reasonable, in order to allow you to complete the purchase.[50]
- **Grants made to buy a home** are ignored for six months, or longer if it is reasonable to do so.[51]

When considering whether it is reasonable to extend the period during which time the value of your property is disregarded, all the circumstances should be considered – eg, your personal circumstances, any efforts made by you to use, or dispose of, the home[52] and the general state of the property market. In practice, periods of around 18 months are not considered unusual.

Note: it is possible for property to be ignored under more than one of the above paragraphs in succession.[53]

Rent that you receive from property which is disregarded is ignored, unless the rent counts as self-employed earnings from a property business (see p130).

The home of a partner, former partner or relative

The value of a home is ignored if it is occupied as her/his home by:[54]

- a close relative who is over pension age or who has limited capability for work; *or*
- your former partner from whom you are not estranged but you are living apart (and are, therefore, not treated as still living together or as living in the same household for universal credit (UC) purposes) – eg, if one of you is living in a care home; *or*
- your former partner from whom you are estranged and who is a lone parent. If your former partner is not a lone parent, the value of the home is ignored for six months for UC from the date you ceased to live in the home.

* *

Definitions

'**Close relative**' includes a parent, son, daughter, step-parent, stepson, stepdaughter, parent-in-law, son-in-law, daughter-in-law, brother or sister, or a partner of any of these people.[55] It also includes half-brothers and -sisters and adopted children.[56]

You are '**estranged**' if you are living apart because your relationship has broken down, even if the separation is amicable.[57]

* *

Personal possessions

All personal possessions, including jewellery, furniture or cars, are ignored.[58] A personal possession has been defined as any physical asset not used for business purposes, other than land.[59] However, a home that you own but do not live in is not normally considered a personal possession and counts as capital (see p141). Personal possessions are not ignored if you have bought them in order to be able to claim or get more benefit. In this case, the sale value, rather than the purchase price, is counted as actual capital and the difference is treated as notional capital (see p148).[60]

An insurance payment for damage to, or the loss of, any personal possessions, which is to be used for their repair or replacement, is ignored for six months, or longer if reasonable.[61]

Business assets

If you are self-employed, your business assets are ignored for as long as you continue to work in that business.[62]

If you cannot work because you are sick or incapacitated, the assets are disregarded for six months from when you stopped work if you can reasonably expect to work in the business again when you recover, or for longer if reasonable in the circumstances.[63]

If you stop working in the business, you are allowed six months (or longer if reasonable) to sell these assets without their value affecting your UC, provided you are taking reasonable steps to sell them.[64]

If the purchase value of an asset was deducted as an expense from your earnings and you later sell or stop using the asset for the business, the sale price (or market value if you were to sell) is treated as a receipt when working out your earnings (see p119).[65]

It is sometimes difficult to distinguish between personal and business assets. The test is whether the assets are 'part of the fund employed and risked in the business'.[66] If the assets of a business partnership (eg, plant and machinery) have been sold but the partnership has not yet been dissolved, the proceeds of sale can still count as business assets.[67] **Note:** letting a single house is not likely to constitute a business.[68]

Personal pension schemes

The value of the right to receive an occupational or personal pension is ignored. The value of a fund held in a personal pension scheme is also intended to be ignored.[69] However, if you are over pension age, you are expected to take your pension and are treated as having a notional income if you do not take it all (see p132).

Insurance policy and annuity surrender values

The surrender value of a life assurance policy is ignored.[70] Some investments include an element of life insurance – eg, endowment policies. If the policy terms include how the payment on death is calculated, the whole investment is ignored.[71] However, you cannot choose to put money in such an investment in order to increase your benefit entitlement, because you are likely to be caught by the notional capital rule if you do (see p148).

Benefits and tax credits

Arrears of benefits and tax credits

Arrears of the following benefits and tax credits, and any compensation you get for late payment of these, are ignored for 12 months from when you receive them, or longer in some cases of arrears of £5,000 or more (see below):[72]

- UC;
- any benefit that is ignored as income for UC – eg, child benefit, disability living allowance and personal independence payment (see p126);
- income support (IS), income-based jobseeker's allowance (JSA), income-related employment and support allowance (ESA), housing benefit (HB), council tax benefit, child tax credit (CTC) and working tax credit (WTC);
- maternity allowance if you received the arrears either during the current UC award or while you were getting IS, income-based JSA, income-related ESA, HB, pension credit, CTC or WTC, they were disregarded in that award and you became entitled to UC within a month of that award ending.

Arrears of £5,000 or more paid to compensate for an official error or error of law are ignored if you receive the arrears during a UC award and they would be disregarded from an award of another means-tested benefit under the rules described on p498 or p522. The arrears are ignored for 12 months from when you receive them but not beyond the end of the UC award in which they were paid. This also applies if you got the arrears while you were getting IS, income-based JSA, income-related ESA, HB, pension credit, CTC or WTC, they were disregarded in that award and you became entitled to UC within a month of that award ending.[73]

> *Example*
> George is on income-related ESA. On 1 November 2020 he gets a payment of £12,000 arrears of ESA due to him because of an official error. In December 2020, he claims UC and his ESA ends. The £12,000 arrears continue to be disregarded in his UC for as long as the award continues.

Note: although arrears are ignored as capital, you may have been paid more UC or other means-tested benefit than you would have been entitled to if benefit had been paid on time. The DWP may deduct the difference from the arrears of the delayed benefit. Otherwise, if the arrears are not reduced, the overpayment is recoverable (see p1237).

Other benefits and payments

- The initial lump sum of bereavement support payment is ignored for 12 months from the date you receive it.[74]
- Social fund payments, Best Start grants and funeral support payments are ignored for 12 months from the date you receive them.[75]
- Any 'transitional SDP amount' of UC (see p29) paid as a lump sum is ignored until your award ends or for 12 months from the date the lump sum is paid if this is longer.[76]

Personal injury and other compensation payments

If you have money in a trust or annuity from a personal injury to you, the value of the trust and any income from the trust or annuity is disregarded. A lump sum from the trust or annuity is, however, taken into account as capital.[77] It should not affect your UC if the trustees give you regular, or even annual, payments, pay your bills instead of giving you a lump sum or buy you something that would be disregarded because it is a personal possession – eg, furniture or a car. If an award is administered by a court (eg, the Court of Protection), its value and income from it is also disregarded. A payment for personal injury to you that is not in a trust is disregarded for 12 months from the date it is paid to you. If the personal injury is to your partner and s/he has since died, you cannot carry over the remainder of the 12-month disregard, or if the payment is in a trust, it is no longer ignored.[78]

> *Personal injury*
> **'Personal injury'** includes not only accidental and criminal injuries, but also any disease and injury as a result of a disease.[79]

Any payment of capital (or income) from certain special compensation schemes approved or set up by the government are ignored if they are:[80]

- to support people with a disability to live independently; *or*
- for you or your partner who has variant CJD (Creutzfeldt-Jacob disease). If you are the parent of someone with variant CJD, the payment is ignored for two years in respect of someone infected from contaminated blood products. If you give money from the payment to your partner, it is ignored for her/his UC claim indefinitely. If you have no partner or children and you give the money to your parent, it is ignored for two years; *or*
- compensation for the London bombings in July 2005, from the London Emergencies Trust or from the We Love Manchester Emergency Fund; *or*
- World War Two compensation (rather than a war pension); *or*
- in respect of someone disabled by thalidomide during her/his mother's pregnancy.[81]

Funeral plan payments

The value of any funeral plan contract is ignored indefinitely.[82] A funeral plan contract is a contract under which:
- you make payments to another person to ensure you are provided with a funeral; *and*
- the sole purpose of the plan is to provide a funeral.

Social services and community care payments

The following payments from a local authority are ignored for 12 months:[83]
- payments for children, young people and families made under: sections 17, 23B, 23C or 24A of the Children Act 1989; section 12 of the Social Work (Scotland) Act 1968; sections 29 or 30 of the Children (Scotland) Act 1995; or sections 37, 38, 109, 110, 114 or 115 of the Social Services and Well-being (Wales) Act 2014;
- payments to meet welfare needs related to old age or disability, unless they are for certain living expenses (eg, food, fuel, clothing, footwear, rent, housing costs or council tax) for you, your partner or dependent child.

See p1001 if you or your partner are involved in a trade dispute.

Miscellaneous payments

The following payments are disregarded:
- 20 per cent of money in a tax-free childcare account (see p871);[84]
- any payments made to holders of the Victoria or George Cross;[85]
- payments under the Windrush Compensation Scheme and Windrush Urgent and Exceptional Payments Scheme (disregarded on an extra-statutory basis);[86]
- victims' payments to people injured in a 'Troubles-related incident'.[87]

5. Notional capital

In certain circumstances, you are treated as having capital that you do not have. This is called **'notional capital'**.[88] There is a similar rule for notional income (see p131). Notional capital counts in the same way as the capital you do have.

You may be treated as having notional capital if:

- you deliberately deprive yourself of capital in order to claim or increase the amount of your universal credit (UC) (see below); *or*
- you are a sole trader or a partner in a business (see p150).

Note: if you are treated as having notional capital because you have deliberately deprived yourself of capital in order to claim or increase benefit, a 'diminishing notional capital rule' (see p149) may be applied so that the value of the notional capital you are treated as having is considered to reduce over time.

Deliberately getting rid of capital

If you deliberately get rid of capital in order to claim or increase your UC, you are treated as still having it.[89] You are not treated as having deprived yourself of capital if:[90]

- you pay off or reduce a debt which you owe; *or*
- you pay for goods or services if the purchase was reasonable in the circumstances of your case.

Paying off debts and bankruptcy

You are not treated as having deprived yourself of capital if you repay or reduce a debt that you owe – eg, you could repay a credit card debt, mortgage, overdraft or loan. It does not matter if the terms of the debt allow you to repay later. However, you may be asked for evidence that you owed the debt, so if you repay a loan from a family member, it may be harder to show that the debt existed.

If you are declared bankrupt, you cannot spend your capital without court approval and cannot usually be considered to have deprived yourself of it if you do. Capital you have (but cannot spend) does not count for benefit purposes from the date of the bankruptcy order.[91] However, if you deliberately go bankrupt or do not take reasonable steps to discharge the bankruptcy in order to get benefit, your capital can still count as notional capital.

Paying for goods and services

If you spend money on goods and services, you are not treated as having deprived yourself of capital if the purchase was reasonable. There is no list of items that are allowed or excluded – it depends on the circumstances. However, you are less likely to be caught by this rule if you spend money on day-to-day necessities or replacing household goods and more likely to be caught if you choose to buy something like an expensive holiday.

Intention to claim or increase universal credit

If you have spent your capital in some way other than paying off a debt or paying for goods and services that are regarded as reasonable, you are only treated as having deprived yourself of capital if you intended to claim UC or increase the amount of UC.

Relevant factors include the following.

- At the time you used your capital, how much choice did you have in spending the money in the way you did?[92]
- How long was it before you needed to claim UC? The longer it was, the less likely it is that you spent the capital in order to get UC. However, there is no set safe period after which you can claim UC without the DWP considering whether you have deliberately deprived yourself of capital.[93]
- Were you mentally capable at the time?[94]

You should not be treated as having deprived yourself of capital if:

- you did not know about the capital limit for UC – you cannot have an intention to get more UC if you do not know about the capital rules. If you are already familiar with the benefit system (eg, you have claimed benefit before and had official information about the capital rules), this is evidence that you did know about the capital limits;[95] *or*
- you told the DWP what you planned to do with your capital and were told that it would not affect your UC. If you went ahead and spent the money the way you said you would, you cannot be said to have intended to get more UC by doing so.[96]

If you use up your resources, you may have more than one motive for doing so. Even if qualifying for benefit is only a less significant motive for your actions and the main motive is something different (eg, ensuring your home is in good condition by spending capital on repairs and improvements), you may still be considered to have deprived yourself of a resource in order to get benefit.[97]

You can deprive yourself of capital, even if you receive another resource in return.[98] For example, if you buy a car so that you can get more benefit, your actual capital includes the value of the car, and the difference between that and the purchase price is treated as notional capital.[99]

The diminishing notional capital rule

If you have deliberately deprived yourself of capital, the value of your notional capital is assumed to reduce over time. This is known as the 'diminishing notional capital rule'.

The notional capital amount is not fixed, but reduces over time at a set rate, as follows.

If you are treated as having notional capital of:[100]

- over £16,000 and your UC entitlement stops, in the following month the amount of UC you would have received but for the notional capital is deducted from the amount of notional capital;
- between £6,000 and £16,000, in the following assessment period the amount of the assumed income from that notional capital is deducted from the amount of notional capital.

Notional capital is reduced in the same way in each subsequent month.

Notional capital is added to any actual capital you may have. This may reduce your UC award because of the amount of assumed monthly income from capital included in the assessment (see p129), or end it altogether.

If your UC stops altogether, make a fresh claim when you think you might become entitled. Ask the DWP to tell you how long it will be before a new claim might succeed. If you have both actual and notional capital, you may need to spend your actual capital to meet your living expenses.

Companies run by sole traders or a few partners

Normally, if you hold shares in a company, their value is taken into account as capital.[101] If, however, your influence in the company is such that you are like a sole trader or like a partner in a small partnership, you are treated accordingly. The value of your shareholding is ignored but you are treated as having a proportionate share of the capital of the company.[102] However, these company assets are not taken into account while you are doing any work on the company's business,[103] even if you only do a little work for the company – eg, taking messages.[104] It has, however, been held that a 'sleeping partner' in a business managed and worked exclusively by others cannot benefit from this disregard. As well as having a financial commitment to the business, you must also be involved or engaged in it in some practical sense as an earner.[105]

Note: income from the company, or your share of it, is regarded as your self-employed earnings. If this is your main employment, it counts as 'gainful employment', so you can be treated as having a minimum level of earnings from that employment if your actual earnings are low (see p121).[106] You may also have employed earnings as a director or employee.

As the value of your shareholding is ignored, dividends are also ignored as income (because actual income that comes from disregarded capital is not in the list of income taken into account for UC – see p130 and 141). Exceptionally, dividends could in reality be earnings and counted as such.[107]

6. How capital is valued

Market value

Your capital is valued at its current market or surrender value.[108] This means the amount of money you could raise by selling it or raising a loan against it. This is the price that would be paid by a willing buyer to a willing seller on a particular date.[109] So if an asset is difficult or impossible to realise, its market value should be heavily discounted or even nil.[110]

If you cannot legally dispose of capital (eg, because of a restraint order), the market value is nil.[111]

In the case of a house, an estate agent's figure for a quick sale is a more appropriate valuation than the district valuer's figure for a sale within three months.[112]

It is not uncommon for an unrealistic assessment to be made of the value of your capital. If you disagree with the decision, you could ask for a revision or appeal (see Chapters 56 and 57).

Expenses of sale

If there would be expenses involved in selling your capital, 10 per cent is deducted from its value (before any debts are deducted) for the cost of sale.[113]

Debts

Deductions are made from the gross value of your capital for any debt or mortgage secured on it.[114] If a creditor (eg, a bank) holds the land certificate to your property as security for a loan and has registered notice of its deposit at the Land Registry, this counts as a debt secured on your property.[115] If a single mortgage is secured on a house and land, and the value of the house is disregarded for benefit purposes, the whole of the mortgage can be deducted when calculating the value of the land.[116]

If you have debts that are not secured against your capital (eg, tax liabilities), these cannot be offset against the value of your capital.[117] However, once you have repaid your debts, your capital may be reduced. **Note:** you can still be treated as having the capital if you deliberately get rid of it in order to get benefit (see p148).

If you have an overdrawn bank account and have savings in another account with the same bank, the amount of the overdraft should be deducted from your savings if the terms of the accounts allow the bank to make these transfers.[118]

Jointly owned capital

If you own any capital asset (except as a partner in a company – see p150) with someone else under a 'joint tenancy', you are treated as owning an equal share of the asset with the other owner(s) – eg, if you own the asset with one other person, you are each treated as having a 50 per cent share of it.[119] This applies regardless of whether the capital asset is in the UK or abroad. See p153 for the rules that apply to assets abroad.[120]

This does not apply if you jointly own the capital asset as 'tenants in common'.[121] In this case, your actual share in the asset is valued.

Joint tenancies and tenancies in common

With a '**joint tenancy**', each co-owner owns the whole of the capital asset 'jointly and severally'. If one of the joint tenants were to die, her/his interest in the asset would pass automatically to the other joint tenant(s).

With a '**tenancy in common**', each co-owner owns a discrete share in the asset. This share can be passed on by the person who has died to whoever s/he wishes.

If you have a joint tenancy, the value of your deemed share is calculated in the same way as your actual capital. However, it is only the value of your deemed share looked at in isolation that counts, and this will usually be worth less than the same proportion of the value of the whole asset. For example, if the asset is a house, the value of any deemed share may be very small or even worthless, particularly if the house is occupied and there is a possibility that the sale of the property cannot be forced. This is because even a willing buyer could not be expected to pay much for an asset s/he would have difficulty making use of.[122] Whether a sale can be forced depends on individual circumstances, and valuations should take into account legal costs and the length of time it could take to gain possession of the property.[123] A valuation should set out details of the valuer's expertise (where relevant), describe the property in sufficient detail to show that all factors relevant to its value have been taken into account, state any assumptions on which it is based and explain what the market is for that type of sale.[124] You may need to challenge any decision (see Chapters 56 and 57) based on an inadequate valuation.

Treatment of assets after a relationship breakdown

When partners separate, assets, such as a former home or bank account, may be in joint or sole names. If, for instance, a bank account is in joint names, you and your former partner are treated as having a 50 per cent share each under the rules on jointly held capital (see p151). On the other hand, a former partner may have a right to some, or all, of an asset that is in your sole name – eg, s/he may have deposited most of the money in a bank account in your name. If this is established, you may be treated as not entitled to the whole of the account but as holding part of it as trustee for your former partner.[125] If an asset such as the matrimonial home belongs to your former partner and you have no share in it, you cannot be treated as having any interest in it under the Matrimonial Causes Act 1973 unless you take divorce or separation proceedings and get a property order.[126]

Shares

Shares are valued at their current market value less 10 per cent for the cost of sale, and after deducting any 'lien' held by brokers for sums owed for purchase or commission.[127] Market value can be worked out from the listed share price. If a more exact value is needed (eg, because your capital is close to the limit), it should be calculated using HM Revenue and Customs guidance, by taking the lowest and highest share prices for the day and using the lowest price plus a quarter of the difference between the two.[128] Fluctuations in price between routine reviews of your award are normally ignored.

Unit trusts

Unit trusts are valued on the basis of the 'bid' price quoted in newspapers. No deduction is allowed for the cost of sale because this is already included in the 'bid' price.[129]

The right to receive a payment in the future

The value of any such right is its market value – what a willing buyer will pay to a willing seller.[130] For something which is not yet realisable, this may be very small.

Overseas assets

If you have assets abroad and there are no exchange controls or other prohibitions to prevent you transferring your capital to the UK, your assets are valued at their current market or surrender value in that country.[131]

If you are not allowed to transfer your capital, you are treated as having capital equal to the amount that a willing buyer in this country would give for those assets (which might not be very much).[132] Deduct any debts or mortgage secured on the assets, 10 per cent for any expenses of sale and any charges for converting the payment into sterling.[133]

Notes

1. The capital limits
1 Regs 18 and 72 UC Regs
2 Reg 51 UC(TP) Regs

2. Whose capital counts
3 s5(2) WRA 2012
4 Reg 18(2) UC Regs

3. What counts as capital
5 para H1020 ADM
6 R v SBC ex parte Singer [1973] 1 WLR 713; reg 46(3) UC Regs
7 R(IS) 3/93
8 para H1050 ADM
9 R(SB) 12/86
10 Barclays Bank v Quistclose Investments Ltd [1970] AC 567; R(SB) 49/83; R(SB) 53/83; R(SB) 1/85; MW v SSWP (JSA) [2016] UKUT 469 (AAC), reported as [2017] AACR 15
11 R(SB) 49/83
12 R(SB) 12/86; for how this works in Scotland, see JK v SSWP (JSA) [2010] UKUT 437 (AAC), reported as [2011] AACR 26; DF v SSWP [2015] UKUT 611 (AAC)
13 MC v SSWP (IS) [2015] UKUT 600 (AAC)
14 CIS/2287/2008
15 R(IS) 1/90; CSIS/639/2006
16 R(SB) 23/85; CSIS/639/2006
17 JC v SSWP [2009] UKUT 22 (AAC)
18 Reg 72(2) UC Regs
19 Gartside v Inland Revenue Commissioners [1968] 1 All ER 121; [1968] AC 553; LG v SSWP (ESA) [2019] UKUT 220 (AAC)
20 Regs 46, 48 and 66(1)(j) UC Regs
21 Thomas v CAO, appendix to R(SB) 17/87
22 CIS/984/2002
23 Reg 72(3) UC Regs

4. Disregarded capital
24 Sch 10 para 1 UC Regs
25 para H2038 ADM
26 Schs 3 para 1(1) and 10 para 1(2) UC Regs
27 R(JSA) 9/03; R(SB) 10/89
28 MM v SSWP (IS) [2012] UKUT 358 (AAC); para H2040 ADM
29 Sch 3 paras 1(4) and 2 UC Regs; para H2039 ADM

30 Reg 48(2) and Sch 10 para 5 UC Regs
31 Reg 48(2) and Sch 10 para 4(1)(b) and (2) UC Regs
32 Sch 10 para 6 UC Regs
33 R(SB) 32/83
34 R(IS) 5/05
35 Reg 48(2) UC Regs
36 SP v SSWP [2009] UKUT 255 (AAC)
37 Reg 48(2) and Sch 10 para 4(1)(c) UC Regs
38 R v London Borough of Tower Hamlets Review Board ex parte Kapur, 12 June 2000, unreported
39 Reg 48(2) and Sch 10 para 4(1)(a) UC Regs
40 Reg 48(2) and Sch 10 para 13(a) UC Regs
41 R(IS) 6/95
42 R(IS) 7/01
43 CIS/685/1992
44 CIS/8475/1995; CIS/15984/1996
45 R(SB) 14/85
46 Reg 48(2) and Sch 10 para 14 UC Regs
47 Reg 48(2) and Sch 10 para 15 UC Regs
48 Barclays Bank v Quistclose Investments Ltd [1970] AC 567; CSB/975/1985
49 Sch 10 para 12 UC Regs
50 Reg 48(2) and Sch 10 para 13(b) UC Regs
51 Reg 48(2) and Sch 10 para 13(c) UC Regs
52 CIS/4757/2003
53 CIS/6908/1995
54 Sch 10 paras 2, 3 and 5 UC Regs
55 Reg 2 UC Regs
56 CSB/209/1986; CSB/1149/1986; R(SB) 22/87
57 R(IS) 5/05; CH/3777/2007
58 Reg 46(2) UC Regs
59 R(H) 7/08
60 CIS/494/1990 and R(IS) 8/04; para H1895 ADM
61 Reg 48(2) and Sch 10 para 14 UC Regs
62 Sch 10 para 7 UC Regs
63 Reg 48(2) and Sch 10 para 8(b) UC Regs
64 Reg 48(2) and Sch 10 para 8(a) UC Regs
65 Reg 57(5) UC Regs
66 R(SB) 4/85
67 CIS/5481/1997

Chapter 8

Capital

68 CFC/15/1990; R(FC) 2/92; *RM v Sefton Council (HB)* [2016] UKUT 357 (AAC)
69 Sch 10 para 10 UC Regs; email from DWP to CPAG, 7 February 2013
70 Sch 10 para 9 UC Regs
71 R(IS) 7/98
72 Sch 10 para 18 UC Regs; reg 10B UC(TP) Regs
73 Reg 10A UC(TP) Regs
74 Sch 10 para 20 UC Regs
75 Sch 10 paras 16, 21 and 22 UC Regs
76 Sch 2 para 7 UC(TP) Regs
77 Reg 75 UC Regs
78 R(IS) 3/03
79 R(SB) 2/89; *KQ v SSWP (IS)* [2011] UKUT 102 (AAC), reported as [2011] AACR 43
80 Reg 76 UC Regs
81 Ignored as a personal injury payment.
82 Sch 10 para 11 UC Regs
83 Sch 10 para 17 UC Regs
84 Memo ADM 26/16
85 Sch 10 para 19 UC Regs
86 Hansard Written question 276279; HB Circular A8/2019
87 Reg 26 VP Regs

5. Notional capital
88 Regs 50(1) and 77(2) UC Regs
89 Reg 50(1) and (2) UC Regs
90 Reg 50(2) UC Regs
91 *KS v SSWP* [2009] UKUT 122 (AAC), reported as [2010] AACR 3
92 R(SB) 12/91; para H1832 ADM
93 CIS/264/1989; R(IS) 7/98
94 para H1830 ADM
95 R(SB) 9/91; R(SB) 12/91
96 *LH v SSWP (IS)* [2014] UKUT 60 (AAC); para H1842 ADM
97 R(SB) 38/85; R(IS) 1/91; R(H) 1/06
98 R(SB) 40/85
99 R(IS) 8/04
100 Reg 50(3) UC Regs
101 para H1020 ADM
102 Reg 77(1) and (2) UC Regs
103 Reg 77(3)(a) UC Regs
104 Vol 5 Ch 29, para 29879 DMG; see also R(IS) 13/93
105 R(IS) 14/98
106 Reg 77(3) UC Regs
107 *HMRC v PA Holdings Ltd* [2011] EWCA Civ 1414

6. How capital is valued
108 Reg 49(1) UC Regs
109 R(SB) 57/83; R(SB) 6/84
110 R(SB) 18/83
111 *CS v SSWP* [2014] UKUT 518 (AAC)
112 R(SB) 6/84
113 Reg 49(1) UC Regs
114 Reg 49(1)(b) UC Regs
115 CIS/255/1989
116 R(SB) 27/84
117 R(SB) 2/83; R(SB) 31/83
118 *JRL v SSWP (JSA)* [2011] UKUT 63 (AAC), reported as [2011] AACR 30
119 Reg 47 UC Regs
120 CIS/2575/1997
121 *Hourigan v SSWP* [2002] EWCA 1890, reported as R(IS) 4/03
122 CIS/15936/1996; CIS/263/1997; CIS/3283/1997 (joint decision); R(IS) 26/95
123 R(IS) 3/96
124 R(IS) 2/02; *Reigate and Banstead Borough Council v GB (HB)* [2018] UKUT 225 (AAC)
125 R(IS) 2/93
126 R(IS) 1/03
127 Reg 49 UC Regs
128 paras H1660-65 ADM
129 para H1673 ADM
130 *Peters v CAO*, appendix to R(SB) 3/89
131 Reg 49(2)(a) UC Regs
132 Reg 49(2)(b) UC Regs
133 Reg 49(3) UC Regs

Part 3

Other means-tested benefits and tax credits

Chapter 9

Income-related employment and support allowance

This chapter covers:
1. Who can get income-related employment and support allowance (p160)
2. The rules about your age (p162)
3. People included in the claim (p162)
4. The amount of benefit (p163)
5. Special benefit rules (p165)
6. Claims and backdating (p166)
7. Getting paid (p168)
8. Tax, other benefits and the benefit cap (p169)

Key facts

- Employment and support allowance (ESA) is a benefit for people who are unable to work because of illness or disability (known as having 'limited capability for work') and who are not entitled to statutory sick pay.
- Entitlement to ESA is assessed by a test called the work capability assessment.
- There are two types of ESA: **contributory ESA**, which is not means tested (but can be affected by certain pensions), and **income-related ESA**, which is means tested.
- You do not have to have paid national insurance contributions to qualify for income-related ESA.
- ESA is administered and paid by the DWP.
- If you disagree with an ESA decision, you can apply for a revision or supersession (see Chapter 56), or appeal against it (see Chapter 57). You must apply for a mandatory reconsideration before you can appeal. All parts of the decision may be looked at.

Part 3: Other means-tested benefits and tax credits
Chapter 9: Income-related employment and support allowance
1. Who can get income-related employment and support allowance

1. Who can get income-related employment and support allowance

You qualify for employment and support allowance (ESA) if you:[1]

- have 'limited capability for work' (see p1010); *and*
- are aged 16 or over but under pension age (see p271); *and*
- are in Great Britain (see p165 if you go abroad); *and*
- are not entitled in your own right to statutory sick pay, income support (IS) or jobseeker's allowance (JSA), and are not in a couple entitled to joint-claim JSA (see p253); *and*
- are not doing any work (except work you can do while claiming – see p1042).

The above conditions apply to both types of ESA. To qualify for income-related ESA, you must also satisfy extra rules (see below).

You may qualify for income-related ESA even if you do not qualify for contributory ESA. You may qualify for both income-related ESA and contributory ESA.

Note: if you are already entitled to contributory ESA and do not come under the universal credit (UC) system, you may be able to top this up with income-related ESA without having to make a new claim (see p26).

Some claimants of ESA (but not those in the 'support group' – see p652) must take part in work-focused interviews and some of those can also be required to undertake 'work-related activity' (see p1140).

Income-related employment and support allowance and universal credit
You can now only make a new claim for income-related ESA in limited circumstances (see p161). Otherwise, when you claim ESA, you will come under the UC system instead (see p23).
If you are already entitled to income-related ESA, you can continue to qualify until:
– you claim UC;
– you become a member of a couple and your partner is getting UC;
– you are affected by the 'managed migration' transfer process (see p30).
The government says that from November 2020, the DWP will begin to transfer existing income-related ESA claims to UC. This transfer process began in July 2019 in pilot areas. When you are affected, your income-related ESA claim ends and you are invited to claim UC. See p30 for further information, and see AskCPAG.org.uk and CPAG's *Welfare Rights Bulletin* for updates.

You cannot usually qualify for income-related ESA if you are pension age or over. However, if you are already getting income-related ESA and you are or become a member of a 'mixed-age' couple (ie, you have reached pension age but your partner has not), in some circumstances, your income-related ESA can continue even though you have reached pension age (see p162).

Who can make a new claim for income-related employment and support allowance

You can only make a new claim for income-related ESA in the following circumstances.[2]

- You are prevented from claiming UC because:[3]
  - you (or your partner) are, or within the last month have been, entitled to IS, income-based JSA, income-related ESA or housing benefit (HB) that includes a severe disability premium (see p346), and if your entitlement to the benefit ended during that month you (or s/he) have continued to satisfy the conditions for that premium; *and*
  - you (and your partner) have not yet been given a 'migration notice' from the DWP that you will be transferred to UC via the 'managed migration' process (see p30).

The above may apply, for example, if you are claiming income-related ESA after a break in your entitlement, you are currently entitled to HB, or you have been getting IS or income-based JSA but no longer qualify.

Note: this rule only applies until 27 January 2021.

- You are prevented from claiming UC because you (or if you are in a couple, you and your partner) are a 'frontier worker' – ie, you work in Great Britain or Northern Ireland, but do not live there.
- You are prevented from claiming UC because you come into some other category of case from whom it has been decided not to accept claims, in order to safeguard or test the efficient administration of UC.

If you cannot make a new claim for income-related ESA under these rules, you can make a claim for UC.

Extra rules for income-related employment and support allowance

You qualify for income-related ESA if, in addition to satisfying the basic rules of entitlement to ESA above:[4]

- your income (see Chapter 20) is less than your applicable amount (see Chapter 17); *and*
- your capital (see Chapter 22) is not over £16,000;[5] *and*
- you are not entitled to pension credit (PC); *and*
- your partner, if you are in a couple (see p319), is not engaged in full-time paid work (p991) or treated as being in full-time paid work (p997); *and*
- your partner is not entitled to income-related ESA, income-based JSA, IS or PC in her/his own right; *and*

Part 3: Other means-tested benefits and tax credits
Chapter 9: Income-related employment and support allowance
3. People included in the claim

- you are not 'receiving education', unless you are entitled to disability living allowance, personal independence payment or armed forces independence payment, in which case you can still qualify for income-related ESA;[6] *and*
- you satisfy the 'right to reside' and 'habitual residence' tests (see Chapter 68);[7] *and*
- you are not a 'person subject to immigration control' (see p1560).[8]

Education

You are in '**education**' if you are a 'qualifying young person' (eg, you are aged under 20 and in full-time, non-advanced education or approved training – see p579) or if you are on a course that is classed as full time.[9] The rules are very similar to those that apply to the definition of full-time courses for IS (see p888). Get advice if you are unsure.

Disqualification from benefit

You can be disqualified from receiving ESA for up to six weeks (or have your benefit paid at a reduced rate if you are a 'person in hardship') in the circumstances described on p649. The rules are the same for both income-related ESA and contributory ESA.

However, the rules for income-related ESA are different from those for contributory ESA if you are:

- absent from Great Britain (see p1651); *or*
- a prisoner or detained in legal custody (see p941).

2. The rules about your age

To satisfy the basic rules for employment and support allowance (ESA), you must be aged at least 16, but under pension age (see p780). However, if you are already getting income-related ESA and are, or become, a member of a 'mixed-age couple' (ie, you have reached pension age but your partner has not) and you are prevented from claiming universal credit (see p161), your income-related ESA continues even though you have reached pension age.[10]

3. People included in the claim

If you are single, you claim income-related employment and support allowance (ESA) for yourself.

If you are a member of a couple (see p319 for who counts), either you claim income-related ESA for both you and your partner or, if your partner meets the qualifying conditions for income-related ESA, s/he can claim for you both instead.

The applicable amount that forms part of the calculation of your benefit includes a personal allowance for a couple and can include premiums based on both your and your partner's circumstances. When your benefit is worked out, your partner's income and capital are usually added to yours. Whichever one of you claims ESA, the other may qualify for national insurance (NI) credits in order to protect her/his NI record. See Chapter 43 for more details.

There are some situations in which you must show that you are 'responsible' for a child who is living in your household – eg:

- to be exempt from compulsory work-focused interviews and work-related activity (see p1136 and p1140);
- for help with your housing costs if you are an owner-occupier (see p363 and p370).

You can count as responsible for any child under 16 and for any qualifying young person (referred to as a 'child' in this *Handbook*). You do not have to be the child's parent. For when you count as responsible for a child and when s/he counts as living in your household, see pp326–27.

4. The amount of benefit

The amount of income-related employment and support allowance (ESA) you get depends on your needs (your 'applicable amount') and how much income and capital you have.

You are paid a limited amount of ESA during an initial 'assessment phase'. See p651 for more information (the rules on when the assessment phase applies are the same as for contributory ESA). After this, there is a 'main phase'. During the main phase you may get an additional component included in your applicable amount. For the calculation, see p164.

Note:

- You are not entitled during the first seven 'waiting days' of your period of limited capability for work, unless an exception applies (see p650 – the rules are the same as for contributory ESA). You may be able to get a short-term advance before your first payment of ESA is due (see p1192).
- If you are appealing against a decision that you do not have limited capability for work and you get ESA pending the outcome of your appeal (see p1038), you are only paid at the assessment phase rate – ie, you do not get an additional component.
- You are entitled to just one award of ESA, but this may be made up of both contributory ESA and income-related ESA.[11] If you are entitled to both types of ESA, the total amount of ESA payable is the same amount as your income-related ESA, but is made up of contributory ESA topped up with income-related ESA.

Part 3: Other means-tested benefits and tax credits
Chapter 9: Income-related employment and support allowance
4. The amount of benefit

Calculating income-related employment and support allowance

Income-related ESA is worked out as follows.

Step one: calculate your applicable amount
Your applicable amount consists of:
- in both the assessment phase (see p651) and the main phase:
  - **a personal allowance** (see p333). Your personal allowance is paid at a lower rate if you are under 25 or, in some cases, if you are under 18, and while you are in the assessment phase (see p651); *and*
  - **premiums** for any special needs (see p339);
- usually in the main phase only: **a support component** (see p652 – the rules are the same as for contributory ESA) or (if you can still get it) **a work-related activity component** (see p653 – the rules are the same as for contributory ESA). **Note:** the work-related activity component was abolished for new claimants from April 2017. In some circumstances (eg, if you are terminally ill), you can be entitled to one of these components during the assessment phase;
- a 'transitional addition' if you were transferred from incapacity benefit, severe disablement allowance or income support (IS) on grounds of disability to ESA, and were entitled to income-related ESA as part of the transfer (eg, because your ESA would have been less than your IS, or on transfer your contributory ESA should have been topped up with income-related ESA). See p27 for more on the transfer process. Although your ESA can continue to include a transitional addition, it is reduced by increases in your ESA.

Note: you cannot get help with your mortgage interest costs in your income-related ESA applicable amount. Instead, you may be able to get a loan from the DWP (see p855).
For more details on applicable amounts, see Chapter 17.

Step two: calculate your income
This is the amount you have coming in each week from, for instance, other benefits, part-time earnings, working tax credit and maintenance (see Chapter 20). If you have capital over £6,000 (£10,000 if you live in a care home), it also includes your tariff income (see p443).

Step three: deduct income from applicable amount
If your income is less than your applicable amount, your income-related ESA equals the difference between the two. If your income is the same as or more than your applicable amount, you are not entitled to ESA.

Example

Terry is aged 35 when he claims ESA. He lives with his wife, Julia, and six-year-old son, Ray. They get child benefit and child tax credit (CTC). Julia works 10 hours a week and earns £80 a week. Terry is assessed as being entitled to a support component. He has not paid enough national insurance contributions to get contributory ESA.

Assessment phase

Applicable amount = £116.80 (personal allowance for couple both aged 18 or over)

Income to be taken into account = £60 (child benefit and CTC are ignored; £20 earnings disregard applies)

Terry's income-related ESA during assessment phase is £116.80 *minus* £60 = £56.80

Main phase

Applicable amount = £180.50 (personal allowance of £116.80 for couple both aged 18 or over *plus* an enhanced disability premium (at the couple rate) of £24.50, *plus* a support component of £39.20)

Income to be taken into account (as above) = £60

Terry's income-related ESA during the main phase is £180.50 *minus* £60 = £120.50

Note:

- If you are not currently entitled to ESA because of the level of your income, but will be when a component is included in your applicable amount, you may be given an '**advance award**'. Under this, you are entitled from the point the additional component is awarded, provided you still satisfy the other conditions, without needing to claim again.[12]
- Earnings you receive for 'permitted work' (see p1042) are disregarded when calculating the amount of your income-related ESA.

Your ESA may be reduced if:

- you do not comply with a requirement to attend work-focused interviews and work-related activity (see p1136 and p1140). **Note:** these requirements do not apply if you are entitled to a support component; *or*
- you are disqualified from ESA but are a person in 'hardship' (see p649 – the rules are the same as for contributory ESA); *or*
- you have committed a benefit offence (see p1278).

5. Special benefit rules

Special rules may apply to:

- people subject to immigration control (see Chapter 67);
- people who have come from abroad (see Chapter 68) or are going abroad (see Chapters 69 and 70);
- people who are living in a care home or other similar accommodation, or people in prison or detention (see Chapter 42).

Part 3: Other means-tested benefits and tax credits
Chapter 9: Income-related employment and support allowance
6. Claims and backdating

6. Claims and backdating

The general rules about claims and backdating are covered in Chapter 50. Most of the specific rules about claiming employment and support allowance (ESA) are described in Chapter 30. **Note:** you can only make a new claim for income-related ESA in limited circumstances (see p252).

To be entitled to ESA, you must usually make a claim for it. However, if you are appealing against a decision that you do not have limited capability for work, you do not need to make a claim, although you must submit a medical certificate.[13] For when ESA can be paid pending an appeal, see p1038.

In most cases (unless you are recognised as exempt straight away), you are required to attend a medical examination to assess whether you have limited capability for work and limited capability for work-related activity. In addition, unless you are in the 'support group' (see p652), you are usually required to attend compulsory work-focused interviews and, in some cases, carry out work-related activity. These interviews can include a 'health and work conversation' (see p1136).

Making a claim

If you are already getting contributory ESA and do not come under the universal credit (UC) system, you can 'top up' your entitlement with income-related ESA without having to make a new claim (see p26). This is because income-related ESA and contributory ESA are two types of the same benefit.[14]

If you can make a new claim for income-related ESA, a claim can be made:[15]

- by telephone. This is the way the DWP prefers you to claim. Telephone a Jobcentre Plus contact centre (Monday–Friday, 8am–6pm, tel: 0800 169 0350; Relay UK (if you cannot hear or speak on the phone): 18001 then 0800 169 0350; Welsh language: 0800 012 1888; textphone: 0800 023 4888); *or*
- in writing by completing the approved claim form. A form can be downloaded from gov.uk (see below for details). Send or take the completed form to your local Jobcentre Plus office. If the DWP has arranged for a local authority to receive claims for ESA, you can also send it to the local authority housing benefit office.

Note:

- You do not have to start your claim by telephone, but it is best to make your claim in the way the DWP prefers if you can. If you claim in writing, keep a copy of your claim form in case queries arise.
- If you are employed, see p659. You should normally be paid statutory sick pay (SSP) (see Chapter 39) for the first 28 weeks of your limited capability for work. After that, you can only get income-related ESA in limited circumstances (see p161).

- If you were getting income-related ESA and then started work but have now become sick again, you can only get income-related ESA again in limited circumstances (see p161). If you can get income-related ESA again and it is within 12 weeks of your previous award ending, you can benefit from rules that link your two awards (see p1041).

You must provide any information or evidence required (see p659). You can amend or withdraw your claim before a decision is made (see p1169). If there is a delay in deciding your claim, you may be able to get a short-term advance of benefit (see p1192).

Forms

The approved claim form is Form ESA1. Get this from gov.uk/government/publications/ employment-and-support-allowance-claim-form, your local Jobcentre Plus office or telephone contact centre.

Who should claim

Usually, you must claim ESA on your own behalf. If you are unable to manage your own affairs, another person can claim ESA for you as your 'appointee' (see p1170).

Information to support your claim

For the general information requirements that apply to all benefits, see p1170.

It is important that you provide any information required when you claim. Until you do, you may not count as having made a valid claim (see p1172). Correct any defects as soon as possible or your date of claim may be affected.

You may also be referred for a medical assessment. If you fail to attend the medical without good cause, your claim can be refused.[16] Face-to-face assessments are suspended during the coronavirus pandemic.

For further details about information or evidence (including medical evidence) that you should provide, see p659. The rules described for contributory ESA also apply to income-related ESA.

Even if you have provided all that was required when you claimed, you may be asked to provide further information to support your claim (see p1174). You may also be asked to provide information after you are awarded ESA and if you fail to do so, your ESA could be suspended or even terminated (see p1200).

The date of your claim

The date of your claim is important as it determines when your entitlement to income-related ESA starts (subject to the rules on waiting days – see p662). This is

Part 3: Other means-tested benefits and tax credits
Chapter 9: Income-related employment and support allowance
7. Getting paid

not necessarily the date from when you are paid. For information about when payment of income-related ESA starts, see below.

The **'date of your claim'** is usually the date of your telephone call starting the claim, or the date your claim form is received. However, there are exceptions (see p660).

Note: you must make sure your claim is valid. If it is 'defective', you are given a short time to correct the defects (see p1173 and p1173). If you do, your claim is treated as having been made when you initially claimed.[17]

In some cases, you can claim in advance (see below), and in some cases your claim can be backdated (see below). If you want this to be done, make this clear when you claim or the DWP might not consider it. If you claimed maternity allowance (MA) or SSP when you should have claimed ESA, see below.

Backdating your claim

Your claim can be backdated for up to three months before the day you actually claim (see p660).

If you claim the wrong benefit

In some circumstances a claim for MA may be treated as a claim for ESA (or vice versa) or your ESA claim can be treated as having been made on the date you applied for SSP (see p660).

Claiming in advance

You can claim ESA up to three months in advance if you are not entitled to it now, but will become entitled within 13 weeks of claiming, unless the reason you do not qualify straight away is because you fail the habitual residence test (see p1586).[18] The date of your claim is the date on which you qualify.[19]

7. Getting paid

As income-related and contributory employment and support allowance (ESA) are two types of the same benefit, the rules described on p661 on getting paid contributory ESA also apply to income-related ESA.

For details of when your income-related ESA might be paid at a reduced rate, see p164.

Income-related employment and support allowance run-on

If you are getting income-related ESA and make a new claim for universal credit (UC) on or after 22 July 2020, your income-related ESA entitlement continues for two weeks (called a 'run-on payment' or a 'transitional income-related ESA payment').[20] You do not have to make a claim for a run-on payment. It should be made automatically. You do not have to pay a run-on payment back and it does not count as a specified benefit for the purposes of the benefit cap (see p1194).[21]

Change of circumstances

You must report changes in your circumstances that you have been told to report, as well as any that you might reasonably be expected to know might affect your right to, the amount of or the payment of your benefit. You should do this as soon as possible, preferably in writing. See p1199 for further information.

Note: if you become a member of a couple with someone entitled to UC, your entitlement to income-related ESA ends (see p32).

8. Tax, other benefits and the benefit cap

Tax

Income-related employment and support allowance (ESA) is not taxable.[22]

Means-tested benefits and tax credits

If you are entitled to income-related ESA:
*   it is an automatic passport to maximum housing benefit (HB). If you are not entitled already, you must make a separate claim (if you still can). It is also an automatic passport to maximum child tax credit (CTC) and usually to maximum working tax credit (WTC);
*   you and your partner may be able to claim WTC if your partner works at least 16 hours but less than 24 hours a week. You and your partner may be able to claim WTC as well as, or instead of, income-related ESA. Get advice about whether you can still make a new claim and, if so, how you would be better off financially;
*   WTC is taken into account as income when working out your income-related ESA, but CTC is not.

If you or your partner have just stopped work or reduced your hours, you may be able to get 'WTC run-on' for a four-week period (see p305).

Non-means-tested benefits

You can be entitled to income-related ESA and contributory ESA at the same time.
While you are on income-related ESA, you get national insurance credits (see p968).
You are not entitled to ESA if you are entitled to statutory sick pay.[23]

Part 3: Other means-tested benefits and tax credits
Chapter 9: Income-related employment and support allowance
8. Tax, other benefits and the benefit cap

Most non-means-tested benefits are taken into account as income when working out the amount of income-related ESA you get. However:

- attendance allowance, disability living allowance, personal independence payment, guardian's allowance and child benefit are not taken into account;
- it can still be worth claiming non-means-tested benefits. If you or your partner qualify for certain of these, you also qualify for certain premiums and, therefore, a higher rate of income-related ESA.

You cannot claim ESA and jobseeker's allowance (JSA) in your own right at the same time. If your partner is entitled to contribution-based JSA, you can claim ESA (if you still can – see p161). Your partner's JSA is taken into account when assessing your income for income-related ESA.

The benefit cap

In some cases, there is a limit on the total amount of specified benefits you can receive (a 'benefit cap'). ESA is one of the specified benefits. However, the benefit cap does *not* apply if you or your partner receive ESA which includes a support component. In other cases, it only applies if you are getting universal credit or HB. See p1194 for further information.

Passports and other sources of help

If you are entitled to income-related ESA, you also qualify for health benefits such as free prescriptions (see Chapter 31) and education benefits such as free school lunches (see p866). You may also qualify for social fund payments (see Chapter 37) or, in Scotland, a Best Start grant (see Chapter 72) or a funeral support payment (see Chapter 73). You may be entitled to a council tax reduction (see p851).

Financial help on starting work

If you stop getting income-related ESA because you or your partner start work, or your partner's earnings or hours in her/his existing job increase, you might be able to get housing costs run-on if you have had those included (see p376) or a mortgage interest run-on if you have been getting a loan for your mortgage interest payments (see p860), or extended payments of HB if you pay rent (see p217). Your local authority may also provide extended help with council tax. See p873 for information about other financial help you might get.

Notes

1. Who can get income-related employment and support allowance
1 ss1 and 20(1) WRA 2007; reg 40(1) ESA Regs
2 Art 5A WRA(No.9)O; Art 6(11) WRA(No.21)O; Art 7 WRA(No.23)O
3 Reg 4A UC(TP) Regs
4 Sch 1 para 6 WRA 2007
5 Reg 110 ESA Regs
6 Reg 18 ESA Regs; Schs 1 para 2 and 2 para 2 ESA(TP)(EA)(No.2) Regs
7 Reg 70 and Sch 5 para 11 ESA Regs
8 s115 IAA 1999
9 Regs 14-17 ESA Regs

2. The rules about your age
10 Art 8 WRA(No.31)O; HB Circular A9/2019

4. The amount of benefit
11 s6 WRA 2007
12 s5 WRA 2007; reg 146 ESA Regs

6. Claims and backdating
13 Reg 3(j) SS(C&P) Regs
14 *LH v SSWP (ESA)* [2014] UKUT 480 (AAC), reported as [2015] AACR 14
15 Regs 4G and 4H SS(C&P) Regs; regs 13 and 15 ESA Regs 2013
16 s19 SSA 1998; reg 23 ESA Regs
17 Regs 4G(5) and 4H(7) SS(C&P) Regs
18 Reg 13(9) SS(C&P) Regs
19 Reg 13(1) SS(C&P) Regs

7. Getting paid
20 Reg 5 UC(MMP&MA) Regs
21 Reg 8B UC(TP) Regs

8. Tax, other benefits and the benefit cap
22 s677 IT(EP)A 2003
23 s20 WRA 2007

Chapter 10

Housing benefit

This chapter covers:

1. Who can get housing benefit (below)
2. The rules about your age (p187)
3. People included in the claim (p189)
4. The amount of benefit (p190)
5. Special benefit rules (p202)
6. Claims and backdating (p202)
7. Getting paid (p213)
8. Tax, other benefits and the benefit cap (p224)

Key facts

- Housing benefit (HB) is a benefit for people on a low income who pay rent.
- The amount of rent used to calculate the HB you get may be restricted, so HB does not necessarily meet the full amount of rent you must pay.
- HB is a means-tested benefit.
- You do not have to have paid national insurance contributions to qualify.
- You can qualify for HB whether you are in or out of work.
- If you need extra financial assistance to meet your housing costs, you can claim discretionary housing payments to top up your HB.
- A benefit cap may be applied if the total amount of certain benefits you receive exceeds a specified amount and your HB can be reduced.
- HB is administered and paid by local authorities, although it is a national scheme and the rules are mainly determined by DWP regulations.
- If you disagree with an HB decision, you can apply for a revision or a supersession (see Chapter 56), or appeal against it (see Chapter 57). You do *not* have to apply for a mandatory reconsideration before you can appeal.

1. **Who can get housing benefit**

You qualify for housing benefit (HB) if:[1]
- your income is low enough (see p190 and Chapter 20 or 21); *and*
- your capital is worth £16,000 or less (unless you or your partner are getting the guarantee credit of pension credit (PC) – see Chapter 22 or 23;[2] *and*

- the payments you make can be met by HB (see p175); *and*
- you or your partner count as liable to pay rent (see p177); *and*
- the payments you make are for the home in which you normally live (see p181) or you are only temporarily absent from it; *and*
- you satisfy the 'right to reside test' and the 'habitual residence test' (see Chapter 68); *and*
- you are not a 'person subject to immigration control' (see p1560). There are exceptions to this rule.

Housing benefit and universal credit

You can now only make a new claim for HB in limited circumstances (see below). If you are already entitled to HB, you can continue to qualify:

– until you claim universal credit (UC) or you become a member of a couple with a partner who is getting UC. **Note:** in both cases, you continue to qualify for HB, even if you are entitled to UC, if the HB is for 'specified accommodation' or 'temporary accommodation' (see p174 for what counts); *or*

– until you and your partner are affected by the 'managed migration' transfer process (see p30); *or*

– for two weeks after you become entitled to UC (called 'HB run-on' – see p220).

The government says that from November 2020, the DWP will begin to transfer existing HB claims to UC or PC. This transfer process began in July 2019 in pilot areas, for a limited number of claimants. When this transfer process happens, your HB claim ends and you will be invited to claim UC (or PC). See p27 for further information, and AskCPAG.org.uk and CPAG's *Welfare Rights Bulletin* for updates.

Which housing benefit rules apply?

There are two sets of HB rules, and thus two different ways you can qualify for HB. You can qualify for what is known as 'working-age HB' or for 'pension-age HB'. See p188 to find out which rules apply to you. **Note:** if you are a member of a 'mixed-age couple' (ie, one of you is at least pension age – see p780 – but not the other), you may qualify for working-age HB instead of pension-age HB, even though one of you is at least pension age.

Who can make a new claim for housing benefit

You can only make a new claim for HB in the following limited circumstances.[3]

- The HB is for 'specified accommodation' or 'temporary accommodation' (see p174 for what counts). **Note:** if you live in either type of accommodation, you can get HB for the rent you pay even if you are getting UC.
- You (and if you are in a couple, you and your partner) are at least pension age (see p779). The DWP intention is that you can make a new claim for pension-age HB in this situation.[4] **Note:** if you are a member of a 'mixed-age couple' (ie,

Part 3: Other means-tested benefits and tax credits
Chapter 10: Housing benefit
1. Who can get housing benefit

one of you is at least pension age but not the other), you cannot normally make a new claim for HB, but see p175 for the exceptions. If you cannot make a new claim under this rule, check whether you can under any of the other rules in this section.

- You are prevented from claiming UC because you are in a specified category where claims are not accepted, or, (or if you are in a couple, you and your partner) are a 'frontier worker' – ie, you work in Great Britain or Northern Ireland but do not live there.
- You are prevented from claiming UC because:
  - you (or your partner) are, or within the last month have been, entitled to HB, income support (IS), income-based jobseeker's allowance (JSA) or income-related employment and support allowance (ESA) that includes a severe disability premium (see p346), and if your entitlement to the benefit ended during that month you (or s/he) have continued to satisfy the conditions for that premium; *and*
  - you (and your partner) have not yet been given a 'migration notice' from the DWP that you will be transferred to UC via the 'managed migration' process.

The above may apply, for example, if you are claiming HB after a break in your entitlement or if you are getting IS, income-based JSA or income-related ESA but not HB. **Note:** this rule only applies until 27 January 2021.

If you cannot make a new claim for HB under any of these rules, or the rules for mixed-age couples below, you can make a claim for UC.

Note:
- If there is a break in your entitlement to HB (eg, you move to a new home in a different local authority area), you can only make a new claim for HB if the rules above, or the rules below that allow claims by mixed-age couples, apply.
- Although you cannot usually make a claim for HB if you are a UC claimant, you can make a new claim in limited cases for a period before your entitlement to UC starts. You must notify the local authority of your intention to claim HB before the date of your UC claim.

Specified and temporary accommodation
'Specified accommodation' is:[5]
- accommodation provided by a relevant body to meet your need for, and where you get, care, support or supervision; *or*
- temporary accommodation provided by a local authority or a relevant body because you have left your home because of domestic violence – eg, a refuge; *or*
- a local authority hostel for homeless people where you get care, support or supervision to assist you to be rehabilitated or resettled within the community; *or*
- 'exempt accommodation' (certain types of supported accommodation – see p403).

For these purposes, a 'relevant body' is a county council in England, housing association, registered charity or voluntary organisation.

Your accommodation is **'temporary accommodation'** if you live in a defined type of homeless accommodation that does not count as 'exempt accommodation' (see p403) and your rent is payable to a local authority or a provider of social housing.[6]

Mixed-age couples

You cannot normally make a new claim for HB if you are a member of a mixed-age couple – ie, if one of you is at least pension age but not the other. If you cannot claim HB under these rules, check whether you can claim under any of the rules on p173. If you cannot make a new claim for HB under any of the rules, you can make a claim for UC.

There are exceptions and you *can* make a new claim for HB if:[7]

- you were at least pension age on 14 May 2019, you were entitled to pension-age HB (see p188) or PC (or both) on that date and have continued to be entitled to some pension-age HB or PC on each day since that date as part of the same mixed-age couple. **Note:** claims for pension-age HB can be backdated by up to three months, so if you claimed backdated pension-age HB by 13 August 2019, you could have been entitled to it on 14 May 2019; *or*
- you are at least pension age and you cannot make a joint claim for UC (see p36) – eg, because your partner does not meet certain conditions or is a prisoner, or you are in a polygamous marriage in specified circumstances. In this case, you can claim pension-age HB as a single person; *or*
- you are in a polygamous marriage but are treated as a couple with one of your partners and both of you are at least pension age. In this case, you or the other member of the couple can claim pension-age HB; *or*
- you are at least pension age and are no longer treated as a couple for UC purposes because your partner is expected to be, or has been, absent from your household for more than six months. In this case, you can claim pension-age HB as a single person.

Note: if you become a member of a mixed-age couple while you are entitled to HB, in some situations your entitlement to HB can end and in some it can continue (see p188).

Payments that can be met by housing benefit

HB can meet any of the following types of payment.[8]

- Rent paid in respect of a tenancy. This can include rent or ground rent payable in respect of a lease of 21 years or less.[9] If your lease is for longer than 21 years, the rent or ground rent may be met by IS, income-based JSA, income-related ESA or PC (see p360).
- Payments in respect of a licence or other permission to occupy premises – eg, if you are a lodger or live in bed and breakfast accommodation.

Part 3: Other means-tested benefits and tax credits
Chapter 10: Housing benefit
1. Who can get housing benefit

- 'Mesne profits' (in Scotland, 'violent profits'), including payments made if you remain in occupation when a tenancy has been ended.
- Other payments for the use and occupation of premises. This does not include boat licence and mooring permit fees if you live in a houseboat.[10]
- Payments for eligible service charges (see p194).
- Rent, including mooring charges, for a houseboat.
- Site rent for a caravan or mobile home (but not a tent, although this may be met by IS, income-based JSA, income-related ESA or PC – see p360).
- Rent paid on a garage or land (unless used for business purposes). Either you must be making a reasonable effort to end your liability for it, or you must have been unable to rent your home without it.[11]
- Contributions made by a resident of a charity's almshouse.
- Payments made under a rental purchase agreement under which the purchase price is paid in more than one instalment and you do not finally own your home until all, or an agreed part of, the purchase price has been paid.
- In Scotland, payments in respect of croft land.

In this *Handbook*, we refer to any of these payments as 'rent'. The payment must be in return for your occupation of the home. This usually means that the payments must be made to the person who has the right to let you occupy it, or someone acting on her/his behalf, but payments to someone else might qualify. This depends on, for example, whether you have a valid tenancy agreement with that person.[12]

Payments that cannot be met by housing benefit

HB cannot meet any of the following types of payments – ie, payments made:[13]
- by an owner or under a long tenancy (ie, you own your accommodation or have a lease of more than 21 years), unless you have a shared ownership tenancy – ie, you are buying part of your home and renting the rest. In this case, you can get HB for your rent. You are treated as the owner of the property if you have the right to sell it, even though you may not be able to do so without the consent of other joint owners;[14]
- for a dwelling owned (or part owned) by your partner;
- by a Crown tenant;
- under a co-ownership scheme under which you receive a payment related to the value of the accommodation when you leave;
- under a hire purchase (eg, for the purchase of a mobile home), credit sale or a conditional sale agreement except to the extent that it is in respect of land.

In some of the above situations, the payments may be met by IS, income-based JSA, income-related ESA or PC instead. See Chapter 18 for further information.
    HB cannot meet payments if you are getting IS, income-based JSA or income-related ESA for these.[15] However, if you are now getting your housing costs met

through IS, income-based JSA or income-related ESA, but were previously getting HB for the same accommodation, your HB continues for your first four weeks on IS, income-based JSA or income-related ESA.[16]

Note: if you live in a care home, you cannot usually get HB for the rent you pay to the home (see p933).

Liability to pay rent

To qualify for HB you must count as liable to pay rent. You count as liable if either you or your partner are liable.[17] You can be treated as liable even if you are not (see p178). You can be treated as not liable even if you are (or can be treated as) liable (see p178). If you pay your rent in advance, you are still treated as liable to pay it, even if you paid it before claiming HB.[18] You can be liable to pay rent by yourself or you can be jointly liable to do so (see p180).

Are you under 18?

People under 18 years old can be liable to pay rent and can therefore qualify for HB, if there is an intention to create legal relations. If you are under 16, an adult or a social services department (social work department in Scotland) is generally responsible for the rent, but HB departments should not decide HB entitlement based on what they think the social services/social work department ought to provide. However, if you are, or have been, looked after by a local authority, you cannot usually qualify for HB (see p947).

For you to be liable to pay rent, your agreement must be legally enforceable.[19] It is not enough if you only have a moral obligation, such as a promise to pay something whenever you can afford to do so. You can count as liable to pay rent even if someone else has been paying it on your behalf, or if your landlord has failed to provide notice of an address so rent is treated as not being due.[20]

Does your agreement have to be in writing?

If you have a written agreement with your landlord, this should establish that you are liable to pay rent, provided the liability is a genuine part of the agreement.[21]

Your agreement can be legally enforceable even if it is not in writing. The fact that you have made a firm promise to pay money to your landlord in return for your occupation of the property should be sufficient to show you are liable to pay rent and so allow you to claim HB.[22] If the local authority refuses to accept that you have a legal liability, apply for a revision or appeal.

Note: even if the local authority accepts that your agreement is legally enforceable, it may still treat you as not liable to pay rent (see p178).

Part 3: Other means-tested benefits and tax credits
Chapter 10: Housing benefit
1. Who can get housing benefit

People treated as liable to pay rent

You are treated as liable to pay rent if:[23]

- you have to pay rent in order to continue to live in your home because the liable person is not doing so; *and*
  - you are the former partner of the liable person; *or*
  - you are not the former partner of the liable person and it is reasonable to treat you as liable.[24] It must be reasonable in all of the circumstances, and in light of the overall purpose of the HB scheme.[25] It does not matter whether or not the landlord is prepared to transfer the tenancy to you or wants to evict you. If the local authority refuses your HB claim, point out that the eligibility rules for HB and for transferring tenancies are separate, and apply for a revision or appeal; *or*
- your landlord allows you a rent-free period as compensation for carrying out repairs or redecoration which s/he would otherwise have had to carry out (for a maximum of eight benefit weeks in a rent-free period). If you expect the work to last longer, arrange with your landlord to schedule the work in periods of eight weeks or less, separated by at least one complete benefit week in which you resume paying rent; *or*
- you are the partner of a full-time student who is treated as not liable to pay rent (see below). This means that you can qualify for HB even if your partner cannot.

Even if you fall into one of these categories, in certain circumstances you can still be treated as not liable to pay rent, and so not entitled to HB (see below).

People treated as not liable to pay rent

Even if you or your partner are liable to pay rent, you can be treated as though you are not liable. In this case, you cannot qualify for HB. This applies if you are in any of the situations below.[26]

- You are a full-time student. This does *not* apply if you are getting pension-age HB (see p188) or if you are a student who can qualify for HB (see p896) and you are getting working-age HB (see p188).
- You do not satisfy the habitual residence test (see p1586).
- You are a member of, and are fully maintained by, a religious order.[27]
- You are living in a care home or an independent hospital (but see p933).[28]
- You pay rent to someone who also lives in the dwelling and who is your (or your partner's) close relative (see p180 for who counts).[29] Your landlord might be regarded as living in your dwelling if you share some accommodation with her/him, other than a bathroom, toilet or a hall or passageway.[30] It does not matter if you use the accommodation at different times or if you pay to use it.[31]
- Your agreement to pay rent is not on a commercial basis.[32] In deciding whether or not your agreement is commercial, the local authority must look at the

whole agreement, taking all the circumstances into account. It must consider, among other things:[33]
- whether your agreement includes terms that are not legally enforceable;
- the rent you must pay under the agreement. It does not have to be a market rent. Paying a low rent does not necessarily mean your agreement is not commercial – eg, if you do chores in exchange for a lower rent. Your agreement can count as commercial even if your landlord is not collecting the full contractual rent from you;
- your relationship to your landlord. However, just because you are a relative of, or have a close friendship with, her/him, or s/he provides you with care and support, does not mean that your agreement is non-commercial.
- You are renting from:[34]
  - any ex-partner of yours and the home is your former joint home with that ex-partner; or
  - any ex-partner of your partner and the home is your partner's former joint home with that ex-partner.
- You or your partner are responsible for a child (under 16) of a person who is your landlord.[35] This only applies if the child is included in your HB claim (see p323).
- You or your partner, or an ex-partner or close relative of either of you, who lives with you, is either:[36]
  - a director or employee of a company which is your landlord; or
  - a trustee or beneficiary of a trust which is your landlord.
  This rule does not apply if you can show the arrangement was not intended to take advantage of the HB scheme (see p180).
- You are renting accommodation from a trustee of a trust, of which your (or your partner's) child (under 16) is a beneficiary.
- You were previously the non-dependant (see p198) of someone who lived, and continues to live, in the accommodation. This rule does not apply if you can show that the agreement was not created to take advantage of the HB scheme (see p180).[37]
- You or your current partner previously owned, or had a long tenancy in (ie, a lease of more than 21 years), the accommodation and less than five years have passed since you last owned it (or the tenancy ceased).[38]
  This rule does not apply if you can show that you could not have continued to occupy the accommodation without giving up ownership (or the tenancy) – eg, the lender was seeking possession of your home. Whether you were legally or practically compelled to give up ownership or the tenancy is relevant, but your motivation for doing so is not.[39] You do not have to be in immediate danger of having to leave your home for this exception to apply.[40] You may need to show that you have taken steps to explore alternatives.[41]
- You or your partner are employed by your landlord and are occupying your accommodation as a condition of employment. This should not apply if you continue to live in the accommodation after ceasing employment.

Part 3: Other means-tested benefits and tax credits
Chapter 10: Housing benefit
1. Who can get housing benefit

- If none of the above apply, the local authority considers that your liability to pay rent has been created to take advantage of the HB scheme (see below).

Close relatives

A **'close relative'** is a parent, parent-in-law (including a civil partner's parent), son, son-in-law (including a son's civil partner), daughter, daughter-in-law (including a daughter's civil partner), brother, sister, step-parent (including a parent's civil partner), stepson (including a civil partner's son), stepdaughter (including a civil partner's daughter), or the partners of any of these.[42] It also includes half-brothers and half-sisters.[43] Relations with in-laws or step-relatives are severed by divorce (or dissolution of a civil partnership) but arguably not by death – eg, a stepchild is still a stepchild after the death of her/his mother.[44]

Agreements taking advantage of the housing benefit scheme

For your agreement to count as 'taking advantage of the HB scheme', it must amount to an abuse of the scheme or to taking improper advantage of it. It must be shown that the main reason you entered into the agreement was to obtain HB.[45] All the circumstances should be taken into account, including what your landlord has to say.[46] An agreement can count as taking advantage of the HB scheme even if it was created from the best of motives.[47] Bear the following in mind.

- You should *not* be seen as taking advantage of the HB scheme just because:
  - your landlord is your parent;[48] *or*
  - you hope to be able to claim HB to help you with your rent – ie, if your main purpose is to get accommodation, not to obtain HB;[49] *or*
  - you seek to find out what rent can be covered by HB before moving in.
- If you are a tenant of a landlord who deliberately charges high rents in order to have them paid by HB, you may be affected by this provision, even though you had no such intention yourself. Argue that a high rent, in itself, does not mean that the liability takes advantage of the HB scheme.[50]
- If your landlord says s/he will evict you if you cannot get HB, this suggests that the agreement does *not* take advantage of the HB scheme.[51]

If the local authority says your agreement is taking advantage of the HB scheme and that you are therefore not entitled to HB, you can appeal.

Joint liability

If you are a member of a couple (see p319) and are jointly liable for the rent, only one of you can claim HB.[52]

The way a group of single people living together and paying rent to their landlord is treated depends on how many of you are liable under the agreement. If all, or some, of you have joint liability for the rent, you can each make a separate claim and be paid HB on your share (unless the local authority thinks the joint tenancy has been created to take advantage of the HB scheme – see p180).

If you live in shared accommodation with people other than your partner and children included in your claim, and are jointly liable for the rent with them, see p192 for information about how your eligible rent is apportioned between you.

Occupying accommodation as your home

HB is paid for the home in which you and your partner and any children included in your claim (see p323) normally live.[53] You cannot usually be paid for any other home. However, there are special rules if you:
- have just moved into your home (see below);
- are temporarily absent from home (see p182);
- are liable to pay rent on more than one home (see p186);
- are in certain other situations (see p187).

Note:
- If you occupy more than one property or room as your home (eg, because you have a large family and rent adjacent flats, or have a live-in carer and rent two adjacent rooms in shared accommodation), you can argue that both properties or rooms count as part of your home – ie, that you only have one home.[54]
- If you have to live in an approved bail or probation hostel or are a prisoner on temporary release, you are treated as not occupying the accommodation in which you are staying.[55] You cannot qualify for HB for any rent you pay for the hostel, but you may be able to qualify for HB for your normal home. See p182 for the rules on temporary absence from home.

Moving home

If you have just moved into your home but were liable to pay rent before moving in, you can get HB on your new home for up to four weeks before you moved in. **Note:** if you must pay rent for your old home as well as your new accommodation, you can only get HB for one of these unless you are covered by the rules described on p186.[56]

You only qualify if the delay in moving was reasonable and:[57]
- you were waiting for a payment from a local welfare assistance scheme or the Scottish Welfare Fund or a social fund payment for a need connected with the move – eg, removal expenses or to help you set up home. This only applies if:
  - you have a child aged five or under living with you; *or*
  - you are getting pension-age HB (see p188); *or*
  - you are getting working-age HB (see p188) and you qualify for a disability, severe disability or disabled child premium, or a support component, or you or your partner are a member of the work-related activity group (see p653); *or*

Part 3: Other means-tested benefits and tax credits
Chapter 10: Housing benefit
1. Who can get housing benefit

- you were waiting for adaptations to be finished to meet needs you, your partner or a child included in your claim (see p323) have because of a disability. The adaptations do not have to involve a change to the fabric or structure of the dwelling, but must be reasonably required and have a clear connection to the disability needs;[58] *or*
- you became liable to make payments on your new home while you were a hospital patient or in residential accommodation (see p185 for the meaning).

Before moving, you must either have claimed HB or have notified the local authority of the move. If you have given up your previous home and have no other home, you can argue that the date you move in is the date you move your furniture and belongings in.[59] Your HB is not paid until you move in. If an earlier claim for HB you made before you moved in was turned down, you must claim again within four weeks of moving to qualify.

If you are not liable to pay rent for your new accommodation

If you move and are not liable to pay rent in your new accommodation (eg, if you are now staying with a relative or are in prison or hospital and you cannot get HB while temporarily absent from home), you can get HB for up to four weeks for your former home if you:[60]

- were liable for rent on it immediately before moving into your new accommodation and continue to be liable – eg, because you have to give notice to your landlord; *and*
- could not reasonably have avoided liability for rent on your former home.

Temporary absence from home

If you are temporarily absent from your normal home, you can qualify for HB for a period, provided you have not rented out your home and you intend to return to it.[61] The length of time you can be away depends on the circumstances and on whether you are absent from home in or outside Great Britain. You can argue that you count as temporarily absent from your home even if you have not yet stayed there – eg, you move your furniture and belongings in, but then have to go into hospital.[62] **Note:** you can claim and qualify for HB while you are temporarily absent from home, even if you were not getting HB before you left.

You can get HB while you are absent from your normal home for up to:

- **13 weeks**, whatever the reason for your absence (see p183); *or*
- **52 weeks**, if you are in any of the situations described on p183.

The period can be shorter if you are, or have been, absent from Great Britain (see p185).

The number of weeks runs from the date you leave home.[63] The day you leave home is included, but not the day you return home.[64] If, for example, you have been away from home for 10 weeks and then have grounds to continue to get HB for 52 weeks, you only get HB for the balance: 42 weeks. However, a new period of absence starts if you return home for even a short stay. A stay of at least 24 hours may be enough.[65] This does not apply if you are a prisoner on temporary release.[66]

Note: if you have someone living with you who is temporarily absent from home (eg, s/he is a student who is away during term time), the local authority may use these rules to decide whether s/he is a non-dependant (see p198).[67] It may also use these rules to decide whether your partner, or a child or young person included in your claim, counts as occupying your home.

Will you be away from home temporarily?

1. Let the local authority know that you are going to be absent from your normal home and the reason for this, as well as if you will be absent from Great Britain, preferably before you go away. Make it clear that your absence will be temporary and that you are unlikely to be away for longer than the period allowed.

2. Your intention to return, and whether or not you are unlikely to be away for longer than the period allowed, should be based initially on the circumstances on the date you leave your home, unless you are in residential accommodation for a trial period.[68]

3. If, at any time after the date you leave your home, you no longer intend to return or it becomes likely that you will be away from home (or absent from Great Britain) for longer than the period allowed, inform the local authority of this change in your circumstances to avoid an overpayment. In this case, the local authority can reconsider your entitlement.[69]

Housing benefit for up to 13 weeks

You can get HB for up to 13 weeks while you are absent from your normal home and you are in Great Britain.[70] It does not matter why you are away from home. You must be unlikely to be away for more than 13 weeks. **Note:** within the 13-week period, you can be absent from Great Britain for up to four weeks. The four-week period can be extended by up to another four weeks in limited cases (see p185).

Housing benefit for up to 52 weeks

You can get HB for up to 52 weeks while you are in residential accommodation (see p185 for the meaning) in Great Britain for a trial period to see whether it suits your needs.[71] On the date you enter the accommodation, you must intend to return home if it is not suitable.[72] You get HB for up to 13 weeks. If the accommodation does not suit your needs, you can have further 13-week trial periods in other accommodation, provided you are not away from home for more than 52 weeks in total.

You can get HB for up to 52 weeks if you are absent from your normal home and you are in Great Britain if you are unlikely to be away for longer than this (or, in exceptional circumstances, unlikely to be away for substantially longer than this) in the situations listed below.[73] **Note:** within the 52-week period, you can be

Part 3: Other means-tested benefits and tax credits
Chapter 10: Housing benefit
1. Who can get housing benefit

absent from Great Britain for up to four or 26 weeks at a time as the case may be (see below and p185). The four-week period can be extended by up to another four weeks in limited cases.

You can get HB for up to 52 weeks if you are absent from home within Great Britain in the following circumstances.[74] **Note:** within the 52-week period, you can get HB while you are temporarily absent from Great Britain for up to 26 weeks (see p185).

- You are resident in a hospital or similar institution as a patient. You cannot get HB after you have been resident in hospital for 52 weeks, even if this is because you are seriously mentally ill. **Note:** a new period of absence starts if you return home for even a short stay.[75]
- You, your partner or a 'dependent child' under 16 are undergoing medical treatment or medically approved convalescence, other than in residential accommodation (see p185 for the meaning). 'Dependent child' is not defined in the rules, so could include children who are not included in your claim.
- You are receiving 'medically approved' care (ie, certified by a medical practitioner), other than in residential accommodation (see below for the meaning).
- You are away from home because of a fear of violence. You need not have experienced actual violence, but you must be in fear of violence in your home or from a former partner, or a child or qualifying young person previously included in your claim. Violence in your home includes violence by neighbours and hate crimes directed at your home. See p186 if you need to claim for two homes and p187 if you do not intend to return to your former home.

You can also get HB for up to 52 weeks if you are absent from home and you are in Great Britain in the following circumstances.[76] **Note:** within the 52-week period, you can get HB while you are temporarily absent from Great Britain for up to four weeks (see p185).

- You are a remand prisoner held in custody pending trial or sentence. Once you are sentenced, you no longer qualify for HB under this rule, but might still qualify under the 13-week rule on p183. The 13 weeks run from the date you were first in prison, so any time you spend in prison awaiting trial or sentence counts towards the 13 weeks. **Note:** you are treated as still in custody if you are a prisoner on temporary release.[77]
- You are required to live in an approved hostel or at an address away from your normal home as a condition of bail.
- You are providing 'medically approved' care – ie, certified by a medical practitioner.
- You are caring for a child under 16 whose parent or guardian is away from home receiving medically approved care or medical treatment.
- You are undertaking a training course (see below).

- You are a student. You must not come into the first category under 'Other situations' on p187, or be entitled to HB on two homes (see p186).
- You are in residential accommodation (see below) for short-term or respite care.

Definitions[78]

'**Residential accommodation**' means a care home, an independent hospital or an Abbeyfield home. It also means an establishment managed or provided by a body incorporated by Royal Charter or constituted by an Act of Parliament, other than a local social services authority.

A '**training course**' is a course of training or instruction provided by or on behalf of, or approved by, a government department, the Secretary of State, Skills Development Scotland, Scottish Enterprise or Highlands and Islands Enterprise.

Absence from Great Britain

You can get HB while you are temporarily absent from Great Britain for up to:

- **four weeks**, whatever the reason.[79] You must be unlikely to be away for longer than four weeks; *or*
- **eight weeks**, but only if you are temporarily absent from Great Britain in connection with the death of your partner or a child or young person included in your claim (see p323), or the death of your or your partner's or child's or young person's close relative. This is because your first four weeks' absence from Great Britain can be extended if the local authority thinks it is unreasonable to expect you to return to Great Britain within the four weeks; *or*
- **four or 26 weeks**, in the situations in which you can get HB while absent from home for up to 52 weeks (see p183). You must be unlikely to be away for longer than this (or, in exceptional circumstances, unlikely to be away for substantially longer than this);[80]
- **26 weeks**, while you are absent from Great Britain as a member of the armed forces posted overseas, a mariner or a continental shelf worker. You must be unlikely to be away for longer than 26 weeks.[81]

The number of weeks runs from the first day of absence from Great Britain.[82] The 13 or 52 weeks you are allowed to be absent from home *in* Great Britain continue to run during any period you are absent from Great Britain.[83] When you return to Great Britain, if you are still away from your normal home, you can continue to get HB for the remainder (if any) of the 13- or 52-week period allowed. However, if your HB ceased because you were no longer treated as occupying your normal home (eg, because you had been absent from Great Britain too long), you cannot qualify for HB until you return home.[84] **Note:** if you are a European Economic

Part 3: Other means-tested benefits and tax credits
Chapter 10: Housing benefit
1. Who can get housing benefit

Area (EEA) national and have a right to reside in the UK and go abroad a EEA state, see p1653.

Examples

Paul visits his mother in London for a week before going on a three-week holiday to France. He lets the local authority know this and also that he plans to visit his sister in Manchester for two weeks on the way home. He can be absent from home for up to 13 weeks and absent from Great Britain for up to four weeks within that period. He gets HB for 1 + 3 + 2 = 6 weeks while he is temporarily absent from home.

Adele travels to Canada to visit her grandmother for two weeks. At the end of the second week, she notifies the local authority that she intends to stay a further three weeks. She is no longer treated as occupying her normal home because she is going to be absent from Great Britain for longer than four weeks. She therefore only gets HB for two weeks.

Mary goes on a training course in Birmingham. She notifies the local authority that she will be away from home for 20 weeks. During the 20-week course, she will be on a placement in France for two weeks. Mary therefore continues to get HB for the 20-week period she is away from home (18 weeks in Great Britain and two weeks outside Great Britain).

Housing benefit for more than one home

You can usually only get HB for one home. **Note:** if you occupy more than one property as a home (eg, you rent adjacent flats because you have a large family or two adjacent rooms in shared accommodation because you have a live-in carer), you can argue that you only have one home.[85]

If you occupy two homes, you can get HB for both:

- **for up to four weeks** for a new and an old home, if:[86]
  - you have moved into the new home and you could not reasonably avoid having to pay rent on your old home.[87] The local authority must consider the reasons why you had to move quickly – eg, if you were forced to move quickly to take advantage of better accommodation, you may not have been able to avoid leaving without giving notice; *or*
  - a move was delayed while you were adapting your new home to meet needs you, your partner or a child included in your claim have because of disability. You can get HB on both homes for the four weeks prior to the date you move. The adaptations do not have to involve a change to the fabric or structure of the dwelling, but must be reasonably required and have a clear connection to the disability needs;[88]
- **for up to 52 weeks** for a temporary home and your normal home, if you have left your home because of a fear of violence (see p184 for the meaning). You must intend to return to your normal home, and it must be reasonable for you to receive payments for both homes. The payments can be either HB or UC. For example, if your temporary home counts as 'specified accommodation' or

'temporary accommodation' (see p174), you can get HB for it, and HB (or a UC housing costs element) for the rent you pay for your normal home;[89]
- **indefinitely** for two normal homes, if:[90]
  - you are a member of a couple and you or your partner are a student eligible for HB (see p896) or are on a training course (see p185 for the meaning), it is necessary for you to live apart and it is reasonable for you to receive HB for both homes; *or*
  - the local authority has housed you in more than one home because your family is large.

Other situations

If you have left your home because of a **fear of violence** (see p184 for the meaning) and you do not intend to return, you can get HB for four weeks for your former home.[91] This only applies if your liability to pay rent was unavoidable – eg, you should have given your landlord notice, but had to leave in a hurry.

If you have two homes, and you are only liable to pay for one of them, you are treated as occupying the home for which you pay and therefore get HB for that home, even when you are not there. This only applies if:[92]
- you are a single claimant or a lone parent, and you are either a student eligible for HB (see p896) or are on a training course (see p185), and you live in one home during periods of study or training and another home at other times – eg, for vacations; *or*
- you had to move into temporary accommodation because essential repairs are being carried out on your main home. 'Essential repairs' means basic works rather than luxuries, but they need not be crucial to making the house habitable.[93]

Note: you cannot get HB under this rule if you pay rent for both homes, or if you pay rent for one and a mortgage on the other.

2. **The rules about your age**

There are no lower or upper age limits for claiming housing benefit (HB). However, if you are:
- under 16, there may be a question about whether you have a legally enforceable liability for rent (see p177);
- 16 or 17 and are being, or have been, looked after by a local authority, you cannot usually qualify for HB. See p947 for further information;
- a single claimant under 35 and are living in private rented accommodation, the amount of your rent that can be met by HB is usually restricted (see Chapter 19).

Part 3: Other means-tested benefits and tax credits
Chapter 10: Housing benefit
2. The rules about your age

Note: some more generous rules may apply if you or your partner are at least pension age (see p780) and qualify for pension-age HB. To work out whether you qualify for pension-age HB or for working-age HB, see below.

Working-age or pension-age housing benefit

You can qualify for HB under two different sets of rules: 'working-age HB' or 'pension-age HB'.[94] Which rules apply usually depends on your (and your partner's) age.

You can qualify for **working-age HB** if:[95]

- you are not yet pension age; *or*
- you are at least pension age but you or your partner are on income support (IS), income-based jobseeker's allowance (JSA), income-related employment and support allowance (ESA) or universal credit (UC). See below if you are a member of a mixed-age couple.

You can qualify for **pension-age HB** if you are at least pension age and neither you nor your partner are on IS, income-based JSA, income-related ESA or UC.[96] You do not have to be getting pension credit (PC) to qualify for pension-age HB. See below if you are a member of a mixed-age couple.

Most of the rules are the same, but there are some differences. For example, if you get pension-age HB, your applicable amount is higher than for working-age HB and the income and capital rules are more generous. Pension-age HB can be backdated for up to three months, but working-age HB can only be backdated for up to one month. **Note:** if you are a member of a 'mixed-age couple' (ie, one of you is at least pension age – see p780 – but not the other), you may have to claim working-age HB or UC instead of pension-age HB, even though one of you is at least pension age (see below).

Mixed-age couples

Since 15 May 2019, if you are a member of 'mixed-age couple' (ie, one of you is at least pension age but not the other), you can only make a new claim for HB and for PC in limited circumstances (see p175 and p271). In addition, in some situations your HB entitlement can end (see below). If you cannot make a new claim for HB or PC, or your entitlement to both HB and PC ends, you can claim UC.

When housing benefit ends if you are in a 'mixed-age couple'

Your entitlement to HB can end if you are, or become, a member of a 'mixed-age couple' – ie, if one of you is at least pension age (see p780), but not the other. This only applies if your entitlement to pension-age HB as a member of that couple would otherwise start on or after 15 May 2019. **Note:** if you were entitled to pension-age HB before 15 May 2019, your entitlement can continue and, in limited cases, you can make a new claim (see p173).

Your entitlement to HB ends when:[97]
- you become a member of a mixed-age couple. This applies if you were not in a mixed-age couple when you were awarded HB – eg, because you were getting working-age or pension-age HB as a single person or because you were getting working-age HB while you and your partner were both under pension age; *or*
- if you are a member of a mixed-age couple and are getting working-age HB because you (or your partner) are on IS, income-based JSA, income-related ESA or UC, entitlement to that benefit ends.

Your HB entitlement ends on the date the change takes effect under under the HB rules (see p223).

Note: your entitlement to HB does *not* end, even if you are or become a member of a mixed-age couple, if:
- the HB is for 'specified accommodation' or 'temporary accommodation' (see p174 for what counts);[98] *or*
- you are prevented from claiming UC for one of the reasons on p174 and, in addition, you cannot qualify for PC or pension-age HB because you are a member of a mixed-age couple. In this case, the member of the couple who is at least pension age is treated as not that age so your award of working-age HB can continue.[99]

3. People included in the claim

You claim housing benefit (HB) for yourself. However, if you are a member of a couple, you or your partner must claim HB for you both. Your applicable amount includes a personal allowance for a couple and can include premiums and components based on both your and your partner's circumstances. When your benefit is worked out, your partner's income and capital are usually added to yours. See p319 for who counts as a couple.

There are some situations in which you must show that you are 'responsible' for a child who is living in your household – eg:
- so your applicable amount can include allowances and premiums for a child(ren);
- to show you are a lone parent so you can benefit from a higher earnings disregard (see p430 and p472);
- to qualify for a disregard of earnings for childcare costs (see p432 and p474);
- for some of the rules about the size of accommodation or the number of bedrooms you are allowed that affect your maximum HB (see Chapter 19).

See p324 for who counts as a child (this includes some qualifying young people). You do not have to be the child's parent. For when you count as responsible for a child, and when s/he counts as living in your household, see pp326–29.

Part 3: Other means-tested benefits and tax credits
Chapter 10: Housing benefit
4. The amount of benefit

4. The amount of benefit

The amount of housing benefit (HB) you get depends on:

- your 'applicable amount' (see Chapter 17). This is made up of personal allowances, as well as premiums and components for any special needs. It may include a transitional addition if you or your partner were transferred to contributory employment and support allowance (ESA), or appealed a decision not to transfer you to ESA (see p355);
- your 'maximum HB' (see below);
- how much capital you have (see p196 and Chapter 22 for working-age HB or Chapter 23 for pension-age HB); *and*
- if you are not on a means-tested benefit, how much income you have (see p196 and Chapter 20 for working-age HB or Chapter 21 for pension-age HB).

For how to calculate HB, if you are on a means-tested benefit see p196, and if you are *not* on a means-tested benefit see p196.

If you do not qualify for HB currently, you may qualify if you can still make a new claim for HB (see p173) and:

- the benefit rates go up; *or*
- you (or your partner or a child included in your claim) become entitled to another benefit (a 'qualifying benefit' – see p211); *or*
- you or your partner reach pension age (see p780). If you qualify for pension-age HB (see p188), your applicable amount is higher and the income and capital rules are also more generous.

If you need help with the costs of your housing in addition to the HB you get, you may qualify for discretionary housing payments (see Chapter 29).

Note: you might get a reduced amount of HB if:

- you are affected by the benefit cap (see p1194); *or*
- your HB is restricted because of a benefit offence (see p1278).

Maximum housing benefit

In order to calculate your HB, you need to know the maximum amount of HB you can get. Your maximum HB is worked out as follows.[100]

- **Step one:** work out the amount of your rent that can be covered by HB (your 'eligible rent') on a weekly basis (see p191). Unless you have any non-dependants for whom a deduction must be made (see p198), this is your maximum HB.
- **Step two:** if you have any non-dependants for whom a deduction must be made, your maximum HB is the figure in Step one, minus the non-dependant

deduction(s) (see p198). This is because it is assumed a non-dependant makes a contribution towards your outgoings, whether or not s/he does so.

Example

Pete and Jenny and their adult son live together in a two-bedroom flat rented from the local authority. Pete is the sole tenant. The rent is £100 a week. This does not include any service charges. Their son earns £150 a week gross.

The amount of rent that can be covered (eligible rent)	£100
Minus non-dependant deduction (see p200)	£36.45
Maximum HB	**£63.55**

Eligible rent

The amount of your rent that can be covered by HB is called your 'eligible rent'. This is not necessarily the rent you pay to your landlord. You need to know your 'eligible rent' to work out your 'maximum HB' (see above).

Your 'eligible rent' is calculated as follows.[101]

- If any of the rent restriction schemes apply to you, your eligible rent is the amount to which your rent is restricted under those rules (known as your 'maximum rent'). See Chapter 19 for details of all the schemes, which one (if any) applies to you and how your rent may be restricted.
- If none of the rent restriction rules apply to you, deduct any ineligible charges (see p193) from the amount of rent you must pay your landlord (your contractual rent). The local authority has general powers to decrease your eligible rent to an amount it considers appropriate (but see p384).

If your rent has been reduced by a 'provider of social housing' under a government-approved tenant incentive scheme, your eligible rent is worked out as if no reduction had been made.[102] A provider of social housing is a local authority, a non-profit registered provider of social housing, a profit-making registered provider of social housing (if you have been housed in social housing) or a registered social landlord.

Note:

- If you are in shared accommodation, your eligible rent might be apportioned between you and the people with whom you share (see below).
- If the rent you pay covers both residential and other accommodation (eg, for business use), your HB only covers the rent you pay for the residential accommodation.[103] You cannot get HB for any part of your accommodation that is used exclusively for business purposes.
- You cannot get HB for rent supplements charged to clear your rent arrears.[104]

Calculating your weekly eligible rent

HB is always paid for a specific benefit week – a period of seven consecutive days beginning with a Monday and ending on a Sunday.[105] If you pay rent at different

Part 3: Other means-tested benefits and tax credits
Chapter 10: Housing benefit
4. The amount of benefit

intervals (eg, monthly or daily), the amount must be converted to a weekly figure before HB can be calculated.[106]

Rent-free periods

If you have a regular rent-free period (eg, you only pay rent 48 weeks a year), you get no HB during your rent-free period. Your applicable amount, weekly income, non-dependant deductions, the set deductions for meals and fuel charges and the minimum amount payable (but not your eligible rent – see p191) are adjusted.[107] This is to ensure that you do not lose or gain benefit by ignoring your circumstances in the weeks that you do not pay rent.

This does not apply if your landlord has temporarily waived the rent in return for your doing repairs (see p178).

If you live in shared accommodation

Unless the local housing allowance or social sector rent restriction rules apply to you (see p384 and p391), if you share accommodation with people other than your partner and children included in your claim and are jointly liable for the rent with them (see p180), the local authority apportions your eligible rent between you. If the rent includes any ineligible service charges, these are apportioned between you on the same basis. If only one of you is liable for the rent, that person is treated as the tenant and the other(s) might count as a non-dependant(s) (see p198).

To work out how to apportion your eligible rent, the local authority considers:[108]
- the number of jointly liable people in the property (including any students who are treated as not liable to pay rent);[109] *and*
- the proportion of the rent actually paid by each liable person; *and*
- any other relevant circumstances, such as:
  - the number of rooms occupied by each jointly liable person; *and*
  - whether any formal or informal agreement exists between you regarding the use and occupation of the home; *and*
  - if one of the jointly liable people has left the accommodation, the demands being made by the landlord on those who remain, or the possibility of finding other accommodation.

In some circumstances, it could be appropriate to apportion the whole of the rent to you, even if you are jointly liable.[110]

Note: if the local housing allowance or social sector rules apply to you, it is not necessary to apportion the eligible rent in this way, but the local authority *does* apportion the rent when looking at whether a restriction applies. See Chapter 19 for details.

Example

Sarah and Maude are friends who rent a two-bedroom housing association flat. They are joint tenants and pay rent of £100 a week and this is the 'eligible rent'. Sarah claims HB. The eligible rent is apportioned between her and Maude and Sarah's HB is based on £50 (£100 divided by two).

Ineligible charges

The local authority normally deducts ineligible charges when it works out the amount of your eligible rent. **Note:** if your rent has been restricted under the local housing allowance rules (see p384), or the rules for hostels, houseboats, mobile homes, caravans and boarders (see p396), an adjustment for ineligible charges is made in this process.

Ineligible charges include:

- water charges for your personal use. Water charges in respect of communal areas (see p194) – eg, in supported or sheltered accommodation – are eligible;[111] *and*
- most fuel charges (see below); *and*
- some service charges (see p194), including charges for meals.

Fuel charges

Fuel charges are ineligible unless they are for communal areas (see p194).[112] If your fuel charge is:

- specified on your rent book or is readily identifiable from your agreement with your landlord, the full amount of the charge is ineligible.[113] However, if your fuel charge is considered to be unrealistically low, a flat-rate amount is ineligible instead (see below). This is also the case if your total fuel charge is specified but contains an unknown amount for communal areas;
- not readily identifiable, a flat-rate amount is ineligible. The amounts are:[114]

If you and your family occupy more than one room:	
For heating (other than hot water)	£34.30
For hot water	£4.00
For lighting	£2.75
For cooking	£4.00
If you and your family occupy one room only:	
For heating alone, or heating combined with either hot water or lighting or both	£20.53
For cooking	£4.00

The above amounts are added together if fuel is supplied for more than one purpose. If you are a joint tenant, all the amounts are apportioned according to your share of the rent (see p192).

Part 3: Other means-tested benefits and tax credits
Chapter 10: Housing benefit
4. The amount of benefit

Note: the local authority must notify you if flat-rate fuel amounts have been used in calculating your HB. It must explain that if you can produce evidence from which the actual or approximate amount of your fuel charge can be estimated, the flat-rate amounts may be varied accordingly.

Do you occupy one room only?

The lower amounts apply if the accommodation you and your partner and children occupy comprises one room only. This is not defined, but the decision maker may say this means that if you only occupy one room but share the use of other rooms (such as a communal lounge), the higher amounts apply.[115] Argue that bathrooms, toilets and shared kitchens are not rooms you occupy. If you are forced to live in one room because the other room(s) in your accommodation are, in practice, unfit to live in (eg, because of severe mould or dampness), argue that the lower amounts apply.

Fuel for communal areas

If you pay a service charge for the use of fuel in communal areas and that charge is separately identified from any other charge for fuel used within your accommodation, it may be included as part of your eligible rent.[116] If you pay a charge for the provision of a heating system (eg, regular boiler maintenance), this is also eligible if the amount is separately identified from any other fuel charge you pay.[117]

Communal areas

'**Communal areas**' include access areas like halls and passageways, but not rooms in common use, except those in sheltered accommodation – eg, a shared TV lounge or dining room.[118]

Service charges

Service charges are only covered by HB if payment is a condition of occupying the accommodation rather than an optional extra. Eligible and ineligible charges are listed below. If the local authority regards any of the eligible charges as excessive, it estimates a reasonable amount given the cost of comparable services. If you are in supported accommodation, see p196.

The following services are eligible for HB:

- services for the provision of adequate accommodation. These include some warden and caretaker services, water charges in respect of communal areas (see above) – eg, in supported or sheltered accommodation, gardens, children's play areas, lifts, entryphones, communal telephone costs, portering and rubbish removal.[119] TV and radio relay charges are covered – eg, satellite or cable, including free-to-view UK channels;[120] *and*

- laundry facilities (eg, a laundry room in an apartment block), but not charges for the provision of personal laundry;[121] *and*
- furniture and household equipment, but not if there is an agreement that the furniture will eventually become yours;[122] *and*
- cleaning of the outside of windows if you or a member of your household cannot clean them yourself, and cleaning of rooms and windows in communal areas, unless your local authority, a county council in England or the Welsh Ministers pays for these.[123]

The following services are not eligible for HB:[124]
- food, including prepared meals (see below);
- sports facilities;
- TV rental, licence and subscription fees (but see above);
- transport;
- personal laundry service;
- provision of an emergency alarm system;
- medical expenses;
- nursing and personal care;
- counselling and other support services;
- any other charge not connected with the provision of adequate accommodation and not specifically included in the list of eligible charges above.

It is the amount of the charge specified in your rent agreement that is not eligible for HB, although local authorities can substitute their own estimate if they consider the amount to be unreasonably low.[125] If the amount is not specified in your rent agreement, the local authority estimates how much is fairly attributable to the service, given the cost of comparable services.[126]

If your housing costs include an amount for meals, set amounts are ineligible regardless of the actual cost.[127] The amount allowed for meals is:

If at least three meals a day are provided:	
For the claimant, partner and each child aged 16 or over included in the claim	£29.05
For each child aged under 16 included in the claim	£14.75
If breakfast only is provided:	
For the claimant, partner and each child included in the claim	£3.60
In all other cases (part board):	
For the claimant, partner and each child aged 16 or over included in the claim	£19.35
For each child aged under 16 included in the claim	£9.70

Part 3: Other means-tested benefits and tax credits
Chapter 10: Housing benefit
4. The amount of benefit

A child only counts as having reached the age of 16 on the first Monday in September following her/his 16th birthday.

The standard amounts are also ineligible for everyone who has meals paid for by you – eg, a non-dependant.[128]

Support services in supported accommodation

If you live in supported accommodation, HB can help with your rent. However, HB is not available for the support services provided with your accommodation. Instead, the local authority funds these (eg, via your landlord or a voluntary organisation) and you may be charged for them.

If you are on a means-tested benefit

Once you have made a claim for HB, being on IS, income-based JSA, income-related ESA, the guarantee credit of PC (or UC) is an automatic passport to maximum HB because all of your income and capital are ignored.[129] The amount of HB you get is always your 'maximum HB' (see p190 for how to work this out).

For these purposes, you are treated as being on:[130]

- income-based JSA when it is payable to you and also:
  - when you satisfy the conditions of entitlement but are not being paid it because of a sanction (see p1145); *and*
  - on your waiting days (see p266); *and*
  - when it is not paid because of the benefit offence rules (see p1278);
- income-related ESA when it is payable to you and also:
  - when you satisfy the conditions of entitlement but are not being paid it because you are disqualified for the reasons on p162; *and*
  - on your waiting days (see p662). The rules are the same as for contributory ESA;
- UC on any day you are entitled to it, whether or not it is being paid to you.

Example

Glen and his partner Craig are the joint housing association tenants of a two-bedroom flat. Glen's aunt lives with them. They pay rent of £150 a week. Glen receives income-related ESA. Glen's aunt receives UC. Glen claims HB. No reduction is made to their rent under the rent restriction rules.

Therefore, the amount of rent that can be covered (their 'eligible rent') is £150 a week. Glen's aunt counts as a non-dependant and so £15.85 a week is deducted.

Therefore, Glen's maximum HB is £134.15 a week (£150 – £15.85).

Because he receives income-related ESA, Glen's HB is £134.15 a week.

If you are not on a means-tested benefit

If you are not on IS, income-based JSA, income-related ESA or the guarantee credit of PC (or UC), follow the steps below to calculate your HB.[131]

Chapter 10

- **Step one:** check that your capital is not too high (see Chapter 22 or 23).
- **Step two:** work out your 'maximum HB' (see p190).
- **Step three:** work out your applicable amount (see Chapter 17).
- **Step four:** work out your income (see Chapter 20 for working-age HB or Chapter 21 for pension-age HB, but also p900 if you are a student and p468 if you are getting the savings credit of PC).
- **Step five:** calculate HB.
  - **If your income is less than or equal to your applicable amount**, HB equals your 'maximum HB'.
  - **If your income is greater than your applicable amount**, work out the difference. HB equals your 'maximum HB' minus 65 per cent of the difference between your income and your applicable amount.

Examples

Justin and Hailey are joint private tenants who pay £160 rent a week. Justin is aged 45. He is unemployed and gets contribution-based JSA of £74.35 a week. Hailey is aged 46 and works 21 hours a week. She is paid £201.75 a week after deductions of tax and national insurance (NI) contributions. Hailey gets working-age HB. A rent restriction is applied and so the amount of rent that can be covered (her 'eligible rent' – see p191) is £120 a week. The couple have no non-dependants. Therefore, Hailey's maximum HB (see p190) is £120 a week. Her applicable amount is £116.80 (the standard rate for a couple).

Income to be taken into account is Justin's JSA and £191.75 of Hailey's earnings a week (because £10 of her earnings are disregarded – see p431).

£74.35 + £191.75 = £266.10

The difference between her income and her applicable amount is £149.30 a week.

65% x £149.30 = £97.05 a week.

Hailey's HB is, therefore, £120 (maximum HB) – £97.05 = £22.95 a week.

Caleb is 67 years old. He lives alone. He gets pension-age HB. He receives an 'old' retirement pension (see Chapter 36) of £134.25 a week. His weekly income from his private pension is £60. His total weekly income is therefore £194.25 (£134.25 + £60). He is a sole tenant of his one-bedroom council flat. His rent of £125 a week includes his heating and hot water. No reduction is made under any rent restriction rules, but deductions are made for heating and hot water so his 'eligible rent' (see p191) is £86.70 a week (£125 – £34.30 and £4). Therefore, his maximum HB (see p190) is £86.70 because he does not have any non-dependants.

His applicable amount is £187.75 (adult personal allowance for a single person at least 65).

The difference between his income and his applicable amount is £6.50.

65% x £6.50 = £4.23 a week.

Caleb's HB is, therefore, £86.70 – £4.23 = £82.47 a week.

Part 3: Other means-tested benefits and tax credits
Chapter 10: Housing benefit
4. The amount of benefit

Deductions for non-dependants

If other people normally live with you in your home, other than your partner and children included in your claim (called 'non-dependants'), a set deduction is usually made from your eligible rent when your 'maximum HB' is calculated (see p190).[132] This is because it is assumed the non-dependant makes a contribution towards your outgoings, whether or not s/he does so. Examples of non-dependants are adult sons or daughters, elderly relatives or friends who share your home.

Non-dependant deductions: checklist

1. Do you have a non-dependant – ie, someone who normally lives with you? If not, no deduction can be made.
2. Even if you have a non-dependant, must a deduction be made?
3. If a non-dependant deduction must be made, what is the correct amount of the deduction?

Who counts as a non-dependant

A person only counts as your non-dependant if s/he normally lives with you.[133] So, for example, if someone is only staying with you temporarily but normally lives elsewhere, or is homeless and is only using your address as a postal address, s/he should not count as a non-dependant. If you think the local authority has wrongly assumed that a person is your non-dependant, ask for a revision or appeal. **Note:** some people do not count as non-dependants even if they normally live with you (see p199).

A person is only living with you if s/he has her/his home with you and shares some accommodation with you.[134] If s/he only shares a bathroom, toilet or a communal area such as a hall, passageway or a room in common use in sheltered accommodation, s/he does not count as living with you. If other areas of the house are shared (including the kitchen, unless it is only used by someone else to prepare food for her/him[135]), the person counts as living with you. This is the case even if you only use them at different times, provided you have a shared right to use them and are living in the same household (see p329 for the meaning of 'household').[136] A person who is separately liable to pay rent to your landlord does not count as living with you for these purposes.

A person should only count as normally living with you if s/he has been there long enough to regard your home as her/his normal home.[137] Factors to be taken into account include:[138]

- the relationship between you;
- how much time s/he spends at your address;
- where s/he has her/his post sent;
- where s/he keeps her/his clothes and personal belongings;

- whether her/his stay or absence from your address is temporary or permanent. The temporary absence rules on p182 may be used to work this out;[139]
- whether s/he has another place that could be regarded as home and if, for instance, s/he pays rent or water charges there, or s/he just travels around.

People who do not count as non-dependants

The following people do *not* count as non-dependants, and no non-dependant deduction is made for them, even if they normally live with you:[140]

- your partner;
- a child or qualifying young person included in your claim;
- a child or qualifying young person living with you who does not count as a member of your household (see p327) – eg, a foster child;
- someone who is staying with you but whose normal home is elsewhere. **Note:** for these purposes, someone can only have one normal home at a time;[141]
- someone who is a resident carer for you or your partner, who is employed by a charitable or voluntary organisation. This applies where a charge is made for her/his services, paid by you or a public body on your behalf;
- any person, or a member of her/his household, to whom you or your partner are liable to pay rent on a commercial basis – eg, a resident landlord;
- someone who jointly occupies your home and is either the joint owner with you or your partner or is liable with you or your partner to make payments in respect of occupying it. You do not jointly occupy the home with someone unless you made a joint agreement with your landlord to do so. The mere fact that you live in the same home does not make you joint occupiers;[142]
- someone who is liable to pay rent on a commercial basis to you or your partner – eg, your tenants or lodgers. However, although no non-dependant deduction can be made for her/him, the rent s/he pays can count as your income (see p442 and p477).

Note: if the person comes within the last three categories above, s/he *does* count as a non-dependant if s/he is treated as not liable for rent under the rules explained on pp178–80 (other than if s/he is a student or a person who has failed the 'habitual residence test').[143]

When a non-dependant deduction is not made

A deduction is not made for any of your non-dependants if either you or your partner:[144]

- are certified as severely sight impaired or blind by a consultant ophthalmologist (or are within 28 weeks of ceasing to be certified); *or*
- receive attendance allowance (AA) (or equivalent benefits paid because of injury at work or a war injury), the care component of disability living allowance (DLA), the daily living component of personal independence payment (PIP) or armed forces independence payment.

Part 3: Other means-tested benefits and tax credits
Chapter 10: Housing benefit
4. The amount of benefit

A deduction is not made for a non-dependant:[145]

- who is staying with you temporarily, but whose normal home is elsewhere;
- who is receiving a training allowance in connection with youth training under specified provisions;[146]
- if you are getting pension-age HB (see p188), who is a full-time student. This includes those getting JSA who count as full-time students while on a specified scheme for assisting people to obtain employment (see p1151);
- if you are getting working-age HB (see p188), who is a full-time student during her/his period of study. This includes those getting JSA who count as full-time students while on a specified scheme for assisting people to obtain employment (see p1151). In addition, no deduction is made during the summer vacation, unless the student is in full-time paid work;
- who usually lives with you, is a member of the armed or reserved forces and is away on operations, irrespective of how long s/he has been away;
- who is in hospital for more than 52 weeks. Separate stays in hospital which are not more than 28 days apart are added together when calculating the 52 weeks;
- who is in prison;
- who is under 18 years old;[147]
- who is under 25 and:
  - entitled to UC, provided s/he does not have any earned income; *or*
  - on IS; *or*
  - on income-based JSA; *or*
  - on income-related ESA, unless s/he receives the support component or s/he has been placed in the work-related activity group (see p653).

  S/he can be treated as being on income-based JSA or income-related ESA for these purposes (see p196);
- who is on PC.

The amount of deductions

If you have a non-dependant living with you who is 18 or over, and for whom a deduction must be made, when working out your maximum HB a fixed amount is deducted from your eligible rent (see p190), whatever s/he pays you. A deduction is made for every non-dependant living in your household, except in the case of a non-dependant couple (see p201).

Unless your non-dependant is in full-time paid work, a £15.85 deduction is made each week. If your non-dependant is in full-time paid work, the amount of the deduction depends on her/his gross weekly income as follows.[148]

Income bands	Deduction
Aged 18 or over and in full-time paid work with a weekly gross income of:	
£469 or more	£102.35
£377–£468.99	£93.25

£283–£376.99	£81.90
£217–£282.99	£50.05
£149–£216.99	£36.45
All others (for whom a deduction is made)	£15.85

The rules on full-time paid work are in Chapter 44. **Note:**

- A non-dependant who is not in (or is treated as not being in) full-time paid work does not attract the higher levels of deduction even if her/his weekly gross income is £149 or more.
- If someone is on IS, or is on (or treated as being on) income-based JSA or income-related ESA (see p196) for more than three days in a benefit week, s/he does not count as being in full-time paid work in that week.[149] This means the lower deduction (£15.85) is made (or, in some cases, no deduction).

Gross income includes wages before tax and NI are deducted, plus any other income the non-dependant has (apart from AA (or equivalent benefits paid because of injury at work or a war injury), DLA, PIP and armed forces independence payment). Also ignored are payments from specified trusts established to compensate victims of medical errors, emergencies and acts of terrorism.[150]

Do you know your non-dependant's income?
If you do not know your non-dependant's income, ask the local authority to consider the circumstances – eg, if your non-dependant is doing a job which is normally very low paid. The local authority should not assume the worst – eg, that your non-dependant is earning the highest amount. It should assess the likely level of her/his income on the evidence available.[151]

Non-dependant couples
Only one deduction is made for a couple (or the members of a polygamous marriage) who are non-dependants. The deduction made is the highest that would have been made if they were treated as individuals.[152] For the purpose of deciding which income band applies (see p200), their joint income counts, even if only one of them is in full-time work.[153]

Non-dependants of joint occupiers
If you share a non-dependant with any other joint occupiers, the deduction is divided between you, taking into account the proportion of housing costs paid by each of you.[154] If the person is a non-dependant of only one of you, the full deduction is made from that person's benefit. No apportionment is made between the members of a couple (or polygamous marriage).

Part 3: Other means-tested benefits and tax credits
Chapter 10: Housing benefit
6. Claims and backdating

If you are getting pension-age HB

If you are getting pension-age HB (see p188), if a non-dependant moves in with you so a deduction should be made, or there has been a change of circumstances in respect of a non-dependant so a higher deduction should be made, the effect of this can be delayed for 26 weeks.[155]

Your non-dependant's income or capital is more than yours

Normally, the income and capital of any non-dependant is only relevant when deciding which non-dependant deduction applies. However, unless you are on IS, income-based JSA, income-related ESA or the guarantee credit of PC, your HB entitlement is assessed on the basis of your non-dependant's income and capital rather than your own if:[156]

- her/his income and capital are both greater than yours; *and*
- the local authority is satisfied you have made an arrangement with your non-dependant to take advantage of the HB scheme (see p180).

Any income and capital normally treated as belonging to you is completely ignored, but the rest of the HB calculation proceeds as normal.

5. Special benefit rules

Special rules may apply to:
- 16/17-year-olds previously looked after by a local authority (see p947);
- people subject to immigration control (see Chapter 67);
- people who have come from or are going abroad (see Chapters 68 and 69);
- people who are studying (see Chapter 41);
- people who are in hospital, living in a care home or other similar accommodation, or people in prison (see Chapter 42).

6. Claims and backdating

To be entitled to housing benefit (HB), you must make a claim for it.[157] Claim HB as soon as you think you might be entitled to it or you may lose benefit. The rules about backdating are explained on p208. To find out when your entitlement to HB starts, see p213.

If you want to claim discretionary housing payments, you must claim these separately (see Chapter 29).

Making a claim

A claim for HB must normally be made in writing on a properly completed claim form.[158] See p205 for information about where to claim. **Note:** if you are claiming another benefit (ie, pension credit (PC), or if you can still make a new claim, income support (IS), income-based jobseeker's allowance (JSA) or employment and support allowance (ESA)), you can claim HB at the same time (see below).

It is always best to claim in writing if you can. However, you may also be able to claim:

- by telephone if:
  - your local authority has published a number for this purpose.[159] If the local authority provides a written statement of your circumstances, you must approve this statement for your claim to be valid. **Note:** even if you cannot claim by telephone, if you phone to ask to be sent a claim form and you return it within one month, your written claim is backdated to the date of your call (see p207); *or*
  - you claim PC (or IS, JSA or ESA) by telephone (see below);
- by electronic communication (eg, online or by email), if your local authority has authorised it.[160]

If you claim in writing, keep a copy in case queries arise. **Note:** the local authority can treat any written document (eg, a letter) as a claim for benefit, provided the written information and evidence you provide is sufficient.[161]

You must provide any information and evidence required (see p206). You can amend or withdraw your claim before a decision is made (see p205). Claim as soon as you can so you do not lose benefit. Ensure your claim is accepted as valid (see p204).

Forms

Claim forms are available free of charge from your local authority.[162] Check your local authority's website to find out where to get a claim form.

Rapid reclaim

You may be able claim HB without having to give as much detail of your circumstances as is usually required (known as 'rapid reclaim') if your circumstances have not changed since the last time you were claiming HB, and you are reclaiming within:[163]

- 26 weeks and you are also reclaiming IS or JSA and are entitled to IS or income-based JSA; *or*
- 12 weeks and you are also reclaiming ESA.

You are given the shortened form by the Jobcentre Plus office but you must send your HB claim to the local authority, *not* to the DWP.

If you are claiming another benefit

If you are claiming PC by telephone, or if you are still able to make a new claim for IS, JSA or ESA and you are claiming by telephone, your HB claim is usually

Part 3: Other means-tested benefits and tax credits
Chapter 10: Housing benefit
6. Claims and backdating

completed at the same time.[164] The DWP takes your details and sends you a statement of your circumstances to check, sign and return to the Jobcentre Plus office, along with evidence to support your claim. It forwards your HB claim to the local authority. You can claim HB by phoning the DWP (using the number specified for this purpose) at any time before a decision is made on your claim for PC (or for IS, JSA or ESA). **Note:** if the local authority or DWP provides a written statement of your circumstances, you must approve this for your claim to be valid.

If you are providing evidence or information that is required or notifying a change of circumstances to the DWP in connection with your PC claim – or if you can still make a new claim, your IS, JSA or ESA claim – eg, by telephone, you can claim HB in the same manner if the DWP agrees. You must claim HB before a decision is made on the award of benefit to which the evidence, information or change of circumstances relates.[165]

You may be asked for further information and evidence (see p206).

Making sure your claim is valid

Where possible, your claim for HB should be accompanied by all the information and evidence needed to assess it.[166] Your claim is 'defective' if you:

- do not complete your claim form properly or you claim in writing, but not on the claim form (eg, by letter or email), and do not provide sufficient information and evidence; or
- claim by telephone and do not provide all the information required by the local authority or DWP during the telephone call.

It is very important that you provide any information or evidence required. Until you do, your claim may be defective and you may not count as having made a valid claim. However, you should not delay your claim just because you do not have all the evidence ready to send.

Correcting a defective claim

If your claim is defective, you are given the opportunity to correct it. If you have:[167]

- not completed the claim form properly, the local authority can return it to you to do so. However, if you sent or gave your claim form to the DWP, it can ask you to provide the local authority with information needed to complete the form; or
- claimed in writing, but not on the claim form (eg, by letter or email), the local authority can send you a claim form to complete properly; or
- claimed by telephone to the local authority, the local authority must give you an opportunity to provide the information required; or
- claimed by telephone to the DWP, the DWP can give you an opportunity to provide the information required. However, if the DWP does not do so, the

local authority *must* give you an opportunity to provide the information, unless it thinks it already has sufficient information. If it does, your claim is treated as though it was received on the date of your original claim.

If you return the form completed properly or provide the information or evidence within one month of the last time you were told your claim is defective, your claim is treated as though it was received on the date of your original claim.[168] The local authority can allow you longer than one month if it thinks this reasonable.

Note: if you are told your claim is defective and it is not accepted as valid, you should be given a decision saying so. You can appeal against the decision.

Amending or withdrawing your claim

You may amend your claim (this includes asking for your claim to be backdated) at any time before a decision is made. You can do this by writing to the local authority, by telephone to the local authority or the DWP on the specified number or by any other manner the local authority or DWP decides or accepts.[169] Amendments are treated as though they were part of your original claim.

You may withdraw your claim at any time before a decision is made.[170] You must do this by writing to the local authority or, if you made your claim by telephone to the local authority, by telephone to the local authority. A notice to withdraw your claim takes effect from the day it is received.

Where to claim

If you claim in writing, you must usually send or give your HB claim to the local authority's designated office for the receipt of HB claims.[171] The address is usually on the claim form or a notice accompanying it. You can check for the address on your local authority's website. It is always best to send or give your claim directly to the local authority and it may speed up your claim if you do so. However, you can also send or give your claim to:[172]

- if you or your partner are also claiming PC (or IS, JSA or, ESA), either your DWP office or the local authority's designated office for HB claims. If you send your HB claim to the DWP, the DWP must usually forward it to the local authority within two working days of receiving it, or as soon as practicable after;[173] *or*
- a county council office, if your local authority has arranged for claims to be received there; *or*
- if you are at least pension age (see p780), any 'authorised office' – ie, an office nominated by the DWP and authorised by the local authority for receiving HB claims.

Keep a copy of your claim form wherever possible. Ask for confirmation that you have delivered it to the relevant office.

If your local authority has authorised it and you are claiming by electronic communication, check the correct address for this with your local authority.[174]

Part 3: Other means-tested benefits and tax credits
Chapter 10: Housing benefit
6. Claims and backdating

If you are allowed to claim by telephone, you must make your claim to the telephone number published or specified for this purpose.[175]

Who should claim

If you are a single person or a lone parent, you claim HB on your own behalf. If you are a member of a couple, you can decide between you who should claim. If you cannot agree who should claim, the local authority can decide for you.[176]

Who should you choose to make the claim?

If you are a member of a couple, the choice of claimant may affect the amount of HB you receive – eg, if one of you is a full-time student and not eligible for HB (see p896) or if one of you is getting ESA and the other is getting personal independence payment (PIP). In addition, if you are considering changing the claim to your partner's name, check whether s/he can make a new claim (see p173) and whether this could result in your becoming subject to harsher rent restriction rules (see Chapter 19) or losing entitlement to any premiums or components (see Chapter 17).

Appointees

If a person is either temporarily or permanently unable to manage her/his own affairs, the local authority must accept a claim made by someone formally appointed to act legally on her/his behalf.[177] If no one has been formally appointed to look after a claimant's affairs, the local authority can decide to make someone aged over 18 an appointee who can act on her/his behalf. For the purpose of the claim, an appointee has the same rights and is responsible for carrying out the same duties as though s/he were the claimant.

You can write to ask to be an appointee, and can resign after giving four weeks' notice. The local authority may terminate any appointment at any time.[178] If someone is given a formal legal appointment, that person automatically takes over from the person appointed by the local authority.[179]

Information to support your claim

When you claim HB, you must:
- satisfy the national insurance (NI) number requirement (see below), unless you are living in a hostel.[180] If you are a member of a couple, your partner must also usually satisfy this requirement; *and*
- provide proof of your identity, if required; *and*
- provide information and evidence required with the claim. Until you do, you may not count as having made a valid claim (see p204). Correct any defects as soon as possible or your date of claim may be affected.

If you or your partner are getting JSA or (if you are claiming working-age HB – see p188) IS, and have notified the DWP that you have started work, the DWP can ask you to provide the local authority with any information or evidence it needs to decide whether you continue to be entitled to HB.[181] This only applies if, as a result of the change, entitlement to IS or JSA will end or the amount of contribution-based JSA will reduce.

The local authority may ask you to provide information *after* you are awarded HB if this is needed to determine whether you are still entitled to HB. You must then supply this within one month, or longer if the local authority thinks this is reasonable.[182] If you fail to do so, your HB could be suspended or even terminated (see p1200). **Note:** you must actually have been notified; proof of posting to your last known address is not sufficient.[183]

The national insurance number requirement

For how you (and your partner) can satisfy the NI number requirement, and for when your partner is exempt, see p1171. The rules are the same as for other benefits. However, note the following.

- You do not have to satisfy the NI number requirement if you live in a hostel.[184]
- If you have claimed HB in association with a claim for PC (or IS or income-based JSA) and the DWP has accepted that you satisfy the NI number requirement, the local authority can accept that you also satisfy it for HB purposes.[185]

The date of your claim

The date of your claim is important because it determines when your entitlement to HB starts. This is not necessarily the date from when you are paid. For information about when payment of HB starts, see p213.

Your date of claim is not necessarily the date it is received by the local authority. It can be an earlier date.

Your '**date of claim**' is usually the earliest of:[186]

- the date you first notify a designated office, DWP office or authorised office (see p205) (or county council office, if the local authority has arranged for claims there) that you want to claim HB, provided a properly completed claim is received in one of those offices within one month. The one-month period can be extended if the local authority thinks it is reasonable; *or*
- the date your valid claim is received by the designated office, DWP office or authorised office (see p205) (or county council office, if the local authority has arranged for claims there).

There are exceptions to the above rules.[187]

- If you or your partner have successfully claimed IS, income-based JSA, income-related ESA or the guarantee credit of PC and your HB claim is made within one month of that claim being received by the DWP, your claim is treated as having been made on the first day of entitlement to that benefit. For example, if your claim for IS is backdated, your date of claim for HB purposes is the date

Part 3: Other means-tested benefits and tax credits
Chapter 10: Housing benefit
6. Claims and backdating

to which your IS claim is backdated. **Note:** for these purposes, you are treated as entitled to JSA or ESA on your 'waiting days'.[188]

- If you are awarded universal credit (UC) and you claim HB within one month of your UC claim or, if you are someone who does not have to make a claim for UC, within one month of being notified that you were awarded UC, your HB claim is treated as having been made on the first day of entitlement to UC.
- If you or your partner are on IS, income-based JSA, income-related ESA or the guarantee credit of PC (or UC), have just become liable to pay rent for your home and your HB claim reaches the local authority's designated office or DWP office within one month of your becoming liable, your claim is treated as having been made on the date that you first became liable to pay rent.
- If you have separated from your partner or s/he has died and s/he was claiming HB for you on the date this happened and you claim within one month of this, your claim is treated as having been made on the date you separated or your partner died.

Note: you must make sure your claim is valid. If it is 'defective', you are given a short time to correct the defects (see p204). If you do, your claim is treated as having been made when you initially claimed.

In some cases, you can claim in advance (see p211) and in some cases your claim can be backdated (see below).

Backdating your claim

It is very important to claim in time. Even if your claim is backdated, the arrears of HB that you can get are limited. Your claim can be backdated:

- for up to three months if you claim pension-age HB (see p188). In this case, you do not have to show good cause for your late claim (see below);
- for up to one month if you claim working-age HB (see p188). In this case, you must show good cause for your late claim (see p209).

For backdated HB to be considered, you must ask for HB for a past period. Do this as soon as possible, preferably at the same time as your claim for HB. Any backdated HB is calculated on the basis of your circumstances and the HB rules as they were over the backdating period.

If you would have been entitled to HB for an earlier period than the backdating rules allow, you could:

- ask for a 'specific grounds' revision if there are grounds (see p1307);
- ask for compensation from the local authority if you were given wrong information or misled by it (see p1439);
- complain to the Ombudsman (see p1446).

If you only qualify for HB when a qualifying benefit is awarded, see p211 for when your claim might be backdated further.

Three months' backdating

If you claim pension-age HB (see p188), your claim can be backdated for up to three months.[189] This applies whatever the reasons were for your delay in claiming and, even if you do not ask for HB for a past period, until some time after you make your claim for HB. You only need to show that you qualified for HB during that period.

You can get backdated HB for the three months before the date of your HB claim (see p207) – eg, the date your claim was received or the date you notified the local authority that you wanted to claim HB.[190] However, if you or your partner successfully claimed the guarantee credit of PC and your claim for HB is received within one month of your PC claim being received by the DWP, your entitlement to HB cannot begin earlier than three months before your claim for PC was made (or treated as having been made).

One month's backdating

If you claim working-age HB (see p188), your claim can be backdated for up to one month.[191]

You must show that you qualified for HB during the period *and* prove you had a continuous 'good cause' for failing to claim or to ask for backdated HB (see below). You can only get backdated HB from the latest of:[192]

- **date one:** the day from which you had continuous good cause for your late claim; *or*
- **date two:** the day one month before your date of claim. Your date of claim is not necessarily the date it is received by the local authority; it can be an earlier date (see p207); *or*
- **date three:** the day one month before you asked for backdated HB.

Example

Rose, aged 41, claimed working-age HB on 8 May 2020. After getting advice, she asked for backdated HB on 18 May 2020.

The local authority accepts that she had a continuous good cause for her late claim from 24 February 2020.

Date one = 24 February 2020.

Date two = 8 April 2020. This is the day one month before her date of claim for HB.

Date three = 18 April 2020. This is the day one month before she asked for backdated HB.

Rose gets backdated HB from 18 April 2020, the latest of the three relevant dates.

If you are claiming HB after a previous entitlement ended, as well as asking for backdated HB, you should see whether you can challenge the local authority's decision to end your entitlement to HB (see Chapters 56 and 57).

You count as having a **'good cause'** for your late claim if you can show there is something that would probably have caused a reasonable person of your age and

Part 3: Other means-tested benefits and tax credits
Chapter 10: Housing benefit
6. Claims and backdating

experience to act (or fail to act) as you did, taking all the circumstances into account (including your state of health and the information which you received and which you might have obtained).[193] The more reasonable your behaviour in not claiming earlier given your circumstances, the more likely it is that you have a good cause.[194] If you have a mental health problem that makes you act unreasonably, this must be borne in mind.[195] If you have difficulty communicating in English or understanding documents, or have little knowledge of the benefits system, this should be taken into account, but these are not usually considered a good cause in themselves.[196]

If you choose not to claim but later change your mind, you must still show that you have a good cause for your late claim. The longer you have delayed in claiming, the harder this may be.[197] However, you may be able to show that you have a good cause – eg, if the reason you did not claim earlier was because you were making real efforts to find work to avoid relying on benefits, and you only chose not to claim for a limited period.

Examples of 'good cause'

1. You sought advice about your rights, but were misled by someone on whom you were entitled to rely – eg, officers from the local authority or the DWP or independent advisers such as solicitors, Citizens Advice offices, trade union officials or accountants.[198] Relying on the advice of work colleagues, friends, or even a doctor, is not enough.[199] The enquiries that you made need not have been specific, provided the situation is such that you ought to have been told about your possible entitlement.

2. You did not seek advice about your rights because you misunderstood them (eg, you believed that you did not need to make a claim), you mistakenly thought that you understood them or you mistakenly thought that you had no entitlement and there was nothing for you to enquire about.[200] Generally, you are expected to find out about your rights, but if it was reasonable for you to form one of these views, you can still have a good cause.

3. The delay was due to something beyond your control (eg, the failure of the post or of someone you asked to help with your claim), provided you checked whether the claim arrived in good time.[201]

4. You were unable to claim because of physical or mental ill health.[202] However, you might reasonably be expected to seek the assistance of friends or relatives if available.

5. You only qualify for HB when a qualifying benefit is awarded (see p211).

If you claim the wrong benefit

There are no rules that allow a claim for another benefit to be treated as a claim for HB.

Claiming in advance

You can claim HB in advance if:

- you become liable for rent for the first time but cannot move into your accommodation until after your liability begins. You must claim HB as soon as you are liable for rent. Once you move in, you may be able to receive HB for the four weeks before moving in (see p181); *or*
- you are not entitled to HB now, but will become entitled within 13 weeks of claiming (17 weeks if you or your partner will be pension age (see p780) within 17 weeks), unless the reason you do not qualify straight away is because you fail the 'habitual residence test' (see p1586). The local authority can treat your claim as having been made in the benefit week immediately before you are first entitled.[203] If this happens, you do not need to make a further claim later.

Housing benefit after an award of a qualifying benefit

You may not be entitled to HB currently, but would be once you, your partner or a child or qualifying young person included in your claim become entitled to another 'qualifying benefit' – eg, DLA, PIP or carer's allowance, because you then qualify for premiums or components. Alternatively, you might be entitled to a higher rate of benefit once the qualifying benefit is awarded. If you are already entitled to HB when the qualifying benefit is awarded, see p1309, p1319 and p1328.

Do you only qualify for housing benefit when a qualifying benefit is awarded?

If you only qualify for HB when a qualifying benefit is awarded, the rules operate in an unfair way so you should do the following.

1. Claim HB (if you still can) while waiting to hear about the claim for a qualifying benefit.

2. If you do not qualify for HB, ask the local authority to wait to make a decision on your claim until the award of the qualifying benefit is made (known as 'stockpiling' your claim). You may have to persuade the local authority that it can do so. If the local authority refuses, argue that its failure to delay making a decision on your claim was an 'error of law' and that there are grounds for a 'specific grounds' revision (see p1307).[204]

3. If you are refused HB but are then awarded a qualifying benefit, claim again and ask for your claim to be backdated. If you need to, argue that you have a good cause for your late claim (see p209).

4. If you lose benefit because of the way the rules operate, ask your local authority for compensation to cover the period before your fresh HB claim.

Notice of the decision

Once the local authority has all the information and evidence required, it must make a decision on your claim for HB within 14 days or as soon as 'reasonably practicable'.[205] If you are a person affected by the decision, you must be notified

Part 3: Other means-tested benefits and tax credits
Chapter 10: Housing benefit
6. Claims and backdating

of it by the local authority without delay or as soon as 'reasonably practicable'.[206] In all other cases (eg, if a decision is made following a change in your circumstances), you (and other people affected by the decision) must be notified within 14 days or as soon as reasonably practicable. You can request reasons for a decision. Your request must be in writing and it must be signed by you.[207]

Person affected by a decision
You are a '**person affected by a decision**' if you are:[208]
– a claimant; *or*
– someone acting for a claimant who is unable to act for her/himself – eg, an appointee; *or*
– someone from whom the local authority decides to recover an overpayment (including a landlord); *or*
– a landlord or agent if the decision concerns whether or not to make a direct payment of HB to you.[209]

Information a decision notice should contain

If the decision is one you can appeal (see p1343), you must be informed of:[210]
- your right to appeal against the decision; *and*
- your right to a written statement of reasons for the decision (if this is not already included – see p1297. The rules are the same as for other benefits).

The other information that must be provided varies with the particular circumstances of your case and includes the following.[211]
- The normal weekly amount of HB to which you are entitled, including the amount of any deductions for non-dependants and fuel. You must be told why fuel deductions have been made and that they can be varied if you provide evidence of the actual amount involved.
- The amount of your rent that can be covered by HB (your weekly 'eligible rent' – see p191).
- If you are a private tenant, the day your HB will be paid and whether payment will be made weekly or monthly.
- The date on which your entitlement starts (see below).
- In some cases, how your applicable amount is calculated, how your income has been assessed and the amount of capital the local authority has taken into account. If the income and capital of a non-dependant has been used instead of yours to calculate your HB (see p202), you must be informed of this and the reasons why.
- If your claim was:
  – successful, your duty to notify the local authority of any change in circumstances which might affect your entitlement and the kinds of changes that should be reported;
  – unsuccessful, a statement explaining exactly why you are not entitled.

- If it has been decided to pay your HB directly to your landlord, information saying how much is to be paid to her/him and when payments will start.

When your entitlement starts

Your entitlement to HB starts:[212]
- if you became liable for rent for the first time, for a home you have moved into, in the week your claim is made or is treated as having been made, from the Monday of that week. This includes if you become liable for daily payments in a hostel or accommodation provided by the local authority on a short-term lease or because you are homeless. This means that your HB starts on the same day your liability to pay rent actually begins;[213] *or*
- in all other cases, from the Monday following your date of claim, or following the date from when you are treated as claiming if your claim is backdated (see pp207–10).

7. Getting paid

How payment of housing benefit (HB) is made depends on whether you are the tenant of the local authority responsible for paying HB or a private or housing association tenant. If you are unable to act for yourself, payment can be made to someone acting on your behalf (see p214). In some circumstances, payment can be made to your landlord (see p215). No HB is payable if the amount would be less than 50 pence a week.[214]

When is housing benefit paid?

You are normally paid in arrears at intervals of a week, two weeks, four weeks or a month, depending on when your rent is usually due. HB can also be paid at longer intervals if you agree.[215] If you are a private or housing association tenant, the local authority can pay your HB weekly to avoid an overpayment or if you are liable to pay rent weekly and it is in your interests for HB to be paid weekly.

Different rules apply if HB is paid direct to your landlord.[216]
Note:
- Your HB might be paid at a reduced rate if you have been sanctioned for a benefit offence (see p1278).
- If payment of your HB is delayed, see p220. You might be able to get a 'payment on account'. If you wish to complain about how your claim has been dealt with or claim compensation, see Chapter 60.
- If payment of your HB is suspended, see p1200.

- If you are overpaid HB, you might have to repay it (see Chapter 53) and, in some circumstances, you may have to pay a penalty (see p1268). If you have been accused of fraud, see Chapter 54.

How your benefit is paid

If your landlord is the local authority responsible for paying HB, your HB is paid in the form of a reduction in your rent. This is called a 'rent rebate'.[217]

If you are a private or housing association tenant, you receive HB in the form of a 'rent allowance'.[218] If you live in a caravan, mobile home or houseboat, this applies even if you are also liable to make payments to a local authority – eg, for site or mooring fees. HB is normally paid to you although, in some cases, it may be paid directly to your landlord or to someone acting on your behalf.

Note: if your rent allowance is:

- less than £1 a week, the local authority can pay your HB up to six months in arrears;[219]
- more than £2 a week, you can insist on two-weekly payments, unless HB is paid directly to your landlord.[220]

The local authority has the discretion to pay you by whatever method it chooses, but, in doing so, it must consider your 'reasonable needs and convenience'.[221] It should not insist on paying your HB into a bank account if you do not have one (but it may encourage you to open one), nor should it make you collect it if it is difficult to reach the office by public transport.[222] If it does, complain to your local councillor. If that has no effect, ask your MP to take up the matter (see p1444) and also complain to the Ombudsman (see p1446).

If the local authority refuses to replace a payment which has never arrived, you could threaten to sue in the county court (sheriff court in Scotland).

Payment to someone acting on your behalf

If an appointee or some other person legally empowered to act for you has claimed HB on your behalf, that person can also receive the HB payments.[223]

If you are able to claim HB for yourself, you can still nominate an agent to receive or collect it for you. To do this, you must make a written request to the local authority. Anyone you nominate must be aged 18 or over.[224]

If a claimant dies, any unpaid HB may be paid to her/his personal representative or, if there is none, to her/his next of kin aged 16 or over.[225] A written application must be received by the local authority within 12 months of the claimant's death. The local authority may allow longer. If HB was being paid to the landlord before the claimant's death, the local authority can pay any outstanding HB to her/him to clear remaining rent due.

Payment direct to a landlord

Your HB can be paid direct to your landlord (or the person to whom you pay rent) but only in specified circumstances. Your landlord could contact the local authority about this.[226] The local authority can suspend payment while it makes enquiries about who should be paid your HB.[227] If the local authority has concerns about your landlord, see p216.

If you have just claimed HB or the local authority has carried out a supersession of your award, and the local authority thinks you have not already paid your rent and that it would be in the interests of the 'efficient administration' of HB, it can make the first payment to your landlord.[228]

Both you and your landlord should be notified if HB is to be paid to your landlord. If it is *not* in your interests to have HB paid directly to your landlord, it is worth trying to persuade the local authority to withhold it rather than paying it to your landlord. Get advice before you do so.

When payment must be made to your landlord

The local authority *must* pay your HB, including payments on account (see p220), directly to your landlord (or the person to whom you pay rent) if:[229]

- you or your partner are on income support (IS), jobseeker's allowance (JSA), employment and support allowance (ESA) or pension credit (PC) and the DWP has decided to pay part of that benefit to your landlord for arrears (see p1205). **Note:** this does not apply if you are on universal credit (UC); *or*
- you have rent arrears equivalent to eight weeks' rent or more, unless you can show that it is in your overriding interest not to make direct payments.[230] Once your arrears have been reduced to less than eight weeks' rent, compulsory direct payments stop. The local authority may then choose to continue direct payments on a discretionary basis (see below).

Payment to your landlord on a discretionary basis

The local authority may pay your HB directly to your landlord (or the person to whom you pay rent):

- if the local housing allowance rent restriction rules do *not* apply to you (see p384):[231]
  - if you have requested or agreed to direct payments; *or*
  - without your agreement, if it decides that direct payments are in your or your family's best interests. You do not have to have any of your family living with you for payment to be made to your landlord under this rule;[232]
- if the local housing allowance rent restriction rules apply to you (see p384), if the local authority:[233]
  - thinks you are likely to have difficulty managing your own financial affairs or that it is improbable that you will pay your rent. The local authority can make direct payments (for a maximum of eight weeks) while it considers the situation; *or*

- thinks it will help you to secure or to keep accommodation. **Note:** the government's intention is that this should only apply if the rent is at a level you can afford; *or*
- has already made direct payments during your current award of HB in any of the situations when direct payments must be made;

- whether or not the local housing allowance rent restriction rules apply to you, without your agreement if you have left the address for which you were getting HB and there are rent arrears. In this case, direct payments of any unpaid HB due in respect of that accommodation can be made, up to the total of the outstanding arrears.[234] If your landlord retained your tenancy deposit to cover any of the rent arrears, the local authority should take this into account when working out how much HB to pay to her/him. It should also deduct any amounts you would be able to offset against what you would owe if your landlord were to take you to court to recover the rent arrears – eg, an amount you paid for repairs that were your landlord's responsibility.[235]

When the local authority has concerns about a landlord

The local authority may refuse to make direct payments to your landlord if it 'is not satisfied that s/he is a fit and proper person'.[236] However, direct payments may still be made if the local authority is satisfied it is in your or your family's best interests.[237]

If the local authority decides not to make payments to your landlord, it can make payments to you (including sending you a cheque payable to the landlord, or paying you in the presence of your landlord) or to a trusted third party, such as a social worker or solicitor.[238]

Continuing payments

Your HB can continue to be paid at the same rate, even though your entitlement might otherwise have changed:

- when you stop claiming:
  - IS, income-based JSA or income-related ESA because you or your partner are moving onto PC. You may be able to continue to receive HB at the same rate for four weeks (see below); *or*
  - IS, income-based JSA, income-related or contributory ESA or severe disablement allowance (SDA) because you or your partner start work or increase your hours or earnings. You may be entitled to extended payments of HB (see p217);
- if you are getting HB when you make a new claim for UC. Your HB may continue for two weeks (called HB run-on – see p220).

Note: if you are now getting your housing costs met through IS, income-based JSA or income-related ESA, but were previously getting HB for the same accommodation, your HB can continue for four weeks (see p176).

Continuing payments on claiming pension credit

To avoid problems caused by delays in reassessing your HB when you move from IS, income-based JSA or income-related ESA onto PC, you can receive pension-age HB for a period (see below), normally at the same rate as the HB you were getting before. Your maximum HB (see p190) is recalculated if your rent increases or there is a change in the non-dependant deductions (see p198) that should be made.[239] **Note:** this rule does *not* apply if you transfer to PC from UC.

You qualify for continuing payments if:[240]

- your partner has claimed PC and the DWP has certified this; *or*
- your IS, income-based JSA or income-related ESA ceased because you reached pension age (see p780). The DWP must certify this and that you are required to claim, or have claimed, PC (or are treated as having done so).

You get continuing payments for:[241]

- a period of four weeks from the day after your IS, income-based JSA or income-related ESA ceases; *or*
- if the four-week period ends other than on a Sunday, until the Sunday after the end of the four-week period.

Extended payments of housing benefit

If you or your partner are on IS, income-based JSA, income-related or contributory ESA or SDA and your entitlement ends because you (or your partner) start work or increase your hours or pay, you may be entitled to continue to receive the same amount of HB as you did before your entitlement ended for up to four weeks. These are called extended payments of HB.

You do not have to make a claim for extended payments of HB; they should be paid automatically.[242] However, your local authority needs to know that your or your partner's entitlement to IS, income-based JSA, ESA or SDA has ceased, so you must notify it.

If you want to get an extended payments decision changed, you can apply for a revision or supersession or appeal (see Chapters 56 and 57).

Who can get extended payments

You qualify for extended payments of HB if you are getting HB, you (or your partner) started work (including self-employed work) or increased your hours or pay, and your (or your partner's) entitlement to:

- IS, income-based JSA or income-related ESA ended.[243] This only applies if you are getting working-age HB (see p188). You (or your partner) must have been entitled to, and in receipt of, either IS, contribution-based, income-based or joint-claim JSA or income-related ESA, or a combination of these, for at least 26 weeks. **Note:** you cannot qualify if, immediately before your entitlement to IS ended, you qualified for housing costs run-on (see p376); *or*

- contributory ESA or SDA ended, and you (or your partner):[244]
  - are *not* getting PC; *and*
  - were not entitled to or in receipt of IS, income-based JSA or income-related ESA; *and*
  - had been continuously entitled to, and in receipt of, contributory ESA or SDA, or a combination of these, for at least 26 weeks.

In all cases, the work, or increase in earnings or hours, must be expected to last at least five weeks.

Do you need to report the change in your circumstances?

1. If you are getting IS, JSA, ESA or SDA and you start work or your hours or pay change, you must report this to the DWP. The end of your entitlement to these benefits is also a change in your circumstances that you must report to the local authority (see p221).

2. If you do not report the end of your entitlement to IS/JSA/ESA/SDA to the local authority, your entitlement to extended payments of HB is not affected, but this could result in an overpayment of HB at the end of the extended payment period.

3. You could be entitled to a higher rate of HB than you were before your entitlement to IS/JSA/ESA/SDA ended. Report the change as soon as possible so it can be taken into account.

If you move home, you can still qualify for extended payments of HB, provided the day you moved was in the same week, or the week before, you or your partner started work or increased your hours or pay.[245] See below for how the amount of the extended payments can be affected.

The amount of the extended payments and how long they last

Extended payments of HB are paid for four weeks unless:[246]

- any of the weeks count as rent-free periods (see p192); *or*
- your liability to pay rent ceases altogether within the four weeks.

The weekly amount of your extended payments (unless you move into local authority accommodation in a different local authority area -- see below) is the higher of the amount of HB:[247]

- you got in the last (non-rent-free) week before your entitlement to IS/JSA/ESA/SDA ended; *or*
- to which you would be entitled based on your new circumstances; *or*
- to which your partner would be entitled if s/he claimed based on her/his circumstances.

However, if the benefit cap is, or was, applied (see p1194), it is the amount of HB you would have got – ie, the amount before any reduction.[248]

Always report any changes in your circumstances during the four-week period. This is because the weekly amount you get is then the highest of the above amounts.[249]

Example

Jill is a local authority tenant with a non-dependant. She gets working-age HB. Her rent is £102 a week. She was getting HB of £66.15 in the week before her entitlement to IS ceased, because a non-dependant deduction of £36.45 was made. Her weekly HB entitlement based on her circumstances in work is £54.37. Her extended payments are therefore £66.15 a week. In the second week of the four-week period, Jill's non-dependant moves out. Her weekly entitlement based on her circumstances in work is now £90.82 (£54.37 + £36.45), because a non-dependant deduction is no longer made. Her extended payments are now £90.82 for the remainder of the four-week period. This is also Jill's HB entitlement from the end of the period.

You may qualify for extended payments of HB for two homes (see p186). However, if your liability to pay rent for either of these ceases within the four-week period, the amount of your extended payments is reduced by the amount of HB payable for that home.[250]

If you were being paid discretionary housing payments (see Chapter 29), ask for these to continue for the extended payment period.

If you move into local authority accommodation in a different local authority area, the weekly amount of your extended payments of HB is the amount of HB you got in the last (non-rent-free) week before your entitlement to IS/JSA/ESA/SDA ended – ie, the amount you got at your old address.[251] The extended payments can be paid to you or to the new local authority landlord. If you or your partner claim HB at your new address, the amount you or your partner get is reduced by the weekly amount of the extended payments. The effect of this is that, if your new HB entitlement is higher, your extended payments are 'topped up'.

If you move house in any other circumstances (eg, to privately rented or housing association accommodation, or within the same local authority area), your extended payments are worked out under the normal rules. If you also claim HB at your new address, it does not appear that the local authority can reduce the amount of HB you get by the weekly amount of your extended payments.[252] It is not clear if this was the intention.

Ongoing entitlement to housing benefit

Your entitlement to HB continues until at least the end of the extended payment period.[253] It can continue after that if you qualify under the normal HB rules, but at the weekly rate based on your new circumstances. You do not have to make a fresh claim. Your HB entitlement is continuous. This means if you have a form of transitional protection that requires continuous entitlement, this continues.

Note: unless you move to local authority accommodation in a different local authority area, if your partner claims HB, this cannot be paid to her/him while you are getting extended payments of HB.[254]

Housing benefit run-on

If you are getting HB and make a new claim for UC, your HB entitlement continues for two weeks (called a 'run-on' or transitional HB payment).[255] You do not have to make a claim for a run-on payment. It should be made automatically. You do not have to pay a run-on payment back, even if you qualify for a UC housing costs element for your rent for the same period. HB run-on counts as a specified benefit for the purposes of the benefit cap.

If your HB is being paid directly to your landlord, your run-on payment is usually also paid to her/him. If this happens, you should ask your landlord to pay you the HB run-on – eg, if you are up to date with your rent payments.

Note:
- Your entitlement to HB can continue indefinitely if this is for 'specified accommodation' or 'temporary accommodation' (see p174 for what counts).
- A benefit cap is not applied to your HB if you are getting UC.[256]

Delays and complaints

The local authority must make a decision on your claim, tell you in writing what the decision is, and pay you any HB to which you are entitled within 14 days or, if that is not reasonably practicable, as soon as possible after that.[257] If you consider a delay to be unreasonable, make a complaint (see p1443). In serious cases, you may want to obtain advice on whether you have grounds for a judicial review (see p1414).

Payments on account

If you are a private or housing association tenant and the local authority has not been able to assess your HB within the required period, the local authority must normally make a 'payment on account' (sometimes called an interim payment) while your claim is being sorted out.[258] The local authority should automatically do this. You should not have to request a payment on account.[259] Bear the following in mind.
- Payments on account are not discretionary. The local authority *must* pay you an amount that it considers reasonable, given what it knows about your circumstances.
- Payments on account can only be refused if it is clear that you will not be entitled to HB, or the reason for the delay is that you have been asked for information or evidence in support of your claim and you have failed, without a good cause, to provide it (see p206).[260] If the delay has been caused by a third

party (eg, the rent officer, your bank or employer), this does not affect your right to a payment on account.

- The local authority must notify you of the amount of a payment on account and that it can recover any overpayment which occurs if your actual HB entitlement is different from the payment.[261]
- If your payment on account is less than your actual entitlement, your future HB can be adjusted to take account of the underpayment.[262]
- If the local authority has not made a payment on account, complain.

Change of circumstances

It is your duty to report any change in your circumstances which you might reasonably be expected to know might affect your right to, the amount of or payment of your HB.[263] You should do this promptly to the office handling your claim. The local authority must tell you in writing about the changes you must report.[264] There may be a number of changes which the local authority requires you to report, depending on the particular circumstances of your case. **Note:** if you are getting PC, you only have to report specified changes (see p222).

If you do not report a change promptly, any resulting overpayment may be recoverable from you (see Chapter 53) and, in some circumstances, you may have to pay a penalty (see p1268). If you are considered to have acted knowingly or dishonestly, you may also be guilty of an offence (see Chapter 54). **Note:**

- It is important to report changes to the right department, not to other parts of the local authority such as social services. Your duty to notify changes is to the HB department, not to the local authority as a whole.[265]
- If your benefit is paid to someone else on your behalf, the duty to report any relevant changes also extends to her/him.[266]

If in doubt, always report changes in circumstances. If you think that the local authority might not have taken a change into account, you should check with it.

How to report a change of circumstances

It is always best to report a change in your circumstances in writing (eg, in a letter) and keep a copy in case of a dispute in the future. However, you can also report a change to the local authority:[267]

- by telephone (unless the local authority says you must report it in writing), if your local authority has published a telephone number for this purpose or allows you to claim HB by telephone (see p203); *or*
- electronically (eg, by email), if your local authority authorises it.[268]

You may report a change in your circumstances to the DWP, instead of the local authority, if the DWP has provided a telephone number for this purpose and:[269]

- you or your partner are getting JSA or (if you are on working-age HB – see p188) IS; *and*

- the change of circumstances is that you or your partner have started work; *and*
- as a result of the change, entitlement to IS or JSA will end or, if you or your partner are getting contribution-based JSA, the amount will reduce.

If the change is a birth or a death, there is a special rule (sometimes called 'Tell Us Once'). You can report such a change in person at a local authority (and, in England, a county council) office, if such an office has been specified.[270] If the change is a death, you can notify it to the DWP electronically, or by telephone if a number has been specified for that purpose. Check with your local authority (eg, at the registrar's office) to see whether it provides this service. More information is available at gov.uk/after-a-death/organisations-you-need-to-contact-and-tell-us-once.

Changes you must report if you get pension credit

If you get PC, the only changes you must report to the local authority are:[271]

- any change to your tenancy, apart from changes in your rent if you are a local authority tenant; *and*
- any changes affecting the residence or income of a non-dependant who normally lives with you; *and*
- any absence from your home which is, or is likely to be, for more than 13 weeks (more than four weeks if you are absent from Great Britain); *and*
- if you are only getting the savings credit of PC:[272]
  - changes affecting a child under 16 who lives with you that could affect how much HB you get. You need not report changes in the child's age; *and*
  - any changes to your capital that do, or could, take it above £16,000; *and*
  - any changes in the income or capital of a non-dependant of yours, if your HB has been assessed on the basis of this instead of your own (see p202), and whether s/he has stopped, or resumed, living with you; *and*
  - any changes in the income or capital of your partner that have not been taken into account since the determination of your PC award, and whether your partner has stopped, or resumed, living with you.

You must report other changes in connection with your PC claim to the DWP. Relevant changes in your circumstances should be passed to the local authority by the DWP.

Changes you must report if you do not get pension credit

The changes you must report if you are getting PC, listed above, are all changes that could affect your right to, the amount of or payment of your HB. So they are also changes you must report if you are *not* getting PC. Examples of other types of change you must report if you do not get PC include changes to:

- your family income or capital;
- the number of boarders you have or the payments made by them;
- your status – eg, marriage, civil partnership, cohabitation or separation.

However, you do *not* have to report:[273]
* any change in your age, or that of your partner or child(ren) or your non-dependant(s). **Note:** you *do* have to report any change that results in a child or young person no longer being included in your claim (see p323);
* if you are on IS, income-based JSA or income-related ESA, any changes that affect the amount of those benefits. **Note:** you *do* have to report entitlement to IS, income-based JSA or income-related ESA ending. Do not assume that the DWP does this on your behalf.

When changes in circumstances take effect
In most cases, a change takes effect from the Monday after it occurred.[274] This applies whether or not a decision is advantageous to you. However, if you are liable to pay rent on a daily basis (eg, in a hostel) and the change means you are no longer entitled to HB, it takes effect on the day it occurs.[275] **Note:**
* If you report a change in circumstances before the local authority has assessed your HB claim, your claim is assessed on the basis of the revised information you have provided.
* Special rules apply if two or more changes occurring in the same benefit week would normally take effect in different benefit weeks.[276]

Exceptions
There are a number of exceptions to the general rule described above, which include the following.
* If the change is one you are required to notify to the local authority (other than one relating to your having to take part in a work-focused interview or, if you are on PC, one of the additional exceptions to the rules described below), it is advantageous to you and you fail to notify the change within the one-month time limit (or any longer period allowed by the local authority – see p1324), the date of notification is treated as if this is the date the change occurred. This means you lose out if you reported the change late.
* If you are getting pension-age HB (see p188) and either a non-dependant comes to live with you or there is a change so that a higher non-dependant deduction should be made, the effect of this can be delayed for 26 weeks.[277]
* If you are entitled to HB (but not UC) when you become a member of a couple with someone getting UC and s/he moves in with you, unless your HB is for 'specified accommodation' or 'temporary accommodation' (see p174 for what counts), your entitlement to HB ends on the day before the day you are jointly entitled to UC with your new partner, or the day before the day you would have been entitled had you met all the financial conditions for UC.[278] **Note:** if instead you move in with your new partner, your HB entitlement ends under the normal HB rules.[279]

Part 3: Other means-tested benefits and tax credits
Chapter 10: Housing benefit
8. Tax, other benefits and the benefit cap

There are additional exceptions to the rules described above:
- if you are being paid PC, the amount of this changes because of a change in your circumstances or a correction of an official error (see p1307), and thus the amount of HB you can be paid changes;[280]
- if there is a change in your rent, if you move to a new home or if you become (or cease to be) entitled to HB for more than one home, and if you or your partner become entitled to ESA which includes a support component or you (or s/he) are put in the work-related activity group.[281]

8. Tax, other benefits and the benefit cap

Tax

Housing benefit (HB) is not taxable.

Means-tested benefits and tax credits

If you are entitled to HB:
- entitlement to income support (IS), income-based jobseeker's allowance (JSA), income-related employment and support allowance (ESA), the guarantee credit of pension credit (PC) or universal credit (UC) acts as an automatic passport to maximum HB (see p190) because all your income and capital are ignored;
- working tax credit counts as income when working out your HB;
- child tax credit counts as income unless you are getting pension-age HB (see p188).

Non-means-tested benefits

Most non-means-tested benefits are taken into account as income when working out the amount of HB you get. However:
- attendance allowance, disability living allowance, personal independence payment, guardian's allowance and child benefit are not taken into account;
- it can still be worth claiming non-means-tested benefits, even if they are taken into account. If you, your partner or your child(ren) qualify for certain of these, you also qualify for certain premiums and components (see Chapter 17) and, potentially, a higher rate of HB. If you think you might qualify, get advice to see whether you would be better off.

You may only qualify for HB once you or your partner, or a child or qualifying young person included in your claim, are awarded another benefit (known as a 'qualifying benefit'). You may be entitled to a higher rate of HB once the qualifying benefit is awarded (see p211).

The benefit cap

In some cases, there is a limit on the total amount of specified benefits you can receive (a 'benefit cap'). HB is one of the specified benefits (but HB for 'specified accommodation' is ignored). The benefit cap only applies if you are getting HB or UC. See p1194 for further information.

Passports and other sources of help

If you have been awarded HB, you may qualify for a Best Start grant (in Scotland – see p1695), a social fund funeral expenses payment (in England and Wales – see p798) or a funeral support payment (in Scotland – see p1703). You may be entitled to a council tax reduction (see p851).

Financial help on starting work

You may be entitled to extended payments of HB (see p217). Your local authority may also offer extended help with council tax. See p873 for information about other financial help you might get.

Notes

1. Who can get housing benefit
1 s130 SSCBA 1992; s115 IAA 1999; reg 10 HB Regs; reg 10 HB(SPC) Regs
2 Reg 26 HB(SPC) Regs
3 Regs 4, 4A and 6 UC(TP) Regs; Art 6 WRA(No.21)O; Art 7 WRA(No.23)O; Art 4 WRA(No.31)O; Art 4(11) WRA(No.32)O
4 Email to CPAG, 30 January 2019
5 Reg 2(1) UC(TP) Regs 2014; Sch 1 para 3A UC Regs
6 Reg 2(1) UC(TP) Regs; Sch 1 para 3B UC Regs
7 Art 6(3)(a) WRA(No.21)O; Art 7(4)(a) WRA(No.23)O; Arts 2(3), 4 and 7 WRA(No.31)O
8 Regs 11(1) and 12(1) HB Regs; regs 11(1) and 12(1) HB(SPC) Regs
9 CH/3110/2003; R(H) 3/07
10 R(H) 9/08; *Kirklees MBC v JM (HB)* [2018] UKUT 219 (AAC)
11 Reg 2(4)(a) HB Regs; reg 2(4)(a) HB(SPC) Regs
12 *R v Cambridge CC ex parte Thomas,* 10 February 1995 (QBD); CH/2959/2006
13 Regs 11(2) and 12(2) HB Regs; reg 12(2) HB(SPC) Regs
14 Reg 2(1) HB Regs and reg 2(1) HB(SPC) Regs, definition of 'long tenancy' and 'owner'; CH/2258/2004; *Burton v New Forest District Council* [2004] EWCA Civ 1510, reported as R(H) 7/05; R(H) 3/07; CH/3586/2005; R(H) 8/07; *CR v Wycombe District Council* [2009] UKUT 19 (AAC); *Blackburn with Darwen BC v DA (HB)* [2014] UKUT 431 (AAC); *GN v Sevenoaks BC (HB)* [2016] UKUT 271 (AAC)
15 Reg 11(2) HB Regs
16 Reg 11(4) HB Regs
17 Reg 8(1)(a) and (b) HB Regs; reg 8(1)(a) and (b) HB(SPC) Regs
18 Reg 8(2) HB Regs; reg 8(2) HB(SPC) Regs

19 *R v Rugby BC HBRB ex parte Harrison*
[1994] 28 HLR 36 (QBD); CH/2959/
2006
20 s48 Landlord and Tenant Act 1987; CH/
3579/2003; CH/257/2005
21 R(H) 3/03
22 *R v Poole BC ex parte Ross* [1995] 28 HLR
351 (QBD); *R v Warrington BC ex parte
Williams* [1997] 29 HLR 872 (QBD)
23 Reg 8(1)(c)-(e) HB Regs; reg 8(1)(c)-(e)
HB(SPC) Regs
24 CSHB/606/2005
25 *FK v Wandsworth BC (HB)* [2016] UKUT
570 (AAC); *Babergh DC v GW (HB)*
[2017] UKUT 40 (AAC)
26 Regs 9, 10 and 56 HB Regs; regs 9 and
10 HB(SPC) Regs
27 *Scott v SSWP* [2011] EWCA Civ 103
28 Reg 9(4) HB Regs; reg 9(4) HB(SPC)
Regs; CH/1326/2004; CH/1328/2004
29 CH/542/2006; R(H) 5/06 decided that
the rule did not conflict with the Human
Rights Act
30 Reg 3(4) HB Regs; reg 3(4) HB(SPC)
Regs; R(H) 5/06; CPC/1446/2008; *RK v
SSWP* [2008] UKUT 34 (AAC)
31 *Thamesdown BC v Goonery* [1995] 1 CLY
2600
32 R(H) 1/03; CH/1171/2002; CH/2899/
2005
33 Reg 9(2) HB Regs; reg 9(2) HB(SPC)
Regs; *R v Poole BC ex parte Ross* [1995]
28 HLR 351 (QBD); CH/1076/2002;
CH/296/2004; CH/1097/2004; paras
A3/3.258-65 GM
34 *DH v Kirklees MBC and SSWP (HB)* [2011]
UKUT 301 (AAC), reported as [2012]
AACR 16; *LB Bexley v KM* [2017] UKUT
354 (AAC)
35 *R (Tucker) v Secretary of State* [2001]
EWCA Civ 1646. The court decided that
the rule did not conflict with the Human
Rights Act; *South Lanarkshire Council v
DG* [2018] UKUT 417 (AAC); para A3/
3.269 GM
36 Reg 9(3) HB Regs; reg 9(3) HB(SPC)
Regs; *SD v London Borough of Brent*
[2009] UKUT 7 (AAC).
37 Reg 9(3) HB Regs; reg 9(3) HB(SPC)
Regs

38 Reg 2(1) HB Regs and reg 2(1),
definition of 'owner' and 'long tenancy',
HB(SPC) Regs; CH/1278/2002; CH/
0296/2003; *MH v Wirral MBC* [2009]
UKUT 60 (AAC); *Bradford MDC v MRC
(HB)* [2010] UKUT 315 (AAC);
Nottingham CC v CJ (HB) [2011] UKUT
392 (AAC); *GN v Sevenoaks BC (HB)*
[2016] UKUT 271 (AAC)
39 CH/3853/2001; CH/396/2002; R(H) 6/
07; *KH v Sheffield CC* [2008] UKUT 11
(AAC)
40 *RS v Fife Council and SSWP* [2018] UKUT
322 (AAC)
41 *CH v Wakefield DC* [2009] UKUT 20
(AAC)
42 Reg 2(1) HB Regs; reg 2(1) HB(SPC)
Regs
43 R(SB) 22/87; *Bristol CC v JKT (HB)* [2016]
UKUT 517 (AAC)
44 paras A3/3.243-45 GM
45 *R v Solihull MBC ex parte Simpson* [1995]
1 FLR 140 (CA); CH/39/2007
46 *R (Mackay) v Barking and Dagenham
HBRB* [2001] EWHC Admin 234
47 CH/2258/2004
48 *R (Mackay) v Barking and Dagenham
HBRB* [2001] EWHC Admin 234
49 *R v Sutton LBC HBRB ex parte Keegan*
[1992] 27 HLR 92 (QBD)
50 *R v Manchester CC ex parte Baragrove
Properties Ltd* [1991] 23 HLR 337 (QBD);
R v Gloucestershire CC ex parte Dadds
[1997] 29 HLR 700 (QBD); CH/39/2007
51 *R v Poole BC ex parte Ross* [1995] 28 HLR
351 (QBD)
52 s134(2) SSCBA 1992; reg 82(1) HB
Regs; reg 63(1) HB(SPC) Regs
53 s130(1) SSCBA 1992; reg 7(1) and (2)
HB Regs; reg 7(1) and (2) HB(SPC) Regs
54 R(H) 5/09; *Birmingham City Council v IB*
[2009] UKUT 116 (AAC)
55 Reg 7(5), (14) and (15)(c) HB Regs; reg
7(5), (14) and (15)(c) HB(SPC) Regs
56 CH/2201/2002
57 Regs 2(1) and 7(8) HB Regs; regs 2(1)
and 7(8) HB(SPC) Regs
58 *Bury MBC v DC (HB)* [2011] UKUT 43
(AAC); *R (Mahmoudi) v LB Lewisham and
Another* [2014] EWCA Civ 284
59 R(H) 9/05
60 Reg 7(7) HB Regs; reg 7(7) HB(SPC)
Regs; para A3/3.430 GM

61 Reg 7(11)(b) and (c), (13)(a) and (b), (13D)(a) and (b), (13G)(a) and (b), (16)(a)-(c) and (18) HB Regs; reg 7(11)(b) and (c), (13)(a) and (b), (13D)(a) and (b), (13G)(a) and (b), (16)(a)-(c) and (18) HB(SPC) Regs
62 R(H) 9/05
63 Reg 7(13) and (17) HB Regs; reg 7(13) and (17) HB(SPC) Regs
64 *KdeS v Camden LB (HB)* [2011] UKUT 457 (AAC)
65 *R v Penwith DC ex parte Burt* [1988] 22 HLR 292 (QBD); para A3/3.460 GM
66 Reg 7(14) and (15)(a) HB Regs; reg 7(14) and (15)(a) HB(SPC) Regs
67 R(H) 8/09; *SK v South Hams DC (HB)* [2010] UKUT 129 (AAC), reported as [2010] AACR 40
68 CH/1237/2004
69 CH/3893/2004
70 Reg 13 HB Regs; reg 13 HB(SPC) Regs
71 Reg 7(11) and (12) HB Regs; reg 7(11) and (12) HB(SPC) Regs
72 *SSWP v Selby DC and Bowman* [2006] EWCA Civ 271, reported as R(H) 4/06
73 Reg 7(16)(d)(i) and (17) HB Regs; reg 7(16)(d)(i) and (17) HB(SPC) Regs
74 Reg 7(16)(c)(ii), (iii), (vii) and (x) HB Regs; reg 7(16)(ii), (iii), (vii) and (x) HB(SPC) Regs
75 *Obrey and Others v SSWP* [2013] EWCA Civ 1584
76 Reg 7(16)(c)(i), (iv)-(vi), (viii)-(ix) and (16A) HB Regs; reg 7(16)(i), (iv)-(vi) and (viii)-(ix) and (16A) HB(SPC) Regs
77 Reg 7(14) and (15)(b) HB Regs; reg 7(14) and (15)(b) HB(SPC) Regs; CSH/499/2006
78 Reg 7(18) HB Regs; reg 7(18) HB(SPC) Regs
79 Reg 7 (13C)-(13E) HB Regs; reg 7 (13C)-(13E) HB(SPC) Regs
80 Reg 7(16)(d)(ii) and (iii), (17C) and (17D) HB Regs; reg 7(16)(d)(ii) and (iii), (17C) and (17D) HB(SPC) Regs
81 Reg 7(13F), (13G) and (18) HB Regs; reg 7(13F), (13G) and (18) HB(SPC) Regs
82 Reg 7(13D), (13G), (17C) and (17D) HB Regs; reg 7(13D), (13G), (17C) and (17D) HB(SPC) Regs; *Slough BC v PK* [2019] UKUT 128 (AAC)
83 Reg 7(13A) and (17A) HB Regs; reg 7(13A) and (17A) HB(SPC) Regs
84 Reg 7(13B) and (17B) HB Regs; reg 7(13B) and (17B) HB(SPC) Regs
85 R(H) 5/09; *Birmingham CC v IB* [2009] UKUT 116 (AAC)
86 Reg 7(6)(d) and (e) HB Regs; reg 7(6)(d) and (e) HB(SPC) Regs
87 CH/1911/2006
88 *R (Mahmoudi) v LB Lewisham and Another* [2014] EWCA Civ 284
89 Reg 7(6)(a) HB Regs; reg 7(6)(a) HB(SPC) Regs
90 Reg 7(6)(b) and (c) HB Regs; reg 7(6)(b) and (c) HB(SPC) Regs
91 Reg 7(10) HB Regs; reg 7(10) HB(SPC) Regs
92 Reg 7(3) and (4) HB Regs; reg 7(3) and (4) HB(SPC) Regs
93 R(SB) 10/81

2. The rules about your age
94 For working-age HB, see the HB Regs. For pension-age HB, see the HB(SPC) Regs.
95 Reg 5 HB Regs
96 Reg 5 HB(SPC) Regs
97 Art 6 WRA(No.31)O
98 Art 6(4) WRA(No.31)O
99 Art 8 WRA(No.31)O

4. The amount of benefit
100 Reg 70 HB Regs; reg 50 HB(SPC) Regs
101 Reg 12B(2) HB Regs; reg 12B(2) HB(SPC) Regs
102 Reg 12(2A) and (2B) HB Regs; reg 12(2A) and (2B) HB(SPC) Regs; reg 12(6A) and (6B) HB Regs, as set out in Sch 3 para 5(1) HB&CTB(CP) Regs
103 Regs 12B(3) and 12C(2) HB Regs; regs 12B(3) and 12C(2) HB(SPC) Regs; reg 12(4) HB Regs and reg 12(4) HB(SPC) Regs, as set out in Sch 3 para 5 HB&CTB(CP) Regs
104 Reg 11(3) HB Regs; reg 11(2) HB(SPC) Regs
105 Reg 2(1) HB Regs; reg 2(1) HB(SPC) Regs
106 Reg 80 HB Regs; reg 61 HB(SPC) Regs
107 Reg 81(3) and Sch 1 para 7(2) HB Regs; reg 62(3) and Sch 1 para 7(2) HB(SPC) Regs
108 Regs 12B(4) and 12C(2) HB Regs; regs 12B(4) and 12C(2) HB(SPC) Regs; reg 12(5) HB Regs and reg 12(5) HB(SPC) Regs, as set out in Sch 3 para 5 HB&CTB(CP) Regs; CH/3376/2002
109 *R (Naghshbandi) v Camden LBC* [2002] EWCA Civ 1038
110 CH/3376/2002

111 Reg 12B(2) HB Regs; reg 12B(2)
HB(SPC) Regs; reg 12(3) HB Regs and
reg 12(3) HB(SPC) Regs, as set out in
Sch 3 para 5 HB&CTB(CP) Regs; *R v
Bristol City Council ex parte Jacobs* [1999]
32 HLR 82 (QBD); *Liverpool City Council v
(1) NM, (2) WD (HB)* [2015] UKUT 532
(AAC), reported as [2016] AACR 19
112 Sch 1 para 5 HB Regs; Sch 1 para 5
HB(SPC) Regs
113 Sch 1 para 6(1) HB Regs; Sch 1 para 6(1)
HB(SPC) Regs
114 Sch 1 para 6(2) and (3) HB Regs; Sch 1
para 6(2) and (3) HB(SPC) Regs
115 paras A4/4.912-13 GM
116 Sch 1 paras 5 and 6(1)(b) HB Regs; Sch 1
paras 5 and 6(1)(b) HB(SPC) Regs
117 Sch 1 para 8 HB Regs; Sch 1 para 8
HB(SPC) Regs
118 Sch 1 para 8 HB Regs; Sch 1 para 8
HB(SPC) Regs. For the meaning of
'sheltered accommodation', see *Oxford
CC v Basey* [2012] EWCA Civ 115,
reported as [2012] AACR 38.
119 para A4/4.730 GM; *CP and Others v
Aylesbury Vale DC v SSWP (HB)* [2011]
UKUT 22 (AAC); *Liverpool City Council v
(1) NM, (2) WD (HB)* [2015] UKUT 532
(AAC), reported as [2016] AACR 19
120 Sch 1 para 1(a)(iii) HB Regs; Sch 1 para
1(a)(iii) HB(SPC) Regs
121 Sch 1 para 1(a)(ii) HB Regs; Sch 1 para
1(a)(ii) HB(SPC) Regs
122 Sch 1 para 1(b) HB Regs; Sch 1 para 1(b)
HB(SPC) Regs
123 Sch 1 para 1(a)(iv) HB Regs; Sch 1 para
1(a)(iv) HB(SPC) Regs
124 Reg 12B(2)(b) and Sch 1 para 1 HB Regs;
reg 12B(2)(b) and Sch 1 para 1 HB(SPC)
Regs; reg 12(3)(b) HB Regs and reg
12(3)(b) HB(SPC) Regs, as set out in Sch
3 para 5 HB&CTB(CP) Regs
125 Reg 12B(2)(c) and Sch 1 para 3(2) HB
Regs; reg 12B(2)(c) and Sch 1 para 3(2)
HB(SPC) Regs; reg 12(3)(c) HB Regs and
reg 12(3)(c) HB(SPC) Regs, as set out in
Sch 3 para 5 HB&CTB(CP) Regs
126 Sch 1 para 3 HB Regs; Sch 1 para 3
HB(SPC) Regs
127 Sch 1 paras 1(a)(i) and 2(1) HB Regs;
Sch 1 paras 1(a)(i) and 2(1) HB(SPC)
Regs
128 Sch 1 para 2(6) and (7) HB Regs; Sch 1
para 2(6) and (7) HB(SPC) Regs

129 s130(3) SSCBA 1992; Schs 4 para 12, 5
para 4, and 6 para 5 HB Regs; reg 26
HB(SPC) Regs; *R v Penwith DC ex parte
Menear* [1991] 24 HLR 120 (QBD); *R v
South Ribble DC HBRB ex parte Hamilton*
[2000] 33 HLR 104 (CA); *DF v LB of
Waltham Forest (HB)* [2017] UKUT 306
(AAC)
130 Reg 2(3), (3A) and (3B) HB Regs; reg
2(3) and (3A) HB(SPC) Regs; *SMcH v
Perth and Kinross Council (HB)* [2015]
UKUT 126 (AAC)
131 s130(3) SSCBA 1992; reg 71 HB Regs;
reg 51 HB(SPC) Regs
132 Reg 70 HB Regs; reg 50 HB(SPC) Regs
133 Reg 3(1) HB Regs; reg 3(1) HB(SPC)
Regs
134 Reg 3(4) and Sch 1 para 8 HB Regs; reg
3(4) and Sch 1 para 8 HB(SPC) Regs;
CPC/1446/2008; *AM v SSWP (IS)* [2011]
UKUT 387 (AAC)
135 CSIS/185/1995
136 *Thamesdown BC v Goonery* [1995] 1 CLY
2600 (CA); *RK v SSWP* [2008] UKUT 34
(AAC)
137 CIS/14850/1996
138 para A5/5.521 GM
139 R(H) 8/09; *SK v South Hams DC (HB)*
[2010] UKUT 129 (AAC), reported as
[2010] AACR 40
140 Reg 3(2) HB Regs; reg 3(2) HB(SPC)
Regs
141 *JP v Bournemouth BC (HB)* [2018] UKUT
75 (AAC), reported as [2018] AACR 30
142 *R v Chesterfield BC ex parte Fullwood*
[1993] 26 HLR 126
143 Reg 3(3) HB Regs; reg 3(3) HB(SPC)
Regs
144 Regs 2(1), definition of 'attendance
allowance', and 74(6) HB Regs; regs
2(1), definition of 'attendance
allowance', and 55(6) HB(SPC) Regs
145 Reg 74(7) and (10) HB Regs; reg 55(7)
and (9) HB(SPC) Regs
146 s2 ETA 1973; s2 Enterprise and New
Towns (Scotland) Act 1990
147 Reg 74(1) HB Regs; reg 55(1) HB(SPC)
Regs
148 Reg 74(1) and (2) HB Regs; reg 55(1)
and (2) HB(SPC) Regs
149 Reg 6(6) HB Regs; reg 6(6) HB(SPC)
Regs
150 Reg 74(9) HB Regs; reg 55(10) HB(SPC)
Regs
151 CH/48/2006
152 Reg 74(3) HB Regs; reg 55(3) HB(SPC)
Regs

153 Reg 74(4) HB Regs; reg 55(4) HB(SPC) Regs
154 Reg 74(5) HB Regs; reg 55(5) HB(SPC) Regs
155 Reg 59(10)-(13) HB(SPC) Regs
156 Reg 26 HB Regs; reg 24 HB(SPC) Regs

6. Claims and backdating

157 s1 SSAA 1992
158 Reg 83(1) and (9) HB Regs; reg 64(2) and (10) HB(SPC) Regs
159 Reg 83(4A) and (4B) HB Regs; reg 64(5A) and (5C) HB(SPC) Regs
160 Reg 83A and Sch 11 HB Regs; reg 64A and Sch 10 HB(SPC) Regs
161 Reg 83(1) HB Regs; reg 64(2) HB(SPC) Regs
162 Reg 83(2) HB Regs; reg 64(3) HB(SPC) Regs
163 paras A2/2.560-65 GM
164 Reg 83(4AA), (4AB) and (4BA) HB Regs; reg 64(5B), (5BA) and (5CA) HB(SPC) Regs
165 Reg 83(4AC)-(4AE) HB Regs; reg 64(5BB)-(5BD) HB(SPC) Regs; Explanatory Memorandum to SI 2008 No.2299
166 Reg 83(1), (4C), (6) and (9) HB Regs; reg 64(2), (5D), (7) and (10) HB(SPC) Regs
167 Reg 83(4D), (4DA), (7) and (7A) HB Regs; reg 64(5E), (5EA), (8) and (8A) HB(SPC) Regs
168 Reg 83(4E), (4F), (8) and (8A) HB Regs; reg 64(5F), (5G), (9) and (9A) HB(SPC) Regs
169 Reg 87(1) and (3) HB Regs; reg 68(1) and (3) HB(SPC) Regs
170 Reg 87(4)-(6) HB Regs; reg 68(4)-(6) HB(SPC) Regs
171 Reg 83(4)(b) HB Regs; reg 64(5)(b) HB(SPC) Regs
172 Regs 2, definition of 'appropriate DWP office', and 83(4)(a), (f) and (g) and (13) HB Regs; regs 2, definition of 'appropriate DWP office', and 64(5)(a), (f) and (g) and (14) HB(SPC) Regs
173 Reg 83(4)(c) HB Regs; reg 64(5)(c) HB(SPC) Regs
174 Reg 83A and Sch 11 HB Regs; reg 64A and Sch 10 HB(SPC) Regs
175 Reg 83(4A) and (4AA) HB Regs; reg 64(5A) and (5B) HB(SPC) Regs
176 Reg 82(1) HB Regs; reg 63(1) HB(SPC) Regs; CH/2995/2006
177 Reg 82(2), (3), (5) and (6) HB Regs; reg 63(2), (3), (5) and (6) HB(SPC) Regs
178 Reg 82(4) HB Regs; reg 63(4) HB(SPC) Regs

179 Reg 82(4)(c) HB Regs; reg 63(4)(c) HB(SPC) Regs
180 s1(1A)-(1C) SSAA 1992
181 Reg 86(1A) HB Regs; reg 67(1A) HB(SPC) Regs; CH v Plymouth City Council and DE [2018] UKUT 215 (AAC)
182 Reg 86(1) HB Regs; reg 67(1) HB(SPC) Regs
183 AA v LB Hounslow [2008] UKUT 13 (AAC)
184 Reg 4(1)(a) HB Regs; reg 4(1)(a) HB(SPC) Regs
185 para A1/1.300 GM
186 Reg 83(5)(d) and (e) HB Regs; reg 64(6)(d) and (e) HB(SPC) Regs
187 Reg 83(5)(a)-(c) and (5A) HB Regs; reg 64(6)(a)-(c) HB(SPC) Regs
188 Leicester CC v LG [2009] UKUT 155 (AAC)
189 Reg 64(1) HB(SPC) Regs
190 Regs 57 and 64(1), (1A) and (6) HB(SPC) Regs; Leicester CC v LG [2009] UKUT 155 (AAC)
191 Reg 83(12) HB Regs
192 Reg 83(12A) HB Regs
193 R(S) 2/63 (T); CH/2659/2002; CH/474/2002; CH/393/2003; A2/Annex A GM
194 UH v LB Islington (HB) [2010] UKUT 64 (AAC)
195 CH/474/2002
196 R(G) 1/75
197 FR v Broadband DC [2012] UKUT 449 (AAC)
198 R(SB) 6/83; CS/50/1950; R(U) 9/74; CI/146/1991; CI/142/1993; FC/39/1993; R v Canterbury CC ex parte Goodman, 11 July 1995, unreported (QBD)
199 R(U) 5/56; R(S) 5/56
200 CI/37/1995
201 R(P) 2/85
202 R(S) 10/59; R(SB) 17/83
203 Reg 83(10) and (11) HB Regs; reg 64(11) and (12) HB(SPC) Regs
204 CG/1479/1999; CIS/217/1999
205 Reg 89 HB Regs; reg 70 HB(SPC) Regs
206 Reg 90 HB Regs; reg 71 HB(SPC) Regs; reg 10 HB&CTB(DA) Regs
207 Reg 90(2) HB Regs; reg 71(2) HB(SPC) Regs; reg 10 HB&CTB(DA) Regs
208 Reg 3 HB&CTB(DA) Regs
209 CH/180/2006
210 Reg 10(1) HB&CTB(DA) Regs
211 Sch 9 paras 9-15 HB Regs; Sch 8 paras 9-15 HB(SPC) Regs; reg 10(1) HB&CTB(DA) Regs

212 Reg 76 HB Regs; reg 57 HB(SPC) Regs; R(H) 9/07; *SL v Renfrewshire Council (HB)* [2014] UKUT 411 (AAC)
213 Regs 2(1), definition of 'benefit week', and 80(2), (3)(a), (4) and (8) HB Regs; regs 2(1), definition of 'benefit week', and 61(2), (3)(a), (4) and (8) HB(SPC) Regs

7. Getting paid
214 Reg 75 HB Regs; reg 56 HB(SPC) Regs
215 Reg 92(1) and (6) HB Regs; reg 73(1) and (6) HB(SPC) Regs
216 Reg 92(3) and (4) HB Regs; reg 73(3) and (4) HB(SPC) Regs
217 s134(1A) SSAA 1992
218 s134(1B) SSAA 1992; regs 91A and 94(1) HB Regs; regs 72A and 75(1) HB(SPC) Regs
219 Reg 91(2) HB Regs; reg 72(2) HB(SPC) Regs
220 Reg 92(5) HB Regs; reg 73(5) HB(SPC) Regs
221 Reg 91(1)(b) HB Regs; reg 72(1)(b) HB(SPC) Regs
222 para A6/6.120 GM
223 Reg 94(2) HB Regs; reg 75(2) HB(SPC) Regs
224 Reg 94(3) HB Regs; reg 75(3) HB(SPC) Regs
225 Reg 97 HB Regs; reg 78 HB(SPC) Regs
226 *R v Haringey LBC ex parte Azad Ayub* [1992] 25 HLR 566 (QBD)
227 R(H) 1/08
228 Reg 96(2) HB Regs; reg 77(2) HB(SPC) Regs
229 Reg 95 HB Regs; reg 76 HB(SPC) Regs; Sch 9 SS(C&P) Regs; *R v Haringey LBC ex parte Azad Ayub* [1992] 25 HLR 566 (QBD)
230 CH 3244/2007; *ST v SCC (CH)* [2019] UKUT 33 (AAC)
231 Reg 96(1)(a) and (b) and (3A)(a) HB Regs; reg 77(1)(a) and (b) and (3A)(a) HB(SPC) Regs
232 *DLT v Eastleigh BC (HB)* [2014] UKUT 242 (AAC)
233 Regs 95(2A) and 96(3A)(b) HB Regs; regs 76(2A) and 77(3A)(b) HB(SPC) Regs
234 Regs 95(2A) and 96(1)(c) HB Regs; regs 76(2A) and 77(1)(c) HB(SPC) Regs
235 *E v Dacorum BC & M* [2017] UKUT 93 (AAC)
236 Regs 95(3) and 96(3) HB Regs; regs 76(3) and 77(3) HB(SPC) Regs
237 Reg 96(3) HB Regs; reg 77(3) HB(SPC) Regs

238 para A6/6.212 GM
239 Reg 54(6) HB(SPC) Regs
240 Reg 54(1) and (2) HB(SPC) Regs
241 Regs 2(1), definition of 'benefit week', and 54(3)-(5) HB(SPC) Regs
242 s32(4) WRA 2007
243 Reg 72 HB Regs
244 Reg 73 HB Regs; reg 53 HB(SPC) Regs
245 Regs 72(4) and 73(2) HB Regs; reg 53(2) HB(SPC) Regs; CH/1762/2004
246 Regs 72A, 72B(6), 73A and 73B(6) HB Regs; regs 53A and 53B(6) HB(SPC) Regs
247 Regs 72B and 73B HB Regs; regs 52 and 53B HB(SPC) Regs
248 Regs 72E and 73E HB Regs
249 Regs 72D(2) and 73D(2) HB Regs; regs 52 and 53D(2) HB(SPC) Regs
250 Regs 72B(5) and 73B(5) HB Regs; reg 53B(5) HB(SPC) Regs
251 Regs 72C and 73C HB Regs; regs 52 and 53C HB(SPC) Regs
252 s34(3) WRA 2007; reg 2(1) HB Regs and reg 2(1), definitions of 'mover' and 'second authority', HB(SPC) Regs
253 s32(1), (2) and (13) WRA 2007; regs 72D and 73D HB Regs; reg 53D HB(SPC) Regs
254 Regs 72B(7) and 73B(7) HB Regs; regs 52(3) and 53B(7) HB(SPC) Regs
255 Regs 8(2A), 8A, 44, 46(1)(a) and 47(2)(a) UC(TP) Regs
256 Reg 75F(1)(g) HB Regs
257 Regs 89(2), 90(1) and 91(3) HB Regs; regs 70(2), 71(1) and 72(3) HB(SPC) Regs
258 Reg 93(1) HB Regs; reg 74(1) HB(SPC) Regs
259 *R v Haringey LBC ex parte Azad Ayub* [1992] 25 HLR 566 (QBD)
260 Reg 93(1) HB Regs; reg 74(1) HB(SPC) Regs; *R v Haringey LBC ex parte Azad Ayub* [1992] 25 HLR 566 (QBD)
261 Reg 93(2) HB Regs; reg 74(2) HB(SPC) Regs
262 Reg 93(3) HB Regs; reg 74(3) HB(SPC) Regs
263 Reg 88(1) HB Regs; reg 69(1) HB(SPC) Regs; reg 4 SS(NCC) Regs
264 Regs 86(2) and 90 and Sch 9 paras 9(1)(g) and 10(a) HB Regs; regs 67(3) and 71 and Sch 8 paras 9(1)(g) and 10(a) HB(SPC) Regs
265 Regs 2(1), 86(3) and 88(1) HB Regs; regs 2(1), 67(3) and 69(1) HB(SPC) Regs
266 Reg 88(1) HB Regs; reg 69(1) HB(SPC) Regs

267 Reg 88(1) HB Regs; reg 69(1) HB(SPC)
Regs

268 Reg 88A and Sch 11 HB Regs; reg 69A
and Sch 10 HB(SPC) Regs

269 Reg 88(6) HB Regs; reg 69(9) HB(SPC)
Regs

270 Reg 88ZA HB Regs; reg 69ZA HB(SPC)
Regs

271 Reg 69(6)-(8) HB(SPC) Regs

272 Reg 69(7) HB(SPC) Regs

273 Reg 88(1), (3) and (4) HB Regs; reg
69(1), (3) and (4) HB(SPC) Regs

274 Regs 2(1), definition of 'benefit week',
and 79(1) HB Regs; regs 2(1), definition
of 'benefit week', and 59(1) HB(SPC)
Regs; reg 8(2) HB&CTB(DA) Regs

275 Reg 79(8) HB Regs; reg 59(8) HB(SPC)
Regs

276 Reg 79(4) and (8) HB Regs; reg 59(4)
and (8) HB(SPC) Regs

277 Reg 59(10)-(13) HB(SPC) Regs

278 Regs 5(2)(a) and 7 UC(TP) Regs

279 Regs 5(2) and 7(5)(b) UC(TP) Regs

280 Reg 60 HB(SPC) Regs

281 Regs 7(2)(o) and 8(14D) HB&CTB(DA)
Regs; reg 79(2), (2A), (2B), (8) and (9)
HB Regs; reg 59(2), (2A), (2B), (8) and
(9) HB(SPC) Regs

3

Chapter 11

Income support

This chapter covers:
1. Who can get income support (below)
2. The rules about your age (p238)
3. People included in the claim (p239)
4. The amount of benefit (p240)
5. Special benefit rules (p241)
6. Claims and backdating (p241)
7. Getting paid (p245)
8. Tax, other benefits and the benefit cap (p247)

Key facts

- Income support (IS) is a benefit for people on a low income who are in one of the specific groups of people who can qualify.
- IS is a means-tested benefit.
- You do not have to have paid national insurance contributions to qualify.
- You cannot qualify for IS if you (or your partner) count as being in full-time paid work.
- IS is administered and paid by the DWP.
- If you disagree with an IS decision, you can apply for a revision or a supersession (see Chapter 56), or appeal against it (see Chapter 57). You must apply for a mandatory reconsideration before you can appeal.

---

1. Who can get income support

You qualify for income support (IS) if:[1]
- you are in one of the specific groups of people who can qualify for IS (see pp234–38); *and*
- neither you nor your partner count as being in full-time paid work (see p238 and Chapter 44); *and*
- you are not studying full time. There are exceptions to this rule (see p890). See p891 if you are studying part time and p885 if you are at school or college in 'relevant education'; *and*

- you are not entitled to jobseeker's allowance (JSA) or employment and support allowance (ESA); *and*
- your partner is not entitled to income-based JSA, joint-claim JSA, income-related ESA or pension credit (PC); *and*
- you are at least 16 and are under pension age (see p779); *and*
- your income is less than your applicable amount (see p240); *and*
- your savings and other capital are worth £16,000 or less. Some capital (including your home) is ignored (see Chapter 22); *and*
- you satisfy the 'habitual residence' and the 'right to reside' tests, and are present in Great Britain. To find out if you are exempt from the tests, see Chapter 68. To see whether you can claim IS during a temporary absence abroad, see p1653; *and*
- you are not a 'person subject to immigration control' (see p1560). There are exceptions to this rule.

In some cases, in order to get IS, you (and your partner) may be required to attend a work-focused interview (see p1136). If the only reason you are getting IS is because you are a lone parent and you do not have any children under the age of three, you may also be required to undertake work-related activity (see p1140).

Income support and universal credit

You can now only make a new claim for IS in limited circumstances (see below).

If you are already entitled to IS, you can continue to qualify until:

– you claim universal credit (UC); *or*

– you become a member of a couple and your partner is getting UC; *or*

– you and your partner are affected by the 'managed migration' transfer process (see p30).

The government says that from November 2020 the DWP will begin to transfer existing IS claims to UC. This transfer process began in July 2019 in pilot areas, for a limited number of claimants. See p30 for further information, and AskCPAG.org.uk and CPAG's *Welfare Rights Bulletin* for updates.

You cannot usually qualify for IS if you are pension age or over. However, if you are already getting IS and you become a member of a 'mixed-age couple' (ie, you have reached pension age but your partner has not), in some circumstances, your IS can continue even though you have reached pension age (see p238).

Who can make a new claim for income support

You can only make a new claim for IS if any of the following apply.[2]

- You are prevented from claiming UC because:
  – you (or your partner) are, or within the last month have been, entitled to IS, income-based JSA, income-related ESA or housing benefit (HB) that includes

Part 3: Other means-tested benefits and tax credits
Chapter 11: Income support
1. Who can get income support

a severe disability premium (see p346), and if your entitlement to the benefit ended during that month you (or s/he) have continued to satisfy the conditions for that premium; *and*
- you (and your partner) have not yet been given a 'migration notice' from the DWP that you will be transferred to UC via the 'managed migration' process (see p30).

The above may apply, for example, if you are claiming IS after a break in your entitlement, you are currently entitled to HB, or you have been getting income-based JSA or income-related ESA but no longer qualify.

Note: this rule only applies until 27 January 2021.

- You are prevented from claiming UC because you (or if you are in a couple, you and your partner) are in a specified category where claims are not accepted, are a 'frontier worker' – ie, you work in Great Britain or Norther Ireland but do not live there.

If you cannot make a new claim for IS under these rules, you can make a claim for UC.

Groups of people who can qualify for income support

Only certain groups of people can qualify for IS. Broadly these are:
- people who are sick or disabled (see p235);
- pregnant women and certain people who are looking after children (see p235);
- carers (see p236);
- certain pupils, students and people on training courses (see p237);
- other groups – eg, people in custody pending trial or sentence, refugees learning English and some people involved in a trade dispute (see p237).

Even if you are in one of the above groups, you must also satisfy the other rules for getting IS described on p232.[3]

Note:
- If you come into one of the groups on any day in a benefit week (see p454), you count as doing so for the whole week.
- If your circumstances change and you no longer come into a particular group, check whether you are in any of the other groups. If so, your entitlement to IS continues.[4]
- If you are a member of a couple and you are not in one of the groups of people who can qualify for IS, but your partner is, s/he could be the claimant. Whichever one of you gets IS, the other may qualify for national insurance (NI) credits to protect her/his NI record (see Chapter 43).
- In the past, there were additional groups of people who could qualify for IS. If you are getting IS on the basis of being in one of these 'transitional groups' (see p238), you may continue to qualify on this basis.

People who are sick or disabled

You can qualify for IS if either of the following applies to you.[5]

- You are entitled to statutory sick pay.
- You are receiving the enhanced rate of the daily living component of personal independence payment (PIP). This only applies if, immediately before you started getting PIP, you were entitled to and in receipt of IS because you were receiving disability living allowance (DLA) highest rate care component and were therefore treated as incapable of work.

Pregnant women and certain people looking after children

You can qualify for IS if any of the following apply to you.[6]

- You are pregnant and:
  - incapable of work because of your pregnancy;[7] or
  - there are 11 weeks or less before the week your baby is due.
- You were pregnant and your pregnancy ended not more than 15 weeks ago – ie, when your baby was born or you had a miscarriage.
- You are a lone parent aged 18 or over and have at least one child under five, or you are a lone parent under the age of 18 and have a child of any age. Your child must be included in your claim (see p323).[8] You do not have to be the child's parent – eg, you could be her/his grandparent or sister or brother.
- You are entitled to and are on 'parental leave' from work under specific provisions (this does *not* include shared parental leave) and:
  - during the period for which you are claiming IS, you are not entitled to any kind of payment from your employer; *and*
  - you and your child(ren) live in the same household (see p327); *and*
  - you were entitled to working tax credit (WTC), child tax credit (CTC) of more than £545 a year or HB on the day before your parental leave began.
- You are entitled to and are on paternity leave[9] and:
  - you are not entitled to statutory paternity pay or to any kind of payment from your employer during the period for which you are claiming IS; *or*
  - you were entitled to WTC, CTC of more than £545 a year or HB on the day before your paternity leave began.
- You are a lone foster parent – ie, a child under 16 has been placed with you by a local authority or voluntary organisation, or because of an order or warrant under the Children's Hearings (Scotland) Act 2011, and you are not a member of a couple. The child must be living with you or accommodated by you.[10]
- A child has been placed with you for adoption by an adoption agency and you are not a member of a couple.

Part 3: Other means-tested benefits and tax credits
Chapter 11: Income support
1. Who can get income support

What happens when you no longer qualify for income support as a lone parent?

1. Unless you are under 18, once your only or youngest child turns five, you cannot qualify for IS unless you are in one of the other groups of people who can qualify – eg, if you are a carer. You can continue to qualify for IS on that basis, even if you can no longer qualify as a lone parent.[11]

2. If you no longer qualify for IS, you may be able to qualify for JSA or ESA (if you can still make a new claim) or for UC. If you qualify for UC or JSA, there are special rules that may help you satisfy the work-related requirements or jobseeking conditions (see Chapters 46 and 48).

You can qualify for IS for a temporary period while any of the following apply to you.[12]

- You are looking after a child under 16 because her/his parent or the person who usually looks after her/him is temporarily ill or temporarily away.[13]
- A child under 16 is included in your claim (see p323) and your partner is temporarily out of the UK.
- You are looking after your partner, or a child (this includes a 'qualifying young person') who is included in your claim (see p323), who is temporarily ill.[14]

Carers

You can qualify for IS if you are a carer and either of the following applies to you.[15]

- You receive carer's allowance (CA), or you would receive it had you not been given a sanction for a benefit offence (see p1278).
- The person you care for:
  - receives attendance allowance (AA), the highest or middle rate care component of DLA, the daily living component of PIP, or armed forces independence payment; *or*
  - has been awarded AA, the highest or middle rate care component of DLA or either rate of the daily living component of PIP on an advance claim, but payments have not yet been made; *or*
  - has claimed AA, DLA, PIP or armed forces independence payment. You can qualify for IS for up to 26 weeks from the date of that claim or until the claim is decided, whichever comes first.

You must be 'regularly and substantially engaged' in providing care. If you do not receive CA, the decision maker must look at the quality and quantity of care you provide. This could be less than the 35 hours a week needed to qualify for CA.[16]

If you stop meeting these conditions or stop being a carer, you can continue to qualify for IS for a further eight weeks.[17] After that, you cannot get IS unless you come into one of the other groups of people who can qualify for IS.

Pupils, students and people on training courses

You can qualify for IS if any of the following apply to you.[18]

- You are in 'relevant education' (see p885) or you are a full-time student who can qualify for IS while studying (see p890).
- You are on a course of full-time, non-advanced education (or were accepted or enrolled on it) and you are under 21, or you are 21 but turned 21 while on such a course. This only applies if:
  - you are an orphan and have no one acting as your parent; *or*
  - you have to live away from your parents and any person acting in their place because you are estranged from them, are in physical or moral danger or there is a serious risk to your physical or mental health; *or*
  - you live away from your parents and any person acting in their place, they are unable to support you financially and:
    - they are chronically sick, or are mentally or physically disabled – ie, they could get a disability or a higher pensioner premium, or they are entitled to ESA including a work-related activity or support component (or would be but for their one-year's entitlement to contributory ESA expiring), or they are 'substantially and permanently disabled'; *or*
    - they are detained in custody under a sentence from the court or while they are awaiting trial or sentence; *or*
    - they are not allowed to come to Great Britain because they do not have leave to enter under the Immigration Rules.
- You are aged 16 to 24 and on a training course provided by the Secretary of State, the Welsh Ministers or, in Scotland, by a local enterprise company. This does not apply if you count as a child for child benefit purposes (see p579), or if you count as being in full-time paid work. If you receive a training allowance while on a course, your income may be too high for you to qualify for IS. However, you may qualify if, for example, you qualify for a disability premium (see p341).

Others

You can qualify for IS if any of the following apply to you.[19]

- You are entitled to, and are on, parental bereavement leave from work and:
  - you are not entitled to statutory parental bereavement pay or to any kind of payment from your employer during the period for which you are on leave and claiming IS; *or*
  - you were entitled to WTC, CTC of more than £545 a year or HB on the day before your parental bereavement leave began.
- You have to go to a court or tribunal as a Justice of the Peace, juror, witness or party to the proceedings.
- You have been remanded in custody, or committed in custody, but only until your trial or until you have been sentenced. You can only get IS for your housing costs – eg, for your ground rent or service charges (see Chapter 18).

Part 3: Other means-tested benefits and tax credits
Chapter 11: Income support
2. The rules about your age

- You are a refugee who is learning English in order to obtain employment. You must be on a course for more than 15 hours a week and, at the time the course started, you must have been in Great Britain for a year or less. You can only get IS for up to nine months under this rule.
- You qualify for 'housing costs run-on' – eg, for ground rent or service charges (see p376 and p998).
- You are involved in a trade dispute or you have been back at work for 15 days or less following a trade dispute (see p1001).

Transitional groups

In the past, there were additional groups of people who could qualify for IS – ie, if you were claiming IS 'on the grounds of disability', as a disabled worker, as a full-time student, in relevant education or as a lone parent of a child aged five or over. If you came into one of these 'transitional groups', you could continue to qualify for IS on this basis even though a new claim could no longer be made by someone in these circumstances. See previous editions of this *Handbook* for further information.

Full-time paid work

You cannot usually qualify for IS if you or your partner are in, or are treated as being in, full-time paid work. If you are the IS claimant, this means 16 hours or more each week. For your partner, this means 24 hours or more each week. If you and your partner work fewer hours than these limits, you may be able to get IS. See Chapter 44 for the rules on work and how your hours are calculated. **Note:** in some situations you are treated as *not* being in full-time work even if you work 16/24 hours or more (see p998).

If you or your partner have just taken up full-time paid work, you may be able to qualify for IS for help with your housing costs (eg, for ground rent or service charges) for the first four weeks (called 'housing costs run-on' in this *Handbook* – see p376).

---

2. The rules about your age

You must be at least 16 to qualify for income support (IS). There are some special rules if you are aged 16 or 17 (see below).

You cannot claim, or continue to get IS, if you are pension age or over (see p779). Instead, you may be able to claim pension credit (see Chapter 13). However, if you are already getting IS and you are, or become, a member of a 'mixed-age couple' (ie, you have reached pension age but your partner has not) and you are prevented from claiming UC (see p233), you are treated as not yet pension age and your IS continues.[20]

16/17-year-olds

If you are 16 or 17, you can qualify for IS in your own right if you satisfy the rules of entitlement described in this chapter.[21] You should not have your claim refused or be turned away by the DWP simply because of your age or because you have been included in someone else's benefit or tax credit claim.

Note:

- If you have been, or are being, looked after by a local authority, you cannot usually get IS. Instead, your local authority should support and accommodate you. See p949 for when you are not excluded from IS.
- In certain circumstances, you may satisfy the rules for both IS and income-based jobseeker's allowance (JSA). You do not have to be available for and actively seeking work and training to qualify for IS and therefore do not risk benefit sanctions. You can still look for work. If you claim IS rather than JSA, however, you might not receive national insurance credits (see Chapter 43).

3. People included in the claim

If you are single, you claim income support (IS) for yourself. If you are a member of a couple, either you can claim IS for both of you or, if your partner also satisfies the qualifying conditions for IS, s/he can claim for you both. If you are in a couple, your applicable amount includes a personal allowance for a couple and can include premiums based on both your and your partner's circumstances. When your benefit is worked out, your partner's income and capital are usually added to yours.

IS does not normally include amounts for your child(ren). However, there are some situations when you must show that you are responsible for a child who is living in your household – eg:

- to be in one of the groups of people who can qualify for IS – eg, to show you are looking after your child who is temporarily ill or that you are a lone parent (see pp235–36);
- to show you are a lone parent so you can benefit from a higher earnings disregard (see p430);
- for some of the rules for help with housing costs – eg, for ground rent or service charges (see Chapter 18).

You do not have to be the child's parent. For who counts as a child, see p324. For when you count as responsible for a child and when s/he counts as living in your household, see pp326–29.

Part 3: Other means-tested benefits and tax credits
Chapter 11: Income support
4. The amount of benefit

4. The amount of benefit

Income support (IS) tops up your income to a level that is set by the government. The amount you get depends on your needs (your 'applicable amount') and on how much income and capital you (and your partner) have.[22] There are three steps involved in working out your IS.

Step one: calculate your applicable amount
Your applicable amount consists of:
- a personal allowance (see p333); *plus*
- premiums (see p339) for any special needs; *plus*
- housing costs – eg, for your ground rent or service charges (see Chapter 18). You cannot get IS for help with your mortgage or loan for repairs and improvements. Instead, the DWP may offer you a loan to help meet your mortgage interest payments (see p855). You cannot get help with your rent. Instead, you may qualify for housing benefit (see Chapter 10).

Note: if it is not possible to assess your housing costs accurately or your entitlement to the severe disability premium (see p346), the DWP can exclude these from your IS until they can be calculated.[23]

Do you have children?
IS does not include allowances and premiums for your children. Instead, you may qualify for child tax credit (CTC) if you can still make a claim (see p285). However, in some cases, you can continue to get allowances and premiums for your children unless you are awarded CTC (see p333). If you *do* get allowances and premiums for your children, there are special rules for how their income and capital are treated (see p420 and p490).

Step two: calculate your income
This is the amount you (and your partner) have coming in each week from, for instance, other benefits, part-time earnings and maintenance (see Chapter 20). If you have capital over £6,000 (£10,000 if you live in a care home), it also includes your 'tariff income' (see p443).

Step three: deduct income from applicable amount

Example
Mr and Mrs Hughes, aged 27 and 29, have a daughter aged 10. Mr Hughes has been caring for his daughter, who is severely disabled. He gets carer's allowance (CA) of £67.25. Mrs Hughes gets child benefit and CTC, as well as disability living allowance (DLA) for her daughter. The couple live in rented accommodation. Their applicable amount is:

Personal allowance	£116.80
Carer premium	£37.50
Total	£154.30

Their income (CA) to be taken into account is £67.25. Child benefit, CTC and DLA are all ignored.

Their IS is £154.30 (applicable amount) *minus* £67.25 (income) = £87.05

If your income is too high for you to qualify for IS currently, you might qualify once you, your partner or a child included in your claim become entitled to another benefit (a 'qualifying benefit') because you are then entitled to premiums. Make your claim for IS at the same time as your claim for the qualifying benefit (see p1180).

You might get a reduced amount of IS if:

- you (or, in some cases, your partner) were required to take part in a work-focused interview and you failed to do so without good cause (see p1157); *or*
- you are a lone parent without any children under three, you were required to undertake work-related activity and you failed to do so without good cause (see p1160); *or*
- you have committed a benefit offence (see p1278).

Different rules for calculating your benefit can apply if you are in one of the groups to whom special rules apply (see below).

5. Special benefit rules

Special rules may apply to:

- 16/17-year-olds who have been, or are being, looked after by a local authority (see p947);
- people subject to immigration control (see Chapter 67);
- people who have come from or are going abroad (see Chapters 68 and 69);
- people who are studying (see Chapter 41);
- people involved in a trade dispute (see p1001);
- people without accommodation, people who (or whose partner or children) are in hospital or living in a care home or other similar accommodation, and people in prison or detention (see Chapter 42).

6. Claims and backdating

The general rules about claims and backdating are covered in Chapter 50. This section explains the specific rules that apply to income support (IS).

Part 3: Other means-tested benefits and tax credits
Chapter 11: Income support
6. Claims and backdating

Making a claim

A claim for IS can be made:

- by phone on 0800 169 0350 (Welsh language: 0800 012 1888; textphone: 0800 023 4888; Relay UK (if you cannot hear or speak on the phone): 18001 then 0800 169 0350), Monday to Friday, 8am to 6pm.[24] You are sent a written statement of your circumstances for you to approve and sign; *or*
- by completing a paper claim form approved by the DWP.[25] Send your completed form to your local Jobcentre Plus office. You may also be able to claim at an alternative office (see p1168). Return the form within one month of your initial contact or you may lose benefit. Keep a copy in case queries arise.

In practice, the DWP prefers you to start your claim by phone. There is no rule that says you must do so, but it is best to make your claim in this way if you can.

You must provide any information or evidence required (see p1170). You can amend or withdraw your claim before a decision is made (see p1169). If there is a delay in making a decision, you may be able to get a short-term advance (see p1192).

Forms

Get Form A1 from a Jobcentre Plus office or download it at gov.uk/income-support/how-to-claim. Phone if you need an alternative format – eg, Braille, large print or audio CD. You may also be able to get the form at your local Citizens Advice, welfare rights service or advice centre.

Note:

- You can make initial contact with the DWP by phone or letter to say you want to claim. The date of your initial contact is important because it usually determines the date on which your claim is treated as having been made (see p243).
- If you download a form, or get one from, for example, an advice centre, it is important to phone the DWP to ensure your date of claim is the earliest possible date (see p243). You are given your date of initial contact to enter on the form.
- If you claim IS by phone, a claim for housing benefit (HB) claim can usually be completed at the same time and passed to the local authority on your behalf. Otherwise, you must make a separate claim to your local authority.

Who should claim

If you are a single person or a lone parent, you claim on your own behalf. If you are one of a couple, you must choose which one of you claims for you both. See p319 for who counts as a couple. If you have a choice about who can claim and you cannot agree, the DWP decides.[26] If you are unable to manage your own affairs, another person can claim IS for you as your 'appointee' (see p1170).

Can you change who claims?

You can change which partner claims, provided the partner previously claiming agrees and the partner who wants to claim is still able to make a new claim (see p233).[27] You should both get advice about how you would be better off financially and on how to protect your national insurance record.

Information to support your claim

For the general information requirements that apply to all benefits, see p1170.

It is important that you provide any information required when you claim. Until you do, you may not count as having made a valid claim (see p1172).[28] Correct any defects as soon as possible or your date of claim may be affected.[29] If you claim IS in writing, you must satisfy what is known as the 'evidence requirement'. See p1174 for further information and to see whether you are exempt.

Even if you have provided all that was required when you claimed, you may be asked to provide further information to support your claim (see p1174). You may also be asked to provide information after you are awarded IS and, if you fail to do so, your IS could be suspended or even terminated (see p1200).

The date of your claim

The date of your claim is important as it determines when your entitlement to IS starts.[30] This is not necessarily the date from when you are paid. For information about when payment of IS starts, see p245.

Your date of claim is not necessarily the date it is received by the DWP. It can be an earlier date.

Your 'date of claim' is usually the earliest of:[31]

- the date you first contact a benefit office (eg, you ask to claim IS by phone) or someone does this on your behalf, so long as a properly completed claim form (if issued) and all the information required are provided within one month; *or*
- if you claim by phone, the date of your call, even if you were given more time to provide information, so long as you have done so;[32] *or*
- the date your properly completed claim form (if issued) and all the information required are received by the benefit office (or, if you can claim at an alternative office, that office).

Note: you must make sure your claim is valid. If it is 'defective', you are given a short time to correct the defects (see p1173 and p1173). If you do, your claim is treated as having been made when you initially claimed.[33]

Part 3: Other means-tested benefits and tax credits
Chapter 11: Income support
6. Claims and backdating

There is an exception to the rules above. If you claim working tax credit (WTC) and are refused because neither you nor your partner are in full-time paid work for WTC purposes (see p299), your date of claim for IS is the date you claimed WTC.[34] However, you must claim IS within 14 days of the decision refusing you WTC. You can ask for your IS claim to start on a later date instead – eg, if your income is currently too high, but is due to decrease.

In some cases you can claim in advance (see below) and in some cases your claim can be backdated (see below). If you want this to be done, make this clear when you claim or the DWP might not consider it.

Backdating your claim

It is very important to claim in time. A claim for IS can normally only be backdated for a maximum of three months and only in limited circumstances. See p1178 for the general rules on when an IS claim can be backdated.

Your claim can be backdated for more than three months if you claim backdated IS after a qualifying benefit has been awarded and an earlier IS claim had been refused (see p1180).[35]

If you might have qualified for IS earlier, but did not claim because you were given the wrong information by the DWP or because you were misled by it, you could ask for compensation (see p1439) or complain to the Ombudsman via your MP (see p1444).

If you claim the wrong benefit

If you claim IS and you should have claimed carer's allowance (CA) instead of, or in addition to, IS, a decision maker can treat your IS claim as a claim for CA.[36] This could help you qualify for a backdated carer premium.

Claiming in advance

If you do not qualify for IS from the date of your claim (unless this is because you fail the habitual residence test – see p1586) but will do so within the next three months, you can be awarded IS from the first date on which you qualify.[37] This gives the DWP time to ensure you receive benefit as soon as you are entitled. The date of your claim is the date on which you qualify.[38] Tell the DWP that you want to claim in advance. You may have to persuade the DWP that it can accept a claim in advance.

You might not be entitled to IS currently, but will be once you (or your partner or a child included in your claim) become entitled to a 'qualifying benefit' (eg, disability living allowance, personal independence payment or CA) because you are then entitled to premiums. You should make your claim for IS at the same time as the claim for the qualifying benefit. If you are:

- refused IS, claim again when you get a decision about the qualifying benefit and ask for your IS to be backdated to the date of your first IS claim or to the date of entitlement to the qualifying benefit, if that is later (see p1180);

- awarded IS, you may be entitled to a higher rate once the outcome of the claim for the qualifying benefit is known. Ask for a revision or a supersession if you think this applies to you (see p1328).

7. Getting paid

The general rules on getting paid are covered in Chapter 51. This section explains the specific rules that apply to income support (IS).

When is income support paid?
You are normally paid fortnightly in arrears.[39] The day you are paid depends on your national insurance number (see p1189).
You are paid in advance if you are returning to work after a trade dispute.[40]

IS is a weekly benefit. However, if you are only entitled to IS for part of a week, you are only paid for the part week.[41]

If you are entitled to less than 10 pence a week (£5 a week if you are getting IS while involved in a trade dispute), you are not paid IS at all, unless you are receiving another social security benefit which can be paid with IS.[42] If you are entitled to less than £1 a week, the DWP can decide to pay you at 13-week intervals in arrears.[43]

Your entitlement to IS usually starts from the date of your claim (see p243).[44]

Note:
- Deductions can be made from your IS to pay to third parties (see p1202).
- Your IS might be paid at a reduced rate if you have been given a sanction for:
  - failing to take part in a work-focused interview (see p1157) or, if you are a lone parent and do not have any children under three, to undertake work-related activity (see p1160); *or*
  - a benefit offence (see p1278).
- For information on missing payments, see p1189. If you cannot get your IS payments because you have lost your bank or post office card or have forgotten your PIN, see p1188. If your payment service card has been lost or stolen, or if you have forgotten your memorable date, see p1189.
- If payment of your IS is delayed, see p1295. If you are waiting for a decision on your claim, or to be paid, you may be able to get a short-term advance (see p1192). If you wish to complain about how your claim has been dealt with or to claim compensation, see Chapter 60.
- If payment of your IS is suspended, see p1200.
- If you are overpaid IS, you might have to repay it (see Chapter 53) and, in some circumstances, you may have to pay a penalty (see p1268). If you have been accused of fraud, see Chapter 54.

Income support run-on

If you are getting IS and make a new claim for universal credit on or after 22 July 2020, your IS entitlement continues for two weeks (called a 'run-on payment' or 'transitional IS payment').[45] You do not have to make a claim for a run-on payment. It should be made automatically. You do not have to pay a run-on payment back and it does not count as a specified benefit for the purposes of the benefit cap (see p1197).[46]

Change of circumstances

You must report changes in your circumstances that you have been told you must report, as well as any that you might reasonably be expected to know might affect your right to, the amount of, or the payment of, your benefit. You should do this as soon as possible, preferably in writing. See p1199 for further information.

When there has been a relevant change of circumstances, a decision maker looks at your claim again and makes a new decision. To see when your IS is then adjusted, see below.

When your income support is adjusted

As a general rule, if you are paid IS in arrears, your IS is adjusted from the beginning of the week in which the change of circumstances takes effect.[47] There are a number of exceptions, including the following.[48]

- If a decision is to your advantage (eg, it means you are entitled to more IS), but you failed to notify the DWP of a change within the time limit (normally one month, but this can be extended – see p1324), your IS is adjusted:
  - if you are paid in arrears, from the beginning of the week in which you notified the change; *or*
  - if you are paid in advance, from the day on which you notified the change if this is the day you are paid benefit or, if it is not, your IS is adjusted from the next week.
- Your IS is adjusted from the date of the change of circumstances (or the day on which this is expected to take place) if:
  - you are paid IS in arrears and the change of circumstances means you no longer qualify for IS, unless this is because your income is too high; *or*
  - you live in a care home for part of the week and are entitled to disability living allowance or personal independence payment when you are staying elsewhere. This means that you can be paid, for example, the severe disability and enhanced disability premiums (see p346 and p343) when you are staying away from the care home.

8. Tax, other benefits and the benefit cap

Tax

Income support (IS) is not taxable except if you are involved in a trade dispute and you are claiming it for your partner.[49]

Means-tested benefits and tax credits

If you are entitled to IS:

- IS is an automatic passport to maximum housing benefit (HB), but if you are not already entitled, you must make a separate claim (if you still can). It is also an automatic passport to maximum child tax credit (CTC) and usually to maximum working tax credit (WTC);
- if you work less than 16 hours a week and your partner works at least 16 hours but less than 24 hours a week, if you still can, you and your partner may be able to claim WTC as well as, or instead of, IS. Get advice to see whether you can still make a new claim and, if so, how you would be better off financially;
- WTC is taken into account as income when working out your IS, but CTC is not.

If you or your partner have just stopped work or reduced your hours, you may be able to get 'WTC run-on' for a four-week period (see p305).

Non-means-tested benefits

In some situations, while you are on IS you get national insurance credits (see p968).

Most non-means-tested benefits are taken into account as income when working out the amount of IS you get. However:

- attendance allowance, disability living allowance, personal independence payment, armed forces independence payment, guardian's allowance and, if you are getting CTC, child benefit, are not taken into account;
- it can still be worth claiming non-means-tested benefits, even if they are taken into account. If you or your partner qualify for certain non-means-tested benefits, you also qualify for certain premiums (see p339) and, therefore, a higher rate of IS.

You may only qualify for IS once you or your partner, or a child included in your claim, are awarded another benefit (known as a 'qualifying benefit'). To make sure you do not lose out while waiting for the outcome of a claim for a qualifying benefit, claim IS at the same time. If your IS claim is refused, once the qualifying benefit is awarded claim IS again and ask for it to be backdated to the date of your first claim (see p1180).

The benefit cap

In some cases, there is a limit on the total amount of specified benefits you can receive (a 'benefit cap'). IS is one of the specified benefits. However, the benefit cap only applies if you are getting universal credit or HB. See p1194 for further information. **Note:** IS run-on (see p246) does not count as a specified benefit.

Passports and other sources of help

If you are entitled to IS, you also qualify for health benefits such as free prescriptions (see Chapter 31) and education benefits such as free school lunches (see p866). You may also qualify for help from your local welfare assistance scheme (see p861), for social fund payments (see Chapter 37) or, in Scotland, a Best Start grant or funeral support payment (see Chapters 72 and 73), and for Healthy Start food and vitamins (see p862) or, in Scotland, Best Start foods (see p865). You may be entitled to a council tax reduction (see p851).

Financial help on starting work

If you stop getting IS because you or your partner start work, or your earnings or hours in your existing job increase, you may be able to continue to get IS for help with your housing costs (eg, ground rent or service charges) for a further four weeks (called 'housing costs run-on' in this *Handbook* – see p376) or extended payments of HB (if you pay rent – see p217). Your local authority may also provide extended help with council tax. If you have a DWP loan for your mortgage interest, this may continue for four weeks (see p860). See p873 for information about other financial help you might get.

Notes

1. Who can get income support
1 s124 SSCBA 1992
2 Regs 4 and 4A UC(TP) Regs; Art 4(11) WRA(No.32)O
3 Reg 4ZA and Sch 1B IS Regs
4 R(IS) 10/05
5 Sch 1B paras 7(d) and 7A IS Regs
6 Sch 1B paras 1-2A, 14, 14A and 14B IS Regs
7 CIS/0542/2001
8 CIS/2260/2002
9 The rules on paternity leave are in Part 2 PAL Regs
10 *JS v SSWP (IS)* [2015] UKUT 306 (AAC), reported as [2016] AACR 13
11 R(IS) 10/05
12 Sch 1B paras 3 and 23 IS Regs
13 CIS/866/2004
14 CIS/4312/2007
15 Sch 1B para IS Regs
16 R(IS) 8/02
17 Sch 1B paras 5 and 6 IS Regs

18   Sch 1B paras 11, 15, 15A and 28 IS Regs
19   Sch 1B paras 9A, 14C and 18-22 and
      Sch 7 para 8(b) IS Regs

2. The rules about your age
20   Art 8 WRA(No.31)O; HB Circular A9/
      2019
21   s124(1)(a) SSCBA 1992

4. The amount of benefit
22   s124(4) SSCBA 1992
23   Reg 13 SS&CS(DA) Regs

6. Claims and backdating
24   Reg 4(11A) and (11B) SS(C&P) Regs
25   Reg 4(1A), (5) and (6) SS(C&P) Regs
26   Reg 4(3) SS(C&P) Regs
27   Reg 4(4) SS(C&P) Regs
28   Reg 4(1A), (7A), (9), (12) and (13)
      SS(C&P) Regs
29   Reg 6(1A) SS(C&P) Regs
30   Reg 19(1) and Sch 4 para 6 SS(C&P)
      Regs
31   Reg 6(1ZA) and (1A) SS(C&P) Regs;
      R(IS) 10/06
32   Reg 6(1)(c) and (d) SS(C&P) Regs
33   Reg 6(1A) SS(C&P) Regs
34   Reg 6(28) SS(C&P) Regs
35   Reg 6(16)-(18) SS(C&P) Regs
36   Reg 9(1) and Sch 1 SS(C&P) Regs; reg
      2(3) ESA(TP) Regs
37   Reg 13(1) and (9) SS(C&P) Regs
38   Reg 13(1) SS(C&P) Regs

7. Getting paid
39   Sch 7 para 1 SS(C&P) Regs
40   Sch 7 paras 2(d) and 6(2) SS(C&P) Regs
41   s124(5) and (6) SSCBA 1992; reg 73 IS
      Regs
42   Reg 26(4) SS(C&P) Regs
43   Sch 7 para 5 SS(C&P) Regs
44   Sch 7 paras 3 and 6 SS(C&P) Regs
45   Regs 8(2A), 46(1) and 47(2) UC(TP)
      Regs
46   Reg 8B UC(TP) Regs
47   Reg 7 and Sch 3A para 1(a) SS&CS(DA)
      Regs
48   Reg 7 and Sch 3A paras 1(b) and 2-6
      SS&CS(DA) Regs

8. Tax, other benefits and the benefit cap
49   s665 IT(EP)A 2003

Chapter 12

Income-based jobseeker's allowance

This chapter covers:
1. Who can get income-based jobseeker's allowance (p251)
2. The rules about your age (p255)
3. People included in the claim (p257)
4. The amount of benefit (p258)
5. Special benefit rules (p259)
6. Claims and backdating (p259)
7. Getting paid (p265)
8. Tax, other benefits and the benefit cap (p266)

Note: unless otherwise stated, references to income-based jobseeker's allowance (JSA) in this chapter also refer to joint-claim JSA.

Key facts

- Jobseeker's allowance (JSA) is a benefit for people who are looking for work.
- There are three types of JSA. **Contribution-based JSA** is a non-means-tested benefit, but it can be affected by earnings and certain pension payments. **Income-based JSA** and **joint-claim JSA** are means-tested benefits.
- You do not have to have paid national insurance contributions to qualify for income-based JSA or joint-claim JSA.
- You cannot qualify for any type of JSA if you count as being in full-time paid work or, for income-based JSA or joint-claim JSA, if your partner counts as being in full-time paid work.
- You must normally be fit for work and satisfy the 'jobseeking conditions'.
- In a number of situations (eg, if you do not take up a job or a place on an employment programme), you may be given a sanction and your JSA may be paid at a reduced (or nil) rate.
- JSA is administered and paid by the DWP.
- If you disagree with a JSA decision, you can apply for a revision or a supersession (see Chapter 56), or appeal against it (see Chapter 57). You must apply for a mandatory reconsideration before you can appeal.

1. Who can get income-based Jobseeker's allowance

You qualify for jobseeker's allowance (JSA) if you:[1]
- are not in full-time paid work (see p254); *and*
- do not have limited capability for work. However, in certain circumstances, people who are sick, have been affected by the coronavirus pandemic or who have gone abroad for NHS hospital treatment can get JSA (see p255); *and*
- are not in 'relevant education' (see p885). In addition, if you are a full-time student, you usually cannot get JSA (see p887); *and*
- satisfy 'jobseeking conditions' (see p1114) – ie, you must:
  - be (or treated as) available for work; *and*
  - be (or treated as) actively seeking work; *and*
  - have a current jobseeker's agreement with the DWP; *and*
- are below pension age (see p780); *and*
- are in Great Britain. JSA can continue to be paid in limited circumstances while you are temporarily away (see p1655).

The above conditions apply to all types of JSA. To qualify for income-based JSA, you must also satisfy extra rules (see p252).

You may qualify for income-based JSA even if you do not qualify for contribution-based JSA. You may qualify for both income-based JSA and contribution-based JSA. You are not usually entitled to JSA for the first seven days of your jobseeking period. These are known as 'waiting days' (see p266). You may be able to get a short-term advance before your first payment of JSA is due (see p1192).

Note: if you are already entitled to contribution-based JSA and do not come under the universal credit (UC) system, you may be able to top this up with income-based JSA without having to make a new claim (see p27).

Income-based Jobseeker's allowance and universal credit
You can now only make a new claim for income-based JSA in limited circumstances (see p252). Otherwise, if you claim JSA, you will come under the UC system instead (see p23).
If you are already entitled to income-based JSA, you can continue to qualify until:
– you claim UC; *or*
– you become a member of a couple and your partner is getting UC; *or*
– you are affected by the 'managed migration' transfer process (see p30).
The government says that from November 2020 the DWP will begin to transfer existing income-based JSA claims to UC. This transfer process began in July 2019 in pilot areas, for a limited number of claimants. See p27 for further information, and AskCPAG.org.uk and CPAG's online service and *Welfare Rights Bulletin* for updates.

Part 3: Other means-tested benefits and tax credits
Chapter 12: Income-based jobseeker's allowance
1. Who can get income-based jobseeker's allowance

You cannot usually qualify for income-based JSA if you are pension age or over. However, if you are already getting income-based JSA and you are or become a member of a 'mixed-age' couple (ie, you have reached pension age but your partner has not), in some circumstances, your income-based JSA can continue even though you have reached pension age (see p255).

Who can make a new claim for income-based jobseeker's allowance

You can only make a new claim for income-based JSA if any of the following apply.[2]

• You are prevented from claiming UC because:
  – you (or your partner) are, or within the last month have been, entitled to income support (IS), income-based JSA, income-related employment and support allowance (ESA) or housing benefit (HB) that includes a severe disability premium (see p346), and if your entitlement to the benefit ended during that month you (or s/he) have continued to satisfy the conditions for that premium; *and*
  – you (and your partner) have not yet been given a 'migration notice' from the DWP that you will be transferred to UC via the 'managed migration' process (see p30).

The above may apply, for example, if you are claiming income-based JSA after a break in your entitlement, you are currently entitled to HB, or you have been getting IS or income-related ESA but no longer qualify.

Note: this rule only applies until 27 January 2021.

• You are prevented from claiming UC because you (or if you are a in a couple, you and your partner) are a 'frontier worker' – ie, you work in Great Britain or Northern Ireland but do not live there.

• You are prevented from claiming UC because you come into some other category of case from whom it has been decided not to accept claims, in order to safeguard or test the efficient administration of UC.

If you cannot make a new claim for income-based JSA under these rules, you can make a claim for UC.

Extra rules for income-based jobseeker's allowance

You qualify for income-based JSA if, in addition to satisfying the rules that apply to all types of JSA (see p251):[3]

• your income is not more than your applicable amount (see p258); *and*
• your savings and other capital are worth £16,000 or less. Some capital (including your home) is ignored (see Chapter 22); *and*
• your partner does not count as being in full-time paid work (see p254); *and*

Chapter 12
Income-based jobseeker's allowance

- you are aged 18 or over. If you are a 16/17-year-old, you might get income-based JSA if you satisfy special rules (see p256); *and*
- if you are a joint-claim couple (see below), at least one of you is aged 18 or over. If one of you is a 16/17-year-old, you can get income-based JSA if the member of the couple who is 16/17 satisfies special rules (see p256); *and*
- neither you nor your partner are entitled to IS, income-related ESA or pension credit (PC), and, if you are not a joint-claim couple (see below), your partner is not entitled to income-based JSA. If you or your partner can qualify for IS or income-related ESA, or your partner can qualify for PC, check whether this would make you better off; *and*
- you are not included as a child in someone else's IS or income-based JSA claim (see p323). However, you can qualify for JSA in your own right in a number of situations (see p256) and you cannot be included in someone's claim for income-based JSA if you are (or would be) entitled to JSA;[4] *and*
- you satisfy the 'habitual residence' and the 'right to reside' tests. To find out if you are exempt from these tests, see Chapter 68; *and*
- you are not a 'person subject to immigration control' (see p1560). There are exceptions to this rule.

Joint-claim couples

If you are a 'joint-claim couple', both you and your partner must usually make a joint claim for JSA and satisfy all the rules for getting income-based JSA. You are a 'joint-claim couple' if you are a member of a couple (see p319) and:[5]

- at least one of you is 18 or over. **Note:** if one of you is 16 or 17, special rules apply (see p256); *and*
- neither of you is responsible for a child in specified circumstances.

Because these rules now apply to very few claimants, they are not described in detail here. See the 2019/20 edition of this *Handbook* for further information. To find out:

- when you count as responsible for a child and what happens if you stop or start being responsible, see pp245–56 of that edition. **Note:** most often, you count as responsible if you are entitled to child benefit for her/him, but there are exceptions;
- whether one of you does not have to satisfy all the conditions for getting JSA, see pp246–47 of that edition. This might apply, for example, if one of you is studying full time, is a carer or is unable to work because of sickness. **Note:** you must still make a joint claim for JSA and satisfy all the other requirements;
- what happens if one of you does not qualify for JSA and how this affects the way your benefit is calculated, see pp247–48 of that edition. This might apply, for example, if one of you is over pension age, or fails to attend the initial interview (see p261), or fails to meet the jobseeking conditions (see p1114), or is subject to immigration control (see p1560).

Part 3: Other means-tested benefits and tax credits
Chapter 12: Income-based jobseeker's allowance
1. Who can get income-based jobseeker's allowance

Jobseeking periods

Your jobseeking period is relevant for a number of reasons, including for whether you satisfy the contribution conditions for contribution-based JSA. You are not usually entitled to JSA for the first seven days of your jobseeking period. These are known as 'waiting days' (see p266).

A '**jobseeking period**' is the period during which you:[6]
- meet the conditions that apply to all types of JSA (see p251); *or*
- do not satisfy the jobseeking conditions, but receive hardship payments (see Chapter 52).

Certain days do not count as part of a jobseeking period.[7] The rules are broadly the same as for contribution-based JSA (see p707). In addition, days for which you lost your entitlement to JSA because you failed to participate in an interview when required or to 'sign on' and days for which you have been refused JSA because you did not provide your partner's national insurance number do not count.

In some cases, two or more jobseeking periods can be linked together and treated as if they were one. Also, certain periods in which you satisfy other conditions can be linked to a jobseeking period (see p707 – the rules are the same as for contribution-based JSA).[8] This means, for example, that:
- if you make a fresh claim for JSA but your jobseeking period links with a previous one, you do not have to serve any waiting days (see p266) to get JSA;
- if the combined jobseeking periods are at least two years, you might be able to get JSA while attending a qualifying course.

Full-time paid work

You cannot usually qualify for income-based JSA if you or your partner are in, or are treated as being in, full-time paid work. If you are the JSA claimant, this means 16 hours or more each week.[9] For your partner, this means 24 hours or more each week.

If you are a joint-claim couple, you cannot get joint-claim JSA if either one of you is in, or treated as being in, full-time paid work. If one of you is not working or is working fewer than 16 hours a week, the other can then work up to 24 hours a week. In this situation, you do not have to make a joint claim.[10] The person working fewer than 16 hours can qualify for income-based JSA.

All the rules on work are covered in Chapter 44. **Note:** in some situations you are treated as not being in full-time paid work even if you work 16/24 hours a week or more (see p998).

If you or your partner have just taken up full-time paid work, you may be able to qualify for IS for help with your housing costs for the first four weeks (housing costs run-on – see p376).

Limited capability for work

Usually, to qualify for JSA you must not have 'limited capability for work'.[11] See Chapter 45 for details about the test that decides this for ESA purposes. If a decision maker has decided that you have (or do not have) limited capability for work for ESA purposes, you are automatically treated as having (or not having) limited capability for work for JSA.[12] This means that if your health improves and you move on to JSA from ESA, you may be asked to provide medical evidence that you no longer have limited capability for work. In all cases, you must still show that you are available for work if you are ill or have a disability. However, there are rules that may allow you to restrict your availability (see p1121).

Even if you have limited capability for work, you can continue to qualify for JSA:
- if you are affected by the coronavirus pandemic; *or*
- for certain short periods of up to 13 weeks; *or*
- if you are temporarily absent from Great Britain to obtain NHS hospital treatment under certain provisions.

See p708 for further information. The rules are the same as for contribution-based JSA.

2. The rules about your age

You cannot usually qualify for:
- **income-based jobseeker's allowance** (JSA) until you are 18. There are special rules that can help you qualify if you are 16 or 17 (see p256). If you do not qualify, check whether you qualify for universal credit (UC), income support (IS) or employment and support allowance (ESA) instead. If you do not come under the UC system, even if you cannot get JSA, IS or ESA, you may qualify for housing benefit (HB);
- **joint-claim JSA** unless you and your partner are both 18. If only one of you is 18 or over, the other must satisfy the conditions for income-based JSA in her/his own right as a 16/17-year-old (see p256).[13] If both of you are under 18, you do not count as a joint-claim couple and so one of you may be able to qualify for income-based JSA for the other.[14]

You cannot qualify for any type of JSA if you are pension age or over (see p780). However, if you are already getting income-based JSA and you are, or become, a member of a 'mixed-age couple' (ie, you have reached pension age but your partner has not) and you are prevented from claiming UC (see p252), you are treated as not yet pension age and your income-based JSA continues.[15]

Part 3: Other means-tested benefits and tax credits
Chapter 12: Income-based jobseeker's allowance
2. The rules about your age

16/17-year-olds

If you are aged 16 or 17, you can qualify for:
- **income-based JSA** if you satisfy the basic rules of entitlement and the additional rules for 16/17-year-olds (see below);
- **joint-claim JSA** if you satisfy the basic rules of entitlement and the additional rules for 16/17-year-olds (see below), and you are a member of a couple and your partner is 18 or over.[16] Usually, both of you must satisfy all the conditions for entitlement, but there are exceptions. If both of you are under 18, you do not count as a joint-claim couple and so one of you may be able to qualify for income-based JSA for both of you.[17]

You should not have your JSA claim refused or be turned away by the DWP simply because of your age or because you have been included in someone else's benefit or tax credits claim. **Note:**
- You can only make a new claim for income-based JSA in limited circumstances (see p252).
- The usual rules about claims and payments apply, but you must usually first register for both work and training at the place specified by the DWP.[18]
- There are special rules for calculating your JSA applicable amount if you are a member of a couple (see p334).
- In general, you are subject to the same jobseeking conditions as people aged 18 or over. However, there are some important differences – eg, you must be actively seeking work *and* training.
- You can be given a sanction in the same way as claimants aged 18 or over. However, there are some special rules.[19]

Note: you can qualify for **contribution-based JSA** if you satisfy the contribution conditions. However, because you are unlikely to have paid sufficient national insurance (NI) contributions before you are 18, it is unlikely you will qualify.

Additional rules for 16/17-year-olds

You can only get income-based JSA while you are 16 or 17 if one of the following applies.[20]
- You come into one of the groups of young people who can qualify before age 18. Broadly, this applies if you come into one of the groups of people who can qualify for IS (see pp234–38), or you have limited capability for work, or you are in a couple and have a child under 16 included in your claim.[21] For full details of the rules, see p251 of the 2019/20 edition of this *Handbook*.
- You qualify during the period of 20 weeks after leaving education or training (called the child benefit 'extension period' – see p581).[22] Broadly, this applies if you are married or in a civil partnership, or you are an orphan with no one acting as your parent, or you are living away from your parents and anyone acting in their place in specified situations – eg, you were in custody or being

looked after by a local authority, you are estranged from them or there is a risk to your mental or physical health. For full details of the rules, see pp251–52 of the 2019/20 edition of this *Handbook*.

- You qualify during certain other periods. Broadly, these are short periods after the end of the child benefit extension period (see above), periods when you are laid off or are on short-term working, or after you accept an offer to enlist in the armed forces.[23] For full details of the rules, see p253 of the 2019/20 edition of this *Handbook*.
- You would be in severe hardship if you are not paid.[24] In this case, you can get what are known as 'severe hardship payments'. These are discretionary. If you want to claim severe hardship payments, state this when you claim JSA and insist on your right to make a claim. For full details of the rules, see pp254–55 of the 2019/20 edition of this *Handbook*. **Note:**
  - Severe hardship payments are payments of JSA, so you are automatically eligible for other benefits – eg, HB.
  - There are special rules about sanctions that only apply to severe hardship payments.

In addition to the situations that apply to claimants aged 18 or over, if you are 16 or 17 you cannot qualify for income-based JSA if you:[25]

- qualify for contribution-based JSA; *or*
- are being, or were previously, looked after by a local authority in the circumstances described on pp947–49. There are exceptions to those rules.

Remember that, in most cases, you cannot qualify for JSA if you are in 'relevant education' (see p885). You may be able to qualify during a period after your education ends (the child benefit 'extension period' – see p581).

3. People included in the claim

If you are single, you claim income-based jobseeker's allowance (JSA) for yourself.

If you are a 'joint-claim couple' (see p253), you and your partner must usually both claim joint-claim JSA. If you are not a joint-claim couple, either you claim income-based JSA for both of you or, if your partner meets the qualifying conditions for income-based JSA, s/he claims for you both. Whichever one of you claims JSA, the other may qualify for national insurance (NI) credits in order to protect her/his NI record. See Chapter 43 for more details about NI credits.

If you are in a couple, your applicable amount includes a personal allowance for a couple and can include premiums based on both your and your partner's circumstances. When your benefit is worked out, your partner's income and capital are usually added to yours.

Income-based JSA does not normally include amounts for your children. However, there are some situations in which you must show that you are responsible for a child who is living in your household – eg:

Part 3: Other means-tested benefits and tax credits
Chapter 12: Income-based jobseeker's allowance
4. The amount of benefit

- in order to take advantage of the special rules to help you meet the jobseeking conditions (see p1114);
- to show you are a lone parent so you can benefit from a higher earnings disregard (see p430);
- for some of the rules for help with housing costs – eg, ground rent or service charges (see Chapter 18).

You do not have to be the child's parent. See p324 for who counts as a child. For when you count as responsible for a child and when s/he counts as living in your household, see pp326–29.

Note: there are different rules about children for deciding whether you must claim joint-claim JSA (see p253).

4. The amount of benefit

Income-based jobseeker's allowance (JSA) tops up your income to a level set by the government. The amount you get depends on your needs (your 'applicable amount') and on how much income and capital you and your partner have.[26] **Note:** if you do not come under the universal credit system and are getting contribution-based JSA, you may qualify for income-based JSA to top this up.

Your applicable amount consists of:

- a personal allowance (see p333); *and*
- premiums (see p339) for any special needs; *and*
- some housing costs (see Chapter 18). **Note:** you can no longer get income-based JSA for help with your mortgage interest or a loan for repairs and improvements. Instead, the DWP may offer you a loan (see p855). You cannot get help with your rent. Instead, you may qualify for housing benefit (see Chapter 10).

Income-based JSA is calculated in the same way as for income support (IS) (see p240).

Note: you are not usually entitled to JSA for the first seven days of your jobseeking period. These are known as 'waiting days' (see p266). You may be able to get a short-term advance before your first payment of JSA is due (see p1192).

Do you have children?

Income-based JSA does not include allowances and premiums for your children. Instead, you may qualify for child tax credit (CTC) if you can still make a claim. However, in some cases, you can continue to get allowances and premiums for your children unless you are awarded CTC (see p333). If you *do* get allowances and premiums for your children, there are special rules for how their income and capital are treated (see p420 and p490).

You might get a reduced amount of JSA if:

- you have been given a sanction (see p1145); *or*
- you are in a joint-claim couple and your partner has not made a joint claim with you (see p253 and pp245–48 of the 2019/20 edition of this *Handbook*); *or*
- you are not in a joint-claim couple, you have a partner and s/he has failed to attend a work-focused interview without good cause (see p1157); *or*
- you are receiving a hardship payment of income-based JSA (see Chapter 52); *or*
- you have committed a benefit offence (see p1278).

Different rules for calculating your JSA may apply if you are in one of the groups to whom special rules apply (see below).

5. Special benefit rules

Special rules may apply to:

- 16/17-year-olds (see p256);
- workers who are laid off or working short time;
- people subject to immigration control (see Chapter 67);
- people who have come from or are going abroad (see Chapters 68, 69 and 70);
- people who are studying (see Chapter 41);
- people involved in a trade dispute (see p1001);
- people without accommodation, people who are (or whose partner or children are) in hospital or living in a care home or other similar accommodation, and people in prison (see Chapter 42).

6. Claims and backdating

The general rules about claims and backdating are covered in Chapter 50. This section explains the specific rules that apply to income-based jobseeker's allowance (JSA). **Note:** you can only make a new claim for income-based JSA in limited circumstances (see p252).

Making a claim

If you are already getting contribution-based JSA and do not come under the universal credit (UC) system, you can top up your entitlement with income-based JSA without having to make a new claim (see p26). This is because income-based JSA and contribution-based JSA are two types of the same benefit.[27]

If you can make a new claim for income-based JSA, a claim can be made:

- at gov.uk/jobseekers-allowance/how-to-claim. **Note:** you cannot claim online if you are claiming JSA when you are prevented from claiming UC because you

Part 3: Other means-tested benefits and tax credits
Chapter 12: Income-based jobseeker's allowance
6. Claims and backdating

(or your partner) get (or within the past month got) a severe disability premium (see p252); *or*

- by telephone on 0800 055 6688 (Welsh language: 0800 012 1888; textphone: 0800 023 4888; Relay UK (if you cannot hear or speak on the phone): 18001 then 0800 055 6688), Monday to Friday, 8am to 6pm. You are sent a written statement of your circumstances to approve, sign and return to the DWP; *or*
- by completing a paper claim form approved by the DWP. JSA claim forms are only available from Jobcentre Plus offices. One must be provided free of charge if you notify the DWP of your intention to claim.[28] Keep a copy in case queries arise.

In practice, the DWP prefers you to start your claim online or by phone. There is no rule that says you must do so, but it is best to make your claim in this way if you can. You must provide any information or evidence required (see p261). You can amend or withdraw your claim before a decision is made (see p1169). If there is a delay in making a decision, you may be able to get a short-term advance (see p1192).

Note:
- If you make initial contact with the DWP by telephone or letter to say you want to claim, the date you do this is important because it usually determines the date on which your claim is treated as having been made (see p261).
- Income-based and contribution-based JSA are two types of one benefit. If you want the DWP to assess your entitlement to both, answer all the relevant questions and provide all the necessary information when making your claim.
- If you claim JSA online or by phone, a claim for housing benefit (HB) can be completed at the same time and passed to the local authority on your behalf. Check that this has happened. If not, you must make a separate claim to your local authority.

Claiming national insurance credits

If you are claiming national insurance (NI) credits but not JSA (see p970), the normal claim procedures for getting JSA apply to you.

Who should claim

If you are a single person or a lone parent, you claim income-based JSA on your own behalf. Unless you must make a joint claim for JSA (see p253), if you are a member of a couple you must choose which one of you claims for you both. See p319 for who counts as a couple. If you cannot agree who should claim, a decision maker decides.[29] If you are not the person claiming JSA, you may wish to claim NI credits to protect your NI record (see p970). If you claim NI credits, you can also qualify for help from the schemes for assisting people to obtain employment.

If you are unable to manage your own affairs, another person can claim JSA for you as your 'appointee' (see p1170).

Information to support your claim

For the general information requirements that apply to all benefits, see p1170. It is important that you provide any information and evidence required when you claim. Until you do, you may not count as having made a valid claim (see p1172). Correct any defects as soon as possible or your date of claim may be affected. If you claim JSA in writing, you must satisfy what is known as the 'evidence requirement'. See p1174 for further information and to see whether you are exempt.

Even if you have provided all that was required when you claimed, you may be asked to provide further information to support your claim (see p1174). You may also be asked to provide information and evidence after you are awarded JSA.

If you fail to do so, your JSA could be suspended, or even terminated (see p1200).

The initial interview

You (or, if you are claiming joint-claim JSA, both you and your partner) must usually attend and participate in an initial interview where, among other things, a jobseeker's agreement (see p1127) is drawn up for you to sign.[30] The DWP telephones or texts you within two days of your claim to arrange your interview. If you do not attend the interview at the right time or place, your date of claim is affected (see p263). If you do not attend the interview at all (and the DWP does not waive the requirement to do so), you have not made a valid claim and so do not qualify for JSA. See p717 for further information. The issues are the same as for contribution-based JSA.

The date of your claim

The date of your claim is important as it determines when your entitlement to JSA starts (subject to the rules on waiting days – see p266). This is not necessarily the date from when you are paid. For information about when payment of JSA starts, see p720. The rules are the same as for contribution-based JSA.

You are not usually entitled to JSA for any day before your date of claim.[31] Your date of claim is not necessarily the date it is received by the DWP. It can be an earlier date. Your claim can be backdated in some circumstances (see p263).

Your 'date of claim' depends on whether or not you are required to attend an initial interview (see above). If you (or you and your partner if you are a joint-claim couple) are required to attend an initial interview, your date of claim is usually:

- the date you first contact the Jobcentre Plus office if you (or both of you) attend the interview at the time specified by the DWP and by that time a properly completed claim is, or has been, provided (on a form or by telephone) with all the information and evidence required. If you (or your partner) fail to attend the interview, see p263;[32] *or*

Part 3: Other means-tested benefits and tax credits
Chapter 12: Income-based jobseeker's allowance
6. Claims and backdating

- if you are a joint-claim couple and only one of you is required to attend an initial interview, the earliest of:[33]
  - the date you or your partner first contacted the Jobcentre Plus office, provided a properly completed claim (on a form or by telephone) with all the information and evidence required is provided within one month of your first contact; or
  - the date on which a properly completed claim (on a form) with all the information and evidence required is received at the Jobcentre Plus office or a claim made by telephone is properly completed, provided the person who is required to attend an interview does so. If you (or your partner) fail to attend the interview, see p263.

Forms
In this section, the term '**form**' refers to a paper form or a claim form completed online.

If you are not required to attend an initial interview and you are not a member of a joint-claim couple, your date of claim is usually the earliest of:[34]
- the date you first contacted the Jobcentre Plus office, so long as a properly completed claim (on a form or by phone) with all the information and evidence required is provided within one month of your first contact; or
- the date on which a properly completed claim (on a form) with all the information and evidence required is received at the Jobcentre Plus office or a claim made by telephone is properly completed.

If you (and your partner) are required to attend an initial interview, the DWP can extend the time you have to provide or make a properly completed claim up to the date one month after the date you first contacted the Jobcentre Plus office to claim JSA.[35] This is discretionary, so provide your claim as required wherever possible.

Note: you must make sure your claim is valid. If the DWP tells you that your claim is 'defective', try to correct the defects as soon as possible so your claim can be treated as having been made when you initially claimed.[36]

There is an exception to the above rules. If you claim working tax credit (WTC) and are refused because neither you nor your partner are in full-time paid work for WTC purposes (see p299), your date of claim for JSA is the date you claimed WTC.[37] However, you must claim JSA within 14 days of the decision refusing you WTC. You can ask for your JSA claim to start on a later date instead – eg, if your income is currently too high, but is due to decrease.

In some cases you may be able to claim in advance (see p264), and in some cases your claim can be backdated (see below). If you want this to be done, make this clear when you claim or the DWP may not consider it.

Have you or your partner claimed contribution-based jobseeker's allowance?

1. If you are a member of a couple and one of you claims contribution-based JSA but is not entitled to it and a subsequent income-based JSA claim is made by the other (or both of you if you are a joint-claim couple), the date of claim for income-based JSA is the date of the earlier claim for contribution-based JSA.[38]

2. If your partner has been claiming contribution-based JSA, this expires and you claim income-based JSA, the date of claim for your income-based JSA is the day after your partner's entitlement expires.[39]

3. If you claim contribution-based JSA as well as joint-claim JSA, you and your partner may be required to attend an initial interview. If you do, but your partner does not, you may be able to argue that your date of claim for contribution-based JSA is the date of your initial contact with Jobcentre Plus.

If you fail to attend the initial interview

If you (or your partner if you are a joint-claim couple) fail to attend your initial interview (see p261) at the time or place specified by the DWP or fail to provide a properly completed claim by the date of the interview and cannot show 'good cause' for this, the rules above do not apply. Instead, so long as a properly completed claim with all the information and evidence required has by then been provided, your date of claim is:

- if you are not a joint-claim couple, the date you eventually go to the Jobcentre Plus office. Your entitlement to JSA cannot start until that date;[40] *or*
- if you are a joint-claim couple and:[41]
  - you are both required to attend an interview, the date one of you eventually goes to the Jobcentre Plus office. Your entitlement to JSA cannot start until that date. However, in this situation, you can only get the single person's rate of JSA until the other attends an interview;[42] *or*
  - only one of you is required to attend an interview, the date the person who is required to attend eventually goes to the Jobcentre Plus office. Your entitlement to JSA cannot start until that date.

'**Good cause**' is not defined. All relevant circumstances must be considered. These may relate to your abilities or to external factors. The general test is whether there is some factor that would probably cause a reasonable person of your age and experience to act, or fail to act, as you did.[43]

Backdating your claim

It is very important to claim in time. A claim for JSA can normally only be backdated for a maximum of three months, and only in limited circumstances.

Part 3: Other means-tested benefits and tax credits
Chapter 12: Income-based jobseeker's allowance
6. Claims and backdating

The general rules on backdating are covered on p1178. See p1135 for the backdating rules if you make a new claim for JSA when your entitlement ends after you failed to sign on or participate in an interview.

Your claim can be backdated for more than three months if you claim after a qualifying benefit is awarded and an earlier JSA claim was refused (see p1180).

If you might have qualified for JSA earlier but did not claim because you were given the wrong information or were misled by the DWP, you could ask for compensation (see p1439) or complain to the Ombudsman via your MP (see p1444).

If you claim the wrong benefit

If you claim WTC when you should have claimed JSA, see p262 to see whether your date of claim can be backdated.

Claiming in advance

If you do not qualify for JSA from the date of your claim (unless this is because you fail the habitual residence test – see p1586), but will do so within the next three months, you can be awarded JSA from the first date on which you qualify.[44] This gives the DWP time to ensure you receive benefit as soon as you are entitled. Tell the DWP you want to claim in advance when you claim and at your initial interview. You might have to persuade the DWP that it can accept a claim in advance.

You might not be entitled to income-based JSA currently, but would be once you (or your partner, or a child included in your claim) become entitled to another 'qualifying benefit' (eg, personal independence payment or carer's allowance) because you are then entitled to premiums. Make your claim for JSA at the same time as the claim for the qualifying benefit. If you are:
- refused JSA, claim again when you get a decision about the qualifying benefit and ask for your JSA to be backdated to the date of your first JSA claim, or to the date of entitlement to the qualifying benefit, if that is later (see p1180);
- awarded JSA, you might be entitled to a higher rate once the outcome of the claim for the qualifying benefit is known. Apply for a revision or a supersession if you think this applies to you (see p1328).

After you are awarded jobseeker's allowance

Once you have been awarded JSA, in order to continue to receive it you (and if you are a joint-claim couple, you and your partner) must:
- attend and participate in regular interviews; *and*
- confirm that you continue to be entitled to JSA – eg, by signing on.

See p1131 for further information about the requirements after you are awarded JSA. **Note:** you are expected to verify your claim for income-based JSA annually by completing a questionnaire and signing a declaration.

If you fail to participate in interviews, you may be given a sanction (see p1145). If you fail to sign on or to participate in interviews, your entitlement to JSA can end (see p1133).

Note: in some cases, if you fail to provide information and evidence when required to do so, your JSA could be suspended or even terminated (see p1200). If you have a partner (and you are not getting joint-claim JSA), s/he may be required to attend a work-focused interview (see p1138). If s/he fails to do so without good cause, your income-based JSA might be paid at a reduced rate.

7. Getting paid

Information about payment of your jobseeker's allowance (JSA) is on p720. The rules are the same as for contribution-based JSA.

If you and your partner are a joint-claim couple, you must nominate which one of you receives payment for both of you. If you cannot agree, a decision maker decides.[45] If your JSA is being paid at a reduced rate because one of you has been given a sanction, it is paid to the other member of the couple.[46] Even if you are not the person nominated to receive the JSA, if you separate from your partner and s/he cannot be traced, you can be paid any arrears of JSA that are due.[47]

Income-based jobseeker's allowance run-on

If you are getting income-based JSA and make a new claim for universal credit (UC) on or after 22 July 2020, your income-based JSA entitlement continues for two weeks (called a 'run-on payment' or 'transitional income-based JSA payment').[48] You do not have to make a claim for a run-on payment. It should be made automatically. You do not have to pay back a run-on payment and it does not count as a specified benefit for the purposes of the benefit cap (see p1197).[49]

Change of circumstances

You must report changes in your circumstances that you have been told you must report, as well as any that you might reasonably be expected to know might affect your right to, the amount of, or the payment of, your benefit, including any that are likely to occur. You should do this as soon as possible, preferably in writing. See p1199 for further information.

If there has been a relevant change of circumstances, a decision maker looks at your claim again and makes a new decision. To see when your JSA is then adjusted, see p721. The rules are the same as for contribution-based JSA.

Note: if you become a member of a couple with someone entitled to UC, your entitlement to income-based JSA ends (see p32).

Part 3: Other means-tested benefits and tax credits
Chapter 12: Income-based jobseeker's allowance
8. Tax, other benefits and the benefit cap

Waiting days

You are not entitled to JSA for the first seven 'waiting days' of any jobseeking period (see p254) unless:[50]

- your claim is linked to a previous claim for JSA so both are treated as part of the same jobseeking period. For joint-claim couples, this includes a previous claim made by either of you separately; *or*
- you (or for joint-claim couples only, either of you) have been entitled to income support (IS), employment and support allowance (ESA) or carer's allowance within the 12 weeks before you become entitled to JSA; *or*
- you are the member of a joint-claim couple nominated to be paid JSA and are in receipt of a training allowance; *or*
- you are 16 or 17 and getting severe hardship payments of JSA.

In addition, you do not have to serve any waiting days if you swap from claiming IS or ESA to claiming JSA, or if you and your partner swap which of you claims IS, ESA or JSA for both of you, and the new claim is for JSA.[51] Before you try to swap, check whether you (or your partner) can still make a new claim for these benefits.
Note:
- If you receive income-based JSA, you are entitled to maximum housing benefit during any waiting days.[52]
- You may be able to get a short-term advance before your first payment of JSA is due (see p1192).

8. Tax, other benefits and the benefit cap

Tax

Jobseeker's allowance (JSA) is taxable.[53] The maximum amount of JSA that is taxable is:
- if you are claiming for yourself, an amount equal to the appropriate personal allowance for a person of your age (see p333); *or*
- if you are a member of a couple, an amount equal to the income-based JSA personal allowance for a couple (half this amount if your partner is unable to claim JSA because s/he is involved in a trade dispute – see p1001).

The tax is not deducted while JSA is being paid but reduces the refund you would otherwise receive through PAYE (pay as you earn) when you return to work.
Any refunds of PAYE payments are paid to you at the end of the tax year to which they relate. Any other tax refund is paid only when you stop getting JSA.

Means-tested benefits and tax credits

If you are entitled to income-based JSA:

- it is an automatic passport to maximum housing benefit (HB), but if you are not already entitled, you must make a separate claim (if you still can). It is also an automatic passport to maximum child tax credit (CTC) and usually to maximum working tax credit (WTC);
- if you work less than 16 hours a week and your partner works at least 16 hours but less than 24 hours a week, you and your partner may be able to qualify for WTC as well as, or instead of, income-based JSA. Get advice to see whether you can still make a new claim, and if so how you would be better off financially;
- WTC is taken into account as income when working out your income-based JSA, but CTC is not.

If you and your partner were getting WTC and you or s/he have just stopped work or reduced your hours, you might get what is known as 'WTC run-on' for a four-week period (see p305).

Non-means-tested benefits

While you are on JSA you are entitled to national insurance (NI) credits (see p970). Most non-means-tested benefits are taken into account when working out the amount of income-based JSA you can get. However:

- attendance allowance, disability living allowance, personal independence payment, armed forces independence payment, guardian's allowance and, if you are getting CTC, child benefit, are not taken into account;
- it can still be worth claiming non-means-tested benefits even if they are taken into account. If you or your partner qualify for certain ones of these, you also qualify for certain premiums (see p339) and, therefore, a higher rate of income-based JSA.

You might only qualify for income-based JSA once you (or your partner or a child included in your claim) are awarded another benefit – known as a 'qualifying benefit'. To make sure you do not lose out while waiting for the outcome of a claim for a qualifying benefit, claim JSA at the same time. If your claim for income-based JSA is refused, once the qualifying benefit is awarded claim JSA again and ask for it to be backdated to the date of your first claim (see p1180).

The benefit cap

In some cases, there is a limit on the total amount of specified benefits you can receive (a 'benefit cap'). JSA is one of the specified benefits. However, the benefit cap only applies if you are getting universal credit or HB. See p1194 for further information. **Note:** income-based JSA run-on (see p265) does not count as a specified benefit.

Part 3: Other means-tested benefits and tax credits
Chapter 12: Income-based jobseeker's allowance
Notes

Passports and other sources of help

If you are entitled to income-based JSA, you also qualify for:
- health benefits such as free prescriptions (see Chapter 31); *and*
- education benefits such as free school lunches (see p866).

You may also qualify for social fund payments (see Chapter 37), Healthy Start food and vitamins – in Scotland, funeral support payment (see Chapter 73), a Best Start grant (see Chapter 72) or Best Start foods (see p865) – and help from your local welfare assistance scheme (see p861). You may be entitled to a council tax reduction (see p851).

Financial help on starting work

If you stop getting JSA because you or your partner start work, or your earnings or your hours in your existing job increase, you may be able to continue to get income-based JSA for help with your housing costs (eg, ground rent or service charges) for a further four weeks (see p376) or extended payments of HB if you pay rent (see p217). Your local authority may also provide extended help with council tax. If you have a DWP loan for your mortgage interest, this may continue for four weeks (see p860). See p873 for information about other financial help you might get.

Notes

1. Who can get income-based jobseeker's allowance
1 s1 JSA 1995
2 Reg 4 and 4A UC(TP) Regs; Art 4(11) WRA(No.32)O
3 ss3, 3A and 13 JSA 1995
4 Reg 76(2)(b) JSA Regs
5 s1(2B)-(2D) and (4) and Sch 1 paras 8A and 9A-9D JSA 1995; regs 3A-(3G) and Sch A1 JSA Regs; CJSA/2633/2004
6 Reg 47(1) and (2) JSA Regs
7 Reg 47(3) JSA Regs
8 Sch 1 para 3 JSA 1995; reg 48 JSA Regs
9 Reg 51 JSA Regs
10 Reg 3E(2)(g) JSA Regs
11 s1(2)(f) JSA 1995
12 Sch 1 para 2 JSA 1995; reg 10 SS&CS(DA) Regs

2. The rules about your age
13 s3A(1)(d) and (e) JSA 1995; reg 58 JSA Regs
14 Reg 3A JSA Regs
15 Art 8 WRA(No.31)O; HB Circular A9/ 2019
16 s3A(1)(d) and (e) JSA 1995
17 Reg 3A JSA Regs
18 Reg 62 JSA Regs
19 ss16 and 17 JSA 1995; regs 63 and 67 JSA Regs
20 ss3(1)(f)(iii) and 3A(1)(e)(ii) JSA 1995
21 Reg 61(1)(b), (c) and (g) and (2)(b) JSA Regs
22 Regs 57 and 59 JSA Regs
23 Regs 60 and 61 JSA Regs

24 ss3(1)(f)(ii), 3A(1)(e)(i) and 16 JSA 1995;
regs 63 and 67 JSA Regs; DWP guidance,
*Jobseekers Allowance For 16 to 17 Year
Olds: making a severe hardship decision*,
available at gov.uk/government/
publications/jsa-for-16-to-17-year-olds-
guidance-for-dwp-staff-making-a-
severe-hardship-decision
25 Reg 57(1), definition of 'young person',
JSA Regs

4. The amount of benefit
26 ss4(3) and (3A) and 13 JSA 1995

6. Claims and backdating
27 *LH v SSWP (ESA)* [2014] UKUT 480
(AAC), reported as [2015] AACR 14
28 Reg 4(5) SS(C&P) Regs
29 Reg 4(3B)(a) SS(C&P) Regs
30 Reg 4(6)(a) SS(C&P) Regs
31 Reg 19(1) and Sch 4 para 1 SS(C&P)
Regs
32 Reg 6(4ZA), (4ZB)(a), (4A)(a)(i) and
(4AA) SS(C&P) Regs
33 Reg 6(4ZC)(a) and (b) SS(C&P) Regs
34 Reg 6(4A)(b) SS(C&P) Regs
35 Reg 6(4AB) SS(C&P) Regs
36 Reg 6(4AB) SS(C&P) Regs
37 Reg 6(28) SS(C&P) Regs
38 Reg 4(3B)(b) SS(C&P) Regs
39 Reg 4(3B)(c) SS(C&P) Regs
40 Reg 6(4A)(a)(ii) SS(C&P) Regs
41 Reg 6(4ZB)(b) and (4ZC)(c) SS(C&P)
Regs
42 Sch 5 para 17A JSA Regs
43 CS/371/1949
44 Reg 13(1) and (9) SS(C&P) Regs

7. Getting paid
45 s3B JSA 1995
46 ss19(7), 19A(10) and 19B(8) JSA 1995
47 Reg 30A SS(C&P) Regs
48 Regs 46(1) and 47(2) UC(TP) Regs; reg 5
The Universal Credit (Managed
Migration Pilot and Miscellaneous
Amendments) Regulations 2019,
No.1152
49 Reg 8B UC(TP) Regs 2014
50 Sch 1 para 4 JSA 1995; reg 46 JSA Regs;
Arts 12 and 13 WRA(No.9)O; Art 11(2)
WRA(No.11)O
51 Reg 14A SS&CS(DA) Regs
52 Reg 2(3)(b) HB Regs

8. Tax, other benefits and the benefit cap
53 ss671-75 IT(EP)A 2003

Chapter 13

Pension credit

3

This chapter covers:
1. Who can get pension credit (p271)
2. The rules about your age (p271)
3. People included in the claim (p272)
4. The amount of pension credit (p273)
5. Special benefit rules (p276)
6. Claims and backdating (p277)
7. Getting paid (p279)
8. Tax, other benefits and the benefit cap (p281)

Key facts
- Pension credit (PC) is a benefit for people on a low income who are at least pension age.
- There are two types of PC: **guarantee credit**, which ensures a minimum level of income, and **savings credit**, which is intended to 'reward' you for making provision for your retirement, such as through savings or an occupational pension. You can be entitled to either guarantee credit, savings credit or both. Savings credit is being phased out.
- PC is a means-tested benefit.
- PC can include an amount for a child or qualifying young person for whom you are responsible.
- You do not have to have paid national insurance contributions to qualify.
- You can qualify for PC whether you are in or out of work.
- PC is administered and paid by the Pension Service, which is part of the DWP.
- If you disagree with a PC decision, you can apply for a revision or supersession (see Chapter 56), or appeal against it (see Chapter 57). You must apply for a mandatory reconsideration before you can appeal.

1. Who can get pension credit

Guarantee credit

You qualify for the guarantee credit of pension credit (PC) if:[1]

- you are at least pension age (see p780). If you have a partner and make a new claim for PC, both of you must usually be pension age. There are exceptions (see p272);[2] *and*
- you are in Great Britain (except for periods of temporary absence – see p1659) and satisfy the 'habitual residence' test and the 'right to reside' test (see Chapter 68);[3] *and*
- your partner (if you have one) is not entitled to PC;[4] *and*
- you have no income, or your income is below a certain amount (known as the 'appropriate minimum guarantee' – see p273);[5] *and*
- you are not a 'person subject to immigration control' (see p1560), although there are exceptions to this rule (see p1565).[6]

Savings credit

You qualify for the savings credit of PC if:[7]

- either:
  - you and your partner (if you have one) reached pension age (see p780) before 6 April 2016; *or*
  - either you or your partner reached pension age before 6 April 2016, you were entitled to savings credit on 6 April 2016 and you have remained entitled to it;[8] *and*
- you or your partner are 65 or over;[9] *and*
- you are in Great Britain (except for periods of temporary absence – see p1659) and satisfy the 'habitual residence' test and the 'right to reside' test (see Chapter 68);[10] *and*
- your partner (if you have one) is not entitled to PC;[11] *and*
- you are not a 'person subject to immigration control', although there are exceptions to this rule (see p1565);[12] *and*
- your 'qualifying income' exceeds the 'savings credit threshold', but is not so high that it produces a nil award (see p276).[13]

2. The rules about your age

Entitlement to pension credit (PC) for both men and women is linked to the minimum qualifying age for state retirement pension.[14] The pension age for men and women has been equalised, and is rising to 66 (by 2020) and will eventually be 68.[15] When you reach pension age depends on your date of birth.

Part 3: Other means-tested benefits and tax credits
Chapter 13: Pension credit
3. People included in the claim

To check your pension age, see gov.uk/state-pension-age. For information about the rules on the qualifying age for PC before pension age was equalised for men and women, see p262 of the 2018/19 edition of this *Handbook*.

If you are a member of a couple and you are at least pension age but your partner is not (called a 'mixed-age couple' in this *Handbook*), you cannot usually qualify for PC.[16] You and your partner may be able to claim universal credit (UC) instead.

There are exceptions to this rule. If you are a member of a mixed-aged couple, you can continue to qualify for PC if, on 14 May 2019 as part of the same couple you were entitled to:[17]

- PC; *or*
- pension-age housing benefit (HB); *or*
- both PC and HB.

You continue to qualify for PC provided you continue to be entitled to some PC or pension-age HB or to both, as part of the same mixed-age couple. You can make a new claim for PC, provided you are entitled to HB on this basis and have been since 14 May 2019.

If you are in a mixed-age couple, you have reached pension age and your partner cannot claim UC because s/he does not satisfy certain UC conditions, you can instead get PC (and HB) as a single person, either until the reason your partner cannot claim UC no longer applies, or s/he reaches pension age. This situation can arise if s/he:

- is under 18, and not someone who is able to claim UC when 16/17 (see p37); *or*
- does not satisfy the habitual residence test (see Chapter 68), or is a person subject to immigration control (see Chapter 67); *or*
- is a prisoner, or is detained in hospital serving a prison sentence (see p937); *or*
- is a member of a religious order and fully maintained by it; *or*
- is absent from Great Britain for more than the permitted period, normally 1 month although there are exceptions (see p1664).

If one of you is temporarily absent from the household and is, or is expected to be, absent for more than six months, you can claim PC (and HB) as a single person until the end of the absence, as you are no longer treated as a couple for UC (see p61).

3. People included in the claim

If you are single, you claim pension credit (PC) for yourself. If you are a member of a couple and both you and your partner are pension age (see above), either of you can claim PC for you both. If only one of you is pension age, see above. See p319 for who counts as a couple.

The 'appropriate minimum guarantee' that forms part of the calculation of your PC includes an allowance for a couple and can include additional amounts based on your and your partner's circumstances. When the amount of your PC is worked out, your partner's income and capital are usually added to yours.

If you are claiming PC but your partner has not yet reached pension age, s/he may qualify for national insurance (NI) credits in order to protect her/his NI record. See Chapter 43 for more details about NI credits.

You can get amounts for a child or qualifying young person for whom you are responsible included in your PC if you are not entitled to tax credits.[18]

4. The amount of pension credit

The amount of pension credit (PC) you receive depends on whether you are claiming as a single person or as a member of a couple, whether you are responsible for any children or qualifying young people, and whether you have any disabilities, caring responsibilities or eligible housing costs. The maximum amount of guarantee credit you could receive is reduced by your income (subject to any applicable disregards). Your savings credit entitlement is based on the amount of your pension(s) and certain other income (see p276). For general information on income and capital, see Chapters 21 and 23. For information on qualifying income for savings credit, see p276.

Guarantee credit

Your maximum guarantee credit is known as the 'appropriate minimum guarantee'[19] and is made up of:
* the standard minimum guarantee; *and*
* where applicable, additional amounts.

Standard minimum guarantee
If you do not have any additional needs, you receive an award of PC which ensures that your weekly income is brought up to a standard minimum guarantee level, depending on your circumstances.

Amount of standard minimum guarantee

Single person[20]	£173.75
Couple[21]	£265.20
Each additional spouse in a polygamous marriage[22]	£91.45

Additional amounts
If you have additional needs (eg, a disability, caring responsibilities or certain housing costs), an additional amount(s) is added to the standard minimum

Part 3: Other means-tested benefits and tax credits
Chapter 13: Pension credit
4. The amount of pension credit

guarantee. The additional amounts broadly correspond to the premiums and housing costs included in income support (IS). There is also a transitional additional amount to ensure you are not worse off as a result of moving on to PC from IS, income-based jobseeker's allowance (JSA) or income-related employment and support allowance (ESA).

Note: you cannot get an amount in your PC for the cost of your mortgage interest payments or for a loan for repairs and improvements. Instead, the DWP may offer you a loan (see p855).

Additional amounts

Severe disability[23]	£66.95	£133.90 (if both
The qualifying rules are broadly the same as for the		partners qualify)
severe disability premium (see p346).		
Carer[24]	£37.50	£37.50 (for each
The qualifying rules are the same as for the carer		partner who qualifies)
premium (see p350).		
Children (see p323).[25]	£64.82	Additional £29.52 for
First child born before 6 April 2017	£54.32	disability, or £92.12
Each subsequent child		for severe disability
Transitional[26]	See below	

Transitional amount

If you were in receipt of IS, income-based JSA or income-related ESA immediately before you first become entitled to PC, in order to ensure you are not worse off by moving onto PC, your appropriate minimum guarantee may include a transitional amount.[27] The transitional amount reduces over time by any increase in your appropriate minimum guarantee and stops when you or your partner are no longer entitled to PC (disregarding any break in entitlement of less than eight weeks).[28]

When your appropriate minimum guarantee may be reduced

Your appropriate minimum guarantee may be reduced in certain circumstances. The most important of these are if:[29]

- you are a couple and one of you is a 'person subject to immigration control' (see p1569);
- you are a prisoner (see p941);
- your partner is abroad (see p1659);
- you are a member of and fully maintained by a religious order. In this case, your appropriate amount is nil.

Chapter 13
Pension credit

The guarantee credit calculation

Step one: calculate your appropriate minimum guarantee
Your appropriate minimum guarantee comprises:
- standard minimum guarantee for you and your partner, if you have one; *plus*
- additional amounts for any special needs and/or certain housing costs.

Step two: calculate your income
This is the amount you have coming in each week – eg, from benefits, private pensions and earnings.[30] Not all income counts (eg, personal independence payment (PIP), disability living allowance, attendance allowance (AA), child tax credit and child benefit are disregarded in full) and some income can be disregarded (see Chapter 21). If you have more than £10,000 capital, you are treated as having income of £1 for every £500 (or part thereof) over £10,000.[31]

Step three: deduct income from appropriate minimum guarantee
The amount of your guarantee credit is your appropriate minimum guarantee less any relevant income you have.[32] If your income is above the appropriate minimum guarantee, you do not qualify for any guarantee credit. You may qualify for guarantee credit if you or your partner become entitled to a qualifying benefit, like AA, which may increase the amount of your appropriate minimum guarantee.

Examples

Barbara is single and aged 68. She is in receipt of AA. She lives alone and no one gets carer's allowance for looking after her. She lives in rented accommodation.
Her appropriate minimum guarantee is:

Standard minimum guarantee (single person rate)	£173.75
Severe disability additional amount	£66.95
Total	**£240.70**

Her weekly income is her basic state pension of £134.25. AA is ignored as income.
She is therefore entitled to £106.45 guarantee credit to bring her total income up to £240.70.
She is also entitled to maximum housing benefit and any other passported benefits that may apply.

Maria and Geoff are a couple. Maria is 67 and Geoff is 68. Their 24-year-old daughter lives with them and she is in receipt of income-based JSA. Maria receives the enhanced rate of the daily living component of PIP and Geoff gets AA.
Their appropriate minimum guarantee is £265.20.
Their joint weekly income for calculating PC is £312.70, made up of basic state pension of £214.70 (Maria £80.45, Geoff £134.25), occupational pension of £95 and £3 deemed income from £11,500 savings. PIP and AA are ignored as income.
They are not entitled to any guarantee credit because their income exceeds their appropriate minimum guarantee of £265.20. Their appropriate minimum guarantee does not include a severe disability addition because their 24-year-old daughter lives with them.

275

Part 3: Other means-tested benefits and tax credits
Chapter 13: Pension credit
5. Special benefit rules

Savings credit

Savings credit is currently being phased out. You can only get savings credit if:
- you or your partner (if you have one) are 65 or over and you both reached pension age (see p780) before 6 April 2016; *or*
- either you or your partner reached pension age before 6 April 2016, and on that date you had an existing award of savings credit and you have remained entitled to it since then.[33]

In addition, the amount of your 'qualifying income' must be above the savings credit threshold.[34]

Savings credit threshold

Single person	£150.47
Couple	£239.17

'Qualifying income' for this purpose is all the income that counts for guarantee credit (see Chapter 21) except:[35]
- working tax credit;
- incapacity benefit;
- contributory ESA;
- contribution-based JSA;
- severe disablement allowance;
- maternity allowance;
- maintenance payments for you, or your partner, from a spouse or former spouse.

The amount of savings credit to which you are entitled is subject to a maximum figure, known as the '**maximum savings credit**'.[36]

Maximum savings credit

Single person	£13.97
Couple	£15.62

For details of how to calculate the amount of savings credit, see pp138–39 of the 2016/17 edition of this *Handbook*.

5. Special benefit rules

Special rules may apply to:
- people subject to immigration control (see Chapter 67);

- people who have come from or are going abroad (see Chapters 68 and 69);
- people who are in hospital or living in a care home or other similar accommodation, and people in prison or detention (see Chapter 42).

6. Claims and backdating

The general rules about claims and backdating are covered in Chapter 50. This section explains the specific rules that apply to pension credit (PC).

Making a claim

A claim can be made:[37]
- by telephone. Call the Pension Service on 0800 99 1234 (textphone: 0800 169 0133) from 8am to 7.30pm, Monday to Friday. This is the Pension Service's 'preferred route' for claiming;
- in writing on the approved form (Form PC1). You ask for this by telephoning the number above. Local authority housing benefit (HB) offices and some other 'alternative offices' (see p1168) can provide this form, but will also encourage you to claim by telephone.

You must provide any information or evidence required (see below). In certain circumstances, the DWP may accept a written application not on the approved form. You can amend or withdraw your claim before a decision is made (see p1169). If there is a delay in dealing with your claim, you may be able to get a short-term advance of benefit (see p1192).

Who should claim

If you are a single person, you must claim on your own behalf. If you are a member of a couple, you must choose which one of you claims for you both (see p319). If you cannot agree who should claim, a decision maker decides.[38]

You can swap who claims, provided you both agree. It may be worthwhile doing so – eg, if one of you is about to go abroad.

If you are unable to manage your own affairs, another person can claim PC for you as your 'appointee' (see p1170).

Information to support your claim

For the general information requirements that apply to all benefits, see p1170.

It is important that you provide any information required when you claim. Until you do, you may not count as having made a valid claim (see p1172). Correct any defects as soon as possible or your date of claim may be affected.

When you claim, you are asked about your circumstances, including details of any income and savings and any housing costs you or your partner have. **Note:**

Part 3: Other means-tested benefits and tax credits
Chapter 13: Pension credit
6. Claims and backdating

you must include details of any personal pension scheme to which you belong. If further information or evidence is needed, see below for when your claim begins.[39]

Once your claim has been decided, you are sent a letter detailing the amount of any award, and the information on which it was based. You are asked to check this and report any omissions or changes.

Even if you provided all that was required when you claimed, you may be asked to supply further information to support your claim (see p1174). You may also be asked to provide further information after you are awarded PC. If you fail to do so, your benefit may be suspended or even terminated (see p1200).

The date of your claim

The date of your claim is important as it determines when your entitlement to PC starts. This is not necessarily the date from when you are paid. For information about when payment of PC starts, see p279.

Your **'date of claim'** (unless the backdating rules apply) is:[40]

- the date your claim, properly completed with all the required information and evidence, is received at the appropriate office (the DWP, local authority HB office or county council office); *or*
- the date you notify the appropriate office of your intention to claim, and you submit a properly completed claim with all the required information and evidence within one month of this date.

Note: you must make sure your claim is valid. If it is 'defective', you are given one month (or longer if considered reasonable) to correct the defects (see p1172). If you do, your claim is treated as having been made when you initially claimed.[41] If you are making an advance claim for PC before you have reached pension age and your claim is defective, you may correct it at any time before the end of the advance period.[42] The one-month time limit runs from the day following the end of the advance period.[43]

In some cases, you can claim in advance (see p279) and in some cases your claim can be backdated (see below). If you want this to be done, make this clear when you claim or the DWP might not consider it.

Backdating your claim

It is important that you claim in time because PC can only be backdated for up to three months. Your claim can be backdated if you satisfy the qualifying conditions over the period for which you require backdating – you do not have to show why your claim was late.[44] If you want your claim to be backdated, it is important that you ask – claims are not automatically backdated. When you make a telephone claim, you should be asked about the date from when you want your claim to start.

If you claim backdated PC within three months of being awarded a qualifying benefit and an earlier PC claim was refused because you did not get a qualifying benefit (see p1180) at that time, your PC can be backdated to the date of your earlier PC claim or the date when the qualifying benefit was first payable, whichever is later.[45]

For general rules on backdating, see p1176.

Claiming in advance

You can make an advance claim for PC to give the DWP time to ensure you receive your benefit as soon as you become entitled. However, you cannot make an advance claim if the reason you do not qualify straight away is because you fail the habitual residence test (see p1587). PC can be claimed up to four months before you qualify, whether this is before you reach pension age and you know you will be entitled then *or* after you reach pension age when you know you will have a future entitlement – eg, because of a drop in income.[46] The date of your claim is the date on which you qualify.

At the time of writing, the government is making extra-statutory payments of universal credit (UC) if you do not make an advance claim for PC and your UC stops in the assessment period immediately before you become entitled to PC and/or housing benefit. The law will change so that you can get UC during the assessment period in which you reach pension age. See AskCPAG.org.uk and CPAG's *Welfare Rights Bulletin* for updates.[47]

7. Getting paid

The general rules on getting paid are in Chapter 51. This section explains the specific rules that apply to pension credit (PC).

When is pension credit paid?

	Qualifying age on or after 6 April 2010	Qualifying age before 6 April 2010
When is PC paid?	The day you are paid depends on your national insurance number (see p1189).[48]	Monday, or the same day as your retirement pension is paid.[49]
How often is PC paid?	Weekly, fortnightly or four-weekly in arrears.	Weekly in advance. If you were entitled to income support immediately before 6 October 2003 and paid in arrears, PC is also paid in arrears.[50]

If you are entitled to less than 10 pence a week, you are not paid PC, unless you are receiving another social security benefit that can be paid with PC.[51] You still have an underlying entitlement. If your entitlement is less than £1 a week, a decision maker can decide to pay you quarterly in arrears.

There may be a delay between the date of your claim and the date PC becomes payable. This is because payment does not normally start until the first payday following the claim.[52] There are exceptions to this rule.[53]

Note:

- Deductions can be made from your PC to pay to third parties (see p1202).
- Your PC might be paid at a reduced rate if you have been sanctioned for a benefit offence (see p1278).
- For information on missing payments, see p1189. If you cannot get your PC payments because you have lost your bank or post office card or have forgotten your PIN, see p1188. If your payment service card has been lost or stolen, or if you have forgotten your memorable date, see p1189.
- If payment of your PC is delayed, see p1295. If you are waiting for a decision on your claim, or to be paid, you may be able to get a short-term advance (see p1192). If you wish to complain about how your claim has been dealt with, or claim compensation, see Chapter 60.
- If payment of your PC is suspended, see p1200.
- If you are overpaid PC, you might have to repay it (see Chapter 53) and, in some circumstances, you may have to pay a penalty (see p1268). If you have been accused of fraud, see Chapter 54.

Change of circumstances

You must report changes in your circumstances that you have been told to report, as well as any that you might reasonably be expected to know might affect your right to, the amount of, or the payment of your benefit. You should do this as soon as possible, preferably in writing. See p1199 for further information.

See below for the circumstances that do not need to be reported during the assessed income period.

If there has been a relevant change of circumstances, a decision maker looks at your claim again and makes a new decision. To find out when the new decision takes effect, see p1320.

If you become a member of a 'mixed-age couple' (see p272), your entitlement to PC stops (see p33). Your partner may be able to claim universal credit instead.

When your pension credit is adjusted

Generally, your PC is adjusted from the day the change occurs or is expected to occur, if this is the day you are paid benefit. If it is not, your PC is adjusted from the start of the next benefit week. However, there are a few exceptions to this general rule.[54]

Assessed income period

If you were already getting PC before 6 April 2016, an assessed income period may have been set. From 6 April 2016, no new assessed income periods have been set.

An 'assessed income period' is a set period during which you are not required to report any changes in certain types of your income, known as 'retirement provision'.[55] 'Retirement provision' means income from:[56]

- a retirement pension (other than state retirement pensions);
- an annuity (other than retirement pension income);
- capital;
- periodic payments from the Pension Protection Fund or the Financial Assistance Scheme.

The effect of this is that if you have an increase in, or subsequently start to receive, retirement provision during your assessed income period, you do not have to report this to the DWP. All other changes in your income that affect your PC entitlement must be reported to the DWP as soon as they occur. During the assessed income period, your PC entitlement may change as a result of 'deemed increases in retirement provision' – eg, periodic increases in an occupational pension. See the 2015/16 edition of this *Handbook* for details.

Before 6 April 2016 an assessed income period could be set for a fixed period, usually five years or, if you were 75 or over, for an indefinite period.[57] All fixed-period assessed income periods have now ended. If an assessed income period has been set for an indefinite period, it continues unless you have a change of circumstances (see below).

Your assessed income period comes to an end if:[58]

- you become a member of a couple; *or*
- you cease to be a member of a couple; *or*
- you or your partner reach the age of 65; *or*
- you are no longer entitled to PC; *or*
- you are single and go to live in a care home on a permanent basis; *or*
- payments of retirement provision due to you stop temporarily or are less than the amount due, and your PC award is superseded as a result.

---

8. Tax, other benefits and the benefit cap

Tax

Pension credit (PC) is not taxable.

Part 3: Other means-tested benefits and tax credits
Chapter 13: Pension credit
8. Tax, other benefits and the benefit cap

Means-tested benefits and tax credits

If you are entitled to PC, the following applies.

- An award of guarantee credit is an automatic passport to maximum housing benefit (HB), but if you are not already entitled, you must make a separate claim (if you still can). If you are only entitled to savings credit, your HB claim is calculated in the usual way. The Pension Service provides the local authority with its assessment of your income.
- If you get guarantee credit, the £16,000 limit on your capital does not apply for HB. It does apply if you only receive savings credit.
- PC is a passport to maximum working tax credit (WTC) and child tax credit (CTC). If you had an award of WTC and/or CTC on 31 January 2019, this can continue. You can claim amounts for a child in your PC, if you are not already getting tax credits. If you are getting an amount for a child(ren) in your PC and are then awarded WTC or CTC retrospectively (eg, following an appeal), entitlement to the amount for a child(ren) in your PC ends.

Non-means-tested benefits

Some non-means-tested benefits are taken into account as income when calculating entitlement to PC. Others have a £10 disregard and some are disregarded entirely. See Chapter 21 for details.

Qualifying for certain non-means-tested benefits can help you qualify for more PC. For example, if you get carer's allowance, you may be entitled to a carer addition with your appropriate minimum guarantee.

The benefit cap

In some cases, there is a limit on the total amount of specified benefits you can receive (a 'benefit cap'). PC is *not* one of the specified benefits. The benefit cap only applies if you are getting HB or universal credit. If you are getting HB, the benefit cap does not normally apply if you are at least the qualifying age for PC.

Passports and other sources of help

If you are entitled to PC, you may also be eligible for:

- a Christmas bonus (see p870);
- health benefits, if you are getting the guarantee credit (see Chapter 31);
- free school lunches, if you are getting the guarantee credit. This only applies in England and Wales – in Scotland, you can qualify via CTC (see p866);
- social fund payments (see Chapter 37) or, in Scotland, a Best Start grant or funeral support payment (see Chapters 72 and 73);
- council tax reduction from your local authority (see p851);
- home insulation grants and discretionary grants from the local authority towards the cost of home improvements (see p872).

Notes

1. Who can get pension credit
1   s2 SPCA 2002
2   ss1(6) and 4(1A) SPCA 2002
3   s1(2)(a) SPCA 2002; regs 2 and 3 SPC Regs
4   s4(1) SPCA 2002
5   s2(2) SPCA 2002; reg 6 SPC Regs
6   s4(2) SPCA 2002
7   s3 SPCA 2002
8   s3 SPCA 2002, as amended by PA 2014; reg 7A SPC Regs
9   s3(1) SPCA 2002
10 s1(2)(a) SPCA 2002; regs 2-4 SPC Regs
11 s4(1) SPCA 2002
12 s4(2) SPCA 2002
13 s3(2)-(4) SPCA 2002

2. The rules about your age
14 s1(6) SPCA 2002
15 s126 and Sch 4 PA 1995
16 s4(1A) SPCA 2002
17 Art 4 WRA(No.31)O; Welfare Reform Act 2012 (Commencement No.31 and Savings and Transitional Provisions (Amendment)) Order 2019 No.935; HB Circular A9/2019 *Mixed-age couples: further guidance (revised)*, 10 July 2019

3. People included in the claim
18 Reg 6(6)(d) and Sch IIA SPC Regs

4. The amount of pension credit
19 s2(3) SPCA 2002
20 Reg 6(1)(b) SPC Regs
21 Reg 6(1)(a) SPC Regs
22 Reg 6 and Sch 3 para 1(5) SPC Regs
23 Reg 6(4) and (5) SPC Regs
24 Reg 6(6)(a) SPC Regs
25 Reg 6(6)(d) and Sch IIA SPC Regs
26 Reg 6(6)(b) SPC Regs
27 Reg 6(6)(b) and Sch 1 para 6 SPC Regs
28 Sch 1 para 6(8) and (9) SPC Regs
29 Regs 5 and 6(2)(b) and (3) SPC Regs
30 s15 SPCA 2002; regs 14-24 SPC Regs
31 Reg 15(6) SPC Regs
32 s2(2) SPCA 2002
33 s3 SPCA 2002, as amended by PA 2014; reg 7A SPC Regs
34 Reg 7(2) SPC Regs
35 Reg 9 SPC Regs
36 s3(7) SPCA 2002; reg 7(1)(a) SPC Regs

6. Claims and backdating
37 Reg 4D SS(C&P) Regs
38 Reg 4D(7) SS(C&P) Regs
39 Reg 7(4) SS(C&P) Regs
40 Reg 4F SS(C&P) Regs
41 Reg 4D(6E) SS(C&P) Regs
42 Regs 4D(12) and 4E(3) SS(C&P) Regs
43 Reg 7(1C) SS(C&P) Regs
44 Reg 19(2) and (3) SS(C&P) Regs
45 Reg 6(16) and (18) SS(C&P) Regs
46 Regs 4E and 13D SS(C&P) Regs
47 Written Statement 146, Dr Thérèse Coffey, House of Commons, 5 March 2020

7. Getting paid
48 Reg 26BA SS(C&P) Regs
49 Reg 26B SS(C&P) Regs
50 Reg 36(6) SPC(CTMP) Regs
51 Reg 13 SPC Regs
52 Reg 16A(1) and (4) SS(C&P) Regs
53 Reg 16A(2) SS(C&P) Regs
54 Reg 7 and Sch 3B SS&CS(DA) Regs
55 ss6-10 SPCA 2002; regs 10-12 SPC Regs
56 s7(6) SPCA 2002
57 s9(1) SPCA 2002
58 s9(4) SPCA 2002; reg 12 SPC Regs

Chapter 14

Child tax credit

3

This chapter covers:
1. Who can get child tax credit (below)
2. The rules about your age (p291)
3. People included in the claim (p291)
4. The amount of child tax credit (p291)
5. Claims and backdating (p292)
6. Getting paid (p294)
7. Tax, other benefits and the benefit cap (p295)

Key facts
- Child tax credit (CTC) is paid to families with children or qualifying young people who have not claimed universal credit (UC).
- You do not have to have paid national insurance contributions to qualify.
- CTC is paid whether or not you or your partner are working.
- CTC does not count as income for income support, income-based jobseeker's allowance, income-related employment and support allowance or pension credit purposes, and can be paid in addition to these benefits.
- CTC is administered and paid by HM Revenue and Customs.
- If you disagree with a CTC decision, you can apply for a mandatory reconsideration and then appeal if you are unhappy with the outcome (see Chapter 66).

1. Who can get child tax credit

You qualify for child tax credit (CTC) if:[1]
- you (or your partner) are 'responsible' for a child or qualifying young person (see p286); *and*
- your income is sufficiently low (see Chapter 62); *and*
- you are 'present' and 'ordinarily resident' in the UK. You can be treated as present and ordinarily resident in the UK in some circumstances – eg, if you are temporarily away. You can be treated as not being in the UK if you claim CTC and do not have a 'right to reside'. You must usually have been living in

the UK for at least three months, although there are exceptions to this rule. See Chapter 68 for further information; *and*
* you are not a 'person subject to immigration control' (see Chapter 67).

Although full-time paid work does not affect your entitlement to CTC, income from work affects the amount you can be paid.

Child tax credit and universal credit

You can now only make a new claim for CTC in limited circumstances (see below). If you are already entitled to CTC, you can continue to qualify until:

– you claim universal credit (UC);[2] *or*

– you become a member of a couple and your partner is getting UC; *or*

– you and your partner are invited to claim UC as part of the 'managed migration' process (see p30).

The government says that, from November 2020, the DWP will begin to notify existing CTC claimants that they must claim UC instead. When this managed migration happens, you will be invited to claim UC and your CTC award will end. See p27 for further information, and AskCPAG.org.uk and CPAG's *Welfare Rights Bulletin* for updates.

Who can make a new claim for child tax credit

You can only make a new claim for CTC in limited circumstances. These are if:[3]
* you already have an award of working tax credit (WTC). If you are then entitled to CTC, this is treated as a change in circumstances and a new claim is not required; *or*
* you were entitled to CTC in 2019/20 and are making a claim for 2020/21; *or*
* you are prevented from claiming UC because:[4]
  – you (or your partner) are, or within the last month have been, entitled to income support (IS), income-based jobseeker's allowance (JSA), income-related employment and support allowance (ESA) or housing benefit (HB) that includes a severe disability premium (see p346), and if your entitlement to the benefit ended during that month, you (or s/he) have continued to satisfy the conditions for that premium; *and*
  – you (and your partner) have not yet been given a 'migration notice' from the DWP that you will be transferred to UC via the 'managed migration' process (see p30); *or*
* you are prevented from claiming UC because you (or if you are in a couple, you and your partner) are a 'frontier worker' – ie, you work in Great Britain or Northern Ireland but do not live there.

If you cannot make a new claim for CTC under these rules, you can make a claim for UC or for pension credit, including an additional amount for a child.

Part 3: Other means-tested benefits and tax credits
Chapter 14: Child tax credit
1. Who can get child tax credit

Children

To qualify for CTC, you must be 'responsible' for at least one child or qualifying young person.[5] The terms 'child' or 'children' in this chapter also refer to qualifying young people. You do not have to be the child's parent – eg, you could be a grandparent, sister or brother. See p288 for when you count as responsible for a child and p289 for when you do not count as responsible.

If you are entitled to CTC for a child and the child dies, you continue to be entitled to CTC for the child for eight weeks immediately following her/his death (or up to the date your child would have turned 20, if this is earlier).[6]

Who counts as a child

Someone counts as a child until her/his 16th birthday.[7] In some circumstances, a young person aged under 20 also counts as a child. HM Revenue and Customs (HMRC) refers to her/him as a '**qualifying young person**'.

A young person counts as a child during any period:[8]

- from her/his 16th birthday until 31 August following that birthday, whether or not s/he is in full-time, non-advanced education or 'approved training' (but see p287 for when s/he may not count as a child); *or*
- from 1 September following her/his 16th birthday (or from 31 August if s/he turns 16 on that date), while s/he is under 20 and in:
  - full-time, non-advanced education (see p580) or in appropriate full-time education (in England only). This does not apply if s/he is getting the education because of her/his employment. A young person counts as being in full-time education during any gaps between the ending of one course and the start of another, if s/he is enrolled on and commences the other course; *or*
  - approved training (see p581 for what counts) or has been enrolled on or accepted to undertake approved training. This does not apply if s/he is getting the training through a contract of employment.

  The course or approved training must have begun before s/he reached 19, or s/he must have been enrolled on or accepted to undertake the course or approved training before that age. **Note:** there is no equivalent to the child benefit 'terminal date rule' (see p582) so, unless the young person is under 18 and the rule in the next bullet point applies, s/he cannot count as a child once the course or training ends. However, HMRC guidance states that if s/he intends to continue full-time education but at an advanced level, payment can continue until the last day of the academic year (31 August) or, if earlier, the date s/he changes her/his mind and decides not to continue in education.[9] Therefore, ensure you notify HMRC when the course or training ends and what your child intends to do next;
- from 1 September following her/his 16th birthday (or from 31 August if s/he turns 16 on that date), while s/he is under 18, has ceased full-time education

or approved training and it is not more than 20 weeks since s/he did so. S/he must notify HMRC within three months of ceasing full-time education or approved training that s/he has registered for work or training with a qualifying body – eg, the place where the local authority provides careers advice for young people or the Ministry of Defence. This rule can apply again if s/he goes back into full-time education or approved training and ceases again.

What should you do when your child turns 16?

Notify HMRC in the September after your child's 16th birthday if s/he is staying on in non-advanced education, appropriate full-time education (in England only), or approved training. In England, this applies even though the school participation age is 17. To be sure that your CTC continues, you should also notify HMRC in the September after your child's 17th, 18th and 19th birthdays that s/he is continuing in education.

When working out whether a young person counts as being in full-time education or approved training, HMRC ignores:[10]
* an interruption of up to six months, whether it began before or after the young person turned 16; *and*
* an interruption of any length which is due to the young person's physical or mental illness or disability.

The interruption is only ignored if HMRC thinks it is reasonable to do so. You should notify HMRC if the above applies.

When a young person does not count as a child

A young person cannot count as a child during any period following her/his 16th birthday in which:[11]
* having ceased full-time education or approved training, s/he is in full-time paid work. This means work of 24 hours or more per week. For information about:
  – what counts as paid work, see p301;
  – how the hours are calculated, see p301;
  – situations when the young person is not treated as being in full-time paid work, see p306.
  The rules are the same as for WTC.
  Remember that, even if a young person has *not* started full-time paid work, s/he cannot count as a child from 1 September after her/his 16th birthday if s/he has ceased full-time education or 'approved training' and has not registered for work or training with a qualifying body; *or*
* s/he gets UC, IS, income-based JSA or income-related ESA in her/his own right.
  Note: you do not count as responsible for a child aged 16 or over if s/he gets CTC, WTC or contributory ESA in her/his own right (see p289).

Part 3: Other means-tested benefits and tax credits
Chapter 14: Child tax credit
1. Who can get child tax credit

Being responsible for a child

For tax credit purposes, a child can only count as the responsibility of one claimant (or joint-claim couple).[12] You are treated as 'responsible' for a child if:[13]

- s/he normally lives with you (see below); *or*
- s/he normally lives with you and also with someone else, but you have the main responsibility for her/him. This only applies if you and another person (or couple) make competing claims for CTC for the same child.

Note:

- Entitlement to child benefit is not a specific factor in working out who is responsible for a child for CTC purposes.
- If a child for whom you are treated as being responsible has a child of her/his own (eg, your grandchild) who normally lives with her/him, you also count as being responsible for that child, but not if your child is 16 or over and is awarded CTC in her/his own right.[14]

Does the child normally live with you?

The rules do not define when a child counts as normally living with you. HMRC says it means that your child 'regularly, usually, typically' lives with you and that this allows for temporary or occasional absences.[15] So if your child counts as normally living with you, s/he should also count as doing so even if s/he is away from home – eg, because s/he is away at school or for a temporary period on holiday or in hospital. You can argue that a child is normally living with you if s/he spends more time with you than with anyone else.[16]

Your child can count as normally living with you even if s/he also lives with someone else, or only lives with you for part of the week and lives for part of the week with someone else – eg, her/his other parent. However, CTC can only be paid to one claimant (or joint-claim couple) – see below. If you are seeking to rely on European Union co-ordination rules to qualify for CTC for a child in another member state, see p1680 for more information.

Do you have main responsibility?

If you (and your partner) and at least one other person (or couple) with whom the child also normally lives claim CTC for the same child, you only qualify for CTC for the child if you can show you have the 'main responsibility' for her/him. This applies if:[17]

- your child normally lives with both you and:
  - at least one other person in another household – eg, with you and with the child's other parent from whom you have separated; *or*
  - someone who is not your partner in the same household – eg, with you and with the child's grandparent where you live together.

  It also applies if it is a combination of these situations. 'Household' is not defined. See p329 for ideas about what might count as a household; *and*

- you and at least one of the other people with whom your child normally lives claim CTC.

You and the other CTC claimant(s) can decide which of you should count as having main responsibility. If you cannot agree, a decision maker decides.[18] You can challenge the decision (see p290).

'**Main responsibility**' is not defined in the rules. The approach for tax credits is different from that for child benefit, HB or child support maintenance, and does not refer to the legal concept of 'parental responsibility'.[19] The decision maker is likely to consider things like:[20]

- whether any court orders exist that set out where your child is to live or who is to care for her/him (although the terms of a court order are not conclusive – what matters is what happens in practice[21]);
- who pays for your child's food and clothes and who is responsible for giving her/him pocket money (but this does not mean that the claimant who spends most on the child always has main responsibility);
- how much of the time the child is living with you (but there is no set threshold of days/nights per week or year);
- where the majority of her/his clothes and belongings are kept and who does her/his laundry;
- who is the main contact or registered address for the school or college, nursery or childcare provider, and who takes most responsibility for your child when s/he is at school;[22]
- who arranges appointments to see a doctor/dentist.

Even though you may be sharing responsibility for a child and s/he normally lives with you for part of the week, HMRC might not treat you as having the main responsibility. There is no provision for allowing CTC to be split between parents if a child divides her/his time between their homes.

Do you share responsibility for a child?
If you share responsibility for your child(ren) equally with other CTC claimant(s), it may be difficult to decide who has the main responsibility. If you and another claimant have more than one child, you can each get CTC for different children – eg, if you have two children, you could get CTC for one child and the other claimant could get CTC for the other.

When you do not count as responsible for a child

Even if a child normally lives with you, you do *not* count as responsible for the child and cannot qualify for CTC for her/him during any period when s/he is:[23]

- provided with, or placed in, accommodation and the accommodation or the child's maintenance is funded wholly or partly by the local authority under specified provisions or out of other public funds. This includes children staying

Part 3: Other means-tested benefits and tax credits
Chapter 14: Child tax credit
1. Who can get child tax credit

with foster carers who get foster payments for them from the local authority. This does not apply if your child is staying in certain forms of residential accommodation and this is only necessary because your child has a disability or because her/his health would be significantly impaired or further impaired if s/he were not staying in the accommodation. You must have been treated as responsible for her/him immediately before s/he went into the accommodation;[24] *or*

- being looked after by a local authority and has been placed with you because you want to adopt her/him. This only applies if the local authority is paying for the child's accommodation or maintenance or both under specified provisions; *or*
- in custody. This only applies if your child:
  - is serving a life or unlimited sentence; *or*
  - is serving a term of more than four months; *or*
  - has been detained 'at Her Majesty's pleasure'; *or*
- at least 16 and:
  - is awarded CTC in her/his own right for a child for whom s/he is responsible; *or*
  - receives WTC in her/his own right (including in a joint claim); *or*
  - is entitled to and receiving contributory ESA in her/his own right; *or*
  - is married, in a civil partnership or living with someone as a couple and her/his partner is not in full-time, non-advanced education or approved training; *or*
  - is your partner and and you are living with her/him.

Note: a young person does not count as a child if s/he gets IS, income-based JSA, income-related ESA or UC in her/his own right (see p287).

Challenging a decision

HMRC may decide that your child does not normally live with you or that you are not the person with main responsibility for her/him, so you are not entitled to CTC. It may also decide that someone else has claimed CTC for your child(ren) and s/he has the main responsibility. In this case, your entitlement to CTC ends and you may have been overpaid, but from no earlier than the date of the competing claim, which should not be backdated.[25]

If you think a decision is wrong and it affects your tax credits, you can request a mandatory reconsideration and then appeal if you are unhappy with the outcome (see Chapter 66). If as a result of a decision or following the outcome of an appeal HMRC says you have been overpaid, you can dispute recovery (see p1522). **Note:** if HMRC has paid two claimants for the same period for the same child who normally lives with both claimants, this is likely to be an official error and so any overpayment should not be recovered.[26]

It is possible that the DWP, the local authority, the Tax Credit Office and the Child Benefit Office might reach different conclusions about whether your child(ren) can be included in your claims. If so, you should appeal *all* the decisions with which you disagree.

2. The rules about your age

You (and your partner) must be aged at least 16 to qualify for child tax credit (CTC).[27] There is no upper age limit. If you are under 16, someone else (eg, your parent or the adult with whom you normally live) may be able to claim CTC for you *and* your child.

3. People included in the claim

You can only qualify for child tax credit (CTC) if you are responsible for one or more children. Some qualifying young people continue to count as children until they are 20. See pp286–90 for who counts as a child and when you count as responsible for her/him.

If you are single, you get CTC yourself.[28] If you are a member of a couple, you get CTC jointly with your partner.[29] For information about who counts as a couple for tax credit purposes, see p1497. **Note:** if you get tax credits jointly with your partner, but then cease to count as a couple (or you get tax credits as a single person, but then become a member of a couple), your entitlement to CTC ends. You should therefore report this change in your circumstances and you will usually then have to claim universal credit as a single person (or a couple).

If you are a couple:
- when working out how much CTC you get, your partner's income is added to yours (see Chapter 62);
- CTC is paid to the person who is the main carer of your children (see p1504).

4. The amount of child tax credit

The amount of child tax credit (CTC) you get depends on:
- your maximum CTC. This is made up of a combination of 'elements':
  – child element (£2,830 a year) – one for each child. **Note:** a child element is not payable for a child born on or after 6 April 2017 if you already have two or more children included in your award. There are exceptions (see p1453);
  – disabled child element (£3,415 a year) – one for each child who qualifies;

Part 3: Other means-tested benefits and tax credits
Chapter 14: Child tax credit
5. Claims and backdating

- severely disabled child element (£1,385 a year) – one for each child who qualifies;
- family element (£545 a year) if the claim includes a child born before 6 April 2017.

For details of how you qualify for the above elements, see Chapter 61;
- how much income you have; *and*
- the 'income threshold figure' that applies to you.

If you are on a means-tested benefit

Being on income support (IS), income-based jobseeker's allowance (JSA), income-related employment and support allowance (ESA) or pension credit (PC) is an automatic passport to maximum CTC.[30] You, therefore, do not need to work out your income or capital. In these circumstances, CTC equals maximum CTC.

If you are not on a means-tested benefit

If you are not on IS, income-based JSA, income-related ESA or PC, follow the steps below to calculate your CTC.
- **Step one:** work out your 'relevant period' (see p1452).
- **Step two:** work out your maximum entitlement (your maximum CTC) for the relevant period (see p1452).
- **Step three:** work out your 'relevant income' (see p1466 and p1474).
- **Step four:** compare your income with the 'income threshold figure' for the relevant period. This is £16,385 a year if you are entitled to CTC only, or £6,530 a year if you are entitled to CTC and your maximum amount of tax credits includes working tax credit (WTC) elements.[31] See p1467 for further information.
- **Step five:** calculate your CTC entitlement for the relevant period (see p1467). If your income is less than the income threshold figure, CTC equals your maximum CTC. If your income exceeds the income threshold figure, your maximum CTC is reduced by 41 per cent of the excess.

You may also be entitled to WTC. Full details of both calculations are in Chapter 61.

---

5. **Claims and backdating**

The general rules on claiming, backdating and how your claim can be renewed at the end of the year are in Chapter 63. This section gives an outline of the rules on claims for child tax credit (CTC).

Making a claim

You can only claim CTC by phoning the Tax Credit Helpline on 0345 300 3900 (textphone: 0345 300 3909).

You can amend or withdraw your claim before you are given notice of the decision on it.[32]

Who should claim

If you are a member of a couple, you must make a joint claim with your partner. If you are not a member of a couple, you claim yourself. For information about who counts as a couple for tax credit purposes, see p1497. If you cannot make your claim yourself, an 'appointee' (see p1499) can claim on your behalf.

Information to support your claim

When you claim CTC, you must:[33]
- satisfy the national insurance number requirement (see p1500);
- provide proof of your identity, if required;
- supply information to support your claim (see p1500).

It is important that you provide all the information required. If you do not do so, a decision might be delayed, or HM Revenue and Customs (HMRC) may decide to reject your claim as not validly made. There is a right of appeal (after mandatory reconsideration) against a decision to reject a tax credit claim that is not made on the correct form or that does not contain all the required information.[34] If HMRC requires further information before it makes a decision on your claim, see p1502 for details of the time you must be given to provide this and what happens if you fail to do so.

When to claim

The general rule is that your claim runs from the date it is received by HMRC.[35] You cannot make a claim in advance of the tax year for which you are claiming. However, you may be able to get your claim backdated.

Backdating your claim

It is important to claim in time. A claim for CTC can only be backdated for a maximum of 31 days.[36] See p1504 for further information.

Note: if you are waiting to hear whether your child or qualifying young person is entitled to disability living allowance (DLA), personal independence payment (PIP) or armed forces independence payment, you should claim CTC, even if you will not qualify for CTC until the disabled child element or severely disabled child element can be included. If you do not qualify, you are given a 'nil award'. A special rule then allows your entitlement to these elements to be backdated for

Part 3: Other means-tested benefits and tax credits
Chapter 14: Child tax credit
6. Getting paid

more than one month (see p1504). You must notify HMRC within one month of the date the DLA, PIP or armed forces independence payment is awarded.

Renewal awards

After the end of the tax year in which you claimed CTC, you (and your partner), receive an 'annual review' from HMRC asking you to confirm or declare your income and your household circumstances for the previous tax year (see p1512). If required, you must reply within a strict time limit. HMRC then makes a final decision, based on your actual income during the tax year. It decides whether you were entitled to CTC and, if so, the amount of your award. HMRC also uses the information about your income and household circumstances for the previous tax year to renew your award for the next tax year.[37] Some awards are finalised and renewed automatically on the information held by HMRC, as shown on your annual review, but you must check this and report any errors or changes. Your tax credit claim can continue to be renewed even though you cannot make a new claim for tax credits anymore because of the introduction of universal credit. **Note:** if you have a 'nil award', you may be given notice that your claim will not be renewed unless you specifically request this.

6. **Getting paid**

This section gives an outline of the rules about payment of child tax credit (CTC). For more information about getting paid, see p1504.

Payment of CTC is normally made in arrears into the bank (or similar) account of whoever you nominate as the main carer of your children (see p1504). If you are unable to act for yourself, payment can be made to someone else on your behalf – called your 'appointee' (see p1499).[38]

When is child tax credit paid?
You are paid every week or every four weeks, whichever you choose, although HM Revenue and Customs (HMRC) can decide how often.[39]

You can be paid by 'payment voucher' at a post office while your account arrangements are being finalised. HMRC no longer issues cheques.
Note:
- Even if you have been sanctioned for a benefit offence, your CTC cannot be paid at a reduced rate.
- If you have forgotten your PIN, see p1188. The issues are the same as for benefits.

- If payment of your CTC is delayed and this is causing hardship, ask HMRC to make an urgent next day/same day payment (see p1506). If you wish to complain about how your claim has been dealt with, see p1441. You might be able to claim compensation (see p1439).
- If payment of your CTC is suspended or postponed, see p1506.
- If you are overpaid CTC, you might have to repay it (see Chapter 64). In some cases, interest can be added to the overpayment. In some circumstances, you may have to pay a penalty (see p1535). If you have been accused of fraud, see Chapter 65.

Change of circumstances

Your initial award of CTC is made on the basis of your (and your partner's) previous year's income and your personal circumstances at the start of the tax year. If your current year's income or your personal circumstances change, your award of CTC can be amended. **Note:**

- There are some changes you *must* report to HMRC (see p1507). If you fail to do so within one month, you might be given a financial penalty. Some changes end your entitlement to CTC and you will usually have to claim universal credit (UC) instead.
- Other changes that affect your maximum entitlement to CTC are not compulsory to report, so you cannot be given a penalty, but they should still be reported to avoid an overpayment or underpayment – eg, when you have a baby or if one of your children stops getting disability living allowance (see p1509). Changes that increase your maximum entitlement to CTC can generally only be backdated one month from when you notify HMRC. Changes that decrease your entitlement generally take effect from the date of change, so may result in an overpayment.
- It is optional to report an estimated change in your current year income (see p1510). Your actual income is always taken into account at the end of the tax year, but you may want to consider reporting an estimate sooner in order to avoid an overpayment or underpayment of CTC.
- Report if you become a member of a couple with someone entitled to UC. Your entitlement to CTC will end (see p32).

Note: if you apply for, and are entitled to, payments under the tax-free childcare scheme, your CTC award is terminated, as you cannot get both at the same time. See p871 for more details.

7. Tax, other benefits and the benefit cap

Tax

Child tax credit (CTC) is not taxable.

Part 3: Other means-tested benefits and tax credits
Chapter 14: Child tax credit
7. Tax, other benefits and the benefit cap

Means-tested benefits and tax credits

If you are entitled to CTC:
- CTC is not taken into account as income for income support (IS), income-based jobseeker's allowance (JSA), income-related employment and support allowance (ESA) or pension credit (PC);
- CTC is not counted as income for universal credit (UC), but there are very limited circumstances when you can be entitled to CTC during an assessment period for UC.[40] This can happen if you become the new partner of a UC claimant (see p32), in which case her/his assessment period continues so that you may receive your last payment of CTC during the first assessment period of your joint UC claim;[41]
- unless you are on IS, income-based JSA or income-related ESA or are at least pension age, the amount of CTC you are paid *is* taken into account as income for housing benefit (HB).

If you get arrears of CTC, these count as capital for means-tested benefits and can be disregarded in some circumstances (see p498 and p522).

If you are in full-time paid work, you may qualify for working tax credit (WTC) in addition to CTC.

Non-means-tested benefits

CTC can be paid in addition to any non-means-tested benefits to which you (or your partner) are entitled, including child benefit, but see Chapter 62 for which of these benefits may be taken into account as income for CTC. If your child qualifies for disability living allowance (DLA), personal independence payment (PIP) or armed forces independence payment, you qualify for the disabled child or severely disabled child elements of CTC and the income from DLA, PIP or armed forces independence payment is ignored.

The benefit cap

In some cases, there is a limit on the total amount of specified benefits you can receive (a 'benefit cap'). CTC is one of the specified benefits. However, the benefit cap only applies if you are getting UC or HB. See p1194 for further information.

Passports and other sources of help

If you are entitled to CTC, you may also qualify for:
- health benefits such as free prescriptions (see Chapter 31). You do not have to satisfy the means test if you are getting CTC and your gross annual income is below a set amount; *and*
- education benefits such as free school lunches (see p866).

Chapter 14

Child tax credit

You may also qualify for a Sure Start maternity grant (Best Start grant in Scotland) or a funeral expenses payment (funeral support payment in Scotland). If you have a low income, you may be entitled to a council tax reduction (see p851).

Note: if you apply for, and are entitled to, payments under the tax-free childcare scheme, your CTC award is terminated, as you cannot get both at the same time. See p871 for more details.

Notes

1. Who can get child tax credit
1 ss3(3) and (7), 8 and 42 TCA 2002; regs 3-5 CTC Regs; reg 3 TC(R) Regs; reg 3 TC(Imm) Regs
2 Reg 8 UC(TP) Regs; *HMRC v LD (TC)* [2018] UKUT 306 (AAC)
3 Art 7(1), (2), (5) and (6) WRA(No.23)O
4 Reg 4A UC(TP) Regs
5 s8(1) TCA 2002
6 s8(5) TCA 2002; reg 6 CTC Regs
7 s8(3) TCA 2002; reg 2(1), definition of 'child', CTC Regs
8 s8(4) TCA 2002; regs 2, definition of 'qualifying young person' and 'full-time education', 4 and 5(1)-(3A) CTC Regs
9 TCTM 02230 and TCM 0114100
10 Reg 5(7) CTC Regs
11 Regs 2, definition of 'remunerative work', and 5(4) CTC Regs
12 Reg 3(1) rule 2.2 CTC Regs
13 s8(2) TCA 2002; reg 3(1) rules 1 and 2 CTC Regs
14 Reg 3(1) rule 4 Case D and (2) CTC Regs
15 TCTM 02202
16 CFC/1537/1995
17 Reg 3(1) rule 2 CTC Regs
18 Reg 3 rule 3 CTC Regs
19 *PG v HMRC (TC)* [2016] UKUT 216 (AAC)
20 TCTM 02204; *PG v HMRC (TC)* [2016] UKUT 216 (AAC)
21 *GJ v HMRC (TC)* [2013] UKUT 561 (AAC)
22 *KN v HMRC (TC)* [2009] UKUT 79 (AAC)
23 Reg 3(1) rule 4.1 CTC Regs
24 Reg 3(1) rule 4.2 CTC Regs; reg 9 CB Regs
25 *LP v HMRC (TC)* [2014] UKUT 533 (AAC)
26 *SH v HMRC and SC (TC)* [2013] UKUT 297 (AAC); *AG v HMRC and AG (TC)* [2018] UKUT 318 (AAC)

2. The rules about your age
27 s3(3) TCA 2002

3. People included in the claim
28 s3(3)(b) TCA 2002
29 s3(3)(a) and (5A) TCA 2002; reg 2(1) CTC Regs; CTC/3864/2004; R(TC) 1/07

4. The amount of child tax credit
30 ss7(2) and 13 TCA 2002; reg 4 TC(ITDR) Regs
31 Reg 3(2) and (3) TC(ITDR) Regs

5. Claims and backdating
32 Reg 5(7) TC(CN) Regs; R(IS) 3/05
33 Reg 5(3)-(6) TC(CN) Regs
34 *CI v HMRC (TC)* [2014] UKUT 158 (AAC)
35 s5(2) TCA 2002
36 Reg 7 TC(CN) Regs
37 Regs 11 and 12 TC(CN) Regs

6. Getting paid
38 s24(3) TCA 2002; reg 6 TC(PC) Regs
39 Regs 8 and 13 TC(PC) Regs

7. Tax, other benefits and the benefit cap
40 Reg 66 UC Regs
41 Reg 5(2)(b)(iii) UC(TP) Regs; reg 21(3B) UC Regs

Chapter 15

Working tax credit

This chapter covers:
1. Who can get working tax credit (below)
2. The rules about your age (p308)
3. People included in the claim (p308)
4. The amount of working tax credit (p308)
5. Claims and backdating (p309)
6. Getting paid (p311)
7. Tax, other benefits and the benefit cap (p313)

Key facts
- Working tax credit (WTC) is paid to some low-paid workers who have not claimed universal credit (UC).
- You do not have to have paid national insurance contributions to qualify.
- WTC is administered and paid by HM Revenue and Customs.
- If you disagree with a WTC decision, you can apply for a mandatory reconsideration and then appeal if you are unhappy with the outcome (see Chapter 66).

1. Who can get working tax credit

You qualify for working tax credit (WTC) if:[1]
- you (or your partner) are in full-time paid work (see p299); *and*
- your income is sufficiently low (see Chapter 62); *and*
- you are 'present' and 'ordinarily resident' in the UK. You can be treated as present and ordinarily resident in the UK in some circumstances – eg, if you are away temporarily. See Chapter 68 for further information; *and*
- you are not a 'person subject to immigration control' (see Chapter 67).

Working tax credit and universal credit

You can now only make a new claim for WTC in limited circumstances (see below). If you are already entitled to WTC, you can continue to qualify until:

– you claim universal credit (UC);[2] *or*

– you become a member of a couple and your partner is getting UC; *or*

– you and your partner become subject to transfer to UC via the 'managed migration' process (see p30).

The government says that, from November 2020, the DWP will begin to notify existing WTC claimants that they must claim UC instead. When this managed migration happens, you will be invited to claim UC and your WTC award will end. See p27 for further information, and AskCPAG.org.uk and CPAG's *Welfare Rights Bulletin* for updates.

Who can make a new claim for working tax credit

You can only make a new claim for WTC in limited circumstances. These are if:[3]

- you already have an award of child tax credit (CTC). If you are then entitled to WTC, this is treated as a change in circumstances and a new claim is not required; *or*

- you were entitled to WTC in 2019/20 and are making a claim for 2020/21; *or*

- you are prevented from claiming UC because:[4]

  – you (or your partner) are, or within the last month have been, entitled to income support (IS), income-based jobseeker's allowance (JSA), income-related employment and support allowance (ESA), or housing benefit (HB) that includes a severe disability premium (see p346), and if your entitlement to the benefit ended during that month you (or s/he) have continued to satisfy the conditions for that premium; *and*

  – you (and your partner) have not yet been given a 'migration notice' from the DWP that you will be transferred to UC via the 'managed migration' process (see p30); *or*

- you are prevented from claiming UC because you (or if you are a couple, you and your partner) are a 'frontier worker' – ie, you work in Great Britain or Northern Ireland, but do not live there.

If you cannot make a new claim for WTC under these rules, you can make a claim for UC.

Full-time paid work

To qualify for WTC, you or your partner must be in full-time paid work. HM Revenue and Customs (HMRC) calls this 'remunerative work'.[5] The number of hours required to be classed as full time for tax credits purposes depends on your circumstances. See below for what counts as full-time work, and p301 for what

Part 3: Other means-tested benefits and tax credits
Chapter 15: Working tax credit
1. Who can get working tax credit

counts as paid work and for how your hours are calculated. 'Work' includes self-employment and work which is done from home.

In some circumstances, you may be treated as not being in full-time paid work even if you are (see p306). In others, you may be treated as if you are in full-time paid work when you are not (see p304). If you are unsure whether you are in full-time paid work, see p992.

Income from work affects your entitlement to WTC. This means that, although your (or your partner's) hours of work are high enough for you to qualify, you might not satisfy the means test.

What counts as full-time work

You count as being in full-time work if any of the following apply.[6]

- You work at least **30 hours** a week and you are aged 25 or over.
- You work at least **16 hours** a week and:
  - you qualify for a disabled worker element; *or*
  - you are aged 60 or over; *or*
  - you are a single claimant and are responsible for at least one child or qualifying young person (see p288); *or*
  - you are a member of a couple, you (or your partner) are responsible for at least one child or qualifying young person (see p288) and your partner either counts as incapacitated for the purposes of the childcare element (see p1461) or s/he is entitled to carer's allowance (CA), or s/he is a hospital inpatient or is in prison.
- You and your partner's combined hours of work are at least **24 hours** a week, and you (or your partner) are responsible for at least one child or qualifying young person (see p288). One of you must work at least 16 hours a week. If only one of you works, that person must work at least 24 hours a week.

If you are under 25, you can only qualify for WTC if you work at least 16 hours a week and qualify for a disabled worker element, or you are responsible for a child in the circumstances above.

If your circumstances change and you are no longer responsible for a child or qualifying young person, or no longer qualify for a disabled worker element, unless you are 60 or over, you may have to increase your weekly hours to at least 30 to continue to qualify for WTC. See Chapter 63 for more information on changes of circumstances and when you must report them.

At the date of your claim, you must be working or have accepted an offer of work which is expected to start within seven days.[7] In the latter case, you only count as being in full-time paid work when the work begins. The work must be expected to continue for at least four weeks after you make your claim (or if you have accepted an offer of work, after the work starts).[8]

Note:
- You can continue to count as being in full-time work for four weeks after you leave work, or your hours reduce to less than the number you (or your partner) need to do. See p305 for information about this 'WTC run-on'.

- If you normally work sufficient hours a week, but are off sick or on maternity, paternity or adoption leave, you may be able to claim WTC as you can be treated as being in full-time paid work (see p304).

What counts as paid work

'Paid work' includes work for which you are paid or expect to be paid.[9] Payment of a benefit (eg, CA) does not count for these purposes. The information on p993 about what counts as paid work for means-tested benefits also applies to WTC.

How your hours are calculated

How you calculate your hours depends on whether you are employed or self-employed.[10]

- If you are employed, include all the hours:
    - you normally work under your contract, if you are an apprentice or employee; *or*
    - you normally perform in the office in which you are employed, if you are an office holder. This includes if you are in an elective office or are a company director; *or*
    - for which you are normally paid by the employment agency with whom you have a contract, if you are an agency worker.
- If you are self-employed, include all the hours you normally do for payment or for which you expect to be paid, and on activities which are necessary to the employment.

Paid meal and refreshment breaks count towards the total hours you work.[11] Also included is any time allowed for medical appointments, but only if this is to treat or monitor your disability and if you are paid, or expect to be paid, for the time.[12] Your total hours from more than one job are added together.

Periods when you are on a customary or paid holiday from work are ignored when calculating your hours.[13] Unpaid meal and refreshment breaks are also ignored.

Employed and self-employed[14]

You count as **'employed'** if you are employed under a contract of service or apprenticeship and your earnings are taxable as employment income under certain provisions of the Income Tax (Earnings and Pensions) Act 2003.

You count as **'self-employed'** if you are carrying out a trade, profession or vocation that is organised and regular, on a commercial basis and with a view to making a profit. A business plan may help to demonstrate this, but the absence of one does not mean you are not self-employed.[15] There is no requirement of actual profitability, and no minimum income floor.[16]

Part 3: Other means-tested benefits and tax credits
Chapter 15: Working tax credit
1. Who can get working tax credit

Hours you normally work

Whether you are employed or self-employed, the measure for WTC purposes is the number of hours you normally work.[17] 'Normally' is not defined in the WTC rules. HMRC says you should calculate your hours based on what you 'regularly, usually or typically' do and that the number of hours you normally work might not be the number of hours specified in your contract of employment.[18] The hours that are relevant are those you *actually* work. If you routinely do paid overtime, argue that these are hours you normally work and that they should be included. See below if your hours fluctuate.

> *Example*
> Jen is a cashier in a supermarket. Her partner stays at home to look after their children. She is contracted to work 21 hours a week over a three-day week but she does 3.5 hours overtime almost every week. She gets an unpaid half-hour lunch break. When Jen and her partner claim WTC, she has just returned from two weeks' paid holiday.
> Jen normally works 21 + 3.5 = 24.5 hours a week. Unpaid lunch breaks and the time she was on paid holiday are not taken into account. As Jen and her partner are responsible for children, one of them needs to work at least 16 hours a week and, between them, they need to work at least 24 hours a week. Jen therefore counts as being in full-time paid work.

When working out your normal hours if you are self-employed, HMRC says you can include not only the hours you spend providing orders or services but also those that are necessary to your self-employment – eg, trips to wholesalers and retailers, visits to potential clients, advertising or canvassing, cleaning the business or vehicles used as part of the business, bookkeeping and research work.[19]

If your hours fluctuate

Working out the number of hours you normally work is straightforward if you do the same number of hours each and every week, or if your hours vary but you always do at least enough hours each week to count as being in full-time paid work.

However, if your weekly hours fluctuate, it can be more complicated. Unless you are a term-time only worker (see p303), there is no rule on how to average your hours. There is no requirement to work the necessary number of hours each and every week, and a common sense approach should be taken.[20] If you have a regular pattern of work (a recognised work cycle), HMRC says the hours you normally work are those that reflect an overall view of the pattern of your hours over a representative period, or over a year.[21] For example, if you always work two weeks on and two weeks off, you could argue that your hours should be averaged over a four-week period.

If you are in any doubt about what your normal hours are, contact HMRC and get advice. To avoid a potential overpayment, it is advisable to report your actual hours every four weeks. If you are unsure whether you are in full-time paid work, see p300.

Examples

Shane works in a residential project. He works three weeks on and one week off. When he is on, he works 40 hours a week. His average hours are 40 x 3 ÷ 4 = 30 hours a week. Shane can try to argue that he normally works 30 hours or more a week. As Shane is aged 45, does not have a physical or mental disability and has no children, he must work at least 30 hours a week. He therefore counts as being in full-time paid work.

Jana is contracted to do 15 hours a week. However, she gets regular overtime of three hours every other week. Her average hours are 15 + 18 ÷ 2 = 16.5 hours. Jana can try to argue that she normally works 16 hours or more a week. As Jana is a lone parent, she need only work 16 hours or more a week. She therefore counts as being in full-time paid work.

If you think your average hours have been calculated unfairly, you can request a mandatory reconsideration and then appeal. You should first work out whether you would be better off claiming UC rather than WTC.

Term-time only workers

If you only work in school term times, periods when you are not working are ignored when deciding whether you are in full-time paid work if:[22]

- you work in a school, an educational establishment or other place of employment; *and*
- you have a recognisable 'work cycle' that lasts for a year; *and*
- your 'work cycle' includes periods of school holidays or similar vacations during which you do not work.

In practice, if the hours of work you do during term time mean you are in full-time paid work during term time, you also count as being in full-time paid work over the holidays. You can get WTC during this period if your normal hours of work each week are sufficient during term time.

Example

Dee is 35 years old and has no children. She is a cleaner at a local college and works 35 hours a week, 36 weeks of the year. She does not work (and is not paid) when the students are on study leave and on holiday. The periods when Dee does not work are ignored. She is in full-time paid work during term time because she works 30 hours or more a week. She therefore counts as being in full-time paid work throughout the year and can get WTC.

Part 3: Other means-tested benefits and tax credits
Chapter 15: Working tax credit
1. Who can get working tax credit

Note:
- It may not be clear whether you have a work cycle that lasts a year – eg, if you have only started your job recently or have a fixed-term contract that finishes at the end of the school term, or are employed on a casual or relief basis.[23] If you have an indefinite contract to work in term time only, you can argue that you have a yearly work cycle from the start.[24]
- If you work casually or intermittently (eg, you are a seasonal worker who works in the summer but you are unemployed the rest of the year), HMRC might say your work cycle is that part of the year in which you are working and that you do not count as being in full-time work when you are unemployed.[25]

People treated as being in full-time paid work

You or your partner are treated as being in full-time paid work in a number of situations.

Maternity, adoption, paternity or shared parental leave

You or your partner are treated as being in full-time paid work when:[26]
- you are being paid statutory maternity pay (SMP), statutory adoption pay (SAP), statutory paternity pay (SPP), statutory shared parental pay (SSPP), statutory parental bereavement pay (SPBP) or maternity allowance (MA); *or*
- you are absent from work during the first 39 weeks of maternity leave, or adoption leave or two weeks of paternity leave; *or*
- you are absent from work during a period of statutory shared parental leave or parental bereavement leave, but only during the period in which you would have been paid SSPP or SPBP had you qualified.

If you are an employee, you are treated as being in full-time paid work from the start of the period above, provided you are in full-time paid work for WTC purposes immediately before the period begins. However, if this is not the case (eg, you are under 25, or are 25 or over but working less than 30 hours a week, and the child you and your partner are having or adopting is your first), you are treated as being in full-time paid work from the date of birth (or adoption), provided you would have counted as being in full-time paid work had you been responsible for a child or qualifying young person immediately before the period begins.[27]

If you are self-employed, you count as being in full-time paid work during any period when the above would have applied had the work done in the week before the period began been as an employee.

If you do not return to work when your SMP, SAP, SPP, SSPP or MA ends, or after the allowed number of weeks of leave, you must notify HMRC, as you are no longer treated as being in full-time paid work under this rule. The statutory entitlement to maternity or adoption leave is 52 weeks, but you are only treated as working for tax credit purposes for the first 39 weeks.

Note: you should notify HMRC if you are in any of the above situations and provide an estimate of your current year's income. This is because any MA and the first £100 a week of any SMP, SAP, SPP and SSPP is ignored as income for WTC.

Periods of ill health

You or your partner are treated as being in full-time paid work when:[28]
- you are being paid statutory sick pay (SSP); *or*
- you are:
  - being paid IS because you are entitled to SSP or because you are incapable of work due to pregnancy; *or*
  - being paid ESA; *or*
  - getting national insurance (NI) credits because you are incapable of work or have limited capability for work.

The period treated as 'in work' while on IS, ESA or NI credits only applies for 28 weeks.

You must have been in full-time paid work for WTC purposes immediately before the period began.

If you are self-employed, you count as being in full-time paid work during any period when the above would have applied had the work done in the week before the period began been as an employee.

If you do not return to work when your SSP ceases (or after 28 weeks on IS, ESA or NI credits), you no longer count as being in full-time paid work under this rule.

Working tax credit run-on

If you or your partner stop work or reduce your hours, you can get 'WTC run-on'. You are treated as being in full-time paid work for the four weeks immediately after you stop work, or your hours reduce to fewer than the number you (or your partner) must do to count as being in full-time paid work.[29] This means you continue to qualify for:
- WTC for the four-week period, even if you would otherwise no longer count as being in full-time paid work;
- all the elements you were previously getting for that period (eg, the 30-hour element and the childcare element), even if the reduction in hours means you would otherwise lose entitlement to these.

You must report the change in your circumstances to HMRC within one month.

Other situations

You or your partner are treated as being in full-time paid work:
- if you were in full-time paid work within the past seven days.[30] This means you can make a new claim or continue to qualify for WTC – eg, during a short period between jobs or when you are on jury service for no more than one week;

Part 3: Other means-tested benefits and tax credits
Chapter 15: Working tax credit
1. Who can get working tax credit

- during any period when you are on strike or are suspended from work while complaints or allegations against you are investigated, provided you were in full-time paid work for WTC purposes immediately before the start of the period. You must not be on strike for longer than 10 consecutive days when you should be working.[31]

Moving between situations in which you are treated as being in full-time work

The rules allow you to be treated as being in full-time paid work for WTC purposes for certain periods in the situations described on p304. If you move from one situation to another (eg, maternity leave followed by sickness leave), HMRC has previously stated that you can continue to be treated as being in work throughout the second period, provided you were treated as being in work immediately before it began.[32] However, the Upper Tribunal has held that you cannot continue to be treated as being in work if you move from a period on SSP to a period on ESA, or if you move from the four-week 'run-on' period (see p305) to a period on MA.[33]

People treated as not being in full-time paid work

You or your partner are treated as *not* being in full-time paid work during any period in which you are receiving pay in lieu of notice after you stop work, unless you continue to qualify under the four-week 'run-on' rule (see p305).[34] In addition, you or your partner are treated as *not* being in full-time paid work if:[35]

- you are a volunteer, or are working for a charity or voluntary organisation and are giving your services free (except for your expenses);
- you are providing care for someone who is staying with you temporarily but who is not normally a member of your household and:
  - the only payment you receive is from a health authority, a local authority, a voluntary organisation, a clinical commissioning group or the person her/himself for caring for her/him; *and*
  - the payment is disregarded as a tax-free payment under HMRC's 'rent-a-room' scheme (see p1487).

  Note: if you are an adult placement carer who has *not* opted for the 'rent-a-room' scheme, you *can* count as being in full-time paid work;[36]
- you are working on a training scheme and are being paid a training allowance (see below), unless the training allowance or the money you are being paid by the DWP is subject to income tax as a profit from work;[37]
- the only payment you receive, or expect to receive, is a sports award from a sports council;
- you are working while you are a sentenced or remand prisoner. This means you cannot qualify for WTC even if the work you do is outside the prison – eg, while you are on temporary release.

Training allowance

A 'training allowance' is an allowance paid to maintain you or a member of your family:[38]
- by a government department or by or on behalf of the Secretary of State, Scottish Enterprise or the Highlands and Islands Enterprise; *and*
- for the period, or part of a period, during which you are on a course provided or approved by, or under arrangements made by, any of the above.

Allowances paid to, or in respect of, you by a government department or by the Scottish government are not included if these are paid because you are a trainee teacher or on a full-time course of education, unless this is under arrangements made under section 2 of the Employment and Training Act 1973.

Students

You are not excluded from getting WTC simply because you are a student. However, you must do sufficient hours of paid work in addition to your studies and the work must be expected to last for four weeks.

Is the work part of your course?

1. If you are paid in return for the work you do (eg, you are paid by an employer during a work placement), you can argue that you are in full-time paid work.

2. Any work you do in studying for a degree or other qualification does not count as full-time paid work – any grant or loan you receive is not paid in return for work done on the course.

3. You are not considered to be in full-time paid work if you are a student nurse, because the grants or loans you get are not payments for work done on the course and do not count as income for tax credit purposes.[39]

When calculating how much WTC you can get, student loans and most other student income are disregarded. See p1485 for what income counts.

Foster carers

If you are working sufficient hours as a foster carer (or approved kinship carer, in Scotland), you can qualify for WTC. HMRC generally accepts that foster carers come under the definition of self-employed (see p301), even if you have no profits and no loss for income tax purposes, and the hours of work you declare should be accepted.[40] If you do more than one job, the total hours are added together. So, if you are doing work in addition to foster caring, the hours from the other work can be added to those spent foster caring.

Fostering allowances (and kinship care allowances, in Scotland) that qualify for tax relief are generally ignored when calculating your WTC. See p1489 for further information.

Part 3: Other means-tested benefits and tax credits
Chapter 15: Working tax credit
4. The amount of working tax credit

2. The rules about your age

You (and your partner) must be aged at least 16 to get working tax credit (WTC).[41] There is no upper age limit.

If you are under 25, you can only qualify for WTC if you work at least 16 hours a week and you are a disabled worker or are responsible for a child in the circumstances described on p300.

3. People included in the claim

If you are a single person, you get working tax credit (WTC) for yourself.[42] If you are a member of a couple (see p1497), you get WTC jointly with your partner.[43] WTC includes elements for you and your partner and for any special needs either of you have (see Chapter 61). When working out how much WTC you get, your partner's income is added to yours (see Chapter 62). **Note:** if you get tax credits jointly with your partner but then no longer count as a couple (or you get tax credits as a single person but then become a member of a couple), your entitlement to WTC ends. You should therefore report this change in your circumstances and you will usually have to claim universal credit (UC) as a single person (or a couple) instead.

If you are responsible for at least one child or qualifying young person:
* you (or your partner) must work at least 16 hours a week to qualify for WTC (although if you are a member of a couple, in most cases your combined hours must be at least 24 a week);
* and you are a couple and one of you works at least 16 hours a week, your hours of work can be added to those of your partner to enable you to qualify for the 30-hour element (see p1458);
* you (and your partner) might qualify for the childcare element in your WTC if you pay for childcare.

See p286 for who counts as a child or qualifying young person. For when you count as responsible for a child, see p288. The rules are the same as for child tax credit (CTC).[44]

4. The amount of working tax credit

The amount of working tax credit (WTC) you get depends on:
* your maximum WTC. This is made up of a combination of 'elements' (see Chapter 61 for how you qualify for these):
  – basic element (£3,040 a year);

- lone parent/couple element (£2,045 a year);
- 30-hour element (£825 a year);
- disabled worker element (£3,220 a year). More than one can be included if you are a member of a couple and you both qualify;
- severe disability element (£1,390 a year). More than one can be included if you are a member of a couple and you both qualify;
- childcare element;
- how much income you have (see Chapter 62); *and*
- the 'income threshold figure'.

If you are on a means-tested benefit

Being on income support (IS), income-based jobseeker's allowance (JSA), income-related employment and support allowance (ESA) or pension credit (PC) is an automatic passport to maximum WTC.[45] You therefore do not need to work out your income. In these circumstances, WTC equals maximum WTC. **Note:** this does not apply while you are getting 'WTC run-on' (see p305).

If you are not on a means-tested benefit

If you are not on IS, income-based JSA, income-related ESA or PC, follow the steps below to calculate your WTC.
- **Step one:** work out your 'relevant period' (see p1452).
- **Step two:** work out your maximum entitlement (your maximum WTC) for the relevant period (see p1466).
- **Step three:** work out your 'relevant income' (see p1466 and p1474).
- **Step four:** compare your income with the 'income threshold figure' for the relevant period – £6,530 a year for WTC.[46]
- **Step five:** calculate your WTC entitlement for the relevant period (see p1467). If your income is less than the 'income threshold figure', WTC equals your maximum WTC. If your income exceeds the 'income threshold figure', your maximum WTC is reduced by 41 per cent of the excess.

You may also be entitled to child tax credit. Full details of both calculations are in Chapter 61.

5. Claims and backdating

The general rules on claiming, backdating and how your claim can be renewed at the end of the year are in Chapter 63. This section gives an outline of the rules on claims for working tax credit (WTC).

Part 3: Other means-tested benefits and tax credits
Chapter 15: Working tax credit
5. Claims and backdating

Making a claim

You can only claim WTC by telephoning the Tax Credit Helpline on 0345 300 3900 (textphone: 0345 300 3909).

You can amend or withdraw your claim before you are given notice of the decision on it.[47]

Who should claim

If you are a member of a couple, you must make a joint claim with your partner. If you are not a member of a couple, you claim for yourself. For information about who counts as a couple for tax credit purposes, see p1497. If you cannot make your claim yourself, an 'appointee' (see p1499) can claim on your behalf.

Information to support your claim

When you claim WTC, you must:[48]

- satisfy the national insurance number requirement (see p1500); *and*
- provide proof of your identity, if required; *and*
- supply information to support your claim (see p1500).

It is important that you provide all the information required. If you do not do so, a decision may be delayed, or HM Revenue and Customs (HMRC) may decide to reject your claim as not validly made. You have a right of appeal (after a mandatory reconsideration) against a decision to reject a tax credit claim that is not made on the correct form or that does not include all the required information, particularly if you have a reasonable excuse for not supplying the information.[49] If HMRC requires further information, see p1502 for details of the time you must be given to provide this and what happens if you fail to do so.

When to claim

The general rule is that your claim runs from the date it is received by HMRC.[50] You cannot make a claim in advance of the tax year in which you are claiming, but you *can* claim WTC in advance of starting work, provided you expect to start work within seven days and will be entitled to WTC within seven days of starting work.[51] However, you may be able to get your claim backdated.

Backdating your claim

It is very important to claim in time. A claim for WTC can usually only be backdated for a maximum of 31 days.[52] See p1504 for further information.

Note: there is a special backdating rule if you claim WTC when you are awarded a qualifying benefit – eg, disability living allowance, personal independence payment or armed forces independence payment (see p1504). Under this rule, your WTC can be backdated more than 31 days.

Renewal awards

At the end of the tax year in which you claimed WTC, you (and your partner if you are a member of a couple) receive an 'annual review' from HMRC asking you to confirm or declare your income and your household circumstances for the previous tax year (see p1512). If required, you must reply within a strict time limit. HMRC then makes a final decision, based on your actual income during the tax year. It decides whether you were entitled to WTC and, if so, the amount of your award. HMRC also uses the information about your income and household circumstances for the previous tax year to renew your award for the next tax year.[53] Some awards are finalised and renewed automatically on the information held by HMRC, as shown on your annual review, but you must check this and report any errors or changes. Your tax credits claim can continue to be renewed even though you cannot usually make a new claim for tax credits because of the introduction of universal credit. **Note:** if you have a 'nil award', you may be given notice that your claim will not be renewed unless you specifically request this.

6. Getting paid

This section gives an outline of the rules on payment of working tax credit (WTC). For more information about getting paid, see p1504.

Payment of WTC is normally made in arrears into your bank (or similar) account. If you make a joint claim, any WTC to which you are entitled towards your childcare expenses is paid to whoever you nominated as the main carer of your child(ren) (see p1504), but cannot be paid directly to the childcare provider. If you are unable to act for yourself, payment can be made to someone on your behalf – called your 'appointee' (see p1499).[54]

When is working tax credit paid?
You are paid every week or every four weeks, whichever you choose, although HM Revenue and Customs (HMRC) can decide how often.[55]

You can be paid by 'payment voucher' at a post office while your account arrangements are finalised. HMRC no longer issues cheques.

Note:
- You can be disqualified from being paid WTC if you have committed a benefit offence (see p1281).
- If you have forgotten your PIN, see p1188. The issues are the same as for benefits.
- If payment of your WTC is delayed and this is causing hardship, ask HMRC to make a next day/same day payment. If you wish to complain about how your

Part 3: Other means-tested benefits and tax credits
Chapter 15: Working tax credit
6. Getting paid

claim has been dealt with, see p1441. You may be able to claim compensation (see p1439).

- If payment of your WTC is suspended or postponed, see p1506.
- If you are overpaid WTC, you might have to repay it (see Chapter 64). In some cases, interest can be added to the overpayment. In some circumstances, you may have to pay a penalty (see p1535). If you have been accused of fraud, see Chapter 65.

Change of circumstances

Your award of WTC is made on the basis of your (and your partner's) previous year's income and your personal circumstances at the start of the tax year. If your current year's income or your personal circumstances change, your award of WTC can be amended. **Note:**

- There are some changes you *must* report to HMRC (see p1507). If you fail to do so within one month, you might be given a financial penalty. Some changes end your entitlement to WTC and you will then usually have to claim universal credit (UC) instead.
- Other changes that affect your maximum entitlement to WTC are not compulsory to report, so you cannot be given a penalty, but they should still be reported to avoid an underpayment or overpayment – eg, when your hours increase to 30 or more so you would qualify for a 30-hour element, or the rate of your partner's personal independence payment award is reduced so you no longer qualify for the severe disability element (see p1509). Changes that increase your maximum entitlement to WTC can generally only be backdated one month from when you notify HMRC. Changes that decrease entitlement generally take effect from the date of change, so may result in an overpayment.
- It is optional to report an estimated change in your current year's income (see p1510). Your actual income is always taken into account at the end of the tax year, but you may want to consider reporting an estimate sooner to avoid an overpayment or underpayment of WTC.

If you are getting WTC and you only qualify for the lone parent or childcare element because you (or your partner) are responsible for a child and the child dies, you are paid WTC for a further eight weeks (or up to the date your child would have turned 20, if this is earlier) as if this had not happened.[56] This is only the case if you would have continued to qualify for the element but for the child's death. After this period, you may continue to qualify for WTC – eg, if you still satisfy the means test and work sufficient hours to count as being in full-time paid work.

Note:

- If you become a member of a couple with someone entitled to UC, your entitlement to WTC ends (see p32).

- If you apply for, and are entitled to, payments under the tax-free childcare scheme, your WTC award is terminated, as you cannot get both at the same time. See p871 for more details.

7. Tax, other benefits and the benefit cap

Tax

Working tax credit (WTC) is not taxable.

Means-tested benefits and tax credits

If you are entitled to WTC:
- WTC counts as income for income support, income-based jobseeker's allowance, income-related employment and support allowance, pension credit (PC) and housing benefit (HB);
- you can get WTC at the same time as PC because there is no rule that prevents you or your partner doing full-time paid work while claiming PC;
- if you qualify for HB, you might get an additional earnings disregard (see p431 and p473);
- WTC does not count as income for universal credit (UC), but there are very limited circumstances when you can be entitled to WTC during an assessment period for UC.[57] This can happen if you become a new partner of a UC claimant (see p32), in which case her/his assessment period continues so that you may receive your last payment of WTC during the first assessment period of your joint UC claim.[58]

If you get arrears of WTC, these count as capital for means-tested benefits and can be disregarded in some circumstances (see p498 and p522).

If you have dependent children (including a 'qualifying young person'), you may qualify for child tax credit (CTC) in addition to WTC.

Non-means-tested benefits

In some situations, while you are receiving WTC you get national insurance credits (see p977).

WTC can be paid in addition to any non-means-tested benefits to which you (or your partner) are entitled, but see Chapter 62 for which of these benefits may be taken into account as income for WTC. Qualifying for certain non-means-tested benefits means you may also qualify for the disabled worker element or severe disability element of WTC.

Part 3: Other means-tested benefits and tax credits
Chapter 15: Working tax credit
Notes

The benefit cap

In some cases, there is a limit on the total amount of specified benefits you can receive (a 'benefit cap'). WTC is *not* one of the specified benefits. The benefit cap does *not* apply if you or your partner are entitled to WTC. See p1194 for further information.

Passports and other sources of help

If you are entitled to WTC, you may also qualify for health benefits, such as free prescriptions (see Chapter 31). You do not have to satisfy the means test if your gross annual income is below a set amount and you are getting WTC which includes a disabled worker element or a severe disability element, or CTC with your WTC.

You may qualify for a Sure Start maternity grant (a Best Start grant in Scotland) or a social fund funeral expenses payment (funeral support payment in Scotland). You may be entitled to a council tax reduction (see p851).

Note: if you apply for, and are entitled to, payments under the tax-free childcare scheme, your WTC award is terminated, as you cannot get both at the same time. See p871 for more details.

Notes

1. Who can get working tax credit
1 ss3(3) and (7), 10 and 42 TCA 2002; regs 4-8 WTC(EMR) Regs; reg 3 TC(R) Regs; reg 3 TC(Imm) Regs
2 Reg 8 UC(TP) Regs; *HMRC v LD (TC)* [2018] UKUT 306 (AAC)
3 Art 7 (1), (2), (5) and (6) WRA(No.23)O
4 Reg 4A UC(TP) Regs
5 s10(1) TCA 2002
6 Reg 4(1) (second condition) WTC(EMR) Regs
7 Reg 4(1) (first condition) WTC(EMR) Regs
8 Reg 4(1) (third condition) WTC(EMR) Regs
9 Reg 4(1) (fourth condition) WTC(EMR) Regs
10 Reg 4(3) WTC(EMR) Regs
11 Reg 4(4)(b) WTC(EMR) Regs
12 Reg 4(5) WTC(EMR) Regs
13 Reg 4(4)(a) WTC(EMR) Regs

14 Reg 2(1) WTC(EMR) Regs
15 *JF v HMRC (TC)* [2017] UKUT 334 (AAC)
16 *JW v HMRC (TC)* [2019] UKUT 114 (AAC)
17 Reg 4(3) WTC(EMR) Regs
18 TCTM 02451-52
19 TCTM 02453
20 CTC/2103/2006
21 TCTM 02457
22 Reg 7 WTC(EMR) Regs; *Stafford and Banks v CAO (TC)* [2001] UKHL 33 (HL), reported as R(IS) 15/01
23 R(JSA) 8/03; CIS/914/1997; CJSA/2759/1998
24 R(JSA) 5/02
25 R(JSA) 1/07; *Saunderson v SSWP* [2012] ScotCS CSIH 10
26 Reg 5 WTC(EMR) Regs
27 Reg 5A WTC(EMR) Regs
28 Reg 6 WTC(EMR) Regs
29 Reg 7D WTC(EMR) Regs
30 Reg 8 WTC(EMR) Regs

31 Regs 7A and 7B WTC(EMR) Regs
32 HMRC Benefits and Credits Consultation Group email to CPAG, 20 December 2007
33 *TK v HMRC (TC)* [2016] UKUT 45 (AAC); *AG v HMRC (TC)* [2017] UKUT 67 (AAC)
34 Reg 7C WTC(EMR) Regs
35 Reg 4(2) WTC(EMR) Regs
36 TCTM 02440
37 Reg 4(2)(c) and (d) and (2A) WTC(EMR) Regs
38 Reg 2(1) WTC(EMR) Regs
39 R(FIS) 1/83; R(FIS) 1/86; TCTM 02431
40 TCTM 02440

2. The rules about your age
41 s3(3) TCA 2002

3. People included in the claim
42 s3(3)(b) TCA 2002
43 s3(3)(a) and (5A) TCA 2002; CTC/3864/2004; R(TC) 1/07
44 Reg 2, definition of 'child' and 'qualifying young person', WTC(EMR) Regs

4. The amount of working tax credit
45 ss7(2) and 13 TCA 2002; reg 4 TC(ITDR) Regs
46 Reg 3(2) TC(ITDR) Regs

5. Claims and backdating
47 Reg 5(7) TC(CN) Regs; R(IS) 5/05
48 Reg 5(3)-(6) TC(CN) Regs
49 *CI v HMRC (TC)* [2014] UKUT 158 (AAC)
50 s5(2) TCA 2002
51 Reg 10 TC(CN) Regs
52 Reg 7 TC(CN) Regs
53 Regs 11 and 12 TC(CN) Regs

6. Getting paid
54 s24(3) TCA 2002; reg 6 TC(PC) Regs
55 Regs 8 and 13 TC(PC) Regs
56 Reg 19 WTC(EMR) Regs; reg 6 CTC Regs

7. Tax, other benefits and the benefit cap
57 Reg 66 UC Regs
58 Reg 5(2)(b)(iii) UC(TP) Regs; reg 21(3B) UC Regs

Part 4

General rules for other means-tested benefits

Chapter 16

....

People included in the claim

This chapter covers:
1. Couples (below)
2. Children (p323)
3. Households (p329)

This chapter covers the rules for means-tested benefits other than universal credit (UC). For UC, see Chapter 4. For child tax credit, see Chapter 14, and for working tax credit, see Chapter 15.

Key facts

- Your partner and, in some cases, your children can be included in your means-tested benefit claim.
- You count as a member of a couple if you are married or in a civil partnership and are living with your partner in the same household. You also count as a couple if you are not married or in a civil partnership, but are living with your partner as if you were living together as a married couple.
- A child or 'qualifying young person' can be included as part of your family if you are responsible for her/him. S/he must also live in your household.
- You can continue to count as a couple, and children and young people can continue to be included in your means-tested benefit, while you are living apart temporarily.

---

1. Couples

Your partner is included in your means-tested benefit claim if you count as a 'couple'. You and your partner count as a 'couple' for means-tested benefit purposes if you are both 16 or over and you are:[1]
- married or civil partners and members of the same household; *or*
- not married or civil partners but 'living together as a married couple or civil partners'.

For when you count as living in the same 'household', see p329. **Note:** for pension credit (PC) only, if your partner is a 'person subject to immigration control' (see p1560), you are treated as *not* being members of the same household and so do not count as a couple.[2]

Part 4: General rules for other means-tested benefits
Chapter 16: People included in the claim
1. Couples

Spouse or civil partner

You can still be treated as part of a couple, even if you are married to someone else or in a civil partnership with someone else.[3]

There are special rules if you are polygamously married.[4] You count as **polygamously married** if you are part of a marriage in which one of you is married to more than one person and your marriages took place in a country that permits polygamy (see also p551).[5] For employment and support allowance (ESA) only, you and all your partners must also be living in the same household (see p329).

You count as someone's **civil partner** if you have been registered as her/his civil partner.

Living together as a married couple or civil partners

You count as a couple if you are 'living together as a married couple or civil partners'. This is referred to as 'cohabiting' in this *Handbook*. This applies to both different and same-sex relationships.[6]

If you are awarded income support (IS), income-based jobseeker's allowance (JSA) or income-related ESA, usually the local authority should not make a separate decision about whether you are cohabiting when considering your claim for housing benefit (HB).[7] However, if the local authority thinks that the benefit claim on which your HB claim is based is fraudulent, it can decide that you are not entitled to HB.[8] If you have not been awarded IS, income-based JSA, income-related ESA or PC, the local authority must consider whether you are cohabiting and may reach a different conclusion from that of the DWP.[9]

The factors below are used as 'signposts' to determine whether or not you are cohabiting.[10] No one factor, in itself, is conclusive, as it is your overall relationship and your particular circumstances that are looked at.[11] The 'emotional aspect' of the relationship (your interdependence, devotion, love and affection) should also be considered.[12] This does not necessarily conflict with the factors below but, like your individual circumstances, should not be regarded as conclusive. For example, if your partner stays with you for three nights or more a week, you should not automatically be treated as living together as a couple.

Are you cohabiting?
1. Do you live in the same household? See p321.
2. Do you have a sexual relationship? See p321.
3. What are your financial arrangements? See p321.
4. Is your relationship stable? See p321.
5. Do you have children? See p321.
6. How do you appear in public? See p322.

Living in the same household

If you live in the same household, you may be treated as cohabiting. For what counts as a 'household', see p329.

Even if you *do* share a household, you may not be cohabiting. It is essential to look at *why* two people are in the same household.[13] For example, if you are living in the same household for 'care, companionship and mutual convenience', you can argue that you are not living together as a husband and wife or civil partners.[14]

Being in a sexual relationship

In practice, a decision maker may not ask you about the existence of a sexual relationship, in which case s/he only has the information if you volunteer it. However, if you are appealing about whether you are a member of a couple, the First-tier Tribunal should consider this and may ask you about it.[15] If you do not have a sexual relationship, you should say so (and perhaps offer to show your separate sleeping arrangements).

Having a sexual relationship is not sufficient, by itself, to prove you are cohabiting. If you have never had a sexual relationship, there is a strong (but not necessarily conclusive) presumption that you are not cohabiting.[16] A couple who abstain from a sexual relationship before marriage should not be counted as cohabiting until they are formally married.[17]

Your financial arrangements

If one person is supported by the other or your household expenses are shared, this may be treated as evidence that you are cohabiting. However, it is important to consider how expenses are shared. There is a difference between, on the one hand, paying a fixed weekly contribution or rigidly sharing bills 50/50 (which does *not* suggest cohabitation) and, on the other hand, a common fund for income and expenditure (which might).

A stable relationship

Marriage and civil partnership are expected to be stable and lasting and so an occasional or brief association should not be regarded as cohabitation. However, the fact that your relationship is stable does not make it cohabitation – eg, you can have a stable relationship as a landlord and lodger, but not be cohabiting.

The way you spend your time together, the activities you undertake together and the things you do for each other are relevant, so questions about how you spend your holidays and how you organise the shopping, the laundry and cleaning may be important.

Children

If you have had a child together and live in the same household as the other parent, there is a strong (but not conclusive) presumption of cohabitation.

Part 4: General rules for other means-tested benefits
Chapter 16: People included in the claim
1. Couples

Your appearance in public

Decision makers may check the electoral roll and awards of other benefits to see whether you present yourselves as a couple. If you do not have a committed emotional loving relationship that is publicly acknowledged, you can argue that you are not living together as a married couple.[18]

Couples living apart

If you separate permanently (ie, you do not intend to resume living with your partner), you no longer count as a couple.[19] When deciding whether you intend to resume living together or not, your intention must be 'unqualified' – ie, it must not depend on something over which you have no control, such as the right of entry to the UK being granted by the Home Office[20] or the offer of a suitable job.[21]

If you and your partner are living apart temporarily, you continue to count as a couple because you are still treated as members of the same household (but see below). If you were not living together in the same household before your time apart, you should not be regarded as living apart temporarily.[22] Your former household need not have been in this country.[23]

However, even if you and your partner are only living apart temporarily, **you no longer count as a couple if:**

- **for IS, income-based JSA, income-related ESA, PC and HB,** you are likely to be separated for more than 52 weeks. However, you still count as a couple if you are unlikely to be separated for 'substantially' longer than 52 weeks and there are exceptional circumstances, such as a stay in hospital, or having no control over the length of the absence;[24]
- **for IS, income-based JSA, income-related ESA and PC:**[25]
  - either of you are in custody;
  - either of you are released on temporary licence from prison;
  - either of you are detained in a high security psychiatric hospital (in Scotland, a 'state hospital') under the mental health provisions;
  - either of you are staying permanently in a care home, an Abbeyfield Home or an independent hospital;
  - you are abroad and do not qualify for benefit while temporarily absent from Great Britain. For when you qualify while temporarily absent and for when your partner is abroad, see p1653 (for IS), p1655 (for income-based JSA), p1651 (for income-related ESA) and p1659 (for PC).

Note: if you and your partner continue to count as a couple while you are temporarily living apart, your partner's income and capital continue to be taken into account. However, in certain situations, your benefit is calculated in a different way (see p934 regarding care homes and p943 regarding approved bail or probation hostels).

Challenging a decision that you are a couple

Your benefit may be stopped or adjusted if the decision maker decides you are a member of a couple.

If you disagree with a decision that you are a couple, you can apply for a revision or supersession (see Chapter 56), or appeal to the First-tier Tribunal (see Chapter 57).

How do you show that you are not a couple?
1. Consider carefully what evidence to submit:
– if you are married or in a civil partnership, to show that you are not living in the same household with your spouse or civil partner;
– if you are not married or in a civil partnership, in relation to each of the six questions on p320, the emotional aspect of your relationship and any other matters you consider relevant.
2. Provide evidence if the other person has another address (eg, a rent book and other household bills), receipts for board and lodging, statements from friends and relatives, or evidence of a formal separation, divorce proceedings or a dissolution application or order.

You do not have to prove that you are not a couple when you first claim benefit, but you must provide any information that is reasonably required to decide your claim.[26] A decision should simply be made on all the evidence available.[27] In contrast, if your benefit as a single person is stopped because it is alleged that you are a couple, the burden of proof is on the decision maker to prove that you are.[28]

If your benefit is stopped because it is decided that you are a couple, challenge the decision and reapply immediately if your circumstances change. Also apply for any other benefits for which you might qualify – eg, HB, as the local authority may reach a different decision to the DWP.[29] You should apply for other benefits for which you previously automatically qualified – eg, health benefits (see Chapter 31).

If you are still entitled to a means-tested benefit as a couple, you should be paid on that basis.

2. Children

A child may count as part of your family and be included in your means-tested benefit. However, you can only get additional amounts in your benefit for her/him in certain circumstances.

For income support (IS), income-based jobseeker's allowance (JSA), income-related employment and support allowance (ESA) and housing benefit (HB), a child is part of your family and is included in your benefit if:
• you or your partner are 'responsible' for her/him (see p326); *and*
• s/he is living in your 'household' (see p327).[30]

Part 4: General rules for other means-tested benefits
Chapter 16: People included in the claim
2. Children

For the guarantee credit of pension credit (PC), a child is part of your family and is included in your PC if:[31]

- you are 'responsible' for her/him (see p326); *and*
- you do not have an award of either child tax credit (CTC) or working tax credit (and you are not treated as having such an award because you are renewing your award and awaiting a decision).

You do not have to be the child's parent.

A child stops being included in your benefit claim if you no longer fulfil the above conditions or if s/he no longer counts as a child (see below).

If a child is part of your family for benefit purposes and is included in your benefit, you can get an additional amount included in your HB and your PC. You can only get an additional amount in your IS or income-based JSA if:

- you already have a current claim for IS or income-based JSA that began before 6 April 2004; *and*
- you had a child included in that claim before 6 April 2004 and you have not been awarded CTC.

Note: usually, you only get additional amounts in your benefit for a maximum of two children. For more information, see p337. However, this does not apply to PC. If an amount for children can be included in your PC, you get an additional amount for each child that qualifies.

ESA does not include additional amounts for children.[32]

Who counts as a child

For IS, income-based JSA, income-related ESA and HB, a person usually counts as a child if:[33]

- s/he is aged under 16; *or*
- s/he is aged 16 or over but under 20 and counts as a 'qualifying young person' for child benefit purposes . This includes, for example, most young people who are at school or college full time studying for GCSEs or A levels (or equivalent), or who are doing approved training. See p579 for who counts as a qualifying young person. A young person can continue to count as a child after s/he has left school or training until the 'terminal date' (see p582) or the end of the child benefit 'extension period' (see p581).

Note: a 19-year-old must have started (or been accepted for or enrolled on) the education or training before reaching 19 in order to count as a qualifying young person.

For PC, a person usually counts as a child if:[34]

- s/he is aged under 16; *or*
- s/he 16 or over but under 20 and is a 'qualifying young person' for PC (see below).

A 'qualifying young person' for PC includes most young people studying for GCSEs or A levels or who are doing approved training. Specifically, it means someone who:[35]

- is aged 16 but who has not reached 1 September following her/his 16th birthday; *or*
- is aged 16–19 but who has not yet reached 1 September following her/his 19th birthday, and has been accepted for (or has enrolled on) approved training or non-advanced education at school or college, or another institution approved by the Secretary of State (see below). During term time there must be more than 12 hours, on average, of tuition, practical work, supervised study and examinations a week. Meal breaks and unsupervised study are not included.

Note: a 19-year-old must have started (or been accepted for or enrolled on) the education or training before reaching 19 in order to count as a qualifying young person.

Approved training and non-advanced education for pension credit
'**Approved training**' is training that is approved by the DWP and provided under section 2(1) of the Employment and Training Act 1973 or section 2(3) of the Enterprise and New Towns (Scotland) Act 1990.
A course is '**non-advanced**' if it is below the level of 'advanced education'. Courses that count as advanced education include university degrees and other courses above GCSE, A level and Scottish National Qualifications above higher or advanced higher level.[36] See p580 for more examples of advanced and non-advanced courses.

Who does not count as a child

For IS, income-based JSA, income-related ESA and HB, a person does *not* count as a child if:[37]

- s/he is getting certain benefits or tax credits in her/his own right and so does not count as a qualifying young person (see p587). For IS and income-based JSA, s/he may not count as a child if s/he is entitled to one of these benefits but is not getting it – eg, because it has been suspended; *or*
- s/he is excluded from entitlement to IS, income-based JSA and HB because s/he is aged 16 or 17, has left local authority care on or after 1 October 2001, and certain other conditions apply (see p947).

For PC, a person does not count as a child if s/he is getting universal credit, ESA (contributory or income-related), JSA (contribution-based or income-based) or IS in her/his own right.[38]

Part 4: General rules for other means-tested benefits
Chapter 16: People included in the claim
2. Children

Responsibility for a child

For IS, income-based JSA, income-related ESA and HB, a child is included in your benefit if you are 'responsible' for her/him and s/he is living in your 'household'.

- **You are treated as responsible for a child for IS** if you get child benefit for her/him (see Chapter 27).[39] If no one gets child benefit, you are responsible if you are the only one who has applied for it. In all other cases, the person responsible is the person with whom the child usually lives.[40] If a child for whom you are responsible gets child benefit for another child, you are also responsible for that child.[41]

- **You are treated as responsible for a child for JSA** if either you get child benefit for her/him or, if no one gets child benefit for her/him, the child 'usually lives' with you or you are the only person who has applied for child benefit.[42] If you share responsibility for the child, even if you do not get child benefit for her/him, you might be regarded as responsible for her/him if you are the 'substantial minority carer' – ie, you have the child with you for at least 104 nights a year.[43] If a child for whom you are responsible gets child benefit for another child, you are also responsible for that child. **Note:** the rules for when you count as responsible for a child for the purposes of deciding whether you must claim joint-claim JSA are different.[44]

- **You are treated as responsible for a child for ESA** if s/he 'usually lives' with you. This is not defined in the rules.[45]

- **You are treated as responsible for a child for HB** if the child is 'normally living' with you.[46] This means that s/he spends more time with you than with anyone else.[47] If it is unclear in whose household the child lives, or if s/he spends an equal amount of time with two parents in different homes (this may not mean literally three and a half days with each parent[48]), you are treated as having responsibility if:[49]
  - you get child benefit for her/him (see Chapter 27);
  - no one gets child benefit, but you have applied for it;
  - no one has applied for child benefit, or both of you have applied, but you appear to have the most responsibility.

  Note: substantial minority carers cannot be regarded as responsible for a child for HB.[50]

For HB, it is only necessary to look at who gets child benefit when it is unclear in whose household the child *normally* lives. **For IS,** it is essential to look first at who gets child benefit, and only if this is not decisive is it relevant to look at where the child *usually* lives.

A child can only be the responsibility of one person in any week for IS, income-based JSA and HB.[51] The rules for ESA do not expressly say this but, in any case, a person can only be responsible for a child if s/he usually lives with her/him.

If benefit is paid for a child, it cannot be split between parents if a child spends her/his time equally between their two homes.

For PC, a child is included if you are 'responsible' for her/him. You are responsible for a child if s/he normally lives with you.[52]

This includes considering the amount of time s/he spends with you, but is not limited to this and should also take into account the nature of the support you provide. If the child normally lives with two (or more) people who are not a couple (eg, if s/he lives in the homes of her/his separated parents), you are responsible if you have the main responsibility. In this situation, you can agree with the other person who this should be. The DWP can, however, decide otherwise or, if you cannot agree, decide which person has the main responsibility. Both the amount of time the child spends with you and the nature of the support you provide should be taken into account.[53] You cannot be treated as responsible for a child during any period in which s/he is:[54]

- looked after by a local authority (including being placed with a foster parent), except during planned short breaks in local authority care to provide respite care for the person who normally looks after her/him, or where s/he is placed with someone who has parental responsibility for her/him; *or*
- a prisoner; *or*
- temporarily absent but in Great Britain, and s/he has been, or is expected to be, absent for more than 52 weeks, unless there are 'exceptional circumstances' (eg, s/he is in hospital) and the absence is unlikely to be substantially more than 52 weeks; *or*
- temporarily absent from Great Britain and s/he has been, or is expected to be, absent from Great Britain for more than four weeks, unless it is for the death of a close relative or medical treatment, when the period of absence may be, respectively, eight weeks or 26 weeks (see p1659).

Living in the same household

In addition to being responsible for her/him, for IS, JSA, ESA and HB a child is only included if s/he is a member of the same household. If you count as responsible for a child, s/he is usually treated as a member of your household, despite any temporary absence. For exceptions to the rule, see below. For what 'household' means, see p329. The requirement for the child to be a member of your household does not apply to PC (but the child must normally be living with you).

When a child does not count as a member of your household

A child does *not* count as a member of your household if:[55]

- **for IS, JSA, ESA and HB**, s/he is not living with you and:
  - s/he has no intention of resuming living with you; *or*
  - s/he is likely to be absent for more than 52 weeks, unless there are exceptional circumstances, such as being in hospital, or if you have no control over the

Part 4: General rules for other means-tested benefits
Chapter 16: People included in the claim
2. Children

length of absence and the absence is unlikely to be substantially longer than 52 weeks;

- **for IS, JSA, ESA and HB:**
  - s/he is being fostered by you or your partner following a formal placement by social services. This does not apply if you are fostering privately or if social services has made a less formal arrangement for the child to live with you; *or*
  - s/he is living with you or your partner prior to adoption and has been placed by social services or an adoption agency; *or*
  - s/he is boarded out with you or your partner, whether or not with a view to adoption (for JSA, ESA and HB only); *or*
  - s/he has been placed with someone else prior to adoption; *or*
  - s/he is in the care of, or being looked after by, the local authority and not living with you. However, s/he counts as a member of your household on the days when s/he comes home – eg, for the weekend or a holiday.[56] Make sure you tell the decision maker in good time. For HB, your child counts as a member of the household for all that week whether s/he returns for all or only part of it;[57]
- **for IS, JSA and ESA,** s/he is not living with you and:
  - s/he has been in hospital or in a local authority home for more than 12 weeks and has not been in regular contact with you or other members of your household. The 12 weeks run from the date s/he went into hospital or the home, or from the date you claim IS/JSA/ESA, if later.[58] However, the 12 weeks run from the date s/he went into the hospital or home if:[59]
    - you were getting income-based JSA immediately before your claim for IS; *or*
    - you were getting IS or income-related ESA immediately before your claim for JSA; *or*
    - you were getting IS or income-based JSA immediately before your claim for ESA;
  - s/he is in custody. **Note:** s/he can still be included in your claim for any periods s/he spends at home;[60] *or*
  - s/he has been abroad for more than four weeks, or for more than eight weeks (26 weeks for ESA) to get medical treatment.[61] The four-/eight-/26-week period runs from the day s/he went abroad, or from the day you claim IS/JSA/ESA, if later. However, the four-/eight-/26-week period is calculated from the day after the child went abroad if:[62]
    - you were getting income-based JSA immediately before your claim for IS; *or*
    - you were getting IS or income-related ESA immediately before your claim for JSA; *or*
    - you were getting IS or income-based JSA immediately before your claim for ESA;

- **for IS and income-based JSA**, s/he is living with you and away from her/his parental or usual home in order to attend school. The child is not included in your claim, but remains a member of her/his parent's household.[63]

3. Households

The term 'household' is not defined. Whether you and another person should be treated as members of the same household is decided on the particular facts of your case. In all cases, you must spend the major part of your time in the same household. For pension credit only, if your partner is a 'person subject to immigration control' (see p1560), you are treated as *not* being members of the same household and so do not count as a couple.[64]

A house or flat can contain a number of separate households and if one person has exclusive occupation of separate accommodation from another, they are not considered to be living in the same household. Physical presence is not, in itself, conclusive. There must be a 'particular kind of tie' binding two people together in a domestic establishment. So, for example, a husband and wife may live in separate households in the same care or nursing home.[65] A household must also involve two or more people living together as a unit and having a reasonable level of independence and self-sufficiency. In one case, it was held that a married couple sharing a room in a residential home because they needed help organising their personal care and domestic activities were not self-sufficient and did not live in a domestic establishment, and, therefore, did not share a household.[66]

Is there a separate household?

If you think you should not be treated as a member of the same household as someone, check whether you can show that you maintain separate households. A separate household may exist if there are:

– independent arrangements for storing and cooking food or separate eating arrangements;

– independent financial arrangements or separate commitments for housing costs;

– no evidence of family life.

You cannot be a member of more than one household at the same time.[67] So if you are a member of one couple, you cannot also be treated as part of another. If two people maintain separate homes (ie, they each have separate addresses where they usually live), they cannot share the same household.[68] Even if you have the right to occupy only part of a room, you may have your own household.[69]

If you are separated from your partner, but living under the same roof, you should not be treated as a couple if you are maintaining separate households. Any

Part 4: General rules for other means-tested benefits
Chapter 16: People included in the claim
Notes

'mere hope' of a reconciliation is not a 'reasonable expectation' if at least one partner has accepted that the relationship is at an end.[70]

If you are still married or in a civil partnership, a shared attitude that the relationship is at an end may not be enough to show there is no shared household.[71]

Notes

4

1. Couples
1 s137(1) SSCBA 1992; CFC/7/1992
   IS Reg 2(1) IS Regs
   JSA s35(1) JSA 1995; reg 1(3) JSA Regs
   ESA Sch 1 para 6(5) WRA 2007; reg 2(1) ESA Regs
   PC s17(1) SPCA 2002; reg 1(2) SPC Regs
   HB Reg 2(1) HB Regs; reg 2(1) HB(SPC) Regs
2 Reg 5(1)(h) SPC Regs
3 R(SB) 8/85
4 **IS** Regs 18 and 23 IS Regs
   JSA Regs 84 and 88(4) and (5) JSA Regs
   ESA Regs 68 and 83 ESA Regs
   PC Reg 8 and Sch 3 SPC Regs
   HB Regs 23 and 25 HB Regs; regs 22 and 23 HB(SPC) Regs
5 **IS** Reg 2(1) IS Regs
   JSA Reg 1(3) JSA Regs
   ESA Reg 2(1) ESA Regs
   PC s12 SPCA 2002
   HB Reg 2(1) HB Regs; reg 2(1) HB(SPC) Regs
6 **IS** Reg 2(1) IS Regs
   JSA s35(1A) JSA 1995; reg 1(3) JSA Regs
   ESA Sch 1 para 6(6) WRA 2007; reg 2(1) ESA Regs
   PC s17(1A) SPCA 2002; reg 1(2) SPC Regs
   HB Reg 2(1) HB Regs; reg 2(1) HB(SPC) Regs
   IS/HB s137(1A) SSCBA 1992
7 *R v Penwith DC HBRB ex parte Menear* [1991] 24 HLR 115 (QBD). However, *AM v Chelmsford Borough Council (HB)* [2013] UKUT 245 (AAC) suggests that this only applies to the assessment of income and capital, and not to cohabitation questions.
8 *R v South Ribble BC HBRB ex parte Hamilton* [2000] 33 HLR 102 (CA)
9 CH/4014/2007
10 *Crake and Butterworth v SBC* [1982] 1 All ER 498; [1981] 2 FLR 264 (QBD)
11 R(SB) 17/81; R(G) 3/71; CIS/87/1993
12 *PP v Basildon District Council (HB)* [2013] UKUT 505 (AAC)
13 *Crake and Butterworth v SBC* [1982]; [1981] 2 FLR 264 (QBD), quoted in R(SB) 35/85
14 R(SB) 35/85
15 CIS/87/1993; CIS/2559/2002; CIS/2074/2008
16 CIS/87/1993
17 CSB/150/1985
18 *JP v SSWP (IS)* [2014] UKUT 17 (AAC)
19 **IS** Reg 16(2)(a) IS Regs
   JSA Reg 78(2)(a) JSA Regs
   ESA Reg 156(3)(a) ESA Regs
   PC Reg 5(1)(a)(i) SPC Regs
   HB Reg 21(2)(a) HB Regs; reg 21(2)(a) HB(SPC) Regs
20 CIS/508/1992; CIS/13805/1996
21 CIS/484/1993
22 **IS** Reg 16(1) IS Regs
   JSA Reg 78(1) JSA Regs
   ESA Reg 156(2) ESA Regs
   PC Reg 5(2) SPC Regs
   HB Reg 21(1) HB Regs; reg 21(1) HB(SPC) Regs
   All *Broxtowe Borough Council v CS (HB)* [2014] UKUT 186 (AAC)
23 CIS/508/1992
24 **IS** Reg 16(2) IS Regs
   JSA Reg 78(2) JSA Regs
   ESA Reg 156(3) ESA Regs
   PC Reg 5(1)(a) SPC Regs
   HB Reg 21(2) HB Regs; reg 21(2) HB(SPC) Regs

Chapter 16

People included in the claim

25 **IS** Reg 16(3) IS Regs
   JSA Reg 78(3) JSA Regs
   ESA Reg 156(4) ESA Regs. This wrongly
   refers to Chapter 4, but correctly refers
   to the rules on temporary absence from
   Great Britain.
   PC Reg 5(1)(b)-(d) and (f) SPC Regs
26 **IS/ESA/PC** Reg 7(1) SS(C&P) Regs
   JSA Reg 24 JSA Regs
   HB Reg 86 HB Regs; reg 67 HB(SPC)
   Regs
27 CIS/317/1994
28 R(I) 1/71
29 R(H) 9/04

2. Children
30 s137 SSCBA 1992
   JSA s35 JSA 1995; reg 77 JSA Regs
   ESA Reg 2(1), definition of 'family', ESA
   Regs
31 Reg 6 and Sch IIA SPC Regs
32 Reg 1 SS(WTCCTC)(CA) Regs
33 **IS** Reg 14 IS Regs
   JSA s35 JSA 1995; regs 1(3) and 76 JSA
   Regs
   ESA Reg 2(1) ESA Regs
   HB Reg 19 HB Regs; reg 19 HB(SPC)
   Regs
   IS/HB s137 SSCBA 1992
34 Reg 4A and Sch IIA SPC Regs
35 Reg 4A and Sch IIA SPC Regs
36 Reg 4A SPC Regs
37 **IS** Reg 14(2) IS Regs
   JSA Reg 76(2) JSA Regs
   ESA Reg 2(1), definition of 'young
   person', ESA Regs
   HB Reg 19(2) HB Regs; reg 19(2)
   HB(SPC) Regs
38 Reg 4A SPC Regs
39 Reg 15(1) IS Regs
40 Reg 15(2) IS Regs
41 Reg 15(1A) IS Regs
42 Reg 77(1)-(3) JSA Regs
43 Reg 77 JSA Regs, as applied in *Hockenjos
   v Secretary of State for Social Security*
   [2004] EWCA Civ 1749, reported as
   R(JSA) 2/05. However, see also CJSA/
   2507/2002.
44 Reg 77(2) JSA Regs
45 Reg 156(10) ESA Regs
46 Reg 20(1) HB Regs; reg 20(1) HB(SPC)
   Regs
47 CFC/1537/1995
48 CFC/1537/1995
49 Reg 20(2) HB Regs; reg 20(2) HB(SPC)
   Regs

50 *JD v SSWP and London Borough of
   Richmond upon Thames (HB)* [2013]
   UKUT 642 (AAC); *JB v SSWP and
   Basingstoke and Deane BC (HB)* [2014]
   UKUT 223 (AAC)
51 **IS** Reg 15(4) IS Regs
   JSA s3(1)(d) JSA 1995; reg 77(5) JSA
   Regs
   HB Reg 20(3) HB Regs; reg 20(3)
   HB(SPC) Regs
52 Sch IIA para 3 SPC Regs
53 Sch IIA para 3(3) and (4) SPC Regs; reg 4
   UC Regs; *MC v SSWP (UC)* [2018] UKUT
   44 (AAC) was about UC but arguably
   should also apply to PC
54 Sch IIA paras 4-8 SPC Regs
55 **IS** Reg 16 IS Regs
   JSA Reg 78 JSA Regs
   ESA Reg 156 ESA Regs
   HB Reg 21 HB Regs; reg 21 HB(SPC)
   Regs
56 **IS** Regs 15(3) and 16(6) IS Regs
   JSA Regs 77(4) and 78(7) JSA Regs
   ESA Reg 156(8) ESA Regs
57 Reg 21(5) HB Regs; reg 21(5) HB(SPC)
   Regs
58 **IS** Reg 16(5)(b) IS Regs
   JSA Reg 78(5)(c) JSA Regs
   ESA Reg 156(6)(c) ESA Regs
59 **IS** Reg 16(5A) IS Regs
   JSA Reg 78(6) JSA Regs
   ESA Reg 156(7) ESA Regs
60 **IS** Regs 15(3) and 16(6) IS Regs
   JSA Regs 77(4) and 78(5)(i) and (7) JSA
   Regs
   ESA Reg 156(6)(h) and (8) ESA Regs
61 **IS** Reg 16(5)(a) and (aa) IS Regs
   JSA Reg 78(5)(a) and (b) JSA Regs
   ESA Reg 156(6)(a) and (b) ESA Regs
62 **IS** Reg 16(5A) IS Regs
   JSA Reg 78(6) JSA Regs
   ESA Reg 156(7) ESA Regs
63 **IS** Reg 16(7) IS Regs
   JSA Reg 78(8) JSA Regs

3. Households
64 Reg 5(1)(h) SPC Regs
65 *Santos v Santos* [1972] 2 All ER 246; CIS/
   671/1992; CIS/81/1993
66 CIS/4935/1997
67 R(SB) 8/85
68 R(SB) 4/83
69 CSB/463/1986
70 CIS/72/1994
71 CIS/2900/1998

Chapter 17

Applicable amounts

This chapter covers:
1. What are applicable amounts (below)
2. Personal allowances (p333)
3. Premiums and additional amounts (p339)
4. Components (p353)
5. Transitional addition (p355)

Key facts
- Applicable amounts are used in some means-tested benefits to help calculate the amount of benefit to which you are entitled.
- Applicable amounts apply in income support, income-based jobseeker's allowance, income-related employment and support allowance (ESA) and housing benefit. There are additional amounts in the guarantee credit of pension credit for people who are severely disabled, carers or people who have a child, which are similar to applicable amounts.
- Applicable amounts differ according to the benefit you are claiming. They are made up of personal allowances, premiums, certain housing costs and, in some cases, components. You may have one or more of these included.

---

1. What are applicable amounts

Your applicable amount for income support (IS), income-based jobseeker's allowance (JSA) and income-related employment and support allowance (ESA) is the amount you are expected to live on each week. Your applicable amount for housing benefit (HB) is the amount used to calculate how much help you need with your rent. This chapter explains how to work out your applicable amount for these benefits. For the way your benefit is calculated, see p240 for IS, p711 for income-based JSA, p164 for income-related ESA and p190 for HB.

What is included in your applicable amount

Your applicable amount is made up of:
- **personal allowances**: the amount the law says you need for living expenses (see p333);

- **premiums**: the amount given for certain extra needs you, your partner or children may have (see p339);
- **a support or work-related activity component** in income-related ESA and, in some circumstances, in HB (see p353);
- certain **housing costs** in IS, income-based JSA and income-related ESA (see p360). **Note:** from 6 April 2018, you cannot get benefit to help with the cost of your mortgage or loan for repairs and improvements. Instead, the DWP may offer you a loan to help meet your interest payments (see p855);
- **a transitional addition** in income-related ESA and HB if you have been transferred to ESA from incapacity benefit, severe disablement allowance or IS on the grounds of disability (see p355).

Can you get allowances and premiums for children?

IS and income-based JSA have not included allowances and premiums for children since 6 April 2004. However, you may continue to have these included if:[1]

– you have a claim which began before 6 April 2004; *and*

– you had a child included in the claim before 6 April 2004; *and*

– you have not yet been awarded child tax credit (CTC).

In these circumstances, personal allowances and premiums for children continue to be included in your claim (and amounts for a new child can be added) unless you claim and are awarded CTC.

You can get allowances and premiums for children in your HB (see p337 and p339). You can get an additional amount for children as part of the guarantee credit of pension credit (see p339).

2. Personal allowances

The amount of your personal allowance in income support (IS), income-based jobseeker's allowance (JSA), income-related employment and support allowance (ESA) and housing benefit (HB) depends on your age and whether you are claiming as a single person or a couple. You also get an allowance for each child included in your HB and, in some circumstances, in IS and income-based JSA.

If you are polygamously married (see p319), you receive an extra amount for each additional spouse in your household.[2] However, unless you are entitled to joint-claim JSA (see p253), if any additional spouse is under the age of 18, you only receive an extra amount for her/him if:[3]

- for IS, income-based JSA and income-related ESA, s/he is either responsible for a child (see p326) or would otherwise meet the special conditions for qualifying for JSA as a 16/17-year-old (see p256); *or*
- for IS and income-related ESA, s/he would qualify for that benefit in her/his own right were s/he not a member of a polygamous marriage.

Rates of personal allowances for people aged 18 or over

Note: some 16/17-year-olds may also be entitled to these rates (see below).

If you have been getting working-age HB (see p188) and this continues even though you are now a member of a 'mixed-age couple ' (ie, if one of you is at least pension age, but not the other) (see p188), your personal allowance remains as for working-age HB, even though one of you has reached pension age.

	IS/JSA/ESA/ working-age HB	pension-age HB only
Single claimant:		
Aged 18–24	£58.90	
Aged 25 or over	£74.35	
Aged 18 or over and ESA includes (or would include) a support component or claimant in work-related activity group (ESA/working-age HB only)	£74.35	
Pension age or over		£187.75
Lone parent:		
Aged 18 or over	£74.35	
Pension age or over		£187.75
Couple:		
Both aged 18 or over	£116.80	
One or both pension age or over		£280.85
One aged under 18 (some IS/JSA/ESA cases only and all HB cases)	£116.80	
One aged under 18 (other IS/JSA/ESA cases):		
either	£74.35	
or	£58.90	
Polygamous marriages (each additional qualifying spouse):		
Partner aged 18 or over, or under 18 in certain circumstances (see p333)	£42.45	
One or more pension age or over		£93.10

Rates of personal allowances for 16/17-year-olds

- For IS and income-based JSA:
  - if you are single and aged 16 or 17 (including if you are a lone parent), you get the same rate as single 18–24-year-olds – ie, £58.90; *or*

- if you are in a couple (unless one of the circumstances below applies) and your partner is also aged under 18, you get £58.90. If your partner is aged 18 or over, see the table on p334.
- For income-related ESA:
  - you get £58.90; *or*
  - if your ESA includes the support component or if you are in the work-related activity group, you get £74.35; *or*
  - if you are in a couple (unless one of the circumstances below applies) and your partner is also under 18, the same amounts as above (£58.90 or £74.35) apply.
- For HB:
  - if you are single (including if you are a lone parent), you get the same rate as 18–24-year-olds – ie, £58.90; *or*
  - if you are entitled to ESA and qualify for the support component or you are in the work-related activity group (see p353), you get £74.35; *or*
  - if you are in a couple and your partner is also under 18, you get £89.00. If your partner is aged 18 or over, or if you are entitled to ESA and either get the support component or are in the work-related activity group, you get £116.80.

For this purpose, you count as qualifying for an ESA component even if your actual award of ESA is nil – eg, because you are only entitled to national insurance contribution credits.

Note: most 16/17-year-olds who have previously been looked after by a local authority cannot claim IS/JSA or HB (see p947).

Young couples in special circumstances

Note: the following rules apply to IS, income-based JSA and income-related ESA only.[4]

If you are a young couple, the amount of personal allowance paid depends on your ages and whether one or both of you are entitled to IS, income-based JSA (including JSA severe hardship payments – see p257) or income-related ESA, or you would be if you were a single person. The amount of your ESA personal allowance depends on whether you are in the ESA assessment phase or the ESA main phase, and on whether you qualify for the support component or are in the work-related activity group (see p353). For some couples, the personal allowance may be no more than that for a single person.

Age	£pw
Both aged 16–17, higher rate:	
ESA assessment phase	89.00
ESA main phase	116.80
IS/JSA	89.00

Both aged 16–17, lower rate:

ESA assessment phase	58.90
ESA main phase	74.35
IS/JSA	58.90

One aged 16–17, one 18 or over, higher rate:

ESA assessment phase	116.80
ESA main phase	116.80
IS/JSA	116.80

One aged 16–17, one 18–24, lower rate:

ESA assessment phase	58.90
ESA main phase	74.35
IS/JSA	58.90

One aged 16–17, one 25 or over, lower rate:

ESA assessment phase	74.35
ESA main phase	74.35
IS/JSA	74.35

If both of you are aged 16 or 17, you get the higher rate personal allowance in the following circumstances.

- For IS:
  - one of you is responsible for a child; *or*
  - both of you would qualify for IS or income-related ESA if you were not a couple; *or*
  - the claimant's partner would qualify for income-based JSA or JSA severe hardship payments if s/he were single.
- For JSA:
  - one of you is responsible for a child; *or*
  - both of you would qualify for income-based JSA if you were not a couple; *or*
  - the claimant would qualify for income-based JSA and her/his partner would qualify for IS or income-related ESA if you were not a couple, or you would both qualify for JSA severe hardship payments if you were single; *or*
  - one of you would qualify for JSA severe hardship payments if you were single and the other for income-based JSA, IS or income-related ESA if s/he were single; *or*
  - you are married or civil partners and you both qualify for income-based JSA, or one does and the other is registered for work or training.
- For ESA:
  - one of you is responsible for a child; *or*
  - both of you would qualify for income-related ESA if you were not a couple; *or*
  - the claimant's partner would qualify for IS if s/he were single; *or*
  - the claimant's partner would qualify for income-based JSA or JSA severe hardship payments as a single person.

The higher rate is paid at the main phase rate if the claimant qualifies for a support or work-related activity component (see pp652–53). Otherwise, it is paid at the assessment phase rate.

If one of you is aged 16 or 17 and the other is 18 or over, you get the higher rate personal allowance in the following circumstances.

- For IS, the younger partner qualifies for IS or income-related ESA (or s/he would do so if s/he were not a member of a couple) or income-based JSA or JSA severe hardship payments.
- For JSA, the younger partner is treated as responsible for a child, or qualifies for income-based JSA or JSA severe hardship payments, or either IS (or s/he would do so were s/he not a member of a couple) or income-related ESA (were s/he to make a claim).
- For ESA, the younger partner would either qualify for IS or income-related ESA (were s/he not a member of a couple), or for income-based JSA or JSA severe hardship payments. It is paid at the same rate in the assessment phase and main phase.

Qualifying for jobseeker's allowance

For these purposes, if you are under 18, you qualify for:

– income-based JSA, if you meet the rules for income-based JSA described on p256; *or*
– JSA severe hardship payments, if you are subject to a severe hardship direction (see p257).

Personal allowances for children

Personal allowances for children are included in your HB applicable amount. IS, income-based JSA and income-related ESA do *not* usually include personal allowances for children. However, if you have been claiming IS or income-based JSA since before 6 April 2004, these can sometimes be included (see p333). You cannot get personal allowances for children in joint-claim JSA, as you cannot claim this type of JSA if you have children. Although there is no personal allowance for a child as part of PC, you may be entitled to an additional amount in your guarantee credit of PC (see p339).

For when children are included in your claim and for who counts as a child, see p323.

Note: your child's income and capital do not affect the amount of HB to which you are entitled. However, if you are still entitled to a personal allowance for your child in your IS or income-based JSA, you do not get an allowance for a child in your IS or income-based JSA if s/he has over £3,000 capital. See p420 for how a child's income may affect IS or income-based JSA.

The two-child limit

You get one personal allowance for each child. However, you cannot get a personal allowance for a third or subsequent child born on or after 6 April 2017, unless an exception applies (see below). Also, for HB only, you do not get a personal allowance for a third or subsequent child who becomes part of your claim (eg, s/he is the child of a new partner) on or after 6 April 2017 or is in a new claim made on or after that date, unless an exception applies. This is known as the 'two-child limit'. The limit applies to children for whom you or your partner are responsible and who are living in your household (see p63).[5]

If you already had a personal allowance for a third or subsequent child included in your HB on 5 April 2017, you continue to get a personal allowance for her/him while that award continues. Also, if you get an element for a child in your child tax credit (CTC), you get a personal allowance for her/him in your HB.

A personal allowance can become payable for a third child who is born on or after 6 April 2017 and to whom this limit applies if an older child leaves the household (so that you are no longer responsible for her/him), or if a young person leaves education (so that s/he no longer qualifies). In these situations, you should report the change as soon as possible so that you continue to get the maximum two personal allowances.

An exception applies, and so a personal allowance is payable, to any child who is living with you and who is being adopted by you from local authority care, or who is living with you under a 'non-parental caring arrangement'. For HB, this means the same as it does for CTC (see p1455). For IS and income-based JSA, this means the same as it does for universal credit (UC) (see p68). In addition, when establishing how many children you have for the two-child limit, such children are ignored. So you can get an element for any such child, plus up to two more children, plus any further (third or subsequent) child to whom an exception also applies.

An exception also applies to a third or subsequent child who is:[6]
- born in a multiple birth, other than the first born if you already have two or more children;
- likely to have been conceived as a result of rape or in a controlling or coercive relationship and you are not living with the alleged perpetrator. For HB, this means the same as it does for CTC (see p1455). For IS and income-based JSA, this means the same as it does for UC (see p68).

For an exception to apply to a child in your HB claim, you must have applied for CTC and have had an exception applied for her/him. See p1455 for more details.

Note: the two-child limit is currently the subject of a legal challenge. See cpag.org.uk/content/two-child-limit-challenge for details, and AskCPAG.org.uk and CPAG's *Welfare Rights Bulletin* for updates.

Rate of personal allowance for children

For HB (and for IS and income-based JSA if still included), there is one rate of personal allowance for children who are included in your claim – £68.27. You get one personal allowance for each child.

3. Premiums and additional amounts

Premiums are added to your personal allowance and are intended to help with the extra expenses you have as a result of your age, having a disability and, in some circumstances, children. Some premiums are not included in some of the means-tested benefits. Pension credit (PC) does not include premiums, but has additional amounts for severe disability, carers and children.

Note: if you or your partner are entitled to 'pension-age' housing benefit (HB) (see p188), your HB can only include the family, disabled child, enhanced disability for a child, severe disability and carer premiums.[7] In these circumstances, your HB cannot include a disability premium. If you (or your partner) are entitled to 'working-age' HB (see p188), that can include the disability premium. If you are in a 'mixed-age' couple (ie, one of you has reached pension age but the other has not), and you are prevented from claiming universal credit (UC) (see p23), you may be entitled to HB – either pension-age HB or working-age HB, depending on your circumstances (see p188). There are no pensioner premiums in either pension-age or working-age HB.

See p352 for information about backdating premiums. See p351 for the premium rates and for which premiums can be paid in addition to other premiums.

Premiums and additional amount for children

Certain premiums can be included in your HB applicable amount if you have children included in your claim. These are the family premium, disabled child premium and the child rate of the enhanced disability premium. Income support (IS), income-based jobseeker's allowance (JSA) and income-related employment and support allowance (ESA) do not usually include these premiums. However, if you have been claiming IS or income-based JSA since before 6 April 2004, see p333.

> **Disability assistance for children and young people**
> In Scotland, a new benefit providing disability assistance for children and young people is due to be introduced in summer 2020 (see p1690). It is expected that there will be changes to refer to this new benefit for some premiums, although, at the time of writing, there is no information available. See AskCPAG.org.uk and CPAG's *Welfare Rights Bulletin* for updates.

For who counts as a child and when children are included in your claim, see p323.
Note: your child's income and capital do not affect the amount of your HB. However, if you are still entitled to premiums for children in your IS or income-based JSA, you do not get a premium (except a family premium) for a child who

Part 4: General rules for other means-tested benefits
Chapter 17: Applicable amounts
3. Premiums and additional amounts

has over £3,000 capital. See p420 for how a child's income may affect IS or income-based JSA.

You can qualify for an additional amount for a child in the guarantee credit of PC if you are not entitled, or treated as entitled, to tax credits, and are responsible for the child (see p323).[8] You get an additional amount for each child who qualifies. The weekly standard amount of the addition is £54.32 for each child born on or after 6 April 2017, or £64.82 for your eldest child if s/he was born before that date. If the child is entitled to disability living allowance (DLA) or personal independence payment (PIP), the standard amount is increased by £29.52. If s/he is entitled to the highest rate of the care component of DLA or the enhanced rate of the daily living component of PIP, or s/he is certified as severely sight impaired or blind by a consultant opthalmologist, the standard rate is increased by £92.12.

If your child dies, you can continue to get the additional amount for up to eight weeks after her/his death (or until s/he would have reached 20 years old, if that is earlier).

Family premium

You cannot get a family premium in any new HB claim made on or after 1 May 2016, or any new IS or income-based JSA claim made on or after 6 April 2004. The family premium cannot be included in any claim for income-related ESA.

Otherwise, you may be entitled to a family premium in your HB, IS or income-based JSA if at least one child is included in your claim (see p323). Only one family premium can be included, irrespective of how many children you have.[9]

The premium can be paid even if you are not the parent of the child.

For HB, if you had a child included in your claim before 1 May 2016, you continue to get the premium, provided you still have a child included in your claim and you do not make a new claim for HB on or after that date.[10]

For IS and income-based JSA, you are only entitled to a family premium in certain circumstances (see p332). If you are entitled, a family premium is included even if you do not receive a personal allowance in your IS or income-based JSA for any child because s/he has capital over £3,000.

If a child who is being looked after by a local authority or who is in custody comes home for part of a week, your IS or income-based JSA includes a proportion of the weekly premium, based on the number of days the child is with you.[11] You can be paid the full premium in your HB if your child who is being looked after by a local authority is part of your household for any part of the week, provided the local authority thinks this is reasonable, given how often and for how long the child is at home with you.[12]

Disabled child premium

You are entitled to a disabled child premium in your HB and, if applicable, your IS and income-based JSA (see p333), for each child included in your claim who gets DLA, PIP, armed forces independence payment if s/he is at least 16, or extra-statutory payments to compensate for non-payment of DLA or PIP, or who is blind.[13] A disabled child premium can still be included for a third or subsequent child, even if you do not get a personal allowance for her/him because of the 'two-child limit' (see p337). Income-related ESA does not include a disabled child premium.

A child is treated as blind if s/he is certified as severely sight impaired or blind by a consultant ophthalmologist, and for the first 28 weeks after s/he has ceased to be certified as such on regaining her/his sight.[14] If DLA or PIP stops because the child has gone into hospital, see p924.

If your child is looked after by a local authority or is in custody for part of the week, the disabled child premium is affected in the same way as the family premium (see above).

Your child's capital does not affect the amount of your HB.[15] For IS and income-based JSA, if your child has over £3,000 capital or has been in hospital for more than 52 weeks, you do not get this premium.[16]

If your child dies

If your child dies, you may be able to continue receiving the disabled child premium for eight weeks.[17] This applies if:
* you get child benefit for the child following her/his death (see p597); *and*
* you were getting the disabled child premium for that child in your applicable amount immediately before her/his death.

Disability premium

Income-related ESA does not include a disability premium.

You qualify for a disability premium if none of the exclusions (see p343) apply and one of the following qualifying conditions applies.[18] The person who satisfies the qualifying condition must be under pension age (see p779). For IS and income-based JSA, if you or your partner have reached pension age, you may get the higher pensioner premium instead (see p345). **Note:** the law refers to the qualifying age for PC rather than pension age, but since December 2018 this has been the same as pension age. There is a single rate and a couple rate, which applies whether one or both of you satisfy the conditions.
* You (or your partner) are getting a qualifying benefit. These are:[19]
  – attendance allowance (AA) (see Chapter 24), DLA (see Chapter 28), PIP (see Chapter 35), armed forces independence payment or an equivalent benefit paid to meet attendance needs because of an injury at work (see Chapter 32) or a war injury;[20] *or*

Part 4: General rules for other means-tested benefits
Chapter 17: Applicable amounts
3. Premiums and additional amounts

- AA, DLA or PIP if you (or your partner) were getting one of these benefits, but payment was suspended when one of you became a hospital patient.[21] In the case of IS and income-based JSA only, you or your partner must previously have qualified for a disability premium; *or*
- for IS and income-based JSA, your partner or, for joint-claim JSA, you or your partner, were getting incapacity benefit paid at the long-term rate which stopped at pension age for income-based JSA (including joint-claim JSA)[22] or when retirement pension/state pension became payable for IS. For IS, you must have been continuously entitled to IS or income-based JSA since that time.[23] If it was your partner who reached pension age or began receiving a retirement pension/state pension, s/he must still be alive.[24] You or your partner must have previously qualified for a disability premium;[25] *or*
- war pensioner's mobility supplement; *or*
- the disabled worker element or severe disability element of working tax credit (WTC); *or*
- severe disablement allowance (SDA). For IS and HB, you must be getting SDA. For income-based JSA, your partner must be getting it. For joint-claim JSA, either you or your partner must be getting it; *or*
- an NHS mobility scooter or private car (for you or your partner) because of a disability;[26] *or*
- extra-statutory payments to compensate you or your partner for not getting any of the above benefits.[27]

Once you qualify for the disability premium, you or your partner are treated as still getting a qualifying benefit if you no longer receive it because of the overlapping benefit rules (see p1190).[28]

- You (or your partner) are certified as severely sight impaired or blind by a consultant opthalmologist. If you (or your partner) regain your sight, you still qualify for 28 weeks after you stop being certified.
- You have incapacity for work (see p683 of the 2013/14 edition of this *Handbook*) and have been incapable of work, or treated as incapable of work (or, for IS and joint-claim JSA only, entitled to statutory sick pay (SSP)) for 364 days or 196 days if you are terminally ill. Your incapacity for work must have started before 27 October 2008. If you become entitled to benefit on the basis of limited capability for work instead of incapacity for work (see Chapter 45), the premium stops.
- For joint-claim JSA only, either you or your partner have (or are treated as having) 'limited capability for work' (see p1010) for a continuous qualifying period of:
  - 196 days if you or s/he are 'terminally ill'; *or*
  - 364 days in all other cases.

For this purpose, gaps in your periods of limited capability for work that last no more than 12 weeks are ignored.[29]

If you undertake training

If you go on a government training course or receive a training allowance for any period, you keep the disability premium even though you may stop receiving one of the qualifying benefits, or cease to be entitled to SSP during the course, provided you continue to be entitled to IS, income-based JSA or HB. After the course, the premium continues if you are getting a qualifying benefit, remain entitled to SSP (for IS only), or remain incapable of work.[30]

Exclusions

You may not be entitled to the disability premium in your IS or income-based JSA once you or your partner have been receiving free treatment as a hospital inpatient for more than 52 weeks (see p917).

You cannot get a disability premium in your HB if:

- you have, or are treated as having, limited capability for work.[31] This applies even if you would otherwise qualify for the premium – eg, if you (or your partner) get DLA, PIP or are certified as blind or severely sight impaired. If your partner is the HB claimant and s/he does not have (and is not treated as having) limited capability for work, the disability premium can be included;[32] or
- you get pension-age HB (see p188).

Do you have limited capability for work?

1. If you claim ESA or national insurance credits on the basis of limited capability for work and you are a member of a couple, it may be beneficial for your partner to be the HB claimant instead of you in order for the disability premium to be be included in your applicable amount.

2. If you have (or are treated as having) limited capability for work, although you cannot qualify for a disability premium, you may qualify for either the support or work-related activity component in your applicable amount, although this is not normally until after the ESA 'assessment phase' has ended. **Note:** the work-related activity component has been abolished for new claims from 3 April 2017.

3. If your partner has limited capability for work but you do not, you can still qualify for the disability premium, which is paid at the couple rate. However, if the disability premium is awarded, you cannot qualify for a support or work-related activity component in your applicable amount.

Enhanced disability premium

The enhanced disability premium can be included in respect of disabled adults and disabled children.[33]

You are entitled to an enhanced disability premium for an adult (at the single rate, or if you are in a couple the couple rate) in your IS, income-based JSA, income-related ESA and HB if:

Part 4: General rules for other means-tested benefits
Chapter 17: Applicable amounts
3. Premiums and additional amounts

- you or your partner receive the highest rate of the DLA care component, the enhanced rate of the daily living component of PIP, or armed forces independence payment. If it is your partner who satisfies this, s/he must be under pension age; *or*
- for income-related ESA, you qualify for the support component (see p652); *or*
- for HB, the decision maker has determined that you have, or can be treated as having, limited capability for work-related activity (see p1028).

This premium can be paid in addition to both the disability and severe disability premiums (see p351). For more details of the premiums with which the enhanced disability premium can be paid, see p351.

The person who qualifies for the premium must usually be under pension age (p779). For HB, if you are single and you reach pension age, you are paid the higher personal allowance (as part of pension-age HB) instead. If you are in a mixed-age couple (ie, one of you has reached pension age and the other has not) and you continue getting working-age HB (see p188), you are treated as both still under pension age and can continue to get the premium. For IS, income-based JSA and income-related ESA, if you are in a mixed-age couple and you remain entitled to the benefit, you are paid a pensioner premium instead.

Note: the law refers to the qualifying age for PC rather than pension age, but since December 2018, this has been the same as pension age.

For HB, you qualify for one enhanced disability premium for each child included in your claim who receives the highest rate of the DLA care component (or extra-statutory payments to compensate for non-payment of this), the enhanced rate of the daily living component of PIP, or armed forces independence payment.

For IS and income-based JSA, you are only entitled to the child rate of this premium in certain circumstances (see p333). If your child dies, the premium continues for eight weeks if you or your partner continue to get child benefit for her/him (see p597).

An enhanced disability premium can still be included for a third or subsequent child, even if you do not get a personal allowance for her/him because of the 'two-child limit' (see p337).

Income-related ESA does not include the child rate of this premium (although you can qualify for the adult rate).

In most cases, you (or your partner or child) are treated as receiving the highest rate of the DLA care component or the enhanced rate of the daily living component of PIP during any period when DLA or PIP is suspended while you are in hospital.

However, the following people cannot qualify:

- for the child rate, for IS and income-based JSA only, children who have been in hospital for more than 52 weeks, or who have more than £3,000 in capital;[34] *and*

- some people who have been in hospital for more than 52 weeks or, in some cases, if their partner has (see p923).

Pensioner premiums

There is a pensioner premium and a higher pensioner premium. They are paid at the same rate.[35]

In most cases, you qualify for a pensioner premium if your partner has reached pension age (see p779). This applies to IS, income-based JSA and income-related ESA only.

Note: the law refers to the qualifying age for PC rather than pension age, but since December 2018 this has been the same as pension age.

You qualify for a higher pensioner premium instead of a pensioner premium in IS or income-based JSA if:

- your partner is aged 80 or over; *or*
- you or your partner are sick or disabled and certain conditions are satisfied.

Note: if you are a member of a mixed-age couple and your IS has continued when you have reached pension age but your partner has not (see p238), you can be entitled to either pensioner premium on the basis of your age, rather than your partner's age.[36]

There are no pensioner premiums in HB. You get a higher personal allowance instead.

Although paid at the same rate as the pensioner premium, qualifying for the higher pensioner premium may be important – eg, because it qualifies you for a £20 earnings disregard (see p430) or because it meets one of the qualifying conditions for the disabled worker element in WTC (see p1458). For joint-claim JSA, there is no pensioner premium or higher pensioner premium on age grounds if your partner is aged 75 or over.

Pensioner premiums are paid at a single or couple rate. The couple rate of the premium is included in your applicable amount even if only one partner fulfils the condition. The rate of the pensioner premium in income-related ESA depends on whether or not you are entitled to the support component or are in the work-related activity group (see p354) and whether you are a member of a couple.

Higher pensioner premium

You qualify for the higher pensioner premium in IS or income-based JSA if:[37]

- your partner is aged 80 or over; *or*
- your partner has reached pension age (see p779) and receives a qualifying benefit (eg, AA, DLA, PIP or SDA), is certified as severely sight impaired or blind, or has an NHS mobility scooter or a private car allowance.

If your AA, DLA or PIP stops because you go into hospital, see p919. If you are getting SDA, see below; *or*

Part 4: General rules for other means-tested benefits
Chapter 17: Applicable amounts
3. Premiums and additional amounts

- for IS, you were getting a disability premium as part of your IS or income-based JSA at some time in the eight weeks before your partner reached pension age and have continued to get IS since then. You are treated as being continuously entitled to benefit if there is a break in your entitlement of eight weeks or less, including the day your partner reached pension age.[38]

Note: if you are a member of a mixed-age couple and your IS has continued when you have reached pension age but your partner has not (see p238), you can be entitled to the higher pensioner premium on the basis of your age, rather than your partner's age.[39]

In the case of couples, the person who was the benefit claimant before s/he reached pension age must continue to claim after that, but the claimant does not need to have been the person who qualified for the disability premium.

Note:
- If you get SDA when you reach 65, you are awarded it for life.[40] This also applies even if it ceases to be paid because you get retirement pension at a higher rate.[41]
- You may not be entitled to the higher pensioner premium once you or your partner have been receiving free treatment as a hospital inpatient for more than 52 weeks (see p923).

Severe disability premium and severe disability addition

You qualify for a severe disability premium or for a severe disability addition in the guarantee credit of PC if *all* the following apply to you.[42]
- You receive a 'qualifying benefit' (see p347). If you are a couple for IS, income-based JSA, income-related ESA or HB, your partner must also be getting a qualifying benefit, or be certified as severely sight impaired or blind by a consultant ophthalmologist (or treated as certified because it is no more than 28 weeks since s/he stopped being certified).[43] For PC, both of you must be getting a qualifying benefit or one must be getting a qualifying benefit and the other certified as severely sight impaired or blind or treated as certified. For PC only, either partner can be the claimant.[44] If you are a member of a couple, you and your partner are treated as getting any of these benefits while one or both of you are in hospital, but only if you are not claiming the premium or additional amount for severe disability on the basis that your partner (or you, for PC) is certified as severely sight impaired or blind or treated as certified.[45] For IS, income-based JSA, income-related ESA and HB, the benefit must be paid for you or your partner. Receipt of benefit for someone else (eg, a child) does not count.[46] It is probably intended that the same rule should apply to PC.
- You do not have a non-dependant aged 18 or over (eg, an adult son or daughter) 'normally residing with you' (see p348). It does not matter whose house it is.[47] Someone is only counted as residing with you if you share accommodation, apart from a bathroom, lavatory or a communal area such as

a hall, passageway or a room in common use in sheltered accommodation. If s/he is separately liable to pay for the accommodation, s/he does not count as residing with you.[48]

- No one gets carer's allowance (CA) or the UC carer element for looking after you or, if you are a couple, no one gets CA or the UC carer element for both of you (but see p921 if you and/or your partner go into hospital). If you are a member of a couple and someone gets CA or the carer element for one (but not both) of you, but you are both disabled, you can get the severe disability premium at the single person's rate. Only actual receipt of CA counts (except if it is not paid because of the loss of benefit rules – see p1278).[49] No account is taken of any underlying entitlement to CA if it is awarded but not paid because of the overlapping benefit rules, or of any extra-statutory payments to compensate for its not being paid. Similarly, no account is taken of any backdated payments or arrears of CA or of the carer element.[50] Also argue that no account should be taken of any overpaid CA or carer element and that, if you have been denied the premium because of a CA or carer element overpayment, it should be repaid to you (see p351).

Receiving a qualifying benefit

A '**qualifying benefit**' is either AA, the middle or highest rate of the DLA care component, the daily living component of PIP, armed forces independence payment, constant attendance allowance or exceptionally severe disablement allowance (or the equivalent war pension).

You are '**treated as receiving**' a qualifying benefit if you receive an extra-statutory payment to compensate you for not receiving that benefit.[51]

Couples

You get the couple rate if both you and your partner get a qualifying benefit and no one gets CA or the carer element of UC for either of you. If CA or the carer element of UC is paid for one of you, or if your partner does not get a qualifying benefit but is certified as severely sight impaired or blind by a consultant ophthalmologist (or treated as certified), you get the single person's rate. In polygamous marriages, the single person's rate is awarded for each eligible spouse who gets a qualifying benefit while CA or the carer element of UC is not paid.

Note:

- You and/or your partner are treated as getting a qualifying benefit, even though it has stopped because you/your partner have been in hospital for more than four weeks, but the severe disability premium is paid at the single person's rate only. Similarly, for IS, income-based JSA, income-related ESA and HB, if you are a couple, you are treated as receiving CA or the carer element of UC even though you are no longer getting it because the person for whom you care has been in hospital for more than four weeks.[52]

Part 4: General rules for other means-tested benefits
Chapter 17: Applicable amounts
3. Premiums and additional amounts

- For couples on IS, JSA and income-related ESA only, if you or your partner temporarily move into a care home, you still count as a couple but your applicable amount is calculated in a different way (see p934).[53] If your applicable amount is calculated as if you and your partner were single claimants, this means that if the person who stays at home gets a qualifying benefit, a severe disability premium is included in the applicable amount of that person.
- For PC, if you or your partner temporarily move into a care home, you still count as a couple if you have not been apart for substantially more than 52 weeks (see p933). So, once the partner in the care home loses her/his AA or DLA care component, no severe disability premium can be paid for either of you, even if the partner at home gets a qualifying benefit, unless the partner in the care home is certified as severely sight impaired or blind (or treated as certified).

Who is not a non-dependant

Non-dependants are adults living with you who are not included in your benefit claim (eg, adult son or daughter, or a parent), but who are regarded as being able to contribute towards your household costs.

The following people who live with you do *not* count as non-dependants.[54]

For IS, income-based JSA, income-related ESA, HB and PC:

- anyone aged under 18;
- anyone else who receives a qualifying benefit for the severe disability premium (see p346);[55]
- anyone who is certified as severely sight impaired or blind by a consultant ophthalmologist (or treated as certified);[56]
- anyone staying in your home who normally lives elsewhere. In deciding whether someone normally lives with you or elsewhere, it may be relevant to consider things like why the residence started, how long it has continued and your relationship;[57]
- any person (and, for IS, income-based JSA, income-related ESA and PC only, her/his partner) employed by a charitable or voluntary body as a resident carer for you or your partner if you pay a charge for that service (even if the charge is only nominal).[58] **Note:** these rules do not apply to a live-in carer employed directly by you (even if, for example, you are paying her/him from direct payments made to you by social services for that purpose).

For IS, income-based JSA, income-related ESA and HB:

- any member of your 'family' (see below for who counts). This may include any child under the age of 20 (see p323) as well as your partner, although your partner must be getting a qualifying benefit (or would be if s/he were not in hospital) or be certified as severely sight impaired or blind, for you to get the severe disability premium (see p346);

- any child or qualifying young person who is living with you but who is not a member of your household (see p327).[59]

For IS, income-based JSA, income-related ESA and PC:
- any person (or her/his partner) who jointly occupies (see p350) your home and is either the co-owner with you or your partner, or jointly liable with you or your partner to make payments to a landlord for occupying it. If this person is a close relative (see p350), however, s/he *does* count as a non-dependant *unless* the co-ownership or joint liability to make payments to a landlord existed either before 11 April 1988 or by the time you or your partner first moved in;
- any person (or any member of her/his household) who is liable to pay you or your partner on a commercial basis (see p350) for occupying the dwelling (eg, tenants or licensees), unless s/he is a close relative of you or your partner;
- any person (or any member of her/his household) to whom you or your partner are liable to make payments on a commercial basis for occupying the dwelling, unless s/he is a close relative of you or your partner.

For PC:
- any child or qualifying young person.[60] This is defined in the same way as for UC (see p324).

Note: for IS, income-based JSA, income-related ESA and PC, if someone comes to live with you in order to look after you (or your partner) and has not lived with you before, your severe disability premium or amount for severe disability remains in payment for the first 12 weeks after the carer moves in, even if s/he would otherwise count as a non-dependant.[61] After that, you lose the premium or the amount for severe disability. The carer should then consider claiming CA (see Chapter 26).

For HB:[62]
- any person who jointly occupies your home and is either the co-owner with you or your partner, or liable with you or your partner to make payments for occupying it. A joint occupier who was a non-dependant at any time within the previous eight weeks counts as a non-dependant if the local authority thinks that the change of arrangements was created to take advantage of the HB scheme;
- any person who is liable to pay you or your partner on a commercial basis for occupying the dwelling unless s/he is a close relative of yours or your partner, or if the local authority thinks that the rent or other agreement has been created to take advantage of the HB scheme (but this cannot apply if the person was otherwise liable to pay rent for the accommodation at any time during the eight weeks before the agreement was made);

Part 4: General rules for other means-tested benefits
Chapter 17: Applicable amounts
3. Premiums and additional amounts

- any person, or any member of her/his household, to whom you or your partner are liable to make payments for your accommodation on a commercial basis unless s/he is a close relative of you or your partner.

Definitions

'**Close relative**' is a parent, parent-in-law (including a civil partner's parent), son, son-in-law (including a son's civil partner), daughter, daughter-in-law (including a daughter's civil partner), brother, sister, step-parent (including a parent's civil partner), stepson (including a civil partner's son), stepdaughter (including a civil partner's daughter), or the partners of any of these.[63]

'**Member of the family**' means your partner and any child who lives in your household and for whom you or your partner count as 'responsible' (see p323).[64]

'**Jointly occupies**' is a legal relationship involving occupation by two or more people (whether as owner-occupiers, tenants or licensees) with one and the same legal right.[65] It does not exist if people merely have equal access to different parts of the premises.

'**Commercial basis**' has no legal meaning, and there is no requirement for there to be an intention to make a profit.[66] It may be sufficient if a 'reasonable' charge is made, even if this does not fully cover the cost of the accommodation and meals being provided.[67] The reasonableness of the charge should be judged just against the cost of occupying the dwelling, not taking into account the additional costs of providing food, clothing and care.[68] A useful, but not conclusive, test to apply is to consider whether the same arrangement might have been entered into with a lodger.[69]

'**Liability**' means a legal or contractual liability. The arrangements need not be in writing.[70]

Carer premium and carer addition

You qualify for a carer premium, or a carer addition in PC, if you or your partner are entitled to CA (see Chapter 26).[71]

You are entitled to CA even if you do not receive it because of the overlapping benefit rules (see p1190) – eg, you get contributory ESA or retirement pension instead.

If the person you or your partner are getting CA for dies, or you or your partner stop being entitled to CA for another reason, your entitlement to a carer premium or carer addition continues for a further eight weeks. The eight-week period runs from the Sunday after the death (or from the date of the death, if the death occurs on a Sunday). In other cases, it runs from the date entitlement to CA stops. If you first claim IS, income-based JSA, income-related ESA or (if you or your partner are below pension age, HB) after the CA stops, you continue to qualify for a carer premium for eight weeks after her/his death or, if it stops for another reason, after entitlement to CA stops.[72]

A double-rate premium is awarded if both you and your partner satisfy the conditions for it.

Should you claim carer's allowance?

1. Before claiming CA, consider how your claim might affect the entitlement to the severe disability premium or severe disability addition of the disabled person for whom you care – particularly if the only financial advantage to you as the carer is the amount of the carer premium/addition, which may be worth considerably less than the severe disability premium (but see p346 for the rules on notional income).

2. Any backdated award of CA does not affect a disabled person's entitlement to the severe disability premium or severe disability addition.[73] You may be able to take advantage of this rule so that you are paid CA or the carer premium/addition for the same period in which the disabled person has already received a severe disability premium or a severe disability addition.

3. Although the severe disability premium or severe disability addition is not payable throughout any period during which a carer is receiving CA, if you are a carer and it is later decided that you have been overpaid CA, the disabled person should ask for the decision refusing her/him the severe disability premium or addition to be revised. You must be both entitled to *and* in receipt of CA for the severe disability premium/addition not to be payable.[74]

4. Other than for HB, if payment of CA stops, the severe disability premium/addition can be backdated to the date the CA stopped.[75]

5. Even if you do not claim CA, if you get UC and your award includes a carer element (see p73), the disabled person for whom you care cannot get the severe disability premium or severe disability addition.

Rates of premiums

Rates of premiums

The following premiums can be paid in addition to any other premium, except that the enhanced disability premium cannot be paid in addition to the pensioner or higher pensioner premium.[76]

Family premium	£17.60
Disabled child premium	£65.52
(for each qualifying child)	
Severe disability premium	
Single (or one partner qualifies)	£66.95
Couple (both partners qualify)	£133.90
Carer premium	
Single (or one partner qualifies)	£37.50
Couple (both partners qualify)	£75.00
Enhanced disability premium	

Part 4: General rules for other means-tested benefits
Chapter 17: Applicable amounts
3. Premiums and additional amounts

Child (for each qualifying child)	£26.60
Single	£17.10
Couple (one or both partners qualify)	£24.50

Only one of the following premiums can be paid. If you qualify for more than one, you get the highest.[77]

Disability premium

Single	£34.95
Couple	£49.80

Pensioner and higher pensioner premium for IS/ income-based JSA

Couple	£148.40

Pensioner premium for income-related ESA

Entitled to support component, couple	£109.20
Entitled to work-related activity component, couple	£118.85
Not entitled to either component, couple	£148.40

Note: you may be entitled to a lone parent increase (£4.60) in the HB family premium if you were entitled to it on 5 April 1998.[78] See p793 of the 2011/12 edition of this *Handbook*.

Backdating premiums

To qualify for the disability, enhanced disability, higher pensioner, severe disability, disabled child or carer premium, you or your partner or child must usually have been awarded a 'qualifying benefit' that applies to each premium. The date you can begin to get your premium may, therefore, depend on the date from when your qualifying benefit is awarded. However, because of the time it may take to deal with your claim for the qualifying benefit, or if your claim is backdated (see p1176) or initially refused but awarded some time later after a revision (see p1303), supersession (see p1315) or appeal (see p1337), you may not get your premium straight away and you may have to apply for it to be backdated.

If you are already getting benefit

If you are already getting IS, JSA, ESA, HB or PC, you should ask for your award of this benefit either to be revised or superseded and for your premium to be backdated to the date from which the qualifying benefit is awarded, or to when you first got (or claimed) IS, JSA, ESA, HB or PC, if that is later. There is no limit to the period for which arrears can be paid to you.[79]

If you were refused benefit or lost entitlement

If you were refused or lost your entitlement to IS, income-based JSA, income-related ESA or HB and you are later awarded a qualifying benefit, in most cases, you can no longer make a new claim for IS, income-based JSA, income-related ESA or HB (but see below) and must now claim UC instead. For when you may still be able to make a new claim, including in cases where you are prevented from claiming UC, see p24. **Note:** unless you are prevented from claiming UC, making a new claim for JSA or ESA will bring you under the UC system (see p23).

If you can still make a new claim for IS, income-based JSA, income-related ESA or HB and your qualifying benefit has been awarded or reinstated, see p341 of the 2018/19 edition of this *Handbook* for details. New claims for PC can still be made after the award of a qualifying benefit. See p278 for the rules on backdating.

If you lose your HB because you lose entitlement to a qualifying benefit, the decision ending your HB can be revised if the qualifying benefit is reinstated. Your HB can be fully backdated in this situation. You must tell the local authority that you have had your qualifying benefit reinstated, but you do not need to make a fresh claim for HB.[80]

4. Components

Your applicable amount for income-related employment and support allowance (ESA) and, in certain circumstances, housing benefit (HB) may include either:[81]
* a support component (see p354); *or*
* if you can still get it, a work-related activity component (see p354).

You cannot be awarded both components at the same time.

You can qualify for one of these components in your HB if either you or your partner meet the conditions for it and have limited capability for work. If you qualify for one component and your partner qualifies for the other, the component for which *you* qualify is awarded.[82]

To qualify for a component in income-related ESA, you must meet the conditions yourself – ie, as the claimant. You cannot qualify on the basis of your partner's limited capability for work alone.

Note:
* You cannot start to qualify for a component in your HB applicable amount if you have reached pension age (see p779), unless you or your partner are on income support, income-based jobseeker's allowance, income-related ESA or universal credit (UC).
* For HB, provided either you or your partner satisfy the conditions for the component and have limited capability for work, it does not matter if ESA is not paid, or if your entitlement to ESA has stopped because of the rules on how long you can be paid contributory ESA.
* For income-related ESA, if you or your partner have been receiving free treatment as a hospital inpatient for a continuous period of more than 52 weeks, you cannot qualify for either component.[83]

Support component

In order to qualify for a support component in your income-related ESA, you must meet the conditions described on p652. The rules are the same as for contributory ESA.

You qualify for a support component in your HB if:[84]

- you or your partner have claimed ESA and you are entitled to the support component (see p652), or you have been refused ESA but you would have been entitled to the component had you been entitled to ESA; *and*
- you are not entitled to a disability premium (p341); *and*
- either you or your partner have limited capability for work-related activity (see p1028 – the rules are the same as for contributory ESA).

Work-related activity component

The work-related activity component has been abolished for new claims from 3 April 2017. For details of who can still get a work-related activity component in ESA, see p653.

You can still get a work-related activity component in your HB if:[85]

- you or your partner have claimed ESA and are entitled to the work-related activity component (see p653), or you have been refused ESA but you would have been entitled to the component had you been entitled to ESA; *and*
- you are not entitled to a disability premium (p341); *and*
- the decision maker has determined that you or your partner have, or can be treated as having, limited capability for work (see p1010).

Note: you keep the maximum work-related activity component in your HB even if you lose it in ESA because of a sanction.[86] The full amount of ESA continues to be taken into account as your income.

Rates of components

Rates of components[87]

Support component	£39.20
Work-related activity component	£29.55

There is no higher rate of the support or work-related activity component paid for couples.

Backdating components

Your entitlement to either the support or work-related activity component in your ESA normally starts once the 'assessment phase' has ended (see p651 – the rules are the same as for contributory ESA). If your assessment phase ends later than 13 weeks after you claim, your entitlement to a component can be backdated to the beginning of the 14th week of your claim.[88] If you make a claim, or request a revision or supersession of your entitlement expressly on the grounds of being terminally ill (see p654 – the rules are the same as for contributory ESA), you do not have to wait for the assessment phase to end to qualify for the support component, but can qualify either from the date of your claim, or from the date on which you became terminally ill if that is later.[89]

If you are getting HB and you become entitled to a support or work-related activity component, you qualify for that component in your applicable amount from the Monday on or after your entitlement to the component began. If your HB entitlement starts after the date your entitlement to the component began, you qualify for the component in your HB applicable amount from the date your entitlement to HB began.[90]

If you only become entitled to HB once a component is awarded to you, you should claim (or reclaim) HB as promptly as you can, as you can only get a maximum of one month's backdating (see p208). **Note:** in most cases, you cannot now make a new claim for HB and will need to claim UC instead. See p172 for when you can make a new claim for HB. Claiming UC brings you under the UC system (see p23).

5. Transitional addition

All awards of incapacity benefit, severe disablement allowance and income support 'on the grounds of disability' have been transferred to employment and support allowance (ESA) (see p655). **Note:** some people were not awarded income-related ESA when they should have been, and are to be paid arrears.

When you transferred, you may have been entitled to a transitional addition included in your income-related ESA or housing benefit applicable amount. For more information, see p356 of the 2019/20 edition of this Handbook.

Notes

1. What are applicable amounts
1 Reg 1(3) and (7) SS(WTCCTC)(CA) Regs

2. Personal allowances
2 **IS** Reg 18(1)(b) IS Regs
   JSA Regs 84(1)(b) and 86B(b) JSA Regs
   ESA Reg 68(1)(b) ESA Regs
   HB Reg 23(b) HB Regs; Sch 3 para 1
   HB(SPC) Regs
3 **IS** Reg 18(2) IS Regs
   JSA Reg 84(2) JSA Regs
   ESA Reg 68(2) ESA Regs
4 **IS** Sch 2 para 1(3) IS Regs
   JSA Sch 1 para 1(3) JSA Regs
   ESA Sch 4 para 1(3) ESA Regs
5 Regs 5, 6 and 9 The Social Security
   (Restrictions on Amounts for Children
   and Qualifying Young Persons)
   Amendment Regulations 2017, No.376;
   reg 22 HB Regs; reg 22 HB (SPC) Regs
6 Regs 5, 6 and 9 The Social Security
   (Restrictions on Amounts for Children
   and Qualifying Young Persons)
   Amendment Regulations 2017, No.376;
   reg 22 HB Regs; reg 22 HB(SPC) Regs

3. Premiums and additional amounts
7 Sch 3 paras 3 and 6-9 HB(SPC) Regs
8 Reg 6(6)(d) and Sch IIA SPC Regs
9 **IS** Sch 2 para 3 IS Regs
   JSA Sch 1 para 4 JSA Regs
   HB Sch 3 para 3 HB Regs; Sch 3 para 3
   HB(SPC) Regs
10 Reg 4 Housing Benefit (Abolition of the
    Family Premium and Date of Claim)
    (Amendment) Regulations 2015,
    No.1857
11 **IS** Regs 15(3) and 16(6) IS Regs
    JSA Regs 74(4) and 78(7) JSA Regs
12 Reg 21(4) and (5) HB Regs; reg 21(4)
    and (5) HB(SPC) Regs
13 **IS** Sch 2 paras 14 and 15(6) IS Regs
    JSA Sch 1 para 16 JSA Regs
    HB Sch 3 paras 16 and 20(7) HB Regs;
    Sch 3 paras 8 and 12(3) HB(SPC) Regs
14 **IS** Sch 2 paras 12(1)(a)(iii) and (2) and
    14(c) IS Regs
    JSA Sch 1 para 14(1)(h) and (2) JSA Regs
    HB Sch 3 paras 13(1)(a)(v) and (2) and
    16(c) HB Regs; Sch 3 para 8(b) HB(SPC)
    Regs

15 Reg 25(3) HB Regs; reg 23(3) HB(SPC)
    Regs
16 **IS** Sch 2 para 14(2)(a) IS Regs
    JSA Sch 1 para 16(2)(a) JSA Regs
17 **IS** Sch 2 para 14 IS Regs
    JSA Sch 1 para 16 JSA Regs
    HB Sch 3 para 16 HB Regs; Sch 3 para 8
    HB(SPC) Regs
18 **IS** Sch 2 para 11 IS Regs
    JSA Sch 1 paras 13, 14, 20G and 20H
    JSA Regs
    HB Sch 3 para 12 HB Regs
19 **IS** Sch 2 para 12(1)(a)(i) IS Regs
    JSA Sch 1 paras 14(1)(a)-(d) and
    20H(1)(a)-(d) JSA Regs
    HB Sch 3 para 13(1)(a)(i) HB Regs
20 **IS** Reg 2(1), definition of 'attendance
    allowance', IS Regs
    JSA Reg 1(3), definition of 'attendance
    allowance', JSA Regs
    HB Reg 2(1), definition of 'attendance
    allowance', HB Regs
21 **IS** Sch 2 para 12(1)(d) IS Regs
    JSA Sch 1 paras 14(1)(g)(ii) and
    20H(1)(h)(ii) JSA Regs
    HB Sch 3 para 13(1)(a)(iii) HB Regs
22 R(IS) 7/02
23 **IS** Sch 2 para 12(1)(c)(i) IS Regs
    JSA Sch 1 paras 14(1)(g)(i) and
    20H(1)(h)(i) JSA Regs
    HB Sch 3 para 13(1)(a)(ii) HB Regs
24 **IS** Sch 2 para 12(1)(c)(i) IS Regs
    JSA Sch 1 para 14(1)(g)(i) and
    20H(1)(h)(i) JSA Regs
25 **IS** Sch 2 para 12(1)(c) IS Regs
    JSA Sch 1 paras 14(1)(g) and 20H(1)(h)
    JSA Regs
26 **IS** Sch 2 para 12(1)(a)(ii) IS Regs
    JSA Sch 1 paras 14(1)(e) and (f) and
    20H(1)(f) and (g) JSA Regs
    HB Sch 3 para 13(1)(a)(iv) HB Regs
27 **IS** Sch 2 para 14A IS Regs
    JSA Sch 1 paras 18 and 20K JSA Regs
    HB Sch 3 para 18 HB Regs
28 **IS** Sch 2 para 7(1)(a) IS Regs
    JSA Sch 1 paras 8(1)(a) and 20D(1)(a)
    JSA Regs
    HB Sch 3 para 7(1)(a) HB Regs
29 Sch 1 para 20H(1)(ee) JSA Regs

30 **IS** Sch 2 paras 7(1)(b) and 12(5) IS Regs
JSA Sch 1 paras 8(1)(b) and 20D(b) JSA Regs
HB Sch 3 paras 7(1)(b) and 13(5) HB Regs
31 The rules only refer to the 'claimant'
32 Sch 3 para 13(9) HB Regs
33 **IS** Sch 2 para 13A IS Regs
JSA Sch 1 paras 15A and 20IA JSA Regs
ESA Sch 4 para 7 ESA Regs
HB Sch 3 para 15 HB Regs; Sch 3 para 7 HB(SPC) Regs
34 **IS** Sch 2 para 13A IS Regs
JSA Sch 1 para 15A JSA Regs
35 **IS** Sch 2 paras 9 and 9A IS Regs
JSA Sch 1 paras 10, 11, 20E and 20F JSA Regs
ESA Sch 4 para 5 ESA Regs
36 Art 8(4) WRA(No.31)O
37 **IS** Sch 2 para 10 IS Regs
JSA Sch 1 paras 12 and 20F JSA Regs
38 Sch 2 para 10(1)(b)(ii), (3) and (4) IS Regs; reg 32 IS(JSACA) Regs
39 Art 8(4) WRA(No.31)O
40 CIS/458/1992
41 **IS** Sch 2 para 7(1)(a) IS Regs
JSA Sch 1 paras 8(1)(a) and 20D(1)(a) JSA Regs
42 **IS** Sch 2 para 13 IS Regs
JSA Sch 1 paras 15 and 20I JSA Regs
ESA Sch 4 para 6 ESA Regs
PC Reg 6(4) and Sch 1 paras 1 and 2 SPC Regs
HB Sch 3 para 14 HB Regs; Sch 3 para 6 HB(SPC) Regs
43 **IS** Sch 2 para 13(2A) IS Regs
JSA Sch 1 paras 15(3) and 20I(2) JSA Regs
ESA Sch 4 para 6(3) and (9) ESA Regs
HB Sch 3 para 14(3) HB Regs; Sch 3 para 6(3) HB(SPC) Regs
44 Sch 1 para 11(b) and (c) SPC Regs
45 **IS** Sch 2 para 13(3A)(a) IS Regs
JSA Sch 1 paras 15(5)(a) and 20I(4)(a) JSA Regs
ESA Sch 4 para 6(5)(a) ESA Regs
PC Sch 1 para 1(2)(b) SPC Regs
HB Sch 3 para 14(5) HB Regs; Sch 3 para 6(7) HB(SPC) Regs
46 **IS** Sch 2 para 14B IS Regs
JSA Sch 1 paras 19 and 20L JSA Regs
ESA Sch 4 para 10 ESA Regs
HB Sch 3 para 19 HB Regs; Sch 3 para 11 HB(SPC) Regs
See also R(IS) 10/94, upheld in *Rider v CAO* [1996] *The Times,* 30 January (CA).
47 *Bate v CAO* [1996] 2 All ER 790, reported as R(IS) 12/96

48 **IS** Reg 3(4) and (5) IS Regs
JSA Reg 2(6) and (7) JSA Regs
ESA Reg 71(6) ESA Regs
HB Reg 3(4) HB Regs; Sch 3 para 6(7) HB(SPC) Regs
49 **IS** Sch 2 para 13(2)(a)(iii) and (b) IS Regs
JSA Sch 1 paras 15(1)(c) and (2)(d) and 20I(1)(d) JSA Regs
ESA Sch 4 para 6(2)(a)(iii) and (b) ESA Regs
PC Sch 1 para 1(1)(a)(iii) SPC Regs
HB Sch 3 para 14(2)(a)(iii) and (b) HB Regs; Sch 3 para 6(2)(a)(iii) and (b) HB(SPC) Regs
50 **IS** Sch 2 para 13(3ZA) IS Regs
JSA Sch 1 paras 15(7) and 20I(6) JSA Regs
ESA Sch 4 para 6(6) ESA Regs
PC Sch 1 para 2(c) SPC Regs
HB Sch 3 para 14(6) HB Regs; Sch 3 para 6(8) HB(SPC) Regs
51 **IS** Sch 2 para 14A IS Regs
JSA Sch 1 paras 18 and 20K JSA Regs
ESA Sch 4 para 9 ESA Regs
PC Sch 1 para 1(2)(a)(ii) SPC Regs
HB Sch 3 para 18 HB Regs; Sch 3 para 10 HB(SPC) Regs
52 **IS** Sch 2 para 13(3A) IS Regs
JSA Sch 1 paras 15(5) and 20I(4) JSA Regs
ESA Sch 4 para 6(5) ESA Regs
PC Reg 6(5) and Sch 1 para 1(2)(b) SPC Regs
HB Sch 3 para 14(5) HB Regs; Sch 3 para 6(7) HB(SPC) Regs
53 **IS** Reg 16(1) and Sch 7 para 9 IS Regs
JSA Reg 78(1) and Sch 5 para 5 JSA Regs
ESA Reg 156 and Sch 5 para 4 ESA Regs
54 **IS** Reg 3 and Sch 2 para 13 IS Regs
JSA Reg 2 and Sch 1 paras 15 and 20I JSA Regs
ESA Reg 71 and Sch 4 para 6 ESA Regs
PC Sch 1 para 2 SPC Regs
HB Reg 3 HB Regs; reg 3 HB(SPC) Regs
55 **IS** Sch 2 para 13(3)(a) IS Regs
JSA Sch 1 paras 15(4)(a) and 20I(3)(a) JSA Regs
ESA Sch 4 para 6(4)(a) ESA Regs
PC Sch 1 para 2(2)(a) SPC Regs
HB Sch 3 para 13(4) HB Regs; Sch 3 para 6(6) HB(SPC) Regs
56 **IS** Sch 2 para 13(3)(d) IS Regs
JSA Sch 1 paras 14(1)(h) and (2), 15(4)(c), 20H(1)(i) and (3) and 20I(3)(c) JSA Regs
ESA Sch 4 para 6(4)(c) and (9) ESA Regs
PC Sch 1 para 2(2)(b) and (c) SPC Regs
HB Sch 3 para 14(4)(b) HB Regs; Sch 3 para 6(6)(b) HB(SPC) Regs

. . . .

57 CIS/14850/1996, para 10
58 **IS** Reg 3(2)(c) and (d) IS Regs
    JSA Reg 2(2)(c) and (d) JSA Regs
    ESA Reg 71(2)(c) and (d) ESA Regs
    PC Sch 1 para 2(d) and (e) SPC Regs
    HB Reg 3(2)(f) HB Regs; reg 3(2)(f)
    HB(SPC) Regs
59 **IS** Reg 3(2)(b) IS Regs
    JSA Reg 2(2)(b) JSA Regs
    ESA Reg 71(2)(b) ESA Regs
    HB Reg 3(2)(c) HB Regs; reg 3(2)(c)
    HB(SPC) Regs
60 Sch 1 para 2(2)(f) SPC Regs
61 **IS** Sch 2 para 13(3)(c) and (4) IS Regs
    JSA Sch 1 paras 15(4)(b) and (6) and
    20I(3)(b) and (5) JSA Regs
    ESA Sch 4 para 6(4)(b) and (7) ESA Regs
    PC Sch 1 para 2(3) and (4) SPC Regs
62 Regs 3 and 9(1) HB Regs; regs 3 and 9(1)
    HB(SPC) Regs
63 **IS** Reg 2(1) IS Regs
    JSA Reg 1(3) JSA Regs
    ESA Reg 2(1) ESA Regs
    HB Reg 2(1) HB Regs; reg 2(1) HB(SPC)
    Regs
    All Definition of 'close relative'
64 **IS/HB** s137(1) SSCBA 1992
    JSA s35(1) JSA 1995
    ESA Reg 2(1) ESA Regs
65 *Bate v CAO* [1996] 2 All ER 790 (HL)
66 R(IS) 11/98, tribunal of commissioners
67 CSIS/43/1989
68 CIS/754/1991; R(IS) 11/98, para 12
69 R(IS) 11/98, para 8
70 CIS/754/1991
71 **IS** Sch 2 para 14ZA IS Regs
    JSA Sch 1 paras 17 and 20J JSA Regs
    ESA Sch 4 para 8 ESA Regs
    PC Reg 6(6)(a) and Sch 1 para 4 SPC
    Regs
    HB Sch 3 para 17 HB Regs; Sch 3 para 9
    HB(SPC) Regs
72 **IS** Sch 2 paras 7 and 14ZA(3) and (4) IS
    Regs
    JSA Sch 1 paras 8, 17(3) and (4) and
    20J(3) and (3A) JSA Regs
    ESA Sch 4 para 8(2)-(4) ESA Regs
    PC Sch 1 para 4(2) and (3) SPC Regs
    HB Sch 3 paras 7 and 17(3) and (4) HB
    Regs; Sch 3 paras 5 and 9(3) HB(SPC)
    Regs
73 **IS** Sch 2 para 13(3ZA) IS Regs
    JSA Sch 1 paras 15(7) and 201(6) JSA
    Regs
    ESA Sch 4 para 6(6) ESA Regs
    PC Sch 1 para 1(2)(c) SPC Regs
    HB Sch 3 para 14(6) HB Regs; Sch 3 para
    6(8) HB(SPC) Regs

74 **IS** Sch 2 para 13(2)(a)(iii) and (b) IS Regs
    JSA Sch 1 paras 15(1)(c) and (2)(d) and
    20I(1)(d) JSA Regs
    ESA Sch 4 para 6(2)(a)(iii) and (b) ESA
    Regs
    PC Sch 1 para 1(1)(ii), (b) and (c)(iv)
    SPC Regs
    HB Sch 3 para 14(2)(a)(iii) and (b) HB
    Regs; Sch 3 para 6(2)(a)(iii) and (b)
    HB(SPC) Regs
75 Reg 7(2)(bc) SS&CS(DA) Regs
76 **IS** Sch 2 para 6(2) IS Regs
    JSA Sch 1 paras 7(2) and 20C(2) JSA
    Regs
    ESA Sch 4 para 3 ESA Regs
    HB Sch 3 para 6 HB Regs
77 **IS** Sch 2 para 5 IS Regs
    JSA Sch 1 paras 6 and 20B JSA Regs
    HB Sch 3 para 5 HB Regs
78 Sch 3 para 3 HB Regs
79 **IS/JSA/ESA** Regs 3(7) and 6(2)(e)
    SS&CS(DA) Regs
    HB Regs 4(7B) and 7(2)(i) HB&CTB(DA)
    Regs
80 Reg 4(7C) HB&CTB(DA) Regs

4. Components
81 **ESA** s4(2), (4) and (5) WRA 2007
    HB Reg 22 and Sch 3 paras 21-24 HB
    Regs
82 Sch 3 para 22(2) HB Regs
83 Reg 69(2) and Sch 5 para 13 ESA Regs
84 Sch 3 paras 22 and 24 HB Regs
85 Sch 3 para 23 HB Regs; Sch 2 Part 1
    ESAUC(MA) Regs
86 Because there is no provision to remove
    it in these circumstances.
87 **ESA** Sch 4 paras 12 and 13 ESA Regs
    HB Sch 3 paras 25 and 26 HB Regs
88 Regs 6(2)(r) and 7(38) SS&CS(DA) Regs
89 Reg 7(1)(a) ESA Regs; regs 3(9)(c),
    6(2)(a) and 7(2)(be) SS&CS(DA) Regs
90 Regs 4(7B), 7(2)(o) and 8(14D)
    HB&CTB(DA) Regs

Chapter 18

· ·

Help with ground rent, service charges and other housing costs

This chapter covers:
1. Who can get help with housing costs (p360)
2. Which housing costs can be met (p360)
3. The amount of housing costs (p362)
4. Waiting periods (p368)
5. Liability to pay housing costs (p369)
6. Occupying accommodation as your home (p370)
7. Linking rules (p375)
8. Housing costs run-on (p376)

This chapter covers the rules for help with ground rent, service charges and other housing costs that can be included in your means-tested benefit if you are an owner-occupier or a long leaseholder. It does not cover the rules on help with these costs for universal credit (see Chapter 6) or for help with your rent in housing benefit (see Chapter 10). It does not cover DWP loans for mortgage interest (see p855).

Key facts
- If you are entitled to income support (IS), income-based jobseeker's allowance (JSA), income-related employment and support allowance (ESA) or pension credit and you own or are buying your home or you are a long leaseholder, your benefit can include help with a variety of housing costs, such as ground rent and service charges.
- Your benefit cannot include help with your mortgage or other loan – eg, for repairs or improvements. Instead, the DWP may offer you a loan.
- If you are entitled to IS, JSA or ESA, you may not get help with your housing costs during an initial 'waiting period'.

· · · ·

Part 4: General rules for other means-tested benefits
Chapter 18: Help with ground rent, service charges and other housing costs
2. Which housing costs can be met

1. Who can get help with housing costs

If you are entitled to income support (IS), income-based jobseeker's allowance (JSA) or income-related employment and support allowance (ESA), help with some of your housing costs can be included in your applicable amount. If you are entitled to pension credit (PC), these costs can be included in your appropriate minimum guarantee.[1] To qualify:

- the housing costs must be a type that can be met (see below) – eg, ground rent or service charges; *and*
- you or your partner must count as liable to pay the housing costs, or be treated as liable (see p369); *and*
- the housing costs must be for the home in which you normally live (see p370).

For information on how to calculate the weekly amount you get, see p362. Deductions might be made if there are other people living in your home (known as non-dependants – see p363).

Note:

- For IS, JSA and ESA only, if you can still make a new claim, you may not get an amount for housing costs during an initial 'waiting period' after you claim (see p368).
- If you or your partner return to work or increase your hours and so count as being in full-time paid work, you may continue to qualify for help with your housing costs for four weeks – called 'housing costs run-on' (see p376).
- If you have a mortgage, the DWP may offer you a loan to help you with your mortgage interest payments (see p855). Get independent financial advice before you accept this.

2. Which housing costs can be met

Your income support (IS), income-based jobseeker's allowance (JSA), income-related employment and support allowance (ESA) or pension credit (PC) can include any of the following housing costs:[2]

- service charges (see p361). **Note:** some service charges are excluded;
- rent or ground rent if you have a lease of more than 21 years. If your lease is of 21 years or less, the rent or ground rent may be met by housing benefit (HB) instead (see p175);[3]
- rentcharge payments (payments by freeholders, similar to ground rent);
- payments under a co-ownership scheme – a type of scheme where the home is let by a housing association and any payment made to a former member is based on the value of the home;[4]
- rent if you are a Crown tenant (in England and Wales, minus any water charges[5]);
- payments for a tent and its pitch if that is your home.

Note: if your home is used for both business and domestic purposes, you can only get help with your housing costs for the part in which you live.[6]

Service charges

Your IS, income-based JSA, income-related ESA or PC can include charges for services. Some service charges are ineligible (see p193 – the rules are the same as for HB).[7] Some service charges can only be met if they relate to the provision of 'adequate accommodation'.[8]

Services

A **'service'** is something that is agreed and arranged on your behalf and for which you are required to pay – eg, if you own a flat and the freeholder arranges for the exterior of the building to be painted, for which you have to pay a share of the cost.

Bear the following in mind.
- Service charges to cover minor repairs and maintenance are eligible. However, those for any of the types of repairs and improvements below are not.
- Payments for support services are not eligible. Instead, you may get help with these through your local authority.
- House insurance paid under the terms of your lease can be a service charge, but insurance required by a bank as a condition of your mortgage is not.[9]
- Services provided by an authority that you arrange yourself are not covered. So, charges for water and sewerage paid to a water company are not met.[10]

Excluded repairs and improvements

You cannot get help with a service charge for the following types of repairs and improvements:[11]
- providing a bath, shower, toilet, wash basin and the necessary plumbing for these, and the provision of hot water not connected to a central heating system;[12]
- repairs to your heating system;
- damp-proof measures;
- providing:
  - ventilation and natural lighting;
  - drainage facilities;
  - facilities for preparing and cooking food (but not for storing it);[13]
  - home insulation;
  - electric lighting and sockets;
  - storage facilities for fuel or refuse;
- repairing unsafe structural defects;
- adaptations for a 'disabled person';[14]

Part 4: General rules for other means-tested benefits
Chapter 18: Help with ground rent, service charges and other housing costs
3. The amount of housing costs

- providing separate sleeping accommodation for a boy and a girl aged 10 or over but under 20 for whom you or your partner are responsible and who live with you.

Note: if you have (or take out) a loan to pay for any of the types of repairs and improvements above, you may be offered a loan by the DWP to help with the interest (see p855). Get independent financial advice before you accept this.

Deductions for fuel charges

Charges for fuel (if they are included in your housing costs) cannot be met.[15] If the charge for fuel is not specified, the set deductions below are made.

Heating	£34.30	Lighting	£2.75
Hot water	£4.00	Cooking	£4.00

3. **The amount of housing costs**

Once you have worked out which housing costs your income support (IS), income-based jobseeker's allowance (JSA), income-related employment and support allowance (ESA) or pension credit (PC) can meet, you can calculate the amount you get. You get the normal weekly charge for the housing costs that can be included in your benefit.[16] If you pay your housing costs annually or irregularly or over 53 weeks, the weekly amount is worked out by dividing what is payable for the year by 52.[17] If your home is used for both business and domestic purposes, only the housing costs for the part in which you live are included.[18]

- **Step one:** calculate the total weekly amount of qualifying housing costs. Remember to deduct any charges that are not eligible – eg, fuel charges (see above).
- **Step two:** deduct any amounts for other people living in your home (known as non-dependants – see p363).

Example

Stan is the owner-occupier of a two-bedroom flat. He does not have a mortgage. His father, who is on contributory ESA, lives with him. Stan is getting income-based JSA. He pays ground rent of £936 a year and a qualifying service charge for caretaker services of £8.50 a week.

Step one: £936 ÷ 52 = £18 a week for ground rent + £8.50 a week for service charges = £26.50 a week housing costs.

Step two: the weekly non-dependant deduction for Stan's father is £15.85. £26.50 – £15.85 = £10.65 a week help with housing costs.

Even if your housing costs have been waived because you or your partner (or, for IS, JSA or ESA only, a child or qualifying young person included in your claim) have paid for repairs or redecoration that are not your responsibility, you can still get IS, income-based JSA, income-related ESA or PC for them for up to eight weeks.[19]

Note:

• For IS, JSA and ESA only, help with housing costs is not usually included during an initial 'waiting period' (see p368).
• You may only get a share of the housing costs if you share liability, or are treated as liable because you share the costs with someone (see p369).
• If you are involved in a trade dispute, see p1003 for when your housing costs can be met.

Deductions for non-dependants

If other people normally live with you in your home who are not part of your family for benefit purposes (called 'non-dependants'), a set deduction is usually made from the amount of benefit you get for housing costs.[20] This is because it is assumed the non-dependant makes a contribution towards your outgoings, whether or not s/he does so. Examples of non-dependants are adult sons or daughters or elderly relatives who share your home. For who counts as a non-dependant, see p198 – the issues are the same as for housing benefit (HB).

The DWP may use the rules on p371 to decide that someone is only temporarily absent from your home.[21] If you think the DWP has wrongly assumed that a person is normally living with you, ask for a revision or appeal (see Chapters 56 and 57).

People who are not non-dependants

The following people do not count as non-dependants, even if they normally live with you, and no deduction is made (although any rent or lodging charges paid to you affect the amount of your IS, income-based JSA, income-related ESA or PC – see p442 and p477).[22]

• Your partner and:
  – for IS, JSA and ESA only, any child or qualifying young person included in your claim and any child or qualifying young person living with you who does not count as a member of your household (see p327) – eg, a foster child or a child placed with you prior to adoption;
  – for PC only, anyone under 20 for whom you or your partner are responsible ('responsible' is not defined in the rules).
• Someone who is liable to pay you or your partner on a commercial basis in order to live in your home (eg, a subtenant, licensee or boarder), along with other members of her/his household. This does not apply if the person is your or your partner's close relative (see p370 for who counts). A low charge does

Part 4: General rules for other means-tested benefits
Chapter 18: Help with ground rent, service charges and other housing costs
3. The amount of housing costs

not necessarily mean that the arrangement is not commercial. You do not have to make a profit. An arrangement between friends can be commercial.[23]

- For IS, JSA and ESA only, someone other than a close relative (see p370 for who counts) to whom you, or your partner, are liable to make payments on a commercial basis (ie, as a subtenant, licensee or boarder) in order to live in her/his property. Other members of her/his household also do not count as non-dependants.

- Someone who jointly occupies your home and is a co-owner or joint tenant with you or your partner. Your joint occupier's partner is also not a non-dependant. For IS, JSA and ESA only, close relatives (see p370 for who counts) who jointly occupy your home are treated as non-dependants unless they had joint liability before 11 April 1988 or joint liability existed on or before the date you first lived in the property (or your partner did, if s/he is the joint owner/tenant). However, a non-dependant deduction is not made for them even though they are non-dependants (see below).

- Someone who is employed by a charitable or voluntary organisation as a resident carer for you, or your partner, and who you pay for that service (even if the charge is nominal). If the carer's partner lives in your home, s/he also does not count as a non-dependant.

When a deduction is not made

No non-dependant deduction is made for any of your non-dependants if either you or your partner:[24]

- are certified as severely sight-impaired or blind by a consultant ophthalmologist (or are within 28 weeks of ceasing to be certified); *or*
- get attendance allowance (AA) (or equivalent benefits paid because of injury at work or a war injury), the care component of disability living allowance (DLA), the daily living component of personal independence payment (PIP) or armed forces independence payment.

In addition, no deduction is made for a non-dependant:[25]

- who is staying with you but whose normal home is elsewhere. **Note:** for these purposes, someone can only have one normal home at a time;[26] *or*
- for whom a deduction is already being made from your HB; *or*
- who is 16 or 17 years old; *or*
- who is under 25 years old and:
  - getting IS or income-based JSA; *or*
  - if s/he is someone who can still get a work-related activity component after 3 April 2017 (see p653), is getting income-related ESA which does not include a work-related activity or support component; *or*
  - if s/he is someone who cannot get a work-related activity component after 3 April 2017 (see p653), s/he is getting income-related ESA and:
    - for ESA, is still in the assessment phase (see p651);

- for IS, is not in the 'work-related activity group' (see p653) or the 'support group' (see p652);
- for JSA and PC, her/his income-related ESA does not include a support component and s/he is not in the 'work-related activity group' (see p653); *or*
- entitled to universal credit, provided s/he does not have any earned income; *or*
- who is getting PC; *or*
- who gets a training allowance in connection with youth training under specific provisions;[27] *or*
- for IS, JSA and ESA, who is a full-time student during her/his period of study (see p887). This includes those getting JSA who count as full-time students while on a specified government scheme for assisting people to obtain employment (see p1151).[28] **Note:** no deduction is made during the summer vacation unless the student is in full-time paid work (see p991); *or*
- for PC, who is a full-time student. This includes those getting JSA who count as full-time students while on a specified government scheme for assisting people to obtain employment (see p1151);[29] *or*
- who is not living with you at present because s/he:
  - has been in hospital for more than 52 weeks. Separate stays in hospital which are not more than 28 days apart are added together when calculating the 52 weeks;
  - is a prisoner (see p941 for who counts); *or*
- for IS, JSA and ESA only, who is a close relative (see p370 for who counts) and a co-owner or joint tenant with you, or your partner. For PC, no deduction is made because co-owners and joint tenants do not count as non-dependants, even if they are close relatives.

The amount of the deduction

If you have a non-dependant living with you who is 18 or over and for whom a deduction must be made, a fixed amount is deducted from the housing costs included in your benefit, whatever s/he pays you. If you also have a loan for mortgage interest from the DWP (see p855), the deduction is apportioned between the help you get with housing costs and your loan payments. The deduction is calculated as follows.[30]

- **Step one:** work out the weekly amount of housing costs that can be included in your benefit (see p362). If you have a loan for mortgage interest from the DWP (see p855), add the weekly amount of your loan payments to the amount of housing costs included in your benefit.
- **Step two:** work out the total amount of non-dependant deductions (see p366). Remember that a deduction is generally made for each of your non-dependants. If you do *not* have a loan for mortgage interest from the DWP, the

Part 4: General rules for other means-tested benefits
Chapter 18: Help with ground rent, service charges and other housing costs
3. The amount of housing costs

amount in this step is the non-dependant deduction made from your housing costs and you do not need to go on to steps three and four.

- **Step three:** if you have a loan for mortgage interest from the DWP, divide the weekly amount of your loan payments by the total from Step one. Multiply the result by the total amount of non-dependant deductions in Step two.
- **Step four:** work out the difference between the amount in Step two and the amount in Step three. If you have a loan for mortgage interest from the DWP, this is the non-dependant deduction made from your housing costs.

Examples

Saira is getting PC. She owns her flat and pays ground rent of £2,002 a year and a service charge of £30 a week. Her sister, aged 45, lives with her. The sister earns £250 a week. Saira does not have a loan for mortgage interest from the DWP.

Step one: the weekly amount of housing costs that can be included in PC is £38.50 (£2,002 divided by 52) + £30 = £68.50

Step two: the weekly non-dependant deduction for her sister is £50.05. As Saira does not have a loan for mortgage interest, this is the non-dependant deduction. Her PC housing costs are, therefore, £18.45 (£68.50 – £50.05).

Hugh is the owner-occupier of a three-bedroom flat. He has been getting income-based JSA for 50 weeks. He pays a mortgage and has a loan for mortgage interest and gets weekly loan payments of £121.90 a week. He pays ground rent of £18 a week and qualifying service charges of £10 a week. Two friends live with him. One is on contributory ESA. The other is in low-paid full-time work and earns £155 a week (gross).

Step one: the weekly amount of housing costs is £28 (£18 + £10).

£28 + £121.90 (weekly loan payment) = £149.90

Step two: the weekly non-dependant deduction for the friend on contributory ESA is £15.85 and for the friend in low-paid work is £36.45. The total amount of non-dependant deductions is £52.30 (£15.85 + £36.45).

Step three: £121.90 (loan payment) divided by £149.90 (the total in Step one) x £52.30 (the total non-dependant deductions) = £42.53

Step four: the non-dependant deduction to be made from Hugh's housing costs is, therefore, £9.77 (£52.30 – £42.53).

So Hugh's income-based JSA includes housing costs of £18.23 a week (£28 – £9.77).

Note: a non-dependant deduction of £42.53 is made from his loan payments.

The deductions

Unless your non-dependant is in full-time paid work, a deduction of £15.85 is made for her/him each week. If your non-dependant is in full-time paid work, the amount of the deduction depends on her/his gross weekly income.[31]

Gross weekly income	Weekly non-dependant deduction
£469 or more	£102.35
£377–£468.99	£93.25
£283–£376.99	£81.90
£217–£282.99	£50.05
£149–£216.99	£36.45
Less than £149	£15.85

The rules on full-time paid work are covered in Chapter 44. **Note:**

- A non-dependant who is not in (or is treated as not in) full-time paid work does not attract the higher level of deduction even if her/his gross weekly income is £149 or more.
- For PC, if someone is getting IS or income-based JSA for more than three days in a benefit week, s/he does not count as being in full-time paid work in that week.[32] This means the lower deduction (£15.85) is made (or, in some cases, no deduction is made).

Gross income includes wages before tax and national insurance are deducted, plus any other income the non-dependant has, but not AA (or equivalent benefits paid because of injury at work or a war injury), DLA, PIP and armed forces independence payment. Also ignored are payments from specified trusts established to compensate victims of medical errors, emergencies and acts of terrorism and, for PC only, payments in kind.[33]

Do you know your non-dependant's income?

You should try to provide information to show which deduction applies. However, if you do not know your non-dependant's income, explain fully why you are unable to get this information. Ask the DWP to consider the circumstances – eg, if your non-dependant is doing a job which is normally very poorly paid. **Note:** the DWP should not assume that your non-dependant is earning the highest amount. It should assess the likely level of your non-dependant's earnings on the evidence available.[34]

A deduction is made for each non-dependant in your home. However, if you have a non-dependant couple and a non-dependant deduction applies to both members, only one deduction is made – the highest applicable.[35] The couple's joint income counts.

If you are a joint occupier with someone other than your partner, any deductions are shared proportionally between you and the other joint occupier(s).[36]

Part 4: General rules for other means-tested benefits
Chapter 18: Help with ground rent, service charges and other housing costs
4. Waiting periods

4. Waiting periods

When you make a claim for income support (IS), income-based jobseeker's allowance (JSA) or income-related employment and support allowance (ESA) (if you still can), your housing costs are not usually included in your benefit until you have been entitled (or treated as entitled) to IS, JSA or ESA for 39 weeks.[37] This is known as a 'waiting period'.[38] There is no waiting period if you claim and qualify for pension credit (PC), and in some other situations (see below).

Note:

- If you are entitled to some IS, JSA or ESA during your waiting period, even though housing costs are not included in your applicable amount, the decision maker should carry out a supersession when your waiting period ends, and your housing costs are then included from the end of that period.[39]
- If you are *not* entitled to some IS, JSA or ESA during your waiting period, help with your housing costs can still be included when it ends if you are *treated* as entitled to IS, JSA or ESA during the waiting period. In some cases, you have to make a new claim for IS, income-based JSA or income-related ESA (when sufficient weeks have passed). For information about when you can be treated as entitled to IS, JSA or ESA (the linking rules), see pp375–76.

If you (or your partner) reclaim IS, income-based JSA or income-related ESA within 26 weeks of a previous award of benefit which included help with housing costs and you (or s/he) have been receiving payments under an employment insurance policy which has since run out, periods between those claims are ignored when calculating the waiting period.[40] Because the number of weeks in the previous award of benefit can be added to the number of weeks in your current award of that benefit, this means that you can requalify for help with housing costs sooner.

No waiting period

Help with your housing costs is included in your benefit without a waiting period if:[41]

- you claim and are awarded PC; *or*
- your partner is at least pension age (see p780); *or*
- you can be treated as entitled to IS, JSA or ESA for sufficient weeks during the period before your claim; *or*
- you have already been entitled to IS, JSA or ESA for sufficient weeks when you agree to pay housing costs; *or*
- you were getting help with your housing costs when the benefit ceased because you:
  - became a 'work or training beneficiary' (see p365 of the 2018/19 edition of this *Handbook*); *or*

– started full-time paid work or training for work or self-employment, or increased your hours or your pay (provided you qualify for a longer linking period – see p368 of the 2018/19 edition of this *Handbook*). You must be able to make a new claim for IS, income-based JSA or income-related ESA and do so within 104 weeks (if you are a 'work or training beneficiary') or 52 weeks (if you qualify for a longer linking period); *or*
- the housing costs are for payments as a Crown tenant, under a co-ownership scheme or for a tent and the site on which it stands.

5. Liability to pay housing costs

You count as liable to pay housing costs if:[42]
- either you, or your partner, are liable to pay them. However, you do not count as liable to pay housing costs if you pay these to someone who is a member of your household (see p329 for the meaning of 'household'). If you or your partner share liability, you might only get help with your share (see below); *or*
- you share the costs with other members of your household and are treated as liable to pay them. You might only get help with your share; *or*
- someone else is liable to pay them but is not paying, so you have to meet the cost yourself in order to continue to live in your home. You must show that it is reasonable in all the circumstances for you to pay instead – eg, if you have given up your home to live with and care for someone and s/he has now gone into a care home, or if you have separated from your partner (even if you have not lived in the home continuously since your partner left[43]).

Shared liability

If you or your partner share liability with someone else, you might only get help with your share. However, if the other person is not paying her/his share, you can argue that you should get help with the full amount.

You are treated as liable to pay housing costs (even if you are not legally liable) if:[44]
- you share the costs with other members of your household; *and*
- at least one of those with whom you share is liable.

You can be paid for your share, provided the people with whom you share are not your or your partner's 'close relatives' and it is reasonable in all the circumstances to treat you as sharing responsibility for the costs.[45]

Part 4: General rules for other means-tested benefits
Chapter 18: Help with ground rent, service charges and other housing costs
6. Occupying accommodation as your home

> **Close relative**
>
> 'Close relative' means a parent, parent-in-law (including a civil partner's parent), son, son-in-law (including a son's civil partner), daughter, daughter-in-law (including a daughter's civil partner), brother, sister, step-parent (including a parent's civil partner), stepson (including a civil partner's son) or stepdaughter (including a civil partner's daughter), or the partners of any of these. 'Sister' or 'brother' includes a half-sister or half-brother. An adopted child ceases to be related to her/his birth family on adoption and becomes the relative of her/his adoptive family.[46]

6. Occupying accommodation as your home

You can get help with housing costs for the home in which you normally live.[47] You cannot usually be paid for any other home. Even if you are liable to pay housing costs for a property, if you have no immediate intention of living there, you cannot get help with the costs.[48] You can argue that a home can consist of more than one building if you occupy more than one dwelling – eg, because your family is too large for one.[49]

> **Your home**
>
> Your 'home' is defined as the building, or part of the building, in which you live. This includes any garage, garden, outbuildings and other premises and land which it is not reasonable or practicable to sell separately.[50]

There are special rules if you:
- have just moved into your home (see below); *or*
- are temporarily absent from home (see p371); *or*
- are liable to pay housing costs on more than one home (see p374).

Moving home

If you have just moved into your home but were liable to pay housing costs before moving in, your income support (IS), income-based jobseeker's allowance (JSA), income-related employment and support allowance (ESA) or pension credit (PC) can include help with the costs for up to four weeks before you moved in if your delay in moving was reasonable. You must have claimed IS, JSA, income-related ESA or PC before moving in.

You must satisfy one of the following conditions.[51]
- You were waiting for adaptations to be finished to meet your or your partner's disability needs or those of:

- for IS, JSA and ESA, a child or qualifying young person included in your claim (see p323); *or*
- for PC, someone under 20 for whom you or your partner are responsible ('responsible' is not defined in the rules).

The adaptations do not need to involve a change to the fabric or structure of the dwelling, but must be reasonably required and have a clear connection to the disability.[52]

- You became responsible for the housing costs while you were in hospital or a similar institution, or you were in a care home or an independent hospital (or, for IS, JSA and ESA only, in an Abbeyfield home).
- You were waiting for local welfare assistance, a payment from the Scottish Welfare Fund or a social fund payment for a need connected with the move – eg, for removal expenses or items to help you set up home.[53] In addition, for IS, JSA and ESA you must:
  - have a child aged five or under living with you, or be getting child tax credit which includes a disabled child or severely disabled child element; *or*
  - for IS and JSA only, qualify for a disability, severe disability, disabled child or pensioner premium; *or*
  - for ESA only, be getting main phase ESA (ie, after the assessment phase has ended) or qualify for a severe disability or pensioner premium.

Note: the amount for housing costs is not actually included in your benefit until you move in. If the earlier IS, JSA, ESA or PC claim you made before you moved was turned down, you must claim again and within four weeks of moving in to qualify.

Temporary absence from home

If you are temporarily absent from home but are still entitled to IS, income-based JSA, income-related ESA or PC, have not rented out your home and intend to return, help with your housing costs continues to be paid for a period. You can argue that you count as temporarily absent even if you have not yet stayed there – eg, you move your furniture and belongings in but then have to go into hospital.[54]
Note: your entitlement to benefit may be affected if you are absent from home outside Great Britain (see Chapter 69).

You can get help with housing costs for up to:
- **13 weeks** while you are away, whatever the reason. You must be unlikely to be away for longer than this;[55]
- **52 weeks** if you are in one of the groups on pp372–73. You must be unlikely to be away for longer than this (or, in exceptional circumstances, unlikely to be away for substantially longer than this).[56]

The 13 and 52 weeks both run from the date you leave home. The day you leave home is included, but not the day you return home.[57] If, for example, you have

Part 4: General rules for other means-tested benefits
Chapter 18: Help with ground rent, service charges and other housing costs
6. Occupying accommodation as your home

been away from home for 10 weeks and then have grounds to continue to get help with housing costs for 52 weeks, you only get this for the balance: 42 weeks. However, a new period of absence starts if you return home even for a short stay – eg, a day or a weekend.[58]

Are you going to be away from home for a period?

1. You must let the DWP know about your absence from home, preferably before you go away.

2. Make it clear that your absence is going to be temporary and how long you are likely to be away.

3. Your intention to return, and whether or not you are unlikely to be away for longer than 13/52 weeks, is considered initially based on the circumstances on the date you leave your home, unless you are in a care home, independent hospital (or, for IS, JSA or ESA, an Abbeyfield home) for a trial period (see below).[59] If at any time after that date, you no longer intend to return or it becomes likely that you will be away from home for more than the 13/52 weeks, your entitlement can be reconsidered.[60]

Note: if you have someone living with you who is temporarily absent (eg, a student who is away during term time), the DWP may use these rules to decide whether s/he is a non-dependant (see p363).[61]

If you have to live in temporary accommodation while essential repairs are done to your normal home and you only have to pay housing costs for one of the homes, your IS, income-based JSA, income-related ESA or PC includes help with the housing costs for that home.[62] This is not subject to the normal limits on temporary absence from home.[63] If you have to pay for both homes, you may be able to get help with housing costs for both for up to four weeks (see p374). However, after the four weeks, you are only paid for one home – your normal home if you are unlikely to be away for more than 13/52 weeks, or your temporary home if you will be away for longer.

Housing costs for up to 52 weeks

You can get help with your housing costs for up to 52 weeks if you are in a care home or an independent hospital (or, for IS, JSA and ESA only, an Abbeyfield home) for a trial period to see if it suits your needs. On the date you enter the accommodation, you must intend to return home if it is not suitable.[64] You can only get your housing costs met for up to 13 weeks.[65] If the accommodation does not suit your needs, you can have further trial periods in other homes, as long as you are not away from home for more than 52 weeks in total.

You can get help with your housing costs for up to 52 weeks if you are unlikely to be away for longer than this (or, in exceptional circumstances, unlikely to be away for substantially longer than this) in the following situations.[66]

- You are resident in a hospital or a similar institution. If you are getting JSA, this must be during a two-week period of sickness when you are treated as capable of work for JSA purposes (see p709 – the rules are the same as for contribution-based JSA). If you are sick for longer than this, claim IS or income-related ESA (if you still can) or PC, or claim universal credit (UC) if you come under the UC system. **Note:** you cannot get help with housing costs after you have been resident in hospital for 52 weeks even if this is because you are seriously mentally ill. However, a new period of absence starts if you return home even for a short stay.[67]
- You are receiving care (approved by a doctor) in the UK or abroad, or you, your partner or a dependent child (for PC, a dependant under 20) are receiving medical treatment or convalescing in the UK or abroad (approved by a doctor). This must not be in a care home or an independent hospital (or, for IS, JSA and ESA only, an Abbeyfield home).
- You are attending a specified 'training course' in the UK or abroad.
- You are required to live in an approved hostel or an address away from your normal home as a condition of bail.
- For IS, ESA and PC only, you are in prison on remand pending trial or sentence. You can argue that this applies even if you are simultaneously serving another sentence.[68] If you were getting JSA before going into prison, to cover your housing costs you must instead claim IS or income-related ESA (if you still can) or PC, or claim UC if you come under the UC system. Once you are sentenced, you are no longer entitled to help with housing costs in IS, ESA or PC. For UC, see p92.
- You are in a care home or an independent hospital (or, for IS, JSA and ESA only, an Abbeyfield home) for short-term or respite care.
- You are providing care for someone living in the UK or abroad (approved by a doctor).
- You are caring for a child under 16 (or, for PC only, someone under 20) whose parent or guardian is receiving medical treatment or care (approved by a doctor) away from home.
- You are away from home because of a fear of violence (see p374 if you need to claim for two homes and for what counts as violence).
- You are a full-time student (see p887) and:
  - living apart from your partner but cannot get help with housing costs for two homes (see p374); *or*
  - a single claimant or a lone parent who is liable to pay housing costs on both a term-time and a home address.

There must be some causal link between your absence from home and being in one of the situations above.[69]

Part 4: General rules for other means-tested benefits
Chapter 18: Help with ground rent, service charges and other housing costs
6. Occupying accommodation as your home

Housing costs for more than one home

In most cases, you can only get help with the housing costs for one home. If you occupy more than one dwelling as a home (eg, because you have a large family), you can argue that you only have one home.[70]

If you have to pay housing costs for two homes, you *can* get IS, income-based JSA, income-related ESA or PC for both:[71]

- **for up to four weeks** if you have moved into a new home and cannot avoid having to pay for the other one as well;[72]

- **indefinitely** if you left your home because of a fear of violence. Provided you left home because of this and are still away from home because of this, it does not matter if you were away from home for some other reason during this period – eg, because you were in prison.[73] You must show that it is reasonable for you to get payment for two homes. So, if you do not intend to return home or someone else is paying the housing costs, you might not get IS, income-based JSA, income-related ESA or PC for both homes.

  'Violence' means violence against you and not caused by you.[74] For the purpose of these rules, it must be fear of violence:[75]
  - in your home. Fear of a racial attack should be covered, provided the attack would take place in your home. Remember that your garden and garage, for example, count (see p370); *or*
  - from a former partner; *or*
  - for IS, JSA and ESA, from a child or qualifying young person who is no longer included in your claim; *or*
  - for PC, from a close relative (see p370 for who counts);

- **indefinitely** if you are one of a couple and you or your partner are a full-time student or on a training course and living away from your home (see below). You have to show that it is reasonable for you to get payment for two homes.

If you have to live in temporary accommodation while essential repairs are done to your normal home and you only have to pay for housing costs for one of the homes, see p372.

If you have to live away from your normal home because you or your partner are a full-time student (see p887) or on a specified training course:[76]

- if you are one of a couple and have to live apart, you can get help with housing costs for both of your homes if it is reasonable for you to get help with both;

- if you are a single person or lone parent and must pay housing costs for *either* your normal home *or* your term-time accommodation but not both, you can get help with housing costs for the home for which you pay.

If neither of the above applies, you may only get help with your usual home for up to 52 weeks during a temporary absence (see p371).[77]

If you have been getting help with housing costs for your term-time accommodation and you stop living there during a vacation, you cannot continue to get this unless you are away because you are in hospital.[78]

7. Linking rules

You are treated as entitled to, or receiving, income support (IS), income-based jobseeker's allowance (JSA) or income-related employment and support allowance (ESA) for certain periods, even though you were not actually entitled to or receiving it. These are known as 'linking rules'. **Note:** periods when you are treated as entitled to IS, income-based JSA or income-related ESA can count towards your waiting period (see p368), so you can get help with housing costs earlier.

You are treated as entitled to and receiving:[79]

- IS for any period when you were entitled to or receiving income-based JSA or income-related ESA;
- JSA for any period when you were entitled to or receiving IS or income-related ESA;
- income-related ESA for any period when you were entitled to or receiving IS, income-based JSA or pension credit (PC);
- IS or JSA for any period when you were receiving JSA as a 'joint-claim couple' (see p253);
- IS, JSA or income-related ESA during a period of no more than 12 weeks between two periods when:
  - for IS and JSA, you were entitled to, receiving or treated as receiving IS, JSA or income-related ESA, or were treated as entitled to one of these while your income or capital was too high in specified circumstances; *or*
  - for ESA, you were entitled to, receiving or treated as receiving IS, income-based JSA, income-related ESA or PC, or were treated as entitled to one of these while your income or capital was too high in specified circumstances.
  The 12 weeks is extended to 104 weeks if you or your partner are a 'work or training beneficiary' (see p365 of the 2018/19 edition of this *Handbook*) or to 52 weeks if you qualify for a longer linking period (see p368 of the 2018/19 edition of this *Handbook*);
- IS or JSA during any period for which you are awarded IS, JSA or income-related ESA after a revision, supersession or appeal;
- income-related ESA during any period for which you are awarded IS, income-based JSA, income-related ESA or PC after a revision, supersession or appeal.

There are other linking rules for periods when:[80]
- you were not entitled to IS, income-based JSA or income-related ESA (or for ESA only, PC) when you claimed because your income was too high or your capital was over £16,000; *or*

Part 4: General rules for other means-tested benefits
Chapter 18: Help with ground rent, service charges and other housing costs
8. Housing costs run-on

- your partner or former partner was receiving or treated as receiving IS, income-based JSA or income-related ESA; *or*
- you stopped getting IS, income-based JSA or income-related ESA (or for ESA only, PC) because you or your partner were on training under specified provisions or were on an employment training rehabilitation course; *or*
- you and a child or young person who is a member of your family counted as the member of a former claimant's family.

For full details of these linking rules, see pp366–67 of the 2018/19 edition of this *Handbook*.

8. Housing costs run-on

When you (or your partner) return to work or increase your hours and so count as being in full-time paid work, you no longer qualify for income support (IS), income-based jobseeker's allowance (JSA) or income-related employment and support allowance (ESA). However, if you qualify for housing costs run-on, you are paid IS for your housing costs for the first four weeks after you go into full-time paid work, even if the benefit you were claiming was income-based JSA or income-related ESA. **Note:**

- You do not have to make a claim to qualify for housing costs run-on; it is paid automatically.[81] However, you must let the DWP know you are starting full-time paid work.
- Housing costs run-on is a payment of IS. Therefore:
  - it is not taxable; *and*
  - it is included in the benefit cap (see p1194); *and*
  - you might get health benefits (see Chapter 31) and education benefits, such as free school lunches (see p866).

Who can get housing costs run-on

You qualify for housing costs run-on if:[82]

- you or your partner take up a new job or increase your weekly hours of work and so count as being in full-time paid work for IS purposes (see p991). You must expect the work to last for at least five weeks; *and*
- throughout the 26 weeks before the day you count as being in full-time paid work, you or your partner were receiving IS, income-based JSA or income-related ESA. Periods when you were receiving housing costs run-on do not count towards the 26 weeks;[83] *and*
- on the day before you or your partner started the work, your IS, income-based JSA or income-related ESA applicable amount included help with any of the

types of housing costs that can be met (see p360) and you or your partner are still liable (or treated as liable) to pay them.

If you qualify, you are paid IS for the housing costs for the first four weeks of full-time paid work.[84]

The amount of housing costs run-on

You are paid the lowest of:[85]
* the weekly amount of IS, income-based JSA or income-related ESA for housing costs that you were getting immediately before you or your partner took up full-time paid work; *or*
* your or your partner's IS, income-based JSA or income-related ESA entitlement in the week before you took up full-time paid work (or the amount to which you would have been entitled had you not been getting a training allowance).

Your earnings from the full-time paid work and any other income you get are disregarded.[86] All of your capital is also disregarded.[87]

Your housing costs run-on can be adjusted if specified changes occur.[88]

Notes

1. Who can get help with housing costs
1 **IS** Regs 17(1)(e) and 18(1)(f) and Sch 3 para 1 IS Regs
JSA Regs 83(7), 84(1)(g) and 86A(d) and Sch 2 para 1 JSA Regs
ESA Regs 67(1)(c) and 69(1)(d) and Sch 6 para 1 ESA Regs
PC Reg 6(6)(c) and Sch 2 para 1 SPC Regs

2. Which housing costs can be met
2 **IS** Sch 3 para 17(1) IS Regs
JSA Sch 2 para 16(1) JSA Regs
ESA Sch 6 para 18(1) ESA Regs
PC Sch 2 para 13(1) SPC Regs
All s1 Rentcharges Act 1977
3 CH/3110/2003; R(H) 3/07
4 paras 23601-3 DMG

5 **IS** Sch 3 para 17(5) IS Regs
JSA Sch 2 para 16(5) JSA Regs
ESA Sch 6 para 18(5) ESA Regs
PC Sch 2 para 13(5) SPC Regs
6 **IS** Sch 3 para 5 IS Regs
JSA Sch 2 para 5 JSA Regs
ESA Sch 6 para 7 ESA Regs
PC Sch 2 para 6 SPC Regs
7 **IS** Sch 3 para 17(2)(b) IS Regs
JSA Sch 2 para 16(2)(b) JSA Regs
ESA Sch 6 para 18(2)(b) ESA Regs
PC Sch 2 para 13(2)(b) SPC Regs
8 R(IS) 4/91; CIS/1460/1995; CIS/15036/1996
9 R(IS) 4/92; R(IS) 19/93
10 CIS/4/1988

Part 4: General rules for other means-tested benefits
Chapter 18: Help with ground rent, service charges and other housing costs
Notes

11 **IS** Sch 3 para 17(2)(c) and (6) IS Regs
JSA Sch 2 para 16(2)(c) and (6) JSA Regs
ESA Sch 6 para 18(2)(c) and (6) ESA Regs
PC Sch 2 para 13(2)(c) and (7) SPC Regs
All CIS/15036/1996; CIS/488/2008
12 *KW v SSWP (IS)* [2012] UKUT 180 (AAC)
13 R(IS) 16/98; *DC v SSWP (JSA)* [2010] UKUT 459 (AAC)
14 **IS** Sch 3 para 1(3) and (4) IS Regs
JSA Sch 2 para 1(3) and (4) JSA Regs
ESA Sch 6 para 1(3) and (4) ESA Regs
PC Sch 2 para 1(2)(a) and (3) SPC Regs
15 **IS** Sch 3 para 17(2) IS Regs
JSA Sch 2 para 16(2) JSA Regs
ESA Sch 6 para 18(2) ESA Regs
PC Sch 2 para 13(2) SPC Regs

3. The amount of housing costs

16 **IS** Sch 3 para 17(1) IS Regs
JSA Sch 2 para 16(1) JSA Regs
ESA Sch 6 para 18(1) ESA Regs
PC Sch 2 para 13(1) SPC Regs
17 **IS** Sch 3 para 17(3) IS Regs
JSA Sch 2 para 16(3) JSA Regs
ESA Sch 6 para 18(3) ESA Regs
PC Sch 2 para 13(3) SPC Regs
18 **IS** Sch 3 para 5 IS Regs
JSA Sch 2 para 5 JSA Regs
ESA Sch 6 para 7 ESA Regs
PC Sch 2 para 6 SPC Regs
19 **IS** Sch 3 para 17(4) IS Regs
JSA Sch 2 para 16(4) JSA Regs
ESA Sch 6 para 18(4) ESA Regs
PC Sch 2 para 13(4) SPC Regs
20 **IS** Reg 3 and Sch 3 para 18 IS Regs
JSA Reg 2 and Sch 2 para 17 JSA Regs
ESA Reg 71 and Sch 6 para 19 ESA Regs
PC Sch 2 paras 1(4)-(9) and 14 SPC Regs
21 R(H) 8/09; *SK v South Hams DC (HB)* [2010] UKUT 129 (AAC), reported as [2010] AACR 40
22 **IS** Reg 3 IS Regs
JSA Reg 2 JSA Regs
ESA Reg 71 ESA Regs
PC Sch 2 para 1(4)-(7) SPC Regs
23 CSB/1163/1988
24 **IS** Sch 3 para 18(6) IS Regs
JSA Sch 2 para 17(6) JSA Regs
ESA Sch 6 para 19(6) ESA Regs
PC Sch 2 para 14(6) SPC Regs
25 **IS** Sch 3 para 18(7) IS Regs
JSA Sch 2 para 17(7) JSA Regs
ESA Sch 6 para 19(7) ESA Regs
PC Sch 2 para 14(7) SPC Regs
26 *JP v Bournemouth BC (HB)* [2018] UKUT 75 (AAC)

27 Made under s2 ETA 1973 or s2 Enterprise and New Towns (Scotland) Act 1990 or by the Secretary of State for people enlisted in HM Forces for any special term of service specified in regulations made under s2 Armed Forces Act 1966
28 Reg 3 JSA(SAPOE) Regs
29 Reg 3 JSA(SAPOE) Regs
30 **IS** Sch 3 para 18(2A) IS Regs
JSA Sch 2 para 17(2A) JSA Regs
ESA Sch 6 para 19(2A) ESA Regs
PC Sch 2 para 14(2A) SPC Regs
All Reg 14 LMI Regs
31 **IS** Sch 3 para 18(1) and (2) IS Regs
JSA Sch 2 para 17(1) and (2) JSA Regs
ESA Sch 6 para 19(1) and (2) ESA Regs
PC Sch 2 para 14(1) and (2) SPC Regs
All Reg 14 LMI Regs
32 Sch 2 para 2(6) SPC Regs
33 **IS** Sch 3 para 18(8) IS Regs
JSA Sch 2 para 17(8) JSA Regs
ESA Sch 6 para 19(8) ESA Regs
PC Sch 2 para 14(8) SPC Regs
34 CH/48/2006
35 **IS** Sch 3 para 18(3) and(4) IS Regs
JSA Sch 2 para 17(3) and (4) JSA Regs
ESA Sch 6 para 19(3) and (4) ESA Regs
PC Sch 2 para 14(3) and (4) SPC Regs
36 **IS** Sch 3 para 18(5) IS Regs
JSA Sch 2 para 17(5) JSA Regs
ESA Sch 6 para 19(5) ESA Regs
PC Sch 2 para 14(5) SPC Regs

4. Waiting periods

37 **IS** Sch 3 paras 1(2) and 8 IS Regs
JSA Sch 2 paras 1(2) and 7 JSA Regs
ESA Sch 6 paras 1(2) and 9 ESA Regs
All CJSA/2028/2000
38 **IS** Sch 3 para 8 IS Regs
JSA Sch 2 para 7 JSA Regs
ESA Sch 6 para 9 ESA Regs
39 *SK v SSWP* [2013] UKUT 138 (AAC); *JR v SSWP* [2018] UKUT 28 (AAC)
40 **IS** Sch 3 para 14(8) and (9) IS Regs
JSA Sch 2 para 13(10) and (11) JSA Regs
ESA Sch 6 para 15(13) and (14) ESA Regs
41 **IS** Sch 3 para 9 IS Regs
JSA Sch 2 para 8 JSA Regs
ESA Sch 6 para 10 ESA Regs

5. Liability to pay housing costs

42 **IS** Sch 3 para 2 IS Regs
JSA Sch 2 para 2 JSA Regs
ESA Sch 6 para 4 ESA Regs
PC Sch 2 para 3 SPC Regs

43 *Ewens v Secretary of State for Social Security*, reported as R(IS) 8/01

44 **IS** Sch 3 para 5(5) IS Regs
JSA Sch 2 para 5(5) JSA Regs
ESA Sch 6 para 7(5) ESA Regs
PC Sch 2 para 6(5) SPC Regs
All R(SB) 22/87; *FK v Wandsworth BC (HB)* [2016] UKUT 570 (AAC); *Babergh DC v GW (HB)* [2017] UKUT 40 (AAC)

45 R(IS) 4/95

46 **IS** Reg 2(1) IS Regs
JSA Reg 1(3) JSA Regs
ESA Reg 2(1) ESA Regs
PC Reg 1(2) SPC Regs
All R(SB) 22/87

6. Occupying accommodation as your home

47 **IS** Sch 3 para 3(1) IS Regs
JSA Sch 2 para 3(1) JSA Regs
ESA Sch 6 para 5(1) ESA Regs
PC Sch 2 para 4(1) SPC Regs

48 CIS/297/1994; *PJ v SSWP (SPC)* [2014] UKUT 152 (AAC)

49 *SSWP v Mohamed Miah*, reported as R(JSA) 9/03; R(H) 5/09

50 **IS** Reg 2(1) IS Regs
JSA Reg 1(3) JSA Regs
ESA Reg 2(1) ESA Regs
PC Reg 1(2) SPC Regs
All Definition of 'dwelling occupied as the home', s137(1) SSCBA 1992 and reg 2(1), definition of 'dwelling', ESA Regs

51 **IS** Sch 3 para 3(7) and (13) IS Regs
JSA Sch 2 para 3(7) and (13) JSA Regs
ESA Sch 6 para 5(7) and (13) ESA Regs
PC Sch 2 para 4(7) SPC Regs

52 *R (Mahmoudi) v LB Lewisham and Another* [2014] EWCA Civ 284, reported as [2014] AACR 14

53 **IS** Reg 2(1) IS Regs
JSA Reg 1(3) JSA Regs
ESA Reg 2(1) ESA Regs
PC Reg 1(2) PC Regs
All Definition of 'local welfare provision'

54 R(H) 9/05

55 **IS** Sch 3 para 3(10) IS Regs
JSA Sch 2 para 3(10) JSA Regs
ESA Sch 6 para 5(10) ESA Regs
PC Sch 2 para 4(10) SPC Regs

56 **IS** Sch 3 para 3(11)-(13) IS Regs
JSA Sch 2 para 3(11)-(13) JSA Regs
ESA Sch 6 para 5(11)-(13) ESA Regs
PC Sch 2 para 4(11)-(13) SPC Regs

57 *KdeS v Camden LB (HB)* [2011] UKUT 457 (AAC)

58 *R v Penwith DC ex parte Burt* [1990] 22 HLR 292 (QBD)

59 CH/1237/2004

60 CH/3893/2004

61 R(H) 8/09; *SK v South Hams DC (HB)* [2010] UKUT 129 (AAC), reported as [2010] AACR 40

62 **IS** Sch 3 para 3(5) IS Regs
JSA Sch 2 para 3(5) JSA Regs
ESA Sch 6 para 5(5) ESA Regs
PC Sch 2 para 4(5) SPC Regs

63 CIS/719/1994

64 *SSWP v Selby DC and Bowman* [2006] EWCA Civ 271, reported as R(H) 4/06

65 **IS** Sch 3 para 3(8) and (9) IS Regs
JSA Sch 2 para 3(8) and (9) JSA Regs
ESA Sch 6 para 5(8) and (9) ESA Regs
PC Sch 2 para 4(8) and (9) SPC Regs

66 **IS** Sch 3 para 3(11)-(13) IS Regs
JSA Sch 2 para 3(11)-(13) JSA Regs
ESA Sch 6 para 5(11)-(13) ESA Regs
PC Sch 2 para 4(11)-(13) SPC Regs

67 *Obrey and Others v SSWP* [2013] EWCA Civ 1584

68 *MR v Bournemouth BC (HB)* [2011] UKUT 284 (AAC)

69 *Torbay BC v RF* [2010] UKUT 7 (AAC), reported as [2010] AACR 26

70 R(H) 5/09

71 **IS** Sch 3 para 3(6) IS Regs
JSA Sch 2 para 3(6) JSA Regs
ESA Sch 6 para 5(6) ESA Regs
PC Sch 2 para 4(6) SPC Regs

72 CH/1911/2006

73 CIS/543/1993

74 CIS/339/1993

75 **IS** Sch 3 para 3(6)(a) IS Regs
JSA Sch 2 para 3(6)(a) JSA Regs
ESA Sch 6 para 5(6)(a) ESA Regs
PC Sch 2 para 4(6)(a) SPC Regs

76 **IS** Sch 3 para 3(3), (6)(b) and (13) IS Regs
JSA Sch 2 para 3(3), (6)(b) and (13) JSA Regs
ESA Sch 6 para 5(6)(b) ESA Regs
PC Sch 2 para 4(6)(b) SPC Regs

Part 4: General rules for other means-tested benefits
Chapter 18: Help with ground rent, service charges and other housing costs
Notes

77 **IS** Sch 3 para 3(11)(c)(viii) IS Regs
JSA Sch 2 para 3(11)(c)(viii) JSA Regs
ESA Sch 6 para 5(11)(c)(viii) ESA Regs
PC Sch 2 para 4(11)(c)(viii) SPC Regs
78 **IS** Sch 3 para 3(4) IS Regs
JSA Sch 2 para 3(4) JSA Regs
ESA Sch 6 para 5(4) ESA Regs
PC Sch 2 para 4(4) SPC Regs

7. Linking rules
79 **IS** Sch 3 para 14(1)(a), (3A) and (15) IS
Regs; reg 32 IS(JSACA) Regs
JSA Sch 2 paras 13(1)(a), (2A) and (4)
and 18(1)(c) JSA Regs
ESA Sch 6 para 15(1)(a), (5), (15) and
(16) and 20(1)(c) ESA Regs
80 **IS** Sch 3 para 14(1)(c), (d), (e) and (f),
(3), (3A), (4), (5), (5A), (5B), (6), (14)
and (15) IS Regs; reg 32 IS(JSACA) Regs
JSA Sch 2 paras 13(1)(c), (d), (dd), (e)
and (f), (3), (4), (5), (6), (7), (8), (9), (16)
and 18(1)(c) JSA Regs; reg 32 IS(JSACA)
Regs
ESA Sch 6 paras 2(9), 15(1)(c), (d), (e),
(g), (3), (5), (8), (9), (10), (11), (12),
(15), (19) and 20(1)(c) ESA Regs

8. Housing costs run-on
81 Reg 3(h) SS(C&P) Regs
82 Reg 6(5) and (8) IS Regs
83 Reg 6(7) IS Regs
84 Reg 6(6) IS Regs; Sch 9A para 3(9)
SS(C&P) Regs
85 Sch 7 para 19A(1) IS Regs
86 Schs 8 para 15C and 9 para 74 IS Regs
87 Sch 10 para 62 IS Regs
88 Sch 7 para 19A(2) and (3) IS Regs

Chapter 19

· ·

Housing benefit rent restrictions

This chapter covers:

1. Which rent restriction rules apply (p382)
2. The local housing allowance rules (p384)
3. The social sector rules: the 'bedroom tax' (p391)
4. Hostels, houseboats, mobile homes, caravans and boarders (p396)
5. Exempt accommodation and claimants: the old scheme rules (p403)
6. Common definitions (p408)
7. Delaying a rent restriction (p412)
8. Challenging a rent restriction (p413)

This chapter covers the rent restriction rules for housing benefit. The rent restriction rules for the universal credit housing costs element are covered in Chapter 6.

Key facts

- If you are a private tenant, your housing benefit (HB) may be based on a rent lower than the one you are liable to pay if it is restricted under one of three rent restriction schemes.
- If you are a local authority or housing association tenant and your home has more bedrooms than the rules allow, the rent used to calculate your HB may be restricted under the social sector rent restriction rules (often called the 'bedroom tax'). In exceptional cases, some housing association tenants have their rent restricted under one of the schemes that apply to private tenants.
- If you are entitled to HB and your rent is restricted, you may be able to get discretionary housing payments from your local authority to help with any shortfall.

Part 4: General rules for other means-tested benefits
Chapter 19: Housing benefit rent restrictions
1. Which rent restriction rules apply

1. **Which rent restriction rules apply**

Your housing benefit (HB) might not cover the full amount of rent you have to pay. This is because, in many cases, the local authority must reduce the rent it uses to calculate your HB by applying a 'rent restriction'. There are four possible rent restriction schemes, depending on the type of tenancy you have and the type of accommodation you occupy. To check which scheme applies to you, see below if you are a private tenant, see p383 if you are a housing association tenant and p384 if you are a local authority tenant. **Note:** if you are a private or housing association tenant, your tenancy may be excluded from some or all of the rent restriction schemes (see below).

Are you thinking of moving home or will there be a break in your claim?
If you are getting HB and are considering a move, or there will be a break in your claim and you can still claim HB, check whether the rent restriction rules that will apply in your new situation will be more or less favourable to you. In some cases, you can check the rent figure that will be used to calculate your HB.

When your tenancy is excluded

If you are a private or housing association tenant, you may have what is known as an 'excluded tenancy'. The following are excluded tenancies.[1]
- A regulated or protected tenancy – ie, a tenancy entered into before 15 January 1989 or, in Scotland, 2 January 1989.
- A tenancy in an approved bail or probation hostel. However, if you are required to live in such a hostel, you cannot qualify for HB towards the rent you pay to the hostel (see p181).
- A former local authority or new town letting which has been transferred to a new owner. However, your tenancy is *not* excluded if there has been a rent increase since the transfer and:
  - the local authority considers your rent to be unreasonably high; *or*
  - if the transfer took place before 7 October 2002, the local authority considers your accommodation to be unreasonably large.
  If this is the case, the rules that apply to hostels, houseboats, mobile homes, caravans and boarders on p396 apply.
- A shared ownership tenancy – ie, you are buying part of your house or flat and renting the rest. However, your tenancy is *not* excluded if your shared ownership tenancy is with a private landlord, in which case the local housing allowance rules on p384 apply.
- A letting by a registered housing association,[2] by a county council (if you live in a caravan or mobile home provided on a travellers' site[3]) or in a caravan, mobile home or houseboat (if you are also liable to make payments to a local

authority – eg, for site or mooring fees). However, your tenancy is *not* excluded if:
- the local authority considers your rent to be unreasonably high; *or*
- you are getting pension-age HB (see p188) and the local authority considers your accommodation to be unreasonably large.

In both cases, the rules that apply to hostels, houseboats, mobile homes, caravans and boarders on p396 apply.

Do you have an excluded tenancy?

If you have an excluded tenancy and you are:
- a private tenant, none of the rent restriction schemes apply to you;
- a housing association tenant, none of the rent restriction schemes apply to you unless your landlord is a registered housing association. If this is the case, the social sector rules on p391 may apply.

If you are a private tenant

If you are a private tenant, and your tenancy is not excluded (see p382), in most cases, the local housing allowance rules on p384 apply. However, there are exceptions. If:
- you live in a specified type of temporary or supported accommodation (called 'exempt accommodation' – see p403) or you have you been getting HB since 1 January 1996 generally for the same property, the old scheme rules on p403 apply; *or*
- your rent includes board and attendance, or you live in a hostel, houseboat, mobile home or caravan, the rules that use rent officer determinations on p396 apply. These rules *may* also apply in other situations if the local authority considers your rent to be unreasonably high or your accommodation to be unreasonably large.

If you are a housing association tenant

If you are a housing association tenant, and your tenancy is not excluded (see p382), in most cases, if neither you nor your partner are at least pension age (see p780), the social sector rules (often called the 'bedroom tax') on p391 apply. However, there are exceptions. If:
- you live in a specified type of temporary or supported accommodation (called 'exempt accommodation' – see p403) or you have been getting HB since 1 January 1996 generally for the same property, the old scheme rules on p403 apply; *or*
- your rent includes board and attendance, or you live in a hostel, houseboat, mobile home or caravan, the rules that use rent officer determinations on p396 apply. These rules *may* also apply in other situations if the local authority

Part 4: General rules for other means-tested benefits
Chapter 19: Housing benefit rent restrictions
2. The local housing allowance rules

considers your rent to be unreasonably high or your accommodation to be unreasonably large; *or*

- if your landlord is not a registered social landlord (in Wales or Scotland) or a non-profit or profit-making provider of registered accommodation (in England), the local housing allowance rules apply (see below).

If you are a local authority tenant

If you are a local authority tenant, and both you and your partner are below pension age (see p780), the social sector rules on p391 (often called the 'bedroom tax') usually apply. **Note:** if you are at least pension age and you have been getting HB since 1 January 1996 generally for the same property, in exceptional cases, the old scheme rules on p403 may apply.

If none of the rent restriction rules apply

Even if none of the rent restriction rules apply to you, the local authority still has discretion to decrease the amount of rent it uses to calculate your HB to an amount it considers 'appropriate'.[4] It should have evidence which justifies doing so and must use its discretion properly. All the circumstances should be taken into account, including your health and financial circumstances, the special housing-related needs of anyone occupying your home and whether alternative accommodation is available to HB claimants.[5] Local authorities should rarely use their powers to decrease your HB in this way. If your HB is reduced under this rule, apply for a revision or appeal (see Chapters 56 and 57).

Has the local authority used rent officer determinations to calculate your HB?
The local authority may say that it can use its discretion to decrease the amount of rent used to calculate your HB, even though it has already restricted your rent under the rules that use rent officer determinations (see p396).[6] If this applies to you, argue that the local authority should only use its discretion in this way if none of the rent restriction rules apply.[7]

2. The local housing allowance rules

If the local housing allowance rules apply, they determine the amount of rent used to calculate your housing benefit (HB) – called your 'maximum rent' in this *Handbook*.[8] Your maximum rent may be lower than the rent you must pay. **Note:** these rules do *not* apply if you have an excluded tenancy (see p382).

The local housing allowance rules apply if you claim HB or move to a new home while you are entitled to HB, and you are:[9]

- a private tenant. This includes if you have a shared ownership tenancy with a private landlord. **Note:** there are exceptions and other rules may instead apply (see p383);

- a housing association tenant. **Note:** there are exceptions and other rules may instead apply (see p383). These include if your landlord is a registered social landlord (in Wales or Scotland) or a non-profit or 'profit-making registered provider of social housing' (in England). In this case, the social sector rules on p391 (the 'bedroom tax') may apply. If your landlord is a profit-making registered provider of social housing, this exception only applies if your accommodation is available at a rent below the market rate.

How your rent is restricted

The local housing allowance rules restrict your rent for HB purposes to an amount (a local housing allowance) that the local authority considers to be appropriate for you. This is your **'maximum rent'** and is the amount of rent used to calculate your HB.

The local housing allowance is based on the number of bedrooms you are allowed under the rules (known as the 'size criteria' – see p386) or, if it is lower, a 'cap rent'.[10]

Cap rent

Your **'cap rent'** is the rent you are liable (or treated as liable) to pay for your home (including service charges).[11] If you share your accommodation with anyone other than your partner and you are jointly liable for the rent with her/him, the local authority apportions the cap rent between you. **Note:** the local authority may say it has general discretion to decrease your cap rent to an amount it considers appropriate under the rules on p384.[12]

Note:

- If you share accommodation and are jointly liable for the rent (eg, you are joint tenants) with someone other than your partner (or a child included in your claim), and you are not members of the same household, your maximum rent is based on the local housing allowance that applies to you personally (see p386), subject to the cap rent rule – ie, it is based on your share of the rent.
- A rent restriction can be delayed in specified circumstances (see p412).
- You may be able to challenge a rent restriction (see p413).

Examples

Phil, aged 28, shares a privately rented house with four friends. Phil claims HB. The appropriate local housing allowance for him is that for one-bedroom shared accommodation: £80 a week. The rent for the house is £300 a week. His cap rent is £60 (£300 ÷ 5). This is lower than the local housing allowance, so Phil's maximum rent is therefore £60 a week.

Part 4: General rules for other means-tested benefits
Chapter 19: Housing benefit rent restrictions
2. The local housing allowance rules

> May and her partner Dev have a joint tenancy of a private flat. May's cousin lodges with them. May claims HB. The appropriate local housing allowance for her is that for two-bedroom accommodation: £150 a week. The rent for the flat is £210 a week. This is her cap rent. This is higher than the local housing allowance, so May's maximum rent is therefore £150 a week.

Which local housing allowance is appropriate

The local housing allowance that is appropriate for you depends on the area in which you live and the category of dwelling that applies to you. To establish the category of dwelling that applies (see p388), you must first know how many bedrooms you are allowed under the rules, known as the 'size criteria'.

The number of bedrooms you are allowed
You are allowed (up to a maximum of four bedrooms):[13]
- one bedroom for each of the following 'occupiers', each coming only into the first category that applies to her/him:
  - a couple (see p319 for who counts);
  - a 'member of a couple who cannot share a bedroom' (see p410 for who counts);
  - a member of a couple whose partner is a 'member of a couple who cannot share a bedroom';[14]
  - a person aged 16 or over;
  - a 'child who cannot share a bedroom' (see p410 for who counts);
  - two children under 16 of the same sex;
  - two children under 10;
  - a child under 16; *and*
- one or two additional bedrooms in specified situations (see p387).

Note: you are only allowed a bedroom for a 'child who cannot share a bedroom' or a 'member of a couple who cannot share a bedroom' if you have a bedroom in your home that is additional to those you would be allowed if the child or the member of the couple *were* able to share a bedroom. 'Bedroom' is not defined, but see p409 for what may count.

You cannot argue that a category is not applicable if there is no room in your home large enough to accommodate the people in that category.[15]

Occupiers
For the local housing allowance rules, an **'occupier'** is:[16]
- you and anyone else living in the dwelling who the local authority is satisfied occupies your dwelling as a home (other than a joint tenant who is not a member of your household); *and*

- your (or your partner's) son, daughter, stepson or stepdaughter who is in the armed forces deployed on operations who was your non-dependant (see p198) before being deployed, provided s/he intends to return home.

'Occupiers' therefore include not only your partner and children, but also other people – eg, a joint tenant who is a member of your household, a non-dependant or a live-in carer. However, a foster child or child placed with you for adoption under specified provisions does not count as an occupier, but you may qualify for an additional bedroom if you or your partner are a 'qualifying parent or carer' or if the child is a 'person who requires overnight care' (see below).[17]

You can argue that someone is an 'occupier' if s/he normally lives with you, but is temporarily away.[18] However, if you share the care of a child, the child is considered to be occupying the home of the parent with whom s/he normally lives.[19] **Note:** the local authority may use the rules described on p182 to decide whether someone counts as occupying your home.

Examples

Will and Zara have two sons, both under age 10. Zara's nephew, aged 20, lives with them. Will claims HB. He is allowed three bedrooms under the rules: one for Will and Zara, one for the two sons and one for the nephew. The appropriate local housing allowance is that for a dwelling with three bedrooms.

Terry, aged 40, lives with his father in the same household. They are joint tenants. He is allowed two bedrooms under the rules, even though he is claiming HB as a single person.

Additional bedrooms

You are allowed one additional bedroom in the following situations. If both apply, you are allowed two additional bedrooms.[20]

- **Non-resident carers.** If you (or your partner), a person who occupies your dwelling as a home (eg, your child or a non-dependant) or a child or young person in respect of whom you or your partner are a 'qualifying parent or carer' (eg, your foster child) are a 'person who requires overnight care' (see p411 for who counts), you are allowed one additional bedroom for a non-resident carer. Even if more than one person requires overnight care, only one additional bedroom is allowed.

- **Fostering, adoption and kinship carers.** If you (or your partner) are a 'qualifying parent or carer' (ie, certain foster parents and people with whom a child has been placed for adoption – see p411 for who counts), you are allowed one additional bedroom. Even if you (or your partner) have more than one foster child or child placed with you for adoption, only one additional bedroom is allowed.

Part 4: General rules for other means-tested benefits
Chapter 19: Housing benefit rent restrictions
2. The local housing allowance rules

Note:

- The rules were amended from 1 April 2017 to allow an additional bedroom for people living with you who require overnight care. If you were already getting HB on that date and had not been allowed an additional bedroom, the local authority should reassess your HB claim and pay you any arrears due.[21]
- If you live in a dwelling adapted for you under a 'sanctuary scheme' (ie, a multi-agency scheme which provides enhanced security measures to enable households at risk of domestic violence to remain safely in their homes), and your rent is restricted because you have more bedrooms than the rules allow, you can argue that the rules discriminate against you.[22] It is not yet clear if the government will amend the rules. See AskCPAG.org.uk and CPAG's *Welfare Rights Bulletin* for updates.
- There are a number of other situations when you may need more bedrooms than shown above – eg, if you need an additional room to store equipment required because of a severe disability, or if you provide accommodation for a disabled person under an adult placement scheme, or if you share the care of your child but s/he counts as normally living with her/his other parent. You should appeal if you are affected, but your appeal may be held up while the courts are considering other cases.

Example

Seamus and Elaine are the foster parents of two children. Their non-dependent son, aged 24, lives with them. They are allowed three bedrooms under the rules: one for Seamus and Elaine, one for their son and one additional room because they are each a 'qualifying parent or carer'. The appropriate local housing allowance is that for a dwelling with three bedrooms.

Categories of dwelling

The category of dwelling that applies to you depends on how many bedrooms you are allowed under the rules (see p386) and whether or not you are living in shared accommodation.

One-bedroom shared accommodation

The one-bedroom shared accommodation category of dwelling applies if you are only allowed one bedroom under the rules) and:[23]

- you are under 35 (even if you do not live in shared accommodation). See below for exceptions; *or*
- you (and your partner) live in shared accommodation. You count as living in shared accommodation if you do not have the exclusive use of at least two rooms, or the exclusive use of one room as well as the exclusive use of a bathroom, a toilet and a kitchen or facilities for cooking. See below for exceptions.

There are exceptions. This category of dwelling does *not* apply (even if you live in shared accommodation) if:[24]

* you have a non-dependant living with you (see p198); *or*
* you (or your partner) qualify for a severe disability premium; *or*
* you are under the age of 22 and:
  - were provided with accommodation by the local authority under specified provisions.[25] **Note:** in some cases, you cannot claim HB if you are being, or were previously, looked after by a local authority (see p948); *or*
  - were looked after by (in the care of), or under the supervision of, a local authority under specific legal provisions after you turned 16; *or*
  - ceased to be subject to a compulsory supervision order under section 83 of the Children's Hearings (Scotland) Act 2011 which had continued after you turned 16. **Note:** there are exceptions; *or*
* you are a single claimant aged at least 25 but under 35 and:
  - have been living in one or more hostels for homeless people for three months or more (this does not have to be continuous) and while living there you have accepted support services to assist you in being rehabilitated or resettled in the community; *or*
  - are an offender subject to specific multi-agency public protection management arrangements. It is understood that this applies if you are a level 2 or 3 offender.[26]

Note: if the shared accommodation category of dwelling does not apply to you, the DWP says that your HB should be based on the local housing allowance for one-bedroom self-contained accommodation (see below).[27] This applies even if you live in shared accommodation.

One-bedroom self-contained accommodation

The one-bedroom self-contained accommodation category of dwelling applies if you are allowed one bedroom under the rules (see p386).[28] You must have:

* the exclusive use of at least two rooms; *or*
* the exclusive use of one room as well as the exclusive use of a bathroom, a toilet and a kitchen or facilities for cooking.

You have the 'exclusive use' of a room if you have the legal right to exclude others from the room.[29]

Rooms

'**Room**' means a bedroom or a 'room suitable for living in', other than one you share with someone who is not a member of your household, a non-dependant or someone who pays rent to you or your partner.[30]

Part 4: General rules for other means-tested benefits
Chapter 19: Housing benefit rent restrictions
2. The local housing allowance rules

Dwellings with two or more bedrooms
If you are allowed more than one bedroom under the rules, the category of dwelling that applies is that for a dwelling with the number of bedrooms you are allowed (see p386), up to a maximum of four.[31] So this category applies, for example, if you are a lone parent or a member of a couple with children, you have a non-dependant living with you, you are a 'person who requires overnight care', someone who lives with you is a 'member of a couple who cannot share a bedroom', you are a 'qualifying parent or carer' (see p411 for who counts), or you are a joint tenant with someone who is a member of your household.

Local housing allowance rates

Local housing allowances for each category of dwelling are normally set by the rent officer annually on the last working day of January, to take effect the following April. From April 2020, the local housing allowance is the lowest of two figures:[32]

- the amount of rent at the 30th percentile point of local market rents for assured tenancies in what is known as a 'broad rental market area'; *or*
- for the specified categories of dwelling below, the amount listed.

Category of dwelling	Maximum local housing allowance
One-bedroom shared accommodation	£295.49
One bedroom self-contained accommodation	£295.49
Two-bedroom accommodation	£365.92
Three-bedroom accommodation	£441.86
Four-bedroom accommodation	£593.75

See lha-direct.voa.gov.uk for the current local housing allowance rates in your area.

How long the restriction applies

The amount of your restricted rent (your 'maximum rent') is based on the local housing allowance that is appropriate at the time your claim is assessed. Your HB is based on this amount until the next time the local authority assesses your claim.[33] This is usually only annually (on 1 April), even if the amount of the local housing allowance changes. When the local authority reassesses your claim, it uses the local housing allowance that is then appropriate. Some changes of circumstance can lead to an earlier reassessment – ie, if:[34]

- there is a change in the category of dwelling that applies to you (see p388) – ie, you are allowed more or fewer bedrooms because, for instance, someone has moved in with you or has moved out, or your child has reached aged 16 and is allowed her/his own bedroom; *or*

- your partner or a child included in your claim (see p323) (or a relative of yours or your partner who lives in the same accommodation as you without a separate right to do so) dies; *or*
- there is a change that affects the amount of your cap rent (see p385) – eg, the rent you pay goes up or down; *or*
- you move to a new home.

Your maximum rent is then based on the local housing allowance that is appropriate on the date of the change.[35]

Example

Cleo rents a three-bedroom house from a private landlord. She pays £170 a week rent. This is her cap rent. She has one son, aged seven. The appropriate local housing allowance is that for a dwelling with two bedrooms. When she claims HB, this is £105. Cleo's maximum rent is therefore £105.

Cleo's sister Sue comes to live with her. As there has been a change in the category of dwelling that applies to Cleo (this is now a dwelling with three bedrooms), the local authority reassesses her claim. The local housing allowance for a dwelling with three bedrooms is now £158. Cleo's maximum rent is now therefore £158.

If you are considering renting accommodation

If you are considering renting accommodation privately, you are likely to claim HB and the local housing allowance rules apply, you may want to find out the rent figure that will be used to calculate it. If you are already claiming benefit, you may wish to find out the rent figure that will be used when your claim is reassessed (usually annually).

Check which category of dwelling applies to you (see p388) and work out the appropriate local housing allowance. Then check the amount of the appropriate local housing allowance in your area at lha-direct.voa.gov.uk.

3. The social sector rules: the 'bedroom tax'

If the social sector rules apply, they determine the amount of rent used to calculate your housing benefit (HB) – called your 'maximum rent' in this *Handbook*.[36] Your maximum rent may be lower than the rent you must pay.

The social sector rules usually apply if you are a local authority or housing association tenant and you are living in accommodation that has more bedrooms than you are allowed under the rules (known as the 'size criteria' – see p394).[37] The social sector rules are commonly referred to as the 'bedroom tax', or by the DWP as the 'removal of the spare room subsidy' or the 'under-occupation charge'.

Part 4: General rules for other means-tested benefits
Chapter 19: Housing benefit rent restrictions
3. The social sector rules: the 'bedroom tax'

Note: there are exceptions. Your rent *cannot* be restricted under the social sector rules if:[38]

- you are getting pension-age HB (see p188); *or*
- you are getting working-age HB (see p188) and you or your partner are at least pension age. **Note:** see below if you are a member of a mixed-age couple – ie, only one of you is at least pension age; *or*
- any of the other rent restriction rules described in this chapter apply. See p384, p396 and p403; *or*
- you are a housing association tenant and your tenancy is one of the excluded tenancies listed on pp382–83 (other than the last one), unless your landlord is a registered housing association; *or*
- you have a shared ownership tenancy – ie, you are buying part of your house or flat and renting the rest; *or*
- your rent is for mooring charges for a houseboat or for identifiable payments for caravan or mobile home site fees;[39] *or*
- you live in specified types of temporary accommodation for homeless people provided by a local authority or a registered housing association.

Are you a member of a mixed-age couple?

If you are a member of a mixed-age couple (ie, only one of you is a least pension age), and one of you is getting working-age HB (see p188), the local authority may say that your rent can be restricted under the social sector rules if you are the one who is at least pension age and are the HB claimant;[40] *and*

– you are prevented from claiming UC for one of the reasons listed on p173 and, in addition, you cannot qualify for PC; *and*

– as you would otherwise be unable to qualify for HB, you are treated as being under pension age for the assessment of your award of HB.

Try to argue that this rule simply allows your award of HB to continue and that, because you are actually at least pension age, the social sector rules do not apply.

How your rent is restricted

If you are the only person liable for the rent for your home (or you are jointly liable, but only with your partner), your 'maximum rent' is determined under the following steps.[41] **Note:** if you are jointly liable for your rent with someone other than your partner (ie, with a joint tenant) the rules are different (see p393).

- **Step one:** establish the number of bedrooms in your home. 'Bedroom' is not defined, but see p409 for what may count.
- **Step two:** work out how many bedrooms you are allowed under the rules for all the people who occupy your home (see p394).
- **Step three:** calculate the amount of rent that can be covered by HB. This is known as your 'eligible rent' (see p191) and is the contractual rent for the

whole dwelling minus any ineligible charges – eg, for fuel or services. If the number of bedrooms in Step one is the same as or lower than the number in Step two, this is your maximum rent – ie, your rent is *not* restricted.

- **Step four:** if the number of bedrooms in Step one is more than the number in Step two, your maximum rent is the amount in Step three reduced by:
  - 14 per cent if you have one too many bedrooms; *or*
  - 25 per cent if you have at least two too many bedrooms.

If it appears to the local authority that the amount in Step four is still too high to be met by HB, it has a general discretion to restrict your maximum rent further.[42]

Note: a restriction can be delayed in specified circumstances (see p412). You may be able to challenge a rent restriction (see p413).

Example

Raj and Indira rent a two-bedroom flat from a housing association. Their rent is £140 a week. Indira claims HB.

Step one: there are two bedrooms in their home.

Step two: they are only allowed one bedroom under the rules (see p394).

Step three: the amount of the rent that can be covered by HB (the 'eligible rent') is £140 a week.

Step four: because they have one more bedroom than the number allowed in Step two, the amount in Step three is reduced by 14 per cent.

14% x £140 = £19.60. Therefore, Indira's maximum rent is restricted to £120.40 (£140 – £19.60).

If you are a joint tenant

If you (and your partner) are liable for the rent with at least one other person (eg, you are a joint tenant with someone other than your partner), the local authority apportions the amount in Step three or Step four (as the case may be) between you, taking all the circumstances into account, including the number of people and the proportion of rent each pays.[43]

Example

Emma and Dave are joint tenants of a four-bedroom council house. They are not a couple. Their rent is £210 a week. Emma pays £140 and Dave pays £70. Emma is an approved foster parent. Dave claims HB.

Step one: the number of bedrooms in Dave's home is four.

Step two: he is allowed three bedrooms under the rules (see p394): one for himself, one for Emma and an additional room because Emma counts as a 'qualifying parent or carer'.

Step three: the amount of the rent that can be covered by HB (the 'eligible rent') is £210.

Part 4: General rules for other means-tested benefits
Chapter 19: Housing benefit rent restrictions
3. The social sector rules: the 'bedroom tax'

Step four: because Dave has one more bedroom than the number allowed in Step two, the amount in Step three is reduced by 14 per cent. 14% x £210 = £29.40
£210 – £29.40 = £180.60
Dave pays one-third of the rent, and the local authority apportions the maximum rent accordingly. One-third of £180.60 = £60.20
Therefore, Dave's maximum rent is £60.20.
Note: if Emma were also to claim HB, her maximum rent would be two-thirds of £180.60 = £120.40.

The number of bedrooms you are allowed

Under the rules (the 'size criteria'), you are allowed:[44]
- one bedroom for each of the following 'occupiers' (see below), each coming only into the first category that is applicable:
  - a couple (see p319 for who counts);
  - a 'member of a couple who cannot share a bedroom' (see p410 for who counts);
  - a member of a couple whose partner is a 'member of a couple who cannot share a bedroom';[45]
  - a person who is aged 16 or over;
  - a 'child who cannot share a bedroom' (see p410 for who counts);
  - two children under 16 of the same sex;
  - two children under 10;
  - a child under 16; *and*
- one or more additional bedrooms in specified circumstances (see p395).

You cannot argue that a category is not applicable if there is no room in your home large enough to accommodate the people in that category.[46]

Unlike the local housing allowance rules, there is no maximum number of bedrooms.

Occupiers

For the social sector rules, an **'occupier'** is anyone who the local authority is satisfied occupies your dwelling as a home.[47] 'Occupiers' therefore include not only you and your partner or children included in your claim but also other people – eg, a joint tenant, a non-dependant or a live-in carer. However, a foster child or child placed with you for adoption under specified provisions does not count as an occupier, but you may qualify for an additional bedroom if you or your partner (or another person jointly liable for the rent with you) are a 'qualifying parent or carer' or if the child is a 'person who requires overnight care' (see p395).[48]

Note:
- The local authority must include a member of the armed forces deployed on operations as an occupier if s/he is your (or your partner's) son, daughter, stepson or stepdaughter who was your non-dependant (see p198) before being deployed and s/he intends to return home.[49]
- You can argue that someone counts as occupying your home if s/he normally lives with you but is temporarily away.[50] However, if you share the care of a child, the child is considered to be occupying the home of only one parent – the parent with whom the child normally lives.[51] **Note:** the local authority may use the rules described on p182 to decide whether someone counts as occupying your home.

Additional bedrooms

You are allowed one additional bedroom in the following situations. If both apply, you are allowed two additional bedrooms.[52]

- **Non-resident carers.** If you (or your partner), a person who occupies your dwelling as a home (eg, your child or a non-dependant) or a child or young person in respect of whom you or your partner are a 'qualifying parent or carer' (eg, your foster child) are a 'person who requires overnight care' (see p411 for who counts), you are entitled to one additional bedroom for a non-resident carer. Even if more than one person requires overnight care, only one additional bedroom is allowed.
- **Fostering, adoption and kinship carers.** If you (or your partner) are a 'qualifying parent or carer' (ie, certain foster parents and people with whom a child has been placed for adoption – see p411 for who counts), you are allowed one additional bedroom. Even if, for example, you (or your partner) have more than one foster child, only one bedroom is allowed.

In addition, if you are jointly liable for the rent with someone other than your partner (eg, a joint tenant), you are allowed an additional bedroom for her/him if s/he (or her/his partner) is a 'person who requires overnight care' or a 'qualifying parent or carer'.[53] You are allowed two additional bedrooms if both conditions are satisfied.

Note:
- The rules were amended from 1 April 2017 to allow an additional bedroom for people living with you who require overnight care. If you were already getting HB on that date and had not been allowed an additional bedroom, the local authority should reassess your HB claim and pay you any arrears due.[54]
- If you live in a dwelling adapted for you under a 'sanctuary scheme' (see p388), and your rent is restricted because you have more bedrooms than the rules allow, you can argue that the rules discriminate against you.[55] It is not yet clear if the government will amend the rules. See AskCPAG.org.uk and CPAG's *Welfare Rights Bulletin* for updates.

Part 4: General rules for other means-tested benefits
Chapter 19: Housing benefit rent restrictions
4. Hostels, houseboats, mobile homes, caravans and boarders

- There are a number of other situations when you may need additional bedrooms – eg, if you need an additional room to store equipment required because of a severe disability, or if you provide accommodation for a disabled person under an adult placement scheme, or if you share the care of your child but s/he counts as normally living with her/his other parent. You should appeal if you are affected, but your appeal may be held up while the courts are considering other cases.[56]

Examples

Angus lives with his wife and child in a four-bedroom council house. He claims HB. Angus gets the daily living component of personal independence payment and needs a carer to stay with him overnight. He is therefore a 'person who requires overnight care'. Under the social sector rules, he is allowed three bedrooms under the rules: one for himself and his wife, one for his child and one for a non-resident carer. He therefore has one too many bedrooms and his rent is restricted.

Bill, an approved foster parent, shares a four-bedroom council house with his mother and father. His foster daughter lives with them. Bill's mother is severely disabled and requires, and receives, overnight care. Bill and his father are joint tenants. Bill claims HB. Bill is allowed two bedrooms under the rules: one for him and one for his mother and father. However, he is allowed one additional bedroom because he is a 'qualifying parent or carer' and one additional bedroom because his mother is a 'person who requires overnight care'. So he is allowed a total of four bedrooms. For the purposes of the social sector rules, he does not have too many bedrooms and his rent is therefore not restricted.

4. **Hostels, houseboats, mobile homes, caravans and boarders**

If you live in certain types of accommodation, the local authority uses 'determinations' made by the rent officer (see p398) to restrict the amount of rent it uses to calculate your housing benefit (HB) – called your 'maximum rent' in this *Handbook*. These are sometimes called the local reference rent rules. Your 'maximum rent' is usually the lowest of the rent officer's determinations, even if the rent you pay is higher.[57] **Note:** these rules do not apply if you have an excluded tenancy (see p382).

These rules apply if:[58]

- you live in a hostel, houseboat, mobile home or caravan; *or*
- your rent includes board *and* attendance.

In rare cases, these rules also apply if:
- your landlord is a registered housing association, or is a county council (if you live in a caravan or mobile home provided on a travellers' site[59]), or you are renting a caravan, mobile home or houseboat (and you are also liable to make payments to a local authority – eg, for the site or mooring fees). However, they only apply if the local authority considers your rent to be unreasonably high (or, in some cases, your accommodation to be unreasonably large). Otherwise, you have an 'excluded tenancy' (see p382); or
- your tenancy was a local authority or new town letting, but it has been transferred to a new owner. However, they only apply if there has been a rent increase since the transfer; *and*
  - the local authority considers your rent to be unreasonably high; *or*
  - if the transfer took place before 7 October 2002, the local authority considers your accommodation to be unreasonably large.

  Otherwise, you have an 'excluded tenancy' (see p382).

Note: if you have been getting HB continuously since before 7 April 2008, these rules may still apply if you live in other types of accommodation – eg, if you rent a private house or flat. See p398 of the 2019/2020 edtion of this *Handbook* for further information.

How your rent is restricted

Under these rules, the local authority asks the rent officer to make determinations about your rent for your home and uses these to establish the amount of rent used to calculate your HB – called your **'maximum rent'** in this *Handbook*. The determinations include:
- a 'claim-related rent', based on the size of your accommodation and the rent you pay (see p399); *and*
- a 'local reference rent', based on average rents for specific types of accommodation in the area in which you live (see p402); *and*
- a 'single room rent', based on average rents for shared accommodation in your area (see p402).

Your maximum rent is then either:[60]
- the lowest of the claim-related rent (see p399) or the local reference rent (see p402); *or*
- if you are a 'young individual' (see p402) and it is relevant, the lowest of the single room rent (see p402) or the claim-related rent (minus any payments for meals).

Part 4: General rules for other means-tested benefits
Chapter 19: Housing benefit rent restrictions
4. Hostels, houseboats, mobile homes, caravans and boarders

> *Example*
>
> Jo and Louis are a couple who rent a three-bedroom mobile home with a living room and separate dining room. They pay rent of £120 a week. The rent officer decides that the accommodation is too big and that the rent is too high, so determines a claim-related rent of £90 and a local reference rent of £80. Their maximum rent is therefore £80 a week.

Note:

- Your maximum rent only covers the rent you pay for residential accommodation.
- If you are in shared accommodation, your maximum rent can be apportioned between you and the people with whom you share.[61]
- A rent restriction can be delayed in specified circumstances (see p412).
- If you have been continuously entitled to, and in receipt of, HB for the same property since 5 October 1997, your maximum rent is the local reference rent plus half the difference between the local reference rent and the claim-related rent.[62]
- If you are considering renting accommodation, the local reference rent rules apply and you are likely to claim HB, you can apply to the local authority for a pre-tenancy determination to find out the rent that will be used to calculate it (see p403).
- The local authority is likely to say it has general discretion to decrease your maximum rent to an amount it considers appropriate (but see p384).[63]
- You may be able to challenge a rent restriction (see p413).

How long the restriction applies

Once your maximum rent is set, your HB is paid on the basis of this until the next time the local authority refers your claim to the rent officer (usually annually). However, if you negotiate with your landlord and s/he agrees a new rent which is lower than the maximum rent, your HB is recalculated using your new rent.[64]

The rent officer's determinations about your rent

In most cases, the local authority must apply to the rent officer and ask her/him to make 'determinations'. The rent officer then makes determinations about the rent for your home (see p399), comparing it with the rent for other private sector tenancies in the area. S/he also makes determinations that indicate the average rents for specific types of accommodation (see p402). **Note:** the local authority *cannot* apply to the rent officer in specified situations.[65] This means that in some cases a determination made for a previous tenant may be valid for your HB claim.

When the local authority must apply to the rent officer

The local authority must apply to the rent officer if you make a new claim for HB or move to a new home while you are entitled to HB, or if the last reference to the rent officer was made in respect of your home at least 52 weeks ago.[66] It must also apply if there has been a specified change in circumstances since the rent officer's last determinations (see below). **Note:** the local authority must also apply to the rent officer if your HB was being restricted under the local housing allowance rules on p384, but these no longer apply – eg, if the home you rent was sold to a housing association and the rules that use rent officer determinations now apply instead.

Specified changes in circumstances

The local authority must apply to the rent officer if there has been one of the following changes in circumstances since a rent officer's determination.[67]

- The number of occupiers has changed (except in a hostel). Argue that this should *not* apply if someone who normally lives with you is only away temporarily.[68]
- There has been a substantial change in the condition of the dwelling or the terms of the tenancy (other than a term relating to the rent).
- There has been an increase in the rent under a term of the tenancy, unless the previous determination was a significantly high, size-related or exceptionally high rent determination (see below).[69]
- A size-related rent determination was made and a child living with you has reached the age of 10 or 16, or there has since been a change in the composition of the household – eg, someone has moved in or moved out, but not if the person is your (or your partner's) son, daughter, stepson or stepdaughter who usually lives with you, who is in the armed forces away on (or who has returned home from) operations.
- The size of accommodation you are allowed under the rules (see p400) is affected because:
  - you or your partner, a person who occupies your dwelling as a home, or or a child or young person in respect of whom you or your partner are a 'qualifying parent or carer' (eg, your foster child) become, or cease to be, a 'person who requires overnight care' (see p411); *or*
  - you or your partner become or cease to be a 'qualifying parent or carer' (see p411); *or*
  - a child becomes, or stops being, a 'child who cannot share a bedroom' (see p410); *or*
  - a person occupying your dwelling as a home becomes, or stops being, a 'member of a couple who cannot share a bedroom' (see p410).

The claim-related rent

The '**claim-related rent**' is the lowest of the determinations below or, if no such determination is made, the rent you are supposed to pay.[70]

- A '**significantly high rent determination**' is made if your rent is significantly higher than that paid for similar tenancies and dwellings in the immediate

Part 4: General rules for other means-tested benefits
Chapter 19: Housing benefit rent restrictions
4. Hostels, houseboats, mobile homes, caravans and boarders

area around your home. It is the amount your landlord might reasonably be paid for your tenancy.[71]

- An 'exceptionally high rent determination' is made if the rent officer considers the 'rent payable' for your home to be exceptionally high. It is the highest amount your landlord might reasonably be paid for an assured tenancy in the neighbourhood for a home that is the same size as yours (or the size you are allowed under the rules – see below).[72]

- A 'size-related rent determination' is made if your accommodation is larger than you are allowed under the rules (see below). It is the amount your landlord might reasonably be paid for a similar tenancy of an appropriate size for you in the vicinity.[73] **Note:** if you are a single person under 35, the rent officer must also identify a single room rent (see p402).

The size of accommodation you are allowed

To work out the size of accommodation you are allowed under the rules (known as the 'size criteria'), the rent officer allows you one bedroom or 'room suitable for living in' for each of the following 'occupiers' (see below), each coming only into the first category for which s/he is eligible:[74]

- a couple (see p319 for who counts);
- a 'member of a couple who cannot share a bedroom' (see p410 for who counts);
- a member of a couple whose partner is a 'member of a couple who cannot share a bedroom';[75]
- a person who is aged 16 or over;
- two children under 16 of the same sex;
- a 'child who cannot share a bedroom' (see p410 for who counts);
- two children under 10;
- a child under 16.

Note: you are only allowed a bedroom for a 'child who cannot share a bedroom' or a 'member of a couple who cannot share a bedroom' if you have a bedroom in your home that is additional to those you would be allowed if the child or the member of the couple *were* able to share a bedroom. 'Bedroom' is not defined, but see p409 for what may count.

You are allowed an **additional bedroom** (or 'room suitable for living in') in the following situations. If both apply, you are allowed two additional bedrooms (or rooms suitable for living in).[76]

- **Non-resident carers.** If you (or your partner), a person who occupies your dwelling as a home (eg, your child or a non-dependant) or a child or young person in respect of whom you or your partner are a 'qualifying parent or carer' (eg, your foster child) are a 'person who requires overnight care' (see p411 for who counts), you are allowed one additional room for a non-resident carer. Even if more than one person requires overnight care, only one additional room is allowed.

- **Fostering, adoption and kinship carers.** If you (or your partner) are a 'qualifying parent or carer' (see p411 for who counts), you are allowed one additional bedroom. Even if, for example, you (or your partner) have more than one foster child, only one additional room is allowed.

Note: unlike the local housing allowance rules, there is no maximum number of bedrooms.

You are also allowed the following number of **'rooms suitable for living in'**.

Number of occupiers	Number of rooms
Fewer than four	One
Four to six	Two
Seven or more	Three

If any of the rooms in your home are not suitable for living in (eg, because of their size or lack of ventilation), argue that they should be ignored.

A person counts as an **'occupier'** if the local authority includes her/him on the form used to refer your tenancy to the rent officer.[77] This can include people in addition to your partner or children included in your claim – eg, a non-dependant or a live-in carer. It does not include a foster child or a child placed with you for adoption under specified provisions, but you may be entitled to an additional bedroom if you (or your partner) are a 'qualifying parent or carer' (see p411) or if the child is a 'person who requires overnight care'.[78]

Note:

- Someone also counts as an occupier if s/he is your (or your partner's) son, daughter, stepson or stepdaughter who usually lives with you and who is in the armed forces, even when s/he is deployed on operations, provided s/he intends to return home.[79]
- You can argue that someone is an occupier if s/he normally lives with you, but is temporarily away.[80] However, if you share the care of a child, the child is considered to be occupying the home of only one parent – the parent with whom s/he normally lives.[81] **Note:** the local authority may use the rules described on p182 to decide whether someone counts as occupying your home.

Example
Alice and Lee have three children: two sons, aged 12 and 14, and a daughter, aged 17. Under the rules, they are allowed one room for themselves, one for their sons and one for their daughter – three bedrooms, as well as two other 'rooms suitable for living in'. They are therefore allowed five rooms, as well as a kitchen, bathroom and toilet.

Part 4: General rules for other means-tested benefits
Chapter 19: Housing benefit rent restrictions
4. Hostels, houseboats, mobile homes, caravans and boarders

The local reference rent and single room rent

The rent officer makes determinations that indicate the average rents for specific types of accommodation in a 'broad rental market area'. These are the following.

- The 'local reference rent' is the mid-point of 'reasonable market rents' for assured tenancies in the broad rental market area appropriate to the size of property in which you live (or the size you are allowed – see p400).[82]
- The 'single room rent' is the midpoint of 'reasonable market rents' for assured tenancies in the broad rental market area in which the tenant has exclusive use of one bedroom only, and other than that only shares a living room, kitchen, toilet and bathroom, and makes no payment for board and attendance.[83] **Note:** it is only used to calculate your HB if you are a 'young individual' (see below).

Young individuals

In general, you count as a 'young individual' if you are a single claimant under 35. If you are a 'young individual', in most cases the rent officer identifies a single room rent. Your 'maximum rent' (see p397) is based on this figure unless you qualify for a severe disability premium as part of your applicable amount or you have a non-dependant living with you (see p198).[84]

Note: you do *not* count as a 'young individual' if:[85]

- your landlord is a registered housing association; *or*
- you are under the age of 22 and:
  - were looked after by (in the care of), or under the supervision of, a local authority under specific legal provisions after you turned 16 or were provided with accommodation by the local authority under specific provisions; *or*
  - ceased to be subject to a compulsory supervision order under section 83 of the Children's Hearings (Scotland) Act 2011 which had continued after you turned 16. **Note:** there are exceptions; *or*
- you are a 'person who requires overnight care' (see p411 for who counts); *or*
- you are a 'qualifying parent or carer' (see p411 for who counts); *or*
- you are at least 25 but under 35 and:
  - have been living in one or more hostels for homeless people for three months or more (this does not have to be continuous) and while living in such a hostel have accepted support services to assist you in being rehabilitated or resettled in the community; *or*
  - are an offender subject to specific multi-agency public protection management arrangements. It is understood that this applies if you are a level 2 or 3 offender.[86]

Service charges

The local authority notifies the rent officer of the amount of rent you are supposed to pay, whether this includes service charges and the amount of the charges that can and cannot be met by HB (see p193).[87] The claim-related rent (see p399) does not include ineligible charges unless you live in one-room accommodation and the landlord provides substantial board and attendance. In this case, the claim-related rent and local reference rent (though not the single room rent) include charges for meals.[88]

If you are considering renting accommodation

If you are considering renting accommodation, the rules that use rent office determinations apply and you are likely to claim HB, you might want to find out the rent figure that will be used to calculate it. In this case, you can apply for a **pre-tenancy determination**.[89] You can also apply if you are already receiving HB and your tenancy is due for renewal, but your tenancy agreement must have started at least 11 months before you apply.[90]

Note:
- You must apply in writing on the form approved by your local authority. Both you and your prospective landlord must sign it.[91]
- A pre-tenancy determination is usually valid for a year.[92] So, if someone else applied for a pre-tenancy determination for your accommodation in the previous 12 months, it also applies to you.
- You cannot appeal against a pre-tenancy determination. However, if you accept the tenancy and claim HB, you can ask for it to be redetermined (see below). If you subsequently negotiate a lower rent with your landlord which is lower than your 'maximum rent', your HB is recalculated using your new rent.[93]

---

5. Exempt accommodation and claimants: the old scheme rules

More generous rent restriction rules (called the 'old scheme' rules in this *Handbook*) apply if you are claiming housing benefit (HB) and you live in specified types of temporary or supported accommodation, known as 'exempt accommodation'. These rules can also apply if you have been getting HB since 1 January 1996, generally for the same property – ie, if you are an 'exempt claimant'. These rules are sometimes called the 'pre-January 1996 rules'.

Note: you cannot usually qualify for HB if you come under the universal credit (UC) system (see p23). However, if you live in 'exempt accommodation', the help you get with your rent for this is not provided in UC. Instead you can claim HB for the rent you pay and the old scheme rules apply.

Exempt accommodation

The old scheme rules apply to you if you live in what is known as 'exempt accommodation', whenever you started living there – eg, even if this was recently.

Part 4: General rules for other means-tested benefits
Chapter 19: Housing benefit rent restrictions
5. Exempt accommodation and claimants: the old scheme rules

Your accommodation is exempt accommodation if it is:[94]

- temporary accommodation (resettlement places) for people without a settled way of life, funded by the government; *or*
- accommodation provided by a housing association, non-metropolitan county council, registered charity or voluntary organisation and that body, or a person acting on its behalf, also provides you with care, support or supervision.[95] You must need the care, support or supervision and it must be more than a token or minimal amount.[96] Even if the care, support or supervision provided by your landlord duplicates other provisions (eg, in a local authority care plan), you can still count as living in exempt accommodation.[97] **Note:** if the person (or body) providing the care, support or supervision has a contract with the local authority to provide these, but is not providing the accommodation, the decision maker is likely to say it is not exempt accommodation.[98]

Exempt claimants: getting housing benefit since 1 January 1996

The old scheme rules also apply to you if you are what is known as an 'exempt claimant' – ie, you are a private tenant (or, in exceptional cases, a local authority or housing association tenant) and you:[99]

- have been continuously entitled to and in receipt of HB since 1 January 1996; *and*
- continue to occupy the same property as your home (except if you are forced to move because fire, flood or natural catastrophe makes it uninhabitable).

Provided that, when you make a new claim for HB, you are *not* someone to whom the local housing allowance rules would now apply (see p384):[100]

- breaks in your HB claim of up to four weeks are ignored; *and*
- an exemption can be transferred to you if you claim HB because:
  - an exempt claimant dies and you are a member of her/his family, or her/his relative (see p412 for who counts) occupying the same accommodation without a separate right to do so. You must continue to occupy the same property and claim within four weeks of the death; *or*
  - your partner (who was exempt) has been detained in custody and is not entitled to HB under the temporary absence rules (see p182). You must continue to occupy the same property and claim within four weeks of her/his detention; *or*
  - your partner (who was exempt) has left the dwelling and you claim within four weeks of the date s/he left.

The exemption can only be transferred if the exempt claimant was in receipt of HB at the time s/he died (or left the dwelling).[101] If it cannot be transferred, other rent restriction rules may apply when you make a new claim.

Note: if you are thinking of making any changes to your claim, check whether this would mean these rules no longer apply. They are usually more generous than the other rent restriction rules.

If you are a local authority or housing association tenant

You cannot count as an exempt claimant if you are a local authority or registered housing association tenant unless:[102]

- you (or your partner) are at least pension age (see p780); *or*
- the old scheme rules applied to you on or before 31 March 2013 – ie, using these rules, the local authority:
  - restricted your rent; *or*
  - decided that your accommodation was too large or your rent was too high, but did not restrict your rent because the rules for those in a protected group applied (see p406), or the restriction was delayed for either of the reasons on p412.

Note: any local authority and registered housing association tenant could count as an exempt claimant before 3 March 2014. Your local authority may have applied the social sector rules to you in error before this date. See p400 of the 2016/17 edition of this *Handbook* for information.

How your rent is restricted

If the old scheme rules apply, they determine the amount of rent used to calculate your HB – called your 'maximum rent' in this *Handbook*. This amount may be lower than the rent you must pay. Your **maximum rent** is either:

- your contractual rent minus ineligible services. It only covers the rent you pay for residential accommodation. If you are in shared accommodation, the rent is apportioned between you and the people with whom you share;[103] *or*
- if the local authority decides your rent should be restricted because your accommodation is unreasonably large (see p406) or your rent is unreasonably high (see p406), the amount it considers appropriate.[104]

If the local authority restricts your rent, it must take into account the cost of suitable alternative accommodation (see p407 for what counts) and other circumstances that are reasonably relevant to the decision – eg, pregnancy, the difficulty of finding other suitable accommodation and whether it would have to rehouse you if you had to move.[105] It should not be unduly influenced by the amount of subsidy it is paid by the government, but can take this into account when deciding on a reasonable level of rent. Your maximum rent cannot be reduced below the amount of rent payable for suitable alternative accommodation.[106]

Part 4: General rules for other means-tested benefits
Chapter 19: Housing benefit rent restrictions
5. Exempt accommodation and claimants: the old scheme rules

Note:
- If you are in a protected group (see below), your rent cannot be restricted unless cheaper suitable alternative accommodation is available and it is reasonable to expect you to move.
- A rent restriction can be delayed in some circumstances (see p412).
- You may be able to challenge a rent restriction (see p413).

Is your accommodation unreasonably large?

Your accommodation counts as unreasonably large if it is larger than what is reasonably needed for you and anyone else who occupies the accommodation.[107] This should include whether you need additional space – eg, because you or someone who lives with you has a disability, or someone who lives elsewhere visits you regularly. When deciding whether your accommodation is unreasonably large, the local authority must take account of suitable alternative accommodation (see p407) occupied by other households of the same size.[108]

Is your rent unreasonably high?

Your rent (including service charges and licence fees) counts as too high if it is unreasonably high for you to have to pay compared with that for suitable alternative accommodation (see p407) elsewhere.[109] In making the comparison, the local authority must consider the full range of rents that could be paid for such accommodation and not just the cheapest.[110] It can consider subsidised rents (eg, by public funding) even if your rent is not subsidised.[111] If your rent is within the range or just above it, the local authority may find it difficult to justify finding your rent to be unreasonably high.[112]

Note: when deciding whether your rent is unreasonably high, the local authority may ask a rent officer to assess what a reasonable rent for your property would be, but the figures are not binding. The local authority (not the rent officer) must decide whether your rent is unreasonably high, using different criteria from that used by the rent officer.[113]

Are you in a protected group?

Even if the the local authority decides that your rent or the size of your accommodation is unreasonable, if you are in a 'protected group', your rent can only be restricted if:[114]
- cheaper suitable alternative accommodation is available to you (see p407); *and*
- it is reasonable to expect you to move (see p408).

You are in a protected group if any of the people the local authority must take into account:[115]
- are at least pension age (see p780); *or*
- satisfy any of the tests for having limited capability for work or being incapable of work;[116] *or*

- have a child (including a 'qualifying young person') living with them for whom they are responsible (see p326).

The local authority must take into account you, your partner, any child(ren) included in your claim and any of your (or your partner's) relatives (see p412 for who counts) who live in the same dwelling as you without a separate right to do so.[117]

Suitable alternative accommodation

'Suitable alternative accommodation' must be suitable for the age and health of all the people that the local authority must take into account, having regard to the nature of the accommodation and the facilities available.[118] The local authority must consider these factors, even if you do not raise your housing needs yourself.[119]

The local authority must take into account you, your partner, any child(ren) included in your claim and any of your (or your partner's) relatives (see p412 for who counts) who live in the same dwelling as you without a separate right to do so.[120] The local authority must compare your home with 'alternative accommodation'.

- It is not sufficient for the local authority simply to show that cheaper or smaller alternative accommodation exists.
- It cannot just compare homes with the same number of bedrooms. It must try to establish what other facilities are available.[121]
- It must compare your home with other properties offering the same security of tenure – eg, if you have an assured tenancy, the local authority cannot rely on comparisons with accommodation that is let on an assured shorthold tenancy, or with council or housing association properties.[122]
- It does not have to exclude properties which you cannot take because the landlord wants a deposit that you cannot afford.[123] However, if you are in a 'protected group', you might be able to argue that the accommodation is not available to you (see below).
- It should not make comparisons with other parts of the country where accommodation costs differ widely from local ones, but it may compare your property with one in a less expensive area within the same city.[124]

Is cheaper suitable alternative accommodation available?

Cheaper suitable alternative accommodation is only 'available' if the local authority proves that it exists and is available to you. It must:

- have sufficient evidence to show there is an active housing market with accommodation of a suitable type, rent and location for you, but it does not need to refer to specific properties;[125] *and*
- take into account personal factors, such as whether you can afford to pay a deposit.[126] If the local authority produces a list of properties that it says are

Part 4: General rules for other means-tested benefits
Chapter 19: Housing benefit rent restrictions
6. Common definitions

available to you, try to show that they are not available because of your
personal circumstances.[127]

Is it reasonable to expect you to move?
In deciding whether it is reasonable to expect you to move, the local authority
must take into account the effects of a move on:[128]
- your ability to retain your job; *and*
- the education of any child or young person living with you. In considering
  this, the local authority must justify any decision that it is reasonable to make
  the child travel to, or move, school.[129]

The local authority may say that it does not need to consider any other factors,
such as your health.[130] However, if there are good reasons why you cannot move
other than those listed above, try to argue that alternative accommodation
cannot be suitable.[131]

If your rent increases

If your landlord increases your rent while you are entitled to HB, the local
authority cannot increase the amount of your rent that can be covered by HB
(your 'eligible rent' – see p191) by the full amount of the increase if it decides that
the increase is:[132]
- unreasonably high compared with increases in suitable alternative
  accommodation (see p407 for what counts). The local authority must consider
  the amount of the increase, as well as the amount of your previous rent and
  what your rent will be, and compare it with the rent in the suitable alternative
  accommodation.[133] It should also consider, for example, the quality of the
  accommodation, your age and state of health, whether you would have to
  move if the increase is not met and how a move would affect you;[134] *or*
- unreasonable because there has been an increase within the preceding 12
  months.

If the local authority considers a rent increase to be unreasonable, it may refuse to
meet all of that increase or meet only so much of it as it considers appropriate. If
your rent has been increased for the second time in under 12 months, but is still
below the market level for suitable alternative accommodation, or the increase
reflects improvements made to your accommodation, argue for the full amount
to be allowed.

6. Common definitions

There are some terms that are the same for some or all of the rent restriction rules.
These are covered in this section and are referred to above where relevant.

What counts as a bedroom

When working out the number of bedrooms you are allowed under the rules, you may need to consider what counts as a bedroom. For example, you may need to argue that a room is a bedroom, or it may be more advantageous for you to argue that a room is not a bedroom.

'Bedroom' is not defined in the rules. It is the ordinary meaning of the word that is relevant. It could be, for example, a lounge or living room, provided it contains a bed or is used for sleeping.[135]

The starting point is whether the room can be used as a bedroom – ie, a room is a bedroom if it is furnished and can be used for sleeping in. How a property is described by the landlord (eg, as a two- or three-bedroom house) or whether a room is designated as a bedroom may be relevant. However, the basis on which your rent is charged (eg, if your flat has two bedrooms but your landlord only charges the rent for a one-bedroom flat) is not relevant.[136]

You may want to argue that the local authority should not count a room in your home as a bedroom and, therefore, that your housing benefit should not be reduced (or reduced as much) under the rent restriction rules. In deciding whether a room is a bedroom, the local authority should, for example, take into account:[137]

* the size of the room (the dimensions and height) – eg, whether it can accommodate a single bed and somewhere to store clothes and whether it has a flat surface on which to place things safely, such as a glass of water, and whether there is space to dress and undress. If a room is too small, provide a measured plan and photographs if you can; *and*
* whether the room is safe to sleep in – eg, if it is contaminated with asbestos; *and*
* access to the room and whether it has adequate natural and electric lighting, heating, ventilation and privacy.

Suggest your personal use of the room should also be taken into account (eg, if you use the room to store equipment you need because of a severe disability), as well as whether your home has been converted or adapted – eg, if two small bedrooms have been converted into one big bedroom, or if a bedroom has been redesignated. However, the local authority is likely to say that in deciding how many bedrooms there are in your home:

* it is the classification and description of the property when it is empty that is relevant and that the classification can only be changed if the property has been structurally altered with the approval of your landlord;[138]
* even if your home could be used in more than one way (eg, as either a one- or two-bedroom property), the local authority can use the way your landlord designates the property to determine how many bedrooms it has.[139]

Part 4: General rules for other means-tested benefits
Chapter 19: Housing benefit rent restrictions
6. Common definitions

Couples who cannot share a bedroom

If you and your partner, or the members of any couple occupying your dwelling as a home (eg, your non-dependants), cannot share a bedroom, you are allowed an additional room under the size criteria. To count as a 'couple who cannot share a bedroom':[140]

- the person who cannot share must be getting the higher rate of attendance allowance (AA), the middle or highest rate of disability living allowance (DLA) care component, the daily living component of personal independence payment (PIP) or armed forces independence payment; *and*
- the local authority must be satisfied that because of her/his disability, the person cannot reasonably share a bedroom with the other member of the couple.

Note:
- Under the local housing allowance rules and the rules that use rent officer determinations, you are only allowed an additional room if you have a bedroom in your home additional to those you would be allowed if the couple were able to share a bedroom (see p386 and p400).
- Before 1 April 2017, a bedroom might not have been allowed (when it should have been) for a disabled member of a couple who cannot share a bedroom. You can still apply for a revision on grounds of official error if you were affected and think you should have been allowed an additional bedroom.[141]

Child who cannot share a bedroom

If a child who cannot share a bedroom is living in your home, you are allowed an additional room for her/him under the size criteria. To count as a 'child who cannot share a bedroom':[142]

- the child must be under 16 and must be entitled to the middle or highest rate of DLA care component, whether or not it is being paid; *and*
- the local authority must be satisfied that because of her/his disability, the child cannot reasonably share a bedroom with another child under 16.

Note:
- Under the local housing allowance rules and the rules that use rent officer determinations, you are only allowed an additional room if you have a bedroom in your home additional to those you would be allowed if the child were able to share a bedroom (see p386 and p400).
- Before 4 December 2013, a bedroom might not have been allowed (when it should have been) for a severely disabled child who cannot share a bedroom. You can still apply for a revision on grounds of official error if you were affected and think you should have been allowed a bedroom for a disabled child.[143]

Person who requires overnight care

If you (or your partner), a person who occupies your dwelling as a home (eg, your child or a non-dependant) or a child or young person in respect of whom you or your partner are a 'qualifying parent or carer' (eg, your foster child) are a 'person who requires overnight care', you are allowed an additional room under the size criteria. Under the social sector rules, you are also allowed an additional bedroom for someone who is jointly liable for the rent with you if s/he (or her/his partner) is a 'person who requires overnight care' (see p395).

A person counts as a 'person who requires overnight care' if:[144]

- s/he is getting AA, the middle or highest rate of DLA care component, the daily living component of PIP or armed forces independence payment; *or*
- s/he has or, if the person is a child, you have provided the local authority with sufficient certificates, documents, information or evidence to satisfy it that overnight care is required.

In addition, arrangements must have been made for one or more people who do not live with you to provide overnight care and to stay overnight regularly in your home for this purpose. You must satisfy the local authority that this care is reasonably required. The carer does not necessarily have to stay overnight on the majority of nights, but the care must be needed often and steadily enough that a bedroom has to be available for the carer.[145] The carer must be provided with the use of a bedroom additional to those used by other people who live with you. 'Bedroom' is not defined, but see p409 for what might count.

Note: a person can count as a 'person who requires overnight care' while away from your home, provided s/he can be treated as occupying it – eg, while temporarily absent.

Qualifying parent or carer

If you (or your partner) are a 'qualifying parent or carer', you are allowed an additional bedroom under the size criteria. Under the social sector rules, you are also allowed an additional bedroom for someone who is jointly liable for the rent with you if s/he (or her/his partner) is a 'qualifying parent or carer' (see p395).

You count as a 'qualifying parent or carer' if:[146]

- a child has been placed (or in Scotland, boarded out) with you under specified provisions – eg, prior to adoption or as a foster parent; *or*
- you are an approved foster parent (in Scotland, this includes foster and kinship carers). This applies even if you do not currently have a child placed with you, provided you have become an approved foster parent, or have fostered a child, within the last 52 weeks.

To come within the definition, you must have a bedroom in your home that is additional to those used by the other people living in your home. 'Bedroom' is not defined, but see p409 for what might count.

Part 4: General rules for other means-tested benefits
Chapter 19: Housing benefit rent restrictions
7. Delaying a rent restriction

Note: you do not count as a qualifying parent or carer if you provide accommodation for a disabled person under an adult placement scheme. However, you can argue that you should still be allowed an additional bedroom.[147]

7. **Delaying a rent restriction**

A rent restriction can be delayed:

- for up to 12 months, if a member of your family (or any of your or your partner's relatives who lived in the same accommodation as you without a separate right to do so) dies and you still live there (temporary absences of up to 13 weeks are allowed);[148]
- for up to 13 weeks, if you, or a member of your family (or any of your or your partner's relatives who live in the same dwelling as you without a separate right to do so) could meet the costs of the dwelling when you took them on (this could include other bills as well as the rent). This only applies if neither you nor your partner were entitled to housing benefit (HB) in the 52 weeks before your current award of HB.[149]

Under the local housing allowance and social sector rent restriction rules, the amount of your rent that can be covered by your HB (your 'eligible rent' – see p191) can change before the end of the 12-month/13-week period if, as calculated under these rules, it is now the same or higher, or you move to a new home or another member of your family (or relative) dies.[150]

Family members and relatives[151]
'Family' means you, your partner and any child or qualifying young person for whom you or your partner are responsible and who lives in your household.
'Relative' means a close relative (see p180 for who counts) or a grandparent, grandchild, uncle, aunt, nephew or niece.

Example
Connor lives in a private three-bedroom flat with his wife and their four-year-old son. They pay rent of £225 a week. Until her recent death, Connor's mother lived with them. Connor's rent was being restricted to the local housing allowance for a three-bedroom property (£190).
When he notifies the local authority of the death of his mother, his rent is restricted to the local housing allowance for a two-bedroom property (£150). However, the decrease is delayed for 12 months from the date of his mother's death.
Connor gets income support. Before his mother's death, his HB was £174.15 a week (£190 *minus* a non-dependant deduction of £15.85).
For 12 months from his mother's date of death, his HB is £190 a week.

Note: in the past, if the local housing allowance rules applied and you qualified for 'transitional protection', a rent restriction could be delayed in a number of circumstances. See earlier editions of this *Handbook* for details: pp282–83 of the 2011/12 edition and pp317–18 of the 2012/13 edition. If you qualified for transitional protection, different rules may apply after a member of your family or a relative dies.

8. Challenging a rent restriction

If you disagree with the local authority's decision to apply a rent restriction (eg, if you think the rules do not apply in your case, or the wrong rules have been applied) or with the factual basis on which the decision was made (eg, you are a 'person who requires overnight care' or a 'member of a couple who cannot share a bedroom' and you should have been allowed more bedrooms under the rules or a room in your home should not count as a bedroom), you can ask for a revision or appeal (see Chapters 56 and 57).[152] However:

- if the local housing allowance rules apply, you cannot appeal against the amount of the local housing allowance;
- if the rules that use rent officer determinations apply (see p396), you cannot appeal against a rent officer's determination, but the local authority can ask for it to be redetermined.[153] The rent officer's redetermination might reduce your maximum rent (and the local authority might restrict your rent further), so consider your position carefully before requesting one – you could end up with less HB. For details of the rules, see p414 of the 2019/20 edition of this *Handbook*.

You can appeal against local authority decisions about your award of housing benefit which involve rent officer determinations – ie, you can challenge the factual basis on which the rent officer made a determination, such as whether you are a 'young individual' or whether someone occupies accommodation with you.[154] If you are in doubt, you may want to appeal *and* ask for a redetermination.

Part 4: General rules for other means-tested benefits
Chapter 19: Housing benefit rent restrictions
Notes

Notes

1. Which rent restriction rules apply

1 Regs 13C(5)(a) and (c) and 14(2)(b) and Sch 2 paras 3-13 HB Regs; regs 13C(5)(a) and (c) and 14(2)(b) and Sch 2 paras 3-13 HB(SPC) Regs

2 Reg 2(1) and Sch 2 para 3(1A) HB Regs; reg 2(1) and Sch 2 para 3(1A) HB(SPC) Regs. Note that in England this means a 'private registered provider of social housing', but if the provider is profit-making, only if the housing is available at a rent below the market rate.

3 The law refers to 'gypsies and travellers': Sch 2 para 3 HB Regs; Sch 2 para 3 HB(SPC) Regs

4 Reg 12B(6) HB Regs; reg 12B(6) HB(SPC) Regs

5 *R on the application of Laali v Westminster CC* [2002] HLR 179; *R v Macclesfield BC HBRB ex parte Temsamani* [1999] unreported (QBD); A4 Annex B GM

6 Reg 12C(2) and (3) HB Regs; reg 12C(2) HB(SPC) Regs; *DC v London Borough of Bromley (HB)* [2018] UKUT 416 (AAC)

7 *AA v Chesterfield BC* [2011] UKUT 156 (AAC)

2. The local housing allowance rules

8 Reg 12D(2)(a) HB Regs; reg 12D(2)(a) HB(SPC) Regs

9 Reg 13C(1), (2)(a)-(c) and (5) HB Regs; reg 13C(1), (2)(a)-(c) and (5) HB(SPC) Regs

10 Reg 13D(5) HB Regs; reg 13D(5) HB(SPC) Regs

11 Reg 13D(4) and (12) HB Regs; reg 13D(4) and (12) HB(SPC) Regs

12 *DC v London Borough of Bromley (HB)* [2018] UKUT 416 (AAC)

13 Reg 13D(2)(c) and (3) HB Regs; reg 13D(2)(c) and (3) HB(SPC) Regs

14 Reg 2(6) HB Regs; reg 2(7) HB(SPC) Regs

15 *SSWP v Hockley and Nuneaton and Bedworth BC* [2019] EWCA Civ 1080

16 Reg 13D(12), definition of 'occupiers', HB Regs; reg 13D(12), definition of 'occupiers', HB(SPC) Regs

17 Reg 21(3) HB Regs; reg 21(3) HB(SPC) Regs; *AA v Chesterfield BC and SSWP (HB)* [2011] UKUT 156 (AAC)

18 *R(H) 8/09; SK v South Hams DC (HB)* [2010] UKUT 129 (AAC), reported as [2010] AACR 40

19 *R v Swale BC HBRB ex parte Marchant* [1999] 1 FLR 1087 (QBD); [2000] 1 FLR 246; *R (Cotton and Others) v SSWP and New Forest DC and Others* [2014] EWHC 3437 (Admin); *PC v SSWP (HB)* [2014] UKUT 467 (AAC); *MR v North Tyneside Council and SSWP* [2015] UKUT 34 (AAC); *SSWP v MM and Northumberland CC* [2015] UKUT 624 (AAC)

20 Reg 13D(3A) and (3B) HB Regs; reg 13D(3A) and (3B) HB(SPC) Regs

21 *R (Carmichael) v SSWP and R (Rutherford) v SSWP* [2016] UKSC 58; *RR v SSWP* [2019] UKSC 52

22 *JD and A v the United Kingdom* [2019] ECHR 753

23 Reg 13D(2)(a) HB Regs; reg 13D(2)(a) HB(SPC) Regs

24 Regs 2(1), definition of 'young individual', (b)-(f) and (i) and (1A)-(1C), and 13D(2)(a) HB Regs; reg 13D(2)(a) and (12) HB(SPC) Regs

25 Regs 2(1), definition of 'young individual', (c) and (f) and 13D(2)(a) HB Regs; reg 13D(2)(a) and (12) HB(SPC) Regs

26 www.justice.gov.uk/downloads/offenders/mappa/mappa-guidance-2012-part1.pdf

27 Ch 2 paras 2.060 and 2.080 *Local Housing Allowance Guidance Manual*

28 Reg 13D(2)(b) HB Regs; reg 13D(2)(b) HB(SPC) Regs

29 *JS v SSWP and Cheshire West and Chester BC (HB)* [2014] UKUT 36 (AAC), reported as [2014] AACR 26

30 Reg 13D(2)(b) HB Regs; reg 13D(2)(b) HB(SPC) Regs

31 Reg 13D(2)(c) HB Regs; reg 13D(2)(c) HB(SPC) Regs

32 Reg 13D(1) HB Regs; reg 13D(1) HB(SPC) Regs; Art 4B(2A) and (2B) and Sch 3B RO(HBF)O; Art 4B(2A) and (2B) and Sch 3B RO(HBF)(S)O

33 Regs 12D(2) and 13C(3) HB Regs; regs 12D(2) and 13C(3) HB(SPC) Regs
34 Regs 2, definition of 'linked person', 12D(2)(b) and 13C(2)(d) HB Regs; regs 2, definition of 'linked person', 12D(2)(b) and 13C(2)(d) HB(SPC) Regs
35 Reg 13D(1) and (12), definition of 'relevant date', HB Regs; reg 13D(1) and (12), definition of 'relevant date', HB(SPC) Regs

3. The social sector rules: the 'bedroom tax'
36 Reg 12BA HB Regs
37 Reg A13(1) HB Regs
38 Regs 2(1), definition of 'registered housing association', and A13(1)-(4) HB Regs
39 *FT v Perth and Kinross Council and SSWP (HB)* [2019] UKUT 43 (AAC)
40 Art 8 WRA(No.31)O; HB Circular A9/2019 *Mixed-age couples: further guidance (revised)*, 10 July 2019
41 Reg B13(2) HB Regs
42 Reg B13(4) HB Regs
43 Reg B13(2)(c) HB Regs
44 Reg B13(5) and (8) HB Regs
45 Reg 2(6) HB Regs
46 *SSWP v Hockley and Nuneaton and Bedworth BC* [2019] EWCA Civ 1080
47 Reg B13(5) HB Regs
48 Reg 21(3) HB Regs
49 Reg B13(8) HB Regs
50 R(H) 8/09; *SK v South Hams DC (HB)* [2010] UKUT 129 (AAC), reported as [2010] AACR 40
51 *R v Swale BC HBRB ex parte Marchant* [1999] 1 FLR 1087 (QBD); [2000] 1 FLR 246; *R (Cotton and Others) v SSWP and New Forest DC and Others* [2014] EWHC 3437 (Admin); *PC v SSWP (HB)* [2014] UKUT 467 (AAC); *MR v North Tyneside Council and SSWP* [2015] UKUT 34 (AAC)
52 Reg B13(6)(a) and (b), (7)(a) and (9)(a), (b) and (e) HB Regs
53 Reg B13(6)(ab) and (b), (7) and (9)(c) and (d) HB Regs
54 *R (Carmichael) v SSWP and R (Rutherford) v SSWP* [2016] UKSC 58; *RR v SSWP* [2019] UKSC 52, 13 November 2019

55 *JD and A v the United Kingdom* [2019] ECHR 753
56 *R (MA and Others) v SSWP* [2014] EWCA Civ 13; *R (Cotton and Others) v SSWP and New Forest DC and Others* [2014] EWHC 3437 (Admin); *PC v SSWP (HB)* [2014] UKUT 467 (AAC); *SSWP v PE and Bolton MBC* [2017] UKUT 393 (AAC)

4. Hostels, houseboats, mobile homes, caravans and boarders
57 Reg 12C HB Regs; reg 12C HB(SPC) Regs
58 Regs 13(1), 13C(5)(a)-(e) and (6) and 14(1) HB Regs; regs 13(1), 13C(5)(a)-(e) and (6) and 14(1) HB(SPC) Regs
59 The law refers to 'gypsies and travellers': Sch 2 para 3 HB Regs; Sch 2 para 3 HB(SPC) Regs
60 Reg 13(2), (3) and (5) HB Regs; reg 13(2), (3) and (5) HB(SPC) Regs
61 Reg 12C(2) and (3) HB Regs; reg 12C(2) HB (SPC) Regs
62 Reg 13(4) HB Regs; reg 13(4) HB(SPC) Regs; Sch 3 para 8 HB&CTB(CP) Regs
63 *DC v London Borough of Bromley (HB)* [2018] UKUT 416 (AAC)
64 Reg 13ZB(1) HB Regs; reg 13ZB(1) HB(SPC) Regs
65 Reg 14(2)(a) and (7) and Sch 2 para 2(1) and (2) HB Regs; reg 14(2)(a) and (7) and Sch 2 para 2(1) and (2) HB(SPC) Regs
66 Reg 14(1) and (8) HB Regs; reg 14(1) and (8) HB(SPC) Regs
67 Reg 14(1) and (8) and Sch 2 para 2(3)(a)-(d) and (f)-(h) and (4) HB Regs; reg 14(1) and (8) and Sch 2 para 2(3)(a)-(g) and (4) HB(SPC) Regs
68 R(H) 8/09; *SK v South Hams DC (HB)* [2010] UKUT 129 (AAC), reported as [2010] AACR 40
69 CH/1556/2006; CH/3590/2007
70 Sch 1 para 6 RO(HBF)O; Sch 1 para 6 RO(HBF)(S)O
71 Sch 1 para 1 RO(HBF)O; Sch 1 para 1 RO(HBF)(S)O
72 Sch 1 para 3 RO(HBF)O; Sch 1 para 3 RO(HBF)(S)O
73 Sch 1 paras 1(4) and 2 RO(HBF)O; Sch 1 paras 1(4) and 2 RO(HBF)(S)O
74 Sch 2 para 1 RO(HBF)O; Sch 2 para 1 RO(HBF)(S)O
75 Reg 2(6) HB Regs; reg 2(7) HB(SPC) Regs
76 Sch 2 paras 1A and 1B RO(HBF)O; Sch 2 paras 1A and 1B RO(HBF)(S)O

Part 4: General rules for other means-tested benefits
Chapter 19: Housing benefit rent restrictions
Notes

77 Art 2(1) RO(HBF)O; Art 2(1) RO(HBF)(S)O. Both, definition of 'occupier'.
78 Reg 21(3) HB Regs; reg 21(3) HB(SPC) Regs
79 Sch 2 para 2(4) HB Regs; Sch 2 para 2(4) HB(SPC) Regs
80 R(H) 8/09; *SK v South Hams DC (HB)* [2010] UKUT 129 (AAC), reported as [2010] AACR 40
81 *R v Swale BC HBRB ex parte Marchant* [1999] 1 FLR 1087 (QBD); [2000] 1 FLR 246; *R (Cotton and Others) v SSWP and New Forest DC and Others* [2014] EWHC 3437 (Admin); *PC v SSWP (HB)* [2014] UKUT 467 (AAC); *MR v North Tyneside Council and SSWP* [2015] UKUT 34 (AAC); *SSWP v MM and Northumberland CC* [2015] UKUT 624 (AAC)
82 Sch 1 paras 4 and 9(2) RO(HBF)O; Sch 1 paras 4 and 9(2) RO(HBF)(S)O
83 Sch 1 para 5 RO(HBF)O; Sch 1 para 5 RO(HBF)(S)O
84 Reg 13(5) and (6) HB Regs
85 Regs 2(1) and (1A)-(1C), definition of 'young individual', HB Regs
86 www.justice.gov.uk/downloads/offenders/mappa/mappa-guidance-2012-part1.pdf
87 Reg 114A(6) and (8)(a) HB Regs; reg 95A(6) and (8)(a) HB(SPC) Regs
88 Sch 1 paras 5(2)(c) and 7(1) RO(HBF)O; Sch 1 paras 5(2)(c) and 7(1) RO(HBF)(S)O
89 Reg 14(1)(e) and (2) HB Regs; reg 14(1)(e) and (2) HB(SPC) Regs
90 Reg 14(8), definition of 'prospective occupier', HB Regs; reg 14(8), definition of 'prospective occupier', HB(SPC) Regs
91 Reg 14(1)(e) and (8), definition of 'specified matters', HB Regs; reg 14(1)(e) and (8), definition of 'specified matters', HB(SPC) Regs
92 Sch 2 para 2(2)(b) HB Regs; Sch 2 para 2(2)(b) HB(SPC) Regs
93 Reg 13ZB(2)-(4) HB Regs; reg 13ZB(2)-(4) HB(SPC) Regs

5. Exempt accommodation and claimants: the old scheme rules
94 Reg 13C(5)(b) HB Regs; reg 13C(5)(b) HB(SPC) Regs; Sch 3 para 4(1)(b) and (10) HB&CTB(CP) Regs; CH/1289/2007
95 R(H) 7/07; R(H) 4/09; CH/3900/2005; CH/2726/2008; *East Hertfordshire DC v KT* [2009] UKUT 12 (AAC); *Bristol CC v AW* [2009] UKUT 109 (AAC)
96 R(H) 7/07; CH/1289/2007; *Salford CC v PF* [2009] UKUT 150 (AAC)
97 *MMcF v Sefton BC (HB)* [2016] UKUT 403 (AAC)
98 R(H) 2/07
99 Sch 3 para 4(1)(a), (2), (3) and (4) HB&CTB(CP) Regs
100 Reg 13C HB Regs; reg 13C HB(SPC) Regs; Sch 3 para 4(2)(a) and (b), (5), (6), (9) and (10) HB&CTB(CP) Regs
101 Sch 3 para 4(10), definition of 'previous beneficiary', HB&CTB(CP) Regs
102 Reg 2(1), definition of 'registered housing association', HB Regs; Sch 3 para 4(2)(aa) HB&CTB(CP) Regs
103 Reg 12(3)-(5) HB Regs and reg 12(3)-(5) HB(SPC) Regs, as set out in Sch 3 para 5(1) HB&CTB(CP) Regs
104 Reg 13(3) HB Regs and reg 13(3) HB(SPC) Regs, as set out in Sch 3 para 5(2) HB&CTB(CP) Regs
105 *R v City of Westminster HBRB ex parte Mehanne* [1992] 2 All ER 317
106 *R v Brent LBC HBRB ex parte Connery* [1989] 22 HLR 40 (QBD)
107 *R v Kensington and Chelsea RBC HBRB ex parte Pirie,* 26 March 1997, unreported (QBD)
108 Reg 13(3)(a) HB Regs and reg 13(3)(a) HB(SPC) Regs, as set out in Sch 3 para 5(2) HB&CTB(CP) Regs
109 Reg 13(3)(b) HB Regs and reg 13(3)(b) HB(SPC) Regs, as set out in Sch 3 para 5(2) HB&CTB(CP) Regs; *R v Beverley DC HBRB ex parte Hare* [1995] 27 HLR 637 (QBD); *R v Kensington and Chelsea RBC ex parte Abou-Jaoude,* 10 May 1996, unreported (QBD)
110 *Macleod v Banff and Buchan District HBRB* [1988] SLT 753 (CS); *Malcolm v Tweedale District HBRB* [1994] SLT 1212 (CS); CH/4970/2002
111 *Birmingham City Council v SSWP and Others* [2016] EWCA Civ 1211
112 *R v Kensington and Chelsea RBC ex parte Abou-Jaoude,* 10 May 1996, unreported (QBD); *R v Coventry CC ex parte Waite,* 7 July 1995, unreported (QBD)
113 *R v Kensington and Chelsea RBC HBRB ex parte Sheikh,* 14 January 1997, unreported (QBD)
114 Reg 13(4) HB Regs and reg 13(4) HB(SPC) Regs, as set out in Sch 3 para 5(2) HB&CTB(CP) Regs
115 Reg 13(4) HB Regs and reg 13(4) HB(SPC) Regs, as set out in Sch 3 para 5(2) HB&CTB(CP) Regs
116 R(H) 3/06

117 Reg 13(10) and (11) HB Regs and reg 13(10) and (11) HB(SPC) Regs, as set out in Sch 3 para 5(2) HB&CTB(CP) Regs
118 Reg 13(9) HB Regs and reg 13(9) HB(SPC) Regs, as set out in Sch 3 para 5(2) HB&CTB(CP) Regs
119 R(H) 2/05
120 Reg 13(10) and (11) HB Regs and reg 13(10) and (11) HB(SPC) Regs, as set out in Sch 3 para 5(2) HB&CTB(CP) Regs
121 *R v Lambeth LBC HBRB ex parte Harrington*, 22 November 1996, unreported (QBD)
122 Reg 13(9)(a) HB Regs and reg 13(9)(a) HB(SPC) Regs as set out in Sch 3 para 5(2) HB&CTB(CP) Regs; *R v Kensington and Chelsea RBC ex parte Pirie*, 26 March 1997, unreported (QBD); *R v Coventry CC ex parte Waite*, 7 July 1995, unreported (QBD)
123 *R v Waltham Forest LBC ex parte Holder* [1996] 29 HLR 71 (QBD); *R v Slough BC ex parte Green*, 15 November 1996, unreported (QBD)
124 *R v Waltham Forest LBC ex parte Holder* [1996] 29 HLR 71 (QBD); *R v Kensington and Chelsea RBC HBRB ex parte Sheikh*, 14 January 1997, unreported (QBD)
125 *R v East Devon DC HBRB ex parte Gibson* [1993] 25 HLR 487 (QBD); CH/4306/2003
126 *R v Waltham Forest LBC ex parte Holder* [1996] 29 HLR 71 (QBD)
127 *R v Oadby and Wigston DC ex parte Dickman* [1995] 28 HLR 806 (QBD)
128 Reg 13(9)(b) HB Regs and reg 13(9)(b) HB(SPC) Regs, as set out in Sch 3 para 5(2) HB&CTB(CP) Regs
129 *R v Kensington and Chelsea RBC HBRB ex parte Sheikh*, 14 January 1997, unreported (QBD)
130 *R v Kensington and Chelsea RBC HBRB ex parte Carney* [1997] *Crown Office Digest* 124 (QBD)
131 *R v Camden LBC HBRB ex parte W* [1999] unreported (QBD); *R v Westminster CC HBRB ex parte Pallas* [1997] unreported (QBD)
132 Reg 13ZA HB Regs and reg 13ZA HB(SPC) Regs, as set out in Sch 3 para 5(3) HB&CTB(CP) Regs
133 *BM v Cheshire West and Cheshire Council* [2009] UKUT 162 (AAC)
134 CH/2214/2003

6. Common definitions

135 *Bolton MBC v BF (HB)* [2014] UKUT 48 (AAC)
136 *CB v Manchester City Council and SSWP (HB)* [2015] UKUT 556 (AAC)
137 *SSWP v Nelson and Nelson* [2014] UKUT 525 (AAC), reported as [2015] AACR 21; *Stevenage BC v ML (HB)* [2016] UKUT 164 (AAC); *M v SSWP* [2017] UKUT 443 (AAC); *Nuneaton and Bedworth BC v RH and SSWP* [2017] UKUT 471 (AAC); *E v Bristol City Council* [2018] UKUT 287 (AAC)
138 *SSWP v the City of Glasgow Council and IB* [2017] CSIH 35, reported as [2017] AACR 29
139 *SSWP v RR (HB)* [2018] UKUT 180 (AAC)
140 Reg 2(1) HB Regs; reg 2(1) HB(SPC) Regs
141 *R (Carmichael) v SSWP and R (Rutherford) v SSWP* [2016] UKSC 58
142 Reg 2(1) HB Regs; reg 2(1) HB(SPC) Regs
143 *Burnip v Birmingham CC and Others* [2012] EWCA Civ 629
144 Reg 2(1) HB Regs; reg 2(1) HB(SPC) Regs
145 *SD v Eastleigh BC (HB)* [2014] UKUT 325 (AAC)
146 Reg 2(1) HB Regs; reg 2(1) HB(SPC) Regs
147 *SSWP v PE and Bolton MBC* [2017] UKUT 393 (AAC)

7. Delaying a rent restriction

148 Regs 2(1), definitions of 'reckonable rent' and 'linked person', 12BA(3)-(5), 12D(3), (4) and (8) and 13ZA(1) and (2) HB Regs; regs 2(1), definitions of 'reckonable rent' and 'linked person', 12D(3), (4) and (8) and 13ZA(1) and (2) HB(SPC) Regs; reg 13(5) HB Regs and reg 13(5) HB(SPC) Regs, as set out in Sch 3 para 5(2) HB&CTB(CP) Regs
149 Regs 12BA(6)-(8), 12D(5), (6) and (8) and 13ZA(3) and (4) HB Regs; regs 12D(5), (6) and (8) and 13|ZA(3) and (4) HB(SPC) Regs; reg 13(7) and (8) HB Regs and reg 13(7) and (8) HB(SPC) Regs, as set out in Sch 3 para 5(2) HB&CTB(CP) Regs

Part 4: General rules for other means-tested benefits
Chapter 19: Housing benefit rent restrictions
Notes

150 Regs 12BA(5) and (8) and 12D(7) HB
Regs; reg 12D(7) HB(SPC) Regs
151 Reg 2(1) HB Regs; reg 2(1) HB(SPC)
Regs

8. Challenging a rent restriction
152 *LB Bexley v LD (HB)* [2010] UKUT 79
(AAC); *SK v South Hams DC (HB)* [2010]
UKUT 129 (AAC), reported as [2010]
AACR 40
153 Regs 15, 16 and 17 HB Regs; regs 15, 16
and 17 HB(SPC) Regs
154 *SK v South Hams DC (HB)* [2010] UKUT
129 (AAC), reported as [2010] AACR 40;
LB Bexley v LD (HB) [2010] UKUT 79
(AAC)

4

Chapter 20

Income: under pension age

This chapter covers:
1. Whose income counts (p420)
2. What counts as income (p420)
3. Earnings (p421)
4. Other income (p435)
5. Notional income (p449)
6. Working out weekly income (p453)

This chapter explains the rules for working out your weekly income for income support, income-based jobseeker's allowance and income-related employment and support allowance. It also covers working-age housing benefit (HB) rules if you and your partner are under pension age. For pension credit and pension-age HB rules if you and your partner are over pension age, see Chapter 21. If you are in a couple and one of you is over pension age but not the other, see p188 for whether the working-age or pension-age HB rules apply. For universal credit, see Chapter 7; for tax credits, see Chapter 62; for carer's allowance, see Chapter 26; and for health benefits, see Chapter 31.

Key facts
- Your entitlement to income support (IS), income-based jobseeker's allowance (JSA), income-related employment and support allowance (ESA) and working-age housing benefit (HB) and the amount you get depend on how much income you have.
- Your own income counts and, if you are a member of a couple, your partner's income also counts.
- Some income may be completely or partly ignored, or it may count in full.
- Some income may be treated as capital and some capital treated as income.
- If you get IS, income-based JSA or income-related ESA (or universal credit), you are entitled to maximum HB, so you do not need to work out your income again for HB.

Part 4: General rules for other means-tested benefits
Chapter 20: Income: under pension age
2. What counts as income

1. Whose income counts

Your income counts and, if you are a member of a couple, your partner's income also counts (see below). The income of your dependent children may also affect your income support (IS) or income-based jobseeker's allowance (JSA) if you have been on benefit since before 6 April 2004 (see below).

Your partner's income

If you are a member of a couple (see p319), your partner's income is added to yours.[1]

Note: if you or your partner are getting IS, income-based JSA or income-related employment and support allowance (ESA) (or universal credit), all your (and your partner's) income is ignored for housing benefit.[2]

If you or your partner are under 18 and so the rate of the IS, income-based JSA or income-related ESA personal allowance for a couple (£116.80) is reduced to £74.35 or £58.90 (see p335), an amount of income equivalent to the reduction is ignored.[3]

A dependent child's income

Maintenance paid to, or for, a child is usually disregarded (see p438).

The income of a dependent child does not affect your means-tested benefits. However, for IS and income-based JSA, if you have been getting benefit since before 6 April 2004 with a child included in your claim and you do not yet have an award of child tax credit, her/his income is counted as yours if s/he does not have capital of over £3,000.[4] Some income may be disregarded.

See p903, p927 and p935 of the 2012/13 edition of this *Handbook* for details.[5]

2. What counts as income

All income is taken into account for income support (IS), income-based jobseeker's allowance (JSA) and income-related employment and support allowance (ESA) unless it is specifically disregarded.

If you get IS, income-based JSA or income-related ESA (or universal credit), all your income is ignored for housing benefit (HB).[6] Otherwise, all income is taken into account for HB, other than income that is specifically disregarded.

Income only counts if it is paid to you for your own use. It does not count if you cannot prevent it being paid to a third party (eg, under an attachment of earnings order), although other payments for you made to a third party might count (see p451).[7]

Income is converted into a weekly amount (see p453).

Income or capital?

The difference between income and capital is not defined. Payments of income are normally made in respect of a specified period and form part of a regular series of payments.[8] However, sometimes a one-off payment can be income depending on what it is paid for – eg, a settlement for underpaid wages under equal pay legislation.[9] Some income is treated as capital (see p493) and some capital is treated as income (see p444).

3. Earnings

How earnings are treated depends on whether you are employed (see below) or self-employed (see p427). In both cases, some of your earnings can be disregarded (see p429).

Employed earnings

This section explains how any earnings received by you or your partner and, in some cases, a dependent child (see p420) are treated. The same rules apply to your (but not your partner's or child's) earnings if you are claiming contribution-based jobseeker's allowance (JSA – see p712).

To work out how earnings are taken into account, do the following.
- Check whether the payments count as earnings (see below). In some cases, payments are treated as capital, as income other than earnings, or ignored altogether.
- Calculate your net earnings (see p423 and p427).
- Work out your weekly net earnings (see p453).
- Deduct the appropriate weekly earnings disregard (see p429).
- Work out the date from when earnings are taken into account (see p456). For income support (IS), income-based JSA and income-related employment and support allowance (ESA), also work out the period covered by the earnings (see p453). Normally, a payment counts from the date it is due to be paid and for the length of time it has been paid – eg, a month's wages count for a month, starting from the day they are due, at the weekly rate as calculated.

There are special rules for how payments affect benefit when you leave a job (see p424).

What counts as earnings

'Earnings' means 'any remuneration or profit derived from ... employment'. As well as your wages, this includes:[10]
- any bonus or commission (including tips);
- holiday pay (but see p424 if your job ends or you are off work);

Part 4: General rules for other means-tested benefits
Chapter 20: Income: under pension age
3. Earnings

- for housing benefit (HB), any statutory sick pay (SSP) or contractual sick pay.[11] For IS, income-based JSA and income-related ESA, all sick pay is treated as 'other income' rather than earnings (and, therefore, does not attract an earnings disregard) and is counted in full, less any tax, class 1 national insurance (NI) contributions and half of any pension contributions;[12]
- for HB, any statutory maternity pay (SMP), statutory adoption pay (SAP), statutory paternity pay (SPP), or statutory shared parental pay (SSPP) or statutory parental bereavement pay (SPBP) or any other payment made to you by your employer while you are on maternity, adoption, paternity, shared parental or parental bereavement leave.[13] For IS, income-based JSA and income-related ESA, all such pay is treated as 'other income' rather than earnings (and, therefore, does not attract an earnings disregard) and is counted in full less any tax that is payable, class 1 NI contributions and half of any pension contributions;[14]
- any payments made by your employer for expenses not 'wholly, exclusively and necessarily' incurred in carrying out your job, including any travel expenses to and from work, and any payments made to you for looking after members of your family. The latter can apply if you are looking after your child, even if s/he cannot be included in your claim;
- a retainer (eg, payments during the school holidays if you work for the school meals service[15]) or a guarantee payment – eg, if you are working short time or laid off;[16]
- certain compensation payments in respect of the termination of your employment, including employment tribunal awards and pay in lieu of notice. See p424 for the way these are treated when you stop work. For IS, JSA and income-related ESA, compensatory refunds of contributions to an occupational scheme[17] are not treated as earnings;
- an equal pay settlement – eg, through a 'single-status agreement';[18]
- any payment of a non-cash voucher which is liable for class 1 NI contributions.[19] Non-cash vouchers that are not liable for contributions are classed as payments in kind (see below).[20]

What does not count as earnings

Examples of payments not counted as earnings include the following.

- Payments in kind (eg, petrol) are ignored,[21] unless you are on IS or income-based JSA and involved in a trade dispute (see p1001), although they may be counted as 'notional income' (see p452).[22] Non-cash vouchers which are not liable for class 1 NI contributions (eg, certain childcare and charitable vouchers) are treated as payments in kind and are disregarded.[23]
- The value of any free accommodation provided as part of your job should be ignored.[24]

- An advance of earnings or a loan from your employer is treated as capital.[25] However, it is treated as earnings for IS or income-based JSA if you or your partner are involved in, or have returned to work after, a trade dispute.
- Payments towards expenses that are 'wholly, exclusively and necessarily' incurred during the course of your work, such as travelling expenses, are ignored.[26] For example, deductions could be made for:
  - tools or work equipment;
  - special clothing or uniforms;[27]
  - postage and telephone costs (including rental);[28]
  - fuel costs (including standing charges);
  - secretarial expenses;[29]
  - running a car (including petrol, tax, insurance, repairs and maintenance and rental on a leased car).[30]

  If any expenditure is for both business and private use, it should be apportioned as appropriate (and any determination by HM Revenue and Customs normally followed).[31]
- If you are a local councillor, travelling expenses and subsistence payments are (and basic allowances may be[32]) ignored as expenses 'wholly, exclusively and necessarily' incurred in your work.
- Earnings payable abroad which cannot be brought into Britain (eg, because of exchange control regulations) are ignored.[33] **Note:** if your earnings are paid in another currency, any bank charges for converting them into sterling are deducted before taking them into account.[34]
- Any occupational pension[35] counts as 'other income', not earnings, and the net amount is taken into account in full.[36] See p713 (and p654) for the occupational pension rules for contribution-based JSA (and contributory ESA).
- If you are a member of the reserve forces, earnings while on training are disregarded for up to 43 days in your first year of training and 15 days thereafter, to allow you to keep a minimum 10 pence a week IS, JSA or income-related ESA entitlement.[37]

Calculating net earnings from employment

Both your 'gross' earnings and 'net' earnings must be calculated.

Gross and net earnings

'**Gross earnings**' means the amount of earnings received from your employer less deductions for any expenses wholly, necessarily and exclusively incurred by you in order to carry out the duties of your employment.[38] See p421 for what counts as earnings and p422 for examples of expenses that can be deducted.

'**Net earnings**' means your gross earnings less any deductions made for:[39]
- income tax; *and*
- class 1 NI contributions; *and*
- half of any contribution you make towards a personal or occupational pension scheme.

Part 4: General rules for other means-tested benefits
Chapter 20: Income: under pension age
3. Earnings

For HB, if your earnings are estimated, the amount of tax and NI contributions you would expect to pay on those earnings is also estimated. This amount, plus half of any pension contribution you are paying, is then deducted.[40]

For HB, the local authority has the discretion to ignore changes in tax or NI contributions for up to 30 benefit weeks. This can be used, for example, if April tax changes are not reflected in your actual income until several months later. When the changes are eventually taken into account and your benefit entitlement is either increased or reduced accordingly, you are not treated as having been underpaid or overpaid benefit during the period of the delay.[41]

4 Payments when you stop work

If you were getting benefit while working, your final earnings are generally taken into account. If you stop work and are not already getting benefit, see p425.

You were getting benefit when working

If your job ends and you were getting benefit while you were in work, any payments made to you when that job ends are taken into account as earnings as follows.[42]

- Final earnings are taken into account as normal (including wages, bonuses and expenses that count as earnings).
- For IS, income-related ESA and HB, pay in lieu of notice is taken into account; for IS and income-related ESA, final earnings are taken into account first, followed by pay in lieu of notice.
- Contractual redundancy pay, ex gratia payments and other types of compensation (other than employment tribunal awards) above the level of entitlement to statutory redundancy pay:
  - are treated as capital for IS and income-related ESA, if you work out your notice or get full pay in lieu of notice. Otherwise, they are taken into account as earnings for one week only;
  - together with pay in lieu of notice, are treated as earnings for JSA, up until the end of the fixed-term contract, if you had one, or until the end of the notice period (sometimes longer if the employer says it covers a longer period). For JSA, if none of the payment covers pay in lieu of notice or early termination of a fixed-term contract, the total of these payments covers a standard number of weeks arrived at by dividing the payment by the weekly maximum statutory redundancy payment (£538) if this is shorter than the notice period;
  - are treated as capital for HB, except any amount representing loss of income, which is taken into account as earnings.
  The weeks the payments count for start after the period covered by final earnings and any pay in lieu of notice.
- Holiday pay normally counts as earnings. However, it counts as capital if it is payable more than four weeks after employment ends or is interrupted – eg, if

you are off sick before your employment ends. For IS, JSA and income-related ESA, it counts for the number of weeks covered by the holiday pay (not the number of working weeks[43]) starting after the period covered by other payments listed in the above three bullet points.

- An employment tribunal award (eg, for unfair dismissal) is taken into account as earnings.
- Arrears of sick, maternity, adoption, paternity, shared parental and parental bereavement pay count as earnings for HB, and as 'other income', rather than earnings, for IS, JSA and income-related ESA.[44]
- Statutory redundancy payments are treated as capital.

Example

Neelam has been getting HB while working part time. She earned £50 a week. She finishes work on 16 July and on that day is given £60, made up of £30 final wages and £30 holiday pay. The £60 wages and holiday pay are taken into account as normal for HB, deducting the earnings disregard.

Note: you cannot usually make a new claim for IS, income-based JSA, income-related ESA or HB (see p24 for exceptions). Instead, you can claim universal credit (UC). In most cases, claiming UC means that awards of any of these benefits (or tax credits) will end (see p25).

Your job ends before benefit starts

If your employment ends before your entitlement to JSA or HB begins, any payments that count as earnings (see p421), including wages, holiday pay (but see below) and pay in lieu of notice, are ignored as income for that benefit, except for the payments below.[45] For IS and income-related ESA, see p415 of the 2018/19 edition of this *Handbook*.

Note: you cannot usually make a new claim for IS, income-based JSA, income-related ESA or HB (see p24 for exceptions). Instead you can claim UC. In most cases, claiming UC means that awards of any of these benefits (or tax credits) will end (see p25).

The following payments are taken into account.

- A retainer counts as earnings.
- If you were in full-time paid work (see p991), certain employment tribunal awards (and 'out-of-court' settlements) count as earnings, including:
  - compensation because of unfair dismissal;[46]
  - a 'protective' award when an employer fails to comply with redundancy procedures and, for JSA, a compensatory award in respect of trade union activity;[47]
  - for HB, pay under a continuation of contract award or for arrears of pay in respect of a reinstatement or re-engagement order.[48]

Part 4: General rules for other means-tested benefits
Chapter 20: Income: under pension age
3. Earnings

If you were in part-time work, the above are all ignored for HB, but count for JSA.

- Guarantee payments for workless days or while suspended on medical or maternity grounds count as earnings, including when awarded by an employment tribunal.[49]
- Arrears of statutory or contractual sick, maternity, adoption, paternity, shared parental and parental bereavement pay and lump-sum advance payments are taken into account for JSA as income, without any earnings disregard, from when they are paid for the same length of time covered by the arrears. They are ignored for HB.[50]
- Statutory redundancy pay counts as capital.[51]
- Contractual redundancy pay (deducting an amount for your statutory entitlement) is ignored completely for JSA.[52] For HB, it counts as capital.[53]
- Some redundancy schemes make periodic payments after leaving work. These are treated as income other than earnings.[54]
- Ex gratia payments and other kinds of compensation (other than employment tribunal awards) are treated in the same way as contractual redundancy pay.
- Holiday pay is usually ignored. However, if your job ends, it counts as capital if your contract provides for it to be payable more than four weeks after termination of employment – eg, in some cases if you leave without giving notice.[55]

If you stop work before your benefit begins but your employment has not ended (eg, you go on sick leave or maternity leave), statutory and contractual sick, maternity, adoption, paternity, shared parental and parental bereavement pay are taken into account as income without any earnings disregard for JSA.[56] For HB, they count as earnings with the usual disregard.[57] If holiday pay is due to be paid more than four weeks after you stopped work, it is treated as capital (unless, for JSA, you are involved in a trade dispute). If it is paid less than four weeks after you stopped work, it is ignored.[58] All other payments that count as earnings are ignored, except for a retainer or guarantee payments for workless days or for medical or maternity suspension.[59] If you are suspended from work, any earnings are taken into account as normal.

Example

Gina has had to leave her home and her job because of domestic abuse. She leaves her full-time job on 31 May with one month's wages, and three days' holiday pay. Both are due to be paid on 31 May. She moves into temporary accommodation and claims HB after her job ends. Her final wages and holiday pay are ignored. She is entitled to HB from 1 June.

Note: if you were getting HB while working and after your job has ended you made a fresh claim for JSA, your final earnings are taken into account for HB (see p424), but disregarded for JSA.

Self-employed earnings

This section explains how any earnings from self-employment received by you or your partner and, in some cases, a dependent child (see p420) are treated. The same rules apply to your (but not your partner's or child's) earnings if you are claiming contribution-based JSA (see p712).

To work out how earnings are taken into account, do the following.

- Calculate net earnings (see below).
- Work out your average earnings (see p428).
- Deduct the appropriate weekly earnings disregard (see p429).

Calculating net earnings

Your **'net profit'** must be worked out. This is your self-employed earnings minus:[60]

- reasonable expenses (see below); *and*
- income tax and NI contributions; *and*
- half of any premium paid in respect of a personal pension scheme which is eligible for tax relief.

Drawings from capital do not count as income, whether or not the business is in profit.[61] If you receive payments for board and lodging, these do not count as earnings,[62] but as other income (less any disregards – see p442).

If you are getting help with your business under a DWP scheme and this is classed as the 'self-employment route' (eg, New Enterprise Allowance), income and expenses are treated differently (see p444).

Reasonable expenses

Expenses must be reasonable and 'wholly and exclusively' incurred for the purposes of your business.[63] This involves similar considerations to those that apply to the allowances permitted in assessing gross earnings of employed earners. If a car or telephone, for example, is used partly for business and partly for private purposes, the costs of it can be apportioned and the amount attributable to business use can be deducted.[64]

Reasonable expenses include:[65]

- repayments of capital on loans for replacing equipment and machinery;
- repayments of capital on loans for, and income spent on, the repair of a business asset, unless this is covered by insurance;
- interest on a loan taken out for the purposes of the business;
- excess of VAT paid over VAT received.

Part 4: General rules for other means-tested benefits
Chapter 20: Income: under pension age
3. Earnings

Reasonable expenses do not include:[66]
- any capital expenditure;
- depreciation;[67]
- money for setting up or expanding the business – eg, the cost of adapting the business premises;
- any loss incurred before the beginning of the current assessment period. If the business makes a loss, the net profit is nil. The losses of one business cannot be offset against the profit of any other business in which you are engaged, or against your earnings as an employee[68] (although if two businesses or employments share expenses, these may be apportioned and offset);[69]
- capital repayments on loans taken out for business purposes;
- business entertainment expenses;
- for HB, debts (other than proven bad debts) – but the expenses of recovering a debt can be deducted.

Working out average earnings from self-employment

For IS, income-based JSA and income-related ESA, the weekly amount is the average of earnings:[70]
- over a period of one year (in practice, normally the last year for which accounts are available);[71] *or*
- over a more appropriate period if you have recently taken up self-employment, there has been a change that will affect your business, or for any other reason if a different period may enable your income and expenditure to be calculated more accurately.

For HB, the amount of your weekly earnings is averaged over an 'appropriate' period (usually based on your last year's trading accounts), which must not be longer than a year.[72]

For all benefits, if your earnings are royalties, copyright payments or payments under the Public Lending Right scheme, the amount of earnings is divided by the weekly amount of benefit that would be payable if you had not received this income plus the amount that would be disregarded from those earnings (for income-related ESA, the amount of benefit that would be payable includes any contributory ESA).[73] For IS, income-based JSA and income-related ESA, you are not entitled to benefit for the resulting number of weeks. For HB, earnings are taken into account for the resulting number of weeks.

If you stop doing self-employed work, any earnings from that work are disregarded except for royalties and copyright and Public Lending Right scheme payments.[74]

Childminders

In practice, childminders are always treated as self-employed. Your net profit is deemed to be one-third of your earnings less income tax, your NI contributions and half of personal pension scheme contributions (see p427).[75] The rest of your earnings are completely ignored.

Disregarded earnings

Some of your earnings from employment or self-employment are disregarded and do not affect your benefit. The amount of the disregard depends on your circumstances. For the amount of disregarded earnings for contribution-based JSA, see p712.

- For HB, there is an additional disregard depending on the hours you work, a childcare costs disregard and a permitted work disregard.
- For income-related ESA, usually £20 a week is disregarded. However, different rules apply if you are doing 'permitted work' (see below).

Disregards for income-related employment and support allowance

Permitted work disregard

- All your earnings from 'permitted work' (see p1043) are disregarded up to whichever earnings limit applies: £20 or £140. (Only £20 can be disregarded from self-employed earnings from royalties, copyright payments or Public Lending Right scheme payments.)[76]
- If your earnings are less than the £20 or £140 limit, up to £20 of what is left can be disregarded from your partner's earnings.[77]

Note: your earnings from any permitted work (for both contributory and income-related ESA) are assessed in the same way as that described in this chapter.[78]

£20 disregard

Twenty pounds of your earnings (including those of your partner) is disregarded if:[79]

- you are doing work you may do while claiming ESA (see p1042), but only if it is:
  - as a councillor; or
  - as a disability member of the First-tier Tribunal. If you are also doing 'permitted work', instead of the £20 disregard, any unused permitted work disregard up to £20 can be deducted from these tribunal earnings; or
  - during an emergency to protect someone or to prevent serious damage to property or livestock; or
  - while receiving assistance in pursuing self-employment under a government scheme; or
- your partner is in part-time employment of under 24 hours a week (but if you are doing permitted work, see above); or
- your partner would be treated as not being in full-time paid work for IS purposes, other than if this is because of qualifying for housing costs run-on (see p998); or

Part 4: General rules for other means-tested benefits
Chapter 20: Income: under pension age
3. Earnings

- your partner is working, but does not count as being in full-time paid work because s/he:
  - is childminding in her/his home; *or*
  - is a carer under the rules for who can qualify for IS (see p236); *or*
  - is receiving assistance under the 'self-employment route' – eg, New Enterprise Allowance; *or*
  - is an auxiliary coastguard, part-time firefighter, part-time member of a lifeboat crew or member of the reserve forces; *or*
  - is working as a councillor; *or*
  - would not qualify for JSA on the grounds that s/he has been involved in a trade dispute (see p1001), or it is the first 15 days following her/his return to work after having been involved in a trade dispute.

Disregards for income support, income-based jobseeker's allowance and housing benefit

£25 disregard

Lone parents on HB have £25 of their earnings ignored.[80] **Note:** if you get IS, income-based JSA or income-related ESA (or UC), all your earnings are disregarded for HB, so this £25 disregard does not apply.

£20 disregard

Twenty pounds of your earnings (including those of your partner) is disregarded if:

- for IS or income-based JSA, you are a lone parent;[81] *or*
- you or your partner qualify for a disability premium (see p341).[82] For IS and income-based JSA, you are treated as qualifying for the premium if you would do so but for the fact that you are in hospital; *or*
- for HB, you or your partner qualify for a severe disability premium (see p346), the support component or work-related activity component (see p354), or you are in the 'work-related activity group' (see p653);[83] *or*
- you or your partner qualify for a carer premium (see p350). The disregard applies to the carer's earnings. If both partners in a couple get the carer premium, £20 is disregarded from their combined earnings. If you are the carer and the claimant, and your earnings are less than £20, up to £5 (£10 for HB) of the disregard can be used on your partner's earnings (or all of what is left of it if your partner's earnings are from one of the services listed in the next bullet point) – but the total disregard cannot be more than £20;[84] *or*
- you or your partner are an auxiliary coastguard, part-time firefighter, part-time member of a lifeboat crew or member of the reserve forces.[85] If you earn less than £20 for doing any of these services, you can use up to £5 (up to £10 for HB, if you have a partner) of the disregard on another job[86] or on a partner's earnings from another job;[87] *or*

- for IS and income-based JSA only, you are a member of a couple, your benefit would include a disability premium but for the fact that one of you qualifies for the higher pensioner premium (see p345), and one of you is under pension age (see p271) and either of you are in employment;[88] *or*
- for IS and income-based JSA only, you or your partner qualify for the higher pensioner premium (see p345) and, immediately before reaching the qualifying age for PC (see p271), you or your partner were in part-time employment and you were entitled to a £20 disregard because of qualifying for a disability premium. Since reaching the qualifying age for PC, you or your partner must have continued in part-time employment, although breaks of up to eight weeks when you were not getting IS, income-based JSA or income-related ESA are ignored.[89]

If you qualify under more than one category, you still have a maximum of only £20 of your earnings disregarded.

Basic £5 or £10 disregard

If you do not qualify for a £25 or £20 disregard (or, for HB, the permitted work disregard – see below), £5 of your earnings is disregarded if you are single. If you claim as a member of a couple, £10 of your total earnings is disregarded – whether or not you are both working.[90]

Permitted work disregard for housing benefit

If you or your partner are doing 'permitted work' (see p1043 for what this means) and getting contributory ESA, severe disablement allowance (SDA) or NI credits for limited capability for work or incapacity, the permitted work earnings limit for that benefit or credit (either £20 or £140) is also disregarded from earnings for HB.[91] This is instead of the usual disregard of £5, £10, £20 or £25.

If your earnings from permitted work are less than the limit, you can use up the rest:

- on your partner's earnings, up to a maximum of £20 or up to the limit if s/he is also doing permitted work, but there is only one disregard between you; *or*
- on your own earnings from other work. See p1042 for other work you may do while claiming one of these benefits. If you are a lone parent, you can also top up the disregard on earnings from other work to £25.

Additional disregard for housing benefit

For HB only, whichever earnings disregard applies is increased by £37.10 if:[92]

- you or your partner receive the 30-hour element as part of your (or your partner's) working tax credit (WTC – see p1458); *or*
- you or your partner are aged 25 or over and work 30 hours or more a week on average; *or*

Part 4: General rules for other means-tested benefits
Chapter 20: Income: under pension age
3. Earnings

- you or your partner work 16 hours or more a week on average and you have a child who is part of your family for benefit purposes (see p323), or your HB includes the family premium (see p340); *or*
- you are a lone parent and work 16 hours or more a week on average; *or*
- you or your partner work 16 hours or more a week on average and your HB includes a disability premium (see p341), the support component or work-related activity component (see p353), or you are in the 'work-related activity group' (see p653). For couples, the partner for whom the premium/component is awarded or who is in the work-related activity group must be working 16 hours or more a week on average.

The additional earnings disregard does not apply if your total earnings are less than the total of £17.10 plus any earnings disregard and childcare costs disregard (see below). In this case, £17.10 is disregarded from any WTC awarded to you or your partner, but the earnings disregard is not increased.

Note: only one additional disregard is allowed from your (or your partner's) earnings.

Example
Owen and Mia are a couple with one child aged eight. Owen gets contributory ESA and HB. Mia works part time for 16 hours a week, earning £160.
The amount of Mia's earnings taken into account for HB is £122.90 a week. From her £160 wages, £20 is disregarded because Owen is in the work-related activity group, and £17.10 is disregarded because they have a child and Mia works sufficient hours for the additional disregard.

Childcare costs disregard for housing benefit

For HB, up to £175 a week for one child, or up to £300 a week for two or more children, can be deducted from your (or your partner's) earnings (from employment or self-employment) for childcare costs if you are:[93]
- a lone parent working 16 hours or more a week; *or*
- a couple and both of you work 16 hours or more a week, or one of you works 16 hours or more a week and the other is 'incapacitated' (see p434), or is in hospital or prison.

The most that can be deducted for one child is £175, even if you pay more. For more than one child, £300 is the maximum even if you pay more or have to pay for more than two children.

It is not necessary for the childcare to be provided only while you are at work, nor for it to be work-related, and there is no requirement for the charges to be reasonable.

You can still get this disregard for childcare costs if you are off work sick, although for lone parents it stops after 28 weeks (see p434).

If you also get WTC or child tax credit (CTC) and your earnings, once other HB disregards have been allowed, are less than the deduction for childcare costs, your earnings and the WTC/CTC are added together before the deduction for childcare costs is made.[94]

The childcare costs disregard only applies to charges you pay for certain types of childcare provided for any child(ren) in your family under the age of 15 (or 16 if s/he is disabled – see below). A child is not treated as having reached the age of 15/16 until the day before the first Monday in September following her/his 15th/16th birthday.[95]

Disabled child

A child is defined as **'disabled'** if s/he is:[96]

– in receipt of disability living allowance (DLA), personal independence payment (PIP), armed forces independence payment; *or*

– certified as severely sight impaired or blind by a consultant ophthalmologist, or stopped being certified before the first Monday in September following her/his 16th birthday, but no more than one year and 28 weeks before then.

The childcare must be provided:[97]

- by a registered childminder or other registered childcare provider (such as a nursery or local authority daycare service); *or*
- out of school hours for children between the ages of eight and 15/16, by a school on school premises or a local authority – eg, an out-of-hours or holiday play scheme; *or*
- by another relevant childcare provider (see p1462 – these are the same as for WTC).

You cannot include charges for care provided by a relative of the child in the child's own home even if s/he is a registered childminder, nor charges paid by you to your partner or by your partner to you for a child in your family. You can include charges for childcare outside the child's home provided by a relative, provided s/he is not your partner and is a registered childminder. The registered childminder could be a former partner who may even be the child's parent. Charges for compulsory education do not count.

If you or your partner are on maternity, adoption, paternity, shared parental or parental bereavement leave, you are treated as working, and so can get the childcare disregard if you (or your partner):[98]

- were working in the week immediately before the leave began; *and*

Part 4: General rules for other means-tested benefits
Chapter 20: Income: under pension age
3. Earnings

- are entitled to SMP, SAP, SPP, SSPP, SPBP (see Chapter 38) or maternity allowance (MA) (see Chapter 34), or are getting IS because you are on paternity leave.

You are no longer treated as working and so cannot get the childcare costs disregard when:
- the maternity, adoption, paternity, shared parental or parental bereavement leave ends; *or*
- if you are not receiving the childcare element of WTC, you or your partner stop getting SMP, SAP, SPP, SSPP, SPBP or MA, or IS because you are on paternity leave; *or*
- if you are receiving the childcare element of WTC when you stop getting SMP, SAP, SPP, SSPP, SPBP or MA or IS because you are on paternity leave, you stop getting the childcare element of WTC.

You can get the childcare costs disregard for the new child in your family while you are still on maternity, adoption, paternity, shared parental or parental bereavement leave.

Childcare costs and ill health or disability
You can still have a childcare costs disregard while off work sick for the first 28 weeks while you are getting SSP, ESA or NI credits for limited capability for work, provided you were working at least 16 hours a week immediately before you started getting one of these benefits.[99]

After 28 weeks, lone parents who are off work sick can no longer get a childcare costs disregard, but couples can do so (before or after 28 weeks) if one of them works 16 hours or more a week and the other is treated as 'incapacitated'.

Incapacitated
You (or your partner) are treated as **'incapacitated'** if:[100]
– you get ESA which includes a support or work-related activity component, or SDA; *or*
– you get attendance allowance, DLA, PIP, armed forces independence payment or constant attendance allowance (or an equivalent award under the war pensions or industrial injuries schemes) or you would receive one of these benefits but for the fact that you (or your partner) are in hospital; *or*
– you have an NHS-provided wheelchair or mobility scooter or similar vehicle; *or*
– your HB includes a disability premium, support component or work-related activity component for the incapacitated person's incapacity or limited capability for work, or that person is in the 'work-related activity group' (see p653); *or*
– you (but not your partner) have been treated either as having limited capability for work or as being incapable of work for a continuous period of 196 days or more (disregarding any break of up to 84 or 56 days respectively).

Calculating childcare costs

The costs to be taken into account are estimated over whatever period, not exceeding a year, that will give the best estimate of the average weekly charge based on information provided by the childminder or care provider.

4. Other income

As well as income from earnings, most other forms of income are taken into account in full, less any tax due. To work out the weekly income to take into account, check whether the payment can be disregarded (in part or in full), deduct any tax due and work out the weekly amount (see p453). Where a taxable benefit or other unearned income is not taxed at source and you have not yet had a tax assessment, ask HM Revenue and Customs for a forecast of the tax due on that income. Otherwise, the DWP calculates how much tax to deduct.[101] For housing benefit (HB), the local authority has discretion to ignore changes in tax rates and in the maximum rate of child tax credit (CTC) and working tax credit (WTC) for up to 30 weeks – eg, where April changes are not reflected in your income until later.[102]

Benefits and tax credits

Benefits and tax credits that are taken into account

The following count in full:

- carer's allowance (CA) – but not CA supplement in Scotland;[103]
- for HB only, CTC. See p438 if your CTC is reduced to recover a tax credit overpayment;
- child's payment under the Armed Forces Compensation Scheme (but if it is paid for a dependent child, it is usually ignored – see p420);
- contribution-based jobseeker's allowance (JSA);
- contributory employment and support allowance (ESA). If ESA is paid at a reduced rate because of a sanction, it is still the full rate that counts;[104]
- severe disablement allowance;
- industrial injuries benefits, except constant attendance allowance and exceptionally severe disablement allowance, which are disregarded;
- maternity allowance;
- retirement pensions;
- statutory sick pay, statutory maternity pay, statutory adoption pay, statutory paternity pay, statutory shared parental pay and statutory parental bereavement pay count for income support (IS), income-based JSA and income-related ESA only, less any class 1 national insurance contributions and half of any pension contributions and any tax.[105] These are treated as earnings for HB and, therefore, may benefit from an earnings disregard (see p429);[106]

Part 4: General rules for other means-tested benefits
Chapter 20: Income: under pension age
4. Other income

- widow's pension;
- WTC:
  - for IS, income-based JSA and income-related ESA;
  - for HB, except if earnings are too low to use the whole £17.10 additional full-time earnings disregard (see p431). In this case, £17.10 is disregarded from your WTC instead of your earnings. You must satisfy the conditions for the additional earnings disregard and have earnings of less than £17.10 plus whichever other earnings disregard applies plus any childcare costs disregard.[107] If earnings are too low to use the full childcare costs disregard, see p433.

  See p438 if a tax credit overpayment is being deducted.

Benefits and tax credits that are not taken into account

The following are ignored completely:

- armed forces independence payment;[108]
- attendance allowance (AA);[109]
- bereavement support payment;[110]
- Best Start grant (in Scotland);[111]
- child benefit.[112] However, for IS and income-based JSA, it is taken into account if you have been getting IS or income-based JSA since before 6 April 2004 and have an amount for that child in your claim (and do not get CTC);[113]
- Christmas bonus;[114]
- constant attendance allowance, exceptionally severe disablement allowance or severe disablement occupational allowance paid because of an injury at work or a war injury;[115]
- CTC is ignored for IS, income-based JSA and income-related ESA;[116]
- disability living allowance (DLA);[117]
- funeral support payment (in Scotland);[118]
- guardian's allowance;[119]
- HB;[120]
- universal credit (UC), IS, income-based JSA and income-related ESA are ignored for HB.[121] There are special HB rules for these (see p196);
- mobility supplement under the War Pension Scheme;[122]
- personal independence payment (PIP);[123]
- any extra-statutory payment made to you to compensate for non-payment of IS, income-based JSA, income-related ESA, UC, mobility supplement, AA, DLA or PIP;[124]
- social fund payments.[125] They are also disregarded as capital indefinitely;[126]
- any supplementary payments to war widows, widowers or surviving civil partners for pre-1973 service;[127]
- any increase for a child dependant is ignored for IS or income-based JSA if you get CTC, and for income-related ESA. For all benefits, any increase for adult or

child dependants who are not members of your family paid with a benefit (eg, IB or retirement pension) or a service pension is ignored;[128]
- any payment made by the DWP to compensate for the loss of HB;[129]
- any payment in consequence of a reduction in liability for council tax, including from a council tax reduction scheme.[130]

Benefits that are partly taken into account

For HB only, widowed parent's allowance has £15 ignored.[131]

The following benefits have £10 ignored (or more for HB – see below):[132]
- for IS, income-based JSA and income-related ESA only, widowed parent's allowance;
- war disablement pension;
- guaranteed income payment and survivor's guaranteed income payment under the Armed Forces Compensation Scheme (or if another pension reduces the payment to below £10, ignore the remainder from the pension);
- war widow's, widower's or surviving civil partner's pension;
- an extra-statutory payment made instead of the above pensions;
- similar payments made by another country;
- a pension from any government paid to the victims of Nazi persecution.[133]

Even if you have more than two payments which attract a £10 disregard, only £20 in all can be ignored.[134] However, the £10 disregard allowed on the above payments is in addition to the total disregard of any mobility supplement or AA (ie, constant attendance allowance, exceptionally severe disablement allowance and severe disablement occupational allowance) paid as part of a war disablement pension.

The £10 disregard may overlap with other disregards, such as on student loans and access funds (see p904 and p907), when a combined maximum of £20 is allowed.

Local authorities may have discretionary local schemes to increase the £10 disregard on war disablement pension, war widow's or widower's pension, and the guaranteed income payment and survivor's guaranteed income payment in your HB. Most increase the disregard or ignore the full amount, so check your local scheme.[135]

Benefit delays

Problems can arise if a decision maker tries to take into account a benefit you are not receiving (such as CA) because it has been delayed. In such a case, the benefit should not be treated as income you have. For IS, income-based JSA and income-related ESA, you should get your full benefit and the DWP deducts the difference from the arrears of the delayed benefit when it is eventually awarded.[136]

For the treatment of payments of arrears of certain benefits and tax credits, see p498.

Part 4: General rules for other means-tested benefits
Chapter 20: Income: under pension age
4. Other income

Benefit deductions and overpayments

Usually, if any deductions are being taken from your benefit (eg, for an overpayment, rent or bills), the full amount of benefit is taken into account before the deduction is taken off.[137] However, if an overpayment of tax credits is being deducted from a tax credits award, it is the amount you actually receive that is taken into account after the deduction to recover the overpayment has been taken off.[138]

Maintenance payments

If you get **child maintenance** for a child who is a member of your family, it is all ignored if it is made by the child's parent (who is not your partner) or by another 'liable relative' (see below).[139] Child maintenance payments include:

- any payment made voluntarily;
- payments under a court order or consent order;
- child support maintenance (assessed by the Child Maintenance Service);
- in Scotland, payments under a registered maintenance agreement.

Note: arrears of regular child support maintenance should be treated as income for a past period. Arrears are ignored as income if, for HB, they cover a period since 27 October 2008 or, for other benefits, since 12 April 2010. Before that, arrears may mean that you have been overpaid benefit, although some overpaid benefits can be deducted from arrears before you get them.[140]

Other kinds of maintenance

If you get another kind of maintenance payment from a former partner (eg, maintenance for yourself):[141]

- £15 is ignored for HB if you have a child who is part of your family for benefit purposes (see p323) or a family premium included in your HB. If you get maintenance from more than one person, only £15 of the total is ignored;
- for other benefits, it is regarded as a 'liable relative' payment and usually counts in full (see below).

Liable relative

A **'liable relative'** is:[142]

– a spouse, civil partner, former spouse or civil partner; *or*

– a parent of a child who is a member of your family; *or*

– someone who can reasonably be treated as the child's father because of the financial support he makes.

For IS, income-based JSA and income-related ESA, any payment from a liable relative other than child maintenance is taken into account in full as income, whether it is paid regularly or as a lump sum, with some exceptions as follows.[143]

- Payments made direct to someone else and not to you (ie, to a third party) are taken into account as maintenance if they are for certain normal living expenses (food, clothing, footwear), for certain bills (fuel, council tax, water charges), for rent met by HB or for housing costs met by IS, JSA or ESA (such as service charges). Payments for other kinds of expenses, such as mortgage repayments paid direct to the mortgage lender or TV licence payments paid direct, are ignored.[144] This means it can be better for you if your ex-partner pays these other kinds of expenses direct rather than to you. If you use your maintenance payments to pay the mortgage yourself, it is taken into account as your income, so you will get less benefit.
- Payments in kind, such as food, holidays and clothing, are ignored (except if you are involved in a trade dispute).
- Gifts (eg, birthday and Christmas presents) of up to £250 in total in any period of 52 weeks are not taken into account as maintenance, but may count as capital.
- If you have already spent a payment before the DWP makes its decision about the effect on your benefit, the payment is ignored, provided you did not deliberately get rid of the money in order to claim or increase your benefit. The issues are the same as the deprivation of income/capital rule on p503.
- A payment from a 'disposition of property' because of divorce, separation, nullity or dissolution of a civil partnership is not taken into account as maintenance (so is not treated as income), but usually counts as capital. This applies, for example, if your former partner buys out your interest in a home so you get a lump-sum settlement instead of a share of the property itself.[145]
- Payments for a child who is not a member of your household (eg, a child looked after by a local authority and not living with you, or a child in custody) do not count as maintenance. They should be ignored if you spend the money on the child, but count as income if you keep the money or spend it on yourself.[146]
- A payment made after the liable relative has died no longer counts as maintenance (so is not automatically treated as income), but is still taken into account as income or capital under the normal rules.

If you get payments towards maintenance from someone who is not a liable relative (eg, a grandparent), this normally counts as a voluntary payment and is ignored (see p441).

If you pay maintenance

If you *pay* maintenance to a former partner or a child not living with you, your payments are not disregarded for the purpose of calculating your income for any benefits.[147] See p506 if part of a personal or occupational pension is paid to a former partner.

Part 4: General rules for other means-tested benefits
Chapter 20: Income: under pension age
4. Other income

Student loans and grants

For the special rules on the treatment of student loans, grants and other types of student support, see Chapter 41.

Adoption, fostering and similar payments

Adoption allowance

An adoption allowance is disregarded in full, except in the following circumstances.[148]

*   If the adoption allowance is paid for a child who is not a member of your family (eg, because the adoption order has not yet been granted), it is fully disregarded in England.[149] In Scotland and Wales, any amount you spend on the child is disregarded and any you keep for yourself is taken into account.[150]
*   For IS and income-based JSA, if you have been getting benefit since before 6 April 2004 with a child included in your claim and do not have an award of CTC, the adoption allowance is taken into account in full up to the level of the adopted child's personal allowance and any disabled child premium.[151] Above that level it is ignored. If the child has capital over £3,000, you get no benefit for that child and all the adoption allowance is disregarded.[152] Get advice to check whether you would be better off claiming UC instead.

Fostering allowance

The way a fostering allowance is treated depends on whether the arrangement is official or private. If a child is placed or boarded out with you by a local authority or a voluntary organisation under specific legal provisions,[153] the child is not counted as a member of your family (see p327) and any fostering allowances you receive while the child is placed with you should be ignored.[154] If the fostering arrangement is a private one, any money you receive from the child's parent(s) is counted as maintenance (see p438).

Child arrangements order allowance and similar payments

If you are paid a child arrangements order allowance by a local authority (in England and Wales), this is treated in the same way as an adoption allowance (see above).[155] Any payments made by the birth parents count as maintenance (see p438). In Scotland, kinship care payments made under section 73 of the Children and Young People (Scotland) Act 2014, section 22 of the Children (Scotland) Act 1995 or regulation 33 of the Looked After Children (Scotland) Regulations 2009 are ignored altogether, but if made under section 50 of the Children Act 1975, they are treated in the same way as an adoption allowance.[156]

Special guardianship allowance

The law treats a special guardianship allowance, payable in England and Wales for a child who is a member of your family, in the same way as an adoption allowance (see above), but official guidance advises that it should be fully disregarded for IS and income-based JSA.[157]

Charitable, voluntary and personal injury payments

Payments from infected blood payment schemes

Any payments from specified schemes for people infected with HIV or hepatitis C through blood products and NHS treatment are disregarded in full.[158]

Payments can still be disregarded if you give them to certain relatives or they inherit them from you after your death.

Any income or capital that derives from any such payments is also disregarded.

Other payments

Most other charitable or voluntary payments that are made irregularly and are intended to be made irregularly are treated as capital and are unlikely to affect your benefit claim unless they take your capital above the limit.[159] However, if you are on IS or income-based JSA, they count as income if you are involved in a trade dispute and, for IS only, for the first 15 days following your return to work after a dispute (see p1001).[160]

Payments made on a regular basis

Charitable and voluntary payments and certain personal injury payments (see below) are ignored if they are made, or are due to be made, regularly.[161]

A '**voluntary payment**' is one given without getting anything back in return.[162]

For IS and income-based JSA, these payments are not disregarded if you are involved in a trade dispute and, for IS only, for the first 15 days following your return to work after a trade dispute.

Payments from a former partner, or the parent of your child, are treated as maintenance (see p438).

Personal injury payments

'**Personal injury payments**' are:[163]

– payments from a trust fund set up out of money paid because of any personal injury to you;

– payments under an annuity purchased either under an agreement or court order set up because of any personal injury to you, or from money paid because of any personal injury to you;

– payments you get under an agreement or court order because of any personal injury to you. This does not include an occupational pension – eg, if you have retired early because of personal injury.[164]

Part 4: General rules for other means-tested benefits
Chapter 20: Income: under pension age
4. Other income

See also p451 for payments made to someone else on your behalf and p448 for payments disregarded under miscellaneous income.

Concessionary coal to former British Coal workers and their surviving partners is ignored (except to strikers). Cash in lieu of coal counts in full.[165]

Income from tenants and lodgers

How income from tenants is treated depends on whether or not you live in the same property.

Lettings without board

If you let out a room(s) in your home to tenants, subtenants or licensees under a formal contractual arrangement, £20 of your weekly charge for each tenant, subtenant or licensee (and her/his family) is ignored.[166] The balance counts as income.

If someone shares your home under an informal arrangement, any payment s/he makes to you for living and accommodation costs is ignored,[167] but a non-dependant deduction may be made from any HB or housing costs paid with IS/income-based JSA/income-related ESA (see p198 and p363).

Boarders

If you have a boarder(s) on a commercial basis in your own home, and the boarder or any member of her/his family is not a close relative of yours, the first £20 of the weekly charge is ignored and half of any balance remaining is then taken into account as your income.[168] For HB, this applies even if the boarder is a close relative and it is not a commercial arrangement. However, a non-dependant deduction may be made for her/him (see p198). This disregard applies for each boarder you have. The charge must normally include at least some meals.[169] If you have a business partner, even though your gross income includes just your share of the weekly charge to boarders, you still get the full disregard of £20 plus half the excess for each boarder.[170]

Note: if you let part of your home, any income left after applying the above disregards which is intended to be used to meet any housing costs of your own which are not met by IS, income-based JSA, income-related ESA or HB, may also be disregarded (see p446).[171]

Tenants in other properties

If you have a freehold interest in a property other than your home and you let it out, the rent is normally treated as capital.[172] This rule also applies if you have a leasehold interest in another property which you are subletting. The full rent counts initially (as well as the capital value of the property itself) but, if you spend some on a debt that is immediately repayable (eg, a monthly mortgage payment) after a period (eg, a month for monthly paid rent), only what remains continues to count as capital. If you spend it on something else to deliberately increase your benefit, the notional capital rules could treat you as still having the money (see p502).[173]

The rent is treated as income if the property you let is in one of the categories where the capital value is disregarded (see p494). In this case, the expenses listed below are deducted from the income.

Income from capital

In general, actual income generated from capital (eg, interest on savings) is ignored as income.[174] It counts as capital from the date you are due to receive it.[175] However, income derived from the following categories of disregarded capital (see p493) is treated as income:[176]

- your home;
- your former home, if you are estranged, divorced or your civil partnership has ended;
- property which you have acquired for occupation as your home, but you have not yet been able to move into;
- property which you intend to occupy as your home, but which needs essential repairs or alterations;
- property occupied wholly or partly by a partner or relative of any member of your family who has reached pension age or who is incapacitated;
- property occupied by your former partner, unless you are estranged, divorced or your civil partnership has ended;
- property for sale;
- property which you are taking legal steps to obtain to occupy as your home;
- your business assets;
- a trust of personal injury compensation.

Some expenses are deducted from this income. Income from property (other than your current home) is ignored up to the amount of the total mortgage repayments (ie, capital and interest, and any payments that are a condition of the mortgage, such as insurance or an endowment policy),[177] council tax and water charges paid in respect of the property for the same period over which the income is received.[178]

Tariff income from capital

If your capital is over a certain level, you are treated as having an assumed income from it, called your '**tariff income**'. You are assumed to have an income of £1 a week for every £250, or part of £250, by which your capital exceeds £6,000 but does not exceed £16,000.[179]

If you are in a care home or similar accommodation (see p489), tariff income applies between £10,000 and £16,000.

Part 4: General rules for other means-tested benefits
Chapter 20: Income: under pension age
4. Other income

Capital that counts as income

The following capital is treated as income:

- instalments of capital outstanding when you claim benefit, if they would bring you over the capital limit. For IS, income-based JSA and income-related ESA, the instalments to be counted are any outstanding, either when your benefit claim is decided or when you are first due to be paid benefit, whichever is earlier, or at the date of any subsequent supersession.[180] For HB, it is any instalments outstanding when your claim is made or treated as made, or when your benefit is revised or superseded.[181] The outstanding instalments count as income by spreading them over the number of weeks between each instalment;[182]
- any payment from an annuity[183] (see p445 for when this is disregarded);
- any professional and career development loan (see p906);[184]
- for IS only, a tax refund if you or your partner have returned to work after a trade dispute (see p1001);[185]
- periodic payments made under an agreement or court order for any personal injury to you (see p441 for when these are disregarded);[186]
- some lump sums from liable relatives (see p438).

Note: capital counted as income cannot also be treated as producing a tariff income (see p443).[187]

Sometimes, you may find that withdrawals from a capital sum are treated as income.[188] This is most likely if the sum was intended to help cover living expenses over a particular period – eg, a bank loan taken out by a student. If this is not the intended use of any capital sum, dispute the decision. Even if the sum is intended for living expenses, argue that, unless it is actually paid in instalments, it should be treated as capital.[189] A loan that you have an obligation to repay immediately should not be treated as your income (or capital), however it is paid.[190]

Income tax refunds

Pay as you earn (PAYE) refunds and self-employment tax refunds are treated as capital.[191]

For IS and JSA, tax refunds paid during a trade dispute are treated as income and taken into account.[192] For IS only, if you or your partner have returned to work after a trade dispute (see p1001), tax refunds are treated as income and are taken into account in full.[193]

Income from employment and training programmes

Payments from employment or training programmes under section 2 of the Employment and Training Act 1973 or section 2 of the Enterprise and New Towns (Scotland) Act 1990 are treated as follows.[194]

The following payments are taken into account:

- for ESA, those made as a substitute for ESA or JSA; for other benefits, payments made as a substitute for IS, JSA or ESA – eg, a training allowance; *and*
- those intended for certain living costs while you are participating in a scheme to enhance your employment prospects. Payments for food, ordinary clothing or footwear, fuel, rent met by HB, housing costs met by IS, JSA or income-related ESA, council tax or water charges are all taken into account.

All other payments are disregarded – eg:

- travel expenses;
- training premium;
- childcare expenses;
- special needs payments;
- expenses for participating in a specified scheme for assisting people to obtain employment (see p1151);[195]
- New Enterprise Allowance weekly allowance.

For ESA, any payment for expenses incurred in complying with a requirement to undertake work-related activity (see p1140) is ignored.[196]

If you have been getting help under the 'self-employment route' (eg, for JSA and HB, the New Enterprise Allowance), any payments to meet expenses 'wholly and necessarily' incurred while trading, or used to repay a loan necessary for the business, are also disregarded if they are from a special account set up for this programme.[197] Income built up in your special account while you are getting this help is treated as capital for HB.[198] At the end of the programme, this is treated as income for IS/JSA/ESA and spread over the same number of weeks in the future for which you have been receiving assistance, less any income tax due on the profits and an earnings disregard appropriate to your circumstances (see p429).[199]

Occupational and personal pensions and annuities

Although you can usually choose to take some, or all, of your occupational or personal pension from age 55, your benefit is not affected if you do not – ie, there is no notional income or capital assumed. Any regular withdrawals from your pension pot or pension income you take count in full as income. If you take a lump sum, this counts as capital, and notional capital rules can apply to how you spend it (see p502).[200] If your partner has reached pension age and chooses not to take income from an occupational or personal pension, you are treated as having notional income. If you (or your partner) have reached pension age, see also p479.

Discretionary payments from a hardship fund are not regarded as an occupational pension, but are treated as charitable or voluntary payments (see p441).[201]

Part 4: General rules for other means-tested benefits
Chapter 20: Income: under pension age
4. Other income

Payments from an annuity count in full unless:

- the annuity is set up with money paid because of personal injury to you, or under an agreement or court order because of personal injury to you (see p441); *or*
- the annuity is set up with money from a home income plan, in which case income from the annuity equal to the interest payable on the loan with which the annuity was bought is ignored if:[202]
  - you used at least 90 per cent of the loan made to you to buy the annuity; *and*
  - the annuity will end when you and your partner die; *and*
  - you or your partner are responsible for paying the interest on the loan; *and*
  - you (if you took out the loan), or your partner (if s/he did), were at least 65 at the time the loan was made; *and*
  - the loan is secured on a property which you or your partner own or in which you have an interest, and the property on which the loan is secured is your home, or that of your partner.

If the interest on the loan is payable after income tax has been deducted, it is an amount equal to the net interest payment that is disregarded. Otherwise, it is the gross amount of the interest payment.

Mortgage and insurance payments

For IS, income-based JSA and income-related ESA only, ignore:

- payments you receive under a mortgage insurance policy which you use to maintain mortgage payments;[203]
- provided you have not already used mortgage protection insurance payments for the same purpose, any money you receive which is given, and which you use, to make the following payments:[204]
  - payments due on a secured loan that does not qualify for a DWP loan for mortgage interest (see p855);
  - capital payments and interest payments on a loan that qualifies for a DWP loan for mortgage interest, but which are not met by the DWP loan;
  - service charges and other eligible housing costs that are not met by the help you get with housing costs in your benefit (see Chapter 18);
- payments of premiums on an insurance policy which you took out to insure against the risk of not being able to make the payments in the above three categories, and premiums on a buildings insurance policy;
- payment of any rent that is not covered by HB (see Chapter 10);
- payment of the part of your accommodation charge in a care home that exceeds that payable by a local authority.

Example

Sami is on income-based JSA. He is an owner-occupier with a mortgage. He gets a DWP loan for mortgage interest, which pays £70 a month towards his interest payments of £100 a month. He still has to pay £30 a month mortgage interest, £90 a month capital repayments and £20 a month premiums on his buildings insurance, which totals £140. He receives £170 a month from an income protection insurance policy. Of this, £140 is ignored and £30 a month counts as his income.

If you are using maintenance from a former partner or parent of your child (but not child maintenance, which is disregarded whatever you use it for) to pay these costs, it may be taken into account as a 'liable relative payment', unless it is paid direct to someone else – eg, a lender (see p438).

For HB only, payments you receive under an insurance policy to insure against the risk of being unable to maintain payments on a loan secured on your home are ignored. However, anything you get above the total of the following counts as your income:[205]

- the amount you use to maintain your payments; *and*
- any premium you pay for the policy; *and*
- any premium for an insurance policy to insure against loss or damage to your home.

Payments you receive under an insurance policy to insure against the risk of being unable to maintain hire purchase or similar payments or other loan payments (eg, credit card debts) are also ignored. However, anything you get above the amount you use to make your payments and the premium for the policy counts as your income.[206]

Social services, community care and other payments

The following payments are ignored:

- local welfare assistance to meet an immediate short-term need or establish or maintain a settled home in certain circumstances (see p861);[207] *and*
- payments from a local authority for children, families and people in need, made under section 17 of the Children Act 1989, section 12 of the Social Work (Scotland) Act 1968, section 22 of the Children (Scotland) Act 1995 or sections 37 or 38 of the Social Services and Well-being (Wales) Act 2014.[208] See p1001 if you or your partner are involved in a trade dispute; *and*
- payments from a local authority for young people who were previously looked after by the local authority, paid under sections 23B or 24A of the Children Act 1989, section 30 of the Children (Scotland) Act 1995 or sections 109, 110, 114 or 115 of the Social Services and Well-being (Wales) Act 2014. A payment under section 23C is also ignored as the young person's income and as yours if

Part 4: General rules for other means-tested benefits
Chapter 20: Income: under pension age
4. Other income

s/he passes it to you, s/he was in your care, is still living with you and is aged 18 or over – eg, under 'staying put' arrangements. In Scotland, this applies to payments under sections 26A and 29 of the Children (Scotland) Act 1995 and includes young people aged 16 or over in 'continuing care'. See p1001 if you or your partner are involved in a trade dispute;[209] *and*

- direct payments to you under an education, health and care plan for a child with special educational needs (paid in England);[210] *and*
- any community care or healthcare direct payments. Local authorities or the NHS pay these to disabled people or carers to buy their own services instead of providing services direct. A direct payment is not ignored as the income of the person you pay for services, even if this is your partner;[211] *and*
- any payment you or your partner receive for looking after someone who is temporarily in your care if it is paid under community care arrangements by the NHS, local authority, voluntary organisation or the person being looked after.[212] Any HB paid to you by a local authority for that person is not ignored, although see p442 for other possible disregards; *and*
- payments under the Supporting People programme for support services to help you live independently are ignored indefinitely.[213] Landlords receiving such payments for providing the services do not benefit from this disregard, although other disregards may apply (see p442); *and*
- if you live in a care home and a local authority arranged your place, local authority payments towards your fees are ignored for IS, JSA and income-related ESA. If a local authority did not arrange your place, any payment intended and used for your maintenance is fully disregarded if it is a voluntary or charitable payment, and partly disregarded if not – up to the difference between the care home fees and your applicable amount;[214] *and*
- a lump-sum payment from a local authority to enable you to make adaptations to your home for a disabled child. This is treated as capital and ignored.[215]

Miscellaneous income

The following income is ignored:
- any discretionary housing payments paid by a local authority;[216] *and*
- education maintenance allowances (paid in Scotland and Wales) and 16 to 19 bursary fund payments (paid in England).[217] These are paid to some young people staying on at school or other non-advanced education; *and*
- any payment to cover your expenses if you are working as an unpaid volunteer, or working unpaid for a charity or voluntary organisation;[218] *and*
- payments in kind (except for IS or income-based JSA, if you or your partner are involved in a trade dispute – see p1001).[219] These may include food, fuel, cigarettes,[220] clothing, holidays, gifts, accommodation, transport or nursery education vouchers. However, see p449 for the rules on notional income and p421 for the rules on non-cash vouchers paid as earnings. Items for essential

living needs provided by the Home Office to an asylum-seeking partner are ignored for IS, income-based JSA and income-related ESA; *and*

- a payment (other than a training allowance) to a disabled person under the Disabled Persons (Employment) Act 1944 to assist her/him to obtain or retain employment;[221] *and*
- any payments, other than for loss of earnings or a benefit, made to jurors or witnesses for attending court;[222] *and*
- Victoria Cross or George Cross payments or similar awards;[223] *and*
- income paid outside the UK which cannot be transferred here;[224] *and*
- if income is paid in another currency, any bank charges for converting the payment into sterling;[225] *and*
- fares to hospital and refunds for prescription or dental charges;[226] *and*
- payments instead of milk tokens and vitamins, or instead of Healthy Start food vouchers;[227] *and*
- payments to assist prison visits;[228] *and*
- for HB, if you make a parental contribution to a student's grant or loan, an equal amount of any 'unearned' income you have for the period the grant or loan is paid. If your 'unearned' income does not cover the contribution, the balance can be disregarded from your earnings. If you are a parent of a student under 25 in advanced education who does not get a grant or loan (or who only gets a smaller discretionary award), up to £58.90 of your contribution to her/his living expenses is ignored from your 'unearned' income (less the weekly amount of any discretionary award the student has). This is only ignored during the student's term. Any balance can be disregarded from your earnings;[229] *and*
- a sports award made by UK Sport from National Lottery funds for living expenses is taken into account. This covers food, ordinary clothing or footwear, fuel, council tax, water charges and rent (less any non-dependant deductions) for which HB could be payable or housing costs that could be met by IS, income-based JSA or income-related ESA. Payments for anything else are ignored – eg, sportswear and dietary supplements to enhance performance;[230] *and*
- any payment for expenses if you are being consulted as a service user by the DWP or a health, care or housing body that provides statutory services (expenses do not count as earnings either);[231] *and*
- victims' payments to people injured in a 'Troubles-related incident'.[232]

5. **Notional income**

In certain circumstances, you may be treated as having income, even if you do not possess it or if you have used it up.

Part 4: General rules for other means-tested benefits
Chapter 20: Income: under pension age
5. Notional income

Deliberately getting rid of income

If you deliberately get rid of income in order to claim or increase your benefit, you are treated as though you still receive that income.[233] The basic issues involved are the same as those for deliberately getting rid of capital (see p503). **Note:** the rule only applies if your intention was to gain benefit for yourself (or your family). It should not apply if, for example, you stop claiming carer's allowance (CA) solely to allow the cared-for person to get a severe disability premium (see p346).[234] However, if you do not claim a benefit which would clearly be paid if you did, it may be argued that you have failed to apply for income (see below).

The rule still applies if you move from one benefit to another in the case of income support (IS), jobseeker's allowance (JSA) and employment and support allowance (ESA). For example, if you got rid of income to increase the amount of your ESA and then claimed JSA instead, you are still treated as having the income for your JSA claim. However, you are not automatically treated as having the income if you claim universal credit (UC) instead, although the income could be considered under the UC rules (see p131).

Failing to apply for income

If you fail to apply for income to which you are entitled without having to fulfil further conditions, you are treated as having it from the date you could have obtained it.[235]

This does not include, for example, income from:
* a discretionary trust;
* a trust set up from money paid as a result of a personal injury;
* funds administered by a court as a result of a personal injury;
* a rehabilitation allowance made under the Employment and Training Act 1973;
* JSA (for IS, JSA and ESA) or ESA (for ESA only);
* if you are under pension age (see p271), a personal or occupational pension scheme or payments from the Pension Protection Fund. However, if you or your partner have reached that age and choose not to take your full pension, you are treated as having an income;[236]
* working tax credit and child tax credit.[237]

It must be certain that the income or benefits would be paid if you were to apply. For example, it may be difficult for the DWP to establish that there was 'no doubt' that CA would be paid to you if you have chosen not to claim it because of the effect on the benefit of the person you are caring for (see p346).[238]

As soon as you apply or make a claim, the rule ceases to apply.[239]

Income due to you that has not been paid

For IS, income-based JSA and income-related ESA only, you are treated as possessing any income that is owing to you – eg:[240]
- wages that are legally due to you, but are not paid;
- an occupational pension payment that is due but has not been received, unless the pension scheme has insufficient funds.[241]

This rule should not apply if:
- any social security benefit has been delayed; *or*
- you are waiting for a late payment of a government training allowance or a benefit from a European Economic Area country; *or*
- money is due to you from a discretionary trust or a trust set up from money paid as a result of a personal injury; *or*
- you are owed earnings when your job has ended because of redundancy but these have not been paid to you.[242]

The income must be due to *you* (or your family) and for your own benefit.[243]

Unpaid wages

For IS, income-based JSA and income-related ESA only, if you have wages due to you, but you do not yet know the exact amount or you have no proof of what they will be, you are treated as having a wage similar to that normally paid for that type of work in that area.[244] If your wages cannot be estimated, you may qualify for a short-term advance (see p1192).[245] For how wages are estimated for housing benefit, see p455.

Income paid to someone else on your behalf

If money is paid to someone on your behalf (eg, a landlord for your rent), this can count as notional income.[246] If so, it is still subject to the usual disregards that would apply if it were actual income – eg, a voluntary or charitable payment of income is ignored whether it is paid direct to you or to someone else on your behalf. See p506 for a description of these third-party rules – they are the same as those for notional capital.

Income in kind given to a third party for you is ignored (eg, a food parcel used to prepare meals for you) unless, for IS or income-based JSA, you or your partner are involved in a trade dispute. However, money given to someone who uses it to buy you goods or services counts as notional income under the usual rules.

Income paid to you for someone else

If you or your partner get a payment for someone not in the 'family' (eg, a relative living with you), it counts as your income if you keep any of it yourself or spend it on yourself or your partner unless it is, for example:[247]

Part 4: General rules for other means-tested benefits
Chapter 20: Income: under pension age
5. Notional income

- from a specified infected blood payment scheme (see p441);
- concessionary coal under the Coal Industry Act 1994;
- a payment for an approved employment-related course of education, or specified scheme for assisting people to obtain employment (see p1151);
- income in kind (eg, a food parcel given to you to make meals for someone else), unless, for IS or income-based JSA, you or your partner are involved in a trade dispute.

Cheap or unpaid labour

If you are helping another person or an organisation by doing work that would normally be paid, or be paid a higher wage, you are deemed to receive a wage similar to that normally paid for that kind of job in that area.[248]

The burden of proving that your work is something for which an employer would pay, and what the comparable wages are, lies with the decision maker in the DWP or local authority.[249]

The rule does not apply if:[250]

- you are on an unpaid approved work placement or work experience; *or*
- you are on a government employment or training programme with no training allowance, or only travel or meals expenses; *or*
- you can show that the person (including a limited company[251]) cannot, in fact, afford to pay, or afford to pay more; *or*
- you work for a charitable or voluntary organisation or as a volunteer, and it is accepted that it is reasonable for you to give your services free of charge.[252]

Sometimes it may also be reasonable to do a job free of charge from a sense of community duty, particularly if the job would otherwise remain undone and there would be no financial profit to an employer.[253]

If you are caring for a sick or disabled relative, it is usually accepted that it is reasonable to do this free of charge rather than expecting her/him to pay you from benefits. However, if you need to show that it is reasonable, you should take into account, for instance:[254]

- how much care you give and what other care options there are;
- your housing arrangements;
- whether you gave up work to care;
- the risk of your losing entitlement to CA if you were paid, or to a social services assessment of your needs;
- whether your relative would actually pay you.

6. Working out weekly income

Income support, income-based Jobseeker's allowance and income-related employment and support allowance

To work out your weekly income for income support (IS), income-based jobseeker's allowance (JSA) and income-related employment and support allowance (ESA), you should do the following.

- Work out the period covered by the income (see below).
- Establish the date from when to start taking the income into account (see below).
- Convert the income into a weekly amount if necessary (see p454). There are special rules on variable income, payments for less than a week and overlapping payments.

These rules apply to earnings from employment and to income other than earnings. See p428 for how self-employed earnings are assessed.

Period covered by a payment

- If a payment of income is made for an identifiable period, it is taken into account for a period of equal length.[255] For example, a week's part-time earnings are taken into account for a week. If you are paid monthly, the payments are taken into account for the number of weeks between the date you are treated as having been paid and the date you are next due to be paid.
- If the payment does not relate to a particular period, the amount of the payment is divided by the amount of the weekly IS, income-based JSA or income-related ESA to which you would otherwise be entitled. If part of the payment should be disregarded, the amount of IS, income-based JSA or income-related ESA is increased by the appropriate disregard. The result of this calculation is the number of weeks that you are not entitled to IS, income-based JSA or income-related ESA.[256] **Note:** if your benefit is stopped, you cannot make a new claim for any of these benefits (see p24 for exceptions). If you claim universal credit (UC) instead, the payment is assessed under UC rules.
- Payments made on leaving a job, if not ignored, are taken into account for a forward period (see p424).

Date from when a payment counts

For IS, income-based JSA and income-related ESA, the date from when a payment of earnings and/or other income counts depends on when it was due to be paid. If it was due to be paid before you claimed IS, income-based JSA or income-related ESA, it counts from the date on which it was due to be paid.[257] Otherwise, it is treated as having been paid on the first day of the benefit week in which it is due,

Part 4: General rules for other means-tested benefits
Chapter 20: Income: under pension age
6. Working out weekly income

or on the first day of the first benefit week after that in which it is practicable to take it into account.[258]

Payments of UC, IS, JSA, ESA and maternity allowance (MA) are treated as paid on a daily basis for each day for which they are paid.[259]

Benefit week

The '**benefit week**' for JSA, and usually also for IS and ESA, although this may vary, is normally the seven days ending with the day allocated to you according to your national insurance number (also your payday).[260] The benefit week for HB is the seven days starting on a Monday.[261]

The date a payment is due may be different from the date of actual payment. Earnings are due on the employee's normal payday. If the contract of employment does not reveal the date of due payment and there is no evidence to indicate otherwise, the date the payment was received should be taken as the date it was due.[262] If your contract of employment is terminated without proper notice, outstanding wages, wages in hand, holiday pay and any pay in lieu of notice are due on the last day of employment and are treated as having been paid on that day, even if this does not happen (although these are usually disregarded).[263]

If you receive compensation (eg, in a sex discrimination equal pay case), there is disagreement as to whether the relevant date is the date when the earnings in question were due to be paid[264] or when the compensation was awarded.[265]

For the treatment of payments at the end of a job, see p424.

Converting income into a weekly amount

To convert income to a weekly amount:

- if the payment is for less than a week, it is treated as the weekly amount;
- if the payment is for a month, multiply by 12 and divide by 52;
- multiply a payment for three months by four and divide by 52;
- divide a payment for a year by 52 (unless it is a working tax credit (WTC) payment, in which case divide by 365 and multiply by seven);
- for any other period, divide the payment by the number of days in the period then multiply by seven.

If you work on certain days but are paid monthly, it is necessary to decide whether the payment is for the days worked or for the whole month. This generally depends on the terms of your contract of employment,[266] but may depend on how your employer has arranged to make payments to you.[267]

Variable income

If your income fluctuates or your earnings vary because you do not work every week, your weekly income may be averaged over the cycle, if there is an identifiable one, or, if there is not, over five weeks, or over another period if this would be more accurate.[268] If the cycle involves periods when you do no work, those periods are included in the cycle, but not other absences – eg, holidays or sickness.

Part weeks

- If income covering a period up to a week is paid before your first 'benefit week' (see p454) and part of it is counted for that week or if, in any case, you are paid for a period of a week or more and only part of it is counted in a particular benefit week, multiply the whole payment by the number of days it covers in the benefit week, then divide the result by the total number of days covered by the payment.[269]
- If any payment of MA falls partly into the benefit week, only the amount paid for those days is taken into account. For any payment of IS, JSA or ESA, that amount is the weekly amount multiplied by the number of days in the part week and divided by seven.[270]

Overlapping payments

If you have regularly received a certain kind of payment of income from one source and in a particular 'benefit week' (see p454) you receive that payment and another of the same kind from the same source (eg, if your employer first pays you sick pay in arrears and this then overlaps with a payment in advance), the maximum amount to be taken into account is the one paid first.[271]

This does not apply if the second payment was due to be taken into account in another week but the overlapping week is the first in which it could practically be counted (see p453).

Housing benefit

To assess your current normal weekly income for HB, you should do the following.
- Average your earnings over a past period (see below for earnings from employment and p428 for self-employed earnings).
- Estimate income other than earnings (see p435 for what income counts) by looking at an appropriate period of up to 52 weeks. The period chosen must give an accurate assessment of your income.[272]
- Convert earnings from employment and income other than earnings into a weekly amount if necessary:
  - count a payment for less than a week as the weekly amount;
  - multiply a monthly payment by 12 and divide by 52;
  - for other periods, divide the payment by the number of days in the period then multiply by seven.
- Deduct the appropriate earnings disregard(s) (see p429).
- Work out the date from when the income is taken into account (see p456).

Part 4: General rules for other means-tested benefits
Chapter 20: Income: under pension age
6. Working out weekly income

Averaging earnings

For HB, earnings as an employee are usually averaged out over the previous:

- five weeks if you are paid weekly; *or*
- two months if you are paid monthly.[273]

If your earnings vary, or if there is likely to be, or has recently been, a change (eg, you usually do overtime but have not done so recently, or you are about to get a pay rise), the local authority may average them over a different period if this is likely to give a more accurate picture of what you are going to earn.[274]

If you are on strike, the local authority should not take into account your pre-strike earnings and average them out over the strike period.[275]

If you have only just started work and your earnings cannot be averaged over the normal period (ie, five weeks or two months), an estimate is made, based on any earnings you have been paid so far if these are likely to reflect your future average wage. If you have not yet been paid or your initial earnings do not represent what you will normally earn, your employer must provide an estimate of your average weekly earnings.[276] If you start work after having been on certain benefits, you may get four weeks' extended payments of HB at the same amount (see p217). If your earnings change during your award, your new weekly average figure is estimated on the basis of what you are likely to earn over whatever period (up to 52 weeks) best allows an accurate estimate.[277] If averaging does not result in a weekly figure, the amount is converted (see above).

Date from when a payment counts

The average weekly earnings from employment are taken into account for HB from the start of a new claim or from the first day of the 'benefit week' (see p454) after you start work if you are already getting HB. If average weekly earnings change, the new amount counts from the date of change, even if you are not paid until later.[278]

Child tax credit and WTC are taken into account instalment by instalment – eg, if paid weekly or four-weekly, each instalment counts for the seven or 28 days ending on the day it is due to be paid.[279] Other benefits are taken into account for the period they are paid for.[280]

Notes

1. Whose income counts
1 **IS/HB** s136(1) SSCBA 1992
JSA s13(2) JSA 1995
ESA Sch 1 para 6(2) WRA 2007; reg 83
ESA Regs
2 Schs 4 para 12 and 5 para 4 HB Regs
3 **IS** Reg 23(4) IS Regs
JSA Reg 88(3) JSA Regs
ESA Reg 83(4) ESA Regs
4 **IS** Reg 23(2) IS Regs
JSA Reg 88(2) JSA Regs
ESA Reg 83(2) ESA Regs
HB Reg 25(3) HB Regs
5 **IS** Reg 44(4) and Sch 8 para 15 IS Regs
JSA Reg 106(4) and Sch 6 para 18 JSA
Regs
Both Reg 1 SS(WTCCTC)(CA) Regs

2. What counts as income
6 Schs 4 para 12 and 5 para 4 HB Regs
7 R(IS) 4/01
8 *R v SBC ex parte Singer* [1973] 1 WLR 713
9 *Minter v Kingston Upon Hull City Council
and Potter v SSWP* [2011] EWCA Civ
1155

3. Earnings
10 **IS** Reg 35(1) IS Regs
JSA Reg 98(1) JSA Regs; reg 58(1) JSA
Regs 2013
ESA Reg 95(1) ESA Regs; reg 80(1) ESA
Regs 2013
HB Reg 35(1) HB Regs
All R(SB) 21/86
11 Reg 35(1)(i)-(j) HB Regs
12 **IS** Regs 35(2)(b) and 40(4) and Sch 9
paras 1, 4 and 4A IS Regs
JSA Regs 98(2)(c) and 103(6) and Sch 7
paras 1, 4 and 5 JSA Regs; reg 58(2)(c)
JSA Regs 2013
ESA Regs 95(2)(b) and 104(8) and Sch
8 paras 1, 4 and 5 ESA Regs; reg
80(2)(b) ESA Regs 2013
13 Reg 35(1)(i)-(j) HB Regs

14 **IS** Regs 35(2)(b) and 40(4) and Sch 9
paras 1 and 4 IS Regs
JSA Regs 98(2)(c) and 103(6) and Sch 7
paras 1 and 4 JSA Regs; reg 58(2)(c) JSA
Regs 2013
ESA Regs 95(2)(b) and 104(8) and Sch
8 paras 1 and 4 ESA Regs; reg 80(2)(b)
ESA Regs 2013
15 **IS** Reg 35(1)(e) IS Regs
JSA Reg 98(1)(d) JSA Regs; reg 58(1)(d)
JSA Regs 2013
ESA Reg 95(1)(e) ESA Regs; reg 80(1)(e)
ESA Regs 2013
HB Reg 35(1)(e) HB Regs
16 R(IS) 9/95
17 **IS** Reg 35(3)(a)(iv) IS Regs
JSA Reg 98(3)(d) JSA Regs; reg 67(4)(d)
JSA Regs 2013
ESA Reg 95(4), definition of
'compensation', ESA Regs; reg 80(4)
ESA Regs 2013
18 *Minter v Kingston Upon Hull City Council
and Potter v SSWP* [2011] EWCA Civ
1155
19 **IS** Reg 35(1)(j) IS Regs
JSA Reg 98(1)(h) JSA Regs; reg 58(1)(i)
JSA Regs 2013
ESA Reg 95(1)(k) ESA Regs; reg 80(1)(k)
ESA Regs 2013
HB Reg 35(1)(k) HB Regs
20 **IS** Reg 35(2A) IS Regs
JSA Reg 98(2A) JSA Regs; reg 58(3) JSA
Regs 2013
ESA Reg 95(3) ESA Regs; reg 80(3) ESA
Regs 2013
HB Reg 35(3) HB Regs
21 **IS** Reg 35(2)(a) and Sch 9 para 21 IS
Regs
JSA Reg 98(2)(a) and Sch 7 para 22 JSA
Regs; reg 58(2)(a) JSA Regs 2013
ESA Reg 95(2)(a) and Sch 8 para 22 ESA
Regs; reg 80(2)(a) ESA Regs 2013
HB Reg 35(2)(a) and Sch 5 para 23 HB
Regs
22 CIS/11482/1995
23 Vol 5 Ch 26, para 26096 DMG

Part 4: General rules for other means-tested benefits
Chapter 20: Income: under pension age
Notes

24 **IS** Reg 35(2)(a) IS Regs
JSA Reg 98(2)(a) JSA Regs; reg 58(2)(a)
JSA Regs 2013
ESA Reg 95(2)(a) ESA Regs; reg 80(2)(a)
ESA Regs 2013
HB Reg 35(2)(a) HB Regs
All Vol 5 Ch 26, para 26040 DMG
25 **IS** Regs 48(5) IS Regs
JSA Reg 110(5) JSA Regs
ESA Reg 112(5) ESA Regs
HB Reg 46(5) HB Regs
26 **IS** Reg 35(2)(c) IS Regs
JSA Reg 98(2)(d) JSA Regs; reg 58(2)(d)
JSA Regs 2013
ESA Reg 95(2)(c) ESA Regs; reg 80(2)(c)
ESA Regs 2013
HB Reg 35(2)(b) HB Regs
27 R(FC) 1/90
28 CFC/26/1989
29 R(FIS) 4/85
30 R(IS) 13/91; R(IS) 16/93; CFC/26/1989
31 R(FIS) 4/85; R(FC) 1/91; R(IS) 13/91
32 CIS/77/1993; CIS/89/1989
33 **IS** Sch 8 para 11 IS Regs
JSA Sch 6 para 14 JSA Regs; Sch para 9
JSA Regs 2013
ESA Sch 7 para 9 ESA Regs
HB Sch 4 para 13 HB Regs
34 **IS** Sch 8 para 12 IS Regs
JSA Sch 6 para 15 JSA Regs; Sch para 10
JSA Regs 2013
ESA Sch 7 para 10 ESA Regs
HB Sch 4 para 14 HB Regs
35 **IS** Reg 35(2)(d) IS Regs
JSA Reg 98(2)(e) JSA Regs; reg 58(2)(e)
JSA Regs 2013
ESA Reg 95(2)(d) ESA Regs; reg
80(2)(d) ESA Regs 2013
HB Reg 35(2)(c) HB Regs
36 **IS** Reg 40(4) and Sch 9 para 1 IS Regs
JSA Reg 103(6) and Sch 7 para 1 JSA
Regs
ESA Reg 104(8) and Sch 8 para 1 ESA
Regs
HB Reg 40(10) and Sch 5 para 1 HB
Regs
37 **IS** Sch 8 para 15A IS Regs
JSA Sch 6 para 19 JSA Regs
ESA Sch 7 para 11A ESA Regs
38 *Parsons v Hogg* [1985] 2 All ER 897 (CA),
appendix to R(FIS) 4/85
39 **IS** Reg 36(3) IS Regs
JSA Reg 99(1) and (4) JSA Regs; reg
59(1) and (3) JSA Regs 2013
ESA Reg 96(3) ESA Regs; reg 81(2) ESA
Regs 2013
HB Reg 36(3) HB Regs
40 Regs 29(2) and 36(6) HB Regs

41 Reg 34 HB Regs; para BW2.34 GM
42 **IS** Reg 35 IS Regs
JSA Reg 98 JSA Regs; reg 58 JSA Regs
2013
ESA Reg 95 ESA Regs
HB Reg 35 HB Regs
43 R(JSA) 1/06
44 **IS** Regs 35(2)(b) and 40(4) IS Regs
JSA Regs 98(2)(c) and 103(6) JSA Regs;
reg 58(2)(c) JSA Regs 2013
ESA Regs 95(2)(b) and 104(8) ESA Regs
45 **JSA** Sch 6 paras 1(1)(a) and (2) and 2
JSA Regs; Sch paras 1(1)(a) and (2) and 2
JSA Regs 2013
HB Sch 4 paras 1(b) and 2(b)(i) HB Regs
46 **JSA** Reg 98(1)(f) JSA Regs; reg 58(1)(f)
JSA Regs 2013
HB Reg 35(1)(g) HB Regs
47 **JSA** Reg 98(1)(g) JSA Regs; reg 58(1)(h)
JSA Regs 2013
HB Reg 35(1)(h) HB Regs
48 **HB** Reg 35(1)(h) HB Regs
49 **JSA** Sch 6 paras 1(1)(a), (2)(a)(ii),
(2)(b)(ii) and 2 JSA Regs; Sch paras
1(1)(a), (2)(a)(ii), (2)(b)(ii) and 2 JSA
Regs 2013
HB Sch 4 paras 1(b)(i)(bb), (b)(ii)(bb)
and 2 HB Regs
50 **JSA** Regs 98(2)(c) and 103(6) and Sch 7
paras 4 and 5 JSA Regs; reg 58(2)(c) JSA
Regs 2013
HB Reg 35(1)(i) to (j) HB Regs
51 **JSA** Reg 98(2)(f) JSA Regs; reg 58(2)(f)
JSA Regs 2013
HB Because not listed as earnings in reg
35 HB Regs
52 Regs 98(1)(b), (3) and 104(4) and Sch 6
para 1(1) JSA Regs
53 **JSA** Reg 98(1)(b) and Sch 6 paras
1(1)(a) and 2 JSA Regs; reg 58(1)(b) and
Sch paras 1(1)(a) and 2 JSA Regs 2013
HB Reg 35 HB Regs
Both CJSA/82/98
54 **JSA** Regs 98(2)(b) and 103(6)(a) JSA
Regs; reg 58(2)(b) JSA Regs 2013
HB Reg 35(1)(b) HB Regs
55 **JSA** Regs 98(1)(c) and 110(3) JSA Regs;
reg 58(1)(c) JSA Regs 2013
HB Reg 35(1)(d) and 46(3) HB Regs
56 **IS** Regs 35(2)(b) and 40(4) IS Regs
JSA Regs 98(2)(c) and 103(6) JSA Regs;
reg 58(2)(c) JSA Regs 2013
ESA Regs 95(2)(b) and 104(8) ESA Regs
57 Reg 35(1)(i)-(j) and Sch 4 paras 1(c) and
2(b)(ii) HB Regs

58 **IS** Regs 35(1)(d) and 48(3) and Sch 8 paras 1(1)(b) and 2 IS Regs
JSA Regs 98(1)(c) and 110(3) and Sch 6 paras 1(1)(b) and 2 JSA Regs; reg 58(1)(c) and Sch paras 1(1)(b) and 2 JSA Regs 2013
ESA Regs 95(1)(d) and 112(3) and Sch 7 paras 1(1)(b) and 2 ESA Regs
HB Regs 35(1)(d) and 46(3) and Sch 4 paras 1(c) and 2(b)(ii) HB Regs
59 **IS** Sch 8 paras 1(1)(b) and 2 IS Regs
JSA Sch 6 paras 1(1)(b) and 2 JSA Regs; Sch paras 1(1)(b) and 2 JSA Regs 2013
ESA Sch 7 paras 1(1)(b) and 2 ESA Regs
HB Sch 4 paras 1(c) and 2(b)(ii) HB Regs
60 **IS** Regs 37(1) and 38(3) IS Regs
JSA Regs 100(1) and 101(4) JSA Regs; regs 60(1) and 61(3) JSA Regs 2013
ESA Regs 97(1) and 98(3) ESA Regs; regs 82(1) and 83(2) ESA Regs 2013
HB Regs 37 and 38(3) HB Regs
61 *AR v Bradford Metropolitan District Council* [2008] UKUT 30 (AAC), reported as R(H) 6/09
62 **IS** Reg 37(2)(a) IS Regs
JSA Reg 100(2)(a) JSA Regs; reg 60(2)(a) JSA Regs 2013
ESA Reg 97(2)(a) ESA Regs; reg 82(2)(a) ESA Regs 2013
HB Sch 5 para 42 HB Regs
63 **IS** Reg 38(3)(a), (4), (7) and (8)(a) IS Regs
JSA Reg 101(4) and (8) JSA Regs; reg 61(3) and (7) JSA Regs 2013
ESA Reg 98(3)(a), (4), (7) and (8)(a) ESA Regs; reg 83(2)(a), (3), (6) and (7)(a) ESA Regs 2013
HB Reg 38(3)(a), (4), (7) and (8)(a) HB Regs
64 R(IS) 13/91; R(FC) 1/91; CFC/26/1989
65 **IS** Reg 38(6) and (8)(b) IS Regs
JSA Reg 101(7) and (9) JSA Regs; reg 61(6) and (8) JSA Regs 2013
ESA Reg 98(6) and (8)(b) ESA Regs; reg 83(5) and (7)(b) ESA Regs 2013
HB Reg 38(6) and (8)(b) HB Regs
66 **IS** Reg 38(5) IS Regs
JSA Reg 101(6) and (8) JSA Regs; reg 61(5) and (7) JSA Regs 2013
ESA Reg 98(5) ESA Regs; reg 83(4) ESA Regs 2013
HB Reg 38(5) HB Regs
67 *SSWP v SK (CA)* [2013] UKUT 12 (AAC), reported as [2014] AACR 24

68 **IS** Reg 38(11) IS Regs
JSA Reg 101(12) JSA Regs; reg 61(11) JSA Regs 2013
ESA Reg 98(11) ESA Regs; reg 83(10) ESA Regs 2013
HB Reg 38(10) HB Regs
All R(FC) 1/93
69 CFC/836/1995
70 **IS** Regs 30 and 38(10) IS Regs; R(JSA) 1/09
JSA Regs 95 and 101(11) JSA Regs; regs 55 and 61(10) JSA Regs 2013
ESA Regs 92 and 98(10) ESA Regs; regs 77 and 83(9) ESA Regs 2013
71 Vol 5 Ch 27, para 27054 DMG, but see *GM v SSWP (JSA)* [2010] UKUT 221 (AAC), reported as [2011] AACR 9
72 Regs 30(1) and 33(2) HB Regs
73 **IS** Reg 30(2) IS Regs
JSA Reg 95(2) JSA Regs; reg 55(2) JSA Regs 2013
ESA Reg 92(2) ESA Regs
HB Reg 37(3) and (4) HB Regs
74 **IS** Sch 8 para 3 IS Regs
JSA Sch 6 para 4 JSA Regs; Sch para 4 JSA Regs 2013
ESA Sch 7 para 4 ESA Regs
HB Sch 4 para 2A HB Regs
75 **IS** Reg 38(9) IS Regs
JSA Reg 101(10) JSA Regs; reg 61(9) JSA Regs 2013
ESA Reg 98(9) ESA Regs; reg 83(8) ESA Regs 2013
HB Reg 38(9) HB Regs
76 Sch 7 paras 5 and 5A ESA Regs
77 Sch 7 para 6 ESA Regs
78 Reg 88 ESA Regs; reg 39(5) ESA Regs 2013
79 Sch 7 paras 7 and 14 ESA Regs
80 Sch 4 para 4 HB Regs
81 **IS** Sch 8 para 5 IS Regs
JSA Sch 6 para 6 JSA Regs
82 **IS** Sch 8 para 4(2) IS Regs
JSA Sch 6 para 5(1) and (2) and 6A para 1(1) and (2) JSA Regs
HB Sch 4 para 3(2) HB Regs
83 Sch 4 para 3(2) HB Regs
84 **IS** Sch 8 paras 6A and 6B IS Regs
JSA Schs 6 paras 7 and 8 and 6A para 2 JSA Regs
HB Sch 4 paras 5 and 6 HB Regs
85 **IS** Sch 8 para 7(1) IS Regs
JSA Schs 6 para 9(1) and 6A para 3 JSA Regs
HB Sch 4 para 8(1) HB Regs

Part 4: General rules for other means-tested benefits
Chapter 20: Income: under pension age
Notes

86 **IS** Sch 8 para 8 IS Regs
    JSA Schs 6 para 10 and 6A para 4 JSA Regs
    HB Sch 4 para 9 HB Regs
87 **IS** Sch 8 para 7(2) IS Regs
    JSA Schs 6 paras 9 and 10 and 6A paras 3 and 4 JSA Regs
    HB Sch 4 para 8(2)(b) HB Regs
88 **IS** Sch 8 para 4(3) IS Regs
    JSA Schs 6 para 5(3) and 6A para 1(3) JSA Regs
89 **IS** Sch 8 para 4(4) and (7) IS Regs
    JSA Schs 6 para 5(4) and (7) and 6A para 1(4) and (5) JSA Regs
90 **IS** Sch 8 paras 6 and 9 IS Regs
    JSA Schs 6 paras 11 and 12 and 6A para 6 JSA Regs
    HB Sch 4 paras 7 and 10 HB Regs
91 Sch 4 para 10A HB Regs
92 Sch 4 para 17 HB Regs
93 Regs 27(1)(c) and 28 HB Regs; reg 30(1)(c) HB(SPC) Regs
94 Reg 27(2) HB Regs; reg 30(2) HB(SPC) Regs
95 Reg 28(6) HB Regs; reg 31(6) HB(SPC) Regs
96 Reg 28(13) HB Regs; reg 31(13) HB(SPC) Regs
97 Reg 28(6)-(8) HB Regs; reg 31(6)-(8) HB(SPC) Regs
98 Reg 28(14) HB Regs; reg 31(14) HB(SPC) Regs
99 Reg 28(2)-(4) HB Regs; reg 31(2)-(4) HB(SPC) Regs
100 Reg 28(11), (12) and (12A) HB Regs; reg 31(11), (12) and (12A) HB(SPC) Regs

4. Other income
101 R(IS) 4/05
102 Reg 34 HB Regs; BW2.34 GM
103 **IS** Sch 9 para 81 IS Regs
    JSA Sch 7 para 77 JSA Regs
    ESA Sch 8 para 69 ESA Regs
    HB Sch 5 para 68 HB Regs
104 **IS** Reg 40(6) IS Regs
    JSA Reg 103(5B) JSA Regs
    HB Reg 40(5A) HB Regs
105 **IS** Reg 35(2) and Sch 9 para 4 IS Regs
    JSA Sch 7 para 4 JSA Regs
    ESA Reg 95(2) and Sch 8 para 4 ESA Regs
106 Reg 35(1)(i) HB Regs
107 Sch 5 para 56 HB Regs
108 **IS** Sch 9 para 76A IS Regs
    JSA Sch 7 para 72A JSA Regs
    ESA Sch 8 para 66 ESA Regs
    HB Sch 5 para 6 HB Regs

109 **IS** Sch 9 para 9 IS Regs
    JSA Sch 7 para 10 JSA Regs
    ESA Sch 8 para 11 ESA Regs
    HB Sch 5 para 9 HB Regs
110 **IS** Sch 9 para 80 IS Regs
    JSA Sch 7 para 76 JSA Regs
    ESA Sch 8 para 68 ESA Regs
    HB Sch 5 para 67 HB Regs
111 **IS** Sch 9 para 82 IS Regs
    JSA Sch 7 para 78 JSA Regs
    ESA Sch 8 para 70 ESA Regs
    HB Sch 5 para 69 HB Regs
112 **IS** Sch 9 para 5B(2) IS Regs
    JSA Sch 7 para 6B(2) JSA Regs
    ESA Sch 8 para 7(2) ESA Regs
    HB Sch 5 para 65 HB Regs
113 **IS** Reg 7(4)-(6) SS(WTCCTC)(CA) Regs
    JSA Reg 8(3)-(5) SS(WTCCTC)(CA) Regs
114 **IS** Sch 9 para 33 IS Regs
    JSA Sch 7 para 35 JSA Regs
    ESA Sch 8 para 37 ESA Regs
    HB Sch 5 para 32 HB Regs
115 **IS** Sch 9 para 9 IS Regs
    JSA Sch 7 para 10 JSA Regs
    ESA Sch 8 para 11 ESA Regs
    HB Sch 5 paras 6 and 9 HB Regs
116 **IS** Sch 9 para 5B(1) IS Regs
    JSA Sch 7 para 6B(1) JSA Regs
    ESA Sch 8 para 7(1) ESA Regs
117 **IS** Sch 9 paras 6 and 9 IS Regs
    JSA Sch 7 paras 7 and 10 JSA Regs
    ESA Sch 8 paras 8 and 11 ESA Regs
    HB Sch 5 para 6 HB Regs
118 **IS** Sch 9 para 83 IS Regs
    JSA Sch 7 para 79 JSA Regs
    ESA Sch 8 para 71 ESA Regs
    HB Sch 5 para 70 HB Regs
119 **IS** Sch 9 para 5A(1) IS Regs
    JSA Sch 7 para 6A(1) JSA Regs
    ESA Sch 8 para 6 ESA Regs
    HB Sch 5 para 50 HB Regs
120 **IS** Sch 9 paras 5 and 52 IS Regs
    JSA Sch 7 paras 6 and 51 JSA Regs
    ESA Sch 8 paras 64 and 65 ESA Regs
    HB Sch 5 para 51 HB Regs
121 Sch 5 para 4 HB Regs
122 **IS** Sch 9 para 8 IS Regs
    JSA Sch 7 para 9 JSA Regs
    ESA Sch 8 para 10 ESA Regs
    HB Sch 5 para 8 HB Regs
123 **IS** Sch 9 paras 6 and 9 IS Regs
    JSA Sch 7 paras 7 and 10 JSA Regs
    ESA Sch 8 paras 8 and 11 ESA Regs
    HB Sch 5 para 6 HB Regs
124 **IS** Sch 9 paras 7 and 8 IS Regs
    JSA Sch 7 paras 8 and 9 JSA Regs
    ESA Sch 8 paras 9 and 10 ESA Regs
    HB Sch 5 paras 7 and 8 HB Regs

125 **IS** Sch 9 para 31 IS Regs
JSA Sch 7 para 33 JSA Regs
ESA Sch 8 para 35 ESA Regs
HB Sch 5 para 31 HB Regs
126 **IS** Sch 10 para 18 IS Regs
JSA Sch 8 para 23 JSA Regs
ESA Sch 9 para 23 ESA Regs
HB Sch 6 para 20 HB Regs
127 **IS** Sch 9 paras 54-56 IS Regs
JSA Sch 7 paras 53-55 JSA Regs
ESA Sch 8 paras 49, 51 and 52 ESA Regs
HB Sch 5 paras 53-55 HB Regs
128 **IS** Sch 9 paras 5B(3) and 53 IS Regs
JSA Sch 7 paras 6B(3) and 52 JSA Regs
ESA Sch 8 paras 7(3) and 50 ESA Regs
HB Sch 5 para 52 HB Regs
129 **IS** Sch 9 para 40 IS Regs
JSA Sch 7 para 42 JSA Regs
ESA Sch 8 para 42 ESA Regs
HB Sch 5 para 36 HB Regs
130 **IS** Sch 9 para 46 IS Regs
JSA Sch 7 para 45 JSA Regs
ESA Sch 8 para 44 ESA Regs
HB Sch 5 para 41 HB Regs
131 Sch 5 para 16 HB Regs
132 **IS** Sch 9 para 16 IS Regs
JSA Sch 7 para 17 JSA Regs
ESA Sch 8 para 17 ESA Regs
HB Sch 5 para 15 HB Regs; Sch Part 2 HB&CTB(WPD) Regs
133 *MN v (1) Bury Council (2) SSWP (HB)* [2014] UKUT 187 (AAC)
134 **IS** Sch 9 para 36 IS Regs
ESA Sch 8 para 39 ESA Regs
JSA Sch 7 para 38 JSA Regs
HB Sch 5 para 34 HB Regs
135 s134(8) SSAA 1992; HB&CTB(WPD) Regs
136 s74(2) SSAA 1992
137 **IS** reg 40(1) and (3) IS Regs
JSA reg 103(1) and (3) JSA Regs
ESA reg 104(1) and (3) ESA Regs
HB reg 40(1) and (5) HB Regs
138 R(IS) 5/99; Vol 5 Ch 28, para 28008 DMG
139 **IS** Sch 9 para 73 IS Regs
JSA Sch 7 para 70 JSA Regs
ESA Sch 8 para 60 ESA Regs
HB Sch 5 para 47A HB Regs
140 *KW v Lancaster City Council v SSWP (HB)* [2011] UKUT 266 (AAC); s74A SSAA 1992
141 Sch 5 para 47 HB Regs
142 **IS** Reg 54 IS Regs
JSA Reg 117 JSA Regs
ESA Reg 119 ESA Regs

143 **IS** Regs 54 and 55 IS Regs
JSA Regs 117 and 118 JSA Regs
ESA Regs 119 and 120 ESA Regs
144 **IS** Reg 42(4)(a) IS Regs
JSA Reg 105(10)(a) JSA Regs
ESA Reg 107(3)(c) ESA Regs
145 R(SB) 1/89
146 **IS** Reg 42(4)(b) IS Regs
JSA Reg 105(10)(b) JSA Regs
ESA Reg 107(4) ESA Regs
147 CIS/683/1993
148 **IS** Sch 9 para 25(1)(a) and (1A) IS Regs
JSA Sch 7 para 26(1)(a) and (1A) JSA Regs
ESA Sch 8 para 26(1)(a) and (2) ESA Regs
HB Sch 5 para 25(1)(a) and (2) HB Regs
149 **IS** Sch 9 para 25(1A) IS Regs
JSA Sch 7 para 26(1A) JSA Regs
ESA Sch 8 para 26(2) ESA Regs
HB Sch 5 para 25(2) HB Regs
150 **IS** Reg 42(4)(b) IS Regs
JSA Reg 105(10)(b) JSA Regs
ESA Reg 107(4) ESA Regs
HB Reg 42(6)(c) HB Regs
All Vol 5 Ch 28, para 28174 DMG
151 **IS** Sch 9 para 25(1)(a) and (2)(b) IS Regs
JSA Sch 7 para 26(1)(a) and (2)(b) JSA Regs
152 **IS** Sch 9 para 25(2)(a) IS Regs
JSA Sch 7 para 26(2)(a) JSA Regs
Both Reg 1 and Schs 1 para 23(c) and 2 para 23(c) SS(WTCCTC)(CA) Regs
153 That is, under ss22C(2) or 59(1)(a) CA 1989 or (in Scotland) s26 C(S)A 1995 or regs 33 or 51 Looked After Children (Scotland) Regulations 2009, No.210
154 **IS** Sch 9 para 26 IS Regs
JSA Sch 7 para 27 JSA Regs
ESA Sch 8 para 28 ESA Regs
HB Sch 5 para 26 HB Regs
155 **IS** Sch 9 para 25(1)(c) and (2) IS Regs
JSA Sch 7 para 26(1)(c) and (2) JSA Regs
ESA Sch 8 para 26(1)(b) ESA Regs
HB Sch 5 para 25(1)(ba) HB Regs
156 **IS** Sch 9 paras 25(1)(ba), 26(a)(iii) and 28(1)(c) IS Regs
JSA Sch 7 paras 26(1)(ba), 27(a)(iii) and 29(1)(c) JSA Regs
ESA Sch 8 para 26(1)(b), 28(a)(iii) and 30(1)(c) ESA Regs
HB Sch 5 paras 25(1)(ba), 26(a)(iii) and 28 HB Regs

Part 4: General rules for other means-tested benefits
Chapter 20: Income: under pension age
Notes

157 **IS** Sch 9 para 25(1)(e) IS Regs; Vol 5 Ch 28, para 28402 DMG
JSA Sch 7 para 26(1)(e) JSA Regs; Vol 5 Ch 28, para 28402 DMG
ESA Sch 8 para 26(1)(d) ESA Regs
HB Sch 5 para 25(1)(d) HB Regs

158 **IS** Sch 9 para 39 IS Regs
JSA Sch 7 para 41(1) JSA Regs
ESA Sch 8 para 41 ESA Regs
HB Sch 5 para 35 HB Regs

159 **IS** Reg 48(9) IS Regs
JSA Reg 110(9) JSA Regs
ESA Reg 112(7) ESA Regs
HB Reg 46(6) HB Regs

160 **IS** Reg 48(10)(a) IS Regs
JSA Reg 110(10) JSA Regs

161 **IS** Sch 9 para 15 IS Regs
JSA Sch 7 para 15 JSA Regs
ESA Sch 8 para 16 ESA Regs
HB Sch 5 para 14 HB Regs

162 R(H) 5/05 explains the difference between a loan and a voluntary payment

163 **IS** Sch 9 para 15(5A) IS Regs
JSA Sch 7 para 15(5A) JSA Regs
ESA Sch 8 para 16(3) ESA Regs
HB Sch 5 para 14 HB Regs

164 *Malekout v SSWP* [2010] EWCA Civ 162, reported as [2010] AACR 28

165 Vol 5 Ch 28, para 28102 DMG

166 **IS** Sch 9 para 19 IS Regs
JSA Sch 7 para 20 JSA Regs
ESA Sch 8 para 20 ESA Regs
HB Sch 5 para 22 HB Regs

167 **IS** Sch 9 para 18 IS Regs
JSA Sch 7 para 19 JSA Regs
ESA Sch 8 para 19 ESA Regs
HB Sch 5 para 21 HB Regs

168 **IS** Sch 9 para 20 IS Regs
JSA Sch 7 para 21 JSA Regs
ESA Sch 8 para 21 ESA Regs
HB Sch 5 para 42 HB Regs

169 **IS** Reg 2(1) IS Regs
JSA Reg 1(3) JSA Regs
ESA Reg 2(1), definition of 'board and lodging', ESA Regs
HB Sch 5 para 42(2) HB Regs
IS/JSA/HB definition of 'board and lodging accommodation'

170 CIS/521/2002

171 CIS/13059/1996

172 **IS** Reg 48(4) IS Regs
JSA Reg 110(4) JSA Regs
ESA Reg 112(4) ESA Regs
HB Reg 46(4) HB Regs
All *CAO v Palfrey and Others, The Times,* 17 February 1995; R(IS) 26/95

173 CIS/563/1991

174 **IS** Sch 9 para 22(1) IS Regs
JSA Sch 7 para 23 JSA Regs
ESA Sch 8 para 23(1) ESA Regs
HB Sch 5 para 17(1) HB Regs

175 **IS** Reg 48(4) IS Regs
JSA Reg 110(4) JSA Regs
ESA Reg 112(4) ESA Regs
HB Reg 46(4) HB Regs

176 **IS** Sch 9 para 22(1) IS Regs
JSA Sch 7 para 23(2) JSA Regs
ESA Sch 8 para 23(2) ESA Regs
HB Sch 5 para 17(1) HB Regs

177 CFC/13/1993

178 **IS** Sch 9 para 22(2) IS Regs
JSA Sch 7 para 23(2) and (3) JSA Regs
ESA Sch 8 para 23(2) and (3) ESA Regs
HB Sch 5 para 17(2) HB Regs

179 **IS** Reg 53 IS Regs
JSA Reg 116 JSA Regs
ESA Reg 118 ESA Regs
HB Reg 52 HB Regs

180 **IS** Reg 41(1) IS Regs
JSA Reg 104(1) JSA Regs
ESA Reg 105(1) ESA Regs

181 Reg 41(1) HB Regs

182 **IS** Reg 29(2) IS Regs
JSA Reg 94(2) JSA Regs
ESA Reg 91(2) ESA Regs
HB Reg 33 HB Regs

183 **IS** Reg 41(2) IS Regs
JSA Reg 104(2) JSA Regs
ESA Reg 105(2) ESA Regs
HB Reg 41(2) HB Regs

184 **IS** Reg 41(6) IS Regs
JSA Reg 104(5) JSA Regs
ESA Reg 105(4) ESA Regs
HB Reg 41(4) HB Regs

185 Regs 41(4) and 48(2) IS Regs

186 **IS** Reg 41(7) IS Regs
JSA Reg 104(6) JSA Regs
ESA Reg 105(5) ESA Regs
HB Reg 41(5) HB Regs

187 **IS** Sch 10 para 20 IS Regs
JSA Sch 8 para 25 JSA Regs
ESA Sch 9 para 25 ESA Regs
HB Sch 6 para 22 HB Regs

188 *R v SBC ex parte Singer* [1973] 1 All ER 931; *R v Oxford County Council ex parte Jack* [1984] 17 HLR 419; *R v West Dorset DC ex parte Poupard* [1988] 20 HLR 295

189 R(H) 8/08

190 *Leeves v Chief Adjudication Officer* [1998] EWCA 1706, reported as R(IS) 5/99; CIS/2287/2008

191 **IS** Reg 48(2) IS Regs
JSA Reg 110(2) JSA Regs
ESA Reg 112(2) ESA Regs
HB Reg 46(2) HB Regs

192 **IS** s126(5) SSCBA 1992
JSA s5(2)(c) JSA 1995
193 Regs 41(4) and 48(2) IS Regs
194 **IS** Sch 9 para 13 IS Regs
JSA Sch 7 para 14 JSA Regs
ESA Sch 8 para 15 ESA Regs
HB Sch 5 para 13 HB Regs
195 **IS** Sch 9 para 1A IS Regs
JSA Sch 7 paras A2 and A3 JSA Regs
ESA Sch 8 para 1A ESA Regs
HB Sch 5 paras A2 and A3 HB Regs
196 Sch 8 para 15A ESA Regs
197 **IS** Sch 9 para 64 IS Regs
JSA Sch 7 para 62 JSA Regs
ESA Sch 8 para 55 ESA Regs
HB Sch 5 para 58 HB Regs
198 Reg 46(7) HB Regs
199 **IS** Regs 39C and 39D IS Regs
JSA Regs 102C and 102D JSA Regs
ESA Regs 102 and 103 ESA Regs
200 DMG Memo 12/15
201 Vol 5 Ch 28, para 28090 DMG
202 **IS** Reg 41(2) and Sch 9 para 17 IS Regs
JSA Reg 104(2) and Sch 7 para 18 JSA Regs
ESA Reg 105(2) and Sch 8 para 18 ESA Regs
HB Reg 41(2) HB Regs
203 **IS** Sch 9 para 29 IS Regs; Vol 5 Ch 28, para 28240 DMG
JSA Sch 7 para 30 JSA Regs
ESA Sch 8 para 31 ESA Regs
204 **IS** Sch 9 para 30 IS Regs
JSA Sch 7 para 31 JSA Regs
ESA Sch 8 para 32 ESA Regs
All R(IS) 13/01
205 Sch 5 para 29 HB Regs
206 **IS** Sch 9 para 30ZA IS Regs
JSA Sch 7 para 31A JSA Regs
ESA Sch 8 para 33 ESA Regs
HB Sch 5 para 29 HB Regs
207 **IS** Sch 9 para 31A IS Regs
JSA Sch 7 para 33A JSA Regs
ESA Sch 8 para 35A ESA Regs
HB Sch 5 para 31A HB Regs
208 **IS** Sch 9 para 28 IS Regs
JSA Sch 7 para 29 JSA Regs
ESA Sch 8 para 30 ESA Regs
HB Sch 5 para 28 HB Regs
209 **IS** Sch 9 para 28(2) and (5) IS Regs
JSA Sch 7 para 29(2) and (5) JSA Regs
ESA Sch 8 para 30(2) and (3) ESA Regs
HB Sch 5 para 28A HB Regs
210 **IS** Sch 9 para 79 IS Regs
JSA Sch 7 para 75 JSA Regs
ESA Sch 8 para 67 ESA Regs
HB Sch 5 para 66 HB Regs

211 **IS** Sch 9 para 58 IS Regs
JSA Sch 7 para 56 JSA Regs
ESA Sch 8 para 53 ESA Regs
HB Sch 5 para 57 HB Regs
All *Casewell v SSWP* [2008] EWCA Civ 524, reported as R(IS) 7/08
212 **IS** Sch 9 para 27 IS Regs
JSA Sch 7 para 28 JSA Regs
ESA Sch 8 para 29 ESA Regs
HB Sch 5 para 27 HB Regs
213 **IS** Sch 9 para 76 IS Regs
JSA Sch 7 para 72 JSA Regs
ESA Sch 8 para 63 ESA Regs
HB Sch 5 para 63 HB Regs
214 **IS** Sch 9 paras 15, 30A and 66 IS Regs
JSA Sch 7 paras 15, 32 and 64 JSA Regs
ESA Sch 8 paras 16, 34 and 56 ESA Regs
215 **IS** Sch 10 para 8(b) IS Regs
JSA Sch 8 para 13(b) JSA Regs
ESA Sch 9 para 12(b) ESA Regs
HB Sch 6 para 10(b) HB Regs
216 **IS** Sch 9 para 75 IS Regs
JSA Sch 7 para 71 JSA Regs
ESA Sch 8 para 62 ESA Regs
HB Sch 5 para 62 HB Regs
217 **IS** Sch 9 para 11 IS Regs
JSA Sch 7 para 12 JSA Regs
ESA Sch 8 para 13 ESA Regs
HB Sch 5 para 11 HB Regs
218 **IS** Sch 9 para 2 IS Regs
JSA Sch 7 para 2 JSA Regs
ESA Sch 8 para 2 ESA Regs
HB Sch 5 para 2 HB Regs
219 **IS** Sch 9 para 21 IS Regs
JSA Sch 7 para 22 JSA Regs
ESA Sch 8 para 22 ESA Regs
HB Sch 5 para 23 HB Regs
220 para BW2 Annex B para 13 GM
221 **IS** Sch 9 para 51 IS Regs
JSA Sch 7 para 50 JSA Regs
ESA Sch 8 para 48 ESA Regs
HB Sch 5 para 49 HB Regs
222 **IS** Sch 9 para 43 IS Regs
JSA Sch 7 para 43 JSA Regs
ESA Sch 8 para 43 ESA Regs
HB Sch 5 para 39 HB Regs
223 **IS** Sch 9 para 10 IS Regs
JSA Sch 7 para 11 JSA Regs
ESA Sch 8 para 12 ESA Regs
HB Sch 5 para 10 HB Regs
224 **IS** Sch 9 para 23 IS Regs
JSA Sch 7 para 24 JSA Regs
ESA Sch 8 para 24 ESA Regs
HB Sch 5 para 24 HB Regs
225 **IS** Sch 9 para 24 IS Regs
JSA Sch 7 para 25 JSA Regs
ESA Sch 8 para 25 ESA Regs
HB Sch 5 para 33 HB Regs

Part 4: General rules for other means-tested benefits
Chapter 20: Income: under pension age
Notes

226 **IS** Sch 9 para 48 IS Regs
JSA Sch 7 para 47 JSA Regs
ESA Sch 8 para 45 ESA Regs
HB Sch 5 para 44 HB Regs
227 **IS** Sch 9 para 49 IS Regs
JSA Sch 7 para 48 JSA Regs
ESA Sch 8 para 46 ESA Regs
HB Sch 5 para 45 HB Regs
228 **IS** Sch 9 para 50 IS Regs
JSA Sch 7 para 49 JSA Regs
ESA Sch 8 para 47 ESA Regs
HB Sch 5 para 46 HB Regs
229 Schs 4 para 11 and 5 paras 19 and 20 HB
Regs
230 **IS** Sch 9 para 69 IS Regs
JSA Sch 7 para 67 JSA Regs
ESA Sch 8 para 57 ESA Regs
HB Sch 5 para 59 HB Regs
231 **IS** Sch 9 para 2A IS Regs
JSA Sch 7 para 2A JSA Regs
ESA Sch 8 para 2A ESA Regs
HB Sch 5 para 2A HB Regs
232 Reg 26 VP Regs

5. Notional income
233 **IS** Reg 42(1) IS Regs
JSA Reg 105(1) JSA Regs
ESA Reg 106(1) ESA Regs
HB Reg 42(1) HB Regs
234 Vol 5 Ch 28, paras 28608-16 DMG; see
also CIS/15052/1996
235 **IS** Reg 42(2) IS Regs
JSA Reg 105(2) JSA Regs
ESA Reg 106(2) ESA Regs
HB Reg 42(2) HB Regs
236 **IS** Reg 42(2ZA) and (2A) IS Regs
JSA Reg 105(2B) and (3) JSA Regs
ESA Reg 106(3) and (4) ESA Regs
237 **IS** Reg 42(2)(e) and (f) IS Regs
JSA Reg 105(2)(d) JSA Regs
ESA Reg 106(2)(e) and (f) ESA Regs
HB Reg 42(2)(f) and (g) HB Regs
238 Vol 5 Ch 28, paras 28608-16 DMG
239 CIS/16271/1996
240 **IS** Reg 42(3) IS Regs
JSA Reg 105(6) JSA Regs
ESA Reg 107(1) ESA Regs
241 **IS** Reg 42(3A) and (3B) IS Regs
JSA Reg 105(7)(a), (8) and (9) JSA Regs
ESA Reg 107(2)(a) and (b) ESA Regs
242 **IS** Reg 42(3C) IS Regs
JSA Reg 105(7)(d) JSA Regs
ESA Reg 107(2)(c) ESA Regs
243 CIS/15052/1996, para 10
244 **IS** Reg 42(5) IS Regs
JSA Reg 105(12) JSA Regs
ESA Reg 108(1) ESA Regs
245 Reg 2 SS(PAOR) Regs

246 **IS** Reg 42(4)(a) IS Regs
JSA Reg 105(10)(a) JSA Regs
ESA Reg 107(3) ESA Regs
HB Reg 42(6)(b) HB Regs
247 **IS** Reg 42(4)(b) and (4ZA) IS Regs
JSA Reg 105(10)(b) and (10A) JSA Regs
ESA Reg 107(4) and (5) ESA Regs
HB Reg 42(6)(c) and (7) HB Regs
248 **IS** Reg 42(6) IS Regs; CIS/191/1991
JSA Reg 105(13) JSA Regs
ESA Reg 108(3) ESA Regs
HB Reg 42(9) HB Regs
249 R(SB) 13/86
250 **IS** Reg 42(6A) IS Regs
JSA Reg 105(13A) JSA Regs
ESA Reg 108(4) ESA Regs
HB Reg 42(10) HB Regs
251 R(SB) 13/86
252 **IS** Reg 42(6A)(a) IS Regs
JSA Reg 105(13A)(a) JSA Regs
ESA Reg 108(4)(a) ESA Regs
HB Reg 42(10)(a) HB Regs
253 CIS/147/1993
254 *Sharrock v CAO*, 26 March 1991 (CA);
CIS/93/1991; CIS/422/1992; CIS/701/
1994

6. Working out weekly income
255 **IS** Reg 29(2) IS Regs
JSA Reg 94(2) JSA Regs; reg 54(2) JSA
Regs 2013
ESA Reg 91(2) ESA Regs; reg 76(2) ESA
Regs 2013
256 **IS** Reg 29(2)(b) IS Regs
JSA Reg 94(2)(b) JSA Regs; reg 54(2)(c)
JSA Regs 2013
ESA Reg 91(2)(c) ESA Regs; reg 76(2)(c)
ESA Regs 2013
257 **IS** Reg 31(1)(a) IS Regs
JSA Reg 96(1)(a) JSA Regs; reg 56(a) JSA
Regs 2013
ESA Reg 93(1)(a) ESA Regs; reg 78(a)
ESA Regs 2013
258 **IS** Reg 31(1)(b) IS Regs
JSA Reg 96(1)(b) JSA Regs; reg 56(b) JSA
Regs 2013
ESA Reg 93(1)(b) ESA Regs; reg 78(b)
ESA Regs 2013
259 **IS** Reg 31(2) IS Regs
JSA Reg 96(2) JSA Regs
ESA Reg 93(2) ESA Regs
260 **IS** Reg 2(1) IS Regs
JSA Reg 1(3) JSA Regs; reg 2(2) JSA Regs
2013
ESA Reg 2(1) ESA Regs; reg 2 ESA Regs
2013
261 Reg 2 HB Regs
262 R(SB) 33/83

263 R(SB) 22/84; R(SB) 11/85
264 CIS/590/1993
265 *SSWP v JP (JSA)* [2010] UKUT 90 (AAC)
266 R(IS) 3/93
267 R(IS) 10/95
268 **IS** Reg 32(6) IS Regs
JSA Reg 97(6) JSA Regs; reg 57(5) JSA
Regs 2013
ESA Reg 94(6) ESA Regs; reg 79(5)(b)
ESA Regs 2013
269 **IS** Reg 32(2) and (3) IS Regs
JSA Reg 97(2) and (3) JSA Regs; reg
57(2) and (3) JSA Regs 2013
ESA Reg 94(2) and (3) ESA Regs; reg
79(2) and (3) ESA Regs 2013
270 **IS** Reg 32(4) IS Regs
JSA Reg 97(4) JSA Regs
ESA Reg 94(4) ESA Regs
271 **IS** Reg 32(5) and Sch 8 para 10 IS Regs
JSA Reg 97(5) and Sch 6 para 13 JSA
Regs; reg 57(4) and Sch para 8 JSA Regs
2013
ESA Reg 94(5) and Sch 7 para 8 ESA
Regs; reg 79(4) ESA Regs 2013
272 Reg 31 HB Regs
273 Reg 29(1)(a) HB Regs
274 Reg 29(1)(b) HB Regs; para BW2/W2.53
GM
275 *R v HBRB of the London Borough of Ealing
ex parte Saville* [1986] 18 HLR 349
276 Reg 29(2) HB Regs
277 Reg 29(3) HB Regs
278 Reg 29A HB Regs
279 Reg 32 HB Regs
280 Reg 31(2) HB Regs

Chapter 21

Income: over pension age

This chapter covers:
1. Whose income counts (p467)
2. What counts as income (p467)
3. Earnings (p469)
4. Income other than earnings (p474)
5. Notional income (p481)
6. Working out weekly income (p483)

This chapter explains the rules for working out your weekly income for pension credit (PC) and for pension-age housing benefit (HB) if you and your partner are over pension age and neither of you are on income support (IS), income-based jobseeker's allowance (JSA), income-related employment and support allowance (ESA) or universal credit (UC). See Chapter 20 for the rules for IS, income-based JSA and income-related ESA and for working-age HB if you and your partner are under pension age. See Chapter 7 for the rules for UC. If you are in a couple and one of you is over pension age but not the other, see p188 for whether the working-age or pension-age HB rules apply.

Note: whenever HB is referred to in this chapter, this only applies to the pension-age rules. The law refers to the qualifying age for PC rather than pension age, but since December 2018 this has been the same as pension age.

Key facts
- Your entitlement to pension credit (PC) and pension-age housing benefit (HB) and the amount you get depends on how much income you have.
- Your own income counts and, if you are a member of a couple, your partner's income also counts.
- Some income may be completely or partly ignored, or it may count in full.
- If you get the guarantee credit of PC, you are entitled to maximum HB, so you do not need to work out your income again for HB.

1. Whose income counts

If you are a member of a couple (see p319), your partner's income is added to yours.[1]

The income of a dependent child does *not* affect pension credit or housing benefit.[2]

2. What counts as income

Pension credit

For pension credit (PC), '**income**' means:[3]

- earnings (see p469 and p471);
- certain benefits and tax credits, including state retirement pensions and war pensions (see p474);
- maintenance (see p477);
- income from tenants and lodgers (see p477);
- income from capital (see p478);
- other specified miscellaneous income, including occupational and personal pensions (see p479);
- notional income (see p481);
- any income paid in lieu of the above.

For each type of income, some income is taken into account and some is ignored (or 'disregarded') in the assessment of PC. If the rules do not specify a type of income as being included in the assessment, it is ignored and does not affect your benefit.

For the rules on qualifying income for the savings credit and the 'assessed income period', see Chapter 13.

Housing benefit

How your income affects your entitlement to housing benefit (HB) depends on whether you are getting PC and, if so, which type of PC.

If you get pension credit guarantee credit

If you (or your partner) get the guarantee credit of PC, all your (and your partner's) income is ignored.[4] This is because entitlement to guarantee credit of PC acts as a passport to maximum HB.

Part 4: General rules for other means-tested benefits
Chapter 21: Income: over pension age
2. What counts as income

If you get pension credit savings credit

If you (or your partner) only get the savings credit of PC, your income for HB purposes is the income (and capital) figure used by the DWP to work out your PC, plus:[5]

- the amount of savings credit of PC; *and*
- any income (and capital) of your partner which was not taken into account in the PC calculation;

minus:[6]

- an amount disregarded from your earnings for childcare charges (see p474);
- the higher amount disregarded from your earnings if you:
  - are a lone parent (see p473);
  - pay maintenance (see p477);
- any additional full-time earnings disregard (see p473);
- any earnings disregarded from 'permitted work' (see p472);
- any discretionary increase to the £10 disregard for war pensions, and war widows' and widowers' pensions (see p476).

If you do not get pension credit

If you or your partner are over pension age (see p271) and do not get the guarantee or savings credit of PC (or universal credit, income support, income-based jobseeker's allowance or income-related employment and support allowance), income is defined in the same way as for PC (see p467).[7] Some income is taken into account and some disregarded, but the rules are not always the same as for PC. The differences are explained in the relevant sections below.

Net weekly income

The income that is taken into account is the amount after deducting any tax or national insurance (NI) contributions.[8]

For HB, the local authority may ignore changes (eg, Budget changes) in tax or NI contributions and the maximum rate of tax credits for up to 30 benefit weeks. When the changes are eventually taken into account, you are not treated as having been underpaid or overpaid benefit during the period of the delay.[9]

Once you have worked out what income should be taken into account, this is converted into a weekly amount (see p483) and the total taken into account in the benefit assessment. See p484 for the date from which a payment is counted. Chapters 10 and 13 explain how income affects the amount of HB or PC you get.

3. Earnings

How earnings are treated depends on whether you are an employed earner (see below) or are self-employed (see p471). In both cases, some of your earnings can be disregarded (see p471).

Employed earnings

What counts as earnings

'**Earnings**' means 'any remuneration or profit derived from... employment'. As well as your wages, this includes:[10]

* any bonus or commission (including tips);
* holiday pay – but this is ignored if your employment ends before your pension credit (PC) or housing benefit (HB) entitlement starts;
* statutory sick pay and contractual sick pay,[11] statutory maternity pay, statutory adoption pay, statutory paternity pay, statutory shared parental pay or statutory parental bereavement pay or any other payment made to you by your employer while you are on maternity leave;[12]
* any payments made by your employer for expenses not 'wholly, exclusively and necessarily incurred' in carrying out your job, such as travel expenses to and from work, and payments made to you for looking after members of your family;
* pay in lieu of notice, or pay in lieu of remuneration except for periodic payments following redundancy. However, all earnings, including pay in lieu, are ignored if your employment ends before your PC or HB entitlement starts;
* a retainer fee (eg, payment during the school holidays if you work for the school meals service[13]) or a guarantee payment;[14]
* an equal pay settlement – eg, through a 'single status agreement';[15]
* any payment of a non-cash voucher which is liable for class 1 national insurance (NI) contributions.[16] Non-cash vouchers that are not liable for contributions (eg, certain childcare and charitable vouchers) are classed as payments in kind and ignored.[17]

What does not count as earnings

Examples of payments not counted as earnings include the following.

* Payments in kind (eg, petrol) are ignored.[18]
* An advance of earnings or a loan from your employer is treated as capital.[19]
* The value of free accommodation provided as part of your job is ignored.[20]
* Payments towards expenses that are 'wholly, exclusively and necessarily incurred', such as travelling expenses during the course of your work, are ignored.[21]

Part 4: General rules for other means-tested benefits
Chapter 21: Income: over pension age
3. Earnings

- If you are a local councillor, travelling expenses and subsistence payments are (and basic allowances may be[22]) ignored as expenses 'wholly, exclusively and necessarily incurred' in your work.
- If your earnings are paid in another currency, any bank charges for converting them into sterling are deducted before taking them into account.[23]
- The net amount of any occupational pension,[24] although not counted as earnings, counts as other income and is taken into account in full.[25]
- Any compensation payments made by an employment tribunal for unfair dismissal or unlawful discrimination do not count as earnings.[26]

4 Calculating net earnings from employment

Both your 'gross' earnings and 'net' earnings must be calculated. It is your 'net' earnings' that are taken into account in the assessment. See p483 for how earnings are converted into a weekly amount.

Gross and net earnings

'**Gross earnings**' means the amount of earnings received from your employer less deductions for any expenses wholly, necessarily and exclusively incurred by you in order to carry out the duties of your employment.[27] See p469 for what counts as earnings and examples of expenses that can be deducted.

'**Net earnings**' means your gross earnings less any deductions made for:[28]

– income tax; *and*

– class 1 NI contributions; *and*

– half of any contribution you make towards a personal or occupational pension scheme.

If your earnings are estimated for HB, the amount of tax and NI you would expect to pay on those earnings is estimated and deducted, together with half of any pension contributions you are paying.[29]

Payments when you stop work

Redundancy payments are treated as capital.[30]

If you leave a job before you claim HB or PC, any earnings should be disregarded as income except certain copyright royalties, and payments for patents, trademarks or under the Public Lending Right scheme.[31]

If you are already getting HB or PC when you leave your job, your earnings are not disregarded for that benefit.

For PC, any final payment is treated as having been paid on the date your next regular payment of earnings would have been paid and taken into account for the same period, unless the final payment is higher than the normal amount. If it is higher, work out over how many normal payment periods it counts – eg, if the final payment is between two and three times as much as normal, it counts over three payment periods.[32]

Example

Sandra has been getting PC and working part time. She earns £90 a week, paid on a Friday. She finishes work on Wednesday 5 August and on that day is given £100, made up of £60 final wages and £40 holiday pay. This £100 is treated as having been paid on Friday 7 August and taken into account for two benefit weeks: £90 in the first week and the remaining £10 in the second week.

Self-employed earnings

Calculating net earnings

Your '**net profit**' over the period before your claim must be worked out. This is your self-employed earnings minus:[33]

- reasonable expenses (see p427 – the rules are the same as those for people under pension age, except that expenses relating to debts are not excluded); *and*
- income tax and NI contributions; *and*
- half of any premium paid in respect of a personal pension scheme which is eligible for tax relief.[34] You must supply certain information about the scheme or annuity contract to the DWP or local authority, if requested.[35]

If you receive payments for board and lodging charges, these do not count as earnings, but as other income (less any disregards – see p477).[36]

Working out average earnings from self-employment

The weekly amount is the average of earnings:[37]

- over a period of one year (in practice, normally the last year for which accounts are available); *or*
- over a more appropriate period if you have recently taken up self-employment or there has been a change which will affect your business.

Childminders

In practice, childminders are always treated as self-employed. Your net profit is deemed to be one-third of your earnings less income tax, NI contributions and half of certain pension contributions.[38] The rest of your earnings are completely ignored.

Disregarded earnings

Some of your earnings from employment or self-employment are disregarded and do not affect your PC or HB. The amount depends on your circumstances. For HB, there is also an additional disregard depending on the hours you work, a childcare costs disregard and a permitted work disregard.

Part 4: General rules for other means-tested benefits
Chapter 21: Income: over pension age
3. Earnings

Pension credit

£20 disregard

Twenty pounds of your earnings (including those of your partner) is disregarded if:

- you are a lone parent;[39] *or*
- you or your partner qualify for an additional amount of PC for being a carer (see p350). If both of you qualify, only £20 is disregarded in total;[40] *or*
- you or your partner are in receipt of:[41]
  - employment and support allowance (ESA) or severe disablement allowance (SDA); *or*
  - attendance allowance (AA), disability living allowance (DLA), personal independence payment (PIP), armed forces independence payment or a mobility supplement; *or*
  - the disabled worker or severe disability element of working tax credit (WTC); *or*
- you or your partner are certified as severely sight impaired or blind by a consultant ophthalmologist;[42] *or*
- you or your partner previously had a £20 earnings disregard in your income support, income-based jobseeker's allowance or income-related ESA and that benefit ended no more than eight weeks before PC entitlement began (the disregard ends if you have a break in employment of more than eight weeks) or, immediately before reaching pension age, there was a £20 disregard in your PC because you or your partner were getting incapacity benefit or SDA. You cannot get this disregard if you have more than an eight-week break in your PC claim;[43] *or*
- you or your partner are an auxiliary coastguard, part-time firefighter, part-time lifeboat crew or in the reserve forces.[44] If your earnings are less than £20 a week, what is left over can be disregarded from your, or your partner's, earnings from any other employment.

Note: if you qualify under more than one category, you still have a maximum of £20 of your earnings disregarded.

Basic £5 or £10 disregard

If you do not qualify for a £20 disregard, £5 of your earnings is disregarded if you are single. If you claim as a member of a couple, £10 of your total income is disregarded, whether or not you are both working.[45]

Housing benefit

Permitted work disregard

For HB only, £20 or £140 is disregarded from earnings if you or your partner are doing 'permitted work' in the circumstances described on p431.[46]

£25 disregard

Lone parents on HB have £25 of their earnings ignored.[47]

£20 disregard

Twenty pounds of your earnings is disregarded if:

- you or your partner qualify for a carer premium. If both of you qualify, only £20 is disregarded in total;[48] *or*
- you or your partner are in receipt of:[49]
  - ESA with a work-related activity or support component or SDA; *or*
  - AA, DLA, PIP, armed forces independence payment or a mobility supplement; *or*
  - the disabled worker or severe disability element of WTC; *or*
- you or your partner are certified as severely sight-impaired or blind by a consultant ophthalmologist;[50] *or*
- you or your partner have (or are treated as having) limited capability for work and the assessment phase has ended;[51] *or*
- you or your partner are (or are treated as) incapable of work and have been for a continuous period of 364 days (196 days if you are terminally ill);[52] *or*
- you or your partner had a £20 earnings disregard in your HB or council tax benefit (CTB) in the eight weeks before you or your partner reached the qualifying age for PC. You cannot get this disregard if you have more than an eight-week break in your employment or in your HB claim (or previously, CTB claim);[53] *or*
- you or your partner are an auxiliary coastguard, part-time firefighter, part-time lifeboat crew or in the reserve forces. If your earnings are less than £20 a week, what is left can be disregarded from your or your partner's earnings from other employment.[54]

Note: if you qualify under more than one category, you still have a maximum of £20 of your earnings disregarded.

Basic £5 or £10 disregard

If you do not qualify for a £25 or £20 disregard, or a permitted work disregard, £5 of your earnings is disregarded if you are single. If you claim as a member of a couple, £10 of your total income is disregarded, whether or not you are both working.[55]

Additional disregard

For HB only, whichever earnings disregard applies is increased by £17.10 if:[56]

- you or your partner receive the 30-hour element as part of your (or your partner's) WTC (see p1458); *or*
- you or your partner work 30 hours or more a week on average; *or*

Part 4: General rules for other means-tested benefits
Chapter 21: Income: over pension age
4. Income other than earnings

- you or your partner work 16 hours or more a week on average and you have a child who is part of your family for benefit purposes (see p323) or your HB includes the family premium (see p340); *or*
- you are a lone parent and work 16 hours or more a week on average; *or*
- you or your partner work 16 hours or more a week on average and one or both of you get ESA which includes a support or work-related activity component, SDA, AA, DLA, PIP, armed forces independence payment, a mobility supplement or the disabled worker or severe disability element in your WTC, or you are certified as severely sight-impaired or blind by a consultant ophthalmologist or have been incapable of work for 364 days (196 days if terminally ill). For couples, the partner who is disabled is the one who must be working 16 hours or more a week on average.

The additional earnings disregard does not apply if your total earnings are less than the total of £17.10, plus any earnings disregard and childcare costs disregard (see below). In this case, £17.10 is disregarded from any WTC awarded to you or your partner, but the earnings disregard is not increased.

Note: only one additional disregard is allowed from your (or your partner's) earnings.

Childcare costs disregard

For HB only, up to £175 a week for one child, or up to £300 a week for two or more children, can be deducted from your (or your partner's) earnings (from employment or self-employment) for childcare costs in certain circumstances.[57] The rules are the same as those for people under pension age (see p432), except you can also have a childcare costs disregard if you are a couple and one of you works 16 hours or more a week and the other is aged 80 or over. There is no childcare costs disregard for PC.

4. Income other than earnings

Benefits and tax credits

Some benefits and tax credits are taken into account as income; others are disregarded, either in full or partly.

Benefits and tax credits that are taken into account

The following benefits and tax credits are taken into account:[58]
- widow's pension;
- carer's allowance (CA) – but not CA supplement in Scotland;
- a war orphan's pension, dependant's allowance or payment under the Armed Forces Compensation Scheme for someone whose parent died and who is still eligible as an adult because of disability;[59]

- contribution-based jobseeker's allowance;
- severe disablement allowance;
- contributory employment and support allowance (ESA). If ESA is paid at a reduced rate because of a sanction, the full rate still counts;[60]
- industrial injuries benefits, except constant attendance allowance and exceptionally severe disablement allowance, which are disregarded;
- maternity allowance;
- retirement pensions;
- statutory sick pay, statutory maternity pay, statutory adoption pay, statutory paternity pay, statutory shared parental pay and statutory parental bereavement pay. These are treated as earnings and may benefit from an earnings disregard (see p471);[61]
- working tax credit (WTC). However, for housing benefit (HB), if your earnings are too low to use the whole £17.10 additional full-time earnings disregard (see p473), £17.10 is disregarded from your WTC instead.[62] If earnings are too low to use the full childcare costs disregard, see p433;
- foreign social security benefits which are similar to the benefits listed above.[63]

Benefits and tax credits that are not taken into account

The following benefits and tax credits are ignored completely:[64]

- armed forces independence payment;
- attendance allowance (AA);
- bereavement support payment;
- Best Start grant (in Scotland);
- child benefit;
- child tax credit;[65]
- Christmas bonus (see p870);
- constant attendance allowance, exceptionally severe disablement allowance or severe disablement occupational allowance paid because of an injury at work or a war injury;
- disability living allowance;
- funeral support payment (in Scotland);
- guardian's allowance;
- HB;
- mobility supplement under the War Pension Scheme;
- personal independence payment;
- social fund payments;
- supplementary payments to pre-1973 war widows or widowers;
- increases for child dependants. Increases for adult dependants are only ignored if the dependant is not your partner.

Part 4: General rules for other means-tested benefits
Chapter 21: Income: over pension age
4. Income other than earnings

Benefits that are partly taken into account

The following benefits have £15 ignored:
- for HB only, widowed parent's allowance.[66]

The following benefits have £10 ignored (or more for HB – see below):
- for PC only, widowed parent's allowance;[67]
- war disablement pension;[68]
- guaranteed income payment and survivor's guaranteed income payment under the Armed Forces Compensation Scheme (if reduced to under £10 by another pension, the remainder is disregarded from the pension);[69]
- war widow's, widower's or surviving civil partner's pension;[70]
- an extra-statutory payment made instead of the above pensions;[71]
- similar payments made by another country;[72]
- a pension from any government paid to the victims of Nazi persecution.[73]

The £10 disregard allowed on the above war pensions is in addition to the total disregard of any mobility supplement or AA (ie, constant attendance allowance, exceptionally severe disablement allowance and severe disablement occupational allowance) paid as part of a war disablement pension.

Local authorities may have discretionary local schemes to increase the £10 disregard on a war disablement, war widow's, widower's or surviving civil partner's pension and on the guaranteed income payment and survivor's guaranteed income payment in your HB.[74] Most increase the disregard or ignore the full amount, so check your local scheme.

Benefit delays

If you have made a claim for benefit but have not yet been paid, the benefit should not be treated as income you have. For PC, you should get your full benefit and the DWP deducts the difference from arrears of the delayed benefit when it is eventually awarded.[75]

For the treatment of payments of arrears of certain benefits and tax credits, see p522.

Benefit deductions and overpayments

Usually, if any deductions are being taken from a benefit (eg, for an overpayment, rent or bills), the full amount of benefit is taken into account before taking off the deduction.[76] However, if an overpayment of tax credits is being deducted from a tax credits award, it is the amount of WTC you actually receive that is taken into account for PC and HB after the deduction to recover the overpayment has been taken off.[77]

Maintenance payments

For **PC**, any maintenance payments for you or your partner made by your (or your partner's) spouse/civil partner or former spouse/civil partner count in full as income. Maintenance for a child is ignored completely.[78]

For **HB**, if you have a child who is part of your family for benefit purposes (see p323) or have a family premium included in your HB, £15 of any maintenance payments for you or your partner made by your (or your partner's) spouse/civil partner or former spouse/civil partner is disregarded.[79] If you receive maintenance from more than one person, only £15 of the total is disregarded. Other kinds of maintenance (eg, for a child) do not count as income and are ignored completely.[80]

If you *pay* maintenance to a former partner or a child not living with you, your payments are not disregarded for the purpose of calculating your income for PC or HB.[81] See p482 if part of a personal or occupational pension is paid to a former partner.

Income from tenants and lodgers

How income from tenants is treated depends on whether or not you live in the same property.

Lettings without board

If you own or are the tenant of your home, and you rent out a room(s) under an agreement, £20 of your weekly charge for each person is ignored. The balance is taken into account.[82]

If someone shares your home under an informal arrangement and is not paying rent under an agreement, any money s/he pays is ignored,[83] but a non-dependant deduction may be made from any HB or housing costs paid with PC.

Boarders

If you have a boarder in your own home, the first £20 a week of the amount s/he pays you is ignored and half of any balance remaining is taken into account as your income.[84] For PC, this does not apply if the boarder is a close relative (see p370) or the arrangement is not commercial.[85] Instead, the whole payment is ignored but there could be a non-dependant deduction from any housing costs paid with PC.[86] For HB, a non-dependant deduction could apply on top of this disregard if the boarder is a close relative or the arrangement is not commercial.[87]

This disregard applies for each boarder you have. The charge must normally include at least some meals.[88] If you have a business partner, even though your gross income includes just your share of the weekly charge to boarders, you still get the full disregard of £20 plus half the excess for each boarder.[89]

Tenants in other properties

Rent from a property other than your home is not taken into account as income.[90] Instead, the value of the property counts as capital and is treated as producing a

Part 4: General rules for other means-tested benefits
Chapter 21: Income: over pension age
4. Income other than earnings

'tariff income' (see below). If the value of the property can be disregarded (see p519), both the rent and the capital value are ignored (there is no tariff income).[91]

Income from capital

The general rule is that capital (unless it is disregarded) is assumed to provide a set rate of income – called 'deemed income' (often called 'tariff income') (see below). *Actual* income generated from capital is ignored as income, except from the types of capital listed below.[92] In these cases, any actual income (but no deemed income) is taken into account.[93] **Note:** for HB, it is only taken into account if the total capital listed below is worth more than £10,000.[94]

Actual income from the following capital is taken into account:
- the value of the right to receive a payment in the future of:
  - income under a life interest or life rent;
  - rent, unless you only have a reversionary (ie, future) interest in the property. For the way the actual rent is treated, see p477;
  - the surrender value or income under an annuity;
- property held in a trust, but not charitable trusts or, for PC, trusts set up out of payments from personal injury to you or your partner or, for HB, from the Independent Living Funds, the London Bombings Relief Charitable Fund, the London Emergencies Trust, the We Love Manchester Emergency Fund or from specified infected blood payment schemes. Income from a discretionary trust can be ignored in some circumstances (see p480).

There are no rules that treat capital of any kind as though it were income.

Deemed income from capital

For PC, if you have capital above £10,000, you are treated as having an assumed income of £1 a week for every £500, or part of £500, by which your capital exceeds £10,000.[95] This is called 'deemed income'. There is no upper capital limit.

For HB, the following applies.
- If you or your partner are getting the guarantee credit of PC, all your (and your partner's) capital is ignored.[96]
- In any other case, there is a capital limit of £16,000.[97] If you have capital above £10,000, you are treated as having an assumed income of £1 a week for every £500, or part of £500, of capital between £10,000.01 and £16,000.[98]

For PC and HB, you are not treated as having any deemed income on capital that is disregarded (see p519).

Example
Samuel, aged 72, has savings of £12,000. Deemed income of £4 a week is taken into account. Any interest from the savings is ignored as income.

Occupational and personal pensions

The following income is taken into account:[99]
- an occupational pension;
- income from a personal pension;
- income from a retirement annuity contract, including an annuity purchased for you or transferred to you on divorce;
- payments from a former employer for early retirement on the grounds of ill health or disability, unless this was under a court order or settlement of a claim;[100]
- an overseas pension;
- a Civil List Act pension;[101]
- payment under an equity release scheme.[102] This provides regular payments from a loan secured on your home. For some home income plans where you buy an annuity, interest on the loan can be disregarded (see p480);
- payments from the Financial Assistance Scheme and periodic payments from the Pension Protection Fund (these help some people with underfunded occupational schemes whose employer has gone out of business).

Some charitable trusts provide discretionary income to people retired from specific occupations. This is ignored for PC and HB.[103]

Occupational and personal pension options

If you have a defined contribution occupational or personal pension (a 'money purchase' pension), for benefit purposes you are generally expected to buy an annuity or take the equivalent income that would be payable through an annuity. Income from an annuity is taken into account. Income that you draw direct from your pension pot is compared to the amount you could get from an annuity and whichever amount is higher is taken into account.[104]

If you also take a lump sum, this counts as your capital.[105] **Note:** if you choose to take a lump sum and spend it in the hope of increasing benefit entitlement, you are likely to be caught by the rules on deprivation of capital (see p503).

If you leave some, or all, of the funds in your pension pot, you are treated as having notional income, usually based on the annuity those funds could yield (see p481).

If you are below pension age, the rules are different (see p445).

Specified miscellaneous income

Any income from copyright royalties and payments for patents, trademarks or under the Public Lending Right scheme are counted in full. Add the payments to your earnings (if any), if you are the first owner of the copyright or patent or author of the book, and deduct the appropriate earnings disregards on p471.[106]

Part 4: General rules for other means-tested benefits
Chapter 21: Income: over pension age
4. Income other than earnings

The following income is ignored:

- income paid outside the UK which cannot be transferred here;[107]
- if income is paid in another currency, any bank charges for converting the payment into sterling;[108]
- income from an annuity is normally taken into account. However, an amount equal to the interest payable on the loan with which the annuity was bought is ignored if:[109]
  - you used at least 90 per cent of the loan made to you to buy the annuity; *and*
  - the annuity will end when you and your partner die; *and*
  - you or your partner are responsible for paying the interest on the loan; *and*
  - you (if you took out the loan) or your partner (if s/he did) were at least 65 at the time the loan was made; *and*
  - the loan is secured on a property which you or your partner own or have an interest in, and the property on which the loan is secured is your home or your partner's home.

  If the interest on the loan is payable after income tax has been deducted, it is an amount equal to the net interest payment that is disregarded, otherwise it is the gross amount of the interest payment;

- any discretionary payment made to you by trustees is ignored altogether, except if the payment is for the purpose of:
  - obtaining food, ordinary clothing or footwear, or household fuel. School uniforms and sportswear are examples of clothing and footwear that are not ordinary; *or*
  - paying rent, council tax or water charges for which you or your partner (if any) are liable. 'Rent' means eligible rent for HB purposes, less any non-dependant deductions; *or*
  - meeting housing costs which could be met by PC.

  In this case, £20 of the payment is disregarded or, if the payment is less than £20, the whole of the payment is disregarded.[110] If this disregard overlaps with certain other disregards (eg, certain war pensions), a combined maximum of £20 is allowed.[111] **Note:** this is a weekly disregard, so payments spread over different or successive benefit weeks attract a £20 disregard for each week;

- periodic payments made to you or your partner under an agreement entered into in settlement of a claim for any injury to you or your partner;[112]
- any payment ordered by a court to be made to you or your partner because of an accident, injury or disease you or your partner (or, for HB only, your child) have.[113]

Other income

Only income that is specified in the rules can affect your benefit (see p467). Any other kind of income is ignored – eg:

- local welfare assistance payments;

- student loans and grants.[114] For HB only, see p449 if you make a parental contribution to a student's grant or loan or towards your under-25-year-old child's expenses in advanced education;
- adoption allowances, fostering allowances, child arrangements order payments and kinship care payments;[115]
- charitable and voluntary payments are not taken into account as income, so if a charity or a person gives you voluntary payments, these do not reduce your benefit. **Note:** maintenance payments can affect your benefit (see p477);
- payments for expenses if you are being consulted as a service user by certain public bodies. Other payments count as earnings but, if you choose not to take them or have them paid to someone else on your behalf, they do not count as your notional income;[116]
- victims' payments to people injured in a 'Troubles-related incident'.[117]

5. Notional income

In certain circumstances, you may be treated as having income that you do not possess.

Note: if you are working but earning less than the going rate, you are not treated as though your wages are higher than those you get, as you are for other means-tested benefits (see p452).

Deliberately getting rid of income

If you deliberately get rid of income in order to claim or increase your benefit, you are treated as though you were still in receipt of that income.[118] The basic issues involved are the same as those for deliberately getting rid of capital (see p526). **Note:** this rule can only apply if your intention was to gain benefit for *yourself* (or your partner). It should not apply if, for example, you stop claiming carer's allowance (CA) solely to allow the cared-for person to get a severe disability premium in her/his benefit (see p346).[119]

If you give up income you get from a small occupational or personal pension to take a lump sum instead, you could be caught by this rule. However, if this is a 'trivial commutation lump sum', you are not treated as still having that income (although the capital counts). There are similar sounding lump sums (eg, 'trivial commutation lump-sum death benefit' which is paid to a dependant), which do not have this protection, so get advice from your pension provider.[120]

Failing to apply for pension income

Sometimes you can be treated as having pension income, even though you have not applied for it.[121]

Part 4: General rules for other means-tested benefits
Chapter 21: Income: over pension age
5. Notional income

Deferring a state pension

If you defer your state pension, category A or B pension, graduated retirement benefit or any shared additional pension paid on divorce, you are *not* treated as having that income for housing benefit (HB) before you claim it. However, you are treated as having that income for pension credit (PC).

The amount that counts for PC is the pension to which you would expect to be entitled were you to claim, less any overlapping benefit you get – eg, CA. If you have a choice of taking a lump sum instead of extra pension income, the amount is based on your taking the lump-sum option (there is no lump-sum choice when claiming a deferred post-April 2016 state pension). To take account of the time it can take to process claims, you are only treated as having this income from the date you could expect to get it were you to make a claim.

For both PC and HB, you are treated as having any amount of category C or D pension and age addition to which you might expect to be entitled if you were to claim. For PC, any overlapping benefit you get is deducted.

Leaving funds in an occupational or personal pension

You are treated as having any income from an occupational pension you have elected to defer beyond the scheme's retirement age,[122] as though you had claimed it. For PC, the time it might take to process it is taken into account and any overlapping benefit is deducted. If you have a defined contribution occupational or personal pension, for benefit purposes you are generally expected to buy an annuity or take the equivalent income that would be payable through an annuity.

If you leave funds in your pension pot, this is disregarded as capital but you are treated as having notional income based on the annuity those funds could yield.[123]If you take one or more lump sums from your pension pot, these count as capital and notional income is worked out on what is left in your pension pot. See p479 for how pension payments are treated.

Income paid to someone else on your behalf

Any money that counts as income and is paid to someone on your behalf is normally treated as being yours and is then either taken into account or ignored as income under the rules described in this chapter. The exception is for payments of income made under an occupational or personal pension scheme (or, for HB only, from the Pension Protection Fund) if you or your partner are bankrupt (or, in Scotland, the subject of a sequestration order). In this case, if the payment is made to the trustee or other person acting on your creditors' behalf and you (and your partner) have no income other than the payment made, it is not treated as being yours.[124]

If you have had a judicial separation rather than a divorce so that usual pension-splitting arrangements are not available, and a court has ordered you to pay part of your pension to your former partner, you could argue this does not count as yours.[125] However, if you pay maintenance from your pension under an agreement out of court, this income is likely to still count as yours.[126]

6. Working out weekly income

To work out your weekly income, you should do the following.
- Work out whether income is taken into account, or fully or partly disregarded (see p467).
- If income varies, work out an average income (see below).
- Convert the income into a weekly amount if necessary (see below).
- Add any deemed weekly income from capital (see p478).

Averaging income

If your earnings vary because you do not work the same hours every week, your weekly income may be averaged over the cycle, if there is an identifiable one.[127] If you do not work a recognisable cycle or your income fluctuates, your income is worked out on the basis of:[128]
- the last two payments before your claim was made or treated as made (or, where applicable, before your claim was superseded) if those payments are at least one month apart; *or*
- the last four payments before your claim was made or treated as made (or, where applicable, before your claim was superseded) if the last two payments are less than a month apart; *or*
- calculating (or estimating for housing benefit – HB) any other payments that would give a more accurate figure for your average weekly income.

In all cases, if the cycle involves periods when you do no work, these are included in the cycle, but not other absences – eg, holidays or sickness.

The payment is treated as if made for a period of a year if you are entitled to:[129]
- royalties or other sums for the use of any copyright, patent or trademark; *or*
- payments for any book registered under the Public Lending Right 1982 scheme; *or*
- payments made on an occasional basis.

Converting income into a weekly amount

Pension credit (PC) and HB are calculated on a weekly basis, so your earnings and other income have to be converted into a weekly amount if necessary. The following rules apply to income from employment and other income.[130] For income from self-employment, see p471.
- If the payment is for less than a week, it is treated as the weekly amount.
- If the payment is for a month, multiply by 12 and divide by 52.

Part 4: General rules for other means-tested benefits
Chapter 21: Income: over pension age
Notes

- Multiply a payment for three months by four and divide by 52.
- Divide a payment for a year by 52.
- Multiply payments for any other periods by seven and divide by the number of days in the period.

Date from when a payment counts

The general rule for PC is that benefits are treated as having been paid on the last day of the PC 'benefit week' in which the benefit is payable, but on the first day if the benefit is paid in advance.[131] Some benefits are treated slightly differently. Contribution-based jobseeker's allowance, contributory employment and support allowance and maternity allowance are treated as having been paid on the day that benefit is payable. For HB, benefits are taken into account over the period for which they are payable.[132]

For other types of income, for PC the general rule is that income counts from the date it is paid for the length of time it has been paid – eg, a month's occupational pension paid on 10 November counts from 10 November to 9 December.[133]

For HB, weekly earnings are taken into account from the start of a new claim or from the first day of the 'benefit week' after you start work. If average weekly earnings change, the new amount counts from the date of change, even if you are not paid until later.[134]

Benefit week

For PC, a **'benefit week'** is the seven days ending on the day PC is payable if paid in arrears, or starting on that day if paid in advance.[135]
For HB, a **'benefit week'** is the seven days starting on a Monday.[136]

Notes

1. **Whose income counts**
1 **PC** s5 SPCA 2002
   HB s136(1) SSCBA 1992
2 Reg 23(3) HB(SPC) Regs

2. **What counts as income**
3 s15 SPCA 2002; reg 15 SPC Regs
4 Regs 25 and 26 HB(SPC) Regs
5 Reg 27(4) HB(SPC) Regs

6 Reg 27(4) HB(SPC) Regs
7 Reg 29 HB(SPC) Regs
8 **PC** Reg 17(10) SPC Regs
   HB Reg 33(12) HB(SPC) Regs
9 Reg 34 HB(SPC) Regs

3. **Earnings**

10 **PC** Reg 17A(2) SPC Regs
    HB Reg 35(1) HB(SPC) Regs
11 **PC** Reg 17A(h) and (k) SPC Regs
    HB Reg 35(1)(h) and (k) HB(SPC) Regs
12 **PC** Reg 17A(h)-(k) SPC Regs
    HB Reg 35(1)(h)-(k) HB(SPC) Regs
13 **PC** Reg 17A(2)(e) SPC Regs
    HB Reg 35(1)(e) HB(SPC) Regs
14 R(IS) 9/95
15 *Minter v Kingston Upon Hull CC and Potter
    v SSWP* [2011] EWCA Civ 1155
16 **PC** Reg 17A(2)(g) SPC Regs
    HB Reg 35(1)(g) HB(SPC) Regs
17 **PC** Reg 17A(4) SPC Regs
    HB Reg 35(3) HB(SPC) Regs
18 **PC** Reg 17A(3)(a) SPC Regs
    HB Reg 35(2)(a) HB(SPC) Regs
19 Vol 14 Ch 86, para 86058 DMG
20 Vol 14 Ch 86, para 86054 DMG
21 **PC** Reg 17A(3)(b) SPC Regs
    HB Reg 35(2)(b) HB(SPC) Regs
22 CIS/77/1993; CIS/89/1989
23 **PC** Sch 6 para 7 SPC Regs
    HB Sch 4 para 10 HB(SPC) Regs
24 **PC** Reg 17A(3)(c) SPC Regs
    HB Reg 35(2)(c) HB(SPC) Regs
25 **PC** s15(1)(c) SPCA 2002
    HB Reg 29(1)(c) HB(SPC) Regs
26 **PC** Reg 17A(3)(e) SPC Regs
    HB Reg 35(2)(e) HB(SPC) Regs
27 *Parsons v Hogg* [1985] 2 All ER 897 (CA),
    appendix to R(FIS) 4/85
28 **PC** Regs 17(10) and 17A(4A) SPC Regs
    HB Reg 36(2) and (4) HB(SPC) Regs
29 Reg 36(5) HB(SPC) Regs
30 Vol 14 Ch 86, para 86162 DMG
31 **PC** Sch 6 para 6 SPC Regs
    HB Sch 4 para 8 HB(SPC) Regs
32 Reg 17ZA SPC Regs
33 **PC** Reg 17B(5) SPC Regs; reg 13(1) and
    (4) SSB(CE) Regs
    HB Reg 39(1)-(3) HB(SPC) Regs
34 **PC** Reg 17B(1) SPC Regs; regs 2 and
    13(4) SSB(CE) Regs
    HB Regs 2(1) and 39(2) and (11)
    HB(SPC) Regs
35 **PC** Reg 32(3) SS(C&P) Regs
    HB Reg 67(5) HB(SPC) Regs
36 **PC** Reg 17B(4)(b) SPC Regs; reg 12(2)
    SSB(CE) Regs
    HB Reg 38(2)(a) HB(SPC) Regs
37 **PC** Reg 17B SPC Regs; reg 11(1)
    SSB(CE) Regs
    HB Reg 37(1) HB(SPC) Regs
38 **PC** Reg 17B(5)(b) SPC Regs; reg 13(10)
    SSB(CE) Regs
    HB Reg 39(8) HB(SPC) Regs

39 Sch 6 para 1 SPC Regs
40 Sch 6 paras 3 and 4A SPC Regs
41 Sch 6 para 4(1)(a) SPC Regs
42 Sch 6 para 4(1)(b) SPC Regs
43 Sch 6 para 4(2)-(4) SPC Regs
44 Sch 6 para 2 SPC Regs
45 **PC** Sch 6 para 5 SPC Regs
    HB Sch 4 para 7 HB(SPC) Regs
46 Sch 4 para 5A HB(SPC) Regs
47 Sch 4 para 2 HB(SPC) Regs
48 Sch 4 para 4 HB(SPC) Regs
49 Sch 4 para 5(1)(a) HB(SPC) Regs
50 Sch 4 para 5(1)(b) HB(SPC) Regs
51 Sch 4 para 5(1)(d) HB(SPC) Regs
52 Sch 4 para 5(1)(c) HB(SPC) Regs
53 Sch 4 para 5(2) HB(SPC) Regs
54 Sch 4 para 3 HB(SPC) Regs
55 **PC** Sch 6 para 5 SPC Regs
    HB Sch 4 para 7 HB(SPC) Regs
56 Sch 4 para 9 HB(SPC) Regs
57 Reg 30(1)(c) HB(SPC) Regs

4. **Income other than earnings**

58 **PC** s15(1)(b) and (e) SPCA 2002; reg
    15(1) SPC Regs
    HB Reg 29(1)(b) and (j) HB(SPC) Regs
59 **PC** Reg 15(5)(a) and (ab) SPC Regs
    HB Reg 29(1)(h) and (l) HB(SPC) Regs
60 **PC** Reg 15(3) SPC Regs
    HB Reg 29(3) HB(SPC) Regs
61 **PC** Reg 17A(2)(h)-(j) SPC Regs
    HB Reg 35(1)(h)-(j) HB(SPC) Regs
62 **PC** s15(1)(b) SPCA 2002
    HB Sch 5 para 21 HB(SPC) Regs
63 **PC** Reg 15(2) SPC Regs
    HB Reg 29(1)(k) HB(SPC) Regs
64 **PC** s15 SPCA; reg 15(1) and Sch 4 paras
    2-6 SPC Regs
    HB Reg 29(1) and Sch 5 paras 2-6
    HB(SPC) Regs
65 s15 SPCA 2002
66 Sch 5 paras 7 and 8 HB(SPC) Regs
67 Sch 4 paras 7 and 7A SPC Regs
68 **PC** Sch 4 para 1(a) SPC Regs
    HB Sch 5 para 1(a) HB(SPC) Regs; Sch
    Part 1 HB&CTB(WPD) Regs
69 **PC** Sch 4 para 1(cc) SPC Regs
    HB Sch 5 para 1(d) HB(SPC) Regs
70 **PC** Sch 4 para 1(b), (ba) and (c) SPC
    Regs
    HB Sch 5 para 1(b) and (c) HB(SPC)
    Regs; Sch Part 1 HB&CTB(WPD) Regs
71 **PC** Sch 4 para 1(d) SPC Regs
    HB Sch 5 para 1(e) HB(SPC) Regs
72 **PC** Sch 4 para 1(e) SPC Regs
    HB Sch 5 para 1(f) HB(SPC) Regs

Part 4: General rules for other means-tested benefits
Chapter 21: Income: over pension age
Notes

73 **PC** Sch 4 para 1(f) SPC Regs
   HB Sch 5 para 1(g) HB(SPC) Regs
   Both *MN v (1) Bury Council (2) SSWP (HB)* [2014] UKUT 187 (AAC)
74 ss134(8) and 139(6) SSAA 1992; *R v South Hams District Council ex parte Ash* [1999] EWHC Admin 418
75 s74(2) SSAA 1992
76 **PC** Reg 15(3) SPC Regs
   HB Reg 29(3) HB(SPC) Regs
77 **PC** Vol 14 Ch 85, para 85022 DMG
   HB Reg 29(5) HB(SPC) Regs
   Both R(IS) 5/99
78 Reg 15(5)(d) SPC Regs
79 Sch 5 para 20 HB(SPC) Regs
80 Reg 29(1)(o) HB(SPC) Regs
81 CIS/683/1993
82 **PC** Sch 4 para 9 SPC Regs
   HB Sch 5 para 10 HB(SPC) Regs
83 **PC** Income from capital under s15(1)(i) SPCA 2002 would count, but is ignored under regs 15(6) and 17(8), Sch 5 para 1A and Sch 4 para 18 SPC Regs.
   HB Reg 29(1)(i) HB(SPC) Regs
84 **PC** Sch 4 para 8 SPC Regs
   HB Sch 5 para 9 HB(SPC) Regs
85 Reg 1(2), definition of 'board and lodging accommodation', SPC Regs
86 Sch 4 para 18 SPC Regs
87 Reg 2(1), definition of 'board and lodging accommodation', HB(SPC) Regs
88 **PC** Reg 1(2), definition of 'board and lodging accommodation', SPC Regs
   HB Reg 2(1), definition of 'board and lodging accommodation', HB(SPC) Regs
89 CIS/521/2002
90 **PC** s15(1)(i) SPCA 2002; Sch 4 para 18 SPC Regs
   HB Reg 29(1)(i) and Sch 5 para 22 HB(SPC) Regs
91 **PC** Reg 17(8) SPC Regs
   HB Regs 29(1)(i) and 44(2) HB(SPC) Regs
92 **PC** Sch 4 para 18 SPC Regs
   HB Sch 5 para 22 HB(SPC) Regs
93 **PC** s15(1)(i) SPCA 2002; reg 15(6) and Sch 4 para 18 SPC Regs
   HB Reg 29(1)(i) HB(SPC) Regs
94 Sch 5 para 24 HB(SPC) Regs
95 s15(2) SPCA 2002; reg 15(6) SPC Regs
96 Regs 25 and 26 HB(SPC) Regs
97 Reg 43 HB(SPC) Regs
98 Reg 29(2) HB(SPC) Regs
99 **PC** ss15(1)(c) and 16(1) SPCA 2002; reg 16 SPC Regs
   HB Reg 29(1)(c) HB(SPC) Regs

100 **PC** Reg 16 SPC Regs
    HB Reg 29(1)(s) HB(SPC) Regs
101 **PC** Reg 16 SPC Regs
    HB Reg 29(1)(t) HB(SPC) Regs
102 **PC** Reg 16 SPC Regs
    HB Reg 29(1)(w) HB(SPC) Regs
103 Vol 14 Ch 85, para 85136 DMG
104 **PC** Reg 18(2)-(10) SPC Regs; Vol 14 Ch 85, para 85460 DMG
    HB Reg 41(4)-(8) HB(SPC) Regs
105 Vol 14 Ch 85, para 85457 DMG
106 **PC** Reg 17(9) SPC Regs
    HB Reg 33(8) HB(SPC) Regs
107 **PC** Sch 4 para 15 SPC Regs
    HB Sch 5 para 16 HB(SPC) Regs
108 **PC** Sch 4 para 16 SPC Regs
    HB Sch 5 para 17 HB(SPC) Regs
109 **PC** Sch 4 para 10 SPC Regs
    HB Sch 5 para 11 HB(SPC) Regs
110 **PC** Sch 4 para 11 SPC Regs
    HB Sch 5 para 12 HB(SPC) Regs
111 **PC** Sch 4 para 11(3)(b) SPC Regs
    HB Sch 5 para 12(3) HB(SPC) Regs
112 **PC** Sch 4 para 14 SPC Regs
    HB Sch 5 para 15 HB(SPC) Regs
113 **PC** Sch 4 para 13 SPC Regs
    HB Sch 5 para 14 HB(SPC) Regs
114 The rules do not include grants and loans in the definition of 'income'.
115 **PC** s15 SPCA 2002; regs 15 and 17B(4) SPC Regs
    HB Regs 29 and 38(2) HB(SPC) Regs
116 **PC** Regs 17A(3)(f), 18(7A) and 24(2) SPC Regs
    HB Regs 35(2)(f), 41(8C) and 42(3) HB(SPC) Regs
117 Reg 26 VP Regs

5. Notional income
118 **PC** Reg 18(6)-(8B) SPC Regs
    HB Reg 41(8)-(8BD) HB(SPC) Regs
119 Vol 5 Ch 28, paras 28608-16 DMG; see also CIS/15052/1996
120 **PC** Reg 18(9) SPC Regs
    HB Reg 41(11) HB(SPC) Regs
121 **PC** Reg 18(1)-(5) SPC Regs
    HB Reg 41(1)-(7) HB(SPC) Regs
122 Vol 14 Ch 85, para 85453 DMG; *BRG v SSWP (SPC)* [2014] UKUT 246 (AAC)
123 **PC** Reg 18(2)-(5) SPC Regs; Vol 14 Ch 85, para 85456 DMG; *SSWP v Goulding* [2019] EWCA Civ 839
    HB Reg 41(4)-(8) HB(SPC) Regs
124 **PC** Reg 24 SPC Regs
    HB Reg 42 HB(SPC) Regs
125 CH/1672/2007
126 *BL v SSWP (SPC)* [2018] UKUT 4 (AAC)

6. Working out weekly income

127 **PC** Reg 17(2)(b)(i) SPC Regs
     HB Reg 33(2)(b)(i) HB(SPC) Regs
128 **PC** Reg 17(2)(b)(ii) SPC Regs
     HB Reg 33(2)(b)(ii) HB(SPC) Regs
129 **PC** Reg 17(4) SPC Regs
     HB Reg 33(4) HB(SPC) Regs
130 **PC** Reg 17(1) SPC Regs
     HB Reg 33(1) HB(SPC) Regs
131 Reg 13B SPC Regs
132 Reg 33(6) HB(SPC) Regs
133 R(PC) 3/08; *PS v SSWP (SPC)* [2016]
     UKUT 21 (AAC)
134 Reg 33(2A) and (3A) HB(SPC) Regs
135 Reg 1(2) SPC Regs
136 Reg 2 HB(SPC) Regs

Chapter 22

Capital: under pension age

This chapter covers:
1. The capital limits (p489)
2. Whose capital counts (p489)
3. What counts as capital (p490)
4. Disregarded capital (p493)
5. Notional capital (p502)
6. How capital is valued (p508)

This chapter explains how capital affects your entitlement to income support, income-based jobseeker's allowance and income-related employment and support allowance. It also applies to working-age housing benefit (HB) rules if you and your partner are under pension age. Chapter 23 explains the rules for pension credit and for pension-age HB rules if you and your partner are over pension age. If you are in a couple and one of you is over pension age but not the other, see p188 for whether the working-age or pension-age HB rules apply. For universal credit, see Chapter 8. For the capital limits for health benefits, see Chapter 31. There are no capital rules for non-means-tested benefits.

Key facts
- If you have more than £16,000 capital, you are not entitled to income support (IS), income-based jobseeker's allowance (JSA), income-related employment and support allowance (ESA) or working-age housing benefit (HB).
- If you have capital above a lower limit of £6,000 (higher if you live in a care home), your benefit is affected because it is assumed that your capital gives you some income – often called 'tariff income'.
- Some kinds of capital are ignored when working out your benefit – eg, the value of the home in which you live.
- Getting IS, income-based JSA or income-related ESA means you always get the maximum amount of HB, so there is no need to work out your capital again for HB.
- If you deliberately get rid of capital in order to get more benefit, you are treated as still having it. This is called 'notional capital'.

1. The capital limits

There is a lower and upper limit.[1]
- The lower limit is £6,000.
- The upper limit is £16,000.

If you have over £16,000 of capital, you are not entitled to benefit. The first £6,000 is ignored and does not affect your weekly benefit. If you have between £6,000.01 and £16,000, you may be entitled to benefit, but it is assumed that you have some income from your capital. This is known as **'tariff income'**.

This 'tariff income' (see p443) is assumed to be £1 a week for every £250, or part of £250, of your capital between £6,000.01 and £16,000.

If you live in a care home, see below.

When working out the value of your capital, some capital is disregarded (see p493). You may also be treated as having some capital which you do not actually have (see p502).

Example
Shane gets income-based jobseeker's allowance. He has £6,900 in savings. He is assumed to have tariff income of £4 a week.

Care homes

If you live permanently in a care home (see p933):
- the lower limit is £10,000;
- the upper limit is £16,000.

Tariff income (see above) starts above £10,000.

Example
Colin gets income-related employment and support allowance (ESA). He has £8,100 in savings. He is assumed to have tariff income of £9 a week. Colin moves permanently into a care home. Because his savings are below the £10,000 limit, they are now disregarded entirely. A few months later he sells his home and gets £80,000. As a result, he is no longer entitled to income-related ESA.

2. Whose capital counts

Your partner's capital

If you are a member of a couple (see p319), your partner's capital is added to yours.[2]

Part 4: General rules for other means-tested benefits
Chapter 22: Capital: under pension age
3. What counts as capital

Your child's capital

Your child's capital is not added to yours and does not affect your benefit.[3] However, if you still have amounts for children included in your income support or income-based jobseeker's allowance (see p333), although your child's capital is not added to yours, if it is over £3,000, you cannot get benefit included for her/him other than the family premium (see p340).[4] If this applies, any income of the child is not counted as yours.[5]

3. **What counts as capital**

All your capital is taken into account, unless it is disregarded (see p493) or is treated as income (see p444).

The term 'capital' is not defined. In general, it means lump-sum or one-off payments rather than a series of payments – eg, it includes savings, property and statutory redundancy payments.[6]

Capital payments can normally be distinguished from income because they are not payable for any specified period and are not part of a regular series of payments (although capital can be paid by instalments).[7]

Note: some capital is treated as income (see p444) and some income is treated as capital (see p493).

Savings

Your savings generally count as capital – eg, cash you have at home, premium bonds, shares, unit trusts and money in a bank account or building society.

If you have put aside money to pay bills, this is still counted as your capital.[8] If your savings are just below the capital limit, you could pay bills by monthly direct debit or use a budget account to keep your capital below the limit.

Savings from past employed earnings and other income (including benefits – see p498) are treated as capital after the period for which the income was paid has lapsed – eg, a weekly payment of child benefit becomes capital a week after it is paid and a monthly occupational pension becomes capital after a month.[9] Beyond that, employed earnings continue to be treated as income until deductions for tax, national insurance and pension contributions have been made.[10]

Fixed-term investments

Capital held in fixed-term investments counts. However, if it is currently unobtainable, it may have little or no value. If you can convert the investment into a form that lets you access it or sell your interest, or raise a loan through a reputable bank using the asset as security, the amount you can get for it counts.

Property and land

Any property or land that you own counts as capital. Many types of property are disregarded (see p493). If there is doubt about who owns the property, see below.

Loans and ownership of capital

Usually it is clear when capital belongs to you and should be taken into account. However, it may be less clear if you are holding money for someone else or if you have been given a loan which you are expected to repay.

A loan to you usually counts as money you possess and, therefore, counts as capital. However, you can argue that a loan, money or other asset you hold for someone else should be disregarded if it is:

- a loan granted on condition that you only use the interest, but do not touch the capital because the capital element has never been at your disposal;[11]
- money you have been paid to be used for a particular purpose on condition that the money must be returned if not used in that way;[12]
- property you have bought on behalf of someone else who is paying the mortgage;[13]
- money held in your bank account on behalf of another person, which is to be returned to her/him at a future date;[14]
- savings from someone else's benefit paid to you as an appointee – eg, your child's disability living allowance;[15]
- a loan and when you get it, you are under an immediate obligation to repay it;[16]
- your own asset but you have expressed a clear intention that it is for someone else's benefit and renounced its use for yourself;[17]
- your interest in a property and you lead someone to believe that you are transferring it to her/him but fail to do so (eg, it is never properly conveyed) and that person acts on the belief that s/he owns it (eg, s/he spends money on repairs). You can argue the asset has been transferred and you are like a trustee.[18] This is called '**proprietary estoppel**'.

See p444 if you find that a loan is taken into account as income even though it is paid as a lump sum.

If you lend money to someone, it could still count as your 'notional capital' (see p502), depending on your reasons for lending it. You usually have a legal right to be repaid and this, in itself, could have a capital value, although the value would normally be less than the amount loaned, and could be nil if you have no expectation of getting the money back.[19]

Trusts

A trust is a way of owning any asset such as money, a house or shares. A 'trustee' looks after the capital and owns the legal title. The trustee uses the capital for the

Part 4: General rules for other means-tested benefits
Chapter 22: Capital: under pension age
3. What counts as capital

benefit of someone else (the 'beneficiary'). If you are a trustee, the capital is not yours to use for yourself unless you are also a beneficiary.

Whether your money is in a discretionary or non-discretionary trust can make a difference to how your benefits are affected.

Payments made from:

- a discretionary trust count as income or capital depending on the nature of the payment.[20] Capital payments are taken into account in full, but income from the trust is generally treated as a voluntary payment and is ignored.[21] The trust asset itself does not normally count as your capital because payments are at the discretion of the trustees and you cannot demand payment (of either income or capital).[22] To be a discretionary trust, the terms of the trust must give trustees discretion over not just when to pay but also whether to make payments at all;[23]
- a non-discretionary trust count in full as capital, whatever the nature of the payment.[24] The trust asset itself also counts as your capital, because in a non-discretionary trust you can obtain the asset from the trustee at any time. For under-18-year-olds who have no right to payment (16 in Scotland, or older if the trust specifies), the value of the trust asset may have a current value which is less than the whole amount;
- a trust set up from money for a personal injury to you or your partner are treated more generously (see p499).

Trustees may have a discretion to use such funds to purchase items that would normally be disregarded as capital, such as personal possessions (eg, a wheelchair, car or new furniture) or to arrange payments that would normally be disregarded as income – eg, ineligible housing costs. Similarly, they may have discretion to clear debts or pay for a holiday, leisure items or educational or medical needs. See p441 for the treatment of voluntary payments, and p441 and p451 for the treatment of payments made to third parties.

Note:

- Putting money in a discretionary trust has the advantage of the value of the trust itself being disregarded. However, if you transfer money into a trust in order to get more benefit, it can still count as yours under the notional capital rules (see p502).
- Capital in a non-discretionary trust is taken into account. If this takes you over the £16,000 capital limit, you are not entitled to benefit.

Money held by your solicitor

Money held by your solicitor normally counts as your capital. This includes compensation payments (but see p499 for when payments for personal injury are disregarded).[25] If you have had legal aid and your solicitor is holding money back while working out the statutory charge to be deducted for legal costs, it does not count as your capital.[26]

Income treated as capital

Certain payments that appear to be income are treated as capital. These are:[27]

- income from capital (eg, interest on a bank account, share dividends and income from property let to tenants (see p442). However, the following count as income, not capital:
  - income from the first five disregarded property bullet points listed on p494;
  - trust funds administered by a court (see p499);
  - income from the home of a partner, former partner or relative in the circumstances described on p496;
  - income from the home in which you normally live;
  - income from business assets or personal injury trusts;
- a lump sum or 'bounty' paid to you not more than once a year as a part-time firefighter, part-time member of a lifeboat crew, auxiliary coastguard or member of the reserve forces. If paid more often, it counts as earnings;
- the following payments:
  - an advance of earnings or loan from your employer;
  - holiday pay which is not payable until more than four weeks after your employment ends or is interrupted;
  - income tax refunds;
  - irregular (one-off) charitable or voluntary payments.

  This does not apply to income support (IS) or income-based jobseeker's allowance (JSA) if you are involved in a trade dispute, or to IS if you are returning to work after a dispute (see p1001);
- for IS, income-based JSA and income-related employment and support allowance only, a discharge grant paid on release from prison;
- for housing benefit (HB) only, any arrears of child tax credit or working tax credit;[28]
- for HB only, the gross receipts from work carried out under New Enterprise Allowance.

4. Disregarded capital

Your home

If you own the home in which you normally live, its value is ignored.[29]

Your home

Your **'home'** includes any garage, garden, outbuildings and land belonging to the property, together with any premises that you do not occupy as your home but which it is impractical or unreasonable to sell separately – eg, croft land.[30]

Part 4: General rules for other means-tested benefits
Chapter 22: Capital: under pension age
4. Disregarded capital

This disregard applies to any home in which you are treated as normally living – eg, because you are only temporarily living away from it (see p371). If you own more than one property, only the one that you normally occupy is disregarded under this rule.[31]

Exceptionally, two separate properties can be regarded as a single home as though one was an annexe of the other, if you personally (rather than a member of your family) normally occupy both properties.[32] This is most likely to be the case for a large family, but other situations are possible where neither property on its own caters for a family's needs – eg, if there is a carer living between two properties.[33]

When the value of the property is disregarded

The value of the property can be disregarded, even if you do not normally live in it, in the following circumstances.

- **If you have left your former home following a relationship breakdown,** the value of the property is ignored for 26 weeks from the date you left. It may also be disregarded for longer if any of the steps below are taken. If it is occupied by your former partner who is a lone parent, its value is ignored for as long as s/he lives there.[34]
- **If you have sought legal advice or have started legal proceedings in order to occupy the property as your home,** its value is ignored for 26 weeks from the date you first took either of these steps.[35] The 26 weeks can be extended if it is reasonable to do so, if you need longer to move in.
- **If you are taking reasonable steps to dispose of a property,** its value is ignored for 26 weeks from the date you first took such steps (which may be before you claim benefit).[36] The steps you take must be 'reasonable'. Advertising at an unrealistic sale price does not count, but placing the property with an estate agent or contacting a possible buyer should,[37] as might taking ancillary proceedings to resolve financial issues in a divorce.[38] The disregard can continue beyond 26 weeks, even for years if it is reasonable – eg, if a court orders that the former matrimonial home should not be sold until the children are grown up. Taking a property off the market and putting it on again does not necessarily begin a new 26-week period, but it may do if the second attempt to sell is quite separate.[39]
- **If you are carrying out essential repairs or alterations which are needed so that you can occupy a property as your home,** the value of the property is ignored for 26 weeks from the date you first began to take steps to carry them out.[40] 'Steps' may include applying for planning permission or a grant or loan to make the property habitable, employing an architect or finding someone to do the work.[41] If you cannot move into the property within that period because the work is not finished, its value can be disregarded for as long as is necessary to allow the work to be carried out.

- **If you have acquired a property and intend to live there as your home but have not yet moved in**, its value is ignored if you intend to live there within 26 weeks of acquiring it.[42] If you cannot move in by then, the value of the property can be ignored for as long as seems reasonable.
- **If you sell your home and intend to use the money from the sale to buy another home**, the capital is ignored for 26 weeks from the date of the sale.[43] This also applies even if you do not own your home but, for a price, you surrender your tenancy rights to a landlord.[44] If you need longer to complete a purchase, your capital can continue to be ignored if it is reasonable to do so. You do not need to have decided within the 26 weeks to buy a particular property. It is sufficient if you intend to use the proceeds to buy some other home within the 26-week (or extended) period,[45] although your 'intention' must involve more than a mere 'hope' or 'aspiration'.[46] There must be an element of 'certainty' which you may be able to show by evidence of a practical commitment to another purchase, although this need not involve any binding obligation.[47] If you intend to use only part of the proceeds of sale to buy another home, only that part is disregarded even if, for example, you have put the rest of the money aside to renovate your new home.[48]
- **If your home is damaged or you lose it altogether**, any payment in consequence of that, including compensation, which is to be used for its repair, or for acquiring another home, is ignored for 26 weeks, or longer if it is reasonable to do so.
- **If you have taken out a loan or been given money for the express purpose of essential repairs or improvements to your home**, it is ignored for 26 weeks, or longer if it is reasonable to do so.[49] If it is a condition of the loan that it must be returned if the improvements are not carried out, you should argue that it should be ignored altogether.[50]
- **If you have deposited money with a housing association as a condition of occupying your home**, this is ignored indefinitely.[51] If money which was deposited for this purpose is now to be used to buy another home, this is ignored for 26 weeks, or longer if reasonable, in order to allow you to complete the purchase.[52]
- **Grants made to buy a home** are ignored for up to 26 weeks if made to local authority tenants to buy a home or do repairs or alterations to it. They can be ignored for longer, if reasonable, to allow completion of the purchase or the repairs/alterations. **Note:** the repairs or alterations must be required to make the property fit for occupation as your home.[53]

When considering whether it is reasonable to extend the period during which time the value of your property is disregarded, all the circumstances should be considered – eg, your personal circumstances, any efforts made by you to use or dispose of the home[54] and the general state of the property market. In practice, periods of around 18 months are not considered unusual.

Part 4: General rules for other means-tested benefits
Chapter 22: Capital: under pension age
4. Disregarded capital

Note: it is possible for property to be ignored under more than one of the above paragraphs in succession.[55]

Some income generated from property which is disregarded is ignored (see p443).

The home of a partner, former partner or relative

The value of a home (see p493) is ignored if it is occupied as her/his home by:[56]
- someone over pension age (see p271), or who has limited capability for work or is incapacitated (see below), who is:
  - a relative of yours or of your partner or dependent child; *or*
  - your spouse or civil partner, provided you are still treated as living in the same household (see p319), or your cohabitee, provided you are still treated as living together as a married couple (see p320); *or*
- your former partner from whom you are not estranged but you are living apart (and are, therefore, not treated as still living together or as living in the same household) – eg, if one of you is living in a care home; *or*
- your former partner from whom you are estranged and who is a lone parent. If your former partner is not a lone parent, the value of the home is ignored for 26 weeks from the date you ceased to live in the home.

Definitions

'**Incapacitated**' is not defined, but guidance suggests it includes anyone who is getting employment and support allowance (ESA), statutory sick pay, attendance allowance (AA) or disability living allowance (DLA) or who would qualify because of her/his health condition or disability.[57] It may also include anyone who is getting personal independence payment (PIP) or universal credit (UC) who has limited capability for work or limited capability for work-related activity. However, you should argue for a broader interpretation, if necessary.

'**Relative**' is a parent, son, daughter, step-parent, stepson, stepdaughter, parent-in-law, son-in-law, daughter-in-law, brother or sister, or a partner of any of these people, half-brother or half-sister, adopted child, grandparent or grandchild, uncle, aunt, nephew or niece.[58]

You are '**estranged**' if you are living apart because your relationship has broken down, even if the separation is amicable.[59]

Personal possessions

All personal possessions, including jewellery, furniture or a car, are ignored.[60] A personal possession has been defined as any physical asset not used for business purposes, other than land.[61] For example, in one case, a static caravan on a non-residential site was treated as a personal possession. However, a home that you own but do not live in is not normally a personal possession and does count as capital (see p494). Personal possessions are not ignored if you have bought them in order to be able to claim or get more benefit. In this case, the sale value, rather than the purchase price, is counted as actual capital and the difference is treated as notional capital (see p502).[62]

Compensation for damage to, or the loss of, any personal possessions, which is to be used for their repair or replacement, is ignored for six months, or longer if reasonable.[63]

Business assets

If you are self-employed, your business assets are ignored for as long as you continue to work in that business.[64]

If you cannot work because you are sick or incapacitated, the assets are disregarded for 26 weeks from the date of claim if you intend to work in the business again when you are able, or for longer if reasonable in the circumstances.[65]

If you stop working in the business, you are allowed a reasonable time to sell these assets without their value affecting your benefit.

It is sometimes difficult to distinguish between personal and business assets. The test is whether the assets are 'part of the fund employed and risked in the business'.[66] If the assets of a business partnership (eg, plant and machinery) have been sold but the partnership has not yet been dissolved, the proceeds of sale can still count as business assets.[67] **Note:** letting a single house is not likely to constitute a business.[68]

For the treatment of business assets if you are taking part in the New Enterprise Allowance, see p501.

Personal pension schemes

The value of a fund held in a personal pension scheme is ignored as capital.[69] The value of the right to receive an occupational or personal pension is also ignored. However, if your partner is over pension age and chooses not to take income from the pension, you are treated as having notional income (see p445).

Insurance policy and annuity surrender values

The surrender value of a life assurance policy is ignored.[70] Some investments include an element of life insurance – eg, endowment policies. If the policy terms include how the payment on death is calculated, the whole investment is ignored.[71] However, you cannot choose to put money in to such an investment in order to increase your benefit entitlement, because you are likely to be caught by the notional capital rule if you do (see p503).

The surrender value of any annuity is also ignored (see p443 and p489),[72] as is the value of the right to receive any payment under an annuity. Any payment under the annuity counts as income[73] (but see p445 for when this is ignored).

Part 4: General rules for other means-tested benefits
Chapter 22: Capital: under pension age
4. Disregarded capital

Future interest in property

A future interest in most kinds of property is ignored.[74] A **'future interest'** is one which will only revert to you, or become yours for the first time, when some future event occurs – eg, where someone else has a life interest in a fund and you are only entitled to it after that person has died.

However, this does not include a freehold or leasehold interest in property which has been let *by you* to tenants. If you did not let the property to the tenant (eg, because the tenancy was entered into before you bought the property), your interest in the property should be ignored as a future interest in the normal way.

The right to receive a payment in the future

If you know that you will receive a payment in the future and you could sell your right to it at any time, it has a market value and, therefore, constitutes an actual capital resource. The value of this is ignored if it is a right to receive:[75]
- income under a life interest or, in Scotland, a life rent; *or*
- an occupational or personal pension; *or*
- any rent if you are not the freeholder or leaseholder. Any actual income which this right generates for you and which is not disregarded as income can be taken into account as income; *or*
- any payment under an annuity (see p448). Any actual income generated by this right and which is not disregarded as income can be taken into account as income; *or*
- any earnings or income that is ignored because it is frozen abroad; *or*
- any outstanding instalments if capital is being paid by instalments; *or*
- any payment under a trust fund set up with money paid because of a personal injury to you or your partner.

Benefits and tax credits

Arrears of benefits and tax credits

Arrears of the following are ignored for 52 weeks after you receive them, or longer in some cases where there has been official error or an error of law (see below):[76]
- AA;
- armed forces independence payment;
- bereavement support payment;
- child tax credit;
- council tax benefit;
- DLA;
- discretionary housing payments;
- income-related ESA;
- housing benefit (HB);
- income support (IS);
- income-based jobseeker's allowance (JSA);

- maternity allowance;
- mobility supplement;
- PIP;
- UC;
- working tax credit;
- concessionary payments instead of any of the above.

If the arrears are £5,000 or more and are paid to compensate for an official error (see p1307) or an error of law, they are ignored until the end of your (or your partner's) award. If you or your partner then reclaim the same benefit, or move from UC, IS, income-based JSA or income-related ESA to another of these four benefits, they continue to be ignored for the whole of this next and any subsequent award(s) if there is no gap between awards.[77]

Note: although arrears are ignored as capital, you may have been paid more IS, income-based JSA, income-related ESA or HB than you would have been entitled to if benefit had been paid on time. Usually, the DWP deducts the difference from the arrears of the delayed benefit. Otherwise, if the arrears are not reduced, the overpayment is recoverable from you (see p1237). For HB, the overpayment is not deducted from the arrears but may be recoverable (see p1253).

Other benefits and payments

The following are ignored for 52 weeks from the date you receive them, or indefinitely where specified:

- initial lump sum of bereavement support payment;[78]
- social fund payments (ignored indefinitely);[79]
- Best Start grant in Scotland (ignored indefinitely);[80]
- fares to hospital, and payments for prescriptions and dental charges;[81]
- funeral support payment in Scotland (ignored indefinitely);[82]
- payments in lieu of milk tokens, vitamins or Healthy Start food vouchers;[83]
- payments to assist prison visits;[84]
- certain payments to war widows, widowers and surviving civil partners;[85]
- any payments by the Secretary of State to compensate for the loss of entitlement to HB (ignored indefinitely).[86]

Charitable, personal injury and other compensation payments

- **Charitable payments.** Any payment in kind by a charity is ignored.[87]
- **Personal injury payments.** If you have money in a trust from a personal injury to you, the value of the trust and any income from it is disregarded.[88] A lump sum from the trust is taken into account as capital. It should not affect your benefit if the trustees give you regular or even annual payments, pay your bills or, instead of giving you a lump sum, buy you something that would be disregarded because it is a personal possession – eg furniture or a car. If an

Part 4: General rules for other means-tested benefits
Chapter 22: Capital: under pension age
4. Disregarded capital

award for damages for personal injury to you is administered by a court (eg, the Court of Protection), its value and income from it is also disregarded.[89] This also applies if the court-administered fund is for children to compensate for the death of a parent. If you have just received a payment for personal injury to you, it is disregarded for 52 weeks from when you receive it.[90] This gives you time to spend it or put it into a trust or annuity before your benefit is affected. There is no 52-week disregard for another payment for the same injury, but it is disregarded as soon as it is in a trust. If the personal injury is to your partner, there is a 52-week disregard for the initial payment and the value of a trust is disregarded, but not income from the trust or annuity. If your partner has since died, you cannot carry over the remainder of the 52-week disregard, or if the payment is in a trust, it is no longer ignored.[91]

Personal injury
'Personal injury' includes not only accidental and criminal injuries, but also any disease and injury as a result of a disease.[92]

- **Special compensation schemes.** Any payment of capital (or income) from certain special schemes approved or set up by the government is ignored if it is:[93]
  - for you or your partner who has variant CJD (Creutzfeldt-Jakob disease). If you are the parent of someone with variant CJD, the payment is ignored for two years. For a dependent child of someone with variant CJD, the payment is ignored until s/he reaches 20, finishes full-time education or for two years, whichever is later; *or*
  - in respect of someone infected from contaminated blood products. If you give money from the payment to your partner or to your dependent child, it is ignored for her/his benefit claim indefinitely. If you have no partner or children and you give the money to your parent, it is ignored for two years; *or*
  - compensation for the London bombings in July 2005, from the London Emergencies Trust or from the We Love Manchester Emergency Fund (for the 2017 terror attacks); *or*
  - World War Two compensation (rather than a war pension); *or*
  - in respect of someone disabled by thalidomide during her/his mother's pregnancy.

Social services, community care and other payments

The following payments from a local authority are ignored indefinitely:[94]
- payments for children and families made under section 17 of the Children Act 1989, section 12 of the Social Work (Scotland) Act 1968 or, for HB, section 22

of the Children (Scotland) Act 1995 and sections 37 and 38 of the Social Services and Well-being (Wales) Act 2014;
- payments to young people who have previously been looked after by the local authority made under sections 23B or 24A of the Children Act 1989, section 30 of the Children (Scotland) Act 1995 or sections 109, 110, 114 or 115 of the Social Services and Well-being (Wales) Act 2014. A payment under section 23C of the Children Act 1989 is also ignored as the young person's capital, and as yours if s/he passes it to you and s/he was in your care, is still living with you and is aged 18 or over – eg, under 'staying put' arrangements. In Scotland, this applies to payments under sections 26A and 29 of the Children (Scotland) Act 1995 and includes young people aged 16 or over in 'continuing care'.

See p1001 if you or your partner are involved in a trade dispute.
Also ignored indefinitely are:
- local welfare assistance to meet an immediate short-term need or establish or maintain a settled home in certain circumstances;[95]
- community care or healthcare direct payments;[96]
- education, health and care plan payments, paid in England for a child with special educational needs;[97]
- payments under the Supporting People programme;[98]
- special guardianship allowances, payable in England and Wales;[99]
- kinship care payments, payable in Scotland;[100]
- payments under sections 2, 3 or 4 of the Adoption and Children Act 2002.[101]

Employment and training programme payments

Some payments are ignored for 52 weeks from the date they are received:[102]
- payment for travel or other expenses from a specified scheme for assisting people to obtain employment (see p1151);
- for income-related ESA, payment for travel or other expenses for undertaking required work-related activity;
- payment under section 2 of the Employment and Training Act 1973 or section 2 of the Enterprise and New Towns (Scotland) Act 1990;
- capital acquired for the purpose of participating under the 'self-employment route' – eg, for income-based JSA and HB, New Enterprise Allowance.[103] Any capital acquired is ignored for as long as you are receiving assistance for taking part in the programme and, after you have ceased trading, for as long as is reasonable in order to dispose of the assets.[104]

Payments to disabled people under the Disabled Persons (Employment) Act 1944 (other than a training allowance) to assist with employment, or local authority payments to assist blind homeworkers, are ignored indefinitely.[105]

For when employment and training programme payments are treated as income, notional income and notional capital, see p444, p451 and p506.

Part 4: General rules for other means-tested benefits
Chapter 22: Capital: under pension age
5. Notional capital

Miscellaneous payments

The following payments are disregarded:

- a sports award made by the UK Sport National Lottery funds, except for any part of the award which is made for ordinary living expenses (see p449). It is disregarded for 26 weeks;[106]
- an education maintenance allowance or a 16 to 19 bursary fund payment are ignored indefinitely;[107]
- for IS, income-based JSA and income-related ESA, any payments made to jurors or witnesses for attending at court, except for payments for loss of earnings or benefit;[108]
- refunds of council tax liability (ignored for 52 weeks from the date you receive the arrears);[109]
- 20 per cent of money in a tax-free childcare account is arguably ignored (see p871);[110]
- any payments made to holders of the Victoria or George Cross;[111]
- payments under the Windrush Compensation Scheme and Windrush Urgent and Exceptional Payments Scheme (disregarded on an extra-statutory basis);[112]
- victims' payments to people injured in a 'Troubles-related incident'.[113]

5. Notional capital

In certain circumstances, you are treated as having capital that you do not have. This is called **'notional capital'**.[114] There is a similar rule for notional income (see p449, p131 and p131). Notional capital counts in the same way as the capital you do have.

You may be treated as having notional capital if:

- you deliberately deprive yourself of capital in order to claim or increase benefit (see p503); *or*
- you fail to apply for capital which is available to you (see p505); *or*
- someone makes a payment of capital to a third party on your behalf or on behalf of a member of your family (see p506); *or*
- you (or a member of your family) receive a payment of capital on behalf of a third party and you (or the member of your family) use or keep the capital (see p507); *or*
- you are a sole trader or a partner in a business which is a limited company (see p507).

Note: if you are treated as having notional capital because you have deliberately deprived yourself of capital in order to claim or increase benefit, a 'diminishing notional capital rule' (see p505) may be applied so that the value of the notional capital you are treated as having is considered to reduce over time.

Deliberately getting rid of capital

If you deliberately get rid of capital in order to claim or increase your benefit, you are treated as still having it.[115] The same applies if your partner got rid of capital, even if s/he did so before you became a couple.[116] You are likely to be affected by this rule if, at the time of using up your money, you knew that you might qualify for benefit (or more benefit), or qualify more quickly as a result. You should not be affected if you knew nothing about the effect of using up your capital (eg, you did not know about the capital limit for claiming benefit)[117] or if you have been using up your capital at a rate which is reasonable in the circumstances. This is because you cannot have the intention if you do not know about the capital rules.[118] Knowledge of capital limits can be inferred from a reasonable familiarity with the benefit system as a claimant,[119] but if you fail to make enquiries about the capital limit, this does not constitute an intention to secure benefit.

In practice, arguing successfully that you have not deprived yourself of capital to get or increase benefit may depend on whether you can show that you would have spent the money in the way you did (eg, to pay off debts or reduce your mortgage) regardless of the effect on your benefit entitlement. If this is unclear, the burden of proving that you did it to get benefit lies with the decision maker.

Your intentions

Even if you did know about the capital limits, it still has to be shown that you intended to obtain, retain or increase your benefit.[120] For example, in one case, a claimant faced repossession of his home and transferred ownership to his daughter (who he feared would otherwise be made homeless), despite having been warned by DWP staff that he would be disqualified from benefit if he did so. It was held that, under the circumstances, he had not disposed of the property with the intention of gaining benefit.[121] The longer the period that has elapsed since the disposal of the capital, the less likely it is for the purpose of obtaining benefit.[122] However, no matter how long it has been since you may have disposed of an asset, there is no set 'safe' period after which benefit can be claimed without the need for further enquiry.[123]

If you use up your resources, you may have more than one motive for doing so. Even if qualifying for benefit is only a lesser motive for your actions and the main motive is something different (eg, ensuring your home is in good condition by spending capital on repairs and improvements), you may still be considered to have deprived yourself of a resource in order to gain benefit.[124]

The test is not what the money has been spent on, but your intention behind the expenditure. However, examples of the kinds of expenditure that could be caught by this rule are expensive holidays and putting money in trust.[125] **Note:** for income support (IS), income-based jobseeker's allowance (JSA) and income-related employment and support allowance (ESA), putting money in trust for yourself does not constitute deprivation if the capital came from compensation paid for a personal injury.[126]

Part 4: General rules for other means-tested benefits
Chapter 22: Capital: under pension age
5. Notional capital

You can deprive yourself of capital, even if you receive another resource in return.[127] For example, if you buy a car so that you can get more benefit, your actual capital includes the value of the car, and the difference between that and the purchase price is treated as notional capital.[128]

Paying off debts and bankruptcy

If you pay off a debt that you are legally required to repay immediately, you may not be counted as having deprived yourself of capital in order to gain benefit.[129] It is the facts of your case that are important: if you paid off an immediately repayable debt when you thought it would not be recalled for some time, you might be considered to have deprived yourself of money in order to get benefit. However, even if you pay off a debt that you are not legally required to repay immediately, the decision maker must still prove that you did so in order to get benefit.[130]

If you are declared bankrupt, you cannot spend your capital without court approval and cannot usually be held to have deprived yourself of it if you do. Capital you have (but cannot spend) does not count for benefit purposes from the date of the bankruptcy order.[131] However, if you deliberately go bankrupt or do not take reasonable steps to discharge the bankruptcy in order to get benefit, your capital can still count as notional capital.

How notional capital is calculated

Notional capital is generally calculated in the same way as actual capital and the same disregards usually apply (see p493).[132] However, you may not be able to rely on the 26-week (or longer) disregard you would otherwise be allowed to take steps to dispose of a property (see p494), even if the new owner is trying to sell it (but there is conflicting caselaw on this).[133]

If more than one benefit is involved

If you have intentionally deprived yourself of capital in order to get IS, it does not necessarily follow that you also intended to get housing benefit (HB). Similarly, deprivation of capital to get income-based JSA cannot be treated as a deprivation for IS, although deprivation for IS can be treated as deprivation for income-based JSA, and deprivation for IS or income-based JSA can be treated as deprivation for income-related ESA. Each decision maker must reach her/his own decision on each benefit. This may result in different conclusions being drawn for each benefit. Even if intent is found in two different benefits, there may be different views about the amount of capital that has been intentionally disposed of.

However, if you are considered to have deprived yourself of capital for the purposes of claiming HB and you then make a successful claim for IS, income-based JSA or income-related ESA, the local authority should put the notional capital rules for HB on hold for as long as the other benefit remains in payment.[134]

The diminishing notional capital rule

The 'diminishing notional capital rule' provides a way of working out how the value of your notional capital may be treated as reducing over time. It only applies if you have deliberately deprived yourself of capital.[135]

It applies from the first week after the week in which it is decided that notional capital is to be taken into account.

- If your benefit is reduced because of tariff income from your notional capital, that capital is diminished by the amount of the reduction each week. For example, if your notional capital is £6,750 (and you have no other capital), giving a tariff income of £3 a week, the reduction is £3 a week until it reaches £6,500, when it will be £2 and so on. For HB, the amount of your notional capital is also reduced by the amount of IS, income-based JSA or income-related ESA you would have had if no notional capital had been taken into account.

- If you have both actual and notional capital, you may have to use your actual capital to meet your living expenses. There is no reason why this should affect the amount by which your notional capital is diminished, even if this effectively results in double counting. Any reduction in your actual capital should be taken into account in calculating any tariff income arising from your combined actual and notional capital, unless you have spent it at such a rate and in such a way that it raises questions of intent, when you may find that the notional capital rules are applied all over again.

- If your benefit award has ended because of notional capital, the amount of notional capital reduces over time. Once it has reduced to a point when a fresh claim might succeed, you cannot usually make a new claim for IS, income-based JSA, income-related ESA or HB (see p24 for exceptions). Instead, you can claim universal credit (UC). If you can make a new claim for IS, income-based JSA, income-related ESA or HB, see p494 of the 2018/19 edition of this *Handbook* for the way notional capital is reduced. **Note:** you are not automatically treated as having the notional capital in a UC claim. If you wish to claim UC, you should do so without delay in order to have the capital considered again under the UC rules (see p148).

Failing to apply for capital

You are expected to apply for any capital that is due to you – eg, if money is held by a court which could be released if you applied, or an unclaimed premium bond win. If you would get capital if you applied for it, you are treated as having that capital.[136]

You are only treated as having such capital from the date you could obtain it. This rule does not apply if you do not apply for:

- capital from a discretionary trust; *or*
- capital from a trust (or fund administered by a court) set up from money paid as a result of a personal injury; *or*

Part 4: General rules for other means-tested benefits
Chapter 22: Capital: under pension age
5. Notional capital

- capital from a personal pension scheme or, if you are under pension age (see p271), from an occupational pension scheme or a payment from the Pension Protection Fund; *or*
- a loan which you could only get if you gave your home or other disregarded capital (see p493) as security; *or*
- for HB only, child tax credit or working tax credit.[137]

Capital payments made to a third party on your behalf

If someone pays an amount to a third party (eg, a fuel company or a building society) for you or your partner (or a child for HB, or for IS or income-based JSA if children are still included in your claim – see p490), this may count as your capital. It counts if the payment is to cover:[138]

- certain normal living expenses – ie, food, household fuel, council tax, water charges or ordinary clothing or footwear. School uniforms and sportswear are not ordinary clothing,[139] nor are special shoes needed because of a disability.[140] Payments made, for instance, for food or clothes for you or your partner count as yours. However, since a child's capital is not counted as belonging to you, a payment to, for example, a clothes shop for your child should count as the child's notional capital and not yours, and, in most cases, is ignored; *or*
- rent which could be met by HB (less any non-dependant deductions); *or*
- for IS, income-based JSA and income-related ESA only, housing costs which could be met by IS, income-based JSA or income-related ESA.

Payments to a third party do *not* count as yours if they are:[141]

- for other kinds of expenses (eg, a TV licence or mortgage repayments), unless they come from a benefit or pension (see below); *or*
- from a specified infected blood payment scheme (see p500); *or*
- for participating in a specified scheme for assisting people to obtain employment (see p1151).

Payments from an occupational or personal pension scheme or from the Pension Protection Fund to a third party count as yours regardless of whether or not the payments are used, or intended to be used, for ordinary living expenses.[142] They are disregarded if:

- you (or your partner) are bankrupt (or in Scotland, the subject of a sequestration order), the payment is made to the trustee or other person acting on your creditors' behalf and you and your partner (or your family for HB, and for IS or income-based JSA if amounts for children are still included in your claim) have no income other than the payment made;[143] *or*
- the payments do not support you financially and, therefore, do not reduce or remove your need to be supported by IS, income-based JSA, income-related ESA or HB – eg, deductions from an occupational pension made under an attachment of earnings order to a former partner.[144] If you have had a judicial

Chapter 22
Capital: under pension age

separation, rather than divorce, so the usual pension-splitting arrangements are not available, and a court has ordered you to pay part of your pension to your former partner, you could argue that this does not count as yours.[145]

For IS, income-based JSA and income-related ESA only, payments *derived* from certain social security benefits (including war disablement pensions, war widows' pensions and Armed Forces Compensation Scheme payments) and paid to a third party count:[146]
- as yours, if you are entitled to the benefit; *and*
- as your partner's, if s/he is entitled to the benefit.

For IS, income-based JSA and income-related ESA, there are different rules if you could be liable to pay maintenance (see p438).

Capital payments made to you for a third party

If you or your partner get a payment for someone not in your family (eg, a relative), it only counts as yours if it is kept or used by you.[147] For HB (and for IS or income-based JSA if amounts for children are still included in your claim – see p490), the same also applies to payments received by a member of your family for someone not in the family. Payments from a specified infected blood payment scheme (see p500), or a specified scheme for assisting people to obtain employment (see p1151), do not count at all. Payments from pension schemes paid for a third party are disregarded in the same circumstances as described on p506.

Companies run by sole traders or a few partners

Normally, if you hold shares in a company, their value is taken into account as capital. If, however, your influence in the company is such that you are like a sole trader or like a partner in a small partnership, you are treated accordingly. For IS, income-based JSA and income-related ESA, the value of your shareholding is ignored but you are treated as having a proportionate share of the capital of the company.[148] However, these company assets are not taken into account while you are doing any work on the company's business,[149] even if you only do a little work for the company – eg, taking messages.[150] It has, however, been held that a 'sleeping partner' in a business managed and worked exclusively by others may not benefit from this disregard. As well as having a financial commitment to the business, you must also be involved or engaged in it in some practical sense as an earner.[151]

For HB, the local authority has discretion about whether to apply the same rules as for IS. If it decides to, it must apply them all.[152]

Part 4: General rules for other means-tested benefits
Chapter 22: Capital: under pension age
6. How capital is valued

6. **How capital is valued**

Market value

Your capital is valued at its current market or surrender value.[153] This means the amount of money you could raise by selling it or raising a loan against it. This is the price that would be paid by a willing buyer to a willing seller on a particular date.[154] So if an asset is difficult or impossible to realise, its market value should be heavily discounted or even nil.[155]

If you cannot legally dispose of capital (eg, because of a restraint order), the market value is nil.[156]

In the case of a house, an estate agent's figure for a quick sale is a more appropriate valuation than the district valuer's figure for a sale within three months.[157]

It is not uncommon for an unrealistic assessment to be made of the value of your capital. If you disagree with the decision, you could ask for a revision or appeal (see Chapters 56 and 57).

Expenses of sale

If there would be expenses involved in selling your capital, 10 per cent is deducted from its value (before any debts are deducted) for the cost of sale.[158]

Debts

Deductions are made from the gross value of your capital for any debt or mortgage secured on it.[159] If a creditor (eg, a bank) holds the land certificate to your property as security for a loan and has registered notice of its deposit at the Land Registry, this counts as a debt secured on your property.[160] If a single mortgage is secured on a house and land, and the value of the house is disregarded for benefit purposes, the whole of the mortgage can be deducted when calculating the value of the land.[161]

If you have debts that are not secured against your capital (eg, tax liabilities), these cannot be offset against the value of your capital.[162] However, once you have repaid your debts, your capital may be reduced. **Note:** you can still be treated as having the capital if you deliberately get rid of it in order to get benefit (see p503).

If you have an overdrawn bank account and have savings in another account with the same bank, the amount of the overdraft should be deducted from your savings if the terms of the accounts allow the bank to make these transfers.[163]

Jointly owned capital

If you own any capital asset (except as a partner in a company – see p507) with someone else under a 'joint tenancy', you are treated as owning an equal share of the asset with the other owner(s) – eg, if you own the asset with one other person, you are each treated as having a 50 per cent share of it.[164] This applies regardless of whether the capital asset is in the UK or abroad. See p510 for the rules that apply to assets abroad.[165]

This does not apply if you jointly own the capital asset as 'tenants in common'.[166] In this case, your actual share in the asset is valued.

Joint tenancies and tenancies in common

With a '**joint tenancy**', each co-owner owns the whole of the capital asset 'jointly and severally'. If one of the joint tenants were to die, her/his interest in the asset would pass automatically to the other joint tenant(s).

With a '**tenancy in common**', each co-owner owns a discrete share in the asset. This share can be passed on by the person who has died to whoever s/he wishes.

If you have a joint tenancy, the value of your deemed share is calculated in the same way as your actual capital. However, it is only the value of your deemed share looked at in isolation that counts, and this will usually be worth less than the same proportion of the value of the whole asset. For example, if the asset is a house, the value of any deemed share may be very small or even worthless, particularly if the house is occupied and there is a possibility that the sale of the property cannot be forced. This is because even a willing buyer could not be expected to pay much for an asset s/he would have difficulty making use of.[167] Whether a sale can be forced depends on individual circumstances, and valuations should take into account legal costs and the length of time it could take to gain possession of the property.[168] A valuation should set out details of the valuer's expertise (where relevant), describe the property in sufficient detail to show that all factors relevant to its value have been taken into account, state any assumptions on which it is based and explain what the market is for that type of sale.[169] You may need to challenge any decision (see Chapters 56 and 57) based on an inadequate valuation.

Treatment of assets after a relationship breakdown

When partners separate, assets, such as a former home or bank account, may be in joint or sole names. If, for instance, a bank account is in joint names, you and your former partner are treated as having a 50 per cent share each under the rules on jointly held capital (see above). On the other hand, a former partner may have a right to some, or all, of an asset that is in your sole name – eg, s/he may have deposited most of the money in a bank account in your name. If this is established, you may be treated as not entitled to the whole of the account but as holding part of it as trustee for your former partner.[170] If an asset such as the matrimonial home belongs to your former partner and you have no share in it, you cannot be treated

Part 4: General rules for other means-tested benefits
Chapter 22: Capital: under pension age
6. How capital is valued

as having any interest in it under the Matrimonial Causes Act 1973 unless you take divorce or separation proceedings and get a property order.[171]

Shares

Shares are valued at their current market value less 10 per cent for the cost of sale, and after deducting any 'lien' held by brokers for sums owed for purchase or commission.[172] Market value can be worked out from the listed share price. If a more exact value is needed (eg, because your capital is close to the limit), it should be calculated using HM Revenue and Customs guidance, by taking the lowest and highest share prices for the day and using the lowest price plus a quarter of the difference between the two.[173] Fluctuations in price between routine reviews of your award are normally ignored. If you have a minority holding of shares in a company, the value of the shares should be based on what you could realise on them, and not by valuing the entire share capital of the company and attributing to you an amount calculated according to the proportion of shares held.[174]

Unit trusts

Unit trusts are valued on the basis of the 'bid' price quoted in newspapers. No deduction is allowed for the cost of sale because this is already included in the 'bid' price.[175]

The right to receive a payment in the future

The value of any such right that is not ignored (see p498) is its market value – what a willing buyer will pay to a willing seller.[176] For something which is not yet realisable, this may be very small.

Overseas assets

If you have assets abroad and there are no exchange controls or other prohibitions to prevent you transferring your capital to the UK, your assets are valued at their current market or surrender value in that country.[177]

If you are not allowed to transfer your capital, you are treated as having capital equal to the amount that a willing buyer in this country would give (which might not be very much).[178] Deduct any debts or mortgage secured on the assets, 10 per cent for any expenses of sale and any charges for converting the payment into sterling.[179]

Notes

1. The capital limits

1 **IS** Regs 45 and 53 IS Regs
JSA Regs 107 and 116 JSA Regs
ESA Regs 110 and 118 ESA Regs
HB Regs 43 and 52 HB Regs

2. Whose capital counts

2 **IS/HB** s136(1) SSCBA 1992
JSA s13(2) JSA 1995
ESA Sch 1 para 6(2) WRA 2007
3 **IS** Reg 23(2) IS Regs
JSA Reg 88(2) JSA Regs
ESA Reg 83(2) ESA Regs
HB Reg 25(3) HB Regs
4 **IS** Reg 17(1)(b) IS Regs
JSA Reg 83(b) JSA Regs
5 **IS** Reg 44(5) IS Regs
JSA Reg 106(5) JSA Regs

3. What counts as capital

6 para BW1.71 GM; Vol 5 Ch 29, para 29020 DMG
7 *R v SBC ex parte Singer* [1973] 1 WLR 713
8 R(IS) 3/93
9 R(IS) 3/93 para 22
10 R(SB) 2/83; R(SB) 35/83; R(IS) 3/93
11 R(SB) 12/86
12 *Barclays Bank v Quistclose Investments Ltd* [1970] AC 567; R(SB) 49/83; R(SB) 53/83; R(SB) 1/85; *MW v SSWP (JSA)* [2016] UKUT 469 (AAC), reported as [2017] AACR 15
13 R(SB) 49/83
14 R(SB) 12/86; for how this works in Scotland, see *JK v SSWP (JSA)* [2010] UKUT 437 (AAC), reported as [2011] AACR 26; *DF v SSWP* [2015] UKUT 611 (AAC)
15 *MC v SSWP (IS)* [2015] UKUT 600 (AAC)
16 CIS/2287/2008
17 R(IS) 1/90; CSIS/639/2006
18 R(SB) 23/85; CSIS/639/2006
19 *JC v SSWP* [2009] UKUT 22 (AAC)
20 CIS/25/1989
21 **IS** Sch 9 para 15 IS Regs
JSA Sch 7 para 15 JSA Regs
ESA Sch 8 para 16 ESA Regs
HB Sch 5 para 14 HB Regs
All Vol 5 Ch 29, para 29239 DMG

22 *Gartside v Inland Revenue Commissioners* [1968] 1 All ER 121; [1968] AC 553
23 *LG v SSWP (ESA)* [2019] UKUT 220 (AAC)
24 **IS** Reg 48(4) IS Regs
JSA Reg 110(4) JSA Regs
ESA Reg 112(4) ESA Regs
HB Reg 46(4) HB Regs
25 *Thomas v CAO*, appendix to R(SB) 17/87
26 CIS/984/2002
27 **IS** Reg 48 IS Regs
JSA Reg 110 JSA Regs
ESA Reg 112 ESA Regs
HB Reg 46 HB Regs
28 Reg 46(9) HB Regs

4. Disregarded capital

29 **IS** Sch 10 para 1 IS Regs
JSA Sch 8 para 1 JSA Regs
ESA Sch 9 para 1 ESA Regs
HB Sch 6 para 1 HB Regs
30 **IS** Reg 2(1), definition of 'dwelling occupied as the home', IS Regs; R(SB) 3/84; CIS/427/1991 and R(IS) 3/96
JSA Reg 1(3), definition of 'dwelling occupied as the home', JSA Regs
ESA Reg 2(1), definition of 'dwelling occupied as the home', ESA Regs
HB Sch 6 para 1 HB Regs
31 **IS** Sch 10 para 1 IS Regs
JSA Sch 8 para 1 JSA Regs
ESA Sch 9 para 1 ESA Regs
HB Sch 6 para 1 HB Regs
32 R(JSA) 9/03; R(SB) 10/89
33 *MM v SSWP (IS)* [2012] UKUT 358 (AAC)
34 **IS** Sch 10 para 25 IS Regs
JSA Sch 8 para 5 JSA Regs
ESA Sch 9 para 5 ESA Regs
HB Sch 6 para 25 HB Regs
35 **IS** Sch 10 para 27 IS Regs
JSA Sch 8 para 7 JSA Regs
ESA Sch 9 para 7 ESA Regs
HB Sch 6 para 27 HB Regs
36 **IS** Sch 10 para 26 IS Regs
JSA Sch 8 para 6 JSA Regs
ESA Sch 9 para 6 ESA Regs
HB Sch 6 para 26 HB Regs
All CIS/6908/1995; R(IS) 4/97
37 R(SB) 32/83
38 R(IS) 5/05
39 *SP v SSWP* [2009] UKUT 255 (AAC)

Part 4: General rules for other means-tested benefits
Chapter 22: Capital: under pension age
Notes

40 **IS** Sch 10 para 28 IS Regs
JSA Sch 8 para 8 JSA Regs
ESA Sch 9 para 8 ESA Regs
HB Sch 6 para 28 HB Regs
41 *R v London Borough of Tower Hamlets Review Board ex parte Kapur*, 12 June 2000, unreported
42 **IS** Sch 10 para 2 IS Regs
JSA Sch 8 para 2 JSA Regs
ESA Sch 9 para 2 ESA Regs
HB Sch 6 para 2 HB Regs
43 **IS** Sch 10 para 3 IS Regs
JSA Sch 8 para 3 JSA Regs
ESA Sch 9 para 3 ESA Regs
HB Sch 6 para 3 HB Regs
44 R(IS) 6/95
45 R(IS) 7/01
46 CIS/685/1992
47 CIS/8475/1995; CIS/15984/1996
48 R(SB) 14/85
49 **IS** Sch 10 para 8(b) IS Regs
JSA Sch 8 para 13(b) JSA Regs
ESA Sch 9 para 12(b) ESA Regs
HB Sch 6 para 10(b) HB Regs
50 *Barclays Bank v Quistclose Investments Ltd* [1970] AC 567; CSB/975/1985
51 **IS** Sch 10 para 9(a) IS Regs
JSA Sch 8 para 14(a) JSA Regs
ESA Sch 9 para 13(a) ESA Regs
HB Sch 6 para 11(a) HB Regs
52 **IS** Sch 10 para 9(b) IS Regs
JSA Sch 8 para 14(b) JSA Regs
ESA Sch 9 para 13(b) ESA Regs
HB Sch 6 para 11(b) HB Regs
53 **IS** Sch 10 para 37 IS Regs
JSA Sch 8 para 9 JSA Regs
ESA Sch 9 para 36 ESA Regs
HB Sch 6 para 38 HB Regs
54 CIS/4757/2003
55 CIS/6908/1995
56 **IS** Sch 10 paras 4 and 25 IS Regs
JSA Sch 8 paras 4 and 5 JSA Regs
ESA Sch 9 paras 4 and 5 ESA Regs
HB Sch 6 paras 4 and 25 HB Regs
57 **HB** BW1/Annex A/A1.01 GM
Other benefits Vol 5 Ch 29, para 29434 DMG
58 **IS** Reg 2(1) IS Regs
JSA Reg 1(3) JSA Regs
ESA Reg 2(1) ESA Regs
HB Reg 2(1) HB Regs
All CSB/209/1986; CSB/1149/1986; R(SB) 22/87
59 R(IS) 5/05; CH/3777/2007; *Bristol City Council v SJP (HB)* [2019] UKUT 360 (AAC)

60 **IS** Sch 10 para 10 IS Regs
JSA Sch 8 para 15 JSA Regs
ESA Sch 9 para 14 ESA Regs
HB Sch 6 para 12 HB Regs
61 R(H) 7/08
62 CIS/494/1990 and R(IS) 8/04
63 **IS** Sch 10 para 8(a) IS Regs
JSA Sch 8 para 13(a) JSA Regs
ESA Sch 9 para 12(a) ESA Regs
HB Sch 6 para 10(a) HB Regs
64 **IS** Sch 10 para 6(1) IS Regs
JSA Sch 8 para 11(1) JSA Regs
ESA Sch 9 para 10(1) ESA Regs
HB Sch 6 para 8(1) HB Regs
65 **IS** Sch 10 para 6(2) IS Regs
JSA Sch 8 para 11(2) JSA Regs
ESA Sch 9 para 10(2) ESA Regs
HB Sch 6 para 8(2) HB Regs
66 R(SB) 4/85
67 CIS/5481/1997
68 CFC/15/1990; R(FC) 2/92; *RM v Sefton Council (HB)* [2016] UKUT 357 (AAC), reported as [2017] AACR 5
69 **IS** Sch 10 para 23A IS Regs
JSA Sch 8 paras 28 and 29 JSA Regs
ESA Sch 9 paras 28 and 29 ESA Regs
HB Sch 6 para 32 HB Regs
70 **IS** Sch 10 para 15 IS Regs
JSA Sch 8 para 20 JSA Regs
ESA Sch 9 para 20 ESA Regs
HB Sch 6 para 17 HB Regs
71 R(IS) 7/98
72 **IS** Sch 10 para 11 IS Regs
JSA Sch 8 para 16 JSA Regs
ESA Sch 9 para 15 ESA Regs
HB Sch 6 para 13 HB Regs
73 **IS** Reg 41(2) IS Regs
JSA Reg 104(2) JSA Regs
ESA Reg 105(2) ESA Regs
HB Reg 41(2) HB Regs
All *Beattie v Secretary of State for Social Security* [2001] EWCA Civ 498, upholding CIS/114/1999, reported as R(IS) 10/01
74 **IS** Sch 10 para 5 IS Regs
JSA Sch 8 para 10 JSA Regs
ESA Sch 9 para 9 ESA Regs
HB Sch 6 para 7 HB Regs
75 **IS** Sch 10 paras 11-14, 16, 23 and 24 IS Regs
JSA Sch 8 paras 16-19, 21, 28 and 30 JSA Regs
ESA Sch 9 paras 15, 16, 18, 19, 21, 28 and 30 ESA Regs
HB Sch 6 paras 13-16, 18, 31 and 33 HB Regs

Chapter 22
Capital: under pension age

76 **IS** Sch 10 para 7 IS Regs
JSA Sch 8 para 12 JSA Regs
ESA Sch 9 para 11 ESA Regs
HB Sch 6 para 9 HB Regs
77 **IS** Sch 10 para 7(2) IS Regs
JSA Sch 8 para 12(2) JSA Regs
ESA Sch 9 para 11(2) ESA Regs
HB Sch 6 para 9(2) HB Regs
78 **IS** Sch 10 para 72 IS Regs
JSA Sch 8 para 65 JSA Regs
ESA Sch 9 para 60 ESA Regs
HB Sch 6 para 62 HB Regs
79 **IS** Sch 10 para 18 IS Regs
JSA Sch 8 para 23 JSA Regs
ESA Sch 9 para 23 ESA Regs
HB Sch 6 para 20 HB Regs
80 **IS** Sch 10 para 75 IS Regs
JSA Sch 8 para 68 JSA Regs
ESA Sch 9 para 63 ESA Regs
HB Sch 6 para 65 HB Regs
81 **IS** Sch 10 para 38 IS Regs
JSA Sch 8 para 36 JSA Regs
ESA Sch 9 para 37 ESA Regs
HB Sch 6 para 40 HB Regs
82 **IS** Sch 10 para 76 IS Regs
JSA Sch 8 para 69 JSA Regs
ESA Sch 9 para 64 ESA Regs
HB Sch 6 para 66 HB Regs
83 **IS** Sch 10 para 39 IS Regs
JSA Sch 8 para 37 JSA Regs
ESA Sch 9 para 38 ESA Regs
HB Sch 6 para 41 HB Regs
84 **IS** Sch 10 para 40 IS Regs
JSA Sch 8 para 38 JSA Regs
ESA Sch 9 para 39 ESA Regs
HB Sch 6 para 42 HB Regs
85 **IS** Sch 10 para 41 IS Regs
JSA Sch 8 para 39 JSA Regs
ESA Sch 9 para 40 ESA Regs
HB Sch 6 para 39 HB Regs
86 **IS** Sch 10 para 31 IS Regs
JSA Sch 8 para 33 JSA Regs
ESA Sch 9 para 33 ESA Regs
HB Sch 6 para 30 HB Regs
87 **IS** Sch 10 para 29 IS Regs
JSA Sch 8 para 31 JSA Regs
ESA Sch 9 para 31 ESA Regs
HB Sch 6 para 34 HB Regs
88 **IS** Schs 9 para 15 and 10 para 12 IS Regs
JSA Schs 7 para 15 and 8 para 18 JSA Regs
ESA Schs 8 para 16 and 9 para 16 ESA Regs
HB Schs 5 para 14 and 6 para 14 HB Regs
All *R v ex parte Singer* [1973] 1 WLR 713

89 **IS** Schs 9 paras 15 and 22, and 10 paras 44 and 45 IS Regs
JSA Schs 7 paras 15 and 23, and 8 paras 42 and 43 JSA Regs
ESA Schs 8 paras 16 and 23, and 9 paras 43 and 44 ESA Regs
HB Schs 5 paras 14 and 17, and 6 paras 45 and 46 HB Regs
90 **IS** Sch 10 para 12A IS Regs
JSA Sch 8 para 17A JSA Regs
ESA Sch 9 para 17 ESA Regs
HB Sch 6 para 14A HB Regs
91 R(IS) 3/03
92 R(SB) 2/89; *KQ v SSWP (IS)* [2011] UKUT 102 (AAC), reported as [2011] AACR 43
93 **IS** Sch 10 paras 22 and 65 IS Regs
JSA Sch 8 paras 27 and 58 JSA Regs
ESA Sch 9 paras 27 and 54 ESA Regs
HB Sch 6 paras 24 and 56 HB Regs
94 **IS** Sch 10 para 17 IS Regs
JSA Sch 8 para 22 JSA Regs
ESA Sch 9 para 22 ESA Regs
HB Sch 6 para 19 HB Regs
95 **IS** Sch 10 para 18A IS Regs
JSA Sch 8 para 23A JSA Regs
ESA Sch 9 para 23A ESA Regs
HB Sch 6 para 20A HB Regs
96 **IS** Sch 10 para 67 IS Regs
JSA Sch 8 para 60 JSA Regs
ESA Sch 9 para 56 ESA Regs
HB Sch 6 para 58 HB Regs
97 **IS** Sch 10 para 71 IS Regs
JSA Sch 8 para 64 JSA Regs
ESA Sch 9 para 59 ESA Regs
HB Sch 6 para 61 HB Regs
98 **IS** Sch 10 para 66 IS Regs
JSA Sch 8 para 59 JSA Regs
ESA Sch 9 para 55 ESA Regs
HB Sch 6 para 57 HB Regs
99 **IS** Sch 10 para 68A IS Regs
JSA Sch 8 para 61A JSA Regs
ESA Sch 9 para 58 ESA Regs
HB Sch 6 para 60 HB Regs
100 **IS** Sch 10 para 74 IS Regs
JSA Sch 8 para 67 JSA Regs
ESA Sch 9 para 62 ESA Regs
HB Sch 6 para 64 HB Regs
101 **IS** Sch 10 para 68 IS Regs
JSA Sch 8 para 61 JSA Regs
ESA Sch 9 para 57 ESA Regs
HB Sch 6 para 59 HB Regs
102 **IS** Sch 10 paras 1A and 30 IS Regs
JSA Sch 8 paras A2, A3 and 32 JSA Regs
ESA Sch 9 paras 1A, 32 and 32A ESA Regs
HB Sch 6 paras A2, A3 and 35 HB Regs

44

Part 4: General rules for other means-tested benefits
Chapter 22: Capital: under pension age
Notes

• •

103 **IS** Sch 10 para 52 IS Regs
JSA Sch 8 para 47 JSA Regs
ESA Sch 9 para 46 ESA Regs
HB Sch 6 para 49 HB Regs
104 **IS** Sch 10 para 6(3) and (4) IS Regs
JSA Sch 8 para 11(3) and (4) JSA Regs
ESA Sch 9 para 10(3) and (4) ESA Regs
HB Sch 6 para 8(3) and (4) HB Regs
105 **IS** Sch 10 paras 42 and 43 IS Regs
JSA Sch 8 paras 40 and 41 JSA Regs
ESA Sch 9 paras 41 and 42 ESA Regs
HB Sch 6 paras 43 and 44 HB Regs
106 **IS** Sch 10 para 56 IS Regs
JSA Sch 8 para 51 JSA Regs
ESA Sch 9 para 47 ESA Regs
HB Sch 6 para 50 HB Regs
107 **IS** Sch 10 para 63 IS Regs
JSA Sch 8 para 52 JSA Regs
ESA Sch 9 para 52 ESA Regs
HB Sch 6 para 51 HB Regs
108 **IS** Sch 10 para 34 IS Regs
JSA Sch 8 para 34 JSA Regs
ESA Sch 9 para 34 ESA Regs
109 **IS** Sch 10 para 36 IS Regs
JSA Sch 8 para 35 JSA Regs
ESA Sch 9 para 35 ESA Regs
HB Sch 6 para 37 HB Regs
110 Memo ADM 26/16
111 **IS** Sch 10 para 46 IS Regs
JSA Sch 8 para 44 JSA Regs
ESA Sch 9 para 45 ESA Regs
HB Sch 6 para 47 HB Regs
112 Hansard Written Question 276279; HB Circular A8/2019
113 Reg 26 VP Regs

5. Notional capital
114 **IS** Reg 51(6) IS Regs
JSA Reg 113(6) JSA Regs
ESA Reg 115(8) ESA Regs
HB Reg 49(6) HB Regs
115 **IS** Reg 51(1) IS Regs
JSA Reg 113(1) JSA Regs
ESA Reg 115(1) ESA Regs
HB Reg 49(1) HB Regs
116 R(IS) 7/07
117 CIS/124/1990; CSB/1198/1989
118 CIS/124/1990
119 R(SB) 9/91
120 CIS/40/1989
121 CIS/621/1991. See also CJSA/3937/2002 and *LH v SSWP (IS)* [2014] UKUT 60 (AAC)
122 CIS/264/1989
123 R(IS) 7/98, para 12(3)
124 R(SB) 38/85; R(IS) 1/91; R(H) 1/06
125 para BW1.714 GM

126 **IS** Reg 51(1)(a) IS Regs
JSA Reg 113(1)(a) JSA Regs
ESA Reg 115(1)(a) ESA Regs
127 R(SB) 40/85
128 R(IS) 8/04
129 R(SB) 12/91; *Verna Jones v SSWP* [2003] EWCA Civ 964; *VW v SSWP (IS)* [2015] UKUT 51 (AAC), reported as [2015] AACR 39
130 CIS/2627/1995; *Verna Jones v SSWP* [2003] EWCA Civ 964
131 *KS v SSWP* [2009] UKUT 122 (AAC), reported as [2010] AACR 3
132 **IS** Reg 51(6) IS Regs
JSA Reg 113(6) JSA Regs
ESA Reg 115(8) ESA Regs
HB Reg 49(7) HB Regs
133 CIS/30/1993, but other commissioners have taken a different view (see, for example, CIS/25/1990 and CIS/81/1991).
134 para BW1.831 GM
135 **IS** Reg 51A(1) IS Regs
JSA Reg 114(1) JSA Regs
ESA Reg 116(1) ESA Regs
HB Reg 49(1) HB Regs
136 **IS** Reg 51(2) IS Regs
JSA Reg 113(2) JSA Regs
ESA Reg 115(2) ESA Regs
HB Reg 49(2) HB Regs
137 Reg 49(2) HB Regs
138 **IS** Reg 51(3)(a)(ii) and (8) IS Regs
JSA Reg 113(3)(a)(ii) and (8) JSA Regs
ESA Regs 2(1) and 115(3)(c) ESA Regs
HB Reg 49(3)(a) and (7) HB Regs
139 **IS** Reg 51(8) IS Regs
JSA Reg 113(8) JSA Regs
ESA Reg 2(1) ESA Regs
HB Reg 49(7)(b) HB Regs
140 Vol 5 Ch 29, para 29867 DMG
141 **IS** Reg 51(3)(a)(ii), (3A)(a) and (ba) IS Regs
JSA Reg 113(3)(a)(ii), (3A)(a), (bb) and (bc) JSA Regs
ESA Reg 115(3)(c), (5)(a) and (ba) ESA Regs
HB Reg 49(3)(b), (4)(a), (bb) and (bc) HB Regs
142 **IS** Reg 51(3)(a)(ia) IS Regs
JSA Reg 113(3)(a)(ia) JSA Regs
ESA Reg 115(3)(b) ESA Regs
HB Reg 49(3)(a) HB Regs
143 **IS** Reg 51(3A)(c) IS Regs
JSA Reg 113(3A)(c) JSA Regs
ESA Reg 115(5)(c) ESA Regs
HB Reg 49(4)(c) HB Regs
144 R(IS) 4/01
145 CH/1672/2007

146 **IS** Reg 51(3)(a)(i) IS Regs
  JSA Reg 113(3)(a)(i) JSA Regs
  ESA Reg 115(3)(a) ESA Regs
147 **IS** Reg 51(3)(b) IS Regs
  JSA Reg 113(3)(b) JSA Regs
  ESA Reg 115(4) ESA Regs
  HB Reg 49(3)(c) HB Regs
148 **IS** Reg 51(4) IS Regs
  JSA Reg 113(4) JSA Regs
  ESA Reg 115(6) ESA Regs
  HB Reg 49(5) HB Regs
149 **IS** Reg 51(5) IS Regs
  JSA Reg 113(5) JSA Regs
  ESA Reg 115(7) ESA Regs
  HB Reg 49(6) HB Regs
150 Vol 5 Ch 29, para 29879 DMG; see also R(IS) 13/93
151 R(IS) 14/98
152 Reg 49(5) HB Regs

6. How capital is valued
153 **IS** Reg 49(a) IS Regs
  JSA Reg 111(a) JSA Regs
  ESA Reg 113 ESA Regs
  HB Reg 47(a) HB Regs
154 R(SB) 57/83; R(SB) 6/84
155 R(SB) 18/83
156 *CS v SSWP* [2014] UKUT 518 (AAC)
157 R(SB) 6/84
158 **IS** Reg 49(a) IS Regs
  JSA Reg 111(a) JSA Regs
  ESA Reg 113(a) ESA Regs
  HB Reg 47(a) HB Regs
159 **IS** Reg 49(b) IS Regs
  JSA Reg 111(b) JSA Regs
  ESA Reg 113(b) ESA Regs
  HB Reg 47(b) HB Regs
160 CIS/255/1989
161 R(SB) 27/84
162 R(SB) 2/83; R(SB) 31/83
163 *JRL v SSWP (JSA)* [2011] UKUT 63 (AAC), reported as [2011] AACR 30
164 **IS** Reg 52 IS Regs
  JSA Reg 115 JSA Regs
  ESA Reg 117 ESA Regs
  HB Reg 51 HB Regs
165 CIS/2575/1997
166 *Hourigan v SSWP* [2002] EWCA 1890, reported as R(IS) 4/03
167 CIS/15936/1996; CIS/263/1997; CIS/3283/1997 (joint decision); R(IS) 26/95
168 R(IS) 3/96
169 R(JSA) 1/02; CH/1953/2003; *Reigate and Banstead Borough Council v GB* [2018] UKUT 225 (AAC)
170 R(IS) 2/93
171 R(IS) 1/03

172 **IS** Reg 49(a) IS Regs
  JSA Reg 111(a) JSA Regs
  ESA Reg 113 ESA Regs
  HB Reg 47(a) HB Regs
173 R(IS) 18/95; Vol 5 Ch 29, paras 29666-71 DMG
174 R(SB) 18/83; R(IS) 2/90
175 R(IS) 18/95; Vol 5 Ch 29, para 29681 DMG
  HB BW1/1.530 GM
176 *Peters v CAO* (appendix to R(SB) 3/89)
177 **IS** Reg 50(a) IS Regs
  JSA Reg 112(a) JSA Regs
  ESA Reg 114(a) ESA Regs
  HB Reg 48(a) HB Regs
178 **IS** Reg 50(b) IS Regs
  JSA Reg 112(b) JSA Regs
  ESA Reg 114(b) ESA Regs
  HB Reg 48(b) HB Regs
179 **IS** Sch 10 para 21 IS Regs
  JSA Sch 8 para 26 JSA Regs
  ESA Sch 9 para 26 ESA Regs
  HB Sch 6 para 23 HB Regs

Chapter 23

Capital: over pension age

This chapter covers:
1. The capital limits (p517)
2. Whose capital counts (p518)
3. What counts as capital (p518)
4. Disregarded capital (p519)
5. Notional capital (p525)
6. How capital is valued (p526)

This chapter explains how capital affects your entitlement to pension credit (PC). It also applies to pension-age housing benefit (HB) if you and your partner are over pension age and neither of you are on income support (IS), income-based jobseeker's allowance (JSA) or income-related employment and support allowance (ESA) or universal credit (UC). If you get IS, income-based JSA, income-related ESA (or UC), your capital is ignored for HB. Chapter 22 explains the rules for IS, income-based JSA, income-related ESA and for working-age HB if you and your partner are under pension age. If you are in a couple and one of you is over pension age but not the other, see p188 for whether the working-age or pension-age HB rules apply. Chapter 8 explains the rules for UC.

Note: whenever HB is referred to in this chapter, this only applies to the rules for people over pension age. The law refers to the qualifying age for PC rather than pension age, but since December 2018 this has been the same as pension age.

Key facts
- There is no upper capital limit for pension credit (PC).
- Generally, you are not eligible for pension-age housing benefit (HB) if your total capital is over £16,000. However, if you get the guarantee credit of PC, there is no capital limit for HB because all your capital is ignored.
- If you have capital over £10,000, this affects the amount of PC or HB you get because it is assumed that your capital gives you some income – called 'deemed income'.
- Capital includes your and your partner's savings, investments and property. Some kinds of capital are ignored when working out your PC or HB – eg, the value of the home in which you live.
- If you deliberately get rid of capital in order to get more benefit, you are treated as still having it. This is called 'notional capital'.

1. The capital limits

Pension credit

There is no upper capital limit for pension credit (PC), beyond which you are excluded from benefit. There is, however, a lower limit of £10,000.

Capital of £10,000 or less is ignored. If you have capital above £10,000, you are treated as having a deemed income (sometimes called 'tariff income') of £1 for every £500, or part of £500, by which your capital exceeds £10,000.[1]

Housing benefit

There is a lower and upper limit.[2]
- The lower capital limit is £10,000.
- The upper limit is £16,000.

The first £10,000 of your capital is ignored. If you have capital above £10,000, you are treated as having a deemed income of £1 for every £500, or part of £500, by which your capital exceeds that amount.[3] If you have over £16,000, you are not entitled to housing benefit (HB) unless you get the guarantee credit of PC, in which case all your and your partner's capital (and income) is ignored for HB.[4] This is because entitlement to PC guarantee credit acts as a passport to maximum HB. Because PC has no upper capital limit, you can get maximum HB even with capital above £16,000.

If you get the savings credit of PC, but not the guarantee credit, the following applies.[5]
- Your capital for HB purposes is the capital figure worked out by the DWP for your PC. This is modified to include any capital belonging to your partner which was not taken into account in the PC calculation.
- During an 'assessed income period' (see p281), an increase in your capital does not affect your PC savings credit, but may affect HB. If capital increases above £16,000 (worked out by the local authority under the HB rules), you are no longer entitled to HB. If your capital increases but is still less than £16,000, the local authority must continue to use the DWP's capital figure.

Example
Amy is 80 and a widow. She has a state pension and a personal pension. She gets HB and the savings credit of PC, but not the guarantee credit. Her PC award letter shows that she has an assessed income period. When she inherits £20,000 her HB stops, but her PC is not affected unless the assessed income period ends because of a change in her circumstances.

Part 4: General rules for other means-tested benefits
Chapter 23: Capital: over pension age
3. What counts as capital

2. Whose capital counts

If you are a member of a couple, your partner's capital is added to yours.

3. What counts as capital

All your capital is taken into account, unless it is disregarded (see p519).

The term 'capital' is not defined. In general, it means lump-sum or one-off payments rather than a series of payments – eg, savings, investments and property.[6] Capital payments can normally be distinguished from income because they are not payable for any specified period and are not part of a regular series of payments (although capital can be paid by instalments).[7]

Savings

Your savings generally count as capital – eg, cash you have at home, premium bonds, stocks and shares, unit trusts and money in a bank account.

Savings from past income (including benefits – see p522) are treated as capital after the period for which the income was paid has lapsed. If you have put aside money to pay bills, this is still counted as your capital.[8] If your savings are just below the capital limit, you could pay bills by monthly direct debit or use a budget account to keep your capital below the limit.

Fixed-term investments

Capital held in fixed-term investments counts. However, if it is currently unobtainable, it may have little or no value. If you can convert the investment into a form that lets you access it or sell your interest, or raise a loan through a reputable bank using the asset as security, the amount you can get for it counts. If it takes time to produce evidence about the nature and value of the investment, you may be able to get a short-term advance of pension credit (see p1192) or a 'payment on account' of housing benefit (see p220).[9]

Property and land

Any property or land that you own counts as capital. Many types of property are disregarded (see p520). If there is doubt about who owns the property, see p491.

Loans

A loan to you usually counts as money you possess and counts as capital. However, in some limited circumstances you can argue that a loan should be disregarded (see p491). If you lend someone money, see p491.

Trusts

Money or property held in a trust for you or your partner is ignored when working out whether you have any deemed income from capital (see p478). You are not assumed to have a fixed income from the trust.[10] This applies to both discretionary and non-discretionary trusts. However, payments actually made from the trust can be taken into account. If made regularly, payments are treated as income. For discretionary trusts, regular payments are either disregarded in full or in part (see p480). If payments are not made regularly, they are taken into account as capital.

The rules are different if the trust is set up from personal injury payments (see p524). Payments made from certain charitable trusts are specifically ignored (see p524).

Money held by your solicitor

Money held by your solicitor normally counts as your capital. This includes compensation payments (but see p524 for when payments for personal injury are disregarded).[11] If you have had legal aid and your solicitor is holding money back while working out the statutory charge to be deducted for legal costs, it does not count as your capital.[12]

4. Disregarded capital

Your home

If you own the home you normally live in, its value is ignored.[13]

Your home

Your '**home**' includes any garage, garden, outbuildings and land belonging to the property, together with any premises that you do not occupy as your home but which it is impractical or unreasonable to sell separately – eg, croft land.[14]

This disregard applies to any home in which you are treated as normally living – eg, because you are only temporarily living away from it (see p371). However, if you own more than one property, only the value of the one normally occupied is disregarded under this rule.[15] Exceptionally, two separate properties can be regarded as a single home, as though one was an annexe of the other, if you personally (rather than a member of your family) normally occupy both.[16] This is most likely to be the case for a large family, but other situations are possible where neither property on its own caters for a family's needs – eg, if there is a carer living between two properties.[17]

Part 4: General rules for other means-tested benefits
Chapter 23: Capital: over pension age
4. Disregarded capital

When the value of the property is disregarded

The value of the property can be disregarded, even if you do not normally live in it, in the following circumstances.

- **If you have left your former home following a relationship breakdown,** the value of the property is ignored for 26 weeks from the date you left. It may also be disregarded for longer if any of the steps below are taken. If it is occupied by your former partner who is a lone parent, its value is ignored for as long as s/he lives there.[18]
- **If you have sought legal advice or have started legal proceedings in order to occupy the property as your home,** its value is ignored for 26 weeks from the date you first took either of these steps.[19] The 26 weeks can be extended, if it is reasonable to do so, if you need longer to move into the property.
- **If you are taking reasonable steps to dispose of any property,** its value is ignored for 26 weeks from the date you first took such steps (which may start before you claimed benefit).[20] See p494 for more details.
- **If you are carrying out essential repairs or alterations which are needed so that you can occupy a property as your home,** the value of the property is ignored for 26 weeks from the date you first began to take steps to carry them out.[21] See p494 for more details.
- **If you have acquired a property to occupy as your home but have not yet moved in,** its value is ignored if you intend to live there within 26 weeks of acquiring it.[22] If you cannot move in by then, the value of the property can be ignored for as long as seems reasonable.
- **Any amounts paid to you or deposited in your name for the sole purpose of buying a home for you to live in or carrying out essential repairs or alterations to your home or the home you intend to occupy** are ignored for a year from the date you were paid them.[23] This includes money from the sale of a home that you earmark to buy another place to live in.[24] For pension credit (PC), if there is an assessed income period (p281) that extends beyond the year's disregard, the rules provide for the disregard to last until the end of that period. However, it is not clear how this applies in all cases. For example, it would not apply if your PC entitlement or assessed income period began only after the year's disregard had expired. Arguably, it should apply in other cases where there is an assessed income period.[25]
- **Any compensation paid under an insurance policy because of loss or damage to your home** is ignored for a year from the date it is paid to you.[26] For PC, if there is an assessed income period, it can be disregarded until the end of that period in the same way as explained in the bullet point above.

When considering whether it is reasonable to increase the period during which time the value of your property is disregarded, all the circumstances should be considered – eg, your personal circumstances, any efforts made by you to use or dispose of the home[27] and the general state of the property market. In practice, periods of around 18 months are not considered unusual.

Note: it is possible for the value of the property to be ignored under more than one of the above paragraphs in succession.[28]

The home of a former partner or relative

The value of a home (see p519) is ignored if it is occupied wholly or partly as her/his home by:[29]

- a relative of yours or of your partner (see p496 for who this includes) who is over pension age (see p271) or who is incapacitated (see below);[30] *or*
- your former partner from whom you are not estranged, divorced or out of a civil partnership – eg, if one of you is living in a care home; *or*
- your former partner from whom you are estranged, divorced or out of a civil partnership if s/he is a lone parent. If s/he is not a lone parent, the value of the home is ignored for 26 weeks from the date you ceased to live in the home.[31]

Definitions

'**Incapacitated**' is not defined, but guidance suggests it includes anyone who is getting employment and support allowance (ESA), statutory sick pay (SSP), attendance allowance (AA) or disability living allowance (DLA), or who would qualify because of her/his health condition or disability.[32]

It may also include anyone getting personal independence payment (PIP) or universal credit (UC) who has limited capability for work or limited capability for work-related activity. However, you should argue for a broader interpretation, if necessary.

You are '**estranged**' if you are living apart because your relationship has broken down, even if the separation is amicable.[33]

Personal possessions

All personal possessions, including items such as jewellery, furniture or a car, are ignored.[34] A personal possession has been defined as any physical asset not used for business purposes, other than land.[35] A home that you own but do not live in is not a personal possession, but counts as capital (see p477).

Compensation paid under an insurance policy for damage to, or loss of, your personal possessions is ignored for a year from the date you were paid the compensation or, for PC only, until the end of the assessed income period (if there is one) if that is longer.[36]

Business assets

If you are self-employed, your business assets are ignored for as long as you continue to work in that business.[37] If you cannot work because of physical or

Part 4: General rules for other means-tested benefits
Chapter 23: Capital: over pension age
4. Disregarded capital

mental illness, but intend to work in the business when you are able, the disregard operates for 26 weeks from the date of claim, or for longer if reasonable in the circumstances.[38] For more about this, see p497.

Insurance policy and annuity surrender values

The surrender value of any life assurance policy is ignored.[39] Some investments include an element of life insurance – eg, endowment policies. If the policy terms include how the payment on death is calculated, the whole investment is ignored.[40] However, you cannot choose to put money into such an investment in order to increase your benefit entitlement, because you are likely to be caught by the notional capital rule if you do (see p525).

The surrender value of any annuity is also ignored for the purposes of the deemed income rule (see p478). Any actual income the surrender value generates for you, and which is not disregarded as income, can be taken into account as income.[41] Any payment under the annuity counts as income (but see p479 for when this is ignored).[42]

Future interests in property

A future interest in most kinds of property is ignored.[43] A '**future interest**' is one which will only revert to you, or become yours for the first time, when some future event occurs. However, this does not include a freehold or leasehold interest in property which has been let by you to tenants. If you did not let the property to the tenant (eg, because the tenancy was entered into before you bought the property), your interest should be ignored as a future interest.

The right to receive a payment in the future

If you know you will receive a payment in the future and you could sell your right to that payment at any time, it has a market value and, therefore, constitutes an actual capital resource. The value of this is ignored if it is a right to receive:[44]
- income under a life interest or, in Scotland, a life rent; *or*
- an occupational or personal pension; *or*
- any rent if you are not the freeholder or leaseholder; *or*
- any payment under an annuity.

Benefits and tax credits

Arrears of benefits and tax credits

Arrears of specified benefits (see below) are ignored as capital:[45]
- for one year after they are received by you; *or*
- for PC, if there is an assessed income period that extends beyond the year's disregard (p281), as the rules provide for the disregard to last until the end of that period. However, it is not clear how this applies in all cases. For example,

it does not apply if your PC entitlement or assessed income period began only after the year's disregard had expired.[46] Arguably, it should apply in other cases where there is an assessed income period;[47] *or*

- for the remainder of the PC or housing benefit (HB) award if the arrears are £5,000 or more and are paid to compensate for an official error or (from 11 September 2018) an error of law, and which you received in full since becoming entitled to PC or HB. If you got the compensation before then, it is still disregarded if your current award follows immediately from a previous award of income support (IS), income-based jobseeker's allowance (JSA), income-related ESA, UC, HB or council tax benefit (CTB) (or PC, for current awards of HB) in which the compensation was disregarded, or it is still being disregarded in an award of one of those benefits.

The **'specified benefits'** are:
- armed forces independence payment;
- AA, constant attendance allowance and exceptionally severe disablement allowance;
- bereavement support payment;
- Best Start grant (in Scotland);
- child tax credit;
- CTB;
- DLA;
- funeral support payment (in Scotland);
- income-related ESA;
- HB;
- IS;
- income-based JSA;
- maternity allowance;
- PC;
- PIP;
- UC;
- for PC only, child benefit and social fund payments;
- for HB only, working tax credit and discretionary housing payments;
- concessionary payments (ie, compensation) made instead of any of the above benefits or payments made in lieu of any of these benefits.

Note: although arrears are ignored as capital, you may have been paid more PC or HB than you would have been entitled to if benefit had been paid on time. For PC, the DWP usually deducts the difference from the arrears of the delayed benefit. Otherwise, if the arrears are not reduced, the overpayment is recoverable from you (see p1237). For HB, the overpayment may be recoverable (see p1253).

Part 4: General rules for other means-tested benefits
Chapter 23: Capital: over pension age
4. Disregarded capital

Other benefits and payments

The following payments are ignored for one year (or, for PC, to the end of the assessed income period) from when you get them:[48]

- refunds of council tax liability, including from a council tax reduction scheme;
- arrears of a supplementary pension to war widows, widowers or surviving civil partners for pre-1973 service.

The initial lump sum of bereavement support payment is ignored for 52 weeks from when you get the payment.[49] Lump-sum state retirement pension, if you deferred your pension and chose a lump sum rather than increased income, is ignored indefinitely.[50]

Personal injury and other compensation payments

- **Personal injury payments.** Any money paid because of a personal injury to you or your partner is ignored, whether or not it has been placed in a trust.[51] Neither deemed income (see p478) nor actual income from the fund is taken into account. If the personal injury was to your partner and s/he has since died, the capital value is no longer ignored.[52] If an award for damages for personal injury to you or your partner is administered by a court (eg, the Court of Protection), its value, and income and capital from it, are disregarded.[53] 'Personal injury' includes not only accidental and criminal injury but also any disease and injury as a result of a disease.[54]
- **Special compensation schemes.** Any payment of capital (or income) from certain special schemes approved or set up by government is ignored if it is:[55]
  - for you or your partner who has variant CJD (Creutzfeldt-Jakob disease). If you are the parent of someone with variant CJD, the payment is ignored for two years; *or*
  - from a specified infected blood payment scheme. You can give money from the payment to your partner and it is ignored indefinitely in her/his benefit claim or, if you have no partner or children, to your parent and it is ignored for two years; *or*
  - compensation for the London bombings in July 2005, from the London Emergencies Trust or from the We Love Manchester Emergency Fund (for the 2017 terror attacks); *or*
  - World War Two compensation (rather than a war pension) if you, your partner or deceased spouse or civil partner were interned as a prisoner of war in Japan, lost a child, suffered injury or forced labour or lost property; *or*
  - in respect of someone disabled by thalidomide during her/his mother's pregnancy.

Funeral plan payments

The value of any funeral plan contract is ignored indefinitely.[56]
A funeral plan contract is a contract under which:
- you make at least one payment to another person; *and*
- that person undertakes to ensure you are provided with a funeral; *and*
- the sole purpose of the plan is to ensure you are provided with a funeral.

Social services, community care and other payments

The following payments are ignored for one year (or for PC, to the end of the assessed income period) from when you get the payments:[57]
- local welfare assistance payments;
- payments under the Supporting People programme.

Ignored indefinitely are:[58]
- community care or health care direct payments;
- payments from a local authority to a young person in Scotland aged 16 or over in 'continuing care' or passed to you by the young person if s/he still lives with you and was in your care;
- for HB, direct payments under an education, health and care plan, paid in England for a child with special educational needs.

Miscellaneous payments

The following payments are disregarded:
- under the Windrush Compensation Scheme and Windrush Urgent and Exceptional Payments Scheme (disregarded on an extra-statutory basis);[59]
- victims' payments to people injured in a 'Troubles-related incident'.[60]

5. Notional capital

In certain circumstances, you are treated as having capital which you do not have. This is called **'notional capital'**.[61] There is a similar rule for notional income (see p481).
You are treated as having notional capital if:
- you deliberately deprive yourself of capital in order to claim or increase benefit (see p526);
- you are a sole trader or a partner in a business (see p526).

Notional capital counts in the same way as capital you do have, except that a 'diminishing notional capital rule' (see p505) may be applied so that the value of the notional capital you are treated as having is considered to reduce over time.

Part 4: General rules for other means-tested benefits
Chapter 23: Capital: over pension age
6. How capital is valued

Deliberately getting rid of capital

If you deliberately get rid of capital in order to claim or increase your benefit, you are treated as still having it (see p503).[62] You are not treated as having deprived yourself of capital if:

- you pay off or reduce a debt which you owe; *or*
- you pay for goods or services if the purchase of those goods or services was reasonable in the circumstances of your case.

The diminishing notional capital rule

The diminishing notional capital rule applies if you are treated as having notional capital because of depriving yourself of capital.

If you are getting pension credit (PC), the amount of the notional capital goes down each week by the extra PC you are losing because of the notional capital – eg, through having 'deemed income' taken into account.[63] For example, if your notional capital is £11,000, you have £2 a week less PC because of deemed income (see p478) so £2 a week is deducted from the notional capital until it reaches £10,500 when it will be £1 a week.

If you are not getting any PC, notional capital goes down, not just by the amount of PC you would have had, but also by any additional housing benefit (HB) you would have had if notional capital had not been taken into account. Ask the DWP for a forecast of when it is worth claiming again. If in doubt, you can claim every 26 weeks (but not more often).

For HB, the same rule applies to reduce your notional capital except that, not only is it reduced by the amount of HB you are losing because of the notional capital, but it is also reduced by any PC you would have been entitled to (or income-based jobseeker's allowance or income-related employment and support allowance), whether or not you are currently getting HB.[64]

Companies run by sole traders or a few partners

The value of shares you hold is normally taken into account as capital, but not if you are treated as a sole owner or partner in the business. Instead, your share of the value of the company itself counts. See p507 – the rules for people over pension age are the same except that local authorities have no discretion but are obliged to follow these rules.[65]

6. How capital is valued

There are a number of issues to consider when valuing capital.

- **Market value.** Capital is valued at its current market or surrender value,[66] which could be very low if it is difficult to sell. See p508 for more information.

- **Expenses of sale.** If there would be expenses involved in selling your capital, 10 per cent is deducted from its value for the cost of sale.[67]
- **Debts.** Deductions are made from the 'gross' value of your capital for any debt or mortgage secured on it.[68] For more information, see p508.
- **Capital that is jointly owned under a joint tenancy.** If you jointly own any capital asset (except as a partner in a company, when the rules explained on p526 apply instead) under a joint tenancy, you are treated as owning an equal share of the asset with all other owners.[69] For example, if two of you own the asset, you are each treated as having a 50 per cent share of it. This rule does not apply, however, if you jointly own the capital asset as 'tenants in common'.[70] For more information, see p508.
- **Treatment of assets after a relationship breakdown.** There are no specific rules about this, but there is some guidance and caselaw (see p509).
- **Shares** are valued at their current market value, less 10 per cent for the cost of sale and after deducting any 'lien' held by brokers for sums owed for the cost of their acquisition and any commission.[71] See p510 for more details.
- **Unit trusts** are valued on the basis of the 'bid' price quoted in newspapers. No deduction is allowed for the cost of sale because this is already included in the 'bid' price.[72]
- **The right to receive a payment in the future.** The value that is not ignored (see p522) is its market value – ie, what a willing buyer would pay to a willing seller.[73] For something which is not yet realisable, this may be very small.
- **Overseas assets.** If you have assets abroad, and there are no exchange controls or other prohibitions that would prevent you transferring your capital to this country, your assets are valued at their current market or surrender value in that country.[74] If you are not allowed to transfer your capital, you are treated as having capital equal to the amount that a willing buyer in this country would give (which might not be very much).[75] Deduct any debts or mortgage secured on the assets, 10 per cent for any expenses of sale and any charges for converting the payment into sterling.[76]
- **Payments in other currencies.** Any payment in a currency other than sterling is taken into account after deducting banking charges or commission payable on conversion.[77]

Part 4: General rules for other means-tested benefits
Chapter 23: Capital: over pension age
Notes

Notes

1. The capital limits
1 s15(2) SPCA 2002; reg 15(6) SPC Regs
2 Reg 43 HB(SPC) Regs
3 Reg 29(2) HB(SPC) Regs
4 Reg 26 HB(SPC) Regs
5 Reg 27 HB(SPC) Regs

3. What counts as capital
6 BP1/P1.71 GM
7 *R v SBC ex parte Singer* [1973] 1 WLR 713
8 R(IS) 3/93; R(PC) 3/08
9 **PC** Reg 2 SS(PAOR) Regs
   HB Reg 74(1) HB(SPC) Regs
10 **PC** Sch 5 para 28 SPC Regs
   HB Sch 6 para 30 HB(SPC) Regs
11 *Thomas v CAO*, appendix to R(SB) 17/87
12 CIS/984/2002

4. Disregarded capital
13 **PC** Sch 5 para 1A SPC Regs
   HB Sch 6 para 26 HB(SPC) Regs
14 **PC** Reg 1(2), definition of 'dwelling occupied as the home', SPC Regs
   HB Reg 2(1), definition of 'dwelling occupied as the home', HB(SPC) Regs
15 **PC** Sch 5 para 1A SPC Regs
   HB Sch 6 para 26 HB(SPC) Regs
16 R(JSA) 9/03; R(SB) 10/89
17 *MM v SSWP (IS)* [2012] UKUT 358 (AAC)
18 **PC** Sch 5 para 6(1) SPC Regs
   HB Sch 6 para 6(1) HB(SPC) Regs
19 **PC** Sch 5 para 2 SPC Regs
   HB Sch 6 para 2 HB(SPC) Regs
20 **PC** Sch 5 para 7 SPC Regs
   HB Sch 6 para 7 HB(SPC) Regs
   Both CIS/6908/1995; R(IS) 4/97
21 **PC** Sch 5 para 3 SPC Regs
   HB Sch 6 para 3 HB(SPC) Regs
22 **PC** Sch 5 para 1 SPC Regs
   HB Sch 6 para 1 HB(SPC) Regs
23 **PC** Sch 5 paras 17 and 19 SPC Regs
   HB Sch 6 paras 18 and 20 HB(SPC) Regs
24 *DG v SSWP (SPC)* [2010] UKUT 241 (AAC); DWP, *A detailed guide to pension credit for advisers PC10S*, page 39
25 *DG v SSWP (SPC)* [2010] UKUT 241 (AAC). But see CPC/206/2005 and CPC/1928/2005, which suggest an assessed income period could be reduced on revision in some cases.

26 **PC** Sch 5 paras 17 and 18 SPC Regs
   HB Sch 6 paras 18 and 19 HB(SPC) Regs
27 CIS/4757/2003
28 CIS/6908/1995
29 **PC** Sch 5 para 4 SPC Regs
   HB Sch 6 para 4 HB(SPC) Regs
30 **PC** Reg 1(2), definition of 'close relative', SPC Regs
   HB Reg 2(1), definition of 'close relative', HB(SPC) Regs
31 **PC** Sch 5 para 6 SPC Regs
   HB Sch 6 para 6 HB(SPC) Regs
32 **PC** para 84444 DMG
   HB para BP1, Annex A1.01 GM
33 R(IS) 5/05; CPC/683/2007; *Bristol City Council v SJP (HB)* [2019] UKUT 360 (AAC)
34 **PC** Sch 5 para 8 SPC Regs
   HB Sch 6 para 8 HB(SPC) Regs
35 R(H) 7/08
36 **PC** Sch 5 paras 17 and 18 SPC Regs
   HB Sch 6 paras 18 and 19 HB(SPC) Regs
37 **PC** Sch 5 para 9 SPC Regs
   HB Sch 6 para 9 HB(SPC) Regs
38 **PC** Sch 5 para 9A SPC Regs
   HB Sch 6 para 10 HB(SPC) Regs
39 **PC** Sch 5 para 10 SPC Regs
   HB Sch 6 para 11 HB(SPC) Regs
40 R(IS) 7/98
41 **PC** Sch 5 para 26 SPC Regs
   HB Sch 6 para 29 HB Regs
42 **PC** s15(1)(d) SPCA 2002
   HB Reg 29(1)(d) HB(SPC) Regs
   Both R(IS) 10/01
43 **PC** Sch 5 para 5 SPC Regs
   HB Sch 6 para 5 HB(SPC) Regs
44 **PC** Sch 5 paras 22 and 24-26 SPC Regs
   HB Sch 6 paras 24 and 27-29 HB(SPC) Regs
45 **PC** Sch 5 paras 17, 20 and 20A SPC Regs
   HB Sch 6 paras 18, 21 and 22 HB(SPC) Regs
46 *DG v SSWP (SPC)* [2010] UKUT 241 (AAC)
47 But see CPC/206/2005 and CPC/1928/2005, which suggest that an assessed income period could be reduced on revision in some cases.

48 **PC** Sch 5 paras 20(1)(f) and 20B SPC Regs
    HB Sch 6 paras 26B and 26E HB(SPC) Regs
49 **PC** Sch 5 para 23E SPC Regs
    HB Sch 6 para 26H HB(SPC) Regs
50 **PC** Sch 5 paras 23A and 23AA SPC Regs
    HB Sch 6 paras 26A and 26AA HB(SPC) Regs
51 **PC** Sch 5 para 16(1) SPC Regs
    HB Sch 6 para 17(1) HB(SPC) Regs
52 R(IS) 3/03
53 **PC** Schs 4 paras 13 and 14, and 5 para 16(2) SPC Regs
    HB Schs 5 paras 14 and 15, and 6 para 17(2) HB(SPC) Regs
54 R(SB) 2/89
55 **PC** Sch 5 paras 12-15 SPC Regs
    HB Sch 6 paras 13-16 HB(SPC) Regs
56 **PC** Sch 5 para 11 SPC Regs
    HB Sch 6 para 12 HB(SPC) Regs
57 **PC** Sch 5 paras 17 and 20(1)(d) and (e) SPC Regs
    HB Sch 6 paras 18 and 21(1)(e) and (f) HB(SPC) Regs
58 **PC** Sch 5 paras 23C and 23D SPC Regs
    HB Sch 6 paras 26D, 26F and 26G HB(SPC) Regs
59 Hansard Written Question 276279; HB Circular A8/2019
60 Reg 26 VP Regs

73 *Peters v CAO* (appendix to R(SB) 3/89)
74 **PC** Reg 20(a) SPC Regs
    HB Reg 46(a) HB(SPC) Regs
75 **PC** Reg 20 SPC Regs
    HB Reg 46(b) HB(SPC) Regs
76 **PC** Sch 5 para 21 SPC Regs
    HB Sch 6 para 23 HB(SPC) Regs
77 **PC** Sch 5 para 21 SPC Regs
    HB Sch 6 para 23 HB(SPC) Regs

5. Notional capital

61 **PC** Reg 21 SPC Regs
    HB Reg 47 HB(SPC) Regs
62 **PC** Reg 21(1) SPC Regs
    HB Reg 47(1) HB(SPC) Regs
63 Reg 22 SPC Regs
64 Reg 48 HB(SPC) Regs
65 **PC** Reg 21(3) and (4) SPC Regs
    HB Reg 47(3) and (4) HB(SPC) Regs

6. How capital is valued

66 **PC** Reg 19(a) SPC Regs
    HB Reg 45(a) HB(SPC) Regs
67 **PC** Reg 19(a) SPC Regs
    HB Reg 45(a) HB(SPC) Regs
68 **PC** Reg 19(b) SPC Regs
    HB Reg 45(b) HB(SPC) Regs
69 **PC** Reg 23 SPC Regs
    HB Reg 49 HB(SPC) Regs
70 R(IS) 4/03
71 **PC** Reg 19(a) SPC Regs
    HB Reg 45(a) HB(SPC) Regs
72 **PC** Vol 14 Ch 84, para 84772 DMG
    HB BP1/P1.530 GM

Part 5

Other benefits

Chapter 24

Attendance allowance

This chapter covers:
1. Who can get attendance allowance (p534)
2. The rules about your age (p534)
3. People included in the claim (p535)
4. The amount of benefit (p535)
5. Special benefit rules (p536)
6. Claims and backdating (p536)
7. Getting paid (p540)
8. Tax, other benefits and the benefit cap (p541)

Key facts

- Attendance allowance (AA) is a benefit for people with disabilities or long-term health problems who have attention or supervision needs and who are pension age or over when they claim.
- AA is a non-means-tested benefit.
- You do not have to have paid national insurance contributions to qualify.
- You can get AA whether or not you work.
- AA can be paid in addition to other benefits and is disregarded as income for means-tested benefits and tax credits.
- AA is administered and paid by the DWP's Disability and Carers Service.
- If you disagree with an AA decision, you can apply for a revision or supersession (see Chapter 56), or appeal against it (see Chapter 57). You must apply for a mandatory reconsideration before you can appeal.

Future changes

From early 2021, it is expected that new claims for AA in Scotland will be replaced by claims for disability assistance for older people (see Chapter 71). The rules for who can get disability assistance for older people and the rates of payment are expected to be similar to AA. Social Security Scotland will be responsible for administering and paying disability assistance for older people. The Scottish government plans to transfer existing AA claimants in Scotland to the new benefit by the end of 2024. See AskCPAG.org.uk and CPAG's *Welfare Rights Bulletin* for updates.

1. **Who can get attendance allowance**

You can get attendance allowance (AA) if:[1]
- you satisfy the residence conditions (see p1629); *and*
- you are not a 'person subject to immigration control', although there are exceptions to this (see p1560); *and*
- you are pension age or over when you first claim (see below); *and*
- you satisfy the disability conditions (see below); *and*
- you are not entitled to the care component of disability living allowance (DLA) (see Chapter 28) or personal independence payment (see Chapter 35).

The disability conditions

AA is paid at a lower or higher rate, depending on your care and supervision needs. You get the lower rate of AA if you satisfy one of the daytime disability conditions *or* one of the night-time disability conditions.[2] You may also get the lower rate of AA if you undergo renal dialysis (see p536). You get the higher rate of AA if you satisfy one of the daytime disability conditions *and* one of the night-time disability conditions.[3] You also get the higher rate of AA if you are terminally ill (see p536).

The **daytime disability conditions** are that you are so severely disabled, physically or mentally, that throughout the day you need:[4]
- frequent attention from another person in connection with your bodily functions; *or*
- continual supervision in order to avoid substantial danger to yourself or others.

The **night-time disability conditions** are that you are so severely disabled, physically or mentally, that at night you need:[5]
- prolonged or repeated attention from another person in connection with your bodily functions; *or*
- another person to be awake for a prolonged period or at frequent intervals to watch over you in order to avoid substantial danger to yourself or others.

The daytime and night-time disability conditions are the same as those for the middle and highest rates of the care component of DLA (see p610).

Unless you are terminally ill, you must have satisfied the disability conditions for six months before the first day of entitlement.[6]

2. **The rules about your age**

You can only claim attendance allowance (AA) if you have reached pension age.[7]
Your pension age will be after you turn 65 if you were born on or after 6 December

1953 (ie, if you reached 65 on or after 6 December 2018), and is due to rise to 66 by October 2020 (see p780).

If you are approaching pension age, it may be better to claim personal independence payment (PIP) if you can rather than AA, since PIP has a mobility component in addition to a daily living component (see Chapter 35). Because the disability tests for PIP are different from those for AA, it may be worth making a claim for AA after you reach pension age if your claim for PIP is refused. Get specialist advice if this applies to you.

Your award continues if you are getting:

- PIP when you reach pension age; *or*
- disability living allowance (DLA) and you turned 65 on or before 8 April 2013.

In these circumstances, you can renew your award of either benefit after you reach pension age instead of having to claim AA. This also means that you can claim, or continue to receive, the mobility component after you reach pension age in certain circumstances if you continue to satisfy the relevant disability conditions (see p621 for DLA and p760 for PIP). You cannot get AA at the same time as either PIP or the care component of DLA. If you are over pension age and have an award of only the mobility component of DLA, you can claim AA in addition to it.

If you have reached pension age and need to renew or change a DLA or PIP award, or have received DLA or PIP within the last 12 months, see p621 for DLA and p760 for PIP.

3. People included in the claim

You claim attendance allowance (AA) for yourself. Your partner may get AA or personal independence payment (PIP – see Chapter 35) or may still have an existing award of disability living allowance (DLA – see Chapter 28) in her/his own right. Your child(ren) may get DLA, or PIP when they reach age 16, in their own right.

4. The amount of benefit

Attendance allowance is paid at one of two weekly rates:[8]

- the lower rate is £59.70;
- the higher rate is £89.15.

5. **Special benefit rules**

Special rules may apply to:
- people on renal dialysis (see below);
- people who are terminally ill (see below);
- people subject to immigration control (see Chapter 67);
- people who have come from or are going abroad (see Chapters 68, 69 and 70);
- people who are in hospital or a hospice, living in a care home or other similar accommodation, or people in prison or detention (see Chapter 42).

Renal dialysis

If you are undergoing renal dialysis on a kidney machine, special rules may apply that entitle you to the lower rate of attendance allowance (AA).[9]

You must have treatment regularly for two or more sessions a week. The dialysis must normally require the attendance or supervision of another person.

If you dialyse in hospital as an outpatient, you must not have help from any member of the staff. Others who dialyse in hospital do not qualify by this special route but can count these spells of hospital dialysis towards the qualifying period. This can help you get AA more quickly for the times you dialyse at home, if you alternate between dialysis in hospital and at home. Even if you do not qualify under this route, you may qualify under the ordinary conditions.

Terminal illness

You are regarded as 'terminally ill' if you have a progressive disease and can reasonably be expected to die within six months as a result.[10] This does not mean that it must be more likely than not that you will die within this period. It simply means that your doctor would not be surprised were you to die within six months. Doctors are expected to take a flexible approach to interpreting this in practice.[11]

If you are terminally ill, you are automatically treated as satisfying the conditions for the higher rate of AA. This is paid straight away without having to serve the six-month qualifying period.[12] These claims are referred to as 'claims under the special rules'. See p537 for how to make a special rules claim. The special rules only apply if your claim, or a request for a revision or supersession of an existing claim, expressly states that you are terminally ill.[13] The DWP can supersede your award if your condition or prognosis improves so that you are no longer regarded as 'terminally ill'.

6. **Claims and backdating**

The general rules about claims and backdating are covered in Chapter 50. This section explains the specific rules that apply to attendance allowance (AA).

Chapter 24

Making a claim

A claim for AA must be in writing. To secure your date of claim (see p538), you should request the approved form (AA1) from the AA helpline. It is usually best to send the completed form to the Attendance Allowance Unit at Mail Handling Site A, Wolverhampton WV98 2AD. You can also take or send it to any other DWP office, and may be able to take or send it to an 'alternative office' (see p1168).

Forms

Form AA1 is available from the AA helpline on 0800 731 0122 (textphone: 0800 731 0317; Relay UK: 18001 then 0800 731 0122).

The form should have a date stamped on it. Keep a record of the date you asked for the form. The DWP may complete a checklist to assess your 'potential benefit entitlement'. This is not part of the claim process and you should always be sent a claim pack.

Claim packs are also available from Citizens Advice and other advice agencies. A version of the form that can be filled in online and then printed is available at gov.uk/attendance-allowance/how-to-claim.

These packs are not date stamped. Send the completed form as soon as possible to secure your date of claim (see p538).

Note: the success of an AA claim can often depend on how well you have completed the claim form, so try to include all the relevant information and use extra pages if necessary. Keep a copy of your claim form in case queries arise. There are useful tips on completing the form in the disability living allowance (DLA) chapter (see pp627–32). Although those pages focus on DLA for children, the disability conditions for the middle and highest rate care component of DLA are the same as the conditions for AA. As there is no mobility component for AA, problems you have with walking outdoors may only be relevant to your AA claim if you need attention or supervision while walking.

You must provide any information or evidence required (see p538). In certain circumstances, the DWP may accept a written application which is not on the approved form.[14] You can amend or withdraw your claim before a decision is made (see p1169).

Claims for terminally ill people are made in a different way (see below).

Who should claim

You normally claim AA for yourself. If you are unable to manage your own affairs, another person can claim AA for you as your 'appointee' (see p1170).

Claiming for terminally ill people

To claim under the special rules for terminal illness (see p536), you must provide Form DS1500, completed by your GP, consultant or specialist nurse, detailing your medical condition. You do not need to fill in the parts of the AA claim form relating to your need for personal care.

When the DWP receives Form DS1500, it decides whether you meet the special rules. If it decides you do not, you can claim in the normal way or request a mandatory reconsideration of the decision.

Someone else can make a claim, apply for a revision or supersession or appeal, on behalf of a terminally ill person without her/his knowledge or permission.[15]

Information to support your claim

For the general information requirements that apply to all benefits, see p1170.

It is important that you provide any information required when you claim. Until you do, you may not count as having made a valid claim (see p1172). Correct any defects as soon as possible or your date of claim may be affected. See p630 for the evidence you might want to provide to help support your claim.

Even if you have provided all that was required when you claimed, you may be asked to provide further information to support your claim (see p1174). You may also be asked to provide information after you are awarded AA and, if you fail to do so, your AA could be suspended, or even terminated (see p1200).

The date of your claim

The date of your claim is important as it determines when your entitlement to AA starts. This is not necessarily the date from when you are paid. For information about when payment of AA starts, see p540.

The **'date of your claim'** is the date your request for a claim pack is received by the DWP or 'alternative office' (see p1168), provided you return the properly completed form within six weeks of the date of your request.[16] If the DWP has issued a form without date stamping it, write and explain when and where it was issued and ask to be paid from that date or six weeks before you sent it in.[17] The DWP can extend the six-week deadline if it considers that it is reasonable, so if you return the form late explain why.[18]

If your claim form was issued by an advice agency or downloaded from the internet, it will not have a date stamp on it and your date of claim is the date the completed form is received by the DWP.

Note: you must make sure your claim is valid. If it is 'defective', you are given a short time to correct the defects (see p1173). If you do, your claim is treated as having been made when you initially claimed.[19]

In some cases, you can claim in advance (see p539). If you want to do this, make this clear when you claim or the DWP might not consider it. If you claimed DLA or personal independence payment (PIP) when you should have claimed AA, or if you claimed industrial injuries disablement benefit, see p539.

Backdating your claim

It is very important to claim as soon as you think you might qualify. A claim for AA *cannot* be backdated.[20]

If you might have qualified for benefit earlier but did not claim because you were given the wrong information or were misled by the DWP, you could ask for a compensation payment (see p1439) or complain to the Ombudsman (see p1444).

If you claim the wrong benefit

A claim for DLA or PIP can be treated as a claim for AA and vice versa, but only if it appears to the DWP that you are not entitled to the benefit you claimed. A claim for an increase of industrial injuries disablement benefit where constant attendance is needed can be treated as a claim for AA and vice versa (see p1182).[21]

Claiming in advance

A claim for AA can be made before you have satisfied the six-month qualifying period (see p534),[22] or any other qualifying condition. Provided you claim no more than six months before you would qualify for AA, a decision can be made on your claim in advance of your date of entitlement. The date of your claim is the date on which you qualify.

Renewal claims

Note: the DWP has announced that some AA awards for fixed periods may be extended due to the coronavirus pandemic. See AskCPAG.org.uk and CPAG's *Welfare Rights Bulletin* for updates.

AA can be awarded for fixed periods (see p541). Renewal claims can be invited up to six months before your old award expires. It is important that you return your completed renewal claim form before your old award expires as no backdating is possible.

The DWP normally treats a renewal claim as a new claim, beginning on the day after your old award ends.[23] However, it may use the information you give in the renewal claim to revise or supersede your existing award, in which case your entitlement may be changed earlier.[24]

If your AA award has ended, you can reclaim the same rate within two years without having to serve the standard six-month qualifying period again.[25]

How your claim is dealt with

The DWP can award AA on the basis of your claim form alone, but may choose to contact someone you have named on the form for more information. It is a good idea to include details of all the medical professionals and other people who know and understand your needs and, if possible, enclose evidence from them. If the DWP cannot obtain sufficient information, it may also arrange for you to be given a medical examination by a healthcare professional acting on behalf of the DWP, who may visit you at home.

If you refuse a medical examination without good cause, the DWP must decide your claim against you.[26]

The DWP may telephone you to ask for further information. If you do not want to be telephoned, state this clearly on the claim form.

The DWP aims to deal with new claims for AA within 40 working days. Claims made under the special rules for terminal illness (see p536) should be decided more quickly.

7. **Getting paid**

The general rules on getting paid are covered in Chapter 51. This section explains the specific rules that apply to attendance allowance (AA).

When is attendance allowance paid?

You are normally paid on a Monday, but the DWP can vary the payday.[27] AA is normally paid every four weeks in arrears. However, AA can be paid:

– at shorter intervals in individual cases;[28]
– weekly in advance.

If you leave hospital or a care home and expect to return within 28 days, AA can be paid at a daily rate for days at home.[29]

Note:
- If you get other DWP benefits, AA may be paid in a single payment with them instead.
- Even if you have been sanctioned for a benefit offence (see p1278), you must be paid your AA.
- For information on missing payments, see p1189. If you cannot get your AA payments because you have lost your bank or post office card or have forgotten your PIN, see p1188. If your payment service card has been lost or stolen, see p1189.
- If payment of your AA is delayed, see p1295. If you wish to complain about how your claim has been dealt with, or claim compensation, see Chapter 60.
- If payment of your AA is suspended, see p1200.
- If you have been overpaid AA, you might have to repay it (see Chapter 53) and, in some circumstances, you may have to pay a penalty (see p1268). If you have been accused of fraud, see Chapter 54.

Length of awards

Awards of AA can be made for either fixed or indefinite periods.[30] The length of an award depends on how long the DWP estimates your current needs may last. If you have an indefinite award, you will not have to make a renewal claim at any stage, but the DWP can reduce or stop your award if it has grounds to revise or supersede it.

There is no legal minimum length for an award.[31] If you think benefit should be awarded for longer, perhaps because your condition is such that your care needs will not decrease, you can consider asking for a revision (see p1303). However, if you challenge the length of your award, the rate of your award may also be reconsidered.

Awards under the special rules for terminal illness (see p536) are normally made for a fixed period of three years.

Change of circumstances

You must report changes in your circumstances that you have been told to report, as well as any that you might reasonably be expected to know might affect your right to, the amount of or payment of your benefit. You should do this as soon as possible, preferably in writing. See p1199 for further information.

If your condition deteriorates so that you become eligible for the higher rate, benefit can be backdated to the day you become eligible, provided you tell the DWP no later than a month after completing the six-month qualifying period. If payment of (but not entitlement to) AA has stopped (eg, while you are in hospital or a care home), still notify the DWP so that the correct rate is paid when payment resumes. If you do not report a change of circumstances within the month, benefit can still be backdated if you do so within 13 months and there were special circumstances that meant it was not practical to report the change earlier.[32]

If your condition improves so that you do not qualify for the higher rate or you lose benefit altogether, the new decision usually takes effect from the date you tell the DWP of the improvement, or from the date of the decision if the DWP changed it without your asking.[33] It only takes effect from an earlier date (and causes an overpayment) if you should have realised earlier that the change should have been reported. It is accepted that it is difficult for claimants to realise when a gradual improvement begins to affect benefit entitlement.[34]

8. **Tax, other benefits and the benefit cap**

Tax

Attendance allowance (AA) is not taxable.[35]

Means-tested benefits and tax credits

AA is not taken into account as income when calculating any of the means-tested benefits. AA is paid on top of these, and if you or your partner get AA, this can increase the amount you get (or mean that you qualify for means-tested benefits for the first time, if your income was previously too high). AA is also ignored when calculating child tax credit and working tax credit (WTC).

You may qualify for one or more of the following extra amounts:

- a limited capability for work-related activity element (see p72) included in your universal credit (UC) if you are entitled to AA, as you are treated as having limited capability for work-related activity (see p1031);
- a higher pensioner premium (see p345) included in your income support (IS) or income-based jobseeker's allowance (JSA), if you have a partner who gets AA;
- a severe disability premium included in your IS, income-based JSA or income-related employment and support allowance if your partner gets AA and you meet the other conditions for this premium;
- a severe disability premium included in your housing benefit (HB), or an addition for severe disability included in the guarantee credit of pension credit if you get AA and meet the other conditions for this premium or addition (see p346);
- a disabled worker element in your WTC if you get AA. If you or your partner get the higher rate of AA, a severe disability element is included in WTC (see Chapter 61).

No housing costs contributions from a non-dependant are taken into account when calculating your UC housing costs element if you, your partner or the non-dependant get AA, or would get it but for being in hospital (see p103). If you or your partner get AA, non-dependant deductions are not made from your HB (see p199), or from any housing costs included in your IS, income-based JSA, income-related ESA or the guarantee credit of PC (see p364).

Non-means-tested benefits

AA may be paid in addition to any other non-means-tested benefits, except that it 'overlaps' with armed forces independence payment (see p868) and constant attendance allowance under the industrial injuries scheme (see p694) or war pensions scheme.[36] See p1190 for details of the overlapping benefits rules. You cannot claim AA if you are entitled to personal independence payment or the care component of disability living allowance.[37]

If you get AA and someone regularly looks after you, that person may be entitled to carer's allowance (CA) (see Chapter 26), and s/he (or her/his partner if claiming as a couple) may also get a carer element in UC (see p73), a carer premium in IS, income-based JSA, income-related ESA or HB, or a carer addition in the guarantee credit of PC (see p350). However, your entitlement to a severe disability premium (or severe disability additional amount) can be affected if s/he gets CA or a carer element in UC, so always get advice.

A young person aged 16, 17 or 18 living in Scotland who cannot get CA may be able to get a young carer grant for looking after you (see Chapter 75).

The benefit cap

In some cases, there is a limit on the total amount of specified benefits you can receive (a 'benefit cap'). AA is *not* one of the specified benefits. The benefit cap does *not* apply if you or your partner get AA (even if it is not paid because you (or s/he) are in hospital or a care home). In other cases, it only applies if you are getting UC or HB. See p1194 for further information.

Passports and other sources of help

You qualify for a Christmas bonus if you get AA at any rate (see p870). You may qualify for council tax reduction (see p851).

If any member of your household gets AA at any rate, you may get a grant for help with insulation and other energy efficiency measures in your home (see p872).

Notes

1. Who can get attendance allowance
1 ss64, 65 and 66 SSCBA 1992; reg 2 SS(AA) Regs
2 s65(3) SSCBA 1992
3 s65(3) SSCBA 1992
4 s64(2) SSCBA 1992
5 s64(3) SSCBA 1992
6 ss65(1)(b) and 66(1)(a)(ii) SSCBA 1992

2. The rules about your age
7 s64(1) SSCBA 1992

4. The amount of benefit
8 Sch 4 Part III SSCBA 1992

5. Special benefit rules
9 s65(2) SSCBA 1992; reg 5 SS(AA) Regs
10 s66(2)(a) SSCBA 1992

11 DWP, *DWP Medical (factual) reports: a guide to completion*, August 2019
12 s66(1) SSCBA 1992
13 Regs 3(9)(b) and 6(6)(c) SS&CS(DA) Regs

6. Claims and backdating
14 Reg 4(1) SS(C&P) Regs
15 s66(2)(b) SSCBA 1992; regs 3(9)(b), 6(6)(c) and 25(b) SS&CS(DA) Regs
16 Reg 6(8), (8A) and (9) SS(C&P) Regs
17 Reg 6(8A) SS(C&P) Regs
18 Reg 6(9) SS(C&P) Regs; *SNN v SSWP (PIP)* [2018] UKUT 210 (AAC), although decided on similar rules for PIP, this case considers circumstances that may be reasonable and the discussion is relevant for AA claims.
19 Reg 6(1)(b) SS(C&P) Regs

20 s65(4) SSCBA 1992
21 Reg 9(1) and Sch 1 SS(C&P) Regs; reg
25(3) and (4) UC,PIP,JSA&ESA(C&P)
Regs
22 s65(6) SSCBA 1992
23 Reg 13C SS(C&P) Regs
24 CDLA/14895/1996
25 s65(1)(b) SSCBA 1992; reg 3 SS(AA)
Regs
26 s19(3) SSA 1998

7. Getting paid
27 Reg 22(3) and Sch 6 SS(C&P) Regs
28 Reg 22 SS(C&P) Regs
29 Reg 25 SS(C&P) Regs
30 s65(1)(a) SSCBA 1992
31 R(DLA) 11/02
32 Regs 7(9)(b) and 8 SS&CS(DA) Regs
33 s10(5) SSA 1998
34 Reg 7(2)(c) SS&CS(DA) Regs; *RD v SSWP
(DLA)* [2011] UKUT 95 (AAC); *DC v SSWP
(DLA)* [2011] UKUT 336 (AAC)

8. Tax, other benefits and the benefit cap
35 s677 IT(EP)A 2003
36 Sch 1 paras 5 and 5a SS(OB) Regs
37 s64(1) and (1A) SSCBA 1992

Chapter 25

• •

Bereavement benefits

This chapter covers:
1. Bereavement support payment (below)
2. Widowed parent's allowance (p547)
3. Definitions (p549)
4. Special benefit rules (p552)
5. Claims and backdating (p553)
6. Getting paid (p556)
7. Tax, other benefits and the benefit cap (p557)

Key facts
- Bereavement benefits are paid to widows, widowers and surviving civil partners. If your spouse or civil partner died on or after 6 April 2017, the relevant bereavement benefit is **bereavement support payment**. If s/he died before this date, and you have dependent children, you may be able to get **widowed parent's allowance.**
- To qualify for all bereavement benefits, your late spouse or civil partner must have either satisfied the national insurance contribution conditions, or been an 'employed earner' and died as a result of an industrial accident or disease.
- You must be under pension age to qualify for bereavement benefits.
- Bereavement benefits are non-means-tested benefits.
- You can get bereavement benefits whether you are in or out of work.
- Beginning a new relationship may affect your entitlement.
- Bereavement benefits are administered and paid by the DWP.
- If you disagree with a bereavement benefit decision, you can apply for a revision or a supersession (see Chapter 56), or appeal against it (see Chapter 57). You must apply for a mandatory reconsideration before you can appeal.

1. Bereavement support payment

Bereavement support payment is a benefit for people whose spouse or civil partner dies on or after 6 April 2017. It comprises monthly payments, payable for a maximum period of 18 months, and a lump-sum payment in the first month.

Who can get bereavement support payment

You can get bereavement support payment if:[1]
* you are a widow, widower or surviving civil partner; *and*
* your spouse or civil partner died on or after 6 April 2017; *and*
* your late spouse or civil partner either:
  – satisfied the national insurance contribution conditions (see p984); *or*
  – was an 'employed earner' and died as a result of an industrial injury or disease (see p552); *and*
* you are under pension age; *and*
* you satisfy the residence condition (see p1627).

Time limits

To get bereavement support payment for the maximum 18-month period, you must make a claim within three months of the date your spouse or civil partner died (see p554).

To get the initial lump-sum payment, you must claim within 12 months of your spouse or civil partner's death.[2]

The rules about your age

There is no lower age limit for bereavement support payment. Anyone who is old enough to legally marry or form a civil partnership may qualify.

Bereavement support payment cannot be paid if you are pension age or over, but you may qualify for state pension (see p778) or a survivor's inherited state pension instead (see p783).

People included in the claim

You claim bereavement support payment for yourself. You cannot get an increase for a new partner, or for your child(ren). If you have a dependent child, you are, however, paid the higher rate of bereavement support payment (see below).[3]

The amount of bereavement support payment

There are two rates of bereavement support payment – a standard rate and a higher rate. You get the higher rate if:[4]
* you were pregnant when your spouse or civil partner died; *or*
* you were entitled to child benefit when your spouse or civil partner died; *or*
* since your spouse or civil partner died, you have become entitled to child benefit for a child or qualifying young person who was residing with you or your late spouse/civil partner immediately before s/he died. This applies even

if you subsequently cease to be entitled to child benefit for that child or qualifying young person.

Rates of bereavement support payment[5]

	Standard rate	Higher rate
Initial lump sum	£2,500	£3,500
Monthly amount	£100	£350

Starting a new relationship

If you start cohabiting with a new partner, enter into a new civil partnership or remarry, this does not affect your entitlement to bereavement support payment.[6]

2. Widowed parent's allowance

Widowed parent's allowance is a benefit for people whose spouse or civil partner died before 6 April 2017. It comprises fortnightly payments, payable for as long as the conditions of entitlement are met.

Who can get widowed parent's allowance

You can get widowed parent's allowance if:[7]
- you are a widow, widower or surviving civil partner; *and*
- your spouse or civil partner died before 6 April 2017; *and*
- your late spouse or civil partner either:
  - satisfied the national insurance (NI) contribution conditions (see p984); *or*
  - was an 'employed earner' and died as the result of an industrial injury or disease (see p552); *and*
- you are under pension age; *and*
- you are entitled to child benefit for at least one 'eligible child' (see below).

Eligible child

A 'child' means both a 'child' and a 'qualifying young person' (see p579 for the definitions). A child counts as an 'eligible child' if:[8]
- s/he is your and your late spouse's/civil partner's child; *or*
- you were residing with your late spouse or civil partner immediately before s/he died and *you* were entitled to child benefit for the child at that time – ie, even if the child is not your late spouse's/civil partner's child; *or*
- immediately before s/he died, your late spouse or civil partner was entitled to child benefit for the child – ie, even if the child is not your child.

Treated as entitled to child benefit

- You still count as entitled to child benefit if it has been awarded to you, but you have elected for it not to be paid to avoid the high-income child benefit charge (see p597).
- If you were residing together, you are treated as entitled to any child benefit to which your late spouse or civil partner was entitled, and vice versa.[9]
- You or your late spouse or civil partner can be treated as entitled to child benefit if you would have been entitled to it had you claimed it, and had the child in question not been abroad.[10]

Treated as residing with your spouse or civil partner

- If you and your spouse or civil partner were living apart at the time of her/his death, you can still be considered to have been residing with her/him if your separation was only intended to be temporary.[11] This depends on the facts of your case.[12]
- If you have been widowed before, or survived a previous civil partner, and this meant that you were left to care for a dependent child(ren), you can qualify for widowed parent's allowance on the basis of the death of your most recent spouse or civil partner, even if you were not residing with her/him when s/he died.[13]

Time limit

Provided you meet all the conditions of entitlement on p547, there is no time limit for claiming widowed parent's allowance after the death of your spouse or civil partner. It then remains payable until you no longer meet one of these conditions – eg, your child is no longer an eligible child because of her/his age.

The rules about your age

There is no lower age limit for widowed parent's allowance. Anyone who is legally old enough to marry or form a civil partnership may qualify.

Widowed parent's allowance cannot be paid if you are pension age or over, but you may qualify for state pension (see p778) or a survivor's inherited state pension instead (see p783).

People included in the claim

You claim widowed parent's allowance for yourself. You cannot claim widowed parent's allowance if you have a new partner (see p549). New claims do not include an increase for your child(ren), although if you have been in receipt of widowed parent's allowance since 5 April 2003, it may still include an addition for a child.

The amount of widowed parent's allowance

Widowed parent's allowance is made up of:
- a basic allowance. The full weekly rate of this is £121.95, but it may be paid at a reduced rate if your late spouse's or civil partner's NI contribution record was incomplete (see below); *and*
- an additional earnings-related payment based on your late spouse's or civil partner's earnings under the additional state pension scheme, if her/his NI contribution record qualifies you for this (see p984). You may be entitled to this even if her/his contribution record is not sufficient for you to qualify for basic widowed parent's allowance.[14]

Reduction if your late spouse or civil partner had an incomplete contribution record

If your late spouse or civil partner had an incomplete NI contribution record, the amount of widowed parent's allowance you receive is reduced proportionately (see p985).[15] You may be able to increase your entitlement to widowed parent's allowance by paying voluntary NI contributions on your spouse's or civil partner's behalf, even though s/he has died. Contact the HM Revenue and Customs helpline (tel: 0300 200 3500; textphone: 0300 200 3519) about this. See p966 for further details and for the time limits for making such payments.

Starting a new relationship

Entitlement to widowed parent's allowance ends if you remarry or enter into a new civil partnership. You cannot requalify for it, even if you subsequently get divorced or if your civil partnership is dissolved. It is suspended if you begin cohabiting (see p551), but can be reinstated if you stop cohabiting.[16]

3. Definitions

Widows, widowers and surviving civil partners

To get bereavement benefits, you must be a widow, widower or surviving civil partner. For this to apply, you must have been married to your spouse (in either a same-sex or opposite-sex marriage), or in a civil partnership with your partner, at the date of her/his death (but see below). The marriage or civil partnership must have been valid under UK law.

A number of court cases have challenged the lawfulness of refusing bereavement benefits to surviving unmarried partners, particularly where there are children. On 30 August 2018, the Supreme Court held that denying widowed parent's allowance to a woman who was not married to her late partner was incompatible with human rights law.[17] Similarly, on 7 February 2020, the High

Court held that denying the higher rate of bereavement support payment to claimants who were not married to their late partner was incompatible with human rights law.[18] See AskCPAG.org.uk and CPAG's *Welfare Rights Bulletin* for updates.

Marriage 'by cohabitation with habit and repute'

In Scotland,[19] you can count as a widow or widower if you were married by 'cohabitation with habit and repute', even if you did not go through a wedding ceremony, provided your cohabitation began before 4 May 2006.[20] For this to apply, your relationship must have been like that of a husband and wife and more than simply living together – there must have been something about it which meant it could be inferred that you and your partner consented to marriage and that nothing existed that would have prevented a valid marriage taking place – eg, one of you being married to someone else.[21] In addition, your relationship must have been such that other people generally believed that you were married.[22]

If you have more than one bereavement

If, following the death of your spouse or civil partner, you remarry or form a new civil partnership and your new spouse or civil partner then dies, your entitlement to bereavement benefits depends on the national insurance contribution record of your most recent spouse or civil partner.

Invalid marriages

A **void** marriage or civil partnership (ie, one in which at least one of the partners was not eligible to marry or form a civil partnership) is invalid. From a legal point of view, it is treated as if it never existed.[23] In England and Wales, a **voidable** marriage or civil partnership is treated as having been valid until a decree absolute of annulment is pronounced.[24] Questions about the validity of marriages or civil partnerships are decided by a special unit at the DWP. If a question arises over the validity of your marriage or civil partnership, get advice from a family law specialist.

Separation, divorce and dissolution

If you were divorced when your former spouse died, or if your civil partnership had been dissolved when your former civil partner died, you are not a widow, widower or surviving civil partner.

A divorce only becomes effective when the decree absolute is pronounced (a decree of divorce, in Scotland), and a civil partnership is dissolved when a final dissolution order is issued (a decree of dissolution, in Scotland). If you were in the process of obtaining a divorce or of dissolving your civil partnership but your spouse or civil partner died before it was finalised, you are still a widow, widower or surviving civil partner (and so may be entitled to bereavement benefits). This is the case even if you were judicially separated.

Polygamous marriages

If your marriage was polygamous, you are not usually entitled to bereavement benefits following the death of your spouse because, generally, the law in England, Wales and Scotland does not treat you as legally married unless your marriage is a monogamous one.[25]

Note:

• If your marriage was *previously* polygamous rather than actually polygamous when your spouse died (eg, if any other spouse had already died), you can qualify.

• A marriage is only considered polygamous if the law of the country where the marriage takes place permits either party to have another wife or husband.[26]

• Whether your marriage is considered polygamous depends on whether you were your spouse's first wife or husband, and on where you and your spouse were 'domiciled' at the time of your marriage and any subsequent marriage. In general terms, 'domicile' means the country in which you have chosen to make your permanent home.[27] In particular, no one who is domiciled in England or Wales is allowed to contract a polygamous marriage anywhere in the world even if the local law allows it.[28]

• If you are the surviving partner but your marriage is considered to have been polygamous and you are refused benefit, depending on the facts of your case (in particular, where the facts suggest that your marriage was actually monogamous), you may be able to argue that you should still be entitled under human rights rules.[29] Seek advice.

Example

At the time of their wedding, Shaznaz and her husband were domiciled in Pakistan and were married under Islamic law. After the wedding they came to live in England, made their permanent home here and had no intention of returning to live in Pakistan at any time. Later, Shaznaz's husband returned temporarily to Pakistan and married a second wife. As her husband was domiciled in England rather than Pakistan at the time of the second marriage, English law does not recognise the second marriage and, therefore, regards Shaznaz as her late husband's only wife. Provided she meets the other conditions of entitlement, she is entitled to bereavement benefits.[30] If her husband had reacquired domicile in Pakistan at the time of his second marriage, and his second wife was still alive, both marriages would be polygamous, and neither wife could claim bereavement benefits.[31]

Cohabitation

'**Cohabiting**' means living with someone as if you are a married couple. Deciding whether or not you are cohabiting may not be straightforward. For futher information, see p320.

If the DWP refuses you widowed parent's allowance because it believes you are cohabiting with a new partner and you do not agree, you can challenge its decision (see Chapters 56 and 57).

Industrial accident or disease

The meaning of 'industrial accident or disease' is discussed on p683 and p687. To qualify for bereavement benefits, the industrial accident or disease must have been a cause of your late spouse or civil partner's death, but it need not have been a direct cause or the only cause.[32] Your late spouse or civil partner must have been an 'employed earner' – ie, an employee, not self-employed (see p962).[33]

4. Special benefit rules

Special rules may apply to:
- widows whose husbands died before 9 April 2001 (see below);
- people who have obtained a gender recognition certificate (see below);
- people who are going abroad (see Chapter 69);
- people in prison or detention (see Chapter 42).

Widows whose husbands died before 9 April 2001

If you are a widow whose husband died before 9 April 2001, you are not entitled to bereavement benefits, but you may still be getting widowed mother's allowance or widow's pension.

For an explanation of the main qualifying conditions for these widows' benefits, see the 2000/01 edition of this *Handbook*.

If your entitlement to widowed mother's allowance ends because you no longer have an eligible child, you may qualify for a widow's pension. This can be paid until you reach 65, provided you satisfy the qualifying conditions.

Once you reach pension age, you may be entitled to both state pension and either widow's pension or widowed mother's allowance. Because of the overlapping benefit rules, you cannot receive both in full at the same time. It is likely to be preferable to claim a state pension, as you are then free to remarry, cohabit or form a new civil partnership, without losing any entitlement.

People who have obtained a gender recognition certificate

If you annulled or dissolved an existing marriage or civil partnership in order to obtain a full gender recognition certificate (which, before 10 December 2014 in England and Wales and 16 December 2014 in Scotland, you had to do),[34] you are not entitled to bereavement benefits on the basis of your ex-spouse's or ex-civil partner's national insurance contribution record, if s/he subsequently dies.

If you are getting widow's pension when a full gender recognition certificate is issued, any entitlement ends. Widowed mother's allowance also ends, but you can qualify for widowed parent's allowance instead.[35]

---

5. Claims and backdating

The general rules about claims and backdating are covered in Chapter 50. This section explains the specific rules that apply to bereavement benefits.

Making a claim

A claim for bereavement support payment or widowed parent's allowance can be made:

- by telephoning the DWP's Bereavement Service on 0800 731 0469 (Welsh language: 0800 731 0453; textphone: 0800 731 0464 (Welsh language: 0800 731 0456); Relay UK: 18001 then 0800 731 0469). After giving information on the telephone, you are sent a statement to approve, sign and return; *or*
- in writing, normally on the approved form (see below); *or*
- online at gov.uk.

If there is a delay in dealing with your claim, you may be able to get a short-term advance of benefit (see p1192).

Forms

Form BSP1 is the approved form for bereavement support payment.

Form BB1 is the approved form for widowed parent's allowance.

When you register the death, you are normally given a Certificate of Registration of Death. If you complete the form on the certificate and send it to the DWP, you should be sent the correct bereavement benefit form. Alternatively, you can get a form by telephoning Jobcentre Plus (tel: 0800 055 6688; Welsh language: 0800 012 1888; textphone: 0800 023 4888) or online at gov.uk.

Who should claim

You must normally claim bereavement benefits yourself. If you are unable to manage your own affairs, another person can claim bereavement benefits for you as your 'appointee' (see p1170).

Information to support your claim

For the general information requirements that apply to all benefits, see p1170.

It is important that you provide any information required when you claim. Until you do, you may not count as having made a valid claim (see p1172). Correct any defects as soon as possible or your date of claim may be affected.

You are normally also expected to provide proof of your spouse's or civil partner's death. If you have reported the death to a local DWP office under the 'Tell Us Once' arrangements (see p1199), you are given a reference number, which you can use as proof of death when you make a claim through the Bereavement Service.

Alternatively, when you register the death you get a death certificate, which can be provided as proof. If you do not have proof that your spouse or civil partner has died, see p555.

You are also usually expected to provide your marriage or civil partnership certificate.[36] Caselaw has provided guidance on assessing evidence from countries where reliable documentary proof of life events, such as marriage, may not be available.[37]

Even if you have provided all that was required when you claimed, you may be asked to provide further information to support your claim (see p1174). You may be asked to provide information after you are awarded bereavement benefits. If you fail to do so, your benefit may be suspended or even terminated (see p1200).

The date of your claim

The date of your claim is important as it determines:

- when your entitlement to bereavement support payment or widowed parent's allowance starts. This is not necessarily the date from when you are paid. For information about when payment of a bereavement benefit starts, see p556; *and*
- whether you qualify for an initial lump sum of bereavement support payment.

The **'date of your claim'** is normally the date of your call, if you claim by telephone, or the date your written claim is received.[38]

You must make sure your claim is valid. If it is 'defective', you are given a short time to correct the defects (see p1173). If you do, your claim is treated as having been made when you initially claimed.[39]

Backdating your claim

Bereavement support payment is automatically backdated to the date of your spouse or civil partner's death, provided you claim within three months of the date of her/his death.[40]

Your bereavement support payment award ends 18 months after your spouse or civil partner died,[41] so you should claim within three months of the date of her/his death to receive the maximum 18-month award.

If you claim more than three months after the date of her/his death, your claim is automatically backdated for three months.[42] Because of this, you can make a claim for bereavement support payment up until 21 months after your spouse or civil partner dies, but you will not receive the maximum award.[43]

Examples

John's wife died on 6 May 2018. He claimed bereavement support payment on 10 July 2018. It is paid for the period 6 May 2018 to 6 November 2019 – ie, he receives the maximum 18-month award.

Susan's civil partner died on 20 August 2018. She claimed bereavement support payment on 4 February 2019. It is paid for the period 4 November 2018 to 20 February 2020. The length of her award is therefore limited to approximately 15.5 months.

Sameena's husband died on 10 July 2017. She claimed bereavement support payment on 28 March 2019. It is paid for the period 28 December 2018 to 10 January 2019. The length of her award is therefore limited to two weeks. She also misses out on the intitial lump-sum payment.

Payment of **widowed parent's allowance** can be backdated for up to three months before the date you make your claim, provided you satisfy the qualifying conditions over that period. You do not need to show reasons why your claim is late.

If you might have qualified for benefit earlier but did not claim because you were given the wrong information or were misled by the DWP, you could make a complaint (see Chapter 60).

If there is a delay in hearing or uncertainty about a death

If you did not find out straight away that your spouse or civil partner had died, but you find out within 12 months of the death, you can apply for bereavement support payment within 12 months of becoming aware of the death, and request that it be backdated to the date of death.[44]

If it is presumed that your spouse or civil partner has died, but this has not been established for certain, you can ask the DWP to make a decision that s/he has died (or is likely to have died) on a particular date. You should provide the information and evidence that has led you to presume s/he has died.

If the DWP decides s/he died *before 6 April 2017*, you can then claim widowed parent's allowance within 12 months of the date of that decision, and have it backdated to the date the DWP has decided your late spouse or civil partner died.[45]

Note: these are also the only circumstances in which you may still qualify for the other two 'old' bereavement benefits (bereavement allowance and/or a bereavement payment). See Chapter 24 of the 2017/18 edition of this *Handbook* for more information about these benefits.

If the DWP decides s/he died *on or after 6 April 2017*, you can claim bereavement support payment within 12 months of the date of that decision, and have it backdated to the presumed date of death.

If you claim the wrong benefit

The decision maker can treat a claim for state pension as a claim for bereavement benefits and vice versa.[46] A claim for bereavement support payment can be treated as a claim for widowed parent's allowance and vice versa. See p1182 for details of interchanging claims in this way.

Claiming in advance

You can claim bereavement benefits up to three months before you expect to qualify. In most circumstances, you will not know of your need to claim benefit in advance, but this may be relevant if, for example, you know that you will no longer be cohabiting.[47] The date of your claim is the date on which you qualify.

6. **Getting paid**

The general rules on getting paid are covered in Chapter 51. This section explains the specific rules that apply to bereavement benefits.

When are bereavement benefits paid?
Bereavement support payment is paid monthly in arrears, on the same day of the month as the date of death of your spouse or civil partner. In months when it cannot be paid on this day because it falls on the 29th, 30th or 31st, it is paid on the last day of the month.[48]
Widowed parent's allowance is normally paid fortnightly, in arrears.

Bereavement support payment and widowed parent's allowance are daily benefits. Payments can be made for part periods at the beginning and end of claims. Part payments are calculated using the daily rate.

Note:
- Your widowed parent's allowance might be paid at a reduced rate in certain circumstances (see p549).
- You may not be paid bereavement benefit if you have received a sanction for a benefit offence (see p1278).
- For information on missing payments, see p1189.

- For what to do if you lose your bank or post office card or forget your PIN, see p1188. If you lose your payment service card, see p1189.
- If payment of your bereavement benefit is delayed, see p1295. If you are waiting for a decision on your claim, or to be paid, you might be able to get a short-term advance (see p1192). If you wish to complain about how your claim has been dealt with, or claim compensation, see Chapter 60.
- If payment of your bereavement benefit is suspended, see p1200.
- If you are overpaid a bereavement benefit, you might have to repay it (see Chapter 53) and, in some circumstances, you may have to pay a penalty (see p1268). If you have been accused of fraud, see Chapter 54.

Change of circumstances

You must report changes in your circumstances that you have been told to report, as well as any that you might reasonably be expected to know might affect your right to, the amount of, or the payment of, your benefit. You should do this as soon as possible, preferably in writing. See p1199 for further information.

If a change of circumstances affects your entitlement to widowed parent's allowance, before your benefit can be stopped or adjusted, the decision maker should first revise or supersede the earlier decision on your entitlement (see Chapter 56).[49] The date from when a new decision takes effect following a supersession normally depends on whether or not it is advantageous to you and whether you reported the change in time (see p1321).

7. Tax, other benefits and the benefit cap

Tax

Bereavement support payment is not taxable.[50] **Widowed parent's allowance** is taxable (except for any increase to widowed parent's allowance for children, which you may still receive, if you have been in receipt of it since 5 April 2003).[51]

Means-tested benefits and tax credits

The initial lump sum of bereavement support payment counts as capital for all means-tested benefits, but it is disregarded for up to 52 weeks. The monthly payments count as income, but are disregarded for all means-tested benefits, including universal credit (UC).[52] Bereavement support payment is ignored when calculating your entitlement to tax credits, as it is not taxable.

Widowed parent's allowance counts as income for means-tested benefits. However:
- £10 of your weekly widowed parent's allowance is disregarded when calculating your entitlement to income support (IS),[53] income-based

jobseeker's allowance (JSA),[54] income-related employment and support allowance (ESA)[55] and pension credit (PC);[56]

- an increase in your widowed parent's allowance for a child is disregarded when calculating your entitlement to income-related ESA and PC, and may be ignored when calculating your entitlement to IS and income-based JSA (see p436 and p475);
- £15 of your weekly widowed parent's allowance is disregarded when calculating your entitlement to housing benefit (HB).[57] However, if you are getting the savings credit (and not the guarantee credit) of PC, the income used to calculate your HB is that used by the DWP to calculate your entitlement to PC (which includes only a £10 disregard from your widowed parent's allowance – see p468).

There are no equivalent widowed parent's allowance disregards for UC.[58]

For tax credits, widowed parent's allowance counts as pension income.

If your partner was entitled to HB when s/he died and you claim HB within a month of her/his death, your HB claim can be treated as having been made on the date your partner died (see p208). In some circumstances, it can be backdated further (see p208).

Non-means-tested benefits

Bereavement support payment does not overlap with contribution-based JSA or contributory ESA – you can be paid bereavement support payment at the same time. However, widowed parent's allowance is affected by the overlapping benefit rules (see p1190).

If you receive an increase in your widowed parent's allowance for a child, the overlapping benefit rules may also affect you. If you get child benefit or guardian's allowance for the same child, see p1192.

Once you reach pension age, your entitlement to bereavement benefits stops. However, you may qualify for state pension (see p778) or a survivor's inherited state pension instead (see p783).

If your bereavement benefit stops before you reach pension age, you may qualify for national insurance credits following bereavement for contributory ESA and contribution-based JSA (see p977).[59]

The benefit cap

In some cases, there is a limit on the total amount of specified benefits you can receive (a 'benefit cap'). Bereavement support payment is not a specified benefit – payments do not count towards the benefit cap.[60] However, widowed parent's allowance is a specified benefit.[61] The benefit cap only applies if you are getting UC or HB. Fifteen pounds of your weekly widowed parent's allowance is ignored if the cap is applied through your HB. See p1194 for further information.

Passports and other sources of help

If you are entitled to widowed parent's allowance, you are also entitled to a Christmas bonus (see p870).

In some circumstances, you may qualify for a social fund funeral expenses payment (see p798). In Scotland, you may qualify for a funeral support payment (see Chapter 73).

If you have low income and capital, you may be entitled to HB (see Chapter 10) and/or council tax reduction (see p851).

For advice about what to do after someone dies, see gov.uk. In Scotland, see also the Scottish government leaflet, 'What to Do After a Death in Scotland', available at gov.scot.

Notes

1. Bereavement support payment
1 s30 PA 2014
2 Reg 3(2) and (5) BSP Regs
3 Reg 4 BSP Regs
4 Reg 4 BSP Regs
5 Reg 3(1)-(6) BSP Regs
6 Bereavement Support Payment Regulations 2017, House of Commons, Hansard, Written Statement, HCWS409, 12 January 2017, para 5

2. Widowed parent's allowance
7 ss39A and 60(2) and (3) SSCBA 1992
8 s39A(3) SSCBA 1992
9 s122(4) SSCBA 1992
10 Reg 16ZA(1)(a) SS(WB&RP) Regs
11 Reg 2(4) SSB(PRT) Regs
12 CIS/1059/2014
13 Reg 16ZA(2) SS(WB&RP) Regs
14 Reg 6(2) SS(WB&RP) Regs
15 Reg 6 SS(WB&RP) Regs
16 s39A(4), (4A) and (5) SSCBA 1992

3. Definitions
17 McLaughlin, Re Judicial Review (Northern Ireland) [2018] UKSC 48
18 Jackson and others v SSWP [2020] EWHC 183
19 But see CAO v Bath [1999] (CA), reported as R(G) 1/00; R(G) 2/70

20 R(G) 5/83; s3 Family Law (Scotland) Act 2006; The Family Law (Scotland) Act 2006 (Commencement, Transitional Provisions and Savings) Order 2006, No.212
21 R(G) 1/71
22 CSG/7/1995; CSG/681/2003; but see also CSG/648/2007
23 R(G) 2/63
24 R(G) 1/73
25 Hyde v Hyde [1866]; reg 2 SSFA(PM) Regs
26 Reg 1(2) SSFA(PM) Regs
27 R(S) 2/92
28 s11(3) MCA 1973
29 NA v SSWP (BB) [2019] UKUT 144 (AAC). The facts included a religious marriage recognised in Pakistan but not recognised in England and Wales, where the late spouse had only ever lived with one other spouse.
30 R(G) 1/95
31 R(G) 1/93; R(P) 2/06
32 CI/142/1949; R(I) 14/51
33 ss2(a) and 60(2) SSCBA 1992

4. Special benefit rules
34 s4 GRA 2004
35 Sch 5 paras 3-5 GRA 2004

5. Claims and backdating
36 Reg 7(1) SS(C&P) Regs
37 CP/4062/2004; see also CP/891/2008
     and *AR v SSWP* [2012] UKUT 467 (AAC)
38 Reg 6(1) and (1ZA) SS(C&P) Regs
39 Regs 4(7), (7ZA), (8), (12) and (13) and
     6(1) SS(C&P) Regs
40 Reg 2(2)(a) BSP Regs
41 Reg 2(3) BSP Regs
42 Reg 2(2)(b) BSP Regs
43 Reg 2(2)(b)(ii) BSP Regs
44 ss1(2) and 3(1)(b)(ii) and (2)(b) SSAA
     1992; s8 SSA 1998; CG/7235/95, para
     13
45 ss1(2) and 3(1)(b)(i), (2)(a) and (3)
     SSAA 1992; s8 SSA 1998; CG/7235/95,
     para 14
46 Reg 9(1) and Sch 1 Part 1 SS(C&P) Regs
47 Reg 13 SS(C&P) Regs

6. Getting paid
48 Reg 3 BSP Regs
49 Reg 17 SS(C&P) Regs

7. Tax, other benefits and the benefit cap
50 s677 IT(EP)A 2003
51 ss577-79, and 676 IT(EP)A 2003
52 **UC** Reg 66 UC Regs
     IS Sch 9 para 80 IS Regs
     JSA Sch 7 para 76 JSA Regs
     ESA Sch 8 para 68 ESA Regs
     HB Sch 5 para 67 HB Regs
53 Reg 40 and Sch 9 para 16(h) IS Regs
54 Reg 103 and Sch 7 para 17(i) JSA Regs
55 Sch 8 para 17(i) ESA Regs
56 Sch IV para 7 SPC Regs
57 Reg 40 and Sch 5 para 16 HB Regs; reg
     29 and Sch 5 para 7 HB(SPC) Regs
58 Regs 22 and 66 UC Regs
59 Reg 8C SS(Cr) Regs
60 s96 WRA 2012
61 Reg 79 UC Regs; regs 75A, 75C and 75G
     HB Regs

Chapter 26
Carer's allowance

This chapter covers:
1. Who can get carer's allowance (p562)
2. The rules about your age (p568)
3. People included in the claim (p569)
4. The amount of benefit (p569)
5. Special benefit rules (p570)
6. Claims and backdating (p570)
7. Getting paid (p573)
8. Tax, other benefits and the benefit cap (p574)

Key facts

- Carer's allowance (CA) is paid to people who care for someone who is severely disabled. A supplement may also be paid if you live in Scotland.
- CA is a non-means-tested benefit.
- You do not have to have paid national insurance contributions to qualify.
- You can qualify for CA whether you are in or out of work, but you must not earn more than £128 a week.
- CA can be paid in addition to other benefits and tax credits, but the overlapping benefit rules may apply. CA counts as income for means-tested benefits.
- CA is administered and paid by the DWP's Carer's Allowance Unit.
- If you disagree with a CA decision, you can apply for a revision or a supersession (see Chapter 56), or appeal against it (see Chapter 57). You must apply for a mandatory reconsideration before you can appeal.
- A young carer grant has been introduced in Scotland (see Chapter 75).

Future changes

From the end of 2021, it is expected that new claims for CA in Scotland will be replaced by claims for carer's assistance. The Scottish government plans to transfer existing CA claimants in Scotland to the new benefit by 2024.

An additional payment for carers of more than one disabled child is expected to be introduced in Scotland from early 2021.

See Chapter 71, and AskCPAG.org.uk and CPAG's *Welfare Rights Bulletin* for updates.

Part 5: Other benefits
Chapter 26: Carer's allowance
1. Who can get carer's allowance

1. Who can get carer's allowance

You qualify for carer's allowance (CA) if:[1]

- you are caring for a 'severely disabled person' (see below). You do not have to be the person's relative, nor do you have to live with her/him; *and*
- the care you give is regular and substantial (see below); *and*
- you are not gainfully employed, which means you earn £128 or less a week (see p563); *and*
- you are not in full-time education (see p899); *and*
- you are aged 16 or over; *and*
- you satisfy the residence conditions (see p1629); *and*
- you are not a 'person subject to immigration control' (see p1560).

Severely disabled person

In this chapter, a **'severely disabled person'** is someone to whom is payable either attendance allowance (AA), the highest or middle rate of disability living allowance (DLA) care component, either rate of the daily living component of personal independence payment (PIP), armed forces independence payment or constant attendance allowance of £71.60 per week or more paid with an industrial injuries benefit or war disablement pension (see p694).[2]

Note:[3]

- Only one person can qualify for CA or the carer's element in universal credit for caring for the same disabled person. If you cannot agree on who this should be, the DWP decides.
- Even if you care for two or more disabled people, you can only qualify for one award of CA for the same day.

Regularly and substantially caring

To qualify for CA, you must be 'regularly and substantially' caring for a severely disabled person. You satisfy this requirement during any week in which you are (or are likely to be) engaged and regularly engaged in caring for her/him for 35 hours or more.[4] A week runs from Sunday to Saturday.[5] Caring can include supervision as well as assistance. If some of the time is spent preparing for the disabled person to come to stay with you or clearing up after her/his visit, this can also count towards the 35 hours.[6]

Note:

- You cannot average the hours if you provide care for more than 35 hours in some weeks and fewer than 35 in others.[7] You must be caring for at least 35 hours in each week of your claim.

- If you are caring for two or more disabled people, you can only qualify for CA if you are caring for at least one of them for 35 hours or more a week.[8] You cannot add together the hours you are caring for both/all of them to make up the 35.

Breaks from caring

You can take a temporary break from caring and continue to qualify for CA. This applies if you have been providing care for at least 35 hours a week in 22 of the last 26 weeks, or for at least 14 of the last 26 weeks if the reason you did not provide care for 22 weeks was that either you or the disabled person were in hospital (or in a similar institution). Weeks before you claimed CA can be counted. Also, in England and Wales (but expected also to apply in Scotland), you can have a temporary break if either you or the disabled person have Covid-19 or are isolating because of coronavirus symptoms.[9]

CA stops if the AA, DLA, PIP or constant attendance allowance of the person for whom you are caring stops because s/he is in hospital or in a similar institution (see p919).[10]

If the person receiving care dies

If the person you care for dies, you continue to be entitled to CA for a further eight weeks, provided you satisfy the other qualifying conditions. This means that you are not entitled if payment of the person's PIP, DLA or AA had stopped because s/he had been in hospital or a care home for more than 28 days when s/he died (see p919 and p928). The eight weeks run from the Sunday following the death, or from the day of the death if this was a Sunday.[11]

Gainfully employed

You cannot qualify for CA if you are 'gainfully employed'. You count as gainfully employed in a week (and cannot qualify for CA in that week) if your earnings from employment and/or self-employment in the previous week were more than £128.[12] For the way earnings are calculated, see below. Your earnings are ignored if you are working during a period when you are not actually caring for the severely disabled person – eg, because s/he is in hospital or you are on a four-week break from caring (see above).[13]

Earnings from employment

To work out how earnings from employment affect your entitlement to CA:
- check whether the payment counts as earnings (see p564) and whether it can be disregarded (see p567);
- work out your weekly net earnings (see p565);
- work out the date from when your earnings count and the period they cover (see p565).

Part 5: Other benefits
Chapter 26: Carer's allowance
1. Who can get carer's allowance

What counts as earnings

For employees, '**earnings**' mean 'any remuneration or profit derived from... employment'. The main type of income which counts as earnings is, therefore, your wages. The following are also included:[14]

- any bonus or commission (including tips);
- holiday pay (but not if it is payable more than four weeks after a job ends or is interrupted);
- compensation for unfair dismissal and certain other types of compensation under the Employment Rights Act 1996 or under trade union legislation;
- an equal pay settlement;[15]
- any payments made by an employer for expenses not 'wholly, exclusively and necessarily' incurred in carrying out the job, including any travel expenses to and from work, and any payments made to you for the cost of arranging care for members of your family;
- a retainer (eg, paid during the school holidays to people who work for the school meals service) or a guarantee payment;
- statutory and/or contractual sick, maternity, adoption, paternity, shared parental and parental bereavement pay;
- certain payments at the end of a job (see below).

This list is not exhaustive and other payments from employment may also count as earnings.[16]

It is the pay you actually receive that is taken into account, rather than what you are legally entitled to,[17] so if you receive less than the minimum wage, it is this lesser amount that counts as 'earnings'.

What does not count as earnings

The following are examples of payments that *do not* count as earnings:

- periodic payments made as part of a redundancy scheme;[18]
- occupational pension payments;[19]
- payments towards expenses that are 'wholly, exclusively and necessarily' incurred in the performance of employment, such as travelling expenses during the course of work;[20]
- payments relating to expenses incurred for participating in a service user consultation.[21]

See p567 for information on earnings disregards.

Payments when you stop work

If you stop work before you claim CA, your final earnings generally do not affect your benefit. Provided your entitlement begins after the employment ends, the following are disregarded:[22]

- final wages, paid or due, including bonuses, commission, tips and expenses that count as earnings;
- holiday pay;
- pay in lieu of notice;
- pay in lieu of remuneration – eg, a loss of earnings payment to a councillor;
- statutory or contractual redundancy pay and other compensation payments (other than from an employment tribunal complaint).

Certain final payments *are* taken into account (unless you are over pension age and they are paid on retirement):[23]
- statutory or contractual maternity, adoption, paternity, shared parental, parental bereavement and sick pay;
- an employment tribunal award or settlement of a complaint to a tribunal or court – eg, compensation for unfair dismissal;
- a retainer.

If you are already entitled to CA when a job ends, any final earnings at the end of that employment are not disregarded.

Calculating net earnings from employment

'Earnings' are net earnings. '**Net earnings**' are gross earnings less any deductions made for income tax, class 1 national insurance (NI) contributions (but not class 3 voluntary contributions[24]) and half of any contribution made towards a personal or occupational pension scheme.[25] It is the amount of weekly earnings that is important; monthly earnings are multiplied by 12 and divided by 52 to arrive at a weekly figure.[26] If payment is for a period of less than a week, it is treated as a payment for a week.[27]

If your earnings fluctuate, your weekly earnings may be averaged as follows.[28]
- If you have a regular pattern of work, your weekly earnings are averaged over one complete 'cycle' of work. This includes periods when no work is done if this forms part of your regular pattern of work – eg, if you regularly work three weeks on and one week off, your earnings are averaged over four weeks.
- In any other case, your earnings are averaged over five weeks, or whatever other period enables the average weekly earnings to be assessed more accurately.[29]

The date from when earnings from employment are counted

Earnings are usually treated as having been received on the first day of the benefit week in which they are due to be paid.[30] If the payment is made on a different date to that on which it is due, see p875 of the 2014/15 edition of this *Handbook*.

> *Benefit week*
>
> The '**benefit week**' is the seven days corresponding to the week for which CA is paid.[31]

Part 5: Other benefits
Chapter 26: Carer's allowance
1. Who can get carer's allowance

The period covered by earnings from employment
Earnings count for a future period starting from the above date. The length of that period is worked out as follows.[32]

- If a payment is made for a particular period, it is taken into account for the number of benefit weeks corresponding to that period. For example, a week's part-time earnings are taken into account for a week. For monthly payments, earnings are taken into account for the number of weeks between the date they are treated as paid and the date the next monthly earnings are treated as paid. If a payment is for a particular period but is a one-off payment (eg, holiday pay on leaving a job if the final payments count – see p564), it is taken into account for the number of weeks from the date it is due to the date the next normal monthly earnings would be treated as paid.[33]

- One-off payments that are not for a specific period are divided by the relevant earnings limit (£128 in 2020/21) plus one penny and any disregard that applies to your earnings to work out the number of weeks for which you will not get benefit.

- If two payments of different types of earnings are made (eg, wages and holiday pay) and the periods worked out as above overlap, they are taken into account consecutively.[34]

Earnings from self-employment
Weekly earnings from self-employment (including any allowance from a DWP scheme to assist with a business[35]) are averaged over a year unless:[36]

- you have recently become self-employed; or
- there has been a change that is likely to affect the normal pattern of the business.

In either case, earnings are averaged over whatever other period the decision maker considers will give the most accurate figure. This means that when you first claim CA, you should provide an up-to-date set of accounts.

For royalties or similar payments (eg, from copyrights), the period for which these payments count is calculated in a similar way to that for payments made for unspecified periods to employees.[37]

See below for the way earnings of childminders, members of a partnership or share fishermen are calculated. Otherwise, it is the net profit from self-employment that is used.

'**Net profit**' is calculated by taking the earnings from self-employment over the period and deducting:[38]

- expenses incurred during the period wholly and exclusively for the purposes of the business. For example, if a car or telephone is used partly for business and partly for private purposes, the costs of it can be apportioned and the amount attributable to business use can be deducted.[39] Certain expenses cannot be deducted, including business entertainment, repayment of capital

on a business loan, capital expenditure and depreciation, and providing board and lodging or renting a room in your home; *and*
- income tax and NI contributions;[40] *and*
- half of any contributions made during the period towards a personal pension scheme or retirement annuity contract.

Childminders are always treated as self-employed and your net profit is deemed to be one-third of your earnings from childminding less income tax, NI contributions and half of certain pension contributions.[41] The rest of your earnings are completely ignored.

For members of a partnership or share fishermen, the relevant share of the 'net profit' is used, and expenses incurred wholly and exclusively for the business are deducted before calculating the share of the profits. After that, income tax, NI contributions and half of any premiums paid into a personal pension or under a retirement annuity contract are deducted from the share.[42]

Notional earnings

You are treated as having 'notional earnings' if it is not possible to work out your actual earnings from employment or self-employment when your claim is decided.[43] This may apply if, for example, the job is new and pay depends on performance, or it is a new business and there is no way of calculating what the profits of that business will be. If so, the 'notional earnings' are an amount that is considered reasonable, taking into account the number of hours worked and the earnings paid for comparable work in the area.

Estimates of the appropriate deductions for income tax and NI contributions and half of any occupational or personal pension contributions are deducted from notional earnings, as are any earnings disregards or, where relevant, allowances for childcare or care costs.

Disregarded earnings

Some income, which might otherwise be classed as earnings, is specifically disregarded and does not affect your CA entitlement. The same earnings disregards apply whether the earnings are from employment or self-employment.

When calculating earnings, the cost of looking after the person you care for, up to a maximum amount, can be deducted from your earnings. If you are getting CA and, because of your work, you have to pay for someone (other than a close relative) to look after the severely disabled person for whom you care (or to look after a child under 16 for whom you or your partner are getting child benefit), these care costs can be deducted when your earnings are calculated (in addition to any disregarded earnings).[44] The maximum deduction is 50 per cent of the figure which would otherwise be your net earnings. Any disregarded income is deducted from your net earnings before calculating the 50 per cent figure.

Part 5: Other benefits
Chapter 26: Carer's allowance
2. The rules about your age

Close relative

'**Close relative**' means a parent, son, daughter, brother, sister or partner (see p319) of you or the severely disabled person for whom you care.

In addition, the following amounts can be disregarded from your earnings:[45]

- any payment made to you by someone who normally lives with you on an informal or non-contractual basis as part of her/his contribution towards shared living expenses;
- the first £20 a week of any income for renting out room(s) in your home;
- the first £20 of any income you receive each week for providing board and lodging in your home. If you get more than £20 a week, 50 per cent of the excess is also disregarded. This disregard applies to each person who lodges with you;
- payments from a local authority or voluntary organisation for fostering or accommodating a child under formal arrangements;
- payments from a health authority, clinical commissioning group, local authority or voluntary organisation for providing temporary care. There is no set time after which care is no longer temporary;[46]
- income tax refunds;
- if you are an employee, any loan or advance of earnings from your employer;
- certain 'bounty' payments made to part-time firefighters, auxiliary coastguards, members of the reserve armed forces and part-time lifeboat crews;
- unless you are abroad yourself, earnings payable abroad which cannot be brought into Great Britain and any bank charges for converting earnings paid in another currency into sterling.

2. The rules about your age

You can claim carer's allowance (CA) if you are aged 16 or over.[47] There is no upper age limit. However, because of the overlapping benefit rules, if you receive retirement pension you may not be paid CA, even if you qualify (see p1190). Even if you are not paid CA, you may qualify for a carer element in your universal credit (see p73), a carer premium in your means-tested benefits or a carer addition in pension credit (see p350). If you are aged 16 to 18 and live in Scotland, you may be able to get a young carer grant (see Chapter 75).

3. **People included in the claim**

You claim carer's allowance (CA) for yourself. You cannot claim any increase in your CA for an adult dependant, or normally claim for a child.

Can you get an increase for a child?

You may continue to qualify for an increase in your CA for a child, if you were entitled to the increase before 6 April 2003 and your entitlement has continued since that date.

If an increase for a child stops being paid for 58 days or less, you may continue to qualify for the increase.[48]

If you are a member of a couple, you may not get an increase for a child if your partner's earnings are at or above the earnings limit. In 2020/21, this is £245 a week for the first child plus £33 for each subsequent child.

If you qualify, you are paid £8 for the eldest child and £11.35 for each subsequent child.

4. **The amount of benefit**

Carer's allowance (CA) is paid at a weekly rate of £67.25.[49]

If you are still entitled to an increase in your CA for a child, see pxviii for the amounts.

Note: if you are a member of a couple, your CA might be paid at a reduced rate if your partner fails to take part in a work-focused interview (see p1138).

Carer's allowance in Scotland

CA is due to be replaced in Scotland by carer's assistance. When it is introduced, it will be paid at the same rate as jobseeker's allowance (JSA). Until carer's assistance is introduced, a CA supplement is paid to people resident in Scotland who are in receipt of CA to increase their amount of CA to the level of JSA.

CA supplement is paid in two lump-sum payments each year and is adjusted annually to take account of inflation. The payments in 2020/21 will be made in June and December, and are £230.10 each.

To qualify, you must be resident in Scotland and be receiving CA on the qualifying date for each payment. The qualifying dates in 2020 are 13 April and 12 October. Anyone getting CA and living in Scotland on these dates will receive a payment. If you are not getting CA on a qualifying date, but are later awarded CA backdated to include the qualifying date, you can get a supplement for that period. You do not get CA supplement if you do not receive CA – eg, if you have an underlying entitlement only, or if you get the carer element of universal credit (UC) without claiming CA. If you get a carer element in your UC, you should

Part 5: Other benefits
Chapter 26: Carer's allowance
6. Claims and backdating

claim CA in order to qualify for the supplement, provided your earnings are not too high to prevent this.

You do not need to get CA and live in Scotland for the whole of a six-month period to qualify; it is enough to be in receipt of CA and resident on the qualifying date.

CA supplement is disregarded as income for means-tested benefits and tax credits.

5. **Special benefit rules**

Special rules may apply if:
- you are subject to immigration control (see Chapter 67);
- you have come from or are going abroad (see Chapters 68, 69 and 70);
- you or the person you are caring for are in hospital or in prison, or the person you are caring for is in a care home or similar accommodation (see Chapter 42).

6. **Claims and backdating**

The general rules on claims and backdating are covered in Chapter 50. This section explains the specific rules that apply to carer's allowance (CA).

If you are claiming a means-tested benefit, see p574 before claiming CA. It is not always advisable for you to claim CA because of the effect it has on your other benefits (and possibly those of the person for whom you care). You do not have to claim CA in order to get the carer element in universal credit (see p73).

Making a claim

A claim for CA must be made in writing. You can do this by completing:
- an online application form at gov.uk/carers-allowance; *or*
- the approved form. Send it to the Carer's Allowance Unit, Mail opening site A, Wolverhampton WV98 2AB. You may also be able to make your claim by taking or sending it to an 'alternative office' (see p1168).

Keep a copy of your claim form in case queries arise.

You must provide any information or evidence required (see p571). In certain circumstances, the DWP may accept a written application not on the approved form.[50] You can amend or withdraw your claim before a decision is made (see p1169). If there is a delay in making a claim, you may be able to get a short-term advance of benefit (see p1192).

Forms

Get Form DS700 (DS700(SP) if you get retirement pension) from your local Jobcentre Plus office, DWP office or telephone contact centre, or from gov.uk/government/publications/carers-allowance-claim-form, or the Carer's Allowance Unit by telephone on 0800 731 0297 (textphone: 0800 731 0317).

Who should claim

You must normally claim CA on your own behalf. However, if you are unable to manage your own affairs, another person can claim CA for you as your 'appointee' (see p1170).

Before claiming, you should be aware of how CA affects your entitlement to means-tested benefits and the means-tested benefit entitlement of the person for whom you care (see p574).

Information to support your claim

For the general information requirements that apply to all benefits, see p1170.

It is important that you provide any information required when you claim. Until you do, you may not count as having made a valid claim (see p1172). Correct any defects as soon as possible or your date of claim may be affected.

The CA claim forms contain a declaration to be completed by the person for whom you care or the person acting for her/him. This asks for confirmation that you provide 35 hours' care a week and explains that her/his benefit may be affected if your claim is successful. Even if this declaration is not completed, the DWP should still make a decision on your claim, although it is likely to be delayed. If the declaration raises questions about the level of care you provide, the DWP may refuse your claim.

Even if your claim is valid, you may be asked to provide further information to support your claim (see p1174). You may also be asked to provide information after you are awarded CA and if you fail to do so, your CA could be suspended, or even terminated (see p1200).

The date of your claim

The date of your claim is important as it determines when your entitlement to CA starts. This is not necessarily the date from when you are paid. For information about when payment of CA starts, see p573.

Your '**date of claim**' is usually the date on which your completed claim form is received by the DWP or a designated 'alternative office' (see p1168).[51] If you

Part 5: Other benefits
Chapter 26: Carer's allowance
6. Claims and backdating

submit your claim online, your date of claim is usually the date it is received, although a decision maker has the discretion to treat it as having been received on an earlier or later date than this.[52]

Note: you must make sure your claim is valid. If it is 'defective', you are given a short time to correct the defects (see p1173). If you do, your claim is treated as having been made when you initially claimed.[53]

In some cases, you can claim in advance (see p573) and, in some cases, your claim can be backdated (see below). If you want this to be done, make this clear when you claim or the DWP may not consider it. If you claimed income support (IS) when you should have claimed CA, see p573.

Backdating your claim

It is very important to claim in time. A claim for CA can usually only be backdated for a maximum of three months.[54] You must satisfy the qualifying conditions over that period. You do not have to show any reasons why your claim was late.

Your claim can be backdated for more than three months in the following situations.[55]

- If you claim CA within three months of a decision to award a 'qualifying benefit' to the person for whom you care (including a decision made by the First-tier Tribunal, the Upper Tribunal or a court), your CA is backdated to the first day of the benefit week in which the qualifying benefit is payable. However, if the decision awarding the qualifying benefit was made following a renewal claim where a fixed period award has ended or is due to end, your CA is only backdated to the first day of the benefit week in which the renewal award became payable.
- Your CA stopped because the 'qualifying benefit' of the person for whom you care was reduced or stopped. This includes if a fixed-term award for the qualifying benefit came to an end or if payment of attendance allowance (AA), disability living allowance (DLA) or personal independence payment (PIP) stopped because the person for whom you care went into hospital, a care home or other similar accommodation. If you make a further claim within three months of the decision to reinstate the qualifying benefit, or of payment starting again, your CA is backdated to the date your earlier claim ended or the date from when the qualifying benefit was re-awarded or became payable again, whichever is later.

Qualifying benefit

A **'qualifying benefit'** is either AA, the middle or highest rate of the DLA care component, either rate of the daily living component of PIP, armed forces independence payment or constant attendance allowance.

If you might have qualified for benefit earlier but did not claim because you were given the wrong information or were misled by the DWP, you could ask for compensation (see p1439) or complain to the Ombudsman via your MP (see p1444).

If you claim the wrong benefit

If you claim IS when you should have claimed CA (either in addition to or instead of IS), a decision maker can treat your IS claim as a claim for CA (see p1182).[56] This applies even if you claim IS 'on the grounds of disability' (see p238). This may enable you to get round the strict time limits on backdating (see p572).

Claiming in advance

You can claim CA up to three months before you qualify.[57] This gives the DWP time to ensure you receive benefit as soon as you are entitled. The date of your claim is the date on which you qualify. The decision maker can award benefit from a future date if s/he believes you will satisfy all the CA qualifying conditions on that date. You should consider claiming in advance – eg, if you are currently earning more than £128 a week, but you plan to stop work or reduce your hours.

7. Getting paid

The general rules on getting paid are covered in Chapter 51. This section explains the specific rules that apply to carer's allowance (CA).

When is carer's allowance paid?

You are paid on a Monday (or Wednesday if the person for whom you care receives constant attendance allowance with an industrial injuries benefit or war pension).[58] CA is paid weekly in advance or four-weekly in arrears (13-weekly in arrears if you agree).[59]

Payments normally run from the first payday after the date of your claim, unless the date of your claim is on your payday, when they run from that day.

Note:
- CA awards are usually made for an indefinite period, but can be made for a fixed period – eg, if a change of circumstances is expected.[60]
- Deductions can be made from your CA to repay certain loans (see p1208) and, in some cases, to pay child support maintenance (see p1207).
- You may not be paid CA if you have been sanctioned for a benefit offence (see p1278).
- For information on missing payments, see p1189. If you cannot get your CA payments because you have lost your bank or post office card or you have

Part 5: Other benefits
Chapter 26: Carer's allowance
8. Tax, other benefits and the benefit cap

forgotten your PIN, see p1188. If you have lost your payment service card or you have forgotten your memorable date, see p1189.

- If payment of your CA is delayed, see p1295. If you are waiting for a decision on your claim, or to be paid, you may be able to get a short-term advance (see p1192). If you wish to complain about how your claim has been dealt with, or claim compensation, see Chapter 60.
- If payment of your CA is suspended, see p1200.
- If you are overpaid CA, you may have to repay it (see Chapter 53) and, in some circumstances, you may have to pay a penalty (see p1268). If you have been accused of fraud, see Chapter 54.

Change of circumstances

You must report changes in your circumstances that you have been told to report, as well as any that you might reasonably be expected to know might affect your right to, the amount of, or the payment of, your benefit. You should do this as soon as possible, preferably in writing. See p1199 for further information. You can also notify your change of circumstances online at gov.uk/carers-allowance.[61]

When there has been a relevant change of circumstances, a decision maker looks at your claim again and makes a new decision. To find out the date from which the new decision takes effect, see p1321.

---

8. Tax, other benefits and the benefit cap

Tax

Carer's allowance (CA) (including an increase for your spouse, civil partner or someone who cares for your child, if you still receive this) is taxable.[62] However, increases for children (if you still receive these) are not taxable.

Means-tested benefits and tax credits

Before you claim CA, consider how your claim might affect your entitlement to means-tested benefits and tax credits. If in doubt, obtain advice.

If you are entitled to CA:

- you may get a carer element included in your universal credit (UC) (see p73) or a carer premium or carer addition included in your other means-tested benefit (see p350);
- you come within one of the groups of people who can claim income support (IS) (see p236) if you receive CA;
- if you are a member of a couple with at least one child or qualifying young person, the other member of the couple only has to work 16 hours a week to qualify for working tax credit (WTC) (see p300). You may also qualify for the childcare element in WTC (see p1460);

- if you are getting UC, you do not have to meet any of the work-related requirements (see p1061). This also applies if you would qualify for CA but for the fact that your earnings are higher than £128 a week;
- if you are a member of a 'joint-claim couple' getting income-based jobseeker's allowance (JSA), you are not required to satisfy the jobseeking conditions.

Note: if the person for whom you care has a severe disability premium/additional amount included in her/his IS, income-based JSA, income-related employment and support allowance (ESA), pension credit (PC) or housing benefit (HB), her/his entitlement to that premium/additional amount can be affected (see p351). Bear in mind that the severe disability premium/additional amount is worth more than the carer premium/additional amount.

Income
CA counts in full as income for all means-tested benefits. However, in some cases an increase in your CA for an adult or child can be ignored. See p126 for UC, p475 for PC and HB if you are at least pension age, and p436 for all other means-tested benefits.

CA counts as qualifying income for the savings credit of PC (see p276).

CA counts in full as income for WTC and child tax credit (CTC). Remember, however, that you cannot get CA if you are in 'gainful employment' (see p563).

Note:
- For IS, income-based JSA and income-related ESA, and, if you are under pension age, HB, if you choose not to claim CA and the DWP decides that you failed to apply for it deliberately, you may be treated as if you receive it (see p450).
- For all means-tested benefits other than UC, if you give up your claim for CA, you can be treated as if you receive it if the DWP decides that you deliberately deprived yourself of it in order to qualify for, or increase your entitlement to, benefit for yourself or your family (but see p450 and p481).

The amount of means-tested benefits
If you are getting UC and:
- you are a member of a couple, you can get a childcare costs element in your UC if one of you is in paid work and the other is not in paid work, is unable to provide childcare and qualifies for CA;
- you (or your partner) qualify for CA, or would do but for the fact that your (or her/his) earnings are higher than £128 a week, a carer element is included in your UC maximum amount. However, if you:
  - have limited capability for work and are a carer, your UC cannot include both a limited capability for work element and a carer element for the same person;

Part 5: Other benefits
Chapter 26: Carer's allowance
8. Tax, other benefits and the benefit cap

- are a single claimant with limited capability for work-related activity, your UC includes a limited capability for work-related activity element instead of a carer element;
- are a member of a couple, your UC includes the limited capability for work-related activity element if one has not already been included for your partner. However, if a limited capability for work-related activity element has been included for you, a carer element can be included for your partner if s/he satisfies the conditions, whether or not s/he would also qualify for a limited capability for work-related activity element.

You may need to work out how you would be better off financially.

If you receive CA (or are entitled to it but do not receive it because of the overlapping benefit rules – see p1190), a carer premium/additional amount is included in your IS, income-based JSA, income-related ESA, PC and HB.

Non-means-tested benefits

For each week you receive CA, you can get national insurance credits (see p975).

CA is subject to the overlapping benefit rules, which means that you may not be paid CA in full if another earnings-replacement benefit (eg, retirement pension) is paid to you (see p1190).

The benefit cap

In some cases, there is a limit on the total amount of specified benefits you can receive (a 'benefit cap'). CA is not one of these specified benefits.[63] If you receive CA (or you would receive it but for the overlapping benefit rules), you are exempt from the cap. See p1194 for further information.

Passports and other sources of help

If you get CA (or would get it but for the overlapping benefit rules), you are entitled to a Christmas bonus (see p870). You may be able to get help, support and services from your local authority – ask for a carer's assessment. If you have a low income, you may be entitled to council tax reduction (see p851).

Notes

1. **Who can get carer's allowance**
   1 s70 SSCBA 1992; reg 9(1) SS(ICA) Regs
   2 s70(2) SSCBA 1992; reg 3 SS(ICA) Regs
   3 s70(7) SSCBA 1992
   4 Reg 4(1) SS(ICA) Regs
   5 s122 SSCBA 1992
   6 CG/6/1990
   7 R(G) 3/91
   8 Reg 4(1A) SS(ICA) Regs
   9 Reg 4(2) SS(ICA) Regs
   10 *SSWP v Pridding* [2002] EWCA Civ 306
   11 s70(1A) SSCBA 1992
   12 Reg 8(1) SS(ICA) Regs
   13 Reg 8(2) SS(ICA) Regs
   14 Reg 9 SSB(CE) Regs
   15 *Minter v Kingston Upon Hull CC and Potter v SSWP* [2011] EWCA Civ 1155
   16 R(IS) 9/95; CIS/743/1992
   17 R(IB) 7/03
   18 Reg 9(1)(b) SSB(CE) Regs
   19 Reg 2(1) SSB(CE) Regs
   20 Reg 9(3) SSB(CE) Regs; *Parsons v Hogg* [1985] 2 All ER 897 (CA), appendix to R(FIS) 4/85
   21 Reg 9(3)(b) SSB(CE) Regs
   22 Sch 1 para 12 SSB(CE) Regs
   23 Sch 1 para 12(2) SSB(CE) Regs
   24 CIS/521/1990
   25 Reg 10(4) SSB(CE) Regs
   26 Regs 6(1) and 8(1)(b)(i) SSB(CE) Regs
   27 Reg 8(1)(a) SSB(CE) Regs
   28 Reg 8(3) SSB(CE) Regs
   29 CG/4941/2003
   30 Reg 7(b) SSB(CE) Regs
   31 Reg 2(1) SSB(CE) Regs
   32 Reg 6(2) SSB(CE) Regs
   33 *Cotton v SSWP* [2009] EWCA Civ 1333, reported as [2010] AACR 17
   34 Reg 6(3) SSB(CE) Regs; *Cotton v SSWP* [2009] EWCA Civ 1333, reported as [2010] AACR 17
   35 Reg 12(1) SSB(CE) Regs
   36 Reg 11(1) SSB(CE) Regs
   37 Reg 11(2) SSB(CE) Regs
   38 Reg 13(1)(a) and (b), (4) and (5) SSB(CE) Regs
   39 R(IS) 13/91; R(FC) 1/91; CTC/26/1989
   40 See also reg 14 SSB(CE) Regs
   41 Regs 13(10) and 14 SSB(CE) Regs
   42 Reg 13(5) SSB(CE) Regs
   43 Reg 4(1) and (3) SSB(CE) Regs and R(IB) 7/03, disapplying reg 4(2) of these Regs
   44 Regs 10(3) and 13(3) and Sch 3 SSB(CE) Regs
   45 Sch 1 SSB(CE) Regs
   46 CG/1752/2006

2. **The rules about your age**
   47 s70(3) SSCBA 1992

3. **People included in the claim**
   48 Art 3 TCA(No.3)O

4. **The amount of benefit**
   49 Sch 4 SSCBA 1992

6. **Claims and backdating**
   50 Reg 4(1) SS(C&P) Regs
   51 Reg 6(1)(a) and (1ZA) SS(C&P) Regs
   52 Reg 4ZC and Sch 9ZC para 4(1) and (2) SS(C&P) Regs
   53 Reg 6(1)(b) SS(C&P) Regs
   54 Reg 19 SS(C&P) Regs
   55 Reg 6(16)-(22), (33) and (34) SS(C&P) Regs
   56 Reg 9(1) and Sch 1 SS(C&P) Regs
   57 Reg 13 SS(C&P) Regs

7. **Getting paid**
   58 Reg 22(3) and Sch 6 SS(C&P) Regs
   59 Reg 22(1) SS(C&P) Regs
   60 Reg 17 SS(C&P) Regs
   61 Reg 32ZA SS(C&P) Regs

8. **Tax, other benefits and the benefit cap**
   62 ss660, 661 and 676 IT(EP)A 2003
   63 Reg 83(1)(i) and (j) UC Regs

Chapter 27

Child benefit and guardian's allowance

This chapter covers:
1. Who can get child benefit (p579)
2. Who can get guardian's allowance (p587)
3. The rules about your age (p589)
4. People included in the claim (p589)
5. The amount of benefit (p590)
6. Special benefit rules (p590)
7. Claims and backdating (p592)
8. Getting paid (p595)
9. Tax, other benefits and the benefit cap (p597)

Key facts

- You may be entitled to child benefit if you are responsible for a child or 'qualifying young person'. You need not be the child's parent.
- You may be entitled to guardian's allowance if you are responsible for a child or qualifying young person and one or both of her/his parents have died. Usually, you must *not* be the child's parent.
- Child benefit and guardian's allowance are non-means-tested benefits.
- You do not need to have paid national insurance contributions to qualify.
- You can qualify whether you are in or out of work.
- If your or your partner's income is over £50,000 a year, one of you may be liable to pay more tax if you get child benefit. Guardian's allowance is not taxable.
- Child benefit and guardian's allowance are administered and paid by HM Revenue and Customs.
- If you disagree with a decision, you can apply for a revision or a supersession (see Chapter 56), or appeal against it (see Chapter 57). You must apply for a mandatory reconsideration before you can appeal.

1. Who can get child benefit

Note: in this chapter the term 'child' is generally used to refer to both a child and a 'qualifying young person'.
You qualify for child benefit for a child if:[1]
- s/he is a 'child' or 'qualifying young person' (see below); *and*
- you are 'responsible' for the child (see p583); *and*
- you have priority over other claimants (see p584); *and*
- you and the child satisfy the residence conditions (see p1628); *and*
- you are not a 'person subject to immigration control' (see Chapter 67).

In some circumstances, even if you meet these conditions, you cannot get child benefit (see p586). If a child you get child benefit for dies, see p597.
Note: guardian's allowance is a separate benefit, but to qualify you must usually get child benefit. For who can get guardian's allowance, see p587.

Who counts as a child

Anyone aged under 16 counts as a 'child'.[2] You can also get child benefit for a child aged 16 or over if s/he counts as a 'qualifying young person'.

Who is a qualifying young person

A 'qualifying young person' is someone aged 16, 17, 18 or 19 who is:[3]
- not in 'relevant education' or training, but only until 31 August (or, if s/he was born on 31 August, 1 September)[4] after her/his 16th birthday; *or*
- 16 or 17, not in *any* education or training, and is in an 'extension period' (see p581); *or*
- undertaking, or enrolled or accepted on, a qualifying type of education (see p580) or 'approved training' (see p581); *or*
- not in relevant education or approved training and it is before the 'terminal date' (see p582).

See p586 for when you cannot get child benefit for a qualifying young person.

Relevant education
'**Relevant education**' is defined as education which is full time and not advanced, so any 'full-time, non-advanced education' (see p580) counts as relevant education. HM Revenue and Customs (HMRC) says that 'appropriate full-time education' in England (see p581) is treated as relevant education.[5]

A child counts as a qualifying young person until none of the above situations apply.[6] If child benefit for a child stops because s/he is not a qualifying young

Part 5: Other benefits
Chapter 27: Child benefit and guardian's allowance
1. Who can get child benefit

person, but s/he later meets the conditions again, you can make a new claim. See p583 if there is a temporary interruption in meeting the conditions.

Education

A child under 20 counts as a qualifying young person if s/he:[7]

- is in 'full-time, non-advanced education' (see below), which s/he started, or was enrolled or accepted on, before turning 19; *or*
- receives 'appropriate full-time education' in England (see p581), which s/he started, or was enrolled or accepted on, before turning 19; *or*
- was previously in one of these types of education, and is enrolled or accepted on another such course.

The education must not be provided as a result of the child's employment or because of an office s/he holds. See p583 if your child's education is interrupted.
Note:

- If a child leaves education before s/he is 20, s/he may still count as a qualifying young person (see p579).
- HMRC sometimes treats a child who starts a course of full-time, non-advanced education while s/he is 19 as having begun the course before turning 19 if s/he has been in full-time, non-advanced education *continuously* since before turning 19. This means s/he counts a qualifying young person during the course, even if s/he was not enrolled or accepted on it before turning 19.

Examples of non-advanced and advanced courses of education[8]

Non-advanced courses	Advanced courses
GCSEs, AS and A levels	A university degree
NVQ and SVQ level 3 and below	NVQ or SVQ level 4 or above
Scottish National Qualifications (up to Higher or Advanced Higher level)	Higher National Diploma or Higher National Certificate
International Baccalaureate	Diploma of Higher Education
BTEC and OCR Nationals	A teaching qualification

Full-time, non-advanced education

To count as 'full-time, non-advanced education', a child's course must normally be provided at a school or college.[9] If a child is educated elsewhere (eg, at home), this also counts if either s/he was being educated in this way before the age of 16 or s/he has a statement of special educational needs that assesses home education as suitable for her/him.[10] HMRC must approve these kinds of education.[11] If s/he starts home education after the age of 16 and this is due to needs related to her/his disability, s/he should satisfy this condition.

To count as full time, the course must be for an average of over 12 hours a week during term time, including tuition, supervised study,[12] exams and practical work, but not meal breaks and unsupervised study.[13]

See p580 for examples of advanced and non-advanced courses.

Appropriate full-time education

To count as 'appropriate full-time education', the education must be suitable for the child, taking into account her/his age, ability and aptitude and any special educational needs s/he has. It cannot be an advanced course.[14]

It does not matter where the education takes place, provided it is in England. If the education is provided at home, it is treated as full time. Education which is not provided at a school is treated as full time if it is tailored activity designed to enable the child to stay in education or training, or if it lasts at least 540 hours a year and was developed by a college, higher education institution or training provider to meet the child's needs.[15]

Approved training

Note: in England, there is no approved training, so you should check whether a child's training counts as 'appropriate full-time education' (see above).

A child under 20 counts as a qualifying young person if s/he:[16]

- is doing approved training, which s/he started, or was enrolled or accepted on, before turning 19; *or*
- was in full-time non-advanced education or approved training, and is now enrolled or accepted on approved training.

Approved training

'Approved training' includes:[17]

– in Scotland, Employability Fund activity;

– in Wales, Traineeships or Foundation Apprenticeships.

The training must not be provided under a contract of employment (but see p582).

See p583 if a child's training is interrupted. If a child leaves approved training before turning 20, s/he may still count as a qualifying young person (see p579).

The extension period

If a child is 16 or 17, s/he continues to count as a qualifying young person during an **'extension period'** if:[18]

- s/he is not in any kind of education or training; *and*
- s/he is registered as available for work, education or training with a careers service or a specified body; *and*
- s/he is not in remunerative work (see p587); *and*

Part 5: Other benefits
Chapter 27: Child benefit and guardian's allowance
1. Who can get child benefit

- you were entitled to child benefit for her/him immediately before the extension period started; *and*
- you apply in writing (or by another method if HMRC accepts this) within three months of the date your child's education or training finished.

The extension period begins on the Monday after the child's course of education or training ends and lasts for 20 weeks. If a child turns 18 during the extension period, child benefit ends unless s/he counts as a qualifying young person on another ground (see p579).

If a child's extension period is interrupted, see p583.

The 'terminal date rule'

If a child leaves qualifying education (see p580) or approved training (see p581) before reaching 20, s/he counts as a qualifying young person until:[19]

- the 'terminal date' if this is a Sunday, or the Sunday after the 'terminal date' (see below); *or*
- if earlier, the Sunday of the week in which s/he turns 20, or the day before her/his 20th birthday if s/he turns 20 on a Monday.

A child does not count as a qualifying young person under this rule if s/he is in remunerative work (see p587).

Terminal date

The '**terminal date**' is the first of the following dates that falls after the date a child left education or training:

– the last day in February; *or*
– 31 May; *or*
– 31 August; *or*
– 30 November.

Note:
- If a child has left education, but returns to sit an exam for her/his previous course, s/he is treated as still being in education until the date of the last exam for which s/he was entered before leaving education.[20]
- A child who has completed her/his Highers or Advanced Highers in Scotland is treated as being in education until a comparable course in England or Wales ends, if this is later.[21]
- A child cannot count as a qualifying young person while in education or training that is provided as a part of her/his job. If s/he is under 20, it is arguable that s/he counts as a qualifying young person from the date s/he leaves such a course until the terminal date, as this rule does not exclude people whose course is provided as part of a job.

Interruptions

If there is a break in a child's satisfying the conditions to be a qualifying young person, this is ignored:[22]

- for up to six months (whether the interruption began before or after the child turned 16) if it is 'reasonable' in the circumstances; *or*
- indefinitely if it is caused by the child's physical or mental illness or disability, and the length of the interruption is 'reasonable' in the circumstances.

This means that a child still counts as a qualifying young person during the interruption. HMRC states that this only applies if there is an interruption during a course of education or training, but it arguably also applies to 16/17-year-olds during the extension period.

However, an interruption cannot be ignored if, immediately afterwards, the child starts or is likely to start:[23]

- a training course which is not 'approved training'; *or*
- a course of advanced education; *or*
- education connected to her/his employment.

Responsible for a child

You are only entitled to child benefit for a child you are 'responsible' for. You count as responsible for a child in any week in which:[24]

- the child is living with you (see below); *or*
- you contribute to the cost of supporting the child (see p584).

A child 'living with' you

To count as living with a child, you must share both a home and 'a settled course of daily living'.[25] This is not the same as 'residing together' or 'presence under the same roof'.[26] A child may be 'living with' you even while s/he is away. There are special rules if a child is looked after by a local authority (see p590).

Living apart

If a child used to live with you, but is now absent, s/he is treated as still living with you if you have not lived apart for more than 56 days in the last 16 weeks.[27] Days a child is absent are ignored if s/he is away *only* to:[28]

- receive education or training (HMRC states that this must be full-time education or approved training); *or*
- stay in certain types of residential accommodation because of her/his disability, or because her/his health would be 'significantly impaired or further impaired' if s/he did not stay there (but see below); *or*
- receive inpatient treatment in a hospital or similar institution (but see below).

In the latter two situations above, a maximum of 12 consecutive weeks' absence can be ignored, unless you regularly incur expenditure in respect of the child, in

Part 5: Other benefits
Chapter 27: Child benefit and guardian's allowance
1. Who can get child benefit

which case the absence can be ignored indefinitely.[29] If you make visits, or give the child pocket money, this rule should be satisfied. Periods in hospital or residential accommodation separated by 28 days or less are treated as one when calculating the 12-week period.

Even if a child is not living with you, you may still qualify for child benefit for her/him if you contribute to the cost of supporting her/him (see below).

See p1648 if your child is abroad.

Example

Amy's son was in hospital for 18 weeks. She regularly took him food and comics. On being discharged, he stayed with his aunt for a month, then returned home. Amy is entitled to child benefit while her son was away from home. He is treated as still living with her while in hospital as she regularly incurred expenditure for him. He also counts as still living with her while staying with his aunt, as he was not absent from home for more than 56 days in the previous 16 weeks – the period in hospital is ignored when calculating the 56 days.

Contributing to the cost of supporting a child

If a child does not live with you, you can still qualify for child benefit if you contribute to the cost of supporting her/him. You must contribute at least the amount of child benefit that would be paid for the child (see p590).[30]

Note:
- Contributions need not be regular, but must total the amount of child benefit that you would qualify for during the period that is being considered.[31]
- Payments in kind, rather than cash, may be counted.[32]
- If you live with your spouse or civil partner, any contribution made by one of you can be treated as a contribution by the other.[33]
- If you and another person(s) each contribute less than the amount of child benefit for the child, but your total contributions are at least the amount of child benefit payable, one of you is treated as contributing the whole sum. If you do not agree who this should be, HMRC decides. If you are awarded child benefit on this basis, you alone must then contribute at least the amount of child benefit paid for the child to remain entitled.[34]

Priority between claimants

More than one person can potentially qualify for child benefit for the same child – eg, if s/he lives with one parent and is maintained by the other. Only one person can be awarded child benefit for a particular child and there is an order of priority for who gets child benefit if two or more people have made a claim.[35]

If two or more people have claimed child benefit for the same child and would qualify for it, the following order of priority applies.[36]
- If you live with the child, you have priority over someone who is contributing to the cost of supporting her/him.

- If you are a woman, you have priority over your male spouse or civil partner if you reside together (see p586).
- If you are the child's parent (including a step-parent, adoptive parent and someone who has legal parental responsibility),[37] you have priority over a non-parent.
- If you are the child's mother or stepmother and are *not* married or in a civil partnership with a man, you have priority over the other parent if you reside together (see p586).
- In any other case, the person agreed between you and the other claimant has priority. If there is no agreement, HMRC chooses who has priority. You cannot appeal against HMRC's choice (but see p1344).[38]

If your claim takes priority over an existing claim, child benefit continues to be paid on the existing claim for the three weeks following the week in which you claim, unless the other claimant withdraws her/his claim or her/his child benefit entitlement ends.[39] Even if your claim has priority, you cannot usually receive child benefit for a period before you made your claim if it has already been paid to someone else for the same child (but see p596).

If you have claimed child benefit and want someone who has equal or lower priority to you to receive it, contact the Child Benefit Office (see p592).[40]

It may be advisable to concede priority to your partner if you spend time abroad, as child benefit normally ends if you have been abroad for more than eight weeks (or 12 weeks in some circumstances – see p1648).

Separation and the priority rules

Problems can arise if there are competing child benefit claims from recently separated parents. Even if a child only lives with one parent, s/he may also be treated as still living with the other parent for a period (usually 56 days) under the rules described on p583. If you are in this situation and a child lives with you, but is still treated as living with her/his other parent, both of you are potentially entitled to child benefit for the child. If neither of you withdraws your claim, the priority rules apply (see p584). In practice, this means that if you are the child's mother, your claim normally takes priority for 56 days after you separate permanently, whoever the child lives with. However, if you are the child's father and you got child benefit before you separated, your claim has priority for three weeks after the week in which the mother claims.[41]

Note: if your ex-partner was getting child benefit when you made your competing claim, see p596.

Part 5: Other benefits
Chapter 27: Child benefit and guardian's allowance
1. Who can get child benefit

Do you share your child's care with her/his other parent?

Separated parents may both potentially be entitled to child benefit. If you do not agree who should receive it, HMRC decides who should be paid. This usually involves looking at who has the greater responsibility of care. In deciding how best to present your case to HMRC, consider the following questions.

1. How many hours each week do you each care for the child?
2. What are the terms of any court orders? Do they reflect the actual care arrangements?
3. Where are the child's possessions kept?
4. At which address is the child registered with services, such as school and her/his doctor?
5. What contributions do each of you make to the cost of bringing up the child? (This may not be conclusive if the resources of one parent are greater than the other.)
6. What impact might the decision have on each parent?
7. Are there other children of the same relationship? In one case involving two parents with almost equal responsibility for their two children, the High Court held that it was reasonable for HMRC to decide that each parent should get child benefit for one child.[42]

These are just examples of the issues to consider – each case depends on its circumstances.

Residing together

It may be important to decide whether you and another person are treated as 'residing together'[43] if you both claim child benefit for the same child (see p584). If you are married, in a civil partnership or a child's parent, you and your spouse/civil partner/the other parent are treated as residing together if your absence from each other:[44]

- is not likely to be permanent (even if you have never actually lived together);[45] or
- is solely because one of you is an inpatient in hospital, or in a similar institution for people with mental health problems, whether this is temporary or permanent.

It is also possible to be absent from one another while you are living under the same roof – eg, if you are maintaining separate households.[46]

When you cannot get child benefit

Even if you meet all the entitlement conditions, you cannot get child benefit if:[47]

- you are the child's spouse, civil partner or partner; or
- the child is married, in a civil partnership or living with her/his partner as if they were married or civil partners[48] unless:
  - the child's spouse, civil partner or partner is in full-time, non-advanced education or approved training; or
  - the child and her/his spouse or civil partner are not 'residing together' (see above – the definition is the same); or

- in some circumstances, the child is in 'remunerative work' (see below); *or*
- the child is aged 16 or over and receiving universal credit, income support, income-based jobseeker's allowance, employment and support allowance, working tax credit or child tax credit; *or*
- the child has spent more than eight consecutive weeks (but see p590):
  - in prison or other custody; *or*
  - being looked after by a local authority.

16–19-year-olds who work

If a child is aged 16 or over and counts as a 'qualifying young person' under the terminal date rule (see p582) or is in an extension period (see p581), you cannot get child benefit for her/him if s/he is in 'remunerative work' – ie, s/he works for 24 hours or more a week in expectation of payment.[49]

If a child is under 16 or a qualifying young person on any other ground (see p579), any work s/he does should not affect your child benefit.

---

2. Who can get guardian's allowance

You qualify for guardian's allowance for a 'child' or 'qualifying young person'(see p579 for who counts – the rules are the same as for child benefit) if:[50]
- you are treated as entitled to child benefit for her/him (see below); *and*
- s/he is an 'eligible child' (see below) and either:
  - s/he lives with you, or is treated as living with you (see p583); *or*
  - you contribute to the cost of providing for her/him (see p589); *and*
- the residence conditions are satisfied (see p1629); *and*
- you are not the child's parent (but see p589).

If a child for whom you get guardian's allowance dies, see p597.

Entitled to child benefit

To get guardian's allowance for a child, you must normally be entitled to child benefit for her/him (see p579). You are treated as entitled to child benefit if:[51]
- you elect not to receive it to avoid the 'high-income child benefit charge' (see p597); *or*
- you live with your spouse and s/he is entitled to child benefit for the child; *or*
- you live in Great Britain and you would be entitled to child benefit for the child were you (or your spouse or civil partner, if you live with her/him) not getting a family benefit from another country.

You are also treated as entitled to child benefit in the week before your entitlement begins. This means guardian's allowance can start on the same day as child benefit.[52]

Part 5: Other benefits
Chapter 27: Child benefit and guardian's allowance
2. Who can get guardian's allowance

Eligible child

A child is an **'eligible child'** if her/his parents (or if s/he was adopted, adoptive parents):[53]
- have both died (or the child was adopted by one person who has now died); *or*
- were not married or in a civil partnership, the mother has died and the father is unknown (but see p589 if the child has been adopted); *or*
- are divorced or their civil partnership has been dissolved, one parent has died and when s/he died, the other parent did not have custody of, and was not maintaining, the child and neither arrangement was required by a court order or child support assessment.

A child is also an eligible child if one of her/his parents (or adoptive parents) has died, and:[54]
- when s/he died the other parent was missing and cannot be found (see below); *or*
- the other parent is in prison or detained in hospital by a court order (but see below).

Missing parents

If one of a child's parents has died, you may qualify for guardian's allowance if, at the date of the death, you did not know the whereabouts of the other parent. Since then, you must have been unable to discover her/his whereabouts, despite making all reasonable efforts to do so – eg, by asking known relatives and friends and checking old addresses.[55] You may not have to make such efforts if there is a risk that you or the child might experience harm or undue distress if you try to trace the missing parent – eg, if s/he is a threat to your, or the child's, physical safety or emotional wellbeing.[56]

If you have had contact with the other parent since the death (but before the decision on the claim), you cannot get guardian's allowance, as her/his whereabouts are known.[57] This may apply even if the contact was only brief (eg, at the funeral), and even if the surviving parent later disappears.

If there has been no contact, but you can communicate with the surviving parent in some way, this is probably sufficient to show that her/his whereabouts are known.[58] 'Whereabouts' is not the same as an address, so showing that you do not know her/his address may not be enough to qualify for guardian's allowance if you have some details of where s/he lives, works or can often be found. However, if all that you know is that the surviving parent is in a large urban area, you can argue that her/his whereabouts are unknown.

Prison sentences

If one of a child's parents has died and the other is in prison, you are only entitled to guardian's allowance if the surviving parent is:[59]

- serving a sentence of imprisonment or detention and, at the date of the death, had at least two years of that sentence remaining; *or*
- detained in hospital by order of a court under specified legislation.

There are detailed rules about what counts as imprisonment or detention, and for calculating whether the length of a sentence amounts to two years, so get advice if you are affected.[60] Guardian's allowance is reduced if the parent in prison contributes to the cost of providing for the child.[61]

Contributing to the cost of providing for a child

To qualify for guardian's allowance for a child who does not live with you, you must contribute at least £17.90 a week to the cost of providing for her/him. This must be in addition to any contribution you make in order to qualify for child benefit for the child (see p584).[62]

When calculating whether you contribute at least £17.90 a week, you can include contributions made by your spouse or civil partner if you live together. If you are not currently making contributions, you are treated as doing so if you state in writing that you will do so once you are awarded guardian's allowance. Any decision to award you guardian's allowance on this basis is revised if you do not actually make the contributions.[63]

Parents, adoptive parents and step-parents

You cannot qualify for guardian's allowance for a child if you are her/his parent, unless one of the following exceptions applies.[64]
- If a child is adopted, her/his adoptive parents count as parents, so if you are her/his biological parent you can claim guardian's allowance (if the qualifying conditions are met).
- If you have adopted a child, you can continue to get guardian's allowance if you were entitled to it immediately before the adoption.
- HM Revenue and Customs says that if you are a child's step-parent you do not count as a parent for guardian's allowance and so can get guardian's allowance for your stepchild.[65]

3. The rules about your age

If you claim child benefit or guardian's allowance, there is no upper or lower age limit to be entitled.

4. People included in the claim

You claim child benefit for each child for whom you are responsible. You claim guardian's allowance for each eligible child (see p588).

Part 5: Other benefits
Chapter 27: Child benefit and guardian's allowance
6. Special benefit rules

5. **The amount of benefit**

Child benefit and guardian's allowance are paid at the following weekly rates.[66]

	£pw
Child benefit – eldest eligible child	21.05
Child benefit – other children (each)	13.95
Guardian's allowance	17.90

The higher rate of child benefit is normally paid for the eldest (or only) child in a family.[67] If you live with your partner and both of you receive child benefit for a child from a previous relationship, the higher rate is only paid to the person who has the eldest child.[68]

6. **Special benefit rules**

Special rules may apply to your child benefit or guardian's allowance if:
* a child is being looked after by a local authority, or is in prison or detention (see below);
* you or the child have come from, or are going, abroad (see Chapters 67, 68, 69 and 70);
* you are in prison or detention (see Chapter 42).

Your child is being looked after by a local authority, or is in prison or detention

Note: the rules in this section prevent you from getting guardian's allowance for an 'eligible child' (see p588) if your child benefit for that child stops.

Special rules apply if a child is:[69]
* looked after by a local authority, is provided with or placed in accommodation under certain legislation and some of the cost of the accommodation or the child's maintenance is met from local authority or public funds (but see p591); *or*
* subject to a compulsory supervision order and lives in residential accommodation under certain legislation; *or*
* in prison or other detention (such as a detention centre or young offenders' institution) as a result of criminal proceedings or non-payment of a penalty imposed on conviction.

If any of these circumstances apply to a child and have done so for at least one day a week in the last eight consecutive weeks, your child benefit entitlement for her/

him ends, unless the child 'ordinarily' lives with you throughout at least one whole day each week (even if s/he is not actually at home in that particular week).[70] A 'day' runs from midnight to midnight, so, in practice, s/he must 'ordinarily' stay with you for two nights during a week for you to qualify.[71] A 'week' means seven days beginning with a Monday.[72]

After the first eight weeks' absence, even if the child does not 'ordinarily' live with you for at least one day a week, you can still get child benefit when the child comes to stay with you for a week or more.[73]

Note:

- Even if a child ordinarily lives with you or comes to stay with you for over a week, if the local authority is making certain payments you may still not qualify for child benefit (see below).
- If a child stops being looked after by a local authority, stops being subject to a supervision order or stops being in prison for at least a week (ie, from Monday to Sunday), but is later in one of those situations again, the eight-week period restarts.
- You can still get child benefit for a child who is looked after by a local authority if s/he is placed in residential accommodation because s/he has a disability or because her/his health would be impaired were s/he not in the accommodation (see p583).[74]
- If a child is detained in a hospital or similar institution because of mental health problems, s/he is only treated as being in prison if s/he was moved there from prison or detention and the expected release date under her/his sentence has not passed. Otherwise, you can continue to get child benefit, provided you meet the normal qualifying conditions.[75]
- If a child was in custody, but is not sentenced to imprisonment or detention, you should be paid child benefit for her/him for the period of her/his detention.[76]

Fostering, adoption and kinship care

If you are a foster carer, a kinship carer or are adopting a child, payments you get from the local authority may affect your child benefit. In many situations, child benefit entitlement is not affected, but it is in the following circumstances.

- *You* cannot get child benefit for a child if a local authority has arranged for her/ him to be placed with you under a placement, or a looking-after or fostering arrangement and the local authority pays for her/his accommodation or maintenance under section 22C(10) of the Children Act 1989, regulation 33 of the Looked After Children (Scotland) Regulations 2009 or section 81(13) of the Social Services and Well-being (Wales) Act 2014.[77]
- *No one* can get child benefit for a child if s/he has been placed with her/his prospective adopters and a local authority pays for the child's accommodation or maintenance under the above provisions.[78]

Part 5: Other benefits
Chapter 27: Child benefit and guardian's allowance
7. Claims and backdating

If these situations do not apply, the normal rules on entitlement apply, including the rules on children who are being looked after by a local authority described on p590 (and the exceptions to these rules described on p591).

Your entitlement to child benefit is not affected if you look after a a child under private fostering arrangements.

7. **Claims and backdating**

The general rules about claims and backdating are covered in Chapter 50. This section explains the specific rules that apply to child benefit and guardian's allowance.

Making a claim

A claim for child benefit must normally be made in writing to the Child Benefit Office. However, you can make a claim by phoning the child benefit helpline if you already get child benefit, you are claiming for an additional child who is aged under six months, that child was born in the UK and the birth has been registered in England, Wales or Scotland.[79]

You must usually get child benefit to be able to get guardian's allowance, but you must make a separate claim. A claim for guardian's allowance should be made in writing to the Guardian's Allowance Unit at the Child Benefit Office.

Forms

The approved child benefit form is Form CH2, which you can get by phoning the Child Benefit Office. The approved guardian's allowance form is Form BG1, which you can get by phoning the Guardian's Allowance Unit (part of the Child Benefit Office). Both forms are also available from gov.uk. They can be completed online, but must be printed, signed and sent by post.[80]

The postal address for enquiries is: Child Benefit Office, PO Box 1, Newcastle upon Tyne NE88 1AA. If your letter is about guardian's allowance you should write 'Guardian's Allowance Unit' at the start of the address. The address is slightly different if you are sending a claim by post, and is written on the claim form. You can also contact HM Revenue and Customs (HMRC) by telephone:
- child benefit helpline: 0300 200 3100; Welsh language: 0300 200 1900 (textphone: 0300 200 3103);
- child benefit intermediaries' helpline (for advisers only): 0300 200 3102;
- guardian's allowance helpline: 0300 322 9080 (textphone: 0300 200 3103).

Keep a copy of your claim form in case queries arise. HMRC has the discretion to accept claims made in another way in individual cases.

You must provide any information and evidence required (see below). You can amend or withdraw your claim before a decision is made (see p1169). If there is a delay in deciding your claim, you can ask for an interim payment (see p596).

Who should claim

You must normally make your own claim for child benefit and guardian's allowance. If you are unable to manage your own affairs, another person can claim for you as your 'appointee' (see p1170).

If someone else also claims child benefit for the same child, you can only get child benefit for that child if your claim has priority (see p584).

If you are a woman and live with your male spouse or civil partner, you are entitled to guardian's allowance rather than him.[81] However, it can be paid to either of you unless you ask for him not to be paid using the approved form.[82]

Information to support your claim

For the general information requirements that apply to all benefits, see p1170.

It is important that you provide any information required when you claim. Until you do, you may not count as having made a valid claim (see p1172). Correct any defects as soon as possible or your date of claim may be affected.

HMRC must see your child's original birth certificate when you claim child benefit, unless:

- child benefit has already been paid for the child (to you or someone else); *or*
- the child was born in Great Britain and the birth has been registered. In this case, you must give details from the birth certificate – the system number in England and Wales or the district, year and entry number in Scotland.

If your child is adopted, you must provide the original adoption certificate. If your child was born abroad, HMRC requires her/his original passport or travel documents used to enter the UK.

If you claim guardian's allowance, you must normally provide the child's original birth certificate, together with the original death certificates of her/his parent(s) and an adoption certificate, if relevant to your claim.

You can send any original documents that you must provide to the Child Benefit Office. You should also be able to take them to your local Jobcentre Plus office, where a certified copy can be made and sent to the Child Benefit Office.[83]

Even if you have provided all that was required when you claimed, you may be asked to provide further information to support your claim (see p1174). You may also be asked to provide information after you are awarded benefit. If you fail to do so, your benefit could be suspended, or even terminated (see p1200).

Part 5: Other benefits
Chapter 27: Child benefit and guardian's allowance
7. Claims and backdating

The date of your claim

The date of your claim is important as it determines when your entitlement to child benefit and guardian's allowance starts. This is not necessarily the date from when you are paid. For information about when payment starts, see p595.

Your '**date of claim**' is normally the date on which your claim form is received at the Child Benefit Office.[84]

Note: you must make sure your claim is valid. If it is 'defective', you are given a short time to correct the defect (see p1173). If you do, your claim is treated as having been made when you initially claimed.[85]

In some cases, you can claim in advance (see below), and in some cases your claim can be backdated (see below). If you want this to be done, make this clear when you claim or HMRC might not consider it. If you initially claimed the wrong benefit, see below.

Backdating your claim

It is very important to claim in time. A claim for child benefit or guardian's allowance can normally only be backdated for up to three months.[86] There are special rules if you are getting benefit and move between Great Britain and Northern Ireland, or if you have been recognised as a refugee (see p1574). You do not have to show any reason why your claim was late. However, if someone else has an award of child benefit for the same child, see p596.

If you might have been entitled to child benefit or guardian's allowance earlier but did not claim as you were given the wrong information or misled by the DWP or HMRC, you could ask for compensation (see p1439) or complain to the Ombudsman through your MP (see p1444).

If you claim the wrong benefit

A claim for guardian's allowance can also be treated as a claim for child benefit for the same child and vice versa.[87] See p1182 for further information.

Claiming in advance

If you do not qualify for child benefit or guardian's allowance when you claim but will do within three months of that date, the decision maker can make an advance award and treat your date of claim as the date on which you first qualify.[88]

8. **Getting paid**

The general rules on getting paid are covered in Chapter 51. This section explains the specific rules that apply to child benefit and guardian's allowance.

When is your benefit paid?

You are normally paid on a Monday (or on a Tuesday), although HM Revenue and Customs (HMRC) can choose any day of the week as your normal payday. Benefit is usually paid four-weekly for three weeks in arrears and one week in advance.

Child benefit and guardian's allowance are weekly benefits. You must normally meet the entitlement conditions at the start of a week (ie, midnight between Sunday and Monday) to be entitled to benefit for that week.[89] Payment begins from the Monday after the date of your claim (see p594) or, if the date of your claim is a Monday, from that date.[90] See p596 if someone else has been getting child benefit for the child.

You can be paid weekly if:[91]
- you are a lone parent; *or*
- you or your partner get universal credit, income support, income-based jobseeker's allowance, income-related employment and support allowance or pension credit; *or*
- HMRC is satisfied that a four-weekly payment 'is causing hardship'.

Your guardian's allowance is always paid at the same time as your child benefit, if you are entitled to both.[92]

Child benefit and guardian's allowance cannot be paid for periods of less than a week.

If your entitlement ends, payment normally continues up to the end of that week.

Your benefit is awarded for an indefinite period unless this would be inappropriate – eg, if a change is expected in the near future.[93]

Note:
- Your benefit can be paid to someone else if this is needed to protect your interests or the interests of the child.[94]
- Even if you have been sanctioned for a benefit offence (see p1278), you must be paid child benefit and guardian's allowance.
- If you have forgotten your PIN, see p1188. If a payment voucher is lost or stolen, see p1189.
- If your payment of child benefit or guardian's allowance is delayed (see p1295), you might be able to get an interim payment (see above). If you want to complain about how your claim has been dealt with, or claim compensation, see Chapter 60.

- If payment of child benefit or guardian's allowance is suspended, see p1200.
- If you are overpaid benefit, you might have to repay it (see Chapter 53) and, in some circumstances, you may have to pay a penalty (see p1268). If you have been accused of fraud, see Chapter 54.

Interim payments

If your claim for child benefit or guardian's allowance is delayed, you can ask HMRC for an interim payment. HMRC does not make an interim payment if you have an appeal pending. An interim payment can be made if it seems that you may be entitled to benefit and:[95]
- there is a delay in you making a claim; *or*
- you have claimed, but not in the correct way – eg, you have filled in the form incorrectly; *or*
- you have claimed correctly, but it is not possible for the claim to be dealt with immediately; *or*
- you have been awarded benefit, but it cannot be paid immediately, other than by an interim payment.

Note:
- There is no right of appeal against a refusal of an interim payment. See the note on p1194 – but it is HMRC that must change the decision, not the DWP.
- An interim payment can be deducted from any later payment of benefit. If it is more than your actual entitlement, the overpayment can be recovered. You should be notified of this in advance.[96]

If someone else has been getting child benefit for the child

If you claim child benefit for a child and someone else is already getting child benefit for her/him, you are only entitled if your claim has priority over the existing claimant's claim (see p584). If so, your benefit starts from the fourth week after the week in which you claim, unless the existing claimant withdraws her/his claim before then or stops getting child benefit for another reason.

Even if your claim has priority, if child benefit has already been paid to someone else for the same child for a period before you claimed, you can only get child benefit for the period before you claimed if:[97]
- a decision maker (or, following an appeal, the First-tier or Upper Tribunal) has decided that the child benefit paid is recoverable because the other person failed to disclose, or misrepresented, a material fact (see p1239) and no appeal against that decision has been made within the time limit. **Note:** if you appeal against a decision refusing your claim under this rule, the tribunal cannot decide that the other person was not entitled for a period before you claimed;[98]
- a decision has been made that the other person was not entitled to child benefit, and s/he has voluntarily repaid the child benefit for that period.

These rules usually prevent you from getting guardian's allowance for a child if someone else gets child benefit for her/him (as you must usually be entitled to child benefit to qualify for guardian's allowance – see p587).

Change of circumstances

You must report any change in your circumstances that you are told to report, as well as any that you might reasonably be expected to know might affect your right to, the amount of, or the payment of your benefit. You should do this as soon as possible, preferably in writing.

You can also report changes of circumstances at gov.uk. See p1199 for further information.

If there has been a relevant change of circumstances, HMRC looks at your claim again and makes a new decision. For when the new decision takes effect, see p1321.

If a child dies

If you were getting child benefit for a child who then dies, your benefit is paid for the next eight weeks, or until the Monday after s/he would have been 20, if that is sooner. If your partner got child benefit for the child and s/he also dies, you are entitled to benefit for the eight-week period if you were living together when s/he died.[99]

If a child is born and dies in the same week, you can also get child benefit for this period if you satisfied the conditions of entitlement during that week.[100]

These rules allow you to also get guardian's allowance for a child during a period after s/he dies, provided s/he continues to count as an 'eligible child'. You do not need to satisfy the conditions about living together or providing for her/his needs (see p587).[101]

---

9. Tax, other benefits and the benefit cap

Tax

Guardian's allowance is not taxable.[102]

If your (or your partner's) 'adjusted net income' in a tax year is over £50,000, you are liable to pay tax on your 'taxable child benefit' for that year. This is called the 'high-income child benefit charge'. For this rule, income is counted on an individual basis – ie, it is *not* the combined income of you and your partner.

Your 'taxable child benefit' includes child benefit for any week that starts in the tax year which is paid to:[103]

- you; *or*
- your partner (but only for weeks when you were partners); *or*

Part 5: Other benefits
Chapter 27: Child benefit and guardian's allowance
9. Tax, other benefits and the benefit cap

- someone who gets child benefit for a child who lives with you, but not with her/him (but only if neither that person nor her/his partner is liable for the charge themselves).

If both you and your partner have income over £50,000, whoever has the highest income is liable for the charge for weeks throughout which you were partners. If you are liable for the charge, you must declare this to HM Revenue and Customs (HMRC) by giving details of your income on a self-assessment tax form within the time limit to do so. See p582 of the 2013/14 edition of this *Handbook* and gov.uk/child-benefit-tax-charge for further details.

Note:[104]

- The high-income child benefit charge is 1 per cent of your taxable child benefit for each complete £100 income you have over £50,000 in a tax year. If your income is over £60,000, the charge equals the amount of taxable child benefit.
- Child benefit awarded for the period after a child dies is not included in your taxable child benefit.

Electing not to be paid child benefit

You (or your partner, if s/he is the claimant) can ask HMRC not to pay child benefit, in order to avoid liability for the high-income child benefit charge. HMRC may not agree to this – eg, if deductions are being made from child benefit to recover an overpayment.[105]

If you elect not to be paid (rather than not claiming child benefit, or ending your claim), your entitlement to child benefit continues. This means that you (or someone with whom you live or who cares for your child) may still qualify for national insurance (NI) credits (see p972 and p974). You can also qualify for guardian's allowance if the child is an 'eligible child' (see p588), or other benefits, such as more generous bereavement benefits (see Chapter 25). For these reasons, consider claiming child benefit, even if you do not want it to be paid.

Note: after electing not to receive child benefit, you have up to two years after the end of the tax year to ask for child benefit to be paid for that year, if you realise that your child benefit would have been more than the charge.

Means-tested benefits and tax credits

If you get child benefit or guardian's allowance:
- means-tested benefits and tax credits can be paid in addition to them;
- they are ignored when calculating your entitlement to universal credit (UC), employment and support allowance, pension credit, housing benefit (HB), working tax credit and child tax credit.[106] They are usually ignored when calculating your entitlement to income support and income-based jobseeker's allowance[107] (but see p436 for when child benefit is taken into account).

Non-means-tested benefits

Increases in non-means-tested benefits for dependent children were abolished in 2003, but some people still get them. You cannot get both guardian's allowance and an increase for the same child.[108] If you still get an increase for a child, it is reduced if you also get the higher rate of child benefit (£21.05) for that child (see p1192).[109]

If you get child benefit for a child aged under 12, you (or, in some circumstances, someone who resides with you or cares for the child) can qualify for NI credits (see p972 and p974).

Your entitlement to any other non-means-tested benefit is not affected by getting child benefit or guardian's allowance.

The benefit cap

In some cases, there is a limit on the total amount of specified benefits you can receive (a 'benefit cap'). Child benefit is one of the specified benefits. However, the benefit cap only applies if you are getting UC or HB.

You are exempt from the benefit cap if you get guardian's allowance.[110]

See p1194 for further information.

Passports and other sources of help

If your income is low, you may be entitled to a council tax reduction (see p851). You may be eligible for free school lunches for your child (see p866).

Children and young people under 19 may qualify for health benefits (see Chapter 31). Young people aged 16 to 19 who are in non-advanced education may qualify for financial help with their studies (see p867).

Notes

1. Who can get child benefit
1 ss141-47 SSCBA 1992; s115 IAA 1999
2 s142(1) SSCBA 1992
3 s142(2) SSCBA 1992; regs 2-7 CB Regs
4 If a child turns 16 on 31 August, HMRC states that s/he is only a qualifying young person up to and including that day but, arguably, this is not correct: compare para 07030 CBTM with reg 4(3) CB Regs.
5 para 07020 CBTM
6 Reg 2(2) CB Regs
7 Reg 3 CB Regs
8 Reg 1(3) CB Regs
9 Reg 3(2)(a)(i) CB Regs
10 Reg 3(3) CB Regs
11 Reg 3(2)(a)(ii) CB Regs

12 'Supervised' study requires the close proximity of a teacher or tutor to enforce discipline, and provide encouragement and help: R(F) 1/93, but see also *Flemming v SSWP* [2002] EWCA Civ 641 (reported as R(G) 2/02) and *SSWP v Deane* [2010] EWCA Civ 699.
13 Reg 1(3) CB Regs
14 Reg 3(2)(ab) CB Regs; s4 Education and Skills Act 2008
15 s4 Education and Skills Act 2008; reg 3 Duty to Participate in Education or Training (Miscellaneous Provisions) Regulations 2013, No.1205
16 Reg 3(2)(c), (d) and (4) CB Regs
17 Reg 1(3) CB Regs
18 Reg 5 CB Regs
19 Reg 7 CB Regs
20 Reg 7(2)2.1 CB Regs
21 Reg 7(2)1.3 CB Regs
22 Reg 6(2) and (3) CB Regs
23 Reg 6(4) CB Regs
24 s143 SSCBA 1992
25 R(F) 2/81
26 R(F) 2/79
27 s143(2) SSCBA 1992
28 s143(3) SSCBA 1992; reg 9 CB Regs; para 06040 CBTM
29 s143(3)(b) and (c) and (4) SSCBA 1992; reg 10 CB Regs
30 s143(1)(b) SSCBA 1992
31 *RK v HMRC (CHB)* [2015] UKUT 357 (AAC), reported as [2016] AACR 4
32 R(U) 3/66
33 Reg 11(4) CB Regs
34 Reg 11 CB Regs
35 s144(3) and Sch 10 SSCBA 1992
36 s13(1) SSAA 1992 and Sch 10 SSCBA 1992
37 s147(3) SSCBA 1992; R(F) 1/08
38 Sch 2 para 4 SSA 1998
39 Sch 10 para 1 SSCBA 1992
40 Regs 14 and 15 CB Regs
41 CF/1771/2003
42 *R (on the application of Ford) v Board of Inland Revenue* [2005] EWHC 1109 (Admin); see also *R (Chester) v Secretary of State for Social Security* [2001] EWHC Admin 1119
43 Or 'residing with' each other – see *Grove v Insurance Officer*, reported as an appendix to R(F) 4/85
44 s147(4) SSCBA 1992; regs 1(3) and 34 CB Regs
45 R(F) 4/85
46 R(F) 3/81
47 Sch 9 SSCBA 1992; regs 8, 12,13 and 16 CB Regs
48 But see *KW v HMRC (CB)* [2011] UKUT 489 (AAC)
49 Regs 1(3), 5(2)(c) and 7(3) CB Regs

2. **Who can get guardian's allowance**
50 ss77 and 122(5) SSCBA 1992
51 s122(4) SSCBA 1992; reg 4A SSB(Dep) Regs
52 Reg 4A(1)(b) and (3) SSB(Dep) Regs
53 s77(2)(a) and (8)(a) SSCBA 1992; regs 4-6 GA(Gen) Regs
54 s77(2)(b) and (c) and (8) SSCBA 1992; reg 7 GA(Gen) Regs
55 s77(2)(b) SSCBA 1992
56 para 12090 CBTM
57 CG/60/1992; R(G) 2/83
58 CG/60/1992; CF/2735/2003
59 Reg 7 GA(Gen) Regs
60 Reg 7 GA(Gen) Regs; para 12050 CBTM
61 s77(8)(c) SSCBA 1992; reg 8 GA(Gen) Regs
62 s77(6)(b) SSCBA 1992
63 Reg 5 SSB(Dep) Regs
64 s77(10) and (11) SSCBA 1992; regs 4 and 6(2) GA(Gen) Regs; R(G) 4/83 (appendix)
65 para 12010 CBTM; and s147(3) SSCBA 1992 only treats a step-parent as a parent for child benefit purposes, but see also R(F) 1/08 which suggests that anyone with parental responsibility is likely to count as a parent.

5. **The amount of benefit**
66 Reg 2(1) CB(R) Regs; Sch 4 Part III SSCBA 1992
67 Reg 2(1) CB(R) Regs
68 Reg 2(2) CB(R) Regs

6. **Special benefit rules**
69 s147(2) and Sch 9 para 1 SSCBA 1992; regs 16-19 CB Regs
70 Reg 16(1)(b)(iv) and (2) CB Regs
71 R(F) 3/85
72 s147(1) SSCBA 1992
73 Reg 16(1)(b)(i)-(iii) CB Regs
74 Regs 9 and 18(b) CB Regs
75 Reg 17(2)-(5) CB Regs
76 Regs 1(3) and 17(1) CB Regs
77 Reg 16(3) CB Regs
78 Reg 16(4) and (5) CB Regs

7. **Claims and backdating**
79 Reg 5 CB&GA(Admin) Regs; gov.uk/ child-benefit/how-to-claim
80 Reg 5 CB&GA(Admin) Regs
81 s77(9) SSCBA 1992

82 Reg 10 GA(Gen) Regs; para 12080
    CBTM
83 Regs 3(2) and 5(5) CB&GA(AA) Regs
84 Reg 5 CB&GA(Admin) Regs
85 Reg 10 CB&GA(Admin) Regs
86 Reg 6 CB&GA(Admin) Regs
87 Reg 11 CB&GA(Admin) Regs
88 Reg 12 CB&GA(Admin) Regs

8. Getting paid
89 s147(2) SSCBA 1992
90 Reg 13 CB&GA(Admin) Regs
91 Regs 18 and 19 CB&GA(Admin) Regs
92 Reg 18(4) CB&GA(Admin) Regs
93 Reg 15 CB&GA(Admin) Regs
94 Reg 33 CB&GA(Admin) Regs
95 Reg 22 CB&GA(Admin) Regs
96 Regs 22(3), 41 and 42 CB&GA(Admin)
    Regs
97 Sch 10 para 1 SSCBA 1992; s13(2) SSAA
    1992; reg 38 CB Regs; CF/2826/2007
98 *CB v HMRC and AE (CHB)* [2016] UKUT
    506 (AAC)
99 s145A SSCBA 1992; reg 20 CB Regs
100 s145A(3) SSCBA 1992
101 s145A(4) SSCBA 1992

9. Tax, other benefits and the benefit cap
102 s677 IT(EP)A 2003
103 ss681B, 681D and 681H IT(EP)A 2003
104 ss681C, 681E and 681H IT(EP)A 2003
105 s13A SSAA 1992; see also HMRC,
    Elections Not to Receive Child Benefit,
    2012, available at gov.uk/government/
    publications/elections-not-to-receive-
    child-benefit
106 **UC** Reg 66 UC Regs
    ESA Sch 8 para 7(2) ESA Regs
    PC Regs 9 and 15(1)(j) SPC Regs
    HB Sch 5 para 65 HB Regs; regs 27 and
    29 HB(SPC) Regs
    TC Reg 7 TC(DCI) Regs
107 Sch 9 para 5B IS Regs; Sch 7 para 6B JSA
    Regs
108 Reg 7(4) SS(OB) Regs
109 Reg 8 SS(OB) Regs
110 **UC** Reg 83(1)(k) UC Regs
    HB Reg 75F(1)(i) HB Regs

Chapter 28

Disability living allowance

This chapter covers:
1. Disability living allowance mobility component (p603)
2. Disability living allowance care component (p610)
3. The rules about your age (p617)
4. People included in the claim (p623)
5. The amount of benefit (p623)
6. Special benefit rules (p623)
7. Claims and backdating (p624)
8. Getting paid (p632)
9. Tax, other benefits and the benefit cap (p634)

New claims for disability living allowance (DLA) can only be made for children under 16. People aged between 16 and pension age who have a disability can claim personal independence payment (PIP) (see Chapter 35). When a child who gets DLA turns 16, s/he is usually invited to claim PIP (see p617).

If you are 16 or over but were under 65 on 8 April 2013 and were already getting DLA, you will be invited to claim PIP (see p617).

Key facts

- Disability living allowance (DLA) is a benefit for people with disabilities or long-term health problems who need help getting around and/or who need supervision or attention.
- You must be under 16 to make a new claim.
- DLA has a care component and a mobility component. You can get either one or both of the components. Each component has different rates.
- DLA is a non-means-tested benefit.
- You can get DLA whether you are in or out of work.
- You do not have to have paid national insurance contributions to get DLA.
- DLA can be paid in addition to other benefits and is disregarded as income for means-tested benefits and tax credits.
- DLA is administered and paid by the DWP's Disability and Carers Service.
- If you disagree with a DLA decision, you can apply for a revision or a supersession (see Chapter 56), or appeal against it (see Chapter 57). You must apply for a mandatory reconsideration before you can appeal.

1. Disability living allowance mobility component

Disability living allowance (DLA) mobility component is for children under 16 who have difficulties when walking. It can be paid at a lower or higher rate.

See p628 for tips on answering the mobility questions on the DLA claim form.

Who can get the mobility component

A child can get DLA mobility component if s/he:[1]
- satisfies the residence conditions (see p1629); *and*
- is not a 'person subject to immigration control', although there are some exceptions (see p1560); *and*
- is under 16 when you first claim (see p617); *and*
- satisfies the 'disability conditions' for either the higher rate (see p604) or the lower rate (see p608); *and*
- unless s/he is terminally ill (see p623), has satisfied the disability conditions throughout the three months immediately before the award begins (see p626 if you are reclaiming) and is likely to continue to satisfy them for the next six months; *and*
- is likely to be able to 'benefit from enhanced facilities for locomotion'.

To benefit from enhanced facilities for locomotion
To get the DLA mobility component, a child must be able to '**benefit from enhanced facilities for locomotion**'. This means s/he must be able to make outdoor journeys from time to time. It is not essential that s/he is interested in or enjoys going out, provided it would be beneficial for her/him to do so. S/he can get DLA mobility component even if s/he has to be carried to a car for a ride.[2]

Part 5: Other benefits
Chapter 28: Disability living allowance
1. Disability living allowance mobility component

Disability conditions for the higher rate mobility component

A child can get the higher rate mobility component if s/he:[3]
- has a disability from a physical cause that means s/he is unable, or virtually unable, to walk (see below); or
- is both blind and deaf (see p606); or
- is blind or severely visually impaired (see p606); or
- was born without feet or is a double amputee (see p607); or
- has a 'severe mental impairment', has 'severe behavioural problems' and qualifies for the highest rate of DLA care component (see p607).

'Unable or virtually unable to walk'

A child can get the higher rate if s/he has a disability from a physical cause that means:[4]
- s/he is unable to walk; or
- her/his ability to walk outdoors is so limited in terms of the distance, speed, length of time, or the manner in which s/he can make progress on foot without severe discomfort that s/he is virtually unable to walk; or
- the exertion required to walk would constitute a danger to her/his life or be likely to lead to a serious deterioration in her/his health.

Personal circumstances, such as the location of the child's home, should not be taken into account. It is not, for instance, relevant if s/he lives a long way from the nearest bus stop,[5] or if s/he cannot use public transport.

Physical disability

A child's inability, or virtual inability, to walk must arise from her/his physical condition.[6] There can be a physical cause, such as pain or dizziness, even without a medically diagnosed origin. It does not matter if the original cause was mental, provided a current physical impairment affects her/his walking. For example, if a child's walking is impaired by weakness due to anorexia nervosa, the cause is physical.[7] Myalgic encephalomyelitis (ME), or chronic fatigue syndrome, should be accepted as having a physical origin unless there is evidence that any mobility restrictions are purely psychological.[8] A child's discomfort from chronic diarrhoea might make her/him virtually unable to walk.[9] Inability to make progress on foot because of behavioural problems may qualify if the cause is physical – eg, Down's syndrome or autism are both accepted as physical disorders of development of the brain.[10]

Unable to walk

A child is unable to walk if s/he cannot move her/his body along by alternate, weight-bearing steps of the feet.[11]

Prostheses, aids and medication

A child's ability to walk is considered taking into account any prosthesis or artificial aid s/he uses, or that would be suitable for her/him.[12] S/he may not qualify if s/he is able to walk with crutches. However, if s/he has one leg and no artificial limb suitable to use, s/he is regarded as 'unable to walk', even if s/he can get around on crutches.[13] If s/he has no feet, s/he qualifies automatically (see p607).[14]

Any medication the child normally and reasonably uses is taken into account – eg, it may not be practical to carry a bulky nebuliser.[15] Her/his walking should be assessed as s/he is now, not how s/he might be after any treatment.[16]

Outdoors

The test is how a child copes with the terrain and environment normally encountered outdoors. If s/he has problems with balance on uneven pavements and roads, or her/his condition is made worse by wind or rain, these should be taken into account.[17] Walking indoors (eg, in a school) is not necessarily an indication of ability to walk outdoors.[18]

Distance

The law does not specify a distance to be used when determining a child's inability to walk. In practice, s/he may be refused benefit if you tick on the claim form that s/he can walk more than 50 metres. However, her/his walking speed, the time it takes to cover the distance and the manner of walking are also relevant, so give details about these on the claim form. Taking more than a minute to walk 50 metres is slow, so if an older child cannot walk this fast without severe discomfort, you should say so.[19]

Without severe discomfort

Any walking that a child can do only with severe discomfort should be ignored when considering whether s/he is virtually unable to walk.[20] This is a lesser test than 'severe pain or distress'.[21] If, when walking, s/he feels severe discomfort (eg, pain or breathlessness brought on by walking), make this clear.[22] S/he may be able to walk a distance without severe discomfort, a further distance that causes severe discomfort, and then have to stop altogether. The test is how far s/he can walk before going any further causes severe discomfort. You should state this distance on the claim, rather than how far s/he can walk before actually having to stop. If s/he can walk further without severe discomfort after a brief rest, this could be taken into account.[23]

If a child is in severe discomfort before s/he starts to walk, even if the pain gets no worse, s/he should count as being virtually unable to walk, provided her/his disability affects the physical act of walking.[24] S/he does not count as being virtually unable to walk if something unconnected with walking (eg, a skin condition affected by sunlight) causes the discomfort.[25]

Part 5: Other benefits
Chapter 28: Disability living allowance
1. Disability living allowance mobility component

The exertion required to walk

A child can get the higher rate mobility component if the exertion required to walk endangers her/his health. If the deterioration in health is sudden, you must show that s/he would never recover, or recovery would take a significant period of time (eg, 12 months) or would require some form of medical intervention. So, a child with ME who needs a few days' rest after walking would not satisfy this test.[26] The fact that walking may cause a child stress, or lead to a deterioration in mental health, does not count.[27]

Blind and deaf

A child can get the higher rate mobility component if:
* the degree of disablement resulting from her/his loss of vision is 100 per cent; *and*
* the degree of disablement resulting from her/his loss of hearing is 80 per cent on a scale where 100 per cent represents absolute deafness;[28] *and*
* the combined effect of the blindness and deafness means that s/he is unable to walk to any intended or required destination while outdoors without the help of another person.[29]

The regulations do not specify how to assess the degree of disablement, but caselaw suggests that the industrial injury provisions should be used (see p689).[30] So 100 per cent disablement through 'loss of vision' means 'loss of sight to such an extent as to render the claimant unable to perform any work for which eyesight is essential'.[31] This is the definition used when someone is registered as severely sight impaired (blind). However, whether or not a child is registered, or the outcome of visual acuity and visual fields tests, is not conclusive of whether s/he satisfies this condition. All evidence of how a child's sight difficulties might affect her/his ability to carry out a real paid job in practice should be considered.[32]

If a child's level of hearing loss, averaged between both ears at 1, 2 and 3 kHz, is at least 87 decibels, s/he satisfies the 80 per cent disablement test.[33] S/he may have to undertake a hearing test. The test takes into account any hearing aid s/he uses or could reasonably be expected to use.[34]

Blind or severely visually impaired

A child must have been certified blind or severely sight impaired and have combined visual accuity, in both eyes, on the 'Snellen scale', while using appropriate corrective lenses if necessary, of:[35]
* less than 3/60; *or*
* 3/60 or more, but less than 6/60, if s/he has a complete loss of peripheral vision and a central visual field of no more than 10 degrees.

'Appropriate' corrective lenses are ones that s/he can wear without discomfort.[36] The test has to be met by both eyes – an average cannot be used if her/his level of vision in one eye is worse than the other.[37]

The Snellen test is taken indoors. This may be discriminatory.[38] If a child does not qualify according to the Snellen scale but her/his vision is significantly worse outdoors, get specialist advice.

Note: in Scotland from 1 April 2018, the system of certifying a person as blind or severely sight impaired no longer applies to children under 16. If this affects a child's ability to get the higher rate mobility component under this rule, seek advice.

People without feet
If a child does not have feet or legs (missing from the ankle or above), s/he is automatically treated as being unable to walk,[39] even if s/he can walk with prostheses.

Severe mental impairment and behavioural problems
A child can get the higher rate mobility component if s/he:[40]
- has a 'severe mental impairment' – ie, arrested development, or incomplete physical development, of the brain, which results in severe impairment of intelligence and social functioning; *and*
- displays severe behavioural problems – ie, the child:
  – exhibits extreme disruptive behaviour; *and*
  – regularly requires someone else to intervene and physically restrain her/him to prevent her/him causing injury to her/himself or others or damage to property; *and*
  – is so unpredictable that another person has to be present and watching over her/him whenever s/he is awake;[41] *and*
- qualifies for the highest rate of the DLA care component (see p610).

If a child does not meet all the above conditions, s/he might still get the higher rate mobility component because a disability prevents her/him from walking effectively, so that s/he is virtually unable to walk (see p604).[42]

Arrested or incomplete development
'Arrested or incomplete development' must occur before the brain reaches its final development. This is during the thirties or early forties for most people, so any condition that affects a child should be accepted as occurring before this.[43] As a result of this arrested or incomplete brain development, s/he must also have a severe impairment of intelligence and of social functioning (see below).[44]

Severe impairment of intelligence and social functioning
An IQ of 55 or less is generally accepted as a 'severe impairment of intelligence'. However, using a crude measure of intelligence based on IQ alone is not appropriate. Some children may have a higher IQ but be unable to apply it practically.[45] A child's 'useful intelligence' (eg, her/his 'degree of judgement in

Part 5: Other benefits
Chapter 28: Disability living allowance
1. Disability living allowance mobility component

relation to everyday living', including factors such as her/his sense of danger) should be considered as a whole and also be taken into account.[46] For example, an autistic child with no awareness of danger may have severely impaired intelligence even if her/his IQ is over 55, and an assessment of language and communication skills (rather than other measures of intelligence) may be particularly important in considering a child's social functioning.[47] Whether a child has 'severe impairment of intelligence and social functioning' should, therefore, be treated as a single test and all the evidence considered as a whole.

Physical restraint

Physical restraint may involve as little as a hand on the arm. You do not need to show that any force is used.[48] If the presence of someone who watches over a child is enough to prevent her/him from being disruptive, or a specially adapted environment allows her/him to be safely left alone, s/he may not pass the test. However, the DWP should not focus only on how s/he is outdoors or in a structured safe environment, and must consider her/his need for, and the nature of, intervention in all environments.[49] Involuntary behaviour, such as falls due to seizures, can be classed as 'disruptive'.[50]

Disability condition for the lower rate mobility component

A child can get the lower rate mobility component if s/he can walk but is 'so severely disabled physically or mentally' that s/he cannot get around outdoors 'without guidance or supervision from another person most of the time'.[51] S/he must also satisfy the 'additional requirements' test (see below).

Any ability s/he may have to use familiar routes without guidance or supervision should be ignored.[52] Getting the lower rate mobility component is based on the child's need for supervision or guidance, rather than any physical difficulty s/he has walking. Any physical difficulty s/he has walking may mean that s/he can get the higher rate.[53]

The 'additional requirements' test

You must show that a child requires guidance or supervision and also that either:[54]
- s/he requires substantially more guidance or supervision than children of her/his age in 'normal' physical and mental health; *or*
- children of the same age in 'normal' physical and mental health would not require such guidance or supervision.

The fact that all young children require some guidance or supervision outdoors is not the point. If a child needs a substantially greater amount of guidance or supervision, or a different type of guidance or supervision, compared to what is normally needed by children of a similar age, s/he should qualify.[55] For example, a child with a visual impairment or learning disability may need an adult to hold, guide or watch over her/him in situations in which most children of a similar age would only require someone to acccompany them. Similarly, a young deaf child may need someone to stay within touching distance, whereas a hearing child would not.[56]

See p627 for tips on how to describe a child's needs on the claim form.

Supervision

'Supervision' can be precautionary (eg, accompanying and watching over a child) in order to monitor a child's physical, mental or emotional state in case s/he needs more assistance to continue walking. It can also be monitoring the route ahead for obstacles or dangers, or places or situations which might upset her/him. Supervision can also be active, such as encouraging, persuading or cajoling a child, or distracting her/him from fears[57] or possibly alarming situations.[58]

Unlike the 'continual supervision' condition for the DLA care component, the child does not need to require supervision to prevent 'substantial danger'.[59] If s/he gets the care component because s/he requires continual supervision, s/he may also get the lower rate mobility component.[60] However, this is not automatic; her/his eligibility must be assessed on the mobility criteria alone.[61]

The supervision does not need to improve the child's walking ability, but should enable her/him to 'take advantage of the faculty of walking'. It is enough that supervision helps, even if it does not remove risks completely or if s/he may not always respond well to the person providing it.[62] If s/he needs to have supervision (eg, to provide help in the event of seizures or a severe asthma attack),[63] even though s/he has no difficulty getting about, s/he can get the lower rate mobility component.[64]

Guidance

'Guidance' can mean physically leading or directing a child, giving oral suggestions or persuasion, helping to avoid obstacles or places that upset her/ him, or leading or persuading a child when s/he becomes disorientated or is anxious. Even if a companion only intervenes occasionally, s/he could still be guiding 'most of the time' if a child would otherwise not know when to change direction. If a child has a visual impairment, s/he may need guidance to follow directions, avoid obstacles or cross roads (even if s/he uses a guide dog or cane). If s/he is deaf and her/his main method of communication is sign language, s/he may require guidance in unfamiliar places if s/he is unable to ask for or follow directions. However, an older child may not qualify if s/he can study maps, read street signs or communicate with passers by.[65]

Fear and anxiety

A child can get the lower rate mobility component because of a mental as well as a physical disablement. If s/he has an anxiety disorder and needs the help of an escort to overcome fear of going outside, s/he is likely to satisfy the 'guidance or supervision' requirement.[66] There is conflicting caselaw, but if no amount of

Part 5: Other benefits
Chapter 28: Disability living allowance
2. Disability living allowance care component

reassurance can persuade her/him to go outside, s/he may not qualify.[67] However, if s/he can just manage a walk into her/his garden, this could be enough to qualify.[68]

Any fear or anxiety that stops a child going out alone must be a symptom of mental disability in order to count. Fear and anxiety arising from a physical disability, such as a fear of having to cope with incontinence while alone, is not sufficient, although s/he may still have a physical need for supervision.[69] If her/his physical disability causes such fear or anxiety that s/he can be said to be mentally disabled, s/he may qualify.

2. **Disability living allowance care component**

Disability living allowance (DLA) care component is for children under 16 who have attention or supervision needs. It can be paid at a lowest, middle or highest rate.

See p627 for tips on completing the DLA claim form.

Who can get the care component

A child can get the DLA care component if s/he:[70]
- satisfies the residence conditions (see p1629); *and*
- is not a 'person subject to immigration control', although there are some exceptions (see p1560); *and*
- is under 16 when you first claim (see p617); *and*
- is not in residential care (see p927); *and*
- satisfies the disability conditions for the lowest, middle or highest rate of the care component (see below) and, unless s/he is terminally ill, satisfies the 'additional requirements' test (see p611); *and*
- unless s/he is terminally ill (see p623), has satisfied the disability conditions throughout the three months immediately before the award begins (see p626 if you are reclaiming) and is likely to continue to satisfy them for the next six months.

The disability conditions

A child can get the **lowest rate care component** if s/he is so severely disabled, physically or mentally, that s/he requires (see p612) attention from another person for a significant portion of the day (whether during a single period or a number of periods) in connection with her/his bodily functions (see p613 and p615).[71]

A child can get the **middle rate care component** if s/he:
- satisfies one of the daytime disability conditions (see p611) *or* one of the night-time disability conditions (see p611);[72] *or*
- undergoes renal dialysis in certain circumstances (see p623).[73]

A child can get the **highest rate care component** if s/he:
- satisfies one of the daytime disability conditions (see below) *and* one of the night-time disability conditions (see below);[74] *or*
- is terminally ill (see p623).[75]

The **daytime disability conditions** are that a child is so severely disabled, physically or mentally, that s/he requires (see p612):[76]
- frequent attention from another person throughout the day in connection with her/his bodily functions (see p613); *or*
- continual supervision throughout the day in order to avoid substantial danger to her/himself or others (see p616).

The **night-time disability conditions** are that a child is so severely disabled, physically or mentally, that s/he requires (see p612):[77]
- prolonged or repeated attention from another person at night (see p616) in connection with her/his bodily functions (see p613); *or*
- another person to be awake at night for a prolonged period or at frequent intervals to watch over her/him (see p617) in order to avoid substantial danger to her/himself or others.

The 'additional requirements' test

You must show not only that a child requires attention or supervision, but also that either:[78]
- the child has attention or supervision requirements 'substantially in excess of the normal requirements' of a child of the same age; *or*
- the child has substantial attention or supervision requirements which younger children in 'normal' physical and mental health may also have, but which children of the same age and in 'normal' physical and mental health would not have. If this is due to 'developmental delay', see below.

This extra test does not apply if you are claiming DLA care component for a child who is terminally ill.[79]

The fact that all young children require assistance throughout the day is not the point. If a child needs substantially more assistance, or assistance of a different type, compared to the assistance normally required by a child of the same age, s/he should qualify.[80] See p627 for tips on how to describe a child's needs on the claim form.

'So severely disabled physically or mentally'

To get the care component, a child must be 'so severely disabled physically or mentally' that s/he needs attention or supervision. S/he does not need to have a specific medical condition. What is important is that s/he is so disabled that s/he

Part 5: Other benefits
Chapter 28: Disability living allowance
2. Disability living allowance care component

has care needs.[81] However, medical evidence can still be important to establish that s/he is disabled and what her/his care needs are.[82]

Problems sometimes arise if, for example, a child has behavioural problems or a developmental delay that have not been attributed to a disability. The test is whether a child has the physical or mental power to control the behaviour.[83]

Attention and supervision

'Requires'

You must show that a child 'requires' attention or supervision from another person. It must be 'reasonably required' rather than 'medically required'.[84] For example, if an incontinent child needs help changing bedding, this help should count as 'reasonably required', even if not actually required to protect her/his skin. Bear in mind that all younger children may be incontinent from time to time, and the attention a child requires must be substantially more than, or different from, the attention normally needed by children of the same age (see p611).

Reasonably requires attention

Attention must be 'reasonably required to enable' a child 'as far as reasonably possible to live a normal life'. Having a social life, recreation and cultural activities are part of normal life. If a child is blind, it is reasonable for you to read to her/him, describe television pictures, or guide her/him during social outings. Similarly, if a child has learning disabilities, it is reasonable to help her/him to travel to, or take part in, social and recreational pursuits. A child's age and interests should be taken into account when deciding what is reasonable.[85]

Reasonably requires supervision

The requirement for supervision need only be reasonable. Most risks can be avoided by staying in a chair all day, but that may be totally unreasonable.[86] A child cannot be expected to avoid every risk of harm (eg, any situation in which s/he might fall) in order to avoid the need for her/him to have supervision.[87]

When considering a child's need for continual supervision (see p616), you can argue that the fact that supervision is provided shows it is needed. Bear in mind that the supervision must be substantially more than, or different from, the supervision a child the same age might normally require (see p611).

Refusing medical treatment

Refusing medical treatment for a child may affect whether or not s/he can get the care component. If treatment offered by her/his doctor would remove the need for help, the attention or supervision a child gets may not be reasonably required. However, it may not be 'reasonably appropriate' for you to agree to the treatment – eg, because of the risks or side effects.[88] Attention or supervision should be accepted as reasonable if you refuse invasive surgery for a child.[89]

Attention

The attention a child requires must be in connection with 'bodily functions' – ie, the normal action of any organ of the body, or a number of organs acting together.

The attention is in connection with bodily functions if it is a substitute method of providing what the function would provide were it not impaired.[90] For example, guiding a visually impaired child so that s/he is able to walk outside should be treated as attention with the bodily function of 'seeing', rather than of 'walking'. A guide assists with 'seeing' by acting 'as the eyes'. Similarly, help to push a child who uses a wheelchair should be treated as attention.[91]

'**Attention**' is 'a service of a close and intimate nature . . . involving personal contact carried out in the presence of the disabled person'.[92] So helping a child to drink counts; carrying the drinks to where s/he is sitting does not.[93] Although attention must usually involve personal contact, it need not be *physical* contact. Contact established by the spoken word may count if, for example, a child is blind.[94] Thus, reading, describing or giving verbal instructions can be attention.

Similarly, if a child needs to be cajoled or stimulated to do routine tasks, s/he may require attention in the form of active stimulation.[95] Spoken reassurance can count if it must be given in the physical presence of a child. Bear in mind that the attention must be substantially more than, or different from, the attention a child the same age might normally require (see p611).

Attention or supervision?

'**Attention**' involves a service of an 'active nature'.[96] '**Supervision**' is passive and 'may be precautionary or anticipatory, yet never result in intervention'.[97] Where supervision does lead to intervention, it becomes attention, so the two categories can overlap. If a child needs to be supervised because s/he is likely to fall and injure her/himself, s/he receives attention when a carer gives her/him a steadying hand or warns of an obstacle.[98] If attention is frequent, a child can get the middle rate care component, even if the supervision is not 'continual' throughout the day. Sometimes an act can be both supervision and attention. It is, therefore, important to emphasise the full extent of a child's needs without trying to fit them neatly into either category at the expense of leaving things out.

Communication

Communication involves several bodily functions, including functions of the brain (such as language processing, or comprehension) or the senses (such as hearing). You need to identify which bodily function is impaired and what attention is needed from another person in connection with that function.[99] If a child is profoundly deaf, s/he may need an interpreter because s/he cannot hear spoken language,[100] or extra effort may be required to initiate a two-way conversation.[101]

Explaining written information to a child with poor literacy skills as a result of deafness[102] or a learning disability may also qualify.[103]

Part 5: Other benefits
Chapter 28: Disability living allowance
2. Disability living allowance care component

Domestic duties

Although attention must normally be carried out in a child's presence, a period of attention can also include incidental activities that could take place without her/him. For example, if a carer strips a soiled bed at night, the additional tasks of wringing out the sheets or hanging them up to dry could count as attention if done on the spot, as would cleaning a soiled carpet in the event of incontinence.[104] Taking the washing away or doing the cleaning at a different time does not qualify as attention.

Domestic tasks performed by a carer outside a child's presence do not normally count as attention. There is conflicting caselaw on whether helping an older child do domestic tasks that children of the same age might normally do for themselves is attention that is reasonably required.[105] Helping a child who has a visual impairment to tidy up around the house is assistance with the bodily function of 'seeing' and can count as attention.[106] Similarly, helping a child with a learning disability to go shopping for clothes may include attention to help her/him communicate her/his requirements. Argue that if an older child can learn to tidy up at home or shop for her/himself, this is part of what constitutes a 'normal life' (see the definition of 'requires' on p612).[107]

Childcare

If an older child is a parent, help to enable her/him to look after her/his children can also count as attention.[108] For example, lifting or holding a baby for feeding is a sufficiently intimate service.[109] It will help if you can identify the bodily function in connection with which the child needs attention. Similarly, assistance to take part in outdoor activities with her/his children allows a young parent to lead a normal social life.[110] However, while help provided to a young parent with a disability may count as attention, help given directly to her/his child does not.[111]

Special diets

Attention only counts if it needs to be given in a child's physical presence, so it is often difficult to include help with food preparation. Arguably though, this type of help may count if it is part of a broader sequence of care tasks. For example, the various parts of the process of regulating the blood sugar levels of a younger diabetic child, some of which require personal contact and some of which do not, should all be treated as attention because they are integral elements of an overall regime.[112] A child with a learning disability or an eating disorder might need similar help to eat properly.

Night and day

A child who needs help using the toilet at 3am, when most people are asleep, clearly needs that help at night. Depending on the age of a child and the amount and type of help required, this may be help that children of the same age do not normally need. Problems showing that help is needed at night can arise when a child needs supervision or attention in the late evening or early morning.

'**Night**' is 'that period of inactivity' which begins when 'the household . . . closes down for the night'.[113] 'Night' is normally assumed to be the period beginning at around 11pm and ending around 7am.[114] The pattern of activities of each household needs to be taken into account. If a carer stays up late to help a child but would otherwise go to bed earlier, that should count as night care.[115] Similarly, if a carer gets up early in the morning to help her/him rather than rise later with the rest of the household, that should count as night care.[116] The definition of 'night' for a child is the same as for an adult, so that help given to a child in the evening before the adults have gone to bed counts only towards satisfying the day condition even if the child is in bed.[117]

'Attention . . . for a significant portion of the day'

If a child needs attention for a 'significant portion of the day', s/he can get the lowest rate care component.[118] This can be attention for either one period or a number of periods – eg, s/he could need help with activities connected with getting up at the beginning of the day, such as dressing and washing, and with activities connected with going to bed at the end of the day, such as undressing and washing, but otherwise not need extra help. Help at night does not count for the lowest rate.[119]

'A significant portion of the day' is often taken to mean an hour or thereabouts.[120] However, if a child's carer spends less time than that in total but has to give help for a number of short periods, that might qualify.[121]

If a carer does not have much time available or the help s/he gives is in spells of particularly concentrated activity, less than an hour's help may be enough. Factors like the amount, importance or effect of the attention may be taken into account.[122]

Frequent attention throughout the day

To satisfy the day attention condition, you must show that a child needs frequent attention throughout the day.[123] Frequency refers to the number and pattern of times attention is needed over a period of time, and should be considered as a whole.[124] A child may still qualify even if the times when attention is needed are not spread evenly throughout the day.[125] The aggregate amount of time taken up is not relevant. So it is possible for a child to need help frequently for a short period each time, and so get the middle rate care component, even if the total amount of time may not be regarded as a 'significant portion of the day', and so s/he might not get the lowest rate.[126]

If a child only needs help at the beginning and end of the day, this is unlikely to be accepted as frequent. Help with toileting (eg, to reach the toilet, use a commode or deal with zips) or help to walk inside the house are both examples of

Part 5: Other benefits
Chapter 28: Disability living allowance
2. Disability living allowance care component

activities that most children usually engage in frequently. Most children who satisfy this condition do so by virtue of a range of different types of care needs.

Prolonged or repeated attention at night

The attention a child needs during the night must be either prolonged or repeated.[127] There is no clear definition of 'prolonged'. An assumption that 20 minutes is prolonged has been accepted as a reasonable starting point, but shorter periods should also be considered.[128] 'Repeated' simply means twice or more.[129] There is no requirement that attention should be needed 'most of the time' – eg, on more than half the nights in a week. A broad overall judgement of a child's needs should be made.[130]

Because sleeping is a 'bodily function', soothing a child back to sleep counts as attention.[131]

Continual supervision

A child satisfies the daytime supervision condition if s/he requires another person to provide 'continual supervision' throughout the day to avoid the risk of substantial danger to the child or to others.[132] Supervision can be precautionary and anticipatory. It does not necessarily involve direct intervention. The supervision test has four aspects.[133]

- **There must be a substantial danger to a child or someone else as a result of her/his medical condition.** What is a 'substantial danger' must be decided on the facts of each case. For example, if a child falls and loses consciousness (eg, due to seizures), s/he would not be able to do anything to save her/himself from injury and so this is more likely to be a 'substantial danger' than if other children fall but only sustain minor bruises.

- **The substantial danger must be one against which it is reasonable to guard.** This involves weighing the remoteness of the risk and the seriousness of the consequences should it arise. For example, the consequences of allowing a child to run out onto the road could be dire, even though such an incident may be isolated.[134] Thus, it can be argued that the child reasonably requires continual supervision.[135] In assessing the likelihood of danger, the DWP must look at what has happened in the past as well as what may happen in the future.[136]

- **There must be a need for the supervision.** What counts is the level of supervision a child 'reasonably requires' (see p612). If s/he has mental health problems and is at risk of harming her/himself, it would be wrong to suggest that no amount of supervision would prevent a determined child from doing this and supervision is, therefore, not required. The correct approach is to decide whether supervision would result in 'a real reduction in the risk of harm' to her/him.[137]

- **The supervision must be continual.** This is less than 'continuous', but supervision which is required only occasionally or spasmodically is insufficient.[138] However, the fact that, for example, a child may need less supervision in a safe structured environment, such as school, does not mean that continual supervision is not required.[139] If it is unavoidable that a child is left alone for a period, s/he can still qualify if you can show that s/he is at risk during this time. A child who is liable to seizures without warning may need continual supervision, although attention for the period between the seizures is not required.[140] Even if s/he has warning of seizures and can prevent her/himself from falling, s/he may require continual supervision if s/he suffers from prolonged periods of confusion, or needs monitoring to make sure s/he comes out of the seizure safely.[141]

Bear in mind that the supervision a child requires must be substantially more than, or different from, the supervision normally needed by children of the same age (see p611).

Watching over
A child satisfies the night-time supervision condition if s/he needs someone to be awake to watch over her/him at night to avoid the risk of substantial danger to her/him or others.[142] The person watching over must be awake for a 'prolonged period' or 'at frequent intervals'. A 'prolonged period' may mean 20 minutes or more.[143] 'At frequent intervals' means more than twice. The frequent intervals need not be spread throughout the night, but can be concentrated in one part of the night.[144]

3. The rules about your age

New claims for disability living allowance (DLA) can only be made for children under 16.

The higher rate mobility component can be paid from age three onwards and the lower rate mobility component from age five.[145] The three months before the child reaches this age can form the qualifying period (see p603), enabling payment to be made from her/his birthday.

There is no lower age limit for DLA care component. However, a baby must still meet the qualifying conditions for three months before DLA becomes payable, unless s/he is terminally ill.[146]

See below for how the introduction of personal independence payment (PIP) affects a child's DLA when s/he turns 16.

Transferring from disability living allowance to personal independence payment

Personal independence payment (PIP) (see Chapter 35) has replaced disability living allowance (DLA) for working-age people.

Part 5: Other benefits
Chapter 28: Disability living allowance
3. The rules about your age

Note:

- the DWP has announced that some DLA awards will be extended due to the coronavirus pandemic, so you may not have to claim PIP as set out in this section.[147] See AskCPAG.org.uk and CPAG's *Welfare Rights Bulletin* for updates.
- if you get DLA and live in Scotland you may not be transferred to PIP as part of this process, unless your award is coming to an end or you report a relevant change in your circumstances (see p1688).[148]

Anyone who is 16 or over, was under 65 on 8 April 2013 and still gets DLA will be invited to claim PIP. You do not need to do anything until you are notified in writing by the DWP. You will also be invited to claim PIP if your DLA award expires or you report a relevant change in your circumstances (unless the change is that you are leaving Great Britain).[149] Always check letters about your DLA carefully to see whether you have been told to claim PIP.

If you are 65 or over when you are told to claim, you are assessed for PIP as if you were under 65 and so you will have access to all the components and rates of PIP.[150] If you are 65 or over and are not awarded any rate of PIP, your claim may be treated as a claim for attendance allowance (see Chapter 24).[151]

If you are 16 or over (and were under 65 on 8 April 2013), you can claim PIP, even if you are entitled to DLA and have not been sent a letter telling you to do so.[152]

Should you claim personal independence payment?

1. If you have received a letter saying that you must claim PIP, you should do so straight away as your DLA award will end (see p620).

2. If you have *not* been told to claim PIP, get specialist advice before claiming PIP, to help you decide whether it is a good idea. This is because the entitlement conditions are different and you may not qualify for PIP. If you claim PIP, your DLA award ends and you cannot change your mind.[153]

3. If you already get the higher rate mobility component and highest rate care component of DLA and have not been told to claim PIP, the DWP will advise you not to proceed with a claim for PIP unless your condition has improved.[154]

Note: if you get DLA and you turned 65 on or before 8 April 2013, you can continue to receive DLA for as long as you meet the qualifying conditions.[155] See p621 for how you can make a renewal claim for DLA or seek a different rate.

Transferring to personal independence payment on reaching age 16

If you are claiming DLA for a child, s/he will normally be invited to claim PIP when s/he reaches 16 and her/his DLA will end.[156] The DWP will normally write to explain this to you when the child is 15 years and seven months old. It will send a further letter when the child is 15 years and 10 months old, and then will write again when the child is 16 to invite her/him to claim PIP. **Note:** if a child gets DLA while s/he is a hospital inpatient, s/he is exempt from the transfer to PIP while s/he remains in hospital. This exemption applies even if you report a relevant change in her/his circumstances (eg, her/his care needs have changed) while s/he is in hospital.[157] **Note also:** if you are claiming DLA for a child in Scotland, her/his transfer to PIP when s/he reaches 16 may be affected by the introduction of new Scottish disability assistance (see Chapter 71).

If your child is about to turn 16 and her/his award of DLA for either component is for a fixed term that is due to end on the day before her/his 16th birthday or within the following six months, the DWP will extend the award until the day before s/he turns 17 or, if earlier, the day her/his DLA ends under the rules on transferring to PIP.[158] These extensions are to give her/him time to claim PIP and have a decision made on entitlement.

If your child gets DLA under the 'special rules' on the basis of terminal illness (see p623), s/he will only be invited to claim PIP when her/his current award expires.[159]

Always check letters about your DLA carefully to see whether you have been asked to claim PIP.

Claims for personal independence payment

If you are sent a written invitation to claim PIP, this must inform you that you have 28 days to make a claim and tell you how to do so. The 28-day time limit can be extended if the DWP thinks it is reasonable to do so.[160] The letter must also tell you that, if you do not claim PIP, your DLA award will end and when this will happen.[161]

You should claim PIP, following the instructions in the letter, as soon as possible, because your DLA award will end whether you claim PIP or not.[162] If you do not claim PIP within the time allowed, your DLA award is suspended from your next payment day.[163] You must be sent a letter explaining that your award has been suspended and will be terminated if you do not claim PIP within 28 days of the date on which it was suspended.[164] If you do so, your award of DLA is reinstated. If you still do not claim PIP, your DLA award ends from the date it was suspended.[165] You should make a new claim for PIP if you satisfy the rules of entitlement (see p740).

If you get DLA and have been invited to claim PIP or are in the process of claiming PIP and notify the DWP of a change of circumstances that may affect your entitlement to DLA, this is treated as a change of circumstances affecting your entitlement to PIP.[166]

See p764 for details of the assessment process once you claim PIP.

If you do not provide information needed to assess your entitlement to PIP (see p763) and do not have a good reason (see p766), your PIP claim will be refused. If

Part 5: Other benefits
Chapter 28: Disability living allowance
3. The rules about your age

this happens, your DLA award ends 14 days after the first DLA payday following the decision refusing your PIP claim.[167] If you win an appeal against the decision that you do not have good reason, your DLA award should be reinstated until a decision on your PIP claim is made.[168] If you are subsequently awarded PIP, it starts from the day after your DLA award ends (see below).[169]

These rules apply if you choose to claim PIP as well as if you are notified that your DLA will stop and invited to claim PIP.[170]

The qualifying conditions for PIP have some similarities to those for DLA, but are also significantly different. See Chapter 35 for details. It is possible that a young person claiming PIP on turning 16 will be awarded a different rate of PIP from the rate of DLA s/he previously received. If this applies to you, get advice and consider seeking a revision and then appealing. Although the qualifying conditions are different, the evidence used to make the previous DLA award may address the same needs for help with daily living and mobility as are relevant to the PIP conditions. The DWP (and the First-tier Tribunal on appeal) should consider this evidence where relevant.[171]

If you have a car through the Motability scheme (see p637) and are not awarded the enhanced rate mobility component of PIP when you transfer from DLA, you will no longer be able to continue in the Motability scheme. Contact Motability for details of support and transitional payments available.

When your disability living allowance ends

If you claim PIP, your DLA award continues until a decision is made on your PIP claim. Your DLA award ends:[172]
- if you are terminally ill (see p762) and your payment of PIP is higher than your payment of DLA was, on either the Tuesday after your PIP claim is decided or the day before your next normal DLA payday, whichever is earlier; *or*
- in any other case, four weeks after the next DLA payday after the decision is made on your PIP claim (whether or not you are awarded PIP).

Your entitlement to PIP starts from the day after your DLA award ends. The rules above also apply if your claim for DLA is refused and you then claim PIP, but the refusal is then overturned following a revision or appeal before your PIP claim is decided.[173] If your PIP claim is decided before the decision on your DLA refusal is changed, any DLA award that is later made to you ends on:[174]
- the day before your PIP award started; *or*
- four weeks after the next DLA payday following the decision to refuse you PIP.

If you withdraw your claim, or notify the DWP that you do not wish to claim PIP when invited to do so, your DLA award ends 14 days after the first DLA payday following the date you notified the DWP.[175]

You must be notified in writing of the date your DLA award ends and the start date of any PIP award.[176]

If you get disability living allowance and turned 65 on or before 8 April 2013

If you get DLA and turned 65 on or before 8 April 2013, you can continue to receive it and are unaffected by the introduction of PIP.

You can make a renewal claim if your DLA award expires, provided you reclaim within a year of the previous award ending.[177] If you are awarded the same rate, you can be paid without having to serve the standard qualifying period again.

If your condition has changed since you turned 65 so that you need more assistance, your award can be increased to the middle or highest rate of the care component. This applies regardless of which component or rate you previously had. You must show that you have met the qualifying conditions for the increased rate for six months (not three months) before it can be awarded, unless you had already completed a three-month qualifying period before you turned 65.[178] This is because the rules about qualifying periods for people in receipt of DLA care component at the age of 65 or over are the same as for attendance allowance (AA).[179] This applies both when a renewal claim is made and when an award is revised or superseded.

If you have an existing award of DLA that was made before you turned 65 (ie, not an award made on a renewal claim, or on a revision or supersession decision, after you turned 65), you can be awarded any rate of either component if you request a revision or supersession of your award after you are 65, provided you show that you have satisfied the disability conditions for the new rate or component since before you turned 65.[180] Otherwise, you cannot qualify for either rate of the mobility component or the lowest rate of the care component for the first time after you turned 65.

If your award was made after you turned 65 (either on a renewal claim or on a revision or supersession of a decision) and you have an award of the lower rate of the mobility component, it cannot be increased to the higher rate of the mobility component after you have turned 65. If you have an award of either rate of the mobility component, you can be awarded the middle or highest rate of the care component on a renewal claim or a revision or supersession, but not the lowest rate.[181]

Examples

Tom turned 65 in 2010, and is now 74. Tom has MS, and has received the middle rate of the care component and the higher rate of the mobility component of DLA since he was 64. Tom's award expires when he turns 75. Because he was 65 before 8 April 2013, Tom can make a renewal claim for DLA. His mobility has not changed, but the DWP accepts that he now needs sufficient care at night to qualify for the highest rate care component. An indefinite award of the highest rate of the care component and the higher rate of the mobility component is made on the renewal claim. The DWP accepts that Tom's night-time needs have existed for six months, and so the new rate is paid from the date his renewal award starts.

Part 5: Other benefits
Chapter 28: Disability living allowance
3. The rules about your age

Sheila turned 65 on 8 March 2013, and is now 72. Sheila has an indefinite award of the middle rate of the care component, which was made in 2001. Sheila's condition has deteriorated steadily since the award was made, and for several years she has been able to walk only very short distances, and only with severe discomfort. She is advised to request a supersession of her award. The DWP accepts that Sheila has been virtually unable to walk since before she turned 65. Her award is superseded to include the higher rate of the mobility component from the date of her supersession request.

If it has been over a year since your last DLA award ended, you must claim AA (see Chapter 24) instead of DLA. If you make a renewal claim for DLA in these circumstances, it will be treated as a claim for AA.

Differences in the rules for adults

There are some important differences between the rules for DLA for adults and those for children that are described in this chapter. See Chapter 27 of the 2015/16 edition of this *Handbook* for full details of the rules for adults.

The most important points are the following.

1. Adults can qualify for the lowest rate of the care component on the basis of a 'cooking test'.[182] This rule does not apply to children. Under the cooking test, you qualify if you are so severely disabled, physically or mentally, that you cannot prepare a cooked main meal for yourself if you have the ingredients. This is not about whether, or how, you actually cook. It is a hypothetical test about what you can reasonably do. It looks at whether you can do all the tasks to cook a labour-intensive, freshly cooked main meal for one using a traditional cooker. It should look at your ability to, for example, plan a meal, chop and prepare food, use kitchen equipment, lift pans and tell when food is cooked properly.

2. The additional requirements test that a child must satisfy before s/he can qualify for the care component (see p611) or the lower rate mobility component (see p608) does not apply to adults. So you just need to show that you satisfy the disability conditions to qualify for benefit. You do not need to show that the attention or supervision you need is more, or of a different type, than assistance other adults might need.

3. The types of assistance an adult needs, and the reason for needing the assistance, may be different from those that apply to a child. The examples explained in this chapter focus on the needs and assistance that are most relevant to children. If you need different types of assistance, or assistance for other reasons, make sure you explain those. Do not assume that you will not qualify for DLA. For example, the types of assistance an adult needs to enjoy a normal life (including a reasonable social life), with domestic tasks or to communicate, will be quite different from a child's needs. If you need attention or supervision because of, for example, alcohol or drug dependency, or to prevent risk of harm because of mental health problems, make sure you explain those. If you live alone and do not get all the attention or supervision you need, remember that it is the help you reasonably require that counts, not the help you actually get.

4. People included in the claim

You claim disability living allowance for a child under 16.

5. The amount of benefit

Disability living allowance (DLA) mobility component is paid at one of two weekly rates:[183]
- the lower rate is £23.60;
- the higher rate is £62.25.

DLA care component is paid at one of three weekly rates:[184]
- the lowest rate is £23.60;
- the middle rate is £59.70;
- the highest rate is £89.15.

6. Special benefit rules

Special rules may apply to children:
- on renal dialysis (see below);
- who are terminally ill (see below);
- subject to immigration control (see Chapter 67);
- who have come from or are going abroad (see Chapters 68, 69 and 70);
- in hospital or a hospice or living in a care home or other similar accommodation, or in a young offenders' institution or other form of detention (see Chapter 42).

Renal dialysis

If a child has renal dialysis on a kidney machine, special rules may allow her/him to get the middle rate of disability living allowance (DLA) care component.[185] The rules are the same as for attendance allowance (AA) (see p536).

Terminal illness

If a child is terminally ill, s/he is automatically treated as satisfying the conditions for the highest rate of the DLA care component and does not need to satisfy the three-month qualifying period.[186] Claims for children who are terminally ill are referred to as 'claims under the special rules' (see p625). The rules are the same as for AA (see p536).[187]

Part 5: Other benefits
Chapter 28: Disability living allowance
7. Claims and backdating

S/he does not automatically get DLA mobility component. S/he must satisfy the usual disability conditions (except the three-month qualifying period) and be likely to continue to satisfy them for the next six months (see p603) until the anticipated date of death.[188]

7. **Claims and backdating**

The general rules about claims and backdating are covered in Chapter 50. This section explains the specific rules that apply to disability living allowance (DLA).

Making a claim

A claim for DLA must be in writing. You should do this by completing the approved claim form (DLA1A Child). It is best to request a form by telephone from the DLA helpline (see below). The DWP may complete a checklist to assess a child's 'potential benefit entitlement'. This is not part of the claim process and you should always be sent a claim form. It is best to send the completed form to the address on it (Disability Benefit Centre 4, Post Handling Site B, Wolverhampton WV99 1BY). You can also take or send it to any other DWP office, and may be able to take or send it to an 'alternative office' (see p1168).

Forms
Form DLA1A Child is available from the DLA helpline on 0800 121 4600; textphone: 0800 121 4523; Relay UK: 18001 then 0800 121 4600.

The form should be date stamped. You have six weeks from the date of your request to return it. If you return it within this time, the date you requested it will be treated as your date of claim.[189] Keep a record of the date you asked for the form.

Claim forms are also available from Citizens Advice or other advice agencies. A version of the form that can be filled in online and then printed is available at gov.uk. These forms are not date stamped. Send in the completed form as soon as possible. Your date of claim is the date your completed form is received by the DWP (see p625 for details).

Note: the success of a DLA claim can often depend on how well you have completed the form. Include all the relevant information and use extra pages if necessary. Keep a copy of the form in case queries arise. For tips on completing the form, see p627.

You must provide any information required (see p625). In certain circumstances, the DWP may accept a written application which is not on the approved form (see p1173).[190] You can amend or withdraw the claim before a decision is made (see p1169).

Claims for terminally ill children are made in a different way (see below).

Who should claim

A claim for a child under 16 is made by an appointee (see p1170). This is usually the child's parent. We use 'you' throughout this chapter to refer to the appointee who is claiming on behalf of a child.

Before a child reaches 16, the DWP should ask whether s/he will continue to need an appointee or will be able to handle her/his own benefits affairs.[191] See p617 for how the introduction of personal independence payment (PIP) affects DLA for a child when s/he turns 16.

Claiming for a child who is terminally ill

If you are claiming on the basis of a child's terminal illness (see p623), you must tick the box on the claim form to say you are claiming under the 'special rules'.[192] In addition to the claim form you must provide Form DS1500, completed by the child's GP, consultant or specialist nurse, detailing her/his medical condition. However, you do not need to fill in the parts of the claim form relating to her/his need for personal care. If you also wish to claim the mobility component for the child, you must answer all the relevant questions on the claim form. If the DWP decides that the child does not meet the special rules, you can claim in the normal way or request a mandatory reconsideration of the decision.

Information to support your claim

For the general information requirements that apply to all benefits, see p1170.

It is important that you provide any information required when you claim. Until you do, you may not count as having made a valid claim (see p1172). Correct any defects as soon as possible or your date of claim may be affected. **Note:** for DLA, there is no requirement to provide a national insurance number for a child under 16.

For suggestions about evidence you might want to provide when completing the claim form, see p627.

Even if you have provided all that was required when you claimed, you may be asked to provide further information to support the claim (see p1174). You may be asked to provide information after DLA is awarded, and if you fail to do so, DLA could be suspended or even terminated (see p1200).

The date of your claim

The date of your child's claim is important as it determines when her/his entitlement to DLA starts. This is not necessarily the date from when DLA is paid. For information about when payment of DLA starts, see p632.

Part 5: Other benefits
Chapter 28: Disability living allowance
7. Claims and backdating

The date of claim is not necessarily the date it is received by the DWP. The **'date of claim'** is the date your request for a claim pack is received by the DWP or an 'alternative office' (see p1168), provided you return the properly completed form within six weeks of the date of your request.[193]

If the DWP has issued a form without date stamping it, write and explain when and where it was issued and ask to be paid from that date or six weeks before you sent it in.[194] The DWP can extend the six-week deadline if it considers that it is reasonable, so if you return the form late, explain why.[195]

If you are using a claim form issued by an advice agency or downloaded from the internet, your date of claim is the date the DWP receives your completed form.

Note: you must make sure the claim is valid. If it is 'defective', you are given a short time to correct the defects (see p1173). If you do, the claim is treated as having been made when you initially claimed.[196]

In some cases, a claim can be made in advance (see below). If you want to do this, make this clear when you claim or the DWP might not consider it. If a claim was made for attendance allowance (AA) or PIP instead of DLA, see p573.

Backdating your claim

It is very important to claim in time. A claim for DLA *cannot* be backdated.[197]

If a child might have qualified for benefit earlier but you did not claim because you were given the wrong information or were misled by the DWP, you could ask for a compensation payment (see p1439) or complain to the Ombudsman through your MP (see p1444).

If you claim the wrong benefit

If you claim AA or PIP by mistake for a child under 16 instead of DLA, the claim for AA or PIP can be treated as a claim for DLA, and vice versa (see p1182).[198]

Claiming in advance

A claim for DLA can be made before a child has satisfied the three-month qualifying period[199] or any other qualifying condition. Provided you claim no more than three months before s/he would qualify for DLA, a decision can be made on the claim in advance of her/his date of entitlement. The date of the claim is the date on which the child qualifies.

Renewal claims

Note: the DWP has announced that some DLA awards may be extended due to the coronavirus pandemic. See AskCPAG.org.uk and CPAG's *Welfare Rights Bulleting* for updates.

DLA can be awarded for fixed periods (see p633). Renewal claims can be invited up to six months before an award expires. Send back your renewal claim form well before the old award expires.

The DWP normally treats a renewal claim as a new claim beginning on the day after an award ends.[200] However, the information you give in the renewal claim may be used to revise or supersede the child's existing award, in which case her/his entitlement may be changed earlier.[201] If you think a child has a strong case for an increased award, return the renewal form early and ask for a revision or supersession. If this is not the case, it is advisable to return the form nearer the date her/his current award runs out, but in time for a decision to be made before it does run out.

On a renewal claim, a child does not have to serve the three-month qualifying period again, provided s/he meets all the other qualifying conditions for the rate s/he previously received. The last three months of the previous award is treated as the qualifying period.[202] However, if s/he qualifies for a different rate when you reclaim, s/he does have to show that s/he has met the qualifying conditions for three months.

When a child approaches age 16, s/he will normally be required to claim PIP, rather than make a renewal claim for DLA. See p617 for details.

See p617 for how the introduction of PIP affects adults who get DLA (including those who turned 65 after 8 April 2013) and p621 for how adults who receive DLA and turned 65 on or before 8 April 2013 can make a renewal claim for DLA.

Completing the claim form

The DLA claim form is long and asks about different aspects of a child's mobility problems and supervision and attention needs. If you find it difficult to complete the form, the DWP can help you by telephone or, in some circumstances, can send a visiting officer to your home. Most advice agencies can also help. The following advice should help you fill in the form as fully as possible.

- **Give as much detail as you can.** Fill in all the pages that are relevant. If the same difficulties apply on more than one page, repeat the information or refer back to earlier in the form. The same help may count towards both the care component and the mobility component – eg, if a child needs attention to deal safely with seizures, this may help satisfy the conditions for the care component but may also mean that s/he needs guidance and supervision when walking outdoors.[203] Do not feel bound by the size of the boxes. If you need extra space to explain the child's situation, use a separate piece of paper. Do not worry if a lot of the questions do not apply to the child. The information you give in just one section could be enough for her/him to get DLA. There is space to include details of people who know about her/his difficulties – include carers and support workers, as well as medical professionals. There is also a statement to be completed by someone who knows the child. If her/his doctor or hospital fills this in, they should not charge for this.[204] If you do not have anyone who can complete it, leave it blank.
- **Aids and adaptions.** The form asks about aids and adaptations the child uses or has been assessed for. If the DWP thinks that a child can use a particular aid or adaptation, it may decide the child does not need attention or supervision.

Part 5: Other benefits
Chapter 28: Disability living allowance
7. Claims and backdating

Therefore, try to explain how useful any equipment actually is, the help the child needs to use it and whether s/he still needs extra help from another person in spite of the equipment. If, for instance, you have had a bath rail fitted, but s/he still finds it very difficult to climb in or out of a bath, explain this. If a child uses picture cards to communicate, explain the amount of help s/he needs to use them, and how long this takes to communicate effectively compared to communication with a non-disabled child.

- **Frequency, variability and duration.** You are asked throughout the form to estimate how long the child needs help for, and how often. You should explain:
  - how long s/he needs help for, to show that s/he needs attention for a 'significant portion of the day' (see p615) or 'prolonged' attention at night (see p616);
  - how often s/he needs help, to show that s/he needs 'frequent attention throughout the day' (see p615) or watching over 'repeatedly' during the night (see p617);
  - how many days a week s/he needs help, to establish her/his overall needs, particularly if s/he has a variable or fluctuating condition. If the child's condition does not vary but s/he only receives all the help s/he needs on certain days, say that s/he needs help seven days a week. It is the help needed, not the help s/he gets, that counts. If s/he only has problems a few days a week, s/he may still get DLA. It is the broad overall picture of needs that counts, not simply comparing the number of 'good' days and 'bad' days.[205] Explain fully the help s/he needs on 'bad' days, but include the help needed on 'good' days as well so that you give an overall picture.

- **Mobility.** See p604 and p608 and the tactics on p630 for how to describe a child's walking ability or the help s/he needs getting about outdoors. Children can only qualify for DLA mobility component from the age of three, but problems with getting around may also indicate care or supervision needs, so explain these even if the child is younger than three. It can be difficult to explain how a child with a disability requires 'substantially more' guidance or supervision outdoors in order to qualify for the lower rate mobility component (see p608). Most young children do not go out, at least in unfamiliar places, on their own. However, a child with a sensory impairment or learning disability may require much more direct or close supervision than a non-disabled child.[206] A child may normally be allowed to walk in the presence of an adult, but a child with a disability may require an adult to hold or guide her/him. Also, even a familiar route may be hazardous to a child whose sight is impaired. It may help to make comparisons with siblings or classmates. A child with attention deficit disorder may need to be accompanied to school or to local shops, whereas other children might be allowed to go alone.[207]

- **Extra attention, supervision or guidance.** When explaining a child's 'extra' requirements, bear in mind that they must be 'substantially in excess' of those required by a child of the same age who does not have a disability (see p608 and p611). It can be difficult to explain what is 'substantially in excess' of the norm. It may be either because of the extra time you devote or the degree of attention, supervision or guidance a child requires.[208] The fact that it may not be unusual for some children of the same age to require similar assistance is the wrong approach. The comparison should be with an 'average child' the same age – ie, a child of average intelligence whose behaviour is neither particularly good nor bad.[209] Children with a disability may need extra help to develop daily living skills, language and social skills. For example, babies with sensory impairments may require more physical stimulation to aid parental bonding and develop communication skills. A child with a disability might need intensive help with eating, whereas children of the same age might be expected to eat unaided or only need certain foods cut up. Similarly, a child with a disability may need supervision to avoid dangers that children would usually be expected to deal with themselves by her/his age. A child with a disability may need help to use toys, may need to be coaxed to explore her/his environment and may develop these skills later than other children. Similarly, you may let a non-disabled child play outdoors and instruct her/him not to cross roads. You may be able to supervise the child indirectly without having to watch her/him all the time. However, you may have to supervise directly a child with sensory impairments or behavioural problems, or keep her/him indoors. Consider also whether certain activities are more difficult for the child than usual – eg, if they cause her/him pain, or make her/him dizzy, tired or breathless. If s/he takes a long time to perform particular tasks, explain this. Also say if s/he is not able to perform a particular activity adequately – eg, if s/he cannot bend to reach her/his feet when washing.

• **Sensory impairments.** There are sections on help with seeing, hearing, speaking and communication. The specific needs of deaf children for an interpreter or other help with communicating or reading, or blind children to have books or correspondence read to them, can be described here. Blind children may need additional help with lots of daily activities. Explain the help required throughout the form. For example, they may need someone to tell them if they have stains on their clothes or if their hands are clean – you should explain these problems in the 'dressing' and 'washing' sections and not just in the 'seeing' section. The help a child with a sensory impairment needs to undertake social and leisure activities should also be explained.

• **Communicating.** Prelingual deaf children whose first language is British Sign Language may need help to understand or communicate in written or spoken English. Blind children will not only need help to understand written information, but may also need help to learn Braille. Children with learning difficulties may need help to express themselves, understand other people or follow instructions or warnings.

Part 5: Other benefits
Chapter 28: Disability living allowance
7. Claims and backdating

- **Mental disabilities.** In the sections on help with communication and on supervision during the day, you should mention any problems caused by anxiety, intrusive thoughts or anger, or learning difficulties. Remember that a child who needs encouraging or prompting to do things can get DLA, as well as one who needs physical help with them. If s/he needs assistance to undertake social or leisure activities, information about that help may also fit in the mobility section of the form. At the end of the form there is a page to 'tell us anything else you think we should know'. It often helps to summarise mental health problems here and explain any other attention or supervision needs the child has.

- **About the child's development.** Describing the extra care or supervision that a child needs compared to others is extremely important. If you are not sure when a child should normally be crawling, walking, speaking, playing with others, understanding instructions, using the toilet independently, feeding her/himself, and so on, ask your health visitor or paediatrician. For example, most children pick up and eat food by 8–12 months. Therefore, if you are still feeding a child after 12 months, you are providing attention that a non-disabled child of the same age would not need. It often helps to make comparisons with other children you know. When completing renewal forms, always describe all the child's needs. Bear in mind that, if you do not mention something, the DWP may suppose that the child no longer needs the same help as s/he did when s/he was younger. However, it is wrong for the DWP to assume that all children with disabilities develop in the same way.

- **Children of nursery or school age.** Children who have a disability, particularly those with sensory impairments or learning disabilities, usually require extra help with learning and school work. This should be explained, as well as other help (eg, help going to the toilet) that they may need at school or nursery. Extra help in the classroom or with homework due to special educational needs can count towards a child's attention needs, as cognition is a bodily function of the brain (see p613).[210] Straightforward teaching would probably not be sufficiently intimate to qualify,[211] but additional help (eg, because of dyslexia) may count.[212]

- **When the child is in bed at night.** Only the needs the child has after the rest of the household has gone to bed count as night-time needs (see p614).

What evidence should you provide?

When making a claim, and especially when preparing for an appeal, ensure that you have as much evidence as possible to support what you say about the child in the claim pack. This can include any of the following.

Evidence that you provide about your knowledge of the child

About her/his care needs. Often the easiest way for the DWP or First-tier Tribunal to get a picture of a child's care needs and their pattern is for you to keep a diary for a week or a month. Use this to record variations in her/his condition and the help s/he needs. This can be particularly useful if s/he has unpredictable care needs or experiences irregular events, such as seizures or falls, which mean that s/he needs extra supervision. Usually this is best presented as a table. The DLA claim form shows an example. You can also ask other carers, friends or other family members to keep a diary, or write letters in support of the claim or appeal.

About her/his walking ability. Walk outdoors with the child to measure the distance s/he can walk without severe discomfort, then write a description of the time it takes to walk this far. It may help to give an example of the distance – eg, 'S/he can walk past five houses – about 40 metres.'

Describe the terrain. Is it rough or uneven? Are there steps or slopes which present her/him with problems?

Explain what sort of discomfort s/he experiences (eg, pain or breathlessness) and how it changes as s/he walks.

Describe her/his manner of walking – eg, s/he may have problems with balance, or may walk with a limp, drag her/his feet or shuffle.

Say if the child needs to stop to rest. Try to explain how far s/he can walk before s/he needs to stop, and for how long s/he needs to rest. Bear in mind that if s/he can walk a further distance without severe discomfort after a brief rest, it is the total distance that counts.

It might help to download a map or satellite picture from the internet and measure the distances on it.

Go somewhere unfamiliar with the child and describe all the difficulty s/he has and the guidance s/he needs.

Evidence from third parties

Doctors' reports. These could be reports which have already been provided by specialists to the child's GP. Often hospital doctors will send copies of reports to the child's parent/guardian when they write them. The GP can be asked for copies of any reports you do not have from the child's medical records. Alternatively, ask the GP or specialist to write a specific letter for the child's claim or appeal. The doctor may charge for writing reports and providing copies from the child's records. It is not usually worth providing hospital appointment letters and other routine documents which do not comment on the child's diagnosis, treatment or disability. The DWP may request a specific report from the child's GP. It can help to make an appointment to discuss the day-to-day problems s/he has before this is written.

Reports from other medical professionals. Reports from health visitors, physiotherapists, psychiatric and other specialist nurses and occupational therapists can often provide more detailed information about a child's disability and how it affects her/his day-to-day life than reports from doctors, who only discuss symptoms and treatment.

Social services and educational reports. If a child has had a social care needs assessment, statement of special educational needs or other care or support plan, this may provide useful supporting evidence of the extra help s/he needs.

> **DWP medical services assessments.** The DWP's decisions can be based on reports prepared by doctors or other healthcare professionals acting on behalf of the DWP to assess your child's entitlement to DLA. These should not necessarily be preferred to your own evidence or to that of your doctor. You should examine any report carefully and explain why any unhelpful findings or assessments are wrong. If, however, the assessment report supports your claim, you should highlight this.

How your claim is dealt with

DLA can be awarded on the basis of the claim form alone, but the DWP may choose to contact someone you have named on the form for more information. It is a good idea to include details of all the medical professionals and other people who know and understand the child's needs and, if possible, enclose evidence from them.

The DWP may telephone you to ask for further information. If you do not want to be telephoned, write this clearly on the claim form.

If the DWP cannot get sufficient information, it may also arrange for the child to be given a medical examination by a healthcare professional acting on behalf of the DWP, who will sometimes visit her/him at home.

If you (or an older child) refuse a medical examination 'without good cause', the claim is likely to be refused.[213]

The DWP aims to deal with new claims for DLA within 40 working days. Claims made under the special rules for terminal illness (see p623) should be decided more quickly. If you disagree with the decision, you can ask for a revision and then appeal (see Chapters 56 and 57) on behalf of the child. See p630 for suggestions about the evidence you can use to support a claim, revision or appeal.

8. Getting paid

The general rules on getting paid are covered in Chapter 51. This section explains the specific rules that apply to disability living allowance (DLA).

As DLA is claimed for a child under the age of 16, it is usually paid to an adult with whom s/he is living. The DWP appoints the adult (an 'appointee') to act on the child's behalf. The appointee is normally the child's parent.[214]

DLA can continue to be paid to the appointee in some circumstances when the child and appointee are not living together, including during a temporary separation of up to 12 weeks, or when the child is absent at a boarding school or in residential care (although other rules may mean that payment stops in such circumstances – see Chapter 42). DLA ceases to be paid to the appointee immediately when the child is in the care of a local authority or any similar arrangement, unless the arrangement is not intended to last for more than 12 weeks.[215]

When is disability living allowance paid?
You are normally paid on a Wednesday, but the DWP can vary the payday.[216] DLA is usually paid every four weeks in arrears. However:
– DLA can be paid at shorter intervals in individual cases;[217]
– DLA under the special rules for terminal illness can be paid weekly.
If the child leaves a care home and expects to return within 28 days, DLA can be paid at a daily rate for days at home.[218]

Note:
- If you get other DWP benefits, DLA may be paid in a single payment with them instead.
- The higher rate of the DLA mobility component can be paid direct to Motability if you are buying a car through the scheme (see p637).
- Even if you have been sanctioned for a benefit offence (see p1278), you must be paid DLA.
- For information on missing payments, see p1189. If you cannot get your DLA payments because you have lost your bank or post office card or you have forgotten your PIN, see p1188. If you have lost your payment service card, see p1189.
- If payment of DLA is delayed, see p1295. If you wish to complain about how your claim has been dealt with, or claim compensation, see Chapter 60.
- If payment of a child's DLA is suspended, see p1200. If you have been overpaid DLA, you might have to repay it (see Chapter 53) and, in some circumstances, you may have to pay a penalty (see p1268). If you have been accused of fraud, see Chapter 54.

Length of awards

Awards of DLA can be made for either fixed or indefinite periods.[219] The length of an award depends on how long the DWP estimates the child's current needs may last.

Awards are usually made for at least six months because of the requirement that a child should satisfy the disability conditions for the next six months. However, there is no legal minimum length for an award.[220] If you think benefit should be awarded for longer, perhaps because the child's condition is such that her/his care or mobility needs will not decrease, consider asking for a revision (see p1303). Bear in mind that if you challenge the length of an award, the rate of the award may also be reconsidered. Even if a child has a longer-term award, the DWP can reduce or stop the award if it has grounds to revise or supersede it.

Part 5: Other benefits
Chapter 28: Disability living allowance
9. Tax, other benefits and the benefit cap

If an award is for a limited period, you will be invited to make a renewal claim up to six months before the award runs out (see p626).

A 'special rules' award (see p623) on the basis of terminal illness is normally made for three years. If there is already a mobility award in place, the length of the special rules award may be adjusted to finish at the same time as the mobility award.

Although DLA has two components, there can only be a single DLA award, consisting of one or both components. If a child has an award of both components, they must be aligned to end on the same day (even if they started at different times).[221]

See p617 for how the introduction of personal independence payment affects DLA when a child reaches 16 (even if s/he currently has an indefinite award of DLA).

Change of circumstances

You must report any change in a child's circumstances that you have been told you must report, as well as any that you might reasonably be expected to know might affect her/his right to, the amount of, or payment of DLA. You should do this as soon as possible, preferably in writing. See p1199 for further information.

If a child's condition deteriorates so that s/he becomes eligible for a higher rate or another component, benefit can be backdated to the day s/he becomes eligible, provided you tell the DWP no later than a month after s/he completes the three-month qualifying period. If payment of (but not entitlement to) DLA has stopped (eg, while a child is in a care home), still notify the DWP of any change so that the correct rate is paid when payment resumes.

If you do not report a change of circumstances within the month, benefit can still be backdated if you do so within 13 months and there were 'special circumstances' that meant it was not practical to report the change earlier.[222]

If a child's condition improves so that s/he should drop down a rate, lose a component or lose benefit altogether, the new decision normally takes effect from the date you tell the DWP of the improvement, or from the date of the decision if the DWP changed it without your asking.[223] It only takes effect from an earlier date (and causes an overpayment) if you should have realised earlier that the change should have been reported. It is accepted that it may be difficult to realise when a gradual improvement begins to affect benefit entitlement.[224]

9. **Tax, other benefits and the benefit cap**

Tax

Disability living allowance (DLA) is not taxable.[225]

Means-tested benefits and tax credits

DLA for a child is not taken into account as income when calculating any of the means-tested benefits or tax credits for a person who has responsibility for the child. DLA is paid on top of these benefits and tax credits, and getting DLA can increase the amount of them (or mean that the person qualifies for them for the first time, if her/his income was previously too high).

If your child is entitled to DLA, you may qualify for one or more of the following extra amounts:

- a disabled child addition in your universal credit (UC) if you come under the UC system (see p23). This is paid at the higher rate if s/he is entitled to the highest rate care component. **Note:** the disabled child addition is included for the child even if the child element is not received because of the 'two-child limit' (see p66);
- a disabled child premium (see p341) in your housing benefit (HB). If s/he gets the highest rate care component, your HB also includes an enhanced disability premium (see p343). These premiums are also included in your income support (IS) and income-based jobseeker's allowance (JSA) if you do not get child tax credit (CTC). **Note:** these premiums are included for the child even if a personal allowance is not received for the child because of the 'two-child limit' (see p66);
- a disabled child element in your CTC for each child who gets DLA (at any rate). If s/he gets the highest rate care component, a severely disabled child element is included in CTC (see p1456). If one or both of these elements should have been included in your CTC but has not been, get advice. **Note:** these elements are included for the child even if the child element is not received because of the 'two-child limit' (see p1456).

If you or your partner receive DLA, you may qualify for one or more of the following extra amounts:

- the disabled worker element in working tax credit (WTC). If you or your partner get the highest rate care component, a severe disability element is included in WTC (two elements are included if you both get the highest rate). See Chapter 61 for further information;
- a disability premium (see p341) in your IS, income-based JSA and, unless you have reached pension age, HB (or for IS and JSA only, higher pensioner premium (see p345) if either of you have reached pension age). If you or your partner are entitled to the highest rate care component and aged under pension age, you also get an enhanced disability premium (see p343). This is also paid with income-related employment and support allowance (ESA) (see p343);
- a severe disability premium/addition is included in your IS, income-based JSA, income-related ESA, the guarantee credit of pension credit (PC) and HB, if you

Part 5: Other benefits
Chapter 28: Disability living allowance
9. Tax, other benefits and the benefit cap

receive the highest or middle rate care component and meet the other conditions for that premium/addition (see p346).

No housing costs contributions from a non-dependant are taken into account when calculating your UC housing costs element if you, your partner or the non-dependant get the DLA middle or highest rate care component, or would get it but for being in hospital (see p103). If you or your partner get any rate of the care component, non-dependant deductions (see p199) are *not* made from any housing costs covered by your HB (see p199), or from any housing costs included in your IS, income-based JSA, income-related ESA or the guarantee credit of PC (see p364).

If you or your partner have reached pension age but you claim UC because the other person has not yet reached this age, and the person over pension age is entitled to DLA, you may still qualify for the limited capability for work element in your UC award (see p70). If the person over pension age is entitled to the highest rate care component, you get the limited capability for work-related activity element in your UC award instead (see p72).

Non-means-tested benefits

You can get DLA in addition to any other non-means-tested benefits, except that:
- DLA overlaps with armed forces independence payment;[226]
- DLA care component overlaps with attendance allowance and constant attendance allowance under the industrial injuries scheme (see p694) or war pensions scheme (see p868);[227] *and*
- DLA mobility component overlaps with the war pensioners' mobility supplement payable under the war pensions scheme (see p868).[228]

See p1190 for details of the overlapping benefits rules.

You cannot be paid both DLA and personal independence payment (see p739).

A person who regularly looks after a child or adult who gets the highest or middle rate care component may be entitled to carer's allowance (CA) (see Chapter 26), and s/he (or her/his partner if claiming as a couple) may also get a carer element in UC (see p73), a carer premium in IS, income-based JSA, income-related ESA or HB, or a carer addition in the guarantee credit of PC (see p350). However, if you are an adult and your carer gets CA or a carer element in UC, it may affect your entitlement to a severe disability premium (or additional amount) so always get advice.

A young person aged 16, 17 or 18 living in Scotland who cannot get CA may be able to get a young carer grant for looking after you (see Chapter 75).

The benefit cap

In some cases, there is a limit on the total amount of specified benefits you can get (a 'benefit cap'). DLA is *not* one of the specified benefits. The benefit cap does *not* apply if you, your partner or child get DLA (even if it is not paid because the person entitled is in hospital or a care home). In other cases, it only applies if you are getting UC or HB. See p1194 for further information.

Passports and other sources of help

You qualify for a Christmas bonus if you receive DLA at any rate (see p870). If you are on a low income, you may be entitled to council tax reduction (see p851).

If you get the higher rate mobility component, you or your carer can be exempt from paying road tax on a car used solely by you or for you. Contact the Disability Benefit Centre (see p624) for an exemption certificate.

If you get the higher rate mobility component, you should qualify for the blue badge scheme of parking concessions, which operates throughout Great Britain and the European Economic Area (with certain local variations). Contact your local authority for further information.

If any member of your household receives DLA at any rate, you can get a grant for help with insulation and other energy efficiency measures in your home (see p872) and may be entitled to other benefits, such as concessionary travel.

Motability

Motability is a charity that runs a scheme to help you lease or buy a car if you receive (or a child for whom you are responsible receives) the higher rate of DLA mobility component for a period of 12 months or more (see p603). DLA mobility component is paid direct to Motability.[229] You may also have to make extra payments. For further information, telephone 0300 456 4566 or visit motability.co.uk.

Notes

1. Disability living allowance mobility component
1 ss71(6) and 73 SSCBA 1992
2 CM/5/1986; *BP v SSWP* [2009] UKUT 90 (AAC)
3 s73 SSCBA 1992; reg 12(1)(b) SS(DLA) Regs
4 Reg 12(1)(a) SS(DLA) Regs
5 R(M) 3/78
6 Reg 12(1)(a) SS(DLA) Regs; R(M) 2/78; R(DLA) 4/06
7 CDLA/1525/2008

8 CDLA/2822/1999; CDLA/4329/2001
9 *MMF v SSWP (DLA)* [2012] UKUT 312 (AAC)
10 R(M) 3/86; CSDLA/202/2007; CDLA/3839/2007; *DM v SSWP (DLA)* [2010] UKUT 375 (AAC)
11 R(M) 2/89; CDLA/97/2001; *Sandhu v SSWP* [2010] EWCA Civ 962
12 Reg 12(4) SS(DLA) Regs
13 R(M) 2/89
14 Reg 12(1)(b) SS(DLA) Regs

15 CDLA/3188/2002; *HJ v SSWP (DLA)* [2010] UKUT 307 (AAC)
16 R(M) 1/95; CSDLA/171/1998
17 CM/208/1989
18 *JK v SSWP (DLA)* [2010] UKUT 197 (AAC)
19 CDLA/1389/1997; CDLA/2195/2008
20 R(M) 1/81
21 R(M) 2/92
22 R(M) 1/83
23 CM/267/93; CDLA/608/1994; R(DLA) 4/03
24 R(DLA) 4/04
25 *Hewitt and Diment v CAO* 29 June 1998, reported as R(DLA) 6/99
26 R(M) 1/98; CDLA/3941/2005 interpreted 'exertion' to mean the activity of walking 'however slight the exertion'
27 *KS v SSWP (DLA)* [2013] UKUT 390 (AAC)
28 Reg 12(2) SS(DLA) Regs
29 Reg 12(3) SS(DLA) Regs
30 R(DLA) 3/95
31 Sch 2 SS(GB) Regs
32 *GB v SSWP (DLA)* [2016] UKUT 566 (AAC)
33 Reg 34(2) and Sch 3 Parts II and III SS(IIPD) Regs
34 Reg 12(2)(b) SS(DLA) Regs
35 s73 (1AB) SSCBA 1992; reg 12(1A) SS(DLA) Regs
36 *NC v SSWP (DLA)* [2012] UKUT 384 (AAC)
37 *SSWP v IK (DLA)* [2014] UKUT 174 (AAC)
38 *SSWP v YR (DLA)* [2014] UKUT 80 (AAC)
39 Reg 12(1)(b) SS(DLA) Regs
40 s73(3) SSCBA 1992; reg 12(5) and (6) SS(DLA) Regs
41 *JH v SSWP (DLA)* [2010] UKUT 456 (AAC); *AH v SSWP (DLA)* [2012] UKUT 387 (AAC); *SSWP v MG (DLA)* [2012] UKUT 429 (AAC)
42 R(M) 3/86; CSDLA/202/2007
43 *N McM v SSWP (DLA)* [2014] UKUT 312 (AAC)
44 R(DLA) 3/98; *MP v SSWP (DLA)* [2014] UKUT 426 (AAC)
45 *M (a child) v CAO* 29 October 1999, reported as R(DLA) 1/00
46 CDLA/95/1995; *DM v SSWP (DLA)* [2015] UKUT 87 (AAC); *EC (by SC) v SSWP (DLA)* [2017] UKUT 391 (AAC)
47 CDLA/3215/2001; *CD v SSWP (DLA)* [2013] UKUT 68 (AAC); *MP v SSWP (DLA)* [2014] UKUT 426 (AAC)
48 CDLA/2054/1998

49 R(DLA) 7/02; R(DLA) 9/02; CDLA/3244/ 2001; CDLA/2955/2008; *SSWP v DM (DLA)* [2010] UKUT 318 (AAC); *SSWP v MG (DLA)* [2012] UKUT 429 (AAC)
50 *TV v SSWP (DLA)* [2013] UKUT 364 (AAC)
51 s73(1)(d) SSCBA 1992
52 R(DLA) 6/03
53 CDLA/42/1994
54 s73(4A) SSCBA 1992
55 *BM v SSWP (DLA)* [2015] UKUT 18 (AAC); *KC-M S (by EC) v SSWP (DLA)* [2015] UKUT 284 (AAC)
56 CDLA/2268/1999
57 R(DLA) 3/04
58 CDLA/42/1994
59 CDLA/42/1994
60 CDLA/42/1994; CDLA/3360/1995; CSDLA/591/1997; CDLA/2643/1998
61 R(DLA) 4/01
62 *IN v SSWP (DLA)* [2013] UKUT 249 (AAC)
63 R(DLA) 6/05
64 R(DLA) 4/01
65 R(DLA) 4/01
66 CDLA/42/1994; R(DLA) 3/04
67 CDLA/2364/1995 and *KH v SSWP (DLA)* [2015] UKUT 8 (AAC), but see CDLA/42/ 1994
68 CDLA/2142/2005
69 Reg 12(7) and (8) SS(DLA) Regs; R(DLA) 3/04; CDLA/2409/2003; R(DLA) 6/05; *SSWP v DC (DLA)* [2011] UKUT 235 (AAC)

2. **Disability living allowance care component**
70 ss71(6) and 72 SSCBA 1992
71 s72(1)(a) and (4)(c) SSCBA 1992
72 s72(4)(b) SSCBA 1992
73 Reg 7 SS(DLA) Regs
74 s72(4)(a) SSCBA 1992
75 s72(5) SSCBA 1992
76 s72(1)(b) SSCBA 1992
77 s72(1)(c) SSCBA 1992
78 s72(1A)(b) SSCBA 1992
79 s72(5) SSCBA 1992
80 R(DLA) 1/05; *BM v SSWP (DLA)* [2015] UKUT 18 (AAC), reported as [2015] AACR 29
81 R(DLA) 3/06, tribunal of commissioners
82 CDLA/4475/04
83 R(DLA) 3/06, tribunal of commissioners
84 R(A) 3/86; *Mallinson v Secretary of State for Social Security*, 21 April 1994 (HL), reported as R(A) 3/94
85 *Secretary of State for Social Security v Fairey (aka Halliday)*, 21 May 1997 (HL), reported as R(A) 2/98
86 R(A) 3/89

87 R(A) 5/90
88 CDLA/3925/1997; *HJ v SSWP (DLA)*
[2010] UKUT 307 (AAC)
89 R(DLA) 10/02
90 *Mallinson v Secretary of State for Social
Security*, 21 April 1994 (HL), reported as
R(A) 3/94
91 *SJ v SSWP (DLA)* [2014] UKUT 222 (AAC)
92 Reg 10C SS(DLA) Regs; *R v National
Insurance Commissioner ex parte
Secretary of State for Social Services*
[1981] 1 WLR 1017 (CA), also reported
as R(A) 2/80
93 R(A) 1/06
94 *Mallinson v Secretary of State for Social
Security*, 21 April 1994 (HL), reported as
R(A) 3/94
95 CA/177/1988; CDLA/14696/1996;
R(DLA) 1/07, tribunal of commissioners
96 R(A) 3/74
97 R(A) 2/75
98 CA/86/1987
99 R(DLA) 1/07, tribunal of commissioners
100 *R v Social Security Commissioner ex parte
Butler*, February 1984, unreported;
*Secretary of State for Social Security v
Fairey (akaHalliday)*, 21 May 1997 (HL),
reported as R(A) 2/98
101 *Secretary of State for Social Security v
Fairey (aka Halliday)*, 21 May 1997 (HL),
reported as R(A) 2/98; R(DLA) 1/02;
R(DLA) 2/02; R(DLA) 3/02; *SSWP v PV
(DLA)* [2010] UKUT 33 (AAC)
102 R(DLA) 2/02
103 CDLA/3607/2001
104 *Cockburn v CAO and Another*, 21 May
1997 (HL), reported as R(A) 2/98;
Ramsden v SSWP, 31 January 2003 (CA),
reported as R(DLA) 2/03
105 CDLA/267/1994, CDLA/11652/1995,
CDLA/3711/1995, CDLA/12381/1996,
CDLA/16996/1996, CDLA/16129/1996
and CDLA/4352/1999 are useful, but
conflict with CSDLA/281/1996 and
CSDLA/314/1997
106 CDLA/267/1994
107 *Secretary of State for Social Security v
Fairey (aka Halliday)*, 21 May 1997 (HL),
reported as R(A) 2/98
108 CDLA/16129/1996, CDLA/16996/1996
and CDLA/4352/1999 are helpful, but
conflict with CSDLA/314/1997
109 CDLA/4352/1999 and CDLA/5216/
1998, the latter being more restrictive
110 CDLA/4352/1999
111 CDLA/5216/1998
112 R(DLA) 1/98

113 *R v National Insurance Commissioner ex
parte Secretary of State for Social Services*
[1974] 1 WLR 1290 (DC), also reported
as R(A) 4/74
114 R(A) 1/04
115 CDLA/2852/2002
116 CDLA/997/2003; *LB v SSWP (DLA)*
[2018] UKUT 445 (AAC)
117 R(A) 1/78
118 s72(1)(a)(i) SSCBA 1992
119 R(DLA) 8/02
120 CDLA/58/1993
121 CSDLA/29/1994
122 *Ramsden v SSWP*, 31 January 2003 (CA),
reported as R(DLA) 2/03; *SO v SSWP
(DLA)* [2019] UKUT 272 (AAC)
123 s72(1)(b)(i) SSCBA 1992
124 R(DLA) 5/05
125 CA/140/1985
126 *AB v SSWP (DLA)* [2015] UKUT 522
(AAC)
127 s72(1)(c)(i) SSCBA 1992
128 R(DLA) 5/05
129 R(DLA) 5/05
130 *AD v SSWP (DLA)* [2017] UKUT 29 (AAC)
131 R(A) 3/78
132 s72(1)(b)(ii) SSCBA 1992
133 R(A) 1/83
134 CA/15/1979, approved in R(A) 1/83
135 R(A) 2/89
136 CA/33/1984
137 R(A) 3/92
138 R(A) 1/73
139 *CP v SSWP (DLA)* [2013] UKUT 230
(AAC)
140 *Moran v Secretary of State for Social
Services, The Times*, 14 March 1987
(CA), reported as R(A) 1/88
141 R(A) 5/81
142 s72(1)(c)(ii) SSCBA 1992
143 Vol 10 Ch 61, para 61165 DMG
144 Vol 10 Ch 61, para 61164 DMG

3. **The rules about your age**
145 s73(1A) SSCBA 1992
146 s72(2) and (5) SSCBA 1992
147 See gov.uk/government/news/
coronavirus-update-benefit-reviews-
and-reassessments-suspended
148 gov.scot/publications/joint-ministerial-
working-group-on-welfare-minutes-
june-2019/
149 Reg 3(5) and (6) PIP(TP) Regs
150 Reg 27 PIP(TP) Regs
151 DWP, *Personal Independence Payment
Handbook*, December 2018, p22,
available at gov.uk
152 Reg 4 PIP(TP) Regs
153 Regs 12, 13 and 15 PIP(TP) Regs

154 DWP, *Personal Independence Payment Handbook,* December 2018, p22, available at gov.uk
155 Reg 4(1)(a) PIP(TP) Regs
156 Reg 3(3) PIP(TP) Regs
157 Reg 3(4A) and (5B) PIP(TP) Regs
158 Reg 18 PIP(TP) Regs
159 Reg 3(4) PIP(TP) Regs; DWP, *Personal Independence Payment Handbook,* December 2018, p43, available at gov.uk
160 Reg 8(4) PIP(TP) Regs
161 Regs 3 and 7 PIP(TP) Regs
162 Regs 9, 11 and 17 PIP(TP) Regs
163 Reg 9 PIP(TP) Regs
164 Reg 10 PIP(TP) Regs
165 Reg 11 PIP(TP) Regs
166 Reg 20 PIP(TP) Regs
167 Reg 13(1) PIP(TP) Regs
168 *OM v SSWP (PIP)* [2017] UKUT 458 (AAC)
169 Regs 13(2) and 17(2)(b) PIP(TP) Regs
170 Reg 12 PIP(TP) Regs
171 R(M) 1/96; *CH and KN v SSWP (PIP)* [2018] UKUT 330 (AAC)
172 Reg 17 PIP(TP) Regs
173 Reg 30 PIP(TP) Regs
174 Reg 17(4) and (5) PIP(TP) Regs
175 Regs 14 and 15 PIP(TP) Regs
176 Reg 17(1) and (3) PIP(TP) Regs
177 Sch 1 paras 3(3), 5(3), 6 and 7 SS(DLA) Regs; see also CSDLA/388/2000
178 Reg 6(3) and (4) SS(DLA) Regs
179 Sch 1 para 3(2) SS(DLA) Regs
180 Sch 1 para 1(3) SS(DLA) Regs
181 Sch 1 paras 2, 6 and 7 SS(DLA) Regs; *DB v SSWP (DLA)* [2016] 205 (AAC)
182 s72(1A)(a) SSCBA 1992

5. The amount of benefit
183 Reg 4(2) SS(DLA) Regs
184 Reg 4(1) SS(DLA) Regs

6. Special benefit rules
185 Reg 7 SS(DLA) Regs
186 s72(5) SSCBA 1992
187 ss66(1) and (2) and 72(5) SSCBA 1992
188 s73(9)(b)(ii) and (12) SSCBA 1992

7. Claims and backdating
189 Reg 6(8), (8A) and (9) SS(C&P) Regs
190 Reg 4(1) SS(C&P) Regs
191 For the process of moving from an appointee for a child getting DLA to one for a person aged 16 or over claiming PIP, see regs 28 and 29 PIP(TP) Regs and *P v SSWP (PIP)* [2018] UKUT 359 (AAC)
192 ss72(5) and 73(12) SSCBA 1992; regs 3(9)(b) and 6(6)(c) SS&CS(DA) Regs

193 Reg 6(8), (8A) and (9) SS(C&P) Regs
194 Reg 6(8A) SS(C&P) Regs
195 Reg 6(9) SS(C&P) Regs; *SNN v SSWP (PIP)* [2018] UKUT 210 (AAC) - although decided on similar rules for PIP, this case considers circumstances that may be reasonable and the discussion is relevant for DLA claims
196 Reg 6(1)(b) SS(C&P) Regs
197 s76(1) SSCBA 1992
198 Reg 9(1) and Sch 1 SS(C&P) Regs; reg 25(3) and (4) UC,PIP,JSA&ESA (C&P) Regs
199 Reg 13A(1) SS(C&P) Regs
200 Reg 13C SS(C&P) Regs
201 CDLA/14895/1996
202 Regs 6 and 11 SS(DLA) Regs
203 R(DLA)4/01; CDLA/333/2005; *DN v SSWP (DLA)* [2016] UKUT 233 (AAC)
204 DWP, *DWP Medical (Factual) Reports: a guide to completion,* August 2019
205 R(A) 2/74; see also *Moyna v SSWP,* 31 July 2003 (HL), reported as R(DLA) 7/03; *DJ v SSWP (DLA)* [2016] UKUT 169 (AAC)
206 CDLA/2268/1999
207 CDLA/4806/2002
208 CSDLA/76/1998
209 CA/92/1992; *DJ v SSWP (DLA)* [2016] UKUT 169 (AAC)
210 *SSWP v Hughes (a minor),* reported as R(DLA) 1/04
211 CDLA/1983/2006
212 *KM v SSWP (DLA)* [2013] UKUT 159 (AAC), reported as [2014] AACR 2
213 s19(3) SSA 1998

8. Getting paid
214 Reg 43 SS(C&P) Regs
215 Reg 43 SS(C&P) Regs
216 Reg 22(3) and Sch 6 SS(C&P) Regs
217 Reg 22 SS(C&P) Regs
218 Reg 25 SS(C&P) Regs
219 s71(3) SSCBA 1992
220 R(DLA) 11/02
221 s71(3) SSCBA 1992; CDLA/2887/2008
222 Regs 7(9) and 8 SS&CS(DA) Regs
223 s10(5) SSA 1998
224 Reg 7(2)(c) SS&CS(DA) Regs; *RD v SSWP (DLA)* [2011] UKUT 95 (AAC); *DC v SSWP (DLA)* [2011] UKUT 336 (AAC)

9. Tax, other benefits and the benefit cap
225 s677 IT(EP)A 2003
226 Art 24C Armed Forces and Reserve Forces (Compensation Scheme) Order 2011, No.517
227 Sch 1 para 5 SS(OB) Regs
228 Reg 42(1)(b)(ii) SS(C&P) Regs
229 Regs 44, 45 and 46 SS(C&P) Regs

Chapter 29

Discretionary housing payments

This chapter covers:
1. Who can get discretionary housing payments (p642)
2. The rules about your age (p643)
3. People included in the claim (p643)
4. The amount of discretionary housing payments (p643)
5. Claims, decisions and getting paid (p644)
6. Tax, other benefits and the benefit cap (p645)

Key facts
- Discretionary housing payments are extra payments that can be made by your local authority if you need help to meet your housing costs – eg, because deductions are being made for non-dependants living with you, you are affected by the benefit cap, or your universal credit (UC) or housing benefit (HB) does not cover your full rent because it has been restricted. They can also be made for lump-sum payments – eg, if you need rent in advance or a deposit for a new home, or if you have removal expenses.
- You must be entitled to help with your rent in UC or to HB to get discretionary housing payments.
- Payments are discretionary. They are paid from a cash-limited budget allocated to your local authority.
- You cannot appeal to the First-tier Tribunal against a discretionary housing payment decision, but you can ask the local authority for a review.

Future changes

The Scottish Parliament has the power to make rules on discretionary housing payments in Scotland. The legal basis for paying discretionary housing payments in Scotland will eventually change. It was not expected that the rules will change significantly when this happens. See AskCPAG.org.uk and CPAG's *Welfare Rights Bulletin* for updates.

Part 5: Other benefits
Chapter 29: Discretionary housing payments
1. Who can get discretionary housing payments

1. **Who can get discretionary housing payments**

A local authority can pay you discretionary housing payments if you are entitled to:[1]

- universal credit (UC) and your maximum amount includes a housing costs element for rent (see Chapter 6), or would include one but for the fact that you live in 'specified' or 'temporary' accommodation (see p85 for what counts); *or*
- housing benefit (HB) (see Chapter 10).

You must also appear to the local authority to require financial assistance, in addition to the benefit to which you are entitled, in order to meet your housing costs. For example, if your UC or HB is being paid at a reduced rate because non-dependant deductions are being made, because of the benefit cap, or under any of the rent restriction rules in Chapter 6 or Chapter 19, you may be able to get discretionary housing payments to make up the difference. Housing costs include rent in advance, deposits and removal expenses, so you may be able to get discretionary housing payments for these.[2] You can get discretionary housing payments even if your benefit is being paid direct to your landlord.[3] **Note:** it is understood that the government in Scotland wants local authorities to use discretionary housing payments to mitigate the effects of the social sector rent restriction rules (the 'bedroom tax').

The local authority has discretion on whether to pay you, the amount to pay you (within certain limits) and over what period to pay you, even if your UC housing costs element or HB is being paid in full direct to your landlord on your behalf.[4] **Note:** the rules do not limit the length of time you can be paid discretionary housing payments. These can be paid indefinitely.

DWP guidance to local authorities in England and Wales is at gov.uk/government/publications/discretionary-housing-payments-guidance-manual. It is understood that separate guidance will be available to local authorities in Scotland.

When discretionary housing payments cannot be made

Discretionary housing payments cannot be made to you if your need for financial assistance arises as a consequence of any of the following:[5]

- ineligible service charges under the UC or HB schemes (see p85 and p193);
- water and sewerage charges;
- liability for council tax. However, you may be able to get help from your local authority's council tax reduction scheme (see p851);
- your rent payments increasing to cover arrears of rent, service charges or other unpaid charges;

- a reduced benefit decision because you refused to co-operate in pursuing maintenance for your child(ren);
- your benefit (eg, income support or employment and support allowance) being reduced because you refused to take part in a work-focused interview;
- your UC or jobseeker's allowance (JSA) being paid at a reduced (or nil) rate because you have been sanctioned under specified rules;
- if you are 16 or 17, your severe hardship payments of JSA (see p257) being reduced because you gave up a place on a training scheme or failed to attend without a good reason;
- any of your benefits being suspended;
- a reduction in your benefit because an overpayment of UC, HB or council tax benefit is being recovered;
- your benefit being restricted because of a benefit offence (see p1278). **Note:** DWP guidance to local authorities in England and Wales wrongly suggests this applies if you are in breach of a community service order.

2. The rules about your age

There are no lower or upper age limits for discretionary housing payments. However, you must be entitled to universal credit (UC) that includes (or would include) a housing costs element for rent or to housing benefit (HB) to qualify for discretionary housing payments and there *are* age rules for UC and HB (see p37 and p187).

3. People included in the claim

You claim discretionary housing payments for yourself. However, your circumstances and needs as well as those of your child(ren) and your partner should be taken into account in deciding whether you can be paid and how much you can get.

4. The amount of discretionary housing payments

Discretionary housing payments are normally paid in weekly amounts. The local authority can decide how much you can be paid, how long you can be paid and how far your payments can be backdated.[6] However, it can only pay discretionary housing payments for periods during which you are (or were) entitled to universal

Part 5: Other benefits
Chapter 29: Discretionary housing payments
5. Claims, decisions and getting paid

credit (UC) and your maximum amount includes (or would include) a housing costs element for rent, or you are (or were) entitled to housing benefit (HB).

You cannot be paid more than:[7]

- if you are entitled to UC and your discretionary housing payments are calculated as a monthly amount, the amount of housing costs element for rent as calculated for your maximum amount (see Chapter 6), or if you are in 'specified' or 'temporary' accommodation (see p85 for what counts), the amount of your rent (other than for your specified or temporary accommodation) and service charges; *or*
- if you are entitled to HB and your discretionary housing payments are calculated as a weekly amount, the amount of your rent and other payments that can be met by HB (see p175), not including any amounts paid for ineligible service charges and rent-free periods.

Any UC or HB you have already received (or will receive) for the period may be deducted.[8]

There is no restriction on the amount of one-off payments.[9] Larger amounts (eg, for rent in advance, a rent deposit or removal expenses) can, therefore, be paid by a lump sum.

Note:

- In deciding whether to pay you discretionary housing payments and, if so, how much to pay you, the local authority can look at what income and capital you have. However, it cannot take disability living allowance into account.[10] You can argue that it also cannot take attendance allowance or personal independence payment into account.[11]
- If you need additional help with housing costs because there is a shortfall between your UC or HB and the rent you are liable to pay, ensure the local authority knows this, in particular if you are getting UC as it may not already have this information.

5. **Claims, decisions and getting paid**

Ask your local authority how to make a claim for discretionary housing payments. It may accept a claim from you, or from someone acting on your behalf, provided you are entitled to universal credit that includes a housing costs element for rent, or housing benefit.[12] Your local authority decides what 'form or manner' your claim should take – eg, in writing or by other means.[13]

You must provide grounds for your claim and provide any other information that the local authority specifies.[14] Provide any evidence that shows why you need discretionary housing payments – eg, a financial statement and evidence of any disability or medical condition affecting you or the people who live with you.

Note:
- If you want your claim to be backdated, tell the local authority.
- You must be given written notice of the local authority's decision on your claim and the reasons for its decision as soon as is 'reasonably practicable'.[15]
- The local authority can pay you or, if reasonable, someone else (eg, your landlord) where appropriate.[16]
- It is your duty to report to the local authority any change in your circumstances that may be relevant to payment of your discretionary housing payments continuing.[17]

Getting a decision changed

You do not have a right to appeal to the First-tier Tribunal against a discretionary housing payment decision. However, you can ask the local authority for a review of its decision.[18] You are entitled to written notice of, and reasons for, the review decision as soon as is 'reasonably practicable'.[19] You may be able to challenge a review decision by judicial review (see p1414). If the local authority's decision involves maladministration (error or wrongdoing) which results in injustice to you, you can also complain to the Ombudsman (see p1444).

6. Tax, other benefits and the benefit cap

Discretionary housing payments are not taxable.

If you get discretionary housing payments:
- they are disregarded as income and capital for the purposes of all the means-tested benefits and tax credits;[20]
- you may also qualify for discretionary council tax reduction (see p851).[21] Ensure you claim both these and discretionary housing payments, if relevant, to avoid missing out.

In some cases there is a limit on the total amount of specified benefits you can receive (a 'benefit cap'). Discretionary housing payments are *not* among the specified benefits. See p1194 for further information.

Notes

1. Who can get discretionary housing payments
1   s69 CSPSSA 2000; reg 2(1) DFA Regs
2   *Discretionary Housing Payments Guidance Manual,* August 2019, para 1.15
3   *Discretionary Housing Payments Guidance Manual,* August 2019, para 2.11
4   Reg 2(2) DFA Regs
5   Reg 3 DFA Regs

4. The amount of discretionary housing payments
6   Reg 5 DFA Regs
7   Reg 4 DFA Regs
8   *Gargett, R (on the application of) v Lambeth LB* [2008] EWCA Civ 1450
9   *Discretionary Housing Payments Guidance Manual,* August 2019, paras 1.182.14 and 2.17
10   *R (Hardy) v Sandwell MBC* [2015] EWHC 890 (Admin)
11   *Discretionary Housing Payments Guidance Manual,* August 2019, para 5.11

5. Claims, decisions and getting paid
12   Reg 6 DFA Regs
13   Reg 6(1)(a) DFA Regs
14   Reg 7 DFA Regs
15   Reg 6(3) DFA Regs
16   Reg 6(2) DFA Regs
17   Reg 7(b) DFA Regs
18   Reg 8 DFA Regs
19   Reg 6(3) DFA Regs

6. Tax, other benefits and the benefit cap
20   **UC** Reg 66 UC Regs
IS Schs 9 para 75 and 10 para 7(1)(d) IS Regs
JSA Schs 7 para 71 and 8 para 12(1)(d) JSA Regs
ESA Schs 8 para 62 and 9 para 11(1)(c) ESA Regs
PC Reg 15 SPC Regs
HB Schs 5 para 62 and 6 para 9(1)(d) HB Regs; reg 29 HB(SPC) Regs
21   s13A(1)(c) LGFA 1992

Chapter 30

Contributory employment and support allowance

This chapter covers:
1. Who can get contributory employment and support allowance (p648)
2. The rules about your age (p650)
3. People included in the claim (p650)
4. The amount of benefit (p650)
5. Special benefit rules (p657)
6. Claims and backdating (p657)
7. Getting paid (p661)
8. Tax, other benefits and the benefit cap (p662)

Key facts

- Employment and support allowance (ESA) is a benefit for people who have 'limited capability for work' (ie, they are unable to work because of illness or disability) and who are not entitled to statutory sick pay.
- Entitlement to ESA is assessed by a test called the 'work capability assessment'.
- There are two types of ESA: **contributory ESA,** which is not means tested (but can be affected by certain pensions), and **income-related ESA,** which is means tested.
- To qualify for contributory ESA, you must have paid sufficient national insurance contributions.
- In some cases, contributory ESA is paid for a maximum of 365 days.
- If you qualify for income-related ESA as well as contributory ESA, you may be able to get your contributory ESA topped up with income-related ESA or with universal credit (UC).
- ESA is administered and paid by the DWP.
- If you disagree with an ESA decision, you can apply for a revision or supersession (see Chapter 56), or appeal against it (see Chapter 57). You must apply for a mandatory reconsideration before you can appeal. All parts of the decision may be looked at.

Part 5: Other benefits
Chapter 30: Contributory employment and support allowance
1. Who can get contributory employment and support allowance

1. **Who can get contributory employment and support allowance**

You qualify for employment and support allowance (ESA) if you:[1]
- have 'limited capability for work' (see p1010); *and*
- are aged 16 or over, but under pension age (see p780); *and*
- are in Great Britain (see Chapters 69 and 70 if you go abroad); *and*
- are not entitled in your own right to income support or jobseeker's allowance (JSA), and are not in a couple entitled to joint-claim JSA (see p253). However, you can get contributory ESA if you are entitled to joint-claim JSA and do not have to satisfy all the JSA conditions; *and*
- are not entitled to statutory sick pay; *and*
- are not engaged in any work, whether it is paid or unpaid, unless it is work you are allowed to do while claiming (called 'permitted work' – see p1043).

In addition to the above, you must satisfy the extra rules that apply to contributory ESA on p649.

Do you come under the universal credit system?

New claims for contributory ESA are usually only possible under the universal credit (UC) system. The DWP may call this 'new-style' ESA. If you make a new claim, usually you will come under the UC system (see p26). However, if you claimed ESA before 12 December 2018 and did not come under the UC system, or you make a new claim for contributory ESA after 12 December 2018 and are prevented from claiming UC (see p23), you do not come under the UC system and your claim is dealt with under the old rules. The DWP may call this 'old-style' ESA.

You are not usually entitled to ESA for the first seven days of your claim (see p1041). However, you may be able to get a short-term advance of ESA paid to you during this waiting period (p1192). You cannot get ESA and certain other benefits at the same time (see p662).

Incapacity benefit and severe disablement allowance

Contributory ESA has, in most cases, replaced awards of two older non-means-tested benefits paid for people unable to work because of ill health. These benefits were incapacity benefit (IB) and severe disablement allowance (SDA). If you were already entitled to SDA and reached pension age before 6 April 2014, you can continue to receive it. In other cases, existing awards of IB and SDA have been transferred to claims for ESA. For more details, see p655.

Extra rules for contributory employment and support allowance

As well as satisfying the basic rules for ESA on p648, you qualify for contributory ESA if:[2]
- you satisfy the national insurance (NI) contribution conditions (see p980); *or*
- you were getting IB or SDA and you have been transferred to contributory ESA (see p655); *or*
- you satisfied the conditions for ESA in youth and you remain entitled (see below).

Employment and support allowance in youth

ESA in youth was abolished for new claimants from 1 May 2012.[3] For details of the rules, see Chapter 10 of the 2012/13 edition of this *Handbook*.

If you lose entitlement to ESA in youth because you have received it for a year, but have still got limited capability for work and are put in the 'support group' (see p652) because your condition has worsened, you can requalify for contributory ESA without having to satisfy the NI contribution conditions.[4]

Disqualification from benefit

You can be disqualified from receiving ESA for up to six weeks if you:[5]
- have 'limited capability for work' because of your own misconduct (but not, for example, if this is due to pregnancy or a sexually transmitted disease); *or*
- have failed without 'good cause' to accept medical treatment (excluding vaccination, inoculation or major surgery) recommended by a doctor treating you and which would be likely to overcome your limited capability for work; *or*
- have failed without 'good cause' to stop engaging in behaviour that would 'retard' your recovery; *or*
- are absent from your home without telling the DWP where you may be found without 'good cause'.

'Good cause' is not defined.

You are not disqualified if you inform the DWP of your circumstances and you are considered to be in hardship – ie, if you are:[6]
- pregnant, or a member of your family is pregnant;
- a single claimant aged under 18, or a member of a couple and both of you are under 18;
- responsible (or your partner is responsible) for a child who lives with you. This does not apply to contributory ESA if you come under the UC system (see p23);
- entitled (or your partner is entitled) to attendance allowance (AA), the middle or highest rate of the care component of disability living allowance (DLA), the

Part 5: Other benefits
Chapter 30: Contributory employment and support allowance
4. The amount of benefit

daily living component of personal independence payment (PIP) or armed forces independence payment;
- waiting (or your partner is waiting) for a decision on a claim for AA, DLA, PIP or armed forces independence payment;
- caring (or your partner is caring) for someone who is entitled to AA, the middle or highest rate care component of DLA, the daily living component of PIP or armed forces independence payment (or who is waiting for a decision on a claim for AA, DLA, PIP or armed forces independence payment);
- at least pension age (see p779), or your partner is at least pension age;
- at risk of hardship (or a member of your family is at risk) if ESA is not paid to you, including if there is a 'substantial risk' that you will not have sufficient essential items such as food, clothing and heating.

In any of the above situations, your ESA is paid at a reduced rate. You get 80 per cent of your basic allowance in contributory ESA, or 80 per cent of your personal allowance in income-related ESA (see p333).[7]

You can also be disqualified from receiving contributory ESA during any period in which you are:
- absent from Great Britain (see p1651); *or*
- a prisoner or detained in legal custody (see Chapter 42).

2. The rules about your age

To satisfy the basic rules for employment and support allowance, you must be aged at least 16 but under pension age (see p780).

3. People included in the claim

You claim contributory employment and support allowance for yourself. You cannot claim any increases for your partner or children.

4. The amount of benefit

You are paid a basic allowance of employment and support allowance (ESA) during an initial 'assessment phase' (see p651). After this, during the 'main phase', you may also get an additional component of ESA. You can get either a 'support component' (see p652) or a 'work-related activity component' (see p653). **Note:** the work-related activity component was abolished for new claimants from 3 April 2017. For who can still get the component, see p653.

There are no increases in contributory ESA for other adults or children. Your contributory ESA may be reduced if:

- you get a pension or a councillor's allowance (see p654); *or*
- the work-related activity component (see p653) applies to you and you do not comply with requirements to attend work-focused interviews and carry out work-related activity (see Chapter 48 or, if you come under the universal credit (UC) system, Chapter 46); *or*
- you have been given a sanction because you have committed a benefit offence (see p1278).

Note:

- If you are appealing against a decision that you do not have limited capability for work and get ESA pending your appeal being heard (see p1038), you are paid at the assessment phase rate – ie, you get the basic allowance only.
- You may also be entitled to income-related ESA. If you are, your contributory ESA is topped up by your income-related ESA. If you come under the UC system (see p23), you cannot get income-related ESA, but your contributory ESA may be topped up by UC.

The assessment phase

The first weeks of your entitlement to ESA are known as the 'assessment phase'. This applies to both contributory and income-related ESA. During this phase, the DWP assesses whether you have limited capability for work. You just get a basic allowance of contributory ESA, the amount of which depends on your age. Your ESA does not usually include an additional component (but see p654 for when a component can be included).

The assessment phase lasts for 13 weeks. If after 13 weeks the DWP has not decided whether you have limited capability for work (eg, because it has not yet completed the work capability assessment – see Chapter 45), the assessment phase continues until the DWP has made its decision.[8] In practice, delays of longer than 13 weeks in completing assessments are common. If you are claiming immediately after an 'extended period of sickness' on jobseeker's allowance (JSA – see p710), the 13-week period starts on the first day of the period of sickness.

If the assessment phase lasts longer than 13 weeks, the additional component is backdated to the 14th week of your claim.[9]

If you are appealing against a decision that you do not have limited capability for work and are getting ESA pending your appeal (see p1038), the assessment phase does not usually end until the First-tier Tribunal has made its decision. However, if you experience a new condition or your condition significantly worsens before your appeal is heard, a new determination on your limited capability for work can be made and it is possible for the assessment phase to end.[10]

Part 5: Other benefits
Chapter 30: Contributory employment and support allowance
4. The amount of benefit

It is possible for your assessment phase to begin on the first day of a period of previous entitlement to ESA (of either kind), so that some, or all, of the 13 weeks are treated as already served.[11] This happens if your current period of limited capability for work is linked to a previous one (see p1041) in which you were entitled to ESA for less than 13 weeks. In these circumstances, your assessment phase ends when your combined entitlement from the previous and current ESA awards amounts to 13 weeks, unless the DWP has not yet completed your assessment, in which case it does not end until the DWP has made its decision.

If you were on JSA during an 'extended period of sickness' (see p710), this counts as time when you had a previous entitlement to ESA.

Calculating your contributory employment and support allowance

Contributory ESA is worked out as follows.
- Add together the basic allowance and the amount of any component to which you are entitled.
  - In the 'assessment phase', you are normally only entitled to a basic allowance.[12] This is £58.90 if you are under 25 or £74.35 if you are 25 or over. In some circumstances, such as if you are terminally ill, you may also be entitled to either a support component (see below) or a work-related activity component (see p653).
  - After the assessment phase is over, you are entitled to a basic allowance of £74.35, irrespective of your age. If you qualify, you can also get a support component of £39.20 a week or (if you can still get it) a work-related activity component of £29.55 a week.
- Deduct from this sum an amount for certain pension payments or for a councillor's allowance, if applicable (see p654).
- Add any transitional addition to which you are entitled if you have been transferred to ESA from incapacity benefit (IB) or severe disablement allowance (SDA) (see p655).[13]

Support component

The support component can be included in your entitlement to both contributory and income-related ESA.[14]

In most cases, you are entitled to the support component if:
- the assessment phase (see p651) has ended (but see p654); *and*
- as well as having limited capability for work, you are also assessed as having 'limited capability for work-related activity' (see p1027).

The support group

If you are assessed as having, or are treated as having, limited capability for work-related activity, the DWP describes you as being in the '**support group**'.

The DWP decides whether or not you have limited capability for work-related activity as part of the work capability assessment (see p1010). You can appeal if you do not agree with the DWP's decision, although you must apply for a mandatory reconsideration first. If you appeal and the First-tier Tribunal finds that you have limited capability for work, it should also consider whether you have limited capability for work-related activity.[15]

If you are in the support group, you do not have to take part in work-focused interviews or associated activity as a condition of getting benefit.[16]

Work-related activity component

The work-related activity component was abolished for new claimants of both contributory and income-related ESA from 3 April 2017.[17] From this date, you can no longer get the component if you are making a new claim for ESA (but see below). You may still be able to get the support component.

You can still get the work-related activity component after 3 April 2017 if:[18]
- your current ESA entitlement started before 3 April 2017 (this includes if you only became entitled to ESA after a mandatory reconsideration or appeal that was after that date);
- you claimed ESA before 3 April 2017 and had limited capability for work (see Chapter 45), you have had a break in your period of limited capability for work, but you have reclaimed ESA within 12 weeks of your previous period ending;
- you were entitled to ESA before 3 April 2017 and then became entitled to maternity allowance (MA), and you have reclaimed ESA within 12 weeks of your MA ending;
- your assessment phase (see p651) for a previous ESA claim began before 3 April 2017, but you were entitled to ESA for no more than 13 weeks and you have reclaimed it within 12 weeks of your previous entitlement ending. **Note:** if you were getting JSA in an 'extended period of sickness' (see p710), this counts as a previous ESA claim;
- you claimed ESA on or after 3 April 2017, but your claim was backdated to before this date, and it is decided that you are in the 'work-related activity group' (see below);
- you were transferred from IB or SDA to contributory ESA, or from income support (IS) to income-related ESA.

The work-related activity group

If you are assessed under the work capability assessment as having limited capability for work, but not for work-related activity (see Chapter 45), the DWP describes you as being in the 'work-related activity group'. This is the case even if you cannot get the work-related activity component. The DWP also describes you as being in the work-related activity group if you are treated as having limited capability for work (see p1011), except if you are waiting for your work capability assessment to be carried out or if you are appealing.[19]

Part 5: Other benefits
Chapter 30: Contributory employment and support allowance
4. The amount of benefit

If you can get it, the work-related activity component can be included in both contributory and income-related ESA if:[20]
- the assessment phase (see p651) has ended (but see below); *and*
- you are not assessed as having 'limited capability for work-related activity' (see p1027) – ie, you are not entitled to the support component; *and*
- you comply with the requirement to attend work-focused interviews and associated activity (see p1136). If you do not, your ESA may be reduced.

You may be required to take part in work-focused interviews and undertake work-related activity (see Chapter 48 or, if you come under the UC system, Chapter 46).

Who can get a component in the assessment phase

You are entitled to the support component (or the work-related activity component, if you can still get it) during the assessment phase if:[21]
- you have requalified for contributory ESA after having previously lost it because of the rules on how long it can be paid (see p656) and now satisfy the conditions for the support component; *or*
- you are terminally ill (ie, you have a progressive disease, as a result of which your death can reasonably be expected within six months) and have either claimed ESA on these grounds, or asked for a revision or supersession and have said that you are terminally ill. In this case, you qualify for the support component automatically and it is included straight away; *or*
- your period of limited capability for work is linked under the 12-week linking rule (see p1041) to an earlier period in which you were entitled to ESA, you were entitled to a component in this earlier claim and it did not end because you were found to be fit for work – ie, you did not fail the work capability assessment. In this case, the component can be included straight away; *or*
- your period of limited capability for work is linked under the 12-week linking rule (see p1041) to an earlier period in which you were entitled to ESA, you were entitled to a component or that award lasted 13 weeks or longer, and it ended either because you failed the work capability asssessment or before you could be assessed. In this case, you can only get the component again once you have been assessed as passing the work capability assessment, although it is dated from the start of your second award; *or*
- your ESA entitlement started within 12 weeks of your losing entitlement to IS, when your IS ended it included the disability premium and the sole reason for your losing entitlement to IS was that you were a lone parent and your youngest child no longer met the age rules (see p235).

Deductions for pension payments and councillor's allowance

A deduction is made from your contributory ESA if you receive certain pension payments of over £85 a week and/or if you are a local councillor and your net allowances are more than £140 a week.[22]

Pension payments taken into account for contributory ESA are periodic payments made under:[23]

- any personal, occupational or public service pension scheme;
- any permanent health insurance policy arranged by your employer that provides payments in connection with ill health or disability after your employment ends. However, if you contributed more than 50 per cent of the pension premiums, the amount you receive from this kind of pension is ignored;
- the Pension Protection Fund and the Financial Assistance Scheme.

If the total amount of the gross pension payments you receive is more than £85 a week, your contributory ESA is reduced by half the pension payments above £85.

Other types of pension payments (including one-off, lump-sum payments) are ignored. The following types of payment are also ignored:[24]

- any part of your pension paid directly to an ex-spouse or ex-civil partner by the pension scheme trustees under a court order (although the DWP may not accept this);[25]
- any payments you receive as a result of the death of the pension holder;
- any shortfall in your pension if it cannot be paid in full because the pension scheme is in deficit or has insufficient funds;
- payments under a pension scheme for death as a result of military or war service under section 639(2) of the Income Tax (Earnings and Pensions) Act 2003, or a guaranteed income payment.

Note: if you were transferred from IB to ESA (see below) and your pension payment was ignored immediately before the transfer, it continues to be ignored in your ESA.[26]

If you are a local councillor and your net allowances are more than £140 a week, your contributory ESA is reduced by the amount by which the net allowances exceed £140.[27]

Transfers to employment and support allowance

Most people who were getting IB, SDA or IS on the grounds of disability on 27 October 2008 have had their claim transferred to a claim for ESA. If you were transferred from IB or SDA but your contibutory ESA would have been less, you were entitled to the difference as a transitional addition to your contributory ESA. But, as ESA is a single benefit, entitlement to income-related ESA should also have been considered. The DWP wrongly failed to consider entitlement in some cases and has been contacting claimants who were underpaid income-related ESA as a result. Those getting IS had their award automatically converted to a claim for income-related ESA. If you get a transitional addition, it is reduced by subsequent increases in your ESA. For more details, see Chapter 31 of the 2016/17 edition of this *Handbook*.

Part 5: Other benefits
Chapter 30: Contributory employment and support allowance
4. The amount of benefit

The transfer process did not apply to people who reached state pension age before 6 April 2014. In particular, if you were getting SDA and reached state pension age before 6 April 2014, you can continue to get SDA as long as you continue to meet the qualifying conditions. See Chapter 4 of the 2000/01 edition of this *Handbook* for the qualifying conditions for SDA.

Duration of contributory employment and support allowance

Contributory ESA is only paid for a maximum of 365 days. However, when calculating this 365-day period, any time when you have limited capability for work-related activity (p1027) and are in in the 'support group' is ignored. So, once you have received contributory ESA for a year and have not been entitled to the support component for that time, you lose your entitlement to contributory ESA. The following applies.[28]

- Time spent in the assessment phase is taken into account when calculating the 365-day period, except if you were assessed as having limited capability for work-related activity (p1027) and put in the support group.
- If you are appealing about not being in the support group, days when you get ESA while you are appealing are taken into account when calculating the 365-day period. This time is then ignored if your appeal is successful.
- If you were transferred from IB or SDA to contributory ESA, your 365-day period is calculated from the date your award was converted to contributory ESA.

You can requalify for contributory ESA again if:[29]

- you remain assessed or treated as having limited capability for work, and you are also assessed as having limited capability for work-related activity for the support component (see p1027); *or*
- the tax years used to decide whether you satisfy the NI contribution conditions (see p980) include at least one year which is later than the last of the relevant tax years which applied to your previous entitlement, and you satisfy the NI contribution conditions again. If you continue to have limited capability for work and still get income-related ESA, under the linking rules (p1041) the tax years remain the same as those that applied to your previous entitlement, so you cannot requalify in this way. However, if you have a break in your ESA entitlement altogether (ie, of both contributory and income-related ESA) of more than 12 weeks (including if you get UC during the break), you start a new period of limited capability for work and the linking rules do not apply.[30]

Example

Ravi is aged 24. He has worked since leaving school and has a full NI contribution record, but in July 2019 had to leave his job because of ill health. He gets the standard rate of the daily living component of personal independence payment. He is not assessed as being in the ESA support group. As Ravi comes under the UC system, he is not entitled to any income-related ESA.

ESA during assessment phase = £58.90 (basic allowance for someone aged under 25).

ESA during main phase = £74.35

Because Ravi is not in the support group, his award of contributory ESA, which began in July 2019, is limited to 365 days.

The relevant tax years for the NI contribution conditions are 2016/17 and 2017/18.

After a year of payment, Ravi's contributory ESA stops on 1 July 2020. His condition has not changed and he still does not qualify for the support component. He still has limited capability for work. As his ESA has stopped completely (ie, he is not entitled to income-related ESA either), after 12 weeks Ravi may requalify for contributory ESA. This is because when he makes a new claim for ESA he starts a new period of limited capability for work which does not link to his previous one. One of the relevant tax years that applies to the new claim (2018/19) is later than the years that applied to Ravi's previous claim. However, he must still satisfy the NI contribution conditions again using the new relevant tax years.

5. Special benefit rules

Special rules may apply to:
- 'people subject to immigration control' (employment and support allowance in youth only) (see Chapter 67);
- people going abroad (see Chapters 69 and 70);
- people in prison or detention (see Chapter 42).

6. Claims and backdating

The general rules about claims and backdating are covered in Chapter 50. This section explains the specific rules that apply to contributory and income-related employment and support allowance (ESA). The rules may be different depending on whether or not you come under the universal credit (UC) system.

Sometimes, you must attend a medical examination to assess whether you have limited capability for work (p1010) or limited capability for work-related activity (p1027). Also, unless you are in the 'support group' (see p652), you may be required to attend compulsory work-focused interviews and, in some cases, carry out work-related activity. These interviews can include a 'health and work conversation' (see p1051 if you come under the UC system, or p1136 if you do not). **Note:** these requirements are suspended during the coronavirus pandemic.

Part 5: Other benefits
Chapter 30: Contributory employment and support allowance
6. Claims and backdating

If you are appealing against a decision that you do not have limited capablity for work, you do not need to make a claim for ESA in order to get ESA pending your appeal, although you must submit a medical certificate.[31] For when ESA can be paid pending an appeal, see p1038.

Note: if you are refused contributory ESA because you do not meet the national insurance (NI) contribution conditions, in some cases it may be worth claiming at a later date that falls in a different benefit year (see p980).

Making a claim

You can start your claim for ESA by telephone or by using the claim form.[32] The DWP refers to contributory ESA paid under the UC system as 'new-style' ESA.

You can claim ESA by telephone on 0800 328 5644 (textphone: 0800 328 1344), Relay UK (if you cannot hear or speak on the phone) 18001 then 0800 328 5644, Welsh language telephone 0800 328 1744, Monday to Friday, 8am to 6pm.[33] Say that you wish to claim 'new-style' contributory ESA. You are then emailed Form NSESAF1. If required, an appointment should also be arranged for you at your local Jobcentre Plus office. Take your completed NSESAF1 claim form and proof of identity with you.

You can download and print a claim form for 'new-style' ESA from gov.uk/ government/publications/new-style-employment-and-support-allowance-esa-claim-form. You still need to book a 'new claims appointment' using the telephone/textphone numbers above. Take your completed claim form, your medical certificate from your doctor, proof of your identity, address and of any pensions or health insurance payments you get to the appointment.

If you want to claim UC to top up your ESA, you must do this separately.

Are you prevented from claiming universal credit?
You might be prevented from claiming UC if you (or your partner) are severely disabled (see p23). If that applies, you do not come under the UC system and can get income-related ESA as well as contributory ESA. In these circumstances, you claim contributory ESA in the same way as you claim income-related ESA (see p166).

You provide information or evidence as required (see p716). You can amend or withdraw your claim before a decision is made (see p1169). If there is a delay in deciding your claim, you may be able to get a short-term advance (see p1192).

Who should claim

You claim contributory ESA on your own behalf. However, if you are unable to manage your own affairs, another person can claim ESA for you as your 'appointee' (see p1170).

If you are employed

If you are employed, you should normally be paid statutory sick pay (SSP) (see Chapter 39) for the first 28 weeks of your limited capability for work. If your employer thinks that you are not entitled to SSP, or if your entitlement to SSP has run out, it should complete and give you Form SSP1. To get contributory ESA, you then need to claim ESA. **Note:** claiming ESA will mean that you come under the UC system (see p23). You are normally expected to include Form SSP1 and a medical certificate with your claim. If your employer refuses you SSP on the grounds that you are not entitled to it, your claim for ESA can be backdated to the date of your SSP claim (see p660). If you disagree with your employer's decision not to pay SSP, you can refer the matter to HM Revenue and Customs (HMRC – see Chapter 59), but do not delay claiming ESA. If you have asked HMRC to decide whether you are entitled to SSP, tell the DWP this when you claim ESA.

Information to support your claim

For the general information requirements that apply to all benefits, see p1170.

It is important that you provide any information required when you claim. Until you do, you may not count as having made a valid claim (see p1172). Correct any defects as soon as possible or your date of claim may be affected.

The DWP may ask you to provide information, including:

- your NI number;
- a medical certificate from your doctor, sometimes called a 'fit note' or 'sick note' (see below);
- your GP's address and telephone number;
- your contact telephone number (if you have one);
- your bank account details;
- details of your employer (if you have one);
- details of other money you are getting, such as benefits, pensions or health insurance payments.

For the first seven days of your limited capability for work, the DWP should accept a self-certificate as medical evidence. After seven days, you must provide a medical certificate from your doctor. If it is unreasonable to expect you to provide this, the DWP can accept other evidence if that is sufficient.[34]

You may be referred by the DWP for a medical assessment. If you do not attend the medical without good cause, your claim can be refused.[35]

Even if you have provided all that was required when you claimed, you may be asked to provide further information to support your claim (see p1174). You may also be asked to provide information after you are awarded ESA and, if you fail to do so, your ESA could be suspended, or even terminated (see p1200).

Part 5: Other benefits
Chapter 30: Contributory employment and support allowance
6. Claims and backdating

The date of your claim

The date of your claim is important as it determines when your entitlement to ESA starts (subject to the rules on waiting days – see p662). This is not necessarily the date from when you are paid. For information about when payment of ESA starts, see p661.

Unless it is backdated, the '**date of your claim**' is usually the date of your telephone call, or the date your claim form is received at a DWP office (or a local authority office – see p658).[36] However, if you notify the DWP that you intend to send a claim form and you send a properly completed form within one month, your date of claim is the date you notified the DWP that you intended to claim.

Note: you must make sure your claim is valid. If it is 'defective', you are given a short time to correct the defects (see p1173). If you do, your claim is treated as having been made when you initially claimed.[37]

In some cases, you can claim in advance (see below) and in some cases your claim can be backdated (see below). If you want this to be done, make this clear when you claim or the DWP might not consider it. If you claimed SSP or maternity allowance (MA) when you should have claimed ESA, see below.

Backdating your claim

Your claim can be backdated for up to three months before the day you actually claim – ie, for time during this period when you were entitled to ESA. You should state from which date you are claiming in that period and ask for it to be backdated. You do not need special reasons for backdating.[38]

If you claim the wrong benefit

If your employer has decided that you are not entitled to SSP and you claim ESA within three months of being notified in writing of this, your ESA claim is treated as having been made on the date of your SSP claim.[39]

A claim for MA can be treated as a claim for ESA and vice versa.[40] If your MA claim is accepted as a claim for ESA, your ESA can be backdated for up to three months before the date you claimed MA if you satisfy the qualifying conditions during that period (see p1182).

Claiming in advance

You can claim ESA up to three months before the date on which you qualify for it.[41] The date of your claim is the date on which you qualify.

Starting work when your claim ends

If you start work, you may be able to benefit from the rules for linking periods of limited capability for work should you fall sick again later (see p1041). If this is the case, provided you claim ESA again within a 12-week linking period, you get the same amount of ESA that you previously received.

7. Getting paid

The general rules on getting paid are covered in Chapter 51. This section explains the specific rules that apply to both contributory and income-related employment and support allowance (ESA).

When is employment and support allowance paid?
The day you are paid depends on your national insurance number (see p1189).[42] ESA is usually paid fortnightly in arrears, although it can be paid at different intervals, including at a daily rate of one-seventh of the weekly amount.[43]
ESA is a weekly benefit, although in some cases it can be paid for a part week.[44]

Note:
- Your contributory ESA might be paid at a reduced rate in some circumstances (see p651).
- Deductions can be made from your ESA to pay to third parties (see p1202).
- You might not be paid ESA, or it might be paid at a reduced rate, if you have been sanctioned for a benefit offence (see p1278). **Note:** you may also be sanctioned for other reasons (see Chapter 49).
- For information on missing payments, see p1189. If you cannot get your ESA payments because you have lost your bank card or you have forgotten your PIN, see p1188. If you have lost your payment service card, or you have forgotten your memorable date, see p1189.
- If payment of your ESA is delayed, see p1295. If you are waiting for a decision on your claim, or to be paid, you might be able to get a short-term advance (see p1192). If you wish to complain about how your claim has been dealt with, or claim compensation, see Chapter 60.
- If payment of your ESA is suspended, see p1200. This includes if you have failed to supply evidence of your limited capability for work.
- If you are overpaid ESA, you might have to repay it (see Chapter 53) and, in some circumstances, you may have to pay a penalty (see p1268). If you have been accused of fraud, see Chapter 54.

Change of circumstances

You must report changes in your circumstances that you have been told you must report, as well as any that you might reasonably be expected to know might affect your right to, the amount of, or the payment of your benefit. You should do this as soon as possible, preferably in writing. See p1199 for further information.

Your ESA is usually adjusted from the beginning of the week in which the change of circumstances takes effect.[45] However, there are exceptions – eg, if you

Part 5: Other benefits
Chapter 30: Contributory employment and support allowance
8. Tax, other benefits and the benefit cap

have notified the DWP that you are terminally ill or if you have failed to notify it of a change about your limited capability for work (see p1320).[46]

Waiting days

You are not entitled to ESA for a period of seven '**waiting days**' at the beginning of your period of limited capability for work (see p1041).[47] This does not apply if:

- your entitlement to ESA starts within 12 weeks of your entitlement to income support, incapacity benefit, severe disablement allowance, pension credit, jobseeker's allowance, carer's allowance, statutory sick pay or maternity allowance coming to an end; *or*
- you have requalified for contributory ESA on the basis of being put in the support group (see p652), having previously lost entitlement because of the rules on how long you can be paid contributory ESA (see p656); *or*
- you are terminally ill, or you have been discharged from the armed forces and three or more days before the discharge were days of sickness absence; *or*
- you have Covid-19, you are isolating because you have symptoms or you are caring for a child in your household for these reasons. See the guidance at nhs.uk/cornoavirus.

You may be able to get a short-term advance before your first payment is due (see p1192).

---

8. **Tax, other benefits and the benefit cap**

Tax

Contributory employment and support allowance (ESA), including ESA in youth, is taxable.[48] If you were transferred from incapacity benefit (IB) or severe disablement allowance (SDA) to contributory ESA (see p655), your contributory ESA is still taxable, even if your IB/SDA was not.

Means-tested benefits and tax credits

If you are entitled to contributory ESA:

- your contributory ESA counts as income for the purposes of means-tested benefits if you do not get income-related ESA;
- if you come under the universal credit (UC) system (see p23), you may be entitled to UC to top up your contributory ESA;
- if you do not come under the UC system, you may be entitled to income-related ESA to top up your contributory ESA, without making a new claim (see p26);
- you may be entitled to an additional component as part of your housing benefit (HB) (see p353).

If you do not come under the UC system, you have a partner and s/he works sufficient hours, you and your partner may be able to claim working tax credit (WTC). ESA counts as a 'qualifying benefit' for the disability element of WTC (see p1458). If you have children, you may be able to claim child tax credit.

You cannot get ESA at the same time as:

- income support (IS) in your own right;[49]
- income-related jobseeker's allowance (JSA) in your own right, including as part of a joint-claim couple. However, you can get contributory ESA if you are part of a JSA joint-claim couple and you do not have to satisfy all the JSA conditions.[50] If your partner is entitled in her/his own right to income-based JSA (and it is not joint-claim JSA – eg, because you have a dependent child), you can get contributory ESA at the same time.

Non-means-tested benefits

While you are on contributory ESA, you may be entitled to national insurance credits (see p968).

Contributory ESA is affected by the rules on overlapping benefits (see p1190), which means that you may not be paid it in full if another earnings-replacement benefit is paid to you.

You are not entitled to ESA if you are entitled to statutory sick pay.[51] You can still get contributory ESA if you get statutory maternity pay (SMP), statutory adoption pay (SAP) or statutory paternity pay (SPP). You can get contributory ESA and statutory shared parental pay (SSPP) if the amount of the SSPP is less than the amount of ESA. Your ESA is reduced by the amount of the SMP, SAP, SPP or SSPP you get.[52] At the time of writing, it appeared that your entitlement to contributory ESA would not be affected if you get statutory parental bereavement pay. However, as the rules had not been finalised this could be subject to change. See AskCPAG.org.uk and CPAG's *Welfare Rights Bulletin* for updates.

You cannot claim ESA and contribution-based JSA in your own right at the same time. If your partner is entitled to contribution-based JSA, you can claim ESA.

The benefit cap

In some cases, there is a limit on the total amount of specified benefits you can receive (a 'benefit cap'). ESA is one of the specified benefits. However, the benefit cap does not apply if you or your partner receive ESA which includes a support component. In other cases, it only applies if you are getting UC or HB. See p1194 for further information.

Passports and other sources of help

If you receive contributory ESA, you may be eligible for a Christmas bonus (see p870).

You may also qualify for health benefits such as free prescriptions (see Chapter 31), and education benefits such as free school lunches (see p866).

You may be entitled to council tax reduction (see p851).

Financial help on starting work

If you stop getting contributory ESA because you start work, you may be able to get extended payments of HB if you pay rent (see p217). Your local authority may provide extended help with council tax. See p873 for information about other financial help you may get.

5 Notes

1. Who can get contributory employment and support allowance

1 ss1 and 20(1) WRA 2007; reg 40(1) and (7) ESA Regs; reg 37(1) and (8) ESA Regs 2013
2 Sch 1 paras 1-4 WRA 2007
3 s53 WRA 2012; s1(3A) WRA 2007
4 s52 WRA 2012
5 s18 WRA 2007; reg 157 ESA Regs; reg 93 ESA Regs 2013
6 Regs 157(3) and 158 ESA Regs; reg 94 ESA Regs 2013
7 Sch 5 para 14 ESA Regs; reg 63 ESA Regs 2013

4. The amount of benefit

8 s24(2) WRA 2007; reg 4 ESA Regs; reg 5 ESA Regs 2013
9 Reg 7(38) SS&CS(DA) Regs; reg 35(7) UC,PIP,JSA&ESA(DA) Regs
10 Regs 4, 5 and 147A ESA Regs; regs 5, 6 and 87 ESA Regs 2013
11 Reg 5 ESA Regs; reg 6 ESA Regs 2013
12 s2(1)(a) WRA 2007; regs 7 and 67(2) and Sch 4 para 1(1)(b) and (c) ESA Regs; regs 7 and 62(1) ESA Regs 2013
13 s2(2) and (3) WRA 2007; reg 67(2) and (3) and Sch 4 paras 1(a), 12 and 13 ESA Regs; Sch 2 para 12 ESA(TP)(EA)(No.2) Regs
14 ss2(2) and 4(4) WRA 2007
15 *PM v SSWP (ESA)* [2012] UKUT 188 (AAC)

16 Reg 54 ESA Regs; ss11 and 11D WRA 2007
17 s15 WRWA 2016
18 Sch 1 Part 1 ESAUC(MA) Regs
19 Reg 2 IS Regs; reg 1 JSA Regs; reg 1 SPC Regs; reg 2 HB Regs; reg 2 HB(SPC) Regs; reg 1 SFCWP Regs
20 ss2(3) and 4(5) WRA 2007
21 Reg 7 ESA Regs; reg 7 ESA Regs 2013
22 Regs 72-79 ESA Regs; regs 64-72 ESA Regs 2013
23 s3 WRA 2007; regs 72, 72A and 74 ESA Regs; regs 64, 65 and 67 ESA Regs 2013
24 Reg 75 ESA Regs; reg 68 ESA Regs 2013
25 R(IB) 1/04 applied this to IB, but it is not followed by the DWP for ESA.
26 Schs 1 para 11 and 2 para 14 ESA(TP)(EA)(No.2) Regs
27 Regs 76(1), 79 and 94(1) ESA Regs; regs 69, 72 and 79 ESA Regs 2013
28 ss51 and 52 WRA 2012; ss1A and 1B WRA 2007
29 ss1A and 1B WRA 2007
30 Vol 8 Ch 41, para 41847 DMG

6. Claims and backdating

31 Reg 3(j) SS(C&P) Regs; reg 7 ESA Regs 2013
32 Regs 13 and 15 UC,PIP,JSA&ESA(C&P) Regs
33 gov.uk/employment-support-allowance/how-to-claim
34 Regs 2 and 5 SS(ME) Regs
35 s19 SSA 1998; reg 23 ESA Regs

36 Reg 6(1F) SS(C&P) Regs; regs 14 and 16
    UC,PIP,JSA&ESA(C&P) Regs
37 Regs 4G(5) and 4H(6) and (7) SS(C&P)
    Regs; regs 13(5) and 15(4)
    UC,PIP,JSA&ESA(C&P) Regs
38 Reg 19 and Sch 4 para 16 SS(C&P) Regs;
    reg 28 UC,PIP,JSA&ESA(C&P) Regs
39 Reg 10(1A) SS(C&P) Regs; reg 17
    UC,PIP,JSA&ESA(C&P) Regs
40 Reg 9 and Sch 1 SS(C&P) Regs; reg 25
    UC,PIP,JSA&ESA(C&P) Regs
41 Reg 13(9) SS(C&P) Regs; reg 34
    UC,PIP,JSA&ESA(C&P) Regs

7. Getting paid
42 Reg 26C(2) SS(C&P) Regs; reg 51
    UC,PIP,JSA&ESA(C&P) Regs
43 Reg 26C SS(C&P) Regs; reg 51(5)
    UC,PIP,JSA&ESA(C&P) Regs
44 Vol 8 Ch 46, para 46011 DMG
45 Reg 7(2)(a) and Sch 3C SS&CS(DA)
    Regs; reg 35 and Sch 1 para 1
    UC,PIP,JSA&ESA(C&P) Regs
46 Reg 7(2) and (25) and Sch 3C
    SS&CS(DA) Regs; reg 35 and Sch 1
    paras 6 and 9 UC,PIP,JSA&ESA(C&P)
    Regs
47 Reg 144 ESA Regs; reg 85 ESA Regs
    2013

8. Tax, other benefits and the benefit cap
48 ss658(4) and 661(1) IT(EP)A 2003
49 s1(3)(e) WRA 2007
50 s1(3)(f) WRA 2007
51 s20 WRA 2007
52 Regs 80-82A ESA Regs; regs 73-75 ESA
    Regs 2013

5

Chapter 31

Health benefits

This chapter covers:
1. Who can get health benefits (below)
2. Prescriptions (p672)
3. Dental treatment and dentures (p673)
4. Sight tests and glasses (p673)
5. Wigs and fabric supports (p675)
6. Fares to receive NHS treatment (p675)
7. Claims and refunds (p676)

Key facts

- Health benefits provide help with the costs of NHS prescriptions, dental treatment, sight tests and glasses, and wigs and fabric supports, as well as fares to receive NHS treatment.
- Some people are exempt from charges and can get full help with NHS costs and fares. Others qualify for full or partial help in specific situations or if their income and capital are below a certain amount (known as the low income scheme).
- Health benefits are administered by the NHS Business Services Authority.

1. Who can get health benefits

Although the NHS generally provides free healthcare, there are fixed charges for some items and services such as prescriptions, dental treatment, sight tests and glasses, and wigs and fabric supports. You may also have fares to pay to get to hospital or another establishment for NHS treatment. However, you may qualify for full help with the charges and fares (ie, you may get the items or services free of charge) or you may get partial help (ie, you get a reduction).

In some cases, you must make a claim (see p676). If you pay for an item or service that you could have received free, or at a reduced cost, you can apply for a refund (see p678).

Chapter 31

Health benefits

Full help

You get full help with charges and fares if you:
- are in an exempt group (see below); *or*
- satisfy specific conditions, depending on the item or service. See p672 for prescriptions, p673 for dental treatment and dentures, p673 for sight tests and glasses, p675 for wigs and fabric supports and p675 for fares to receive NHS treatment; *or*
- get full help with health costs under the low income scheme (see p668). **Note:** if you do not qualify for full help with health costs, you may qualify for partial help under the low income scheme.

Exempt groups

You qualify for full help with charges and fares if you are in an exempt group. You are in an exempt group if:[1]
- you, or a member of your family (see p668 for who counts), get any of the following qualifying benefits:
    - universal credit (UC). In the assessment period (see p39) before the health cost was incurred, you must either have:
        - no earnings; *or*
        - earnings no greater than £435 (or £935, if you have a limited capability for work, or if the child element is included in your UC).
    Note: if you claim as a couple, these limits apply to your and your partner's combined income (see p70).
    - income support (IS), income-based jobseeker's allowance (JSA), income-related employment and support allowance (ESA) or the guarantee credit of pension credit (PC); *or*
    - child tax credit (CTC), or both CTC and working tax credit (WTC), or WTC that includes a disabled worker or severe disability element. Your gross annual income for tax credits must not exceed £15,276;
- you, or a member of your family, are an asylum seeker who gets asylum support (see p1573). Dependants for whom you are claiming asylum support count as members of your family;
- you are aged 16 or 17 and you get support from a local authority after being looked after (in Scotland, getting support under section 29(1) of the Children (Scotland) Act 1995 after leaving care). This does not appear to apply for sight tests in England and Wales or for vouchers for glasses and contact lenses in England.

If you are exempt on the grounds that you get tax credits, HM Revenue and Customs sends you an exemption certificate which you should present when you collect your prescription. If you do not receive your certificate, present your letter of entitlement to tax credits.

If you are exempt on the grounds that you get UC, you should show a statement of your entitlement in the last assessment period. If you get any of the other DWP benefits listed in the bullet points on p667, show your letter of entitlement when you collect your prescription.

Even if you are not in one of the exempt groups, note the following.

- If you are a war disablement pensioner, you may qualify for free prescriptions and wigs and fabric supports. You may also be able to claim money back for dental treatment, sight tests, glasses or contact lenses or fares to hospital. You must have a valid war pension exemption certificate, and you must need the items or treatment, or to travel, because of your war disability. See p676 for where to claim.
- If you are a hospital inpatient, all medication and NHS treatment is provided free of charge (including glasses and contact lenses if prescribed through the hospital eye service). If you are an outpatient or are at a walk-in centre, medication taken and treatment given while you are in the hospital or walk-in centre is also provided without charge (but you may be charged for dentures and bridges).

Member of the family
'**Family**' means you and your partner and any child or qualifying young person included in your claim for the qualifying benefit or tax credit (see p323 for means-tested benefits and p286 for tax credits).

Partial help

If you do not qualify for full help with charges and fares, you may still qualify for partial help under the low income scheme.

The low income scheme

You and members of your family (see above for who counts) may be entitled to full or partial help with NHS charges under the low income scheme, even if you do not qualify for full help on other grounds. You must make a claim (see p676). The low income scheme is administered by the NHS Business Services Authority.

You (and members of your family) qualify for full help under the low income scheme if:

- you have capital of less than £16,000 (or if you live permanently in a care home, less than £23,250 in England and Scotland, or £24,000 in Wales).[2] Your capital is calculated as for IS (see Chapter 22); *and*
- your income (see p671) does not exceed your 'requirements' (see p669) by more than 50 per cent of the current cost of an English prescription (currently 50 per cent of £9.15 = £4.57).[3] If your income exceeds your requirements by

more than this amount, see below to find out whether you qualify for partial help with charges.

If you are entitled to full help with NHS charges under the low income scheme, you are issued with an HC2 certificate. If you are entitled to partial help, you are issued with an HC3 certificate.

Partial help with items and services

If you do not qualify for full help with NHS charges, you (and members of your family) may qualify for partial help with these under the low income scheme. You may get:[4]

- reduced-cost dental treatment (including check-ups) and appliances (including dentures); *and*
- reduced-cost sight tests. There is no set charge for sight tests, so it is worth shopping around if you are not entitled to a free test; *and*
- vouchers towards the cost of glasses and contact lenses; *and*
- in England, reduced-cost wigs and fabric supports (these are free in Wales and Scotland); *and*
- partial help with fares to receive NHS treatment.

Note: in England, you cannot qualify for reduced-cost prescriptions under the low income scheme, only free prescriptions. If you cannot qualify for free prescriptions, see p673 for information about prepayment certificates. In Wales and Scotland, prescriptions are free of charge.

You are expected to pay up to a set amount towards the charges. The set amount is:[5]

- for dental charges and charges for wigs and fabric supports, three times the amount by which your income exceeds your requirements (your 'excess income');
- for glasses or lenses, twice the amount of your excess income;
- for a sight test or fares to receive NHS treatment, the amount of your excess income.

Example

Martin's income exceeds his requirements by £6 so he cannot qualify for full help under the low income scheme. However, he may get partial help. He has to pay the first £18 of dental charges and charges for wigs and fabric supports, the first £6 of the cost of a sight test, the first £12 towards the cost of glasses and lenses and the first £6 of his fares to receive NHS treatment. If he lives in England, he must pay the full cost of prescriptions.

Calculating your requirements

Your 'requirements' are similar to the IS 'applicable amount' (see Chapter 17). The most significant elements and differences are set out below. There are no reductions in the applicable amounts of people who are subject to immigration control or who are not habitually resident in the UK, or for students, people engaged in a trade dispute or people without accommodation.

Your requirements are made up of the following elements.[6]

- **Personal allowance(s):**

Single person aged under 25	£58.90
Single person aged under 25, entitled to ESA work-related activity or support component, or incapable of work for at least 28 weeks starting on or after 27 October 2008	£74.35
Single person aged 25–59 or lone parent aged under 60	£74.35
Single person or lone parent aged 60 or over	£173.75
Couples, both partners aged under 60	£116.80
Couples, one or both partners aged 60 or over	£265.20

- **Premiums:** the disability, enhanced disability, severe disability and carer premiums are added to your requirements if you would qualify for them under the IS rules (see p339).

A disability premium can also be included if you or your partner have been incapable of work for 28 weeks. It can also be included if you (or your partner) have been awarded ESA which includes a work-related activity or support component, or if you (or s/he) have been getting ESA for at least 28 weeks. You (and your partner) must be under 60.

If you are a single claimant or a lone parent, the amount of the disability premium is increased to £39.20 if you qualify for an ESA support component or if you are getting the middle or highest rate care component of disability living allowance (DLA), either rate of the daily living component of personal independence payment (PIP) or armed forces independence payment, and have been getting ESA or have been incapable of work, for at least 28 weeks.

An enhanced disability premium can be included if you (or your partner) are getting the DLA highest rate care component, the enhanced rate of the daily living component of PIP, armed forces independence payment or ESA which includes a support component. You (and your partner) must be under 60.

- **Weekly council tax.**
- **Weekly rent** *less* **any housing benefit** (HB) and any non-dependant deductions, applied broadly in the same way as the deductions under the rules on IS housing costs (see p363). Deductions for fuel and ineligible service charges are made in accordance with the HB rules.
- **Weekly mortgage interest and capital payments on loans** secured on a home, to buy a home or to adapt a home for the special needs of a disabled person, and payments on an endowment policy relating to the purchase of a home. Some other housing costs can be included. Deductions are made for non-dependants.

If you live permanently in a care home, your requirements are your weekly accommodation charge, including meals and services, and a personal expenses allowance. If your place is being funded by a local authority (fully or in part), you are exempt from some charges.

Calculating your income

Your income is calculated as for IS (see Chapter 20), with modifications. These include the following.[7]

- Your income is normally taken into account in the week in which it is paid. If you are affected by a trade dispute, your normal earnings are taken into account.
- You are entitled to an earnings disregard of £20 if you get a disability premium (see p341), or if you or your partner are aged 60 or over.
- If you (or your partner) are doing permitted work while claiming ESA (see p1043), the amount of earnings that can be disregarded is the same as for income-related ESA (see p429). If you *and* your partner are both doing permitted work, the disregard is applied to your joint income.
- The full amount of your (or your partner's) contributory ESA is taken into account, even if it is paid at a reduced rate because you failed to take part in a work-focused interview. This does not appear to apply if you come under the UC system (see p23).
- Regular liable relative payments (see p438) count as weekly income. Irregular payments are averaged over the 13 weeks prior to your claim. Lump-sum payments are treated as capital.
- Student loans and grants are divided by 52, unless you are in your final year or are doing a one-year course, in which case the loan is divided by the number of weeks you are studying. The £10 disregard from student loans only applies if you are eligible for a premium, you receive an allowance because of deafness, or you are not a student but your partner is. In addition, in England and Wales, sums in excess of a specified amount of a maintenance grant and certain loans paid to Scottish students studying in England or Wales are disregarded. Also, if a voluntary payment is taken into account, up to £20 of it is disregarded.
- Insurance policy payments for housing costs that cannot be met by IS count as income, but payments for unsecured loans for repairs and improvements (including premiums) are ignored.
- If you live permanently in residential or nursing care:
  - in Wales, no tariff income from any capital is taken into account;
  - in England and Scotland, the lower threshold for tariff income is £14,250. Remember that if your place is being funded by a local authority (in full or in part), you are exempt from some charges.
- The savings credit of PC is ignored as income.

2. **Prescriptions**

Prescriptions are free in Wales and Scotland. You qualify for free prescriptions in England (and you can get an English prescription free of charge in Wales and Scotland) if:[8]

- you are in one of the exempt groups listed on p667; *or*
- you qualify under the low income scheme (see p668); *or*
- you are aged 60 or over; *or*
- you are aged under 16, or you are under 19 and in full-time education; *or*
- you are pregnant or have given birth in the last 12 months; *or*
- you are a permanent resident in a care home and your place is being partly or wholly funded by a local authority; *or*
- you are prescribed or given specific medicines in respect of a pandemic disease; *or*
- you are in prison or a young offenders' institution or other secure accommodation (or were given the prescription while you were); *or*
- you are detained under the Immigration Act 1971 or section 62 of the Nationality, Immigration and Asylum Act 2002; *or*
- you have:
  - a continuing physical disability, which prevents you leaving your home except with the help of another person;
  - epilepsy requiring continuous anticonvulsive therapy;
  - a permanent fistula, including a caecostomy, ileostomy, laryngostomy or colostomy, needing continuous surgical dressing or an appliance;
  - diabetes mellitus (except where treatment is by diet alone);
  - diabetes insipidus and other forms of hypopituitarism;
  - myxoedema;
  - hypoparathyroidism;
  - forms of hypoadrenalism (including Addison's disease), for which specific substitution therapy is essential;
  - myasthenia gravis;
  - a sexually transmitted disease; *or*
- you are undergoing treatment for cancer, the effects of cancer or the effects of cancer treatment.

If you have any of the conditions listed in the last two bullet points, ask your GP for Form FP92A to apply for a medical exemption certificate which you should present when you collect your prescription. Medical exemption certificates are valid for no more than five years.

If you are exempt from NHS charges on the basis that you are pregnant or have given birth in the last 12 months, ask your midwife, health visitor or GP for a maternity exemption form.

Prepayment certificates

In England, if you are not exempt from charges and you need more than three prescription items in three months or 12 items in a year, you can save money by buying a prepayment certificate.

Apply online, by post, by telephone or at a registered chemist on Form FP95, which you can get from chemists, some surgeries and relevant health bodies. You can download Form FP95, buy a prepayment certificate and apply for a refund of prescription charges you have already paid at nhsbsa.nhs.uk/help-nhs-prescription-costs/prescription-prepayment-certificates or by calling 0300 330 1341. You can pay by credit or debit card or in monthly instalments by direct debit.

A refund can be claimed in certain circumstances – eg, if you buy a prepayment certificate and then qualify for free prescriptions.

3. Dental treatment and dentures

NHS dental check-ups are free in Scotland. In England, Wales and Scotland, you qualify for free NHS dental treatment (including check-ups) and appliances (including dentures) if, when your treatment is arranged or charges are made:[9]
- you are in one of the exempt groups listed on p667; or
- you qualify under the low income scheme (see p668); or
- you are under 18, or you are under 19 and in full-time education; or
- in Wales, for free check-ups only, you are under 25 or are 60 or over; or
- you are pregnant or have given birth within the last 12 months; or
- you are a permanent resident in a care home and your place is being partly or wholly funded by a local authority; or
- in England and Wales, you are in prison or a young offenders' institution; or
- you are a patient of the community dental service (available if you have difficulty getting treatment because of a disability or for other reasons – contact your health authority for details) or an NHS hospital dental service. **Note:** there may be a charge for dentures and bridges.

4. Sight tests and glasses

Free sight tests

NHS sight tests are free in Scotland. In England and Wales you qualify for a free NHS sight test if:[10]
- you are in one of the exempt groups listed on p667; or
- you qualify under the low income scheme (see p668); or

- you are aged 60 or over; *or*
- you are under 16, or you are under 19 and in full-time education; *or*
- you are registered blind or partially sighted; *or*
- you have been prescribed complex or powerful lenses; *or*
- you have been diagnosed as having diabetes or glaucoma or are at risk of getting glaucoma; *or*
- you are aged 40 or over and are the parent, brother, sister or child of someone with glaucoma; *or*
- you are a patient of the hospital eye service; *or*
- in England, you are on leave from prison or a young offenders' institution.

Vouchers for glasses and contact lenses

If you are given a prescription for glasses following an eye test, you may be entitled to a voucher that you can use to buy glasses or contact lenses if you need these for the first time, or because your previous ones have worn out through fair wear and tear, or your new prescription differs from your old one. You qualify if:[11]
- you are in one of the exempt groups listed on p667; *or*
- you qualify under the low income scheme (see p668); *or*
- you are under 16, or under 19 and in full-time education; *or*
- you are a hospital eye service patient needing frequent changes of glasses or contact lenses; *or*
- in England, you are on leave from prison or a young offenders' institution; *or*
- you have been prescribed complex or powerful lenses.

In addition, you may be entitled to a voucher when your glasses or lenses need to be replaced or repaired if, because of illness (illness or disability in Scotland), you have lost or damaged them and the cost of repair or replacement is not covered by insurance or warranty. This only applies if:[12]
- you are under 16, or under 19 and in full-time education. **Note:** the requirement for the loss or damage to have been caused by illness (illness or disability in Scotland) does not apply to children under 16 and, in England, to young people under 18 who were previously looked after by a local authority;[13] *or*
- you or a member of your family (see p668 for who counts) are covered by the first bullet point listed under 'Exempt groups' on p667; *or*
- you qualify under the low income scheme (see p668); *or*
- you have been prescribed complex or powerful lenses.

You can redeem the voucher at any supplier when you buy your glasses or contact lenses (or have glasses repaired). Vouchers are, however, only valid for two years.[14] Vouchers might not cover the full cost of the glasses or lenses you choose to buy. Prices vary; you may need to shop around if you do not want to pay the extra cost.

5. Wigs and fabric supports

Wigs and fabric supports are free in Scotland and Wales. You qualify for free wigs and fabric supports in England if:[15]

- you are in one of the exempt groups listed on p667; *or*
- you qualify under the low income scheme (see p668); *or*
- you are a hospital inpatient; *or*
- you are aged under 16, or under 19 and in full-time education; *or*
- you are a permanent resident in a care home and your place is being partly or wholly funded by a local authority; *or*
- you are in prison or a young offenders' institution or are detained under the Immigration Act 1971 or section 62 of the Nationality, Immigration and Asylum Act 2002.

6. Fares to receive NHS treatment

You qualify for full help with your fares to attend a hospital or any other establishment for NHS treatment or services if:[16]

- you are in one of the exempt groups listed on p667; *or*
- you qualify under the low income scheme (see p668); *or*
- you are a permanent resident in a care home and your place is being partly or wholly funded by a local authority; *or*
- you live in the Isles of Scilly or the Scottish Islands or Highlands and have to travel more than a specified distance. Special rules, including maximum costs, apply.[17]

The travel expenses of a companion can also be covered – eg, if your child is attending a hospital and you need to accompany her/him, or if you need to be accompanied for medical reasons. You get help with the cost of travelling by the cheapest means of transport that is reasonable and, in Scotland, if necessary, the cost of overnight accommodation. This usually means standard-class public transport. If you have to travel by car or taxi, you should be paid a mileage allowance and road and toll charges, or taxi fares.

Claim at the place where you receive NHS treatment. You may be able to request payment in advance of travelling if this is necessary.

Travel expenses can be covered if you are travelling abroad to receive NHS treatment if the means and cost of travel, as well as any requirements for a companion, have been agreed in advance with the health service body that has arranged the treatment. In England and Wales, you are entitled to payment for the cost of travel to and from the airport, ferry port or international train station if you are in one of the above groups. You are also entitled to payment or repayment of onward travelling expenses to the treatment centre, whether or not you come into one of the above groups. In Scotland, the rules do not specify what can be covered.

7. **Claims and refunds**

In some situations, you do not have to make a claim for help with charges.

- If you are exempt on the grounds of your age, receipt of a qualifying benefit or because you are a full-time student under 19, complete the back of the prescription form (if required), or complete the appropriate form at your dentist, optician or hospital. See below if you get universal credit (UC).
- If you are an asylum seeker receiving asylum support, an HC2 certificate is issued by the Home Office. For further advice, phone Migrant Help on 0808 801 0503.
- You need an exemption certificate (which you should be sent automatically) if you are exempt because you receive tax credits. This could be up to eight weeks after you are awarded tax credits. If you have not yet received your exemption certificate, sign the prescription form, or other appropriate form, to say you do not have to pay, and use your tax credits award notice as proof.
- If you are exempt because you are pregnant or have given birth in the last 12 months, you need an exemption certificate. Obtain one by completing a form, which you can get from your doctor, midwife or health visitor.
- If you are entitled to free prescriptions because you have one of the conditions listed on p672 or you are undergoing treatment for cancer, the effects of cancer or the effects of cancer treatment, you need an exemption certificate. Apply on Form FP92A, which you can get from your GP.

In other cases, you must make a claim. **Note:** if you are a war disablement pensioner, contact the Veterans UK helpline on 0808 1914 2 18 or see gov.uk/government/publications/war-pension-scheme/war-pension-scheme-what-you-need-to-know.

Claiming if you get universal credit

Not all help with health costs claim forms have a tick box for UC. In this situation, the official NHS information suggests that you tick the box for income-based jobseeker's allowance instead.[18] If you are unsure whether you are entitled to help with health costs because you do not know how much you earned in your last complete assessment period before the day you apply for help with health costs, check your online journal or call the UC helpline (tel: 0800 328 5644). If you cannot get a figure for your last month's earned income and you think it might exceed the threshold, you should pay the relevant charge and ask for a refund form at the same time. For prescription charges, you will not be able to get the refund form (Form FP57) at a later stage. If you receive help with health costs when you are not entitled, you may have to pay a penalty (see p678).

Claiming under the low income scheme

To get full or partial help with charges and fares under the low income scheme, you must make a claim. This includes if you are an asylum seeker but you are not receiving asylum support. If you *are* receiving asylum support, see above. This also includes if you are exempt because you live in a care home or you are aged 16 or 17 and were previously looked after by a local authority.

Claim on Form HC1, available from Jobcentre Plus offices or NHS hospitals, some chemists, GP practices, dentists, opticians or advice centres. At nhsbsa.nhs.uk/nhs-low-income-scheme you can order a form (in England only) or you can download it. You can also get a form by phoning 0300 330 1343 (England), 0345 603 1108 (Wales) or 0131 275 6386 (Scotland). Another person can apply on your behalf if you are unable to act for yourself.

If you live in a care home or you are aged 16 or 17 and were previously looked after by a local authority, you can use a shorter Form HC1(SC).

Getting a certificate and when it expires

If you qualify for:
- full help, you are sent an HC2 certificate;
- partial help, you are sent an HC3 certificate which tells you the contribution you must make towards the charges.

Certificates are normally valid for 12 months. However, they are usually valid for:[19]
- five years if you are a single person aged 65 or over, or one of a couple, one aged 60 or over and the other aged 65 or over. This only applies if you do not receive earnings, or payments from an occupational pension, a personal pension or an annuity, and you do not have a dependent child or young person as a member of your household; *or*
- six months from the date of claim if you are receiving asylum support; *or*
- until the end of your course or the start of the next academic year if you are a full-time student.

Make a repeat claim on Form HC1 shortly before the expiry date. If you have a five-year certificate, you must notify the issuing authority of any changes in the composition of your family or household. In other cases, changes of circumstances (eg, starting work and increases in income) do not affect the validity of a certificate. However, if the change could result in increased help (eg, your income has *decreased*), you can reapply for a fresh assessment before the certificate expires.

Proof of entitlement

You are normally asked for proof that you are entitled to full or partial help with charges, although you should not be denied an item or service if you are unable to provide the required evidence. If you have an HC2 or HC3 certificate, show this to the dentist, optician, hospital or pharmacist (you may also have to enter details on the appropriate form). In other cases, you may need to show evidence of your date of birth, student status or exemption certificate.

Overpayments and fraud

If you receive help to which you were not entitled, you can be issued with a penalty notice requiring you to pay the charge you should have paid plus a penalty, unless you can show that you did not act 'wrongfully' or with 'any lack of care'. The penalty can be increased if you do not pay it within 28 days, and court proceedings can be taken to recover the debt. Anyone wrongly claiming help with charges on your behalf can be liable to pay a penalty charge. You can also be prosecuted if you obtain help wrongly, on the basis of a false statement or representation.[20]

Delays and complaints

For general queries or to make an informal complaint, telephone 0300 330 1343. If you are unhappy with the decision on your claim or how it has been dealt with, or there are delays in obtaining a certificate, you can make a formal complaint by telephone, in writing or email to the head of the relevant service at the NHS Business Services Authority. See nhsbsa.nhs.uk/contact-us/complaints for more details.

If necessary, you could pay for the treatment or items you need and, after the outcome of your complaint, try to obtain a refund.

Refunds

If you pay for an item or service that you could have got free, or at reduced cost, you can apply for a refund. Do this within three months of paying the charge, although the time limit can, in some cases, be extended if you can show good cause for applying late – eg, you were ill.[21]

Apply for a refund of a prescription charge (in England) on Form FP57, which you must obtain when you pay as one cannot be supplied later. For other items and services, apply on the relevant Form HC5 specific to that item/service, available to download at nhsbsa.nhs.uk or by phoning 0300 330 1343 (England), 0345 603 1108 (Wales) or 0131 275 6386 (Scotland), or from a Jobcentre Plus office or NHS hospital. You must submit a receipt or other documents to show that you have paid the charge. If you need an HC2 or HC3 certificate and have not applied for one, send a Form HC1 with your application for a refund.

Notes

1. Who can get health benefits

1 **E** Regs 2-5 NHS(TERC) Regs; reg 3 POS Regs; reg 8 NHS(OCP) Regs 2013
   S Regs 2 and 4 NHS(TERC)(S) Regs; regs 3 and 8 NHS(OCP)(S) Regs
   W Regs 2-5 NHS(TERC)(W) Regs; reg 13 NHS(GOS) Regs; regs 3 and 8 NHS(OCP) Regs

2 **E** Sch 1 Table A NHS(TERC) Regs
   S Sch Part 1 NHS(TERC)(S) Regs
   W Sch 1 Table A NHS(TERC)(W) Regs

3 **E** Reg 5(2)(e) and (f) NHS(TERC) Regs; reg 3(2)(c) and (d) POS Regs; regs 3(2) and 8(3)(b) and (c) NHS(OCP) Regs 2013
   S Reg 4(2)(c) and (d) NHS(TERC)(S) Regs; regs 3(2) and 8(3)(e) and (f) NHS(OCP)(S) Regs
   W Reg 5(2)(e) NHS(TERC)(W) Regs; reg 13(2)(e) and (f) NHS(GOS) Regs; regs 3(2) and 8(3)(e) and (f) NHS(OCP) Regs

4 **E** Reg 6 NHS(TERC) Regs; regs 3 and 8 NHS(OCP) Regs 2013
   S Reg 5 NHS(TERC)(S) Regs; regs 3 and 8 NHS(OCP)(S) Regs
   W Reg 6 NHS(TERC)(W) Regs; regs 3 and 8 NHS(OCP) Regs

5 **E** Reg 6 NHS(TERC) Regs; regs 7, 15 and 20 NHS(OCP) Regs 2013
   S Reg 6 NHS(TERC)(S) Regs; regs 14 and 19 NHS(OCP)(S) Regs
   W Reg 6 NHS(TERC)(W) Regs; regs 7, 14 and 19 NHS(OCP) Regs

6 **E** Reg 17 and Sch 1 Table B NHS(TERC) Regs
   S Reg 8 and Sch Part 2 NHS(TERC)(S) Regs
   W Reg 16 and Sch 1 Table B NHS(TERC)(W) Regs

7 **E** Reg 16 and Sch 1 Table A NHS(TERC) Regs
   S Reg 8 and Sch Part 1 NHS(TERC)(S) Regs
   W Reg 15 and Sch 1 Table A NHS(TERC)(W) Regs

2. Prescriptions

8 **E** Regs 10-13 NHS(CDA) Regs; regs 4 and 5 NHS(TERC) Regs
   S Regs 3 and 4 NHS(FP&CDA)(S) Regs
   W Regs 3, 4 and 8 NHS(FP&CDA)(W) Regs; regs 4 and 5 NHS(TERC)(W) Regs

3. Dental treatment and dentures

9 **E** s177 NHSA 2006; regs 3 and 7 and Sch 5 NHS(DC) Regs; regs 4 and 5 NHS(TERC) Regs
   S Sch 11 NHS(S)A 1978; reg 5 and Sch 2 NHS(DC)(S) Regs; regs 3 and 4 NHS(TERC)(S) Regs
   W s126 NHS(W)A 2006; regs 3 and 7 and Sch 5 NHS(DC)(W) Regs; regs 4 and 5 NHS(TERC)(W) Regs

4. Sight tests and glasses

10 **E** Reg 3 POS Regs; regs 3 and 8 NHS(OCP) Regs 2013
   W Reg 13 NHS(GOS) Regs; regs 3 and 8 NHS(OCP) Regs

11 **E** Regs 8 and 9 NHS(OCP) Regs 2013
   S Regs 8 and 9 NHS(OCP)(S) Regs
   W Regs 8 and 9 NHS(OCP) Regs

12 **E** Regs 8 and 16 NHS(OCP) Regs 2013
   S Regs 8 and 15 NHS(OCP)(S) Regs
   W Regs 8 and 15 NHS(OCP) Regs

13 **E** Reg 16(3) NHS(OCP) Regs 2013
   S Reg 15(1) NHS(OCP)(S) Regs
   W Reg 15(1) NHS(OCP) Regs

14 **E** Reg 12(1) NHS(OCP) Regs 2013
   S Reg 12(1) NHS(OCP)(S) Regs
   W Reg 12(1) NHS(OCP) Regs

5. Wigs and fabric supports

15 **E** Regs 10,11 and 12 NHS(CDA) Regs; regs 4 and 5 NHS(TERC) Regs
   S Regs 3 and 4 NHS(FP&CDA)(S) Regs
   W Regs 3, 4 and 8 NHS(FP&CDA)(W) Regs

6. Fares to receive NHS treatment

16 **E** s183(a) NHSA 2006; regs 3 and 5
      NHS(TERC) Regs
      S s75A(1)(b) NHS(S)A 1978; regs 3 and
      4 NHS(TERC)(S) Regs
      W s131(a) NHS(W)A 2006; regs 3 and 5
      NHS(TERC)(W) Regs
17 **E** Reg 9 NHS(TERC) Regs
      S Reg 7 NHS(TERC)(S) Regs

7. Claims and refunds

18 nhs.uk/using-the-nhs/help-with-health-
      costs/help-with-health-costs-for-people-
      getting-universal-credit
19 **E** Reg 8 NHS(TERC) Regs
      S Reg 10 NHS(TERC)(S) Regs
      W Reg 8 NHS(TERC)(W) Regs
20 **E** ss193 and 194 NHSA 2006
      S ss99ZA and 99ZB NHS(S)A 1978
      W ss141 and 142 NHS(W)A 2006
21 **E** Reg 11 NHS(TERC) Regs; reg 18
      NHS(CDA) Regs; regs 6 and 24
      NHS(OCP) Regs 2013
      S Reg 11 NHS(TERC)(S) Regs; reg 5
      NHS(FP&CDA)(S) Regs; reg 20
      NHS(OCP)(S) Regs
      W Reg 10 NHS(TERC)(W) Regs; regs
      3(10) and 11A NHS(FP&CDA)(W) Regs;
      regs 6 and 20 NHS(OCP) Regs

Chapter 32

Industrial injuries benefits

This chapter covers:
1. Who can get industrial injuries benefits (p682)
2. Industrial injuries disablement benefit (p693)
3. Reduced earnings allowance (p695)
4. Retirement allowance (p696)
5. Special benefit rules (p697)
6. Claims and backdating (p697)
7. Getting paid (p699)
8. Tax, other benefits and the benefit cap (p700)

Key facts
- Industrial injuries benefits are paid if you are disabled as a result of an accident at work or a disease caused by your job (but not if this is self-employment).
- The main industrial injuries benefit is **disablement benefit**, but you may also qualify for **reduced earnings allowance** or **retirement allowance**.
- All industrial injuries benefits are non-means-tested benefits.
- You do not have to have paid national insurance contributions to qualify.
- You can qualify whether you are in or out of work.
- Industrial injuries benefits are administered and paid by the DWP.
- If you disagree with an industrial injuries benefit decision, you can apply for a revision or a supersession (see Chapter 56), or appeal against it (see Chapter 57). You must apply for a mandatory reconsideration before you can appeal.

Future changes

In Scotland, industrial injuries benefits will be replaced by employment-injury assistance from autumn 2022. Social Security Scotland will then be responsible for administering and paying this benefit. See Chapter 71, and AskCPAG.org.uk and CPAG's *Welfare Rights Bulletin* for updates.

Part 5: Other benefits
Chapter 32: Industrial injuries benefits
1. Who can get industrial injuries benefits

1. **Who can get industrial injuries benefits**

You can qualify for industrial injuries benefits if you satisfy the **'industrial injury condition'** – ie:[1]

- you have had a 'personal injury' in an 'industrial accident' (see p683) or you have a 'prescribed industrial disease' (see p687); *and*
- at the time of the injury you were an employed earner (see below); *and*
- as a result of that accident or disease, you have had a 'loss of faculty' (see p689); *and*
- as a result of that 'loss of faculty', you are 'disabled'.

Industrial injuries benefits include industrial injuries disablement benefit, reduced earnings allowance (REA) and retirement allowance. You can only qualify for REA or retirement allowance if your accident or disease occurred before October 1990.

If you have been injured by your work, you may also have the right to sue your employer. Legal help may be available and you may be able to get a free consultation with a solicitor. Your right to compensation from your employer is separate from your rights to benefit under the industrial injuries scheme (although your compensation may be reduced if you have received benefits from the DWP – see p1212).

Employed earners

You can only get industrial injuries benefits if you were an 'employed earner' (see p962) and your accident or disease was caused by your employment.[2] If you are self-employed, you are excluded from the scheme.

If you pay, or ought to pay, class 1 national insurance (NI) contributions (see p962) as an employed earner, you can qualify for industrial injuries benefits. This includes if you pay class 1 (and, in the case of volunteer development workers, class 2 – see p963) contributions while abroad.[3] You can also qualify if your earnings are too low to pay contributions.

Certain workers are treated as employed earners – eg, apprentices, agency workers, taxi drivers, office cleaners and various others.[4] You can also be treated as an employed earner if you are participating in a government course or training scheme which forms part of a mandatory work scheme. The person or organisation providing the training is treated as the employer for the purposes of making a claim.[5]

You are treated as *not* being an employed earner if:[6]

- you are employed by your spouse or civil partner and either your employment is not for the purpose of her/his business or profession (eg, if your partner employs you as her/his carer) or your earnings are normally below the lower earnings limit (see p962); *or*

- you are employed by a close relative (parent, step-parent, grandparent, son, daughter, stepchild, grandchild, brother, sister, half-brother or half-sister) in a private house where you both live, and your employment is not for your relative's trade or business carried out there; or
- you are a member of, or a civilian employed by, visiting armed forces, unless (in the case of a civilian employee) you are normally resident in the UK.

If you were not lawfully employed in the work in which you had the accident or contracted the disease which gave rise to your claim for benefit, you can still be treated as an employed earner. This is at the DWP's discretion.[7]

Personal injury

Personal injury includes the obvious, such as broken legs or arms, but also covers the less obvious, such as strains and psychological injury.[8] An assault at work causing slight physical injury may cause a far greater psychological injury resulting in agoraphobia, for example. The question is whether or not you have experienced a physiological or psychological change for the worse. It is not enough just to be in pain if the pain is merely a symptom of an existing condition and does not make that condition substantially worse.[9] The damage must be to you or part of you. Dislocation of an artificial hip joint counts as a personal injury,[10] but damage to a pair of spectacles does not.[11]

Accident

The term 'accident' has been defined as an unlooked-for mishap or occurrence.[12] However, an accident need only be unexpected from your point of view.[13] It does not matter if it could have been anticipated by an expert. If you do a heavy or dangerous job where accidents are common, a resulting injury is just as much an accident as if your job is sedentary and comparatively safe. A heart attack can be an injury but there needs to be some external event or series of events causing it, such as heavy lifting or work-related stress.[14] Deliberate acts by third parties can be accidents – eg, assaults on security workers or on staff in shops and hospitals.[15]

An accident is 'industrial' if you can show a connection with your work. This connection is established if the accident arose 'out of and in the course of your employment'.[16] It is not only industrial workers who can have 'industrial accidents'; all employees can. For example, if you are an office worker and a badly loaded filing cabinet tilts and falls on you, this should count as an 'industrial accident'. There need not be a dramatic event; any accident sustained while you are doing your job can qualify – eg, spilling a hot drink and scalding yourself. An illness brought on by conversation could count as being caused by an industrial accident.[17]

Part 5: Other benefits
Chapter 32: Industrial injuries benefits
1. Who can get industrial injuries benefits

Accident or process?

Benefit is payable for an 'accident', but not for a 'process' (unless it causes a 'prescribed disease' – see p687). Falling from a ladder and breaking your leg is an accident, but developing back pain as the result of years of heavy manual work is a process, as is breathing in dust over many years.[18] However, sometimes a series of events, over a period of time, can be treated as an accident for benefit purposes.[19] The cumulative effect of a series of incidents can also result in an accident.[20] Your claim for benefit should not be refused simply because you cannot identify which incidents caused the injury.[21]

Example

Cyril's job is trimming excess plastic from electrical cables with a pair of clippers. A particularly rigid batch comes through and each cut requires greater strength. Over two or three days he suffers a strain injury in his hand. The series of cuts constitutes a series of accidents that meets the definition.

It is easier to establish the series of events as an accident if the period of time is fairly short,[22] or if it is noticed at an identifiable moment.[23] An accident is proved if you can establish that an identifiable occurrence must have happened, even if it is impossible to prove when.[24]

In the course of employment

The accident must arise 'in the course of employment'.

Generally, when you arrive at your employer's workplace and are on her/his private property, you are 'in the course of your employment'. You do not have to have clocked in or have reported to your workplace. If you arrive early (eg, to get ready for work or to have a meal in the canteen),[25] you are covered, although if you arrive early for your own convenience, you are not.[26] You are probably covered during breaks from working if you remain on the employer's property,[27] but probably not if you go elsewhere. So if, during a tea break, you go to a local shop to buy a snack, you are outside the course of your employment.[28] If you are allowed to have a snack either at home or at work while still on duty, you are covered.[29]

While at work, most activities are considered to be in the course of employment.[30] Chatting[31] or attending union meetings,[32] for example, are 'reasonably incidental' to the employment, provided they are not done in breach of instructions.[33] Even if you were doing something in breach of instructions, you may still be covered if:

- the accident would have been taken as arising out of, and in the course of, your employment if you had not been acting in breach of those instructions; *and*

- what you were doing was for the purposes of, or in connection with, your employment.[34]

Example
Clara works in a paper factory where there is an absolute ban on riding on the load of a forklift truck. She is seen riding on the load, falls off and is injured. Usually she would not be covered, but she saw the load was slipping and rode on the truck in order to hold it on. This was done for the purposes of her employment and so on this occasion she is covered.

Even if you are at home, depending on your contract, you may be covered.[35] You may be covered when you are off on sick leave, if you are engaged in contractual duties.[36]

Example
While on sick leave with stress, John is seen relaxing in the park by a former colleague he had reported for theft. He is assaulted and his jaw is broken. This is an industrial accident arising *out of* his employment (see p686) but not in the course of it, as he was not engaged in any contractual duties, or any activities related to his work, at the time of the assault.

In putting forward your claim (see p697) or arguing your case at an appeal (see Chapter 57), consider all aspects of your employment, including the wording of your contract and the degree of flexibility in the arrangements between you and your employer.[37]

Accidents while travelling
You are not in the course of your employment (see p684) during ordinary journeys to and from work, unless you are travelling on transport operated by or on behalf of your employer, or arranged by your employer, and not being operated in the ordinary course of a public transport service.[38]

Many employees have no set place of work – eg, lorry drivers, home helps, fuel company employees. A lorry driver is at work when driving her/his lorry, but gas company workers travelling directly from home to their first job of the day are not always in the course of employment (see p684), even if driving a company van. It depends on the circumstances, including the rules for the use of the van.[39] In one case, a home help was found to be in the course of her employment travelling between jobs, but not going to the first job or from the last. This is because she became engaged in her employment once she started at the first job and remained engaged until the end of the day.[40]

Some employees with no fixed hours of work may be regarded as covered from the moment of leaving home.[41] Caselaw has eased the rules on travelling – eg, to conferences or meetings. So, you can be treated as being at your place of work

Part 5: Other benefits
Chapter 32: Industrial injuries benefits
1. Who can get industrial injuries benefits

while attending a meeting at a site where you do not work.[42] You must look at all the factors when deciding whether or not you were in the course of your employment. For example, a police officer who had to travel about 40 miles from home to a training course was in the course of his employment while travelling.[43] Provided you go reasonably directly, with no marked deviation from a proper route, and do not embark on activities unrelated to the journey, you may be covered.

One important factor in deciding whether you are in the course of your employment is whether you receive wages for travelling.[44] However, if you receive a flat-rate travelling allowance as compensation for having to work at a workplace other than your normal base, this may not be enough to make your journey to your alternative workplace part of your work.[45]

Out of employment

As well as arising in the course of your employment (see p684), the accident (see p683) must arise 'out of' your employment, so that in some way the employment contributed to it. For example, the fact that you suffered a detached retina at work is not sufficient to show it arose 'out of' the employment, but medical evidence which shows that it was caused by sudden head movements while inspecting a production line enables you to establish that an industrial accident (see p683) took place. An unexplained fracture while walking at work is not an industrial accident,[46] but it is if you slip and the fracture occurs while you are falling. You are covered even if you are more susceptible to injury because, for example, your bones are brittle[47] or your eyesight is poor.

Example
Joe, a farm worker, suffers sudden pain in the groin while doing his normal job of digging. It is found that a previous hernia, which had been surgically repaired, has given way again. The DWP says that this could have happened at any time and so did not arise 'out of' the employment. Joe's doctor says it could have happened at any time but probably did so at that time because of the heavy digging. The First-tier Tribunal awards him benefit.

An accident also arises out of your employment if it arises in the course of employment (see p684) and it is caused by:[48]
- another's misconduct, 'skylarking' or negligence; *or*
- the behaviour or presence of an animal (including a bird, fish or insect); *or*
- your being struck by any object or by lightning.

In all cases, you must not have contributed to the accident by your conduct, either outside your employment or by any act 'not incidental to' the employment. (This involves looking at what you are employed to do, then at whether you were discharging a duty when the accident occurred, or whether what you were doing was reasonably incidental to that duty.) If you are skylarking at work and are injured as a result, for example, this is not incidental to your employment. If you act to deter someone else from doing so, however, this does not take you out of the course of your employment.[49]

An accident is deemed to arise out of, and in the course of, your employment if you are helping people in an emergency, or trying to save property at or near where you are employed.[50]

Prescribed industrial disease

It is necessary for the disease to be a 'prescribed industrial disease'. This means it is on a list,[51] set out in regulations, of diseases that are known to have a link to a particular 'prescribed' occupation (see below).[52] Each prescribed disease has a statutory definition and you must fit within that. It is not sufficient simply to have a medical diagnosis that you have a particular condition.[53] From time to time new diseases are added to the list. However, you cannot claim for a disease for any period before it was added to the list.[54] Each prescribed industrial disease has a letter and number to identify it – eg, prescribed disease A12 is carpal tunnel syndrome and prescribed disease D1 is pneumoconiosis. The complete list is in Appendix 5.

If the DWP accepts that you have a prescribed industrial disease, other diseases which result from it are included when assessing your 'loss of faculty' and disablement.[55] See p689 for how your disablement is assessed.

Prescribed occupations

Different diseases are 'prescribed' for specific types of jobs because particular jobs have different health risks. To qualify for benefit on grounds of a prescribed industrial disease, you must have a disease which is on the list and prove that:
- you have worked in one or more of the jobs for which that disease is prescribed ('prescribed occupations'); *and*
- your job caused the disease.

If the DWP refuses to accept that you have worked in a prescribed occupation, you should obtain advice, preferably from your trade union or an advice agency. An expert's report may help to prove your case.

Time limits

For most prescribed diseases, you do not have to have worked in a prescribed occupation for any minimum length of time. You can also claim at any time, even if it is many years since you worked in that occupation. However, there are exceptions to these general rules. For example, if you have occupational deafness (prescribed disease A10), you must have worked in a prescribed occupation for 10 years and claim within five years of having done so.[56] If you have occupational asthma (prescribed disease D7), you must claim within 10 years of working in a

Part 5: Other benefits
Chapter 32: Industrial injuries benefits
1. Who can get industrial injuries benefits

prescribed occupation.[57] If you have cataracts (prescribed disease A2), you must have worked in a prescribed occupation for five years or more in aggregate.[58] Appendix 5 lists relevant time limits or qualifying periods for other prescribed diseases.

Cause

For some diseases, unless the contrary can be proved, it is assumed that, if you have the disease within a particular interval (one, two, six or 12 months, depending on the disease) of working in the prescribed occupation (see p687), the occupation caused it.[59] With other diseases, there is a presumption that a specific type of occupation caused them, regardless of when you last worked in that occupation.[60] There are also diseases where no assumed link exists (eg, dermatitis – prescribed disease D5), and you must establish the link 'on a balance of probabilities' – ie, that it is more likely than not that there is a connection.[61] The DWP investigates the connection issue, and you may need to ask your GP or consultant for a report linking the disease to your occupation. DWP guidance says that, for some prescribed diseases, barring exceptional circumstances, the presumption that the disease was caused by the occupation should be automatic.[62]

There are different time conditions for carpal tunnel syndrome (prescribed disease A12[63]), in respect of some occupations, tuberculosis (prescribed disease B5), pneumoconiosis (prescribed disease D1), and diseases due to chemical agents.[64]

Example
Fern has been a farm worker for 10 years and has developed osteoarthritis of the hip (prescribed disease A13). She also broke her hip on a climbing holiday three years ago. The climbing accident does not alter the presumption that her prescribed disease was caused by her occupation.

Onset and recrudescence

The 'onset' (date of starting) of a prescribed disease is taken as the date you first had a relevant 'loss of faculty' (see p689). In deafness cases, it is the later of either the date you first experienced the loss of faculty or the date you successfully claimed benefit.[65]

In diseases other than deafness, asthma and respiratory conditions, you can improve and then worsen again. It is important to know whether it is a 'recrudescence' (fresh outbreak of the existing disease) or a completely new attack. The first is deemed to be a continuation of the existing prescribed disease;[66] with the second, you have to wait 15 weeks before disablement benefit can be claimed. If a further attack starts during a current period of assessment, it is assumed to be a recrudescence unless proved otherwise.

Loss of faculty and disablement

In addition to showing the link between your injury or disease and your occupation, you must also establish that you have had a 'loss of faculty' and are 'disabled'.

'**Loss of faculty**' is the damage or impairment of part of the body or mind caused by the industrial accident or disease. '**Disability**' is the inability to do something as a result of that damage or impairment. The total of all of your disabilities, taken together, amount to a '**disablement**'. This disablement is expressed as a percentage.

In assessing your disablement, the DWP considers three questions.

- Has the relevant industrial accident (see p683) or prescribed disease (see p687) resulted in a loss of faculty (see below)?
- What is the extent of disablement resulting from a loss of faculty (this is expressed as a percentage – see below)?
- What period is to be taken into account by the assessment (see p692)?

A loss of faculty

A 'loss of faculty' is an 'impairment of the proper functioning of part of the body or mind'[67] caused by an accident or disease. A 'loss of faculty' is not the same as disablement. It includes disfigurement, even if the disfigurement is not accompanied by a loss of physical faculty.[68] A decision that there has been a personal injury resulting from an industrial accident (see p683) does not prevent the DWP or the First-tier Tribunal from finding that there is no loss of faculty.[69]

The extent of disablement

The extent of your disablement is assessed on a percentage basis. In order to qualify for disablement benefit (see p693), generally you must reach a threshold of at least 14 per cent disablement. However, a finding of at least 1 per cent may permit a claim for REA (see p695).

Any assessment between 14 and 19 per cent is treated as being 20 per cent.[70] If the total disablement from all industrial accidents and diseases is more than 20 per cent, it is rounded to the nearest multiple of 10 per cent, with multiples of 5 per cent being rounded upwards.[71] For example, an assessment of 22 per cent is rounded down to 20 per cent and an assessment of 25 per cent is rounded up to 30 per cent, as is an assessment of 26 per cent.

Some assessments of disablement are set out in regulations.[72] These are known as 'prescribed degrees of disablement' and include various amputations (eg, loss of a hand or a leg) and degrees of hearing loss (see Appendix 4). However, even in these cases, the DWP must take into account the real disablement resulting from an injury and increase or decrease the figure to arrive at a reasonable assessment[73] – eg, the loss of a right hand is more disabling for a right-handed person than for a left-handed person. The full extent of your disablement caused by the injury

Part 5: Other benefits
Chapter 32: Industrial injuries benefits
1. Who can get industrial injuries benefits

must be taken into account. A further disablement or condition which arises at a later date, but which can be shown to be caused by the industrial accident or disease, must be included in the assessment.[74]

Impaired function of the pleura, pericardium or peritoneum caused by diffuse mesothelioma automatically has an assessment of 100 per cent disablement.[75]

Apart from age, sex and physical and mental condition, your personal circumstances must be ignored, so that particular problems you may have, like the location of your office or the distance to the nearest bus stop, are not taken into account.

Your disablement should be assessed by comparing you with a person of the same age and sex whose physical and mental condition is 'normal'.[76]

When there is no prescribed degree of disablement, reference may be made to the prescribed percentages to help with the assessment.[77] Although you may suggest that your assessment should be a particular percentage, the DWP makes its own judgement.[78]

What happens at the assessment?

It is important that you are straightforward with the examining healthcare professional. There are checks to establish that your symptoms are consistent with the injury, and that your movements are consistent with the disablement you claim you have. Therefore, how you walk into the room and how you undress are also considered. Make sure that the person examining you is aware of all the things that you now cannot do as a result of your injury or disease.

Offsets if your disability has more than one cause

If a disability is congenital or arose before an industrial one, it is deducted from the total disablement.[79] The reduction is often called the 'offset'. Mistakes are sometimes made because the DWP incorrectly offsets for medical conditions that have not caused any disability.

Examples

Sam loses a hand, which would normally be 60 per cent, but he had previously lost the index finger. So 14 per cent is deducted, leaving 46 per cent (rounded up to 50 per cent).

Rhian has a back injury as a result of an industrial accident. The DWP has reduced her assessment by 5 per cent on the grounds of a pre-existing disability of which she knew nothing. Many people have spines that are slightly curved as a result of lifting things. The DWP may have looked at an x-ray, correctly considered that her curved spine was not due to the relevant accident and then incorrectly reduced her assessment.

In the second example, the DWP should have considered whether the pre-existing loss of faculty (see p689), the curved spine, really had (or would have) led to disablement that would have occurred regardless of the industrial accident. It should have considered, among other things, whether the loss of faculty led to disablement before the industrial accident occurred. There is no physical disablement if you do not have any pain or restriction of movement and it is, therefore, wrong to reduce your assessment unless there is a good reason for deciding that disablement would have arisen during the period of assessment even if the industrial accident had not occurred.

In the second example, depending on the medical opinion:

- there may be no offset; *or*
- it may be appropriate to make a life award (see p692) with some uniform offset over the whole period in respect of any future back problems Rhian is likely to have; *or*
- it may be appropriate to make a stepped assessment, making no offset initially but bringing one in at some future date, or applying different levels of offset for different parts of the period covered by the award.[80]

No reduction is made if your injury is one for which the regulations award 100 per cent and this is considered a reasonable assessment for the industrial accident.[81]

The DWP should also bear in mind that, even if you had a pre-existing problem which caused a disability, the accident may worsen the effects of it, as well as cause a new problem. In such a case, the assessment should reflect the increase in the original problem as well as the new disability.[82]

If another disability arose after an industrial accident, the DWP first has to assess the disablement arising from the industrial injury. If it is less than 11 per cent, any disability from the other cause is ignored. If it is more than 11 per cent, any extra disablement caused by the effect of the industrial injury on the other disability is added.[83]

Examples

Ali loses a little finger in an industrial accident and is assessed as 7 per cent disabled as a result. He then loses the other fingers of that hand in a non-industrial accident. He continues to be assessed as 7 per cent disabled because of the industrial accident.

Paul loses the middle, ring and little fingers of one hand in an industrial accident and is assessed as 30 per cent disabled as a result. He then loses the index finger of that hand in a non-industrial accident. His total disablement is now 50 per cent. But loss of the index finger only would have been 14 per cent. The disablement resulting from his industrial accident may, therefore, be reassessed at 36 per cent (50 per cent *minus* 14 per cent), which is rounded up to 40 per cent.

Two or more industrial accidents or diseases

If you have more than one industrial accident, the percentages of disablement (see p689 and Appendix 4) can be added together and may entitle you to benefit,

Part 5: Other benefits
Chapter 32: Industrial injuries benefits
1. Who can get industrial injuries benefits

even if neither accident would do so on its own. If you have two or more industrial accidents, you may end up in a situation where the second or later accident is made worse by the interaction with the effect of the previous accident(s). Your most recent assessment should include an increase for any such interaction.[84] This also applies if an industrial disease (see p687) interacts with the effects of an industrial accident.

Example
Divij has a fall at work and seriously injures his left leg. He receives a life assessment of 10 per cent. Years later, he has a further fall and seriously injures the other leg. He is assessed as 10 per cent disabled for that accident, with a further 5 per cent for the extra disability he has as a result of the interaction between the two injuries. The total of 25 per cent is rounded up, resulting in payment of a 30 per cent pension.

There are special rules if you have pneumoconiosis. The rules allow for certain conditions to be taken into account in order to increase the assessment, even though these conditions did not arise from the pneumoconiosis. Any effect of tuberculosis is assessed with the effects of the pneumoconiosis.[85] If your disability is assessed at 50 per cent because of the pneumoconiosis, any additional disability because of chronic obstructive pulmonary disease is added.[86] If you have made such a claim for pneumoconiosis, you cannot then make a separate claim for chronic obstructive pulmonary disease.[87]

The period covered by the assessment

The DWP or the First-tier Tribunal decides how long you are likely to be affected by a relevant loss of faculty and how long you have already been affected (see p689). Percentage assessments are usually made for six months, or for one or two years, or are given for life,[88] but definite dates must be given.

An assessment is either final or provisional.[89] You get a provisional assessment when there is doubt about what will happen in the future, and you are automatically called for another assessment at the end of the period.[90] Life assessments are final.

If you are given a final assessment for a fixed period, this means that the DWP believes you will no longer be affected by your accident or disease by the end of that period. If you think that the effects of the accident or disease will last for longer, consider an appeal against that assessment (see Chapter 57).

If your condition deteriorates during a period of assessment, or if you still have a disability at the end of a period for which you have been given a final assessment, you should apply for a supersession (see p1315).

An assessment of disablement for occupational deafness is for life.[91]

2. Industrial injuries disablement benefit

The main benefit linked to industrial accidents and diseases is industrial injuries disablement benefit (IIDB). You may qualify for additional amounts of benefit paid along with or as increases to IIDB. These are:
- constant attendance allowance (see p694);
- exceptionally severe disablement allowance (see p695);
- reduced earnings allowance (see p695).[92]

Who can get industrial injuries disablement benefit

You can qualify for IIDB if:[93]
- you satisfy the industrial injury condition (see p682) as a result of one or more industrial accidents (see p683) or prescribed diseases (see p687); *and*
- your resulting disablement is assessed as being at least 14 per cent (1 per cent in the case of pneumoconiosis, byssinosis and diffuse mesothelioma) (see p689 and Appendix 4); *and*
- 90 days (excluding Sundays) have elapsed since the date of the accident or of the onset of the prescribed disease or injury (if you have mesothelioma, you can be paid without serving this waiting period).

Disqualification

You may be disqualified for up to six weeks if you do not provide the required information or notify changes in your circumstances, or do not have a medical examination or treatment. You cannot, however, be disqualified for refusing to have an operation, unless it is a minor one.[94]

The rules about your age

There are no specific age rules or requirement to have paid national insurance contributions. You must simply be under a contract of employment. Therefore, a child who is working is covered, as well as a person over pension age.

People included in the claim

You claim IIDB for yourself. You cannot claim any increases for an adult or your child(ren) unless you are getting unemployability supplement (abolished for new claims after 5 April 1987).

Part 5: Other benefits
Chapter 32: Industrial injuries benefits
2. Industrial injuries disablement benefit

The amount of benefit

The amount of benefit you get depends on the extent of your disablement.[95] See p689 for how this is assessed.

Extent of disablement	£ per week
100%	182.00
90%	163.80
80%	145.60
70%	127.40
60%	109.20
50%	91.00
40%	72.80
30%	54.60
11% – 20%	36.40

IIDB can be paid if the assessment of your disablement is at least 14 per cent,[96] except in the cases of pneumoconiosis, byssinosis and diffuse mesothelioma, when it must be at least 1 per cent.[97] Before 1 October 1986, IIDB was paid for an assessment of disablement of at least 1 per cent. The old rules are still in force for claims made before this date.[98] If you are getting a payment as a result of such a small percentage assessment, see p176 of the 17th edition of CPAG's *Rights Guide to Non-Means-Tested Benefits*.

You may be able to get an increase of benefit (see below).

Increases of industrial injuries disablement benefit

You get increased IIDB if you qualify for constant attendance allowance or exceptionally severe disablement allowance.

Constant attendance allowance

You qualify for constant attendance allowance if:[99]

- you are entitled to IIDB based on a degree of disablement assessed at 100 per cent; *and*
- you require constant attendance as a result of the relevant loss of faculty (see p689).

Disablement as a result of pre-1948 industrial accidents and diseases, war injuries and injuries incurred while on police or fire duty, may be taken into account in considering the degree of your disablement.

The amount you get depends on your disability and the amount of attendance you need.[100]

- The higher weekly rate of £145.60 is paid if you are so 'so exceptionally severely disabled as to be entirely, or almost entirely dependent on (constant) attendance for the necessities of life and [are] likely to remain so dependent for a prolonged period and the attendance so required is whole-time'.

- The lower weekly rate of £72.80 is paid if you are 'to a substantial extent dependent on (constant) attendance for the necessities of life, and [are] likely to remain so dependent for a prolonged period'. This amount can be increased by up to £109.20 a week if 'the extent of such attendance is greater by reason of the beneficiary's exceptionally severe disablement'. If attendance is part time only, the amount payable is 'such sum as may be reasonable in the circumstances' (usually £36.40 a week).

Some people will be better off claiming disability living allowance, personal independence payment or attendance allowance instead, where this is paid at a higher rate.

Exceptionally severe disablement allowance
This is paid at the weekly rate of £72.80 if you are entitled to constant attendance allowance (or would be if you were not in hospital) at the higher or intermediate rate and you are likely to remain so permanently.[101]

3. Reduced earnings allowance

Reduced earnings allowance (REA) is available if you had an accident or started to have a disease before 1 October 1990. A successful first claim can still be made now if you had an accident or disease before this date.

The amount of REA you get depends on whether your current earnings, or earnings in a job which it is considered you could do, are less than the current earnings in your previous 'regular occupation'. This involves looking at your work history and the content of your job, rather than at your job title.

See Chapter 31 of the 2015/16 edition of this *Handbook* for the qualifying conditions for REA.

Who is still entitled to reduced earnings allowance
You qualify for REA if:[102]

- you satisfy the industrial injury condition (see p682) because of an industrial accident (see p683) before 1 October 1990 or an industrial disease (see p687), the onset of which was before that date (see p688); *and*
- your resulting disablement is assessed as being at least 1 per cent (see p689 and Appendix 4); *and*
- as a result of a relevant loss of faculty, either:
  - you are incapable and likely to remain permanently incapable of following your regular occupation and are incapable of following employment of an equivalent standard which is suitable in your case; *or*

- you are, and have been at all times since the end of the 90-day qualifying period for industrial injuries disablement benefit (IIDB), incapable of following your regular occupation or employment of an equivalent standard which is suitable in your case. (If you did return to your former, regular occupation – eg, to see whether you were capable of carrying on – this will not necessarily prevent a later claim for REA from succeeding.[103])

For more details, see p695 of the 2015/16 edition of this *Handbook*.

The amount of benefit

The amount of REA you get is the amount by which your current earnings, or earnings in a job which it is considered you could do, are less than the current earnings in your previous regular occupation (see p697 of the 2015/16 edition of this *Handbook*).[104]

If you are unemployed, the DWP's healthcare professional is asked for your limitations, a DWP disability employment adviser is asked what job s/he thinks you could do and Jobcentre Plus is asked to quote a wage which such a job would pay in your area.

Once the first assessment has been made, the amount is usually increased in line with earnings in that industry or workplace, unless that regular occupation has ceased to exist.[105] In this case, it is calculated as rising in line with the nearest 'occupational group' as defined by the DWP. You can ask for a fresh assessment to take into account your prospects of advancement, but you must show that promotion would have happened (eg, at the end of a period of employment or training), not just that it might have happened had you been particularly diligent.[106]

The maximum amount you can receive for any one award is £72.80 a week.[107] The total you can receive from IIDB and REA (whether for one or more awards) is 140 per cent of the standard rate of IIDB.[108] If you were over pension age and retired before 6 April 1987, your allowance is reduced if it would otherwise mean you would be receiving more than 100 per cent of the standard rate of IIDB.[109] If you qualified for REA and were retired or treated as retired on either 10 April 1988 or 9 April 1989, you continue to receive the allowance at the same 'frozen' rate. Its value, therefore, erodes over time.

4. Retirement allowance

Retirement allowance is a reduced rate of reduced earnings allowance (REA – see p695) for people over pension age, paid for life.

You qualify for retirement allowance if:[110]

- you are over pension age (see p780);
- you have given up regular employment;

- you were entitled to REA at a rate of at least £2 a week (in total, if you had more than one award) immediately before you gave up regular employment;
- you are not entitled to REA.

You can only get one award of retirement allowance, even if you had more than one award of REA.[111]

The amount of retirement allowance you get is £18.20 a week or 25 per cent of the amount of REA you were receiving, whichever is the lower. There are no increases for dependants.

5. Special benefit rules

Special rules may apply to:
- people who are going abroad (see Chapters 69 and 70);
- people in prison or detention (see Chapter 42).

6. Claims and backdating

The general rules about claims and backdating are covered in Chapter 50. This section explains the specific rules that apply to industrial injuries benefits.

Making a claim

Claims for industrial injuries benefits (other than retirement allowance – see below) must be made in writing.[112] You can download a claim form from gov.uk, or call to request a form (tel: 0800 121 8379; textphone: 0800 169 0314; Relay UK: 18001 then 0800 121 8379). The notes you get with the claim form tell you the address to which you should send your completed claim form. Keep a copy in case queries arise.

You must provide any information or evidence required (see p698). In certain circumstances, the DWP may accept a written application not on the approved form.[113] You can amend or withdraw your claim before a decision is made (see p1169). If there is a delay in making a claim, you may be able to get a short-term advance of benefit (see p1192).

Note: you do not have to make a claim for retirement allowance.[114]

Forms

There are different forms depending on the benefit claimed and whether you are claiming for an accident or a disease. You can download the IIDB form from gov.uk/industrial-injuries-disablement-benefit/how-to-claim.[115] You need to call to request the REA form (tel: 0800 121 8379; textphone: 0800 169 0314; Relay UK: 18001 then 0800 121 8379).

Part 5: Other benefits
Chapter 32: Industrial injuries benefits
6. Claims and backdating

Who should claim

You claim for yourself. If you are unable to manage your own affairs, another person can claim industrial injuries benefits for you as your 'appointee' (see p1170).

Information to support your claim

For the general information requirements that apply to all benefits, see p1170.

It is important that you provide any information required when you claim. Until you do, you may not count as having made a valid claim (see p1172). Correct any defects as soon as possible or your date of claim may be affected.

Even if your claim is valid, you may be asked to provide further information to support your claim (see p1174). You may also be asked to provide information after you are awarded industrial injuries benefits and if you fail to do so, your benefit could be suspended, or even terminated (see p1200).

The date of your claim

The date of your claim is important, as it determines when your entitlement to industrial injuries benefits starts. This is not necessarily the date from when you are paid. For information about when payment of benefit starts, see p699.

The **'date of your claim'** is the date it is received at the industrial injuries disablement benefit (IIDB) centre.

Note: you must make sure your claim is valid. If it is 'defective', you are given a short time to correct the defects (see p1173). If you do, your claim is treated as having been made when you initially claimed.[116]

In some cases, you can claim in advance (see p699) and in some cases, your claim can be backdated (see below). If you want this to be done, make this clear when you claim or the DWP may not consider it. If you claimed disability living allowance (DLA), personal independence payment (PIP) or attendance allowance (AA) instead of constant attendance allowance, see below.

Backdating your claim

It is important to claim in time. Your claim can be backdated for up to three months if you satisfy the qualifying conditions over that period. You do not have to show any reasons why your claim was late. The rules on backdating are covered on p1177.

If you might have qualified for benefit earlier but did not claim because you were given the wrong information or were misled by the DWP, ask for compensation (see p1439) or complain to the Ombudsman via your MP (see p1444).

If you claim the wrong benefit

In some circumstances, it is possible for a claim for one benefit to be treated as a claim for a different benefit (see p1182). However, for industrial injuries benefits it is only possible to 'interchange' constant attendance allowance with DLA, PIP and AA.

Claiming in advance

An advance claim can be made for IIDB if you have had an accident or have a prescribed disease and you are within the 90-day waiting period. The date of your claim is the date on which you qualify. Otherwise it is not possible to claim industrial injuries benefits in advance.

Renewal claims

Assessments can be provisional or final, and for a limited period or for life. A provisional assessment means that the DWP considers that your medical condition has not yet settled down, and may get worse or better. At the end of a provisional assessment, you are invited to be re-examined. A final assessment means that the DWP believes that your condition has settled down and your case is dealt with once and for all. At the end of a period of award, you must therefore apply for a renewal of benefit. **Note:** from 19 March 2020, assessments are suspended for at least three months.

If you get IIDB for a particular disease, you may recover at some point but subsequently have a further attack. If there is a continuation (or recrudescence) of the old disease, you do not have to wait 90 days before becoming entitled to IIDB.

7. Getting paid

The general rules on getting paid are covered in Chapter 51. This section explains the specific rules that apply to industrial injuries benefits.

When are industrial injuries benefits paid?

You are paid on a Wednesday,[117] weekly in advance or four weeks in arrears.[118]

Note:
- You might not be paid your industrial injuries benefit if you have been sanctioned for a benefit offence (see p1278).
- For information on missing payments, see p1189. If you cannot get your payments because you have lost your bank or post office card or you have forgotten your PIN, see p1188. If you have lost your payment service card, see p1189.
- If payment of your industrial injuries benefit is delayed, see p1295. If you are waiting for a decision on your claim, or to be paid, you may be able to get a short-term advance (see p1192). If you wish to complain about how your claim has been dealt with, or claim compensation, see Chapter 60.
- If payment of your industrial injuries benefit is suspended, see p1200.

Part 5: Other benefits
Chapter 32: Industrial injuries benefits
8. Tax, other benefits and the benefit cap

- If you are overpaid industrial injuries benefit, you may have to repay it (see Chapter 53) and, in some circumstances, you may have to pay a penalty (see p1268). If you have been accused of fraud, see Chapter 54.

Change of circumstances

You must report any change of circumstances that you have been told you must report, as well as any that you might reasonably be expected to know might affect your right to, the amount of, or the payment of your benefit. You should do this as soon as possible, preferably in writing. See p1199 for further information.

8. **Tax, other benefits and the benefit cap**

Tax

Industrial injuries benefits are not taxable.[119]

Means-tested benefits and tax credits

Industrial injuries disablement benefit (IIDB), reduced earnings allowance (REA) and retirement allowance are taken into account in full for all the means-tested benefits. Constant attendance allowance and exceptionally severe disablement allowance are disregarded. Industrial injuries benefits are ignored as income for tax credits.

Non-means-tested benefits

In general, the overlapping benefits rule does not apply to industrial injuries benefits. It is possible, for example, to get full disablement benefit as well as full employment and support allowance.

Carer's allowance (see Chapter 26) may be paid to someone who is 'regularly and substantially caring' for you while you are getting constant attendance allowance (see p694).[120]

If your spouse or civil partner died as a result of an industrial accident or disease, you may qualify for a bereavement benefit even though the national insurance contribution conditions are not satisfied (see Chapter 25).[121]

The benefit cap

In some cases, there is a limit on the total amount of specified benefits you can receive (a 'benefit cap'). Industrial injuries benefits are *not* specified benefits. The benefit cap only applies if you are getting universal credit or housing benefit. It does *not* apply if you or your partner get IIDB, REA or retirement allowance. See p1194 for further information.

Passports and other sources of help

You qualify for a Christmas bonus if you get disablement benefit, but only if it includes unemployability supplement or constant attendance allowance (see p870). If you are on a low income, you may be entitled to council tax reduction (see p851).

If you have (or are a dependant of someone who has died and who had) pneumoconiosis (including asbestosis, silicosis and kaolinosis), byssinosis, diffuse mesothelioma, diffuse pleural thickening, or primary carcinoma of the lung if accompanied by asbestosis or diffuse pleural thickening, and you cannot get compensation from your employer (eg, because s/he has ceased trading), or you do not have a realistic chance of obtaining damages from that employer, you may be able to get a one-off lump-sum payment from the DWP in addition to any industrial injuries benefit. You must make a claim within 12 months of the decision awarding IIDB.[122] Similarly, you can be entitled to a one-off lump-sum payment from the DWP for diffuse mesothelioma (including if you are a dependant of someone who had that condition immediately before s/he died), without the need to have worked.[123] The time limit for claiming is 12 months (from the date of diagnosis or death). The time limit may be extended if there is good cause. All these lump-sum payments may be recovered (ie, deducted) from compensation (see p1212).

Notes

1. Who can get industrial injuries benefits
1 ss94 and 103 SSCBA 1992
2 ss94(1) and 108(1) SSCBA 1992
3 Reg 10C(5) and (6) SSB(PA) Regs
4 Regs 2, 4 and 6 SS(EEEIIP) Regs
5 Regs 2 and 3 IIB(ETSC) Regs; s95A SSCBA 1992
6 Reg 3 SS(EEEIIP) Regs
7 s97 SSCBA Act 1992
8 R(I) 49/52
9 R(I) 1/76
10 R(I) 5/81
11 R(I) 1/82
12 *Fenton v Thorley* [1903] AC 443 (HL)
13 CI/123/1949
14 *Jones v Secretary of State for Social Services* [1972] AC 944 (HL), also reported as an appendix to R(I) 3/69; *SSWP v Scullion* [2010] EWCA Civ 310

15 *Trim Joint District School Board of Management v Kelly* [1914] AC 667 (HL)
16 s94(1) SSCBA 1992
17 CI/105/1998; CI/142/2006
18 *Roberts v Dorothea Slate Quarries Co. Ltd* [1948] 2 All ER 201 (HL)
19 R(I) 24/54; R(I) 43/55
20 CI/3370/1999
21 *Mullen v SSWP* [2002] Session Case 251; SLT 149; SCLR 475; *Greens Weekly Digest* 3-121, IH (2DIV)
22 R(I) 43/61; R(I) 4/62
23 R(I) 18/54
24 CI/159/1950
25 *R v National Insurance Commissioner ex parte East* [1976] ICR 206 (DC), also reported as an appendix to R(I) 16/75
26 R(I) 1/59; R(I) 45/55

27 *R v Industrial Injuries Commissioner ex parte AEU* [1966] 2 QB 31 (CA), also reported as an appendix to R(I) 4/66
28 R(I) 10/81
29 *R v National Insurance Commissioner ex parte Reed* (DC), reported as an appendix to R(I) 7/80
30 s94(3) SSCBA 1992
31 R(I) 46/53
32 R(I) 9/57
33 *R v Industrial Injuries Commissioner ex parte AEU* [1966] 2 QB 31 (CA), also reported as an appendix to R(I) 4/66
34 s29(6)(b) SSA 1998; CI/210/1950
35 R(I) 64/51
36 R(I) 1/99
37 *Nancollas v Insurance Officer* [1985] 1 All ER 833 (CA), also reported as an appendix to R(I) 7/85
38 s99 SSCBA 1992
39 R(I) 1/88
40 R(I) 12/75
41 R(I) 4/70
42 R(I) 1/93
43 *Nancollas v Insurance Officer* [1985] 1 All ER 833 (CA); *Ball v Insurance Officer* [1985] 1 All ER 833 (CA); both also reported as an appendix to R(I) 7/85
44 *Smith v Stages* [1989] 2 WLR 529 (HL)
45 R(I) 1/91
46 R(I) 6/82
47 R(I) 12/52
48 s101 SSCBA 1992
49 R(I) 3/67
50 s100 SSCBA 1992
51 Sch 1 SS(IIPD) Regs
52 Reg 2 SS(IIPD) Regs
53 R(I) 3/03
54 R(I) 2/03; R(I) 4/96
55 Reg 3 SS(IIPD) Regs
56 Regs 2(c) and 25 SS(IIPD) Regs
57 Reg 36 SS(IIPD) Regs
58 Reg 2(e) SS(IIPD) Regs
59 Reg 4(1), (4) and (5) SS(IIPD) Regs
60 Reg 4(2) and (6) SS(IIPD) Regs
61 Reg 4(1) SS(IIPD) Regs
62 para 67186 DMG
63 Reg 4(5) SS(IIPD) Regs
64 Reg 4(1) SS(IIPD) Regs
65 Reg 6(2)(c) SS(IIPD) Regs
66 Reg 7 SS(IIPD) Regs
67 *Jones v Secretary of State for Social Services* [1972] AC 944 (HL), also reported as an appendix to R(I) 3/69
68 CI/499/2000; s122(1) SSCBA 1992
69 s30 SSA 1998
70 s103(3) SSCBA 1992

71 s103(2) and (3) SSCBA 1992; regs 15A and 15B SS(IIPD) Regs
72 Sch 2 SS(GB) Regs; Sch 3 SS(IIPD) Regs
73 Reg 11(6) SS(GB) Regs
74 *JL and DO v SSWP (II)* [2011] UKUT 294 (AAC), reported as [2012] AACR 15
75 Reg 20A SS(IIPD) Regs
76 Sch 6 para 1 SSCBA 1992
77 Reg 11(8) SS(GB) Regs; R(I) 5/95; R(I) 1/04
78 CI/636/1993. In some cases, it may be an error of law to arrive at a different figure without giving reasons for this (para 10).
79 Reg 11(3) SS(GB) Regs
80 CI/34/1993
81 Reg 11(7) SS(GB) Regs
82 R(I) 3/91
83 Reg 11(4) SS(GB) Regs
84 R(I) 3/91
85 Reg 21 SS(IIPD) Regs
86 Reg 22 SS(IIPD) Regs
87 Reg 2(d) SS(IIPD) Regs
88 Sch 6 para 6 SSCBA 1992
89 Sch 6 para 7 SSCBA 1992
90 Sch 6 para 6(2)(b) SSCBA 1992
91 Reg 29 SS(IIPD) Regs

2. Industrial injuries disablement benefit
92 s94(2) SSCBA 1992
93 ss94, 103 and 108 SSCBA 1992
94 Reg 40 SS(GB) Regs
95 Sch 4 SSCBA 1992
96 s103(1) SSCBA 1992
97 Reg 20(1) SS (IIPD) Regs
98 Sch 7 para 9(1)(a) SSCBA 1992; reg 14 SS(II&D)MP Regs
99 s104 SSCBA 1992
100 s104 SSCBA 1992; reg 19 SS(GB) Regs
101 s105 SSCBA 1992

3. Reduced earnings allowance
102 Sch 7 paras 11 and 12(1), (2) and (7) SSCBA 1992
103 *SSWP v RD (II)* [2017] UKUT 481 (AAC)
104 Sch 7 para 11(10) SSCBA 1992
105 Sch 7 para 11(14) SSCBA 1992
106 Sch 7 para 11(6) SSCBA 1992
107 Regs 2 and 3 Social Security (Industrial Injuries) (Reduced Earnings Allowance and Transitional) Regulations 1987 No.415; Sch 7 para 11(13) SSCBA 1992
108 Sch 7 para 11(10) SSCBA 1992
109 Sch 7 para 11(11) SSCBA 1992

4. Retirement allowance
110 Sch 7 para 13 SSCBA 1992
111 *TA v SSWP (II)* [2010] UKUT 101 (AAC)

6. Claims and backdating
112 Reg 4(1) SS(C&P) Regs
113 Reg 4(1) SS(C&P) Regs
114 Reg 3(e) SS(C&P) Regs
115 s68(1) WRA 2012
116 Reg 6(1)(b) SS(C&P) Regs

7. Getting paid
117 Sch 6 para 3 SS(C&P) Regs
118 Reg 22 SS(C&P) Regs

8. Tax, other benefits and the benefit cap
119 s667 IT(EP)A 2003
120 Regs 14, 17 and 21 SS(IB)(T) Regs
121 s60(2) and (3) SSCBA 1992
122 Industrial Injuries Disablement Benefits:
     technical guidance, Section 11.5
123 Part 4 CMOPA 2008; Vol 11 DMG

5

Chapter 33

Contribution-based jobseeker's allowance

This chapter covers:

1. Who can get contribution-based jobseeker's allowance (p705)
2. The rules about your age (p711)
3. People included in the claim (p711)
4. The amount of benefit (p711)
5. Special benefit rules (p715)
6. Claims and backdating (p715)
7. Getting paid (p720)
8. Tax, other benefits and the benefit cap (p721)

Key facts

- Jobseeker's allowance (JSA) is a benefit for people who are looking for work.
- There are three types of JSA: **contribution-based JSA** (a non-means-tested benefit, but it can be affected by earnings and certain pension payments), **income-based JSA** (a means-tested benefit) and **joint-claim JSA** (a means-tested benefit paid if you must make a joint claim with your partner).
- You may be able to get your contribution-based JSA topped up with universal credit (UC), or if you can still claim, income-based JSA or joint-claim JSA.
- To qualify for contribution-based JSA, you must have paid sufficient national insurance contributions.
- You cannot qualify for any type of JSA if you count as being in full-time paid work.
- You must normally be fit for work and meet work-related requirements, or if you do not yet come under the UC system, satisfy the jobseeking conditions.
- In a number of situations (eg, if you fail to attend a job interview or do not take up a job or a place on an employment programme), you may be given a sanction and your JSA may be paid at a reduced or nil rate.
- JSA is administered and paid by the DWP.
- If you disagree with a JSA decision, you can apply for a revision or a supersession (see Chapter 56), or appeal against it (see Chapter 57). You must apply for a mandatory reconsideration before you can appeal.

Chapter 33

Contribution-based jobseeker's allowance

1. Who can get contribution-based jobseeker's allowance

You qualify for jobseeker's allowance (JSA) if you:[1]
- are not in full-time paid work (see p708); *and*
- do not have limited capability for work. However, in certain circumstances, people who are sick, have been affected by the coronavirus pandemic or who have gone abroad for NHS hospital treatment can get JSA (see p708); *and*
- are not in 'relevant education'. In addition, if you are a full-time student you usually cannot get JSA (see p899). **Note:** different rules apply if you do not come under the universal credit (UC) system (see p885 and p887); *and*
- are below pension age (see p780); *and*
- accept a 'claimant commitment'. **Note:** different rules apply if you do not come under the UC system (see below); *and*
- are in Great Britain. JSA can continue to be paid in limited circumstances while you are temporarily away (see p1655). Contribution-based JSA can be paid if you are unemployed and looking for work in a European Economic Area country (see p1657). For changes expected when the UK leaves the European Union, see p1670.

In addition to the rules above, you must satisfy the extra rules on p706. You can be required to meet work-related requirements, as well as some requirements connected to these – ie:[2]
- work-focused interviews;
- work preparation;
- work search;
- work availability.

You can be given a sanction if you fail to do so. See Chapter 46 for full details of these requirements. **Note:** different rules apply if you do not come under the UC system (see below).

You are not usually entitled to JSA for the first seven 'waiting days' in any jobseeking period (see p721). You may be able to get a short-term advance before your first payment of JSA is due (see p1192).

If you do not come under the universal credit system
From 12 December 2018, new claims for contribution-based JSA are usually only possible under the UC system. If you make a new claim, usually you will come under the UC system (see p26). However, if you make a new claim for contribution-based JSA on or after 12 December 2018 and are prevented from claiming UC because you or your partner qualify for a severe disability premium, or you or your partner are a 'frontier worker' (see p252) –

Part 5: Other benefits
Chapter 33: Contribution-based jobseeker's allowance
1. Who can get contribution-based jobseeker's allowance

the rules are the same as for income-based JSA), you do not come under the UC system and your claim is dealt with under old rules. The DWP may call this 'old-style' JSA.

If you do not come under the UC system, you must still satisfy the extra rules for contribution-based JSA on below. However, instead of accepting a claimant commitment, you must have a current jobseeker's agreement with the DWP (but the DWP also calls this a 'claimant commitment'). Instead of meeting work-related requirements, you must be available for work and actively seek work.[3]

Your entitlement ends if you fail to meet these 'jobseeking conditions' and, in some cases, you can be given a sanction if you claim again. See p1114 for full details of these conditions.

Many of the rules for contribution-based JSA for those who do not come under the UC system are the same as the rules for income-based JSA. For this reason, these rules are not explained in full this chapter. You should also refer to Chapter 12 for the rules about jobseeking periods and claims and backdating.

Extra rules for contribution-based jobseeker's allowance

In addition to satisfying the rules that apply to all types of JSA , you must:[4]

- satisfy the contribution conditions (see p980). This depends on your record of national insurance (NI) contributions and credits in the two tax years (6 April to 5 April) immediately before the benefit year in which your jobseeking period begins (or in which a period linked to a jobseeking period begins, if earlier). For example, if you claim JSA immediately after a period of limited capability for work, the contribution test is applied using the date on which you first had limited capability for work; *and*
- not have earnings from part-time work above a prescribed amount (see p712).

Example
Reggie was working full-time until he was injured in a car accident on 5 November 2019 and claimed employment and support allowance (ESA). On 28 April 2020, he is fit for work and claims contribution-based JSA. Because the period during which he had limited capability for work links to his current jobseeking period (see the rules for linked periods on p707), he must have sufficient NI contributions in the two tax years before 2019 – ie, 2016/2017 and 2017/2018.

Note: if you do not come under the UC system, you cannot qualify for contribution-based JSA if you are entitled to income support (IS).

Jobseeking periods

Your 'jobseeking period' is relevant for a number of reasons, including for whether you satisfy the contribution conditions for JSA. You are not usually entitled to JSA for the first seven days of your jobseeking period. These are known as 'waiting days' (see p721). **Note:** if you do not come under the UC system, see p254.

Jobseeking period

A 'jobseeking period' is the period during which you meet the conditions that apply to all types of JSA (see p705).[5]

What does not count as part of a jobseeking period
The following do not count as part of a jobseeking period:[6]
- days for which you do not claim (or are not treated as claiming) JSA;
- a period for which you claimed backdated benefit which has been refused;
- any week (Sunday to Saturday) for which you are not entitled to JSA because you were involved in a trade dispute (see p1001) for all or part of that week;
- days on which you are not entitled to JSA because you have not provided your NI number (see p1171).

How jobseeking periods link
In some cases, two or more jobseeking periods can be linked together and treated as if they were one period. Also, certain periods in which you satisfy other conditions ('linked periods' – see below) can be linked to a jobseeking period. This means, for example, that:
- the question of whether you satisfy the NI contribution conditions for contribution-based JSA is decided by looking at your situation at the beginning of the first jobseeking period (or the beginning of a period linked to a jobseeking period, if earlier) and not at the beginning of your current claim;[7]
- if you make a fresh claim for JSA but your jobseeking period links with a previous one, you do not have to serve any waiting days (see p721) to get JSA;
- if the jobseeking periods together are longer than 182 days, you cannot get any more contribution-based JSA (see p714).

Two jobseeking periods are treated as linked if they are separated by one or any combination of the following:[8]
- any period of no more than 12 weeks; *or*
- a period during which you are doing jury service; *or*
- a 'linked period' (see below); *or*
- any period of no more than 12 weeks which comes between two linked periods or between a jobseeking period and a 'linked period'.

Linked periods

A '**linked period**' is any period during which you:[9]
– are entitled to carer's allowance, but only if this allows you to get contribution-based JSA when you would not otherwise satisfy the contribution conditions; *or*

Part 5: Other benefits
Chapter 33: Contribution-based jobseeker's allowance
1. Who can get contribution-based jobseeker's allowance

– have, or are treated as having, limited capability for work (see Chapter 45); *or*

– are incapable of work or treated as incapable of work; *or*

– are entitled to maternity allowance; *or*

– are undergoing training for which a training allowance is payable.

You cannot argue that a period spent taking time out of work to look after children is a linked period for these purposes.[10]

Full-time paid work

You cannot usually qualify for contribution-based JSA if you are in full-time paid work. This means 16 hours or more each week.[11] All the rules on work are covered in Chapter 44.

In some situations, you are treated as *not* being in full-time work even if you work 16 hours or more (see p998). In others, you are treated as being in full-time work when you are not (see p997). See p993 for how your hours are calculated and p993 for what counts as paid work.

Even if your partner is in full-time paid work, you (and s/he) may qualify for UC (see Chapter 3).

Limited capability for work

To qualify for JSA, usually you must not have 'limited capability for work'.[12] See Chapter 45 for details about the test that decides this. If your health improves and you move onto JSA from UC or ESA, you may be asked to provide medical evidence that you no longer have limited capability for work. In all cases, you must still show that you are available for work if you are ill or have a disability. However, there are special rules that may help you meet the work-related requirements (see p1057).

Note: if you do not come under the UC system and a decision maker has decided that you have (or do not have) limited capability for work for ESA, you are automatically treated as having (or not having) limited capability for work for JSA.[13]

Periods of sickness when you can claim jobseeker's allowance

Even if you have limited capability for work, or you are affected by the coronavirus pandemic, you can be treated as not having limited capability for work:

- indefinitely if you have Covid-19, are isolating or are caring for a child who is; *or*
- during a short period of up to two weeks (see p709); *or*
- during an extended period of up to 13 weeks (see p710); *or*
- while you are getting NHS hospital treatment abroad (see p710).

In all cases, you can continue to claim JSA if the *only* reason why you would not otherwise qualify is that you are unable to work because of ill health.[14]

You do not have to continue to claim JSA in these situations and may qualify for UC or ESA. If you are only going to be unable to work for a short time, it may be better to continue to claim JSA. Get advice if you are unsure. Take the following into account.

- Switching from JSA to ESA and then back again when you are no longer sick means you must make a succession of benefit claims. You could be without income while these are being processed. You may start to come under the UC system if you do not do so already. However, switching from JSA allows you to escape the pressure of being fully available for, and looking for, work.
- If you can still qualify for income-based JSA (see p251), the amount you get can be higher than the amount you get on income-related ESA – eg, if you qualify for a disability premium in JSA, and do not qualify for a component in ESA.
- If you qualify for contribution-based JSA, you can only receive this for 182 days in any jobseeking period (see p714). If you qualify for contributory ESA, it is paid indefinitely if you are in the support group. Otherwise, it is paid for 365 days (see p656).

Two-week periods of sickness

You are allowed up to two two-week periods of sickness in a jobseeking period (see p706) or, if your jobseeking period has lasted more than 12 months, in any successive 12-month period.[15] You must make a written declaration that you have been unfit for work from a specific date or for a specific period on a form available at the Jobcentre Plus office.[16] You are *not* allowed a two-week period of sickness if you state in writing that you are going to claim (or have claimed) UC or ESA.

If you are sick more often than this, or for a longer period, you may be able to claim JSA during an 'extended period of sickness' (see p710). Otherwise, you must claim UC or ESA instead of JSA for the time you are unable to work.

Note:
- The two-week periods do not include any period when you qualify for an 'extended period of sickness' or, in some cases, you are affected by coronavirus.[17]
- You are *not* allowed a two-week period of sickness if you were getting statutory sick pay (SSP) in the eight weeks before you were sick, or if the period of sickness follows immediately after an 'extended period of sickness' under the rules on p710.[18] Instead, you can claim benefit on the basis of having limited capability for work without having to serve any 'waiting days' (see p662).

You do not normally have to meet a work search requirement and a special rule helps you meet the work availability requirement (see p1069).[19] If you are sick for more than seven days, you must provide a medical certificate from a doctor. **Note:** if you do not come under the UC system, you are treated as being available for, and actively seeking, work during the period of sickness.[20]

Part 5: Other benefits
Chapter 33: Contribution-based jobseeker's allowance
1. Who can get contribution-based jobseeker's allowance

Extended periods of sickness

You are allowed an 'extended period of sickness' if you state that you:[21]

- have been, or expect to be, unable to work for more than two weeks, but not for more than 13 weeks; *or*
- have already been unable to work for two two-week periods of sickness under the rules described above and you have been, or expect to be, unable to work for two weeks or less.

You are not allowed an extended period of sickness if you state in writing that you are going to claim (or have claimed) UC or ESA.

You must satisfy the DWP that you are unable to work by providing evidence as required, including a medical certificate from a doctor.

You are treated as not having limited capability for work for up to 13 weeks from the first day you are sick, or until you are no longer sick if this is sooner.[22] You are only allowed one extended period of sickness in the 12 months that start on the first day of sickness (not counting, in some cases, when you are affected by the coronavirus pandemic).[23] If you are sick for longer, you must claim UC or ESA instead of JSA for the time you are unable to work.

You are not allowed an extended period of sickness if you were getting SSP in the eight weeks before you were sick.[24] Instead, you can claim benefit on the basis of having limited capability for work without having to serve any waiting days (see p662).

You do not have to meet a work search requirement if the DWP is satisfied that it would be unreasonable to require you to comply with one, and special rules help you meet the work availability requirement if the DWP is satisfied it would be unreasonable to apply the normal rules.[25] **Note:** if you do not come under the UC system, you are treated as available for work during the period of sickness.[26] You are treated as actively seeking work in any week in which you are allowed an extended period of sickness, unless it would be reasonable for you to take steps to seek employment, and you have not taken such steps. Whether it is reasonable is at the discretion of your work coach.

NHS treatment abroad

You are treated as not having limited capability for work if you are temporarily absent from Great Britain for the purpose of getting NHS hospital treatment under certain provisions.[27] You can claim for an indefinite period. This does not apply if you stated in writing before the period of absence began that you claimed ESA immediately before the beginning of the period.

You must make a written declaration that you will be unfit for work from a specific date or for a specific period on a form available at the Jobcentre Plus office.[28]

You do not have to meet a work search requirement and a special rule helps you meet the work availability requirement.[29] **Note:** if you do not come under the

UC system, you are treated as being available for, and actively seeking, work during the period of sickness.[30]

2. The rules about your age

There is no minimum age for entitlement to contribution-based jobseeker's allowance (JSA). However, in practice, because you can only qualify if you satisfy the national insurance contribution conditions, you are unlikely to qualify before you are 18. You cannot claim any type of JSA if you are pension age or over (see p780). However, see p255 if you are getting income-based JSA, you are (or become) a mixed-age couple (ie, you have reached pension age but your partner has not) and you are prevented from claiming universal credit in specified circumstances.

3. People included in the claim

You claim contribution-based jobseeker's allowance for yourself. You cannot claim any increases for your partner or child(ren).

4. The amount of benefit

Contribution-based jobseeker's allowance (JSA) is paid at the following weekly rates.[31]

Age of claimant	£pw
Under 25	58.90
25 or over	74.35

These amounts are reduced penny for penny if you receive certain pension payments of more than £50 in any week or any part-time earnings. For more on how these types of income affect contribution-based JSA, see p712. Other types of income and any capital, including any earnings and capital of your partner, do not affect your contribution-based JSA.

Note:

- Contribution-based JSA is only paid for a limited period (see p714).
- You may qualify for universal credit (UC) to top up your contribution-based JSA if you satisfy the means test – eg, if you have a partner or a child, if you, your partner or child have a disability so you qualify for elements, or if you pay

Part 5: Other benefits
Chapter 33: Contribution-based jobseeker's allowance
4. The amount of benefit

rent, service charges or ground rent, or for childcare. **Note:** if you do not come under the UC system, you may instead qualify for income-based JSA.

- Your JSA might be paid at a reduced (or nil) rate if you are given a sanction or if you have committed a benefit offence (see p1278).

Deductions for earnings and pension payments

Earnings and pension payments you receive can affect your entitlement to contribution-based JSA.[32] Any other income you receive does *not* affect your contribution-based JSA (but see p1190 for the rules on overlapping benefits).

Note:

- You cannot qualify for JSA if you are in full-time paid work (see p708), so it is earnings from part-time work that are taken into account.
- Any savings you have and the income and savings of your partner and children do not affect your contribution-based JSA, but do affect UC and income-based JSA.

Earnings

Your earnings from part-time work can affect your entitlement to contribution-based JSA. The rules on the following are the same as for income-based JSA:

- what counts as earnings (p421);
- calculating net earnings from employment (p423);
- payments when you stop work (p424);
- calculating net earnings from self-employment (p427);
- working out average earnings from self-employment (p428);
- childminders (p428);
- how weekly earnings from employment are assessed (p453).

There are different rules on how your earnings affect your contribution-based JSA.

How earnings affect your contribution-based jobseeker's allowance

Your contribution-based JSA is reduced by the full amount of any earnings you receive over a disregarded amount.[33] For contribution-based JSA, normally £5 a week of your earnings are disregarded. However, if you are an auxiliary coastguard, a part-time firefighter, a part-time lifeboat crew member or a member of the reserve forces, £20 a week is disregarded.[34] If you earn less than £20 for doing any of these services, you can use up to £5 of the disregard on earnings from another job.

You are not entitled to contribution-based JSA for any week in which your earnings exceed a prescribed amount.[35] However, the days in any week when your earnings exceed this amount do not count towards your maximum 182 days of contribution-based JSA (see p714). The prescribed amount is not the same for everyone. It is calculated by adding together the amount of the relevant earnings disregard and the rate of contribution-based JSA paid to someone your age (see p711), and then deducting one penny.

Example

Maggie, aged 35, is entitled to contribution-based JSA of £74.35 a week. She works part time and her net earnings are £45 a week. Her earnings disregard is £5 a week. Maggie therefore gets £34.45 contribution-based JSA a week (£74.35 – £40). Applying the formula: (£74.45 + £5) – £0.01 = £79.44. So if Maggie were to earn more than £79.44 a week, she would not be entitled to contribution-based JSA.

Pension payments

Certain pension payments you receive may affect your contribution-based JSA.[36] The gross amount of your pension payments is taken into account – ie, the amount before tax is deducted, and this is converted into a weekly amount.[37]

Any pension payments you receive because of the death of a person who was a member of a pension scheme are ignored.[38] For example, if your late partner was a member of a scheme, any payment made to you following her/his death does not affect your contribution-based JSA.

Fifty pounds of your weekly pension payments (or if you get more than one pension, of the total of your weekly pensions) is disregarded, and your contribution-based JSA is reduced by the remainder.[39]

Any pension payment you receive is counted from the first day of the benefit week in which the payment is made to you.[40]

Example

Brian claims JSA and is entitled to contribution-based JSA from Wednesday 22 April 2020. His benefit week begins on a Friday. He starts receiving a personal pension of £68 a week from Monday 27 April 2020. £18 a week (£68 – £50) is deducted from his contribution-based JSA from the benefit week starting Friday 24 April 2020.

If your pension is increased when you are on contribution-based JSA, the change should be taken into account from the first day of the benefit week in which the increase is paid.[41] **Note:**

* The amount of your pension payments may mean that you are not paid any JSA. However, unless your earnings also exceed the prescribed amount (see p712), you remain *entitled* to contribution-based JSA (provided you also satisfy the other conditions for getting JSA).
* Any day on which you are entitled to JSA (even if it is not paid) counts towards your 182 days' entitlement to contribution-based JSA (see p714).
* A combination of earnings and pension payments may mean that you are not paid any JSA, even though you may remain entitled to it.

Part 5: Other benefits
Chapter 33: Contribution-based jobseeker's allowance
4. The amount of benefit

Duration of contribution-based jobseeker's allowance

You cannot receive more than 182 days of contribution-based JSA in any jobseeking period (see p706) or in two or more jobseeking periods if your entitlement is based on national insurance (NI) contributions in the same two contribution years.[42] The 182 days can include days both before and after you come under the UC system (see p23).[43]

You can have another 182 days of contribution-based JSA for a later claim if:[44]

- you satisfy the contribution conditions; *and*
- at least one of the two contribution years used to decide whether you satisfy the contribution conditions is later than the second contribution year used to decide your previous entitlement. This can only apply if you are in a later jobseeking period than the one during which you exhausted your entitlement to contribution-based JSA.

Days that count towards the 182-day total

Each day for which you are entitled to contribution-based JSA, even if you are not paid, counts, including days when the amount of JSA you are paid has been reduced to nil because you have been given a sanction, or because you are getting a pension or a combination of pension and earnings.

Days on which you are *not* entitled to contribution-based JSA can also count. This applies to days within a jobseeking period on which you are not entitled to contribution-based JSA because:[45]

- your contribution-based JSA is not payable either because you have been given a sanction (see Chapters 47 and 49) or because you have committed a benefit offence, so long as you satisfy the contribution conditions for JSA; *or*
- if you do not come under the UC system, you do not meet the jobseeking conditions and you are receiving a JSA hardship payment (see p1223).

Days on which you are not entitled to JSA and which do *not* count include:

- waiting days (see p721);
- days in any benefit week in which you are not entitled to JSA because you earn more than the prescribed amount (see p712) – but see above if you have been given a sanction; *or*
- if you do not come under the UC system, days when you are refused contribution-based JSA because you do not meet the jobseeking conditions and you are *not* getting a JSA hardship payment.

Note: if you do not come under the UC system and you are a laid-off or short-time worker, days for which you claim contribution-based JSA count towards your 182 days of entitlement, even if your benefit is reduced to take account of your earnings. So, if you think you are likely to become fully unemployed in the near future and you are not claiming income-based JSA, you might gain more JSA overall by not claiming it until you are fully unemployed. However, if your earnings drop below the lower earnings limit (see Appendix 6), you cease to be treated as paying NI contributions. You may then wish to claim JSA, which entitles you to NI credits.

5. Special benefit rules

Special rules may apply to:
* people who have come from or are going abroad (see Chapters 67, 68, 69 and 70);
* people who are are studying (see Chapter 41);
* people involved in a trade dispute (see p1001).

6. Claims and backdating

The general rules about claims and backdating are covered in Chapter 50. This section explains the specific rules that apply to contribution-based jobseeker's allowance (JSA). **Note:** if you do not come under the universal credit (UC) system, see also p259.

Note: in rare cases, it may be beneficial for you to delay your claim for contribution-based JSA so that you can draw on a different year's record of national insurance (NI) contributions.

JSA claims are dealt with by DWP decision makers (see p1288) and work coaches (see p1048 and p1114).

Making a claim

You can start your claim for contribution-based JSA online, by telephone or by completing a paper claim form approved by the DWP.[46] The DWP sometimes calls it 'new-style' JSA. A claim for contribution-based JSA can be made:
* online at gov.uk/jobseekers-allowance/how-to-claim; *or*
* by telephone on 0800 055 6688 (Welsh language: 0800 012 1888; textphone: 0800 023 4888; Relay UK (if you cannot hear or speak on the phone): 18001 then 0800 055 6688), Monday to Friday, 8am to 6pm. Say that you want to claim 'new-style' JSA. You may be sent Form UCJSA 1 to complete.

The DWP prefers you to start your claim online, or by telephone if you cannot claim online.[47] There is no rule that says you must do this, but it is best to make your claim in the way the DWP prefers if you can. If you cannot do either, you may be asked to attend the Jobcentre Plus office to make your claim in person. Get advice if you are unable to claim online or use a telephone and the Jobcentre Plus office tells you that you cannot start your claim in any other way. **Note:** you

Part 5: Other benefits
Chapter 33: Contribution-based jobseeker's allowance
6. Claims and backdating

can make initial contact with the DWP by telephone or letter to say you want to claim. The date of your initial contact is important because it usually determines the date on which your claim is treated as having been made (see p717).

The DWP telephones or texts within two days of your claim to arrange for you to attend the Jobcentre Plus office to complete your claim at an initial interview.[48] See p717 for further information and for what you must bring with you.

You may be sent or given a form to complete about the work you will be looking for and how you intend to go about getting it. The information you give forms the basis of your claimant commitment (or jobseeker's agreement).

If you want to claim UC to top up your contribution-based JSA, you must do this separately.

Are you prevented from claiming universal credit?

You might be prevented from claiming UC to top up your JSA if you (or your partner) get (or within the past month got) a severe disability premium (see p23) or if you are a 'frontier worker'. In this situation, you *can* make a new claim and qualify for income-based JSA. In this case, you must claim contribution-based JSA under the rules that apply for income-based JSA. See p259 for how to claim.

You must provide information or evidence as required (see below). You can amend or withdraw your claim before a decision is made (see p1169). If there is a delay in deciding your claim, you may be able to get a short-term advance (see p1192).

Claiming national insurance credits

If you are claiming NI credits but not JSA (see p970), the normal claim procedures for getting JSA apply to you.

Who should claim

You claim contribution-based JSA on your own behalf. If you are unable to manage your own affairs, another person can claim JSA for you as your 'appointee' (see p1170).

Information to support your claim

For the general information requirements that apply to all benefits, see p1170.

It is important that you provide any information required when you claim. Until you do, you may not count as having made a valid claim (see p1172).

Correct any defects as soon as possible or your date of claim may be affected. **Note:** if you do not come under the UC system, you may have to meet what is known as the 'evidence requirement'. See p1174 for this and to see whether you are exempt.

Even if you have provided all that was required when you claimed, you may be asked to provide further information to support your claim (see p1174). You may also be asked to provide information after you are awarded JSA and if you fail to do so, your JSA could be suspended, or even terminated (see p1200).

The initial interview

You must usually attend and participate in an initial interview.[49] If you do not attend the interview at the right time or place, your date of claim is affected (see p718). If you do not attend the interview at all (and the DWP does not waive the requirement to do so), you have not made a valid claim and so do not qualify for JSA.

The DWP telephones or texts you within two days of your claim to arrange your initial interview.

If attending the Jobcentre Plus office would mean that you would have to be away from home for too long, arrangements can be made for your interview to be carried out elsewhere.

The DWP says you should take one form of identification to the interview (eg, your passport, biometric residence permit or driving licence), proof of your date of birth (eg, your birth or marriage certificate or NHS medical card) and proof of your address (eg, a utility bill or bank statement) along with your P45 if you have one.[50]

If you have been sent a claim form, complete it before your interview. If you do not provide all the evidence and information required, your interview might not go ahead.

At the interview:

- you are told what is expected from you while you are receiving JSA;
- you and your work coach discuss what work you are looking for and what you intend to do to find it;
- a claimant commitment (or jobseeker's agreement) is drawn up for you to sign;
- you may be referred to a job vacancy immediately. However, a claimant commitment (or jobseeker's agreement) should still be completed to establish your entitlement in case you do not get the job.

The interview also covers what you were doing before you became unemployed and, in particular, why you left your previous job. If the person who interviews you thinks that you may have left voluntarily or been dismissed for misconduct, your case is referred to a decision maker who will probably make further enquiries before deciding whether to give you a sanction.

The date of your claim

The date of your claim is important as it determines when your entitlement to JSA starts (subject to the rules on waiting days – see p721).[51] This is not necessarily the date from when you are paid.

Part 5: Other benefits
Chapter 33: Contribution-based jobseeker's allowance
6. Claims and backdating

Your date of claim is not necessarily the date it is received by the DWP. It can be an earlier date (see below).

Your '**date of claim**' depends on whether or not you are required to attend an initial interview.

- If you are required to attend an initial interview, your date of claim is the date you first contact the Jobcentre Plus office if you attend your initial interview at the time specified by the DWP and by that time a properly completed claim is, or has been, provided (on a form, online or by telephone). The DWP can extend the time you have to provide or make a properly completed claim up to the date one month after the date of first contact. This is discretionary, so provide your claim as required wherever possible. If you fail to attend your initial interview, see below.[52]

- If you are not required to attend an initial interview, your date of claim is the earliest of:[53]
  - the date you first contact the Jobcentre Plus office, so long as a properly completed claim (on a form, online or by telephone) with all the information and evidence required is provided within one month of your first contact or, if you come under the UC system (see p23), a longer period that the DWP thinks is reasonable; *or*
  - the date on which a properly completed claim (on a form, online or by telephone) with all the information and evidence required is received at the Jobcentre Plus office; *or*
  - if you are notified that your claim is defective and you supply all the information required within one month of this, or a longer period that the DWP thinks is reasonable, the date your claim is received.

In some cases, you can claim in advance (see p719) and in some cases your claim can be backdated (see p719). If you want this to be done, make this clear when you claim or the DWP might not consider it.

Note: if you do not come under the UC system, there is an exception to the above rules if you claim working tax credit and you are refused (see p262).

If you fail to attend the initial interview

If you fail to attend your initial interview at the time specified by the DWP, or you fail to provide a properly completed claim by the date of the interview and cannot show good cause for this, the rules above do not apply. Instead, so long as a properly completed claim is provided, your date of claim is the date you eventually go to the Jobcentre Plus office. Your entitlement to JSA cannot start until that date.[54]

'**Good cause**' is not defined. All relevant circumstances must be considered. These may relate to your abilities, or to external factors. The general test is whether there is some factor that would probably cause a reasonable person of your age and experience to act, or fail to act, as you did.[55]

Backdating your claim

It is very important to claim in time. A claim for JSA can be backdated for a maximum of three months, and only in limited circumstances (see p1178).

If you might have qualified for JSA earlier but did not claim because you were given the wrong information or were misled by the DWP, you could ask for compensation (see p1439) or complain to the Ombudsman through your MP (see p1444).

Note: if you do not come under the UC system (see p23) and you make a new claim for JSA after your previous JSA entitlement ended when you failed to sign on or participate in an interview, see p1135 for the special backdating rules that apply.

If you claim the wrong benefit

There are no rules that allow a claim for another benefit to be treated as a claim for JSA.

Claiming in advance

If you do not qualify for JSA from the date of your claim, but will do so within the next three months, you can be awarded JSA from the first date on which you qualify.[56] This gives the DWP time to ensure you receive benefit as soon as you are entitled. Let the DWP know you want to claim in advance when you claim and at your initial interview. You might have to persuade the DWP that it can accept a claim in advance.

After you are awarded jobseeker's allowance

Once you have been awarded JSA, in order to continue to receive it you must provide any evidence and information required by the DWP. If you do not do so, your JSA could be suspended or even terminated (see p1200). In addition, you must:

- attend and participate in regular interviews; *and*
- confirm that you continue to qualify for JSA – eg, by signing on.

In some cases, if you fail to participate in interviews, you may be given a sanction (see p1087). You are required to meet work-related requirements and you can be given a sanction if you fail to do so. See Chapter 46 for further information about the requirements after you are awarded JSA, and Chapter 47 for information about sanctions.

Note: if you do not come under the UC system, see p264 for some additional information.

7. **Getting paid**

The general rules on getting paid are covered in Chapter 51. This section explains the specific rules that apply to jobseeker's allowance (JSA). **Note:** the rules in this section apply to all types of JSA.

When is jobseeker's allowance paid?
JSA is normally paid fortnightly in arrears.[57]

JSA is a weekly benefit, although in some cases it can be paid for part weeks.[58] Most questions about entitlement and payment are decided in relation to a particular 'benefit week' – ie, the period of seven days ending on the day of the week allocated to you according to your national insurance (NI) number.[59]

If you are entitled to less than 10 pence a week, you are not paid JSA at all,[60] but you are still eligible for NI credits (see p970). If you are entitled to less than £1 a week, the DWP can decide to pay you at longer intervals of not more than 13 weeks.[61]

Note:
- Deductions can sometimes be made from your JSA to pay to third parties (see p1203).
- Your JSA might be paid at a reduced (or nil) rate if you have been sanctioned for a benefit offence (see p1278). You may also be given a sanction for other reasons (see Chapter 47 and p1145).
- For information on missing payments, see p1189. If you cannot get your JSA payments because you have lost your bank or post office card or you have forgotten your PIN, see p1188. If you have lost your payment service card, see p1189.
- If payment of your JSA is delayed, see p1295. If you are waiting for a decision on your claim, or to be paid, you may be able to get a short-term advance (see p1192). If you wish to complain about how your claim has been dealt with, or claim compensation, see Chapter 60.
- If payment of your JSA is suspended, see p1200.
- If you are overpaid JSA, you might have to repay it (see Chapter 53) and, in some circumstances, you may have to pay a penalty (see p1268). If you have been accused of fraud, see Chapter 54.

Change of circumstances

You must report changes in your circumstances that you have been told you must report, as well as any that you might reasonably be expected to know might affect your right to, the amount of or the payment of your benefit, including any that

Chapter 33
Contribution-based jobseeker's allowance

are likely to occur. You should do this as soon as possible, preferably in writing. See p1199 for further information.

When there has been a relevant change of circumstances, a decision maker looks at your claim again and makes a new decision.

As a general rule, your JSA is adjusted from the first day of the benefit week in which the change occurs or is expected to do so.[62] There are a number of exceptions to this rule.[63] In particular, if a decision is to your advantage, but you failed to notify the DWP of a change within the time limit (normally one month, but this can be extended – see p1324), your JSA is adjusted:

- if you are paid in arrears, from the first day of the benefit week in which you notified the change; *or*
- if you do not come under the UC system and you are paid in advance, from the day on which you notified the change, if this is the first day of the benefit week. If it is not, your JSA is adjusted from the next week.

Waiting days

You are not entitled to JSA for the first seven 'waiting days' in any jobseeking period (see p706) unless:[64]

- your claim is linked to a previous claim for JSA, so both are treated as part of the same jobseeking period; *or*
- you were entitled to income support (IS), employment and support allowance (ESA) or carer's allowance in the 12 weeks before you became entitled to JSA.

In addition, you do not have to serve any waiting days if you swap from claiming IS or ESA to claiming JSA.[65]

You may be able to get a short-term advance before your first payment of JSA is due (see p1192).

---

8. Tax, other benefits and the benefit cap

Tax

Jobseeker's allowance (JSA) is taxable.[66] The maximum amount of JSA that is taxable is:

- an amount equal to the weekly rate of JSA for a person of your age (see p711); *or*
- if you are a member of a couple, an amount equal to the income-based JSA applicable amount for a couple which would be included if you were getting income-based JSA.

The tax is not deducted while JSA is being paid, but reduces the refund you would otherwise receive through pay as you earn (PAYE) when you return to work.

Part 5: Other benefits
Chapter 33: Contribution-based jobseeker's allowance
8. Tax, other benefits and the benefit cap

Any tax refunds of PAYE payments are paid to you at the end of the tax year to which they relate. Any other tax refund is paid only when you stop getting JSA.

Means-tested benefits and tax credits

If you are entitled to contribution-based JSA, it counts as income for the purposes of means-tested benefits unless you (or your partner) get universal credit (UC), income support (IS), income-based JSA, income-related employment and support allowance (ESA) or pension credit (PC), in which case it is ignored for housing benefit (HB) purposes.

If you need more income, you (and your partner) may be able to claim UC (or you may be able to claim income-based JSA if you do not come under the UC system) to top up your contribution-based JSA. You cannot claim JSA and IS at the same time. If you have a partner, s/he may be able to claim IS, income-related ESA or PC and you can claim contribution-based JSA (but not income-based JSA).

If you or your partner have just stopped work or reduced your hours, you might get 'WTC run-on' for a four-week period (see p305).

Non-means-tested benefits

While you are on JSA, you are entitled to national insurance credits (see p970). Contribution-based JSA is affected by the overlapping benefit rules (see p1190).

The benefit cap

In some cases, there is a limit on the total amount of specified benefits you can receive (a 'benefit cap'). JSA is one of the specified benefits. The benefit cap only applies if you are getting UC or HB. See p1194 for further information. **Note:** income-based JSA run-on (see p265) does *not* count as a specified benefit.

Passports and other sources of help

If you are entitled to UC or income-based JSA in addition to contribution-based JSA you may also qualify for:
- health benefits such as free prescriptions (see Chapter 31); *and*
- Healthy Start food and vitamins (see Chapter 40); in Scotland, Best Start foods (see p865); *and*
- social fund payments (see Chapter 37); in Scotland, funeral support payment or a Best Start grant (see Chapters 72 and 73); *and*
- education benefits such as free school lunches (see p866).

If you are not entitled to one of those benefits, you may qualify for health benefits under the low income scheme (see p668). Whether or not you are entitled to one of those benefits, you may qualify for council tax reduction (see p851). You may also qualify for help from your local welfare assistance scheme (see p861).

Financial help on starting work

If you stop getting income-based JSA because you or your partner start work, or your earnings or hours in your existing job increase, you may be able to continue to get help with your housing costs (eg, service charges or ground rent) for four weeks (see p376) or extended payments of HB if you pay rent (see p217). Your local authority may also provide extended help with council tax. See p873 for information about other financial help you might get.

Notes

1. Who can get contribution-based jobseeker's allowance
1 s1 JSA 1995
2 ss60-6I JSA 1995
3 s1(2)(a)-(c) JSA 1995 prior to amendments made by the Welfare Reform Act 2012
4 s2 JSA 1995
5 Reg 47(1) and (2) JSA Regs; reg 37(1) JSA Regs 2013
6 Reg 37(2) JSA Regs 2013
7 s2(1) and (4) JSA 1995
8 Reg 39 JSA Regs 2013; reg 48 JSA Regs
9 Reg 39(2) and (4) JSA Regs 2013; reg 48(2) and (3) JSA Regs
10 LE v SSWP [2009] UKUT 166 (AAC). The judge decided that the rule indirectly discriminated against women but that the discrimination was justified.
11 Reg 42 JSA Regs 2013
12 s1(2)(f) JSA 1995
13 Reg 10 SS&CS(DA) Regs
14 Regs 46(1), 46A(1) and 47(1) JSA Regs 2013; regs 55(1), 55ZA(1) and 55A(1) JSA Regs
15 Reg 46(1) and (3) JSA Regs 2013; reg 55(1) and (3) JSA Regs
16 Reg 46(2) JSA Regs 2013; reg 55(2) JSA Regs
17 Reg 46(7) JSA Regs 2013; reg 55(7) JSA Regs
18 Reg 46(4) and (6) JSA Regs 2013; reg 55(4) and (6) JSA Regs
19 Reg 16(5) JSA Regs 2013
20 Regs 14(1)(l) and 19(1)(l) JSA Regs

21 Reg 46A(1), (3) and (3A) JSA Regs 2013; reg 55ZA(1), (3) and (3A) JSA Regs
22 Reg 46A(4) JSA Regs 2013; reg 55ZA(4) JSA Regs
23 Reg 46A(5) JSA Regs 2013; reg 55ZA(5) JSA Regs
24 Reg 46A(6) JSA Regs 2013; reg 55ZA(6) JSA Regs
25 Reg 16A JSA Regs 2013
26 Regs 14(1)(l) and 19(1)(lzl) JSA Regs
27 Reg 47 JSA Regs 2013; reg 55A JSA Regs
28 Reg 47(2) JSA Regs 2013; reg 55A(2) JSA Regs
29 Reg 16(3)(b)(iii) JSA Regs 2013
30 Regs 14(1)(l) and 19(1)(ll) JSA Regs

4. The amount of benefit
31 s4(1) and (2) JSA 1995; reg 49 JSA Regs 2013; reg 79 JSA Regs
32 s4(1) JSA 1995
33 s4(1)(b) JSA 1995; reg 50 JSA Regs 2013; reg 80 JSA Regs
34 Regs 59(2) and 61(2) and Sch JSA Regs 2013; reg 99(3) and 101(3) and Sch 6 JSA Regs
35 s2(1)(c) JSA 1995; reg 48 JSA Regs 2013; reg 56(1) and (2) JSA Regs
36 ss4(1) and 35(1) JSA 1995; R(JSA) 1/01
37 Reg 51 JSA Regs 2013; reg 81 JSA Regs; R(U) 8/83
38 Reg 51(4) JSA Regs 2013; reg 81(2)(c) and (d) JSA Regs
39 Reg 51(1) JSA Regs 2013; reg 81(1) JSA Regs
40 Reg 51(2) JSA Regs 2013; reg 81(1A) JSA Regs

41 Reg 51(3) JSA Regs 2013; reg 81(1B) JSA
   Regs
42 s5(1) JSA 1995
43 Arts 12 and 13 WRA(No.9)O; Arts 10(2)
   and 11(2) WRA(No.11)O
44 s5(2) JSA 1995
45 Reg 37(3) JSA Regs 2013; reg 47(2) and
   (4) JSA Regs; Arts 12 and 13
   WRA(No.9)O; Arts 10(2) and 11(2)
   WRA(No.11)O

6. Claims and backdating
46 Regs 3, 21 and 23 and Sch 2
   UC,PIP,JSA&ESA(C&P) Regs
47 gov.uk/guidance/new-style-jobseekers-
   allowance
48 Reg 19 UC,PIP,JSA&ESA(C&P) Regs
49 Reg 19 UC,PIP,JSA&ESA(C&P) Regs
50 gov.uk/jobseekers-allowance/how-to-
   claim
51 Reg 29(1) UC,PIP,JSA&ESA(C&P) Regs
52 Reg 20 UC,PIP,JSA&ESA(C&P) Regs
53 Regs 21, 22 and 24
   UC,PIP,JSA&ESA(C&P) Regs
54 Reg 20(2) UC,PIP,JSA&ESA(C&P) Regs
55 CS/371/1949
56 Reg 34 UC,PIP,JSA&ESA(C&P) Regs

7. Getting paid
57 Reg 52 UC,PIP,JSA&ESA(C&P) Regs; reg
   26A SS(C&P) Regs
58 s1(3) and Sch 1 para 5 JSA 1995; reg 64
   JSA Regs 2013; reg 150 JSA Regs
59 Reg 2(2) JSA Regs 2013; reg 1(3) JSA
   Regs
60 Reg 52 JSA Regs 2013; reg 87A JSA Regs
61 Reg 52(3) UC,PIP,JSA&ESA(C&P) Regs;
   reg 26A(3) SS(C&P) Regs
62 Reg 35 and Sch 1 UC,PIP,JSA&ESA(DA)
   Regs; reg 7 and Sch 3A para 7
   SS&CS(DA) Regs
63 Reg 35 and Sch 1 Part 1
   UC,PIP,JSA&ESA(DA) Regs; reg 7 and
   Sch 3A paras 8-13 SS&CS(DA) Regs
64 Sch 1 para 4 JSA 1995; reg 36 JSA Regs
   2013
65 Reg 48(5) UC,PIP,JSA&ESA(DA) Regs

8. Tax, other benefits and the benefit cap
66 ss671-75 IT(EP)A 2003

Chapter 34

Maternity allowance

This chapter covers:
1. Who can get maternity allowance (below)
2. The rules about your age (p731)
3. People included in the claim (p731)
4. The amount of benefit (p732)
5. Special benefit rules (p732)
6. Claims and backdating (p733)
7. Getting paid (p735)
8. Tax, other benefits and the benefit cap (p736)

Key facts

- Maternity allowance (MA) is a benefit for women who are pregnant or have recently given birth and who are not entitled to statutory maternity pay.
- MA is a non-means-tested benefit.
- You do not need to have paid national insurance (NI) contributions to qualify although, in some circumstances, your entitlement may depend on your spouse's or civil partner's NI contribution record and if you are self-employed, your NI contribution record may affect the amount of MA you receive.
- MA is affected by the overlapping benefit rules, so you may not be able to get MA and another earnings-replacement benefit at the same time.
- You may be disqualified from MA if you work.
- MA is administered and paid by the DWP.
- If you disagree with a decision on MA, you can apply for a revision or supersession (see Chapter 56), or appeal against it (see Chapter 57). You must apply for a mandatory reconsideration before you can appeal.

1. Who can get maternity allowance

You qualify for maternity allowance (MA) if:[1]
- you are pregnant or have recently given birth; *and*
- you are not entitled to statutory maternity pay (SMP) for the same pregnancy or birth; *and either*

- you meet the conditions relating to your employment or self-employment – ie:
  - you have been employed or self-employed in at least 26 weeks in your 'test period' (see below). This is called the 'employment condition' (see p727); *and*
  - your average weekly earnings in 13 weeks of your test period (or, if you are self-employed, the average weekly earnings you are treated as having – see p728) are at least £30 a week. This is called the 'earnings condition' (see p727); *and*
  - you are within your 39-week 'maternity allowance period' (MA period – see p728); *or*
- you meet the conditions relating to having helped your spouse or civil partner with her/his self-employment – ie:
  - your spouse or civil partner was a self-employed earner in at least 26 weeks in your test period and s/he has paid class 2 national insurance (NI) contributions for those 26 weeks (s/he can pay class 2 contributions early to help you meet this condition – see p964);[2] *and*
  - for at least part of each of those 26 weeks you took part in, or assisted, your spouse or civil partner with her/his self-employment, but you were not employed by, or in partnership with, her/him; *and*
  - you are within your 14-week 'qualifying period' (see p729); *and*
  - you do not qualify for MA on the basis of your own employment or self-employment.

If you qualify for MA on the basis of your own employment or self-employment, your MA can be paid over a longer period and may be paid at a higher weekly rate than if you qualify for MA on the basis of having helped your spouse or civil partner with her/his self-employment.

In certain circumstances, you may be disqualified from receiving MA if you work or fail to attend a medical examination (see p730).

Note: if you get SMP (or if you would have got SMP but for having reduced your maternity pay period in connection with a claim for shared parental leave or statutory shared parental pay (SSPP – see Chapter 38)), you cannot receive MA for the same week for the same baby, even if you have more than one job or have been self-employed as well as employed.[3]

Definitions

Your **'expected week of childbirth'** (EWC) is the week, starting on a Sunday, in which your baby is due to be born.

Your **'test period'** is the 66 weeks immediately before your EWC. For the date on which your test period starts, see Appendix 8.

Employment condition

To qualify for MA on the basis of your employment or self-employment, you must have been employed or self-employed for at least 26 weeks in your test period.[4] If you are employed or self-employed for part of a week, the whole of that week counts. The 26 weeks do not need to be consecutive and you do not need to have worked in the same job for the whole period. You need only show that you have been employed and/or self-employed for any part of each of the 26 weeks. For MA, to count as employed or self-employed you must be an employed or self-employed earner (see p962).

When you become self-employed, you are normally required to register with HM Revenue and Customs (HMRC) for NI and tax purposes. If you delay registering, the DWP may consider the date on which you registered as the date your self-employment started, rather than the date you became a self-employed earner. If, as a consequence, the DWP decides you do not meet the employment condition for MA, get advice.

See p732 if you have worked abroad.

Note: even if you do not meet this employment condition, you may still qualify for MA if you have helped your spouse or civil partner with her/his self-employment (see p726).

Example

Rita's baby is due on Saturday 4 July 2020.

Rita's EWC begins on Sunday 28 June 2020 and her 66-week 'test period' runs from Sunday 24 March 2019 to Saturday 27 June 2020. In this period, Rita was a self-employed earner from Tuesday 14 May 2019 until Thursday 1 August 2019 and was employed from Monday 6 January 2020 until Friday 10 April 2020. As the weeks in which she started and ended her self-employment and employment count, Rita meets the 26-week employment condition.

Earnings condition

To qualify for MA on the basis of your employment or self-employment, your average weekly earnings in 13 weeks of your test period (or, if you are self-employed, the average weekly earnings you are treated as having – see below) must be at least £30 a week. This is known as the 'MA threshold'. For how earnings are averaged, see p732.[5]

Note: even if you do not meet this earnings condition, you may still qualify for MA if you have helped your spouse or civil partner with her/his self-employment (see p726).

Earnings from employment

If you are employed, your gross earnings are used to calculate your average weekly earnings. What counts as earnings is the same as for SMP (see p819).[6] If you get a backdated pay rise for the period over which your earnings are averaged, this is included in the calculation.[7]

Earnings from self-employment

The amount you actually earn from self-employment is not taken into account. Instead, you are treated as earning a certain amount based on whether or not you have paid class 2 NI contributions, and this figure is used to calculate your average weekly earnings. For each week:[8]

- for which you have paid a class 2 NI contribution, you are treated as having earnings of an amount 90 per cent of which is equal to the maximum amount of MA that can be paid for that week. In 2020/21, this is £168;[9]
- for which you could have paid a class 2 contribution but have not done so, you are treated as having earnings of £30 a week – ie, equal to the MA threshold.

Note: if you are self-employed, your liability to pay class 2 contributions is calculated after the end of the tax year through the income tax self-assessment procedure. To help you meet the condition in the first bullet point (which qualifies you for a higher rate of MA – see p732), you can pay class 2 contributions early, on a voluntary basis (see p964).[10] If you would benefit from this, after you have claimed MA you should get a letter from HMRC telling you the amount to pay and how to pay it, should you want to pay early.

Maternity allowance period

MA awarded on the basis of your employment or self-employment can only be paid for weeks in the MA period.[11] This is a period of 39 consecutive weeks that normally starts on the day your maternity pay period would have begun had you been entitled to SMP (see p811). However:[12]

- if you are not employed or self-employed at the beginning of the 11th week before your EWC (see p726), your MA period starts from the beginning of that week (but if your baby was born before this, it starts from the day after the birth); *and*
- if you are not entitled to MA during the 11th week before your EWC, but you become entitled to it before your baby is born (perhaps because you then meet the earnings or employment condition), provided you have stopped work, the earliest day on which your MA period can start is the day you become entitled to MA, and the latest it can start is the day after the birth.

To calculate the 11th week before your EWC, see Appendix 8.

Reducing your maternity allowance period and statutory shared parental pay

If you get MA on the basis of your own employment or self-employment (rather than on the basis you help your spouse or civil partner with her/his self-employment), you can end your MA period early, relinquishing up to 37 weeks of your MA, so that the father of your child or your partner can qualify for SSPP from her/his employer (see p814) and/or shared parental leave from work. If s/he meets the qualifying conditions, s/he can then get SSPP for the number of weeks of MA that you have chosen to give up.

To reduce your MA period in this way, you must give the DWP a 'curtailment notification' stating the date you want your MA period to end (called your 'curtailment date'). Your curtailment date must fall at least two weeks after the birth of your baby (or four weeks after it, if you are employed in a factory or workshop) and at least one week before what would have been the last day of your MA period. The curtailment notification should be given to the DWP office that deals with your MA claim at least eight weeks before your curtailment date (although the DWP has discretion to accept less notice than this).[13] It is always advisable to give a curtailment notification in writing, although the DWP cannot insist on this.

Think carefully before giving up your MA in this way as it is only possible to cancel a curtailment notification if you do so before your curtailment date and if:[14]

- you gave the curtailment notification before your child was born. In this situation, you must inform the DWP that you want to cancel it within six weeks of the birth, but can subsequently give another curtailment notification; *or*
- your partner dies. In this situation, you must inform the DWP within a reasonable time after the death and must provide the date of death.

14-week qualifying period

MA awarded on the basis that you have helped your spouse or civil partner with her/his self-employment can be paid for a maximum of 14 consecutive weeks, called the 'qualifying period'. Your qualifying period starts:[15]

- if you stopped working with your spouse or civil partner before the beginning of the 11th week before your EWC, on the first day of the 11th week before your EWC;
- if you stopped working with your spouse or civil partner during or after the 11th week before your EWC (but before the day your baby is born), on the day after you stop work. Once you have reached the fourth week before your EWC, this applies even if you just refrain from working with your spouse or civil partner (eg, because you are unwell), if this is at least in part because of your pregnancy or childbirth;
- otherwise, it starts on the day after you have your baby.

'Stopping work' means either stopping permanently or until after the birth. To calculate the 11th week before your EWC, see Appendix 8.

Note: if you are not entitled to MA during the 11th week before your EWC but you become entitled to it before your baby is born, provided you have stopped working with your spouse or civil partner, the earliest day your 14-week qualifying period can start is the day you become entitled to MA and the latest is the day after the birth.[16]

Disqualification from maternity allowance

In some circumstances, you can be disqualified from MA if you work or if you fail to attend a medical examination.

If you work

It is important to tell the DWP of any work that you do. This is because the DWP can disqualify you from receiving MA for as long as is reasonable given the circumstances if:[17]

- you are entitled to MA on the basis of your own employment or self-employment (see p726) and you work for more than 10 days during your MA period. The disqualification must be for at least the number of days you worked in excess of these 10 days. Both employed and self-employed work counts and the 10 days do not need to be consecutive. If you work for part of a day, it counts as a full day. If you work for 10 days or less, your MA is unaffected, even if you are paid for that work; *or*
- you are entitled to MA on the basis of helping with your spouse or civil partner's self-employment (see p726) and you do *any* work during your 14-week qualifying period. This applies if the work is helping your spouse or partner with her/his business or work you do as an employee or as a self-employed earner. The disqualification must be for at least the number of days you worked.

You can challenge the DWP's decision, including its decision on the length of the disqualification period (see Chapters 56 and 57).

Example
Before going on maternity leave, Grace, who is self-employed, worked full time. She qualifies for MA of £151.20 a week (because she paid class 2 NI contributions for 13 weeks in her test period) but while on maternity leave still does small amounts of administrative work, such as responding to enquires with information about when she will return to work after her maternity leave. She also took on a contract that meant she worked for three hours a day over an 11-day period. The DWP decides that the small amounts of administrative work she does, which are minimal and necessary to maintain her business while she is on leave, can be ignored. However, each of the days on which she worked for three hours count as a full day of work. Although the first 10 such days do not affect her entitlement to MA, the 11th does. The DWP decides that in the circumstances it is reasonable to disqualify her from MA for one day and deducts £21.60 from her weekly MA (one-seventh of £151.20).[18]

Note:
- If you are employed and on maternity leave, working for your employer for more than 10 days may affect your continued entitlement to leave. If you do not want your maternity leave to end, get employment advice before agreeing to such work.
- If you have been disqualified from MA because you have returned to work and have worked for more than 10 days, provided you have not brought your MA period to an end by submitting a curtailment notification (see p728), you may be able to get MA again if you stop work and are still within your MA period. If you are employed and your maternity leave has ended because of your return to work, this could be during a period when you are on sick leave or when you take shared parental leave. It is not necessary for you to end your MA period in order to qualify for shared parental leave (but it may be necessary to submit a curtailment notification for your partner to qualify for SSPP and/or shared parental leave).

If you fail to attend a medical

You are disqualified from receiving MA if, before the birth of your baby, you fail to attend a medical examination without good cause. For this to apply, you must have been given written notice of the examination at least three days beforehand by the DWP or someone acting on its behalf. The DWP can disqualify you for as long as is reasonable given the circumstances, but the disqualification cannot start until the day of the missed examination and cannot continue once you have given birth.[19]

Whether or not you have good cause for failing to attend depends on your circumstances. You can challenge the DWP's decision on whether you have good cause or on the length of the disqualification period (see Chapters 56 and 57).

2. The rules about your age

There are no upper or lower age limits for receiving maternity allowance.

3. People included in the claim

You claim maternity allowance for yourself. You cannot claim any increase for your partner or child(ren).

4. **The amount of benefit**

Type of maternity allowance	Maximum period of payment	Weekly amount
Entitlement arising from your own employment or self-employment (see p726)	39 weeks	£151.20 or 90 per cent of your average weekly earnings, whichever is less.[20]
Entitlement arising from helping your spouse or civil partner with her/his self-employment (see p726)	14 weeks	£27[21]

Calculating average weekly earnings

If you qualify for maternity allowance (MA) on the basis of your own employment or self-employment, your average weekly earnings are used to determine both whether you meet the earnings condition (see p727) and the amount of your MA. They are calculated as follows.[22]

- If you have paid class 2 national insurance contributions as a self-employed person (see p963) for at least 13 weeks in your 66-week test period, no calculation is needed – you automatically qualify for the maximum weekly amount of MA of £151.20 a week.
- Otherwise, add together your earnings (or the earnings you are treated as having from self-employment – see p728) in the 13 weeks in your 66-week test period when your earnings are highest and divide the total by 13. If you have more than one job, the earnings from all your jobs, including earnings you are treated as having from self-employment, are counted.

In both cases, the 13 weeks do not need to be consecutive. If you are not paid weekly, work out your weekly earnings by dividing the payments you receive by the nearest number of weeks in the period for which they are paid.[23]

5. **Special benefit rules**

Special rules may apply to:
- people who are going abroad (see Chapters 69 and 70);
- people in prison or detention (see Chapter 42).

There are also special rules if you have been employed abroad.
- If, following a period of employment abroad, you have returned to Great Britain and you remained ordinarily resident in Great Britain while you were

away, you may be able to rely on periods of employment abroad to satisfy the employment and earnings condition for maternity allowance (MA).[24]

- In some circumstances, you may be able to rely on periods you have worked in a European Economic Area country to qualify for MA (see p1633). This applies at least until the end of the transition period (following the UK leaving the European Union) and, for some people, after that (see p1670).

6. **Claims and backdating**

The general rules about claims and backdating are covered in Chapter 50. This section explains the specific rules that apply to maternity allowance (MA).

If you are (or have recently been) employed, you may be entitled to statutory maternity pay (SMP) (see Chapter 38) from your employer (or ex-employer) instead of MA. If you were employed in the 15th week before your expected week of childbirth (EWC), the DWP expects you to have applied for SMP. If your employer has decided you are not entitled to SMP, it should give you Form SMP1 explaining why and you should send this to the DWP to support your claim for MA. If you disagree with your employer's decision, or your employer fails to give you a decision, also ask HM Revenue and Customs to make a decision on your entitlement to SMP (see Chapter 59).

Making a claim

A claim for MA must be made in writing, normally on the approved form. Send your completed form to the DWP using the address which is included on the form. Keep a copy of your claim form in case queries arise. Your claim will not be accepted unless it is received after the 15th week before your EWC.[25]

You must complete the form in accordance with the instructions on it. See p734 for the information and evidence you are expected to provide in connection with your claim. The decision maker at the DWP may accept a written application not on the approved form.[26] You can amend or withdraw your claim before a decision is made (see p1169). If you are waiting for a decision on your claim or you are waiting to be paid, you may be able to get a short-term advance of benefit (see p1192).

Forms

The approved form is Form MA1, which you can get from the Jobcentre Plus national contact centre (tel: 0800 055 6688; textphone: 0800 023 4888) or from gov.uk/maternity-allowance/how-to-claim.

Who should claim

You must normally claim MA for yourself. However, if you are unable to manage your own affairs, another person can claim MA for you as your 'appointee' (see p1170).

Information to support your claim

For the general information requirements that apply to all benefits, see p1170.

It is important that you provide any information required when you claim. Until you do, you may not count as having made a valid claim (see p1172). Correct any defects as soon as possible as your date of claim may be affected.

The DWP also expects you to provide:

- a certificate from your doctor or a registered midwife, giving the expected date of birth of your child (Form MAT B1) and, if you are claiming MA after your baby is born, giving the date of the baby's birth.[27] This certificate is not accepted as evidence of your EWC if it is issued before the 20th week before your EWC. If you cannot obtain Form MAT B1, other evidence can be accepted, if it is sufficient in the circumstances;
- if you have been employed, pay slips or some other written proof of your earnings and Form SMP1 from any employer for whom you worked during the 15th week before your EWC. Do not delay sending your claim for MA because you are waiting for your SMP1 or evidence of your earnings; you can send these in later;
- if you are claiming MA on the basis you help your spouse or civil partner with her/his self-employment, your marriage or civil partnership certificate.

Even if you have provided all that was required when you claimed, you may be asked to provide further information to support your claim (see p1174). You may also be asked to provide information after you are awarded MA. If you fail to do so, your MA could be suspended, or even terminated (see p1200).

The date of your claim

The date of your claim is important as it can determine when your entitlement to MA starts. This is not necessarily the date from when you are paid. For information about when payment of MA starts, see p735.

The **'date of your claim'** is normally the date it is received at a DWP office.[28]

Note: you must make sure your claim is valid. If it is 'defective', you are given a short time to correct the defect (see p1173). If you do, your claim is treated as having been made when you initially claimed.[29]

In some cases, you can claim in advance (see p735) and in some cases your claim can be backdated (see p735). If you want this done, make this clear when you claim or the DWP may not consider it. If you claimed employment and support allowance (ESA) instead of MA, or if you have been refused SMP, see below.

Backdating your claim

A claim for MA can be backdated for up to three months if you satisfy the qualifying conditions over that period. You do not have to show any reasons why your claim was late.[30]

If you might have qualified for benefit earlier but did not claim because you were given the wrong information or were misled by the DWP, you could ask for compensation (see p1439) or complain to the Independent Case Examiner or to the Ombudsman through your MP (see p1440 and p1444).

If you claimed ESA instead of MA, or if you have been refused SMP, see below.

If you claim the wrong benefit

A claim for ESA may also be treated as a claim for MA and vice versa (see p1182).[31] This may allow you to get your claim for MA backdated for more than the usual three months.

If your employer (or former employer) has decided that you are not entitled to SMP and you claim MA within three months of being notified of your employer's decision in writing, your claim for MA is treated as having been made either on the date you gave your employer notice of when you wanted the maternity pay period to start or at the beginning of the 14th week before your EWC, whichever is later.[32]

Claiming in advance

You cannot make a claim for MA until after the 15th week before your EWC (ie, until week 26 of pregnancy), but you should claim as soon as possible after that.[33] However, if you qualify for MA on the basis of your own employment or self-employment, it may be worth waiting a few weeks before claiming if this means you will have higher average earnings, and these would increase the amount of your MA.

7. Getting paid

The general rules on getting paid are covered in Chapter 51. This section explains the specific rules that apply to maternity allowance (MA).

When is maternity allowance paid?

The day you are paid depends on your national insurance number (see p1189). MA is normally paid fortnightly or four-weekly in arrears.[34]

If you have claimed in time and are entitled to MA, payment normally runs from the first day of your MA period (see p728) or 14-week qualifying period (see p729) until that period ends. To calculate the amount of MA due for a period of less than a week, the daily rate of MA is used, which is one-seventh of the weekly amount.[35]

Note:

- In some circumstances, you can be disqualified from receiving MA (see p730).
- Even if you have been sanctioned for a benefit offence (see p1278), you must be paid your MA.
- For information on missing payments, see p1189. If you cannot get your MA payments because you have lost your bank or post office card or you have forgotten your PIN, see p1188. If you have lost your payment service card, see p1189.
- If payment of your MA is delayed, see p1295. If you are waiting for a decision on your claim, or to be paid, you might be able to get a short-term advance (see p1192). If you wish to complain about how your claim has been dealt with, or claim compensation, see Chapter 60.
- If payment of your MA is suspended, see p1200.
- If you are overpaid MA, you might have to repay it (see Chapter 53) and, in some circumstances, you may have to pay a penalty (see p1268). If you have been accused of fraud, see Chapter 54.

Change of circumstances

You must report any change in your circumstances that you have been told you must report, as well as any that you might reasonably be expected to know might affect your right to, the amount of, or the payment of, your benefit. You should do this as soon as possible, preferably in writing. See p1199 for further information.

If the change affects your entitlement to MA, a decision maker looks at your claim again and makes a new decision (see p1315). The date from which the new decision takes effect depends on whether or not it is advantageous to you and whether you reported the change in time (see p1321).

8. Tax, other benefits and the benefit cap

Tax

Maternity allowance (MA) is not taxable.[36]

Means-tested benefits and tax credits

If you are entitled to MA:

- you may also qualify for universal credit (UC) (see Chapter 3), but see p23 for circumstances when you are prevented from claiming UC. If you are already getting a 'legacy benefit' (ie, those listed on p21), seek advice before claiming UC. This is because claiming UC is likely to end your entitlement to any legacy benefits and it is advisable first to check you will be better off on UC;

- the MA you get is taken into account in full as income when calculating your entitlement to UC, income support, income-based jobseeker's allowance, income-related employment and support allowance (ESA), the guarantee credit of pension credit and housing benefit (HB). However, when calculating the amount of your capital for these benefits, any arrears of MA paid on the basis of your employment or self-employment are ignored for 52 weeks from the date you receive them (12 months for UC) unless the arrears amount to £5,000 or more when, in some circumstances, they can be ignored for longer (see pp145, 498 and 522);
- MA is ignored when calculating your entitlement to working tax credit (WTC) and child tax credit and sometimes you can be treated as being in full-time work for WTC purposes while getting MA (see p304).

Note: the fact that MA is treated as unearned income for UC, and so is taken into account in full when calculating UC entitlement, is the subject of a test case[37] (see AskCPAG.org.uk and CPAG's *Welfare Rights Bulletin* for further information and updates).

Non-means-tested benefits

MA is affected by the overlapping benefit rules (see p1190).

For details of how your entitlement to MA affects your entitlement to statutory sick pay, see p843.

If you get MA on the basis of your own employment or self-employment, reducing your MA period may allow the father of your baby or your partner to get statutory shared parental pay and/or shared parental leave (see Chapter 38).

You can get national insurance credits for each week for which you get MA (because you are treated as having limited capability for work in those weeks – see p971).

You may qualify for both MA and contributory ESA (because you can be treated as having limited capability for work during the period when you are entitled to MA) but you cannot receive both benefits in full because of the overlapping benefit rules. In some circumstances, contributory ESA may be more than your MA entitlement. A claim for MA may be treated as a claim for ESA (see p1182).

The benefit cap

In some cases, there is a limit on the total amount of specified benefits you can receive (a 'benefit cap'). MA is one of the specified benefits. However, the benefit cap only applies if you are getting UC or HB. See p1194 for further information.

Passports and other sources of help

For details of whether you may qualify for:

- a Sure Start maternity grant from the social fund if you live in England or Wales, see p796, or, if you live in Scotland, a Best Start grant pregnancy and baby payment, see p1696;
- Scottish child payment if you live in Scotland (expected to be introduced by Christmas 2020), see Chapter 74;
- certain health benefits, see Chapter 31;
- Healthy Start food vouchers, see p862, or, if you live in Scotland, Best Start foods, see p865;
- Healthy Start vitamins, see p865;
- council tax reduction, see p851;
- tax-free childcare, see p871.

Notes

1. Who can get maternity allowance

1 ss35(1) and (2) and 35B(1), (2) and (4) SSCBA 1992
2 Reg 90ZA SS(Con) Regs
3 ss35(1)(d) and (3E) and 35B(1)(d) SSCBA 1992
4 s35(1)(b) SSCBA 1992
5 ss35(1)(c) and (6A) and 35A(4) SSCBA 1992
6 s35A(4)(a) SSCBA 1992; reg 2 SS(MatA)(E) Regs
7 Reg 6(2) SS(MatA)(E) Regs
8 Reg 3 SS(MatA)(E) Regs
9 s35A(5)(c), (5A) and (5B) SSCBA 1992; reg 5 SS(MatA)(E) Regs
10 Reg 90ZA SS(Con) Regs
11 ss35(2) and 165 SSCBA 1992; reg 2(2)SMP Regs
12 ss35(2) and 165 SSCBA 1992; reg 2 SMP Regs; reg 3 SS(MatA) Regs
13 Regs 3-5 MA(C) Regs
14 Reg 6 MA(C) Regs
15 s35B(4)-(8) SSCBA 1992
16 Reg 3(2B) and (2C) SS(MatA) Regs
17 Reg 2(1)-(4) SS(MatA) Regs
18 Paras 62592-9 DMG
19 Reg 2(7) and (8) SS(MatA) Regs

4. The amount of benefit

20 ss35(1) and 35A SSCBA 1992
21 ss35(6A) and 35B(3) and (10) SSCBA 1992
22 Regs 4 and 6 SS(MatA)(E) Regs
23 Reg 6(3) SS(MatA)(E) Regs

5. Special benefit rules

24 SS(MatA)(WA) Regs

6. Claims and backdating

25 Reg 14(1) SS(C&P) Regs
26 Reg 4(1) SS(C&P) Regs
27 Reg 2(3) SS(ME) Regs
28 Reg 6(1) SS(C&P) Regs
29 Regs 4(7) and (7ZA) and 6(1) SS(C&P) Regs
30 Reg 19(2) SS(C&P) Regs
31 Regs 9 and 11 and Sch 1 Part I SS(C&P) Regs; regs 18 and 25 UC,PIP,JSA&ESA(C&P) Regs
32 Reg 10(3) and (4) SS(C&P) Regs
33 Reg 14 SS(C&P) Regs

7. Getting paid

34 Reg 24 SS(C&P) Regs
35 s35(5) SSCBA 1992

8. Tax, other benefits and the benefit cap

36 s677 IT(EP)A 2003
37 *Moore and Others v SSWP*, CO/4081/2019

Chapter 35

Personal independence payment

This chapter covers:

1. Who can get personal independence payment (p740)
2. The rules about your age (p760)
3. People included in the claim (p761)
4. The amount of benefit (p761)
5. Special benefit rules (p761)
6. Claims and backdating (p762)
7. Getting paid (p768)
8. Tax, other benefits and the benefit cap (p770)

Key facts

- Personal independence payment (PIP) is a benefit for adults with a disability or long-term health problem who have difficulty with getting around or daily living activities.
- PIP has daily living and mobility components. You can qualify for one or both components.
- PIP is a non-means-tested benefit.
- You do not have to have paid national insurance contributions to qualify.
- You can get PIP whether or not you work.
- PIP is administered and paid by the DWP.
- If you disagree with a PIP decision, you can apply for a revision or a supersession (see Chapter 56), or appeal against it (see Chapter 57). You must apply for a mandatory reconsideration before you can appeal.

. . . .

Future changes

From some time in 2021, it is expected that new claims for PIP in Scotland will be replaced by claims for disability assistance. Social Security Scotland will administer the new benefit. The Scottish government plans to transfer existing PIP claimants in Scotland to the new benefit by 2025. Chapter 71 has more details of the plans, and see AskCPAG.org.uk and CPAG's *Welfare Rights Bulletin* for updates.

. . . .

Part 5: Other benefits
Chapter 35: Personal independence payment
1. Who can get personal independence payment

1. Who can get personal independence payment

Note: if you are entitled to disability living allowance (DLA), see p618 to help you decide whether to claim personal independence payment (PIP).

You can get PIP if you:

- meet the age rules (see p760); *and*
- are not a 'person subject to immigration control' (see Chapter 67); *and*
- meet the residence conditions (see p1629); *and*
- meet the disability conditions for the daily living component, the mobility component or both (see below); *and*
- meet the required period condition (see p759), unless you are terminally ill.

The disability conditions

A points-based test is used to assess how your physical or mental condition (see below) affects your ability to undertake specific daily living activities (see p741) and mobility activities (see p753).[1] Each activity has a list of statements (called 'descriptors') which describe different difficulties with the activity or types of help you might need to manage it.

The test is what help you reasonably need, not what help you have available.[2] Restrictions to your lifestyle due to your condition (eg, when you are able to go out, or whether you must avoid noisy environments) should not result in you scoring fewer points.[3] However, the fact that you do not need, or choose not to, do some activities cannot help you to score points. For example, if you have never learned to cook, the assessment considers whether you *would* have difficulty preparing and cooking food due to your condition.

Each descriptor has a points score, and you get points for one descriptor for each activity – the one which best describes the difficulties you have with that activity. See p757 if your difficulties with the activities vary on different days, or if more than one descriptor in an activity applies to you.

The points you score for each activity relevant to a component are then added together. You qualify for a component at:[4]

- the standard rate if you score eight points or more; *or*
- the enhanced rate if you score 12 points or more.

You automatically qualify for the enhanced rate of the daily living component if you are terminally ill (see p762).

Physical or mental condition

Your difficulties must be due to your 'physical or mental condition'.[5] This does not require an additional test of whether you have a specific medical diagnosis.[6] However, there must be a physical or mental cause of your difficulty with carrying out a particular activity.[7] For example, if you are illiterate, you cannot score points for this reason unless you have a condition that affects your ability to learn to read.[8] Drug or alcohol dependency can count as a mental condition.[9]

The daily living activities

There are 10 daily living activities. This section does not cover every kind of disability or health problem, so think carefully about how your condition affects your ability to undertake each activity.

Note: the law is evolving as the Upper Tribunal decides cases that affect the interpretation of the descriptors (see p1383). See AskCPAG.org.uk and CPAG's *Welfare Rights Bulletin* for updates.

The assessment of your ability to manage the activities distinguishes between different kinds of help you may need. You do not score any points if you can manage an activity 'unaided'. This means without the use of an 'aid or appliance' (see p742), or without 'supervision', 'prompting' or 'assistance' (see below).[10]

The highest scoring descriptor for most of the activities applies if you cannot undertake the activity at all, even with these kinds of help. Arguably if you need so much assistance with an activity that someone else is effectively doing it for you, any contribution that you can make should be ignored and you should score points for a 'cannot' descriptor.[11]

Assistance, supervision and prompting[12]

'**Assistance**' means 'physical intervention by another person' to help you carry out an activity. It does not include someone doing the whole activity for you,[13] or giving verbal instructions, which counts as 'prompting'.

'**Supervision**' means the continuous presence of another person throughout the activity to ensure your safety. You need supervision if there is a 'real risk' of harm while carrying out the activity, considering both the likelihood and seriousness of the harm.[14] This means that you may score points even if you would not come to any harm most days if left unsupervised. This interpretation was not previously accepted, and the DWP's former interpretation was less generous. The DWP is looking again at PIP decisions made since 9 March 2017 to check they are correct and will change any awards it discovers are wrong.[15] Get advice if you think that you should have scored more points.

The risk does not need to be caused by doing the activity; it is enough that you need continuous supervision to carry it out (see p756).[16] If someone is also supervising other people at the same time, you can still satisfy a supervision descriptor.[17]

'**Prompting**' means another person reminding or encouraging you to carry out an activity, or explaining how to do it. You can score points even if you can sometimes manage unaided if there is a specific or urgent need to undertake the activity. Whether you can manage the activity on a normal day when there is not such an urgent need must also be considered.[18] The person prompting you does not necessarily need to be in your presence, so prompting by telephone, or arguably in the form of someone leaving you notes or reminders,[19] can allow you to score points, if you need this to be able to carry out an activity.

Part 5: Other benefits
Chapter 35: Personal independence payment
1. Who can get personal independence payment

For how your ability to carry out the activities with these kinds of help is assessed, see p756.

For how to decide which descriptor you satisfy if your difficulties vary, see p757.

You automatically qualify for the enhanced rate of the daily living component if you are terminally ill (see p762), even if you have no problems with any of the activities.

Aids and appliances

You score points for most of the daily living activities if you do not need help from another person, but need an 'aid or appliance' to carry out the activity. This is something that improves, provides or replaces a mental or physical function (including a prosthesis).[20] Some examples are an artificial leg, walking stick, wheelchair, modified cutlery needed because of your disability, or adaptations to your home like grab rails in the bathroom or a shower seat. It is unlikely to include surgical implants like hip replacements, retinal implants and heart valves.[21] If you have such an implant, think carefully about whether the effects of your condition with it in place mean that you should still score points in the assessment.

An aid or appliance that you do not use is is still taken into account if you could 'reasonably be expected' to use it to manage the activity.[22]

Could you use an aid or appliance?

When you could reasonably be expected to use an aid or appliance is not set out in the regulations. Some factors that may be relevant to whether it is reasonable for you to use an aid or appliance include whether:

– you have been advised to use it by a medical professional;

– it is available to you (this might include affordability if the NHS does not provide it); *and*

– it is practical for you to use it – eg, whether you can store it in your home.

If you are assessed as needing an aid or appliance to manage an activity and you think this is not reasonable, try to get evidence to show that you cannot use it, or you still need help from someone, despite using it.

To be awarded points in the assessment for needing an aid or appliance, you must need to use it because of your physical or mental condition. The aid need not be something that only people with a disability use,[23] or designed to help with the task that you need it for. However, it must improve, provide or replace a function that is vital to managing the specific activity, not just to managing it in a particular way.[24] For example, many people sit down to dress, so you will not score points for needing to do this because of your condition if, apart from your need to sit down to do so, you are able to dress unaided (see p756). However, if you need an aid to perform an essential part of the activity (eg, a crutch to stand up while dressing), you should still score points for it.[25] Something that you must use before you can manage an activity (eg, to warm up your hands, improving your manual dexterity) can also count as an aid.[26]

Your ability to use reasonably practicable alternatives may mean that you are assessed as managing an activity 'unaided'. Any alternatives that significantly restrict your choices arguably still count as aids to help you manage the activity.[27]

Examples

Bill needs to wear slip-on shoes because it takes him more than twice as long to tie his shoelaces as it used to before he had problems with manual dexterity. He can manage all his other clothing unaided. As slip-on shoes are a reasonable adjustment for Bill to make, he can dress and undress unaided.

Ben has severely restricted motor function following a stroke. He must wear slip-on shoes to manage alone. He must also wear loose-fitting clothing, cardigans without buttons and trousers with elasticated waistbands to dress within a reasonable time. The clothes that Ben must wear in order to dress without help amount to using aids to dress and undress, even though someone without Ben's difficulties may also choose to wear them.

Activity one: preparing food

Descriptors	Points
a. Can prepare and cook a simple meal unaided.	0
b. Needs to use an aid or appliance to be able to either prepare or cook a simple meal.	2
c. Cannot cook a simple meal using a conventional cooker but is able to do so using a microwave.	2
d. Needs prompting to be able to either prepare or cook a simple meal.	2
e. Needs supervision or assistance to either prepare or cook a simple meal.	4
f. Cannot prepare and cook food.	8

Definitions[28]

'**Simple meal**' means a cooked one-course meal for one person, using fresh ingredients.
'**Prepare**' means make food ready for cooking or eating.
'**Cook**' means to heat food at or above waist height. This means that your ability to bend down and get food from a low oven is irrelevant.[29]
See also the definitions common to all the daily living activities on p741.

This is an objective test of your ability to manage the tasks involved in preparing ingredients and cooking a reasonable range of simple meals, so takes no account of your specific dietary needs,[30] religious beliefs or cultural preferences.[31] Similarly, the impact of things such as childcare responsibilities or family size on your ability to prepare a meal is not relevant.[32]

Part 5: Other benefits
Chapter 35: Personal independence payment
1. Who can get personal independence payment

Descriptor 1c only looks at whether you can *cook* using a microwave – your ability to *prepare* the ingredients for a simple meal must also be considered.[33] To 'prepare' food, you must be able to peel and chop vegetables.[34] If you must use pre-prepared vegetables, you score points for needing assistance to prepare or cook a meal, unless you could prepare them with an aid or appliance. Aids to help you prepare and cook food could include specialist cooking utensils or a spiked chopping board. Lever arm taps and lightweight pans are less likely to be accepted as aids,[35] and a perching stool arguably does not count as an aid unless your condition means that you are only able to stand for very short periods.[36]

If you cannot read, tell the time or use timers because of your condition, this is relevant to whether you score points for this activity. However, you do not automatically score any points due to reading difficulties, as it is possible to cook without being able to read.[37]

It is arguable that you satisfy descriptor 1f if you are completely unable to either prepare or cook food, no matter how much help you get, even though you can manage the other task unaided.[38]

Activity two: taking nutrition

Descriptors	Points
a. Can take nutrition unaided.	0
b. Needs:	2
(i) to use an aid or appliance to be able to take nutrition; *or*	
(ii) supervision to be able to take nutrition; *or*	
(iii) assistance to be able to cut up food.	
c. Needs a therapeutic source to be able to take nutrition.	2
d. Needs prompting to be able to take nutrition.	4
e. Needs assistance to be able to manage a therapeutic source to take nutrition.	6
f. Cannot convey food and drink to her/his mouth and needs another person to do so.	10

Definitions[39]

'**Take nutrition**' means to cut food into pieces, convey food and drink to your mouth and chew and swallow food and drink, or to take nutrition using a therapeutic source.

'**Therapeutic source**' means parenteral or enteral tube feeding, using a rate-limiting device such as a delivery system or feed pump.

See also the definitions common to all the daily living activities on p741.

This activity focuses on the mechanical actions involved in eating and drinking (or using a therapeutic source), so the nutritious quality of what you consume is not relevant.[40] However, if your condition means that you need prompting to eat at all,[41] or your condition means that you need to eat lots of calories and you need prompting to eat enough, you can satisfy descriptor 2d.[42] You must be able to manage every aspect of taking nutrition without a theraputic source to manage this acitvity unaided, so difficulty swallowing solid foods can potentially allow you to score points for this activity.[43]

If you spill so much food that you need to change your clothes after eating, this is arguably not taking nutrition to an acceptable standard. Unless an aid or appliance (eg, adapted cup or cutlery), help to cut up your food or prompting from someone else means you can manage this, you should satisfy descriptor 2f.

Specially designed cutlery (eg, which is easier to grip) counts as an aid for this activity.

If you need help to set up or put away therapeutic feeding equipment due to your condition, you should satisfy descriptor 2e, even if you do not need help to use it once it has been set up. If you use such equipment overnight, you count as using it on two days for the purpose of deciding how many points you score, if your needs vary on different days (see p757).[44]

Activity three: managing therapy or monitoring a health condition

Descriptors	Points
a. Either:	0
(i) does not receive medication or therapy or need to monitor a health condition; *or*	
(ii) can manage medication or therapy or monitor a health condition unaided.	
b. Needs any one or more of the following:	1
(i) to use an aid or appliance to be able to manage medication;	
(ii) supervision, prompting or assistance to be able to manage medication;	
(iii) supervision, prompting or assistance to be able to monitor a health condition.	
c. Needs supervision, prompting or assistance to be able to manage therapy that takes no more than 3.5 hours a week.	2
d. Needs supervision, prompting or assistance to be able to manage therapy that takes more than 3.5 but no more than 7 hours a week.	4
e. Needs supervision, prompting or assistance to be able to manage therapy that takes more than 7 but no more than 14 hours a week.	6
f. Needs supervision, prompting or assistance to be able to manage therapy that takes more than 14 hours a week.	8

Part 5: Other benefits
Chapter 35: Personal independence payment
1. Who can get personal independence payment

Definitions[45]

'**Manage medication**' means take medication, where a failure to do so is likely to result in a deterioration in your health.

'**Medication**' means medication taken at home, which is prescribed or recommended by a registered doctor, nurse or pharmacist.

'**Monitor a health condition**' means detect significant changes in your condition which are likely to lead to a deterioration in your health, and take action advised by a registered doctor or nurse, or a health professional regulated by the Health and Care Professions Council, without which your health is likely to deteriorate.

'**Manage therapy**' means to undertake therapy, where a failure to do so is likely to result in a deterioration in your health.

'**Therapy**' means therapy to be undertaken at home which is prescribed or recommended by a registered doctor, nurse or pharmacist, or a health professional regulated by the Health and Care Professions Council. It does not include taking or administering medication, or any action which, in your case, comes within the definition of 'monitor a health condition'.

See also the definitions common to all the daily living activities on p741.

Examples of 'therapy' include needing help with dialysis, to fit prescribed bandages,[46] to undertake specialist massage treatment at home or to manage a special diet.[47] You cannot score points for help with therapy if there is a specific descriptor in another activity that describes exactly the same kind of help.[48] For example, needing assistance to self-catheterise scores points under Activity 5 (see p748),[49] and needing assistance to take nutrition using a therapeutic device scores points under Activity 2 (see p744).[50] **Note:** needing supervision or prompting with these things may arguably score you points for this activity.[51] General supervision provided in supported accommodation is not 'therapy'.[52] Smoking cessation treatment and weight loss counselling do not count as therapy if there is no evidence that smoking or obesity are making your condition worse.[53] It is arguable that if you need help with exercises to *improve* some aspect of how your condition affects you or to make you more comfortable, your health would deteriorate without it and so it counts as 'therapy'.[54]

As your need for therapy will itself result from your condition, you do not need to show that your condition is connected to the specific help that you need with it, just that you need help.[55] When deciding which descriptor is satisfied, the amount of time you need help with therapy is relevant, not the length of time the therapy takes.[56] The help you need to set up a machine you use for therapy (eg, a TENS machine) counts, even if you can manage unaided once it has been set up.[57]

As the descriptors about therapy refer to the amount of help you need during 'a week', you should not be excluded by the rule on fluctuating conditions (see p757) if you only need help with therapy on a minority of days.

Monitoring your health condition could include someone checking on how you are – eg, if you have schizophrenia which is normally controlled by medication.

Aids and appliances to help you manage medication could include a dosette box to organise pills if you are forgetful due to your condition, or a specialist device to help you to inject yourself, if you have difficulty with manual dexterity. However, an inhaler or syringe does not count as an aid, as it is a way of delivering medication, not something you need to use to help you manage your medication independently.[58]

Activity four: washing and bathing

Descriptors	Points
a. Can wash and bathe unaided.	0
b. Needs to use an aid or appliance to be able to wash or bathe.	2
c. Needs supervision or prompting to be able to wash or bathe.	2
d. Needs assistance to be able to wash either her/his hair or body below the waist.	2
e. Needs assistance to be able to get in or out of a bath or shower.	3
f. Needs assistance to be able to wash her/his body between the shoulders and waist.	4
g. Cannot wash and bathe at all and needs another person to wash her/his entire body.	8

Definitions[59]
'**Bathe**' includes getting into or out of an unadapted bath or shower.
See also the definitions common to all the daily living activities on p741.

If you cannot get into an unadapted bath without help, you satisfy descriptor 4e, even if you have a wet room at home so never need to do this.[60] A bath seat counts as an aid for this activity.[61]

If you are at risk if you bathe alone, whether you need supervision depends on the seriousness of the harm and how likely it is (see p741). You should not be expected to reduce the time you spend in the bath or shower to avoid the risk.[62]

To wash to an acceptable standard, you should be clean (and arguably, dry)[63] when you have finished. If it takes you a long time to wash and bathe without help, you can argue that you need assistance to do so.

If you can only motivate yourself to have a bath or shower if you have something important to do that day, it is arguable that you still need prompting to wash or bathe if you would not manage this unprompted on a normal day.[64]

Part 5: Other benefits
Chapter 35: Personal independence payment
1. Who can get personal independence payment

Activity five: managing toilet needs or incontinence

Descriptors	Points
a. Can manage toilet needs or incontinence unaided.	0
b. Needs to use an aid or appliance to be able to manage toilet needs or incontinence.	2
c. Needs supervision or prompting to be able to manage toilet needs.	2
d. Needs assistance to be able to manage toilet needs.	4
e. Needs assistance to be able to manage incontinence of either bladder or bowel.	6
f. Needs assistance to be able to manage incontinence of both bladder and bowel.	8

Definitions[65]

'**Manage incontinence**' means manage involuntary evacuation of the bowel or bladder, including using a collecting device or self-catheterisation, and clean yourself afterwards.
'**Toilet needs**' means getting on and off an unadapted toilet, evacuating the bladder and bowel, and cleaning yourself afterwards.
See also the definitions common to all the daily living activities on p741.

Even if you only have difficulty with one of the three things included in the definition of 'toilet needs' above, you can still score points for this activity.[66] However, you must have difficulty with an aspect of the activity as defined, so following a strict hygiene regime to avoid infections does not mean that you score points, unless your ablity to do one of these three things is affected by your condition.[67]

Examples of aids and appliances include a raised toilet seat, grab rails near the toilet,[68] a stoma and colostomy bag,[69] incontinence pads,[70] or a shower head used to clean yourself.[71] If it is *reasonable* for you to use incontinence pads most days (this includes using pads overnight) as a precaution, you satisfy descriptor 5b, even if you are only actually incontinent on a minority of days,[72] or do not actually use pads.[73] A commode can count as an aid for this activity, but only if part of the reason you must use it is that your condition means you have difficulty with toilet needs or incontinence (not if you only use it because of problems managing the stairs at home, for example).[74] You score more points if you need help from someone else to use one of these things.

Difficulty dressing and undressing to use the toilet does not allow you to score points for this activity.[75]

Activity six: dressing and undressing

Descriptors	Points
a. Can dress and undress unaided.	0
b. Needs to use an aid or appliance to be able to dress or undress.	2
c. Needs either:	2
(i) prompting to be able to dress, undress or determine appropriate circumstances for remaining clothed; *or*	
(ii) prompting or assistance to be able to select appropriate clothing.	
d. Needs assistance to be able to dress or undress her/his lower body.	2
e. Needs assistance to be able to dress or undress her/his upper body.	4
f. Cannot dress or undress at all.	8

Definitions[76]

'Dress and undress' includes putting on and taking off socks and shoes.
See also the definitions common to all the daily living activities on p741.

To score points for this activity, it is only necessary that you have difficulty with dressing or undressing, not both. Similarly, having difficulty with either your socks or shoes is sufficient for you to score points.[77]

If you must wear them because of your condition, clothes that are easier to manage, such as slip-on shoes, cardigans rather than jumpers or zips rather than buttons, may count as aids to help you dress, depending on the extent to which your choices are restricted by your condition(s).[78] If you only need one of these things (eg, your only difficulty is with tying shoelaces), this may, nonetheless, allow you to dress and undress unaided.[79]

If you must sit down to dress or undress, this does not count as needing an aid or appliance.[80] However, if you must use an aid to get up after getting dressed sitting down, you satisfy descriptor 6b.[81]

Selecting appropriate clothing includes choosing the right clothes for the weather, and also not reusing clothing which is dirty.[82] If you take a long time to choose clothes due to your condition, you may satisfy descriptor 6c.[83]

Part 5: Other benefits
Chapter 35: Personal independence payment
1. Who can get personal independence payment

Activity seven: communicating verbally

Descriptors	Points
a. Can express and understand verbal information unaided.	0
b. Needs to use an aid or appliance to be able to speak or hear.	2
c. Needs communication support to be able to express or understand complex verbal information.	4
d. Needs communication support to be able to express or understand basic verbal information.	8
e. Cannot express or understand verbal information at all even with communication support.	12

Definitions[84]

'Basic verbal information' means information in your native language conveyed verbally in a simple sentence.

'Complex verbal information' means information in your native language conveyed verbally in either more than one sentence or one complicated sentence.

'Communication support' means support from a person trained or experienced in communicating with people with specific communication needs, including interpreting verbal information into a non-verbal form and vice versa.

See also the definitions common to all the daily living activities on p741.

If you have problems speaking English because you have never learned the language, this does not count. If strangers find it hard to understand you (due to your condition affecting your speech rather than your accent), you may need help to communicate to an acceptable standard and within a reasonable time.

Your ability to read, write or send text messages is not relevant. Your ability to lip-read is not taken into account in deciding whether you can understand speech.[85] If you have difficulty using a phone or understanding speech in a noisy environment due to your condition, you can potentially score points.[86]

The definition of 'communication support' includes both someone with specialist training, like a British Sign Language interpreter, and someone who knows you and is experienced in helping you to communicate.[87] How many points you score depends on whether you need help with even a single simple sentence, or whether you can manage this but need help with anything more complicated. If you have problems speaking or understanding speech because of a mental health problem or cognitive impairment, you can score points for this activity if your problems are with the act of speaking, hearing or understanding speech – ie, not just a reluctance to speak because you are shy in social situations.[88]

Activity eight: reading and understanding signs, symbols and words

Descriptors	Points
a. Can read and understand basic and complex written information either unaided or using spectacles or contact lenses.	0
b. Needs to use an aid or appliance, other than spectacles or contact lenses, to be able to read or understand either basic or complex written information.	2
c. Needs prompting to be able to read or understand complex written information.	2
d. Needs prompting to be able to read or understand basic written information.	4
e. Cannot read or understand signs, symbols or words at all.	8

Definitions[89]

'**Basic written information**' means signs, symbols and dates written or printed in standard size text in your native language.

'**Complex written information**' means more than one sentence of written or printed standard size text in your native language.

'**Read**' includes reading signs, symbols and words, but does not include Braille. The exclusion of Braille from the definition of 'read' means that if you have no effective sight at all, you are assessed as being unable to read.

See also the definitions common to all the daily living activities on p741.

If your ability to read is affected so that you satisfy a descriptor at certain times of the day, you should score points for this activity, even if you can read unaided at other times of the day.[90] Similarly, it is arguable that you should only be assessed as needing an aid or appliance to read (rather than someone to help) if you can read both outside and inside using aids.

If you can read to the standard required with one eye (including using glasses), then a problem with your other eye does not mean you score points.[91]

If you have a mental or cognitive impairment and, because of this, need help to understand the meaning of written information, you should score points for this activity. If you have never learned to read in English, you only score points for this activity if this is because of a physical or mental condition.[92]

Part 5: Other benefits
Chapter 35: Personal independence payment
1. Who can get personal independence payment

Activity nine: engaging with other people face to face

Descriptors	Points
a. Can engage with other people unaided.	0
b. Needs prompting to be able to engage with other people.	2
c. Needs social support to be able to engage with other people.	4
d. Cannot engage with other people due to such engagement causing either:	8
(i) overwhelming psychological distress to the claimant; *or*	
(ii) the claimant to exhibit behaviour which would result in a substantial risk of harm to the claimant or another person.	

Definitions[93]

'Psychological distress' means distress related to an enduring mental health condition or an intellectual or cognitive impairment.

'Social support' means support from a person trained or experienced in assisting people to engage in social situations.

See also the definitions common to all the daily living activities on p741.

This activity looks at your ability to interact with individuals or small groups,[94] and in social situations.[95] 'Engage with other people' means to 'interact in a contextually and socially appropriate manner', 'understand body language' and 'establish relationships'.[96] All three of these factors should be considered.[97] Your ability to interact with strangers, as well as people you know, should be considered. The test is whether you can engage with adults generally, not just with particular groups of people, such as women or young people.[98]

'Establish relationships' does not refer to any particular type of relationship, but means something more than just the ability to respond to questions.[99] Both mental and physical conditions are relevant to this activity, so a visual impairment may affect your ability to understand body language, for example.[100] Even if you undertake social activities (eg, going to a pub), you may still score points for this activity if you cannot engage with other people without help.[101]

The person helping you does not always need to be physically present.[102] While the descriptors distinguish between 'prompting' and 'social support', there is some overlap between them. To satisfy descriptor 9c, you must show that the prompting (or other social support) needs to be provided by someone trained or experienced (but this could include a family member or friend experienced in helping you).[103]

Activity 10: making budgeting decisions

Descriptors	Points
a. Can manage complex budgeting decisions unaided.	0
b. Needs prompting or assistance to be able to make complex budgeting decisions.	2
c. Needs prompting or assistance to be able to make simple budgeting decisions.	4
d. Cannot make any budgeting decisions at all.	6

Definitions[104]

'Complex budgeting decisions' means decisions involving calculating household and personal budgets, managing and paying bills and planning future purchases.
'Simple budgeting decisions' means decisions involving calculating the cost of goods and calculating the change required after a purchase.
See also the definitions common to all the daily living activities on p741.

The focus of this activity is on difficulty making decisions because of your physical or mental condition, rather than poor money management skills. But if your condition means that you are very impulsive, you can satisfy descriptor 10b if this would prevent you from budgeting effectively.[105] Similarly, if your condition (eg, a mental health problem or an autism spectrum disorder) means that you cannot manage your own finances, you could score points for descriptor 10b regardless of your level of intelligence.[106]

It is unlikely that you will be awarded points for this activity based solely on a physical condition.[107] However, if you have difficulty *making decisions* because of a physical condition (eg, you need someone to read information repeatedly to be able to make a decision because you have a visual impairment), you may arguably satisfy descriptor 10b.[108]

The mobility activities

There are two mobility activities in the assessment. Remember that your difficulties with the activities must be caused by a physical or mental condition (see p740) for you to score points. This section does not cover every kind of disability or health problem, so think carefully about how your condition affects your ability to manage each of the activities.

Note: the law is evolving as the Upper Tribunal decides cases that affect the interpretation of the descriptors (see p1383). See AskCPAG.org.uk and CPAG's *Welfare Rights Bulletin* for updates.

For how your ability to carry out an activity as described by a descriptor is assessed, see p756.

For which descriptor you satisfy if your difficulties vary, see p757.

Part 5: Other benefits
Chapter 35: Personal independence payment
1. Who can get personal independence payment

Activity one: planning and following journeys

Descriptors[109]	Points
a. Can plan and follow the route of a journey unaided.	0
b. Needs prompting to be able to undertake any journey to avoid overwhelming psychological distress to the claimant.	4
c. Cannot plan the route of a journey.	8
d. Cannot follow the route of an unfamiliar journey without another person, assistance dog or orientation aid.	10
e. Cannot undertake any journey because it would cause overwhelming psychological distress to the claimant.	10
f. Cannot follow the route of a familiar journey without another person, an assistance dog or an orientation aid.	12

Definitions[110]

'**Assistance dog**' means a dog trained to guide or assist a person with a sensory impairment.

'**Orientation aid**' means a specialist aid designed to assist disabled people to follow a route safely. A standard satnav does not count as an orientation aid, although one designed or modified for disabled people might.[111]

'**Prompting**' means reminding, encouraging or explaining by another person.

'**Psychological distress**' means distress related to an enduring mental health condition or an intellectual or cognitive impairment.

'**Unaided**' means without the use of an aid or appliance, or without supervision, prompting or assistance.

If you need prompting to leave the house as the thought of going out causes overwhelming psychological distress, you can satisfy descriptor 1b even if once you start a journey you do not need to be accompanied by someone else.[112] Prompting by telephone is arguably sufficient, if it is needed for you to leave the house.[113] It is arguable that you can satisfy descriptor 1b or 1e if you need prompting to, or cannot, go out during part of a day, if your 'lifestyle is restricted to more than a trivial extent'.[114]

The use of the words 'follow the route' means that you can satisfy descriptors 1d and 1f if you need someone to help you get to your destination (this could include help to navigate, supervision to keep you safe, or help to deal with unexpected diversions), but not if you only need help to communicate with people you meet during a journey.[115] It is possible to satisfy descriptor 1d or 1f if you sometimes manage a specific journey alone, as long as you generally need one of the kinds of help described.[116] If you can manage part of a journey (eg, in your car) by yourself, you can still score points if you need someone else with you at the start or end of the journey.[117] Your ability to manage a range of journeys, not just a short or local journey, should be considered.[118]

You can only satisfy descriptors 1d and 1f due to anxiety if you need someone with you to avoid *overwhelming* psychological distress.[119] That person does not need to be taking action to help you if their presence alone is enough to relieve the distress.[120]

DWP guidance suggests that if you satisfy descriptor 1e as you cannot leave the house at all on the majority of days, you cannot also satisfy descriptor 1f.[121] This is arguably not correct (eg, if you also have a visual impairment and would need a guide dog if you were able to go out), but the Upper Tribunal has held that if you satisfy descriptor 1e, whether you also satisfy descriptor 1f should be decided without taking account of any psychological distress that you experience.[122]

Note: the DWP's interpretation of this activity used to be less generous. It is contacting claimants who get PIP (or who have been refused it since 28 November 2016) who might score more points for this activity.[123] Get advice if you think you would have scored more points for this activity or been entitled to PIP, but the effects of psychological distress were not taken into account.

Activity two: moving around

Descriptors	Points
a. Can stand and then move more than 200 metres, either aided or unaided.	0
b. Can stand and then move more than 50 metres but no more than 200 metres, either aided or unaided.	4
c. Can stand and then move unaided more than 20 metres but no more than 50 metres.	8
d. Can stand and then move using an aid or appliance more than 20 metres but no more than 50 metres.	10
e. Can stand and then move more than one metre but no more than 20 metres, either aided or unaided.	12
f. Cannot, either aided or unaided:	12
(i) stand; *or*	
(ii) move more than one metre.	

Definitions[124]

'**Aided**' means with the use of an aid or appliance, or with supervision, prompting or assistance.

'**Stand**' means to stand upright with at least one biological foot on the ground, so double amputees are treated as unable to stand and satisfy descriptor 2f.

'**Unaided**' means without the use of an aid or appliance, or without supervision, prompting or assistance.

See also the definitions of 'supervision', 'prompting' and 'assistance' on p741.

Part 5: Other benefits
Chapter 35: Personal independence payment
1. Who can get personal independence payment

This activity looks at your ability to 'stand and then move', so any movement you can manage using a wheelchair is ignored. The descriptors assess your ability on the usual type of surfaces you might encounter outdoors, including your ability to manage kerbs, but not flights of steps or steep slopes.[125]

The points you score for this activity should take account of how often you want to go out, but cannot due to your condition (as long as this is reasonable). So, for example, you should not be assessed on the basis that you only *need* to go out once a day to a local shop unless you do not *want* to go out at other times.[126]

The number of points you score depends on the distance you can move, and whether you can move aided or unaided. If you can manage more than 50 metres using an aid or appliance or with help, you can only satisfy descriptors 2a and 2b, even if you can only manage less than 50 metres unaided.[127]

It is not necessary for you to be able to manage the distance mentioned in one go, as brief stops do not mean that you cannot move this distance.[128]

However, the length and duration of any stops are relevant to whether you can move that distance repeatedly and within a reasonable time period (see p757). If you can manage to move a particular distance 'within a reasonable time period', the fact that you can only move slowly is not relevant to whether you are managing the activity to an acceptable standard.[129] However, pain,[130] dizziness and breathlessness are all relevant to whether you are able to move to an acceptable standard (or safely).

If moving around causes you significant pain, its impact on how far you can walk can be considered, even if the pain has no known physical cause.[131] However, if your physical difficulties walking are caused by psychological distress, this is considered under Activity 1 (see p754), and not this activity.[132]

Can you carry out an activity?

If a descriptor describes help you need to carry out an activity, unless you can manage an activity in the way described by a descriptor in *all* of the following ways, you must be awarded a higher scoring descriptor.[133]

- **Safely.** This is defined as being in a manner that is unlikely to cause harm to you or anyone else, either during or after the activity. This means that there is 'a real possibility that cannot be ignored of harm occurring'. This involves considering both the likelihood of any harm occurring, and the severity of the consequences if it did occur.[134] You should not be expected to restrict the way in which you carry out an activity (eg, how long you shower for) in order to do it safely.[135]
- **To an acceptable standard.** This is not defined in the regulations, and what it means is closely linked to the activity in question. What is an acceptable standard will depend to an extent on your experience of doing the activity, making the test a subjective one.[136] The level of pain you experience when managing an activity is one factor that should be considered.[137]

- **Repeatedly.** This is defined as being as often as it is reasonably required for you to carry out the activity. This means that if you have problems with an activity at some point during a day, you should satisfy a scoring descriptor on that day.[138] In considering how often you 'reasonably' need to undertake an activity, your own choices should generally be respected, so think carefully about what you would want to do if you did not have your condition.[139]
- **Within a reasonable time period.** This is defined as being no more than twice the maximum time normally taken by someone with no health problems or disabilities to complete the activity. Time you spend thinking about the activity (eg, choosing clothes) can be taken into account if the hesitation is due to your condition.[140]

These four factors should be considered separately. For example, if you can manage the activity within a reasonable time period as defined, the fact that you are doing it slowly is not relevant to the question of whether you can manage to an acceptable standard.[141]

These definitions still leave a lot of discretion to the DWP. If you think you have not been given enough points because of this rule, you can ask for a mandatory reconsideration and then appeal. Explain which factor means you cannot carry out the activity as described by the descriptor you were awarded, and which descriptor you think you should satisfy.

Example

Conrad has a condition that means he has no perception of danger and is very impatient. Having a friend prompt him while he prepares and cooks food does not allow him to manage this activity safely. Even using a microwave leaves him at risk of harm from knives or eating undercooked food. He satisfies descriptor 1e (see p743).

Fluctuating conditions

If a scoring descriptor applies to you at some point in a day (ie, 24 hours, starting from midnight), you should be accepted as satisfying it on that day, unless the amount of help you need is so minimal that it can be ignored.[142]

Example

Archie has a visual impairment, which causes him dififculties in poor light. If it is dark outside, he needs another person to be able to follow the route of an unfamiliar journey. At other times during the day, he can normally follow journeys by himself. He should satisfy descriptor 1d in the planning and following journeys activity (see p754).

Part 5: Other benefits
Chapter 35: Personal independence payment
1. Who can get personal independence payment

Which descriptor you are awarded for an activity also depends on how your condition affects you on different days. You are normally assessed over a one-year period starting from three months before you claim PIP, or the date your condition starts to affect you if that is later.[143] If you reclaim PIP after a gap and the 'special rule' on p759 applies, the assessment looks at the last three months of your previous award and the nine months from the date of your new claim.[144]

The descriptor you score points for is decided as follows.[145]

- If only one descriptor in the activity applies to you on over 50 per cent of the days, that descriptor is used.
- If two or more descriptors each apply to you on over 50 per cent of the days, the one that scores the most points is used.
- If neither of the above bullet points apply, but the number of days on which you satisfy two or more scoring descriptors totals more than 50 per cent of the days, the scoring descriptor that applies most often is used. If two descriptors apply on the same number of days, the highest scoring one is used.

Example

Aisha makes a new claim for PIP on 5 May 2020. She has arthritis, which has affected her ability to dress for more than three months, so the period considered is from 5 February 2020 to 4 February 2021 (three months before the date she claimed and nine months after that date). Her condition is not deteriorating, but affects her differently on different days. On about two days a week (or 104 days a year), she can dress and undress unaided. Three days a week (or 156 days a year), she manages to dress using loose clothes with no buttons, slip-on shoes and a grabber to help with her socks. On a further two days a week (104 days a year), she also needs assistance from a family member to dress her upper body. The third bullet point above applies, as no single descriptor is satisfied on over half the days. Aisha is awarded points for descriptor 6b (see p749) as she satisfies one or other of the scoring descriptors on over half of the days, and this descriptor applies most often.

It can be very difficult to decide which descriptors you satisfy if your condition fluctuates. It may be helpful for you to keep a diary over several weeks to help explain how your condition affects you.

When calculating which descriptor you should satisfy under this rule, it is important to think about how the effects of your condition vary, bearing in mind that you may not need to attempt some activities every day. For example, if your mental health condition means you can only go out or make budgeting decisions on good days, a couple of times a week, this does not mean that you should not score any points for these activities, even if you do all your shopping and pay your bills on good days as you have no one to help you on bad days. Similarly, the fact that you can sometimes manage activities if there is a specific reason you must do so does not mean that you do not need prompting to manage them on other days.[146]

Note: if you have more than one fluctuating condition and these affect your ability to manage a particular activity independently of each other, you may be affected on more than half of the days in the period considered, even if each condition only affects you on a minority of days.[147]

The required period condition

Unless you are terminally ill (see p762),[148] you cannot get PIP unless you satisfy the 'required period condition'.[149] This normally means that you must be expected to meet the disability conditions for over one year in total. The required period condition is made up of two separate periods.[150]

If it is likely that you have met the disability conditions for three months ('the past period') when you claim PIP, it can be awarded from that date. You must also be likely to continue to meet them for at least another nine months from that date ('the prospective period').

If you do not satisfy the past period condition when you claim, a PIP award can be made starting up to three months after the date your claim is decided, if you will satisfy both parts of the required period condition by then.[151]

For how the required period condition affects an ongoing award of PIP, see p769.

Note:
- A special rule applies if:
  - you used to get PIP; *and*
  - your award ended less than two years ago (one year if you are over pension age); *and*
  - you make a new claim on the basis of the same condition(s) or a new condition that developed as a result of a previous one.

  In this situation, if you met the disability conditions for a component at a particular rate during the last three months of your previous award, you qualify for the same component from the date of your new claim, if your needs are expected to last for at least nine months from that date.[152]
- If you claim PIP and either you get DLA and are being transferred to PIP (see p617) or your DLA award ended under two years ago (one year if you are over pension age), you do not have to satisfy the past period test. You must still satisfy the prospective period test.[153]

Part 5: Other benefits
Chapter 35: Personal independence payment
2. The rules about your age

2. **The rules about your age**

You must be aged 16 or over to claim personal independence payment (PIP).[154]

The upper age limit for making a new PIP claim is normally the day you reach pension age (see p780).[155]

There are several exceptions to the upper age limit.

- If you were under 65 on 8 April 2013 and either you are entitled to disability living allowance (DLA) or your etitlement ended less than a year ago, you can claim PIP even if you are over pension age.[156] See p618 if you get DLA and are thinking about claiming PIP.
- If you claimed PIP before reaching pension age, an award can be made to you.[157]
- If you are entitled to PIP when you reach pension age, your award continues to its end date, if you still meet the entitlement conditions.[158]
- Your PIP award can be revised or superseded after you reach pension age (see Chapter 56).[159]
- If your PIP award has a fixed end date, you can make a renewal claim up to six months before this date, even if you are over pension age (see p769). Also, if you have been entitled to PIP, you can reclaim it within one year of your previous award ending, even if you are now over pension age. Your new claim must be on the basis of the same disability or health condition(s) as your former award, or a new condition that has developed as a result of the original one(s).

Note: in the latter two situations above, your entitlement to the mobility component is restricted.[160]

Mobility component for older people

If you are entitled to the mobility component when you reach pension age, you continue to get it, provided you still meet the entitlement conditions. However, if you make a PIP claim (including a renewal claim) after reaching pension age, your entitlement to the mobility component must be due to the same condition(s) as your previous award, or a new condition that has developed as a result of the original one(s).[161] Special rules restrict the rate you can get.[162]

- You only get the enhanced rate of the mobility component if you meet the normal entitlement conditions and you got the enhanced rate in an award which ended less than one year before you claim.
- You can get the standard rate if you meet the entitlement conditions and you got either rate of the mobility component in an award which ended less than one year before you claim.

If your existing award of PIP is revised or superseded due to a change that happens after you reach pension age, you can only get the mobility component if you currently get it, or it stopped less than a year before the date on which the decision takes effect.[163] Also, to get the mobility component at the same rate, your entitlement must be due to substantially the same condition(s) as your previous award.[164] You can move from the enhanced rate to the standard rate (even if your mobility needs result from a new condition),[165] but you cannot get the mobility component for the first time or move from the standard rate to the enhanced rate.[166]

There are no restrictions on your entitlement to the mobility component due to your age if:[167]
- you make a claim for PIP; *and*
- you were under 65 on 8 April 2013; *and*
- either you are entitled to DLA and claiming PIP as part of the transfer process (see p617), or your entitlement to DLA ended less than a year ago.

3. People included in the claim

You claim personal independence payment (PIP) for yourself. Your partner may get PIP or attendance allowance (AA) her/himself, or still get disability living allowance (DLA). Your child may get DLA in her/his own right, or PIP when s/he turns 16. See Chapter 24 for information about AA and Chapter 28 for information about DLA.

4. The amount of benefit

The daily living component of personal independence payment (PIP) is paid at one of two weekly rates:[168]
- the standard rate is £59.70;
- the enhanced rate is £89.15.

The mobility component of PIP is paid at one of two weekly rates:[169]
- the standard rate is £23.60;
- the enhanced rate is £62.25.

5. Special benefit rules

Special rules may apply to:
- people who are terminally ill (see p762);
- people subject to immigration control (see Chapter 67);
- people who have come from or are going abroad (see Chapters 68, 69 and 70);

Part 5: Other benefits
Chapter 35: Personal independence payment
6. Claims and backdating

- people who are in hospital or living in a care home or other similar accommodation, or people in prison or detention (see Chapter 42).

Terminal illness

You are regarded as 'terminally ill' if you have a progressive disease from which your death can reasonably be expected within six months.[170] If you claim personal independence payment (PIP) and you are terminally ill, you are automatically entitled to the enhanced rate of the daily living component.[171] You must satisfy the disability conditions for the mobility component (see p753), but you do not need to satisfy the required period condition (see p759).[172] If you claim PIP and are terminally ill, it does not matter how long you have lived in the UK.[173] However, there are other residence tests that you must satisfy (see p1629).

Claims from terminally ill people are referred to as 'special rules' claims. If you want to claim PIP, or you are requesting a revision or supersession, on the basis of being terminally ill, you should expressly state this.[174] Someone else can claim PIP on behalf of a terminally ill person without her/his knowledge or authority.[175]

Note: the process of claiming PIP is different if you are terminally ill (see p763).

---

6. Claims and backdating

The general rules about claims are covered in Chapter 50. This section explains the specific rules that apply to personal independence payment (PIP).

Note: if you get disability living allowance (DLA) and have received a letter telling you to claim PIP, you should do so straight away, as your DLA award will end. If you have *not* been sent a letter telling you to claim PIP, get specialist advice to help you decide whether it is a good idea to do so. See p618 for further details.

Making a claim

It is usually best to claim PIP by telephone. If you are unable to claim by telephone, you can ask for form PIP1 to be sent to you.[176] A video relay service for British Sign Language users is available at gov.uk/pip/how-to-claim.

Forms

Form PIP1 is available from the PIP claims line on 0800 917 2222 (textphone: 0800 917 7777; Relay UK (if you cannot hear or speak on the phone): 18001 then 0800 917 2222).

If you cannot use the phone and there is no one to help you, write asking for a claim form to Personal Independence Payment New Claims, Post Handling Site B, Wolverhampton WV99 1AH. This will delay your date of claim.

If you need to submit your claim form via email as your condition means that you cannot claim by telephone or in writing, you should be able to request an email address to send your claim to as a reasonable adjustment to the process.[177] If you have a query about an existing PIP claim, contact the PIP helpline on 0800 121 4433 (textphone: 0800 121 4493; Relay UK: 18001 then 0800 121 4433).

You must provide any information or evidence required (see below). You can amend or withdraw your claim before a decision is made (see p1169).

If you get PIP already and your award ends within the next year, see p769.

If your entitlement to PIP ended because you were abroad (see p1629), but you return to Great Britain less than 12 months later, a new PIP claim can be assessed on the basis of information held about your claim if your needs have not changed.[178] The DWP refers to this as a 'rapid reclaim'.

People who are terminally ill

The PIP claims process is different if you are terminally ill. You should explain that the claim is on the grounds of terminal illness when making it. Your GP, consultant or specialist nurse should complete Form DS1500, giving details of your condition and prognosis.

You are asked questions about mobility needs as part of the claim. If you are accepted as terminally ill, you are not asked to complete a separate questionnaire or attend a consultation.[179]

Someone else can claim PIP on behalf of a terminally ill person without her/his knowledge or authority.[180] If you have claimed PIP on someone else's behalf, you can also ask for a revision or supersession (see p1301) and appeal against the decision without her/his knowledge or authority.[181]

Who should claim

You must normally make a claim for PIP yourself. If you are unable to manage your affairs, another person can claim PIP for you as your 'appointee' (see p1170). Someone else can also claim PIP for a person who is terminally ill (see above).

Information to support your claim

For the general information requirements that apply to all benefits, see p1170.

It is important that you provide any information required when you claim. Until you do, you may not count as having made a valid claim (see p1172). Correct any defects as soon as possible or your date of claim may be affected.

Once you have claimed, there is a separate assessment process (see p764).

Even if your claim is valid, you may be asked to provide further information to support your claim (see p1174). You may also be asked to provide information after you are awarded PIP and, if you fail to do so, your PIP could be suspended, or even terminated (see p1200).

Part 5: Other benefits
Chapter 35: Personal independence payment
6. Claims and backdating

The assessment process

If you claim PIP and meet the basic entitlement conditions (see p740), you are assessed to see whether you meet the disability conditions (see p740) and the required period condition (see p759). You are also assessed if your PIP award is being reviewed (see p769) or you report a change in your circumstances (see p769). The assessment process can include requirements to:[182]

- provide information or evidence (normally in the form of a questionnaire about how you manage daily living and mobility activities); *and*
- attend and participate in a consultation with a health professional.

The questionnaire

You are sent a questionnaire, which asks for contact details of professionals who know how your condition affects you. You have one month from the day it was sent to you to return it. You may be allowed longer, if this is considered reasonable.[183] If you do not return the questionnaire (or other information that is requested) without good reason (see p766), a 'negative determination' is made, and your claim is refused (or your existing award ends).[184]

If you need to ask for extra time to complete your questionnaire, contact the DWP as soon as possible. If your request is refused, and a negative determination made, see p766.

If you have made a new claim, the questionnaire (PIP2) asks for details of people who know how your condition affects you, and information about your condition(s) and any treatment you get. See below for how to complete it.

If your award is being reviewed (see p769), you are sent a different questionnaire (AR1). It asks if anything has changed since you were awarded PIP, roughly when this happened and how you are affected now. See below for help in completing the questionnaire.

You are asked questions relating to the 10 daily living activities (see p741) and two mobility activities (see p753).

How should you complete the questionnaire?

1. Read the notes on the form before answering the questions. It may help to draft your answers on a separate sheet of paper first.

2. Many advice agencies can help you to complete the questionnaire. If you have difficulties with English, reading or writing, you should get help.

3. If someone else has to fill in the questionnaire for you, or you are only able to do so yourself slowly, or with pain, explain this.

4. Compare your answers with the information on pp741–56 to work out your likely score. Your answers should not be exaggerated, but check that you have not underestimated any of your problems and have given all the details you can.

5. Remember that many of the terms in the assessment have special definitions. For example, 'dressing and undressing' includes putting on, or taking off, shoes or socks.

6. If you have good and bad days, explain this. You may need different help (see p741) with an activity on different days or at different times of day. If so, try to explain how often you need each kind of help, as this is also relevant to the points that you score (see p757).

7. List any aids or appliances (see p742) that you need to help you complete an activity, and any problems you have using them.

8. Explain if an activity takes you a long time or puts you at risk, or if you cannot complete it as often as you need to, only to a low standard or with pain (see p756).

9. It might be a good idea to ask someone who knows you well to check that your answers fully explain your difficulties with the activities.

10. If you have other information that is relevant to your difficulties with daily living or mobility activities, send a copy of it with the questionnaire. This could include a report from an occupational therapist or consultant, or information from your doctor, a support worker or carer. You could also send a statement from a friend or family member. If you are unsure whether evidence is helpful, check how closely it relates to the activities in the assessment. Evidence that confirms the severity of your condition may also be useful – eg, x-rays, test results or a Certificate of Vision Impairment.

11. Make a copy of the completed questionnaire before returning it to the DWP, and keep a copy of any additional information that you send with it.

On receiving a completed questionnaire, the DWP sends it to a health professional who decides what other evidence s/he thinks is needed. This is likely to include asking you to participate in a consultation.

The consultation

You can be asked to take part in a consultation with a health professional to assess whether you satisfy the disability conditions (even if you already have a PIP award). Two companies, Independent Assessment Services and Capita, carry out consultations,[185] and should contact you to explain what you need to do. You can find more information in letters they send to you, or on their websites.[186] The DWP also publishes a guide to carrying out assessments for health professionals.[187]

Before arranging a consultation, the health professional decides whether to ask for evidence from someone who knows you. It is possible that a health professional will prepare a report without a consultation.[188]

You must normally be sent written notice of the date and time of a consultation (and, for face-to-face consultations, where it will be) at least seven days in advance.[189] However, this rule does not apply if you accept less notice or notice by phone.[190]

Consultations are normally face to face in an assessment centre.

Recordings of assessments

If you want a recording of your consultation you can request permission to make an audio recording of it. You must give the health professional a copy of the recording at the consultation, on CD or cassette. There are restrictions on the equipment that you can use – eg, using a computer is not considered acceptable.[191]

Part 5: Other benefits
Chapter 35: Personal independence payment
6. Claims and backdating

You can take someone along to support you, and s/he can also give information to the health professional. In order to produce a report for the decision maker, the health professional asks you questions about your condition and how you manage different daily living and mobility activities.

What should you do at the consultation?

1. Explain as much as possible about how you are affected by your condition(s).

2. Remember that the assessment report can also include informal observations of your behaviour – eg, whether you have attended the consultation by yourself. If you were dropped off outside the assessment centre, you should explain this, and any difficulties travelling by yourself would have caused you.

3. If you need to take additional painkillers to attend the consultation, explain this, and also what you can and cannot do taking your normal dose.

4. If you have good and bad days, make sure that you explain this, and how your needs are different on a bad day. This is especially important if you are assessed on a good day.

5. If you are not fluent in English, it is vital that someone who can interpret for you attends. Contact the assessment provider as soon as possible if you need an interpreter.

You can ask for an assessment at home or at a local healthcare centre. However, you should try to provide medical evidence explaining why you cannot attend an assessment centre.[192] If your request is refused and you do not attend, your claim may be refused (see below).

If you fail to complete part of the assessment process

If you do not return a questionnaire on time or do not participate in a consultation, and the DWP does not accept that you had good reason for the failure, it makes a 'negative determination'. This results in a new PIP claim being refused,[193] or an existing award being superseded and removed from the date of the decision (see p1319).[194]

If the DWP decides that you are not entitled to PIP due to a negative determination, you can ask for a mandatory reconsideration (see p1339), and appeal if the decision is not changed. You should also make a new claim, in case your challenge is not successful.

Check carefully any letters that you received telling you what to do. It may be arguable that the information you were sent was not sufficient to make you aware of the requirement to return the questionnaire or attend a consultation.[195]

Good reason

In deciding whether you have '**good reason**', the DWP must consider the state of your health and the nature of your disability, along with any other reasons why you did not do what was required.[196] Guidance suggests a number of other things *may* amount to good reason, including domestic emergencies and not having received notifications.[197] The guidance suggests that telling the assessment provider what has happened as soon as possible is relevant to whether you have good reason or not. You should contact the assessment provider as soon as you can to explain why you will not be able to (or did not) attend a consultation. Guidance to health professionals suggests that a negative determination should not be made if you have a mental or cognitive impairment and do not return a questionnaire, so if you have this kind of condition you should explain any effect it had on your ability to return it.[198]

You should try to get supporting evidence – eg, confirmation of postal problems at your address, or medical evidence of the impact of the request to attend a consultation on your condition. You can argue that the unsuitability of the location of a consultation you were required to attend was good reason for not attending it.[199]

The date of your claim

The date of your claim is important as it determines when your entitlement to PIP starts. For information about when payment of PIP starts, see p768.

If you claim by telephone, your **'date of claim'** is usually the date of your call.[200] If you request a paper claim form, your date of claim is the date your request is received by the DWP, provided you return the properly completed form so it is received within one month (or longer if reasonable).[201]

Note: you must make sure your claim is valid. If it is 'defective', you are given a short time to correct the defects (see p1172). If you do, your claim is treated as having been made when you initially claimed.[202]

In some cases, you can claim in advance (see below). If you claimed DLA or attendance allowance (AA) when you should have claimed PIP, see below.

Backdating your claim

You cannot backdate a claim for PIP.[203]

If you might have qualified for PIP sooner but did not claim because you were given the wrong information or misled by the DWP, you could ask for compensation (see p1439) or complain to the Ombudsman via your MP (see p1444).

If you claim the wrong benefit

A claim for DLA or AA can be treated as a claim for PIP and vice versa.[204] In both cases, this only applies if the DWP thinks you are not entitled to the benefit you actually claimed. See p1182 for further information.

Claiming in advance

You can claim PIP in advance if you do not satisfy the entitlement conditions, but will do so within three months of the date your claim is decided.[205] This may be relevant if you do not satisfy the required period condition (see p759) when you first claim. In this situation, the date you first qualify is your date of claim.

If you already get PIP, you can make a renewal claim up to six months before your award ends (see p769).

7. **Getting paid**

The general rules on getting paid are in Chapter 51. This section explains the specific rules that apply to personal independence payment (PIP).

When is personal independence payment paid?

PIP is usually paid on the same day of the week as the decision was made on your claim, but this can be changed by the DWP.[206] PIP is usually paid every four weeks in arrears, or if you are terminally ill, weekly in advance.[207]

Payment of PIP normally starts from your date of claim (see p767).

Note: the enhanced rate of the mobility component can be paid direct to Motability (see p772) if you are buying or leasing a car through the scheme.[208]

- Payment of PIP may be made to someone else on your behalf, if this is needed to protect your interests.[209]
- Even if you have been sanctioned for a benefit offence (see p1278), you must be paid PIP.
- For information on missing payments, see p1189. If you have lost your bank or post office card or you have forgotten your PIN, see p1188. If you have lost your payment service card, see p1189.
- If payment of your PIP is delayed, see p1295. If you wish to complain about how your claim has been dealt with, or claim compensation, see Chapter 60.
- If payment of your PIP is suspended, see p1200.
- If you are overpaid PIP, you may have to repay it (see Chapter 53) and, in some circumstances, you may have to pay a penalty (see p1268). If you have been accused of fraud, see Chapter 54.

Length of awards

PIP is normally awarded for a fixed period – eg, two or five years. The length of award depends on how likely it is that your needs will change over time. You are normally awarded PIP for three years if you are terminally ill.[210]

An indefinite award can be made if a fixed-term award would be inappropriate.[211] Most indefinite awards are reviewed every 10 years, to check they are still correct.[212]

If you think that you should have been given a longer award, you can ask for a mandatory reconsideration (see p1303), and appeal if the decision is not changed.[213] If you do this, the amount of your benefit may also be reconsidered.

Note: your entitlement to PIP can be reassessed at any time after it has been awarded.[214] For what happens if your award is coming to an end, see below.

Reviews and renewal claims

If you already get PIP, you can make a renewal claim up to six months before your award ends.[215] However, you may not need to do this, as your award may be reviewed by the DWP one year before it ends (see below).[216] If your award is not reviewed, the DWP may not contact you until three months before it ends, to remind you to make a new claim. **Note:** due to the coronavirus pandemic, the DWP has announced it is suspending PIP reviews until June 2020. See AskCPAG.org.uk and CPAG's *Welfare Right Bulletin* for updates.

Is your personal independence payment award ending?

If you are awarded PIP for a fixed period, you may be referred for a review a year before your award ends. The process of reviewing your award is similar to the assessment process for new claims (see p764). Return the questionnaire and take part in any consultation, as otherwise a negative determination may be made, ending your PIP award (see p766). A decision maker then decides whether to carry out a supersession (see p1315). A supersession decision could extend, change or remove your PIP award.

If your award is due to end in less than six months and the DWP has not contacted you, consider making a renewal claim or requesting a supersession (see p1315) so you get a decision before your award ends. Get advice about the impact on your current award.

Change of circumstances

You must report any changes in your circumstances that you have been told you must report, as well as any that you might reasonably be expected to know might affect your right to, the amount of, or the payment of, PIP. To continue to qualify for PIP, your needs must be expected to last for a further nine months on any day of your award.[217] So, if a change means that your needs are no longer expected to last at least this long, you should report it. Get advice if you think that your condition has improved so much that your entitlement to PIP might be affected.

You should report any changes in your circumstances as soon as possible, preferably in writing. See p1199 for further information.

If payment of (but not entitlement to) PIP has stopped (because you are in hospital, a care home or prison – see Chapter 42), still notify the DWP of any changes so the correct rate is paid when payment resumes.

If there has been a relevant change of circumstances, a decision maker looks at your award again and makes a new decision. To find out the date from which the new decision takes effect, see p1320.

Part 5: Other benefits
Chapter 35: Personal independence payment
8. Tax, other benefits and the benefit cap

8. **Tax, other benefits and the benefit cap**

Tax

Personal independence payment (PIP) is not taxable.[218]

Means-tested benefits and tax credits

PIP is not taken into account as income when calculating means-tested benefits and tax credits, and is paid in addition to them. Getting PIP can increase the amount you get, or can mean that you qualify for means-tested benefits or tax credits for the first time, if your income was previously too high.

If you or your partner are entitled to PIP, you may qualify for:

- a limited capability for work-related activity element in your universal credit (UC) if you or your partner are entitled to the enhanced rate of the PIP daily living component and are over pension age (see p72). Alternatively, a limited capability for work element is included in your UC if you or your partner are entitled to PIP, but not the enhanced rate of the daily living component, and are over pension age, in some circumstances (see p70);
- a disability premium in income support (IS), income-based jobseeker's allowance (JSA) or housing benefit (HB) if you are under pension age (see p341);
- a higher pensioner premium in IS or income-based JSA if you have a partner and either of you have reached pension age (see p345);
- an enhanced disability premium in IS, income-based JSA, income-related employment and support allowance (ESA) or HB if you or your partner are entitled to the enhanced rate of the daily living component and are under pension age (see p343);
- a severe disability premium/addition in IS, income-based JSA, income-related ESA, the guarantee credit of pension credit (PC) or HB if you or your partner receive the daily living component and meet other conditions (see p346);
- a disabled worker element in working tax credit (WTC) if you or your partner receive PIP, work 16 hours a week or more and meet other conditions (see p1458); *and*
- a severe disability element in WTC if you or your partner are entitled to the enhanced rate of the daily living component (see p1460).

If your child is entitled to PIP and still counts as part of your household (even if you do not get a basic amount for her/him because of the 'two-child limit'), you may qualify for:

- a disabled child addition in UC, which is paid at a higher rate if s/he is entitled to the enhanced rate of the daily living component (see p67);
- a disabled child premium in HB and, if you do not get child tax credit (CTC), in IS or income-based JSA (see p341);

- an enhanced disability premium in HB if s/he is entitled to the enhanced rate of the daily living component and (if you do not get CTC) in IS or income-based JSA (see p343);
- a disabled child element in CTC (see p1456);
- a severely disabled child element in CTC if s/he is entitled to the enhanced rate of the daily living component (see p1456);
- an additional amount in your PC (if you do not get CTC), which is paid at a higher rate if s/he is entitled to the enhanced rate of the daily living component (see p339).

If you or your partner receive the daily living component, non-dependant deductions are not made from your HB (see p198), or from any housing costs included in your IS, income-based JSA, income-related ESA or the guarantee credit of PC (see p363).

No housing costs contributions from a non-dependant are taken into account when calculating your UC housing costs element if you, your partner or the non-dependant receive the PIP daily living component, or are entitled to it but payment is suspended as you are in hospital (see p102).

Non-means-tested benefits

PIP may be paid in addition to any other non-means-tested benefits, except that:
- if you are entitled to PIP, you cannot claim disability living allowance[219] or attendance allowance;[220]
- PIP overlaps with some war pension payments for constant attendance or mobility, and armed forces independence payment (see p868);[221]
- PIP daily living component overlaps with constant attendance allowance under the industrial injuries scheme (see p694);[222]
- PIP mobility component is not paid if you get a grant for the use of a vehicle from the NHS.[223]

If you get the daily living component of PIP and someone regularly looks after you, that person may be entitled to carer's allowance (CA) (see Chapter 26) and the carer element of UC (see p73). However, any severe disability premium/addition you get will stop if s/he gets CA or the carer element, so always get advice.

If you get the daily living component, a young person living in Scotland may be able to get a young carer grant for looking after you (see Chapter 75).

The benefit cap

In some cases, there is a limit on the total amount of specified benefits you can receive (a 'benefit cap'). PIP is *not* one of the specified benefits. The benefit cap does *not* apply if you, your partner or child get PIP (even it is not paid because the person entitled is in hospital or a care home). In other cases, it only applies if you are getting UC or HB. See p1194 for further information.

Passports and other sources of help

You qualify for a Christmas bonus if you get PIP (see p870).

If you get PIP, you may be entitled to other 'passported' benefits such as a 'blue badge' parking concession or a concessionary travel card. Contact your local authority for more information.

If you receive the enhanced rate of the PIP mobility component and you or your carer have a car used only by you or for you, you are exempt from vehicle excise duty (road tax). If you receive the standard rate, you get a 50 per cent reduction to your vehicle excise duty.[224]

If you have a low income, you may be entitled to council tax reduction (see p851).

Motability

Motability is a charity that runs a scheme to help you lease or buy a car, scooter or powered wheelchair. You are eligible if you get the enhanced rate of the PIP mobility component and have 12 months or more left to run on your award.

If you use the scheme, your PIP mobility component is paid direct to Motability.[225] You may also have to make extra payments. For further information, telephone 0300 456 4566 (textphone: 0300 037 0100) or see motability.co.uk. If you are a British Sign Language user, see motability.co.uk/contact/british-sign-language-service.

Notes

1. Who can get personal independence payment
1   ss77-80 WRA 2012; Part 2 and Sch 1 SS(PIP) Regs
2   *MB v SSWP (PIP)* [2016] UKUT 250 (AAC)
3   *PM v SSWP (PIP)* [2017] UKUT 154 (AAC); *EG v SSWP (PIP)* [2017] UKUT 101 (AAC)
4   Regs 5 and 6 SS(PIP) Regs
5   ss78-9 WRA 2012
6   *MR v SSWP (PIP)* [2017] UKUT 86 (AAC)
7   *TK v SSWP (PIP)* [2020] UKUT 22 (AAC)
8   *KP v SSWP (PIP)* [2017] UKUT 30 (AAC)
9   *SD v SSWP (PIP)* [2017] UKUT 310 (AAC)
10 Sch 1 Part 1 SS(PIP) Regs
11 *JT v SSWP (PIP)* [2018] UKUT 101 (AAC); *CP v SSWP (PIP)* [2018] UKUT 5 (AAC)
12 Sch 1 Part 1 SS(PIP) Regs
13 *GM v SSWP (PIP)* [2017] UKUT 268 (AAC)
14 *RJ, GMcL and CS v SSWP v RJ (PIP)* [2017] UKUT 105 (AAC), reported as [2017] AACR 32

15 gov.uk/government/publications/
personal-independence-payment-
changes/safety-and-supervision-
changes-to-pip-law-from-
9-march-2017
16 *SSWP v IM (PIP)* [2015] UKUT 680 (AAC)
17 *LB v SSWP (PIP)* [2017] UKUT 436 (AAC)
18 *GG v SSWP (PIP)* [2016] UKUT 194
(AAC); *PM v SSWP (PIP)* [2017] UKUT
502 (AAC)
19 *SSWP v MMcK* [2017] CSIH 57. The
Supreme Court made no comment on
this suggestion in the appeal against this
decision (*SSWP v MM (Scotland)* [2019]
UKSC 34, reported as [2019] AACR 26).
20 Reg 2 SS(PIP) Regs
21 *MR v SSWP (PIP)* [2017] UKUT 86 (AAC),
although the comments were not
strictly necessary to the decision in that
case
22 Reg 4(2) SS(PIP) Regs
23 *CW v SSWP (PIP)* [2016] UKUT 197
(AAC), reported as [2016] AACR 44; *NA
v SSWP (PIP)* [2015] UKUT 572 (AAC)
24 *CW v SSWP (PIP)* [2016] UKUT 197
(AAC), reported as [2016] AACR 44; *AP v
SSWP (PIP)* [2016] UKUT 501 (AAC)
25 *MR v SSWP (PIP)* [2019] UKUT 293 (AAC)
26 *RB v SSWP (PIP)* [2019] UKUT 186 (AAC)
27 *PE v SSWP (PIP)* [2015] UKUT 309 (AAC),
reported as [2016] AACR 10; *JM v SSWP
(PIP)* [2016] UKUT 542 (AAC)
28 Sch 1 Part 1 SS(PIP) Regs
29 *RH v SSWP (PIP)* [2015] UKUT 281 (AAC)
30 *SSWP v KJ (PIP)* [2017] UKUT 358 (AAC)
31 *ZI v SSWP (PIP)* [2016] UKUT 572 (AAC),
reported as [2018] AACR 1
32 *SC v SSWP (PIP)* [2017] UKUT 317 (AAC)
33 *AI v SSWP (PIP)* [2016] UKUT 322 (AAC)
34 *LC v SSWP (PIP)* [2016] UKUT 150 (AAC)
35 *GB v SSWP (PIP)* [2015] UKUT 546 (AAC)
accepted that lever arm taps were an
aid, but the DWP no longer believes that
this decision is correct, so this may not
be accepted: see *AP v SSWP (PIP)* [2016]
UKUT 501 (AAC). *YW (deceased) by MM
v SSWP (PIP)* [2017] UKUT 42 (AAC)
suggested that lightweight pans are not
aids, but note that this view was not
necessary to the decision.
36 *DR v SSWP (PIP)* [2018] UKUT 209
(AAC), but see also *EG v SSWP (PIP)*
[2015] 275 UKUT AAC, which came to
the opposite view
37 *SSWP v DT (PIP)* [2017] UKUT 272 (AAC)
38 *AI v SSWP (PIP)* [2016] UKUT 322 (AAC)
39 Sch 1 Part 1 SS(PIP) Regs

40 *MM and BJ v SSWP (PIP)* [2016] UKUT
490 (AAC), reported as [2017] AACR 17
41 *JW v SSWP (PIP)* [2018] UKUT 169 (AAC)
42 *TK v SSWP (PIP)* [2020] UKUT 22 (AAC)
43 *PA v SSWP (PIP)* [2019] UKUT 270 (AAC)
44 *SSWP v KS (PIP)* [2018] UKUT 102 (AAC)
45 Sch 1 Part 1 SS(PIP) Regs
46 *PM v SSWP (PIP)* [2018] UKUT 138 (AAC)
47 *SSWP v LB (PIP)* [2015] UKUT 612 (AAC).
The DWP interprets this aspect of the
decision as still applying to the current
definition of 'therapy' - see gov.uk/
government/publications/personal-
independence-payment-changes/
special-diet-as-therapy-changes-to-pip-
law-from-28-november-2016.
48 *KM v SSWP (PIP)* [2018] UKUT 296 (AAC)
49 *AS v SSWP (PIP)* [2017] UKUT 104 (AAC),
reported as [2017] AACR 31
50 *SSWP v TMcl (PIP)* [2016] UKUT 574
(AAC)
51 *SSWP v KS (PIP)* [2018] UKUT 102 (AAC)
52 *DC v SSWP (PIP)* [2016] UKUT 11 (AAC)
53 *AH v SSWP (PIP)* [2016] UKUT 276
(AAC). While this case was the subject of
a further appeal to the Court of Appeal
(*Hickey v SSWP* [2018] EWCA Civ 851),
this aspect of the Upper Tribunal's
decision was not considered in the
court's judgment.
54 *MM v SSWP (PIP)* [2018] UKUT 193
(AAC), but note that the point was not
finally decided
55 *TK v SSWP (PIP)* [2020] UKUT 22 (AAC)
56 *MF v SSWP (PIP)* [2015] UKUT 554
(AAC), reported as [2016] AACR 20
57 *RH v SSWP (PIP)* [2015] UKUT 281 (AAC)
58 *RB v SSWP (PIP)* [2016] UKUT 556 (AAC)
59 Sch 1 Part 1 SS(PIP) Regs
60 *SP v SSWP (PIP)* [2015] UKUT 190 (AAC),
reported as [2016] AACR 43
61 *AP v SSWP (PIP)* [2016] UKUT 501 (AAC)
62 *SH v SSWP (PIP)* [2018] UKUT 251 (AAC);
RJ, GMcL and CS v SSWP v RJ (PIP) [2017]
UKUT 105 (AAC), reported as [2017]
AACR 32
63 *MB v SSWP (PIP)* [2018] UKUT 139 (AAC)
64 *GG v SSWP (PIP)* [2016] UKUT 194 (AAC)
65 Sch 1 Part 1 SS(PIP) Regs
66 *GW v SSWP (PIP)* [2015] UKUT 570
(AAC)
67 *DA v SSWP (PIP)* [2019] UKUT 320 (AAC)
68 *FK v SSWP (PIP)* [2017] UKUT 375 (AAC)
69 *JM v SSWP (PIP)* [2016] UKUT 296 (AAC)
70 *BS v SSWP (PIP)* [2016] UKUT 456 (AAC)
71 *GW v SSWP (PIP)* [2015] UKUT 570
(AAC)
72 *SSWP v NH (PIP)* [2017] UKUT 258 (AAC)

73 *KO v SSP (PIP)* [2018] UKUT 78 (AAC)
74 *KW v SSWP (PIP)* [2017] UKUT 54 (AAC)
75 *GP v SSWP (PIP)* [2015] UKUT 498 (AAC)
76 Sch 1 Part 1 SS(PIP) Regs
77 *JM v SSWP (PIP)* [2016] UKUT 542 (AAC)
78 *PE v SSWP (PIP)* [2015] UKUT 309 (AAC), reported as [2016] AACR 10
79 *JM v SSWP (PIP)* [2016] UKUT 542 (AAC)
80 *CW v SSWP (PIP)* [2016] UKUT 197 (AAC), reported as [2016] AACR 44; *AP v SSWP (PIP)* [2016] UKUT 501 (AAC)
81 *MR v SSWP (PIP)* [2019] UKUT 293 (AAC)
82 *DP v SSWP (PIP)* [2017] UKUT 156 (AAC)
83 *ML v SSWP (PIP)* [2017] UKUT 171 (AAC)
84 Sch 1 Part 1 SS(PIP) Regs
85 *P v SSWP (PIP)* [2018] UKUT 376 (AAC)
86 *EG v SSWP (PIP)* [2017] UKUT 101 (AAC)
87 *TC v SSWP (PIP)* [2016] UKUT 550 (AAC)
88 *SSWP v AS (PIP)* [2017] UKUT 454 (AAC)
89 Sch 1 Part 1 SS(PIP) Regs
90 *TR v SSWP (PIP)* [2015] UKUT 626 (AAC), reported as [2016] AACR 23
91 *MR v SSWP (PIP)* [2017] UKUT 86 (AAC)
92 *KP v SSWP (PIP)* [2017] UKUT 30 (AAC)
93 Sch 1 Part 1 SS(PIP) Regs
94 *SM v SSWP (PIP)* [2019] UKUT 292 (AAC); *AM v SSWP (PIP)* [2017] UKUT 7 (AAC)
95 *DV v SSWP (PIP)* [2017] UKUT 244 (AAC); *SF v SSWP (PIP)* [2016] UKUT 543 (AAC)
96 *SF v SSWP (PIP)* [2016] UKUT 543 (AAC); *SSWP v AM (PIP)* [2015] UKUT 215 (AAC)
97 *HA v SSWP (PIP)* [2018] UKUT 56 (AAC)
98 *HA v SSWP (PIP)* [2018] UKUT 56 (AAC); *RC v SSWP (PIP)* [2017] UKUT 352 (AAC)
99 *RC v SSWP (PIP)* [2017] UKUT 352 (AAC)
100 *DV v SSWP (PIP)* [2017] UKUT 244 (AAC)
101 *HJ v SSWP (PIP)* [2016] UKUT 487 (AAC)
102 *SSWP v MM (Scotland)* [2019] UKSC 34, reported as [2019] AACR 26
103 *SSWP v MM (Scotland)* [2019] UKSC 34, reported as [2019] AACR 26; *SL v SSWP (PIP)* [2016] UKUT 147 (AAC)
104 Sch 1 Part 1 SS(PIP) Regs
105 *DP v SSWP (PIP)* [2017] UKUT 156 (AAC)
106 *PR v SSWP (PIP)* [2015] UKUT 584 (AAC); *JW v SSWP (PIP)* [2018] UKUT 169 (AAC)
107 *RB v SSWP (PIP)* [2016] UKUT 393 (AAC)
108 *SSWP v LB (PIP)* [2016] UKUT 530 (AAC)
109 In 2017, the DWP amended the wording of some descriptors in this activity, but the High Court quashed the changes in *R (RF) v SSWP* [2017] EWHC 3375 (Admin). The changes are not included in the descriptors, as they never had any effect (see *AH v SSWP (PIP)* [2018] UKUT 262 (AAC)).

110 Sch 1 Part 1 SS(PIP) Regs
111 *SSWP v NF (PIP)* [2017] UKUT 480 (AAC)
112 *AA v SSWP (PIP)* [2018] UKUT 339 (AAC)
113 The definition of 'prompting' does not require the physical presence of the person who is prompting you.
114 *TR v SSWP (PIP)* [2015] UKUT 626 (AAC), reported as [2016] AACR 23; *PM v SSWP (PIP)* [2017] UKUT 154 (AAC); *AA v SSWP (PIP)* [2018] UKUT 339 (AAC). Note that PIP AG part 2 suggests that this argument may not be accepted, although it does suggest that only being able to go out in darkness is not managing this activity to an acceptable standard.
115 *MH v SSWP (PIP)* [2016] UKUT 531 (AAC), reported as [2018] AACR 12
116 *AA v SSWP (PIP)* [2018] UKUT 339 (AAC)
117 *JB v SSWP (PIP)* [2019] UKUT 203 (AAC); *SB v SSWP (PIP)* [2019] UKUT 274 (AAC)
118 *MC v SSWP (PIP)* [2019] UKUT 264 (AAC); *SSWP v IV (PIP)* [2016] UKUT 420 (AAC)
119 *MH v SSWP (PIP)* [2016] UKUT 531 (AAC), reported as [2018] AACR 12
120 *AA v SSWP (PIP)* [2018] UKUT 339 (AAC)
121 PIP AG part 2
122 *MH v SSWP (PIP)* [2016] UKUT 531 (AAC), reported as [2018] AACR 12, although note that the view that descriptors 1e and 1f are not mutually exclusive was not necessary to the decision
123 ADM Memo 16-18 explains the process for DWP staff; information for the public is available at gov.uk/government/publications/personal-independence-payment-changes/overwhelming-psychological-distress-and-journeys-changes-to-pip-law-from-28-november-2016
124 Sch 1 Part 1 SS(PIP) Regs
125 *DT v SSWP (PIP)* [2016] UKUT 240 (AAC)
126 *PM v SSWP (PIP)* [2017] UKUT 154 (AAC); *BM v SSWP (PIP)* [2017] UKUT 486 (AAC)
127 *AP v SSWP (PIP)* [2016] UKUT 501 (AAC), but note that *KL v SSWP (PIP)* [2015] UKUT 612 (AAC) came to a different conclusion and interprets the law more generously
128 *KN v SSWP (PIP)* [2016] UKUT 261 (AAC); *TF v SSWP (PIP)* [2015] UKUT 661 (AAC)
129 *KL v SSWP (PIP)* [2016] UKUT 545 (AAC)
130 *LH v SSWP (PIP)* [2018] UKUT 57 (AAC)
131 *NK v SSWP (PIP)* [2016] UKUT 146 (AAC)

132 *MH v SSWP (PIP)* [2016] UKUT 531 (AAC), reported as [2018] AACR 12
133 Reg 4(2A) and (4) SS(PIP) Regs; *TF v SSWP (PIP)* [2015] UKUT 661 (AAC)
134 *RJ, GMcL and CS v SSWP v RJ (PIP)* [2017] UKUT 105 (AAC), reported as [2017] AACR 32
135 *SH v SSWP (PIP)* [2018] UKUT 251 (AAC)
136 *PA v SSWP (PIP)* [2019] UKUT 270 (AAC); *PM v SSWP (PIP)* [2017] UKUT 154 (AAC)
137 *PS v SSWP (PIP)* [2016] UKUT 326 (AAC)
138 *TR v SSWP (PIP)* [2015] UKUT 626 (AAC), reported as [2016] AACR 23
139 *PM v SSWP (PIP)* [2017] UKUT 154 (AAC)
140 *ML v SSWP (PIP)* [2017] UKUT 171 (AAC)
141 *KL v SSWP (PIP)* [2016] UKUT 545 (AAC)
142 *TR v SSWP (PIP)* [2015] UKUT 626 (AAC), reported as [2016] AACR 23, which held that this is essentially a question of whether an activity can be undertaken 'repeatedly' (para 34)
143 Regs 2, 7(3) and 14 SS(PIP) Regs; reg 24 PIP(TP) Regs; *AB v SSWP (PIP)* [2017] UKUT 217 (AAC)
144 Regs 2, 7(3) and 15 SS(PIP) Regs
145 Reg 7 SS(PIP) Regs
146 *GG v SSWP (PIP)* [2016] UKUT 194 (AAC)
147 *AK v SSWP (PIP)* [2015] UKUT 620 (AAC)
148 s82(2) and (3) WRA 2012
149 s81 WRA 2012; regs 12-14 SS(PIP) Regs
150 *AH v SSWP (PIP)* [2016] UKUT 541 (AAC)
151 Reg 33(1) UC,PIP,JSA&ESA(C&P) Regs
152 Regs 15 and 26 SS(PIP) Regs
153 Reg 23 PIP(TP) Regs; *AH v SSWP (PIP)* [2016] UKUT 541 (AAC). Note that *EB v SSWP (PIP)* [2017] UKUT 311 (AAC) came to a different conclusion, holding that this rule can only apply to the effects of a condition that existed when you were last awarded DLA. Arguably, this is an incorrect interpretation as Sch 10 para 5(b) and (c) WRA 2012 permits regulations to take account of periods of entitlement to DLA in deciding whether the required period condition is satisfied. This provision was not mentioned in *EB*, and it is arguably a more natural reading of the regulations that current or recent DLA entitlement means that the 'past period test' is automatically satisfied.

2. The rules about your age
154 Reg 5 PIP(TP) Regs
155 s83 WRA 2012; s126 and Sch 4 PA 1995
156 Reg 27 PIP(TP) Regs
157 Reg 25(b) SS(PIP) Regs
158 Reg 25(a) SS(PIP) Regs
159 Reg 27 SS(PIP) Regs
160 Regs 15 and 26 SS(PIP) Regs
161 Regs 15 and 26 SS(PIP) Regs
162 Reg 26(2)(c) SS(PIP) Regs
163 Reg 27 SS(PIP) Regs
164 Reg 27(3)(a)(ii) and (3)(b) SS(PIP) Regs
165 Reg 27(3) SS(PIP) Regs
166 Reg 27(3)(a)(i) and (4) SS(PIP) Regs
167 Reg 27 PIP(TP) Regs. The definitions of 'previous award' and 'component' in reg 2 SS(PIP) Regs mean that regs 15 and 26 of those regulations only apply to people who have had a previous PIP award.

4. The amount of benefit
168 Reg 24(1) SS(PIP) Regs
169 Reg 24(2) SS(PIP) Regs

5. Special benefit rules
170 s82(4) WRA 2012
171 s82(2) WRA 2012
172 s82(3) WRA 2012
173 Reg 21 SS(PIP) Regs
174 s82(1)(b) WRA 2012; regs 5(2)(c) and 23(2) UC,PIP,JSA&ESA(DA) Regs
175 s82(5) WRA 2012

6. Claims and backdating
176 Reg 11(1) UC,PIP,JSA&ESA(C&P) Regs; DWP, *Personal Independence Payment Handbook*, December 2018, p25
177 House of Commons, *Hansard*, Written Question 121453, answered 18 January 2018
178 House of Commons, *Hansard*, Written Statement HCWS603, 20 April 2017. The DWP confirmed the introduction of this process by email to CPAG on 5 January 2018.
179 DWP, *Personal Independence Payment Handbook*, December 2018, pp41-43; PIP AG paras 1.7.1-30
180 s82(5) WRA 2012
181 Reg 49(c) UC,PIP,JSA&ESA(DA) Regs
182 s80 WRA 2012; regs 8 and 9 SS(PIP) Regs
183 Reg 8(1) and (2) SS(PIP) Regs
184 Reg 8(3) SS(PIP) Regs
185 Broadly speaking, if you live in Scotland, northern England or southern England, the contractor is Independent Assessment Services. If you live in the Midlands or Wales, it is Capita. There is a map showing postcode areas covered by each contractor at gov.uk/government/publications/pip-postcode-map-uk.

· ·

186 capita-pip.co.uk or
mypipassessment.co.uk
187 See gov.uk/government/publications/
personal-independence-payment-
assessment-guide-for-assessment-
providers ('PIP AG' below)
188 Reg 9(1) SS(PIP) Regs says that you
'may' be asked to attend a consultation
189 Reg 9(3)(a) and (4) SS(PIP) Regs
190 Reg 9(3)(b) SS(PIP) Regs
191 PIP AG, paras 1.6.57-60
192 PIP AG, paras 1.6.70-74
193 s80(4)-(6) WRA 2012; regs 8(3) and 9(2)
SS(PIP) Regs
194 Reg 26(2) UC,PIP,JSA&ESA(DA) Regs; *KB
v SSWP (PIP)* [2016] UKUT 537 (AAC)
195 *IR v SSWP (PIP)* [2019] UKUT 374 (AAC)
196 Reg 10 SS(PIP) Regs
197 Ch P6 ADM
198 PIP AG para 1.1.7
199 *OM v SSWP (PIP)* [2017] UKUT 458
(AAC); *TC v SSWP (PIP) (No.2)* [2018]
UKUT 286 (AAC)
200 Reg 12(1)(b) UC,PIP,JSA&ESA(C&P)
Regs
201 Reg 12(1)(c) UC,PIP,JSA&ESA(C&P)
Regs
202 Regs 11(6) and 12
UC,PIP,JSA&ESA(C&P) Regs
203 Reg 27 UC,PIP,JSA&ESA(C&P) Regs
204 Reg 25(3) and (4)
UC,PIP,JSA&ESA(C&P) Regs
205 Reg 33(1) UC,PIP,JSA&ESA(C&P) Regs

7. Getting paid
206 Reg 49 UC,PIP,JSA&ESA(C&P) Regs
207 Reg 48 UC,PIP,JSA&ESA(C&P) Regs
208 Reg 62 UC,PIP,JSA&ESA(C&P) Regs
209 Reg 58(2) UC,PIP,JSA&ESA(C&P) Regs
210 para P2079 ADM
211 s88(2) and (3) WRA 2012
212 para P2062 ADM
213 *RS v SSWP (PIP)* [2016] UKUT 85 (AAC)
214 Reg 11 SS(PIP) Regs
215 Reg 33(2) UC,PIP,JSA&ESA(C&P) Regs
216 para P2063 ADM
217 Reg 14(b) SS(PIP) Regs; *BM v SSWP (PIP)*
[2017] UKUT 486 (AAC)

8. Tax, other benefits and the benefit cap
218 s677(1) IT(EP)A 2003
219 Reg 22(1) PIP(TP) Regs
220 s64(1) and (1A) SSCBA 1992

221 Sch 1 paras 5 and 5a SS(OB) Regs; reg
61 UC,PIP,JSA&ESA(C&P) Regs
222 Sch 1 para 5 SS(OB) Regs
223 Reg 61 UC,PIP,JSA&ESA(C&P) Regs
224 gov.uk/financial-help-disabled/vehicles-
and-transport
225 Regs 62, 63 and 64
UC,PIP,JSA&ESA(C&P) Regs

Chapter 36

. . . .

Retirement pensions

This chapter covers:
1. Who can get state pension (p778)
2. The rules about your age (p779)
3. People included in the claim (p780)
4. The amount of benefit (p780)
5. Special benefit rules (p785)
6. Claims and backdating (p786)
7. Getting paid (p789)
8. Tax, other benefits and the benefit cap (p790)

This chapter covers the rules that apply to people who reach pension age on or after 6 April 2016 and who are eligible for the new state retirement pension, known as 'state pension'. People who reached pension age before 6 April 2016, including those who had already claimed their state retirement pension and those who had deferred claiming it, continue on the previous retirement pension scheme. In this chapter, these pensions are referred to as 'old' retirement pensions. For more details about these, see the 2015/16 edition of this *Handbook*.

Key facts
- State pension is a non-means-tested, contributory benefit, paid to people who reach pension age on or after 6 April 2016.
- State pension is an individual pension based solely on your own national insurance contributions (although there are some limited exceptions).
- You can qualify whether you are in or out of work.
- State pension is affected by the overlapping benefit rules.
- State pension is administered and paid by the Pension Service, which is part of the DWP.
- If you reached pension age before 6 April 2016, you cannot get state pension, but you may be entitled to an 'old' retirement pension instead.
- If you disagree with a decision on your state pension, you can apply for a revision or a supersession (see Chapter 56), or appeal against it (see Chapter 57). You must apply for a mandatory reconsideration before you can appeal.

1. **Who can get state pension**

You can get state pension if you reach pension age (see p780) on or after 6 April 2016. Whether you qualify, and the amount you receive, depends on your national insurance (NI) contribution record. If you do not have any qualifying years (ie, years in which you paid or were credited with sufficient NI contributions) before 6 April 2016, you must have 35 qualifying years to receive a state pension at the full rate. If you have at least 10 qualifying years of contributions, you may receive a reduced rate of state pension.[1] If you have qualifying years from before 6 April 2016, your state pension is paid at the transitional rate (see p782). This may be more or less than, or the same as, the full rate. You normally need at least 10 qualifying years to receive any state pension. See Chapter 43 for full details of the contribution conditions for state pension.

Did you reach pension age before 6 April 2016?
If you reached pension age before 6 April 2016, you cannot claim state pension. However, you may be entitled to an 'old' retirement pension – ie, a category A, category B or category D retirement pension. This applies even if you reached pension age before 6 April 2016 but deferred claiming your retirement pension until after that date.

The rules for 'old' retirement pensions are not explained in detail in this chapter. See Chapter 36 of the 2015/16 edition of this *Handbook* for full details.

From 12 October 2015, existing claimants of the 'old' retirement pension, and people who reached pension age before 6 April 2016 but have not yet claimed, may be able to pay class 3A NI contributions. This can increase their entitlement to additional state pension as part of their 'old' retirement pension. See p964 for details.

You do not automatically become entitled to state pension just by reaching pension age. You must make a claim, unless you are a widow in certain situations (see p787). If you do not claim, you are treated as having deferred your state pension (see below).

You do not have to retire from work if you reach pension age and claim state pension. If you decide to carry on working, your earnings do not reduce the state pension you receive and you no longer pay NI contributions. However, the amount of tax you pay may increase because state pension is taxable.

There are some groups of claimants to whom special rules apply (see p785).

Deferring your state pension

Once you reach pension age, you can choose to defer your entitlement to state pension. In return, you later become entitled to a higher rate of pension. **Note:** you do not have the option of taking a taxable lump-sum payment plus interest.

You can defer your state pension by simply not claiming it when you reach state pension age. If you are already claiming, you can choose to stop getting it in order to get more later on, but you can only do this once. To stop claiming, you must notify the Pension Service by telephone or in writing.[2] You can specify a future date on which you want to stop claiming, provided this is within four weeks of your notifying the Pension Service.[3] You can cancel the deferment at any time by making a claim for state pension, and can backdate that cancellation by up to 12 months.[4]

Your state pension is increased by one-ninth of 1 per cent for each week of deferment.[5] For example, if you defer your pension for one year, it increases by approximately 5.8 per cent, which increases a full state pension by approximately £9.78 a week. You are not entitled to any increase unless you defer your pension for long enough to earn an increase of at least 1 per cent.[6]

The increase is calculated on the amount you would have received immediately before the end of the deferral period if you had not deferred claiming. If your entitlement changes during the deferral period (eg, because you become entitled to an inherited amount on the death of your spouse or civil partner – see p783), the calculation takes this into account so that it is based on the rates of pension to which you would have been entitled throughout the deferral period.[7]

You do not receive an increase in state pension for any whole week in the period of deferral in which:[8]

- you get severe disablement allowance, incapacity benefit, carer's allowance, widow's pension, widowed mother's allowance or unemployability supplement, or your spouse, civil partner or anyone you are residing with is receiving an increase in any of these benefits for you; *or*
- you would have been disqualified from receiving state pension because you were a prisoner; *or*
- you are, or your partner is, in receipt of pension credit, universal credit, income support, income-based jobseeker's allowance or income-related employment and support allowance.

If you die either while you are deferring your state pension or after you have started to receive your state pension, your deferral increase is not inheritable.

If you are going to live abroad and have deferred your state pension, see p785.

2. The rules about your age

State pension can be claimed when you reach pension age (see p780) if this is on or after 6 April 2016. If you reached pension age before this date, you may be entitled to an 'old' retirement pension instead (see Chapter 36 of the 2015/16 edition of this *Handbook*). You can claim state pension:

- from 6 March 2020, if you were born between 6 June 1954 and 5 July 1954;

- from 6 May 2020, if you were born between 6 July 1954 and 5 August 1954;
- from 6 July 2020, if you were born between 6 August 1954 and 5 September 1954;
- from 6 September 2020, if you were born between 6 September 1954 and 5 October 1954;
- from your 66th birthday, if you were born between 6 October 1954 and 5 April 1960.

Pension age

Pension age for men and women has equalised since November 2018.

Since December 2018, the pension age for men and women has been rising by one month every two months, reaching 66 by October 2020. Between 2026 and 2028 it will rise to 67.[9] A person born after 5 October 1954 but before 6 April 1960 will reach pension age at 66. A person born between 6 April 1960 and 5 March 1961 will reach pension age at up to 66 years and 11 months, depending on her/his date of birth. Someone born after 5 March 1961 but before 6 April 1977 will reach pension age at 67.[10] The government has announced that an increase in the pension age to 68 will now take place between 2037 and 2039. Men and women born between 6 April 1970 and 5 April 1978 are affected.[11]

You can check when you will reach pension age using the official calculator at gov.uk/state-pension-age.

3. **People included in the claim**

You claim state pension for yourself. You do not get an increase in your state pension for an adult dependant or your child(ren).

If you are entitled to an 'old' retirement pension and already have an increase included for a child, the increase can continue to be paid in certain circumstances. See Chapter 33 of the 2012/13 edition of this *Handbook* for details of who continues to qualify for an increase. You do not get the increase for your child if your partner's earnings are at or above the earnings limit. In 2020/21, this is £245 a week for the first child, increased by £33 for each subsequent child. If you qualify, you are paid £8 a week for the eldest child for whom child benefit is also paid, and £11.35 a week for each subsequent child. Adult dependency increases were abolished from April 2020.

4. **The amount of benefit**

The full weekly rate of state pension is £175.20. In addition, you may receive a higher pension if you deferred your entitlement to state pension (see p778). Some

Chapter 36

Retirement pensions

people may receive a transitional rate of state pension that is higher than £175.20 (see p782). You can request a statement estimating your state pension entitlement from the Future Pension Centre by telephone on 0800 731 0175 (textphone: 0800 731 0176), by writing to the Pension Service or at gov.uk/check-state-pension.

You are not entitled to any increase in state pension for an adult or child dependant.

The amount of 'old' retirement pensions

If you reached pension age before 6 April 2016, you cannot get state pension but may instead be entitled to an 'old' retirement pension.

Category A retirement pension is paid at a weekly rate of £134.25.

Category B retirement pension for a spouse or civil partner is paid at a weekly rate of £80.45.

Category B retirement pension for a widow, widower or surviving civil partner is paid at a weekly rate of £134.25.

Category D retirement pension is paid at a weekly rate of £80.45.

The above amounts are the full rates. If you have not paid or been credited with sufficient national insurance (NI) contributions to qualify for the full rate, you get a reduced rate.

If you receive one of these retirement pensions, you receive an age addition of 25 pence a week if you are over 80.

Depending on which pension you are entitled to, you may also receive:

– graduated retirement benefit, based on earnings between 1961 and 1975;

– an additional state pension, based on earnings after 5 April 1978;

– a higher pension if entitlement was deferred;

– an amount equivalent to the age-related addition to long-term incapacity benefit if you were receiving this within eight weeks of reaching pension age (see p780). If you have an additional state pension, this amount is offset against it;

– an increase for a child (see p780).

See Chapter 36 of the 2015/16 edition of this *Handbook* for full details of when you may be entitled to these additional amounts.

State pension is an individual pension based solely on your own contributions (except in the circumstances described on p782) – ie, you cannot count the contributions of your spouse or civil partner towards your pension. State pension is based on NI contributions made wholly for tax years from 2016/17 onwards, has a single rate and is not inheritable. If your spouse or civil partner reached state pension age before 6 April 2016, s/he may be entitled to an 'old' retirement pension based on your NI contributions up to 5 April 2016.

If you do not have the required qualifying years (see p979) for the full rate of state pension, you get a reduced rate. This is calculated by multiplying 1/35th of the full rate by the number of qualifying years (which must be at least 10 to receive any state pension).[12] For example, if you have 17 qualifying years, you

receive a state pension of £85.09 a week (17 x £175.20/35). Only people whose qualifying years are all from 2016/17 onwards have their state pension calculated this way.

For many years, people are likely to have a mix of contributions made before and after 6 April 2016. NI contributions and credits for years before 6 April 2016 count towards your state pension. There are transitional rules that aim to ensure that anyone reaching pension age after this date receives at least the same level of entitlement as they would have done under the 'old' retirement pension scheme based on their own NI contributions.

There are transitional provisions for:
- people who have paid, been treated as having paid, or been credited with contributions for tax years before the introduction of state pension (see below); *and*
- women who, before 1977, elected to pay a reduced rate of contributions (see p783); *and*
- inheriting entitlement from a late spouse or civil partner who had made contributions for tax years before the introduction of state pension (see p783).

Transitional rate of state pension

If you have qualifying years (see p979) before 6 April 2016, the amount of your state pension is worked out to ensure that your 'starting amount' is at least as much as you would have received under the 'old' retirement pension rules.[13] You must have at least 10 qualifying years to receive a transitional rate of state pension.[14]

Your 'starting amount' is the higher of:
- your entitlement to 'old' retirement pension. This takes account of your entitlement to basic category A retirement pension, additional pension and graduated retirement benefit. See Chapter 36 of the 2015/16 edition of this *Handbook*; *and*
- your entitlement under the new state pension rules as if they had applied throughout your working life.

In each case, a deduction is made if you were contracted out from the additional state pension scheme.

If you were entitled to a substantial amount of additional pension, your starting amount may be higher than the full rate of state pension. If so, the difference between your starting amount and the full rate is called your 'protected payment'. Your protected payment is paid on top of your full state pension and is increased each year in line with inflation. Your transitional rate of state pension up to the level of the full state pension is increased each year at the same rate as the state pension.[15] Any further qualifying years you have do not add more to your state pension.

If your starting amount is lower than the full state pension, you can add additional qualifying years up to the amount needed to qualify for a full-rate state pension or until you reach pension age, whichever is first. You may wish to do this even if you already have more than 35 qualifying years – eg, if, despite having more than 35 qualifying years, you do not qualify for the full rate because a deduction has been applied to reflect contracting out.[16] You may be able to pay NI contributions to fill in gaps in your record (see Chapter 43). Each qualifying year beginning on or after 6 April 2017 adds £175.20/35 (ie, approximately £5) a week to your state pension.

Women who paid reduced-rate contributions

Before 1977, married women and widows could opt out of gaining entitlement to retirement pension in their own right by electing to pay reduced-rate NI contributions (see Chapter 43). Their entitlement to retirement pension was based on the contributions of their spouse.

State pension is based on an individual's own contribution record, but there are special transitional rules for women who reach pension age on or after 6 April 2016 and who have paid reduced-rate contributions. These apply if you still had the right to pay reduced-rate NI contributions at the start of the period of 35 years ending in the tax year before you reach pension age – ie, if you reached pension age in May 2016, you had a 'reduced-rate election' in force at the beginning of the 1981/82 tax year.

If you have any qualifying years from having paid or been credited with sufficient NI contributions in some tax years before 2016/17, there is an alternative calculation if this would be more beneficial than the transitional rate to which you would otherwise be entitled. This is at least equivalent to the combination of:[17]

- the standard rate of basic 'old' retirement pension based on the NI contributions of a spouse or civil partner (£77.45 if you are married or in a civil partnership and your spouse or civil partner has also reached state pension age, or £129.20 if you are widowed, divorced or if your civil partnership is dissolved); *and*
- any additional pension to which you are entitled based on your own contribution record.

If you have no qualifying years from before 6 April 2016, you receive a transitional rate of state pension equivalent to the full category B retirement pension if both you and your spouse have reached pension age, or to the full category A retirement pension if you are no longer married or in a civil partnership.[18]

Widows, widowers and surviving civil partners

If you reach pension age on or after 6 April 2016, there are transitional rules that may allow you to qualify for an amount of state pension (known as a 'survivor's inherited state pension') based on the additional pension that your late spouse or civil partner would have been entitled to under the 'old' retirement pension scheme. This only applies if you were married or in a civil partnership before 6 April 2016 and your spouse or civil partner died while you were married or civil partners. If you were under pension age when s/he died and you remarry or enter a new civil partnership before you reach pension age, you do not qualify.[19]

If your spouse or civil partner reached pension age, or died below pension age, before 6 April 2016, you may be entitled to an inherited amount based on the amount of additional pension you would have been entitled to under the 'old' category B retirement pension rules.[20]

You may be entitled to an inherited amount of half of the difference between your spouse or civil partner's transitional rate and the full rate of state pension, if:[21]

- s/he reached pension age, or died below pension age, on or after 6 April 2016; *and*
- s/he was entitled to the transitional rate of state pension immediately before s/he died (or would have been if s/he had reached pension age before s/he died or on the same day as you reached pension age); *and*
- her/his transitional rate was, or would have been, more than the full rate of state pension.

Your survivor's pension is paid in addition to any state pension or transitional rate of state pension (including one paid to women who elected to pay reduced-rate NI contributions – see p783).

You do not lose this amount if you marry or form a civil partnership again after reaching pension age. However, as this new marriage or civil partnership takes place after 6 April 2016, you cannot get an inherited amount from your new spouse/civil partner if s/he subsequently dies, even if this would have been a higher amount.

Note: if you reached pension age before 6 April 2016 and your spouse or civil partner dies after this date, you may still be able to qualify for a category B retirement pension based on her/his contributions in the tax years before the tax year beginning 6 April 2016. See Chapter 36 of the 2015/16 edition of this *Handbook* for more details. This applies whether or not s/he reached pension age before 6 April 2016.

For how your entitlement to bereavement benefits affects entitlement to state pension, see Chapter 25.

Inheriting a deferred 'old' retirement pension

You may inherit an amount of state pension equivalent to an inherited deferred amount of 'old' retirement pension if:[22]

- your spouse or civil partner reached pension age before 6 April 2016; *and*

- s/he had either claimed her/his 'old' retirement pension and was receiving a weekly increase from having deferred it, or was still deferring her/his 'old' retirement pension when s/he died; *and*
- at the time of her/his death you were over pension age or, if you were under pension age, you had not remarried or entered a new civil partnership before reaching pension age.

If your spouse or civil partner was deferring her/his 'old' retirement pension when s/he died and had deferred it for at least 12 months, you can choose to claim this amount as a lump sum or as a weekly state pension (a 'widowed person's or surviving civil partner's lump sum or pension'). If you do not make a choice within three months of being notified by the DWP of your right to do so (or a longer period if the DWP allows this), you are paid a lump sum. In certain circumstances, you can change your mind, provided you do so within three months of making a choice.[23] If your spouse or civil partner was already getting her/his 'old' retirement pension or s/he had deferred it for less than 12 months, you receive the inherited deferral payment as an extra weekly amount.

These rules mean that you have the same options as you would have had under the old retirement pension system, so it applies regardless of when you reach pension age.

Inherited graduated retirement benefit
You may be entitled to an amount of inherited survivor's state pension based on the graduated retirement benefit entitlement of your late spouse or civil partner. This is based on graduated contributions s/he may have paid between 1961 and 1975. You have the option of choosing a lump sum or a weekly amount if s/he had deferred her/his entitlement to graduated retirement benefit for at least 12 months at the time of her/his death.[24]

5. **Special benefit rules**

Special rules may apply to:
- people who have come from or are going abroad (see below);
- people in prison or detention (see Chapter 42).

People coming from or going abroad

If you have lived elsewhere than the UK during your working life, your state pension may be affected – eg, it may be paid at a reduced rate. However, there are reciprocal arrangements with many countries that may help you qualify for a full pension. If you have worked in another European Economic Area (EEA) state, you may benefit from the European Union (EU) co-ordination rules (see Chapter 70). If you are covered by these, your employment in another EEA state and contributions paid there can count towards your overall national insurance contribution record used to determine your entitlement to state pension (see p1678). If you are not covered by the EU co-ordination rules, you may be able to benefit from a reciprocal agreement or an association or co-operation agreement (see p1581).

If you go to live abroad, your pension can be paid in any other country. However, unless you move to live in another EEA state, Switzerland, Gibraltar or a country with which the UK has a reciprocal agreement for pensions, you are not entitled to uprating increases, so the amount of pension you receive is frozen at the rate at which it was paid when you went abroad. Similarly, if you claim a deferred pension abroad, the uprating increases that occurred while you were abroad are ignored when calculating both the deferral increase and rate payable.[25] **Note:** arrangements with other EEA states may be affected when the UK leaves the EU (see p1670).

6. **Claims and backdating**

The general rules about claims and backdating are covered in Chapter 50. This section explains the specific rules that apply to state pension.

Making a claim

You must usually make a claim for state pension (but see below if you are a widow). A claim for state pension can be made:[26]

- in writing by completing the approved form. Send it to the Pension Service. Find your local pension centre at gov.uk/find-pension-centre. You may be able to make your claim by taking or sending it to an alternative office (see p1168); *or*
- by telephone on 0800 731 7898 (textphone: 0800 731 7339); *or*
- online at gov.uk/state-pension.

If you claim in writing, keep a copy of your claim form in case queries arise.

You must provide any information or evidence required (see p787). In certain circumstances, the DWP may accept a written application not on the approved form.[27] You can amend or withdraw your claim before a decision is made (see p1169). If there is a delay in making a claim, you may be able to get a short-term advance of benefit (see p1192).

Forms

The state pension claim form (Form BR1NSP) is normally sent to you by the DWP about four months before you reach pension age. Otherwise, you can get it from the state pension claim line on 0800 731 7898 (textphone: 0800 731 7339) or at gov.uk/state-pension/how-to-claim.

If you are a widow

If you are a widow, you do not need to make a claim for state pension if either:[28]
- you are over 65 when you stop getting widowed mother's allowance; *or*
- you are getting a widow's pension immediately before your 65th birthday.

You must make a claim for state pension if you want to start receiving it before your widow's pension or widowed mother's allowance stops. If your widow's pension or widowed mother's allowance includes additional state pension, you receive this as an extra amount on top of your state pension, provided you do not remarry or form a new civil partnership before you reach pension age. If your state pension, plus any inherited amount, is less than your widow's pension or widowed mother's allowance, you are paid the difference until those benefits come to an end.

If you make a claim for state pension, your pension should be calculated under the rules (including the various transitional rules) as they apply to you. You do not need to identify and claim for the different elements that apply to you.[29]

Who should claim

You must normally claim state pension on your own behalf. However, if you are unable to manage your own affairs, another person can claim state pension for you as your 'appointee' (see p1170).

Information to support your claim

For the general information requirements that apply to all benefits, see p1170.

It is important that you provide any information required when you claim. Until you do, you may not count as having made a valid claim (see p1172). Correct any defects as soon as possible or your date of claim may be affected.

When you claim state pension, you must prove you have reached pension age. For most people, it is sufficient to produce your birth certificate, but problems can occur if you were born in a country which did not have a formal system of registering births. Other evidence that can prove your birth date includes:
- passport or identity card; *or*
- school or health records; *or*
- army records; *or*
- statements from people who know you.

Even if you have provided all that was required when you claimed, you may be asked to provide further information to support your claim (see p1174). You may also be asked to provide information after you are awarded state pension and if you fail to do so, your state pension could be suspended, or even terminated (see p1200).

The date of your claim

The date of your claim is important as it determines when your entitlement to state pension starts. This is not necessarily the date from when you are paid. For information about when payment of state pension starts, see p789.

The '**date of your claim**' is the date your written or telephone claim, properly completed with all the required evidence and information, is received at the appropriate office (the DWP, local authority housing benefit office or other designated office). A claim made by telephone is made on the date of the telephone call. **Note:** telephone claims cannot be made at designated offices.[30]

Note: you must make sure your claim is valid. If it is not, you are given a short time to correct the defects (see p1172). Your claim is then treated as having been made when you initially claimed.[31]

In some cases, you can claim in advance (see p789) and in some cases your claim can be backdated (see below). If you want this to be done, make this clear when you claim or the DWP might not consider it. If you claimed the wrong benefit when you should have claimed state pension, see below.

Backdating your claim

It is very important to claim in time, because the maximum period for backdating is 12 months. You cannot backdate your claim for any period before the date you would have first become entitled to state pension.[32] You do not have to show any reason why your claim is late. The rules on backdating are covered on p1176.

If you claim more than 12 months after you became entitled to state pension, you are treated as having deferred your entitlement. You can still request that your claim is backdated but you should consider the impact on your deferral amount when requesting backdating. If you backdate your claim, it reduces the amount of time you deferred claiming your pension, which reduces the amount of your weekly increase. Weigh up the financial implications of your options when considering backdating – if necessary, get advice.

If you might have qualified for state pension earlier but did not claim because you were given the wrong information or were misled by the DWP, you could ask for compensation (see p1439) or complain to the Ombudsman via your MP (see p1444).

If you claim the wrong benefit

If you have claimed the wrong benefit, in certain circumstances it is possible for your claim to be interchanged with another benefit.[33] For state pension, this interchange is only possible with bereavement allowance. If you make a claim for state pension, your pension should be calculated under the rules (including the various transitional rules) as they apply to you. You do not need to identify and claim for the different elements that apply to you. If you claim state pension on the wrong form (eg, you complete a claim form for 'old' retirement pension), it is likely to be treated as a valid claim if the form is properly completed.[34]

Claiming in advance

Claims for state pension (including a claim where you have deferred your entitlement – see p778) can be made up to, but no more than, four months in advance.[35] You should take advantage of this, as it can take a long time to sort out your contribution record. The date of your claim is the date on which you qualify.

7. **Getting paid**

The general rules on getting paid are covered in Chapter 51. This section explains the specific rules that apply to state pension. **Note:** rules on payment of 'old' retirement pension are very similar to rules on payment of state pension. See p781 of the 2015/16 edition of this *Handbook*.

When is state pension paid?

The day you are paid depends on your national insurance number (see p1189).[36] State pension is normally paid weekly, fortnightly or four-weekly in arrears. It can be paid every 13 weeks if you agree, or at longer intervals of up to a year if the DWP directs and you are entitled to less than £5 a week.[37]

State pension is payable from the date on which you reach pension age. If this is a day other than your payday, part-week payments are made.

Note:

- Deductions can be made from your state pension to pay third parties (see p1202).
- Even if you have been sanctioned for a benefit offence (see p1278), you must be paid your state pension.
- For information on missing payments, see p1189. If you cannot get your pension payments because you have lost your bank or post office card or have forgotten your PIN, see p1188. If your payment service card has been lost or stolen, or if you have forgotten your memorable date, see p1188.
- If payment of your state pension is delayed, see p1295. If you are waiting for a decision on your claim, or to be paid, you may be able to get a short-term advance (see p1192). If you wish to complain about how your claim has been dealt with, or claim compensation, see Chapter 60.
- If payment of your state pension is suspended, see p1200.
- If you are overpaid state pension, you may have to repay it (see Chapter 53) and, in some circumstances, you may have to pay a penalty (see p1268). If you have been accused of fraud, see Chapter 54.

Change of circumstances

You must report changes in your circumstances that you have been told you must report, as well as any that you might reasonably be expected to know might affect your right to, the amount of, or the payment of, your state pension. You should do this as soon as possible, preferably in writing. See p1199 for further information.

8. Tax, other benefits and the benefit cap

Tax

State pension (and 'old' retirement pension) is taxable.[38] This includes inheritable lump-sum payments of deferred 'old' retirement pension and graduated retirement benefit.[39]

Means-tested benefits and tax credits

State pension (and 'old' retirement pension) is taken fully into account for the purposes of means-tested benefits, but pensioners receive a higher rate of some means-tested benefits. They are partially taken into account as income for tax credits (see Chapter 62).

You may qualify for pension credit (PC) to top up your state pension income (see p271).

Non-means-tested benefits

State pension (and 'old' retirement pension) is affected by the overlapping benefit rules (see p1190).

The benefit cap

In some cases, there is a limit on the total amount of specified benefits you can receive (a 'benefit cap'). State pension (and 'old' retirement pension) is *not* a specified benefit.[40] The benefit cap only applies if you are getting universal credit or housing benefit (HB). If you are getting HB, the benefit cap normally only applies if you are below pension age. See p1194 for further information.

Passports and other sources of help

You qualify for a Christmas bonus (see p870) if you receive state pension (or 'old' retirement pension).[41] People aged 60 or over qualify for free prescriptions and eye tests regardless of their income. If you are on a low income, you may be entitled to council tax reduction (see p851).

Notes

1. Who can get state pension
1 s2(1)-(3) PA 2014; reg 13(1) SP Regs
2 Reg 7 SP Regs
3 Reg 8 SP Regs
4 Reg 9 SP Regs
5 s17(4) PA 2014; reg 10 SP Regs
6 s17(2) PA 2014
7 Reg 12A SP Regs
8 Regs 11 and 12 SP Regs

2. The rules about your age
9 s126 and Sch 4 PA 1995; s26 PA 2014
10 Memo DMG 18/14
11 'New timetable for state pension changes to maintain fair and sustainable pension', DWP press release, 19 July 2017

4. The amount of benefit
12 s3(2) PA 2014
13 s5 and Sch 1 PA 2014
14 s4 PA 2014; reg 13(2) SP Regs
15 Sch 2 PA 2014; ss148AC and 151A SSAA 1992
16 PA 2014 Explanatory Notes, para 61
17 s11 and Sch 6 PA 2014
18 s12 and Sch 7 PA 2014
19 s7 and Schs 3 and 4 PA 2014
20 Sch 3 paras 2-4 PA 2014
21 Sch 3 paras 5-8 PA 2014
22 s8 PA 2014
23 ss8 and 9 PA 2014; regs 4-6 SP Regs
24 s10 PA 2014; regs 15-20 SP Regs

5. Special benefit rules
25 ss18(3) and 20 PA 2014; s179 SSAA 1992; regs 21-23 SP Regs

6. Claims and backdating
26 Regs 4 and 4ZC SS(C&P) Regs
27 Reg 4(1) SS(C&P) Regs
28 Reg 3(d) SS(C&P) Regs
29 Reg 3(ja) SS(C&P) Regs
30 Reg 6 SS(C&P) Regs
31 Reg 6(1)(b) SS(C&P) Regs
32 Reg 19(1) and Sch 4 SS(C&P) Regs
33 Reg 9(1) and Sch 1 SS(C&P) Regs
34 Reg 4(1) SS(C&P) Regs
35 Regs 15 and 15B(2) SS(C&P) Regs

7. Getting paid
36 Reg 22CA(4) SS(C&P) Regs
37 Reg 22CA(2) and (3) SS(C&P) Regs

8. Tax, other benefits and the benefit cap
38 s577(2)(za) IT(EP)A 2003
39 s8(4B) Finance (No.2) Act 2005
40 s96(11)(za) WRA 2012
41 s150(2) SSCBA 1992

Chapter 37

· ·

Social fund payments

This chapter covers:
1. Budgeting loans (below)
2. Sure Start maternity grants (p796)
3. Funeral expenses payments (p798)
4. Cold weather payments (p805)
5. Winter fuel payments (p806)
6. Tax, other benefits and the benefit cap (p808)

Key facts

- The social fund provides one-off loans and payments for specific expenses or circumstances.
- **Budgeting loans** are interest-free loans. **Sure Start maternity grants, funeral expenses payments, cold weather payments and winter fuel payments** are non-repayable.
- Social fund loans and payments are administered and paid by the DWP.
- If you disagree with a budgeting loan decision, there is an internal review system and then a further review to the Independent Case Examiner.
- If you disagree with a decision on a Sure Start maternity grant, funeral expenses payment, cold weather payment or winter fuel payment, you can apply for a revision (see Chapter 56) or appeal against it (see Chapter 57). You must apply for a mandatory reconsideration before you can appeal.

1. Budgeting loans

Budgeting loans are available in England, Wales and Scotland. To be eligible, you must satisfy all the following conditions. **Note:** if you come under the universal credit (UC) system (see p23), you cannot apply for a budgeting loan and must apply for a budgeting advance of your UC payments instead (see p51).

- **You must be in receipt of a 'qualifying benefit'** when your budgeting loan application is determined.[1] Qualifying benefits are: income support (IS), income-based jobseeker's allowance (JSA), income-related employment and support allowance (ESA) and pension credit (PC) (guarantee or savings credit). Payments on account and hardship payments are included. You are treated as being in receipt of a qualifying benefit if it is being paid to you, or to an appointee on your behalf. You are eligible if you receive a backdated award of a qualifying benefit, covering the date your application is determined. **Note:** you are not 'in receipt of' a qualifying benefit if your partner or another member of your family is the claimant.[2] If you are a member of a 'joint-claim couple' for JSA, you are only eligible for a budgeting loan if you are the partner being paid JSA.

- **You and/or your partner, between you, must have been receiving a qualifying benefit throughout the 26 weeks before the date on which your application is determined**, disregarding any number of breaks of 28 days or less.[3] If you are in receipt of PC, any time when you were in receipt of UC can count when calculating the 26 weeks and any breaks of up to one calendar month are ignored. A period covered by a payment of arrears should count, as should any benefit received while in Northern Ireland. The waiting days at the start of a claim for JSA or ESA (see p721 and p662) do not count. More than one partner could help you satisfy the qualifying period.

- **You must not have too much capital.**[4] Any budgeting loan award is reduced by the amount of capital you have in excess of £1,000 (£2,000 if you or your partner are 63 or over). Capital is calculated as for the qualifying benefit that you are receiving (see Chapters 22 and 23). Payments made from the Family Fund to you, your partner or child, and refugee integration loans are ignored. Capital held by your child(ren) should be disregarded.

- **You, or your partner, must not be involved in a trade dispute** (see p1001).[5]

- **You must not be a 'person subject to immigration control'** (there are exceptions to this rule) – see p1560.

- **The loan must be for one or more of the following categories of allowable expenses**, the need for which occurs in the UK:[6]
  - furniture and household equipment;
  - clothing and footwear;
  - maternity expenses;
  - funeral expenses;
  - rent in advance and/or removal expenses to secure accommodation;
  - improvement, maintenance and security of the home;
  - travelling expenses;
  - expenses associated with seeking or re-entering work;
  - hire purchase and other debts for any of the above items.

  You are required to tick the category of expense for which you need the loan on the application form. You do not have to specify the particular items you need – eg, a bed or a winter coat.

- **The loan must be a minimum of £100.**[7] You must state how much you are asking for on your application form. You cannot be awarded more than the maximum amount (see p794).

- **You must be likely to be able to repay the loan** (see p795).[8]

The maximum amount you can be awarded is:
- £348 if you are a single person;
- £464 if you have a partner;
- £812 if you or your partner claim child benefit.

You may get less, depending on the amount you requested and the capital rules. Any loan may also be reduced by the amount of any social fund debt you or your partner have. You cannot be liable to repay more than £1,500 in total.

Applying and getting paid

Applications can be made online at gov.uk, or in writing on the approved Form SF500 available online or from your local job centre, or in any other written form accepted by the Secretary of State. An application can be made on your behalf by your appointee, or by another person, provided you give your written consent.[9]

Your application is treated as made on the day it is received by the DWP.[10] If your application was incomplete and you comply with a request for additional information, it is treated as having been made on the day it was originally received.

Payments are generally made into the account into which your qualifying benefit is paid or, if you do not have an account, in the same way as your qualifying benefit is paid.

Challenging a decision

The DWP may inform you of the decision of your application by telephone, and if offered a loan you can accept it then. However, you should still receive a written decision, with an explanation if it has been refused or partly refused, together with a notification of your right to request a review.

If you want to challenge the decision, the review is carried out by a different decision maker. However, a decision is only likely to be changed if it was based on incorrect information about your circumstances, or if the amount you are allowed to borrow has increased.

You must apply for a review of a decision by writing to the office where the decision was made within 28 days of the date the decision was issued to you.[11] Your application must include your grounds for requesting a review.[12] If someone is making an application on your behalf, it must be accompanied by your written permission (unless the person is your appointee – see p1170).[13]

Late applications can be accepted for 'special reasons'.[14] Special reasons are not defined, but if you cannot apply in time, it may be quicker to submit a new application.

If a decision is not wholly revised in your favour, the reviewing officer must either telephone or write to you to explain why and ask further questions if necessary.

If you are still unhappy with the decision, you can ask the Independent Case Examiner (see p1440) to carry out a second-tier review.[15] Do this in writing within 28 days, although the time limit may be extended if there are special reasons.

Repayments

All loans must be repaid to the DWP.[16]

The decision maker may give you more than one option for repaying a loan, depending on whether you have any other outstanding social fund loans and your other financial commitments. S/he may offer an option of a higher loan with an increased repayment rate, but you cannot be asked to repay at a rate higher than 20 per cent of your IS, income-based JSA or income-related ESA applicable amount or PC appropriate minimum guarantee plus any child tax credit or child benefit you receive. The loan must be repaid within 104 weeks.

The details of the loan offer and repayment terms are included in the written decision (see p794). You have 14 days from the date the decision was sent to return the declaration agreeing to one of the offers made to you. This time limit can be extended for 'special reasons'.[17]

Methods of repayment

Budgeting loans are usually recovered by direct deductions from your benefit, although you can make a payment at any time to pay off all, or part, of the debt. Deductions can only be made from the following benefits:[18]

- bereavement benefits (except bereavement support payment);
- carer's allowance;
- disablement benefit, reduced earnings allowance and industrial death benefit;
- ESA (contributory or income-related);
- incapacity benefit;
- IS;
- JSA (contribution-based or income-based);
- maternity allowance;
- PC;
- retirement pensions;
- severe disablement allowance;
- UC.

A loan can be recovered from:[19]

- you (the applicant) or the person who the loan was for;
- your partner, if you are living together as a couple (see p319);
- a person who is liable to maintain either the person who made the application or the person on whose behalf it was made.

Part 5: Other benefits
Chapter 37: Social fund payments
2. Sure Start maternity grants

Rescheduling repayment terms

You cannot request a review of a decision relating to repayment terms or recovery. If you have accepted a loan, however, and the repayment terms are causing hardship (eg, because your financial situation has deteriorated), you can ask the DWP to reschedule the loan so that the weekly repayment rate is reduced.

2. Sure Start maternity grants

Sure Start maternity grants are available in England and Wales. If you live in Scotland, you may qualify for a Best Start grant (see Chapter 72).

You qualify for a Sure Start maternity grant if you satisfy all the following conditions.

- **You or your partner have been awarded one of the following qualifying benefits** (including payments on account and hardship payments) in respect of the day you claim a maternity grant:[20]
  - universal credit;
  - income support (IS);
  - income-based jobseeker's allowance;
  - income-related employment and support allowance;
  - child tax credit which includes a child, disabled child or severely disabled child element (see p1453);
  - working tax credit, including the disabled worker or severe disability element (see p1458);
  - pension credit (guarantee or savings credit).

  You are treated as receiving one of these benefits if you are entitled to a DWP loan for help with your mortgage interest (see p855), even if you are not actually entitled to the benefit. You are eligible if you receive a backdated award of a qualifying benefit covering the date you claim a maternity grant. If you are waiting for a decision on a claim for a qualifying benefit, the DWP may defer making a decision on your maternity grant claim until the qualifying benefit claim has been decided. If your maternity grant claim is refused while you are waiting for a decision on a qualifying benefit, you should reclaim a maternity grant within three months of being awarded the qualifying benefit. **Note:** if you do not claim a maternity grant within the time limits (see p798), a backdated award of a qualifying benefit does not qualify you for a grant. If you are not entitled to a qualifying benefit in your own right because you are under 16 (or under 19 and in 'relevant education' – see p885), a member of your family can claim a maternity grant for you if s/he is getting a qualifying benefit in respect of you.
- **You live in England or Wales.**[21]
- **One of the following applies:**[22]

- you or a member of your family are pregnant or have given birth in the last six months (including stillbirth after 24 weeks of pregnancy);
- you are the parent (but not the mother and not the mother's partner) of a child who is less than 12 months old, or you are responsible for that parent, and you are responsible for the child;
- you are the guardian of a child who is less than 12 months old;
- you or your partner have a child who is less than 12 months old placed with you for adoption and you are responsible for the child;
- you have adopted a child who is less than 12 months old under a recognised adoption which takes place outside the UK;
- you or your partner have been granted a child arrangements order, parental order (following a surrogate pregnancy) or adoption order for a child who is less than 12 months old.

In the last five cases, you are entitled to a payment even if one has already been made to the birth mother or a member of her family.[23]

- **There is no other member of your family who is under 16 at the time of claim** (excluding any child you adopted or became responsible for as a kinship carer or foster carer, provided s/he was over 12 months old when you became responsible for her/him). However, a grant can be awarded for each child of a multiple birth, but the number of grants is reduced if there are other children in the family who are under 16. For example, if you give birth to triplets and already have one or more children under 16 in the family (and none of them are multiple births) two grants are awarded, or if you already have twins you are awarded one grant. If you are under 20 and another member of your family claims for you, the grant is payable, provided you do not have other children under 16.[24]

- **You or your partner are not involved in a trade dispute** (see p1001), unless specified circumstances apply.[25]

- **You claim within the time limits** (see p798).

- **You have received health and welfare advice from a healthcare professional** (see p798).[26]

- **You are not a 'person subject to immigration control'** (there are exceptions to this rule) – see p1560.

The terms 'partner' and 'family' in the above rules have almost the same meanings as they do for IS purposes (see Chapter 16).[27]

The amount

You are entitled to a grant of £500 for each qualifying child or expected qualifying child.[28] The payment is not affected by any capital you have and is not repayable.

Part 5: Other benefits
Chapter 37: Social fund payments
3. Funeral expenses payments

Claiming and getting paid

Claim on Form SF100, which you can get from your local Jobcentre Plus office or from gov.uk, or by telephone (0800 169 0140). There are strict time limits for claiming. You can claim a maternity grant at any time from 11 weeks before the first day of your expected week of childbirth until six months after the actual date of the birth. If you adopt a child, have a child arrangements order for a child or have a child by a surrogate mother, you can claim up to six months following the date of the adoption, child arrangements order or parental order, provided the child is under 12 months when the claim is made. You cannot make a successful claim outside these time limits.[29]

The back of your claim form must be signed by a healthcare professional (eg, a midwife, health visitor or doctor) to confirm that you have received health and welfare advice about your baby or your maternal health.

Your date of claim is normally the date your form is received by the DWP.[30] If you make a written claim in some other way, you should be sent the appropriate form to complete. If you return it within one month, or a longer period if the DWP considers this reasonable, your date of claim is the date the DWP received your initial application.[31] See p796 for when your claim can be backdated if you are subsequently awarded a qualifying benefit.

If you are overpaid a maternity grant, you may have to repay it (see Chapter 53) and, in some circumstances, you may have to pay a penalty (see p1268).

3. **Funeral expenses payments**

Funeral expenses payments are available in England and Wales. If you live in Scotland, you may qualify for a funeral support payment (see Chapter 73).

You qualify for a funeral expenses payment if you satisfy all the following conditions.

- **You or your partner have been awarded one of the following qualifying benefits** (including payments on account and hardship payments) in respect of the day you claim a funeral expenses payment:[32]
  - universal credit;
  - income support (IS);
  - income-based jobseeker's allowance;
  - income-related employment and support allowance;
  - housing benefit (HB);
  - child tax credit, which includes a child, disabled child or severely disabled child element (see p1452);
  - working tax credit, which includes the disabled worker or severe disability element (see p1457);
  - pension credit (guarantee or savings credit).

You are treated as receiving one of these benefits if you are entitled to a DWP loan for help with your mortgage interest (see p855), even if you are not actually entitled to the benefit. You are eligible if you receive a backdated award of a qualifying benefit which covers the date you claim a funeral expenses payment. If you are waiting for a decision on a claim for a qualifying benefit, the DWP may defer making a decision on a claim for a funeral expenses payment until the qualifying benefit claim has been decided. If your claim for a funeral expenses payment is refused while you are waiting for a decision on a qualifying benefit claim, reclaim within three months of being awarded the qualifying benefit. **Note:** if you do not claim a funeral expenses payment within the time limit, a backdated award of a qualifying benefit does not qualify you for a grant.

- **You live in England or Wales.**[33]
- **You or your partner are in one of the categories of eligible people** listed below who can be treated as responsible for the funeral expenses.
- **You or your partner accept responsibility for funeral expenses** (see p802).[34] If you are claiming as a 'close relative' or 'close friend', it must also be reasonable for you to accept responsibility.
- **The funeral takes place in the UK,**[35] unless you or your partner are covered by specified European Union (EU) legislation, in which case the funeral can take place in any European Economic Area (EEA) state or Switzerland (see p802).[36]
- **A social fund funeral payment has not already been made in respect of the person who has died** (but the amount of a previous award can be revised up to the maximum allowed under the rules).[37]
- **The person who died was 'ordinarily resident' in the UK** (see p1585).[38]
- **You are not a 'person subject to immigration control'** (there are exceptions to this rule) – see p1560.
- **You claim within the time limits** (see p804).

In addition in England, there is a **children's funeral fund payment**.[39] This is available for the funeral of a child aged under 18 or a stillborn child born after the 24th week of pregnancy. The payment covers 'reasonable' burial or cremation fees and 'reasonable' associated expenses, including a coffin or casket, but not costs exclusively related to religious requirements. The payment is available for all such funerals, and does not depend on low income, entitlement to benefit or on satisfying residence conditions. No children's funeral fund payment can be made if a funeral expenses payment has already been paid to cover the same items. In most cases, you do not need to apply for a children's funeral fund payment as the application is made by the person providing the funeral – eg, the funeral director.

Part 5: Other benefits
Chapter 37: Social fund payments
3. Funeral expenses payments

Eligible people

You are only eligible for a funeral expenses payment if you or your partner are in one of the following groups of people who can be treated as responsible for the funeral costs.[40]

- You were the 'partner' of the person when s/he died.
- The deceased was a 'child' for whom you were responsible when s/he died and there is no 'absent parent', or there is an absent parent but s/he (or her/his partner) was getting a qualifying benefit (see p798) when the child died. If there is an absent parent who was not getting a qualifying benefit when the child died, you may qualify for a payment as a close relative of the child. If the deceased was a stillborn child, you are eligible for a funeral expenses payment if you were the parent or the parent's partner – it does not matter whether there is an absent parent.
- You were a parent, son or daughter of the person who died and it is reasonable for you to accept responsibility for the funeral expenses (see p802), and you are not excluded by the rules below.
- You were a 'close relative' or a 'close friend' of the person who died and it is reasonable for you to accept responsibility for the funeral expenses (see p802), and you are not excluded by the rules below.

Definitions[41]

'**Child**' is defined as for IS purposes (see p323). You are 'responsible' for a child if you get, or could get, child benefit for her/him (see p326).

'**Stillborn child**' means a child born dead after 24 weeks of pregnancy.

'**Absent parent**' means a parent of a deceased child, where the child:

– was not living in that parent's household at the date of death; *and*

– was living with another person who was responsible for her/him.

'**Close relative**' means parent, parent-in-law, son, son-in-law, daughter, daughter-in-law, step-parent, stepson, stepson-in-law, stepdaughter, stepdaughter-in-law, brother, brother-in-law, sister, sister-in-law.

'**Close friend**' is not defined in the law. It can include a relative who is not a close relative – eg, a grandparent or grandchild.[42]

'**Partner**' has the same meaning as for IS (see p319). You also count as a partner, however, if you were living in a care home when the person died and:[43]

– you and your spouse or civil partner were living in the same home; *or*

– you were a member of a couple before one or both of you moved into the home.

This rule is designed to enable a surviving partner to claim a funeral expenses payment if one or both partners were in a home at the date of death.

Exclusion of certain close relatives and friends

If you claim as a close relative or close friend of the person who died (see p802), you cannot get a funeral expenses payment if:

- the person who died had a partner (unless that partner died before the funeral without making a claim for a funeral payment);[44] *or*
- the deceased was a child or stillborn child and a responsible person or parent is able to claim a funeral payment under the above rules;[45] *or*
- there is (other than you) a parent, son or daughter of the person who died, unless s/he is:[46]
  - under the age of 18; *or*
  - aged 18 or 19 and counts as a qualifying young person for child benefit purposes (see p579); *or*
  - getting (or her/his partner gets) a qualifying benefit (see p798); *or*
  - estranged from the deceased when s/he died ('estranged' is not defined); *or*
  - a student aged 18 on a full-time course of advanced education (see p887), or aged 19 to pension age on any full-time course; *or*
  - a member of a religious order which fully maintains her/him; *or*
  - a prisoner (including in youth custody or a remand centre) who (or whose partner) was getting a qualifying benefit immediately before being detained; *or*
  - resident in a care establishment and the costs are met in whole or in part by a local authority; *or*
  - an inpatient receiving free treatment in a hospital or similar institution and s/he (or her/his partner) received a qualifying benefit immediately before becoming a patient; *or*
  - an asylum seeker receiving asylum support from the Home Office or a local authority; *or*
  - ordinarily resident (see p1585) outside the UK; *or*
- there is a close relative of the deceased who was in *closer contact* with the deceased than you were, taking into account the nature and extent of such contact;[47] *or*
- there is a close relative of the deceased who was in *equally close contact* with the deceased as you were and who (or whose partner) is not getting a qualifying benefit (see p798).[48]

Note: the last two bullet points do not apply if the close relative was under the age of 18 when the person died, or was a student, member of a religious order, prisoner, inpatient or asylum seeker as set out above, or was ordinarily resident outside the UK.[49]

If you are refused a payment on this ground, the DWP (not you) must establish whether there is another close relative who is not getting a qualifying benefit.[50]

Examples

Jane is not entitled to a funeral expenses payment because, although she looked after her brother for many years before he died, he had a son who is not getting a qualifying benefit (see p798). Although the son rarely saw his father, they were not estranged.

Part 5: Other benefits
Chapter 37: Social fund payments
3. Funeral expenses payments

> Yuri is entitled to a funeral expenses payment when his close friend Robert dies because, although Robert had two surviving close relatives, a son and a sister-in-law, the son is getting HB and Yuri was in closer contact with Robert than either of them were.

Accepting responsibility for funeral costs

To qualify for a funeral payment, you or your partner must 'accept responsibility' for funeral expenses.[51] This means you must be liable to pay the costs of a funeral, even if you do not make the arrangements.[52]

If the funeral director's account or contract is in your name, you should normally be treated as having accepted responsibility. If it is in someone else's name (or another person has paid the bill), you can still be 'responsible' if:

- s/he is acting as your agent – eg, because you are too distressed to act on your own behalf;[53] *or*
- s/he transfers liability to you, prior to full payment, with the consent of the funeral director.[54]

If you are a close relative (see p800) or close friend of the person who died, it must also be 'reasonable' for you to accept responsibility for the funeral expenses, in the light of the nature and extent of your contact with her/him.[55] In one case, it was held reasonable for a person to have accepted responsibility for his father's funeral even though he had not seen him for 24 years.[56]

European Economic Area nationals

You can get a funeral expenses payment for a funeral that takes place in any member state of the EEA or Switzerland (see p1668) if:[57]

- you are a 'worker' or self-employed, or you retain that status; *or*
- you are a member of the family of a worker – ie:
  - her/his spouse or civil partner;
  - the worker's/spouse's/civil partner's child, grandchild or other descendant who is either under 21 or dependent;
  - a dependent relative of the worker, spouse or civil partner in the ascending line – eg, a parent or grandparent; *or*
- you have a permanent right to reside in the UK.

For more details on the benefit rights of EEA nationals, see Chapter 70.

If you have been refused a payment for a funeral that took place in an EEA state and you satisfied the above rules, you should ask for a revision (see p1307).

Note: following the UK leaving the EU on 31 January 2020, these rules may change at the end of the transition period (see p1596).

The amount

You are entitled to a payment that is sufficient to cover:[58]
- the necessary costs of purchasing a new burial plot and necessary burial fees, including any medical references or other required documents. The burial of ashes following cremation is not, however, covered;
- the necessary cremation fees, including medical references, certificates and removing a pacemaker (restricted to £20 if not carried out by a doctor);
- the costs of documentation necessary for the release of the assets of the person who died;
- the reasonable cost of transport for the portion of journeys in excess of 80 kilometres (50 miles), undertaken to:
  - transport the body within the UK to a funeral director's premises or to a place of rest;
  - transport the coffin and bearers in a hearse and the mourners in another vehicle from the funeral director's premises or place of rest to the funeral. The cost of this plus burial in an existing plot cannot exceed the cost of such transport plus the purchase and burial costs of a new plot;[59]
- the necessary expenses of one return journey for the responsible person to arrange or attend the funeral. The maximum allowed is the cost of a return journey from home to where the burial or cremation costs are incurred;
- up to £700 for any other funeral expenses – eg, funeral director's fees, religious costs, flowers and other transport costs. The government has announced that this is to increase to £1,000 from spring 2020. See AskCPAG.org.uk and CPAG's *Welfare Rights Bulletin* for updates.

Note:
- The cost of any items or services provided under a prepaid funeral plan or equivalent arrangement cannot be met. Expenses not covered by the plan can be met if they fall into the above categories, but the maximum allowed under the last category is restricted to £120.[60]
- Costs relating to religious requirements cannot be included in the amount allowed for burial and transport.[61]

If the amount awarded does not cover your funeral expenses, you may be able to claim a budgeting loan (see p792).

Deductions from awards

The following are deducted from an award of a funeral expenses payment:[62]
- the assets of the person who died which are available to you or a member of your family (defined as for IS purposes) without probate or letters of administration. However, if you have a joint account with the person who died, those assets become yours at the point of death and cannot be deducted.[63] Assets at the date of death count, even if you have spent or distributed them

Part 5: Other benefits
Chapter 37: Social fund payments
3. Funeral expenses payments

before your claim for a funeral payment.[64] However, arrears of most benefits and tax credits payable to the deceased at the date of death are excluded from the assets;[65]
- a lump sum legally due to you or a member of your family from an insurance policy, occupational pension scheme, burial club or equivalent source on the person's death;
- a funeral grant paid by the government for a war disablement pensioner;
- an amount paid or payable under a prepaid funeral plan or equivalent arrangement (whether or not the plan was fully paid).

Any capital you have apart from the above does not affect the amount of the funeral payment. Any payments from the Macfarlane Trust, the Macfarlane (Special Payments) Trusts, MFET Ltd, the Fund, the Eileen Trust, the CJD Trusts, the Skipton Fund, the Caxton Foundation, the London Bombings Relief Charitable Fund, the London Emergencies Trust and the We Love Manchester Emergency Fund are not deducted from an award of a funeral payment.[66]

Claiming and getting paid

Claim on Form SF200, which you can get from your local Jobcentre Plus office or from gov.uk or by telephone (via the Bereavement Service on 0800 731 0469; textphone 0800 731 0464). There are strict time limits for claiming. You can claim at any time from the date of death to up to six months after the date of the funeral.[67] There is no provision for late claims.

When completing the form, bear in mind the rules about accepting responsibility for the funeral expenses and your contact with the person who died.

Your date of claim is normally the date the form is received by the DWP or the date you make your telephone claim.[68] If you do not complete Form SF200 properly or apply in writing but not on the form, you should be sent the form to complete or correct. If you submit it within one month (or a longer period if the DWP considers this reasonable), your claim is treated as being made on the date you originally applied.[69] See p799 for when your claim can be backdated if you are subsequently awarded a qualifying benefit.

Payment is normally made directly to the funeral director, unless you have already paid the bill.[70]

If you are overpaid a funeral expenses payment, you may have to repay it (see Chapter 53) and, in some circumstances, you may have to pay a penalty (see p1268). However, see below for recovery from the estate of the person who died.

Recovery from the estate

The DWP is entitled to recover funeral expenses payments from the estate of the person who died and usually attempts to do so.[71] Funeral expenses are a first charge on the estate and have priority over anything else (although there may be insufficient assets for full repayment).[72]

4. **Cold weather payments**

Cold weather payments are available in England, Wales and Scotland.

Future changes

From 2021, it is expected that cold weather payments will be replaced by coldspell heating assistance for some claimants in Scotland. See Chapter 71, and AskCPAG.org.uk and CPAG's *Welfare Rights Bulletin* for updates.

You qualify for a cold weather payment if you satisfy all the following conditions.
- **There is a period of cold weather** in the area where you have your usual home. This is defined as seven consecutive days during which your designated local weather station either forecasts or records a temperature at or below zero degrees celsius.[73]
- **You have been awarded pension credit** (guarantee or savings credit) for at least one day during the period of cold weather. **You also qualify if you have been awarded universal credit (UC), income support (IS), income-based jobseeker's allowance (JSA), or income-related employment and support allowance (ESA)** for at least one day during the period of cold weather[74] and:
  - your UC includes an increase for a disabled or severely disabled child, or you have been assessed as having, or are treated as having, limited capability for work or limited capability for work and work-related activity, and you are not in employment or gainful self-employment during the period of cold weather or on the day it is forecast; *or*
  - your IS or income-based JSA applicable amount includes a disability, severe disability, enhanced disability, disabled child, pensioner or higher pensioner premium (see p339); *or*
  - your income-related ESA applicable amount includes the pensioner premium, severe disability premium or enhanced disability premium, or you have been assessed as having, or are treated as having, limited capability for work or limited capability for work-related activity; *or*
  - you are responsible for a child under five; *or*
  - you are getting child tax credit (CTC) which includes a disabled child or severely disabled child element (see p1452).
  You are treated as receiving one of the above benefits if you are entitled to a DWP loan for help with your mortgage interest (see p855), even if you are not actually entitled to the benefit.

Part 5: Other benefits
Chapter 37: Social fund payments
5. Winter fuel payments

- **You are not living in a care home, independent hospital or Abbeyfield Society establishment** unless you are responsible for a child under five or getting CTC which includes a disabled child or a severely disabled child element.[75]
- **You are not a 'person subject to immigration control'** (there are exceptions to this rule) – see p1560.

The amount

The sum of £25 is paid for each week of cold weather.[76]

Claiming and getting paid

You do not need to make a claim for a cold weather payment. The DWP should automatically pay you if you qualify. Your district DWP should publicise when there are periods of cold weather in your area. If you do not receive payment and you think you are entitled, submit a written claim and ask for a written decision. A payment cannot be made more than 26 weeks from the last day of the winter period (1 November to 31 March) in which the cold weather period fell.[77] If you are overpaid a cold weather payment, you might have to repay it (see Chapter 53) and, in some circumstances, you may have to pay a penalty (see p1268).

5. **Winter fuel payments**

Winter fuel payments are available in England, Wales and Scotland. From 2020, it is expected that some families with disabled children in Scotland will be able to get winter heating assistance from Social Security Scotland (see p1688).

Future changes

From 2021, it is expected that winter fuel payments will be replaced by winter heating assistance for some claimants in Scotland. The Scottish government plans to transfer existing winter fuel payment claimants in Scotland to the new benefit by 2024. See Chapter 71, and AskCPAG.org.uk and CPAG's *Welfare Rights Bulletin* for updates.

You qualify for a winter fuel payment if you satisfy all the following conditions.[78]
- **You have reached pension age** in the 'qualifying week'.
- **You are ordinarily resident in Great Britain** (see p1585) **or you are habitually resident in a European Economic Area country with an average winter temperature that is not higher than that of the warmest part of the UK, or in Switzerland. Note:** following the UK leaving the EU on 31 January 2020, these rules may change at the end of the transition period (see p1596).

- **You claim in time** (see p808), if a claim is required.
- **You are not excluded from a payment under the rules below.**

The qualifying week

The **'qualifying week'** is the week beginning on the third Monday in September.

Who cannot get a winter fuel payment

You are excluded from entitlement to a payment if, throughout the qualifying week (see above):[79]

- you are serving a custodial sentence;
- you have been receiving free inpatient treatment for more than 52 weeks in a hospital or similar institution (see p918);
- you are receiving pension credit (PC), income-based jobseeker's allowance (JSA) or income-related employment and support allowance (ESA) and you are living in residential care (see below);[80]
- you are a 'person subject to immigration control' (there are exceptions) – see p1560.

Living in residential care

You count as **'living in residential care'** if you are living in a care home (ie, an independent home which is registered or exempt from registration, or a local authority home which provides board) or independent hospital throughout the qualifying week and the 12 preceding weeks, disregarding temporary absences.

The amount

Subject to the rules below, you are entitled to a winter fuel payment of:[81]

- £200 if you are aged between pension age and 79 (inclusive) in the qualifying week (see p806); *or*
- £300 if you are aged 80 or over in the qualifying week.

If you do not get PC, income-based JSA or income-related ESA and you share your accommodation with another qualifying person (whether as a partner or friend), you get £100 if you are both between pension age and 79 or £150 if you are both aged 80 or over. If only one of you is aged 80 or over, s/he gets £200 and the other person gets £100.

If you get PC, income-based JSA or income-related ESA, you (and your partner if you have one) get £200 if one or both of you is between pension age and 79, or £300 if one or both of you is aged 80 or over, regardless of whether there is anyone else in your household who qualifies.

Part 5: Other benefits
Chapter 37: Social fund payments
6. Tax, other benefits and the benefit cap

If you are living in residential care (see p807) in the qualifying week and are not getting PC, income-based JSA or income-related ESA, you are entitled to a payment of £100 if you are aged between pension age and 79, or £150 if you are aged 80 or over.

Claiming and getting paid

You should automatically receive a payment without having to make a claim if you received a payment the previous year, or if you are getting retirement pension or any other social security benefit (except child benefit, universal credit, council tax reduction and housing benefit) in the qualifying week.[82]

Otherwise, you must claim a winter fuel payment on or before 31 March following the qualifying week.[83] To ensure you receive your payment before Christmas, submit your claim before the qualifying week. You can claim via the winter fuel payment helpline on 0800 731 0160 (textphone: 0800 731 0464), or you can download a claim form from gov.uk/winter-fuel-payment.

You should get a written decision.

If you are a member of a couple and your partner is receiving income support, the payment can be made to either of you (even though your partner is under pension age).[84]

The government aims to make payments between mid-November and Christmas.

6. **Tax, other benefits and the benefit cap**

Social fund loans and payments are not taxable.

They are disregarded as income and capital for the purposes of means-tested benefits and tax credits, and do not affect entitlement to any non-means-tested benefits.

In some cases, there is a limit on the total amount of specified benefits you can receive (a 'benefit cap'). Social fund loans and payments are *not* one of the specified benefits. The benefit cap only applies if you are getting universal credit or housing benefit.

Chapter 37

Notes

1. Budgeting loans
1 Dir 8 BLG
2 *R v SFI ex parte Davey,* 19 October 1998
   (HC), unreported
3 Dir 8 BLG
4 Dir 9 BLG
5 Dir 8 BLG
6 Dir 2 BLG
7 Dir 53 BLG
8 Dir 11 BLG
9 Reg 4 SF(AM) Regs
10 Reg 5 SF(AM) Regs
11 Reg 2(1)(a) and (2)(a) SF(AR) Regs
12 Reg 2(4) SF(AR) Regs
13 Reg 2(6) SF(AR) Regs
14 Reg 2(3) SF(AR) Regs
15 para 132 Part 4 BLG
16 s78(1) SSAA 1992
17 Reg 6(3) and (4) SF(AM) Regs
18 Reg 3 SF(RDB) Regs
19 s78(3) SSAA 1992

2. Sure Start maternity grants
20 Reg 5(2) SFM&FE Regs
21 Reg 5(6) SFM&FE Regs
22 Reg 5(3) SFM&FE Regs
23 Reg 3A SFM&FE Regs
24 Reg 5A SFM&FE Regs
25 Reg 6 SFM&FE Regs
26 Reg 5(4) SFM&FE Regs
27 Reg 3(1) and (2) SFM&FE Regs
28 Reg 5(1) SFM&FE Regs
29 Reg 19 and Sch 4 para 8 SS(C&P) Regs
30 Reg 6(1)(a) SS(C&P) Regs
31 Regs 4(7) and 6(1)(b) SS(C&P) Regs

3. Funeral expenses payments
32 Reg 7(3) and (4) SFM&FE Regs
33 Reg 7(9A) SFM&FE Regs
34 Reg 7(7) SFM&FE Regs
35 Reg 7(9)(b) SFM&FE Regs
36 Reg 7(9)(a) SFM&FE Regs
37 Reg 4(1) and (2) SFM&FE Regs
38 Reg 7(5) SFM&FE Regs
39 The Social Fund (Children's Funeral
   Fund for England) Regulations 2019,
   No.1064
40 Reg 7(8)(a)-(e) SFM&FE Regs
41 Reg 3(1) SFM&FE Regs
42 CIS/788/2003

43 Reg 3(2) SFM&FE Regs
44 Regs 7(8)(e) and 8(4) SFM&FE Regs
45 Reg 7(8)(e) SFM&FE Regs; R(IS) 7/04
46 Reg 8(1) and (2) SFM&FE Regs
47 Reg 8(7)(a) SFM&FE Regs
48 Reg 8(7)(b) SFM&FE Regs
49 Reg 8(8) SFM&FE Regs
50 *Kerr v Department for Social Development
   (NI)* [2004] All ER(D) 65, reported as
   [2004] UKHL 23
51 Reg 7(7) SFM&FE Regs
52 CSB/488/1982
53 CIS/12344/1996; R(IS) 6/98
54 CIS/85/1991
55 Reg 7(8)(e) SFM&FE Regs
56 CIS/12783/1996
57 Reg 7(10) SFM&FE Regs
58 Reg 9(1), (2) and (3) SFM&FE Regs
59 Reg 9(8) SFM&FE Regs
60 Reg 9(10) SFM&FE Regs
61 Reg 9(7) SFM&FE Regs
62 Reg 10(1) SFM&FE Regs
63 Vol 7 Ch 39, para 39404 DMG
64 R(IS) 14/91
65 Reg 10(1A) SFM&FE Regs
66 Reg 10(2) SFM&FE Regs
67 Sch 4 para 9 SS(C&P) Regs
68 Reg 6(1)(a) SS(C&P) Regs
69 Regs 4(7) and 6(1)(b) SS(C&P) Regs
70 Reg 35(2) SS(C&P) Regs
71 s78(4) SSAA 1992; CIS/616/1990
72 R(SB) 18/84

4. Cold weather payments
73 Reg 2(1) and (2) SFCWP Regs
74 Regs 1A(2), (3) and (6) SFCWP Regs
75 Reg 1A(4) SFCWP Regs
76 Reg 3 SFCWP Regs
77 Reg 2(6) SFCWP Regs

5. Winter fuel payments
78 Reg 2 SFWFP Regs
79 Reg 3 SFWFP Regs
80 Reg 1(2) and (3) SFWFP Regs
81 Reg 2 SFWFP Regs
82 Reg 4 SFWFP Regs
83 Reg 3(1)(b) and (2) SFWFP Regs
84 Reg 36(2) SS(C&P) Regs

Chapter 38

Statutory maternity, adoption, paternity and other parental pay

5

This chapter covers:
1. Who can get a payment (p811)
2. The rules about your age (p822)
3. People included in the claim (p822)
4. The amount of benefit (p823)
5. Special benefit rules (p823)
6. Claims (p826)
7. Getting paid (p827)
8. Tax, other benefits and the benefit cap (p828)

Key facts

- Statutory maternity pay (SMP), statutory adoption pay (SAP), statutory paternity pay (SPP) and statutory shared parental pay (SSPP) are payments made to certain employees by their employers for the birth or adoption of a child.
- Statutory parental bereavement pay (SPBP) is a payment made to certain employees by their employers following the death of a child or a stillbirth.
- SMP, SAP, SPP SSPP and SPBP are not means tested, although they have employment and earnings conditions.
- You do not need to intend to return to work to qualify for SMP, SAP, SPP, SSPP or SPBP, and you do not have to repay any of these payments if you do not return.
- You may be entitled to more maternity, adoption, paternity, shared parental pay or pay in connection with a bereavement under your employment contract.
- If you disagree with your employer's decision on your entitlement, or if your employer has failed to make a decision, you can challenge this (see Chapter 59).

1. **Who can get a payment**

Statutory maternity pay

You qualify for statutory maternity pay (SMP) from your employer if you are pregnant or have recently given birth and:

- you have been continuously employed by the same employer for at least 26 weeks (see p817) by the end of the week which is 15 weeks before the week in which your baby is due (the 'expected week of childbirth');[1] *and*
- your average gross weekly earnings are at least the 'lower earnings limit' (£120 a week in 2020/21). Your earnings are looked at over a 'relevant perod' which depends on the expected week of childbirth (see p819);[2] *and*
- you are in the 'maternity pay period' (see below);[3] *and*
- you give your employer at least 28 days' notice of the date you want payment of your SMP to start,[4] and a certificate (Form MAT B1) from your doctor or midwife, confirming the expected date of birth.[5]

If you do not qualify for SMP, you may be able to get maternity allowance (MA) instead (see Chapter 34).

The maternity pay period

SMP is paid for 39 consecutive weeks. You can usually choose to start to receive SMP at any point between 11 weeks before your baby is due and the day after your baby is born. However, if you have to stop work earlier than planned, your maternity pay period may begin earlier than the date given in your notice to your employer.[6]

- If your baby is born early, your maternity pay period begins on the day after the birth. You should let your employer know about the birth as soon as you can (if possible, within 28 days). Your employer can ask you to confirm this in writing.[7]
- If you are off work because of your pregnancy within four weeks of your due date, your SMP starts on the day after the first day of your absence.
- If you leave your job, see p823.

You may decide to reduce your maternity pay period – eg, if this would allow the father of the child/your partner to claim statutory shared parental leave and/or pay (see p814). The earliest your maternity pay period can end is two weeks after the birth (four weeks if you are employed in a factory).

Statutory adoption pay

You qualify for statutory adoption pay (SAP) from your employer if you are adopting a child under UK law and:

Part 5: Other benefits
Chapter 38: Statutory maternity, adoption, paternity and other parental pay
1. Who can get a payment

- you have been continuously employed by the same employer for at least 26 weeks (see p817) when you are notified that you have been matched with a child for adoption;[8] *and*
- your average gross weekly earnings are at least the 'lower earnings limit' (£120 a week in 2020/21). Your earnings are looked at over a 'relevant period' which depends on the date you are matched with a child – see p819;[9] *and*
- you are in the 'adoption pay period' (see below);[10] *and*
- you give your employer at least 28 days' notice of when you want payments of SAP to start (this can simply be 'on the day of placement' – ie, without specifying a date), the 'matching certificate' from the adoption agency confirming the placement date and the date you were notified of it, and a written declaration that you want to receive SAP rather than statutory paternity pay (SPP).[11]

Note: you will usually be better off claiming SAP, as it is paid for longer.

If you are jointly adopting a child, only one of you can claim SAP. It may be preferable for the person whose average earnings are higher to apply, as this determines the amount paid (see p823). The person who is not claiming SAP may be able to claim SPP (adoption), see below.

See p825 if you are adopting a child from abroad.

The adoption pay period

SAP is paid for 39 consecutive weeks. You can choose to start to receive SAP at the earliest 14 days before the day you expect the child to be placed with you and, at the latest, on the date of placement (or the day after if you are at work that day). When giving notice, you can choose a date which relates to the expected placement date. You need to inform your employer when the child is actually placed with you if you asked for your SAP to start on that day or the following day.[12]

The adoption pay period ends early if the child is not placed with you, or if the adoption ends because the child dies or s/he is returned to the adoption agency.[13] In these circumstances, payment of SAP continues for eight weeks, then stops.

You may decide to reduce the adoption pay period yourself – eg, if this would allow your partner to claim statutory shared parental leave and/or pay (see p814). The earliest date your adoption pay period can end is two weeks after it started.

Statutory paternity pay

You qualify for SPP from your employer if you are taking time off work to care for a child or to support your partner, and you satisfy the conditions below. You can be:

- the child's father, if you expect to have responsibility for her/his upbringing; *or*

- the partner of the child's mother, if you expect to share the main responsibility for the child's upbringing with her;[14] *or*
- the person adopting a child; *or*
- the adopter's partner, if you expect to share the main responsibility for the child's upbringing with her/him.[15]

Note: you may have a choice between SAP and SPP if you are adopting with your partner. Bear in mind that SPP can be worth more to begin with, depending on your earnings, and has a longer maximum pay period (see p823).

You qualify for SPP if:

- you have been continuously employed by the same employer for at least 26 weeks (see p817):
  - by the end of the week which is 15 weeks before the week the baby is due (the 'expected week of childbirth');[16] *or*
  - by the end of the week in which you (and/or your partner) are notified that you have been matched with a child for adoption;[17]
- your average gross weekly earnings are at least the 'lower earnings limit' (£120 a week in 2020/21). Your earnings are looked at over a 'relevant period' which depends on the expected week of childbirth or the date you are matched with a child for adoption (see p819);[18]
- you are in the 'paternity pay period' (see below);[19] *and either*
- at least 15 weeks in advance of the date the baby is due, you notify your employer of this due date and of the date you want payment of your SPP to start (see below), and provide a declaration that you are entitled to claim;[20] *or*
- within seven days of notification of the adoption match, you notify your employer of the date you expect the child to be placed for adoption and of the date you want payment of your SPP to start (this can simply be 'on the day of placement' – ie, without specifying a date), and provide a declaration that you are entitled to claim.[21]

SPP can be paid at the same time as SMP or MA, but not SAP or statutory shared parental pay (SSPP).

The paternity pay period

SPP is paid for two consecutive weeks. The earliest SPP can be paid is the child's date of birth or the date of the child's placement for adoption, and the latest is eight weeks after that date. For SPP for a birth, you can choose whether you want it to start on the day the child is born, the following day, or a specified number of days after the birth. In this case, you must inform your employer of the date the child is born as soon as you can after the birth. Alternatively, you can request that SPP starts on a specific date as long as this is after the first day of the week in which the child is expected. In this case, you only need to let the employer know if the

Part 5: Other benefits
Chapter 38: Statutory maternity, adoption, paternity and other parental pay
1. Who can get a payment

child has not arrived by the date you specified for your SPP to begin, as this will have to be changed.[22]

For SPP for an adoption, you can choose whether you want SPP to start on the day the child is placed with you and your partner, the following day, or a specified number of days after the placement. In this case, you must inform your employer when the child is placed with you as soon as you can. Alternatively, you can request that SPP starts on a specific date as long as this is later than the expected date of placement. In this case, you only need to let your employer know if the child has not been placed with you by the date you have asked SPP to start, as this will have to be changed.[23]

Statutory shared parental pay

You may qualify for SSPP from your employer if your partner has chosen to give up her SMP or MA, or her/his SAP, early.

You may also qualify if you have recently given birth or adopted a child and you choose to give up your SMP or SAP early. You might choose to do this because the rules on when SSPP can be paid are more flexible and it could allow you to return to work for a longer period than would otherwise be possible without losing your right to more paid leave. If you are doing this as a mother/adopter, bear in mind that SMP/SAP is worth more than SSPP for the first six weeks.

Note:
- SMP, SAP or MA must have been paid for at least two weeks before it can be given up early.[24]
- If you or your partner change your mind about swapping to SSPP, any 'curtailment' (ie, early ending) of SMP, SAP or MA can be cancelled before the payments end.[25]

You qualify for SSPP if:
- you have been continuously employed by the same employer for at least 26 weeks (see p817) by the end of either the week that is 15 weeks before the week the baby is due (the 'expected week of childbirth')[26] or when you (and/or your partner) are notified that you have been matched with a child for adoption.[27] You also need to continue in this employment at least until the week before your SSPP starts;
- your average gross weekly earnings are at least the 'lower earnings limit' (£120 a week in 2020/21). Your earnings are looked at over a relevant period which depends on the expected week of childbirth or the date you are matched with a child for adoption (see p819);[28]
- you are in the 'shared parental pay period' (see p815);[29]
- your partner has sent a 'curtailment notice' to her/his employer at least eight weeks before s/he wants payment of her/his SMP, SAP or MA to stop,[30] or you have sent your employer a curtailment notice if you want your own SMP or SAP to stop[31] and you have given your employer:

- at least eight weeks' notice of the date you want payments of SSPP to start;
- notification of the baby's due date, the date of birth or the date of the adoption placement;
- confirmation of the total number of weeks and the period(s) for which you intend to claim SSPP;
- declaration from your partner confirming that s/he consents to your claiming SSPP and that you will share the main responsibility for the care of the child with her/him, and a declaration from you, confirming that you are entitled to claim.[32]

If you are the mother or the SAP claimant and you want to claim SSPP, your partner in the application (this can be the father of the child, your spouse, civil partner or your partner who lives with you and the child) must:[33]
- have the main responsibility of the child (apart from you); *and*
- have been employed for 26 weeks in the 66 weeks before the expected week of childbirth or before the week you are notified that you have been matched with a child for adoption; *and*
- have average weekly earnings of at least £30 in 13 of those 66 weeks.

The shared parental pay period

When you or your partner give notice that you wish to 'curtail' your SMP, SAP or MA (after it has been paid for at least two weeks – see above), SSPP is payable for the remaining number of weeks in the 39-week period. If both you and your partner qualify for SSPP, and you both intend to claim it, you can share the available weeks of SSPP between you in whatever proportion you choose. If you are going to do this, you must both give at least eight weeks' notice of your intention to take SSPP. You can get SSPP for the same or different weeks. Alternatively, either one of you can get all the available weeks of SSPP. The weeks of SSPP can be paid over one continuous period, or over a number of shorter periods (if your employer agrees to this). It cannot be paid for any day falling after the child's first birthday, or after the first anniversary of her/his adoption placement. You can give your employer notice of your intention to take SSPP and then follow this up with notice of specific periods of SSPP (and leave) you wish to book, or do both these at the same time (see p826), but you must usually give at least eight weeks' notice before any period of SSPP.

Statutory parental bereavement pay

Statutory parental bereavement pay (SPBP) is paid for up to two weeks to employees who meet certain conditions in respect of the death of a child or a stillbirth. It applies only where the death or stillbirth happens on or after 6 April 2020.[34] You qualify for SPBP if a child under 18 dies or is stillborn after 24 weeks of pregnancy (see p824) and you:[35]
- are a bereaved parent; *and*

Part 5: Other benefits
Chapter 38: Statutory maternity, adoption, paternity and other parental pay
1. Who can get a payment

- have been continuously employed by the same employer for at least 26 weeks (see p817) ending with the week immediately before the week in which the child died, and continue to be employed by that employer from that point to the day of the child's death; *and*
- your average gross weekly earnings are at least the 'lower earnings limit' (£120 in 2020/21). Your earnings are looked at over a 'relevant period' which depends on the week in which the death occurred (see p819); *and*
- you give your employer notice of the week or weeks you want the payment to be made.

A bereaved parent includes all legal parents (including adoptive parents), natural (biological) parents whose children have been adopted where the adopter was required to allow them to be in contact with the child, and intended parents (who have applied for, or intend to apply for, a parental order in respect of a child under a surrogacy arrangement).[36]

You are also a bereaved parent if you had day to day responsibility for the child, and s/he was living in your own home, for at least four weeks ending with the day the child died. However, you are not a parent if an actual parent of the child, or someone else who had responsibility for the child, is also living in the premises where the child is cared for. You are also not a parent if you are entitled to receive any remuneration in respect of the care of the child, although some payments do not count (eg, a fostering allowance paid by a local authority is not remuneration).

The partner of a bereaved parent is also entitled to SPBP if s/he meets the other conditions. A partner means someone who lives with the parent and the child in an enduring family relationship and is not a close relative of the parent.[37]

You must give your employer notice of the SPBP you want to take. The maximum number of weeks of SPBP for the death of one child is two (however, you can be entitled to SPBP in respect of more than one child[38]). You can choose to be paid for either one week or two, or you can take two separate weeks at different times. SPBP can only be paid within 56 weeks beginning with the date of the child's death.[39] You are supposed to give notice of at least 28 days before the first day for which you want to receive SPBP, but if this is not reasonably practicable, you should give it as soon as you can do so.[40]

With your notice, you should include the following in writing:[41]
- the name of the person claiming SPBP; *and*
- the date of the child's death; *and*
- a declaration that you meet one of the conditions for being a bereaved parent (eg, you are the child's parent or the partner of a bereaved parent).

If you later change your mind about your weeks of SPBP, you can withdraw your notice. You must give notice to withdraw no later than the first day of a week of SPBP if you were going to be taking it within 56 days of the child's death, and at least a week before a week of SPBP if you were going to be taking it later than that.[42]

Continuous employment

To satisfy the continuous employment rule, you must have been employed by an employer who was liable to pay employer's national insurance (NI) contributions for you, or would have been if your earnings had been high enough (see p963) or you had been older (if you are under 16).[43] For all statutory payments in this chapter, you need to have been employed for 26 weeks by the end of the week which is 15 weeks before the expected week of childbirth (see p811), for adoption, by the date you (and/or your partner) are notified that you have been matched with a child, or for the death of a child, by the end of the week before the week in which your child died. Any work, even for only part of a week, counts as a week of work. A week for SMP, SAP, SPP, SSPP or SPBP usually runs from Sunday to Saturday, so you need to check which week the date falls into and count backwards. Tables to help you do this for SMP, SPP for a birth and SSPP for a birth are in Appendix 8.

For SPBP, if you have been employed in each of the 26 weeks (but no more) ending with the week before the week of the child's death, the first week of your employment for counting the 26 weeks starts on the first day you were employed by your employer, even if this is not a Sunday. For any subsequent weeks, as with the other statutory payments, you do not have to work full time, as work in all or part of a week counts as a week of work.

If you are an 'employed earner' for NI purposes (see p962), you normally count as an employee.[44] If you are employed under a contract of apprenticeship, you count as an employee.[45] Agency workers count, if someone is liable to pay employer's NI contributions, as do company directors who are paid a salary.

You do not need to have a written contract of employment to count as an employee.

Periods of employment in a European Economic Area country may count towards your period of continuous employment if you were employed by the same employer in Great Britain in the 15th week before your baby was due, or the week you were notified that you had been matched with a child for adoption.[46] In addition, if you were working outside Great Britain but your employer was liable to pay Class 1 NI on your earnings, then your period of employment may count.

Even if you are an employee, you may not be entitled to SMP, SAP, SPP or SSPP if your employer is based outside Great Britain (see p1661). See p1661 if you are employed abroad.

If the baby is born early (in or before the 15th week before your expected week of childbirth), you satisfy the continuous employment rule if you would have done so (for SMP or SPP for a birth) had the baby been born on the expected date or (for SSPP for a birth) if the baby had been born after the 15th week before the

Part 5: Other benefits
Chapter 38: Statutory maternity, adoption, paternity and other parental pay
1. Who can get a payment

expected week of childbirth. For SSPP, you must also continue to be employed by the same employer from the date of the baby's birth until the week before your first period of SSPP begins.[47]

For SMP, if you are employed for only part of the 15th week before your expected week of childbirth, the whole week still counts towards your continuous employment. For SAP, the same applies if you are employed for only part of the week in which you received notification that you have been matched with a child. For SPBP, if you have been employed for each of the 26 weeks (but no more) before the week of the child's death, the first of those 26 weeks does not need to be a complete week. For the purposes of counting the weeks, the first week starts on the first day of your employment and ends at midnight on the following Saturday (or ends at midnight on the start date if you started employment on a Saturday).[48]

Breaks in employment

If you return to work for the same employer following a break in your employment, certain weeks when you were not employed can still count towards your 26 weeks' continuous employment. These include weeks in which you were:[49]

- incapable of work because of sickness or injury; *or*
- absent because your employer temporarily had no work to offer you – eg, you are an agency worker and the agency is unable to find you work in any particular week; *or*
- absent from work, but because of an arrangement or custom, you are regarded as continuing in employment – eg, if you are a teacher employed on a term-by-term contract.

Note: the above rules are only relevant when there is a *break* in your employment with your employer. So, for example, sickness absence should count towards your continuous employment if you remain employed by your employer while off sick, as should absence because of adoption, paternity, shared parental, parental bereavement or parental leave.

For SMP only, if you have gaps between contracts with the same employer of no more than 26 weeks during which you are absent from work wholly or partly because of pregnancy, and you are employed both before and after your baby is born but not while you are off work due to childbirth, the weeks in between the contracts can still count towards your continous employment.[50]

If your employer offers contracts of up to 26 weeks, at least twice a year, to people who have worked there before, and you are absent from work due to pregnancy (for SMP), disease or disability, you do not need to return to work to benefit from these rules.[51]

If your employment is legally transferred from one employer to another, your employment is unbroken.[52] If you have been reinstated or re-engaged following an unfair dismissal claim, any period between your dismissal and your reinstatement or re-engagement counts towards your 26 weeks' continuous employment.[53] If you have been dismissed without being reinstated or re-engaged, see p823.

If being on strike has affected the weeks which count towards your continuous employment, see p1005.

Earnings

What counts as earnings

As well as your gross wages, bonuses and any overtime pay you receive during the relevant period, your earnings include payments such as:[54]

- other statutory payments (although, at the time of writing, it was not known if statutory parental bereavement pay will count as earnings when assessing your entitlement to statutory adoption, paternity or shared parental pay, this is likely to be the intention – see AskCPAG.org.uk and CPAG's *Welfare Rights Bulletin* for updates);
- arrears of pay following reinstatement or re-engagement in your job or a continuation of your contract of employment under the Employment Rights Act 1996.

Certain payments (eg, some payments in kind) are ignored.[55]

How earnings are averaged

For births, earnings are averaged over a 'relevant period' ending with the last normal payday which falls either in or before the 15th week before the expected week of childbirth, and going back to the day after the last normal payday which fell at least eight weeks before that (ie, roughly 23 weeks before the baby is due). See Appendix 8 for help working out dates. For adoptions, the relevant period ends with the last normal pay day that falls in or before the week you are notified of being matched with a child for adoption, and goes back to the day after the last normal pay day which falls at least eight weeks before that. For the death of a child, the relevant period ends with the last normal payday which falls before the first day of the week in which the child dies, and goes back to the day after the last normal payday which falls at least eight weeks before that. In the case of a stillbirth, you may also be entitled to SMP (see p824).

A week for SMP, SPP, SAP, SSPP and SBPB runs from a Sunday to Saturday. If you are paid at intervals of one or more calendar months, weekly earnings are calculated by dividing earnings received in the relevant period by the number of calendar months in that period (to the nearest whole number), multiplying by 12 and dividing by 52.[56] If you are not paid monthly or weekly, or there is not an exact number of weeks in the relevant period that applies to you, your weekly earnings are calculated by taking the total of your earnings in the relevant period, dividing by the number of days in the relevant period and multiplying by seven.

Part 5: Other benefits
Chapter 38: Statutory maternity, adoption, paternity and other parental pay
1. Who can get a payment

Pay rises

For **SMP**, if you are awarded a pay rise that affects your wages for any part of the period from the first day of your 'relevant period' (see p819) until the last day of your statutory maternity leave, your employer should reassess your average earnings during the relevant period as if your earnings for each of the weeks in that period had included the pay increase, and pay any arrears of SMP due to you. This is the case, even if the pay rise did not happen until after the relevant period.[57] If you become entitled to SMP as a result of the pay rise, your employer should deduct any payments of MA that you may have received for the same period from the SMP you are owed.[58]

For **SAP, SPP and SSPP**, only a backdated pay rise that is paid in respect of the relevant period used to calculate your SAP, SPP or SSPP will lead to your employer recalculating the average and paying any arrears of SAP, SPP or SSPP due to you.[59]

The lower earnings limit

For births, the lower earnings limit used is the one in force at the end of the 15th week before the expected week of childbirth. For adoptions, the lower earnings limit used is the one in force at the end of the week in which you or the adopter are notified of being matched with the child for adoption. For deaths, the lower earnings limit is the one in force at the end of the week immediately before the week in which the child dies. For the tax year 2020/21, the lower earnings limit is £120 a week. See Appendix 6 for the amounts for other years.

Working while getting statutory payments for the birth, adoption or death of a child

Your entitlement to SMP, SAP, SPP, SSPP or SPBP is not affected by any work you do on a self-employed basis. However, your entitlement may be affected if you work for an employer.

Working for the employer who is paying you

You can do up to 10 'keeping in touch' days' work for the employer who pays you SMP or SAP, and up to 20 for SSPP, without your entitlement to these payments being affected. However, if you do any work for that employer in excess of these 10/20 days, you lose a week's payment for every week in which you do that further work.[60] **Note:** HM Revenue and Customs seems to interpret the rules about 'keeping in touch' days for SSPP as meaning that, if you work for 20 days or more, your SSPP ends altogether. Arguably, this is incorrect and can be challenged. Seek specialist advice if you are affected.

If you do any work during the paternity pay period for an employer who is paying you SPP, that employer is not liable to pay you SPP for the week in which you work.[61] If you do any work during the parental bereavement pay period for an employer who is paying you SPBP, that employer is not liable to pay you SPBP for the week in which you work.[62]

These rules apply even if you are working for the employer under a new contract which did not exist before your maternity, paternity or adoption pay period began.

For SMP, if you return to work for your employer but you are then off sick during what would otherwise be your maternity pay period, you are not entitled to statutory sick pay (SSP). Instead, you can get SMP for each week in which you are off for a whole week. This does not apply if you have curtailed your maternity pay period and you are past the curtailment date (see p814), when you would be able to get SSP as usual. If you had returned to work before giving a curtailment notice, any additional weeks' SMP you are paid while off work sick are ignored when calculating the number of weeks for which SSPP can be paid.[63] This may allow you or your partner to book SSPP.

Working for more than one employer who is liable to pay you

If you work for more than one employer and you meet the conditions of entitlement to SMP (see p811), SAP (see p811), SPP (see p812) or SPBP (see p815) in respect of the work you do for each, you can get SMP, SAP, SPP or SPBP from each job. However, if your earnings from any of your jobs are aggregated when calculating your liability to pay NI contributions, the jobs are counted as one and the amount of SMP, SAP or SPP your employers must pay is apportioned between them.

If more than one employer is liable to pay you SMP, SAP, SPP or SPBP, unless the payments are just one award apportioned between them, any work you do for one of them does not affect your entitlement to SMP, SAP SPP or SPBP from the other.

If more than one employer is liable to pay you SSPP, you do not need to be on shared parental leave from all your jobs at the same time. The number of weeks of SSPP you can get from each employer is calculated without looking at how many weeks of SSPP you get from any other employer. However, *all* the weeks you get SSPP, from any employer, are counted when calculating the number of weeks of SSPP which would be left for your partner to take. There is no double counting of the same week(s) though, so if you get SSPP from more than one employer for one week, that week is only counted once, meaning you may be better off claiming SSPP from all your liable employers for the same weeks if your partner intends to take some SSPP as well.[64]

Working for another employer

If you work for another employer not liable to pay you SMP, SAP, SPP, SSPP or SPBP, this brings your statutory payments to an end early. You also cannot get SMP, SAP and SPP for the remainder of your maternity, paternity or adoption pay period.[65] This means that if you start working for a new employer, your SMP, SAP, SPP or SSPP comes to an end. However, there are two exceptions.

Part 5: Other benefits
Chapter 38: Statutory maternity, adoption, paternity and other parental pay
3. People included in the claim

- For SMP, if the work is done while you are on maternity leave but before your baby is born, your entitlement to SMP is unaffected.[66]
- Your SMP, SAP, SPP, SSPP or SPBP is not affected by any work you do for an employer who is not liable to pay you SMP, SAP, SPP, SSPP or SPBP if you also worked for that employer in the:
  - 15th week before the expected week of confinement, for SMP, SPP (birth) and SSPP (birth); *or*
  - week in which you or the adopter were notified that you had been matched with a child for adoption, for SAP and SPP (adoption); *or*
  - 15th week before the expected week of the child's placement for adoption, for SSPP (adoption);
  - week immediately before the week of the child's death.[67]

If you work for an employer who is not liable to pay you, and for whom you did not work in the relevant week, you must notify the employer who is paying you within seven days of the first day on which you do the work. It is advisable to inform your employer in writing and for SAP, SPP, SSPP and SPBP, your employer has the right to request the information in writing.[68]

2. The rules about your age

There are no upper or lower age limits for statutory maternity pay, statutory adoption pay, statutory paternity pay, statutory shared parental pay or statutory parental bereavement pay.

3. People included in the claim

You claim statutory maternity pay, statutory adoption pay, statutory paternity pay, statutory shared parental pay or statutory parental bereavement pay for yourself. You cannot claim any increase for your partner or child(ren).

4. **The amount of benefit**

	Maximum period of payment	Gross amount
Statutory maternity pay and statutory adoption pay	39 weeks	First six weeks: 90% of average weekly earnings Remaining 33 weeks: Lesser of £151.20 or 90% of average weekly earnings
Statutory paternity pay	Two weeks	Lesser of £151.20 or 90% of average weekly earnings
Statutory shared parental pay	37 weeks	Lesser of £151.20 or 90% of average weekly earnings
Statutory parental bereavement pay	Two weeks	Lesser of £151.20 or 90% of average weekly earnings

If you meet the conditions of entitlement with more than one employer, see p821.

5. **Special benefit rules**

Special rules may apply to:
- people who give up their job or who have been dismissed (see below);
- stillbirths, multiple births or adoption (see p824);
- people who have adopted a child from abroad (see p825);
- foster parents approved as adopters (see p825);
- people whose baby is born with the help of a surrogate (see p825);
- people in prison or detention (see p937);
- people who are abroad or going abroad (see Chapter 69);
- people involved in a trade dispute (see p1005).

If you give up your job or are dismissed

Your employer is still liable to pay you statutory maternity pay (SMP), statutory adoption pay (SAP), statutory paternity pay (SPP) or SSPP if:
- you give up your job or are dismissed after you start receiving your statutory payments (but see p1436 if your employer is insolvent);[69]
- your employer dismisses you at any time, provided HM Revenue and Customs or an employment tribunal finds this was 'solely or mainly' to avoid paying SMP, SAP, SPP, SSPP or SPBP, and you had been employed by that employer for

Part 5: Other benefits
Chapter 38: Statutory maternity, adoption, paternity and other parental pay
5. Special benefit rules

at least eight continuous weeks. In this situation, the amount you are paid for SMP, SAP, SPP or SPBP is calculated using your average earnings during the eight-week period ending with the last day in respect of which you are paid.[70] For the amount of SSPP, your average earnings are calculated over the period ending on the last day you are paid and going back to the day after the last payday which falls at least eight weeks before that.[71]

- you satisfy the qualifying conditions and your job ends for any reason at any time after:
  - **for SMP**, the beginning of the 15th week before your baby is due;[72] *or*
  - **for SAP**, the beginning of the week in which you were notified of being matched with a child for adoption;[73] *or*
  - **for SPP**, the day on which the child is born,[74] or placed for adoption;[75] *or*
  - **for SSPP**, the beginning of the week in which your first period of SSPP starts;[76]
  - **for SPBP**, the day on which the child dies.[77]

If you qualify for SMP but your job ends before your maternity pay period was due to start, your SMP starts at the beginning of the 11th week before the date your baby is due or, if your job ends after this, on the day after you finish work, unless your baby is born before these dates (in which case it begins the day after the birth).[78]

If you qualify for SAP but your job ends before your adoption pay period was due to start, it starts 14 days before the expected date of placement or, if your job ends after this, on the day after you finish work, unless your child is placed with you before this (in which case it begins on the date of placement).[79]

If you are dismissed while pregnant or in connection with maternity, adoption, paternity, shared parental or parental bereavement leave or pay, get advice about your employment rights urgently.

Stillbirths, multiple births and adoptions

If your baby is stillborn after 24 weeks' pregnancy, SMP and SPP are payable in the same way as for a live birth, so if you have a stillbirth certificate, you can qualify.[80] If the baby is stillborn before you have completed 24 full weeks of pregnancy, this is treated as a miscarriage, and SMP and SPP are not payable. You may, however, qualify for statutory sick pay, employment and support allowance or universal credit. It may be possible to argue that a week for the purposes of this rule means seven days and not the Sunday to Saturday definition used for the employment or earnings conditions (see p819).[81] You should get advice if you are close to 24 weeks and miss out due to the way the weeks are counted.

If the baby is born alive but then dies (even after only a moment), this is a live birth and you can get SMP or SPP, even if it happens before 24 weeks' of pregnancy. Even if SMP has been awarded for the birth, SSPP can only be paid if the child's death occurs after you have given notice to your employer of your intention to claim SSPP.

You may be entitled to SPBP as well as SMP, SPP or SSPP. You can take this in addition as long as you do so within 56 weeks of the stillbirth, and give the required notice (see p816). The 'relevant period' for averaging earnings is different for the death of a child (see p819), but if you are already on SMP when your baby is stillborn, you will usually qualify for SPBP as well, unless your SMP is very low. If you were on SSP in the period before a stillbirth you may not qualify for SPBP but could still qualify for SMP.

If you do qualify for both SMP and SPBP, remember that SMP has to be taken immediately after the stillbirth (unless it has already started). SPBP will need to be taken at some point after the SMP ends, but this does not have to be immediately afterwards (as long as it is within the 56-week period), and you will need to give your employer separate notice for this.

No additional SMP, SAP, SPP or SSPP is payable if you or your partner give birth to more than one baby, or have more than one child placed with you for adoption, unless this happens as part of a different adoption arrangement.[82] You are entitled to SPBP in respect of each child if you satisfy the conditions in respect of the death of more than one child.[83]

If you are adopting a child from abroad

If you are adopting a child from abroad, you may be entitled to SAP, SPP or SSPP. To qualify, you must still satisfy the usual rules of entitlement (see p811, p811 and p814), but with certain modifications.[84] Although you must have 'official notification' that you have been approved for adoption from the UK authorities (sometimes called a 'certificate of eligibility and suitability to adopt'), you will not have been matched with a child for adoption by UK authorities under UK law, and so you will not be able to provide the date of placement or the date of notification of being matched for adoption. You should therefore use Form SC6 (for SAP) or Form SC5 (for SPP), available from gov.uk, to apply for SAP or SPP from your employer for an overseas adoption. At the time of writing, there is no official form for SSPP.

Foster parents approved as adopters

In England, if you are a local authority foster parent who has been approved as a prospective adopter and you are fostering the child in the meantime (sometimes called a 'fostering for adoption' placement), you may qualify for SAP, SPP or SSPP before the actual adoption.[85]

If your baby is born with the help of a surrogate

If you have had a child with the help of a surrogate mother, you may qualify for SAP, SPP or SSPP if:[86]

- you have obtained a parental order from the court; *or*
- on the date of the child's birth you intend to apply for a parental order from the court within six months of the baby's birth, and you expect your application to be successful.

If this applies, your entitlement to SAP, SPP and SSPP can start from the due date or the date of birth of the child, instead of the date of the adoption match or adoption placement. If a child born with the help of a surrogate dies, you may be entitled to SPBP (see p816).

6. Claims

Making a claim

It is not necessary for you to complete a claim form to qualify for statutory maternity pay (SMP), statutory adoption pay (SAP), statutory paternity pay (SPP), statutory shared parental pay (SSPP) or statutory parental bereavement pay (SPBP), but you must give your employer the required notice and evidence with the relevant time limit.

Forms

For SPP, you may use Form SC3 to provide the information and notice to your employer for a birth, or Form SC4 for an adoption. These forms are available from gov.uk/paternity-pay-leave.

Forms to request SSPP and leave are available from gov.uk/shared-parental-leave-and-pay.

Note: it is advisable to use these forms to ensure all the information and notice requirements are met.

Notification sent to your employer in a properly addressed and prepaid letter is treated as having been given on the day it is posted.[87] For SMP, SAP, SPP and SPBP, you should provide notice in writing and supply evidence at the same time, if you are able to do so, or as soon as possible afterwards. For SSPP, you can send notice and information to your employer electronically, if your employer has agreed to this.

Time limits

You must give your employer notice of when you want your SMP, SAP, SPP SSPP or SPBP to start within a certain period of time 'or as soon as reasonably practicable after that'. There is also a time limit for providing the required evidence (which may sometimes be required at the same time as the notice) and this can be extended if there is a 'good cause' for the delay. These terms are not defined – you must show that any delay was reasonable, given your circumstances. If time limits are missed, your employer may not pay you. If you think your employer's decision is wrong, you can challenge it (see Chapter 59).

If your employer has its own maternity, adoption, paternity, shared parental or parental bereavement pay scheme, the notice requirements for this scheme may be different. Check this with your employer.

Who should claim

If you are entitled to SMP, SAP, SPP, SSPP or SPBP but are not well enough to deal with your own affairs, HM Revenue and Customs (HMRC) can appoint someone else to act for you.[88] This person must apply in writing to be your 'appointee' (see p1170). For further information, contact the HMRC helpline (tel: 0300 200 3500; textphone: 0300 200 3519).

If you claim the wrong benefit

In some circumstances where you claim statutory sick pay but you are close to your due date, your employer may be able to start your maternity leave and pay you SMP instead (see p830).

You may get a claim for maternity allowance backdated if your employer has informed you that you are not entitled to SMP (see p735).

7. Getting paid

Statutory maternity pay (SMP), statutory adoption pay (SAP), statutory paternity pay (SPP), statutory shared parental pay (SSPP) and statutory parental bereavement pay (SPBP) are usually paid by your employer in the same way and at the same intervals as your normal wages or salary.[89]

Note:
- If you are also entitled to contractual maternity, adoption, paternity, shared parental or parental bereavement pay (or any other contractual remuneration) from your employer, SMP, SAP, SPP, SSPP or SPBP forms part of your payments. Your employer can offset any payment of SMP, SAP, SPP, SSPP or SPBP from its contractual liability to pay you for the same period.[90]
- Your employer cannot pay you SMP, SAP, SPP, SSPP or SPBP by making a payment in kind, or by providing board and lodging, or by providing a service or some other facility.[91]
- If you become entitled to SMP because of a pay rise, your employer can deduct any maternity allowance (MA) you received for the same period from the SMP you are owed.[92]

Part 5: Other benefits
Chapter 38: Statutory maternity, adoption, paternity and other parental pay
8. Tax, other benefits and the benefit cap

- If your entitlement has been decided by a decision maker from HM Revenue and Customs (HMRC), or by the First-tier or Upper Tribunal, your employer may be required to pay you within a certain time limit (see p1436). If your employer cannot or will not pay you, see p1436 for when payment can be made by HMRC.[93]
- The rules on overpayments described in Chapter 53 do not apply to SMP, SAP, SPP, SSPP or SPBP. If your employer tells you that you have been overpaid SMP, SAP, SPP, SSPP or SPBP, get advice on your entitlement. You may also need debt advice. If your employer decides you have been paid SMP in error, consider claiming MA. You may be able to get this backdated (see p735).
- If your employer becomes insolvent, see p1436.
- For SAP, SSPP and SPBP, HMRC, not your employer, pays you if you are entitled for a period after you were imprisoned or detained, or if you were subsequently released without charge, found not guilty or given a non-custodial sentence (see p937).[94]

Change of circumstances

You must keep your employer informed of any change of circumstances that may affect your entitlement, such as if you start work for someone else while your employer is paying you SMP, SAP, SPP, SSPP or SPBP. For SSPP, you must inform your employer if the person getting SMP, MA or SAP decides to revoke the agreement to end these payments early and continue to receive SMP, MA or SAP, as this means you will not qualify for SSPP.

If you qualify for SMP, SAP, SPP, SSPP or SPBP, your entitlement is not affected if you go abroad.

8. Tax, other benefits and the benefit cap

Tax

Statutory maternity pay (SMP), statutory adoption pay (SAP), statutory paternity pay (SPP), statutory shared parental pay (SSPP) and statutory parental bereavement pay (SPBP) are treated as earnings, and you pay tax and national insurance (NI) contributions as appropriate.[95]

Means-tested benefits and tax credits

If you come under the universal credit (UC) system (see p23), you may qualify for UC as well as SMP, SAP, SPP, SSPP and SPBP.

For UC and contributory employment and support allowance (ESA), in some circumstances you can be treated as having limited capability for work-related activity while pregnant (see p1031).

If you do not come under the UC system and are entitled to SMP, SAP, SPP, SSPP or SPBP:

- being pregnant or on maternity, adoption or paternity leave may allow you to qualify for income support (IS) (see p235). However, most people cannot make new claims for IS;
- you can be treated as having limited capability for work while you are pregnant (see p1012) and so may qualify for income-related ESA. However, most people cannot make new claims for income-related ESA;
- you cannot qualify for income-based jobseeker's allowance (JSA) if you are getting SMP or if you are on adoption, paternity or shared parental leave, because you are treated as being unavailable for work. Your partner may qualify, but most people cannot make new claims for income-based JSA;[96]
- if you are a member of a 'joint-claim couple' for JSA (see p253) and you are pregnant, in some circumstances you do not need to meet all the conditions to qualify and, in some circumstances (including if you get SMP), only your partner needs to claim. However, most people cannot make new claims for income-based JSA;
- in some circumstances, you can be treated as being in full-time work for working tax credit (WTC) (see Chapter 15) while you are getting SMP, SAP, SPP or SSPP (or for some periods when you are on maternity, adoption, paternity or shared parental leave – see p304). You may also qualify for child tax credit (CTC) (see Chapter 14). If you are entitled to WTC, you may be able to get help with the cost of childcare, even before you return to work (see p1460). Most people cannot make new claims for tax credits, but you can start to get CTC if you already get WTC, or WTC if you already get CTC, and you can add children to your tax credit award. It is probable that you can be treated as in full-time work while you are getting SPBP, though this is not confirmed at the time of writing.

When calculating your entitlement to means-tested benefits and tax credits, SMP, SAP, SPP and SSPP are:

- treated as employed earnings for UC;
- treated in full as income for IS and income-based JSA;
- treated as earnings for housing benefit (HB) and pension credit. You may be able to get an allowance for certain childcare charges deducted from your earnings when calculating your entitlement to HB;
- treated as employment income for CTC and WTC. The first £100 of your weekly SMP, SAP, SPP or SSPP is disregarded.

Although not confirmed at the time of writing, it is likely that SPBP will be treated in the same way as SMP, SAP, SPP and SSPP for the purposes of benefits and tax credits.

Part 5: Other benefits
Chapter 38: Statutory maternity, adoption, paternity and other parental pay
8. Tax, other benefits and the benefit cap

Non-means-tested benefits

If you come under the UC system, provided you do not have limited capability for work and are not treated as having limited capability for work (but see p705), you may qualify for contribution-based JSA while getting SMP, SAP, SPP, SSPP or SPBP. As you must accept a claimant commitment to qualify for JSA, get advice before claiming if you are still employed – the DWP may contact your employer and this may jeopardise your employment. If you do not come under the UC system, you cannot get contribution-based JSA if you are receiving SMP or if you are on adoption, paternity or shared parental leave, as you are treated as being unavailable for work. It is likely that SPBP or parental bereavement leave would have the same effect.

You cannot get statutory sick pay (SSP) when you are receiving SMP. If you are sick with a pregnancy-related illness (or an existing condition made worse by your pregnancy) in the four weeks before the week your baby is due, your employer can start your maternity leave (even if it is sooner than you had planned) and pay you SMP rather than SSP. It cannot do this if your illness is *not* pregnancy related.

You cannot receive SAP, SPP, SSPP or SPBP for any week in which you are entitled to SSP.[97]

If you get SMP, you cannot also get maternity allowance (MA) for the same period in respect of the same pregnancy.[98]

If you are getting SMP, SAP or SSPP, you may qualify for NI credits (see p976). It may be important to claim credits in order to protect your future entitlement to contributory benefits, such as state pension.

Contributory employment and support allowance

You can qualify for contributory ESA as well as SPP if you satisfy the conditions for contributory ESA during your paternity pay period.

You can also qualify for contributory ESA while you are getting SMP, SAP or SSPP if you satisfy the NI contribution conditions and had limited capability for work (or you could be treated as having limited capability for work) on the day before your statutory payments started.[99]

However, your contributory ESA is reduced by the amount of SMP, SAP or SSPP you receive for the same week.

In some circumstances, if you are pregnant or have recently given birth, you can be treated as having limited capability for work or as having limited capability for work-related activity if you are pregnant (see p1011 and p1031).

The benefit cap

In some cases, there is a limit on the total amount of specified benefits you can receive (a 'benefit cap'). SMP, SAP, SPP, SSPP and SPBP are *not* specified benefits.

The benefit cap only applies if you are getting UC or HB. See p1194 for further information.

Other sources of help

For details of:

- in England and Wales, Sure Start maternity grants, see p796. In Scotland, Sure Start grants have been replaced with Best Start grants (see Chapter 72). In some circumstances, you may qualify for a maternity grant even if you are not the mother of the child. You do not have to be a person who has given birth to a child to qualify for these grants;
- in England and Wales, funeral expenses payments, see p798. In Scotland, funeral support payments, see p1703;
- free prescriptions and free NHS dental treatment, see Chapter 31;
- Healthy Start food vouchers and vitamins, see p862. In Scotland, new claims should be made to the Best Start foods scheme (see p865);
- council tax reduction, see p851;
- tax-free childcare, see p871.

Notes

1. Who can get a payment
1 s164(2)(a) SSCBA 1992
2 s164(2)(b) SSCBA 1992
3 s165 SSCBA 1992; reg 2 SMP Regs
4 s164(4) and (5) SSCBA 1992
5 Reg 22 SMP Regs
6 Reg 2 SMP Regs
7 Reg 23 SMP Regs
8 s171ZL(2)(b) and (3) SSCBA 1992
9 ss171ZL(2)(d) and 171ZS(6)-(8) SSCBA 1992
10 s171ZN(2) SSCBA 1992; reg 21 SPPSAP(G) Regs
11 s171ZL(6) and (7) SSCBA 1992; regs 23 and 24 SPPSAP(G) Regs
12 Regs 21 and 23 SPPSAP(G) Regs
13 Reg 22 SPPSAP(G) Regs
14 s171ZA(2)(a) SSCBA 1992; reg 4 SPPSAP(G) Regs
15 s171ZB(2)(a) SSCBA 1992; reg 11 SPPSAP(G) Regs
16 s171ZA(2)(b) and (3) SSCBA 1992
17 s171ZB(2)(b) and (3) SSCBA 1992

18 **Father/mother's partner**
ss171ZA(2)(c) and 171ZJ(6)-(8) SSCBA 1992
Adopter/adopter's partner
ss171ZB(2)(c) and 171ZJ(6)-(8) SSCBA 1992
19 **Father/mother's partner** s171ZE(2) SSCBA 1992; reg 6 SPPSAP(G) Regs
Adopter/adopter's partner
s171ZE(2) SSCBA 1992; reg 12 SPPSAP(G) Regs
20 s171ZC(1) and (3)(c) SSCBA 1992; reg 9 SPPSAP(G) Regs
21 s171ZC(1) and (3)(c) SSCBA 1992; reg 15 SPPSAP(G) Regs
22 Regs 6 and 7 SPPSAP(G) Regs
23 Regs 12 and 13 SPPSAP(G) Regs
24 Regs 7(2)(b), (3) and (6) and 12(2)(c) and (5) SMP&SAP(C) Regs
25 Regs 8 and 13 SMP&SAP(C) Regs

26 **Father/mother's partner**
s171ZU(4)(d) and (g) SSCBA 1992; reg
30 SSPP(G) Regs
Mother s171ZU(2)(c) and (f) SSCBA
1992; reg 30 SSPP(G) Regs

27 **Adopter** s171ZV(2)(c) and (f) SSCBA
1992; reg 31 SSPP(G) Regs
Adopter's partner s171ZV(4)(d) and
(g) SSCBA 1992; reg 31 SSPP(G) Regs

28 **Father/mother's partner**
ss171ZU(4)(f) and 171ZZ4(6)-(8)
SSCBA 1992; reg 30 SSPP(G) Regs
Mother ss171ZU(2)(e) and 171ZZ4(6)-
(8) SSCBA 1992; reg 30 SSPP(G) Regs
Adopter ss171ZV(2)(e) and
171ZZ4(6)-(8) SSCBA 1992; reg 31
SSPP(G) Regs
Adopter's partner ss171ZV(4)(f) and
171ZZ4(6)-(8) SSCBA 1992; reg 31
SSPP(G) Regs

29 **Father/mother's partner/mother**
Reg 10 SSPP(G) Regs
Adopter/adopter's partner Reg 22
SSPP(G) Regs

30 **Father/mother's partner** Regs 5 and
7 SMP&SAP(C) Regs
Adopter's partner Regs 10 and 12
SMP&SAP(C) Regs

31 **Mother** Regs 4 and 7 SMP&SAP(C)
Regs
Adopter Regs 9 and 12 SMP&SAP(C)
Regs

32 **Father/mother's partner**
ss171ZU(4)(j)-(p) and 171ZW(1)(b)
SSCBA 1992; reg 7 SSPP(G) Regs
Adopter's partner ss171ZV(4)(j)-(p)
and 171ZW(1)(b) SSCBA 1992; reg 20
SSPP(G) Regs
Mother ss171ZU(2)(i)-(o) and
171ZW(1)(b) SSCBA 1992; reg 6
SSPP(G) Regs
Adopter ss171ZV(2)(i)-(o) and
171ZW(1)(b) SSCBA 1992; reg 19
SSPP(G) Regs

33 Regs 4(1) and (3), 17(1) and (3) and 29
SSPP(G) Regs

34 Reg 2 SPBP(G) Regs

35 ss171ZZ6 and 171ZZ7 SSCBA 1992

36 Reg 4 SPBP(G) Regs

37 Reg 4(1)(g) and (8)(b), (c) and (d)
SPBP(G) Regs

38 s171ZZ6(6) SSCBA 1992

39 Reg 7 SPBP(G) Regs

40 Reg 8(1) SPBP(G) Regs

41 Reg 8(2), (3), (4) and (5) SPBP(G) Regs

42 Reg 8(6), (7), (8) and (9) SPBP(G) Regs

43 **SMP** s171(1) SSCBA 1992; reg 17 SMP
Regs
SAP&SPP ss171ZJ(1) and (2) and
171ZS(1) and (2) SSCBA 1992; reg 32
SPPSAP(G) Regs
SSPP s171ZZ4(1) SSCBA 1992; reg 33
SSPP(G) Regs
SPBP s171ZZ8(1) SSCBA 1992; reg 11
SPBP(G) Regs

44 **SMP** Reg 17 SMP Regs
SAP&SPP Reg 32 SPPSAP(G) Regs
SSPP Reg 33 SSPP(G) Regs
SPBP Reg 11 SPBP(G) Regs

45 **SMP** Reg 17(2) SMP Regs
SAP&SPP Reg 32 SPPSAP(G) Regs
SSPP Reg 33(4) SSPP(G) Regs
SPBP Reg 114) SPBP(G) Regs

46 **SMP** Regs 2 and 5 SMP(PAM) Regs
SAP&SPP Regs 3, 5 and 6
SPPSAP(PAM) Regs
SSPP Regs 5 and 7 SSPP(PAM) Regs

47 **SMP** Reg 4(2)(a) SMP Regs
SAP&SPP Reg 5(a) SPPSAP(G) Regs
SSPP Reg 30(2) and (3) SSPP(G) Regs

48 Reg 15 SPBP(G) Regs

49 **SMP** Reg 11 SMP Regs
SAP&SPP Reg 33 SPPSAP(G) Regs
SSPP Reg 34 SSPP(G) Regs
SPBP Reg 12 SPBP(G) Regs

50 Reg 11(1)(d) and (3) SMP Regs

51 **SMP** Reg 11(3A) SMP Regs
SAP&SPP Reg 33(3) SPPSAP(G) Regs
SSPP Reg 34(4) SSPP(G) Regs
SPBP Reg 11(4) SPBP(G) Regs

52 **SMP** Reg 14 SMP Regs
SAP&SPP Reg 36 SPPSAP(G) Regs
SSPP Reg 37 SSPP(G) Regs
SPBP Reg 16 SPBP(G) Regs

53 **SMP** Reg 12 SMP Regs
SAP&SPP Reg 34 SPPSAP(G) Regs
SSPP Reg 35 SSPP(G) Regs
SPBP Reg 13 SPBP(G) Regs

54 **SMP** Reg 20 SMP Regs
SAP&SPP Reg 39 SPPSAP(G) Regs
SSPP Reg 32(7) and (8) SSPP(G) Regs
SPBP Reg 19 SPBP(G) Regs

55 **SMP** Reg 20(2)(a) SMP Regs
SAP&SPP Reg 39(2)(a) SPPSAP(G) Regs
SSPP Reg 32(7)(a) SSPP(G) Regs
SPBP Reg 19(2) SPBP(G) Regs

56 **SMP** Reg 21(5) SMP Regs
SAP&SPP Reg 40(5) SPPSAP(G) Regs
SSPP Reg 32(4) SSPP(G) Regs
SPBP Reg 19(6) SPBP(G) Regs

57 Reg 21(7) SMP Regs

58 Reg 21B SMP Regs

59 **SAP&SPP** Reg 40(7) SPPSAP(G) Regs
    SSPP Reg 32(6) SSPP(G) Regs
    SPBP Reg 19(8) SPBP(G) Regs
60 **SMP** s165(4) and (5) SSCBA 1992; reg
    9A SMP Regs
    SAP s171ZN(3) and (4) SSCBA 1992;
    reg 27A SPPSAP(G) Regs
    SSPP Regs 4(2)(g), 5(2)(e), 12, 15,
    17(2)(g), 18(2)(e), 24, 27 SSPP(G) Regs
61 s171ZE(5) and (6) SSCBA 1992
62 s171ZZ9(6) SSCBA 1992
63 Regs 10(1)(a)(i) and 22(1)(a)(i) SSPP(G)
    Regs
64 ss171ZU(2)(n) and (o) and (4)(o) and
    (p) and 171ZV(2)(n) and (o) and (4)(o)
    and (p) SSCBA 1992; regs 10(7) and (8)
    and 22(5) and (6) SSPP(G) Regs
65 **SMP** s165(6) SSCBA 1992; reg 8(2)
    SMP Regs
    SAP s171ZN(5) SSCBA 1992; reg 26(1)
    SPPSAP(G) Regs
    SPP s171ZE(7) SSCBA 1992; reg 17(1)
    SPPSAP(G) Regs
    SSPP ss171ZU(2)(n) and (4)(o),
    171ZV(2)(n) and (4)(o) and 171ZY(4)
    SSCBA 1992; regs 12, 15, 24 and 27
    SSPP(G) Regs
66 s165(6) SSCBA 1992
67 **SMP** Reg 8(1) SMP Regs
    SAP Reg 25 SPPSAP(G) Regs
    SPP Regs 10 and 16 SPPSAP(G) Regs
    SPP Regs 12, 15, 24 and 27 SSPP(G)
    Regs
    SPBP Reg 10 SPBP(G) Regs
68 **SMP** Reg 24 SMP Regs
    SAP Reg 26(2) and (3) SPPSAP(G) Regs
    SPP Reg 17(2) and (3) SPPSAP(G) Regs
    SSPP Regs 12(2) and (3) and 24(2) and
    (3) SSPP(G) Regs
    SPBP Reg 10 (2) and (3) SPBP(G) Regs

5. Special benefit rules

69 **SMP** s164(2)(a) and (3) SSCBA 1992
    SAP s171ZM SSCBA 1992
    SPP s171ZD SSCBA 1992
    SSPP s171ZX SSCBA 1992
70 **SMP** s164(8) SSCBA 1992; reg 3(1)
    SMP Regs
    SAP s171ZM(2) SSCBA 1992; reg 30
    SPPSAP(G) Regs
    SPP s171ZD(2) SSCBA 1992; reg 20
    SPPSAP(G) Regs
    SPBP Reg 22 SPBP(G) Regs
71 s171ZX(2) SSCBA 1992; reg 42 SSPP(G)
    Regs
72 s164(2)(a) SSCBA 1992
73 s171ZL(2)(b) and (3) SSCBA 1992
74 s171ZA(2)(b) and (d) SSCBA 1992

75 s171ZB(2)(b) and (d) SSCBA 1992
76 Regs 30(2)(a) and (c) and 31(2)(a) and
    (c) SSPP(G) Regs
77 s171ZZ6(2)(e) SSCBA 1992
78 s165(2) SSCBA 1992; reg 2(3) and (5)
    SMP Regs
79 Reg 29 SPPSAP(G) Regs
80 **SMP, SAP, SPP, SSPP** s171(1) SSCBA
    1992
    s171ZA(5) SSCBA 1992
81 para 62025 DMG. This guidance relates
    to MA but it is arguable that a similar
    approach could be taken for SMP.
82 **SMP** s171(1) SSCBA 1992
    SAP s171ZL(5) SSCBA 1992
    SPP ss171ZA(4) and 171ZB(6) SSCBA
    1992
    SSPP ss171ZU(16) and 171ZV(16)
    SSCBA 1992
83 s171ZZ6(6) SSCBA 1992
84 SSCBA(AAO) Regs;
    SPP(A)&SAP(AO)(No.2) Regs; Statutory
    Paternity Pay (Adoption) and Statutory
    Adoption Pay (Adoption from Overseas)
    (Administration) Regulations 2003,
    No.1192; Statutory Shared Parental Pay
    (Adoptions from Overseas) Regulations
    2014, No.3093
85 Reg 2(2)(c) and (d), (3) and (4)
    SPPSAP(G) Regs; reg 2 SSPP(G) Regs
86 **SPP** ss171ZA, 171ZB and 171ZE SSCBA
    1992; SPPSAP(G) Regs
    SAP ss171ZL and 171ZN SSCBA 1992;
    SPPSAP(G) Regs
    SSPP s171ZV SSCBA 1992; SSPP(G)
    Regs

6. Claims

87 **SMP** Regs 22(4) and 23(3) SMP Regs
    SAP&SPP Reg 47 SPPSAP(G) Regs
    SSPP Reg 49(3)(b) SSPP(G) Regs
88 **SMP** Reg 31 SMP Regs
    SAP&SPP Reg 46 SPPSAP(G) Regs
    SSPP Reg 48 SSPP(G) Regs
    SPBP Reg 28 SPBP(G) Regs

7. Getting paid

89 **SMP** Reg 27 SMP Regs
    SAP&SPP Reg 41 SPPSAP(G) Regs
    SSPP Reg 43 SSPP(G) Regs
    SPBP Reg 23 SPBP(G) Regs
90 **SMP** Sch 13 para 3 SSCBA 1992
    SAP s171ZP(5) SSCBA 1992
    SPP s171ZG(2) SSCBA 1992
    SSPP s171ZZ1 SSCBA 1992
    SPBP s171ZZ11 SSCBA 1992 and reg
    21 SPBP(G) Regs

91 **SMP** Reg 27 SMP Regs
   SAP&SPP Reg 41 SPPSAP(G) Regs
   SSPP Reg 43 SSPP(G) Regs
   SPBP Reg 23 SPBP(G) Regs
92 Reg 21B SMP Regs
93 **SAP** Reg 44 SPPSAP(G) Regs
   SSPP Reg 46 SSPP(G) Regs
   SPBP Reg 24 SPBP(G) Regs
94 **SAP** Reg 44 SPPSAP(G) Regs
   SSPP Reg 46 SSPP(G) Regs
   SPBP Reg 26 SPBP(G) Regs

8. Tax, other benefits and the benefit cap
95 s4(1)(a)(ii)-(vii) SSCBA 1992
96 Reg 15(bc) and (c) JSA Regs
97 **SAP** Reg 27(1)(a) SPPSAP(G) Regs
   SPP Reg 18(a) SPPSAP(G) Regs
   SSPP Regs 14(1)(a) and 26(1)(a)
   SSPP(G) Regs
   SPBP Reg 9(1)(a) SPBP(G) Regs
98 s35(1)(d) SSCBA 1992
99 s20(2)-(5), (6) and (7) WRA 2007; regs
   80, 81, 82A ESA Regs; regs 73, 74 and
   75A ESA Regs 2013

Chapter 39

Statutory sick pay

This chapter covers:
1. Who can get statutory sick pay (below)
2. The rules about your age (p841)
3. People included in the claim (p841)
4. The amount of benefit (p842)
5. Special benefit rules (p843)
6. Claims and backdating (p844)
7. Getting paid (p846)
8. Tax, other benefits and the benefit cap (p847)

Key facts

- Statutory sick pay (SSP) is paid by employers to certain employees who are unfit for work.
- SSP can be paid for up to 28 weeks.
- SSP is a non-means-tested benefit.
- Your entitlement to SSP is not based on your national insurance contribution record, but your usual earnings must be above a certain amount to qualify.
- If you qualify, SSP is the minimum amount your employer should pay while you are sick. You may be entitled to more under your contract.
- If you disagree with your employer's decision on your entitlement to SSP, or if your employer has failed to make a decision, you can challenge this (see Chapter 59).

Future changes

The government has said it is proposing to extend statutory sick pay to those earning less than the lower earnings limit (see p839) and to make it more flexible so that it would also be payable to those on a phased return to work. See AskCPAG.org.uk and CPAG's *Welfare Rights Bulletin* for updates.

Part 5: Other benefits
Chapter 39: Statutory sick pay
1. Who can get statutory sick pay

1. **Who can get statutory sick pay**

You qualify for statutory sick pay (SSP) if:[1]

- you are an employee (see below); *and*
- you are incapable of work (see below); *and*
- you are within a period of incapacity for work (see p838); *and*
- you are within your period of entitlement to SSP (see p838); *and*
- the day is a qualifying day (see p840); *and*
- your normal earnings are at least the lower earnings limit for national insurance (NI) contributions (see p839).

There are some groups of people to whom special rules apply (see p843). Certain people do not qualify for SSP (see p839). See below if your employer has dismissed you solely or mainly to avoid paying SSP.

Employees

To be entitled to SSP you must be an employee. If you count as an 'employed earner' for NI purposes (see p962), or you would do so but for being under 16, you normally count as an employee for SSP purposes – eg, you may count as an employee if you are an agency worker.

You do not have to have a written contract of employment. It is the fact that you are employed that matters. Your right to SSP cannot be taken away by any document, whether you sign it or not. If your employer dismisses you to avoid paying SSP, see below.[2]

Even if you are an employee, you are treated as if you are not (and so your employer does not have to pay you SSP) if your employer is:[3]

- not resident and not present in Great Britain, and does not have a place of business in Great Britain (and is not treated as having one); *or*
- exempt from social security legislation because of an international treaty.

Dismissal from work

If your employer dismisses you during your period of entitlement to SSP solely or mainly to avoid paying you SSP, it is still liable to pay you SSP. In these circumstances, your employer should continue to pay you SSP until either your period of entitlement to SSP ends or until your contract would have ended had you not been dismissed, whichever occurs first.[4] If your employer dismisses you for another reason (ie, not solely or mainly to avoid paying you SSP), you are not normally entitled to SSP from that employer once your contract ends.

Incapable of work

To qualify for SSP, you must be 'incapable of work'. This has a specific meaning for SSP. Other tests, such as that of 'limited capability for work' described in Chapter 45, do not apply to SSP.

To be 'incapable of work' for SSP purposes, you must be:[5]
- incapable of doing work that you could reasonably be expected to do under the terms of your contract because you have a specific disease, or a physical or mental disability; *or*
- treated as incapable of such work (see below).

Usually, after seven days of absence your employer expects you to provide a medical certificate (a 'fit note') from a doctor. During the coronavirus pandemic, you may be able to get an 'isolation note' instead.

On the medical certificate your doctor can state either that you are not fit for work, or that you 'may be fit for work taking account of the following advice'. These statements are not related to your specific job. If your doctor thinks you may be fit for some work, s/he can include a description of the effects of your condition on your ability to work and specify whether s/he thinks you may benefit from a phased return to work, altered hours, amended duties or workplace adaptations to facilitate your return to work.[6]

Does your employer doubt your incapacity for work?

1. It is up to your employer to decide whether it accepts that you are incapable of work. If it does not, it does not pay you SSP, although you can challenge its decision.

2. Your employer can get further advice. It may consult its own medical officer (if it has one), your doctor (with your permission) or HM Revenue and Customs (HMRC).

3. If the matter is not resolved and your employer consults HMRC, HMRC may involve its Medical Service (MS) and, with your permission, the MS may contact your doctor to arrange for you to have a medical examination with an MS doctor (or other healthcare professional). Your employer is then given only the MS's view on whether you are fit for work in the job you do. It is still your employer's decision whether or not to pay you SSP.

4. If your employer refuses to pay you SSP, ask HMRC to make a decision (see Chapter 59).

Treated as incapable of work

Even if you are not actually incapable of work, your employer may treat you as incapable of work if:[7]
- you have been officially excluded or prevented from working because you have (or it is suspected that you have) an infection, disease or contamination detailed under public health legislation, or you have been in contact with someone who has; *or*
- you are under medical care in connection with a specific disease or physical or mental disability; *and*
  - a doctor has stated that you should not work as a precautionary measure or in order to convalesce; *and*
  - you do not go in to work for your employer; *or*
- during the coronavirus pandemic, you have been advised to self-isolate, or you are caring for a person with symptoms and has been told to self-isolate.

Part 5: Other benefits
Chapter 39: Statutory sick pay
1. Who can get statutory sick pay

If you are incapable of work for just part of a day, you must be treated as incapable of work for the whole day provided you do not do any work on that day. If you are a shift worker and you are incapable of work for part of a day but you do some work on that day, you should still be treated as incapable of work for the whole day if you only finish a shift that began the day before and you do not do any work on a shift that starts on that day and ends the next.

Period of incapacity for work

For SSP to be paid, you must be within a 'period of incapacity for work'.[8] This is defined as four or more consecutive days of incapacity for work (see p836). This means that you can only qualify for SSP if you are incapable of work for at least four days in a row. Every day of the week (including Sunday) counts, even if it is not a day on which you would normally work. Days of incapacity for work that fall before or after the period covered by your contract can still be included in your period of incapacity for work (but see p840 if you have not yet started work).

Two or more periods of incapacity for work are 'linked' and treated as a single period if they are separated by eight weeks or less.

Period of entitlement to statutory sick pay

You only qualify for SSP if you are within 'a period of entitlement'. In certain circumstances, a period of entitlement cannot arise and so you do not qualify for SSP (see p839).

When entitlement to statutory sick pay starts

A period of entitlement normally starts on the first day of your period of incapacity for work, unless your contract of employment starts either during your period of incapacity for work or between two linked periods (see below).[9]

When entitlement to statutory sick pay ends

A period of entitlement to SSP ends (and so your SSP stops) if:[10]

- your period of incapacity for work ends; *or*
- you reach your maximum 28 weeks' entitlement to SSP from a particular employer (see p842); *or*
- your contract of employment ends (unless it has been brought to an end by your employer solely or mainly to avoid paying SSP – see p836); *or*
- in some circumstances, you are pregnant or have just had a baby (see p843); *or*
- you reach the third anniversary of the start of the period of entitlement; *or*
- you are in prison or detained in legal custody (see p937).

Two or more periods of incapacity for work that are separated by eight weeks or less are linked and treated as a single period.[11] It may therefore be possible for you to have a period of entitlement which lasts for three years and not to have exhausted your 28 weeks' entitlement to SSP over that period.

If you have received your maximum 28 weeks' entitlement to SSP from a particular employer and you are still incapable of work, see p842.

If your employer stops paying you SSP because it decides your period of entitlement has ended, see p846.

When statutory sick pay is not paid

In certain circumstances, a period of entitlement to SSP cannot arise. As a result, you do not qualify for any SSP during your period of incapacity for work.

A period of entitlement cannot arise if:[12]

- your normal weekly earnings are below the lower earnings limit (see below); *or*
- at some time in the 85 days before the date on which your period of entitlement would have begun you were entitled to employment and support allowance (ESA) or, in some circumstances, you would have been entitled. For this to apply, you must have claimed ESA (or made a claim for another benefit that was treated as a claim for ESA). If you have limited capability for work, you may qualify for universal credit (UC) and/or ESA instead of SSP; *or*
- at the time when your period of entitlement would have begun there is a strike at your workplace (but see p1004); *or*
- you have not yet started work under your contract of employment (but see p840 if you had an earlier contract with the same employer); *or*
- you are in prison or legal custody (see p937); *or*
- at the time when your period of entitlement would have begun, you were entitled to statutory maternity pay (SMP) or, in some circumstances, maternity allowance (see p843); *or*
- you are within the period immediately before or after you give birth (see p843).

If your employer decides not to pay you SSP on any of the above grounds, see p846.

Note: if you qualified for either incapacity benefit or severe disablement allowance in the 57 days before your period of entitlement to SSP would have started, you may not qualify for SSP. Instead, if you have limited capability for work, you may qualify for UC and/or ESA. See p619 of the 2012/13 edition of this *Handbook* for details.

People with low earnings

You cannot get SSP if your 'normal weekly earnings' are less than the lower earnings limit for NI contributions (£120 a week in 2020/21 – see p962).

Your **'normal weekly earnings'** are calculated by averaging your gross earnings from your employer (ie, before tax and NI contributions are deducted) over the period between:[13]

Part 5: Other benefits
Chapter 39: Statutory sick pay
1. Who can get statutory sick pay

- your last normal payday before your period of entitlement to SSP began (see below); *and*
- the day after the last normal payday that falls at least eight weeks before this.

Only payments actually made in this period count, even if, in theory, you should have been paid more.[14] However, if your employer has unlawfully withheld *all* of your wages for the period over which your earnings are averaged, you should not be excluded from entitlement to SSP on the basis that you have low earnings if you otherwise would have qualified.[15]

If you are paid every one or more calendar months, your average earnings are calculated by dividing your earnings over the above period by the number of calendar months in the period (to the nearest whole number), multiplying by 12 and dividing by 52. If you are paid at other intervals and the period is not an exact number of weeks, the average is calculated by dividing your earnings by the number of days in the above period and multiplying by seven.

As well as your wages, your gross earnings include payments such as:[16]
- SSP, SMP, statutory adoption pay, statutory paternity pay, statutory shared parental pay and statutory parental bereavement pay;
- maternity pay;
- arrears of pay following reinstatement or re-engagement in your job or a continuation of a contract of employment under particular legislation.

Certain payments (eg, some payments in kind) are ignored.[17]

There are special rules to calculate your earnings if you have not been employed sufficiently long to have been paid wages over this eight-week period.[18]

See p842 if you have more than one job.

People who have not yet started work

If you have agreed to work for an employer but have not started work when your period of incapacity for work begins, you are not entitled to SSP from that employer for any day during your period of incapacity for work, unless your current contract of employment can be linked to a previous one with the same employer. Your employment is linked if there are eight weeks or less between the date your new contract starts and the date your last contract with the employer ended.[19] You do not have to have written contracts for this to apply.

Qualifying days

You can only be entitled to SSP for 'qualifying days'. SSP is not paid for your first three qualifying days, which are known as 'waiting days' (see p841).[20] **Note:** at the time of writing, the government announced plans for workers self-isolating due to the coronavirus to be paid SSP from their first day off work – ie, with no waiting days.[21] This will be a temporary measure. See AskCPAG.org.uk and CPAG's *Welfare Rights Bulletin* for updates.

Qualifying days are usually those days of the week on which you normally work. Other days may be selected as qualifying days by agreement between you and your employer if they would better reflect your contract of employment – eg, if you work a complicated shift pattern. For this purpose, a week begins on Sunday and there must be a minimum of one qualifying day in each week.[22]

If you and your employer cannot agree which days are qualifying days, they are presumed to be:[23]

- the days on which it is agreed that you are required to work; *or*
- Wednesday, if it is agreed that you are not required to work on any day in that week – eg, offshore oil workers, who may work two weeks 'on' and then two weeks 'off'; *or*
- if you cannot agree about which days you are or are not required to work, every day in the week, except days on which you and your employer agree that no employee works.

Required to work
'**Required to work**' means required by the terms of your contract of employment.[24] Days when you can choose whether or not to work do not count – eg, voluntary overtime shifts.

Waiting days

SSP is not paid for the first three qualifying days in a period of entitlement.[25] These are called '**waiting days**' and, as they must be qualifying days, they are not necessarily the first three days of your sickness.

If your period of incapacity for work can be linked to an earlier one in your period of entitlement with the same employer (see p838), any waiting days you served in the earlier linked period(s) do not have to be served again and you can get SSP from your first qualifying day in your present one.

2. The rules about your age

There are no lower or upper age limits for entitlement to statutory sick pay.

3. People included in the claim

You claim statutory sick pay for yourself. You cannot claim any increases for your partner or child(ren).

Part 5: Other benefits
Chapter 39: Statutory sick pay
4. The amount of benefit

4. **The amount of benefit**

Statutory sick pay (SSP) is not paid for the first three qualifying days in a period of entitlement (see p841). After that, it is payable at a rate of £95.85 a week. If you qualify, the weekly amount of SSP is the same irrespective of the number of hours you normally work for your employer each week when you are not sick.[26]

SSP is a daily benefit so it can be paid for periods of less than a week. The daily rate is calculated by dividing the weekly amount by the number of qualifying days you have in that week. A week for these purposes runs from Sunday to Saturday.

Example

Zofia is employed in a shop and works four days a week (Wednesday to Saturday). These are her qualifying days. After injuring her hand, she is incapable of work for just over two weeks. In the week of her injury, she works on Wednesday and is off sick for the rest of the week. Her period of entitlement to SSP begins on Thursday, the first day of her absence, but she is not entitled to SSP for that week as the first three qualifying days in her period of entitlement (Thursday to Saturday) are waiting days. As she is incapable of work for all her qualifying days in the next week she gets £95.85 SSP. In the following week, she is off sick on Wednesday, Thursday and Friday and returns to work on Saturday. She receives £71.89 SSP (£95.85 divided by her four qualifying days to give a daily rate paid for three days).

People with more than one job

If you cannot work, you are entitled to SSP from any job for which you fulfil the qualifying conditions. So, you can get payments of SSP from two different employers or payments for more than one contract with the same employer – eg, if you are both a daytime teacher and an evening tutor with a local authority. However, if your earnings from any of your different jobs are added together when calculating your liability to pay class 1 national insurance contributions (which usually means you contribute less than if they had been treated separately), you can only receive a total of £95.85 a week from those jobs. In these circumstances, your employers' liability to pay you SSP is apportioned by agreement between them or, if they cannot agree, in proportion to their share of your combined earnings.[27]

It is possible for you to be unable to work on one contract and be entitled to SSP, but be able to work on a different contract – eg, if you perform different tasks for each.

Maximum entitlement to statutory sick pay

You are entitled to a maximum of 28 weeks of SSP from a particular employer in any one period of entitlement (see p838) – ie, 28 times the weekly rate of SSP.[28]

Once you have reached your maximum 28 weeks' entitlement with a particular employer, you cannot qualify for SSP again from that employer for the same contract until your current period of incapacity for work ends and a new one arises. Previous periods of incapacity for work are linked to your current one if they are separated by eight weeks or less.[29] However, see p839 if you got employment and support allowance (ESA) in the intervening period.

If you are still incapable of work after you have received your 28-week entitlement to SSP, consider claiming ESA and/or universal credit if you are not already claiming it (see Chapters 3, 9 and 30).

5. **Special benefit rules**

Special rules may apply to:
- people who are going abroad (see p1661);
- women who are pregnant or who have recently given birth (see below);
- people involved in a trade dispute (see p1001) and people in prison or detention (see p937).

Women who are pregnant or who have recently given birth

If you are entitled to statutory maternity pay (SMP – see p811), you cannot get statutory sick pay (SSP) during the maternity pay period. If you are entitled to maternity allowance (MA) on the basis of your own employment or self-employment (see p725), you cannot get SSP during the MA period.[30] Within the limits set out on p728 and p811 (and unless your baby is born early), you can choose when your maternity pay or MA period begins. So, for example, your employer cannot insist that you claim SMP or MA at the earliest possible date in order to limit the period for which it has to pay SSP.

Even if you are not entitled to SMP or MA, or if you are entitled to MA on the basis that you have helped your spouse or civil partner with her/his self-employment (see p726):[31]
- you cannot get SSP (because a period of entitlement cannot arise) if your period of incapacity for work started at some time during the 18 weeks which run from the first of the following dates:
  - the beginning of the week in which you had your baby (but see below); *or*
  - if you are incapable of work either wholly or partly because of your pregnancy on a day that falls in the four weeks before your 'expected week of childbirth', the beginning of the week that contains the first such day;
- if SSP is already being paid to you (because your period of entitlement started before the above period, or because your incapacity for work was not initially linked to your pregnancy), it stops from the first of the following dates:[32]

Part 5: Other benefits
Chapter 39: Statutory sick pay
6. Claims and backdating

- the first day falling on or after the beginning of the fourth week before your expected week of childbirth when you are incapable of work wholly or partly because of your pregnancy; *or*
- the date on which you have your baby.

For the above purposes, a week begins on a Sunday. If your baby is stillborn before you have completed 24 weeks of pregnancy, you qualify for SSP if you satisfy the other conditions of entitlement.

6. **Claims and backdating**

To qualify for statutory sick pay (SSP), you must notify your employer of your incapacity for work, rather than notifying the DWP or HM Revenue and Customs (HMRC).

Making a claim

You do not need to complete a claim form to qualify for SSP – just inform your employer that you are sick (see below). Your employer should then decide whether you are entitled to SSP.

Telling your employer that you are sick

Your employer can decide the time limit by when it wants to be notified of your sickness absence and the way in which it should be told. Your employer must take reasonable steps to inform you of how and when it wants to be notified of your absence. However, for SSP purposes, your employer cannot insist that you notify it of your sickness:[33]

- earlier than the first qualifying day (which is not necessarily your first day of sickness – see p840), or by a specific time on the first qualifying day;
- personally;
- by providing medical evidence;
- more than once a week;
- on a printed form or other document it provides.

Time limits

The following time limits apply for notifying your employer.[34]

- You must notify your employer of your incapacity for work within the time limit set by your employer, if it has taken reasonable steps to inform you of this (unless it requires you to give notice earlier than the first qualifying day).
- If your employer has not taken reasonable steps to inform you, or if it has made no arrangements about the notification it requires, you must notify your employer of your incapacity for work in writing on or before the seventh day after your first qualifying day (see p840).

- This seven-day time limit, or your employer's time limit, can be extended by one month if you have good cause for the delay. What is 'good cause' is not defined in the regulations, but you must show that your delay was reasonable given the circumstances.
- If it is not practical for you to inform your employer within that time, the time limit can be extended further, provided you have notified it as soon as is reasonably practicable and you have notified it on or before the 91st day after your first qualifying day.

Notice sent in a properly addressed pre-paid letter is treated as having been given on the day it was posted. If you do not notify your employer of your absence within the above time limits, you can still be entitled to SSP (and qualify for a total of 28 weeks' payment in your period of entitlement if you are off work for that long), but your entitlement starts from a later date.[35]

Information to support your claim

Your employer can require you to provide 'such information as may reasonably be required' to determine your claim for SSP.[36]

Medical evidence

For the first seven days of your incapacity for work you are only required to provide a self-certificate as evidence of your incapacity for work. Your employer cannot insist on your obtaining a medical certificate.[37] After the first seven days, employers usually expect you to provide a medical certificate from a doctor. During the coronavirus pandemic, you may be able to get your own 'isolation note' instead. If you provide a certificate from someone else, such as an osteopath or chiropractor, this can be accepted if your employer considers it sufficient.[38] Whatever type of medical evidence you provide, it is up to your employer to decide whether or not to accept it. See Chapter 59 if you want to challenge your employer's decision. See p837 for information on evidence of your incapacity for work.

Who should claim

As your employer cannot insist that you personally notify it of your incapacity for work, someone else can notify your employer on your behalf.

If you cannot deal with your own affairs, HMRC can appoint someone else to act for you (an 'appointee' – see p1170). For further information, contact the HMRC helpline (tel: 0300 200 3500; textphone: 0300 200 3519).

If you claim the wrong benefit

A claim for another benefit cannot be treated as a claim for SSP. However, if you have notified your employer of your sickness, but you are not entitled to SSP, you may be able to get a claim for employment and support allowance (ESA) backdated more than the usual three months (see p660).

Backdating your entitlement

To qualify for SSP, you must notify your employer of your sickness (see p844). Even if you have not notified your employer promptly, your entitlement can still be backdated if you do so within the time limits on p844.

If statutory sick pay ends or is refused

If your employer decides that you are not entitled to SSP or stops paying you, it should provide you with a statement (usually on Form SSP1) within certain time limits, giving you the reasons for its decision.[39] If you do not agree with your employer's decision, see Chapter 59 for how to challenge it.

Whether or not you agree with your employer's decision, you should consider claiming other benefits. If you are not well enough to work, consider claiming ESA and/or universal credit (see Chapters 3, 9 and 30). The DWP usually asks HMRC to make a decision on your entitlement to SSP before it makes a decision on your claim for ESA.

7. **Getting paid**

Statutory sick pay (SSP) is usually paid in the same way and at the same intervals as your wages or salary.

SSP is a daily benefit, so if you qualify for it, it can be paid for periods of less than a week. See p842 for the way the daily rate is calculated.

Note:

- If you are entitled to contractual sick pay from your employer, SSP forms part of your pay. Your employer can deduct the amount of SSP you are entitled to from the contractual sick pay it is liable to pay you for the same period.[40]
- Your employer cannot pay you SSP by making a payment in kind or by providing board and lodging, a service or other facilities.[41]
- Deductions that can be made from your wages (eg, union subscriptions) can also be made from your SSP.[42]
- If your entitlement to SSP has been decided by HM Revenue and Customs (HMRC) or by the First-tier Tribunal or Upper Tribunal, your employer may be required to pay your SSP within a certain time limit (see p1436).
- If your employer cannot or will not pay you, see p1436 for details of when payment of SSP can be made by HMRC.
- The rules on overpayments and recovery of overpaid benefit described in Chapter 53 do not apply to SSP. If your employer pays you SSP and later decides that you were not entitled to it, it may attempt to recover the sum it considers

overpaid by making a deduction from your wages. If this happens, get advice. If your employer decides that you have been overpaid SSP in error, consider claiming employment and support allowance. You may be able to get your claim backdated (see p660).

Change of circumstances

Notify your employer of any change in your circumstances that may affect your entitlement to SSP.

8. Tax, other benefits and the benefit cap

Tax

Statutory sick pay (SSP) is treated like any other earnings. You pay tax and, depending on the amount of your earnings in the same week, national insurance (NI) contributions by pay as you earn (PAYE) in the normal way.[43]

Means-tested benefits and tax credits

If you come under the universal credit (UC) system (see p23), you may qualify for UC as well as SSP.

For the purpose of qualifying for help with the cost of childcare in your UC, you can be treated as still in paid work while getting SSP (see p74).

If you are prevented from claiming UC because you are severely disabled (see p23):
- you may qualify for income support (IS) as well as SSP (see p235);
- you cannot qualify for employment and support allowance (ESA) during your period of entitlement to SSP.

In some circumstances, you can be treated as being in full-time work for working tax credit (WTC) while you are getting SSP (see p305). Entitlement to SSP can help you qualify for the disabled worker element (see p1458) and/or a childcare element (see p1460) in your WTC.[44] However, if you are not already claiming WTC, you cannot make a new claim unless you are prevented from claiming UC because you are severely disabled (see p23). You may be able to claim UC instead.

When calculating your entitlement to means-tested benefits and tax credits, SSP is:
- treated as employed earnings for UC. When calculating your entitlement to UC, it is your net earnings that are taken into account, so certain amounts may be deducted before applying the work allowance (see p118 and p41);
- treated in full as income for IS and income-based jobseeker's allowance (see p435);

Part 5: Other benefits
Chapter 39: Statutory sick pay
8. Tax, other benefits and the benefit cap

- treated as earnings for pension credit and housing benefit (HB) (see Chapters 20 and 21). If you get SSP, an allowance for certain childcare charges may be deducted from your earnings when calculating your entitlement to HB (see p432);
- treated as employment income for WTC and child tax credit (see p1481).

Non-means-tested benefits

If you are getting SSP, you cannot get:
- ESA; *or*
- statutory adoption pay (SAP); *or*
- statutory paternity pay (SPP); *or*
- statutory shared parental pay (SSPP); *or,*
- statutory parental bereavement pay (SPBP).[45]

You cannot qualify for SSP during your maternity pay period or, if your entitlement is based on your own employment or self-employment, during your maternity allowance (MA) period (see p728).[46] If you get MA on the basis of your spouse's or partner's employment or self-employment, see p843.

SSP may affect your entitlement to some non-means-tested benefits.
- SSP counts towards the earnings condition for MA, statutory maternity pay, SAP, SPP, SSPP and SPBP.
- SSP counts as earnings for carer's allowance, increases in non-means-tested benefits for dependants and reduced earnings allowance.

SSP does not affect your entitlement to other non-means-tested benefits.

Unless you have other earnings, such as occupational sick pay, you do not have to pay NI contributions while on SSP as the weekly rate of SSP is below the NI lower earnings limit. Instead, you are entitled to class 1 NI credits (see p971).[47]

The benefit cap

In some cases, there is a limit on the total amount of specified benefits you can receive (a 'benefit cap'). SSP is *not* a specified benefit. The benefit cap only applies if you are getting UC or HB. The benefit cap may not apply if you or your partner have worked recently and you may count as in work while receiving SSP. See p1194 for further information.

Other sources of help

If you are on a low income, you may be entitled to certain health benefits (see Chapter 31). You may be entitled to council tax reduction (see p851).

Notes

1. Who can get statutory sick pay
1 ss151-154 SSCBA 1992
2 ss151 and 163(1) SSCBA 1992
3 Reg 16(2) SSP Regs
4 Reg 4 SSP Regs
5 s151(4) SSCBA 1992
6 Sch 1 SSP(ME) Regs
7 Reg 2 SSP Regs
8 s152 SSCBA 1992
9 s153(2), (7) and (8) SSCBA 1992
10 ss153(2) and (12) and 155 SSCBA 1992;
    reg 3(1), (3) and (4) SSP Regs
11 s152(3) SSCBA 1992
12 s153(3) and Sch 11 SSCBA 1992; reg 3
    SSP Regs
13 s163(2) SSCBA 1992; regs 17 and 19
    SSP Regs
14 CSSP/2/1984; CSSP/3/1984
15 *Seaton v HMRC* [2011] UKUT 297 (TCC)
16 Reg 17 SSP Regs
17 Reg 17(2) SSP Regs
18 Reg 19(7) and (8) SSP Regs
19 Sch 11 para 6 SSCBA 1992
20 ss154 and 155(1) SSCBA 1992
21 DWP press release, *Sick pay from day one
    for those affected by coronavirus,* 4 March
    2020
22 s154(3) SSCBA 1992
23 Reg 5(2) and (3) SSP Regs
24 R(SSP) 1/85
25 s155(1) SSCBA 1992

4. The amount of benefit
26 s157 SSCBA 1992
27 Regs 20 and 21 SSP Regs
28 s155(2)-(4) SSCBA 1992
29 s152(3) SSCBA 1992

5. Special benefit rules
30 s153(2)(d) and (12) SSCBA 1992
31 Reg 3(5) SSP Regs
32 Reg 3(4) SSP Regs

6. Claims and backdating
33 Reg 7(1), (4) and (5) SSP Regs
34 Reg 7(1)-(3) SSP Regs
35 s156(3) SSCBA 1992
36 s14(1) SSAA 1992
37 Reg 2(2) SSP(ME) Regs
38 Reg 2(1) SSP(ME) Regs
39 Reg 15 SSP Regs

7. Getting paid
40 Sch 12 para 2 SSCBA 1992
41 Reg 8 SSP Regs
42 s151(3) SSCBA 1992

8. Tax, other benefits and the benefit cap
43 s4(1) SSCBA 1992
44 Regs 6, 9 and 13 WTC(EMR) Regs
45 s20(1) WRA 2007; regs 18 and 27
    SPPSAP(G) Regs; regs 14(1)(a) and
    26(1)(a) SSPP(G) Regs; reg 9(1)(a)
    SPBP(G) Regs
46 s153(2)(d) and (12) SSCBA 1992
47 Reg 8B(2)(a)(iii) SS(Cr) Regs

5

Chapter 40

Other payments

This chapter covers:
1. Council tax reduction (p851)
2. Loans for mortgage interest (p855)
3. Local welfare assistance schemes (p861)
4. Healthy Start food and vitamins (p862)
5. Education benefits (p866)
6. Free milk for children (p868)
7. Payments for former members of the armed forces (p868)
8. Christmas bonus (p870)
9. Other financial help (p870)

Key facts

- There are a number of payments you may be able to get in addition to your benefits. For some of these you must be receiving a 'qualifying benefit'.
- You may be able to get financial help from your local authority – eg, your council tax may be reduced, you may qualify for help under its welfare assistance scheme or your child may be able to get help with certain costs of education, such as free school lunches.
- If you are an owner-occupier and getting universal credit or another means-tested benefit, you may be offered a loan from the DWP to help with your mortgage interest payments.
- Under the Healthy Start scheme, you can get vouchers for milk, fruit and vegetables, and coupons for free vitamins. A similar scheme, Best Start foods, operates in Scotland. Free milk is also available to children in daycare under the welfare food scheme.
- You can get a £10 Christmas bonus if you are entitled to a qualifying benefit in the relevant week.
- Other sources of financial help are available – eg, if you are on a low income, starting work, have children, are an older person, have an illness or disability, need help with home improvements or have other special needs.

1. **Council tax reduction**

If you need help to pay your council tax, you may be able to get a reduction under your local authority's council tax reduction scheme. In some areas, this is known as council tax support or rebate. **Note:** a council tax reduction is *not* a social security benefit or a tax credit and the rules for benefits and tax credits in this *Handbook* do not apply.

In:[1]

- England and Wales, local authorities may devise their own local schemes which must meet minimum requirements. In Wales, if a local authority does not adopt its own scheme, a default scheme applies. Check with your local authority whether it has its own local scheme or whether the default scheme applies;
- Scotland, there is a national scheme, administered by local authorities.

Check with your local authority whether you qualify for a council tax reduction. Ensure the rules are being applied correctly in your case. If your local authority has adopted its own scheme, check that it meets the minimum requirements. **Note:**

- You may be able to get extended help for a period if you take up paid work, more paid work or better paid work.
- In England and Scotland, but not in Wales, there is an alternative maximum council tax (known as 'second adult rebate') designed to help you if you share your home with anyone on a low income.
- In Scotland, if your property is in Bands E to H, you may be entitled to additional council tax reduction if your income is below a certain level.

Can you get a discretionary reduction from your local authority?

In England and Wales, in addition to its council tax reduction scheme, your local authority has a discretionary power to reduce your council tax bill.[2] Local authorities can reduce the council tax payable in indivudual circumstances (eg, if you are in financial hardship) and in group cases (eg, during a local emergency, such as flooding). You should apply for a discretionary reduction in writing, stating that you are applying for a reduction under section 13A of the Local Government Finance Act 1992, and provide any supporting evidence. If the local authority refuses, you can appeal against its decision to a valuation tribunal.

You may also qualify for a council tax discount (eg, a 25 per cent discount if you are the only resident) or exemption (eg, if only students occupy the dwelling), which is not means tested and depends on your circumstances. For further information, see CPAG's *Council Tax Handbook*.

Common rules for all applicants

The following basic conditions apply in England, Wales and Scotland for all applicants, whether you are under or over pension age.

- You must be liable for council tax on the dwelling in which you are a resident.[3]
- You must not be a 'person subject to immigration control' (see p1560) and you must satisfy the habitual residence test (see p1587).[4]
- You must make an application for a council tax reduction.[5] You can apply in writing. You can also apply by telephone or online if your local authority allows this. If your claim is 'defective', you must be notified and given at least one month to correct it.
  - If you or your partner have been awarded universal credit (UC), income support (IS), income-based jobseeker's allowance (JSA), income-related employment and support allowance (ESA) or pension credit (PC) and apply for council tax reduction within one month of applying for that benefit, the date of your application is the date of your benefit claim.
  - If you or your partner are on UC, IS, income-based JSA, income-related ESA or PC and apply for council tax reduction within one month of becoming liable to pay council tax for the first time, the date of your application is the date you became liable for council tax.
- Your council tax reduction is generally applied by reducing your council tax bill.
- If you disagree with a council tax reduction decision, you can appeal, initially to the local authority. Appeals must be in writing and made within one month of your being sent the decision in Wales or within two months in Scotland. There are no formal time limits for appeals in England.
- If you are not satisfied with the outcome of the appeal, you can make a further appeal to a valuation tribunal (in England and Wales) or the council tax reduction review panel (in Scotland). In England and Wales, you must appeal within two months of the date of the local authority's response. In Scotland, you must appeal within 42 days of the date of the response.[6]

Common rules for applicants over pension age

The following rules apply in England, Wales and Scotland for applicants of pension age or over. These rules apply if your partner is under pension age, but they do not apply if you or your partner are entitled to UC, IS, income-based JSA or income-related ESA.[7]

- If you or your partner are getting the guarantee credit of PC, you are entitled to the maximum council tax reduction, which is 100 per cent of your council tax liability less any non-dependant deductions.
- You cannot qualify for council tax reduction if you have capital over £16,000, unless you getting the guarantee credit of PC. Capital under £10,000 is ignored.

If you have capital between £10,000 and £16,000, a tariff income is counted of £1 a week for every £500, or part of £500, over £10,000.

- If you are not on PC, your applicable amount, income and capital are calculated in a broadly equivalent way to housing benefit (HB) (see Chapters 17, 21 and 23).
- If your income is below your applicable amount, you are entitled to the maximum council tax reduction, which is 100 per cent of your council tax liability, less any non-dependant deductions.
- If your income is above your applicable amount, your maximum council tax reduction is reduced by 20 per cent of your excess income.
- A non-dependant deduction may be made for another adult living in your home. The rules for who counts as a non-dependant and when a deduction is made are the same as for HB (see p198), but the amounts are different.
- Your application can be backdated for three months.

If you are under pension age

England

In England, the support available for working-age people varies from one local authority to another. Some of the main features and the minimum requirements of council tax reduction schemes for people under pension age in England are as follows.[8]

- The capital limit may be less than £16,000.
- If you get IS, income-based JSA or income-related ESA, you are entitled to the maximum council tax reduction, but this may be less than 100 per cent of your council tax liability.
- Your local authority may set rules to allow your application to be backdated, but is not obliged to do so.
- Your local authority must make a decision within 14 days of receiving your properly completed application, or as soon as reasonable.

Wales

Some of the main features of the minimum requirements and the default scheme in Wales are as follows.[9]

- You cannot qualify for council tax if you have capital over £16,000. Capital under £6,000 is ignored. If you have capital between £6,000 and £16,000, a tariff income is counted of £1 a week for every £250, or part of £250, over £6,000.
- If you get IS, income-based JSA or income-related ESA, you are entitled to maximum council tax reduction, which is 100 per cent of your council tax liability less any non-dependant deductions.
- If you get UC, your applicable amount is your maximum UC, and your income is the figure used by the DWP plus the amount of UC payable. Monthly

amounts are converted to weekly amounts by multiplying by 12 and dividing by 52.

- If you do not get UC, your applicable amount is calculated in a similar way as for means-tested benefits, but all personal allowances and premiums have increased in line with inflation since 2013, even if the equivalent allowances in social security payments have been frozen.

- If your income is below your applicable amount, you are entitled to maximum council tax reduction, which is 100 per cent of your council tax liability less any non-dependant deductions.

- If your income is more than your applicable amount, your maximum council tax reduction is reduced by 20 per cent of your excess income.

- Your application may be backdated for up to three months if you had continuous good cause for not applying earlier.

Scotland

Some of the main features of the council tax reduction scheme in Scotland are as follows.[10]

- You cannot qualify for council tax reduction if you have capital over £16,000. Capital under £6,000 is ignored. If you have capital between £6,000 and £16,000, a tariff income is counted of £1 a week for every £250, or part of £250, over £6,000.

- If you get IS, income-based JSA or income-related ESA, you are entitled to maximum council tax reduction, which is 100 per cent of your council tax liability less any non-dependant deductions.

- If you get UC, your applicable amount is based on your maximum UC, and your income is either the figure used by the DWP or, if your income changes frequently, the local authority may estimate your income over an appropriate period. An additional £17.07 is included in respect of each child, and £54.32 is added to your applicable amount for each child for whom a UC child element is not payable due to the two-child limit.[11] Your income also includes the amount of UC payable excluding any transitional severe disability premium amount (see p29), or if the local authority has used an estimate because your income changes, an estimate of the amount of UC payable. Monthly amounts are converted to weekly amounts by multiplying by 12 and dividing by 52.[12]

- If you do not get UC, your applicable amount is calculated in a similar way as for means-tested benefits, but the amount for a child has been increased above inflation and there is no two-child limit.

- If your income is below your applicable amount, you are entitled to maximum council tax reduction, which is 100 per cent of your council tax liability.

- If your income is more than your applicable amount, your maximum council tax reduction is reduced by 20 per cent of your excess income.

- Your application may be backdated for up to six months if you had continuous good cause for not applying earlier.

2. Loans for mortgage interest

If you have a mortgage, the DWP may offer you loan payments to help with the interest payments. You are only eligible for the offer of a loan if you are entitled to universal credit (UC), income support (IS), income-based jobseeker's allowance (JSA), income-related employment and support allowance (ESA) or pension credit (PC). The DWP calls these loans support for mortgage interest loans.

If you accept a loan for your mortgage interest, regular payments are made, usually directly to your lender.[13] Payments are made monthly (for UC) or four-weekly (for IS, income-based JSA, income-related ESA or PC). The amount of each loan payment is calculated with a formula and is not necessarily what you have to pay (see p858).

Getting advice

It is vital to get independent legal and financial advice (eg, from a financial adviser or solicitor) before accepting a loan for mortgage interest from the DWP. **Note:** the information about the loan you get from the DWP or its agent (currently in a telephone call from Serco) is *not* independent advice.

Note:

- A loan for mortgage interest is *not* a social security benefit.
- You normally have to repay the loan (see p860). There are exceptions.
- A charge on your property (a standard security in Scotland) is made in favour of the DWP. This enables the DWP to recover what you owe it, if there is sufficient equity in your property.
- The DWP adds interest to the total amount you owe until the earliest of the date the loan is paid back (or written off), or you have died (or until both you and your partner have died) or, in some cases, you are sent a statement of what you owe the DWP so you can repay in full.[14] The rate of interest charged by the DWP is set out in the rules and is currently 1.3 per cent.[15]

Even though a loan for mortgage interest is not benefit, if you disagree with a decision about a loan, you can apply for a revision or a supersession, or appeal against the decision under the rules that apply to benefits.[16] You must apply for a mandatory reconsideration before you can appeal. See Chapters 56 and 57.

Note: if you have other housing costs (eg, ground rent or service charges), help with these *can* be included in your UC, IS, income-based JSA, income-related ESA or PC. See Chapter 6 for UC and Chapter 18 for the other means-tested benefits.

Who can get a loan for mortgage interest

You can get a loan for mortgage interest if:[17]

- you are entitled to UC, and you (and your partner) do not have any earned income (see p116).[18] This includes earnings from work you can do while claiming contributory ESA (see p1042) or work of less than 16 hours a week you can do while claiming contribution-based JSA (see p991). The nature and duration of the work is not relevant – eg, it does not matter if your job is part time or temporary; *or*
- you are entitled (or treated as entitled – see below) to IS, income-based JSA, income-related ESA or PC.

In either case, you must also meet the following conditions:

- your loan qualifies (see below); *and*
- you (or your partner) count as liable to pay your loan (see p857); *and*
- your loan is for the home in which you normally live (see p857); *and*
- the DWP offers you a loan for mortgage interest and you accept the offer. You (and your partner) must sign and return the loan agreement. You must also create a legal charge (in England and Wales) or a standard security (in Scotland) in favour of the DWP. If you have a partner and both of you are the legal owners of your home, you must both do this. If only one of you is the legal owner, the other must give her/his written consent.

The DWP must provide you with specified information within six months of your accepting the offer of a loan for mortgage interest.[19] This includes a summary of the terms and conditions of the DWP loan agreement and information about where you and your partner can get further information and independent legal and financial advice about the loan. The information may be provided by a third party on the DWP's behalf. Currently, the third party is Serco. The DWP says this information will be provided by telephone. **Note:** this information is *not* independent advice.

Note: you are treated as entitled to IS, JSA, ESA or PC if you have claimed it and you are not entitled solely because your income is the same as, or more than, your applicable amount (your standard minimum guarantee for PC), but is less than this amount plus the weekly loan payments you would receive if you were entitled.[20] You cannot be treated as entitled to UC in this way – you must actually be entitled to UC.

Which loans qualify

Depending on which benefit you are entitled to, the loan for mortgage interest can cover: [21]

- for UC, interest payments on a loan that is secured on the accommodation you occupy, or are treated as occupying, as a home (see p91), whatever the purpose of the loan; *and*

- for IS, JSA, ESA or PC, mortgages and other loans for house purchase and loans used to pay for specified repairs and improvements or to meet a service charge for these. The types of repairs and improvements are those on p361 that are excluded from help with housing costs; *and*
- for UC or PC, 'alternative finance payments' – ie, payments made under alternative finance arrangements to enable you to acquire an interest in the accommodation you occupy, or are treated as occupying, as a home (see below), such as a Sharia-compliant mortgage.

The rules for the type of loans that qualify are broadly the same as for the housing costs rules before 6 April 2018. See the 2017/18 edition of this *Handbook* for details. For UC, see pp488–89 and for IS, JSA, ESA and PC, see pp46–52. For IS, JSA, ESA and PC, restrictions might be made if you took out or increased your home loan or loan for repairs and improvements while entitled to IS, income-based JSA, income-related ESA or PC, or in a period between claims.[22]

Liability for payments

To get a loan for mortgage interest, you (or your partner) must be liable to make payments on a loan that qualifies, or you (or s/he) must be treated as liable.[23] **Note:** you (or your partner) can be treated as *not* liable to make payments even if you are, in specified situations, or if you are entitled to UC, if the DWP considers the liability to be contrived.[24]

For UC, the rules for who counts as liable for payments are broadly the same as for the housing costs rules before 6 April 2018. See p490–94 of the 2017/18 edition of this *Handbook*. For IS, JSA, ESA and PC, the rules for who counts as liable are broadly the same as for the housing costs rules in Chapter 18 (see p369).

Note: if you are jointly liable to make payments with someone other than your partner, you are only treated as liable for the proportion of the payments for which you (and your partner) are responsible.[25]

Occupying the accommodation as a home

To get a loan for mortgage interest, you must normally occupy the accommodation as your home.[26] You cannot usually get a loan for mortgage interest for any other home. However, there are special rules if you:[27]

- have just moved into your home;
- are liable to make payments for more than one dwelling, including if you have left your home because of a fear of domestic violence;
- are temporarily absent from home, including if you are away from home because of a fear of domestic violence;
- are a student or on a training course;
- are in temporary accommodation while repairs are carried out on your home.

For UC, the rules on occupying accommodation are broadly the same as for the housing costs rules before 6 April 2018. See pp494–98 of the 2017/18 edition of this *Handbook*. For IS, JSA, ESA and PC, the rules on occupying accommodation are broadly the same as for the housing costs rules in Chapter 18 (see p370).

The amount of loan payments

If you accept a loan, regular payments are made usually directly to your lender. Your monthly (for UC) or weekly (for IS, income-based JSA, income-related ESA or PC) loan payments are worked out by applying a standard percentage rate to the amount you owe to your lender, subject to an upper limit, and dividing by 12 or 52 as the case may be.[28] Any income above your applicable amount (for IS/ESA/JSA) or above your appropriate minimum guarantee (for PC) or any unearned income above your maximum amount (for UC) is deducted. Also deducted is the amount of any payment you get under a mortgage protection insurance policy. The standard rate is the average mortgage rate published by the Bank of England and changes when this differs by 0.5 percentage points or more.[29] The current rate is at gov.uk/support-for-mortgage-interest and, at the time of writing, was 2.61 per cent.

Example

Eileen is an owner-occupier with a mortgage. The amount she owes her mortage lender is £175,000. She is unemployed and her only income is UC. She accepts a loan for mortgage interest from the DWP. Her loan payments are worked out as follows.

£175,000 x 2.61% = £4,567.50

£4,567.50 ÷ 12 = £380.63

Eileen's monthly loan payments are therefore £380.63. Her debt to the DWP comprises each loan payment she gets, along with the interest that accrues on that debt. So, for example, if Eileen gets loan payments for 10 months, she will owe the DWP £3,806.30 plus interest (this is different from the average mortgage rate and is currently 1.3 per cent).

Note: even if there is a reduction in the amount you owe your lender, your regular loan payments are usually only recalculated annually, on the anniversary of the date you started getting them.[30]

If the amount you owe your lender is more than an upper limit, the amount of your loan payments is usually calculated using this.[31] The upper limit is usually £200,000 if you are entitled to UC, IS, JSA or ESA.

If you are entitled to PC, the upper limit is usually £100,000. However, if you are entitled to IS, JSA or ESA with an upper limit of £200,000, but you then claim PC, this higher upper limit continues to apply.

Deductions for non-dependants

If you are entitled to IS, income-based JSA, income-related ESA or PC, a set deduction is made from your weekly loan payments for people who normally live with you in your home who are not part of your family for benefit purposes (called 'non-dependants').[32] The rules for who counts as a non-dependant, and when a deduction is made, are broadly the same as for the housing costs rules in Chapter 18 (see pp363–65). To calculate the amount of the deduction, see p365. If you have other housing costs (eg, ground rent or service charges) and help with these is included in your benefit, the non-dependant deduction is apportioned between the help you get with housing costs and your loan payments.

When loan payments start and end

Once you have accepted a loan for mortgage interest, your regular loan payments start:[33]

- if you are entitled to PC, from the first day of the first benefit week after your first date of entitlement (there is no 'waiting period' for PC); or
- if you are entitled to UC, from the first day of the first assessment period after an initial 'waiting period' of nine consecutive assessment periods in which you are entitled to UC. If you were getting loan payments while entitled to (or treated as entitled to) IS, income-based JSA or income-related ESA and claim UC within one month of that claim ending, you do not have to serve the waiting period again for UC; or
- if you are entitled to (or treated as entitled to) IS, income-based JSA or income-related ESA, after an initial 'waiting period' of 39 consecutive weeks in which you are entitled to (or treated as entitled to) one of those benefits; or
- if you were entitled to (or treated as entitled to) IS, income-based JSA or income-related ESA but had not completed the waiting period, and claim UC within one month of that claim ending, from the first day of the first assessment period after a waiting period of 273 days when you were entitled to (or treated as entitled to) those benefits or UC; or
- a later start date if you request.

Loan payments are always made in arrears.

Once loan payments start, you can ask to stop getting them at any time. Loan payments end if:[34]

- you are no longer entitled to UC. If you become entitled to UC again, you will only be eligible for loan payments after the waiting period of nine consecutive months in which you are entitled to UC; or
- you are entitled to UC and you (or you partner) have any earned income – eg, if you start a job. If you are still entitled to UC and in a subsequent assessment period you have no earnings, you should qualify for loan payments without having to serve the nine-month waiting period again. The rules do not stipulate that you must have no earnings during the waiting period. DWP guidance is not clear on this point – you can request a mandatory reconsideration of a decision that you are not eligible for an offer of a loan in this situation; or

- you are no longer entitled (or treated as entitled) to IS, income-based JSA, income-related ESA or PC. However, if you have been getting IS, JSA or ESA, check whether you qualify for mortgage interest run-on (see below). If you become entitled to IS, income-based JSA or income-related ESA again within 52 weeks (although you will only be able to make a new claim for these benefits in very limited circumstances), you can be offered loan payments without having to serve the 39-week waiting period again (there is no 'waiting period' for PC); *or*
- you are no longer liable (or treated as liable) to pay your loan; *or*
- you are no longer occupying (or treated as occupying) your home; *or*
- your loan for mortgage interest agreement ends in accordance with its terms.

Check whether you have to repay your loan for mortgage interest (see below).

Are you moving onto universal credit?
If you have been getting loan payments in IS, income-based JSA or income-related ESA and move onto UC, you can only get loan payments in UC if you have no earned income. So, for example, if you have been working within the 'permitted work' limits for ESA and are still working when you move onto UC, your loan payments will stop.

Mortgage interest run-on

When you (or your partner) return to work or increase your hours and so count as being in full-time paid work, you no longer qualify for IS, income-based JSA or income-related ESA and therefore no longer qualify for a loan for mortgage interest. However, if you qualify for mortgage interest run-on, your weekly loan payments continue to be paid for the first four weeks after you go into full-time paid work.[35] **Note:** you do not have to make a claim to qualify for mortgage interest run-on; it is paid automatically. However, you must let the DWP know you are starting full-time paid work. The rules are broadly the same as they were before 6 April 2018. See pp474–75 of the 2017/18 edition of this *Handbook* for details.

Repaying the loan

The amount of your loan (ie, the total of all the loan payments you have received) and any interest you owe the DWP must normally be repaid in full in any of the following situations.[36]

- You sell your home (although the government has announced that if you have bought a new home, you can request that a loan balance can be transferred to your new home).[37]

- Ownership of your home is transferred, assigned or otherwise disposed of. This does not apply if this is to:
  - you, following your partner's death, or your partner, following your death, provided you or your partner live in the home; *or*
  - you, from a former spouse or civil partner under a court order or an agreement for maintenance, provided you live in the home.
- You have died, or, if you have a partner s/he is the owner and s/he has died, or if you are both owners, both of you have died.

In the first two situations, repayment is made from the proceeds of the sale, transfer or assignment. In the third situation, repayment is made from the person's estate.

Interest is charged on the amount of loan payments at the average gilt rate published by the Office for Budget Responsibility (at the time of writing, 1.3 per cent) and is set for six-month periods starting on 1 January and 1 July.[38] You can repay some, or all, of what you owe before any of the above situations occur, provided you pay at least £100 at a time. **Note:** if your home is transferred, assigned or otherwise disposed of at less than the market value, it is treated as if this happened at market value for the purposes of the repayment rules.[39]

Note: if the DWP has a legal charge (in England or Wales) or a standard security (in Scotland) on your home and there is not enough equity to cover the amount you owe, repayment is limited to the amount that is available after other prior ranking charges or securities (eg, your outstanding mortgage) have been paid.[40] This means that if there is insufficient left, or nothing left, after repayment of the prior rankings, any remaining loan for mortgage interest and any interest you owe the DWP are written off and are considered to be fully repaid.

3. **Local welfare assistance schemes**

Help may be available under local welfare assistance schemes set up by your local authority (in England) or by the devolved administrations (the Discretionary Assistance Fund in Wales and the Scottish Welfare Fund in Scotland). The DWP may refer to this as 'local welfare provision'.

You may qualify if you need help, for example:
- with immediate short-term needs in a crisis – eg, if you do not have sufficient resources, or you need help with expenses in an emergency or as a result of a disaster, such as a fire or flood in your home;
- to establish yourself in the community following a stay in institutional or residential accommodation, or to help you remain in the community;
- to set up a home in the community as part of a planned resettlement programme;
- to ease exceptional pressure on your family;

- to enable you to care for a prisoner or young offender on temporary release;
- with certain travel expenses – eg, to visit someone in hospital, to attend a funeral, to ease a domestic crisis, to visit a child living with her/his other parent or to move to suitable accommodation.

In England, the local scheme is at your local authority's discretion. Check with your local authority to find out what help is available, whether you qualify and how to apply.

The Discretionary Assistance Fund for Wales offers non-repayable emergency assistance payments and individual assistance payments.

The Scottish Welfare Fund provides community care grants and crisis grants. The basic rules for the scheme are set by the Scottish government, with each local authority having some discretion. You should apply to your local authority.[41]

4. **Healthy Start food and vitamins**

In England and Wales, if you qualify for Healthy Start food and vitamins, you get free vitamins as well as vouchers that can be used to buy specified types of food. In Scotland, the Healthy Start scheme has been replaced by Best Start foods (see p865).

Healthy Start food vouchers

If you qualify for Healthy Start food, you:[42]
- get fixed-value vouchers (worth £3.10 each) that can be exchanged for 'Healthy Start food' at registered food outlets; *or*
- are paid an amount equal to the value of the vouchers to which you are entitled, if there is no registered food outlet within a reasonable distance of your home.

Healthy Start food

'Healthy Start food' means liquid cow's milk and cow's milk-based infant formula, fresh or frozen fruit and vegetables including loose, pre-packed, whole, sliced, chopped or mixed fruit or vegetables (but not fruit or vegetables to which fat, salt, sugar, flavouring or any other ingredients have been added).[43] From 1 October 2020, it also includes canned, fruit and vegetables, and fresh dried or canned pulses.

Who can claim

You qualify for Healthy Start food vouchers:[44]
- **if you are at least 10 weeks pregnant** and you are:
  - 18 or over and are entitled to (or are a partner or member of the family of someone who is entitled to) a 'qualifying benefit' (see p864);

- under 18, whether or not you are entitled to a qualifying benefit (but not if you are excluded from these because you are a 'person subject to immigration control' – see p1560); *or*
- **if you are a mother** who has 'parental responsibility' for a child and:
  - you are 16 or over and entitled to (or you are a partner or member of the family of someone who is entitled to) a qualifying benefit other than income-related employment and support allowance (ESA). If you are entitled to universal credit (UC) or pension credit (PC), your child must be under one year old. For other benefits, your child must be under one or it is less than a year since her/his expected date of birth. This means you can continue to qualify for vouchers for a period after your child is one – ie, if s/he was born prematurely; *or*
  - it is less than four months since your baby's expected date of birth and you have not yet notified Healthy Start that s/he was born. You must have been entitled to a qualifying benefit before your baby was born. This allows your entitlement to vouchers to continue until you notify the birth. Once you do, you can then qualify under the rule above (if you are 18 or over). **Note:** as long as you provided the notification within the four-month period, you can also get extra vouchers for your child from her/his date of birth.

  If you qualify for vouchers for more than one child under this rule (eg, you have twins), you get a voucher for each. If you do not have 'parental responsibility' but would otherwise qualify for vouchers, your child qualifies instead of you;[45]
- **if you are responsible for a child under four** who is a member of your family. You or a member of the family must be entitled to a qualifying benefit (see p864) other than income-related ESA.

In practical terms, this means that each week you get one voucher for each of your children aged between one and four, two vouchers for each of your children under one (or within one year of their expected date of birth), plus one voucher if you are pregnant.

Example

Vera is 17 weeks pregnant. She has three children: twin girls aged two and a boy aged seven. She is getting income support (IS). She qualifies for a voucher because she is more than 10 weeks pregnant. Her twins each qualify for a voucher as they are under four. Her son does not qualify for a voucher. Vera gets three vouchers each week totalling £9.30. When the baby is born, Vera will be entitled to two vouchers for a child under one, plus one voucher for each of the twins aged under four. She will get four vouchers each week, totalling £12.40.

Definitions

The '**qualifying benefits**' are IS, income-based jobseeker's allowance (JSA), PC and, in some cases, income-related ESA. Child tax credit (CTC) is also a qualifying benefit, provided that gross income for CTC purposes does not exceed £16,190 and there is no entitlement to working tax credit (WTC), other than if this is during the four-week WTC run-on period (see p305). UC is a qualifying benefit if during the last complete assessment period or the assessment period before that you (and your partner) earned £408 or less. If you subsequently cease to be entitled to UC or your earnings exceed the £408 threshold, you continue to qualify for Healthy Start food vouchers for a further eight weeks after the last complete assessment period.[46]

'**Parental responsibility**' means parental responsibility as defined in section 3(1) of the Children Act 1989 (in England or Wales).[47]

'**Family**' means a person and her/his partner and any child or qualifying young person who is a member of her/his household and for whom s/he or her/his partner counts as being responsible.[48] So, for example, if you are not entitled to a qualifying benefit but are included in your mother's or father's claim for one of these, you can qualify for Healthy Start food vouchers.

To count as the member of a family of someone entitled to UC, s/he must be 'responsible' for you under the UC rules (see p326) and must also satisfy the £408 earnings rule described above.

If you are an asylum seeker receiving asylum support, you get an extra amount to help you buy healthy food if you are pregnant or have a child under three.

Claims

You must make an initial claim for Healthy Start food vouchers in writing and must provide specified information and evidence.[49] You can:

- complete the form in the Healthy Start leaflet (HS01), available from midwives, health visitors, maternity clinics and some doctors' surgeries or from 0345 607 6823;
- download a form or complete it online and print it off, or email yourself a form at www.healthystart.nhs.uk.

If you are under 16, your claim must also be signed by your parent or carer. Send the completed form to: Healthy Start Issuing Unit, Freepost RRTR-SYAE-JKCR, PO Box 1067, Warrington WA55 1EG.

If you are getting Healthy Start food vouchers while you are pregnant and then inform Healthy Start of your baby's birth by telephone while s/he is under four months old, you can get extra vouchers for her/him from her/his date of birth.[50] You may need to make a claim for UC for her/him (or add her/him to your existing UC or tax credits claim) to ensure that you continue to get the vouchers.

You are still entitled to Healthy Start vouchers for a child even if a child element is not payable in UC/CTC/IS/JSA because of the 'two-child limit'.

If you do not get vouchers to which you think you are entitled, or have any other problems with these, contact the Healthy Start Issuing Unit on 0345 607 6823.

Note: paper vouchers may be replaced with a prepayment card in the future.

Healthy Start vitamins

If you qualify for Healthy Start food vouchers, you also qualify for Healthy Start vitamins.[51] Ask your local health professional what the local arrangements are for getting these.

You do not have to make a separate claim for Healthy Start vitamins; you are sent Healthy Start vitamin coupons with your Healthy Start food vouchers. However, you must show evidence to the vitamin supplier that you are entitled (ie, the letter to which your most recent Healthy Start vouchers were attached) and, if requested, proof of your child's age.[52] In Scotland, all pregnant women are eligible for free vitamins, regardless of income.[53] If you are entitled to Best Start foods in Scotland, you can also get free vitamins from your health board.[54]

Best Start foods in Scotland

The Best Start foods payment card has replaced the Healthy Start voucher scheme in Scotland.[55] If you qualify, you will get a payment of £4.25 for yourself if you are pregnant, £8.50 for a child aged under one and £4.25 for each child aged one or two. Payments are made by credits to a payment card.

Best Start foods are administered by Social Security Scotland. Best Start foods include cow's milk, first infant formula milk, fresh, frozen or tinned fruit and vegetables, fresh or tinned pulses and eggs.

You qualify for Best Start foods if you are pregnant or responsible for a child under three and you are:[56]
- 18 or over and are entitled to (or are a member of the family of someone who is entitled to) a 'qualifying benefit'; *or*
- under 18, whether or not you are entitled to a 'qualifying benefit'. You continue to qualify until the end of your pregnancy if you turn 18 during pregnancy, or until your child's first birthday if you turn 18 while responsible for her/him.

The qualifying benefits for Best Start foods are:[57]
- IS, income-based JSA, income-related ESA or PC;
- CTC (if not entitled to WTC) if you have an annual income of £16,190 or less;
- WTC if you have an annual income of £7,320 or less;
- housing benefit if your weekly income is £311 or less; *and*

- UC if you, or you and your partner together, have an earned income of £610 or less in either of the last two complete monthly assessment periods. If you stop getting UC, or your earned income exceeds this limit, you continue to be entitled to Best Start foods for eight weeks after the end of the most recent assessment period.

If you are pregnant, you can apply from the start of your pregnancy. You will usually only be asked for evidence when around 24 weeks' pregnant. You must report the child's birth within four months to get the payment from the child's date of birth.[58] Responsibility for a child is defined in the same way as for Best Start grants (see p1698). You are still entitled to Best Start foods for a child even if a child element is not payable in UC/CTC/IS/JSA because of the 'two-child limit'.

If you were getting Healthy Start vouchers for a child aged at least two and you apply for Best Start foods by 31 March 2020, you continue to be entitled to Best Start foods until the child reaches age four.[59] If you were previously entitled to Best Start foods within 12 weeks, and you think you are eligible again, you can contact Social Security Scotland and become entitled again without having to make a new claim.[60]

5. **Education benefits**

Financial help is available from your local authority if you are in school or are a student, or if you have children in school or college.

Free school lunches

School children are entitled to free school lunches if their families get:[61]
- universal credit (UC). In Scotland, your earnings (and those of your partner, if you make a joint claim) must not be more than £610 in the UC assessment period before your application. In England and Wales, your earnings (and those of your partner, if you make a joint claim) must not exceed:
  - £616.67 in the UC assessment period immediately before the date you claim free school lunches; *or*
  - £1,233.34 in the two UC assessment periods immediately before the date you claim free school lunches; *or*
  - £1,850 in the three UC assessment periods immediately before the date you claim free school lunches;
- income support (IS), income-based jobseeker's allowance or income-related employment and support allowance (ESA);
- child tax credit and have annual taxable income of £16,190 (in England and Wales) or £16,105 (in Scotland), or less. However, this does not apply if the family is entitled to working tax credit (WTC) unless:

– this is during the four-week 'WTC run-on' period (see p305); *or*
– in Scotland only, the WTC award is based on annual taxable income of £6,900 or less;
- in England and Wales only, guarantee credit of pension credit (PC).

Note: pupils eligible for free school lunches in England on 31 March 2018 or in Wales on 31 March 2019 and those who become eligible after this date remain so until 31 March 2022 in England or 31 December 2023 in Wales, whether or not they (or their parents) continue to be entitled to a qualifying benefit. Those entitled to free school lunches on 31 March 2022 in England or on 31 December 2023 in Wales continue to be entitled until they finish their current stage of education – eg, primary or secondary school.[62]

Also entitled are:

- 16–18-year-olds getting the above benefits or tax credits in their own right;[63]
- asylum seekers in receipt of asylum support;
- in Scotland, a child attending pre-school nursery (or similar) who is entitled under any of the first three bullet points on p866, or if her/his family gets PC, incapacity benefit or severe disablement allowance, or if since the age of two the child is being, or has been, looked after by a local authority or is the subject of a kinship care or guardianship order.[64]

Note: in England and Scotland, free school lunches are provided to all children during the first three years of primary school. In Wales, free school breakfasts are provided to all children in primary schools maintained by the local authority.[65]

School transport and school clothes

Local authorities must provide **free transport to school** for pupils aged five to 16 if it is considered necessary to enable the pupil to get to the 'nearest suitable school'. This applies if the pupil lives more than a set distance from that school. However, if there is no safe walking route, a pupil must be given free transport no matter how far away s/he lives from the nearest suitable school. Free school transport must also be be provided to pupils with special educational needs and to those whose parents are on a low income – ie, if they qualify for free school lunches or their parents are on the maximum rate of WTC.

Local authorities can give **grants for school uniforms and other school clothes**. Each authority determines its own eligibility rules. Some school governing bodies or parents' associations also provide help with school clothing.

Education maintenance allowance and 16 to 19 bursaries

An education maintenance allowance is a means-tested payment for young people aged 16 to 19 who stay on in further education and who live in Wales or

Scotland. Payments are made directly to the young person and are conditional on regular course attendance. The young person gets a weekly allowance during term time. The amount depends on the household income. For further details, see studentfinancewales.co.uk or mygov.scot/ema.

16 to 19 bursaries are payments for young people aged 16 to 19 who stay on in further education or training in England. These are available through the school, college or training provider. Certain young people in need (eg, young people in care, care leavers, young people without parental support who get UC or IS, or who get UC or ESA and either disability living allowance or personal independence payment) can get the maximum bursary. Discretionary bursaries are available to those in financial difficulty. See gov.uk/1619-bursary-fund for further information.

Neither payment counts as income for any benefits or tax credits the parent may be getting. They are also not affected by any income the young person has from part-time work.

Note: if you are a student, to find out what help is available to finance your studies, contact your local authority or college or university, or see gov.uk/ student-finance. Also see CPAG's *Student Support and Benefits Handbook* and *Benefits for Students in Scotland Handbook*.

6. **Free milk for children**

Children under five are entitled to 189–200 millilitres of free milk on each day they are looked after for two hours or more:[66]
- by a registered childminder or daycare provider; *or*
- in a school, playcentre or workplace nursery which is exempt from registration; *or*
- in local authority daycare.

Children under one are allowed fresh or dried milk. This is provided by the welfare food scheme.

7. **Payments for former members of the armed forces**

If you are a former member of the armed forces, you can claim under the following schemes, administered by the Ministry of Defence.

You can qualify for **war pension disablement benefits** if you have ill health or a disablement caused by service before 6 April 2005. The degree of your disablement is assessed on a percentage scale, with 100 per cent being the level of disablement that qualifies for the maximum award. If you are assessed at 20 per cent or more, you receive a pension, and if you are assessed at under 20 per cent, you get a lump sum (gratuity). You can also qualify for a number of supplementary allowances. Two of these are particularly important.

- **Constant attendance allowance.** You qualify for this if your disablement is assessed at 80 per cent or more, and because of your disablement you require 'constant attendance'. This has the same meaning as either 'attention' or 'supervision' for attendance allowance (AA) or disability living allowance (DLA) care component (see p612). The allowance is paid at four different rates depending on the number of hours for which you require constant attendance and whether this is in the daytime or at night. If you claim AA, DLA care component or the daily living component of personal independence payment (PIP), any constant attendance allowance to which you are entitled is deducted from these benefits. **Note:** the top two rates of constant attendance allowance are considerably more than the highest rates of AA, DLA care component or PIP daily living component.

- **Mobility supplement.** You qualify for this if your disablement is assessed at 40 per cent or more, and because of your disablement your ability to walk is 'of little or no practical use'. This is, in effect, the same test as for the higher rate of the mobility component of DLA. There is a single rate of benefit currently worth £68.35 a week. If you claim DLA mobility component or PIP mobility component, any mobility supplement to which you are entitled is deducted from your DLA or PIP entitlement. **Note:** unlike DLA and PIP, there is no upper age limit for claiming mobility supplement.

You can qualify for help under the **Armed Forces Compensation Scheme** if you have ill health or a disablement caused by service on or after 6 April 2005. The main benefit is a lump-sum payment. To qualify, you must have had an injury or ill health that comes within one of the specified 'descriptors'. Each descriptor is assigned to a 'tariff level', running from one (the most severe) to 15, which determines the amount payable. If you receive an award of at least tariff level 11, you also qualify for a 'guaranteed income payment', calculated as a percentage of your salary on the day your service in the armed forces ended. Awards are at 30, 50, 75 or 100 per cent, depending on your tariff level.

Armed forces independence payment is payable to those entitled to a guaranteed income payment under the Armed Forces Compensation Scheme at the 50 per cent rate or more. It is payable at a rate equivalent to the total of the enhanced rates of both the daily living and mobility components of PIP.

For more information, see gov.uk/government/organisations/veterans-uk or call Veterans UK on 0808 1914 2 18.

8. Christmas bonus

You qualify for a Christmas bonus of £10 if you are entitled (or treated as being entitled) to any of the qualifying benefits for at least part of the 'relevant week' (even if the benefit is paid later).[67] The relevant week is usually the week beginning with the first Monday in December.[68]

Qualifying benefits[69]

Armed forces independence payment; attendance allowance; carer's allowance; disability living allowance; contributory employment and support allowance which includes either the support or the work-related activity component; long-term incapacity benefit; industrial death benefit for widows or widowers; industrial injuries disablement benefit (if it includes unemployability supplement or constant attendance allowance); pension credit (PC); personal independence payment; severe disablement allowance; state pension or retirement pensions; war disablement pension (if it includes the mobility supplement, constant attendance allowance or unemployability supplement, or if you are at least pension age – see p780);[70] war widow's or surviving civil partner's pension; and widowed parent's allowance.

You may also qualify for an extra bonus for your partner (a further £10) if s/he has not received a bonus in her/his own right, and:[71]

- you are both at least pension age (see p780) and you are entitled, or may be treated as entitled, to an increase in one of the qualifying benefits in respect of her/him; *or*
- you are both at least pension age (see p271) and the only qualifying benefit you get is PC.

The bonus is not taxable and has no effect on other benefits or tax credits.

It is paid automatically. However, you should contact the DWP within a year if you have not obtained your bonus, otherwise your right is lost.[72]

9. Other financial help

This *Handbook* is mainly concerned with information about social security benefits and tax credits. However, there is other financial help, or help in kind, to which you may be entitled, especially if you are on a low income, have children, have an illness, disability or other special needs, or are an older person.

See the *Disability Rights Handbook*, published by Disability Rights UK, for help for those with care needs.

Food banks

If you are experiencing severe financial hardship (eg, caused by debt or benefit delays), you may be able to get vouchers for food which can be redeemed at a food bank. Vouchers are available from front-line care professionals such as doctors and social workers. Jobcentre Plus staff may also give out vouchers. Further information and contact details for many food banks can be found at trusselltrust.org or by contacting your local authority.

You may be able to get help with food or meals through local community groups which are part of the FareShare network. Further information is available at fareshare.org.uk.

Tax-free childcare

Tax-free childcare is a government scheme to help parents with the cost of childcare. Parents of children aged under 12 (under 17, if they are disabled) can apply.[73]

The government tops up each payment of 80 pence you make into an online childcare account by 20 pence. The maximum annual top-up for each child in qualifying childcare is £2,000 (£4,000 for each disabled child). Payments from the account are debited to a registered childcare provider.

Payments can be made up until 1 September after the child's 11th birthday (16th birthday, if s/he is disabled). There is no limit on the number of children for whom you can make payments.

You (and your partner) must usually both be working and each earning at least 16 times the minimum wage for your age, and your individual earnings are not expected to exceed £100,000 a year each. One of a couple does not have to be in work if s/he is entitled to carer's allowance or contributory employment and support allowance (ESA) or credits for limited capability for work.[74]

Note: you cannot be in the tax-free childcare scheme and still get universal credit (UC) or tax credits.[75] If you are entitled to UC, you are not eligible for the scheme. If you are getting tax credits, your award stops once you register for tax-free childcare – ie, you lose all your entitlement, not just the childcare element. The government may introduce rules that mean you lose all your UC entitlement if you register for the scheme.

If you are considering tax-free childcare, you should therefore check whether or not you will be better off. In most cases, you will be better off continuing to claim UC or tax credits. If you are any doubt, get advice. **Note:**
- The maximum amount of top-up payments in the tax-free childcare scheme may be considerably less than what you can get in UC or tax credits.
- Tax-free childcare does not include any other amounts, and must be spent on childcare. UC and tax credits include amounts for adults, children and disability as well as a childcare element (in UC and working tax credit (WTC)), and UC may include an amount for your housing costs.

- You must reconfirm your circumstances with the tax-free childcare scheme every three months, whereas UC uses a monthly assessment period and tax credits are assessed on annual income and finalised annually.
- If you leave the tax-free childcare scheme and claim UC again, you may be disqualified from applying for tax-free childcare again for up to three years, unless there has been a relevant change of circumstances – eg, a change in the make-up of your household or a change in your work.

See childcarechoices.gov.uk for more information.

Help to Save

Help to Save is a UK-wide government scheme offering a top-up to working people on low incomes who open a new type of savings account and pay into it regularly. To be eligible, you must be getting either:[76]
- UC with earnings of at least £604.59 a month (the monthly equivalent of 16 hours a week at the 'national living wage'); *or*
- WTC. You must either get WTC at more than a nil rate, or be eligible for WTC and get child tax credit at more than a nil rate.

Help to Save accounts last for four years. You can pay in up to £50 a month. After two years, the government will pay in a bonus of 50 per cent of your highest balance, and again at the end of the four years. The government bonus is disregarded as capital for UC, other means-tested benefits and tax credits. Your account can remain open, and you can keep paying into it and receive bonuses, even if you are no longer entitled to the benefit or tax credit that made you eligible to open it. Help to Save is administered by HM Revenue and Customs. See gov.uk/get-help-savings-low-income for more information. You can withdraw money at any time, but it will affect the amount of bonus you can get. You can close your account at any time, but if you close your account early, you will not get a bonus and will not be able to open another account.

Repairs, improvements and energy efficiency

Your local authority may be able to provide you with a grant to help with the cost of improving your home. The main types of grants available are:
- home improvement grants; *and*
- disabled facilities grants.

You may also be able to get:
- assistance from a home improvement agency (a local not-for-profit organisation) to repair, improve, maintain or adapt your home, sometimes called 'care and repair' or 'staying put' schemes, or with small repairs, safety checks and odd jobs from a handyperson service. For information see, in

England, foundations.uk.com, in Wales, careandrepair.org.uk and in Scotland, careandrepairscotland.co.uk;
- a one-off discount of £140 on your energy bill under the Warm Home Discount scheme if you get the guarantee credit of pension credit, or you are on a low income and get other qualifying means-tested benefits and meet your energy supplier's criteria. This does not affect your entitlement to a cold weather payment (see p805) or winter fuel payment (see p806). For further information, visit gov.uk/the-warm-home-discount-scheme;
- a grant for help with insulation and other energy efficiency measures in your home. Different schemes operate in England, Wales and Scotland. For further information, visit energysavingtrust.org.uk. For more details, see CPAG's *Fuel Rights Handbook*.

Special funds for sick or disabled people

A range of help is available for people with an illness or disability to assist with things like paying for care services in their own home, equipment, holidays, furniture and transport needs, and for people with haemophilia or HIV contracted via haemophilia treatment. Grants are also available for practical support to help people do their jobs – eg, to pay for specialist equipment and travel. For more information, see the *Disability Rights Handbook*, published by Disability Rights UK.

Help from social services

Local authority social services departments have statutory duties to provide a range of practical and financial help to families, children, young people, older people, people with disabilities, carers and asylum seekers. Contact your local authority children's services.

Charities

There are many charities that provide various types of help to people in need. Your local authority social services department or local advice centre may know of appropriate charities that could assist you, or you can consult publications, such as *A Guide to Grants for Individuals in Need* and the *Charities Digest*, in your local library. Turn2us has details of charities that can provide financial help on its website turn2us.org.uk. In many cases, applications for support can be made directly from the website. Information on grants available for individuals can also be found at fundsonline.org.uk.

Financial help when preparing for and starting work

If you are looking for work, you may be eligible for a Jobcentre Plus travel discount card, which entitles you to a 50 per cent reduction on selected rail fares, and on other public transport in some areas. This is available if you have been unemployed and claiming UC or jobseeker's allowance (JSA) for three to nine months if you are aged under 25, or three to 12 months if you are aged 25 or over. You may also qualify if you are claiming other benefits and are 'actively engaged' with a Jobcentre Plus adviser.[77] Some information is available at gov.uk/government/publications/support-to-help-with-the-cost-of-transport/support-to-help-with-the-cost-of-transport.

If you are attending training/education, a job interview or starting work, you may be able to get some financial support from the Flexible Support Fund, administered by Jobcentre Plus, to help your transition into work after a period of time on benefit – eg, for childcare costs, travel expenses and new clothes for interviews, and training course fees. You are expected to fund travel costs for fortnightly work search interviews yourself, but travelling expenses for additional appointments can be refunded.[78] Payments are discretionary. The government has said that the Flexible Support Fund can be used more widely for upfront childcare costs before the claimant receives her/his first wage.[79] Check with your Jobcentre Plus office or employment scheme or programme provider to see what is available. Do this before you start work, because you may have to apply before your job starts or within a short period of starting it.

If you are aged at least 18 and starting or developing your own business, you may be eligible for the New Enterprise Allowance. You may be able to get mentoring to help set up a business plan, a weekly allowance worth up to £1,274 over 26 weeks and be able to apply for a start-up loan. You or your partner must be getting UC, JSA or ESA, or you must be getting income support (IS) as a lone parent. Ask your Jobcentre Plus work coach for more information.

In Scotland, it is expected that a Job Start Payment will be introduced for young people starting work averaging at least 12 hours a week over a four-week period. You qualify if you are aged 16 to 24 and have been out of work and claiming UC, IS, income-based JSA or income-related ESA for six months, or if you are a care leaver aged 16 to 25 and getting one of those benefits when you are offered the job. The Job Start Payment will be a one-off grant of £250, or £400 if you are responsible for a child. You cannot receive another Job Start Payment within two years of getting one. The Job Start Payment will be administered by Social Security Scotland.

Notes

1. Council tax reduction
1 s13A LGFA 1992
   E CTRS(DS)E Regs; CTRS(PR)E Regs
   W CTRS(DS)W Regs; CTRSPR(W) Regs
   S CTR(S) Regs; CTR(SPC)S Regs
2 s13A(1)(c) LGFA 1992
3 ss13A(1) and 80 LGFA 1992
4 **E** Regs 12 and 13 CTRS(PR)(E) Regs
   W Regs 28 and 29 CTRSPR(W) Regs
   S Regs 16 and 17 CTR(S) Regs; regs 16
   and 17 CTR(SPC)(S) Regs
5 **E** Sch 7 para 1 CTRS(PR)(E) Regs
   W Sch 12 paras 1-7 CTRSPR(W) Regs
   S Regs 82-88 CTR (S) Regs; regs 61-68
   CTR(SPC)(S) Regs
6 **E** Sch 7 para 2 CTRS(PR)E Regs
   W Sch 12 paras 8-10 CTRSPR(W) Regs
   S Regs 90A-90D CTR(S) Regs; regs 70A-
   70C CTR(SPC)(S) Regs
7 **E** Reg 3 CTRS(PR)(E) Regs
   W Reg 3 CTRSPR(W) Regs
   S Reg 12 CTR(SPC)(S) Regs
8 CTRS(PR)(E) Regs
9 CTRSPR(W) Regs
10 CTR(S) Regs
11 Reg 23(2A) CTR(S) Regs
12 Reg 26 CTR(S) Regs

2. Loans for mortgage interest
13 Reg 17 LMI Regs
14 Reg 15 LMI Regs
15 Reg 15(5) and (6) LMI Regs
16 s8(3)(bc) SSA 1998
17 Regs 2(1), 3, 4 and 5 LMI Regs
18 Reg 3(4) LMI Regs
19 Regs 5(2)(d) and 6 LMI Regs
20 Reg 2(1), definition of 'claimant', 'joint
   claimant' and 'single claimant', and
   (2)(aa) LMI Regs
21 Regs 2 and 3(2)(a) and Sch 1 LMI Regs
22 Reg 2(2)(aa) and Sch 1 para 3 LMI Regs;
   *Saleem v Secretary of State for Social
   Security*, reported as R(IS) 5/01; *SSWP v
   Mohammed* [2011] EWCA Civ 1358,
   reported as [2012] AACR 29
23 Reg 3(2)(b) and Sch 2 LMI Regs
24 Sch 2 paras 3 and 6 LMI Regs
25 Reg 3(3) LMI Regs
26 Reg 3(2)(c) and Sch 3 LMI Regs
27 Sch 3 paras 4-10 and 13-18 LMI Regs

28 Regs 2(1), 7, 11, 12, 13 and 14A LMI
   Regs
29 Reg 13 LMI Regs
30 Regs 2(1), 11(4) and (5) and 12(4) and
   (5) LMI Regs; reg 7(12B) SS&CS(DA)
   Regs
31 Regs 11(1), (2) and (3) and 12(1) and
   (2) LMI Regs
32 Reg 14 LMI Regs
33 Regs 2, definition of 'qualifying period',
   8 and 9(7) LMI Regs
34 Reg 9(1)-(3) LMI Regs
35 Reg 9(4)-(6) LMI Regs
36 Reg 16 LMI Regs
37 DWP press release, 12 June 2019
38 Reg 15 LMI Regs
39 Reg 16(7) LMI Regs
40 Reg 16(4), (5) and (6) LMI Regs

3. Local welfare assistance schemes
41 Welfare Funds (Scotland) Act 2015; The
   Welfare Funds (Scotland) Regulations
   2016, No.107

4. Healthy Start food and vitamins
42 Regs 5(2) and 8 HSS&WF(A) Regs
43 Regs 2(1) and 5(1) and Sch 3
   HSS&WF(A) Regs; HSS(DHSF)(W) Regs
44 Reg 3 HSS&WF(A) Regs
45 Reg 3(5) HSS&WF(A) Regs
46 Reg 3(8)-(11) HSS&WF(A) Regs
47 Reg 2(1) HSS&WF(A) Regs
48 Reg 2(1) HSS&WF(A) Regs
49 Reg 4 and Sch 2 HSS&WF(A) Regs
50 Reg 4(2) HSS&WF(A) Regs
51 Reg 3 HSS&WF(A) Regs
52 Reg 8A HSS&WF(A) Regs
53 gov.scot/policies/maternal-and-child-
   health/free-vitamins-for-all-pregnant-
   women
54 Scottish Government, *Protecting
   Scotland's Future: the government's
   programme for Scotland 2019-20*,
   September 2019, p104
55 WF(BSF)(S) Regs
56 Reg 6, 7 and 8 WF(BSF)(S) Regs
57 Reg 10 WF(BSF)(S) Regs
58 Reg 11 WF(BSF)(S) Regs
59 Reg 20 WF(BSF)(S) Regs
60 Reg 11 WF(BSF)(S) Regs

5. **Education benefits**
61 **E** s512ZB Education Act 1996; The
   Education (Free School Lunches)
   (Prescribed Tax Credits) (England)
   Order 2003, No.383; The Free School
   Lunches and Milk (Universal Credit)
   (England) Order 2013, No.650
   W s512ZB Education Act 1996; The
   Education (Free School Lunches)
   (Prescribed Tax Credits) (Wales) Order
   2003, No.879 (W.110); The Free School
   Lunches and Milk (Universal Credit)
   (Wales) Order 2019 No.187 (W.47)
   S s53(7) and (8) Education (Scotland)
   Act 1980; Reg 4A The Education (School
   Lunches) (Scotland) Regulations 2009,
   No.178
62 Art 3 Welfare Reform Act 2012
   (Commencement No.30 and Transitory
   Provisions) Order 2018, No.145; Art 3
   The Free School Lunches and Milk
   (Universal Credit) (Wales) Order 2019,
   No.187 (W.47)
63 For CTC, the legislation only provides for
   this in Scotland
64 The Education (School Lunches)
   (Scotland) Regulations 2015, No.269
65 s88 School Standards and Organisation
   (Wales) Act 2013

6. **Free milk for children**
66 Reg 18 WF Regs

8. **Christmas bonus**
67 ss148(1) and 149(1) SSCBA 1992
68 s150(4) SSCBA 1992
69 s150(1) SSCBA 1992
70 s149(4) SSCBA 1992
71 ss148(2) and (5) and 150(2) SSCBA
   1992
72 Reg 38 SS(C&P) Regs

9. **Other financial help**
73 childcarechoices.gov.uk
74 Reg 15 Childcare Payments (Eligibility)
   Regulations 2015 No.448

75 ss30 and 31 Childcare Payments Act
   2014
76 The Savings (Government
   Contributions) Act 2017; The Help-to-
   Save Accounts Regulations 2018 No.87
77 See response to Freedom of Information
   request 'Job Centre Discount Card', 2
   August 2015 on whatdotheyknow.com
78 See esearchbriefings.parliament.uk/
   ResearchBriefing/Summary/SN06079
   and data.parliament.uk/
   DepositedPapers/Files/DEP2019-0980/
   52._Flexible_Support_Fund_v5.0.pdf
79 Parliamentary Written Question 275211
   answered on 17 July 2019

Part 6

Special benefit rules

Chapter 41

Benefits for students

This chapter covers:
1. Universal credit (p880)
2. Income support and jobseeker's allowance (p885)
3. Employment and support allowance (p894)
4. Housing benefit (p896)
5. Other benefits (p899)
6. Student income and means-tested benefits (p900)
7. Giving up, changing or taking time out from your course (p908)

England, Scotland and Wales have separate education systems with different student funding.

This chapter covers only those benefits which are potentially affected if you are studying.

Key facts

- If you are a part-time student, your benefits are not usually affected by your studying, although there are extra conditions to meet for jobseeker's allowance and, for some students, universal credit.
- Most full-time students are excluded from claiming means-tested benefits. There are some exceptions, including for parents, disabled students and some young people on further education courses.
- Even if you can claim means-tested benefits, most student funding for living costs counts as income and reduces or stops your benefit.
- If you are a full-time student and are taking time out from your course but have not abandoned it completely, you still count as a student and cannot usually claim benefits, but there are some exceptions.
- Child tax credit, working tax credit and certain benefits, including maternity allowance, statutory sick pay, child benefit, disability living allowance and personal independence payment, have no special eligibility rules for full-time students, so you can claim these in the same way as anyone else, although your student income may affect your entitlement to tax credits in some cases.

Part 6: Special benefit rules
Chapter 41: Benefits for students
1. Universal credit

1. **Universal credit**

Universal credit (UC) is being introduced gradually over the next few years. For more information about when you come under the UC system, see p23.

Undertaking a course of study (the law refers to this as 'receiving education') may mean that you are not eligible for UC, unless you are in one of the groups of people for whom an exception is made (see p881). In general, these are students with children, some disabled students and young students in non-advanced education who have no parental support.

Receiving education

If you are 'receiving education', in most cases you are not eligible for UC.[1] There are exceptions (see p881).

You are 'receiving education' if you are:[2]

- undertaking a full-time course of advanced education. This is education above the level of advanced NVQ, AS/A level or a Scottish national qualification (higher or advanced higher), and includes degree-level or postgraduate-level courses, and HNDs; *or*
- undertaking another full-time course of study or training for which a loan or grant is provided for your maintenance.

In addition, you are treated as receiving education if:

- you are a 'qualifying young person'. You must be enrolled on, or accepted on, a course of non-advanced education or approved training of more than 12 hours a week, and you must have been enrolled on, accepted on or have started the course before you turned 19. You can continue to be a qualifying young person until 31 August after your 19th birthday (see p324).[3] A qualifying young person on a 'relevant training scheme' is not treated as receiving education. This includes someone on a traineeship,[4] or on certain courses or schemes of work or voluntary work preparation; *or*
- none of the above three bullet points apply, but you are on a course that is not compatible with your work-related requirements (see p882).[5]

You count as receiving education from the day you start, to the last day of your course, or sooner if you abandon it or are dismissed from it.[6]

If you are undertaking a part of a modular course (one that consists of two or more modules, and your college or university requires you to complete successfully a specific number of modules before it considers you to have completed the course), you count as undertaking it for the period beginning on the day that part of the course starts, and ending on the last day on which you are registered with your college or university as attending or undertaking that part of your course. This includes any vacations, unless that vacation follows the last day on which you are required to attend or undertake your course, or on such earlier date that you finally abandon or are dismissed from that part of the course.[7]

If you have failed examinations or failed to complete a module, any period in which you undertake the course in order to retake those examinations or modules is classed as part of the course and you are treated as undertaking a course (even if your college or university registers you as a part-time student during your re-sit period).

Who is entitled to universal credit while receiving education

You are eligible for UC while receiving education (although at least some of your student funding may count as income) if you are:[8]

- under 21 on a non-advanced course (or you are aged 21 and turned 21 on the course) and are 'without parental support' (see below);
- responsible for a child or qualifying young person (p324);
- a single foster parent;
- a member of a couple, both of you are full-time students and one of you is responsible for a child or is a foster parent;
- assessed as having limited capability for work (see p1010) and you also get attendance allowance, disability living allowance or personal independence payment;
- over pension age (see p271);
- a student with a partner who is not a student, or who is a student but would be entitled to UC her/himself while receiving education;[9]
- waiting to return to your course after taking time out because of illness or caring responsibilities (see p884).[10]

Without parental support

'Without parental support' means you are not looked after by a local authority and you:[11]
– have no parent; *or*
– cannot live with your parents because you are estranged from them, or because there is a serious risk to your physical or mental health, or you would suffer significant harm if you lived with them; *or*
– are living away from your parents, and they cannot support you financially because they are ill or disabled, in prison or not allowed to enter Britain.
'**Parent**' includes someone acting in place of a parent.

When someone else can claim for you

If you cannot get UC yourself, someone may be able to claim for you if you are a 'qualifying young person' – ie, generally, if you are under 20 and in non-advanced education (see p62 and p324).

Part 6: Special benefit rules
Chapter 41: Benefits for students
1. Universal credit

Your work-related requirements

Most people claiming UC have work-related requirements as a condition of getting benefit, which may involve undertaking work-related activity or looking for work (see p1050). You have no work-related requirements if you are receiving education and are eligible for UC (unless you are only eligible under the last bullet point on p881 – waiting to return to your course) and you are:[12]

- under 21 (or 21 and you turned 21 on your course) in non-advanced education and 'without parental support' (see p881); *or*
- in receipt of student income which is taken into account for UC – ie, a student loan or a maintenance grant (see below). **Note:** over the summer vacation, when student income is ignored, you may have work-related requirements.

Note: even if you do not fit into one of the groups on p881, you may have no work-related requirements under the general rules – eg, if you are responsible for a child under one, or if you are severely disabled (see p1061).

If you are receiving education but do not get a loan or grant, you may, therefore, be subject to all work-related requirements, and must be available for and actively seeking work (see p1069). This is more likely to be the case if you are in non-advanced education or on some postgraduate courses.

Studying part time

If you are on a part-time course, you may still be treated as 'receiving education' if the course is not compatible with your work-related requirements.[13] So if you are subject to all work-related requirements, you must show that you meet these despite being on a part-time course. In some cases, it may be possible to argue that the course should be seen as 'voluntary work preparation', and, therefore, reduce your work search requirements (see p1053).[14]

If you are on a part-time course that is accepted as being compatible with your work-related requirements, you can get UC.

How student income affects universal credit

If you (or your partner) have any student income, it may count as income for UC.[15]

You are counted as having student income if you are undertaking a course and have a student loan or grant in respect of that course.[16]

Grants

The term 'grant' means an educational grant or award. It does not include a grant paid to someone under 21 in non-advanced education to enable them to finish a course.[17] This means that education maintenance allowance payments and 16 to 19 bursary fund payments do not count as student income. Access or discretionary fund payments are likely to count as student income (as an 'educational grant'), unless they can be disregarded under the rules below.

If you get a grant but do not get a loan, the grant income is taken into account for UC. Certain amounts of your grant are disregarded as your income if they are:[18]

- for tuition fees or exams;
- in respect of your disability;
- for extra costs of residential study away from your usual place of study during term time;
- to pay for the costs of your normal home (if you live somewhere else during your course), unless these are met by your UC;
- for the maintenance of someone who is not included in your UC claim;
- for books, equipment, course travel costs or childcare costs.

If you get a grant and also get a loan and your grant is paid for the same period, it is completely disregarded unless it is for the maintenance of someone who is part of your UC claim (eg, a partner or a child) or for rent payments that are met by UC.[19]

Student loans

Student loans for maintenance[20] count as income if you could get a loan by taking 'reasonable steps', even if you choose not to apply for one. The maximum loan you could be entitled to (or 30 per cent of the maximum, for a postgraduate master's degree or doctoral loan in England or Wales[21]) is taken into account as income.

This is the case even if the loan is reduced by an assessed parental (or partner) contribution, or if part of the loan is replaced by a grant. However, if you are eligible for a special support element as part of your maintenance loan in England, this is disregarded, as it is paid for books, travel, equipment and childcare.[22] You may need to get a statement from Student Finance England explaining your entitlement. In Scotland, a student loan includes a young student's bursary.[23]

Calculating student income

UC is paid for an 'assessment period' of one month (see p49). Student income counts as income in assessment periods that fall during the course, as well as in the assessment period in which the course, and any subsequent year of the course, begins.[24] Student income is ignored in the assessment period in which the last week of the course or the start of the long vacation falls. The long vacation is the longest holiday, lasting at least a month, in a course which is at least two years long. Student income is also ignored in any other assessment period that falls completely within the long vacation.[25]

In each assessment period, £110 of student income is disregarded.

Part 6: Special benefit rules
Chapter 41: Benefits for students
1. Universal credit

To work out how much of your student income is taken into account:

- **Step one:** calculate your annual loan or grant or, if the course lasts for less than a year, the amount of loan or grant for the course.
- **Step two:** work out how many assessment periods apply for that year, or for the course if it is less than a year long.
- **Step three:** divide the amount from Step one by the number of assessment periods in Step two.
- **Step four:** deduct £110.

Example

Holly gets a student loan of £10,194 in total. This includes a special support element of £3,783, which is disregarded, leaving £6,411. Year one of her course runs from 30 September 2019 to 15 May 2020. Her assessment periods run from the 20th of the month to the 19th of the following month. Her loan counts as income for seven assessment periods.

£6,411 ÷ 7 = £915.86

£915.86 – £110 = £805.86

Holly's UC is calculated on student income of £805.86 a month from 20 September 2019 to 19 April 2020.

Taking time out from your course

During a period of temporary absence from your course, you usually still count as receiving education, so the student rules apply. Therefore, if you take time out because you have to re-sit exams or because you are ill, you still count as receiving education and are only eligible for UC if you are in one of the eligible groups (see p881) – eg, you are a parent.

You do not count as 'receiving education' and can claim UC if you have taken time out from your course because of illness or caring responsibilities, you have now recovered or your caring responsibilities have ended, you are not eligible for a grant or student loan, and you are waiting to return to your course.[26] Your institution must have agreed to your taking time out, and you must have recovered from your illness or your caring responsibilities must have ended within the last year.

If you leave your course completely, you no longer count as receiving education, so the normal UC rules apply. Student income is taken into account up to the end of the assessment period before the one in which you leave the course.

If you take time out of a modular course, which amounts to time out of 'a part' of such a course, it may be argued that you do not count as undertaking a course during that period.[27]

2. **Income support and jobseeker's allowance**

You cannot usually make a new claim for income support (IS) or income-based jobseeker's allowance (JSA), unless you are severely disabled and are prevented from claiming universal credit (UC) (see p24).

If you are studying, you may count as being in 'relevant education' (see below), or as a 'full-time student' (see p887). You cannot usually qualify for IS or JSA (either contribution-based or income-based). There are some exceptions, however, which are outlined in this section. You may also be able to qualify if you are studying part time (see p891).

Note: this section deals with the rules for income-based JSA, and for contribution-based JSA if claiming under the old mean-tested benefit system. The rules are different for contribution-based JSA if you come under the UC system (see p899).

Relevant education

If you are in relevant education, you can only get IS in some circumstances and you cannot usually get JSA.[28] **Note:** for JSA, a young person on a traineeship does not count as being in relevant education. For this purpose, traineeship is a course of up to six months which helps 16–24-year-olds to prepare for work and is funded or arranged by the Secretary of State under section 14 of the Education Act 2002.[29]

You count as being in '**relevant education**' if you are a 'qualifying young person' for child benefit purposes (see p579) – ie, you are under 20 and in full-time, non-advanced education or approved training on which you were accepted, enrolled or started when you were under 19.[30] For these purposes, 'full-time' means more than 12 hours a week in term time, not including meal breaks and unsupervised study. 'Non-advanced' means anything below degree, HNC or HND level.

You can continue to count as being in relevant education for a period after your education or training ends – eg, if you have enrolled on another course or during what is known as the child benefit 'extension period' (see p579).

Who is entitled to income support while in relevant education
You can qualify for IS while in relevant education if:[31]
- you are the parent of a child for whom you are treated as responsible and who is a member of your household (see p326); *or*
- you are a refugee who is learning English to obtain employment (see p238); *or*
- you are an orphan and have no one acting in place of your parents; *or*
- you have left local authority care and you have to live away from your parents and any person acting in their place (see p886). **Note:** if you are a care leaver

Part 6: Special benefit rules
Chapter 41: Benefits for students
2. Income support and jobseeker's allowance

aged 16 or 17 (see p948), you can only qualify for IS while you are in relevant education if you are a lone parent and treated as responsible for a child;[32] *or*
- you have to live away from your parents and any person acting in their place (see below) because:
  - you are estranged from them; *or*
  - you are in physical or moral danger; *or*
  - there is a serious risk to your physical or mental health.

The physical or moral danger does not have to be caused by your parents. Therefore, a young person who is a refugee and cannot rejoin her/his parents can claim IS while at school;[33] *or*
- you live apart from your parents and any person acting in their place, they are unable to support you and:
  - they are in prison; *or*
  - they are unable to come to Britain because they do not have leave to enter under the Immigration Rules;[34] *or*
  - they are chronically sick, or are mentally or physically disabled. This covers people who could get a disability premium or higher pensioner premium, get employment and support allowance (ESA) including a work-related or support component (or who would be entitled to contributory ESA including a work-related component but this has stopped being paid after 52 weeks), have an armed forces grant for car costs because of disability, or who are substantially and permanently disabled.

You may be able to claim IS under some of the above rules beyond age 20 if you are in one of the groups of full-time students who can claim (see p890).

Definitions

A 'person acting in place of your parents' can include a local authority or voluntary organisation if you are being cared for by them, or foster carers, but only until you leave care.[35] It does not include a person who is your sponsor under the Immigration Rules.[36] In the last bullet point above, however, a person acting in place of your parents includes the person with whom you are placed, but does not expressly include the local authority.[37]

'Estrangement' implies emotional disharmony,[38] where you have no desire to have any prolonged contact with your parents or they feel similarly towards you. It is possible to be estranged even though your parents are providing some financial support or you still have some contact with them. If you are being cared for by a local authority, it is also possible to be estranged from the local authority. If you are, you could qualify for IS if you have to live away from accommodation provided by a local authority.[39]

Who is entitled to jobseeker's allowance while in relevant education

You cannot qualify for JSA while in relevant education unless you are someone who can qualify for IS while in relevant education (see p885),[40] or you are treated as not being in relevant education. If you *can* qualify for IS while in relevant education, it may be better for you to claim IS.

In some cases, if you were previously on certain benefits and are now on a non-advanced course, which would be part time according to the rules for full-time students (ie, over 12 but not over 16 hours), you do not count as being in relevant education and can get JSA.[41]

When someone else can claim for you

If you cannot qualify for IS or JSA because you are in relevant education, someone else may be able to get child benefit, and UC or child tax credit (CTC) and working tax credit if s/he is treated as 'responsible' for you.

When you leave relevant education

Once you have left relevant education, you may be able to get IS or JSA if you satisfy the rules for getting those benefits (see Chapters 11 and 12). You can continue to count as being in relevant education for a period after your education or training ends – eg, if you have enrolled on another course or during the child benefit 'extension period' (see p581). While you continue to be treated as in relevant education, you are only entitled to IS in the circumstances on p885.

Full-time students

If you are a full-time student, you cannot usually qualify for IS or JSA for the duration of your course, including vacations.[42] See p890 for exceptions to this rule. See p908 if you give up, change or take time out from your course and p891 if you are studying part time.

You count as a full-time student if you are not in relevant education (see p885), you are not getting a training allowance, and:[43]

- you are under 19 and attending or undertaking a full-time course of 'advanced education'. '**Advanced education**' means degree- or postgraduate-level qualifications, teaching courses, diplomas of higher education, HND or HNC and all other courses above advanced GNVQ or equivalent, OND, A levels or a Scottish national qualification (higher or advanced level). See p888 for what counts as a full-time course; *or*
- you are 19 or over but under pension age (see p780) and attending or undertaking a full-time course of study. If your course is full time, you are treated as a full-time student regardless of the level of the course, unless you are aged under 20 and can still be treated as being in 'relevant education' (see p885). See p888 for what counts as a full-time course; *or*
- you are on a sandwich course (see p888).

You are treated as a student until either the last day of your course or until you abandon or are dismissed from it.[44] The 'last day of the course' is the date on which the last day of the final academic year is officially scheduled to fall.[45]

Part 6: Special benefit rules
Chapter 41: Benefits for students
2. Income support and jobseeker's allowance

For JSA, the period of study includes periods during which you are doing work connected to the course, even if this is after the normal end of your study.[46]

Full-time courses

In England and Wales, your course counts as full time and you are treated as a full-time student if:[47]

- it is fully or partly funded by the Secretary of State under section 14 of the Education Act 2002, section 100 of the Apprenticeships, Skills, Children and Learning Act 2009 or the Welsh government, and your personal 'learning agreement' involves more than 16 hours of 'guided learning' each week. Courses include academic or vocational courses leading to a recognised qualification. The Secretary of State and the Welsh government also fund basic literacy and numeracy courses, English as a Second or Other Language (ESOL) programmes, Access and similar courses that prepare you to move on to qualification-bearing courses, and courses developing independent living skills for people with learning difficulties. The number of guided learning hours you do each week is set out in your learning agreement. This is signed by you and the college. The DWP uses this agreement to decide whether or not you are on a full-time course;[48] *or*
- it is not funded by the Secretary of State under section 14 of the Education Act 2002, section 100 of the Apprenticeships, Skills, Children and Learning Act 2009 or the Welsh government and is a 'full-time course of study'.

In Scotland, your course counts as full time and you are treated as being a full-time student if:[49]

- it is totally or partly funded by the Scottish Ministers at a college of further education, is not higher education *and* your personal learning document states that your course:
  - involves more than 16 hours a week of classroom-based or workshop-based programmed learning under the guidance of a teacher; *or*
  - involves more than 21 hours' study a week, 16 hours or less of which involve classroom-based or workshop-based programmed learning, and the rest of which involve using structured learning packages with the help of a teacher. The number of hours of 'learning' you do each week is set out in your learning document. This is signed by you and the college. The DWP uses this document to decide whether or not you are on a full-time course; *or*
- it is a course of higher education which is funded wholly or in part by the Scottish Ministers and is a full-time course of study; *or*
- it is not funded by the Scottish Ministers and is a full-time course of study.

Sandwich courses

A course is a 'sandwich course' if it consists of alternate periods of full-time study at your educational institution and periods of industrial, professional or work experience organised so that, taking the course as a whole, you attend the periods of full-time study for an average of at least 18 weeks in each year.[50] This does not apply if it is a course of initial teacher training. If your periods of full-time study and work experience alternate within any week of your course, the days of full-time study are aggregated with each other and with any weeks of full-time study to determine the number of weeks of full-time study in each year.

Work experience includes periods of employment abroad for modern language students whose course is at least half composed of modern language study.

Health-related courses

If you attend a health-related course for which you are entitled to receive an NHS bursary, you are treated as a full-time or part-time student as appropriate, and not an employee.[51]

Modular courses

A modular course consists of two or more modules, and your college or university requires you to complete successfully a specific number of modules before it considers you to have completed the course.[52] You are treated as a full-time student if you are currently attending part of a modular course that would be classed as a full-time course.[53] You are treated as a full-time student for the period beginning on the day your course is defined as a full-time course and ending on the last day on which you are registered with your college or university as attending or undertaking that part of your course. This includes any vacations, unless that vacation follows the last day on which you are required to attend or undertake your course, or on such earlier date that you finally abandon or are dismissed from that part of the course.[54]

If you have failed examinations or failed to complete a module, any period in which you attend or undertake the course in order to retake those examinations or modules is classed as part of the full-time course and you are treated as a full-time student (even if your college or university registers you as a part-time student during your re-sit period).[55]

Because the rules do not define what is a full-time course, unless funded by the Secretary of State under section 14 of the Education Act 2002, section 100 of the Apprenticeships, Skills, Children and Learning Act 2009 or Scottish Ministers (see p888), you may be able to argue that you are not attending a full-time course, regardless of your attendance, if your course is not defined as full time or part time by your college or university.[56]

Note: if you take time out of a complete 'part' of a modular course, you may not count as undertaking a course during this time.[57]

Other courses

If your course does not automatically count as full time under the rules above, whether it counts as a 'full-time course of study' depends on the college or

Part 6: Special benefit rules
Chapter 41: Benefits for students
2. Income support and jobseeker's allowance

university. Definitions are often based on local custom and practice within educational institutions. The college or university's definition is not absolutely final, but if you want to challenge it, you will have to produce a good argument showing why it should not be accepted.[58] If your course is only for a few hours each week, argue that it is not full time. However, a course could be full time even though you only have to attend a few lectures a week.[59]

Full-time students who are entitled to income support

Even if you are a full-time student, you can qualify for IS (although most student funding counts as income) if you are:[60]

- a lone parent under age 18 (regardless of the age of your child/ren), or a lone parent of a child under five; *or*
- a lone foster carer of a child under 16; *or*
- single, or are one of a couple and both of you are full-time students and:
  - you fit into one of the groups of people who can claim IS (see Chapter 11); *and*
  - you (or, if you are one of a couple, either one or both of you) are responsible for a child or young person (see p583); *and*
  - it is the summer vacation;
- a refugee who is learning English to obtain employment (see p238); *or*
- in, enrolled on or accepted for full-time non-advanced education and you are aged under 21, or you are 21 and you reached that age while in such education. In addition, you must:
  - have no parents (or anyone acting in their place); *or*
  - have to live away from your parents (or anyone acting in their place) because you are estranged from them, or are in physical or moral danger or there is a serious risk to your physical or mental health; *or*
  - be living away from your parents (or anyone acting in their place) and they cannot support you financially and they are:
    - chronically sick or mentally or physically disabled; *or*
    - in prison; *or*
    - prohibited from entering or re-entering Great Britain.

Full-time students who are entitled to jobseeker's allowance

Even if you are a full-time student, you can qualify for JSA (although most student funding counts as income) if you are:

- single and responsible for a child or, if you are one of a couple, both of you are full-time students and either one or both of you is responsible for a child (see p583). This exception only applies during the summer vacation and if you are available for work, or treated as available because you are on either of the courses in the next bullet point;[61] *or*

- on an employment-related course of up to two weeks that has been approved in advance by the DWP,[62] or a Venture Trust training programme of up to four weeks.[63] In either case, only one course is allowed in any 12-month period; *or*
- participating in a scheme for assisting people to obtain employment (eg, Skills Conditionality – see p1151) – ie, you have been required to attend full-time training under it;[64] *or*
- aged 25 or over and on a qualifying course;[65] *or*
- waiting to go back to your course, having taken approved time out because of an illness or caring responsibility and that has now come to an end (see p908).

Maintaining two homes

In some cases, if you qualify for IS or income-based JSA, you may be entitled to help with the costs of more than one home if you have to live away from your normal home to attend a course. For further details, see p374.

Part-time students

If you are studying but are not in relevant education (see p885) or attending a full-time course (see p888), you are treated as attending a part-time course and classed as a part-time student.

Who is entitled to income support while studying part time

You can get IS while studying part time if you are not on a full-time course and you satisfy the other rules for getting IS (see Chapter 11).

If you are currently studying part time on a course you previously attended full time, the DWP may argue that you are attending a full-time course and should, therefore, be treated as a full-time student. It may be possible to challenge this interpretation.[66] Get specialist advice if you are in this situation.

Who is entitled to jobseeker's allowance while studying part time

You count as a part-time student if your course is not full time.[67] You can get JSA while studying part time if you meet the jobseeking conditions – ie, you are available for work, actively seeking work and you have a valid jobseeker's agreement (see p1114). If you have agreed restrictions with the DWP on the hours that you are available for work, there are special rules that can help you claim JSA and study part time (see p892).

When you claim JSA you may be asked to fill in a 'student questionnaire'. Your answers are taken into account when deciding whether you are available for and actively seeking work. The DWP must be satisfied that you are genuinely available for and actively seeking work while you are studying part time.

Availability for work and part-time study

Your availability for work should not be affected by your part-time course if your hours of study or training are at times outside your agreed pattern of availability

Part 6: Special benefit rules
Chapter 41: Benefits for students
2. Income support and jobseeker's allowance

(see p1122) – ie, they do not clash with the times you are willing and able to work. If the hours of your course *do* clash with the times you say you are available for work (as set out in your jobseeker's agreement – see p1127), you are only accepted as available for work if either:[68]

- you are able to rearrange the hours of the course or study to fit around your job; *or*
- you are willing and able to give up the course should a job become available.

Deciding whether you are available for work

A number of factors should be considered when deciding whether you are available for work while you are studying part time. If, for example, it appears you are not willing or able to give up your course or that you cannot confine your study to times that would fit in with employment, you are treated as not being available for work. The factors that may be relevant include:[69]

- if you are studying or training away from home, whether you can be contacted if a job becomes available;
- the extent of your efforts to find employment;
- how important the successful completion of the course is to your future career, including whether it will enhance your chances of finding employment;
- whether you gave up a job or training to do the course;
- the days and hours you are required to attend the course;
- whether the times of attendance could be changed to fit in with any job you might obtain or whether successful completion of the course is possible if you miss some of the scheduled attendances;
- the duration of the study or training;
- whether a fee was paid and, if so, the amount and whether any of the fee could be refunded or transferred if you abandoned or interrupted your studies. If you have paid a fee, it may be more difficult (depending on the amount) to convince the DWP that you are prepared to abandon the course;
- whether you received a grant and, if so, the source, the amount and whether you would have to repay any or all of it if you interrupted or abandoned the course.

The guidance for decision makers states that where a number of claimants are following the same course, some may be able to show that they are available, but others may not.[70] The DWP should consider each claim individually and not operate a blanket policy. The DWP assumes that you may be less willing to leave a course if you are near its end or as the chance of obtaining a qualification approaches.[71]

Restricting your availability for work

There are special rules that can help you qualify for JSA if you are a part-time student. These say that, in certain circumstances, the fact that you are on your course is ignored when deciding whether you are available for work if the hours of your course fall wholly or partly within the times you say you are available for work. However, you still have to be available for and actively seeking work during the rest of the week when you are not on your course.

These rules apply to you if you are a part-time student, and you are willing and able to rearrange the hours of your course to take up a job and the restrictions on your hours of availability have been agreed with the DWP because:[72]
- of your physical or mental condition (see p1121); *or*
- of your caring responsibilities (see p1123); *or*
- you are working 'short time'; *or*
- they leave you available for work for at least 40 hours a week (see p1122).

You must also satisfy one of two conditions.
- For the three months immediately before the date you started the course, you were unemployed and getting JSA, or you were incapable of work and getting IS, incapacity benefit (IB) or ESA, or you were on a course of 'training'.
- In the six months immediately before you started the course, you were unemployed and getting JSA, or you were incapable of work and getting IS, IB or ESA, or you were on a course of training for a total of at least three months and, for any remaining part of the six months, you were working full time or earning too much to qualify for benefit.

The three-month and six-month periods can only begin after you have reached your terminal date (see p582) and are treated as having ceased to be in relevant education (see p582).

Training

'**Training**' means training for which young people aged under 18 are eligible, or for which a person aged 18–24 may be eligible, provided or arranged by the Secretary of State under section 14 of the Education Act 2002, the Welsh government or Skills Development Scotland.[73]

How student income affects income support and jobseeker's allowance

There are special rules for assessing your income from your student grant, loan or other types of student support (see p900), including for people claiming IS while in 'relevant education'.[74] These rules do not apply if you are receiving a training allowance.

The normal rules for assessing your other income and capital apply (see Chapters 20 and 22).

Part 6: Special benefit rules
Chapter 41: Benefits for students
3. Employment and support allowance

3. **Employment and support allowance**

Whether you can qualify for employment and support allowance (ESA) while studying full time depends on the type of ESA.

You can qualify for contributory ESA as a full-time or part-time student (see p649).

You cannot qualify for income-related ESA if you are 'receiving education' unless you are getting disability living allowance (DLA), personal independence payment (PIP) or armed forces independence payment (see below). You may be able to qualify if you are studying part time (see p895).

Note: in certain circumstances, if you are attending a training course and are paid a training allowance, you cannot qualify for ESA because you do not count as having limited capability for work (see p1015).[75]

Who is entitled to income-related employment and support allowance

You cannot usually make a new claim for income-related ESA, unless you are severely disabled and are prevented from claiming universal credit (UC) (see p25).

However, if you currently get contributory ESA and do not come under the UC system, you can also qualify for income-related ESA if your income is low enough.

If you are 'receiving education', you can only qualify for income-related ESA if you are getting DLA, PIP or armed forces independence payment.[76] This usually applies for the duration of your course, including vacations. See p895 if you have finished studying and p908 if you give up, change or take time out from your course.

For income-related ESA purposes, you count as 'receiving education' if you are:
- a 'qualifying young person' for child benefit purposes (see p579), but not if you are on a traineeship;[77] *or*
- undertaking a 'course of study'.[78] The DWP may refer to you as a 'full-time student'. The definition is the same as the definition of full-time student for income support (IS) and jobseeker's allowance (JSA) (see p887). A course of study is similar to a full-time course for IS and JSA, except, for ESA, it also includes a sandwich course (see p888) and does not include a traineeship. Note that if you take time out of a complete part of a modular course, you may not count as undertaking a course during that time.[79]

Note:
- The term 'full-time student' is used in the rest of this section to refer to someone who is receiving education for income-related ESA purposes.
- Unless you are a 'qualifying young person' for child benefit purposes, if you qualify for income-related ESA as a full-time student because you are getting

DLA, PIP or armed forces independence payment, you automatically count as having limited capability for work (see p1011).[80]

Maintaining two homes

In some cases, if you are a full-time student and you qualify for income-related ESA, you may be entitled to help with the costs of more than one home if you have to live away from your normal home to attend a course. For further details, see p374.

When you stop being a full-time student

Once you stop being a full-time student, you may be able to get income-related ESA (see Chapter 9). However, bear the following in mind.

- If you were a 'qualifying young person' for child benefit purposes (eg, you were under 20 and on a full-time course of non-advanced education – see p579), you continue to count as a qualifying young person for a period after your education or training ends – eg, if you have enrolled on another course or during the child benefit 'extension period' (see p581). While you continue to be treated as a qualifying young person, you can only qualify for income-related ESA if you are receiving DLA, PIP or armed forces independence payment. If you cannot qualify for ESA in your own right, your parents may be able to continue to claim child benefit and tax credits for you.
- If you counted as a full-time student other than because you were a 'qualifying young person' for child benefit purposes (see p579), you continue to be treated as a full-time student until the last day of your course, or until you abandon the course or are dismissed from it (see p908).

Studying part time

You can qualify for income-related ESA if you do not count as a full-time student under the rules described on p894.

When someone else can claim for you

If you are under 20, a 'qualifying young person' for child benefit purposes (see p579) and cannot qualify for ESA because you are 'receiving full-time education' (see p894) or are a full-time student (see p894), someone else may be able to qualify for child benefit, and UC or child tax credit and working tax credit if s/he is treated as 'responsible' for you.

How student income affects employment and support allowance

There are special rules for assessing your income from your student grant, loan or other types of student support (see p900).

Part 6: Special benefit rules
Chapter 41: Benefits for students
4. Housing benefit

The normal rules for assessing your other income and capital apply (see Chapters 20 and 22).

4. **Housing benefit**

You cannot usually make a new claim for housing benefit (HB) (but see p24 for the exceptions).

Note: if you are eligible for HB, have reached pension age and neither you nor your partner are in receipt of income support (IS), income-based jobseeker's allowance (JSA) or income-related employment and support allowance (ESA), the student rules for HB do not apply and there are no restrictions on your studying and qualifying for HB.[81]

Whether you can get HB depends on whether you are classed as a full-time or a part-time student.

The rules for deciding whether you are a full-time student are similar to the rules for IS and JSA (see p887), except that there is no separate rule in HB if you are in 'relevant education' (see p885).

If you are a full-time student (see p887), you cannot usually qualify for HB, but there are some exceptions (see below).

Full-time students who are entitled to housing benefit

You can qualify for HB (although most student funding counts as income) if:[82]

- you are on IS, income-based JSA, income-related ESA or universal credit (UC) except if your UC includes an amount for housing costs (see Chapter 6); *or*
- you are under 21, not following a course of higher education (higher education includes degree courses, teacher training, HND, HNC and postgraduate courses), or are aged 21 and you reached that age while on such a course and are still on it, or you are a child or a 'qualifying young person' for child benefit purposes (see p579); *or*
- you and your partner are both full-time students and either or both of you are responsible for a child or qualifying young person (see p579). **Note:** unlike for IS and JSA, this provision applies throughout the year; *or*
- you are a lone parent responsible for a dependent child or qualifying young person aged under 20 (see p579); *or*
- you are a lone foster carer and the child has been formally placed with you; *or*
- you meet the conditions for the disability premium (see p341). **Note:** you cannot qualify for a disability premium if you have limited capability for work; *or*
- you have been (or have been treated as) incapable of work (see p683 of the 2013/14 edition of this *Handbook*) for 196 days (28 weeks); *or*

- you have had (or have been treated as having) limited capability for work (see p1010) for 196 days (28 weeks) and you continue to have it. Two or more periods are joined to form a single period if they are separated by 12 weeks or less. **Note:** claims from 27 October 2008 are assessed under these rules rather than the incapacity for work rules in the bullet point above, unless, broadly, you already get incapacity benefit or IS because of incapacity for work; *or*
- you meet the conditions for the severe disability premium (see p346); *or*
- you qualify for a disabled students' allowance because you are deaf; *or*
- you are waiting to go back to your course, having taken approved time out because of an illness or caring responsibility and this has now come to an end (see p909).

Note: even if you are a full-time student who comes into one of the above groups, you cannot qualify for HB if the circumstances under the two headings below apply to you.

Being away from your term-time accommodation

Even if you are a full-time student who can qualify for HB (see p896), if your main reason for occupying your home is to enable you to attend your course, you cannot qualify for HB on that home for any full week when you are absent from it outside your period of study (see p901).[83]

This rule does not apply if:

- you are away from home because you are in hospital;[84]
- the main reason for occupying your home is *not* to enable you to attend your course but for some other purpose – eg, to provide a home for your children or for yourself because you do not have a home elsewhere to live when you are not attending your course. If this applies, any absences outside your period of study are dealt with under the temporary absence rules (see p182).

Accommodation rented from an educational establishment

If you are a full-time student who can qualify for HB (see p896), you can usually get HB even if you rent your accommodation from your educational establishment.[85] If you are a part-time student, this rule applies if you would be able to qualify for HB if you were treated as a full-time student.

You cannot, however, get HB if you are a:

- full-time student waiting to go back to your course, having taken approved time out because of illness or caring responsibilities (see p909) and your illness or caring responsibilities have not yet ended; *or*
- part-time student whose only basis of entitlement to HB if you were a full-time student would be that you are receiving IS, income-based JSA or income-related ESA.

Part 6: Special benefit rules
Chapter 41: Benefits for students
4. Housing benefit

The above two exceptions do not apply if:

- your educational establishment itself rents the accommodation from a third party other than on a long lease or where the third party is an education authority providing the accommodation as part of its functions; *or*
- the accommodation is owned by a separate legal body – eg, a company established to build halls of residence.

You cannot get HB if the local authority decides that your educational establishment has arranged for your accommodation to be provided by a person or body other than itself in order to take advantage of the HB scheme.

Maintaining two homes

The rules about claiming HB for two homes are explained on p186. If you are one of a couple and receive HB for two homes, the assessment of HB for each home is based on your joint income and your applicable amount as a couple.

Part-time students

You may be able to qualify for HB if you are studying part time. The rules for deciding whether you are a part-time student are similar to the rules for IS and JSA (see p891), except that there is no separate rule in HB if you are in 'relevant education' (see p885).

Partners of students

If your partner is not a student, s/he can qualify for HB if s/he meets the qualifying conditions.[86] The claim is assessed in the normal way, except that the rules about being away from term-time accommodation (see p897) apply to your partner's claim.[87] Additionally, the special rules for assessing any income you receive from a grant, loan and other types of student support for students apply (see p900).

How student income affects housing benefit

If you or your partner are on IS, income-based JSA, income-related ESA, UC or the guarantee credit of pension credit (PC), you are entitled to maximum HB (see Chapter 10).

If you are not on UC, IS, income-based JSA, income-related ESA or the guarantee credit of PC but you or your partner are eligible for HB, your entitlement is calculated in the same way as for other claimants (see Chapters 20 and 22), except that there are special rules for assessing the amount of your income from grants, loans and other types of student support (see p900). **Note:** for courses lasting more than one year, in many cases loans and grants are not counted as income over the summer vacation. You may find, therefore, that your HB entitlement is higher over this period, and that you need to check that your entitlement is reviewed at that time.

Payments

Students are covered by all the normal rules on the administration and payment of HB (see Chapter 10). However, there is a provision that can apply specifically to students. The local authority may decide to pay a rent allowance once each term, although students have the same right as other claimants to insist on fortnightly payments if their entitlement is more than £2 a week.[88]

5. **Other benefits**

Carer's allowance

You cannot qualify for carer's allowance (CA) (see Chapter 26) if you are in full-time education.[89] Usually, if the course you are attending is described by the university, college or school as full time, you are regarded as being in full-time education, although there may be exceptions – eg, if you are exempted from parts of the course.[90] So the actual hours you attend may not be crucial. However, if you are attending for 21 hours a week or more (as specified by the institution), you are treated as being in full-time education. When calculating the 21 hours, include only hours spent in 'supervised study' (see below). Ignore any time spent on meal breaks or unsupervised study undertaken on or off the premises of the educational establishment.[91]

You are treated as still being in full-time education during vacations and any temporary interruption of the course, but not if you have abandoned the course or been dismissed from it. If an interruption is not temporary (eg, if you have agreed with your institution to take a whole year out of your course), you may be able to claim CA.[92]

Supervised study

'**Supervised study**' does not depend on whether your supervisor (ie, teacher, tutor, lecturer) is present with you.[93] If your study is directed to your course of education and the curriculum of your course and it is undertaken to meet the reasonable requirements of your course, it normally counts as supervised study. It counts regardless of whether that study is undertaken on or off the premises of the educational institution you attend.

'**Unsupervised study**' means work beyond the reasonable requirements of your course. In assessing your hours of attendance, evidence from your educational institution about the amount of time you are expected to study to complete your course is important.

Contribution-based jobseeker's allowance

If you come under the universal credit (UC) system (see p23) and are claiming contribution-based jobseeker's allowance (JSA), the rules in this section apply. If

Part 6: Special benefit rules
Chapter 41: Benefits for students
6. Student income and means-tested benefits

you do not come under the UC system and are claiming contribution-based JSA, the rules on p887 apply.

Students who are in 'relevant education' cannot claim contribution-based JSA. You are in relevant education if you are:[94]

- a qualifying young person (see p579);
- on a full-time course of advanced education;
- on another full-time course for which a loan or grant is provided for your maintenance;
- on a course which is not compatible with your work-related requirements.

Note: you can claim contribution-based JSA, even if you are in relevant education, if you took time out because of illness or caring responsibilities, you have now recovered or the caring responsibilities have ended, and you are waiting to rejoin your course.

National insurance credits

You may be able to receive national insurance credits (see Chapter 43) for a tax year in which you were on a full-time course.

6. **Student income and means-tested benefits**

The rules in this section apply to income support (IS), income-based jobseeker's allowance (JSA), income-related employment and support allowance (ESA) and housing benefit (HB). They apply if you are a part-time or a full-time student. If you are claiming universal credit, see p882.

There are many types of financial support available for students, paid as either grants or loans. Some types of grant or loan are available to all students who meet the conditions of entitlement. Others are available on a discretionary basis. The support varies depending on whether you live in England, Wales or Scotland. For more information, see gov.uk/student-finance, studentfinancewales.co.uk, saas.gov.uk or CPAG's *Student Support and Benefits Handbook* and *Benefits for Students in Scotland Handbook*.

If you (or your partner) are a student, some of your (or your partner's) income from your grant, loan and certain other forms of student support is taken into account when calculating the amount of your benefit.[95] Your other income and capital are dealt with under the normal rules (see Chapters 20 and 22).

Note: the DWP has issued guidance to decision makers on how student support should be treated. Often this guidance only covers some of the benefits to which this section refers. For example, guidance may have been issued for HB purposes, but no equivalent guidance has been issued for IS, JSA or ESA. In addition, the legislation and guidance may not cover all sources of student support across the UK, particularly as new sources of support are introduced.

- The information in this section applies to support available to new students for the 2019/20 academic year. For how grants and loans are treated for students who started their course in previous academic years, see the previous editions of this *Handbook*.
- Grant and loan income do not affect your contribution-based JSA or contributory ESA.
- Any student income you have from a grant or loan is not taken into account as income if you are claiming HB and you:
  - are getting IS, income-based JSA, income-related ESA or the guarantee credit of pension credit (PC); *or*
  - have reached pension age and you (or your partner) are not getting IS, income-based JSA or income-related ESA.[96]

Grants

Student grants include any kind of educational grant or award, bursary (such as those paid by the NHS for certain health-related courses), scholarship, studentship, exhibition or supplementary allowance.[97] Payments from access funds (see p906), education maintenance allowances or similar payments are not treated as grants.

Some grants are ignored as income (see p902) and others are taken into account. When calculating income from a grant, certain amounts can be disregarded.

If you are assessed as entitled to a parental or partner's contribution to your grant, it counts as income, whether or not it has been paid to you.[98] However, only the amount of contribution you actually receive counts if:

- for IS, you are a lone parent, a lone foster carer or a disabled student (see p890); *or*
- for JSA, you qualify for a disability premium (see p341); *or*
- for ESA, you are a lone parent or a full-time student who gets disability living allowance (DLA) or personal independence payment (PIP).

Calculating grant income

Your grant income is apportioned:[99]

- if it is payable for your period of study (unless you are attending a sandwich course), over the number of benefit weeks in your period of study;
- if it is payable for a period other than your period of study, over the number of benefit weeks in the period for which the grant is payable.

In most cases, the former applies and your grant income is assessed over a period starting from the 'benefit week' which coincides with (or immediately follows) the first day of your 'period of study' (see p902) and ending with the benefit week, the last day of which coincides with (or immediately precedes) the last day of

Part 6: Special benefit rules
Chapter 41: Benefits for students
6. Student income and means-tested benefits

your period of study. In this context, 'benefit week' means the week for which benefit is paid.[100]

This means your grant income is apportioned over the number of complete benefit weeks in your period of study. Any part weeks at the beginning or end of that period are ignored. **Note:** this rule does not apply to an NHS bursary.

Period of study

'Period of study' means:[101]

– for a course of one year or less, from the start of the course to the last day of the course;

– for a course of more than one year, in the first and subsequent years (but not the final year), from the start of the course or the start of the year of the course to:

– if the grant is payable for a period of 12 months, the day before the start of the next year of the course; *or*

– in any other case, the day before the start of your normal summer vacation;

– in the final year of a course lasting more than one year, from the start of the final year of the course to the last day of the course.

Dependants' grants are taken into account over the same period as the student loan if you have a student loan or you are eligible for one.[102]

If you are attending a sandwich course, your grant income is taken into account over a different period. Any periods spent on placement or work experience in your period of study are excluded and your grant is apportioned over the remaining benefit weeks in your period of study. **Note:** this only applies if your grant is payable for your period of study. If your grant is payable for a different period, it is taken into account over the number of benefit weeks in the period for which it is payable.

Grant income that is ignored

The following grant income is ignored:[103]

- any allowance for tuition and examination fees;
- disabled students' allowance;
- any allowance to meet the cost of residential study away from your normal educational establishment during term time;
- any allowance for the cost of your normal home (away from college) but, for IS, JSA and ESA, only up to the amount of your rent that is not met by HB;
- any amount for a partner or child living abroad;
- for IS/JSA/ESA only, any amount intended to maintain a dependent child (unless you still have amounts for children included in your IS/JSA and do not get child tax credit);
- any amount for the childcare costs of a dependent child;
- any amount for the cost of books and equipment;
- any amount for travel costs related to course attendance;

- parents' learning allowance;
- special support payment in Wales;[104]
- if you have been required to make a contribution to your own grant (eg, because you have other income, such as maintenance), an amount equivalent to that contribution is disregarded.[105] In the case of a couple, the amount of any contribution that one member has been assessed to pay to her/his partner who is a student is disregarded from the non-student's income;[106]
- an education maintenance allowance, 16 to 19 bursary or similar payments, including a Care to Learn payment or a Welsh government learning grant;[107]
- higher education bursary for care leavers in England.

In addition to the above amounts, the following fixed sums are ignored.[108] These disregards apply only to the grant you receive for your period of study and not to any supplementary allowances you may be paid during the long vacation.[109]

- A fixed amount of £390 for books and equipment (2019/20 academic year). If your grant includes a specific amount to cover the cost of books and equipment, that amount is ignored in addition to this fixed amount.
- A fixed amount of £303 for the cost of travel (2019/20 academic year). If your grant includes a specific amount to cover the cost of travel expenses for attending your course, that amount is ignored in addition to this fixed amount. If your actual travel costs are higher than any sum specified in your grant for travel (which is ignored under the rules above) plus this fixed amount, the additional costs are not ignored and are taken into account.[110]

Note:
- If you also receive a student loan, the fixed amounts for books and equipment and for travel are not disregarded when calculating your grant income, but are disregarded from your loan income instead (see p904).
- For the purpose of these fixed amounts, the 2019/20 academic year began on 1 August 2019 if your period of study (see p901) began in August 2019. If your period of study began on or after 1 September 2019, the fixed sums apply from that date. At the time of writing, the amounts for 2020/21 were not available. See AskCPAG.org.uk and CPAG's *Welfare Rights Bulletin* for updates.

Loans

Student loans are treated as income, but certain amounts can be disregarded. **Note:** some supplementary allowances paid under the student loan provisions are paid as non-repayable grants and are treated as grant income (see p901).

Calculating income from a student loan

How your, or your partner's, student loan is treated depends on whether your course lasts for one year or less, or for a longer period (see p906).[111]

Part 6: Special benefit rules
Chapter 41: Benefits for students
6. Student income and means-tested benefits

The maximum amount of available loan is taken into account as income, even if you do not apply for a loan or for the maximum amount.[112] If you get a postgraduate master's degree or doctoral degree loan, 30 per cent of the maximum is taken into account. However, for ESA only, if you do not get a loan while you are taking time out because of ill health, there is no assumed loan taken into account.[113] The special support element in a maintenance loan for full-time undergraduate students in England is ignored as income[114] – you may need to get a statement from Student Finance England showing the breakdown of your loan entitlement.

You are treated as having a parental or partner's contribution to your loan and this is taken into account as income, whether or not it has been paid to you. However, only the amount of contribution you actually receive counts if:[115]

- for IS, you are a lone parent, a lone foster carer or a disabled student (see p890); *or*
- for JSA, you qualify for a disability premium (see p341); *or*
- for ESA, you are a full-time student who gets DLA or PIP (see p894).

A student loan for maintenance and a supplementary allowance paid to a student on a Postgraduate Certificate in Education course are treated in the same way as student loans and supplementary allowances for undergraduate students.

If you are on a health-related course funded by the NHS, only the lower maximum loan rate should be taken into account.

Loan income that is ignored

The following are ignored.

- Loans paid for tuition fees (known as a 'fee loan' or a 'fee contribution loan').[116]
- If you have been required to make a contribution to your own loan (eg, because you have other income, such as maintenance), an amount equivalent to that contribution is disregarded as income.[117]
- In the case of a couple, the amount of any contribution that one member has been assessed to pay to her/his partner who is a student is disregarded from the non-student's income.[118]

Also ignored is a fixed amount of:[119]

- £390 for the cost of books and equipment (2019/20 academic year); *and*
- £303 for the cost of travel (2019/20 academic year).

Note: for the purpose of the above fixed amounts, the 2019/20 academic year began on 1 August 2019 if your period of study (see p901) began in August 2019. If your period of study began on or after 1 September 2019, the fixed sums apply from that date. At the time of writing, the amounts for 2020/21 were not available.

£10 a week is ignored for each week in the period over which your loan income is taken into account (see p905). This amount may overlap with other disregards applied to certain war pensions (see p437) and access funds (see p906). A combined maximum sum of £20 a week can be ignored.

The period over which loan income is taken into account

Loan income is apportioned over a period of 'benefit weeks'.

The first benefit week may fall before the start of your actual academic year and the last benefit week may fall either before or after the last day of your academic year (academic years vary between educational institutions). This may mean your benefit is recalculated several times depending on when your actual academic year falls in relation to the relevant benefit weeks. You must make a new claim (if you still can) or check that your entitlement is revised at these times.

Academic year

The rules give a definition of an 'academic year' for the purposes of calculating student loan income. This definition may be different from the actual academic year of the educational institution you attend. '**Academic year**' means a period of 12 months beginning on 1 January, 1 April, 1 July or 1 September according to whether your course begins in the winter, the spring, the summer or the autumn respectively. If you are required to begin attending your course during August or September and to continue attending through the autumn, the academic year of your course is treated as beginning in the autumn rather than summer – ie, from 1 September.[120]

If you are required to start attending your course in August, or your course is for less than one academic year, the period begins with the benefit week, the first day of which coincides with, or immediately follows, the first day of the course.[121]

If your academic year does not start on 1 September, your loan payable for that academic year is apportioned equally between the benefit weeks in the period beginning with the benefit week, the first day of which coincides with, or immediately follows, the first day of that academic year and ending with the benefit week, the last day of which coincides with, or immediately precedes, the last day of that academic year. Excluded from that are any benefit weeks falling entirely within the quarter during which, in the opinion of the decision maker, your longest vacation falls.[122]

Quarters

'**Quarter**' means one of the periods from 1 January to 31 March, 1 April to 30 June, 1 July to 31 August, or 1 September to 31 December.[123]

In the first, or only, year of your course, your loan income (calculated under the rules below) is ignored for each benefit week that falls before the start of your

Part 6: Special benefit rules
Chapter 41: Benefits for students
6. Student income and means-tested benefits

'period of study' (the first day of the first term). This is because you cannot be treated as a student until you actually start your course.[124]

A course lasting for one academic year or less

Your loan is apportioned over the benefit weeks beginning with the benefit week, the first day of which coincides with or immediately follows the first day of the 'academic year' (or, if a course begins in August, from the first day of the first benefit week on or after the first day of the course) and ending with the benefit week, the last day of which coincides with or immediately follows the last day of the course.

A course lasting for more than one academic year

Unless it is your final year (see below), your loan is apportioned over the period from the earlier of:

- the first day of the first benefit week in September; *or*
- the first benefit week, the first day of which coincides with or immediately follows the first day of the autumn term.

It is taken into account until the last day of the benefit week that coincides with or immediately precedes the last day of June.

Final year of a course

Your loan is taken into account over the period beginning with either:

- if the final academic year starts on 1 September, the benefit week, the first day of which coincides with or immediately follows the earlier of 1 September or the first day of the autumn term; *or*
- the benefit week, the first day of which coincides with or immediately follows the first day of the academic year.

It is taken into account until the benefit week, the last day of which coincides with or immediately precedes the last day of the course.

Income from other types of loan

Any financial support you receive in the form of a loan (other than a student loan), including a loan received from an overseas source, does not count as a student loan or a grant.[125] It is taken into account as 'other income' (see p435).

Discretionary funds and other payments

Access funds (which include the discretionary learner support funds available to some students in further education, any discretionary hardship funds offered by higher education institutions in England or Wales, the 16 to 19 bursary fund in England and discretionary funds in Scotland) are administered by colleges and universities.[126] Individual educational institutions may call all or part of these funds by other names – eg, access bursary, mature students' bursary and childcare support. Payments from access funds should be distinguished from payments with similar names from other sources – eg, hardship loans.

How a payment from access funds is treated depends on whether it is paid as a single lump sum, in instalments or to bridge the period before you start your course or receive a student loan payment.

A single lump-sum payment

A single lump-sum payment is treated as capital, but is disregarded for 52 weeks if the payment is intended for, and used for, any items, expenses or charges which you or your partner may incur (other than 'daily living expenses').[127] However, if the payment is intended for but not used for these items, expenses or charges, it is taken into account as capital immediately. A single lump-sum payment made for 'daily living expenses' counts as capital immediately.

Daily living expenses
'Daily living expenses' are:
– food;
– ordinary clothing or footwear – ie, for normal daily use, but not including school uniforms or any that are used solely for sporting activities;
– household fuel;
– for IS/JSA/ESA only, rent for which HB is payable;
– for HB, your 'eligible rent', minus any non-dependant deductions;
– for IS/JSA/ESA only, housing costs met by IS, income-based JSA or income-related ESA;
– council tax;
– water charges.

Payments made in instalments

Payments made in instalments are treated as income, but are disregarded in full.[128] However, if the payment is intended and used for daily living expenses (see above), it is taken into account as income for each week it is intended to cover, except for the first £20 a week, which is disregarded. This amount may overlap with other disregards applied to certain war pensions (see p437) and student loans (see p904). A combined maximum sum of £20 a week can be ignored.

Payments before course starts or student loan received

A payment (whether paid as a single payment or in instalments) is ignored, even if it is for 'daily living expenses', if it is made:[129]
- on or after whichever is the earlier of 1 September or the first day of your course, if it is intended to bridge the period before you receive your student loan; or

Part 6: Special benefit rules
Chapter 41: Benefits for students
7. Giving up, changing or taking time out from your course

- before the first day of your course, if it is made in anticipation of your becoming a student.

Other sources of income intended to cover study costs

If you receive a payment from any source other than a grant or student loan, which is intended to cover items or expenses that would be ignored when calculating grant income, the payment made from that other source for those items or expenses is also ignored.[130] You must show that the payment is necessary for you to be able to attend the course. Any sum paid which is not necessary (or is likely to exceed the sum necessary) for you to attend the course counts as income. For example, if your grant or student loan does not cover all your tuition fees, any money received from another source such as a parent, intended to make up the difference, is ignored as income. However, if the amount you receive is greater than is likely to be necessary to pay the difference, the amount above that sum counts as income.

6 Once you have completed your course

For IS/JSA/ESA only, any grant income, student loan, or assessed contribution made by a parent or spouse/civil partner as part of the loan or grant, that you received no longer counts as income once you have completed your course.[131] It should also be ignored as income for HB once you have completed the course.

Any student financial support you have left once you have completed your course counts as capital (see Chapter 22), as there are no provisions to disregard it under the rules about capital.

---

7. Giving up, changing or taking time out from your course

This section only applies to income support (IS), contribution-based and income-based jobseeker's allowance (JSA), income-related employment and support allowance (ESA) and housing benefit (HB). It does *not* apply if (for IS and JSA) you are (or were) in 'relevant education' (see p885 and p887 instead), or (for ESA) you are (or were) a 'qualifying young person' for child benefit purposes (see p894 and p895 instead). For the rules for universal credit, see p884.

Note: most people cannot make a new claim for IS, income-based JSA, income-related ESA or HB (see p24).

If you abandon your course or are dismissed from it, you can qualify for IS, JSA or income-related ESA from the day after that date, provided you satisfy the other rules for getting these benefits (see Chapters 11, 12 and 9). If you are on a sandwich course (see p888), or your course includes a compulsory or optional period on placement, you count as a full-time student during the sandwich or placement period, even if you have been unable to find a placement or your placement comes to an end prematurely.[132]

If you attend a course at an educational institution that provides training or instruction to enable you to take examinations set and marked by an entirely different and unconnected body (ie, a professional institution) and you abandon or take time out from it because you fail the examinations set by the other body (or you finish the course at the educational institution but fail the exams), you may be able to argue that you are not a student from the date you left the course at your educational institution, even if you intend to re-sit the examinations set by the other body at a later date.[133]

If you are taking time out from your course for any other reason and for however long a period, you cannot qualify for IS, JSA or income-related ESA during your period of absence,[134] except in the limited circumstances set out below (but if you are taking time out from a modular or similar course, see also p889).

You may retain entitlement to some student support on a statutory or discretionary basis – eg, through student loans or hardship funds. You should get specialist advice.

If you complete one course and start a different course, you are not treated as a student in any period between the courses.[135]

Changing from full-time to part-time attendance

If, for personal reasons, you have to change from full-time to part-time attendance on a 'traditional' full-time course, you may be able to argue that you have abandoned your full-time course and are registered on a part-time course and, therefore, that you are not a full-time student.[136]

If, because of exam failure or any other reason, you change to a different course, or your college requires you to change the level of course (eg, from A level to GCSE) and this involves a change from full-time to part-time study, argue that you are a part-time student.[137]

However, changing your attendance may affect your entitlement to any student support you may be receiving. Get advice on this before acting.

Time out to be a carer

If you are a full-time student and you have taken time out from your course to care for someone, you cannot qualify for IS, JSA or income-related ESA unless you are someone who can qualify while studying (see p890 and p894). In some cases, you may be able to get carer's allowance (see p899).

You can qualify for JSA and HB, but not IS or income-related ESA, when your caring responsibilities have come to an end.[138] **Note:** the rules do not provide a definition of caring responsibilities or when they come to an end. You can then

Part 6: Special benefit rules
Chapter 41: Benefits for students
7. Giving up, changing or taking time out from your course

qualify for a maximum period of one year, provided you are not eligible for a student grant or loan during the period, until whichever is the earlier of:

- the day you rejoin your course; *or*
- the first day from which your educational institution has agreed you can rejoin your course.

Time out because of illness

If you are a full-time student and you have taken time out from your course because you are ill, you cannot qualify for income-related ESA unless you get disability living allowance, personal independence payment or armed forces independence payment.

Once your illness has ended, you can qualify for JSA and HB. The rules are the same as for when caring responsibilities have ended (see p909).

Time out because you are pregnant

If you are a full-time student and you have taken time out from your course because you are pregnant, you cannot qualify for IS, JSA or income-related ESA, unless you are someone who can qualify while studying (see p890 and p894). Note:

- Check to see whether you qualify for statutory maternity pay or maternity allowance.
- Once your baby is born, you may then qualify for IS (eg, if you are a lone parent) or you or your partner may qualify for HB.

Calculating student income

Grants

For IS, income-based JSA and income-related ESA, if you cease to be a full-time student before your course finishes, any grant you have received is taken into account as if you were still a student (see p901) until the earliest of:[139]

- the date you repay the grant; *or*
- the last date of the academic term or vacation in which you ceased to be a full-time student; *or*
- if the grant is paid in instalments, the day before the date the next instalment would have been paid had you still been a full-time student.

For HB, it is not taken into account as if you were still a student.[140] Instead, it is taken into account until the grant provider asks you to repay it. Until then, it should be calculated over an appropriate period.[141] It could be argued that your grant should be taken into account as income only to the end of the period which your last instalment was meant to cover.

Loans

For income-related ESA, if you suspend attendance on your course because of illness or disability and this is confirmed in writing by the educational institution, you are not treated as having any part of a student loan which has not been paid to you.

If you abandon or are dismissed from your course before it finishes, there are special rules on how your student loan is treated for IS, income-based JSA, income-related ESA and HB.

If you abandon your course before you have received the final instalment of your student loan, it is taken into account using the formula:[142]

$$A - \frac{(B \times C)}{D}$$

A = the maximum amount of student loan available to you (see p903), including any amount paid as a grant intended to maintain your dependants, that you would have received had you remained a student until *the last day of the academic term* in which you abandoned or were dismissed from your course, less any disregards that apply (see p904). This amount is the 'relevant payment'. If, however, you were paid in two or more instalments in a quarter (eg, monthly, as is currently the case for Scottish students studying in Scotland), A = the relevant payment that you would have received, calculated in the same way except that it is the amount that you would have received had you remained a student up until *the day you abandoned or were dismissed from your course.*

B = the number of benefit weeks immediately following the benefit week which includes the first day of your academic year to the benefit week immediately before that which includes the day on which you abandoned or were dismissed from your course (for HB, calculate up until the week that includes the one in which you left the course).

C = the weekly amount of student loan for the academic year which would have been taken into account to calculate your benefit under the normal rules (see p903) but without applying the £10 a week disregard (see p904). This applies regardless of whether you were actually entitled to benefit before you abandoned or were dismissed from your course.

D = the number of benefit weeks beginning with the benefit week which includes the day on which you abandoned or were dismissed from your course and ending with the benefit week which includes the last day of the last 'quarter' for which your relevant payment (see A) would have been payable to you had you remained on your course, or to the day before which you would have been due your next loan payment, if earlier.

Part 6: Special benefit rules
Chapter 41: Benefits for students
7. Giving up, changing or taking time out from your course

Example

Bhavna abandons her three-year degree course at a university outside London on 25 October 2019 during the first term of her second year. Her benefit week starts on a Tuesday. Her assumed maximum loan income (ignoring any special support element) would have been taken into account for 43 weeks (first complete benefit week in September to last complete benefit week in June).

Step one: calculate the relevant payment

Loan instalment paid for first term (33% x £6,411)	£2,115.63
less deduction for books and travel	£693.00
Total taken into account	**£1,422.63**

Step two: calculate the benefit weeks prior to leaving the course

3 September 2019 to 21 October 2019	= 7 weeks

Step three: calculate maximum loan for the academic year

Maximum loan	£6,411
less deduction for books and travel	£693
Total loan	£5,718
Weekly amount	**= £132.98**
(£5,718 ÷ 43 weeks)	

Step four: calculate complete benefit weeks from the benefit week including the date of abandonment to the end of the benefit week including the end of the quarter

22 October 2019 to 6 January 2020	= 11 weeks

$$\frac{1,422.63 - (7 \times 132.98)}{11} = £44.71$$

Therefore, £44.71 a week is taken into account from 22 October 2019 to 6 January 2020 (11 weeks) and nothing thereafter.

Note: this formula can result in a nil loan income figure depending on the exact date in your term that you abandon, or are dismissed from, your course.

If you voluntarily repay your student loan, for IS, income-based JSA and income-related ESA you are treated as still having that loan income calculated under the above rules.[143] However, for all the benefits, guidance to decision makers says you should not be treated as having any loan income if the Student Loans Company demands you repay the loan instalment immediately.[144]

Notes

1. Universal credit
1 s4(1)(d) WRA 2012
2 Reg 12 UC Regs
3 Reg 5 UC Regs
4 para H6035 ADM
5 Reg 12(4) UC Regs
6 Reg 13 UC Regs
7 Reg 13(1)(b), (2) and (3) UC Regs
8 Reg 14 UC Regs
9 Reg 3(2)(b) UC Regs
10 Reg 13(4) UC Regs
11 Reg 8(3) UC Regs
12 Reg 89 UC Regs
13 Reg 12(4) UC Regs
14 Reg 95(4) UC Regs
15 Regs 68-71 UC Regs
16 Reg 68(1) UC Regs
17 Reg 68(7) UC Regs
18 Reg 70 UC Regs
19 Reg 68(3) UC Regs
20 Reg 68(7) UC Regs
21 Reg 69(1A) UC Regs
22 www.practitioners.slc.co.uk/media/
   1153/201617-student-finance-
   arrangements-for-new-full-time-
   students-eligible-for-benefits.pdf
23 Reg 68(7) UC Regs
24 Reg 68(1) UC Regs
25 Reg 68(7) UC Regs
26 Reg 13(4) UC Regs
27 *RVS v SSWP* [2019] UKUT 102 (AAC)

2. Income support and jobseeker's allowance
28 s124(1)(d) SSCBA 1992; s1(2)(g) JSA
   1995
29 Reg 54(4A) JSA Regs
30 **IS** Reg 12 IS Regs
   JSA Reg 54 JSA Regs
31 Regs 4ZA and 13(2)(a)-(e) IS Regs
32 Reg 2(1)(b)(i)&(ii) C(LC)SSB Regs; reg
   13(2)(a) and (b) IS Regs; Vol 6 Ch 30,
   para 30525 DMG
33 R(IS) 9/94
34 R(IS) 9/94
35 CIS/11766/1996
36 R(IS) 9/94
37 Reg 13(3)(a)(ii) IS Regs
38 R(SB) 2/87
39 CIS/11441/1995

40 s1(2)(g) JSA 1995; regs 54, 57(2) and
   (4)(a) and 61(1)(c) JSA Regs
41 Reg 54(3) and (4) JSA Regs
42 **IS** Reg 4ZA(2) IS Regs
   JSA Reg 15(a) JSA Regs
43 **IS** Reg 61(1), definition of 'student', IS
   Regs
   JSA Reg 1(3), definition of 'student', JSA
   Regs
44 **IS** Reg 2(1), definition of 'period of
   study', IS Regs
   JSA Reg 1(3A) JSA Regs
   HB Reg 53(2)(b) HB Regs
45 **IS** Reg 61(1), definition of 'last day of the
   course', IS Regs
   JSA Reg 130, definition of 'last day of
   the course', JSA Regs
   HB Reg 53(1), definition of 'last day of
   the course', HB Regs
46 Reg 4, definition of 'period of study', JSA
   Regs
47 **IS** Reg 61(1), definitions of 'full-time
   course of advanced education' and 'full-
   time course of study', IS Regs; Vol 6 Ch
   30, para 30148 DMG
   JSA Reg 1(3), definition of 'full-time
   student', JSA Regs
   HB Reg 53(1), definition of 'full-time
   course of study', HB Regs
48 Vol 6 Ch 30, paras 30197-98 DMG
49 **IS** Reg 61, definitions of 'full-time course
   of advanced education' and 'full-time
   course of study', IS Regs; Vol 6 Ch 30,
   para 30149 DMG
   JSA Reg 1(3), definition of 'full-time
   student', JSA Regs
   HB Reg 53(1), definitions of 'full-time
   course of study' and 'higher education',
   HB Regs
50 **IS** Reg 61(1), definition of 'sandwich
   course', IS Regs
   JSA Reg 1(3), definition of 'sandwich
   course', JSA Regs
   HB Reg 53(1), definition of 'sandwich
   course', HB Regs
51 R(IS) 19/98
52 **IS** Reg 61(4) IS Regs
   JSA Reg 1(3C) JSA Regs
   HB Reg 53(4) HB Regs

6

Part 6: Special benefit rules
Chapter 41: Benefits for students
Notes

53 **IS** Reg 61(2)(a) IS Regs
    JSA Reg 1(3A)(a) JSA Regs
    HB Reg 53(2)(a) HB Regs
54 **IS** Reg 61(3)(b) IS Regs
    JSA Reg 1(3B)(b) JSA Regs
    HB Reg 53(3)(b) HB Regs
55 **IS** Reg 61(3)(a) IS Regs
    JSA Reg 1(3B)(a) JSA Regs
    HB Reg 53(3)(a) HB Regs
56 R(IS) 15/98; R(IS) 7/99; CJSA/836/1998;
    R(IS)1/00; *Chief Adjudication Officer v
    Webber* [1997] 4 All ER 274
57 *RVS v SSWP* [2019] UKUT 102 (AAC)
58 R(SB) 40/83; R(SB) 41/83
59 **IS** Reg 61, definitions of 'full-time course
    of advanced education' and 'full-time
    course of study', IS Regs
    JSA Reg 1(3), definition of 'full-time
    student', JSA Regs
60 Reg 4ZA and Sch 1B IS Regs
61 Reg 15(2) and (3) JSA Regs
62 Reg 14(1)(a) JSA Regs
63 Reg 14(1)(k) JSA Regs
64 Reg 7(2) JSA(SAPOE) Regs
65 Regs 17A and 21A JSA Regs
66 CIS/152/1994; R(IS) 15/98; CJSA/836/
    1998; R(IS) 1/00
67 Reg 1(3), definition of 'part-time
    student', JSA Regs
68 Vol 4 Ch 21, para 21241 DMG
69 Vol 4 Ch 21, para 21242 DMG
70 Vol 4 Ch 21, para 21243 DMG
71 Vol 4 Ch 21, para 21244 DMG
72 Reg 11 JSA Regs
73 Reg 11(3) JSA Regs
74 Regs 2(1) and 61(1), definitions of
    'student' and 'course of study', IS Regs

3. Employment and support allowance
75 Reg 32(2) and (3) ESA Regs
76 Sch 1 para 6(1)(g) WRA 2007; reg 18
    ESA Regs
77 Reg 15 ESA Regs
78 Reg 14 ESA Regs
79 *RVS v SSWP* [2019] UKUT 102 (AAC)
80 Regs 14 and 33(2) ESA Regs

4. Housing benefit
81 There are no student rules in the
    HB(SPC) Regs
82 Reg 56(2) HB Regs
83 Reg 55(1) HB Regs
84 Reg 55(2) HB Regs
85 Reg 57 HB Regs
86 Reg 8(1)(e) HB Regs
87 Reg 58 HB Regs
88 Reg 92(7) HB Regs

5. Other benefits
89 Reg 5 SS(ICA) Regs
90 *SSWP v Deane* [2010] EWCA Civ 699
91 Reg 5(2) SS(ICA) Regs
92 *SM v SSWP* [2016] UKUT 406 (AAC)
93 R(G) 2/02
94 Reg 45 JSA Regs 2013

**6. Student income and means-tested
   benefits**
95 **IS** Regs 2(1), definition of 'student', and
    61(1), definition of 'course of study', IS
    Regs
    JSA Regs 1(3), definition of 'full-time
    student', and 130, definition of 'course
    of study', JSA Regs
    ESA Reg 131, definition of 'full-time
    student', ESA Regs
    HB Reg 53(1), definition of 'student'
    and 'course of study', HB Regs
96 Reg 29 HB(SPC) Regs
97 **IS** Reg 61(1), definition of 'grant', IS
    Regs
    JSA Reg 130, definition of 'grant', JSA
    Regs
    ESA Reg 131(1), definition of 'grant',
    ESA Regs
    HB Reg 53(1), definition of 'grant', HB
    Regs
98 **IS** Reg 61(1), definition of 'grant
    income', IS Regs
    JSA Reg 130, definition of 'grant
    income', JSA Regs
    ESA Reg 131(1), definition of 'grant
    income', ESA Regs
    HB Reg 53(1), definition of 'grant
    income', HB Regs
99 **IS** Reg 62(3) IS Regs
    JSA Reg 131(4) JSA Regs
    ESA Reg 132(4) ESA Regs
    HB Reg 59(5) HB Regs
100 Sch 7 para 4 SS(C&P) Regs
101 **IS** Reg 61(1), definition of 'period of
    study', IS Regs
    JSA Reg 1(3), definition of 'period of
    study', JSA Regs
    ESA Reg 131(1), definition of 'period of
    study', ESA Regs
    HB Reg 53, definition of 'period of
    study', HB Regs
102 **IS** Reg 62(3B) IS Regs
    ESA Reg 132(6) ESA Regs
    HB Reg 59(7) HB Regs
103 **IS** Reg 62(2) and (2A) IS Regs
    JSA Reg 131(2) and (3) JSA Regs
    ESA Reg 132(2) and (3) ESA Regs
    HB Reg 59(2) and (3) HB Regs

104 **IS/JSA** Vol 6 Ch 30, para 30329 DMG
ESA Vol 9 Ch 51, paras 51919-20 DMG
HB paras C2/2.170-73 GM

105 **IS** Reg 67A IS Regs
JSA Reg 137A JSA Regs
ESA Reg 141 ESA Regs
HB Reg 67 HB Regs

106 **IS** Reg 67 IS Regs
JSA Reg 137 JSA Regs
ESA Reg 140 ESA Regs
HB Reg 66 HB Regs

107 **IS** Schs 9 para 11 and 10 para 63 IS Regs
JSA Schs 7 para 12 and 8 para 52 JSA Regs
ESA Schs 8 para 13 and 9 para 52 ESA Regs
HB Schs 5 para 11 and 6 para 51 HB Regs

108 **IS** Reg 62(2A) IS Regs
JSA Reg 131(3) JSA Regs
ESA Reg 132(3) ESA Regs
HB Reg 59(3) HB Regs

109 CIS/91/1994

110 R(IS) 7/95

111 **IS** Reg 61(1), definition of 'student loan', IS Regs
JSA Reg 130, definition of 'student loan', JSA Regs
ESA Reg 131(1), definition of 'student loan', ESA Regs
HB Reg 53(1), definition of 'student loan', HB Regs

112 **IS** Reg 66A(3) and (4) IS Regs
JSA Reg 136(3) and (4) JSA Regs
ESA Reg 137(4) and (5) ESA Regs
HB Reg 64(3) and (4) HB Regs

113 Reg 137(4A) ESA Regs

114 **IS** Reg 66D IS Regs; Vol 6 Ch 30, para 30330 DMG
ESA Reg 139A ESA Regs
JSA Reg 136C JSA Regs
HB Reg 64B HB Regs

115 **IS** Reg 66A(4) IS Regs
ESA Reg 137(5) ESA Regs
JSA Reg 136(4) JSA Regs

116 **IS** Reg 66C IS Regs
JSA Reg 136B JSA Regs
ESA Reg 139 ESA Regs
HB Reg 64A HB Regs

117 **IS** Reg 67A IS Regs
JSA Reg 137A JSA Regs
ESA Reg 141 ESA Regs
HB Reg 67 HB Regs

118 **IS** Reg 67 IS Regs
JSA Reg 137 JSA Regs
ESA Reg 140 ESA Regs
HB Reg 66 HB Regs

119 **IS** Reg 66A(2) and (5) IS Regs
JSA Reg 136(2) and (5) JSA Regs
ESA Reg 137(3) and (6) ESA Regs
HB Reg 64(2) and (5) HB Regs

120 **IS** Reg 61(1), definition of 'academic year', IS Regs
JSA Reg 130, definition of 'academic year', JSA Regs
ESA Reg 131(1), definition of 'academic year', ESA Regs
HB Reg 53(1), definition of 'academic year', HB Regs

121 **IS** Reg 66A(2)(a) IS Regs
JSA Reg 136(2)(a) JSA Regs
ESA Reg 137(3)(a) ESA Regs
HB Reg 64(2)(a) HB Regs

122 **IS** Reg 66A(2)(aa) IS Regs
JSA Reg 136(2)(aa) JSA Regs
ESA Reg 137(3)(b) ESA Regs
HB Reg 64(2)(b) HB Regs

123 **IS** Reg 66A(2)(aa) IS Regs
JSA Reg 136(2)(aa) JSA Regs
ESA Regs 104(6) and 137(3)(c) ESA Regs
HB Reg 64(2)(b) HB Regs
All The Education (Student Support) (No.2) Regulations 2008, No.1582

124 CIS/3734/2004

125 R(IS) 16/95

126 **IS** Reg 61(1), definition of 'access funds', IS Regs
JSA Reg 130, definition of 'access funds', JSA Regs
ESA Reg 131(1), definition of 'access funds', ESA Regs
HB Reg 53(1), definition of 'access funds', HB Regs

127 **IS** Reg 68(3) and (4) IS Regs
JSA Reg 138(3) and (4) JSA Regs
ESA Regs 2(1) and 142(3) ESA Regs
HB Regs 2(1) and 68(3) and (4) HB Regs

128 **IS** Reg 66B IS Regs
JSA Reg 136A JSA Regs
ESA Regs 2(1) and 138 ESA Regs
HB Regs 2(1) and 65 HB Regs

129 **IS** Reg 66B(4) IS Regs
JSA Reg 136A(4) JSA Regs
ESA Reg 138(4) ESA Regs
HB Reg 65(5) HB Regs

130 **IS** Reg 66(1) IS Regs
JSA Reg 135(1) JSA Regs
ESA Reg 136(1) ESA Regs
HB Reg 63 HB Regs

131 **IS** Sch 9 paras 13 and 61 IS Regs
JSA Sch 7 paras 14 and 59 JSA Regs
ESA Sch 8 paras 15 and 54 ESA Regs

Part 6: Special benefit rules
Chapter 41: Benefits for students
Notes

7. **Giving up, changing or taking time out
   from your course**
132 CIS/368/1992; R(IS) 6/97
133 R(JSA) 2/02; CJSA/1965/2008
134 R(IS) 7/99
135 R(IS) 1/96
136 Vol 6 Ch 30, paras 30230-33 DMG;
     paras C2/2.41-42 GM
137 CIS/152/1994; R(IS) 15/98
138 **JSA** Reg 1(3D) and (3E) JSA Regs
     HB Reg 56(6) and (7) HB Regs
139 **IS** Regs 29(2B) and 32(6A) IS Regs
     JSA Regs 94(2B) and 97(7) JSA Regs
     ESA Regs 91(4) and 94(7) ESA Regs
140 para C2/2.425 GM
141 *Leeves v Chief Adjudication Officer*,
     reported as R(IS) 5/99; reg 31(1) HB
     Regs
142 **IS** Reg 40(3A), (3AA), (3AAA) and (3AB)
     IS Regs
     JSA Reg 103(5), (5ZA), (5AZA) and
     (5ZB) JSA Regs
     ESA Reg 104(4)-(6) ESA Regs
     HB Reg 40(7)-(9) HB Regs
143 Reg 6(6)(a) SS&CS(DA) Regs; CJSA/
     549/03
144 Vol 6 Ch 30, para 30470 DMG; para C2/
     2.421 GM

Benefits in hospital, care homes, prison and in other special circumstances

This chapter covers:

1. Hospital patients (below)
2. People in care homes and similar accommodation (p927)
3. Prisoners (p937)
4. 16/17-year-old care leavers (p947)
5. People without accommodation (p949)

Key facts

- Your benefit entitlement may be affected if you (or your partner, child or non-dependant) go into hospital, a care home or prison. It may also be affected if you are without accommodation, or if you are aged 16 or 17 and were previously looked after by a local authority.
- Some benefits are not payable, or are payable at a reduced rate, either immediately or after a specified period.
- You should always notify the relevant benefit authority as soon as possible if any of the above circumstances apply, or cease to apply, to avoid being overpaid or underpaid.

1. Hospital patients

Some benefits are affected after you, your partner or child have been a patient in a hospital, or in an institution similiar to a hospital, for a period of time. In some cases, benefit is no longer paid. In other cases, it is paid at a reduced rate.

See p926 for information on paying for your normal home while you are a patient.

You can arrange for someone else to collect your benefit while you are a patient (see p1188). If you are unable to manage your affairs, someone else can act as your appointee (see p1170).

Part 6: Special benefit rules
Chapter 42: Benefits in hospital, care homes, prison and in other special circumstances
1. Hospital patients

Always inform the DWP, HM Revenue and Customs (HMRC) and/or the local authority as soon as you can if your benefits may be affected by the rules described below, to avoid being overpaid or underpaid.

Who counts as a patient

For benefits other than personal independence payment (PIP), you count as a 'patient' if you are being maintained free of charge while undergoing medical or other treatment as an inpatient in a hospital or 'similar institution'. The treatment must be provided and funded under NHS legislation or in a hospital or similar institution which is maintained or administered by the Defence Council.[1] You do *not* count as a patient if you are getting treatment as a private patient, you are meeting the cost of your treatment in a private hospital or the local authority has organised the placement.[2]

For PIP, you count as a 'patient' if you are undergoing medical or other treatment as an inpatient at a hospital or 'similar institution' and any of the costs of your treatment, accommodation and any related services are paid for out of public funds. The costs count as being paid for 'out of public funds' where you are being provided with medical or other treatment under NHS legislation, or you are in a hospital or similar institution which is maintained or administered by the Defence Council. You do *not* count as a patient for PIP if you are getting treatment as a private patient or you are meeting the cost your treatment in a private hospital.[3]

Definitions

'Hospitals' include all NHS hospitals, armed forces hospitals and special hospitals such as Broadmoor, Rampton and the State Hospital in Scotland. Prison hospital wings do not count as hospitals.

A **'similar institution'** to a hospital is not defined in the law, but can include some care homes, and rehabilitation units that provide medical or nursing care.[4]

'Medical or other treatment' is treatment by a doctor, dentist or professionally qualified or trained nurse, or by someone under the supervision of such a person.[5]

If you are in a care home and receiving medical or nursing care which is more than 'incidental and ancillary' to your other care needs, the NHS is responsible for meeting your care home costs in full. In this situation, you count as a patient. For PIP, if you are in a care home which is deemed to be a 'similar institution' to a hospital (ie, because you are provided with medical or nursing care), you count as a patient if the NHS is paying for *any* of your care, treatment, accommodation or related services.[6][7]

The days on which you count as a patient

You count as a patient from the day after the day you enter hospital (or a similar institution) up to and including:

- for attendance allowance (AA), disability living allowance (DLA) and PIP, the day before the day you leave (unless, for PIP only, you go straight into a care home or prison, in which case you count as a patient until the day you leave hospital);[8] *or*
- for other benefits, the day you leave.[9]

Example

Hilda is claiming PIP and employment and support allowance (ESA). She is taken ill and admitted to hospital on 1 January. After successful treatment, she is discharged on 21 January.

For PIP purposes, she counts as a patient from 2 January up to and including 20 January = 19 days.

For ESA purposes, she counts as a patient from 2 January up to and including 21 January = 20 days.

Disability benefits

If you were under 18 when you went into hospital, you continue to be paid DLA or PIP regardless of how long you are in hospital, even if you turn 18 while you are still a hospital in-patient.[10] This applies whether or not you were entitled to DLA or PIP when you went into hospital, so if you were under 18 when you became a patient, you can claim DLA or PIP while you are in hospital and if it is awarded, you will be paid it. If you are under 16 and were entitled to DLA when you went into hospital, you can continue to get DLA after the age of 16 (and have your DLA renewed) while you remain in hospital – you do not have to claim PIP.[11] DLA for children will be replaced in Scotland by child disability payment, starting in summer 2020 (see p1690). It is expected that you will continue to be paid this benefit if you are under 18 when you become a hospital patient.

If you are aged 18 or over when you become a hospital patient, you are not paid AA, DLA or PIP after you have been a patient for 28 days.[12] Even if your payment of AA, DLA or PIP stops because of these rules your *entitlement* continues. This means that payment can begin again following your discharge from hospital without your having to make a new claim. Payment can be at a daily rate if you are expected to be readmitted within 28 days.[13]

There is a 28-day 'linking rule'.[14]

- Different periods spent as a patient that are separated by 28 days or less are linked together and treated as one period.
- Periods spent as a resident in a care home (or, for PIP only, as a prisoner) link with periods spent as a patient if they are 28 days or less apart.

Example

Horace is claiming AA. He goes into hospital for an operation on 16 July and is discharged on 30 July. He counts as a patient from 17 July up to and including 29 July = 13 days. His AA is not affected by his stay in hospital.

Part 6: Special benefit rules
Chapter 42: Benefits in hospital, care homes, prison and in other special circumstances
1. Hospital patients

> Horace has to go back into hospital for further treatment on 10 August. He counts as a
> patient again from 11 August. As there are less than 28 days between his discharge and
> readmission, the two spells in hospital are linked. When he has been a patient for a further
> 15 days, he cannot be paid AA.

Note:
- If you are terminally ill, you can be paid AA, DLA or PIP while you are in a hospice, provided the DWP has been informed that you are terminally ill.[15] In most cases, the DWP must be informed in writing. This applies unless the hospice is an NHS hospital.
- If you are awarded AA, DLA or PIP while you are a patient aged 18 or over, payment cannot begin until you are discharged.[16]
- You can continue to be paid the mobility component of DLA while you are a patient if you have been a patient since 31 July 1995 (other than if you are detained under the Mental Health Act). You are paid at the lower rate (even if you would otherwise qualify for the higher rate). This transitional protection ends if you cease to be a patient for more than 28 consecutive days.[17]
- You continue to be exempt from the benefit cap (see p1194) even if you or your partner are no longer receiving AA, DLA or PIP after being a patient for 28 days.[18]

Carer's allowance

You no longer qualify for carer's allowance (CA) if the person you care for no longer receives AA, DLA or PIP – ie, if s/he is aged 18 or over and has been a patient for 28 days. If the person you care for is discharged and payment of AA, the DLA care component or the daily living component of PIP resumes, you should reclaim CA if you satisfy the rules for entitlement. Your claim can be backdated to the date from when AA or DLA is payable again, provided you reclaim CA within three months of that date.[19]

Once you have been caring for a disabled person for a while, a temporary break in caring does not affect your CA (see p563), including if you (or the person you care for) are a hospital patient. You can remain entitled to CA during a temporary break (or breaks) of up to four weeks in any period of 26 weeks. This can be extended for up to 12 weeks in any 26-week period if you or the person you care for has been in hospital for at least eight of those 12 weeks.[20] This can be useful if you (or the person you care for) are going in and out of hospital. However, if the person you care for is 18 or over when s/he goes into hospital, has been a patient for 28 days and is therefore no longer receiving AA, DLA or PIP (see p919), your entitlement to CA ends, even though you have not yet had a temporary break of 12 weeks.

Universal credit

Your universal credit (UC) is not normally affected until you (or your partner or child) have been in hospital for more than six months. However, you are no longer entitled to a carer element if the AA, DLA or PIP of the person you care for stops because s/he is aged 18 or over when s/he goes into hospital and s/he has been in hospital for more than 28 days.[21] See p926 for information on paying for your usual home.

Single claimants

You can continue to get UC while you are in hospital. However, the housing costs element stops if your stay in hospital exceeds, or is expected to exceed, six months.[22] If you receive a loan from the DWP to help you with your mortgage interest, payments will stop if your stay in hospital exceeds, or is expected to exceed, six months.[23]

Couples

You and your partner continue to count as a couple for UC while one of you is temporarily absent from the household, including when one of you is in hospital. You must continue to make a joint claim with your partner and UC is paid as usual. If the partner who is not in hospital is working, you may qualify for a childcare costs element (see p74). However, if the absence exceeds, or is expected to exceed, six months, you no longer count as a couple.[24] If you no longer count as a couple:

- you can no longer make a joint claim for UC;
- the calculation of your benefit no longer includes amounts for your partner;
- you should notify the DWP as you may both have to reclaim UC as single people.

Children

A child continues to be included in your UC claim while s/he is temporarily absent from your household because s/he is in hospital. However, s/he is no longer included in your claim if the absence exceeds, or is expected to exceed, six months.[25] If your child is no longer included in your claim:

- the calculation of your benefit no longer includes amounts for her/him;
- your work allowance (see p41) and the work-related requirements you must meet may change (see Chapter 46).

Jobseeker's allowance

You cannot qualify for jobseeker's allowance (JSA) if you have limited capability for work (see p1010). You must also be available for, and actively seeking, work (see p1114). If you cannot satisfy these conditions because you are in hospital,

Part 6: Special benefit rules
Chapter 42: Benefits in hospital, care homes, prison and in other special circumstances
1. Hospital patients

you may need to claim a different benefit such as UC or employment and support allowance (ESA) instead. However, you can continue to get JSA:[26]

- for up to 13 weeks during a period of sickness; *or*
- indefinitely, if you are absent from Great Britain for NHS hospital treatment.

In these circumstances, you are treated as not having limited capability for work and as satisfying the jobseeking requirements for JSA. See p708 for further information.

Other means-tested benefits

If you are getting income support (IS), income-related ESA, housing benefit (HB) or pension credit (PC) when you go into hospital, these benefits can often continue, although the amount to which you are entitled might change (see below). See p921 for how UC is affected. See p926 for information on paying for your ususal home.

If your, or your partner's, disability benefit stops

If payment of your (or your partner's) AA, DLA or PIP stops because you (or your partner) is 18 or over when you (or your partner) go into hospital and you (or your partner) have been in hospital for 28 days, the severe disability premium included in your IS, income-based JSA, income-related ESA or HB or the severe disability addition in your PC is affected.

- If you are a single claimant, you are no longer entitled to the severe disability premium in your IS, income-based JSA, income-related ESA or HB, or to the PC severe disability addition.
- If you are a member of a couple, you (or your partner) are treated as getting AA, DLA or PIP if the only reason it is not being paid is because you (or s/he) are a patient. This means that you continue to get the severe disability premium/ addition in your means-tested benefit. However, it is paid at the single rate instead of the couple rate. For the purposes of entitlement to the severe disability premium/addition, your carer is also treated as getting CA if s/he would be entitled to and receiving it, but for the fact that you (or your partner) have been a patient for longer than 28 days.[27]

Entitlement to the disability premium in IS, income-based JSA and HB, the enhanced disability premium in IS, income-based JSA, income-related ESA and HB, and the higher pensioner premium in IS and income-based JSA, are not affected when payment of AA, DLA or PIP stops after 28 days.[28] However, these premiums can be affected if you (or your partner) are a patient for 52 weeks (see p923).

For HB, if you are a member of a couple, a deduction for childcare charges can be made from earnings if one of you is in full-time paid work and the other is in hospital (see p432 and p474).

Note: for IS only, if you are only in hospital for part of the week and are entitled to PIP when you are not in hospital, you can be paid the severe disability and enhanced disability premiums when you are staying away from the hospital from the date the change occurs (or is expected to occur).[29]

If your carer's allowance stops

You no longer qualify for CA when payment of the AA, DLA or PIP of the person you are caring for stops. In this situation, the carer premium in your IS, income-based JSA, income-related ESA and HB or the carer addition in PC can continue to be paid for eight weeks after your entitlement to CA stops (see p350). After this, you are no longer entitled to a carer premium or addition. If your CA stops because *you* are a patient, the person you were caring for may become entitled to the severe disability premium or addition (see p346 for more information on the severe disability premium).

Pension credit child amounts

If you get PC which includes an amount for a child (see p323), the amount for the child can continue while s/he is in hospital – providing the hospital stay is not expected to exceed, or has not exceeded, 52 weeks or, in exceptional circumstances, it is unlikely to be substantially more than 52 weeks.[30] There is no 'linking rule' in this provision. This means that if your child is discharged from hospital and is then re-admitted, a new period as a patient starts.

If you have been in hospital for 52 weeks

You still count as a couple for IS, JSA, ESA, PC and HB while you and your partner are temporarily apart. However, you no longer count as a couple if you are likely to be separated for more than 52 weeks or, in exceptional circumstances (including a stay in hospital), not substantially more than 52 weeks.[31] If you no longer count as a couple, you are both treated as a single claimant (or lone parent) for these benefits.

If your child has been in hospital for more than 52 weeks, s/he may no longer count as living with you (see p327) and no longer be included in your claim.

Note:

- HB and help with your housing costs may no longer be payable once you have been away from home for 52 weeks – eg, if you live alone. For information about paying for your usual home while you are a patient, see p926.
- If you have a non-dependant living with you and s/he has been a patient for 52 weeks, non-dependant deductions made for her/him stop (see p927).

The rate of IS, income-based JSA or income-related ESA may be lower if you (or your partner) have been a patient for a continuous period of more than 52 weeks, because you are no longer entitled to certain premiums (see p924). You may have

Part 6: Special benefit rules
Chapter 42: Benefits in hospital, care homes, prison and in other special circumstances
1. Hospital patients

already lost the severe disability and carer premiums (see p922). The calculation of HB may also be affected if you are not 'passported' to the maximum amount.

There are no 'linking rules' with these provisions. This means that if you are discharged from hospital and are then re-admitted, a new period as a patient starts and you can again be entitled to IS, income-based JSA, income-related ESA, PC or HB premiums at the rate you were getting before your admission to hospital. If you have completely lost your entitlement to IS, income-based JSA, income-related ESA or HB, you are likely to have to claim UC instead. See p21 for when you might have to claim UC.

Premiums and components: single claimants and lone parents

If you are a single claimant or a lone parent and you have been a patient for more than 52 weeks:[32]

- the disability premium is not included in your IS or income-based JSA and the enhanced disability premium is not included in your IS, income-based JSA or income-related ESA;
- the work-related activity component and the support component are not included in your income-related ESA.

Premiums and components: couples

If you are a member of a couple and:

- both you and your partner have been a patient for more than 52 weeks, but you still count as a couple:[33]
  - the higher pension premium and enhanced disability premium are not included in your IS, income-based JSA or income-related ESA. **Note:** the pensioner premium is included in your IS if your partner qualifies, or in your income-based JSA or income-related ESA if you or your partner qualify;
  - the disability premium is not included in your IS or income-based JSA;
  - the work-related activity component and the support component are not included in your income-related ESA;
- one of you has been a patient for more than 52 weeks, but you still count as a couple:
  - you are paid the normal rate of IS and income-based JSA, but without any premiums for the patient, other than the pensioner premium;[34]
  - you are paid the normal rate of income-related ESA. Premiums may be affected by changes to other benefits (see p923).[35]

Premiums: children

If you have a child and s/he is (or you are) a patient, s/he may no longer be included in your claim if s/he no longer counts as living with you (see p323). If this happens, you can no longer get allowances and premiums for her/him in your HB (and in your IS or income-based JSA, if still included). If s/he **is** still included in your claim:

- you continue to be entitled to the normal HB premiums, including the disabled child and enhanced disability premiums – these are not affected if you or your child have been a patient for more than 52 weeks;[36]
- if your child is the patient, you are no longer entitled to the disabled child premium and enhanced disability premium for her/him in IS and income-based JSA.[37]

Other benefits

Child benefit

Your entitlement to child benefit can be affected if your child is not living with you. However, periods of up to 84 days when your child is receiving inpatient treatment in a hospital or similar institution are ignored. If your child has been in hospital for 84 days or longer, you remain entitled to child benefit if:

- you are regularly incurring expenditure in respect of the child; *or*
- you are contributing at least the amount of child benefit to the cost of supporting the child.

See p583 for details of these rules.

Child tax credit

Child tax credit (CTC) remains payable for a child, provided s/he normally lives with you.[38] Guidance from HMRC says this means that the child 'regularly, usually, typically' lives with you, and that this allows for temporary absences.[39] You remain entitled to CTC if your child is in hospital on a temporary basis.

Contributory employment and support allowance

You are not entitled to a work-related activity or support component in your contributory ESA once you have been a patient for a continuous period of more than 52 weeks.[40]

Increases for an adult or a child in non-means-tested benefits

If you are still entitled to an increase in a non-means-tested benefit for an adult or child (eg, with CA), this is no longer payable once you (or both you and the adult or child) have been a patient for 52 weeks, unless you apply to the DWP to pay the increase on your behalf to:[41]

- the person for whom the increase is paid; *or*
- someone else approved by the DWP. The DWP must be satisfied that the payment will be used for the benefit of:
  - the person for whom the increase is paid, if you are a patient; *or*
  - at least one of your children, if both you and the person are patients.

There are no 'linking rules' with this provision. This means that if you (or the person for whom you are paid the increase) are discharged from hospital and are

Part 6: Special benefit rules
Chapter 42: Benefits in hospital, care homes, prison and in other special circumstances
1. Hospital patients

then readmitted, a new period as a patient starts and you can be paid the increase again. **Note:** if you cease to satisfy the conditions for an increase for an adult, or an increase for a child stops being paid for more than 58 days, you lose your entitlement to it.

Winter fuel payment

You are not entitled to a winter fuel payment if you have been a patient for more than 52 weeks.[42]

Paying for your usual home

The benefit you can get to help pay for your usual home may be affected while you, or your partner, child or non-dependant, are temporarily in hospital (whether as an NHS or private patient). **Note:** if you leave your home permanently, you are no longer entitled to benefit for it.

- You can get a UC housing costs element for up to six months, provided your absence from home does not exceed (or is not expected to exceed) six months (see p92).[43] If you are on UC and are getting a DWP loan to help pay your mortgage interest, payments stop if you have been absent for six months (or if your absence is likely to exceed six months).[44]
- You can get HB, or help with your housing costs (service charges and ground rent for owner-occupiers) in your IS, income-based JSA, income-related ESA or PC, provided you have not been absent (or are not likely to be absent) from home for more than 52 weeks or, in exceptional circumstances, not substantially longer than 52 weeks (see p182 and p371).[45] You can get HB or help with housing costs for a maximum of 52 weeks. If you are on IS, income-based JSA, income-related ESA or PC and you get a DWP loan to help with your mortgage interest, you can continue to get this provided you have not been absent (or are not likely to be absent) for more than 52 weeks, or in exceptional circumstances, not substantially longer than 52 weeks. You can continue to get the DWP loan for a maximum of 52 weeks.[46]

Note:
- Another person (eg, your partner) might be able to qualify for these benefits (or for the DWP loan to help pay mortgage interest – see p857) instead of you if s/he is (or can be treated as) liable to pay the rent or housing costs (see p87, p177 and p369).
- There are no 'linking rules' with these provisions. This means that if a new period as a patient starts, you can again be entitled to HB or an amount in your UC, IS, income-based JSA, income-related ESA or PC – eg, if you are discharged from hospital and then are readmitted.
- For HB, you can be treated as occupying, but temporarily absent from, a new dwelling, even if you have not yet stayed there, if you move your furniture and belongings in but cannot move in yourself – eg, because you have to go into hospital.[47]

Partners, children and non-dependants

If your partner, child or non-dependant is away from home because s/he is in hospital, this could affect the amount of your HB or housing costs paid with your UC, IS, income-based JSA, income-related ESA or PC. This could apply, for example, if s/he no longer counts as living with you or, for UC, s/he no longer counts as a member of your 'extended benefit unit' (see p96). Bear the following in mind.

- If you live in rented accommodation, you may no longer be allowed the same number of bedrooms under the size criteria (see p386, p394, p400 and p97) and your UC or HB may be reduced. For UC, this only applies if your partner, child or non-dependant is absent (or expected to be absent) from home for more than six months.[48]
- If your non-dependant is absent, check whether a deduction for housing costs contributions or a non-dependant deduction should still be made for her/him (see p198, p363 and p102).

---

2. People in care homes and similar accommodation

Most benefits are paid as normal if you live in a care home or similar type of accommodation. However, some benefits are no longer payable and some may be paid at a reduced rate. The benefits affected are covered on pp928–35, but see p583 for how your child benefit could be affected if you or your child are resident in a care home.

Always inform the DWP, HM Revenue and Customs and/or the local authority promptly if your benefits may be affected by the rules described on pp928–35, to avoid being overpaid or underpaid.

- -

Care homes and similar accommodation

There is not sufficient space in this *Handbook* to cover all the different kinds of care homes and similar accommodation, and the funding arrangements for people living in them. The rules covered in this section mainly apply to homes which provide you with accommodation and personal and/or nursing care. They do not apply to other types of supported or sheltered accommodation, even if you are receiving personal care services from your local authority social services department (social work department in Scotland). Some homes are run by the NHS, some by local authorities and some are independent. If your place is funded by the NHS, you may count as a 'patient' in a hospital or similar institution, in which case the rules on p917 apply to you. If you are in a local authority-funded or independent home, you may have to contribute part of the cost.

- -

Part 6: Special benefit rules
Chapter 42: Benefits in hospital, care homes, prison and in other special circumstances
2. People in care homes and similar accommodation

Attendance allowance, disability living allowance and personal independence payment

You cannot usually be paid attendance allowance (AA), the disability living allowance (DLA) care component or the personal independence payment (PIP) daily living component once you have been a resident in a care home for 28 days if any of the 'costs of any qualifying services' provided for you are met out of public or local funds under specified provisions (see below).[49] Until then, AA, the DLA care component and the PIP daily living component are paid as normal. See p929 for exceptions to these rules.

DLA for children will be replaced in Scotland by child disability payment starting in summer 2020. It is expected that the rules for payment of this benefit in a care home will be the same as for DLA.

Care homes, qualifying services and specified provisions
For these purposes a **'care home'** is an establishment that provides you with accommodation as well as nursing or personal care.[50]
'Qualifying services' are the costs of accommodation, board and personal care.[51] For AA and DLA, the 'costs of any qualifying services' do *not* include the cost of:[52]
– domiciliary services (including personal care) provided in a private dwelling;
– improvements to, or furniture or equipment provided for, a private dwelling because of the needs of a disabled person, or for a care home, for which a grant or payment was made out of public funds, except if the grant or payment is of a regular or repeated nature;
– social and recreational activities outside the care home;
– buying or running a motor vehicle used in connection with any qualifying service provided in the care home.
The **'specified provisions'** are:[53]
– Part III of the National Assistance Act 1948, sections 59 and 59A of the Social Work (Scotland) Act 1968, the Mental Health (Care and Treatment) (Scotland) Act 2003, the Community Care and Health (Scotland) Act 2002, the Mental Health Act 1983, section 57 of the Health and Social Care Act 2001, Part 1 of the Care Act 2014, and Part 4 of the Social Services and Well-being (Wales) Act 2014; *or*
– any other Acts relating to people with disabilities or (in the case of DLA and PIP only) young people, education or training – eg, in some special residential schools.
In most cases, a local authority pays for the services in a care home under one of these provisions, but it is always worth checking. Local authorities also have powers to provide accommodation under housing legislation and the Local Government Act 1972, in which case AA, DLA and PIP are not affected.[54] **Note:** the First-tier Tribunal can decide that your placement is being funded under a different legal power than the one the local authority has stated.[55]

Note:
- The DLA mobility component, PIP mobility component and armed forces independence payment are paid as normal however long you are a resident in a care home.
- If your entitlement to AA, the DLA care component or PIP daily living component begins while you are in a care home, you cannot be paid for days when you count as resident in the care home (including the first 28 days).[56]
- Entitlement to AA, DLA or PIP continues while you are in a care home, even after payment stops. This means that payment can begin again when you are no longer resident in a care home. If you expect to return within 28 days, you can be paid at a daily rate from when you leave.[57]
- You continue to be exempt from the benefit cap (see p1194), even if you or your partner or child are no longer receiving AA, DLA or PIP after being resident in a care home for 28 days.[58]
- If the NHS provides nursing services in a care home and your nursing needs are more than 'merely incidental and ancillary' to other care needs, you may be treated as a 'patient' for AA, DLA and PIP purposes (see p918).[59]
- If you think the DWP has refused payment of AA, DLA or PIP wrongly, you can appeal (see Chapter 57). You must apply for a mandatory reconsideration first.

Exceptions

There are exceptions to the rules. You can continue to be paid AA, the DLA care component and the PIP daily living component after you have been resident in a care home for 28 days if:
- you are terminally ill and are in a hospice, provided the DWP has been informed that you are terminally ill. In most cases, the DWP must be informed in writing.[60] This applies unless the hospice is an NHS hospital; *or*
- for DLA and PIP only, you are a student and the cost of your accommodation is wholly or partly met from a student grant or loan, or from a grant made to educational institutions under specified legislation;[61] *or*
- you are under 16 (for DLA) and being looked after by a local authority, or under 18 (for DLA and PIP) and receiving services from your local authority because of your disability or health, but only if you have been placed by the local authority in a private dwelling with a family, a relative or some other suitable person;[62] *or*
- for DLA and PIP, your accommodation is outside the UK and the costs of any qualifying services are being met by a local authority under specified legislation relating to education – eg, at the Higashi School;[63] *or*
- you are 'self-funding' (see below).

If you are self-funding

You can continue to be paid AA, the DLA care component and the PIP daily living component if you are meeting the whole cost of all the 'qualifying services' from

Part 6: Special benefit rules
Chapter 42: Benefits in hospital, care homes, prison and in other special circumstances
2. People in care homes and similar accommodation

your own resources, or with the help of another person or a charity – known as 'self-funding'.[64] This applies whether you are in an independent or local authority home. You count as self-funding even if:

- you are claiming benefits, such as universal credit (UC), income support (IS), employment and support allowance (ESA), pension credit (PC), AA, DLA or PIP; *or*
- a local authority has arranged and contracted to pay for your placement, provided you are paying the whole cost of all the 'qualifying services'; *or*
- a local authority is temporarily funding your placement while you sell a property (eg, your former home), or if you have entered into what is known as a 'deferred payment agreement'. You must be liable and able to repay the local authority in full when the property is sold, or when payment under the deferred agreement falls due. This is known as 'retrospective self-funding'.[65]

Are you likely to become self-funding?

If you move into a care home and are initially receiving help with the fees from the local authority, the DWP should suspend payment of your AA, DLA or PIP if you are likely to become self-funding in the future – eg, if you are only getting local authority help while you sell your former home, or your capital is likely to increase above the limit of the local authority's means test. When you repay the local authority and become self-funding, payment can resume and any arrears can be paid to you. If the DWP terminated payment of your AA, DLA or PIP and refuses to pay you arrears when you become self-funding, you can argue that the decision to terminate payment should be revised on the grounds of 'official error'.[66]

Days on which you count as being resident in a care home

The general rule is that you do not count as resident in a care home on the day you enter and the day you leave.[67] However, if you:[68]

- are a patient in a hospital or similar institution (or, for PIP only, a prisoner) and enter a care home, you count as a resident in the care home from:
  – for AA and DLA, the day you enter;
  – for PIP, the day after the day you enter; *and*
- leave a care home and enter a hospital or similar institution as a patient (or, for PIP only, become a prisoner), you cease to count as a resident in the care home on the day after you leave.

There is a 28-day 'linking rule'. This means that different periods as a resident in a care home separated by 28 days or less link together for the purpose of calculating the 28 days when you can continue to be paid AA, the DLA care component or the PIP daily living component. Periods spent as a patient in a hospital or similar institution (or, for PIP only, as a prisoner) also count towards the 28-day limit on payment if they are separated by 28 days or less from periods when you are resident in a care home in the circumstances described above.[69]

It can be important to plan periods of respite care in the light of the linking rules so that you can continue to be paid AA, the DLA care component or the PIP daily living component for as long as possible. This can also enable your carer to keep her/his carer's allowance (CA).

How other benefits are affected

If payment of AA, the DLA care component or the PIP daily living component stops, CA is affected in the same way as for hospital patients (see p919). The carer premium, paid with IS, income-based jobseeker's allowance (JSA), income-related ESA and housing benefit (HB), and the carer addition paid with PC can continue to be paid for eight weeks after CA stops (see p350).[70] The UC carer element stops as soon as the relevant disability benefit stops because you no longer satisfy the conditions of entitlement for CA.[71]

Once payment of AA, the DLA care component or the PIP daily living component stops because you have been resident in a care home for 28 days, you are no longer entitled to the severe disability premium or addition paid with IS, income-based JSA, income-related ESA, HB and PC. In addition, you may no longer be entitled to the disability, enhanced disability or higher pensioner premium if the only reason you qualified was because you were receiving AA, DLA care component or PIP daily living component.

Note:
- For IS and ESA only, if you only live in a care home for part of the week and are entitled to DLA when you are staying elsewhere, you can be paid, for example, the severe disability and enhanced disability premiums when you are staying away from the care home from the date the change occurs (or is expected to occur).[72] For ESA, this also applies if you are entitled to PIP when you are staying elsewhere.
- For ESA only, you qualify for the enhanced disability premium if you are getting the ESA support component, even if you are not receiving the DLA care component or PIP daily living component.
- If you are still being paid AA, DLA care component or PIP daily living component (eg, because you have not yet been in a care home for 28 days), you may be entitled to a severe disability premium, even if you were not before – eg, if you are no longer treated as living with a non-dependant or a partner.

Universal credit

You cannot get the UC housing costs element for the rent you pay to your care home.[73] If you are in a care home, the lower capital threshold for the tariff income rule remains £6,000 (see p137) unlike in benefits such as IS, income-based JSA,

Part 6: Special benefit rules
Chapter 42: Benefits in hospital, care homes, prison and in other special circumstances
2. People in care homes and similar accommodation

income-related ESA and HB for people under pension age, where the lower capital threshold increases if you are resident in a care home (see p933).

Care home

A 'care home' means:[74]

– a care home (a care home service in Scotland) as defined in section 3 of the Care Standards Act 2000, paragraph 2 of Schedule 12 to the Public Services Reform (Scotland) Act 2010 or Part I of the Regulation and Inspection of Social Care (Wales) Act 2016. If the home comes within the definition, it counts as a care home even if it also has some other function, such as an educational institution;[75]

– an independent hospital (an independent healthcare service in Scotland) as defined in section 275 of the National Health Service Act 2006 (in England) other than a health service hospital, section 2 of the Care Standards Act 2000 (in Wales) or section 10F(1)(a) and (b) of the National Health Service (Scotland) Act 1978 (in Scotland).

If you are not sure whether you live in a care home which falls within this definition, get advice.

Single claimants

You can continue to get UC while in a care home. The housing costs element for your normal home can continue if your stay in a care home is temporary. However, the housing costs element stops if your stay in a care home exceeds, or is expected to exceed, six months.[76] If your stay is temporary and you receive a loan from the DWP to help with your mortgage interest, payments stop if your stay in a care home exceeds, or is expected to exceed, six months.[77]

Couples

You and your partner continue to count as a couple while one of you is temporarily absent from the household, including when one of you is in a care home. You must continue to make a joint claim and UC is paid as normal. If the person who is not living in a care home is working, you may qualify for the childcare costs element (see p74). However, if the absence is permanent or it exceeds, or is likely to exceed, six months, you no longer count as a couple.[78] If you no longer count as a couple:

- you can no longer make a joint claim for UC;
- the calculation of your benefit no longer includes amounts for your partner;
- you may both need to reclaim UC as single claimants.

Children

A child continues to be included in your claim while s/he is temporarily absent from your household because s/he is in a care home. However, s/he is no longer included in your claim if the absence exceeds, or is expected to exceed, six months.[79] If your child is no longer included in your claim:

- the calculation of your benefit no longer includes amounts for her/him;
- the work-related requirements you must meet may change (see Chapter 46).

Other means-tested benefits

How your IS, income-based JSA, income-related ESA, PC and HB are affected depends on whether you (or your partner or child) are temporarily or permanently living in a care home. If you are in a care home (on either basis), these benefits are generally calculated in the usual way, although if payment of your AA, DLA care component or PIP daily living component stops, you may no longer be entitled to certain premiums (see p931). For information about paying for your usual home, see p935.

For the definition of 'care home', see p932. The meaning is the same as for UC, except it also includes an Abbeyfield home.

Note:

- If you have a partner, you may no longer count as a couple if you (or your partner) are resident in a care home. If your child is resident in a care home, s/he may no longer be included in your claim (see p934).
- For PC, if you have an 'assessed income period' (see p281), it comes to an end if you do not have a partner and are provided with accommodation in a care home (other than in an Abbeyfield home) on a permanent basis. This means your income may be reassessed.[80]

Housing benefit for your care home

You cannot usually get HB for the rent you pay to your care home.[81] For these purposes, a care home does *not* include an Abbeyfield home. There are exceptions if you were entitled to HB for your care home when the rules changed at various times in the past and you have transitional protection.[82]

Note: if you are on a placement under the adult placement scheme (a scheme similar to fostering, but for adults) living with an approved carer, the normal conditions of entitlement to HB apply and you may be able to get HB.[83]

Tariff income from savings

For IS, income-based JSA, income-related ESA and, if you and your partner are under pension age, for HB, if you are permanently resident in a care home, the threshold for calculating your tariff income from any capital is increased to £10,000 (see p489), instead of £6,000. This also applies if you live in Polish resettlement accommodation (certain care homes for Polish people who came to the UK as refugees after the Second World War). Some temporary absences from the care home or resettlement accommodation are ignored.[84] For HB, the £10,000 threshold is only relevant (and only applies) in the limited situations in which

Part 6: Special benefit rules
Chapter 42: Benefits in hospital, care homes, prison and in other special circumstances
2. People in care homes and similar accommodation

you can get HB while living in a care home. For PC (and for HB, if you or your partner are at least pension age), the threshold is always £10,000 (see p517).

Partners and children

- If you or your partner move into a care home permanently (for PC only, other than to an Abbeyfield home), you no longer count as a couple.[85] This also applies if you and your partner are both in care homes permanently, even if you are in the same home and the same room.[86] If you do not count as a couple, your benefit, and that of your partner, is calculated as if you were single claimants.

- If you or your partner move into a care home temporarily, you still count as a couple if you intend to live together again. This only applies if you are unlikely to be apart for more than 52 weeks or your time apart is longer than 52 weeks, but there are exceptional circumstances and the time apart is unlikely to be substantially longer than 52 weeks.[87] If you still count as a couple:
  - your PC and HB continue to be assessed under the normal rules. This means that, once the person in the care home stops getting AA, the DLA care component or the PIP daily living component, no severe disability premium (or additional amount) for either of you can be included in your applicable amount unless you can receive it on the basis that the person who is in the care home is severely sight impaired or blind (see p346);
  - your applicable amount for IS, income-based JSA and income-related ESA is calculated in a special way. You receive the amount for two single claimants if this is higher than the amount you receive as a couple. This can include the severe disability premium in respect of either or both of you, as if you were single claimants, even if you are not normally entitled to it at home.[88]

If child benefit stops because your child lives in a care home or is being looked after by a local authority, this may affect whether s/he is included in your claim (see p323). If your child is no longer included, you can no longer get a personal allowance and premiums for her/him in your HB (or your IS or income-based JSA, if amounts for your child are still included in these benefits – see p333). Entitlement to premiums for your child is also affected if s/he is no longer paid DLA or PIP.

Pension credit child amounts

If you get PC which includes an amount for a child (see p323) and s/he is in a care home, what happens to the child amount depends on whether the child is looked after by the local authority. If s/he is not looked after by the local authority, the amount for the child can continue while s/he is in a care home providing the stay is not expected to exceed, or has not exceeded, 52 weeks or, in exceptional circumstances, the stay is unlikely to be substantially more than 52 weeks.[89] The extra amount that you may get if the child has a disability (see p339) continues during a temporary absence even if her/his DLA or PIP has stopped being paid.[90] There is no 'linking rule' in this provision. This means that if the child comes home from a care home and then goes back in, a new period as a patient starts. If s/he is in a care home and counts as 'looked after' by the local authority, you no longer get the child amount in your PC, unless it is a 'planned short break' (respite).[91]

Social fund payments

Some social fund payments are affected if you are in a care home. You cannot get:
- a cold weather payment (see p805) if you are in a care home (see p927) or Polish resettlement accommodation, unless you are responsible for a child under five or you are getting child tax credit which includes a disabled child or severely disabled child element;[92]
- a winter fuel payment(see p806) if you are getting income-based JSA, income-related ESA or PC and are (and for a period have been) in a care home or Polish resettlement accommodation (see p807). If you are not getting one of these benefits, you are entitled to a winter fuel payment of £100 if you are aged between pension age and 79 and £150 if you are aged 80 or over.[93]

Paying for your usual home

The benefit you can get to help pay for your usual home may be affected while you, or your partner, child or non-dependant, are temporarily in a care home. **Note:** if you leave your home permanently (eg, you become a permanent resident in a care home), you are no longer entitled to benefit for it.

If you are temporarily away from home, you can qualify for:
- UC housing costs element for up to six months, provided your absence from home does not exceed (or is not expected to exceed) six months (see p92). If you are on UC and are getting a DWP loan to help pay your mortgage interest, payments stop if you have been absent for six months (or your absence is likely to exceed six months);[94]
- HB, or help with your housing costs (service charges and ground rent for owner-occupiers) in your IS, income-based JSA, income-related ESA or PC for up to 52 weeks, provided your absence from home does not exceed (or is not likely to exceed) 52 weeks, you intend to return to your home and you do not sub-let it. In exceptional circumstances, the absence may be expected to be longer than 52 weeks, provided it is not likely to last substantially longer than 52 weeks. HB or housing costs are still only payable for a maximum of 52 weeks (see p182 and p371). If you are on IS, income-based JSA, income-related ESA or PC and you get a DWP loan to help with your mortgage interest, you can continue to get this for up to 52 weeks if your absence from home does not exceed (or is not likely to exceed) 52 weeks, you intend to return to your home and you do not sub-let it. In exceptional circumstances, the absence may be

Part 6: Special benefit rules
Chapter 42: Benefits in hospital, care homes, prison and in other special circumstances
2. People in care homes and similar accommodation

expected to be longer than 52 weeks, provided it is not expected to last substantially longer than 52 weeks. The loan to help with mortgage interest is still only payable for a maximum of 52 weeks. [95]

Note:

- Another person (eg, your partner) might be able to qualify for these benefits (or for the DWP loan to help with mortgage interest – see p857) instead of you if s/he is (or can be treated as) liable to pay the rent or housing costs (see p87, p177 and p369).
- There are no 'linking rules' with these provisions. This means that, if a new period in a care home starts, you can again be entitled to HB or an amount in your UC, IS, income-based JSA, income-related ESA or PC.
- For HB, you can be treated as occupying, but temporarily absent from, a new dwelling, even if you have not yet stayed there, if you move in your furniture and belongings but cannot move in yourself – eg, because you are in hospital or a care home[96] on a temporary basis.[97]
- There are special rules if you are a temporary resident in a care home for a trial period. If you intend to return home, you can get HB and help with your housing costs in your IS, income-based JSA, income-related ESA and PC for up to 13 weeks for each trial period (in different care homes) subject to an overall maximum of 52 weeks (see p182 and p371).[98] This does not apply to UC.

Partners, children and non-dependants

If your partner, child or non-dependant is away from home because s/he is in a care home, this could affect the amount of your HB or housing costs paid with your UC, IS, income-based JSA, income-related ESA or PC. This could apply, for example, if s/he no longer counts as living with you or, for UC, s/he no longer counts as a member of your 'extended benefit unit' (see p96). Bear the following in mind.

- If you live in rented accommodation, you may no longer be allowed the same number of bedrooms under the size criteria (see p386, p394, p400 and p97) and your UC or HB may be reduced. For UC, this only applies if your partner, child or non-dependant is absent (or expected to be absent) from home for more than six months.[99]
- If your non-dependant is absent, check whether a deduction for housing costs contributions or a non-dependant deduction should still be made for her/him (see p198, p363 and p102).

3. **Prisoners**

Most benefits are affected if you are a prisoner. Some are not payable, some are suspended and some are only payable for a temporary period. There are also issues to consider if you are given an alternative sentence to prison.

Always inform the DWP, HMRC and/or the local authority as soon as you, or a member of your family, enter or leave prison to avoid any underpayment or overpayment of benefit. If you are being held on remand and are then sentenced, notify the benefit authorities as soon as this happens. Do not assume that the prison will do this for you.

Non-means-tested benefits

You are disqualified from getting most non-means-tested benefits while you are a prisoner. For statutory sick pay (SSP), statutory maternity pay (SMP), statutory adoption pay (SAP), statutory paternity pay (SPP), statutory shared parental pay (SSPP) and statutory parental bereavement pay (SPBP), see below. For other non-means-tested benefits, see p938. In some cases, payment of your benefit is only suspended pending the outcome of your trial or sentence (see p939). For benefits that are payable, see p939.

Prisoners

You count as a **'prisoner'** for **non-means-tested benefits** if you are in prison or detained in legal custody.[100] This includes if you are remanded in custody awaiting trial or sentencing as well as if you are serving a custodial sentence. You do *not* count as a prisoner if you are on bail or living in approved premises (eg, a bail or probation hostel), or if you are released on parole, temporary licence or under a home detention curfew (electronic tagging).

See p942 if you are detained in a hospital or similar institution as a person with a mental disorder.

Statutory sick, maternity, adoption, paternity, and other parental pay

If you are a prisoner you:[101]
- are not entitled to SSP. If you are getting SSP your entitlement ends;
- cannot be paid SMP or SPP. Even if you are then released from prison during the maternity or paternity pay period, you do not get SMP or SPP for the rest of that period. If you cannot be paid SMP, check whether you can be paid maternity allowance (MA) (see p725) instead on your release from prison;
- cannot be paid SAP, SSPP or SPBP for the time you are a prisoner, unless you are subsequently released without charge or after being found not guilty, or you are convicted but do not receive a custodial sentence. If one of these exceptions apply, you should receive arrears for the period you were detained

Part 6: Special benefit rules
Chapter 42: Benefits in hospital, care homes, prison and in other special circumstances
3. Prisoners

and payment should also resume for any period of entitlement after your release.

Other non-means-tested benefits

If you are a prisoner, you cannot be paid attendance allowance (AA), bereavement benefits, disability living allowance (DLA), carer's allowance (CA), contributory employment and support allowance (ESA), incapacity benefit (IB), MA, reduced earnings allowance (REA), retirement allowance, retirement pensions or severe disablement allowance (SDA).[102] Pending trial or sentencing, these benefits are only suspended, which means that you may be owed arrears if you do not receive a prison sentence (see p939).

You are paid **personal independence payment** (PIP) for the first 28 days that you count as a prisoner, whatever the outcome of the proceedings against you.[103] However, this does not apply if you are awarded PIP while you are a prisoner, in which case you are not paid PIP until your release from prison.[104] There is a 'linking rule' which means that different periods spent as a prisoner separated by one year or less are linked together and treated as one period.[105] Periods spent in a care home or hospital are also linked with periods spent as a prisoner (see p919 and p930).

DLA for children will be replaced in Scotland by **child disability payment** starting in summer 2020. It is expected that you will continue to be entitled to the care component for the first 28 days that you are a prisoner and that you will continue to be entitled to the mobility component during any period that you are a prisoner.

You cannot be paid an **increase in CA or retirement pensions for your spouse or civil partner** if s/he is a prisoner.[106]

If you do not come under the universal credit (UC) system (see p21), you are unable to satisfy the jobseeking conditions for **jobseeker's allowance** (JSA) while you are in prison. In addition, you are treated as being unavailable for work if you are a prisoner on temporary release. This means that you cannot qualify for (and, therefore, cannot be paid) JSA. However, unless you count as a prisoner, you are treated as available for and actively seeking work during temporary police detention (legal custody in Scotland) of up to 96 hours (see Chapter 48).[107]

If you come under the UC system, you are unable to meet the work-related requirements for JSA while you are in prison. In addition, you are treated as not having met the work availability requirement if you are a prisoner on temporary release under specified provisions.[108] However, you may be able to satisfy the DWP that you should not have to meet a work search requirement during temporary police detention (legal custody in Scotland).

For non-means-tested benefits that are payable while you are a prisoner, see p939.

Benefits that are suspended

If you are a remand prisoner awaiting trial or sentence, payment of contributory ESA, IB, SDA, AA, DLA, CA, MA, REA, retirement pensions, retirement allowance and bereavement benefits is suspended pending the outcome. An increase of CA or retirement pension for your spouse or civil partner is suspended if s/he is a remand prisoner. If you (or s/he) subsequently receive a sentence of imprisonment or detention (including a suspended sentence), you are not paid the benefits for the whole period you are (or s/he is) in prison.[109]

If you (or your spouse or civil partner) do not receive a sentence of imprisonment or detention, or your conviction is quashed, full arrears of any of the benefits that have been withheld are payable when you are released.[110] Arrears are only payable if the normal conditions of entitlement for benefit were met while you (or your spouse/civil partner) were a remand prisoner. For contributory ESA, you are treated as not having limited capability for work once you have been disqualified as a prisoner for six weeks.[111] This rule does not apply if contributory ESA is suspended and subsequently reinstated because you do not receive a custodial sentence.[112] This is because you are not actually 'disqualified' in this situation.

For the purpose of entitlement to an increase in your benefit for a spouse or civil partner, you should be treated as still 'residing with' her/him while s/he is in prison, unless your marriage/partnership has broken down and your separation is likely to be permanent.[113]

Benefits payable

You are entitled to **industrial injuries disablement benefit** (but not any of the increases on p694) for periods when you are a prisoner. However, you are not paid until you are released and you can only get a maximum of 12 months' arrears.[114] If you are in prison for more than a year, you should be paid for the 12-month period which gives you the most benefit.[115] You are entitled to full arrears for any period you were on remand, provided you are not subsequently sentenced to imprisonment or detention.[116]

You are entitled to **child benefit** and **guardian's allowance**:[117]

- while you are a prisoner. You must continue to be 'responsible' for the child (see p583). If you are in prison for some time, you may want to arrange for child benefit to be paid to the person looking after your child;
- while your child is a prisoner, but entitlement to child benefit usually ends after eight weeks.[118] There are exceptions to the rules (see p590). Full arrears are payable at the end of any period of remand if your child is not sentenced to imprisonment or detention. Once entitlement to child benefit ends, entitlement to guardian's allowance in respect of the child also ends.

Note: if child benefit stops because your child is a prisoner, this may affect whether you can get an increase for her/him with your non-means-tested benefits,

Part 6: Special benefit rules
Chapter 42: Benefits in hospital, care homes, prison and in other special circumstances
3. Prisoners

and personal allowances and premiums for her/him with your housing benefit (HB) (and income support (IS) or income-based JSA if these amounts are still included). For increases for a child, see the chapter in this *Handbook* about the benefit you are claiming. For IS and JSA, see p333.

Universal credit

If you are a single person and you become a prisoner (see below), you can get the housing costs element in your UC for up to six months. To be entitled, you must have been getting the housing costs element immediately before you were a prisoner.[119] You do not get any other elements of UC. See p945 for details of housing costs element.

Prisoners

You count as a **'prisoner'** if you are:[120]

– detained in custody (eg, in prison or a young offenders' institution) awaiting trial or sentence (on remand) or following a sentence of imprisonment; *or*
– on temporary release under specific provisions (this does not include parole licence).

If your partner or a child included in your claim is a prisoner, see below. If you have a non-dependant who is a prisoner, no deduction is made from your housing costs element (see p103), but you may no longer qualify for a bedroom for her/him after a period (see p100).[121]

Couples

If you are a member of a couple and one of you is a prisoner, or is serving a prison sentence while detained in hospital, the other partner can claim UC as a single claimant.[122] Provided you still count as a couple, your and your partner's income and capital are still assessed jointly, but the amount of your UC is that for a single person.[123] If the partner who is not a prisoner is working, you may qualify for a childcare costs element (see p74). In any case, if the absence from the household exceeds, or is expected to exceed, six months, you no longer count as a couple.[124] The amount of your housing costs element for your rent may be affected (see p947).

Children

If your child is a prisoner, s/he can no longer be included in your claim (see p62).[125] If your child is no longer included in your claim:
• the calculation of your benefit no longer includes amounts for her/him;
• the amount of your housing costs element for your rent may be affected (see p947);

- the work allowance which applies to you (see p41) and work-related requirements you must meet may change if, for example, you no longer have a dependent child living with you (see Chapter 46).

Other means-tested benefits

If you are a prisoner (see below):
- you cannot qualify for income-based JSA as you are unable to satisfy the jobseeking conditions;
- IS, income-related ESA and PC guarantee credit usually stop immediately. The only exception to this is if you get IS, income-related ESA or PC guarantee credit which includes an amount for housing costs (service charges and ground rent for owner-occupiers – see p359). In this situation, you can get the benefit for up to 52 weeks while you are detained in custody awaiting trial or sentence, but you only get your housing costs paid. If you have continued to be entitled to one of these benefits (because you get housing costs), it will stop once you have been sentenced;[126]
- you can qualify for HB for a limited period (see p946);
- you cannot get any savings credit of PC.[127]

If you have a non-dependant who is a prisoner, no non-dependant deduction is made for her/him.[128] However, for HB you may no longer qualify for a bedroom for her/him after a period. See p198 and p363 for further information about non-dependant deductions.

For information about UC if you (or your partner or child) are a prisoner, see p940.

Prisoner

For IS, JSA, ESA, PC and HB, you count as a **'prisoner'** if you are:[129]
- detained in custody (eg, in prison or a young offenders' institution) awaiting trial or sentence (on remand) or following a sentence of imprisonment; *or*
- on temporary release under specific provisions (this does not include parole licence).

You do not count as a prisoner if you are detained in hospital under specific mental health provisions (but see p942 if you received a prison sentence as a result of a criminal conviction). Check to see whether your benefit is affected by the special rules for hospital patients instead (see p922). In addition, you do not count as a prisoner if you are:
- released on licence or parole; *or*
- on bail or living in approved premises – eg, a bail or probation hostel; *or*
- released under a home detention curfew (electronic tagging).

Part 6: Special benefit rules
Chapter 42: Benefits in hospital, care homes, prison and in other special circumstances
3. Prisoners

Partners and children

If you have a partner and one of you is a prisoner:

- you no longer count as a couple for IS, income-based JSA, income-related ESA or PC;[130]
- you continue to count as a couple for HB, provided you intend to live together again and the prisoner is unlikely to be away for substantially longer than 52 weeks.[131] If the partner who is not a prisoner is working, s/he may be able to have childcare costs deducted from her/his earnings (see p432 and p474).[132]

If you no longer count as a couple, the partner who is *not* a prisoner may be able to claim benefit as a single person (or lone parent).

If child benefit stops because your child is a prisoner, s/he may no longer be included in your claim for HB, IS or income-based JSA, in which case your entitlement to a personal allowance and premiums for her/him might be affected.

Child tax credit (CTC) continues to be paid for your child, unless s/he has been sentenced to more than four months in prison, in which case CTC stops and s/he no longer counts as a dependant for working tax credit (WTC).[133]

If you get PC which includes an amount for a child (see p323), the amount for the child stops if s/he becomes a prisoner.[134]

Social fund payments

You cannot get a winter fuel payment if you are serving a custodial sentence (see p807). You cannot get other social fund payments if you are not getting a qualifying benefit (see Chapter 37).[135]

If you are detained under mental health legislation

Special rules apply for non-means-tested benefits (other than contribution-based JSA, SSP, SMP, SAP, SPP and SSPP) and for UC, IS, income-related ESA and PC, if, although you received a prison sentence as a result of a criminal conviction, you are currently detained in a hospital or similar institution as a person with a mental disorder under sections 45A or 47 of the Mental Health Act 1983, section 59A of the Criminal Procedure (Scotland) Act 1995 or section 136 of the Mental Health (Care and Treatment) (Scotland) Act 2003. This applies if you are:[136]

- ordered to be detained in hospital by a court after you are convicted, where the court specifies a length of sentence; *or*
- sent to prison, but later transferred to hospital by order.

If this applies, although you are a hospital patient, you are treated as a prisoner for the above benefits, but only until you would have been entitled to be released under your original sentence or, if you are held under an indeterminate sentence (eg, you are a life prisoner), until your release is authorised.[137] After that, if you are still in hospital, your benefit might be affected under the rules that apply to hospital patients (see p917).

Note:

- The rules do not apply to JSA, but in this situation you are unable to satisfy the jobseeking conditions (or, if you come under the UC system, the work-related requirements).
- If you are detained in a hospital or similar institution under provisions other than those listed above (eg, you were convicted of a criminal offence but were ordered to be detained in hospital and were not given a prison sentence), you may be paid non-means-tested benefits, or you may qualify for UC, IS, income-related ESA or PC. Check whether your benefit is affected under the rules that apply to hospital patients (see p917).

Community sentences

If you have been given a community sentence that involves punishment or supervision in the community, you do not count as a prisoner. However, bear the following in mind.

- There might be a question about whether you satisfy the jobseeking conditions for JSA (or the work-related requirements for UC if you come under the UC system). Guidance for JSA suggests that Jobcentre Plus should liaise with the Probation Service (in Scotland, Criminal Justice Social Work Services) to avoid any problems.[138] Guidance for UC suggests that any restrictions caused by a community sentence or order should be taken into account when setting a work search requirement.[139]
- If you undertake basic skills training and are treated as a full-time student, this may affect your entitlement to benefits (see Chapter 41).

If you are on bail or living in approved premises

Your non-means-tested benefits are paid as normal if you are on bail or living in approved premises (eg, a bail or probation hostel) or other accommodation as a condition of bail. However, special rules can apply for means-tested benefits.

For UC, you and your partner continue to count as a couple while one of you is temporarily absent from the household. You must continue to make a joint claim and UC is paid as normal. However, if the absence exceeds, or is expected to exceed, six months, you no longer count as a couple.[140] If you no longer count as a couple, you can no longer make a joint claim for UC and the calculation of your benefit no longer includes amounts for your partner. Each partner must make a claim for UC as a single person if appropriate.

For IS, income-based JSA, income-related ESA, PC and HB, if you have a partner and you are temporarily separated because one of you is living away from home, you still count as a couple if you intend to live together again, but only if you are unlikely to be apart for more than 52 weeks or, in exceptional

Part 6: Special benefit rules
Chapter 42: Benefits in hospital, care homes, prison and in other special circumstances
3. Prisoners

circumstances, not substantially longer than 52 weeks.[141] For IS, income-based JSA and income-related ESA only, if one of you is living in an approved bail or probation hostel, your applicable amount is calculated in a special way – at either the single rate for each of you added together or the couple rate, whichever is the greater.[142]

If you are required to live away from home in an approved bail or probation hostel or another address that you are bailed to:

- you cannot get the UC housing costs element for the hostel.[143] You can get the housing costs element for your normal home for up to six months, provided you are not expected to be away for longer;[144]
- you cannot get HB for the rent you pay for the hostel;[145]
- you can continue to get HB and help with your housing costs in IS, income-based JSA, income-related ESA or PC for your normal home for up to 52 weeks, provided you intend to return home and you are unlikely to be away for longer than this (or, in exceptional circumstances, not substantially longer than this);[146]
- you can get a DWP loan for your mortgage interest on your normal home for up to six months (UC) or 52 weeks (other benefits), provided you are not expected to be away for longer than this and you continue to satisfy the other conditions of entitlement.[147]

If you are no longer entitled to the UC housing costs element or HB for your normal home (or the DWP loan to help with mortgage interest – see p857), these can be paid to another person if s/he is (or can be treated as) liable (see p87, p369 and p177).

Benefits on release

If you are **temporarily released** (on temporary licence), you no longer count as a prisoner for non-means-tested benefits. You still count as a prisoner for means-tested benefits (unless you are released on parole licence).

When you are **permanently released** from prison, you should claim any benefits to which you are entitled as soon as possible. The prison gives you a discharge form that can help you prove your identity. You may also be interviewed by a DWP liaison officer before you leave prison, who should point out which benefits you might be able to claim.

- As UC, IS, income-based JSA and income-related ESA are generally paid in arrears, you may need to apply for a budgeting advance (see p51) or a short-term advance (see p1192).
- For JSA, you are treated as satisfying the jobseeking conditions for the first seven days after your release.[148] **Note:** this does not apply if you come under the UC system (see p23).

- If you are at least 25 and are an offender who is subject to multi-agency risk management arrangements, you are exempt from the private sector rent restriction rules for single claimants under 35 (see p402).
- You may receive a discharge grant from the Prison Service, which counts as capital for IS, income-based JSA and income-related ESA purposes.[149] The rules do not say how it should be treated for UC, PC or HB.
- If you are released without being sentenced to imprisonment or detention, you should receive any arrears of your non-means-tested benefits that were suspended (see p939).
- If you are released following the quashing of a conviction, you are entitled to national insurance credits for the period you were imprisoned or detained (see p978).

Help with travelling expenses

The Help with Prison Visits scheme can help a partner or close relative (or another person if s/he is your only visitor) with the cost of visiting you in prison, or the cost of someone bringing your children to visit you. S/he must be getting 'qualifying income'.

Claim online at gov.uk/help-with-prison-visits or contact Help with Prison Visits, PO Box 17594, Birmingham B2 2QP (tel: 0300 063 2100). You can also email HelpwithPrisonVisits@justice.gov.uk.

Qualifying income
'Qualifying income' is UC, IS, income-based JSA, income-related ESA and PC, and health benefits on low-income grounds, as well as CTC or WTC. The WTC must include a disabled worker element, or you must be getting CTC and WTC. If your qualifying benefit is UC, you must have a monthly income of less than £1,250. If your qualifying income is tax credits, your annual income must be less than £17,474.

Paying for your usual home

The benefit you can get to help pay for your normal home may be affected while you, or your partner, child or non-dependant, are temporarily in prison. **Note:** if you leave your home permanently, you are no longer entitled to benefit for it.

Universal credit housing costs

If you are a prisoner, whether you are awaiting trial or sentence or are serving a custodial sentence, you can continue to qualify for a UC housing costs element for your normal home for up to six months.[150] However, you can only qualify following a sentence of imprisonment if you have not been sentenced to a term that is expected to go beyond the six-month period. The six-month period includes any time you have already been in prison before being sentenced – eg, if

Part 6: Special benefit rules
Chapter 42: Benefits in hospital, care homes, prison and in other special circumstances
3. Prisoners

you were remanded in custody.[151] You can only get the housing costs element if you were entitled to it immediately before becoming a prisoner.[152] If you are on UC and get a DWP loan for your mortgage interest, payments may continue for up to six months, providing your absence is not expected to last for more than six months.[153]

The UC housing costs element (or the DWP loan to help with mortgage interest – see p857) can be paid to another person (eg, your partner) if s/he is (or can be treated as) liable to pay the rent or housing costs (see p88).

Housing benefit and other means-tested benefits

While you are detained in custody awaiting trial or sentence, you can get HB and help with your housing costs (service charges and ground rent for owner-occupiers) paid with IS, income-related ESA or PC for your normal home for up to 52 weeks, provided you intend to return home, you are unlikely to be away for longer than this (or, in exceptional circumstances, unlikely to be away for substantially longer than this) and you do not sub-let your home.[154]

If you get a DWP loan for your mortgage interest and you are on a benefit other than UC, payments may continue while you are detained in custody awaiting trial or sentence for up to 52 weeks, provided you intend to return home, you are unlikely to be away for longer than this (or in exceptional circumstances, unlikely to be away for substantially longer than this) and you do not sub-let your home.[155]

If you are serving a custodial sentence, you can get HB for up to 13 weeks, provided you are unlikely to be away from your normal home for longer than this – ie, you are serving a short sentence.[156] The 13 weeks run from the date you were first in prison.[157] So any time you spend in prison awaiting trial or sentence counts towards the 13 weeks. If you are serving a sentence of more than 13 weeks, you may still be entitled to HB, as prisoners serving short sentences are often released early under a home detention curfew (electronic tagging).

If you are on temporary release under specific provisions, you continue to be treated as a prisoner.[158] This means that, even if you return home, you are still treated as if you are away from home.

In this situation, if you are a convicted prisoner, you are not entitled to IS, income-based JSA, income-related ESA or PC and cannot get help with your housing costs.

For HB, you are still treated as if you are away from home and these periods count towards the 13/52 weeks for which HB may be payable.[159]

When calculating how long you have been absent from home for HB, the day you go into prison is counted as a day of absence but the day you return home is not.[160]

Note:
- You should report any change in your circumstances as soon as possible – ie, when you are remanded in custody, begin a custodial sentence or are being released from custody.

- If you do not qualify for HB for 52 or 13 weeks under the rules described above, you may be able to continue to get HB for a former home for up to four benefit weeks if you are still liable to pay rent for it, and you could not reasonably have avoided this liability – eg, because your tenancy agreement required you to give notice.[161]
- HB and housing costs paid with IS, income-based JSA, income-related ESA or PC can be paid to another person (eg, your partner), if s/he is (or can be treated as) liable to pay the rent or housing costs (see p369, p87 and p177). There is a similar rule for mortgage interest loans.[162]

Partners, children and non-dependants

If your partner, child or non-dependant is away from home because s/he is in prison, this could affect the amount of your HB or housing costs paid with your UC, IS, income-based JSA, income-related ESA or PC. This could apply, for example, if s/he no longer counts as living with you or, for UC, s/he no longer counts as a member of your 'extended benefit unit' (see p96). Bear the following in mind.

- If you live in rented accommodation, you may no longer be allowed the same number of bedrooms under the size criteria (see p386, p394, p400 and p97) and your UC or HB may be reduced. For UC, this only applies if your partner, child or non-dependant is absent (or expected to be absent) from home for more than six months.[163]
- If your non-dependant is absent, check whether a deduction for housing costs contributions or a non-dependant deduction should still be made for her/him (see p198, p363 and p102).

---

4. 16/17-year-old care leavers

You cannot usually qualify for universal credit (UC), income support (IS), income-based jobseeker's allowance (JSA) or housing benefit (HB) if you are aged 16 or 17 and count as a 'care leaver' for these purposes (although there are exceptions – see p949[164]). Entitlement to other benefits is not affected by being a care leaver.

Being a care leaver means that you were previously 'looked after' by the local authority and certain other conditions apply. Your local authority must assess and meet your needs for maintenance, accommodation and support. In addition, you cannot be treated as a child member of the family of a person claiming IS, income-based JSA, income-related employment and support allowance (ESA) or HB. So, for example, s/he cannot get allowances and premiums for you with her/his HB.[165]

Part 6: Special benefit rules
Chapter 42: Benefits in hospital, care homes, prison and in other special circumstances
4. 16/17-year-old care leavers

Being looked after

Being '**looked after**' means, for example, that you were subject to a care, supervision or permanence order, or provided with accommodation by the local authority under specified legal provisions.

Note:

- If you are *currently* being looked after by a local authority:
  - for UC purposes, you generally cannot be treated as the responsibility of a person, so, for example, s/he cannot get child elements for you in her/his UC. However, there are exceptions to this (see p63);[166]
  - for PC purposes, you generally cannot be treated as the responsibility of a person, so, for example, s/he cannot get child elements for you in her/his PC. However, there are exceptions to this (see p326);[167]
  - you cannot be included as a child in another person's claim for IS, income-based JSA, income-related ESA or HB if you are not living with her/him (see Chapter 16);
  - a person cannot usually qualify for child benefit or child tax credit for you (see p586 and p289).
- In England and Wales, if you are aged 16 or 17 and *currently* being looked after by a local authority and have been looked after for at least 13 weeks starting after your 14th birthday, you cannot qualify for IS, income-based JSA or HB unless any of the exceptions on p949 apply.[168] Similar rules apply to UC in England, Wales and Scotland.[169]
- Local DWP and social services offices should liaise to ensure any disputes about who is responsible for supporting you are quickly resolved. If you are refused both benefit and social services support, get specialist advice.

Who is excluded from means-tested benefits

You are excluded from UC, IS, income-based JSA and HB as a care leaver if you are no longer being looked after, you are aged 16 or 17 and:[170]

- you were looked after by a local authority (and, in Scotland, were provided with accommodation) for at least 13 weeks (or for UC, in Scotland, three months). The 13-week/three month period must have started after your 14th birthday and, in England and Wales, ended after you turn 16. In Scotland, you must have been looked after and accommodated for at least 13 weeks (or for UC, three months) since your 14th birthday and have been looked after, but not necessarily accommodated, by the local authority at or beyond your 16th birthday.[171] The local authority must be obliged to provide you with aftercare services;[172] *or*
- in Scotland, you are in a 'continuing care' placement under section 26A of the Children (Scotland) Act 1995, you were being looked after and accommodated for at least 13 weeks (or for UC, three months) since your 14th birthday and

were looked after, but not necessarily accommodated, by the local authority at or beyond your 16th birthday; *or*

• in England or Wales, you are not subject to a care order, but you were in hospital, or detained in a remand centre or a young offenders' or similar institution when you became 16 and, immediately before you were in hospital or detained, you were being looked after by a local authority (in Wales, accommodated) for at least 13 weeks since your 14th birthday.[173]

The 13 weeks or three months do not have to be continuous. Some pre-planned short-term placements, after which you return to the care of your parent, or person acting as your parent, do not count towards the 13 weeks or three months.[174] For UC, in Scotland, any period when you have been placed with a member of your family does not count towards the three months.[175]

Note: in England and Wales, you are not excluded from UC, IS, income-based JSA or HB if you have been in a family placement (ie, living with your parent, someone with parental responsibility for you or someone who had a child arrangements order for you before you were looked after) for at least six months (unless the placement has broken down).[176]

Who is not excluded from means-tested benefits

Even if you fall within the definition of care leaver , you can get UC if you (or your partner if you have one) are responsible for a dependent child or if you have limited capability for work. However, you cannot get the housing costs element for your rent.[177]

You can qualify for IS or income-based JSA (but not HB) if you are a lone parent, a lone foster parent or getting statutory sick pay, even though you count as a care leaver.[178]

Care leavers are not excluded from ESA, so if you are not able to work due to ill health you may be able to claim ESA.

In Scotland, you are not excluded from IS, income-based JSA and HB if you are living with your family or another person who has parental responsibility for you, unless you are receiving regular financial assistance from the local authority under section 29(1) of the Children (Scotland) Act 1995.[179]

5. People without accommodation

Entitlement to non-means-tested benefits, universal credit (UC) and pension credit (PC) is unaffected if you do not have accommodation. However, income support (IS), income-based jobseeker's allowance (JSA) and income-related employment and support allowance (ESA) may be paid at a reduced rate (see

Part 6: Special benefit rules
Chapter 42: Benefits in hospital, care homes, prison and in other special circumstances
5. People without accommodation

p951). If you do not have accommodation, you may have problems satisfying the jobseeking conditions for JSA or the claimant responsibilities for UC – see below.

If you become homeless and have no money, you can apply for a budgeting advance or a short-term advance (see p51 and p1192). It is possible to get help at any time in an emergency. You may also be able to claim local welfare assistance (see p861).

If you are homeless, the local authority may have a duty to assist you with accommodation or advice. A child or young person may be entitled to help from social services.

Note:
- If you are at least 25, have been living in a homeless hostel for at least three months and have accepted rehabilitation or resettlement support, you are exempt from the private sector rent restriction rules in housing benefit and UC for single people under 35. The three-month period does not need to be continuous.[180]
- You can qualify for help with payments for a tent and its pitch (if that is your home) with IS, income-based JSA, income-related ESA and PC (see p360). You cannot get a UC housing costs element for rent payments you make for a tent or the site on which a tent stands.[181]

Jobseeking conditions and claimant responsibilities

Even if you are homeless, to qualify for UC (and contribution-based JSA and contributory ESA if you come under the UC system), you must accept a claimant commitment and, to avoid being sanctioned, meet your work-related requirements (see Chapter 46). To qualify for JSA if you do not come under the UC system, you must satisfy jobseeking conditions (see Chapter 48)

Being homeless may reduce your prospects of finding work, but personal circumstances that reduce your chances of being employed should not prevent you from getting UC or JSA. You can be available for work even if you do not have accommodation. However, it must be possible for you to be contacted at short notice in order to satisfy the requirement that you are willing and able to take up any job immediately, or after the amount of notice allowed (see p1056 and p1116). You may satisfy this requirement by daily visits to the Jobcentre Plus office, or a drop-in centre or support group where a message can be left for you – eg, to notify you of vacancies.

Note:
- The fact that you are homeless should be taken into account when deciding whether you are actively seeking work or whether you satisfy the work search requirement. For JSA, when deciding what steps it is reasonable for you to take to find work, the DWP is specifically required to take into account the fact that you have no accommodation and the steps you need to take (and took) to find a home.[182]

- If you come under the UC system, the DWP can agree deductions from your expected hours of work search for time you spend dealing with a domestic emergency or other temporary circumstances, which can include homelessness.[183] See p1054 for further information.

Income support, income-based jobseeker's allowance and income-related employment and support allowance

The amount of your IS, income-based JSA and income-related ESA may be lower than normal if you are a person 'without accommodation'.[184] You get the personal allowance for you (and your partner, if you have one) and any additional component in income-related ESA that you are entitled to, but do not get any premiums.[185] **Note:** there are no special rules about the amount of UC payable if you do not have accommodation.

Having no fixed address is *not* the same as being 'without accommodation'. If you have accommodation, but are staying in different places on different nights (eg, with different friends or relatives), your IS, income-based JSA or income-related ESA should be paid as normal.[186]

Accommodation

'**Accommodation**' is not defined in the rules and should be interpreted widely and flexibly. The DWP says that, to count as having accommodation, you must have 'an effective shelter from the elements which is capable of being heated, in which occupants can sit, lie down, cook and eat, and which is reasonably suited for continuous occupation. The site of the accommodation may alter from day to day, but it is still accommodation if the structure is habitable.'[187]

Examples include tents, caravans and other substantial shelters. However, the DWP is likely to say that cardboard boxes, bus shelters, sleeping bags and cars do not qualify.[188]

Note: if you are temporarily absent from the accommodation you normally occupy as your home, even if you are living a lifestyle as though you have no accommodation (eg, you are sleeping rough), you should be treated as having accommodation.[189]

Part 6: Special benefit rules
Chapter 42: Benefits in hospital, care homes, prison and in other special circumstances
Notes

Notes

1. Hospital patients

1 Reg 2(4) SS(HIP) Regs; reg 6 SS(AA) Regs; regs 8 and 12A SS(DLA) Regs
2 Vol 3 Ch 18, paras 18021 and 18059 DMG; R(DLA) 2/06
3 s86(2) and (3) WRA 2012; reg 29(2) SS(PIP) Regs; para P3062 ADM
4 Vol 3 Ch 18, paras 18028-33 and 18041 DMG; para P3001 ADM
5 R(DLA) 2/06, vol 3 paras 18031-33 DMG; P3061-62 ADM
6 *SSWP v Slavin* [2011] EWCA Civ 1515, reported as [2012] AACR 30; *JP v SSWP* [2013] UKUT 524 (AAC)
7 s86(2) and (3) WRA 2012, reg 29(2) SS(PIP) Regs; Vol 3 Ch 18, para 18060-63; DMG para P3062 ADM
8 **AA** Reg 6(2A) SS(AA) Regs
   DLA Regs 8(2A) and 12A(2A) SS(DLA) Regs
   PIP Reg 32(2) SS(PIP) Regs
9 Reg 2(5) SS(HIP) Regs
10 Reg 8(2B) SS(DLA) Regs
11 Regs 3(4A) and (5B) and 19 PIP(TP) Regs
12 **AA** Reg 8(4) SS(AA) Regs
   DLA Regs 10(6) and (7) and 12B(9A) and (12) SS(DLA) Regs
   PIP Reg 30(3) and (4) SS(PIP) Regs
13 **AA/DLA** Reg 25 SS(C&P) Regs
   PIP Reg 50 UC,PIP,JSA&ESA(C&P) Regs
14 **AA** Reg 8(2) SS(AA) Regs
   DLA Regs 10(5) and 12B(3) SS(DLA) Regs
   PIP Reg 32(4) and (5) SS(PIP) Regs
15 **AA** Reg 8(4) and (5) SS(AA) Regs
   DLA Regs 10(6) and (7) and 12B(9A) and (12) SS(DLA) Regs
   PIP Reg 30(3) and (4) SS(PIP) Regs
16 **AA** Reg 8(3) SS(AA) Regs
   DLA Regs 10(3) and 12B(2) SS(DLA) Regs
   PIP Reg 30(2) SS(PIP) Regs
17 Regs 12B(4)-(6) and 12C SS(DLA) Regs
18 Reg 75F(1)(f) HB Regs; reg 83(1)(h) UC Regs
19 Reg 6(19)-(21) SS(C&P) Regs
20 Reg 4(2) SS(ICA) Regs
21 Regs 29(1) and 30 UC Regs
22 Sch 3 para 9 UC Regs
23 Sch 3 para 18 LMI Regs
24 s39 WRA 2012; reg 3(6) UC Regs
25 s10 WRA 2012; reg 4(7) UC Regs
26 Regs 46A(1), (3) and (3A) and 47 JSA Regs 2013; regs 55ZA(1), (3) and (3A) and 55A JSA Regs
27 There is no such deeming rule in the SPC Regs. It is not needed because the SPC Regs set out the benefit rates in a different way than for other benefits.
28 **IS** Sch 2 paras 12(1)(d) and 13A(1) IS Regs
   JSA Sch 1 paras 14(1)(g)(ii) and 15A(1) JSA Regs
   ESA Sch 4 para 7 ESA Regs
   HB Sch 3 paras 13(1)(a)(iii) and 15(1) HB Regs; Sch 3 para 7 HB(SPC) Regs
29 Sch 3A para 3(i) SS&CS(DA) Regs
30 Reg 6 and sch IIA para 6 SPC Regs
31 **IS** Reg 16(1) and (2) IS Regs
   JSA Reg 78(1)-(2) JSA Regs
   ESA Reg 156(1)-(3) ESA Regs
   PC Reg 5(1)(a) SPC Regs
   HB Reg 21(1) and (2) HB Regs; reg 21(1) and (2) HB(SPC) Regs
32 **IS** Reg 2(1), definition of 'long-term patient', and Sch 2 paras 11(2)(a) and 13A(2)(b) IS Regs
   JSA Reg 1(3), definition of 'long-term patient', and Sch 1 paras 13(2)(a) and 15A(2)(b) JSA Regs
   ESA Schs 4 para 7(2)(a) and 5 para 13 ESA Regs
33 **IS** Reg 2(1), definition of 'long-term patient', and Sch 2 paras 10(6), 11(2)(b) and 13A(2)(c) IS Regs
   JSA Reg 1(3), definition of 'long-term patient', and Sch 1 paras 12(5)(b) and 20IA(2)(b) JSA Regs
   ESA Schs 4 para 7(2)(b) and 5 para 13 ESA Regs
34 **IS** Reg 2(1), definition of 'long-term patient', and Sch 2 paras 10(6), 11(2)(c) and 13A(2)(d) IS Regs
   JSA Reg 1(3), definition of 'long-term patient', and Sch 1 paras 12(5)(c), 13(2)(c), 15A(2)(c), 20F(5), 20(G)(a) and 20IA(2)(a) JSA Regs
35 Schs 4 paras 5, 6, 7, and 5 para 13 ESA Regs

36 Sch 3 paras 15(1) and 16(a) HB Regs; Sch 3 paras 7 and 8(a) HB(SPC) Regs
37 **IS** Reg 2(1), definition of 'long-term patient', and Sch 2 paras 13A(2)(a) and 14(2) IS Regs
    JSA Reg 1(3), definition of 'long-term patient', and Sch 1 paras 15A(2)(a) and 16(2) JSA Regs
38 Reg 3 CTC Regs
39 TCTM 02202
40 Sch 5 para 13 ESA Regs; reg 63(1) ESA Regs 2013
41 Reg 2(2) and (3) SS(HIP) Regs
42 Reg 3 SFWFP Regs
43 Sch 3 para 9 UC Regs
44 Sch 3 para 18 LMI Regs
45 **IS** Sch 3 para 3(11) IS Regs
    JSA Sch 2 para 3(11) JSA Regs
    ESA Sch 6 para 5(11) ESA Regs
    PC Sch II para 4(11) SPC Regs
    HB Reg 7(16) HB Regs; reg 7(16) HB(SPC) Regs
46 Sch 3 para 10 LMI Regs
47 R(H) 9/05
48 Sch 4 para 11 UC Regs

2. People in care homes and similar accommodation

49 **AA/DLA** ss67(2) and 72(8) SSCBA 1992; regs 7 and 8(1) SS(AA) Regs; regs 9 and 10(1) SS(DLA) Regs
    PIP s85 WRA 2012; regs 28 and 30(1) SS(PIP) Regs
50 ss67(3) and 72(9) SSCBA 1992; s85(3) WRA 2012
51 **AA/DLA** ss67(4) and 72(10) SSCBA 1992
    PIP s85(4) WRA 2012
52 Reg 7(3) SS(AA) Regs; reg 9(6) SS(DLA) Regs
53 **AA** Reg 7(2) SS(AA) Regs
    DLA Reg 9(2) SS(DLA) Regs
    PIP Reg 28(2)-(4) SS(PIP) Regs
54 CDLA/1465/1998; CDLA/2127/2000
55 CA/2985/1997
56 **AA** Reg 8(3) SS(AA) Regs
    DLA Reg 10(3) SS(DLA) Regs
    PIP Reg 30(2) SS(PIP) Regs
57 **AA/DLA** Reg 25 SS(C&P) Regs
    PIP Reg 50 UC,PIP,JSA&ESA(C&P) Regs
58 **UC** Reg 83(1)(h) UC Regs
    HB Reg 75F(1)(f) HB Regs
59 R(DLA) 2/06
60 **AA** Reg 8(4) and (5) SS(AA) Regs
    DLA Reg 10(6) and (7) SS(DLA) Regs
    PIP Reg 30(3) SS(PIP) Regs
61 **DLA** Reg 9(3) SS(DLA) Regs
    PIP Reg 28(2)(f) SS(PIP) Regs

62 **DLA** Reg 9(4)(a) and (b) and (5) SS(DLA) Regs
    PIP Reg 28(3)(a) and (4) SS(PIP) Regs
63 **DLA** Reg 9(4)(c) SS(DLA) Regs
    PIP Reg 28(3)(b) SS(PIP) Regs
64 **AA** Reg 8(6) SS(AA) Regs
    DLA Reg 10(8) SS(DLA) Regs
    PIP Reg 30(5) SS(PIP) Regs
    Steane v CAO and Secretary of State, 24 July 1996, reported as R(A) 3/96
65 R(A) 1/02; CA/3800/2006; *CAO v Creighton and Others,* 15 December 1999 (NICA), reported as R 1/00 (AA); *SSWP v DA* [2009] UKUT 214 (AAC)
66 *SSWP v JL (DLA)* [2011] UKUT 293 (AAC)
67 **AA** Reg 7(4) SS(AA) Regs
    DLA Reg 9(7) SS(DLA) Regs
    PIP Reg 32(1) and (2) SS(PIP) Regs
68 **AA** Reg 7(5) and (6) SS(AA) Regs
    DLA Reg 9(8) and (9) SS(DLA) Regs
    PIP Reg 32(3) SS(PIP) Regs
69 **AA** Reg 8(2) SS(AA) Regs
    DLA Reg 10(5) SS(DLA) Regs
    PIP Reg 32(4) SS(PIP) Regs
70 **IS** Sch 2 para 14ZA IS Regs
    JSA Sch 1 para 17(3) JSA Regs
    ESA Sch 4 para 8(4) ESA Regs
    PC Sch 1 para 4 SPC Regs
    HB Sch 3 para 17(2) HB Regs; sch 3 para 9(2) HB(SPC) Regs
71 Regs 29(1) and 30 UC Regs
72 **IS** Sch 3A para 3(h) and (i) SS&CS(DA) Regs
    ESA Sch 3C para 3(f) and (g) SS&CS(DA) Regs
73 Sch 1 para 3(d) UC Regs
74 Sch 1 para 1 UC Regs
75 *SA v SSWP (IS)* [2010] UKUT 345 (AAC), reported as [2011] AACR 16
76 Sch 3 para 9 UC Regs
77 Sch 3 para 18 LMI Regs
78 s39 WRA 2012; reg 3(6) UC Regs
79 s10 WRA 2012; reg 4(7) UC Regs
80 Reg 12(c) SPC Regs
81 Reg 9(1)(k) HB Regs; reg 9(1)(k) HB(SPC) Regs
82 Sch 3 para 9 HB&CTB(CP) Regs
83 HB/CTB Circular A20/05
84 **IS** Reg 53(1A), (1B) and (1C) IS Regs
    JSA Reg 116(1A), (1B) and (1C) JSA Regs
    ESA Reg 118(2), (3) and (4) ESA Regs
    HB Reg 52(3)-(5), (8) and (9) HB Regs
85 **IS** Reg 16(3)(e) IS Regs
    JSA Reg 78(3)(d) JSA Regs
    ESA Reg 156(4)(d) ESA Regs
    PC Reg 5(1)(b) SPC Regs
    HB Reg 21(2) HB Regs; reg 21(2) HB(SPC) Regs

Part 6: Special benefit rules
Chapter 42: Benefits in hospital, care homes, prison and in other special circumstances
Notes

86 Appendix to CIS/4934/1997; CIS/4965/ 1997; CIS/5232/1997; CIS/3767/1997
87 **IS** Reg 16(1) and (2) IS Regs
JSA Reg 78(1)-(2) JSA Regs
ESA Reg 156(1)-(3) ESA Regs
PC Reg 5(1)(a) SPC Regs
HB Reg 21(1) and (2) HB Regs; reg 21(1) and (2) HB(SPC) Regs
88 **IS** Sch 7 paras 9 and 10 IS Regs
JSA Schs 5 paras 5 and 6 and 5A paras 4 and 5 JSA Regs
ESA Sch 5 paras 4 and 5 ESA Regs
All CIS/1544/2001
89 Reg 6 and Sch IIA para 6 SPC Regs
90 Sch IIA para 9 SPC Regs
91 Sch IIA para 4 SPC Regs
92 Reg 1A(4) and (5) SFCWP Regs
93 Regs 1 and 2 SFWFP Regs
94 Sch 3 para 18(1) LMI Regs
95 Sch 3 para 10 LMI Regs
96 R(H) 9/05
97 R(H) 9/05
98 **IS** Sch 3 para 3(8)-(12) IS Regs
JSA Sch 2 para 3(8)-(12) JSA Regs
ESA Sch 6 para 5(8)-(12) ESA Regs
PC Sch 2 para 4(8)-(12) SPC Regs
HB Reg 7(11)-(13), (16) and (17) HB Regs; reg 7(11)-(13), (16) and (17) HB(SPC) Regs
99 Sch 4 para 11 UC Regs

3. Prisoners
100 **ESA** s18(4)(b) WRA 2007
PIP s87 WRA 2012
Statutory payments Reg 3(1) and (2) SSP Regs; reg 9 SMP Regs; regs 18(c) and 27(1)(c) SPPSAP(G) Regs; regs 14 and 26 SSPP(G) Regs
Other benefits s113(1)(b) and Sch 9 para 1 SSCBA 1992; reg 2(9) and (10) SS(GB) Regs; reg 10(2)(d) and Sch 2 para 7(b)(ii) SSB(Dep) Regs; R(S) 8/79
101 Reg 3(1) and (2) SSP Regs; reg 9 SMP Regs; regs 18(c) and 27(1)(c) and (2) SPPSAP(G) Regs; regs 14 and 26 SSPP(G) Regs; reg 9(1)(c) and (2) SPBP(G) Regs
102 **ESA** s18(4)(b) WRA 2007; reg 160 ESA Regs; reg 96 ESA Regs 2013
Other benefits s113(1)(b) SSCBA 1992; reg 2 SS(GB) Regs; s19 PA 2014; regs 2 and 3 SP Regs
103 s87 WRA 2012; reg 31(1) SS(PIP) Regs
104 Reg 31(2) SS(PIP) Regs
105 Reg 32(1) and (5) SS(PIP) Regs
106 s113(1)(b) SSCBA 1992
107 Reg 14(1)(s) JSA Regs
108 Reg 13(1)(b) JSA Regs 2013

109 **ESA** Reg 160(1), (2) and (5)(c) ESA Regs; reg 96(1), (2) and (6)(c) ESA Regs 2013
Other benefits Reg 2(2) and (8)(c) SS(GB) Regs; reg 14 SS(ICA) Regs; s19 PA 2014; regs 2 and 3 SP Regs
All R(S) 1/71
110 **ESA** Reg 161 ESA Regs; reg 97 ESA Regs 2013
Other benefits Reg 3 SS(GB) Regs; reg 14 SS(ICA) Regs
111 Reg 159(1) ESA Regs; reg 95 ESA Regs 2013
112 Reg 160 ESA Regs; reg 96 ESA Regs 2013
113 CS/541/1950
114 Regs 2(6) and (7) and 3(1) SS(GB) Regs
115 Reg 2(7) SS(GB) Regs; Vol 3 Ch 12, para 12091 DMG
116 Reg 2(2) and (7) SS(GB) Regs
117 **CB** s113(1)(b) SSCBA 1992. Child benefit is not in Parts 2-5 of that Act.
GA Reg 2(5) SS(GB) Regs
118 Sch 9 para 1(a) SSCBA 1992; regs 16 and 17 CB Regs
119 Reg 19 UC Regs
120 Reg 2 UC Regs
121 Sch 4 paras 11 and 16(2)(h) UC Regs
122 Reg 3(3)(c) UC Regs
123 Regs 18, 22(3) and 36(3) UC Regs
124 s39 WRA 2012; reg 3(6) UC Regs
125 Reg 4(6)(b) UC Regs
126 **IS** Sch 1B para 22, Sch 3 para 3(11) and (12) and Sch 7 para 8 IS Regs
ESA Schs 5 para 3 and 6 para 5(11) and (12) ESA Regs
PC Reg 6(2)(a), (3), (6)(c), (7), (9) and (10) SPC Regs
127 Reg 7(3) SPC Regs
128 **IS** Sch 3 para 18(7)(g) IS Regs
JSA Sch 2 para 17(7)(g) JSA Regs
ESA Sch 6 para 19(7)(g) ESA Regs
PC Sch 2 para 14(7)(e) SPC Regs
HB Reg 74(7)(f) HB Regs; reg 55(7)(f) HB(SPC) Regs
129 **IS** Reg 21(3) IS Regs
JSA Reg 85(4) JSA Regs
ESA Reg 69(2) ESA Regs
PC Reg 1(2) SPC Regs
HB Reg 7(14) and (16)(c)(i) HB Regs; reg 7(14) and (16)(c)(i) HB(SPC) Regs
130 **IS** Reg 16(3)(b) IS Regs
JSA Reg 78(3)(b) JSA Regs
ESA Reg 156(4) ESA Regs
PC Reg 5(1)(c)(ii) and (iii) SPC Regs
131 Reg 21(2) HB Regs; reg 21(2) HB(SPC) Regs
132 Reg 28 HB Regs; reg 31 HB(SPC) Regs

133 Reg 3, Rule 4.1 Case C, CTC Regs; reg 2(2) WTC(EMR) Regs
134 Sch IIA para 5 SPC Regs
135 *Stewart v SSWP* [2011] EWCA Civ 907 decided that the exclusion of prisoners from entitlement to a funeral expenses payment did not breach the HRA 1998
136 **UC** Reg 19(1)(c) and (4) UC Regs
   IS Reg 21(3ZA)-(3ZC) and Sch 7 para 2A IS Regs
   ESA Regs 69(3)-(5) and 160(3)-(4A) and Sch 5 para 12 ESA Regs; reg 96(3)-(5) ESA Regs 2013
   PC Reg 8 and Sch 3 para 2 SPC Regs
   PIP Reg 31(3) and (4) SS(PIP) Regs
   Other benefits Reg 2(3), (4) and (4A) SS(GB) Regs
   All CSS/239/2007; *JB v SSWP (IS)* [2010] UKUT 263 (AAC)
137 **UC** Reg 19(1)(c) and (4) UC Regs
   IS Reg 21(3ZA)-(3ZC) and Sch 7 para 2A IS Regs
   ESA Regs 69(3)-(5) and 160(3)-(4A) and Sch 5 para 12 ESA Regs; reg 96(3)-(5) ESA Regs 2013
   PC Reg 8 and Sch 3 para 2 SPC Regs
   PIP Reg 31(3) and (4) SS(PIP) Regs
   Other benefits Reg 2(3)-(4A) SS(GB) Regs
   All CSS/239/2007; *JB v SSWP (IS)* [2010] UKUT 263 (AAC)
138 Vol 4 Ch 21 paras 21198-02 DMG
139 para J3086 ADM
140 s39 WRA 2012; reg 3(6) UC Regs
141 **IS** Reg 16(2) IS Regs
   JSA Reg 78(2) JSA Regs
   ESA Reg 156(3) ESA Regs
   PC Reg 5(1)(a) SPC Regs
   HB Reg 21(1) and (2) HB Regs; reg 21(1) and (2) HB(SPC) Regs
142 **IS** Sch 7 para 9(a)(v) IS Regs
   JSA Schs 5 para 5(a)(vi) and 5A para 4(a)(vi) JSA Regs
   ESA Sch 5 para 4(a)(v) ESA Regs
143 Schs 1 paras 1 and 3(c) and 3 para 1(1) UC Regs
144 Sch 3 para 9 UC Regs
145 Reg 7(5) HB Regs; reg 7(5) HB(SPC) Regs
146 **IS** Sch 3 para 3(11)(c)(i) and (12) IS Regs
   JSA Sch 2 para 2(11)(c)(i) and (12) JSA Regs
   ESA Sch 6 para 5(11)(c)(i) and (12) ESA Regs
   PC Sch 2 para 4(11)(c)(i) and (12) SPC Regs
   HB Reg 7(16)(c)(i) and (17) HB Regs; reg 7(16)(c)(i) and (17) HB(SPC) Regs

147 Sch 3 paras 10(2)(c) and 18 LMI Regs
148 Regs 14(1)(h) and 19(1)(h) JSA Regs
149 **IS** Reg 48(7) IS Regs
   JSA Reg 110(7) JSA Regs
   ESA Reg 112(6) ESA Regs
150 Reg 19(2) and (3) UC Regs
151 Reg 19(2)(b) UC Regs
152 Reg 19(2)(a) UC Regs
153 Sch 3 para 18 LMI Regs
154 **IS** Schs 1B para 22, 3 para 3(11) and (12) and 7 para 8 IS Regs
   ESA Schs 5 para 3 and 6 para 5(11) and (12) ESA Regs
   PC Reg 6(2)(a), (3), (6)(c), (7), (9) and (10) and Sch 2 para 4(11) and (12) SPC Regs
   HB Reg 7(16)(c)(i) and (17) HB Regs; reg 7(16)(c)(i) and (17) HB(SPC) Regs
155 Sch 3 para 10(1) and (2) LMI Regs
156 Reg 7(13) HB Regs; reg 7(13) HB(SPC) Regs
157 CSH/499/2006
158 **UC** Reg 2(1) UC Regs
   IS Reg 21(3) and Sch 7 para 8(a) IS Regs
   JSA Reg 85(4) JSA Regs
   ESA Reg 69(2) and Sch 5 para 3(a) ESA Regs
   PC Regs 1(2) and 6 SPC Regs
159 Reg 7(14) and (15) HB Regs; reg 7(14) and (15) HB(SPC) Regs; R(IS) 17/93
160 *KdeS v Camden LB (HB)* [2011] UKUT 457 (AAC)
161 Reg 7(7) HB Regs; reg 7(7) HB(SPC) Regs; Ch A3, paras 3.430-32 GM
162 Sch 2 para 2 LMI Regs
163 Sch 4 para 11 UC Regs

4. 16/17-year-old care leavers
164 **UC** Reg 8(1), (2) and (4) UC Regs
   IS Reg 4ZA(3A) IS Regs
   JSA Reg 57, definition of 'young person', JSA Regs
   IS/JSA/HB ss6 and 8(6) C(LC)A 2000; C(LC)SSB(S) Regs
165 **IS** Reg 14(2)(c) IS Regs
   JSA Reg 76(2)(d) JSA Regs
   ESA Reg 2(1), definition of 'young person', ESA Regs
   HB Reg 19(2)(c) HB Regs; reg 19(2)(c) HB(SPC) Regs
166 Regs 4(6)(a) and 4A UC Regs
167 Sch IIA para 4 SPC Regs
168 s6 C(LC)A 2000
169 Reg 8(1) and (4) UC Regs

Part 6: Special benefit rules
Chapter 42: Benefits in hospital, care homes, prison and in other special circumstances
Notes

● ●

170 **UC** Reg 8(4) UC Regs
   IS Reg 4ZA(3A) IS Regs
   JSA Reg 57, definition of 'young
   person', JSA Regs
   IS/JSA/HB ss6 and 8(6) C(LC)A 2000;
   C(LC)SSB(S) Regs
171 Reg 2(2)(b) C(LC)SSB(S) Regs; reg
   8(4)(b) UC Regs
172 s6 C(LC)A 2000; reg 3 CL(E) Regs; reg
   40(1) CPP&CR(E) Regs; regs 3 and 4
   C(LC)(W) Regs; C(LC)SSB(S) Regs
173 Reg 3 CL(E) Regs; reg 4(1) and (2)
   C(LC)(W) Regs
174 ss6 and 8(6) C(LC)A 2000; regs 40(2)
   and 48 CPP&CR(E) Regs; reg 3(3) CL(E)
   Regs; regs 3(2) and 4(2A) C(LC)(W)
   Regs; reg 2(4)(a) C(LC)SSB(S) Regs
175 Reg 8(4)(b) UC Regs. 'Member of your
   family' is not defined. Arguably, the
   intention is to exclude periods of time
   when you are living with a person who
   has parental responsibilities for you.
176 Reg 3(5) and (6) CL(E) Regs; reg 4(4)-(6)
   C(LC)(W) Regs
177 Sch 4 para 4 UC Regs
178 Reg 2 C(LC)SSB Regs; reg 2(3)
   C(LC)SSB(S) Regs. The C(LC)SSB Regs
   have been amended to include
   entitlement to income-related ESA, but
   this is not needed because the C(LC)A
   2000 was not amended.
179 Reg 2(2) C(LC)SSB(S) Regs

5. People without accommodation
180 **UC** Sch 4 para 29(4) UC Regs
   HB Reg 2(1), definition of 'young
   individual', HB Regs
181 Sch 1 paras 1 and 3(b) UC Regs
182 Reg 18(3)(j) JSA Regs
183 **UC** Reg 95(2) UC Regs
   JSA Reg 12(2) and (3) JSA Regs 2013
184 This rule was challenged under the HRA
   1998, but the court decided the rules
   did not conflict with it: *R(RJM) v SSWP*
   [2008] UKHL 63
185 **IS** Sch 7 para 6 IS Regs
   JSA Schs 5 para 3 and 5A para 2 JSA
   Regs
   ESA Sch 5 para 1 ESA Regs
186 Vol 4 Ch 24, para 24157 and Vol 9 Ch
   54, para 54157 DMG
187 Vol 4 Ch 24, paras 24158-59 and Vol 9
   Ch 54, paras 54158-59 DMG
188 Vol 4 Ch 24, paras 24159-60 and Vol 9
   Ch 54, paras 54159-60 DMG; R(IS) 23/
   98
189 Vol 4 Ch 24, para 24162 and Vol 9 Ch
   54, para 54162 DMG

● ● ● ● ●

Part 7

National insurance, work and work-related rules

Chapter 43

National insurance contributions

This chapter covers:
1. Contributions and contributory benefits (p960)
2. Paid contributions (p961)
3. National insurance credits (p968)
4. Contribution conditions for benefits (p979)

This chapter explains the national insurance (NI) contribution rules relevant to contributory benefits. For details of the NI number requirement that applies to most benefits, see p1171.

Key facts

- Entitlement to contributory benefits, and sometimes the amount paid, depends on your national insurance (NI) contribution record. For some benefits, it depends on the contribution record of your spouse or civil partner, or your late spouse or civil partner.
- If you are employed or self-employed, you may be liable to pay NI contributions. If you are not liable to pay contributions, in some circumstances you can be awarded NI 'credits', or you may be able to pay contributions voluntarily.
- There are different types of NI contributions (called 'classes'). Not all classes of NI contributions or all types of NI credits count for all contributory benefits.
- NI contributions are collected by HM Revenue and Customs.

Part 7: National insurance, work and work-related rules
Chapter 43: National insurance contributions
1. Contributions and contributory benefits

1. Contributions and contributory benefits

Benefits that have national insurance (NI) contribution conditions are:
- contribution-based jobseeker's allowance; *and*
- contributory employment and support allowance; *and*
- bereavement support payment and widowed parent's allowance; *and*
- state pension and 'old' retirement pensions – ie, category A and B retirement pensions; *and*
- incapacity benefit (but see p648); *and*
- widows' benefits (but see p552).

These are known as '**contributory benefits**'.

Entitlement to contributory benefits normally depends on NI contribution conditions being met. For the detailed rules on the contribution conditions for these benefits, see pp979–985.

In some circumstances, you may be liable to pay NI contributions. If you are not, in order to help you meet the contribution conditions for some contributory benefits, you may either be credited with earnings or with contributions, or you can choose to pay contributions. For details of NI 'credits', see p968.

Note:
- It may be possible for you to rely on the contributions you have paid in other European Economic Area states to qualify for contributory benefits (see p1678 and for the way this may be affected by the UK leaving the European Union, see p1670).
- Your NI contribution record is based on the NI contributions you have paid, or the NI credits you have received, for each tax year – ie, 6 April to 5 April.
- If you are self-employed, your entitlement to maternity allowance (MA) and the amount you receive may be affected by whether you have paid class 2 NI contributions (see p728). For you to qualify for MA on the basis that you help your spouse or civil partner with her/his self-employment, s/he must meet conditions relating to class 2 NI contributions (see p726).

How decisions are made

Most decisions on NI contributions are made by an officer of HM Revenue and Customs (HMRC). Appeals against such decisions can be decided by an HMRC review or by the First-tier Tribunal (Tax).[1] The process is similar to appealing against an HMRC decision on your entitlement to a statutory payment (see p1430).

Decisions relating to entitlement to NI credits are made either by HMRC or the DWP, depending on the type of NI credit.

If you disagree with a decision on your entitlement to NI credits, you can apply for a revision or supersession (see Chapter 56), or you can appeal against it (see

Chapter 57). You must apply for a mandatory reconsideration before you can appeal. Your appeal is decided by the First-tier Tribunal (Social Security and Child Support).[2]

---

2. **Paid contributions**

There are seven different types ('classes') of paid national insurance (NI) contribution.[3] Three of these (classes 1, 2 and 3) can help you to qualify for contributory benefits, but only class 1 contributions count for *all* contributory benefits. Class 3A contributions, which could only be paid if you reached pension age before 6 April 2016, count towards entitlement to additional state pension. See p782 of the 2015/16 edition of this *Handbook* for details of additional state pension.

If you are an 'employed earner', you may be liable for class 1 contributions, depending on the amount you earn. If you are a 'self-employed earner', you are normally liable to pay class 2 contributions, unless your profits are low or you are exempt from payment (and you may also be liable for class 4 contributions). If you are not liable to pay contributions, you may choose to pay class 2 (if you are self-employed) or class 3 contributions voluntarily. These are known as 'voluntary contributions'.

Class of contribution	Payable by	Giving entitlement to
Class 1	Employed earners and their employers	All benefits with contribution conditions
Class 1A and 1B	Employers of employed earners	No benefits
Class 2	Self-employed earners	All benefits with contribution conditions, except contribution-based jobseeker's allowance (JSA)
Class 3	Voluntary contributors	State pension, category A and B retirement pensions and widowed parent's allowance
Class 3A	Voluntary contributors	An amount (a 'unit') of additional state pension
Class 4	Self-employed earners	No benefits

The rules about your age

- You are not liable for class 1 or 2 contributions if you are under 16 years old or over pension age (see p780).[4]

Part 7: National insurance, work and work-related rules
Chapter 43: National insurance contributions
2. Paid contributions

- You cannot pay class 3 contributions if you are under 16 (and sometimes if you are 17 or 18) or for the tax year in which you reach pension age or any subsequent tax year.[5]

Employed earners and self-employed earners

Your liability to pay class 1, 2 or 4 NI contributions depends on whether you are an employed or self-employed earner.[6] It is normally clear whether you are employed or self-employed. If there is a dispute, it usually concerns whether you are employed under a *contract of service* (in which case, you are an employee) or a *contract for services* (in which case, you are self-employed).[7] **Note:**

- To be an employed or self-employed earner, you must be 'gainfully employed'.
- Office holders, including people in elective office, who receive earnings are classed as employed earners. Office holders include judges, registrars of births, marriages and deaths and most company directors. (If you are a company director and pay yourself a wage from which class 1 NI is deducted, this may help you to claim both statutory payments and contributory benefits. You will need to register as an employer.)
- Certain people are deemed to be employed earners. These include office cleaners, many agency workers and people employed by their spouse or civil partner for the purposes of their spouse's or civil partner's employment.[8]
- Examiners, moderators and invigilators are deemed to be self-employed.[9]
- If you have two or more jobs, it is possible to be both employed and self-employed.
- You do not have to pay NI contributions on earnings from certain kinds of employment – eg, if you are employed by your spouse or civil partner and it is not for the purpose of her/his employment, or if you are employed in your home by a close relative who lives with you and the job is not for a trade or business that is carried out there.[10]

More than one job

If you are employed as an employed earner in more than one job, the basic rule is that your liability to pay class 1 contributions is calculated for each job as if the other(s) did not exist, although the total you pay is subject to a maximum.[11] There are some exceptions – eg, if you have two different jobs for the same employer or employers who carry on business in association with each other. In this situation, to stop employers avoiding liability, earnings from these jobs are normally added together and your NI contributions are based on your total earnings.[12]

If you are self-employed and also have a job as an employed earner, you may be liable to pay both class 1 and class 2 contributions, subject to a maximum.[13]

Class 1 contributions

Class 1 contributions have two elements: primary contributions (paid by employed earners) and secondary contributions (paid by employers).[14]

The amount of primary class 1 contributions you pay depends on the amount you earn in relation to the upper and lower earnings limit for the tax year, and to the amount of that year's 'primary threshold'. See Appendix 6 for details of the earnings limits and the primary threshold.

If your earnings are equal to or below the primary threshold (£183 a week in 2020/21), you do not have to pay NI contributions on them. If they are between the lower earnings limit (£120 a week in 2020/21) and the primary threshold, you are treated as if you had paid class 1 NI contributions on those earnings.[15]

If you earn more than the primary threshold, you are liable to pay class 1 contributions of 12 per cent of your earnings between the primary threshold and upper earnings limit (£962 a week in 2020/21), plus 2 per cent of the earnings you have above the upper earnings limit.[16] If you are a married woman or widow with reduced liability for contributions (see p965), you pay lower class 1 contributions.[17]

It is your employer's responsibility to deduct your contributions from your earnings and pay them with its own contributions to HM Revenue and Customs (HMRC).[18] If your employer has failed to pay your contributions to HMRC, you are treated as though they had been paid, unless you have been negligent, or consented to or connived in that arrangement.[19]

Class 2 contributions

You must pay class 2 contributions for each week in a tax year in which you are a self-employed earner (see p962), unless your taxable profits in that year are below the 'small profits threshold' or you are exempt from payment. The small profits threshold for 2020/21 is £6,475. The main grounds for being exempt from payment of class 2 contributions are that you receive certain benefits – eg, maternity allowance (MA) or employment and support allowance (ESA) for the week to which the contribution relates, or carer's allowance for at least part of that week.[20]

Your liability for class 2 contributions is calculated annually after the end of the tax year using the income tax self-assessment procedure. They are payable with any income tax and class 4 contributions for which you are liable in the same year (but see below if you are claiming MA).[21]

Even if you are not liable to pay class 2 contributions, provided you are a self-employed earner, you may still choose to pay voluntary class 2 contributions to protect your NI contribution record (see p966).[22]

Class 2 contributions are payable at a flat rate.[23] The current and previous year's rates are:

2020/21	£3.05 a week
2019/20	£3.00 a week

Part 7: National insurance, work and work-related rules
Chapter 43: National insurance contributions
2. Paid contributions

Note:
- The self-assessment procedure was not used to collect class 2 contributions in tax years before 2015/16. For details, see the 2014/15 edition of this *Handbook*.
- Married women and widows with reduced liability for contributions (see p965) are not liable for class 2 contributions and cannot pay them voluntarily.[24]
- Volunteer development workers employed abroad and share fishermen pay class 2 contributions at special rates, which count towards contribution-based JSA, unlike other class 2 contributions.[25]

Class 2 contributions and maternity allowance

Payment of class 2 contributions becomes due on 31 January after the end of the tax year for which they are paid. You can pay class 2 contributions early, on a voluntary basis, in order to increase your entitlement to MA (see p728), or your spouse or civil partner can pay them early to enable you to qualify for MA on the basis that you help with her/his self-employment (see p726). In either situation, the contributions may be paid at any time from the week to which they relate. If you (or your spouse or civil partner) pay them early and are later assessed as liable to pay class 2 contributions for the same weeks under the self-assessment procedure, these voluntary contributions are converted to cover that liability, so you do not pay twice.[26]

If you employ yourself (eg, if you are a company director) and pay yourself a wage, you should check to see whether you are liable for class 1 contributions, as you may be able to claim statutory maternity pay instead.

Class 3 contributions

Payment of class 3 contributions is voluntary.[27] They only give entitlement to state pension, category A and B retirement pensions and widowed parent's allowance.[28] To help you decide whether to pay class 3 contributions, see p966.

Class 3 contributions are paid at a flat rate. The current and previous year's rates are:[29]

2020/21	£15.30 a week
2019/20	£15.00 a week

Class 3A contributions

Class 3A contributions were voluntary national insurance contributions for people who would reach pension age before April 2016. For more information, see the 2016/17 edition of this *Handbook*.

Pre-1975 contributions

The present contribution system was introduced on 6 April 1975. Between 5 July 1948 and 5 April 1975, class 1 contributions were paid by a 'flat-rate stamp' in the same way as class 2 and class 3 contributions.

Before 6 April 1975, contribution years were not the same as tax years, as they are now. Transitional arrangements in both 1948 and 1975 may have resulted in your having a contribution year that was not 12 months long, which may explain what would otherwise be anomalies in your contribution record.

Reduced liability for married women and widows

Women who were married or widowed on 6 April 1977 could choose to pay reduced class 1 or no class 2 contributions, provided they applied to do so before 12 May 1977.[30]

If you 'elected' to pay at this reduced rate, you can continue to do so until you either apply to pay the full rate again (called 'revoking an election') or until the right to pay reduced contributions is automatically lost.[31] These reduced-rate contributions do not help you build up entitlement to contributory benefits.

If you have paid reduced-rate NI contributions and reach pension age on or after 6 April 2016, see p783 for how your state pension may be calculated. If you reached pension age before 6 April 2016 and you do not qualify for a retirement pension based on your own contributions, you may qualify for a category B retirement pension instead. See Chapter 36 of the 2015/16 edition of this *Handbook* for details.

To pay the full rate again, complete the form in HMRC leaflet CF9 for married women or CF9A for widows (available from gov.uk/reduced-national-insurance-married-women).

Coming from abroad and going abroad

The rules on liability for NI contributions when you have come to the UK from abroad, or if you go abroad, are complex. In particular, the rules described below may not apply if you are covered by the European Union co-ordination rules (see p1672) or if you move from or to a country which has a reciprocal agreement with the UK (see p1582). In some circumstances, contributions paid in other countries count towards British benefits. In particular, this may apply if you have paid contributions in the European Economic Area (see p1668). You may also be entitled to benefits from other countries while you are in this country.

If you have come from abroad and are employed or self-employed in Great Britain, you may be liable for class 1 or 2 (and 4) contributions.[32] If you are self-employed but not liable to pay contributions, you may be able to pay class 2 contributions voluntarily. If you are not liable to pay contributions, you can choose to pay class 3 contributions if you are resident (see p1585) in Great Britain throughout the course of the tax year in respect of which you wish to pay

Part 7: National insurance, work and work-related rules
Chapter 43: National insurance contributions
2. Paid contributions

contributions and, in some circumstances, even if you have not been resident for the whole tax year.[33]

If you are abroad working as an employee and your employer has a place of business in Britain, in some circumstances for the first year you must still pay class 1 contributions. If you are not liable, or are no longer liable, to pay class 1 contributions, it may be worth paying class 3 contributions (see below).[34]

If you are self-employed outside Great Britain, you may pay class 2 contributions if you wish, provided you were employed or self-employed immediately before you left Britain and either:

- you have been resident in Great Britain for a continuous period of at least three years at some time in the past; *or*
- you have paid contributions producing an earnings factor of at least 52 times the lower earnings limit in each of three years in the past. Each set of 52 flat-rate contributions paid before April 1975 counts as satisfying that condition in respect of one year.[35]

Certain volunteer development workers who are employed abroad may also be allowed to pay class 2 contributions.[36]

Normally, class 3 contributions may be paid while you are abroad if you satisfy either of the conditions which would allow you to pay class 2 contributions (but you do not need to have been employed or self-employed before you left Britain or while abroad). You may also pay them if you paid class 1 contributions for the first year you were employed abroad.[37]

For information on payment of NI contributions while abroad, see gov.uk or telephone the HMRC helpline (tel: 0300 200 3500 or from abroad: +44 191 203 7010; textphone: 0300 200 3519).

Northern Ireland and Isle of Man contributions count towards British benefits.

Improving your contribution record

If there are years for which you do not have a full contribution record, it may be beneficial to pay voluntary class 2 contributions (if you are self-employed but not liable to pay class 2 contributions – see p963) or class 3 contributions (see p964). These are called 'voluntary contributions'. Before paying voluntary contributions in respect of a tax year, check whether you qualify for NI credits in that year. (In any event, you are not entitled to pay class 3 contributions if you would instead be entitled to class 3 credits – see p968.[38]) You can request an NI statement to check whether there are gaps in your contribution record by completing an online form (available at gov.uk), or by telephoning or writing to the National Insurance Contributions and Employer Office, HM Revenue and Customs, BX9 1AN (tel: 0300 200 3500).

If it is more than 30 days before you reach pension age, you can also request a state pension statement to help you decide whether to pay voluntary contributions. You can do this online (at gov.uk/check-state-pension), by telephoning the Future Pension Centre (tel: 0800 731 0175; Welsh language: 0800 731 0453; textphone: 0800 731 0176) or by post using Form BR19 (available at gov.uk/check-state-pension). If you are within 30 days of pension age, contact the Pension Service for details of your state pension (tel: 0800 731 7898; Welsh language: 0800 731 7936; textphone: 0800 731 7339).

Should you make voluntary contributions?

1. Both class 2 and 3 contributions may help you qualify for state pension, or qualify for a higher rate of state pension. Class 2 contributions also count for contributory ESA.

2. Class 2 contributions count for bereavement support payment; class 3 contributions and NI credits do not.

3. Both class 2 and 3 contributions count for widowed parent's allowance.

4. Voluntary contributions may be paid on behalf of a contributor after her/his death, provided they are paid no later than s/he would have been allowed to pay them.[39]

5. Consider the cost of paying voluntary contributions and compare this to the additional amount of benefit that might be awarded.

6. Class 2 and 3 contributions paid late do not always count for benefit purposes (see below).

7. If you have overpaid contributions for a particular year, or have paid voluntary contributions in error, you may be able to get a refund.

8. Get advice before paying voluntary contributions for years in which you have paid contributions abroad. In some cases, these can count towards British benefits (see p965).

9. If in doubt about paying the contributions, get advice.

Late payment of contributions

Payments of class 1, 2 or 3 NI contributions are considered late if they are paid after the date on which they are due to be paid.

If you are liable for class 1 contributions, your employer is responsible for paying them to HMRC. If your employer failed to pay these or has paid them late, you are treated as if the contributions had been paid (usually on the date they were due to be paid), unless you have been negligent or consented to, or connived in, the failure to pay.[40]

Class 2 contributions (including voluntary class 2 contributions) are due on 31 January after the end of the tax year for which they are paid. Class 3 contributions are due 42 days after the end of the tax year for which they are paid.[41]

Contributions paid after these dates normally cannot help you to qualify for contributory benefits for any period before you pay them and they can usually only count towards your benefit entitlement for the period from the date they have been paid if:[42]

Part 7: National insurance, work and work-related rules
Chapter 43: National insurance contributions
3. National insurance credits

- for class 1 contributions, they were paid by the end of the second tax year after the tax year for which the contributions are paid; *or*
- for class 2 or 3 contributions, they are paid by the end of the sixth tax year after the tax year in which you are liable to pay them or, if they are voluntary contributions, in which you are entitled to pay them (although special rules apply if you make late payments of class 2 contributions through PAYE (pay as you earn)); *or*
- for class 3 contributions (for any tax year in which, for at least six months, you were a full-time apprentice, in full-time education or training or a prisoner, and for the year before and after such a year in which you met this condition but for less than six months), they are paid by the end of the sixth complete tax year after the end of a period of education, apprenticeship or imprisonment.

Even if paid within these time limits, class 2 contributions paid late cannot count for the second contribution condition for contribution-based JSA and contributory ESA, until six weeks after they have been paid.[43] This also applies to class 1 contributions which are paid after the start of the relevant benefit year, unless they can be treated as paid earlier in the circumstances described above.

In limited circumstances, contributions paid after the above time limits can still count for benefit purposes.[44] For example:

- If you reached pension age between 6 April 2008 and 5 April 2015, you can pay additional class 3 contributions for any six tax years (but not tax years before 1975/76), provided you already have at least 20 years that count as qualifying years for retirement pension. If you reached pension age before 6 April 2010, years of home responsibilities protection can count towards the 20 years (see p973), but at least one of those 20 years must comprise paid (not just credited) contributions. You must pay the additional contributions within six years of reaching pension age. Any additional contributions paid on or after 6 April 2011 count for benefit purposes from the date they are paid.[45]
- If you reach pension age on or after 6 April 2016, you have until 5 April 2023 to pay voluntary contributions for any of the tax years from 2006/07 to 2015/16.[46]

3. **National insurance credits**

In some circumstances, you can be 'credited' with earnings (sometimes known as class 1 credits) or with class 3 contributions. 'Credits' can help you satisfy:

- the second contribution condition for benefits with two contribution conditions – ie, contribution-based jobseeker's allowance (JSA), contributory employment and support allowance (ESA) and, if your spouse or civil partner died before 6 April 2017, widowed parent's allowance; *and*
- the contribution conditions for retirement pensions (see p969).

Not all types of credits count for all these contributory benefits, although many class 1 credits do. Class 3 credits count for widowed parent's allowance and state pension. They also count for category A and B retirement pensions.

Note:

- You can only receive sufficient credits in any tax year to meet the contribution condition for that year.[47]
- Some credits are awarded automatically; others you must claim. To help you decide whether to claim credits or to see whether you have been awarded credits, you can check your national insurance (NI) contribution record at gov.uk/check-national-insurance-record or you can apply for a statement of your NI record at tax.service.gov.uk/shortforms/form/NIStatement or by telephoning the number below.
- Credits cannot help you to satisfy the first contribution condition for benefits with two contribution conditions, or to qualify for bereavement support payment, which has a single contribution condition.
- If you are a married woman with reduced liability for contributions (see p965), you can only qualify for credits for universal credit (UC) (see p971), for certain parents and carers (see p972), for family members providing childcare (see p974), for official error (see below), starting credits (but see p975) or credits following bereavement (see p977). You are not entitled to other types of credits.
- Some people were credited with earnings for the tax years from 1993/94 to 2007/08 following an official error arising from discrepancies between the DWP and HM Revenue and Customs (HMRC) computer systems.[48] These credits were awarded automatically. See the 2009/10 edition of this *Handbook* for details.

Enquiries about credits can be made to the NI helpline (tel: 0300 200 3500; textphone: 0300 200 3519), or by writing to the National Insurance Contributions and Employer Office, HM Revenue and Customs, BX9 1AN.

Retirement pensions and credits

If you reach pension age on or after 6 April 2016, you may qualify for state pension. If you reached pension age before this date, you may qualify for category A or B retirement pension.

Most types of credits (including class 3 credits) can help you meet the contribution conditions for these benefits, and help determine the amount you receive.

For transitional rate state pension (see p782), most kinds of credits for tax years before 6 April 2016 can be taken into account when calculating your 'starting amount'.

Part 7: National insurance, work and work-related rules
Chapter 43: National insurance contributions
3. National insurance credits

Credits for unemployment

These credits can help you meet the contribution conditions for all contributory benefits (see p960), except bereavement support payment.

If you are entitled to UC and do not receive any JSA, these credits do not apply. However, you can get credits for UC (see p971).

You can be credited with earnings equal to the lower earnings limit for either:[49]

- each complete week (ie, the seven days from Sunday to Saturday) for which you receive JSA (or for which you would have received JSA but for the loss of benefit for benefit offences rules – see p1278); or
- each complete week in which you are not entitled to UC (to be entitled, you normally must have claimed it) but for which you satisfy, or can be treated as satisfying, the following qualifying conditions for JSA – ie, you:
  – are not engaged in full-time paid work (see p991); *and*
  – are not in relevant education (see p885); *and*
  – do not have limited capability for work (see Chapter 45); *and*
  – are under pension age; *and*
  – are either available for and actively seeking work (see p1115 and p1124) or, if you come under the UC system, satisfy the work search and work availability requirements (see p1053 and p1056), or you would have satisfied the availability and actively seeking work requirements or the work search and work availability requirements in that week but for having limited capability for work (see p708) or being incapable of work for part of the week.

You may also qualify for credits for weeks before 29 October 2013 in which you would have satisfied the above conditions for JSA but were treated as being in full-time paid work because you received a compensation payment. See pp885–86 of the 2013/14 edition of this *Handbook* for details.

Credits for unemployment are awarded automatically if you get JSA. Otherwise, you must apply in writing to Jobcentre Plus, either on the first day for which you are claiming them or within a reasonable period of time after that. You must provide the DWP with the evidence it requires to show that you satisfy the conditions. Even if you are not entitled to JSA, it may be important to continue to 'sign on' at the Jobcentre Plus office in order to get credits for unemployment and protect your right to contributory benefits.

However, you do not get credits for weeks in which:[50]

- you would not have been entitled to JSA (whether or not you actually claimed it) because you are involved in a trade dispute; *or*
- your JSA is reduced (or not paid) because you have been sanctioned. See p1079 and p1145 for the circumstances when this may apply; *or*
- you are receiving hardship payments of income-based or joint-claim JSA (see p1222); *or*
- you are a 16/17-year-old receiving JSA severe hardship payments.

Credits for limited capability for work or incapacity for work

These credits can help you meet the contribution conditions for all contributory benefits, except bereavement support payment.

You can be credited with earnings equal to the lower earnings limit for each complete week during which you either:[51]

- were entitled to statutory sick pay (SSP); *or*
- had limited capability for work; *or*
- would have had limited capability for work had you been entitled to contributory ESA (even if the reason you are not entitled to contributory ESA is because of the 365-day limit – see p656) or had you claimed ESA or maternity allowance (MA); *or*
- were incapable of work or could be treated as incapable of work, or you would have been had you made a claim for incapacity benefit (IB) or MA. For information on incapacity for work, see p683 of the 2013/14 edition of this *Handbook*.

You cannot qualify for these credits for weeks in which you are entitled to UC, unless you are also entitled to ESA, SSP, MA, IB or severe disablement allowance in those weeks (to be entitled to UC, you normally must claim it). You also cannot qualify for these credits for days on which you were treated as not having limited capability for work (see p1015) or not being incapable of work (or days on which you would have been, had you otherwise been entitled to ESA or IB).

These credits are awarded automatically if you get ESA or MA. You can apply for ESA, even if you are not entitled to the benefit, and maintain a 'credits only' claim for limited capability for work. To apply for credits on the basis that you get SSP, write to the National Insurance Contributions and Employer Office, HM Revenue and Customs, BX9 1AN. In other circumstances, you must apply to Jobcentre Plus. Unless the credits are awarded automatically, you must apply for them before the end of the benefit year (ie, by the first Saturday in January – see p980) following the tax year in which you are entitled to the credit. This time limit can be extended if it is considered reasonable to do so, given your circumstances.[52]

Credits for universal credit

These credits can help you meet the contribution conditions for widowed parent's allowance and state pension. They also count for category A and B retirement pensions. They are awarded automatically.

If you are entitled to UC for at least part of a week, you can be credited with a class 3 contribution for that week.[53]

If you are not entitled to UC because your income and/or capital is too high and you are looking for work or have limited capability for work, you should consider making a 'credits only' claim for JSA (see p970) or ESA (see above).

Part 7: National insurance, work and work-related rules
Chapter 43: National insurance contributions
3. National insurance credits

Credits for certain parents and carers

These credits can help you meet the contribution conditions for widowed parent's allowance and state pension. They also count for category A and B retirement pensions.

You can be credited with a class 3 contribution for each week which falls after 6 April 2010 if:

- for any part of the week, you are awarded child benefit for a child under the age of 12;[54] *or*
- you reside with someone who, for any part of the week, is awarded child benefit for a child aged under 12 and:
  - you share responsibility with that person for a child under 12; *and*
  - in the tax year to which the credit relates, the person awarded child benefit has paid, or been credited with, NI contributions with an earnings factor of more than 52 times that year's lower earnings limit (see Appendix 6). In calculating this, any credits s/he gets on the basis of the child benefit award are ignored.[55]

  Note: in this situation, for weeks from 6 April 2016, the rules on when you qualify for a class 3 credit for state pension are different and indicate only that you must be the partner of someone who gets child benefit for a child, you must reside with your partner and you both must share the responsibility for the child. The rules do not expressly state that the child must be under 12 (although your partner still must have paid, or been credited with, sufficient NI contributions);[56] *or*
- in that week you are caring for someone for at least 20 hours, or for more than one person for a total of at least 20 hours and:[57]
  - the person(s) for whom you care is entitled to a qualifying benefit (see below); *or*
  - the decision maker considers that the level of care provided is appropriate.

  You can continue to qualify for these credits for 12 weeks after the week in which you stop satisfying this condition – this allows you to have breaks in caring of up to 12 weeks without losing credits; *or*
- in that week you satisfy the conditions for carers who may qualify for income support (IS) described on p236 (the rules do not state that you must get IS to qualify for credits in this situation);[58] *or*
- for any part of the week, you are an approved foster parent or foster carer (including a kinship carer in Scotland);[59] *or*
- the week falls in the 12 weeks:[60]
  - before the date you become entitled to carer's allowance (CA); *or*
  - following the week in which you stop being entitled to CA (unless you already qualify for credits for CA for that week – see p975).

Qualifying benefit

A **'qualifying benefit'** includes the daily living component of personal independence payment, attendance allowance, the middle or highest rate of disability living allowance care component, armed forces independence payment, constant attendance allowance in respect of an industrial or war disablement and certain payments under the Pneumoconiosis, Byssinosis and Miscellaneous Diseases Benefit Scheme or Workmen's Compensation (Supplementation) Scheme.[61]

Unless you are entitled on the basis that you are awarded child benefit for a child under 12, in most circumstances you must be ordinarily resident in Great Britain and not in prison or in legal custody to qualify for these credits.[62]

If you get child benefit, IS or CA, the credits are awarded automatically. If you qualify because you are caring for someone for at least 20 hours, apply to the DWP using a carer's credit application form (Form CC1). Otherwise apply to HMRC on Form CF411A. Both forms are available at gov.uk. Your application must be received before the end of the tax year following the tax year to which the credits relate. This time limit can be extended if the DWP or HMRC considers it reasonable in the circumstances.[63]

Note: you can qualify for these credits on the basis of an award of child benefit even if you (or the person with whom you reside) have elected not to receive the child benefit because of the high-income child benefit tax charge (see p598).

Credits for home responsibilities protection

Home responsibilities protection, which helped a contributor satisfy the contribution conditions for widowed parent's allowance and category A or B retirement pension, was abolished on 6 April 2010 and was replaced with NI credits for certain parents and carers (see p972).

Any year of home responsibilities protection awarded up to and including 2009/10 is converted into 52 class 3 NI contributions:

- for widowed parent's allowance, if the contributor died on or after 6 April 2010;
- for category A retirement pension, if you reached pension age on or after that date;
- for calculating your entitlement to the transitional rate of state pension, if you qualify for it.

However, for widowed parent's allowance, this conversion can only be done for half the requisite number of years needed to qualify for a full basic widowed parent's allowance (see p985). For category A retirement pension and for calculating the transitional rate of state pension, it can be done for a maximum of 22 years.[64]

Part 7: National insurance, work and work-related rules
Chapter 43: National insurance contributions
3. National insurance credits

If the contributor reached pension age or died before 6 April 2010, see the 2009/10 edition of this *Handbook* for how years of home responsibilities protection affect the contribution conditions for category B retirement pension.

Credits for family members providing childcare

If you do not qualify for credits as a parent or a carer (see p972), these credits can help you meet the contribution conditions for widowed parent's allowance and state pension. They also count for category A retirement pension if you reached pension age on or after 6 April 2012 and for category B retirement pension in certain circumstances. See the 2015/16 edition of this *Handbook* for details.

From 6 April 2011, you can be credited with a class 3 contribution for each week during which you provide childcare for a child aged under 12, if:[65]

- you are a specified 'family member' of the child (you do not need to be a blood relative and many ex-family members count – see below); *and*
- someone has been awarded child benefit for the child for that week and, in the tax year in which that falls, her/his contribution record is sufficient for the year to count as a qualifying year for state pension (see p986). In calculating this, any credits s/he gets on the grounds of receiving child benefit for a child under 12 are ignored; *and*
- you are ordinarily resident in Great Britain (see p1585).

There is no set number of hours for which you must care for the child to qualify. Only one person can qualify for these credits for a particular week for the same child(ren) covered by a child benefit award. The credits are in respect of the child benefit award, and not per child. However, if childcare is shared, it may be possible for someone else to get credits for different weeks in a tax year.

You must apply to HMRC for these credits after the end of the tax year in question. There is no time limit for claiming.[66] Use Form CA9176 (for specified adult childcare credits), available at gov.uk.

Note: if you satisfy the qualifying conditions, you can still get these credits, even if the person entitled to child benefit elects not to receive it because of the high-income child benefit tax charge (see p598).

Family member

You count as a **'family member'** if you are:[67]
- the child's parent (from 6 April 2016 for state pension only, if you are her/his non-resident parent, but see p972 if you reside together), grandparent, great or great-great-grandparent, sibling, aunt or uncle (including if you are an adopted, step- or half-sibling of the child or of the child's parent);
- a spouse or civil partner, or former spouse or civil partner, of any of the above relatives, or her/his son or daughter;
- a partner or former partner of any of the above (including, for instance, a former partner of a former spouse of one of the above relatives), or her/his son or daughter;
- the child's niece, nephew or first cousin;

– a spouse, civil partner or partner (or former spouse, civil partner or partner) of the child's first cousin.

A 'partner' is someone with whom the relative lives as if they were married.

Credits for carer's allowance

These credits can help you meet the contribution conditions for all contributory benefits, except bereavement support payment. They are awarded automatically.

You can be credited with earnings equal to the lower earnings limit for each week in which you receive CA (see Chapter 26), or would receive it but for the loss of benefit for benefit offences rules (see p1278).[68] You also receive credits if the only reason why you do not receive CA is because you are receiving widowed parent's allowance, bereavement allowance or a widow's benefit instead. **Note:** this does not apply to bereavement support payment, as you receive both CA and bereavement support payment at the same time.

If you are caring for someone but are not entitled to these credits, you may qualify for credits for certain carers (see p972).

Starting credits

These credits can help you meet the contribution conditions for widowed parent's allowance. They also count for category A and B retirement pensions and for calculating the transitional rate of state pension (see p987). They are awarded automatically.

You can receive class 3 credits for the tax years in which you reach the age of 16, 17 and 18 if you would otherwise have had an insufficient contribution record for those years to count towards the contribution conditions for the above benefits.[69]

However, for category A and B retirement pensions (and for calculating the transitional rate of state pension), you could only qualify for these credits:

- for tax years falling before 6 April 2010; *and*
- if you had to make an application for an NI number to be allocated to you, if your application for an NI number was made before 6 April 2010.

No credits were made under this provision for years before 6 April 1975.

Education and training credits

For the purpose of qualifying for contribution-based JSA and contributory ESA, you can be credited with earnings equal to the lower earnings limit for either one of the two complete tax years that fall before the relevant benefit year (see p980) if:

- for any part of those tax years you were on:[70]
  - a course of full-time training, including training to acquire occupational or vocational skills (or, if you are disabled, a part-time course of at least 15 hours a week); *or*

Part 7: National insurance, work and work-related rules
Chapter 43: National insurance contributions
3. National insurance credits

– a course of full-time education; *or*
– an apprenticeship; *and*
- in the other tax year in which you must satisfy the second contribution condition for the benefit (see p982), you have an earnings factor of 50 times the lower earnings limit without relying on this provision; *and*
- you were at least 18 (or you reached 18) in the tax year in question; *and*
- you were under 21 when the course or apprenticeship started; *and*
- your course of education, training or apprenticeship has finished.

You can receive credits which count for all contributory benefits (except bereavement support payment) for each week in which you are undertaking a training course approved by a DWP decision maker if:[71]
- in that week you were not entitled to UC – but see p971 for credits if you were entitled to UC. To be entitled to UC, you normally must have claimed it; *and*
- the training is full time (or at least 15 hours a week if you are disabled) or it is an introductory course; *and*
- the training is not part of your job; *and*
- the training is intended to last for one year or less (except in certain circumstances, if it is a course for disabled people); *and*
- you were 18 or over at the beginning of the tax year in which the week falls.

If the course was arranged by Jobcentre Plus, you get the credits automatically. Otherwise, you must apply to the National Insurance Contributions and Employer Office, HM Revenue and Customs, BX9 1AN.

Credits for statutory maternity, adoption, additional paternity, shared parental and parental bereavement pay

These credits can help you meet the contribution conditions for all contributory benefits, except bereavement support payment.

You can be credited with earnings equal to the lower earnings limit for each week for which you receive statutory maternity pay, statutory adoption pay, statutory shared parental pay or statutory parental bereavement pay or for which you received additional statutory paternity pay.[72]

To apply for these credits, write to the National Insurance Contributions and Employer Office, HM Revenue and Customs, BX9 1AN. Your application must be received before the end of the benefit year (see p980) following the tax year in which the week falls, but this time limit may be extended if it is reasonable to do so.

Credits for jury service

These credits can help you meet the contribution conditions for all contributory benefits, except bereavement support payment.

You are entitled to be credited with earnings equal to the lower earnings limit for each week after 6 April 1988 during which you spend at least part of the week on jury service, unless you are self-employed in that week.[73]

To apply for these credits, write to the National Insurance Contributions and Employer Office, HM Revenue and Customs, BX9 1AN. Your application must be received before the end of the benefit year (see p980) following the tax year in which the week falls (or such further period as is reasonable).

Credits following bereavement

These credits help you meet the contribution conditions for contribution-based JSA and contributory ESA. They are awarded automatically.

If you were entitled to bereavement payment, widowed parent's allowance or bereavement allowance, you can be credited with sufficient earnings for each year up to and including the one in which your entitlement to any of those benefits stopped, to enable you to satisfy the second contribution condition for contribution-based JSA or contributory ESA.[74]

For the purpose of satisfying the second contribution condition for contributory ESA, you are also entitled to credits for each year up to and including the one in which your entitlement to widow's allowance (abolished in April 1988) or widowed mother's allowance ended.[75]

Credits for tax credits

These credits are awarded automatically.

For each week for which you receive, for any part of the week, the disabled worker element or severe disability element in working tax credit (WTC), you are entitled to be credited with earnings equal to the lower earnings limit. These credits count for all contributory benefits, except bereavement support payment.[76]

Alternatively, for each week for which you are paid WTC (without the disabled worker element or the severe disability element), you are credited with earnings equal to the lower earnings limit to help you satisfy the contribution conditions for widowed parent's allowance and state pension. They also count for category A and B retirement pensions. In this case, if WTC was paid to you as a member of a couple but only one of you has earnings, the credits are awarded to that person. If you both have earnings, they are awarded to the person to whom WTC is paid.[77]

You can only qualify for either of these credits during any week in which you were:[78]

- employed and earning less than the lower earnings limit (see p962); *or*
- self-employed but not liable to pay class 2 contributions because your profits were below the small profits threshold (see p963) or you had a small earnings exception. (It is not possible to have a small earnings exception for tax years from 2015/16. See the 2014/15 edition of this *Handbook* for further details); *or*

Part 7: National insurance, work and work-related rules
Chapter 43: National insurance contributions
3. National insurance credits

- self-employed but exempt from paying class 2 contributions because you were getting a particular benefit (see p963). However, this does not apply for category A and B retirement pensions and only applies for state pension for weeks which fall in a tax year from 6 April 2016 (provided you did not qualify for the disabled worker or severe disability element in your WTC), otherwise it applies for state pension and the other benefits for weeks from 1 January 2017.

If you used to get working families' tax credit, disabled person's tax credit, family credit or disability working allowance, see the 1999/00 and 2002/03 editions of this *Handbook* for details of similar credits.

Credits for a quashed conviction

These credits can help you meet the contribution conditions for all contributory benefits, except bereavement support payment.

If you were imprisoned or detained in legal custody after being convicted of an offence, and that conviction has subsequently been quashed by the courts, you can be credited with earnings for each week during at least part of which you were imprisoned or detained.[79]

To apply for these credits, write to the National Insurance Contributions and Employer Office, HM Revenue and Customs, BX9 1AN.

Credits for service families

These credits can help you meet the contribution conditions for all contributory benefits, except bereavement support payment.

From 6 April 2010, you can be credited with earnings equal to that year's lower earnings limit for each week during any part of which you were:[80]

- the spouse or civil partner of a member of the armed forces (or someone treated as such for the purpose of occupying accommodation); *and*
- accompanying, or were treated as accompanying, her/him on an assignment outside the UK.

You must usually apply for these 'class 1' credits on the approved form (Form MODCA1, available at gov.uk), once you have a confirmed date for the end of the overseas posting and before the end of the tax year following the tax year in which the overseas assignment ended. This time limit can be extended if it is reasonable, given your circumstances.

The decision maker has discretion to accept an application made before you receive confirmation of the end date of the overseas assignment. If your application is accepted, you can be awarded credits for the period before your application, but you must make a further application under these rules for credits for any subsequent period.

Alternatively, to help you meet the contribution conditions for state pension only, you can be credited with a class 3 contribution for each week in any tax year from 6 April 1975 in which, for at least part of the week, you meet the above conditions, provided the member of the armed forces you were accompanying had paid or been credited with sufficient NI contributions for that year to count as a qualifying year (see p986).[81] In this situation, you must normally apply for the credits on the approved form. There is an online form at gov.uk. Applications can only be made for a past period.

Note: in respect of years from 6 April 2010, claim the class 1 credits if you satisfy the conditions for them, as they count towards the contribution conditions for more benefits – the class 3 credits only count for state pension.

4. **Contribution conditions for benefits**

Entitlement to contributory benefits normally depends on the national insurance (NI) contribution conditions being met.

- **For state pension**, your entitlement is based on your own NI contribution record. However, in some cases, for the transitional rate of state pension, the amount you receive depends on the contribution record of your spouse or civil partner (or your late or former spouse or civil partner) (see p782).
- **For contribution-based jobseeker's allowance (JSA) and contributory employment and support allowance (ESA)**, your entitlement is based on your own NI contribution record (unless you qualify for contributory ESA without needing to satisfy the contribution conditions).
- **For bereavement support payment and widowed parent's allowance**, the relevant 'contributor' is your late spouse or civil partner.

You may be credited with earnings or contributions to fill gaps in your contribution record (see p968).

NI contributions normally cannot count for benefit purposes until after they have been paid (if they are paid late, see p967). However, in some circumstances, your entitlement to benefit, or the amount of benefit you are entitled to, may depend on class 2 or 3 contributions which you have not yet paid because the due date for their payment has not been reached (see p967). In this situation, provided you pay the contributions by the due date, they can be treated as having being paid earlier.[82] If you claimed benefit before paying the contributions, once you have paid them the earlier decision on your claim can be revised to take account of the contributions.[83] See p983 for details of this rule in relation to contribution-based JSA and contributory ESA. For other benefits, this may not apply if you are late in notifying HM Revenue and Customs (HMRC) of your self-employment.

If you reached pension age before 6 April 2016, see the 2015/16 edition of this *Handbook* for the contribution conditions for category A and B retirement

Part 7: National insurance, work and work-related rules
Chapter 43: National insurance contributions
4. Contribution conditions for benefits

pensions. The contribution conditions for bereavement payment, bereavement allowance, incapacity benefit and widow's pension are covered in previous editions of this *Handbook*.

It may be possible for you to rely on the contributions you have paid in other European Economic Area states to qualify for contributory benefits (see p1668).

If you are a woman who has paid reduced-rate NI contributions, see p783 for how your state pension is calculated.

Jobseeker's allowance and employment and support allowance

Contribution-based JSA and contributory ESA have two contribution conditions relating to the two complete tax years falling immediately before the 'relevant benefit year'. If you claim in 2020, you must satisfy the contribution conditions for the tax years 2017/18 and 2018/19.

Tax and relevant benefit years

A '**tax year**' runs from 6 April to 5 April the following year.

A '**benefit year**' is almost the same as a calendar year and runs from the first Sunday in January.[84]

The '**relevant benefit year**' is usually the calendar year during which you meet the entitlement conditions and submit a claim for contribution-based JSA or contributory ESA. However:

– for contribution-based JSA, if it is earlier than the year in which you make your claim, the relevant benefit year is the benefit year in which a period that is linked to the current jobseeking period began (see p706);

– for contributory ESA, if you otherwise would not meet the contribution conditions for contributory ESA, your relevant benefit year can be any benefit year which includes any part of your current period of limited capability for work (or any part of any period(s) of limited capability for work that can be linked to your current period – see p1041). **Note:** a period of limited capability for work cannot include a period that falls before the three-month time limit for backdating an ESA claim.[85]

When the contribution conditions do not apply

You can qualify for contributory ESA without having to satisfy the contribution conditions if:[86]

- your contributory ESA ended because you had received it for 365 days in the circumstances described on p656, you continued to have (or be treated as having) limited capability for work after your entitlement ended and you now have, or are treated as having, limited capability for work-related activity (see p1027). In this situation, you can qualify for contributory ESA again without having to satisfy the contribution conditions; *or*

- you are transferred to contributory ESA, having previously received incapacity benefit (IB) or severe disablement allowance (SDA) (see p655). In this situation,

when you are transferred, the contribution conditions for contributory ESA are waived (but if your contributory ESA is subsequently stopped because of the 365-day limit and you want to reclaim it, you must meet the usual contribution conditions to get contributory ESA again unless the previous bullet point applies); *or*
- you were getting IB or SDA but, following a determination that you do not have limited capability for work, your IB or SDA is not converted into contributory ESA and you have appealed against the decision. In this situation, you are treated as satisfying the contribution conditions for contributory ESA while you are pursuing your appeal (see p1038).

The first condition: paid contributions

You must have paid, or be treated as having paid, at least 26 weeks' contributions on earnings at the lower earnings limit in one of the last two complete tax years immediately before the relevant benefit year (see p980).

Lower earnings limits

2017/18	£113
2018/19	£116
2019/20	£118
2020/21	£120

Example
If Lexi makes a claim in 2020, she meets the first condition if she earned at least £113 a week for 26 weeks between 6 April 2017 and 5 April 2018, or at least £116 a week for 26 weeks between 6 April 2018 and 5 April 2019.

Note:
- The 26 weeks do not need to be consecutive, but they must fall in a single tax year.
- For contribution-based JSA, only class 1 contributions count towards meeting this condition (unless you are a share fisherman or volunteer development worker, when special class 2 contributions also count). For ESA, both class 1 and class 2 contributions count.[87]

When the first condition is relaxed

In some situations, the first contribution condition is relaxed, so that sufficient contributions paid in *any* one tax year are enough to satisfy the condition, provided they were paid, or treated as paid (see p983), before the week for which you are claiming the benefit.

For contribution-based JSA and contributory ESA, this applies if you were entitled to credits for service families (see p978) in at least one week in the tax year before the relevant benefit year (see p980).[88]

For contributory ESA, it also applies if you:[89]

Part 7: National insurance, work and work-related rules
Chapter 43: National insurance contributions
4. Contribution conditions for benefits

- were entitled to carer's allowance (CA) in the last complete tax year before the relevant benefit year (even if it was not paid because of the overlapping benefit rules – see p1190); *or*
- were entitled to NI credits for a quashed conviction at some time in any tax year before the relevant benefit year (or you would have been entitled to such credits had you claimed them); *or*
- were in full-time paid work (see p300) for more than two years immediately before your period of limited capability for work began and you were entitled to working tax credit which included a disabled worker or severe disability element (see p1458 and p1460).

The second condition: paid or credited contributions

You must have paid contributions or received NI credits on earnings of at least 50 times the lower earnings limit in each of the two complete tax years immediately before the relevant benefit year.

Example

If Theo makes a claim in 2020, he meets the second condition if he paid contributions on total earnings of at least £5,650 (50 x £113) in 2017/18, and of at least £5,800 (50 x £116) in 2018/19.

Note:
- Only certain NI credits count towards meeting this condition – eg, credited class 3 contributions do not count (see pp968–978).
- To count, any paid contributions must be class 1 contributions (or special class 2 contributions – see p981) for contribution-based JSA, or class 1 or 2 contributions for contributory ESA.[90]
- For class 2 contributions, you must have paid at least 50 contributions in each of the two complete tax years – this condition cannot be satisfied by having reached this earnings level over fewer weeks.
- To satisfy this condition with NI credits, you must have been awarded them for at least 50 weeks during each of the two years.

The timing of your claim

In rare cases, it may be beneficial for you to delay a claim for contribution-based JSA so that you can draw on a different year's contribution record. This is because the years in which you must meet the contribution conditions depend on the benefit year in which your jobseeking period starts. So, for example, if your current jobseeking period is not linked to an earlier one (see p707) and you claim before 5 January 2021, you must meet the contribution conditions in the tax years 2017/18 and 2018/10, whereas if you claim on or after 5 January 2021, you must meet them in 2018/19 and 2019/20.

Any day for which you do not claim does not count as part of your jobseeking period (see p707),[91] so it is easy to postpone when that period begins. However, if you claim and are refused benefit because the contribution conditions are not satisfied, your jobseeking period will have started. You must then normally wait for more than 12 weeks to make a fresh claim. The 12-week gap breaks the jobseeking period.

The situation is different for contributory ESA. If your claim for contributory ESA is refused only on the grounds that you do not meet the contribution conditions, in some cases it can be worth making a later claim that falls in a different benefit year (see p980).

Example

Shanti lives with her partner who works full time. Shanti was self-employed and paid class 2 NI contributions throughout the tax years 2017/18 and 2018/19 (in the tax year 2016/17 she did not pay NI contributions or get NI credits). In December 2019, she became ill and claimed contributory ESA for the first time. The relevant benefit year was 2019 and the two complete tax years falling before that are 2016/17 and 2017/18. Having no contributions or credits for 2016/17, Shanti was refused contributory ESA. If she claims again in the 2020 benefit year (which started on 6 January 2020), the contributions she paid in 2017/18 and 2018/19 are counted and she may qualify for contributory ESA. The rules allow 2020 to count as her relevant benefit year because part of her period of limited capability for work falls in that year.

Class 2 contributions treated as paid earlier

Since 6 April 2015, because the deadline for payment of class 2 contributions for a tax year is 31 January after the end of that year, your entitlement to contributory ESA (or contribution-based JSA on the basis of special class 2 contributions) may depend on class 2 contributions that are not yet due to be paid. If you claim benefit before paying the contributions, your claim may be refused because you do not meet the contribution conditions. You can choose to pay class 2 contributions early to try to avoid this problem – if you do, write to HMRC to ensure it knows the payment you are making is intended to be an early payment of class 2 contributions. Alternatively, provided you pay the contributions by 31 January, they can be treated as having been paid on an earlier date to enable you to qualify for contribution-based JSA or contributory ESA from a date before they were actually paid.[92]

Example

Sonja is self-employed and lives with her partner who works full time. Sonja becomes ill and unable to work on 8 January 2020 and claims ESA on the same day. Her relevant benefit year is 2020. The tax years in which she must have met the contribution conditions for contributory ESA are 2017/18 and 2018/19. Although she paid class 2 contributions

Part 7: National insurance, work and work-related rules
Chapter 43: National insurance contributions
4. Contribution conditions for benefits

for each week in 2017/18, her claim for contributory ESA is refused because she has not yet submitted her self-assessment tax return for 2018/19 and has not paid class 2 contributions for that tax year. On 29 January 2020 she submits her self-assessment return and pays class 2 contributions for 2018/19. She asks the DWP to reconsider the decision to refuse her contributory ESA. As Sonja paid her class 2 contributions by the due date (31 January 2020), they can be treated as having been paid before 8 January 2020. The earlier decision to refuse her claim is revised and she is awarded contributory ESA from 15 January 2020 (she is not entitled for the first seven days of her period of limited capability for work – see p648).

Bereavement support payment

To satisfy the contribution condition for bereavement support payment, your late spouse or civil partner must have paid NI contributions on earnings of at least 25 times that year's lower earnings limit – eg, £3,000 in 2020/21: 25 x £120.

This condition must be met in any one tax year in your late spouse's or civil partner's working life, but only class 1 or 2 NI contributions count (see p985 for the meaning of 'working life').[93]

If your spouse or civil partner died before 6 April 2017, you may be entitled to widowed parent's allowance (or may have been entitled to bereavement payment and bereavement allowance). For details of the contribution conditions for bereavement payment and bereavement allowance, see the 2017/18 edition of this *Handbook*.

Widowed parent's allowance

There are two contribution conditions for widowed parent's allowance. **Note:** you can only qualify for this benefit if your late spouse or civil partner died before 6 April 2017.

The first condition

In any one tax year before s/he died or reached pension age, your late spouse or civil partner must have paid class 1, 2 or 3 NI contributions on earnings of at least 52 times that year's lower earnings limit – eg, £5,824 in 2016/17: 52 x £112.[94] The payment of 50 flat-rate contributions for any time before 6 April 1975 also satisfies this condition.[95]

The first condition is deemed to be satisfied if the contributor was receiving the support or work-related activity component of ESA (see p652 and p653) or long-term IB either:[96]

- in the year in which s/he died (if s/he died before reaching pension age) or in which s/he reached pension age; *or*
- in the preceding year.

The second condition

To qualify for the maximum basic rate of widowed parent's allowance, in the required number of tax years during your late spouse's or civil partner's working life s/he must have paid class 1, 2 or 3 NI contributions, or received NI credits, on earnings of at least 52 times that year's lower earnings limit – eg, £5,824 in 2016/17: 52 x £112.[97] Most, but not all, NI credits count towards meeting this condition (see pp968–978).

Working life

The contributor's **'working life'** is the period from the beginning of the tax year in which s/he reached the age of 16 up to, but excluding, the year in which s/he reached pension age or in which s/he died (if s/he died before reaching pension age).[98] If s/he was over 16 on 5 July 1948, her/his working life may have started on a different date.[99]

The required number of years needed to satisfy this condition depends on the length of your late spouse or civil partner's 'working life', and is calculated as follows.[100]

Length of working life	Required number of years
1–10 years	Length of working life minus one
11–20 years	Length of working life minus two
21–30 years	Length of working life minus three
31–40 years	Length of working life minus four
41–50 years	Length of working life minus five

Note:
- A reduced rate of benefit may be paid if you have not met the second contribution condition for the required number of years (see below).
- If your spouse or civil partner died before 6 April 2010, past years of home responsibilities protection may reduce the required number of years over which you must meet the second contribution condition. See the 2009/10 edition of this *Handbook* for details.
- To calculate the number of years before 6 April 1975 in which you satisfied the contribution condition, add together all the contributions paid or credited before 6 April 1975, and divide the answer by 50, rounding up if the result is not a whole number, provided that does not produce a number greater than the number of years of your working life before 6 April 1975.

Reduced benefit because of insufficient contributions

Benefit can be paid at a reduced rate if the second contribution condition is not satisfied for the required number of years, provided it is satisfied in at least 25 per

Part 7: National insurance, work and work-related rules
Chapter 43: National insurance contributions
4. Contribution conditions for benefits

cent of the required number. The benefit is paid at a percentage of the amount which would otherwise be paid. The percentage is calculated by expressing the number of years in which the condition is satisfied as a percentage of the required number of years and rounding it up to the nearest whole number.[101] So, if you are a widow and your husband's working life was 12 years, so that the required number of years is 10, and he only satisfied the condition in eight years, you receive 80 per cent of the basic rate of widowed parent's allowance.

If you still qualify for them, increases for children are paid in full.[102]

It may be possible for you to pay class 3 contributions to increase the number of years in which the second contribution condition is satisfied, but see p966 for what to consider before doing so.

Retirement pensions

If you reached pension age before 6 April 2016, you are not entitled to state pension but may be entitled to category A or B retirement pension instead.[103] For the NI contribution conditions for category A and B retirement pensions, see the 2015/16 edition of this *Handbook*.

State pension

If you reach pension age on or after 6 April 2016 (ie, if you are a woman born on or after 6 April 1953 or a man born on or after 6 April 1951), you may be entitled to state pension (see Chapter 36).

Your entitlement to state pension and the amount you receive depends on the number of NI 'qualifying years' you have.

Qualifying years[104]

A **'qualifying year'** is a tax year in your working life in which you have paid class 1, 2 or 3 NI contributions or received NI credits which, in total, produced an earnings factor of at least 52 times that year's lower earnings limit – eg, £6,240 in 2020/21: 52 x £120. Most, but not all, kinds of NI credits can be counted. For tax years before 6 April 1978, contributions or credits must have been paid on earnings of at least 50 times that year's lower earnings limit for the year to count as a qualifying year.[105]

To qualify for state pension, you must have at least 10 qualifying years (but see below if you paid a reduced rate of NI contributions as a married woman).[106]

If one of your qualifying years is a tax year before 6 April 2016, your entitlement to state pension is calculated at the transitional rate (see p987).[107]

Note:
- If you have paid reduced-rate NI contributions as a married woman or widow and your election to pay at a reduced rate was in force at the start of the 35-year period which ends in the tax year before you reach pension age, you do not

need to have 10 qualifying years to qualify for state pension.[108] See p783 for how your entitlement is calculated.

- If your spouse or civil partner has died, you may qualify for an amount of state pension based on her/his contribution record. See p783 for details.

The transitional rate of state pension

If at least one of your qualifying years (see above) falls before 6 April 2016, your entitlement to state pension is assessed at the transitional rate. The amount you receive depends on your 'starting amount'. Your starting amount is based on your contribution record up to 6 April 2016. Your starting amount is the greater of either:[109]

- the weekly amount of basic category A retirement pension, additional state pension and graduated retirement benefit you would have qualified for had you reached pension age on 6 April 2016 and had the new state pension scheme not been introduced. See below for how your basic category A retirement pension is calculated and the 2015/16 edition of this *Handbook* for details of additional state pension and graduated retirement benefit; *or*

- the weekly amount of state pension you would be entitled to on 6 April 2016 if you reached pension age on that date, using the number of qualifying years you had up to that date (see p986). You are entitled to the full rate of state pension if you have at least 35 qualifying years in your working life. If you have less than 35 qualifying years (but at least 10), you build up one thirty-fifth of the full weekly rate of state pension for each of your qualifying years.

If you have been contracted out of the state second pension scheme, the above amounts are adjusted to reflect this.

See p782 for further details of how the transitional rate of state pension is calculated. If your starting amount is less than the full rate of state pension, it can be increased if you have further qualifying years falling after 5 April 2016. Each further qualifying year adds one thirty-fifth of the full weekly rate of state pension to your starting amount up to the maximum of the full weekly rate of state pension. You may be able to increase your number of qualifying years by claiming NI credits and/or making voluntary NI contributions (see p966).

You can get an estimate of your starting amount by applying for a state pension statement (see p966).

Note: if your spouse or civil partner has died, you may qualify for an inherited amount of state pension based on her/his contribution record (see p783).

Part 7: National insurance, work and work-related rules
Chapter 43: National insurance contributions
Notes

Notes

1. Contributions and contributory benefits

1 s11 SSC(TF)A 1999; Part III SSC(DA) Regs; Arts 6(c)(i) and 7 First-tier Tribunal and Upper Tribunal (Chambers) Order 2010, No.2655
2 Sch 3 para 17 SSA 1998; s17 SSC(TF)A 1999; Arts 2-4 National Insurance Contribution Credits (Transfer of Functions) Order 2009, No.1377

2. Paid contributions

3 s1(2) SSCBA 1992
4 ss6(1) and (3) and 11(7) SSCBA 1992
5 s13 SSCBA 1992; regs 48(1) and 49(1)(f) and (2A)-(2C) SS(Con) Regs
6 s2(1) SSCBA 1992
7 *Ready Mix Concrete South East Ltd v Ministry of Pensions and National Insurance* [1968] 2 QB 497 (QBD); *Global Plant v Secretary of State for Health and Social Security* [1971] 3 All ER 385 (QBD)
8 Sch 1 paras 1-5A SS(CatE) Regs; *ITV Services Ltd v HMRC* [2012] UKUT 47 (TCC)
9 Sch 1 paras 6 SS(CatE) Regs
10 Sch 1 paras 7-12 SS(CatE) Regs
11 Regs 13, 14, 15 and 21 SS(Con) Regs
12 Sch 1 para 1 SSCBA 1992; regs 13, 14, 15 and 21 SS(Con) Regs
13 Reg 21 SS(Con) Regs
14 ss6 and 7 SSCBA 1992
15 ss6 and 6A SSCBA 1992
16 s8 SSCBA 1992
17 Reg 131 SS(Con) Regs
18 Sch 1 para 3 SSCBA 1992
19 Reg 60 SS(Con) Regs
20 s11 SSCBA 1992; reg 43 SS(Con) Regs
21 s11(5) SSCBA 1992
22 s11(6) SSCBA 1992; reg 43 SS(Con) Regs
23 s11(2) SSCBA 1992
24 Reg 127(1) SS(Con) Regs
25 Regs 125, 149, 151 and 152 SS(Con) Regs
26 Regs 1(2) and 90ZA SS(Con) Regs
27 s13 SSCBA 1992
28 s14 SSCBA 1992; reg 49 SS(Con) Regs
29 s13(1) SSCBA 1992
30 Reg 127 SS(Con) Regs
31 Regs 128(1) and 130 SS(Con) Regs
32 ss2(1), 6 and 11 SSCBA 1992; reg 145(1)(a), (c), (d) and (2) SS(Con) Regs
33 Reg 145(1)(c) and (e) SS(Con) Regs
34 Reg 146 SS(Con) Regs
35 Regs 147 and 148 SS(Con) Regs
36 Regs 149 and 151 SS(Con) Regs
37 Regs 146(2)(b), 147 and 148 SS(Con) Regs
38 s11(6) SSCBA 1992; regs 43(3), 48 and 49 SS(Con) Regs
39 Reg 62 SS(Con) Regs
40 Reg 60 SS(Con) Regs; reg 5 SS(CTCNIN) Regs
41 Reg 1(2) SS(CTCNIN) Regs
42 Reg 4 SS(CTCNIN) Regs; reg 48(3)(b) SS(Con) Regs
43 Reg 4(7) and (8) SS(CTCNIN) Regs
44 Regs 50 and 61 SS(Con) Regs; regs 4(11), 5A, 6, 6A and 6B SS(CTCNIN) Regs
45 s13A SSCBA 1992; reg 3(8D) SS&CS(DA) Regs; reg 6C SS(CTCNIN) Regs
46 Regs 50C and 61B SS(Con) Regs

3. National insurance credits

47 Reg 3 SS(Cr) Regs; reg 25(2) SP Regs
48 Regs 8D, 8E and 8F SS(Cr) Regs
49 Reg 8A SS(Cr) Regs; regs 26 and 29 SP Regs
50 Reg 8A(5) SS(Cr) Regs; regs 26 and 29 SP Regs
51 Reg 8B SS(Cr) Regs; regs 26 and 29 SP Regs
52 Reg 8B(4) SS(Cr) Regs; regs 26 and 29 SP Regs
53 Reg 8G SS(Cr) Regs; regs 26 and 31 SP Regs
54 s23A(2) and (3)(a) SSCBA 1992; regs 27 and 34(1)(a) SP Regs
55 s23A(2) and (3)(c) SSCBA 1992; regs 2, 5(1)(a), 6 and 9 SS(CCPC) Regs; reg 27 SP Regs
56 Reg 34(1)(b) and (2)-(4) SP Regs
57 s23A(2) and (3)(c) SSCBA 1992; regs 5(1)(b) and 7(1)(c) SS(CCPC) Regs; regs 27, 37(1) and (2)(a) and 38(1)(c) SP Regs

58 s23A(2) and (3)(c) SSCBA 1992; reg 5(1)(c) SS(CCPC) Regs; reg 37(1) and (2)(b) SP Regs

59 s23A(2) and (3)(b) SSCBA 1992; reg 4 SS(CCPC) Regs; reg 36 SP Regs

60 Reg 7 SS(CCPC) Regs; reg 38(1)(a) and (b) and (2) SP Regs

61 Reg 2 SS(CCPC) Regs; reg 37(4) SP Regs

62 Reg 8 SS(CCPC) Regs; regs 34(2), 36(1) and 37(3) SP Regs

63 Regs 9-12 SS(CCPC) Regs; regs 34(2)(e), 36(3), 37(5) and (6) and 39(a) SP Regs

64 s23A(5)-(7) SSCBA 1992; reg 27 SP Regs

65 Reg 9F SS(Cr) Regs; reg 26 and 35 SP Regs

66 Reg 9F(8) SS(Cr) Regs; reg 39(b) SP Regs

67 Sch SS(Cr) Regs; reg 35(6)-(8) SP Regs

68 Reg 7A SS(Cr) Regs; regs 26 and 29 SP Regs

69 Reg 4 SS(Cr) Regs; reg 26 SP Regs

70 Reg 8 SS(Cr) Regs

71 Reg 7 SS(Cr) Regs; regs 26 and 29 SP Regs

72 Reg 9C SS(Cr) Regs; regs 26 and 29 SP Regs

73 Reg 9B SS(Cr) Regs; regs 26 and 29 SP Regs

74 Reg 8C SS(Cr) Regs

75 Reg 3(1)(b) SSB(MW&WSP) Regs

76 Reg 7B SS(Cr) Regs; regs 26 and 29 SP Regs

77 Reg 7C SS(Cr) Regs; regs 26 and 30 SP Regs

78 Regs 7B(2) and 7C(1) SS(Cr) Regs; regs 26, 29 and 30(1) SP Regs

79 Reg 9D SS(Cr) Regs; regs 26 and 29 SP Regs

80 Reg 9E SS(Cr) Regs; regs 26 and 29 SP Regs

81 Regs 28 and 33 SP Regs

4. Contribution conditions for benefits

82 Regs 7(1) and 7A SS(CTCNIN) Regs

83 Reg 3(8J) and (8K) SS&CS(DA) Regs

84 s21(6) SSCBA 1992; s2(4) JSA 1995; Sch 1 para 3 WRA 2007

85 Sch 1 para 3(1)(f) WRA 2007; regs 2(1) and 13 ESA Regs; regs 2 and 14 ESA Regs 2013

86 s1B WRA 2007; Sch 2 paras 2 and 15 ESA(TP)(EA)(No.2) Regs

87 **JSA** ss1(2)(d) and 2 JSA 1995; regs 45A, 158 and 167 JSA Regs; regs 34, 69 and 75 JSA Regs 2013

ESA Sch 1 para 1 WRA 2007; reg 7 ESA Regs; reg 8 ESA Regs 2013

88 Reg 45B JSA Regs; reg 8(2)(ca) ESA Regs; reg 35 JSA Regs 2013; reg 9(2)(d) ESA Regs 2013

89 Reg 8 ESA Regs; reg 9 ESA Regs 2013

90 s2 JSA 1995; Sch 1 para 2 WRA 2007; regs 158 and 167 JSA Regs; regs 69 and 75 JSA Regs 2013

91 Reg 47(3)(a) JSA Regs; reg 37(2)(a) JSA Regs 2013

92 Reg 7A SS(CTCNIN) Regs; reg 3(8E) SS&CS(DA) Regs; reg 17(3) UC,PIP,JSA&ESA(DA) Regs

93 s31 PA 2014

94 Sch 3 para 5 SSCBA 1992

95 Reg 6 SS(WBRP&OB)(T) Regs

96 Sch 3 para 5(6) and (6A) SSCBA 1992

97 Sch 3 para 5(3) SSCBA 1992

98 Sch 3 para 5(8) SSCBA 1992

99 Reg 7(7) SS(WBRP&OB)(T) Regs; s20 and Sch 3 para 5(5) SSCBA 1992

100 Sch 3 para 5(5) SSCBA 1992

101 Reg 6 SS(WB&RP) Regs

102 s60(4)-(6) SSCBA 1992; reg 6(3) SS(WB&RP) Regs

103 s1 PA 2014

104 s2(4) PA 2014

105 s4(4) and (5) PA 2014

106 Reg 13 SP Regs

107 s4(1)(c) PA 2014

108 s11(1) PA 2014

109 s5 and Sch 1 PA 2014

Chapter 44

Work and benefits

This chapter covers:
1. How work affects your benefits (p991)
2. People treated as in full-time paid work (p997)
3. People treated as not in full-time paid work (p998)
4. Self-employed people (p999)
5. Non-means-tested benefits (p1000)
6. People involved in a trade dispute (p1001)

This chapter explains how any paid work carried out by you, your partner or anyone living with you affects your entitlement to income support (IS), jobseeker's allowance (JSA), employment and support allowance (ESA), housing benefit (HB) and pension credit (PC). See Chapter 7 for how your earnings affect the amount of your universal credit and Chapters 20 and 21 for how they affect the amount of your IS, income-based JSA, income-related ESA, HB and PC.

Key facts
- Your eligibility for universal credit is not affected if you or your partner are in full-time paid work. However, you cannot get a housing costs element for any payments you must make as an owner-occupier if you or your partner have any earnings, no matter how low these are, or whatever hours you work.
- You cannot usually qualify for income support (IS) or income-based jobseeker's allowance (JSA) if you or your partner are in full-time paid work, or for income-related employment and support allowance (ESA) if your partner is in full-time paid work. You cannot qualify for contribution-based JSA if you are in full-time paid work.
- You cannot qualify for IS on the basis that you are incapable of work or for any type of ESA if you do any work, unless it is work you are permitted to do while claiming.
- Your eligibility for housing benefit and pension credit is not affected if you or your partner are in full-time paid work.
- Entitlement to some non-means-tested benefits may be affected by work.
- If you, your partner or a non-dependant are involved in a strike or trade dispute, this can affect the calculation of your benefits or tax credits.

1. **How work affects your benefits**

Which benefits you can claim when working

Paid work affects your universal credit (UC), income support (IS), jobseeker's allowance (JSA), employment and support allowance (ESA), housing benefit (HB) and pension credit (PC) in different ways.

The rules on work for working tax credit (WTC) are different (see p299). If you or your partner are in full-time paid work, you may be able to receive WTC. In some circumstances, you may be able to choose between getting WTC or a means-tested benefit. Sometimes, you can receive both. For more information, see pp1019–20 in the 2017/18 edition of this *Handbook*. **Note:** there are now very few situations in which you can make a new claim for IS, income-based JSA, income-related ESA, HB or or tax credits (see p24), but you may, for instance, be able to claim WTC on starting full-time work if you already receive child tax credit, or claim income-related ESA if you are are already getting contribution-based ESA.

Which means-tested benefit or tax credit should you choose?

1. If you can choose between getting UC, IS, JSA or ESA and WTC, check which passported benefits you gain or lose (see p12).

2. If you receive UC, IS, JSA or ESA, you can get help with some housing costs (see Chapter 18). You cannot get help with housing costs in WTC.

3. You cannot get a housing costs element in your UC for payments you make as an owner-occupier if you or your partner have any earnings (see Chapter 6).

4. If you (or your partner) are responsible for children or have limited capability for work, a work allowance will be disregarded when calculating your earnings for UC (see p41).

5. There is a capital limit for UC, IS, income-based JSA and income-related ESA, but not for WTC.

6. You can get help with your childcare costs if you receive UC or WTC, though not if you receive IS, JSA or ESA.

The full-time work rule

If you or your partner (or a non-dependant) work full time for payment, the DWP often calls this 'remunerative work'. It is called 'full-time paid work' in this *Handbook*. The number of hours that count as being 'full time' depends on the benefit concerned and whether the work is done by you, your partner or a non-dependant.

- Your eligibility for UC, HB and PC is not affected if you or your partner are in full-time paid work. For HB, however, work can affect the way your income is calculated – eg, whether you can get an additional earnings disregard (see p431 and p473) or a childcare costs disregard (see p432 and p474). You cannot get a

Part 7: National insurance, work and work-related rules
Chapter 44: Work and benefits
1. How work affects your benefits

housing costs element in your UC for payments you make as an owner-occupier if you or your partner have any earnings, no matter how low these are, or whatever hours you work (see p84).

- If you do any paid work (unless it is work that you can do while claiming – see p1042), you are not entitled to ESA.[1]
- If your partner is in full-time paid work, you cannot usually qualify for IS, income-based JSA or income-related ESA.[2] Your partner's working hours do not affect your entitlement to contribution-based JSA or contributory ESA.
- In some situations, a young person who is aged 16 or over and does paid work for 24 hours a week or more does not count as a 'qualifying young person' who can be included in your claim (see p323 and p579). In this case, you might not be able to get an allowance or premiums in your HB for her/him (or, if still included, in your IS or income-based JSA).
- If you have a non-dependant living with you, the amount of the non-dependant deduction made from your IS, income-based JSA, income-related ESA or PC housing costs, and from your HB, can be higher if s/he is in full-time paid work (see p365 and p200).

See p993 for what counts as paid work and p993 for how the hours are calculated. 'Work' includes self-employment and work which is done from home. In some circumstances, you may be treated as not being in full-time paid work even if you are (see p998). In others, you may be treated as if you are in full-time paid work when you are not (see p997).

What counts as full-time work

For IS, JSA and HB, **you** count as being in 'full-time work' if you work 16 hours or more a week.[3] See p993 for how the hours are calculated. You cannot qualify for ESA if you do *any* number of hours of work, unless it is work you can do while claiming (see p1042).

Your partner counts as being in 'full-time work':
- for IS, income-based JSA (but not joint-claim JSA) and income-related ESA, if s/he works 24 hours or more a week;[4]
- for HB, if s/he works 16 hours or more a week.[5]

For IS, JSA, ESA, PC and HB, **your non-dependant** counts as being in full-time paid work if s/he works 16 hours or more a week.[6]

Note:
- For PC, there is no rule for when you or your partner count as being in full-time work because it is not affected by the the number of hours worked.
- For joint-claim JSA, you do not have to make a joint claim with your partner if s/he works 16 or more hours a week.[7]

- For HB, you and your partner may have to work more than 16 hours a week to benefit from an additional earnings disregard (see p431 and p473).

Example

Della works 15 hours a week. She can get income-based JSA, provided her earnings are not too high. If she works an additional five hours, she would be in full-time work and would no longer be entitled to JSA. She would still be able to get HB, but her earnings might affect the amount she receives.

What counts as paid work

'Paid work' is work for which you are paid, or for which it is expected that you will be paid – ie, there is an expectation that you get payment, now or in the future, even if no payment is finally made.[8] Whether or not you are paid or are working in expectation of payment should be decided at the time the work is done, not, for example, at the end of the year or accounting period.[9]

Note:

- You must have a real prospect of payment, not just a hope or desire to make money – eg, a self-employed writer who has never sold a manuscript and has no publisher's contract may have no real expectation of payment and so is not in paid work even if s/he spends a lot of time writing.[10]
- Paid work includes work for which you receive payment in kind – eg, free meals, accommodation or produce.[11]

How your hours are calculated

Include all hours actually worked for which payment is made or which you work in expectation of payment. If you do more than one job, add the hours from each together. If routine paid overtime is done, include those hours. If work is casual or intermittent (eg, you are a seasonal worker who works in the summer, but you are unemployed for the rest of the year), you can argue that only the hours when you are in work are relevant (but see p995 for 'term-time' workers).[12] Your word should be accepted unless there is reason for doubt.

Note:

- If your hours fluctuate, there are rules on how they should be averaged (see p994).
- For IS, JSA and income-related ESA only, paid lunch hours and breaks count towards the total hours.[13]
- For PC and HB, the rules do not say how to calculate the hours of work unless these fluctuate. However, for PC, the DWP says that you should only count the hours for which payment is made or which are worked in expectation of payment, including overtime, but not including paid breaks – eg, lunch or tea breaks.[14]

Part 7: National insurance, work and work-related rules
Chapter 44: Work and benefits
1. How work affects your benefits

- For JSA only, any hours spent caring for someone for whom it would be possible to qualify for IS as a carer (see p236) are ignored, unless the carer is employed and paid to act as a carer.[15] For IS and ESA, although hours spent caring are not ignored, you and your partner (for IS), or your partner (for ESA), are treated as not being in full-time paid work in this situation (see p998).

If you are unsure whether you (or your partner) are in full-time paid work, see p996. If you think the average hours have been calculated wrongly so you cannot get the benefit you want, you can appeal. Work out whether you are better off receiving IS/JSA/ESA or WTC if you have a choice (see p991). You can also appeal if your non-dependant's hours have been calculated unfairly and the DWP or local authority is making a non-dependant deduction that is too high. **Note:** except for HB, you must apply for a mandatory reconsideration before you can appeal (see Chapters 56 and 57).

If your hours fluctuate

If your (or your partner's or your non-dependant's) hours fluctuate, an average of the weekly hours is calculated as follows.

Regular pattern of work

If there is a regular pattern of work (a 'work cycle'), the average hours worked throughout each cycle are used – eg, if you regularly work three weeks on and one week off, your hours are the average over the four-week period (the 'work cycle').[16] Weeks when you are on paid holiday, off sick, or on maternity, paternity, shared parental, adoption or parental bereavement leave, or are absent from work without a good reason, are disregarded – ie, the hours you would otherwise have worked are included when calculating the average hours.[17]

Note:

- If you work casually or intermittently (eg, you are a seasonal worker and work in the summer but you are unemployed during the rest of the year), you can argue that your work cycle is that part of the year in which you are in work and that you do not count as being in work when you are unemployed.[18]
- If you (or your partner or non-dependant) have a work cycle that lasts a year with periods in which you do not work – eg, in a school:
  - for JSA and ESA, if the average hours of work you do over the whole cycle means you are not in full-time paid work, you can get JSA or income-related ESA. However, you may only qualify during periods when your income is sufficiently low – eg, during unpaid summer holidays. You could also get WTC if you (or your partner) work sufficient hours each week during term time (see Chapter 15);
  - for IS, PC and HB, the 'term-time only' worker rule applies (see below).

Example

Eduardo, a shop worker, works two seven-and-half hour shifts each week, on Monday and Wednesday. Every three weeks he works two additional weekend shifts. These are also seven-and-half hours each.

Over his work cycle of three weeks, Eduardo works a total of 60 hours. So his average working week is 20 hours.

Eduardo's partner can get income-related ESA because Eduardo is not in full-time paid work for this purpose (although his earnings will be included in the ESA calculation). However, Eduardo cannot claim JSA himself, even though he is available for and actively seeking more work, because his work is regarded as full time for JSA purposes.

No regular pattern of work

If there is no regular pattern of work (no recognisable work cycle), an average of your hours is used. This is the average over the five weeks immediately before the date of your claim (or of a supersession decision), or the average over a longer or a shorter period if this would give a more accurate figure.[19] The five-week period may not be appropriate if the average is distorted – eg, if you have done a short period of overtime that is not typical.[20]

No work pattern yet established

If you (or your partner or non-dependant) have not yet established a recognisable work cycle, the number of hours or average number of hours you are expected to work each week is used.[21] This may apply, for example, if you have just started work or if your working arrangements have changed and your previous work cycle no longer applies. Once there is sufficient evidence to calculate your average hours, the decision can be revised or superseded.

'Term-time only' workers

For IS, PC and HB, if you have a recognisable work cycle, with periods when you do not work, that lasts for a year, the 'term-time only' worker rule applies. The average number of hours in the periods when you are actually working (eg, during term time) determines whether you are in full-time paid work throughout the year.[22] People who work in schools, colleges or similar institutions are affected by this rule, but it could also apply in any other seasonal job. In practice, if your average hours of work during term time mean you are in full-time paid work during term time, you also count as being in full-time paid work over the school holidays, even if you do no work and are not paid. This means:

- if you or your partner count as being in full-time paid work, you cannot receive IS during the school holidays. You might be able to claim JSA or ESA. You can get WTC if you normally work sufficient hours each week (see p299);

Part 7: National insurance, work and work-related rules
Chapter 44: Work and benefits
1. How work affects your benefits

- if a non-dependant counts as being in full-time paid work, higher rate non-dependant deductions may continue to be made from your HB or your IS, JSA, ESA or PC housing costs (see p200 and p365) throughout the year.

Although this rule may apply to other seasonal workers, if you work casually or intermittently and are unemployed the rest of the year, you can argue that it does not apply to you.[23] If your contract comes to an end before a period of absence from work, you should not count as a term-time only worker, unless there is an understanding with your employer that you are expected to start work again.[24]

Sometimes it might not be clear whether you have a work cycle that lasts a year (eg, if you have only started your job recently or have a fixed-term contract that finishes at the end of the school term), or you are employed on a casual or relief basis.[25] It takes time before it can be said that you have a yearly work cycle.[26] However, if you have an indefinite contract to work in term time only, the decision maker may say that you have a yearly work cycle from the start.[27]

Example

Sheila is a school meals worker. She works 20 hours a week, 38 weeks of the year. She gets four weeks' paid holiday, but otherwise is not paid when she is not working at the school. Her average hours are calculated as follows:

20 hours x 38 weeks = 760 hours. 52 weeks – 4 weeks' paid holiday = 48 weeks.

760 hours divided by 48 weeks = 15.84 average hours a week.

Sheila can get JSA as she is not in full-time paid work for JSA purposes. She might also qualify for WTC. She cannot qualify for IS as the term-time only worker rule applies and her hours during term time are too high.

If you are unsure whether you are in full-time paid work

If your (or your partner's) circumstances change while you are claiming:

- IS, JSA or ESA, you may be uncertain about whether the paid work is now full time – eg, if your average weekly hours change or your partner now gets regular overtime. If it appears that you (or your partner) are now working 16/24 hours or more a week, report this to the DWP to avoid an overpayment. Also check to see whether you can claim WTC or UC. Remember, you cannot qualify for ESA if *you* do *any* paid work, unless it is work you can do while claiming (see p1042);
- HB, report this to the local authority. A change in your hours of work may affect your entitlement to an additional earnings or a childcare costs disregard (see p431 and p432).

In all cases, increases or decreases in your earnings can affect the amount of benefit to which you are entitled.

If your non-dependant's circumstances change while you are claiming HB (or help with housing costs in IS, JSA, ESA or PC), report this to the local authority (or DWP) to enable your non-dependant deduction to be adjusted.

2. People treated as in full-time paid work

You or your partner can be treated as being in full-time paid work, even if you are not, if:

- for income support (IS), jobseeker's allowance (JSA) and housing benefit (HB), you or your partner (or for employment and support allowance (ESA), your partner) normally work full time, but are on holiday and you intend to resume work once the holiday is over.[28] Whether you count as being on holiday depends on your contractual or legal entitlement to holiday. You can argue that you only count as being on holiday if you are paid for it.[29] However, for JSA, even if you do not count as being in full-time paid work because you are on unpaid leave, you are likely to have difficulty persuading the DWP that you are available for and actively seeking work (see Chapter 48). For IS and HB, in some cases, if you are a full-time 'term-time only' worker and your cycle of work lasts a year, you are treated as being in full-time work during the school holidays (see p995);
- for IS, JSA and HB, you or your partner (or, for ESA, your partner) are absent from full-time paid work without a good reason.[30] All your circumstances should be taken into account. If your employer has authorised your absence, it is likely that the decision maker will accept you have a good reason;
- for IS and JSA, you or your partner stopped full-time paid work, but you are still within the period covered by payment in lieu of earnings or wages, or certain holiday pay (unless they can be disregarded). For ESA, this rule applies if you stopped paid work or if your partner stopped full-time paid work.[31] See p424 for when payments when you stop work count as income.

For IS, JSA, PC and HB, your non-dependant can also be treated as being in full-time paid work under the rules above. For ESA, your non-dependant can also be treated as being in full-time paid work if s/he normally works full time but is on holiday, or is away from work 'without good cause'.

You or your partner can be treated as in being full-time paid work for the first seven days you (or s/he) are involved in a trade dispute. See p1001 for information about entitlement to, and the amount of, IS or JSA during a trade dispute.

Part 7: National insurance, work and work-related rules
Chapter 44: Work and benefits
3. People treated as not in full-time paid work

3. **People treated as not in full-time paid work**

There are situations when you (or your partner or non-dependant) are treated as not being in full-time paid work, even if you actually are. For income support (IS), jobseeker's allowance (JSA) and employment and support allowance (ESA), see below. For housing benefit (HB) and pension credit (PC), see p999.

Income support, jobseeker's allowance and employment and support allowance

You (and your partner and your non-dependant) are treated as not being in full-time paid work in the following circumstances. Unless indicated, this applies to you for IS and JSA, and to your partner for IS, income-based JSA and income-related ESA, if you (or s/he):[32]

- are working on a training scheme and are being paid a training allowance under specific provisions; *or*
- for JSA only, are on work experience or, if you do not come under the universal credit system, are participating in a specified scheme for assisting people to obtain employment – eg, the Work and Health Programme (see p1151); *or*
- are a volunteer (other than for a relative) or are working for a charity or voluntary organisation and are giving your services free (except for your expenses); *or*
- are providing care for someone:
  - who is staying with you but who is not normally a member of your household and you receive payments from a health authority, local authority or voluntary organisation, or from the person concerned under section 26(3A) of the National Assistance Act 1948 for caring for her/him;
  - for IS and ESA, in the circumstances described on p236. This means that any hours of work you do are ignored, not just the hours you spend caring. For JSA, the hours you spend caring are ignored in this situation (see p994); *or*
- are a foster carer (or, in Scotland only, a kinship carer) receiving a payment from a local authority or voluntary organisation for a child you are looking after. For working tax credit purposes, you can count as being in full-time paid work (see p307); *or*
- work as a part-time firefighter, auxiliary coastguard, member of the Reserve Army or reserve forces, or member of a lifeboat crew; *or*
- are performing duties as a local authority councillor; *or*
- for IS and ESA only, are working as a childminder in your own home; *or*
- are engaged in an activity for which you (or s/he) receive, or expect to receive, a sports award from UK Sport and no other payment is made; *or*
- for IS only, qualify for housing costs run-on (see p376); *or*
- are a student and are doing work in connection with your course of education;[33] *or*

- are on maternity, adoption, paternity, shared parental or parental bereavement leave or are absent from work because you are sick, even if you normally work 16/24 hours or more each week.[34]

Note:
- For ESA, *you* do not count as being in paid work if you are doing work you can do while claiming (see p1042).
- You, your partner or your non-dependant can also be treated as not in full-time paid work if you (or s/he) are involved in a trade dispute or, for IS or ESA, have recently returned to work following one. See p1001 for more about IS or JSA during a trade dispute.

Housing benefit and pension credit

You (or your partner or non-dependant) are treated as *not* being in full-time paid work if:[35]
- you (or s/he) are on maternity, adoption, paternity, shared parental or parental bereavement leave or are absent from work because you are sick, even if you normally work 16 hours or more each week. However, for HB, you and your partner *can* count as being in full-time paid work on such leave to enable you to get an earnings disregard for childcare costs (see p432 and p474); *or*
- the only payment you (or s/he) receive is a sports award from UK Sport.

In addition, you (or your partner or non-dependant) are treated as *not* being in full-time paid work in a benefit week, if in that week you (or s/he) are on IS or income-based JSA (or for HB only, income-related ESA) for more than three days.[36]

4. Self-employed people

All work in expectation of payment counts as paid work. If you work sufficient hours, you therefore count as being in full-time paid work, even if your income is low. The DWP counts payments from the business to meet living expenses (in cash or in kind) as payment for work unless the drawings are from the business capital.[37] If you simply invest in a business and do not help to run it, you are not treated as self-employed.[38]

It may be difficult to establish whether or not you are in full-time paid work – eg, if there are periods when you have no work, or if you only work part of the year (eg, seasonally) on a regular basis. Whether or not you are in work depends on whether you are carrying out activities in connection with self-employment. Whether or not you are in full-time paid work depends on how many hours you are doing in expectation of payment (using the rules described earlier in this chapter). During periods when you are not in work, or if you have ceased trading, you should not count as being in paid work.[39]

Part 7: National insurance, work and work-related rules
Chapter 44: Work and benefits
5. Non-means-tested benefits

When calculating the number of hours you work each week, the decision maker counts all those necessary to run your business, including time spent visiting potential customers, providing estimates, advertising, bookkeeping, visiting wholesalers and retailers, cleaning the premises and doing research work – eg, if you are a writer.[40] The hours spent on services for which you are paid count, as well as other time which is essential for your business – eg, preparation time and finding new customers.[41] The decision maker should accept your statement unless there is a reason for doubt.[42]

Note:

- Some of the initial work necessary to set up a business may not count as paid work if it is unpaid preparatory work done in the hope of further paid work.[43]
- If your business is not yet making money or has ceased to make a profit, you may count as working in expectation of payment if you are taking drawings against future profit or if the business is a viable one and is likely to yield profit in the future. With no prospect of a profit, the decision maker is likely to want to know why you are working for nothing.[44]

5. **Non-means-tested benefits**

Entitlement to some non-means-tested benefits is affected by issues to do with work and employment. For the rules for a specific benefit, see the relevant chapter in this *Handbook*.

- You cannot qualify for:
  - carer's allowance if you are 'gainfully employed' – ie, you earn more than £128 each week (see p563 for how this is calculated);
  - benefits based on your limited capability for work (eg, contributory employment and support allowance) in any week you do any work, unless this is work you can do while claiming (see p1042);
  - contribution-based jobseeker's allowance (JSA) if you are in full-time paid work. The income-based JSA rules described in this chapter apply.
- To qualify for:
  - industrial injuries benefits, you must have been an employed earner when you had an accident or contracted a disease;
  - maternity allowance, you must satisfy an employment condition.
- Statutory sick pay, statutory maternity pay, statutory adoption pay, statutory paternity pay, statutory shared parental pay and statutory parental bereavement pay are linked to your being employed (not self-employed).
- Whether you are an employed earner or self-employed affects your national insurance contributions (see Chapter 43).

6. People involved in a trade dispute

If you (or your partner) are involved in a trade dispute, your universal credit (UC), income support (IS) and jobseeker's allowance (JSA) are affected, as well as benefits paid to you by your employer, increases for an adult paid with non-means-tested benefits and some social fund payments. You can still qualify for housing benefit (HB), income-related employment and support allowance (ESA) and pension credit (PC), but there are issues to consider (see p1006).

Note: trade dispute law is complex. If there is any doubt about whether you are involved in a trade dispute, get specialist employment advice.

Universal credit

You remain entitled to UC if you are involved in a trade dispute. However, if you (or your partner) have withdrawn your labour in support of a trade dispute, you are treated as having the same earnings you would have received were it not for the trade dispute, even if you are not getting these. This does not apply if your contract of employment has been terminated.[45] The definiton of 'trade dispute' is the same as in employment law.[46] **Note:** any strike pay you receive (eg, from your trade union) does not count as income.[47]

Income support and jobseeker's allowance

You can qualify for IS while you are involved in a trade dispute, and for the first 15 days after you return to work (see p238).

You are not entitled to JSA (including hardship payments) for the whole of any week (seven days from Sunday) if you (or if you are a joint-claim couple, both of you) are involved in a trade dispute for one or more days during that week.[48] Weeks when you are not entitled to JSA do not count as part of your 'jobseeking period' (see p706).[49] This means, for instance, that they do not count towards your 26-week entitlement to contribution-based JSA. If you have a partner and only one of you is involved in a trade dispute, unless you are a joint-claim couple (see p253), the partner who is not involved can receive income-based JSA. If you are a joint-claim couple, you can both get income-based JSA.[50] The partner involved in the trade dispute does not have to satisfy the jobseeking conditions.

For IS, you are (and, for IS and income-based JSA, your partner is) treated as being in full-time paid work for the first seven days you are involved in a trade dispute.

You (and your partner) cannot qualify for IS or income-based JSA for this period.[51] This does not apply if your partner was already entitled to IS or income-based JSA, or you were already entitled to IS, when you became involved in the dispute. If the trade dispute causes a series of stoppages, this only applies for seven days from the start of the first stoppage.[52] After the seven-day period, you are not

Part 7: National insurance, work and work-related rules
Chapter 44: Work and benefits
6. People involved in a trade dispute

treated as being in full-time paid work, but your IS or your partner's IS or income-based JSA is calculated under special rules (see p1003).[53]

Trade disputes

A 'trade dispute' is any dispute between employers and employees or between employees and employees connected with terms or conditions of employment, or the employment or non-employment of anyone.[54] **Note:** this definition is wider than that of 'lawful industrial action' for employment law purposes.

You count as being involved in a trade dispute if:[55]

- you are not working because of a 'stoppage of work' caused by a trade dispute at your 'place of work' (see below). This applies until the stoppage ends, even if you are not a party to the dispute or your contract has been terminated as part of the dispute (but see below);[56] *or*
- you withdraw your labour to further a trade dispute, whether or not there is a stoppage of work at your place of work.

For IS and income-based JSA, you can be awarded benefit at a reduced rate, pending a decision on whether you are involved in a trade dispute.[57] You cannot appeal to the First-tier Tribunal against this decision.[58] However, the decision maker should then carry out a revision of the decision once full information and evidence is available and you can appeal against the new decision.

Stoppage of work and place of work

A '**stoppage of work**' could be due to a strike, lock-out or any other stoppage caused by a trade dispute. The stoppage does not have to involve everyone, or to stop all work.[59] The DWP says that there is no 'stoppage' if normal work continues through the employment of replacement workers or reorganisation.[60]

'**Place of work**' means the place or premises where you are employed, but it does not include a separate department carrying out a different branch of work, which is commonly undertaken as a separate business elsewhere. For example, a colliery canteen worker laid off during a miners' strike was not 'involved in a trade dispute at her place of work'.[61] It can be difficult to establish that separate branches are separate businesses.[62]

You do *not* count as being involved in a trade dispute if:

- you can prove you are not directly interested in the dispute – ie, you will not be affected by its outcome.[63] This could apply if your terms and conditions will not be affected by the outcome of the dispute. It could also apply if your employment has permanently ended and you will not gain anything from the dispute, but it may be difficult to convince the DWP that your employment has permanently ended, because when a dispute is settled it is common for the employer to agree to re-employ those who were dismissed during it;[64] *or*

- you can prove that during a stoppage of work:[65]
  - you have been made redundant; *or*
  - you have become genuinely employed elsewhere – ie, not just to avoid the trade dispute rules;[66] *or*
  - you genuinely resume employment with your employer and then leave for a reason other than the trade dispute. **Note**: if you claim JSA, you may be given a sanction if you leave (see p1082 and p1146).

For income-based JSA (if your partner is the claimant) and IS, even if you are (or count as) involved in a trade dispute, the special rules for those involved in a trade dispute do not apply:[67]

- while you have limited capability for work or are incapable of work; *or*
- from the sixth week before the week you are due to have a baby to the end of the seventh week after the week the baby is born; *or*
- from the day you return to work with the same employer, even if the dispute is continuing or you are doing a different job.

Amount of income support or income-based jobseeker's allowance

Even if you can qualify for IS or income-based JSA while you (or your partner) are involved in a trade dispute, the amount that is payable is reduced and may mean that you are not actually entitled to any IS or income-based JSA. Your applicable amount is calculated in a special way and it is assumed that you have a set level of strike pay. Certain income is taken into account, even if this would be disregarded were you (or your partner) not involved in a trade dispute. **Note**: if you are entitled to IS of less than £5 a week, you are only paid if you are receiving another benefit that can be paid together with IS as a single payment.[68]

Applicable amount

Your IS or income-based JSA applicable amount is calculated as follows.

If you are a single claimant, or a member of a couple (without children) both involved in a trade dispute:

- your applicable amount for IS is reduced to nil;[69]
- you are not entitled to any JSA.[70]

If you are a lone parent, or a member of a couple (with children) both involved in a trade dispute:

- your IS applicable amount only includes:[71]
  - personal allowances for your children, the family premium and any premiums for your children (if still included); *and*
  - housing costs (service charges and ground rent for owner-occupiers);
- you are not entitled to any JSA.[72]

If you are a member of a couple (with or without children) and only one of you is involved in a trade dispute, your applicable amount only includes:[73]

Part 7: National insurance, work and work-related rules
Chapter 44: Work and benefits
6. People involved in a trade dispute

- half the normal personal allowance for a couple and half of any premiums paid at the couple rate, rounded down to the nearest multiple of 5 pence;
- any premiums payable solely in respect of the person *not* involved in the trade dispute;
- personal allowances for your children, the family premium and premiums for your children (if still included); *and*
- housing costs (service charges and ground rent for owner-occupiers).

Actual and assumed strike pay

If you (or your partner) are involved in a trade dispute, £40.50 a week is deducted from your IS or income-based JSA as 'assumed strike pay', whether or not you or your partner receive any payments.[74] Any payments you or your partner do receive from a trade union in excess of £40.50 a week count as income (actual payments of up to £40.50 are ignored). If you and your partner are both involved in a trade dispute, only £40.50 in total is ignored.[75]

Example
Cliff is on strike. His partner is not involved in the dispute. Their only income is £50 a week strike pay.

Applicable amount	£58.40	(half normal amount)
less income	£9.50	(strike pay over £40.50)
	= £48.90	
less	£40.50	(assumed strike pay)
IS payable =	**£8.40**	

Other income and capital

Other income and capital are generally treated as normal for IS and income-based JSA. However, certain voluntary payments and payments from your employer which would usually be disregarded are taken into account as income. For a full list of these, see p944 of the 2018/19 edition of this *Handbook* or consult the regulations.[76]

Benefits paid to you by your employer

Statutory sick pay

You cannot qualify for statutory sick pay (SSP) unless you are within a 'period of entitlement'. A period of entitlement cannot arise if, on the date it would begin, there is a stoppage of work because of a trade dispute at your place of work (ie, you became incapable of work during the trade dispute), unless you can prove that you did not have a direct interest in the dispute on or before that date.[77] You are not entitled to SSP throughout your period of sickness, even if the trade dispute ends. You may, however, qualify for ESA. **Note:** you can continue to qualify for SSP if you were already entitled to SSP when the trade dispute began.

'Stoppage of work' and 'trade dispute' are not defined in the SSP rules. However, an overtime ban or working to grade does not count as a stoppage of work.[78]

Statutory maternity, adoption, paternity, shared parental and parental bereavement pay

To qualify for statutory maternity pay (SMP), statutory adoption pay (SAP), statutory paternity pay (SPP), statutory shared parental pay (SSPP) or statutory parental bereavement pay (SPBP), you must have been employed for a continuous period of at least 26 weeks ending on a specified date (see p818). For this purpose, any week in which you are not working because of a stoppage of work due to a trade dispute at your place of work does not break your continuity of employment. However, unless you can prove that at no time did you have a direct interest in the trade dispute:

- any such week does not count towards the total of 26 weeks' employment you need to qualify for SMP, SAP, SPP, SSPP or SPBP; *and*
- if you are dismissed during the stoppage of work, your continuity of employment ends on the day you stopped work.[79]

Tax credits

For working tax credit (WTC) you can continue to be treated as being in full-time paid work while you are on strike for up to 10 consecutive days when you should be working, providing you were in full-time paid work before you went on strike (see p299).[80] You can continue to get child tax credit (CTC) while you are on strike.

Social fund payments

Involvement in a trade dispute does not affect your entitlement to a funeral expenses, cold weather or winter fuel payment. You cannot, however, qualify for a budgeting loan if you or your partner are involved in a trade dispute.[81]

For information about when you count as being involved in a trade dispute, see p1002. The rules are the same as for JSA.

You do not count as being involved in a trade dispute during a period when you are incapable of work, or from the sixth week before the week you are due to have a baby to the end of the seventh week after the week the baby is born.[82]

Sure Start maternity grant

If you or your partner are involved in a trade dispute, your entitlement to a Sure Start maternity grant is not affected if your qualifying benefit is UC, income-related ESA or PC. However, you can only qualify for a Sure Start maternity grant if your qualifying benefit is:[83]

- IS or income-based JSA, if the trade dispute has been going on for at least six weeks when you claim a maternity grant; *or*
- WTC or CTC, if you claimed the relevant tax credit before the trade dispute began.

Part 7: National insurance, work and work-related rules
Chapter 44: Work and benefits
6. People involved in a trade dispute

The above restrictions do not apply to a Best Start grant pregnancy and baby payment in Scotland.

Housing benefit, income-related employment and support allowance and pension credit

There are no rules that reduce the amount of your HB, income-related ESA and PC if you or your partner are involved in a trade dispute. However, bear the following in mind.

- For income-related ESA, your partner is treated as not being in full-time paid work if s/he is involved in a trade dispute, and for the first 15 days following her/his return to work after having been involved in a trade dispute.[84]
- For HB and PC, it does not matter if you or your partner are treated as being in full-time paid work.
- You may become entitled to HB, income-related ESA or PC (or an increased amount of these) if your (or your partner's) income drops because of a trade dispute.
- For HB, if your earnings are reduced due to a trade dispute, the local authority should take this into account and not just consider your pre-strike earnings.[85] Your earnings can be averaged over a different period than normal if this results in a more accurate estimate (see p456 and p483).
- For income-related ESA and PC, you can apply to have your award reassessed under the rules on variable earnings (see p454 and p483).

Non-dependants

Non-dependant deductions made from your IS, JSA, ESA or PC housing costs and from HB are usually higher if your non-dependant is in full-time paid work. However, if your non-dependant is involved in a trade dispute, this may mean that the non-dependant deduction should be reduced. See p200 and p365 for further information.

Income support loans on your return to work

If you return to work with the same employer, whether or not the trade dispute has ended, you can qualify for IS in the form of a loan for the first 15 days back at work.[86] You fit into one of the groups of people who can claim IS and are not treated as being in full-time paid work for this period.[87] As no new claims for IS can now be made, a loan is only available if you or you partner already receive IS. Your income and capital are calculated as if you were still involved in the trade dispute, except that the rules about actual and assumed strike pay, and other payments received because you or your partner are not working (see p1004), do not apply.[88] For more about these loans and the rules for repaying them, see p947 in the 2018/19 edition of this *Handbook*.

Notes

1. How work affects your benefits

1 Sch1 para 6 (1)(e) WRA 2007; regs 40 and 41 ESA Regs; reg 37 ESA Regs 2013
2 s124(1)(c) SSCBA 1992; s3(1)(e) JSA 1995; Sch 1 para 6(1)(f) WRA 2007
3 **IS** Reg 5 IS Regs
JSA Reg 51 JSA Regs; reg 42 JSA Regs 2013
HB Reg 6(1) HB Regs; reg 6(1) HB(SPC) Regs
4 **IS** Reg 5(1A) IS Regs
JSA Reg 51(1)(b) JSA Regs
ESA Reg 42(1) ESA Regs
5 Reg 6(1) HB Regs; reg 6(1) HB(SPC) Regs
6 **IS** Regs 2(1) and 5 IS Regs
JSA Reg 51(1)(c) JSA Regs
ESA Sch 6 para 2(1) ESA Regs
PC Sch 2 para 2(1) SPC Regs
HB Reg 6(1) HB Regs; reg 6(1) HB(SPC) Regs
7 Reg 3E(2)(g) JSA Regs
8 R(IS) 5/95; *Fiore v CAO*, 20 June 1995
9 *CAO v Ellis* [1995] (CA), reported as R(IS) 22/95; CTC/626/2001
10 R(IS) 1/93
11 CFC/33/1993; R(FIS) 1/83
12 R(JSA) 1/07; *Saunderson v SSWP* [2012] ScotCS CSIH 10
13 **IS** Reg 5(7) IS Regs
JSA Reg 51(3)(a) JSA Regs; reg 42(3)(a) JSA Regs 2013
ESA Regs 42(2) and 45(9) and Sch 6 para 2(7) ESA Regs
14 Ch 78 App 5, paras 21, 23, 30 and 47 DMG
15 Reg 51(3)(c) JSA Regs; reg 42(3)(c) JSA Regs 2013
16 **IS** Reg 5(2)(b)(i) IS Regs
JSA Reg 51(2)(b)(i) JSA Regs; reg 43(2)(b)(i) JSA Regs 2013
ESA Regs 42(2) and 45(8)(b)(i) and Sch 6 para 2(2)(a) ESA Regs
PC Sch 2 para 2(4) SPC Regs
HB Reg 6(2)(a) HB Regs; reg 6(2)(a) HB(SPC) Regs
17 R(JSA) 5/03
18 R(JSA) 1/07; *Saunderson v SSWP* [2012] ScotCS CSIH 10
19 para 20322 DMG
IS Reg 5(2)(b)(ii) IS Regs
JSA Reg 51(2)(b)(ii) JSA Regs; reg 42(2)(b)(ii) JSA Regs 2013
ESA Regs 42(2) and 45(8)(b)(ii) and Sch 6 para 2(2)(b) ESA Regs
PC Sch 2 para 2(2)(b) SPC Regs
HB Reg 6(2)(b) HB Regs; reg 6(2)(b) HB(SPC) Regs
20 CFC/2963/2001; *NS v SSWP (IS)* [2015] UKUT 423 (AAC)
21 **IS** Reg 5(2)(a) IS Regs
JSA Reg 51(2)(a) JSA Regs; reg 42(2)(a) JSA Regs 2013
ESA Regs 42(2) and 45(8)(a) and Sch 6 para 2(3) ESA Regs
PC Sch 2 para 2(4) SPC Regs
HB Reg 6(4) HB Regs; reg 6(4) HB(SPC) Regs
All R(IS) 8/95
22 **IS** Regs 2(2)(b)(i) and 5(3B) IS Regs
PC Sch 2 para 2(3) SPC Regs
HB Reg 6(3) HB Regs; reg 6(3) HB(SPC) Regs
All *Stafford and Banks v CAO* [2001] UKHL 33, reported as R(IS) 15/01
23 R(JSA) 1/07; *Saunderson v SSWP* [2012] ScotCS CSIH 10; *MC v SSWP (IS)* [2013] UKUT 384 (AAC) provides a useful summary of the equivalent rules on earnings
24 CJSA/3832/2006
25 R(JSA) 8/03
26 CIS/914/1997; CJSA/2759/1998
27 R(JSA) 5/02

2. People treated as in full-time paid work

28 **IS** Reg 5(3) IS Regs
JSA Reg 52(1) JSA Regs; reg 43(1) JSA Regs 2013
ESA Reg 42(3) and Sch 6 para 2(4) ESA Regs
PC Sch 2 para 2(5) SPC Regs
HB Reg 6(5) HB Regs; reg 6(5) HB(SPC) Regs
All R(U) 1/62
29 R(JSA) 5/03; Vol 4 Ch 20, para 20309 DMG

Part 7: National insurance, work and work-related rules
Chapter 44: Work and benefits
Notes

● ●

30 **IS** Reg 5(3) IS Regs
JSA Reg 52(1) JSA Regs; reg 43(1) JSA Regs 2013
ESA Reg 42(3) and Sch 6 para 2(4) ESA Regs
PC Sch 2 para 2(5) SPC Regs
HB Reg 6(5) HB Regs; reg 6(5) HB(SPC) Regs

31 **IS** Reg 5(5) and (5A) IS Regs
JSA Reg 52(3) and (3A) JSA Regs; reg 43(2) and (3) JSA Regs 2013
ESA Regs 41(2) and (3) and 42(4) and (5) ESA Regs

3. People treated as not in full-time paid work
32 **IS** Reg 6(1) and (5) IS Regs
JSA Reg 53(a)-(f) and (i)-(m) JSA Regs; reg 44 JSA Regs 2013
ESA Reg 43 and Sch 6 para 2(6) and (8) ESA Regs

33 R(FIS) 1/86; CDWA/1/1992

34 **IS** Reg 5(3A) IS Regs
JSA Reg 52(1) JSA Regs; reg 43(1) JSA Regs 2013
ESA Reg 43(3) and Sch 6 para 2(5) ESA Regs
All CIS/621/2004

35 **PC** Sch 2 para 2(7) and (8) SPC Regs
HB Reg 6(7) and (8) HB Regs; reg 6(7) and (8) HB(SPC) Regs

36 **PC** Sch 2 para 2(6) SPC Regs
HB Reg 6(6) HB Regs; reg 6(6) HB(SPC) Regs

4. Self-employed people
37 Vol 4 Ch 20, para 20238 DMG
38 CIS/649/1992
39 R(JSA) 1/09; GM v SSWP (JSA) [2010] UKUT 221 (AAC), reported as [2012] AACR 9; Saunderson v SSWP [2012] ScotCS CSIH 10
40 Vol 4 Ch 20, para 20265 DMG
41 R(FIS) 6/85; Kazantzis v CAO [1999], reported as R(IS) 13/99
42 Vol 4 Ch 20, para 20267 DMG
43 Kevin Smith v CAO [1994] (CA), reported as R(IS) 21/95
44 CAO v Ellis [1995] (CA), reported as R(IS) 22/95; CIS/434/1994

6. People involved in a trade dispute
45 Reg 56 UC Regs
46 Reg 2, definition of 'trade dispute' (as defined in s244 of the Trade Union and Labour Relations (Consolidation) Act 1992), UC Regs
47 Reg 66 UC Regs

48 ss14, 15A and 35(1), definition of 'week', JSA 1995
49 Reg 47(3)(e) JSA Regs; reg 37(2)(d) JSA Regs 2013
50 ss15 and 15A JSA 1995; reg 3D and Sch A1 para 17 JSA Regs
51 **IS** Reg 5(4) IS Regs
JSA Reg 52(2) and (2A) JSA Regs
52 Vol 6 Ch 32, paras 32678-79 DMG
53 **IS** Reg 6(4)(b) IS Regs
JSA Reg 53(g) and (gg) JSA Regs
54 s126 SSCBA 1992; ss14 and 35(1), definition of 'trade dispute', JSA 1995
55 s14(1) and (2) JSA 1995; s126 SSCBA 1992
56 R(U) 1/65; Vol 6 Ch 32, paras 32121-25 and 32160-61 DMG
57 Regs 13(2)(a)(i) and 15(a)(i) SS&CS(DA) Regs
58 Sch 2 paras 13 and 19 SS&CS(DA) Regs
59 R(U) 7/58; R(U) 1/87
60 Vol 6 Ch 32, para 32107 DMG
61 s14(4) and (5) JSA 1995; CU/66/1986(T)
62 R(U) 4/62; R(U) 1/70
63 s14(1)(b) JSA 1995
64 Presho v Insurance Officer [1984] (see R(U) 1/84); Cartlidge v CAO [1986] 2 All ER 1; R(U) 1/87
65 s14(3) JSA 1995
66 R(U) 6/74
67 **IS** ss126(1) and (2) and 127(a) SSCBA 1992
JSA s15(4) JSA 1995; reg 171 JSA Regs
68 Reg 26(4) SS(C&P) Regs
69 s126(3)(a) and (d)(i) SSCBA 1992
70 ss14 and 15A JSA 1995
71 s126(3)(b) and (d)(ii) SSCBA 1992
72 s14 JSA 1995
73 **IS** s126(3)(c) SSCBA 1992
JSA ss15(2)(a) and (b) and 15A(4) and (5) JSA 1995
74 **IS** s126(5)(b) and (7) SSCBA 1992
JSA ss15(2)(d) and 15A(5) JSA 1995; reg 172 JSA Regs
75 **IS** Sch 9 para 34 IS Regs
JSA Sch 7 para 36 JSA Regs
76 **IS** s126(5)(a) SSCBA 1992; regs 35(1)(d), 41(3), 42(4) and 48(2), (5), (6), (9), (10)(a) and (c), and Sch 9 paras 15(3)(b), 21, 28 and 39, and Sch 10 paras 17 and 22 IS Regs
JSA ss15(2)(c) and 15A(5) JSA 1995; regs 98(1)(c), 104(3), 105(10) and 110(2), (5), (6), (9) and 110(a) and (c), and Sch 7 paras 15(3)(b), 22, 29 and 41, and Sch 8 paras 22 and 27 JSA Regs
77 Sch 11 paras 2(g) and 7 SSCBA 1992

78 R(SSP) 1/86
79 **SMP** Reg 13 SMP Regs
   SAP/SPP Reg 35 SPPSAP(G) Regs
   SSPP Reg 36 SSPP(G) Regs
   SPBP Reg 14 SPBP(G) Regs
80 Reg 7A WTC(EMR) Regs
81 SF Dir 8(1)(b); s14 JSA 1995
82 s126(1) and (2) SSCBA 1992; s14 JSA
   1995; reg 171 JSA Regs; reg 3 SFM&FE
   Regs; SF Dir 8
83 Regs 3(1) and 6 SFM&FE Regs; s126
   SSCBA 1992; s14 JSA 1995
84 Reg 43(2)(b) ESA Regs
85 *R v HBRB London Borough of Ealing ex
   parte Saville* [1986] HLR 349
86 s127 SSCBA 1992
87 Reg 6(4)(b) and Sch 1B para 20 IS Regs
88 s127(a) SSCBA 1992; regs 35(1)(d),
   41(3) and (4), 42(4) and 48(6) and (10)
   and Sch 9 paras 15, 21, 28 and 39 and
   Sch 10 para 17 IS Regs

Chapter 45

Limited capability for work

This chapter covers:
1. The work capability assessment (below)
2. Challenging a decision (p1036)
3. Periods of limited capability for work (p1041)
4. Work you can do while claiming employment and support allowance (p1042)

Key facts

- If you are too disabled or ill to be expected to work, you may be entitled to benefit and national insurance credits on the basis of having 'limited capability for work'. The main benefits this affects are universal credit and employment and support allowance.
- Whether or not you have limited capability for work is assessed by a 'work capability assessment'. This also tests whether you have 'limited capability for work-related activity'. If so, you are not required to attend work-focused interviews or prepare to return to work, and are entitled to a higher amount of benefit.
- If you work, you may be regarded as not having limited capability for work or work-related activity.
- If you disagree with the decision about your limited capability for work or work-related activity, you can apply for a revision or supersession (see Chapter 56), or appeal against it (see Chapter 57). You must apply for a mandatory reconsideration before you can appeal.

1. The work capability assessment

The work capability assessment is a test used by the DWP to decide whether:

- you have 'limited capability for work' – ie, whether you can get benefit on the basis of being unable to work; *and*
- you have 'limited capability for work-related activity' – ie, whether your health condition is so severe that, in addition to not being able to work, you are not required to engage in activity such as attending interviews about looking for work or retraining.

The assessment is used to decide whether you can get extra amounts included in your universal credit (UC) and your work-related responsibilities if you come under the UC system. It is also used to decide your entitlement to employment and support allowance (ESA).

In addition, the work capability assessment is used to decide whether you are entitled to national insurance (NI) credits for limited capability for work (see Chapter 43) and whether you can still get a work-related activity component in your housing benefit (HB) (see p353). **Note:** this component was abolished for new claims from 3 April 2017. For NI credits and HB, whether you have limited capability for work is decided under the rules for ESA.

You satisfy the work capability assessment if you score sufficient points (see p1017) or you do not but an exceptional circumstance applies (see p1015). You also satisfy the test without actually undergoing the assessment if you are treated as having limited capability for work (see below). In some circumstances, you can be treated as not having limited capability for work even though you have passed the assessment (see p1015).

Treated as having limited capability for work

You are automatically treated as having limited capability for work (without undergoing the work capability assessment) in certain circumstances. In other circumstances, you may be treated as having limited capability for work because of your health.[1]

Universal credit

You are automatically treated as having limited capability for work for UC if:

- you have already been assessed as having limited capability for work for 'new-style' ESA (ie, contributory ESA paid under the UC system);[2] *or*
- you are transferring to UC from ESA and you were assessed as having limited capability for work for ESA, or you were entitled to NI contribution credits for limited capability for work when you claimed UC.[3]

You are treated as having limited capability for work for UC because of your health if:[4]

- you have Covid-19, or you are isolating because of symptoms, or you are caring for a child in your household who is affected in this way. See guidance at nhs.uk/coronavirus. You do not need a medical certificate; *or*
- you are at least pension age (see p779) and get disability living allowance (DLA) or personal independence payment (PIP); *or*
- you are terminally ill – ie, your death can reasonably be expected within six months; *or*
- you are receiving chemotherapy or radiotherapy treatment for cancer, recovering from such treatment or are likely to receive such treatment within

Part 7: National insurance, work and work-related rules
Chapter 45: Limited capability for work
1. The work capability assessment

six months from the date the DWP determines whether or not you pass the work capability assessment; *or*

- you have been given official notice not to work because of being in contact with an infectious disease; *or*
- you are an inpatient in hospital where you have been medically advised to stay for at least 24 hours, or are recovering from treatment as an inpatient (and the DWP is satisfied that your condition remains sufficiently serious), including if you are attending a residential programme of rehabilitation for drug or alcohol addiction; *or*
- you are receiving plasmapheresis, regular weekly treatment for haemodialysis for chronic renal failure, or regular weekly treatment for total parenteral nutrition for gross impairment of enteric function, or are recovering from such treatment; *or*
- you are pregnant and there is a serious risk to your health or your baby's health if you do not refrain from work.

Note: unlike for ESA, there is no UC rule that treats you as having limited capability for work while you are waiting for the work capability assessment to be carried out.

Are you transferring to universal credit from employment and support allowance?

If you were getting ESA but then claim UC, you automatically have limited capability for work. However, the DWP may wrongly overlook this rule and insist that you have to be assessed again. If this affects you, do the following.

1. Point out the rule and insist that you should be treated as having limited capability for work for UC. If necessary, challenge the decision on your UC entitlement.

2. The DWP may say that it needs to check that you were getting ESA – complain if this is taking a long time. Ultimately, an unreasonably long delay might be challenged by judicial review (see p1446).

3. If you were getting the support component in your ESA, the limited capability for work-related activity element should be included in your UC from your first monthly assessment period.[5]

4. If you were getting the work-related activity component in your ESA, the limited capability for work element should be included in your UC from your first monthly assessment period.[6]

5. Remember that, despite these rules, the DWP can still apply the work capability assessment to you again.

Employment and support allowance

You are automatically treated as having limited capability for work for ESA if:[7]

- you are affected by coronavirus – the same rules apply as for UC (see p1011); *or*
- you are waiting for an assessment or appeal (see p1014); *or*
- you get the support component for one of the eating and drinking descriptors (see p1027); *or*
- you get statutory sick pay for the purpose of the 196-day qualifying period (see p649) for ESA in youth; *or*
- for income-related ESA only, you are in education, you are not a 'qualifying young person' (see p579) and you get income-related ESA because you receive DLA, PIP or armed forces independence payment;[8] *or*
- for contributory ESA only, you get UC and have been assessed as having limited capability for work for UC.[9]

You are treated as having limited capability for work because of your health for ESA if:[10]

- you are pregnant or have recently given birth, you are not entitled to maternity allowance (MA) or statutory maternity pay, you have a medical certificate giving the expected or actual date of birth, and you are within the period beginning with the first day of the sixth week before the expected week of childbirth (or the actual day of childbirth if earlier) and ending on the 14th day after you have the baby; *or*
- you are pregnant and entitled to MA; *or*
- you are pregnant and there is a serious risk to your health or your baby's health if you do not refrain from work; *or*
- you are terminally ill – ie, your death can reasonably be expected within six months; *or*
- you are receiving chemotherapy or radiotherapy treatment for cancer, recovering from such treatment or are likely to receive such treatment within six months from the date the DWP determines whether or not you pass the work capability assessment; *or*
- you have been given official notice not to work because of being in contact with an infectious disease; *or*
- you are an inpatient in hospital where you have been medically advised to stay for at least 24 hours, or are recovering from treatment as an inpatient (and the DWP is satisfied that your condition remains sufficiently serious), including if you are attending a residential programme of rehabilitation for drug or alcohol addiction; *or*
- you are receiving plasmapheresis, regular weekly treatment for haemodialysis for chronic renal failure, or regular weekly treatment for total parenteral nutrition for gross impairment of enteric function, or are recovering from such treatment. The DWP must be satisfied that you should continue to be treated as having limited capability for work. In the first week of such treatment, you

Part 7: National insurance, work and work-related rules
Chapter 45: Limited capability for work
1. The work capability assessment

must be receiving it or recovering from it for at least two days. You continue to be treated as having limited capability for work if your treatment later goes down to one day a week. However, you cannot get income-related ESA in any week in which you work (apart from work you can do while claiming – see p1042), although you can claim contributory ESA for the days of treatment and recovery.[11]

If you are waiting for an assessment or you are appealing

You are treated as having limited capability for work if:[12]

- you are applying for ESA and have provided a current medical certificate, but the work capability assessment has not yet been carried out. You can get ESA while waiting for your assessment. However, this does not apply if you are reclaiming ESA after having failed the work capability assessment, unless your condition has significantly worsened or you have a new health condition. Your condition has significantly worsened if it is considered that you would now be likely to pass the work capability assessment;[13]
- you are appealing against a decision that you have failed the work capability assessment (ie, you were found not to have limited capability for work) and you have submitted a medical certificate. However, unless your current claim for ESA was made before 30 March 2015, this only applies if:
  - this is the first time you have failed the work capability assessment; *or*
  - this the first time you have failed the work capability assessment since a previous decision that you satisfied it (see p1038);
- you are reclaiming ESA and have provided a current medical certificate, after being treated as failing the work capability assessment because you failed to return the ESA50 questionnaire or failed to attend the medical. You can get ESA while waiting for your assessment. However, this only applies if:
  - you have now returned the questionnaire; *or*
  - it is more than six months since the decision treating you as not having limited capability for work; *or*
  - your condition has significantly worsened. Your condition has significantly worsened if it is considered that you would now be likely to pass the work capability assessment;[14] *or*
  - you have a new health condition.

Examples

Julie had back pain and so applied for ESA, but failed the work capability assessment. Later, she develops depression and reclaims ESA, supplying a medical certificate. The DWP accepts that Julie has a new condition, and so treats her as having limited capability for work and pays her ESA while a new work capability assessment is arranged.

Dom claims ESA, but fails the work capability assessment. He requests a mandatory reconsideration of the decision, but it is not changed, so Dom appeals. As this is the first time Dom has failed the work capability assessment and he has supplied a current medical certificate, he is treated as having limited capability for work and so can get ESA while his appeal is pending.

Exceptional circumstances

If you have been assessed under the work capability assessment but do not score sufficient points to have limited capability for work, you are treated as doing so for UC and ESA if:[15]

- you have an uncontrolled or uncontrollable life-threatening disease, and there is medical evidence to show this. There must be reasonable cause for the disease not to be controllable by a recognised therapeutic procedure; or
- because of your illness, there would be a substantial risk to the mental or physical health of any person were you to be found not to have limited capability for work. The 'substantial risk' is one that could arise from the sort of work you may be expected to do, or from the journey to or from work, although it is not necessary to go into the detail of individual job descriptions or potential jobseeker's agreements.[16] However, this exceptional circumstance does not apply to you if the risk could be significantly reduced by reasonable adjustments in your workplace, or by your taking medication prescribed by your doctor.

Treated as not having limited capability for work

Universal credit

For UC, you are treated as *not* having limited capability for work if:[17]

- you have previously failed the work capability assessment, either for UC or for contributory ESA under the UC system ('new-style' ESA). The DWP does not reassess you unless the decision was made in ignorance of, or based on a mistake about, a material fact, or there has been a relevant change in your condition; or
- you do not return the UC50 questionnaire (see p1033), or you do not attend the medical (see p1034) and do not have good reason (see p1033) for this; or
- you work, none of the exceptions in the bullets below apply and your earnings are at or above a certain threshold. This threshold is the level of earnings you would receive for 16 hours' work a week paid at the rate of the national minimum wage for people aged 25 and over, converted to a monthly amount – ie, in 2020/21 earnings at or above £604.58 a month.[18]

You can work and earn above this threshold without automatically being treated as not having limited capability for work if:

- you are entitled to attendance allowance (AA), DLA or PIP (but the DWP may apply the work capability assessment to you); or

Part 7: National insurance, work and work-related rules
Chapter 45: Limited capability for work
1. The work capability assessment

- you have already been assessed as having limited capability for work or as having limited capability for work-related activity (see p1027) under the UC system (not for ESA outside the UC system) (but the DWP may reapply the work capability assessment to you); *or*
- you have been treated under the UC system as having limited capability for work, or for work-related activity, because of your health (see p1011 and p1027), or because an exceptional circumstance applies (see p1015). The DWP cannot apply or reapply the work capability assessment to you.

Are you transferring to universal credit from employment and support allowance?

If you were getting ESA and doing 'permitted work' (see p1043), but then claim UC, it is not clear whether the rules about work described above should apply to you. Bear in mind the following.

1. UC does not have a permitted work rule, but there is no general rule that prevents you from having limited capability for work if you are doing some work.

2. In many situations, your earnings from permitted work will be below the earnings threshold (see above), you are getting PIP or DLA, or you are treated as having limited capability for work (or for work-related activity) because of your health or because an exceptional circumstance applies. In any of these situations, you are *not* automatically treated as not having limited capability for work.

3. In practice, it is understood that the DWP usually accepts that you have limited capability for work at the point you transfer to UC from ESA, but it may consider reapplying the work capability assessment to you.

Employment and support allowance

For ESA, you are treated as *not* having limited capability for work, even if you have been assessed as satisfying the work capability assessment, if you:
- do not return the ESA50 questionnaire (see p1033) or attend the medical (see p1034) while the work capability assessment applies to you, and you do not have good cause (see p1033 and p1034); *or*
- do any work, except certain work you can do while claiming (see p1042);[19] *or*
- are disqualified from receiving contributory ESA for more than six weeks because you are a prisoner. If this applies, but you are entitled to income-related ESA (ie, pending trial, or sentence pending conviction), you are only treated as not having limited capability for work after your entitlement has ended;[20] *or*
- attend a training course and receive a training allowance or premium, unless your ESA claim is for a period beginning after you stopped attending the course, or if the training allowance or premium was only for travelling or meal expenses;[21] *or*

- are (or were) a member of the armed forces and the day in question is a day of sickness absence from duty.[22]

Scoring points

The assessment does not take into account actual jobs, your education or training, or any language or literacy problems. It is a test of your ability to perform certain activities, taking account of a 'specific bodily disease or disablement' or a 'specific mental illness or disablement', and the direct results of medical treatment (from a registered doctor) for these.[23] There are two lists of activities: one physical (see p1018), one mental (see p1023). Under each activity, there is a further list of statements, called 'descriptors', which describe different levels of difficulty in carrying out the activity. Attached to each descriptor is a points score. You are awarded the highest scoring descriptor in each activity that applies to you.

For the physical activities, this takes into account your ability when wearing or using any aid, appliance or prosthesis that you normally wear or use, or any aid or appliance that you could reasonably be expected to wear or use.[24]

To score enough points to satisfy the test, you must score a total of 15 points or more. The points can be scored in one or more activities, and scores from the physical and mental activities can be combined. For example, you can score nine points in the physical test and six points in the mental test.

Good days and bad days, pain and tiredness

Generally, what counts is your capability as it is 'most of the time'. If you cannot repeat an activity without a reasonable degree of regularity, you should be considered unable to perform it. The following points apply.

- Your ability to perform an activity with some degree of repetition should be considered and a 'broad-brush' approach applied, rather than just a day-by-day approach.[25]
- A descriptor should apply to you if you cannot perform the activity most of the time. The severity of your condition, the frequency of your good and bad days and the unpredictability of the bad days are all relevant.[26]
- If you have long periods of remission, you may be considered capable of work during these periods. This depends on the severity of your condition and on the length of your periods of ill health and your periods of remission.[27]
- Pain, fatigue and the increasing difficulty you may have in performing an activity on a repeated basis compared with someone in good health should be taken into account.[28] 'Pain' may include nausea and dizziness.[29]
- Any risk to your health in performing an activity should be considered, particularly if carrying it out is against medical advice. If the risk is sufficiently serious, you may be considered incapable of the activity.[30]

Part 7: National insurance, work and work-related rules
Chapter 45: Limited capability for work
1. The work capability assessment

Physical disabilities

To score points in the physical test, your incapacity must arise from a 'specific bodily disease or disablement'.[31]

Activity one: mobilising

Mobilising unaided by another person with or without a walking stick, manual wheelchair or other aid if such aid is normally used, or could reasonably be worn or used.

Descriptors	Points
a. Cannot, unaided by another person:	15
(i) mobilise more than 50 metres on level ground without stopping in order to avoid significant discomfort or exhaustion; *or*	
(ii) repeatedly mobilise 50 metres within a reasonable timescale because of significant discomfort or exhaustion.	
b. Cannot, unaided by another person, mount or descend two steps even with the support of a handrail.	9
c. Cannot, unaided by another person, either:	9
(i) mobilise more than 100 metres on level ground without stopping in order to avoid significant discomfort or exhaustion; *or*	
(ii) repeatedly mobilise 100 metres within a reasonable timescale because of significant discomfort or exhaustion.	
d. Cannot, unaided by another person, either:	6
(i) mobilise more than 200 metres on level ground without stopping in order to avoid significant discomfort or exhaustion; *or*	
(ii) repeatedly mobilise 200 metres within a reasonable timescale because of significant discomfort or exhaustion.	
e. None of the above applies.	0

Your ability to use a walking stick or manual wheelchair (but not an electric one) or another aid can be taken into account if you normally use one or could 'reasonably' use one. Issues such as your ability to propel and handle a manual wheelchair, and whether one is medically suitable for you, should be taken into account.[32] Official guidance stresses the importance of considering things like fatigue and breathlessness.[33] **Note:** if descriptor 1(a) applies, you also have limited capability for work-related activity (see p1027).

Activity two: standing and sitting

Standing and sitting

Descriptors	Points
a. Cannot move between one seated position and another seated position located next to one another without receiving physical assistance from another person.	15
b. Cannot, for the majority of the time, remain at a work station:	9
(i) standing unassisted by another person (even if free to move around); *or*	
(ii) sitting (even in an adjustable chair); *or*	
(iii) a combination of (i) and (ii), for more than 30 minutes, before needing to move away in order to avoid significant discomfort or exhaustion.	
c. Cannot, for the majority of the time, remain at a work station:	6
(i) standing unassisted by another person (even if free to move around); *or*	
(ii) sitting (even in an adjustable chair); *or*	
(iii) a combination of (i) and (ii),	
for more than an hour before needing to move away in order to avoid significant discomfort or exhaustion.	
d. None of the above applies.	0

Official guidance says that in transferring from one seated position to another, it is reasonable to take into account a transfer board, but not something more specialised, such as a hoist. Your ability to stand does not require you to stand absolutely still, but you must have at least one hand free, so if you need two crutches to stand, this would not count as ability to stand.[34] **Note:** if descriptor 2(a) applies, you also have limited capability for work-related activity (see p1027).

Activity three: reaching

Reaching

Descriptors	Points
a. Cannot raise either arm as if to put something in the top pocket of a coat or jacket.	15
b. Cannot raise either arm to top of head as if to put on a hat.	9
c. Cannot raise either arm above head height as if to reach for something.	6
d. None of the above applies.	0

This activity is about your ability to reach with either arm above waist height. It is not a test of your ability to use your hands or fingers.[35] **Note:** if descriptor 3(a) applies, you also have limited capability for work-related activity (see p1027).

Part 7: National insurance, work and work-related rules
Chapter 45: Limited capability for work
1. The work capability assessment

Activity four: picking up, moving and transferring things

Picking up and moving or transferring by the use of the upper body and arms

Descriptors	Points
a. Cannot pick up and move a 0.5 litre carton full of liquid.	15
b. Cannot pick up and move a one litre carton full of liquid.	9
c. Cannot transfer a light but bulky object such as an empty cardboard box.	6
d. None of the above applies.	0

This activity is about picking up and moving specified objects, but is not a test of your ability to carry them. Problems with your shoulders, neck or back, as well as with your arms, should be taken into account.[36] It may be that you can transfer a bulky cardboard box with just one arm, but this will depend on all the circumstances of your condition.[37] **Note:** if descriptor 4(a) applies, you also have limited capability for work-related activity (see p1027).

Activity five: manual dexterity

Manual dexterity

Descriptors	Points
a. Cannot press a button (such as a telephone keypad) with either hand or cannot turn the pages of a book with either hand.	15
b. Cannot pick up a £1 coin or equivalent with either hand.	15
c. Cannot use a pen or pencil to make a meaningful mark with either hand.	9
d. Cannot single-handedly use a suitable keyboard or mouse.	9
e. None of the above applies.	0

This activity is about your hand and wrist function with work-related tasks, such as using a keypad, or a computer keyboard or mouse. It is not a test of your computer literacy. A 'meaningful mark' can be something very simple such as a signature or tick.[38] Official guidance says that to score points for inability to use a suitable keyboard or mouse, you must be unable to use both the keyboard and mouse. However, there is a conflict in the caselaw about this, and you may be able to argue that your inability to use one of them means you should score points.[39] **Note:** if descriptor 5(a) applies, you also have limited capability for work-related activity (see p1027).

Activity six: making yourself understood

Making self understood though speaking, writing, typing, or other means which are normally or could reasonably be used, unaided by another person

Descriptors	Points
a. Cannot convey a simple message, such as the presence of a hazard.	15
b. Has significant difficulty conveying a simple message to strangers.	15
c. Has some difficulty conveying a simple message to strangers.	6
d. None of the above applies.	0

This activity is about expressing yourself so that you can be understood, but is not restricted to speech. Official guidance mentions brain injury, motor neurone disease, Parkinson's disease and stroke as among possible relevant conditions. If you have communication problems arising from a panic disorder or chronic fatigue syndrome, the guidance suggests scoring points under the mental health assessment instead if your problems are 'purely due to mental health problems'.[40] **Note:** if descriptor 6(a) applies, you also have limited capability for work-related activity (see p1027).

Acitivity seven: understanding communication

Understanding communication by:

(i) verbal means (such as hearing or lip reading) alone;

(ii) non-verbal means (such as reading 16-point print or Braille) alone; *or*

(iii) a combination of (i) and (ii),

using any aid that is normally or could reasonably be used, unaided by another person.

Descriptors	Points
a. Cannot understand a simple message, such as the location of a fire escape, due to sensory impairment.	15
b. Has significant difficulty understanding a simple message from a stranger due to sensory impairment.	15
c. Has some difficulty understanding a simple message from a stranger due to sensory impairment.	6
d. None of the above applies.	0

You may score points in this activity if you have a hearing impairment, a visual impairment or both a hearing and a visual impairment that means you have problems understanding simple communication. Your ability is assessed taking account of things like hearing aids, Braille and large print communication. You may score points if you have problems in understanding either spoken or written communication – you do not need to have problems with both.[41] **Note:** if

Part 7: National insurance, work and work-related rules
Chapter 45: Limited capability for work
1. The work capability assessment

descriptor 7(a) applies, you also have limited capability for work-related activity (see p1027).

Activity eight: navigation and maintaining safety

Navigation and maintaining safety using a guide dog or other aid if either or both are normally or could reasonably be used.

Descriptors	Points
a. Unable to navigate around familiar surroundings, without being accompanied by another person, due to sensory impairment.	15
b. Cannot safely complete a potentially hazardous task such as crossing the road, without being accompanied by another person, due to sensory impairment.	15
c. Unable to navigate around unfamiliar surroundings, without being accompanied by another person, due to sensory impairment.	9
d. None of the above applies.	0

This is a test of your ability to get about safely, if you have a 'sensory impairment'. This usually means impaired sight or hearing, but could include impairment of other senses, or possibly if you have serious balance problems due to Meniere's disease.[42] Your ability is assessed taking into account your guide dog, or other aid if normally used or if it could reasonably be used. This means normally used by you or by people in your situation, acting reasonably in all the circumstances.[43] Official guidance says that you are not assessed as using a guide dog unless you actually have one, and that GPS devices are not considered.[44]

Activity nine: incontinence

Absence or loss of control while conscious leading to extensive evacuation of the bowel and/or bladder, other than enuresis (bedwetting), despite the wearing or use of any aids or adaptations which are normally or could reasonably be worn or used.

Descriptors	Points
a. At least once a month experiences: (i) loss of control leading to extensive evacuation of the bowel and/or voiding of the bladder; *or* (ii) substantial leakage of the contents of a collecting device, sufficient to require cleaning and a change in clothing.	15
b. The majority of the time is at risk of loss of control leading to extensive evacuation of the bowel and/or voiding of the bladder, sufficient to require cleaning and a change in clothing, if not able to reach a toilet quickly.	6
c. Neither of the above applies.	0

This activity is about managing incontinence. Because 'extensive' evacuation of the bowel or bladder is referred to, minor leakage or dribbling do not count. Incontinence that occurs while you are asleep or having a fit or seizure is not covered.[45] The test is meant to deal with issues of personal dignity, so if you have an incontinence problem and because of mobility problems you are unable to reach a toilet before you lose control, you score points, provided this is frequent enough.[46] **Note:** to be assessed as also having limited capability for work-related activity on this activity, you must lose control at least once a week (see p1027).

Activity 10: consciousness during waking moments

Consciousness during waking moments	
Descriptors	Points
a. At least once a week, has an involuntary episode of lost or altered consciousness resulting in significantly disrupted awareness or concentration.	15
b. At least once a month, has an involuntary episode of lost or altered consciousness resulting in significantly disrupted awareness or concentration.	6
c. Neither of the above applies.	0

This activity is about involuntary lost or altered consciousness that results in 'significantly disrupted awareness or concentration'. Because it is in the context of 'during waking moments', it is about problems that occur when you are normally awake. 'Altered' consciousness is regarded as a 'definite clouding of mental faculties resulting in loss of control of thoughts or action'.[47] Official guidance says that dizziness or vertigo are not relevant, unless it is in the context of an epileptic or similar seizure.[48]

Mental disabilities

To score points in the mental disabilities test, your incapacity must arise from a 'specific mental illness or disablement'.[49]

Activity 11: learning tasks

Learning tasks	
Descriptors	Points
a. Cannot learn how to complete a simple task, such as setting an alarm clock.	15
b. Cannot learn anything beyond a simple task, such as setting an alarm clock.	9
c. Cannot learn anything beyond a moderately complex task, such as the steps involved in operating a washing machine to clean clothes.	6
d. None of the above applies.	0

Part 7: National insurance, work and work-related rules
Chapter 45: Limited capability for work
1. The work capability assessment

This is about your ability to learn new tasks – but note that the specified tasks are just examples. If you cannot repeat a task or have to be shown how to do it again, you have not learned it. Official guidance mentions learning disability, organic brain disorder including stroke and receptive dysphasia among possible relevant conditions.[50] **Note:** if descriptor 11(a) applies, you also have limited capability for work-related activity (see p1027).

Activity 12: awareness of everyday hazards

Awareness of everyday hazards (such as boiling water or sharp objects)	
Descriptors	*Points*
a. Reduced awareness of everyday hazards leads to a significant risk of:	15
(i) injury to self or others; *or*	
(ii) damage to property or possessions,	
such that the claimant requires supervision for the majority of the time to maintain safety.	
b. Reduced awareness of everyday hazards leads to a significant risk of:	9
(i) injury to self or others; *or*	
(ii) damage to property or possessions,	
such that the claimant frequently requires supervision to maintain safety.	
c. Reduced awareness of everyday hazards leads to a significant risk of:	6
(i) injury to self or others; *or*	
(ii) damage to property or possessions,	
such that the claimant occasionally requires supervision to maintain safety.	
d. None of the above applies.	0

This activity is about your ability to recognise risks from common hazards, such as boiling water or sharp objects. A wide range of conditions could be relevant here: learning difficulties or conditions affecting concentration, including the detrimental effects of medication, or from brain injury or other neurological conditions affecting self-awareness. It may also apply if you have a severe depressive illness or a psychotic disorder and as a result of that have a significant reduction in your attention and concentration, although the official guidance says it is unlikely to apply to anxiety disorders.[51] **Note:** if descriptor 12(a) applies, you also have limited capability for work-related activity (see p1027).

Activity 13: initiating and completing personal action

Initiating and completing personal action (which means planning, organisation, problem solving, prioritising or switching tasks)

Descriptors	Points
a. Cannot, due to impaired mental function, reliably initiate or complete at least two sequential personal actions.	15
b. Cannot, due to impaired mental function, reliably initiate or complete at least two sequential personal actions for the majority of the time.	9
c. Frequently cannot, due to impaired mental function, reliably initiate or complete at least two sequential personal actions.	6
d. None of the above applies.	0

The 'personal action' is about planning, organisation, problem solving, prioritising and switching tasks. There is no definition of 'personal action' and a common sense approach should be taken, so it should include things like cooking, dressing, washing and brushing your teeth, planning a simple meal, and dealing with finances and appointments.[52] You must be able to carry out the personal action 'reliably'. In one case, someone with obsessive compulsive disorder who took an excessive amount of time to complete at least two actions was found not to be able to 'reliably' complete them.[53] **Note:** if descriptor 13(a) applies, you also have limited capability for work-related activity (see p1027).

Activity 14: coping with change

Coping with change

Descriptors	Points
a. Cannot cope with any change to the extent that day to day life cannot be managed.	15
b. Cannot cope with minor planned change (such as a pre-arranged change to the routine time scheduled for a lunch break), to the extent that, overall, day to day life is made significantly more difficult.	9
c. Cannot cope with minor unplanned change (such as the timing of an appointment on the day it is due to occur), to the extent that, overall, day to day life is made significantly more difficult.	6
d. None of the above applies.	0

Official guidance says that this activity is about your ability to deal with changes in routine. Possible relevant conditions include moderate/severe learning disability, autistic spectrum disorder, brain injury, obsessive compulsive disorder, severe anxiety or psychotic illness.[54] Inability to cope could be indicated by a

Part 7: National insurance, work and work-related rules
Chapter 45: Limited capability for work
1. The work capability assessment

number of responses, including stress reactions and the need for another person to intervene.[55] **Note:** if descriptor 14(a) applies, you also have limited capability for work-related activity (see p1027).

Activity 15: getting about

Getting about	
Descriptors	*Points*
a. Cannot get to any place outside the claimant's home with which the claimant is familiar.	15
b. Is unable to get to a specified place with which the claimant is familiar, without being accompanied by another person.	9
c. Is unable to get to a specified place with which the claimant is unfamiliar without being accompanied by another person.	6
d. None of the above applies.	0

This activity is about your ability to go out without being helped by someone else. It takes account of problems from conditions like learning difficulties, severe anxiety and agoraphobia, rather than physical health problems which are considered in Activities one and eight. Use of a mobile phone app should not be taken into account.[56]

Activity 16: coping with social engagement

Coping with social engagement due to cognitive impairment or mental disorder	
Descriptors	*Points*
a. Engagement in social contact is always precluded due to difficulty relating to others or significant distress experienced by the claimant.	15
b. Engagement in social contact with someone unfamiliar to the claimant is always precluded due to difficulty relating to others or significant distress experienced by the claimant.	9
c. Engagement in social contact with someone unfamiliar to the claimant is not possible for the majority of the time due to difficulty relating to others or significant distress experienced by the claimant.	6
d. None of the above applies.	0

The problems taken into account in this activity are those arising from 'cognitive impairment or mental disorder'. To score points, your social engagement must be restricted due to 'difficulty relating to others or significant distress'. Autism could be relevant here, but so could other conditions – eg, anxiety, depression and personality disorder. The activity is supposed to be a test of your ability to engage with others in a working environment, so should not be limited to socialising, but should include things like reciprocity, give and take, initiation and response.[57] **Note:** if descriptor 16(a) applies, you also have limited capability for work-related activity (see below).

Acitivity 17: appropriateness of behaviour with other people

Appropriateness of behaviour with other people, due to cognitive impairment or mental disorder

Descriptors	*Points*
a. Has, on a daily basis, uncontrollable episodes of aggressive or disinhibited behaviour that would be unreasonable in any workplace.	15
b. Frequently has uncontrollable episodes of aggressive or disinhibited behaviour that would be unreasonable in any workplace.	15
c. Occasionally has uncontrollable episodes of aggressive or disinhibited behaviour that would be unreasonable in any workplace.	9
d. None of the above applies.	0

This activity considers problems due to 'cognitive impairment or mental disorder'. Merely being disinhibited or angry is not enough. Alcohol abuse, for example, does not count by itself, but if you are assessed as having alcohol (or drug) dependency, or a condition like autism or psychotic illness, the consequences for your behaviour may count.[58] All the descriptors look at whether you have 'uncontrollable episodes of aggressive or disinhibited behaviour which would be unreasonable in any workplace'. The behaviour could be physical but also verbal – eg, serious verbal aggression.[59] **Note:** if descriptor 17(a) applies, you also have limited capability for work-related activity (see below).

Limited capability for work-related activity

The work capability assessment includes an assessment of whether you have limited capability for work-related activity. This is to decide whether your disability is so severe or your health is so poor that, in addition to not being able to work, you cannot be expected to do things like attend work-focused interviews or retraining. For UC, if you have limited capability for work-related activity, you are said to have 'limited capability for work and work-related activity'.[60]

The test decides whether you are entitled to a limited capability for work-related activity element in your UC (see p72) and whether you are in the 'support group' for ESA (see p652). If you have claimed HB as well as ESA, it is used to decide whether you are entitled to a support component in your HB (see p354). See below for details of the assessment.

You may automatically count as having limited capability for work-related activity, or you may be required to complete a questionnaire and/or attend a

Part 7: National insurance, work and work-related rules
Chapter 45: Limited capability for work
1. The work capability assessment

medical. If you do not return the questionnaire or take part in the medical and do not have 'good reason' ('good cause' for ESA), you are treated as not having limited capability for work-related activity.

When deciding whether you have good reason/good cause, the DWP must take into account:[61]
- whether you were outside Great Britain at the time you were notified;
- your state of health;
- the nature of any disability you have;
- any other matter it thinks appropriate.

Assessing limited capability for work-related activity

To have limited capability for work-related activity, your mental or physical condition must be such that one or more statements (or 'descriptors') describing a severe limitation in certain activities could be applied to you (see below).

A descriptor applies if it applies to you for the majority of the time(s) you try to do the activity described. You are assessed wearing any prosthesis that you are normally fitted with or wear, and/or using any aid or appliance that you normally wear or use, or could reasonably be expected to wear or use.[62]

Some descriptors are about physical incapacity. To have them applied to you, your incapacity must arise from 'a specific bodily disease or disablement'. Other descriptors are about mental incapacity. To have them applied to you, your incapacity must arise from 'a specific mental illness or disablement'.[63]

The DWP may retest you to find out whether there has been a relevant change of circumstances, to see whether a previous finding was wrong or mistaken, or (for ESA only) if it is three months or more since your last test.[64]

You may be required to complete a questionnaire and/or attend a medical examination.

Activity	Descriptors
1. Mobilising unaided by another person with or without a walking stick, manual wheelchair or other aid if such aid is normally, or could reasonably be, worn or used.	Cannot either: (a) mobilise more than 50 metres on level ground without stopping in order to avoid significant discomfort or exhaustion; or (b) repeatedly mobilise 50 metres within a reasonable timescale because of significant discomfort or exhaustion.
2. Transferring from one seated position to another.	Cannot move between one seated position and another seated position located next to one another without receiving physical assistance from another person.

Activity	Descriptors
3. Reaching.	Cannot raise either arm as if to put something in the top pocket of a coat or jacket.
4. Picking up and moving or transferring by the use of the upper body and arms (excluding standing, sitting, bending or kneeling and all other activities specified in this Schedule).	Cannot pick up and move a 0.5 litre carton full of liquid.
5. Manual dexterity.	Cannot press a button (such as a telephone keypad) with either hand or cannot turn the pages of a book with either hand.
6. Making self understood through speaking, writing, typing, or other means which are normally, or could reasonably be, used unaided by another person.	Cannot convey a simple message, such as the presence of a hazard.
7. Understanding communication by: (i) verbal means (such as hearing or lip reading) alone; (ii) non-verbal means (such as reading 16 point print or Braille) alone; *or* (iii) a combination of (i) and (ii), using any aid that is normally, or could reasonably be, used unaided by another person.	Cannot understand a simple message, such as the location of a fire escape, due to sensory impairment.
8. Absence or loss of control while conscious leading to extensive evacuation of the bowel and/or voiding of the bladder, other than enuresis (bed-wetting), despite the wearing or use of any aids or adaptations which are normally, or could reasonably be, worn or used.	At least once a week experiences: (a) loss of control leading to extensive evacuation of the bowel and/or voiding of the bladder; *or* (b) substantial leakage of the contents of a collecting device, sufficient to require the individual to clean themselves and change clothing.
9. Learning tasks.	Cannot learn how to complete a simple task, such as setting an alarm clock, due to cognitive impairment or mental disorder.

Part 7: National insurance, work and work-related rules
Chapter 45: Limited capability for work
1. The work capability assessment

Activity	Descriptors
10. Awareness of hazard.	Reduced awareness of everyday hazards, due to cognitive impairment or mental disorder, leads to a significant risk of: (a) injury to self or others; *or* (b) damage to property or possessions, such that the claimant requires supervision for the majority of the time to maintain safety.
11. Initiating and completing personal action (which means planning, organisation, problem solving, prioritising or switching tasks).	Cannot, due to impaired mental function, reliably initiate or complete at least two sequential personal actions.
12. Coping with change.	Cannot cope with any change, due to cognitive impairment or mental disorder, to the extent that day to day life cannot be managed.
13. Coping with social engagement, due to cognitive impairment or mental disorder.	Engagement in social contact is always precluded due to difficulty relating to others or significant distress experienced by the claimant.
14. Appropriateness of behaviour with other people, due to cognitive impairment or mental disorder.	Has, on a daily basis, uncontrollable episodes of aggressive or disinhibited behaviour that would be unreasonable in any workplace.
15. Conveying food or drink to the mouth.	(a) Cannot convey food or drink to the claimant's own mouth without receiving physical assistance from someone else; (b) Cannot convey food or drink to the claimant's own mouth without repeatedly stopping or experiencing breathlessness or severe discomfort; (c) Cannot convey food or drink to the claimant's own mouth without receiving regular prompting given by someone else in the claimant's physical presence; *or* (d) Owing to a severe disorder of mood or behaviour, fails to convey food or drink to the claimant's own mouth without receiving: (i) physical assistance from someone else; *or* (ii) regular prompting given by someone else in the claimant's presence.

Activity	Descriptors
16. Chewing or swallowing food or drink.	(a) Cannot chew or swallow food or drink; (b) Cannot chew or swallow food or drink without repeatedly stopping, experiencing breathlessness or severe discomfort; (c) Cannot chew or swallow food or drink without repeatedly receiving regular prompting given by someone else in the claimant's presence; *or* (d) Owing to a severe disorder of mood or behaviour, fails to: (i) chew or swallow food or drink; *or* (ii) chew or swallow food or drink without regular prompting given by someone else in the claimant's presence.

Treated as having limited capability for work-related activity

You are treated as having limited capability for work-related activity because of your health if:[65]

- you have a terminal illness – ie, your death can reasonably be expected within six months; *or*
- you are receiving chemotherapy or radiotherapy treatment for cancer, or are recovering from that treatment, or you are likely to receive such treatment within six months from the date the DWP determines whether or not you have limited capability for work-related activity. In any of these circumstances, the DWP must be satisfied that you have limited capability for work-related activity. When deciding this, the decision maker should take into account the medical evidence to see if your cancer treatment has side effects which are likely to limit your ability to carry out work-related activity;[66] *or*
- because of a specific disease or disablement, there would be a substantial risk to your mental or physical health or to the mental or physical health of someone else if you were found not to have limited capability for work-related activity; *or*
- you are pregnant and there would be a serious risk of damage to your health or to your baby's health if you do not refrain from work-related activity and, for UC only, from work; *or*
- for UC only, you have reached pension age (see p271) and are entitled to AA, the highest rate of the DLA care component or the enhanced rate of the PIP daily living component.

Part 7: National insurance, work and work-related rules
Chapter 45: Limited capability for work
1. The work capability assessment

In addition, for UC only, you are automatically treated as having limited capability for work-related activity if you are transferring to UC from ESA and you had, or were treated as having, limited capability for work-related activity for ESA – ie, you were entitled to the support component in your ESA.[67]

Are you transferring to universal credit from employment and support allowance?

If you were getting ESA and were assessed as having limited capability for work-related activity, but then claim UC, you automatically have limited capability for work-related activity. However, the DWP may wrongly overlook this rule and insist that you have to be assessed again. If this affects you, do the following.

1. Point out the rule and insist that you should be automatically treated as having limited capability for work-related activity for UC. If necessary, challenge the decision on your UC entitlement.

2. The DWP may say that it needs to check that you were getting ESA – complain if this is taking a long time. Ultimately, an unreasonably long delay might be challenged by judicial review (see p1446).

3. The limited capability for work-related activity element should be included in your UC from your first monthly assessment period.[68]

4. Remember that, despite these rules, the DWP can still apply the work capability assessment to you again.

The work capability assessment process

Information is sought from your doctor and, unless you are treated as having limited capability for work (see p1011), you are sent a questionnaire (UC50 or ESA50) to complete. In most cases, you are required to attend a medical examination at an assessment centre with a doctor (or other approved healthcare professional) from the DWP medical service. Assessments are carried out on behalf of the DWP medical service by the Health Assessment Advisory Service. For official information about the assessment, such as having an audio recording of your medical, using an interpreter and the location of assessment centres, see chdauk.co.uk. For advice about the questionnaire and medical, see p1033 and p1034.

As part of the work capability assessment, the doctor (or other approved healthcare professional) also carries out an assessment of whether you have limited capability for work-related activity.

There are no rules on how often you are reassessed. Usually, this is decided by the DWP medical service. If you are assessed as having limited capability for work-related activity (see p1027) and having a 'severe, lifelong' disability or condition and are 'unlikely to ever be able to move into work', you will not be reassessed.[69]

The questionnaire

Unless it is already accepted that you have limited capability for work, or you are treated as having limited capability for work, you are sent a questionnaire (UC50 or ESA50) to complete.

How do you complete the questionnaire?

1. Read the notes on the form before answering the questions. It may be helpful to draft your answers on a separate sheet of paper first.

2. If someone has to complete the questionnaire for you, or if you can only do so yourself slowly or with pain, explain this.

3. Make sure to list all your symptoms. If you have to appeal, the First-tier Tribunal may be less likely to believe you have symptoms if you did not mention them on the questionnaire. Ask someone who knows you well to check your answers.

4. If you have good and bad days, explain this. If possible, give a rough estimate of how often you could perform the activity and how often you could not.

5. Compare the draft of your answers with the list beginning on p1018 and work out your score. Your answers should not be exaggerated, but check that you have not underestimated any of your problems and that you have given all the detail you can.

6. If you have any difficulties with English or with reading and writing, get independent help before you submit the form.

7. If someone has helped you fill out the form, include her/his details at the end where the form asks about this.

8. Always make a copy of your questionnaire with your answers before returning it.

You have four weeks from the date the questionnaire is sent to complete and return it. A reminder must be sent to you at least three weeks after the questionnaire was sent. You must then be given a further week from the date the reminder was sent to return the questionnaire. If you still do not return it in time, you are treated as not having limited capability for work, unless you can show that you had a good reason (for ESA, good cause) for not returning it on time.[70]

Good cause and good reason

When deciding whether you have **'good cause'**, the DWP must consider all the circumstances, including whether you were outside Great Britain at the relevant time, your state of health and the nature of your disability.[71] There is no equivalent rule for deciding whether you have **'good reason'** for UC, but in practice the same sort of issues should be taken into account.

If you are late in completing and returning the questionnaire, do so as soon as you can and explain why you were late. If your benefit stops because you are considered not to have had good reason/cause, but you think you did, consider

Part 7: National insurance, work and work-related rules
Chapter 45: Limited capability for work
1. The work capability assessment

challenging the decision (see p1036). It is understood that 'safeguarding' procedures apply if you are considered to be 'vulnerable' – eg, if you have a serious mental health condition. The safeguarding procedures are not a legal requirement, but involve extra checks before treating you as not having limited capability for work. If you think you are vulnerable, ask whether the safeguarding procedures were applied to you. You should also make a fresh claim for benefit. If the DWP decides that you did not have a good reason/cause, you can appeal (see Chapter 57).

On receiving your completed questionnaire, the DWP considers whether you should be treated as having limited capability for work or whether you clearly score enough points to satisfy the test. If neither of these apply, a medical examination is arranged.

Medical examinations

You may be required to attend a medical examination as part of the work capability assessment. Bear in mind the following.

- If you fail to attend a medical examination without a good reason (for ESA, good cause), you are treated as not having limited capability for work.
- If you cannot attend the medical, contact your assessment centre immediately to explain why and ask for another appointment.
- If you are too ill to travel, ask to be examined at home.
- You can claim your travel expenses for going to the medical. If you have to attend by taxi or minicab, you cannot claim for your fares unless your assessment centre agrees to this before you travel.
- You can take a friend or adviser to the medical with you.
- The medical examiner takes into account the information on your questionnaire, what you tell her/him, and your appearance and behaviour during the assessment.

In order to complete the medical report, the medical examiner asks about your condition and assesses whether, in her/his opinion, you have limited capability for work. S/he considers your abilities in each of the specific areas of activity.

The medical examiner asks about your typical day and uses the information to assess your ability to perform the activities in the work capability assessment. Make sure to tell the examiner about things like good and bad days and what medication you are taking. S/he then completes a report (a UC85 or ESA85), indicating which descriptors s/he thinks apply to you, and sends it to the DWP.

Failing to attend a medical examination

If you do not attend a medical examination without a good reason (good cause for ESA), you are treated as not having limited capability for work – ie, you fail the work capability assessment. You must have been sent notice of the date and time of the medical at least seven days beforehand, unless you agreed to accept less than this.[72]

Good reason and good cause

When deciding whether you have **'good cause'** for ESA, the DWP must consider all the circumstances, including those that apply to the questionnaire (see p1033). 'Good cause' may also include being too ill or distressed on the day of the medical, or wishing to be examined by someone of the same sex and this was not possible. You may also be able to show that you had good cause if your refusal to attend was based on a firm religious conviction.[73] In practice, the same sort of things should be taken into account when deciding whether you have **'good reason'** for UC.

If your benefit stops because you are considered not to have good reason/cause for failing to attend the medical, but you think you did, consider challenging the decision (see p1036). It is understood that 'safeguarding' procedures apply if you are considered to be 'vulnerable' – eg, if you have a serious mental health condition. The safeguarding procedures are not a legal requirement, but involve extra checks before treating you as not having limited capability for work. If you think you are vulnerable, ask whether the safeguarding procedures were applied to you. You should also make a fresh claim for benefit. If the DWP does not accept that you had good cause/reason, consider appealing (see Chapter 57).

The decision

The decision on whether or not you have limited capability for work is made by a DWP decision maker. The decision maker can disagree with the medical report, although in practice this is unusual. The medical examiner includes in the medical report a suggested date when the work capability assessment should be applied to you again in order to retest your capability. You cannot appeal about how often you are retested.

If the decision maker does not consider that you have limited capability for work, you may still be entitled to some UC if your claim was for UC. If your claim was for ESA, you are not entitled to ESA. If you have been getting ESA, your award is revised or superseded (see Chapter 56) and your benefit is stopped.

What should you do next?

1. If you have been refused ESA (but do not want to challenge the decision) and do not have a job to return to, to get means-tested help in most cases you will need to claim UC. A claim for UC ends your entitlement to any other means-tested benefits you are getting. For more on when you come under the UC system, see p23.

2. For both UC and ESA, if you think you are not well enough to work, you may be able to challenge the decision by appealing to the First-tier Tribunal (see Chapter 57). You must apply for a mandatory reconsideration first.

Part 7: National insurance, work and work-related rules
Chapter 45: Limited capability for work
2. Challenging a decision

3. If you challenge the decision and your claim was for UC, you may still be entitled to some UC, but will not get elements for limited capability for work or work-related activity. If your claim was for ESA, you cannot get ESA while your request for a mandatory reconsideration is being considered, but you may subsequently be able to get ESA pending an appeal. In most cases, you cannot make a new claim for IS or income-based JSA, and will need either to wait to get ESA pending an appeal, or claim UC instead (see p23). If you claim UC (or make a new claim for JSA), this terminates any entitlement you may have to income-related ESA, even if your challenge is successful. Once you have appealed, if this is the first time you have been found not to have limited capability for work because you have failed the work capability assessment, or the first time since a previous decision that you pass it, and you have also submitted a medical certificate, you can get ESA again (instead of UC, JSA or IS) pending the appeal, without having to make a new claim. However, if this is the second or subsequent time that you have failed the work capability assessment, see p1037.

2. Challenging a decision

You can challenge a decision by applying for a revision or supersession (see Chapter 56), or by making an appeal (see Chapter 57). You must apply for a mandatory reconsideration before you can appeal.

Initially, the DWP makes a 'determination' on your limited capability for work.[74] The determination should then be incorporated into a decision about your entitlement to benefit or national insurance (NI) credits for limited capability for work. You only have a right of appeal once this is included in a decision.[75]

Appeals are considered by the First-tier Tribunal, which must include a medically qualified person (see p1370). The tribunal does not have to follow either the UC85 or ESA85 medical report or the DWP's decision.

When you appeal against a decision, the whole decision can be looked at again if it is considered right to do so. So the tribunal might decide to look at an aspect of the decision that you are happy with and do not want changed. This could result in your losing some, or even all, of your entitlement. The tribunal should give you a warning if it wants to look at an aspect of the decision that you do not want changed.

Are you appealing?
1. Get advice from one of the organisations listed in Appendix 1.
2. Remember that there are only certain circumstances in which you can work and still be regarded as having limited capability for work (see p1010). If you work while you are appealing, you may lose entitlement to benefit, even if you eventually win your appeal.

3. Request a copy of the medical evidence that the DWP holds on your file. If you appeal, a copy of the medical report should be included in the appeal papers that the DWP sends to you and HM Courts and Tribunals Service.

4. Request an oral hearing of your appeal. This will give the tribunal the opportunity to hear from you first hand about how your condition affects you, and what happened at the medical examination.

5. Discuss your limited capability for work with your own doctor. In practice, it can be very difficult to win an appeal if your GP or consultant does not support you.

6. Get medical evidence to support your appeal, if you can. This could be from your GP or your consultant, or from both. It is more helpful if this comments on the things at issue in your appeal rather than just setting out your diagnosis and treatment. Check whether your doctor insists on charging you.

7. If you cannot get medical evidence yourself, consider using previous medical reports if you passed the work capability assessment and getting evidence from other sources – eg, a community nurse or an occupational therapist. You could ask the tribunal to obtain further medical evidence, although in practice, it may refuse.[76]

8. The tribunal should make a decision based on all the evidence – medical and non-medical. If necessary, point out that it can prefer your own or your doctor's evidence to that of the medical examiner.[77]

9. DWP medical reports are in electronic form. These may have inconsistencies or errors in them. The tribunal must deal with any discrepancies and take these into account when considering the weight to be given to different sources of evidence.[78]

10. The tribunal cannot carry out its own examination of you.[79] However, be aware that it may observe your conduct in the room – eg, how you walk or sit.

11. Consider asking a person who lives with you or who knows you well to attend the hearing to describe the day-to-day problems you have.

12. Take a list of any medication you are taking to the hearing.

Getting benefit while challenging a decision

You can continue to get universal credit (UC) while your request for a mandatory reconsideration is being considered and while your appeal is pending.

If you have been refused employment and support allowance (ESA) because you have failed the work capability assessment, you cannot get ESA while your request for a mandatory reconsideration is being considered. You may be able to get one of the following instead – but also see the note below:

- UC (see p1040); *or*
- jobseeker's allowance (JSA) (see p1040); *or*
- income support (IS) (see p1040).

Note: unless you are prevented by law from claiming UC (and so cannot come under the UC system), you cannot make a new claim for income-based JSA or IS

Part 7: National insurance, work and work-related rules
Chapter 45: Limited capability for work
2. Challenging a decision

(see p23). If you are not prevented from claiming UC, a claim for UC or for JSA or ESA (of any kind) will bring you under the UC system (see p23). That will mean that you can no longer get income-based JSA or income-related ESA, even if your challenge of the ESA decision is successful.

Once you have appealed, you may be able to get ESA while your appeal is pending (see below) – you do not need to make a new claim. This is usually the best option, if you are able to get ESA. You cannot get income-related ESA pending your appeal if you have claimed UC or JSA (income-based or contribution-based) and so have come under the UC system. Getting ESA pending your appeal does *not* mean that you come under the UC system, as it does not require a new claim to be made,[80] although there are cases where the DWP has wrongly said that it does involve a new claim.

Example

Jim was getting income-related ESA, but this stops when he fails the work capability assessment. Jim requests a mandatory reconsideration of the decision, and decides to claim JSA in the meantime. Jim is not prevented from claiming UC. As Jim has made a new claim for JSA, he now comes under the UC system, cannot get income-based JSA, and must claim UC instead.

Jim then appeals and gets UC while his ESA appeal is pending. Jim's appeal against the work capability assessment is eventually successful, but he remains on UC and does not go back to income-related ESA. If Jim had decided not to claim JSA, once he appealed he may have been able to get income-related ESA pending his appeal instead of having to claim UC.

Getting employment and support allowance while appealing

If (after your mandatory reconsideration) you appeal against a decision that you do not have limited capability for work for ESA and it is the first such decision you have had, or the first since a previous decision that you have limited capability for work, and you have submitted a medical certificate, you are entitled to ESA until the First-tier Tribunal makes its decision.[81] You cannot get ESA pending an appeal if you are being *treated as* not having limited capability for work because you did not return the questionnaire or attend the medical (see p1033 and p1034).

Once you have appealed, the government has said that your ESA pending an appeal can cover the period when your request for a mandatory reconsideration was being considered.[82]

However, you cannot get ESA pending an appeal if the decision that you do not have limited capability for work is the second, or a subsequent, such decision you have had in a row and the decision you are appealing against is about a claim made on or after 30 March 2015.

Examples

Megan claims ESA in June 2020. She is found not to have limited capability for work – ie, she fails the work capability assessment. Megan challenges this by asking for a mandatory reconsideration, but the decision is not changed. She then appeals and sends in a medical certificate. Megan gets ESA pending the appeal as this is the first time she has failed the work capability assessment, and has not made a new claim for UC or JSA.

Alex claimed ESA in June 2019. He was found not to have limited capability for work (ie, he failed the work capability assessment), but he appealed and successfully challenged this. The tribunal decided that he had limited capability for work and he was paid ESA. In May 2020, Alex has another work capability assessment, and fails it. After a mandatory reconsideration, Alex appeals again and sends in a medical certificate. Alex gets ESA pending the appeal: although he has failed the work capability assessment for a second time, it is the first time that he has done so since a prevous decision (ie, that of the tribunal) that he does have limited capability for work, and he has not made a new claim for UC or JSA.

If you have limited capability for work, but are appealing about whether or not you should be put in the support group, you remain entitled to ESA while your request for a mandatory reconsideration is being considered and while your appeal is pending. However, the amount you are paid does not include the support component.

Note:
- To get ESA pending an appeal, you must continue to submit medical certificates. You do not need to make a new claim for ESA.[83]
- ESA pending an appeal does not include an additional component, although it can include any premiums and housing costs to which you are entitled.[84]
- You are treated as having limited capability for work while you are appealing, so usually the DWP does not assess you in this period. However, if you develop a new condition or your condition significantly worsens, the DWP can assess you again. If it determines that you have limited capability for work, you can get ESA in the normal way (including either of the additional components) from that point on. The First-tier Tribunal still considers your appeal for the period up until then. Even if the DWP determines that you do not have limited capability for work, you remain entitled to ESA pending the appeal.[85]
- If your appeal is successful, the original decision about your limited capability for work is changed so that you are entitled to ESA. Your ESA continues in the normal way, and you can qualify for an additional component.
- If your appeal is successful but the DWP considers that your condition improved while the appeal was pending, it might decide that you do not have limited capability for work now.[86] You can appeal against this decision, and should be able to get ESA pending the appeal again.[87]

Part 7: National insurance, work and work-related rules
Chapter 45: Limited capability for work
2. Challenging a decision

- If you lose your appeal, the original decision that you do not have limited capability for work is not changed. From the week after the week in which the First-tier Tribunal notifies the DWP of its decision, the DWP treats you as not having had limited capability for work while you were getting ESA pending your appeal.[88] Your entitlement to ESA therefore stops, although you keep the ESA that was paid to you pending the appeal. Although you can appeal against the decision to treat you as not having limited capability for work, the prospect of success is likely to be limited, as the rules allow the DWP to do this when you have lost your appeal. To continue to get ESA in this situation, whether you appeal or not, you must make a fresh claim.[89]
- If you lose your appeal and make a new claim for ESA, you cannot be treated as having limited capability for work (and so get ESA while waiting for a work capability assessment) unless your condition has significantly worsened or you have a new health condition.

Getting jobseeker's allowance or income support while challenging a decision

Generally, it is not possible to make a new claim for income-based JSA or IS. However, you can make a new claim (and get IS or income-based JSA during both your mandatory reconsideration and your appeal) if you are are prevented by law from claiming UC (see p23). If you are not prevented from claiming UC, then if you claim JSA (income-based or contribution-based) you will come under the UC system (see p23), so that you cannot get income-based JSA or income-related ESA, even if you win your appeal.

Getting universal credit while challenging a decision

Generally, you can get UC while challenging a decision. If you make a new claim for UC, you come under the UC system (see p23) and you cannot get income-related ESA again, even if your challenge is successful and you were originally on income-related ESA.

You can get UC while you are waiting for your request for a mandatory reconsideration to be considered and once you have appealed. You may still be able to get contributory ESA or contribution-based JSA under the UC system. You may be subject to work-related requirements while you are appealing (see Chapter 46). If your challenge is successful, your UC can then include a limited capability for work element, if you can still get it, or a limited capability for work-related activity element if that applies.[90] If your challenge is unsuccessful, you may still be able to get UC, but will not be entitled to a limited capability for work or limited capability for work-related activity element.

If your condition worsens

For UC, once there has been a decision that you do not have limited capability for work, there is no further work capability assessment, unless there is evidence to suggest that the decision was made in ignorance of, or based on a mistake about, a material fact, or there has been a relevant change in circumstances regarding your condition.[91]

For ESA, if your condition has significantly worsened since the decision, or you have a new condition, and you are not already getting ESA pending the appeal, you could make a new claim for ESA – but see the note below. In this situation, you should be treated as having limited capability for work until a new work capability assessment is carried out (see p1011).

Note: if you make a new claim for ESA, you come under the UC system unless you are prevented from claiming UC (see p23). If you come under the UC system, you cannot get income-related ESA. You can get UC instead. You may still be able to get contributory ESA.

If you are already getting ESA pending the appeal, you could inform the DWP and ask it to make a determination on your limited capability for work. If the DWP thinks that you still fail the work capability assessment, your entitlement to ESA after the appeal has been decided could be affected, even if you win your appeal.

3. **Periods of limited capability for work**

A 'period of limited capability for work' for employment and support allowance (ESA) generally means a period in which you have, or are treated as having, limited capability for work. It does not include any period not covered by your claim for ESA.[92] However, see the linking rules below. There are no rules on periods of limited capability for work for universal credit.

Linking rules

Different periods of limited capability for work can be joined or 'linked' to form one continuous period for ESA. The effect is that you are treated as having had limited capability for work throughout the whole of the linked period. Different periods are linked if they are not more than 12 weeks apart.[93]

If periods of limited capability for work are linked, it means that:

- the question of whether or not you satisfy the national insurance contribution conditions for ESA may be decided at the beginning of the first period (see p980);[94]
- you do not have to serve further 'waiting days' (see p662) before becoming entitled to ESA because you have already served them;
- you may get one of the additional ESA components straight away, or once you have been reassessed as passing the work capability assessment;
- for the purposes of the rules on housing costs, certain linking rules apply (see p375).

Part 7: National insurance, work and work-related rules
Chapter 45: Limited capability for work
4. Work you can do while claiming employment and support allowance

4. **Work you can do while claiming employment and support allowance**

The general rule is that you cannot work and be entitled to employment and support allowance (ESA) at the same time.[95] With certain exceptions (see below), in any week in which you work (paid or unpaid), you are not entitled to ESA and you are automatically treated as not having limited capability for work, even if it has previously been decided that you do.[96]

However, you are only treated as not entitled to ESA on the actual days that you work, rather than the whole week, if you work:

- during the first week of your claim; *or*
- during the last week in which you had limited capability for work or were treated as having limited capability for work.[97]

It is arguable that work that is so minimal that it can be regarded as trivial or negligible[98] should be ignored.

You can do certain work without automatically being treated as not having limited capability for work. For how earnings from this may affect income-related ESA, see p429. **Note:** earnings under the 'permitted work' rules (see p1043) that are under the relevant earnings limit are ignored for ESA.

You can do the following:[99]

- work as a local councillor;
- work (for a maximum of one day or two half days a week) as a member of the First-tier Tribunal if you have been appointed because of your experience of disability issues;
- domestic work (eg, cooking and cleaning) in your own home;
- caring for a relative (see p1043);
- caring for another person living with you under specific legislation relating to accommodating children or temporarily caring for someone else if you are paid for this;
- caring for someone provided with 'continuing care' by a local authority under section 26A of the Children (Scotland) Act 1995, where you get payments for that;
- work you do to protect someone or prevent serious damage to property or livestock during an emergency;
- work done while receiving assistance in pursuing self-employment under section 2 of the Employment and Training Act 1973 or section 2 of the Enterprise and New Towns (Scotland) Act 1990 (test-trading);
- voluntary work that is not for a relative (see p1043), provided the only payment you receive is to cover your reasonable expenses and it is considered reasonable for you to work free of charge;

- work done in the course of a work placement (unpaid work experience with an employer), approved in writing by the DWP before the placement starts;
- for contributory ESA, any work you do in a week in which you are treated as having limited capability for work because you are receiving plasmapheresis, regular weekly treatment for haemodialysis for chronic renal failure, regular weekly treatment for total parenteral nutrition, or are recovering from such treatment (see p1013);[100]
- 'permitted work' (see below).

Relatives

A '**relative**' is a grandparent, grandchild, uncle, aunt, nephew, niece, and includes '**close relatives**' – ie, parent, parent-in-law, son, son-in-law, daughter, daughter-in-law, step-parent, stepson, stepdaughter, brother, sister, or the partner of any of these.

Note: you can work and still be entitled to universal credit (UC). However, if you earn more than a set monthly amount from work, you may be treated as not having limited capability for work or the DWP may reassess you (see p1015). If you are doing permitted work for contributory ESA and also also claiming UC, for UC your earnings from that work are treated in the same way as any other earnings from work (see p116).

Permitted work

'Permitted work' (sometimes called 'exempt' work) is work of any kind, which you can do while on ESA:[101]

- as part of a treatment programme done under medical supervision while you are in hospital or regularly attending hospital as an outpatient, provided you do not earn more than £140 a week; *or*
- for an unlimited period, provided you do not earn more than £20 a week. This is called the 'permitted work lower limit'; *or*
- for an unlimited period, provided you do not earn more than £140 a week and you are in 'supported (sometimes called 'supervised') work' (see below); *or*
- for an unlimited period, where you work on average less than 16 hours a week and in any week you do not earn more than £140 a week. This is called the 'permitted work higher limit'. For how your hours are calculated, see p993.

Supported work

'**Supported work**' is work which is supervised by someone employed by a public or local authority, or by a voluntary organisation or community interest company, whose job it is to find work for people with disabilities. This could include work in a sheltered workshop or with help from social services. The DWP usually says that you need not have the person working alongside you, although the support should be ongoing and regular. Where possible, check in advance that the DWP agrees that the work counts as supported work.

Part 7: National insurance, work and work-related rules
Chapter 45: Limited capability for work
Notes

If your earnings in any week are higher than the relevant limit, you are not entitled to ESA for that week.[102] Your earnings are worked out for this purpose in the same way as for income-related ESA (see p421), except that only your own earnings count, not those of your partner. Only your earnings count, not any other kind of income.

Although there are no special rules, you must inform the DWP, in advance if possible, about any permitted work you do. The DWP asks you to complete Form PW1ESA, available at gov.uk/government/publications/employment-and-support-allowance-permitted-work-form. If the particular activities you carry out in your work suggest that your limited capability for work might have changed, the DWP might reassess this.

Notes

1. The work capability assessment
1   **UC** Reg 39 and Schs 8 and 9 UC Regs
    ESA Regs 20, 25 and 26 ESA Regs; regs 16, 22 and 26 ESA Regs 2013
2   Reg 39(1)(a) UC Regs
3   Regs 19(2) and 21(2) UC(TP) Regs
4   Reg 39(6) and Sch 8 UC Regs
5   Reg 19(4) UC(TP) Regs
6   Reg 19(2) UC(TP) Regs, with savings regarding pre-April 2017 as in the ESAUC(MA) Regs
7   Regs 20, 25 and 26 ESA Regs; regs 16, 22 and 26 ESA Regs 2013
8   Reg 33(2) ESA Regs
9   Reg 16(1)(h) ESA Regs 2013
10 Regs 20, 25, 26 and 33 ESA Regs; regs 16, 22 and 26 ESA Regs 2013
11 Regs 26, 44 and 46 ESA Regs; regs 22, 38 and 40 ESA Regs 2013; Vol 8 Ch 42, paras 42049-58 DMG
12 Reg 30 ESA Regs; reg 26 ESA Regs 2013
13 *EI v SSWP (ESA)* [2016] UKUT 397 (AAC)
14 *EI v SSWP (ESA)* [2016] UKUT 397 (AAC)
15 **UC** Sch 8 paras 4 and 5 UC Regs
    ESA Reg 29 ESA Regs; reg 25 ESA Regs 2013
16 *Charlton v SSWP* [2009] EWCA Civ 42; *JW v SSWP* [2011] UKUT 416 (AAC)
17 Regs 41, 43 and 44 UC Regs
18 Reg 41(2) and (3) UC Regs
19 Reg 44 ESA Regs; reg 37 ESA Regs 2013

20 Reg 159 ESA Regs; reg 95 ESA Regs 2013
21 Reg 32(2) ESA Regs; reg 27 ESA Regs 2013
22 Reg 32(1) ESA Regs; reg 27(1) ESA Regs 2013
23 **UC** Regs 39 and 42 UC Regs
    ESA Reg 19 ESA Regs; reg 15 ESA Regs 2013
24 **UC** Reg 42(2) UC Regs
    ESA Reg 19(4) ESA Regs; reg 15(4) ESA Regs 2013
25 *AF v SSWP (ESA)* [2011] UKUT 61 (AAC); *SAG v Department for Social Development (ESA)* [2011] NICom 171
26 CIB/14534/1996
27 CIB/2620/2000
28 CIB/14587/1996; CIB/14722/1996; CIB/13161/1996; CIB/13508/1996
29 CIB/14722/1996
30 CSIB/12/1996
31 **UC** Reg 39(4) UC Regs
    ESA Reg 19(5) ESA Regs; reg 15(5) ESA Regs 2013
32 *SI v SSWP (ESA)* [2014] UKUT 308 (AAC), reported as [2015] AACR 5; *AR v SSWP (ESA)* [2013] UKUT 417 (AAC)
33 WCA Handbook para 3.2.2
34 WCA Handbook para 3.2.3
35 WCA Handbook para 3.2.4

36 *TO'B v SSWP (ESA)* [2011] UKUT 461
   (AAC); *AG v SSWP (ESA)* [2018] UKUT
   137 (AAC)
37 *KH v SSWP (ESA)* [2014] UKUT 455 (AAC)
38 *SSWP v LH (ESA)* [2017] UKUT 475 (AAC)
39 WCA Handbook para 3.2.5; *CL v SSWP
   (ESA)* [2013] UKUT 434 (AAC) holds that
   inability to use keyboard or a mouse is
   sufficient, *DG v SSWP (ESA)* [2014] UKUT
   100 (AAC) holds that inability to use
   both is required.
40 WCA Handbook para 3.2.8
41 WCA Handbook para 3.2.9
42 *SSWP v AI* (rule 17) (ESA) [2017] UKUT
   346 (AAC)
43 CIB/1499/1996
44 WCA Handbook para 3.2.7
45 WCA Handbook para 3.2.10
46 *EM v SSWP (ESA)* [2014] UKUT 34 (AAC)
47 *CB v SSWP (ESA)* [2015] UKUT 287
   (AAC)
48 WCA Handbook para 3.2.11
49 **UC** Reg 39(4) UC Regs
   ESA Reg 19(5) ESA Regs; reg 15(5) ESA
   Regs 2013
50 WCA Handbook para 3.5.2
51 WCA Handbook para 3.5.3
52 *MP v SSWP (ESA)* [2015] UKUT 458
   (AAC); WCA Handbook para 3.5.4
53 *MW v SSWP (ESA)* [2014] UKUT 112
   (AAC)
54 WCA Handbook para 3.5.5
55 *GV v SSWP (ESA)* [2013] UKUT 405
   (AAC)
56 WCA Handbook para 3.5.6; *TM v SSWP
   (ESA)* [2018] UKUT 9 (AAC)
57 *JC v SSWP (ESA)* [2014] UKUT 352 (AAC),
   reported as [2015] AACR 6
58 WCH Handbook para 3.5.8; *DR v SSWP
   (ESA)* [2014] UKUT 188 (AAC); [2014]
   AACR 38
59 *WC v SSWP (ESA)* [2014] UKUT 363
60 Reg 40 UC Regs
61 Regs 36-39 ESA Regs; regs 34-36 ESA
   Regs 2013
62 **UC** Reg 42(2) UC Regs
   ESA Reg 34(3) ESA Regs; reg 30(3) ESA
   Regs 2013
63 **UC** Reg 40(3) UC Regs
   ESA Reg 34(6) ESA Regs; reg 30(6) ESA
   Regs 2013
64 **UC** Reg 41 UC Regs
   ESA Reg 34 ESA Regs; reg 30 ESA Regs
   2013
65 **UC** Sch 9 UC Regs
   ESA Reg 35 ESA Regs; reg 31 ESA Regs
   2013
66 paras 42057 and 42365 DMG

67 Reg 19(4) UC(TP) Regs
68 Reg 19(4) UC(TP) Regs
69 DWP, *Employment and Support
   Allowance and Universal Credit: changes
   to the work capability assessment from 29
   September 2017*, September 2017
70 **UC** Reg 43 UC Regs
   ESA Reg 22 ESA Regs; reg 18 ESA Regs
   2013
71 Reg 24 ESA Regs; reg 18 ESA Regs 2013
72 **UC** Reg 44 UC Regs
   ESA Reg 23 ESA Regs; reg 19 ESA Regs
   2013
73 R(S) 9/51; CIB/3117/2008

2. Challenging a decision
74 **UC** Reg 39 UC Regs
   ESA Reg 19 ESA Regs; reg 15 ESA Regs
   2013
75 Vol 1 Ch 6, para 06041 DMG
76 s20 SSA 1998; R(S) 3/84
77 CIB/407/1998; CIB/1149/1998; R(M)
   1/93; CIB/3074/2003
78 CIB/511/2005
79 s20(3) SSA 1998
80 Reg 3(j) SS(C&P) Regs
81 Reg 30(1) and (3) ESA Regs; reg 26(1)
   and (3) ESA Regs 2013
82 House of Commons, *Hansard*, Written
   Answers, 16 December 2013, col 486W
83 Reg 30(3) ESA Regs; reg 26(3) ESA Regs
   2013; reg 3(j) SS(C&P) Regs; reg 7
   UC,PIP,JSA&ESA(C&P) Regs
84 Reg 5(4) ESA Regs; reg 6(5) ESA Regs
   2013 provides that the assessment
   phase applies, pending the First-tier
   Tribunal's decision.
85 Reg 147A(2) and (4) ESA Regs; reg 87(2)
   and (4) ESA Regs 2013
86 Reg 147A(6) and (7) ESA Regs; reg 87(7)
   and (8) ESA Regs 2013
87 This is because the DWP will have made
   a determination that you do not have
   limited capability for work, and not
   merely treated you as not having limited
   capability for work, so reg 30(3) ESA
   Regs and reg 26(3) ESA Regs 2013
   should apply.
88 Reg 147A(5) ESA Regs; reg 87(5) ESA
   Regs 2013
89 Reg 3(j) SS(C&P) Regs; Memo DMG 33/
   10, para 52; reg 7
   UC,PIP,JSA&ESA(C&P) Regs
90 Art 24 WRA(No.9)O
91 Reg 41(4) UC Regs

Part 7: National insurance, work and work-related rules
Chapter 45: Limited capability for work
Notes

3. Periods of limited capability for work
92 Reg 2, definition of 'period of limited
    capability for work', ESA Regs
93 Regs 2 and 145 ESA Regs; regs 2 and 86
    ESA Regs 2013
94 paras 1-3 Sch 1 WRA 2007

4. Work you can do while claiming
   employment and support allowance
95 Reg 40 ESA Regs; reg 37 ESA Regs 2013
96 Regs 40 and 44 ESA Regs; regs 37 and
    38 ESA Regs 2013
97 Reg 40(4) ESA Regs; reg 37(4) ESA Regs
    2013
98 CIB/5298/1997; CIB/6777/1999
99 Regs 40 and 45 ESA Regs; regs 37 and
    39 ESA Regs 2013
100 Reg 46 ESA Regs; reg 40 ESA Regs 2013
101 Reg 45 ESA Regs; reg 39 ESA Regs 2013
102 Regs 40(1) and (2)(f) and 45 ESA Regs;
    regs 37(2)(f) and 39 ESA Regs 2013

Chapter 46

Universal credit work-related requirements

This chapter covers:
1. The claimant commitment (below)
2. The work-related requirements (p1050)
3. Which requirements apply (p1059)

This chapter covers your responsibilities if you come under the universal credit (UC) system. If you do not come under the UC system, see Chapter 48.

Key facts
- If you come under the universal credit (UC) system, to qualify for UC, contribution-based jobseeker's allowance or contributory employment and support allowance, you must usually accept a 'claimant commitment'.
- There are work-related requirements, some or all of which you may have to meet. These are: work-focused interviews, work preparation, work search and work availability.
- If you do not meet the work-related requirements which apply to you, you may be given a sanction. Your benefit is then paid at a reduced (or nil) rate. However, you may qualify for UC hardship payments (see Chapter 52).

1. The claimant commitment

If you come under the universal credit (UC) system (see p23), you must usually accept a claimant commitment to qualify for UC, contribution-based jobseeker's allowance (JSA) and contributory employment and support allowance (ESA).[1] If you are claiming UC jointly with your partner, both of you must usually accept a claimant commitment.[2] If you are required to accept one and do not do so, you are not entitled to UC, JSA or ESA.

You *can* qualify for UC, contribution-based JSA or contributory ESA without accepting a claimant commitment if the DWP considers that you cannot accept one because you lack the capacity to do so, or there are exceptional circumstances

Part 7: National insurance, work and work-related rules
Chapter 46: Universal credit work-related requirements
1. The claimant commitment

which mean it would be unreasonable to expect you to accept one at the moment – eg, you are likely to be in hospital for several weeks or there is a domestic emergency. If you are terminally ill, you should not be required to accept a claimant commitment.[3] If you lack capacity, the DWP may refer your claim to see whether an appointee is needed (see p1170). Your appointee is not required to accept a claimant commitment on your behalf. If you already have an appointee, this does not automatically mean that you lack capacity, though it may indicate that you do.[4] The DWP should make a decision based on all the available evidence.[5]

The claimant commitment is a record of your responsibilities while you are receiving benefit.[6] It must include:[7]

- the work-related requirements you must meet (see p1059); *and*
- any other information the DWP thinks is appropriate to include.

Note:

- Specific work-related requirement actions may be stated elsewhere on your online account – ie, not only in your commitments section. If so, it should always be made clear what is mandatory.
- Even if you do not have to meet any work-related requirements, your claimant commitment explains your other responsibilities – eg, to report changes in your circumstances.

Work coaches

Job centre staff who support and interview you if you are claiming benefits under the UC system are called '**work coaches**'. Your work coach draws up your claimant commitment and discusses your responsibilities with you. Decisions about what you have to do to meet your work-related responsibilities cannot be changed by a revision, supersession or an appeal, but you can negotiate, ask for a second opinion and/or a review or ask to speak to a manager. If necessary, you can complain. From 19 March 2020 for at least three months, you will not usually be required to meet you work coach in person.

Accepting your claimant commitment

You must accept the most up-to-date version of your claimant commitment using the method specified by the DWP. This could be online, by telephone or in writing.[8] Be sure to use the method specified or you may not count as accepting the claimant commitment. For example, even if you have attended a commitments meeting, you may still need to accept your claimant commitment via your online journal.

If no work-related requirements are to be imposed on you, or you only have to attend work-focused interviews, your first claimant commitment is usually accepted as part of the normal claims process.[9] Otherwise, your claimant commitment is drawn up by your work coach for you to accept. Most claimants need to attend a commitments meeting to discuss their circumstances. Ensure that you inform your work coach of any problems you may have in meeting the work-related requirements and that any limitations you are allowed (see p1057) are put on record.

Note:

- You should be given a 'cooling-off' period of up to seven days if you refuse to accept a claimant commitment, to give you the chance to reconsider.[10]
- If you are not happy with your claimant commitment, you may be able to get it reviewed (see p1050).

The DWP specifies a time within which you must accept your claimant commitment. If you accept it within that time, you are usually treated as accepting it on the date of your claim (or any date to which your claim has been backdated).[11] However, if you are awarded UC or ESA without making a claim, you are treated as accepting it on the first day of the first assessment period (for UC) or the first benefit week (for ESA) of your benefit award. You can request a second opinion on whether the requirements in your commitment are reasonable before you accept them.[12]

The time within which you must accept your claimant commitment (including one that has been updated) can be extended, if:

- for UC and JSA, you ask the DWP to review any action that it has been proposed you take as a work search or work availability requirement, or whether there should be any limitations on these requirements;[13]
- for ESA, you ask for an extension.[14]

The DWP must be satisfied that your request is reasonable. Be careful not to miss any time limits specified by the DWP for accepting your claimant commitment as this may delay the start of your entitlement to benefit. Even if you are not happy with your claimant commitment, it may be better to agree to it and make it clear that you will comply. You can then ask for a review (see p1050).

Has your claim been closed because you have not attended a commitments meeting?

If your claim is closed because you have failed to attend a commitments meeting, this is a decision that you are not entitled to UC. You should contact the DWP as soon as possible to avoid your claim being refused in this way and explain any additional needs you have. Otherwise, your claim may be closed on the day after the appointment. If you have additional needs (eg, English is not your first language, or you have literacy difficulties or a disability), the DWP should help you to rebook your appointment.[15] If your claim is closed, this is a refusal to award you UC and you can ask for a written explanation of the decision. You should be advised of your right to challenge the decision by mandatory reconsideration and appeal.[16] You should also consider submitting a new claim in the meantime.

Part 7: National insurance, work and work-related rules
Chapter 46: Universal credit work-related requirements
2. The work-related requirements

Reviewing your claimant commitment

Your claimant commitment can be reviewed and updated as the DWP thinks fit.[17] This is done on an ongoing basis to record any changes to the expectations placed on you and the consequences for failing to comply with them. See p1049 for when the time for accepting your claimant commitment can be extended if you ask for a review.

Guidance suggests your claimant commitment should be reviewed after any change in your circumstances.[18] You can ask for your claimant commitment to be reviewed and updated at any time. If the DWP agrees to review it, you should do everything possible to comply with the work-related requirements that have been imposed on you while a review is being considered. It is important to make it clear that you intend to do so. Keep a record of what you have done and any reasons you have for not being able to comply fully.

You cannot appeal a decision about your claimant commitment. If you think a decision is unreasonable, you can complain and continue to negotiate. See cpag.org.uk/welfare-rights/judicial-review for a template letter you may be able to use if the commitments are unreasonable for your circumstances.

2. The work-related requirements

If you come under the universal credit (UC) system (see p23), you may have to meet work-related requirements, even if you are in paid work.[19] There are some situations when no work-related requirements can be imposed on you (see p1061). See pp1059–74 for which (if any) requirements may apply.

If you do not meet the requirements, you continue to be entitled to benefit, but you may be given a sanction and your benefit may be paid at a reduced (or nil) rate (see Chapter 47). For information on avoiding a sanction, see p1079. **Note:** if you are entitled to UC and also to contribution-based jobseeker's allowance (JSA) or contributory employment and support allowance (ESA), you only need to meet one set of work-related requirements – those for UC.[20]

The work-related requirements are:
- work-focused interviews (see p1051);
- work preparation (see p1051);
- work search (UC and JSA only – see p1053); *and*
- work availability (UC and JSA only – see p1056).

Note: you may also have to attend other interviews connected to the work-related requirements while you are entitled to UC, contribution-based JSA or contributory ESA (see p1059).

Your work-related requirements and the specific actions you must take may be set out in your claimant commitment, or may be notified to you in some other way.[21] You should not be sanctioned if the DWP has not given you proper notification of a requirement which allows you to understand what you have to do and the consequences of not complying.[22]

Work-focused interviews

If a work-focused interview requirement is imposed on you, you must take part in one or more work-focused interviews – ie, interviews relating to work or work preparation.[23] You may also have to participate in other interviews for any purpose connected to the work-related requirements (see p1059).

For UC and ESA, you are usually required to have a 'health and work conversation' with your work coach before your work capability assessment (see p1010). The health and work conversation is a type of work-focused interview about the help you may need to get into work in the future. You do not need to have a health and work conversation in certain circumstances where it would not be appropriate – eg, if you have a terminal illness. The conversation can also be deferred – eg, because of medical treatment.

The DWP tells you how, when and where a work-focused interview is to take place. It should also tell you the reason for the interview, in basic terms, and the consequences of failing to participate.[24] A work-focused interview may:[25]

- assess your prospects for obtaining or remaining in work (and/or, for UC, more or better paid work);
- assist or encourage you to obtain or remain in work (and/or, for UC, more or better paid work);
- identify activities you can undertake and opportunities for training, education or rehabilitation that will make it more likely that you will obtain or remain in work (and/or, for UC, more or better paid work);
- for UC, determine whether you are in gainful self-employment (see p123) or whether you are in a 'start-up period' (see p123);
- identify current or future work opportunities that are relevant to you.

Note: for at least three months from 19 March 2020, all requirements to attend the job centre are suspended. All the interviews mentioned in this chapter will be carried out in other ways where possible. Do not attend the job centre unless your appointment explicitly tells you to do so.

Inform the DWP if you have any particular needs – eg, you have literacy difficulties, English is not your first language or you are disabled. You should be offered a home visit or telephone interviews if appropriate.

Work preparation

If a work preparation requirement is imposed on you, you must take 'particular action' specified by the DWP that makes it more likely that you will obtain paid work, more paid work or better paid work.[26]

Part 7: National insurance, work and work-related rules
Chapter 46: Universal credit work-related requirements
2. The work-related requirements

> ### Particular action
>
> For these purposes, **'particular action'** includes attending a skills assessment, improving personal presentation, participating in training or in an employment programme, undertaking work experience or a work placement and developing a business plan.[27] The DWP must make it clear if you are required to participate in any work preparation activity, and explain the consequences if you fail to participate. **Note:** employment programmes provided by, or for, the Scottish government are voluntary and you cannot be sanctioned if you do not participate.

If you have a disability

If you have a disability or health condition that affects the work you can do, you may be able to get specialist employability support for 12 months. This is intensive support and training to help disabled people into work. For further information, see gov.uk/specialist-employability-support. You need to contact Jobcentre Plus to be assessed for the scheme. Your work-related requirements are not affected by participation in the scheme, although your work coach may agree that it counts towards your work preparation. The Work and Health Programme (see p1152) is also available to disabled people (the DWP says this is voluntary unless you have been out of work and claiming unemployment benefits for two years[28]). In Scotland, there are voluntary programmes you can consider under the Fair Start Scotland scheme. You cannot be sanctioned if you fail to participate in an employment support scheme provided by, or for, the Scottish government.

Your health condition or disability should always be considered when deciding what you have to do as work preparation, including any adjustments you need.

If you are aged 18 to 21

If you are 18 to 21 years old, unemployed and must meet all the work-related requirements for UC (see p1069), you receive intensive support from the first day of your claim. Once you have been getting UC for six months, if you are still unemployed, you will be offered a traineeship (or equivalent in Scotland or Wales), a place on a sector-based work academy (work experience with local employers) or other work experience. This activity does not prevent you from receiving UC.[29] The options are voluntary, although if you choose the sector-based work academy option there are mandatory elements to participation, which should be explained to you. The DWP refers to the scheme for 18–21-year-olds as the 'Youth Obligation Support Programme'.

Your work-related requirements (including the Youth Obligation) can be temporarily suspended in certain circumstances[30] – eg, if you are handing in fit notes, or you have recently been bereaved or experienced domestic violence. If you choose to take part in employment support services provided by, or for, the Scottish government, these are voluntary and you cannot be sanctioned if you do not participate. However, your work coach may refer you to work-related activity which is mandatory as part of the Youth Obligation.

Work search

If a work search requirement is imposed on you, you are expected to take 'all reasonable action' (see below) to obtain paid work, more paid work or better paid work. You must also take any 'particular action' specified by the DWP.[31]

Particular action

For these purposes, '**particular action**' includes carrying out work searches, applying for jobs, creating and maintaining an online profile, registering with an employment agency and seeking references.[32] The DWP can specify the amount of time you must spend doing any 'particular action'.

Note: if you are told to apply for a particular job vacancy, you are treated as failing to meet the work search requirement if you are offered an interview for the vacancy and do not participate.[33] The DWP must give you adequate notice of what you are required to do, and explain the consequences of failing to comply. You do not have to be available for work for a minimum of three months from 30 March 2020.

All reasonable action

In general, you are expected to look for work, regardless of its type or the salary. However, certain limitations can apply to the work you are available for and seeking to do (see p1057).

To count as taking 'all reasonable action' to find paid work, more paid work or better paid work, you must take action that gives you the best prospects of obtaining work. If you are unemployed, this will usually include making job applications. You must normally spend a specified number of hours in each week seeking work – ie:[34]

- at least the weekly number of hours you are expected to work (your 'expected hours' – see p1054), minus any deductions the DWP allows (see p1054); *or*
- fewer hours than your 'expected hours', provided the DWP is satisfied that you have taken all reasonable action. For example, if you have been offered a job to start the following week, you may have completed all reasonable action despite having spent fewer than your expected hours on searching for work. Alternatively, you may have an unavoidable situation which has prevented you from spending more hours on your work search.[35] Make sure the DWP is aware of any particular circumstances that affected your work search.

Part 7: National insurance, work and work-related rules
Chapter 46: Universal credit work-related requirements
2. The work-related requirements

Your expected hours

You are normally expected to spend 35 hours a week looking for work (your 'expected hours'). However, a lower number of expected hours applies in some cases. This is the number that the DWP thinks is:[36]

- for UC, compatible with your caring responsibilities, if you are a 'responsible carer' (see p1063) of a child who has not yet reached compulsory school age – ie, aged three or four. The DWP says that the expectation will normally be 16 hours a week;[37]
- compatible with your child's normal school hours (including travelling time to and from school), if you are a 'responsible carer' (or, for JSA only, a 'responsible foster carer') for a child under 13. For UC, your child must have reached compulsory school age. The DWP says that the expectation will normally be 25 hours a week.[38] 'Responsible foster carer' is not defined, but it should apply if you are a 'responsible foster parent' (see p1063);
- compatible with your caring responsibilities, if you are a 'relevant carer', a 'responsible carer' (for UC, for a child aged 13 or over) or a 'responsible foster parent (see p1062 for the definitions), and the DWP is satisfied that you have reasonable prospects of obtaining paid work, more paid work or better paid work;
- reasonable in the light of your 'physical or mental impairment'.

If you think that your expected hours are too high given your health, disability or caring responsibilities, you can negotiate with your work coach and ask for a review (see p1050). Make it clear that you will comply with your current hours if at all possible. You cannot appeal a decision about your expected hours of work search. If negotiation is unsuccessful, you can complain, but get advice first if possible. If negotiation and complaining are not successful, it may be appropriate to consider sending a judicial review pre-action letter (see p1418).[39] Keep a record of the requests you make to vary your expected hours (eg, by asking via your online journal and taking a screenshot), even if they are not changed.

The DWP can agree deductions from your expected hours of work search for time you spend:[40]

- carrying out paid work; *or*
- carrying out voluntary work. You can do as much voluntary work as you wish, but this can only ever count towards 50 per cent of your expected hours; *or*
- carrying out a work preparation requirement or 'voluntary work preparation' – ie, action that you agree with the DWP to take on a voluntary basis to make it more likely you will obtain paid work, more work or better paid work; *or*
- dealing with temporary childcare responsibilities, a domestic emergency, funeral arrangements or other temporary circumstances. You should not be sanctioned if you temporarily reduce your hours of work search because of this type of unavoidable circumstance,[41] but you should try to agree this with your work coach or inform the DWP as soon as possible. In some cases, your work

coach could decide to suspend your work search requirement completely for a temporary period (see p1073).

Examples

Kathy is getting contribution-based JSA. She is looking for shop work. To get relevant experience, she volunteers in a charity shop for 10 hours a week. Her expected hours are 35 hours a week. However, she need only spend 25 hours a week looking for work because the DWP agrees to deduct the 10 hours during which she is doing voluntary work.

Jim and Bill are joint UC claimants. Jim spends a lot of time caring for Bill who is on long-term sick leave. All of the work-related requirements are imposed on Jim. No work-related requirements are imposed on Bill because he has limited capability for work-related activity. Jim counts as a 'relevant carer' (see p1063) and his expected hours are 16 hours a week (the hours the DWP is satisfied are compatible with his caring responsibilities). He is therefore meant to look for work for 16 hours a week.

Proving you are searching for work

Always keep careful records of the steps you take to find work or get more hours/pay. The DWP may give you a form on which to do this, or you may be expected to keep a record of your activity on your UC account. The DWP may require you to verify what you have done.[42]

How do you prove you are searching for work?

1. Check your claimant commitment to ensure you understand what the DWP expects you to do each week. You must be able to give details of the action you have taken (eg, at an interview with your work coach), so it is extremely important that you keep a record of your attempts to get a job. However, the DWP should accept that it will not always be possible to provide evidence of your work search – eg, employers do not always respond and some of your work search may be done via face-to-face conversations which you cannot prove took place.[43]

2. Make a note every time you do anything that may count as work search. Include the dates and times, who you spoke to and what was said. You should do this online if you have been asked to do so as part of your UC journal.

3. Keep copies of any letters or emails you send, of any advertisements to which you reply and of any job applications you make. If you deliver your CV or a job application by hand, ask for a receipt as proof. Make notes of job searches you do online, including when you use the government's online 'Find a job' service. If your job search is mainly recorded online, take screenshots of relevant activity.

4. Tell the DWP if you have difficulty using a computer, or in reading or writing, or with the English language. You should still try to present proof of your work search – eg, by getting a friend or relative to help you compile your record of jobseeking steps. The DWP should

Part 7: National insurance, work and work-related rules
Chapter 46: Universal credit work-related requirements
2. The work-related requirements

consider what is reasonable for you in the light of all your circumstances and consider whether you need additional support.[44]

5. Sometimes your activities to seek work may be looked at more intensively than usual, possibly over several previous weeks, so ensure they are always sufficient. Do not rely on the fact that your activities have so far not been challenged by the job centre.

6. The 'Find a job' service shows the jobs that have been suggested for you and the jobs for which you have applied. The DWP may ask you to allow it to access your account to check on what you have been doing. Although using 'Find a job' is not a requirement of UC or JSA, if you do not use it the DWP may decide that you are not taking 'all reasonable action'.

7. If the DWP has suggested jobs that you have not applied for, your work coach may question whether you meet the work search requirement. It is therefore best to follow up suggestions and apply for jobs, even if you think they are not appropriate. If you do not meet the requirements of a job (eg, it requires a driving licence and you do not have one), you should point this out to your work coach and could also consider a complaint, but it is still best to apply to avoid a sanction.

Work availability

If a work availability requirement is imposed on you, you must be able and willing immediately to:[45]

- take up paid work, more paid work or better paid work; *and*
- attend an interview in connection with obtaining paid work, more paid work or better paid work.

You may be able to limit the work you are available for and seeking to do.

Note: for JSA, you are treated as *not* having met the work availability requirement if you are a prisoner on temporary release under specified provisions.[46] You do not have to be available for work for a minimum of three months from 30 March 2020.

Able and willing to take up work or attend an interview immediately

Being *willing* to work is essentially a test of your attitude – your desire and willingness to work. You must usually be immediately willing and able to attend an interview offered to you in connection with obtaining paid work.[47] It must be lawful for you to work in Great Britain.[48] There must be nothing to prevent you from receiving offers of interviews or job offers (eg, because you are away from home for a short time), and nothing to prevent you from acting on them straight away, with the following exceptions. You are allowed:[49]

- **up to one week** to take up work if you are doing voluntary work, if the DWP is satisfied you need longer;
- **up to one month** to take up work if you are a 'responsible carer' or a 'relevant carer' (see p1063 for the definitions), if the DWP is satisfied you need longer, taking into account alternative care arrangements;

- **until after your notice period** has passed if you are working and you have a duty under employment law, or under the terms of your contract, to give your employer notice that you are leaving work.

In all the situations above, you can also be given **up to 48 hours' notice to attend an interview** in connection with obtaining work. If you cannot arrange to attend an interview because you are employed, you should argue that the law only requires you to attend an interview if you are able to do so.

Even if no work search requirement can be imposed on you for a period, you must still be able and willing to take up paid work or attend an interview immediately, once the circumstances that exempt you from the work search requirement no longer apply, and, in some cases, if the DWP thinks it is reasonable, *before* the circumstances that exempt you from looking for work no longer apply. See p1069 for periods of sickness and p1073 for other circumstances where no work search requirement can be imposed.

Holidays

There is no provision for taking a holiday from work search and work availability in UC or in JSA under the UC system.

Limitations on availability and search for work

You can limit the work you are available for and seeking to do, provided the DWP is satisfied that certain conditions apply. You can limit:[50]
- the type of work (see below);
- the number of hours a week, or the times, you can work (see p1058);
- the rate of pay (see p1058);
- the location of the work (see p1058).

You may be able to agree limits on your availability for either an indefinite or a limited period.

The type of work

You can limit the type of work in the following circumstances.[51]
- If you have previously done work of a particular type, you can limit your work search and availability to work of a similar type for up to three months from your date of claim (or, if you were exempt from work-related requirements while getting UC because you had sufficient earnings, from the date you cease paid work if this is later). The DWP must be satisfied that you still have a reasonable prospect of getting work despite the limitation. Ensure you understand when the period starts and ends.
- If you have a 'physical or mental impairment' that has a substantial adverse effect on your ability to do work of a particular type or in particular locations,

Part 7: National insurance, work and work-related rules
Chapter 46: Universal credit work-related requirements
2. The work-related requirements

you do not have to be available for or look for such work. You do not have to show that you have a reasonable prospect of getting work.

DWP guidance says that you can also limit the type of work you look for because of sincerely held beliefs – eg, on religious or conscientious grounds. However, you must show you have reasonable prospects of finding work despite the restriction.[52]

The number of hours

You are normally expected to search for work for at least 35 hours a week (see p1054 for the rules about your 'expected hours' of work search), but you may be expected to be *available* for work of up to 48 hours. However, if you are a 'relevant carer' or a 'responsible carer' (see p1063 for the definitions), or you have a 'physical or mental impairment', your expected hours are lower, and in this situation the hours you are expected to search for work and to be available for work are the same.[53]

There may be times when you have taken 'all reasonable action' (see p1053) to find work even though your hours of work search are lower than the expected number, providing you can show what you have done gives you the best prospects of finding work.[54]

The rate of pay

If you have previously done work at a particular rate of pay, you can limit your work search and availability to work for a similar rate of pay for up to three months from your date of claim (or if you were exempt from work-related requirements while getting UC because you had sufficient earnings, from the date you cease paid work if this is later), if the DWP is satisfied that you still have a reasonable prospect of getting work despite the limitation.[55] Ensure you understand when the period starts and ends.

The location of the work

You can limit the location of the work you must search for and be available to do.[56] However, in general, the following apply.
- You need only be available for, and to look for, work in locations that are no more than 90 minutes travel time from your home in either direction. When looking at travel time, the DWP should take into account the frequency of public transport and any disability or health condition you have, which may mean travelling independently takes you longer than it would do otherwise. Your ability to travel may also be affected by your caring responsibilities. In the case of responsible carers of young children, DWP guidance suggests that travel-to-work time should be proportionate to work search requirements – eg, reduced to 60 minutes each way if your expected hours are 16 a week.[57] As the responsible carer of a child, you can negotiate an even shorter expected travel

time based on your circumstances if you can show that you still have a reasonable prospect of work.

- If you have a 'physical or mental impairment' that has a substantial adverse effect on your ability to do work in particular locations (eg, you cannot manage stairs), you do not have to be available for work or to look for work in those locations.

The effect of the rules on minimum working conditions

The rules about minimum working conditions (see Appendix 7) can affect your claim for UC or JSA if you are looking for work. You can insist that you are only available for work that meets these conditions (ie, that you will not accept a job if the terms do not comply with the legal requirements) – eg, if an employer is offering a job at less than the minimum wage. However, the DWP says that you can be sanctioned for failing to apply for a zero-hour contract, as these are not unlawful as long as the employer allows you to take work with other employers.[58] However, you should consider a complaint if you are told to apply for job without guaranteed hours which is inappropriate for your circumstances – eg, because you have childcare responsibilities.

Other interviews

The DWP can require you to participate in an interview for any purpose connected to any of the work-related requirements – ie, to:[59]
- impose a work-related requirement on you; or
- verify that you have complied with a work-related requirement; or
- assist you to comply with a work-related requirement.

At the interviews, you may be asked to provide evidence and information. You may also be asked to report any changes in your circumstances that are relevant to your work-related requirements and your compliance with them. You must be informed of an interview and made aware of the consequences of failing to attend and take part (you cannot be sanctioned for failing to attend or participate unless you received proper notification).[60] This can be provided in a written document (letter or claimant commitment), online (eg, via your UC journal), face to face, by text, by email or by telephone. The DWP should keep a record of how and when you were notified and what you were told in case there is a dispute about whether you were correctly informed.[61]

---

3. **Which requirements apply**

Many people must meet *all* the work-related requirements (see p1069). However:
- in some cases, work-related requirements cannot be imposed on you (see p1061); *or*

Part 7: National insurance, work and work-related rules
Chapter 46: Universal credit work-related requirements
3. Which requirements apply

- you may only have to meet a work-focused interview requirement (see p1066); *or*
- you may only have to meet a work-focused interview and a work preparation requirement (see p1068); *or*
- you may not have to meet a work search or a work availability requirement for a period (see p1069).

Note: if you are entitled to universal credit (UC) and also to contribution-based jobseeker's allowance (JSA) or contributory employment and support allowance (ESA), you only need to meet one set of work-related requirements – those for UC.[62]

Your work-related requirements depend on your circumstances (see below). If you are responsible for a child, your work-related requirements usually depend on her/his age, and if you are in a couple, whether you are the 'responsible carer' (see p1063). You cannot appeal a decision about which work-related responsibilities apply to you, so if you think they are unreasonable, you should negotiate with your work coach and, if necessary, complain. Where negotiation and complaining are not successful, you could consider a judicial review pre-action letter (see p1418).[63] To avoid a sanction, make it clear that you will comply with your work-related responsibilities in the meantime. Keep a record of your attempts to negotiate and/or complain. If you are sanctioned, you can appeal this decision (see p1108) – eg, if your work-related requirements were not reasonable (see p1100).

Which work-related requirements apply?

Your circumstances	Work-related requirement
Sick or disabled (see p1064)	No work-related requirements. You do not
Looking after a very young child(ren) or	have to look for work, be available for work
caring for someone with a disability (see	or participate in activity or conversations
p1062)	about preparing for work or improving your
Threat or history of domestic violence (see	skills. However, you must usually still agree
p1061)	a claimant commitment (see p1047), and
On UC and earning a sufficient amount (see	you must report changes in your
p1064)	circumstances.
At least pension age (see p1066)	
In education (see p1066)	
Looking after a child(ren) aged one	Work-focused interviews only (see p1066).
On ESA as a lone parent with a child(ren)	
aged at least one but under three	
Foster parent or 'friend and family carer' for	
a child(ren) over one and under 16 (see	
p1067)	

Looking after a child(ren) aged two (see p1068)

Limited capability for work (see p1068)

All other claimants (see p1069)

Work preparation (see p1051) and work-focused interviews (see p1051).

All the work-related requirements apply if you are not in any of the above groups. This could include some people with responsibility for children, some disabled people and some people in work. However, there may be temporary circumstances when the work search and work availability requirements do not apply to you, including if you are sick (see p1069), bereaved or have experienced domestic violence (see p1071), are working (see p1072) and in other temporary circumstances (see p1073). At other times, you may be able to restrict your availability for work and the type of work you have to look for (see p1057).

AskCPAG has a useful tool on identifying UC conditionality level at askcpag.org.uk/link/200329/identifying-the-correct-level-of-universal-credit-conditionality.

No work-related requirements

No work-related requirements *at all* can be imposed on you if:
- you are a recent victim of domestic violence (see below); *or*
- for UC and contributory ESA (or if you are getting *both* contribution-based JSA *and* UC), you fit into a specified group – ie, you are:
  - looking after children or have other caring responsibilities (see p1062);
  - sick or disabled (see p1064);
  - for UC only, in work and earning enough (see p1064);
  - in other specified situations (see p1066).

If your situation changes so that you are covered by the above, any requirements that have already been imposed cease to have effect.[64]

Domestic violence

If you notify the DWP that you have experienced, or been threatened with, domestic violence from your partner, your former partner or a family member and you satisfy specified conditions (see below), all work-related requirements

Part 7: National insurance, work and work-related rules
Chapter 46: Universal credit work-related requirements
3. Which requirements apply

that have been imposed on you cease to have effect for 13 consecutive weeks from the date of notification.[65] In addition, no new work-related requirements can be imposed on you during this period. For UC, if but for the domestic violence rules you would have to meet all the work-related requirements and you are the 'responsible carer' of a child under 16 (see p1063), no work availability or work search requirements can be imposed for a further 13 consecutive weeks (ie, for 26 weeks in total), although you could be required to attend work-focused interviews and/or engage in work preparation after the first 13 weeks.[66]

You must satisfy all the following conditions.

- This rule must not have applied to you on any earlier occasion in the 12 months before you notify the DWP.
- The domestic violence (or threat of domestic violence) must have taken place within the six months before you notify the DWP.
- When you notify the DWP, you must not be living at the same address as the person who was violent or threatened violence.
- As soon as possible, and no later than one month after you notify the DWP, you must provide evidence from a person acting in an official capacity that shows that your circumstances are consistent with those of a person who has experienced, or been threatened with, domestic violence in the six months before you notified the DWP, and that you have made contact with the person acting in an official capacity about an incident that occurred in that six-month period.

Domestic violence[67]

'Domestic violence' means any incident or pattern of incidents of controlling behaviour, coercive behaviour, violence or abuse, including physical, sexual, psychological, financial or emotional abuse, regardless of your gender or sexuality.

'Family member' for these purposes means the following members of your family, or of the family of your partner or your former partner: grandparent, grandchild, parent, parent-in-law, son, son-in-law, daughter, daughter-in-law, step-parent, stepson, stepdaughter, brother, brother-in-law, sister, sister-in-law, or the partner of any of these.

A **'person acting in an official capacity'** means a healthcare professional, a police officer, a registered social worker, your employer or your trade union representative. It also means any public, voluntary or charitable body with which you have had direct contact in connection with domestic violence.

Looking after children and other caring responsibilities

If you are getting UC or contributory ESA, no work-related requirements can be imposed on you if:[68]

- for UC, you are the 'responsible carer' (see p1063) of a child under one; *or*

- for ESA, you are not a member of a couple and you are responsible for a child under one – eg, you are a lone parent. The rules do not define when you count as responsible for a child; *or*
- you are the 'responsible foster parent' (see below) of a child under one; *or*
- you are an 'adopter' (see p1064) and it is not more than 12 months (for UC) or 52 weeks (for ESA) since your child was placed with you for adoption. You can elect for the 12 months (or 52 weeks) to start in the 14 days before your child was expected to be placed with you;
- you are pregnant and there are 11 weeks or less before the week your baby is due; *or*
- you had a baby not more than 15 weeks ago (including if this was a stillbirth); *or*
- you have 'regular and substantial caring responsibilities for a severely disabled person' (see p1064); *or*
- you have caring responsibilities for one or more severely disabled people for at least 35 hours a week, but do not satisfy the qualifying conditions for carer's allowance (CA). For UC, this only applies if the DWP is satisfied that it is unreasonable for you to meet a work search requirement and a work availability requirement, even if these are limited.

Definitions

You are a **'responsible carer'**:[69]

– for UC, if you are a single person, or a member of a couple claiming as a single person, who is responsible for a child under 16 (see p323) – eg, you are a lone parent, or you claim as a single person because your partner does not meet the basic conditions of UC;

– for JSA and ESA, if you are the only person responsible for a child under 16.

If you are a member of a couple and you are joint claimants, you are a responsible carer for UC if you or your partner (for JSA and ESA, you *and* your partner) are responsible for a child under 16 and you and your partner have nominated you as being responsible for the child. Only one of you can be nominated. The nomination applies to all your children. It can only be changed once in the 12 months after the nomination or if there has been a change of circumstances which the DWP considers relevant. If the DWP does not allow you to change a nomination, get advice. You cannot appeal a decision about who is the responsible carer.

You are a **'relevant carer'** if:[70]

– you are the parent of a child, have caring responsibilities for her/him but are not the 'responsible carer'; *or*

– you have caring responsibilities for someone who has a 'physical or mental impairment' (and for JSA only, the impairment means s/he needs such care).

You are a **'responsible foster parent'** if you are the child's only foster parent or, if you are a member of a couple who are both foster parents, you and your partner have nominated you as the 'responsible foster parent'.[71] Only one of you can be nominated. The nomination applies to all your children. It can only be changed once in the 12 months after the nomination or if there has been a relevant change of circumstances.

Part 7: National insurance, work and work-related rules
Chapter 46: Universal credit work-related requirements
3. Which requirements apply

You are an **'adopter'** if you have been matched with a child by an adoption agency and you are, or are intended to be, the 'responsible carer' of the child.[72] This does not apply if you are the foster parent or a close relative of the child.

A person is **'severely disabled'** if s/he is someone to whom attendance allowance, the highest or middle rate of disability living allowance care component, the daily living component of personal independence payment, armed forces independence payment or constant attendance allowance under the industrial or war disablement schemes (see p694) is payable.[73]

You have **'regular and substantial caring responsibilities'** if you satisfy the qualifying conditions for CA (see Chapter 26), or you would do but for the fact that your earnings are higher than allowed for CA (currently £128 a week – see p563).[74] However, you must not receive any earnings at all from your caring responsibilities. You do not have to be getting CA. If you are not covered by these rules, you may still be a 'relevant carer' which may reduce your work-related requirements.

Sick and disabled people

If you are getting UC or contributory ESA, no work-related requirements can be imposed on you if:[75]

- you have both limited capability for work and limited capability for work-related activity – ie, you are in the support group for ESA and/or have limited capability for work-related activity for UC (see Chapter 45); *or*
- you are entitled to ESA, but it is paid at a nil rate – eg, because you are getting an occupational pension.

Do you have limited capability for work-related activity?
If you are on ESA and in the support group, or you were in the support group on ESA and are moving to UC, the same limited capability for work-related activity decision should be applied to your UC. You can be reassessed at any time, but if you have recently had a work capability assessment, you should point this out to your work coach. If you were told that you should not be reassessed after your last work capability assessment, but you are referred to be assessed again, you could also consider making a complaint or contacting your MP.

You are earning enough

If you are getting UC, no work-related requirements at all can be imposed on you if you are:[76]

- a single claimant, or a member of a couple, and your own average monthly earnings are at least your individual earnings threshold (see below); *or*
- a member of a couple and your combined average monthly earnings are at least your joint earnings threshold (see below). No work-related requirements

can be imposed on you even if you are not working but your partner earns enough to meet this threshold;[77] *or*

- self-employed and are treated as having a minimum earnings level (see p121); *or*
- an apprentice and your average monthly earnings are at least the amount you would be paid at the rate of the national minimum wage (see Appendix 7) for 30 hours work (or, if lower, for your weekly 'expected hours' – see p1054).

Your monthly earnings are calculated using your gross actual or estimated earned income in the current assessment period – ie, before income tax, national insurance (NI) contributions and pension contributions have been deducted.[78] If your earnings fluctuate, these are averaged over one cycle of work or, if there is no cycle, over three months or the period that enables the average to be worked out more accurately. The DWP can disregard earnings from employment that has ended if this enables it to determine your monthly earnings more accurately. This means that if you are no longer working and receive a final payment of wages, the DWP can decide that you must meet work-related requirements, but does not have to.

Note: usually, if you are getting UC and earn a certain amount each month (excluding self-employed earnings) – called the 'administrative earnings threshold' – you are not expected to look for more work (see p1072). Other work-related requirements (eg, attending work-focused interviews) can be imposed on you. The DWP may refer to this as being in the 'light touch' regime. At the time of writing, however, the DWP has the power to select you for an 'in-work pilot scheme'. If you are selected, you can be required to look for more work or work that pays up to the thresholds below (called the 'conditionality earnings threshold').

Earnings thresholds

- **To work out your individual earnings threshold**, multiply the amount you would earn at the hourly rate of the national minimum wage (see Appendix 7) by the relevant number of hours for you (see below). Multiply this amount by 52 and divide it by 12.[79]
- **To work out your joint earnings threshold if you are a member of a couple**, work out the sum of your and your partner's individual earnings thresholds and add these together.[80] However, if you are claiming as a single person (see p36), your joint earnings threshold is the sum of your individual threshold and the amount someone would be paid at the rate of the minimum wage for 35 hours work (multiplied by 52 and divided by 12).

Fractions of a pound are ignored.[81]

For your individual threshold, the relevant hours are:[82]

- 16 hours a week, but only if (even though you are exempt from any work-related requirements under this rule) you would otherwise be someone who

Part 7: National insurance, work and work-related rules
Chapter 46: Universal credit work-related requirements
3. Which requirements apply

only has to meet a work-focused interview requirement (see below) or a work-focused interview requirement and a work preparation requirement (see p1068); *or*

- the hours you are expected to work each week (your 'expected hours') – usually 35 a week. A lower number of hours can apply (see p1054).

Example

Raj and Sunita are joint UC claimants. They have three children, the youngest of whom is of compulsory school age and under 13. They agree that Sunita should be the 'responsible carer'. Raj's 'expected hours' are 35 a week. The DWP has agreed that Sunita's 'expected hours' are 25 a week as these are compatible with their youngest child's school hours (see p1054).

Raj works 30 hours a week and earns £1,800 a month.

35 hours x £8.72 = £305.20

£305.20 x 52 ÷ 12 = £1322.53

His individual earnings threshold is therefore £1322.53.

Sunita works 15 hours a week and earns £780 a month.

25 hours x £8.72 = £218

£218 x 52 ÷ 12 = £944.67

Her individual earnings threshold is therefore £944.67.

Their joint earnings threshold is therefore £1322.53 + £944.67 = £2267.20

Their joint earnings (£2,580) exceed their joint earnings threshold. No work-related requirements can be imposed on either of them.

Other situations

If you are getting UC or contributory ESA, no work-related requirements can be imposed on you if:[83]

- for UC, you are at least pension age. This is only relevant if you are a member of a couple and your partner is not yet that age; *or*
- you are in full-time, non-advanced education or training and you have no parental support (see p38). For ESA, this also applies if you have been enrolled or accepted for the education or training. For both UC and ESA, you must be under 21, or be aged 21 and have reached that age while on the course; *or*
- for UC, you are eligible for UC while receiving education (see p881) and you have student income (see p882) for your course which is taken into account when calculating your UC. If your student income is a postgraduate master's degree loan, this only applies if your course is full time.

Work-focused interview requirement only

If you are in the work-focused interview 'regime', you are required to participate in interviews to discuss work and consider steps to prepare for it, but all action other than participating in the interviews is voluntary.

A work-focused interview requirement, and no other work-related requirements, can be imposed on you if you are getting UC or contributory ESA and:[84]

- for UC, you are the 'responsible carer' (see p1063) of a child aged one; *or*
- for ESA, you are a single person who is responsible for a child aged at least one but under three; *or*
- you are a foster parent, and you:
  - are the 'responsible foster parent' (see p1063) of a:
    - child aged at least one but under 16; *or*
    - qualifying young person (see p324). The DWP must be satisfied that s/he has care needs which make it unreasonable for you to have to meet a work search requirement or a work availability requirement even if these were limited (for UC), or a work preparation requirement (for ESA); *or*
  - are not the 'responsible foster parent' (see p1063) of a child under 16 or a qualifying young person, but the DWP is satisfied that the child or young person has care needs which make it unreasonable for you to have to meet a work search requirement or a work availability requirement even if these were limited (for UC), or a work preparation requirement (for ESA); *or*
  - do not have a child or qualifying young person placed with you currently, but intend to have one placed with you, and within the past eight weeks:
    - for UC, you have been in any of the situations described above applying to foster parents; *or*
    - for ESA, you have been the 'responsible foster parent' of a child aged at least one but under 16; *or*
- you have become a 'friend or family carer' (see below) for a child under 16 in the past 12 months, and you are her/his 'responsible carer' (see p1063).

Note: if your child is under one and you are the 'responsible foster parent', or for UC, the 'responsible carer', or for ESA, a single person who is responsible for the child, no work-related requirements can be imposed on you (see p1062).

Friend or family carer[85]

You are a **'friend or family carer'** if you are responsible for a child under 16 but are not her/his parent or step-parent. You must be taking care of the child because:

- s/he has no parents, or has parents who are unable to care for her/him. For when you count as responsible for a child for UC, see p63. 'Responsible for a child' is not defined in the ESA rules; *or*
- it is likely that s/he would otherwise be looked after by a local authority because there are concerns about her/his welfare.

If you have been getting UC or ESA on the basis that you have to meet additional work-related requirements but you now fit into one of the groups above, any requirements previously imposed on you cease to apply.[86]

Part 7: National insurance, work and work-related rules
Chapter 46: Universal credit work-related requirements
3. Which requirements apply

If you have young children, your work-focused interviews should be arranged taking childcare availability into account. You should be told that you can rearrange your interview if you have a good reason why you cannot attend – eg, childcare, social services or medical appointments.[87]

Work-focused interview and work preparation requirement only

If a work-focused interview requirement *and* a work preparation requirement (but no other work-related requirements) can be imposed on you, you are only expected to prepare for a move into paid work, more paid work or better paid work – eg, by participating in a training or employment scheme. You do not have to look for work or be available for work.

For UC, this requirement applies if you are the 'responsible carer' (see p1063) of a child aged two. It also applies if you are entitled to contributory ESA or UC and you have limited capability for work (see Chapter 45).[88] You do not automatically count as having limited capability for work until this has been decided in a work capability assessment (see p1011 for some exceptions). If you are providing medical evidence (usually fit notes), after 28 days you should be referred for a work capability assessment if this has not already been done.[89] Until you have a decision about your limited capability for work, the DWP has discretion about which work-related requirements to apply (see p1070). Any work search requirements must take your condition(s) into account.

Do you have limited capability for work?
If you have a limited capability for work decision, make sure your work coach knows how your illness affects what you can do and ask her/him to use her/his discretion in deciding which requirements to impose on you. If you were on ESA when you claimed UC and had been found to have limited capability for work, or you had NI credits for limited capability for work when you claimed UC, that limited capability for work decision applies to your UC.[90] You also have limited capability for work for UC if you already have limited capability for work in an ongoing ESA award. You may have to point this out to your work coach. Having a limited capability for work decision for ESA or NI credits does not prevent the DWP from referring you for another work capability assessment for UC, but if you have had a limited capability for work decision recently and it has been recommended that you should not be reassessed for some time (eg, by the health professional in her/his report to the DWP or by a tribunal), you should make sure your work coach is aware of this and consider making a complaint if you are referred again.

If you have limited capability for work, reasonable adjustments for your health needs must be offered when carrying out work-focused interviews (eg, offering telephone interviews where appropriate) and in determining what you should do to prepare for work. If you are the responsible carer of a child aged two, interviews must be accommodated around childcare availability and you should only be expected to carry out work preparation when another responsible adult is looking after your child(ren).[91]

Note:

- In some situations (eg, if you are in the ESA 'support group'), no work-related requirements at all can be imposed on you (see p1061).
- If you have been getting UC on the basis that you have to meet other work-related requirements, but you are now in one of the above groups, any requirements previously imposed cease to apply.[92]

All work-related requirements

If you do not come into any of the other work-related requirement groups (see p1073) and none of the temporary circumstances apply to you (see below), the DWP *must* impose a work search requirement and a work availability requirement on you for UC and JSA. It can also impose a work-focused interview requirement or a work preparation requirement, or both, and is likely to do so.[93] **Note:** if you are getting ESA, a work search and work availability requirement can *never* be imposed on you.

Consider negotiating with your work coach and complaining if necessary, if you think you should have been covered by any of the exceptions, but have been told you must meet all the requirements. You cannot appeal against your work-related requirements, but if negotiation and complaining fail, you could consider a judicial review pre-action letter (see p1418).[94] If you are given a sanction for failing to meet a requirement, you can appeal. You must apply for a mandatory reconsideration first.

No work search or work availability requirement for a period

If you are getting UC or contribution-based JSA or both, a work search and a work availability requirement cannot be imposed on you for a period (but you may have to meet other work-related requirements) in a number of situations. **Note:** for ESA, a work search or work availability requirement can *never* be imposed on you.

Sick and disabled people

If you are getting UC or contribution-based JSA, a work search requirement cannot be imposed on you for certain specified periods if you are unfit for work. This usually applies for a maximum of 14 days and no more than twice in any 12-month period.[95] For the first seven days, you must provide a declaration that you are unfit for work. For any further days, you must provide a fit note from your doctor (for UC only, this only applies if requested by the DWP). However, if you have previously failed a work capability assessment while under the UC system, or you have been treated as not having limited capability for work for UC because

Part 7: National insurance, work and work-related rules
Chapter 46: Universal credit work-related requirements
3. Which requirements apply

you failed to provide information or attend an assessment, the DWP can decide not to suspend your work search requirement. This should only apply if you are unfit for work because of the same condition (or substantially the same condition) and you are not being referred to a new work capability assessment.[96]

In several situations, the DWP has discretion whether or not to impose a work search requirement. This applies:[97]

- for UC, if you are unfit more than twice, or for longer than 14 days if the DWP thinks it would be unreasonable to require you to meet a work search requirement even if it were limited. This could apply, for example, if you are waiting for a work capability assessment. If it is not possible to meet even limited requirements, or your requirements do not reflect your condition, you should negotiate with your work coach and complain if necessary;
- for UC and JSA, if you have failed a previous work capability assessment or were treated as not having limited capability for work, and your medical evidence shows that you currently have the same, or substantially the same, condition as you had before those decisions were made. Even if the DWP does not refer you for a new work capability assessment, it can decide that it is unreasonable to require you to meet a limited work search requirement. However, it does not have to do so. This means that you can be expected to meet a limited work search requirement even though you are unwell or disabled – eg, while you are appealing a work capability assessment outcome. You should negotiate with your work coach and complain if it is not possible for you to meet your requirements and/or it affects your health;
- for JSA, if you are allowed an 'extended period of sickness' of up to 13 weeks under the rules described on p710 and the DWP thinks it would be unreasonable to require you to meet a work search requirement. If you are sick for longer than 13 weeks, you can no longer claim JSA.

You must provide a fit note from your doctor. For UC only, this only applies if requested by the DWP.

For the purposes of the work availability requirement, you only need to be willing and able to take up work and attend an interview for UC when the above circumstances no longer apply or, for JSA, when the period of sickness has ended.[98] However, if the DWP thinks it is reasonable to require you to attend an interview, you must be able and willing to attend one before the period of sickness has ended.

You cannot appeal against your work-related requirements but if negotiation and complaining are not successful, you could consider a judicial review pre-action letter (see p1418). Keep a record of everything you do to try to change your work-related requirements and explain clearly why you cannot meet them if this is the case.

If you continue to provide fit notes for UC, the DWP should refer you for a work capability assessment from day 29 of your sickness or declared disability, if it has not already done so.[99] However, if you have previously failed a work capability assessment, the DWP cannot refer you to a further assessment unless there is evidence to suggest that there has been a relevant change of circumstances (eg, your condition has deteriorated), or the previous decision was made without being aware of the facts, or was based on a mistake about facts.[100] If you have failed a work capability assessment, the DWP should still take your condition into account when putting together your work-related requirements, and can take into account medical evidence to do so (this applies whether or not you are challenging the decision that you are capable of work).

Bereavement and domestic violence

If you are getting UC or contribution-based JSA, a work search requirement cannot be imposed on you if it is less than six months since the death of your partner or a child under 16 (or, for UC only, a 'qualifying young person').[101] You or your partner must have been responsible for the child or qualifying young person, or you must have been the child's parent. For when you count as responsible for a child for UC, see p63. 'Responsible for a child' is not defined in the JSA rules.

For UC only, a work search requirement cannot be imposed on you if you are the 'responsible carer' of a child under 16 (see p1063 for who counts), and there has been a 'significant disruption' in your normal childcare responsibilities because in the last 24 months:[102]

- a parent, sister or brother, or a person who was the previous responsible carer, of the child has died; *or*
- any person who normally lived in the same accommodation as the child has died. The person does not have to have been a relative or carer. S/he must have being living in the accommodation at the time of her/his death, and must not be liable to make payments for the accommodation on a commercial basis; *or*
- the child has been a victim of, or witness to, a violent or abusive incident. This does not apply if you are the perpetrator of that violence or abuse.

This can apply for one month in each of the four consecutive six-month periods after the event occurs, beginning on a date specified by the DWP after you have notified it of the circumstances, and provided that the DWP is satisfied that the circumstances apply.[103] If the death affecting the child is that of your partner or another child or of a qualifying young person and the rules described above apply, or if *you* are the victim of the domestic violence and the rules on p1061 apply, the month runs at the same time as any period you have been allowed under those rules – ie, you do not get any extra time.

For the purposes of the work availability requirement, you only need to be willing and able to take up work and attend an interview once the circumstances no longer apply.[104]

Part 7: National insurance, work and work-related rules
Chapter 46: Universal credit work-related requirements
3. Which requirements apply

You have sufficient earnings from employment

If you are getting UC, a work search requirement cannot be imposed on you, but you may have to meet other work-related requirements, if:[105]

- you are a single claimant and your employed earnings (see p117) are at least £343 a month (from April 2020); *or*
- you are in a couple and your joint employed earnings (see p117) are at least £549 a month (from April 2020).

The DWP calls these earnings levels the 'administrative earnings threshold' and may refer to people as being in the 'light touch' regime.[106] The 'light touch' regime does not apply if you are selected to participate in an 'in-work pilot scheme' (a scheme testing which work-related requirements are likely to help you retain work or obtain more or better paid work if you have a job). If you are selected for a scheme, a work search requirement can be imposed on you, even if your monthly employed earnings are at least £343 or £549.[107] In this case, you continue to have a work search requirement until you reach the earnings threshold that applies to you (see p1064). You must be notified in writing (this includes electronic communication) if you are selected for the scheme. **Note:** at the time of writing, the DWP was not running an in-work pilot scheme, but has the power to do so until 19 February 2021.[108] The government has indicated its intention to use these powers and so it may reintroduce trials of in-work conditionality. See AskCPAG.org.uk and CPAG's *Welfare Rights Bulletin* for updates.

Note: if your monthly earnings are above your individual or joint earnings threshold (the 'conditionality earnings threshold'), no work-related requirements can be imposed on you (see p1064), so this rule only applies if your monthly employed earnings are at least £343 or £549, but lower than your earnings threshold, and you have not been selected for an in-work pilot scheme.

> #### Example
> Nicole, aged 27, is working part time. Her gross pay is £870 a month. Under the UC rules, she is expected to work 35 hours a week. 35 x £8.72 = £305.20. £305.20 x 52 ÷ 12 = £1,322.53. Her individual earnings threshold is therefore £1,322.53. Although she is not exempt from all the work-related requirements, because her take-home pay is more than £343 a month, a work search requirement cannot be imposed on her.

For the purposes of the work availability requirement, you only need to be willing and able to take up work and attend an interview once the circumstances no longer apply – ie, once your earnings reduce to below the relevant limit.[109] If your earnings fluctuate, an average over a representative period can be used.[110] However, the DWP can ignore earnings in respect of a job which has finished.

Other temporary circumstances

If you are getting UC or contribution-based JSA, a work search requirement cannot be imposed on you if:[111]

- you are attending a court or tribunal as a witness or party to the proceedings; *or*
- you qualify for UC or JSA while you are temporarily absent from Great Britain (see p1655 and p1663) because you are:
  - for JSA only, attending a job interview; *or*
  - for JSA only, receiving, or taking your child under 16 for, medical treatment; *or*
  - for UC only, receiving, or taking your child under 16 (or your partner or a qualifying young person) for, medical treatment or convalescence or care; *or*
- you are receiving and participating in a course of treatment for alcohol or drug addiction and have been for no more than six months; *or*
- you are under police protection while involved as a witness in a criminal investigation or proceedings; *or*
- for UC only, you are a prisoner (see p940); *or*
- for UC, you are carrying out a 'public duty'. This is not defined, but should include being on jury service, crewing a lifeboat or carrying out duties as a volunteer firefighter or special constable.[112] For JSA, see below.

For the purposes of the work availability requirement, you only need to be willing and able to take up work and attend an interview once the circumstances no longer apply.[113]

If the DWP is satisfied that it would be unreasonable for you to have to meet a work search requirement even if this were limited, a work search requirement cannot be imposed on you if:[114]

- for JSA only, you are carrying out a public duty; *or*
- you are carrying out a work preparation requirement (see p1051) or 'voluntary work preparation' – ie, action agreed with the DWP that makes it more likely that you will get paid work; *or*
- you have temporary childcare responsibilities; *or*
- there are other temporary circumstances. These could include anything that makes it unreasonable for you to have to seek work – eg, becoming homeless, caring for a relative, or a flood, fire or other disaster at your home. For UC, dealing with domestic emergencies and funeral arrangements are specifically included, but other situations may also make it unreasonable – eg, a child's exclusion from school.[115]

If any of the temporary circumstances apply to you, you should explain why you are not currently able to look for work and make sure that there is a record of your circumstances. You may be able to argue you should not be sanctioned if

Part 7: National insurance, work and work-related rules
Chapter 46: Universal credit work-related requirements
Notes

temporary circumstances applied and the DWP did not consider suspending your work search requirement.[116]

For the purposes of the work availability requirement, you only need to be willing and able to take up work and attend an interview when the circumstances no longer apply.[117] However, for UC, if the DWP thinks it is reasonable to require you to attend an interview, you must be able and willing to attend one before the circumstances cease to apply.

Notes

1. The claimant commitment
1 **UC** s4(1)(e) WRA 2012
 JSA s1(2)(b) JSA 1995
 ESA s1(3)(aa) WRA 2007
2 s3(2) WRA 2012
3 **UC** Reg 16 UC Regs
 JSA Reg 8 JSA Regs 2013
 ESA Reg 45 ESA Regs 2013
 All para J1026 ADM
4 See also DWP, *Universal Credit Guidance*, 'Appointees personal acting bodies and corporate acting bodies', v8.0 and *'Claimant commitment – Overview'*, v2.0, House of Commons library deposited papers, available at rightsnet.org.uk/ universal-credit-guidance
5 para J1022 ADM
6 **UC** s14(1) WRA 2012
 JSA s6A(1) JSA 1995
 ESA s11A(1) WRA 2007
7 **UC** s14(1)-(4) WRA 2012
 JSA s6A(1)-(4) JSA 1995
 ESA s11A(1)-(4) WRA 2007
8 **UC** s14(5) WRA 2012; reg 15 UC Regs
 JSA s6A(5) JSA 1995; reg 7 JSA Regs 2013
 ESA s11A(5) WRA 2007; reg 44 ESA Regs 2013
9 para J1011 ADM
10 para J1010 ADM
11 **UC** Reg 15(1) and (2) UC Regs
 JSA Reg 7(1) JSA Regs 2013
 ESA Reg 44(1) and (2) ESA Regs 2013

12 DWP, *Universal Credit Guidance*, 'Claimant commitment – commitment not accepted', v.20, House of Commons library deposited papers, available at rightsnet.org.uk/universal-credit-guidance
13 **UC** Reg 15(3) UC Regs
 JSA Reg 7(2) JSA Regs 2013
14 Reg 44(3) ESA Regs 2013
15 DWP, *Universal Credit Guidance*, 'Fail to attend', v14.0, House of Commons deposited papers, available at rightsnet.org.uk/universal-credit-guidance
16 You may be able to challenge the decision by arguing that you accepted your default claimant commitment when you made your UC claim and this has not yet been replaced by a personalised commitment, so the DWP cannot show that you do not meet the basic conditions of UC.
17 **UC** s14(2) WRA 2012
 JSA s6A(2) JSA 1995
 ESA s11A(2) WRA 2007
18 DWP, *Universal Credit Guidance*, 'Claimant commitment overview', v2.0, House of Commons library deposited papers, available at rightsnet.org.uk/ universal-credit-guidance

2. The work-related requirements

19 **UC** s13 WRA 2012
   JSA ss6 and 6F JSA 1995
   ESA s11 WRA 2007
20 **JSA** Reg 5(2) JSA Regs 2013
   ESA Reg 42(2) ESA Regs 2013
21 **UC** s24(4) WRA 2012
   ESA s11H(4) WRA 2007
   JSA s6H(4) JSA 1995
22 *JB v SSWP* [2018] UKUT 360 (AAC)
23 **UC** s15 WRA 2012
   JSA s6B JSA 1995
   ESA s11B WRA 2007
24 para J3031 ADM
25 **UC** Regs 87 and 93 UC Regs
   JSA Reg 10 JSA Regs 2013
   ESA Reg 46 ESA Regs 2013
26 **UC** s16(1) and (2) WRA 2012
   JSA s6C(1) and (2) JSA 1995
   ESA s11C(1) and (2) WRA 2007
27 **UC** s16(3)-(6) WRA 2012
   JSA s6C(3) JSA 1995
   ESA s11C(3)-(6) WRA 2007
28 see gov.uk/work-health-programme
29 Reg 12(1B) UC Regs
30 DWP, *Universal Credit Guidance,* 'Youth
   Obligation Support Programme', v12.0,
   House of Commons deposited papers,
   available at rightsnet.org.uk/universal-
   credit-guidance
31 **UC** s17(1) WRA 2012
   JSA s6D(1) JSA 1995
32 **UC** s17(2) and (3) WRA 2012
   JSA s6D(2) and (3) JSA 1995
33 **UC** Reg 94 UC Regs
   JSA Reg 11 JSA Regs 2013
34 **UC** Reg 95(1) UC Regs
   JSA Reg 12(1) JSA Regs 2013
35 *RR v SSWP (UC)* [2017] UKUT 459 (AAC)
36 **UC** Reg 88 UC Regs
   JSA Reg 9 JSA Regs 2013
37 para J3058 ADM
38 para J3058 ADM
39 cpag.org.uk/welfare-rights/judicial-
   review/judicial-review-pre-action-
   letters/claimant-commitment-uc
40 **UC** Reg 95(2)-(4) UC Regs
   JSA Regs 4(1) and 12(2) and (3) JSA
   Regs 2013
41 *RR v SSWP (UC)* [2017] UKUT 459 (AAC)
42 **UC** s23(3) WRA 2012
   JSA s6G(3) JSA 1995
43 para J3103 ADM
44 paras J3253-56 ADM
45 **UC** s18(1) and (2) WRA 2012; regs 87
   and 96(1) UC Regs
   JSA s6E(1) and (2) JSA 1995; regs 3(7)
   and 13(1) JSA Regs 2013

46 Reg 13(1)(b) JSA Regs 2013
47 **UC** Reg 96(1) UC Regs 2013
   JSA Reg 13(1)(a) JSA Regs 2013
48 *Shaukat Ali v CAO,* Appendix to R(U) 1/
   85
49 **UC** Reg 96(2)-(5) UC Regs
   JSA Regs 2 and 13(2)-(5) JSA Regs 2013
50 **UC** s17(4) and (5) WRA 2012
   JSA s6D(4) and (5) JSA 1995
51 **UC** Reg 97(4)-(6) UC Regs
   JSA Reg 14(3) and (4) JSA Regs 2013
   paras J3163- J3165 ADM
52 DWP, *Universal Credit Guidance,*
   'Claimant commitment – availability for
   work', v2.0, House of Commons library
   deposited papers, available at
   rightsnet.org.uk/universal-credit-
   guidance
53 **UC** Reg 97(2) UC Regs
   JSA Reg 14(5) JSA Regs 2013
54 **UC** Reg 95 (1) UC Regs
   JSA Reg 12(1) JSA Regs 2013
55 **UC** Reg 97(4) and (5) UC Regs
   JSA Reg 14(3) JSA Regs 2013
56 **UC** Reg 97(3) and (6) UC Regs
   JSA Reg 14(2) and (4) JSA Regs 2013
57 DWP, *Universal Credit Guidance,*
   'Intensive work search regime', v16.0,
   House of Commons library deposited
   papers, available at rightsnet.org.uk/
   universal-credit-guidance
58 para K2301 ADM
59 **UC** s23 WRA 2012
   JSA s6G JSA 1995
   ESA s11G WRA 2007
60 para K1171 ADM; *JB v SSWP (UC)* [2018]
   UKUT 360 (AAC)
61 para J3001 ADM

3. Which requirements apply

62 **JSA** Reg 5(2) JSA Regs 2013
   ESA Reg 42(2) ESA Regs 2013
63 cpag.org.uk/welfare-rights/judicial-
   review/judicial-review-pre-action-
   letters/claimant-commitment-uc
64 **UC** s19(5) WRA 2012
   JSA Reg 15(1)(a) JSA Regs 2013
   ESA s11D(3) WRA 2007
65 **UC** Reg 98 UC Regs
   JSA Regs 5 and 15 JSA Regs 2013
   ESA Reg 49 ESA Regs 2013
66 Reg 98(1A) UC Regs
67 **UC** Reg 98(4) UC Regs
   JSA Reg 15(5) JSA Regs 2013

Part 7: National insurance, work and work-related rules
Chapter 46: Universal credit work-related requirements
Notes

68 **UC** s19(2)(b) and (c) WRA 2012; reg 89(1)(b), (c), (d) and (f) UC Regs
JSA Reg 5 JSA Regs 2013
ESA s11D(2)(b) and (c) WRA 2007; reg 47(1)(a), (b), (c), (f) and (g) ESA Regs 2013

69 **UC** s19(6) WRA 2012; reg 86 UC Regs
JSA Reg 4 JSA Regs 2013
ESA Reg 41 ESA Regs 2013

70 **UC** Reg 85 UC Regs
JSA Reg 4(1) JSA Regs 2013

71 **UC** Regs 85 and 86 UC Regs
JSA Reg 4 JSA Regs 2013
ESA Reg 41 ESA Regs 2013

72 **UC** Reg 89(3) UC Regs
ESA Reg 47(5) ESA Regs 2013

73 **UC** Reg 89(2) UC Regs
ESA Reg 47(5) ESA Regs 2013

74 **UC** Reg 30 UC Regs
ESA Reg 47(2) and (3) ESA Regs 2013

75 **UC** s19(2)(a) WRA 2012
ESA s11D(2)(a) WRA 2007; reg 47(1)(e) ESA Regs 2013

76 Reg 90 UC Regs

77 DWP, *Universal Credit Guidance,* 'Working enough regime', v6.0, House of Commons library deposited papers, available at rightsnet.org.uk/universal-credit-guidance

78 Reg 90(6) UC Regs

79 Reg 90(2) UC Regs

80 Reg 90(3) UC Regs

81 Reg 6(1A) UC Regs

82 Regs 88 and 90(2) UC Regs

83 **UC** s19 WRA 2012; reg 89(1)(a), (da) and (e) UC Regs
ESA s11D WRA 2007; reg 47(1)(d) ESA Regs 2013

84 **UC** s20 WRA 2012; reg 91 UC Regs
ESA s11E WRA 2007; reg 48 ESA Regs 2013

85 **UC** Reg 91(3) UC Regs
ESA Reg 48(3) ESA Regs 2013

86 **UC** s20(3) WRA 2012
ESA s11E(3) WRA 2007

87 DWP, *Universal Credit Guidance,* 'Work-focused interview regime', v.6.0, House of Commons library deposited papers, available at rightsnet.org.uk/universal-credit-guidance

88 **UC** s21 WRA 2012
ESA s11F WRA 2007

89 DWP, *Universal Credit Guidance,* 'Health conditions and disabilities – day 1 to day 29', v11.0, House of Commons library deposited papers, available at rightsnet.org.uk/universal-credit-guidance

90 Regs 19 and 21 UC(TP) Regs; reg 39(1)(a) UC Regs (if there was a credits-only claim for 'new- style' ESA before UC was claimed)

91 DWP, *Universal Credit Guidance,* 'Work preparation regime', v12.0, House of Commons library deposited papers, available at rightsnet.org.uk/universal-credit-guidance

92 s21(4) WRA 2012

93 **UC** s22 WRA 2012
JSA s6F JSA 1995

94 cpag.org.uk/welfare-rights/judicial-review/judicial-review-pre-action-letters/claimant-commitment-uc

95 **UC** Reg 99(1)(a) and (4) UC Regs
JSA Reg 16(1)(a) and (5) JSA Regs 2013

96 **UC** Reg 99(4ZA) and (4ZB) UC Regs
JSA Reg 16(5A) and (5B) JSA Regs 2013

97 **UC** Reg 99(5)(c) and (d) UC Regs
JSA Regs 16(5B) and 16A(1) and (2) JSA Regs 2013

98 **UC** Reg 99 (1)(b), (2B), (2C), (5A) and (5B) UC Regs
JSA Regs 16 (1)(b) and 16A(4)-(6) JSA Regs 2013

99 DWP, *Universal Credit Guidance,* 'Health conditions and disabilities day 1 to day 29', v11.0, House of Commons library deposited papers, available at rightsnet.org.uk/universal-credit-guidance

100 Reg 41(4) UC Regs

101 **UC** Reg 99(1) and (3)(d) UC Regs
JSA Reg 16(3)(c) JSA Regs 2013

102 Reg 99(1) and (4A) UC Regs

103 Reg 99(4B) and (4C) UC Regs

104 **UC** Reg 99(1)(b) UC Regs
JSA Reg 16(1)(b) JSA Regs 2013

105 Regs 6(1A) and 99(1), (6) and (6A) UC Regs

106 DWP, *Universal Credit Guidance,* 'Light touch regime', v9.0, House of Commons library deposited papers, available at rightsnet.org.uk/universal-credit-guidance

107 The Universal Credit (Work-Related Requirements) and In Work Pilot Scheme Amendment Regulations 2015, No.89, as amended by SI 2020/152

108 The Universal Credit (Work-Related Requirements) In Work Pilot Scheme (Extension) Order 2020, No.152

109 Reg 99(1)(b) UC Regs

110 Regs 2, definition of 'monthly earnings', 90(6) and 99(6) and (6A) UC Regs

111 **UC** Reg 99(1) and (3)(a)-(c) and (e)-(g)
UC Regs
JSA Regs 4(1) and 16(1) and (3)(a), (b),
(d) and (e) JSA Regs 2013
112 para J3208 ADM
113 **UC** Reg 99(1)(b) UC Regs
JSA Reg 16(1)(b) JSA Regs 2013
114 **UC** Reg 99(2A) and (5)(a) and (b) UC
Regs
JSA Reg 16(1) and (4) JSA Regs 2013
115 paras J3068-72 ADM
116 *RR v SSWP (UC)* [2017] UKUT 459 (AAC)
117 **UC** Reg 99(2B), (2C), (5A) and (5B) UC
Regs
JSA Reg 16(1)(b) JSA Regs 2013

Chapter 47

Universal credit system sanctions

This chapter covers:
1. When you can be sanctioned (p1079)
2. How your benefit is reduced (p1088)
3. The sanction period (p1093)
4. Good reasons for your actions (p1100)
5. Sanction decisions (p1106)
6. Challenging a sanction decision (p1108)

The rules on sanctions in this chapter apply if you are getting universal credit (UC). They also apply if you come under the UC system and are getting jobseeker's allowance (JSA) or employment and support allowance (ESA) (see p23). If you get JSA or ESA and you do not come under the UC system, see Chapter 49.

Key facts

- If you are getting universal credit, jobseeker's allowance or employment and support allowance and you do not meet your work-related requirements, you may be given a sanction.
- If you are given a sanction, your benefit is paid at a reduced (or sometimes nil) rate for a period.
- Whether or not you can be sanctioned, and for how long, depends on what you have done, or failed to do, in relation to your work-related requirements.
- You may be able to avoid a sanction if you can show that you have a good reason for your actions.
- You may qualify for hardship payments if you have been given a sanction.
- You can apply for a revision or supersession (see Chapter 56), or appeal (see Chapter 57) against a sanction decision. You must apply for a mandatory reconsideration before you can appeal.
- From 30 March 2020, for a minimum of three months, you cannot be required to look for work or be available for work and, therefore, a new sanction cannot be imposed if you fail to do so.

1. **When you can be sanctioned**

You can be given a sanction if you do not meet the work-related requirements you have as a condition of getting universal credit (UC) and, if you come under the UC system (see p23), jobseeker's allowance (JSA) and employment and support allowance (ESA). See Chapter 46 for the work-related requirements.

Note: you cannot be sanctioned if you do not have any work-related requirements, including if you are in the 'support group' for ESA (see p1061).

What can you do to avoid a sanction?

1. If you think that any work-related activity you are being asked to do is unreasonable, talk to your work coach about it. Explain why it is unreasonable – eg, because of your health or caring responsibilities. You should keep a record (a note of the date, time, and what was said) of your attempts to negotiate with your work coach, as this could be important if you have to show you had a good reason at a later date. If necessary, you could consider a pre-action letter about an unreasonable claimant commitment (template letters are available from cpag.org.uk/welfare-rights/judicial-review).

2. If there is a possibility that you will be given a sanction, make sure you give full details of your side of the story. Check all the relevant sections in this chapter to work out what information and evidence you should provide. Make sure the DWP is aware of any needs you have which could make it difficult for you to fulful your work-related requirements.

3. If, to avoid being given a sanction, you must show you had a good reason for what you did or did not do, make sure you explain your reasons fully, and provide these in time. See pp1100–06 for what may (or may not) count.

4. If you left or were dismissed from a job and it appears there may have been misconduct or that you left voluntarily without a good reason, your former employer is asked for a statement. You should be given an adequate chance to comment on what s/he says. Your remarks may be passed to her/him for further comments. Make sure you explain why you disagree with an allegation of misconduct or why you had a good reason for leaving your job. If you are going to an employment tribunal (eg, to claim unfair dismissal), say so. Discuss your reply with whoever is advising you on this, as you may be asked questions at the employment tribunal hearing by your former employer about what you have said.

5. If you refused to apply for or accept a job, what the potential employer says might be taken into account. Make sure you explain what enquiries you made about the nature of the job, and your reasons for not applying for or accepting it. For example, if you assumed the employer would not make adjustments but you did not ask her/him about this, you may not have a good reason.

6. If you are taking part in a training scheme or employment programme, it will probably be the provider who raises doubts about your compliance or attendance. Before a sanction is imposed, you should be given an adequate chance to comment on any statements made against you. Bear in mind that even if the scheme or programme provider is satisfied that you have done what was required of you, or that you had a good reason for failing to do so, the DWP may reach a different conclusion.

Part 7: National insurance, work and work-related rules
Chapter 47: Universal credit system sanctions
1. When you can be sanctioned

7. Information, queries or declarations you send to the DWP can be posted on your online journal, if you have one. If you are unable to post on your journal or do not have one, you should communicate with the DWP in any way accessible to you – eg, by telephone or in person. In any case, you should keep a record of all your interactions with the DWP, irrespective of how they take place – eg, by taking a screenshot of messages you post on your journal.

If you are given a sanction, your UC, JSA or ESA is paid at a reduced (or nil) rate during a set 'sanction period'. There are four levels of sanctions (see below). The amount of the benefit reduction and the length of the sanction period depend on which work-related requirement you have failed to meet. Some special rules apply to the length of the sanction period if you are aged 16 or 17.

If you are entitled to UC, the reduction in your benefit is applied to your UC, even if the sanction was in respect of your JSA or ESA claim. See p1092 for information about applying a sanction to another benefit if your circumstances change. The days in your sanction period count towards your days of entitlement to contribution-based JSA or contributory ESA, even if you are not actually paid any benefit. For example, if you are entitled to 365 days of contributory ESA and you are sanctioned for 14 days, in total you will only receive contributory ESA for 351 days.

Work-related requirement	Level of sanction
Failing to apply for or to accept paid work (UC and JSA only)	High
Ceasing paid work or losing pay for specified reasons (UC and JSA only)	High
Failing to be available for paid work or to take all reasonable action to get paid work (UC and JSA only)	Medium
Failing to meet a work-focused interview requirement (where other requirements also apply)	Low
Failing to meet a requirement connected to a work-related requirement	Low
Failing to meet a work preparation requirement	Low
Failing to take a particular action to get paid work (UC and JSA only)	Low
Failing to meet a work-related interview requirement (where no other requirements apply) (UC and ESA only)	Lowest

We refer to things that can lead to a sanction (eg, leaving work voluntarily) as 'sanctionable actions'. The DWP may refer to the cause of a sanction as a 'sanctionable failure'.[1]

In some cases, you cannot be given a sanction if you can show you had a good reason for your actions (see p1100). You may be able to get UC hardship payments (including if you are getting JSA or ESA) if you have been sanctioned.

If you disagree with a sanction decision, see p1108 for information about challenging it.

Note: different rules apply if you have been given a sanction because of a benefit offence (see p1278).

High level sanctions

If you are getting UC or JSA, you can be given a high level sanction if you are in the all work-related requirements group (see p1069) and you:[2]
- fail to apply for a particular vacancy or accept an offer of paid work without a good reason (see below); or
- cease paid work or lose pay voluntarily without a good reason or because of 'misconduct' (see p1082);
- fail to take part in a prescribed work placement. At the time of writing, the only prescribed scheme (Mandatory Work Activity) is closed, but other schemes may be prescribed in the future.

Failing to apply for or to accept paid work
You can be given a high level UC or JSA sanction if, without a good reason:[3]
- you are told to apply for a particular vacancy for paid work and you do not do so, or you fail to take up paid work when it is offered to you (see p1056). **Note:** if the vacancy was available because of a strike, you cannot be given a sanction;[4] or
- you failed to take up an offer of paid work before you claimed UC (or JSA). For UC, you must be subject to all the work-related requirements (see p1069) when you are awarded UC. For both UC and JSA, no reduction in your benefit can be made if the number of days between the date you failed to take up the offer and your date of claim for UC (or JSA) is more than the sanction period that would otherwise apply.[5]

Paid work
'**Paid work**' for these purposes means work done for payment or for which you expect to be paid.[6]

The DWP might treat you as having refused to apply for or accept paid work if you do not arrive on time, go to the wrong place, ask an employer for unreasonable conditions or behave in such a way as to put off a prospective employer.[7] It is not a 'good reason' to refuse paid work or fail to apply for it because you are not sure of the effect on your benefits.[8]

Part 7: National insurance, work and work-related rules
Chapter 47: Universal credit system sanctions
1. When you can be sanctioned

Note:
- You only have to be available for work and to look for work in locations that are no more than 90 minutes from your home.[9] You may find it difficult to show you have a good reason if your travel time is shorter than this, but if you have agreed (or tried to agree) a shorter travel to work time with your work coach, you should make this clear when you challenge the sanction (see p1058).
- You may be able to show that you have a good reason for refusing a job if you have previously done work of a particular type or at a particular rate of pay, you have been allowed to limit your work search to looking for work of a similar type or rate of pay (see p1057), and you refuse a job that does not meet these conditions.
- The DWP says that if you are getting UC and you refuse to accept a job with a zero-hour contract without a good reason, you can be given a sanction if the contract allows you to take up work with other employers that will lift your earnings above your individual earnings threshold (see p1065). However, you should not be given a sanction if the zero-hour contract has an exclusivity clause – ie, if you are prevented by the employer from working for any other employer or from being self-employed.[10] Exclusivity clauses are unenforceable in law,[11] but DWP guidance suggests that such a requirement from a potential employer could mean you cannot be required to take up the job – eg, if the hours offered restrict your flexiblity to increase your earnings with other employers, you should not be sanctioned for refusing.[12] You are likely to be asked for proof that your employer would prevent you from doing other work, but a contract does not necessarily have to be in writing. If you are reluctant to take a zero-hour contract because of fluctuating earnings which would make it difficult for you to budget, make your work coach aware of this and get independent advice.

Ceasing paid work or losing pay

Unless any of the exceptions on p1083 apply, you can be given a high level UC or JSA sanction if you cease paid work (see p1081) or lose pay:[13]
- 'voluntarily' (see p1084) and without a good reason (see p1102). You have not left work voluntarily if there is a genuine redundancy situation or your contract of employment ends, even if you volunteer for redundancy (see below); or
- because of misconduct (see p1085). You can also be sanctioned if you are suspended from work for misconduct or if you resigned rather than be dismissed.[14]

For UC, you can be given a sanction on this ground even if you had no work-related requirements imposed on you at the time the event occurred because you were earning a sufficient amount (see p1065 for the earnings thresholds), provided your ceasing work or losing pay means you are now subject to all the work-related requirements. However, if you currently have no work search requirement because you are still earning enough to have this requirement removed and you have not been selected for an 'in-work pilot scheme' (see p1072), you cannot be sanctioned (see below).

For both UC and JSA, you can be given a sanction on this ground if you ceased the paid work or you lost pay before your claim for UC (or JSA). For UC, you must be subject to all the work-related requirements when you are awarded UC. However, for both UC and JSA, no reduction in your benefit can be made if the number of days between the date you ceased work or lost pay and your date of claim for UC (or JSA) is more than the sanction period that would otherwise apply.[15]

If you are self-employed, you will not be sanctioned for giving up paid work or losing pay.[16] The DWP decides whether you are still gainfully self-employed, looking at all the circumstances – eg, whether a drop in income is part of your normal pattern of work.[17] If it decides that you are still self-employed, you may be treated as having more income than you actually earn (see p121). If you stop self-employment completely because of the application of this rule (the 'minimum income floor'), you should not be sanctioned.

For what may happen if you take retirement, see p1086.

Exceptions

For UC only, you cannot be given a sanction on this ground (even if you cease paid work or lose pay voluntarily or because of misconduct) if your monthly earnings (or, if you are a joint claimant, your joint monthly earnings) are still above the amount that means a work search requirement cannot be imposed on you at the present time (see p1072), unless you have been selected to take part in an 'in-work pilot scheme'. If you are in an in-work pilot scheme, you can be sanctioned for ceasing work or losing pay which takes your earnings below a higher amount (see p1064).[18]

For both UC and JSA, you cannot be given a sanction (even if you cease paid work or lose pay voluntarily) if:[19]

- you volunteer or accept your employer's proposal for redundancy (see p1084); or
- you are allowed to limit the number of hours you are available for work and are looking for work (see p1054), you take up paid work (or more hours of paid work) for more hours than that limit and you cease that paid work (or doing the higher hours) or lose pay within a trial period. 'Trial period' is not defined in the rules, but the DWP says it is a period of 56 days starting on the 29th day and ending on the 84th day on which you took up paid work (or more hours).[20] You can argue that anything that can reasonably be described as a trial period should count; or
- you ceased paid work or lost pay because of a strike; or

Part 7: National insurance, work and work-related rules
Chapter 47: Universal credit system sanctions
1. When you can be sanctioned

- you ceased paid work as a member of the regular or reserve armed forces, or lost pay in that capacity; *or*
- you have been laid off or kept on short-time work by your employer for at least four consecutive weeks (or for six weeks in a 13-week period). You must have applied for redundancy pay within a specified time.[21]

Leaving a job or losing pay voluntarily

If you are getting UC or JSA, you can be given a high level sanction if you leave your job or lose pay 'voluntarily' without a good reason (see p1102).

Voluntarily

'**Voluntarily**' is not defined in the rules, but the DWP says it means that you have brought the situation about by your own acts and of your own free will.[22] You have not left your employment (or lost pay) voluntarily if you had no choice in the matter or there is convincing evidence (eg, medical evidence from your GP) that you were not responsible for your actions. You have not lost pay voluntarily if your hours under a zero-hour contract are reduced because you worked for another employer to gain more hours.[23]

If you are thinking of reducing your hours for a good reason (eg, because of your caring responsibilities or health), speak to your work coach first and make a written record of your conversations. It is not clear whether you would be regarded as having lost pay voluntarily in this situation. You may be expected to explore other options first – eg, investigating the availability and costs of childcare.

You are likely to be treated as giving up your job voluntarily if:

- you resign giving notice. If you genuinely believed that your employer was about to end your employment or you were given the 'choice' of resignation or dismissal, you have not left your job voluntarily, but the DWP may then consider whether you lost your job through misconduct (see p1085);
- your employer gives you notice to end your employment but then cancels or suspends it, but you decide not to continue in the employment, if it is clear that you have a genuine choice to remain.[24] However, the circumstances may mean you have a 'good reason'.

You have *not* left your job voluntarily if:

- you volunteer, or accept your employer's proposal, for redundancy, even if you were offered, or could have applied for, alternative jobs with the same employer.[25] This only applies if there is a redundancy situation at your workplace – eg, if a whole factory or department is closing down or if there is a cut in the number of people needed to carry out certain tasks. **Note:** if you refuse other work, you might be sanctioned for another reason – eg, refusing employment or 'neglecting to avail' yourself of an opportunity of employment;

- your employer ends your contract of employment.[26] **Note:** if you left your job because your employer imposed a change in your terms or conditions without your agreement and the new terms are less favourable than before, you may be able to argue that you have not left voluntarily, or that you had a good reason for leaving.[27] However, a cut in pay is not a good reason to leave if your pay remains at or above the national minimum wage (see Appendix 7).

Misconduct

'Misconduct' is not defined in the rules. However, bear the following in mind.

- You are only guilty of misconduct if your actions or omissions are 'blameworthy'. You do not have to have done anything dishonest or deliberately wrong; serious carelessness or negligence may be enough.[28]
- Everyone makes mistakes or is inefficient from time to time. So, for example, if you are a naturally slow worker who, despite making every effort, cannot produce the output required by your employer, you are not guilty of misconduct even if the poor performance may justify your dismissal.
- The misconduct must have some connection with your employment but it does not have to take place during working hours to count. However, a sanction cannot be imposed if the actions or omissions took place before your employment began – eg, you gave inaccurate information about yourself when applying for the job.[29]

Some behaviour is clearly misconduct – eg, dishonesty (whether or not connected with your work) if it causes your employer to dismiss you because s/he no longer trusts you.[30] However, some behaviour is not necessarily misconduct.

- A refusal to carry out a reasonable instruction by an employer is not misconduct if you had a good reason or you refused because of a genuine misunderstanding.[31]
- You should not be treated as losing a job because of misconduct if you are dismissed for 'whistleblowing' – ie, for disclosing wrongful behaviour which it was in the public interest to disclose. However, if you have not reported the matter through the proper channels, you might be guilty of misconduct.[32]
- Bad timekeeping and failing to report in time that you are sick might amount to misconduct – eg, if you were persistently late or failed to report that you were sick on a number of occasions.
- Breaking rules covering personal conduct might amount to misconduct, depending on the seriousness of the breach. A breach of a trivial rule might not be misconduct.[33]
- Refusing to work overtime is misconduct if you were under a duty to work overtime when required and the request to do it was reasonable.

Although evidence from your employer is taken into account, the fact that s/he did not describe your actions as 'misconduct' does not guarantee that you will not be given a sanction.

Part 7: National insurance, work and work-related rules
Chapter 47: Universal credit system sanctions
1. When you can be sanctioned

If there is medical evidence that you had a mental illness and you were not responsible for your actions at the time of the alleged misconduct, the DWP decision maker should not impose a sanction.[34]

Whether misconduct caused the loss of employment or pay

Your misconduct need not be the only cause of the loss of your employment or pay, but it must be an immediate and substantial reason.[35] If your misconduct was not the real reason for your dismissal (eg, your employer used this as an excuse but really only wanted to reduce staff numbers), you should not be sanctioned.

If you believe that your dismissal was unreasonable or an overreaction on your employer's part, get advice to see whether you might have a case for unfair dismissal at an employment tribunal. You should tell the DWP if you are seeking advice and/or taking action against your employer.

If there was misconduct, the exact way in which you lost your employment is not important. You may be summarily dismissed, be dismissed with notice or resign as an alternative to possible dismissal.[36]

Relationship with unfair dismissal and other proceedings

Sometimes the same facts have to be considered by other bodies – eg, employment tribunals and the criminal courts. The questions and legal tests that other bodies use may not be the same as those which apply to benefits.

DWP decision makers, the First-tier Tribunal and employment tribunals are independent of each other; decisions by one are not binding on the other. This means:

- a finding by an employment tribunal that a dismissal was fair does not prevent the DWP decision maker or the First-tier Tribunal from concluding that you did not lose your job through misconduct;[37]
- although the First-tier Tribunal normally accepts a criminal conviction as proof that you have done what is alleged, it must go on to consider whether this was connected with your employment, whether it amounts to misconduct and whether the misconduct was the reason why you lost your employment;
- the DWP decision maker or the tribunal does not have to wait for the outcome of other proceedings before making a decision, but they are more likely to do so if there is a conflict of evidence.

Taking retirement

If you take retirement, you might be treated as having left your job voluntarily.[38] Under employment law, your employer cannot usually make you retire at any particular age, so taking retirement is something you do of your own choice. However, you might be able to show you have a good reason – eg, if you can show that the work was getting too much for you because of your age or your health. If you have retired early due to ill health you may need to submit sick notes at the beginning of your claim while you are waiting for a work capability assessment (see p1069).

Employers sometimes have special early retirement schemes allowing you to take your occupational pension at an earlier age than normal, often in order to deal with a redundancy situation. In this case, you come under the special rules about redundancy (see p1084). Employers often try to avoid using the word 'redundancy' and you may have to prove that a redundancy situation existed.

If you take early retirement under some other special scheme, you cannot show you have a good reason merely because your action was in your employer's interest.[39]

Medium level sanctions

If you are getting UC or JSA, you can be given a medium level sanction if you have a work search and/or work availability requirement (see p1069) and, without a good reason, you:[40]

- do not take all reasonable action to get paid work, more paid work or better paid work (see p1053); *or*
- are not available for work (see p1056).

You should keep detailed records of your work search and be able to prove what you have done to look for work (see p1055). If there are particular reasons why you cannot take your expected steps to seek work (eg, because of illness or caring responsibilities), or you think your work-related responsibilities are unreasonable for your circumstances, make you sure you tell the DWP as soon as possible and keep a record of this. For more tactics to avoid sanctions, see p1079.

Low level sanctions

If you are getting UC, JSA or ESA, you can be given a low level sanction if, without a good reason, you:[41]

- fail to meet a work-focused interview requirement (see p1051). **Note:** for UC and ESA, this does not apply if you are *only* required to meet a work-focused interview requirement and have no other work-related requirements. In this case, you can be given a lowest level sanction instead (see p1088); *or*
- fail to meet a requirement to participate in interviews, provide information or evidence, confirm your compliance (eg, by completing a task on your online 'to do' list) or report a change in your circumstances that is relevant to whether work-related requirements can be imposed on you or to your compliance with a work-related requirement; *or*
- fail to meet a work preparation requirement (see p1051) – eg, you refuse to do a community work placement or to go on a training scheme or employment programme. Failure to participate, even if you attend a work preparation activity, could also be a failure to meet a work preparation requirement – eg, if

Part 7: National insurance, work and work-related rules
Chapter 47: Universal credit system sanctions
2. How your benefit is reduced

you fail to confirm your identity without a good reason, this could be a failure to participate;[42] *or*

- for UC and JSA only, fail to take any particular action specified by the DWP to get paid work, more paid work or better paid work (see p1053).

For ESA, to be given a low level sanction, you must be someone who can be required to meet a work preparation requirement *and* a work-focused interview requirement (see p1068). For UC, you must be someone who can be required to meet all the work-related requirements, or to meet a work preparation requirement and a work-focused interview requirement.

A low level sanction should not be applied unless you have been notified clearly about what you have to do and the consequences of not complying with your requirements.[43] Details of the specific appointment for a work-focused interview and its purpose (ie, the type of interview), including the date, time and place, as well as the consequences of failing to attend, must have been given to you.[44]

How quickly do you have to contact the DWP?

The rules do not specify a time within which you must contact the DWP to explain your reasons if you have failed to do any of the above. However, to avoid a sanction decision being made, you should contact the DWP as soon possible and provide as much information as you can to show you had a good reason. The DWP may contact you (this may be via your journal if you are on UC) and ask for additional information, which you should provide if possible. If it was not clear what your work-related requirements were (eg, you did not realise you had to participate in an interview), make sure you state this and also consider making a complaint.

Lowest level sanctions

If you are getting UC or ESA, you can be given a lowest level sanction if you can only be required to meet a work-focused interview requirement (see p1066) and you fail to participate in a work-focused interview without a good reason.[45] Details of the interview and the consequences of failing to attend must have been given to you. If you fail to attend or to participate, contact the DWP as soon as possible to explain.

2. **How your benefit is reduced**

If you are given a sanction, your benefit is paid at a reduced (or nil) rate until the sanction period (see p1093) ends. The reduction for each universal credit (UC)

assessment period or each benefit week for jobseeker's allowance (JSA) and employment and support allowance (ESA) is calculated as follows.[46]
- **Step one:** take the number of days in the assessment period or benefit week (or, if lower, the total number of outstanding days in the sanction period). Deduct any days in the assessment period/benefit week for which the sanction period has been suspended because you have also been given a sanction for a benefit offence (see p1092).
- **Step two:** multiply the number of days in Step one by the relevant daily reduction rate. See below for UC, p1092 for JSA and p1090 for ESA.

For UC, the amount in Step two is adjusted so that it is not more than your standard allowance (see p66) or, if you are a joint claimant and only one of you has been sanctioned, so that it is not more than 50 per cent of your standard allowance. The reduction in your UC is made after the benefit cap has been applied, if relevant (see p1194).

Universal credit

For UC, the daily reduction rate is normally the amount of standard allowance that applies to you multiplied by 12 and divided by 365 (the 'high rate').[47] However, the daily reduction is 40 per cent of this amount (the 'low rate') if, at the end of the assessment period for which the reduction is being calculated:[48]
- you do not have to meet any work-related requirements (see p1061) because you:
  – are the responsible carer or responsible foster parent of a child under one;
  – are pregnant and there are 11 weeks or less before the week your baby is due;
  – had a baby not more than 15 weeks ago (including if the baby was stillborn);
  – are adopting a child and it is no more than 52 weeks since the child was placed with you; *or*
- you can only be required to meet a work-focused interview requirement (see p1066); *or*
- you are 16 or 17 years old.

If you are in a couple and are a joint claimant, the daily rate using the calculation above is divided by two.[49] If your partner is also given a sanction, the daily reduction rate that applies to her/him is also divided by two. The chart below shows the daily reduction rate for a couple if only one of you has been sanctioned.

The daily reduction rate is nil if, at the end of the assessment period for which the reduction is being calculated, you are someone who does not have to meet any work-related requirements because you have limited capability for work and work-related activity (see p1064).[50]

Part 7: National insurance, work and work-related rules
Chapter 47: Universal credit system sanctions
2. How your benefit is reduced

The daily reduction rates are rounded down to the nearest 10 pence.[51]

Daily reduction rates

	High rate £ per day	Low rate £ per day
Single		
Under 25	11.20	4.40
25 or over	13.40	5.30
Couple		
Both under 25	8.00	3.20
Either 25 or over	9.70	3.80

Note: you may still be entitled to some UC during the assessment period – ie, if you qualify for elements for children or any other elements, such as for childcare or housing costs. However, any deductions from benefit will still apply (see p1202).

Example
Tim and his partner are both aged 35 and are getting UC as joint claimants. They live in rented accommodation. Tim was given a 182-day high level sanction. There are 150 days outstanding in Tim's sanction period. This month is a 30-day assessment period. His partner was not given a sanction.
Step one: the relevant number of days is 30, as this is lower than the number of outstanding days in Tim's sanction period.
Step two: the daily rate is £9.70. The reduction is therefore 30 x £9.70 = £291.
Fifty per cent of Tim's standard allowance is £297.02 (£594.04 ÷ 2). This is higher than the reduction.
Tim and his partner's UC is therefore reduced by £291 over the assessment period. They continue to get the amount to which they are entitled that exceeds £291, including the help they get with their rent.

Employment and support allowance

For ESA, the daily reduction rate is normally the weekly amount of ESA to which you are entitled (not including any component or premium(s)) multiplied by 52 and divided by 365, rounded down to the nearest 10 pence (the 'high rate').[52]

The daily reduction rate is 40 per cent of the amount as calculated above (the 'low rate') if, at the end of the benefit week for which the reduction is being calculated:[53]

- you are a lone parent responsible for a child under one or the responsible foster parent of a child under one (see p1063);

- you are pregnant and there are 11 weeks or less before the week your baby is due;
- you had a baby not more than 15 weeks ago (including if the baby was stillborn);
- you are adopting a child and it is no more than 52 weeks since the child was placed with you (see p1063);
- you can only be required to meet a work-focused interview requirement (see p1066).

The daily reduction rate is nil if, at the end of the benefit week for which the reduction is being calculated, you do not have to meet any work-related requirements because you have limited capability for work and for work-related activity (see p1064).[54]

Note:
- The ESA work-related activity component was abolished for new claims from 3 April 2017. This means the impact of a sanction is greater for those who do not get the component. If this affects you, you may be able to apply for a higher hardship payment (see p1226).
- If you are getting a reduced rate of ESA because you have been disqualified from receiving ESA for any of the reasons on p649 (eg, because of failure to accept treatment), the daily reduction rates are also reduced.

Daily reduction rates

	High rate £ per day	Low rate £ per day
Entitled to main phase ESA	10.50	4.20
Under 25, not entitled to main phase ESA	8.30	3.32
25 or over, not entitled to main phase ESA	10.50	4.20
Reduced rate ESA due to disqualification:		
Entitled to main phase	8.40	3.36
Under 25, not entitled to main phase ESA	6.70	2.68
25 or over, not entitled to main phase ESA	8.40	3.36

Example

Julie, aged 30, claimed ESA recently. She is getting £74.35 a week ESA. She fails to participate in a work-focused interview, but participates three days later. She is given a low level sanction. Her total sanction period is nine days (see p1096): two days before she complies plus seven days = nine days.

For the first benefit week, the reduction is calculated as follows.

Step one: the relevant number of days is seven (the number of days in the benefit week).

Step two: 7 x £10.50 = £73.50

Julie's ESA is reduced by £73.50 for one benefit week. She is paid the remainder (£0.85).

For the second benefit week, the reduction is calculated as follows.

Part 7: National insurance, work and work-related rules
Chapter 47: Universal credit system sanctions
2. How your benefit is reduced

Step one: the relevant number of days is two (the number of days in the sanction period still outstanding).

Step two: 2 x £10.50 = £21.00

Julie's ESA for the week is reduced by £21.00. She is paid the remainder (£53.35). For the following weeks, she is paid as normal.

Jobseeker's allowance

For JSA, the daily reduction rate is the weekly amount of JSA to which you are entitled multiplied by 52 and divided by 365, rounded down to the nearest 10 pence.[55] The daily reduction rates are therefore as follows. If you are:

- under 25: £8.30;
- 25 or over: £10.50.

Example
Maya is a JSA claimant aged 24. She was given a seven-day low level sanction.
Step one: the relevant number of days is seven.
Step two: 7 x £8.30 = £58.10
Maya's JSA for the benefit week is reduced by £58.10. She is paid the remainder (£0.80). The following benefit week, she is paid the full rate of JSA (£58.90) because the sanction period has ended.

If your benefits change

- If you are given a UC sanction, your UC is being paid at a reduced rate when your entitlement ends, you still come under the UC system and you are entitled to JSA or ESA, the reduction is then made to your JSA or ESA.[56] The reduction is calculated as for JSA or ESA (see above) and is made for the remainder of the UC sanction period. Any days between the day your entitlement to UC ends and the day your entitlement to JSA or ESA starts are deducted from the period.
- If you are given a JSA or ESA sanction under the UC system and you become entitled to UC, the reduction is made to your UC instead of your JSA or ESA.[57] It is calculated as for UC (see p1089) and is made for the remainder of the JSA or ESA sanction period. If your award of JSA or ESA has ended, any days between the day your award of JSA or ESA ends and the day your award of UC starts are deducted from the period.

Special rules apply if you were given a sanction while entitled to JSA (or ESA) before you came under the UC system. In this case, if you are now entitled to:

- JSA (or ESA) under the UC system, but not UC, you are treated as if you were given a JSA (or ESA) sanction under the UC system;[58]
- UC, you are treated as if you were given a UC sanction.[59]

In both cases, the reduction is made for the remainder of the former JSA (or ESA) sanction period, minus any days between the day your former JSA (or ESA) entitlement ended (if relevant) and your current UC, JSA or ESA entitlement starts.

If you were originally given a sanction while entitled to JSA or ESA before coming under the UC system, you then came under the UC system, but later left it and claimed JSA or ESA outside the UC system, your original 'old system' sanction is not taken into account.[60] This is very unlikely to apply as there are only limited circumstances in which you can make new claims for JSA or ESA outside the UC system (see p23).

3. **The sanction period**

Length of the sanction period

Sanctions can be given for various periods, depending on your work-related requirements for universal credit (UC) or jobseeker's allowance (JSA) and employment and support allowance (ESA) under the UC system, and what you have done or failed to do. A sanction period may be longer if you have previously been sanctioned at the same level.

Sanction	Sanction period
High level sanctions (UC and JSA only)	91 or 182 days
Failing to apply for or to accept paid work	
Ceasing paid work or losing pay for specified reasons	
Medium level sanctions (UC and JSA only)	28 or 91 days
Failing to be available for paid work or to take all reasonable action to get paid work	
Low level sanctions (UC, JSA and ESA)	Until you comply with a requirement, plus a fixed period of seven, 14 or 28 days
Failing to meet a work-focused interview requirement (where other requirements also apply)	
Failing to meet a requirement connected to a work-related requirement	
Failing to meet a work preparation requirement	
Failing to take a particular action to get paid work (UC and JSA only)	

Part 7: National insurance, work and work-related rules
Chapter 47: Universal credit system sanctions
3. The sanction period

Lowest level sanctions (UC and ESA only)	Until you comply with a requirement
Failing to meet a work-related interview requirement (where no other requirements apply)	

High level sanctions

If you are given a high level sanction, it is usually imposed for 91 days. However, it is imposed for 182 days if you have previously had a 91-day high level sanction (see below).[61]

If you are given a high level UC sanction and you are 16 or 17 years old, a fixed sanction period is imposed for:[62]

- 14 days; *or*
- 28 days, if you have previously had a 14- or 28-day high level sanction (see below).

Longer sanction periods if you have previously been sanctioned

You can be given a longer sanction period of 182 days (28 days if you are a 16/17-year-old) if you have previously had a high level sanction. For the longer sanction period to apply, your previous sanctionable action must have taken place at least 14 days, but less than 365 days, before your current sanctionable action. If you have already had more than one high level sanction, only the most recent one is considered when deciding the length of a new sanction.

The 365 days run from the date of the previous sanctionable action, not from the date of the decision imposing the previous sanction, which could be some time later. If the previous sanctionable action was within 14 days of the current one, the length of the new sanction period is the same as the previous one. If it was 365 days or more before the current one, the length of the new sanction period is the same as if you were given a sanction for the first time.

For JSA, a high level UC sanction, and for UC, a high level JSA sanction which has been applied to your UC, also counts for these purposes.[63]

Sanctions you received when you were getting JSA but not under the UC system also count.

If you are getting JSA under the UC system, any previous JSA sanctions (both under the UC system and not) are not taken into account if you have been entitled to JSA or ESA not under the UC system, or to income support, at some point since the reduction to your JSA began.[64]

Note: if you are given a longer sanction period, but later a previous sanction is removed (eg, by the First-tier Tribunal), ask the DWP decision maker to reduce the sanction period if relevant.[65] Appeal if s/he fails to do so. If you have already appealed against the later sanction, the tribunal should take this into account and ensure that if it upholds the later sanction decision, the sanction period is for 91 days.[66]

Reduced sanction periods

If you are given a high level sanction because you failed to accept paid work, ceased paid work or lost pay voluntarily or because of misconduct before the date of your claim, your sanction period is reduced to take account of days when you did not claim UC (or JSA). It is calculated as follows and is the shorter of the following.[67]

- **Step one:** if the job was only due to last for a limited period, work out the number of days starting with the day after the date of your current sanctionable action and ending on the day the paid work would have ended. 'Limited period' is not defined.
- **Step two:** in any other case, work out the sanction period that would normally apply.
- **Step three:** reduce the amount in Step one or Step two, as relevant, by the number of days between the date of your current sanctionable action and your date of claim (see p47 and p717).

In practical terms, this means that if you claim UC (or JSA) after the job would have ended, or you delay your claim for UC (or JSA) long enough, your benefit is not paid at a reduced (or nil) rate.[68]

Example

Glynis quits her job on 7 October. It was only due to last until 1 November. She claims JSA on 16 November. She is given a high level sanction for the first time, so a 91-day sanction period would normally apply. However, her job was only due to last for a limited period. The number of days from 8 October to 1 November is 25 days. The number of days between 7 October and 16 November is 39 days. Glynis's sanction period is therefore reduced to nil and her JSA is not paid at a reduced rate.

Medium level sanctions

Medium level sanctions are usually imposed for 28 days. However, a medium level sanction is imposed for 91 days if you have previously had a 28-day or 91-day medium level sanction (see below).[69]

If you are given a medium level UC sanction and you are 16 or 17 years old, a fixed sanction period applies of:[70]

- seven days; *or*
- 14 days, if you have previously had a seven- or 14-day medium level sanction (see below).

Longer sanction periods if you have previously been sanctioned

You can be given a longer sanction period of 91 days (14 days if you are a 16/17-year-old) if you have previously had a medium level sanction.

Part 7: National insurance, work and work-related rules
Chapter 47: Universal credit system sanctions
3. The sanction period

For the longer sanction periods to apply, the previous sanctionable action must have taken place at least 14 days, but less than 365 days, before your current sanctionable action. The 365 days run from the date of the previous sanctionable action, not from the date of the decision imposing the previous sanction, which could be some time later. If you have already had more than one medium level sanction, only the most recent one is considered when deciding on the length of a new sanction.

If the previous sanctionable action was within 14 days of the current one, the length of the new sanction period is the same as the previous one. If it was 365 days or more before the current one, the length of the new sanction period is the same as if you were given a sanction for the first time.

For JSA, a medium level UC sanction also counts for these purposes. For UC, a medium level JSA sanction which was applied to your UC also counts for these purposes. If you were given a JSA sanction when you did not come under the UC system, and you are then given another sanction under the UC system, the previous sanctionable action can count when the new sanction period is determined.

If you are given a sanction but later a previous sanction is removed (eg, by the First-tier Tribunal), ask the DWP decision maker to reduce the sanction period if relevant. Appeal if s/he fails to do so. If you have already appealed against the later sanction, the tribunal should take the removal of the previous sanction into account and ensure that if it upholds the later sanction decision, the sanction period is for 28 days.

Low level sanctions

If you are given a low level UC, JSA or ESA sanction, it is imposed for a period made up of the period until you comply with the work-related requirement plus a fixed period as follows.

Step one: work out the number of days, starting on the date your sanctionable action took place and ending on the earliest of the following:[71]

- the day before the date you meet a 'compliance condition' (see below) specified by the DWP; *or*
- for UC and ESA only, the day before the date you come into a category in which you no longer have to meet any work-related requirements (see p1061); *or*
- the day before the date you are no longer required to take particular action specified in a work preparation requirement; *or*
- the date your entitlement to UC (or JSA or ESA) ends. For UC, this does not apply if this is because you cease to be, or become, a member of a couple.

Compliance condition

A 'compliance condition' is:[72]

– a condition that you stop a sanctionable action – eg, if you failed to participate in an employment programme, a condition that you must participate; *or*

– a condition relating to your future compliance with a work-related requirement (or a requirement connected to one) – eg, if you failed to attend a training scheme, a condition that you must attend and participate in an interview to discuss what training may be suitable.

For example, the DWP says that the compliance condition required following failure to attend a work-focused interview is to arrange and attend another work-focused interview.[73] The DWP should inform you of the consequences of not meeting the condition immediately.

Step two: work out the fixed sanction period.
- For UC if you are at least 18 years old, and for JSA or ESA, this is usually for seven days. However, the period is:[74]
  - 14 days, if you have previously had a seven-day low level sanction (see below); *or*
  - 28 days, if you have previously had a 14-day or 28-day low level sanction (see below).
- For UC if you are 16 or 17 years old, this is for seven days, but only if you have been given a low level sanction previously (see below).[75] If you have not been given a low level sanction previously (or it is not taken into account – see below), there is no fixed period and your sanction lasts only until you meet the compliance condition.

Step three: add the number of days in Steps one and two together. This is your low level sanction period.

What can you do to limit the length of a low level sanction period?

If the DWP does not make a decision to give you a sanction until some time after your sanctionable action, you might not have a compliance condition to meet until you are given the sanction. The DWP is still likely to say that your indefinite sanction period runs from the assessment period in which it decides to give you the sanction and lasts for the relevant number of days, starting from the date your sanctionable action took place. Try to argue that you have already complied with the condition before you were given the sanction – eg, if you are given a sanction because you failed to provide your CV on a specified date, but you provided one later. Provide any relevant information and evidence to prove you have already complied. You could also make a complaint about the time the DWP took to decide to give you a sanction (see Chapter 60). If there was any confusion about what you were required to do at the time of the sanctionable action and in the period before the DWP accepts that you complied with the condition, explain this when challenging the sanction and/or complaining.

Part 7: National insurance, work and work-related rules
Chapter 47: Universal credit system sanctions
3. The sanction period

Longer sanction periods if you have previously been sanctioned

You can be given a longer sanction period if you have previously had a low level sanction. For the longer sanction periods to apply, the previous sanctionable action must have taken place at least 14 days, but less than 365 days, before your current sanctionable action. If you have already had more than one low level sanction, only the most recent one is considered when making a decision about the length of a new sanction.

The 365 days run from the date of the previous sanctionable action, not from the date of the decision imposing the previous sanction, which could be some time later. If the previous sanctionable action was within 14 days of the current one, the length of the new sanction period is the same as the previous one. If it was 365 days or more before the current one, the length of the new sanction period is the same as if you were given a sanction for the first time.

For UC, a low level JSA or ESA sanction that has been applied to your UC also counts for these purposes. For JSA, a low level UC or ESA sanction, and for ESA, a low level UC or JSA sanction, also count for these purposes.[76]

If you were given a JSA or ESA sanction when you did not come under the UC system and you are then given another sanction under the UC system, the previous sanctionable action can count when the new sanction period is determined.[77]

Note: if you are given a sanction but later a previous sanction is removed (eg, by the First-tier Tribunal), ask the DWP decision maker to reduce the sanction period if relevant.[78] Appeal if s/he fails to do so. If you have already appealed against the later sanction, the tribunal should take the removal of the previous sanction into account.[79]

Lowest level sanctions

If you are given a lowest level sanction, it can be imposed indefinitely. It is imposed for the number of days starting on the date your sanctionable action took place and only ends on the earliest of:[80]

- the day before the date you meet a 'compliance condition' specified by the DWP (see p1096 for the meaning). If it was not made clear to you what you had to do, or it was difficult to rearrange the work-focused interview, you should include that in your good reason when challenging the length of the sanction, and complain; *or*
- the day before the date you come into a category in which you no longer have to meet any work-related requirements (see p1061); *or*
- the date your entitlement to UC (or ESA) ends. For UC, this does not apply if this is because you cease to be, or become, a member of a couple.

When the sanction period starts and ends

For all levels of sanction, the sanction period starts:[81]

- for UC, on the first day of the assessment period in which the decision is made to give you a sanction or, if your UC was not reduced for the sanction during that period, from the first day of the next assessment period;
- for JSA, if you have not been paid any JSA for the benefit week in which the sanctionable action took place, on the first day of that benefit week, or if you have been paid for that week, the first day of the benefit week after the last benefit week for which you were paid JSA;
- for ESA, if you have not been paid any ESA for the benefit week in which the DWP decision maker decides you should be sanctioned, on the first day of that benefit week, or if you have been paid for that week, the first day of the benefit week after the last benefit week for which you were paid ESA.

However, if your benefit is already being paid at a reduced rate because of a previous sanction, it is not reduced for a new sanction until the previous reduction ends.

Once a sanction period has begun, it continues unbroken until the sanction period comes to an end.[82] This means, for example, that if you take a job for a short period but then claim UC (or JSA or ESA) again during the period of the sanction, although you are still caught by the sanction, this is only for any days still outstanding in the sanction period.

If your UC (or JSA or ESA) entitlement ends before the DWP decision maker has decided to give you a sanction, but the decision to do so is made when you are again entitled to the benefit, the decision is treated as having been made on the day before your previous entitlement ended.[83] So, in practice, the number of days between the two awards of benefit are deducted from the sanction period.

A sanction is suspended for any period during which you are sanctioned for a benefit offence (see p1278).[84]

If you have more than one sanction at the same time

Your sanction period is worked out for each sanction you are given. If more than one decision to sanction you is made at the same time, or you are sanctioned when your benefit is already reduced because of a sanction, the sanction periods run consecutively. If your benefit is already being paid at a reduced rate because of a previous sanction, it is not reduced for a new sanction until the previous reduction ends.[85]

The maximum outstanding sanction period for all sanctions is 1,095 days. So if a new sanction is imposed when you already have an existing sanction, the sanction period is adjusted to ensure that the outstanding period for all your sanctions will not go over the 1,095-day limit.[86]

Part 7: National insurance, work and work-related rules
Chapter 47: Universal credit system sanctions
4. Good reasons for your actions

When a sanction is terminated

All sanctions terminate and your benefit is no longer paid at a reduced (or nil) rate if, since the date of the most recent sanctionable action, you have been in paid work for (or for periods that total) at least six months (for UC) or 26 weeks (for JSA or ESA).[87] You count as being in paid work if:

- for UC, your monthly earnings during the six months are at least the amount of your individual earnings threshold (see p1065). This includes if you are treated as having a minimum level of self-employed earnings under the rules described on p121;
- for UC, you are someone who does not have to satisfy any work-related requirements for any of the reasons listed on p1061 and p1066 (other situations) and your monthly earnings during the six months are at least 16 times the minimum wage for a person of your age multiplied by 52 and divided by 12;
- for JSA, your weekly earnings are at least what you would earn for the number of hours you are expected to work (see p1054) at the minimum wage for a person of your age;
- for ESA, your weekly earnings are at least 16 times the minimum wage for a person of your age.

4. **Good reasons for your actions**

In a number of situations, a sanction cannot be imposed if you have a good reason for your actions. **'Good reason'** is not defined in the rules, but caselaw on sanctions in the universal credit (UC) system, as well as caselaw on 'good cause' and caselaw on 'good reason' for jobseeker's allowance (JSA) sanctions outside the UC system (see p1155), can be applied.[88] In addition, what may count as good reason is set out in guidance.[89] If you appeal against the sanction decision, the guidance is not binding on the First-tier Tribunal; it must make up its own mind about what counts as a good reason.

It is up to you to show you have a good reason, but the DWP decision maker should take all the circumstances into account.

How much time are you given to explain your good reasons?
You should always be given the opportunity to provide your reasons for what you did or did not do. You should be given sufficient time to explain your reasons and to provide relevant evidence. There are no specified time limits, but the DWP says you should be given at least five working days if the information is requested by post. You may be given less time than this if you can be contacted by telephone, face to face or by electronic means. The DWP says that you should be given more time if you have to get information or evidence from someone else, you have a representative, or you have a health condition or there are other temporary circumstances (eg, caring responsibilities) that prevent you

from replying.[90] The time you are given should reflect your circumstances. If the time you are given seems unreasonable, you should mention this when you challenge the sanction decision and/or complain.

For ideas about what might count as a good reason, see below.

Circumstances that should be taken into account

The DWP decision maker should take all your circumstances into account when deciding whether you have a good reason for any sanctionable action. This should include the following.

- Any restrictions or limitations you have been allowed to place on your availability for work, including reductions to your expected hours of work (see p1054), or restrictions which should have been made if your circumstances had been fully taken into account.[91] You may have taken all 'reasonable action' given your circumstances at the time (see p1053). You do not necessarily have a good reason for refusing to apply for a job which does not meet your restrictions or limitations, but your restrictions are very significant factors to take into account.[92]
- Any condition you have or any personal circumstances that suggest that a particular job or activity would be likely to cause you unreasonable physical or mental stress or significant harm to your health.
- A disease or physical/mental disability that affects your ability to work or to meet your work-related requirements, or which means your health (or the health of others) would have been at risk.
- You misunderstood what you had to do because of language, learning or literacy difficulties, or because you were misled by the DWP. Instructions about work preparation and work-related activity must be clear.[93] There must be notification of the work-related requirement and an explanation of the consequences of non-compliance.[94] Ignorance of the law may sometimes mean that you have a good reason, but you are expected to make reasonable enquiries of your work coach if you do not understand what you have to do.[95] If you do not know about a requirement (eg, you do not receive notification of a work-focused interview), you have good reason for not complying with it.[96] However, you are expected to check your UC online account, including messages on your journal, where reasonable. If you were unable to do this, you should explain why.
- You (or someone for whom you care) were attending a medical, dental or other important appointment which it would have been unreasonable to rearrange.
- You have experienced domestic violence or bullying or harassment.
- A sincerely held religious or conscientious objection.[97]
- Caring responsibilities that make it unreasonable for you to meet your work-related requirements or continue in work, including whether suitable childcare

Part 7: National insurance, work and work-related rules
Chapter 47: Universal credit system sanctions
4. Good reasons for your actions

would have been (or was) reasonably available.[98] You are expected to consider available options for childcare and give reasons if you believe they are not suitable.

- You are homeless.[99] You may also be able to argue that your work coach should have suspended your work-related requirements during a period of homelessness.
- Any transport difficulties.
- Excessive travelling time involved, including where this is excessive because of your health or caring responsibilities (but see below for when this does not count as a good reason).
- Unreasonably high expenses (eg, for childcare or travel) that were (or would be) unavoidable.[100]

Account should also be taken of any other factor that appears relevant. See, in particular, p1106 for when the terms of a job on offer break the law on minimum working conditions.

Note: there are situations where the work search requirement for UC and JSA should be suspended temporarily (see p1073). If this should have applied to you, you may not have to argue that you had a good reason for your actions. Instead, you should show why your work-related requirements were not reasonable at the time. You may still have been required to take part in work preparation (see p1051), but you may be able to argue that you have a good reason for failing to do so because of the same temporary circumstances.

When might you not have a good reason?

You may find it difficult to show that you have a good reason for failing to apply for, or accept, paid work on the grounds of distance if your travel time is shorter than 90 minutes. This is because you have to be available for work and to look for work in locations that are up to 90 minutes from your home.[101] However, there could be other factors such as childcare or high travelling expenses, which can be considered when deciding whether you had a good reason, and in some cases the DWP should consider whether a shorter travel to work time should be allowed (see p1058). Although not specified, it is probable that travel time of up to 90 minutes to attend work-related activity or an interview would also not be seen as a good reason, but all the other relevant factors (including childcare, expenses and the effect on your health) should be taken into account.

Leaving a job or reducing your hours

You may be able to show you have a good reason for leaving a job or reducing your hours in the following situations.

- Your chances of getting other employment, including self-employment, were good, there were strong reasons for leaving your job and you acted reasonably in doing so.[102]
- You genuinely did not know or were mistaken about the conditions of the job (eg, it was beyond your physical or mental capacity, or was harmful to your health), you gave it a fair trial before leaving and it was reasonable for you to leave when you did.[103]
- You left your job or reduced your hours for personal or domestic reasons – eg, to look after a sick relative.[104] Explain why you left your job before looking for, or getting, alternative employment. It could be helpful to show that you tried to negotiate an arrangement with your employer to resolve the problem – eg, for a reduction in your hours or time off work.
- You left your job to move with your partner who has taken a job elsewhere.[105] Relevant factors may include how important it was to your partner's career to make the move and how good your chances are of finding work in the new area.
- Your employer made a change in the terms and conditions of your employment that does not amount to your contract of employment ending. You are expected to use any grievance procedure first. In some situations (eg, with a zero-hour contract), a reduction in hours may be part of your contract of employment because your hours are not guaranteed. You should not be sanctioned if the reduction in hours is not voluntary (see p1084).
  If you leave your job because your employer cuts your wages unilaterally, you might not be able to show you have a good reason. The DWP will not consider a cut unless it takes you below the national minimum wage (see Appendix 7), but a cut in wages may be a good reason if, for example, you are not given proper notice of an imposed change to your pay, or your work-related expenses are now an unreasonably high proportion of your pay. If you stay in your job, a cut in wages is a reduction in pay, but may not be voluntary (see p1084).
- You left your job because of a firm offer of alternative employment, but claimed benefit because the offer fell through. However, the DWP may say you do not have a good reason if the offer was cancelled before you left your previous employment or you changed your mind and did not take the new job and you could have stayed in the existing employment, or you did not ask your employer if you could stay.

The DWP decision maker should take into account:
- any caring responsibilities you have which made it unreasonable for you to stay in your job and whether suitable childcare was (or could have been) available; *and*
- any childcare expenses you had to pay as a result of being in the job, if they were an unreasonably high proportion of the income you received.

Part 7: National insurance, work and work-related rules
Chapter 47: Universal credit system sanctions
4. Good reasons for your actions

What should you do before you give up a job or reduce your hours?

1. Do everything possible to resolve problems before you give up your job. If the conditions of a job are poor, try to sort out any problems (eg, by raising them with your employer, or using any grievance procedure) rather than leaving immediately, and to look for another job seriously before giving one up. Keep a record of your negotiations with your employer. You may have difficulty showing you have a good reason if you do not do so.

2. Employers are required to provide certain minimum working conditions and pay the minimum wage (see Appendix 7). These could help to show that you have a good reason for giving up work. Point out that the intention of the Working Time Regulations is to protect the health and safety of workers, so conditions that do not comply with them should be regarded as unacceptable. Your employer should also comply with the Equality Act 2010 and make reasonable adjustments if you are disabled.

3. If you need to reduce your hours because of your health or caring responsibilities, make sure that you have a record of your request to your employer and any other adjustments you have asked for before the reduction in hours. You should try to negotiate with your employer rather than leaving the job, if possible.

4. You are likely to have difficulty showing you have a good reason for leaving a job or reducing your hours just because the pay is low (although your work-related expenses should be taken into account).[106] However, you can argue that this does not apply if you left your job because your employer refused to pay the national minimum wage.[107]

Leaving or failing to participate in work preparation or work-related activity

You should be given clear instructions about where you have to attend for work-related activity and the consequences of failing to participate. For example, if it is not clear that the activity is mandatory, or you do not understand what you are supposed to do and when, you may have a good reason for failing to participate. You may not have a good reason simply because you consider that the work preparation or work-related activity is not useful or not relevant to your needs, but you could consider complaining. You are likely not to have a good reason for failing to participate if you refuse to confirm your identity because of data protection concerns and you do not offer another acceptable form of evidence of identity.[108]

You may be able to show you have a good reason for leaving a particular work-related activity (eg, a training scheme or employment programme) or for failing to participate in work preparation or work-related activity (see p1101). The DWP decision maker should consider the following.

- Your continued participation would have put your health and safety, or that of others, at risk.
- The travelling time to or from the scheme or programme was excessive (although not listed as a good reason in guidance, this could relate to other good reasons such as your health).

- You had caring responsibilities, no one else was available to provide the care, and it was not practical to make other arrangements.
- Temporary circumstances made it difficult for you to participate – eg, you were attending court as a party to the proceedings, a witness or a juror, you were crewing or launching a lifeboat, or you were on duty as a part-time member of a fire brigade.
- You were arranging or attending the funeral of a close relative or a close friend.
- You had to deal with a domestic emergency.
- You were having structured alcohol or drug dependency treatment.

Note: there are temporary circumstances in which the work search requirement in UC should be lifted[109] and you may not be expected to be available for work (see p1074). However, you may still have been required to take part in work preparation. If this applied to you, you may be able to argue that your good reason relates to the same temporary circumstances, and/or that the temporary circumstances should have been taken into account in limiting the work preparation you were required to do.

Refusing or failing to apply for a job

You may be able to show you have a good reason for refusing a job – eg:
- if the travelling time to or from the job was more than 90 minutes or more than the maximum travelling time agreed with your work coach;
- if you are within your 'permitted period' (see p1121) and have restricted the type of work for which you are available to your usual occupation or to at least your usual rate of pay, or both, and you refuse a job that does not meet these conditions;
- if you have been laid off or are on short-time working, have been accepted as available only for casual employment and you refuse to take some other type of work;[110]
- if you come under the rules that exempt you from having to be able to start work immediately, and you refuse to take a job which you would have to start immediately (see p1116).

You can be sanctioned for refusing to accept a job which does not have guaranteed hours (a zero-hour contract), but you should not be sanctioned if:[111]
- your employer reduces your hours because you have taken work with another employer in order to gain more hours of work (or arguably, because you look for other work); *or*
- the hours offered by your employer would restrict the opportunity for you to increase your paid work with other employers.

Part 7: National insurance, work and work-related rules
Chapter 47: Universal credit system sanctions
5. Sanction decisions

Note: you cannot be given a sanction if you refuse a job because it is vacant because of a trade dispute.[112]

What should you do before refusing or failing to apply for a job?

Employers are required to provide certain minimum working conditions and pay the minimum wage (see Appendix 7). Try to argue that you have a good reason for not applying for any job where the terms do not comply with the legal requirements. Make sure that this is the case, particularly where the Working Time Regulations 1998 are concerned, as there are many exceptions and opt-outs that might apply. If the terms offered break the rules about the limit on the number of hours in the average working week, the DWP may suggest that you agree to an 'individual opt-out'. Argue that this would be unreasonable, as the working time rules are intended to protect the health and safety of workers. The DWP accepts that you have a good reason for refusing a job if you do so because it does not pay at least the national minimum wage that applies to you.[113] However, you are unlikely to have a good reason simply because you are not sure of the effect of work and pay on your benefits.[114] You may not have a good reason for not applying for a job simply because you believe you are unlikely to be successful. You should ask your work coach to reconsider, explaining why you think you will not get the job and suggesting other actions you could take. You are especially unlikely to have a good reason if you have previously agreed to apply for the job and did not attempt to negotiate with your work coach.[115]

5. **Sanction decisions**

A DWP decision maker decides whether you should be given a sanction, often some time after the sanctionable action took place. Do not assume that because you have not yet been informed of any sanction, the DWP has decided not to sanction you.

You should be issued with notice, telling you that you have been given a sanction.[116] This information should either be sent in a letter or be posted on your universal credit (UC) online account.

It is possible that you will not know you have been given a sanction until your benefit is paid at a reduced (or nil) rate. You should contact the DWP as soon as you are aware of the reduction in your benefit to find out what sanctionable action is involved, give a good reason, if possible, and comply with your work-related requirements if applicable. For example, with a low level sanction (which runs until you comply with the requirement), you must be given formal notification of the decision and then, in theory, you could comply on the same day – eg, if you fail to attend an appointment, you could phone and remake the appointment on the same day.

If the sanction decision is made some time after the sanctionable action, you could complain as well as challenge the sanction decision. Your 'good reason' may be affected by whether your work-related requirements were made clear to you at the time of the sanctionable action. Any compliance condition you need to meet to stop a sanction period from increasing must also be made clear to you. This may be a different requirement if the original is no longer appropriate – eg, if you failed to attend a training day which is no longer available. If your work-related requirements or the compliance condition (see p1096) were not made clear, you should complain as well as challenge the sanction decision.

If you have complex needs (see below), you should be contacted by telephone (or another method which is accessible to you) about what led to the sanction and any good reason you may have, before the sanction decision is made.

Only a DWP decision maker can decide whether you have a good reason for the sanctionable action and whether a sanction should be applied. However, if an employment or training scheme provider requires you to do something on behalf of the DWP,[117] failure to comply may result in a sanction. If a provider alerts the DWP about a possible sanctionable action, the DWP should ask you, in writing, whether you have a good reason for what happened.

People who are vulnerable

If you have complex needs, special procedures apply before your case is referred for a sanction decision. 'Complex needs' procedures may apply if you are considered to be 'vulnerable'. This may be if you have a serious mental health condition, but can also apply if there is a language barrier, you have an addiction or are homeless. These procedures involve extra checks before you are given a sanction, to make sure you understand your work-related requirements and to gather any reasons for what you did or did not do.

If you think that you are vulnerable because of your condition or situation, but have been given a sanction, ask whether the 'complex needs' procedures were applied to you. If you have a disability and the DWP does not follow these procedures (eg, it does not make sure that you were able to comply with your work-related requirements without your health being affected), this could be a breach of the Equality Act 2010. If you have failed to comply with a work-related requirement, the DWP should check whether you have complex needs before referring your case for a sanction decision.[118] If you have a health condition which affects your ability to leave your home, at least two attempts should be made to make a home visit, and a sanction referral should not be considered unless the home visit and all other attempts to contact you have failed.[119] If the sanction decision is passed to a decision maker and the evidence shows the requirements were unreasonable at the time of your sanctionable action, the decision maker should accept that you had a good reason and return the case to the DWP for your requirements to be reduced.[120]

Part 7: National insurance, work and work-related rules
Chapter 47: Universal credit system sanctions
6. Challenging a sanction decision

6. Challenging a sanction decision

If you are given a sanction, your benefit is paid at a reduced rate, often for a lengthy period. It is, therefore, always worth challenging a sanction decision.

You can challenge:

- the decision to give you a sanction, including:
  - whether you have lawfully been required to do something: whether you have been properly notified of any requirements and the consequences of not complying – eg, to attend an interview or participate in work-related activity. Your work-related requirements must have been made clear to you,[121] and you should also make it clear if you considered your requirements to be unreasonable given your circumstances;
  - whether you failed to do something, or did something, as alleged by the DWP;
  - whether you have a good reason (see p1100) for what you did or did not do;
- the length of the sanction period – eg, if there is a dispute about the number of times you have been sanctioned, or you are challenging a previous decision to give you a sanction.

You should also consider complaining if the actions of the DWP contributed to the sanction and/or the length of the sanction – eg, if your work-related requirements were not made clear to you, or you did not get notification until some time after the sanctionable action, which made it difficult for you to comply and end the sanction period. You can apply for a revision or appeal against a sanction decision in the usual way (see Chapters 56 and 57).

If you have been given a sanction more than once, you should challenge *all* the decisions if possible. Apply for a mandatory reconsideration of all the sanction decisions, asking for the time limit for doing so to be extended if relevant. If you are not sure about the number or length of the sanctions, ask the DWP to clarify what decisions have been made.

If a previous sanction is removed (eg, by a decision maker or the First-tier Tribunal), the sanction period for a later sanction of the same type can be reduced.[122] If you have appealed against the later sanction, the tribunal should take the removal of the previous sanction into account.[123]

You must apply for a mandatory reconsideration before you can appeal. You can ask for a sanction decision to be revised, even if it was made a long time ago, as universal credit (UC) sanctions, and jobseeker's allowance and employment and support allowance sanctions under the UC system, can be revised at any time (see p1308).

You must be given written notice of the sanction decision, setting out your appeal rights.[124] Although notification of sanction decisions is meant to happen automatically when the sanction is applied to your benefit, this does not always happen. If you were given a sanction but did not receive written notice of the decision, get advice. You may still be able to ask for a mandatory reconsideration and then appeal, even if the decision was made a long time ago.

If you have received a decision letter with a postal address, you can send your request for a mandatory reconsideration to the address on the letter and/or hand it in to the job centre (if possible, do both). If you are a UC claimant, you can state that you want a mandatory reconsideration on your online account, if you have one. However, it is advisable to follow this up by phone and in writing if possible – eg, you may not be able to upload all the evidence you want to send via your online account. Ensure that your request for a mandatory reconsideration is acknowledged and keep a copy of your application (including a screenshot if you request the mandatory reconsideration via your online account). Even if you post it on your journal, provide a copy to the job centre as soon as possible, making a note of the date and time that you do so. If you do not have an online account, you can request a mandatory reconsideration by telephone or in writing. You should make it clear that you are formally requesting a mandatory reconsideration and keep proof of your request.

You should apply for a revision of *all* outstanding sanction decisions made against you, including those which will not be applied until your existing sanction period is over. If you decide to appeal once you have a mandatory reconsideration notice (see p1339), you can ask for related sanction decisions to be considered in the same appeal hearing.

How can you increase your chances of getting a decision changed?

1. An appeal to the First-tier Tribunal gives you a chance to challenge the DWP's version of events, including the evidence it is using from your former employer or a work-related activity scheme provider. You should ask the DWP for all the information and documents that were used in the process of making the sanction decision. If the DWP does not provide these, the tribunal can be asked to direct it to do so (see p1358). As you must request a mandatory reconsideration first, any information you can supply to the DWP at that point is useful, in case you can get the decision changed quickly. If a mandatory reconsideration is refused, you can still use the same arguments at an appeal.

2. Attend the appeal hearing if you can. Explain your case fully and, if relevant, the good reasons for what you did or failed to do (see p1100), including any factors relating to your own situation and/or how the sanction was notified to you.

3. Provide as much evidence as you can to support your case – eg, medical evidence or evidence about your caring responsibilities. The tribunal can allow witnesses (eg, family members or former work colleagues) to give evidence on your behalf.

Note: if you do not attend the appeal hearing and further evidence or information about you is submitted by the DWP, the tribunal should consider an adjournment to allow you to attend, or to respond to the information/evidence.

Part 7: National insurance, work and work-related rules
Chapter 47: Universal credit system sanctions
Notes

AskCPAG has a useful tool to create a note to put in your journal requesting a mandatory reconsideration of a sanction decision at askcpag.org.uk/link/200331/universal-credit-sanctions--mandatory-reconsideration.

Notes

1. When you can be sanctioned
1 **UC** Reg 100(1) UC Regs
 JSA Reg 17 JSA Regs 2013
 ESA Reg 50 ESA Regs 2013
2 **UC** s26 WRA 2012; reg 114 UC Regs
 JSA s6J JSA 1995; reg 29 JSA Regs 2013
3 **UC** s26(2)(b) and (c) and (4)(a) WRA 2012
 JSA s6J(2)(b) and (c) and (3)(a) JSA 1995
4 **UC** Reg 113(1)(a) UC Regs
 JSA Reg 28(1)(a) JSA Regs 2013
5 **UC** Reg 113(1)(e) UC Regs
 JSA Reg 28(1)(c) JSA Regs
6 R(IS) 5/95; *Fiory v CAO,* 20 June 1995
7 para K3057 ADM
8 *S v SSWP* [2017] UKUT 477 (AAC)
9 **UC** Reg 97(3) UC Regs
 JSA Reg 14(2) JSA Regs 2013
10 paras K3271-75 ADM
11 s27A Small Business, Enterprise and Employment Act 2015
12 para K2301 ADM
13 **UC** s26(2)(d), (3) and (4) WRA 2012
 JSA s6J(2)(d) and (3) JSA 1995
14 R(U) 10/71; R(U) 2/76
15 **UC** Reg 113(1)(e) UC Regs
 JSA Reg 28(1)(c) JSA Regs 2013
16 para K2224 ADM
17 para H4055 ADM
18 Reg 113(1)(g) UC Regs
19 **UC** Reg 113(1)(b)-(d) and (f) and (2) UC Regs
 JSA Reg 28(1)(b) and (d)-(f) and (2) JSA Regs 2013
20 para K3213 ADM
21 s148 Employment Rights Act 1996
22 para K3203 ADM
23 para K2031 ADM
24 para K3236 ADM
25 **UC** Reg 113(1)(f) UC Regs
 JSA Reg 28(1)(f) and (2) JSA Regs 2013
26 R(U) 25/52

27 para K2241 ADM
28 R(U) 8/57, para 6
29 R(U) 26/56; R(U) 1/58
30 R(U) 10/53
31 R(U) 14/56
32 *AA v SSWP (JSA)* [2012] UKUT 100 (AAC), reported as [2012] AACR 42
33 R(U) 24/56
34 K3073 ADM
35 R(U) 1/57; R(U) 14/57; CU/34/1992
36 R(U) 2/76
37 R(U) 2/74
38 R(U) 26/51; R(U) 20/64; R(U) 4/70; R(U) 1/81
39 R(U) 3/81
40 **UC** s27 WRA 2012; reg 103(1) UC Regs
 JSA s6K JSA 1995; reg 17 JSA Regs 2013
41 **UC** s27 WRA 2012; reg 104(1) UC Regs
 JSA s6K JSA 1995; reg 17 JSA Regs 2013
 ESA s11J WRA 2007; reg 50 ESA Regs 2013
42 *CS v SSWP (JSA)* [2019] UKUT 218 (AAC)
43 *JB v SSWP* [2018] UKUT 360 (AAC)
44 paras K1181-82 ADM
45 **UC** s27 WRA 2012; reg 105 UC Regs
 ESA s11J WRA 2007; reg 50 ESA Regs 2013

2. How your benefit is reduced
46 **UC** Regs 101(5) and 110 UC Regs
 JSA Regs 17 and 26 JSA Regs 2013
 ESA Regs 50 and 58 ESA Regs 2013
47 Reg 111(1) UC Regs
48 Reg 111(2) UC Regs
49 Reg 111(5) UC Regs
50 Reg 111(3) UC Regs
51 Reg 111(4) UC Regs
52 Reg 59 ESA Regs 2013
53 Reg 60(1) ESA Regs 2013
54 Reg 60(2) ESA Regs 2013
55 Reg 27 JSA Regs 2013

56 **JSA** Reg 30 JSA Regs 2013
   ESA Reg 61 ESA Regs 2013
57 **UC** Reg 112 and Sch 11 paras 1 and 2
   UC Regs
   JSA Reg 6 JSA Regs 2013
   ESA Reg 43 ESA Regs 2013
58 Arts 14, 15, 17 and 18 WRA(No.9)O
59 Regs 30 and 32 UC(TP) Regs
60 **UC** Reg 33(3)(b) UC(TP) Regs
   JSA Art 19(3)(b) WRA (No.9)O
   ESA Art 16(3)(b) WRA (No.9)O

3. The sanction period
61 Reg 102(2)(a) UC Regs
62 Reg 102(2)(b) UC Regs
63 **UC** Sch 11 para 3 UC Regs
   JSA Reg 19 JSA Regs 2013
64 Art 19(3) WRA(No.9)O
65 Reg 14 UC,PIP,JSA&ESA(DA) Regs
66 CJSA/2375/2000
67 **UC** Reg 102(4) and (5) UC Regs
   JSA Regs 17 and 19(3) JSA Regs 2013
68 **UC** Reg 113(1)(e) UC Regs
   JSA Reg 28(1)(c) JSA Regs 2013
69 **UC** Reg 103(2)(a) and 112 and Sch 11
   para 3 UC Regs
   JSA Reg 20 JSA Regs 2013
70 Reg 103(2)(b) UC Regs
71 **UC** Reg 104(2)(a) and (3)(a) UC Regs
   JSA Reg 21(2) JSA Regs 2013
   ESA Reg 52(a) ESA Regs 2013
72 **UC** s27(6) and (7) WRA 2012
   JSA s6K(6) and (7) JSA 1995
   ESA s11J(5) and (6) WRA 2007
73 DWP, *Universal Credit Guidance,* 'Fail to
   attend', v14.0, House of Commons
   library deposited papers, available at
   www.rightsnet.org.uk/universal-credit-
   guidance
74 **UC** Regs 104(2)(b) and 112 and Sch 11
   para 3 UC Regs
   JSA Reg 21(3) JSA Regs 2013
   ESA Reg 52(b) ESA Regs 2013
75 Reg 104(3)(b) UC Regs
76 **UC** Sch 11 para 3 UC Regs
   JSA Reg 21 JSA Regs 2013
   ESA Regs 50 and 52 ESA Regs 2013
77 Regs 31 and 33 UC(TP) Regs; Arts 16-19
   WRA(No.9)O
78 Reg 14 UC,PIP,JSA&ESA(DA) Regs
79 CJSA/2375/2000
80 **UC** Reg 105(2) UC Regs
   ESA Reg 53 ESA Regs 2013
81 **UC** Reg 106 UC Regs
   JSA Reg 22 JSA Regs 2013
   ESA Reg 54 ESA Regs 2013

82 **UC** Reg 107(1) UC Regs
   JSA Reg 23(1) JSA Regs 2013
   ESA Reg 55(1) ESA Regs 2013
83 **UC** Reg 107(2) UC Regs
   JSA Reg 23(2) and (3) JSA Regs 2013
   ESA Reg 55(2) and (3) ESA Regs 2013
84 **UC** Reg 108 UC Regs
   JSA Reg 24 JSA Regs 2013
   ESA Reg 56 ESA Regs 2013
85 **UC** Reg 106(c) UC Regs
   JSA Reg 22(c) JSA Regs 2013
   ESA Reg 54(c) ESA Regs 2013
86 **UC** Reg 101(1)-(3) UC Regs
   JSA Reg 18(1)-(3) JSA Regs 2013
   ESA Reg 51(1)-(3) ESA Regs 2013
87 **UC** Reg 109 UC Regs
   JSA Reg 25 JSA Regs 2013
   ESA Reg 57 ESA Regs 2013

4. Good reasons for your actions
88 *S v SSWP* [2017] UKUT 477 (AAC)
89 Ch K2 ADM
90 paras K2011-14 ADM
91 *RR v SSWP* [2017] UKUT 459 (AAC)
92 *HS v SSWP* [2009] UKUT 177 (AAC),
   reported as [2010] AACR 10
93 *SSWP v DC (JSA)* [2017] UKUT 464
94 *JB v SSWP* [2018] UKUT 360 (AAC)
95 *S v SSWP* [2017] UKUT 477 (AAC)
96 *SP v SSWP* [2018] UKUT 227
97 R(JSA) 7/03 discusses the meaning of
   'conscientious objection' in this context.
98 para K2142 ADM
99 paras K2091-95 ADM
100 para K2157 ADM
101 **UC** Reg 97(3) UC Regs
    JSA Reg 14(2) JSA Regs 2013
102 R(U) 4/73
103 R(U) 3/73
104 R(U) 14/52
105 R(U) 19/52; R(U) 4/87; CJSA/2507/
    2005
106 para K2157 ADM
107 para K2238 ADM
108 *CS v SSWP (JSA)* [2019] UKUT 218 (AAC)
109 Reg 99(3) UC Regs
110 paras K2175-76 ADM
111 para K2301 ADM
112 **UC** Reg 113(1)(a) UC Regs
    JSA reg 28(1)(a) JSA Regs 2013
113 para K2213 ADM
114 *S v SSWP* [2017] UKUT 477 (AAC)
115 *KB v SSWP (UC)* [2019] UKUT 408 (AAC)

5. Sanction decisions
116 Reg 51 UC,PIP,JSA&ESA(DA) Regs
117 s29 WRA 2012
118 para J3257 ADM

Part 7: National insurance, work and work-related rules
Chapter 47: Universal credit system sanctions
Notes

119 DWP, *Universal Credit Guidance,* Home
visit, v7.0, House of Commons library
deposited papers, available at
www.rightsnet.org.uk/universal-credit-
guidance
120 paras K2054-58 ADM

6. Challenging a sanction decision
121 *JB v SSWP (UC)* [2018] UKUT 360 (AAC)
122 Reg 14 UC,PIP,JSA&ESA(DA) Regs
123 CJSA/2375/2000
124 Reg 51 UC,PIP,JSA&ESA(DA) Regs

Chapter 48

Claimant responsibilities: other benefits

This chapter covers:
1. The jobseeking conditions for jobseeker's allowance outside the universal credit system (p1114)
2. Work-focused interviews for other benefits (p1136)
3. Work-related activity for income support and employment and support allowance (p1140)

This chapter covers the work-related responsibilities you, and in some cases your partner, may have in order to get income support (IS), jobseeker's allowance (JSA) and employment and support allowance (ESA). If you come under the universal credit (UC) system (see p23), including if you are claiming contribution-based JSA or contributory ESA under the UC system, the rules in this chapter do not apply to you. See Chapter 46 instead. For your responsibilities for incapacity benefit and severe disablement allowance, or if you are still claiming IS on the basis of incapacity for work, see Chapter 46 in the 2017/18 edition of this *Handbook*.

Key facts
- To qualify for jobseeker's allowance (JSA) outside the universal credit (UC) system, you must usually satisfy jobseeking conditions.
- If you do not meet the jobseeking conditions, your JSA may end and you may be given a sanction when you reclaim. This means your JSA is paid at a reduced or nil rate. However, you may qualify for hardship payments.
- You and your partner may have to take part in work-focused interviews for income support (IS), JSA (as the partner of the claimant) or employment and support allowance (ESA).
- Some claimants of IS or ESA may be required to undertake work-related activity.
- If you do not take part in work-focused interviews or undertake work-related activity and you cannot show a good cause, you may be given a sanction.
- If you disagree with a decision that you are not entitled to benefit and/or to impose a sanction, you can apply for a revision or a supersession (see Chapter 56) or appeal against the decision (see Chapter 57). You must apply for a mandatory reconsideration before you can appeal.

Part 7: National insurance, work and work-related rules
Chapter 48: Claimant responsibilities: other benefits
1. The jobseeking conditions for jobseeker's allowance outside the universal credit system

1. The jobseeking conditions for jobseeker's allowance outside the universal credit system

To qualify for jobseeker's allowance (JSA) if you do not come under the universal credit (UC) system, you must usually satisfy three jobseeking conditions. You must:

- be (or be treated as) available for work; *and*
- be (or be treated as) actively seeking work; *and*
- have (or be treated as having) a current jobseeker's agreement with the DWP. In practice, the job centre calls this a claimant commitment.

You can also be required to attend a scheme for assisting people to obtain employment (see p1115).[1]

There are special rules if:

- you are a lone parent (see p1116);
- you have experienced or been threatened with domestic violence (see p1118);
- you have a disability (see p1125);
- you are a laid-off or short-time worker. For more information, see pp1085–86 of the 2019/20 edition of this *Handbook;*
- you are in full-time training or study, or, in limited circumstances, you are participating in a specified scheme for assisting people to obtain employment. For more information, see pp1086–88 of the 2019/20 edition of this *Handbook;*
- you are 16 or 17. Most people under 18 cannot claim JSA outside the UC system. If you are 16 or 17 and get JSA outside the UC system, see p1096, p1103 and p1107 of the 2019/2020 edition of this *Handbook.*

If you do not satisfy the jobseeking conditions, or there is doubt about whether you do, you may be able to get hardship payments (see Chapter 52).

Work coaches

The Jobcentre Plus staff who support and interview people seeking work are usually called 'work coaches'. For JSA outside the UC system, their legal title is employment officers. They are sometimes also called personal advisers. An employment officer means an officer of the Secretary of State for Work and Pensions, or someone officially designated as an employment officer by her/him.[2] The job of a work coach is to agree with you the steps you will take to get back to work, keep a check on those steps, offer practical help and advice, and notify you of job vacancies. You cannot apply for a revision or supersession, or appeal, against decisions made by your work coach – eg, decisions about what you must do to look for work. A decision that you are not entitled to JSA, or a decision to sanction you, is made by a DWP decision maker. You can ask for these decisions to be changed by a revision and appeal.

Schemes for assisting people to obtain employment

If you are participating in a specified scheme for assisting people to obtain employment (eg, the Work and Health Programme, see p1152), you usually have to be available for work and actively seek work as well as attend the scheme. If you have been directed to attend, you can be sanctioned if you do not participate. You must be told in writing that you are required to participate, when the scheme starts, what you have to do and what will happen if you fail to participate. Even if you do not think the scheme is reasonable activity for you (eg, because of your work experience), it may still be reasonable if it will provide recent evidence of good attendance and dealing with people in the workplace, and you have been out of work for a long time.

You do not have to actively seek work if you are establishing a business with the help of a government scheme called New Enterprise Allowance.

In some limited circumstances (if you are a full-time student or you have very recently been released from detention), you do not have to be available for work or actively seek work while participating in a scheme. For more information, see p1087 of the 2019/20 edition of this *Handbook*.

Available for work

To qualify for JSA, you must be available for work. The general rule is that to be available for work you must be:[3]

- 'willing and able' to take up work 'immediately' (see p1116); *and*
- available at any time of the day and on any day of the week; *and*
- prepared to take a job that would involve working for *at least* 40 hours a week; *and*
- prepared to work for *less than* 40 hours a week if required to do so. In practice, this means that you must be prepared to work part time.

However, you may be able to place restrictions on your availability for work (see p1120), such as the type of work or the days and times you are available.

In some circumstances:

- you do not have to be available for work if you are getting a training allowance or if you are participating in a specified scheme for assisting people to obtain employment (see above);
- you can be treated as being available for work even if you are not (see p1117);
- you can qualify for joint-claim JSA even if you or your partner (but not both of you) are not available for work (see p253).

Your availability for work is considered at an initial interview when you first claim JSA (see p261 and p717). Your jobseeker's agreement (called a 'claimant commitment' by the DWP) contains details of the particular days and times that

Part 7: National insurance, work and work-related rules
Chapter 48: Claimant responsibilities: other benefits
1. The jobseeking conditions for jobseeker's allowance outside the universal credit system

you are available for work (your 'pattern of availability') as well as any other restrictions you may place on your availability.

Note:

- The DWP can decide that you are not available for work without having to show that you have turned down a job.[4] However, the fact that you turn down a job does not necessarily mean that you are not available.
- If your entitlement to JSA ends because you have not complied with the requirement to be available for work, you may be given a sanction when you claim JSA again (see p1149).
- If you are not available or treated as being available for work, you cannot get JSA under the normal rules, but you may be able to get hardship payments (see Chapter 52).

If you are a lone parent or have temporary additional childcare responsibilities

If you are a lone parent and have childcare responsibilities, you must be available for work to qualify for JSA. This also applies in general (whether you are a lone parent or not) if you are looking after children under 16, even during the school holidays. However, some special rules can apply which may treat you as available for work, allow you to restrict your availability or give you more time to take up a job. For more information, see p1089 and p1091 of the 2019/20 edition of this *Handbook*.

Willing and able to take up work immediately

Being *willing* to work is essentially a test of your attitude – your desire and willingness to work. What you do in practice to display this willingness is usually dealt with under the rules for actively seeking work.

You must be prepared to take up work as an employed person – being only available for self-employment is not sufficient.[5] However, this means that you do not count as being unavailable for work if you refuse to work as a self-employed person.

In order to be *able* to work, it must be lawful for you to work in Great Britain.[6] Your immigration status may affect this – eg, if a condition of your entry is that you do not work. In addition, there must be nothing to prevent you from receiving job offers (eg, because you are away from home for more than a short time) and nothing to prevent you from acting on them straight away – eg, because you have other commitments that you cannot easily abandon.

Being able to take up work *immediately* means that you must usually be able to start work without any delay, with little more than the time needed to get washed and dressed and have breakfast.[7] You can be allowed more time than this in some situations.

When you are allowed more time

You do not have to be available for work immediately in the following situations. You only need to be available for work:

- **on one week's notice** if you are doing voluntary work or have caring responsibilities (see below for what counts).[8] You must be willing and able to attend a job interview on 48 hours' notice. However, if you have caring responsibilities for a child under 16 and you can show these make it unreasonable for you to take up a job or attend an interview within these periods, you only have to be available on **28 days' notice** and be willing and able to attend an interview on seven days' notice;
- **on 24 hours' notice** if you are providing a paid or unpaid service (other than if you are doing voluntary work or have caring responsibilities).[9] This includes services you provide for family or friends on a non-commercial basis, such as giving someone a regular lift to work in your car.[10] It could also include activities that are of service to the community in general (eg, offenders working in the community as part of their punishment) and tribunal members;
- **after your notice period** has passed if you are working part time. This applies if you have a duty to give your employer notice that you are leaving work under employment law.[11] If under the terms of your contract you must give longer notice, argue that the longer notice period should apply.

Note: if the DWP agrees that you are only available to work at certain times (see p1122), you are not required to be able to take up employment at times when you are not available.[12] However, you must be willing and able to take up the offer as soon as you reach the next period in your pattern of availability (the days and times you are available).

Definitions[13]

'Voluntary work' is work which is done for a charity or other not-for-profit organisation or for anyone other than your partner or a child who is included in your claim, for which you receive no payment other than for your reasonable expenses.

'Caring responsibilities' means responsibility for looking after a member of your 'household' (see p329 for the meaning of household) or a close relative who is a child under 16, someone over pension age or someone who needs care because of her/his mental or physical condition. This applies even if you share the responsibilities with someone – eg, with your partner.

Treated as available for work

Even if you are not actually available for work, you can be treated as if you are for periods during your claim. You must still satisfy the other conditions of entitlement to JSA. The rules which treat you as available for work cover lone parents, some people looking after a child under 16, people undertaking certain

Part 7: National insurance, work and work-related rules
Chapter 48: Claimant responsibilities: other benefits
1. The jobseeking conditions for jobseeker's allowance outside the universal credit system

studying and training, people doing certain community activities and those affected by bereavement and other domestic emergencies. For more information on being treated as available for work in these situations, see pp1091–94 of the 2019/20 edition of this *Handbook*.

In addition, you can be treated as available for work during some periods of temporary absence from Great Britain (see below), if you are affected by domestic violence (see below), during certain periods of sickness (see p708) and in some other situations (see below).

Note: for a minimum of three months from 30 March 2020, you are treated as available for work.

Temporary absence from Great Britain

You are treated as being available for work when you are temporarily absent from Great Britain and you are:[14]

- taking a child who is included in your claim (see p323) abroad temporarily for specified medical treatment (for a maximum of eight weeks);[15] *or*
- attending a job interview (for a maximum of seven days). You must tell your work coach in advance and confirm it in writing if required to do so; *or*
- a member of a couple and the pensioner, enhanced pensioner, higher pensioner, disability or severe disability premium is being paid for your partner and you are both away from Great Britain (for a maximum of four weeks); *or*
- abroad for the purpose of getting NHS hospital treatment (see p710); *or*
- a member of a joint-claim couple on the date of your claim and, on the day your partner makes the claim for JSA, you are:
  - in Northern Ireland (for a maximum of four weeks) but only if you are unlikely to be away for more than 52 weeks; *or*
  - attending a job interview (for a maximum of seven days).

Domestic violence

If you notify the DWP that you have experienced, or been threatened with, domestic violence from your partner, former partner or certain family members, you can be treated as being available for work for up to four weeks from the date of notification.[16] This only applies if you are not living at the same address as the person and if the domestic violence (or threat) took place within the 26 weeks before you notified the DWP.

The four-week period is extended to 13 weeks if you provide relevant evidence during the four weeks from a person acting in an official capacity. You can only be treated as available for work under this rule once in any 12-month period.

For more information about being treated as available for work due to domestic violence, see p1093 of the 2019/20 edition of this *Handbook*.

Other situations when you can be treated as available for work

As well as the situations listed above, you are treated as being available for work:[17]

- if you have been discharged from detention in prison, a remand centre or a youth custody institution and you are not required to participate in a specified scheme for assisting people to obtain employment (for one week from the date of discharge). If you have been required to participate in a scheme, you are instead exempt from being available for work. For more information, see p1087 of the 2019/20 edition of this *Handbook*;
- during temporary police detention (legal custody in Scotland) of up to 96 hours, but not if you come within the definition of 'prisoner' (see p941);[18]
- during a two-week (see p709) or extended (see p710) period of sickness, or if you are temporarily absent from Great Britain for the purpose of getting NHS hospital treatment (see p710);
- if you were recently found not to have limited capability for work, and your time limit for claiming JSA is extended because you were not told promptly enough that your entitlement to ESA had ended so you could not claim JSA in time (during the period for which the time limit is extended);
- during any part of a week at the beginning of your claim if, in respect of all the days concerned, you satisfy some specified rules for being available for work;[19]
- during any part week at the end of your claim.

Treated as unavailable for work

Even if you are (or can be treated as) available for work, you are nevertheless treated as unavailable for work if:[20]

- you are a full-time student (see p887). **Note:** there are exceptions;
- you are on temporary release from prison;
- you are receiving maternity allowance or statutory maternity pay;
- you are on adoption, paternity, shared parental or parental bereavement leave;
- it is during any part of a week at the beginning of your claim. You are treated as being unavailable for work unless you satisfy specified rules for being treated as available for that period.

Unavailable for part of a week

On occasion, you might be unavailable for work for a short period during a benefit week – eg, because you are away from home.

If this happens and you have put restrictions on the times that you are available (see p1122):[21]

- your JSA is not affected if the period during which you are not available comes entirely outside the particular days and times that you are available for work (your 'pattern of availability'); *or*
- you lose JSA for the whole of that benefit week if all or part of the period during which you are not available comes within your pattern of availability.

If you have not put any restrictions on the times you are available, you may lose benefit for that week because you are not available to take up work immediately.[22]

Part 7: National insurance, work and work-related rules
Chapter 48: Claimant responsibilities: other benefits
1. The jobseeking conditions for jobseeker's allowance outside the universal credit system

For this reason, it is best to avoid signing a jobseeker's agreement with totally unrestricted times that you are available.

If you are arrested and held by the police for a short time but then released, you can be treated as being available for work for up to 96 hours while you are detained.

If you are doing voluntary work and have placed restrictions on the total number of hours you are available to work (see p1122), any voluntary work you do (see p1117 for what counts) within your pattern of availability must be ignored when deciding whether you are available, provided you are willing and able to rearrange the voluntary work with:[23]

- one week's notice, in order to take up any job whose hours fall within your pattern of availability;
- 48 hours' notice, to attend an interview in connection with an opportunity for work at a time that falls within your pattern of availability.

There is a similar rule in certain cases if you are a part-time student (see p891).

Restrictions on availability for work

You can restrict your availability for work *in any way* if the restrictions are reasonable in light of your physical or mental condition and, in some cases, if you have specified caring responsibilities for a child under 16 (see p1121). Otherwise, if you can prove that you still have a reasonable prospect of securing employment (see below), you can place some restrictions on the work you are available to do. These are:[24]

- the type of work for which you are available (see p1121);
- the number of hours, days and times you are available (see p1122);
- the terms and conditions of employment for which you are available, including the rate of pay (see p1123);
- the location of the job (see p1124).

Any restrictions are entered in your jobseeker's agreement. If you and your work coach have not agreed in advance that there are certain types of work which you cannot, or are unwilling to, do, it may prove difficult to justify not being available for it in the future. If you are 16 or 17, you may be able to restrict your availabilty for work to jobs where the employer provides training. For more information, see p1096–97 of the 2019/20 edition of this *Handbook*.

A reasonable prospect of securing employment

You must usually show that you have a 'reasonable prospect' of securing employment, despite any restrictions you are allowed to place on your availability. This does not apply if you can restrict your availability in any way (see below), if you are a lone parent who can restrict your availability to your child's normal school hours (see p1122), or if you are 16 or 17 and can restrict your availability to jobs offering suitable training (see p1120).[25] When considering restrictions, your work coach should consider all the relevant evidence, including your skills and experience and the type of vacancies available.[26] Negotiating restrictions on your availability can help to avoid a sanction, but it is important not to be too restrictive if this is likely to limit your reasonable prospect of finding work.

Restricting your availability in any way

You can restrict your availability for work in any way if:[27]

- the restrictions are reasonable in light of your physical or mental condition (see below); *or*
- you have caring responsibilities (see p1117) for a child under 16 and you are the subject of a parenting order or have entered into a parenting contract in respect of the child under specific provisions.

You can restrict anything about the work, including the type, hours, location and terms and conditions. If the restrictions you impose are reasonable in light of your physical or mental condition, or the terms of the order or contract, you do not have to show that you have reasonable prospects of securing employment. For example, it may be reasonable to refuse to consider work which requires travel away from home because of your caring responsibilities for a child who needs supervision under the terms of a parenting order.

To restrict your availability because of your physical or mental condition, you usually need to provide medical evidence. If you have not already done so, you may want to consider whether you have limited capability for work (see p1010) and can claim a different benefit (ESA and/or UC). However, get advice before doing so as you may end up worse off on UC.

The type of work

The general rule is that you must be available for any type of employment, but you are allowed to place restrictions on the sort of jobs for which you are available, provided you have a reasonable prospect of securing employment (see p1120).[28] In addition, special rules allow you to make restrictions:

- during your 'permitted period' if you have one (see below);
- if you are a laid-off or short-time worker;
- because of a sincerely held religious belief or conscientious objection (see p1122).

Permitted periods

If you have previously done work of a particular type (a 'usual occupation'), you can be allowed a 'permitted period' of between one and 13 weeks from the date you claim JSA during which you are allowed to be available only for vacancies in your usual occupation or which pay at least what you would normally receive, or both.[29] Whether you are allowed a permitted period depends on the nature of

Part 7: National insurance, work and work-related rules
Chapter 48: Claimant responsibilities: other benefits
1. The jobseeking conditions for jobseeker's allowance outside the universal credit system

your previous occupation, including how long you have worked in it and whether jobs are available locally.[30] If you are allowed a permitted period, it should be noted in your jobseeker's agreement.[31] If you were previously self-employed, looking for work in your previous occupation can count as 'actively seeking work' (see p1125).

Religious belief or conscientious objection

You do not have to be available for work that offends a sincerely held religious belief or a sincere conscientious objection – eg, a job in a company associated with live animal exports if you have a conscientious objection to these.[32] You must still have reasonable prospects of securing employment despite those restrictions and any other restrictions you may have imposed (see p1120).[33]

The number of hours, days and times

You can restrict the total number of hours you are available, provided you are available for at least 40 hours a week and:[34]

- you have agreed with your work coach the particular days and times that you are available for work (a 'pattern of availability') and this has been recorded in your jobseeker's agreement; *and*
- you still have reasonable prospects of securing employment despite the restrictions (see p1120) and they do not *considerably* reduce your prospects of securing employment.

You are allowed to restrict the total number of hours you are available to less than 40 in some situations if you are a lone parent (see below) or if you have caring responsibilities (see p1123). You may also be allowed to restrict your availability in any way, including the number of hours, if you have a physical or mental condition (see p1121).

Note: you must be prepared to work for the maximum number of hours for which you are available, but you must also be prepared to accept jobs that offer fewer hours than you would wish.

If you are a lone parent

If you are a lone parent and you have a child under 13 included in your claim (see p323), you only need to be available for work during her/his normal school hours.[35] You do not have to show that you still have reasonable prospects of securing employment. You may be able to restrict your total hours further depending on how your caring responsibilities affect your availability. The DWP says you cannot restrict your availability to school hours during school holidays[36] but, as a person with caring responsibilities, you may be able to restrict your hours in other ways and/or look only for temporary work.

Caring responsibilities

If you have caring responsibilities (see p1117), you can restrict the total hours you are available for work to less than 40 hours a week if:[37]

- you are available for employment for at least 16 hours a week and for as many hours as your caring responsibilities permit, taking into account relevant factors, including the particular hours and days you spend caring, whether your caring responsibilities are shared with someone else, and the age and physical and mental condition of the person for whom you care; *and*
- you have a reasonable chance of securing employment (see p1120) despite the restricted hours. You do not have to show you have a reasonable chance if you have caring responsibilities for a child under 16 and your work coach considers that you would not satisfy the condition because of the type and number of job vacancies within travelling distance.

If you are a carer and you cannot be available for work for at least 16 hours a week, you may be able to claim IS (see p233) or UC, depending on your circumstances, the circumstances of the person you care for and how much time you spend caring. You should get advice before claiming a different benefit as, if you have to claim UC, it is unlikely to be possible for you to return to JSA outside the UC system.

The terms and conditions of employment

You can put restrictions on the terms and conditions of employment for which you are available (including the rate of pay – but see below), provided you can show that you still have reasonable prospects of securing employment despite those restrictions and any other restrictions you may have imposed (see p1120).[38]

The rules about minimum working conditions (see Appendix 7) can affect your claim for JSA. The DWP should not object to your placing a restriction on your availability for work – ie, that you will not accept a job if the terms do not comply with the legal requirements, such as if an employer is offering a job at less than the national minimum wage.

Note: the DWP says you should *not* be told to apply for jobs that include a zero-hour contract or an 'employee shareholder contract' and that you should not be given a sanction if you refuse or fail to apply for, or to accept, such a vacancy.[39]

The rate of pay

You can restrict the rate of pay:

- during your permitted period (see p1121), if you have one, to the rate you are accustomed to receiving in your usual occupation;[40]
- for six months from the date you claimed JSA, provided you still have reasonable prospects of securing employment (see p1120).[41]

Any restrictions you may place on the rate of pay should be agreed at your initial interview. These should be recorded in your jobseeker's agreement.

Part 7: National insurance, work and work-related rules
Chapter 48: Claimant responsibilities: other benefits
1. The jobseeking conditions for jobseeker's allowance outside the universal credit system

The location of the job

You can put restrictions on the localities within which you are available for work, provided you can show that you still have reasonable prospects of securing employment in the selected areas (see p1120).[42] Your travel-to-work time may also be a factor, especially if it is combined with caring responsibilities or physical or mental conditions that limit your travel.

Actively seeking work

To qualify for jobseeker's allowance (JSA), you must actively seek work. Special rules apply if you have been allowed a 'permitted period' (see p1125). In some cases you:

- do not have to actively seek work if you are participating in a specified scheme to obtain employment or you are getting a training allowance (see p1117);
- can be treated as if you are actively seeking work even if you are not (see p1125);
- can qualify for joint-claim JSA even if you or your partner (but not both of you) are not actively seeking work (see p253).

There are special rules about what you must do when looking for work if you are 16 or 17. For more information, see p1103 of the 2019/20 edition of this *Handbook*.

Note: if your entitlement to JSA ends because you failed to comply with the requirement to actively seek work, you may be given a sanction when you claim JSA again (see p1149).

What you must do

To count as actively seeking work, you must do the following.

- In each benefit week (and part week at the beginning of your claim) you must take such 'steps' as you can reasonably be expected to have to take in order to have the best prospects of securing employment in Great Britain.[43]
- You are expected to take a minimum of three steps, unless taking fewer steps is all that is reasonable.[44] **Note:** it is possible that, in some weeks, there may be no steps that you could reasonably be expected to take.[45] On the other hand, the minimum number of steps may not be enough to show you have done what can reasonably be expected.

Your jobseeker's agreement (called a 'claimant commitment' by the DWP) records what steps you have agreed to take to find work. Your work coach is likely to suggest that you take considerably more than three steps each week. Bear in mind that by signing the agreement you are accepting that it is reasonable for you to take the number of steps specified. Unspecified steps are unlikely to be accepted as reasonable.[46] In the event of a dispute, point out if you felt you had no option but to agree to what was proposed. Any changes to your jobseeker's agreement should be recorded (see p1130).

Your work coach is likely to look at whether or not you have kept to your jobseeker's agreement in deciding whether you are actively seeking work.[47] S/he will review the steps you have taken at your regular interview. You do not necessarily have to take all the steps in your jobseeker's agreement each week to prove you are actively seeking work: the test is what you did, not what you did not do.[48] However, if there is a dispute, the DWP decision maker is likely to say that what is in your jobseeker's agreement is a good indication of what you could reasonably have been expected to do. Your work coach will expect you to spend a considerable amount of time looking for work, and, unless there are specific reasons, will expect seeking work to take up the same amount of time as a full-time job. It is your responsibility to show that you are actively seeking work based on steps you have taken, even if you consider that you are not receiving adequate support from the job centre.[49] If a DWP decision maker decides that you are not actively seeking work, your entitlement to JSA ends. If you then claim JSA again, you can be given a sanction (see p1149).

For more information on showing that you have taken sufficient 'steps' and what steps are reasonable, see pp1101–3 of the 2019/20 edition of this *Handbook*.

If you have a disability

If you have a disability or health condition that affects the work you can do, you may be able to get specialist support to help you get into work. For further information, see gov.uk/specialist-employability-support. You need to contact Jobcentre Plus to be assessed for the scheme. Make sure you are clear about what is voluntary, and what you have agreed to do as part of your jobseeking conditions.

Actively seeking work during your permitted period

If you have been allowed a permitted period (see p1121), you count as actively seeking work during that period even if you are only looking for jobs in your normal line of work or at your normal level of pay, or both.[50] If you have been self-employed in your usual occupation at any time within the 12 months before you claim JSA, you count as actively seeking work if you are seeking self-employment in that occupation.

Treated as actively seeking work

Even if you are not actively seeking work, you can be treated as if you are.

- If you are attending a 'qualifying course' with the approval of your work coach and are treated as being available for work (see p1117), you are also treated as actively seeking work.[51] If this is in any week that falls entirely in a vacation, you must take such steps as can reasonably be expected in order to have the best prospects of securing temporary employment.
- You are allowed two weeks (longer in some circumstances) during which time you are regarded as actively seeking work while away from home (see p1126).

Part 7: National insurance, work and work-related rules
Chapter 48: Claimant responsibilities: other benefits
1. The jobseeking conditions for jobseeker's allowance outside the universal credit system

Other situations in which you can be treated as actively seeking work generally mirror those where you are treated as being available for work and have the same maximum lengths (see p1117).[52] In most cases, you are only considered to be actively seeking work if the situation affects you for at least three days in the 'benefit week' (see p454 for the definition). However, you are treated as actively seeking work in any week:[53]

- in which you are allowed an extended period of sickness under the rules described on p710. However, this does not apply if it would be reasonable for you to take steps to seek employment in that week, and you have not taken such steps;
- which is part of a period in which you are taking active steps to set yourself up as self-employed under a scheme to assist people to do so (for up to eight weeks). This can only apply once in any period of entitlement to JSA. The scheme must be provided or funded by a specified government agency. **Note:** if you are participating in New Enterprise Allowance, you do not have to actively seek work;[54]
- in which you spend at least three days on a government-sponsored employment or training course or programme for which you are not paid a training allowance. This does not apply if you are on Work Experience, or on any of the schemes for assisting people to obtain employment listed on p1152.

Note: for a minimum of three months from 30 March 2020, you are treated as actively seeking work.

You are *not* treated as actively seeking work just because you have caring responsibilities for a child under 16 and are looking after her/him during the school holidays or at a time when s/he is excluded from school, although you may be treated as being available for work. For more information, see p1091 of the 2019/20 edition of this *Handbook*.

Holidays and other absences from home

While you are on JSA, you can be treated as actively seeking work while away from home – eg, on holiday.[55] You still must be available for work, so you are expected to give an assurance that you are willing and able to cut your absence short if notified of a job. In any 12-month period, you can be away from home for up to:[56]

- three weeks, if during each week you spend at least three days on an Outward Bound course; *or*
- if you are blind, two weeks, plus up to four other weeks spent attending training in the use of guide dogs for at least three days a week; *or*
- two weeks, in any other case.

If you are away for longer than this and so cannot be treated as actively seeking work, you must show that you are looking for work while you are away.

You must usually be in Great Britain to qualify for JSA. To check whether you can get JSA while temporarily away, see p1655, and whether you can be treated as available for work, see p1118. If you are unemployed and want to look for work in another European Economic Area country, see p1657 to see whether you can be paid your contribution-based JSA. Even if you cannot get JSA while you are away, you might be able to get national insurance credits (see p970).

What should you do before you go away?

1. Inform your work coach before you go away from home, even if you will be in Great Britain. You can be required to give notice in writing.[57] Make sure you keep a record of your notification.

2. You must be available for work and be able to receive information about job offers. You must, therefore, provide details of how you can be contacted or how you plan to contact your work coach while you are away.[58]

3. Check with your Jobcentre Plus office when you must 'sign on' when you return home (see p1131). This could be a day that is not your usual signing day. If you do not sign on when you are supposed to, you may lose benefit for the whole of the period you were away unless you can show you had a good reason for failing to sign on (see p1133).

The jobseeker's agreement

To qualify for JSA, you must agree and sign a 'jobseeker's agreement'.[59] This enables your work coach to monitor and direct your search for a job and gives you a chance to put any agreed restrictions on your availability for work on record. It is discussed with you during your initial interview (see p261 and p717). **Note:** the DWP calls your jobseeker's agreement a 'claimant commitment'. However, the rules are not the same as for claimant commitments under the UC system. If you are claiming JSA under the UC system, see Chapter 46.

Until you have agreed the contents of the jobseeker's agreement with your work coach, your claim for JSA is not passed to a decision maker to decide whether you are entitled to JSA. However, see p1129 for situations when you can be treated as having signed an agreement. If a decision on your claim is delayed or JSA is refused because you have not entered into a jobseeker's agreement, you may be able to get hardship payments (see Chapter 52).

The agreement is not valid until it has been signed by you and your work coach.[60] It can be in electronic form and can be signed by an electronic signature.[61] You must be given a copy.[62] To find out when your agreement can be backdated, see p1130. For what happens if you cannot agree, see p1129.

Note: some people getting a training allowance do not have to have a current jobseeker's agreement (see p1117). In some cases, you can qualify for joint-claim JSA even if you or your partner (but not both of you) do not have a current jobseeker's agreement (see p253).

Part 7: National insurance, work and work-related rules
Chapter 48: Claimant responsibilities: other benefits
1. The jobseeking conditions for jobseeker's allowance outside the universal credit system

What is in the jobseeker's agreement

A jobseeker's agreement must contain specific information, such as your name and the date of the agreement. It must also include:[63]

- the type of job you are going to actively seek. If you are allowed to place restrictions on the type of work for which you are available, these are entered in a separate box;[64] *and*
- the total number of hours that you are available for work each week (unless you say that you are prepared to work at any time), with a breakdown of what hours you are available each day. This is known as your 'pattern of availability'. For information on restricting the number of hours and the times for which you are available, see p1122; *and*
- how quickly you must be available for work (see p1116), and other restrictions you are placing on the work for which you are available – eg, the level of pay or the distance you are prepared to travel; *and*
- the steps you are to take to seek work or to improve your chances of work – eg, preparing a CV, registering on job websites and attending relevant courses; *and*
- if you have been allowed a 'permitted period' (see p1121), the dates on which it starts and ends; *and*
- a statement of your right to have a proposed jobseeker's agreement referred to a decision maker (see p1129 and p1130) who can decide whether it is reasonable, and to apply for a revision or supersession or appeal against her/his decision if you and your work coach cannot agree on what should be in the agreement; *and*
- if you are 16 or 17, your jobseeker's agreement must explain any special rules which apply to you. For more information, see p1107 of the 2019/20 edition of this *Handbook*.

It also advises you to keep a record of what you do to find work and states that if you do not do enough, your JSA might be affected.

Your jobseeker's agreement is not binding on you or the DWP;[65] there is no automatic penalty if you fail to keep it.[66] However, the contents of the agreement and whether you have abided by it are important evidence if there is a dispute about whether you are available for or actively seeking work, and also if you are accused of refusing a suitable job offer.[67] If you have done everything in your jobseeker's agreement, try to argue that you should not be accused of not being available for or actively seeking work.[68]

Do you think your jobseeker's agreement is unreasonable?

You may think that what your jobseeker's agreement says you are expected to do to find work is unreasonable – eg, you are expected to take too many steps, or you are expected to be available for work for too many hours or at unreasonable times. You may consider that specific steps are unreasonable for you . However, whether something is unreasonable depends on all the circumstances,[69] including what other steps you are taking to find work.

You can ask for your jobseeker's agreement to be referred to a decision maker. However, you risk losing benefit if you refuse to sign it.

Rather than refusing to sign the jobseeker's agreement proposed by your work coach, it may be better to sign it and then write to the DWP saying that you would like it changed (see p1130). You should not lose JSA, provided you comply with the original agreement while the variation is being considered. It is important to make it clear that you intend to do so. If your agreement is revised, unless you can show it is unreasonable, it is better to comply with it (and make it clear that you are doing so) even if you want to seek a further change. Broad statements that you will do everything you can to seek employment may not be reasonable by themselves, and you can be expected to give details of what you have done to find employment.[70]

Treated as signing a jobseeker's agreement

There are rules that treat you as signing a jobseeker's agreement when you have not yet done so. These are mainly to deal with situations where there is an unavoidable delay between the date you claim JSA and the date of your initial interview (see p261 for income-based JSA and p717 for contribution-based JSA), and so enable JSA to be paid before the interview. You can also be treated as having signed a jobseeker's agreement:[71]

- for as long as you are treated as being available for work because of circumstances that arose between your date of claim and your initial interview;
- if there are circumstances affecting the normal procedures for claiming, awarding or paying JSA (eg, a computer failure at the DWP, a strike by staff or severe weather), which make it impracticable or unduly difficult for you to comply with them;[72]
- during a period of up to 13 weeks during which you are treated as available for work because you have experienced, or been threatened with, domestic violence (see p1118), if you have not signed a jobseeker's agreement before the period begins;
- during a temporary absence from Great Britain for up to seven days if you are a member of a joint-claim couple attending an interview abroad when your partner makes the claim.

Disputes about a jobseeker's agreement

You and your work coach may disagree about what should be in your jobseeker's agreement. Your work coach is not allowed to sign your jobseeker's agreement unless s/he is satisfied that you will qualify as being available for and actively seeking work if you comply with its terms.[73] If s/he thinks you are placing unreasonable restrictions on your availability for work, or that the steps you propose to take to actively seek work are not sufficient, s/he will not sign an agreement based on your proposals. In this situation:[74]

Part 7: National insurance, work and work-related rules
Chapter 48: Claimant responsibilities: other benefits
1. The jobseeking conditions for jobseeker's allowance outside the universal credit system

- the work coach may refer a proposed jobseeker's agreement (including one proposed by you) to a decision maker; *or*
- if you ask your work coach to do so, s/he *must* refer a proposed agreement to a decision maker immediately.

You can apply for hardship payments while you are waiting for the decision (see p1223). However, you risk losing benefit if you refuse to sign the agreement while it is being considered. For more information about what happens when a jobseeker's agreement is referred to a decision maker, see p1108 of the 2019/20 edition of this *Handbook*.

If you are unhappy with a decision about your jobseeker's agreement, you can ask for a revision or appeal (see Chapters 56 and 57). You must apply for a mandatory reconsideration before you can appeal.

Backdating the jobseeker's agreement

A jobseeker's agreement is automatically backdated to the first day you claimed JSA, provided you and your work coach can agree about what it should contain, but the date may be different if it is referred to a decision maker.[75] The backdating of the agreement should cover any date to which your claim has been backdated (see p1178).

If the agreement is referred to a decision maker, it is only backdated if s/he makes a direction ordering this.[76] S/he must consider all the relevant circumstances.[77]

Changing your jobseeker's agreement

The terms of your jobseeker's agreement can be changed by agreement between you and your work coach. Any change must be in writing and signed by both of you.[78] This can be in electronic form and can be signed by an electronic signature.[79]

Both you and your work coach can propose changes at any time. Put your proposals in writing (keeping a copy) and explain how they give you a reasonable chance of finding a job. If the work coach changes your jobseeker's agreement, you should consider what it requires and if it is reasonable for you to comply with it (see p1128).[80] Bear in mind that if you do not agree to it, your JSA may end.

A work coach cannot agree to a change unless s/he considers that the terms mean that you satisfy the jobseeking conditions.[81] If you and the work coach:

- agree the proposed changes, you must be given a copy of the new jobseeker's agreement;[82]
- do not agree the proposed changes, these can be referred to a decision maker.[83] They *must* be referred to a decision maker if you request this. For more information on what happens when changes to a jobseeker's agreement are referred to a decision maker, see pp1109–10 of the 2019/20 edition of this *Handbook*.

If you are unhappy with a decision maker's decision, you can request a revision or appeal (see Chapters 56 and 57). You must apply for a mandatory reconsideration before you can appeal.

Interviews and signing on

While you are getting jobseeker's allowance (JSA), you (or both of you if you are a joint-claim couple) must normally participate in regular interviews and may be asked to sign a declaration ('sign on') regularly, usually at the Jobcentre Plus office.[84] This is to enable the DWP to check that you have satisfied the jobseeking conditions and that you continue to qualify for JSA. You can be required to provide information and evidence about your circumstances, your availability for work and how you have been actively seeking work.[85] You can be notified of the manner, time and place of an interview by telephone, post or electronic means.[86] If you:

- fail to sign on, your entitlement to JSA may end (see p1133);
- fail to participate in an interview, your entitlement to JSA may end (see p1133) or you may be given a sanction.

Note: when you first claim JSA, you must attend an initial interview (see p261 for income-based JSA and p717 for contribution-based JSA). If you do not attend the interview at the right time, your date of claim is affected (see p263 for income-based JSA and p718 for contribution-based JSA). If you do not attend the interview at all (and the DWP does not waive the requirement to do so), you have not made a valid claim and so do not qualify for JSA.

Note: for at least three months from 19 March 2020, all requirements to attend the jobcentre in person are suspended. All the interviews mentioned in this chapter will be carried out in other ways where possible. Do not attend the jobcentre unless your appointment explicitly tells you to do so.

Travel expenses

Your travel expenses to and from the Jobcentre Plus office to participate in interviews and to 'sign on' are generally not reimbursed. If travelling to sign on is causing you hardship, ask whether you can sign on by post (see p1132).

Signing on

At your regular interview, you may be asked to sign a declaration (known as 'signing on') that:[87]

- you have been available for and actively seeking work or could be treated as if you were and, for most 16/17-year-olds, that you have been actively seeking suitable training. You may be asked for evidence that you continue to meet these conditions; *and*

Part 7: National insurance, work and work-related rules
Chapter 48: Claimant responsibilities: other benefits
1. The jobseeking conditions for jobseeker's allowance outside the universal credit system

- there has been no change in your circumstances that might affect the amount of, or your right to, JSA (other than those you may have already notified to the DWP).

If you fail to sign on, your entitlement to JSA can end (see p1133) or you may be given a sanction under the rules that apply to interviews (see p1150).

You are normally told your regular signing-on day and time at the start of your claim. Generally, you are told you must sign on every two weeks, but it can be more or less frequently.

You may be required to sign on or attend interviews more frequently in certain circumstances – eg, if your work coach thinks you need more help to find work, if you are suspected of not meeting the jobseeking conditions or of fraud, or if you have no fixed abode. Because decisions about how often you have to sign on are made by your work coach, you cannot appeal. However, you can ask for the frequency to be altered – eg, if your circumstances change or the cost of travel causes hardship. It is always best to continue to sign on as required by the DWP, even if your JSA is stopped, so that you can be paid arrears if the decision is changed.[88] If you are struggling to sign on as frequently as required (eg, because of travel costs or disability), discuss this with your work coach.

Signing on by post

The DWP may allow you to sign on by post – eg, if you live a long way from the Jobcentre Plus office, or the cost of travel to the job centre causes you hardship, or you have a disability which restricts your mobility. Even so:
- you must attend, and participate in, any further interviews required. You could try to get an interview arranged nearer your home, if attending at the Jobcentre Plus office would result in your being away from home for a long time;
- you must send a signed declaration and show that you are available for and actively seeking work. If this is not received at the time specified by the DWP, your entitlement to JSA ends, unless you can show a good reason for the delay (see p1133). If you cannot show this, you must make a fresh claim for JSA.

Further interviews

If you remain unemployed for a period of time, you must participate in a number of additional interviews. If you fail to do so, your entitlement to JSA can end (see p1134) or you can be given a sanction.

Some interviews take place at set intervals. However, you can be required to participate in an interview at any time – eg, if your work coach thinks you need more help with your search for work or there is a question about whether you fulfil the jobseeking conditions.

You may be asked to agree to a change of your jobseeker's agreement (see p1130) to record any change in the type of work for which you are looking or the steps you will take to find it.

When your entitlement to jobseeker's allowance ends

Your entitlement to JSA can end if:

- you fail to 'sign on' on the day you were notified to do so (see below). However, it does not end if you contact the Jobcentre Plus office within five working days of your failure and show you had a 'good reason';[89] *or*
- you fail to participate in an interview when you are required to do so (see p1134). However, it does not end if you contact the Jobcentre Plus office within five working days of your failure.[90] You may instead be given a sanction if you cannot show you had a 'good reason' (see p1155).

Ensure that you contact the Jobcentre Plus office within five working days of your failure to participate in an interview or to sign on. Explain why you have a good reason – eg, if you did not receive notice that you were supposed to attend, or genuinely misunderstood when you were supposed to attend.

What should you do if your entitlement ends?

1. If a decision is made to stop your entitlement, ask for the decision to be revised, or appeal against it. You must apply for a mandatory reconsideration before you can appeal.

2. To protect your position, make a new claim for JSA if you are able to do so. Get advice before claiming if you want to make sure that your original benefit can be reinstated. If it can, ask for it to be backdated under the normal rules, or if you are allowed to sign on by post under the special rule on p1135. You may not be able to reclaim income-based JSA unless you are severely disabled. If you cannot claim income-based JSA, you may have to consider claiming UC. You will not be able to return to income-based JSA if you successfully claim UC. If you reclaim contributory JSA, in most circumstances, you will come under the UC system for the purpose of your work-related responsibilities (see Chapter 46). However, if you are severely disabled, you may not come under the UC system (see p705).

3. If you have missed signing on or attending an interview, ask the Jobcentre Plus office to accept the information about your search for work that is available on your 'Find a job' account, or any other information that you would have provided on your signing-on day or at your appointment. If this is accepted, the decision maker should revise the decision that stopped your benefit so that you are at least paid up to the date you did not sign on.[91]

Failure to sign on

Your entitlement to JSA can end if you do not provide a signed declaration on the day you were notified to do so, unless you can show a good reason within five working days of your failure.[92] You must be given five days before a decision is made to end your entitlement.[93] 'Good reason' is not defined in the rules, but for information about what may count, see p1155. See above for how you can minimise your loss. **Note:** your signing-on day is usually the day of your regular interview. If that is the case then you may instead lose your entitlement or be given a sanction under the rules about participating in interviews (see p1134) – ie,

Part 7: National insurance, work and work-related rules
Chapter 48: Claimant responsibilities: other benefits
1. The jobseeking conditions for jobseeker's allowance outside the universal credit system

if you failed to sign on because you did not show up at the Jobcentre Plus office for your regular interview.[94]

If your entitlement to JSA ends, you must make a fresh claim. However, unless you are severely disabled, it may not be possible for you to reclaim JSA and/or you may come under different jobseeking rules (see p1133). You lose JSA for the whole period between the date on which your entitlement ends and the date on which you are treated as having claimed again. If you failed to sign on, the date on which your entitlement to JSA ends is the earliest of:[95]

- the day after the last day for which you have provided information or evidence that shows you continue to be entitled to JSA – eg, at your regular fortnightly interview. In many cases, this is the day after the last day on which you signed on. Ask the Jobcentre Plus office to accept the information that you would have provided on your signing-on day. If this is accepted, you can be paid up to the day you did not sign on;[96] *or*
- the day on which you should have signed on.

If you are severely disabled and able to reclaim JSA under the rules in this chapter, the date on which you are treated as having claimed JSA again is normally the first day on which you contact the Jobcentre Plus office again. See p1135 to see whether your new claim can be backdated.

The effect of this is that, if you fail to sign on, you may lose JSA for the full period for which you would have been paid had you signed on at the right time. In addition, you lose JSA for the days between the day you missed signing on and the day you next contact the Jobcentre Plus office.

Failure to participate in an interview

Your entitlement to JSA can end if you do not participate in an interview when you are required to do so – eg, if you are late for or miss the appointment, or you turn up but refuse to answer questions. Notification of your regular interviews is normally given when you first claim JSA. Notification of these, and of further interviews, can be sent or given in writing, by telephone or by electronic means.[97] If you did not receive confirmation, you should argue that you were not properly notified. The law assumes that if a letter has been addressed correctly and full postage paid, it will be received, so if you do not receive postal notification, you will need to give good reasons why this happened – eg, there are problems receiving post at your address.[98]

If you are notified that you must participate in an interview on a specified date, unless you contact your work coach within five working days (see below), your entitlement to JSA ends if you fail to participate in the interview:[99]

- at the right time – eg, you attend on the right day, but are late. This only applies if, when you failed to participate in an interview on a previous occasion, the DWP gave or sent you a written notice warning you that, if you fail to participate the next time you are required to do so, your entitlement to JSA could cease or you could be given a sanction. **Note:** if you failed to sign on because you were late for the interview, you may instead lose your entitlement under the rules about failing to sign on (see p1133). Under those rules, you do not have to have been given a warning; *or*

- on the right day. You do not have to have been given a warning.

Your entitlement to JSA can only end if you do not contact the work coach within five working days of the date you failed to participate in an interview.[100] You must be given five days before a decision is made to end your entitlement.[101] **Note:** you may be given a sanction if you cannot show a good reason (see Chapter 49).

If you contact the work coach more than five days from the date you failed to participate in an interview, your entitlement to JSA ends and you must make a fresh claim. You lose JSA for the whole period between the date on which your entitlement ends and the date on which you are treated as having claimed again. The date on which your entitlement to JSA ends can never be earlier than the day after the last time you participated in an interview. Otherwise, it is the earliest of:[102]

- the day after the last day for which you have provided information that shows you continue to be entitled to JSA – eg, at your regular fortnightly interview. In many cases, this means the day after the last day on which you signed on. Ask the Jobcentre Plus office to accept the information that you would have provided at the interview. If this is accepted, you can be paid up to the day you did not participate in the interview;[103] *or*
- the day on which you should have participated in an interview.

Only people getting a severe disability premium in a means-tested benefit can reclaim JSA under the jobseeking rules in this chapter. If this applies to you, the date on which you are treated as having claimed JSA again is usually the first day on which you contact the Jobcentre Plus office again. However, if this was the same day as the failure to participate in an interview, you are treated as having made your fresh claim on the *following* day.[104] See below to check whether your new claim can be backdated.

Note:

- If you fail to attend and participate in your initial interview (ie, when you claim JSA), you might not be awarded JSA or your date of claim might be affected.
- If the requirement to attend or participate in an interview is for a training or employment scheme or programme, your entitlement does not end, but you can be given a sanction under other rules (see p1145).[105]

Backdating your new claim

If your entitlement to JSA has ceased because you failed to participate in an interview or to 'sign on' and you are able to make a new claim under the same

Part 7: National insurance, work and work-related rules
Chapter 48: Claimant responsibilities: other benefits
2. Work-focused interviews for other benefits

system because you are severely disabled (see p23), in limited circumstances it may be possible to get your new claim backdated and so avoid some, or all, of the loss of JSA. Your claim can be backdated:

- under any of the normal rules (see p1178); *or*
- if you are not normally required to attend the Jobcentre Plus office (eg, you sign on by post) and you did not receive the notice to attend, to the day after your entitlement to JSA ended, provided you make a new claim for JSA immediately after you are informed that your entitlement ended.[106]

2. **Work-focused interviews for other benefits**

If you are getting certain specified benefits, you (or, in some cases, your partner) can be required to take part in work-focused interviews. Claimants who are not required to attend an interview can still take part in the schemes on a voluntary basis.

At the interview, job opportunities, education, training and rehabilitation are discussed. There is no requirement to take action based on the discussions.

There are currently a number of ways you can be required to take part in work-focused interviews:

- interviews for employment and support allowance (ESA) (see below). You may also have to attend a 'work and health conversation' with a Jobcentre Plus work coach before your work capability assessment;
- interviews for lone parents entitled to income support (IS) (see p1137);
- interviews for certain other IS claimants, including some lone parents (see p1137);
- interviews for the partners of people entitled to certain specified benefits (see p1138).

You may be required to take part in interviews by decision makers at the DWP or by advisers contracted by the DWP – eg, as part of the Work and Health Programme (see p1152).[107] If you (or your partner) do not take part, you could be given a sanction and your benefit could then be paid at a reduced rate (see p1157). For some claimants of IS, if you fail to take part when you claim, you may be treated as not having made a claim (see p1137) and, therefore, cannot qualify for IS.

There have been many changes to the rules on work-focused interviews since they were introduced. See previous editions of this *Handbook* for details.

Interviews for employment and support allowance

Unless you are exempt (see p1137), you may be required to take part in work-focused interviews if you are entitled to ESA or you have been given an 'advance award' of ESA (see p165), in order to receive the full rate of benefit.[108] You may also be required to take part in an interview at around week four of your claim – called a 'health and work conversation'. This is a type of work-focused interview with your work coach and is part of your claim for ESA.

Note:

- There are no limits on the frequency or timing of ongoing work-focused interviews.
- The requirement to take part in an interview can be deferred to another date if it is considered that an interview would not be of assistance or appropriate.[109] There is no right of appeal about this, but you can complain.
- If you fail to take part in a work-focused interview without good cause, you may be given a sanction and your benefit is then paid at a reduced rate.

Exemptions

You are not required to take part in work-focused interviews if:[110]

- you are a lone parent and responsible for a child under one who is a member of your household (see p326 and p327); *or*
- the decision maker thinks that an interview would not be (or would not have been) of assistance because you are (or were likely to be) starting or returning to work; *or*
- the decision maker has decided that you have, or are treated as having, limited capability for work-related activity – ie, you are in the 'support group' (see p652); *or*
- you are only entitled to contributory ESA at a nil rate – eg, because of your pension income.

Interviews for income support

Unless you are exempt (see p1138), you must take part in work-focused interviews if you are entitled to, or claim, IS. This can apply regardless of why you are on IS, including if you are a lone parent responsible for and living in the same household as a child (see p326), if you claim IS with statutory sick pay (SSP) or if you are someone who can claim IS as a lone parent and on another basis – eg, you also get carer's allowance (CA).[111]

You may have to attend a work-focused interview when you make a new claim for IS. This does not apply if you are a lone parent responsible for a child under five or a lone parent under 18, or someone claiming IS with SSP (see p235). If you fail to take part in an interview when you claim IS, you are treated as not having made a claim and are, therefore, not entitled to benefit.[112] You can ask for your interview to be deferred (or not carried out at all) if it is not appropriate. If your interview is deferred to a later date when you claim IS, you are treated as complying and paid IS in the meantime. However, if you then fail to take part in the interview, your entitlement is terminated.[113]

Part 7: National insurance, work and work-related rules
Chapter 48: Claimant responsibilities: other benefits
2. Work-focused interviews for other benefits

You may also have to attend work-focused interviews on an ongoing basis as a condition of continuing to receive the full amount of IS. The frequency and timing of the interviews depends on whether you are claiming IS solely as a lone parent or if you are claiming on another basis.[114] The requirement to take part in an interview can be deferred to another date (and in some cases waived) if it is considered that it would not be of assistance or appropriate.[115]

If you fail to take part in a work-focused interview as part of your ongoing conditions of receiving IS, and you cannot show good cause, you may be given a sanction and your IS is then paid at a reduced rate (see p1157).

Note: if you ask for an interview to be deferred or waived and the DWP refuses, there is no right of appeal, but you can complain.

Exemptions

You are not required to take part in work-focused interviews if you are:[116]
- a lone parent under 18; *or*
- a lone parent responsible for a child aged under one who is a member of your household; *or*
- already subject to the work-related requirements for ESA (see p1136).

Interviews for partners

If you are a member of a couple and you are entitled to IS, income-based JSA (but not joint-claim JSA) or income-related ESA, unless s/he is exempt, your partner may be required to take part in work-focused interviews if:[117]
- you are both aged 18 or over, but under pension age; *and*
- you have been continuously entitled to one of these benefits for 26 weeks or more; *and*
- the benefit is paid to you at a higher rate because of your partner – eg, you get the couple rate of income-based JSA.

Note:
- Your partner must take part in one work-focused interview as a condition of your receiving the full amount of your benefit. However, if you are claiming income-based JSA and you or your partner are responsible for a child aged one or over who is a member of your household, your partner must take part in further interviews every six months.[118]
- The requirement to take part in an interview can be waived or deferred to another date if it is considered that it would not be of assistance or appropriate.[119] There is no right of appeal about this, but you can complain.
- If your partner fails to take part in a work-focused interview and cannot show good cause, you may be given a sanction and your benefit is then paid at a reduced rate (see p1157).

Exemptions

Your partner is not required to take part in a work-focused interview under these rules if:[120]

- s/he is entitled to one of the above benefits in her/his own right. However, in this case, s/he may be required to take part in a work-focused interview under one of the other sets of rules described in this chapter; or
- you or your partner are responsible for a child under one who is a member of your household.

Taking part in an interview

For at least three months from 19 March 2020, all work focused interviews take placy by telephone or in some other way which avoids you leaving your home.[121] There is no right of appeal about how the interview takes place, but you should complain if you think that a reasonable request for an adjustment has not been taken into account. If you have a disability, a failure to make reasonable adjustments for your interview may be a breach of the Equality Act 2010.[122]

'**Taking part**' in an interview means that you must do the following.[123]

- Turn up at the time and place notified. For ESA, if you are not required to attend an interview in person, you must be available (eg, by telephone) on the date and at the time notified and respond to any contact made.
- 'Participate in discussions' with your work coach about your employability and about any reasonable activity you are willing to do (or have done) which may enhance your employment prospects. **Note:** this does not apply if it is your partner who is required to take part in an interview. If you are on IS under the interviews for IS rules (see p1137), this only applies if you are a lone parent or are claiming IS with statutory sick pay (SSP).
- Answer questions about your educational qualifications, employment history, any current work and your future hopes for working, vocational training, employment skills and abilities and medical conditions that affect your chances of getting a job, and your caring or childcare responsibilities.
- Discuss and assist in completing an 'action plan'. This includes any action you and the work coach agree is reasonable and you are willing to take. There is nothing to say you must take the steps in the action plan. **Note:**
  - This does not apply for ESA (where an action plan is only drawn up if it is decided that you must undertake 'work-related activity' – see below) or for work-focused interviews for partners.
  - If you are on IS under the interviews for IS rules (see p1137), this only applies if you are a lone parent or are claiming IS with SSP.
- In further interviews, discuss your progress, how the action plan might be amended and any further support that might be available to you.

Part 7: National insurance, work and work-related rules
Chapter 48: Claimant responsibilities: other benefits
3. Work-related activity for income support and employment and support allowance

3. Work-related activity for income support and employment and support allowance

Unless you are exempt, you may be required to undertake some 'work-related activity'. If the DWP decides that you are required to do so, you must be notified properly in a written action plan which is given to you, telling you what you have to do.[124] Any requirement must be reasonable, taking into account your circumstances.[125] You may be required to undertake work-related activity if you are required to take part in work-focused interviews and you are entitled to:[126]

- income support (IS), the only reason you are entitled is because you are a lone parent and you do not have any children under three; *or*
- employment and support allowance (ESA). **Note:** you are exempt from the requirement to take part in work-focused interviews if you have, or are treated as having, limited capability for work-related activity – ie, you are in the 'support group' (see p652).

You may be required to undertake the work-related activity by decision makers at the DWP as well as by advisers contracted by the DWP – eg, in the Work and Health Programme (see p1152).[127] If the DWP refers you to a scheme, the scheme manager decides what, if any, work-related activity you are required to undertake. If you fail to take part in work-related activity without good cause, you may be given a sanction (see p1160). However, this does not apply to employment support schemes delivered by or for the Scottish government, which are voluntary (you cannot be sanctioned for failing to participate).

The main features are as follows.

- 'Work-related activity' is activity that makes it more likely that you will get a job or remain in work.[128] The exact activity is at the discretion of your work coach. For ESA, it specifically includes work experience and work placements. However, the DWP says you cannot be required to undertake work experience; this is voluntary.[129] So if you do not undertake work experience, you should *not* be given a sanction.
- You cannot be required to apply for a job or undertake work (as an employee or otherwise).[130] If you are put under pressure to do so, get advice.
- For ESA, you cannot be required to undergo medical treatment.[131]
- All work-related activity must be recorded in an 'action plan', which must be in writing and specify the activity you are required to undertake.[132] You must be given a copy. An action plan must be reconsidered if you request it, and a written decision issued following the request.[133]
- A requirement about the time when, or by which, you must undertake work-related activity can be lifted if the DWP considers it would be (or would have been) unreasonable.[134]

For IS, you can restrict the times you are required to be available to undertake work-related activity, but you must be available during your child's normal school hours, or during periods in which you have entrusted someone over 18 to supervise your child on a temporary basis (other than for healthcare) – eg, a babysitter or member of your family.[135] For ESA, if you are the lone parent of a child under 13, you can only be required to undertake work-related activity during your child's normal school hours.[136]

If you have a disability

If you have a disability or health condition that affects the work you can do, you may be able to get specialist employability support for 12 months. This is intensive support and training to help disabled people into work. Involvement in this scheme does not alter what you need to do to get your full benefit, but your work coach may agree that it fulfils the requirement to undertake 'work-related activity' if this applies to you. However, taking part in employability support delivered by or for the Scottish government is always voluntary and you cannot be sanctioned if you do not participate. For further information, see gov.uk/specialist-employability-support. You need to contact Jobcentre Plus to be assessed for the scheme.

Exemptions

You cannot be required to undertake work-related activity if:[137]

- you are a lone parent who is responsible for a child under three who is a member of your household (see p326 and p327); *or*
- you are exempt from the requirement to take part in work-focused interviews; *or*
- for IS, as well as being a lone parent, you come within any of the other groups of people who can claim IS (see p234); *or*
- for ESA, you are entitled to carer's allowance, or your ESA includes a carer premium (p350).

Part 7: National insurance, work and work-related rules
Chapter 48: Claimant responsibilities: other benefits
Notes

Notes

1. The jobseeking conditions for jobseeker's allowance outside the universal credit system

1 s17A JSA 1995
2 ss9(1) and 35(1) JSA 1995
3 s6(1) JSA 1995; reg 6 JSA Regs
4 R(U) 44/53
5 s6(1) and (9) JSA 1995
6 *Shaukat Ali v CAO*, appendix to R(U) 1/85
7 *Secretary of State for Social Security v David*, 15 December 2000, reported as R(JSA) 3/01
8 Regs 4 and 5(1)-(1B) and (6) JSA Regs
9 Reg 5(2) JSA Regs
10 CU/96/1994
11 Reg 5(3) JSA Regs
12 Reg 5(4) JSA Regs
13 Reg 4 JSA Regs
14 Reg 14(1)(c), (m), (n), (nn), (p) and (q) JSA Regs
15 Reg 14(4) JSA Regs
16 Reg 14A JSA Regs
17 Reg 14(1)(h), (i), (j), (l), (o) and (s) JSA Regs
18 CJSA/5944/1999
19 Reg 14(2A) JSA Regs; R(JSA) 2/07
20 Reg 15 JSA Regs
21 Reg 7(3) JSA Regs
22 *Secretary of State for Social Security v David*, 15 December 2000, reported as R(JSA) 3/01
23 Reg 12 JSA Regs
24 s6(2) and (3) JSA 1995; regs 6, 7, 8, 13 and 13A JSA Regs
25 Regs 10 and 64(3) JSA Regs
26 Reg 10(1) JSA Regs
27 Reg 13(3) and (3A) JSA Regs
28 Reg 8 JSA Regs
29 s6(5), (7) and (8) JSA 1995; reg 16 JSA Regs
30 Reg 16(2) JSA Regs
31 Reg 31(f) JSA Regs
32 Vol 4 Ch 21, para 21451 DMG
33 Reg 13(2) JSA Regs
34 Reg 7 JSA Regs
35 Reg 13A JSA Regs
36 Vol 4 Ch 21, para 21454 DMG
37 Regs 4 and 13(4)-(7) JSA Regs
38 Reg 8 JSA Regs

39 Vol 6 Ch 34, paras 34415-18 DMG
40 Reg 16(1) JSA Regs
41 Regs 8 and 9 JSA Regs
42 Reg 8 JSA Regs
43 s7(1) JSA 1995; reg 18A JSA Regs; *GP v SSWP (JSA)* [2015] UKUT 476 (AAC), reported as [2016] AACR 14
44 Reg 18(1) JSA Regs
45 CJSA/2162/2001
46 *RL v SSWP (JSA)* [2018] UKUT 177 (AAC)
47 *R (Smith) v SSWP (JSA)* [2015] EWHC 2284 (Admin)
48 CJSA/1814/2007
49 *PC v SSWP (JSA)* [2016] UKUT 277 (AAC)
50 Reg 20 JSA Regs
51 Reg 21A JSA Regs
52 Regs 19 and 21B JSA Regs
53 Regs 1(3) and 19(1)(lzl), (q) and (r) and (3) JSA Regs
54 Reg 7 JSA(SAPOE) Regs
55 Reg 19(1)(p) JSA Regs
56 Reg 19(2) JSA Regs
57 Reg 19(1)(p) JSA Regs
58 R(U) 4/66
59 s1(2)(b) JSA 1995
60 s9(3) JSA 1995
61 s9(3A) JSA 1995
62 s9(4) JSA 1995
63 s9(1) JSA 1995; reg 31 JSA Regs
64 *HS v SSWP (JSA)* [2009] UKUT 177 (AAC), reported as [2010] AACR 10
65 *RL v SSWP (JSA)* [2017] UKUT 282 (AAC)
66 CJSA/1814/2007
67 *R (Smith) v SSWP (JSA)* [2015] EWHC 2284 (Admin)
68 CJSA/2162/2001
69 *PG v SSWP (JSA)* [2017] UKUT 388 (AAC); *CH v SSWP (JSA) (No. 2)* [2018] UKUT 320 (AAC)
70 *RL v SSWP (JSA)* [2018] UKUT 177 (AAC)
71 Reg 34 JSA Regs
72 CJSA/935/1999
73 s9(5) JSA 1995
74 s9(6) JSA 1995
75 Reg 35 JSA Regs
76 s9(7)(c) JSA 1995
77 s9(8)(a) JSA 1995; reg 32 JSA Regs
78 s10(1) and (2) JSA 1995
79 s10(2A) JSA 1995
80 *PG v SSWP (JSA)* [2017] UKUT 388 (AAC)

81 s10(4) JSA 1995
82 s10(3) JSA 1995
83 s10(5) JSA 1995
84 s8 JSA 1995; regs 23 and 23A JSA Regs
85 Reg 24(1)-(5A) JSA Regs; *RL v SSWP (JSA)* [2017] UKUT 282 (AAC)
86 Regs 23 and 23A JSA Regs
87 s8 JSA 1995; regs 24(6) and (10) and 65A JSA Regs
88 CJSA/1080/2002; *GM v SSWP (JSA)* [2014] UKUT 57 (AAC)
89 Regs 25(1)(c) and 27 JSA Regs
90 Reg 25(1)(a) JSA Regs
91 R(JSA) 2/04
92 Regs 25(1)(c) and (1A) and 27 JSA Regs; *SSWP v Michael Ferguson* [2003] EWCA Civ 536, reported as R(JSA) 6/03
93 *DL v SSWP (JSA)* [2013] UKUT 295 (AAC)
94 R(JSA) 2/04
95 Reg 26 JSA Regs; *SSWP v Michael Ferguson* [2003] EWCA Civ 536, reported as R(JSA) 6/03; R(JSA) 2/04
96 R(JSA) 2/04
97 Regs 23 and 23A JSA Regs
98 Regs 23 and 23A JSA Regs; s7 Interpretation Act 1978; R(JSA) 1/04
99 s8(2) JSA 1995; reg 25(1)(a) and (b) and (1A) JSA Regs
100 Reg 25(1)(a) and (b)(iii) JSA Regs
101 *DL v SSWP (JSA)* [2013] UKUT 295 (AAC)
102 Reg 26 JSA Regs; *SSWP v Michael Ferguson* [2003] EWCA Civ 536, reported as R(JSA) 6/03; R(JSA) 2/04
103 R(JSA) 2/04
104 Reg 6(4C) SS(C&P) Regs
105 Reg 25(1A) JSA Regs
106 Reg 6(4B) SS(C&P) Regs

2. Work-focused interviews for other benefits

107 **ESA** Reg 62 ESA Regs
Other benefits Reg 3(1) SS(JPI) Regs; reg 2(1) SS(WFILP) Regs; reg 3(1) SS(JPIP) Regs; reg 5 SS(IBWFI) Regs
108 Reg 54(2)(a) ESA Regs
109 Reg 59 ESA Regs
110 Regs 54(2) and 60 ESA Regs
111 Regs 2-2ZB SS(WFILP) Regs; regs 4, 4ZA and 4A SS(JPI) Regs
112 Reg 12(2)(a) SS(JPI) Regs
113 Regs 7(3) and 12(2)(b) SS(JPI) Regs
114 Regs 2(4), (2ZA)(2) and 2ZB(5) and (6) SS(WFILP) Regs; regs 4, 4ZA and 4A SS(JPI) Regs
115 Regs 5 and 6 SS(WFILP) Regs; regs 4, 4ZA and 4A SS(JPI) Regs
116 Reg 4 SS(WFILP) Regs; s2A(2A)(b) SSAA 1992; reg 8(4) SS(JPI) Regs

117 s2AA SSAA 1992; regs 2, 'definition of partner', 3 and 7 SS(JPIP) Regs
118 Reg 3A SS(JPIP) Regs
119 Regs 5 and 6 SS(JPIP) Regs
120 Reg 7 SS(JPIP) Regs
121 DWP press release, 23 March 2020
122 s29 Equality Act 2010
123 Reg 11(2)-(2B) SS(JPI) Regs; reg 3 SS(WFILP) Regs; regs 6 and 7 SS(IBWFI) Regs; reg 57 ESA Regs; reg 10(1) and (2) SS(JPIP) Regs

3. Work-related activity for income support and employment and support allowance

124 **IS** Reg 3 IS(WRA) Regs
ESA Reg 5 ESA(WRA) Regs
125 **IS** Reg 2(3)(a) IS(WRA) Regs
ESA Reg 3(4)(a) ESA(WRA) Regs
126 **IS** s2D SSAA 1992; reg 2 IS(WRA) Regs
ESA s13 WRA 2007; reg 3 ESA(WRA) Regs
127 **IS** Reg 11 IS(WRA) Regs
ESA Reg 9 ESA(WRA) Regs
128 **IS** s2D(9)(d) SSAA 1992
ESA s13(7) and (8) WRA 2007
129 Vol 9 Ch 53, para 53073 DMG
130 **IS** Reg 2(3)(b) IS(WRA) Regs
ESA Reg 3(4)(b)(i) ESA(WRA) Regs
131 Reg 3(4)(b)(ii) ESA(WRA) Regs
132 **IS** Reg 3 IS(WRA) Regs
ESA Reg 5 ESA(WRA) Regs
133 **IS** Reg 5 IS(WRA) Regs
ESA Reg 7 ESA(WRA) Regs
134 **IS** Reg 4 IS(WRA) Regs
ESA Reg 6 ESA(WRA) Regs
135 Reg 10 IS(WRA) Regs
136 Reg 3(5) ESA(WRA) Regs
137 **IS** Reg 2(2) IS(WRA) Regs
ESA Reg 3(2) ESA(WRA) Regs

Chapter 49

Sanctions: other benefits

This chapter covers:
1. Jobseeker's allowance (p1145)
2. Other benefit sanctions (p1156)
3. Sanction decisions (p1161)
4. Challenging a sanction decision (p1161)

This chapter covers the sanction rules if you do not come under the universal credit (UC) system. Information on sanctions if you come under the UC system is in Chapter 47.

Note: it is always advisable to avoid a sanction before a sanction decision is made. If a sanction decision is made, you should challenge it if possible.

Key facts

- If you are getting jobseeker's allowance (JSA), you can be given a sanction if you do not meet certain work-related requirements – eg, if you fail to participate in interviews, you leave work voluntarily or because of misconduct, you do not accept a job or a place on a training scheme or employment programme, or you are found not to be available for work or actively seeking work.
- You can be given a sanction if you are getting income support (IS) or employment and support allowance (ESA) and you do not take part in work-focused interviews or, in some cases, work-related activity. If your partner is entitled to IS, income-based JSA or income-related ESA, you can be sanctioned for not taking part in work-focused interviews.
- You may be able to avoid a sanction if you can show that you have a good reason or good cause for your actions.
- If you are given a sanction, your benefit is paid at a reduced (or nil) rate for a period.
- You may qualify for hardship payments if you have been given a sanction.
- You can apply for a revision or supersession (see Chapter 56), or appeal (see Chapter 57) against a sanction decision. You must apply for a mandatory reconsideration before you can appeal.

1. Jobseeker's allowance

If you get jobseeker's allowance (JSA) and you do not come under the universal credit (UC) system, you can be given a sanction if you do not meet your jobseeking conditions. If you come under the UC system and are getting contribution-based JSA, different rules apply (see Chapter 47).

Note: from 30 March 2020, for a minimum of three months, you are treated as meeting the jobseeking conditions and, therefore, a new sanction cannot be imposed if you fail to meet them.

If you are given a sanction, your JSA is paid at a reduced (or nil) rate. There are high level sanctions (see p1146), low level sanctions (see p1150) and sanctions if you are found not to be available for work or to be actively seeking work (also known as 'intermediate level' sanctions – see p1149). The amount of the benefit reduction and the length of your sanction period depends on your situation. If you are given a sanction, you might be able to get hardship payments (see p1222).

Note: we refer to things that can lead to your being given a sanction as 'sanctionable actions'. The DWP may call these 'sanctionable failures'.[1]

Jobseeking requirement	Sanction period
High level sanctions	13 or 26 weeks
Losing a job because of misconduct (see p1146)	
Leaving a job voluntarily (see p1146)	
Refusing or failing to apply for or accept a job (see p1146)	
'Neglecting to avail' yourself of a job opportunity (see p1147)	
Intermediate level sanctions	Four or 13 weeks
Found not to be available for or actively seeking work (see p1149)	
Low level sanctions	Four or 13 weeks
Failing to participate in interviews (see p1150)	
Failing to participate in a specified scheme for assisting people to obtain employment (see p1151)	
Other training scheme or employment programme sanctions (see p1152)	
Failing to carry out a jobseeker's direction (see p1153)	

Note:
- The days in your sanction period count towards your 182 days of entitlement to contribution-based JSA (see p714), even if you are not actually paid any benefit.
- If you disagree that you should be given a sanction or disagree with the sanction period, you can challenge the decision (see p1161).
- For housing benefit (HB) purposes, if you satisfy the conditions for entitlement to income-based JSA, you are treated as being on it even if you are not being

Part 7: National insurance, work and work-related rules
Chapter 49: Sanctions: other benefits
1. Jobseeker's allowance

paid it because of a sanction.[2] In this situation, the local authority should *not* end your entitlement to HB. You remain entitled to maximum HB.

Different rules apply if you have been given a sanction because of a benefit offence (see p1278).

High level sanctions

You can be given a high level sanction if you:[3]
- lose a job because of 'misconduct' (see the 2018/19 edition of this *Handbook*); *or*
- leave a job voluntarily without a good reason (see the 2018/19 edition of this *Handbook*); *or*
- refuse or fail to apply for, or accept, a job without a good reason (see below); *or*
- 'neglect to avail' yourself of a job without a good reason (see p1147).

A **'job'** for these purposes does not include employment while participating in an employment programme (see p1151) or self-employment.[4] When considering whether you should be given a sanction, the decision maker should only look at your last employment preceding your claim and your subsequent actions.[5]

Refusing or failing to apply for, or to accept, a job

You can be given a high level sanction if you are informed of a job vacancy by your work coach (including someone officially designated as an employment officer, who may not work for the DWP – see p1114), and you refuse or fail to apply for the job or to accept it when it is offered to you.[6] This does not apply if you can show you have a good reason (see p1155).

To be sanctioned, you must have been informed of a job vacancy by a work coach. You can try to argue that this does not include an appointment with a recruitment agency.[7] You may be informed verbally, in writing or by other means – eg, by text or email. No sanction should be imposed if you did not receive the notification. The DWP says you should be clearly informed of the specific vacancy, what you are expected to do and by when, and the consequence of failing to comply.[8]

If you are informed of a vacancy and are unsure about what your financial situation would be, get advice about the amount of financial help you would get if you took the job, including in-work benefits, passported benefits and free childcare. However, it may be difficult to show you have a good reason for refusing a job because of your income or the rate of pay. It is best to apply for jobs, even if you think they are not appropriate, to avoid the risk of losing your benefit.

Note:
- The decision maker cannot give you this sanction if the job was vacant because of a stoppage of work caused by a trade dispute.[9]

- The DWP says you should *not* be told to apply for jobs that have a 'zero-hour contract' or an 'employee shareholder contract' and that you should *not* be given a sanction if you refuse or fail to apply for, or to accept, such a vacancy.[10]
- You can be expected to apply for and accept temporary work. You cannot escape a sanction on the grounds that a job is temporary.
- If you repeatedly fail to take jobs that are offered to you, a decision maker may also decide that you are not available for or actively seeking work and end your entitlement to JSA altogether. You may then be sanctioned when you claim JSA again (see p1149).

The DWP may treat you as having refused to apply for or accept a job if you behave in any way which means you lose a job opportunity or an offer of employment is withdrawn – eg, you do not arrive on time for an interview or go to the wrong place without a good reason.[11]

'Neglecting to avail' yourself of a job

You can be given a high level sanction if you fail to take up a reasonable opportunity of employment without a good reason (see p1155).[12] This is called 'neglecting to avail' yourself of a job. You do not have to be informed of a vacancy by a work coach for this sanction to apply.

In practice, this sanction usually only applies where the opportunity for employment is with your current or former employer – eg, if you do not return to work with a former employer after what was originally intended to be a temporary break, such as maternity leave, or you refuse an offer of alternative employment in a redundancy situation. However, it may be applied more generally.[13]

The DWP is likely to give a sanction if, for example, you knew you had a reasonable chance of getting the job and did not take the necessary steps to get it. However, it cannot give a sanction if:

- the job was vacant because of a stoppage of work caused by a trade dispute;[14] *or*
- the 'opportunity' is for further work with an employer you have been working for during a trial period.

Trial periods

In certain circumstances, you may take a job for a trial period and leave it without the risk of being sanctioned for leaving voluntarily or for 'neglecting to avail' yourself of a reasonable opportunity of employment.[15] You can only use these rules if you are claiming JSA outside the UC system after leaving a job within the trial period rules. For more information, see the 2018/19 edition of this *Handbook*.

Length of the sanction period

If you are given a high level sanction, it is usually imposed for 13 weeks. However, it can be imposed for 26 weeks, if you have been given a high level sanction previously (but see below) for a sanctionable action of yours (not your partner's).[16]

Part 7: National insurance, work and work-related rules
Chapter 49: Sanctions: other benefits
1. Jobseeker's allowance

For the 26-week sanction period to apply, the most recent previous sanctionable action must have taken place at least two weeks, but less than 52 weeks, before your current sanctionable action. The 52 weeks run from the date of the previous sanctionable action, not from the date of the decision imposing the previous sanction, which could be some time later. If the most recent previous sanctionable action was within two weeks of the current one, the length of the new sanction is the same as the previous one. If it was 52 weeks or more before the current one, the length of the new sanction period is the same as if you were given a sanction for the first time.

Losing a job because of misconduct (see p1146), leaving a job voluntarily (see p1146) and 'neglecting to avail' yourself of a job (see p1147) *before* your date of claim (see p261 and p717) do not count as sanctionable actions for the purpose of working out whether a 26-week sanction period should be applied.[17]

For when your sanction period could be reduced, see below. For what happens if you stop claiming JSA, see p1156.

Note: if you are given a 26-week sanction but later a previous sanction is removed (eg, by the First-tier Tribunal), ask a decision maker to reduce the sanction period if relevant.[18] If s/he fails to do so, appeal. If you have already appealed against the later sanction, the tribunal should take the removal of the previous sanction into account.[19]

When sanction periods can be reduced after leaving work

If you are sanctioned because, before the day you claim JSA, you lost a job because of misconduct, you left a job voluntarily or you 'neglected to avail' yourself of a job (see p1147):[20]

- if the job was only due to last for a 'limited period' that ends on or before the end of the sanction period that would normally apply, the sanction period ends on the day the job would have ended, and is reduced by the number of days between the date of the sanctionable action and your date of claim (see p261 and p717). A 'limited period' is a specific length of time that is either fixed or which can be ascertained before it begins by reference to some relevant circumstance;[21] *or*
- in other cases, the sanction period that would normally apply is reduced to take account of days on which you did not claim JSA – ie, by the number of days between the date of the sanctionable action and your date of claim (see p261 and p717).

In practical terms, this means that if you claim JSA after the job would have ended, your benefit is not paid at a reduced (or nil) rate.[22]

When the sanction period starts

The sanction period normally starts on the first day of the benefit week (see p454) after the last benefit week for which you were paid JSA.[23] However, if you have not been paid any JSA since the sanctionable action, the sanction period starts on the first day of the benefit week in which it took place.

Intermediate level sanctions

If you were previously entitled to JSA outside the UC system and that entitlement ended because you (or, if you are a member of a joint-claim couple, your partner or both of you) did not comply with the requirement to be available for or to be actively seeking work, you can be given an intermediate level sanction if you are able to make a new claim for JSA outside the UC system, which for most people will not be possible (see p23).[24]

Even if a previous entitlement to JSA ended in the circumstances above, you cannot be given a sanction for this reason if:[25]

- you were treated as being available for work (see p1117) or as actively seeking work (p1125), but the reason for this no longer applied; *and*
- you then failed to comply with the requirement to be available for or to actively seek work and as a result your entitlement to JSA ended; *and*
- the DWP considers that, in your circumstances, it is not appropriate to sanction you.

Length of the sanction period

If you are given an intermediate level sanction because a previous entitlement to JSA ended when you (or if you are a member of a joint-claim couple, your partner) were found not to be available for work or to be actively seeking work, it is normally imposed for:[26]

- four weeks if entitlement has only ended once for this reason; *or*
- 13 weeks, if entitlement has ended two or more times for this reason and the most recent time is at least two weeks, but less than 52 weeks, since the time before. If the most recent previous sanctionable action was within two weeks of the current one, the length of the new sanction is the same as the previous one. If it was 52 weeks or more before the current one, the length of the new sanction period is the same as if you were given a sanction for the first time.

Any period that is more than 13 weeks since your (or your partner's) entitlement to JSA ended cannot be included in the sanction period.[27] For when your sanction period could be reduced, see p1150. For what happens if you stop claiming JSA, see p1156.

Note: if you are given a 13-week sanction but later the previous sanction is removed (eg, by the First-tier Tribunal), ask a decision maker to reduce the sanction period if relevant.[28] If s/he fails to do so, appeal. If you have already appealed against the later sanction, the tribunal should take the removal of the previous sanction into account.[29]

Part 7: National insurance, work and work-related rules
Chapter 49: Sanctions: other benefits
1. Jobseeker's allowance

Reduced sanction periods

The four- or 13-week sanction period is reduced by the number days on which you were not paid JSA. This is the number of days starting on the first day of the benefit week (see p454) following the benefit week in which you were last paid JSA on your previous claim and ending with the day before your date of claim (see p261 and p717), or if your JSA was suspended because there was a question about whether you were available for or actively seeking work, the date the suspension ends.[30]

When the sanction period starts

The sanction period starts on your date of claim (see p261 and p717) or, if your JSA was suspended because there was a question about whether you were available for or actively seeking work, on the date the suspension ends.[31]

Low level sanctions

You can be given a low level sanction if you:[32]
- fail to participate in an interview without a good reason (see below); *or*
- fail to participate in a specified scheme for assisting people to obtain employment without a good reason (see p1151); *or*
- refuse or fail to apply for or to accept, give up, fail to attend or 'neglect to avail' yourself of a place on a training scheme or employment programme without a good reason (see p1152); *or*
- lose a place on a training scheme or employment programme through misconduct (see p1152); *or*
- refuse or fail to carry out a jobseeker's direction without a good reason (see p1153).

Failure to participate in an interview

You can be given a low level sanction if you are given a notice by your work coach (see p1114) that you must participate in an interview on a specified date and you fail to do so without a good reason (see p1155). Notice can be given in writing, by telephone or by electronic means.[33] This applies if you fail to participate:[34]
- at the right time – eg, you attend on the right day but are late. There must have been a previous occasion in which you failed to participate in an interview at the right time and the work coach must have given or sent you a written notice warning you that, if you failed to participate at the right time the next time you were required to do so, your entitlement to JSA could cease or you could be sanctioned; *or*
- on the right day.

To avoid being given a sanction on this ground, you must contact the work coach within five working days and show you had a good reason for your failure.

Note:
- In some cases, if you fail to participate in an interview, your entitlement to JSA could instead end (see p1133) – ie, if you do not contact the work coach within five working days. If this happens, you may not be able to reclaim JSA outside the UC system.
- If you attend and participate in an interview but do not 'sign on', your entitlement to JSA could end (see p1133).

Schemes for assisting people to obtain employment

You can be given a low level sanction if you fail to participate in a specified scheme for assisting people to obtain employment (see p1152 for which schemes) without a good reason (see p1155).[35] For other training scheme and employment programme low level sanctions, see p1152.

You must be given notice in writing.[36] The notice must give you specified information, including the day on which your participation will begin, what you must do to participate and the consequences of failing to do so. The hours, where you are to participate and the likely nature of the tasks you will be expected to do should be included. You cannot simply be told that you must carry out any activities required by the scheme provider.

You may be able to argue that before a notice requiring you to participate is given, you should be provided with enough information about the scheme and the criteria for being placed on it to enable you to make informed and meaningful representations on why you should not be required to participate.[37] You should also be able to make such representations about any activity you are required to undertake once you have been required to participate. Your conduct is relevant to your participation in a scheme, not just attendance. A refusal to confirm your identity to the scheme provider due to data protection concerns, for example, could be a failure to participate if you do not offer to confirm it in another way.[38]

If you were not given proper notice, including if you did not receive notice (eg, because it was sent to the wrong address), or the notice is not sufficiently clear, you can argue that you cannot be given a sanction if you failed to participate in the scheme.[39] **Note:** scheme providers can notify you that you are required to participate in a particular scheme, but they cannot decide to give you a sanction if you do not do so. Only a DWP decision maker can do this.[40] Designated employment officers (see p1114) working for scheme providers can also direct you to apply for or accept jobs, but only a DWP decision maker can make a high level sanction decision (see p1146) in relation to a failure to apply for or accept these jobs.

Part 7: National insurance, work and work-related rules
Chapter 49: Sanctions: other benefits
1. Jobseeker's allowance

Specified schemes[41]

The Work Programme: this was a scheme involving up to two years of back-to-work support to avoid the risk of long-term unemployment. Referrals stopped in March 2017. Although no one is on the Work Programme any more, you may have had a sanction relating to it.

The Work and Health Programme: this scheme is compulsory for long-term (24 months or more) unemployed claimants in England and Wales. It provides support and activities for up to 456 days to assist claimants to obtain and retain employment. Activity and support must be considered reasonable in your circumstances, in the view of the provider. Some claimants may be on the programme on a voluntary basis – eg, disabled people. If this applies to you, you cannot be sanctioned for failing to participate

Skills Conditionality: skills training.

The sector-based work academy: up to six weeks of pre-employment training, a work experience placement for an agreed period and a guaranteed job interview or support in the application process. **Note:** the DWP says that it is voluntary to agree to participate in this scheme, but if you agree, it can be compulsory to attend the training element and job interview and you can be given a sanction if you fail to do so.[42] However, sanctions should not be given for failing to take part in the work experience except in cases of misconduct.

New Enterprise Allowance: self-employment support. **Note:** if you are claiming JSA or employment and support allowance (ESA), your partner can also join this scheme.

Full-time Training Flexibility: training for 16 to 30 hours a week for those on JSA continuously for at least 26 weeks.

Schemes may be added to or deleted from the above list, so get advice if you are in doubt about whether a scheme is specified. Remember that even if a scheme is not specified, other sanction rules may apply (see below).

If you have completed a specified scheme and are still claiming JSA, you may be expected to undertake other activities in order to improve your job prospects. You can be given a low level sanction for failing to participate in an interview (see p1150) or failing to carry out a jobseeker's direction (see p1153). You may be expected to attend the job centre every day, participate in unpaid community work placements or attend intensive support and training.

Other training scheme and employment programme sanctions

You can be given a low level sanction in connection with 'training schemes' or 'employment programmes' if you:[43]

- lose your place because of 'misconduct'. See the 2018/19 edition of this *Handbook* for information on misconduct; *or*
- give up or fail to attend without a good reason (see p1155). You might be treated as failing to attend if you have been absent without authorisation, even if the absence is only for one day, or if you arrive late and are not allowed to attend;[44] *or*

- are informed by a work coach of a place and you refuse or fail to apply for, or to accept, it without a good reason (see p1155). See the information in the section about refusing or failing to apply for or accept a job on p1146. References to an employer should be read as references to your scheme or programme provider; *or*
- 'neglect to avail' yourself of a reasonable opportunity of a place without a good reason (see p1155).

Training schemes and employment programmes

A '**training scheme**' is any scheme or course designed to help you gain skills, knowledge or experience that will make it more likely that you will obtain work, or be able to do so.[45]
An '**employment programme**' is any programme or scheme designed to assist you to prepare for, or move into, work.[46]

If you refuse to start a scheme or programme or if you fail to attend or leave a scheme or programme without a good reason, you can be given a sanction under these rules. If it is a specified scheme for assisting people to obtain employment, once you have begun, you may be given a sanction if you fail to participate in it (see p1151).

Note:
- Training schemes and work experience placements do not count as 'remunerative work'.[47]
- You may not have a good reason for failing to participate or refusing to accept a place because of your previous work experience if this was some time ago.[48]
- You may be offered voluntary work experience or work placements via the job centre. If you decide to participate, you will have a good reason for leaving, unless you leave as a result of misconduct after you have been informed in writing of the requirement to behave appropriately in the workplace.[49]

Jobseeker's direction sanctions

You can be given a low level sanction if you refuse or fail to carry out a jobseeker's direction, without a good reason (see p1155).[50]

A '**jobseeker's direction**' is a direction given by your work coach aimed at assisting you to find a job or increase your chances of employment.[51]

A jobseeker's direction must be reasonable. It would not be reasonable, for example, if it would not help you find a job or increase your chances of being employed, was at odds with your sincere conscientious or religious beliefs or if it might unlawfully discriminate against you on grounds such as gender, disability, religion or nationality.

Any jobseeker's direction must be relevant to *your* needs and to the circumstances of the local labour market. If your work coach accepts that a

Part 7: National insurance, work and work-related rules
Chapter 49: Sanctions: other benefits
1. Jobseeker's allowance

jobseeker's direction was unreasonable, or could not be carried out in the time required, s/he cancels it.

A jobseeker's direction might, for example, direct you to apply for a specific job vacancy, to use the government's 'Find a job' website, to attend a training or employment scheme, or to improve your appearance or behaviour in order to present yourself better to potential employers. You can be given an opportunity to take the action voluntarily before any direction is given. It must be clear that you are being given a jobseeker's direction.[52]

A jobseeker's direction can be given at any time and more than once. It states the time within which you are expected to comply with it, and checks are made to ensure that you have done so. Each refusal to carry out a direction could result in your being sanctioned.

Note: you cannot appeal against a work coach's decision to issue a jobseeker's direction. However, if you are sanctioned for failing to carry one out, you can challenge this on the basis that the direction that led to the sanction was not given to you, was not reasonable, or that you did not fail to carry it out or you have a good reason for not carrying it out.[53]

Length of the sanction period

If you are given a low level sanction, it is imposed for:[54]
- four weeks; *or*
- 13 weeks, if you have been given one or more of this type of low level sanction for a sanctionable action of yours (not your partner's), the most recent of which took place at least two weeks, but less than 52 weeks, before your current sanctionable action. If the most recent previous sanctionable action was within two weeks of the current one, the length of the new sanction is the same as the previous one. If it was 52 weeks or more before the current one, the length of the new sanction period is the same as if you were given a sanction for the first time.

The 52 weeks run from the date of the previous sanctionable action, not from the date of the decision imposing the previous sanction, which could be some time later.

For what happens if you stop claiming JSA, see p1156.

If you are given a 13-week sanction but later the previous sanction is removed (eg, by the First-tier Tribunal), ask a decision maker to reduce the sanction period if relevant.[55] If s/he fails to do so, appeal. If you have already appealed against the later sanction, the tribunal should take the removal of the previous sanction into account.[56]

When the sanction period starts

The sanction period normally starts on the first day of the benefit week after the last benefit week (see p454) for which you were paid JSA.[57] However, if you have not been paid any JSA since the sanctionable action, the sanction period starts on the first day of the benefit week in which it took place.

How your jobseeker's allowance is reduced

JSA is paid at a reduced (or nil) rate during the sanction period.[58]

If you are a:

- single person, a member of a couple (other than a joint-claim couple) or a member of a joint-claim couple and both of you are given a sanction, your JSA is reduced by 100 per cent of the amount of JSA that is payable to you – ie, you are not paid any JSA during the sanction period; *or*
- member of a joint-claim couple and only one of you is given a sanction, your JSA is paid at the rate of:
  - contribution-based JSA, if the person who has not been given a sanction qualifies for it; *or*
  - hardship payments, if you and your partner qualify (see p1222); *or*
  - in any other case, income-based JSA calculated as if the person who has not been given the sanction is a single person. However, any income or capital either of you have is taken into account in the calculation.

In this situation, the joint-claim JSA is paid to the person who has not been given a sanction.[59]

If your JSA is paid at a reduced (or nil) rate, you might be able to get hardship payments (see p1222). You may be able to claim other benefits, but be aware that a sanction from JSA outside the UC system will carry over if you claim UC or contribution-based JSA under the UC system (see p1092).

If you are given more than one sanction

No benefit reduction can be made for a new sanction for any days when your JSA is already being paid at a reduced (or nil rate) because of a previous sanction.[60] If you are a member of a joint-claim couple, this only applies if both the new and the previous sanctions are as a result of a sanctionable action by the same member of the couple. Because of the rules for when a sanction period starts, this means that if you are given more than one sanction for the same period, the sanctions effectively overlap.[61]

Good reasons for your actions

In a number of situations, you cannot be given a sanction if you have a good reason for your actions. 'Good reason' is not defined in the rules, but what may count is set out in guidance.[62] If you appeal against the sanction decision, the guidance is not binding on the First-tier Tribunal; it must make up its own mind about what counts as a good reason.

Part 7: National insurance, work and work-related rules
Chapter 49: Sanctions: other benefits
2. Other benefit sanctions

It is up to you to show you have a good reason, but the DWP decision maker should take all the circumstances into account. The factors that may mean you have a good reason depend on the sanction.

For good reason that may be relevant to leaving a job, see the 2018/19 edition of this *Handbook*. For good reason that may be relevant to other sanction situations, see the 2019/20 edition of this *Handbook*.

How much time are you given to explain your good reasons?
You should be given the opportunity to explain your reasons and to provide relevant evidence. For example, if the DWP thinks you have lost a job because of your misconduct, you should be given a chance to comment on any statements made by your employer.[63] If you fail to participate in an interview (see p1150), you must be given at least five working days. However, in all cases, the sooner you give your reasons, the more likely you are to avoid a sanction. If there are circumstances which prevent you giving your reasons immediately, you should explain these – eg, you have to get evidence from someone else. If you are sanctioned, you can request a mandatory reconsideration of a sanction decision and then appeal if necessary.

If you stop claiming jobseeker's allowance

If you stop claiming JSA before the end of your sanction period, the sanction can be applied to JSA outside the UC system again, if you are able to reclaim (unless you are severely disabled and meet certain conditions, you cannot reclaim outside the UC system) (see p23). For the rules if you can claim JSA outside the UC system, see the 2018/19 edition of this *Handbook*. If you claim UC or JSA under the UC system, the JSA sanction can be applied to JSA/UC under the UC system – see p1092.

2. **Other benefit sanctions**

You can also be sanctioned if you are getting income support (IS) or employment and support allowance (ESA) not under the universal credit (UC) system. If you come under the UC system (see p23), different rules apply (see Chapter 47).

You can be given a sanction if, without 'good cause':
- you (or, in some cases, your partner) fail to take part in a work-focused interview in certain situations (see below); *or*
- you fail to take part in work-related activity when required to do so while entitled to ESA or IS (see p1160). For IS, this only applies if the only reason you are on IS is because you are a lone parent and if you do not have any children under three.

For ideas about what might be good cause for failing to take part in a work-focused interview and/or work-related activity, see the 2019/20 edition of this *Handbook*. You should be given at least five days to show you have good cause before any decision to impose a sanction is made.[64]

Work-focused interview sanctions

There are currently a number of situations when you can be required to take part in work-focused interviews while you are entitled to benefit – ie, if you:
- are entitled to or claim ESA (see p1136); *or*
- are entitled to or claim IS (see p1137); *or*
- are the partner of someone entitled to IS, jobseeker's allowance (JSA) (but not joint-claim JSA) or income-related ESA (see p1138).

If you (or your partner) fail to take part without a 'good cause', you are given a sanction and your benefit is paid at a reduced rate. **Note:**
- The amount of the reduction, and how long it lasts, depends on the benefit you are getting and the rules under which you are required to take part in work-focused interviews.
- If you are getting ESA and you experience hardship as a result of a sanction, you may qualify for hardship payments (see p1225).
- If you are getting housing benefit (HB), your entitlement should continue. However, let the local authority know about the change in your circumstances to ensure it has all the information it requires.

For ESA, you have a right of appeal against a decision imposing a sanction.[65] For other benefits, you can appeal against a decision that you did not take part in an interview and a decision that you have not shown good cause for your failure within five working days.[66] If you are given a sanction because your partner fails to take part in an interview, both of you are notified of the decision and both of you have the right to appeal.[67]

How your benefit is reduced

The amount by which your benefit is reduced depends on the benefit you are claiming and the rules that apply to you. For ESA, see below. For other benefits, see p1158.

Employment and support allowance

If you are entitled to ESA and you are given a sanction, your benefit is reduced by 100 per cent of the personal allowance that applies for a single person who qualifies for a support component (ie, the personal allowance for main phase ESA) – currently £74.35 a week.[68] Your weekly benefit cannot be reduced by more than this amount and you must be left with at least 10 pence a week. This means that

Part 7: National insurance, work and work-related rules
Chapter 49: Sanctions: other benefits
2. Other benefit sanctions

you are paid any remaining ESA to which you are entitled – ie, if a component, amounts for a partner or premiums are included in your applicable amount.

Note: if you experience hardship as a result of the reduction, you may qualify for hardship payments (see Chapter 52).

Examples

Bernie is getting ESA of £116.80 a week for himself and his partner. When he is sanctioned, his benefit is reduced by £74.35 a week and he is paid £40.50 a week for the duration of the sanction period.

Lisa is a single claimant aged 23 living in rented accommodation. She has only been claiming income-related ESA for 10 weeks, so is getting £58.90 a week. When she is sanctioned, her benefit is reduced to 10 pence a week for the duration of the sanction period.

Other benefits

Unless you are getting ESA, if you are given a sanction, your benefit is reduced by £14.87 a week.[69] This also applies if it is your partner who fails to take part in an interview.[70] You must be left with at least 10 pence a week. If your benefit is reduced because your partner fails to take part in an interview and you are getting more than one of the specified benefits (see p1138), any means-tested benefit is reduced first, followed by carer's allowance if applicable.[71]

Note: your IS cannot be reduced under these rules if it is already being reduced because you failed to take part in a work-focused interview or in work-related activity, and the last reduction was made in the two weeks before your current failure to take part in a work-focused interview.[72]

Length of the sanction period

The length of the sanction period depends on the benefit you are claiming and the rules you come under. For ESA, see below. For other benefits, see p1159.

Employment and support allowance

For ESA, the sanction period is worked out as follows.[73]

- **Step one:** an indefinite-length sanction period is given. This is normally one week for each seven-day period during which you fail to take part in an interview or agree a date when you will do so with the DWP – ie, it lasts until you comply. However, if within one week after you fail to take part in an interview, you take part in one, or agree a date when you will do so, your ESA is only reduced for the relevant fixed period under Step two below. If you agree a date to take part with an organisation acting for the DWP (eg, an employment programme provider), make sure the date you agree to take part is passed on to the DWP (this may be earlier than the date of your rescheduled interview).

- **Step two:** an additional fixed-period sanction is given as follows:
  - one week, if it is the first time you have been sanctioned; *or*
  - two weeks, if you failed to take part in an interview at least two weeks, but less than 52 weeks, before a previous failure to take part that resulted in a sanction; *or*
  - four weeks, if you failed to take part in an interview at least two weeks, but less than 52 weeks, before a previous failure to take part that resulted in a two- or four-week sanction.

Note: if the most recent sanctionable action was within two weeks of the current one, the length of the new sanction is the same as the previous one. If it was 52 weeks or more before the current one, the length of the new sanction period is the same as if you were given a sanction for the first time. Note also that a sanction ceases to apply if you are no longer someone required to take part in work-focused interviews.[74]

Examples

Sandra does not take part in a work-focused interview with her employment scheme provider and is given a sanction by the DWP. This is the first time she has failed to take part in an interview. After two days, she agrees to take part in an interview with her scheme provider. She takes part in the interview 10 days later. Her benefit is only paid at a reduced rate for a fixed period of one week because she agreed to take part in an interview within one week of her failure.

Alison does not take part in a work-focused interview. This is the second time she has been given a sanction: she failed to take part in an interview 15 weeks ago. Her ESA starts to be paid at a reduced rate. Three weeks later, she agrees to take part in an interview. The ongoing sanction ends, but her ESA continues to be paid at a reduced rate for a further fixed period of two weeks.

If you are given a sanction but later the previous sanction is removed (eg, by the First-tier Tribunal), ask a decision maker to reduce the fixed sanction period if relevant.[75] If s/he fails to do so, appeal. If you have already appealed against the later sanction, the tribunal should take the removal of the previous sanction into account.[76]

Other benefits

For benefits other than ESA, you are sanctioned for an indefinite period. However, the sanction ceases to apply if:[77]

- you (or your partner) take part in a work-focused interview; *or*
- for IS only, you take part in work-related activity; *or*
- you (or your partner) are no longer required to take part in work-focused interviews under the relevant scheme or you reach pension age.

Part 7: National insurance, work and work-related rules
Chapter 49: Sanctions: other benefits
2. Other benefit sanctions

In addition, if you are given a sanction because your partner failed to take part in a work-focused interview, the sanction ceases to apply if you cease to be partners, or you cease to get additional benefit for her/him.[78]

Work-related activity sanctions

If you are entitled to IS or ESA, you can be required to undertake work-related activity (see p1140). However, for IS, you can only be required to do so if the only reason you are on IS is because you are a lone parent and if you do not have any children under three.

If you fail to undertake work-related activity without good cause, you are given a sanction and your benefit is paid at a reduced rate. You must be given at least five days to show good cause – ie, you must show good cause within five working days of the date you are notified by the DWP that you failed to take part.[79] For IS only, you may still be able to demonstrate good cause up to a month after you are notified that you did not take part, if the facts you rely on could not reasonably have been brought to the DWP's attention within five days.[80] **Note:** if you do not contact the DWP in time to show you have good cause, you can still try to argue that you should not be given a sanction if the requirement to undertake work-related activity was unreasonable.[81]

For IS, the rules for what might count as 'good cause' are the same as for work-focused interview sanctions (see the 2019/20 edition of this *Handbook*).[82] 'Good cause' is not defined in the ESA rules, but the DWP should consider factors that are broadly the same. For IS and ESA, the rules for the amount of the benefit reduction are the same as for work-focused interview sanctions (see p1157).

Note:

- For IS, when deciding whether you have good cause, the availability of childcare can be taken into account as well as other reasons.[83]
- Your IS cannot be reduced under these rules if it is already being reduced because you failed to take part in a work-focused interview or to undertake work-related activity, and the last reduction was made in the two weeks before your current failure.[84]
- For ESA, if you experience hardship as a result of a sanction, you may qualify for hardship payments (see p1225).
- If you are getting HB, your entitlement should continue. However, let the local authority know about the change in your circumstances to ensure it has all the information required.

You have a right of appeal against a decision imposing a sanction.

Length of the sanction period

For ESA, the sanction period is normally one week for each seven-day period during which you fail to:[85]

- undertake the work-related activity set out in your 'action plan' (see p1140); *or*

* undertake alternative work-related activity notified by the DWP; *or*
* make an agreement with the DWP to undertake the work-related activity set out in your action plan or alternative work-related activity on an agreed date. If you make the agreement with an organisation acting for the DWP (eg, an employment programme provider), make sure the information is passed on to the DWP.

A further fixed period is added (see p1158 – the rules are the same as for ESA work-focused interview sanctions). Your ESA cannot be paid at a reduced rate if you are no longer required to undertake work-related activity or the DWP decides it is no longer appropriate to require you to undertake it at that time.[86]

For **IS**, the sanction period lasts until either you meet a requirement to undertake work-related activity or take part in a work-focused interview, or you are no longer required to undertake work-related activity.[87]

3. **Sanction decisions**

A DWP decision maker decides whether you should be given a sanction, often some time after the 'sanctionable action' took place. Do not assume that because you have not yet been informed of any sanction, the DWP has decided not to sanction you.

You should be issued with a notice, telling you that you have been given a sanction automatically. This means that you should know you have been given a sanction before your benefit is paid at a reduced (or nil) rate and you have a chance to contact the DWP urgently if a mistake has been made.

It is understood that 'safeguarding' procedures apply if you are considered to be 'vulnerable' – eg, if you have a serious mental health condition. The safeguarding procedures are not a legal requirement, but involve extra checks before you are given a sanction. If you think that you are vulnerable because of your condition but have been given a sanction, ask whether the safeguarding procedures were applied to you.

For tips on avoiding sanctions, see the 2019/20 edition of this *Handbook*.

4. **Challenging a sanction decision**

If you are given a sanction, your benefit is paid at a reduced rate, often for a lengthy period. It is, therefore, always worth challenging a sanction decision. You can apply for a revision or appeal against it in the usual way. For benefits other than employment and support allowance, see p1157 for special rules about work-focused interview sanctions.

Part 7: National insurance, work and work-related rules
Chapter 49: Sanctions: other benefits
4. Challenging a sanction decision

You must apply for a mandatory reconsideration before you can appeal. You should apply within the time limit for an 'any grounds' revision if you can (see p1341). Ask for the time limit to be extended if your application is late. In some cases, there is no time limit for applying for a mandatory reconsideration – ie, if you can show grounds for an 'any time' revision (see p1307). See p1308 for the specific situations in which a sanction decision can be revised at any time.

You must be given written notice of the sanction decision, setting out your appeal rights.[88] Although notification of sanction decisions is meant to happen automatically, this does not always happen. If you were given a sanction but did not receive written notice of the decision, get advice. You may still be able to ask for a mandatory reconsideration and then appeal, even if the decision was made a long time ago. If possible, you should hand in your application for a revision to the job centre office to ensure it is received as soon as possible, but you should also post it to the address on your sanction decision letter. You can also request a revision by telephone, though it is a good idea to follow this up in writing. Keep a copy of your application. If your mandatory reconsideration is not successful, but you still believe the sanction decision is wrong, it is often worth appealing as this provides an independent assessment of events.

Sanction decisions you can challenge

You can challenge:
- the decision to give you a sanction – eg:
  - whether you failed to do something or did what it is alleged you did;
  - whether you have been properly notified of any requirements and the consequences of non-compliance – eg, to attend an interview or participate in a scheme;
  - for jobseeker's allowance, if you are given a sanction for failing to carry out a jobseeker's direction, whether the jobseeker's direction was reasonable;
  - whether you have a good reason (see p1155) or good cause (for what you did or did not do);
- the length of the sanction period – eg, if there is a dispute about the number of times you have been sanctioned, or you are challenging a previous decision to give you a sanction.

If you have been given a sanction more than once, you should challenge *all* the decisions if possible. Apply for a mandatory reconsideration of all the sanction decisions, asking for the time limit for doing so to be extended if relevant.

If a previous sanction is removed (eg, by a DWP decision maker or the First-tier Tribunal), the sanction period for a later sanction should be reduced.[89] If you have appealed against the later sanction, the tribunal should take the removal of the previous sanction into account.[90]

Notes

1. **Jobseeker's allowance**
1 Reg 75(5) JSA Regs
2 Reg 2(3)(a) HB Regs
3 s19(2) JSA 1995
4 Reg 75(4) JSA Regs
5 CJSA/3304/1999
6 s19(2)(c) JSA 1995
7 *MT v SSWP (JSA)* [2016] UKUT 72 (AAC)
8 Vol 6 Ch 34, para 34729 DMG
9 s20(1) JSA 1995
10 Vol 6 Ch 34, paras 34415-18, 34335-38 and 34743 DMG
11 Vol 6 Ch 34, para 34732 DMG; CJSA/ 2082/2002; CJSA/2692/1999
12 s19(2)(d) JSA 1995
13 *MT v SSWP (JSA)* [2016] UKUT 72 (AAC)
14 s20(1) JSA 1995
15 s20(3) JSA 1995
16 Reg 69(1) and (2) JSA Regs
17 Reg 69(3) JSA Regs
18 Reg 3(6) SS&CS(DA) Regs
19 CJSA/2375/2000
20 Reg 69(4) JSA Regs
21 Reg 69(5) JSA Regs
22 Reg 70A(1) JSA Regs
23 Reg 69(6) JSA Regs
24 s19B JSA 1995; reg 69B JSA Regs
25 Reg 69B(5) JSA Regs
26 Reg 69B(6) JSA Regs
27 s19B(5) JSA 1995
28 Reg 3(6) SS&CS(DA) Regs
29 CJSA/2375/2000
30 Reg 69B(7) JSA Regs
31 Reg 69B(8) JSA Regs
32 s19A(2) JSA 1995
33 Regs 23 and 23A JSA Regs
34 s19A(2)(a) JSA 1995; reg 70A(2)-(4) JSA Regs
35 s19A(2)(b) JSA 1995
36 Reg 5 JSA(SAPOE) Regs
37 *R (Reilly and Another) v SSWP* [2013] UKSC 68, reported as [2014] AACR 9; *SSWP v TJ (JSA)* [2015] UKUT 56 (AAC). *SSWP v TJ* was appealed in *Reilly and Hewstone and Jeffrey & Bevan v SSWP* [2016] EWCA Civ 413 and the court upheld this aspect of the decision.
38 *CS v SSWP (JSA)* [2019] UKUT 218 (AAC)

39 *PL v SSWP (JSA)* [2013] UKUT 227 (AAC); *DD v SSWP (JSA)* [2015] UKUT 318 (AAC); *SSWP v DC (JSA)* [2017] UKUT 464 (AAC)
40 Reg 17 JSA(SAPOE) Regs
41 Reg 3 JSA(SAPOE) Regs
42 Vol 6 Ch 34, para 34852 DMG
43 s19A(2)(d)-(g) JSA 1995
44 R(JSA) 2/06
45 Reg 75(1)(b) JSA Regs
46 Reg 75(1)(a) JSA Regs
47 *AW v SSWP* [2016] UKUT 387 (AAC)
48 *AW v SSWP* [2016] UKUT 387 (AAC)
49 s17A JSA 1995; reg 5 JSA(SAPOE) Regs; para 34954 DMG
50 s19A(2)(c) JSA 1995
51 s19A(11) JSA 1995
52 *DM v SSWP (JSA)* [2015] UKUT 67 (AAC)
53 *SA v SSWP (JSA)* [2015] UKUT 454 (AAC)
54 Reg 69A(1) and (2) JSA Regs
55 Reg 3(6) SS&CS(DA) Regs
56 CJSA/2375/2000
57 Reg 69A(3) JSA Regs
58 ss19(1), 19A(1) and 19B(1-(3) JSA 1995; reg 70 JSA Regs
59 ss19(7), 19A(10) and 19B(8) JSA 1995
60 Reg 70(2) JSA Regs
61 Regs 69(6), 69A(3) and 69B(8) JSA Regs
62 Vol 6 Ch 34, paras 34200-503 DMG
63 Vol 6 Ch 34, para 34571 DMG

2. **Other benefit sanctions**
64 *DL v SSWP (JSA)* [2013] UKUT 295 (AAC)
65 There is no specific appeal provision, but the DWP confirmed there is a normal right of appeal against such a decision in an email to CPAG, 21 January 2008.
66 s2B SSAA 1992; Sch 2 para 5A SSA 1998; reg 15 SS(JPI) Regs; reg 9 SS(WFILP) Regs; reg 10 SS(IBWFI) Regs; reg 14 SS(JPIP) Regs
67 Reg 14 SS(JPIP) Regs
68 Reg 63 ESA Regs
69 Reg 12(2)(c)-(7) SS(JPI) Regs; reg 8 SS(WFILP) Regs
70 Reg 11 SS(JPIP) Regs
71 Reg 11(4) SS(JPIP) Regs
72 Reg 12A SS(JPI) Regs; reg 7(5A) and (5B) SS(WFILP) Regs
73 Reg 63(6)-(11) ESA Regs

Part 7: National insurance, work and work-related rules
Chapter 49: Sanctions: other benefits
Notes

74 Reg 64(2) ESA Regs
75 Reg 3(5C) and (6A) SS&CS(DA) Regs
76 CJSA/2375/2000
77 Regs 12(9), (9A) and (12) and 13 SS(JPI) Regs; reg 9(8) and (11) SS(IBWFI) Regs; regs 7(2) and 8(3) and (4) SS(WFILP) Regs; regs 11(9) and (11) and 12 SS(JPIP) Regs
78 Reg 12 SS(JPIP) Regs
79 Reg 8(1) ESA(WRA) Regs; reg 6(1) IS(WRA) Regs; *DL v SSWP (JSA)* [2013] UKUT 295 (AAC)
80 Reg 6(3) IS(WRA) Regs
81 **IS** Regs 2(3)(a) and 4 IS(WRA) Regs
ESA Regs 3(4)(a) and 6 ESA(WRA) Regs
All *LM v SSWP (ESA)* [2016] UKUT 360 (AAC)
82 **IS** Reg 8 IS(WRA) Regs
ESA Reg 8 ESA(WRA) Regs; regs 63 and 64 ESA Regs
83 Reg 7 IS(WRA) Regs
84 Reg 8(4) IS(WRA) Regs
85 Reg 63(6)-(11) ESA Regs
86 Reg 64(1)(b) and (c) ESA Regs
87 Reg 9 IS(WRA) Regs

7

4. Challenging a sanction decision
88 Regs 3ZA and 28 SS&CS(DA) Regs
89 Reg 3(6) SS&CS(DA) Regs
90 CJSA/2375/2000

Part 8

Claiming benefits and getting paid

Chapter 50

· ·

Claims

This chapter covers:
1. Making a claim (p1168)
2. Who should claim (p1169)
3. Information to support your claim (p1170)
4. The date of your claim (p1176)

This chapter covers the general rules on claims and backdating. See the chapter about the benefit you are claiming for the specific rules about that benefit. This chapter does not cover the rules for the Scottish social security benefits (see Chapter 76). If you are getting any of these, see the chapter about the benefit you are getting for the rules that apply. It also does not cover tax credits (see Chapter 63), statutory sick pay (see Chapter 39), statutory maternity, adoption, paternity, shared parental and parental bereavement pay (see Chapter 38), social fund budgeting loans (see p792), health benefits (see Chapter 31), the other payments in Chapter 40 or discretionary housing payments (see Chapter 29). Generally, the rules for housing benefit (HB) are not covered (see Chapter 10), although the national insurance number requirement described in this chapter also applies to HB.

Key facts
- To be entitled to a benefit, you must usually make a claim for it.
- Depending on the benefit, you may be able to claim by telephone, online, on a paper claim form or in person.
- You must usually provide your national insurance number and any other evidence considered reasonable.
- Once you have made a valid claim, a decision must be made by a decision maker at the DWP or HM Revenue and Customs (see Chapter 55).

Part 8: Claiming benefits and getting paid
Chapter 50: Claims
1. Making a claim

1. Making a claim

In most cases, to be entitled to benefit, you must make a claim for it.[1] If you cannot claim for yourself, an 'appointee' can claim on your behalf (see p1170).

How to make a claim

Each benefit has its own rules for how to make a claim. See the chapter in this *Handbook* about the benefit you want to claim. You may be able to claim in writing, including online, or by telephone. You may also have to attend an interview to complete your claim, or be sent a written statement to sign and return.

During the coronavirus pandemic, the DWP is encouraging all claims to be made online, or where that is not possible, by telephone. Attendance at jobcenters is by appointment only.

Child benefit and guardian's allowance are normally claimed in writing. If you need help, you can ask for a visit from HM Revenue and Customs (HMRC), usually by contacting the helpline (tel: 0300 200 3100 for child benefit or 0300 322 9080 for guardian's allowance).

Is making a claim impractical or impossible for you?

If starting a claim is difficult for you, explain this and ask to claim in a different way. For example:

- if speaking in English is difficult, an interpreter can be arranged;
- another person may be able to phone on your behalf, especially if you are there to help;
- if you cannot claim by telephone, you may be able to claim online;
- if you cannot claim by telephone or online, a face-to-face interview could take place at a local Jobcentre Plus office;
- a home visit could be arranged;
- you may be able to claim in person at an 'alternative office' (see below);
- except for UC, a claim form could be completed and sent.

Alternative offices

The DWP has made arrangements to enable you to get help to claim some benefits at an 'alternative office'. You can claim carer's allowance, disability living allowance, income support, employment and support allowance (ESA), pension credit and retirement pension at an alternative office. If you are over pension age (see p779), you can also claim attendance allowance, bereavement benefits and winter fuel payment at these offices.[2] **Note:** you cannot claim contributory ESA in this way if you come under the UC system (see p23).

Alternative offices[3]

'Alternative offices' may include designated DWP offices, designated local authority housing benefit offices and some English county councils. Also included are some local advice centres. If you want to claim at an alternative office, ask whether it has been designated to accept your claim.

Amending or withdrawing your claim

You can amend your claim at any time before a decision is made by writing to the office handling it.[4] In some circumstances, your claim may be treated as having been amended from the date it was originally made. For example, if you claimed ESA but did not request that it be backdated, you can amend your claim to include this and your request should be treated as having been made at the date of your claim. However, if you amend your claim to say that your circumstances have changed since you claimed (eg, a partner has moved in with you), this amendment would only take effect from the date the change happened (in this example, the date s/he moved in).

You can withdraw your claim at any time before a decision is made by writing to the office handling it.[5] Notice to withdraw your claim takes effect from the day it is received.

You can also amend or withdraw your claim online if you do so in an approved way.[6]

Note: a claim for universal credit (UC) affects any existing claims you have for the benefits and tax credits which UC replaces (see p21). Withdrawing your claim for UC before a decision is made on it will not enable you to continue to get the benefits and tax credits you previously claimed. Get advice before claiming UC if you already receive benefits and/or tax credits.

For other benefits, you can also withdraw your claim by phoning the DWP or HMRC office handling it.

In practice, you should also be able to withdraw a claim for a benefit you have already been awarded and your award will be superseded (see p1315), as you should not be forced to continue receiving benefit when you have indicated that you no longer wish to do so.[7]

2. **Who should claim**

The general rule is that a claim must be made by you, the claimant. For most means-tested benefits, although you usually receive an extra amount because you have a partner, your partner is not a claimant and does not have to make the claim with you. The chapters on individual benefits explain who must make the claim for each benefit.

Part 8: Claiming benefits and getting paid
Chapter 50: Claims
3. Information to support your claim

Appointees

Someone else (eg, a friend or relative, or a solicitor or the representative of an organisation) can be authorised to act on your behalf if s/he is aged at least 18 and you cannot claim for yourself – eg, if you have a mental illness or a learning disability.[8] S/he is called an 'appointee'. The appointee takes on your rights and responsibilities as a claimant – eg, s/he can make claims for benefit on your behalf, and must notify changes in your circumstances. S/he signs claim forms and other statements on your behalf, and must spend the benefit in your best interests. If benefit is overpaid, the appointee may be responsible for repaying it. Normally, the appointeeship applies from the date of the appointment, but if someone acts on your behalf and later becomes your appointee, these actions can be validated in retrospect.[9]

To apply to be made an appointee, the potential appointee should contact the helpline for the benefit in question – eg, for attendance allowance (AA), the AA helpline. The DWP arranges for someone to visit to assess if an appointee is needed for you, and to make sure s/he is a suitable appointee. The application form (Form BF56) can be completed by the visiting officer during the assessment. If the DWP agrees with the application, it will send Form BF57 to the appointee, confirming her/his appointment. The appointment is effective from this time.

Note: only one person at any one time can be an appointee for a claimant's DWP benefits.

The appointment continues until you are clearly able to manage your affairs or the appointee no longer wishes to act for you (s/he should contact the DWP straight away and inform it of this). It can also be stopped if the appointee is not acting properly.

If you are an appointee for a claimant who dies, you should reapply for appointee status to settle any outstanding benefit matters.[10] An executor of a will can pursue an outstanding claim or appeal on behalf of a claimant who has died, even if the decision was made before probate is granted.[11]

Note: if someone is your appointee for housing benefit purposes, the DWP can make her/him an appointee without a written application if s/he agrees to this.[12]

---

3. Information to support your claim

When you claim benefit, you must:
- satisfy the national insurance (NI) number requirement (see p1171); *and*
- prove your identity, if required (see p1172); *and*
- provide sufficient information to ensure your claim is valid (see p1172).

If you claim in the right way (see p1168) and satisfy the above criteria, you have made a 'valid claim'. It is important that you make a valid claim as it affects your 'date of claim' (see p1176).

If your claim is accepted as valid, it is then referred to a decision maker to decide whether you are entitled to benefit (see Chapter 55).

Note: even if your claim is accepted as valid, you can be asked for additional information and evidence before a decision is made on it (see p1174).

If your claim is not accepted as valid, you should be given a decision saying so. You can ask for a mandatory reconsideration of the decision, and then appeal if the decision is not changed (see p1339).[13]

The national insurance number requirement

To be entitled to benefit, you must usually satisfy the NI number requirement by:[14]

- providing an NI number and information or evidence showing it is yours; *or*
- providing evidence or information to enable your NI number to be traced, if you do not know it; *or*
- applying for an NI number if you do not have one and providing sufficient information and evidence to allow one to be allocated. This does not necessarily mean that you must be allocated an NI number. In general, you have done enough if you have supplied all the information that you could reasonably have been expected to with your application.[15]

If you are claiming a means-tested benefit, your partner must usually also satisfy the NI number requirement (but see above).[16] This also applies if you are getting benefit and your partner has started living with you and so your benefit award must be superseded.[17]

Note:

- If you do not need to make a claim for the benefit (eg, in some circumstances for retirement pension), the NI number requirement should not apply.
- If you cannot satisfy the NI number requirement straight away, you may be able to ask for a short-term advance of benefit (see p1192).
- If you are refused benefit because you do not satisfy the NI number requirement, you can ask for a mandatory reconsideration of the decision, and then appeal if the decision is not changed.[18]

Who is exempt

You are exempt from the NI number requirement if the benefit is:

- disability living allowance (DLA) and you are under 16;[19]
- housing benefit (HB) and you live in a hostel.[20]

If a child (including a qualifying young person – see p579) is included in your claim for universal credit (UC) or HB, or can still be included in your award of income support (IS) or income-based jobseeker's allowance (JSA) (see p323), s/he is exempt from the NI number requirement.[21] If you are claiming a means-tested benefit as a couple (see p319) and your partner is a 'person subject to immigration

Part 8: Claiming benefits and getting paid
Chapter 50: Claims
3. Information to support your claim

control', s/he could be exempt from the NI number requirement in some situations (see p1571).

Proof of identity

You may be asked to produce further documents or evidence that prove your identity. If you are claiming for your partner, you must also prove her/his identity.

You can prove your identity with a passport, a biometric residence card, a permanent residence card, an identity card issued by a European Economic Area state, a certificate of naturalisation as a British citizen or a letter from the Home Office. You could also produce your birth certificate, driving licence, a travel pass with a photograph, a local council rent card or tenancy agreement, or even paid fuel or telephone bills.

Note:
- Provide details of any other people who can confirm what you have stated – eg, your solicitor or other legal representative or official organisation.
- You should not be refused benefit simply because you do not have a document, especially if it is unreasonable for you to have or obtain it. Ask the decision maker to make a decision on your claim. You can ask for a mandatory reconsideration of the decision, and then appeal if the decision is not changed (see p1339).

In some cases, the available evidence that you are who you say you are may not be accepted. Some claimants may have particular difficulty getting evidence. Ask for an explanation of exactly what is required and why. Complain if you consider any requests for information are unreasonable (see Chapter 60). If you think you have experienced discrimination, get advice – eg, from the Equality Advisory and Support Service.[22]

Providing sufficient information

Before making a decision on whether you are entitled to benefit, the decision maker can ask you to provide further information or evidence to support your claim, including proof of your identity (see above). You must provide sufficient information to ensure your claim is valid.

You must normally attend an interview for a JSA claim to be valid (see below).

For other benefits, or for JSA if you do not have to attend an interview, if you claimed by telephone, see p1173. If you claimed in writing or online, see p1173.

Note: if you claim UC, you may be required to agree your claimant commitment at an interview (see p1047).

Claims for jobseeker's allowance if you must attend an interview

In order for your JSA claim to be valid, you must usually attend an interview at a Jobcentre Plus office. Your claim is then treated as having been made on the date you first notified your intention to claim, or the first date you are claiming for if this is later.[23]

If you fail to attend the interview without good cause or do not submit a properly completed form at or before the interview, you are treated as not having made a valid claim until the date you do so. The DWP has the discretion to allow you up to one month from the date you first notified your intention to claim to rectify the situation.[24]

Claims by telephone

A claim made by telephone is valid if you provide all the information needed during the phone call. If you do not do this, your claim is 'defective'. You are given a chance to remedy the defect.[25] For employment and support allowance (ESA) and pension credit only, you must also approve a written statement of your circumstances if asked to.[26]

For IS, and JSA if you do not come under the UC system (see p23) and do not have to attend an interview to complete your claim, you must supply the necessary information within a month of first notifying your intention to make a claim.[27]

For other benefits (and contribution-based JSA if you come under the UC system), if you supply the necessary information within a month of the date you are first notified of the defect, your claim is treated as having been made when you first notified your intention to claim. The decision maker can extend this one-month period if s/he thinks it is reasonable.[28]

Claims in writing or online

Note: different rules apply to IS claims, and to JSA claims if you do not come under the UC system (see p1174).

For other benefits, if you initially made your claim in writing on the approved form (this includes claiming online if you are able to do so for the particular benefit), it is valid if it is completed in accordance with the instructions on the form. If you do not do this, your claim is defective. You should be given a chance to remedy the defect.[29] If you supply the necessary information within one month of the date you are first notified of the defect, your claim is treated as having been made when it was first received. The decision maker can extend this one-month period if s/he thinks it is reasonable.[30]

Note: if you claim online, the system may not allow you to submit a claim if essential information is not entered. Without the required information it is generally not possible to make a claim for UC, as the system will not accept it. If your claim for UC is not accepted, you should complete your claim the same day if possible to avoid losing benefit. For other benefits, you should try to claim in another way as soon as you can, otherwise you may lose benefit.[31]

To be valid, written claims for JSA, ESA, IS and personal independence payment (PIP) *must* be made on an approved form.[32] For other benefits, any letter or other

Part 8: Claiming benefits and getting paid
Chapter 50: Claims
3. Information to support your claim

written communication may be treated as being a valid claim for benefit.[33] In practice, if you make a written claim that is not on the approved form, you are likely to be sent it to complete. If you properly complete and return the form within one month (or longer, if the decision maker considers it reasonable) of its being sent to you, you count as having made a valid claim on the date of your first letter or other written communication.[34]

Written claims for income support and jobseeker's allowance

Unless you are exempt (see below), a written claim for IS or JSA is not valid unless you:[35]

- claim on the approved form; *and*
- complete the claim form according to the instructions; *and*
- produce all the information and evidence required (the 'evidence requirement').

If you do not meet the evidence requirement, the DWP must notify you that your claim is defective. If you complete the form and return it within one month, along with any necessary information or evidence, your claim is treated as having been made on the date you first notified your intention to claim.[36]

You are exempt from the evidence requirement if the information or evidence required does not exist, or it is not reasonably practicable for you to meet the requirement because:[37]

- you have a disability, and you cannot find someone to help you complete the form or get the proof. You can argue that someone else is not expected to proactively offer you help;[38]
- you cannot get evidence without serious risk of harm;
- you can only get evidence from a third party;
- there is sufficient evidence that you are not entitled (eg, because your capital or income is too high), so it is inappropriate to require further information.

If you cannot complete the form or provide the required information or evidence for one of the reasons listed above, tell the office handling your claim as soon as possible. Ideally, explain your circumstances on the claim form or by telephoning the office. You can provide supporting letters – eg, from a social worker or a solicitor. If the DWP exempts you from the evidence requirement, it might:

- help you to fill in the form or give you longer to complete it; *or*
- collect evidence or information on your behalf; *or*
- tell you that you do not have to provide the information.

Further information to support your claim

Even if your claim has been accepted as valid, you may still be required to provide additional documentation and evidence.[39] Provided you have made a valid claim, your date of claim should not be affected if you fail to do so.[40]

If you must travel to provide the evidence, you may be able to claim your travelling expenses.[41]

You must provide the information or evidence within one month of the request, or within seven days of the request for JSA. A decision maker can allow longer than this if it is reasonable. If you do not provide the information, adverse conclusions are likely to be drawn and your claim decided on that basis. In some circumstances, decisions must be made in a certain way if the required information is not available (see p1289).

It is best to send evidence and documents to the office handling your claim. For some benefits, an 'alternative office' (see p1168) may also be able to accept evidence and documents. If a local authority has used information on your claim for HB and has passed it to the DWP because it is relevant to your claim for another benefit, in most cases the DWP must use that information without checking it further.[42]

If you are asked to provide evidence which you do not have, ask what other evidence would be acceptable. Ask what is required and why, and complain (see Chapter 60) if you think any requests for information are unreasonable. Ask for a decision to be made on your claim. You can appeal against this decision (see Chapter 57).[43] You must request a mandatory reconsideration first.

Contacting the benefit office

1. Writing to the DWP or HMRC is the best way to have your case dealt with. It ensures there is a record of what you said and enables you to cover all the points you want to make.

2. Always keep a copy of the letters, forms and other documents you send, as well as copies of those sent to you. This may help you or your adviser to challenge decisions.

3. It is often necessary to telephone the DWP or HMRC. If you do this, make a note of the date, the name and location of the person you spoke with and what is said. If the information is important, follow up the phone call with a letter confirming what was said.

4. If you need to visit an office (eg, because your case cannot be dealt with by telephone) and you cannot get there (eg, because of your age, health or a disability), an officer may be able to make a home visit. If you are refused a visit and are not satisfied with the reason you are given, ask to speak to a supervisor or the customer services manager.

Note:

- If your claim involves medical issues, you may have to provide evidence in the form of a questionnaire. In most cases, the decision maker can refer you to a 'healthcare professional' or, for PIP only, a 'health professional' (see p1176) for an examination and/or a report. If you fail to have an examination and are not accepted as having 'good cause' or 'good reason', your claim will be decided against you.[44] See the chapter in this *Handbook* about the benefit that you have claimed for more details.

- NI contribution issues can be referred to HMRC.

Part 8: Claiming benefits and getting paid
Chapter 50: Claims
4. The date of your claim

Healthcare and health professionals

A **'healthcare professional'** is a registered medical practitioner (eg, a doctor), registered nurse, or registered occupational therapist or physiotherapist, or for DLA mobility component for a severe visual impairment only, a registered optometrist or orthoptist.[45]

The rules for who counts as a **'health professional'** for PIP are not set out in regulations. Guidance states that paramedics are included, along with doctors, registered nurses, occupational therapists and physiotherapists.[46]

4. **The date of your claim**

Usually, your date of claim is the date on which a valid claim (see p1170) is received by the DWP, local authority or HM Revenue and Customs (HMRC). Once a decision is made that you are entitled to benefit, the date from when it is awarded, and the date from when you are paid, is determined by the date of claim. Check the relevant chapter for the specific rules about the date of claim for that benefit and the date from when you are paid.

The date of claim is earlier than the date a valid claim is made if:

- your claim is 'backdated' (see below);
- the claim you made for one benefit is treated as a claim for a different benefit instead (see p1182).

In some situations, you may be able to claim a benefit in advance. See the relevant chapter for the specific rules on the benefit you want to claim.

Backdating your claim

In general, you should claim benefit as soon as you think you qualify. There are strict time limits for making a claim.[47] If you miss the time limit, you may be able to have your claim backdated. If you want your claim to be backdated, you must ask for this to happen, otherwise (except for bereavement support payment) it is not considered.[48] If you satisfy the conditions for getting benefit, it should be paid from your date of claim, even if backdating is refused. If backdating is refused, you can ask for a mandatory reconsideration of the decision, and then appeal if the decision is not changed. Payment should not be held up because you are challenging a decision on backdating.

If you have not asked for backdating, you can ask for your claim to be amended to include backdating before a decision on it is made (see p1169). If a decision has been made on your claim, in order to have a request for backdating considered, you must make a new claim for the past period – your request for backdating runs from when you make this new claim.

The rules for backdating are different, depending on your circumstances and the benefit you have claimed.

- Claims for attendance allowance (AA), disability living allowance (DLA) and personal independence payment (PIP) can never be backdated.[49]
- Claims for some benefits can be backdated without special reasons (see below).
- Claims for income support (IS) and jobseeker's allowance (JSA) can only be backdated in limited circumstances (see p1178).
- For the universal credit (UC) backdating rules, see p47.
- The backdating period is longer for some benefits if you are reclaiming following an award of a 'qualifying benefit' (see p1180).
- Special rules apply if you are reclaiming backdated JSA after your JSA stopped when you failed to attend an interview or sign on (see p1133).
- For the rules on backdating Scottish social security benefits, see p1700, p1708, p1715 and p1720.

If you are prevented from receiving backdated benefit because of an error of the DWP or, in child benefit and guardian's allowance cases, HMRC, write and request compensation (see p1439). The intervention of an MP or the Ombudsman (see p1444) may help.

Benefits that can be backdated without special reasons

Claims for some benefits can be backdated for up to three months, regardless of the reason why you did not claim earlier. State pension can be backdated for up to 12 months without needing to have special reasons.[50] If you want benefit for a period before the date you make your claim, you must show that you would have qualified for the benefit had you claimed at the time. The benefits that can be backdated without special reasons are:

- bereavement support payment (see p554);
- carer's allowance (CA) (see p572);
- child benefit and guardian's allowance (see p594);
- contributory and income-related employment and support allowance (ESA) (see p660);
- industrial injuries benefits (see p698);
- maternity allowance (MA) (see p735);
- pension credit (PC) (see p278);
- retirement pension (see p788).

There are exceptions to the rules.

- The time limit for claiming bereavement support payment can be extended in some cases – eg, when you did not know your partner had died (see p555).
- If you are claiming backdated child benefit or guardian's allowance after being awarded refugee status, see p1574.

Part 8: Claiming benefits and getting paid
Chapter 50: Claims
4. The date of your claim

- If you miss the time limit to claim disablement benefit for occupational deafness or occupational asthma (see p687), you may lose your right to benefit altogether.

Backdating income support and jobseeker's allowance

Your IS or JSA claim can be backdated for up to one or three months in some circumstances, if these circumstances mean you could not reasonably claim sooner. It is important to explain why you are claiming late. In some cases, your claim can be backdated for longer periods after an award of a qualifying benefit (see p1180).

Why are you claiming late?

1. If you can, provide evidence or information that backs up why you are making a late claim – eg, a copy of the letter from your adviser or information from your employer which misled you (see p1180).

2. If you have been misled, misinformed or given insufficient advice by an officer of the DWP, explain how and when this happened and, where possible, give the name and a description of the officer concerned.

3. If relevant, explain why there was no one else who could have helped you to claim.

If a person has been formally appointed by a court or the DWP to act on your behalf, your appointee (see p1170), not you, must show that it was not reasonable to expect her/him to claim sooner than s/he did.[51]

If someone is informally acting on your behalf, you must show that s/he was acting for you. You must also show that it was reasonable for you to delegate responsibility for your claim and that you took care to ensure that the person helping you claimed properly.[52]

One month's backdating

The decision maker must backdate your claim for up to one month if one or more of the following applies (or has applied), and because of this you could not reasonably have been expected to make your claim any earlier.[53]

- The office where you were supposed to claim was closed (eg, because of a strike) and there were no other arrangements for claims to be made.
- You could not get to the DWP office because there were difficulties with the type of transport you normally use and there was no reasonable alternative.
- There were adverse postal conditions – eg, bad weather, a postal strike, or the post office failed to act under its agreement to deliver under-stamped mail to the DWP.[54]
- If you come under the UC system, you could not make an online claim for contribution-based JSA because the DWP's computer system was not working.

- You (or your partner) stopped getting another benefit, but were not informed before your entitlement ceased, so you could not claim IS or JSA in time. **Note:** if you come under the UC system (see p23), this only applies if you stopped getting contributory ESA but were not informed before your entitlement ceased.
- For joint-claim JSA, your partner failed to attend her/his initial interview at Jobcentre Plus.
- You claimed IS or JSA in your own right within one month of separating from your partner.
- A close relative of yours died in the month before your claim. 'Close relative' means your partner, parent, son, daughter, brother or sister.
- You were unable to notify the DWP of your intention to claim because the telephone lines to the office were busy or not working.

Three months' backdating

Your claim can be backdated for up to three months if you can show it was not reasonable to expect you to claim earlier than you did for one of the following reasons.[55] If more than one reason applies, the combined effect of all of them must be considered in deciding whether it was reasonable for you to claim earlier.[56]

- You were given information by an officer of the DWP or HMRC and, as a result, thought your claim would not succeed. 'Information' includes general information produced by the DWP or HMRC staff and placed on government websites. It does not have to be tailored to your circumstances or involve personal communication between you and an officer.[57] **Note:** once you come under the UC system (see p23), the information must be from a DWP officer to allow your JSA claim to be backdated for this reason. The information that is relevant includes if:
  – you were given incorrect information or the wrong claim form and this led you to claim the wrong benefit;
  – someone with authority to act on your behalf was given incorrect information;[58]
  – you were told your claim would not be accepted;[59]
  – you were told you did not have to fill in a claim form;[60]
  – the refusal of, or failure to respond to,[61] an earlier claim for the same[62] or a different[63] benefit led you to believe that you were not entitled;
  – the information was incomplete and had not included advice on claiming when it should have done.[64]

  '**Officer**' includes anyone carrying out public functions at the benefit office – eg, a security guard.[65] It does not matter if the information you received was correct or reasonable on the basis of any information that you gave to the officer about your circumstances, provided the officer's advice caused you to think that a claim would fail.[66]

Part 8: Claiming benefits and getting paid
Chapter 50: Claims
4. The date of your claim

- You were given advice in writing by Citizens Advice or another advice service, a solicitor or other professional adviser (eg, an accountant), a doctor or a local authority and, as a result, thought your claim would not succeed. 'Advice in writing' includes leaflets, emails[67] or information on a website, provided it is directed at claimants in your position. Your claim should be backdated if you are given written confirmation of advice that was originally given to you orally,[68] provided this is done before the decision maker decides whether you are entitled to backdating.[69] The written advice must also be given to you. It is not enough for your adviser to record a note of verbal advice unless you are provided with a copy.[70]
- You or your partner were given written information about your income or capital by your employer or former employer, or a bank or building society, and, as a result, you thought your claim would not succeed. **Note:** this does not apply once you come under the UC system.
- You could not get to the DWP office because of bad weather.

In addition, your claim can be backdated for up to three months if:
- you have learning, language or literacy difficulties, or you are deaf or blind; *or*
- you were sick or disabled (but not if you are claiming JSA); *or*
- you were caring for someone who is sick or disabled; *or*
- you were dealing with a domestic emergency that affected you.

In addition, it must have not been 'reasonably practicable' for you to seek help from anyone else to make your claim.[71] If you are mentally ill, this does not necessarily mean you cannot be expected to seek assistance.[72] However, another person is not expected to proactively offer help.[73]

Backdating after an award of a qualifying benefit

If your claim for benefit is refused, it can be backdated if you reclaim it after an award of a 'qualifying benefit'.

Note:
- More generous rules apply for CA (see p572).
- Different rules apply for Sure Start maternity grants and funeral expenses payments (see p799).
- This rule does not apply to backdating claims for JSA if you come under the UC system (see p23), or to claims for UC and ESA.

Qualifying benefit

A **'qualifying benefit'** is any benefit (except PIP) awarded to you or someone else, which gives you entitlement to another benefit, or makes another benefit payable at a higher rate. PIP is only a qualifying benefit in relation to backdating entitlement to CA.[74] If you will *only* qualify for a means-tested benefit if you are awarded PIP, you should claim it immediately and ask the DWP not to decide your claim until your PIP claim has been decided. You should also get specialist advice.

You can get backdating if:[75]
- your original claim (eg, for PC) is refused; *and*
- you, or your partner or dependent child, claimed a qualifying benefit (eg, AA for your partner) no later than 10 working days after your original claim; *and*
- the qualifying benefit is awarded; *and*
- you make a further claim (eg, for PC) within three months of the decision awarding the qualifying benefit and are now entitled to the award of the original benefit.

In these circumstances, benefit is backdated to the date of your original claim or the date on which the qualifying benefit was first paid, whichever is later.

An additional rule applies if your IS or income-based JSA is terminated. A further claim can be backdated either to the date of the termination, or the date when a qualifying benefit was awarded (whichever date is later) if:[76]
- you, a family member or a person being cared for claim a qualifying benefit; *and*
- you claim IS or income-based JSA within three months of the qualifying benefit being awarded.

Note:
- The qualifying benefit rule also applies if the claim for the qualifying benefit was originally refused, but later awarded after a revision, supersession or appeal.[77]
- If you lost entitlement to benefit (eg, CA), or payment of it stopped because the award of a qualifying benefit (eg, DLA) was terminated or reduced, your benefit is backdated if you reclaim within three months of the reinstatement of the qualifying benefit. This also applies if you lost entitlement to a benefit (eg, you lost your IS because your income increased) but a claim for a qualifying benefit had not yet been decided and, had it been awarded, you would have been entitled again. In this case, your benefit is backdated if you claim within three months of the date the qualifying benefit is awarded.[78]
- If you lost entitlement to your benefit because AA or DLA stopped being paid because the person entitled was in hospital, a care home or other special accommodation, your benefit is backdated if you reclaim it within three months of payment of AA or DLA restarting.[79] **Note:** this rule does not apply when PIP stops in these circumstances.

If you are already entitled to UC, IS, JSA, ESA, PC or housing benefit, you might get a higher rate once you, a family member or a non-dependant qualifies for another benefit. See p1328 for backdating additional benefit in this situation.

Part 8: Claiming benefits and getting paid
Chapter 50: Claims
4. The date of your claim

If you claim the wrong benefit

If you claim one benefit when you are entitled to another benefit, your claim can sometimes be treated as a claim for that other benefit. This can be a way round the strict rules about your date of claim and backdating, as your claim for the benefit you should have claimed is treated as having been made on the date you claimed the wrong benefit.

A claim for:[80]

- ESA can be treated as a claim for MA and vice versa;
- bereavement benefits (but not bereavement support payment) can be treated as a claim for state pension and vice versa;
- bereavement support payment can be treated as a claim for other bereavement benefits and vice versa;
- IS can be treated as a claim for CA;
- AA, DLA or an increase in disablement pension for constant attendance (see p694) can be treated as a claim for any of the others;
- PIP can be treated as a claim for either DLA or AA and vice versa, but only if it appears that you are not entitled to the benefit that you actually claimed;
- child benefit can be treated as a claim for guardian's allowance and vice versa.

Note:

- The decision maker does not have to accept your claim for one benefit as a claim for another. You cannot appeal if this is refused. You can request a revision (see p1303) but your only remedy if the decision maker refuses to change the decision is to seek a judicial review (see p1414).[81]
- For all benefits, except UC, IS, JSA, ESA and PIP, there is a general power to treat any written document as a claim for benefit, which could arguably include if you filled in the wrong claim form.[82]
- For some benefits, although you cannot be treated as having claimed the right benefit, there are special rules about the date your claim is treated as having been made if you first claimed the wrong benefit and later claim the right one when your claim is refused. For more details, see 'The date of your claim' in the chapter of this *Handbook* about the benefit you should have claimed.
- If you claimed the wrong benefit as a result of incorrect information given to you by an employee of the DWP or HMRC and the above rules cannot help you, see p1439 for information about how to ask for compensation.

Notes

1. Making a claim
1 s1(1) SSAA 1992
2 Regs 4(6A)-(6CC), 4D and 4H SS(C&P) Regs
3 Regs 4(6B), 4D(3A) and (4) and 4H(3) SS(C&P) Regs
4 **UC/PIP/JSA&ESA under UC** Reg 30 UC,PIP,JSA&ESA(C&P) Regs
  CB/GA Reg 8 CB&GA(Admin) Regs
  Other benefits Reg 5(1) and (1A) SS(C&P) Regs
5 **UC/PIP/JSA&ESA under UC** Reg 31 UC,PIP,JSA&ESA(C&P) Regs
  CB/GA Reg 9 CB&GA(Admin) Regs
  Other benefits Reg 5(2) SS(C&P) Regs
6 **UC/PIP/JSA&ESA under UC** Reg 2 and Sch 2 UC,PIP,JSA&ESA(C&P) Regs
  CB/GA Reg 2 and Sch 2 CB&GA(Admin) Regs
  Other benefits Reg 4ZC and Sch 9ZC SS(C&P) Regs
7 CJSA/3979/1999; CJSA/1332/2001; CDLA/1589/2005

2. Who should claim
8 **UC/PIP/JSA&ESA under UC** Reg 57 UC,PIP,JSA&ESA(C&P) Regs
  CB/GA Reg 28 CB&GA(Admin) Regs
  Other benefits Reg 33 SS(C&P) Regs
9 R(SB) 5/90
10 CIS/642/1994
11 CIS/379/1992
12 **UC/PIP/JSA&ESA under UC** Reg 57(6) UC,PIP,JSA&ESA(C&P) Regs
  Other benefits Reg 33(1A) SS(C&P) Regs

3. Information to support your claim
13 Sch 2 SS&CS(DA) Regs, Sch 3 UC,PIP,JSA&ESA(DA) Regs and Sch 2 CB&GA(DA) Regs do not include such decisions in the list of decisions against which there is no right of appeal
14 **CB/GA** s13(1A) and (1B) SSAA 1992
  Other benefits s1(1A) and (1B) SSAA 1992
15 CH/4085/2007
16 s1(1A) SSAA 1992
17 *SSWP v Wilson* [2006] EWCA Civ 882, reported as R(H) 7/06

18 CH/1231/2004; CH/4085/2007
19 Reg 1A SS(DLA) Regs
20 Reg 4(a) HB Regs; reg 4(a) HB(SPC) Regs
21 **UC** Reg 5 UC,PIP,JSA&ESA(C&P) Regs
  IS and JSA Reg 2A(a) IS Regs and reg 2A(a) JSA Regs, which still apply in these cases because of the transitional protection in reg 1 SS(WTCCTC)(CA) Regs
  HB Reg 4(b) HB Regs; reg 4(b) HB(SPC) Regs
22 www.equalityadvisoryservice.com or phone 0808 800 0082 (textphone: 0808 800 0084)
23 **JSA under UC** Regs 19 and 20 UC,PIP,JSA&ESA(C&P) Regs
  JSA Regs 4(6)(a) and 6(4ZB), (4ZC), (4A)(a) and (4AA) SS(C&P) Regs
24 **JSA under UC** Reg 20(3) UC,PIP,JSA&ESA(C&P) Regs
  JSA Reg 6(4AB) SS(C&P) Regs
25 **UC/PIP/JSA&ESA under UC** Regs 8(4) and (5), 11(4) and (5), 13 and 23 UC,PIP,JSA&ESA(C&P) Regs
  Other benefits Regs 4(11)-(13), 4D(6A)-(6E) and 4G SS(C&P) Regs
26 **ESA under UC** Reg 13(2) UC,PIP,JSA&ESA(C&P) Regs
  Other benefits Regs 4D(6B) and 4G(2) SS(C&P) Regs
27 Regs 4(7A) and (7B) and 6(1A) and (4A)(b) SS(C&P) Regs
28 **UC/PIP/JSA&ESA under UC** Regs 8(5) and (6), 11(5) and (6), 13(4) and (5) and 23(3) and (4) UC,PIP,JSA&ESA(C&P) Regs
  Other benefits Regs 4(7) and (13), 4D(6D) and (6E) and 4G(4) and (5) SS(C&P) Regs
29 **UC/PIP/JSA&ESA under UC** Regs 8(3), 11(3), 15(2) and 21(3) UC,PIP,JSA&ESA(C&P) Regs
  CB/GA Reg 10 CB&GA(Admin) Regs
  Other benefits Regs 4 (7) and (8), 4D(2) and 4H(2) SS(C&P) Regs

8

30 **UC/PIP/JSA&ESA under UC** Regs 8(5) and (6), 11(5) and (6), 15(3) and (4) and 21(4) and (5)
UC,PIP,JSA&ESA(C&P) Regs
CB/GA Reg 10 CB&GA(Admin) Regs
Other benefits Regs 4(7)(b), 4D (10) and (11) and 4H(6) and (7) SS(C&P) Regs
31 *CW v SSWP (JSA)* [2016] UKUT 114 (AAC)
32 **UC/PIP/JSA&ESA under UC** Regs 8(1), 11(1)(a), 15(1) and 21(1)
UC,PIP,JSA&ESA(C&P) Regs
Other benefits Reg 4H(2) SS(C&P)Regs
33 **CB/GA** Reg 5 CB&GA(Admin) Regs
Other benefits Regs 4(1) and 4D(2) SS(C&P) Regs
34 **CB/GA** Reg 10 CB&GA(Admin) Regs
Other benefits Reg 4(7ZA) SS(C&P) Regs
35 Reg 4(1A) SS(C&P) Regs
36 Regs 4(7A) and (7B) and 6(1A) and (4AB) SS(C&P) Regs
37 Reg 4(1B) SS(C&P) Regs
38 CIS/2057/1998
39 **UC/PIP&ESA under UC** Reg 37
UC,PIP,JSA&ESA(C&P) Regs
JSA Reg 24 JSA Regs; reg 31 JSA Regs 2013
CB/GA Reg 7 CB&GA(Admin) Regs
Other benefits Reg 7 SS(C&P) Regs
40 R(IS) 4/93; CIS/51/2007; *MS v SSWP (JSA)* [2016] UKUT 206 (AAC)
41 ss180 and 180A SSAA 1992
42 The Social Security (Claims and Information) Regulations 2007, No.2911
43 CIS/51/2007
44 **PIP** s80 WRA 2012
ESA ss8-9 WRA 2007
IIDB Reg 12(3) SS&CS(DA) Regs; s19 SSA 1998
Other benefits s19 SSA 1998
45 s39(1) SSA 1998; reg 3 SS(DLA)A Regs
46 PIP AG, p122

4. The date of your claim
47 **UC/PIP/JSA&ESA under UC** Regs 26-29 UC,PIP,JSA&ESA(C&P) Regs
CB/GA Reg 6 CB&GA(Admin) Regs
Other benefits Reg 19 and Sch 4 SS(C&P) Regs
48 R(SB) 9/84
49 ss65(4) and 76 SSCBA 1992; reg 27 UC,PIP,JSA&ESA(C&P) Regs

50 **ESA under UC** Reg 28
UC,PIP,JSA&ESA(C&P) Regs
CB/GA Reg 6 CB&GA(Admin) Regs
Other benefits Reg 19(1)-(3B) and Sch 4 SS(C&P) Regs
51 R(SB) 17/83; R(IS) 5/91; CIS/812/1992
52 R(P) 2/85
53 **JSA under UC** Reg 29(4) and (5)
UC,PIP,JSA&ESA(C&P) Regs
Other benefits Reg 19(6) and (7) SS(C&P) Regs
54 CIS/4901/2002
55 **JSA under UC** Reg 29(2) and (3)
UC,PIP,JSA&ESA(C&P) Regs
Other benefits Reg 19(4) and (5) SS(C&P) Regs
56 CIS/2484/1999
57 *SSWP v PG (JSA)* [2015] UKUT 616 (AAC), but see also *S K-G v SSWP (JSA)* [2014] UKUT 430 (AAC), which earlier came to the opposite conclusion, holding that 'information' must be tailored to your circumstances in some way
58 CJSA/4573/1999
59 CJSA/4066/1998
60 CIS/610/1998
61 CJSA/3084/2004
62 R(IS) 3/01
63 CIS/4490/1998
64 CJSA/0580/2003
65 CIS/610/1998
66 CIS/3994/1998; CSIS/815/2004
67 CIS/5430/1999
68 CJSA/1136/1998
69 CIS/5430/1999
70 CIS/5430/1999
71 **JSA under UC** Reg 29(3)
UC,PIP,JSA&ESA(C&P) Regs
Other benefits Reg 19(5) SS(C&P) Regs; C12/98 (IS)
72 C12/98 (IS)
73 CIS/2057/1998
74 Reg 6(22) SS(C&P) Regs. PIP does not count for the general rule, as it is not defined as a 'relevant benefit' for the purpose of this regulation.
75 Reg 6(16)-(26) SS(C&P) Regs
76 Reg 6(30) SS(C&P) Regs
77 Reg 6(26) SS(C&P) Regs
78 Reg 6(19) SS(C&P) Regs
79 Reg 6(19)-(21A) SS(C&P) Regs
80 **UC/PIP/JSA&ESA under UC** Reg 25
UC,PIP,JSA&ESA(C&P) Regs
CB/GA Reg 11 CB&GA(Admin) Regs
Other benefits Reg 9 and Sch 1 SS(C&P) Regs

8

81 **UC/PIP/JSA&ESA under UC** Sch 3
para 1(b) UC,PIP,JSA&ESA(DA) Regs
CB/GA Sch 2 para 6(d) CB&GA(DA)
Regs
Other benefits Sch 2 para 5(g)
SS&CS(DA) Regs
See also R(A) 3/81
82 **CB/GA** Reg 5(1)(b) CB&GA(Admin)
Regs
Other benefits Regs 4(1) and 4D(2)
SS(C&P) Regs

Chapter 51

. . . .

Getting paid

This chapter covers:
1. Who is paid (p1187)
2. How and when you are paid (p1187)
3. Overlapping benefits (p1190)
4. Advance payments (p1192)
5. The benefit cap (p1194)
6. Change of circumstances after you claim (p1199)
7. When payments can be suspended (p1200)
8. When your entitlement is terminated (p1202)
9. Deductions and payments to third parties (p1202)
10. Recovery of benefits from compensation payments (p1212)

This chapter covers the general rules for most benefits. See the chapter about the benefit you are getting for the specific rules about that benefit. This chapter does not cover the rules for Scottish social security benefits (see Chapter 76 and the chapter about the benefit you are claiming), statutory sick pay (see Chapter 39), statutory maternity, adoption, paternity, shared parental and parental bereavement pay (see Chapter 38), social fund payments (see Chapter 37), the health benefits in Chapter 31, the other types of financial help in Chapter 40 or discretionary housing payments (see Chapter 29). For information about payment of tax credits, see Chapter 63.

Key facts
- The DWP, local authority or HM Revenue and Customs (HMRC) decides how benefit is paid to you. There is no right of appeal.
- You are usually paid by direct credit transfer into a bank or similar account.
- If your claim or payment of your benefit is delayed, you may be able to get an advance payment.
- A benefit cap may restrict the total amount of benefit you receive.
- You must report certain changes in your circumstances.
- Deductions can be made from your benefit. In certain circumstances, payment of your benefit can be suspended. In addition, your benefit might not be paid, or might be paid at a reduced rate, as a result of a sanction or a penalty.

1. **Who is paid**

Payment is usually made direct to you, but there are some circumstances when payments can be made to other people or organisations on your behalf.

- If you are unable to manage your own money or if you die, your benefit is paid to a person appointed to act on your behalf – called an 'appointee' (see p1170).[1]
- You can choose to have child benefit, guardian's allowance, joint-claim jobseeker's allowance (JSA) or universal credit (UC) paid to your partner.
- Your benefit (except housing benefit (HB)) can be paid to someone else if it is in the interests of you or your partner, or any of your children for whom you are getting benefit.[2] This includes paying your UC housing costs for rent to someone who then makes payments to your landlord.
- Your HB can be paid direct to your landlord (or the person to whom you pay rent) on your behalf in certain circumstances (see p215). Your UC housing costs for rent are not paid direct to your landlord, unless the DWP thinks the 'alternative payment arrangements' should apply. If you live in Scotland, you can request direct payment (see p49).
- Deductions can be made from certain benefits (usually UC, income support, JSA, employment and support allowance or pension credit) for certain payments to be made to someone else on your behalf (see p1202).[3]

2. **How and when you are paid**

The DWP or HM Revenue and Customs (HMRC) decides how and when your benefit is paid. There is no right of appeal about this. For how and when housing benefit is paid, see p214.

Note:

- You are usually paid your benefit by direct credit transfer into a bank or similar account.
- If you cannot open or manage an account, payment can sometimes be made by the payment exception service (see p1188). Child benefit and guardian's allowance can be paid by a payment voucher (see p1189).
- You can check your universal credit payments online. If you are unable to do this, ask the DWP for help in accessing your online account. It may be possible to do this by telephone, or possibly in person at a Jobcentre Plus office.

Direct payment

You are usually paid by direct credit transfer into a bank account, building society account or similar account (including a post office card account and some credit union accounts). This is called 'direct payment'. If this is not suitable for you, you may be able to get your benefit paid by the payment exception service , or your

Part 8: Claiming benefits and getting paid
Chapter 51: Getting paid
2. How and when you are paid

child benefit or guardian's allowance paid by voucher (see below). **Note:** the DWP and HMRC prefer you to have a bank account or building society account, and will encourage you to move to one of these rather than use a post office card account. Post office card accounts will be phased out by 30 November 2021. The government says it will introduce an alternative payment service for those unable to open a 'mainstream account'.[4]

Your benefit is paid into an account nominated by you or by your appointee.[5]

If you experience difficulty accessing your money as a result of these arrangements, complain to the DWP or HMRC. You could contact your MP (see p1444).

If someone collects your benefit for you

It should be possible, if necessary, to arrange for someone else to be able to access your account in order to collect your benefit for you. Ask your bank or building society about this. If you use a post office card account, a second card can be issued to the person who collects your benefit.

If you lose your card or forget your PIN

If you lose your bank card or forget your PIN, contact the bank and ask for a replacement card or new PIN to be issued as soon as possible.

If you use a post office card account and you lose your card, call 0800 389 2101. If you forget your PIN, call the customer service helpline on 0345 722 3344 (typetalk: 0345 722 3355). You should get a replacement card or PIN within four working days.

If you cannot access your benefit while waiting for a new card or PIN, contact the office that pays your benefit for advice.

If all else fails, you may be able to get a payment from your local authority while the problem is sorted out (see p861). If you cannot get access to your benefit, and the DWP or HMRC refuses to remedy the situation, get advice (see Appendix 1).

Payment by the payment exception service, voucher or cheque

If you cannot open or manage an account, your DWP benefits are paid by the government's payment exception service at a PayPoint outlet. The DWP sends you an information pack about the payment exception service and identifies two PayPoint outlets near your home which you could use. To withdraw your benefit at the PayPoint outlet, you must produce your payment service card, or text message or emailed voucher from the payment exception service, a memorable date agreed with the DWP and proof of your identity. The voucher is valid for 30 days. If you do not use it in time, ask the DWP to reissue it. If someone regularly gets your benefit for you, s/he can be issued with her/his own payment service card. See gov.uk/payment-exception-service for more information.

If you lose your payment service card, contact the office that pays your benefit. Your card will be blocked and you will be sent a new one. You may be sent a voucher or text message to get your benefit in the meantime. In an emergency, you may be given a telephone number to call for a reference number which will enable you to get your benefit.

If you cannot open or manage an account, HMRC may pay your child benefit or guardian's allowance by issuing you with a payment voucher. This can be cashed at a post office, using a code and reference number which HMRC sends you. The local authority may arrange to pay your housing benefit by another method, including by cheque.

When you are paid

When and how often your benefit is paid depends on the benefit you have claimed.[6] You are sometimes paid in advance and sometimes in arrears. Some benefits have specific paydays. For others, the day you are paid depends on your national insurance number. See the chapter for the benefit you are claiming.

Last two numbers of your NI number	Day of payment
00–19	Monday
20–39	Tuesday
40–59	Wednesday
60–79	Thursday
80–99	Friday

Missing payments

If you are entitled to benefit, you must be paid it.[7] If your benefit is not paid into your account, your payment service card does not allow you to collect your benefit or you are not issued with a cheque, the DWP or HMRC must rectify this.

If there is a long delay, the DWP or HMRC may say that your entitlement to payment is lost 12 months after the date it was due to be paid into your account. However, this should not apply if you have not been paid.[8] If necessary, get advice (see Appendix 1).

Emergencies

If you have lost all your money or there has been a crisis, it is possible to get help at any time. Your local police station should have a contact number for DWP staff on call outside normal office hours.

If you are unable to contact the DWP, or it does not help, you may be able to get a payment from your local authority in a crisis (see p861). The police station should have a contact number.

If you need money urgently, you should provide as much information as you can to support your claim. It may help if you can get an advice agency or third party (eg, a health visitor, social worker, doctor or MP) to support you.

3. **Overlapping benefits**

Sometimes you cannot be paid more than one non-means-tested benefit in full at the same time. This is because of the overlapping benefit rules. These may also apply if:
- more than one person is claiming an increase for the same child or adult (see p1192);
- you are getting child benefit, guardian's allowance or an increase in your non-means-tested benefit for your child (see p1192);
- you are entitled to an increase in your non-means-tested benefit for an adult who is getting one or more of certain benefits her/himself (see p1192).

Disability living allowance (DLA) care component, the daily living component of personal independence payment (PIP), attendance allowance (AA) and armed forces independence payment overlap with constant attendance allowance.[9] Otherwise AA, DLA, PIP, disablement benefit (see p693), reduced earnings allowance (see p695) and retirement allowance (see p696) can be received in addition to any of the other benefits described in this *Handbook* – eg, you can receive employment and support allowance (ESA), both components of PIP and disablement benefit at the same time.

Earnings-replacement benefits

Some benefits compensate you for your inability to work because of unemployment, sickness, pregnancy or old age. These are 'earnings-replacement' benefits. You cannot usually receive more than one of the following earnings-replacement benefits at the same time.
- Contributory benefits:
  - contribution-based jobseeker's allowance;
  - contributory ESA;
  - maternity allowance (which counts as contributory for the purposes of this rule);
  - retirement pension;
  - widow's pension;
  - widowed parent's allowance.
- Non-contributory benefits:
  - severe disablement allowance;
  - carer's allowance (CA).

If more than one of the earnings-replacement benefits listed above is payable to you, the following applies.[10]

- A contributory benefit is paid in preference to a non-contributory benefit. This is then topped up by any balance of a non-contributory benefit due.
- If the above does not apply, weekly benefits are paid and topped up by any balance of a daily benefit (unless you make an application to receive the daily benefit in full). See the chapter in this *Handbook* about the benefit you are claiming to see if it is a daily or a weekly benefit.
- If neither of the above bullet points applies, the highest rate benefit is paid or, if the rates are the same, one benefit is paid.

Retirement pensions

You cannot usually get more than one retirement pension at a time.[11] However, there are special rules if you are married or in a civil partnership and at least one of you reached pension age after 6 April 1979, or you are a surviving spouse or civil partner entitled to both an old category A and an old category B retirement pension (see Chapter 36 of the 2015/16 edition of this *Handbook*), and your category A pension would be paid at a reduced rate because you have not paid sufficient contributions (see p986). In this situation, your basic category A pension is increased by whichever is less of either:[12]

- the amount of the shortfall between your category A pension and the full category A pension of £134.25; *or*
- the amount of your category B pension.

You are also entitled to an additional pension on your own contribution record and one on that of your spouse or civil partner up to the maximum additional pension a person could theoretically receive on one contribution record.[13]

Additional pensions under the old additional state pension scheme and graduated retirement benefit do not overlap with non-means-tested benefits. However, if two or more such benefits are payable with an additional pension and graduated retirement benefit, the benefits are calculated as if the additional pension or graduated retirement benefit is part of the benefit, and the overlapping benefit rule is then applied to the benefits.[14] For more information about additional state pension and graduated retirement benefit, see Chapter 36 of the 2015/16 edition of this *Handbook*.

There are exceptions to this rule if you are a category B retirement pensioner whose own contribution record would entitle you to a category A retirement pension. See p278 of the 2008/09 edition of this *Handbook*. Also, an additional pension paid with widow's pension (see p552) overlaps with the new state pension (see p778).[15]

An age addition paid with retirement pension overlaps with another age addition.[16]

Increases in non-means-tested benefits for adults

An increase in a non-means-tested benefit for an adult overlaps with certain earnings-replacement benefits (see p1190) or training allowances which are payable to that adult – eg, an increase of retirement pension for your partner is not paid if s/he is being paid CA in her/his own right.[17] If the increase is less than or equal to the benefit payable to the adult, the increase is not paid. If the increase is greater than the basic benefit, you get the difference. This does not apply if the adult is not residing with you and is employed by you to care for a child.

Increases in non-means-tested benefits for children

Only one person can receive child benefit or an increase in a non-means-tested benefit for the same child.

The standard rate of child benefit (see p590) does not overlap with any other benefit. However, if you receive the higher amount payable for your eldest child (see p590), any other non-means-tested benefit for the same child (except DLA, PIP and guardian's allowance) or increase paid for the same child is reduced by £3.45.[18] All increases for children overlap with guardian's allowance and are reduced by the amount of guardian's allowance you get for the child.[19]

4. Advance payments

If you are waiting for a decision on your claim or you are waiting to be paid and you are in 'financial need' (see below for what this means), you may be able to get an advance loan of your benefit.[20] This is called a 'short-term advance' of benefit or, for universal credit (UC), a 'universal credit advance'. You must repay the advance by deductions from future payments of your benefit, but you are not charged interest.

> *Financial need*
> '**Financial need**' means that because you have not received your benefit, there is a serious risk of damage to the health or safety of you or a member of your family. 'Family' means your partner and any children for whom you or your partner are responsible (see p583).[21]

You may be in financial need in various circumstances – eg, if you have no money for food or for your gas or electricity meter, or during a 'waiting period' that applies before you are entitled to benefit, or while you are waiting for an increase in benefit after a change in your circumstances. For UC, if you have transferred from any of the benefits or tax credits that UC replaces (see p21) in the last month, the DWP treats you as being in financial need.[22]

You can get an advance payment of most benefits. See p1194 for the exceptions.

If you are in financial need because you are waiting for a decision on your claim, you may be able to get an advance payment if the decision maker considers it likely that you are entitled to the benefit and:

- you have made a claim, but the claim has not yet been decided; *or*
- you are not required to make a claim for the benefit, but you have not yet been awarded it.

If you are in financial need because you are waiting to be paid, you may be able to get an advance payment if you have been awarded the benefit and:

- you are waiting for your first payment; *or*
- you have received your first payment, but it was for a shorter period than subsequent payments will be paid for, and you are waiting for your next payment; *or*
- you have had a change of circumstances which increases your entitlement, but your benefit has not yet been increased and paid to you; *or*
- you are entitled to a payment but it is 'impracticable' to pay all or some of it on the date on which it is due.

Note:

- You can request an advance payment at your local Jobcentre Plus office, or use the telephone number for the specific benefit at gov.uk/short-term-benefit-advance. For UC, the DWP encourages you to apply using your online UC account or via your Jobcentre Plus work coach. If you need help, telephone the UC helpline on 0800 328 5644 (textphone: 0800 328 1344; Relay UK if you cannot hear or speak on the phone: 18001 then 0800 328 5644; Welsh language: 0800 328 1744).
- There are no rules on how much a short-term advance should be. The DWP considers how much you have asked for, how much you can afford to repay and what your benefit entitlement will be. For UC, you can get up to 100 per cent of your estimated award within five days of requesting an advance – but in urgent cases payment can be made faster, including on the same day as your request.
- The DWP says that you must ask for a UC advance no later than three working days before the end of your monthly assessment period (see p39), unless you are claiming within a month of coming off another means-tested benefit or tax credit.
- You are usually contacted about your application on the day you apply or early the next day. If you are to be offered an advance payment, you are asked to accept the amount and the repayment terms. You should explain any problems with this. If you do not accept the offer, you are not given the advance.

Part 8: Claiming benefits and getting paid
Chapter 51: Getting paid
5. The benefit cap

- There is no right of appeal against a refusal to award an advance payment.[23] You can ask the DWP to reconsider the decision, but after that the only legal remedy is judicial review (see p1414). You could contact your MP to see whether s/he can help to get the decision reconsidered (see p1444). You may be able to get help in a crisis from your local authority (see p861). You could also try using the emergency service (see p1189).

- You must be notified of your liability to repay the advance.[24] Advances of benefit paid outside the UC system are recovered by deductions from subsequent payments of your benefit. Usually, the DWP wants to recover the advance within 12 weeks, at no more than 25 per cent of your benefit. If you need longer to repay, tell the DWP and explain why. You can ask the DWP to reconsider the decision about repayment, and (for benefits other than UC) if you remain unhappy you can can appeal.[25]

- The DWP usually wants to recover a UC advance within 12 months. In practice, the DWP often wants to recover at a rate of 30 per cent of your monthly UC standard allowance. Arguably, the correct rate is either 15 per cent or, if you have earnings, 25 per cent of your standard allowance.[26] However, note that when you apply for an advance, if you tell the DWP that you will refuse to repay at the 30 per cent rate, it may decide not to offer you an advance in the first place, and you will not be able to appeal. If you need longer to repay, tell the DWP and explain why.

- You cannot appeal against the decision about the repayment of an advance of UC, including the rate of recovery. You can ask the DWP to reconsider the decision, but after that the only legal remedy is judicial review (see p1414).[27]

Benefits for which you cannot get a short-term advance

You cannot get a short-term advance of:[28]
- housing benefit (HB). If your HB is delayed and you are a private or housing association tenant, you might be able to get an interim payment known as a 'payment on account' (see p220);
- attendance allowance;
- disability living allowance;
- personal independence payment;
- child benefit or guardian's allowance (but see p596);
- statutory sick, maternity, adoption, paternity, shared parental pay or parental bereavement.

5. **The benefit cap**

The 'benefit cap' may limit the total amount of benefit you can be paid.[29] If the total amount of your benefits is capped, the cap is applied:

- by reducing the amount of your universal credit (UC) (see p1197); *or*
- by reducing the amount of your housing benefit (HB) (see p1197).

See p1197 for the 'specified' benefits that are taken into account when deciding whether the cap applies.

Note: there are a number of situations when the benefit cap does not apply, or when it is not applied immediately (see below).

You can appeal (see Chapter 57) against having the benefit cap applied through your HB.[30] There is no right of appeal against a decision to apply the benefit cap through UC. Instead, you must ask for a revision or a supersession (see Chapter 56).

The Supreme Court has rejected arguments that the cap breaches the human rights of lone parents.[31]

When the benefit cap does not apply

The benefit cap does not apply if:
- you are not getting UC or not getting working-age HB (see p188);
- you or your partner are working and get working tax credit (WTC – see below);
- you or your partner (or, in some cases, your child and arguably any other member of your family) are entitled to one of the disability or carer benefits listed on p1196;
- it would be applied through your UC, you and/or your partner work and your combined earnings are high enough (see below).

In addition, if you or your partner have been working recently, there may be a 'grace period' during which the cap does not apply (see below).

If you get a relatively high amount of HB, the cap is especially likely to apply. If the amount of your HB decreases (eg, because you move to cheaper accommodation), this may mean that the cap no longer applies.

Work-related exceptions

If the benefit cap should be applied through your **UC**, it is not applied if:[32]
- you or your partner are working (either employed or self-employed) and have net monthly earnings of at least £604 in your UC monthly assessment period. Your partner's earnings are added to yours; *or*
- you are within a nine-month 'grace period'.

The benefit cap is not applied through your UC for a 'grace period' of nine consecutive months, if:[33]
- your earnings (or your and your partner's combined earnings) from employed or self-employed work are now less than £604 a month but, immediately before the first day on which this applies, they had been at least £604 a month in each of the preceding 12 months; *or*

Part 8: Claiming benefits and getting paid
Chapter 51: Getting paid
5. The benefit cap

- before your current period of entitlement to UC, you stopped paid employed or self-employed work and, before you stopped work, your earnings (or your and your partner's combined earnings) had been at least £604 a month in each of the preceding 12 months.

The grace period begins on the most recent day on which either condition applies. For how earnings from work are calculated for UC, see Chapter 7.

Although not explicitly stated in the UC rules, it is arguable that you count as still in work while on maternity, adoption, paternity, shared parental or parental bereavement leave, or while receiving statutory sick pay (SSP). If you are in this position, get advice.

If the benefit cap should be applied through your **HB**, it is not applied if:[34]

- you (or your partner) are entitled to WTC. This includes if you have claimed WTC but have a nil award because of your income (see p1499); *or*
- you are within a 39- week 'grace period' after finishing work (see below).

The benefit cap is not applied through your HB for a 'grace period' of 39 weeks if:[35]

- you or your partner were previously in work (either employed or self-employed) for at least 50 weeks out of the 52 weeks before the last day of work; *and*
- in that 50 weeks, the person in work was not entitled to income support (IS), jobseeker's allowance (JSA) or employment and support allowance (ESA).

The grace period begins on the day after the last day of work.

You count as still in work while on maternity, adoption, paternity, shared parental or parental bereavement leave, or while receiving SSP.[36]

Benefits for disabled people and carers

The benefit cap does not apply if you or your partner get:[37]

- ESA that includes the support component;
- UC that includes the limited capability for work-related activity element;
- carer's allowance, guardian's allowance, or UC that includes the carer element;
- attendance allowance (or you are entitled to it, but are not paid it while you are in hospital or a care home);
- disability living allowance, personal independence payment or armed forces independence payment. This exemption also applies if the person entitled is a child for whom you or your partner are responsible. The exemption continues while the person entitled is not paid benefit while s/he is in hospital or a care home;
- industrial injuries disablement benefit, reduced earnings allowance or retirement allowance;
- a war pension (or you are entitled to it but are not paid while you are in hospital or a care home).

When the benefit cap applies

The benefit cap only applies if:
- you get UC or you get working-age HB (see p188); *and*
- none of the exceptions apply (see p1195); *and*
- the total amount of certain specified benefits you (and your partner, if you are a member of a couple) receive is above a certain level (see below).

When calculating the amount of benefit you receive, the general rule is that your full benefit entitlement is taken into account. Deductions for repayment of overpayments, payments to third parties, council tax debts, fines and sanctions are generally ignored (but see p1198 for some exceptions if the cap is applied through your HB and you get child tax credit (CTC) or widowed parent's allowance).[38]

If you get universal credit

The cap applies once your (and, if you are in a couple, your partner's) monthly entitlement to specified benefits exceeds a certain amount. The amount is:
- if you live outside Greater London: £1,116.67 a month (£257.69 a week) if you are single, or £1,666.67 a month (£384.62 a week) if you are a couple or a lone parent; *or*
- if you live in Greater London: £1,284.17 a month (£296.35 a week) if you are single, or £1,916.67 a month (£442.31 a week) if you are a couple or a lone parent.

Your benefit payments are converted into monthly amounts for this calculation.

Specified benefits

If you get UC, the **'specified benefits'** taken into account for the benefit cap are:[39]
- UC;
- JSA;
- ESA, if neither you nor your partner are in the support group (ESA is not taken into account while you are disqualified from receiving it);
- child benefit;
- maternity allowance (MA);
- widowed parent's allowance;
- widow's pension.

If you get housing benefit

The cap applies once your (and, if you are in a couple, your partner's) weekly entitlement to specified benefits exceeds a certain amount. The amount is:
- if you live outside Greater London: £257.69 a week if you are single, or £384.62 a week if you are a couple or a lone parent; *or*

Part 8: Claiming benefits and getting paid
Chapter 51: Getting paid
5. The benefit cap

- if you live in Greater London: £296.35 a week if you are single, or £442.31 a week if you are a couple or a lone parent.

Specified benefits

If you get HB, the **'specified benefits'** taken into account for the benefit cap are:[40]

- IS;
- JSA;
- ESA, if neither you nor your partner are in the support group (ESA is not taken into account while you are disqualified from receiving it);
- HB, except for 'specified accommodation'. This means: 'exempt accommodation' (see p403) or accommodation provided by a housing association, charity, voluntary organisation or English county council to meet your need for care, support or supervision; temporary accommodation provided by one of these bodies or a local authority because you have left home because of domestic violence; or a local authority hostel where you get care, support or supervision;
- child benefit;
- incapacity benefit;
- MA;
- severe disablement allowance;
- widowed parent's allowance (after the £15 disregard);
- widow's pension;
- CTC (but if you are repaying an overpayment from the previous tax year, the amount of CTC taken into account is reduced by the amount deducted for the repayment).

The local authority does not have to decide whether or not to apply the cap, unless it is told by the DWP that it may apply in your case or that you have had a change in your benefit entitlement. However, it can decide to apply the cap on the basis of information or evidence suggesting that it should do so.[41]

How the benefit cap is applied

If the cap is applied through your UC, the DWP reduces your UC by the amount by which the total amount of the specified benefits you receive exceeds the cap. However, if you are entitled to the childcare costs element in your UC (see p74) and this is more than the amount by which your specified benefits exceeds the cap (the 'excess'), your UC is not reduced. If it is not more than the excess, your UC is reduced, but the excess is reduced by your childcare costs element before the reduction is applied.[42]

If the cap is applied through your HB, the local authority reduces your HB by the amount by which the total amount of the specified benefits you receive exceeds the cap. You must be left with at least 50 pence a week HB, so that you can still access discretionary housing payments and other passported payments.[43]

6. Change of circumstances after you claim

You have a duty to report certain changes in your circumstances. The DWP or HM Revenue and Customs (HMRC) should inform you of the main kinds of changes that you must report, but might not list them all. It is also your duty to report *any* change in your circumstances that you might reasonably be expected to know might affect your right to, the amount of, or the payment of, your benefit.[44] For the rules on changes of circumstances that apply to housing benefit, see pp221–24.

You must notify changes promptly to the DWP or HMRC office handling your claim. Check the information sent to you about your benefit award, but get advice if you are in doubt. The rules say that the office handling your claim for child benefit or guardian's allowance includes the HMRC Child Benefit Office (PO Box 1, Newcastle Upon Tyne NE88 1AA), or any office specified by HMRC.

You must notify the changes in writing or by telephone.[45] It is best to notify changes in writing so that you have a record of what you have reported. If you report a change by telephone, note the time and date of your call, the name of the person you spoke with, and confirm what was said in writing. Keep a copy of any letters you send and take screenshots if reporting online. If you give the original to an officer, ask her/him to stamp your copy to confirm s/he has received the original.

There are additional ways you can report a change of circumstances.
- For child benefit and guardian's allowance, you may be able to report the change in person,[46] either at the HMRC Child Benefit Office or another office specified by HMRC. However, it is always better to do so in writing.
- Except for child benefit and guardian's allowance, if the change is a death, there is a special rule (sometimes called 'Tell Us Once'). For information see gov.uk/after-a-death/organisations-you-need-to-contact-and-tell-us-once. You can also report a birth or a death in person at a local authority (and, in England, a county council) office specified for that purpose. If the change is a death, you can notify it by telephone to the DWP if a number has been specified for that purpose.[47]

Note:
- If you do not promptly report a change which you have a duty to notify, any resulting overpayment may be recoverable from you (see Chapter 53).
- If you are considered to have acted 'knowingly' or dishonestly, you may also be guilty of an offence, which may lead to prosecution or a benefit penalty. Even if you have not committed an offence, a civil penalty may be applied (see Chapter 54).

Part 8: Claiming benefits and getting paid
Chapter 51: Getting paid
7. When payments can be suspended

7. **When payments can be suspended**

Payment of part or all of your benefit can be suspended in certain circumstances. This means that the suspended benefit is not paid to you.

Suspension while an appeal is pending

Your benefit can be suspended if the DWP, the local authority or HM Revenue and Customs (HMRC) is appealing (or considering an appeal) against:[48]

- a decision of the First-tier Tribunal, Upper Tribunal or court to award you benefit; *or*
- a decision of the Upper Tribunal or court about someone else's case if the issue in the appeal could affect your claim. For housing benefit (HB) only, the other case must also be about an HB issue.

The DWP, the local authority or HMRC must give you written notice that it intends to request the statement of reasons from the First-tier Tribunal, or that it intends to apply for leave to appeal, or to appeal. It must do this as soon as is 'reasonably practicable'.[49]

The decision maker must then do one of these things within the usual time limits for doing so (see Chapter 57 and 58).

If s/he does not, the suspended benefit must be paid to you.[50] The suspended benefit must also be paid to you if the decision maker withdraws an application for leave to appeal, withdraws the appeal or is refused leave to appeal and cannot renew the application for leave to appeal.

Suspension for not providing information and evidence

You can be required to supply information or evidence if the decision maker needs this to determine whether your award of benefit should be revised or superseded (see p1303 and p1315).[51]

Payment of your benefit can be suspended if you do not provide the information and evidence.[52]

You must be notified in writing if the decision maker wants you to provide information or evidence. Within 14 days, or seven days for contribution-based jobseeker's allowance (JSA) if you come under the universal credit (UC) system (see p23), or one month for child benefit, guardian's allowance and HB, of being sent the request, you must:

- supply the information or evidence.[53] You can be given more time than this if you satisfy the decision maker that this is necessary; *or*
- satisfy the decision maker that the information does not exist or you cannot obtain it.[54]

If the decision maker has not already done so, your benefit can be suspended if you do not provide the information or evidence within the relevant time limit.[55] See below for whether your entitlement to benefit can be terminated.

Suspension for not taking part in a medical examination

Most benefits can be suspended if you do not take part in a medical examination on two consecutive occasions without 'good cause'.[56] This applies if:

- the decision maker is looking at whether you should still be getting a benefit (or whether you are getting it at the correct rate); *or*
- you apply for a revision or a supersession and the decision maker thinks a medical examination is necessary in order to make a decision.

This rule does not apply if the issue is whether you have limited capability for work. For information on these medicals and the consequences of failing to take part in them, see p1034. It also does not apply to personal independence payment. However, if you do not take part in a medical, the DWP may still suspend your benefit because of a doubt about your entitlement (see below).

Suspension in other circumstances

Your benefit can also be suspended in various other circumstances, including if:[57]

- a question has arisen about your entitlement, or if the DWP, HMRC or (for HB) the local authority thinks you are being or have been overpaid;[58]
- you have been getting JSA and a question has arisen about whether you are meeting your jobseeking conditions. Your JSA must be suspended until this matter is resolved. **Note:** this does not apply to contribution-based JSA if you come under the UC system (see p23).[59]

Challenging decisions to suspend benefit

You cannot appeal to the First-tier Tribunal against the decision to suspend your benefit. The only ways to change the decision are to negotiate to get your benefit reinstated or to challenge the decision in the courts by judicial review (see p1414). You could also ask for an advance payment of benefit (see p1192). Get advice.

The decision maker may be willing to continue to pay your benefit, or at least some of it, if you can show that you will experience hardship otherwise. If you receive a letter telling you that your benefit has been suspended, reply and explain how the suspension affects you and ask for it to be reconsidered. It may be wise to get advice first (see Appendix 1).

Part 8: Claiming benefits and getting paid
Chapter 51: Getting paid
9. Deductions and payments to third parties

8. **When your entitlement is terminated**

Your entitlement to benefit can be terminated if:

- your benefit was suspended in full, you are then required to provide information or evidence to determine whether the decision awarding you benefit should be revised or superseded, and you fail to do so within one month of the request;[60] *or*
- your benefit was suspended in full because you did not provide information or evidence required to determine whether the decision awarding you benefit should be revised or superseded and it is more than one month since your benefit was suspended.[61]

The termination of your entitlement to benefit takes effect from the date payment was suspended (or an earlier date if you ceased to be entitled for another reason).[62]

Your entitlement to most benefits may also be terminated if you do not take part in a medical examination and it is more than one month since your benefit was suspended on this ground.[63]

If you disagree with a decision to terminate your benefit, you can ask for a revision (see p1303) and then appeal (see Chapter 57).

9. **Deductions and payments to third parties**

Your benefits are usually paid direct to you, but there are some circumstances when money can be deducted and paid to another person (a third party) on your behalf.

What deductions can be made

Amounts can be deducted from your benefit to pay third parties for:[64]

- housing costs (see p1204);
- rent arrears (see p1205);
- fuel (see p1205);
- water charges (p1206);
- council tax arrears (see p1207);
- child support maintenance (see p1207); *and*
- other payments – eg, loan repayments, fines and other charges (see p1208).

Note: in addition to the above deductions to third parties, you may also have deductions to the DWP or HM Revenue and Customs (HMRC) made to recover budgeting loans from the social fund (see p795) and overpayments (see p1247) and regarding fraud and penalties (Chapter 54). Your benefit may also be reduced if you have been sanctioned (see Chapter 47 for the universal credit (UC) system and Chapter 49 for other benefits) or because the DWP is recovering a hardship payment (see Chapter 52).

From which benefits can deductions be made

Deductions for payments to third parties are usually made from UC, income support (IS), income-based jobseeker's allowance (JSA), income-related employment and support allowance (ESA) and pension credit (PC). In some circumstances, they can also be made from contribution-based JSA and contributory ESA (see below).

Deductions can only be made from other benefits to repay eligible loans (see p1208) and child support maintenance that you owe (see p1207).

Deductions from contribution-based jobseeker's allowance and contributory employment and support allowance

Deductions to third parties can be made from your contribution-based JSA or your contributory ESA for the payments listed above if you have an 'underlying entitlement' to income-based JSA or income-related ESA – ie, if you were not entitled to contribution-based JSA or contributory ESA, you would be entitled to income-based JSA or income-related ESA at the same rate.[65]

Deductions can also be made from contribution-based JSA and contributory ESA even if you have no underlying entitlement to income-based JSA or income-related ESA for council tax arrears and for fines.

When deductions can be made

Deductions and direct payments to third parties can only be made if you or your partner are liable to make the payments.[66] Deductions should only be made if there is evidence that you are liable – eg, the bill is in your or your partner's name.

Your consent is required before direct payments (including for arrears) are made for fuel costs and water charges from your UC if the total amount deducted for these payments exceeds 25 per cent of your UC standard allowance and child elements (see Chapter 5).[67]

Otherwise, the DWP can make deductions from your UC without your consent.

Your written consent is required before deductions for tax credit overpayments and self-assessment tax debts can be made from your IS, income-based JSA, income-related ESA or PC. Your consent is also required before deductions are made for rent arrears, service charges for fuel and water, fuel costs (including arrears), water charges (including arrears) and repayment of integration loans if:[68]

- you (or your partner) do not get child tax credit (CTC) and the total to be deducted for these payments exceeds 25 per cent of your family's applicable amount (see Chapter 17) or, in the case of PC, 25 per cent of your minimum guarantee (see p273);

Part 8: Claiming benefits and getting paid
Chapter 51: Getting paid
9. Deductions and payments to third parties

- you (or your partner) get CTC, and the total to be deducted for these payments exceeds 25 per cent of the total sum of your CTC and child benefit plus your family's applicable amount (see Chapter 17) (or, in the case of PC, your minimum guarantee) (see p273).

The DWP can make deductions from these benefits without your consent if they are made for:
- council tax arrears;
- fines;
- current housing costs;
- nursing home charges or hostel charges not included in housing benefit (HB).

The deductions

Deductions to third parties are made before you receive your regular benefit payment. If you want to have deductions made to help you clear any arrears or debts, ask the DWP office dealing with your claim. If you disagree with a decision about deductions, you can challenge it by applying for a mandatory reconsideration (see p1339) and then by appealing (see Chapter 57).

Housing costs

Deductions can only be made for the housing costs that can be included in your benefit – this does not include rent payments. For which housing costs can be included, see p83 for UC (in effect, just service charges, as deductions for rent payments cannot be made) and p360 for other benefits. For the amount of the deductions, see p1208. If you are in rent arrears, see p1205 for the separate deductions which can be made.[69]

To have deductions made from your UC, you must be in arrears with your service charges. Your earnings (or your combined earnings with your partner) must also be below the UC work allowance that applies to you (see p41). If your earnings (or combined earnings) are equal to, or exceed, the work allowance for three monthly assessment periods, the deduction must stop.

If your current IS, income-based JSA, income-related ESA or PC includes amounts for housing costs and you are in arrears (excluding payments for ground rent or rent charge payments, unless paid with your service charges or for a tent[70]), deductions can be made from your IS, JSA, ESA or PC to clear the debt and to meet current payments. Deductions are made if it would be 'in the interests' of you or your family to do so.

You only qualify for direct deductions from IS, income-based JSA, income-related ESA and PC if you owe more than half of the annual total of the relevant housing cost. This condition can be waived if it is in the 'overriding interests' of you or your family that deductions start as soon as possible – eg, repossession of your home is imminent.[71]

Rent arrears

Deductions can be made from your **UC** for rent arrears if you are in debt with your rent (including water, service and other charges included in it), if:[72]

- you are entitled to UC housing costs for rent payments or occupy 'exempt' accommodation' and get HB for that (p403); *and*
- you occupy the accommodation to which the rent applies; *and*
- your earnings (or if you make a joint claim with your partner, your combined earnings) for the previous UC monthly assessment period (see p39) are below the level of the work allowance that applies to you (see p41). If your earnings (or joint earnings) equal or exceed the work allowance for three monthly assessment periods, the deduction must stop.

The DWP can make a monthly deduction from your UC equivalent to between 10 per cent and 20 per cent of the standard allowance (see p66) that applies in your case and pay it to your landlord. The DWP should take your circumstances into account in deciding how much the deduction will be.

If you are in arrears with your rent while on **HB**, or are £100 or more in arrears of hostel payments, an amount can be deducted from your **IS, income-based JSA, income-related ESA or PC** and paid direct to your landlord. This can also apply if (in England and Wales) you are in approved premises under section 13 of the Offender Management Act 2007 and have built up arrears of service charges rather than rent arrears.[73] For the amount of the deductions, see p1208.

Rent arrears do not include the amount of any non-dependant deductions (see p198), but can cover any water charges or service charges payable with your rent and not met by HB. Fuel charges included in your rent cannot be covered by direct deductions if they change more than twice a year.

To qualify for direct deductions for rent arrears, your arrears must be equal to at least four times your full weekly rent. If you have not paid your full rent for eight weeks or more, direct deductions can be made automatically if your landlord asks the DWP to make them.[74] If your arrears relate to a shorter period, deductions can only be made if it is in the overriding interests of your family to do so.[75] In either case, the decision maker must be satisfied that you are in rent arrears. Even if you are, you can ask her/him not to make direct deductions – eg, if you are claiming compensation from your landlord because of the state of repair of your home.[76] Once your arrears are paid off, direct payments can continue for any fuel and water charges included in your rent.[77]

Fuel

If you are in debt with your mains gas or electricity, the DWP can make deductions from your **UC** and pay it to the fuel company. It can deduct a monthly amount equal to 5 per cent of your standard allowance (see p66), plus an additional amount that the DWP considers to be equal to the average monthly fuel costs, except if you are paying for that by other means – eg, a prepayment meter.[78]

Part 8: Claiming benefits and getting paid
Chapter 51: Getting paid
9. Deductions and payments to third parties

If you are in debt for any gas or electricity (including reconnection or disconnection charges), deductions can be made from your UC if your earnings (or, if you are claiming jointly with your partner, your combined earnings) for the previous monthly UC assessment period (see p39) are below the level of the work allowance that applies in your case (see p41).[79] If your earnings equal or exceed the work allowance for three monthly assessment periods, the deduction must stop.

For IS, income-based JSA, income-related ESA and PC, an amount can be deducted each week and paid to the fuel company in instalments – usually once a quarter.[80] This is sometimes called 'Fuel Direct'. For the amount of the deduction, see p1208. Deductions can be made if:[81]

- the amount you owe is £74.35 or more (including reconnection or disconnection charges if you have been disconnected); *and*
- you continue to need the fuel supply; *and*
- it is in your, or your family's, interests to have deductions made.

An amount is deducted for the fuel you use each week (your current consumption) as well as for the arrears you owe. The amount deducted for current consumption is whatever is necessary to meet your current weekly fuel costs. This is adjusted if the cost increases or decreases. Deductions for current consumption can be continued after the debt has been cleared.[82]

See CPAG's *Fuel Rights Handbook* for help if you have fuel debts.

Water charges

If you are in debt with charges for water and sewerage (including reconnection charges), deductions may be made from your UC if your earnings (or, if you are claiming jointly with your partner, your combined earnings) for the previous monthly UC assessment period (see p39) are below the level of the work allowance that applies in your case (see p41). If your earnings equal or exceed the work allowance for three monthly assessment periods, the deduction must stop.

The DWP can make a deduction from your UC and pay it to the water company. It can deduct a monthly amount equal to 5 per cent of your standard allowance (see p66), plus an additional amount that the DWP considers necessary to meet your continuing monthly water costs.

If you are in debt with charges for water and sewerage, direct deductions can be made from your **IS, income-based JSA, income-related ESA and PC.**[83] Debt includes any disconnection, reconnection and legal charges. For the amount of the deductions, see p1208. If you pay your landlord for water with your rent, deductions are made under the arrangements for rent arrears (see p1205).[84]

Deductions can be made if you failed to budget and it is in the interests of you or your family to make deductions.[85] If you are in debt to two water companies, you can only have a deduction for arrears made to one at a time. Your debts for water charges should be cleared before your debts for sewerage costs, but the amount paid for current consumption can include both water and sewerage charges.[86]

Council tax arrears

Deductions for council tax arrears can be made from **UC, IS, JSA, ESA or PC** if the local authority gets a liability order from a magistrates' court (in Scotland, a summary warrant or decree from a sheriff court) and applies to the DWP for recovery to be made in this way.[87] Deductions can be made for arrears and any unpaid costs or penalties imposed. For the amount of the deductions, see p1208. See CPAG's *Council Tax Handbook* for help if you have council tax arrears.

Child support maintenance

Some child support maintenance is paid under the official child support scheme (often referred to as the '2012 rules' scheme) operated by the DWP through the Child Maintenance Service whereby deductions from a non-resident parent's benefit can be made to enforce payment. For full details of child support maintenance, see CPAG's *Child Support Handbook*.

If you are liable to pay child support maintenance under the official scheme at the flat rate, a deduction of £8.40 a week (this includes the addition of the DWP 'collect and pay' service) can be made from your:[88]

- UC (at a rate of £36.40 a month), IS, income-based JSA, income-related ESA or PC, including if your partner is liable;
- carer's allowance (CA);
- contributory ESA;
- industrial injuries benefit;
- contribution-based JSA;
- retirement pension;
- war widow's or war disablement pension;
- widowed parent's allowance;
- widow's pension;
- training allowance (other than Work-Based Learning for Young People or Skillseekers).

The whole of the child support may be deducted from the above benefits.[89] If more than one partner in a couple or polygamous marriage is liable to pay child support maintenance at the flat rate, it is deducted from any UC, IS, income-based JSA, income-related ESA or PC they jointly receive, with the deduction paid equally. So, for example, if both partners in a couple are liable for child support at a flat rate of £8.40, they each pay £4.20.

A deduction of £8.40 a week can also be made from any of the above benefits for any arrears of child support. Deductions for arrears can only be made if there are no deductions for ongoing child support liablity being made. Once a person's ongoing liability for child support ends (eg, when the youngest or only child for

Part 8: Claiming benefits and getting paid
Chapter 51: Getting paid
9. Deductions and payments to third parties

whom they are paying child support is no longer a qualifying child), a deduction of £8.40 can continue to be made towards any arrears due.

If you come under the UC system (see p23), a deduction for arrears can be made from your UC, or contribution-based JSA or contributory ESA. The deduction for arrears in all cases is £8.40 a week (£36.40 a month).[90]

Other deductions

Other deductions can be made from your benefit for the following.

- **Residential accommodation charges.** Deductions can be made from your IS, JSA, ESA or PC (not UC) to meet your accommodation charges if you have failed to budget for them and it is considered to be in your interests for deductions to be made.[91]
- **Hostel payments.** If you (or your partner) live in a hostel or (in England and Wales) approved premises under section 13 of the Offender Management Act 2007, you have claimed HB to meet your accommodation costs and your payments cover fuel, meals, water charges, laundry and/or cleaning of your room, part of your IS, JSA, ESA or PC (not UC) can be paid direct to the hostel for these items.[92]
- **Court fines.** Magistrates' courts (any court in Scotland) can apply to the DWP for a fine, costs or compensation order to be deducted from your UC, IS, JSA, ESA or PC.[93]
- **Eligible loans.** Deductions can be made from your UC, IS, JSA, ESA or PC and (if necessary) your retirement pension or CA towards repaying 'eligible' loans if you have not kept up with the repayments.[94] 'Eligible loans' are loans made by certain not-for-profit lenders, such as community development financial institutions, credit unions and charities, but do not include business loans.
- **Integration loans.** Deductions can be made to repay an integration loan – ie, loans paid to refugees and people granted humanitarian protection and their dependants. Deductions can be made from your UC, IS, JSA, ESA or PC.[95]
- **Tax credit overpayments and self-assessment tax debts.** Deductions can be made from your IS, JSA, ESA or PC to repay these. The deduction is paid to HMRC. Your written consent is required.[96] Deductions can also be made from your UC (or contributory ESA or contribution-based JSA paid under the UC system – ie, where you are no longer getting tax credits and have come under the UC system). The overpayment is treated as a UC overpayment. Your consent is not required.[97]

How much can be deducted

If deductions to third parties (see p1202) are made from your **UC**, in most cases they are made at a fixed rate of 5 per cent of your standard allowance (see p66), with the following exceptions:

- Deductions for child support maintenance are made at a flat rate of £8.40 a week (£36.40 a month) for ongoing liability or £8.40 a week (£36.40 a month) for arrears.
- Deductions for rent arrears are made at a rate of at least 10 per cent but not more than 20 per cent of your standard allowance.
- Deductions for court fines are made at a minimum of at least 5 per cent of your standard allowance and a maximum of £108.35 a month.

In practice, deductions of any kind from your UC will usually not exceed 30 per cent of your standard allowance (see p66). For how this limit applies if you have more than one deduction, see p1210. Third-party deductions cannot leave you with less than one pence of UC.[98]

If deductions to third parties are made from your **IS**, **income-based JSA, income-related ESA or PC**, the maximum deductions are shown below.

Type of arrears	Deduction for arrears	Deduction for ongoing cost
Housing costs	£3.75 for each housing debt (maximum of £11.25)	Current weekly cost
Rent arrears and hostel payments	£3.75	Nil (met by UC or HB)
Residential accommodation charges	Nil	The accommodation allowance (for those in local authority homes); all but £26.05 of your IS, JSA, ESA or PC (for those in private or voluntary homes)
Hostel payments	Nil	Weekly amount assessed by local authority
Fuel	£3.75 for each fuel debt (maximum of £7.50 payable)	Estimated amount of current consumption
Water charges	£3.75 (adjusted every 26 weeks)	Estimated costs
Council tax arrears	£3.75	Nil
Fines	Nil	£5 (lower amount £3.75)
Repayment of eligible loans	Nil	£3.75
Repayment of integration loans	Nil	£3.75
Child support maintenance	£8.40	£8.40
Repayment of tax credit overpayments and self-assessment tax debts	Nil	Maximum £11.25

Part 8: Claiming benefits and getting paid
Chapter 51: Getting paid
9. Deductions and payments to third parties

More than one deduction

More than one deduction can be made from your **UC**. No more than three of the following deductions for third parties may be made from UC at any one time,[99] and you must be left with at least one pence of UC:[100]

- housing costs;
- rent arrears;
- fuel debts;
- water charges;
- repayment of eligible loans;
- repayment of integration loans;
- council tax arrears;
- fines, costs and compensation orders.

The total amount payable for fuel debts and water charges combined cannot exceed an amount equal to 25 per cent of your standard allowance plus any child elements to which you are entitled (see Chapter 5) without your consent.[101]

In practice, the DWP usually does not deduct more than 30 per cent of your standard allowance (see p66).[102] This maximum applies to the total of most deductions from your UC, not just those for third parties. The total includes all those mentioned in the priority between deductions rules (see p1211), as well as those for sanctions (see Chapter 47), benefit offences (p1278) and to recover overpayments of UC, JSA or ESA and advances of UC. If the total deductions would exceed 30 per cent of your standard allowance, then the deductions mentioned in the priority between deductions rules are reduced (using the priority rules – see p1211). However, deductions for ongoing costs (as opposed to arrears) of fuel or water charges are ignored when calculating the total. Deductions of more than the limit may still be made for housing costs, rent arrears or fuel debts, if the DWP considers it would be in your best interests.[103]

More than one third-party deduction can be made from your **IS, income-based JSA, income-related ESA and PC**. You must be left with at least 10 pence of benefit.[104] If you are also having an overpayment recovered from your benefit, having agreed to pay a penalty, admitted fraud or been found guilty of fraud (see p1248), the total amount of the deductions cannot exceed £30 a week.[105] Otherwise, if you are having an overpayment recovered from your benefit, the deductions for third parties described in this chapter should have priority – ie, they are applied first.[106]

Note: for IS, income-based JSA, income-related ESA and PC:

- deductions for the total of housing costs, rent arrears, fuel arrears, water arrears, council tax arrears, court fines and repayment of integration loans cannot exceed £11.25 a week;[107]
- if the combined cost of deductions for arrears and current consumption for fuel, rent, water charges, housing costs arrears and repayment of integration

loans is more than 25 per cent of a certain limit, the deductions cannot be made without your consent. If you (or your partner) do not get CTC, this limit is your total applicable amount (see p332) or, for PC, more than 25 per cent of your minimum guarantee (see p273) before housing costs. If you (or your partner) get CTC, this limit is increased by the amount of child benefit and CTC paid to you.

Priority between deductions

For UC, an order of priority applies to certain deductions if your UC is 'insufficient' to meet all the deductions that apply to it. Your award of UC is 'insufficient' if the total amount of deductions would be more than 40 per cent of the standard allowance that applies to you (see p66). The following deductions are paid in the following order of priority:[108]

- housing costs;
- rent arrears (and related charges), if the amount of the deduction is 10 per cent of your standard allowance;
- fuel;
- council tax arrears;
- fines, if the amount of the deduction is 5 per cent of the standard allowance;
- water charges;
- child support maintenance;
- repayment of social fund payments;
- recovery of hardship payments;
- penalties instead of prosecution for benefit offences;
- recovery of overpayments of benefits or tax credits caused by fraud;
- civil penalties;
- recovery of overpayments of benefits or tax credits not caused by fraud;
- repayment of integration loans;
- repayment of eligible loans;
- rent arrears (and related charges), if the amount of the deduction is more than 10 per cent of your standard allowance;
- fines, costs and compensation orders, if the amount of the deduction is more than 5 per cent of the standard allowance.

If you have more debts or current charges than can be met from your benefit (see p1208), the following deductions are paid in the following order of priority from your **IS, income-based JSA, income-related ESA and PC**:[109]

- housing costs;
- rent arrears (and related charges);
- fuel charges;
- water charges;
- council tax arrears;

Part 8: Claiming benefits and getting paid
Chapter 51: Getting paid
10. Recovery of benefits from compensation payments

- unpaid fines, costs and compensation orders;
- repayment of integration loans;
- repayment of eligible loans;
- repayment of tax credit overpayments and self-assessment tax debts.

Deductions for child support are always payable.

If you owe both gas and electricity arrears, the DWP chooses which one to pay first, depending on your circumstances.[110]

If you have been overpaid benefit or given a social fund loan, you may also have to repay these through deductions from your benefit.[111] Argue that these deductions should take a lower priority than the deductions set out above.

---

10. Recovery of benefits from compensation payments

If you are seeking compensation from someone (the 'defendant') through the courts (eg, because you have been unfairly dismissed or because you have had a personal injury), you might be awarded damages to compensate you for your loss. However, if, as the result of a defendant's action, you have had to claim benefit, the amount of damages awarded is reduced by the amount of benefit you received.

Employment cases

In an employment case such as wrongful or unfair dismissal, your claim for compensation for loss of earnings may be reduced by the amount of benefit (eg, jobseeker's allowance (JSA)) you receive.[112] Get specialist employment law advice. Also, the DWP is able to recover payments of JSA, income support (IS) or income-related employment and support allowance (ESA) from your employer by deductions from your compensation if it is an unfair dismissal or protective award case dealt with in an employment tribunal. In such cases, the DWP sends a 'recoupment notice' to the employer, and a copy to you, setting out the benefit to be deducted before the compensation is paid to you. You may give notice to the DWP that you do not accept the amount recouped within 21 days of the recoupment notice (or longer if allowed), and can appeal to the First-tier Tribunal against the decision that the DWP makes in response.[113]

Personal injury cases

If you are paid compensation for an accident, injury or disease after 6 October 1997, those compensating you can reduce the amount paid to you when you have received benefit in respect of the same loss. They must then pay the money back to the Compensation Recovery Unit (CRU), which is part of the DWP. It does not matter whether the payment is voluntary, with or without legal proceedings, or by order of a court. A reduction is not made if the compensation is paid for pain and suffering, because benefits are not paid for this.

The CRU can only recover the benefit in the right-hand column of the table on p1214, and only if you were paid it as a consequence of the accident, injury or disease.

Note: the CRU can also recover, under a similar scheme with its own rules, certain lump-sum payments made by the DWP to you or a dependant.[114] The lump-sum payments that can be recovered are those made by the DWP for lung diseases under the Pneumoconiosis etc. (Workers' Compensation) Act 1979 (or as compensation if you have had a claim under that Act rejected) or payments under the Diffuse Mesothelioma Payment Scheme.

A guide to the procedures, *Recovery of Benefits and Lump Sum Payments and NHS Charges: technical guidance*, is available at gov.uk/government/collections/cru.

Which benefits can be recovered

All benefits paid to you 'in consequence' of the injury or disease from which you have suffered during the 'relevant period' are recoverable.

The relevant period

The **'relevant period'** is usually the period of five years from the day:[115]

– after the day of your accident or injury if you are claiming compensation for an accident or injury; *or*

– you first claimed a recoverable benefit because of the disease if you are claiming compensation in respect of a disease.

The relevant period ends if those compensating you make a final payment of compensation or an agreement is made under which compensation already paid is accepted as being in final payment.[116]

Before you are paid compensation, those compensating you must apply to the DWP for a 'certificate of recoverable benefits'.[117] This tells them which benefits are recoverable.

Those compensating you become liable to pay the DWP for the total amount of recoverable benefit 14 days after the certificate is issued.[118] It is the compensator's obligation, not yours, and so if the compensator fails to pay, the CRU cannot pursue you for the money. The compensator remains liable even if it fails to apply for a certificate.[119]

Part 8: Claiming benefits and getting paid
Chapter 51: Getting paid
10. Recovery of benefits from compensation payments

Offsetting against your compensation

Before the compensator pays your compensation, it can deduct the recoverable benefits paid during the relevant period from certain types of compensation.[120]

Compensation	Recoverable benefits
Loss of earnings	Universal credit, disablement benefit, ESA, incapacity benefit, IS, invalidity allowance, invalidity pension, JSA, reduced earnings allowance, severe disablement allowance, sickness benefit, statutory sick pay (paid before 6 April 1994), unemployment benefit, unemployability supplement
Cost of care	Attendance allowance, disability living allowance (DLA) care component, disablement benefit paid for constant attendance (see p694) or exceptionally severe disablement (see p695), personal independence payment (PIP) daily living component
Loss of mobility	Mobility allowance, DLA mobility component, PIP mobility component

Example
Gary receives a £30,000 compensation payment consisting of £15,000 for loss of earnings, £5,000 for pain and suffering, and £10,000 for the cost of care. By the time the award is made, he has received £20,000 of ESA and £5,000 of PIP daily living component. The award for loss of earnings is reduced to nil. Gary receives the full award for pain and suffering, but his award for the cost of care is reduced by £5,000. The compensator is liable to pay the DWP recoverable benefits of £25,000, and pays Gary a net award of £10,000 (£5,000 pain and suffering, plus £5,000 care).

Any compensation reduced by this method is treated as being paid to you. Those compensating you must give you a statement showing how the payment has been calculated, even if the recovery of benefits reduces a particular type of compensation to nil. If the recoverable benefit exceeds the compensation paid to you for a particular loss, those compensating you still have to pay the balance to the DWP.

Exempt payments

The recovery rules apply to all claims, no matter how small. However, certain compensation payments are exempt.[121] These include:
- payments under the Fatal Accidents Act 1996, the Vaccine Damage Payments Act 1979 and the NHS industrial injury scheme;
- payments under the Pneumoconiosis Compensation Scheme and certain payments for loss of hearing;
- criminal injuries compensation and certain disaster/emergency relief funds – eg, the London Bombing Relief Charitable Fund;

- contractual sick pay and redundancy payments;
- payments from insurance companies from policies agreed before the accident;
- payments from certain trusts – eg, an approved scheme regarding infected blood such as the Macfarlane Trust or Eileen Trust, the UK Asbestos Trust, the EL Scheme Trust and the Thalidomide Trust.

Challenging a recovery decision

A decision maker may look at a certificate of recoverable benefit again (this is called a review) if s/he is satisfied that there was an error in its preparation, or that it recovers too much benefit, or that the person who applied for the certificate supplied incorrect or insufficient information, as a result of which the amount of benefit recovered is less than it should be.[122] You and those compensating you can both appeal to the First-tier Tribunal (see Chapter 57) against the certificate, but not until the compensation payment has been made and the benefit paid back to the DWP.[123] Also, the person appealing must apply for a review before s/he can appeal. It is best to apply for a review as soon as possible, but there is no absolute time limit.[124] Further appeals can be made to the Upper Tribunal in the usual way (see Chapter 58).[125]

Notes

1. Who is paid

1 **UC/PIP/JSA&ESA under UC** Regs 57 and 58 UC, PIP, JSA&ESA(C&P) Regs
HB Reg 94(2) HB Regs; reg 75(2) HB(SPC) Regs
CB/GA Regs 27 and 28 CB&GA(Admin) Regs
Other benefits Regs 30 and 33 SS(C&P) Regs

2 **UC/PIP/JSA&ESA under UC** Reg 58 UC, PIP, JSA&ESA(C&P) Regs
CB/GA Reg 34 CB&GA(Admin) Regs
Other benefits Reg 34(1) and (2) SS(C&P) Regs

3 **UC/PIP/JSA&ESA under UC** Reg 60 UC, PIP, JSA&ESA(C&P) Regs
Other benefits Reg 35 SS(C&P) Regs

2. How and when you are paid

4 House of Commons, *Hansard*, Written questions and answers 215600, 11 February 2019

5 **UC/PIP/JSA&ESA under UC** Reg 46 UC, PIP, JSA&ESA(C&P) Regs
CB/GA Reg 16 CB&GA(Admin) Regs
Other benefits Reg 21 SS(C&P) Regs

6 **UC/PIP/JSA&ESA under UC** Reg 51 UC, PIP, JSA&ESA(C&P) Regs
CB/GA Regs 16-20 CB&GA(Admin) Regs
Other benefits Regs 22-26C SS(C&P) Regs

7 **UC/PIP/JSA&ESA under UC** Reg 45
UC,PIP,JSA&ESA(C&P) Regs
HB Reg 91 HB Regs; reg 72 HB(SPC)
Regs
CB/GA Reg 18 CB&GA(Admin) Regs
Other benefits Reg 20 SS(C&P) Regs
8 **UC/PIP/JSA&ESA under UC** Reg 55
UC,PIP,JSA&ESA(C&P) Regs
CB/GA Reg 25 CB&GA(Admin) Regs
Other benefits Reg 38(1)(bb)
SS(C&P) Regs
All CDLA/2609/2002 commented on
the way a similar rule applied to
payment by giro/order book

3. **Overlapping benefits**
9 Reg 6 SS(OB) Regs
10 Reg 4(5) SS(OB) Regs
11 s43(1) SSCBA 1992; s1 PA 2014; reg
4(5) SS(OB) Regs
12 ss51A and 52(2) SSCBA 1992
13 s16(1), (2) and (6) SSCBA 1992; reg 2
SS(MAP) Regs
14 Reg 4(2)(f) and (4) SS(OB) Regs
15 Reg 4(4A) SS(OB) Regs
16 Reg 4(3) SS(OB) Regs
17 Reg 10 SS(OB) Regs
18 Reg 8 SS(OB) Regs
19 Reg 7 SS(OB) Regs

4. **Advance payments**
20 Regs 5 and 6 SS(PAB) Regs
21 Reg 7 SS(PAB) Regs
22 Reg 17 UC(TP) Regs does not refer to
'financial need' in this situation
23 **UC/PIP/JSA&ESA under UC** Sch 3
para 14 UC,PIP,JSA&ESA(DA) Regs
Other benefits Sch 2 para 20A
SS&CS(DA) Regs
24 Reg 8 SS(PAB) Regs
25 Advances under the UC system are
recovered under regs 3, 10 and 11
SS(OR) Regs, and there is no right of
appeal about recovery under those
rules. For other advances, Sch 2 para
20A SS&CS(DA) Regs allows a right of
appeal against decisions on deductions
under reg 10 SS(PAB) Regs.
26 Arguably, recovery of UC advances are
subject to the rates in reg 11 SS(OR)
Regs
27 Advances under the UC system are
recovered under regs 3, 10 and 11
SS(OR) Regs, and there is no right of
appeal about recovery under those rules
28 Reg 3, definition of 'benefit', SS(PAB)
Regs

5. **The benefit cap**
29 ss96 and 97 WRA 2012
30 Under Sch 2 para 8A SSA 1998 there is
no right of appeal for UC, but at the time
of writing the relevant rule for HB
appeals at Sch 7 para 6 CSPSSA 2000
had not been amended
31 *R (DA and others) and R (DS and others) v
SSWP* [2019] UKSC 21
32 Reg 82(1) UC Regs
33 Reg 82(2) UC Regs
34 Reg 75E HB Regs; HB Circular A15/2013
35 Reg 75E(3) HB Regs
36 Reg 75E(4) HB Regs
37 Reg 75F HB Regs; reg 83 UC Regs
38 Reg 75C HB Regs; reg 80 UC Regs
39 s96(5A) WRA 2012; reg 79 UC Regs
40 s96(5A) WRA 2012; regs 75A, 75C and
75G HB Regs
41 Reg 75B HB Regs
42 Reg 81 UC Regs
43 Reg 75D HB Regs

6. **Change of circumstances after you
claim**
44 **UC/PIP/JSA&ESA under UC** Reg 38
UC,PIP,JSA&ESA(C&P) Regs
JSA Reg 24 JSA Regs
CB/GA Reg 23 CB&GA(Admin) Regs
Other benefits Reg 32 SS(C&P) Regs
45 **UC/PIP/JSA&ESA under UC** Reg
38(5) UC,PIP,JSA&ESA(C&P) Regs
JSA Reg 24(7) JSA Regs
JSA and other benefits Regs 2, 3 and
5 SS(NCC) Regs, which apply for fraud,
allow notification by telephone (unless it
is specifically required to be in writing)
Other benefits Reg 32(1B) SS(C&P)
Regs
46 Reg 23(5) CB&GA(Admin) Regs
47 **UC/PIP/JSA&ESA under UC** Reg 39
UC,PIP,JSA&ESA(C&P) Regs
JSA Reg 24 JSA Regs
Other benefits Reg 32ZZA SS(C&P)
Regs

7. **When payments can be suspended**

48 **UC/PIP/JSA&ESA under UC** Reg 44(2)(b) and (c) UC,PIP,JSA&ESA(DA) Regs
HB Reg 11(2)(b) HB&CTB(DA) Regs
CB/GA Sch 7 para 13(2) CSPSSA 2000
Other benefits s21(2)(c) and (d) SSA 1998; reg 16(3)(b) SS&CS(DA) Regs

49 **UC/PIP/JSA&ESA under UC** Reg 44(5) UC,PIP,JSA&ESA(DA) Regs
HB Reg 11(3) HB&CTB(DA) Regs
CB/GA Reg 18(4) and (5) CB&GA(DA) Regs
Other benefits Reg 16(4) SS&CS(DA) Regs

50 **UC/PIP/JSA&ESA under UC** Reg 46(c) UC,PIP,JSA&ESA(DA) Regs
HB Reg 12(1)(b) HB&CTB(DA) Regs
CB/GA Reg 21 CB&GA(DA) Regs
Other benefits Reg 20(2) and (3) SS&CS(DA) Regs

51 **UC/PIP/JSA&ESA under UC** Reg 38(2) UC,PIP,JSA&ESA(C&P) Regs; reg 45 UC,PIP,JSA&ESA(DA) Regs
HB Reg 86(1) HB Regs; reg 67(1) HB(SPC) Regs
CB/GA Reg 23 CB&GA(Admin) Regs
Other benefits Reg 32(1) SS(C&P) Regs

52 **UC/PIP/JSA&ESA under UC** Reg 45(6) UC,PIP,JSA&ESA(DA) Regs
HB Reg 13 HB&CTB(DA) Regs
CB/GA Reg 19 CB&GA(DA) Regs
Other benefits Reg 17(2) SS&CS(DA) Regs

53 **UC/PIP/JSA&ESA under UC** Reg 45(4)(a) UC,PIP,JSA&ESA(DA) Regs
HB Reg 13(4)(a) HB&CTB(DA) Regs
CB/GA Reg 19(2) CB&GA(DA) Regs
Other benefits Reg 17(4)(a) SS&CS(DA) Regs

54 **UC/PIP/JSA&ESA under UC** Reg 45(4)(b) UC,PIP,JSA&ESA(DA) Regs
HB Reg 13(4)(b) HB&CTB(DA) Regs
CB/GA Reg 19(2)(b) CB&GA(DA) Regs
Other benefits Reg 17(4)(b) SS&CS(DA) Regs

55 **UC/PIP/JSA&ESA under UC** Reg 45(6) UC,PIP,JSA&ESA(DA) Regs
HB Reg 13(4) HB&CTB(DA) Regs
CB/GA Reg 19(5) CB&GA(DA) Regs
Other benefits Reg 17(5) SS&CS(DA) Regs

56 s24 SSA 1998; reg 19(2) SS&CS(DA) Regs

57 **HB** Sch 7 para 13(2)(a) CSPSSA 2000
CB/GA Reg 18(2) CB&GA(DA) Regs
Other benefits ss21(2)(a) and (b), 22 and 24 SSA 1998

58 **UC/PIP/JSA&ESA under UC** Reg 44(2)(a)(i) and (iii) UC,PIP,JSA&ESA(DA) Regs
HB Reg 11(2)(a)(i) and (c) HB&CTB(DA) Regs
CB/GA Reg 18(2)(a) and (c) CB&GA(DA) Regs
Other benefits Reg 16(3)(a)(i) and (iii) SS&CS(DA) Regs

59 Reg 16(2) SS&CS(DA) Regs; reg 44(2) UC,PIP,JSA&ESA(C&P) Regs does not include this provision

8. **When your entitlement is terminated**

60 **UC/PIP/JSA&ESA under UC** Reg 47(1)(a) UC,PIP,JSA&ESA(DA) Regs
HB Reg 14(1)(a) HB&CTB(DA) Regs
CB/GA Reg 20(1)(a) CB&GA(DA) Regs
Other benefits Reg 18(1)(a), (2) and (4) SS&CS(DA) Regs

61 **UC/PIP/JSA&ESA under UC** Reg 47(1)(b) UC,PIP,JSA&ESA(DA) Regs
HB Reg 14(1)(b) HB&CTB(DA) Regs
CB/GA Reg 20(1)(b) CB&GA(DA) Regs
Other benefits Reg 18(1)(b), (3) and (4) SS&CS(DA) Regs

62 **UC/PIP/JSA&ESA under UC** Reg 47(2) UC,PIP,JSA&ESA(DA) Regs
HB Reg 14(1) HB&CTB(DA) Regs
CB/GA Reg 20(2) CB&GA(DA) Regs
Other benefits Reg 18(1) SS&CS(DA) Regs

63 Reg 19(3) and (4) SS&CS(DA) Regs

9. **Deductions and payments to third parties**

64 **UC/PIP/JSA&ESA under UC** Regs 59 and 60 and Schs 6 and 7 UC,PIP,JSA&ESA(C&P) Regs
Other benefits Regs 34A and 35 and Sch 9 SS(C&P) Regs; CC(DIS) Regs; CT(DIS) Regs; F(DIS) Regs

65 Sch 9 para 1(2) and (3) SS(C&P) Regs

66 Sch 9 para 2(1) SS(C&P) Regs; Sch 6 para 2(1) UC,PIP,JSA&ESA(C&P) Regs

67 Sch 6 para 3(3) UC,PIP,JSA&ESA(C&P) Regs

68 Sch 9 para 8(2) and (4) SS(C&P) Regs

69 **UC/PIP/JSA&ESA under UC** Sch 6 para 6(6) UC,PIP,JSA&ESA(C&P) Regs
Other benefits Sch 9 para 3(5) SS(C&P) Regs

70 **UC/PIP/JSA&ESA under UC** Sch 5
para 5(7) UC,PIP,JSA&ESA(C&P) Regs
Other benefits Sch 9 para 1, definition
of 'housing costs', SS(C&P) Regs
71 Sch 9 para 3(4) SS(C&P) Regs
72 Sch 6 para 7 UC,PIP,JSA&ESA(C&P)
Regs
73 Sch 9 para 5 SS(C&P) Regs
74 Sch 9 para 5(1)(c)(i) SS(C&P) Regs
75 Sch 9 para 5(1)(c)(ii) SS(C&P) Regs
76 Sch 9 para 5(6) SS(C&P) Regs; R(IS) 14/
95
77 Sch 9 para 5(7) SS(C&P) Regs
78 Sch 6 para 8 UC,PIP,JSA&ESA(C&P)
Regs
79 Sch 6 para 8 UC,PIP,JSA&ESA(C&P)
Regs
80 Sch 9 para 6 SS(C&P) Regs
81 Sch 9 para 6(1) SS(C&P) Regs
82 Sch 9 para 6(4)(b) SS(C&P) Regs
83 Sch 9 paras 1 and 7 SS(C&P) Regs
84 Sch 9 para 7(1) SS(C&P) Regs
85 Sch 9 para 7(2) SS(C&P) Regs
86 Sch 9 para 7(7) SS(C&P) Regs
87 CC(DIS) Regs; CT(DIS) Regs; CIS/
11861/1996
88 **UC/PIP/JSA&ESA under UC** Sch 7
paras 1 and 2 UC,PIP,JSA&ESA(C&P)
Regs
Other benefits Sch 9B para 2 SS(C&P)
Regs
89 **UC/PIP/JSA&ESA under UC** Sch 7
para 2 UC,PIP,JSA&ESA(C&P) Regs
Other benefits Sch 9B para 2 SS(C&P)
Regs
90 **UC/PIP/JSA&ESA under UC** Sch 7
para 3 UC,PIP,JSA&ESA(C&P) Regs
Other benefits Sch 9B para 3 SS(C&P)
Regs
91 Sch 9 para 4 SS(C&P) Regs
92 Sch 9 para 4A SS(C&P) Regs
93 F(DIS) Regs
94 **UC/PIP/JSA&ESA under UC** Sch 6
para 11 UC,PIP,JSA&ESA(C&P) Regs
Other benefits Sch 9 para 7C SS(C&P)
Regs
95 **UC/PIP/JSA&ESA under UC** Sch 5
para 12 UC,PIP,JSA&ESA(C&P) Regs
Other benefits Sch 9 para 7D SS(C&P)
Regs; reg 9 The Integration Loans for
Refugees and Others Regulations 2007
No.1598
96 Sch 9 para 7E SS(C&P) Regs
97 Reg 12 UC(TP) Regs; The Tax Credits
(Exercise of Functions) Order 2014,
No.3280
98 Sch 6 para 3(1)(a)
UC,PIP,JSA&ESA(C&P) Regs

99 Sch 6 para 3(1)(b)
UC,PIP,JSA&ESA(C&P) Regs
100 Sch 6 para 3(1)(a)
UC,PIP,JSA&ESA(C&P) Regs
101 Sch 6 para 3(3) UC,PIP,JSA&ESA(C&P)
Regs
102 The legal limit is actually 40 per cent.
Sch 6 para 4 UC,PIP,JSA&ESA(C&P)
Regs; 'Universal credit: debt and
deductions that can be taken from
payment', DWP guidance online at
gov.uk/guidance/universal-credit-debt-
and-deductions-that-can-be-taken-
from-payments
103 Sch 6 para 4 UC,PIP,JSA&ESA(C&P)
Regs
104 Sch 9 para 2(2) SS(C&P) Regs
105 Reg 16(5ZA) SS(PAOR) Regs
106 Reg 16(5ZB) SS(PAOR) Regs
107 Sch 9 para 8(1) SS(C&P) Regs
108 Sch 6 para 5 UC,PIP,JSA&ESA(C&P)
Regs
109 Sch 9 para 9 SS(C&P) Regs
110 Reg 4 CC(DIS) Regs; reg 8 CT(DIS) Regs
111 Regs 15 and 16 SS(PAOR) Regs; reg 3
SF(RDB) Regs

10. **Recovery of benefits from
compensation payments**
112 *Nabi v British Leyland (UK) Ltd* [1980] 1
WLR 529 (CA)
113 The Employment Protection
(Recoupment of Jobseeker's Allowance
and Income Support) Regulations 1996,
No.2349
114 The Social Security (Recovery of
Benefits) (Lump Sum Payments)
Regulations 2008, No.1596
115 s3 SS(RB)A 1997
116 s3(4) SS(RB)A 1997
117 s4 SS(RB)A 1997
118 s6(4) SS(RB)A 1997
119 s7 SS(RB)A 1997
120 s8 and Sch 2 SS(RB)A 1997
121 s1 and Sch 1 SS(RB)A 1997; reg 2 SS(RB)
Regs
122 s10 SS(RB)A 1997; reg 9 SS&CS(DA)
Regs
123 ss11 and 12 SS(RB)A 1997
124 s11(2A) SS(RB)A 1997; reg 9ZB
SS&CS(DA) Regs. Neither provide a
time limit for review. See the official
guidance at gov.uk/government/
publications/repaying-compensation-
to-dwp-what-to-do-if-you-think-our-
decision-is-wrong.
125 s13 SS(RB)A 1997; reg 13 SS(RB)App
Regs

8

Chapter 52

Hardship payments

This chapter covers:
1. Hardship payments of universal credit (below)
2. Hardship payments of jobseeker's allowance (p1222)
3. Hardship payments of employment and support allowance (p1225)
4. Deciding hardship (p1226)
5. Applying for hardship payments (p1230)
6. Getting paid (p1230)
7. Challenging a hardship payment decision (p1230)
8. Tax, other benefits and the benefit cap (p1231)

Key facts
- Hardship payments are reduced-rate payments of universal credit (UC), jobseeker's allowance (JSA) and employment and support allowance (ESA) that are made in limited circumstances, including if you have been sanctioned.
- You or your partner or children must be experiencing hardship. In some cases for JSA, you must be in a 'vulnerable group'.
- You must apply for hardship payments and demonstrate on a regular basis that you are experiencing hardship.
- You must pay back hardship payments of UC. You do not have to pay back hardship payments of JSA or ESA.

---

1. Hardship payments of universal credit

You may be able to get hardship payments of universal credit (UC) if your UC is being paid at a reduced (or nil) rate because you have been given a sanction or because you have committed a benefit offence. You must pay back hardship payments of UC (see p1221). Hardship payments of UC are not made automatically. You must apply for them (see p1230).

If you come under the UC system (see p23) and your contribution-based jobseeker's allowance (JSA) or contributory employment and support allowance (ESA) is paid at a reduced (or nil) rate and you experience hardship, you may qualify for hardship payments of UC.

Part 8: Claiming benefits and getting paid
Chapter 52: Hardship payments
1. Hardship payments of universal credit

When you can get hardship payments

If you (or your partner) are given a sanction, you can get hardship payments of UC if:[1]

- you are 18 or over and are given a sanction (or your partner is 18 or over and has been given a sanction) and, as a result, your UC has been paid at a reduced (or nil) rate using the 'high rate' daily reduction (see p1089). **Note:** if you are aged 16 or 17, or your partner is given a sanction and s/he is 16 or 17, you cannot qualify for hardship payments because your UC is paid at a reduced rate using the 'low rate' daily deduction (see p1089); *and*
- for low level sanctions only, you (or your partner, or both of you if both of you have been given a sanction) have complied with any condition specified by the DWP – eg, you have now taken part in a work-focused interview or have agreed to attend training; *and*
- you (or your partner) apply for hardship payments in the approved manner, or in a way that the DWP accepts is sufficient, and provide any information or evidence required by the DWP; *and*
- you (and your partner) accept that the hardship payments are recoverable; *and*
- the DWP is satisfied that:
  - you (and your partner) have met all the work-related requirements that were in force in the seven days before you applied for hardship payments; *and*
  - you (and your partner) are experiencing hardship (see p1227).

If your UC has been reduced because of a benefit offence (see p1278), you can qualify for hardship payments of UC if:[2]

- you (and your partner) meet all the conditions of entitlement to UC; *and*
- you (and your partner) apply for hardship payments in the approved manner, or in a way that the DWP accepts is sufficient, and provide any information or evidence required by the DWP; *and*
- you (and your partner) accept that the hardship payments are recoverable; *and*
- the DWP is satisfied that you (and your partner) are experiencing hardship (see p1227).

Note: you can qualify under the benefit offences rules even if you (or your partner) are aged 16 or 17.

Hardship payment periods

Each hardship payment is paid at a daily rate for the period starting on the date you satisfy all the conditions for getting one and ending on the day before your next normal UC payday.[3] You cannot get a UC hardship payment until after the first assessment period in respect of which you are paid reduced UC. If the period your hardship payment can be made for is seven days or less, a hardship payment is made until the next normal payday for the following assessment period or, if sooner, the last day in respect of which your UC is paid at a reduced (or nil) rate.[4]

How do you ensure you get maximum hardship payments?

You must apply for hardship payments of UC in each assessment period in which you need one – ie, in each assessment period in which your UC is paid at a reduced rate. The hardship payment period starts when you apply for one and ends on the day before your UC payday. DWP guidance says you cannot apply for a hardship payment before your normal UC payday.[5] To ensure you get the maximum amount, apply for hardship payments on every UC payday you are paid a reduced rate of UC.

The amount of hardship payments

The amount of hardship payments is worked out as follows.[6]
- **Step one:** determine the amount of the reduction made from your UC for the sanction (see p1089) or the benefit offence (see p1279) in the assessment period before the one in which you apply for hardship payments.
- **Step two:** multiply the amount in Step one by 12 and divide by 365. Take 60 per cent of this amount, rounding to the nearest penny.
- **Step three:** multiply the amount in Step two by the number of days for which hardship payments can be made to you.

Example

Dan is a single claimant aged 40. His normal UC payday is the 3rd of the month. He was given a 91-day medium level sanction on 17 September, in a 30-day assessment period. When his UC starts to be paid at a reduced rate, he applies and qualifies for hardship payments on 7 October. He therefore gets hardship payments for the period starting on 7 October and ending on 2 November (27 days).

Step one: the relevant amount is £318 (£10.60 daily reduction x 30 days).

Step two: £318 x 12 ÷ 365 x 60% = £6.27

Step three: Dan can be paid hardship payments for 27 days.

£6.27 x 27 days = £169.29

Dan's hardship payments for that assessment period are £169.29. He gets these in addition to any UC he can be paid – eg, if he qualifies for a housing costs element.

If Dan is still experiencing hardship, he should apply for hardship payments on the day he gets his next payment of UC (ie, 3 November) to ensure he gets maximum hardship payments.

Recovery of hardship payments

You must usually pay back hardship payments of UC.[7] However, hardship payments:
- are *not* recoverable during any assessment period in which you have sufficient monthly earnings (see p1222); *and*

Part 8: Claiming benefits and getting paid
Chapter 52: Hardship payments
2. Hardship payments of jobseeker's allowance

- *stop* being recoverable (ie, are 'written off') if, for at least six months since the last day on which your UC was paid at a reduced (or nil) rate (or for two or more periods that total at least six months), you (and your partner if you are a joint claimant) have had sufficient monthly earnings.[8]

You have sufficient monthly earnings if you (or, if you are a joint claimant, you and your partner) are someone who does not have to meet any work-related requirements:

- because your earnings (your combined earnings if you are a joint claimant) are the same as, or above, your earnings threshold (see p1065); *or*
- for any of the other reasons listed on p1061 and p1066 (other situations). If you are a joint claimant, both you and your partner must be someone who does not have to meet any work-related requirements for one of these reasons. In this case, your monthly earnings (your combined monthly earnings if you are a joint claimant) must be at least 16 times the minimum wage for a person of your age (or your partner's age if s/he is younger than you) multiplied by 52 and divided by 12.

Hardship payments can normally only be recovered from the person to whom they were paid. However, if you are a joint claimant, an amount paid to your partner is treated as paid to you, and vice versa.[9]

All the methods used to recover overpayments described on p1248 can be used to recover hardship payments.[10] Recovery rates for hardship payments from ongoing UC are the same as for the recovery of overpayments of UC (see p1248). These are the maximum rates of recovery, which can be reduced if you can show that you cannot afford them.

2. Hardship payments of jobseeker's allowance

If you do not come under the universal credit (UC) system (see p23), you may be able to get hardship payments of income-based jobseeker's allowance (JSA) – eg, if your JSA is being paid at a reduced (or nil) rate or has been suspended. You do not have to pay them back.[11] Hardship payments of JSA are not made automatically. You must apply for them (see p1230).

When you can get hardship payments

You can qualify for hardship payments of income-based JSA if:
- it is not clear that you satisfy the jobseeking conditions (see p1223); *or*
- your JSA has been reduced because of a sanction (see p1224).

You cannot qualify for hardship payments if you (or your partner) are entitled to income support (IS) or income-related employment and support allowance (ESA), or are in one of the specific groups of people who could have claimed IS (see Chapter 11).[12] **Note:** If you are unable to claim hardship payments because you are in one of these specific groups, you may be able to claim UC instead. However, if you claim UC you will usually not be able to return to JSA once the sanction period has ended.

If, after getting hardship payments, you are awarded full income-based JSA, IS, income-related ESA or pension credit (PC) for the same period, the income-based JSA, IS, income-related ESA or PC is reduced by the amount of hardship payments you were paid.[13]

Whether you satisfy the jobseeking conditions

If there are doubts about whether you satisfy the jobseeking conditions, you may be able to get hardship payments in the following situations.

- At the beginning of a claim for JSA, if you are waiting for a decision about whether you (or if you are a member of a joint-claim couple, you or your partner) satisfy the 'jobseeking conditions' (see p1114).[14] If there is any other reason for the delay in deciding your claim, you are not eligible under this rule. You get hardship payments until the DWP makes a decision on your claim, provided you (or if you are a member of a joint-claim couple, both of you) continue to satisfy the other conditions for getting income-based JSA.
- If your JSA is suspended because there is doubt about whether you (or if you are a member of a joint-claim couple, you or your partner) satisfy the 'jobseeking conditions' (see p1114).[15] You get hardship payments until the DWP makes a decision, provided you satisfy the other conditions for getting income-based JSA. If you are a member of a joint-claim couple, both of you must satisfy these conditions (or one of you, if the other is in an exempt group).
- If the DWP decides that you do not satisfy the jobseeking conditions and you are in a 'vulnerable group' (see p1224). However, you cannot qualify if you (or, if you are a joint-claim couple, either of you) are treated as unavailable for work for one of the reasons listed on p1119.[16]

You normally cannot start getting hardship payments until the 15th day after your date of claim (not including any waiting days which may apply – see p266) or the 15th day of the suspension. If you are in a vulnerable group (see p1228), they start sooner (see p1224).[17] If you are subject to successive 14-day suspensions (eg, at each signing-on day, your work coach doubts that you have taken sufficient steps to find work) and so never reach the 15th day of any suspension period, get advice as this may be unlawful.

Part 8: Claiming benefits and getting paid
Chapter 52: Hardship payments
2. Hardship payments of jobseeker's allowance

If you are in a vulnerable group

If you are in a vulnerable group (see p1228), you get hardship payments:[18]

- from the beginning of a claim, subject to the waiting days rules on p266, or if later, the date the DWP decides you are in a vulnerable group; *or*
- if your JSA is suspended, from the date that the suspension begins; *or*
- from the date the DWP decides that you do not satisfy the 'jobseeking conditions'. You (or if you are a member of a joint-claim couple, both of you) must continue to satisfy the other conditions for getting income-based JSA.

Jobseeker's allowance is reduced because of a sanction

If you are given a sanction (see p1145), you can qualify for hardship payments.[19] **Note:** if you have committed a benefit offence, your benefit may be paid at a reduced rate (see p1278). If you are not entitled to a reduced payment of benefit, you may be able to get a hardship payment.

If you are in a vulnerable group (see p1228), you get hardship payments from the first day of the period when JSA is not paid. **Note:** this does not apply if your sanction is due to a benefit offence and the only reason you would be considered 'vulnerable' is because you or your partner are homeless or because your (or your partner's) functional capacity is limited by a 'mental illness without physical impairment'.[20]

If you are not in a vulnerable group, you cannot get hardship payments until the 15th day of the period. The DWP says that if during a sanction period another sanction is imposed for a different reason, you cannot get hardship payments for the first 14 days of the period of the new sanction.[21] If this happens, you should appeal and argue this is wrong.

Hardship payments continue until the end of the sanction period, provided you satisfy the other conditions for getting income-based JSA. If you are a member of a joint-claim couple, both of you must satisfy these conditions unless one of you is exempt.

The rules about your age

You cannot usually get hardship payments until you are 18. However, if you are 16 or 17 and your JSA is sanctioned, see p1219 of the 2019/20 edition of this *Handbook*.

The amount of hardship payments

The weekly amount of hardship payments you get depends on your needs. Your personal allowance, premiums and housing costs are calculated as for income-based JSA. The usual disregards for capital and income are applied. However, your applicable amount is normally reduced by 40 per cent of:[22]

- if you are not a member of a couple, the appropriate personal allowance for a single person of your age;

- if you are a member of a couple (other than a joint-claim couple), the appropriate personal allowance for a single person:
  - aged under 25, if both of you are aged 16 or 17, or if one of you is between age 18 and 25 and the other is a 16/17-year-old who would not be eligible for income-based JSA in her/his own right;
  - aged 25 or over in all other cases, provided one of you is 18 or over;
- if you are a member of a joint-claim couple, the appropriate personal allowance for a single person aged 25 or over.

The reduction is only 20 per cent if you or your partner, or a child included in your claim (see p323), are pregnant or 'seriously ill' (not defined). In all cases, the reduction is rounded to the nearest five pence.

3. Hardship payments of employment and support allowance

If you do not come under the universal credit system (see p23), you may be able to get hardship payments of income-related employment and support allowance (ESA) if your ESA is being paid at a reduced (or nil) rate because you have been given a sanction or because you have committed a benefit offence. You do not have to pay them back. Hardship payments of ESA are not made automatically. You must apply for them (see p1230).

Note: different hardship rules apply if you could be disqualified from getting ESA (eg, because you have limited capability for work through your own misconduct, or you have failed to accept treatment without 'good cause'), but you are experiencing hardship (see p649).

When you can get hardship payments

You can qualify for hardship payments of income-related ESA if:[23]
- your ESA is being paid at a reduced (or nil) rate:
  - because you have been given a sanction for failing to take part in a work-focused interview (see p1157) or for failing to undertake work-related activity (see p1160); or
  - because you have committed a benefit offence (see p1278); and
- you, your partner or a child for whom you or your partner are responsible (see p326) would experience hardship if payments were not made. See p1229 for what is taken into account in deciding whether you would experience hardship.

You must satisfy the rules for entitlement to income-related ESA (see Chapter 9).

The amount of hardship payments

The weekly amount of hardship payments is a percentage of the ESA personal allowance that applies for a single person whose ESA includes a support component (ie, the personal allowance for main-phase ESA), rounded to the nearest five pence. The percentage is:[24]

- 80 per cent, if your ESA does not include a work-related activity component and you or your partner, or a child or qualifying young person for whom you or your partner are responsible and who lives in your household, are pregnant or seriously ill. For 2020/21, this is 80 per cent of £74.35 = £59.48 a week. **Note:** this does *not* apply if your ESA is being paid at a reduced (or nil) rate because you have committed a benefit offence; *or*
- 60 per cent in all other cases. For 2020/21, this is 60 per cent of £74.35 = £44.61 a week.

This is paid in addition to any amounts of ESA you are still being paid despite the reduction for the sanction (eg, a component if you qualify), as well as premiums and housing costs, if relevant.

4. **Deciding hardship**

When you apply for hardship payments, explain anything that is causing you hardship, or which makes it more likely that you will experience hardship. This includes health, disability, pregnancy and any needs you, your partner and children have.

Hardship

'Hardship' is not defined in the rules. The DWP says that it means 'severe suffering or privation' (meaning 'a lack of the necessities of life').[25] For universal credit (UC), the DWP expects you to investigate other sources of support and reduce non-essential expenditure. Hardship should be decided by looking at whether you can cover your essential needs for accommodation, heating, food and hygiene.[26]

When deciding whether or not you are experiencing hardship, the DWP must consider certain things. For UC, see p1227; for jobseeker's allowance (JSA), see p1227; and for employment and support allowance (ESA), see p1229. If your claim is refused, consider applying for a revision or appealing (see Chapters 56 and 57).

In all cases, the DWP looks at the resources available to you.

- The DWP normally takes into account income and capital that is disregarded when calculating your benefit – eg, personal independence payment (PIP), disability living allowance (DLA) and savings below £6,000.

- You should only be treated as having resources that are likely to be actually available to you. For example, if you have savings in a bank account but they are subject to a notice period for withdrawal, you should not be treated as having this capital until you can access it. You may be expected to ask your family for help, and investigate sources of free help, but you are not expected to rely on charity.
- You should not be treated as having resources if these are only available on credit, or you would have to sell any of your possessions.

Universal credit

The DWP only considers you to be in hardship if both the following apply.[27]
- Because your UC has been reduced as a result of a sanction using the 'high rate' daily reduction (see p1089) or because you have committed a benefit offence (see p1279), you (and your partner) cannot meet your immediate and most basic and essential needs, or those of a child for whom you (or your partner) are responsible (see p326). '**Needs**' means accommodation, heating, food and hygiene – eg, products to keep you and your home clean, or nappies for your baby.
- You (and your partner) have made every effort to get alternative sources of support (eg, from your family) to meet (or partly meet) your needs and to stop incurring any expenditure not related to your basic and essential needs. The DWP says that this should not include expenditure on things you need to help you look for work, such as a telephone and internet access, or to maintain your child(ren)'s access to education.[28] The DWP must consider what is reasonable in your case, but you should not be required to sell or pawn anything (other than stocks and shares) or take out credit. The DWP should not force you to request or accept help from charities if you choose not to do so, but may expect you to investigate and consider what help might be available.[29]

See p1226 for information about what resources might be taken into account.

Jobseeker's allowance

For JSA, you cannot get hardship payments unless the DWP is satisfied that you are in a 'vulnerable group' or that you or your partner would experience hardship if payments were not made.[30]

In some situations, you can only get hardship payments if you are in a vulnerable group.

When deciding whether or not you would experience hardship, the DWP must consider the following.[31]
- Whether you or your partner, or a child included in your claim (see p323), qualify for a disability premium or the disabled child or severely disabled child element of child tax credit (CTC).

- The resources likely to be available to you or your partner, or a child included in your claim (see p323), if no hardship payments are made, how far these fall short of your reduced applicable amount (see p1224) and the length of time this is likely to be the case. Also included are any resources that may be available from others in your household – eg, your parents. CTC and child benefit cannot be taken into account.[32] See p1226 for what resources might be taken into account.
- Whether there is a 'substantial risk' that you, your partner or a child included in your claim (see p323) would be without essential items (eg, food, clothes, heating or accommodation) or whether they would be available at considerably reduced levels and, if so, for how long.

Vulnerable groups

You are in a vulnerable group if:[33]

- you or your partner are **pregnant** and would experience hardship if no payment were made;
- you or your partner are **responsible for a child** who would experience hardship if no payment were made. See p326 for when you count as responsible for a child. **Note:** if you are a lone parent and are responsible for a child under five, or you are a lone parent under 18, you cannot claim hardship payments (see p1223);
- your income-based JSA includes a **disability premium** or would include one if your claim were to succeed and the person for whom the premium is paid would experience hardship if no payment were made;
- you or your partner have a **chronic medical condition** and as a result your (or your partner's) functional capacity is 'limited or restricted by physical or mental impairment', and the DWP is satisfied that:
  - it has lasted or is likely to last for at least 26 weeks; *and*
  - if no payment were made, the health of the person with the condition would decline further than that of a 'normal healthy adult' within the next two weeks and the person would experience hardship;
- you or your partner:
  - are, for a considerable portion of the week, **caring for someone** who:
    - is getting attendance allowance (AA), the highest or middle rate of the care component of DLA, either rate of the daily living component of PIP or armed forces independence payment. If the person has claimed one of these benefits, you count as being in a vulnerable group for up to 26 weeks from the date of the claim or until the claim is decided, whichever is first; *or*
    - has been awarded AA, the highest or middle rate of DLA care component, the daily living component of PIP or armed forces independence payment but it is not yet in payment; *and*

– would not be able to continue caring if no hardship payment were made. You do not have to show that the person you are caring for would experience hardship.

This rule does not apply if the person who is being cared for lives in a care home, an Abbeyfield home or an independent hospital;[34]

- you or your partner are a **16/17-year-old** who can claim income-based JSA (see p256) and would experience hardship if no payment were made (or if you are a joint-claim couple, you both would experience hardship);

- you or your partner are a 16/17-year-old claiming JSA on the basis of a **severe hardship direction** (see p256). You do not have to show that you would experience hardship. However, you do not count as being in a vulnerable group if the person subject to the direction does not satisfy the jobseeking conditions;

- you (or if you are a joint-claim couple, at least one of you) are under 21 at the date of your hardship statement (see p1230) and within the last three years were **being looked after by the local authority** (see p947), were someone the local authority had a duty to keep in touch with, or you qualified for advice and assistance from the local authority.[35] **Note:** the law does not cover local authorities in Scotland, but in practice it is the DWP's intention that this rule does cover you in Scotland;

- you or your partner are **homeless**.

Employment and support allowance

For ESA, when deciding whether or not you would experience hardship, the DWP must consider the following.[36]

- Whether you or your partner, or a child included in your claim (see p323), qualify for a severe disability premium or an enhanced disability premium, or the disabled child or severely disabled child element of CTC.

- The resources likely to be available to your household (including from people who are not included in your claim for benefit – see p329) if no hardship payments were to be made, and how far these fall short of the amount of hardship payments to which you would be entitled. Also included are any resources that may be available from people who are not members of your household. For ESA sanctions, CTC or child benefit paid to you or your partner for a child who is included in your claim (see p323) or who is a member of your household cannot be taken into account.[37] See p1226 for information about what resources might be taken into account.

- Whether there is a 'substantial risk' that your household would be without essential items (eg, food, clothes, heating or accommodation) or whether they would be available at considerably reduced levels.

The length of time any of the above factors are likely to continue must also be considered.[38]

Part 8: Claiming benefits and getting paid
Chapter 52: Hardship payments
7. Challenging a hardship payment decision

5. **Applying for hardship payments**

Hardship payments are not made automatically. You must apply for them in the approved manner, or in such other form as the DWP accepts is sufficient. Check with the Jobcentre Plus office, the universal credit (UC) helpline or post an enquiry in your journal about how you should apply. You must provide information and evidence if required.[39] For jobseeker's allowance (JSA), the DWP calls this a '**hardship statement**'.

Although you cannot get JSA or employment and support allowance (ESA) hardship payments until you have made your application, there is no general rule to prevent you from getting these for a period before the date on which you made it.

The likelihood of being able to convince the DWP that you are experiencing hardship increases over time. Apply for hardship payments at any time you are without your normal payment of UC, JSA or ESA. **Note:** you cannot qualify for hardship payments of UC in the first assessment period in which you are given a sanction – ie, before you have actually been paid UC at a reduced rate (see p1220). You must wait until the beginning of the next assessment period before you can apply – because this is the first assessment period after the one in respect of which you were given a reduced payment.

Note:
- For JSA, while you are getting hardship payments, you (or if you are a joint-claim couple, one of you) must normally make a 'hardship declaration' at the Jobcentre Plus office each time you 'sign on' to confirm that you are still in hardship.[40]
- For UC, you must make a fresh application for hardship payments in each assessment period. See p1221 for how to ensure maximum payments.

6. **Getting paid**

The general rules on getting paid are covered in Chapter 51. Hardship payments of jobseeker's allowance (JSA) and employment and support allowance (ESA) are made on the day that your JSA or ESA would normally be paid. Hardship payments of universal credit should be made as quickly as possible, once the application has been allowed. Where practical, this should be on the day the application is accepted.[41]

7. **Challenging a hardship payment decision**

If you are refused hardship payments, you can appeal to the First-tier Tribunal (see Chapter 57). You must apply for a mandatory reconsideration first. Ask for a written statement of reasons for the decision if this has not already been provided (see p1297).

Remember to tell the DWP if your circumstances worsen while you are applying for a reconsideration or appealing. Ask it to consider whether hardship payments can now be paid based on your new circumstances.

8. **Tax, other benefits and the benefit cap**

Tax

Hardship payments of jobseeker's allowance (JSA) are taxable in the same way as income-based JSA (see p266). Hardship payments of employment and support allowance (ESA) and universal credit (UC) are not taxable.

Claiming other benefits or tax credits

If you have a partner, s/he could claim income support, income-based JSA, income-related ESA or pension credit instead of you. See p1226 of the 2019/20 edition of this *Handbook* for details. However, in most cases s/he will come under the UC system (see p23) so will be unable to claim these benefits.

Passported benefits

Hardship payments are a type of UC, income-based JSA and income-related ESA and so you are still entitled to passported benefits, such as help with health costs, in the usual way.

If you get hardship payments of income-based JSA, income-related ESA or, if you live in 'specified' or 'temporary' accommodation (see p85), UC, you are still entitled to full housing benefit (HB). You can also get HB on the basis of having no income. So, whether or not you are getting hardship payments, payment of your HB should not be affected if you have been given a sanction. If it is, contact the local authority immediately. You may also be entitled to a council tax reduction from your local authority (see p851).

Notes

1. Hardship payments of universal credit
1   Reg 116(1) UC Regs
2   Regs 16D(1) and (2)(a) and 16E(a)-(c) SS(LB) Regs
3   Reg 117 UC Regs; reg 16F SS(LB) Regs
4   Reg 117(2) UC Regs
5   para L1146 ADM
6   Regs 6 and 118 UC Regs; reg 16G SS(LB) Regs
7   s71ZH(1)(a) and (e) SSAA 1992; s28(2)(f) WRA 2012; reg 119 UC Regs; reg 16H SS(LB) Regs
8   Reg 119 UC Regs
9   s71ZH(4) SSAA 1992
10 s71ZH(5) SSAA 1992

2. Hardship payments of jobseeker's allowance
11 s71ZH(1)(b)-(d) SSAA 1992; s19C(2)(f) JSA 1995 came into force on 19 June 2017, but there are currently no regulations providing for the recovery of JSA hardship payments
12 Regs 140(3) and 146A(3) JSA Regs
13 Regs 146 and 146H JSA Regs; reg 5(2) Cases 1 and 2 SS(PAOR) Regs
14 Regs 141(2), 142(2), 146C(2) and 146D(2) JSA Regs
15 Regs 141(5), 142(3), 146C(5) and 146D(3) JSA Regs
16 Regs 141(4) and 146C(4) JSA Regs
17 Regs 141(3), 142(2) and (4), 146C(3), and 146D(2) and (4) JSA Regs
18 Regs 141 and 146C JSA Regs
19 Regs 141(6), 142(5), 146C(6) and 146D(5) JSA Regs
20 Regs 5-16 SS(LB) Regs
21 Vol 6 Ch 35, para 35304 DMG
22 Regs 145 and 146G JSA Regs

3. Hardship payments of employment and support allowance
23 Regs 2(1), definition of 'hardship payment', 64A(a)-(c) and 64B ESA Regs; reg 16A(1) SS(LB) Regs
24 Reg 64D ESA Regs; reg 16C SS(LB) Regs

4. Deciding hardship
25 Vol 6 Ch 35, para 35155 DMG
26 Ch L1, paras L1002-03 ADM

27 Reg 116(2) and (3) UC Regs; reg 16D(2)(b)-(d) and (3) SS(LB) Regs; Ch L1 ADM
28 paras L1099 and L1100 ADM
29 paras L1084-93 ADM
30 Regs 140(1) and (2) and 146A(1) and (2) JSA Regs
31 Regs 140(5) and 146A(6) JSA Regs
32 Reg 140(6) JSA Regs
33 Regs 140(1) and 146A(1) JSA Regs
34 Regs 140(4) and 146A(4) JSA Regs
35 These are specific duties in the Children Act 1989 in England and the Social Services and Well-being (Wales) Act 2014 in Wales
36 Reg 64C ESA Regs; reg 16A(2) SS(LB) Regs
37 Reg 64C(2) ESA Regs
38 Reg 64C(1)(e) ESA Regs; reg 16A(2)(e) SS(LB) Regs

5. Applying for hardship payments
39 **UC** Reg 116(1)(c) and (d) UC Regs; reg 16E(a) and (b) SS(LB) Regs
    JSA Regs 143 and 146E JSA Regs
    ESA Reg 64A(d) and (e) ESA Regs; reg 16B SS(LB) Regs
40 Regs 144 and 146F JSA Regs

6. Getting paid
41 DWP, *Universal Credit Full Service Guidance,* Recoverable hardship payments, House of Commons library, available at data.parliament.uk/ DepositedPapers/Files/DEP2019-0980/ 103._Recoverable_Hardship_ Payments_v5.0.pdf

Chapter 53

Overpayments

This chapter covers:
1. Introduction (below)
2. Overpayments that are always recoverable (p1234)
3. Overpayments that are sometimes recoverable (p1238)
4. Recovery of overpaid benefit (p1247)
5. Overpayments of housing benefit (p1253)

For overpayments of tax credits, see Chapter 64. For overpayments of Scottish social security benefits, see Chapter 76.

References in this chapter to HM Revenue and Customs apply to overpayments of child benefit and guardian's allowance.

Key facts

- If you are paid more benefit than you are entitled to, this is called an overpayment.
- If you are overpaid benefit under the universal credit (UC) system, you can always be required to repay it, regardless of how it was caused.
- In other situations, except for housing benefit (HB), the general rule is that you must repay the overpayment if it arose because you did not disclose something or you misrepresented something, regardless of whether this was your fault.
- All overpayments of HB must be repaid, except those caused by official error which you also could not have reasonably known were overpayments.
- The DWP, HM Revenue and Customs and local authorities have the discretion not to recover an overpayment in certain situations.

1. Introduction

An 'overpayment' occurs when you are paid more benefit than you should have been paid. If you are told that you must repay an overpayment, do the following.

- Use the relevant chapters in this *Handbook* to check whether or not you were entitled to some, or all, of the amount that the DWP, HM Revenue and Customs or local authority says is an overpayment. If you were entitled to

Part 8: Claiming benefits and getting paid
Chapter 53: Overpayments
2. Overpayments that are always recoverable

some, or all, of the amount, you should challenge the decision about your entitlement.
- If some, or all, of the amount should not have been paid, check whether:
  - for benefits other than housing benefit (HB), the overpayment is always recoverable (see below);
  - for benefits other than HB, the overpayment is sometimes recoverable, depending on the circumstances. Check whether all three conditions that allow the overpayment to be recovered are met (see p1239 and p1243), and also whether the overpayment can be reduced under the rules described on p1244;
  - the overpayment of HB is recoverable (see p1253). If so, check whether it can be recovered from you (p1257) and whether any amount can be offset against the sum claimed (see p1256).
- If you are not the person whose benefit was overpaid, check whether the overpayment can be recovered from you (see p1245 and p1257).
- Consider whether it is worth asking for the overpayment not to be recovered. For overpayments of HB, see p1257, and for other benefits, see p1247.
- If you must repay an overpayment, check that the method of recovery used is correct and whether you should ask for the money to be recovered in a different way. For overpayments of HB, see p1257, and for other benefits, see p1247.

Note:
- For benefits other than HB, if you are overpaid and this was because you made an incorrect statement or failed to provide information, you may also have to pay a penalty (p1268). If it is considered that an overpayment was made because of fraud, in addition to the overpayment being recovered, you may be prosecuted or given the option of paying a penalty instead of going to court. See Chapter 54 for further information.
- If an overpayment has been included in a debt relief order, it cannot be recovered.[1] Similarly, if you are subject to a bankruptcy order, any overpayment that is notified to you as recoverable before the order was made is not recoverable. However, once the order ceases to have effect, any overpayment caused by fraud becomes recoverable.

2. **Overpayments that are always recoverable**

Except for overpayments of housing benefit (HB – see p1253), the DWP or HM Revenue and Customs (HMRC) can always recover the following overpayments.
- You come under the universal credit (UC) system (see p23) and you have been paid too much UC, contribution-based jobseeker's allowance (JSA) or contributory employment and support allowance (ESA) (see p1235).

- You have been paid too much income support (IS), income-based JSA, income-related ESA or pension credit (PC) because you were owed income that you have now received (see p1237).
- Too much mortgage interest was paid directly to your lender (see p1237).
- Too much benefit has been paid into your bank account by mistake (see p1238).

Although the above overpayments are always recoverable, you may still be able to argue that you were entitled to some, or all, of the amount, or that some or all of the overpayment does not fall into one of the above categories. The decision maker in the DWP, HMRC or local authority also has the discretion not to recover in certain circumstances (see p1247).

Overpayments if you come under the universal credit system

If you come under the UC system (see p23) and you are overpaid UC, contribution-based JSA or contributory ESA, the DWP can recover any amount of overpaid benefit, regardless of the cause of the overpayment.[2] See p1247 for how the overpayment can be recovered.

Note:
- If you are overpaid, the amount recovered can be reduced (see below).
- In general, the DWP must first change the decision awarding you benefit before it can decide whether the overpayment can be recovered (see p1243).[3]
- The overpayment is usually recovered from the person to whom it is paid, but see p1236 for more details.
- You can appeal against a decision that you have been overpaid, or about the amount of an overpayment. You must request a mandatory reconsideration before you can appeal (see p1338). You cannot appeal against a decision to recover an overpayment.[4]
- You can ask the DWP to use its discretion not to recover the overpayment (see p1247).

The amount recovered

The amount recovered is the difference between what you received and the amount to which you were entitled after the decision awarding you benefit has been changed.[5] This amount can be reduced in the following circumstances.

Offsetting universal credit

If you were overpaid JSA or ESA, the amount that can be recovered may be reduced by the amount of any UC you could have received. For this to happen, you must have made a claim for UC. The overpaid amount is reduced by the amount of UC you would have got:[6]
- had you notified any change of circumstances that affected your JSA or ESA entitlement (other than a change of dwelling) to the DWP at the time it occurred; *or*

Part 8: Claiming benefits and getting paid
Chapter 53: Overpayments
2. Overpayments that are always recoverable

- had you not misrepresented or failed to disclose something before the award of JSA or ESA; *or*
- had a mistake by the decision maker not occurred.

You are overpaid universal credit because of a mistake about your capital

If you are overpaid UC because of a mistake about your savings for a period of more than three months, the amount that can be recovered is reduced to take into account the fact that you would have been spending your capital had you not been receiving UC.

At the end of each three-month period for which you have been overpaid, the amount of capital you are regarded as having is reduced by the amount of UC that you were overpaid in those three months.[7] The overpayment for the next three months is then calculated as if you had this reduced amount of capital.

You are overpaid because you moved home

If you are overpaid the housing element of UC because you moved home, but payments continued being made for your previous home, the decision maker may reduce the amount to be recovered by an amount equal to what you would have received in respect of your new home.[8]

S/he can only do this if the payments for your previous home are made to the same person as those for your new home.[9] If the decision maker reduces the amount to be recovered in this way, the reduction in the overpaid amount is treated as if it were paid in respect of your new home.[10]

From whom can an overpayment be recovered

An overpayment of UC, contribution-based JSA or contributory ESA is usually recoverable from the person to whom it was paid. However, it can be recovered from someone else in the following circumstances.[11]

- If the overpaid amount was paid to an appointee or to someone other than you because it was not in your interest to pay you directly (see p1187), the overpayment can also be recovered from you, the claimant.
- If an overpaid amount was paid to a third party under the rules about deductions and payments to third parties (see p1202), the amount is recoverable from you, the claimant. However, amounts paid to the third party in excess of the amounts allowed by those rules are only recoverable from the third party.
- If the overpaid amount includes an amount for housing costs paid to another person (eg, your landlord) and:
  - the overpayment occurred because someone failed to disclose or misrepresented a material fact (see p1239 and p1243), it is recoverable from that person, not the person to whom it was paid;
  - the overpayment occurred because you moved home, it is recoverable from you, as well as from the person to whom it was paid;

– the overpayment occurred because the payment exceeded the housing costs for which you are liable (eg, it was more than your rent), it is recoverable from the person to whom it was paid – eg, your landlord;
– the overpayment did not occur for any of the above three reasons, it is recoverable from you, the claimant, not the person to whom it was paid.

You were owed income that you have now received

If you are owed money while you are getting IS, income-based JSA, income-related ESA or PC, this may result in your being overpaid benefit. This is because when you receive the money you are owed, your income for benefit purposes is calculated afresh and you must repay any IS, income-based JSA, income-related ESA or PC to which you would not have been entitled had the money been paid on time.[12]

This rule applies to any income that affects the amount of IS, income-based JSA, income-related ESA or PC you get, including:[13]

- earnings;
- other social security benefits. **Note:** arrears of some benefits are treated as capital and ignored for 52 weeks (see Chapters 22 and 23);
- benefits paid by other European Economic Area member states.[14]

If you are owed arrears of benefit, the DWP can reduce (or 'abate') those arrears before they are paid to you, if not doing so would mean that you have then been overpaid UC, IS, income-based JSA, income-related ESA or PC. If the arrears are not reduced and you are overpaid, the DWP can recover the overpayment from you.[15]

Note: you can appeal about whether an overpayment has occurred and how it has been calculated.[16] You must apply for a mandatory reconsideration before you can appeal (see p1339). You cannot appeal against the decision to recover any overpayment that has occurred, but you can ask the DWP to use its discretion not to recover it (see p1247).

See p1247 for how the overpayment can be recovered.

Too much mortgage interest has been paid to your lender

Before April 2018, if you were getting help with your housing costs in your IS, income-based JSA, income-related ESA or PC (see Chapter 18), your mortgage interest was usually paid directly to your lender. From April 2018, help with your mortage interest is no longer included in your IS, income-based JSA, income-related ESA or PC (or UC). You are offered a loan instead (see p855).

If it is decided that you were overpaid mortgage interest in the past, see p1239 of the 2018/19 edition of this *Handbook* for details of when it is recoverable.

Part 8: Claiming benefits and getting paid
Chapter 53: Overpayments
3. Overpayments that are sometimes recoverable

Too much benefit has been credited to your account

Your benefit may be paid by direct credit transfer into a bank or building society account. If you are credited with too much money because of the direct credit transfer system itself, the excess can be recovered in certain circumstances.[17]

The overpayment can only be recovered if it was caused by the direct credit transfer system and:[18]

- you were notified in writing before you agreed to your benefit being paid into a bank or other account that any excess benefit could be recovered; *and*
- it has been certified that you were paid excess benefit because of the direct credit transfer system.

If the excess benefit cannot be recovered under the rules described above, it may be recoverable under the rules described below, or those for recovery following late payment of income (see p1237).

You can appeal to the First-tier Tribunal against a decision to recover excess benefit credited to your bank or other account.[19] You must apply for a mandatory reconsideration before you can appeal (see p1339).

Even if the overpayment is recoverable, you can ask the DWP or HMRC to use its discretion not to recover it (see p1247).

3. **Overpayments that are sometimes recoverable**

Except for the overpayments described on p1234 and overpayments of housing benefit (HB – see p1253), some overpayments can only be recovered if:[20]

- you failed to disclose, or you misrepresented, a 'relevant material fact' (see p1239) and this caused the overpayment (see p1243); *and*
- the decision awarding you benefit has been changed (see p1243).

If you have been overpaid and all the above conditions do not apply to the whole of the overpayment, only that part of the overpayment to which they all apply is recoverable from you. For example, if you were paid too much benefit over a two-year period, but you told the DWP about all the relevant facts after the first year, the overpayment made after this was not caused by your failure to disclose and is, therefore, not recoverable from you.

Example

Seamus was receiving income support (IS) as a carer. The person he was caring for stopped getting personal independence payment (PIP) in 2018. Seamus informed the DWP of this in 2019, but the DWP continued to pay Seamus his IS until 2020. This overpayment from 2019 onwards is not recoverable.

Note:
- Even if an overpayment can be recovered, in some situations amounts must be deducted from the recoverable sum (see p1244).
- This type of overpayment can sometimes be recovered from you, even if you are not the claimant (see p1245).
- You can appeal against a decision that the overpayment is recoverable from you (see p1246). You must apply for a mandatory reconsideration first (see p1339).
- Even if an overpayment is recoverable under these rules, you can ask the DWP or HM Revenue and Customs (HMRC) to use its discretion not to recover it (see p1247).

You failed to disclose, or you misrepresented, a material fact

For an overpayment to be recoverable, you must have:
- failed to disclose a relevant 'material fact' (see below); or
- misrepresented a relevant 'material fact' (see p1241).

A material fact

A **'material fact'** is one which influences how much benefit you should be paid.[21] Sometimes there can be a difference between your honest opinion and a material fact.[22] For example, a statement about the distance you can walk should be taken as your honest opinion of your ability, rather than as a statement of fact.[23] If the decision maker comes to a different conclusion about the facts, you can argue that an overpayment should not be recovered.[24]

Facts	Conclusions about the facts
You have arthritis	You have limited capability for work
A friend is sharing your flat	You are living together as husband and wife or civil partners
You have a bad back	Your mobility is severely restricted most of the time

Failure to disclose

You count as having failed to disclose a relevant material fact if:[25]
- you knew about a fact (see below);
- you had a legal duty to disclose that fact (see p1240); and
- you did not comply with that legal duty (see p1240).

Knowledge of a fact

If you did not know about a fact, including if it was a change in your circumstances, you have not 'failed' to disclose it.[26] You cannot fail to disclose something you did not know about unless:
- there was a reason why you should have been aware of it;[27] or

Part 8: Claiming benefits and getting paid
Chapter 53: Overpayments
3. Overpayments that are sometimes recoverable

- it was reasonable for you to make enquiries, which would have revealed the information to you;[28] *or*
- you had been aware of it, but simply forgot.[29]

Legal duty to disclose

You have two different legal duties to disclose facts: a specific duty and a general duty.

You have a **specific duty** to disclose a fact that you know about (see p1239) and which is a type of fact that you have clearly been told by the DWP or HMRC that you must disclose – eg, in your benefit award letter or in the notes which accompanied it.[30]

You do not have a specific legal duty to disclose something unless the instruction is clear and there is no room for doubt about whether or not you are required to report it.[31]

If you were not clearly told that you must report a certain fact, this specific duty to disclose does not apply. If, despite there being a clear instruction to disclose a particular fact in a letter or accompanying notes, you are subsequently told by an officer of the DWP that you do not need to disclose this type of fact, this can mean that you no longer have a duty to disclose it.[32]

You also have a **general duty** to disclose any change in your circumstances since the decision awarding you benefit was made, if you could reasonably be expected to know that your benefit may be affected.[33]

What you can reasonably be expected to know depends on the details of your case. For example, if you were told by the DWP or a lawyer that your benefit would not be affected, or if you were too ill to have realised that it might be, it is arguable that you could not reasonably have been expected to have known that your benefit could be affected.[34] If there is no obvious connection between the fact and the overpaid benefit, argue that it was not reasonable for you to have known that your benefit might be affected.

Complying with your duty to disclose

Generally, to make a valid disclosure, you must tell the 'relevant office' in sufficiently clear terms so that the effect on your claim can be examined.

If you have a specific duty to disclose (see above), the 'relevant office' is the one that handles the benefit you are claiming.[35] This may be a benefit delivery centre (eg, for IS) or a central office (eg, for PIP). For special rules on reporting a birth or death (sometimes called 'Tell Us Once'), see p1199.

If you have a general duty to disclose (see above), the 'relevant office' is any DWP office or, in jobseeker's allowance (JSA) cases, a specified DWP office. However, it is always best to tell the office handling your claim if you can. For child benefit and guardian's allowance, you can disclose changes in your circumstances to the Child Benefit Office, or any office specified to you by HMRC.[36] Again, it is best to ensure that you tell the Child Benefit Office, as it administers your claim. You only count as having failed to disclose once the time by when it was reasonably practicable for you to have done so has passed – eg, if it was impossible for you to make the disclosure earlier than you did, you have not failed to comply with the general duty to disclose.

If the office already knew about the fact and you were aware it knew, it is strongly arguable that you have not failed to disclose.[37] Even if you were not aware that the office already knew, it may be possible to argue that its knowledge means that any failure on your part did not actually cause the overpayment (see p1243). This is especially so if the office would not have acted any differently, even if you had reported the fact to it.[38]

You can usually notify changes in writing or by telephone, but it is best to do so in writing.[39]

If you completed a form while giving information, whether you count as having failed to disclose depends not just on what you said on the form, but also on whether you gave the necessary information in another way.[40] If you do not complete a form correctly and give the relevant information in the wrong place, you have disclosed the facts.[41]

If you made a statement in person or by telephone, but the decision maker says there is no record of this, you should appeal and give as much information as possible about the circumstances in which the disclosure was made – eg, when you called, who you spoke to and what was said. A record of the telephone number called, if you have it, is likely to be helpful.

You should usually make the disclosure yourself, unless you have an appointee acting for you (see p1170).[42] If someone else discloses the fact on your behalf, it must be made to the correct office with your knowledge and you must believe that there is no need to repeat it yourself. If someone else makes the disclosure to an office not handling your claim, but s/he reasonably believes that the information will be passed to the correct office, this may count as disclosure.[43]

Once you have made a proper disclosure to the office handling your claim, you are not expected to repeat it.[44] However, if you give the information to a different office and subsequently become aware that it has not been acted on, you must take further steps to make a proper disclosure.[45] A short time may elapse before you can reasonably be expected to realise that the original information has not been acted on.[46]

Misrepresentation

Misrepresentation occurs if you have provided information that is inaccurate – eg, you gave a wrong answer to a specific question on the claim form. It does not apply if you have not given information, unless this was deliberately intended to mislead.[47] The following apply.

- It does not matter whether a reasonable person would also have given innaccurate information. No 'failure' on your part needs to be shown.[48]

Part 8: Claiming benefits and getting paid
Chapter 53: Overpayments
3. Overpayments that are sometimes recoverable

- It does not matter if you honestly believed that the information you gave was correct – once it is shown to be incorrect, you have misrepresented it. However, you have not misrepresented if you added the phrase 'not to my knowledge' to your statement.[49]
- A written statement may be qualified by an oral one. If you fill in a form incorrectly but explain the situation to an officer when handing in the form, your explanation must be taken into account when deciding whether what is stated on the form is misrepresentation.[50] Similarly, if you give incorrect information in one document but correct information in another, there may not be a misrepresentation.[51] However, if you have declared a fact on a previous claim, but inadvertently give incorrect information on a later claim, you have misrepresented it. The decision maker is not required to check the information you gave on the earlier claim for you.[52]
- If you are incapable of managing your affairs, but nevertheless sign a claim form which is incorrectly completed, you cannot argue later that you were not capable of making a true representation of your circumstances.[53] However, it is arguable that benefit cannot be recovered from you if you:[54]
  – have a disability or you cannot read or write English very well; *and*
  – thought you were signing something different from what you were, or you did not understand the effect of your signature; *and*
  – took precautions to understand what you were signing – eg, you checked the form for accuracy before you signed it.[55]
- If you sign a declaration on a claim form that states, 'I declare that the information I have given is correct and complete', but you left out relevant information because you were unaware of it, this is not misrepresentation unless you knew (or ought reasonably to have known) the information was incomplete.[56]

Note:
- If you did not declare a fact because you were unaware of it, signing the declaration does not amount to a misrepresentation because all you are declaring is that you have correctly disclosed those facts *which were known to you*.[57]
- If you were told by the DWP or HMRC that certain facts are irrelevant to your claim, signing the declaration cannot be a misrepresentation if you fail to disclose these facts.[58]
- If someone else disclosed a fact to an office not handling your claim but s/he reasonably believed it would be passed to the correct office, it may be that disclosure has been made, and therefore your signing the declaration does not amount to a misrepresentation.[59]

Your failure to disclose, or your misrepresentation, has caused the overpayment

An overpayment is only recoverable if it was caused by your failure to disclose (see p1239), or your misrepresenting (see p1241), a material fact (see p1239). **Note:** it is possible that if you have a duty to disclose a fact in respect of one benefit and you fail to do so, this could be regarded as the cause of an overpayment of another benefit.[60]

You may be able to argue that the overpayment was not caused by your failure to disclose or your misrepresentation.

- If the relevant office has been given the correct information to decide your claim by someone else, but does not act on it, you could argue that the overpayment did not arise because of your failure.[61] However, if one DWP office does not inform another about *other* changes in your circumstances (eg, an increase in your earnings), this does not prevent the overpayment resulting from your failure to disclose the information yourself to the second office.[62]
- If the relevant office has obtained information from another source that leads it to think you may be being overpaid but it does not suspend your benefit while it makes enquiries to establish this for certain, it is still possible that the cause of the overpayment is your failure to disclose or your misrepresentation.[63]
- If you have not disclosed a relevant fact to the relevant office and you then sign a declaration that you have reported the relevant facts (eg, when you sign on), this is a misrepresentation.
- If what you say on your claim form is obviously incorrect and the decision maker does not check this, the overpayment will have been caused by official error, not your misrepresentation, and it is not recoverable.[64]

The decision awarding you benefit has been changed

If the decision to award you benefit is considered to be incorrect, it must be changed before any overpayment can be recovered.[65] The only exception to this rule is when the circumstances of the overpayment mean that there is no decision that needs to be revised in order for an overpayment to exist – ie, if you were actually paid more than the amount the original decision awarded to you.[66]

A decision to change your benefit award is made by a decision maker, who then carries out a revision or a supersession (see p1303 and p1315). The new decision should state the new amount payable (if any).[67]

During the period when you were overpaid, there may have been more than one decision on your benefit award. Unless *all* these decisions are changed, *all* of the overpayment cannot be recovered.[68]

Note: in practice, there are therefore two decisions that must be made before an overpayment can be recovered from you: the decision that changes a previous decision about your benefit, and the decision that the overpayment is recoverable.[69] Both decisions may be included in one decision letter, but it must

Part 8: Claiming benefits and getting paid
Chapter 53: Overpayments
3. Overpayments that are sometimes recoverable

be clear that both have been made.[70] It is also possible that your benefit award has been changed, but you are not notified about this until you are also notified that the overpayment is recoverable.[71]

If the decision(s) about your benefit has not been changed and/or the new decision(s) has not been notified to you (or it appears that it may not have been), appeal to the First-tier Tribunal (see p1337) against the decision that the overpayment is recoverable. You must apply for a mandatory reconsideration first (see p1339).

The amount that is recovered

The amount of the overpayment is the difference between what you were paid and what you should have been paid.[72] Check that the amount of the overpayment is correct by:
- checking the period of the overpayment;
- working out the total amount of benefit you were paid over the period;
- establishing the correct amount of benefit you should have received during the period;
- deducting this from the total amount of benefit you were paid.

No interest charges may be added to the amount of the overpayment.

The decision maker works out what you should have been paid using the information you originally gave her/him, plus any facts you misrepresented or did not disclose.

If you have been overpaid, the decision maker should deduct from the overpayment any universal credit (UC), IS, income-based JSA, income-related employment and support allowance (ESA) or pension credit (PC) to which you or your partner would have been entitled had benefit been paid correctly.[73]

If additional facts are needed to prove you were underpaid UC, IS, income-based JSA, ESA or PC, you cannot offset the underpayment of these benefits against the overpayment.[74] However, if you have been getting one of these benefits, you can ask the DWP to revise or supersede your award (see p1303 and p1315). It could then withhold any arrears owed to you to reduce the overpayment.

If you were overpaid UC, IS, income-based JSA, income-related ESA or PC because you had too much capital, the overpayment is calculated taking account of the fact that, had you received no benefit, you would have had to use your capital to meet everyday expenses. For each 13-week period, the DWP assumes your capital is reduced by the amount of overpaid benefit.[75] This is known as the 'diminishing capital' rule. If your capital goes below the capital limit, any subsequent overpayment is not recoverable. However, if there are any increases or decreases in your actual capital during the overpayment period, these are also taken into account.[76]

Example

Nina received IS of £100 a week for a period of 30 weeks. She has capital of £20,000. After 13 weeks, the diminishing capital rule means that she is treated as having spent 13 x £100 = £1,300 and her capital is deemed to be £18,700. After a further 13 weeks, her capital is deemed to be £17,400.

After 26 weeks, Nina has paid £5,000 towards her credit card arrears after the credit card company threatened her with court proceedings. As long as obtaining benefit was not the significant purpose for making this payment (see p502), her capital is now deemed to be £12,400.

In addition to checking that the overpayment has been calculated correctly, you should claim any other benefits or tax credits to which you may be entitled and ask for these to be backdated (see p1176 for benefits and p1504 for tax credits) so you can repay the overpayment. Do not delay making the claims or you could lose out.

If you were overpaid a benefit which overlaps with another benefit you claimed but were not paid (see p1190), ask for a revision or supersession of that benefit and ask for it to be paid instead (see p1303).

If you were overpaid a benefit but, in fact, were entitled to another, check whether the claim for the benefit you were overpaid can be treated as a claim for the other (see p1182).

Example

Maxine should not have been receiving IS because her partner is in full-time paid work. However, she is caring for her aunt who is disabled and receiving attendance allowance. Maxine should ask the DWP to treat her claim for IS as a claim for carer's allowance (CA) and offset arrears of CA against the IS she has been overpaid.

From whom can an overpayment be recovered

An overpayment can be recovered from you if it was caused by your failing to disclose or your misrepresenting a material fact (see p1239).[77] The DWP or HMRC may argue that it can recover the overpayment from you, even if you are not the claimant or you were not paid the benefit. However, it is arguable that only a claimant, an 'appointee' or a person with power of attorney to whom the benefit was paid can fail to disclose a material fact.[78]

If you are an appointee (see p1170), the overpayment can be recovered from you or the claimant (or both of you), depending on your circumstances and the facts of the case – ie, which one of you misrepresented or failed to disclose a material fact. The DWP or HMRC should issue a decision that deals with both your liabilities.[79] However:

Part 8: Claiming benefits and getting paid
Chapter 53: Overpayments
3. Overpayments that are sometimes recoverable

- if the overpaid benefit has not been given to the claimant, the overpayment cannot be recovered from her/him, unless s/he contributed to the misrepresentation or s/he did not disclose a material fact;
- the overpayment cannot be recovered from you if you used 'due care and diligence' in making any statements that led to the overpayment.

Whether the overpayment can be recovered from you if you have **power of attorney** depends on whether the benefit was paid to you. If benefit was paid to you on behalf of the claimant, the overpayment is recoverable from you in the same way as from appointees.[80] If benefit was not paid to you, it cannot be recovered from you.[81]

An overpayment can be recovered from a claimant's estate if s/he dies.[82] Recovery can only begin after either probate or letters of administration have been granted.[83]

Challenging an overpayment decision

If you disagree that an overpayment has been made, or that an overpayment can be recovered (ie, because the required conditions are not met) or with the amount to be recovered (ie, because you were entitled to some, or all, of the payments), you can appeal. You must ask for a mandatory reconsideration first.

If you have missed the time limit for a mandatory reconsideration (see p1341), you can apply for a supersession and then appeal against any refusal to supersede.[84]

The First-tier Tribunal can consider whether you were entitled to some, or all, of the money (the amount of the overpayment), as well as whether the overpayment is recoverable from you on the basis that it was caused by your failure to disclose or misrepresentation. Both issues can also be considered, even if you have only challenged the decision about whether the overpayment is recoverable (and not the decision about your entitlement to benefit during the period of overpayment).[85]

Do not pay back any of the money until your appeal has been decided. If you do so and then successfully appeal, the DWP or HMRC should reimburse you. If it does not, you may be entitled to recover the money in court proceedings because you repaid the money on the basis of a mistake. Write to the DWP or HMRC and explain that you do not intend to repay any of the money until your appeal has been decided. Official guidance says that, except for overpayments of UC, recovery of overpaid benefit should be suspended while you are challenging the decision about the overpayment.[86] If the DWP or HMRC is already making deductions from your benefit (see p1248 and p1250), ask it to stop doing so straight away.

Note: even if the tribunal decides that an overpayment is recoverable, the decision maker has the discretion not to recover, so it can still be worth asking for it not to be recovered (see p1247).

4. **Recovery of overpaid benefit**

Note: this section does *not* apply to recovery of overpayments of housing benefit (HB – see p1253).

If an overpayment can be recovered (see p1234 and p1238), the DWP or HM Revenue and Customs (HMRC) must decide whether to recover it (see below) and, if so, the method to use. The recovery method depends on the type of overpayment. If you come under the universal credit (UC) system and have been overpaid UC, contribution-based jobseeker's allowance (JSA) or contributory employment and support allowance (ESA), see p1248. For all other overpayments, see p1250.

Note: except when seeking to recover overpaid benefit through the courts, there is no time limit within which the DWP or HMRC must begin recovery action.

The discretion not to recover

Even if an overpayment is recoverable, the DWP and HMRC have the discretion not to recover all or part of it. The DWP has two policies that set out the situations when recovery is not made.

- Guidance for overpayments of UC, contribution-based JSA and contributory ESA if you come under the UC system (see p1235) used to state that the DWP can use its discretion not to recover an overpayment if it would cause you hardship.[87] Although this guidance has been withdrawn, the discretion should still apply. You can also ask the DWP not to recover if the reason you were overpaid was because of a mistake on the part of the DWP.[88]
- Guidance for all other overpayments emphasises that it is only in exceptional cases that recovery is not pursued.[89] However, the DWP and HMRC can use their discretion to decide not to recover the overpayment, particularly if you acted in good faith and recovery would cause you hardship or be detrimental to your health or the health of your family.

If you agree to repay the overpayment or you do not ask for recovery not to be made, in almost all cases the DWP or HMRC recovers the overpayment from you. If an overpayment is recoverable from you, but repaying it is difficult or you think there is a reason why recovery should not take place, contact the DWP or HMRC debt management section. The details should be on the letters you receive about the overpayment. Each case is decided on its merits. You should emphasise that you acted in good faith, point out any misleading advice you received (particularly from the DWP or HMRC) and how repaying would cause you hardship. To demonstrate hardship on financial grounds, you must usually provide full income and expenditure details for you and your family.

Part 8: Claiming benefits and getting paid
Chapter 53: Overpayments
4. Recovery of overpaid benefit

If the DWP or HMRC refuses to use its discretion not to recover, you cannot appeal against this decision. Your only possible legal recourse is judicial review (see p1414), but it may also help to involve your MP. The First-tier Tribunal cannot 'write off' part of the overpayment, even if there are mitigating circumstances. It can only decide whether it is recoverable and, if so, how much is repayable.

If you have been underpaid in the past but cannot now get arrears (eg, because of the rules on backdating – see p1176), ask the DWP or HMRC to reduce the amount to be recovered by this sum if it will not write it off altogether.

Methods of recovery: universal credit system

This section applies to the recovery of overpayments of UC, and of contribution-based JSA or contributory ESA if you come under the UC system (see p1235).

Note: the methods of recovery described in this section can also be used to collect or recover court costs incurred in recovering overpayments, advance payments of UC (see p1192), budgeting advances of UC (see p51), hardship payments of UC (see p1219), financial penalties for benefit offences (see p1275), civil penalties for incorrect statements (see p1268) and overpayments of tax credits if the debt has been transferred to the DWP (see p1528).

Deductions from benefit

Overpayments of UC, and contribution-based JSA or contributory ESA if you come under the UC system, can be recovered through deductions from all the benefits in this *Handbook* except income support (IS), HB, social fund payments, child benefit and guardian's allowance.[90] **Note:** at the time of writing, there was no mechanism in place to recover overpayments from Scottish social security benefits. See p1725, and AskCPAG.org.uk and CPAG's *Welfare Rights Bulletin* for updates.

Maximum deductions from universal credit

Note: the maximum amounts below apply to *all* overpayments being recovered by deductions from your UC – eg, an overpayment of IS that occurred before you came under the UC system.[91]

If an overpayment is being recovered from your UC, at the time of writing the regulations provide that the maximum amount that can be deducted each month is 40 per cent of the appropriate UC standard allowance.[92] The government has stated that, in practice, the maximum amount that will be recovered is 30 per cent of the appropriate UC standard allowance.[93] This means that the deduction will be the highest of:

- if you or your partner are found guilty of an offence, or have accepted a caution or agreed to pay a penalty in connection with the overpayment (see p1267), or if UC hardship payments are being recovered:
  - £76.82 if you are single and under 25;

- £96.97 if you are single and 25 or over;
- £120.58 if you and your partner are both under 25;
- £152.21 if you or your partner are 25 or over;
- if you have some earned income:
  - £64.01 if you are single and under 25;
  - £80.81 if you are single and 25 or over;
  - £100.48 if you and your partner are both under 25;
  - £126.84 if you or your partner are 25 or over;
- in all other cases:
  - £38.41 if you are single and under 25;
  - £48.48 if you are single and 25 or over;
  - £60.29 if you and your partner are both under 25;
  - £76.11 if you or your partner are 25 or over.

You must be left with at least one penny of UC each month after the deduction.[94] The above maximum amounts do not apply if:

- you are being paid arrears of UC (other than if they are as a result of payments being restored following a suspension of your benefit), so the whole of the arrears can be used to recover an overpayment;[95] *or*
- the overpayment is of UC housing costs to cover rent and it is being recovered from someone else – eg, your landlord.[96]

Maximum deductions from jobseeker's allowance or employment and support allowance

The maximum weekly deduction that can be made to recover an overpayment from your JSA is an amount equal to 40 per cent of your JSA.[97]

The maximum weekly deduction that can be made to recover an overpayment from your ESA is 40 per cent of the basic allowance that applies to you (see p650).[98]

In both cases, if the 40 per cent figure is not a multiple of five pence, the amount is rounded up to the next highest multiple of five pence.

Maximum deductions from pension credit

The maximum weekly amount that can be deducted from pension credit (PC) to repay an overpayment under these rules (ie, if you were overpaid under the UC system and are now getting PC) is:[99]

- £18.65 if the overpayment is one for which you were found guilty of an offence, you were cautioned or you agreed to pay a penalty as an alternative to prosecution; *or*
- £11.20 in all other cases.

You must be left with at least 10 pence of PC after any deductions.

Part 8: Claiming benefits and getting paid
Chapter 53: Overpayments
4. Recovery of overpaid benefit

Deductions from earnings

Overpayments can be recovered by your employer deducting amounts from your wages or salary.[100] The rules are the same as those outlined on p1251.

Recovery through the courts

The rules for recovering overpayments through the courts are similar to those for the recovery of HB (see p1260).[101]

Methods of recovery: other benefits

This section applies to all recoverable overpayments, except overpayments of UC, and contribution-based JSA or contributory ESA if you come under the UC system. For these, see p1248.

Deductions from benefit

If you have a recoverable overpayment of benefit and you are now getting UC, the overpayment can be transferred to your UC claim and treated as an overpayment of UC. It is then recovered under the rules for UC (see p1248).

Recoverable overpayments can usually be repaid through deductions from most of the benefits in this *Handbook*. There are some exceptions. **Note:** at the time of writing, there was no mechanism to recover overpayments from Scottish social security benefits. See CPAG's online service and *Welfare Rights Bulletin* for updates.

- Overpayments of child benefit and guardian's allowance can be recovered by deductions from either of these benefits,[102] but overpayments of other benefits cannot be deducted from them.[103]
- No deductions can be made from HB, except for HB or council tax benefit (see p125) overpayments.[104]

Deductions can only be made from the benefit of the person who must repay the overpayment. However, if you are a member of a couple, overpayments of IS, income-based JSA, income-related ESA and PC can be recovered from benefits either of you receive, provided you are married or living together as if you were married.[105]

Overpayments can also be recovered from arrears of benefit you are owed, except arrears of a benefit that has been suspended (see p1200).[106]

If an overpayment of IS, income-based JSA, income-related ESA or PC occurred because of a duplication of payment, the DWP usually deducts it from the arrears owing to you.[107] However, if it does not do so, you can still be asked to repay it even if you have spent the money.

Note: overpaid benefit cannot be recovered by making deductions from tax credits.

Maximum deductions

The maximum weekly amounts that can be deducted from **IS, income-based JSA, contribution-based JSA** (if you would be entitled to income-based JSA at the same rate), **income-related ESA, contributory ESA** (if you would be entitled to income-related ESA at the same rate) and **PC** are:[108]

- £30 if you have agreed to pay a penalty (see p1275), admitted fraud or been found guilty of fraud; *or*
- £11.25 in any other case.

The deduction can be increased by half of any:[109]

- £5, £10 or £20 earnings disregard (see p429); *or*
- charitable income paid on a regular basis subject to a disregard (see p441); *or*
- benefit subject to a £10 disregard (see p429).

If you have been overpaid contribution-based JSA but are not entitled to income-based JSA, the maximum deduction is one-third of the personal allowance for someone of your age (see p334).[110]

The above amounts are maximum amounts. You might be able to persuade the DWP to deduct less. If other deductions are also being made from your benefit, see p1210 for the total maximum amount that can be deducted.

If an overpayment is being recovered from a benefit other than IS, income-based JSA, income-related ESA or PC, the rules limiting the maximum payment that can be deducted do not apply. See p1248 if the overpayment is being recovered from your UC.[111] The DWP usually wants to deduct one-third of your weekly benefit. However, you can argue that your rate of repayment should be less than this.

Deductions from earnings

If you work for an organisation with 10 or more employees, an overpayment can be recovered by your employer deducting amounts from your earnings.[112] If this happens, you and your employer should be sent a notice setting out that deductions from your earnings are to be made and the rules for calculating how much to deduct.[113] You must inform the DWP if you leave your employment and you must give the DWP details of any new employment.[114] Failure to notify the DWP of these is a criminal offence.[115] Your employer should inform you, in writing, of how much the deductions are and how they were calculated no later than the day on which you are given a payment which has had a deduction made from it (or, if that is impractical, no later than the following payday).[116]

The maximum that can be deducted each week is worked out as a percentage of your net earnings – ie, earnings after income tax, class 1 national insurance contributions and pension contributions have been deducted.[117] The maximum is higher if you have been found guilty of an offence.[118]

Part 8: Claiming benefits and getting paid
Chapter 53: Overpayments
4. Recovery of overpaid benefit

Maximum deductions from earnings

Net monthly earnings (if paid monthly)	Net weekly earnings (if paid weekly)	Deduction	Deduction if found guilty of an offence
Less than £430	£100 or less	Nil	5%
£430.01 to £690	£100.01 to £160	3%	6%
£690.01 to £950	£160.01 to £220	5%	10%
£950.01 to £1,160	£220.01 to £270	7%	14%
£1,160.01 to £1,615	£270.01 to £375	11%	22%
£1,615.01 to £2,240	£375.01 to £520	15%	30%
£2,240.01 or over	£520.01 or over	20%	40%

If you would be left with less than 60 per cent of your net earnings after the deductions (eg, because amounts are being deducted from your wages or salary for other things), the deduction should be reduced so that you are left with 60 per cent of your net earnings.[119] There are rules on the order of priority in which deductions should be made (see p1211).[120] **Note:** the decision maker can reduce the amount to be deducted below the above percentages by issuing a new notice to your employer with the reduced amount.[121]

Recovery through the courts

Recoverable overpayments of benefit may be recovered by enforcement proceedings in the county court in England or Wales or the sheriff court in Scotland.[122] The DWP or HMRC may use these proceedings if you are no longer claiming benefit.

Once there is a decision from a decision maker, the First-tier Tribunal or Upper Tribunal, the court must enforce it, unless you persuade it to delay enforcement (known as a 'stay of execution') while you appeal against the relevant decision. If you are in this situation, get advice.

Note: recovery action through the courts in England and Wales must be taken within six years of the decision to recover or, if later, any written acknowledgement of the overpayment or voluntary repayment.[123] In Scotland, the DWP regards the time limit as being 20 years from the date of the decision to recover (or, if there was no such decision, five years from the decision that there was an overpayment).[124] Get advice about how these limits apply to you.

Can the DWP rely on common law?

The DWP cannot recover overpayments of benefit using 'common law.' This means that if the DWP cannot recover an overpayment under the rules described in this chapter (see p1238) because, for example, it was not caused by misrepresentation or a failure to disclose, it cannot reclaim it through the courts.[125]

5. Overpayments of housing benefit

Note: council tax benefit (CTB) was abolished on 1 April 2013. However, it is possible that there may be decisions after this date about CTB overpayments made before this date. You may also still be repaying an overpayment of CTB. The rules on calculating the amount and the recoverability of overpayments of CTB were similar to those for housing benefit (HB). For further details, see p1094 of the 2012/13 edition of this *Handbook*.

If you have been overpaid income support (IS), income-based jobseeker's allowance (JSA) or income-related employment and support allowance (ESA), you may also have been overpaid HB. This is because your automatic passport to maximum HB ceases when you are no longer entitled to these benefits. If you are in this situation, inform the local authority dealing with your HB claim. Although it cannot change the decision about your other benefit, the local authority should still go on to make its own decision on your entitlement to HB.

What is an overpayment

An 'overpayment' is an amount of HB which has been paid and to which the local authority decides you were not entitled under the HB rules.[126] Being 'paid' includes payment to you, your landlord or someone else, including HB credited to your local authority rent account (see p214).[127]

Overpayments that are always recoverable

An overpayment of HB is always recoverable if:
- it is the result of the local authority's overestimating your HB when making a payment on account (see p220). When the local authority decides how much HB you should get, it must recover any excess you were paid from future HB payments.[128] However, if you stop getting HB before the local authority decides, the overpayment can only be recovered under the other rules (see below); *or*
- it is a future payment that has been credited to your rent account. In this case, the overpayment can be recovered even if it was made as a result of an 'official error'.[129] If an overpayment of HB caused by an official error has been credited to your account for a *past* period, see p1254.

Overpayments that are not recoverable

An overpayment that is not covered by either of the bullet points above is not recoverable if you can show that:[130]
- it was caused by an 'official error' (see p1254); *and*
- no 'relevant person' contributed to making the official error (see p1255); *and*

Part 8: Claiming benefits and getting paid
Chapter 53: Overpayments
5. Overpayments of housing benefit

- no 'relevant person' could reasonably have been expected to realise that an overpayment was being made (see p1255).

Overpayments to which all these criteria apply are sometimes referred to as 'official error' overpayments.

Was the overpayment caused by an official error?

For the overpayment not to be recoverable, it must have been caused by an 'official error'. **Note:** the official error does not have to be the sole cause of the overpayment, but if the substantial cause of the overpayment was something that you did or failed to do, the overpayment is likely to be recoverable.[131]

An 'official error' is a mistake (either an act or omission) by:[132]

- the local authority responsible for HB; *or*
- an officer of the authority; *or*
- a person acting for that authority – eg, an employee of a contractor providing HB services; *or*
- an officer of the DWP or HM Revenue and Customs (HMRC) acting as such.

Examples of 'official error' include the following.

- A mistake made by the local authority in calculating your entitlement.
- A failure by the local authority to reduce your HB when you inform it of a change of circumstances. It is always best to notify changes in writing to the office you have been told to report changes to, and keep a copy. If you have reported a move into work to the DWP by telephone under the arrangements where it passes this on to the local authority (see p221) and have provided all the information and evidence needed, any overpayment that occurs is due to official error. However, if you did not provide all that was needed, the local authority does not treat any overpayment as official error.[133]
- Using a claim form that does not ask a question relevant to your entitlement. Whether or not this counts as an official error depends on the particular facts of your case. Leaving out a particular question is more likely to be an official error if the information omitted is likely to be relevant in a large number of cases, and if it is reasonable for the question to have been asked.[134]
- A failure by another department of the local authority to pass on details of a change of circumstances when it promised to do so. This is an official error because the definition does not require the mistake to be made by the HB office. If you have not been given a particular office to report a change to, you may have fulfilled your duty by reporting the change to any local authority office, and there may be an official error if that office fails to pass it to the HB office.[135]
- A mistake made by the DWP in calculating your entitlement to IS, income-based JSA or income-related ESA which results in an incorrect calculation of your entitlement to HB. However, it is not an official error if the local authority

failed to check your entitlement with the DWP, unless it has information that shows the award is wrong or fraudulent.[136]
- A failure by the DWP to pass on information to the local authority.[137]
- Incorrect advice given to you by an officer of the local authority, the DWP or HMRC, provided s/he is acting as an officer at the time (rather than as a friend giving you informal advice).

The list above is not exhaustive.

Did a relevant person contribute to making the offical error?

Even if the overpayment was caused by an official error, if a 'relevant person' contributed to that mistake being made, the overpayment can still be recovered.

Relevant person

A '**relevant person**' is:

– the HB claimant; *or*

– a person acting on the claimant's behalf, either because the claimant is unable to deal with her/his affairs or because the claimant has asked the authority in writing to deal with the other person on her/his behalf; *or*

– a person to whom the payment was made, including a different person acting on the claimant's behalf or a landlord.

The relevant person must have caused the *error*, not the overpayment.[138]

The local authority might say that it only needs to show that *any* relevant person caused the official error, but it does not have to pursue that person for the overpayment.[139] If a relevant person caused the official error, the overpayment is recoverable. However, you may still be able to argue that it is not recoverable from you – eg, it was caused by a failure to disclose a relevant fact, but it was not you who failed to disclose. See p1257 for information about from whom overpayments can be recovered.

Did a relevant person realise that an overpayment was being made?

Even if the official error was not caused by a relevant person, an overpayment is still recoverable if any relevant person knew, or ought reasonably to have known, that an overpayment had been made. The test is whether or not you could reasonably have been be expected to *know* (not merely suspect) that an overpayment had occurred. Much depends on what could reasonably have been expected of you given the information available to you, in particular the extent to which the local authority advised you about the scheme, your duties and obligations (especially your duty to notify changes of circumstances).[140]

Part 8: Claiming benefits and getting paid
Chapter 53: Overpayments
5. Overpayments of housing benefit

If you or another relevant person could only have realised that there was an overpayment at some point during the period of the overpayment, the overpayment is only recoverable from that date.

The amount that is recovered

Check the amount of an overpayment to ensure the local authority has calculated it correctly. The local authority should distinguish between parts of an overpayment that are recoverable and those that are not. To calculate the amount of the overpayment, it should:
- determine the period over which you have been paid too much benefit;
- identify the period(s) over which it is entitled to recover;
- work out the total amount of HB you were paid over the period(s) during which it can recover;
- work out the correct amount of HB you should have received during the period(s) of the overpayment. The local authority must award you the amount of HB you (or your partner) would have received if it had been aware of your true circumstances. If necessary, it should ask you for any required information or evidence to do this. However, the local authority does not include a change of your address when doing this;[141]
- deduct the HB you should have been paid from what you were paid.[142]

The local authority must not add any interest charges to the amount of the overpayment.[143]

Deductions from the overpayment

As well as any amount of HB which you should have been paid, the local authority must consider deducting other amounts from the overpayment (this is known as 'offsetting'). These are:
- if you are a council tenant, extra rent paid into your rent account. If you have been getting HB during the overpayment period and, for some reason, have paid more into your rent account than you should have paid according to your original (incorrect) benefit assessment, the extra rent you have paid can be deducted from any overpayment made during that period. The local authority might not apply this rule if you paid extra rent to repay rent arrears;[144]
- reductions under the 'diminishing capital rule' (see below).

No other amounts can be deducted.

If you were overpaid HB because you had too much capital, the overpayment is calculated taking into account the fact that, had you received no HB, you would have used your capital. This is known as the **'diminishing capital rule'**. It only applies if you were overpaid for more than 13 weeks and either:[145]
- the overpayment was caused by a misrepresentation of, or a failure to disclose, the amount of your capital (see p1239); *or*

- the overpayment was caused by an error (other than an 'official error' – see p1254) about your capital (or that of a member of your family).

For each 13-week period, the local authority assumes that your capital is reduced by the amount of overpaid HB.[146]

From whom can an overpayment be recovered

The general rule is that a recoverable overpayment can be recovered from the person to whom it was paid – eg, a landlord.[147] However, this does not apply if someone else misrepresented or failed to disclose a material fact, or if someone else should have realised that there was an overpayment at the time.

An overpayment can be recovered from someone other than the person to whom it was paid, including the claimant, if:[148]

- the overpayment was caused by misrepresentation or failure to disclose a material fact (see p1238). In this case, it can be recovered from the person who misrepresented or failed to disclose the fact, but not the person to whom the payment was made; *or*
- the overpayment was caused by an official error (see p1253) and the claimant (or someone acting on the claimant's behalf) or any other person to whom the HB was paid could reasonably have been expected to realise that there was an overpayment at the time. In this case, it can be recovered from whoever should have realised, but not the person to whom it was paid; *or*
- neither of the above two bullet points apply, in which case the overpayment is also recoverable from the claimant. Therefore, if you are the claimant, the overpayment may be recovered from you, as well as the person to whom it was paid.

If you are the claimant and the overpayment is recoverable from you, no matter how it was caused, the local authority can also recover the overpayment by deducting any HB paid to your partner, provided you were a couple both at the time of the overpayment and when the deduction is made.[149]

If you think you have been wrongly chosen under these rules (eg, because you did not fail to disclose a material fact), you can appeal to the First-tier Tribunal. However, if the overpayment can be recovered from you under these rules, you cannot appeal simply because you think the local authority should recover from another person instead.[150]

In the event of the death of the person from whom recovery is being sought, the local authority may consider recovering any outstanding overpayment from her/his estate.[151]

Methods of recovery

A local authority can decide how much, if any, of a recoverable overpayment it will recover (but see p220 if the overpayment was of a payment on account).[152]

Part 8: Claiming benefits and getting paid
Chapter 53: Overpayments
5. Overpayments of housing benefit

This is similar to the discretion that the DWP and HMRC have to recover overpayments (see p1247).

If the local authority decides to recover, it can ask for the whole amount or recover it by instalments. When an overpayment is recovered from your landlord, note how this affects your liability to pay rent (see p1262). Overpayments of HB can be recovered:

- from payments of HB (see below);
- from other benefits (see p1259);
- by adjusting your rent account if you are a local authority tenant (see p1260);
- by your employer deducting amounts from your wages or salary (see p1260);
- through the courts (see p1260).

The methods used and the rates of recovery should be consistent between groups of claimants. For example, council tenants should not be required to repay an overpayment in a lump sum if private tenants can repay by instalments.

Note: except when seeking to recover overpaid benefit through the courts, there is no time limit within which a local authority must begin recovery action.

Deductions from housing benefit

A local authority can recover an overpayment by deducting amounts from HB payable to any person from whom an overpayment can be recovered (see p1245).[153] As well as yourself, this could be your partner (see below) or your landlord (see p1259). Deductions can be made from both future payments of HB and any arrears that are owing.

If you have moved home, the local authority may be able to recover an overpayment of HB from your previous home by adjusting the HB paid at your new home. It can decide to do this if:[154]

- the overpayment occurred after you moved, and occurred because you were no longer living at your previous home; *and*
- the same local authority that paid you the overpayment is paying your HB at your new home.

In these circumstances, the local authority can deduct all the weekly HB owing to you for your new home to recover the overpayment, for however many weeks you were overpaid at your previous home.

Deductions from your partner's housing benefit

If you were the claimant and the overpayment, no matter how it was caused, is recoverable from you, the local authority can also recover it by deductions from any HB later awarded to your partner, provided you were a couple at both the time of the overpayment and when the deduction is made.[155]

Deductions from your landlord's housing benefit

The local authority may recover the overpayment from:

- HB paid to your landlord if s/he is claiming HB her/himself;[156]
- HB paid directly to your landlord on your behalf.[157] The notification of the overpayment (see p1261) should make it clear from whom the authority is recovering;
- HB paid directly to your landlord on behalf of other claimants.[158]

When HB is recovered from a landlord in this way, there are special rules on how this affects your liability to pay rent (see p1262).

Maximum deductions

The maximum weekly amount that can be deducted is £18.75 if you have agreed to pay a penalty (see p1275), admitted fraud or been found guilty of fraud, or £11.25 in any other case.[159]

The rate of recovery can be increased by up to half of any amount of earned income which is disregarded as income in the calculation of your HB (see p429 and p471).[160] Amounts of income disregarded for childcare costs cannot be used to increase the rate of recovery in this way.

However, you can argue that the rate will cause you hardship and a lesser amount should be recovered instead. You must be left with at least 50 pence of HB per week.[161]

Deductions from other benefits

The local authority can ask the DWP to recover an overpayment of HB by making deductions from most of the benefits in this *Handbook* (except guardian's allowance and, arguably, child benefit).[162] **Note:** at the time of writing, there was no mechanism in place to recover overpayments from Scottish social security benefits. See AskCPAG.org.uk and CPAG's *Welfare Rights Bulletin* for updates. If the overpayment is recoverable from your partner (see p1257), it can be recovered by deductions from her/his universal credit (UC), IS, income-based JSA, income-related ESA, pension credit or personal independence payment.

An overpayment can also be recovered from any benefits paid to your landlord in her/his own right.[163]

Deductions can only be made if:[164]

- a recoverable overpayment has been made as a result of a misrepresentation of, or failure to disclose (see p1239), a material fact by you, on your behalf or by or on behalf of another person to whom HB has been paid; *and*
- the local authority is unable to recover that overpayment from any HB; *and*
- the person who is to repay the overpayment is receiving a sufficient amount of at least one of the relevant benefits to allow deductions to be made.

Except for UC (see p1248), there are no rules limiting the maximum amount that can be deducted. However, you can argue that your rate of repayment should be

Part 8: Claiming benefits and getting paid
Chapter 53: Overpayments
5. Overpayments of housing benefit

reasonable. If you are on IS, income-based JSA or income-related ESA, argue that the weekly maximums for these benefits should apply (see p1251). Ask the DWP to use its discretion to reduce the amounts if the deductions will cause you hardship.

If deductions stop because you are no longer entitled to a particular benefit, or the amount to which you are entitled is insufficient for deductions to be made, the DWP notifies the local authority which, once again, becomes responsible for any further recovery action.

Adjusting your rent account

If you are a local authority tenant, the local authority can recover an overpayment by adding it as a debt to your rent account. If a local authority recovers overpaid HB in this way, the overpayment should be separately identified and you should be informed that the amount being recovered does not represent rent arrears.[165]

If the local authority is seeking to evict you because you have rent arrears, you should get advice. It cannot argue you owe it rent arrears if you have only been overpaid HB. Local authorities are reminded in DWP guidance that overpayments of HB paid to their own tenants are not rent arrears and should not be treated as such.[166]

An overpayment cannot be recovered in this way if you have a private or housing association landlord. However, an overpayment can be recovered from your landlord (see p1259). If the local authority recovers from your landlord, you might count as being in rent arrears (see p1241).

Deductions from earnings

The local authority can order your employer to deduct amounts from your (but not your partner's) wages or salary in order to recover the overpayment.[167] The rules for this are explained on p1251.

Court action

If a local authority cannot use any of the methods of recovery listed on p1257 and you cannot agree on repayments, it can try to recover the money you owe through the county court (sheriff court in Scotland) if it thinks you can afford to make repayments. It should not start proceedings until your time for challenging the decision has passed.

A local authority should not use court proceedings to recover an overpayment if it has not followed the correct procedure (see p1252) – eg, if it has not issued the correct notification.[168]

A local authority can:
- sue you for the debt created by the overpayment. If the correct procedure has not been followed, you can use this as a defence.[169] You may also be able to claim compensation in certain circumstances. However, you cannot say that you should have received more HB;[170] or

- use the special rules to register the overpayment as a debt which can then be recovered using a court procedure.[171] Get advice if you think the local authority is not entitled to do this.

Note: recovery action through the courts in England and Wales must be taken within six years of the decision to recover or, if later, any written acknowledgement of the overpayment or voluntary repayment.[172] In Scotland, the DWP regards the time limit as being 20 years from the date of the decision to recover (or, if there was no such decision, five years from the decision that there was an overpayment). Get advice about how these limits apply to your case.[173]

If the local authority is successful in its court proceedings against you, you may have to pay legal costs and interest, as well as the overpayment. Remember that court procedures often require you to take action within a very short period of time. If the local authority is threatening to use court proceedings, get advice.

Notification of an overpayment

If the local authority decides that a recoverable overpayment has occurred, it must write to the person from whom repayment is being sought (see p1257) within 14 days if possible, notifying her/him of this.[174]

This notification must state:[175]

- that there is an overpayment which is legally recoverable;
- the reason why there is a recoverable overpayment;
- the amount of the recoverable overpayment;
- how the amount of the overpayment was calculated;
- the benefit weeks to which the overpayment relates;
- if recovery is to be made from future benefit, the amount of the deductions;
- if recovery is to be made from your landlord by deductions from someone else's HB, your identity and the claimant from whose HB the deduction will be made;[176]
- your right to ask for a further written explanation of any of the decisions the local authority has made about the overpayment, how you can do this and the time limit for doing so;
- that you have a right to ask the local authority to reconsider any of the decisions it has made about the overpayment, how you can do this and the time limit for doing so.

It may also include any other relevant matters.

Guidance states that the local authority should issue a single notification to all relevant parties (eg, landlord and tenant), saying from whom the overpayment is recoverable and from whom it is not.[177]

If you write and ask the local authority for a more detailed written explanation of any of the decisions it has made about an overpayment, it must send you this within 14 days or, if this is not reasonably practicable, as soon as possible.[178]

Part 8: Claiming benefits and getting paid
Chapter 53: Overpayments
5. Overpayments of housing benefit

If a notification sent to you is a clear decision that there is an overpayment which is recoverable from you, but does not contain all the matters above, it is only valid if the omissions do not put you at a disadvantage.[179] If, for example, it does not set out your right to apply for a revision so that you do not do so until it is too late, you have been put at a disadvantage and so can argue that the overpayment is not recoverable. However, if the decision is not about recoverability and is only about the fact that you have been overpaid, you can argue that there is no decision saying that you must repay the overpayment.[180]

No recovery should be sought until after you have been notified and the one-month time period for asking for a revision or appealing has passed.[181]

The effect of recovery from your landlord

If you are a private or housing association tenant, an overpayment of HB recovered from your landlord (see p1259) could mean that s/he tries to obtain money from you. The landlord could argue that you are in rent arrears as a result and could seek possession of your home.

Whether or not HB was paid directly to your landlord, s/he may still try to argue that, even if you owe no rent, you nevertheless owe a debt under common law. This is probably not correct. If s/he threatens to sue you, get advice straight away.

If you are a local authority tenant, these rules do not apply. However, the local authority can recover an overpayment of HB by making deductions from your rent account (see p1259).

If you were overpaid HB and HB was paid directly to your landlord, the following rules apply.

- If you are overpaid and the local authority recovers the overpayment from your landlord by making deductions from direct payments of other tenants' HB (see p1258), the other tenants are treated as having paid the amount of the deduction towards their rent.[182]
- If you are overpaid and the local authority recovers the overpayment from your landlord by making deductions from direct payments of your HB, you are treated as having paid the amount of the deduction towards your rent if your landlord is convicted of an offence or agrees to pay a penalty (see p1275) in relation to that overpayment.[183] If the local authority decides to recover under this rule, it must notify both your landlord and you that you are to be treated as having paid your rent.[184]

In these situations, your landlord cannot argue that you are in arrears of rent. It is also much easier to argue that your landlord cannot sue you under common law for a debt.

Challenging an overpayment decision

You can apply for a revision or appeal (see Chapters 56 and 57) if you want to dispute:

- the decision that you have been overpaid HB;
- the amount of the overpayment;
- the decision that it can be recovered;
- that the overpayment is to be recovered from you under the rules set out on p1257.

Do not pay back any of the money until your challenge has been dealt with. Local authority guidance states that overpayments should not be recovered while under appeal.[185] If the local authority is already making deductions from your HB (see p1256) or deductions are being made from your other benefits (see p1259), ask it to stop this straight away.

Notes

1. **Introduction**
1 *SSWP v Payne and Another* [2011] UKSC 60

2. **Overpayments that are always recoverable**
2 s71ZB(1) SSAA 1992; Art 5(3A) WRA(No. 8)O
3 s71ZB(3) SSAA 1992
4 *LP v SSWP* [2018] UKUT 332 (AAC)
5 Reg 16 SS(OR) Regs
6 Reg 8(3) SS(OR) Regs
7 Reg 7 SS(OR) Regs
8 Reg 9(1)(a) and (b) and (2) SS(OR) Regs
9 Reg 9(1)(c) SS(OR) Regs
10 Reg 9(3) SS(OR) Regs
11 Reg 4 SS(OR) Regs
12 s74 SSAA 1992
13 Reg 7(1) SS(PAOR) Regs
14 R(SB) 3/91
15 s74(2) and (4) SSAA 1992
16 See, for example, the appeals in R(SB) 28/85 and R(IS) 6/02
17 s71(4) SSAA 1992; reg 11 SS(PAOR) Regs; reg 35 CB&GA(Admin) Regs

18 Reg 11 SS(PAOR) Regs; reg 35 CB&GA(Admin) Regs
19 Sch 2 para 20(d) SS&CS(DA) Regs

3. **Overpayments that are sometimes recoverable**
20 s71(1) and (5A) SSAA 1992; R(SB) 34/83
21 R(SB) 2/92
22 CDLA/5803/1999
23 CDLA/1823/2004
24 R(S) 4/86; R(I) 3/75
25 *B v SSWP* [2005] EWCA Civ 929, reported as R(IS) 9/06. The effect of the decision is that recovery is under reg 32 SS(C&P) Regs and, presumably, under the equivalent rules in reg 24 JSA Regs and reg 23 CB&GA(Admin) Regs.
26 R(SB) 21/82
27 R(SB) 54/83; CSB/296/1985
28 CG/160/1999
29 R(SB) 21/82
30 Reg 32(1A) SS(C&P) Regs; reg 24(1)-(5A) JSA Regs; reg 38(3) UC,PIP,JSA&ESA(C&P) Regs
31 *Hooper v SSWP* [2007] EWCA Civ 495, reported as R(IB) 4/07. See also official guidance in Memo DMG 26/07.

32 R(A) 2/06
33 Reg 32(1B) SS(C&P) Regs; reg 24(7) JSA Regs; reg 38(4) UC,PIP,JSA&ESA(C&P) Regs
34 CSB/510/1987; CIS/545/1992; CIS/1769/1999. These decisions arose from the old test of failure to disclose and it is not clear they apply now. However, the point seems to have been adopted in *DG v SSWP* [2009] UKUT 120 (AAC).
35 R(SB) 15/87; *Hinchy v SSWP* [2005] UKHL 16, reported as R(IS) 7/05
36 Reg 23(5) CB&GA(Admin) Regs
37 *LH v SSWP (RP)* [2017] UKUT 249 (AAC)
38 CG/5631/1999; CIS/1887/2002; *WA v SSWP* [2009] UKUT 132 (AAC); *GJ v SSWP (IS)* [2010] UKUT 107 (AAC)
39 Reg 32(1B) SS(C&P) Regs requires notification in writing or by telephone, unless the DWP specifically requires otherwise
40 R(SB) 18/85
41 CWSB/2/1985
42 R(SB) 15/87
43 CDLA/6336/1999
44 R(SB) 15/87; CIS/3529/2008
45 R(SB) 54/83
46 CSB/393/1985
47 CIS/5117/1998
48 R(SB) 9/85
49 *Jones and Sharples v CAO* [1994] 1 All ER 225 (CA); R(SB) 9/85
50 R(SB) 18/85
51 R(SB) 2/91
52 R(SB) 3/90
53 *Sheriff v CAO* [1995] (CA), reported as R(IS) 14/96
54 CG/4494/1999 suggests the principle may apply in social security; R(IS) 4/06 is more doubtful, but does not rule it out.
55 CIS/3846/2001
56 *Jones and Sharples v CAO* [1994] 1 All ER 225 (CA); *Franklin v CAO* [1995] (CA); CIS/674/1994; CIS/583/1994; CIS/674/1994
57 *Franklin v CAO* [1995] (CA)
58 CIS/583/1994
59 CDLA/6336/1999
60 *TM v SSWP (ESA)* [2015] UKUT 109 (AAC)
61 CIS/159/1990; CS/11700/1996; CSIS/7/1994; CG/5631/1999; *GJ v SSWP (IS)* [2010] UKUT 107 (AAC)
62 *Duggan v CAO* [1989] (CA); CG/662/1998; CG/4494/1999; *Hinchy v SSWP* [2003] EWCA Civ 138
63 *JM v SSWP (IS)* [2011] UKUT 15 (AAC)
64 CIS/222/1991

65 s71(5A) SSAA 1992; CIS/3228/2003; R(IS) 13/05. See CPC/3743/2006 for when not all the overpayment period has been covered by the change of the award.
66 Reg 12 SS(PAOR) Regs
67 CIS/3228/2003
68 CSIS/45/1990
69 R(SB) 7/91
70 *LL v SSWP* [2013] UKUT 208 (AAC)
71 This was the case in *Hamilton v Department for Social Development* [2010] NICA 46, but it is clear from *SSWP v AD (IS)* [2011] UKUT 184 (AAC) that whether this is the case depends on the specific decision-making history in your case.
72 R(SB) 20/84; R(SB) 24/87
73 Reg 13(1)(b) and (1A) SS(PAOR) Regs
74 *Commock v CAO*, reported as an appendix to R(SB) 6/90; CSIS/8/1995
75 Reg 14 SS(PAOR) Regs
76 CIS/5825/1999
77 s71(3) SSAA 1992
78 *B v SSWP* [2005] EWCA Civ 929, reported as R(IS) 9/06, which says that overpayments for failure to disclose are recoverable because of a breach of duty by a claimant of reg 32 SS(C&P) Regs; CIS/1996/2006; CIS/2125/2006; *PA v SSWP (DLA)* [2016] UKUT 428 (AAC)
79 R(IS) 5/03. This tribunal of commissioners' decision was intended to resolve the conflict between the earlier CIS/332/1993 and R(IS) 5/00, and preferred the latter.
80 *PA v SSWP (DLA)* [2016] UKUT 428 (AAC)
81 CA/1014/1999; CSDLA/1282/2001
82 *Secretary of State for Social Services v Solly* [1974] 3 All ER 922; R(SB) 21/82
83 CIS/1423/1997
84 *PA v SSWP (DLA)* [2016] UKUT 428 (AAC)
85 *MC v SSWP (IS)* [2015] UKUT 600 (AAC)
86 DWP, *Benefit Overpayment Recovery Guide*, Chapter 4, available at gov.uk/government/uploads/system/uploads/attachment_data/file/616116/benefit-overpayment-recovery-guide.pdf

4. Recovery of overpaid benefit

87 gov.uk/government/publications/what-happens-if-you-are-overpaid-universal-credit-jobseekers-allowance-or-employment-and-support-allowance. At the time of writing, this guidance remains withdrawn.

88 When the Welfare Reform Bill (which introduced these rules) was being debated, the minister said it was the intention not to recover many overpayments which had been caused by official error – see House of Commons, *Hansard*, 19 May 2011, col 1019

89 DWP, *Benefit Overpayment Recovery Guide*, available at gov.uk

90 Reg 10 SS(OR) Regs

91 Reg 16(7A) and (7B) SS(PAOR) Regs

92 Reg 11 SS(OR) Regs

93 The 30 per cent rate is provided for in guidance

94 Reg 11(7) SS(OR) Regs

95 Reg 11(8) SS(OR) Regs

96 Reg 11(9) SS(OR) Regs

97 Reg 12 SS(OR) Regs

98 Reg 13 SS(OR) Regs

99 Reg 14 SS(OR) Regs. The maximum recoverable weekly amounts stated in this rule are calculated as percentages of a monthly figure of UC. It is assumed that these are converted to weekly figures.

100 Reg 29A SS(PAOR) Regs

101 s71ZE SSAA 1992

102 Reg 42A CB&GA(Admin) Regs

103 Reg 16(1) and (2) SS(PAOR) Regs

104 Regs 15 and 16 SS(PAOR) Regs

105 Reg 17 SS(PAOR) Regs

106 Reg 16(3) SS(PAOR) Regs

107 s74(2)(b) SSAA 1992

108 Reg 16(4), (4A), (5) and (6) SS(PAOR) Regs

109 Reg 16(6) SS(PAOR) Regs

110 Reg 16(5A) SS(PAOR) Regs

111 Reg 16(7A) and (7B) SS(PAOR) Regs

112 Reg 18 SS(OR) Regs

113 Reg 19 SS(OR) Regs

114 Reg 23 SS(OR) Regs

115 Reg 30 SS(OR) Regs

116 Reg 21 SS(OR) Regs

117 Reg 20(3) SS(OR) Regs

118 Reg 20(3A)-(3B) SS(OR) Regs

119 Regs 17(1) and 20(7) SS(OR) Regs

120 Reg 29 SS(OR) Regs

121 Reg 25 SS(OR) Regs

122 s71(10) SSAA 1992

123 s9(1) Limitation Act 1980

124 DWP, *Benefit Overpayment Recovery Guide*, based on the provisions of the Prescription and Limitation (Scotland) Act 1973, available at gov.uk

125 *CPAG v SSWP* [2010] UKSC 54, upholding the decision of the Court of Appeal in *CPAG, R (on the application of) v SSWP* [2009] EWCA Civ 1058

5. Overpayments of housing benefit

126 Reg 99 HB Regs; reg 80 HB(SPC) Regs

127 Reg 99 HB Regs; reg 80 HB(SPC) Regs

128 Reg 93(3) HB Regs; reg 74(3) HB(SPC) Regs

129 Reg 100(4) HB Regs; reg 81(4) HB(SPC) Regs

130 Reg 100(2) HB Regs; reg 81(2) HB(SPC) Regs

131 *Duggan v CAO* [1989] (CA); *R on the application of Sier v Cambridge CC* [2001] EWCA Civ 1523; CH/571/2003; CH/3761/2005

132 Reg 100(3) HB Regs; reg 81(3) HB(SPC) Regs

133 HB/CTB Circular A23/2009

134 *MB v Christchurch BC (HB)* [2014] UKUT 201 (AAC), reported as [2014] AACR 39

135 CH/2567/2007; HB/CTB Circular A15/2009

136 CH/571/2003; CH/5485/2002

137 CH/939/2004; see also *R on the application of Sier v Cambridge CC* [2001] EWCA Civ 1523; CH/3761/2005

138 *R on the application of Sier v Cambridge CC* [2001] EWCA Civ 1523

139 *Warwick DC v Freeman* [1994] 27 HLR 616 (CA); CH/4918/2003

140 *R v Liverpool City Council ex parte Griffiths* [1990] 22 HLR 312; CH/2554/2002; CH/2567/2007

141 Reg 104 HB Regs; reg 85 HB(SPC) Regs; *Adan v London Borough of Hounslow and SSWP* [2004] EWCA Civ 101, reported as R(H) 5/04; CH/4943/2001; HB/CTB Circular A13/2006; *JM v London Borough of Tower Hamlets* [2015] UKUT 460 (AAC)

142 Reg 104(1) HB Regs; reg 85 HB(SPC) Regs

143 *R v Kensington and Chelsea RBC ex parte Brandt* [1995] 28 HLR 528 (QBD), at 537

144 Reg 104(3) HB Regs; reg 85(3) HB(SPC) Regs

145 Reg 103 HB Regs; reg 84 HB(SPC) Regs

146 Reg 103(1)(a) and (b) HB Regs; reg 84(1)(a) and (b) HB(SPC) Regs

147 s75(3)(a) SSAA 1992

148 Reg 101(2) HB Regs; reg 82(2) HB(SPC)
Regs
149 Reg 102(1ZA) HB Regs; reg 83(1ZA)
HB(SPC) Regs
150 R(H) 6/06
151 DWP, *Housing Benefit Overpayments
Guide,* paras 4.43(k) and 4.210-4.289,
available at gov.uk
152 s75(1) SSAA 1992
153 Reg 102 HB Regs; reg 83 HB(SPC) Regs;
s75 SSAA 1992
154 Reg 104A HB Regs; reg 85A HB(SPC)
Regs
155 Reg 102(1ZA) HB Regs; reg 83(1ZA)
HB(SPC) Regs
156 s75(5)(a) SSAA 1992; reg 106 HB Regs;
reg 87 HB(SPC) Regs
157 s75(5)(b) SSAA 1992; reg 106 HB Regs;
reg 87 HB(SPC) Regs
158 s75(5)(c) SSAA 1992; reg 106 HB Regs;
reg 87 HB(SPC) Regs
159 Reg 102 HB Regs; reg 83 HB(SPC) Regs;
HB/CTB Circular A42/00
160 Reg 102(4) HB Regs; reg 83(4) HB(SPC)
Regs
161 Reg 102(5) HB Regs; reg 83(5) HB(SPC)
Regs
162 Reg 105(1)(a) HB Regs
163 s75(5)(a) SSAA 1992; reg 106 HB Regs;
reg 87 HB(SPC) Regs
164 Regs 102 and 105 HB Regs; regs 83 and
86 HB(SPC) Regs
165 *R v Haringey LBC ex parte Azad Ayub*
[1992] 25 HLR 566 (QBD)
166 DWP, *Housing Benefit Overpayments
Guide,* para 4.90
167 Reg 106A HB Regs; reg 87A HB(SPC)
Regs; *LA Welfare Direct Bulletin* 9/2019
168 *Warwick DC v Freeman* [1994] 27 HLR
616 (CA)
169 *Warwick DC v Freeman* [1994] 27 HLR
616 (CA)
170 *Plymouth CC v Gigg* [1997] 30 HLR 284
(CA)
171 s75(7) SSAA 1992
172 s9(1) Limitation Act 1980
173 DWP, *Benefit Overpayment Recovery
Guide,* based on the provisions of the
Prescription and Limitation (Scotland)
Act 1973, available at gov.uk
174 Reg 90(1)(b) HB Regs; reg 71(1)(b)
HB(SPC) Regs
175 Sch 9 paras 2, 3, 6 and 15 HB Regs; Sch
8 paras 2, 3, 6 and 15 HB(SPC) Regs;
para A7.222 GM
176 Sch 9 para 15(2) HB Regs; Sch 8 para
15(2) HB(SPC) Regs
177 HB/CTB Circular A13/2006

178 Reg 90(4) HB Regs; reg 71(4) HB(SPC)
Regs
179 *Haringey LBC v Awaritefe* [1999] 32 HLR
517 (CA)
180 CH/1395/2006
181 DWP, *Housing Benefit Overpayments
Guide,* Part 4, paras 4.240-4.242,
available at gov.uk
182 s75(6) SSAA 1992
183 s75(6) SSAA 1992; reg 107 HB Regs; reg
88 HB(SPC) Regs
184 Reg 107(3) HB Regs; reg 88(3) HB(SPC)
Regs
185 DWP, *Housing Benefit Overpayments
Guide,* Part 4, paras 4.240-4.242,
available at gov.uk

Chapter 54

Fraud and penalties

This chapter covers:
1. Civil penalties (p1268)
2. Investigating benefit claims (p1269)
3. Prosecution of offences (p1273)
4. Administrative penalties for benefit offences (p1275)
5. Sanctions for benefit offences (p1278)

This chapter covers the rules on fraud for benefits administered by the DWP, housing benefit, child benefit and guardian's allowance. For tax credits and fraud, see Chapter 65. For the rules on the Scottish social security benefits and fraud, see Chapter 76. This chapter does not cover the rules for statutory sick, maternity, adoption, paternity, shared parental and parental bereavement pay.

Key facts

- When you claim benefit, you must give correct and complete information to the DWP, HM Revenue and Customs or the local authority. You might commit an offence if you deliberately mislead the agency dealing with your claim.
- You must report changes in your circumstances that could affect your entitlement. You may commit an offence if you do not notify the relevant office of changes promptly.
- Even if you are not suspected of an offence, you may get a fine (known as a 'civil penalty') if you provide incorrect information and you are considered to have acted negligently, or if you have not notified a change of circumstances promptly and do not have a reasonable excuse.
- If it is believed that you have committed fraud, you may be prosecuted. Alternatively, you may be given the option of paying an administrative penalty. Your benefit could be suspended or you could be given a sanction, even if you are not prosecuted.
- If you are suspected or accused of fraud, get advice before taking any action or making any statements.

Part 8: Claiming benefits and getting paid
Chapter 54: Fraud and penalties
1. Civil penalties

1. Civil penalties

You can be given a civil penalty if you or someone acting on your behalf have acted carelessly in relation to your claim but are not considered to have committed fraud.

Civil penalties are different from the 'administrative penalties' imposed for benefit offences (see p1275). You cannot be given a civil penalty if you have been charged in connection with, or accepted a formal caution for, the same benefit offence, or have received a notice about an administrative penalty for that offence.

A civil penalty of £50 may be given if:[1]

- you 'negligently' make an incorrect statement or representation, or negligently give incorrect information or evidence, about a claim for, or an award of, a benefit, and you do not take 'reasonable steps' to correct the error; *or*
- you do not provide information or evidence, or you fail to notify a 'relevant change of circumstances', and you do not have a 'reasonable excuse'; *and*
- your negligence or failure results in your being overpaid benefit of more than £65.[2] The overpayment period must start on or after 1 October 2012.

Definitions

A **'relevant change of circumstances'** is one that affects entitlement to benefit.[3]

'Reasonable excuse' means something that would have caused a reasonable person of a similar age and experience to act as you did.[4] Your state of health and the information which you received or might have obtained may be relevant, as may any advice you have received.[5]

Other terms used are not defined in the legislation but the DWP has produced guidance on the meaning of the following.[6]

'Negligently' is acting carelessly, not paying attention to, or disregarding the importance of, anything that needs to be done in relation to your claim. It is more than a simple mistake.

'Reasonable steps' is doing something which is sensible or practicable to correct an error.

The penalty is added to the overpayment and recovered in the same way (see p1250).[7] If you are claiming jointly with your partner and the penalty is for negligently making or giving incorrect statements, representations, information or evidence, it can be recovered from your partner instead of you, unless s/he was not (and could not reasonably be expected to be) aware of the error.

You can appeal against the imposition of a civil penalty (see Chapter 57)[8] – eg, you can argue that you did not behave negligently or that you had a 'reasonable excuse' for not declaring a change in your circumstances. **Note:** you may also want to consider appealing the overpayment decision (see Chapter 53).

2. Investigating benefit claims

Investigation of suspected benefit fraud covered by this chapter is carried out by the DWP's Counter Fraud and Compliance Directorate. It does not have to tell you straight away about any enquiries it is making. It usually waits until it has collected more information and then asks you to attend an interview.

Collecting information

There are special rules allowing the release of information to the DWP from:
- HM Revenue and Customs (HMRC);[9]
- government departments – eg, on issues about passports, immigration, emigration, nationality and prisoners;[10]
- the Registration Service – eg, about age, death, marriage and civil partnership;[11]
- local authorities.[12]

Local authorities may also be supplied with information held by the DWP or HMRC, and may share information with other local authorities.[13]

Local authorities, HMRC and the DWP can require information about redirected post and have undelivered social security post returned to them.[14]

All information acquired is confidential to the bodies concerned with the administration of benefit, including private companies contracted to carry out such functions. Unauthorised disclosure of this information is a criminal offence.[15]

Are you unhappy about the use of your personal information?
The Data Protection Act 2018 restricts the use of personal data held about you. If a local authority, the DWP or HMRC makes a request for information which you think is inappropriate or unreasonable, refer the matter to the Information Commissioner (see ico.org.uk).

Powers of investigation

As 'authorised officers', fraud investigators have certain powers to obtain information.[16] **'Authorised officers'** can be:
- officials of any government department (not just the DWP);
- employees of local authorities carrying out housing benefit (HB) functions; *or*
- employees of organisations that perform contracted-out HB functions.

Authorised officers should use a code of practice when obtaining information.[17] Information that is the subject of 'legal privilege' (ie, confidential communication between a legal adviser and her/his client) cannot be requested.[18]

Part 8: Claiming benefits and getting paid
Chapter 54: Fraud and penalties
2. Investigating benefit claims

Authorised officers have powers to enter, at a reasonable time, premises which they have reasonable grounds for suspecting are:[19]
- a person's place of employment;
- where a trade or business is carried out or documents relating to it are kept;
- where a personal or occupational pension scheme is administered or documents relating to it are kept;
- where someone operating a compensatory scheme for an industrial accident or disease may be found;
- where a person on whose behalf a compensatory payment for an industrial accident or disease has been made may be found.

The above may include someone's home. The authorised officer must show a certificate of appointment if asked for it. S/he can question anyone on the premises and require, if reasonable, any documents or copies of documents.

Authorised officers cannot come into your home without your permission (except if you run a business from your home) and they cannot detain you. They cannot make you give information or answer questions in such a way as to confess that you, or your partner, are guilty of an offence.[20]

Authorised officers may access certain electronic records, including those kept by:[21]
- any bank or person whose business is providing credit to the public – eg, credit card companies and building societies;
- the Director of National Savings;
- any insurer;
- any credit reference agency;
- any money transfer service;
- any ultilities company;
- any telephone company;
- any educational institution;
- the Student Loans Company.

All fraud investigators can use surveillance to investigate social security fraud – eg, observing people entering or leaving premises. Any surveillance must be authorised by an officer of the appropriate level.

Fraud investigators in England and Wales are bound by codes of practice under the Police and Criminal Evidence Act 1984.[22] In Scotland, fraud investigators must work to the common law principle of the 'test of fairness'. If these are breached, this may restrict the use of evidence they have obtained.[23] If you think the officers have acted unfairly, get advice.

Interviews under caution

If you are suspected of fraud, fraud investigators should carry out a formal interview, known as an 'interview under caution'. You should receive reasonable advance notification in writing (uploaded to your journal if you are claiming UC) of around 10 to 15 days informing you specifically that you must attend an interview under caution. You may receive a reminder telephone call before the interview confirming your attendance and to check whether any special arrangements are needed.[24] Note that an interview under caution is not the same as other types of interviews conducted by the DWP such as 'compliance interviews' which are not fraud related.

You should always be cautioned before the interview. If the fraud officer fails to do so, the interview may not be admissible in court. If you do not understand the caution, its meaning should be explained to you. If you appear unable to understand the significance of the interview or the questions being put to you (eg, due to incapacity or a learning disability), you should be asked if you want someone to assist or attend with you (such as a relative, other 'appropriate adult' or solicitor) and the interview may be suspended if you do.[25]

You do not have to answer any questions put to you, but if you do not answer questions, this might be taken as a sign of guilt. If you decide not to answer questions, you could instead prepare a written statement to give to the investigators.

You might not be told why the interview is happening. If you have not been informed of the purpose of the interview, it may be inadmissible as evidence in court.

The interview is normally recorded and you can request a copy. A transcript is produced for use at any trial or appeal hearing.

If you have extra travel costs to attend the interview, these should be reimbursed. If you need someone to accompany you because you are vulnerable (eg, you are under 18, have a learning disability or other complex needs), her/his travel expenses can also be reimbursed.

Are you suspected of fraud?

1. If you think fraud officers may interview you, get advice before you attend the interview. Free legal advice may be available from a solicitor.

2. Take someone (eg, a solicitor, adviser or friend) to the interview with you. Although s/he cannot speak for you, s/he can support you and take notes. A solicitor is also allowed to advise you during the interview, ask for clarification of questions and challenge improper questioning.

3. Try to remain calm and listen carefully to the questions you are asked. If you do not understand anything, ask for clarification. You must answer the questions yourself. Think carefully about the implications of the answers you give.

4. If you think you can explain why the situation has arisen, you should mention it at the interview, as any explanation you give later is less likely to be believed if you are prosecuted.[26] If you can explain matters, your benefit is less likely to be taken away.

5. Do not confess to something that you did not do just to finish the interview or to prevent your benefit from being stopped.

Part 8: Claiming benefits and getting paid
Chapter 54: Fraud and penalties
2. Investigating benefit claims

6. Consider making a complaint (see Chapter 60) if you feel the interview was not conducted fairly or you were treated in a way which failed to take into account issues such as disability.

The effect of a fraud investigation on your benefit

If the DWP, HMRC or local authority have doubts about your entitlement to benefit, other procedures may also be applied at the same time as a fraud investigation.

- In some circumstances, your benefit may be suspended (see p1200) – eg, if there are doubts about your entitlement or if there is a possibility that you are being overpaid.
- You may be asked to provide additional information and evidence. If you do not do so within a specified time limit, your award can be terminated (see p1202). If you still believe that you are entitled to benefit, make a new claim.

If a fraud investigation is taking a long time to complete, your benefit may be suspended for a long time. However, the DWP, HMRC or local authority should not withhold your benefit indefinitely without making a decision on whether or not you are entitled to it. Complain if you think an investigation is taking too long (see Chapter 60). If that brings no results, seek legal advice about forcing the DWP, HMRC or local authority to make a decision (see p1446).

The decision on whether you should be prosecuted is separate from a decision to recover any overpayment of benefit (see Chapter 53). The two processes are independent and have different tests. Therefore:

- a decision or appeal on your claim does not have to be delayed while you wait for the outcome of a criminal prosecution;[27]
- a court fine does not prevent recovery of an overpayment. However, if you have to make payments under a compensation order made by a court to the DWP, HMRC or local authority, it cannot also recover that amount as an overpayment.[28]

Acquittal in a fraud case does not necessarily mean that the decision on your benefit entitlement was wrong. Whatever the result of an investigation or prosecution, it may take longer to assess your future claims because your circumstances may be checked more thoroughly. Complain if it takes too long (see Chapter 60). You should not be prevented from making a fresh claim during a fraud investigation if your circumstances change. You can also apply for an advance payment (see p1192) or help from a local welfare assistance scheme (see p861).

3. **Prosecution of offences**

Benefit offences can broadly be divided into two categories, based on the severity of the penalty you can be given.

- Making false representations in order to claim benefit is the less serious of the benefit offences (see below).
- Making dishonest representations in order to claim benefit is the more serious benefit offence (see p1274).

In the most serious cases in England and Wales, you may be charged with the criminal offences of theft or fraud, and in Scotland, with common law offences, instead.[29] These offences carry more severe penalties.

If found guilty, you can be fined or imprisoned, or both. Any fine that you have to pay is in addition to any recoverable overpayment (see Chapter 53). You can also be given a sanction for a period (see p1278).

In England and Wales, DWP and HM Revenue and Customs (HMRC) prosecutions are carried out by the Crown Prosecution Service, which also conducts prosecutions on behalf of many local authorities. In Scotland, prosecutions are conducted by the Crown Office and Procurator Fiscal Service.

False representations

You commit the offence of making false representations if you:[30]
- make a statement which you know to be false or give information or produce documents that you know to be false (or knowingly cause or allow someone else to do so) in order to claim a benefit or payment for yourself or someone else, or for any other purpose relating to the benefit rules. It does not have to be shown that you intended to obtain benefit to which you were not entitled;[31] *or*
- fail to notify the DWP, HMRC or local authority promptly of a change of circumstances which you know affects your entitlement to benefit or another payment. This also applies to appointees and other third parties receiving benefit on your behalf, and landlords receiving direct payments of housing benefit. You count as notifying a change promptly if you do so as soon as reasonably practicable after the change occurs; *or*
- cause or allow another person to fail to notify a change of circumstances to the DWP, HMRC or local authority promptly which you know affects her/his entitlement to benefit or other payment.

For an offence to have been committed, you must have acted 'knowingly'. You do not 'know' something if you are merely careless about whether or not something is true, or if you fail to find out.[32] You have not committed an offence if you do not notify a change of circumstances that did not affect your entitlement to

Part 8: Claiming benefits and getting paid
Chapter 54: Fraud and penalties
3. Prosecution of offences

benefit or if there was already no entitlement to benefit.[33] To have acted 'knowingly', you must have been made aware of where any change must be reported and the manner in which it must be reported.[34]

The maximum penalty for these offences is a £5,000 fine or three months in prison, or both.[35]

Duty to report a change in circumstances

The rules on fraud and your duty to report a change of circumstances are different to those outlined on p1199. For fraud purposes, you only commit an offence if you do not report promptly a change that you *know* affects your benefit. However, to avoid potential allegations of fraud or prosecution, you should report *all* changes promptly. It is always advisable to report the change in a way that allows you to show that you have done so – eg, if in writing, date and retain a copy or get a receipt, keep records of telephone calls and take screenshots if reporting online. For more information about reporting changes of circumstances, see p1199.

Duties of advisers and other third parties

If you are an adviser, you are not under a duty to notify the DWP, HMRC or local authority about a claimant's change of circumstances, provided you have fully advised her/him of the law and her/his requirement to notify changes in her/his circumstances and provide truthful information. In order to commit an offence of allowing or causing someone to fail to notify a change of circumstances, or knowingly allowing or causing someone to give false information, there must be some sort of implied permission given to the person to not report the change or to give false information.[36] You do not 'allow' someone to do something unless you can stop them doing it.[37] You should do nothing to help facilitate a misrepresentation or failure to notify a change of circumstances – eg, help to complete a claim or review form which you know is inaccurate. If you – as an adviser – know that a claimant is being overpaid, you should make sure you advise her/him of her/his duty to notify the relevant benefit authority of the overpayment and you should do nothing that facilitates the overpayment continuing.

Dishonest representations

You commit the offence of making dishonest representations if you make any of the false representations on p1273 in order to claim benefit and you act dishonestly ('knowingly' in Scotland) in doing so.[38] This means that you did something that most people would consider dishonest and that you must have known it was dishonest.[39]

The maximum penalty if you are convicted in a magistrates' court (sheriff court in Scotland) is a £5,000 fine or six months in prison (12 months in Scotland[40]), or both. If you are convicted in the Crown Court (High Court in

Scotland), you can receive an unlimited fine or up to seven years in prison, or both.[41]

Prosecutions

Not all cases in which there is evidence to justify a prosecution are taken to court. Instead, you may be given the chance to pay an 'administrative penalty' (see p1276). In some cases, no action is taken at all. The factors taken into account include the strength of the evidence, the amount of benefit involved, whether an offence was planned and your personal circumstances. The decision about whether or not to prosecute is normally taken by the Crown Prosecution Service or Crown Office and Procurator Fiscal Service, who, in exceptional cases, can recommend an 'administrative caution' instead.[42] **Note:** you may be given a sanction, even if you are not prosecuted (see p1278).

There are time limits for bringing a prosecution for making false representations in order to claim benefit (see p1273). A prosecution must be started either within three months of the date the DWP, HMRC or local authority (or, in Scotland, the Crown Office and Procurator Fiscal Service) thinks it has sufficient evidence to prosecute you, or within 12 months of the date you committed the offence, whichever is later.[43]

There are no time limits for bringing a prosecution for making dishonest representations in order to claim benefit.

Are you being prosecuted?

If you are being prosecuted, get advice. You may be entitled to free legal help from a solicitor and representation in court. Check carefully that the Counter Fraud and Compliance Directorate is able to prove all the parts of the offence with which you are charged. Do not plead guilty until you have obtained advice. You should also get specialist welfare rights advice about challenging any overpayment decision and whether it is recoverable separately, as the solicitor helping with any fraud allegations may not be a welfare rights specialist.

4. Administrative penalties for benefit offences

The Counter Fraud and Compliance Directorate (CFCD) may offer you the option of paying an administrative penalty under civil law instead of being prosecuted for a benefit offence under criminal law. These administrative penalties are not the same as the civil penalties described on p1268. You can still be sanctioned if you accept an administrative penalty (see p1278).

Part 8: Claiming benefits and getting paid
Chapter 54: Fraud and penalties
4. Administrative penalties for benefit offences

The amount of the penalty depends on when the offence was committed.

- For offences committed wholly after 7 May 2012, the penalty is 50 per cent of any amount overpaid, subject to a minimum of £350 even if you were not actually overpaid, and:[44]
  - a maximum of £2,000 if committed partly or wholly before 1 April 2015; *or*
  - a maximum of £5,000 if committed wholly after 31 March 2015.
- For offences committed partly or wholly before 8 May 2012, the amount of the penalty is 30 per cent of the overpayment.

The overpayment must have been caused by an offence you committed on or after 18 December 1997.[45]

The penalty is added to any overpayment of benefit and is recoverable in the same way (see p1250 and p1257).[46]

Note: the DWP no longer offers cautions for offences committed wholly or partly after 1 April 2012. Penalties may be offered instead.[47] For more details about DWP cautions, see the 2012/13 edition of this *Handbook*. However, an 'administrative caution' may still be recommended by the Crown Prosecution Service or Crown Office and Procurator Fiscal Service as an alternative to prosecution.

The option of paying a penalty

You can be offered the option of paying a penalty if:[48]

- an overpayment has been found to be recoverable from you, or, for offences committed wholly after 7 May 2012, would have been if an award had been made. The DWP, HMRC or local authority must have revised or superseded your award of benefit and issued a decision that any overpayment is recoverable (see Chapter 53); *and*
- the overpayment was due to an act or omission on your part. This must have occurred on or after 18 December 1997;[49] *and*
- there are grounds for prosecuting you for an offence relating to the overpayment.

The CFCD issues you with a notice setting out how the scheme works, how to agree to pay a penalty and how to withdraw your agreement.[50] If you are not issued with a proper notice, it may not be possible to enforce the penalty.

The notice is sent with an invitation to an interview to discuss accepting the penalty. The interview is only about whether to offer you a penalty. The interview should not be carried out by an officer who was present during the interview under caution (see p1270).[51] You cannot use it to add to or alter any statement you made about the alleged offence in an interview under caution. If you are unable to decide whether or not to accept the penalty at the interview, you can ask for up to five days to make up your mind provided the DWP considers the request reasonable in your circumstances.[52]

What happens if you accept a penalty?[53]

1. If you agree to pay a penalty, you cannot be prosecuted for any offence relating to the overpayment. However, you can still be prosecuted in the future if you commit another offence or one relating to a different overpayment.

2. If it is found on revision, supersession or appeal that the overpayment is *not due or not recoverable*, any penalty you have paid must be repaid to you. This does not change the fact that you have agreed to pay a penalty in exchange for immunity from prosecution, so you still cannot be prosecuted for the offence.

3. If *the amount of the overpayment is changed* following a revision, supersession or appeal, the agreement is cancelled, so you lose your immunity from prosecution, and any penalty you have paid must be repaid to you. However, if you make a fresh agreement to accept a penalty, you are again immune from prosecution and the amount of penalty you have already paid can be offset against the new penalty rather than being repaid to you.

If you do not accept the penalty, the CFCD *may* pass the case to the Crown Prosecution Service or Crown Office and Procurator Fiscal Service to consider whether to prosecute you.

Changing your mind

If you agree to pay a penalty, you can change your mind, provided you notify the CFCD within 14 days (28 days for offences committed partly or wholly before 8 May 2012) in the manner it specifies.[54] If you change your mind after the end of this period, there is no right of appeal against the imposition of the penalty, but you can complain (see Chapter 60) if you think you should not have been offered a penalty – eg, if it turns out there was insufficient evidence to prosecute you. Note that if any overpayment is later found not to be due or recoverable, any penalty you have already paid must be repaid to you but you remain immune from prosecution for the same offence. If you decide not to accept the penalty, you lose your immunity from prosecution. If you have already paid any part of it, this must be refunded to you.

Should you agree to pay a penalty?

1. Get advice and consider your options carefully.

2. If you are not prosecuted, your case does not go to court and you cannot get a prison sentence.

3. If you accept a penalty, you may still be given a sanction (see p1278).

4. You may be invited to pay a penalty when there is insufficient evidence to prosecute you. The fraud officer can only recommend that your case be considered for prosecution. The Crown Prosecution Service, Crown Office and Procurator Fiscal Service or local authority legal department decides whether or not to prosecute (see p1273). You are not automatically prosecuted if you refuse to accept a penalty.

Part 8: Claiming benefits and getting paid
Chapter 54: Fraud and penalties
5. Sanctions for benefit offences

5. If you are prosecuted and found guilty, the court might offer you a caution or community service rather than a fine. On the other hand, you could get a large fine or even a prison sentence.

6. A penalty may be a substantial amount of money. For minor offences, the amount of a fine imposed by the court could be less.

---

5. Sanctions for benefit offences

If you get certain benefits, known as 'sanctionable benefits' (see p1279), you can be sanctioned if:[55]

- you are convicted of one or more benefit offences in a set of proceedings; *or*
- you agree to pay an administrative penalty for a benefit offence instead of being prosecuted (see p1275).

If you are sanctioned, your benefit is usually not paid or sometimes paid at a reduced rate (see p1279).

Note: these sanctions are different to those imposed for failing to comply with work-related requirements described in Chapters 47 and 49.

Under what is sometimes referred to as the 'one-strike rule' (because it can apply after just one offence), a conviction is not always required as your benefit can be sanctioned by just agreeing to pay an administrative penalty for an offence.

If you are convicted of a benefit offence and have already committed an earlier offence(s), a longer sanction may be imposed under the 'two-strikes rule' instead. This applies if:[56]

- you are convicted of one or more benefit offences in the current set of proceedings; *and*
- within five years of the date you *committed* any of the current offences, you committed an earlier benefit offence, including an offence for which you accepted an administrative penalty or caution; *and*
- the current offence has not been previously treated as a current offence, and the earlier offence has not been previously treated as an earlier offence, under the two-strikes rule in relation to a reduction of your benefits, a joint claim for jobseeker's allowance (JSA) or a family member's benefit under these sanction rules.

The benefit offence(s) must have been committed after 1 April 2010 (for the one-strike rule) or on or after 1 April 2002 (for the two-strikes rule) and be:[57]

- in connection with a 'disqualifying' benefit; *or*
- to attempt, conspire or aid the committing of a benefit offence.

Disqualifying benefits [58]

All social security benefits and tax credits are **'disqualifying benefits'** for the purposes listed above, except statutory sick pay, statutory maternity pay, statutory adoption pay, statutory paternity pay and maternity allowance.

See below for details of the sanctions that can be applied.

Sanctionable benefits

'Sanctionable benefits' are :[59]
- universal credit (UC);
- employment and support allowance (ESA);
- housing benefit (HB);
- income support (IS);
- JSA (joint-claim JSA is not a 'sanctionable benefit' but can still be removed or reduced);[60]
- pension credit (PC);
- bereavement benefits (except bereavement support payment);
- carer's allowance;
- industrial injuries benefits (except constant attendance and exceptionally severe disablement allowances);
- war pensions (except constant attendance allowance, exceptionally severe disablement allowance and mobility supplement).

Under separate rules, you lose your working tax credit (WTC) if you have committed a benefit offence on or after 5 April 2012 (see p1281).

Payment of any other benefits cannot, therefore, be stopped or reduced under these rules.

The sanctions

Usually, sanctionable benefits are not paid during a sanction period (see p1280). In some cases, however, your benefit may be paid at a reduced rate.
- UC is usually reduced by the rate of your UC standard allowance calculated on a daily basis. This is the same amount as when a sanction for failing to meet your work-related requirements applies (see p1089).[61] However, the 'low rate' only applies if you are subject to no work-related requirements because you are a responsible carer or foster parent for a child under the age of one, an adopter or are pregnant, and the 'high rate' still applies if you are subject to no work-related requirements only because you have been found to have limited capability for work and work-related activity. Only half of the applicable rate is applied to individual joint claimants.

Part 8: Claiming benefits and getting paid
Chapter 54: Fraud and penalties
5. Sanctions for benefit offences

If your UC is reduced, you may be able to get hardship payments in the same way as when you are sanctioned for not meeting your claimant responsibilities, except that 16/17-year-olds *can* get hardship payments in these circumstances (see p1219).[62]

- **IS, income-based JSA, joint-claim JSA, PC and HB** are usually reduced by 40 per cent of the appropriate personal allowance for a single person of your age (see p334), or 20 per cent if you or a member of your family are pregnant or seriously ill.[63] However:
  - if you are a member of a joint-claim JSA couple (see p253), one of you is sanctioned for a benefit offence and the other is not subject to *any* type of sanction (including the sanctions described in Chapter 49), JSA is paid at the rate of:[64]
    - contribution-based JSA, if the person who has not been sanctioned qualifies for it; *or*
    - hardship payments, if you and your partner qualify (see p1224);[65] *or*
    - in any other case, income-based JSA calculated as if the partner who has not been sanctioned were a single person. However, any income or capital of either of you is taken into account;
  - if you are a member of a joint-claim JSA couple, one or both of you are sanctioned for a benefit offence and either both of you are also sanctioned under the rules described in Chapter 49 or one of you would qualify for IS, JSA is not paid. However, you may still qualify for hardship payments under the rules described on p1224;[66]
  - if you are claiming income-based JSA in any circumstances other than those of a joint-claim couple as described in the bullet points above, you are not paid at the reduced rate unless you qualify under rules which are the same as those that apply for JSA hardship payments as described on p1224.[67] If you are also sanctioned under the rules described in Chapter 49, you do not qualify for a reduced rate of JSA under these rules but can still qualify under the rules in Chapter 52;
  - HB is unaffected if you or a member of your family are entitled to IS, income-based JSA, income-related ESA or PC during the sanction period.[68]
- **Income-related ESA** is reduced by 100 per cent of the appropriate personal allowance for a single person of your age (see p333), or 40 per cent if you or a member of your family are subject to no work-related requirements, or 20 per cent if you or a member of your family are pregnant or seriously ill.[69] You may be able to get hardship payments if your income-related ESA is reduced in this way (see p1225).

The sanction period

The sanction period under the one-strike rule (see above) is **three years** if:[70]

- you are convicted for serious fraud or conspiracy to defraud; *or*
- the overpayment is at least £50,000; *or*

- you are given a sentence of at least a year; *or*
- the offence is committed over a period of at least two years.

The sanction period under the one-strike rule is **13 weeks** if you are convicted in less serious cases and **four weeks** if you pay an administrative penalty (see p1275).[71]

Sanction periods under the two-strikes rule are **26 weeks** (except for serious fraud, for which the sanction period is three years) or **three years** if the earlier offence is within five years of a previous one.[72]

The sanction period starts at least 28 days after the determination that a restriction on payment of benefits should apply.[73]

Note: sanctions under these rules prevent payment of a benefit during the sanction period, not entitlement, which ensures the link between benefits and other entitlements (eg, free school lunches and free prescriptions) remains.[74] However, a minimal 10 pence a week entitlement to IS, PC and income-related ESA remains in place while you are sanctioned.[75]

Loss of working tax credit for a benefit offence

You are disqualified from being paid WTC for a set period of time if you have committed a benefit offence.[76] You do not need to have been convicted.

You are disqualified from WTC if:

- you commit a benefit offence concerning a 'disqualifying benefit' (see p1279) on or after 5 April 2012; *and*
- you would be entitled to WTC if it were not for this rule, either as a single person or as part of a joint claim. If you have a joint claim, but only one of you is disqualified from WTC, WTC remains payable, but the amount is reduced by 50 per cent.[77]

The 'one-strike' and 'two-strikes' rules and the definition of a sanctionable offence that apply to sanctionable benefits (see p1278) apply. The sanction periods are also the same (see p1279).

You are not disqualified from receiving child tax credit under this rule.

Part 8: Claiming benefits and getting paid
Chapter 54: Fraud and penalties
Notes

Notes

1. Civil penalties
1 ss115C-115D SSAA 1992; SS(CP) Regs
2 Vol 3 Ch 9, para 09420 DMG; Ch D1
  para D1271 ADM
3 s115D(6) SSAA 1992
4 *VT v SSWP (IS)* [2016] UKUT 178 (AAC),
  reported as [2016] AACR 42
5 *JP v SSWP* [2017] UKUT 505 (AAC)
6 Vol 3 Ch 9, paras 09425-29 and 09436-
  37 DMG; Ch D1 paras D1276-80 and
  D1287-88 ADM
7 Reg 15 SS(PAOR) Regs; reg 3 SS(OR)
  Regs
8 *VT v SSWP (IS)* [2016] UKUT 178 (AAC),
  reported as [2016] AACR 42

2. Investigating benefit claims
9 s127 WRA 2012
10 s122B SSAA 1992
11 ss124, 124A, 124B and 125 SSAA 1992
12 ss122D and 122E SSAA 1992
13 ss122C and 122E SSAA 1992
14 ss182A and 182B SSAA 1992
15 s123 and Sch 4 SSAA 1992
16 ss109A, 109B and 109C SSAA 1992
17 s3 SSFA 2001; DWP, *Code of Practice on
  Obtaining Information*, November 2016,
  available at gov.uk
18 s109B(5)(b) SSAA 1992
19 s109C SSAA 1992
20 ss109B(5) and 109C(6) SSAA 1992
21 ss109BA and 109B(2A) SSAA 1992
22 s67(9) PACEA 1984
23 s78(1) PACEA 1984; *DHSS v McKee*
  [1995] 6 *Bulletin of NI Law* 17 (NI Crown
  Court)
24 DWP, May 2019, *Fraud investigations:
  staff guide part 1*, p511, 'Planning the
  interview' available at gov.uk
25 DWP, May 2019, *Fraud investigations:
  staff guide part 1*, p521-22, paras 74-76
  available at gov.uk
26 s34 CJPOA 1994
27 *Mote v SSWP and Chichester District
  Council* [2007] EWCA Civ 1324,
  reported as R(IS) 4/08
28 CIS/683/1994; *KP v RB of Kensington and
  Chelsea* [2014] UKUT 393 (AAC)

3. Prosecution of offences
29 *Osinuga v Director of Public Prosecution*
  [1997] 30 HLR 853
30 s112(1)-(1F) SSAA 1992
31 *Clear v Smith* [1981] 1 WLR 399
32 *Taylor's Central Garages v Roper* [1951]
  115 JPR 445
33 *R v Passmore* [2007] EWCA Crim 2053; *R
  v Laku* [2008] EWCA Crim 1745
34 *Coventry City Council v Vassell* [2011]
  EWHC 1542 (Admin)
35 s112(2) SSAA 1992
36 *R v Chainey* [1914] 1 KB 137 at 142 (DC)
37 *R v Tilley* [2009] EWCA Crim 1426
38 s111A SSAA 1992
39 *R v Ghosh* [1982] EWCA Crim 2
40 s45 Criminal Proceedings etc (Reform)
  (Scotland) Act 2007
41 s111A(3) SSAA 1992
42 DWP, *Penalties Policy: in respect of social
  security fraud and error*, August 2017,
  para 4.5, available at gov.uk
43 s116(2), (2A) and (7) SSAA 1992;
  Bennett v SSWP [2012] EWHC 371
  (Admin)

4. Administrative penalties for benefit offences
44 s115A(3)-(3A) SSAA 1992
45 s25(7) SSA(F)A 1997; Art 2(1)(b)
  SSA(F)AO No.5
46 s115A(4)(a) SSAA 1992
47 DWP, *Penalties Policy: in respect of social
  security fraud and error*, August 2017,
  para 4.5.1, available at gov.uk
48 s115A(1)-(1A) SSAA 1992
49 s25(7) SSA(F)A 1997; Art 2(1)(b)
  SSA(F)AO No.5
50 s115A(2) SSAA 1992
51 DWP, *Fraud investigations: staff guide
  part 1*, p67, 'Officers who may issue the
  Administrative Penalty notice and
  interview people' para 6, May 2019,
  available at gov.uk
52 DWP, *Fraud investigations: staff guide
  part 1*, pp76-77, 'Additional time
  allowed to consider Administrative
  Penalty Offer advising the person of the
  conditions' paras 6-12, May 2019,
  available at gov.uk

53 s115A(4)(b), (6) and (7) SSAA 1992
54 s115A(5) SSAA 1992

5. Sanctions for benefit offences

55 s6B(1) SSFA 2001
56 s7(1) SSFA 2001
57 ss6B(13) and 7(8), definition of 'benefit offence', SSFA 2001
58 s6A(1), definition of 'disqualifying benefit', SSFA 2001; reg 19A, definition of 'disqualifying benefit', SS(LB) Regs
59 s6A(1), definition of 'sanctionable benefit', SSFA 2001; reg 19 SS(LB) Regs
60 s8 SSFA 2001
61 Reg 3ZB SS(LB) Regs
62 Regs 16D-16H SS(LB) Regs
63 ss6B, 7, 8 and 9 SSFA 2001; regs 3, 3A, 5-10, 17 and 18 SS(LB) Regs
64 Regs 4 and 11-13 SS(LB) Regs
65 Regs 11-16 SS(LB) Regs. These are hardship payments under the loss of benefit rules but the qualifying conditions are the same as those described in Chapter 52.
66 Reg 11(4) SS(LB) Regs excludes joint-claim JSA couples with both partners sanctioned under the rules described in Chapter 49, or if one is entitled to IS, from hardship payments under the loss of benefit rules, but this does not prevent them from qualifying under the hardship payment rules in Chapter 52.
67 ss7(2) and (4) and 8(2) and (4) SSFA 2001; regs 5-8 and 10 SS(LB) Regs
68 Reg 18 SS(LB) Regs
69 Reg 3ZA SS(LB) Regs
70 s6B(11A)(a) and (14) SSFA 2001
71 s6B(11A)(b) and (c) SSFA 2001
72 s7(6A) SSFA 2001
73 s6B(11) SSFA 2001; reg 1A SS(LB) Regs
74 s6B(4) and (5) SSFA 2001
75 Regs 3(2), 3ZA(4) and 3A(3) SS(LB) Regs
76 ss36A and 36B TCA 2002
77 Reg 3 The Loss of Tax Credits Regulations 2013, No.715

Part 9

Getting a benefit decision changed

Chapter 55

Decisions

This chapter covers:
1. When a decision must be made (below)
2. Decisions on claims (p1293)
3. Decisions on other issues (p1295)
4. Delays in getting a decision (p1295)
5. Information about decisions (p1296)

This chapter covers the rules for decisions about benefits (including housing benefit), the social fund payments in Chapter 37 (except budgeting loans) and decisions about DWP loans for mortgage interest (see p855). It does not cover the rules for Scottish social security benefits (see Chapter 76), statutory payments (see Chapter 59) or the health benefits in Chapter 31.

References in this chapter to HM Revenue and Customs (HMRC) only apply to decisions about child benefit and guardian's allowance. HMRC also makes decisions about tax credits. For the rules for tax credits, see Chapter 63.

Key facts
- The benefits system is a 'decision-based system'.
- Decisions are needed to create awards of benefit and set the amounts and dates of those awards.
- Decisions are also needed to decide if you have been overpaid.
- Decisions should be made within a reasonable time.
- You should be notified of decisions which carry a right of appeal.

1. When a decision must be made

A decision must be made about your entitlement when you submit a claim for benefit. However, there are additional situations where a decision must be made. This is because the benefits system is a 'decision-based system'. This means is that there must be a formal and identifiable decision on questions such as:
- whether, and when, a valid claim for benefit has been made;
- when a claim for benefit has been made, whether or not you are entitled to an award of that benefit;

Part 9: Getting a benefit decision changed
Chapter 55: Decisions
1. When a decision must be made

- the date from which your award should start;
- the amount you should be awarded;
- whether amounts to which you are entitled can be paid;
- whether you need to repay an overpayment.

Decisions are made by decision makers in the agency that deals with that particular benefit (see below). In order to make a decision, the decision maker must first determine the facts of your case and then establish which rules apply to someone in your situation (see below). This might involve deciding other issues as part of coming to a full decision. Sometimes, the decision maker is bound to accept the ruling of another body on a particular issue (see p1292). There can only ever be a single decision in respect of your entitlement to benefit on a particular day (see p1290). In making initial decisions, the decision maker must consider the situation at the time of her/his decision (see p1294).

Who makes decisions

Decisions about child benefit and guardian's allowance are made by officers of HM Revenue and Customs (HMRC). Decisions about housing benefit (HB) are made by officers at the local authority. Decisions about all other benefits are made by officers of the DWP in the name of the Secretary of State for Work and Pensions (the government minister responsible for the DWP). In this *Handbook*, we refer to these officers as 'decision makers'.

The DWP refers to personal independence payment (PIP) decision makers as 'case managers', although their role is the same.

Decisions about whether you have limited capability for work or are terminally ill for benefit purposes are made by the DWP, even if the main benefit decision is made by another authority – eg, the local authority.[1]

You may have to attend your local Jobcentre Plus office to discuss your jobseeking conditions or claimant responsibilities (see Chapters 46 and 48). In practice, the person you meet is extremely unlikely to be a decision maker, although s/he may make recommendations to the decision maker – eg, about whether you should be given a sanction.

How decisions are made

In order to make a decision about your benefit, a decision maker first needs to know the facts of your case. To do this, the decision maker should consider the evidence and decide whether it is more likely to be the situation than not.

A decision maker can take account what you say and accept that as evidence, even if you do not have other evidence confirming this is the case. If there is a range of evidence about a particular point which could lead to different conclusions, the decision maker has to weigh the evidence.

Once the decision maker has decided what facts the evidence establishes, s/he considers what the facts mean for your entitlement to benefit. S/he does this by looking at the benefit entitlement rules for someone in your situation.

It is helpful to think about a decision as made up of a number of building blocks (sometimes called 'determinations').[2] For example, a decision that you are not entitled to income support (IS) could be based on determinations that:

- you are responsible for a child aged under five;
- you are a member of a couple;
- you are not subject to immigration control;
- you satisfy the habitual residence test;
- you do not have too much income or capital.

These determinations do not themselves have legal force and affect your entitlement to IS until they are incorporated into an 'outcome decision' about whether or not you are entitled to IS. As your right to challenge a decision (see p1293) attaches to a decision and not a determination, if you disagree with the individual determinations, you can challenge them when they are incorporated into a decision which is notified to you.

Guidance used by decision makers

Decision Makers' Guide: staff guide: for DWP decision makers on all DWP benefits except those covered by the *Advice for Decision Making: staff guide.*[3]

Advice for Decision Making: staff guide: for DWP decision makers on universal credit (UC), PIP, contribution-based jobseeker's allowance (JSA) and contributory employment and support allowance (ESA) for people who come under the UC system.[4]

Universal Credit Guidance: operational guidance for DWP decision makers on all aspects of UC.[5]

Personal Independence Payment Assessment Guide: for assessment providers.[6] This comes in several parts and should be read with the assessment provider's guidance, where it exists.[7] See also the *Personal Independence Payment Handbook,* aimed at claimants and advisers.[8]

Work Capability Assessment Handbook: for healthcare professionals who carry out work capability assessments.[9]

Housing Benefit Guidance Manual.[10] See also housing benefit bulletins and urgent bulletins and the *Discretionary Housing Payment Guidance Manual.*[11] Local authorities also have their own guidance.

Decisions made with limited information

The decision maker can make a decision in certain circumstances, even if s/he is waiting for you to provide more evidence or information.

Part 9: Getting a benefit decision changed
Chapter 55: Decisions
1. When a decision must be made

A decision is always made on the basis that the evidence or information needed is adverse to you if:[12]

- for IS and JSA only, it is needed to decide:
  - whether you should be paid benefit (or less benefit) because you (or a member of your family) are involved in a trade dispute (see p1001). This does not apply to JSA if you come under the UC system (see p23); *or*
  - whether you are in relevant education (see p885);
- for IS, ESA, pension credit (PC) and social fund payments only, it is needed to decide whether you are entitled to a severe disability premium (additional amount for PC).

In both of these cases, if you request an 'any grounds' revision (see p1303) and provide the missing information, the decision can be revised to take account of it.

Special rules apply if, when you claim your retirement pension, you have not yet elected whether to take a lump sum or an increased pension (for state pension, this must be because your late partner deferred claiming her/his pension). The decision maker can choose whether or not to decide your claim immediately. If s/he does make a decision on your claim, for state pension s/he *may* revise it when you make the election, and for category A or B retirement pension, s/he *must* revise it when you make the election (see p1311).[13]

For PIP, if you are in a care home and evidence or information is required to decide whether the cost of your accommodation will be met from local or public funds, if the decision maker makes 'reasonable enquiries', s/he can make a decision on the evidence or information s/he has.[14]

For UC, if further evidence or information is needed to decide whether you qualify for a DWP loan to help with your mortgage interest (see p855), the decision maker has discretion to make a decision.[15] If you are entitled to IS, ESA or PC, the decision maker can also make a decision on the basis of the evidence or information s/he already has.[16]

In all of these cases, if you request an any grounds revision (see p1303) and provide the missing information, then the decision can be revised to take account of it.

Decisions are final

Decisions about benefits are final. This is important because it means that once a decision has been made about your entitlement to a particular benefit for a particular day, then there cannot be another decision about your entitlement on that day.[17] If this were not the case, there would be a question about which of the two decisions was the correct one.

Example

Example

Elke claims PIP on 10 June. Her claim is refused on 20 August. She appeals. While she is waiting for that appeal to be dealt with, she makes a new claim for PIP on 7 September. On 11 October, PIP is awarded at the standard rate starting from 7 September. When the tribunal comes to deal with Elke's appeal, it cannot award PIP for any date after 6 September as the decision on the second PIP claim is final. If Elke is not happy with the decision on her second claim, she must also challenge that decision.

This means that if you think there is something wrong with your entitlement to a particular benefit on a particular day, you need to get the decision which deals with that benefit for that day changed (see p1293). Similarly, it means that if a decision maker thinks there is something wrong with your entitlement on a particular day, s/he cannot simply make a completely new decision about this. Instead, s/he needs to change the decision that applies to that day.

If, in the course of making a particular decision, the decision maker has determined a particular fact is true (eg, that you were living with a partner on a particular date), the rule about decisions being final does not mean that particular fact has to be accepted for the purposes of other decisions (although in practice it is likely to be). It simply means that the outcome of the decision (ie, its effect on your entitlement to benefit) for that day is final.

Example

A decision maker decides you were not entitled to IS on a particular date because you had too much capital. It is possible for it later to be decided that no overpayment of IS for that day is recoverable from you because you did not in fact have the capital.[18]

Similarly, if the decision maker has decided a particular fact in respect of a particular period, then another decision maker, dealing with a different period, does not have to accept that fact is correct.[19]

There are, however, some exceptions to these rules where certain findings about facts made for one decision must be adopted in respect of other decisions.

- If in making a decision, the decision maker has determined that you have or do not have limited capability for work (or are treated as having or not having limited capability for work), then that finding about your limited capability for work (or lack or it) must also be applied in respect of any further decisions unless a new decision is made on this question.[20]
- A finding about the date of onset of an industrial disease made for industrial injuries benefits is conclusive for further decisions about industrial injuries benefits.[21]

Part 9: Getting a benefit decision changed
Chapter 55: Decisions
1. When a decision must be made

Decisions not made by decision maker who decides your benefit entitlement

There are some situations in which the decision maker who is making the decision about a benefit you have claimed, or for which you have an award, is not the one who decides a particular issue. These include:

- for HB, decisions about whether you have income or capital when you get IS, income-related ESA, income-based JSA, PC or UC (see below);
- for HB and tax credits, decisions about limited capability for work (see below);
- decisions about national insurance (NI) contributions (see below).

Housing benefit decisions on income and capital where you get certain benefits

If you get IS, income-related ESA, income-based JSA, PC (although not if you get the savings credit of PC only) or UC, all of your income and capital is ignored when calculating HB entitlement.[22]

The HB decision maker should not, therefore, consider your income or capital. There are two exceptions to this rule.

- If the decision maker has evidence about your income and capital that has not already been considered by the DWP decision maker which raises a doubt about whether your benefit award is correct, s/he may inform the DWP. The decision maker can suspend your HB while s/he waits to see if the DWP makes a new decision (see p1201).
- If the decision maker has strong and clear evidence you are fraudulently concealing evidence from the DWP about your income and capital, s/he can make her/his own decision on the issue.[23]

Decisions about limited capability for work

Only a DWP decision maker can decide whether you have limited capability for work, and her/his decision is binding for decision makers for other benefits and tax credits.[24]

Decisions about national insurance contributions

Certain questions about NI contributions and a person's employment are dealt with by a special procedure – eg:[25]

- whether you were an 'employed earner' for the purposes of paying contributions or entitlement to industrial injuries disablement benefit; or
- whether you were liable to pay a particular class of contributions or have paid contributions for a particular period; or
- the amount of contributions you were liable to pay.

These matters are referred to HMRC for a decision, which is then binding on the decision maker.[26] The decision maker can continue to deal with other aspects of your claim, but can defer making a decision on it. The decision maker should also refer matters to HMRC if s/he decides your claim on the basis of facts which do not appear to be disputed (eg, if it appears you do not satisfy the contribution conditions for a benefit), but you apply for a revision or supersession, or appeal against the decision because you dispute the facts – eg, you think your contribution record is wrong.

When HMRC makes a decision, you can appeal against it.[27] The appeals process is similar to appealing against an HMRC decision on your entitlement to statutory payments (see Chapter 59).

The First-tier Tribunal can also require the DWP to refer matters that are HMRC's responsibility, but which are relevant to a benefit appeal, to HMRC for a decision.[28] The DWP may revise the decision on your claim as a result. If not, the matter goes back to the tribunal.

Note: the decision maker can make arrangements for some issues concerning whether you can be credited with earnings or contributions to be decided by HMRC.[29] You can appeal against these decisions in the same way as against DWP decisions. You must first request a mandatory reconsideration of the decision (see p1339).

Correcting a decision

Unless the benefit is child benefit or guardian's allowance, if the decision maker makes an accidental error in her/his decision (eg, a typing error or a miscalculation in the arithmetic), this can be corrected.[30] You must be sent or given written notice of the correction as soon as practicable. To see how the time limit for applying for an 'any grounds' revision of the decision can be extended when a decision has been corrected, see p1304.

If you disagree with a decision maker's decision

If you think a decision is wrong, you may be able to:
- apply for a revision of the decision (see p1303); *or*
- apply for a supersession of the decision (see p1315).

In most cases, you also have the right to appeal to the First-tier Tribunal (see Chapter 57). You must apply for a mandatory reconsideration first (see p1339).

The time limit for applying for what is known as an 'any grounds' revision is strict – normally only one month from the date on the decision letter (see p1304).

2. Decisions on claims

Once you have made a valid claim for benefit (see p1172), your claim is referred to a decision maker to decide whether you are entitled. A decision maker must

Part 9: Getting a benefit decision changed
Chapter 55: Decisions
2. Decisions on claims

normally make a decision on the claim,[31] but may sometimes withhold making a decision if there is a 'test case' pending (see p1330).

Before making a decision, the decision maker may request further information (see p1174). If there is a question about the facts of your claim that needs special expertise, the decision maker can get assistance from experts.[32]

Once a valid claim has been made, it is not possible for a decision maker to refuse to make a decision on the claim.[33] Sometimes, decision makers say that they have 'closed' a claim – eg, because after claiming UC, you did not book or attend an interview to establish your identity. There is no power allowing them to do this – a decision to 'close' a claim is a decision to refuse to make an award in respect of that claim and booking an interview is not a condition of entitlement to UC.

Circumstances at time of decision

When deciding a claim for benefit, the decision maker must consider your circumstances at the date s/he is making the decision. The decision maker cannot later change a decision to take account of new circumstances which did not exist at the time of the decision.

That means that if your claim for benefit was refused and you want to have new circumstances taken into account, you must make a new claim for benefit.

Example
Fahad had capital worth £17,750 when he made a claim for UC. His claim was refused on the basis that he had too much capital. He now has capital worth £12,000. He must make a new claim to allow the decision maker to take into account his new circumstances.

If your circumstances have changed between when you made your claim for benefit and when your claim is decided, the decision maker should decide whether you met the conditions of entitlement on each of the days between when you made the claim and when it is decided. For example, if you claimed contributory ESA but your health improved and you commenced work for over 16 hours a week before the claim was decided, then the decision should award you ESA for the period from the date of claim to the day before you started work. Similarly, if you did not meet the rules for entitlement when you made your claim but you start to meet them before the claim is decided, the decision can award you benefit from the day you started to meet the rules for entitlement.[34]

Once a decision has been made about a claim for benefit that claim ceases to exist.[35] If the decision was that you were entitled and you have an *award* of benefit, quite often this is still called a 'claim', but strictly speaking that is wrong.

3. **Decisions on other issues**

In addition to decisions about whether to make an award of benefit where a claim has been made, decisions are needed about other issues. These include decisions about:

- whether an overpayment is recoverable (see p1233);
- whether an overpayment should be recovered (see p1247);
- whether you have to pay a penalty (see p1268);
- whether you are entitled to hardship payments (see p1219);
- whether you can get an advance payment (see p1192);
- whether deductions should be made from your payment (see p1202);
- whether payment of benefit under an award should be suspended (see p1200);
- whether payment under an award should cease because you are in hospital or a care home (see p917);
- about what work-related requirements apply to your universal credit award (see p1059).

4. **Delays in getting a decision**

The government website states that new claims for child benefit can take up to 12 weeks to process (or longer for claimants from abroad).[36] The DWP no longer publishes official targets, but all claims should be dealt with as soon as is reasonably practicable.[37]

Is there a delay?

1. If you have been waiting a long time for a decision, check that your claim has been received. If it has not, if possible send a copy or claim again, and refer to the claim you made earlier.

2. If the decision maker denies receiving your claim, you should claim again and ask for backdating and refer to your previous claim. If the decision maker makes a decision that your award only starts from when the second claim was received, you can challenge that decision and argue that you made the earlier claim – in an appeal, the tribunal can accept that an earlier claim was made.

3. If your claim has been received but not dealt with, ask why. If you are not satisfied with the explanation for the delay, complain (see Chapter 60). If the claim is not decided within a reasonable time, it might be possible to send a letter before action for judicial review (see p1418).

4. If a decision cannot be made on your claim straight away, ask the office to make a short-term advance of benefit if these are payable for the benefit you have claimed (see p1192), or an interim payment of child benefit or guardian's allowance (see p596).

Part 9: Getting a benefit decision changed
Chapter 55: Decisions
5. Information about decisions

5. You may be able to claim a means-tested benefit or, for housing benefit, a payment on account while a decision is being made on your claim for a non-means-tested benefit. The amount paid may be deducted from arrears of the other benefit(s) you subsequently receive, or you may be asked to repay the amount (see p1237).

6. You may be able to get help from your local authority for any short-term needs in a crisis (see p861).

---

5. **Information about decisions**

You must be given written notice of a decision against which you can appeal (see p1343 for which decisions). This is usually called a '**decision notice**'. You must be informed of:[38]

- your right to appeal against the decision; *and*
- your right to a written statement of reasons for the decision, if this is not already included (see p1297).

You are also told that you must apply for a mandatory reconsideration before you can appeal against the decision (see p1339).

If a decision has not been notified to you, then it may not have legal effect.[39] That could mean that other decisions which depend on that decision cannot be enforced. For example, if a decision reducing your entitlement for a past period was not notified to you, then a subsequent decision that the resultant overpayment was recoverable is invalid.[40]

Explanations

Sometimes the decision maker may claim that you must ask for an explanation before you can apply for a revision or a supersession, or to appeal. This is wrong. Although you can ask for an explanation of any decision, you do not have to do so before you challenge the decision. If you want an explanation, contact the office that made the decision.

At the end of the explanation, you should be asked whether you are happy with the decision. If you are not happy, say so. The decision maker should then advise you about your right to apply for a revision (see p1303). S/he may refer to this as a dispute or a mandatory reconsideration.

Explanations are usually given orally. You may also have the right to request a written statement of reasons for a decision (see p1297) if it is one against which you can appeal.

The time limit for applying for a revision is very strict. It runs from the date you are sent or are given the decision with which you disagree (*not* the date of the explanation) and can only be extended in limited circumstances (see p1304).

Therefore, ensure you apply for a revision within the time limit, even if the decision has not yet been explained to you.

Written reasons

You may want to see the reasons for a decision in writing. You only have a right to a written statement of reasons for a decision if this has not already been provided with the decision and it is a decision against which you can appeal. You must ask for the written statement of reasons within one month of the date of the notification of the decision. The decision maker must then provide the statement within 14 days, or as soon as practicable afterwards.[41]

Note: the time limit to apply for a revision is extended if you ask for a written statement of reasons, but only if this has not already been provided. See p1304 for further information.

Month

'**Month**' means a complete calendar month running from the day after the day you were sent or given a decision.[42] For example, a decision sent on 24 July has a time limit that expires at the end of 24 August.

The DWP says that a written statement of reasons is provided automatically with decisions about universal credit, employment and support allowance, personal independence payment, bereavement benefits, maternity allowance, retirement pension and social fund payments. For other benefits, if you are in any doubt about whether there is a statement of reasons for the decision, apply for a revision within the time limit.

You may believe that a written statement of reasons has not been included with your decision or is inadequate, but the DWP, HMRC or local authority could disagree. In these cases, the decision maker is likely to argue that your time limit for applying for a revision cannot be extended.

If you are in any doubt, you should assume that the time limit for applying for a revision has *not* been extended. If you miss the time limit in this situation, argue that the rules that allow a late application for a revision apply (see p1305). You may also be able to apply for a revision if you have specific grounds (see p1307).

Notes

1. When a decision must be made

1 **UC/PIP/JSA&ESA under UC** Reg 40 UC,PIP,JSA&ESA(DA) Regs
Other benefits Reg 11 SS&CS(DA) Regs
2 CIB/2338/2000
3 gov.uk/government/collections/ decision-makers-guide-staff-guide
4 gov.uk/government/publications/ advice-for-decision-making-staff-guide
5 Deposited at www.parliament.uk/ business/publications/business-papers/ commons/deposited-papers/ and available at rightsnet.org.uk/universal-credit-full-service-guidance
6 gov.uk/government/publications/ personal-independence-payment-assessment-guide-for-assessment-providers
7 For Independent Assessment Services (Atos), see mypipassessment.co.uk/. For Capita, see capita-pip.co.uk/en/ assessment-process.html.
8 gov.uk/government/publications/ personal-independence-payment-fact-sheets
9 gov.uk/government/publications/work-capability-assessment-handbook-for-healthcare-professionals
10 gov.uk/government/collections/ housing-benefit-and-council-tax-benefit-manual
11 gov.uk/government/collections/ housing-benefit-for-local-authorities-bulletins; gov.uk/government/ publications/housing-benefit-urgent-bulletins-2019; gov.uk/government/ publications/discretionary-housing-payments-guidance-manual
12 **UC/PIP&ESA under UC** Reg 39 UC,PIP,JSA&ESA(DA) Regs
Other benefits Regs 13(2) and (3) and 15 SS&CS(DA) Regs
13 Regs 13A and 13B SS&CS(DA) Regs
14 Reg 39(5) UC,PIP,JSA&ESA(DA) Regs
15 Reg 39(4) UC,PIP,JSA&ESA(DA) Regs
16 Reg 13(1) SS&CS(DA) Regs
17 s17 SSA 1998
18 *MC v SSWP (IS)* [2015] UKUT 600 (AAC); *SSWP v AM (IS)* [2010] UKUT 428 (AAC)
19 *MW v Leeds CC (HB)* [2018] UKUT 319 (AAC)
20 Reg 10 SS&CS(DA) Regs; reg 40(1)-(2) UC,PIP,JSA&ESA Regs
21 Reg 6(1) SS(IIPD) Regs; R(I)2/04
22 Sch 4 para 12 and Sch 6 para 5 HB Regs; regs 25-26 HB(SPC) Regs
23 *DF v LB Waltham Forest (HB)* [2017] UKUT 161 (AAC)
24 Reg 11 SS&CS(DA) Regs; reg 40(3) UC,PIP,JSA,ESA(DA) Regs
25 s8 SSC(TF)A 1999
26 s10A SSA 1998; reg 42 UC,PIP,JSA&ESA(DA) Regs; reg 11A SS&CS(DA) Regs
27 s11 SSC(TF)A 1999
28 s24A SSA 1998; reg 43 UC,PIP,JSA&ESA(DA) Regs; reg 38A SS&CS(DA) Regs
29 s17 SSC(TF)A 1999; Sch 3 para 17 SSA 1998; National Insurance Contribution Credits (Transfer of Functions) Order 2009, No.1377
30 **UC/PIP/JSA&ESA under UC** Reg 38 UC,PIP,JSA&ESA(DA) Regs
Other benefits Reg 9A SS&CS(DA) Regs

2. Decisions on claims

31 R(SB) 29/83; CIS/807/1992; R(H) 3/05
32 s11(2) SSA 1998
33 R(H) 3/05
34 *SSWP v KK (JSA)* [2019] UKUT 313 (AAC)
35 s8(2) SSA 1998

4. Delays in getting a decision

36 See gov.uk/child-benefit/how-to-claim
37 *R (C and W) v SSWP and Zacchaeus 2000 Trust* [2015] EWHC 1607 (Admin)

5. **Information about decisions**

38 **UC/PIP/JSA&ESA under UC** Reg 51
UC,PIP,JSA&ESA(DA) Regs
CB/GA Reg 26(1) CB&GA(DA) Regs
Other benefits Reg 28(1) SS&CS(DA)
Regs
39 *R (Anufrijeva) v SSHD* [2003] UKHL 26
40 *SM v SSWP (SPC)* [2017] UKUT 336
(AAC)
41 **UC/PIP/JSA&ESA under UC** Regs 3
and 51 UC,PIP,JSA&ESA(DA) Regs
CB/GA Regs 3 and 26(1)(b) and (2)
CB&GA(DA) Regs
Other benefits Regs 2 and 28(1)(b)
and (2) SS&CS(DA) Regs
42 R(IB) 4/02

9

Revisions and supersessions

This chapter covers:
1. Getting a decision changed (p1301)
2. Revisions (p1303)
3. Supersessions (p1315)
4. Revisions and supersessions after a 'qualifying benefit' award (p1328)
5. The 'anti-test case rule' (p1330)

This chapter covers the rules for benefits, the social fund payments in Chapter 37 (except budgeting loans) and decisions about DWP loans for mortgage interest (see p855). It does not cover the rules for Scottish social security benefits (see Chapter 77), statutory payments (see Chapter 59) or the health benefits in Chapter 31.

References in this chapter to HM Revenue and Customs (HMRC) only apply to decisions about child benefit and guardian's allowance. HMRC also makes decisions about tax credits. For the rules for tax credits, see Chapter 66.

Key facts

- If a decision is wrong or no longer correct, it can be changed by a new decision – called either a 'revision' or a 'supersession'.
- You can apply for a revision or a supersession, or the DWP, local authority or HM Revenue and Customs can carry one out because it wants to change your award.
- In some cases, you do not need to show any grounds for a revision, but you must ask for one within a set time limit. In other cases, you can ask for a revision at any time, but you must show there are specific grounds.
- The date on which a revision or a supersession takes effect determines the date from when you are paid arrears if you are entitled to more benefit, or the date from when you have been overpaid if you are entitled to less benefit.
- You can also challenge a decision by appealing to the First-tier Tribunal. Unless the benefit is housing benefit, you must apply for a mandatory reconsideration first and the decision maker considers whether to carry out a revision.

1. **Getting a decision changed**

The DWP, the local authority and HM Revenue and Customs (HMRC) make many decisions about your entitlement to benefits – eg, whether you are entitled to a benefit, the date from when you are entitled and the amount you should be paid. Other issues, such as whether benefit is payable or whether an overpayment is recoverable, are also the subject of decisions. Once a decision has been made, it can only be changed by a further decision.[1] These further decisions are called revisions (see pp1303–15) and supersessions (see pp1315–27).

To get more information about a decision, ask for an explanation or a written statement of reasons if this has not already been provided (see p1297).

In many cases, decisions can also be changed by appealing to the First-tier Tribunal (see Chapter 57). However, unless the benefit is housing benefit (HB), you must apply for a mandatory reconsideration before you can appeal (see p1339). In terms of the law, a 'mandatory reconsideration' is a request for a revision – the term simply emphasises that the decision maker must have considered whether or not to revise the decision (ie, it is mandatory) before an appeal can be made.

You can apply for a revision or a supersession of a decision that you cannot appeal (see p1344 for some examples). If such a decision is not changed following your application, you may be able to apply for a judicial review in the High Court or the Court of Session in Scotland (see p1414).

Note: it is important that you keep within any time limit (see p1304 for revisions and p1346 for appeals).

Revisions and supersessions

Revisions and supersessions are both ways of changing a decision about your benefit entitlement. Broadly:

- **A revision** is the way of changing a decision that was wrong at the time it was made – ie, the decision maker wrongly refused to award you benefit, or awarded you an incorrect amount – eg, because s/he thought you had savings which you did not have. A revision takes effect from the date the original decision took effect.
- **A supersession** is usually the way of changing a decision which was correct at the time it was originally made, but which has subsequently become wrong – eg, because your circumstances have now changed and you no longer meet a condition of entitlement. A supersession does not take effect from the date the original decision took effect – it takes effect from a later date.

You can apply for a revision or a supersession and the decision maker at the DWP, local authority or HMRC can also initiate one.

Note: you must apply for a revision within a certain time (unless one of the specific grounds allowing revisions to be carried out without meeting a time limit

Part 9: Getting a benefit decision changed
Chapter 56: Revisions and supersessions
1. Getting a decision changed

apply). If you miss the time limit or you do not have speciifc grounds, it may be possible to get a decision that was wrong when it was originally made changed via a supersession. However, as you generally get less arrears of benefit after a supersession, make sure you apply within the time allowed if you can.

In some cases, if the decision maker is reducing or removing your entitlement, it may be in your interests to argue that this can only be done by carrying out a supersession, rather than a revision.

The risks of applying for a revision or supersession

Following a revision or a supersession, the original decision may remain the same – ie, your application for a revision or supersession is refused. It may also be revised or superseded so as to either increase *or* decrease the amount of your benefit, or to take away your entitlement altogether. There are particular issues if you apply for a revision or supersession of a disability living allowance (DLA) or a personal independence payment (PIP) decision (see below).

Note: you may apply for a revision or supersession in the hope that your benefit will be increased, but the outcome could be that you get less benefit, and you could be required to repay an overpayment (see Chapter 54). This is because (although s/he does not have to do so) the decision maker can consider issues that are not raised in your application for a revision or supersession.[2] Therefore, before you apply for a revision or supersession consider whether it is possible that less or no benefit could be awarded for all, or some, of the period in question. If you apply for a revision or supersession and the decision maker makes a decision which is less advantageous to you than the original decision, s/he must show that there was a specific ground to do so and that the outcome of the revision or supersession is related to that ground. However, this does not apply if the decision maker starts taking action to revise the decision within a month of the original decision having been made. In this case, s/he can make an 'any grounds' revision (see p1303).[3]

Disability living allowance and personal independence payment

If you apply for a revision or supersession because you have not been awarded one component of DLA or PIP when you are already in receipt of the other, or because you are not happy with the rate of a component of DLA or PIP that you have been awarded, although s/he does not have to do so, the decision maker may consider:

– the component which is not the subject of the revision or supersession;
– whether to reduce the rate of a component, or end your entitlement to it, even if you asked for a higher rate;
– whether to reduce the length of the period for which you have been awarded a component, even if it was originally awarded for an indefinite period.

If you are aged over 16 and report a change of circumstances that is relevant to the rate of DLA to which you are entitled, you are likely to be invited to claim PIP (see p617). Your entitlement to DLA will then end, even if you do not claim PIP.

2. **Revisions**

If you think a decision is wrong, you can apply for a revision.[4] The decision maker must then look at the decision again to see whether it can be changed. The DWP, the local authority and HM Revenue and Customs (HMRC) often refer to your request as a 'dispute' or a 'request for a reconsideration'.

Mandatory reconsideration

Unless the benefit is housing benefit (HB), you must apply for a mandatory reconsideration of a decision before you can appeal against it (see p1339). When the DWP or HMRC deals with your application, it looks at its decision again – ie, it considers whether to carry out a revision. The rules and advice on revisions in this chapter therefore apply in full when you apply for a mandatory reconsideration. Once the DWP or HMRC has considered your application, it issues a mandatory reconsideration notice (see p1342). You need this notice to appeal to the First-tier Tribunal.

When a decision can be revised

A decision can be revised either following your request for a revision or because the decision maker decides to carry out a revision.[5] There are two types of revision:
- 'Any grounds' revisions. You (or the decision maker) do not have to show that specific grounds apply (see below), but you (or the decision maker) must apply or start the process within a strict time limit (see p1306 for the time limit that applies to the decision maker and p1304 for the time limit that applies to you).
- 'Specific grounds' revisions. You (or the decision maker) must show that one of the specific permitted grounds exists (see p1307). If this is the case, the decision can be revised, even if it was made a long time ago.

Decisions of the First-tier (or Upper) Tribunal cannot be revised. In some cases, these decisions can be superseded. Otherwise, they can only be changed by appealing further to the Upper Tribunal or a court (see Chapter 58).

'Any grounds' revisions

If action to get a decision changed is started within a specific time limit, the decision can be changed on 'any grounds'. This means that it can be changed simply because a new decision maker takes a different view of the same evidence.

The time limits for getting a decision changed by a revision on 'any grounds' are different depending on whether:
- you are applying for a decision to be revised (see p1304); *or*
- the revision is started by the decision maker (see p1306).

Part 9: Getting a benefit decision changed
Chapter 56: Revisions and supersessions
2. Revisions

A revision on 'any grounds' is a completely fresh look at the decision. The decision maker can do any or all of the following:

- simply form a different opinion about the same evidence – eg, the first decision maker may have decided that the money in your bank account belonged to you and so meant you had too much capital to qualify for benefit, but the new decision maker might accept your explanation that the money belonged to someone else;
- take into account any new evidence which shows what your circumstances were at the time of the original decision – eg, you have a new medical report, showing that you have limited capability for work;
- take into account any omissions in the information you gave at the time – eg, if you failed to mention in your claim for universal credit (UC) that you had housing costs;
- correct any misunderstanding of the law which affected the previous decision – eg, by accepting you do not need to receive child benefit for a child in order to count as responsible for her/him for the purposes of UC.

A decision maker can only revise a decision on any grounds on the basis of your circumstances at the time:[6]

- the decision took effect; *or*
- in the case of advance awards for benefits other than HB, the decision was made.

If your circumstances have since changed, make a fresh claim or ask for a supersession (see p1315) instead.

Note: if you apply for an 'any grounds' revision of a decision about employment and support allowance (ESA), attendance allowance (AA), disability living allowance (DLA) or personal independence payment (PIP) because you (or the person on whose behalf you are claiming) are terminally ill, you must state this explicitly.[7] If you do not do so, the decision maker cannot revise the decision on this ground.

Time limit for applying for an 'any grounds' revision

You must apply for an 'any grounds' revision:

- **in the case of a Sure Start maternity grant or a social fund funeral expenses payment**, within one month of the date you were sent or given the decision or, if later, within the time limit for claiming the payment (see p798 and p804);[8]
- **in the case of a cold weather payment or a winter fuel payment**, within one month of the date you were notified of the decision. For these purposes, you are generally assumed to have been notified seven days after the decision was made, but there are exceptions;[9]

- **in the case of HB**, within one month of the date you were sent or given the decision.[10] If a written statement of reasons has not already been included with the decision, days from the date your request for the statement is received by the local authority to the date on which it is provided to you are ignored when calculating the one month;[11]
- **in all other cases:**[12]
  - within one month of the date you were sent or given the decision; *or*
  - within one month and 14 days of the date you were sent or given the decision, if you requested a written statement of reasons (see p1297) and it is provided within the month; *or*
  - within 14 days of a written statement of reasons being provided, if you requested one within one month of the date you were sent or given the decision, but it is not provided within that one-month period.

For benefits (other than a Sure Start maternity grant or a social fund funeral expenses payment, child benefit or guardian's allowance), if an accidental error in a decision has been corrected (see p1293), any day falling before the day on which the correction is notified to you is ignored when calculating the one-month period.[13]

Late requests

You can apply for an 'any grounds' revision outside the time limit in limited circumstances, provided this is within an absolute time limit.

The absolute time limit

In most cases, you must apply for an 'any grounds' revision within **13 months** of the date you were notified of the decision.[14]

If you requested a written statement of reasons (see p1297):

– for HB, days from the date you requested the statement to the date on which it was provided are ignored when calculating the 13 months; *or*

– for other benefits, if the statement of reasons is provided within one month of the date you were notified of the decision, the 13 months are extended by 14 days. If it is provided during a period later than one month after that date, the 13 months are extended by 14 days, plus the number of days in that period.

In all cases, for a late request for an 'any grounds' revision to be accepted:[15]

- your application must contain:
  - sufficient details about the decision with which you disagree for it to be identified. Say which benefit you are disagreeing about and the date the DWP, HMRC or the local authority sent you the decision; *and*
  - a summary of your reasons for applying late; *and*

Part 9: Getting a benefit decision changed
Chapter 56: Revisions and supersessions
2. Revisions

- you must show that:
  - it is reasonable to grant your application; *and*
  - there are special circumstances which mean that it was not practicable for you to apply for a revision within the time limit. Any special circumstances can count. The longer you have delayed applying for a revision, the more compelling these must be.

In addition, for child benefit, guardian's allowance and HB:[16]

- you must show that your application has merit – ie, that there is a prospect the decision can be changed if time is extended; *and*
- when deciding whether it is reasonable to grant your application, the decision maker cannot take account of the fact that:
  - a court or the Upper Tribunal has interpreted the law in a different way than previously understood and applied;
  - you (or anyone acting for you) misunderstood or were unaware of the relevant law, including the time limits for applying for a revision.

If your late request for an 'any grounds' revision is refused, you cannot appeal against that refusal.[17] However:

- For benefits other than HB, you may still be able to appeal against the original decision. Under the rules on mandatory reconsiderations, you only have a right of appeal against a decision if the decision maker has considered whether to revise it. If you applied for an 'any grounds' revision within the absolute time limit, by refusing to accept that time should be extended, the decision maker *has* considered whether to revise the decision, so you can appeal.[18] If you have missed the absolute time limit for an 'any grounds' revision, you only have a right of appeal if you can show that one of the specific grounds for a revision applied. In practice, decision makers at the DWP rarely refuse to accept a late request for a revision made within the absolute time limit.
- For HB, you may be able to make a late appeal against the original decision. A late appeal must be admitted if the decision maker does not object or if the First-tier Tribunal thinks it is fair and just to do so, it is more likely that you will have your request for a late appeal accepted than your request for an 'any grounds' revision accepted.

Time limit for decision makers

For benefits other than HB, the decision maker can revise a decision her/himself on any grounds provided s/he starts action within one month of the date you are sent or given a decision.[19] For HB, a decision maker can also decide to revise a decision her/himself, but only if, within one month of the date you are sent or given it, s/he has information which shows that there was a mistake about the facts of your case or the decision was made in ignorance of relevant facts.[20]

If these conditions are not met, the decision maker can only carry out a revision if there are specific grounds.

'Specific grounds' revisions

A revision can be carried out at any time (even years after the original decision was made) in specific situations. So, if you can show there are specific grounds, you can apply for a revision at any time. The decision maker at the DWP, HMRC or local authority can also carry out a revision at any time if s/he thinks one of the specific grounds exists. 'Specific grounds' revisions are often referred to as 'any time' revisions. If a decision maker refuses to consider a 'specific grounds' revision, see p1314.

In practice, if you apply for a revision (including a mandatory reconsideration) and it is within one month of your being sent or given the decision, the DWP, the local authority or HMRC treats your application as one for an 'any grounds' revision (see p1303). If your application is late and reasons for lateness are not accepted by the DWP, the local authority or HMRC, the decision maker should go on to consider whether any of the specific grounds exist to allow a revision on that basis.

There are a number of grounds for a 'specific grounds' revision. The main ones are where there has been:
- an official error (see below);
- a sanction decision (see p1308);
- an award of a 'qualifying benefit' (see p1309);
- an appeal against a decision (see p1310);
- a mistake about or ignorance of facts (see p1310).

Some other specific grounds are summarised on p1311.

Official error

A decision can be revised at any time if there was an official error.[21]

For benefits, other than child benefit and guardian's allowance, this means:[22]
- an error made by an officer of the DWP or HMRC; *or*
- for HB only, errors made by the local authority or by a person authorised to carry out any function of the local authority or provide services relating to HB; *or*
- other than for HB, errors made by a person employed by someone providing services to the DWP; *or*
- other than for HB, PIP, UC and, if you come under the UC system (see p23), contribution-based jobseeker's allowance (JSA) and contributory ESA, errors made by an employee of a local authority (or an employee of a person acting on behalf of, or providing services to, a local authority).

Part 9: Getting a benefit decision changed
Chapter 56: Revisions and supersessions
2. Revisions

For child benefit and guardian's allowance, it means an error made by an officer of HMRC or a person employed by someone providing services to HMRC.[23]

Note:

- If the error is that the decision maker got the law wrong, this does not count as an official error if this is only shown to be the case because of a later decision from the Upper Tribunal or a court.[24] If a legal mistake was made in your case that was only later shown to be a legal mistake because of a subsequent decision in another case, you could make a fresh claim (or apply for a supersession), and the 'anti-test case rule' could apply (see p1330).
- If someone else (eg, you, your partner or your representative) caused or contributed to the error, it does not count as an official error.[25] This includes if the way your claim form was completed contributed to the error.[26]

Official error: examples

The following can count as official errors.

Getting the law wrong (unless this is only established by a subsequent Upper Tribunal or court decision in another case – see above).

The decision maker (or local authority) had specific evidence which s/he failed to take into account, even though it was relevant. You should argue that this applies even if the evidence does not conclusively prove your entitlement, so long as it raised a strong possibility that you were entitled.

The DWP, the local authority or HMRC had documentary or other written evidence of your entitlement, but failed to give it to the decision maker dealing with your claim when the earlier decision was made.

No reasonable decision maker having established the facts could have made the decision that was made.[27]

The decision maker failed to ask you about something that was relevant to the decision and which was reasonably obvious would need to be asked in order to be able to ensure the decision was correct.[28]

Sanction decisions

A decision can be revised at any time if:[29]

- for UC and JSA, and, if you come under the UC system, ESA, it is a decision to give you a sanction for any reason; *or*
- you do not come under the UC system and it is a decision to give you a sanction because:
  - you (or in some cases your partner) failed to take part in a work-focused interview without good cause (see p1157). This only applies if the decision contained an error and, for ESA only, if you did not materially contribute to the error; *or*

– for ESA and income support (IS) only, you failed to undertake work-related activity without good cause (see p1160). This only applies if the decision contained an error to which you did not materially contribute.

This means that you can apply for a revision (including a mandatory reconsideration) even if the decision to give you a sanction was made a long time ago. This is useful if you did not realise you could challenge the decision at the time it was made and, for example, you can show you had good cause or a good reason for your actions, or you did not do (or fail to do) what is alleged. If you have been given a sanction more than once, you should apply for a revision of all the decisions if possible and then appeal if you do not get all that you want. If you are applying for a mandatory reconsideration before you can appeal (see p1339), make this clear in your application. See p1108 and p1161 for further information about challenging a sanction decision.

Note: for JSA if you do not come under the UC system, a decision can also be revised at any time to begin a sanction on the grounds that you were previously entitled to JSA and that entitlement ended because you were found not to be available for or actively seeking work (see p1149).[30] In practice, this means that if you are awarded and paid JSA while a decision maker considers whether you should be sanctioned, the sanction applies from the date you were awarded JSA.

Awards of a 'qualifying benefit'

A decision can be revised at any time if:

- you are awarded a benefit (eg, UC, IS, income-based JSA, income-related ESA, pension credit (PC) or HB) and, for a period which includes the date that award took effect, you (or your partner, or a child included in your claim – see p323) are awarded another benefit or an increase in its rate. This can work to your advantage if the other benefit is a 'qualifying benefit' (eg, DLA or carer's allowance – see p1328);[31] *or*
- for IS, JSA, ESA and PC only, if you have a non-dependant living with you (see p363) and since you were awarded IS, income-based JSA, income-related ESA or PC, your non-dependant has been awarded a qualifying benefit (see p1328) for a period that includes the date your award took effect and this means that you are now entitled to a severe disability premium (for IS, JSA or ESA) or a severe disability addition (for PC).[32]

A decision to end your entitlement to HB because your (or your partner's or child's) qualifying benefit ceases can also be revised at any time. This only applies if the qualifying benefit is later reinstated following a revision, supersession or appeal.[33]

See p1328 for further information. If you are only entitled to a benefit once a qualifying benefit is awarded, see p211 and p1180.

Part 9: Getting a benefit decision changed
Chapter 56: Revisions and supersessions
2. Revisions

A decision that has been appealed

If you appealed against a decision, and you:

- appealed within the time limit or were allowed a late appeal (see p1346 and p1347) and the appeal has not yet been determined, a decision maker can look at the decision again and revise it.[34] This includes if the First-tier Tribunal has adjourned the hearing or if the Upper Tribunal has sent a case back to the First-tier Tribunal to make a new decision. This enables the decision maker to take new information that has come to light in the appeal process into account. **Note:** your appeal could lapse if a decision maker revises the decision, even if you do not get everything you want (see p1356); *or*
- make a fresh claim or request a supersession when your circumstances change (see p1375) and, as a result, a new decision about your entitlement is made, a decision maker can revise the new decision once your appeal has been decided. This only applies if you appealed against a decision to the First-tier Tribunal (or, for HB only, to the Upper Tribunal or a court) and:[35]
  - a fresh claim is decided or the decision is superseded before your appeal is determined; *and*
  - the appeal is then determined; *and*
  - the decision maker would have made her/his decision differently had s/he been aware of the appeal decision at the time her/his decision was made.

Mistake about or ignorance of facts

A decision can be revised at any time if there was a mistake about the facts of your case or the decision was made in ignorance of relevant facts, provided, as a result of the mistake or ignorance about the facts, the decision was more favourable to you than it would have been – eg, you were awarded too much benefit.[36] If you have been overpaid, the decision maker may seek to recover the overpayment (see Chapter 54). Because this specific ground only arises when the decision was more generous to you than it would have been without the mistake or ignorance about a fact, in practice this ground is only used when a decision maker wants to revise a decision. **Note:** there must have been a mistake about or ignorance of facts, not conclusions or opinions about the facts. See p1239 for some examples.

The rules are different if there was a mistake about, or ignorance of, facts relating to a 'disability determination' or a 'limited capability for work determination'.[37] In this case, it must be shown that, at the time the decision that you were entitled to a benefit (eg, DLA or ESA) was made, you knew, or could reasonably have been expected to know, about the fact and that it was relevant to your benefit. Otherwise, a decision cannot be revised on this ground and you will not have been overpaid benefit, although there may be grounds for a supersession.

Disability and limited capability for work determinations[38]

A **'disability determination'** is a decision about whether you satisfy the disability conditions for AA or DLA, are disabled for the purposes of severe disablement allowance

(SDA), or whether the existence or extent of your disablement is sufficient for you to be entitled to industrial injuries disablement benefit or to be paid at the same rate as that paid immediately before the decision. It does *not* include decisions about PIP.

A **'limited capability for work determination'** is a decision about whether you have, or can be treated as having, limited capability for work under any of the first six bullet points on p1013 or because you get the support component on the basis that you meet one of the eating and drinking descriptors in the test for limited capability for work-related activity (see Appendix 4). This does *not* apply if you come under the UC system.

If the mistake about or ignorance of facts means you should be entitled to *more* benefit:

- a decision can be superseded on this ground (see p1317);
- a decision can be revised on any ground if you satisfy the rules for an 'any grounds' revision (see p1303).

Other grounds for revision

There are many other situations when a decision maker can carry out a 'specific grounds' revision at any time. This includes if the decision is one against which you have no right of appeal (see p1344 for which decisions).[39]

Other decisions that can be revised at any time include a decision:

- to reduce your UC or your HB under the benefit cap rules (see p1194);[40]
- to end your entitlement to contributory ESA because you have been receiving it for 365 days, but it is subsequently found that you had, or can be treated as having had, limited capability for work-related activity before your entitlement ended;[41]
- to refuse you PIP because you are resident in a care home and the costs of any qualifying services (see p928) provided for you are met by public funds, the decision was made with incomplete evidence (see p1290) and, after the decision, any of the costs of the qualifying services are recovered from you;[42]
- to treat you as not satisfying the disability conditions for the daily living component or the mobility component of PIP because you did not return your questionnaire or you failed to participate in your assessment consultation. However, this only applies if the decision was made because of an error to which you did not contribute;[43]
- to increase the amount of rent used for the housing costs element (for UC) or your maximum rent (for HB) because of a rent officer's redetermination, or because a local housing allowance rate or broad rental market area has been amended because of a rent officer's error;[44]
- about state pension (or an 'old' retirement pension), PC or HB, where you or your partner deferred claiming a pension, then changed your option from a higher pension to a lump sum (or, for state pension and retirement pension only, vice versa).[45]

Part 9: Getting a benefit decision changed
Chapter 56: Revisions and supersessions
2. Revisions

Note: this list is not exhaustive. There are a number of other decisions that can be revised at any time.[46]

How to apply for a revision

For UC, you can apply for a revision by requesting this in your online journal – this gives you a record you can access, proving you have made the request. If you also need to submit evidence, speak to your work coach or telephone the UC helpline and ask for a facility to enable you to upload the relevant documents. You do not have to apply for a revision online. You can also telephone or send a letter by post or take a written request to the job centre. It is always worth phoning the UC helpline after you have submitted an application, either via your journal or in writing, to confirm that it is being dealt with as a request for revision.

For HB, you must apply for a revision (including a late application) in writing.[47]

For benefits other than HB, you do not have to apply for a revision in writing, although it is always best to do so. This ensures that the decision maker understands that you are asking for one, not just seeking an explanation or complaining about the rules.

In all cases, it is worth checking that an application sent by post has been received and is being dealt with appropriately.

When establishing whether an 'any grounds' revision is made within the time limit (see p1304), your application counts as having been received on the day it arrives at an 'appropriate office'.[48] Note: if you are applying for a mandatory reconsideration before you can appeal (see p1339), make this clear in your application.

The appropriate office

The '**appropriate office**' is the office specified on the notice of the decision with which you disagree or, for JSA if you do not come under the UC system (see p23), the office where you have to sign on.[49] For benefits (other than child benefit, guardian's allowance, HB and, if you come under the UC system, contribution-based JSA, contributory ESA and UC), if you are a person who is, or would be, required to attend a work-focused interview as a condition of getting benefit, the Jobcentre Plus office is also an appropriate office.

A decision maker does not have to consider any issues other than those raised in your application.[50] To ensure the decision maker considers everything you want her/him to, you should:

- make it clear what sort of revision you are applying for. Show how you meet the specific grounds for a 'specific grounds' revision or the time limit for an 'any grounds' revision;
- set out all the points about the decision with which you disagree;

- provide any information or evidence that supports your case. This includes, for example, medical evidence from a GP, consultant or other health worker if this is relevant. If the benefit is AA, DLA or PIP, evidence or information from your carer or a diary of your walking, supervision or care needs over a period may be useful. The decision maker may ask you for further information or evidence (see below).

The DWP, the local authority or HMRC can treat an application for a supersession as an application for a revision and an application for a revision as an application for a supersession.[51] In addition, any correspondence in which you make it clear that you are unhappy with a decision and want it changed, even if you do not use the term 'revision' or 'mandatory reconsideration' should be treated as a request for a revision. For example, a claim for benefit accompanied by a request for it to be backdated to the date a previous award ended can be treated as an application for a revision of the decision to end that previous award.[52] Although you do not have to use the correct terminology, doing so ensures that there can be no doubt about what you are asking for.

How do you get evidence of previous decisions to support your application?

1. If the decision you are trying to get changed was made a long time ago, it can be difficult to identify the grounds. You can obtain information held by the DWP, the local authority or HMRC by making a 'subject access request' under the Data Protection Act 1998. See the Information Commissioner's website at ico.org.uk for details.

2. In some cases, the DWP, the local authority or HMRC may say it has destroyed old papers relating to your claim. Ask whether your papers have simply been archived, rather than actually destroyed. You can try to argue that missing papers should be presumed to contain information that is favourable to your case. However, this is unlikely to be accepted unless you can show that the papers should have been retained because they could have been relevant to any potential appeal, or that they were destroyed deliberately to thwart your case.[53]

Providing further evidence and information

The decision maker can ask you for more evidence or information if s/he thinks this is needed to consider all the issues raised by your application for a revision.[54] You must provide this within one month of the request. The decision maker can allow longer. If you do not provide the information, your application is decided on the basis of the information and evidence the decision maker already has. The DWP can also ask you to have a medical examination – eg, if the decision concerns whether you have limited capability for work.

Note: in some cases if you fail to provide information in a specified time period or have a medical examination, payment of your benefit could be suspended, which may lead to your entitlement being terminated (see p1200).

Part 9: Getting a benefit decision changed
Chapter 56: Revisions and supersessions
2. Revisions

Similar rules allow the decision maker to ask for evidence or information if you apply for a supersession. If the benefit is UC, you must provide this within 14 days.[55]

When a revision takes effect

The date a revision takes effect is important. This is the date from when you are paid arrears if you are entitled to more benefit, or from when you have been overpaid if you are entitled to less benefit. In all cases, a revision takes effect from:

- the date the decision being revised took (or would have taken) effect[56] – eg, your date of claim if you are challenging a decision on a claim; *or*
- the correct date, if the date on which the decision being revised took effect was found to be wrong.[57]

It is important to make it clear that you want payment for the past period. You may get less backdating if the 'anti-test case rule' applies (see p1330).

Note: if a decision is revised on the grounds that there was a mistake about, or ignorance of, facts relating to a 'disability determination' or a 'limited capability for work determination' in the circumstances described on p1310, if the benefit is a qualifying benefit for another benefit (see p1328) and the revision means your entitlement to the other benefit is affected, the decision about the other benefit takes effect on the same date.[58]

Challenging a revision

If the original decision is one against which you have a right of appeal (see p1343 for which decisions), you can appeal to the First-tier Tribunal against that decision *as revised*. If the decision maker refuses to revise a decision, you can appeal against the original decision *as made*. In both cases, therefore, the appeal is against the original decision. You must be notified in writing of whether the decision maker has revised the decision or whether s/he has refused to revise it. For UC, the written notification can be given in your online journal. For benefits other than HB, if you applied for a mandatory reconsideration, this is called a 'mandatory reconsideration notice' (see p1342).

The time limit for appealing (see p1346) depends on the benefit involved and whether it was an 'any grounds' or a 'specific grounds' revision.[59]

For HB, the time limit for appealing runs from the date:

- you were sent or given notification of the revision or the refusal to revise an 'any grounds' revision and your application for a revision was made within the time limit (or a late application was accepted);
- of the original decision if a decision maker has refused to do a 'specific grounds' revision (see p1307) – eg, because s/he does not accept that an official error was made.[60]

If the decision maker refuses to do an 'any grounds' revision because your application was late and s/he did not accept your reasons for why it was late, arguably the time runs from the date you are notified that the revision is not to be considered. However, it is arguable that this is wrong and the time runs from the date of the notice of the original decision. If you are in this situation, try to appeal within 13 months of the original decision.

If the time for appealing runs from the date of the original decision, you may be able to apply for a judicial review in the High Court/Court of Session (see p1421) against the refusal to carry out a 'specific grounds' revision or the refusal to accept your reasons for applying late for an 'any grounds' revision. Alternatively, you may be able to make a late appeal (see p1347). If you want to appeal against the original HB decision, the time limit runs from the date you were sent or given notice of it, so if you are outside the absolute time limit, you cannot appeal.

For benefits other than HB, the time for appealing runs from the date you were sent or given notification of the revision/refusal to revise. The only exception to this is if you were seeking a 'specific grounds' revision, you were notified of the original decision more than 13 months ago and your application for a revision is refused. In this case, you can appeal if the tribunal accepts that the decision could have been revised as there was a specific ground.[61] **Note:** in this case, it is not clear whether your application needs to clearly raise a specific ground revision or whether it is sufficient that a revision on a specific ground was available. Get advice if this affects you.

3. Supersessions

A decision that is wrong or which is no longer correct can be changed by a supersession, but there must be grounds to do so.[62] The most common ground for a supersession is that your circumstances have changed since the decision was made

You can apply for a supersession even if the decision was made a long time ago, but the arrears of benefit you are paid can be limited (see p1320 for when a supersession takes effect). It is usually better to apply for a revision or appeal.

When a decision can be superseded

You can ask for a decision maker's decision (and in some cases a First-tier Tribunal's or an Upper Tribunal's decision) to be superseded or the decision maker can decide to do this her/himself.[63] There must be grounds for a supersession. There are many grounds for supersession. The main ones are:
- a change of circumstances (see p1316);
- mistakes about or ignorance of facts (see p1317);

Part 9: Getting a benefit decision changed
Chapter 56: Revisions and supersessions
3. Supersessions

- where a decision is legally wrong (see p1318);
- capability for work and disability conditions (see p1318);
- after a qualifying benefit has been awarded (see p1319).

Some other grounds for a supersession are summarised on p1319.

Note: if a decision could be revised, it cannot be superseded unless there are grounds for a supersession that are not covered by the revision rules.[64]

Change of circumstances

A decision maker's or a tribunal's decision can be superseded if:[65]

- your circumstances have changed since it had effect; *or*
- in the case of advance awards (other than for housing benefit (HB)), your circumstances have changed since it was made; *or*
- it is anticipated that your circumstances will change.

There must be a relevant change of circumstances (see below).

Note:

- The decision maker may say that a change of circumstances you have reported is a change that could not possibly result in a supersession and so refuse to consider a supersession. If this happens, see p1327.
- If there is doubt about whether a change of circumstances has occurred (eg, whether your medical condition has improved or worsened), it is necessary to compare the circumstances as they were at the time the decision took effect with the circumstances as they were at the time the supersession would take effect.[66]
- Some changes in your capability for work or the effects of your disability are dealt with under different rules (see p1318).

Relevant changes of circumstances

The change must be what is known as a 'relevant change of circumstances' – ie, it must mean that the original decision (eg, to award you benefit) may no longer be correct. What is relevant can depend on the benefit. Examples include changes in your income or your medical or physical condition, moving home or being absent from home, becoming or ceasing to be a member of a couple, or having a child or a child leaving home. Bear the following in mind.

- An amendment to the law counts as a relevant change of circumstances, but a decision of a court or the Upper Tribunal that the law has been wrongly interpreted does not.[67]
- Although a new medical opinion does not count, a new medical report following an examination may provide evidence of a relevant change.[68] Note: a new medical report might mean there is a a separate ground for a supersession (see p1318).

- Becoming terminally ill counts for universal credit (UC), employment and support allowance (ESA), attendance allowance (AA), disability living allowance (DLA) and personal independence payment (PIP), but you or the person claiming on your behalf must state explicitly that you are terminally ill in the supersession application.[69]

Change of circumstances after benefit is refused

If you were correctly refused benefit but your circumstances are now different, you *cannot* seek a supersession on the grounds of a change of circumstances. You must instead make a fresh claim (unless you are seeking a supersession because there has been a 'recrudescence' of a prescribed disease – see p688).[70] Even if you are appealing against the decision refusing or stopping your benefit, make a fresh claim when your circumstances change, and appeal if you are still refused. You could lose out if you do not do so, because the tribunal cannot take a change of circumstances into account if it happens after the decision with which you disagree (see p1375).

Mistake about or ignorance of facts

A decision maker's or a tribunal's decision can be superseded if there was a mistake about the facts of your case or if it was made in ignorance of relevant facts. However, in the case of a decision maker's decision, this only applies if:[71]

- for HB, a revision on the same ground cannot be done. **Note:** the local authority can revise a decision if, within one month of your being sent or given it, it has information that shows that there was a mistake about the facts of your case or the decision was made in ignorance of relevant facts;[72] *or*
- for other benefits, the time limit for applying for an 'any grounds' revision (or any longer period allowed) has passed (see p1304) or, if the decision maker decides to do a supersession her/himself, it is more than one month since you were sent or given the decision.

In practice, this ground for supersession generally only applies if, as a result of a mistake or ignorance about the facts, a decision was less favourable to you than it would have been (eg, you were awarded too little benefit) and you have missed the time limit for applying for an 'any grounds' revision. If a decision is more favourable to you than it would have been (ie, you were being overpaid), a decision maker can initiate a 'specific grounds' revision (see p1310).

Note:

- There must have been a mistake about the facts or the decision maker (or the tribunal) must not have had all the facts, but it does not matter how the mistake came about or whether you could have produced evidence sooner than you did or failed to give the information on your claim form.
- The mistake or ignorance must be in respect of facts, not conclusions or opinions about the facts.[73] See p1239 for some examples.

Part 9: Getting a benefit decision changed
Chapter 56: Revisions and supersessions
3. Supersessions

- Sometimes it is possible to argue that the decision maker's mistake was an 'official error' (see p1307). If so, a 'specific gounds' revision on this ground may be possible. If superseding the decision would give you an increased award, this is the better option, as full arrears of benefit are payable.

Decisions that are legally wrong

A decision maker's decision can be superseded if it was legally wrong (known as an error of law)[74] and:

- for HB, a revision on the same basis cannot be done; *or*
- for other benefits, the time limit for seeking an 'any grounds' revision (or any longer period allowed) has passed (see p1304) or, if the decision maker decides to carry out a supersession her/himself, it is more than one month since you were sent or given the decision.

In many cases, if there has been an error of law, a 'specific grounds' revision on the basis of official error is also possible (see p1307). If the new decision is to your advantage, a revision is the better option, as full arrears of benefit are payable.

Note: if a decision of the First-tier or Upper Tribunal is legally wrong, this is not a ground that allows it to be changed by a supersession (it can only be changed by appealing against it).

Capability for work and disability conditions

A decision maker's or a tribunal's decision can be superseded if it is a decision to award you UC, ESA or national insurance (NI) credits on the basis that you have, or are treated as having, limited capability for work (see Chapter 45), or it is a decision to award you PIP on the basis that you satisfy one of the disability conditions. The decision can be superseded if:

- since the decision was made:[75]
  - a healthcare professional (see p1176 for who counts) or, for PIP and ESA under the UC system, an 'other person' approved by the Secretary of State, has provided medical evidence – eg, on your capability for work (or on whether you satisfy the disability conditions for PIP); *or*
  - the decision maker has decided that you can be treated as having limited capability for work (or, for UC, for work and work-related activity) under specified provisions.

The rules, therefore, allow the decision maker to consider your entitlement to UC, ESA, NI credits or PIP without identifying a specific change of circumstances (see p1316).[76] The rate of benefit may be increased or reduced, or your entitlement may end. However, your entitlement should *only* end if s/he decides on the basis of the evidence that you no longer have limited capability for work, or no longer satisfy the conditions for PIP.[77]

If you have told the decision maker that your condition has not improved since your last assessment or you have a variable condition, you can argue that reference should be made to earlier assessments and decisions on your claim;[78] *or*

- it is a decision to award you PIP and there has been a determination that, because you did not return your questionnaire or you failed to participate in your assessment consultation, you do not satisfy the disability conditions for the daily living component or the mobility component.[79]

Awards of qualifying benefits

A decision maker's or a tribunal's decision awarding you benefit can be superseded if:

- you are awarded the benefit (eg, IS, ESA or HB) but, from a later date than the entitlement began, you or your partner (or a child included in your claim – see p323) are awarded another benefit or an increase in its rate. This can work to your advantage if the other benefit is a 'qualifying benefit' (eg, DLA, PIP or carer's allowance – CA) (see p1328);[80] *or*
- for IS, income-based JSA, income-related ESA and PC only, if you have a non-dependant living with you (see p348) and since you were awarded the benefit, your non-dependant has been awarded a qualifying benefit (see p1328) for a period beginning after the date your award took effect, and this means that you are now entitled to a severe disability premium (for IS, JSA or ESA) or a severe disability addition (for PC).[81]

See p1328 for further information. If you are only entitled to a benefit once a qualifying benefit is awarded, see p211 and p1180.

Other grounds for supersession

There are other situations when a decision can be superseded, including if the decision is one against which you have no right of appeal (see p1344).[82] Other decisions that can be superseded include those:

- where the amount of rent for the purposes of the housing costs element (for UC) or your maximum rent (for HB) decreases because of a rent officer's redetermination. **Note:** for HB, a decrease in your maximum rent because a local housing allowance rate or a broad rental market area has been amended due to a rent officer's error, is a change of circumstances;[83]
- which reduced your HB under the benefit cap rules (see p1194), or increased or reduced the reduction;[84]
- about PC and HB, where you or your partner deferred claiming a retirement pension or a state pension and you are paid a lump sum or repay it because you change your option to a pension increase;[85]
- of the First-tier or Upper Tribunal made while a test case was pending, where the test case is eventually decided in your favour (see p1364).[86]

The list above is not exhaustive. Other decisions can be superseded.[87]

Part 9: Getting a benefit decision changed
Chapter 56: Revisions and supersessions
3. Supersessions

How to apply for a supersession

For HB, you must apply for a supersession in writing.[88] **For benefits other than HB**, you do not have to apply for a supersession in writing, although it is always best to do so. This ensures that the decision maker understands that you are asking for one, not just seeking an explanation or complaining about the rules. **For UC**, in practice the DWP may refuse to deal with an application for a supersession unless you have indicated that there is a 'change of circumstances' on your online journal. **Note:** the date of your application for a supersession may be before this – eg, if at an earlier date you wrote about the change on your journal.

The application counts as received when received at an appropriate office. This is the same as for revisions (see p1312).

A notification of a change in circumstances can be treated as an application for a supersession, so if you are reporting a change of circumstances, check that your application is received. The date of receipt is important as it can affect the date from when your benefit is changed.

When you apply for a supersession, include any information and evidence that supports your case and that may enable the decision maker to change the decision in your favour. For how to get evidence and for providing further information, see p1313. The issues are the same as for revisions. **Note:**
- The DWP, the local authority or HMRC can treat an application for a supersession as an application for a revision and an application for a revision as an application for a supersession.[89]
- A claim for benefit or a question about your entitlement can be treated as an application for a supersession.[90]

When a supersession takes effect

If a decision is superseded, the date the new decision (the supersession) takes effect is important. This is the date from when you are paid arrears if you are entitled to more benefit, or the date from when you have been overpaid if you are entitled to less benefit. It is important to make it clear that you want payment for a past period. For how the 'anti-test case rule' may affect the amount of backdated benefit you can receive, see p1330.

The general rule

There is a general rule that applies in many cases. This is that if a decision is superseded, the new decision takes effect from:[91]
- the date you applied for the supersession; *or*
- if the decision maker decides to carry out a supersession on her/his own initiative, the date the decision is made.

There are many exceptions when the general rule does not apply. For these, the date a supersession takes effect depends on the ground for the supersession. For the exceptions, see below and the chapter in this *Handbook* about the benefit you are claiming.

Changes in your circumstances

If the ground for supersession is a change in your circumstances, when the supersession takes effect usually depends on whether or not it is advantageous to you.

There are also some special rules that apply in particular situations, including the following.

- For benefits other than UC, child benefit and guardian's allowance, if there has been a change in the legislation that affects your benefit, the supersession takes effect from the date the legislation takes effect (for UC, the change takes effect from the start of the next assessment period unless the legislation took effect on the first day of an assessment period).[92]
- For IS, income-based JSA, income-related ESA and PC, if your carer (or your partner's carer) has stopped being paid carer's allowance (CA), the supersession takes effect from the day after the last day for which CA was paid, provided this was to someone other than you or your partner. This means that if you are now entitled to the severe disability premium in your IS, income-based JSA or income-related ESA or the severe disability addition in your PC, your award can be increased from when the carer stopped getting CA for looking after you (or your partner).[93]
- For ESA and UC, if the change is that you are terminally ill (you must state this in the application for a supersession), the supersession takes effect from the date you became terminally ill.[94]

If a supersession is not advantageous

If the decision maker decides to carry out a supersession her/himself or you apply for a supersession and it is *not advantageous* to you, the supersession usually takes effect from:

- for UC, the start of the assessment period in which the change takes place or is expected to take place. There is an exception if the decision is one you were required to notify and is about limited capability for work (see p1322);[95]
- if you come under the UC system (see p23), for contribution-based JSA and contributory ESA, the start of the benefit week in which the change takes place or is expected to take place.[96] There is an exception if the decision is one you were required to notify and is about limited capability for work (see p1322);
- for HB, the Monday after the week in which the change occurs.[97] For the exceptions to this rule, see p223;
- for PIP, the date on which the change takes place or is expected to take place.[98] There is an exception if the change is one you were required to notify and relates to the disability conditions for PIP (see p1322);

Part 9: Getting a benefit decision changed
Chapter 56: Revisions and supersessions
3. Supersessions

- for other benefits, the date of the change of circumstances.[99] There is an exception if the change is one you were required to notify and relates to a disability or limited capability for work determination (see below).

Note: if a supersession is not advantageous to you, you may have been overpaid. The DWP, the local authority or HMRC may seek to recover the overpayment.

Disability and limited capability for work

Different rules apply if the decision is *not advantageous* to you, it concerns a change you were required to notify and it related to:

- if you come under the UC system, limited capability for work; *or*
- if you do not come under the UC system, a disability or limited capability for work determination (see p1310 for what counts); *or*
- the disability conditions for PIP.

In this case, if you (or the person being paid the benefit) failed to notify the change when you knew that you should have, or could reasonably be expected to have known that you should have, the supersession takes effect from the date you (or the person being paid the benefit) ought to have notified the change.[100] However, if you (or the person being paid) could not have reasonably been expected to know that you should have reported the change, the supersession usually takes effect from:[101]

- for UC, the start of the assessment period in which the DWP makes the decision; *or*
- for ESA if you come under the UC system and PIP, the date you applied for the supersession, or if the decision maker decides to do a supersession on her/his own, the date the decision is made; *or*
- for other benefits, from the date on which the supersession decision is made.

So if your condition is found to have improved in the past, and you could not have been expected to report this, you will not have been overpaid, or be expected to repay any overpayment.

Note: if you do not come under the UC system, the benefit is a 'qualifying benefit' (see p1328 for what counts) and the supersession means your entitlement to another benefit is affected, the decision about the other benefit takes effect on the same date.[102]

If a supersession is advantageous

If the supersession is *advantageous* to you, when it takes effect depends on whether the decision maker initiated the supersession, or you applied for one.

If the decision maker initiated a supersession, it usually takes effect from:

- for UC, the start of the assessment period in which s/he first took action with a view to carrying out a supersession;[103]

- for HB, the Monday after the week in which the change occurs.[104] However, if the change is one you are required to notify to the local authority (other than, if you get PC and the rate of this changes as described in the first bullet point on p224), you must have notified the local authority of the change within one month of the change.[105] For further information on when changes in circumstances take effect and exceptions to this rule, see p223;
- for AA, DLA and PIP, the date on which s/he first took action with a view to carrying out a supersession;[106]
- for other benefits, the start of the benefit week in which s/he first took action with a view to carrying out a supersession.[107]

If you apply for the supersession, it usually takes effect from:
- for UC, the start of the assessment period in which the change takes place or is expected to take place. You must have notified the DWP of the change within that assessment period;[108]
- for JSA and ESA if you come under the UC system (see p23), the start of the benefit week in which the change takes place or is expected to take place. You must have notified the DWP of the change within one month of the change;[109]
- for HB, the Monday after the week in which the change occurs.[110] However, if the change is one you are required to notify to the local authority (other than if you get PC and the note on , listed on p224), you must have notified the local authority of the change within one month of the change;[111]
- for PIP, the date the change takes place, or is expected to take place. You must notify the DWP of the change within one month of the change.[112] However, if the change means you are now entitled to a higher rate of benefit, the supersession takes effect from the day you satisfy the conditions of entitlement for that rate (this includes the 'required period condition' – see p759).[113] In this case, you must have notified the DWP within one month of satisfying the conditions of entitlement;
- for AA or DLA, if the change:[114]
  - means you are now entitled to a higher rate of benefit, the day you satisfy the conditions of entitlement to that rate (this includes the qualifying period condition – see p534, p603 and p610). You must have notified the DWP of the change within one month of doing so;
  - makes a difference to whether benefit is payable to you (eg, you leave hospital or a care home), the day of the change. You must have notified the DWP of the change within one month of the change;
- for other benefits, from the date the change takes place, or is expected to take place. You must have notified the DWP (or HMRC) of the change within one month of the change.[115] There are exceptions to this rule for IS and PC and, if you do not come under the UC system, JSA and ESA.[116]

The one-month periods can be extended. If your application for an extension is refused, see p1324 for when the supersession takes effect.

Part 9: Getting a benefit decision changed
Chapter 56: Revisions and supersessions
3. Supersessions

Late notification of a change of circumstances

If the supersession is *advantageous* to you and you fail to notify a change within the one-month periods above (or, for UC, within the assessment period), you can apply for an extension of time in limited circumstances, to a **maximum of 13 months**.[117] Your application must contain:[118]

- details of the relevant change of circumstances; *and*
- the reasons why you failed to notify the change in time. You must show that:
  - it is reasonable to grant your request; *and*
  - the change of circumstances is relevant to the decision you want changed; *and*
  - there are special circumstances that mean it was not practicable for you to notify the change within the time limit. The longer you have delayed, the more compelling the special circumstances must be.

When deciding whether it is reasonable to grant your application, the decision maker cannot take account of the fact that:[119]

- a court or the Upper Tribunal has interpreted the law in a different way than was previously understood and applied;
- you (or anyone acting for you) misunderstood or were unaware of the relevant law, including the time limits for applying for a supersession.

If your application for an extension of time is refused, or your application was made outside the maximum time limit, arrears are limited. The supersession takes effect:

- for UC, from the start of the assessment period in which you notified the change;[120] *or*
- for AA or DLA, from the date you applied for the supersession;[121] *or*
- for IS, JSA, ESA and PC:[122]
  - if you are paid in arrears, from the start of the benefit week in which you notified the change; *or*
  - if you are paid in advance and you notified the change on the first day of the benefit week, from that day. Otherwise it takes effect from the start of the benefit week following the week in which you notified the change; *or*
- for HB, usually from the Monday after the date when you notified the change (see p223);[123] *or*
- for other benefits, from the date you notified the change.[124]

Mistake about or ignorance of facts

If there has been a mistake about or ignorance of facts, the general rule on p1320 usually applies. So even if you are entitled to more benefit, arrears are limited. There are exceptions.

Exceptions to the general rule

If the First-tier or Upper Tribunal made a decision in ignorance of relevant facts or made a mistake about the facts and, as a result, it was more *advantageous* to you than it would otherwise have been (eg, you have been overpaid benefit), the supersession takes effect:[125]

- for UC and ESA if you come under the UC system (see p23), from the start of the assessment period (for UC) or the start of the benefit week (for ESA) in which the tribunal's decision took effect; *or*
- for other benefits, from the date the tribunal's decision took effect.

However, the First-tier or Upper Tribunal decision is only superseded from this earlier date if you knew, or you could reasonably have been expected to know, the fact in question and that it was relevant to the decision and:[126]

- the decision related to a disability determination (see p1310 for the definition); *or*
- it is a decision about your limited capability for work or whether you can be treated as having limited capability for work.

If you did not know (or could not be expected to know), the general rule on p1320 applies.

For HB, if a decision maker's decision was made in ignorance of facts or there was a mistake about the facts and the new decision is *advantageous* to you, the supersession takes effect from the start of the benefit week in which:[127]

- you applied for the supersession; *or*
- if you did not apply for a supersession, the local authority first had sufficient information to show that the original decision was made in ignorance of, or based on a mistake about, the facts.

The list above is not exhaustive. There are other exceptions to the general rule.[128]

Awards of qualifying benefits

If you are entitled to a benefit at a higher rate because you (or your partner, your child or a non-dependant) were awarded a qualifying benefit (see p1328 for what counts), the supersession takes effect on the date of entitlement to the qualifying benefit or to an increase in its rate. For IS, JSA, ESA and PC only, if you had a non-dependant living with you while you were waiting for a decision on your claim for a qualifying benefit, your IS, JSA, ESA or PC award can be superseded to include a severe disability premium (additional amount with PC) from the date the non-dependant can be ignored (or ceased to live with you). See pp1328–30 for further information.

Test cases

If a decision about your benefit is being superseded because of a decision by the Upper Tribunal or a court in another case (a 'test case'), the supersession is

Part 9: Getting a benefit decision changed
Chapter 56: Revisions and supersessions
3. Supersessions

effective from the date of the tribunal's or court's decision, even if you did not realise it was relevant to your case until some time later.[129] This could help you get considerable arrears of benefit. For the special rule for the period before the date the test case is decided, see p1330.

If, while an appeal against the initial decision in a test case was pending:

- for benefits other than HB, a decision was made on your claim for benefit or to make a revision or a supersession, but your benefit was suspended and if the test case is eventually decided against you (in whole or in part), the supersession takes effect from the date the earlier decision took effect;[130]
- you appealed to the First-tier or Upper Tribunal, it determined your appeal as if the test case had been decided in the way most unfavourable to you and the test case eventually goes in your favour (see p1364), the supersession takes effect from the date it would have taken effect had the tribunal made its decision in accordance with the decision in the test case.[131] For UC, the date is the start of the assessment period (for IS, JSA, ESA and PC, the start of the benefit week) in which it would have taken effect had the tribunal made its decision in accordance with the decision in the test case.[132]

Other grounds for supersession

There are a large number of other exceptions to the general rule on p1320. These include if:

- your rent for the purposes of the housing costs element (for UC) or your maximum rent (for HB) has decreased because of a rent officer's redetermination;[133]
- for UC and ESA, a healthcare professional (see p1176 for who counts) approved by the Secretary of State has provided medical evidence on your capability for work or a decision maker has decided that you can be treated as having limited capability for work or work-related activity;[134]
- for PC and HB, you or your partner deferred claiming a retirement pension or state pension and you are paid a lump sum or change your option to a pension increase;[135]
- entitlement to a benefit depends on your NI contribution record, and the decision needed to be changed because additional contributions have been added to the record.[136]

The list above is not exhaustive. There are many other exceptions to the general rule.[137]

Challenging a supersession

Following your application for a supersession, or a decision maker initiating a supersession, a new decision is issued in writing. If you do not get all that you wanted, you can apply for a revision of the new decision. If the decision is one against which you have a right of appeal (see p1343), you can appeal to the First-tier Tribunal. Unless the benefit is HB, you must apply for a mandatory reconsideration first (see p1339). If you have a right of appeal against the decision, you must be told about this.

If the decision maker has said there are no grounds for a supersession, you must show why there are, and say what you think the new decision should be. If the decision maker has conducted a supersession, but you do not agree that s/he had grounds for this, you should explain why.

If a decision maker refuses to consider a supersession

When you apply for a supersession, a decision maker must make a decision if your application contains a ground for supersession that is potentially relevant to the amount of benefit you can be paid or the length of time you can be paid it. There are two possibilities.

- The decision maker agrees that there is a reason to change your award. For example, you are claiming HB and notify the decision maker that your non-dependant has moved out and so are entitled to more benefit. In this situation, the decision maker carries out a supersession.
- The decision maker does not think there is a reason to change your award. For example, you are getting the standard rate of the PIP daily living component, feel your condition has deteriorated and want to claim the enhanced rate instead. However, the decision maker thinks you do not qualify for the enhanced rate. In this situation, the decision maker issues a decision refusing to carry out a supersession.

In either situation, you can apply for a revision of the decision maker's decision or appeal against it.[138] Unless the benefit is HB, you must apply for a mandatory reconsideration before you can appeal (see p1339).

The only situations in which a decision maker does not have to make a decision are if an application has not been made properly and therefore cannot possibly lead to a supersession, or if an application is clearly not on a potentially relevant ground or is otherwise misconceived. In these cases, there is no decision against which you can seek a revision or appeal, but you may be able to apply for a judicial review (see p1414).

Part 9: Getting a benefit decision changed
Chapter 56: Revisions and supersessions
4. Revisions and supersessions after a 'qualifying benefit' award

4. Revisions and supersessions after a 'qualifying benefit' award

Some of the rules for revisions and supersessions can help you if you (or your partner, your child or a non-dependant) become entitled to a 'qualifying benefit'.

Qualifying benefits

A **'qualifying benefit'** is, in general, any benefit which gives you entitlement to another benefit, or makes another benefit payable at a higher rate.

For example, the rules can help if there was a delay in assessing your entitlement to a qualifying benefit (eg, attendance allowance (AA), disability living allowance (DLA), personal independence payment (PIP), carer's allowance (CA) or child benefit) and so:

- you did not get an element in your universal credit (UC), a disability- or carer-related premium in your means-tested benefit or an additional amount in your pension credit (PC), or allowances for your children. For income support (IS), jobseeker's allowance (JSA), employment and support allowance (ESA) and PC only, this includes where there are delays in assessing your non-dependant's entitlement to a qualifying benefit (see p1329); *or*
- a non-dependant deduction was made from your means-tested benefit.

Note: these rules can help you get arrears of benefit, even if the qualifying benefit was awarded some time ago, and you did not report the change in your circumstances at the time.[139]

Do you have to be entitled to a means-tested benefit?

You can only apply for a revision or supersession on this ground if you are already entitled to UC, IS, JSA, ESA, PC or housing benefit (HB).[140] It is, therefore, essential to make a claim, if you are not prevented from doing so by the introduction of UC, at the same time as the claim for a qualifying benefit. If you only qualify for one of these when the qualifying benefit is awarded, see p1329.

You or a family member are awarded a qualifying benefit or an increased rate

If you, or your partner or a child included in your claim (see p323), are awarded a qualifying benefit, or are awarded an increase in its rate (eg, you were getting the standard rate of the daily living component of PIP and are awarded the enhanced rate of that component), and arrears of the qualifying benefit are payable, your award of UC, IS, JSA, ESA, PC or HB can be increased on revision or supersession and arrears paid for the same length of time.[141] This applies if:

- you are now entitled to premiums/components/elements/additional amounts or, if the qualifying benefit is child benefit, to allowances or premiums for your children paid with your benefit; *or*
- no non-dependant deduction, or for UC, a deduction for housing costs contributions, should now be made from your means-tested benefit because you or your partner are now entitled to a qualifying benefit – eg, AA, the care component of DLA or the daily living component of PIP.

Note: for IS, JSA, ESA and PC only, if you had a non-dependant living with you while you were waiting for a decision on your claim for a qualifying benefit, your IS, JSA, ESA or PC award can be superseded to include the severe disability premium (or additional amount), from the date s/he can be ignored (or from the date s/he ceased to reside with you) if this is after the date from which the qualifying benefit is payable.[142]

Example

Gus has been getting income-related ESA and HB for two months. His ESA does not include any premiums and, because his uncle lives with him and his partner, Tanya, a non-dependant deduction is being made from his HB. He claims PIP and Tanya claims CA on 15 July. Six months later, Gus is awarded the enhanced rate of the daily living component of PIP and Tanya is awarded CA, both payable from 15 July. Gus is now entitled to the enhanced disability and carer premiums in his ESA and a non-dependant deduction should not be made from his HB. His ESA and HB awards are superseded and he is paid arrears, backdated to 15 July.

Your non-dependant is awarded a qualifying benefit or an increased rate

For IS, JSA, ESA and PC only, if you have a non-dependant (see p363) living with you and, but for this, a severe disability premium (or additional amount for PC) would be paid, your award of IS, income-based JSA, income-related ESA or PC can be increased on revision or supersession to include this premium (or additional amount) from the date the non-dependant is awarded a qualifying benefit.[143]

You only qualify when the qualifying benefit is awarded

If you make an unsuccessful claim for a benefit, and only qualify when the qualifying benefit is awarded, you should make a second claim as soon as you hear about the qualifying benefit. See p1180 for further information.

Part 9: Getting a benefit decision changed
Chapter 56: Revisions and supersessions
5. The 'anti-test case rule'

If you only qualify for HB when the qualifying benefit is awarded, see p211. If you lose benefit because of the way the rules operate, ask the local authority for compensation.

If you only claim for the first time *after* you hear about the qualifying benefit, you can only qualify for backdated benefit under the normal backdating rules. See Chapter 50 and the chapter about the benefit you are claiming.

See p572 for a similar rule that helps you get extra backdated CA when the person for whom you care becomes entitled to a qualifying benefit.

5. **The 'anti-test case rule'**

A special rule applies when a case is going through the appeals system that will determine a point of social security law (a 'test case'), which can affect how the decision on that point in the test case is applied in your case.

The rule applies if the Upper Tribunal or a court decides in an appeal that a decision maker in a different case (the test case) has made an error of law (see p1397 for what counts), and you make a claim, or apply for a revision or a supersession (either before or after the test case decision). In this situation, your decision maker must decide any part of your claim (or revision or supersession) which relates to the period before the test case decision as if the decision that was under appeal in the test case had been found by the tribunal or court not to have been wrong.[144] **Note:**

- The anti-test case rule only applies if the test case is the first authoritative decision on the issue, and not merely a later decision confirming an earlier decision.[145]
- The test case decision only has to be disregarded for the period before it was made if it found the decision maker to have been wrong, not if it found her/ him to be right.

For housing benefit (HB), you can avoid the anti-test case rule by appealing rather than seeking a revision or supersession if the rules allow you to do so. Unless the benefit is HB, you must apply for a mandatory reconsideration before you can appeal (see p1339).

What happens while a test case is pending

If an appeal (a test case) is pending against a decision of the Upper Tribunal or a court, the decision maker can postpone making a decision on your claim or request for a supersession or revision.[146] The decision maker can only do this if s/he thinks that a possible result of the test case is that you will have no entitlement to benefit. This prevents you appealing until a decision is made in the test case. If the decision is postponed, once a decision has been made in the test case, the decision maker makes the decision in your case.[147]

If you would be entitled to benefit even if the test case were decided against you, the decision maker can make a decision on the assumption that the test case has been decided in the way that is most unfavourable to you.[148] However, this means that you can at least be paid something while you wait for the result of the test case. Then, if the decision in the test case is in your favour, the decision maker revises her/his decision. **Note:**

- If you already have a decision in your favour, the decision maker can suspend payment of your benefit (see p1200).
- If you have already appealed to the First-tier Tribunal, see p1364.

Notes

1. **Getting a decision changed**
1 **HB** Sch 7 para 11 CSPSSA 2000
Other benefits s17 SSA 1998
2 **HB** Sch 7 paras 3(2) and 4(3) CSPSSA 2000
Other benefits ss9(2) and 10(2) SSA 1998
3 *Wood v SSWP* [2003] EWCA Civ 53

2. **Revisions**
4 **HB** Sch 7 para 3 CSPSSA 2000
Other benefits s9 SSA 1998
5 **UC/PIP/JSA&ESA under UC** s9(1) SSA 1998; regs 5 and 8 UC,PIP,JSA&ESA(DA) Regs
HB Sch 7 para 3(1) CSPSSA 2000; reg 4 HB&CTB(DA) Regs
CB/GA s9(1) SSA 1998; regs 5, 8, 10 and 11 CB&GA(DA) Regs
Other benefits s9(1) SSA 1998; reg 3 SS&CS(DA) Regs
6 **UC/PIP/JSA&ESA under UC** Reg 5(2)(a) UC,PIP,JSA&ESA(DA) Regs
HB Reg 4(10) HB&CTB(DA) Regs
CB/GA Reg 5(3) CB&GA(DA) Regs
Other benefits Reg 3(9)(a) SS&CS(DA) Regs
7 **UC/PIP/JSA&ESA under UC** Reg 5(2)(c) UC,PIP,JSA&ESA(DA) Regs
Other benefits Reg 3(9)(b) and (c) SS&CS(DA) Regs

8 Reg 3(3) SS&CS(DA) Regs
9 Regs 1(3), definition of 'date of notification', and 3(1)(b) SS&CS(DA) Regs
10 Regs 2 and 4(1)(a) HB&CTB(DA) Regs
11 Reg 4(4) HB&CTB(DA) Regs
12 **UC/PIP/JSA&ESA under UC** Regs 2, 3(2) and 5(1)(b) UC,PIP,JSA&ESA(DA) Regs
CB/GA Regs 3 and 5(2)(b) CB&GA(DA) Regs
Other benefits Regs 1(3), 2(b) and 3(1)(b) SS&CS(DA) Regs
13 **UC/PIP/JSA&ESA under UC** Reg 38(4) UC,PIP,JSA&ESA(DA) Regs
HB Reg 10A(3) HB&CTB(DA) Regs
Other benefits Reg 9A(3) SS&CS(DA) Regs
14 **HB** Regs 4(4) and 5(3)(b) HB&CTB(DA) Regs
UC/PIP/JSA&ESA under UC Reg 6 UC,PIP,JSA&ESA(DA) Regs
CB/GA Reg 6(3)(c) CB&GA(DA) Regs
Other benefits Reg 4 SS&CS(DA) Regs

Part 9: Getting a benefit decision changed
Chapter 56: Revisions and supersessions
Notes

15 **UC/PIP/JSA&ESA under UC** Reg 6(3)-
(6) UC,PIP,JSA&ESA(DA) Regs
HB Reg 5(3)(a), (4) and (6)
HB&CTB(DA) Regs
CB/GA Reg 6(3)(a) and (b), (4) and (5)
CB&GA(DA) Regs
Other benefits Reg 4(3)(a), (4) and (5)
SS&CS(DA) Regs

16 **HB** Reg 5(4)(b) and (5) HB&CTB(DA)
Regs
CB/GA Reg 6(4)(b) and (6)
CB&GA(DA) Regs
Other benefits Reg 4(4)(b) and (6)
SS&CS(DA) Regs

17 R(TC) 1/05

18 *R(CJ) and SG v SSWP (ESA)* [2017] UKUT
324 (AAC); Memo DMG 17/17; Memo
ADM 21/17

19 **UC/PIP/JSA&ESA under UC** Reg
5(1)(a) UC,PIP,JSA&ESA(DA) Regs
CB/GA Reg 5(2)(a) CB&GA(DA) Regs
Other benefits Reg 3(1)(a)
SS&CS(DA) Regs

20 Reg 4(1)(b) HB&CTB(DA) Regs

21 **UC/PIP/JSA&ESA under UC** Regs 8
and 9(a) UC,PIP,JSA&ESA(DA) Regs
HB Reg 4(2)(a) HB&CTB(DA) Regs
CB/GA Reg 10(2)(a) CB&GA(DA) Regs
Other benefits Reg 3(5)(a)
SS&CS(DA) Regs

22 **UC/PIP/JSA&ESA under UC** Reg 2
UC,PIP,JSA&ESA(DA) Regs
HB Reg 1(2) HB&CTB(DA) Regs
Other benefits Reg 1(3) SS&CS(DA)
Regs

23 Reg 10(3) CB&GA(DA) Regs

24 **UC/PIP/JSA&ESA under UC** Reg 2
UC,PIP,JSA&ESA(DA) Regs
HB Reg 1(2) HB&CTB(DA) Regs
CB/GA Reg 10(3) CB&GA(DA) Regs
Other benefits Reg 1(3) SS&CS(DA)
Regs

25 **UC/PIP/JSA&ESA under UC** Reg 2
UC,PIP,JSA&ESA(DA) Regs
HB Reg 1(2) HB&CTB(DA) Regs
CB/GA Reg 10(3) CB&GA(DA) Regs
Other benefits Reg 1(3) SS&CS(DA)
Regs

26 CDLA/393/2006

27 CDLA/1707/2005

28 *R (Smith) v SSWP* [2018] UKUT 270
(AAC)

29 **UC/JSA&ESA under UC** Reg 14(1)(a)-
(c) UC,PIP,JSA&ESA(DA) Regs
Other benefits Reg 3(5C), (6), (6A)
and (7CD) SS&CS(DA) Regs

30 Reg 3(6B) SS&CS(DA) Regs

31 **UC/PIP/JSA&ESA under UC** Regs 8
and 12 UC,PIP,JSA&ESA(DA) Regs
HB Reg 4(7B) HB&CTB(DA) Regs
CB/GA Reg 11 CB&GA(DA) Regs
Other benefits Reg 3(7) SS&CS(DA)
Regs

32 Reg 3(7ZA) SS&CS(DA) Regs

33 Reg 4(7C) HB&CTB(DA) Regs

34 **UC/PIP/JSA&ESA under UC** Regs 8
and 11(1) UC,PIP,JSA&ESA(DA) Regs
HB Reg 4(1)(c) HB&CTB(DA) Regs
CB/GA Reg 8(2) CB&GA(DA) Regs
Other benefits Reg 3(4A) SS&CS(DA)
Regs

35 **UC/PIP/JSA&ESA under UC** Regs 8
and 11(2) UC,PIP,JSA&ESA(DA) Regs
HB Reg 4(7) HB&CTB(DA) Regs
CB/GA Reg 8(3) CB&GA(DA) Regs
Other benefits Reg 3(5A) SS&CS(DA)
Regs

36 **UC/PIP/JSA&ESA under UC** Regs 8
and 9(b) UC,PIP,JSA&ESA(DA) Regs
HB Reg 4(2)(b) HB&CTB(DA) Regs
CB/GA Reg 10(2)(b) CB&GA(DA) Regs
Other benefits Reg 3(5)(b) and (d)
SS&CS(DA) Regs

37 Regs 3(5)(c)and 7A(1) SS&CS(DA) Regs

38 Reg 7A SS&CS(DA) Regs

39 **UC/PIP/JSA&ESA under UC** Regs 8
and 10 UC,PIP,JSA&ESA(DA) Regs
HB Reg 4(6) HB&CTB(DA) Regs
CB/GA Reg 9 CB&GA(DA) Regs
Other benefits Reg 3(8) SS&CS(DA)
Regs

40 **UC/PIP/JSA&ESA under UC** Regs 8
and 19(1) UC,PIP,JSA&ESA(DA) Regs
HB Reg 4(7H) HB&CTB(DA) Regs

41 **UC/PIP/JSA&ESA under UC** Reg
15(5) UC,PIP,JSA&ESA(DA) Regs
Other benefits Reg 3(5I) SS&CS(DA)
Regs

42 Regs 8 and 18(2) UC,PIP,JSA&ESA(DA)
Regs

43 Regs 8 and 18(3) UC,PIP,JSA&ESA(DA)
Regs

44 **UC/PIP/JSA&ESA under UC** Regs 8
and 19(2) UC,PIP,JSA&ESA(DA) Regs
HB Reg 4(3) HB&CTB(DA) Regs; reg
18A(1) and (3) HB Regs; reg 18A(1) and
(3) HB(SPC) Regs

45 **State pension** Reg 3(7DB) SS&CS(DA)
Regs
RP Reg 3(7E) SS&CS(DA) Regs
PC Reg 3(7D) and (7DA) SS&CS(DA)
Regs
HB Reg 4(7D) and (7DA) HB&CTB(DA)
Regs

46 **UC/PIP/JSA&ESA under UC** Regs 8, 13, 15(2)-(4) and (4A), 16, 17 and 18(1) UC,PIP,JSA&ESA(DA) Regs
HB Reg 4(7A) and (7DB) HB&CTB(DA) Regs
Other benefits Reg 3(5D)-(5H), (5J), (7A), (7EA), (7EB), (8B)-(8K) SS&CS(DA) Regs

47 Regs 4(8) and 5(2) HB&CTB(DA) Regs

48 **UC/PIP/JSA&ESA under UC** Reg 5(1)(b) UC,PIP,JSA&ESA(DA) Regs
CB/GA Reg 5(1)(b) CB&GA(DA) Regs
Other benefits Reg 3(1)(b) SS&CS(DA) Regs

49 **UC/PIP/JSA&ESA under UC** Reg 2 UC,PIP,JSA&ESA(DA) Regs
HB Reg 4(8) HB&CTB(DA) Regs
CB/GA Reg 2(1), definition of 'appropriate office', CB&GA(DA) Regs
Other benefits Reg 3(11) SS&CS(DA) Regs

50 **HB** Sch 7 paras 3(2) and 4(3) CSPSSA 2000
Other benefits ss9(2) and 10(2) SSA 1998

51 **UC/PIP/JSA&ESA under UC** Regs 20(1) and 33(1) UC,PIP,JSA&ESA(DA) Regs
HB Regs 4(9) and 7(6) HB&CTB(DA) Regs
CB/GA Regs 7(1) and 14(1) CB&GA(DA) Regs
Other benefits Regs 3(10) and 6(5) SS&CS(DA) Regs

52 R(JSA)2/04

53 R(IS) 11/92; *SSWP v TJ (JSA)* [2015] UKUT 56 (AAC), paras 213-15

54 **UC/PIP/JSA&ESA under UC** Regs 20(2) and (3) and 33(2) and (3) UC,PIP,JSA&ESA(DA) Regs
HB Regs 4(5) and 7(5) HB&CTB(DA) Regs
CB/GA Regs 7(2) and (3) and 14(3) CB&GA(DA) Regs
Other benefits Regs 3(2) and 6(4) SS&CS(DA) Regs

55 Reg 33(4) UC,PIPJSA&ESA(DA) Regs

56 **HB** Sch 7 para 3(3) CSPSSA 2000
Other benefits s9(3) SSA 1998

57 **UC/PIP and JSA/ESA under UC** Reg 21 UC,PIP,JSA&ESA(DA) Regs
HB Reg 6 HB&CTB(DA) Regs
CB/GA Reg 12 CB&GA(DA) Regs
Other benefits Reg 5(1) SS&CS(DA) Regs

58 Reg 7A(2) SS&CS(DA) Regs

59 s9(5) SSA 1998; Sch 7 para 3(5) CSPSSA 2000; rr22(2)(d)(I) and 23 TP(FT) Rules

60 R(IS) 15/04; *Beltekian v Westminster City Council and Another* [2004] EWCA Civ 1784, reported as R(H) 8/05; *AS v SSWP (CSM)* [2012] UKUT 448 (AAC), reported as [2013] AACR 18

61 *PH & SM v SSWP (DLA)(JSA)* [2018] UKUT 404 (AAC)

3. Supersessions

62 **HB** Sch 7 para 4 CSPSSA 2000
Other benefits s10 SSA 1998

63 **UC/PIP/JSA&ESA under UC** Reg 22 UC,PIP,JSA&ESA(DA) Regs
HB Reg 7(2) HB&CTB(DA) Regs
CB/GA Reg 13(1) CB&GA(DA) Regs
Other benefits Reg 6(2) SS&CS(DA) Regs

64 **UC/PIP/JSA&ESA under UC** Reg 32 UC,PIP,JSA&ESA(DA) Regs
HB Reg 7(4) HB&CTB(DA) Regs
CB/GA Reg 15 CB&GA(DA) Regs
Other benefits Reg 6(3) SS&CS(DA) Regs

65 **UC/PIP/JSA&ESA under UC** Reg 23 UC,PIP,JSA&ESA(DA) Regs
HB Regs 7(2)(a) and 7A(4) HB&CTB(DA) Regs
CB/GA Reg 13(2)(a) CB&GA(DA) Regs
Other benefits Reg 6(2)(a) SS&CS(DA) Regs; Sch 2 para 25A(2) ESA(TP)(EA) No.2 Regs
All *Wood v SSWP* [2003] EWCA Civ 53, reported as R(DLA) 1/03

66 CSDLA/637/2006; CSDLA/822/2006

67 *CAO v McKiernon*, 8 July 1993 (CA), reported as an attachment to R(I) 2/94

68 *Cooke v Secretary of State for Social Security* [2001], reported as R(DLA) 6/01; R(S) 4/86; R(IS) 2/98; CIB/7899/1996; CIS/856/1994

69 **UC/PIP/JSA&ESA under UC** Reg 23(2) UC,PIP,JSA&ESA(DA) Regs
Other benefits Reg 6(6)(c) SS&CS(DA) Regs

70 **HB** Sch 7 para 2 CSPSSA 2000
Other benefits s8(2) SSA 1998; reg 12A SS&CS(DA) Regs

71 **UC/PIP/JSA&ESA under UC** Regs 24 and 31(a) UC,PIP,JSA&ESA(DA) Regs
HB Reg 7(2)(b) and (d) HB&CTB(DA) Regs
CB/GA Reg 13(2)(b) and (c)(i) CB&GA(DA) Regs
Other benefits Reg 6(2)(b) and (c) SS&CS(DA) Regs

72 Reg 4(1)(b) HB&CTB(DA) Regs

73 R(I) 3/75; CSDLA/251/2007

Part 9: Getting a benefit decision changed
Chapter 56: Revisions and supersessions
Notes

74 **UC/PIP/JSA&ESA under UC** Reg 24
UC,PIP,JSA&ESA(DA) Regs
HB Reg 7(2)(b) HB&CTB(DA) Regs
CB/GA Reg 13(2)(b) CB&GA(DA) Regs
Other benefits Reg 6(2)(b)
SS&CS(DA) Regs

75 Reg 26(1) UC,PIP,JSA&ESA(DA) Regs;
regs 6(2)(r) and 7A(1) SS&CS(DA) Regs;
CIB/4033/2003; R(IB) 2/05

76 *SF v SSWP (PIP)* [2016] UKUT 481 (AAC);
DS v SSWP (PIP) [2016] UKUT 538
(AAC), reported as [2017] AACR 19

77 CSIB/377/2003; CIB/1509/2004; R(IB)
5/05; *JB v SSWP (IB)* [2010] UKUT 246
(AAC); *ST v SSWP (ESA)* [2012] UKUT
469 (AAC)

78 CIB/1972/2000; CIB/3179/2000; CIB/
3985/2001; *ST v SSWP (ESA)* [2012]
UKUT 469 (AAC); *FN v SSWP (ESA)*
[2015] UKUT 670 (AAC), reported as
[2016] AACR 24

79 s80(5) and (6) WRA 2012; regs 8 and 9
SS(PIP) Regs; reg 26(2)
UC,PIP,JSA&ESA(DA) Regs; *KB v SSWP
(PIP)* [2016] UKUT 537 (AAC)

80 **UC/PIP/JSA&ESA under UC** Reg 23
UC,PIP,JSA&ESA(DA) Regs. For these
benefits, although this counts as a
change of circumstances, it takes effect
differently to most such changes.
HB Reg 7(2)(i) HB&CTB(DA) Regs
CB/GA Reg 13(2)(e) CB&GA(DA) Regs
Other benefits Reg 6(2)(e)
SS&CS(DA) Regs

81 Reg 6(2)(ee) SS&CS(DA) Regs

82 **UC/PIP/JSA&ESA under UC** Reg 25
UC,PIP,JSA&ESA(DA) Regs
HB Reg 7(2)(e) HB&CTB(DA) Regs
CB/GA Reg 13(2)(d) CB&GA(DA) Regs
Other benefits Reg 6(2)(d)
SS&CS(DA) Regs

83 **UC** Reg 30 UC,PIP,JSA&ESA(DA) Regs
HB Reg 7(2)(c) HB&CTB(DA) Regs; reg
18A(2) HB Regs; reg 18A(2) HB(SPC)
Regs

84 Reg 7(2)(r) HB&CTB(DA) Regs

85 **PC** Reg 6(2)(o) and (oa) SS&CS(DA)
Regs
HB Reg 7(2)(j), (ja) and (jb)
HB&CTB(DA) Regs

86 **UC/PIP/JSA &ESA under UC** Reg
31(b) UC,PIP,JSA&ESA(DA) Regs
HB Reg 7(2)(d)(ii) HB&CTB(DA) Regs
CB/GA Reg 13(2)(c)(ii) CB&GA(DA)
Regs
Other benefits Reg 6(2)(c)(ii)
SS&CS(DA) Regs

87 **UC/PIP/JSA&ESA under UC** Regs 27,
28 and 29 UC,PIP,JSA&ESA(DA) Regs
HB Regs 7(2)(g), (h), (q), (r) and (s) and
7A(2) and (3) HB&CTB(DA) Regs
Other benefits Reg 6(2)(f), (fa), (h),
(j), (k), (p), (q), (s), (sa), (t) and (u)
SS&CS(DA) Regs

88 Reg 7(7) HB&CTB(DA) Regs

89 **UC/PIP/JSA&ESA under UC** Regs
20(1) and 33(1) UC,PIP,JSA&ESA(DA)
Regs
HB Regs 4(9) and 7(6) HB&CTB(DA)
Regs
CB/GA Regs 7(1) and 14(1)
CB&GA(DA) Regs
Other benefits Regs 3(10) and 6(5)
SS&CS(DA) Regs

90 R(I) 50/56

91 **HB** Sch 7 para 4(5) CSPSSA 2000
Other benefits s10(5) SSA 1998

92 **UC/PIP/JSA&ESA under UC** Reg
35(1) and Sch 1 paras 32 and 33
UC,PIP,JSA&ESA(DA) Regs
HB Reg 8(10) HB&CTB(DA) Regs
Other benefits Reg 7(9)(a)(ii), (30)
and (30A) SS&CS(DA) Regs

93 Reg 7(2)(bc) SS&CS(DA) Regs

94 **UC/PIP/JSA&ESA under UC** Reg
35(1) and Sch 1 paras 9 and 28
UC,PIP,JSA&ESA(DA) Regs
Other benefits Reg 7(2)(be)
SS&CS(DA) Regs

95 Sch 1 para 20 UC,PIP,JSA&ESA(DA) Regs

96 Sch 1 para 1 UC,PIP,JSA&ESA(DA) Regs

97 Reg 8(2) HB&CTB(DA) Regs

98 Sch 1 para 12 UC,PIP,JSA&ESA(DA) Regs

99 **AA/DLA** Reg 7(2)(c)(iv) SS&CS(DA)
Regs
CB/GA Reg 16(5) CB&GA(DA) Regs
Other benefits Reg 7(2)(c)(v)
SS&CS(DA) Regs

100 **UC/PIP/JSA/ESA under UC** Sch 1
paras 7, 8, 11, 16, 17, 19, 23, 24 and 30
UC,PIP,JSA&ESA(DA) Regs
Other benefits Regs 7(2)(c)(ii) and
7A(1) SS&CS(DA) Regs

101 **UC/PIP/JSA&ESA under UC** s10(5)
SSA 1998; Sch 1 paras 2, 13 and 25
UC,PIP,JSA&ESA(DA) Regs
Other benefits s10(5) SSA 1998 as
none of the other heads of reg 7(2)(c)
SS&CS(DA) Regs apply

102 Reg 7A(2) SS&CS(DA) Regs

103 Sch 1 para 29 UC,PIP,JSA&ESA(DA) Regs

104 Reg 8(2) HB&CTB(DA) Regs

105 Reg 8(3) HB&CTB(DA) Regs

106 **AA/DLA** Reg 7(9)(a) SS&CS(DA) Regs
PIP Sch 1 para 18 UC,PIP,JSA&ESA(DA) Regs
107 **JSA&ESA under UC** Sch 1 para 10 UC,PIP,JSA&ESA(DA) Regs
CB/GA Reg 16(4) CB&GA(DA) Regs
Other benefits Reg 7(2)(bb) SS&CS(DA) Regs
108 Sch 1 paras 20 and 21 UC,PIP,JSA&ESA(DA) Regs
109 Sch 1 paras 1 and 6 UC,PIP,JSA&ESA(DA) Regs
110 Reg 8(2) HB&CTB(DA) Regs
111 Reg 8(3) HB&CTB(DA) Regs
112 Sch 1 paras 12 and 14 UC,PIP,JSA&ESA(DA) Regs
113 Sch 1 para 15 UC,PIP,JSA&ESA(DA) Regs
114 Reg 7(9) SS&CS(DA) Regs; *SSWP v DA* [2009] UKUT 214 (AAC)
115 **CB/GA** Reg 16(3)(a) CB&GA(DA) Regs
Other benefits Reg 7(2)(a) SS&CS(DA) Regs
116 Schs 3A, 3B and 3C SS&CS(DA) Regs
117 **UC/PIP/JSA&ESA under UC** Reg 36 UC,PIP,JSA&ESA(DA) Regs
HB Reg 9 HB&CTB(DA) Regs
CB/GA Reg 17 CB&GA(DA) Regs
Other benefits Reg 8 SS&CS(DA) Regs
118 **UC/PIP/JSA&ESA under UC** Reg 36(3)-(7) UC,PIP,JSA&ESA(DA) Regs
HB Reg 9(2)-(4) HB&CTB(DA) Regs
CB/GA Reg 17(3)-(5) CB&GA(DA) Regs
Other benefits Reg 8(3)-(5) SS&CS(DA) Regs
119 **UC/PIP/JSA&ESA under UC** Reg 36(7) UC,PIP,JSA&ESA(DA) Regs
HB Reg 9(5) HB&CTB(DA) Regs
CB/GA Reg 17(6) CB&GA(DA) Regs
Other benefits Reg 8(6) SS&CS(DA) Regs
120 Sch 1 para 21 UC,PIP,JSA&ESA(DA) Regs
121 Reg 7(9)(d) SS&CS(DA) Regs
122 Reg 7(2)(b)(i) and (ii) SS&CS(DA) Regs; Sch 1 para 6 UC,PIP,JSA&ESA(DA) Regs
123 Reg 8(3) HB&CTB(DA) Regs; reg 79(1) HB Regs; reg 59(1) HB(SPC) Regs
124 **UC/PIP/JSA&ESA under UC** Sch 1 para 14 UC,PIP,JSA&ESA(DA) Regs
CB/GA Reg 16(3)(b) CB&GA(DA) Regs
Other benefits Reg 7(2)(b)(iii) SS&CS(DA) Regs
125 **UC/PIP/JSA&ESA under UC** Reg 37(1)-(3) UC,PIP,JSA&ESA(DA) Regs
HB Reg 8(7) HB&CTB(DA) Regs
CB/GA Reg 16(7) CB&GA(DA) Regs
Other benefits Reg 7(5) SS&CS(DA) Regs

126 **UC/ESA** Regs 2 and 37 (1) and (3) UC,PIP,JSA&ESA(DA) Regs
Other benefits Reg 7(5) and Sch 3C, para 8 SS&CS(DA) Regs
127 Reg 8(4) HB&CTB(DA) Regs
128 **UC/PIP/JSA&ESA under UC** Reg 35(2)-(4) UC,PIP,JSA&ESA(DA) Regs
Other benefits Reg 16(2) SS(C&P) Regs; Schs 3A para 12, 3B para 7, and 3C para 9 SS&CS(DA) Regs
129 **UC/PIP/JSA&ESA under UC** Reg 35(5) UC,PIP,JSA&ESA(DA) Regs
HB Reg 8(8) HB&CTB(DA) Regs
CB/GA Reg 16(9) CB&GA(DA) Regs
Other benefits Reg 7(6) SS&CS(DA) Regs
All *MP v SSWP (DLA)* [2010] UKUT 130 (AAC)
130 **UC/PIP/JSA&ESA under UC** Reg 37(5) and (6) UC,PIP,JSA&ESA(DA) Regs
CB/GA Reg 16(9A) CB&GA(DA) Regs
Other benefits Reg 7(6A) SS&CS(DA) Regs
131 **HB** Reg 8(11) HB&CTB(DA) Regs
CB/GA Reg 16(8) CB&GA(DA) Regs
PIP Reg 37(4)(a) UC,PIP,JSA&ESA(DA) Regs
Other benefits Reg 7(33) SS&CS(DA) Regs
132 **UC/PIP/JSA&ESA under UC** Reg 37(4)(b) and (c) UC,PIP,JSA&ESA(DA) Regs
Other benefits Schs 3A para 12, 3B para 7, and 3C para 8 SS&CS(DA) Regs
133 **UC** Reg 35(14) UC,PIP,JSA&ESA(DA) Regs
HB Reg 8(2) and (6) HB&CTB(DA) Regs
134 Reg 35(6)-(9) UC,PIP,JSA&ESA(DA) Regs; reg 7(38)-(40) SS&CS(DA) Regs
135 **PC** Reg 7(7A) SS&CS(DA) Regs
HB Reg 8(14A) HB&CTB(DA) Regs
136 Reg 35(13) UC,PIP,JSA&ESA(DA) Regs; reg 7(8A) SS&CS(DA) Regs
137 **UC/PIP/JSA&ESA under UC** Reg 35(10)-(12) UC,PIP,JSA&ESA(DA) Regs
HB Reg 8(6A), (9), (14D), (14E), (14F), (14G) and (15) HB&CTB(DA) Regs
Other benefits Reg 7(8), (8ZA), (11), (12A)-(12G), (24), (25), (28), (29), (29A)-(29C), (34)-(37) and (41)-(43) SS&CS(DA) Regs
138 *Wood v SSWP* [2003] EWCA Civ 53, reported as R(DLA) 1/03

Part 9: Getting a benefit decision changed
Chapter 56: Revisions and supersessions
Notes

4. Revisions and supersessions after a 'qualifying benefit' award

139 *HR v Wakefield DC* [2009] UKUT 72 (AAC); *OL v SSWP (ESA)* [2018] UKUT 135 (AAC)

140 **IS/JSA/ESA/PC/UC** s8(2) SSA 1998
HB Sch 7 para 2 CSPSSA 2000

141 **UC/PIP/JSA&ESA under UC** Regs 12 and 23 and Sch 1 para 31 UC,PIP,JSA&ESA(DA) Regs
IS/JSA/ESA/PC Regs 3(7), 6(2)(e) and 7(7) SS&CS(DA) Regs
HB Regs 4(7B) and (7C), 7(2)(i) and 8(14) HB&CTB(DA) Regs; CIS/1178/2001
All *BB v SSWP (ESA)* [2017] UKUT 280 (AAC)

142 Reg 7(7)(b) SS&CS(DA) Regs

143 Regs 3(7ZA), 6(2)(ee) and 7(7) SS&CS(DA) Regs

5. The 'anti-test case rule'

144 **HB** Sch 7 para 18 CSPSSA 2000
Other benefits s27 SSA 1998
All *CAO and Another v Bate* [1996] 2 All ER 790 (HL)

145 R(FC) 3/98; R(I) 1/03

146 **HB** Sch 7 para 16 CSPSSA 2000
Other benefits s25 SSA 1998

147 **HB** Sch 7 para 18(2) CSPSSA 2000
Other benefits s27(2) SSA 1998

148 **UC/PIP/JSA&ESA under UC** s25(3) and (4) SSA 1998; reg 53 UC,PIP,JSA&ESA(DA) Regs
HB Sch 7 para 16(3) and (4) CSPSSA 2000; reg 15 HB&CTB(DA) Regs
CB/GA s25(3) and (4) SSA 1998; reg 22 CB&GA(DA) Regs
Other benefits s25(3) and (4) SSA 1998; reg 21 SS&CS(DA) Regs

9

Chapter 57

Appealing to the First-tier Tribunal

This chapter covers:
1. Before you appeal (p1338)
2. How to appeal (p1345)
3. After you send or deliver your appeal (p1352)
4. Hearings (p1366)
5. Proving your case (p1376)
6. The tribunal's decision (p1385)

This chapter covers the rules for appeals to the First-tier Tribunal about benefits, the social fund payments in Chapter 37 (except budgeting loans), decisions about DWP loans for mortgage interest (see p855) and national insurance credits. It does *not* cover the rules for statutory payments (see Chapter 59), the health benefits in Chapter 31 or the Scottish social security benefits (see Chapter 77).

References in this chapter to HM Revenue and Customs only apply to decisions about child benefit and guardian's allowance. For information about appeals about tax credits, see Chapter 66.

Key facts

- If you disagree with certain decisions made by the DWP, the local authority or HM Revenue and Customs, you can appeal to the First-tier Tribunal.
- For benefits other than housing benefit, you must apply for a mandatory reconsideration before you can appeal.
- There is an absolute time limit for appealing.
- Appeals can take time. You may need to make a fresh claim for benefit or seek a supersession while you are waiting for your appeal to be heard.
- The tribunal can allow or reject your appeal, and replace the decision about which you appealed with any decision it thinks is right. This could be more or less favourable to you.
- If your appeal is unsuccessful, you may be able to appeal to the Upper Tribunal.

Part 9: Getting a benefit decision changed
Chapter 57: Appealing to the First-tier Tribunal
1. Before you appeal

Future changes

The government intends that, eventually, all appeals will be made online, and progress of the case will be tracked by text, email or online. Currently, this is only possible for appeals about employment and support allowance, personal independence payment (PIP) and universal credit.

There will be hearings by telephone or video conference. Online submission of appeals and other online procedures are currently being tested along with a text and email notification service.

Online dispute resolution is being tested on PIP appeals, where appellants and decision makers upload documents and submissions, and answer questions posed by the tribunal online. The tribunal may allow your appeal on the basis of this information, but if it cannot, you can still have an oral hearing.

The government also says that, in future, there will no longer be an automatic right to an oral hearing, but oral hearings will still be possible where needed. See AskCPAG.org.uk and CPAG's *Welfare Rights Bulletin* for updates.

1. **Before you appeal**

You can appeal against some decisions of the DWP, the local authority or HM Revenue and Customs (HMRC). Appeals are dealt with in the Social Entitlement Chamber of the First-tier Tribunal (Social Security and Child Support) – referred to as the First-tier Tribunal in this *Handbook* (except in Chapter 59). Appeals are dealt with by a judge (and, in some cases, members) assigned to the First-tier Tribunal. The administration of the work of all tribunals is the responsibility of HM Courts and Tribunals Service (HMCTS), part of the Ministry of Justice. HMCTS officials deal with the day-to-day work of the First-tier Tribunal through a network of regional offices. See p1352 for who may deal with your appeal.

Before you appeal, you should do the following.

- Make sure you have sufficient information about the decision you are unhappy about. Ask for a written statement of reasons if this has not already been provided (see p1297).
- Check whether you must apply for a mandatory reconsideration before you can appeal and apply within the time limit if relevant (see p1339).
- Check whether you would be better off applying for a revision or supersession instead of appealing (see p1339).
- In some cases, you should get advice before you appeal. If you apply for a mandatory reconsideration, the DWP or HMRC looks at your case afresh. So does the First-tier Tribunal when you appeal. There is, therefore, a risk you could lose benefit. For example, if your appeal is about a benefit that can be paid at different rates (eg, personal independence payment (PIP)), the rate

could go down. If you are appealing about an overpayment, the amount could increase.

Revision, supersession or appeal?

1. Unless the benefit is housing benefit (HB), you must apply for a mandatory reconsideration before you can appeal (see below).

2. For HB, if you are not yet sure if you want to appeal it can be worth applying for a revision before you appeal. You get two bites at the cherry, because if your application for a revision is turned down, you can still appeal against the original decision.

3. There is no time limit for applying for certain revisions but you must show specific grounds (see p1307). You can ask for a 'specific grounds' revision even if the time limit for applying for what is known as an 'any grounds' revision or appealing has expired. However, you might not be able to appeal against a refusal to do a 'specific grounds' revision (see p1314).

4. In most cases, there is no time limit for applying for a supersession – eg, if there has been a mistake about the facts or if a test case is decided in your favour but you do not become aware of this until some time later. However, you generally get less arrears of benefit if you apply for a supersession. See pp1320–26 for information about when a supersession takes effect.

5. If the 'anti-test case' rule applies to you (see p1330), and all that you did before the test case was decided was apply for a revision or a supersession, the arrears of benefit you get could be limited. This is not the case if you appealed.

Mandatory reconsideration

Unless the benefit is HB, before you can appeal you must ask for the decision you are unhappy with to be looked at again – ie, you must apply for a mandatory reconsideration. The officer reconsidering the decision must then consider whether to revise the decision. There are useful tools for generating mandatory reconsideration letters at AskCPAG.org.uk.

If mandatory reconsideration applies

You can only appeal against a decision if:

- for child benefit and guardian's allowance, you have applied for a mandatory reconsideration and HMRC has decided not to revise the decision. **Note:** if it revises the decision, you can appeal against the original decision, as revised;[1] *or*
- for other benefits, you have been notified properly (see p1340), in writing, that you must apply for a revision before you can appeal (the DWP uses the term 'mandatory reconsideration'), you have done so, and the DWP has considered whether to revise the decision.[2]

Part 9: Getting a benefit decision changed
Chapter 57: Appealing to the First-tier Tribunal
1. Before you appeal

Bear in mind that it is the First-tier Tribunal that decides whether you have a right of appeal, *not* the DWP or HMRC. However, the easiest way to prove to the tribunal that you have a right of appeal is to apply for a mandatory reconsideration and send the tribunal the 'mandatory reconsideration notice' that you are given by the DWP or HMRC (see p1342).

Have you been notified properly?

For benefits other than child benefit and guardian's allowance, you only have to apply for a mandatory reconsideration if the decision notice (see p1296) includes a statement that you only have a right of appeal if the DWP has considered an application for a revision of the decision. The notice must also inform you of the time limit for applying for an 'any grounds' revision (see p1304) and that you can ask for a statement of reasons for the decision (if one has not been included) within one month of being notified of the decision (see p1297). If the DWP does not notify you properly (this is only likely to happen in limited cases), you do *not* have to apply for a mandatory reconsideration before you can appeal, although it may be easier to do so. If you have not applied for a mandatory reconsideration, make it clear on your appeal form that you have *not* been notified properly and provide proof.

Time limits for applying for a mandatory reconsideration

When you apply for a mandatory reconsideration, you are applying for a revision. There are two types of revision: 'any grounds' revisions (p1303) and 'specific grounds' revisions (see p1307). **Note:** if you are disputing a decision that was made:

- recently, it is always best to apply for an 'any grounds' revision. You must do so within a strict time limit. In most cases, you must apply within **one month** of being sent or given the decision (see p1304). If you can show there are special circumstances, you can apply outside this limit so long as you do so within the absolute time limit (usually 13 months – see p1305);
- some time ago, and you have missed the time limits for an 'any grounds' revision, you need to apply for a 'specific grounds' revision. You must show grounds (see p1307) – eg, that there has been an official error.

If you miss the time limit for an 'any grounds' revision

If the decision maker refuses to accept your application for a mandatory reconsideration because you missed the one-month time limit for an 'any grounds' revision, but you have applied within the absolute time limit, the decision maker has considered whether to revise the decision so you have a right to appeal.[3] The DWP says the decision maker should make a decision refusing to revise and issue you with a mandatory reconsideration notice.[4]

Note: if the decision maker:[5]
- refuses to consider your application for an 'any grounds' revision because it was made outside the absolute time limit for doing so (see p1304), s/he should go on to consider whether there are grounds for a 'specific grounds' revision;
- decides there are no grounds for a revision, s/he should consider whether to do a supersession.

In both cases, you should argue that the decision maker has considered whether to revise the decision and that you now have a right of appeal.

An application for a 'specific grounds' revision can count as an application for a mandatory reconsideration even if you apply outside the time limit for an 'any grounds' revision.[6] If the DWP says your application does not count, appeal to the First-tier Tribunal and point out that the DWP has considered whether to revise the decision, so you have satisfied the mandatory reconsideration rules and have a right to appeal.

Applying for a mandatory reconsideration

It is always best to apply for a mandatory reconsideration in writing (by letter or on a form), although you can make a verbal application – eg, by telephone. If you apply by telephone, all calls should be noted, but this may not always happen. If you are appealing about universal credit (UC), you can also apply on your UC online account (your journal). In all cases, make it clear that you are applying for a mandatory reconsideration.

Forms

For child benefit and guardian's allowance, you can use Form CH24A available at gov.uk/government/publications/child-benefit-and-guardians-allowance-appeal-form. For other benefits you can use Form CRMR1 available at gov.uk/mandatory-reconsideration/how-to-ask-for-mandatory-reconsideration.

Explain why you disagree with the decision and provide any additional information and evidence that supports your case. It is important to follow up your application to ensure that it has been received.

If you sent or delivered your appeal to the First-tier Tribunal when you should have applied for a mandatory reconsideration first, the tribunal may say your appeal is not valid and return it to you to resolve the issue. If you do not do so, it can 'strike out' your appeal (see p1360).

If you send your appeal to the DWP before first applying for a mandatory reconsideration, the DWP can (but does not have to) treat your appeal as an application for a mandatory reconsideration.[7] If the DWP does not do this, apply for a mandatory reconsideration as soon as possible, explaining why your application is late if relevant. Although there is no equivalent rule for child benefit

Part 9: Getting a benefit decision changed
Chapter 57: Appealing to the First-tier Tribunal
1. Before you appeal

and guardian's allowance, there is nothing to prevent HMRC from treating an appeal as an application for a mandatory reconsideration.

The mandatory reconsideration notice

The DWP or HMRC gives or sends you a mandatory reconsideration notice telling you the result of your application. This notice is proof that the DWP or HMRC has accepted and considered your application. If you are still unhappy with the decision, you can then appeal to the First-tier Tribunal. You must send a copy of the notice to the tribunal when you appeal.[8] Although the tribunal can waive this requirement, this is discretionary and it may instead 'strike out' your appeal (see p1360).[9] **Note:** the tribunal *cannot* waive the requirement to apply for a mandatory reconsideration.

> *What if you do not have a mandatory reconsideration notice?*
>
> If you have applied for a mandatory reconsideration, but have not been sent or given a mandatory reconsideration notice, try to provide the tribunal with as much evidence as you can that you did apply, and that the DWP or HMRC has considered your application. Provide a copy of your application along with proof you posted or delivered it, if possible. Also provide copies of any correspondence with the DWP or HMRC and any notes of telephone calls or personal contact with the DWP or HMRC since you made the application.

If the DWP or HMRC only provides a mandatory reconsideration notice after a long delay, this may put you at a disadvantage – eg, if it is now difficult to obtain evidence to support your appeal. Tell the First-tier Tribunal if you think this improves the DWP's or HMRC's chances, or reduces your chances, of winning your appeal. The tribunal should then consider whether it can do something to remedy the situation – eg, obtain medical evidence.[10]

Who can appeal

You can appeal to the First-tier Tribunal if you are the claimant. However, certain other people can also appeal (see below and p1343).

Appeals about benefits other than housing benefit

If you are appealing about a benefit other than HB, you have a right to appeal if you are:[11]
- a claimant; *or*
- an appointee claiming on someone's behalf (see p1170); *or*
- claiming attendance allowance, disability living allowance or PIP on behalf of someone who is terminally ill, even if this is without her/his knowledge; *or*
- a person from whom an overpayment of a benefit or one of the regulated social fund payments in Chapter 37 (other than a budgeting loan) or a duplication of

payment of income support, income-based jobseeker's allowance (JSA), income-related employment and support allowance (ESA), pension credit or UC can be recovered (see Chapter 53). This is the case even if you were not the person who claimed the benefit that was overpaid;[12] *or*

- someone from whom a short-term or budgeting advance, or hardship payments, can be recovered; *or*
- the partner of a claimant, if the decision concerns whether you failed to take part in a work-focused interview without good cause;[13] *or*
- a person appointed by the DWP or HMRC to make a benefit claim for, or proceed with a claim made by, someone who has died.

Appeals about housing benefit

If you are appealing about HB, you have a right to appeal if you are a person affected by the decision – ie, your rights, duties or obligations are affected by the decision, and you are:[14]

- a claimant; *or*
- someone acting for a claimant who is unable to act for her/himself – eg, an appointee (see p206); *or*
- someone from whom the local authority decides an overpayment can be recovered (including a landlord or agent);[15] *or*
- a landlord or agent, if the decision concerns whether or not to make a direct payment of HB to you; *or*
- a person appointed by the local authority to proceed with the appeal.

Decisions you can appeal

You can appeal to the First-tier Tribunal against most decisions taken by the Secretary of State for Work and Pensions (the DWP), a local authority officer or an officer of HMRC (known as decision makers – see p1288).[16] Unless the benefit is HB, you must apply for a mandatory reconsideration before you can appeal (see p1339). You can appeal against an original decision or a decision made after a supersession. You cannot appeal against a decision to do a revision (or not to do a revision), but you can appeal against the original decision, as revised.

Has the decision maker refused to make a decision?

If a decision maker refuses to make a decision on your claim, this effectively prevents your having the right to appeal. You should remind the decision maker that s/he *must* make a decision on every valid claim.[17] Even if the decision maker does not accept that a claim made on the correct claim form is valid, you should be given a decision saying so. You can then appeal and ask the tribunal to decide whether your claim is valid.[18] If a decision maker refuses to consider your application for a supersession, see p1327.

Note: a decision maker can sometimes postpone making a decision if there is a test case pending (see p1330).

Part 9: Getting a benefit decision changed
Chapter 57: Appealing to the First-tier Tribunal
1. Before you appeal

You must be given a written notice of any decision that you can appeal.[19] This:
- must give you information about your right to appeal and your right to request a written statement of reasons for it if this has not been included; *and*
- for benefits other than HB, child benefit and guardian's allowance, normally includes information about applying for a mandatory reconsideration before you can appeal.

Examples of decisions you can appeal

Whether you are entitled to a benefit.

Whether an overpayment is recoverable (unless you come under the UC system and it is an overpayment of UC, contribution-based JSA or contributory ESA), and the amount of an overpayment.

Whether to impose a civil penalty (see p1268).[20]

Whether your claim has been validly made or can be backdated.

Whether benefit is payable under the overlapping benefit rules.[21]

Whether you should be given a sanction, and whether you had good cause or a good reason for your actions or your failure to take action.

Whether you have limited capability for work or limited capability for work-related activity.

Whether you satisfy the habitual residence test.

Whether you satisfy the disability conditions for benefit.

Whether you can be paid hardship payments.

Whether your award of contributory ESA should end because you have been paid it for 365 days (see p656).[22]

Whether you are available for, or actively seeking, work.

Whether a jobseeker's agreement is reasonable or you had a good reason for refusing or failing to carry out a jobseeker's direction.

Decisions you cannot appeal

You cannot appeal against some decisions.[23] You *can* ask for a 'specific grounds' revision or a supersession of a decision about which you do not have a right of appeal, whatever your reason for thinking it is wrong.[24] However, if the decision maker refuses to revise or supersede the decision, your only legal remedy is to apply for a judicial review (see p1414).

Examples of decisions you cannot appeal

Who should be the claimant when a couple is unable to decide.

Who should be entitled to child benefit when two people whose claims have equal priority cannot agree.

Whether a claim for one benefit can be treated as a claim for (or in addition to) another benefit.

Whether to demand recovery of an overpayment, and the amount of weekly deductions.

Whether to suspend payment of benefit.

Whether to appoint a person as an appointee (see p1170).

Whether to make a short-term advance, a budgeting advance or a payment on account.

How much benefits are increased (uprated) every year.[25]

2. How to appeal

You must appeal in writing. This is known as a 'notice of appeal'. **Note:** unless it is an appeal about housing benefit (HB), you must usually apply for a mandatory reconsideration before you can appeal (see p1339).

Can you submit your appeal online?

If you are appealing about employment and support allowance, personal independence payment or universal credit, you can submit your appeal online at www.appeal-benefit-decision.service.gov.uk/benefit-type. Online submission of appeals will be introduced for other benefits so check at that address to see whether you can do so.

You must appeal within a strict time limit (see p1346). See p1350 to find out what information your notice of appeal must contain to ensure your appeal is valid.

You should use the appropriate form wherever possible. If you do not use the appropriate form, your appeal can be accepted as valid provided it is in writing and includes all the information required (see p1350).

Appeal forms

For HB, use the form approved by your local authority.[26]

For benefits other than child benefit and guardian's allowance, use the appeal form (SSCS1) in the leaflet *Notice of Appeal Against a Decision of the Department for Work and Pensions*. It is available in large print.

For child benefit and guardian's allowance, use the appeal form (SSCS5) in the leaflet *Notice of Appeal Against a Decision of HM Revenue and Customs*.

Both forms are available from gov.uk. They are both available in Welsh.

Note: if you want the First-tier Tribunal to deal with your appeal quickly, make this clear when you appeal, explaining why. For HB, because you have to send or deliver your notice of appeal to the local authority, you could write to the tribunal, asking it to intervene.

Part 9: Getting a benefit decision changed
Chapter 57: Appealing to the First-tier Tribunal
2. How to appeal

Where to send your appeal

You must send or deliver your notice of appeal:
- for HB, to the local authority office that sent you the decision.[27] It passes your appeal to the First-tier Tribunal;
- for other benefits, direct to the First-tier Tribunal at the appeal centre in Bradford (if you live in England or Wales) or in Glasgow (if you live in Scotland).[28] The address to use is on the appeal form. The appeal centre checks whether your appeal is valid and if so, passes it to the appropriate regional office.

The time limit for appealing

The time limit for appealing depends on whether or not you had to apply for a mandatory reconsideration before you could appeal. If you miss the time limit, it can be extended (see p1347), but there is an absolute time limit within which you must appeal (see p1349).

If you had to apply for a mandatory reconsideration

If you had to apply for a mandatory reconsideration before you could appeal (see p1339), your appeal, including all the information described on p1350, must arrive at the First-tier Tribunal within one month after you are sent the mandatory reconsideration notice (see p1342).[29]

Month

'**Month**' means a complete calendar month running from the day after the day you have been sent or given a decision.[30] For example, a decision sent on 24 July has an appeal time limit that expires at the end of 24 August.

When calculating time, if something has to be done by a certain day, it must be done by 5pm that day. If a time limit ends on a day other than a working day, you have until the next working day to meet the time limit.[31] A 'working day' is any day other than Saturday, Sunday, Christmas Day, Good Friday or a bank holiday.

If you did not have to apply for a mandatory reconsideration

If you did not have to apply for a mandatory reconsideration (this generally only applies to HB), your appeal, including all the information described on p1350, must arrive at the relevant office (for HB, this is the office that sent you the decision and for other benefits, this is the First-tier Tribunal) by the latest of the following:[32]
- one month after the date the written decision was sent to you; *or*
- if you ask for a written statement of reasons for the decision (if one has not already been given to you – see p1297), 14 days after the latest of:

– the end of that month – ie, if the written statement of reasons is provided within the one-month period, you get one month plus 14 days to appeal; *or*

– the date the written statement of reasons is provided.

You must ask for a written statement of reasons within one month of being given notice of a decision.

If you applied for a revision before you appealed and the decision maker revises the decision, but you still want to appeal because you did not get all you want, the one-month time limit runs from the date you are sent the new decision.[33] If you applied for an 'any grounds' revision and the decision maker refused to do a revision, you must appeal no later than one month after the date you are sent notice of the refusal.[34]

If the decision maker refuses to do a 'specific grounds' revision and says you cannot appeal, you should appeal against the original decision within the time limit (if this has not already passed). If this is not possible, get advice.

If you miss the time limit

If you miss the time limit for appealing, your appeal is still treated as made in time if neither the decision maker nor any other person with a right of appeal against the decision (or anyone who has been added as a party to the appeal – eg, the other parent if you are disputing who counts as responsible for your child) does not object.[35] Often, the DWP or HM Revenue and Customs (HMRC) does not object. However, for benefits other than HB, the tribunal can look at the issue of lateness even if the decision maker (or party to the appeal) has not raised an objection. **Note:** for HB appeals only, there are special rules that set out when the decision maker can treat your appeal as made in time and so should not object (see p1348).

If the decision maker (or other person) *does* object, the tribunal can still extend your time limit.[36] There is no guarantee that it will do so, so keep within the time limit wherever possible. There is an absolute time limit for appealing after which you cannot appeal (see p1349).

In addition to the information you must provide on your appeal form (see p1350), you must include the reasons why your appeal is late.[37] The tribunal can extend the time limit for appealing if this will enable it to deal with your appeal fairly and justly, so give details of any special circumstances that mean this would be the case. See p1348 for some ideas about what may be relevant.

Note:
- The First-tier Tribunal decides whether your appeal has been made within the time limit, *not* the DWP, the local authority or HMRC. If you think there may be a dispute about whether your appeal has been made within the time limit, explain why you think it was when you appeal.
- If you miss the time limit and the First-tier Tribunal does not extend it, you can appeal to the Upper Tribunal against the decision.[38]

Part 9: Getting a benefit decision changed
Chapter 57: Appealing to the First-tier Tribunal
2. How to appeal

- The tribunal can also shorten time limits, but should only do this if this will enable it to deal with your appeal fairly and justly.
- If you are appealing a decision about HB and are required to provide information you did not include with your appeal, your time limit can be extended under separate rules (see p1351).

Housing benefit appeals

A decision maker can treat your HB appeal as made in time if it is in the 'interests of justice'.[39] For these purposes, it is *not* in the interests of justice unless it was not practicable for you to appeal in time because:[40]

- your partner or a dependant died or had a serious illness; *or*
- the person who appealed died or had a serious illness; *or*
- you are not resident in the UK; *or*
- normal postal services were disrupted; *or*
- there are other special circumstances that are 'wholly exceptional'. The longer you have delayed appealing, the more compelling the special circumstances must be.[41]

When deciding whether it is in the interests of justice, account cannot be taken of the fact that:[42]

- a court or the Upper Tribunal has interpreted the law in a different way than was previously understood and applied; *or*
- you (or anyone acting for you) misunderstood or were unaware of the relevant law, including the time limits for appealing.

If the decision maker objects to your appeal being treated as made within the time limit, s/he must refer it to the First-tier Tribunal immediately.[43] The tribunal then decides whether your time limit can be extended.

Why your time limit should be extended

Your reasons and circumstances need to show it would be fair and just to extend your time limit for appealing. What may or may not be such a reason or circumstance cannot be defined in advance, but the following are all relevant.

- **The reasons for the delay.** Explain these as clearly and as fully as possible. Do not worry if some or all of the delay is your fault. Any explanation is better than none at all. Even if you knew the time limit, but simply ignored it, it may be possible to say something favourable. Say if things have been difficult at home or you were confused by the rules or just assumed that the DWP (or the local authority or HMRC) was the expert and had got it right until, for example, you were advised otherwise or read an article in a newspaper. Reasons for the delay could include the fact that:
  - you did not receive the decision;
  - you made a reasonable mistake in calculating the time limit;

- you posted your appeal in time, but it went astray in the post;
- you were ill;
- a mistake was made by your advisers. It should not make any difference that you might be able to sue them for negligence;
- you were given wrong advice or otherwise misled by the DWP (or the local authority or HMRC) – eg, you were discouraged from appealing by a decision maker who advised you incorrectly that an appeal would be doomed to fail. If you lose money because you are refused a late appeal, consider claiming compensation (see p1439).

- **The length of the delay.** The usual approach is that time limits have to be kept to, and there has to be good reason for not doing so. Short delays are likely to be easier to justify than long delays, but a good reason is still needed.
- **The merits of your appeal.** The more likely your appeal is to succeed, the greater the injustice in refusing to extend the time limit. A strong case is particularly useful if there has been a very long delay and a time limit is usually extended where there has been a 'clear error', which would have long-term continuing effects unless corrected.[44]
- **The amount of money at stake.** Even if there has been no clear error, a time limit may be extended if there is a lot of money at stake.[45]
- **A decision in a test case.** A decision in a test case, establishing that an earlier decision was incorrect, can amount to a reason to extend a time limit, in some circumstances.[46] Such appeals often involve large sums of money and (given the test case) a clear error in the decision which is being appealed against.

The absolute time limit for appealing

You cannot appeal if it is more than 12 months after the date your time limit for appealing expired.[47] **Note:** in very exceptional circumstances (eg, if you did not receive notice of the decision you want to appeal), you can argue that the tribunal should waive the absolute time limit and allow you to appeal if this is absolutely necessary to protect your right to a fair hearing under human rights law.[48] However, this is unlikely to apply unless you have done all that you could to appeal in time.

For HB, if the decision maker thinks your appeal has been made outside the absolute time limit, s/he must refer it to the First-tier Tribunal immediately.[49] The tribunal decides whether your appeal has been made in time, not the local authority.

If the First-tier Tribunal decides that you cannot appeal because your appeal was made outside the absolute time limit, but you think it was made in time, or it refuses to waive the absolute time limit, you can appeal to the Upper Tribunal against the decision.[50]

Part 9: Getting a benefit decision changed
Chapter 57: Appealing to the First-tier Tribunal
2. How to appeal

Making sure your appeal is valid

The First-tier Tribunal decides whether your appeal is valid, *not* the DWP, the local authority or HMRC. For your appeal to be valid:

- you must provide all the information required (see below). **Note:** even if you do not use the correct appeal form, your appeal can still be valid; *and*
- you must sign your notice of appeal.[51] However, if you have provided written notice that you have appointed a representative, s/he can sign it on your behalf. If your solicitor signs your notice of appeal on your behalf, it should be accepted that s/he is authorised to do so;[52] *and*
- your notice of appeal must be in English or Welsh.

The information you must provide
You must provide:[53]

- your name and address and that of your representative, if you have one; *and*
- the address where documents can be sent or delivered – eg, to you or your representative; *and*
- if you are appealing about HB, details about the decision with which you disagree, sufficient for it to be identified; *and*
- if you are appealing about benefits other than HB:
  - the name and address of any other person who has a right of appeal against the decision (see p1342); *and*
  - a copy of the mandatory reconsideration notice (see p1342) or, if you did not have to apply for a mandatory reconsideration before the appeal, a copy of the decision you want to appeal. **Note:** if you were not given written notice that you had to apply for a mandatory reconsideration before you could appeal, state this clearly on the appeal form and enclose a copy of the decision notice as proof; *and*
  - any statement of reasons for the decision that you have; *and*
  - any documents in support of your appeal that you have not already supplied to the decision maker; *and*
- a summary of your reasons for believing the decision is wrong (your grounds for appeal). Do not simply say you think the decision is wrong, but explain why.

It is also helpful to include information and evidence that supports your appeal because a decision maker may look at the decision again before the appeal hearing and might revise it.

Examples of grounds for appeal
'The decision says I have been overpaid income support because I failed to disclose that my wife had started working part time, but I wrote to the DWP as soon as she started work and told it what her take-home pay would be.'

'The DWP says I am not entitled to a housing costs element for my rent because my tenancy agreement is contrived. It says this is because I am paying rent to a relative. My landlord is my aunt, but she owns a number of properties that she lets commercially, including the one she lets to me.'

'HMRC says I should not get child benefit for my son because he left school in June. This decision is wrong because my son stayed on at school to do his A levels.'

'You say I cannot get personal independence payment daily living component. This decision is wrong because you have not taken into account the amount of help I need because of my incontinence problems.'

If you had to apply for a mandatory reconsideration before you could appeal and the DWP or HMRC only provided a mandatory reconsideration notice after a long delay, this may put you at a disadvantage – eg, if it is now difficult to obtain evidence to support your appeal. Point out if you think this improves the DWP's or HMRC's chances, or reduces your chances, of winning your appeal. The tribunal should then consider if it can do something to remedy the situation.[54]

What happens if you do not provide sufficient information

If you are appealing about HB and you do not include the information required on your appeal form or in your appeal letter, the local authority can ask you to provide the information you left out.[55] If you used an appeal form, this is returned to you to complete. Be sure to provide the information within the time allowed, otherwise you may not have made your appeal within the time limit.

Your time limit for appealing (see p1346) is extended by:[56]

- 14 days from the date your appeal form is returned to you for completion, if the completed form is received back within 14 days; *or*
- 14 days from the date you are asked for further information, if you provide this within 14 days of the request; *or*
- the length of time you are given to complete the form or provide information, if this is longer than 14 days.

If you do not complete the form properly or provide the information required in time, your appeal, along with any relevant documents and evidence, is forwarded to the First-tier Tribunal by the local authority. It then considers whether your appeal is valid and can go ahead.[57] **Note:** if you complete and return the form or provide the information:

- after the expiry of the time limit, but before your appeal is forwarded to the tribunal, the local authority should accept that your appeal is valid and then consider whether to object to it being treated as made in time (see p1347);[58]
- before the tribunal makes a decision, any further details you provide must be taken into account.[59]

Part 9: Getting a benefit decision changed
Chapter 57: Appealing to the First-tier Tribunal
3. After you send or deliver your appeal

If your appeal is not accepted as valid, try to make a fresh appeal, giving reasons why your appeal is late if relevant (see p1347).

If you are appealing about benefits other than HB and you do not include the information or documents (including the mandatory reconsideration notice) required on the appeal form, the tribunal clerk (see p1353) can waive the requirement, or require you to provide what you left out and then 'strike out' your appeal (see p1360) if you fail to do so.[60] You can ask the tribunal to reconsider the clerk's decision. You must apply in writing within 14 days after the date you are sent notice of the decision.[61] The tribunal can give you longer, but there is no guarantee of this, so keep within the time limit wherever possible. If your appeal is struck out, it can be reinstated by the clerk – eg, if you later provide the mandatory reconsideration notice (see p1361).

Note: if you had to (and did) apply for a mandatory reconsideration before you could appeal, but you have not been sent or given a mandatory reconsideration notice, see p1342.

---

3. After you send or deliver your appeal

If you sent your appeal direct to the First-tier Tribunal, it sends a copy to the DWP or HM Revenue and Customs (HMRC). In all cases, the DWP, the local authority or HMRC prepares its case – known as the 'decision maker's response' (see p1354). For housing benefit (HB) appeals, you are sent an enquiry form (see p1353) to complete and return to the tribunal. **Note:** you may find that your appeal is not dealt with if there is a test case or a lead case pending that deals with the same issues (see p1364).

Can you sign up for the 'Track Your Appeal' service?

If you live in England or Wales, you are appealing about universal credit, employment and support allowance or personal independence payment, you appealed after 30 April 2018 and you have opted for an oral hearing, you can sign up for an email and text notification service called 'Track Your Appeal' by phoning 0300 123 1142, Monday to Friday, 8am to 8pm or Saturday, 8am to 2pm. You then get regular updates on the progress of your appeal – eg, notices confirming evidence you sent to the tribunal office has been received, and reminding you of your hearing date.

Who deals with your appeal

Any of the following may be be involved with your appeal at some time.

- **A judge.** S/he is always legally qualified. As well as hearing and making the decision on your appeal, s/he carries out various other functions – eg, s/he decides whether you have made your appeal in time, and whether to extend a time limit or to issue directions.

- **A member of the First-tier Tribunal.** S/he could be a doctor, a person with experience of disability or an accountant. S/he hears and makes the decision on your appeal with the judge. To see which members hear and decide your appeal, see p1370.

- **An expert.** If your appeal involves issues that require specialist expertise, an expert (the tribunal may call her/him an 'assessor') may be used.[62] If s/he provides a written report, it should be sent to every party involved in the appeal. The expert cannot take part in making the decision on your appeal.

- **A registrar** (s/he must be legally qualified) or a **tribunal caseworker** (s/he must be appropriately trained). A registrar or a tribunal caseworker can carry out any of the functions of the First-tier Tribunal, under the supervision of a judge. S/he can make all the decisions a judge can make other than the final decision on your appeal.[63]

- **A clerk to the First-tier Tribunal.** S/he can carry out specified functions, including waiving a requirement for you to provide information with your notice of appeal, requiring you to provide information and in some cases striking out your appeal (see p1360). S/he attends the appeal hearing in an administrative capacity – eg, to pay expenses. S/he cannot take part in making the decision on your appeal and should not express any views on the case.[64]

You must be given 14 days to ask a judge to reconsider a registrar's, a tribunal caseworker's or a clerk's decision.[65] You must apply in writing within 14 days after the date you are sent notice of the decision.[66] The tribunal can give you longer, but there is no guarantee of this, so keep within the time limit wherever possible.

The enquiry form

In some cases, the First-tier Tribunal sends you a questionnaire (called an enquiry form). For appeals about:

- a benefit other than HB, if you sent your appeal direct to the First-tier Tribunal, you are unlikely to be sent an enquiry form if you have already provided this information on your appeal form. However, if you did not use an appeal form (eg, you appealed by letter), you *are* sent an enquiry form;

- HB, you are sent an enquiry form when the First-tier Tribunal receives your appeal papers from the local authority.

The enquiry form asks you whether you want an oral hearing and, if so, when you and your representative (if you have one) are available to attend, if you have not already provided this information. If you want an oral hearing, you must state this. It is always best to opt for an oral hearing. You should always consult your representative before completing and returning the enquiry form.

Part 9: Getting a benefit decision changed
Chapter 57: Appealing to the First-tier Tribunal
3. After you send or deliver your appeal

Return the enquiry form within 14 days. If you do not return it in time, the tribunal can 'strike out' your appeal (see p1360) or automatically deal with your appeal at a paper hearing. However, you are entitled to receive a ruling on the merits of your appeal, so it should only be struck out on this ground in exceptional cases.[67] For information about oral and paper hearings, see p1366.

The decision maker's response

The DWP, the local authority or HMRC must prepare a bundle of papers relevant to your appeal (called the 'decision maker's response') and forward this to the First-tier Tribunal:

- for HB, as soon as reasonably practicable. You are entitled to have your appeal heard within a reasonable period of time, so the decision maker should prepare the response and send it to the tribunal without delay. Following a complaint, an Ombudsman said the local authority should forward an appeal to the First-tier Tribunal within 28 days;[68]
- for other benefits, within 28 days of receiving the notice of appeal.[69]

Both you and your representative (if any) are normally sent a copy.[70] However, check with your representative as this might not always happen.[71]

If the decision maker opposes your appeal, the response must include any reasons for this that are not in the documents the First-tier Tribunal has already been given.[72] It must refer to the law on which the decision was based and explain the legal basis on which the decision was made in a way that enables the tribunal to ensure that you are able to participate fully in the appeal.[73] The decision maker must also provide:[74]

- a copy of any written record of, and statement of reasons for, the decision with which you disagree, if you did not send these with your appeal form; *and*
- copies of all documents s/he has that may be relevant, unless the tribunal directs otherwise. The decision maker should treat as relevant anything that the tribunal might rely on to make findings about the facts, irrespective of what s/he considers to be relevant.[75] If the tribunal thinks that the decision maker may have other relevant evidence, it can direct her/him to produce this. If your appeal involves a medical issue or one about your disability:
  - any recent medical reports there have been in connection with your claim are usually included; *and*
  - if the decision you are appealing followed from a report by a health care professional (eg, your benefit was reduced or stopped following such a report), that report should be included; *and*
- for HB appeals only, a copy of your appeal form (or letter) along with all the documents you provided with it and, unless already provided to the First-tier Tribunal, the name and address of your representative.

Read through the whole response carefully to find out the case being made against you. Be sure to take it with you to the hearing.

Has your appeal been held up by the decision maker?

You cannot usually bypass the normal procedures. However, note the following.

1. Although you cannot usually expect the First-tier Tribunal to deal with your appeal before the decision maker has had a chance to prepare her/his response, it is free to allow matters to be handled differently if circumstances require it.[76]

2. Ask the tribunal to require the decision maker to provide documents, information and evidence by a specified date (make a direction – see p1358), or make a direction setting a hearing date.[77]

3. If you are appealing about HB and the decision maker does not forward your appeal within a reasonable period, forward a copy of it to the First-tier Tribunal yourself and proceed as above.

Note: in some circumstances, the tribunal can bar the decision maker from taking any further part in the appeal (see p1362), in which case your appeal could be decided without a response being made. However, it can lift the bar if the response is eventually received.

Providing other information

Make sure that everything you want to say in support of your appeal has been put in writing and that there are no other documents and evidence that you would like the tribunal to see. **Note:**

- It is always good to provide a written submission and additional evidence or information to support your appeal (known as a 'reply') – eg, independent medical evidence or supporting statements from witnesses.
- You (or your representative) must provide your reply within one month after the date you are sent the decision maker's response.[78] The tribunal can give you longer (or shorter) than one month.[79] There is no guarantee that you will be given longer, so keep within the time limit wherever possible.

Do you intend to send a reply to the decision maker's response?

Tribunal staff often want to fix a hearing date as soon as they can after the decision maker's response has been received. As a result, they sometimes overlook the need to allow you time to reply. To avoid this happening, inform the tribunal office that you intend to send a reply as soon as possible after you receive the response.

Note: your reply and any further documents and submissions that are sent to the tribunal by you (or the DWP, local authority or HMRC) are added to the decision maker's response forming what is known as the 'appeal bundle'.

Part 9: Getting a benefit decision changed
Chapter 57: Appealing to the First-tier Tribunal
3. After you send or deliver your appeal

At this stage, your appeal is likely to be considered ready for a hearing (see p1366). The tribunal may issue directions (see p1358) requiring you (or the DWP, the local authority or HMRC) to provide a submission, further information or documents within a specific period. You (or the decision maker) can also ask it to issue directions. If you are given a direction, it is important that you comply with it. If you do not, your appeal can be struck out (see p1360).

When your appeal can lapse

After you appeal, a decision maker may look at the decision you are appealing about again and revise it – eg, on the basis of any facts, information or evidence you provided with your appeal form. This is the case, even if the decision maker had already considered a revision when you applied for a mandatory reconsideration. If the decision maker revises the decision, your appeal could lapse, even if you do not get everything you want, and you have to appeal again.[80]

Your appeal lapses if the revised decision is more advantageous to you than the original decision – eg, the decision:[81]

- awards you benefit at a higher rate or for a longer period; *or*
- lifts a refusal or disqualification of benefit or a sanction (in whole or in part); *or*
- reverses a decision to pay benefit to a third party (see p1202); *or*
- means you gain financially from the revised decision; *or*
- says an overpayment of benefit is not recoverable or that less should be recovered.

Note: the DWP says you should be contacted by a decision maker to see if you would still want to appeal if the decision were revised to your advantage. If you would still want to appeal, it says it should not revise the decision.[82] You can accept this 'offer' and ask the decision maker to revise the decision. Although in this case your appeal lapses, you can still appeal – eg, you did not get all that you wanted or if you change your mind.

If your appeal lapses, you must make a fresh appeal. You do not have to apply for another mandatory reconsideration before you can appeal in this situation.[83] Your time limit for appealing (see p1346) runs from the date the revised decision is sent to you.[84]

If the First-tier Tribunal decides that your appeal has lapsed, you can appeal against that decision to the Upper Tribunal. However, it is better, if you can, to make a fresh appeal against the original decision.

If the decision is revised and is not more advantageous to you, your appeal must go ahead, but against the revised decision.[85] You have one month from the date the decision is sent or given to you to make further representations.[86] At the end of that period (or earlier if you agree in writing), your appeal proceeds unless the decision is revised again and is now more advantageous to you.[87]

What the First-tier Tribunal can do

There are procedural rules that the First-tier Tribunal must follow when dealing with your appeal. The aim (known as the 'overriding objective') is to enable it to deal with cases fairly and justly.[88] This includes avoiding delay (provided the issues can be considered properly), avoiding unnecessary formality, seeking flexibility in the proceedings and ensuring that all the parties can participate fully. You, the DWP, the local authority and HMRC must help the First-tier Tribunal further this objective and co-operate with it. This involves ensuring, as far as possible, that your case is ready by the time of the hearing.[89]

The First-tier Tribunal can:[90]

- extend or shorten any time limits (see below); *and*
- issue directions (see p1358); *and*
- postpone or adjourn your appeal hearing (see p1359); *and*
- 'strike out' your appeal (see p1360) or bar the decision maker or another party to the appeal from taking part (see p1362); *and*
- summon witnesses to attend a hearing, answer questions or produce documents. If someone fails to comply, the First-tier Tribunal can refer the matter to the Upper Tribunal. The Upper Tribunal can punish the person for contempt of court.[91] **Note:** you cannot be required to give evidence or produce any document that you could not be compelled to give by a court;[92] *and*
- suspend the effect of its decision while any application for permission to appeal, or any appeal against or review of that decision, is outstanding.[93]

Note: the rules for what the Upper Tribunal can do are generally the same as for the First-tier Tribunal. The endnotes in this section, therefore, also refer to Upper Tribunal rules where relevant.

Extending or shortening time limits

Time limits can be extended or shortened.[94] The rules do not specify when this should (or must) be done, but the overriding objective of all the tribunal rules is to enable the tribunal to deal with appeals fairly and justly (see above).[95]

The tribunal may shorten your and the DWP's, the local authority's or HMRC's time limits if it thinks that delay should be avoided, provided the issues can be considered properly.[96] You might want to ask for the DWP's (or the local authority's or HMRC's) time limits (eg, to comply with a direction) to be shortened if your situation is urgent or your circumstances are exceptional.

If you know that you are going to miss (or have missed) a time limit, you should ask for it to be extended by the tribunal. Always ask in writing for a time limit to be extended and apply in advance if you can. Give the reasons why you are going to be (or are) late in meeting the time limit, as well as any special circumstances which mean your time limit should be extended so that your appeal can be dealt with fairly and justly.

Part 9: Getting a benefit decision changed
Chapter 57: Appealing to the First-tier Tribunal
3. After you send or deliver your appeal

Note:
- The tribunal does not have to extend any particular time limit, so there is no guarantee that you will be given more time. Keep within the time limits wherever possible.
- For the rules about extending your time limit for appealing, see p1347. For some ideas about what may count as a good reason for a late appeal, see p1348.

Directions

In the course of your appeal, the First-tier Tribunal might issue directions – eg, requiring you (or the DWP, the local authority or HMRC) to provide a submission, further information or documents, or requiring you or a presenting officer (see p1369) to attend a hearing.[97] It must send you and the decision maker (and anyone affected by the direction) notice of any direction it issues, unless it thinks there is a good reason not to do so.[98] You can challenge a direction (eg, if you think insufficient time has been given to comply with it) by applying for another direction to amend, suspend or set aside the first one.[99]

If you are given a direction, it is important that you comply with it. If you fail to comply with a requirement or a direction, the tribunal can take any action it thinks is 'just' – eg, it can:[100]

- waive the requirement; *or*
- require you to remedy the failure; *or*
- strike out your appeal (see p1360); *or*
- conclude that any information or evidence required was adverse to you.[101] However, it should not use this as a way to punish you. It should only decide information or evidence was adverse to you if it is probable that the reason it was not provided was that it did not exist or would harm your case.[102] The tribunal should not decide information or evidence was adverse to you because you refuse your consent to disclose your medical records, but you may have more difficulty proving your case.[103]

The tribunal can also take the above action if it is the DWP, the local authority or HMRC that is given a direction. The tribunal can also bar the DWP, the local authority or HMRC from taking further part in your appeal (see p1362).

If you miss the deadline in a direction, try to provide what has been requested as soon as possible. The tribunal may still consider the information or evidence – eg, if you provide it at the hearing.[104] However, remember that it can decide *not* to consider evidence if it is late or if it would otherwise be unfair to do so.[105]

You or the decision maker can also apply to the First-tier Tribunal to ask it to issue directions. This can be useful, for example, if you are having trouble getting documents or information from the decision maker. You can apply in writing, or orally at the hearing.[106] In either case, you must give reasons for your application.

Postponements and adjournments

The First-tier Tribunal can postpone or adjourn a hearing.[107] The decision can be made by the judge. However, if the issue arises at a hearing and the panel comprises more than one member, the judge should consult the other member(s).[108] The decision must be recorded properly. **Note:** if a hearing is postponed or adjourned, this does not mean that you cannot get another postponement or adjournment if you need one – eg if there is a good reason why the next hearing should not take place. The tribunal making the decision to postpone or adjourn should, therefore, not tie the hands of the next tribunal by directing it to proceed when the appeal is listed again.[109] The next tribunal must consider any further application for a postponement or adjournment on its merits, although the fact that there has been a previous one is something it can take into account.

Remember that if you do not attend a hearing, the tribunal can decide not to adjourn the hearing and hear the appeal without you (see p1368).[110] Your appeal is less likely to succeed if you do not attend.

Your case might be postponed or adjourned if there is a test case or lead case pending which deals with the same issues as your appeal (see p1364).

Getting a hearing postponed

If the hearing date you are given is inconvenient or you want more time to prepare your case, you can ask for the hearing to be postponed to another date. You should apply in writing to the First-tier Tribunal before the hearing date, as soon as you decide you want a postponement, saying why you want your appeal to be postponed. Make it clear that you do not want the hearing to go ahead in your absence. If you have not provided enough information about why you want your appeal to be postponed (eg, you simply say you have an appointment, but not that it is an important medical appointment), the clerk to the tribunal should ask you for more information rather than simply referring your request for a decision.[111]

Bear the following in mind.

- Do not presume that a postponement will be granted. Telephone before the hearing is due to take place to check whether it has been agreed. Be ready to attend the hearing if it goes ahead. If you have a representative, s/he should warn you that your application might not be successful.[112]
- The judge conducting the hearing should consider whether it should be adjourned, even if you have been refused a postponement.[113]

The tribunal can postpone your oral hearing even if this is not requested.

Getting a hearing adjourned

If a hearing (either oral or paper) is under way, it can be adjourned – eg, if you or the DWP, the local authority or HMRC asks for an adjournment or if the First-tier

Part 9: Getting a benefit decision changed
Chapter 57: Appealing to the First-tier Tribunal
3. After you send or deliver your appeal

Tribunal thinks this is the best course – eg, if more evidence is required or you need time to consider the law. You should consider asking for an adjournment if the tribunal says it is going to consider whether you should get a lower rate of benefit than you are getting currently, to allow you to prepare your case and make representations. If you no longer want to pursue your appeal, you may be able to withdraw it (see p1363).

The tribunal should consider the benefit of an adjournment, why you (or the DWP, the local authority or HMRC) are not ready to go ahead and what the impact would be on the other party and the tribunal system.[114] It should adjourn a hearing:

- if you are not there and there is doubt about whether you received notice of the oral hearing;[115] *or*
- if you have advised it that you cannot attend, have a good reason for not attending and have asked for another hearing date;[116] *or*
- if you are unable to attend the hearing (eg, you are in prison or hospital), but your evidence could play an important part in its reaching a decision;[117] *or*
- if you want to be represented at the oral hearing, but your representative is not available on the date it has been listed and has made a reasonable request for a postponement. Your representative should explain why s/he cannot attend and why no one else can represent you in her/his place;[118] *or*
- if you need to get a representative – eg, because it is difficult for you to represent yourself, you have mental health problems or the decision with which you disagree concerns a large overpayment;[119] *or*
- to enable you to get additional evidence which you could not until then have reasonably been expected to realise was needed.[120]

If a hearing is not postponed or adjourned

If the hearing is not postponed or adjourned and the tribunal makes a decision with which you disagree, in limited circumstances you can apply for the decision to be 'set aside' (see p1388). Alternatively, you may be able to appeal to the Upper Tribunal against the First-tier Tribunal's final decision on the grounds that its refusal to postpone or adjourn the hearing was an error of law.

When your appeal can be struck out

If you fail to comply with a direction, or in a limited number of other circumstances, your appeal can be 'struck out', in whole or in part. This cancels your appeal, or part of your appeal, and it does not go ahead. If your appeal is struck out because you failed to comply with a direction, see p1361 for when you can get your appeal reinstated.

If you fail to comply with a direction

If you fail to comply with a direction given to you by the tribunal – eg, you do not provide the required information or documents:[121]

- your appeal is struck out automatically if you were notified in the direction that a failure to comply *would* lead to your appeal being struck out;
- there is discretion to strike out your appeal if you were notified in the direction that a failure to comply with it *could* lead to your appeal being struck out. Before deciding to do so, the tribunal should consider carefully why the direction was given and whether it can still make a fair and just decision – eg, without the information you were supposed to provide.[122]

Can your appeal be reinstated?

If your appeal is struck out because you failed to comply with a direction, you can apply for your appeal to be reinstated.[123] You must apply in writing. Your application must be received by the tribunal within one month of your being sent notice that your appeal was struck out. It can give you longer (or shorter) than one month. There is no guarantee that you will be given longer, so keep within the time limit wherever possible. Explain why you think your appeal should not have been struck out – eg, why you think you *did* comply with the direction, or why you were unable to do so or to comply in time.

Other circumstances

Your appeal *must* be struck out if the tribunal does not have 'jurisdiction' to deal with it – eg, you do not have a right to appeal against the decision or you have appealed to the wrong tribunal.[124]

In addition, there is *discretion* to strike out your appeal if:[125]

- you failed to co-operate with the tribunal to such an extent that it cannot deal with your appeal fairly and justly; *or*
- the tribunal considers your appeal has no reasonable prospect of success. It should only do so if the result of the appeal is clear and incontestable. It should generally not do so if the facts of the case are in dispute.[126]

In all cases:

- you must be given an opportunity to comment. You should always take this opportunity and explain why you think your appeal should not be struck out – eg, why you had a good reason for failing to co-operate or why you think you have a chance of winning your appeal;
- you cannot apply for your appeal to be reinstated, but may be able to challenge the decision to strike it out.

Challenging a decision to strike out your appeal

If the tribunal strikes out your appeal or refuses to reinstate your appeal after it has been struck out, you may be able to make a fresh appeal against the decision maker's decision.[127] See p1346 for the time limit for doing so. Otherwise, you can appeal to the Upper Tribunal against the decision to strike out your appeal or to refuse to reinstate it.[128]

Part 9: Getting a benefit decision changed
Chapter 57: Appealing to the First-tier Tribunal
3. After you send or deliver your appeal

Being barred from taking part in an appeal

The decision maker and any person (other than you) who is taking part in the appeal because s/he has a right of appeal against the decision you are challenging (see p1342) or s/he has been added as a party to the appeal by the tribunal (eg, the other parent if you are disputing who counts as responsible for your child) can be barred from taking further part in the appeal in the same circumstances in which your appeal can be struck out.[129] In practice, this is likely to apply mainly if the decision maker (or other person with a right of appeal):

- fails to comply with a direction; or
- fails to co-operate with the tribunal to such an extent that it cannot deal with your appeal fairly and justly.

The decision maker (or other person) can apply for the bar to be lifted in the same circumstances in which you can apply for an appeal to be reinstated (see p1361). If the bar is not lifted, the tribunal does not have to consider any response or other submission made by her/him.[130] It can decide any or all of the issues against her/him and can deal with her/his case more briefly than would otherwise be required. However, the decision maker (or person) still has a right of appeal against the tribunal's decision and a right to apply for a statement of reasons for the decision.[131]

Representatives

You can have a representative to help you with your appeal and to be with you at the hearing.[132] S/he can explain the procedures, present your case to the tribunal and ensure it is aware of all the relevant issues and the law. Bear in mind that, even if you have a representative, you may have to answer questions from the tribunal; your representative is not normally allowed to answer for you.

You must send or give the tribunal written notice of your representative's name and address or s/he must do this on your behalf.[133] This does not apply for HB if you provide this notice to the local authority before your appeal is forwarded to the tribunal. If your representative is providing the notice, unless s/he is a solicitor, s/he should also provide an authorisation signed by you.

Once you have given notice that you have a representative, s/he is presumed to be acting for you unless you (or your representative) give notice in writing that this is no longer the case.[134] Your representative must be sent any documents required to be sent to you. These then do not have to be sent to you.[135] However, do not presume this always happens. If you receive documents, check that your representative has also received them.

Even if you have not previously notified the tribunal that you have a representative, someone can attend the hearing with you (eg, a friend or relative) and act as one, or assist you at the hearing, if the tribunal agrees.[136]

Meeting the costs

Free legal help is only available in limited cases.

- In England and Wales, you cannot get free legal help to cover preparatory work, such as obtaining medical reports and writing submissions. However, if you have a solicitor acting for you in an industrial injury or personal injury claim, s/he may have medical and other reports and evidence which you can use for your benefit appeal. In Scotland, you may be able to get free legal help for preparatory work.
- You cannot *normally* get free legal help from a lawyer to cover representation at an oral hearing. In England and Wales, you may be able to get this in very exceptional cases, if it is necessary to make these services available to you because a failure to do so would be a breach of your human rights or your rights under European Union law.[137]

If you are not eligible for free advice and assistance, or you want to be represented by a lawyer at an oral hearing, you are likely to have to pay. However, you may be able to get free help from a law centre, advice centre or Citizens Advice. There are a number of agencies that can advise you and help you prepare your case, and even represent you (see Appendix 1). Remember that many non-lawyer advisers know more about social security law than lawyers, and their advice and representation is usually free.

Withdrawing an appeal

If you change your mind about appealing, you can withdraw your appeal.[138]

- If you are appealing about HB and your appeal has not yet been passed to the First-tier Tribunal, write to the local authority office dealing with your appeal, saying that you do not wish your appeal to go ahead. Your representative can write on your behalf.
- In any other case (ie, once your appeal is lodged with the tribunal), you can withdraw your appeal:
  - by sending or giving written notice to the tribunal. You can withdraw your appeal before the hearing, and also if a hearing has taken place but was adjourned without the tribunal reaching a decision. The withdrawal takes effect immediately. Normally, you do not need the tribunal's agreement to withdraw in this way, but in some cases it may notify you that you can only do so if it agrees. This might happen, for example, if the tribunal thinks it possible that you are entitled to less benefit, adjourns a hearing to allow you time to consider counter arguments, but does not think you should be allowed to avoid the issue by withdrawing your appeal in the meantime; *or*
  - at an oral hearing, but only if the tribunal agrees. The withdrawal takes effect when it agrees.

Part 9: Getting a benefit decision changed
Chapter 57: Appealing to the First-tier Tribunal
3. After you send or deliver your appeal

The tribunal must notify you that the withdrawal of your appeal has taken effect. It must also notify any other party to the appeal.

If you tell the tribunal that you want to withdraw your appeal before the hearing (eg, you telephone the tribunal office), but then you fail to confirm this in writing, the tribunal clerk can waive the requirement to provide written notice.[139] You can ask the tribunal to reconsider the clerk's decision – eg, if you did not send written notice because you changed your mind and no longer wanted to withdraw your appeal. You must apply in writing within 14 days after the date you are sent notice of the decision.[140] The tribunal can give you longer (or shorter) than this. There is no guarantee you will be given longer, so keep within the time limit wherever possible.

If you withdraw your appeal but then decide that you want it to go ahead, you can apply for it to be reinstated.[141] The other parties can also apply for your appeal to be reinstated. The application must be in writing and it must be received by the tribunal within one month after the earliest of the following:

- the date the applicant was sent notice that the withdrawal of your appeal had taken effect; *or*
- if your appeal was withdrawn at an oral hearing and the applicant was present at the hearing when this happened, the date of the hearing.

The tribunal can give you longer (or shorter) than one month. There is no guarantee that you will be given longer, so keep within the time limit wherever possible.

Consent orders

If all the parties to the appeal agree what the solution to your dispute should be, you can ask the tribunal judge to make a 'consent order' and to make any other appropriate provision you have agreed.[142] This procedure is unlikely to be relevant in most cases and is only likely to be of use if you are effectively giving up your appeal, but the DWP, the local authority or HMRC promises you something in return for this. The First-tier Tribunal only deals with your appeal in this way if it considers it appropriate. It may simply make a decision on your appeal in the usual way.

If a consent order is made, there does not have to be a hearing and no reasons for the order need to be given. Get independent advice *before* agreeing to a consent order.

Test cases and lead cases

Sometimes appeals to the First-tier Tribunal are made by more than one person about the same issues of fact or law. When this happens, appeals dealing with the same issues may be delayed until a decision has been made in a test case or a lead case.

Test cases

If a case is pending against a decision of the Upper Tribunal or a court that deals with issues raised in your case (a 'test case'), the DWP, the local authority or HMRC can suspend payment of your benefit (see p1200) or even postpone making a decision about your claim (see p1330), pending the outcome of the appeal in the test case. In addition, for benefits other than HB, if a test case is pending and you have already appealed to the First-tier Tribunal (your appeal is then known as a 'look alike' case), the decision maker can serve notice requiring the First-tier Tribunal in *your* appeal:[143]

- not to make a decision and to refer your case back to her/him; *or*
- to deal with your appeal by either:
  - postponing making a decision until the test case is decided. Once a decision has been made in the test case, the decision is made on your appeal; *or*
  - deciding your appeal as if the test case had been decided in the way most unfavourable to you, but only if this is in your interests. If this happens, and the test case eventually goes in your favour, the decision maker has to make a new decision superseding the tribunal's decision in the light of the decision in the test case.[144]

Lead cases

If appeals are made to the First-tier Tribunal by more than one person about the same issues of fact or law (eg, a number of appeals about service charges from tenants in the same block of flats), the tribunal can specify one or more of the appeals as a 'lead case'. It can then postpone making a decision on all the other related appeals.[145]

The tribunal can also order that when it makes its decision in the lead cases(s), the decision applies to (and is binding on) all the other related appeals. You must be sent a copy of the decision.

If your appeal is not the lead case, you can apply to the tribunal for a direction that the decision does not apply to, and is not binding on, your appeal. You must apply in writing within one month after the date you are sent a copy of the decision. The tribunal can give you longer (or shorter) than this. There is no guarantee that you will be given longer, so keep within the time limit wherever possible.

Part 9: Getting a benefit decision changed
Chapter 57: Appealing to the First-tier Tribunal
4. Hearings

4. **Hearings**

Appeals can be dealt with either at a paper or an oral hearing. Your appeal *must* be dealt with at an oral hearing, unless:[146]

- both you and the DWP or the local authority or HM Revenue and Customs (HMRC) have consented (or both of you have not objected) to the appeal being dealt with at a paper hearing. **Note:** if you (or the DWP, local authority or HMRC) state you want an oral hearing, there must be one; *and*
- the First-tier Tribunal considers that it can decide the matter without an oral hearing. It should explain this in its statement of reasons if you ask for one.

If you want an oral hearing, state this on the appeal form or the enquiry form. Otherwise, the tribunal presumes that you do not object to a paper hearing.

If there is not an oral hearing, the tribunal makes its decision by looking at what you said on your appeal form, any evidence or other information you provided and the decision maker's response. This is known as a paper hearing (see p1367).

Note:
- There may be online appeal hearings in the future (see p1338).
- In some cases, the tribunal may consider your appeal at what is known as a 'triage session'. If it considers that your appeal should be decided in your favour, it may make its decision without you having to attend a hearing but not unless you and the DWP, local authority or HMRC consent. If, during the triage session, the tribunal thinks that your appeal might be successful if you were to give favourable answers to a limited number of questions, it may use online dispute resolution (see p1338) in areas where this is being tested.

Should you choose an oral hearing?

You may not want to attend an oral hearing – eg, because you are worried about speaking for yourself or about the cost or difficulty in attending. Get advice before you decide what to do. Bear the following in mind.

1. You are more likely to win your appeal if you attend an oral hearing, particularly if it concerns a medical issue or your disability, or if the facts of your case are in dispute.

2. If you attend an oral hearing, you can explain your side of the story.

3. You can ask someone to represent you at the hearing (see p1362) and your chances of winning are likely to be higher if you do.[147] You can also take a friend, relative or adviser with you for support.

4. The First-tier Tribunal aims to provide a qualified interpreter if you need one.

5. You, an interpreter and any witnesses may be able to get expenses paid. You can claim for travel (including the extra costs involved for disabled people), meals, loss of earnings and childcare costs.[148]

6. If you or your representative cannot attend an oral hearing at a particular venue (eg, because of a disability), a hearing might be arranged at an alternative venue, or you might be able to participate via a video link or telephone (see p1369).[149]

Paper hearings

You are not sent notice of a paper hearing. The tribunal makes its decision in your absence and you are then notified of its decision.

If you opt for a paper hearing, send the tribunal your arguments about your appeal in writing and any information and evidence you can get to support it (called a 'reply'). Write to the tribunal to let it know you intend to send a reply and state how long it may take to do so.

You must provide your reply within one month after the date you were sent the decision maker's response.[150] If you need longer than this, ask for an extension. If your paper hearing takes place before the month is up and you could (and would) have provided further evidence within that period, you can challenge the tribunal's decision on the ground that it made an error of law.[151]

If you opt for a paper hearing, can there be an oral hearing?

1. If you opt for a paper hearing, your appeal could still be dealt with at an oral hearing. This could happen, for example, if the other party wants an oral hearing or the tribunal decides there should be one because it can only deal with your appeal fairly and justly by having one – eg, it needs to ask you questions about the facts of your case. It could also happen if, during a paper hearing, it is uncertain whether or not anyone has asked for an oral hearing, or if the tribunal suspects that you opted for a paper hearing due to a misunderstanding.[152]

2. If you get unexpected notice of an oral hearing, contact the tribunal to check the reasons for this. You should attend the hearing.

3. If you opt for a paper hearing but then decide you want an oral hearing, you may be able to change your mind. You must tell the tribunal before it makes its decision.

Oral hearings

You must be given reasonable notice of an oral hearing – at least 14 days' notice, unless you agree to less notice than this or there are urgent or exceptional circumstances.[153] The hearing normally takes place at an appeal venue in your area. You can see where the appeal venues are at sscs.venues.tribunals.gov.uk/venues/venues.htm. If you are unable to attend a hearing at the venue, see p1369.

If you have not been given the correct notice (you can argue that this includes the decision maker's response as well as the time and date of the hearing[154]), you

Part 9: Getting a benefit decision changed
Chapter 57: Appealing to the First-tier Tribunal
4. Hearings

can object to the hearing going ahead. If the tribunal decides to proceed with the hearing, attend and explain why your case will be prejudiced (eg, you did not have adequate time to prepare it) and ask for an adjournment (see p1359).

Can an oral hearing go ahead without you?

The tribunal can go ahead with an the oral hearing even if you are not there if:[155]

– it is satisfied that you were notified of the hearing, or that reasonable steps have been taken to notify you. However, it does not normally have to find out why you have not attended – eg, by getting the clerk to the tribunal to telephone you.[156] It *should* attempt to contact you (eg, if your case is complex or your evidence is needed to allow the tribunal to decide your appeal fairly) if this would ensure, so far as is practicable, that you are able to participate fully in the proceedings;[157] *and*

– it thinks that it is in the interests of justice. It should always consider the alternative of adjourning the hearing to give you another opportunity to attend (see p1359).

The tribunal should only go ahead with the hearing if it considers that it has sufficient evidence to decide the appeal fairly.[158] **Note:** if the panel hearing your appeal comprises more than one member, the decision whether or not to go ahead with the hearing should be made by all of the members, not just by the judge alone.[159]

If you turn up late, after the tribunal has decided to proceed in your absence, it should still consider whether to allow you to participate, and whether it should adjourn the hearing to give you another opportunity to attend.[160]

An appeal is heard in public unless the tribunal thinks it should be in private.[161] The tribunal can exclude specific people from hearings in some circumstances. If you want your hearing to be in private, ask for this to be considered. In practice, it is extremely rare for members of the public to attend.

The tribunal can postpone or adjourn a hearing (see p1359).

Child, vulnerable adult and sensitive witnesses

The First-tier Tribunal must consider how to assist any children under 18, vulnerable adults (eg, severely physically or mentally disabled people aged 18 or over) and 'sensitive witnesses' to give evidence.[162] This includes allowing them to give evidence by telephone, video link or other means, or appointing someone with special expertise to help the person give evidence and adopting a less robust style of questioning. You are a 'sensitive witness' if the quality of evidence you give is likely to be diminished because of your fear or distress in connection with giving evidence. If you are a child, vulnerable adult or sensitive witness, and you need special arrangements to be made, you or your representative should let the tribunal know as soon as possible in advance of the hearing. The tribunal should make a note in its record of proceedings that it has considered how to assist you.

Other ways to participate in an oral hearing

If you are unable to attend a hearing at a venue, you may be able to participate via a video link, telephone or other means of instantaneous two-way electronic communication (a remote hearing).[163] There may be more of these during the coronavirus pandemic. If you opted for a paper hearing, the tribunal should take note of any reasons that you give for this choice. If these suggest that you might be happy to give your evidence by telephone, the tribunal should consider adjourning the hearing to give you an opportunity to ask for a telephone hearing.[164]

Alternative venues

Most appeal venues have access for disabled people, and the First-tier Tribunal may meet the cost of special transport to get there. It may also arrange the hearing at another venue – eg, a hotel meeting room near where you live. However, if you are unable to attend a hearing at any of the venues, in rare cases it is possible to hold the hearing in your home (known as a 'domiciliary hearing'), although the tribunal may say this is not necessary if you can use special transport.[165] Include a letter from your doctor with your request for a domiciliary hearing, confirming that you are unable to travel at all – eg, even by private ambulance. Explain why it would not be an adequate solution for you to give your evidence by telephone. You can appeal against a decision to refuse you a domiciliary hearing.[166] Alternatively, if the refusal meant that the way your appeal was dealt with was unfair, you may be able to appeal against the decision on your appeal to the Upper Tribunal.[167]

At the hearing

Any of the following may be present at your appeal hearing.
- **A judge** (see p1352). S/he always acts as the chair of the hearing.
- **A member of the First-tier Tribunal** (see p1353). To see which members hear and decide your appeal, see p1370.
- **An expert** (see p1353). S/he cannot take part in making the decision.
- **A tribunal clerk** (see p1353). S/he cannot take part in making the decision.

A **presenting officer** may be present to represent the decision maker. S/he explains the reasons for the decision, but is not there to defend it at all costs and may provide information which helps your case. Presenting officers often only attend if an appeal is considered complicated. The tribunal can issue a direction requiring a presenting officer to attend the hearing.

The judge and up to two other members hear and decide your appeal. The judge makes a note of what is said by everyone at the hearing. To see which members decide your appeal, see below.

You can have a **representative** with you at the hearing.[168] S/he can explain the procedures, present your case and ensure that the tribunal is aware of all the relevant issues and the law. If you have one, see p1362 for the notice you must

Part 9: Getting a benefit decision changed
Chapter 57: Appealing to the First-tier Tribunal
4. Hearings

send or give to the tribunal. You can also be accompanied by someone at the hearing – eg, a friend or relative. The tribunal can give permission for her/him to act as your representative or assist you in presenting your case.[169]

The First-tier Tribunal aims to provide a qualified **interpreter** if you need one. If you do, tell it in advance of the hearing. If an official interpreter is not available, on rare occasions, it might allow a relative to act as your interpreter if s/he understands that s/he should simply translate accurately and give your answers in your own words, without comment or explanation.[170]

The judge and members

Those who decide a particular kind of appeal are as follows.[171]

- **A judge, a doctor and a person with experience of disability** decide attendance allowance (AA), disability living allowance (DLA) and personal independence payment (PIP) appeals.

  However, if your appeal only raises issues of law, a judge hears your appeal (or a judge and a member whose experience and qualifications are needed to make the decision).

- **A judge and a doctor** decide appeals:
  - about whether you have limited capability for work under the work capability assessment or have limited capability for work-related activity; *and*
  - about industrial injuries benefits or severe disablement allowance (SDA).

  However, if your appeal only raises issues of law (eg, it concerns your failure to attend a medical examination), a judge hears your appeal (or a judge and a member whose experience and qualifications are needed to make the decision).[172]

- **A judge** decides all other appeals on her/his own.

Note: during the coronavirus pandemic, a judge alone may hear your appeal.

Unless your appeal is about AA, DLA or PIP, an additional judge can be included in specified cases, an accountant may be included (if the examination of financial accounts is required) or there can be an additional doctor (if there are complex medical issues). However, there can never be more than three deciding an appeal.

If the group deciding your appeal is comprised incorrectly, you can appeal to the Upper Tribunal and argue that this was an error of law.[173]

Note:

- If your appeal is meant to be heard by two or more members but some of these are absent, the hearing can still go ahead, but only if you and the DWP, or the local authority or HMRC, agree.[174]

- If you have both a DLA (or PIP) and an employment and support allowance appeal, they should not be heard together or consecutively by the same members. They should be heard completely separately, by entirely different members.[175]

- If your appeal is only partly heard by a judge and at least one member, the group deciding your appeal at a new hearing should generally be the same, or completely different.[176]
- You cannot argue that a doctor should not decide your appeal even if s/he regularly provides medical reports about benefit claimants to the DWP.[177]
- You can argue that the tribunal should not rely on evidence from a DWP doctor with whom any of the members hearing your appeal sit at other times. This depends on how often and how recently this has happened.[178]

Procedure at an oral hearing

When the tribunal is ready to hear your case, you (and your representative) are taken in with any presenting officer. There are no strict rules of procedure. The judge decides how the hearing is conducted.[179] The tribunal's overriding objective is that your appeal be dealt with fairly and justly.[180] This includes ensuring that you are able to participate fully.

What happens at an oral hearing?

1. The judge should introduce everyone present.

2. The judge (and members) often starts by asking you (and the presenting officer) questions. Even if you have a representative, you are usually expected to give your own evidence (see p1377). Be prepared for some searching questions.

3. The presenting officer may be asked to summarise the decision maker's case.

4. You should be given the opportunity to explain your case. It is the tribunal's job to help you to say everything you want by putting you at your ease and asking the right questions. If you think there are mistakes in the papers, point them out. You can call witnesses and ask questions of the presenting officer's witnesses. If you forget to say something when it is your turn to speak, do not hesitate to add it at the end of the hearing. See p1376 for help with proving your case.

5. The tribunal considers all the facts, evidence and law before it makes a decision. It should not bargain with you by 'offering' to allow part of your appeal if you agree to drop other parts – eg, by offering you one component of PIP if you agree not to argue for the other.[181]

Appeals about disability or limited capability for work

If your appeal concerns your disability or your limited capability for work, the tribunal considers all the medical and other relevant evidence, and tries to draw out the evidence about your disabilities, listening to all you have to say with the help of questioning from the doctor member(s). The doctor member is there to help the tribunal understand the medical evidence and provide medical information. However, s/he should not give her/his clinical opinion.[182] The evidence may confirm the opinions expressed in medical reports with which you

Part 9: Getting a benefit decision changed
Chapter 57: Appealing to the First-tier Tribunal
4. Hearings

disagree, or it may support your view. See p1378 for information about medical evidence. Consider the following.

- Tell the tribunal how your disability or limited capability for work affects you at work or in your daily life at home. You should be completely straightforward, neither underplaying nor overplaying your symptoms. If you feel better on some days than others, explain how and how often, and say whether you are being seen on a good day or a bad day.
- The tribunal should not restrict itself to accepting the medical evidence about you given in written reports.[183] If there is conflict between what is said in a report and what you have said in writing (eg, on your claim form), it should not accept the evidence in the report without first listening to what you have to say about how your condition affects you.[184] Ensure that you explain any inconsistencies. The tribunal should be particularly careful not to accept automatically the findings in medical reports produced with the assistance of a computer programme.[185]

Medical examination at the oral hearing

The tribunal cannot usually carry out physical examinations.[186] Studying x-ray evidence does not count as a physical examination, so you can ask the tribunal to consider this.[187]

It *can* carry out a physical examination if your appeal relates to the assessment of your disablement for SDA or industrial injuries disablement benefit, or whether you have a prescribed disease or injury.[188] It should let you know during the hearing if it thinks a physical examination is not necessary so you can make representations.[189]

You are examined by the medical member(s) of the tribunal.[190] You can have someone with you as a chaperone or if, for instance, you need help undressing. Make sure you tell the medical member(s) if you are in pain or discomfort. It is also a good idea to provide a full list of any medicines you are taking. After the examination, you should be invited to make further representations to the tribunal if you wish.

Can the tribunal take its observations of you into account?

The tribunal may observe your abilities and behaviour at the hearing and take these into account when making its decision – eg, if your appeal concerns your ability to walk, but it cannot subject you to a walking test.[191] It should not attach undue weight to its observations[192] and you should usually be given the opportunity to comment on them.[193] Remind the tribunal that what it sees may only be relevant to your physical or mental condition on that day and not in general.[194] Tell it, for instance, whether you have just taken medication or have been resting for some time in the waiting area. **Note:** the tribunal can use information about walking distances it obtains itself – eg, from Google maps. However, the evidence should be presented to you so that you can comment on, or refute, it.[195]

Referral for a medical report

The tribunal can adjourn the hearing and refer you to a healthcare professional approved by the DWP (see p1176) for a medical examination and report if your appeal concerns:[196]

- whether you are entitled to AA, DLA or PIP, the appropriate rate of benefit or the period for which you are entitled; *or*
- whether you are entitled to SDA; *or*
- whether you have limited capability for work or for work-related activity; *or*
- the extent of your disablement for SDA or industrial injuries disablement benefit purposes; *or*
- whether you have a loss of faculty as a result of an industrial accident (see p689).

The tribunal can specify the type of healthcare professional to whom you should be referred.[197] The medical examination may take place in your home or at a DWP medical examination centre. **Note:** athough you cannot be compelled to undergo a medical examination, the tribunal may draw negative conclusions if you refuse.

A report or medical notes may also be requested from your GP or other medical adviser with your permission.

The written decision to adjourn for a report should make clear why the tribunal adjourned and what sort of medical evidence is being sought.

What the tribunal considers

The tribunal's job is to decide whether the decision you are appealing about was correct. It must look at the law and issues afresh, taking into account any new evidence or information you (and the DWP, the local authority or HMRC) provide. The tribunal considers all the evidence.[198] It should decide your appeal in an investigative way, but the members should generally not make their own enquiries into the facts of your case before the hearing.[199] **Note:**

- You (or the DWP, the local authority or HMRC) can raise an issue at the hearing.[200] However, the tribunal might then adjourn to give the other side a chance to address the point.
- The tribunal should consider an issue if it is in the appeal papers or in any representations you make, or if the evidence should lead it to believe it is relevant to your appeal.[201] It does not have to consider issues that are 'not raised by' your appeal.[202] **Note:**
  - You do not necessarily have to raise an issue with the tribunal for it to be something it should consider, even if you have a representative, but the issue must be one which in some way obviously demands attention – eg, from evidence included in the appeal papers.[203] Even if you say that you do not want an issue to be considered, the tribunal can still exercise its discretion to consider it.[204] However, if you have a representative, the

Part 9: Getting a benefit decision changed
Chapter 57: Appealing to the First-tier Tribunal
4. Hearings

tribunal may decide not to investigate matters that s/he does not raise on your behalf or that s/he says s/he does not want to be considered.[205]
– The tribunal can consider issues even if no one has raised them.[206] This could include whether the amount of benefit you are currently receiving is correct. It should use its discretion fairly.

Are you appealing about a disability benefit?

If you are appealing because you were not awarded one component of DLA or PIP when you are in receipt of the other, or you ask for a higher rate of DLA, PIP or AA than you are already getting, the tribunal does not have to consider issues which are not the subject of your appeal. However, it may decide to consider both components of DLA or PIP, or to consider whether you should get a lower rate of DLA, PIP or AA than you are already getting. **Note:**
– You should be given warning of this, and a chance to prepare your case properly and make representations or to consider withdrawing your appeal.[207]
– Ask for the oral hearing to be adjourned if you need time or want someone to advise or represent you.
– If your appeal is being dealt with at a paper hearing, you should be given the opportunity to attend an oral hearing or to withdraw your appeal.[208]
– You should be given an explanation of why the tribunal decided to use its discretion in this way in the statement of reasons for its decision.[209]

If you are concerned about what might happen in your appeal, you may be able to withdraw it (see p1363). You need permission if you ask to withdraw your appeal at the hearing, or if you are notified that you can only withdraw your appeal if the tribunal agrees. **Note:** the DWP (or the local authority or HMRC) can apply for your appeal to be reinstated (see p1364).

Appeals involving revisions and supersessions

If your appeal involves a revision or a supersession decision, the tribunal can make any decision that the decision maker could have taken.[210] This includes where the decision maker carried out a supersession:
• but failed to state the grounds or to identify the correct grounds for doing so; *or*
• when s/he should have conducted a revision (and, in some cases, vice versa).

In addition, the tribunal can decide that a 'specific grounds' revision should be done where no decision has been made on the matter by a decision maker (either to revise the decision or refuse to do so) – ie, if you are appealing because the decision maker refused to carry out a supersession.[211]

If there are errors in the decision, argue that the tribunal should correct the decision. However, it can adjourn the hearing, point out the errors to the decision maker and invite the decision maker to reconsider, rather than making any corrections itself.[212]

Changes of circumstances after the decision under appeal

When the tribunal hears your appeal, it considers whether the decision with which you disagree was correct for the period up to and including the date it was made. If your circumstances change after the decision, it cannot take this into account.[213]

Any evidence you get after the decision with which you disagree could still be relevant to your appeal. If the evidence relates to the period before the decision you are disputing was made, or to a past event that was relevant to the decision, it must be taken into account.[214] In some situations, events that happen after the date of a decision can throw light on the situation at or before that date, in which case evidence of such events may also be taken into account – eg, if the tribunal needs to decide whether an improvement in your health was likely to happen.

What you should do if your circumstances change

As a general rule, you should consider making a fresh claim (or seeking a supersession) every time your circumstances change, and appeal if you are unhappy with the subsequent decision, particularly if your appeal is about:

- whether you have limited capability for work, have limited capability for work-related activity or qualify for AA, DLA or PIP, or the rate of AA, DLA or PIP to which you are entitled and your condition has worsened; *or*
- whether you satisfy the 'habitual residence test' (see p1586); *or*
- how much income or capital you have, and this changes.

If you wait until the tribunal makes its decision and this goes against you, you could lose out. You can only get arrears from the date your circumstances changed if a fresh claim (or the effect of a supersession) can be backdated. This is only possible in limited circumstances.

Example

Ravi has been getting PIP mobility component. A decision maker decides his condition has improved so stops his PIP. He appeals. While waiting for his appeal hearing, his condition deteriorates, he makes a fresh claim and is awarded PIP mobility component. When the tribunal hears his appeal against the original decision, it upholds the decision maker's decision. However, because Ravi made a fresh claim when his circumstances changed, he has not lost out.

If you make a fresh claim (or seek a supersession), you can ask the decision maker to wait until your appeal has been determined before making a decision. However,

Part 9: Getting a benefit decision changed
Chapter 57: Appealing to the First-tier Tribunal
5. Proving your case

if the decision maker decides the fresh claim (or supersession) and you disagree with the decision:

- you can appeal against the new decision. All the appeals may be heard together by the tribunal, but it may be better for them to be heard separately;[215] *or*
- whether or not you appeal against the new decision, you can ask the decision maker to revise it once your first appeal is determined (see p1310).

Example

Henry claims pension credit (PC) but the decision maker says he does not satisfy the habitual residence test and refuses his claim. He appeals against the decision and makes a fresh claim for PC on 10 May 2020. The new claim is refused. Henry wins his appeal. Because there has been a fresh decision on his entitlement, the tribunal can only award PC up to 10 May 2020. However, the decision maker does a 'specific grounds' revision and awards PC from that date as well.

5. **Proving your case**

Appeals to the First-tier Tribunal are taken on many issues – disputes about facts or the law, or both – so the advice given here can only be general. You usually need to think about both the facts and the law because they are connected.

Sorting out the facts

You are likely to know more than anyone else about the facts of your case. Your key task is to pass your knowledge on to the tribunal. It rehears your case completely, so fresh facts and arguments can be put by either side.

How do you ensure the tribunal has all the facts?

1. Check through the appeal papers carefully to work out what evidence the decision maker used in support of the decision. This helps you decide what evidence you need to win your case.

2. Study the decision maker's evidence and think about your arguments – eg, to show how the decision maker may have got the wrong impression.

3. Gather evidence and information to back up your arguments. Send it to the tribunal as soon as possible before your oral hearing. Otherwise, it might decide to adjourn your appeal (see p1359) or even decide not to take the evidence or information into account.[216] The tribunal sends a copy to the DWP, the local authority or HM Revenue and Customs (HMRC), which might then decide to support your appeal.

4. Ask any witnesses who support your case to attend the hearing.

The tribunal can issue directions (see p1358) on how you (or the DWP, the local authority or HMRC) should provide evidence and submissions or on how witnesses should give evidence – eg, orally at a hearing, or by making a written submission or a witness statement within a set period of time.[217] It can accept evidence from you (or the DWP, the local authority or HMRC) even if it was not available to a previous decision maker.[218]

Evidence includes:

- oral evidence – what you (and any witnesses or others) actually say at the hearing (see below). The tribunal cannot dismiss oral evidence without a proper explanation of why it has done so;[219] *and*
- written evidence – any documents you (or the DWP, the local authority or HMRC) provide, including medical evidence (see p1378 and p1378); *and*
- filmed evidence (see p1379).

Oral evidence

You, the presenting officer and witnesses can give your oral evidence at the hearing. You are usually expected to give your own oral evidence at the hearing, if you can. Your representative is generally not allowed to give this for you. However, s/he can assist the tribunal in gathering evidence from you (eg, by asking you questions)[220] and can give her/his *own* evidence based on her/his observations, or factual evidence within her/his own knowledge.[221]

If s/he is at the hearing, the presenting officer can put forward arguments as to why s/he thinks the tribunal should confirm that the DWP's (or the local authority's or HMRC's) decision was correct. However, s/he is not necessarily the person who actually made the decision on your claim.

You or the DWP (or the local authority or HMRC) can call witnesses to give evidence. However, the tribunal can limit the number.[222] The tribunal can refuse to hear witnesses who are not relevant, but it should always be fair to you and generally allow witnesses to speak, even if it looks like they may have nothing useful to say.[223] The tribunal itself can summon witnesses.[224]

Hearsay evidence

If you, your representative, the presenting officer or witnesses report what other people have said, this is known as 'hearsay evidence'. The tribunal must carefully weigh up its value, given that the person who originally made the statement is not present at the hearing.[225]

Unless the presenting officer is giving her/his own evidence (eg, because s/he was directly involved in the decision on your claim), any factual statements s/he makes are hearsay evidence, but the tribunal might not doubt the accuracy of the evidence.[226]

Part 9: Getting a benefit decision changed
Chapter 57: Appealing to the First-tier Tribunal
5. Proving your case

Written evidence

Written evidence includes letters, medical and other reports, wage slips, bank statements, birth certificates and anything else that helps prove the facts. If, for example, the DWP (or the local authority or HMRC) says you failed to disclose an increase in your earnings and you have been overpaid, you could explain how and when you did so. It is even better to produce a copy of the letter you sent informing the decision maker of the change, or a letter you received confirming you reported the change or if you telephoned the DWP (or local authority or HMRC) to report the change on a specific day, an itemised phone bill confirming that you called the DWP (or local authority or HMRC) on that day. It is not unknown for the DWP (or the local authority or HMRC) to fail to include copies of relevant documents in the decision maker's response. Check the response carefully and submit copies of any missing documents to the tribunal as soon as you can. If you do not have copies, insist that the decision maker provides these. The tribunal can issue a direction requiring the decision maker to do so (see p1358).

Is the person who provided written evidence absent from the hearing?

1. Argue that the tribunal should not place any weight on the written evidence of someone who is not at the hearing as you have not had the opportunity to question her/him. It should not place weight on the written evidence of an interviewing officer if you are disputing the interview, or an investigating officer if you are disputing what s/he heard or saw. However, the tribunal may still decide that there is no reason to doubt the truth of the officer's statement.

2. The evidence of an anonymous witness cannot be relied on without the consent of the tribunal, and consent should only be given in exceptional circumstances.[227]

Medical evidence

You can ask your doctor to provide medical evidence, or ask an advice agency to write to your doctor. Your doctor may charge for such evidence, but an advice agency or solicitor might be able to get a report free. Your medical evidence should deal with the points in dispute and also with the dates relevant to the decision with which you disagree. If your doctor does not know about the effect of your disability on your everyday life, tell her/him about it and ask her/him to confirm that this is consistent with the degree of your disability. Your evidence, or that of a friend or relative, may also be of use.

If you obtain a medical report, send it to the tribunal in advance of the hearing, with a copy of the letter to your doctor as this helps to show that s/he is expressing her/his own opinion about your case. You could also ask your doctor to supply a copy of her/his notes about you over the last few years.

Note: the tribunal can refer you for an examination and obtain a report if it thinks this is necessary (see p1373). If the lack of medical evidence is causing you difficulties at the hearing, remind the tribunal of its power to obtain one.

Do you disagree with the medical evidence?

1. If the DWP has obtained a report from your GP's surgery which is provided by a doctor you do not usually see, point this out to the tribunal. In all cases if the evidence is unfavourable, point out how long the doctor has known you and what s/he knows about your day-to-day living activities or walking ability. If a doctor does not know you (or know you well) or know how you are affected by your condition, this should be taken into account.

2. If a medical report is provided by a healthcare professional, tell the tribunal about any relevant issues with the examination – eg, if you were not examined or were only given a very short examination, if you were not allowed to explain how you are affected by your condition properly, or if the person examining you has not recorded your answers to her/his questions correctly. Try to point out anything in the content of the report that confirms what you say.

3. Argue that the tribunal should not rely on evidence from a DWP doctor who also sits as a tribunal member with whom any of the members hearing your appeal sit at other times. This depends on how often and on how recently this has happened.[228]

Filmed evidence

The DWP, the local authority or HMRC might use evidence filmed during the course of an investigation – eg, if you are appealing about entitlement to employment and support allowance (ESA), disability living allowance or personal independence payment (PIP). You cannot prevent it doing so.[229] The tribunal should always find out if the surveillance was properly authorised. If it was not authorised, argue that any evidence obtained should be ignored.

You must be given time to view and consider the evidence in advance of the hearing. You should be allowed to be present when the tribunal views it and must be given the opportunity to comment on the issues and evidence.[230] If relevant, insist that the person who did the filming be called as a witness. If the filming was only intermittent and if filming in the intervening periods would have provided evidence favourable to you, point this out to the tribunal.

Checking the law

If you know what the law says, you know what facts you have to prove. The primary sources of social security law are statute law and caselaw decided by the Upper Tribunal and courts. It is easy to find both, once you know what you are looking for. The endnotes in this *Handbook* point you in the right direction. There are also a number of books that explain the law and refer you to relevant legislation and cases (see Appendix 2).

Part 9: Getting a benefit decision changed
Chapter 57: Appealing to the First-tier Tribunal
5. Proving your case

Look carefully at the decision maker's response (see p1354), as this refers to the statute law and caselaw which s/he thinks is relevant. The DWP, the local authority or HMRC does not always get the law right and you should emphasise a point that it has overlooked or got wrong.

Statute law

Statute law comprises Acts of Parliament and regulations (and rules for procedure in the First-tier Tribunal and Upper Tribunal). The Acts set out the main framework and allow regulations and rules covering the details to be made. These regulations and rules are known as statutory instruments. The legislation is often amended, so you must confirm that what you are referring to is up to date.

The best way to look up the relevant statute law is in one of the annotated volumes of legislation listed in Appendix 2. Remember that, in rare cases, the books do not contain all the regulations and rules that are relevant. Acts, regulations and rules are also available at legislation.gov.uk and amended versions are usually available.

Note: benefit law is complicated and the staff who administer benefits are issued with guidance manuals and circulars. The DWP, the local authority, HMRC and the First-tier and Upper Tribunals, are only bound by what the law says, not by the guidance. Nevertheless, it is sometimes useful to check the guidance. See Appendix 2 for a list of what is available.

If the statute law is ambiguous

If the statute law is ambiguous, the First-tier Tribunal, the Upper Tribunal and the courts can look at statements made to parliament by ministers when the law was first made.[231] You can check the House of Commons' and House of Lords' official reports (known as *Hansard*) to see what was said in parliament when the law was first introduced, and the transcripts of debates in the Delegated Legislation Committee (who examine some statutory instruments) at hansard.parliament.uk. You can also check the Explanatory Memorandum that accompanies most statutory instruments. Another source of information is the Social Security Advisory Committee (gov.uk/government/organisations/social-security-advisory-committee).

European legislation

Social security benefits are not governed by British law alone and European Union (EU) law continues to apply during the transition period that began when the UK left the EU (see p1670). During this period, regulations and Directives made by the EU continue to apply in the UK and throughout the European Economic Area (EEA). See Chapter 70 for further information.

Human rights

The Human Rights Act 1998 incorporates into UK law most of the Articles of the European Convention on Human Rights. All legislation must be applied, *so far as it is possible to do so*, in a way which is compatible with this Convention.[232] If a provision of secondary legislation (eg, a regulation), even as so interpreted, results in a breach of Convention rights (eg, it is discriminatory), a tribunal must disapply it, unless it is prevented from doing so by a provision in primary legislation.[233] A tribunal does not have the power to disapply primary legislation and, unlike the courts, it does not have any power to make a declaration of incompatibility.

The First-tier Tribunal must take into account any relevant caselaw of the European Court of Human Rights (ECtHR), but if there is a conflict between a UK court and the ECtHR, the decision of the UK court should generally be followed.[234]

The articles of the Convention most likely to be relevant in social security cases are:

- Article 6(1): right to a fair hearing before an independent and impartial tribunal;
- Article 8: right to respect for private and family life;
- Article 1 of the First Protocol: right to protection of property;
- Article 14: prohibition of discrimination.

If your case is one in which a Human Rights Act argument arises, get specialist advice. Challenges in social security cases using the Human Rights Act and the Convention are difficult and need specialist input.

Caselaw

The decision maker's response often refers to decisions of the Upper Tribunal and the courts (known as 'caselaw'). You should also use caselaw to support your appeal if possible. To help you decide which cases to use, see p1383.

Note: before 3 November 2008, decisions now made by the Upper Tribunal were made by social security commissioners.

Identifying Upper Tribunal and commissioners' decisions

All Upper Tribunal decisions have file numbers – eg, CDLA/2195/2008.

- The last numbers indicate the year in which the appeal was lodged.
- The letters after the 'C' indicate the benefit involved in the decision. An extra 'S' after the 'C' denotes a Scottish case, as in CSIB/721/2004.

Upper Tribunal decisions that are published on the official websites (see p1384) are given a 'citation number' (sometimes called a 'neutral citation') – eg, *JP v SSWP (ESA)* [2016] UKUT 48 (AAC).

- First, the parties to the appeal are identified. The benefit claimant is identified by initials. The first name (or initials) is the party who appealed and the second is the other party. **Note:** 'SSWP' stands for Secretary of State for Work and Pensions – ie, the DWP.
- Next is the year the decision was given (in square brackets) and the letters 'UKUT' (meaning United Kingdom Upper Tribunal).

Part 9: Getting a benefit decision changed
Chapter 57: Appealing to the First-tier Tribunal
5. Proving your case

- The final number is the appeal number.
- Since 2010, letters to indicate the type of benefit involved in the decision are usually included before the year in the citation.

The most important Upper Tribunal decisions are chosen to be reported and are given a new number. All reported decisions:

- from 1951 to 2010 begin with an 'R' – eg, CU/255/1984 became R(U) 3/86. The following letter(s) denote(s) the type of benefit. The last numbers indicate the year in which the decision was published;
- from 2010 begin with the citation number. This is followed by the year the decision is reported (in square brackets), then the letters AACR (meaning Administrative Appeals Chamber Reports) and the reported decision number. In this *Handbook*, a reported decision is shown as follows: eg, *Torbay BC v RF (HB)* [2010] UKUT 7 (AAC), reported as [2010] AACR 26.

Identifying court decisions

Court decisions are identified by the names of the parties involved in the appeal. The first name is usually the party who has appealed and the second name is the other party. In judicial review cases, the case citation begins with 'R', which stands for 'Regina' (the Queen).

Examples of court decisions

Hockenjos v Secretary of State for Social Security [2004] EWCA Civ 1749, 21 December 2004 is a decision of the England and Wales Court of Appeal Civil Division.

R v South Tyneside MBC ex parte Tooley [1997] QBD and *R (Reynolds) v Secretary of State for Work and Pensions* [2002] EWHC Admin 426 are decisions of the England and Wales High Court, formerly known as the Queen's Bench Division and now as the Administrative Court, following applications for judicial review.

Saunderson v SSWP [2012] CSIH 10 is a decision of the Court of Session Inner House in Scotland.

Identifying decisions of the Court of Justice of the European Union

The Court of Justice of the European Union (CJEU) ensures that European law is interpreted and applied in the same way across the EU. Its cases include those that decide one or more questions that have been referred by a national court where there is doubt as to how an EU law should be interpreted. The CJEU also decides cases brought by the European Commission, or another member state, against the failure of a member state to comply with EU law. Decisions are identified by the names of the parties involved. The first name is usually the party who has brought the case, and the second name is the other party in that case. These names are then followed by a unique reference number and the year that the case was decided.

Examples of decisions of the Court of Justice of the European Union

Gusa v Minister for Social Protection, C-442/16 [2017]

Commission of the European Communities v Kingdom of Belgium, C-408/03 [2006]

Precedent

When the Upper Tribunal or a court decides an appeal, the decision sets a precedent, which a decision maker or the First-tier Tribunal deciding a similar case must follow.[235] Unreported decisions must be followed in the same way as reported ones.[236] **Note:** commissioners' decisions also set a precedent.

If there is an irreconcilable conflict between two or more decisions, the First-tier Tribunal has to choose which decision to follow.[237]

- It normally follows a reported decision of the Upper Tribunal (or a commissioner) in preference to an unreported one.
- It must follow an Upper Tribunal decision made by a three-judge panel (or the decision of a tribunal of commissioners) in preference to a decision of a single judge (or commissioner).
- Decisions of the Supreme Court, House of Lords, the Court of Appeal or the Court of Session (or the Court of Justice of the European Union) take precedence over all decisions of the Upper Tribunal (and commissioners).[238]

The Upper Tribunal has more freedom than the First-tier Tribunal.

- It does not have to follow an Upper Tribunal decision made by a single judge (or the decision of a single commissioner) if satisfied that the earlier decision was wrong.[239]
- It follows an Upper Tribunal decision made by a three-judge panel (and the decision of a tribunal of commissioners) unless there are compelling reasons not to. If the judge thinks it may be wrong, s/he can ask the President of the Administrative Appeals Chamber for the case to be transferred to another three-judge panel in the Upper Tribunal to reconsider the point.
- If an appeal is heard by a three-judge panel in the Upper Tribunal, the panel does not have to follow the decision of another similarly comprised panel (or tribunal of commissioners), but usually does so.[240]

Which cases to use

Caselaw can seem less precise than statute law, and frequently cases seem to contradict each other. Very often there are small differences in the facts of the cases, which justify the different results. To find cases relevant to your own, use the endnotes in this *Handbook* or the references to cases in the publications listed in Appendix 2. Bear the following in mind.

Part 9: Getting a benefit decision changed
Chapter 57: Appealing to the First-tier Tribunal
5. Proving your case

- Find cases where the facts are similar to yours. If cases appear to be against you, look at the facts of those cases carefully and see whether any differences justify a different decision in your case (known as 'distinguishing' cases). One distinction may simply be that what seemed reasonable in the 1950s does not seem fair in the 2010s and 2020s.[241]
- Most appeals before April 1987 were decided when there was a right of appeal to commissioners on questions of fact as well as law, so the First-tier Tribunal may not necessarily be erring in law if it takes a different view from a commissioner in a pre-April 1987 decision.
- Ensure that the caselaw is still relevant to the decision you are appealing – ie, check whether there have been amendments to the statute law since the caselaw was decided.
- Check the decisions referred to in the decision maker's response (see p1354). Think of arguments why the decisions should not apply in your case. Sometimes the response relies on only part of a decision and fails to mention another part which is more favourable to you.

Obtaining Upper Tribunal, commissioners' and court decisions

Many of the **Upper Tribunal and commissioners' decisions** made before January 2016 are available at administrativeappeals.decisions.tribunals.gov.uk/Aspx/default.aspx. Many Upper Tribunal decisions made from January 2016 are available at gov.uk/administrative-appeals-tribunal-decisions. Some decisions are also available at bailii.org and an archive of older decisions is at rightsnet.org.uk. Decisions may also be obtained from the Upper Tribunal Offices (see gov.uk/courts-tribunals/upper-tribunal-administrative-appeals-chamber).

Reported decisions are published from time to time in bound volumes, which are sometimes available in law libraries. The bound volumes of decisions from 2010 onwards are called Administrative Appeals Chamber Reports and contain reports of social security cases as well as those from other jurisdictions.

Summaries of reported and other important Upper Tribunal and commissioners' decisions and important court decisions are published in CPAG's *Welfare Rights Bulletin*. However, it is important to use the full decision, not just the summary, at the appeal hearing.

If an unreported decision is to be used at a hearing in the First-tier Tribunal by the DWP, the local authority or HMRC, a copy should be supplied to you. Similarly, if you wish to use one, you should supply copies to everyone, preferably by sending one to the tribunal in advance of the hearing.

Many **court decisions** are available online. See, for example, judiciary.uk/judgments, scotcourts.gov.uk and supremecourt.uk/decided-cases/index.html. Also, a useful link to court decisions is at bailii.org.

Presenting your case at the hearing

Each case is different and hearings are informal, so there is no set pattern for presenting cases. If you want to make a presentation on your appeal, make this clear to the First-tier Tribunal as soon as possible – eg, before the hearing starts, because the tribunal often expects to go straight into asking you questions. This is the way hearings are commonly conducted. Always send any detailed submissions, medical reports and other evidence *before* the hearing.

How should you present your case?

1. You can use a written submission at the hearing and read directly from it. However, the tribunal usually asks questions, so be prepared to talk about your case without the script.

2. Make it clear at the start what you think the outcome of the appeal should be and why – eg, what rate of PIP you think you qualify for, or which ESA descriptors you think you satisfy, or that your claim for housing benefit should be backdated.

3. Tell the tribunal which parts of the decision maker's response you dispute and the parts with which you agree.

4. It is usually best to set out the facts and call any witnesses before turning to legal arguments.

5. It is the tribunal's job to help you to say everything you want by putting you at your ease and asking the right questions. However, you must also be prepared for some searching questions. If you forget to say something when it is your turn to speak, do not hesitate to add it at the end of the hearing.

6. The tribunal's decision

You may be told the tribunal's decision at the hearing and you are given a **decision notice** confirming it. If it is not given at the hearing or you opted for a paper hearing, the decision notice is sent to you later. It may include a summary of the tribunal's reasons for its decision. You *must* be informed of:[242]

- your right to request a statement of reasons for the decision (see p1386); *and*
- the conditions for appealing to the Upper Tribunal, including the time limit for doing so.

Note:
- If the tribunal is unable to come to a unanimous decision, it makes a majority decision. The judge has the casting vote.[243] However, if the tribunal consists of two members and there is complete disagreement about the facts, the judge should not use her/his casting vote, but instead should adjourn the appeal to be heard by different tribunal members.[244]

Part 9: Getting a benefit decision changed
Chapter 57: Appealing to the First-tier Tribunal
6. The tribunal's decision

- A decision can be corrected, superseded, reviewed or set aside (see p1387). You, or the DWP, the local authority or HM Revenue and Customs (HMRC) can also appeal against it to the Upper Tribunal.

Record of proceedings

A record of the tribunal proceedings is made by the judge that indicates the evidence taken and submissions made, as well as any procedural applications.[245] This could be a recording of the hearing or a written record.[246] If you are considering an appeal to the Upper Tribunal, it is a good idea to get a copy. If you foresee disputes about what happened at the hearing, keep your own notes.

The record is kept by the tribunal for six months from the date of its decision or for six months from various other specific dates, including the date you are sent written reasons for its decision. So, if you applied for a statement of reasons for the decision, the record of proceedings should not be destroyed until six months after the statement has been provided.[247]

You can apply for a copy of the record of proceedings. You must do so in writing within the relevant six-month period. The tribunal can give you longer (or shorter) than this. There is no guarantee that you will be given longer, so keep within the time limit wherever possible. Bear in mind that if you apply after the six-month period, the record may have been destroyed. You can apply for a typed copy of a written record – eg, if the written copy is difficult to read, but the tribunal may refuse to provide one. However, if you appeal to the Upper Tribunal, you can ask an Upper Tribunal judge to make a direction that a typed version is to be prepared.

The statement of reasons

The First-tier Tribunal may give the reasons for its decision at the oral hearing, or give or send you a written statement of reasons, prepared by the judge.[248] If you are not provided with a written statement of reasons, you have a right to apply for one.[249] **Note:** the judge may say that the decision notice (see p1385) is to stand as the written statement of reasons, so check it carefully.

You must generally have a statement of reasons if you want to appeal to the Upper Tribunal. You must show that the First-tier Tribunal made an error of law (see p1397) and it may be difficult to do so without a statement of reasons.

Your request for a statement of reasons must be:[250]
- in writing; *and*
- received by the First-tier Tribunal within one month (see p1346) of your being sent or given its decision notice. It can give you longer (or shorter) than this.[251] There is no guarantee that you will be given longer, so keep within the time limit wherever possible.

The written statement of reasons must then be sent to you within one month or as soon as it is reasonably practicable after that.[252] There are, however, often long delays.

Note:

- If you mistakenly ask the First-tier Tribunal for permission to appeal to the Upper Tribunal instead of asking for a statement of reasons, it should treat this as a request for a statement of reasons.[253]
- If the judge refuses wrongly to provide a statement of reasons, you may have grounds for appeal to the Upper Tribunal.[254]
- If there is a long delay in getting a statement of reasons, you could apply for permission to appeal to the Upper Tribunal. The Upper Tribunal can require the First-tier Tribunal to provide reasons for its decision.[255]

The DWP, the local authority or HMRC can also ask for a statement of reasons. If this happens, it usually means it is considering appealing to the Upper Tribunal.

If you win your appeal

If you win your appeal, the DWP, local authority or HMRC should carry out the First-tier Tribunal's decision straight away. It can do this on the basis of the decision notice (see p1385). However, if the DWP, the local authority or HMRC:

- disagrees with the decision, it might consider appealing against it to the Upper Tribunal. In this case, you are not normally paid while it decides what to do. See p1200 for what the DWP, the local authority or HMRC must do before it can suspend payment of your benefit. If the DWP, local authority or HMRC decides to appeal, you are not normally paid until the Upper Tribunal decides the case.[256] However, you can ask the DWP, the local authority or HMRC to pay you if you are in financial hardship;
- applies for permission to appeal to the Upper Tribunal, the First-tier Tribunal may be able to suspend the effect of its decision until the application is determined (by either tribunal), and then until any review of, or appeal against, the decision is determined.[257]

The First-tier Tribunal can also suspend the effect of its decision if *you* apply for permission to appeal to the Upper Tribunal.

If you disagree with the tribunal's decision

If you disagree with the First-tier Tribunal's decision, you cannot simply ask it to look at the decision again – eg, if you have additional evidence. However:

- if the decision contains a clerical mistake or other accidental slip or omission, this can be corrected by the tribunal. This only applies if it is a genuine error such as a typing or spelling mistake or a mathematical miscalculation, not an error of law on an important issue in your appeal. **Note:** the tribunal cannot

Part 9: Getting a benefit decision changed
Chapter 57: Appealing to the First-tier Tribunal
6. The tribunal's decision

use this rule to amend or add to its reasons for the decision, but can amend these if it reviews its decision (see p1401);[258]
- the decision can be superseded by the DWP, the local authority or HMRC, if there are grounds (see p1315), though arrears can be limited. However, if the tribunal made a mistake about the law, you must appeal to the Upper Tribunal;
- you (or the DWP, the local authority or HMRC) can appeal to the Upper Tribunal against the decision (see Chapter 58);
- if you (or the DWP, the local authority or HMRC) seek permission to appeal to the Upper Tribunal against a decision, the First-tier Tribunal can review it (see p1401);
- the decision can be set aside, which means the decision is cancelled and your appeal is heard again (see below).

If you are considering an appeal to the Upper Tribunal, ask for the First-tier Tribunal's statement of reasons (if one has not yet been provided) within the one-month time limit (see p1386), even if you are first going to apply for the decision to be set aside.

Setting aside a decision on procedural grounds

A First-tier Tribunal decision can only be set aside on procedural grounds if the judge thinks it is 'in the interests of justice' to do so and:[259]
- you, your representative or the DWP, the local authority or HMRC:
  - were not sent, or did not receive, appeal papers or other relevant documents, at an appropriate time – eg, in sufficient time before the hearing; *or*
  - were not present at the oral hearing. However, if you (or they) chose not to attend, it might not be 'in the interests of justice' to set the decision aside; *or*
- the tribunal was not sent appeal papers or other documents relating to the proceedings at an appropriate time – eg, in sufficient time before the hearing; *or*
- there was some other procedural irregularity.

You must apply in writing to the First-tier Tribunal. The application must be received no later than one month after the date you are sent the decision notice (see p1385).[260] The tribunal can give you longer (or shorter) than this.[261] There is no guarantee that you will be given longer, so keep within the time limit wherever possible. The rules do not say what the time limit is if you are given the decision notice at the hearing but you should apply within the time limit above to protect your position.
Note:
- Applications are normally decided without a hearing.[262] Make sure you give a full explanation of your reasons when you apply. If you could not attend the hearing (eg, because you were ill), provide evidence of this – eg, a note from your doctor. If your application is late, explain the reasons for this.

- If the decision is set aside, your appeal is heard again and a new decision is made. You should be given the opportunity to ask for an oral hearing, even if your appeal was originally decided at a paper hearing.[263]
- If a decision is wrongly set aside, any subsequent rehearing by the First-tier Tribunal is invalid.[264]

In some circumstances, a decision can also be set aside by agreement (see below).

If the decision is not set aside

If the First-tier Tribunal refuses to set aside a decision, you can appeal to the Upper Tribunal against the refusal.[265] You can often argue that the circumstances you mentioned in your application for a set aside also show that the tribunal made an error of law. So it might be better to try to appeal to the Upper Tribunal against the original decision *and* the refusal. If your application for the First-tier Tribunal's decision to be set aside is refused, the time limit for applying for permission to appeal to the Upper Tribunal can run from the date you are sent notice of this.[266] However, this only applies if you applied for the decision to be set aside within the one-month time limit (or any longer period allowed by the First-tier Tribunal).

Note: the First-tier Tribunal can treat your application for a decision to be set aside as an application for permission to appeal to the Upper Tribunal, or as an application for a correction of the decision.[267]

Setting aside a decision by agreement

The First-tier Tribunal must set aside a decision if an application is made for permission to appeal against it to the Upper Tribunal, and you and the DWP, the local authority or HMRC agree that the First-tier Tribunal made an 'error of law' (see p1397).[268] Bear in mind that the First-tier Tribunal does not send copies of applications for permission to appeal to the other party. If you think that the DWP, the local authority or HMRC might agree that the tribunal made an error of law, you should send it a copy of your application. However, there is no guarantee that it will take any action on this.

Part 9: Getting a benefit decision changed
Chapter 57: Appealing to the First-tier Tribunal
Notes

Notes

1. Before you appeal

1 s12(1), (2) and (3D) SSA 1998
2 s12(2)(b) and (3A)-(3C) SSA 1998; reg 3ZA SS&CS(DA) Regs; reg 7 UC,PIP,JSA&ESA(DA) Regs
3 *R (CJ) and SG v SSWP (ESA)* [2017] UKUT 324 (AAC), reported as [2018] AACR 5
4 Memo DMG 5/19; Memo ADM 8/19
5 Memo DMG 5/19; Memo ADM 8/19
6 *PH and SM v SSWP* [2018] UKUT 404 (AAC)
7 **UC/PIP/JSA&ESA under UC** Reg 7(5) UC,PIP,JSA&ESA(DA) Regs
   Other benefits Reg 3ZA(5) SS&CS(DA) Regs
8 r22(4)(a) TP(FT) Rules
9 r7 TP(FT) Rules
10 *MM v SSWP (PIP)* [2016] UKUT 36 (AAC)
11 **UC/PIP/JSA&ESA under UC** Reg 49 UC,PIP,JSA&ESA(DA) Regs
   CB/GA Reg 24 CB&GA(DA) Regs
   Other benefits Reg 25 SS&CS(DA) Regs
   All s12 SSA 1998
12 s12(4) SSA 1998
13 Reg 14 SS(JPIP) Regs
14 Sch 7 para 6(3) and (6) CSPSSA 2000; regs 3 and 21 HB&CTB(DA) Regs; *Wirral MBC v Salisbury Independent Living Ltd* [2012] EWCA Civ 84, reported as [2012] AACR 37
15 R(H) 3/04; R(H) 10/07
16 **UC/PIP/JSA&ESA under UC** s12 and Schs 2 and 3 SSA 1998; reg 50(1) and Sch 2 UC,PIP,JSA&ESA(DA) Regs
   HB Sch 7 para 6 CSPSSA 2000
   CB/GA s12 and Schs 2 and 3 SSA 1998; reg 25(2) CB&GA(DA) Regs
   Other benefits s12 and Schs 2 and 3 SSA 1998; reg 26 SS&CS(DA) Regs
17 R(SB) 29/83; R(SB) 12/89; CIS/807/1992; R(H) 3/05
18 R(IS) 6/04
19 **UC/PIP/JSA&ESA under UC** Regs 7(3) and 51 UC,PIP,JSA&ESA(DA) Regs
   HB Reg 10 HB&CTB(DA) Regs
   CB/GA Reg 26 CB&GA(DA) Regs
   Other benefits Regs 3ZA and 28 SS&CS(DA) Regs
20 *VT v SSWP (IS)* [2016] UKUT 178 (AAC), reported as [2016] AACR 42

21 *SSWP v Adams* [2003] EWCA Civ 796, reported as R(G) 1/03
22 *MC and JH v SSWP (ESA)* [2014] UKUT 125 (AAC), reported as [2014] AACR 35
23 **UC/PIP/JSA&ESA under UC** Sch 2 SSA 1998; reg 50(2) and Sch 3 UC,PIP,JSA&ESA(DA) Regs
   HB Sch 7 para 6(2) CSPSSA 2000; reg 16 and Sch HB&CTB(DA) Regs
   CB/GA Sch 2 SSA 1998; reg 25 and Sch 2 CB&GA(DA) Regs
   Other benefits Sch 2 SSA 1998; reg 27 and Sch 2 SS&CS(DA) Regs
24 **UC/PIP/JSA&ESA under UC** Regs 10 and 25 UC,PIP,JSA&ESA(DA) Regs
   HB Regs 4(6) and 7(2)(e) HB&CTB(DA) Regs
   CA/GA Regs 9 and 13(2)(d) CB&GA(DA) Regs
   Other benefits Regs 3(8) and 6(2)(d) SS&CG(DA) Regs
25 *RL v SSWP (JSA)* [2017] UKUT 282 (AAC)

2. How to appeal

26 Reg 20(1) HB&CTB(DA) Regs
27 Reg 20(1) HB&CTB(DA) Regs; r23 TP(FT) Rules
28 r22 TP(FT) Rules
29 r22(2)(d)(i) TP(FT) Rules
30 CIB/3937/2000; *SSWP v SC (SF)* [2013] UKUT 607 (AAC)
31 r12 TP(FT) Rules
32 **HB** r23(2)(a)(i) and (ii) TP(FT) Rules
   Other benefits r22(2)(d)(ii) and Sch 1 para 5(a) and (b) TP(FT) Rules
   All r12 TP(FT) Rules
33 s9(5) SSA 1998; Sch 7 para 3(5) CSPSSA 2000
34 r23(2)(a)(iii) and Sch 1 para 5(c) TP(FT) Rules
35 rr22(8)(a) and 23(4) and (5) TP(FT) Rules
36 r5(3)(a) TP(FT) Rules
37 rr22(6) and 23(3) TP(FT) Rules
38 *LS v Lambeth LB (HB)* [2010] UKUT 461 (AAC), reported as [2011] AACR 27
39 Reg 19(5A) HB&CTB(DA) Regs
40 Reg 19(6) and (7) HB&CTB(DA) Regs
41 Reg 19(8) HB&CTB(DA) Regs
42 Reg 19(9) HB&CTB(DA) Regs
43 r23(7)(a) TP(FT) Rules

44 R(M) 1/87; R(I) 5/91
45 R(M) 1/87
46 CIS/147/1995
47 rr22(8) and 23(5) and (8) TP(FT) Rules
48 *KK v Sheffield City Council (CTB)* [2015]
   UKUT 367 (AAC); *PM v SSD (AFCS)*
   [2015] UKUT 647 (AAC)
49 r23(7)(b) TP(FT) Rules
50 *LS v Lambeth LB (HB)* [2010] UKUT 461
   (AAC), reported as [2011] AACR 27
51 rr22(3) and 23(6) TP(FT) Rules
52 r11(5) TP(FT) Rules; *CO v LB Havering
   (HB)* [2015] UKUT 28 (AAC)
53 rr22(3), (4) and (9) and 23(6) TP(FT)
   Rules
54 *MM v SSWP (PIP)* [2016] UKUT 36 (AAC)
55 Reg 20(2)-(6) HB&CTB(DA) Regs
56 Reg 20(6) HB&CTB(DA) Regs
57 Reg 20(7) HB&CTB(DA) Regs
58 para C7/7.128-29 GM
59 Reg 20(8) HB&CTB(DA) Regs
60 rr4 and 7(2) TP(FT) Rules; Practice
   Statement: *Delegation of Functions to
   Staff in Relation to the Social Entitlement
   Chamber of the First-tier Tribunal on or
   after 1 October 2014,* 18 September
   2014, paras 5-7
61 r4(3) TP(FT) Rules

3. After you send or deliver your appeal
62 s28 TCEA 2007
63 Practice Statement: *Delegation of
   Functions to Registrars First-tier Tribunal
   (Social Entitlement Chamber),* 1
   December 2016; *Practice Statement
   authorising Tribunal Caseworkers First-tier
   Tribunal (Social Entitlement Chamber) to
   carry out functions of a judicial nature,* 16
   July 2018
64 Practice Statement: *Delegation of
   Functions to Staff in Relation to the Social
   Entitlement Chamber of the First-tier
   Tribunal on or after 1 October 2014,* 18
   September 2014
65 *T v SSWP (ESA)* [2019] UKUT 59 (AAC)
66 r4(3) TP(FT) Rules
67 *DTM v Kettering BC (CTB)* [2013] UKUT
   625 (AAC)
68 r24(1A) TP(FT) Rules; Art 6 European
   Convention on Human Rights; s6 HRA
   1998; CH/3497/2005; *MB v Wychavon
   DC* [2013] UKUT 67 (AAC); Local
   Government Ombudsman, Complaint
   01/C/13400 against Scarborough BC
69 r24(1)(c) TP(FT) Rules
70 r24(5) TP(FT) Rules
71 r11(6)(a) TP(FT) Rules
72 r24(2) TP(FT) Rules

73 *LH v SSWP (PIP)* [2018] UKUT 57 (AAC);
   TM v SSWP (PIP) [2019] UKUT 204 (AAC)
74 r24(4) TP(FT) Rules; *ST v SSWP (ESA)*
   [2012] UKUT 469 (AAC); *FN v SSWP
   (ESA)* [2015] UKUT 670 (AAC), reported
   as [2016] AACR 24
75 *FI v HMRC* [2018] UKUT 226 (AAC)
76 R(H) 1/07
77 rr5 and 6(1)-(3) TP(FT) Rules
78 r24(6) and (7) TP(FT) Rules
79 r5(3)(a) TP(FT) Rules
80 **HB** Sch 7 para 3(6) CSPSSA 2000
   Other benefits s9(6) SSA 1998
81 **UC/PIP/JSA&ESA under UC** Reg
   52(1) and (5) UC,PIP,JSA&ESA(DA) Regs
   HB Reg 17(1) and (2) HB&CTB(DA)
   Regs
   CB/GA Reg 27(1) and (5) CB&GA(DA)
   Regs
   Other benefits Reg 30(1) and (2)
   SS&CS(DA) Regs
82 Vol 1 Ch 6, para 6160-6183 DMG; para
   A5159-5161 ADM; *'An offer you can't
   refuse?',* article in *Welfare Rights Bulletin*
   273, December 2019, p4
83 *AI v SSWP (PIP)* [2019] UKUT 103 (AAC);
   para 4 Memo DMG 20/13
84 **HB** Sch 7 para 3(5) CSPSSA 2000;
   r23(2) TP(FT) Rules
   Other benefits s9(5) SSA 1998; Sch 1
   para 5 TP(FT) Rules
85 **UC/PIP/JSA&ESA under UC** Reg
   52(2) UC,PIP,JSA&ESA(DA) Regs
   HB Reg 17(3) HB&CTB(DA) Regs
   CB/GA Reg 27(2) CB&GA(DA) Regs
   Other benefits Reg 30(3) SS&CS(DA)
   Regs
86 **UC/PIP/JSA&ESA under UC** Reg
   52(3) UC,PIP,JSA&ESA(DA) Regs
   HB Reg 17(4) HB&CTB(DA) Regs
   CB/GA Reg 27(3) CB&GA(DA) Regs
   Other benefits Reg 30(4) SS&CS(DA)
   Regs
87 **UC/PIP/JSA&ESA under UC** Reg
   52(4) UC,PIP,JSA&ESA(DA) Regs
   HB Reg 17(5) HB&CTB(DA) Regs
   CB/GA Reg 27(4) CB&GA(DA) Regs
   Other benefits Reg 30(5) SS&CS(DA)
   Regs
88 r2 TP(FT) Rules; r2 TP(UT) Rules
89 *MA v SSWP* [2009] UKUT 211 (AAC)
90 rr5, 6, 8, 15 and 16 TP(FT) Rules; rr5-7,
   8, 15 and 16 TP(UT) Rules

Part 9: Getting a benefit decision changed
Chapter 57: Appealing to the First-tier Tribunal
Notes

91 s25 TCEA 2007; r7(3) TP(FT) Rules; r7(3) and (4) TP(UT) Rules; *MD v SSWP (Enforcement Reference)* [2010] UKUT 202 (AAC), reported as [2011] AACR 5; *CB v Suffolk CC (Enforcement Reference)* [2010] UKUT 413 (AAC), reported as [2011] AACR 22

92 r16(3) TP(FT) Rules; r16(3) TP(UT) Rules

93 r5(3)(l) TP(FT) Rules; r5(3)(l) and (m) TP(UT) Rules

94 r5(3)(a) TP(FT) Rules; r5(3)(a) TP(UT) Rules

95 r2 TP(FT) Rules; r2 TP(UT) Rules

96 r2(2)(e) TP(FT) Rules; r2(2)(e) TP(UT) Rules

97 rr5, 6 and 15 TP(FT) Rules; rr5, 6 and 15 TP(UT) Rules; *SR v Bristol CC* [2008] UKUT 7 (AAC)

98 r6(4) TP(FT) Rules; r5(4) TP(UT) Rules

99 r6(5) TP(FT) Rules; r6(5) TP(UT) Rules

100 r7 TP(FT) Rules; r7 TP(UT) Rules

101 R(H) 3/05; CCS/3757/2004

102 *SSWP v HS (JSA)* [2016] UKUT 272 (AAC), reported as [2017] AACR 29

103 *AP v SSWP (ESA)* [2017] UKUT 304 (AAC)

104 CIB/4253/2004

105 r15(2)(b) TP(FT) Rules; r15(2)(b) TP(UT) Rules

106 r6(2) and (3) TP(FT) Rules; r6(2) and (3) TP(UT) Rules

107 r5(3)(h) TP(FT) Rules; r5(3)(h) TP(UT) Rules; *MA v SSWP* [2009] UKUT 211 (AAC); Practice Statement: *Composition of Tribunals in Social Security and Child Support Cases in the Social Entitlement Chamber on or after 1 August 2013*, 31 July 2013, para 10

108 *GC v SSWP (ESA)* [2012] UKUT 60 (AAC)

109 *LJT v SSWP (PIP)* [2019] UKUT 21 (AAC)

110 r31 TP(FT) Rules; r38 TP(UT) Rules

111 *BV v SSWP (PIP)* [2018] UKUT 444 (AAC)

112 CDLA/1290/2004

113 CDLA/3680/1997; *JC v SSWP (PIP)* [2018] UKUT 110 (AAC)

114 *MA v SSWP* [2009] UKUT 211 (AAC)

115 CDLA/5413/1999

116 CIS/566/1991; CS/99/1993

117 CIS/2292/2000; *DC v SSWP (ESA)* [2015] UKUT 150 (AAC)

118 CIS/6002/1997; *R v Social Security Commissioner ex parte Angora Bibi* [2000] unreported (HC); CIB/1009/2004; CIB/2058/2004

119 CIS/3338/2001; *DC v SSWP* [2014] UKUT 218 (AAC)

120 *MH v Pembrokeshire (HB)* [2010] UKUT 28 (AAC)

121 r8(1), (3)(a) and (5) TP(FT) Rules; r8(1), (3)(a) and (5) TP(UT) Rules

122 *DTM v Kettering BC (CTB)* [2013] UKUT 625 (AAC)

123 r8(5) and (6) TP(FT) Rules; r8(5) and (6) TP(UT) Rules

124 r8(2) and (4) TP(FT) Rules; r8(2) and (4) TP(UT) Rules

125 r8(3)(b) and (c) and (4) TP(FT) Rules; r8(3)(b) TP(UT) Rules

126 *AW v IC and Blackpool CC* [2013] UKUT 30 (AAC)

127 R(IS) 5/94

128 *LS v Lambeth LB (HB)* [2010] UKUT 461 (AAC), reported as [2011] AACR 27

129 rr1(3), definition of 'respondent', and 8(7) TP(FT) Rules; rr1(3), definition of 'respondent', and 8(7) TP(UT) Rules

130 r8(8) TP(FT) Rules; r8(8) TP(UT) Rules

131 *ZB v SSWP (CSM)* [2013] UKUT 367 (AAC); *SL v SSWP and KL (CSM)* [2014] UKUT 128 (AAC); *CW v SSWP and Another (CSM)* [2014] UKUT 290 (AAC)

132 r11 TP(FT) Rules; r11 TP(UT) Rules; CIB/1009/2004; CIB/2058/2004

133 r11(2) TP(FT) Rules; r11(2) TP(UT) Rules

134 r11(6)(b) TP(FT) Rules; r11(4)(b) TP(UT) Rules

135 r11(6)(a) TP(FT) Rules; r11(4)(a) TP(UT) Rules; *MP v SSWP (DLA)* [2010] UKUT 103 (AAC)

136 r11(7) and (8) TP(FT) Rules; r11(5) and (6) TP(UT) Rules

137 s10 Legal Aid, Sentencing and Punishment of Offenders Act 2012

138 **HB** Reg 20(9) HB&CTB(DA) Regs; r17 TP(FT) Rules
Other benefits r17 TP(FT) Rules
All *WM v SSWP (DLA)* [2015] UKUT 642 (AAC)

139 rr4 and 7(2)(a) TP(FT) Rules; Practice Statement: *Delegation of Functions to Staff in Relation to the Social Entitlement Chamber of the First-tier Tribunal on or after 1 October 2014*, 18 September, paras 3 and 4

140 r4(3) TP(FT) Rules

141 r17(4) and (5) TP(FT) Rules

142 r32 TP(FT) Rules; r39 TP(UT) Rules

143 s26 SSA 1998

144 s26(5) SSA 1998

145 rr5(3)(b) and 18 TP(FT) Rules

4. Hearings

146 r27(1) TP(FT) Rules; *MH v Pembrokeshire CC (HB)* [2010] UKUT 28 (AAC); *AT v SSWP (ESA)* [2010] UKUT 430 (AAC); *MM v SSWP (ESA)* [2011] UKUT 334 (AAC)

147 r11 TP(FT) Rules

148 r21 TP(FT) Rules

149 r1 TP(FT) Rules, definition of 'hearing'
150 r24(6) and (7) TP(FT) Rules
151 *MP v SSWP (DLA)* [2010] UKUT 103 (AAC)
152 r5(3)(f) TP(FT) Rules; *DT v SSWP (UC)* [2019] UKUT 268 (AAC)
153 r29 TP(FT) Rules
154 CH/3594/2002
155 r31 TP(FT) Rules; *WT v SSWP (DLA)* [2011] UKUT 93 (AAC)
156 *PS v SSWP (ESA)* [2017] UKUT 55 (AAC)
157 *KD v SSWP (ESA and IS) and KD and HMRC (TC)* [2020] UKUT 9 (AAC)
158 *LR v SSWP (ESA)* [2017] UKUT 412 (AAC)
159 *RK v SSWP (ESA)* [2018] UKUT 436 (AAC)
160 *AK v HMRC (TC)* [2016] UKUT 98 (AAC)
161 r30 TP(FT) Rules
162 Practice Direction: *Child, Vulnerable Adult and Sensitive Witnesses,* 30 October 2008; *SW v SSWP (DLA)* [2015] UKUT 319 (AAC); *LO'L v SSWP (ESA)* [2016] UKUT 10 (AAC), reported as [2016} AACR 31; *RT v SSWP (PIP)* [2019] UKUT 207 (AAC)
163 r1(3) TP(FT) Rules, definition of 'hearing'
164 *LO'L v SSWP (ESA)* [2016] UKUT 10 (AAC), reported as [2016] AACR 31
165 *KO v SSWP (ESA)* [2013] UKUT 544 (AAC); *LS v SSWP (DLA)* [2015] UKUT 638 (AAC); *DB v SSWP (DLA)* [2016] UKUT 205 (AAC)
166 *LS v Lambeth LB (HB)* [2010] UKUT 461 (AAC), reported as [2011] AACR 27
167 CIB/2751/2002; CDLA/1350/2004
168 r11 TP(FT) Rules; CIB/1009/2004; CIB/2058/2004
169 r11(7) and (8) TP(FT) Rules
170 *ZO v SSWP (IB)* [2010] UKUT 143 (AAC); AS v SSWP (ESA) [2019] UKUT 261 (AAC)
171 r2 The First-tier Tribunal and Upper Tribunal (Composition of Tribunal) Order 2008 SI No.2835; Practice Statement: *Composition of Tribunals in Social Security and Child Support Cases in the Social Entitlement Chamber on or after 1 August 2013,* 31 July 2013
172 *CH v SSWP (ESA)* [2017] UKUT 6 (AAC)
173 *MB and Others v SSWP (ESA & DLA)* [2013] UKUT 111 (AAC), reported as [2014] AACR 1
174 Sch 4 para 15(6) TCEA 2007; *SB v SSWP (DLA)* [2013] UKUT 531 (AAC); *PF v SSWP (ESA)* [2015] UKUT 553 (AAC)
175 *PJ v SSWP (ESA)* [2011] UKUT 224 (AAC); *MB and Others v SSWP (ESA & DLA)* [2013] UKUT 111 (AAC), reported as [2014] AACR 1

176 R(U) 3/88; *JH v SSWP and MH* [2016] UKUT 158 (AAC)
177 *Gillies v SSWP* [2006] UKHL 2, reported as R(DLA) 5/06
178 *SSWP v Cunningham* [2004] ScotCS 211, reported as R(DLA) 7/04; R(DLA) 3/07
179 Practice Statement: *Composition of Tribunals in Social Security and Child Support Cases in the Social Entitlement Chamber on or after 1 August 2013,* 31 July 2013, para 12
180 r2 TP(FT) Rules
181 CSDLA/606/2003
182 *PM v SSWP (PIP)* [2017] UKUT 154 (AAC)
183 CM/527/1992; CIB/3074/2003
184 CIB/5586/1999
185 CIB/476/2005; CIB/511/2005
186 s20(3) SSA 1998
187 R(IB) 2/06
188 s20(3) SSA 1998; r25(2) TP(FT) Rules; R(DLA) 5/03
189 CI/3384/2006
190 Practice Statement: *Composition of Tribunals in Social Security and Child Support Cases in the Social Entitlement Chamber on or after 1 August 2013,* 31 July 2013, para 14
191 r25(4) TP(FT) Rules
192 R(DLA) 1/95, qualified by CM/2/1994; *GL v SSWP* [2008] UKUT 36 (AAC)
193 *ID v SSWP (PIP)* [2015] UKUT 692 (AAC); *KMN v SSWP (PIP)* [2019] UKUT 42 (AAC)
194 R(DLA) 8/06
195 *HI v SSWP* [2014] UKUT 238 (AAC)
196 ss20(2) and 39 SSA 1998; r25(3) and Sch 2 TP(FT) Rules; *SSWP v DB (PIP)* [2016] UKUT 212 (AAC)
197 s20(2A) SSA 1998
198 CDLA/2014/2004
199 *GL v SSWP* [2008] UKUT 36 (AAC); *HI v SSWP* [2014] UKUT 238 (AAC)
200 CH/1229/2002
201 *Mongan v Department for Social Development* [2005] NICA 16, reported as R3/05 (DLA)
202 **HB** Sch 7 para 6(9)(a) CSPSSA 2000
Other benefits s12(8)(a) SSA 1998
203 *Mooney v SSWP* [2004] SLT 1141, reported as R(DLA) 5/04; *Mongan v Department for Social Development* [2005] NICA 16, reported as R3/05 (DLA); *SSWP v Hooper* [2007] EWCA Civ 495, reported as R(IB) 4/07; *KKL v SSWP (CPIP)* [2018] UKUT 17 (AAC)
204 *KKL v SSWP (CPIP)* [2018] UKUT 17 (AAC)
205 CSDLA/336/2000; CSIB/160/2000; R(H) 1/02

Part 9: Getting a benefit decision changed
Chapter 57: Appealing to the First-tier Tribunal
Notes

206 CH/1229/2002; R(IB) 2/04; *AP-H v SSWP (DLA)* [2010] UKUT 183 (AAC)
207 CI/531/2000; CDLA/1000/2001; CH/1229/2002; R(IB) 2/04; CDLA/884/2008; *ET v SSWP (PIP)* [2017] UKUT 478 (AAC); *LJ v SSWP (PIP)* [2017] UKUT 455 (AAC)
208 CDLA/4184/2004
209 R(IB) 2/04
210 R(IB) 2/04; CH/3009/2002
211 CDLA/1707/2005
212 R(IB) 2/04; R(IB) 7/04; CIS/1675/2004
213 **HB** Sch 7 para 6(9)(b) CSPSSA 2000
Other benefits s12(8)(b) SSA 1998; R(DLA) 4/05
214 R(DLA) 2/01; R(DLA) 3/01; CJSA/2375/2000
215 R(SB) 4/85

5. **Proving your case**
216 r15(2) TP(FT) Rules
217 r15(1)(e) and (f) TP(FT) Rules
218 r15(2) TP(FT) Rules
219 R(SB) 33/85; R(SB) 12/89
220 CIB/2058/2004
221 r11(5) TP(FT) Rules; CDLA/1138/2003; CDLA/2462/2003; *SK v SSWP (ESA)* [2014] UKUT 141 (AAC)
222 r15(1)(d) TP(FT) Rules; CDLA/2014/2004
223 R(SB) 6/82
224 r16 TP(FT) Rules
225 CIS/4901/2002
226 *Walsall MBC v PL* [2009] UKUT 27 (AAC)
227 *JM v SSWP* [2012] UKUT 472 (AAC)
228 *SSWP v Cunningham* [2004] ScotCS 211, reported as R(DLA) 7/04; R(DLA) 3/07
229 R(DLA) 4/02; CIS/1481/2006; *DG v SSWP (DLA)* [2011] UKUT 14 (AAC); *BS v SSWP (DLA)* [2016] UKUT 73 (AAC)
230 *AF v SSWP (DLA) (No.2)* [2017] UKUT 366 (AAC)
231 *Pepper v Hart* [1992] UKHL 3, reported as 3 WLR 1032, *The Times,* 30 November 1992
232 s3(1) HRA 1998
233 *RR v SSWP* [2019] UKSC 52
234 *Leeds CC v Price* [2006] UKHL 10
235 R(I) 12/75; *Dorset Healthcare Trust v MH* [2009] UKUT 4 (AAC)
236 R(SB) 22/86
237 R(I) 12/75; *Dorset Healthcare Trust v MH* [2009] UKUT 4 (AAC)
238 *CSBO v Leary,* reported as R(SB) 6/85; see generally CS/140/1991
239 R(G) 3/62; R(U) 4/88
240 R(U) 4/88
241 *Nancollas v Insurance Officer* [1985] 1 All ER 833 (CA), reported as R(I) 7/85

6. **The tribunal's decision**
242 r33 TP(FT) Rules
243 Art 8 First-tier Tribunal and Upper Tribunal (Composition of Tribunal) Order 2008, No.2835
244 *PF (Nigeria) v Secretary of State for the Home Department* [2015] EWCA Civ 251, reported as 1 WLR 5235
245 Practice Statement, *Record of Proceedings in Social Security and Child Support Cases in the Social Entitlement Chamber on or after 3 November 2008,* 30 October 2008
246 *MK v SSWP (CI)* [2014] UKUT 323 (AAC)
247 *DT v SSWP* [2015] UKUT 509 (AAC)
248 r34(2) TP(FT) Rules
249 r34(3) TP(FT) Rules; CCS/1664/2001
250 r34(4) TP(FT) Rules; CIB/3937/2000
251 r5(3)(a) TP(FT) Rules
252 r34(5) TP(FT) Rules
253 r38(7)(a) TP(FT) Rules
254 *RU v SSWP (ESA)* [2014] UKUT 532 (AAC)
255 r5(3)(n) TP(UT) Rules
256 **UC/PIP/JSA&ESA under UC** s21 SSA 1998; reg 44 UC,PIP,JSA&ESA(DA) Regs
HB Sch 7 para 13 CSPSSA 2000; reg 11 HB&CTB(DA) Regs
CB/GA s21 SSA 1998; reg 18 CB&GA(DA) Regs
Other benefits s21 SSA 1998; reg 16 SS&CS(DA) Regs
257 r5(3)(l) TP(FT) Rules
258 r36 TP(FT) Rules; CI/3887/1999; CSDLA/168/2008; *AS v SSWP (ESA)* [2011] UKUT 159 (AAC)
259 r37(1) and (2) TP(FT) Rules
260 r37(3) TP(FT) Rules
261 r5(3)(a) TP(FT) Rules
262 r27(2) TP(FT) Rules; CSB/172/1990
263 CIB/4193/2003
264 CI/79/1990; CIS/373/1994
265 *LS v Lambeth LB (HB)* [2010] UKUT 461 (AAC), reported as [2011] AACR 27
266 r38(3) and (4) TP(FT) Rules
267 r41 TP(FT) Rules
268 **HB** Sch 7 para 7(3) and (4) CSPSSA 2000
Other benefits s13(3) and (4) SSA 1998

Chapter 58

Appealing to the Upper Tribunal and the courts

This chapter covers:
1. Appealing to the Upper Tribunal (p1396)
2. How to appeal (p1399)
3. After you get permission to appeal (p1404)
4. Oral hearings (p1408)
5. The decision (p1409)
6. Appealing to the Court of Appeal or Court of Session (p1411)
7. Applying for judicial review (p1414)

This chapter does not cover the rules for appeals to the Upper Tribunal for Scotland about the Scottish social security benefits (see Chapter 77).

Key facts

- If your appeal to the First-tier Tribunal is unsuccessful, you may be able to appeal to the Upper Tribunal, but only if the First-tier Tribunal made an error of law. You must first get permission to appeal from the First-tier or Upper Tribunal.
- If your Upper Tribunal appeal is unsuccessful, you may be able to appeal to the Court of Appeal or the Court of Session.
- The DWP, local authority and HM Revenue and Customs can also appeal to the Upper Tribunal or the courts.
- Occasionally, if you cannot appeal, you may be able to challenge a decision by a judicial review in the Upper Tribunal or in the High Court or the Court of Session.
- There are strict time limits for appealing and for applying for judicial review. They can sometimes be extended.
- Appeals can take time. If your circumstances change while you are waiting for your appeal to be heard, you may need to make a fresh claim for benefit or request a supersession.

Part 9: Getting a benefit decision changed
Chapter 58: Appealing to the Upper Tribunal and the courts
1. Appealing to the Upper Tribunal

1. **Appealing to the Upper Tribunal**

You have a right of appeal against any First-tier Tribunal decision (except an excluded decision – see below) to the Administrative Appeals Chamber of the Upper Tribunal.[1] Your appeal is dealt with by a judge (or judges). HM Courts and Tribunals Service (HMCTS) is responsible for the administration of the tribunal's work.

Excluded decisions[2]
'Excluded decisions' are certain decisions taken by the First-tier Tribunal when it considers a review (see p1401) – ie, decisions:
– to review, or not to review, an earlier decision; *or*
– to take no action, or not to take any particular action, in the light of a review of an earlier decision; *or*
– to set aside an earlier decision on review (the decision that is set aside is also excluded); *or*
– to refer, or not to refer, a matter to the Upper Tribunal.

You can only appeal to the Upper Tribunal if the First-tier Tribunal made an 'error of law' (see p1397).[3] You must first apply for, and obtain, permission to appeal and there is a strict time limit for applying (see p1401 and p1404). The DWP, the local authority and HM Revenue and Customs (HMRC) have the same appeal rights as you.

If you have evidence not known by the First-tier Tribunal, you may be able to ask the DWP, the local authority or HMRC for a supersession of the tribunal's decision on the grounds that there was a mistake about or ignorance of the facts (see p1317). You can do this while you are waiting for your appeal to be heard. Bear in mind that the amount of arrears you can get with a supersession is usually limited, so you need to continue with your appeal at the same time.

Note:
- If a decision in a test case is pending that deals with issues raised in your appeal, the Upper Tribunal may delay your appeal. For when the decision maker can serve a notice requiring the tribunal to delay your appeal, see p1365 – the rules are the same as for the First-tier Tribunal.
- Some Upper Tribunal decisions can be made by legally qualified HMCTS staff (called 'registrars').[4] You can ask an Upper Tribunal judge to reconsider a registrar's decision. You must apply in writing within 14 days after the date you are sent notice of the decision. The tribunal can give you longer (or shorter) than this. There is no guarantee you will be given longer, so keep within the time limit wherever possible.

- You can apply for a judicial review by the Upper Tribunal of a First-tier Tribunal decision against which you do not have a right of appeal (see p1422). You can appeal against most First-tier Tribunal decisions. However, if you are unsure whether you should apply to appeal against a decision or for a judicial review, you can apply for both. The Upper Tribunal decides which is the proper route.

Error of law

The First-tier Tribunal made an error of law in the following situations.[5] The error must have made a difference to the outcome of the appeal.

- The tribunal got the law wrong or misinterpreted it – eg, it misunderstood the particular benefit rule concerned. **Note:** if the tribunal gives the reasons for its decision in its decision notice (see p1385) and these indicate that it did not apply the law correctly, the decision notice is likely to be a more reliable statement of its reasons than a later conflicting explanation in a statement of reasons.[6]
- The tribunal gave you a physical examination when it was not permitted to do so (see p1372) and based its decision on evidence obtained from this.[7]
- There was a breach of the rules of natural justice (see below).
- The tribunal failed to make proper findings of fact or did not make use of those findings correctly in coming to its decision (see p1398).
- The tribunal did not provide adequate reasons for its decision (see p1399).

What if a different tribunal would have made a different decision?
The First-tier Tribunal has not made an error of law simply because a different First-tier Tribunal (or the Upper Tribunal) might have reached a different conclusion.[8] An appeal to the Upper Tribunal is *not* another opportunity for you to argue about the facts of the case.[9]

Breach of the rules of natural justice

The First-tier Tribunal made an error of law if there was a breach of the rules of natural justice. This includes where:

- the procedure followed by the tribunal leads to unfairness. However, the judge may say that this is not an error of law if it had no effect on the outcome of the case. Examples of procedural unfairness include if:
  - the person presenting the DWP case (the presenting officer) is allowed to be in the room with the tribunal members without you;[10]
  - you are not allowed to call witnesses who are likely to be able to give relevant evidence to support you;
  - the tribunal has unreasonably refused to postpone or adjourn a hearing (see p1359), even though you notified it that you could not attend and had a good reason;
  - the tribunal failed to include you as a party to the appeal when it should have been obvious that you had an interest in the outcome of the case – eg,

Part 9: Getting a benefit decision changed
Chapter 58: Appealing to the Upper Tribunal and the courts
1. Appealing to the Upper Tribunal

in your child's other parent's appeal if there is a dispute about who should receive child benefit for the child;[11]

– the tribunal failed to act on a request for an interpreter and, as a result, it was unable to understand your evidence correctly;[12]

– the standard of interpretation was not adequate and the tribunal did not take appropriate action;[13]

– the tribunal pressurises you into giving up your right to a fair hearing – eg, it bargains with you by 'offering' you one component of personal independence payment if you agree not to argue for the other. **Note:** if you decide to carry on with the appeal and the tribunal decides not to award the component 'offered', it should warn you before the hearing ends to allow you to consider this and make representations. This should be recorded in the statement of reasons for its decision;[14]

• you did not get notice of the hearing through no fault of your own and so you lost the appeal without having had a chance to put your case properly, even if you could have applied for the tribunal's decision to be set aside instead;[15]

• an oral hearing was requested but one did not take place;[16]

• you did not receive the decision maker's response or did not receive it in sufficient time before the hearing, or you did not receive advance notice of documentary evidence that you had not seen before, and were not given an opportunity to read it properly;[17]

• the tribunal made a decision at a paper hearing that was more unfavourable to you than the one you had appealed – eg, it removed your entitlement to benefit without warning you or giving you the chance to make representations.[18]

Errors concerning the facts

The First-tier Tribunal made an error of law if:

• there is no evidence to support its decision; *or*

• when making its conclusions from the facts, it took things into account which it should not have, or refused or failed to take things into account which it should have (see p1373). However, the tribunal has not necessarily made an error of law if it fails to take account of evidence that was not before it at the hearing – ie, evidence only produced when your appeal is before the Upper Tribunal; *or*

• the facts are inconsistent with the decision – eg, the tribunal accepted that a man and a woman live in separate households, but then decided that they are living together as a married couple;[19] *or*

• it does not give proper findings of fact. The tribunal must show there are sufficient facts to support its decision.[20] It can rely on the summary of the facts given in the decision maker's response (see p1354), provided these are not in dispute and they cover all the relevant issues.[21] If you and the DWP, the local authority or HMRC disagree about the facts, the tribunal must explain which version it prefers and why. It should refer to the main evidence on which it has relied. However, it is not necessarily an error of law if it does not mention every item of evidence put forward. The tribunal should give an adequate explanation of why it rejected any piece of evidence as untrue;[22] *or*

- it made a mistake about a fact that would have made a difference to the outcome of your appeal, there was unfairness as a result, and the fact could have been established by objective and uncontentious evidence. This only applies if you and your adviser were not responsible for the mistake.[23]

The reasons for the decision

The First-tier Tribunal made an error of law if it does not provide adequate reasons for its decision.[24] The tribunal must not simply say what its decision is; it must give sufficient reasons so that you can see why it reached the conclusion it did. If the summary of the reasons given in the decision notice are inconsistent with those given in its written statement of reasons, this is an error of law.[25] If a delay in writing the reasons indicates that they are unreliable as an accurate statement of the tribunal's reasoning, you can argue that the reasons are inadequate.[26]

Note: the tribunal does not have to give its reasons for refusing to adjourn an appeal hearing.[27] However, a refusal to adjourn may be so obviously unfair that it constitutes an error of law.

2. **How to appeal**

You must obtain permission to appeal to the Upper Tribunal.[28] This means you must show that the First-tier Tribunal has possibly made an error of law (see p1397) and you have the beginnings of a case. You must first apply to the First-tier Tribunal for permission. If it refuses (or rejects) your application, you can then apply for permission directly to the Upper Tribunal. There is a strict time limit for applying for permission to appeal (see p1401 and p1404).

Note: because of the length of time you usually have to wait before your case is dealt with, you should make a fresh claim for benefit (or request a supersession) – eg, if your circumstances change. See p1375 for the advantages of doing this (the issues are similar to those for First-tier Tribunal appeals).

Applying to the First-tier Tribunal

You must apply for permission to appeal, in the first instance, to the First-tier Tribunal.[29] Before applying, you should obtain a statement of reasons for its decision (see p1386). If you do not have a statement of reasons, see p1400.

Your application for permission to appeal must:[30]

- be in writing; *and*

Part 9: Getting a benefit decision changed
Chapter 58: Appealing to the Upper Tribunal and the courts
2. How to appeal

- contain:
  - details of your grounds for appeal (ie, the error(s) of law you think the tribunal made); *and*
  - sufficient information about the decision for it to be identified; *and*
  - if you are making a late application, your reasons for this; *and*
- state the result you are seeking – eg, say what you think the tribunal's decision should have been, or how it should have dealt with your appeal.

Bear in mind that the person considering your application is often the same judge who decided your appeal, although this is not always the case.[31] Applications for permission to appeal are normally decided without a hearing, so make sure you give a full explanation of your grounds for appeal when you apply.[32]

The First-tier Tribunal must send you a record of its decision on your application as soon as practicable.[33] If your application is refused, you must also be sent a statement of reasons for the refusal and notice of your right to make a fresh application to the Upper Tribunal for permission to appeal, along with information about how to apply, and the time limit for doing so. You should study the First-tier Tribunal's reasons for refusal carefully; be prepared to rethink your arguments before applying to the Upper Tribunal.

Note: if you, the DWP, the local authority or HM Revenue and Customs (HMRC) apply for permission to appeal to the Upper Tribunal, the First-tier Tribunal can review its decision (see p1401) or treat the application for permission to appeal as an application for the decision to be corrected or 'set aside'.[34] If you and the other party agree that the tribunal made an error of law, its decision *must* be set aside (see p1389).

If you do not have a statement of reasons

You may find it difficult to show that the First-tier Tribunal made an error of law if you do not have a statement of reasons for its decision. **Note:** if you do not have a statement of reasons because:[35]

- you did not apply for one, the First-tier Tribunal must treat your application for permission to appeal as an application for a statement of reasons. Once the statement of reasons is provided, unless the tribunal decides to give you permission to appeal, you must then apply for permission to appeal again;
- your application for one was refused when you missed the time limit (see p1386), the First-tier Tribunal can only allow your application for permission to appeal to go ahead ('admit' your application) if it thinks it is in the interests of justice.[36] It then decides whether or not to give you permission. If it rejects your application (ie, refuses to admit it) or refuses to give you permission, you can still apply directly to the Upper Tribunal for permission.

Time limit for applying

Your application for permission to appeal must be received by the First-tier Tribunal no later than one month (see below) after the latest of the following dates – ie, the date you were sent:[37]

- the decision notice; *or*
- a written statement of reasons (see p1386) for the tribunal's decision. See p1400 if you do not have a statement of reasons; *or*
- notice that, following a review (see below), the reasons for the tribunal's decision were amended, or the decision was corrected; *or*
- notice that an application for the tribunal's decision to be set aside (see p1388) was unsuccessful, but only if that application was made within the time limit for applying for a set aside (or any longer period allowed).

The tribunal can extend (or shorten) your time limit.[38] There is no absolute time limit for applying, but the longer you delay, the harder it may be to show that the time limit should be extended. There is no guarantee that you will be given longer, so keep within the one-month time limit wherever possible. See p1348 for when it might be fair and just to extend your time limit. The issues are the same as for appeals to the First-tier Tribunal.

If your time limit is not extended, the First-tier Tribunal must reject your application.[39] If your application is rejected, you can still apply directly to the Upper Tribunal for permission (see p1402). However, the Upper Tribunal can only allow your application to go ahead (admit your application) if it considers it is in the interests of justice to do so.[40]

Month

'Month' means a complete calendar month running from the day after the day you have been sent or given a decision.[41] For example, a decision sent on 24 July has an appeal time limit that expires at the end of 24 August.

When calculating time, if something has to be done by a certain day, it must be done by 5pm that day. If a time limit ends on a day other than a working day, you have until the end of the next working day to meet the time limit.[42]

When the First-tier Tribunal can review its decision

When the First-tier Tribunal receives an application for permission to appeal to the Upper Tribunal, it must first consider whether or not to review its own decision.[43] It should not go on to consider the application until it has decided not to review its decision, or decided to review it but to take no action. However, if it does go on, that does not necessarily make its decision about permission invalid.[44] You do not have a right to apply for a review yourself, but if you do, your application can be treated as an application for permission to appeal.[45]

Part 9: Getting a benefit decision changed
Chapter 58: Appealing to the Upper Tribunal and the courts
2. How to appeal

The First-tier Tribunal can only review a decision if it is satisfied that there is an error of law in it (see p1397).[46] If it decides to carry out a review, it should consider whether to give you and the decision maker an opportunity to comment. This means that if the DWP, local authority or HMRC has applied for permission to appeal, you have the chance to say why the decision should not be changed. If the tribunal *does* review the decision, it can:[47]

- correct any accidental errors in the decision or the record of the decision; *and*
- amend the reasons given for the decision – eg, if it considered matters, but inadvertently did not include them in the statement of reasons. However, the tribunal should not add reasons which were not part of its thinking at the time it made its decision;[48] *and*
- 'set aside' the decision. This means the decision is cancelled. The tribunal must then either make a new decision or refer your appeal to the Upper Tribunal to make a decision.

You must be notified in writing of the outcome of the review and your right of appeal (if any).[49] If the First-tier Tribunal has taken any action and you were not given an opportunity to comment before the review, you must also be notified that you can apply for the action to be cancelled and for the decision to be reviewed again.

If the First-tier Tribunal decides not to review its decision, or reviews it but takes no action, it must consider whether to give you permission to appeal to the Upper Tribunal against the decision.[50]

Applying to the Upper Tribunal

Before you can apply to the Upper Tribunal for permission to appeal, you must first apply to the First-tier Tribunal.[51] If the First-tier Tribunal refuses you permission or rejects your application (eg, because it was late), you can then make a fresh application to the Upper Tribunal. You must apply in writing.

Forms

Use Form UT1 (Social Entitlement). This is available from the regional office of HM Courts and Tribunals Service (HMCTS) (see sscs.venues.tribunals.gov.uk/venues/venues.htm for your local office), the Upper Tribunal Office (see gov.uk/administrative-appeals-tribunal for the addresses) or at gov.uk/government/collections/administrative-appeals-chamber-upper-tribunal-forms.

Your application must include:[52]
- your name and address and the name and address of your representative (if any). You must also give the address where documents can be sent or delivered; *and*

- details of the decision you want to appeal. You should include the First-tier Tribunal reference number; *and*
- the grounds for your appeal – ie, the error(s) of law you think the First-tier Tribunal made; *and*
- if your application is late, a request for your time limit to be extended and the reasons why you are applying late; *and*
- whether you want your application to be dealt with at an oral hearing; *and*
- copies of the First-tier Tribunal's decision, its statement of reasons (see below if you do not have one) and the notice of its refusal or rejection of your application for permission. If your application to the First-tier Tribunal was rejected because it (or your application for a statement of reasons) was late, you must also include the reasons for the lateness.

The Upper Tribunal can waive any irregularities in your application in some cases.[53] If your application to the First-tier Tribunal for permission to appeal was rejected because it was late or your application for a statement of reasons was late, the Upper Tribunal can only allow your application for permission to appeal to go ahead ('admit' your application) if it thinks it is in the interests of justice to do so.[54] If your application is admitted, the tribunal then goes on to decide whether to give you permission to appeal.

The appeal form asks whether you want an oral hearing of your application.

What if you do not have a statement of reasons?

If you do not have a statement of reasons for the First-tier Tribunal's decision, you are not prevented from applying to the Upper Tribunal for permission to appeal. However, you must be able to show that the First-tier Tribunal made an error of law (see p1397) without it – eg, from what is said in the decision notice.[55] It is an error of law if the First-tier Tribunal fails to provide a statement of reasons where it has a duty to do so – eg, you apply for one in time, but the tribunal says your application was late and refuses to provide one.[56]

You can send your application to the Upper Tribunal office by post, fax or document exchange, or deliver it in person. The tribunal can also permit you to send it by other methods – eg, email.[57] The appeal form tells you where to send or deliver it.

The Upper Tribunal obtains the file of your appeal papers from the regional office of HMCTS. It considers these as well as what you say in your application before reaching a decision. The DWP, local authority or HMRC normally plays no part in the procedure at this stage, although the tribunal sometimes asks it to make a submission in cases of particular difficulty. If this happens, you are given an opportunity to reply.

You are sent a written notice of the tribunal's decision on your application, usually including the reasons for the decision.[58] You cannot appeal against a

Part 9: Getting a benefit decision changed
Chapter 58: Appealing to the Upper Tribunal and the courts
3. After you get permission to appeal

refusal to admit your application to appeal or to give you permission to appeal, but you might be able to apply for the decision to be set aside (see p1410) or to a court for judicial review (see p1421).[59]

Time limit for applying

Your application for permission to appeal must be received by the Upper Tribunal no later than one month (see p1401) after the date the First-tier Tribunal's refusal (or rejection) was sent to you.[60] The Upper Tribunal can extend (or shorten) your time limit.[61] There is no guarantee that you will be given longer, so keep within the one-month time limit wherever possible.

The decision whether or not to allow a late appeal to the Upper Tribunal must be made bearing in mind the merits of the appeal and the consequences for you (and the DWP, the local authority or HMRC).[62] See p1348 for when it might be fair and just to extend your time limit. The issues are the same as for appeals to the First-tier Tribunal. If your time limit is not extended, the Upper Tribunal rejects your application to appeal and your appeal does not go ahead.

3. **After you get permission to appeal**

If you have been given permission to appeal by the First-tier Tribunal, you must send the Upper Tribunal:[63]

- a 'notice of appeal', so that it is received within one month after you are sent notice of the permission. You are sent a form on which to do this; *and*
- if you are sending the notice of appeal late, a request for an extension of time and the reasons why your notice is late; *and*
- a copy of the notice that you have been given permission to appeal; *and*
- a copy of the First-tier Tribunal's decision and its statement of reasons (if you have one); *and*
- your details; *and*
- your reasons for appealing against the decision.

The Upper Tribunal can extend (or shorten) the time limit for receipt of your notice of appeal.[64] There is no guarantee that you will be given longer, so keep within the time limit wherever possible. See p1348 for when it might be fair and just to extend your time limit. The issues are the same as for appeals to the First-tier Tribunal. If your time limit is not extended, the Upper Tribunal rejects your appeal and it does not go ahead.

Note: if you have applied for permission to appeal directly to the Upper Tribunal on Form UT1, unless you are told otherwise, your application is treated as a notice of appeal. In this case, you do not need to send in another.[65]

Chapter 58

What the Upper Tribunal can do

There are procedural rules that the Upper Tribunal must follow when dealing with your appeal. The 'overriding objective' of these is to enable it to deal with cases fairly and justly.[66] This includes avoiding delay (provided the issues can be considered properly), avoiding unnecessary formality, allowing flexibility in the proceedings and ensuring that all the parties can participate fully. You, the DWP, the local authority and HM Revenue and Customs (HMRC) must help the tribunal further the objective and co-operate with it. This involves ensuring, as far as possible, that your case is ready by the time of any hearing.[67] The rules are generally the same as for the First-tier Tribunal, so where relevant, these are referred to below.

The Upper Tribunal can do the following.[68]

- Extend or shorten any time limits (see p1357). For the rules about extending your time limit for applying for permission to appeal, see p1401 and p1404.
- Issue directions (see p1358).
- Postpone or adjourn your appeal hearing (see p1359).
- 'Strike out' an appeal (see p1360). **Note:** the Upper Tribunal does *not* have the discretion to strike out your appeal on the grounds that there is no reasonable prospect of success.
- Bar people from taking part in an appeal (see p1362). **Note:** *you* can be barred from taking part in an appeal if the other party appealed.
- Require the First-tier Tribunal to provide reasons for its decision, or other information or documents relating to its decision or the proceedings.[69]
- Summons witnesses to attend a hearing, answer questions and produce documents. If someone fails to comply, the tribunal can punish her/him for contempt of court.[70] **Note:** you cannot be required to give evidence or produce any document that you could not be compelled to give by a court.[71]
- Suspend the effect of its decision while considering any application for permission to appeal against, or review of, that decision. It can also suspend the effect of a First-tier Tribunal decision while an application for permission to appeal against the decision is being considered, and pending that appeal being determined.[72]

Representatives

You can have a representative to help you with your appeal.[73] S/he can explain the procedures, present your case and produce a written submission to ensure the Upper Tribunal is aware of all the relevant issues and the law. You must send or give the tribunal written notice of your representative's name and address, or s/he must do this on your behalf. Unless s/he is a solicitor or barrister, if your representative is providing the notice, s/he should also provide an authorisation signed by you.

Part 9: Getting a benefit decision changed
Chapter 58: Appealing to the Upper Tribunal and the courts
3. After you get permission to appeal

Note: even if:

- your representative acted for you in your appeal to the First-tier Tribunal, you must still authorise her/him to act for you in your appeal to the Upper Tribunal – you may have already done this at an earlier stage. Once you have given notice that you have a representative, s/he is presumed to be acting for you unless you give (or s/he gives) notice in writing that this is no longer the case.[74] Your representative must be sent any documents that are required to be sent to you; these then do not have to be sent to you.[75] However, do not assume that this always happens. If you receive documents, check that your representative has also received them;
- you have not previously notified the tribunal that you have a representative, someone can attend the hearing with (or for) you and act as your representative and help you present your case, if the tribunal agrees.[76]

Can your representative or adviser get help with your appeal?

If you live in England or Wales, your representative, adviser or support worker may be able to get advice about, and assistance with, your appeal to the Upper Tribunal from CPAG under its Upper Tribunal Assistance Project. This can include advice on procedure and the merits of your case, as well as help making your application for permission to appeal. In some cases, CPAG may be able to provide representation. See cpag.org.uk/upper-tribunal-assistance-project for further information and an online referral form.

Meeting the costs of representation

Free legal help from a solicitor is available in limited cases. This is means tested. If you cannot qualify, you may be able to get free help from your local Citizens Advice office, law centre, welfare rights service or advice centre.

If you are resident in England or Wales, free legal help is available for advice and assistance with appealing to the Upper Tribunal, including applications for permission to appeal that are made directly to the Upper Tribunal, but you will only qualify for help from a lawyer to cover representation at an oral hearing in very exceptional cases – if it is necessary to make these services available to you because a failure to do so would be a breach of your right to have legal representation as provided under human rights law or European Union law.[77]

If you are resident in Scotland, free legal help is currently available for Upper Tribunal appeals, including for help preparing for paper, as well as oral, hearings. If the Scottish Legal Aid Board approves, you can get help with representation, but only if the Upper Tribunal is sitting in Scotland. The Board only gives approval if it is satisfied that your case is arguable, it is reasonable for representation to be made available and your case is too complex for you to be able to present it efffectively yourself in person – eg, if there is likely to be procedural difficulty or a substantial question of law, or if the evidence is complex or difficult, or if you may be unable to understand the proceedings or to state your own case because of mental illness, a disability, or because of your age or knowledge of English.[78]

If you are granted funding for legal help, you must send a copy of the funding notice (in Scotland, the legal aid certificate) to the Upper Tribunal as soon as practicable.[79] You must also let the other parties involved in your appeal know that you have been granted funding.

Withdrawing an appeal

If you change your mind about appealing, you can withdraw your appeal.[80] However, once you have been given permission to appeal, you must have the Upper Tribunal's consent. You must give notice to the tribunal that you want to withdraw your appeal in writing or at an oral hearing.

If you withdraw your appeal but then decide that you want it to go ahead, you can apply for it to be reinstated.[81] You must apply in writing. Your application must be received by the Upper Tribunal within one month after the date it received written notice that you wanted to withdraw your appeal, or, if you withdraw your appeal at an oral hearing, within one month (see p1401) after the date of the hearing. The tribunal can give you longer (or shorter) than one month.[82] There is no guarantee that you will be given longer, so keep within the time limit wherever possible.

The written procedure

When permission to appeal has been given, the Upper Tribunal sends you a copy of the appeal file. This is the file that was used by the First-tier Tribunal plus any documents added since you first contacted the Upper Tribunal. You and the DWP, local authority or HMRC are asked for a response and are told the timetable for providing one.[83]

The decision maker is usually asked to provide a response first. DWP and HMRC responses are written by specialist staff working from national centres. They often take a different view than decision makers who have been involved previously and may even support your appeal.

You are given the chance to reply to the response and are usually given one month in which to do so, although the tribunal may extend (or shorten) the time limit.[84] There is no guarantee that you will be given longer, so keep within the time limit wherever possible. If you have nothing to add and do not want to reply at any stage, tell the tribunal.

If the decision maker supports your appeal, the tribunal may give its decision without reasons if you agree to this.[85]

Has the decision maker been given permission to appeal?

If you won your appeal at the First-tier Tribunal, the DWP, local authority or HMRC may have obtained permission to appeal to the Upper Tribunal. If so, you are asked to provide

Part 9: Getting a benefit decision changed
Chapter 58: Appealing to the Upper Tribunal and the courts
4. Oral hearings

a response under the rules described above. It is very important to provide one. Consider the decision maker's arguments carefully and explain why you think the First-tier Tribunal did not make an error of law and why you think its decision was correct. Bear in mind that if the decision maker wins the appeal to the Upper Tribunal, the First-tier Tribunal's decision could be overturned and you could, for example, lose the benefit that it awarded to you, or have to repay an overpayment it said was not recoverable.

4. **Oral hearings**

The Upper Tribunal decides whether or not there should be an oral hearing of the appeal.[86] It must take your views, and those of the DWP, the local authority or HM Revenue and Customs (HMRC), into account. The form you are sent on which to provide your submission asks you whether you want an oral hearing and, if so, why. The tribunal can decide to hold an oral hearing, even if you have not asked for one. However, it normally only holds one if the case involves complicated issues of law that cannot easily be resolved by written arguments. If there is no oral hearing, the tribunal reaches a decision on the basis of the written responses and other documents provided.

If the tribunal decides there should be an oral hearing, you must be given at least 14 days' notice, although you may get less notice than this if you agree, or your appeal is urgent or there are exceptional circumstances.[87]

Oral hearings are held on a regular basis in Cardiff, Edinburgh, London and Manchester, but can be held in other locations if necessary. Your fares are paid in advance. If you live in Wales, you can give your evidence in Welsh.[88]

A hearing closer to your home can be arranged in exceptional circumstances – eg, if you have difficulty travelling because of a disability. A judge decides whether or not to hold a local hearing based on, for example, medical evidence and why a local hearing is needed.

You and your representative may be able to participate in the oral hearing via a video link – eg, if your disability makes it difficult for you to travel, or to avoid travel costs and time.[89] You may also be able to participate in the hearing by telephone or other means of instantaneous two-way electronic communication.

Usually, one judge hears your appeal. However, if there is a 'question of law of special difficulty', an important point of principle or practice, or it is otherwise appropriate, two or three judges may hear your appeal,[90] but the procedure is the same.

Note:
- The tribunal may ask you to provide a summary of the arguments you are going to make (a 'skeleton argument') in advance of the hearing. If it does, you must provide one.[91] You should do this within the time you are allowed, and ensure it reaches the tribunal at least a week before the hearing.[92]

- The hearing is more formal than First-tier Tribunal hearings, but the judge lets you say everything you want to. Judges usually intervene a lot and ask questions, so be prepared to argue your case without your script.
- A full set of Upper Tribunal decisions and the statute law (see p1379) are available for your use.
- The decision maker is usually represented by a lawyer, so you should also consider obtaining representation – eg, from a solicitor, your local Citizens Advice or advice centre. See p1406 for meeting the costs of representation.

5. **The decision**

There are two stages to an Upper Tribunal decision.[93]
- **Stage one:** the tribunal decides whether the First-tier Tribunal made an error of law. If it decides that it did, the First-tier Tribunal's decision is normally 'set aside' and no longer has any effect. However, in some cases, the Upper Tribunal may decide that the error of law had no practical effect on the outcome of your appeal and so the decision does not have to be set aside.
- **Stage two:** if the First-tier Tribunal's decision is set aside, the Upper Tribunal decides how to deal with the case.
  - If it agrees that the First-tier Tribunal's decision was wrong, the case is often sent back to the First-tier Tribunal to hear your appeal again and make a new decision. The Upper Tribunal usually makes an order stating that the new tribunal should not include the judge or any of the members from the original appeal hearing and gives directions on how it should reconsider the issues. **Note:** at the new hearing, the First-tier Tribunal will not necessarily decide your appeal in your favour. However, you may be able to appeal to the Upper Tribunal again if there is another error of law.
  - If the Upper Tribunal thinks the First-tier Tribunal's statement of reasons for its decision contains all the material facts, or it has been able to make any necessary extra findings of fact, it may make the final decision. This might, or might not, be in your favour.

The Upper Tribunal's decision is usually given in writing, but may be given orally at the hearing.[94] You are normally not referred to by name in the decision.[95] Detailed reasons are given. You must be sent a decision notice as soon as is reasonably practicable, as well as notice of your right of appeal, how to appeal and the time limit for doing so. Decisions are often lengthy as they may need to explain difficult issues of law. So it may take time for the judge to prepare the decision. If there is undue delay, you can complain to the Adminstrative Appeals Chamber President.

Part 9: Getting a benefit decision changed
Chapter 58: Appealing to the Upper Tribunal and the courts
5. The decision

If you disagree with the Upper Tribunal's decision

If you disagree with the Upper Tribunal's decision, you cannot simply ask it to look at the decision again – eg, if you have additional points to make. However, the following may be done.

- The tribunal may correct any clerical mistake or an accidental slip or omission in a decision or record of a decision.[96]
- The tribunal may 'set aside' its decision on procedural grounds – ie, how it handled your appeal.[97] If it sets aside a decision, this means the decision is cancelled. A decision can be set aside if the tribunal thinks it is in the interests of justice and:
  - you, your representative or the DWP, the local authority or HM Revenue and Customs (HMRC) were not sent papers or other documents relating to the proceedings, or did not receive them at an appropriate time, or the tribunal was not sent them at an appropriate time; or
  - you, your representative or the DWP, local authority or HMRC were not present at a hearing; or
  - there has been some other procedural irregularity in the proceedings in the Upper Tribunal.

  You must apply in writing for a decision to be set aside. Your application is dealt with by the judge who made the original decision. It must be received by the tribunal no later than one month after you were sent notice of the decision. The tribunal can extend (or shorten) this time limit. However, there is no guarantee that you will be given longer, so keep within the time limit wherever possible.[98] If you think the tribunal made a legal error, you must instead appeal to the Court of Appeal or Court of Session, or, if relevant, apply for a judicial review.
- The decision can be superseded by the DWP, local authority or HMRC if there are grounds – eg, if there was a mistake about, or ignorance of, the facts (see p1315). However, if the tribunal made a mistake about the law, you must appeal to a court.
- You or the DWP, local authority or HMRC can appeal to the Court of Appeal (in Scotland, the Court of Session) – see p1411.
- If you (or the decision maker) seek permission to appeal to the Court of Appeal or Court of Session, the tribunal can review its decision (see p1412).

The Upper Tribunal can treat an application for a decision to be corrected, set aside or reviewed, or for permission to appeal against a decision, as an application for any other of these.[99]

6. Appealing to the Court of Appeal or Court of Session

You may appeal against an Upper Tribunal decision (except an excluded decision – see below) to the Court of Appeal (or in Scotland, the Court of Session). You can only do this if the Upper Tribunal made an error of law (see p1397 for what may count) and you must first obtain permission to appeal.[100] The DWP, the local authority and HM Revenue and Customs (HMRC) have the same appeal rights as you.

Excluded decisions

'**Excluded decisions**'[101] are decisions taken by the Upper Tribunal on an application for permission to appeal against a First-tier Tribunal decision and certain decisions taken when it considers a review (see p1412) – ie, decisions:

– to review, or not to review, an earlier decision;

– to take no action, or not to take any particular action, in the light of a review of an earlier decision;

– to set aside an earlier decision on review (the decision that is set aside is also excluded).

Permission to appeal to the Court of Appeal or the Court of Session cannot be given unless the Upper Tribunal or the Court of Appeal/Court of Session considers that the appeal would raise some important point of principle or practice or there is another compelling reason to hear the appeal.[102]

You should obtain advice before appealing. See p1413 for information about meeting the cost of going to court. Before making any application, get advice about whether you could be liable for the other side's costs.

The procedure in the Court of Appeal/Court of Session is strict, formal and far less flexible than the procedure before the tribunals. The DWP, local authority or HMRC is represented by a solicitor and a barrister.

Note: in England and Wales, if the Upper Tribunal decision involves a point of law of general public importance, in exceptional cases, it can grant you a certificate that allows you to apply for permission to appeal directly to the Supreme Court, rather than appealing to the Court of Appeal first.[103]

Applying to the Upper Tribunal

You must apply for permission to appeal, in the first instance, to the Upper Tribunal. Your application must:[104]

• be in writing; *and*

• contain sufficient information about the tribunal's decision for it to be identified; *and*

Part 9: Getting a benefit decision changed
Chapter 58: Appealing to the Upper Tribunal and the courts
6. Appealing to the Court of Appeal or Court of Session

- state the error(s) of law you think the tribunal made. These must be identified clearly;[105] *and*
- if your application is late, include a request for an extension of time and the reasons why the application was not made in time; *and*
- state the result you are seeking – eg, what you think the tribunal's decision should have been.

You must be sent a record of the decision on your application as soon as practicable.[106] If your application is refused, you must also be sent a statement of reasons for the refusal and notice of your right to apply to the Court of Appeal/Court of Session for permission to appeal, along with information about how to apply and the time limit for doing so.

The time limit for applying

Your application must be received by the Upper Tribunal within three months after the date you were sent:[107]

- written notice of the decision; *or*
- notice that the reasons for the decision have been amended, or the decision has been corrected, following a review; *or*
- notice that an application for the tribunal's decision to be set aside was unsuccessful, but only if that application was made within the time limit for applying for a set-aside (or any longer period allowed).

The tribunal can extend (or shorten) your time limit for applying for permission to appeal to the Court of Appeal/Court of Session.[108] However, there is no guarantee that you will be given longer, so keep within the time limit wherever possible. If your time limit is not extended, the tribunal must refuse your application.[109]

When the Upper Tribunal can review its decision

The Upper Tribunal can review its own decision (other than an excluded decision – see p1411) if an application has been made for permission to appeal to the Court of Appeal or Court of Session.[110] You do not have a right to apply for a review yourself, but if you do, your application can be treated as an application for permission to appeal.[111]

The tribunal can review its decision if:[112]

- when it made the decision, it overlooked a legal provision, or a court or tribunal decision it was required to follow, which could have had a 'material effect' on the decision; *or*
- since the decision, a court has made a decision which the tribunal must follow. This only applies if the court's decision could have had a 'material effect' on the tribunal's decision had it been made at the time.

If the tribunal *does* review the decision, it can:[113]
- correct accidental errors in the decision or the record of the decision; *and*
- amend the reasons given for the decision; *and*
- 'set aside' the decision. If it does this, it must make a new decision.

You must be notified in writing of the outcome of the review and your right of appeal (if any).[114] If the tribunal has taken any action and you were not given an opportunity to comment before the review, you must also be notified that you can apply for the outcome to be set aside and for the decision to be reviewed again.

If the tribunal does not review its decision, or reviews it but takes no action, it must consider whether to give you permission to appeal to the Court of Appeal/Court of Session.[115]

Applying to the court

If the Upper Tribunal refuses you permission to appeal, you can make a fresh application to the Court of Appeal or Court of Session.[116] The tribunal's statement of reasons for the refusal must specify the relevant court.[117] It tells you the time limit for applying: this is very short, so you should lodge your application as soon as possible. You should seek advice *before* you make your application. Because the requirements and procedures are complicated, you should contact the relevant court to find you what you need to do, and when you need to serve notices on the relevant parties.

In England and Wales, the Court of Appeal considers your application for permission to appeal without an oral hearing. It can direct that there is an oral hearing, and must do so if it thinks your application cannot be determined fairly without one.[118] If it refuses you permission to appeal, you cannot appeal further or apply for a judicial review.

In Scotland, the procedure for appealing to the Court of Session is similar to that for England and Wales, but there are a number of differences. The Court of Session hears applications for permission to appeal at an oral hearing rather than making the decision simply by reading the papers. The application for permission and the appeal itself can be heard at the same time.

Meeting the cost of going to court

Free legal help from a solicitor is currently available for appeals on a point of law in the Supreme Court, the Court of Appeal, the High Court and the Court of Session, and you should consider obtaining legal advice and representation for these. Free legal help is means tested. You usually have to pay court fees unless you are eligible for free legal help or you are exempt from paying court fees – eg, because of your financial circumstances. If you want to be represented by a lawyer and do not have free legal help, you also have to pay her/his fees and, if you lose

Part 9: Getting a benefit decision changed
Chapter 58: Appealing to the Upper Tribunal and the courts
7. Applying for judicial review

your case, the other side's costs. Before making *any* application to a court, get advice about whether you could be liable for the other side's costs.

7. **Applying for judicial review**

Judicial review is a form of legal challenge to the lawfulness of a decision, action or a failure to act (referred to as 'decisions' in this section). It is generally a challenge to the *way* in which a decision has been reached, rather than to the decision itself.

A claim for judicial review can be brought by an individual with a 'sufficient interest' in the decision (you will always have a sufficient interest in a decision about your own benefit claim) or an organisation which has established standing in the courts – eg, CPAG.[119] A claim can only be brought against a decision of a 'public nature'. Decisions of the DWP, HM Revenue and Customs (HMRC) or a local authority about benefit entitlement are of a 'public nature'.

Judicial review is a 'remedy of last resort' and only available when you do not have an alternative remedy (see p1415).

A claim for judicial review is brought in the High Court in England and Wales, or the Court of Session in Scotland (see p1421). Unlike tribunals, these courts have the power to make costs orders – ie, you can be ordered to pay the other side's costs as well as your own. If you are successful in a claim for judicial review, the court will rarely substitute its own view of what the correct decision is but will leave it to the original decision maker to remake the decision, this time following the correct procedure.

In England and Wales, before you can apply for a judicial review in the High Court you must follow a 'pre-action protocol' (see p1418). This is designed to avoid expensive litigation, and the majority of straightforward cases where there has clearly been unlawfulness on the part of the decision maker are resolved at this stage. It is, therefore, a valuable way of getting a decision changed when you cannot appeal against it. This protocol does not apply in Scotland, but it is good practice to avoid litigation and sending a 'letter before claim' can provide a way of doing so.

Judicial review can be used to challenge a decision of the Upper Tribunal to refuse permission to appeal against a First-tier Tribunal decision, and occasionally to challenge First-tier Tribunal decisions in the Upper Tribunal (see p1422).

Note: get advice if you are considering a judicial review. You are unlikely to be successful without the help of a solicitor or welfare rights adviser.

Time limit

In England and Wales, you must make your claim for judicial review in the High Court promptly and, in any event, no later than three months from the date the grounds to make the claim first arose – ie, the date of the decision you want to challenge.[120] This means that the whole pre-action stage must be completed within three months. The High Court may extend the time limit where there are good reasons for doing so.

In Scotland, you must apply to the Court of Session within three months of the decision you want to challenge (or a longer period that it considers equitable).[121] **Note:** there is no pre-action protocol in Scotland.

To challenge a decision of the Upper Tribunal refusing you permission to appeal against a First-tier Tribunal decision, you must apply to the court no more than 16 days from the date on which the Upper Tribunal's decision was sent (see p1422).[122] You do not need to follow a pre-action protocol.

When to consider judicial review

Judicial review is only possible in limited circumstances.
- **If there is no right of appeal.** Judicial review is appropriate when there is no right of appeal and any other available remedies are not 'effective' (see below). There is no right of appeal against an increasing number of benefit decisions. These include discretionary decisions (eg, discretionary housing payments) and decisions which specifically exclude a right to appeal (eg, whether to split benefit payments between members of a couple, or the amount offered to you as a benefit advance).[123]
- **If it is a last resort.** Judicial review is known as a 'remedy of last resort'. If there is another way of challenging a decision, you are expected to use it. This might include appealing to the First-tier or Upper Tribunal, complaining or using an Ombudsman service (see Chapter 60). If there is a right of appeal, or an internal dispute process (eg, within a local authority to review discretionary housing payment decisions), you must use it. However, the alternative remedy must be both 'effective and appropriate'.[124] Using a complaints process or an Ombudsman will rarely be an effective alternative if a quick decision is needed. Even if you have a right of appeal, you may still be able to start the judicial review process with a 'letter before claim' (see p1418) if the appeal will not be effective or if is not appropriate. If this applies to you, ask for a mandatory reconsideration/appeal and send a 'letter before claim' at the same time.

Is the appeal 'effective and appropriate'?

An appeal might not be effective and appropriate for a number of reasons.

– There is a need for speed. Your circumstances may mean that an appeal is not 'effective' because it will take too long. If you are homeless and/or destitute, or if you are facing eviction for rent arrears and have no income for food or heating, and you have been refused benefits to which you are legally entitled, it may not be effective to wait for an appeal to be heard.

Part 9: Getting a benefit decision changed
Chapter 58: Appealing to the Upper Tribunal and the courts
7. Applying for judicial review

– It is a matter of public importance. If you are an adviser, you may be aware of instances where decision makers have routinely misinterpreted or misapplied the law. Starting judicial review proceedings with a 'letter before claim' can improve future decision making, as well as resolving the issue for an individual claimant.
– The remedy you are seeking is not available from an appeal. For example, you might want a change made to the decision makers' guidance, staff training or damages under the Human Rights Act, none of which a tribunal can award.

Grounds for judicial review

The reasons for asking for a decision to be judicially reviewed are known as 'grounds for judicial review'. Common grounds for judicial review include the following.

Failure to follow the law

The most common ground for judicial review is a failure to apply the law. This is similar to one of the grounds for appeal (see p1397), so if there is a right of appeal, you must use it or explain why it is ineffective.[125]

Failure to make a decision or to make a decision within a reasonable time

Decision makers have a duty to consider all claims for benefit within a 'reasonable time'.[126] This applies to both new claims and to revisions and mandatory reconsiderations. What counts as 'reasonable' depends on all the circumstances, including the impact on you and the complexity of the case.

Failure to exercise discretion

It is unlawful for decision makers to operate a 'blanket policy' when they have a discretion.[127] Examples of blanket policies include:
- the same decision being made in all cases in your area, regardless of individual factors;
- a local authority policy which has eligibility criteria for a benefit which is not provided for in the governing legislation and consequently restricts its ability to consider each application on a case-by-case basis.

Failure to take into account relevant evidence, or taking irrelevant evidence into account

You may have grounds for a judicial review if no account has been taken of relevant evidence or information (eg, medical evidence or proof of earnings) in reaching a decision. If the decision maker has made no reference to particular evidence or information that you have provided, or has not provided an explanation as to why the evidence has not been taken into account, this may be an indication that no account has been taken of it. You must be able to demonstrate how, had the information/evidence been properly taken into account, a different decision would have been reached.[128]

Note: if the DWP or a tribunal fails to give *any* reasons for a decision (rather than failure to explain exclusion of particular evidence), the usual remedy is to appeal. For judicial review, failure to provide reasons primarily indicates 'failure to take account of relevant evidence' but you may also be able to argue that, as a matter of public law, you are entitled to know what was taken into account.

You may also have grounds for judicial review if the decision maker has taken irrelevant evidence or information into account – eg, if incorrect criteria have been used (such as length of residence for council tax reduction[129]).

Failure to make enquiries

You have a duty to provide information and evidence in connection with your benefit claim and the DWP, HMRC and local authority have a duty to make enquiries if information or evidence is available to them which is not available to you.[130]

Example

Ana left an abusive relationship and has no contact with her estranged spouse who is a European Economic Area worker. She could challenge the DWP's failure to seek information from HMRC and the Home Office to establish her right to reside based on her spouse's worker status.

Failure to follow guidance, or applying unlawful guidance

There is extensive guidance for decision makers to use when making decisions (see p1289). It is useful to identify what the guidance says, how it corresponds to the law, and whether it has been followed correctly.

If the guidance corresponds to the legislation, but has not been followed in practice, the ground for judicial review is 'failure to follow the law and own guidance'. If the guidance does not correspond to the law and has been followed in preference to the law to your detriment, your ground is 'failure to follow the law and unlawful guidance'.[131]

Discrimination and breach of human rights

Decision makers must comply with both the Equality Act 2010 and the Human Rights Act 1998, which provide duties not to discriminate directly or indirectly.

The Equality Act can be useful where you can demonstrate that in failing to apply the law or guidance, the decision maker has discriminated against you because of your age, disability, gender reassignment, marriage or civil partnership, pregnancy or maternity, race, religion or belief, gender or sexual orientation – ie, the protected characteristics under the Act. Section 20 of the Equality Act also imposes a duty on public authorities to make reasonable adjustments to avoid

Part 9: Getting a benefit decision changed
Chapter 58: Appealing to the Upper Tribunal and the courts
7. Applying for judicial review

substantial disadvantage to disabled people, and failure to make reasonable adjustments is a ground for judicial review.

Article 14 of the European Convention on Human Rights (brought into UK law by the Human Rights Act) provides protection from discrimination in the enjoyment of the other rights set out in the Convention. Protocol 1, Article 1 provides a right to enjoy property peacefully, and welfare benefits are accepted as 'property' for these purposes.[132] The Human Rights Act provides broader protection from discrimination than the Equality Act as it makes it unlawful to discriminate on a wider range of grounds.

The pre-action protocol

In England and Wales, before you can apply for judicial review in the High Court, you must usually use the pre-action protocol.[133] In exceptional circumstances (eg, if the time limit is pending or the matter is urgent), you do not have to comply, but you will have to explain the circumstances.

There are no court fees and no risk having to pay the other side's costs during the pre-action stage. The only costs at this stage are any charges made by your adviser or solicitor (which may be eligible for legal help). Failure to comply with the pre-action protocol can result in sanctions against the non-compliant party if the matter reaches the High Court, the costs of which are potentially high. The risk of costs if the matter reaches the High Court provides a strong incentive for both parties to comply with the pre-action protocol and to resolve the issue without court action.

The majority of cases where there is clear unlawfulness on the part of the decision maker are resolved at the pre-action stage. It is important to get advice before sending a pre-action letter, as it is only likely to be successful if sent on your behalf by a solicitor or advice agency.

Note:
- If your issue is not resolved at the pre-action stage, there is no requirement to pursue the matter to the next stage (ie, actual litigation) if you do not want to go to court.
- The pre-action protocol does not apply in Scotland, but it is good practice to try to avoid litigation and sending a 'letter before claim' as described in the pre-action protocol can provide a way of doing so.
- You do not need to use the pre-action protocol if you wish to challenge a decision of the Upper Tribunal refusing you permission to appeal against a First-tier Tribunal decision.[134]

The letter before claim

The pre-action protocol requires you (the 'claimant') to send a 'letter before claim' to the decision maker (the 'defendant') before initiating judicial review proceedings. The letter must contain:[135]

- the name and address of the 'defendant' – ie, the legal department of the DWP, HMRC or your local authority; *and*
- your full name and address; *and*
- your reference details – this will usually be your national insurance number, but could also be your housing benefit reference number, or any other reference which will assist the relevant benefit authority to identify you; *and*
- the name, address and reference details of your legal advisers (if any); *and*
- details of the matter being challenged; *and*
- details of any interested parties who need to be sent a copy of the paperwork. An 'interested party' is 'any person (other than the claimant and defendant) who is directly affected by the claim' (in benefit cases, there are not usually interested parties);[136] *and*
- a brief summary of the facts and relevant legal principles, the date and details of the decision being challenged, and why you consider it to be wrong; *and*
- details of the remedy you are seeking; *and*
- proposals for any alternative way of resolving the dispute. Both parties should consider whether alternative dispute resolution or using a complaints procedure would be more suitable than litigation. This is unlikely to be the case, but you must demonstrate that you have considered this; *and*
- details of any information sought from the benefits authority; *and*
- details of any relevant documents; *and*
- the address to be used for all the court documents. This will usually be the address of the advice agency or legal firm assisting you; *and*
- a proposed reply date. This will depend on the circumstances of your case, but in most circumstances, 14 days is a reasonable time to allow. The benefit authority should normally respond within 14 days. Failure to do so will be taken into account by the court and sanctions may be imposed if the matter proceeds to litigation.

The letter before claim should be sent by post and email to:
- DWP Legal Advisers, Government Legal Department, 2nd Floor, Caxton House, Tothill Street, London SW1H 9NA; email: legal.queries@dwp.gov.uk; *or*
- HMRC Solicitor's Office, South West Wing, Bush House, Strand, London WC2B 4RD; email: mailbox.litigation@hmrc.gov.uk; *or*
- the local authority's legal department.

If you are writing on behalf of a client, you must include her/his signed form of authority to act.

Part 9: Getting a benefit decision changed
Chapter 58: Appealing to the Upper Tribunal and the courts
7. Applying for judicial review

'Letter before claim'

Use the following structure when drafting your 'letter before claim' and ensure you include all the above information required by the pre-action protocol.

Background facts

What are your circumstances? Give relevant details of your family, your health and housing.

What has happened? Include relevant dates.

What action has already been taken to try to resolve the dispute?

What has been the effect on you of the decision or action being challenged?

Legal background

What does the legislation say should have happened?

What does any caselaw say should have happened?

What does any guidance say should have happened?

How is this different to what, in fact, has happened – ie, to the decision/action you are challenging?

Grounds for judicial review

What are your reasons for requesting judicial review? These are your 'grounds for judicial review' (see p1416 and also p1397 – the rules are the same as for appealing to the Upper Tribunal).

Alternative remedies

If there is an alternative remedy, explain how you have exhausted it, or use this section to justify why you are not using it.

Details of the action you expect the benefit agency to take

Explain what you are asking for. This will depend on what your grounds for judicial review are. If you have challenged the decision maker's failure to do something, your request will be for her/him to do that thing and might also include a request to improve future decision making. For example, you might want to ask:

– for your claim to be decided and paid without further delay from (including from the date you first made your application);

– that the decision maker takes into account all the relevant evidence you supplied and exercises her/his discretion. For example, you could ask her/him to: 'waive recovery of an overpayment' or 'reduce the level of the deductions from my benefit to [amount]';

– that the decision maker follows the law and its own guidance and awards you benefit from and including [date];

– for Human Rights Act damages;

– that staff guidance be issued and staff training provided to ensure all members of staff are aware of the discretion available to them and the relevant regulations and guidance;

– for guidance to be amended where it does not comply with the law.

CPAG has 'letters before claim' templates available at cpag.org.uk/welfare-rights/judicial-review/judicial-review-pre-action-letters. You can use these to challenge commonly occuring benefit problems where there is no effective alternative remedy.

If you send a letter before claim and do not receive a reply within the time requested, contact the benefit authority's legal department to request a response without further delay. Point out that 14 days is considered a reasonable time by the judicial review pre-action protocol.

If you receive a response saying that 'judicial review is not appropriate', check whether the decision has, in fact, been changed by a revision. If so, and you are satisfied with this, no further action is needed.

If you receive a negative response that you do not think addresses your challenge and the decision has not been changed, you can:

- make further representations to the benefit authority's legal department; *or*
- drop the matter and take no further action; *or*
- refer the matter to a solicitor to issue judicial review proceedings in the High Court or Court of Session (making sure you are within the strict time limit – see below).

Judicial review in the High Court or Court of Session

Judicial review in the High Court in England and Wales or Court of Session in Scotland is a means of challenging a decision where there is no alternative means for challenging the decision and, in England and Wales, you have exhausted the pre-action stage on p1418 (there is no pre-action protocol in Scotland). The grounds for your challenge are those in your pre-action correspondence (see p1418).

You cannot usually apply to the High Court/Court of Session for a judicial review if you have another independent means of resolving the problem (see p1415).

England and Wales

To start a claim for judicial review in the High Court of England and Wales, you have to submit form N461 together with supporting documents and the court fee or a request for a fee remission.

Once your claim has been 'issued' by the court (ie, it has been allocated a court number and been stamped), send a copy of it and the supporting documents to the body whose decision you are challenging. It has 21 days to file with the court and send you an acknowledgement of service and a very basic defence to the claim (known as 'summary grounds of defence').

Once a claim for judicial review is started in the courts, it involves a two-stage process. First, you must get permission from the High Court to apply for judicial review. Your application for permission is initially decided on the papers. If it is refused, you have the opportunity of renewing your application at an oral hearing. If permission is refused at the oral hearing, you have a right of appeal to the Court of Appeal. Permission to apply for judicial review is only given if the case has reasonable prospects of success. If permission is granted (whether on the papers or at a renewed oral hearing), the second stage is a substantive hearing of the case.

Part 9: Getting a benefit decision changed
Chapter 58: Appealing to the Upper Tribunal and the courts
7. Applying for judicial review

You should always consider obtaining legal advice from a solicitor or legal advice centre before starting judicial review proceedings in the court as there are likely to be significant costs involved and it is important that your claim is presented clearly and cogently, particularly when the decision maker will be legally represented. However, legal aid is available for many judicial review cases, subject to conditions. Check whether you are eligible.[137]

If you are looking for a solicitor to pursue judicial review in the High Court, note that legal firms and law centres which undertake judicial review work often do so under a public law contract as there are very few welfare benefits legal aid contracts available. There is a map of legal firms which have confirmed they are able to consider referrals from advice agencies in England and Wales for judicial review litigation at cpag.org.uk/welfare-rights/judicial-review/map-solicitors – the majority of these hold public law legal aid contracts. Some city firms also take referrals on a pro bono basis if you are not eligible for legal aid or if you cannot obtain a legal aid solicitor.

A claim for judicial review can typically take between six and 12 months to go through all the High Court stages.

Scotland

The procedure is similar in Scotland, except there is no pre-action protocol. Court action for judicial review starts using a document known as a 'petition'.

You must obtain 'leave' (permission) from the court to bring a judicial review action. The court may grant permission where there is 'sufficient interest' in the subject matter and the application has a real prospect of success.

If permission is refused by the court, you have a right to an oral hearing before a different judge, as well as a further right of appeal to the Inner House of the Court of Session.[138]

Judicial review in the Upper Tribunal

Challenging a decision of the First-tier Tribunal

Occasionally, you can challenge a First-tier Tribunal decision by applying for a judicial review by the Upper Tribunal. You cannot usually do so if you have a right of appeal to the Upper Tribunal against the decision. You may need the services of a solicitor or legal advice centre to apply for a judicial review. Check what you might have to pay – you may qualify for free legal help.

Note: if you are in any doubt about whether you have a right of appeal against a decision you want to challenge, you can apply for both permission to appeal and for a judicial review. The Upper Tribunal decides which is the proper route.

In England and Wales, you can apply for a judicial review of a First-tier Tribunal decision if it is a decision against which you have no right of appeal to the Upper Tribunal and it is a decision:[139]

- made under any of the First-tier Tribunal procedural rules; *or*

- to review (or not to review) a decision following an application for permission to appeal to the Upper Tribunal, or a decision as to what action to take in the light of the review.

You must first apply for permission in writing and must include specified information.[140] You can use Form JR1, available at gov.uk/government/collections/court-and-tribunal-forms. You must apply promptly and your application must be received by the Upper Tribunal no later than three months after the date of the decision you want to challenge.[141] Provided you apply promptly, the time limit can be extended to:
- one month after the date you were sent written reasons for the First-tier Tribunal's decision; *or*
- one month after the date you were sent notice that an application to set aside the decision was unsuccessful, provided the application was made within the time limit for applying for a set-aside (or longer period allowed).

In Scotland, you can challenge a First-tier Tribunal decision by a judicial review if it is a procedural decision or ruling, including procedural omissions or oversights.[142] You cannot apply directly to the Upper Tribunal; you must first apply to the Court of Session. You must apply within three months of the decision you want to challenge (or a longer period that the Upper Tribunal considers equitable).[143] If specified conditions are satisfied, your case is transferred to the Upper Tribunal.[144] The Upper Tribunal then decides whether your application was made in time and whether to give you permission.[145]

Transferring judicial review cases to the Upper Tribunal
The High Court and the Court of Session can transfer judicial review claims to the Upper Tribunal.[146] It may be appropriate to request a transfer if you think your case would benefit from being decided by an Upper Tribunal judge experienced in social security law rather than a High Court/Court of Session judge.

Challenging refusal of permission to appeal to the Upper Tribunal
There is no right of appeal against a decision by the Upper Tribunal to refuse permission to appeal from the First-tier Tribunal. This type of decision can only be challenged by way of a judicial review. Judicial review is only available to challenge refusal of permission to appeal where:[147]
- the proposed appeal would raise an important point of principle; *or*
- there is another compelling reason for the court to hear the appeal.

The procedure is the same as issuing proceedings in the High Court or Court of Session (see p1421), except that the time limit is 16 days from the date the decision letter was sent[148] and you do not need to follow the pre-action protocol.

Part 9: Getting a benefit decision changed
Chapter 58: Appealing to the Upper Tribunal and the courts
Notes

Notes

1. Appealing to the Upper Tribunal

1 s11 TCEA 2007; *LS v Lambeth LB (HB)* [2010] UKUT 461 (AAC), reported as [2011] AACR 27
2 s11(5)(d) and (e) TCEA 2007
3 s11 TCEA 2007
4 r4 TP(UT) Rules; Practice Statement, *Delegation of Functions to Staff on or after 3 November 2008*, 30 October 2008
5 R(A) 1/72; R(SB) 11/83; R(IS) 11/99; R(I) 2/06; *R (Iran) v Secretary of State for the Home Department* [2005] EWCA Civ 982
6 CIS/2345/2001; CH/4065/2001
7 CDLA/433/1999
8 CDLA/1456/2002; R(H) 1/03
9 *Basildon DC v AM* [2009] UKUT 113 (AAC)
10 *TA v LB of Islington (HB)* [2014] UKUT 71 (AAC)
11 *GC v HMRC and DC (CHB)* [2018] UKUT 223 (AAC)
12 *DS v SSWP (ESA)* [2013] UKUT 572 (AAC)
13 CDLA/2748/2002
14 CSDLA/606/2003; *KMN v SSWP (PIP)* [2019] UKUT 42 (AAC)
15 CS/1939/1995; CDLA/5413/1999; CIB/303/1999
16 CDLA/3224/2001
17 CH/3594/2002; *RC (Dec'd) v Maldon DC (HB)* [2012] UKUT 333 (AAC)
18 CDLA/1480/2006
19 CDLA/7980/1995; CH/5221/2001; CH/396/2002; CIB/2977/2002
20 *ES v SSWP* [2009] UKUT 6 (AAC)
21 R(IS) 4/93
22 *JH v HMRC* [2015] UKUT 397 (AAC)
23 *R (Iran) v Secretary of State for the Home Department* [2005] EWCA Civ 982
24 R(DLA) 3/08; *SP v SSWP* [2009] UKUT 97 (AAC)
25 *LA v SSWP (ESA)* [2014] UKUT 482 (AAC)
26 CJSA/322/2001; R(IS) 5/04
27 *Carpenter v SSWP* [2003] EWCA Civ 33, reported as R(IB) 6/03

2. How to appeal

28 s11(3) TCEA 2007
29 s11(4)(a) TCEA 2007; r21(2) TP(UT) Rules
30 r38(2), (5) and (6) TP(FT) Rules

31 Practice Statement, *Composition of Tribunals in Social Security and Child Support Cases in the Social Entitlement Chamber on or after 1 August 2013*, 31 July 2013, para 11
32 r27(2) TP(FT) Rules; CSB/172/1990
33 r39(3)-(5) TP(FT) Rules
34 r41 TP(FT) Rules
35 r38(7) TP(FT) Rules
36 *HP v SSWP (ESA)* [2014] UKUT 491 (AAC)
37 r38(3) and (4) TP(FT) Rules
38 r5(3)(a) TP(FT) Rules
39 r38(5) TP(FT) Rules
40 r21(7)(b) TP(UT) Rules
41 CIB/3937/2000; *SSWP v SC (SF)* [2013] UKUT 607 (AAC)
42 r12 TP(FT) Rules; r12 TP(UT) Rules
43 s9 TCEA 2007; r39(1) TP(FT) Rules
44 *GA v SSWP* [2017] UKUT 416 (AAC)
45 r41 TP(FT) Rules
46 r40(2) TP(FT) Rules
47 s9(4) and (5) TCEA 2007
48 *SE v SSWP* [2009] UKUT 163 (AAC); *AM v SSWP (IB)* [2009] UKUT 224 (AAC); *JS v SSWP* [2013] UKUT 100 (AAC), reported as [2013] AACR 30
49 r40(3) and (4) TP(FT) Rules; *SSWP v AM and Northumberland County Council (HB)* [2015] UKUT 360 (AAC)
50 r39(2) TP(FT) Rules
51 s11(4)(a) TCEA 2007; r21(2) TP(UT) Rules
52 r21(4), (5), (6)(a) and (7) TP(UT) Rules; CSDLA/1207/2000
53 r7(1) and (2)(a) TP(UT) Rules
54 r21(7)(b) TP(UT) Rules
55 R(IS) 11/99; CDLA/5793/1997
56 CCS/1664/2001
57 r13(1) TP(UT) Rules
58 r22(1) and (2) TP(UT) Rules
59 s13(8)(c) TCEA 2007
60 r21(3)(b) TP(UT) Rules
61 r5(3)(a) TP(UT) Rules
62 R(M) 1/87; *R (Birmingham City Council) v Birmingham County Court* [2009] EWHC 3329 (Admin), reported as [2010] 1 WLR 1287

3. **After you get permission to appeal**
63 r23 TP(UT) Rules
64 r5(3)(a) TP(UT) Rules
65 r22(2)(b) TP(UT) Rules
66 r2 TP(UT) Rules
67 *MA v SSWP* [2009] UKUT 211 (AAC)
68 rr5-7, 8, 15 and 16 TP(UT) Rules
69 r5(3)(n) TP(UT) Rules
70 s25 TCEA 2007
71 r16(3) TP(UT) Rules
72 r5(3)(l) and (m) TP(UT) Rules
73 r11 TP(UT) Rules; CIB/1009/2004; CIB/2058/2004
74 r11(4)(b) TP(UT) Rules
75 r11(4)(a) TP(UT) Rules; *MP v SSWP (DLA)* [2010] UKUT 103 (AAC)
76 r11(5) TP(UT) Rules
77 s10 Legal Aid, Sentencing and Punishment of Offenders Act 2012
78 Regs 5A(d) and 13 Advice and Assistance (Assistance by Way of Representation) (Scotland) Regulations 2003, No.179
79 r18 TP(UT) Rules
80 r17 TP(UT) Rules
81 r17(4) and (5) TP(UT) Rules
82 r5(3)(a) TP(UT) Rules
83 rr24 and 25 TP(UT) Rules
84 rr5(3)(a) and 25(2) TP(UT) Rules
85 r40(3)(b) TP(UT) Rules

4. **Oral hearings**
86 r34 TP(UT) Rules
87 r36 TP(UT) Rules
88 Practice Direction, *First-Tier and Upper Tribunals: use of the Welsh language in tribunals in Wales,* 30 October 2008
89 r1(3) TP(UT) Rules, definition of 'hearing'
90 r3 The First-tier Tribunal and Upper Tribunal (Composition of Tribunal) Order 2008 SI No.2835; Practice Statement, *Composition of Tribunals in Relation to Matters that Fall to be Decided by the Administrative Appeals Chamber of the Upper Tribunal on or after26 March 2014,* 26 March 2014
91 R(I) 1/03
92 *R(IS) 2/08; NA v SSWP (ESA)* [2018] UKUT 399 (AAC)

5. **The decision**
93 s12 TCEA 2007
94 r40 TP(UT) Rules
95 *Adams v SSWP and Green (CSM)* [2017] UKUT 9 (AAC), reported as [2017] AACR 28
96 r42 TP(UT) Rules

97 r43 TP(UT) Rules; *SK v SSWP* [2016] UKUT 529 (AAC), reported as [2017] AACR 25
98 r5(3)(a) TP(UT) Rules
99 r48 TP(UT) Rules

6. **Appealing to the Court of Appeal or Court of Session**
100 s13 TCEA 2007
101 s13(8)(c)-(e) TCEA 2007
102 s13(6) and (6A) TCEA 2007; Appeals from the Upper Tribunal to the Court of Appeal Order 2008, No.2834; r41.57 Rules of the Court of Session 1994
103 ss14A-14C TCEA 2007
104 r44(1), (6)(a) and (7) TP(UT) Rules
105 *Fryer-Kelsey v SSWP* [2005] EWCA Civ 511, reported as R(IB) 6/05
106 r45(3)-(5) TP(UT) Rules
107 r44(2), (3) and (5) TP(UT) Rules
108 r5(3)(a) TP(UT) Rules
109 r44(6) TP(UT) Rules
110 r46(1) TP(UT) Rules
111 r48 TP(UT) Rules
112 s10 TCEA 2007; r45(1) TP(UT) Rules
113 s10(4) and (5) TCEA 2007
114 r46(2) and (3) TP(UT) Rules
115 r45(2) TP(UT) Rules
116 s13(3)-(5) TCEA 2007
117 s13(11)-(13) TCEA 2007; r45(4)(b) TP(UT) Rules
118 r52.5 CPR

7. **Applying for judicial review**
119 **EW** s31(3) Senior Courts Act 1981
    S s 27B(2)(a) Court of Session Act 1988
120 r54.5(1) CPR
121 s27A Court of Session Act 1988
122 r54.7A(3) CPR
123 Sch 2 SS&CS(DA) Regs
124 *Glencore Energy UK Limited v Commissioners of HMRC* [2017] EWHC 1476 (Admin)
125 For an example of the successful use of this, see cpag.org.uk/welfare-rights/judicial-review/judicial-review-pre-action-letters/carers-following-death
126 *R (C and W) v SSWP* [2015] EWHC 1607 (Admin)
127 *R (S) v SSHD* [2007] EWCA Civ 546
128 For an example of use, see 'JR12 Real Time Information incorrectly reported' at cpag.org.uk/welfare-rights/judicial-review/judicial-review-pre-action-letters/disputed-earnings-uc
129 *R (Winder and Ors) v Sandwell MBC* [2012] EWHC 2617 (Admin)

9

Part 9: Getting a benefit decision changed
Chapter 58: Appealing to the Upper Tribunal and the courts
Notes

130 *Kerr v Department for Social Development (Northern Ireland)* [2004] UKHL 23, para 62
131 For an example of a challenge to unlawful guidance, see cpag.org.uk/ welfare-rights/judicial-review/judicial-review-pre-action-letters/deductions-uc
132 *Stec v United Kingdom* [2006] 43 EHRR 47, para 53
133 justice.gov.uk/courts/procedure-rules/ civil/protocol/prot_jrv
134 r54.7A CPR
135 Annex A of the pre-action protocol for judicial review, justice.gov.uk/courts/ procedure-rules/civil/protocol/ prot_jrv#annexa
136 r54.1(f) CPR
137 gov.uk/legal-aid/eligibility
138 ss27B-27D Court of Session Act 1988
139 s18 TCEA 2007; *Practice Direction (Upper Tribunal: Judicial Review Jurisdiction)* [2009], 1WLR 327
140 r28 TP(UT) Rules
141 r28(2) and (3) TP(UT) Rules; *CICA v First-tier Tribunal and CB (CIC)* [2015] UKUT 371 (AAC)
142 ss20, 20A and 21 TCEA 2007; Act of Sederunt (Transfer of Judicial Review Applications from the Court of Session) 2008, No.357; *Currie, Petitioner* [2009] CSOH 145, reported as [2010] AACR 8
143 s27A Court of Session Act 1988
144 *EF v SSWP* [2009] UKUT 92 (AAC), reported as R(IB) 3/09
145 s20A(2) TCEA 2007
146 s31A Senior Courts Act 1981; s20 TCEA 2007
147 *R (Cart) v the Upper Tribunal and Others* [2011] UKSC 28; *Eba v Advocate General for Scotland* [2011] UKSC 29
148 r54 7A(30) CPR

Chapter 59

. . . .

Challenging decisions on statutory payments

This chapter covers:
1. Notification of your employer's decision (p1428)
2. Involving HM Revenue and Customs (p1428)
3. Appealing against a decision (p1430)
4. Appeals to the Upper Tribunal (p1434)
5. Appeals to the courts (p1435)
6. Payment if your challenge is successful (p1436)

This chapter explains the rules for challenging decisions on entitlement to statutory payments. These rules do not apply to challenging decisions on other benefits (except some decisions on national insurance contributions – see p960).

In this chapter, when the term First-tier Tribunal is used, it means the First-tier Tribunal (Tax) and when the term Upper Tribunal is used, it means the Upper Tribunal (Tax and Chancery).

Key facts

- Your employer should make the initial decision on your entitlement to statutory sick pay, statutory maternity pay, statutory adoption pay, statutory paternity pay, statutory shared parental pay and statutory parental bereavement pay.
- If you disagree with your employer's decision, or your employer has failed to make a decision, you can ask HM Revenue and Customs (HMRC) to decide whether you are entitled.
- If you disagree with HMRC's decision on your entitlement, you can ask for it to be reviewed. If you are unhappy with the outcome of the review, you can appeal to the First-tier Tribunal.
- If you disagree with the First-tier Tribunal's decision, you may be able to appeal to the Upper Tribunal. If you disagree with the Upper Tribunal's decision, you may be able to appeal to a court.

Part 9: Getting a benefit decision changed
Chapter 59: Challenging decisions on statutory payments
2. Involving HM Revenue and Customs

1. **Notification of your employer's decision**

If you have taken the necessary steps to request statutory sick pay (SSP), statutory maternity pay (SMP), statutory adoption pay (SAP), statutory paternity pay (SPP) or statutory shared parental pay (SSPP) from your employer (see Chapters 38 and 39), but your employer decides it is not liable to pay you, it should notify you of its decision within:[1]

- seven days for SSP or SMP;
- 28 days for SAP, SPP or SSPP.

This also applies to a former employer for SMP, SAP, SPP and SSPP.

For SSP, your employer should normally provide this information on Form SSP1, or on its own computerised form if it contains the same information. For SMP, SAP and SPP, it is normally given on Form SMP1, SAP1 or SPP1 respectively. There is no official form for SSPP. If you have given your employer certain evidence to establish your entitlement, it should be returned to you – eg, Form MAT B1 for SMP.

Note: at the time of writing, the rules on the time within which your employer should notify you if it has decided it is not liable to pay you statutory parental bereavement pay, and details of whether there will be an official form for your employer to use to notify you of this, had not been published.

2. **Involving HM Revenue and Customs**

If you disagree with your employer's decision on your entitlement to statutory sick pay (SSP), statutory maternity pay (SMP), statutory adoption pay (SAP), statutory paternity pay (SPP), statutory shared parental pay (SSPP) or statutory parental bereavement pay (SPBP), or if your employer has failed to make a decision, you can request that HM Revenue and Customs (HMRC) makes a formal decision on your entitlement.[2] You must do so within six months of the earliest date for which your entitlement is in dispute.[3] It is likely that this six-month deadline will apply to SPBP but, at the time of writing, the rules had not been published.

Call HMRC's Statutory Payments Disputes Team to initiate your request on 0300 056 0630. You may be sent a form to use or HMRC may suggest you write a letter.

Forms

You should normally apply on Form SSP14 (for SSP), SMP14 (for SMP), SAP14 (for SAP), SPP14 (for SPP) or ShPP14 (for SSPP), which can be obtained from, and should be returned to, HMRC's Statutory Payments Disputes Team, HMRC, PT Operations NE England, BX9 1AN. At the time of writing, details of the form for SPBP had not been published.

On either the form or in your letter, you must provide details of the period for which your entitlement to SSP, SMP, SAP, SPP or SSPP is at issue and the grounds on which your employer has refused payment, if you know them.[4] It is likely this will also apply to requests for a decision from HMRC on entitlement to SPBP but, at the time of writing, the rules had not been published.

If possible, you should also send a copy of Form SSP1, SMP1, SAP1 or SPP1 your employer has given you, or the information your employer has given you about its decision on your entitlement to SSPP, and evidence of your entitlement – eg, a medical certificate (if you have been sick for more than seven days), Form MAT B1, or the 'matching certificate' from the adoption agency. However, do not delay your application if you do not have this information.

It can take some time to get a final decision on your entitlement, so consider whether there are other benefits which you can claim in the interim (see Chapter 1). However, if you claim employment and support allowance (ESA) while waiting for a decision on your entitlement to SSP, or maternity allowance (MA) while waiting for a decision on your entitlement to SMP, the DWP does not normally make a decision on your ESA/MA claim until HMRC has made a decision on your entitlement to SSP or SMP (because you do not qualify for ESA if you are entitled to SSP, nor for MA if you are entitled to SMP). For this reason, the DWP can request that HMRC make a formal decision on your entitlement to SSP or SMP, if you have not already done so. If you would qualify for ESA or MA, do not delay claiming or you may lose out financially if the final decision is that you do not qualify for SSP or SMP.

Note: if you are thinking of challenging your employer's decision on your entitlement to a statutory payment, you should tell your employer that you intend to contact HMRC. Your employer can get advice on statutory payments from HMRC's Employers' Helpline: 0300 200 3200.

Requests for further information

HMRC may contact you and/or your partner for further information, and can also require your employer to provide information relating to your entitlement – eg, the reasons for its decision. HMRC can impose a financial penalty on your employer if it fails to provide the information. If your employer fails to comply with requests for information, press HMRC to make its own decision on your entitlement.

Part 9: Getting a benefit decision changed
Chapter 59: Challenging decisions on statutory payments
3. Appealing against a decision

HMRC can also impose a financial penalty on you for not providing information or documents that you have been reasonably required to provide to decide your entitlement.[5] However, this is only likely to happen if HMRC believes that you have acted fraudulently or have been negligent.

HM Revenue and Customs' decision

In order to resolve your dispute, HMRC may send both you and your employer a written opinion on your entitlement before it issues a formal decision on your application. It may give you a deadline before which both you and your employer can object to its written opinion before it issues a formal decision.

This decision is legally binding on your employer. If HMRC decides you are entitled to be paid by your employer (and your employer does not appeal), it should pay you on or before your first payday after the 30-day appeal time limit (see below) expires.[6]

Varying or superseding a decision

HMRC can change its own decision by varying or superseding it.[7] It can **vary** its decision if it now believes that the decision was wrong at the time it was made. It must tell you and your employer of the new decision in writing. The new decision takes effect from the date that the original decision would have had effect if the reason for the variation had been known. If you or your employer have appealed against a decision, HMRC may vary that decision at any time before the appeal is determined.

HMRC can **supersede** an earlier decision if it has become incorrect for any reason – eg, if your circumstances have changed. The new decision takes effect from the date of your change of circumstances.

If HMRC varies or supersedes an earlier decision, either you or your employer can appeal against the new decision.

3. Appealing against a decision

Both you and your employer can appeal against a decision made by HM Revenue and Customs (HMRC).[8]

Your appeal should be made in writing to HMRC and should include your reasons for appealing.[9] Send your appeal to: The Statutory Payments Disputes Team, HM Revenue and Customs, PT Operations NE England, BX9 1AN. You have a choice about how your appeal is dealt with (see p1431).

Time limit for appealing

Your appeal should reach HMRC within 30 days of the date on which HMRC made its formal decision.[10] This time limit may be extended by HMRC if the reason you are late is considered reasonable.[11] If HMRC does not accept your late appeal, you can apply to the First-tier Tribunal for permission to appeal late. However, you cannot be certain that a late appeal will be accepted, so it is preferable to keep within the time limit.

Choosing how your appeal is dealt with

You can choose whether you would like your appeal to be decided by the First-tier Tribunal or by HMRC conducting a review. To make this choice, in addition to sending your written appeal to HMRC, you should notify:[12]

- the tribunal in writing that you want it to consider your appeal (see p1433); *or*
- HMRC in writing that you want it to conduct a review. (If HMRC conducts a review and you disagree with its decision, you can still apply to the tribunal for a decision on your appeal, provided you apply within the time limits below.)

If, having made your appeal, you do not ask either the tribunal to consider your appeal or HMRC to review its decision, HMRC should write to you, offering to review its decision (called an 'HMRC-initiated review' in this chapter). Before HMRC initiates a review, it may try to settle the appeal (see below). However, until HMRC has issued a notification offering you a review, you can still notify the tribunal that you want it to decide your appeal or inform HMRC yourself that you want it to conduct a review.

Settling or withdrawing your appeal

HMRC can try to settle your appeal at any time before the determination of the appeal. If, before the appeal is decided, you reach an agreement with HMRC (or if an agreement is reached between your employer and HMRC, if your employer has appealed), the matter is treated as settled by agreement and the appeal lapses.[13]

You can withdraw your appeal at any time before it is decided by notifying HMRC and your employer that you wish to do so. Your employer and HMRC have 30 days to object and, if no objection is made, your appeal will lapse.[14]

Review by HM Revenue and Customs

Initial view on entitlement

If you have asked for your appeal to be decided by an HMRC review, or if HMRC has initiated a review, HMRC first informs you of its 'initial view on your entitlement'.

If you have requested an HMRC review, HMRC should send you its initial view on your entitlement within 30 days, beginning with the date it receives your written request for a review, although it can send it later than this if it is reasonable.[15] The same rules apply if it is your employer who has initiated the review.

Part 9: Getting a benefit decision changed
Chapter 59: Challenging decisions on statutory payments
3. Appealing against a decision

If HMRC has initiated the review, HMRC should send its initial view on your entitlement with its offer of a review.[16] You then have 30 days, starting on the date of HMRC's letter to inform in writing:[17]

- HMRC, that you want it to conduct the review (see below); *or*
- the First-tier Tribunal, that you want it to decide your appeal (see p1433). In some circumstances, the tribunal can consider your appeal even if you apply after the 30-day time limit (see p1434).

If HMRC has initiated the review but you neither accept the offer of a review nor notify the tribunal that you want it to consider your appeal within the above time limit, HMRC proceeds as if you have agreed to its initial view on your entitlement and treats the matter as settled by agreement. Notification of this should be sent to you and your employer, and your appeal lapses.[18]

The review

After HMRC has issued its initial view on your entitlement (and, for HMRC-initiated reviews, provided you have accepted HMRC's offer of a review), a review is carried out by an HMRC decision maker who was not involved in making the original decision.

If you disagree with HMRC's initial view, it is important to write to explain why. The decision maker must consider any information you provide, if you provide it at a stage that gives her/him a reasonable opportunity to do so.[19]

HMRC should notify you of its review decision and the reasons for it within 45 days beginning with the date it:[20]

- notified you of its initial view of the matter, if you requested the review; *or*
- received your acceptance of its offer of a review, if HMRC initiated the review.

In either case, these time limits can be changed if you agree.

If HMRC does not notify you of its review decision within this time limit, its decision is taken to be the same as its initial view on your entitlement and HMRC must inform you of this.[21]

If you do not agree with the review decision

If you or your employer do not agree with HMRC's review decision, you may notify the First-tier Tribunal that you want it to consider your appeal. The time limit for doing so is 30 days, beginning with the date of either:[22]

- HMRC's letter notifying you of its review decision; *or*
- if HMRC did not notify you of its review decision within the time limit, the date of its letter telling you it has adopted its initial view on your entitlement as its decision.

In the latter situation, you can appeal before receiving HMRC's letter, provided your appeal is made after the expiry of the time limit for making the review decision.

If you do not notify the tribunal within the time limit, your appeal can only be considered if the tribunal gives permission (see p1434).[23]

Alternative dispute resolution

If either you or your employer have notified the First-tier Tribunal that you want it to consider your appeal, HMRC may invite you to apply for alternative dispute resolution. If alternative dispute resolution is suggested before this, do not delay notifying the tribunal of your appeal, as the time limits for notifying the tribunal are not put on hold while you consider or take part in alternative dispute resolution. If alternative dispute resolution is used, an HMRC officer who has not been involved in the decision acts as a mediator to try to resolve the dispute. If you reach an agreement, you and your employer are sent written confirmation and, if it is different from HMRC's earlier decision on your entitlement, HMRC may vary its earlier decision (see p1430). For alternative dispute resolution to be used, both you and your employer must agree to it. If you are offered alternative dispute resolution, get advice.

Appeals to the First-tier Tribunal

You can request that the First-tier Tribunal considers your appeal if:[24]
- you have appealed against HMRC's original decision on your entitlement and want your appeal to be decided by the tribunal, rather than by an HMRC review (see p1430); *or*
- you have appealed and HMRC has initiated a review (see p1431). Rather than accept the offer of a review, you can notify the tribunal that you want it to decide your appeal. See p1431 for the time limits for notifying the tribunal, and p1434 if you miss the time limit; *or*
- your appeal against HMRC's original decision has been decided by an HMRC review and you disagree with the decision, or if HMRC has not notified you of its review decision within the time limits; *or*
- you missed the time limit for appealing against HMRC's original decision on your entitlement and HMRC does not agree to accept your late appeal (but see p1434).

Notifying the First-tier Tribunal

If you want the First-tier Tribunal to consider your appeal, you must notify it in writing or submit the appeal online. See p1431 for the time limit for doing so. Your written notice must contain certain information, including the details of the decision you are appealing against, the result you want and your grounds for appealing. If you miss the time limit, you must also ask for permission to make a late application and explain why your request is late.[25]

Use Form T240 'Notice of Appeal (tax)', available from gov.uk (search for 'Form T240') or telephone 0300 123 1024. Your notice should be sent to HM Courts and

Part 9: Getting a benefit decision changed
Chapter 59: Challenging decisions on statutory payments
4. Appeals to the Upper Tribunal

Tribunals Service, First-tier Tribunal (Tax Chamber), PO Box 16972, Birmingham B16 6TZ, either by post or electronically. You must include a copy of the written record of the decision you are appealing against and any statement giving the reasons for that decision (eg, the notification HMRC sent informing you of its decision), unless you do not have this information and cannot reasonably obtain it.

Alternatively, you can submit your appeal through the HM Courts and Tribunals Service online service at gov.uk/tax-tribunal/appeal-to-tribunal.

Note: when completing Form T240, be aware that statutory payments are described as 'direct taxes' by HMRC.

Missed time limits

If you miss the relevant time limit for notifying the First-tier Tribunal that you want it to determine your appeal or the time limit for appealing against HMRC's original decision on your entitlement (and HMRC does not agree to accept your late appeal), you can still ask the First-tier Tribunal to consider your appeal. It must give its permission for the time limit to be extended. Although there are no specific rules about when the time limit can be extended,[26] the overriding objective of the rules is to enable tribunals to deal with cases fairly and justly.[27] Whether the First-tier Tribunal extends the time limit depends on the circumstances, so give detailed reasons why your appeal is late. As you cannot be certain of success, it is essential to keep within the time limits if you can.

How the First-tier Tribunal decides your case

The First-tier Tribunal allocates your case to be considered in one of four ways.[28] Further details of the procedures can be obtained from the First-tier Tribunal (Tax) leaflet T242 *Making an Appeal: explanatory leaflet*, available from gov.uk.

The tribunal can confirm HMRC's decision or change it.[29] It must send you a notice informing you of its decision, which may include its full written findings and the reasons for its decision.[30] If you disagree with the tribunal's decision, you may be able to appeal against it to the Upper Tribunal (see below).

In certain circumstances, you can apply for the First-tier Tribunal's decision to be 'set aside' (there is a time limit for doing so), or the tribunal can correct its own decision.[31] The tribunal can also review its decision if you have applied for permission to appeal to the Upper Tribunal and it considers there was an error of law in the decision.[32]

4. **Appeals to the Upper Tribunal**

You and your employer can appeal to the Upper Tribunal (Tax and Chancery Chamber) against a decision of the First-tier Tribunal, but only on the grounds that the First-tier Tribunal has made an 'error of law' (see p1397).[33] The rules for making an appeal are almost the same as those for making an appeal to the Upper Tribunal (Administrative Appeals Chamber) described in Chapter 58, although there are differences in the procedure for lodging an appeal and in the time limit for applying. You must first apply to the First-tier Tribunal (Tax) for permission to appeal. Your application must normally be received no later than 56 days after the latest of the dates listed on p1401 (usually the date the tribunal sent you its full written reasons for the decision). In some circumstances, the First-tier Tribunal can give permission for you to appeal later than this.[34] Use Form T247 to apply to the First-tier Tribunal for permission to appeal to the Upper Tribunal (available from gov.uk – search for 'Form T247').

If you have not been sent the First-tier Tribunal's full written findings and reasons, you must obtain these before applying for permission to appeal. Write to the First-tier Tribunal to request these – your request must be received within 28 days of the date it sent you its decision notice. In some circumstances, this time limit can be extended.[35] If the First-tier Tribunal gives permission for you to appeal, you must submit a 'notice of appeal' and certain other information to the Upper Tribunal within the time limit. For details, see p1404. Use Form FTC1 available from gov.uk.

If the First-tier Tribunal refuses permission for you to appeal or only gives permission on limited grounds, you can apply to the Upper Tribunal for permission. Use Form FTC1. See p1404 for the time limits for applying.[36] If, without a hearing, the Upper Tribunal refuses you permission to appeal or to appeal late, or gives permission to appeal subject to conditions or on limited grounds, you can apply for this decision to be reconsidered at a hearing. An application to do so must be made in writing and be received by the Upper Tribunal within 14 days of the date it sent you notice of its decision, although the Upper Tribunal has discretion to extend this time limit.[37] The Upper Tribunal has the power to make an order for costs (expenses in Scotland), so before making any application get advice about whether you could be liable for costs if you lose your case.

See Chapter 58 for further information on Upper Tribunal procedures.

5. Appeals to the courts

You and your employer can appeal against the decision of the Upper Tribunal to the Court of Appeal (the Court of Session in Scotland) if the tribunal made an 'error of law' – ie, it interpreted the law incorrectly.[38]

You must apply for permission to appeal, which is only granted if certain conditions are met (see p1411). Your application should normally be made to the Upper Tribunal within one month of the date it sent you written reasons for its decision. This time limit can be extended with the tribunal's permission.[39] See p1411 for further details on appealing to the courts.

Part 9: Getting a benefit decision changed
Chapter 59: Challenging decisions on statutory payments
6. Payment if your challenge is successful

6. **Payment if your challenge is successful**

If it is decided that your employer should pay you a statutory payment, your employer should pay you within a certain time limit. If your employer has appealed or is within the time limit for doing so, it does not have to pay you until a final decision is given on appeal, or until the time limit for the appeal or a further appeal has passed. If no appeal against the decision has been made (or if the matter has been finally determined), your employer should pay you on or before the first payday after:[40]

- the day the employer is notified that the appeal has been finally determined; *or*
- the day the employer receives notification that leave to appeal has been refused, and there is no further opportunity to apply for leave; *or*
- in any other case, the day the time limit for appeal expires.

If, because of your employer's payroll methods, it is not practical for you to be paid at this time, your employer should pay you on or before your next payday after this date.

If your employer does not pay

If your employer does not pay you within the above time limit, HM Revenue and Customs (HMRC) should pay you (although HMRC states it will first contact your employer to try to get it to pay).[41] Write to HMRC's Statutory Payments Disputes Team (see p1429) asking for payment. This applies even if your employer is insolvent, but only for payment owed for the period before the date of insolvency. For any period that falls after the date of insolvency, HMRC, rather than your employer, is automatically liable to pay you any statutory payment for which you are eligible.[42]

Notes

1. **Notification of your employer's decision**
   1 **SSP** s130 SSAA 1992; reg 15 SSP Regs
     SMP s132 SSAA 1992; reg 25A SMP Regs
     SPP&SAP Reg 11 SPPSAP(A) Regs
     SSPP Regs 2(2) and 11 SSPP(A) Regs
     SPBP Reg 11 SPBP(A) Regs

2. **Involving HM Revenue and Customs**
   2 s8 SSC(TF)A 1999
   3 **SSP/SMP** Reg 3 SSP&SMP(D) Regs
     SPP/SAP Reg 13 SPPSAP(A) Regs
     SSPP Reg 13 SSPP(A) Regs
     SPBP Reg 13 SPBP(A) Regs
   4 **SSP/SMP** Reg 3 SSP&SMP(D) Regs
     SPP/SAP Reg 13 SPPSAP(A) Regs
     SSPP Reg 13 SSPP(A) Regs
     SPBP Reg 13 SPBP(A) Regs
   5 **SSP/SMP** s113A SSAA 1992
     SPP/SAP/SSPP/SPBP s11(1) and (2) Employment Act 2002
   6 **SSP** Reg 9 SSP Regs
     SMP Reg 29 SMP Regs
     SPP/SAP Reg 42 SPPSAP(G) Regs
     SSPP Reg 44 SSPP(G) Regs
     SPBP Reg 24 SPBP(G) Regs
   7 s10 SSC(TF)A 1999; regs 5 and 6 SSC(DA) Regs

3. **Appealing against a decision**
   8 s11(2)(a) SSC(TF)A 1999
   9 s12 SSC(TF)A 1999
   10 s12(1) SSC(TF)A 1999
   11 s49 TMA 1970; reg 9 SSC(DA) Regs
   12 ss49A, 49B, 49D and 49I TMA 1970; reg 7 SSC(DA) Regs
   13 s49A(4) TMA 1970; regs 7(2) and 11 SSC(DA) Regs
   14 Reg 11(5) SSC(DA) Regs
   15 s49B(2) and (5) TMA 1970
   16 s49C(2) TMA 1970
   17 ss49C(3) and (8) and 49H TMA 1970
   18 s49C(4) TMA 1970; reg 11 SSC(DA) Regs
   19 s49E(4) TMA 1970
   20 s49E(6) and (7) TMA 1970
   21 s49E(8) and (9) TMA 1970
   22 s49G TMA 1970
   23 s49G(3) TMA 1970

24 ss49D, 49G and 49H TMA 1970
25 r20 TP(FT)(TC) Rules
26 s49(2)(b) TMA 1970; r20(4) TP(FT)(TC) Rules
27 r2 TP(FT)(TC) Rules
28 r23 TP(FT)(TC) Rules
29 Reg 10 SSC(DA) Regs
30 r35 TP(FT)(TC) Rules
31 rr37 and 38 TP(FT)(TC) Rules
32 r41 TP(FT)(TC) Rules

4. **Appeals to the Upper Tribunal**
   33 s11 TCEA 2007; reg 12(2) SSC(DA) Regs
   34 r39 TP(FT)(TC) Rules
   35 rr5(3)(a) and 35(4) and (5) TP(FT)(TC) Rules
   36 r21(3)(b) TP(UT) Rules
   37 rr5(3)(a) and 22(3)-(5) TP(UT) Rules

5. **Appeals to the courts**
   38 s13(2) TCEA 2007; reg 12(2) SSC(DA) Regs
   39 r44 TP(UT) Rules

6. **Payment if your challenge is successful**
   40 **SSP** Reg 9 SSP Regs
     SMP Reg 29 SMP Regs
     SPP/SAP Reg 42 SPPSAP(G) Regs
     SSPP Reg 44 SSPP(G) Regs
     SPBP Reg 24 SPBP(G) Regs
   41 **SSP** s151(6) SSCBA 1992; reg 9A SSP Regs
     SMP s164(9)(b) SSCBA 1992; reg 7 SMP Regs
     SPP/SAP ss171ZD(3) and 171ZM(3) SSCBA 1992; reg 43 SPPSAP(G) Regs
     SSPP s171ZX(3) SSCBA 1992; reg 45 SSPP(G) Regs
     SPBP s171ZZ8(3) SSCBA 1992; reg 25 SPBP(G) Regs
   42 **SSP** Reg 9B SSP Regs
     SMP Reg 7(3) and (4) SMP Regs
     SPP/SAP Reg 43(2) and (3) SPPSAP(G) Regs
     SSPP Reg 45(3)-(5) SSPP(G) Regs
     SPBP Reg 25 (2)-(4) SPBP(G) Regs

Chapter 60

Complaints

This chapter covers:
1. Grounds for a complaint (p1439)
2. Compensation payments (p1439)
3. Complaining about the DWP (p1440)
4. Complaining about HM Revenue and Customs (p1441)
5. Complaining about a local authority (p1443)
6. Complaining about HM Courts and Tribunals Service (p1443)
7. Using your MP (p1444)
8. Complaining to the Ombudsman (p1444)
9. Legal action (p1446)

This chapter covers the rules for making complaints about benefits administered by the DWP and HM Revenue and Customs. It also covers the rules for making complaints about housing benefit and HM Courts and Tribunal Service. See Chapter 77 for how to make a complaint about a Scottish social security benefit.

Key facts

- You can complain about any government or local authority department, and anyone contracted to provide a service on its behalf.
- Your complaint can be about a delay in dealing with your claim, poor administration, the behaviour of staff, or the way in which a particular policy or practice has impacted on you.
- It is best to put your complaint in writing, even if you have to start the process by telephone.
- If your complaint is not resolved satisfactorily, you may be able to complain to an Ombudsman or Adjudicator.

1. Grounds for a complaint

If you are unhappy with how you have been treated by a government or local authority department, or someone providing a service on its behalf, you can complain.

Your complaint can be about any issue concerning how your claim has been handled or how you have been treated. This includes matters such as delays, discourtesy, poor administration, the behaviour of staff, bad advice, or the way in which a particular department's policy or practice impacts on you. You can also ask for compensation for any loss you incur related to your complaint (see below).

If you disagree with a decision about your benefit or tax credit entitlement, see Chapters 56, 57 and 66 instead.

2. Compensation payments

You should expect prompt, courteous and efficient service from staff dealing with your claim. If you are unhappy with the way your claim has been administered, you can ask for compensation. Compensation payments are discretionary.

The DWP, HM Revenue and Customs (HMRC) and local authorities sometimes pay compensation if you can show that you have lost out through their error or delay and the loss cannot be made good by a revision, supersession or appeal (see Chapters 56, 57 and 66) or by backdating your claim. For instance, if you did not claim carer's allowance because you were misled by the DWP and you could not have the benefit backdated for more than three months, you can claim compensation. You may also receive 'consolatory payments' if you are considered to have experienced injustice, hardship or distress.

The DWP should automatically consider whether compensation should be paid if you are owed arrears of benefit, but you should still write to your local DWP office and ask. If you do not get a sympathetic response, ask your MP (see p1444) to write on your behalf or to take up your case with the social security minister.

The DWP uses a guide, *Financial Redress for Maladministration*, to help it decide when and how much compensation (known as 'extra-statutory' or ex gratia payments) should be paid.[1] HMRC's *Complaints and Remedy Guidance* sets out when it makes 'financial redress'.[2]

You should ask for a payment equal to the money you have lost. You can also ask for additional amounts to cover interest on arrears and any extra expenses you had, and to compensate you for any injustice, hardship or distress experienced because of the mistake. If your loss was as a clear result of incorrect advice or negligence on the part of the agency, you may be able to bring a court action for damages. Get legal advice promptly if this is the case.

Part 9: Getting a benefit decision changed
Chapter 60: Complaints
3. Complaining about the DWP

3. **Complaining about the DWP**

The DWP has a complaints procedure that applies to all its agencies including:
- the Pension Service;
- Jobcentre Plus;
- Debt Management.

The DWP does not deal with complaints about contracted providers – eg, employment programme providers and those carrying out medical assessments on its behalf. To complain about a contracted provider, use its internal complaints procedure. If you are still not satisfied, you can complain to the Independent Case Examiner (see below) and the Parliamentary and Health Service Ombudsman (see p1445).

You can find information about standards and complaints on the DWP website.[3]

The DWP's preferred method of dealing with complaints is by telephone, but you can also make complaints in person or in writing. If the DWP cannot contact you by telephone, it should respond in writing. You can also request that any response is made in writing.

The DWP has an online complaints service for jobseeker's allowance and universal credit claimants at https://makeacomplaint.dwp.gov.uk/.

The DWP has a three-stage internal complaints procedure for its agencies.
- **Stage one.** You should first contact the office that dealt with your claim.
- **Stage two.** If you are still unhappy, your complaint can be passed to a complaints resolution manager. S/he should contact you by telephone to discuss the complaint and how they will investigate it. Your complaint should normally be dealt with within 15 working days.
- **Stage three.** If you remain unhappy, your complaint can be passed to a senior manager who should normally deal with your complaint within 15 working days.

If you are still unhappy, you can complain to the Independent Case Examiner (see below). You may also have grounds to make a complaint to the Ombudsman (see p1445) if the DWP has not dealt with your complaint within a reasonable timescale.

Complaining to the Independent Case Examiner

The Independent Case Examiner (ICE) deals with complaints about DWP agencies and its contracted providers. ICE also carries out second-tier reviews of budgeting loan decisions (see p795).

ICE's role is to consider whether there has been maladministration. It cannot deal with matters of law or cases that are subject to judicial review or other legal procedures (other than appeals).

You can only make a complaint to ICE if you have already completed the complaints procedure of the particular agency concerned. This usually means that you have had a final response to your complaint. A complaint should be made to ICE no later than six months after the final response from the agency you are complaining about.

Complaints to ICE can be made in writing to PO Box 209, Bootle L20 7WA or by telephone on 0800 414 8529. An appointed representative can act on your behalf. You must provide all relevant information, including the final response to your complaint from the agency you are complaining about.

ICE should tell you within two weeks if it can accept your complaint. If accepted, ICE then attempts to resolve the complaint within eight weeks by mediating an agreement between you and the agency concerned. If this fails, an investigation case manager can ask for all the relevant information from the parties and attempt to settle the complaint. If this is not possible, an investigation is carried out and a formal report prepared, setting out how the complaint arose and how it believes it should be settled. This should be completed within 15 weeks or 20 weeks in more complex cases. If you remain unhappy, ask your MP to consider referring your complaint to the Parliamentary and Health Service Ombudsman (see p1445).

Is it worth complaining?

The ICE's 2019 annual report shows that it resolved, settled or investigated 1,185 cases about the DWP in 2018/19, 32 per cent of which were resolved or settled without investigation. 806 cases were investigated, of which 44 per cent were partially or fully upheld. ICE recommendations in upheld cases include apologies, corrective action and financial redress. This shows that, if your case is accepted by ICE, you are likely to get a satisfactory outcome in just under two-thirds of cases. However, for complaints about working-age benefits, this rises to a satisfactory outcome in nearly three-quarters of cases.

If you are unhappy with the way ICE dealt with your case, use its own complaints process.

4. Complaining about HM Revenue and Customs

You can complain about how HM Revenue and Customs (HMRC) has dealt with your tax credit, child benefit or guardian's allowance claim, or with your national

Part 9: Getting a benefit decision changed
Chapter 60: Complaints
4. Complaining about HM Revenue and Customs

insurance credits or contributions. You can do this online if you have, or set up, a Government Gateway account, by telephone or in writing to HMRC (see gov.uk/complain-about-hmrc). If you want to dispute the recovery of a tax credit overpayment, HMRC has a different process you need to follow (see p1522).

If you are not happy with the initial response, ask HMRC to review your complaint. The review should be carried out by a different customer service adviser, who will give you HMRC's final reply to your complaint.

If you are not happy with HMRC's final reply, you can ask the Adjudicator to look into it.

Complaining to the Adjudicator

The Adjudicator deals with complaints about HMRC and is similar in nature to the Independent Case Examiner (see p1440). The Adjudicator only investigates a complaint if you have already completed the HMRC internal complaints procedure. You cannot complain direct to the Adjudicator about an HMRC-contracted service provider; you must complain via HMRC first. A complaint should be made within six months of the final response from HMRC.[4]

A complaint to the Adjudicator should be made in writing or using the form available at gov.uk/guidance/how-to-complain-to-the-adjudicators-office. If you have problems, you can phone the Adjudicator's Office on 0300 057 1111. You can appoint someone to act on your behalf by completing a form available from the Adjudicator's Office website. You must provide the final response to your complaint from HMRC.

Complaints can be made about delays, inappropriate staff behaviour, misleading advice, the use of discretion or any other form of maladministration. The Adjudicator cannot investigate disputes about matters of law. If it can accept the complaint, the Adjudicator starts an investigation and attempts to resolve the issue by mediating an agreement between you and HMRC. If this fails, it can make recommendations, including that compensation be paid. HMRC has undertaken to follow the Adjudicator's recommendations in all but exceptional circumstances.

Is it worth complaining?

The Adjudicator's 2019 annual report shows that 42.8 per cent of complaints about tax credits resolved by the Adjudicator were upheld in 2018/19. This means that where cases are not resolved using HMRC's internal complaints procedure, a referral to the Adjudicator has a good chance of producing a successful outcome. For all the complaints about HMRC in 2018/19, just over £0.28 million of redress was recommended.

If you are unhappy with the Adjudicator's response, ask your MP to put your complaint to the Parliamentary and Health Service Ombudsman (see p1445). As well as looking at your complaint about HMRC, the Ombudsman may also look into the way in which the Adjudicator has investigated your complaint. Further information about the Adjudicator can be found at gov.uk/government/organisations/the-adjudicator-s-office.

5. **Complaining about a local authority**

If you are unhappy about the actions of your local authority or someone providing services on its behalf and wish to make a complaint, ask for a copy of its complaints policy. Local authorities are required to have an effective complaints procedure, which should be made available to the public. If you are unable to obtain the policy, write to the supervisor of the person dealing with your claim, making it clear why you are dissatisfied. If you do not receive a satisfactory reply, complain to the principal officer. Send a copy of the letter to your ward councillor and to the councillor who chairs the relevant local authority committee – local authority officers are always accountable to the councillors. If this does not produce results, or if the delay is causing you hardship, consider a complaint to the Ombudsman (see p1446) or legal action (see p1446).

Government departments also monitor local authorities, so you could contact your MP or write to the relevant minister – eg, the Secretary of State for Work and Pensions.

6. **Complaining about HM Courts and Tribunals Service**

Complaints about the administration of your appeal

If you are dissatisfied with the administration of your appeal, complain to HM Courts and Tribunals Service (HMCTS). Raise your complaint initially with the person who has been dealing with the administration of your appeal in person, by email or telephone. Her/his name and contact details should be on all the correspondence you have received. Alternatively, you can complain about HMCTS at complain-about-a-court-or-tribunal.form.service.justice.gov.uk. You should receive a response to your complaint within 10 working days. If you are not happy with the response, you can ask that your complaint is reviewed. You should receive a response within 10 working days.

If you think the matter has still not been resolved satisfactorily, ask the Customer Investigations Team to carry out a further review (the senior manager who dealt with your complaint should give you contact details). The Customer Investigations Team aims to respond within 15 days.

If you are still dissatisfied, you can complain to the Parliamentary and Health Service Ombudsman (see p1445).

Part 9: Getting a benefit decision changed
Chapter 60: Complaints
8. Complaining to the Ombudsman

HMCTS's complaints procedure can be found at gov.uk/government/organisations/hm-courts-and-tribunals-service/about/complaints-procedure.

Complaints about the conduct of tribunal members

If you are unhappy about the way in which you were treated by a tribunal judge or member (eg, because s/he was rude, discourteous or racist), raise the matter initially by writing to the relevant tribunal president within three months of the incident. The name of the appropriate president can be found at judicialconduct.judiciary.gov.uk/contact-a-tribunal-president.

If your complaint is about the conduct of a tribunal president, it should be made to the Judicial Conduct Investigations Office (see complaints.judicialconduct.gov.uk).

If you are not happy with the response to your complaint about a tribunal judge, member or president, you can complain to the Judicial Appointments and Conduct Ombudsman (see gov.uk/guidance/judicial-conduct-complain-to-the-ombudsman). The Ombudsman's decision is final.

7. Using your MP

If you are not satisfied with the response from the officers to whom you have complained, you may wish to take up the matter with your MP. Your MP may also be able to help if you are getting no response to your complaint.

To find out who your MP is and how to contact her/him, call the House of Commons Enquiry Service on 0800 112 4272 (Freephone) or 020 7219 4272, or go to members.parliament.uk/constituencies.

Your MP will probably want to write to the benefit authority for an explanation of what has happened. If you wish to make a complaint to the relevant Ombudsman, you must usually do so through your MP. This does not apply if you are complaining to the Ombudsman about a local authority or tribunal members.

8. Complaining to the Ombudsman

The role of the Ombudsman is to investigate complaints of maladministration by government departments, including avoidable delays, failure to advise about appeal rights or refusal to answer reasonable questions or respond to correspondence, discourteousness, racism or sexism. The Parliamentary and Health Service Ombudsman deals with complaints about central government departments and the Local Government and Social Care Ombudsman (in

England) or the Public Services Ombudsman (in Scotland and Wales) hears complaints about local government.

Should you ask for compensation first?

It is probably better to pursue a compensation payment before making a complaint to the Ombudsman. This is because, if the Ombudsman does not uphold your complaint, the benefit authority is unlikely to compensate you. Wherever possible, get and keep receipts for expenses such as postage, telephone calls, travel and professional advice to help prove the cost of any delay or maladministration.

The Ombudsman does not usually investigate a complaint unless you have exhausted the internal complaints procedure. However, if the authority is not acting on your complaint, or there are unreasonable delays, this delay may also form part of your complaint. The time limit for lodging a complaint with the Ombudsman is normally 12 months from the date you were notified of the matter complained about. However, a delay in bringing a complaint does not necessarily prevent a complaint being investigated if there are good reasons for the delay.

The Ombudsman can look at documents on your claim held by benefit authorities. You may be interviewed to check any facts. The Ombudsman can recommend financial redress if you have been unfairly treated or experienced a loss as a result of the maladministration.

A public body, such as the DWP or a local authority, is required to follow the recommendations of a complaints panel unless there are good reasons not to. If it has failed to do so, you may have grounds to complain to the Ombudsman and, in some circumstances, may have grounds for a judicial review (see p1414).

The Parliamentary and Health Service Ombudsman

The Parliamentary and Health Service Ombudsman deals with complaints about all central government departments. This includes the DWP, HM Revenue and Customs, HM Courts and Tribunals Service and any agencies carrying out functions on behalf of these departments. Complain for Change is a website launched by The Parliamentary and Health Service Ombudsman to encourage and help people to complain about government departments.

To make a complaint, you must write to your MP, who then refers the complaint to the Ombudsman. See p1444 for how to contact your MP. Remember, the Ombudsman can only investigate complaints of maladministration and not complaints about entitlement, which should be dealt with by the First-tier Tribunal.

The Local Government and Social Care Ombudsman/Public Services Ombudsman

If you have tried to sort out your complaint with the local authority but you are still not satisfied with the outcome, you can apply to the Local Government and Social Care Ombudsman (in England) or the Public Services Ombudsman (in Wales and Scotland). The Ombudsman can investigate any cases of maladministration by local authorities, but not matters of entitlement, which are dealt with by the First-tier Tribunal.

You can complain to the Ombudsman either by completing an online form, by post or by telephone (in England see lgo.org.uk/make-a-complaint, in Wales see ombudsman.wales/making-a-complaint, in Scotland see spso.org.uk/making-a-complaint). The Ombudsman may take up to 12 months to complete its investigation but straightforward cases can be dealt with more quickly. A complaint may make the authority review its procedures, which could benefit other claimants.

One outcome of your complaint may be a 'local settlement'. This is where the local authority agrees to take some action that the Ombudsman considers is a satisfactory response to your complaint and the investigation is discontinued. If you are unhappy with the way in which the Ombudsman has dealt with your complaint, you can ask that it is reviewed internally by the Ombudsman or take legal action.

9. **Legal action**

In some circumstances, you may have grounds for judicial review against a benefit authority if, for example, it refuses to process your claim or has made a decision against which you have no right of appeal. For further information about judicial reviews, see p1414.

It is not possible to sue a benefit authority for negligence in the way it decides your claim.[5] However, you can seek compensation through the courts if there has been:

- 'misadvice' – ie, if an employee of a benefit authority or HM Courts and Tribunals Service gives wrong advice which leads to some financial loss for you;
- unpaid benefit – ie, if your benefit claim has been determined, but you have not been paid;
- discrimination, victimisation or harassment under the Equality Act 2010;
- a breach of human rights (see p1380).

Although it is possible to seek compensation through the courts, it should never be your first course of action and should only ever be considered after seeking legal advice.

Notes

2. **Compensation payments**
    1 gov.uk/government/publications/
      compensation-for-poor-service-a-guide-
      for-dwp-staff
    2 gov.uk/hmrc-internal-manuals/
      complaints-and-remedy-guidance

3. **Complaining about the DWP**
    3 gov.uk/government/organisations/
      department-for-work-pensions/about/
      complaints-procedure

4. **Complaining about HM Revenue and
   Customs**
    4 For further details, see CPAG's *Tax
      Credits and Complaints* factsheet at
      cpag.org.uk/content/tax-credits-and-
      complaints.

9. **Legal action**
    5 *Jones v Department of Employment*
      [1989] QB 1

Part 10

General rules for tax credits

Chapter 61

Tax credit amounts

This chapter covers:
1. The relevant period (p1452)
2. The maximum amount of child tax credit (p1452)
3. The maximum amount of working tax credit (p1457)
4. How to calculate the amount of tax credits (p1465)
5. Change of circumstances (p1470)

Key facts

- The amount of tax credits to which you are entitled depends on your family circumstances and your income.
- There are no limits on the amount of savings or other capital that you can have.
- If you get income support (IS), income-based jobseeker's allowance (JSA), income-related employment and support allowance (ESA) or pension credit (PC), you automatically get the maximum amount of tax credits that you could receive.
- If you do not get IS, income-based JSA, income-related ESA or PC, you may get less than your maximum amount of tax credits, depending on the level of your income.
- Your maximum amount of child tax credit depends on how many children you have, and whether any child in your family has a disability.
- The amount of working tax credit depends on whether you are single with no dependants, a lone parent or a member of a couple, the hours you work, whether you (or your partner) are disabled, and whether you have eligible childcare costs.

Part 10: General rules for tax credits
Chapter 61: Tax credit amounts
2. The maximum amount of child tax credit

1. **The relevant period**

The amount of tax credits you can get is based on your entitlement during a 'relevant period'. Tax credit awards are calculated using a maximum annual amount that you could receive.

- Your award is usually calculated on the basis that you will be entitled to tax credits for the whole tax year (6 April to 5 April), and your relevant period is therefore one year.[1] Your annual entitlement is calculated and then paid to you over the course of that year.
- If your circumstances change in the course of the year, and your award is amended, a new relevant period begins. The new relevant period is calculated on the basis that it will end at the end of the tax year.[2] In both cases, you are entitled to tax credits for less than a year, and so only a proportion of the annual amount can be paid.

In order to work out your maximum amount of tax credits exactly, therefore, you must know the length of your relevant period.

Relevant period
A '**relevant period**' for child tax credit (CTC) is the number of days in a period of an award during which your maximum amount remains the same.[3]
A '**relevant period**' for working tax credit (WTC) is the number of days in a period during which the elements making up your maximum amount of tax credit (apart from the childcare element) remain the same and your average weekly childcare charge does not change by £10 or more or reduce to nil.[4]
If you are entitled to both CTC and WTC, a '**relevant period**' is one during which both of the above conditions are satisfied.[5]

2. **The maximum amount of child tax credit**

The maximum amount of child tax credit (CTC) you can get is calculated by adding together the 'elements' that apply to you.[6] The amount of each element is set at an annual rate. The annual rate is converted to a daily rate by dividing it by the number of days in the tax year (365 in 2020/21) and rounding *up* to the nearest penny. To calculate entitlement, the daily rate of each element is then multiplied by the number of days in the relevant period. The effect of this is that entitlement in a whole year is always slightly higher than the annual rates listed below – eg, the family element (£1.50 x 365) works out as £547.50 in 2020/21. If you are entitled to CTC for a period of less than a year, or if your entitlement changes part way through the year, the amount of each of these elements is adjusted so that the correct proportion of your annual maximum amount is paid to you.[7] How entitlement is calculated when entitlement changes part way through a tax year is explained on p1470.

Element	Annual rate	Daily rate
Family element	£545	£1.50
Child element	£2,830	£7.76
Disabled child element	£3,415	£9.36
Severely disabled child element	£1,385	£3.80

Family element

One family element is payable if you are responsible for a child or young person born before 6 April 2017.[8] The family element is not payable in claims that only include children born on or after 6 April 2017. If you are getting CTC for a child born on or after 6 April 2017, without the family element, and then become responsible for another child born before 6 April 2017, the family element is added from the date you became responsible for the older child. If you are responsible for a child born before 6 April 2017, the family element is still payable. You do not have to have been entitled to CTC before 6 April 2017. Only one family element is payable, regardless of how many children you have.

Child element

You get a child element for each child or young person you are responsible for (see p288). However, a child element is not payable for a child born on or after 6 April 2017, if you have two or more other children already included in your CTC award (unless an exception applies – see p1455).[9] This is known as the 'two-child limit' (see below). You get a child element for each child born before 6 April 2017. You do not have to have been entitled to CTC before 6 April 2017.

The two-child limit

In general, you cannot get a child element for a child born on or after 6 April 2017 if you already have two or more other children included in your award, unless an exception applies. You can always get an element for a child born before 6 April 2017.

When establishing the number of children you have for this purpose, a child who is covered by the first two exceptions on p1455 (ie, you have adopted her/him or s/he is living with you under a 'non-parental caring arrangement') is ignored.

So you can get an element for the following:
- any child born before 6 April 2017; *and*

Part 10: General rules for tax credits
Chapter 61: Tax credit amounts
2. The maximum amount of child tax credit

- a child born on or after 6 April 2017 who is not counted as your third or subsequent child; *and*
- a third or subsequent child born on or after 6 April 2017 to whom an exception applies.

Examples

Amy has four children. Three were born before 6 April 2017, and one was born on 6 May 2017. No exceptions apply to the children. Amy gets three child elements for the three children born before 6 April 2017.

Shakira and Josh have three children. Two were born before 6 April 2017 and are Josh's nephews, who have been living with them for several years under a child arrangements order. The other child was born on 6 May 2017. They are entitled to three child elements for all three children. An element is included for the two older children because they were born before 6 April 2017. Because Josh's nephews do not count for the purposes of the two-child limit, an element is also included for the child born on 6 May 2017.

The order of children (ie, whether a child is the first, second, third or subsequent child) is determined by allocating each child a date:
- if you or your partner are the child's parent, according to the child's date of birth; *or*
- in any other case, according to the date you or your partner became responsible for her/him. **Note:** from 28 November 2018, a child who is covered by the first two exceptions on p1455 (ie, you have adopted her/him or s/he is living with you under a non-parental caring arrangement) is not counted.[10] Before 28 November 2018, the High Court held that it was unlawful for you to be affected by the two-child limit because such a child was counted towards the number of your children.[11] If you were affected in this way, HM Revenue and Customs (HMRC) has said that it will pay the child element retrospectively.[12]

The order of children is usually decided according to the earliest of these dates – ie, the child with the earliest allocated date is the 'first child', and so on. However, if the date for two or more children is the same, the order of children must be decided in order to ensure you receive the highest number of child elements.

The child element can become payable for a third child to whom the two-child limit would apply when an older child leaves the household (as you are no longer responsible for her/him) or when a young person leaves education (as s/he no longer qualifies). In these situations, you should report the change as soon as possible so that you continue to get the maximum two child elements. You should always notify the Tax Credit Office of the birth of a third or subsequent child so that the child element can become payable if there is a change, and because other elements for disabled children (see p1456) and childcare costs in working tax credit (see p1460) remain payable.

Note: the two-child limit is currently the subject of a legal challenge. See cpag.org.uk/welfare-rights/legal-test-cases/two-child-limit-challenge for details, and AskCPAG.org.uk and CPAG's *Welfare Rights Bulletin* for updates.

Exceptions

The 'two-child limit' does not apply to the following children.[13]

- A child born in a multiple birth, other than the first born if you already have two or more children. So, if you have:
  - no older children, you get the child element for all children in a multiple birth;
  - one older child, you get the child element for all children in a multiple birth;
  - two or more older children, you get the child element for all but one of the children in a multiple birth.
- A child living with you under a 'non-parental caring arrangement'. This means:
  - a child whose parent is a child or qualifying young person for whom you are responsible; *or*
  - where the child is living with you on a long-term basis because s/he is unable to live with her/his parents and you are caring for her/him as a family member or friend. You or your partner must not be the child's parent or step-parent and you must:
    - be named in a child arrangements order under section 8 of the Children Act 1989 or a residence order under Article 8 of the Children (Northern Ireland) Order 1995 as a person with whom the child is to live; *or*
    - be the appointed or special guardian, or be entitled to guardian's allowance, for the child; *or*
    - have a kinship care order under section 72(1) of the Children and Young People (Scotland) Act 2014, or parental responsibilities or rights under section 80 of the Adoption and Children (Scotland) Act 2007 for the child; *or*
    - continue to be responsible for the child if any of the above bullet points applied immediately before the child's 16th birthday; *or*
    - be caring for the child because otherwise it is likely s/he would be taken into the care of the local authority. You must provide evidence from a social worker (see gov.uk/government/publications/support-for-a-child-who-is-informally-living-with-you).
- A child who is being adopted by you from local authority care or who has been placed with you for adoption. This exception does *not* apply if:
  - you or your partner were the child's step-parent immediately before the adoption;
  - you or your partner have been the child's parent (other than by adoption) at any other time;
  - the child is being adopted directly from abroad.

Part 10: General rules for tax credits
Chapter 61: Tax credit amounts
2. The maximum amount of child tax credit

- A child who is likely to have been conceived as a result of rape, or in a controlling or coercive relationship ('non-consensual conception'). You must not be living at the same address as the alleged perpetrator for this exception to apply, even though you might have been living with the alleged perpetrator at the time of conception. A controlling or coercive relationship includes behaviour that causes you to fear, on at least two occasions, that violence will be used against you, or that causes you serious alarm or distress which has a substantial adverse effect on your day-to-day activities. You must provide evidence from an 'approved person' that you have had contact with her/him or another approved person about the rape or relationship. A list of 'approved persons' is in official guidance and includes healthcare professionals, social workers and approved organisations such as specialist rape charities (see gov.uk/government/publications/support-for-a-child-conceived-without-your-consent/approved-third-party-professionals-who-can-complete-these-forms). Third-party evidence is not required if there has been a conviction for rape or coercive, controlling behaviour in the UK, or for a similar offence abroad, or if you have been awarded criminal injuries compensation after a sexual offence, physical abuse or mental injury, and it is likely that the offence or injury resulted in the conception. You can be treated as having provided evidence if you have already provided it to the DWP for universal credit, income support or jobseeker's allowance purposes.

If you are the step-parent of the child but are no longer part of a couple with the child's parent, the exception can continue to apply if you have continuously been entitled to CTC and responsible for the child. Get advice.[14]

Disabled child element

You get a disabled child element for each child you are responsible for who gets disability living allowance (DLA) (or child disability payment in Scotland), or young person who gets personal independence payment (PIP) or armed forces independence payment, or who is certified as blind or severely sight impaired by a consultant ophthalmologist, or was certified in the last 28 weeks. The element still applies if DLA or PIP has stopped because your child or young person is in hospital.[15] It is paid in addition to the child element for that child. You can get the disabled child element for a third or subsequent child born on or after 6 April 2017 who is disabled, even if you are not getting a child element for her/him.[16] If you were getting CTC in 2016/17 and your child was entitled to DLA or PIP, but you were not getting a disabled child element, the government announced that it would pay the element even if you had not notifed HMRC of the DLA/PIP award.[17]

Severely disabled child element

You get a severely disabled child element for each child you are responsible for who gets the highest rate of the care component of DLA (or the higher rate of child disability payment), the enhanced rate of the daily living component of of PIP or armed forces independence payment. The element still applies if DLA or PIP has stopped because your child or young person is in hospital.[18] It is paid in addition to the child element and disabled child element for that child. You can get the severely disabled child element for a third or subsequent child born on or after 6 April 2017, even if you are not getting a child element for her/him. If you were getting CTC in 2016/17 and your child was entitled to DLA highest care component or PIP enhanced daily living component, but you were not getting a severely disabled child element, the government announced that it would pay the element even if you had not notified HMRC of the DLA/PIP award, or a change in the award.[19] The way the elements are set out in this *Handbook* reflects tax credit award notices, which show that you get a severely disabled child element in addition to a disabled child element.

3. **The maximum amount of working tax credit**

The maximum amount of working tax credit (WTC) you get is calculated by adding together the 'elements' that apply to you.[20] The amount of each element, except the childcare element, is set at an annual rate. The annual rate is converted to a daily rate by dividing by the number of days in the tax year (365 in 2020/21) and rounding up to the nearest penny. To calculate entitlement, the daily rate of each element is then multiplied by the number of days in the relevant period. The effect of this is that entitlement in a whole year is always slightly higher than the annual rates listed below – eg, the lone parent or couple element works out as £2,047.65 in 2020/21 (£5.61 x 365). The amount of the childcare element is set using your average *weekly* childcare costs.[21] See p1460 for how your childcare element is calculated.

If you are entitled to WTC for a period of less than a year, or if your entitlement changes part way through the year, the amount of the elements is adjusted so that the correct proportion of your annual maximum amount is paid.[22] See p1470 for how your entitlement is calculated when it changes part way through a tax year.

Element	Annual rate	Daily rate
Basic element	£3,040	£8.33
Lone parent element	£2,045	£5.61
Couple element	£2,045	£5.61
30-hour element	£825	£2.27
Disabled worker element	£3,220	£8.83
Severe disability element	£1,390	£3.81
Childcare element. For this, see p1460.		

Part 10: General rules for tax credits
Chapter 61: Tax credit amounts
3. The maximum amount of working tax credit

Basic element

One basic element is paid with each award of WTC. To be entitled to this element, you must be engaged in 'qualifying remunerative work'. In this *Handbook* we call this 'full-time paid work' (see p299).[23] Unless you qualify for the basic element of WTC, you cannot qualify for any of the other elements.[24]

Lone parent element

You get the lone parent element if you claim as a single person and are responsible for a child or qualifying young person.[25]

Couple element

You get the couple element if you are a couple making a joint claim (see p1496).[26] If you are not responsible for a child or qualifying young person, you cannot get the couple element if your partner is serving a prison sentence of more than 12 months or is a 'person subject to immigration control' (see p1560), but you must still make a joint claim.[27] You can only have one couple element included in your maximum amount.[28] For when you count as a couple, see p1497.

30-hour element

You get a 30-hour element if you are:[29]
- a single claimant who works for at least 30 hours a week; *or*
- making a joint claim and either or both of you work for at least 30 hours a week; *or*
- making a joint claim, responsible for a child or qualifying young person and:
  – you are both working; *and*
  – one of you works at least 16 hours a week; *and*
  – your joint hours of work total at least 30 hours a week.

You can only have one 30-hour element included in your maximum amount.[30]

Disabled worker element

You get a disabled worker element if you:[31]
- work at least 16 hours a week; *and*
- have a disability which puts you at a disadvantage in getting a job; *and*
- receive, or have recently received, a qualifying benefit for sickness or disability.

If you are claiming as a couple, at least one of you must satisfy all these conditions – ie, the element is not payable if only you are working and your partner is disabled.

If both you and your partner meet all these conditions, two disabled worker elements can be paid.[32]

Having 'a disability which puts you at a disadvantage in getting a job' means you must meet any one of the conditions listed in Appendix 3.[33] For initial claims only (where there has been no entitlement to the disabled worker element in the preceding two years), this can include undergoing a period of rehabilitation as a result of an illness or accident, but only for the remainder of the tax year in which you claim.

In order to count as receiving a 'qualifying benefit', you must satisfy one of the following conditions. A disabled worker element can be included in the calculation of your maximum amount in a new claim or added to an existing tax credit award at any time during the tax year if your award is revised (see p1470). You must:

- for at least one day in the 182 days immediately preceding the date your award is calculated or revised, have been in receipt of:
  - incapacity benefit (IB) at the long-term or short-term higher rate; *or*
  - severe disablement allowance (SDA); *or*
  - employment and support allowance (ESA) for at least 28 weeks (including linked periods); *or*
  - credits for limited capability for work following time limiting of contributory ESA, for at least 28 weeks (including periods on ESA and linked periods); *or*
  - ESA or credits (as above), together with IB, SDA or statutory sick pay (SSP) for at least 28 weeks (including linked periods); *or*
- for at least one day in the 182 days immediately preceding the date your award is calculated or revised, have been in receipt of a disability premium paid for you with income support (IS), income-based jobseeker's allowance (JSA) or housing benefit (HB), or a higher pensioner premium with IS or JSA; *or*
- have received for at least 140 days forming a single period of incapacity for work (see p838) or limited capability for work (see Chapter 45) (the last of which must have fallen within 56 days of the date your award is calculated or revised) SSP, occupational sick pay, ESA or credits for limited capability for work for a period of 20 weeks; *and*
  - have a disability at the date of the claim which is likely to last for at least six months (or for the rest of your life if your death is expected within that time); *and*
  - have gross earnings that are less than they were before the disability began by at least the greater of 20 per cent and £15 a week; *or*
- have undertaken 'training for work' for at least one day in the 56 days immediately preceding the date your award is calculated or revised *and* were receiving one of the benefits or credits listed in the first bullet point above within the 56 days before that training started. 'Training for work' means training provided under the Employment and Training Act 1973, or, in Scotland, the Enterprise and New Towns (Scotland) Act 1990, or training which you attend for 16 hours or more a week if its primary purpose is teaching occupational or vocational skills;[34] *or*
- get disability living allowance (DLA), personal independence payment (PIP), attendance allowance (AA), armed forces independence payment or a mobility

Part 10: General rules for tax credits
Chapter 61: Tax credit amounts
3. The maximum amount of working tax credit

supplement or constant attendance allowance payable with a war pension or industrial injuries disablement benefit (IIDB). If your qualifying benefit stops or is not payable (eg, because you are in hospital), you are no longer entitled to the disability element on these grounds;[35] *or*

- have an invalid carriage or similar vehicle; *or*
- have been entitled to WTC with the disabled worker element under one of the above first four bullet points and still have a disability which puts you at a disadvantage in getting a job (see Appendix 3). In this case, you can continue to be entitled to the disabled worker element indefinitely. **Note:** this does not apply if you previously only qualified through DLA or PIP, but if you were getting HB with a disability premium, you can remain entitled even though DLA or PIP has stopped.[36]

Renewals or linked claims

If you renew or make a further claim for WTC within 56 days of the day your previous award ended, *and* in that earlier claim you qualified for the disabled worker element under any of the first four bullet points above, you are treated as though you still meet those conditions and can continue to get the disabled worker element in your new award. You must also still have a disability which puts you at a disadvantage in getting a job (see Appendix 3 – for renewals and new claims within two years of a previous entitlement to the disabled worker element, this must be under Part 1[37]).

You can still benefit from this linking rule if your income was too high for you to get any WTC within the previous 56 days, provided your maximum amount of WTC would have included the disabled worker element on one of the above grounds.[38]

Severe disability element

You get a severe disability element if you get the highest rate of the care component of DLA, the enhanced rate of the daily living component of PIP, the higher rate of AA, or armed forces independence payment (including if payment of these has been suspended because you are in hospital).[39] If you have a partner who meets this condition, a severe disability element can be included for her/him, whether or not s/he is in work.

If both you and your partner meet the condition, two severe disability elements can be paid.[40]

Childcare element

Your maximum amount of WTC can include a childcare element to help meet the cost of 'relevant childcare' (see p1462).[41] This element is 70 per cent of your actual childcare costs of up to £175 a week for one child or £300 a week for two or more children – ie, up to £122.50 or £210 a week.[42]

To get the childcare element of WTC, you or your partner must be 'responsible for' at least one child.[43] You can include childcare costs for a third or subsequent child born on or after 6 April 2017, even if you do not get the child element for her/him because of the 'two-child limit'. You do not have to be the child's parent. 'Responsible for' has the same meaning for WTC as it does for child tax credit (CTC) (see p288).[44]

The childcare element is part of the maximum WTC calculation and cannot be claimed on its own or as part of CTC.[45]

You must be:[46]

- a lone parent working at least 16 hours a week; *or*
- a member of a couple and:
  - you are both working at least 16 hours a week; *or*
  - one of you is working at least 16 hours a week, and the other is incapacitated (see below), entitled to carer's allowance (including an underlying entitlement) or is in hospital or in prison (serving a sentence or remanded in custody).

You are still entitled to the childcare element during periods throughout which you are treated as being in work for WTC purposes – eg, during the first 39 weeks of maternity leave or the four-week run-on period (see p304).[47]

Incapacitated

You or your partner are treated as being '**incapacitated**' if you (or your partner, if s/he is the one who is not working):[48]

- get IB or SDA; *or*
- have been getting contributory ESA for at least 28 weeks; *or*
- get contributory ESA after a period on SSP, which adds up to at least 28 weeks, provided you satisfied the national insurance contribution conditions for contributory ESA (the 28 weeks can have been in one period or in periods that can be linked together); *or*
- get contributory ESA after being transferred from IB or SDA; *or*
- are entitled to credits for limited capability for work only because your contributory ESA has stopped after 52 weeks; *or*
- get AA, DLA, PIP or armed forces independence payment (or an equivalent award paid as an increase under the war pensions or industrial injuries disablement scheme), or would get it but for the fact that you are in hospital; *or*
- get IIDB with constant attendance allowance; *or*
- have an award of HB which includes a disability premium or a childcare earnings disregard, because the non-working member of the couple is incapacitated; *or*
- were treated as incapacitated solely on the basis of being paid council tax benefit on 31 March 2013 that included a disability premium because the non-working member of the couple was incapacitated, but only if your entitlement to WTC remains continuous from 1 April 2013; *or*
- have an invalid carriage or similar vehicle; *or*
- get an equivalent benefit from a European Economic Area (EEA) country.[49]

Part 10: General rules for tax credits
Chapter 61: Tax credit amounts
3. The maximum amount of working tax credit

You can claim the childcare element for a new baby as well as for any other children for whom you are responsible while you are on statutory maternity, adoption, paternity or shared parental leave (for the first 39 weeks only), or while you are paid maternity allowance. See p304 for these and other situations when you are treated as being in full-time work.

Relevant childcare charges can be for any child in your family up to the last day of the week in which 1 September falls, following the child's 15th birthday or her/his 16th birthday if s/he qualifies for the disabled child element (see p1456).[50]

You can only include the charges that you pay. If you get childcare vouchers from your employer, your WTC cannot include the childcare element for the amount covered by the voucher.

You cannot get tax-free childcare and tax credits at the same time, and your entire tax credit claim will end if you apply for, and are awarded, tax-free childcare payments.[51]

You cannot get the childcare element for free early years' entitlement or for charges in respect of the child's compulsory education or, in England, for childcare during school hours for a child of compulsory school age. If you have made an agreement for the provision of future childcare, you can include charges which you will pay and you can notify HM Revenue and Customs (HMRC) of the charges up to a week in advance.[52]

Relevant childcare

In England, in order to be 'relevant childcare', the childcare must be:[53]
- provided by a childcare provider correctly registered by Ofsted; *or*
- provided by a childminder who is registered with a childminder agency registered with Ofsted; *or*
- provided to a child who is three or four years old by a school under the direction of the school's governing body (or equivalent) on school premises or premises that may be inspected as part of an inspection of the school by the Chief Inspector; *or*
- out-of-school-hours childcare or supervised activity-based childcare provided for a child aged between five and 15 years (16 if disabled) by a school on the school premises or premises that may be inspected as part of an inspection of the school by the Chief Inspector; *or*
- provided for a child by a person registered with the Care Quality Commission as a service provider in relation to the regulated activity of personal care; *or*
- provided by a foster parent who is also registered with Ofsted, but not in respect of the child who is being fostered by that foster parent.

In Wales, in order to be 'relevant childcare', the childcare must be:[54]
- provided by a childcare provider registered by the Care Inspectorate Wales; *or*
- provided by an approved foster parent, who is providing daycare or childminding for a child aged eight or over, but not for a child who is being

fostered by that foster parent. If the child is under eight, the foster parent must also be registered by the Care Inspectorate Wales; *or*
- out-of-school-hours childcare provided by a school on the school premises or by a local authority; *or*
- provided in the child's home by a person approved under the Tax Credits (Approval of Child Care Providers) (Wales) Scheme 2007 or, if several children are being looked after, in one of the children's homes; *or*
- provided by a domiciliary worker or nurse from an agency registered under the Regulation and Inspection of Social Care (Wales) Act 2016 in the child's home.

In Scotland, in order to be 'relevant childcare', the childcare must be:[55]
- provided by a childcare provider registered by the Care Inspectorate; *or*
- in an out-of-school-hours childcare club registered by the Care Inspectorate; *or*
- provided in the child's home by, or introduced through, a childcare agency, sitter service or nanny agency registered by the Care Inspectorate.

If you are a member of the armed forces or a civil servant working for the Ministry of Defence in another country, you can include childcare costs approved by the Department for Education.[56] If you use a childcare provider in another EEA country, you can include childcare costs approved under that country's equivalent registration scheme.[57]

You cannot get help with the costs of childcare provided in your own home if that care is provided by a relative of your child.

'**Relative**' means parent, grandparent, aunt or uncle, brother or sister, whether related by blood, marriage, civil partnership or 'affinity'.[58] By 'affinity', we understand that HMRC means people who are related through a partner, rather than a spouse or civil partner. For example, if childcare is provided in your home by your partner's mother, she is related to the child by affinity, even if your partner is not the child's parent, and so you cannot claim for the cost of paying her.

You can claim help with the costs of childcare provided by a relative away from your home, but s/he must also be a registered or approved childminder. In practice, it is unlikely that a childminder would be able to remain registered for long if only looking after a child to whom s/he was related – contact the relevant agency for advice in this situation. If approved under the Tax Credits (Approval of Child Care Providers) (Wales) Scheme 2007, s/he must also care for at least one other child who is not related to her/him.[59]

The amount of the childcare element

Step one: work out your relevant period

Add up the number of days in your relevant period (see p1452). If you are making or renewing a claim for tax credits for a new tax year, your award is usually based

Part 10: General rules for tax credits
Chapter 61: Tax credit amounts
3. The maximum amount of working tax credit

on entitlement at the same rate for a whole tax year, and your relevant period is one year. The tax year 2020/21 has 365 days.

Step two: calculate your relevant childcare charge

Your 'relevant childcare charge' is your average weekly charge. The way in which your average weekly charge is calculated depends on whether you pay for childcare weekly, monthly or at some other interval, and on whether the amount you pay varies over time.[60]

- If you pay for childcare on a weekly basis and the charge is a fixed weekly amount, add together the charges in the most recent four weeks before the claim and divide by four.
- If you pay for childcare on a weekly basis, have paid for childcare for at least 52 weeks and the charge varies over time, add together the charges in the last 52 weeks and divide by 52.
- If you pay on a monthly basis and the charge is a fixed monthly amount, multiply that monthly amount by 12 and divide the total by 52.
- If you pay on a monthly basis and the charge varies from month to month, add together the charges for the last 12 months and divide the total by 52.
- If there is insufficient information for HMRC to establish your average weekly charge by any of the above methods, the charge is calculated on the basis of information you provide about your childcare costs, using any method which, in its opinion, is reasonable.
- If you have entered into an agreement to pay for childcare that will be provided during the period of your award, your average weekly childcare costs are calculated on the basis of your own written estimate of these. In practice, you provide this estimate on your tax credit claim form.
- If you are only paying childcare costs for a fixed period (eg, over the summer holidays), your relevant childcare charge can be averaged and paid over that period rather than over the whole year.

When you have calculated your average weekly childcare charges by one of these methods, round the figure up to the nearest whole pound. This is the figure that you should notify to HMRC. If this weekly amount is less than the maximum of £175 a week for one child, or £300 a week for two or more children, your actual childcare costs are used, as in Step three. If your actual childcare costs are more than these limits, the maximum amounts are used, as in Step four. There is no minimum amount of childcare charges that can be included.

Step three: calculate your actual childcare costs for the relevant period

The weekly amount from Step two is converted to an amount covering your relevant period. Multiply the weekly charge by 52 to calculate the annual amount. Divide this figure by the number of days in the current tax year to find the daily rate, and then multiply this daily rate by the number of days in your relevant period. This gives your childcare costs for the relevant period. There is no rounding up or down for actual childcare costs at this stage.[61]

Step four: calculate your maximum eligible childcare costs for the relevant period
The maximum eligible weekly amounts are divided by seven and rounded up to the nearest penny to find the daily rate. This daily rate is then multiplied by the number of days in the relevant period.

Maximum childcare costs	Weekly rate	Daily rate
One child	£175	£25.00
Two or more children	£300	£42.86

Step five: calculate the childcare element for the relevant period
Take the lower of the two figures from Steps three and four, and calculate 70 per cent of that figure. Round the amount up to the nearest penny. This gives your childcare element for the relevant period.

Example
Tracy pays a fixed amount of £200 every week in eligible childcare costs for her two children. Her childcare element for the whole of the tax year is calculated as follows.
Step one: work out her relevant period
Tracy's relevant period is one year (365 days).
Step two: calculate her relevant childcare charge
Her relevant childcare charge is £200 a week for two children. This is below the maximum of £300 a week, so her actual childcare costs are used.
Step three: calculate her actual childcare costs for the relevant period
£200 x 52 = £10,400
(£10,400 ÷ 365) x 365 = £10,400
Step four is not necessary because actual childcare costs are below the maximum.
Step five: calculate the childcare element for the relevant period
Childcare element is 70% x £10,400 = £7,280
Tracy's childcare element for the relevant period (in this case, one whole tax year) is £7,280.

4. **How to calculate the amount of tax credits**

If you get certain benefits

If you or your partner get income support (IS), income-based jobseeker's allowance (JSA), income-related employment and support allowance (ESA) or pension credit

Part 10: General rules for tax credits
Chapter 61: Tax credit amounts
4. How to calculate the amount of tax credits

(PC), you are automatically entitled to the maximum amount of child tax credit (CTC) or working tax credit (WTC). **Note:** this does not apply to WTC during the four-week 'run-on' period after stopping work (see p305).[62] You calculate the maximum amount by adding together the elements of each tax credit for which you qualify over your relevant period, as described on pp1452–65. Your maximum amount is not subject to any reduction during the period you are getting IS, income-based JSA, income-related ESA or PC, regardless of your income in the rest of the current or previous tax year (but see Chapter 64 if an overpayment is being recovered from your award).

If you do not get certain benefits

If you or your partner do *not* get IS, income-based JSA, income-related ESA or PC, your entitlement is worked out as described below.

Step one: work out your relevant period

Add up the number of days in your relevant period (see p1452). If you are making a claim for tax credits at the beginning of a new tax year, your award is based on entitlement at the same rate for a whole tax year, and your relevant period is one year. The tax year 2020/21 has 365 days.

Step two: calculate your maximum entitlement for the relevant period

First, identify the different elements of each tax credit for which you are eligible. Take the daily rate (see p21) of each element, apart from the childcare element of WTC.

Multiply this daily rate by the number of days in the relevant period. Add the adjusted amounts of each element together. Next, calculate your childcare element for the relevant period as described on p1463.

Add the childcare element for the relevant period to the other elements for the relevant period to find your maximum entitlement for the relevant period.

Step three: work out your relevant income

The income used in the tax credit calculation is called your 'relevant income' (see Chapter 62).

HM Revenue and Customs (HMRC) begins by using your previous tax year's income to calculate your award for the current year. To finalise your entitlement at the end of the tax year, it requires details of your income in the year that has just ended (the current year's income) and compares this with the previous year's income. If your income has not changed, the current year's income is used. If your income has changed by a disregarded amount or less, your entitlement is still based on the previous year's income. If your income has changed by more than a disregarded amount, your entitlement is based on the current year's income after the disregard. Your relevant income is calculated as follows.[63]

- If your current year's income is more than your previous year's income and the difference is not more than £2,500, your previous year's income is used.
- If your current year's income is more than your previous year's income and the difference is more than £2,500, your current year's income minus £2,500 is used.
- If your current year's income is less than your previous year's income and the difference is not more than £2,500, your previous year's income is used.
- If your current year's income is less than your previous year's income and the difference is more than £2,500, your current year's income plus £2,500 is used.

Divide this income by the number of days in the tax year to which your claim for tax credits relates (365 in 2020/21) to find the daily rate, then multiply this by the number of days in the relevant period. Round this amount down to the nearest penny. This is your income in the relevant period. See p1474 for more on relevant income, including if your tax credit award is finalised during the year because you become entitled to universal credit.

Step four: compare your income with the threshold

Find the annual threshold that applies to you.
- If you are entitled to WTC only, the annual threshold is £6,530.
- If you are entitled to WTC *and* CTC, the annual threshold is £6,530.
- If you are entitled to CTC only, the annual threshold is £16,385.

Divide the threshold that applies to you by the number of days in the current tax year, then multiply this figure by the number of days in the relevant period. Round this amount up to the nearest penny. This figure is your threshold for the relevant period.

Step five: calculate tax credit entitlement for the relevant period

- If your income is less than the threshold that applies to you, you get the maximum amount of tax credit(s).
- If your income is greater than the threshold that applies to you, subtract the threshold figure from your relevant income to find your excess income. Calculate 41 per cent of this excess income and round this figure down to the nearest penny. Finally, reduce your maximum amount of tax credit(s) by this amount.
- The different elements of your maximum tax credit are tapered away in a set order.
  - First, the elements of WTC, except for the childcare element, are reduced.
  - Second, the childcare element is reduced.
  - Third, the child elements of CTC plus any disabled or severely disabled child elements for your children are reduced.
  - Finally, the family element is reduced.

Part 10: General rules for tax credits
Chapter 61: Tax credit amounts
4. How to calculate the amount of tax credits

If you get CTC only, or WTC only, and the calculation results in entitlement of less than £26, no tax credit award is made. If you get both CTC and WTC and the total entitlement is less than £26, no award is made.[64]

To find out the amount of your weekly payment, divide the above total by the number of days in your relevant period to find the daily rate and then multiply this daily rate by seven. If your tax credit is paid four-weekly, multiply the daily rate by 28 to calculate the amount of your payments.

Example

Tracy has been getting tax credits for several years. During 2019/20, she worked 20 hours a week and earned £8.21 an hour gross. During the tax year 2020/21, she expects to continue to work the same hours, with a rise in pay to £8.72 an hour.

Step one: work out the relevant period

Tracy's relevant period is 365 days in 2020/21.

Step two: calculate her maximum entitlement for the relevant period

		Daily rate	x 365
CTC	Family element	£1.50	£547.50
	Child element for two-year-old child	£7.76	£2,832.40
	Child element for four-year-old child	£7.76	£2,832.40
WTC	Basic element	£8.33	£3,040.00
	Lone parent element	£5.61	£2,047.65
	Childcare element		£7,280.00
Maximum amount of tax credits			**£18,580.40**

Step three: work out her relevant income

In 2019/20, Tracy earned £8,585.31 ((£8.21 x 20 hours) ÷ 7 days) x 366 (rounded down to the nearest penny).

She continues at the same hours, with a small rise in pay during 2020/21.

In 2020/21, she expects to earn £9,093.71 ((£8.72 x 20 hours) ÷ 7 days) x 365 (rounded down to the nearest penny).

During the year in which tax credits are paid (2020/21), as the increase is below the disregard, her income for the year 2019/20 is used.

Tracy's income for the relevant period is therefore:

(£8,585.31 ÷ 365) x 365 = £8,585.31 (rounded down to the nearest penny)

Step four: compare her income with the threshold for the relevant period

As Tracy is eligible for both WTC and CTC, her annual threshold figure is £6,530.

The threshold for the relevant period is therefore:

(£6,530 ÷ 365) x 365 = £6,530 (rounded up to the nearest penny)

Step five: calculate tax credit entitlement for the relevant period

Tracy has excess income of £2,055.31 (income of £8,585.31 minus the threshold figure of £6,530).

Apply the taper of 41 per cent to this excess income:

41% x £2,055.31 = £842.67 (rounded down to the nearest penny)

Tracy's maximum tax credit (£18,580.40) is reduced by this amount. Her total tax credit entitlement is:

£18,580.40 – £842.67 = £17,737.73

The reduction is first applied to the elements of her WTC, apart from the childcare element. Tracy's tax credit entitlement for the tax year 2020/21 is:

WTC (not including childcare element)	£4,245.43
Childcare element	£7,280.00
CTC	£6,212.30
Total tax credits	**£17,737.73**

Tax credits are paid weekly or four-weekly. To find the approximate weekly rate of payment, this figure is divided by 365 (the number of days in Tracy's relevant period) and multiplied by 7.

(£17,737.73 ÷ 365) x 7 = £340.18

Calculating the amount of tax credits: a quick way

For a rough projection of an award, you can use the annual rates as follows.

Step one: calculate maximum tax credits

Add together the annual rates of CTC and WTC elements to which you are entitled. For the childcare element, multiply 70 per cent of the weekly cost by 52 to give an annual amount.

Step two: work out relevant income

This is either your income in the previous tax year, or an estimate of your current year's income after a disregard, if it has increased or decreased by more than the disregarded amounts (see p1466).

Step three: compare income with threshold

The threshold is £6,530 if you are eligible for WTC only, or to WTC and CTC. The threshold is £16,385 if you are eligible for CTC only – ie, you are not working sufficient hours to qualify for WTC.

If your income is below the threshold, the maximum tax credit in Step one is payable.

If your income is above the threshold, the difference is used for Step four.

Step four: work out tax credits payable

The maximum amount of tax credits in Step one is reduced by 41 per cent of your income above the threshold in Step three. This gives an annual figure for a complete tax year, which can be misleading as circumstances may change. It may be more helpful to divide by 52 to give a weekly income figure.

Part 10: General rules for tax credits
Chapter 61: Tax credit amounts
5. Change of circumstances

Note: a new calculation must be made if your circumstances change or if your income goes up or down by more than you estimated.

Example

As in the previous examples, Tracy is a lone parent with two children, working 20 hours a week, earning £8.72 an hour (in 2020/21), paying £200 a week for childcare.

Step one: calculate maximum tax credits

Maximum CTC = £545 (family element) + £5,660 (two child elements) = £6,205

Maximum WTC = £3,040 (basic element) + £2,045 (lone parent element) + £7,280 (childcare element £200 x 70% x 52 weeks) = £12,365

Total = £18,570

Step two: work out relevant income

Relevant income = £8,538.40 (£8.21 x 20 x 52 weeks in 2019/20)

Step three: compare income with threshold

£8,538.40 (income) – £6,530 (threshold) = £2,008.40

Step four: work out tax credits payable

£18,570 (maximum tax credits) – £823.44 (£2,008.40 x 41%) = £17,746.56 tax credits payable for complete tax year = £341.28 a week.

5. Change of circumstances

There are different ways in which a change in your circumstances can affect your entitlement to tax credits.

- If your circumstances change in a way that affects your maximum entitlement, a new relevant period begins. For example, if a disability benefit which gives entitlement to a disability element is awarded to you or someone included in your award, this changes your maximum amount of tax credit and starts a new relevant period.
- Other changes, such as becoming single or part of a couple, bring your award to an end. You usually have to claim universal credit (UC) instead.
- Changes in income do not affect your maximum entitlement and do not bring your existing award to an end, but can affect the amount of tax credit which is payable to you. For example, if your existing award has been based on your current tax year's income and you have a significant rise in your income during that tax year, you may be overpaid tax credit, unless you report the change at once, enabling your award to be recalculated.

See p1507 for more information about how these changes affect your award.

In any of these circumstances, your tax credit award must be recalculated. Work through Steps one to five on pp1466–67, for each relevant period.

Example

Tracy claims disability living allowance (DLA) for her four-year-old child and the middle rate of the care component is awarded from day 201 of the tax year 2020/21. She therefore has two relevant periods during this tax year. The first is 200 days long, and the second, from the date her daughter is awarded DLA, is 165 days long. Two calculations must be done.

The first calculation

Step one: work out the relevant period

Tracy's relevant period is 200 days without the disabled child element.

Step two: calculate maximum entitlement for the relevant period

		Daily rate	x 200
CTC	Family element	£1.50	£300
	Child element for two-year-old child	£7.76	£1,552
	Child element for four-year-old child	£7.76	£1,552
WTC	Basic element	£8.33	£1,666
	Lone parent element	£5.61	£1,122
	Childcare element		£3,989.05
Maximum tax credits			**£10,181.05**

Step three: work out her relevant income

Relevant income is (£8,585.31 ÷ 365) x 200 = £4,704.27 (rounded down to the nearest penny)

Step four: compare her income with the threshold for the relevant period

Threshold for the relevant period is (£6,530 ÷ 365) x 200 = £3,578.09 (rounded up to the nearest penny)

Step five: calculate tax credit entitlement for the relevant period

Tracy has excess income of £1,126.18 (income £4,704.27 minus threshold £3,578.09).

41% x £1,126.18 = £461.73 (rounded down to the nearest penny)

Maximum tax credit £10,181.05 reduced by £461.73 = £9,719.32

Tracy's tax credit entitlement for the first relevant period of 200 days is £9,147.32.

Part 10: General rules for tax credits
Chapter 61: Tax credit amounts
5. Change of circumstances

The second calculation

Step one: work out the relevant period

Tracy's relevant period is 165 days with the disabled child element.

Step two: calculate maximum entitlement for the relevant period

		Daily rate	x 165
CTC	Family element	£1.50	£247.50
	Child element for two-year-old child	£7.76	£1,280.40
	Child element for four-year-old child	£7.76	£1,280.40
	Disabled child element	£9.36	£1,544.40
WTC	Basic element	£8.33	£1,374.45
	Lone parent element	£5.61	£925.65
	Childcare element		£3,290.96
Maximum tax credits			**£9,943.76**

Step three: work out her relevant income

Relevant income is (£8,585.31 ÷ 365) x 165 = £3,881.03 (rounded down to the nearest penny)

Step four: compare her income with the threshold for the relevant period

Threshold for the relevant period is (£6,530 ÷ 365) x 165 = £2,951.92 (rounded up to the nearest penny)

Step five: calculate tax credit entitlement for the relevant period

Tracy has excess income of £929.11 (income £3,881.03 minus threshold £2,951.92).

41% x £929.11 = £380.93 (rounded down to the nearest penny)

Maximum tax credit £9,943.76 reduced by £380.93 = £9,562.83

Tracy's tax credit entitlement for the second relevant period of 165 days is £9,562.83.

The final amount of tax credits if you claim universal credit

10

If your tax credits claim is finalised during the year (see p1516) because you claim or become entitled to UC, your income is treated differently. This may happen if you become part of a couple with someone who is already getting UC, or if you make a claim for UC. In this situation, your part-year income up to the date you become entitled to UC is required. Your income in the part year is divided by the number of days in that part year, and then multiplied by the number of days in the tax year (365) to find your 'notional current year income'. This figure is then compared with your income in the previous year. If your notional current year income in 2020/21 has increased or decreased compared to 2019/20 by more than £2,500, your notional current year income is used, after applying the disregard. Your notional current year income is divided by 365 and then multiplied by the number of days in the relevant period and rounded down to the nearest penny to find your income in the relevant period.[65] See p1477 for more information.

Notes

1. The relevant period
1. s5(1) TCA 2002
2. s5(2) TCA 2002
3. Reg 8(2) TC(ITDR) Regs
4. Reg 7(2) TC(ITDR) Regs
5. Reg 8(2) TC(ITDR) Regs

2. The maximum amount of child tax credit
6. Reg 7 CTC Regs
7. Regs 7 and 8 TC(ITDR) Regs
8. s13 WRWA 2016
9. s13 WRWA 2016
10. Reg 9(1)(a)(ii) CTC Regs
11. *SC and Others v SSWP* [2018] EWHC 864 (Admin)
12. Email to CPAG, 15 November 2018
13. Regs 9-13 CTC Regs
14. Reg 14 CTC Regs
15. Reg 8(1) and (2) CTC Regs
16. s13(3) WRWA 2016
17. Autumn Statement 2016
18. Reg 8(1) and (3) CTC Regs
19. Autumn Statement 2016; HMRC email to CPAG, 18 December 2018

3. The maximum amount of working tax credit
20. Reg 20 WTC(EMR) Regs
21. Reg 15 WTC(EMR) Regs
22. Regs 7 and 8 TC(ITDR) Regs
23. Reg 4 WTC(EMR) Regs
24. Reg 3(2) WTC(EMR) Regs
25. Reg 12 WTC(EMR) Regs
26. Reg 11(1) WTC(EMR) Regs
27. Reg 11 WTC(EMR) Regs
28. Reg 3 WTC(EMR) Regs
29. Reg 10 WTC(EMR) Regs
30. Reg 3 WTC(EMR) Regs
31. Reg 9 WTC(EMR) Regs
32. Reg 3(3) WTC(EMR) Regs
33. For further guidance on the terms used, see TCM 0122060
34. Reg 9B WTC(EMR) Regs
35. R(TC) 1/06
36. HMRC, Helpsheet TC956, *How to Qualify for the Disability Elements of Tax Credits*, October 2019, p4; *PW v HMRC (TC)* [2018] UKUT 12 (AAC)
37. Reg 9A WTC(EMR) Regs
38. Reg 9(8) WTC(EMR) Regs
39. Reg 17 WTC(EMR) Regs
40. Reg 3(3) WTC(EMR) Regs
41. Regs 3 and 13 WTC(EMR) Regs
42. Reg 20(3) WTC(EMR) Regs
43. Reg 14(1) WTC(EMR) Regs
44. Reg 14(1) WTC(EMR) Regs
45. Reg 20 WTC(EMR) Regs
46. Reg 13(1) WTC(EMR) Regs
47. Regs 5-8 WTC(EMR) Regs; Explanatory Memorandum to The Working Tax Credit (Entitlement and Maximum Rate) (Amendment) Regulations 2009, No.1829
48. Reg 13(4) WTC(EMR) Regs
49. *AS v HMRC (TC)* [2017] UKUT 361 (AAC)
50. Reg 14(3) WTC(EMR) Regs
51. s30 Childcare Payments Act 2014
52. Reg 14(6) WTC(EMR) Regs; reg 27(2A) and (5B) TC(CN) Regs
53. Reg 14(2) WTC(EMR) Regs; see also HMRC leaflet WTC5, *Working Tax Credit: help with the costs of childcare*
54. Reg 14(2)(f) WTC(EMR) Regs
55. Reg 14(2)(b) WTC(EMR) Regs
56. Reg 4(2)(d)(ii) WTC(EMR) Regs
57. Reg 4(2)(d)(i) WTC(EMR) Regs
58. Reg 14(1A)(a) and (1B)(a) WTC(EMR) Regs
59. Reg 14(1A)(d) WTC(EMR) Regs
60. Reg 15 WTC(EMR) Regs
61. Reg 7(3) TC(ITDR) Regs, steps 7-10

4. How to calculate the amount of tax credits
62. ss7(2) and 13 TCA 2002; reg 4 TC(ITDR) Regs
63. s7(3) TCA 2002; reg 5 TC(ITDR) Regs
64. Reg 9 TC(ITDR) Regs

5. Change of circumstances
65. Reg 12A and Sch UC(TP) Regs, as amended by UC(TP)(A) Regs

10

Chapter 62

Income: tax credits

This chapter covers:
1. Relevant income (below)
2. Whose income counts (p1478)
3. What income counts (p1478)
4. Notional income (p1491)

Key facts
- The amount of tax credits to which you are entitled depends on how much income you have.
- In general, most taxable income is taken into account and non-taxable income is ignored, but there are exceptions.
- The assessment is usually based on income for a full tax year, 6 April to 5 April.
- The amount to which you are entitled changes if your income increases or decreases by more than £2,500 in the current year compared with the previous year.
- Your savings or other capital are not taken into account, and you are eligible for tax credits whatever the level of your capital. However, interest and other income earned from savings or capital do count.

10

1. Relevant income

Tax credits are calculated using your 'relevant income'.
- If your income has not changed by more than £2,500, your relevant income is your income in the complete tax year before your claim (the previous year's income).
- If your income has changed by more than £2,500, your relevant income is your income in the complete tax year of your claim (the current year's income) after a disregard has been applied.
- If you have become entitled to universal credit (UC), your relevant income is determined by comparing your previous year's income with your income in the part of the year up to the date your entitlement to tax credits stops (the part-year income) spread over the full year. If this has changed by more than

£2,500, your relevant income is the part-year income, after a disregard has been applied.

The tax credit assessment is based on income over a full tax year (6 April to 5 April) except during a time when you are getting income support (IS), income-based jobseeker's allowance (JSA), income-related employment and support allowance (ESA) or pension credit (PC). If the tax credit award only runs for part of the year, the full year's income is reduced on a pro rata basis (see p1466), unless your tax credit claim has ended because you are entitled to UC.

Note: while you are on IS, income-based JSA, income-related ESA or PC, you are entitled to maximum tax credits, so the level of your income in the previous or current year does not matter. When your benefit stops, the tax credit award is again based on your relevant income.

Previous year's income

Tax credit awards are initially based on your income in the tax year before the year of the award. This is referred to as the 'previous year's income'. So, for a tax credit award made from 6 April 2020, the previous year is 2019/20. Your tax credit entitlement is finalised at the end of the year by comparing this figure with your income in the year of the award (the current year's income – see below). Your income can increase or decrease by up to £2,500 compared with the previous year without it affecting your final entitlement in the current year. If your income has not changed by more than £2,500, your final tax credit entitlement is still based on the previous year's income. Changes of less than £2,500 do not affect your award until the following year.

If HM Revenue and Customs (HMRC) does not receive any information about a change in your income, your award continues to be based on the previous year's income until the end of the tax year.

Current year's income

Your final tax credit entitlement is based on a comparison of your income in the previous year with your income in the year of the award (the current year's income). So, for a tax credits award made from 6 April 2020, the current year is 2020/21. An annual amount for a complete tax year is required, which you may not know for certain until the end of the tax year, but you can provide an estimate during the year. At the end of each tax year, HMRC finalises your entitlement by comparing your previous year's income with your current year's income, and applying a disregard of £2,500 for an increase or decrease in income. This process is called the 'annual review'.

If your income in the current year (2020/21):[1]
- has not changed since the previous year, the current year's income is used;
- has decreased by £2,500 or less, the previous year's income is used;

Part 10: General rules for tax credits
Chapter 62: Income: tax credits
1. Relevant income

- has decreased by more than £2,500, the current year's income plus £2,500 is used;
- has increased by £2,500 or less, the previous year's income is used;
- has increased by more than £2,500, the current year's income minus £2,500 is used.

If you tell HMRC during the year about an increase in income of more than £2,500 compared with the previous year, your award can be revised based on an estimate of the current year's income less a disregard of £2,500. This is advisable if you want to reduce the risk of overpayments at the end of the year.

If you expect your income in the current year to decrease by more than £2,500 compared with the previous year, tell HMRC. It may adjust your award, basing it on your estimate plus £2,500. Tell HMRC quickly if you later think your estimate was too low so it can readjust your award. If you do not, you could end up with an overpayment. HMRC may also use a figure for your earnings it obtains via 'real-time information' from your employer for PAYE (pay as you earn) tax purposes.

You can phone the Tax Credit Helpline or write to the Tax Credit Office with details of your current year's income. There is no special form to complete, so make sure you provide full details of *all* your (and your partner's) relevant income for the current year. At the end of the year, HMRC carries out an annual review and you are usually required to declare your income for the year that has just ended.

Examples

From 6 April 2019 to 5 April 2020, Izzy worked part time and earned a total of £8,000. Since then, she has increased her hours and expects to earn £12,500 in the current year of the award, from 6 April 2020 to 5 April 2021. Her tax credit award is initially based on income of £8,000. Because her income is expected to increase by £4,500 in the current year (ie, above the £2,500 disregard), her final entitlement is based on an income of £10,000 (£12,500 – £2,500). She should report this change during the year to avoid an overpayment.

From 6 April 2019 to 5 April 2020, Marsha and Bill, who are claiming as a couple, had a total income of £27,000. In the current year of the award, from 6 April 2020 to 5 April 2021, Marsha stops work and they expect to earn £11,000 between them. Their tax credit award is initially based on the previous year's income of £27,000. Because their income is expected to decrease by £16,000 in the current year (£27,000 – £11,000), their final entitlement is based on income of £13,500 (£11,000 + £2,500). For the next year, 6 April 2021 to 5 April 2022, if they are still getting tax credits, their award will initially be based on an income of £11,000.

Part-year income

If your tax credit award has ended because you are entitled to UC, your income for part of that year is used. This allows your tax credits claim to be finalised during the year, so that you do not get an annual review at the end of the tax year (see p1516). This can happen if you become a couple with someone who is entitled to UC or if you make a claim for UC. HMRC may decide to wait until the end of the year to finalise an award, if it decides it is not practical to do so during the year.[2]

If your tax credit award is finalised during the tax year because you claim UC, you are asked to provide details of your income in the earlier part of the year, up to the date you become entitled to UC. Your income from 6 April to the date your tax credit award ends is divided by the number of days in that part of the year, and multiplied by the number of days in the tax year (365 in 2020/21), then rounded down to the nearest pound. This is referred to as 'notional current year income' in the legislation.[3] The result is compared with your 2019/20 income, applying the disregard of £2,500 for an increase or decrease.

Example

From 6 April 2019 to 5 April 2020, Jo received tax credits as a lone parent working 16 hours a week at £12 an hour, with an income of £9,984. From 6 April 2020 to 12 October 2020, she continues to claim tax credits as a lone parent in the same job, although she takes on extra shifts, working 28 hours a week. On 13 October 2020 she moves in with her partner, Sam, who is getting UC. Jo's tax credit claim ends and Sam's UC claim becomes a joint claim. HMRC asks Jo to provide details of her earnings from 6 April 2020 to 12 October 2020, a period of 190 days. She calculates the gross taxable amount she has earned in this period, including the extra shifts, which she works out as £9,072. HMRC takes this figure, divides it by 190 and multiplies it by 365, then rounds down to the nearest pound, which works out as £17,427. As this exceeds Jo's 2019/20 income by more than £2,500, the notional current year's income after applying the disregard is £14,927. This is the relevant income for the final tax credits assessment (see p1466, Step 3). There is no reassessment at the end of the tax year, even though she earns much less in the latter part of the year.

Estimating income

There are no special rules for how to estimate income. Using, for instance, payslips and benefit award letters, work out how much income you have already received in the current year and estimate how much you will receive for the remainder of the year. Tax credits are always worked out using annual income (unless you claim UC – see p1516), so you must include all income received or estimated for the whole tax year, 6 April to 5 April, even if you are asking for an award to be adjusted part way through the year.

Part 10: General rules for tax credits
Chapter 62: Income: tax credits
3. What income counts

If you are self-employed, HMRC's self-assessment helpline (tel: 0300 200 3310; textphone: 0300 200 3319) can advise you how to work out your business profits. You must estimate your profits for the accounting period that ends in the current tax year. This might be different from your current earnings, particularly if your accounting year end is early in the tax year.

You should always make it clear that you are using an estimate. There is a box to tick on the annual declaration to do this. If you provide an estimate in response to an annual declaration, you must be notified that this is to be treated as your actual income unless you rectify your estimate by a specified date, which must be at least 30 days after the notice and no later than 31 January.[4]

2. **Whose income counts**

If you are a member of a couple (see p1497), your partner's income is added to yours.[5] Otherwise, only your own income counts.

If you were previously getting tax credits as a couple, but you are now a single claimant, only your individual income in the previous and current year counts in your new single tax credits award, not that of your former partner. In your old award as a couple, your joint income in the previous and current year counts – ie, including the remainder of the tax year after you stopped being a couple.[6] The income in the complete tax year is used and then apportioned on a pro rata basis for the period of the claim (see p1466).

If you were a single claimant but are now in a couple, your joint income in the previous and current year counts in the new joint claim, even if you were not in a couple in the previous year.[7]

10 Children's income

Children's income is ignored. However, if you have transferred money under a trust to your child and tax rules treat that income as still belonging to you, it may also be treated as yours for tax credits.[8]

3. **What income counts**

In general, taxable social security benefits are taken into account, and gross earnings (before tax and national insurance (NI)) and business profits are taken into account less your pension contributions. Most other income, such as pensions and interest on savings, is added together and is only taken into account if the total is more than £300 a year. The rules specify what income must be taken into account and what is disregarded. Although based on income tax rules, there are some differences for tax credits.

If you have a special exemption from income tax, your income is calculated as though you were liable for tax.[9] Foreign military personnel, officials of international organisations or consular staff may have such an exemption.

Types of income

The sources of your income fall into certain categories and within each category certain amounts can be disregarded. There is also a general list of income that is disregarded (see p1489).

The income taken into account in the tax credits assessment is worked out as follows.[10]

Add together your income, or your joint income if you are a couple, from the following categories:
- social security benefits (see p1480);
- income from employment (see p1481);
- taxable profits from self-employment (see p1484);
- student income (see p1485);
- miscellaneous income (see p1485).

Add together your income, or your joint income if you are a couple, from:
- pension income (see p1485);
- income from investments (see p1486);
- income from property (see p1487);
- foreign income (see p1488);
- notional income (see p1491).

If the total income in the last group of five categories is £300 or less, it is ignored completely. Otherwise, deduct £300 and add the remainder to your income from the first group of five categories. **Note:** couples share one £300 disregard.[11]

This gives you the total income that is taken into account – subject to any disregards (see p1489).

Example

Carl and Ellie renew their claim for child tax credit (CTC) and working tax credit (WTC) from April 2020. HM Revenue and Customs (HMRC) assesses their claim on their joint income for the year 6 April 2019 to 5 April 2020. In 2019/20, Ellie earned £13,500 before tax and NI contributions. Carl received contributory employment and support allowance (ESA) totalling £4,700 and an occupational pension of £500. Income taken into account is:

Employment income = £13,500

ESA = £4,700

Occupational pension = £200 (ie, £500 *minus* £300 disregard)

Total income = £18,400

Part 10: General rules for tax credits
Chapter 62: Income: tax credits
3. What income counts

Benefits

Generally, benefits are taken into account if they are taxable, and ignored if they are not.

Disregarded benefits

The following benefits are disregarded:[12]
- armed forces independence payment;
- attendance allowance;
- bereavement support payment;
- Best Start grants in Scotland;
- carer's allowance (CA) supplement in Scotland;
- child benefit;
- Christmas bonus;
- disability living allowance;
- discretionary housing payments;
- funeral support payment in Scotland;
- guardian's allowance;
- housing benefit (HB);
- income support (IS), except to strikers;
- income-based jobseeker's allowance (JSA) (even though this is taxable);
- income-related ESA, including a transitional addition;[13]
- industrial injuries benefit (except industrial death benefit);
- maternity allowance;
- pension credit;[14]
- personal independence payment;
- Scottish Welfare Fund payments;[15]
- severe disablement allowance;
- short-term lower rate incapacity benefit (IB);
- social fund payments;
- tax-free childcare payments;[16]
- transitional long-term IB (paid if you transferred from invalidity benefit in 1995);
- universal credit (UC);[17]
- any payment to compensate for the loss of IS, JSA or HB;
- any payment in lieu of Healthy Start vouchers or vitamins;
- increases for a child[18] or adult[19] paid with any of the above.

Tax credits themselves are disregarded. Local welfare assistance scheme payments are not specifically disregarded, but they are not taxable so do not count as income. New Scottish benefits to replace any of the above, job start payment, Best Start foods, the young carer's grant and the Scottish child payment do not count as income.[20] Statutory sick pay (SSP), statutory maternity pay (SMP), statutory adoption pay (SAP), statutory paternity pay (SPP), statutory shared parental pay (SSPP) and statutory parental bereavement pay (SPBP) are treated as employment income (see below). Retirement pensions, widowed mother's allowance, widowed parent's allowance, widow's pension, industrial death benefit and war pensions are treated as pension income (see p1485).

Benefits taken into account

Any benefits not in the list above are taken into account in full. These include:

- CA;
- contribution-based JSA;[21]
- contributory ESA, including a transitional addition;
- long-term IB (except the non-taxable transitional long-term IB – see p1480);
- increases for a child or adult (even if not taxable) paid with any of the above.

It is the amount of benefit payable that is taken into account. Arrears of benefit or any ex gratia payment in connection with a benefit are taken into account as income for the year in which the payment of arrears is made.[22]

Each year the DWP should give you a statement of the taxable benefits you received in the previous tax year. You can ask the local benefit office for a replacement if you did not get one. If you get any increase for a child paid with CA or IB (or widowed mother's or widowed parent's allowance), this is not included in the statement but is taken into account as income, so you should declare it for tax credits purposes.

Employment income

For tax credits, it is your 'gross' taxable pay that is taken into account.[23] This means your pay before any income tax or NI contributions are deducted, but after pension contributions are deducted.

Income counts whether received in the UK or elsewhere, unless it has been classed as not taxable because it cannot be transferred to or realised in the UK.[24]

What counts as employment income

'Employment income' means the following income received in the tax year:[25]

- any earnings from an office or employment, including:[26]
  - wages and overtime pay;
  - holiday pay and occupational sick pay;
  - bonuses and commission (including tips or gratuities);
  - 'benefits in kind' – ie, goods or assets that can be converted into money, such as gifts of drink, clothes and fuel;
  - payments made on your behalf – eg, rent paid by your employer direct to your landlord;
  - earnings from work you can do while claiming ESA ('permitted work' – see p1043);

Part 10: General rules for tax credits
Chapter 62: Income: tax credits
3. What income counts

- taxable expenses (see below for expenses that do not count as earnings);[27]
- any taxable cash voucher, non-cash voucher or credit token – eg, company credit card.[28] Vouchers spent on allowable expenses are ignored;[29]
- taxable payments in connection with the termination of your employment or with a change in your duties or wages, including non-statutory and statutory redundancy payments, pay in lieu of notice and employment tribunal awards for unfair dismissal. With the exception of pay in lieu of notice (except in some cases involving damages for breach of contract or practice),[30] the first £30,000 of the total of such payments is ignored;[31]
- SSP;[32]
- SMP, SAP, SPP, SSPP and SPBP above £100 a week. The first £100 a week is ignored;[33]
- strike pay from your trade union (even though this is non-taxable);[34]
- the cash equivalent of the benefit of a company car for private use and car fuel benefits.[35] Other expenses in connection with the car are ignored.[36] If you enter into a salary sacrifice arrangement for a company car on or after 6 April 2017, the amount included as earnings is the higher of the amount given up or the cash equivalent benefit of the car, unless it is an 'ultra-low emissions vehicle', in which case it is the cash equivalent benefit that counts.[37] However, if you are a disabled employee with an adapted or automatic company car, the car is exempt from income tax and ignored for tax credits;[38]
- payments for agreeing to restrict your future conduct or activities;[39]
- taxable income from an employee share scheme;[40]
- payment for work done while sentenced or on remand in prison;[41]
- the amount of earnings given up under a salary sacrifice scheme entered into from 6 April 2017 which is not tax exempt, or the cash equivalent of the benefit, whichever is higher. Ongoing arrangements made before 6 April 2017 for cars, accommodation and school fees can continue under old rules until 6 April 2021.[42]

The taxable value of goods and vouchers is shown on Form P11D, given to you by your employer at the end of the tax year.

Payments not counted as earnings

Some payments do not count as earnings and are disregarded in the tax credits assessment. Payments from your employer that are not taxable generally do not count as income for tax credits.

Note: if you use a salary sacrifice arrangement, the taxable income figure should be used, so the exemption or value of the benefit is the same for tax credits and income tax purposes.[43] The following payments are ignored (provided they are exempt from income tax):[44]

- expenses incurred 'wholly, exclusively and necessarily' in the course of your employment.[45] **Note:** if you are a volunteer with a charity or voluntary organisation, all your expenses are ignored.[46] However, any that are taxable are taken into account – eg, 'round-sum' expense allowances payable irrespective of how you might spend it;[47]

- certain other expenses – eg, for removal benefits, cars or transport for disabled employees, travel and subsistence, mileage allowance, car parking expenses, tax-free mobile phone and fixed deductions for repairing and maintaining work tools;[48]
- non-taxable vouchers, benefits or credit tokens, such as for recreational facilities, subsidised meals, transport, entertainment or hospitality;[49]
- small gifts or vouchers from third parties, not made in recognition of particular services (not exceeding £250 in total);[50]
- tax-free cycles and equipment under Cyclescheme;[51]
- homeworkers' additional household expenses;[52]
- childcare vouchers or credit tokens for 'relevant childcare' (see p1462);[53]
- tax-free award under a staff suggestion scheme;[54]
- certain professional fees – eg, to approved professional bodies, for indemnity insurance or registration;[55]
- any charity payments under a payroll giving scheme;[56]
- payment for work-related training, individual learning account training and retraining expenses when leaving employment;[57]
- certain discretionary payments made by the DWP to help you into work (but in-work payments made by a third-party provider, including non-cash items such as clothing or travelcards, are not exempt from income tax and are likely to be treated as employment income);[58]
- tax-free benefits and payments under PAYE (pay as you earn) settlement agreements and special arrangements;[59]
- tax exempt bonus payments of up to £3,600 paid to employees, or former employees, by an employee ownership trust;[60]
- the amount given up under certain salary sacrifice arrangements which are tax-exempt, including for benefits listed above and for independent pension advice, counselling and other outplacement services;[61]
- the first £30,000 of payments to compensate for the termination of your employment or a change in your duties or wages.[62]

Some groups of workers have special income tax exemptions. The following are ignored as earnings for tax credits:

- certain armed forces' allowances – eg, for travel to and from leave, food, accommodation, certain operational allowances, council tax relief, continuity of education and reserve forces' training;[63]
- free coal to miners, or former miners, or cash in lieu;[64]
- if you are an actor or performer, the tax-free amount of agents' fees;[65]
- expenses for mainland transfers for offshore oil and gas workers;[66]
- Crown employees' foreign service allowance;[67]

Part 10: General rules for tax credits
Chapter 62: Income: tax credits
3. What income counts

- expenses of a minister of religion, including a rent deduction;[68]
- European Commission daily subsistence allowance to seconded national experts.[69]

Deduct pension contributions

Deduct any contributions you make to a personal or occupational pension approved by HMRC.[70]

If you pay contributions through your employer, your P60 or P45 should show your wages after the contributions have been deducted, so there is no further deduction to make.

If you pay the pension contributions direct, deduct the gross annual contributions. Because tax relief is given on personal pension contributions, your actual contributions are less than the gross amount included in the pension plan. It is the higher gross amount that you should deduct from your employment income. Your pension provider should supply you with annual statements of contributions received.

If you have no income from employment but are still making pension contributions, deduct the contributions from any other income you may have.

Income from self-employment

Your taxable profits from any 'trade', 'profession' or 'vocation' are taken into account for the relevant year.[71] If you have a business partner, it is taxable profits from your share of the business income that count.[72] This includes trading outside the UK. It also includes profits from renting out property if this is conducted as a business. (If property income comes from a 'trade', income counts without the £300 disregard that would otherwise apply to such income.) If renting property is not conducted as a business, see p1487. You may be asked to provide evidence that your self-employment is organised and regular, on a commercial basis, with a view to making a profit.

Payments under the New Enterprise Allowance scheme to help you start a new business are not counted as income for working out your trading profits.[73] Taxable profits are shown on your tax return for the relevant year. You should deduct allowable business expenses from the annual turnover to arrive at a profit figure. HMRC's self-assessment helpline (tel: 0300 200 3310; textphone: 0300 200 3319) should be able to give advice. See also p1477.

Business losses

If your business is run on a commercial basis and has made a loss, your income is nil for that tax year unless you have other income that counts in the assessment. If you do have other income, you should deduct the amount of the loss from that income (from joint income if you are claiming as a couple).[74] If you do not have enough income to offset the full amount, any left over can be carried forward and deducted from profits of the same trade in the next and later tax years.

Deductions from self-employment

Deduct the gross amount of personal pension contributions (see p1484) and any gift aid donation to charity (see p1490).

Student income

The following income is taken into account:[75]
- adult dependants' grant;
- in Scotland, lone parents' grant;
- professional and career development loans, but only any amount applied for or paid in respect of living expenses for the period supported by the loan.[76]

All other kinds of student support are disregarded, including student loans, childcare grants, discretionary grants and hardship funds.

Note: unlike most means-tested benefits, becoming a student does not affect your entitlement to WTC and CTC. Provided you satisfy the eligibility rules, you can continue to qualify.

Miscellaneous income

Any income that does not fit into any of the other nine categories on p1479 is taken into account if it is taxable under the HMRC 'sweep-up' provisions in Part 5 of the Income Tax (Trading and Other Income) Act 2005.[77] This includes copyright royalties if your writing does not amount to a trade or profession.

Pension income

Pension income taken into account

The following pension income is taken into account. The first £300 a year is ignored from the total of your pension and any income from savings, investments, property or foreign or notional income.

- **State retirement pensions and graduated retirement benefit.**[78] (The Christmas bonus and winter fuel payment are ignored.) HMRC says that, as well as your pension, it takes into account any additional state pension, and any increase for an adult or child paid with your pension.[79] Include as income any lump sum to which you become entitled through deferring your state pension.
- **Personal and occupational pensions.**[80] It is the gross amount before tax is deducted that counts. Your pension provider should give you a certificate each year showing how much pension was paid and how much tax deducted. If you retired because of work-related illness or disability caused by injury on duty, only count the amount of pension that you would have been paid if you had retired on non-work-related ill-health grounds. Any extra amount paid is ignored.[81] Tax-free lump sums paid under a personal pension scheme, retirement annuity contract or tax-exempt pension scheme are ignored

Part 10: General rules for tax credits
Chapter 62: Income: tax credits
3. What income counts

completely.[82] If you have the option of taking a lump sum from a pension because you are aged 55 and over, the tax-free amount (usually up to 25 per cent of the total value of the pension pot) is ignored, but other payments count as income. If you choose not to take an income or lump sum from a personal or occupational pension, regardless of your age, this cannot be counted as notional income (see p1491). If you cash in a small pension or the fund is too small to pay a pension, the lump sum you get counts. If you get a winding-up lump sum when your occupational pension scheme winds up, this counts.

- **Widow's pension, widowed mother's and widowed parent's allowance,** including any increases for a child or adult dependant.[83]
- **Industrial death benefit.**[84]
- **Survivor's guaranteed income payment and child's payment** under the Armed Forces Compensation Scheme.[85]

Pension income disregarded

Ignore the following **war pensions:**[86]

- war disablement pension, including constant attendance allowance and mobility supplement;
- annuity or additional pension to holders of the Victoria Cross, George Cross and certain other medals;
- wounds, injury or disablement pensions to members of the armed forces – eg, guaranteed income payment;
- death in service pensions for service in the armed forces. If the death in service pension is overlapped by another pension, ignore an equivalent amount from the other pension.

Investment income

There is no capital limit in the tax credit assessment as there is with means-tested benefits. The value of your savings is ignored completely. However, taxable *income* from savings and investments is taken into account. For example, the amount of savings in a bank account is ignored, but the interest on those savings is taken into account.

Investment income is taken into account as described below. The first £300 a year is ignored from the total of your investment income and any income from pensions or property, or foreign or notional income.

Investment income taken into account

Take into account the following amounts before tax is deducted:[87]

- interest on invested money, including outside the UK – eg, interest on savings in a bank account;
- dividends from shares of a company resident in the UK (including the tax credit payable by the company with the dividend);
- income from government stocks and bonds;

- taxable payments from a life assurance policy, life annuity contract or capital redemption policy;
- discounts on securities – ie, the profit from trading in securities such as government stocks and bonds;
- interest, annuity or other annual payment payable as a charge on a property or as a reservation out of it;
- payments from the estate of someone who has died;
- interest arising from a debt owed to you.

Investment income disregarded

Certain investment income is disregarded:

- interest, a dividend or bonus from an individual savings account (ISA);[88]
- government bonus payments into a lifetime ISA or a help-to-save account;[89]
- interest under a certified save as you earn (SAYE) scheme;[90]
- income from savings certificates ;[91]
- tax-exempt annual payments made by an individual in the UK not for commercial reasons – eg, from a covenant;[92]
- winnings from betting, pools, lotteries and games with prizes;[93]
- certain compensation payments to Second World War victims;[94]
- tax-free periodical payments of damages for personal injury, disease or death awarded through a court, out-of-court settlement or agreement, and interest on such damages;[95]
- periodical payments from the Thalidomide Trust;[96]
- annuity payments under a Criminal Injuries Compensation Scheme award;[97]
- interest on the first £30,000 of a home income plan loan taken out before 9 March 1999 to buy a life annuity;[98]
- interest on compensation to a child under 18 for the loss of a parent;[99]
- payments from the variant Creutzfeldt-Jakob disease government-funded trust, the Macfarlane Trusts, Independent Living Funds and the Eileen Trust. These are disregarded for the lifetime of the disabled person or a partner who receives the payment or inherits from the estate, or for two years if paid to or inherited by a parent;[100]
- tax-exempt capital element of a purchased life annuity;[101]
- tax-exempt health and employment insurance payments (eg, permanent health insurance or employment protection policies) or immediate-needs annuity payments.[102]

Property income

The capital value of property is ignored, but rental income is taken into account unless this is exempt from tax under the 'rent-a-room' scheme.[103] This scheme allows you to rent furnished accommodation in your own home, earning up to £7,500 a year tax free.[104]

Part 10: General rules for tax credits
Chapter 62: Income: tax credits
3. What income counts

If you are not covered by the 'rent-a-room' scheme (eg, you rent out a property that you do not live in yourself), you can deduct expenses wholly and exclusively incurred in running the property – eg, repairs, water charges, insurance premiums and mortgage interest (but not capital repayments of a mortgage).[105] This may be different from how the property is treated for tax purposes.

The first £300 a year is ignored from the total of your property income and any pensions, investment income, foreign or notional income.

If you rent out property as a business (eg, you run a hotel or guesthouse), count this as income from self-employment (see p1484).[106]

Income from property outside the UK counts as 'foreign income' (see below).

Income from outside the UK

Although earnings from abroad are taken into account in the same way as UK earnings, other 'foreign income' (eg, from pensions, property or investments) is taken into account subject to the following rules.[107]

The following are disregarded:[108]
- a banking charge or commission for converting currency to sterling;[109]
- social security payments from outside the UK that are equivalent to tax-free UK benefits (see p1480);
- certain pensions or compensation for victims of persecution during World War Two;
- tax-free lump-sum payments under an overseas pension scheme;
- personal injury damages from a court outside the UK;
- certain education allowances payable to workers in the public sector of some countries outside the UK;
- property losses in one tax year that can be offset against property income in the following year;[110]
- maintenance payments;
- income that you are prevented from transferring to the UK by law or by the government of the country where the income arises or because you cannot get foreign currency in that country. Other income that remains abroad is counted.[111]

The first £300 a year is disregarded from the total of your foreign income and any pensions, investment, property or notional income.

Income from outside the UK is still taken into account even if you would normally have tax relief on that income in the UK to avoid double taxation in both countries (such income is treated as though it were taxable in the UK in the normal way).[112]

Converting currency

If your income is in another currency, HMRC expects you to convert it to sterling using an average of the exchange rates over 12 months ending on 31 March for the tax year in which the income is paid.[113] These rates are published on gov.uk/ government/collections/exchange-rates-for-customs-and-vat. If your tax credit award is based on an estimate of the current year's income, the rate of conversion is adjusted once the exchange rate average is available at the end of the tax year.

General income disregards

All of the following income is disregarded in the tax credit assessment.[114]

Employment and training programmes

Ignore the following income:

- travelling expenses, a living-away-from-home allowance and a training grant if you are participating in training under section 2 of the Employment and Training Act 1973 or, in Scotland, under section 2 of the Enterprise and New Towns (Scotland) Act 1990, or attending a course at an employment rehabilitation centre (where these are not taxable as profits);[115]
- if you are aged 25 or over and getting JSA while on a 'qualifying course', a discretionary payment to help meet your special needs;[116]
- a payment to a disabled person under section 2 of the Employment and Training Act 1973 or section 15 of the Disabled Persons (Employment) Act 1944 to assist disabled people to get or keep employment;[117]
- education maintenance allowance;[118]
- certain DWP payments from former employment programmes. Payments from Work Programme providers are not specifically disregarded and are likely to be treated as employment income.[119]

See also p1483 for other disregarded payments.

Maintenance and children

Any maintenance you receive from an ex-partner, or that your partner receives from her/his ex-partner, is ignored, whether it is paid under a court order or not. Any maintenance for a child or qualifying young person which you receive from her/his other parent (if the parent is not currently your partner) is also ignored.[120]

If you *pay* maintenance, you cannot deduct this from income.

If you foster a child placed with you by a local authority or independent fostering provider, all your income from foster care (eg, the fostering allowance) is ignored, provided the annual amount is no more than £10,000 plus £200 a week for each child under 11 and £250 a week for each child aged 11 or over. If your fostering income is over this limit, only the taxable amount is taken into account – ie, the amount above this limit or the actual net profit.[121] There is a similar disregard for local authority payments if a child or adult is placed with you under an adult placement scheme or 'staying put' care for care leavers, or you are a kinship carer of a looked-after child.[122] **Note:** a foster child or looked-after child

Part 10: General rules for tax credits
Chapter 62: Income: tax credits
3. What income counts

may not count as a member of your family for tax credits, so you may not get CTC for her/him (see p289).

An adoption allowance,[123] or special guardianship payment, for a child who is a member of your household is ignored completely. For a child who lives with you under a residence order, a residence order allowance and any payments made by a local authority under section 17 of the Children Act 1989 or, in Scotland, under section 22 of the Children (Scotland) Act 1995 or section 50 of the Children Act 1975 are ignored.[124]

Other income

The following is ignored from your income:

- any contribution you make to an approved personal or occupational pension scheme (see p1484);[125]
- payments for fares to hospital or to assist prison visits;[126]
- community care direct payments;[127]
- payments under the Supporting People programme;[128]
- asylum support payments or vouchers for a former asylum seeker or dependant;[129]
- trade union provident benefits – eg, sickness or accident benefit or funeral payment;[130]
- payment for expenses incurred if you are an unpaid volunteer with a charity or voluntary organisation;[131]
- jury or witness payments, if this is not compensation for loss of earnings or loss of benefit;[132]
- a payment for someone you are caring for temporarily made to you by a health authority, local authority, voluntary organisation, clinical commissioning group, NHS England, or by the person her/himself under the local authority's financial assessment. This disregard only applies if the payment would be tax free under HMRC's 'rent-a-room' scheme (see p1487);[133]
- any payment under an insurance policy taken out to insure against the risk of being unable to maintain mortgage repayments or other payments on a loan secured on your home. However, any payment you get above the amount you use to maintain the repayments, plus the premiums on that policy or buildings insurance premiums required as a condition of the mortgage, count as your income;[134]
- any payment under an insurance policy taken out to insure against the risk of being unable to maintain repayments under a hire purchase, regulated or conditional sale agreement. However, any payment above the amount you use to maintain the repayments and the premiums on that policy counts as your income;[135]
- the gross amount of any 'gift aid' donation to charity;[136]
- a sports award for anything other than living expenses. Living expenses count as your income. Ignore parts of the award for dietary supplements and living-away-from-home accommodation costs;[137]

- any payment made under, or in connection with, the Home Office Windrush Compensation Scheme (interest on such a payment is disregarded for 52 weeks from the date you receive it);[138]
- any payment in connection with the Scottish Child Abuse Inquiry;[139]
- any payment made by the National Emergencies Trust;[140]
- victims' payment made by the Northern Ireland in respect of injury as a result of a Troubles related incident.[141]

4. **Notional income**

Sometimes you are treated as though you have income that you do not actually have. This is called '**notional income**'.[142] There are four kinds of notional income.

- **Income you have deprived yourself of to get, or increase, tax credits.**[143] See p503 for details of when this rule might affect you (the basic rules are similar to those that apply to deprivation of capital for benefits).
- **Income that you have failed to apply for.** You are treated as having income that would become available to you if you applied for it.[144] This does not include:
  - income under a trust set up from a personal injury payment;
  - income from a personal pension scheme, regardless of your age;
  - interest on damages awarded through the courts for personal injury;
  - a rehabilitation allowance;
  - state pension;
  - category A or B retirement pension;
  - graduated retirement benefit;
  - shared additional pension.
- **Cheap or unpaid labour.** If you work or provide a service for less than the going rate, you are treated as getting a reasonable rate for the job if the person has the means to pay.[145] This does not affect you if you are a volunteer and it is reasonable for you to provide your services free of charge. Nor does it apply if you are on an approved employment or training programme.

  Sometimes carers looking after disabled people have been expected to charge the person they care for under a similar provision affecting means-tested benefits. If you are in this position, see p452 for more details.
- **Income treated as yours under certain tax avoidance provisions or where tax law treats capital as income**. It also counts as your income for tax credits, although there is a difference to income tax provisions for a claimant who receives property income through an estate rather than directly.[146]

Part 10: General rules for tax credits
Chapter 62: Income: tax credits
Notes

Notes

1. Relevant income

1 s7(3) TCA 2002; reg 5 TC(ITDR) Regs
2 Reg 12A(3) UC(TP) Regs
3 s7(4A) TCA 2002, as added by reg 12A and Sch UC(TP) Regs
4 s17(8) TCA 2002; reg 33 TC(CN) Regs

2. Whose income counts

5 s7(5) TCA 2002
6 *PD v HMRC (TC)* [2010] UKUT 159 (AAC)
7 R(TC) 1/08
8 Reg 14(2)(b)(vii) TC(DCI) Regs

3. What income counts

9 Reg 3(6) TC(DCI) Regs
10 Reg 3(1) TC(DCI) Regs
11 Reg 3(1) Step 1 TC(DCI) Regs
12 Reg 7(3) TC(DCI) Regs
13 A transitional addition is part of the ESA applicable amount under reg 67(1)(d) ESA Regs, inserted by Sch 2 para 52 ESA(TP)(EA)(No.2) Regs.
14 Pension credit paid under SPCA 2002 is, by definition, not counted as social security income under reg 7(1) TC(DCI) Regs
15 Reg 19 Table 6 (19 to 22) TC(DCI) Regs. Scottish Welfare Fund payments are paid under the Welfare Funds (Scotland) Act 2015 so cannot count as social security income under reg 7 TC(DCI) Regs.
16 s66 Childcare Payments Act 2014
17 Reg 7(1) TC(DCI) Regs (UC is paid under WRA 2012)
18 Reg 7(4) TC(DCI) Regs
19 The regulations do not mention the treatment of increases for adults. However, these are non-taxable if paid with a non-taxable benefit and the intention is that tax credits follow suit. See HMRC, *Employment Income Manual*, para 76102.
20 Reg 19 Table 6 paras 25, 26 and 28-31 TC(DCI) Regs
21 s674 IT(EP)A 2003
22 Reg 7(1)(c) and (d) TC(DCI) Regs; TCM 0120040
23 Reg 4 TC(DCI) Regs
24 Reg 3(3)-(5) TC(DCI) Regs

25 Reg 4 TC(DCI) Regs
26 Regs 2(2) and 4(1)(a) TC(DCI) Regs; HMRC, *Employment Income Manual*, para 00520
27 Reg 4(1)(b) TC(DCI) Regs
28 Reg 4(1)(c)-(e) TC(DCI) Regs
29 ss362-63 IT(EP)A 2003; reg 4(4) Table 1 para 11D and (5) TC(DCI) Regs
30 HMRC, *Employment Income Manual*, paras 12975-79
31 Reg 4(1)(f) TC(DCI) Regs; see also TCTM 04111
32 Reg 4(1)(g) TC(DCI) Regs
33 Reg 4(1)(h) TC(DCI) Regs
34 Reg 4(1)(k) TC(DCI) Regs
35 Reg 4(1)(i) TC(DCI) Regs
36 Reg 4(4) Table 1 paras 14B, 14C and 14D TC(DCI) Regs
37 Reg 4(1)(ia) TC(DCI) Regs
38 Reg 4(4) Table 1 para 2B TC(DCI) Regs
39 Reg 4(1)(j) TC(DCI) Regs
40 Reg 4(1)(l) TC(DCI) Regs
41 Reg 4(1)(m) TC(DCI) Regs; reg 4(2)(g) WTC(EMR) Regs
42 Reg 4(6)-(10) TC (DCI) Regs
43 Explanatory Memorandum to Tax Credits (Definition and Calculation of Income) (Amendment) Regulations 2017, No.396
44 Reg 4(4) TC(DCI) Regs; for a full list, see TCTM 04200-04229
45 Reg 4(5) TC(DCI) Regs; s336 IT(EP)A 2003
46 Reg 19 Table 7 para 1 TC(DCI) Regs
47 Reg 4(1)(b) TC(DCI) Regs; HMRC, *Employment Income Manual*, para 05100
48 Regs 4(4) Table 1 paras 1, 2A, 2C, 4, 6, 11F and 13, and 4(5) TC(DCI) Regs
49 Reg 4(4) Table 1 paras 5, 11D and 11E TC(DCI) Regs
50 Reg 4(4) Table 1 para 14 TC(DCI) Regs
51 Reg 4(4) Table 1 para 11D TC(DCI) Regs; ss244 and 266 IT(EP)A 2003
52 Reg 4(4) Table 1 para 17 TC(DCI) Regs
53 Reg 4(4) Table 1 para 15 TC(DCI) Regs
54 Reg 4(4) Table 1 para 12 TC(DCI) Regs
55 Regs 4(4) Table 1 para 21 and 4(5) TC(DCI) Regs; ss343 and 346 IT(EP)A 2003

10

56 Reg 4(5) TC(DCI) Regs; s713 IT(EP)A 2003
57 Reg 4(4) Table 1 paras 11C and 18 TC(DCI) Regs
58 Reg 4(4) Table 1 para 16 TC(DCI) Regs; DWP, *Provider Guidance, Generic Guidance,* Ch13
59 Reg 4(4) Table 1 para 20 TC(DCI) Regs
60 Reg 4(4) Table 1 para 22 TC(DCI) Regs
61 Reg 4(6), (8) and (9) TC(DCI) Regs
62 Reg 4(1)(f) TC(DCI) Regs; see also TCTM 04111
63 Reg 4(4) Table 1 paras 3, 3A, 3B, 3C and 7 TC(DCI) Regs
64 Regs 4(4) Table 1 para 9 and 5(2) Table 2 para 11 TC(DCI) Regs
65 Reg 4(5) TC(DCI) Regs; s352 IT(EP)A 2003
66 Reg 4(4) Table 1 para 11A TC(DCI) Regs
67 Reg 4(4) Table 1 para 11B TC(DCI) Regs
68 Reg 4(5) TC(DCI) Regs; s351 IT(EP)A 2003
69 Reg 4(4) Table 1 para 11 TC(DCI) Regs
70 Reg 3(7)(c) TC(DCI) Regs
71 Reg 6(a) TC(DCI) Regs
72 Reg 6(b) TC(DCI) Regs
73 HMRC, *Business Income Manual,* para 40401
74 Reg 3(1) Step 4 TC(DCI) Regs
75 Reg 8 TC(DCI) Regs
76 Reg 19(c) Table 8 para 2 TC(DCI) Regs
77 Reg 18 TC(DCI) Regs
78 Reg 5(1)(a) TC(DCI) Regs
79 TCTM 04301; HMRC, *Employment Income Manual,* para 76102
80 Reg 5(1)(b)-(o) TC(DCI) Regs
81 Reg 5(2) Table 2 para 9 TC(DCI) Regs
82 Reg 5(2) Table 2 para 10 TC(DCI) Regs
83 Reg 5(1)(a) TC(DCI) Regs
84 Reg 5(1)(a) TC(DCI) Regs
85 Reg 5(1)(b) TC(DCI) Regs; HMRC, *Employment Income Manual,* para 74306
86 Reg 5(2) Table 2 paras 1-8 TC(DCI) Regs
87 Reg 10(1) TC(DCI) Regs
88 Reg 10(2)(a) Table 4 para 1(a) and (b) TC(DCI) Regs
89 Reg 10(2)(a) Table 4 para 15 TC(DCI) Regs
90 Reg 10(2)(a) Table 4 para 3 TC(DCI) Regs
91 Reg 10(2)(c) TC(DCI) Regs
92 Reg 10(2)(e) TC(DCI) Regs
93 Reg 10(2)(a) Table 4 para 4 TC(DCI) Regs
94 Reg 10(2)(a) Table 4 paras 5-7 TC(DCI) Regs

95 Reg 10(2)(a) Table 4 para 8 TC(DCI) Regs (a lump-sum payment of personal injury compensation or damages is not taxable under s51(2) Taxation of Chargeable Gains Act 1992)
96 TCTM 04608
97 Reg 10(2)(a) Table 4 para 9 TC(DCI) Regs
98 Reg 10(2)(a) Table 4 para 10 TC(DCI) Regs
99 Reg 10(2)(a) Table 4 para 11 TC(DCI) Regs
100 Reg 10(2)(b) Table 5 TC(DCI) Regs
101 Reg 10(2)(a) Table 4 para 12 TC(DCI) Regs
102 Reg 10(2)(a) Table 4 para 13 TC(DCI) Regs; TCTM 04612
103 Reg 11 TC(DCI) Regs
104 Income Tax (Limit for Rent-a-Room Relief) Order 2015, No.1539; see HMRC, Helpsheet HS223, *Rent-a-Room Scheme*
105 TCTM 04006; HMRC, *Property Income Manual,* paras 2020-40 and 2105
106 TCTM 04006
107 Reg 12(1) TC(DCI) Regs
108 Reg 12(3) TC(DCI) Regs
109 Reg 3(7)(a) TC(DCI) Regs
110 Reg 12(4) TC(DCI) Regs
111 Reg 3(3) TC(DCI) Regs
112 Reg 3(5A) TC(DCI) Regs
113 Reg 3(6A) TC(DCI) Regs
114 Reg 19 TC(DCI) Regs
115 Reg 19 Table 7 para 2(a)-(c) TC(DCI) Regs
116 Reg 19 Table 8 para 1 TC(DCI) Regs
117 Reg 19 Table 6 para 2 TC(DCI) Regs
118 Reg 19 Table 6 para 5 TC(DCI) Regs
119 Reg 19 Table 6 para 3 TC(DCI) Regs; DWP, *Provider Guidance, Generic Guidance,* Chapter 13
120 Reg 19 Table 6 para 10 TC(DCI) Regs
121 Reg 19 Table 6 para 9 TC(DCI) Regs
122 Reg 19 Table 6 para 9 TC(DCI) Regs; The Qualifying Care Relief (Specified Social Care Schemes) Order 2011, No.712; s806A IT(TOI)A 2005
123 Reg 19 Table 6 para 11(a) TC(DCI) Regs
124 Reg 19 Table 6 para 11(a) and (b) TC(DCI) Regs
125 Reg 3(7)(c) TC(DCI) Regs
126 Reg 19 Table 6 paras 12 and 13 TC(DCI) Regs
127 Reg 19 Table 6 para 14 TC(DCI) Regs
128 Reg 19 Table 6 para 14A TC(DCI) Regs
129 Reg 19 Table 6 para 15 TC(DCI) Regs
130 Reg 19 Table 6 para 16 TC(DCI) Regs
131 Reg 19 Table 7 para 1 TC(DCI) Regs

10

Part 10: General rules for tax credits
Chapter 62: Income: tax credits
Notes

132 Reg 19 Table 8 para 6 TC(DCI) Regs
133 Reg 19 Table 8 paras 3 and 4 TC(DCI)
      Regs
134 Reg 19 Table 8 para 5(a) TC(DCI) Regs
135 Reg 19 Table 8 para 5(b) TC(DCI) Regs
136 Reg 3(7)(b) TC(DCI) Regs
137 Reg 19 Table 8 para 7 TC(DCI) Regs
138 Regs 10(2)(f) and 19 Table 6 para 24
      TC(DCI) Regs
139 Reg 19 Table 6 para 27 TC(DCI) Regs
140 Reg 19 Table 6 para 32 TC(DCI) Regs
141 Reg 19 Rable 6 para 33 TC(DCI) Regs

4. **Notional income**
142 Reg 13 TC(DCI) Regs
143 Reg 15 TC(DCI) Regs
144 Reg 16 TC(DCI) Regs
145 Reg 17 TC(DCI) Regs
146 Reg 14 TC(DCI) Regs

10

Chapter 63

Claims, decisions and getting paid: tax credits

This chapter covers:
1. Who can get tax credits (p1496)
2. How and when to make a claim (p1499)
3. Decisions (p1503)
4. Backdating your claim (p1504)
5. Getting paid (p1504)
6. Change of circumstances (p1507)
7. Annual reviews (p1512)
8. Contacting HM Revenue and Customs (p1516)

Key facts

- Tax credits are administered and paid by HM Revenue and Customs' Tax Credit Office.
- Tax credits are dealt with differently from social security benefits. Tax credits are dealt with over a tax year, using annual income, and entitlement is finalised at the end of the tax year.
- Your tax credits may be affected by changes in your circumstances or income.
- Tax credit claims are finalised between April and July each year. This annual review also acts as a renewal claim for the new tax year.

Future changes

The government says that from November 2020 (or earlier, under a pilot for up to 10,000 claimants), the DWP will begin to transfer existing tax credits claimants to universal credit. See p23 for further information, and AskCPAG.org.uk and *Welfare Rights Bulletin* for updates.

Part 10: General rules for tax credits
Chapter 63: Claims, decisions and getting paid: tax credits
1. Who can get tax credits

1. **Who can get tax credits**

You must be at least 16 years old to be entitled to tax credits.[1] You must meet the qualifying conditions for child tax credit (CTC – see p284) or working tax credit (WTC – see p298). You can be entitled to either tax credit or both. You must not be a universal credit (UC) claimant (see p1508). If you are already getting tax credits and you claim UC, your tax credits will stop.[2]

If you are a member of a married couple or registered civil partnership, or live with someone as if you are married, you get tax credits jointly with your partner. This is known as a 'joint claim' and 'joint award', based on you and your partner's circumstances and income.[3] HM Revenue and Customs (HMRC) has the discretion to treat a claim by one member of a couple as having also been made by the other, but usually only uses this power to accept renewal claims by telephone.[4] See p1497 for when you are treated as a couple.

If you are not part of a couple, you have a single claim and single award, solely based on your circumstances and income.

If you made a joint claim and are no longer in a couple, or if you made a single claim and are now in a couple, your entitlement ends. You must usually make a new claim for UC instead.[5] You should tell the Tax Credit Office as soon as possible. If you do not, you could be overpaid. You could also be given a financial penalty if you fail to notify the change within one month (see p1507).[6]

Who can make a new claim for tax credits

You can only make a new claim for tax credits in limited circumstances. These are if:[7]

- you already have an award of one type of tax credit and you become entitled to the other one – eg, if you are already getting CTC, you can start to get WTC. This is treated as a change in circumstances and a new claim is not required;
- you were entitled to WTC in 2019/20 and are making a claim for 2020/21 (ie, a renewal);
- you are prevented from claiming UC because:
  - you (or your partner) are, or within the last month have been, entitled to income support (IS), income-based jobseeker's allowance (JSA), income-related employment and support allowance (ESA) or housing benefit (HB), that includes a severe disability premium (see p346) and if your entitlement to the benefit ended during that month you (or s/he) have continued to satisfy the conditions for that premium in that month; *and*
  - you (or your partner) have not yet been given a 'migration notice' from the DWP that you will be transferred to UC via the 'managed migration' process (see p30); *or*
- you are prevented from claiming UC because you (or if you are in a couple, you and your partner) are a 'frontier worker' – ie, you work in Great Britain or Northern Ireland but do not live there.

Couples

You and your partner count as a 'couple' if you are:[8]
- married or registered civil partners, unless you are separated and this is under a court order or is likely to be permanent (see below); *or*
- not married or registered civil partners, but are living together as if you are (see below).[9]

Note: if you are entitled to tax credits and become part of a couple with someone who is entitled to UC (see p23), your tax credit award ends and you are treated as making a joint UC claim.[10]

Married couples and civil partners

You have a joint tax credits award with your partner if you are married to her/him or you are registered as civil partners. You still count as a couple for tax credits purposes if you are married or are registered civil partners and are still in a relationship but are not living together – eg, because of work or housing reasons. You continue to count as a couple while you and your partner are temporarily separated. It does not matter how long the temporary separation lasts (but see p1498 if you or your partner go abroad).

If you and your partner are permanently separated or are separated under a court order, your joint tax credit award ends and you will usually have to claim UC instead. This is the case even if you are still living under the same roof and whether or not you are taking steps to divorce your partner or dissolve your civil partnership.[11] The test is whether you are 'separated in circumstances in which the separation is likely to be permanent' and this depends on your (and your partner's) intentions, and should also take into account the context of cultural attitudes to separation and divorce.[12] The focus is on the state of the relationship, not exclusively whether you are living in the 'same household', which differs from the rule for means-tested benefits (see p319).[13] If you are having a trial separation and there is at least a 50 per cent chance of reconciliation, HMRC is likely to say you still count as a couple.[14]

Special rules apply if you are a member of a polygamous unit.[15]

Living together as a couple

You must claim tax credits jointly with your partner if you are living together as if you are married or in a registered civil partnership. In determining whether or not you count as living together as a couple, HMRC is likely to consider the same factors as the DWP does for means-tested benefits.[16] See p320 and p323 for more information.

If you and your partner stop living together, your joint tax credits award ends and you will usually have to claim UC instead. However, if you and your partner are only temporarily living apart (eg, one of you is in hospital or in respite care), you may still be treated as a couple.

Part 10: General rules for tax credits
Chapter 63: Claims, decisions and getting paid: tax credits
1. Who can get tax credits

Note: HMRC often applies too narrow an interpretation of the test. For example, there is no rule that says that if your partner stays with you for three nights or more a week you are *automatically* to be treated as a couple living together.

Challenging a living together decision

If you get tax credits as a single person, HMRC may investigate your award if it suspects that you are living with a partner (see Chapter 65). HMRC may ask you for information or evidence and may suspend payments if you have not responded by the specified date (you must be given at least 30 days). If it decides that you are not entitled as a single person, you can request a mandatory reconsideration and, if you are unhappy with the outcome, appeal against such a decision (but not against a suspension of payments) (see Chapter 66). **Note:** HMRC often relies on information it obtains from credit reference agencies, but such information on its own is unlikely to be sufficient. In the event of an appeal, HMRC must usually produce all the evidence it used to make the decision.[17] HMRC sometimes makes standard requests for a list of evidence, including a legal separation order and utility bills showing the alleged partner's address is elsewhere. However, if you explain why such evidence does not exist or is not available to you, the fact that you cannot provide it should not go against you when making a decision.[18]

If you think a decision about whether or not you count as a couple is wrong and it affects your tax credits, consider requesting a mandatory reconsideration and then appealing. It is possible that the DWP, the local authority and HMRC might reach different conclusions about whether you are a couple. If so, appeal *all* the decisions with which you disagree.

Couples and residence rules

If you or your partner go abroad, either permanently or for more than a set period of time, and cannot be treated as being in the UK (see p1662), you cease to satisfy the residence conditions. In this case, you must terminate your joint tax credits claim. If you do not do so, you may be given a financial penalty (see p1535). The person still in the UK will usually have to claim UC instead.

If your partner does not have a right to reside in the UK (see p1591), s/he is treated as not being present in the UK for CTC, so you can get CTC as a single person.[19] The requirement to have a right to reside only applies to CTC, not WTC. In some cases, HMRC may treat you as a single claimant for CTC and joint claimants for WTC. It is advisable to ensure that HMRC is fully aware of your circumstances.

You can get tax credits as a couple even though your partner is a 'person subject to immigration control' (see p1560) and would not be able to get tax credits in her/his own right.[20]

Appointees

The following people can act on your behalf if you are unable to manage your claim yourself:[21]

- a receiver appointed by the Court of Protection with power to make a claim for tax credits on your behalf;
- in Scotland, a tutor, curator or other guardian acting or appointed in terms of the law who is administering your estate;
- a person who is your 'appointee' (see p1170) for social security purposes; *or*
- if none of the above applies, a person aged 18 or over who applies to HMRC in writing to act on your behalf and is appointed by HMRC in that capacity – see gov.uk/getting-help-with-your-tax-credits-claim/appointees.

2. How and when to make a claim

You can only make a new claim for tax credits in limited circumstances (see p1496). You must usually claim tax credits by telephone. You have no entitlement to tax credits unless you make a claim.[22] You claim both child tax credit (CTC) and working tax credit (WTC) together. HM Revenue and Customs (HMRC) has discretion to accept an application made by other means, but in practice this rarely happens.[23] HMRC no longer issues claim forms.

If you are renewing a claim, this may be done by telephone, online or automatically in specific cases (see p1502).

You claim by contacting the Tax Credit Helpline (see p1516).

The Tax Credit Helpline may also ask you questions about your identity and eligibility for tax credits, to confirm that you are prevented from claiming universal credit (UC).

Note: the date of your claim is the date of your telephone call if you provide sufficient information as accepted by HMRC. Your claim can be backdated in certain circumstances (see p1504).

When to claim

If you are severely disabled and prevented from claiming UC (see p23), you should claim tax credits as soon as you think you are eligible. You cannot make a claim for tax credits in advance of the tax year for which you are claiming.[24] The general rule is that a claim for tax credits runs from the date it is received by the Tax Credit Office until the end of the tax year in which the claim is made.[25]

If you were entitled to tax credits before the date your claim is received by the Tax Credit Office, your claim can be backdated for up to 31 days. Backdating of WTC is possible for a longer period if you are entitled to a disabled worker element and only become entitled to WTC following an award of a qualifying benefit (see p1504).

Part 10: General rules for tax credits
Chapter 63: Claims, decisions and getting paid: tax credits
2. How and when to make a claim

Once a claim for tax credits has been made, it can be renewed at the end of that tax year (see p1502).

Should you renew a nil award?[26]

Tax credits are always based on annual income. HMRC bases the initial award on your (and your partner's) *previous* tax year's income (see p1475). If your income in the previous year was too high to qualify for tax credits, but you think your income in the current year may be substantially lower and you will qualify (eg, if you are self-employed with a fluctuating income, or your income is going to fall because your work is seasonal, you are going on maternity leave or you might be made redundant), you may have a 'nil award'.[27] This means that you are eligible for tax credits and your claim is in the system, but you are currently not paid anything because your previous year's income was too high. This protects your position because, once your current year's income is known, HMRC can amend the nil award to make a payment for the whole period of your claim. The nil award can be amended during the year or at the end of the tax year, and the new award runs from your original date of claim (or the date to which your claim was backdated).

Information to support your claim

You must provide all the information required by HMRC, unless HMRC decides otherwise.[28] If you do not supply all the requested information, a decision may be delayed, or HMRC may decide to 'reject' your claim as not validly made. You can appeal against a decision to reject a claim that is not made in an accepted manner or does not contain all the required information.[29] If you need advice about the information required, contact the Helpline (see p1516).

National insurance number requirement

Your claim must include the following for each person:[30]
- your (and your partner's if you are claiming as a couple) national insurance (NI) number plus information or evidence establishing that the number is yours (or your partner's); *or*
- information or evidence to enable HMRC to find your (and your partner's) NI number; *or*
- an application for an NI number, with the necessary evidence or information to allow one to be allocated (this does not necessarily mean that you must actually be allocated an NI number).

You do not need to meet the above NI number requirement if HMRC believes you have a reasonable excuse.[31] 'Reasonable excuse' is not defined, but HMRC says it varies from case to case and discretion must be used fairly.[32] You can appeal against a decision that you do not have a reasonable excuse for not meeting the NI number requirement.[33] If someone has not been given an NI number, you can argue this is a reasonable excuse.

If you or your partner are a 'person subject to immigration control' (see p1560), see p1572 for the NI number requirement and p1564 for how tax credits are affected by your immigration status.

Child benefit reference number

You may be asked for the child benefit reference number for any child(ren) for whom you are claiming. You do not have to provide one if you do not have one. There is no legal requirement to claim child benefit in order to be entitled to CTC. If you do not have a child benefit reference number (eg, because you are waiting for your child benefit claim to be processed), do not delay claiming CTC. Child benefit can be backdated for three months, but CTC can only be backdated for 31 days, and it usually takes longer than this for a child benefit claim to be made and processed. HMRC has confirmed that tax credit claims will not be rejected because the child benefit reference number is missing.[34]

If you do not have a child benefit reference number, it may take longer to confirm the identity of the child, and that you are responsible for her/him. However, the tax credit award will still be made from the date of claim, with up to 31 days' backdating. As long as your tax credit claim is received within 31 days of the date of birth of a new baby, or the date you became responsible for a child, it will be awarded from that date, even if it takes longer than this to process.

Income

If you are receiving income support, income-based jobseeker's allowance (JSA), income-related employment and support allowance (ESA) or pension credit when you claim tax credits, you must confirm this. You do not need to provide any other income details.[35] HMRC expects you to know which type of JSA or ESA you are getting.[36]

Otherwise, when you make a claim for tax credits, you must provide a figure for your income during the previous tax year. If you are part of a couple and making a joint claim, your award is based on your joint income during the previous tax year. This applies even in situations in which you may not have been living as a couple in the previous year, so income before the relationship began still counts as joint income.[37] For what counts as income, see Chapter 62.

If you think that your current tax year's income is going to be substantially different from the previous tax year's income, you must still provide details of your previous tax year's income. When HMRC makes a decision on your claim, you are sent an award notice informing you how to notify it of your estimated income for the current year. You can also request that your award be adjusted at any time during the year of the award. Where appropriate, HMRC adjusts your award of tax credits, using your estimated figure of your current year's income (see p1475).

If you worked as an employee throughout the previous tax year, your P60 for that year has details of your taxable income. If you received any payments in kind

Part 10: General rules for tax credits
Chapter 63: Claims, decisions and getting paid: tax credits
2. How and when to make a claim

from your employer, you should have details of these on Form P11D, which your employer should give you. If you were self-employed throughout the previous tax year, you can use your tax return as the basis for your taxable income. If you were in receipt of taxable social security benefits, you should be able to get a statement of taxable benefit income from the DWP.

Bank account details

You are required to provide details of a bank, building society or post office card account into which the tax credits can be paid. This is because entitlement depends on having a bank or other account.[38] See p1505 if you do not have an account.

Further information and evidence

HMRC might need further information or evidence before making a decision on your claim or renewal or when considering whether to revise a decision. The information or evidence can be required from you or from your employer or childcare provider. If material is required, HMRC gives notice to provide it within a specified time limit. In all cases, this must be at least 30 days.[39] The basic rule is that you can be required to provide any further information or evidence that HMRC considers necessary. If you do not provide the material requested, your claim should be decided on the information available and you might be refused tax credits. If you provide incorrect information or fail to comply with requirements to provide information or evidence, you may be given a financial penalty or, if you are considered to have acted fraudulently, a fine or imprisonment, or both (see Chapter 65).

Renewing your award

From 6 April each year, HMRC reviews all tax credit awards (see p1512). This annual review, and your response, is also your renewal claim for the new tax year. If you were entitled to either tax credit in 2019/20, you can make a renewal claim for 2020/21.[40] Tax credits continue to be paid on a provisional basis during the annual review (see p1506).

Withdrawing your award

If you no longer wish to receive tax credits, you can withdraw your claim during the annual review (see p1512). However, if you have been receiving 'provisional payments' (see p1506) since the start of the new tax year, these become overpayments if there is no renewal claim. If you have a nil award because your income is too high for an award to be made, HMRC seeks to withdraw your claim. HMRC writes to you at least 35 days before the annual review to notify you that your claim will not be renewed unless you respond within 30 days that you want your claim to continue.[41] Renewing a nil award protects your future entitlement and may prove valuable if income drops unexpectedly later in the year.[42]

3. **Decisions**

Once you have made a valid claim for tax credits (see p1499), HM Revenue and Customs (HMRC) must make a decision on whether you are entitled to either of the tax credits and, if so, at what rate.[43] HMRC must decide your entitlement to both child tax credit and working tax credit. HMRC may first require you, or your partner if you are making a joint claim, to provide any information or evidence that it needs to make a decision.[44]

You can amend, either verbally or in writing, the details you provided when making your claim at any time until HMRC makes its initial decision and your date of claim will remain the same.[45]

An '**initial decision**' is made at the start of your claim or renewal, and is based on an estimate of your tax credit award for the whole year (6 April to 5 April) or the remainder of the year if you claim during the year. You are notified of the initial decision in an award notice (Form TC602). You are asked to check the details on your award notice using a checklist (Form TC602(SN)). Contact the Tax Credit Office if any of the details shown on the award notice are wrong or have changed. If you do not and an overpayment results, HMRC may expect you to pay it back (see p1523).

You must be notified of the initial decision. The notice must include the date on which it is given and your right to request a mandatory reconsideration, and subsequent right to appeal.[46] If you had already claimed tax credits in the previous year, your initial decision for the coming year may be included in the annual review (see p1512).[47]

A '**revised decision**' may be made during the tax year – eg, following certain changes of circumstances (see p1507). Decisions can be revised at any time during the tax year, and as many times as is required. Each revised decision is notified on a tax credits award notice (Form TC602).

A '**final decision**' is made after the end of the tax year, as part of the annual review (see p1515). It is based on your circumstances during the year and is the decision that confirms what your entitlement actually was. You are sent a tax credits award notice (Form TC602). A final decision can only be changed in limited circumstances (see p1545).

Unless the decision on your award is changed after a revision, mandatory reconsideration or appeal, the initial decision and the final decision are the only decisions on your claim that you receive.

If you think an initial decision, revised decision or final decision is wrong, you can request a mandatory reconsideration and then appeal (see Chapter 66).

Part 10: General rules for tax credits
Chapter 63: Claims, decisions and getting paid: tax credits
5. Getting paid

4. **Backdating your claim**

In general, your claim for tax credits can be backdated for up to 31 days (but see below), provided you satisfied the rules of entitlement throughout the 31-day period.[48] This cannot include a period in which you were entitled to universal credit (UC), or when you were receiving tax-free childcare payments (see p871), unless you were registered for tax-free childcare but no payments were made from your tax-free childcare account and the account has now been closed.

It is best to ask for your claim to be backdated to when you think your entitlement began (subject to the 31-day limit), either in writing or in a subsequent telephone call. You do not need to give any reasons.

A renewal claim can be backdated for a longer period, depending on when you make your annual declaration (see p1513).

If you were entitled to tax credits but no payment was made because you did not provide sufficient details of an account into which payments could be made and you subsequently provide the necessary details, payment can be backdated for up to three months from the date you supply the information, (but no more than 31 days before the date you claimed).[49]

A new claim for working tax credit (WTC) can be backdated for more than 31 days if you have a disability and you have been waiting to hear about a disability benefit. If your claim includes the disabled worker element (see p1458) and you claim within 31 days of being awarded a qualifying disability benefit (usually personal independence payment (PIP)), your WTC claim can be backdated to the date from which your PIP was awarded, provided you were working at least 16 hours throughout the period and did not qualify for WTC without the award of the disability benefit, including because your income was too high.[50]

A new claim for child tax credit (CTC) cannot be backdated for more than 31 days, even if a disability benefit has been awarded for the child. If you have an existing award of WTC or CTC and want to be awarded the disability or severe disability elements following an award of a qualifying disability benefit, see p1509.

See p1574 for backdating if you are granted refugee status.

5. **Getting paid**

Who is paid

If you have a joint award, child tax credit (CTC) and the childcare element of working tax credit (WTC) are paid into the account of the 'main carer' of the child(ren), as nominated when you claim.[51] The **'main carer'** can be either you or your partner, depending on who you both agree should be paid. If both live at the same address and either you do not identify who should be paid, or you cannot agree, HM Revenue and Customs (HMRC) decides. If you and your partner are not currently living at the same address or one of you is temporarily absent, HMRC decides which of you will be paid. If the main carer changes following an award of tax credits, HMRC can make the payments to that person instead if it considers it reasonable.

If you have a joint award of WTC and one of you is working, the payment (apart from any amount for childcare) is made to the person who is in full-time paid work (see p299). If you are both in full-time paid work, you can decide who will receive the payment. If you cannot agree, HMRC decides. If you both agree who should be paid, write to the Tax Credit Office requesting that payment be made to that person.[52]

If you make a joint claim and your partner dies, you receive any outstanding amount of tax credits that would have been paid to you and your partner up to the date of death, after which you must usually claim UC instead.[53]

If an appointee (see p1170) is acting on your behalf, payment is normally made to her/him.[54]

How and when payments are made

HMRC makes payments of tax credits by direct credit transfer into a bank, building society (or similar) or post office card account.[55] The government is writing to people with post office card accounts asking them to switch to a bank, building society or credit union account, but post office card accounts remain available for the time being. You can request that the payments be made into your account every week or every four weeks, but HMRC has the discretion to make payments weekly or four-weekly as it sees fit. CTC and the childcare element of WTC must be paid at the same time and at the same intervals.[56] Generally, tax credits payments are made in arrears.[57]

If you are entitled to less than £2 tax credits a week, your award may be paid as a single lump sum for the year, payable at such time as HMRC considers appropriate.[58]

If it is not considered appropriate for payments to be made into an account, HMRC can decide on the manner and timing of payment by other means, such as by 'payment voucher' at a post office (but it no longer issues cheques).[59]

If you do not provide account details, HMRC should write to you, requesting that you supply the information within four weeks, after which your payments may be postponed.[60] If you then require an authority from HMRC to open an account, you have three weeks from the date it supplies you with this to provide details of your account. If you do not provide details of an account within three months of your payments being postponed (or by the end of the relevant tax year if this is earlier), your entitlement may cease from the date payments were postponed. These periods can be extended if there are exceptional circumstances

Part 10: General rules for tax credits
Chapter 63: Claims, decisions and getting paid: tax credits
5. Getting paid

or you have a 'reasonable excuse' for not being able to provide the details within the time limits.[61]

If you lose your bank or post office account card or forget your PIN, see p1188.

Payments of tax credits may be reduced if an overpayment is being recovered. See Chapter 64 for more information.

Urgent payments

There is no provision in the tax credits legislation for payments to be made before a decision has been made on entitlement. However, once a decision has been made to award tax credits, there is official guidance on making payments urgently when requested. Urgent payments should be made if you or your child are experiencing hardship, especially in cases of domestic violence, identity fraud or immediate risk of eviction. These payments are referred to in the *Tax Credits Manual* as 'manual payments', 'interim payments' and 'user-requested payments'. Payment can be made by the next day into an account.[62]

When payment is postponed or suspended

Payment of tax credits may be postponed or suspended if:[63]
- you have failed to provide correct account details (see p1502); *or*
- you have failed to respond to a request for information or evidence by a specified date (see p1502); *or*
- you are receiving 'provisional payments' (see below); or
- there is an appeal pending against a decision of the First-tier Tribunal, Upper Tribunal or a court either in your case or in another case that might affect your award (including if HMRC is considering whether to make a further appeal or request a statement of reasons).

If your income drops during the year, your tax credits may be increased and you may appear to be due some arrears of tax credits for the earlier part of the year. HMRC refers to this as a 'potential payment', and it may be held back until the end of the year when your final income is known. If the underpayment is confirmed at the end of the tax year, it must be paid to you.[64]

Provisional payments

Your claim is renewed by the annual review process from April to July, during which time your tax credits may continue to be paid on a provisional basis.[65]

Provisional payments can be made while you are waiting to renew your claim and have not had a final decision on the previous year. Provisional payments can also continue if you have renewed your claim but not yet received an initial decision on the new tax year. Provisional payments are discretionary and can be made, adjusted or suspended without a formal decision being made, but you may receive a letter which is referred to as a 'statement like an award notice' (Form TC602(J)).[66]

If HMRC does not have up-to-date income details, these payments are based on the assumption that your income for the tax year just ended increased in line with average earnings.[67] If your income increased by more than this, you may be overpaid until the review is complete. Therefore, it is best to provide details of your income as soon as possible and not wait for the annual review. If you withdraw or fail to renew your claim, any provisional payments since the start of the year will become an overpayment because there is no claim for the new tax year.

6. **Change of circumstances**

Changes in your family circumstances, childcare charges or income during your award may lead to changes in your tax credit entitlement. If changes do affect your entitlement, this can be altered either soon after the change has occurred, or at the end of the year when the final decision is made and HM Revenue and Customs (HMRC) makes a final check on your details. Certain changes must be notified to the Tax Credit Office within one month or you may incur a penalty (see below). You should report other changes which increase your entitlement within one month of the date of change, for your increased award to be backdated for up to one month.

Changes that must be notified

Some changes must be notified to the Tax Credit Office within one month of the date of the change or the date you became aware of the change, if this was later. The notification must be 'given' to the appropriate office (see p1512).[68] If you do not do this, you may receive a penalty decision notice (see p1535).

If you have any of the following changes in your circumstances, the way your tax credits are calculated changes.[69] Either your entitlement to tax credits ceases or a new 'relevant period' starts from the date the change is treated as having taken effect. A new relevant period means that a new calculation of your tax credit entitlement is made. See p1452 for more on the relevant period and details of the calculation.

You must notify the Tax Credit Office within one month if:[70]

- you were claiming as a single person but are now part of a couple. Your tax credit entitlement comes to an end from the date the change occurred, and you must usually claim universal credit (UC) instead;
- you were claiming as a couple but are no longer part of that couple. Your entitlement comes to an end from the date the change occurred, and you must usually claim UC instead;

Part 10: General rules for tax credits
Chapter 63: Claims, decisions and getting paid: tax credits
6. Change of circumstances

- you or your partner leave the UK permanently or for more than eight weeks (12 if due to illness or bereavement) and cannot be treated as being in the UK (see p1662). Entitlement comes to an end and you must usually claim UC instead;
- for child tax credit (CTC) only, you lose your right to reside in the UK (see p1591);
- there has been a decrease of £10 a week or more over four consecutive weeks in your or your partner's average weekly childcare charge (as calculated on p1463) or the childcare costs have stopped. This change takes effect on the day after the four consecutive weeks. If you have been awarded childcare costs for a fixed period that was known when the costs were awarded, the change takes effect from the week following the end of the period of the award, instead of the usual four-week period;[71]
- you or your partner stop normally working at least 16 or 30 hours a week (see p299 for rules about work). You can still count as being in work in some situations – eg, in some cases of illness or maternity and during the four-week run-on of working tax credit (WTC) (see p305). For a couple, you do not need to report a change in which partner is working, provided this does not affect your entitlement or maximum rate;[72]
- you are a couple with children, and you and your partner stop normally working a combined total of 24 or 30 hours a week;
- you or your partner cease to be responsible for one or more of your children (see p288 for when you count as responsible);
- a child for whom you or your partner are responsible dies (see p286 for who counts as a child);
- a child for whom you or your partner are responsible stops counting as a child or qualifying young person, other than by reaching age 20 (see p286 for who counts as a child). You must notify the Tax Credit Office within one month of the date the change actually occurred, rather than when you became aware of the change.

Changes that terminate your tax credits award

Your tax credit award automatically terminates in the following situations.

- You become a UC claimant. This may happen if you make a claim for UC or become part of a couple with someone who is already entitled to UC. The DWP issues a 'stop notice' to HMRC, notifying it that you have claimed and meet the basic conditions for UC.[73] Your tax credit award is terminated, even if you do not receive any UC because your income or capital is too high. Your tax credits claim usually ends on the day before your entitlement to UC begins. However, if you become part of a couple with a UC claimant, your new joint UC claim begins from the start of your partner's assessment period in which you became a couple.[74] In this case, you are still entitled to tax credits up to the actual date you became a couple.[75]

- You apply for, and are entitled to, tax-free childcare payments (see p871). Check whether you will be better off on tax-free childcare before applying. This is only likely to be the case if you are entitled to a small amount of tax credits. Your entire tax credits claim, not just the childcare element, ends on the day before your entitlement period for tax-free childcare begins.[76]

Changes that affect your maximum entitlement

In addition to the changes outlined above, other changes in your circumstances can also affect your entitlement to tax credits. Some changes can be notified up to a week in advance (see p1512). However, most changes which *increase* your entitlement are only backdated for a maximum of one month from the time that you notify the Tax Credit Office of the change (except a change that affects your entitlement to one of the disability elements – see below).[77]

Changes that *decrease* your entitlement always take effect from the date of change, irrespective of when you notify the Tax Credit Office. Delaying notifying these changes can, therefore, lead to an underpayment or overpayment, so tell the Tax Credit Office as soon as possible. Overpayments are usually recovered from you (see Chapter 64).

The changes in your circumstances that affect your tax credit entitlement include if:

- you have a new baby, or another child joins your family (you should still report this change even if you may be affected by the two child limit – see p1453);
- your child is staying on in full-time non-advanced education after 31 August following his/her 16th birthday (HMRC considers this to be a change, as the default position is that CTC will stop unless you notify it of this);
- you or your partner start normally working at least 16, 24 or 30 hours a week;
- your childcare costs increase by £10 or more a week for at least four weeks in a row. The change takes effect from the first week in which your costs increase.[78] You can report an increase of £10 or more a week as soon as one occurs, provided you expect it to last for at least four weeks. For how your childcare costs are calculated, see p1463.

Backdating your entitlement to a disabled worker, severe disability, disabled child or severely disabled child element

The disabled worker and severe disability elements of WTC can be backdated for more than one month if you notify the Tax Credit Office that you have been awarded a qualifying disability benefit (usually personal independence payment (PIP)), within one month of that award being made.[79] The elements can be backdated to the date from which the disability benefit was awarded. This includes after an appeal or supersession from a previous tax year. If the award means that you become entitled to WTC for the first time, see p1504.

Part 10: General rules for tax credits
Chapter 63: Claims, decisions and getting paid: tax credits
6. Change of circumstances

A similar rule applies to CTC entitlement. If a child for whom you are responsible is awarded DLA (child disability payment in Scotland) or a young person is awarded PIP, you are entitled to the disabled child element. If the child is awarded the DLA care component at the highest rate, child disability payment higher rate or the enhanced rate of the PIP daily living component, you are also entitled to the severely disabled child element in your CTC award. The elements can be backdated for more than one month, to the date from which DLA or PIP was awarded, if you notify the Tax Credit Office of the award of DLA or PIP within one month of the DLA or PIP decision.[80] This includes after an appeal or supersession from a previous tax year.

You should report changes to a qualifying disability benefit, as failure to do so may result in an underpayment or overpayment. However, as it is not listed as a change that you are legally obliged to report, you cannot be given a penalty for failing to report a change in entitlement to a disability benefit during a tax year (but if you fail to notice it is incorrectly recorded in your circumstances at the annual review, you could be given a penalty for a false declaration).[81]

If you are now getting UC, but have been awarded a qualifying disability benefit for a period when you were on tax credits, you can still get arrears of tax credits up to the date of your UC claim. You should notify HMRC within one month of the disability benefit decision and request that the final decision on your tax credits is revised.

Changes in income

The initial decision on your award of tax credit is usually based on your previous year's income. Your award can be changed to reflect:
- an expected fall in your annual income of more than £2,500 compared with the previous year (see below); *and*
- an expected rise in your annual income of more than £2,500 compared with the previous year (see p1511).

You are not required to report a change in income during the year and a penalty cannot be imposed on you if you fail to do so, unless it is a formal request for information (see p1534). However, it is often worth reporting a change when it occurs to avoid overpayments or underpayments. HMRC may use 'real-time information' on wages obtained from your employer for tax purposes. HMRC always requires a figure for your annual income in the complete tax year, so be careful to keep an in-year estimate accurate and up to date.

If you expect your annual income to fall by more than £2,500
- If you notify the Tax Credit Office of an estimated decrease in your annual income of more than £2,500 during the year, your tax credit payments may be increased. However, the first £2,500 of the decrease is disregarded, so it is only any decrease over that amount that makes a difference. HMRC adds £2,500

onto the current year's income and bases your award on the result. For example, if your 2019/20 income was £10,000 and your 2020/21 income is £6,000, your tax credits award for 2020/21 is based on £8,500.[82]

- An increase in tax credits means that if you get housing benefit (HB), the amount could be reduced because tax credits count as income.
- At the end of the year, it may be that your income did not fall as you predicted and, as a result, you have been overpaid tax credits, which you may have to repay. For example, if your 2019/20 income was £9,000 and you ask for your tax credits to be based on an estimate that your 2020/21 income will be £6,000 but, at the end of 2020/21, your actual income is £8,000, your tax credit award should not have been increased and you will have been overpaid.
- HB takes into account the amount of tax credits you actually *receive*. If you have been overpaid tax credits, HB is *not* increased for the period during which you should have received a lower amount of tax credits. Not only will you usually have to repay the overpaid tax credits, you may have lost out on the additional HB which you would have been able to claim had you been receiving a lower award of tax credits.
- If the Tax Credit Office is not aware of a fall in income of more than £2,500 during the year, your tax credit entitlement is not adjusted until the final decision at the end of the year. In this instance, you will have been underpaid tax credits for the year, and this should be paid to you as a lump sum. This lump sum counts as capital for HB and is ignored for 52 weeks after you have received it.[83] You will not, therefore, have been overpaid HB as a result of receiving these arrears and you will not have been overpaid or lost out on tax credits.

If you expect your annual income to rise by more than £2,500

- If you notify the Tax Credit Office that you expect your income to increase by more than £2,500 during the year, your tax credit award is decreased. This may mean that you prevent an overpayment of tax credits building up further during the year (see Chapter 64). Your HB (if you are entitled to any) can then be increased to take account of the lower award of tax credits.
- If the Tax Credit Office is not aware of an expected rise in your income during the year, you keep being paid the 'extra' tax credits during the year and will incur an overpayment. The overpaid tax credits are usually recoverable from you by reducing the amount of tax credits you are paid in the following year, in which case your HB in that year is likely to increase.
- There is no penalty for incurring an overpayment of tax credits on the basis of an increase in income.
- If you have overestimated your income, and it does not rise as expected, you may have been underpaid tax credits and you can receive a lump sum at the end of the year.

Part 10: General rules for tax credits
Chapter 63: Claims, decisions and getting paid: tax credits
7. Annual reviews

Notifying changes of circumstances

You can notify any changes in your circumstances by telephone, in writing or online through a government gateway account. The notification must be given to any office specified in writing by HMRC – eg, the Tax Credit Office address on your award notice.[84] This could include the government's 'Tell Us Once' service following a death.

If you notified the DWP or another part of HMRC of a change which affects your tax credit entitlement and this was not passed on and resulted in an underpayment or overpayment, you should raise this in *any* dispute (see p1522). In practice, to be safe, you should ensure that the Tax Credit Office has been informed. HMRC encourages claimants to telephone the Tax Credits Helpline (see p1516) with queries or to report a change. However, it is advisable to confirm the notification in writing to the Tax Credit Office and to keep a copy so you have a record of what you have said and when you said it.

Notification must be given by the person who claimed the tax credit. In joint claim cases, it can be given by either member of the couple.[85]

Some changes of circumstances can be notified up to a week in advance. These are if:[86]
- you have accepted an offer of work and expect to start work within seven days;
- you have arranged childcare and will incur childcare costs during the current tax year;
- your weekly childcare costs are going to change by £10 a week or more.

You can also notify HMRC in advance if you expect your child to stay on in full-time, non-advanced education or approved training from 1 September after her/his 16th birthday.[87]

You can amend the notification at any time before the initial award is revised, in which case the amended notification is taken as being notified at the time that your original notification was sent.[88]

If you notify a change of circumstances, HMRC should send you a new award notice (if the change affected your award) within 30 days.[89] If you do not receive one within 30 days, HMRC's leaflet asks you to call the Tax Credits Helpline again. However, provided you can prove the original notification was made, it is HMRC's responsibility to act on the information provided (see p1523).

7. **Annual reviews**

The annual review is the process by which HM Revenue and Customs (HMRC) finalises your entitlement for the year that has just ended, and makes an initial decision on your award for the year that has just begun. By responding to the annual review, you renew your claim for tax credits for the new tax year.

If you had an award of tax credits for the tax year 2019/20, HMRC should write to you between April and July 2020 enclosing an annual review form (Form TC603R). This is referred to in the legislation as the 'final notice'.[90]

If you had more than one award for tax credits during the previous tax year (eg, because of a gap in eligibility), you receive a separate annual review form and annual declaration form, if required, for each award. If you are sent more than one set of forms covering different awards, check and reply to each separately, even if they ask for the same information.

If you are sent an annual review form, but not an annual declaration form, you are asked to check that all the details about your award for the previous year are correct and to notify the Tax Credit Office of any changes in your circumstances. You are then deemed to have confirmed that all the details in the form are correct.[91] The final decision on the award for 2019/20 and an initial decision on the award for 2020/21 are as set out on the annual review form and you do not receive another notice of the final decision when it is made on or after 31 July. However, always check the form and the notes accompanying it carefully to see whether you need to return the forms or report a change or error.

If the details on the forms sent to you about your award and income are not correct and you fail to reply within the time allowed, you may not receive the correct amount of tax credits. If you are overpaid as a result, you may have to repay the overpayment. If you fail to notify certain changes of circumstances promptly, you may be given a penalty (see p1535).

If your tax credit award ends because you become entitled to universal credit (UC), see p1516.

Automatic renewal

If you have been receiving income support, income-based jobseeker's allowance, income-related employment and support allowance or pension credit throughout 2019/20 and are still getting one of those benefits, the annual review may tell you that your award will be renewed automatically on the information shown on the notice, unless you report a change or error. This automatic renewal process may also apply if HMRC uses 'real-time information' on earnings provided by your employer for PAYE (pay as you earn) purposes, but you must still check that this is correct. In other cases, you may also receive an annual declaration form (Form TC603D – see below).

The annual declaration

You may receive an annual declaration form (Form TC603D) that asks for details of your income in the previous tax year. You must also tell the Tax Credit Office of any changes in your personal circumstances that are different from those set out in the annual review form.

Part 10: General rules for tax credits
Chapter 63: Claims, decisions and getting paid: tax credits
7. Annual reviews

If you are sent an annual declaration form, you must always respond to it on or before the date specified – usually 31 July, unless it was issued after 1 July, in which case you must be given at least 30 days to respond. If you are returning the annual declaration form by post, this is the date by which it must be received by the Tax Credit Office.

Responses must usually be on a form provided by HMRC (Form TC603RD). Alternatively, you can call the Tax Credit Helpline (see p1516) or renew your award online at gov.uk/manage-your-tax-credits. If you are unable to respond to the annual declaration (eg, because of illness), responses can be accepted from receivers and people who are appointees for tax credit or benefit purposes.[92]

If you respond in writing but do not use the annual declaration form, HMRC has discretion whether to accept it.[93]

If you do not respond to the annual declaration, your tax credit payments will stop, you may have to repay any tax credits paid since 6 April and you may have to pay a penalty.

For a joint award, one member of a couple can make the declaration by telephone or online on behalf of her/his partner; if it is in writing, both partners must sign it.[94] If a couple separate during the renewal period, a declaration by one partner allows the claim to be renewed up to the date of separation.[95] Both members of a separated couple are expected to make signed declarations for the previous year to allow the award for that year to be finalised. However, if only one signs the declaration, the award can be finalised, based on the information held by HMRC about the other member.[96]

If you do not know your total income for the period in question, do not delay making your annual declaration. Instead, provide an estimate and send details of your actual income as soon as you can. The annual declaration form allows for this, and there is a box to tick to show that you have given an estimate. You must provide your actual income figure by a second deadline, usually 31 January at the latest. The annual declaration form notifies you that if you do not do so, you are treated as having declared that your final income was as estimated, and your estimate is used to finalise your entitlement.[97]

Responding to the annual declaration, if required, is how your award is renewed for the new tax year, and failure to meet the deadline can mean that you lose out on tax credits. Unless you are single and are now part of a couple or you were in a couple and are now single, the following apply.

- If you make your annual declaration by the 31 July deadline, your renewal claim is backdated to 6 April 2020.[98]
- If you do not make your annual declaration by 31 July, HMRC sends you a notice that your payments of tax credits have ceased. If you make your annual declaration within 30 days following the date on this notice, your renewal claim is backdated to 6 April 2020.[99]
- If neither of the above applies, but you make your annual declaration by 31 January 2021 and have 'good cause' for making a late declaration, your renewal

claim is backdated to 6 April 2020.[100] 'Good cause' is not defined, but HMRC says it will look at each case on its individual merits. It will consider whether you were not able to complete the form because of exceptional circumstances and could not make arrangements for someone else to handle your affairs.[101]

- If you make your annual declaration late without good cause, or after 31 January in any case, this can still be treated as a new claim and it can only be backdated for 31 days.[102] Unless you are prevented from claiming UC, you will have to argue that this can be treated as a new claim for tax credits because the wording of the renewal provision still applies to you (see p1496).

Note: if you are not accepted as having good cause for making a late declaration, you should request a mandatory reconsideration, and then appeal to the First-tier Tribunal if you are unhappy with the outcome.[103] Remember that your late declaration should be treated as a new claim in any case.

The final decision

After the annual review has been completed, HMRC must make a final decision on whether you were entitled to tax credits for the tax year in question and, if so, the amount of your entitlement for that year.[104] The final decision can, therefore, establish that:
- the initial decision was correct and you received the right amount;
- you were underpaid tax credits;
- you were overpaid tax credits.

If you are underpaid tax credits, HMRC must pay you, usually in a lump sum.[105] If you are overpaid, HMRC asks you to pay back the overpayment (see Chapter 64).

If you do not agree that you have been overpaid, it is important that you request a mandatory reconsideration of the lower award notified to you in the final decision.

HMRC aims to deal with your review within eight weeks of receiving your declaration.[106] If you did not have an annual declaration form to complete, the final decision is as set out in your annual review form (unless, having read your annual review form, you find that you have a change of circumstances to report, in which case HMRC sends you details of your new award after it has dealt with the reported change). If your annual review told you what the final decision will be, and when it will be made, and you do not report any changes, the final decision can be made without further notification.[107] Any other decision must be notified to you in writing, stating the date on which it is made and including details of your right to request a mandatory reconsideration and your subsequent right of appeal.[108] If a decision does not include these details, it is 'defective' and the time limit for requesting a mandatory reconsideration does not start to run.[109]

A final decision must not be made before you have been given the chance to respond to the annual review and/or make your annual declaration on or before

Part 10: General rules for tax credits
Chapter 63: Claims, decisions and getting paid: tax credits
8. Contacting HM Revenue and Customs

the deadline (usually 31 July). Once you have made your annual declaration, HMRC may make a final decision before the deadline. However, you can still change your declaration by the deadline, in which case HMRC may revise the final decision.[110] If you do not make your annual declaration by the deadline, the final decision can be made after that date, based on the information held by HMRC at that time.[111] If you have given an estimate, HMRC may make a final decision, but can revise it if you give details of your actual income by the second deadline (usually 31 January).

HMRC also sends you an initial decision notice (Form TC602), setting out your award for the tax year 2020/21.

Note: if your tax credit award ends because you become entitled to UC, the final decision may be made during the tax year (see below).

In-year finalisation

If your tax credits award ends because you become entitled to UC, your tax credits award is finalised during the year, rather than at the end of the tax year.[112] This may happen if you become part of a couple with someone who is already entitled to UC, or if you make a claim for UC. HMRC may decide to wait until the end of the tax year to finalise an award if it decides it is not practical to do so during the year. If in-year finalisation applies, you do not get another annual review at the end of the year. You are asked to confirm or declare your income up to the date that your tax credits award ended, and your award is based on part-year income (see p1477). If you do not know your exact income, you can provide an estimate within 30 days. However, your estimated part-year income is used to finalise your award and you are not given an opportunity to rectify the estimate later.[113] If you disagree with the final decision following in-year finalisation for any reason, including the income figure used, you can request a mandatory reconsideration and, if you are unhappy with the outcome, appeal (see Chapter 66).

8. **Contacting HM Revenue and Customs**

You can telephone the Tax Credit Helpline (tel: 0345 300 3900; or textphone via Relay UK 18001 then 0345 300 3900). Be ready to give your name, address and national insurance (NI) number. Always keep a note of the date and time of your call, with a brief note of what is said and, if possible, the name and title of the person you speak to. HM Revenue and Customs (HMRC) aims to record all calls, but a small number may not be recorded because of technical difficulties.[114] In the event of a dispute, you can request the recording of your call. If the recording is not available, and you can show that you made a call on a certain date, HMRC has agreed that you should be given the benefit of the doubt about what was said.[115]

It is best to follow up your call with a letter confirming the information you have provided and the advice given. Write to the Tax Credit Office at the address on the award notice and include your name, address, NI number and the date. Always keep a copy of your letter. If you are requesting a mandatory reconsideration, appealing, disputing recovery of an overpayment or making a complaint, it is best to use the relevant form or put it in writing. HMRC has an online service (gov.uk/manage-your-tax-credits) to check details of your claim and report changes of circumstances. HMRC's policy is to retain images of claim forms, documents and recordings of telephone calls for five years plus the tax year or from the date of the last decision on that claim.[116]

There is also a separate intermediaries line for use by approved advice agencies (see gov.uk/getting-help-with-your-tax-credits-claim/authorisation) and an MPs' hotline for exclusive use by MPs' offices, which in some cases can get quicker results.

If things go wrong

If a decision is wrong, you can request a mandatory reconsideration and, if you are unhappy with the outcome, appeal against it (see Chapter 66). If you are given wrong advice by an employee of HMRC, you may be able to seek compensation either through the internal complaints procedure (see p1441) or judicial review. If you are given wrong information by HMRC or the DWP which led to an overpayment, this may be grounds for its recovery to be waived (see p1522). Official guidance states that in some cases, if HMRC has given you incorrect advice in the past, it may be bound by it if applying the correct legal position retrospectively would cause you real harm or loss and be so unfair as to constitute an abuse of power.[117]

If your claim has been received but not dealt with, ask why. If you are not satisfied with the explanation, make a complaint to HMRC (see p1441). You can also complain if, for example, you have been treated badly or your case has been mishandled. In some cases, you can seek a judicial review (see p1414). If you are unhappy with the way HMRC handles your complaint, you can take it to the Adjudicator's Office and, if still unhappy, ask your MP to take it to the Parliamentary and Health Service Ombudsman (see p1442). It is not possible to sue HMRC for negligence in the way your award is decided.[118]

Part 10: General rules for tax credits
Chapter 63: Claims, decisions and getting paid: tax credits
Notes

Notes

1. Who can get tax credits
1 s3(3) TCA 2002
2 Reg 8 UC(TP) Regs; *HMRC v LD (TC)* [2018] UKUT 306 (AAC)
3 s3(3)(a) and (8) TCA 2002
4 Reg 13(3) TC(CN) Regs
5 s3(4) TCA 2002; regs 5 and 6 UC(TP) Regs
6 s32(3) TCA 2002; reg 21(2)(a) TC(CN) Regs
7 Art 7(1), (2), (5) and (6) WRA(No.23)O
8 s3(5A) TCA 2002
9 s48(2) TCA 2002. Tax credits legislation has not been amended to reflect same-sex marriage. HMRC says this is not necessary because the legal interpretation of a married couple is changed via Sch 3 M(SSC)A 2013 and s4 Marriage and Civil Partnership (Scotland) Act 2014.
10 Regs 5 and 6 UC(TP) Regs; reg 9(8) UC,PIP,JSA&ESA(C&P) Regs
11 *HMRC v PD (TC)* [2012] UKUT 230 (AAC)
12 s3(5A)(a)(ii) and (c)(ii) TCA 2002; *UA v HMRC (TC)* [2019] UKUT 113 (AAC)
13 *DG v HMRC (TC)* [2013] UKUT 631 (AAC)
14 R(TC) 2/06
15 TC(PM) Regs
16 *Crake and Butterworth v SBC* [1982] 1 All ER 498; R(SB) 17/81; CTC/3864/2004
17 *TM v HMRC (TC)* [2013] UKUT 444 (AAC); *NI v HMRC (TC)* [2015] UKUT 490 (AAC)
18 *SS v HMRC (TC)* [2014] UKUT 383 (AAC)
19 Reg 3(5) and (6) TC(R) Regs
20 Reg 3(2) TC(Imm) Regs; reg 11(4) WTC(EMR) Regs
21 Regs 17 and 18 TC(CN) Regs

2. How and when to make a claim
22 s3(1) TCA 2002
23 Reg 5(2) TC(CN) Regs
24 Reg 9 TC(CN) Regs
25 s5(2) TCA 2002; reg 4 TC(CN) Regs
26 See 'If you know your income will go down' at gov.uk/claim-tax-credits/when-to-claim
27 s14(3) TCA 2002
28 Reg 5(3) TC(CN) Regs

29 *CI v HMRC (TC)* [2014] UKUT 158 (AAC), which rejects the decision saying there is no such right in *ZM and AB v HMRC (TC)* [2013] UKUT 547 (AAC)
30 Reg 5(4) TC(CN) Regs
31 Reg 5(6) TC(CN) Regs
32 TCTM 06110
33 *CI v HMRC (TC)* [2014] UKUT 158 (AAC), which rejects the decision saying there is no such right in *ZM and AB v HMRC (TC)* [2013] UKUT 547 (AAC)
34 HMRC reply to CPAG email, 11 April 2012
35 s7(2) TCA 2002; Form TC600, Part 5; reg 4 TC(ITDR) Regs
36 HMRC leaflet WTC8, *Child Tax Credit and Working Tax Credit: why overpayments happen*, pp5-6
37 s7(5)(a) TCA 2002; R(TC) 1/08
38 Reg 14 TC(PC) Regs
39 ss14, 15, 16, 17,18,19 and 22 TCA 2002; regs 30-33 TC(CN) Regs
40 Art 7(6) WRA(No.23)O
41 Reg 12(8) TC(CN) Regs
42 s14(3) TCA 2002

3. Decisions
43 s14(1) TCA 2002
44 s14(2) TCA 2002
45 Regs 5 and 6 TC(CN) Regs
46 s23 TCA 2002
47 s23(3) TCA 2002

4. Backdating your claim
48 Reg 7 TC(CN) Regs
49 Reg 14(2) TC(PC) Regs
50 Reg 8 TC(CN) Regs; *MMB v HMRC (TC)* [2014] UKUT 221 (AAC)

5. Getting paid
51 Reg 3 TC(PC) Regs
52 Reg 4 TC(PC) Regs
53 Reg 5 TC(PC) Regs
54 Reg 6 TC(PC) Regs
55 Reg 13(1) TC(PC) Regs
56 Reg 8(2), (2A) and (2B) TC(PC) Regs
57 TCTM 08102
58 Reg 10 TC(PC) Regs
59 Regs 9 and 13 TC(PC) Regs
60 Reg 11(2A) TC(PC) Regs

61 Reg 14(3) and (4A)-(4E) TC(PC) Regs;
TCM 0212200
62 TCM 0212160
63 Reg 11 TC(PC) Regs; HMRC leaflet
WTC/FS9, *Tax Credits: suspension of
payments*
64 Reg 12(3) TC(PC) Regs; s30 TCA 2002
65 s24(4) TCA 2002; reg 7 TC(PC) Regs
66 TCTM 09490
67 Reg 12(4) TC(PC) Regs

6. Change of circumstances
68 ss6(3) and 32(3) TCA 2002; regs 2, 21
and 22 TC(CN) Regs
69 Regs 7(2) and 8(2) TC(ITDR) Regs
70 Reg 21(2) TC(CN) Regs
71 Reg 16(5) WTC(EMR) Regs
72 *JL v HMRC (TC)* [2013] UKUT 325 (AAC)
73 *HMRC v LH* [2018] UKUT 306 (AAC)
74 Reg 21(3B) UC Regs
75 Regs 5, 7 and 12A UC(TP) Regs
76 s30 Childcare Payments Act 2014
77 Regs 20 and 25 TC(CN) Regs
78 Reg 16(5)(a) WTC(EMR) Regs
79 Reg 26 TC(CN) Regs
80 Reg 26A TC(CN) Regs
81 Reg 21 TC(CN) Regs
82 s7(3)(d) TCA 2002; reg 5(b) TC(ITDR)
Regs
83 Sch 6(9) HB Regs
84 Regs 2 and 22 TC(CN) Regs
85 Reg 23 TC(CN) Regs
86 Reg 27 TC(CN) Regs
87 Reg 27(2B) TC(CN) Regs
88 Reg 24 TC (CN) Regs
89 HMRC leaflet COP26, *What Happens If
We've Paid You Too Much Tax Credits?*

7. Annual reviews
90 s17(1) TCA 2002
91 s17(2)(b) and (6)(b) TCA 2002
92 Regs 34-36 TC(CN) Regs
93 *SG v HMRC (TC)* [2011] UKUT 199 (AAC)
94 Reg 34 TC(CN) Regs
95 Reg 13 TC (CN) Regs
96 s18(3) TCA 2002
97 s17(8) TCA 2002; reg 33(b) TC(CN)
Regs
98 Reg 11(3)(a) TC(CN) Regs
99 Reg 11(3)(b) TC(CN) Regs
100 Reg 11(3)(c) TC(CN) Regs
101 TCM 0136160
102 Reg 11(3)(d) TC(CN) Regs; Art 7
WRA(No.23)O
103 *SG v HMRC (TC)* [2011] UKUT 199
(AAC), in particular para 84
104 s18 TCA 2002
105 s30 TCA 2002

106 HMRC leaflet TC603RD, *Renew Your Tax
Credits Now*
107 s23(3) TCA 2002
108 s23(2) TCA 2002
109 *NA v HMRC (TC)* [2016] UKUT 404
(AAC), para 11
110 s18(5) TCA 2002
111 s18(8) TCA 2002
112 Reg 12A UC(TP) Regs, as amended by
UC(TP)(A) Regs
113 Sch para 2 UC(TP) Regs, as amended by
UC(TP)(A) Regs; HMRC leaflet
TC603URD, *Ending Your Tax Credits
Award Because of a Claim for Universal
Credit*

8. Contacting HM Revenue and Customs
114 Response to a Freedom of Information
request, 12 January 2009
115 HMRC Benefits and Credits Consultation
Group minutes, 4 December 2008
116 *AG v HMRC (TC)* [2013] UKUT 530 (AAC)
117 Adjudicator's Office, *Annual Report
2019*, p11; HMRC's *Admin Law Manual*
(ADML1300)
118 *Jones v Department of Employment*
[1989] QB 1 (CA)

10

Chapter 64

Overpayments of tax credits

This chapter covers:
1. What is an overpayment of tax credits (below)
2. Disputing recovery (p1522)
3. Recovery of overpayments (p1526)
4. Interest on overpayments (p1530)

Key facts
- The rules on the recovery of tax credit overpayments are different from those that apply to most social security benefits.
- All tax credit overpayments are recoverable, however they are caused, but HM Revenue and Customs (HMRC) has the discretion to decide whether or not to do so.
- There are rules on the amount that may be recovered and guidance on the way in which HMRC should recover an overpayment.
- There is no right to request a mandatory reconsideration by HMRC or appeal to an independent tribunal about a decision on whether or not to recover an overpayment of tax credits. However, you can ask HMRC to look at it again and use its discretion not to recover (known as a 'dispute').
- If you do not agree that you were overpaid, you can request a mandatory reconsideration by HMRC of the decision on your entitlement and appeal to an independent tribunal.

1. What is an overpayment of tax credits

The main rules on overpayments are the same for child tax credit (CTC) and working tax credit (WTC).[1] If you (and your partner if you are making a joint claim) are paid more tax credits for a tax year than you are entitled to, the extra amount is regarded as an overpayment.

HM Revenue and Customs (HMRC) can decide to adjust your award during the year of your current tax credit award to prevent an overpayment building up (an 'in-year overpayment') and/or recover all or some of the overpayment from you after the end of the tax year (an 'end-of-year overpayment').

Note: you cannot request a mandatory reconsideration by HMRC or appeal to the First-tier Tribunal against the decision to recover the overpayment. However, you can ask HMRC to use its discretion not to recover. This is referred to as a 'dispute'.

If you do not accept that you received more tax credits than you should have (ie, you were not overpaid because you were correctly entitled to some or all of the amount that HMRC says was an overpayment), you can request a mandatory reconsideration of the decision on your entitlement by HMRC. If you are unhappy with the outcome, you can appeal to the tribunal. See Chapter 66 for more information. If your challenge is successful and the decision on your tax credit entitlement is changed, there is no overpayment (or a lower amount of overpayment) to be recovered.

When an overpayment occurs

The most likely causes of an overpayment are the following.
- Your income falls or rises by more than £2,500 (see p1510) in the current year, compared with the previous tax year.[2]
- You did not tell the Tax Credit Office in time about a change of circumstances, or the change was not acted on (see p1507).
- The information you gave the Tax Credit Office was incorrect, or inaccurately recorded.
- None of the above applies, but an overpayment occurred anyway because of the way the rules on income and changes in circumstances work.

In-year overpayments

In-year overpayments arise during the year of your current tax credit award. Decisions on in-year overpayments can be made during the course of the tax year concerned in the following circumstances.[3]
- If HMRC thinks there is likely to be an overpayment, it can adjust the award (or an award of another tax credit) to reduce or wipe out the overpayment. This may mean that your award is reduced for the rest of the year.
- If an award is terminated on the grounds that you did not satisfy the basic conditions of entitlement, HMRC may decide that the amount already paid to you, or some of it, is to be regarded as an overpayment. The basic conditions of entitlement are, for CTC, that you are responsible for a child (see p286) and, for WTC, that you are engaged in full-time work (see p300).

End-of-year overpayments

End-of-year overpayments are overpayments that are identified after the end of the tax year concerned – ie, after your award for that year has been finalised.

Part 10: General rules for tax credits
Chapter 64: Overpayments of tax credits
2. Disputing recovery

HMRC can decide that there has been an end-of-year overpayment when it makes:[4]
- a final decision (see p1515);
- an enquiry decision (see p1545);
- a decision on discovery (see p1546).

Notification of overpayments

HMRC must change the decision on your entitlement and notify you of the new decision.[5] **Note:** you have the right to request a mandatory reconsideration by HMRC and then appeal against any decision about your entitlement (see p1548). If you think that the new decision is wrong and that, therefore, you have not been overpaid as much as HMRC says, or that you have not been overpaid at all, request a mandatory reconsideration. If you are unhappy with the outcome, appeal to the First-tier Tribunal.

You may only find out about an in-year overpayment when HMRC writes to you to say that your entitlement has changed and your payment has been adjusted. If HMRC intends to recover an end-of-year overpayment from you, it must also give you notice of that, how much it is and how it is to be recovered from you. It usually does this at the same time as it writes to you about the final decision on your entitlement for the tax year. **Note:** you cannot request a mandatory reconsideration or appeal against the decision to recover an overpayment.[6]

2. **Disputing recovery**

You cannot request a mandatory reconsideration by HM Revenue and Customs (HMRC) or appeal to the First-tier Tribunal against the decision to recover the overpayment. However, you can ask HMRC to look again at its decision again and use its discretion to recover. This is referred to as a 'dispute'.

You should dispute recovery if you accept that you received more tax credits than you were correctly entitled to, but you do not think you should have to pay back the money. To dispute recovery, complete Form TC846 at gov.uk/government/publications/tax-credits-overpayment-tc846 (or contact the Tax Credit Helpline for a copy) or write to the Tax Credit Office. Recovery of the overpayment usually begins immediately and is not suspended during the dispute, although if your dispute is successful, the amount already recovered is refunded to you.[7] There is no legal time limit for disputing recovery, but HMRC expects you to do so within three months of notification of the overpayment or of the outcome of a mandatory reconsideration or an appeal deciding that you have been overpaid.[8] HMRC says it will consider exceptions to this if you could not reasonably have been expected to act within three months – eg, if you were in hospital. It is arguable that a late dispute should also be allowed if you have been waiting for an explanation of the overpayment. HMRC has discretion on this, but if it applies the time limit too rigidly, this may be unlawful.

What should you do?

1. If you do not agree that you have been overpaid and you think you were entitled to all, or part, of the amount of tax credit you received, request a mandatory reconsideration by HMRC of the decision on your entitlement that gave rise to the alleged overpayment, using Form WTC/AP. If you are unhappy with the outcome, you can appeal to the First-tier Tribunal on Form SSCS5. Recovery of the overpayment is suspended during the mandatory reconsideration and appeal process.

2. If you have been overpaid because your claim should have ended, but you would have been entitled to some, or all, of the amount you received if you had claimed correctly, ask for the overpayment to be reduced by offsetting your notional entitlement (see p1524).

3. If you accept that you were overpaid, but you do not think you should have to repay some, or all, of the money because you met your responsibilities and some (or all) of the overpayment was caused by an error on the part of HMRC, dispute the decision to recover, using Form TC846. If there were exceptional circumstances that meant you were unable to meet your responsibilities, tell HMRC about this on the form. The dispute is an internal HMRC process and recovery continues during the dispute. HMRC says that you can only dispute recovery once, unless you provide new information within 30 days of being notified of the outcome of the dispute (or later, in exceptional circumstances).

4. If you cannot afford to repay the money, ask for the rate of recovery to be reduced, or for recovery to be written off altogether on hardship grounds. Form TC846 does not allow you to raise this in the dispute, so raise this separately via the Tax Credit Helpline or in writing to the address on your notice to pay.

5. If you have mental health problems and recovery may cause you distress, supply evidence in writing and ask for the overpayment to be written off in line with HMRC guidance.

6. If you are still unhappy with the decision to recover, consider applying for a judicial review or making a complaint.

The responsibilities test

The way in which HMRC uses its discretion whether or not to recover tax credit overpayments is set out in its leaflet *What Happens If We've Paid You Too Much Tax Credits?* (COP26), which is used if you dispute recovery. If an overpayment has been caused by a mistake or failure to act by HMRC (ie, it has not met its responsibilities), it may decide not to recover all or part of the overpayment.

However, for the overpayment not to be recovered, you must also show that you have acted correctly in relation to your claim for tax credits – ie, you have met your responsibilities. Your 'responsibilities' are not defined in the law, only in guidance.

Part 10: General rules for tax credits
Chapter 64: Overpayments of tax credits
2. Disputing recovery

If HMRC thinks it has met all its responsibilities but you have not met all of yours, it normally recovers the overpayment. If it thinks that both itself and you have failed to meet responsibilities, it looks at the circumstances and may write off part of the overpayment. An overpayment can still occur even though both you and HMRC have met these responsibilities, in which case HMRC is still likely to seek recovery.

HMRC regards its responsibilities as:

- giving you correct advice based on your information;
- accurately recording your information and paying the correct amount;
- putting right mistakes you tell it about and sending you a corrected award notice;
- accurately recording your notification of changes in your circumstances;
- sending you a new award notice within 30 days of having all the necessary information.

HMRC regards your responsibilities as:

- providing accurate, complete and up-to-date information;
- reporting changes of circumstances throughout the year;
- using the checklist (TC602(SN)) sent with your award notice to tell it if anything is wrong or incomplete;
- checking that your payments match the amount given on the award notice;
- reporting any errors on your award notice, normally within one month.

Note: if there were exceptional circumstances (eg, illness) which meant that you were unable to meet your responsibilities at the time, explain this and HMRC may write off the overpayment. HMRC must take into account your circumstances and your ability to comply.[9] Remember that it is best to dispute the decision to recover the overpayment on Form TC846, and attach additional pages if necessary.

Reducing the overpayment

HMRC may reduce ('offset') the amount of the overpayment by the amount of any tax credit to which you would have been entitled had you claimed correctly – ie, by your 'notional entitlement'. This process is referred to in HMRC guidance as 'offsetting notional entitlement' and is applied if the overpayment was caused by:[10]

- your ceasing to count as a single claimant and becoming part of a couple (you need details of your partner's income); *or*
- your ceasing to count as part of a couple and claiming instead as a single claimant.

Previous guidance stated that a new claim for tax credits must be made in order to calculate notional entitlement. However, it is generally no longer possible to make a new claim for tax credits and you usually have to claim universal credit (UC) (see p1496). Instead, you should provide HMRC with all the information that would have been needed for a new tax credits claim following the change in your status, so that your notional entitlement can be calculated up to the date that you claimed UC. HMRC says that offsetting your notional entitlement will be applied in all cases to any overpayment which has occurred as a result of a change in single/couple status in the current year, regardless of why you did not notify the change.[11] For previous years, HMRC says that notional entitlement will be applied unless there is evidence of fraudulent behaviour that has resulted in financial gain.[12]

HMRC says that it will proactively identify such cases but, as this cannot be guaranteed, you should contact it yourself if you think you may benefit from offsetting. If your claim was incorrect from the start, or you made a false statement, notional entitlement can still be applied, but in such cases HMRC may consider imposing a penalty or prosecution. Notional entitlement should not be withheld as a consequence of late or non-reporting of a change of circumstances.[13]

Although the guidance only refers to single person/couple claims, you should request that the amount of the overpayment is offset in other circumstances – eg, if you were overpaid because you left the UK for more than the permitted period but you would have been entitled to tax credits on your return. In some cases, a refusal by HMRC to offset may be challenged by judicial review in the courts. Get further advice if you are affected.

Hardship and mental ill health

Hardship is not defined, but HMRC leaflet *What Happens If We've Paid You Too Much Tax Credits?* (COP26) refers to financial hardship in terms of family circumstances that lead to extra living costs, such as looking after someone who is chronically ill or disabled, and an inability to pay for essential living expenses such as rent, gas or electricity. In cases of hardship, HMRC may put recovery on hold, extend the period over which the overpayment is repaid, partially remit or, in exceptional circumstances, write off the overpayment altogether. Other guidance suggests that consideration should also be given to reducing or writing off your overpayment if you have no means to repay, no assets and recovery would cause hardship.[14]

The guidance also states that if you have a mental health problem, HMRC should deal with your case carefully and sympathetically to avoid causing you distress. It may require a letter from a healthcare professional or mental health social worker explaining the nature of your illness, prognosis and prospects for recovery. If your mental health problem existed at the time the overpayment occurred, this may be considered to be exceptional circumstances and so HMRC should consider writing off the overpayment. If you have a mental health problem at the time the overpayment is being recovered, HMRC may decide not to continue with the recovery.[15]

Part 10: General rules for tax credits
Chapter 64: Overpayments of tax credits
3. Recovery of overpayments

The guidance on hardship and mental health applies whether you are repaying directly or by deductions from an ongoing award, but it may not be commonly known to all helpline staff.

There is a special payment helpline (tel: 0345 302 1429; textphone: 0345 300 3909) to discuss hardship. You may also write, with a financial statement, to the HMRC office dealing with repayment. You should *not* use Form TC846 (see p1529) if you want more time to repay. If you remain unhappy with the decision, see p1523 for what you can do.

Taking your dispute further

If HMRC has considered your dispute and you still think you should not have to pay back an overpayment, you can ask HMRC to review its decision, provided you give new information within 30 days (or later in exceptional circumstances). HMRC says that you can only do this once.[16]

The only legal way to challenge a decision on recovering an overpayment (ie, either after a dispute or an attempt to negotiate repayment) is by judicial review in the courts. Usually, this is only possible in extreme cases – eg, if HMRC insists on your repaying an overpayment that was clearly caused by an error or failure on its part, you met all your responsibilities and it is urgent that HMRC changes its decision. For more about judicial review, see p1414.

The only other way of persuading HMRC to change its mind is by making a complaint. You first need to use HMRC's own complaints procedure. If you remain dissatisfied, you can complain to the Adjudicator's Office and then to the Parliamentary and Health Service Ombudsman via your MP. Both can recommend action and order financial compensation, but are likely to take time to complete their investigations. You may wish to involve your MP at an earlier stage of your complaint, as this can produce quicker results. See Chapter 60 for details about making a complaint.

3. **Recovery of overpayments**

HM Revenue and Customs (HMRC) can recover either all or part of any overpayment.[17] It usually recovers the overpayment by:
- adjusting (ie, reducing) your current award; *or*
- transferring the debt to the DWP to recover from you; *or*
- requiring you to repay the overpayment.

Note: although all overpayments are legally recoverable, HMRC can use its discretion not to recover and you can dispute recovery (see p1522).

You must be given notice that you must repay an end-of-year overpayment. The notice must also say how much the overpayment is, and how it is to be recovered from you.[18]

HMRC usually begins recovery immediately after it notifies you of the overpayment. It does not ask you whether recovering an overpayment will cause you hardship or if you think it should not be recovered from you. It is, therefore, important to contact the Tax Credit Office if you do not think the overpayment should be recovered. HMRC refers to this as a 'dispute' (see p1522). Recovery is not suspended during the dispute process, but if the dispute is found in your favour, the amount already recovered is refunded to you.[19]

Note: if you do not agree that you have been overpaid, request a mandatory reconsideration by HMRC of the decision about your entitlement and, if you are unhappy with the outcome, appeal to the First-tier Tribunal (see Chapter 66). Recovery is suspended during the mandatory reconsideration and appeal process.[20]

Overpayments and award notices

If you have been overpaid, you should be sent an award notice outlining the revised decision on your entitlement. Award notices can be very complicated. You should also be sent a checklist (Form TC602(SN)) with information used in the calculation, for you to check. You can request an award calculation notice (Form TC647) from HMRC, which gives more details about how your payment has been worked out. If it is still unclear, write to the Tax Credit Office (its address is at the top of the award notice) requesting an individual explanation. However, do not delay sending in your dispute form while you are waiting for the explanation, as a dispute should usually be made within three months. You can send further details once you have received the full explanation.

If you still do not receive a satisfactory response, consider taking up the matter with your MP or making a complaint (see Chapter 60).

From whom can an overpayment be recovered

In-year overpayments are recovered from you by reducing the ongoing tax credit award. An end-of-year overpayment can be recovered from the person(s) to whom the tax credit award was made. This means:[21]

- if you made a claim as a single person, the overpayment can be recovered from you;
- if you made a joint claim with your partner, the overpayment can be recovered from one or both of you. If you have separated from your partner, HMRC's practice is first to ask you both to repay the overpayment equally. If you wish, you and your ex-partner may agree to pay different amounts. Although HMRC has the power to ask one person to repay the whole amount, guidance states that usually each person is asked to repay a maximum of half the overpayment, unless one partner has acted fraudulently or negligently and the other is seen to be an 'innocent partner'.[22]

Part 10: General rules for tax credits
Chapter 64: Overpayments of tax credits
3. Recovery of overpayments

How the overpayment is recovered

You must be notified of the new decision on your entitlement.[23] For end-of-year overpayments, HMRC must notify you (and your partner, if it is a joint overpayment) of the amount to be repaid, and how the overpayment is to be repaid.[24] Tax credit overpayments are treated as unpaid tax debts. If the debt is transferred to the DWP, it is treated as an overpayment of universal credit (UC) and all methods of recovery used by the DWP may apply.[25]

HMRC can require you to repay:[26]

- by deductions from ongoing payments of any tax credit (see below). This is HMRC's preferred method of repayment. The amount that is deducted is usually limited;
- direct to HMRC. You should receive a notice showing the full amount to be repaid. You are offered a standard repayment period of 12 monthly instalments, although up to 10 years may be negotiated;
- by transferring the debt to the DWP to make deductions from UC or certain other benefits (see p1248 – your overpayment is treated as an overpayment of UC). This can happen without your agreement, but you must be notified. The debt should not be transferred to DWP while there is an outstanding dispute about recovery, or ongoing mandatory reconsideration or appeal about the decision that gave rise to the overpayment;[27]
- with your agreement, by deductions from certain benefits paid by the DWP (see p1208). Note that if HMRC transfers the debt to the DWP to recover, this method can be used without your agreement;[28]
- with your agreement, via pay as you earn (PAYE) by altering your tax code to allow deductions from your wages. Note that if HMRC transfers the debt to the DWP to recover, this method can be used without your agreement;[29]
- by deduction from your bank account, in some cases, or court action (see p1529).[30]

Deductions from ongoing awards

HMRC can adjust your tax credit payments so that you receive less money and so, in effect, repay the overpayment. It only does this if you or your partner have previously been overpaid either as single claimants or as part of the same couple. It does not recover an overpayment in this way if you or your partner have previously been overpaid in a joint award with a different partner. You should be notified of the amount being deducted. There is a maximum amount by which HMRC can reduce your tax credit award to recover an end-of-year overpayment:[31]

- 10 per cent of the award if you are receiving the maximum tax credits to which you could be entitled – ie, with no reduction for income;
- 100 per cent of the award if you receive only the family element of child tax credit (CTC);

- 50 per cent of the award if your income is over £20,000 (this is the figure being treated at the time as your actual current year's income);
- 25 per cent of the award if none of the above apply.

Note: these are maximum amounts, although HMRC applies them automatically. If you accept that you should repay but cannot afford to repay at the above rates, ask HMRC to accept repayment at a lower rate. You may need to show why it would cause you hardship (see p1523) to pay at the maximum rate.

The maximum amounts only apply to end-of-year overpayments. For an in-year overpayment, HMRC may stop or reduce your ongoing payments by more than the above limits, so that you only receive your estimated remaining entitlement (if any) for the rest of the year.[32] HMRC says that this is to prevent a further overpayment building up, but you can request hardship payments if this leaves you unable to meet your basic living expenses.

HMRC considers adjusting recovery or making payments on hardship grounds if requested.[33] In-year recovery is adjusted to the limits used for end-of-year recovery if you are accepted as being in hardship, or the amount you get may be increased further in exceptional cases.[34] You may be asked to provide details of your income and expenditure. In urgent cases, HMRC says a decision on adjusting payments due to hardship should be made within two working days.[35]

Revised notices of overpayments, changing the method of recovery, can be issued at any time.[36]

Direct payment to HM Revenue and Customs

If you are no longer entitled to tax credits, or you were overpaid as part of a couple and you have now separated, you must repay your overpayment by direct payment to HMRC. HMRC suspends direct recovery if you are already repaying another overpayment (at the 10, 25 or 50 per cent rate described above) through your current tax credit award – but you may need to ask for this.[37] The notice to pay (Form TC610) asks you to contact HMRC to pay in full or negotiate repayment. If the overpayment has not been repaid and you have not contacted HMRC within 42 days, a reminder letter is sent, followed by a more strongly worded warning letter. If you fail to respond to this letter, HMRC may use a debt collection agency or start legal proceedings to recover the debt.

Other methods of recovery

HMRC may ask the DWP to recover tax credit overpayments by deduction from specified benefits with your written consent (see p1208).[38] However, HMRC has begun the process of transferring old tax credits debt to the DWP to recover as if it were an overpayment of UC, which can be recovered without your consent through deductions from UC or other benefits, or by any other methods of recovery available to the DWP (see p1248).[39] HMRC may recover tax credit overpayments from your wages via PAYE, but only with your agreement.[40]

Part 10: General rules for tax credits
Chapter 64: Overpayments of tax credits
4. Interest on overpayments

HMRC may recover tax credit debts direct from bank and building society accounts and individual savings accounts (ISAs). In England and Wales, it can only do so if the debt is £1,000 or more, and you must usually be left with a minimum of £5,000 in your account or accounts.[41] HMRC guidance includes safeguards, including a guaranteed face-to-face visit, before this method is used and there is a right of appeal to the county court.[42] In Scotland, it can apply for bank arrestment under a 'summary warrant'.

If HMRC cannot recover by any other methods, or you do not respond to requests for recovery, it may consider taking legal action. Further action will follow if HMRC considers that you are refusing to repay, or neglecting to keep to an agreement to repay. All the circumstances are taken into account before taking such action, but HMRC may:

- take enforcement proceedings to take control of your goods (England and Wales) or seize and sell your possessions (Scotland). Unless you let HMRC officials or agents into your property, they cannot enter your home and take control of/seize your personal possessions without a warrant from the court; *or*
- take court action against you, including bankruptcy proceedings.

Note: recovery action through the courts in England and Wales must be taken within six years of the decision that there has been an overpayment, or, if later, any written acknowledgement of the overpayment or voluntary repayment.[43] In Scotland, HMRC regards the time limit for court action as being five years from the last effective action.[44]

Negotiating repayment

If you have difficulty repaying, HMRC may agree to your repaying the overpayment over a longer period than normal by making an instalment plan. In cases of hardship, or if your mental health is a factor (see p1523), the overpayment may be written off. Contact the Tax Credit Payment Helpline on 0345 302 1429 (textphone: 0345 300 3909), or write to HMRC at the address on the notice to pay, or complete Form TC1133 online using a government gateway account. Usually, you are asked to pay something straight away, and the rest over a later period. HMRC takes into account all the relevant circumstances, including your income, savings, other debts and outgoings. You must show how the repayments will cause you hardship by providing evidence of your income and expenditure and showing, for example, how you will be unable to meet your essential living expenses, or providing evidence of your mental health problems.

4. **Interest on overpayments**

Interest may be added to an overpayment being recovered from you (and/or your partner, if you have a joint claim) if HM Revenue and Customs (HMRC) considers that the overpayment is due to 'fraud or neglect' on the part of you (and/or your partner).[45]

Interest is added 30 days after whichever of the following dates apply:[46]

- if you (or your partner) were treated during the tax year concerned as being overpaid as a result of your award being terminated because you did not satisfy the basic conditions of entitlement (see p1521), the date of the decision terminating the award; *or*
- if the above did not apply, the date in the final notice that you were given to confirm your actual income for the tax year.

When added to the overpayment, the interest is treated as if it were part of the overpayment. This means that it is subject to the same rules as the overpayment itself.[47]

The amount of interest added to the penalty is 6.5 per cent a year or, if it is different from the average lending rate of the main banks, the bank lending rate plus 2.5 per cent.[48]

You can request a mandatory reconsideration of the decision to add interest to an overpayment and, if you are still unhappy, appeal (see Chapter 66). For example, you might wish to argue that you did not act fraudulently or negligently, or that the amount of the interest is wrong. You (and/or your partner, if s/he is subject to the decision) must be given notice of a decision adding interest to an overpayment. The notice must be dated and include details of your right to request a mandatory reconsideration of the decision.[49]

Notes

1. What is an overpayment of tax credits
1 s28 TCA 2002
2 Reg 5 TC(ITDR) Regs
3 s28(5) and (6) TCA 2002
4 s28(1) TCA 2002
5 s23 TCA 2002
6 ss29(1) and (2) and 38 TCA 2002

2. Disputing recovery
7 HMRC leaflet COP26, *What Happens If We've Paid You Too Much Tax Credits?*
8 HMRC leaflet COP26, *What Happens If We've Paid You Too Much Tax Credits?*
9 Adjudicator's Office, *Annual Report 2014*, p20

10 *Pre-Budget Report 2009*; TCM 0228220; HMRC leaflet COP26, *What Happens If We've Paid You Too Much Tax Credits?*
11 Benefits and Credits Consultation Group email, 16 February 2017
12 HMRC email to CPAG, 1 August 2018
13 Adjudicator's Office, *Annual Report 2017*, p17
14 HMRC, *Debt Management and Banking Manual*, 555090
15 HMRC, *Debt Management and Banking Manual*, 555600
16 HMRC leaflet COP26, *What Happens If We've Paid You Too Much Tax Credits?*

Part 10: General rules for tax credits
Chapter 64: Overpayments of tax credits
Notes

3. **Recovery of overpayments**
17 s28(1) TCA 2002
18 ss28(1) and 29 TCA 2002
19 HMRC leaflet COP26, *What Happens If We've Paid You Too Much Tax Credits?*
20 HMRC leaflet COP26, *What Happens If We've Paid You Too Much Tax Credits?*
21 s28(3) and (4) TCA 2002
22 HMRC leaflet COP 26, *What Happens If We've Paid You Too Much Tax Credits?;* CCM 8290
23 s23 TCA 2002
24 s29 TCA 2002
25 The Tax Credits (Exercise of Functions) Order 2014, No.3280; The Tax Credits (Exercise of Functions in relation to Northern Ireland and Notices for Recovery of Tax Credit Overpayments) Order 2017, No.781
26 s29(3)-(5) TCA 2002
27 s28(1)(b) TCA 2002; reg 12 UC(TP) Regs; The Tax Credits (Exercise of Functions in relation to Northern Ireland and Notices for Recovery of Tax Credit Overpayments) Order 2017 No.781; government response to the Public Accounts Committee, March 2018
28 Sch 9(7E) SS(C&P) Regs
29 s29(5) TCA 2002
30 Sch 8 Finance (No.2) Act 2015
31 Reg 12A TC(PC) Regs; HMRC leaflet COP26, *What Happens If We've Paid You Too Much Tax Credits?*
32 Autumn Statement *2013*, para 1.317
33 TCM 0216120; HMRC leaflet COP26, *What Happens If We've Paid You Too Much Tax Credits?*
34 TCM 0214120
35 Benefits and Credits Consultation Group, email 27 November 2016
36 s29(2) TCA 2002
37 HMRC leaflet COP26, *What Happens If We've Paid You Too Much Tax Credits?*
38 Sch 9(7E)(3) SS(C&P) Regs
39 s28(1)(b) TCA 2002; reg 12 UC(TP) Regs; The Tax Credits (Exercise of Functions) Order 2014, No.3280 and The Tax Credits (Exercise of Functions in relation to Northern Ireland and Notices for Recovery of Tax Credit Overpayments) Order 2017, No.781
40 Reg 4 Income Tax (Pay As You Earn) (Amendment No.4) Regs 2014, No.2689
41 Sch 8 Finance (No.2) Act 2015
42 Autumn Statement *2014*, para 2.165

43 s9(1) Limitation Act 1980
44 HMRC, *Debt Management and Banking Manual*, 595080

4. **Interest on overpayments**
45 s37(1) TCA 2002
46 s37(2)-(3) TCA 2002
47 s37(6) TCA 2002
48 Reg 4 TC(IR) Regs
49 ss37(4) and 38(1)(d) TCA 2002

10

Chapter 65

Investigations, penalties and fraud: tax credits

This chapter covers:
1. Investigating awards (below)
2. Penalties (p1535)
3. Prosecution for fraud (p1539)

Key facts

- HM Revenue and Customs has wide powers to investigate your tax credits award and require information from you.
- In certain circumstances, including if you supply incorrect information or do not comply with other requirements, a financial penalty may be imposed.
- If you are considered to have acted fraudulently, you may be prosecuted and fined or imprisoned, or both.

1. Investigating awards

HM Revenue and Customs (HMRC) can require you to supply information and evidence to help it check whether your award is correct. HMRC refers to investigations into the accuracy of awards as 'examinations' and 'enquiries'. Examinations are carried out on some awards *during* the year in order to check that they are correct. Enquiries may be carried out *after* the year concerned to check that you were paid the correct amount. More serious investigations into fraud may also be carried out.

HMRC might ask you to provide things like bank statements or your rent book. You can appoint someone else to deal with HMRC on your behalf – eg, an adviser, accountant or a relative. HMRC requires a signed letter from you confirming this is what you want (or use Form TC689 at gov.uk/ government/publications/tax-credits-and-child-benefit-allow-someone-else-to-act-for-you-tc689). However, you are still treated as responsible for the information provided.

HMRC does not currently undertake face-to-face meetings with tax credit claimants as part of a routine examination or enquiry.

Part 10: General rules for tax credits
Chapter 65: Investigations, penalties and fraud: tax credits
1. Investigating awards

Not all examinations or enquiries are fraud investigations. Fraud investigations tend only to happen in the more serious cases and, in such cases, HMRC has additional powers (see p1535).

Examinations

During the tax year of your award, HMRC may telephone or write to you requiring information or evidence.[1] Normally, it writes to you to say that it is examining your award, but this is not a legal requirement. There is no limit on the number of examinations that can take place during the same tax year. If the examination is started while you are already receiving tax credits, usually you continue to be paid while the examination is being carried out. Payments can only be suspended in specific circumstances (see p1506). An examination may end without a new decision but you should be notified that it has been completed.[2] See p1543 for more information on decisions made following an examination.

You cannot stop an examination taking place, but if you are unhappy with the way you are being treated, you can make a complaint (see Chapter 60).

Enquiries

After your tax credit award is finalised at the end of the tax year, HMRC may carry out an enquiry into the award. It may request further information or evidence in connection with your award. An enquiry can only be opened within one year of the final decision, and only once in respect of a tax year. HMRC must notify you in writing that it is opening an enquiry. When it has completed the enquiry, it must make a decision on your entitlement.[3] See p1545 for more details about decisions made following an enquiry.

You can apply to HMRC to complete its enquiry by making a decision on your tax credit entitlement for the year in question. If HMRC wishes to continue with the enquiry, it passes your request to the First-tier Tribunal, which must give a direction that the enquiry is completed unless it is is satisfied that there are reasonable grounds for it to continue.[4] If you are unhappy with the decision following the enquiry, you can request a mandatory reconsideration and then appeal.

Powers to seek information

HMRC can require you (and/or your partner if you have a joint award) to provide information or evidence during the tax year if it believes your award may be wrong (for an examination). It can also require information or evidence after your award has been finalised (for an enquiry).

It can also do this if it is necessary for a revision during an award or a final notice and final decision (see Chapter 63).[5] You must be given at least 30 days to provide the information.[6] HMRC does not have to suspect you of fraud in order to require information or evidence from you.

It is important that you co-operate with requests for information or evidence as far as you can. Even though you may not be the subject of a fraud investigation, HMRC might suspend your payments or apply for a financial penalty if you refuse to supply information and evidence (see below). If the information or evidence is not available, explain why.

HMRC can also require your employer or childcare provider to provide information. They must be given at least 30 days to do so. If they are subject to these requirements, they can also be subject to penalties (see below). They can be required to provide information and evidence relating to your award or for the purpose of a revision during an award or an enquiry (see p1542).[7]

If fraud is suspected

If you are suspected of fraud, HMRC may undertake an investigation to consider whether or not to give you a financial penalty (see below). In serious cases, it undertakes a criminal investigation with a view to prosecution (see p1539). Fraud investigations in serious cases may be carried out by an HMRC criminal investigation officer and may be linked to investigations by other sections of HMRC, or by the DWP and local authorities. You are usually told why your award is being investigated and that you can seek legal advice from someone who can attend any interview with you. It is advisable to get legal advice as quickly as possible (eg, from a solicitor) if you are being investigated. You are likely to be interviewed under caution (see p1270).

In addition to the powers described above and in Chapter 54, HMRC has specific powers when investigating fraud.[8] If HMRC has 'reasonable grounds' for suspecting serious fraud, a court can make an order requiring you (or any other person) to provide documents containing relevant evidence within a specified time. Falsifying, concealing, destroying or disposing of the documents is an offence.[9]

2. Penalties

You can be given a financial penalty if you have:[10]
- fraudulently or negligently made an incorrect statement or declaration, or supplied incorrect information or evidence; *or*
- failed to comply with requirements.

These penalties are civil penalties. You do not have to be prosecuted for a criminal offence. If you do not think a penalty should be imposed (eg, because you had a reasonable excuse for not declaring a change in circumstances or you could not obtain the information asked for), tell HM Revenue and Customs (HMRC). You must be notified of the penalty, including the date of the decision and your right

Part 10: General rules for tax credits
Chapter 65: Investigations, penalties and fraud: tax credits
2. Penalties

to request a mandatory reconsideration and subsequent appeal (see p1550).[11] A penalty cannot be imposed more than one year after an enquiry decision, or more than one year after the end of the enquiry window (see p1545), whichever is later.[12]

In certain circumstances, these rules can also apply in the same way to your employer or your childcare provider (see p1534).

Incorrect statements and information

HMRC can impose a penalty of up to £3,000 on you if you have acted fraudulently or negligently and you have:[13]
- made an incorrect statement or declaration in connection with an award, a notification of a change of circumstances (see p1507) or in a response to a final notice (see p1515); *or*
- given incorrect information or evidence in connection with an initial decision (see p1503), a requirement to provide information or evidence during the course of your award, a revision during an award (see p1543), a final decision (see p1515) or an enquiry (see p1545).

There is no definition of 'negligence' but, in practice, HMRC considers what you could reasonably be expected to have known and how careful you were.[14]

Penalties for incorrect statements and information

The maximum penalty is £3,000, although HMRC need not impose the maximum. For a deliberate and wrong new claim, the penalties are set at £600 for the first time, £1,000 for a second wrong new claim and £1,500 for further claims. For a deliberate and wrong declaration in the course of an award, HMRC sets penalties at 30 per cent of the amount over-claimed for a first incorrect declaration, 50 per cent for a second incorrect declaration, or 100 per cent for a third, subject to the £3,000 maximum.[15] The decision maker must consider whether there are any aggravating or mitigating factors, and that the maximum penalty is reserved for the worst offences.[16] The penalty is payable 30 days after the date you were notified of it.[17] The amount of the penalty may be increased by the addition of interest (see p1538).

If you are a member of a joint-claim couple (see p1496), a penalty may be imposed on both you and your partner. However, a penalty cannot be imposed on you if you are an 'innocent partner' – ie, if you were not, and could not reasonably have been expected to have been, aware that your partner had fraudulently or negligently made an incorrect statement or provided incorrect information or evidence.[18] In this case, the penalty is imposed solely on your partner. However, even if a penalty is imposed, or partly imposed, on you and your partner, the total penalty for the same incorrect statement cannot amount to more than £3,000.

If you are acting for someone else and you fraudulently or negligently make an incorrect statement, the penalty applies to you as well as that person.[19]

Failing to comply

A financial penalty of up to £300 (it does not have to be the maximum) may be imposed for:[20]

- failing to provide information or evidence requested by HMRC by a specified date in connection with an initial claim (see p1503), a revision during an award (see p1543), a final decision (see p1515) or for an enquiry (see p1545). HMRC cannot impose such a penalty itself, but may start proceedings in the First-tier Tribunal to do so;[21] *or*
- failing to comply with a requirement to declare your circumstances or income by a specified date in your annual review (see p1512). HMRC can impose such a penalty itself, but you have the right to request a mandatory reconsideration and then appeal;[22] *or*
- failing to notify a specified change of circumstances within one month of the change or of the date you became aware of the change, if that is later.[23] HMRC can impose such a penalty itself, but you have the right to request a mandatory reconsideration and then appeal. The specified changes are listed on p1507.

A penalty is not imposed if you had a 'reasonable excuse' for not telling HMRC about the change. Tell HMRC if you think this applies. However, HMRC does not accept the fact that you did not know you had to inform it as a reasonable excuse.[24]

Penalties for failing to comply

The maximum penalty for failing to comply is £300. If the penalty is for failing to comply with a request to provide information or evidence, or for failing to comply with a requirement to declare circumstances or income by the date specified in the annual review, there may be a further daily penalty of up to £60 a day for each day you continue to fail to comply. You must be notified of the penalty, including the date on which it is given, and your right to a mandatory reconsideration. The penalty is payable 30 days after the date you were notified of it.[25] The amount of the penalty may be increased by the addition of interest (see p1538).

However, if the penalty is for failing to comply with a request to provide information or evidence, HMRC cannot apply the penalty itself. Instead, it must write to HM Courts and Tribunals Service, which then summons you to the First-tier Tribunal, which decides whether the penalty should be applied.[26] You can appeal against the tribunal's decision to the Upper Tribunal (see p1555).

A penalty cannot be imposed after you have provided the information or evidence requested.[27] You have not failed to provide information or evidence if you did so within any time that HMRC has allowed you to, or if you had a

Part 10: General rules for tax credits
Chapter 65: Investigations, penalties and fraud: tax credits
2. Penalties

'reasonable excuse' for the failure, or if, having had a reasonable excuse, you later provided the information or evidence without unreasonable delay.[28]

If you are a member of a couple and a £300 penalty has been imposed for failing to comply with a requirement about a final notice or for failing to report the specified change of circumstances, the total of that penalty applied to either or both of you is a maximum of £300 for each failure.[29]

Interest added to penalties

HMRC may apply interest to a penalty, even if you are not considered to have acted fraudulently or negligently – ie, if the penalty is for failing to comply. The amount of the interest becomes part of the penalty and is recoverable in the same way as the penalty itself.[30]

The amount of interest added to the penalty is 6.5 per cent a year or, if that is different from the average lending rate of the main banks, the bank lending rate plus 2.5 per cent.[31]

You can appeal against the penalty itself and the amount of the penalty. However, there is no right of appeal about the addition of interest to a penalty (although there is a right of appeal if interest has been added to an overpayment – see p1548).[32]

Recovery of penalties

HMRC has discretion about whether to impose a penalty and, subject to the maximum amounts, the amount. Also, although the penalty itself can only be altered on appeal, HMRC has discretion about whether to insist that you pay all or some of it.[33] If you tried your best to fulfil all your obligations, or if the penalty would cause you hardship, tell HMRC and ask it to use its discretion not to recover all or some of the amount.

If you have not paid or made an arrangement to pay, HMRC may take enforcement proceedings or court action against you to recover the amount owed. **Note:** enforcement proceedings do not require court action. See CPAG's *Debt Advice Handbook* for more information.

Challenging a penalty

You can tell HMRC that you disagree with the penalty and/or the addition of interest to it – eg, when it contacts you to tell you that you are liable for a penalty. In some cases, it may warn you about a possible penalty before a formal decision is made. It can remove the penalty and/or the interest.

Once a formal decision has been made, you can request a mandatory reconsideration and then appeal, including against the amount of the penalty, but not against any addition of interest (see Chapter 66).

Note: be aware that, subject to the maximum, the tribunal considering your appeal can increase, as well as decrease, the amount of the penalty.

For more information on mandatory reconsiderations and appeals, see p1548, and for more on penalty appeals, see p1550.

Have you been given a penalty?

1. Explain to HMRC why you think a penalty should not be imposed – eg, if you acted with reasonable care or had a reasonable excuse for failing to report a change in circumstances.

2. If you get a decision imposing a penalty, you can request a mandatory reconsideration and then appeal. Remember that if the penalty is for failing to provide information requested by HMRC, it can only be imposed by a First-tier Tribunal and you have a right of appeal to the Upper Tribunal against this decision.

3. If you accept that a penalty can be imposed, you can still negotiate with HMRC about the amount. You could argue that the maximum amount should not be imposed in your case – eg, because you acted innocently and to the best of your knowledge or abilities.

4. If HMRC has used its discretion to mitigate or waive a penalty, check whether this means that a new decision on the penalty will be issued. If a decision is not issued, you may lose your right to challenge the penalty.

3. **Prosecution for fraud**

You are regarded as having committed the offence of fraud if you knowingly take part in fraudulent activity in order to get a tax credit for you or anyone else.[34] If you are prosecuted and then convicted by a court, you are liable to be fined or imprisoned, or both.

Will you be prosecuted?

Whether or not you will be prosecuted is a discretionary decision. Not all cases of fraud end in prosecution. HM Revenue and Customs (HMRC) may investigate your award under civil investigation procedures – ie, without a view to prosecuting you, but with a view to charging a penalty (see p1535). You are usually told about this. However, this does not mean that HMRC cannot change its mind and decide to refer you to the Crown Prosecution Service (the Crown Office and Procurator Fiscal Service in Scotland) for prosecution.

The factors that it may take into account are likely to include the strength of the evidence, the amount of tax credits involved, whether an offence was planned and your personal circumstances.

Official HMRC policy indicates that criminal investigations are more likely if:[35]

- there is organised or systematic fraud, including conspiracy;
- false statements are made or false documents given during a civil investigation;
- deliberate concealment, deception, conspiracy or corruption is suspected;
- false or forged documents have been used;

Part 10: General rules for tax credits
Chapter 65: Investigations, penalties and fraud: tax credits
3. Prosecution for fraud

- you have committed previous offences or there is a repeated course of unlawful conduct or previous civil action;
- there is a link to suspected wider criminality.

This is not a complete list and, ultimately, everything depends on the circumstances of your case.

What should you do if you are prosecuted?

1. The most important thing to do is to get advice. You may be entitled to legal help and have a solicitor or barrister represent you in court.

2. Check carefully that HMRC can prove all the parts of the offence with which you are charged. Do not plead guilty until you have obtained advice.

Fines and imprisonment

If a court convicts you of fraud in connection with tax credits and:[36]

- you are convicted in a moderately serious case (summary procedure), usually in a magistrates' court (sheriff court in Scotland), you can be given a maximum of six months' imprisonment or a fine of an unlimited amount in England and Wales (or in Scotland, a maximum fine of £10,000), or both; *or*
- you are convicted in a very serious case (on indictment), usually in the Crown Court (High Court in Scotland), you can be given a maximum of seven years' imprisonment or a fine of an unlimited amount, or both.

Future changes

At some point, the rules on fines and imprisonment will change as follows.[37]

If your offence is in connection with no more than £20,000 of tax credits, you may be tried only under summary procedure in the magistrates' court (sheriff court in Scotland). If you are convicted, you are liable to a maximum of 51 weeks' (England and Wales) or six months' (Scotland) imprisonment, or a fine of an unlimited amount in England and Wales (or in Scotland, a maximum fine of £10,000).

If the offence is in connection with more than £20,000 of tax credits, you may be tried either under summary procedure or on indictment in either the magistrates' court (sheriff court in Scotland) or the Crown Court (High Court in Scotland). If you are tried under summary procedure, you are liable to a maximum of 12 months' imprisonment or a fine of an unlimited amount in England and Wales (or in Scotland, a maximum fine of £10,000), or both. If you are convicted on indictment, you are liable to a maximum of seven years' imprisonment or a fine of an unlimited amount, or both. See AskCPAG.org.uk and CPAG's *Welfare Rights Bulletin* for updates.

10

Loss of benefit

If you have committed an offence in connection with working tax credit (WTC) or child tax credit, you can be sanctioned or disqualified from certain other benefits (see p1279). If you have committed an offence in connection with tax credits or other benefits, you can be disqualified from receiving WTC (see p1281).

Notes

1. Investigating awards

1   ss14(2) and 16(3) TCA 2002
2   Sch 2 TCA 2002; HMRC leaflet WTC7, *Tax Credits Penalties: what happens at the end of a tax credits check,* available at gov.uk
3   s19(3) and (8) TCA 2002
4   ss19(9) and (10) and 63(3) TCA 2002
5   ss14(2),15(2),16(3), 18(10), 19(2) and 22 TCA 2002
6   Reg 32 TC(CN) Regs
7   ss14(2)(b),15(2)(b),16(3)(b) and 19(2)(b) TCA 2002; regs 30 and 31 TC(CN) Regs
8   s36 TCA 2002
9   s20BB TMA 1970, as applied by s36 TCA 2002

2. Penalties

10   ss31 and 32 TCA 2002
11   Sch 2 TCA 2002; HMRC leaflet WTC7, *Tax Credits Penalties: what happens at the end of a tax credits check,* available at gov.uk
12   Sch 2, para 6, TCA 2002
13   s31 TCA 2002
14   HMRC leaflet WTC7, *Tax Credits Penalties: what happens at the end of a tax credits check,* available at gov.uk
15   HMRC leaflet WTC7, *Tax Credits Penalties: what happens at the end of a tax credits check,* available at gov.uk
16   *SP v HMRC* [2016] UKUT 238 (AAC), reported as [2016] AACR 46
17   Sch 2 para 1 TCA 2002; HMRC leaflet WTC7, *Tax Credits Penalties: what happens at the end of a tax credits check,* available at gov.uk
18   s31(3) TCA 2002

19   s31(5) TCA 2002
20   s32 TCA 2002
21   s32(1)(a) and Sch 2 paras 1 and 3 TCA 2002
22   s32(1)(b) TCA 2002
23   ss3(4) and (7), 6(3) and 32(3) TCA 2002; reg 21(2) TC(CN) Regs
24   s32(5)(b) TCA 2002; CCM 10170
25   Sch 2 para 1 TCA 2002
26   Sch 2 paras 1 and 3 TCA 2002; CCM 10220
27   s32(4) TCA 2002
28   s32(5) TCA 2002
29   s32(6) TCA 2002
30   s37(5) and (6) TCA 2002
31   Reg 4 TC(IR) Regs
32   ss37(5)-(6) and 38 TCA 2002
33   Sch 2 paras 1 and 5 TCA 2002

3. Prosecution for fraud

34   s35(1) TCA 2002
35   HMRC criminal investigation policy, available at gov.uk
36   s35(2) TCA 2002
37   s124 WRA 2012. At the time of writing, there was no commencement order.

10

Chapter 66

Getting a tax credit decision changed

This chapter covers:
1. Revisions (below)
2. Mandatory reconsiderations (p1548)
3. Appealing to the First-tier Tribunal (p1552)
4. Appealing to the Upper Tribunal (p1555)
5. Appealing to the Court of Appeal or Court of Session (p1555)

Tax credit appeals are heard by the First-tier Tribunal Social Entitlement Chamber, which also deals with social security benefits. Chapters 57 and 58 cover appeals about benefit decisions. This chapter refers you to these when the tax credit rules are the same as the benefit rules.

Key facts
- Decisions on your tax credit entitlement can be changed by a revision by HM Revenue and Customs, provided certain grounds are met.
- If you think a decision is wrong, you can ask for it to be looked at again (reviewed). This is called a mandatory reconsideration.
- If you are unhappy with the outcome of a mandatory reconsideration, you can appeal to an independent tribunal – the First-tier Tribunal.
- There are strict time limits for carrying out a revision, applying for a mandatory reconsideration and appealing.

1. Revisions

A decision may be revised by HM Revenue and Customs (HMRC). How a revision is made depends on whether the decision with which you disagree is:
- an 'initial decision' on a claim or renewal (see p1543); *or*
- a 'final decision' after the tax year has ended following an annual review (see p1545); *or*
- a decision of the First-tier Tribunal (see p1555).

The revision process is used when HMRC uses its power to change a decision – eg, after notification of a change of circumstances. If *you* disagree with a decision, including a revised decision, you should request a mandatory reconsideration and then appeal.

Revising an initial decision during an award

When you claim or renew a tax credit, HMRC must decide whether to make an award and the rate at which to award it.[1] This is called an 'initial decision'. If you disagree with it, you can request a mandatory reconsideration and then appeal (see p1548).

The initial decision can be revised if:

- your circumstances have changed so that you should get an additional or higher element (see below); *or*
- HMRC has reasonable grounds for believing that you are entitled to a different rate of tax credit or that you are not entitled to a tax credit at all (see p1544); *or*
- there has been an official error (see p1545).

If your claim has been turned down altogether or your award has been terminated, you cannot ask for the decision to be revised, unless it is on grounds of official error. Instead, you should usually request a mandatory reconsideration within 30 days if you want the decision to be changed.

If your income in the previous year is too high to qualify for a tax credit, but you satisfy the other qualifying conditions, you are awarded a tax credit at a nil rate. This nil-rate award can be revised if your income is estimated to be lower in the current year.[2]

Your circumstances have changed

If you notify the Tax Credit Office that your circumstances have changed so that you should now get an element that you were not previously getting, HMRC must decide whether to amend your award and, if so, how.[3] For example, if you report that you have started to pay childcare costs, your working tax credit (WTC) award can be revised to include the childcare element. HMRC may request further information or evidence before making a revised decision.

If you notify the Tax Credit Office of the change within one month, the increase in your award can be fully backdated.[4] There are specific rules on backdating if your award is recalculated following a change in childcare charges or childcare provided (see p1509) or if you have been awarded a disability benefit (see p1509).

The increase in your award cannot be backdated for more than one month before the date you notify HMRC of the change, except if the change is that you have been awarded a disability benefit (see p1509).

If you disagree with a revised decision, you can request a mandatory reconsideration and then appeal to the First-tier Tribunal (see p1548). A revised

Part 10: General rules for tax credits
Chapter 66: Getting a tax credit decision changed
1. Revisions

decision may be revised as many times as necessary, either following another change, if HMRC has 'reasonable grounds' for believing your entitlement has changed (see below) or because of an official error (see p1546).

Reasonable grounds for believing your entitlement has changed

HMRC can amend or terminate an award if it has 'reasonable grounds' for believing that you are:[5]

- entitled to a different rate of tax credit; *or*
- not entitled to WTC or not entitled to child tax credit.

This could happen, for example, because you tell the Tax Credit Office about a change in your income or because incorrect information was used to decide your claim. It could also happen following an examination into your award (see p1534).

If the rate of tax credit is changed, HMRC revises your award, taking into account any change in circumstances from the date it arose unless:

- it is a change that increases your entitlement to tax credit elements, which can only be backdated for up to one month (see p1543);
- your childcare charges decrease by £10 a week or more. In this case, there is a four-week 'run-on' at the same rate before the award is reduced (see p1507);[6]
- there is a four-week 'run-on' because you stop work or reduce your hours below 16, 24 or 30 a week (see p305).

Decisions can only be revised in this way during the period of the award, not after an award has been terminated, nor after a final decision has been made.[7]

10

- -
Example
Pauline provides an estimate of her income for the current year. This has decreased by more than £2,500 compared with the previous year's income on which her award was based. The initial decision can be revised and her award recalculated based on the current year's income plus £2,500. The estimate she provides must be sufficient to give HMRC reasonable grounds for believing that her entitlement should change.
- -

HMRC is not obliged to revise your award, even when there are grounds. It could leave the changes to be dealt with at the annual review – eg, if it is late in the year and the change is minor.[8]

If you disagree with the revised decision, you can request a mandatory reconsideration and then appeal (see p1548). The burden of proof is on HMRC to set out the reasonable grounds for its decision and the evidence used to support it.[9]

Official error

An initial decision can be revised in your favour if it is incorrect because of an official error (see p1546).[10]

Revising a final decision

After 5 April, HMRC carries out the annual review (see p1512) for the year just ended and makes a final decision on your entitlement for that year. It sends you an annual review form which details the circumstances on which the award was based and usually an annual declaration form, giving your income for the tax year just passed.

If HMRC sends you an annual declaration form, you must complete and return it by the deadline given (31 July in most cases). HMRC finalises your entitlement for the year just passed. A final decision is conclusive unless it is changed on mandatory reconsideration or appeal, or in the following circumstances.

- If you change your statement about your income or circumstances before the deadline, the final decision can be changed (see below).
- Once a final decision is made, there is a period during which HMRC can open an enquiry into your entitlement (see below). This is known as a 'revision on enquiry'.
- Outside the period of enquiry, a final decision can be revised on 'discovery' of certain information about your tax liability or in relation to fraud or neglect (see p1546). This is known as a 'revision on discovery'.
- A final decision can be revised in your favour because of an official error (see p1546).

Changing your statement

If you reply to the annual review notice but then wish to change your statement, you may do so. If it is on or before the deadline given in the notice for replying (31 July in most cases), but HMRC has already made a final decision, the final decision may be revised.[11]

If HMRC only had an estimate of your income for the current year (eg, because you are self-employed and have not yet finalised your accounts), you have a later deadline (usually 31 January) by which to give details of your actual income for that year. If you do so, HMRC must make a new final decision.[12] It can revise the new decision if you change your statement on or before the later deadline.[13] If you do not give further details of actual income, HMRC must nevertheless make a new final decision once the later deadline is passed.

'Revision on enquiry'

HMRC does not need any particular grounds to open an enquiry into your entitlement, and some awards are selected for enquiry at random.[14] It must begin its enquiry by giving you written notice. An enquiry can only be opened for a particular tax year after the final decision for that year has been made, and within

Part 10: General rules for tax credits
Chapter 66: Getting a tax credit decision changed
1. Revisions

a limited period of time. This is known as the 'enquiry window'. It begins immediately after the final decision and ends a year after the deadline by when you had to reply to the annual review notice, or a year after the later deadline for self-employed people and others to supply actual income details if only an estimate was provided.[15] If you are required to submit an income tax return, the enquiry must begin by the day your tax return becomes final.

When the enquiry is completed, HMRC makes a fresh decision on whether you are entitled and how much the award should be. There is no time limit in which HMRC should conclude an enquiry, but you can apply to the First-tier Tribunal for a direction to bring the enquiry to an end.[16]

Only one enquiry into entitlement can be conducted for any one tax year.[17] For more details, see p1534.

If you disagree with the decision, you can ask for a mandatory reconsideration and then appeal (see p1548). It can also be revised if it is incorrect because of an official error (see below).[18] HMRC can also revise an enquiry decision by a 'revision on discovery' (see below).

'Revision on discovery'

'Discovery' is a power to revise your entitlement in earlier years. If it is too late to 'enquire' into your entitlement, HMRC can still revise a final decision in specific circumstances. A final decision or an enquiry decision may be revised within five years if HMRC has 'reasonable grounds' for believing that your tax credit entitlement is wrong:

- because of a revision of your income tax liability. The revision of your tax credit entitlement must take place within a year of your income tax liability being revised;[19] *or*
- because of fraud or neglect.[20] The fraud or neglect may be on your part, or your partner's if it is a joint claim, or on the part of anyone acting for you (see p1499). Your tax credit entitlement in a tax year cannot be revised on this ground after five years from the end of the tax year – eg, a tax credit award for 2014/15 (or earlier) cannot be revised after 5 April 2020.[21]

There is nothing to stop HMRC going through this process more than once.[22] If a final decision, enquiry decision or discovery decision has been revised because of an official error, this can be further revised in this way.[23]

If you disagree with a discovery decision, or do not think HMRC has shown grounds to revise using this power, you can request a mandatory reconsideration and then appeal (see p1548). Alternatively, the decision may be revised if it is incorrect because of an official error.

Official error

An initial decision, final decision, enquiry decision or discovery decision can be revised in your favour if it is incorrect because of an official error.[24] The decision can be revised at any time up to five years after the date of the decision. An official error can include opening an enquiry (see p1545) without notice, and it is arguable that there is an official error if you have not been given the opportunity to contribute to an enquiry.[25]

Official error

'Official error' means an error relating to a tax credit made by an HMRC or DWP officer or a person providing tax credit services for them. If you, or someone acting for you, contributed to the error, it is *not* an official error. An error of law can be an official error, but not if it is only shown to be an error of law because of a later Upper Tribunal or court decision.

How to request a revision

If your circumstances change, there are rules on how HMRC should be notified (see p1512). In other cases, there are no set rules to follow. If you disagree with a decision, you should usually request a mandatory reconsideration, then appeal if you are unhappy with the outcome rather than ask HMRC to use one of its powers to revise a decision. If you are outside the absolute time limit for a mandatory reconsideration or appeal and want a decision to be revised on grounds of official error, you should request this in writing. If HMRC refuses to revise a decision on official error grounds, it is arguable that you have a right of appeal against this decision.[26]

Keep a copy of any letter you send to HMRC. If you call the Tax Credit Helpline, keep a log of your calls: the date and time you made the call, the name of the person you spoke with, the information provided and what was agreed.

What happens after you request a revision

Before making its decision, HMRC may ask you to provide more information or evidence if it needs this to help with the decision.[27] HMRC may contact your employer or childcare provider if it also needs information from them.[28]

It is important that you respond to a request for information by the date given in the letter. If you do not provide the required information, HMRC may take proceedings to the First-tier Tribunal to impose a penalty of up to £300, and if you still do not comply, a further daily penalty of up to £60 a day could be imposed. See p1535 for how these penalties are applied.

HMRC must give notice of the decision to you, and to your partner if it is a joint claim. This must include details of your right to appeal.[29]

Part 10: General rules for tax credits
Chapter 66: Getting a tax credit decision changed
2. Mandatory reconsiderations

2. **Mandatory reconsiderations**

HM Revenue and Customs (HMRC) must carry out a review if you have made a valid request for one, and it must notify you of the outcome. You must be notified of the outcome of the review before you can appeal. A review is known as a 'mandatory reconsideration', and applies to all tax credit decisions made on or after 6 April 2014.[30]

Who can request a mandatory reconsideration

The following people can request a mandatory reconsideration:[31]
- you, the tax credit claimant. For joint claimants, only one partner needs to make the request;
- for decisions about penalties, the person subject to the penalty;
- an appointee, if you are unable to make the request yourself (see p1499). If you do not have an appointee, the person (who must be 18 or over) who is to act on your behalf should write to HMRC asking to be appointed;
- another person with the power to make a tax credit claim for you – ie, a receiver appointed by the Court of Protection, a judicial factor or guardian.

The law does not specify who can request a mandatory reconsideration, but Form WTC/AP (see p1550) requires a signature from the tax credit claimant or appointee. It also asks whether you are getting help from a representative, and requires your signature to authorise that person to act for you. You may be able to argue that your representative has the right to request a mandatory reconsideration on your behalf with your prior signed authority, but it may be simpler to ensure you sign the request where possible. HMRC does not accept photocopied signatures.

Which decisions can be reconsidered

You can request a mandatory reconsideration of:[32]
- an initial decision;
- a final decision;
- a revised decision (after a change in circumstances, on reasonable grounds or for official error);
- an enquiry decision;
- a discovery decision;
- a decision imposing a penalty;
- a decision charging interest on an overpayment.

Caselaw has established that there is a right to have a mandatory reconsideration and then appeal against the following decisions (but, in practice, HMRC may not accept this):

- a decision to reject a claim that is not made on the approved form, or that does not contain all the information requested on the form, including the national insurance (NI) number requirement (see p1500);[33]
- a decision that you do not have good cause for making a late annual declaration (see p1513);[34]
- a refusal to revise a decision on the grounds of official error (see p1546);[35]
- a decision contained in a 'statement like an award notice' (see p1506);[36]
- a decision to terminate your tax credit award because you are a universal credit claimant (although this decision may be contained within the final decision on your tax credits) (see p1508).[37]

In these situations, you should request a mandatory reconsideration, quoting the relevant caselaw. If HMRC refuses to carry out a mandatory reconsideration, you should ask for confirmation of this in writing and then appeal to the First-tier Tribunal on Form SSCS5, asking it to decide whether you have a right of appeal.

Which decisions cannot be reconsidered

You cannot request a mandatory reconsideration or appeal against:
- a decision to recover all or part of an overpayment (see below);
- a decision about the rate or method of recovery of an overpayment;
- a decision to postpone payments (see p1506);
- a decision not to accept a late request for a mandatory reconsideration (although this is subject to a legal challenge);
- a decision to open an enquiry into your entitlement (but you can apply to the tribunal for a direction to bring an enquiry to an end – see p1534);
- a decision to terminate your tax credit award because you have successfully applied for, and are entitled to, payments under the tax-free childcare scheme (see p871).

Decisions to recover overpayments

There is a different process if you want to dispute a decision to recover an overpayment – ie, if you accept that you were overpaid, but do not think you should have to repay any money. If HMRC decides you have been overpaid tax credits, it can recover all or part of them at its discretion, and you cannot request a mandatory reconsideration or appeal against this decision. You can, however, request a mandatory reconsideration of the decision on your entitlement – ie, if you do not agree that you were overpaid, or disagree with the amount. In some cases, HMRC may use its discretion not to recover an overpayment, or to reduce the amount – eg, if recovery would cause hardship (see p1525). Complain to HMRC if you are unhappy with the way your award has been handled. If your complaint is not resolved to your satisfaction, you can ask the Adjudicator to look into it (see p1441). See Chapter 64 for more information on tax credit overpayments.

Part 10: General rules for tax credits
Chapter 66: Getting a tax credit decision changed
2. Mandatory reconsiderations

How to request a mandatory reconsideration

A mandatory reconsideration must be requested in writing and must identify you (eg, your name and NI number) and the decision in question. It is advisable (but not essential) to use Form WTC/AP, *What To Do If You Think Your Child Tax Credit Or Working Tax Credit Is Wrong,* available at gov.uk. If you telephone HMRC to ask for a decision to be reconsidered, this is not a formal request for a mandatory reconsideration. You must still put your request in writing. If your representative requests the mandatory reconsideration on your behalf, your signed authority should be included.

Send your request to HMRC at the address given on the decision notice.

Time limit

Your request for a mandatory reconsideration must be received by HMRC within 30 days of the date given on the decision letter.[38]

You may not get a separate initial or final decision notice if the annual review notice states what the decision will be and the date on which it will be made – usually 31 July. This may apply if your claim has been automatically renewed. In this case, your request for a mandatory reconsideration must be received within 30 days of the date specified as the date on which the decision is made on the annual review notice – eg, by 30 August if the decision date is given as 31 July.

Late requests

If your request for a mandatory reconsideration is received by HMRC outside the 30-day time limit, you must explain why it is late. HMRC may accept a late request within 13 months of the original decision if it is satisfied that there were special circumstances that meant it was not practical for you to meet the time limit. HMRC must also be satisfied that it is reasonable, given all the circumstances, to accept the late request. The longer the delay, the more compelling the reasons must be.[39] Reasons listed as acceptable in the HMRC guidance are if:[40]

- you, your partner or dependant had a serious illness, or have died;
- you are not resident in the UK;
- there has been a disruption in normal postal services.

This list is not exhaustive and other reasons for lateness may be accepted.

If your application to extend the time limit is refused, you cannot ask for this decision to be reconsidered. You do not have a right of appeal against this or the original decision. **Note:** HMRC's refusal to allow the right of appeal following a late request is currently the subject of a legal challenge. See AskCPAG.org.uk and CPAG's *Welfare Rights Bulletin* for updates.[41]

Penalty decisions

You can request a mandatory reconsideration of most decisions to impose a penalty. HMRC can impose a penalty for making incorrect statements, failing to report a required change of circumstances or failing to comply with the annual review. You can request a mandatory reconsideration in the normal way, then appeal to the First-tier Tribunal if necessary.[42]

However, if you fail to comply with a request for information or evidence, HMRC cannot decide to impose a penalty of up to £300 itself, but must take 'proceedings' to the First-tier Tribunal. You have an opportunity to attend a hearing where the tribunal decides whether or not you should be given a penalty. You can then appeal to the Upper Tribunal.[43] Unlike most appeals to the Upper Tribunal, you do not need to show that there has been an 'error of law'.[44] The usual time limits and procedures for applying for permission to appeal apply. For information on penalties, see p1535.

After you request a mandatory reconsideration

If a written request is received within the time limit, or a late request is accepted, HMRC must carry out a mandatory reconsideration of the decision in question. The mandatory reconsideration must be carried out as soon as is reasonably practical, and HMRC's stated target is 42 days.[45] If you are still waiting for the outcome of a mandatory reconsideration by the time the final decision is made (usually 31 July) (see p1515), you should also request a mandatory reconsideration against the final decision, because your mandatory reconsideration or appeal against the in-year decision lapses.[46] If your annual review told you what the final decision would be and when it would be made, you may not get another notice, but you should still request a mandatory reconsideration within 30 days of the date you were told it would be made (usually 31 July).

HMRC may request further information or evidence from you. This must be in writing and specify a date by when it should be provided. If you do not provide the information or evidence by the date specified, HMRC may proceed with the mandatory reconsideration. New information or evidence does not have to be provided as a pre-condition for a mandatory reconsideration.

A penalty cannot be imposed on you for failing to provide information or evidence requested in connection with a mandatory reconsideration.

HMRC must issue a **'mandatory reconsideration notice'**, containing sufficient information for you to understand the outcome, details of any change to the decision and the reasons for its conclusion. The outcome must be one of the following.[47]

- The decision is upheld. There is no change to the original decision with which you disagree, and you have the right of appeal.
- The decision is varied. In this case, the original decision is changed. If the decision is changed in your favour but you still disagree with part of it, you can appeal against the decision as varied. You do not have to go through the mandatory reconsideration process again.

Part 10: General rules for tax credits
Chapter 66: Getting a tax credit decision changed
3. Appealing to the First-tier Tribunal

- The decision is cancelled. You are left in the position you were in before the decision was made. There does not appear to be a right of appeal in this situation, as this would be against a decision that has been cancelled.

3. **Appealing to the First-tier Tribunal**

You can only appeal against a tax credits decision after a mandatory reconsideration has been carried out and the outcome has been notified to you in writing. Tax credit appeals are heard by the same First-tier Tribunal that deals with social security benefits, which is administered by HM Courts and Tribunals Service (HMCTS).[48] Many of the rules are the same as those for social security benefits (see Chapter 57). This chapter refers you to Chapter 57 where the tax credit rules are the same as the benefit rules.

Who can appeal

The following people have the right of appeal:[49]
- you, the tax credit claimant. For joint claimants, both or either of you can make the appeal. If only one appeals, the First-tier Tribunal decision still applies to both, provided you are both given the right to a hearing;[50]
- for appeals about penalties, the person subject to the penalty;
- an appointee, if you are unable to appeal yourself (see p1499). If you do not have an appointee, the person (who must be 18 or over) who is to act on your behalf in the appeal should write to HM Revenue and Customs (HMRC) asking to be appointed;
- another person with the power to make a tax credit claim for you – ie, a receiver appointed by the Court of Protection, a judicial factor or guardian.[51]

The tribunal rules state that you must sign the appeal, but also state that you can appoint a representative who can do anything that you are required to do, except sign a witness statement. Your representative may sign the appeal on your behalf with your signed consent, but it may be simpler to ensure you sign the appeal yourself if possible.[52]

How to appeal

You should appeal on the appropriate form – Form SSCS5 (*Notice Of Appeal Against A Decision Of HM Revenue and Customs*), which must be signed by you or by your representative. If your representative signs the appeal, s/he must send your signed authority to act on your behalf. Enclose a copy of the mandatory reconsideration notice and send Form SSCS5 to HMCTS. Alternatively, you can write a letter. You must include:

- your signature (on the appeal request itself, or on a signed authority for your representative to act on your behalf);
- your name and address;
- the name and address of your representative, if you have one;
- the grounds for appeal – ie, the reasons why you disagree with the decision;
- a copy of the mandatory reconsideration notice.

Time limit

Your appeal must be received by HMCTS within one month of the date on the mandatory reconsideration notice.[53]

Late appeals

If your appeal is received outside the one-month time limit but within the absolute time limit of 13 months, it is accepted, provided HMRC does not object and unless the First-tier Tribunal directs otherwise. If HMRC objects, the tribunal can still accept your appeal if it is in the interest of justice.[54] In very exceptional circumstances (eg, if you did not receive notice of the decision you want to appeal), you can argue that the tribunal has the discretion to allow you to appeal outside the absolute time limit.[55] However, this is unlikely to apply unless you have done all you could to appeal in time.

What happens after you appeal

HMRC must prepare its response (a submission) within 28 days of receiving notice of your appeal from the tribunal.[56] This should include the law used to make its decision, and all relevant information and evidence.[57]

Settling the appeal

HMRC may want to settle the appeal without going to the tribunal. You can point out to HMRC where you think its decision is wrong and supply information or arguments you want it to consider. Even though HMRC has already had the opportunity to reconsider its decision, once you have lodged your appeal it may offer you terms on which to settle the appeal. Your appeal can only be settled with your consent. If you do not agree, the appeal must proceed to the tribunal.

If you are asked to settle the appeal, check first whether the proposed agreement gives you everything to which you think you are entitled. Get advice if you are not sure whether or not to agree. If in doubt, continue with the appeal. If you agree to settle, HMRC must write to you setting out the terms of the agreement – eg, giving you a new amount. Your appeal then lapses unless you write to HMRC within 30 days of the date of the written notice of agreement saying you have changed your mind and wish to proceed with your appeal.[58]

Part 10: General rules for tax credits
Chapter 66: Getting a tax credit decision changed
3. Appealing to the First-tier Tribunal

If your appeal has not been heard by the end of the year

If your appeal has not been heard by the time you get HMRC's final decision on your entitlement at the end of the year, request another mandatory reconsideration and appeal against the final decision. This is because an appeal against an in-year decision lapses once a final decision is made on that year.[59]

Withdrawing an appeal

You can ask to withdraw the appeal if you decide not to go ahead with it. See p1363 for details of withdrawing and reinstating an appeal if you change your mind.

When your appeal can be struck out

Your appeal may be 'struck out' before the hearing in certain circumstances. The rules are the same as those for benefits (see p1360). Your appeal may be struck out if it was against an in-year decision and a final decision has since been made on the same year.[60]

The hearing

The tribunal holds an oral hearing if you have asked for one. Otherwise, there is a paper hearing in your absence (see p1366). For information on asking for the hearing to be postponed or adjourned to a later date, see p1359. The tax credit rules are the same as those for benefits, except that there are no special 'test case' provisions for tax credits that can block your appeal or affect its outcome (although payment can be postponed while there is an appeal pending in another case that could affect your own award).[61] The rules on 'lead cases' described on p1365 also apply to tax credits.

Procedures for tax credit appeals

There are procedural rules that the tribunal must follow when dealing with your appeal. See pp1369–89 and pp1357–64 for details. The tax credit rules are the same, with the following exceptions.
- **Medical examinations.** The tribunal cannot refer you to a doctor for a medical examination.[62] However, if your appeal concerns a disability question, it may be important to get your own medical evidence (see p1378).
- **Change in circumstances after you appeal.** The rules apply to tax credits in the same way as they do to benefits except:
  - wherever Chapter 57 refers to 'supersession', read 'revision' for tax credits;
  - if you reclaim or ask for a revision because of a change in circumstances after you appeal, there is no specific provision for a decision maker to revisit her/his decision on that claim or revision once the appeal has been heard on the grounds that s/he would have made a different decision had s/he known what the tribunal's decision would be.

- **After the hearing.** If HMRC is considering appealing to the Upper Tribunal, you are normally not paid until the Upper Tribunal decides the case. HMRC can postpone payment in these circumstances, without notifying you of its intention.[63]
- **If you disagree with the First-tier Tribunal's decision.** The decision cannot be superseded (because supersessions do not apply to tax credits), but it can be revised in any of the ways described in this chapter except for official error (see p1542).

  If the First-tier Tribunal made an error of law, you can appeal to the Upper Tribunal as you can in benefit appeals. For tax credits, HMRC is not prevented from revising the First-tier Tribunal's decision on 'reasonable grounds', which could also include an error of law (if it is still within the tax year of the award).
- **When a decision can be set aside.** If you appeal to the Upper Tribunal, there is no provision obliging the First-tier Tribunal to set aside the decision if both you and HMRC agree that the First-tier Tribunal made an error of law.[64]

4. Appealing to the Upper Tribunal

You can appeal to the Upper Tribunal against a decision of the First-tier Tribunal if the First-tier Tribunal made an error of law. In some penalty appeals, you can also appeal about the amount of the penalty (see p1550), without having to show an error of law.

Chapter 58 explains what an error of law is and how to appeal (see p1397). The rules for tax credits are the same as those for benefits, except that if you disagree with the Upper Tribunal decision, it cannot be superseded but it can be revised in any of the ways described on p1542, except because of an official error.

5. Appealing to the Court of Appeal or Court of Session

You can appeal to the Court of Appeal (in England and Wales) or to the Court of Session (in Scotland) against a decision of the Upper Tribunal, but only if there has been an error of law (see Chapter 58).

Part 10: General rules for tax credits
Chapter 66: Getting a tax credit decision changed
Notes

Notes

1. Revisions

1 s14(1) TCA 2002
2 s14(3) TCA 2002
3 s15(1) TCA 2002
4 Reg 25 TC(CN) Regs; reg 16(5)(a) WTC(EMR) Regs
5 s16(1) TCA 2002
6 Reg 16(5)(b) WTC(EMR) Regs
7 s16(1) TCA 2002
8 CTC/2662/2005; CTC/3981/2005
9 *SB v HMRC (TC)* [2014] UKUT 543 (AAC); *NI v HMRC (TC)* [2015] UKUT 490 (AAC)
10 s21 TCA 2002
11 s18(5) TCA 2002
12 s18(6) TCA 2002
13 s18(9) TCA 2002
14 s19(1) TCA 2002
15 s19(4) TCA 2002
16 s19(9) TCA 2002
17 s19(11) TCA 2002
18 s21 TCA 2002
19 s20(1) and (3) TCA 2002
20 s20(4) TCA 2002
21 s20(5) TCA 2002
22 s20(6)(a) TCA 2002
23 s20(6)(b) TCA 2002
24 s21 TCA 2002; reg 3 TC(OE) Regs
25 *JI v HMRC (TC)* [2013] UKUT 199 (AAC), para 53
26 *JI v HMRC (TC)* [2013] UKUT 199 (AAC), para 50
27 ss15(2)(b),16(3)(b) and 19(2)(b) TCA 2002
28 Regs 30 and 31 TC(CN) Regs
29 s23 TCA 2002

2. Mandatory reconsiderations

30 Footnote to Art 2 Tax Credits, Child Benefit and Guardian's Allowance Reviews and Appeals Order 2014, No.886
31 See HMRC leaflet WTC/AP, *What To Do If You Think Your Child Tax Credit Or Working Tax Credit Is Wrong*
32 s38 TCA 2002
33 *CI v HMRC (TC)* [2014] UKUT 158 (AAC) held that there is a right of appeal, but this disagrees with the earlier *ZM and AB v HMRC (TC)* [2013] UKUT 547 (AAC), which held there there is no such right

34 *SG v HMRC (TC)* [2011] UKUT 199 (AAC)
35 *JI v HMRC (TC)* [2013] UKUT 199 (AAC), para 50
36 *TM v HMRC (TC)* [2016] UKUT 512 (AAC), but see also *DG v HMRC (TC)* [2016] UKUT 505 (AAC)
37 *HMRC v LH (TC)* [2016] UKUT 306 (AAC)
38 ss23(2) and 39(1) TCA 2002
39 s21A TCA 2002
40 TCM 0014020
41 Sch 2 para 4(1) TCA 2002
42 s38 TCA 2002
43 s63 and Sch 2 para 4(1) TCA 2002
44 Sch 2 para 4(1) TCA 2002; see also *SP v HMRC (No.2)* [2017] UKUT 329 (AAC)
45 David Gauke MP, Exchequer Secretary to the Treasury, Eighth Delegated Legislation Committee, 26 March 2014
46 *LS and RS v HMRC* [2017] UKUT 257 (AAC)
47 s21A(3) TCA 2002

3. Appealing to the First-tier Tribunal

48 s63(2) TCA 2002
49 s12 SSA 1998, as applied by reg 4 TC(A) Regs under the power in s63(8) TCA 2002
50 CTC/2612/2005
51 Reg 3 TC(A)(No.2) Regs
52 rr11 and 22 TP(FT) Rules
53 r22(2)(d)(i) TP(FT) Rules
54 rr2 and 5(3)(a) TP(FT) Rules
55 *KK v Sheffield City Council (CTB)* [2015] UKUT 367 (AAC)
56 r24(1)(c) TP(FT) Rules
57 *CS v HMRC (TC)* [2015] UKUT 407 (AAC)
58 s54 TMA 1970, as applied by Tax Credits (Settlement of Appeals) Regulations 2014, No.1933
59 *LS and RS v HMRC (TC)* [2016] UKUT 257 (AAC)
60 *LS and RS v HMRC (TC)* [2017] UKUT 257 (AAC)
61 Reg 11 TC(PC) Regs
62 The power to refer to a doctor in s20 SSA 1998 does not apply to tax credits
63 Reg 11 TC(PC) Regs
64 s13(3) SSA 1998, as applied by reg 5(2) TC(A) Regs under the power in s63(8) TCA 2002

10

Part 11

Immigration and residence rules for benefits and tax credits

transition period, which, at the time of writing, was due to be 31 December 2020 (see p1596).

You require leave to enter or remain but do not have it

You are a 'person subject to immigration control' if you require leave to enter or remain but do not have it.[4]

If you are not an EEA national, you require leave to enter or remain in the UK *unless* you are:

- a British citizen or person with the right of abode; *or*
- a person with a European free movement right of residence – eg, if you are:
  - a family member of an EEA, or Swiss (or in very limited circumstances British – see p1616) national who has a right to reside in the UK (see p1614);[5]
  - a Swiss national with a right to reside. Swiss nationals, in general, have the same residence rights as EEA nationals and do not require leave to enter or, if they have a right to reside, leave to remain in the UK;[6]
  - the primary carer of a British citizen who is in the UK, and it is necessary for you to have a right to reside in the UK so that s/he can continue to reside within the EU.[7] **Note:** in most cases, having a right to reside on this basis does not entitle you to any benefits that require a right to reside (see p1591), but you can still be entitled to other benefits that do not require a right to reside, such as personal independence payment (PIP) and carer's allowance (CA).[8]

Examples of when you require leave to enter or remain but do not have it include if you:

- are an asylum seeker on immigration bail;
- have overstayed your limited leave to enter or remain. **Note:** if you apply for further leave on the same or a different basis before your current leave expires, your leave is extended from the date it would have expired until your application is decided or withdrawn. While your leave is extended in this way, you are not someone who requires leave and does not have it;[9]
- have entered the UK without either immigration leave, or a right to enter under EU law, and since then have not obtained leave to remain;
- you previously had a right of residence under EU law (eg, as the family member of an EEA national with a right to reside) but this has now ceased and you have not obtained any leave to remain;
- are subject to a deportation order.

Note:

- If you came to live in the UK before 1973 (and you are a Commonwealth citizen), or before 1989 (and you are now British or have a right of abode or indefinite leave), you may be entitled to compensation from the Windrush Compensation Scheme if you experienced losses, including loss of benefits,

Part 11: Immigration and residence rules for benefits and tax credits
Chapter 67: Coming from abroad: immigration status
1. Immigration status

due to a lack of documentary evidence of your status.[10] DWP guidance states that payments under this scheme, or the previous Windrush Exceptional Payments scheme, should be disregarded for all means-tested benefits 'on an extra-statutory basis'.[11] However, the council tax reduction regulations have been amended to disregard these payments as income and capital. Interest on payments made under the scheme are ignored as income for tax credits for 52 weeks.[12]

- If you are unsure of your immigration status, get independent immigration advice before contacting the Home Office.
- There are close links between the benefit authorities and the Home Office. Making a claim for benefit could alert the immigration authorities to your presence and status in the UK. Get specialist immigration advice before claiming benefits if you are unsure about your immigration status.

Your leave has a 'no recourse to public funds' condition

You are a 'person subject to immigration control' if you have leave to enter or remain in the UK that is subject to the condition that you do not have recourse to 'public funds'.[13]

Most people admitted to the UK with time-limited leave, such as spouses/civil partners, students or visitors, are given limited leave to stay which is subject to the condition they do not have recourse to public funds.

Public funds

'Public funds' are defined in the Immigration Rules as:[14]

- attendance allowance;
- CA;
- child benefit;
- child tax credit;
- council tax benefit (now abolished);
- council tax reduction;
- disability living allowance;
- income-related employment and support allowance;
- homelessness assistance and housing provided under specific provisions;
- housing benefit (HB);
- income support;
- income-based jobseeker's allowance;
- local welfare assistance (except the Discretionary Assistance Fund for Wales);
- pension credit;
- PIP;
- severe disablement allowance;
- social fund payments;
- universal credit;
- working tax credit.

Only the benefits, tax credits and assistance listed in the Immigration Rules are public funds. Therefore, if you get any other benefit or other assistance, you are not in breach of the no recourse to public funds condition.

If you have recourse to public funds when your leave prohibits you from doing so, you have breached a condition of your leave. This may affect your right to remain in the UK: you could be liable to be deported, have further leave refused and/or be prosecuted for committing a criminal offence.[15]

If your leave is subject to a no recourse to public funds condition, you are defined as a 'person subject to immigration control' and (unless you are covered by one of the exceptions – see pp1565–67) you are not entitled to the benefits and tax credits defined as public funds. However, if you *are* covered by one of the exceptions, you can claim and receive that public fund benefit, as you are not regarded as having recourse to public funds under the Immigration Rules.[16]

You are regarded as having recourse to public funds if someone else's benefit is increased because of your presence – eg, if the amount of your partner's HB is greater because you are included in her/his claim. If this happens, you have breached the condition not to have recourse to public funds. Obtain specialist immigration advice before making a claim.

Your leave was given as a result of a maintenance undertaking

If your leave to enter or remain was given as a result of a maintenance undertaking, you are a 'person subject to immigration control'.[17] For example, if an elderly relative is seeking to join family in the UK, it is usual to require a maintenance undertaking.

Maintenance undertaking

A '**maintenance undertaking**' means a written undertaking given by another person under the Immigration Rules to be responsible for your maintenance and accommodation.[18] There are specific Home Office forms on which an undertaking can be given. However, no official form need be used, provided the undertaking is sufficiently formal and definite.[19] The document must contain a promise or agreement that the other person will maintain and accommodate you in the future. If it merely contains a statement about her/his present abilities and intentions, it does not amount to an undertaking.[20]

Your leave is considered to be 'as a result of a maintenance undertaking' if this was a factor in granting it. It does not need to have been the only, or even a major, factor.[21] However, if the maintenance undertaking was not relevant to your being granted leave, its existence does not make you a person subject to immigration control. If you are in doubt about whether you have leave given as a result of an undertaking, get specialist immigration advice.

Part 11: Immigration and residence rules for benefits and tax credits
Chapter 67: Coming from abroad: immigration status
2. Benefits and tax credits affected by immigration status

You are appealing a refusal to vary your previous leave

If you have leave solely because you have appealed against a decision to refuse an application to vary the leave you previously had, you are a 'person subject to immigration control'.[22]

> *Example*
> Sayf is an Iraqi national who has been granted two and a half years' discretionary leave. Just before this expires, he applies for a further period of discretionary leave. His application is refused and he immediately appeals against this decision. His previous discretionary leave is extended while the appeal is pending. From the refusal of his application and while the appeal is pending, he is a 'person subject to immigration control'.

If you have leave solely because you requested an administrative review of a decision refusing to vary your leave, it is arguable that this does not bring you within the definition of 'person subject to immigration control'.[23] Get specialist advice.

2. Benefits and tax credits affected by immigration status

The general rule is that if you are defined as a 'person subject to immigration control' (see p1560), you are excluded from council tax reduction[24] and the following benefits and tax credits:[25]

- attendance allowance (AA);
- carer's allowance (CA);
- child benefit;
- child tax credit (CTC);
- disability living allowance (DLA);
- funeral support payment (in Scotland);[26]
- income-related employment and support allowance (ESA);
- ESA in youth;[27]
- housing benefit (HB);
- incapacity benefit (IB) for incapacity in youth;[28]
- income support (IS);
- income-based jobseeker's allowance (JSA);
- pension credit (PC);
- personal independence payment (PIP);
- severe disablement allowance (SDA);
- social fund payments;
- universal credit (UC);
- working tax credit (WTC).

Chapter 67

Coming from abroad: immigration status

However, there are limited exceptions when some people subject to immigration control can claim means-tested benefits (see below), some can claim non-means-tested benefits (see p1566) and some can claim tax credits (see p1567).

A person subject to immigration control is only excluded from the above benefits and tax credits and can therefore claim any other benefit. For example, if you have paid sufficient national insurance (NI) contributions, you can claim any of the contributory benefits – eg, retirement pensions, contribution-based JSA and contributory ESA. You can also claim benefits that depend on employment – eg, maternity allowance (MA), industrial injuries benefits or statutory payments.

Exceptions

Means-tested benefits

If you are in any of the exempt groups below, being a 'person subject to immigration control' does not exclude you from entitlement to the following means-tested benefits:[29]

- UC;
- IS;
- income-based JSA;
- income-related ESA;
- PC;
- HB.

You are not excluded if:

- you are a national of North Macedonia or Turkey[30] and you are lawfully present in the UK – eg, during a period in which you have leave to enter or remain in the UK (you are very unlikely to be assisted by this exemption if you are an asylum seeker because although you are lawfully present, you still need a right to reside for each of these benefits – see p1591[31]). **Note:** if you receive a means-tested benefit because this exempt group applies to you, the Home Office does not regard you as having recourse to public funds.[32] You are also not excluded from council tax reduction, although receiving it does count as having recourse to public funds and so breaches any no recourse to public funds condition attached to your leave;[33]
- you have leave to enter or remain given as a result of a maintenance undertaking and have been resident in the UK for at least five years (beginning on either the date you entered the UK or when the maintenance undertaking was signed, whichever is later). If there are gaps in your residence as a result of your going to live for a period in another country, the periods of residence in the UK can be added together to make the five years.[34] However, depending on your circumstances, you may not have ceased to be resident during the short periods of absence, and each absence must be considered individually (see p1585);[35]

Part 11: Immigration and residence rules for benefits and tax credits
Chapter 67: Coming from abroad: immigration status
2. Benefits and tax credits affected by immigration status

- you have leave to enter or remain given as a result of a maintenance undertaking and the person (or, if more than one, all the people) who gave the undertaking has died.

Social fund and other payments

If you are defined as a 'person subject to immigration control', this does not exclude you from entitlement to:

- social fund payments *if* you are in any of the exempt categories for means-tested (see p1565) or non-means-tested benefits (see p1565);[36] *or*
- funeral support grants *if* you are in any of the exempt categories for non-means-tested benefits (see below);[37] *or*
- Best Start grants.

However, you must meet the other conditions of entitlement, including (except for Best Start grants if you are under 20, and winter fuel payments) being in receipt of a qualifying benefit.

Non-means-tested benefits

If you are in any of the exempt groups below, being a person subject to immigration control does not exclude you from getting the following non-means-tested, non-contributory benefits:[38]

- AA;
- CA;
- child benefit;
- DLA;
- ESA in youth;
- funeral support payment in Scotland;
- IB for incapacity in youth;
- PIP;
- SDA.

You are not excluded if:

- you have leave to enter or remain given as a result of a maintenance undertaking;
- you are a member of a European Economic Area national's family (see p1669).[39] For further information on when this exemption should apply, including if your family member is a British citizen, see CPAG's *Benefits for Migrants Handbook*;
- you are a national of Algeria, Morocco, San Marino, Tunisia or Turkey and either you are currently lawfully working (see p1567) in Great Britain, or you have ceased to be lawfully working in Great Britain for a reason such as pregnancy, childcare, illness or accident, or because you have reached retirement age;[40]

Chapter 67

- you are living with a member of your family (see p1673) who is covered by the above bullet point;
- for DLA, PIP, AA and child benefit only, you are covered by a reciprocal agreement. In practice, this is most helpful for child benefit and, in particular, if you are covered by the agreement with former Yugoslavia which applies to Bosnia-Herzegovina, Kosovo, North Macedonia, Montenegro and Serbia.[41] See p1582 for more information about reciprocal agreements.

Lawfully working

You should be accepted as '**lawfully working**' if you have been insured (by paying, or being credited with, NI contributions),[42] and any work you have done has not breached any conditions attached to your leave. If you are an asylum seeker, you should be accepted as lawfully working if you have permission to work from the Home Office.

Tax credits

If you are a 'person subject to immigration control', this does not exclude you from getting CTC or WTC in the following circumstances.[43]

- You have leave to enter or remain given as a result of a maintenance undertaking and you have been resident in the UK for at least five years (beginning on either the date you entered the UK or when the maintenance undertaking was signed, whichever is later).
- You have leave to enter or remain given as a result of a maintenance undertaking and the person (or, if more than one, all the people) who gave the undertaking has died.
- For CTC only, you are a national of Algeria, Morocco, San Marino, Tunisia or Turkey and either you are lawfully working (see above) in the UK, or you have ceased lawfully working for a reason such as pregnancy, childcare, illness or accident, or because you have reached retirement age.[44]
- For WTC only, you are a national of North Macedonia or Turkey and you are lawfully present in the UK – eg, during a period in which you have leave to enter or remain in the UK.
- For CTC only, you transferred to CTC from IS or income-based JSA that included amounts for a child and you were entitled to that IS or JSA because you came into the first bullet point on p1565.[45]

If you are a person subject to immigration control, but your partner is not (or s/he comes into one of the above groups), you can receive tax credits on the basis of a joint claim (see p1571).

Part 11: Immigration and residence rules for benefits and tax credits
Chapter 67: Coming from abroad: immigration status
3. Partners and children

3. **Partners and children**

Some benefits and tax credits have special rules that apply if any partner or child who lives with you is subject to immigration control. These rules vary, so check the rules for the relevant benefit or tax credit.

Means-tested benefits

Universal credit

If you live with your **partner** and claim universal credit (UC), you are generally required to make a joint claim. If your partner is a 'person subject to immigration control' and is not in one of the exempt groups who can get UC (see p1564), your joint claim is treated as a claim for UC as a single person and:[46]

- your award is based on the maximum amount for a single person;[47] *and*
- your partner does not have to accept a claimant commitment or comply with any work-related requirements because s/he is not a claimant;[48] *and*
- your partner's income and capital are taken into account (see p36);[49] *and*
- your partner does not affect your being the 'responsible carer' of a child (see p1062) – eg, to determine your work-related requirements, or to enable you to be entitled to UC when you are receiving education;[50] *and*
- the couple rate of the earnings threshold applies for determining when no work-related requirements apply to you (see p1065), and in calculating any self-employed 'minimum income floor' that may apply if you are self-employed (note the 'minimum income floor' does not apply to your partner if s/he is self-employed) (see p121).[51]

These claims described above do not include additional amounts for your partner. Therefore, if her/his leave is subject to a 'no recourse to public funds' condition, your claim for UC does not breach this condition because it does not result in your receiving increased public funds as a result of her/his presence (see p1562). If your UC claim includes a housing costs element, in almost all circumstances this will not be higher as a result of your partner's presence, as s/he is not a claimant and is therefore ignored in the housing costs calculation.[52] However, if you and your partner are joint tenants, the amount of rent used to calculate your housing costs element includes your partner's share (see p104 and p109). If this results in an additional amount of UC housing costs element being paid, this will breach any no recourse to public funds condition attached to your partner's leave. The only scenario that CPAG is aware of in which this can arise is if you and your partner are joint tenants with one or more other joint tenants. Obtain specialist immigration advice before claiming a housing costs element if you have concerns about breaching a no recourse to public funds condition.

Note: if you have reached pension age and your partner is under pension age, but is not entitled to UC because s/he is a 'person subject to immigration control', your claim is *not* treated as a single claim for UC. Instead, you must claim pension credit (PC) and housing benefit (HB) and you are treated as a single person for these claims.[53]

If you are entitled to UC, you can include any **child** you are responsible for in your claim, regardless of the child's immigration status. However, if the child's leave is subject to a no recourse to public funds condition, receiving UC amounts for her/him will breach that condition and could affect her/his right to remain in the UK (see p1562). Obtain specialist immigration advice before making a claim.

Income support, income-based jobseeker's allowance and income-related employment and support allowance

If your partner is a 'person subject to immigration control' (see p1560), s/he is included in your claim for income support (IS), income-based jobseeker's allowance (JSA), including if you are a joint-claim couple, or income-related employment and support allowance (ESA). However, you are only paid a personal allowance at the single person's rate, unless s/he is in one of the exempt groups of people who can get the means-tested benefits listed on p1565, in which case, you are paid at the couple rate.[54]

In all cases, your partner is still treated as part of your household and part of your claim. Therefore, her/his work, income and capital can all affect your benefit entitlement. Her/his presence means you cannot be entitled to IS as a lone parent (see p235) and may mean you are not entitled to a severe disability premium (see p346).

Premiums are payable if either you or your partner satisfy the qualifying conditions (see p339) and should be paid at the couple rate.

Note: if your partner's leave to enter or remain in the UK is subject to a no recourse to public funds condition, receiving an additional (or a couple rate of a) premium for her/him can be regarded as having additional recourse to public funds and affect her/his right to remain in the UK (see p1562). Obtain specialist immigration advice before claiming the benefit that would result in the premium being paid.

Pension credit

If your partner is a 'person subject to immigration control' (whether or not s/he is in one of the exempt groups listed on p1565), s/he is treated as not being part of your household.[55] This means that you are paid as a single person and your partner's income and capital do not affect your claim. Your partner's presence may mean you cannot get the additional amount for severe disability as the DWP treats her/him as 'normally residing with' you for this purpose unless an exemption applies (see p346).[56]

If you are entitled to PC, you can include any child you are responsible for in your claim, regardless of the child's immigration status. However, if the child's leave is subject to a no recourse to public funds condition, receipt of PC amounts

Part 11: Immigration and residence rules for benefits and tax credits
Chapter 67: Coming from abroad: immigration status
3. Partners and children

for her/him will breach that condition and can affect her/his right to remain in the UK (see p1562). Obtain specialist immigration advice before making a claim.

Housing benefit

If your partner and/or child for whom you are responsible is a 'person subject to immigration control', this does not affect the amount you are paid. Unless the exception below applies, your partner is included in your claim and your applicable amount includes the couple rate of the personal allowance and any premiums to which either of you are entitled.

Similarly, your child is included in your claim and your applicable amount includes a personal allowance for each child (subject to the 'two-child limit' – see p337), together with any premiums for which s/he qualifies.

Therefore if your partner's and/or child's leave is subject to a no recourse to public funds condition, a claim for HB can result in additional public funds being paid as a result of her/his presence. This can affect her/his right to remain in the UK (see p1562). Obtain specialist immigration advice before making a claim.

The only **exception** is if you are of pension age and your partner is under pension age and is a 'person subject to immigration control' (and not covered by an exempt group). You are not required to make a joint claim for UC (see p1568), but, instead claim HB (and PC) and you are treated as single for your HB (and PC) claim.[57]

Non-means-tested benefits

Non-means-tested benefits include both contributory benefits (based on your national insurance (NI) contribution record) and non-contributory benefits.

Your immigration status, and that of your partner or child, does not affect your entitlement to either contributory benefits (eg, contributory ESA) or benefits based on current or past employment (eg, maternity allowance and statutory payments).

Your entitlement to non-contributory benefits is affected by your immigration status if you are the claimant, but is not affected by the immigration status of any partner or child included in your claim. Therefore, for **child benefit**, if you are not a 'person subject to immigration control', or you are but you are in one of the exempt groups (see p1566), you can claim for any child for whom you are responsible, regardless of the child's immigration status. However, if the child's leave is subject to a no recourse to public funds condition, receiving child benefit for her/him may be regarded as recourse and could affect her/his right to remain in the UK. Obtain specialist immigration advice before making a claim.

Similarly, if your child is not a person subject to immigration control, or s/he is but is in one of the exempt groups on p1566, s/he can claim **disability living allowance** even if you are a person subject to immigration control.

Tax credits

If your partner is a 'person subject to immigration control' and you are not (or you are but are in one of the exempt groups on p1567), your joint claim for tax credits (see p1496) is treated as if your partner were *not* subject to immigration control.[58] However, unless you or your partner are responsible for a child, or your partner is a national of North Macedonia or Turkey and lawfully present in the UK, your WTC does not include the couple element.[59]

There are no immigration status conditions for children, so your CTC and/or WTC includes amounts for any child for whom you are responsible (subject to the 'two-child limit' see p1453).

If your partner's leave is subject to the condition that s/he does not have recourse to public funds, s/he is *not* regarded as having recourse by receiving tax credits on the basis of a joint claim as described above. Therefore, the claim does not breach that condition. If such a joint claim includes a child whose leave is subject to the condition that s/he does not have recourse to public funds, any tax credits awarded in respect of that child are also not regarded as recourse.[60]

If your claim for CTC or WTC is *not* a joint claim as described above (ie, one partner is a person subject to immigration control) and it includes an amount for a child whose leave is subject to a no recourse to public funds condition, this may be regarded as recourse and could affect her/his right to remain in the UK. Obtain specialist immigration advice if this could apply.

4. National insurance numbers and contributions

Exemption from the national insurance number requirement

In general, the national insurance (NI) number requirement (see p1171) applies, regardless of immigration status, to you and any partner included in your claim (even if you are not going to receive any extra benefit for her/him because s/he is a 'person subject to immigration control' – see p1568).

However, if you are the benefit claimant, your partner does not have to satisfy the NI number requirement if:[61]

- s/he is a 'person subject to immigration control' because s/he requires leave to enter or remain in the UK, but does not have it (see p1561); *and*
- s/he has not previously been given an NI number; *and*
- you are claiming income support, income-based jobseeker's allowance, income-related employment and support allowance or pension credit and your partner is not entitled to that benefit her/himself, or you are claiming housing benefit and your partner fails the habitual residence test (see p1586).

Part 11: Immigration and residence rules for benefits and tax credits
Chapter 67: Coming from abroad: immigration status
4. National insurance numbers and contributions

However, in practice, it is difficult to see who could satisfy the first bullet point and not satisfy this.

You may still be asked for information about an NI number application for your partner, even though s/he is exempt, but a refusal to allocate an NI number does not prevent you from being entitled to benefits or tax credits, or council tax reduction.

Note: this exemption is not relevant to universal credit (UC) because you do not need an NI number to *make* a claim for UC and the DWP only requests it later. If your partner is a 'person subject to immigration control', your joint claim is treated as a claim for UC by you as a single person (see p1568) and, therefore, your partner is not a claimant and does not need an NI number.[62]

Tax credits

The NI number requirement for tax credits is similar to the requirement for benefits (and includes the above exemption for partners who require leave but do not have it).[63]

In addition, the NI number requirement does not apply if the Tax Credit Office is satisfied that you (and/or your partner if it is a joint claim) have a 'reasonable excuse' for not complying with the requirement – eg, if you are unable to prove your identity because the Home Office has all your documents and you can prove this (eg, with a letter from your solicitor).[64]

If your claim was refused because you have not satisfied the NI number requirement, you can appeal on the grounds that either your partner is exempt or you had a 'reasonable excuse'.[65] You must apply for a mandatory reconsideration before you can appeal.

National insurance contributions

If you have worked and paid contributions in an European Economic Area country and you are covered by the European Union co-ordination rules (see p1672), these can be taken into account when working out your entitlement to UK contributory benefits (see p1678). Similar rules apply if you have worked and paid contributions in a country with which the UK has a reciprocal agreement (see p1582).[66] You may also be able to make up a shortfall in your contribution record by making voluntary contributions (see p964). Get advice to check whether this is worth doing. Being a 'person subject to immigration control' (see p1564) does not exclude you from any of the contributory benefits.

5. Asylum seekers and refugees

Asylum seekers

You are referred to as an 'asylum seeker' while you are waiting for a Home Office decision on an application for refugee status. If you are a non-European Economic Area (EEA) national seeking asylum in the UK, you generally come within the definition of a 'person subject to immigration control' as someone who requires leave, but does not have it (see p1561). You are, therefore, excluded from the social security benefits listed on p1564 unless you are in one of the exempt groups on pp1565–67.

If benefit can be paid for you either because you are in an exempt group or because your partner can include you in her/his claim, this does not affect your asylum application. You can receive any benefit defined as a 'public fund' (see p1562) because asylum seekers are not subject to any condition not to have recourse to public funds.

If you are excluded from social security benefits because you are a 'person subject to immigration control', you may be entitled to alternative forms of state support. If you are destitute, you may be eligible for asylum support from the Home Office. **Note:** asylum support is not taken into account as income for universal credit (UC). It is disregarded for income support (IS), income-based jobseeker's allowance (JSA) and income-related employment and support allowance (ESA) if it is 'income in kind'. If your partner claims housing benefit (HB), asylum support is taken into account as income unless your partner is 'passported' onto maximum HB due to receiving UC, IS, income-based JSA, income-related ESA or pension credit.[67]

However, any benefit your partner receives is taken into account as income when calculating your asylum support, unless you can show it would not reasonably be available to you – eg, a disability benefit.

If you are not eligible for asylum support or benefits, you may be able to get assistance from your local authority under one or more of the community care provisions, particularly if you have additional needs as a result of your age, sickness or disability. If you have children, or you are a child, you may be eligible for support under the Children Act 1989 or Children (Scotland) Act 1995. Get independent legal advice about what you are entitled to, if possible before you apply, and always if you are refused.

For more information about asylum support, see CPAG's *Benefits for Migrants Handbook*.

Refugee and other leave granted after an asylum application

If, following your asylum application, you are granted leave that is not subject to a condition that you do not have recourse to public funds (eg, refugee leave or

Part 11: Immigration and residence rules for benefits and tax credits
Chapter 67: Coming from abroad: immigration status
5. Asylum seekers and refugees

humanitarian protection), you are no longer a 'person subject to immigration control'. During this period of leave, you can claim all benefits, provided you meet the usual rules of entitlement. If you are granted leave that *is* subject to a condition that you do not have recourse to public funds, you *are* defined as a 'person subject to immigration control' and you are excluded from the benefits listed on p1564, unless you are in an exempt group (see pp1565–67).

If you are granted refugee leave or humanitarian protection, you can be joined by certain family members under family reunion provisions. A family member who is given leave to enter or remain in the UK under these provisions is not a 'person subject to immigration control' during her/his period of leave and can claim all benefits, provided s/he meets the usual rules of entitlement. In Scotland, you can also claim a Scottish Welfare Fund family reunion crisis grant from your local authority if your family members have been granted permission to join you in this way. Contact the British Red Cross if you want help to apply for this grant.

If you (or the family member you have joined) have refugee leave or humanitarian protection, you do not need to satisfy the past presence test for the disability and carers benefits (see p1630).

If you are granted refugee status, humanitarian protection or discretionary leave, you are exempt from the habitual residence test (see p1586) and exempt from the requirement to have lived in the UK for three months for child benefit and child tax credit (see p1584).

Income support and universal credit for refugees studying English

If you are entitled to IS or are in one of the limited groups that can make a new claim for IS (see p233), then being a refugee studying English is one of the categories that can qualify for IS (see p237). If you have been granted refugee leave, you can get IS for up to nine months while you are studying if you:[68]

- attend, for more than 15 hours a week, a course (in practice, a combination of courses are accepted) for the purpose of learning English so you may obtain employment; *and*
- have been in Great Britain for not more than 12 months on the date the course began.

There is no equivalent rule for UC. If you are attending a part-time course to learn English, to be entitled to UC the course must be accepted as compatible with your work-related requirements (see Chapter 46).[69]

Backdating child benefit, guardian's allowance and tax credits

If you have been granted refugee leave, or leave as an unaccompanied child relocated from Europe (known as 'section 67 leave'), you can claim child benefit, guardian's allowance and, in limited circumstances, tax credits and have them backdated to the date of your asylum application.[70]

You must claim backdated child benefit and guardian's allowance within three months, and tax credits within one month, of receiving the Home Office letter granting you leave.[71] If the Home Office letter is sent to a solicitor acting for you, the three- or one-month period starts from the date your solicitor receives the letter.[72] The amount of child benefit and guardian's allowance paid is not reduced by any asylum support you may have received.

In practice, it is very hard to claim backdated tax credits. Your claim is treated as having been made on the date you claimed asylum, and is renewed each subsequent April. Therefore, you can only claim tax credits if you applied for asylum before UC was introduced in your area. If you have received any asylum support for essential living needs this reduces your tax credits over that period and often completely cancels out entitlement.[73] HM Revenue and Customs (HMRC) can accept a claim by telephone or letter, but it must contain all the information required and must satisfy the NI number requirement.[74] However, the expectation is that you will make your claim by telephone.[75] Be clear that you are making a claim and ask HMRC to take all the information required for your claim to be accepted.[76] If HMRC refuses to accept your claim, see cpag.org.uk/welfare-rights/judicial-review/judicial-review-pre-action-letters/tax-credits for the next steps and ask an advice centre to help you.

Note: there is no provision to pay backdated UC.

Integration loans

If you (or someone upon whom you are dependent) are granted refugee leave or humanitarian protection and you are aged 18 or over, you may be eligible for an integration loan.[77] This is a discretionary loan of at least £100, paid for expenses associated with your integration into UK society, including for employment, education and housing. Claims are decided by the Home Office and so these loans are not covered in this *Handbook*. The application form and guidance notes are available at gov.uk.

Before applying for, or in addition to, an integration loan, you may want to consider accessing help from your local welfare assistance scheme (see p861) or applying for other financial help (see p870).

Part 11: Immigration and residence rules for benefits and tax credits
Chapter 67: Coming from abroad: immigration status
Notes

Notes

1. Immigration status

1 s115(9) IAA 1999
2 s7 IA 1988
3 Sch 3 para 1 I(EEA) Regs
4 s115(9)(a) IAA 1999
5 s7 IA 1988; regs 11 and 14(2) I(EEA) Regs
6 *The Agreement Between the European Community and its Member States, of the one part, and the Swiss Confederation, of the other, on the Free Movement of Persons*, Luxembourg, 21 June 1999, Cm 5639; reg 2 I(EEA) Regs defines Switzerland as an EEA state; reg 11 provides that no EEA national requires leave to enter the UK and Part 2 of I(EEA) Regs provides residence rights.
7 *Zambrano*, C-34/09 [2011] ECR I-01177; *Dereci and Others*, C-256/11 [2011] ECR I-11315; also in UK law: reg 16 I(EEA) Regs
8 See, for example, *DM v SSWP (PIP)* [2019] UKUT 26 (AAC)
9 s3C IA 1971; Vol 2 para 073202 DMG; paras C1679 and C2017 ADM
10 gov.uk/guidance/windrush-compensation-scheme
11 HB Adjudication Circular A8/2019, paras 13-14
12 Regs 10(2)(f) and 19 (table 6, para 23) TC(DCI) Regs
13 s115(9)(b) IAA 1999
14 para 6 Immigration Rules, HC395
15 s24(1)(b)(ii) IA 1971
16 para 6B Immigration Rules, HC395
17 s115(9)(c) IAA 1999
18 s115(10) IAA 1999
19 *R (Begum) v Social Security Commissioner* [2003] EWHC 3380 (Admin)
20 *Ahmed v SSWP* [2005] EWCA Civ 535
21 CIS/3508/2001; see also *SJ v SSWP (SPC)* [2015] UKUT 505 (AAC), reported as [2016] AACR 17
22 s115(9)(d) IAA 1999 referred to Sch 4 para 17 IAA 1999, which was repealed by Sch 9 para 1 NIAA 2002. It has been held that the reference should be read as if to s3C(1) and (2)(b) and (c) IA 1971 (as s17(2) Interpretation Act 1978 applies) – *EE v City of Cardiff (HB)* [2018] UKUT 418 (AAC). See also *GO v HMRC (CHB)* [2018] UKUT 328 (AAC).
23 s3C(2)(d) IA 1971 was only inserted from 20 October 2014 and so the reasoning of *EE v City of Cardiff (HB)* [2018] UKUT 418 (AAC) does not apply.

2. Benefits and tax credits affected by immigration status

24 Reg 13 CTRS(PR)E Regs; reg 19 CTR(SPC)S Regs; reg 19 CTR(S) Regs; reg 29 CTRSPR(W) Regs; Sch para 20 CTRS(DS)W Regs
25 s115 IAA 1999; s42 TCA 2002; reg 3 TC(Imm) Regs
26 reg 9(5) FEA(S) Regs
27 Reg 11(1)(b) ESA Regs; reg 12(1)(b) ESA Regs 2013
28 Reg 16(1)(b) SS(IB) Regs
29 Reg 2(1) and Part 1 of Sch SS(IA)CA Regs; para C1060 ADM; Vol 2 para 070835 DMG
30 Confirmed in *OD v SSWP (JSA)* [2015] UKUT 438 (AAC)
31 *Szoma v SSWP* [2005] UKHL 64, reported as R(IS) 2/06; *Yesiloz v LB Camden and Another* [2009] EWCA Civ 415. These arguments about temporary admission are likely to apply equally to immigration bail.
32 para 6B Immigration Rules
33 Reg 13(1A) CTRS(PR)E Regs; reg 19(2) CTR(S) Regs; reg 19(2) CTR(SPC)S Regs; reg 29(2) CTRSPR(W) Regs; Sch para 20(2) CTRS(DS)W Regs; para 6A Immigration Rules. Council tax reduction is not included in the regulations referred to in para 6B Immigration Rules, which disregards claims made as a result of exemptions.
34 R(IS) 2/02
35 CPC/1005/2005
36 Reg 2 SS(IA)CA Regs

37 Reg 9(5) FEA(S) Regs
38 **All** Reg 2(2), (3) and (4)(b) and Sch Part
   II SS(IA)CA Regs; Vol 2 paras 070836-37
   DMG; para 10140 CBTM
   AA Reg 2(1)(a)(ib) SS(AA) Regs
   CA Reg 9(1)(ia) SS(ICA) Regs
   DLA Reg 2(1)(a)(ib) SS(DLA) Regs
   ESA Reg 11(1)(b) and (3) ESA Regs; reg
   12(1)(b) and (3) ESA Regs 2013
   FSP Reg 9(5) FEA(S) Regs
   IB Reg 16(1)(b) and (5) SS(IB) Regs
   PIP Reg 16(d)(ii) SS(PIP) Regs
   SDA Reg 3(a)(ib) SS(SDA) Regs
   YCG Reg 7(7) CA(YCG)(S) Regs
39 *JFP v DSD (DLA)* [2012] NICom 267,
   which declined to follow the more
   restrictive approach of CDLA/708/2007.
   However, see also *MS v SSWP (DLA)*
   [2016] UKUT 42 (AAC). See also para
   10140 CBTM.
40 *Krid v Caisse Nationale d'Assurance
   Vieillesse des Travailleurs Salariés
   (CNAVTS)*, C-103/94 [1995] ECR I-
   00719, para 26. This exempt group
   continues after Brexit due to reg 2 The
   Social Security, Child Benefit and Child
   Tax Credit (Amendment) (EU Exit)
   Regulations 2019, No 1431.
41 The Family Allowances, National
   Insurance and Industrial Injuries
   (Yugoslavia) Order 1958, No.1263
42 *Sürül v Bundesanstalt für Arbeit*, C-262/
   96 [1999] ECR I-02685
43 Reg 3 TC(Imm) Regs; TCTM 02105,
   02107 (North Macedonia instead of
   Croatia should be listed) and 02108
44 *Krid v Caisse Nationale d'Assurance
   Vieillesse des Travailleurs Salariés
   (CNAVTS)*, C-103/94 [1995] ECR I-
   00719, para 26. This exempt group
   continues after Brexit due to reg 4 The
   Social Security, Child Benefit and Child
   Tax Credit (Amendment) (EU Exit)
   Regulations 2019, No 1431.
45 Regs 3 and 5 TC(Imm) Regs

3. Partners and children
46 ss3 and 4(1)(c) and (2) WRA 2012; reg
   3(3) UC Regs; reg 9(1)
   UC,PIP,JSA&ESA(C&P) Regs
47 Regs 3(3) and 36(3) UC Regs
48 ss3 and 4(1)(e) WRA 2012; reg 3(3) UC
   Regs; reg 9(1) UC,PIP,JSA&ESA(C&P)
   Regs
49 Regs 3(3), 18(2) and 22(3) UC Regs
50 ss4(1)(d) and 19(6) WRA 2012; regs
   14(c) and 86 UC Regs

51 s39 WRA 2012; regs 62(1), (3) and (4)
   and 90(3) UC Regs; ADM para H4077
52 S/he must be a claimant to be defined as
   a joint renter or joint owner-occupier:
   Schs 4 para 1 and 5 para 1 UC Regs
53 Art 7(2)(b) and (3)(b) WRA(No.31)O;
   HB Circular A9/2019, paras 15-17;
   Memo DMG 07/19, para 12
54 **IS** Reg 21(3) and Sch 7 para 16A IS Regs
   JSA Reg 85(4) and Sch 5 para 13A JSA
   Regs
   ESA Reg 69 and Sch 5 para 10 ESA Regs
55 Reg 5(1)(h) SPC Regs
56 Sch 1 paras 1(1)(a)(ii) and 2 SPC Regs;
   Vol 13 para 78946 DMG
57 Art 7(2)(b) and (3)(b) WRA(No.31)O;
   HB Circular A9/2019, paras 15-17
58 Reg 3(2) TC(Imm) Regs
59 Reg 11(4) and (5) WTC(EMR) Regs
60 para 6B Immigration Rules, HC395. The
   TC(Imm) Regs are made under s42 TCA
   2002.

4. National insurance numbers and contributions
61 **IS** Reg 2A IS Regs
   JSA Reg 2A JSA Regs
   ESA Reg 2A ESA Regs
   PC Reg 1A SPC Regs
   HB Reg 4(c) HB Regs; reg 4(c) HB(SPC)
   Regs
   **Bereavement benefits and
   retirement pensions** Reg 1A(c)
   SS(WB&RP) Regs
   TC Reg 5(8) TC(CN) Regs
62 paras A2153-54 ADM
63 Reg 5 TC(CN) Regs
64 Reg 5(6) TC(CN) Regs
65 *ZM and AB v HMRC (TC)* [2013] UKUT
   547 (AAC); *CI v HMRC (TC)* [2014] UKUT
   158 (AAC)
66 Under orders made in powers conferred
   by s179 SSAA 1992

5. Asylum seekers and refugees
67 **UC** Reg 66 UC Regs
   IS Sch 9 para 21 IS Regs
   JSA Sch 7 para 22 JSA Regs
   ESA Sch 8 para 22 ESA Regs
   HB Sch 5 para 23 HB Regs
68 Reg 4ZA(3)(b) and Sch 1B para 18 IS
   Regs
69 Reg 12(4) UC Regs
70 **CB/GA** Reg 6(2)(d) and (e)
   CB&GA(Admin) Regs
   TC Regs 3(4)-(10) and 4 TC(Imm) Regs

11

Part 11: Immigration and residence rules for benefits and tax credits
Chapter 67: Coming from abroad: immigration status
Notes

71 **CB/GA** Reg 6(2)(d) and (e)
CB&GA(Admin) Regs
TC Reg 3(5) TC(Imm) Regs
72 *Tkachuk v SSWP* [2007] EWCA Civ 515;
CIS/3797/2003
73 Reg 3(9) TC(Imm) Regs; CTC/3692/
2008
74 Reg 5 TC(CN) Regs
75 gov.uk/claim-tax-credits/backdate-a-
claim
76 Reg 5(2)(b) TC(CN) Regs; see also *MR v
HMRC (TC)* [2018] UKUT 238 (AAC)
77 s13 Asylum and Immigration
(Treatment of Claimants, etc) Act 2004;
The Integration Loans for Refugees and
Others Regulations 2007, No.1598

Chapter 68

Coming from abroad: residence rules

This chapter covers:
1. Introduction (p1580)
2. The different residence and presence tests (p1583)
3. Habitual residence (p1586)
4. Right to reside (p1591)
5. Who has a right to reside (p1594)
6. Rules for specific benefits and tax credits (p1625)

This chapter describes the residence and presence rules that affect your entitlement while you are in Great Britain. If you go abroad, see Chapter 69.

If you or your partner are not a European Economic Area (EEA) national, before using this chapter check Chapter 67 for information on how your immigration status can affect your entitlement to benefits and tax credits. If you are an EEA national, the European Union co-ordination rules may help you to satisfy the residence and presence tests when you are in the UK. These rules are outlined in Chapter 70.

Key facts
- Different types of residence conditions apply to many benefits and tax credits. These are: **residence, ordinary residence, right to reside and habitual residence.**
- Entitlement to most benefits and tax credits also depends on your being **present** in Great Britain or the UK.
- Some benefits require you to have been present for a certain period of time (known as **past presence**) or to have been **living in** the UK or common travel area for three months prior to your claim.
- The rules on residence and presence vary between different benefits and tax credits. If you satisfy the conditions for one, it does not mean you satisfy the conditions for another.

Part 11: Immigration and residence rules for benefits and tax credits
Chapter 68: Coming from abroad: residence rules
1. Introduction

Brexit
Further to the UK leaving the European Union on 31 January 2020, the rules descibed in
this chapter continue until the end of the transition period, which, at the time of writing,
was due to end on 31 December 2020. For more information, including the rules after this
period, see p1596.

1. **Introduction**

Many benefits have residence and/or presence conditions. The rules vary between
different benefits and tax credits. Whether you meet the conditions can depend
on how long you have been in Great Britain, your nationality, your immigration
status and whether you are covered by the provisions of European law (while it
applies – see p1581).

Although many presence and residence rules refer to Great Britain rather than
the UK, there is a reciprocal agreement between Britain and Northern Ireland,
which means that, in general, you can satisfy the residence conditions if you
move between Great Britain and Northern Ireland.

There are residence conditions for the following benefits and tax credits:
- attendance allowance (see p1629);
- Best Start grant (in Scotland) (see p1635);
- bereavement support payment (see p1627);
- carer's allowance (see p1629);
- child benefit (see p1628);
- child tax credit (see p1635);
- disability living allowance (see p1629);
- contributory employment and support allowance (ESA) in youth (see p1629);
- income-related ESA (see p1625);
- funeral expenses payment (see p1634);
- funeral support payments (in Scotland) (see p1634);
- guardian's allowance (see p1629);
- housing benefit (see p1625);
- incapacity benefit in youth (see p1629);
- income support (see p1625);
- income-based jobseeker's allowance (JSA) (see p1625);
- pension credit (see p1625);
- personal independence payment (see p1629);
- category D retirement pension (see p1634);
- Scottish child payment (in Scotland, expected to be introduced by Christmas
  2020) (see p1629);
- severe disablement allowance (see p1629);

- Sure Start maternity grant (see p1635);
- universal credit (see p1625);
- winter fuel payment (see p1635);
- working tax credit (see p1635);
- young carer grant (in Scotland) (see p1629).

Council tax reduction also has residence conditions.

Contributory benefits, such as contribution-based JSA, contributory ESA and retirement pensions (except category D), as well as the employment-related benefits (maternity allowance and industrial injuries benefits) do not have residence conditions. However, they have presence requirements, which mean that if you go abroad, some benefits cease and others are not increased unless exceptions apply (see Chapter 69). Industrial injuries benefits also have conditions related to your presence in Great Britain at the time you had your accident or contracted your disease. There are no residence or presence requirements for statutory sick pay, statutory maternity pay, statutory adoption pay, statutory paternity pay, statutory shared parental pay and statutory parental bereavement pay paid by your employer (but see p1661).

Which rules apply

Your rights are affected by the rules that apply to you. This *Handbook* uses terms 'UK law', 'European Union (EU) law' and 'reciprocal agreements'.

In general, if you are covered by EU law, more generous EU law provisions apply. If they do not apply, but you are covered by a reciprocal agreement, the reciprocal agreement provisions apply. If you are not covered by either EU law or a reciprocal agreement, or in some cases if UK law is more generous, UK law applies.

UK law refers to UK legislation and caselaw. The UK benefits and tax credits legislation contains rules about the residence and presence conditions that you must satisfy to be entitled to certain benefits. These rules are set out in this chapter.

EU law refers to EU legislation and caselaw. Following the UK leaving the EU, this EU law continues to apply during the transition period (also called the implementation period). At the time of writing, the transition period was due to end on 31 December 2020, but could be extended until 31 December 2022. In general, for EU law to apply you must be an EEA national (see p1669) or the family member of an EEA national, and your circumstances must involve more than one EEA state – eg, you are a French national living in the UK. For information on changes resulting from the UK leaving the EU, see p1596.

There are two main areas of EU law which affect benefit and tax credit entitlement that are covered in this *Handbook*.

Part 11: Immigration and residence rules for benefits and tax credits
Chapter 68: Coming from abroad: residence rules
1. Introduction

- If you or your family member are an EEA national, EU law may give you a right of residence that enables you to satisfy the right to reside requirement (see p1591).
- If you are covered by the co-ordination rules (see p1672), these can help you get benefits or tax credits in the UK (eg, by enabling you to count periods of residence in any EEA state to satisfy the past presence requirements (see p1583) for UK benefits), but they can also prevent you from claiming a UK benefit – eg, if the UK is not the 'competent state' to pay that benefit.

Note: it is not usually necessary to understand how the co-ordination rules may affect you in order to know whether you have a right of residence in EU law, or vice versa. However, it can be helpful to know whether you are covered by the co-ordination rules (see p1672) if you would not otherwise satisfy a requirement to be present, have been present, have been 'living in' for a past period or be ordinarily resident.

Reciprocal agreements exist between the UK and some other countries that can assist in similar ways to EU law.

Reciprocal agreements with the UK

EEA states: Austria, Belgium, Croatia, Cyprus, Denmark, Finland, France, Germany, Iceland, Ireland, Italy, Luxembourg, Malta, Netherlands, Norway, Portugal, Slovenia, Spain and Sweden. In general, the reciprocal agreement applies if the EU co-ordination rules do not apply.

Non-EEA states: Barbados, Bermuda, Bosnia-Herzegovina, Canada, Chile, Guernsey, Isle of Man, Israel, Jamaica, Jersey, Kosova, North Macedonia, Mauritius, Montenegro, New Zealand, Philippines, Serbia, Turkey and the United States of America.

There are 'association' and 'co-operation' agreements with Algeria, Morocco, San Marino, Slovenia, Tunisia and Turkey.

There are also reciprocal agreements between Great Britain and Northern Ireland.

The scope of the reciprocal agreements differs greatly, in terms of the people covered, the benefits covered and the provisions made. It is, therefore, crucial to check the individual agreement. You can find the agreements at legislation.gov.uk – search under the relevant country and check for subsequent amendments. See also CPAG's *Benefits for Migrants Handbook*.

2. **The different residence and presence tests**

The presence and residence conditions you are required to satisfy vary between the different benefits and tax credits. You may be required to satisfy tests for your:
- presence (see below);
- past presence (see below);
- 'living in' for three months (see p1584);
- residence (see p1585);
- ordinary residence (see p1585);
- habitual residence (see p1586);
- right to reside (see p1591).

Presence

You must usually be present in Great Britain at the time you make your benefit or tax credit claim, and continue to be present. There are specific rules that allow you to be treated as present during temporary absences (see Chapter 69). If you are covered by the European Union (EU) co-ordination rules (see p1672), these can also mean that you do not need to be present. See the rules for the relevant benefits and tax credits starting on p1625 and p1647.

Being present means being physically present in Great Britain. For the DWP, HM Revenue and Customs or local authority to disqualify you from benefit because you were absent from Great Britain, it must show that you were absent throughout that day. This means that on the day you leave Great Britain and the day you arrive in Great Britain you count as present.

Past presence

The following benefits require that, in addition to being present at the time you make your claim, you must also have been present in Great Britain for a period of time before you become entitled:
- attendance allowance;
- carer's allowance (CA);
- disability living allowance;
- personal independence payment.

If you are covered by the EU co-ordination rules (see p1672), these may exempt you from this requirement, or enable you to satisfy it by adding certain periods of residence in an European Economic Area (EEA) country to periods of presence in Great Britain (under the 'aggregation principle' – see p1630).

For details of the past presence test, including exceptions, see p1629.

Part 11: Immigration and residence rules for benefits and tax credits
Chapter 68: Coming from abroad: residence rules
2. The different residence and presence tests

'Living in' for three months

There is a requirement to have been living for the past three months in:

- the common travel area (the UK, the Republic of Ireland, the Channel Islands and the Isle of Man) in order to satisfy the habitual residence test for **income-based jobseeker's allowance (JSA)** (for exceptions, see the 2019/20 edition of this *Handbook* or CPAG's *Benefits for Migrants Handbook*);[1] *or*
- the UK, for **child benefit and child tax credit (CTC)** (see below).

The phrase 'living in' is not defined in the regulations and should therefore have its ordinary, everyday meaning. It does not have the same meaning as 'presence' and you may satisfy this condition despite having been temporarily absent.

When deciding whether your absence means you ceased living in the common travel area/UK, the following factors are relevant:[2]

- the reasons for, and the intended and actual length of, your absence;
- the duration and connectedness (including your family ties, education, work, bank account, GP and accommodation) of your previous residence in the common travel area/UK;
- whether you maintained any of these connections, particularly your accommodation, while you were gone and the nature of your accommodation abroad.

See p1647 for more information about temporary absences. For child benefit and CTC only, also check whether you are exempt from this requirement (see below).

If you are covered by the EU co-ordination rules (see p1672) and have moved to the UK from an EEA country, you may be able to use certain periods of residence there to satisfy this condition (under the 'aggregation principle' – see p1678).

Child benefit and child tax credit

To be treated as present in Great Britain for child benefit and present in the UK for CTC, you must have been living in the UK for the three months before your first day of entitlement.[3] This requirement does not apply if you:[4]

- are an EEA national and a 'worker' in the UK (see p1607), including if you have retained that status;
- are an EEA national and a 'self-employed person' in the UK (see p1608), including if you have retained that status;
- are a non-EEA national who would be classed as a 'worker' or 'self-employed person' if you were an EEA national;
- are a family member (see p1614) of someone in any of the three bullet points above;
- are a refugee;
- have humanitarian protection;
- were granted leave as an unaccompanied child relocated from Europe (known as 'section 67 leave');
- have leave under the displaced persons provisions;

- have leave granted outside the Immigration Rules with no restriction on accessing public funds;
- have leave to remain in the UK pending an application for indefinite leave to remain as a victim of domestic violence;
- have been deported or otherwise legally removed from another country to the UK;[5]
- are returning to the UK after a period working abroad and, other than for the last three months of your absence, you were paying UK class 1 or class 2 NI contributions;
- are returning to the UK after an absence of less than 52 weeks, and either:
  – before departing the UK you were ordinarily resident for three months; *or*
  – you were covered by the rules that treat you as present during a temporary absence for eight or 12 weeks during payment of child benefit (see p1648) or CTC (see p1662).

Residence

The requirement to be simply 'resident', rather than 'ordinarily resident' or 'habitually resident', is only a condition for the old category D retirement pension. However, it is a necessary part of being ordinarily resident (see below) or habitually resident (see p1586). Residence is more than mere physical presence in a country and you can be resident without being present – eg, if you are away on holiday. You are usually resident in the country in which you have your home for the time being. You can remain resident during a temporary absence, depending on your circumstances, including the length of your absence, your intentions to return, your accommodation, and where your family and your personal belongings are.[6]

Note: you must be 'resident' in Scotland for the CA supplement (see p569) and the universal credit payment options (see p49) that only apply in Scotland. In general, this will apply if your address has a postcode in Scotland. Other Scottish benefits require you to be ordinarily resident in Scotland (see below).

Ordinary residence

The benefits and tax credits that have an ordinary residence requirement are:
- bereavement support payment;
- Best Start grant (in Scotland);
- child benefit;
- CTC;
- employment and support allowance in youth;
- funeral support payment (in Scotland);
- incapacity benefit in youth;
- category D retirement pension;
- Scottish child payment (in Scotland, expected to be introduced by Christmas 2020);

Part 11: Immigration and residence rules for benefits and tax credits
Chapter 68: Coming from abroad: residence rules
3. Habitual residence

- severe disablement allowance;
- social fund funeral expenses payment and winter fuel payment;
- working tax credit;
- young carer grant (in Scotland).

The term 'ordinary residence' is not defined in the legislation, and caselaw has confirmed that the words should have their natural and ordinary meaning.[7] You are ordinarily resident in a country if you are living there for a settled purpose for the time being (whether for a short or long duration).[8] The Upper Tribunal has held that the residence must be lawful.[9] There are some exceptions to the requirement to be ordinarily resident, and if you are covered by the EU co-ordination rules, these may assist you in satisfying it (see pp1625–37). In practice, claims are rarely refused on the basis of ordinary residence.

3. **Habitual residence**

The requirement to be habitually resident applies to:[10]
- attendance allowance (AA);
- Best Start grant (in Scotland);
- carer's allowance (CA);
- disability living allowance (DLA);
- housing benefit (HB);
- income support (IS);
- income-based jobseeker's allowance (JSA);
- income-related employment and support allowance (ESA);
- pension credit (PC);
- personal independence payment (PIP);
- universal credit (UC);
- young carer grant (in Scotland).

To be entitled to one of the above benefits, you must be habitually resident in the **'common travel area'** (ie, the UK, the Republic of Ireland, the Channel Islands and the Isle of Man) or, for a Best Start grant or a young carer grant, the UK, the Channel Islands, Isle of Man or the European Economic Area (EEA), or be exempt from the requirement (see p1589).

Note:
- You are also excluded from council tax reduction if you do not satisfy (and are not exempt from) the habitual residence test (see p1586).[11] See CPAG's *Benefits for Migrants Handbook* for details.
- You may be entitled to a winter fuel payment from the social fund if, instead of being ordinarily resident in Great Britain, you are habitually resident in an EEA country or Switzerland (see p1635).

The habitual residence test

To satisfy the habitual residence test for **AA, CA, DLA and PIP** you must be 'habitually resident in fact' in the common travel area.

To satisfy the habitual residence test for a **young carer grant** or, if you are aged under 20 and neither you nor your partner receive a qualifying benefit, a **Best Start grant**, you must be 'habitually resident in fact' in the UK, Channel Islands, Isle of Man, Switzerland or the EEA.

To satisfy the habitual residence test for **UC, IS, income-based JSA, income-related ESA, PC and HB**, you must:

- be 'habitually resident in fact' in the common travel area; *and*
- have a right to reside in the common travel area (see p1592); *and*
- for income-based JSA only, have been living in the common travel area for the past three months (see p1584).

For details on establishing that you are 'habitually resident in fact', see p1590.

Some groups of people are exempt from the habitual residence test (see p1589). If you are in one of these groups, you are treated as satisfying the requirement to be 'habitually resident in fact', and (for the means-tested benefits) the requirement to have a right to reside and (for income-based JSA) the requirement to have been living here for the past three months. Your residence is not examined further and, provided you meet the other conditions of entitlement, you are eligible for benefit. Whether or not you are exempt is not always considered, so if you come into one of these groups, make it clear to the DWP or local authority that you are exempt, if you might not otherwise be accepted as habitually resident.

The habitual residence test applies to the benefit claimant.

If you are making a joint claim for UC, both you and your partner must satisfy, or be exempt from, the test. If your partner fails the test, your joint claim is treated as a claim for UC as a single person. Your UC award is based on the maximum amount for a single person, but your partner's income and capital are taken into account (see p1626).[12] For other means-tested benefits, if you are the claimant and you satisfy (or are exempt from) the habitual residence test, whether or not your partner satisfies it does not affect your entitlement, unless you are a joint-claim couple for JSA. In this case, if you satisfy the test, but your partner does not, you are entitled to JSA without your partner making a joint claim with you and you are paid as a couple (see p253).

If you fail the habitual residence test

If you fail the habitual residence test, you are not paid any benefit.

- For UC and PC, you are treated as not present in Great Britain.[13]
- For IS, income-based JSA, income-related ESA and HB, you are classed as a 'person from abroad'. This means for IS, income-based JSA and income-related ESA, you have an applicable amount of nil,[14] and for HB, you are treated as not liable for rent.[15]

Part 11: Immigration and residence rules for benefits and tax credits
Chapter 68: Coming from abroad: residence rules
3. Habitual residence

- For AA, CA, DLA, PIP, young carer grant and Best Start grant, you have failed to meet the prescribed residence requirements.[16]

Have you failed the habitual residence test?

1. If you are refused benefit because you have failed the habitual residence test, consider challenging this decision (see Chapters 56, 57 and 77). You may want to contact a local advice agency for help with this.

2. The decision maker must consider whether you satisfied the habitual residence test on your date of claim and also whether you did so on any subsequent date until the date of her/his decision.[17]

3. While challenging the decision, you should make a further claim. If this is refused, also challenge that decision and claim again and so on. This is because when the decision refusing your initial claim is looked at again, the decision maker (or First-tier Tribunal) cannot take account of things that have changed since the decision was made. So, if the decision maker considers that you were not habitually resident at the time benefit was originally refused, but you are now (eg, because you have been resident for an appreciable period of time), s/he cannot take this into account when looking again at the previous decision in your case. However, s/he can take it into account if sufficient residence had been completed by the date of the decision on your second, or subsequent, claim. Sometimes, the benefit authorities say that you cannot make another claim while your appeal (or request to have the first decision looked at again) is pending. This is wrong and you should, with the help of an adviser if possible, insist on making a further claim.

4. Check whether you are exempt from the habitual residence test (see p1589).

5. Establish which part of the test the decision maker considers you have failed.

6. If you have claimed a means-tested benefit and the decision maker considers you do not have a right to reside, use the section in this chapter starting on p1594 to check the ways in which you can have a right to reside.

7. If you made a joint claim for UC and the decision maker found that you failed the habitual residence test but your partner satisfied it, your joint claim is treated as a claim by your partner as a single person (see p1626). S/he can continue to be paid UC while you challenge the decision on your entitlement.

8. If you have been receiving IS, HB, child tax credit (CTC) and/or working tax credit (WTC) and you make a claim for UC which the DWP refuses on the basis that you fail the habitual residence test, this does *not* terminate your award of any of these benefits. These only end if you have claimed UC *and* the DWP is satisfied that you meet the first four basic conditions for UC (see p36).[18] Your IS, HB, CTC and/or WTC should continue while you challenge the refusal of your UC claim.

9. If you can claim HB, the local authority must make its own decision and not just follow the DWP's decision that you have failed the habitual residence test.

10. Although the onus of proof is on the benefit authorities to establish that you are *not* habitually resident,[19] produce as much evidence as possible to show that you *are*. All decisions should be made on the balance of probabilities.[20]

Who is exempt from the habitual residence test

You are exempt from the habitual residence test for **means-tested benefits** if you:[21]

- are a refugee;
- have humanitarian protection;
- have discretionary leave;
- have destitution domestic violence concession leave;
- have temporary protection granted under the displaced persons' provisions;
- have been deported, expelled or legally removed from another country to the UK and you are not a 'person subject to immigration control' (see p1560);
- are an EEA national and are a 'worker' (see p1607), including if you have retained this status;
- are an EEA national and a 'self-employed person' (see p1608), including if you have retained this status;
- are a family member (see p1614), other than an 'extended family member', of someone in either of the above two bullet points;
- are an EEA national with a permanent right of residence as a retired or permanently incapacitated worker or self-employed person, or you are a family member of such a person (see p1624);
- (for income-related ESA only) are being transferred from an award of IS which was transitionally protected from the requirement to have a right to reside (see p1592);
- (for HB only) receive IS, income-related ESA or PC;
- (for HB only) receive income-based JSA and either:
  - you have a right to reside other than one that is excluded for HB (see p1592); *or*
  - you have been receiving both HB and income-based JSA since 31 March 2014. Entitlement on this basis ends when either that entitlement to income-based JSA ceases or you make a new claim for HB.[22]

For a young carer grant, you are exempt from the requirement to be habitually resident if you are in one of the first six bullet points listed above.[23]

For a Best Start grant, you are exempt from the requirement to be habitually resident if you or your partner are receiving a qualifying benefit (see p1696) or you are in one of the first six bullet points listed above.[24]

For AA, CA, DLA and PIP, the above exemptions do not apply, but you are treated as being habitually resident (as well as treated as present – see p1649) if you are abroad in your capacity as a serving member of the forces, or you are living with someone who is and s/he is your spouse, civil partner, son, stepson, daughter, stepdaughter, father, stepfather, father-in-law, mother, stepmother or mother-in-law.[25]

Part 11: Immigration and residence rules for benefits and tax credits
Chapter 68: Coming from abroad: residence rules
3. Habitual residence

Establishing you are 'habitually resident in fact'

You are required to be habitually resident in the 'common travel area' (ie, the UK, the Republic of Ireland, Channel Islands and the Isle of Man) for all the benefits that have this requirement with only three exceptions.

- For a **young carer grant**, you must be a habitually resident in the common travel area or Switzerland or an EEA country.
- For a **Best Start grant**, if you are aged under 20 and you or your partner are not getting a qualifying benefit, you must be habitually resident in the common travel area or Switzerland or an EEA country.
- For AA, CA, **the care component of DLA or the daily living component of PIP**, if you are covered by the European Union (EU) co-ordination rules and can show a genuine and sufficient link to the UK, you can be entitled if you are habitually resident in an EEA state or Switzerland (see p1650).

There is no definition of 'habitual residence' in the legislation. However, there is a considerable amount of caselaw on its meaning, and from this certain principles have emerged.

- There is no comprehensive list of factors that are relevant, so all the facts of your situation should be considered.[26]
- To be habitually resident, you must be resident (see p1585). It is not enough merely to intend to reside in the future.[27]
- You must have a settled intention to reside in the relevant area. It does not need to be permanent; it is enough if you intend to make the relevant area your home for the time being.[28] You must provide evidence of your intention, including your reasons for moving there, the strength of your ties (or your 'centre of interest') and the viability of your residence. Factors that could be relevant include arranging or seeking employment, education or training, joining and/or bringing your family, arranging accommodation, bringing possessions, registering with a doctor, joining clubs and associations, and breaking ties with the place of your previous residence. The viability of your continued residence, although a relevant factor, is not an additional requirement.[29]
- In most cases, you must have an 'appreciable period' of actual residence. How long this period must be is not fixed and depends on your circumstances.[30] The DWP or local authority must not set a standard period of time for which all claimants must be resident before they can become habitually resident, and any such policy should be challenged by judicial review (see p1414). There is a large amount of caselaw on what constitutes an appreciable period of residence. Periods of between one and three months are frequently cited,[31] but no general rule can be derived from any one case and your appreciable period may be longer or shorter.[32] The stronger your settled intention to make your home in the common travel area for the time being, the shorter your period of actual

residence needs to be before you can be accepted as habitually resident (and vice versa).[33]

You may not need an appreciable period of actual residence, or the period may be very short, if you are:

– a returning resident. This applies if you have been habitually resident in the relevant area previously, you left in circumstances which meant you ceased to be habitually resident and you then return to live in the area again. The decision on how long a period of residence you need to have in order to resume your previous habitual residence depends on the circumstances in which you left, your links with the relevant area while you were away and the circumstances of your return.[34] You can be found to be habitually resident on the day of your return;

– covered by the EU co-ordination rules (see p1672) and are claiming income-based JSA, income-related ESA or PC (since these are listed as special non-contributory benefits – see p1676). If this applies, you cannot be denied benefit solely because your period of residence is considered to be too short. Your period of residence is one of the factors that should be taken into account in assessing habitual residence, but it is not an absolute requirement and may be outweighed by other factors.[35]

- A temporary absence, such as a holiday, should not mean that you cease to be habitually resident. This should be accepted if you have a definite date of return[36] or you are abroad for a temporary reason such as a Voluntary Service Overseas placement.[37]
- When deciding whether you are habitually resident, the DWP or local authority must consider the whole period from your date of claim down to the date the decision is made, since at some point during this period you may have become resident for an appreciable period and your entitlement would begin from that date.[38]

4. Right to reside

The right to reside requirement applies to:
- universal credit (UC);
- income support (IS);
- income-based jobseeker's allowance (JSA);
- income-related employment and support allowance (ESA);
- pension credit (PC);
- housing benefit (HB);
- child benefit;
- child tax credit (CTC).

Part 11: Immigration and residence rules for benefits and tax credits
Chapter 68: Coming from abroad: residence rules
4. Right to reside

You are also excluded from council tax reduction if you do not have a right to reside.[39] See CPAG's *Benefits for Migrants Handbook* for details.

Means-tested benefits

You must have a right to reside in the common travel area (ie, the UK, the Republic of Ireland, the Channel Islands and the Isle of Man) in order to satisfy the habitual residence test for UC, IS, income-based JSA, income-related ESA, PC and HB. If you (or your partner, for UC) do not satisfy the habitual residence test because you do not have a right to reside, see p1587.

The type of residence right you need

Any right of residence in the common travel area (see p1586) enables you to satisfy the right to reside requirement for each of the means-tested benefits, unless your *only* right of residence is:[40]

- limited leave granted under the EU Settlement Scheme (also known as 'pre-settled status') (see p1597). See below for a challenge to this; *or*
- as a European Economic Area (EEA) national with an initial right of residence during your first three months in the UK (see p1605); *or*
- as a family member of the above; *or*
- as the primary carer of a British citizen who is dependent on you and would have to leave the EU if you left the UK (see p1619);[41] *or*
- (except for income-based JSA) as an EEA jobseeker; *or*
- (except for income-based JSA) as a family member of an EEA jobseeker. **Note:** this exclusion does not apply if you are a former family member of a jobseeker and have retained your right to reside – eg, following the departure of the jobseeker from the UK (see p1617).[42]

If you are an EU national with pre-settled status but no other right to reside, it is arguable that excluding you from means-tested benefits (and child benefit and CTC) is unlawful. At the time of writing, this argument had been made in the High Court and judgment was due.[43] For updates and a template letter to use until the judgment, see cpag.org.uk/welfare-rights/judicial-review/judicial-review-pre-action-letters/eu-pre-settled-status.

If you have been receiving benefits since April 2004

You do not need a right to reside to be entitled to any of the means-tested benefits, except UC, if you have been receiving any combination of IS, income-based JSA, PC, HB, income-related ESA (since 31 October 2011 and including periods linked by the 12-week linking rule – see p1041) or council tax benefit (until it was abolished from 1 April 2013) *continuously* since 30 April 2004. This transitional protection means you do not need a right to reside in order to continue to receive that benefit or if you make a new claim for one of these benefits, provided the periods of entitlement have been continuous since 30 April 2004.[44]

Example

Delphine is French. She came to the UK in 2003 with her baby and claimed IS as a lone parent while living with friends. In 2008, she had another child, moved into a rented flat and made a new claim for HB. In 2012, her partner moved in and so her IS stopped, but she continued to receive HB. In 2015, her partner moved out and she claimed income-related ESA as she had several health problems.

Delphine has not needed a right to reside for any of these benefit claims because she has been receiving one of the five benefits on each day since 30 April 2004. However, if Delphine were to claim UC, because UC is not covered by this transitional protection, she would not be entitled unless she had a right to reside. If Delphine were to obtain settled status under the EU Settlement Scheme (see p1597), this would give her a right to reside and she could then be entitled to UC.

Child benefit and child tax credit

If you (and your partner for CTC) do not have a right to reside in the UK, you are treated as not present in Great Britain for child benefit and CTC and, therefore, are not entitled to these benefits.[45]

If you are claiming CTC and you (or your partner, if it is a joint claim) lose your (or her/his) right to reside, this is a change of circumstances that you must notify to HM Revenue and Customs within one month (see p1507). If your partner lost her/his right to reside, unless you can make a single claim for CTC (see p1496), you may be entitled to claim UC as a single person.

The right to reside requirement was introduced on 1 May 2004. You do not need a right to reside to continue to receive child benefit or CTC if you have been receiving it since before this date.

The type of residence right you need

Any right of residence in the UK enables you to satisfy the requirement for child benefit and CTC, unless your *only* right of residence is:[46]

- limited leave granted under the EU Settlement Scheme (also known as 'pre-settled status') (see p1597). See p1592 for a challenge to this; *or*
- as the primary carer of a British citizen who is dependent on you and would have to leave the EU if you left the UK (see p1619).[47] However, you are not excluded on this basis if you are a national of Algeria, Morocco, San Marino, Tunisia or Turkey and working in the UK as you are covered by agreements that override this exclusion (see p1566).[48] To date, all other legal challenges to this exclusion have failed.[49]

Part 11: Immigration and residence rules for benefits and tax credits
Chapter 68: Coming from abroad: residence rules
5. Who has a right to reside

Note: if you are not entitled to child benefit for a child living with you, someone else who contributes to the cost of that child may be able to claim child benefit instead (see p584).

5. **Who has a right to reside**

Whether or not you have a right to reside can depend on your nationality, immigration status and the circumstances of you and your family members. You may have more than one right of residence, or you may not have any.

Any residence right is sufficient to satisfy the right to reside requirement, unless it is specifically excluded (see p1591).

You have a right to reside if you are:

- a British citizen; *or*
- an Irish citizen. Irish citizens have a right to reside in Ireland, which is part of the common travel area (the area within which you need to have a right to reside for means-tested-benefits – see p1592); *or*
- a Commonwealth citizen with a right of abode; *or*
- a person with leave to enter or remain. Any form of immigration leave satisfies the right to reside requirement, with the exception of limited leave granted under the EU Settlement Scheme (also called 'pre-settled status') (see p1597), which is excluded (see p1591). **Note:** if you have leave which is subject to a condition that you do not have recourse to public funds, or indefinite leave granted as the result of a maintenance undertaking, you are a 'person subject to immigration control' (see p1560) and, therefore, excluded from benefits on that basis unless you are in an exempt group (see p1564); *or*
- a person with a European free movement right of residence (see p1599) other than one that is excluded for the benefit you are claiming (see p1591).

British and Irish citizens

If you are a **British citizen**, including if you also hold another nationality, you have an automatic right to reside in the UK. If you are the family member of a British citizen or you are the primary carer of a British citizen, see p1619.

If you are an **Irish citizen**, you have a right to reside in Ireland, which satisifies the requirement of means-tested benefits to have a right to reside in the common travel area. As an Irish citizen, you are not required to obtain leave under the EU Settlement Scheme (see p1597), but you can if you wish. At the time of writing, legislation was being passed which states that Irish citizens do not require leave to enter or remain in the UK.[50]

If you are the **family member of an Irish citizen** in the UK, your residence rights as a family member depend on the Irish citizen having a relevant right to reside in the same way as family members of other EEA nationals (see p1614), and you will need to obtain leave under the EU Settlement Scheme before the deadline (see p1597).

European Economic Area nationals, their family members and carers

If you are an EEA national or a non-EEA national who is a family member or carer of an EEA national, you have a right to reside if:

- you have leave granted under the EU Settlement Scheme (see p1597); *or*
- you have any other leave to enter or remain in the UK (but if you are a non-EEA national check whether you are a 'person subject to immigration control' (see p1560) as this could exclude you from entitlement to benefit); *or*
- you have a European free movement right of residence (see p1599).

Any residence right satisfies the right to reside requirement for each of the benefits that have it, *unless* the right to reside is specifically excluded for the benefit you are claiming (see p1591).

Main legal sources of residence rights for EEA nationals, their family members and carers:
Free movement rights are provided under both EU law and UK law. Although the UK left the EU on 31 January 2020, EU law continues to apply in the UK, during the transition period. At the time of writing, this was due to end on 31 December 2020, but could be extended up to 31 December 2022 (see 1596).

Free movement rights come from EU treaties, in particular the **Treaty on the Functioning of the EU (TFEU)** and, for Norway, Iceland and Liechenstein, **the EEA Agreement.** However, the details of residence rights are set out in the **EU Directive 2004/38.** This sets out most of the situations in which an EEA national or her/his family member has a right to reside in the UK. This came into force from 30 April 2006 and was extended to cover nationals of Norway, Iceland and Liechtenstein from 1 March 2009.[51] Swiss nationals and their family members are covered by a separate agreement which provides similar rights.[52]

The **Immigration (European Economic Area) Regulations 2016** (called 'the EEA Regulations' in this *Handbook*) apply to all EEA nationals (except British citizens – see p1594) and Swiss nationals.[53] These give similar rights of residence to those contained in the above EU Directive. Where these rules conflict with, or do not completely incorporate, Directive 2004/38, you can rely on whichever is more favourable to you. The current EEA Regulations replaced the the previous, very similar, EEA Regulations 2006, from 1 February 2017.[54]

Immigration Rules, Appendix EU sets out the EU Settlement Scheme. This provides the basis for EEA citizens and their family members and carers to apply for indefinite leave (settled status) or limited leave (pre-settled status) – see p1597.

If you are a family member of a British citizen, see p1616.

Part 11: Immigration and residence rules for benefits and tax credits
Chapter 68: Coming from abroad: residence rules
5. Who has a right to reside

Changes due to the UK leaving the European Union

The UK left the EU on 31 January 2020. However, EU law continues to apply in the UK during the transition period (see below), in generally the same ways as it did before the UK left the EU. Therefore, the European free movement rights described in this chapter continue until the end of the transition period.

Transition period

The transition period (also called the 'implementation period') is the period from the UK leaving the EU at 11pm on 31 January 2020 to 31 December 2020.[55]

During the transition period, in general, EU law continues to have effect as it did before 31 January 2020.

On 31 January 2020, all EU legislation and caselaw was converted into UK law and all EU-derived law (eg, the EEA Regulations) continues to have effect the day after as it did the day before.[56] For the purposes of this retained EU law and EU-derived law, during the transition period, the UK is treated as if it were still a member state of the EU and EEA and European free movement rights continue to apply the in the UK.[57]

The Withdrawal Agreement allows, if agreed by 1 July 2020, for this period to be extended once, up to 31 December 2022.[58] Although UK legislation prohibits an extention,[59] the UK government could pass further legislation enabling the transition period to be extended in accordance with the Withdrawal Agreement.

Until the end of the transition period, if you are an EEA national, or the family member or primary carer of an EEA national, you may either have a right to reside under the EU Settlement Scheme (see p1597), or one or more European free movement rights of residence, or both. Note your residence right(s) will only satisfy the right to reside requirement for those benefits that have it, if that residence right is not excluded for the benefit you want to claim (see p1591).

At the end of the transition period, since European free movement rights are part of UK law, they will continue *until* legislation is introduced to end or amend them by the UK government. At the time of writing, a bill to end free movement rights in the UK after the transition period had been introduced (see below).

If you are an EEA national, coming to live in the UK after the end of the transition period, or the family member of such an EEA national, you will not be able to apply for leave under the EU Settlement Scheme. At the time of writing, it was not clear what immigration leave you will be able to apply for, and it was not clear what your rights to benefits will be.

The UK government has introduced new legislation to:[60]
- end free movement within UK law; *and*
- enable EEA nationals arriving after the end of the transition period to be made subject to the same immigration controls as non-EEA nationals; *and*

- enable the benefit entitlements of EEA nationals arriving after the end of the transition period to be aligned to those of non-EEA nationals.

However, the details will be in subsequent legislation.

For details of rights after the end of the transition period, see AskCPAG.org.uk and CPAG's *Welfare Rights Bulletin* for updates.

Note: the UK leaving the EU also affects the EU co-ordination rules (see p1670).

Settled and pre-settled status

The EU Settlement Scheme is set out in the Immigration Rules.[61] It was established to enable EEA nationals, and their non-EEA family members, already living in the UK to continue doing so lawfully after free movement rights end. Some key points are covered below and summaries of the scheme are available on gov.uk.

To be eligible for leave under the EU Settlement Scheme, you must be an EEA national who began residing in the UK before the end of the transition period, or the family member of such an EEA national, or have been residing in the UK with a derivative right to reside (see p1619) before the end of the transition period. At the time of writing, the transition period was due to end 31 December 2020, but could be extended up to 31 December 2022.[62]

You may be eligible for:

- **indefinite leave under the EU Settlement Scheme (also called settled status)** if you can show you have been residing in the UK:
  - for five years as an EEA national, or family member (see below) of an EEA national or with a derivative right to reside (see p1619). Certain gaps abroad are disregarded (these are the same as those disregarded for acquiring permanent residence see p1621); *or*
  - for less than five years and you satisfy the conditions for obtaining permanent residence in less than five years (see p1624);
- **limited leave for five years (also called pre-settled status)** if you can show you have been residing in the UK for less than five years as an EEA national or family member (see below) of an EEA national, or with a derivative right to reside. Before this leave expires, you will need to apply for settled status once you can show you have resided in the UK for five years as above.

Note: if you are an EEA national, your residence in the UK does not have to have been with a right to reside – actual residency is sufficient.

If you are a non-EEA family member of an EEA national resident in the UK, you must provide evidence of being covered by the definition of 'family member' on p1614 (including if you are an 'extended family member' and have been issued with the relevant residence document that remains in force).

If you are a non-EEA national with a derivative right to reside, you will need to provide evidence of this (see p1619) and you should get an immigration adviser to assist you to apply.

Part 11: Immigration and residence rules for benefits and tax credits
Chapter 68: Coming from abroad: residence rules
5. Who has a right to reside

If you are an Irish citizen or you have indefinite leave to remain in the UK, you do not need to obtain settled or pre-settled status, but you can do.

If you are the family member an Irish citizen you need to obtain leave under the EU Settlement Scheme before the deadline.

The deadline for applying under the EU Settlement Scheme, at the time of writing, was 30 June 2021. There are limited exceptions for some exisiting family members to join EEA nationals already living in the UK, and be granted leave after this date.

If you only start to live in the UK after the end of the transition period, you are not eligible to apply for leave under the EU Settlement Scheme, unless you are joining your EEA family member already residing in the UK before that date. At the time of writing, no details were available of the immigration options for those arriving after the end of the transition period. See AskCPAG.org.uk and CPAG's *Welfare Rights Bulletin* for updates.

You lose your settled status if you are outside the UK for more than five years.

Before applying under the EU Settlement Scheme, check the rules that are in place at that time as the Immigration Rules change frequently. Get immigration advice before applying if you are a non-EEA national, or you have a criminal conviction, or you have been subject to a deportation, exclusion or removal decision, or your situation is in any way complicated. You should also get advice if your application is refused, or if you have lived in the UK for at least five years but have only been granted pre-settled status, or if you are having difficulty proving your residence in the UK.

Evidence of your status

If you are granted indefinite or limited leave under the EU Settlement Scheme (also called settled or pre-settled status), you are not issued with a physical document, unless you are a non-EEA national family member of an EEA national and did not already have a biometric residence card when you applied. Instead, you confirm your settled or pre-settled status by accessing your online profile. You can get a 'share code' to allow others, including the DWP, HM Revenue and Customs (HMRC) or local authority, to view your status online.[63]

Alternatively, you can provide the benefit authority with a copy of the Home Office document emailed to you when you were granted leave under the EU Settlment Scheme. Although this is not proof of status by itself, the decision maker should accept this as supporting evidence and can then verify your status directly with the Home Office.[64]

Benefit entitlement

If you have indefinite leave granted under the EU Settlement Scheme (also called settled status) you have a right to reside that satisfies the right to reside requirement of all benefits that have this requirement.[65]

However, if you have limited leave granted under the EU Settlement Scheme (also called pre-settled status) this right to reside is excluded for all benefits that require a right to reside. Therefore you will be excluded from these benefits unless you have another right of residence, other than one that is excluded for the benefit you are claiming. For details of the excluded residence rights and a legal challenge to the exclusion of pre-settled status, see p1591. **Note:** limited leave granted under the EU Settlement Scheme has been added to the list of excluded residence rights for council tax reduction in England and Wales since 1 April 2020.

If you are a non-EEA national and have either settled status or pre-settled status, you are not defined as a 'person subject to immigration control' (see p1560) and therefore not excluded from any benefits on this basis.

European free movement rights: checklist

As European free movement rights can be affected by many things, it can be helpful to work through the following steps.

- **Step one:** are you an EEA national with a right to reside as a 'qualified person'[66] – ie, are you an EEA national in the UK as a:
  - jobseeker (see p1605);
  - worker (see p1607), including if you have retained this status (see p1609);
  - self-employed person (see p1608), including if you have retained this status (see p1609);
  - self-sufficient person (see p1613);
  - student (see p1614).
- **Step two:** are you a 'family member' (see p1614) of someone covered in Step one? If so, you have a right to reside whether or not you are an EEA national yourself.
- **Step three:** do you have a permanent right of residence (see p1621)? This is normally after five years of 'legal residence' (see p1622).
- **Step four:** do you have a 'derivative' right to reside through someone else's right to reside, but not as her/his family member? This covers certain children and carers (see p1619).

Note:
- If you have been granted indefinite leave to remain under the EU Settlement Scheme (also known as settled status – see p1597), you have a right to reside for all benefits that have this requirement and so do not need to also show you have any free movement rights.

Part 11: Immigration and residence rules for benefits and tax credits
Chapter 68: Coming from abroad: residence rules
5. Who has a right to reside

- If you are a Croatian, A2 or A8 national (see p1601 for who are A2 and A8 nationals), or a family member of a Croatian, A2 or A8 national, needing to rely on past periods of residence, check whether additional restrictions applied (see p1601).
- You can have more than one right to reside at a time.[67] For example, you may be both a self-employed person and also the family member of someone with a permanent right of residence.
- European free movement rights may end or change after the end of the transition period (see p1596).

Residence documents

If you have a European free movement right of residence, you can be issued with a residence document. **Note:** except to have residence rights as an 'extended family member', you do not need a residence document to have a right to reside. In order to have a right of residence as an 'extended family member' (see p1616), you must have a family permit, registration certificate or residence card, which remains in force.[68] If you have any other European free movement right of residence, you can also obtain a residence document, but it is not necessary. A residence document does not, in itself, give you a right to reside – eg, if your right to reside ceases.[69]

You can be issued with the following residence documents.

- **A registration certificate** if you are an EEA national with a right of residence provided under the EEA Regulations.[70]
- **A residence card** if you are a non-EEA national and you have a right to reside as the family member of an EEA 'qualified person' (see p1599) or an EEA national with a permanent right of residence.[71]
- **A derivative residence card** if you have a derivative right to reside (see p1619).[72]
- **A document certifying permanent right of residence** if you are an EEA national with a permanent right of residence, or a **permanent residence card** if you are a non-EEA national with a permanent right of residence.[73]
- **A residence document** issued, or treated as issued, under previous regulations. These are treated as if they were issued under the current EEA Regulations.[74]
- **A family permit** for entry to the UK if you are a non-EEA family member of an EEA national and do not have any of the other residence documentation.[75]

Forms and further information, including about application fees, are available on the Home Office website.

Note:

- The above documents will cease to be valid from a future date, which is expected to be 30 June 2021 (the deadline for obtaining leave under the EU Settlement Scheme).
- If you need to prove that you have been granted leave under the EU Settlement Scheme, see p1598.

Croatian, A2 and A8 nationals

Croatia, A2 and A8 states

Croatia joined the EU on 1 July 2013.

Restrictions applied until 30 June 2018.

The A2 states are: Bulgaria and Romania.

These states joined the EU on 1 January 2007.

Restrictions applied until 31 December 2013.

The A8 states are: Czech Republic, Estonia, Hungary, Latvia, Lithuania, Poland, Slovakia and Slovenia.

These states joined the EU on 1 May 2004.

Restrictions applied until 30 April 2009 (see below).

The treaties under which the above 'accession' states joined the EU allowed existing member states to restrict accession state nationals' access to their labour markets and their residence rights as workers and jobseekers (see below). The duration of these restrictions was limited to five years from the date the states joined the EU, but could be extended for a further two years if certain conditions were met. The UK government imposed the restrictions for five years and then extended the A8 and A2 restrictions for the additional two-year period. However, this extension of the A8 restrictions from 1 May 2009 to 30 April 2011 was held to be unlawful. This means that A8 nationals were *not* subject to restrictions during that two-year period.[76]

Restrictions on employment and residence rights

Although the restrictions on Croatian, A2 and A8 nationals have now ended, the restrictions remain relevant if your current or future residence rights are affected by the residence rights you or your family member had during the period of restriction – eg, when establishing permanent residence.

If you are a Croatian or an A2 national, and were not in one of the exempt groups listed on p1602, during the period of restrictions, you had restrictions on your employment and residence rights. Before taking up employment, you were required to obtain an 'accession worker authorisation document' (in most cases, an accession worker registration certificate, specifying the employer you could work for), and then work in accordance with it.[77] Your residence rights were restricted as follows.[78]

- You did not have a right to reside as a jobseeker.
- You were only defined as a 'worker' if you had an accession worker authorisation document and were working in accordance with it.
- You could not retain your worker status when you stopped work in the ways other workers could (see p1609).

Part 11: Immigration and residence rules for benefits and tax credits
Chapter 68: Coming from abroad: residence rules
5. Who has a right to reside

If you are an A8 national, and were not in one of the exempt groups listed on p1603, during the period of restrictions, you had restrictions on your employment and residence rights.

You had to work for an 'authorised employer',[79] which broadly meant you had to register each job you took with the Worker Registration Scheme within the first month (but see p1604 for the precise meaning, as it can affect your residence rights). Your residence rights were restricted as follows.[80]

- You did not have a right to reside as a jobseeker.
- You were only defined as a 'worker' if you were working for an 'authorised employer' (see p1604).
- You could not retain your worker status when you stopped work in the ways other workers could (see p1609). However, if you lost your job within the first month of employment, you could retain your status in those ways, but only until the end of the month.[81]

The restrictions do not affect other residence rights you may have, or had, as an EEA national (eg, as a self-employed or self-sufficient person)[82] or other rights you may have under EU law.

Note: depending on your circumstances, it may be possible to argue that it would be disproportionate to enforce all the requirements of the restrictions.[83] This will only apply in limited circumstances and you should get specialist assistance to make this argument.

Croatian and A2 nationals who were exempt from restrictions

If you are a Croatian or an A2 national, during the relevant period of restrictions (see p1601), you were not subject to worker authorisation and did not have the above restrictions on your residence rights if you:[84]

- had on 30 June 2013 (Croatian) or 31 December 2006 (A2) leave to enter or remain with no restriction on employment; *or*
- were legally working (see p1604) in the UK for a 12-month period, without breaks of more than 30 days (in total), up to and including 31 December 2006 (A2) or 30 June 2013 (Croatian); *or*
- had legally worked in the UK for a 12-month period (beginning before or after 31 December 2006 (A2) or 30 June 2013 (Croatian), without breaks of more than 30 days (in total); *or*
- were a 'posted worker' – ie, you were working in the UK for an employer who is not established in the UK; *or*
- were a member of a diplomatic mission (or the family member of such a person) or someone otherwise entitled to diplomatic immunity; *or*
- had dual nationality with the UK or another (non-A2/Croatian) EEA state; *or*
- were the spouse/civil partner (or, Croatian only, unmarried or same-sex partner) of a UK national or of a person settled in the UK; *or*

- were the spouse/civil partner (or, Croatian only, unmarried or same-sex partner) or child under 18 of a person with leave to enter or remain in the UK that allowed employment; *or*
- had a permanent right of residence (see p1621); *or*
- were a student with a registration certificate which stated that you could not work more than 20 hours a week (unless it was part of vocational training, during vacations or, for Croatians only, for up to two years as a student union sabbatical officer) and you complied with this. If the certificate confirmed you could work during the four months after the course ended, the exemption continued for this period; *or*
- were a family member of an EEA national who had a right to reside, unless the EEA national was an A2 (or, Croatian only, a Croatian) national subject to worker authorisation (or, A2 only, the only reason s/he was not an A2 national subject to worker authorisation was because s/he was covered by the group below); *or*
- were a family member of an A2 (or, if you are Croatian, a Croatian) national subject to worker authorisation who had a right to reside (for an A2 national only, as a worker, student, self-employed or self-sufficient person). If you are a Croatian national (or an A2 national relying on an A2 worker), you were a 'family member' if you were the descendant and either under 21 or dependent, or the spouse/civil partner or (Croatians only) the unmarried or same-sex partner; *or*
- were a 'highly skilled person' – ie, you:[85]
  - met the points-based criteria set out in the Immigration Rules for entering the UK on this basis; *or*
  - had a qualification at degree level or higher in the UK, or Higher National Diploma in Scotland and, within 12 months of this award, you applied for a registration certificate confirming your unconditional access to the labour market.

A8 nationals who were exempt from restrictions

If you are an A8 national, during the relevant period of restrictions (see above), you were not required to register your work with the Worker Registration Scheme and were not subject to the above restrictions on your residence rights if you:[86]

- had leave to enter or remain on 30 April 2004 which had no restriction on employment; *or*
- were legally working (see p1604) in the UK for a 12-month period, without breaks of more than 30 days (in total), up to and including 30 April 2004; *or*
- had legally worked in the UK for a 12-month period[87] (beginning before or after 30 April 2004), without breaks of more than 30 days (in total); *or*
- were the spouse/civil partner or child under 18 of a person with leave to enter or remain in the UK that allowed employment; *or*

Part 11: Immigration and residence rules for benefits and tax credits
Chapter 68: Coming from abroad: residence rules
5. Who has a right to reside

- had dual nationality with the UK or another (non-A8/A2) EEA state or Switzerland; *or*
- were a family member of another EEA or Swiss national who had a right to reside under the EEA Regulations (other than an A8/A2 national subject to registration/authorisation if her/his only right to reside was for the first three months in the UK); *or*
- were the member of a diplomatic mission (or the family member of such a person) or someone otherwise entitled to diplomatic immunity; *or*
- were a 'posted worker' – ie, you were working in the UK for an employer who is not established in the UK.

Legally working

The phrase 'legally working' has a specific meaning and only refers to employment, not self-employment. It is relevant for determining whether you have completed 12 months of legal work in order to be exempt from the restrictions, and whether at a particular time you were a 'worker'.

If you are a Croatian or A2 national, during the period of restrictions (see p1601) you were 'legally working' if:[88]
- you were working in accordance with your worker authorisation document; *or*
- you were working during a period when you were in one of the exempt groups on p1602 (other than posted workers); *or*
- the work was done before 1 July 2013 (for Croatian nationals) or before 1 January 2007 (for A2 nationals), either in accordance with any leave you had under the Immigration Act 1971 or when you did not require leave. This does not apply to work done with permission from the Home Office while you were an asylum seeker.[89]

If you are an A8 national, during the period of restrictions (see p1601) you were 'legally working' if:[90]
- you were working for an authorised employer (see below); *or*
- you were working during a period when you were in one of the exempt groups on p1603 (other than if you were the spouse/civil partner or child of a person whose leave to enter or remain in the UK allowed employment); *or*
- the work was done before 1 May 2004 either in accordance with any leave you had under the Immigration Act 1971 or when you did not require leave. This does not apply to work done with permission from the Home Office while you were an asylum seeker.[91]

Authorised employer for A8 nationals
If you were an A8 national subject to restrictions, you were working for an **'authorised employer'** if you:[92]

– were working within the first month of employment;

– applied for a worker's registration certificate within the first month of work, but did not yet have a certificate or refusal;

– had a valid worker's registration certificate for that employer;

– had been legally working for that employer since 30 April 2004; *or*

– began work at an agricultural camp between 1 May 2004 and 31 December 2004, and before 1 May 2004 you had been issued with leave under the Immigration Act 1971 as a seasonal worker at such a camp.

If you only applied for a registration certificate after the first month of work, you only count as working for an authorised employer from the date it was issued. It does not apply retrospectively.[93]

If you were a Croatian, A2 or A8 national subject to restrictions and your employment ended during the period of restrictions (see p1601), you stopped legally working, stopped being a 'worker' and, unless you are in an exempt group, could not retain your worker status. However, if you were still under a contract of employment, you continued to be legally working and a worker – eg, if you were on maternity leave, holiday leave, sick leave or compassionate leave (including if the leave was unpaid).[94]

Initial right of residence

If you are an EEA national, you generally have an initial right of residence for the first three months of your stay in the UK, provided you have a valid identity card or passport and are not an unreasonable burden on the social assistance system of the UK.[95]

You also have a right of residence if you are a family member of an EEA national who has an initial right of residence (even if you are not an EEA national), provided you have a valid passport and are not an unreasonable burden on the social assistance system of the UK.[96]

If this is your only right of residence:

• it does not satisfy the right to reside requirement for universal credit (UC), income support (IS), income-based jobseeker's allowance (JSA), income-related employment and support allowance (ESA), pension credit (PC) or housing benefit (HB). To be entitled to these benefits, you need another residence right (see p1592);

• it can count towards meeting the five years' residence required for permanent residency (see p1621).[97]

Jobseekers

If you are an EEA national, you have a right to reside as a jobseeker if:[98]

• you are in the UK and you provide evidence that you are seeking employment and have a 'genuine chance of being engaged'. **Note:** (under the EEA

Part 11: Immigration and residence rules for benefits and tax credits
Chapter 68: Coming from abroad: residence rules
5. Who has a right to reside

Regulations only) after 91 days this evidence must be compelling (see below); *and*

- you entered the UK in order to seek employment, or (EEA Regulations only) you are present in the UK seeking employment immediately after having a right to reside as a worker (except if you retained worker status while involuntarily unemployed – see p1609), a student or self-sufficient person.

There is no time limit on how long you can have a right to reside as a jobseeker. It continues for as long as you continue to satisfy the above requirements (but see below).[99]

If you are a Croatian, A2 or A8 national who was subject to restrictions, you did not have a right to reside as a jobseeker.[100] For details of the periods of these restrictions and who they affect, see p1601.

Providing evidence

To have a right to reside as a jobseeker, you must provide evidence that you are seeking employment and have a genuine chance of being engaged.[101]

The most straightforward way of demonstrating this is to 'sign on' for contribution-based JSA or national insurance (NI) credits on the basis of unemployment, and provide evidence that you are available for work and actively seeking work (see p1115 and p1124) or that you satisfy the work search and work availability requirements (see p1069) if you come under the UC system (see p23). There would only be a few unusual circumstances in which you would satisfy these conditions and not be accepted as having a genuine chance of being engaged.[102] However, it is not necessary to claim or receive JSA if you can provide evidence that you are seeking employment and have a genuine chance of being engaged in another way.[103]

Under the EEA Regulations, the evidence that you are looking for work and have a genuine chance of being engaged must be 'compelling':[104]

- to continue to have a right to reside as a jobseeker for more than 91 days, or from the start of your period of residence as a jobseeker (unless you have since been absent from the UK for a period of at least 12 months) if you previously had a right to reside as a jobseeker for a total of 91 days or you previously retained worker or self-employed status while involuntarily unemployed (see p1609) for at least six months; *and*
- since then you have had an absence from the UK. **Note:** the benefit authorities have not been enforcing this requirement, except in very occasional cases.

The requirement for your evidence to be compelling is known as the the 'genuine prospects of work test'. The introduction of UC has reduced the relevance of this test for benefit claimants who are jobseekers (as this right to reside does not satisfy the requirement for UC – see p1592). If the 'genuine prospects of work test' is applied to you while are a jobseeker, check it has been applied at the right time (see above) and see the points on p1610.

Benefit entitlement

If you have a right to reside as a jobseeker and this is your only right to reside:

- it does not satisfy the right to reside requirement for UC, IS, income-related ESA, PC or HB – you must have some other right to reside for these benefits;
- it does satisfy the right to reside requirement for income-based JSA, child benefit and child tax credit (CTC). **Note:** to get income-based JSA, child benefit or CTC, unless you are in an exempt group, you must have been living here for the past three months (see p1584) and, for income-based JSA, be 'habitually resident in fact' (see p1587);
- it can count towards meeting the five years' residence requirement for permanent residency (see p1621).

Workers

If you are an EEA national and a 'worker' in the UK, you have a right to reside.[105] You satisfy the right to reside requirement for all the benefits that have this requirement and you are exempt from the habitual residence test (see p1589).

You are a 'worker' if:

- you are in an employment relationship. This means you must:[106]
  - provide services; *and*
  - work in return for remuneration; *and*
  - work under the direction of another person; *and*
- the work you do entails activities that are 'genuine and effective', rather than 'marginal and ancillary'.

Is your work genuine and effective?

All the relevant factors must be taken into account when deciding whether your work is genuine and effective, including the following.

1. The duration of the employment. The longer the period of time your employment lasts, the more likely it is that you have established worker status. However, in specific cases, two weeks has been held to be sufficient to establish worker status.[107]

2. The number of hours worked. There is no minimum threshold. Someone working 10 hours a week was held to be a worker,[108] as was an au pair working 13 hours a week for a modest wage plus board and lodging.[109] The European Court of Justice (ECJ) held that 5.5 hours' work is potentially capable of making someone a worker.[110]

3. The level of your earnings. There must be some remuneration (although it can be in kind, such as board and lodgings[111]), and voluntary work does not result in worker status.[112] Provided the work done is genuine and effective, earnings that are so low that you need to subsidise them with benefits do not prevent you from being a worker.[113]

4. The regularity of the work. The more regular and less erratic the work, the more likely it is that worker status will be established. It is possible to be a worker while undertaking work through an agency,[114] or while working 'cash in hand' without tax and NI being deducted.[115]

Part 11: Immigration and residence rules for benefits and tax credits
Chapter 68: Coming from abroad: residence rules
5. Who has a right to reside

Although guidance to decision makers advises that someone is automatically a worker if s/he has been earning, on average, a 'minimum income threshold' (£183 a week or £792 per month in 2020/21) for three months, it confirms that, in all other cases, an individual assessment must be made, taking the above factors into account.[116]

Note: if you are a Croatian or A2 national who, during the period of restrictions, was subject to those restrictions, you only count as a 'worker' if you had an accession worker authorisation document and worked in accordance with it. Similarly, if you were an A8 national who, during the period of restrictions, was subject to those restrictions, you only counted as a 'worker' if you were working for an 'authorised employer' (see p1604). For details of the periods of these restrictions and who is affected, see p1601.

You only cease to be a worker when the employment relationship ends. While you are still under a contract of employment, you continue to be a worker. Consequently, you are still a worker if you are a woman on maternity leave (including unpaid maternity leave),[117] or if you are on holiday leave or sick leave (including if it is unpaid).[118]

If you have ceased to be a worker, you may retain your worker status in certain circumstances (see p1609).

Self-employed people

If you are an EEA national and a 'self-employed person' in the UK, you have a right to reside[119] and therefore satisfy the right to reside requirement for all the benefits that have this requirement (see p1591). You are also exempt from the habitual residence test (see p1589).

You are a self-employed person if you provide services in return for remuneration, but not under the direction of another person. The work you do must entail activities that are 'genuine and effective' rather than 'marginal and ancillary' (see p1607).[120]

You count as being self-employed when you are established in the UK in order to pursue self-employed activity.[121] You must provide evidence of the steps you have taken or the ways in which you have set yourself up as self-employed.[122] It helps if you have registered with HMRC as self-employed. However, if you have not registered, this does not necessarily mean you cannot be accepted as self-employed.[123]

If you are a Croatian, A2 or A8 national and during the periods of restrictions (see p1601) you were self-employed, you had the same rights as other EEA nationals; no additional restrictions applied.

If you stop working, you do not necessarily cease to be self-employed. You may be in a temporary lull, and it is accepted that you can continue to be self-employed during such times, depending on your particular circumstances and the evidence you provide – eg, the amount of work you have, any steps you are taking to develop your business or find new work, and your marketing and business administration. Account must also be taken of your motives and intentions.[124]

You can continue to be self-employed if you stop work for a period of maternity leave, but intend to return to self-employment afterwards (see p1612).[125]

If you have ceased to be self-employed, you may be able to retain your self-employed status in certain circumstances (see below).

Retaining worker or self-employed status

You can retain the status of 'worker' or 'self-employed', even though you are no longer working, if:[126]

- you are involuntarily unemployed and registered as a jobseeker (see below);
- you are temporarily unable to work because of an illness or accident (see p1612);
- you are undertaking vocational training (see p1612);
- you are unable to work because you are in the late stages of pregnancy or you have just given birth (see p1612).[127]

Before arguing that you have retained your worker or self-employed status, check whether you have ceased to be a worker (see p1607) or self-employed (see p1608). For example, if you are off work on unpaid sick leave but you can return to your job when you are better, you are still a worker and so you do not need to argue that you have retained your worker status.

Note: if you are a Croatian, A2 or A8 national who, during the relevant period of restrictions, was subject to those restrictions, you could not retain your worker status in the ways described in this section, unless you are an A8 national and you stopped working during the first month of employment. In this case, you could retain your worker status in the ways described in this section for the remainder of that month.[128] There were no restrictions on retaining self-employed status for Croatian, A2 or A8 nationals. For details of the restriction periods and who they affect, see p1601.

You are involuntarily unemployed and registered as a jobseeker

Under EU Directive 2004/38, you retain your status as a worker or self-employed person if you:[129]

- are recorded as involuntarily unemployed (see p1610); *and*
- have registered yourself as a jobseeker with the relevant employment office.

Under the EEA Regulations, in addition to the above, you must provide evidence that you are seeking employment (or, to retain self-employed status, seeking either employment or self-employment) and have a genuine chance of being engaged. To retain your worker or self-employed status while involuntarily unemployed beyond six months, the EEA Regulations require that this evidence must be 'compelling' (see p1610). The EEA Regulations also include requirements that are not enforced by benefit authorities. These are that you must have entered

Part 11: Immigration and residence rules for benefits and tax credits
Chapter 68: Coming from abroad: residence rules
5. Who has a right to reside

the UK in order to seek employment (or self-employment if you are retaining self-employed status) and you must be in the UK seeking employment (and self-employment if you are rertaining self-employed status) immediately after having a right to reside as a student or a self-sufficient person or a worker, other than if you retained your worker status on this basis (or a self-employed person, other than if you retained your self-employed status on this basis).[130]

Note: at the time of writing, all these additional requirements of the EEA Regulations had been held by the Upper Tribunal to be unlawful and of no effect as they are not required under EU law. However, it was not known if the case would be appealed further.[131] See AskCPAG.org.uk and CPAG's *Welfare Rights Bulletin* for updates.

You are '**involuntarily unemployed**' if you are seeking, and are available to take up, employment (or self-employment, to retain your status as a self-employed person). This depends on your remaining in the labour market. The circumstances in which you left your last job, or ceased your self-employment, are just one factor in determining this, and your actions and circumstances since ceasing work must also be taken into account.[132]

The best way to register as a jobseeker is to claim UC and/or JSA, and show that you continue to satisfy the work search and work availability requirements (or the requirements to be available for and actively seeking work for JSA), even if you are not entitled to benefit.[133] If you are claiming a benefit that does not require you to look for work, you can satisfy the requirement to register as a jobseeker (and thereby retain your worker status) if you declare to the job centre that you are looking for work before your claim is determined, and provide evidence of seeking work.[134] If there was a gap between your ceasing work and registering as a jobseeker, see p1613.

If you were employed or self-employed for less than a year, the EEA Regulations limit the period during which you can retain your worker or self-employed status while registered as a jobseeker to a maximum of six months.[135] The EU Directive allows you to retain worker status for no less than six months.[136]

If you were employed or self-employed for more than a year (not necessarily in one continuous job), you can retain your worker or self-employed status on this basis indefinitely, unless there is an event that indicates you have withdrawn from the labour market entirely.[137]

After six months, the EEA Regulations require that the evidence that you are continuing to seek employment and have a genuine chance of being engaged must be 'compelling'.[138] This requirement is known as the 'genuine prospects of work test' and at the time of writing had just been held by the Upper Tribunal to be an unlawful requirement.

Do you satisfy the genuine prospects of work test?

1. At the time of writing, the Upper Tribunal had just held that the regulations requiring 'compelling' evidence in order to retain worker (or self-employed) status are unlawful as

EU law only requires you to be involuntarily unemployed and registered as a jobseeker.[139] Unless this decision is appealed, further the genuine prospect of work test should not be applied to you if you are retaining worker or self-employed status. Note this recent judgment does not apply to the requirement for compelling evidence if you only have a right to reside as a jobseeker (see p1605).

2. The 'genuine prospects of work test' does not apply to you if you have a right to reside *other than* as someone retaining worker or self-employed status on the basis of being involuntarily unemployed (or as a jobseeker).[140] Tell the decision maker you have an alternative right to reside that will satisfy the requirement for the benefit you are claiming.

3. Check that the requirement has not been applied before you have retained your worker or self-employed status on the basis of being involuntarily unemployed for six months. If it has been applied after 91 days, this is likely to be because the decision maker is treating you as only having a right to reside as a jobseeker. Guidance lists examples of periods that can be disregarded when counting the six months, including periods of sickness, periods of temporary absence when you are treated as being in Great Britain (see p1655), and up to 13 weeks when you are treated as being available for work due to domestic violence.[141]

4. If the requirement to provide compelling evidence has been applied to you after six months of retaining worker or self-employed status on the basis of being involuntarily unemployed then, in addition to following the points below, you should challenge any decision that your evidence is not 'compelling' (and that you, therefore, fail the 'genuine prospects of work test') and ask for your appeal to be stayed pending the outcome of the further appeal from the recent Upper Tribunal case (see point 1 above).

5. The term 'compelling' is not defined in the legislation and so should have its ordinary, everyday meaning. Your evidence must show, on the balance of probabilities, that you are seeking employment and have a genuine chance of being engaged.[142]

6. If you have been looking unsuccessfully for work for at least six months, this is relevant when considering whether you have a genuine chance of being engaged, but it is only one factor.[143] Ensure that the evidence of your genuine chance of being engaged is strong and extensive. Include details of the work you were doing that gave you worker or self-employed status, together with all other work you have done (paid and unpaid, both in and out of the UK), all your qualifications, and all your skills and abilities that make you employable.

7. The decision maker should consider your *chances* of being engaged within a reasonable period, and so changes in your circumstances (such as qualifications you are expected to obtain) in that future period are relevant.[144] If you have appealed against a decision that you have not provided compelling evidence, the First-tier Tribunal is not prevented from drawing inferences from events that occurred after the time of the decision about circumstances at, or before, that time. For example, obtaining a job six weeks after the decision is evidence of your *chance* of being engaged on the date of the decision.[145]

8. Refer to the decision makers' guidance if it is helpful. However, the examples it includes are not exhaustive and, as guidance, it is not legally binding.[146]

Part 11: Immigration and residence rules for benefits and tax credits
Chapter 68: Coming from abroad: residence rules
5. Who has a right to reside

You are temporarily unable to work because of an illness or accident

To retain your worker or self-employed status, your inability to work must be temporary. This simply means not permanent.[147] This can apply if you have a permanent health condition that fluctuates and causes temporary periods when you are unable to work.[148] You are considered to be temporarily unable to work if there is a realistic prospect of your being able to work again in the foreseeable future.[149] You do not need to have claimed ESA or another benefit on the grounds of inability to work, nor do you need to pass the test of limited capability for work. The test is a factual one of whether you are unable to do the work you were doing or, if it follows a period in which you were seeking work, the sort of work you were seeking.[150] Your inability to work must be caused by an illness or accident which *you* have – eg, you are not covered if you are unable to work because you are looking after a child who is ill.[151]

If you are unable to work because of pregnancy, see below.

You are undertaking vocational training

You retain your worker or self-employed status if you are undertaking a vocational training course. Unless you are involuntarily unemployed, the training must be related to your previous employment. If it is not, you must be accepted as being 'involuntarily unemployed'. You should be accepted as 'involuntarily unemployed' if there is no employment available to you that is reasonably equivalent to your last employment.[152]

Pregnancy and childbirth

If you have established worker or self-employed status and you are now not working because of late pregnancy or childbirth, you may still count as a worker or self-employed person, or you may be able to retain your worker or self-employed status.

You do not cease to be a worker while you are still under a contract of employment, so you are still a worker while on maternity leave, whether or not it is paid. This also applied to Croatian, A2 and A8 nationals who established worker status during the periods of restrictions (see p1601).[153]

You can continue to be a self-employed person if you stop work for a period of maternity leave, but intend to resume your self-employment.[154]

You can retain your worker or self-employed status if you have a pregnancy-related illness that prevents you from working (see p1609).[155]

You can retain worker or self-employed status if you gave up work (or seeking work, if you retained your worker or self-employed status while involuntarily unemployed – see p1609) because of the physical constraints of the late stages of pregnancy or the aftermath of childbirth, provided you start work again (or start seeking work and thereby retain your worker status while involuntarily unemployed) within a 'reasonable period' after giving birth.[156] Other than in unusual cases, 52 weeks is a 'reasonable period' and the period will usually start 11 weeks before the due date.[157]

Moving between groups and gaps

You can retain your worker or self-employed status if you are in one of the groups on p1609 and continue to do so if you move into another category.[158] For example, you may have been involuntarily unemployed and registered as a jobseeker, then you became ill and were temporarily unable to work, and then you got better and started vocational training. You retain your worker or self-employed status throughout.

You may be able to retain your worker or self-employed status if there is a gap between your ceasing work and registering as a jobseeker with the DWP.[159] If the delay is more than a few days, all your circumstances, including the reasons for the gap and what you did during it, should be considered to establish whether there was undue delay[160] and whether you withdrew from the labour market during that period.[161] Arguably, you should also be able to retain your worker or self-employed status if there is a gap between your ceasing work and being temporarily unable to work because of illness or an accident, since there is no requirement for the illness or accident to be the reason for your ceasing work. You should also still retain your worker or self-employed status during a short gap between two different circumstances applying, provided you remain in the labour market during that time.

Self-sufficient people

You have a right of residence as a self-sufficient person if you are an EEA national and you, and any family members whose right to reside depends on their being your family member, have:[162]

- sufficient resources not to become an unreasonable burden on the social assistance system of the UK during your period of residence;[163] *and*
- comprehensive sickness insurance.

The UK government cannot set a fixed amount that is regarded as 'sufficient resources' and must take account of your personal situation.[164] You have **'sufficient resources'** if they:[165]

- exceed the maximum level you (and your family) can have to be eligible for 'social assistance' (see below); *or*
- do not exceed that level, but the decision maker considers that you still have sufficient resources, taking into account your (and your family's) personal situation.

The 'maximum level' is the equivalent of your means-tested benefit applicable amount, including any premiums. Your resources also include your accommodation, so if your resources are more than your applicable amount plus your rent, or if friends or family provide you with free and stable accommodation, they should be 'sufficient'.[166]

11

Part 11: Immigration and residence rules for benefits and tax credits
Chapter 68: Coming from abroad: residence rules
5. Who has a right to reside

You cannot automatically be regarded as not self-sufficient just because you make a claim for a means-tested benefit. All your circumstances, including the likely duration of your claim, must be assessed to determine whether or not your benefit claim makes you an unreasonable burden on the social assistance system of the UK.[167]

The source of the resources does not matter.[168] However, you cannot rely on your earnings from employment in the UK to give you self-sufficient status.[169] Check instead whether the employment gives you 'worker' status (see p1607). You can, however, rely on the earnings of your non-EEA national spouse/civil partner,[170] or if you are a child, the earnings of your non-EEA parent (even if derived from employment that is unlawful due to a lack of residence card and work permit[171]).

The requirement to have **comprehensive sickness insurance** cover is satisfied if you have private health insurance.[172] It is also satisfied if the UK can be reimbursed by another state for any NHS costs you incur while in the UK. This usually applies if you are covered by the EU co-ordination rules (see p1672) and another state continues to be your 'competent state' (see p1676) after you come to the UK.[173] For further information, see CPAG's *Benefits for Migrants Handbook*.

Students

You have a right to reside as a student if you are an EEA national and you:[174]
- are enrolled as a student in a government-accredited college; *and*
- provide an assurance that you have sufficient resources for you, and any family members whose right to reside depends on their being your family member, not to become a burden on the UK social assistance system during your intended period of residence (see above); *and*
- together with any family members who do not have an independent right to reside, have comprehensive sickness insurance (see above).

Family members

You have a right to reside if you are a 'family member' of an EEA national who has either a right to reside in the UK as a 'qualified person' (see p1599), a permanent right to reside (see p1621) or an initial right to reside (see p1605). This applies whether or not you are an EEA national yourself. You have a right to reside for as long as the EEA national has a right to reside and for as long as you remain her/his family member.

Family members[175]

You are a **'family member'** if you are the EEA national's:

– spouse or civil partner; *or*

– child, grandchild or great-grandchild, or the child, grandchild or great-grandchild of the EEA national's spouse/civil partner, and you are under 21; *or*

– child, grandchild or great-grandchild, or the child, grandchild or great-grandchild of the EEA national's spouse/civil partner, and you are her/his dependant; *or*

– parent, grandparent or great-grandparent, or the parent, grandparent or great-grandparent of the EEA national's spouse/civil partner, and you are her/his dependant.

You remain a spouse or civil partner even if you are separated. You only cease to be a spouse or civil partner on divorce or dissolution of the civil partnership.[176]

'Dependence' is not defined in the legislation, but caselaw has established a number of principles.[177] To be dependent, you must receive support from the other person. The support must be 'material', although not necessarily financial, and must contribute towards your basic necessities. Translation, emotional and social support do not count.[178] It is irrelevant if there are alternative sources of support, including employment, available.[179]

If you only became dependent on the EEA national in the UK, this does not prevent you from being classed as a family member, unless you are an 'extended family member' (see p1616), in which case you must have already been dependent (or a member of her/his household) in the country you have come from.[180]

Note:

- If your only right to reside is as a family member of an EEA national who only has a right to reside for her/his initial three months (see p1605), this does not enable you to satisfy the right to reside requirement for UC, IS, income-based JSA, income-related ESA, PC and HB (see p1592).
- If your only right to reside is as a family member of an EEA national who has a right to reside as a jobseeker, this does not enable you to satisfy the right to reside requirement for UC, IS, income-related ESA, PC, and HB (see p1592).

Are you unable to prove your right to reside?

If you are relying on your family member for your right to reside and you cannot prove what s/he is doing (eg, if you have separated from your spouse and have no evidence that s/he is a worker), ask the DWP, HMRC or local authority to investigate this – eg, by using the database of NI contributions to establish that your spouse is a worker. Provide information about your spouse to enable it to do so. If it is refused and you appeal, you can ask the First-tier Tribunal to issue a direction (see p1358) to the DWP, HMRC or local authority to make these investigations and argue that otherwise it has not shown that you do not have a right to reside.[181]

Part 11: Immigration and residence rules for benefits and tax credits
Chapter 68: Coming from abroad: residence rules
5. Who has a right to reside

Extended family members

If you do not count as a family member, but you have a partner or relative in the UK who is an EEA national, you may be treated as her/his family member if you are her/his 'extended family member' and you have been issued with an EEA family permit, a registration certificate or a residence card, which remains in force (see p1600).[182]

Extended family member

You are an **'extended family member'** of an EEA national if s/he is your:[183]

– partner and you are in a durable relationship with her/him (or you are the child, under 18, of the partner); *or*

– non-adoptive legal guardian (under the country in which the guardianship order was granted), you are under 18, dependent on her/him and have lived with her/him since s/he became your legal guardian; *or*

– relative; *and*

– you meet the requirements of the Immigration Rules (other than those relating to entry clearance) for indefinite leave as her/his dependent relative; *or*

– you have serious health problems that require her/his (or her/his spouse or civil partner's) care; *or*

– you previously were dependent on her/him, or were a member of her/his household, in a country other than the UK and you are accompanying her/him to, or wish to join her/him in, the UK, or you have joined her/him in the UK and continue to be dependent on her/him or to be a member of her/his household.[184]

Family members of British citizens

British citizens do not automatically give residence rights to their family members.

However, if you are a family member (including an extended family member with the relevant residence document[185]) of a British citizen, you have a free movement right to reside under EU law if:[186]

- s/he resided with a right to reside as a worker, self-employed person, self-sufficient person or self-sufficient student, or having acquired a right of permanent residence, in an EEA state (not including the UK when it was part of the EEA); *and*

- you resided with the British citizen as her/his family member in that EEA state and your joint residence in that EEA state was 'genuine' (which has been held to mean real, substantive and effective, and more than mere physical presence[187]).

On return to the UK, the British citizen confers EU law residence rights on you. The EEA Regulations (see p1595) contain these rights, but interpret them more restrictively than the CJEU has done.[188] Get specialist advice if any of these restrictions affect you.

- The EEA Regulations list the following as relevant to whether your residence in the EEA state is, or was, genuine:[189]
  - whether the British citizen transferred her/his 'centre of life' there;
  - the length of joint residence there;
  - the nature and quality of the joint accommodation there and whether it was her/his principal residence;
  - the degree of your and the British citizen's integration;
  - whether it was your first lawful residence in the EU.
  These factors go beyond the findings of the CJEU which, when considering whether residence is 'genuine', focused on whether the conditions for the relevant residence rights were satisfied.[190]
- The EEA Regulations only give you a right to reside if the British citizen currently has a right to reside under these regulations (with certain mitigations – eg, if s/he is a self-sufficient person, s/he need not be covered by comprehensive sickness cover). However, the CJEU has held that it is not necessary for a person who had been a worker in another EEA state to carry out economic activity on her/his return in order for her/his family member to have a right of residence.[191]
- The EEA regulations require the British citizen to have transferred her/his centre of life to the EEA state, but EU law does not.[192]
- If you are a non-EEA national, the EEA Regulations exclude you from having a right to reside on this basis if the purpose of your residence in the EEA state was to circumvent the immigration laws.[193]

Family members of dual citizens

If you are the family member of a British citizen who also has citizenship of an EEA country, you can have a right to reside in the same circumstances as if you were the family member of a non-British EEA national. The British citizen must have moved to the UK and resided as an EEA national with a right to reside as a 'qualified person' (see p1599), or with a permanent right to reside at the time s/he acquired British citizenship. If s/he currently has a right to reside as a qualified person, s/he must have had such a right continuously since acquiring British citizenship.[194]

A dual British/EEA national does not have rights under EU law if s/he has lived all her/his life in the UK. In this case, you cannot derive any rights from her/him.[195]

Former family members who retain their right to reside

In general, if you are the family member of an EEA national who has a right to reside, you lose your right to reside if s/he ceases to be your family member or to have a right to reside. However, there are some exceptions which mean you can retain your right to reside if the EEA national dies or leaves the UK, or if your marriage or civil partnership ends. These rights are in EU Directive 2004/38, but

Part 11: Immigration and residence rules for benefits and tax credits
Chapter 68: Coming from abroad: residence rules
5. Who has a right to reside

they are not exactly reproduced in the UK EEA Regulations. The benefit authorities accept the rights set out in the EEA Regulations (listed below), but do not always accept those in the Directive (see p1619). If you only have a right to reside under the Directive and are refused benefit, you should challenge the decision and get specialist advice.

You retain your right to reside under the EEA Regulations if you are a family member of an EEA national who is a 'qualified person' (see p1599) or a person with a permanent right to reside (see p1621) and:[196]

- the EEA national dies and you are:
  - not an EEA national, but if you were, you would be a worker, or a self-employed or self-sufficient person (or you are the family member of such a non-EEA national), and you resided in the UK with a right to reside under the EEA Regulations for at least a year immediately before s/he died; *or*
  - her/his child or grandchild (or the child or grandchild of her/his spouse or civil partner) and you were in education (see p1621) immediately before her/his death and you remain in education; *or*
  - the parent with custody of a child in the previous bullet point; *or*
- the EEA national leaves the UK and you are:
  - her/his child or grandchild (or the child or grandchild of her/his spouse or civil partner) and you were in education (see p1621) immediately before s/he left the UK and you remain in education; *or*
  - the parent with custody of a child in the previous bullet point; *or*
- your marriage or civil partnership to the EEA national is terminated, and s/he was a qualified person or had a permanent right to reside at least until the termination proceedings began,[197] and you are not an EEA national, but if you were, you would be a worker, or a self-employed or self-sufficient person (or you are the family member of such a non-EEA national), and you were residing in the UK with a right to reside under the regulations at the date of the termination and:
  - prior to the termination, the marriage/civil partnership had lasted for at least three years with you both residing in the UK for at least one of those years; *or*
  - you have custody of the EEA national's child; *or*
  - you have a right of access to the EEA national's child, which a court has said must take place in the UK; *or*
  - your continued right of residence in the UK is warranted by particularly difficult circumstances, such as your (or another family member's) being subject to domestic violence during the period of the marriage/civil partnership.

You have a right to reside on this basis for as long as the conditions apply to you,[198] until you can acquire a permanent right of residence (see p1621).[199]

Note:
- If your only right of residence is as the primary carer of a dependent British citizen who would otherwise have to leave the whole of the EEA, you do not satisfy the right to reside requirement for any means-tested benefits (see p1592) and only satisfy it for child benefit and CTC if you are a national of Algeria, Morocco, San Marino, Tunisia or Turkey and working in the UK (see p1593).
- Periods with a right to reside under any of the bullet points on p1620 do not count towards the period of residence required for acquiring a permanent right to reside (see below).

Child in education

To have a right to reside as a worker's child in education and as a primary carer of a child in education, there must have been a common period when the child was in the UK and the parent (or step-parent[219]) was a worker in the UK. The child need not have entered education while the parent (or step-parent) was a worker.[220]

These rights also apply if the worker was an A8 national working during the period of restrictions for an authorised employer (see p1601), even if it was for less than 12 months.[221] As the first month of work would have always been for an authorised employer, the A8 national's child who was in the UK during that first month of work and who is now in education can also have these rights.[222] These rights also apply in the same way if the worker was a Croatian or an A2 national working in accordance with her/his worker authorisation document during the period of restrictions.

Your right to reside as a primary carer of a worker's child in education ends when the child reaches 18, unless s/he continues to need your presence and care in order to be able to pursue and complete her/his education.[223]

Education

'**Education**' excludes nursery education, but includes education before the compulsory school age if it is equivalent to that received at or after compulsory school age – eg, education received by a child under five in a school reception class.[224]

If you are the primary carer of a child of a self-employed EEA national,[225] or of a pre-school age child of a worker,[226] you are not currently accepted as deriving a right to reside from that child.

People with a permanent right of residence

You have a permanent right of residence if you have 'resided legally' (see p1622) in the UK for a 'continuous period of five years' (see p1622) or in limited circumstances after a shorter period (see p1624).[227] Once you have this permanent right of residence, you satisfy the right to reside requirement for all benefits that have that requirement.[228]

Part 11: Immigration and residence rules for benefits and tax credits
Chapter 68: Coming from abroad: residence rules
5. Who has a right to reside

Once acquired, you only lose your permanent right of residence if you are absent from the UK for more than two consecutive years.[229] However, in exceptional circumstances, your residence rights can be revoked or cancelled on grounds of public policy, public security or public health.[230]

Note: if you are an EEA national, in most cases you will eligible for indefinite leave under the EU Settlement Scheme (also known as settled status) if either:

- you can show at least five years' residence in the UK, whether or not you had a right to reside during that time; *or*
- you satisfy the requirements for permanent residence in less than five years (see p1624).

From the day you are granted this leave it will satisfy the right to reside requirement for all benefits that require it. For more information on settled status, see p1597.

A continuous period of five years

When calculating whether you have 'five years' continuous residence', temporary absences from the UK do not affect the continuity of your residence (and you can count the time spent abroad as part of your five years[231]) if:[232]

- they are not more than a total of six months a year; *or*
- they comprise one absence of up to 12 consecutive months for important reasons, such as pregnancy and childbirth, serious illness, study or vocational training, or a posting abroad; *or*
- they are for compulsory military service.

It may be arguable that some periods of residence when you remain in the UK, but are not 'residing legally' do not interrupt your 'continuity of residence', provided the total period of 'residing legally' is at least five years.[233] However, in other circumstances, continuous residence during which you are 'residing legally' is required.[234]

Guidance to decision makers states that cumulative gaps of up to 30 days in any one year do not break your continuity of residence if they are between two periods when you have different residence rights, but not if they separate two periods when you have the same residence right.[235] Refer to this guidance if it is helpful, but remember it is not legally binding.

If you spend time in prison[236] or if you are removed from the UK under the EEA Regulations or subject to a deportation or expulsion order,[237] this interrupts the continuity of your residence and you cannot count this time towards your five years.

What counts as 'resided legally'

You have 'resided legally' in any period during which you had a right of residence as a:

- worker (see p1607) (including if you retain your worker status – see p1609);

- self-employed person (see p1608) (including if you retain your self-employed status – see p1609);
- self-sufficient person (see p1613);
- student (see p1614);
- jobseeker (see p1605) since 30 April 2006 (see below);
- person with an initial right of residence since 30 April 2006 (see below);
- family member (see p1614) of any of the above.

If you have a continuous period of five years' residence on the basis of one or more of the above, you have a right of permanent residence under both the EEA Regulations and (other than an initial right of residence or as a jobseeker, or family member of either) the EU Directive 2004/38.

The **EEA Regulations** allow you to count continuous residence 'in accordance with these regulations' (or in accordance with previous regulations), other than with a 'derivative right to reside' (see p1619).[238] This includes periods since 30 April 2006 when you had an initial right to reside or a right to reside as a jobseeker (or family member of either). (These rights were not included in the EEA Regulations before this date.)[239]

Under **EU Directive 2004/38**, you must have 'resided legally for a continuous period of five years'.[240] This means that you must have had a residence right under the Directive or under any of the earlier EU legislation that it replaced.[241] This covers all the groups listed above, except for jobseekers and their family members.

You are not counted as having 'resided legally' during periods when your right to reside was as the primary carer of either a worker's child in education or a self-sufficient child,[242] or when your right of residence was only in accordance with UK law – eg, a period during which you had leave to remain under the Immigration Rules.[243]

If you are an A8, A2 or a Croatian national, you count as having 'resided legally' during periods before your state joined the EU if you would have come into one of the groups above (other than a jobseeker), or you would have resided in accordance with the EEA Regulations were it not for the fact that you were not an EU national at that time.[244] Once your state joined the EU, the periods when you count as having resided legally are as above, except they were subject to the additional restrictions for A8, A2 and Croatian nationals (see p1601).

Family members

If you are the family member (including extended family member with the relevant residence document[245]) (see p1614) of a person with a permanent right of residence, you have a right to reside for as long as you remain a family member.[246] After five years of being the family member of an EEA national with a permanent right of residence, you acquire a permanent right of residence yourself. You can also add periods as a family member of a person with a permanent right of residence to other periods when you count as 'residing legally' (see p1622) to make up your five years, and so acquire a permanent right of residence.[247]

Part 11: Immigration and residence rules for benefits and tax credits
Chapter 68: Coming from abroad: residence rules
5. Who has a right to reside

Permanent residence in less than five years

In the circumstances listed below you can acquire a permanent right of residence before five years.[248] If so, you are exempt from the habitual residence test (see p1589).

- You were a worker (see p1607) or self-employed person (see p1608) in the UK, but have now stopped working in the UK and:
  - at the time you stopped working, you had reached pension age or (workers only) taken early retirement and:
    - your spouse or civil partner is a British citizen (or s/he lost that nationality by marrying you); *or*
    - you worked in the UK for the preceding year and resided (whether or not you had a right to reside[249]) in the UK continuously for more than three years; *or*
  - you stopped working as a result of a permanent incapacity (this means it is not a temporary incapacity – see p1612, but it may follow temporary incapacity – see first note below[250]) and:
    - your spouse or civil partner is a British citizen (or s/he lost that nationality by marrying you); *or*
    - you have resided (whether or not you had a right to reside[251]) in the UK continuously for more than two years (under the EEA Regulations only: immediately before you stopped working); *or*
    - the incapacity was because of an accident at work or occupational disease that resulted in benefit entitlement; *or*
  - you are a worker or self-employed in another EEA country while residing in the UK and returning, as a rule, at least once a week, following (under the EEA Regulations only: immediately following) three years of continuous employment or self-employment and residence in the UK.
- You are the family member of a worker or self-employed person in any of the above bullet points and both of you are residing in the UK.[252] **Note:** the EEA Regulations require that you had a right to reside on the basis of being her/his family member at the point s/he ceased working.[253]
- You are the family member of a worker or self-employed person who died while still working and who did not acquire a permanent right of residence in one of the above ways and:
  - s/he had lived in the UK for two years; *or*
  - the death resulted from an accident at work or an occupational disease; *or*
  - you lost your UK nationality as a result of marrying her/him.

Note:
- You can count as periods of employment any period in which you were not working because of illness or accident, or some reason not of your own making, or (workers only) periods of involuntary unemployment (subject to the same limitations as those retaining worker status this way – see p1609).[254]

- The Upper Tribunal has held that no restrictions were imposed on A8 nationals in order to limit their rights to permanent residence in under five years.[255]

Other residence rights

If you do not have one of the rights of residence under the EEA Regulations or EU law outlined on pp1594–1624, it may be possible to argue that you should still have a right of residence by applying principles that have been accepted in other cases. In particular, it has been accepted that you may have residence rights directly from the Treaty on the Functioning of Europe if these are necessary for someone else's rights not to be infringed.[256] For further details, see CPAG's *Benefits for Migrants Handbook*.

You should also check whether you can obtain settled or pre-settled status under the EU Settlement Scheme (see p1597).

---

6. Rules for specific benefits and tax credits

This section explains the residence and presence rules for each benefit. It includes which residence and presence tests apply and how you may be assisted by the European Union (EU) co-ordination rules.

For the rules on being paid while you are abroad, see Chapter 69.

Universal credit and other means-tested benefits

To be entitled to universal credit (UC), income support (IS), income-based jobseeker's allowance (JSA), income-related employment and support allowance (ESA), pension credit (PC) and housing benefit (HB), you (and your partner, for UC) must:
- (except HB – see below) be present in Great Britain (see p1583);[257] *and*
- be habitually resident (see p1586), including having a right to reside (see p1591) and, for income-based JSA only, have been living for the past three months (see p1584) in the 'common travel area' – ie, the UK, the Republic of Ireland, the Channel Islands and the Isle of Man (unless you are exempt – see p1589).[258]

In certain circumstances, the rules treat you as being present in Great Britain during a temporary absence, so you can continue to receive these benefits while you are abroad for limited periods (see Chapter 69).

For UC, if your partner fails the habitual residence test, your joint claim is treated as a claim for UC as a single person (see p1626).

To be entitled to the carer element in your UC (see p73), you must satisfy the past presence test as it applies to carer's allowance (see p1629).

Part 11: Immigration and residence rules for benefits and tax credits
Chapter 68: Coming from abroad: residence rules
6. Rules for specific benefits and tax credits

If you are receiving HB, IS, child tax credit (CTC) or working tax credit (WTC) and claim UC and the DWP decides you do not satisfy the above residence or presence tests, this does *not* terminate your existing award of any of these four benefits (see p1588, point 8).

For HB, although being present in Great Britain is not a condition of entitlement, going abroad can still affect your entitlement (see p1652).

Note: if you are are moving, or have moved, to Great Britain from Northern Ireland or vice versa and are claiming income-related ESA, see p1631.

Couples claiming universal credit

If you live with your partner and claim UC, you are generally required to make a joint claim, and you and your partner must both satisfy, or be exempt from, the habitual residence test. If your partner fails the habitual residence test, your joint claim is treated as a claim for UC as a single person and:[259]

- the maximum amount of UC is that for a single person;[260]
- your partner does not have to accept a claimant commitment or comply with any work-related requirements because s/he is not a claimant;[261]
- your partner's income and capital are taken into account (see p36);[262]
- your partner does not affect your being the 'responsible carer' of a child (see p1062) – eg, to determine your work-related requirements, or to enable you to be entitled to UC when you are receiving education;[263]
- the couple rate of the earnings threshold applies for determining when no work-related requirements apply to you (see p1065), and in calculating any self-employed 'minimum income floor' that may apply if you are self-employed (note the 'minimum income floor' does not apply to your partner if s/he is self-employed) (see p121).[264]

Note: if you have reached pension age and your partner is under pension age but is not entitled to UC because s/he fails the habitual residence test, your claim is *not* treated as a single claim for UC. Instead, you must claim PC and HB and you are treated as a single person for these claims.[265]

If your partner is abroad

If you have a partner who is abroad, you may continue to receive benefit that includes an amount for her/him for a limited period if you are only temporarily living apart. The rules vary between the benefits (see Chapter 69).

If these rules do not apply, or at the end of the limited period:

- you cease to be entitled to UC as joint claimants. You must claim as a single person. Your award is based on the maximum amount for a single person, but your partner's income and capital are taken into account until you have been, or you expect to be, apart for six months (as then you cease to be treated as a couple).[266] However, if you are of pension age, but your partner is under pension age, once s/he stops being treated as part of your household for the purposes of PC, due to being abroad for more than the specified periods (see p1659), you can claim PC and pension-age HB as a single person. If you do not switch from UC to PC, your UC will continue to be paid until you cease to be treated as a couple with your partner (when you have, or expect to be, apart for six months);[267]

- your applicable amount for IS, income-based JSA, income-related ESA, PC and HB no longer includes an amount for your partner. However, your partner's capital, income and work are still taken into account when working out how much benefit you get. This is because s/he is still treated as being part of your household, despite temporarily living away from you, unless you are in any of the situations listed on p322.[268]

Where questions of 'intention' are involved (eg, when deciding whether you or your partner intend to resume living with your family), the intention must be 'unqualified'. This means it must not depend on a factor over which you have no control – eg, the right of entry to the UK being granted by the Home Office,[269] or the offer of a suitable job.[270]

If your child is abroad

If you have a child who is abroad, your benefit entitlement could be affected if s/he ceases to be treated as part of your household (see p327).[271]

If your child is abroad, s/he is only included in your applicable amount for UC, IS, income-based JSA and PC for a limited period, and her/his absence can also affect your HB (see Chapter 69).

Bereavement benefits

You must be ordinarily resident (see p1585) in Great Britain on the date your spouse or civil partner died to be entitled to bereavement support payment.[272]

You do not need to satisfy any residence or presence rules to be entitled to widowed parent's allowance.

European Union co-ordination rules

If the EU co-ordination rules apply to you (see p1672) and the UK is your 'competent state' (see p1676):[273]

- you can, if necessary, rely on national insurance (NI) contributions paid by your late spouse/civil partner in EEA states to calculate your entitlement to bereavement benefits (under the 'aggregation principle' – see p1678); *and*
- for bereavement support payment, the requirement to be ordinarily resident in Great Britain on the date your spouse or civil partner died does not apply if you were resident in an EEA state on that date.

Part 11: Immigration and residence rules for benefits and tax credits
Chapter 68: Coming from abroad: residence rules
6. Rules for specific benefits and tax credits

Reciprocal agreements

If you are covered by a reciprocal agreement (see p1582), these can assist in similar ways to the EU co-ordination rules in respect of the relevant country. If the agreement treats you as being present in the UK while in the other country and you were ordinarily resident in that country on the date your spouse or civil partner died, you are treated as ordinarily resident in Great Britain on that date.[274]

Child benefit and guardian's allowance

Child benefit

To be entitled to child benefit, you and your child(ren) must be present in Great Britain (see p1583).[275]

To be treated as present, you (but not your child/ren) must also:[276]
- be ordinarily resident in the UK (see p1585); *and*
- have a right to reside in the UK (see p1593), unless your current claim began before 1 May 2004; *and*
- have been living in the UK for the three months prior to your date of claim (unless you are exempt – see p1584).

You are treated as present if you are:[277]
- a Crown servant posted overseas and:
  - you are, or immediately before your posting abroad you were, ordinarily resident in the UK; *or*
  - immediately before your posting, you were in the UK in connection with that posting; *or*
- the partner of a Crown servant posted overseas and in the same country as her/him or temporarily absent from that country under the same exceptions that enable child benefit to continue during a temporary absence from Great Britain (see p1648); *or*
- a person who is in the UK as a result of your being deported or legally removed from another country.

You and/or your child can be treated as present for limited periods during a temporary absence (see p1648).

While you are treated as present, you continue to satisfy that condition of entitlement. This means that you can continue to receive child benefit if it is already being paid and you can also make a fresh claim during your, or your child's, absence. If you, or your child, spend longer abroad than the permitted periods (see p1648), you (or s/he) cease to satisfy the presence condition and your entitlement to child benefit ends. **Note:** if you or your child are treated as being present, you must satisfy all the other conditions of entitlement including, if your child is not living with you, contributing to the costs of that child (see p584).

Note: Scottish child payment, which is due to be introduced in Scotland by Christmas 2020, is expected to require that you are ordinarily resident in Scotland (see Chapter 74).

Guardian's allowance

Entitlement to guardian's allowance depends on entitlement to child benefit, so you must meet the conditions for child benefit on p1628.

In addition, at least one of the child's parents must have:[278]

- been born in the UK; *or*
- at some time after reaching the age of 16, spent a total of 52 weeks in any two-year period in Great Britain.

In order to satisfy the second condition above, you are treated as being present in Great Britain during any absence abroad which is due to your employment as a serving member of the forces, an airman or airwoman, mariner or continental shelf worker.

European Union co-ordination rules

If the EU co-ordination rules apply to you (see p1672), you may be able to:

- use certain periods of residence in one or more EEA countries to satisfy the child benefit requirement to have been living in the UK for the past three months under the 'aggregation principle' (see p1678);
- be paid child benefit and guardian's allowance for a child who is resident in an EEA country without her/him needing to satisfy the rules on temporary absences, provided you satisfy all the other conditions of entitlement, including contributing to the costs of the child (see p584).[279] See p1680 for more details;
- use time spent in one or more EEA states to satisfy the requirement for guardian's allowance to have spent 52 weeks in any two-year period in Great Britain (see p1678). It may also be arguable that this condition should not apply if you have a 'genuine and sufficient link to the UK' (see p1630).[280]

Disability benefits and carer's allowance

For attendance allowance (AA), disability living allowance (DLA), personal independence payment (PIP) and carer's allowance (CA), you must:[281]

- be present in Great Britain at the time of your claim; *and*
- have been present in Great Britain for at least 104 weeks in the last 156 weeks (the 'past presence test'). See p1583, but see also the exceptions below; *and*
- be habitually resident in the common travel area (see p1586).

A challenge to the legality of the past presence test when applied to British children with strong connections to the UK was, at the time of writing, due to be heard.[282]

Part 11: Immigration and residence rules for benefits and tax credits
Chapter 68: Coming from abroad: residence rules
6. Rules for specific benefits and tax credits

For ESA in youth, incapacity benefit (IB) in youth and severe disablement allowance (SDA), see the 2017/18 edition of this *Handbook* or CPAG's *Benefits for Migrants Handbook*.[283]

To be entitled to the **CA supplement**, you must be in receipt of CA and resident (see p1585) in Scotland.

To qualify for a **young carer grant**, on the day of your application you must be:[284]
- ordinarily resident in Scotland (unless you satisfied this requirement for a previous award and since then you became, and continue to be, ordinarily resident in an EEA country or Switzerland); *and*
- habitually resident in the UK, Channel Islands, Isle of Man, Switzerland or the EEA (see p1587) or be exempt from this requirement (see p1589).

When you can be treated as present

You are treated as being present during certain absences (see p1649). Any period when you are treated as present can be counted to satisfy both the presence and the past presence tests.

Exceptions to the past presence test

If you are claiming the DLA care component for a baby under six months old, there is a shorter 13-week past presence test. If covered by this, it continues to apply until your child's first birthday. If your child becomes entitled to DLA at between six and 36 months, the past presence test is 26 weeks in the last 156 weeks.[285]

For AA, DLA and PIP, the 104-week (or 26-week or 13-week) past presence test does not apply if you are terminally ill.[286]

If you have refugee leave or humanitarian protection (or you have leave as the dependent family member of someone who has such leave), the past presence test does not apply.[287]

European Union co-ordination rules

If you are covered by the co-ordination rules (see p1672), you can only be entitled to AA, DLA care component, the daily living component of PIP and CA if the UK is your 'competent state'.[288] This might not be the case if you (or your family member who brings you within the co-ordination rules) receive a 'pension' from another member state.[289] For further details, see p1676 and CPAG's *Benefits for Migrants Handbook*.

The EU co-ordination rules can make it easier to claim AA, DLA, PIP and CA in the UK and can also enable you to make a new claim if you live in an EEA state.

The past presence test does not apply to AA, DLA, PIP and CA if:[290]
- you are habitually resident in Great Britain; *and*
- you are covered by the co-ordination rules (see p1672); *and*
- you can demonstrate 'a genuine and sufficient link to the UK ' (see p1631).

If you are covered by the co-ordination rules (see p1672), but are not exempt from the past presence test because you do not have 'a genuine and sufficient link to the UK', you may be able to count certain periods of residence in one or more EEA states to satisfy the past presence test for these benefits (under the 'aggregation principle' – see p1678).[291]

Do you have a genuine and sufficient link to the UK?

Factors that are relevant when demonstrating that you have a 'genuine and sufficient link to the UK' (not to the 'UK social security system' as specified in the regulations[292]) can include:[293]

– whether you have worked in the UK;

– whether you have spent a significant part of your life in the UK;

– whether you have been present in the UK for a reasonable period;

– whether you are receiving a UK contributory benefit;

– evidence of your motives, intentions and expectations;

– the benefit you are claiming and if you are claiming a disability benefit, whether your carer would be entitled to CA;

– the duration of your presence in Great Britain;

– whether you are dependent on a family member who has worked in the UK and/or who receives a UK contributory benefit. 'Family member' in this context is not limited to people covered by the definition of 'member of the family' in the co-ordination rules (see p1673), and can, for example, include your sister.[294]

Contributory employment and support allowance

To be entitled to contributory ESA, you must be in Great Britain.[295] The rules on when you can be paid during a temporary absence are in Chapter 69. There are no residence conditions, except for contributory ESA in youth (see the 2017/18 edition of this *Handbook* or CPAG's *Benefits for Migrants Handbook*).

European Union co-ordination rules

If the EU co-ordination rules apply to you (see p1672) and the UK is your 'competent state' (see p1676), you can, if necessary, rely on NI contributions paid in one or more EEA states to entitle you to contributory ESA in the UK (under the 'aggregation principle' – see p1678). You may also be able to 'export' (ie, continue to receive) a 'sickness' or 'invalidity' benefit from another EEA state (see p1679).

Reciprocal agreements

If you have lived and worked in a country with which the UK has a reciprocal agreement (see p1582), you may be able to count periods of insurance paid in that country towards your entitlement to contributory ESA in the UK.

If you have moved from Northern Ireland to Great Britain (or vice versa), reciprocal arrangements mean your ESA (both income-related and contributory)

Part 11: Immigration and residence rules for benefits and tax credits
Chapter 68: Coming from abroad: residence rules
6. Rules for specific benefits and tax credits

should be paid at the same rate.[296] For further details, see CPAG's *Benefits for Migrants Handbook*.

Industrial injuries benefits

To be entitled to any of the industrial injuries benefits, you must have:
- been in Great Britain when the accident at work happened;[297] *or*
- been engaged in Great Britain in the employment that caused the disease (even if you have also been engaged outside Great Britain in that employment);[298] *or*
- been paying UK class 1 or class 2 NI contributions when the accident at work happened or you contracted the disease. Benefit is not payable until you return to Great Britain.[299]

There are exceptions, which mean that you can qualify for benefit in respect of an accident which happens, or a disease which is contracted, outside Great Britain while you are:[300]
- employed as a mariner or airman or airwoman; *or*
- employed as an apprentice pilot on board a ship or vessel; *or*
- on board an aircraft on a test flight starting in Great Britain in the course of your employment.

In these cases, there are also more generous rules for defining when accidents arise 'out of and in the course of' your employment, and for complying with time limits under benefit rules.[301]

European Union co-ordination rules

If the EU co-ordination rules apply to you (see p1672) and the UK is your 'competent state' (see p1676), you can, if necessary, rely on periods of employment and NI paid in one or more EEA states in order to qualify for industrial injuries benefits in the UK (under the 'aggregation principle' – see p1678).

If you have an accident while travelling abroad in an EEA country state, this can be deemed to have occurred in the state liable to pay industrial injuries benefits.[302] If you have worked in two or more EEA states in a job that gave you a prescribed industrial disease, you get benefit from the state in which you last did work that, by its nature, is likely to cause that disease and which recognises that disease under its industrial injuries scheme.[303]

Contribution-based jobseeker's allowance

To be entitled to contribution-based JSA, you must be in Great Britain.[304] The rules on when you can be paid during a temporary absence are covered in Chapter 69. There are no residence conditions.

European Union co-ordination rules

In most cases, if the EU co-ordination rules apply to you (see p1672), you may be able to count NI contributions paid in one or more EEA states to entitle you to contribution-based JSA in the UK (under the 'aggregation principle'). However, this is usually only possible if your most recent period of paying, or being credited with, contributions was in the UK (see p1678).[305]

If you are coming to, or returning to, the UK to look for work and have been working in an EEA state, you may be able to obtain, before you leave, a U2 form authorising you to export your unemployment benefit from that EEA state. You can continue to receive that state's unemployment benefit for up to three months if:[306]

- you were getting it immediately before coming to the UK; *and*
- you have been registered as available for work for four weeks (or less, if that state's rules allow) in that EEA state; *and*
- you claim JSA within seven days after you were last registered in the other member state; *and*
- you satisfy the JSA jobseeking conditions (if you do not come under the UC system – see p23), or you accept a claimant commitment and you meet your work-related requirements (if you come under the UC system – see p1047).

The three months can be extended to a maximum of six months if the state from which you are claiming the unemployment benefit agrees.[307]

Reciprocal agreements

If you have lived and worked in a country with which the UK has a reciprocal agreement (see p1582), you may be able to count periods of insurance paid in that country towards your entitlement to contribution-based JSA. If you are covered by the agreements between Great Britain and Northern Ireland, you can be treated as in Great Britain if you go to Northern Ireland (see p1655)

Maternity allowance

Entitlement to maternity allowance (MA) is based on past employment, generally in Great Britain.[308] There are no residence requirements. However, in general you are disqualified if you are absent from Great Britain.[309] See p1657 for the rules allowing you to be paid during a temporary absence.

European Union co-ordination rules

If the EU co-ordination rules apply to you (see p1672) and the UK is your 'competent state' (see p1676), you can, if necessary, rely on periods of employment in other EEA states in order to qualify for MA in the UK (under the 'aggregation principle' – see p1678).

Part 11: Immigration and residence rules for benefits and tax credits
Chapter 68: Coming from abroad: residence rules
6. Rules for specific benefits and tax credits

Retirement pensions

Retirement pensions, other than category D retirement pension, do not have any residence or presence entitlement conditions. They can be paid without a time limit, whether or not you are present in Great Britain. However, going abroad can mean you are not paid the annual uprating, can be relevant to decisions on deferring your retirement and can prevent you from 'de-retiring' while you are abroad (see p1660).[310]

To be entitled to category D retirement pension, you must have been:[311]

- resident in Great Britain for at least 10 years in any continuous period of 20 years ending on or after your 80th birthday; *and*
- ordinarily resident (see p1585) in Great Britain on either:
  – your 80th birthday; *or*
  – the date on which you claimed category D pension, if later.

European Union co-ordination rules

If the co-ordination rules apply to you (see p1672) and the UK is your 'competent state' (see p1676), you can, if necessary, rely on NI contributions paid, or for category D retirement pension certain periods of residence completed, in EEA states to calculate your entitlement to retirement pensions in the UK (under the 'aggregation principle' – see p1678). However, your award may be reduced to reflect the proportion of years of contributions paid, or periods of residence completed, in the UK out of the total years of contributions paid or periods of residence completed in all states.[312] The requirement to be ordinarily resident for category D retirement pension may not apply to you if you can show that you have a 'genuine and sufficient link to the UK' (see p1630).[313]

Reciprocal agreements

If you have lived and worked in a country with which the UK has a reciprocal agreement (see p1582), you may be able to count periods of residence or insurance paid in that country towards your UK retirement pension entitlement.

Social fund and other payments

Funeral payments

To qualify for a **funeral support payment** in Scotland you must be ordinarily resident in Scotland at the date you make you application.[314]

To qualify for a **funeral expenses payment** from the social fund you must live in England or Wales.[315]

To qualify for either a **funeral expenses payment** or a **funeral support payment**:

- the person who has died must have been ordinarily resident (see p1585) in the UK at the date of death (this does not apply in Scotland if s/he was a stillborn child);[316]

- the funeral must usually take place in the UK. However, it can take place in any EEA state if you or your partner are:[317]
  - an EEA national and a worker (see p1607) or self-employed (see p1608), including if you have retained either status (see p1609);
  - a family member of one of the above (see p1614);
  - an EEA national with a permanent right of residence acquired in less than five years (see p1624);
  - arguably, a person with any other right of residence in the UK under EU law. For further details, see CPAG's *Benefits for Migrants Handbook*.[318]

To qualify for a **children's funeral fund payment**, the funeral must take place in England on or after 23 July 2019, and be for a child aged under 18 or stillborn. There are are no residence (or immigration status) requirements.[319]

Maternity grant payments

To qualify for a **Sure Start maternity grant** from the social fund you must live in England or Wales.[320]

To qualify for a **Best Start grant**, you must:
- be ordinarily resident in Scotland;[321] *and*
- if neither you nor your partner receive a qualifying benefit (a means-tested benefit or tax credits), but you qualify for a grant because you are aged under 20 (see p1699), you must be habitually resident in the UK, Channel Islands, Isle of Man, Switzerland or the EEA (see p1587) or be exempt from this requirement (see p1589).[322]

Winter fuel payments

To qualify for a winter fuel payment, you must be ordinarily resident (see p1585) in Great Britain on any day in the qualifying week (see p806).[323]

European Union co-ordination rules

You are not required to be ordinarily resident in Great Britain in order to be entitled to a winter fuel payment if, on any day in the qualifying week, you are:[324]
- covered by the EU co-ordination rules (see p1672); *and*
- habitually resident in Switzerland or an EEA country (other than Cyprus, France, Gibraltar, Greece, Malta, Portugal, Spain or the UK); *and*
- can demonstrate a 'genuine and sufficient link to the UK' (see p1630).

Tax credits

To be entitled to **child tax credit** (CTC), you (and your partner, if you have made a joint claim) must:[325]
- be present in the UK (see p1583); *and*
- be ordinarily resident in the UK (see p1585); *and*

Part 11: Immigration and residence rules for benefits and tax credits
Chapter 68: Coming from abroad: residence rules
6. Rules for specific benefits and tax credits

- have a right to reside in the UK (see p1594), unless you have been receiving CTC since before 1 May 2004; *and*
- have been living in the UK for the three months prior to your date of claim (unless you are exempt – see p1584).

To be entitled to **working tax credit** (WTC), you (and your partner, if you have made a joint claim) must be:[326]
- present in the UK (see p1583); *and*
- ordinarily resident in the UK (see p1585).

There are limited exceptions for Crown servants posted overseas, and exceptions from the requirement to be ordinarily resident (although in practice, claims are rarely refused on the latter basis).[327]

For the rules on when you can be treated as present, and can therefore either continue to receive tax credits (or make a fresh claim if you are in one of the groups on p1496), see p1662.

Being absent (except when you are treated as being present), ceasing to be ordinarily resident or losing your right to reside are all changes that you must notify to HM Revenue and Customs (HMRC) within one month. If you do not, HMRC may recover any overpaid tax credits (see Chapter 64) and impose a penalty (see Chapter 65).

Couples

If you are a member of a couple and have made a joint tax credit claim, both of you must satisfy the residence requirements. Your entitlement to tax credits as a couple ends if HMRC considers that you and your partner have separated and this is likely to be permanent,[328] or if either you or your partner:
- are abroad for longer than a permitted temporary absence (see p1662);
- (for CTC only) lose the right to reside;
- cease to be ordinarily resident.

If your entitlement to tax credits as a couple ends, you and/or your partner may be entitled to UC (or may be able to make a single claim for tax credits if you are in one of the groups on p1496).

If you receive tax credits on the basis of a single claim, but then your partner returns to the UK or becomes ordinarily resident or acquires a right to reside, you cease to be entitled to tax credits. You may then be entitled to UC (or may be able to make a joint claim for tax credits if you are in one of the groups on p1496).

If you or your partner are abroad (even during a period while treated as being present) and you (or s/he) were the only partner in full-time work, you may lose entitlement to WTC if the requirement to be in full-time work is no longer satisfied (see p300).

You have a duty to notify HMRC of any of the above changes within one month (see p1507). If you fail to do so, HMRC may recover any overpaid tax credits (see Chapter 64) and impose a penalty (see Chapter 65).

European Union co-ordination rules

If the EU co-ordination rules apply to you (see p1672), you may be able to be paid CTC for a partner or child who is resident in an EEA country (see p1680). WTC is not a social security benefit under the EU co-ordination rules (see p1674) and so if your partner is in an EEA state, *you* can be entitled to CTC on the basis of a joint CTC claim, but entitled to WTC on the basis of a single WTC claim.[329]

Notes

2. The different residence and presence tests

1 Reg 85A(2) JSA Regs
2 *AEKM v Department for Communities (JSA)* [2016] NICom 80, paras 21, 46-48 and 61; *TC v SSWP (JSA)* [2017] UKUT 222 (AAC); Vol 2 para 072996 DMG; TCTM 02035; CBTM 10025
3 **CB** Reg 23(5) CB Regs
  CTC Reg 3(6) TC(R) Regs
4 **CB** Reg 23(6) CB Regs
  CTC Reg 3(7) TC(R) Regs
5 **CB** Reg 23(3) CB Regs
  CTC Reg 3(3) TC(R) Regs
6 R(IS) 6/96, para 19; R(P) 2/67; CPC/1035/2005; see also *TC v SSWP (JSA)* [2017] UKUT 222 (AAC)
7 R(M) 1/85
8 *R v Barnet London Borough Council ex parte Shah* [1983] 2 AC 309; *GC v HMRC (TC)* [2014] UKUT 251 (AAC); *Arthur v HMRC* [2017] EWCA Civ 1756, paras 16, 31 and 32
9 *MS v SSWP (DLA)* [2016] UKUT 42 (AAC)

3. Habitual residence

10 **UC** Reg 9 UC Regs
  IS Regs 21 and 21AA IS Regs
  JSA Regs 85 and 85A JSA Regs
  ESA Regs 69 and 70 ESA Regs
  PC Reg 2 SPC Regs
  HB Reg 10 HB Regs; reg 10 HB(SPC) Regs
  AA Reg 2(1)(a)(i) SS(AA) Regs
  DLA Reg 2(1)(a)(i) SS(DLA) Regs
  PIP Reg 16(c) SS(PIP) Regs
  CA Reg 9(1)(a) SS(ICA) Regs
11 Reg 12 CTRS(PR)E Regs; reg 16 CTR(SPC)S Regs; reg 16 CTR(S) Regs; reg 28 CTRSPR(W) Regs; Sch para 19 CTRS(DS)W Regs
12 Regs 3(3), 18(2), 22(3) and 36(3) UC Regs; reg 9(1) UC,PIP,JSA&ESA(C&P) Regs
13 **UC** Reg 9 UC Regs
  PC Reg 2 SPC Regs
14 **IS** Regs 21 and 21AA and Sch 7 para 17 IS Regs
  JSA Regs 85 and 85A and Sch 5 para 14 JSA Regs
  ESA Regs 69 and 70 and Sch 5 para 11 ESA Regs
15 Reg 10(1) HB Regs; reg 10(1) HB(SPC) Regs

Part 11: Immigration and residence rules for benefits and tax credits
Chapter 68: Coming from abroad: residence rules
Notes

16 **AA** s35(1) SSA 1975; reg 2(1) SS(AA)
Regs
DLA s71(6) SSCBA 1992; reg 2(1)
SS(DLA) Regs
PIP s77(3) WRA 2012; reg 16 SS(PIP)
Regs
CA s70(4) SSCBA 1992; reg 9(1) SS(ICA)
Regs
YCG regs 3 and 8 CA(YCG)(S) Regs
BSG Sch 1 paras 1(c) and 4 EYA(BSG)(S)
Regs
17 See, for example, *GE v SSWP (ESA)*
[2017] UKUT 145 (AAC), reported as
[2017] AACR 34, paras 52-58 and *SSWP
v KK (JSA)* [2019] UKUT 313 (AAC), para
8
18 Reg 8 UC(TP) Regs
19 R(IS) 6/96
20 See, for example, DMG Memo 8/18,
para 11; ADM Memo 14/18, para 11 in
relation to claimants of the Windrush
generation, but it applies in all cases.
21 **UC** Reg 9(4) UC Regs
IS Reg 21AA(4) IS Regs
JSA Reg 85A(4) JSA Regs
ESA Reg 70(4) ESA Regs
PC Reg 2(4) SPC Regs
HB Reg 10(3B) HB Regs
22 Reg 3 HB(HR)A Regs
23 reg 8(2) CA(YCG)(S) Regs
24 Sch 2 para 4(1)(b) and (2) EYA(BSG)(S)
Regs
25 **AA** Reg 2(3A) SS(AA) Regs
DLA Reg 2(3A) SS(DLA) Regs
PIP Reg 20 SS(PIP) Regs
CA Reg 9(3) SS(ICA) Regs
26 R(IS) 6/96, paras 17 and 20; CIS/13498/
96, para 17
27 CIS/15927/1996
28 *R v Barnet London Borough Council ex
parte Shah* [1983] 2 AC 309, para 344;
CIS/13498/1996
29 R(IS) 2/00; CIS/4474/2003
30 *Nessa v Chief Adjudication Officer* [1999]
UKHL 41
31 CIS/4474/2003
32 CIS/1972/2003
33 CIS/1304/97; CJSA/5394/98
34 CIS/1304/1997; CJSA/5394/1998
35 Art 70 EU Reg 883/04; Art 10a EU Reg
1408/71; *Swaddling v Adjudication
Officer*, C-90/97 [1999] ECR I-01075
36 CIS/12703/1996
37 *KS v SSWP (SPC)* [2010] UKUT 156
(AAC); see also *TC v SSWP (JSA)* [2017]
UKUT 222 (AAC)
38 R(IS) 2/00; CIS/11481/1995

4. Right to reside
39 Reg 12 CTRS(PR)E Regs; reg 16
CTR(SPC)S Regs; reg 16 CTR(S) Regs;
reg 28 CTRSPR(W) Regs; Sch para 19
CTRS(DS)W Regs
40 **UC** Reg 9(3) UC Regs
IS Reg 21AA(2) and (3) IS Regs
JSA Reg 85A(2) and (3) JSA Regs
ESA Reg 70(2) and (3) ESA Regs
PC Reg 2(2) and (3) SPC Regs
HB Reg 10(3) and (3A) HB Regs; reg
10(3) and (4) HB(SPC) Regs
41 To date all legal challenges to this
exclusion have failed – most recently, *R
(on the application of HC) v SSWP and
Others* [2017] UKSC 73.
42 *Slezak v SSWP* [2017] CSIH 4, reported
as [2017] AACR 21
43 *Fratila and Tanase v SSWP*, CO/3632/
2019, heard 18 and 19 February 2020
44 Reg 6 SS(HR)A Regs; reg 11 SS(PA)A
Regs; see also *AP v SSWP (IS)* [2018]
UKUT 307 (AAC)
45 **CB** Reg 23(4) CB Regs
TC Reg 3(5) TC(R) Regs
46 **UC** Reg 9(3) UC Regs
IS Reg 21AA(2) and (3) IS Regs
JSA Reg 85A(2) and (3) JSA Regs
ESA Reg 70(2) and (3) ESA Regs
PC Reg 2(2) and (3) SPC Regs
HB Reg 10(3) and (3A) HB Regs; reg
10(3) and (4) HB(SPC) Regs
47 **CB** Reg 23(4) CB Regs
TC Reg 3(5) TC(R) Regs
48 **CB** Reg 23(4)(b) and (4A) CB Regs
CTC Reg 3(5)(b)(ii) and (5A) TC(R) Regs;
Regs 5 and 6 Social Security, Child
Benefit and Child Tax Credit
(Amendment) (EU Exit) Regulations
2019, No 1431.
HMRC v HEH and SSWP (TC and CHB)
[2018] UKUT 237 (AAC)
49 Most recently, *R (on the application of
HC) v SSWP and Others* [2017] UKSC 73

5. Who has a right to reside
50 Immigration and Social Security
Coordination (EU Withdrawal) Bill 2019-
21
51 Decision of the EEA Joint Committee
No.158/2007
52 Swiss nationals: *Agreement between the
European Community and its Member
States, of the one part, and the Swiss
Confederation, of the other, on the Free
Movement of Persons*, 21 June 1999,
Cmd 5639. In force from 1 June 2002.
53 Reg 2(1) I(EEA) Regs

54 Reg 1 I(EEA) Regs – except reg 9, which was replaced from 25 November 2016
55 Arts 2(e), 126 and 127 WA 2019; ss1A, 1B, 8A and Sch 2 part 1A EU(W)A 2018
56 ss2-7 EU(W)A Act 2018
57 s1B(3)(d) and (e) EU(W)A 2018
58 Art 132 WA 2019
59 s15A EU(W)A 2018
60 Immigration and Social Security Co-ordination (EU Withdrawal) Bill 2019-21
61 Appendix EU IR
62 Arts 2(e), 126 and 127 Withdrawal Agreement; ss1A and 1B EU(W) 2018
63 gov.uk/view-prove-immigration-status
64 ADM Memo 09/19 para 6; DMG Memo 6/19 para 6
65 confirmed in ADM Memo 09/19 para 7; DMG Memo 6/19 para 7; HB circular A7/2019 para 9
66 Regs 6 and 14(1) I(EEA) Regs. The same groups are covered in Arts 7 and 14 EU Dir 2004/38 but the term 'qualified person' is not used in the Directive.
67 *SSWP v JB (JSA)* [2011] UKUT 96 (AAC)
68 Reg 7(3) I(EEA) Regs
69 *SSWP v Dias*, C-325/09 [2011] ECR I006387; *EM and KN v SSWP* [2009] UKUT 44 (AAC); *MD v SSWP (SPC)* [2016] UKUT 319 (AAC); regs 17(8), 18(7), 19(4) and 20(5) I(EEA) Regs
70 Reg 17 I(EEA) Regs
71 Reg 18 I(EEA) Regs
72 Reg 20 I(EEA) Regs
73 Reg 19 I(EEA) Regs
74 Reg 45 and Sch 6 para 2 I(EEA) Regs
75 Reg 12 I(EEA) Regs
76 *SSWP v Gubeladze* [2019] UKSC 31; see also DMG Memo 11/19 and ADM Memo 14/19 and *AM v SSWP (ESA)* [2019] UKUT 215 (AAC)
77 **Croatia** Reg 8 AC(IWA) Regs
    A2 Reg 9 A(IWA) Regs
78 **Croatia** Regs 4 and 5 AC(IWA) Regs
    A2 Reg 6 A(IWA) Regs
79 Reg 7 A(IWR) Regs
80 Reg 5 A(IWR) Regs
81 The CJEU recently held that this restriction was lawful: *Prefeta v SSWP*, C-618/16 [2018]
82 CIS/1042/2008; *SSWP v JB* [2011] UKUT 96 (AAC)
83 *JK v SSWP (SPC)* [2017] UKUT 179 (AAC); see also *SSWP v LM (ESA) (Interim Decision)* [2017] UKUT 485 (AAC), paras 22-24
84 Reg 2 AC(IWA) Regs; reg 2 A(IWA) Regs
85 Reg 4 A(IWA) Regs; reg 3 A(IWA) Regs
86 Reg 2 A(IWR) Regs

87 Reg 2(8) A(IWR) Regs; *SSWP v LM (ESA) (Interim Decision)* [2017] UKUT 485 (AAC) paras 20-21
88 Reg 2(5) AC(IWA) Regs; reg 2(12) A(IWA) Regs
90 Reg 2(7) A(IWR) Regs
91 *Miskovic and Another v SSWP* [2011] EWCA Civ 16
92 Reg 7 A(IWR) Regs
93 *SSWP v ZA* [2009] UKUT 294 (AAC); *Szpak v SSWP* [2013] EWCA Civ 46
94 *BS v SSWP* [2009] UKUT 16 (AAC)
95 Reg 13(1) and (3) I(EEA) Regs; Arts 6(1) and 14(1) EU Dir 2004/38
96 Reg 13(2) and (3) I(EEA) Regs; Art 6(2) EU Dir 2004/38
97 *GE v SSWP (ESA)* [2017] UKUT 145 (AAC), reported as [2017] AACR 34
98 Art 45 TFEU; Arts 14 and 24 EU Dir 2004/38; reg 6 I(EEA) Regs
99 *The Queen v Immigration Appeal Tribunal, ex parte Antonissen*, C-292/89 [1991] ECR I-00745
100 **Croatia** Reg 5 AC(IWA) Regs
    A2 Reg 6 A(IWR) Regs
    A8 Regs 4(2) and (4) and 5(2) A(IWR) Regs
101 *The Queen v Immigration Appeal Tribunal, ex parte Antonissen*, C-292/89 [1991] ECR I-00745
102 R(IS) 8/08
103 *GE v SSWP (ESA)* [2017] UKUT 145 (AAC), reported as [2017] AACR 34, para 46; see also *Cardiff CC v HM (HB)* [2019] UKUT 271 (AAC), paras 6 and 18 and *SSWP v KK (JSA)* [2019] UKUT 313 (AAC), para 9
104 Reg 6(1) and (7)-(10) I(EEA) Regs
105 Regs 6(1) and 14 I(EEA) Regs; Arts 7(1) and 14 EU Dir 2004/38
106 *Lawrie-Blum v Land Baden-Württemberg*, C-66/85 [1986] ECR 02121
107 *Barry v LB Southwark* [2008] EWCA Civ 1440; *Tarola v Minister for Social Protection*, C-483/17 [2019]
108 *Rinner-Kühn v FWW Spezial-Gebäudereinigung GmbH and Co. KG*, 171/88 [1989] ECR 02743
109 R(IS) 12/98
110 *Genc v Land Berlin*, C-14/09 [2010] ECR I-00931
111 *Steymann v Staatssecretaris van Justitie*, 196/87 [1988] ECR 06159
112 CIS/1837/2006; CIS/868/2008

11

Part 11: Immigration and residence rules for benefits and tax credits
Chapter 68: Coming from abroad: residence rules
Notes

113 *Kempf v Staatssecretaris van Justitie*, C-
139/85 [1986] ECR 1741; *Bettray v
Staatssecretaris van Justitie*, C-344/87
[1989] ECR 01621; *Genc v Land Berlin*, C-
14/09 [2010] ECR I-00931
114 CIS/1502/2007
115 *JA v SSWP (ESA)* [2012] UKUT 122 (AAC),
cited with approval in *EP v SSWP (JSA)*
[2016] UKUT 445 (AAC), para 21
116 Vol 2 paras 073038-40 DMG; paras
C1487-89 ADM; HB A3/2014, para 15;
'*Child Benefit and Child Tax Credit: right to
reside establishing whether an EEA
national is/was a worker or a self-
employed person under EU law*', para 7;
RF v LB Lambeth [2019] UKUT 52 (AAC)
117 CIS/4237/2007
118 *BS v SSWP* [2009] UKUT 16 (AAC)
119 Regs 6(1) and 14 I(EEA) Regs; Arts 7(1)
and 14 EU Dir 2004/38
120 *Jany and Others v Staatssecretaris van
Justitie*, C-268/99 [2001] ECR I-08615
121 Reg 4(1)(b) I(EEA) Regs
122 R(IS)6/00, para 31
123 *TG v SSWP* [2009] UKUT 58 (AAC)
124 *SSWP v JS (IS)* [2010] UKUT 240 (AAC)
125 CIS/1042/2008; *HMRC v GP* [2017]
UKUT 11 (AAC)
126 Art 7(3) EU Dir 2004/38; *Gusa v Minister
for Social Protection (Ireland)*, C-442/16
[2017]; reg 6 I(EEA) Regs
127 *Saint Prix v SSWP*, C-507/12 [2014];
HMRC v Dakneviciute, C-544/18 [2019];
see also ADM Memo 21/19 and DMG
Memo 17/19
128 Reg 5(4) A(IWR) Regs; reg 7A(4) I(EEA)
Regs 2006, as saved by reg 45 and Sch 4
para 2 I(EEA) Regs
129 Art 7(3)(b) and (c) EU Dir 2004/38; *Gusa
v Minister for Social Protection (Ireland)*,
C-442/16 [2017]
130 Reg 6(2)(b) and (c), (3), (4)(b) and (c),
(4A)-(4C) and (5)-(7) I(EEA) Regs
131 *KH v Bury MBC and SSWP* [2020] UKUT
50 (AAC) – permission to appeal must
be requested by 25 May 2020.
132 CH/3314/2005, para 11; *SSWP v MK*
[2013] UKUT 163 (AAC); *SB v SSWP (UC)*
[2019] UKUT 219 (AAC), paras 8-13
133 See, for example, *SSWP v WN (rule 17)*
[2018] UKUT 268 (AAC)
134 *SSWP v Elmi* [2011] EWCA Civ 1403
135 Reg 6(2)(c), (3), (4)(c), (4A), (4B), (4C),
(5) and (6) I(EEA) Regs
136 Art 7(3)(c) EU Dir 2004/38; see, for
example, *Tarola v Minister for Social
Protection*, C-483/17 [2019] and *SB v
SSWP (UC)* [2019] UKUT 219 (AAC)

137 Art 7(3)(b) EU Dir 2004/38; reg 6(2)(b),
(4)(b), (4B), (4C), and (5)-(7) I(EEA)
Regs; *SSWP v MM* [2015] UKUT 128
(AAC), para 54, see also *KH v Bury MBC
and SSWP* [2020] UKUT 50 (AAC), paras
40-41
138 Reg 6(2)(b), (4)(b) and (7) I(EEA) Regs
139 *KH v Bury MBC and SSWP* [2020] UKUT
50 (AAC) – permission to appeal must
be requested by 25 May 2020
140 Confirmed in Vol 2 para 073080 DMG
and para C1403 ADM
141 Vol 2 para 073108 DMG and para
C1422 ADM
142 *KS v SSWP* [2016] UKUT 269 (AAC) and
caselaw cited; Vol 2 paras 073096-
073100 DMG; paras C1412-16 ADM
143 *SSWP v MB and others (JSA)* [2016] UKUT
372 (AAC), reported as [2017] AACR 6,
paras 49-60, especially paras 49 and 57
144 *SSWP v MB and others (JSA)* [2016] UKUT
372 (AAC), reported as [2017] AACR 6,
para 47
145 *OS v SSWP (JSA)* [2017] UKUT 107
(AAC), paras 5-7 and caselaw cited
146 Vol 2 Part 3 DMG; Ch C1 ADM
147 *SSHD v FB* [2010] UKUT 447 (IAC); *LM v
HMRC (CHB)* [2016] UKUT 389 (AAC);
SSWP v LM (ESA) (Interim decision)
[2017] UKUT 485 (AAC), paras 31-34
148 CIS/3890/2005
149 *De Brito v SSHD* [2012] EWCA Civ 709;
Konodyba v RB of K&C [2012] EWCA Civ
982; *Samin v SSHD* [2012] EWCA Civ
1468; *SSWP v LM (ESA) (Interim decision)*
[2017] UKUT 485(AAC), paras 31-34;
see also *BL SSWP (ESA)* [2019] UKUT 364
(AAC), paras 20-23
150 CIS/4304/2007; *HK v SSWP* [2017]
UKUT 421 (AAC), paras 4-6 and 8
151 CIS/3182/2005
152 *SSWP v EM* [2009] UKUT 146 (AAC); see
also *OB v SSWP (ESA)* [2017] UKUT 255
(AAC), para 32
153 CIS/4237/2007
154 CIS/1042/2008; *HMRC v GP* [2017]
UKUT 11 (AAC); see also *HMRC v HD
(CHB) (Second interim decision)* [2018]
UKUT 148 (AAC), paras 2 and 3
155 CIS/731/2007
156 *Saint Prix v SSWP*, C-507/12 [2014];
HMRC v Dakneviciute, C-544/18 [2019];
see also ADM Memo 21/19 and DMG
Memo 17/19
157 *SSWP v SFF and others* [2015] UKUT 502
(AAC); *Weldemichael and Another v SSHD*
[2015] UKUT 540 (IAC)

158 CIS/4304/2007; *SSWP v IR* [2009] UKUT 11 (AAC); *SSWP v SFF and others* [2015] UKUT 502 (AAC), para 40
159 CIS/1934/2006
160 *SSWP v MK* [2013] UKUT 163 (AAC); *VP v SSWP (JSA)* [2014] UKUT 32 (AAC), paras 56-61; *SSWP v MM* [2015] UKUT 128 (AAC), paras 47-52; *SSWP v LM (ESA) (Interim decision)* [2017] UKUT 485 (AAC), para 23
161 *SSWP v IR* [2009] UKUT 11 (AAC)
162 Art 7(1) EU Dir 2004/38; regs 4(1)(c) and (2)-(4), 6(1) and 14(1) I(EEA) Regs
163 *Pensionsversicherungsanstalt v Brey*, C-140/12 [2013], paras 54-57
164 Art 8(4) EU Dir 2004/38
165 Reg 4(4) I(EEA) Regs
166 *SG v Tameside MBC (HB)* [2010] UKUT 243 (AAC)
167 *Pensionsversicherungsanstalt v Brey*, C-140/12 [2013]; *AMS v SSWP (PC) (Final Decision)* [2017] UKUT 381 (AAC), reported as [2018] AACR 27; *AS v SSWP (UC)* [2018] UKUT 260 (AAC), para 43
168 *Commission of the European Communities v Kingdom of Belgium*, C-408/03 [2006] ECR I-02647; *Zhu and Chen v SSHD*, C-200/02 [2004] ECR I-09925; *Alokpa v Ministre du Travail, de l'Emploi et de l'Immigration*, C-86/12 [2013], para 27
169 *VP v SSWP (JSA)* [2014] UKUT 32 (AAC), reported as [2017] AACR 25, paras 88-97
170 *Singh and Others v Minister of Justice and Equality* C-218/14 [2015]
171 *Bajratari v SSHD* C-93/18 [2019]
172 *W (China) and Another v SSHD* [2006] EWCA Civ 1494
173 *SG v Tameside MBC (HB)* [2010] UKUT 243 (AAC); *SSWP v GS (PC)* [2016] UKUT 394 (AAC), reported as [2017] AACR 7
174 Art 7(1) EU Dir 2004/38; regs 4(1)(d) and (2)-(4), 6(1) and 14(1) I(EEA) Regs
175 Art 2(2) EU Dir 2004/38; reg 7(1) I(EEA) Regs
176 *Diatta v Land Berlin*, 267/83 [1985] ECR 00567
177 CIS/2100/2007, which considers the findings of *Centre Public d'Aide Sociale de Courcelles v Lebon*, C-316/85 [1987] ECR 02811; *Zhu and Chen v SSHD*, C-200/02 [2004] ECR I-09925; and *Jia v Migrationsverket*, C-1/05 [2007] ECR I-00001
178 *SSWP v MF (SPC)* [2018] UKUT 179 (AAC)

179 *Reyes v Migrationsverket* C-423/12 [2014]; *Centre Public d'Aide Sociale de Courcelles v Lebon*, C-316/85 [1987] ECR 02811; *ECO v Lim (EEA dependency)* [2013] UKUT 437 (IAC)
180 *Pedro v SSWP* [2009] EWCA Civ 1358; *Jia v Migrationsverket*, C-1/05 [2007] ECR I-00001; *SSHD v Rahman and Others*, C-83/11 [2012]; *Oboh and Others v SSHD* [2013] EWCA Civ 1525
181 *Kerr v DSDNI* [2004] UKHL 23, paras 62-69; para A1405 ADM; Sch 2 para 5(3) Data Protection Act 2018
182 Reg 7(3) I(EEA) Regs; CPC/3588/2006; *SS v SSWP (ESA)* [2010] UKUT 8 (AAC); *SSWP v LZ (SPC)* [2014] UKUT 147 (AAC); *Macastena v SSHD* [2018] EWCA Civ 1558; *SSHD v Aibangbee* [2019] EWCA Civ 339; *MW v SSWP (UC)* [2019] UKUT 184; *AM v SSWP and CC Swansea Council* [2019] UKUT 361 (AAC), paras 19-21
183 Reg 8 I(EEA) Regs. Most of these groups are covered in Art 3 EU Dir 2004/38, but the term is not used.
184 See also *AA (Algeria) v SSHD* [2014] EWCA Civ 1741; *Dauhoo (EEA Regs – Reg 8(2)) v SSHD* [2012] UKUT 79 (IAC)
185 EEA Regs were amended by regs 3 and 4 Immigration (EEA Nationals) (EU Exit) Regs 2019, No.486 following *SSHD v Banger*, C-89/17 [2018]
186 Art 21(1) TFEU; *R v IAT et Surinder Singh ex parte SSHD*, C-370/90 [1992] ECR I-4265; *O and B v Minister voor Immigratie, Integratie en Asiel*, C-456/12 [2014]; *Coman v Inspectoratul General pentru Imigrari*, C-673/16 [2018]
187 *ZA (Reg 9 EEA Regs; abuse of rights) Afghanistan* [2019] UKUT 281 (IAC), para 75; *VW v SSWP (PC)* [2014] UKUT 573 (AAC)
188 Regs 1, 7(4) and 9 I(EEA) Regs since 1 February 2017 and reg 4 and Sch 5 I(EEA) Regs for the prior period from 25 November 2016.
189 Reg 9(4) I(EEA) Regs
190 *O and B v Minister voor Immigratie, Intergratie en Asiel*, C-456/12 [2014]
191 *Minister voor Vreemdelingenzaken en Integratie v Eind*, C-291/05 [2007] ECR I-10719; for a summary of *Eind*, see *B v SSWP* [2017] UKUT 472 (AAC), paras 33-39
192 *ZA (Reg 9 EEA Regs; abuse of rights) Afganistan* [2019] UKUT 281 (IAC)
193 Reg 9(4) I(EEA) Regs

Part 11: Immigration and residence rules for benefits and tax credits
Chapter 68: Coming from abroad: residence rules
Notes

194 Regs 2(1) (see definition of 'EEA national') and 9A I(EEA) Regs; reg 3 I(EEA)A Regs 2018; *Lounes v SSHD*, C-165/16 [2017]; Art 21(1) TFEU; *AS v SSWP (UC)* [2018] UKUT 260 (AAC); *Kovacevic (British Citizen – Art 21 TFEU) Croatia* [2018] UKUT 273 (IAC); *ODS v SSWP (UC)* [2019] UKUT 192 (AAC); DMG Memo 15/18, paras 11-18; ADM Memo 21/18, paras 11-18

195 *McCarthy v SSHD*, C-434-09 [2011] ECR I-03375

196 Reg 10 I(EEA) Regs

197 *Baigazieva v SSHD* [2018] EWCA Civ 1088

198 Reg 14(3) I(EEA) Regs

199 Reg 10(9) I(EEA) Regs

200 Art 12 EU Dir 2004/38

201 Art 12(3) EU Dir 2004/38

202 *Baigazieva v SSHD* [2018] EWCA Civ 1088

203 Art 13 EU Dir 2004/38

204 *Singh and Others v Minister of Justice and Equality*, C- 218/14 [2015]

205 *SSHD v NA*, C-115/15 [2016]

206 Arts 12(1) and 13(1) EU Dir 2004/38

207 *JP v SSWP (ESA)* [2018] UKUT 161 (AAC), paras 12-21; *GA v SSWP (SPC)* [2018] UKUT 172 (AAC), paras 27-44

208 Arts 12, 13 and 18 EU Dir 2004/38

209 Reg 16 I(EEA) Regs

210 *Baumbast and R v SSHD*, C-413/99 [2002] ECR I-07091, para 57; *IP v SSWP (IS)* [2015] UKUT 691 (AAC)

211 See also *London Borough of Harrow v Ibrahim and SSHD*, C-310/08 [2010] ECR I-01065; *Teixeira v London Borough of Lambeth and SSHD*, C-480/08 [2010] ECR I-01107; *GBC Echternach and A Moritz v Minister van Onderwijs en Wetenschappen*, joined cases C-389/87 and C-390/87 [1989] ECR 00723; *Baumbast and R v SSHD*, C-413/99 [2002] ECR I-07091

212 See also *London Borough of Harrow v Ibrahim and SSHD*, C-310/08 [2010] ECR I-01065; *Teixeira v London Borough of Lambeth and SSHD*, C-480/08 [2010] ECR I-01107; *GBC Echternach and A Moritz v Minister van Onderwijs en Wetenschappen*, joined cases C-389/87 and C-390/87 [1989] ECR 00723; *Baumbast and R v SSHD*, C-413/99 [2002] ECR I-07091

213 See also *Zhu and Chen v SSHD*, C-200/02 [2004] ECR I-09925; *SSHD v NA*, C-115/15 [2016]

214 See also *Zambrano v ONEm*, C-34/09 [2011] ECR I-01177; *Dereci and Others v Bundesministerium für Inneres*, C-256/11 [2011] ECR I-11315; see also *DM v SSWP (PIP)* [2019] UKUT 26 (AAC)

215 *Chavez-Vilchez v Raad van bestuur van de Sociale verzekeringsbank* C-133/15 [2017] and caselaw cited

216 Reg 16(8)-(11) I(EEA) Regs. See also *MA v DSD (JSA)* [2011] NICom 205

217 Reg 16(7)(c) I(EEA) Regs

218 linked cases CUC/1190/2019 and CUC/1035/2019

219 *Baumbast and R v SSHD*, C-413/99 [2002] ECR I-07091, para 57; *IP v SSWP (IS)* [2015] UKUT 691 (AAC)

220 *Teixeira v London Borough of Lambeth and SSHD*, C-480/08 [2010] ECR I-01107, para 74; *Bolton MBC v HY (HB)* [2018] UKUT 103 (AAC) and caselaw cited

221 *SSWP v JS (IS)* [2010] UKUT 347 (AAC)

222 *DJ v SSWP* [2013] UKUT 113 (AAC)

223 *Teixeira v London Borough of Lambeth and SSHD*, C-480/08 [2010] ECR I-01107, para 87; see also *Alarape and Tijani v SSHD*, C-529/11 [2013]

224 Reg 16(7(a) I(EEA) Regs; DMG Memo 24/16, para 15; see also CIS/3960/2007; *Shabani v SSHD* [2013] UKUT 315 (IAC)

225 joined cases of *Czop* (C-147/11) and *Punakova* (C-148/11) [2012]; *Hrabkova v SSWP* [2017] EWCA Civ 794 – permission to appeal to UKSC refused

226 *AM v SSWP and CC Swansea Council* [2019] UKUT 361 (AAC), paras 49-64

227 Arts 16 and 17 EU Dir 2004/38; regs 5 and 15 I(EEA) Regs

228 See, for example, *MW v SSWP (UC)* [2019] UKUT 184

229 Art 16(4) EU Dir 2004/38; reg 15(3) I(EEA) Regs - note that the words 'only' and 'consecutive' were removed from these regulations from 1 February 2017, but EU law has not changed and should be followed.

230 Part 4 I(EEA) Regs

231 *Idezuna v SSHD* [2011] UKUT 474 (IAC); *Babajanov v SSHD* [2013] UKUT 513 (IAC)

232 Art 16(3) EU Dir 2004/38; reg 3 I(EEA) Regs

233 *OB v SSWP (ESA)* [2017] UKUT 255 (AAC), paras 29-30 and 34; endorsed in *AP v SSWP (IS)* [2018] UKUT 307 (AAC), paras 15-18

234 *SSHD v Ojo* [2015] EWCA Civ 1301, para 20; *Cardiff City Council v HM (HB)* [2019] UKUT 271(AAC)
235 Vol 2 paras 073433-35 DMG; paras C1812-14 ADM
236 *Nnamdi Onuekwere v SSHD*, C-378/12 [2014]; reg 3(3) I(EEA) Regs
237 Reg 3(3) I(EEA) Regs
238 Reg 15(1) and (2) I(EEA) Regs; Sch 6 para 8 I(EEA) Regs
239 Regs 6(1)(a), 7, 13, 14(1) and (2), 15(1) and Sch 6 para 8 I(EEA) Regs; *GE v SSWP (ESA)* [2017] UKUT 145 (AAC), reported as [2017] AACR 34; Vol 2 para 073428 DMG; para C1807 ADM
240 Art 16(1) EU Dir 2004/38
241 *SSWP v Taous Lassal*, C-162/09 [2010] ECR I-09217; *SSWP v Dias*, C-325-09 [2011] ECR I-06387
242 *Oakafor and Others v SSHD* [2011] EWCA Civ 499; *Alarape and Tijani v SSHD*, C-529/11 [2013]; *Bee and Another v SSHD* [2013] UKUT 83 (IAC)
243 *Ziolkowski* (C-425/10) and *Szeja* (C-425/10) *v Land Berlin* [2011] ECR I-14035
244 *Ziolkowski* (C-425/10) and *Szeja* (C-425/10) *v Land Berlin* [2011] ECR I-14035; Sch 6 para 8(3) I(EEA) Regs
245 See, for example, *MW v SSWP (UC)* [2019] UKUT 184 (AAC)
246 Reg 14(2) I(EEA) Regs
247 Regs 14(2) and 15(1)(a) and (b) I(EEA) Regs
248 Regs 5 and 15 I(EEA) Regs; Art 17 EU Dir 2004/38
249 *SSWP v Gubeladze* [2019] UKSC 31
250 *De Brito v SSHD* [2012] EWCA Civ 709
251 *SSWP v Gubeladze* [2019] UKSC 31; *SSWP v NZ (ESA) (Final decision)* [2019] UKUT 250 (AAC)
252 Art 17(3) EU Dir 2004/38; *PM (EEA – spouse - 'residing with') Turkey* [2011] UKUT 89 (IAC)
253 Reg 15(1)(d) I(EEA) Regs
254 Art 17(1) EU Dir 2004/38; reg 5(7) I(EEA) Regs
255 Art 17(1) EU Dir 2004/38; regs 5(7) and 6(2), and Sch 4 para 2 I(EEA) Regs preserving regs 7A(3) and 7B(4) I(EEA) Regs 2006; *NZ v SSWP (ESA) (Third interim decision)* [2017] UKUT 360 (AAC); see also *SSWP v NZ (ESA)(Final decision)* [2019] UKUT 250 (AAC)
256 Arts 20 and 21 TFEU

6. Rules for specific benefits and tax credits

257 **UC** s4(1)(c) WRA 2012
   IS s124(1) SSCBA 1992
   JSA s1(2)(i) JSA 1995
   ESA s1(3)(d) WRA 2007
   PC s1(2)(a) SPCA 2002
258 **UC** Reg 9 UC Regs
   IS Regs 21-21AA IS Regs
   JSA Regs 85-85A JSA Regs
   ESA Regs 69-70 ESA Regs
   HB Reg 10 HB Regs; reg 10 HB(SPC) Regs
   PC Reg 2 SPC Regs
259 ss3 and 4(1)(c) and (2) WRA 2012; regs 3(3) and 9 UC Regs
260 Regs 3(3) and 36(3) UC Regs
261 ss3 and 4(1)(e) WRA 2012; reg 3(3) UC Regs; reg 9(1) UC,PIP,JSA&ESA(C&P) Regs
262 Regs 3(3), 18(2) and 22(3) UC Regs
263 ss4(1)(d) and 19(6) WRA 2012; regs 14(c) and 86 UC Regs
264 s39 WRA 2012; Regs 62(1),(3) and (4) and 90(3) UC Regs
265 Art 7(2)(b) and (3)(b) WRA(No.31)O; HB Circular A9/2019, paras 15-17; Memo DMG 07/19, para 12
266 s39 WRA 2012; Regs 3, 18(2), 22(3) and 36(3) UC Regs
267 Art 7(2)(b) and (3)(b) WRA(No.31)O; HB Circular A9/2019, paras 15-17; DMG Memo 7/19, para 12
268 **IS** Reg 16 IS Regs
   JSA Reg 78 JSA Regs
   ESA Reg 156 ESA Regs
   PC Reg 5 SPC Regs
   HB Reg 21 HB Regs; reg 21 HB(SPC) Regs
269 CIS/508/1992; CIS/13805/1996
270 CIS/484/1993
271 **UC** Reg 4(7) UC Regs
   IS Reg 16 IS Regs
   JSA Reg 78 JSA Regs
   ESA Reg 156 ESA Regs
   PC Reg 5 SPC Regs
   HB Reg 21 HB Regs; reg 21 HB(SPC) Regs
272 s30(1) PA 2014
273 Arts 5, 6, 7, 42 and 43 EU Reg 883/04
274 Sch 1 para 4 The Social Security (Reciprocal Agreements) Order 2017, No.159; DMG Memo 15/17 para 6
275 s146 SSCBA 1992
276 Reg 23 CB Regs
277 Regs 23, 30 and 31 CB Regs
278 Reg 9 GA(Gen) Regs

Part 11: Immigration and residence rules for benefits and tax credits
Chapter 68: Coming from abroad: residence rules
Notes

279 *RK v HMRC (CHB)* [2015] UKUT 357 (AAC); *JL v HMRC (CHB)* [2017] UKUT 193 (AAC), paras 30-32 and 49
280 *Stewart v SSWP*, C-503/09 [2011] ECR I-06497
281 **AA** Reg 2 SS(AA) Regs
DLA Reg 2 SS(DLA) Regs
PIP Reg 16 SS(PIP) Regs
CA Reg 9 SS(ICA) Regs
282 Linked cases CDLA/2019/2018 and CDLA/2208/2018, hearing listed for 22-24 April 2020
283 **ESA** Reg 11 ESA Regs; reg 12 ESA Regs 2013
IB Reg 16 SS(IB) Regs
SDA Reg 3 SS(SDA) Regs
284 Reg 8 CA(YCG)(S) Regs
285 Reg 2(6) and (7) SS(DLA) Regs
286 **AA** Reg 2(3) SS(AA) Regs
DLA Reg 2(4) SS(DLA) Regs
PIP Reg 21 SS(PIP) Regs
287 **AA** Reg 2C SS(AA) Regs
DLA Reg 2C SS(DLA) Regs
PIP Reg 23A SS(PIP) Regs
CA Reg 9C SS(ICA) Regs
288 ss65(7), 70(4A) and 72(7B) SSCBA; s84 WRA 2012
289 Arts 23-32 EU Reg 883/04
290 **AA** Reg 2A SS(AA) Regs
DLA Reg 2A SS(DLA) Regs
PIP Reg 22 SS(PIP) Regs
CA Reg 9A SS(ICA) Regs
291 Art 6 and Annex XI UK entry para 2 EU Reg 883/04; *SSWP v MM and BK v SSWP* [2016] UKUT 547 (AAC)
292 *Kavanagh and Another v SSWP* [2019] EWCA Civ 272, para 68 – see also para 32: the DWP dropped this part of its appeal against *SSWP v MM and BK v SSWP* [2016] UKUT 547 (AAC), paras 28-31.
293 *Stewart v SSWP*, C-503/09 [2011]; *Kavanagh and Another v SSWP* [2019] EWCA Civ 272; *SSWP v JG (IS)* [2013] UKUT 298 (AAC); *SSWP v Garland* [2014] EWCA Civ 1550. See also ADM Memos 20/17 and 11/19 and DMG Memos 16/17 and 8/19
294 *PB v SSWP (DLA)* [2016] UKUT 280 (AAC)
295 ss1(3)(d) and 18(4)(a) WRA 2007
296 SS(NIRA) Regs; SS(GBRA)NI Regs
297 s94(5) SSCBA 1992
298 Reg 14 SS(IIPD) Regs
299 Reg 10C(5) and (6) SSB(PA) Regs
300 Reg 2 SS(II)(AB) Regs; reg 2 SS(II)(MB) Regs
301 Regs 3, 4, 6 and 8 SS(II)(MB) Regs; regs 3 and 6 SS(II)(AB) Regs

302 Art 5 EU Reg 883/04
303 Art 38 EU Reg 883/04; Art 36 EU Reg 987/09; *SSWP v OF (by MF) (II)* UKUT [2011] 448 (AAC)
304 s1(2)(i) JSA 1995
305 Art 61(2) EU Reg 883/04
306 Art 64 EU Reg 883/04
307 Art 64(3) EU Reg 883/04
308 s2(1) and s35(1) SSCBA 1992. For exceptions, see the Social Security (Maternity Allowance) (Work Abroad) Regulations 1987, No.417; Vol 2 Ch 7, paras 075570-73 DMG
309 s113(1) SSCBA 1992
310 s113 SSCBA 1992; reg 4(1) SSB(PA) Regs
311 Reg 10 SS(WB&RP) Regs
312 Art 52 EU Reg 883/04
313 *Stewart v SSWP*, C-503/09 [2011] ECR I-06497; *SSWP v Garland* [2014] EWCA Civ 1550, paras 14 and 28
314 Reg 9(1) FEA(S) Regs
315 Reg 7(9A) SFM&FE Regs
316 Reg 7(5) SFM&FE Regs; reg 9(2)(a) and (6) FEA(S) Regs
317 Reg 7(9) and (10) SFM&FE Regs; reg 9(2)(b) FEA(S) Regs
318 *John O'Flynn v Adjudication Officer*, C-237/94 [1996] ECR I-02617 (R(IS) 4/98); Art 24 EU Dir 2004/38
319 The Social Fund (Children's Funeral Fund for England) Regulations 2019, No.1064; ADM Memo 13/19 and DMG Memo 10/19
320 Reg 5(6) SFM&FE Regs
321 Sch 2 para 4(1)(a) EYA(BSG)(S) Regs
322 Sch 2 para 4(1)(b) and (2) EYA(BSG)(S) Regs
323 Reg 2 SFWFP Regs
324 Reg 2 SFWFP Regs
325 s3(3) TCA 2002; reg 3(1) and (5) TC(R) Regs
326 s3(3) TCA 2002; reg 3(1) TC(R) Regs; *GC v HMRC (TC)* [2014] UKUT 251 (AAC) contains a useful discussion of these requirements
327 Reg 3 TC(R) Regs
328 s3(5A) TCA 2002
329 CCM 20090, 20160 and 20170; TCTM 09374 and 09376

11

Chapter 69

Going abroad

This chapter covers:
1. The rules on getting paid abroad (below)
2. Rules for specific benefits and tax credits (see p1647)

Key facts
- Most benefits and tax credits are affected if you, or your partner or child, go abroad.
- In certain circumstances, you can continue to receive benefit for a set number of weeks while you are away for a temporary period.
- You may be entitled to receive UK benefits for a longer (or indefinite) period if you go to an European Economic Area (EEA) country.

Brexit
Further to the UK having left the European Union (EU), the rules described in this chapter on your benefit entitlements if you go to an EEA country continue until the end of the transition period which, at the time of writing, was due to end on 31 December 2020. For more information, including the rules after this period, see p1670.

1. The rules on getting paid abroad

Most benefits and tax credits are affected if you, or your partner or child, go abroad. Some can always be paid abroad, some can only be paid in certain circumstances and for limited periods, and some have rules affecting the amount that can be paid if you are abroad.

Your entitlement abroad depends on:
- the benefit or tax credit you are claiming (see p1647);
- the reason why you are going abroad;
- whether your absence is temporary or permanent;
- the length of time you intend to be abroad;
- the country you are going to;

Part 11: Immigration and residence rules for benefits and tax credits
Chapter 69: Going abroad
1. The rules on getting paid abroad

- whether you are covered by the European Union (EU) co-ordination rules;
- whether you are covered by a reciprocal agreement.

Which rules apply

The UK benefit and tax credit legislation contains rules about how your absence affects your entitlement (see below). If these allow your entitlement to continue when you are abroad, you do not need to check the other rules.

The EU co-ordination rules may apply if you are a European Economic Area (EEA) national or a British citizen, or a family member of an EEA national or a British citizen, and you are going to an EEA country. The rules can enable you to be paid your benefits or tax credits when you go to an EEA country for longer than would be the case under UK law. They can also enable you to be paid certain benefits for a family member living in an EEA country.

See pp1647–64 for information on individual benefits and see Chapter 70 for further information on the co-ordination rules.

Note: following the UK leaving the EU, the co-ordination rules continue to apply to you if you go to an EEA country during the transition period which, at the time of writing, was due to end on 31 December 2020. For more information, including the rules after this period, see p1670.

Reciprocal agreements exist between the UK and some other countries, and can assist in similar ways to the EU co-ordination rules. In general, these only apply if the EU co-ordination rules do not assist you. Great Britain and Northern Ireland also have reciprocal agreements. See p1582 for the countries with agreements and see CPAG's *Benefits for Migrants Handbook* for more information on how they can assist.

UK law

Ordinary residence

You must be 'ordinarily resident' in Great Britain (the UK, for child benefit and tax credits) in order to receive some benefits and tax credits (see p1585). If, by going abroad, you cease to be ordinarily resident, your entitlement stops. However, if your absence abroad is temporary and you intend to return to Great Britain (or the UK), your ordinary residence is not usually affected.[1] In practice, it is very rare that ceasing to be ordinarily resident is the reason why your entitlement ends when you go abroad. It is more likely that your entitlement ends simply because you are absent (see below). If you receive a decision that your entitlement to a benefit or tax credit has ended because you have ceased to be ordinarily resident, ask for the decision to be looked at again and get specialist advice.

Presence and absence

Most benefits require you to be **present** in Great Britain (the UK, for tax credits). There are rules that allow you to be treated as present and therefore still entitled to the benefit or tax credit in specified circumstances during a temporary absence. Some benefits also have a rule that disqualifies you from entitlement if you are **absent** from Great Britain. There are specified exemptions to this rule for each benefit.

'**Presence**' means being physically present in Great Britain (the UK, for tax credits) and '**absence**' means not physically present in Great Britain. You count as present on the day you arrive or return from an absence. In general, you also count as present on the day you go abroad.[2] However, for housing benefit the day of departure counts as your first day of absence from Great Britain.[3]

Temporary absence

In specified circumstances, you can be treated as present, and therefore entitled to benefit, during a temporary absence.

For tax credits, child benefit (for your, not the child's, absence), attendance allowance (AA), disability living allowance (DLA) and personal independence payment (PIP), you are defined as being temporarily absent from Great Britain (the UK, for tax credits), if, at the beginning of the period of absence, you are unlikely to be absent for more than 52 weeks.[4]

For all other benefits, temporary absence is not defined and you must demonstrate that your absence will be temporary.[5] Provide full details of why you are going abroad, how long you intend to be away, and what you intend to do while abroad. **Note:** although your intentions are relevant, they are not decisive.[6] If your circumstances change while you are abroad (eg, you go abroad for one reason and decide to stay abroad for a different purpose), your absence may no longer be regarded as temporary.[7] Although there is no set period for a temporary absence (except for tax credits, child benefit, AA, DLA and PIP), as a general rule absences of more than 12 months are not considered to be temporary unless there are exceptional circumstances.[8] If the purpose of the trip abroad is obviously temporary (eg, for a holiday, to visit friends or relatives or for a particular course of medical treatment) and you buy a return ticket, your absence should be viewed as temporary.

2. Rules for specific benefits and tax credits

Bereavement benefits

In general, bereavement benefits are payable while you are abroad. However, your benefit is not uprated each year if you have ceased to be ordinarily resident in Great Britain on the day before the annual uprating takes place,[9] unless you have gone to a European Economic Area (EEA) country and you are covered by the European Union (EU) co-ordination rules (see p1648) or can rely on a reciprocal agreement (see p1628).

Part 11: Immigration and residence rules for benefits and tax credits
Chapter 69: Going abroad
2. Rules for specific benefits and tax credits

If you were abroad on the date your spouse or civil partner died, you are only entitled to a bereavement support payment if, despite your absence, you were ordinarily resident in Great Britain on that date (see p1627), or the EU co-ordination rules apply or a reciprocal agreement applies.

European Union co-ordination rules

If you are covered by the EU co-ordination rules (see p1672):[10]

- and you go to stay or live in an EEA country, you can be paid your bereavement support payment or widowed parent's allowance for as long as you would receive them if you remained in Great Britain, including any annual uprating. See p1679 for more information on exporting benefits;
- for bereavement support payment, if the UK is your 'competent state' (see p1676), the requirement to be ordinarily resident in Great Britain on the date your spouse or civil partner died does not apply if you were resident in an EEA country on that date.

Child benefit and guardian's allowance

Child benefit

You and your child can be treated as being present in Great Britain during a temporary absence (see p1647).

Provided you are ordinarily resident, you continue to be entitled to child benefit for:[11]

- **the first eight weeks;** *or*
- **the first 12 weeks** of any period of absence, or any extension to that period, which is in connection with:
  - the treatment of an illness or disability of you, your partner, a child for whom you are responsible, or another relative of you or your partner; *or*
  - the death of your partner, a child or qualifying young person for whom you or your partner are responsible, or another relative of you or your partner.

Relative

'**Relative**' means brother, sister, parent, grandparent, great-grandparent, child, grandchild or great-grandchild.[12]

Your child is treated as being present during a temporary absence for:[13]

- the first 12 weeks; *or*
- any period during which s/he is absent for the specific purpose of being treated for an illness or disability which began before her/his absence began; *or*
- any period when s/he is in Northern Ireland; *or*
- any period during which s/he is absent because s/he is:
  - receiving full-time education at a school or college in an EEA country or in Switzerland; *or*

– engaged in an educational exchange or visit made with the written approval of the school or college which s/he normally attends; *or*

– a child who normally lives with a Crown servant posted overseas who is either in the same country as her/him or is absent from that country for one of the reasons in the above two bullet points.[14]

If a child is born outside the UK during the eight- or 12-week period in which you could be treated as being present in Great Britain, s/he is treated as being in the UK for up to 12 weeks from the start of your absence.[15]

While you and your child are present, or treated as present, you can continue to receive child benefit that was already in payment and can also make a fresh claim during your, or her/his, absence.

Guardian's allowance

Entitlement to guardian's allowance depends on entitlement to child benefit, so you can be paid guardian's allowance abroad for the same period as child benefit.

However, your guardian's allowance is not uprated each year if you have ceased to be ordinarily resident in Great Britain on the day before the annual uprating takes place,[16] unless you have gone to an EEA country and you are covered by the EU co-ordination rules (see below) or you can rely on a reciprocal agreement.

European Union co-ordination rules

Child benefit and guardian's allowance are classed as 'family benefits' under the EU co-ordination rules. If you are covered by these rules (see p1672):

* you can be paid child benefit and guardian's allowance for a child resident in an EEA country. S/he does not have to be in education; *and/or*

* you can be paid child benefit and guardian's allowance if you are an EEA national and you go to stay or live in an EEA country. Your benefit is uprated in the normal way.

See p1680 for more information.

Disability benefits and carer's allowance

You can be treated as present in Great Britain, and therefore continue to be entitled to (or begin a period of entitlement to, or count the period towards the past presence required for) attendance allowance (AA), disability living allowance (DLA), personal independence payment (PIP) or carer's allowance (CA), during an absence abroad:[17]

* (for AA, DLA and PIP only) for the first **13 weeks** of a 'temporary absence' (see p1647);

Part 11: Immigration and residence rules for benefits and tax credits
Chapter 69: Going abroad
2. Rules for specific benefits and tax credits

- (for AA, DLA and PIP only) for the first **26 weeks** of a 'temporary absence' (see p1647) if the absence is solely in connection with medical treatment for your illness or disability that began before you left Great Britain;
- (for CA only) for up to **four weeks** if your absence is, and was when it began, for a temporary purpose and does not exceed four weeks. If you are not accompanied by the person for whom you are caring, you must satisfy the rules that entitle you to CA during a break from caring (see p563);
- (for CA only) if your absence is temporary and is for the specific purpose of caring for someone who is also absent from Great Britain and who continues to receive AA, DLA care component paid at the highest or middle rate, the daily living component of PIP, armed forces independence payment or constant attendance allowance;
- if you are an airman or airwoman, mariner or continental shelf worker;
- while you are a serving member of the armed forces, or you are living with your spouse, civil partner, son, daughter, stepson, stepdaughter, father, father-in-law, stepfather, mother, mother-in-law or stepmother who is a serving member of the armed forces.

You must also continue to be habitually resident (see p1586). You are treated as being habitually resident if you are covered by the last bullet point above.

If your entitlement to PIP ended because you went abroad and the rules above did not apply for the whole period you were away, and you return to Great Britain within 12 months, a new claim for PIP can be assessed on the basis of the information held about your last claim if your needs have not changed. The DWP refers to this as a 'rapid reclaim'.[18]

You can continue to be paid an increase in your CA for your spouse/civil partner or dependent adult while s/he is abroad, provided you continue to be entitled to CA and reside with her/him. **Note:** you can be treated as residing together during a temporary absence from each other.[19]

You can claim a **young carer grant** while you are ordinarily resident in an EEA country or Switzerland if you previously received a young carer grant when ordinarily resident in Scotland (see p1629).

European Union co-ordination rules

If you move to an EEA country and are covered by the EU co-ordination rules (see p1672), you can continue to be paid (or make a new claim for) AA, the care component of DLA, the PIP daily living component and CA without having to satisfy the presence, past presence and habitual residence tests (see p1629) if:[20]

- you are habitually resident in an EEA country or Switzerland; *and*
- you can demonstrate a 'genuine and sufficient link to the UK' (see p1630).

You can continue to be paid for as long as the UK continues to be your 'competent state' (see p1676).[21]

The above rule has only been in force since April 2013. For the circumstances in which you could be paid in an EEA country before this date, see CPAG's *Benefits for Migrants Handbook*.

DLA mobility component and PIP mobility component are classed as 'special non-contributory benefits' and so can only be paid when you are resident in the UK.[22]

If you receive CA while in the UK and the EU co-ordination rules apply to you, you may be able to continue to be paid an addition for an adult or child who goes to stay or live in an EEA country. See p1680 for more information.

Employment and support allowance

You cannot normally get employment and support allowance (ESA) if you are not in Great Britain.[23] However, provided you meet the other conditions of entitlement, if you were entitled to ESA immediately before leaving Great Britain and are temporarily absent, you can continue to be entitled:[24]

- **indefinitely** if:
  - your absence is for NHS treatment at a hospital or other institution outside Great Britain; *or*
  - you are living with your spouse, civil partner, son, stepson, daughter, stepdaughter, father, father-in-law, stepfather, mother, mother-in-law or stepmother who is a serving member of the armed forces; *or*
- **for the first four weeks**, if your absence is unlikely to exceed 52 weeks; *or*
- **for the first 26 weeks**, if your absence is unlikely to exceed 52 weeks and is solely in connection with arrangements made to treat:
  - your disease or disablement which is directly related to your limited capability for work which began before you left Great Britain; *or*
  - the disease or disablement of a dependent child who you are accompanying.

The treatment must be carried out by, or under the supervision of, a person qualified to provide medical treatment, physiotherapy or similar treatment.

If you are going to Northern Ireland from Great Britain (or vice versa), see p1631.

Note: there are also rules on when you can receive housing costs in your income-related ESA if you are temporarily absent from your home (see p371).

If your partner is abroad

If you are the claimant and you stay in Great Britain, your income-related ESA includes an amount for your partner for:[25]

- the first four weeks s/he is abroad; *or*
- the first 26 weeks if s/he is accompanying a child abroad for treatment in line with the 26-week rule above.

Part 11: Immigration and residence rules for benefits and tax credits
Chapter 69: Going abroad
2. Rules for specific benefits and tax credits

If both you and your partner are abroad, your income-related ESA includes an amount for your partner for the first 26 weeks if both of you are accompanying a child abroad for treatment in line with the 26-week rule above.[26]

After this four- or 26-week period, your benefit is reduced because your applicable amount is calculated as if you have no partner. However, your partner is still treated as being part of your household, and therefore her/his work, income and capital affect your income-related ESA entitlement, unless you are no longer treated as a couple (see p322).[27]

European Union co-ordination rules

If you are covered by the co-ordination rules (see p1672) and the UK is your 'competent state' (see p1676), you can, if you go to live in an EEA country, continue to be paid contributory ESA after the assessment phase, when it is classed as an 'invalidity benefit' (and, in most cases, also during the assessment phase – see p1674).

If the UK continues to pay your contributory ESA while you are resident in an EEA country, the DWP continues to assess your limited capability for work and your limited capability for work-related activity. However, any checks and medicals take place in the state in which you live and the reports are sent to the DWP.[28]

Income-related ESA is listed as a 'special non-contributory benefit' (see p1676) and the EU co-ordination rules cannot help you to be paid abroad. You can only be paid income-related ESA abroad under the UK rules on p1655.

Housing benefit

You cannot normally get housing benefit (HB) if you are not in Great Britain due to the requirements for you to be occupying your home.[29] However, provided you meet the other conditions of entitlement, HB can be paid when you are temporarily absent from Great Britain for:[30]

- **up to four weeks**, if your absence is not expected to exceed this; or
- **up to eight weeks**, if your absence is not expected to exceed that and is in connection with the death of your partner, your child or qualifying young person who normally lived with you or your (or her/his) close relative and the local authority considers it unreasonable for you to return to Great Britain within four weeks; or
- **up to 26 weeks**, if your absence is not expected to exceed this and it is solely in connection with your (or your partner's or child's or qualifying young person's) medical treatment, or medically approved convalescence.

Note:
- The periods for which you can continue to be entitled to HB while you are absent abroad are shorter than if you were absent from your home but remain in Great Britain (see p182).

- The period of absence starts on the day you leave Great Britain.[31]
- If you are (or you are a family member of) an EEA national with a right to reside in the UK (see p1595) and go abroad to an EEA country, it is arguable that the shorter period for which you can be entitled while abroad is discriminatory under EU law and should not apply (see p1678).[32]

If your partner or child is abroad

Whether or not you have amounts included in your HB for your partner or child who is abroad depends on whether s/he is treated as part of your household (see p322 and p327). The amount of HB you are entitled to may also depend on whether s/he is treated as occupying the home (see p182).[33]

European Union co-ordination rules

HB is not a social security benefit under the EU co-ordination rules (see p1674). This means that the EU co-ordination rules cannot assist you and, if you go to an EEA country, you can only be paid under the UK rules above.

Income support

You cannot normally get income support (IS) if you are not in Great Britain.[34] However, IS can be paid when you are temporarily absent from Great Britain, provided you meet the other conditions of entitlement:[35]

- **indefinitely** if your absence is for NHS treatment at a hospital or other institution outside Great Britain; or
- **during the first four weeks** of your absence, if it is unlikely to exceed 52 weeks and:
  - you are in Northern Ireland; or
  - you and your partner are both abroad and s/he satisfies the conditions for one of the pensioner premiums, the disability premium or the severe disability premium (see p339); or
  - you are enititled to statutory sick pay (SSP) and are abroad for the sole purpose of receiving treatment (see p1653) for the incapacity that entitles you to SSP; or
  - you have been continuously entitled to SSP for 364 days before you go abroad (or for 196 days if you are terminally ill or receiving the highest rate of DLA care component, the enhanced rate of the daily living component of PIP or armed forces independence payment). Two or more periods of entitlement to SSP are treated as continuous if the break between them is not more than 56 days each time; or
  - you are not in one of the following groups of people who can claim IS (see p234):
    - a person in 'relevant education'; or

Part 11: Immigration and residence rules for benefits and tax credits
Chapter 69: Going abroad
2. Rules for specific benefits and tax credits

- involved in a trade dispute, or have returned to work for 15 days or less following the dispute; *or*
- entitled to SSP (other than in the situation above); *or*
- **during the first eight weeks** of your absence, if it is unlikely to exceed 52 weeks and is solely in connection with arrangements made for the treatment (see below) of a disease or disablement of a child or qualifying young person. The child or young person must be a member of your family (see p323).

'Treatment' must be carried out by, or under the supervision of, a person qualified to provide medical treatment, physiotherapy or similar treatment.

Note: there are also rules on when you can receive housing costs in your IS if you are temporarily absent from your home (see 371).

If your partner is abroad

If you are the IS claimant and you stay in Great Britain, your IS applicable amount includes an amount for your partner who is abroad for:[36]

- the first four weeks; *or*
- the first eight weeks if s/he meets the conditions of the eight-week rule above.

If both you and your partner are abroad, your IS includes amounts for your partner for the first eight weeks if you both meet the conditions of the eight-week rule above.[37]

After this four- or eight-week period, your benefit is reduced because your applicable amount is calculated as if you have no partner. However, your partner is still treated as being part of your household and therefore her/his work, income and capital affect your IS entitlement, unless you are no longer treated as a couple (see p322).[38]

If your child is abroad

If you were getting an amount in your IS for your child before s/he went abroad, you can continue to be paid for her/him for:[39]

- the first four weeks; *or*
- the first eight weeks, if your child meets the conditions of the eight-week rule above.

European Union co-ordination rules

IS is not a social security benefit under the EU co-ordination rules (see p1674). This means that the EU co-ordination rules cannot assist you and if you go to an EEA country, you can only be paid under the UK rules above.

Industrial injuries benefits

Disablement benefit and retirement allowance are not affected if you go abroad.[40]

Constant attendance allowance and exceptionally severe disablement allowance are payable for the first six months of a temporary absence, or a longer period that the DWP may allow.[41]

Reduced earnings allowance (REA) can be paid while you are temporarily absent abroad for the first three months, or longer if the DWP allows, if:[42]

- your absence from Great Britain is *not* in connection with employment, trade or business; *and*
- your claim was made before you left Great Britain; *and*
- you were entitled to REA before going abroad.

Note: REA has now been abolished. If you break your claim, you may no longer be eligible for benefit.

European Union co-ordination rules

Industrial injuries benefits, except retirement allowance, are classed as 'benefits for accidents at work and occupational diseases' under the EU co-ordination rules (see p1674). If you are covered by these rules (see p1672) and you go to stay or live in an EEA country, you can be paid industrial injuries benefits (except retirement allowance) without any time limit and they are fully uprated each year. See p1679 for more details.

Jobseeker's allowance

You cannot normally get jobseeker's allowance (JSA) if you are not in Great Britain.[43] However, provided you meet the other conditions of entitlement, JSA can be paid when you are temporarily absent:[44]

- **indefinitely**, if you are entitled to JSA immediately before leaving Great Britain and your absence is for NHS treatment at a hospital or other institution outside Great Britain; *or*
- **for up to four weeks**, if you are entitled to JSA immediately before leaving Great Britain and:
  - your absence is unlikely to exceed 52 weeks, you continue to satisfy the conditions of entitlement and you are in Northern Ireland. **Note:** the reciprocal agreements between Great Britain and Northern Ireland can mean that after four weeks, the administration of your claim transfers to Northern Ireland – you do not need to make a new claim;[45] *or*
  - (except if you come under the universal credit (UC) system – see p23) the absence is unlikely to exceed 52 weeks, you continue to satisfy the conditions of entitlement and your partner is also abroad with you and satisfies the conditions for one of the pensioner premiums, the disability premium or the severe disability premium (see p339); *or*

Part 11: Immigration and residence rules for benefits and tax credits
Chapter 69: Going abroad
2. Rules for specific benefits and tax credits

- – (except if you come under the UC system) you are in receipt of a training allowance;[46] *or*
- **for up to eight weeks,** if you are entitled to JSA immediately before leaving Great Britain and your absence is unlikely to exceed 52 weeks and is solely in connection with arrangements made to treat a disease or disablement of a child or qualifying young person. The treatment must be carried out by, or under the supervision of, a person qualified to provide medical treatment, physiotherapy or similar treatment and the child or young person must be a member of your family (see p323); *or*
- **for an absence of up to seven days,** if you are attending a job interview and you notified your work coach before you left (in writing if required). On your return, you must satisfy her/him that you attended the interview as stated; *or*
- **for an absence of up to 15 days,** to train as a member of the reserve forces.

You can be treated as being available for work and actively seeking work or, if you come under the UC system (see p23), you are exempt from the work search requirement and are treated as 'able and willing immediately to take up work' during certain temporary absences abroad. These are similar to, but more limited than, those listed above (see p1118, p1126 and p1073).[47]

Note: there are also rules on when you can receive housing costs in your income-based JSA if you are temporarily absent from your home (see p371).

Joint-claim jobseeker's allowance if your partner is abroad

If you are a joint-claim couple (see p253) and your partner is temporarily absent from Great Britain **on the date you make your claim,** you are paid as a couple for:[48]

- **an absence of up to seven days,** if your partner is attending a job interview;
- **up to four weeks,** if your partner is:
  - – in Northern Ireland and the absence is unlikely to exceed 52 weeks; *or*
  - – getting a training allowance in the circumstances above.

If you are a joint-claim couple and your partner goes abroad **after you claimed** JSA, and her/his absence is for NHS treatment at a hospital or other institution outside Great Britain, you continue to be paid as a couple for up to four weeks.[49]

After this seven-day/four-week period, your JSA is reduced because your applicable amount is calculated as if you have no partner.[50] However, your partner is still treated as part of your household if s/he is abroad for treatment in the circumstances above. Therefore, her/his work, income and capital affects your joint-claim JSA entitlement, unless s/he ceases to be treated as part of your household for another reason (see p322).[51]

Income-based jobseeker's allowance if your partner is abroad

If you are the income-based JSA claimant and you stay in Great Britain, your applicable amount includes an amount for your partner while s/he is abroad for:[52]

- **the first four weeks** of a temporary absence; *or*
- **the first eight weeks** if your partner meets the conditions of the eight-week rule on p1656.

If both you and your partner are abroad, your applicable amount includes an amount for your partner for the first eight weeks if both of you meet the conditions of the eight-week rule on p1656.[53]

After this four- or eight-week period, your benefit is reduced because your applicable amount is calculated as if you have no partner. However, your partner is still treated as being part of your household, and therefore her/his work, income and capital affect your income-based JSA entitlement unless you are no longer treated as a couple (see p322).[54]

Income-based jobseeker's allowance if your child is abroad

If you were getting JSA for your child before s/he went abroad, you can continue to be paid for her/him for:[55]

- **the first four weeks**; *or*
- **the first eight weeks** if your child meets the conditions of the eight-week rule on p1655.

European Union co-ordination rules

Contribution-based JSA is classed as an 'unemployment benefit' under the EU co-ordination rules (see p1674). If you are covered by these rules (see p1672) and the UK is your 'competent state' (see p1676), you can continue to be paid contribution-based JSA for up to three months if:[56]

- you satisfied the conditions for contribution-based JSA for at least four weeks before you left the UK, unless the DWP authorised you to go abroad before then; *and*
- you register as unemployed in the EEA state you go to within seven days and comply with its procedures.

Income-based JSA is classed as a 'special non-contributory benefit' under the EU co-ordination rules (see p1676) and, therefore, these rules cannot assist you to be paid income-based JSA abroad. You can only be paid income-based JSA abroad under the UK rules on p1655.

Maternity allowance, incapacity benefit and severe disablement allowance

If you are temporarily absent from Great Britain, you can continue to be paid maternity allowance (MA), incapacity benefit (IB) and severe disablement allowance (SDA) if:[57]

- you are receiving AA, DLA, PIP or armed forces independence payment (see p1649); *or*

Part 11: Immigration and residence rules for benefits and tax credits
Chapter 69: Going abroad
2. Rules for specific benefits and tax credits

- the DWP agrees. You can then receive the benefit for the first 26 weeks of your temporary absence; *or*
- you are the spouse, civil partner, son, stepson, daughter, stepdaughter, father, stepfather, father-in-law, mother, stepmother or mother-in-law of a serving member of the armed forces, and you are abroad only because you are living with her/him.

In addition:
- when you left Great Britain, you must have been continuously incapable of work for six months and have been continuously incapable since your departure; *or*
- your absence from Great Britain must be for the specific purpose of being treated for an incapacity which began before you left Great Britain; *or*
- for IB only, the incapacity for work is the result of a personal injury caused by an accident at work (see p683) and your absence from Great Britain is for the specific purpose of receiving treatment for it.

If you are due to have a medical examination, this can be arranged abroad.

Note: most IB and SDA claims have been transferred to ESA (see p655). If you lose entitlement to IB or SDA by going abroad, you are not entitled to contributory ESA on your return if you do not satisfy the contribution conditions at that time.

You can continue to be paid an increase for your spouse/civil partner or dependent adult in your IB or SDA while s/he is abroad if you are entitled to IB/SDA and you are residing with her/him. You can be treated as residing together during a temporary absence from each other.[58]

European Union co-ordination rules

If you are covered by the EU co-ordination rules (see p1672) and the UK is your 'competent state' for the payment of this benefit (see p1676):
- you can be paid MA if you go to stay or live in an EEA country, as MA is classed as a 'maternity benefit' under the EU co-ordination rules (see p1674);[59]
- you can continue to be paid your IB and SDA if you go to live in an EEA country, as both are classed as 'invalidity benefits' under the EU co-ordination rules (see p1674). Provided you continue to satisfy the rules of entitlement, benefit is paid without any time limit and at the same rate as if you were still in the UK, including your annual uprating. The state from which you claim benefit is the one that determines your degree of invalidity, but any checks and medicals take place in the country in which you are living and the reports are then sent to the paying state;[60]
- if you remain in the UK, you may be able to continue to be paid an increase in your IB or SDA for an adult or child if s/he goes to stay or live in an EEA coountry (see p1680).

See p1679 for more details on exporting benefits.

Pension credit

You cannot normally get pension credit (PC) if you are not in Great Britain.[61] However, provided you meet the other conditions of entitlement, PC can be paid when you are temporarily absent from Great Britain for:[62]

- **up to four weeks**, if your absence is not expected to exceed this; *or*
- **up to eight weeks**, if your absence is not expected to exceed that and is in connection with the death of your partner, your child or qualifying young person who normally lived with you or your (or her/his) close relative and the DWP considers it unreasonable for you to return to Great Britain within four weeks; *or*
- **up to 26 weeks**, if your absence is not expected to exceed this and it is solely in connection with your (or your partner's or child's or qualifying young person's) medical treatment, or medically approved convalescence.

'Qualifying young person' is defined as it is for UC (see p62) but someone receiving UC, IS, JSA or ESA is not a qualifying young person.[63]

'Close relative' is defined as it is for UC (see p90).[64]

Note: there are also rules on when you can receive housing costs in your PC if you are temporarily absent from your home (see p371).

If your partner is abroad

If you are entitled to PC and your partner is abroad, your PC only includes an amount for her/him if s/he is covered by the rules above.[65] After this, s/he is not treated as being part of your household and you are paid as a single person. Your partner can also stop being treated as part of your household in the circumstances on p322.[66] **Note:** if your partner is under pension age and ceases to be treated as part of your household, when s/he returns you will not be able to include her/him in your PC claim, but may instead be able to claim UC (see p271).

If your child is abroad

You are treated as not responsible for your child or qualifying young person, and therefore not entitled to an amount for her/him within your PC, if s/he is temporarily absent from Great Britain for more than:[67]

- **four weeks**, if her/his absence is not expected to exceed this; *or*
- **eight weeks**, if her/his absence is not expected to exceed this and is in connection with the death of your partner, a child or qualifying young person who normally lives with you, a close relative of hers/his, yours or your partner's, and the DWP considers it unreasonable for her/him to return to Great Britain within four weeks; *or*
- **up to 26 weeks**, if her/his absence is not expected to exceed this and it is solely in connection with her/his or your or your partner's medical treatment, or medically approved convalescence.

Part 11: Immigration and residence rules for benefits and tax credits
Chapter 69: Going abroad
2. Rules for specific benefits and tax credits

'Qualifying young person' is defined as it is for UC (see p62) but someone receiving UC, IS, JSA or ESA is not a qualifying young person.[68]

'Close relative' is defined as it is for UC (see p90).[69]

European Union co-ordination rules

PC is classed as a 'special non-contributory benefit' under the EU co-ordination rules (see p1676) and, therefore, these rules cannot assist you to be paid PC abroad.

You can only be paid PC abroad under the UK rules on p1659.

Retirement pension

All retirement pensions are payable without time limit while you are abroad.[70] However, unless you have gone to an EEA country and you are covered by the EU co-ordination rules or you can rely on a reciprocal agreement (see p1661), if you are not ordinarily resident (see p1585) in Great Britain:[71]

- on the day before the annual uprating takes place, your benefit is not uprated each year;
- for state pension only, when you claim a pension that you have deferred, the upratings that occurred while you were abroad are ignored when calculating both the deferral increase and rate payable;
- for 'old' retirement pensions only, you cannot stop claiming your pension ('de-retire') in order to accrue a deferral payment.[72]

Although category D retirement pension is payable if you are abroad, you must meet the residence requirements at the date you claim, see p1634.

You can continue to be paid an increase in your category A retirement pension for your spouse/civil partner or dependent adult while s/he is abroad if you are entitled to the pension and residing with her/him.[73] You can be treated as residing together during a temporary absence from each other.[74]

European Union co-ordination rules

Retirement pensions are classed as 'old age benefits' under the EU co-ordination rules (see p1674). If you are covered by these rules (see p1672) and the UK is your 'competent state' (see p1676):

- if you go to stay or live in an EEA country, you can continue to be paid your retirement pension without time limit and it is paid at the same rate as if you were still in the UK, including your annual uprating (see p1679);
- you can opt to stop claiming your pension ('de-retire') in order to accrue a deferral payment while living in an EEA country;
- if you remain in the UK, you may be able to continue to be paid an increase for an adult or child if s/he goes to stay or live in an EEA country (see p1680).

At the time of writing, UK government guidance stated that if you were living in an EEA country by the end of the transition period (which was due to end 31 December 2020), your retirement pension would be paid and uprated each year, even if you did not start claiming your pension until after the end of the transition period.[75] If you are living in Ireland before or after the end of the transition period, your retirement pension will be paid and uprated due to a new Convention on Social Security between the UK and Ireland. Your entitlements if you move to an EEA country after the end of the transition period will depend on the terms of any new agreements. For more details on the transition period and the rules afterwards, see p1670.

Reciprocal agreements

If you are covered by a reciprocal agreement (see p1581) that provides for uprating, you can be paid your pension at the same rate as if you were still in the UK, including your annual uprating.

Note: the agreements with Canada and New Zealand, and the former agreement with Australia, do not provide for uprating.

Statutory payments

There are no presence or residence rules for SSP, statutory maternity pay (SMP), statutory adoption pay (SAP), statutory paternity pay (SPP), statutory shared parental pay (SSPP) and statutory parental bereavement pay (SPBP). You remain entitled to these benefits if you go abroad, provided you meet the normal rules of entitlement, including those relating to being an employee (see Chapters 38 and 39).[76]

Although you are generally required to be employed in Great Britain to count as an 'employee', you count as an employee even while employed abroad in certain circumstances, including if:[77]

- your employer is required to pay secondary class 1 national insurance (NI) contributions for you; *or*
- you are a continental shelf worker or, in certain circumstances, an airman or airwoman or mariner; *or*
- you are employed in an EEA country and, had you been employed in Great Britain, you would have been considered an employee, and the UK is the competent state under the EU co-ordination rules (see p1676).

Your employer is not required to pay you SSP, SMP, SAP, SPP or SSPP if:[78]

- your employer is not required by law to pay employer's class 1 NI contributions (even if those contributions are in fact made) because, at the time they become payable, your employer:
  - is not resident or present in Great Britain; *and*
  - has (or is treated as having) no place of business in Great Britain; *or*

Part 11: Immigration and residence rules for benefits and tax credits
Chapter 69: Going abroad
2. Rules for specific benefits and tax credits

- because of an international treaty or convention, your employer is exempt from the Social Security Acts or those Acts are not enforceable against your employer.

European Union co-ordination rules

It is arguable that SSP is a 'sickness benefit' and SMP, SAP, SPP, SSPP and SPBP are 'maternity/paternity benefits' under the co-ordination rules (see p1674). This can be relevant if you need add together periods of employment under the 'aggregation principle' (see p1678) or export one of these benefits to an EEA state (see p1679).

Tax credits

Provided you are ordinarily resident, you can be treated as present and therefore entitled to child tax credit (CTC) and working tax credit (WTC) during a 'temporary absence' (see p1647) for:[79]
- **the first eight weeks**; or
- **the first 12 weeks** of any period of absence, or any extension to this period of absence, which is in connection with:
  - treating an illness or disability of you, your partner, a child for whom you are responsible, or another relative (see below) of either you or your partner; or
  - the death of your partner, a child or qualifying young person for whom you or your partner are responsible, or another relative (see below) of you or your partner.

Relative

'Relative' means brother, sister, parent, grandparent, grandchild, great-grandparent or child.[80]

You are also treated as present if you are:[81]
- a Crown servant posted overseas and:
  - you are, or immediately before your posting abroad you were, ordinarily resident in the UK; or
  - immediately before your posting you were in the UK in connection with that posting; or
- the partner of a Crown servant posted overseas and in the same country as her/ him or temporarily absent from that country under the same exceptions that enable tax credits to continue during a temporary absence from Great Britain.

While you are treated as present in any of the above ways, you can continue to receive any tax credits that are already in payment, renew your award and, if you are receiving CTC or WTC, make a new claim for the other (see p1496) during your absence.

If you (or your partner, if you have a joint claim) spend longer abroad than the permitted periods, you cease to satisfy the presence condition and your tax credit entitlement ends. If you do not notify this to HM Revenue and Customs within one month (see p1507), you may be overpaid (see Chapter 64) and could be given a penalty (see Chapter 65). On your return to the UK, unless you are entitled to claim tax credits (see p1496) you will need to claim UC.

See p1636 for considerations if you are making a joint claim as a couple.

European Union co-ordination rules

CTC is classed as a 'family benefit' under the EU co-ordination rules. If you are covered by these rules (see p1672), you can, if you satisfy the other conditions (including that the child is 'normally living with' you), be paid CTC:

- for a child resident in an EEA country; *and/or*
- if you are an EEA national and you go to stay or live in an EEA country.

See p1680 for more details.

WTC is not a social security benefit under the EU co-ordination rules (see p1674). This means that the EU co-ordination rules cannot assist you and, if you (or your partner) go to an EEA country, you can only be paid under the UK rules above.

Universal credit

You cannot normally be paid UC if you (and your partner, if it is a joint claim) are not in Great Britain.[82] However, provided you were entitled immediately before the period of absence and you continue to meet the other conditions of entitlement, UC can be paid when you are temporarily absent from Great Britain for:[83]

- **one month**, if your absence is not expected to exceed, and does not exceed, one month; *or*
- **two months**, if your absence is in connection with the death of your partner or child, or a 'close relative' (see p90) of yours or of your partner or child, and it would be unreasonable for you to return to Great Britain within the first month; *or*
- **six months**, if your absence is not expected to exceed, and does not exceed, six months and you are a mariner or continental shelf worker; *or*
- **six months**, if your absence is not expected to exceed, and does not exceed, six months and is solely in connection with the medically approved care, convalescence or treatment of you, your partner or child. If this applies to you, you are automatically exempt from the work search requirement and also treated as 'able and willing immediately to take up work' during your absence (see p1069).[84]

Part 11: Immigration and residence rules for benefits and tax credits
Chapter 69: Going abroad
2. Rules for specific benefits and tax credits

Note: to be entitled to the carer element in your UC while you are abroad, you must satisfy the rules for CA (see p1649).

If your partner is abroad

If you have a joint claim for UC and you both go abroad, UC continues to be paid while both of you meet one of the above conditions. If you both remain abroad for longer than the relevant period, your entitlement ends.

If you stay in Great Britain while your partner is abroad, her/his absence does not affect your entitlement during the one-, two- or six-month period if one of the above circumstances applies to her/him. After this time, you cease to be entitled as joint claimants and must claim as a single person. However, if you have been, and expect to be, apart for less than six months, although your award is based on the maximum amount for a single person, your partner's income and capital are taken into account until you have been (or expect to be) apart for six months, when you then stop being treated as a couple.[85] However, if you are of pension age, but your partner is under pension age, once s/he stops being treated as part of your household for the purposes of PC, due to being abroad for more than the specified periods (see p1659), you can claim PC and pension-age HB as a single person. If you do not switch from UC to PC, your UC will continue to be paid until you cease to be treated as a couple with your partner (when you have, or expect to be, apart for six months).[86]

If your child is abroad

If your child is abroad, you are treated as no longer responsible for her/him if her/his absence abroad is, or is expected to be, longer than the one-, two- or six-month period allowed in the circumstances above (the circumstances must apply to your child).[87]

European Union co-ordination rules

The DWP considers UC not to be a social security benefit under the EU co-ordination rules (see p1674). This means that the EU co-ordination rules cannot assist you and, if you go to an EEA country, you can only be paid under the UK rules above.

Notes

1. The rules on getting paid abroad

1 *R v Barnet LBC ex parte Shah* [1983] 2 AC 309 (HL), Lord Scarman at p342D; see also *GC v HMRC (TC)* [2014] UKUT 251 (AAC)

2 vol 2 pt 1 ch7 para 070642 DMG; para C1122 ADM

3 *Slough BC v PK* [2019] UKUT 128 (AAC)

4 **CB** Reg 24(2) CB Regs
AA Reg 2(3C) SS(AA) Regs
DLA Reg 2(3C) SS(DLA) Regs
PIP Reg 17(2) SS(PIP) Regs
TC Reg 4(2) TC(R) Regs

5 *Chief Adjudication Officer v Ahmed and Others*, 16 March 1994 (CA), reported as R(S) 1/96

6 *Chief Adjudication Officer v Ahmed and Others*, 16 March 1994 (CA), reported as R(S) 1/96

7 R(S) 1/85

8 R(U) 16/62

2. Rules for specific benefits and tax credits

9 Reg 5 SSB(PA) Regs

10 Arts 5, 7, 42 and 43 EU Reg 883/04

11 Reg 24 CB Regs

12 Reg 24(1) CB Regs

13 Reg 21 CB Regs

14 Reg 32 CB Regs

15 Reg 21(2) CB Regs

16 Reg 5 SSB(PA) Regs

17 **AA** Reg 2(2), (3B) and (3C) SS(AA) Regs
DLA Reg 2(2), (3B) and (3C) SS(DLA) Regs
PIP Regs 17-20 SS(PIP) Regs
CA Reg 9(2) and (3) SS(ICA) Regs

18 *Disability*, House of Commons, *Hansard*, Written Statement, HCWS603, 20 April 2017

19 Reg 13 SSB(PA) Regs; Sch 2 para 7 SSB(Dep) Regs; reg 2(4) SSB(PRT)Regs

20 **AA** Reg 2B SS(AA) Regs
DLA Reg 2B SS(DLA) Regs
PIP Reg 23 SS(PIP) Regs
CA Reg 9B SS(ICA) Regs

21 **AA** s65(7) SSCBA 1992
DLA s72(7B) SSCBA 1992
PIP s84 WRA 2012
CA s70(4A) SSCBA 1992

22 *Bartlett and Others v SSWP*, C-537/09 [2011] ECR I-03417; *SSWP v DS* [2019] UKUT 238 (AAC); Art 70 EU Reg 883/04; *Swaddling v AO*, C-90/97 [1999] ECR I-01075

23 ss1(3)(d) and 18(4)(a) WRA 2007

24 Regs 151-55 ESA Regs; regs 88-92 ESA Regs 2013

25 Reg 156 and Sch 5 paras 6 and 7 ESA Regs

26 Reg 156 and Sch 5 para 7 ESA Regs

27 Reg 156 ESA Regs

28 Arts 5, 46 and 82 EU Reg 883/04; Arts 27 and 46 EU Reg 987/2009

29 s130(1)(a) SSCBA 1992

30 Reg 7 HB Regs; reg 7 HB(SPC) Regs

31 *Slough BC v PK* [2019] UKUT 128 (AAC)

32 Art 18 TFEU; Art 24 EU Dir 2004/38; *O'Flynn v Adjudication Officer*, C-237/94 [1996] ECR I-02617; R(IS) 4/98

33 Regs 7 and 21 HB Regs; regs 7 and 21 HB(SPC) Regs

34 s124(1) SSCBA 1992

35 Reg 4 IS Regs

36 Reg 21 and Sch 7 paras 11 and 11A IS Regs

37 Reg 21 and Sch 7 para 11A IS Regs

38 Reg 16 IS Regs

39 Reg 16(5) IS Regs

40 Reg 9(3) SSB(PA) Regs

41 Reg 9(4) SSB(PA) Regs

42 Reg 9(5) SSB(PA) Regs

43 s1(2)(i) JSA 1995

44 s21 and Sch 1 para 11 JSA 1995; reg 50 JSA Regs; reg 41 JSA Regs 2013

45 Sch para 2 SS(NIRA) Regs; Sch para 2 SS(GBRA)NI Regs

46 Regs 50(4) and 170 JSA Regs

47 Regs 14 and 19 JSA Regs; reg 16 JSA Regs 2013

48 Regs 3E(1) and (2)(c), 50(6B), 86C and 170 and Sch 5A para 7 JSA Regs; Vol 4 paras 24146-49 DMG

49 Regs 3E(1) and (2)(c), 50(6B) and 86C JSA Regs

50 Regs 50(6B) and 78(1A) and (3)(c) and Sch 5A para 7 JSA Regs

51 Reg 78 JSA Regs

52 Reg 85 and Sch 5 paras 10 and 11 JSA Regs

11

53 Reg 85 and Sch 5 para 11 JSA Regs
54 Reg 78 JSA Regs
55 Reg 78(5) JSA Regs
56 Art 64 EU Reg 883/04
57 Reg 2 SSB(PA) Regs
58 Reg 13 SSB(PA) Regs; reg 14 SS(IB-ID) Regs; reg 2(4) SSB(PRT) Regs
59 Arts 7 and 21 EU Reg 883/04
60 Arts 5 and 46 EU Reg 883/04; Art 87 EU Reg 987/2009
61 s1(2)(a) SPCA 2002
62 Reg 3 SPC Regs
63 Reg 4A SPC Regs
64 Reg 1 SPC Regs
65 Reg 5 SPC Regs
66 Reg 5 SPC Regs
67 Sch 2IIA para 7 SPC Regs; DMG Memo 14/18, paras 21-24
68 Reg 4A SPC Regs
69 Reg 1 SPC Regs
70 s113 SSCBA 1992; reg 4(1) SSB(PA) Regs
71 Regs 4(3) and 5 SSB(PA) Regs; ss18 and 20 PA 2014; regs 21-23 SP Regs
72 Reg 6 SSB(PA) Regs
73 Reg 2(4) SSB(PRT) Regs
74 Reg 13 SSB(PA) Regs; reg 10 SSB(Dep) Regs
75 gov.uk/guidance/benefits-and-pensions-for-uk-nationals-in-the-eea-or-switzerland
76 **SSP** Reg 10 SSP(MAPA) Regs
   SMP Reg 2A SMP(PAM) Regs
   SAP/SPP Reg 4 SPPSAP(PAM) Regs
   SSPP Reg 6 SSPP(PAM) Regs
   SPBP Reg 6 SPBP(PAM) Regs
77 **SSP** s163(1) SSCBA 1992; reg 16 SSP Regs; regs 5-10 SSP(MAPA) Regs
   SMP s171(1) SSCBA 1992; regs 2, 2A, 5, 7 and 8 SMP(PAM) Regs
   SAP/SPP ss171ZJ(2)-(3) and 171ZS(2)-(3) SSCBA 1992; regs 3, 4, 8 and 9 SPPSAP(PAM) Regs
   SSPP s171ZZ4(2) SSCBA 1992; regs 5, 6, 7, 9, 10 SSPP(PAM) Regs
   SPBP s171ZZ14(2)-(3) SSCBA; regs 5-10 SPBP(PAM) Regs
78 **SSP** Reg 16(2) SSP Regs
   SMP Reg 3 SMP(PAM) Regs; reg 17(3) SMP Regs
   SAP/SPP Reg 2 SPPSAP(PAM) Regs; reg 32(3) SPPSAP(G) Regs; reg 24(4) ASPP(G) Regs
   SSPP Reg 33(5) SSPP(G) Regs; reg 4 SSPP(PAM) Regs
   SPBP Reg 4 SPBP(PAM) Regs
79 Reg 4 TC(R) Regs
80 Reg 2(1) TC(R) Regs

81 Regs 3, 5 and 6 TC(R) Regs
82 ss3 and 4(1)(c) WRA 2012
83 Reg 11 UC Regs
84 Reg 99(1)-(3) UC Regs
85 Regs 3, 18, 22 and 36 UC Regs
86 Art 7(2)(b) and (3)(b) WRA(No.31)O; HB Circular A9/2019, paras 15-17; DMG Memo 7/19, para 12
87 Reg 4(7) UC Regs

Chapter 70

European Union co-ordination rules

This chapter covers:
1. Introduction (below)
2. Changes due to the UK leaving the European Union (p1670)
3. Who is covered (p1672)
4. Which benefits are covered (p1674)
5. Principles of co-ordination (p1676)
6. Family benefits (p1680)

Key facts
- The co-ordination rules are most relevant when you have moved to the UK from a European Economic Aread (EEA) country or vice versa.
- If you are a British citizen you are treated as an EEA national, and the UK is treated as an EEA member state, for the purposes of the European Union (EU) co-ordination rules until the end of the 'transition period' (see below).
- If you are an EEA national (or British citizen), or the family member of an EEA national (or British citizen), and your circumstances involve more than one EEA state (or the UK and an EEA state), your benefit entitlements may be affected by the EU co-ordination rules.

Brexit
Further to the UK leaving the EU, the rules described in this chapter will continue until the end of the transition period which, at the time of writing, was due to end on 31 December 2020. For more information, including the rules after this period see p1670.

Part 11: Immigration and residence rules for benefits and tax credits
Chapter 70: European Union co-ordination rules
1. Introduction

1. **Introduction**

If you are a British citizen or European Economic Area (EEA) national (see p1669) or a member of a British citizen's or EEA national's family (see p1673), your benefit entitlement may be affected by European Union (EU) law.

There are two main areas of EU law affecting benefit and tax credit entitlement that are covered in this *Handbook*: the residence rights that enable you to satisfy the right to reside requirement outlined in Chapter 68 and the social security co-ordination rules, which are summarised in this chapter. In general, you do not need to know whether you have a right to reside in order to understand how the co-ordination rules affect you.

The co-ordination rules can affect whether you qualify for benefits in the UK. In most cases, they make it easier to satisfy the UK rules – eg, by enabling you to count periods of residence, insurance and employment in any EEA country to meet the conditions of entitlement for a UK benefit. However, in limited circumstances, the co-ordination rules can prevent you from claiming a UK benefit if, for example, the UK is not the competent state to pay that type of benefit. The co-ordination rules can also help you to be paid a UK benefit while you are abroad in an EEA country for longer than you would be able to do under UK law alone.

European Union law

Although the UK left the EU on 31 January 2020, EU legislation and caselaw continues to apply in the UK during the transition period (see p1670). In general, for EU law to apply, you must be an EEA national or British citizen or the family member of an EEA national or British citizen and your circumstances must involve more than one EEA country or the UK and one or more EEA countries – eg, if you have moved between countries, you live in one and work in another, or you live in one but are the national of another.[1]

Member states of the European Union

Austria	Estonia	Italy	Portugal
Belgium	Finland	Latvia	Romania
Bulgaria	France	Lithuania	Slovakia
Croatia	Germany	Luxembourg	Slovenia
Cyprus	Greece	Malta	Spain
Czech Republic	Hungary	The Netherlands	Sweden
Denmark	Ireland	Poland	

. . . .

. . . .

Member states of the European Economic Area

The EEA consists of the EU countries plus Iceland, Liechtenstein and Norway.

From 1 June 2002, an agreement with Switzerland means that, in general, Swiss nationals are treated the same as EEA nationals. Any references to EEA nationals, therefore, also include Swiss nationals.[2]

Note: during the transition period, references within the EU co-ordination rules to EU or EEA member states are treated as if the UK continued to be a member state, and references to EU or EEA nationals are treated as if they included references to British citizens (see p1670).

. . . .

EU law has been extended to the three EEA countries outside the EU so that, in general, EEA nationals are covered by EU law to the same extent as nationals of EU states.

EU law applies beyond the actual territory of the EEA states to territories 'for whose external relations a member state is responsible'.[3]

The co-ordination rules

EU law co-ordinates all the social security systems within the EEA. The intention is that people should not lose out on social security protection simply because they move to another member state.

Note: during the transition period, for the purpose of the EU co-ordination rules, the UK is treated as if it is still a member of the EU and EEA (see p1670).

The co-ordination rules contain the following principles.

- **The single state principle.** You can generally, at any one time, only claim a particular category of benefit from one member state, referred to as the 'competent state' (see p1676).
- **Equal treatment of people.** Discrimination on nationality grounds in terms of access to, the rate of and payment of the benefits covered is prohibited (see p1678).
- **Equal treatment of benefits, income, facts or events.** If receipt of a benefit or a fact or an event has a legal consequence in one member state, this must be recognised in the same way by other member states (see p1678).
- **Aggregation.** Periods of residence, insurance and employment in any EEA country can be used towards entitlement to benefit in another (see p1678).
- **Exportability of certain benefits.** You can continue to be paid certain benefits if you go to another EEA country (see p1679).
- **Administrative co-operation.** Member states undertake to co-operate in the administration of the co-ordination rules.

The current co-ordination rules succeed, but do not repeal, the previous set of rules (referred to in this *Handbook* as the 'old co-ordination rules'). See p1674 for who is covered by the old rules.

Part 11: Immigration and residence rules for benefits and tax credits
Chapter 70: European Union co-ordination rules
2. Changes due to the UK leaving the European Union

Using the co-ordination rules

In order to rely on the co-ordination rules, check:

- whether you are covered by the current or the old co-ordination rules (see p1674);
- whether you are personally covered (see p1672);
- whether the benefit you want to claim is covered and into which category it falls (see p1674);
- which state is the 'competent state' to pay the benefit (see p1676);
- the individual benefit and tax credit rules in Chapter 68 for your entitlement in the UK, or in Chapter 69 if you want to be paid when you or a member of your family is in an EEA country.

The co-ordination rules are complex and this chapter only provides an overview. For more information, see CPAG's *Benefits for Migrants Handbook*.

---

2. Changes due to the UK leaving the European Union

The UK left the European Union (EU) on 31 January 2020. However, EU law continues to apply in the UK during the transition period (see below), in generally the same ways as it did before the UK left the EU. Therefore, the EU co-ordination rules described in this chapter continue to apply in the UK and throughout the European Economic Aread (EEA) and to British citizens and EEA nationals who are covered by these rules (see p1672), until the end of the transition period.

Transition period

The transition period (also called the 'implementation period') is the period from the UK leaving the EU at 11pm on 31 January 2020 to 31 December 2020.[4]

During the transition period, in general, EU law continues to have effect as it did before 31 January 2020.

On 31 January 2020, all EU legislation and caselaw was converted into UK law and all EU derived law (eg, the EEA Regulations) continues to have effect the day after as it did the day before.[5] For the purposes of this retained EU law and EU derived law, during the transition period, the UK is treated as if it were still a member state of the EU and EEA, and so the EU co-ordination rules continue to apply to the UK and to British citizens who move to, or live, or work, in an EEA country.[6]

The Withdrawal Agreement provides, if the decision is made by 1 July 2020, for this period to be extended once for a period up to 31 December 2022.[7] While UK legislation prohibts an extension,[8] the UK government could pass further legislation enabling the transition period to be extended in accordance with the Withdrawal Agreement.

Note: the UK leaving the EU also affects residence rights (see p1596).

After the transition period

At the end of the transition period, if you are within the personal scope of the withdrawal agreements (see below) at the end of the transition period, the co-ordination rules will continue to apply to you for as long as you continue, 'without interruption', to be in one of the situations listed in that personal scope – eg, you continue to be an EEA national residing and working or claiming social security benefits in the UK or a British citizen residing and working or claiming social security benefits in an EEA country.

You are covered by the **'personal scope'** of the withdrawal agreements if, at the end of the transition period, you are:[9]

- an EEA or Swiss national 'subject to the legislation' (see p1673) of the UK – eg: a polish national working in the UK; *or*
- a UK national 'subject to the legislation' of an EEA state or Switzerland; *or*
- an EEA national 'subject to the legislation' of an EEA state or Switzerland while residing in the UK – eg: a French national living in the UK receiving a French social security benefit; *or*
- a UK national 'subject to the legislation' of the UK while residing in an EEA state or Switzerland; *or*
- a refugee or stateless person residing in the UK or an EEA state or Switzerland and 'subject to the legislation' of the UK or an EEA state or Switzerland; *or*
- a member of the family (see p1673) or survivor of one of the above; *or*
- if none of the above apply, you are an EEA national with an EU free movement right to reside in the UK (see p1599) or a UK national with an EU free movement right to reside in an EEA state or Switzerland; *or*
- a family member (see p1614) of a person in the group immediately above.

Note:
- If you are within the personal scope because you are covered by one of the last two bullets, the co-ordination rules continue to apply after the end of the transition period for as long as you continue to have an EU free movement right to reside, or a right to work, in the relevant EEA country or Switzerland or UK, or you continue to be a family member of the person who does.[10]
- The personal scope set out in the withdrawal agreements (summarised above) is not exactly the same as the personal scope of the EU co-ordination rules (see p1672), although there is considerable overlap.
- Until new caselaw is established on the meaning of an 'interruption' to your situation, it may be relevant to refer to the caselaw on the meaning of the 'relevant situation remains unchanged' which can determine when the new co-ordination rules apply in place of the old (see p1674).

If you are not covered by personal scope of the withdrawal agreements, your benefit entitlements will be determined by UK law, unless you are covered by a

Part 11: Immigration and residence rules for benefits and tax credits
Chapter 70: European Union co-ordination rules
3. Who is covered

new agreement made between the UK and one or more EEA countries, either individually or as a group.

A new **Convention on Social Security has been agreed between the UK and Ireland** to ensure the rights described in this chapter continue to apply after the transition period to British and Irish citizens, refugees and stateless people (and members of their families) who are residing in either country and who have been 'subject to the legislation' (see below) of either or both states.[11] This Convention mirrors the structure of the EU co-ordination rules (see p1669) and broadly reproduces their principles and effects, but is limited to the UK and Ireland and to specified benefits of each country. It is expected to come into force from the end of the transition period.[12]

At the time of writing, the UK government had introduced new legislation to enable changes to the social security co-ordination rules after the transition period. However, many of the changes will be in subsequent legislation.[13]

For updates on new UK legislation and new agreements with other EEA states, see AskCPAG.org.uk and CPAG's *Welfare Rights Bulletin*.

3. **Who is covered**

Changes due to the UK leaving the Eropean Union

The UK left the European Union (EU) on 31 January 2020. However, the EU co-ordination rules continue to operate until the end of the transtion period, which, at the time of writing, was due to end 31 December 2020, but could be extended (see p1670). The rules below describe who is covered by the co-ordination rules until the end of the transition period. In general, if you are covered by the co-ordination rules at the end of the transition period, these rules can continue beyond that period if your situation continues to be one that is covered.

In order to be covered by the co-ordination rules, you must come within their **'personal scope'**.

You are within the personal scope of the co-ordination rules if you are:[14]
- residing in the UK or a European Economic Area (EEA) country and you have been 'subject to the legislation of one or more member states' (see p1673) and you are:
  - an EEA national; *or*
  - a British citizen; *or*
  - a refugee; *or*
  - a stateless person; *or*
- a member of the family (see p1673) or a 'survivor' of one of the above (in the UK, a widow, widower or surviving civil partner).

In addition, for the co-ordination rules to apply, your situation must involve more than one member state. This usually means that you must have moved between EEA countries, or you live in one and work in another, or you live in one and are the national of another.[15]

Subject to the legislation of a member state

During the transition period, the UK is treated as a 'member state' for the purpose of the EU co-ordination rules.

You have been **'subject to the legislation of a member state'** if you have worked in and paid (or should have paid) national insurance (NI) contributions to, or received any social security or special non-contributory benefit (see p1674) from, that state. You may also be subject to the legislation if you are potentially eligible for any social security benefit or special non-contributory benefit.[16]

'Legislation' is defined as 'in respect of each member state, laws, regulations and other statutory provisions and all other implementing measures relating to the social security branches covered by Article 3(1) of the Regulation'.[17]

The 'social security branches' referred to in this definition include UK benefits that are intended to assist you in the event of one of the risks on p1674.

Member of the family

A member of the family of someone covered by the co-ordination rules can also rely on the rules that cover that person (which can vary depending on the type of benefit claimed). **Note:** the consequences of being a member of someone's family are not always favourable – eg, if it changes which state is competent to pay your benefit (see p1676).

Members of the family

You are a **'member of the family'** of a person covered by the co-ordination rules if you are:[18]

– someone defined or recognised as a member of the family, or designated as a member of the household, by the legislation under which benefits are provided; or

– if the legislation under which benefits are provided does not distinguish between members of the family and other people to whom the legislation applies, the person's spouse or child either under the age of 'majority' (18 in England and Wales; 16 in Scotland) or older but dependent on the person covered.

If under the legislation you are only considered to be a member of the family or member of the household if you are living in the same household as the person, this condition is considered satisfied if you are mainly dependent on her/him.

Part 11: Immigration and residence rules for benefits and tax credits
Chapter 70: European Union co-ordination rules
4. Which benefits are covered

When the old co-ordination rules apply

There are two sets of co-ordination rules, as the current rules did not repeal the previous ones. The current rules[19] apply to the majority of benefit claimants. However, the old co-ordination rules[20] may continue to apply to you if you have already been relying on them to receive your benefit,[21] and your 'relevant situation remains unchanged'.[22]

Note: as most claims are now covered by the current co-ordination rules, this *Handbook* does not include the old ones. For more information on when the old co-ordination rules apply, see CPAG's *Benefits for Migrants Handbook,* and for the old rules, see the 2012/13 edition of this *Handbook.*

4. **Which benefits are covered**

The benefits to which the co-ordination rules apply are referred to as being within the '**material scope**' of the rules.

Individual benefits are not directly referred to. Instead, the rules have broad categories of benefits (eg, 'old age' or 'maternity') designed to cover certain 'risks'. Any social security benefit designed to provide assistance in the event of a particular risk comes into that particular category. Each state must list the benefits it considers to be designed to assist with that risk.

Benefits are also divided into the following types, depending on the conditions of eligibility:
- social security benefits (see below);
- special non-contributory benefits (see p1676);
- social and medical assistance (see p1676).

Those benefits deemed to be social security benefits have the most rights, and special non-contributory benefits provide fewer rights. Social and medical assistance is not covered by the co-ordination rules.

Social security benefits

Risk	UK benefit
Sickness	Attendance allowance (AA)
	Carer's allowance (CA)
	Disability living allowance (DLA) care component
	Personal independence payment (PIP) daily living component
	Statutory sick pay
	Contributory employment and support allowance (ESA) in the assessment phase (but see p1676)

Maternity and paternity	Maternity allowance
	Statutory maternity, adoption, paternity, shared parental and parental bereavement pay (but see below)
Invalidity	AA, DLA care and mobility component and CA if you were in receipt of benefit before 1 June 1992. If you claimed after this date, see the note below.
	Long-term incapacity benefit
	Severe disablement allowance
	Contributory ESA after the assessment phase
	Arguably, contributory ESA during the assessment phase (see below)
	State pension
Old age	Category A, B and D retirement pensions
	Additional pension
	Graduated retirement benefit
	Winter fuel payments
	Increments – eg, to pensions
	Increases of retirement pension for an adult
	Age addition in pensions
Pre-retirement	None
Survivors	Bereavement benefits
Death grants	Bereavement support payment
Accidents at work and occupational diseases	Industrial injuries disablement benefit
	Constant attendance allowance
	Exceptionally severe disablement allowance
	Reduced earnings allowance
Unemployment	Contribution-based jobseeker's allowance (JSA)
Family benefits (see p1680)	Child benefit
	Child tax credit
	Increases in other benefits for an adult or a child
	Guardian's allowance

Note: AA, CA and DLA care component are categorised as sickness benefits.[23] However, they have previously been categorised differently at different times. For information on how these changing categories affected when these benefits could be paid in another EEA country before April 2013, see CPAG's *Benefits for Migrants Handbook*.

The mobility component of DLA has been listed as, and the mobility component of PIP is accepted as, a special non-contributory benefit (see p1676).

Part 11: Immigration and residence rules for benefits and tax credits
Chapter 70: European Union co-ordination rules
5. Principles of co-ordination

Note:

- If you have a long-term or permanent disability, it is arguable that contributory ESA during the assessment phase, as well as after, should be regarded as an invalidity benefit.[24] However, in most cases it makes no difference to when it can be paid.
- The DWP considers that statutory maternity, adoption, paternity, shared parental and parental bereavement pay should be treated as pay, rather than as social security or special non-contributory benefits.[25]
- The DWP considers universal credit to be neither a social security benefit nor a special non-contributory benefit.[26]

Special non-contributory benefits

The UK government has only listed pension credit, income-related ESA, income-based JSA and DLA mobility component as special non-contributory benefits.[27] However, the the mobility component of PIP is also accepted as a special non-contributory benefit.[28]

Special non-contributory benefits can only be paid by, and under the legislation of, the state in which you are resident.[29] See below for details of how residence is determined. However, although you cannot 'export' special non-contributory benefits, all the other co-ordination principles apply.[30]

Social and medical assistance

Benefits that are neither social security nor special non-contributory benefits are considered to be social assistance and are excluded from the co-ordination rules.[31] The UK does not specify which benefits it considers to be social assistance.

---

5. Principles of co-ordination

The single competent state

In general, under the co-ordination rules, you can only claim a particular category of benefit from one member state, and are only liable to pay national insurance (NI) contributions to one member state, at any one time. This is expressed as the general principle that you can only be subject to the legislation of a single member state.[32]

The '**competent state**' is the one responsible for paying your benefit and to which you are liable to pay NI contributions.[33] In general, it is the state in which you are:[34]

- employed or self-employed (even if you are not currently earning enough to pay NI[35]); or
- resident, and from which you receive an unemployment benefit; or

- a conscripted member of the armed forces or doing compulsory civilian service; *or*
- a civil servant.

If none of the above apply, the competent state is the state in which you are 'resident' (see below).[36]

You are treated as still employed or self-employed if, as a result of that activity, you are receiving cash benefits (other than for the risks of invalidity, sickness, old age, being a survivor or accidents at work).[37]

There are exceptions to this general rule – eg, in the payment of 'sickness benefits' (see p1674), if you (or the member of your family who brings you within the co-ordination rules) receive a 'pension' (which can include state benefits other than retirement pensions) from a European Economic Area (EEA) state other than the one in which you live then the competent state will generally be the state that pays the pension.[38]

If the DWP decides that a member of your family affects your competent state (eg, because s/he works in another state), get specialist advice.[39]

'**Residence**' means habitual residence.[40] If there is a difference of views between two states or institutions about where you are 'resident', they must agree where your centre of interest is, taking into account all your circumstances. If there is still a dispute, your intentions, especially the reasons why you moved, will be decisive in establishing where you are resident.[41]

If the state in which you claim benefit decides it is not the competent state to pay that category of benefit, it must pass your claim to the state it considers competent without delay. The date you submitted a claim (or appeal) to a state that is not competent is treated as your date of claim (or appeal) by the state that is competent.[42]

If two or more states take a different view on which is competent to pay a benefit, you can get provisional payments from your state of residence or, if you are not resident in any, the state to which you first applied, while the issue is resolved.[43]

For further information on how the competent state is determined, including when exceptions apply, see CPAG's *Benefits for Migrants Handbook*.

When the UK remains the competent state

If you are subject to the legislation of the UK, either because you last worked in the UK or you are resident in the UK, you remain subject to this (ie, the UK remains your competent state) until:[44]

- you start to work in an EEA state;[45] *or*
- in some circumstances, you move to an EEA state and become resident there (see above).

Note: these general rules can be supplemented by other rules specific to the category of benefit being paid.[46] For example, if you start receiving a pension from

Part 11: Immigration and residence rules for benefits and tax credits
Chapter 70: European Union co-ordination rules
5. Principles of co-ordination

an EEA state, this will generally mean that state becomes competent to pay your sickness and family benefits (see CPAG's *Benefits for Migrants Handbook*).

In general, if you continue to be entitled to a UK benefit when you move to an EEA state, the UK remains the competent state for paying that benefit until either you become employed/self-employed in the other state or, in certain circumstances, you start to receive a benefit from it.[47]

Equal treatment

If you are covered by the co-ordination rules, you are entitled to the same benefits under the legislation of the competent state (see p1676) as a national of that state.[48] Both direct discrimination based on your nationality and (if it cannot be justified as proportionate and in pursuit of a legitimate aim) indirect discrimination based on your nationality are prohibited.

The legal effects of facts or events, including receipt of a particular benefit or income, must also be treated equally.[49] The Upper Tribunal has held that although this does not apply to the effects on working tax credit (WTC) (because WTC is not covered by the co-ordination rules – see p1674), other EU equal treatment provisions[50] mean that the WTC rules on entitlement to the childcare element must be interpreted so as to accept receipt of Dutch invalidity benefit as evidence of a claimant's incapacity.[51] In a recent Upper Tribunal case, the DWP accepted that a Polish disability benefit was equivalent to the care component of disability living allowance and therefore had the same effect for the purpose of entitlement to carer's allowance.[52]

See CPAG's *Benefits for Migrants Handbook* for further information on equal treatment.

Aggregation

The principle of **'aggregation'** enables you to add together periods of insurance, residence or employment/self-employment completed under the legislation of one or more EEA states to satisfy the requirements of a benefit.[53] This may be necessary if your entitlement to benefit depends on your fulfilling a certain period of residence, employment or insurance. For example, if you want to claim a UK contribution-based benefit, such as contributory employment and support allowance, but you have not paid sufficient NI contributions in the UK, you can rely on contributions paid in one or more EEA states to satisfy the UK contribution rules. To be entitled to a UK benefit, the UK must be the competent state to pay the category of benefit you are claiming. The competent institution (eg, in the UK, the DWP and HM Revenue and Customs) must contact the institutions in the relevant state(s) to determine the periods completed under their legislation.[54] What constitutes a period of residence, employment or insurance is determined by the legislation of the state under which it took place.[55] **Note:** the Upper

Tribunal has held that 'mere residence' in an EEA country cannot be used to satisfy the past presence test in disability and carers' benefits (see p1630).[56]

Example

Sancha is a Portuguese national who worked for many years in Portugal. She leaves her job in Portugal and moves to the UK. She works for two weeks before being made redundant. Sancha is expecting a baby in two months' time and claims maternity allowance (MA). She is entitled to MA because the UK is her competent state and she can add her periods of employment in Portugal to her employment in the UK to satisfy the condition of having worked for 26 out of the last 66 weeks.

Note: for unemployment benefits, your periods of insurance (or, if required for entitlement, employment or self-employment) can only be aggregated if you were last insured (or worked) in the state from which you claim. However, this additional condition does not apply if, during your last period of work, you resided in a state other than your competent state (eg, because you worked in another state) *and* you claim in that state where you still reside or have returned to.[57]

Exporting benefits

The co-ordination rules allow you to 'export' certain benefits to an EEA country if you cease to be resident in the EEA country in which your entitlement arose.

This means that certain benefits may not be reduced, modified, suspended, withdrawn or confiscated just because you go to live in an EEA country.[58] The rules for exporting vary according to the benefit concerned: some are fully exportable, some may be exportable on a temporary basis, and some are not exportable at all.

Check the individual benefit rules in Chapter 69 to see whether the benefit can be exported. If it can, you should contact the office that pays your benefit well in advance, so that arrangements can be made to pay you in the EEA country you are going to.

Under the co-ordination rules, all benefits categorised as social security benefits are exportable. See p1674 for a list of the UK benefits covered.

The following benefits are fully exportable and can be exported indefinitely:

- invalidity benefits;
- old age benefits;
- survivors' cash benefits;
- pensions for accidents at work or occupational diseases;
- death grants.

The following benefits can be exported for a limited period or subject to certain restrictions:

Part 11: Immigration and residence rules for benefits and tax credits
Chapter 70: European Union co-ordination rules
6. Family benefits

- unemployment benefits;
- sickness, maternity and paternity benefits (although, in most cases, these are exportable in a similar way to the fully exportable benefits).[59]

Special non-contributory benefits (see p1676) cannot be exported. They are paid only in the country in which you are resident.[60]

Overlapping benefit rules

A general principle of the co-ordination rules is that you should not use one period of compulsory insurance to obtain more than one benefit.[61] In general, you are only insured in one EEA state for any one period, so you cannot use insurance from that period to obtain entitlement to benefits of the same kind from two states. Usually, benefits are adjusted to ensure that either only one state pays the benefit, taking into account periods of insurance in other countries, or that the benefit is paid pro rata according to the lengths of the periods of insurance in different EEA countries.

In certain cases, however, you may be paid both the full level of a UK benefit and a proportion of a benefit from one or more EEA states, accrued as a result of having paid insurance contributions there. EEA states are not allowed to apply provisions preventing the overlapping of their own benefits with those of other EEA states if it would reduce what you would have received from your years of contributions in the first state alone.[62]

6. **Family benefits**

Under the co-ordination rules, family benefits in the UK include child benefit, child tax credit (CTC), guardian's allowance and child dependants' additions in other benefits.

You can export family benefits without any time limit, provided the competent state to pay your family benefits has not changed.[63] Exported family benefits are uprated in the normal way. You can also be paid for members of your family (see p1673) living in an EEA state.[64] However, you must satisfy the other conditions for that benefit, including for CTC that the child is 'normally living with' you, and for child benefit, if the child is not living with you that you are contributing to the costs of that child at least the amount of child benefit that would be payable.[65]

Generally, you are entitled to receive family benefits from your competent state, under the rules on p1676.[66] However, if you are receiving a pension, you claim family benefits from the state which is the competent state for paying your pension.[67]

To ensure that equivalent family benefits are not paid by more than one state in respect of the same family member for the same period, there are detailed rules to determine which state has priority to pay.[68] **Note:** these priority rules only need to be considered if there is an actual overlap of entitlement because claims have been made in more than one state (unless entitlement does not require a claim to have been made).[69] If the state with priority pays family benefits at a lower rate than a state with lower priority, the latter pays a 'top-up' to supplement the amount paid by the priority state. However, this top-up need not be paid for children residing in another state where entitlement to the family benefit is based on residence only (rather than on employment or receipt of a pension).[70] For further information on family benefits, including the priority rules, see CPAG's *Benefits for Migrants Handbook*.

Notes

1. Introduction
1 *Petit*, C-153/91 [1992] ECR I-04973; Art 3(1) EU Dir 2004/38
2 *The Agreement between the European Community and its Member States, of the one part, and the Swiss Confederation, of the other, on the Free Movement of Persons*, Luxembourg, 21 June 1999, Cmd 5639 (in force 1 June 2002). Note also that reg 2 I(EEA) Regs defines Switzerland as an EEA state.
3 Art 355(3) TFEU; Vol 2 para 070040 DMG; para C1005 ADM

2. Changes due to the UK leaving the European Union
4 Arts 2(e), 126 and 127 WA 2019; ss1A, 1B, 8A and Sch 2 part 1A EU(W)A 2018
5 ss2-7 EU(W)A 2018
6 s1B(3)(d) and (e) EU(W)A 2018
7 Art 132 WA 2019
8 s15A EU(W)A 2018
9 Title III, WA 2019; Title III UK-EFTA Agreement; Part 3 UK-Swiss Agreement
10 Arts 10, 13, 24, 25 and 30(3)-(4) WA 2019; Arts 12, 23, 24, 19(3)-(4) UK-EFTA Agreement; Arts 10, 20 and 25(3)-(4) UK-Swiss Agreement

11 Art 3 Convention on Social Security Between the Government of the United Kingdom of Great Britain and Northern Ireland and the Government of Ireland, 1 February 2019
12 Art 65 and Explanatory Memo Convention on Social Security Between the Government of the United Kingdom of Great Britain and Northern Ireland and the Government of Ireland, 1 February 2019
13 Immigration and Social Security Co-ordination (EU Withdrawal) Bill 2019-21

3. Who is covered
14 Art 2 EU Reg 883/04
15 *Petit*, C-153/91 [1992] ECR I-04973
16 See also Vol 2 Ch 7, Part 1 Appendix, para 5 DMG
17 Art 1(l) EU Reg 883/04; see also para C2115 ADM
18 Arts 1(i) and 2 EU Reg 883/04; *PB v SSWP (DLA)* [2016] UKUT 280 (AAC), paras 8-10
19 EU Reg 883/04
20 EU Reg 1408/71

Part 11: Immigration and residence rules for benefits and tax credits
Chapter 70: European Union co-ordination rules
Notes

21 Art 87(8) EU Reg 883/04; *Recital (2), Decision H1 of 12 June 2009 of the Administrative Commission for the Co-ordination of Social Security Systems* [2010] OJ C-106/13; *SSWP v PW (CA)* [2013] UKUT 296 (AAC); *KG v SSWP (DLA)* [2015] UKUT 146 (AAC)

22 *SSWP v SO* [2019] UKUT 55 (AAC); *KR v SSWP (DLA)* [2019] UKUT 85 (AAC), paras 10-12; *SSWP v MC (DLA)* [2019] UKUT 84 (AAC), paras 6 and 21

4. Which benefits are covered

23 *Commission of the European Communities v European Parliament and Council of the European Union,* C-299/05 [2007] ECR I-08695; *SSWP v Tolley,* C-430/15 [2017]; *LD v SSWP* [2017] UKUT 65 (AAC)

24 *Stewart v SSWP,* C-503/09 [2011] ECR I-06497

25 Vol 2 para 070153 DMG

26 SSAC, *Universal Credit and Related Regulations Report and Government Response,* December 2012

27 Art 70 and Annex X EU Reg 883/04

28 Ch C2, para C2097 and Appendix para 4 ADM; *SSWP v DS* [2019] UKUT 238 (AAC)

29 Art 70 EU Reg 883/04; *Swaddling v AO,* C-90/97 [1999] ECR I-01075

30 Art 3(3) EU Reg 883/04; *Dano v Jobcenter Leipzig,* C-333/13 [2014], paras 46-55

31 Art 3(5) EU Reg 883/04

5. Principles of co-ordination

32 Art 11 EU Reg 883/04

33 Art 1(q) and (s) EU Reg 883/04

34 Art 11 EU Reg 883/04

35 *JS v SSWP* [2019] UKUT 239 (AAC); ADM Memo 1/20; DMG Memo 3/20

36 Art 11(3)(e) EU Reg 883/04

37 Art 11(2) EU Reg 883/04

38 Arts 23-32 EU Reg 883/04; Vol 2, Ch 7, Pt 2 Appendix 3 DMG; Ch C2 Appendix 1 ADM

39 *AM v SSWP* [2017] UKUT 26 (AAC); but see *SSWP v TG (DLA)* [2019] UKUT 86 (AAC), paras 7-8 and 13-18; *GK v SSWP (CA)* [2019] UKUT 87 (AAC), paras 6-7 and 12-17 and pending cases: CSDLA/136/2017 and CSG/95/2017

40 Art 1(j) EU Reg 883/04

41 Art 11 EU Reg 987/2009

42 Art 81 EU Reg 883/04; Art 2 EU Reg 987/2009; *SSWP v AK (AA)* [2015] UKUT 110 (AAC), reported as [2015] AACR 27; see also *MGL v SSWP (ESA)* [2018] UKUT 352 (AAC); Vol 2 Ch 7, Part 2 Appendix 4 DMG; Ch C2 Appendix 2 ADM

43 Art 6(2) and (3) EU Reg 987/2009; *SSWP v HR (AA)* [2014] UKUT 571 (AAC); *SSWP v Fileccia* [2017] EWCA Civ 1907; Vol 2 Ch 7, Part 2 Appendix 4 DMG; Ch C2 Appendix 2 ADM

44 Arts 11-16 EU Reg 883/04

45 See, for example, *SSWP v MC (DLA)* [2019] UKUT 84 (AAC); ADM Memo 20/19 and DMG Memo 16/19

46 Title III EU Reg 883/04

47 See, for example, *Kuusijärvi v Riksförsäkringsverket,* C-275/96 [1998] ECR I-03419; *HB v HMRC (CHB)* [2014] UKUT 554 (AAC); *SSWP v Tolley,* C-430/15 [2017]; see also *KR v SSWP (DLA)* [2019] UKUT 85 (AAC) and ADM Memo 20/19 and DMG Memo 16/19

48 Art 4 EU Reg 883/04

49 Art 5 EU Reg 883/04

50 Art 7(1) and (2) EU Reg 492/11

51 *AS v HMRC* [2017] UKUT 361 (AAC), reported as [2018] AACR 14, resulting in the inclusion of reg 13(6)(K) in the WTC(EMR) Regs

52 CG/1346/2018; DMG Memo 02/20

53 Art 6 EU Reg 883/04

54 Art 12 EU Reg 987/2009

55 Arts 1(t)(u) and (v) and 6 EU Reg 883/04; *Decision H6 of 16 December 2010 of the Administrative Commission for the Co-ordination of Social Security Systems* [2011] OJ C-45/04

56 *SSWP v MM and BK v SSWP* [2016] UKUT 547 (AAC) – note the appeal against this part of the decision was not pursued when it went to the Court of Appeal – *Kavanagh and Another v SSWP* [2019] EWCA Civ 272; see also DMG Memo 16/17 and ADM Memo 20/17

57 Arts 61 and 65(5)(a) EU Reg 883/04

58 Art 7 EU Reg 883/04

59 Art 7 EU Reg 883/04

60 Art 70 EU Reg 883/04

61 Art 10 EU Reg 883/04

62 *Teresa and Silvana Petroni v Office National des Pensions Pour Travailleurs Salariés (ONPTS), Bruxelles* 24-75 [1975] ECR 01149

6. **Family benefits**

63 Art 67 EU Reg 883/04; *HB v HMRC (CHB)*
[2014] UKUT 554 (AAC)

64 Art 67 EU Reg 883/04; *HMRC v Ruas*
[2010] EWCA Civ 291; *JL v HMRC (CHB)*
[2017] UKUT 193 (AAC)

65 *RI v HMRC (TC)* [2019] UKUT 306 (AAC);
s143(1)(b) SSCBA 1992; *RK v HMRC
(CHB)* [2015] UKUT 357 (AAC), reported
as [2016] AACR 4; *JL v HMRC (CHB)*
[2017] UKUT 193 (AAC)

66 *Bogatu v Minister for Social Protection*, C-
322/17 [2019]

67 Art 67 EU Reg 883/04, second sentence

68 Art 68 EU Reg 883/04

69 *Bundesagentur für Arbeit – Familienkasse
Sachsen v Trapkowski*, C-378/14 [2015];
JL v HMRC (CHB) [2017] UKUT 193
(AAC); *WC v HMRC (CF)* [2019] UKUT
289 (AAC)

70 Art 68(2) EU Reg 833/04

Part 12

Scottish social security benefits

Chapter 71

The Scottish social security system

This chapter covers:
1. Overview of the Scottish social security system (see p1688)
2. How this part of the *Handbook* is organised (see p1692)

Key facts

- Several one-off payments and benefits for disabled people and carers will eventually be different in Scotland.
- Social Security Scotland (part of the Scottish government) administers and pays the new benefits.
- Three Best Start grants, a funeral support payment and young carer grant have already been introduced.
- In 2020, it is expected that disability living allowance for children will be replaced by child disability payment for new claims and that a new Scottish child payment will be introduced.
- The rules about how to claim Scottish benefits and challenge decisions are different from the rules for the other benefits in this *Handbook*.
- The rules on some other payments, including the Scottish Welfare Fund, council tax reduction and discretionary housing payments, are also different in Scotland, but these are *not* covered in this part of the *Handbook*.

Part 12: Scottish social security benefits
Chapter 71: The Scottish social security system
1. Overview of the Scottish social security system

1. Overview of the Scottish social security system

Responsibility for some benefits has been devolved to Scotland.[1] They are delivered by Social Security Scotland (SSS), which is part of the Scottish government. The way you apply for, and challenge decisions about, benefits delivered by SSS is different to the benefits they replace (which are administered by the DWP). There are common rules for some Scottish benefits about:

- how a decision (known as a 'determination' – see p1724) about your entitlement is made and can be challenged;[2]
- when and how overpayments are recovered;[3]
- criminal offences.[4]

In some cases, the language used in the law is different to that used to describe other benefits, even when the concepts are similar.

The Scottish benefits

SSS administers and pays a number of benefits. Some of these have common rules – eg, about how your entitlement is determined, how you are paid and how you can challenge a determination. The law refers to these benefits as coming under the 'Scottish social security system'.[5] In this *Handbook*, we refer to them as 'Scottish benefits'.

Note: at the time of writing, the Scottish government intended that the rules for Scottish child payment would be the same as the common rules for other Scottish benefits, but the law does not require this and the rules are still in draft form.[6] See AskCPAG.org.uk and CPAG's *Welfare Rights Bulletin* for updates.

The Scottish benefits that have already been introduced are:

- Best Start grants (see Chapter 72); *and*
- funeral support payment (see Chapter 73); *and*
- young carer grant (see Chapter 75).

It was expected that the following changes would be made by April 2021.[7] However, these plans have been delayed by the coronavirus pandemic.

- Disability living allowance (DLA) will be replaced by 'child disability payment' for new claims for children living in Scotland. See p1690 for more details.
- If you get the DLA highest rate care component (or the same rate of child disability payment) for a child who lives in Scotland during a qualifying week, you may get a single £200 payment of winter heating assistance at some point in the winter of 2020. It is expected that you will not have to apply separately for this payment.[8]

- If you get a means-tested benefit or tax credit and live in Scotland, you will be able to get Scottish child payment if you are responsible for a child under 6, probably by December 2020 (see Chapter 74).
- From spring 2021, your carer's allowance (CA) may be increased if you live in Scotland and care for more than one disabled child. At the time of writing, nothing more was known about this policy. It is not clear whether the common rules in this part of the *Handbook* will apply to the new payment or not.[9]

Note: it appears that the Scottish government and the DWP have agreed that if you get DLA and live in Scotland you may no longer be transferred to personal independence payment (PIP), unless your award is coming to an end or you report a change in your circumstances.[10] However, at the time of writing, the law had not changed. So if you are invited to claim PIP you must do so, as your DLA award will eventually end, whether you claim PIP or not. See p617 for details.

Future changes

It is expected that the following benefits will be replaced *for new claims* by the dates shown below.[11] However, these may be delayed due to the coronavirus pandemic. The common rules described in this part of the *Handbook* will then apply to them.

- Attendance allowance (AA) will be replaced by disability assistance for older people and PIP will be replaced by disability assistance for working-age people during 2021. It is expected that the two new benefits will be introduced at different times, with the working-age benefit introduced first.
- CA will be replaced by carer's assistance from early 2022.
- Cold weather payments will be replaced by cold-spell heating assistance and winter fuel payments will be replaced by winter heating assistance by the end of 2021 (perhaps only for some claimants).
- Industrial injuries benefits will be replaced by employment-injury assistance from autumn 2022.

The transfer of existing claimants to the new Scottish benefits is not expected to be complete until 2025. During the transitional period, some claimants will continue to get the existing benefits from the DWP and others will get the new Scottish benefits from SSS. Severe disablement allowance will continue to be delivered by the DWP indefinitely if you still get it. It will not be part of the Scottish social security system.

See AskCPAG.org.uk and CPAG's *Welfare Rights Bulletin* for updates.

Note: some other benefits are also administered and paid by SSS or local authorities, and have different rules in Scotland, but these *do not* come under the Scottish social security system (see p1692).

Part 12: Scottish social security benefits
Chapter 71: The Scottish social security system
1. Overview of the Scottish social security system

Child disability payment

Note: the rules described in this section are all in draft form and may change. See AskCPAG.org.uk and CPAG's *Welfare Rights Bulletin* for updates.

Child disability payment will replace DLA *for new claims*. Most of the entitlement conditions and the rates of the new benefit will be the same as those for DLA.[12] However, the definition of terminal illness will be different (see below). See Chapter 28 for details of the current DLA entitlement conditions.

If a child's entitlement to child disability payment starts before s/he turns 16, it will be able to continue until her/his 18th birthday.[13] References to a 'child' in this section also apply to a young person aged 16 and over who is able to get child disability payment under this rule.

The care component of child disability payment will not normally be paid if a child is in prison or a care home for more than 28 days. The rules are expected to be similar to the rules for DLA (see Chapter 42). However, in the draft regulations:[14]

- the mobility component is not affected by periods in prison or custody; *and*
- child disability payment will be paid in full for the first 28 days in legal custody; *and*
- if payment of child disability payment stops completely because a child is in a care home or prison, entitlement to it also ends. This means that a new claim may be required each time a child who does not get the mobility component leaves residential care or prison.

There will be a number of ways to claim child disability payment, but it will be important to do so as soon as possible, as entitlement will not normally be backdated.[15] It is likely that you will be allowed six weeks to complete a claim after starting it, and that information about how to claim will be published online at mygov.scot.

If a child is awarded child disability payment but it is later stopped or reduced, short-term assistance may be payable (see p1691).

Terminal illness rules for child disability payment

For child disability payment, the definition of 'terminal illness' will be different to the definition for DLA. A child will be treated as terminally ill if a doctor or nurse ('the health professional')[16] believes that s/he has a progressive disease that can reasonably be expected to cause her/his death.[17] In making this judgement, the health professional must consider guidance produced by the Chief Medical Officer for Scotland. At the time of writing, this guidance had not yet been published. See AskCPAG.org.uk and CPAG's *Welfare Rights Bulletin* for updates.

It is expected that SSS will use a new form called Benefits Assessment under Special Rules in Scotland (BASRiS) to verify whether a child is terminally ill.[18]

If SSS accepts that a child is terminally ill and the claim has been made on that basis, the following rules are expected to apply.[19]

- The child will be entitled to the highest possible rate of child disability payment that is payable. This includes the high rate of the mobility component, if s/he is aged three or over.
- If a statement verifying that a child is terminally ill is dated up to 26 weeks before the date of claim, the child disability payment will be backdated to the date of the statement.
- SSS will not ask for any other evidence of how a child's condition affects her/him, or for the child to attend an assessment.
- Someone else will be able to claim child disability payment on behalf of the child without her/his knowledge.[20]

From 2021, it is expected that similar rules will apply if you claim the Scottish benefits that will replace PIP and AA (see p1689), and you are terminally ill.

Short-term assistance

If a child is awarded child disability payment but that award is later removed or reduced by another determination, it may be possible to continue to get the same level of payments in the form of 'short-term assistance' while challenging the decision.

It is expected that:[21]

- a separate claim for short-term assistance will be required; *and*
- it will be possible to get short-term assistance for the periods:
  - between requesting a redetermination and your entitlement being redetermined; *and*
  - after appealing to the First-tier Tribunal, until it decides your appeal; *and*
  - during which the First-tier Tribunal is considering whether to admit a late appeal; *and*
- short-term asistance will not be paid if SSS believes that the previous award of child disability payment was made as a result of fraud; *and*
- short-term assistance will not be paid if child disability payment is stopped or reduced because a child is in residential care or prison.

See AskCPAG.org.uk and CPAG's *Welfare Rights Bulletin* for updates.

In the future, it is likely that simlar rules will allow you to get short-term assistance if you get a replacement for PIP, AA, CA or an industrial injuries benefit under the Scottish social security system, your award is later reduced or stopped, and you are challenging this decision.

Universal credit payment rules

Although UC is administered and paid by the DWP, the Scottish government has the power to change the UC payment arrangements and the amount of the housing costs element.[22] The common rules in this part of the *Handbook* do not apply to these arrangements.

Part 12: Scottish social security benefits
Chapter 71: The Scottish social security system
2. How this part of the *Handbook* is organised

- If you live in Scotland, you can request that your UC is paid twice monthly, or the housing costs element is paid to your landlord, unless the DWP has already made a similar 'alternative payment arrangement'. For details, see p49.
- In the future, members of a couple will be able to split their UC payment into two separate payments.[23]
- In the future, the rules about how the UC housing costs element is calculated will be changed in Scotland to abolish the 'bedroom tax' for social sector tenants.[24] For details of the current rules, see p107. Until this change is made, if you are affected by the bedroom tax you should apply for a discretionary housing payment from your local authority (see Chapter 29).

Benefits that do not come under the Scottish social security system

The majority of benefits described in this *Handbook* have the same rules, wherever you live in the UK. See Chapter 1 for an overview of which benefits may be relevant to your circumstances.

Some benefits are administered and paid by SSS (or will be in the future) or by local authorities, and there are different rules in Scotland, but they are *not* part of the Scottish social security system. The information in this part of the *Handbook* does *not* cover the following benefits.[25]

- **Carer's allowance supplement.** This is a payment made twice a year by SSS to people who are living in Scotland and getting CA. For details, see p569.
- **Best Start foods.** This scheme has replaced the Healthy Start scheme in Scotland. See p865 for details.
- **Job Start Payment.** This new payment has not yet been introduced. See p874 for details of the plans.
- **Benefits delivered by local authorities.** These include:
  - discretionary housing payments (see Chapter 29);
  - the Scottish Welfare Fund (see p861); *and*
  - council tax reduction (see p851).

---

2. **How this part of the *Handbook* is organised**

This part contains information about individual benefits and the common rules for Scottish benefits that are part of the Scottish social security system (see p1688). For detailed information about how to use this *Handbook*, see Chapter 1.

Rules for individual Scottish benefits

For information about who can get the Scottish benefits, how to apply and how they are paid, see:

- Chapter 72 for Best Start grants;

- Chapter 73 for funeral support payment;
- Chapter 74 for Scottish child payment;
- Chapter 75 for young carer grant.

For some information about the proposed rules for child disability payment, see p1690.

Note: at the time of writing, child disability payment and Scottish child payment had not yet been introduced, so the rules may change. See AskCPAG.org.uk and CPAG's *Welfare Rights Bulletin* for updates.

Common rules for all Scottish benefits

Chapters 76 and 77 describe the common rules that apply to all Scottish benefits. This information will also apply to those Scottish benefits expected to be introduced in future years (see p1689). At the time of writing, the Scottish government intended that these common rules will apply to Scottish child payment.[26] See:

- Chapter 76 for the common rules for claims, overpayments, fraud and complaints;
- Chapter 77 for how to get a determination changed, including how to appeal to the First-tier Tribunal.

Notes

1. Overview of the Scottish social security system
1 Sch 5, Part 2 sF1 SA 1998
2 ss24-27 and 37-62 SS(S)A 2018
3 ss63-70 SS(S)A 2018
4 ss71-76 SS(S)A 2018
5 s23 SS(S)A 2018

6 Schedule to the SCP Regs (draft). Note that the Scottish government intends to amend the SS(S)A 2018 before Scottish child payment is introduced, which may affect the final rules. For further details, see the letter from Shirley-Ann Somerville MSP to Bob Doris MSP on the upcoming Social Security Bill (21 February 2020), available from parliament.scot/S5_Social_Security/General%20Documents/20200221_CabSecSSOP_to_Convener_Social_Security_Bill.pdf

Part 12: Scottish social security benefits
Chapter 71: The Scottish social security system
Notes

7 Scottish government, *Delivery of devolved Social Security benefits: Stakeholder Toolkit*, February 2020, available from gov.scot/publications/devolved-social-security-benefits-stakeholder-engagement-toolkit-2
8 Reg 17 DACYP(S) Regs (draft)
9 Scottish government, *Policy Position Paper: Support for Carers*, 28 February 2019, available from gov.scot/publications/support-carers-policy-position-paper
10 gov.scot/publications/joint-ministerial-working-group-on-welfare-minutes-june-2019
11 Scottish government, *Delivery of devolved Social Security benefits: Stakeholder Toolkit*, February 2020, available from gov.scot/publications/devolved-social-security-benefits-stakeholder-engagement-toolkit-2
12 DACYP(S) Regs (draft)
13 Regs 22(4) and 36 DACYP(S) Regs (draft)
14 Regs 11-15 DACYP(S) Regs (draft)
15 Reg 24 DACYP(S) Regs (draft)
16 While the SS(S)A 2018 currently only allows a doctor to make a judgement of whether a child is terminally ill, the Scottish government intends to amend this rule before child disability payment is introduced. For details, see the letter from the Cabinet Secretary for Social Security and Older People to the Convener of the Social Security Committee on the upcoming Social Security Bill (21 February 2020), available from parliament.scot/S5_Social_Security/General%20Documents/20200221_CabSecSSOP_to_Convener_Social_Security_Bill.pdf
17 Sch 5 para 1(2) SS(S)A 2018; reg 9 DACYP(S) Regs (draft)
18 Reg 9(8) DACYP(S) Regs (draft)
19 Sch 5 paras 9-12 SS(S)A 2018; reg 9 DACYP(S) Regs (draft)

20 The Scottish government intends to amend the SS(S)A 2018 to make this clear before child disability payment is introduced. For details, see the letter from Shirley-Ann Somerville MSP to Bob Doris MSP on the upcoming Social Security Bill (21 February 2020), available from parliament.scot/S5_Social_Security/General%20Documents/20200221_CabSecSSOP_to_Convener_Social_Security_Bill.pdf
21 s36 and Sch 10 SS(S)A 2018; regs 18-21 DACYP(S) Regs (draft)
22 ss29 and 30 SA 2016
23 Letter from Shirley-Ann Somerville MSP to Bob Doris MSP, 12 February 2019, available from parliament.scot/S5_Social_Security/General%20Documents/20190212_CabSecSSOP_to_Conv_UC-_split_payments.pdf
24 See for example, Scottish Parliament, *Official Report*, 19 September 2017, col 12
25 s23 SS(S)A 2018

2. **How this part of the *Handbook* is organised**
26 SCP Regs (draft)

Chapter 72

Best Start grants

This chapter covers:
1. Who can get a Best Start grant (below)
2. The rules about your age (p1699)
3. The amount of benefit (p1699)
4. Claims and getting paid (p1700)
5. Tax, other benefits and the benefit cap (p1701)

Key facts
- Best Start grants include a payment for women who are pregnant or who have recently given birth – called a **pregnancy and baby payment** – and amounts to help with the costs of young children – called an **early learning payment** and a **school-age payment**.
- Best Start grants are not means tested, but you must usually receive a qualifying benefit to qualify.
- You do not need to have paid national insurance contributions to qualify.
- Best Start grants are administered and paid by Social Security Scotland.
- If you disagree with a decision about a Best Start grant, you can request a redetermination and then appeal against it (see Chapter 77). You must request a redetermination before you can appeal.

1. Who can get a Best Start grant

You qualify for a Best Start grant if:[1]
- you or your partner are aged under 18. In some circumstances, 18/19-year-olds can qualify (see p1699); *or*
- on the date of your application, you or your partner are receiving a qualifying benefit (see p1696).

You must also:
- claim within the time limit (see p1700);
- be ordinarily resident in Scotland (see p1585);

Part 12: Scottish social security benefits
Chapter 72: Best Start grants
1. Who can get a Best Start grant

- be 'habitually resident' in the UK, Channel Islands, Isle of Man, European Economic Area or Switzerland. You do not need to meet this condition if you are receiving a qualifying benefit or you are exempt from it (see p1589).

In addition, you must meet the conditions for the pregnancy and baby payment below, the early learning payment (see p1697) or the school-age payment (see p1697).

Qualifying benefits

To qualify for a Best Start grant, you or your partner must be getting one of the following:[2]
- universal credit (UC);
- income-based jobseeker's allowance (JSA);
- income-related employment and support allowance (ESA);
- income support (IS);
- housing benefit (HB);
- pension credit (PC);
- child tax credit (CTC);
- working tax credit (WTC).

You must be getting UC in the assessment period that includes the date of your claim for a Best Start grant, or getting UC in the assessment period before that. For the other benefits, you must be getting the benefit on the date of your claim for a Best Start grant. See p1700 for when your claim is made or can be treated as made.

You must be getting one of the above qualifying benefits at a rate of more than £0 before any third-party deductions or sanctions are applied. You do not count as getting a qualifying benefit if it was paid in error, including an official error.[3]

Who can get a pregnancy and baby payment

In addition to the basic rules for a Best Start grant above, to qualify for the pregnancy and baby payment:[4]
- either:
  - you (or your partner) must be (or have been) more than 24 weeks' pregnant, or you gave birth to a child before or during the 24th week of pregnancy; or
  - you (or your partner) have become responsible for a baby under the age of one and you (or your partner) are not the child's mother (see p1698); and
- you have not received, and are not due to receive, a Sure Start maternity grant (see p796) for the same child; and
- no one else has received, and is not due to receive, a Best Start grant pregnancy and baby payment or a Sure Start maternity grant (see p796) for the same child, unless:

- you became responsible for the child for the first time after someone else claimed or was awarded a payment or grant;
- you have not been that person's partner or dependant, and s/he has not been your or your partner's dependant, since that person claimed or was awarded a payment or grant; *and*
- the child does not normally live with the person who has already received a payment or grant.

If your child dies, or is stillborn, after the 24th week of pregnancy, you are still entitled to the pregnancy and baby payment and do not have to pay it back.

You are not entitled to the pregnancy and baby payment if the child is living in a residential establishment (ie, a local authority-approved children's home) on the date of your claim.

Who can get an early learning payment

In addition to the basic rules for a Best Start grant above, you qualify for the early learning payment if:[5]

- you or your partner are responsible for the child (see p1698) on the day you claim, which must be within the period from the child's second birthday to six months after the child's third birthday; *and*
- no one else has received, or is due to receive, an early learning payment for the child, unless:
  - you became responsible for the child for the first time after someone else applied for, or was awarded, a payment; *and*
  - you have not been that person's partner at any time since s/he applied for, or was awarded, an early learning payment for the child; *and*
  - the child does not normally live with the person who has already received an early learning payment.

You are not entitled to the early learning payment if the child is living in a residential establishment (ie, a local authority-approved children's home) on the date of your claim. You can qualify for an early learning payment whether or not you have received a pregnancy and baby payment for the child. It does not matter whether your child is actually in early learning (eg, nursery, childcare or with a childminder) or not.

Who can get a school-age payment

In addition to the basic rules for a Best Start grant above, you qualify for the school-age payment if:[6]

- you or your partner are responsible for a child (see p1698) born between 1 March 2015 and 29 February 2016 inclusive, and you claim from 1 June 2020 to 28 February 2021; *and*

Part 12: Scottish social security benefits
Chapter 72: Best Start grants
1. Who can get a Best Start grant

- no one else has received, or is due to receive, a school-age payment for the child unless:
  - you became responsible for the child for the first time after someone else claimed or was awarded a payment;
  - you have not been that person's partner at any time since s/he claimed or was awarded a school-age payment for the child; *and*
  - the child does not normally live with the person who has already received a school-age payment.

You are not entitled to the school-age payment if the child is living in a residential establishment (ie, a local authority-approved children's home) on the date of your claim. You can qualify for a school-age payment whether or not you have received a pregnancy and baby payment or an early learning payment for the child. It does not matter whether your child has actually started school or not.

Responsible for a child

You count as responsible for a child if you meet any of the following conditions on the day you claim a Best Start grant.[7]

- The child is your dependant. S/he is your dependant if:
  - you are getting child benefit for her/him;
  - you are getting CTC and s/he is included in your award (**Note:** it does not matter if a child element is not payable because of the 'two-child limit');
  - you are getting UC and s/he is included in your award in the assessment period which includes the date of your Best Start grant claim, or the one before that (**Note:** it does not matter if a child element is not payable because of the 'two-child limit'); *or*
  - you are getting a child amount for her/him in your PC.
- You are under 20, the parent of the child, you normally live with her/him, and you are a dependant in someone else's child benefit, CTC, UC or PC award (see above).
- You have been granted a parental order following a surrogate pregnancy.
- You have adopted the child under Scottish law, or the law of any other country or jurisdiction recognised under Scottish law.
- The child has been placed with you for adoption by an approved adoption agency in the UK.
- You are the appointed guardian of the child.
- You are an approved kinship carer for the child, and the child lives with you (exclusively or predominantly) under the terms of a kinship care order, or of an agreement with a local authority in the UK for a looked-after child.

2. **The rules about your age**

There are no age limits for a Best Start grant. However, you qualify for a Best Start grant without being awarded a qualifying benefit if:[8]
- you are aged under 18 on the date of your claim;
- you are aged 18 or 19 on the date of your claim, and you are the dependant of another person. You are a dependant of another person if:
  - s/he is getting child benefit for you;
  - s/he is getting child tax credit and you are included as a 'qualifying young person' (see p286 for who counts) in the award (**Note:** it does not matter if a child element is not payable because of the 'two-child limit');
  - s/he is getting universal credit and you are included as a 'qualifying young person' (see p62 for who counts) in the award in the assessment period which includes the date of your claim for a Best Start grant, or the one before that (**Note:** it does not matter if a child element is not payable because of the 'two-child limit');
  - s/he is getting an amount in her/his pension credit for you; *or*
  - s/he is an approved kinship carer for you (see p1698).

3. **The amount of benefit**

The pregnancy and baby payment is £600 if there are no other children aged under 16 living in your household, or £300 if there is another child aged under 16 living in your household. You still get the £600 payment if the only other child(ren) in your household is:
- a parent of the child for whom a Best Start grant is being made;
- a sibling of a parent of the child;
- a child for whom you are not responsible;
- a sibling born as a result of the same birth, but this only applies to one payment of £600 (see example below).

There is a multiple pregnancy supplement of £300 if more than one child is born, or is to be born, as a result of the same pregnancy.

Example
Olivia is pregnant with triplets. She has no other children living in her household. She is entitled to £600 for one child, £300 each for the other two children, and a multiple pregnancy supplement of £300. Her total Best Start grant is £1,500.

The early learning payment is £250 for each child.
The school-age payment is £250 for each child.

Part 12: Scottish social security benefits
Chapter 72: Best Start grants
4. Claims and getting paid

4. **Claims and getting paid**

The general rules on claims and getting paid are covered in Chapter 76. This section explains the specific rules that apply to Best Start grants.

Making a claim

You can claim a Best Start grant:
- online at mygov.scot/best-start-grant;
- by telephone on 0800 182 2222; *or*
- in writing on the approved form.

Forms

You can download the form from mygov.scot/best-start-grant-form or request it by telephone.

If you claim by post, your completed form should be returned to Best Start grant, PO Box 10300, Dundee DD1 9FU – a prepaid envelope is available on request.

Information to support your claim

You do not need to send any evidence with your claim for a pregnancy and baby payment if you are getting a qualifying benefit and you have received a 'baby box' from the Scottish government for your baby. If you are aged 18 or 19 and not getting a qualifying benefit in your own right, you must send a letter from your school or college confirming the course you are on. If you have responsibility for a child under a legal order but the child is not included as your dependant in a benefit claim, you are asked to send a copy of the legal order.

You do not need to send any other evidence with your claim but it may be requested.

The date of your claim

You must usually claim a Best Start grant within a time limit (known as the 'application window'). This is:
- for the pregnancy and baby payment, between being 24 weeks pregnant and six months after the birth if you, or your partner or dependant, have been pregnant with the child, or if you have become responsible for a child in other circumstances, the day before her/his first birthday;
- for the early learning payment, from the child's second birthday to six months after her/his third birthday;
- for the school-age payment, from 1 June in the calendar year in which the child's fifth birthday falls (or if the child is born in January or February, the

calendar year in which her/his fourth birthday falls), to the last day in February in the following year.

Your claim is usually treated as having been made on the day it is received by Social Security Scotland (SSS). If you are not eligible on that date, but you would be eligible within 10 days, your claim can be treated as having been made up to 10 days later. If you are waiting for a backdated award of a qualifying benefit and you apply for a Best Start grant within 20 working days after the end of the application window, your claim can be treated as having been made on a day that falls within the application window.[9] If you were previously turned down for a Best Start grant but are awarded a qualifying benefit on appeal, which is backdated to include the date of your Best Start grant claim, a Best Start grant can be awarded without a new claim.[10]

If you claim the wrong payment

If you have claimed one type of payment (eg, a pregnancy and baby payment), and SSS finds that you will be entitled to a payment for another child (eg, a school-age payment for an older child) within 10 days, it can decide your entitlement without your having to make a claim.[11]

Getting paid

A Best Start grant is paid into the bank or other account you nominate when you make your claim. If you do not have an account, and have arranged for other benefits to be paid by the government's payment exception service (see p1188), the Best Start grant can be paid in the same way. Some, or all, of a Best Start grant payment can be made in a form other than money (eg, a voucher) if you accept an offer from SSS to receive it in this way. If you withdraw your agreement before the grant is given, it must be paid as money.

5. Tax, other benefits and the benefit cap

Tax, benefits and tax credits

Best Start grants are not taxable.[12]

They are not counted as income or capital for means-tested benefits or tax credits.[13] You cannot qualify for a Sure Start maternity grant if you have received a Best Start grant pregnancy and baby payment for the same child.[14]

The benefit cap

In some cases, there is a limit on the total amount of specified benefits you can receive (a 'benefit cap'). Best Start grant payments are not specified benefits. The benefit cap only applies if you are getting universal credit or housing benefit. See p1194 for further information.

Notes

1. Who can get a Best Start grant
1 EYA(BSG)(S) Regs
2 Regs 11 and 12 and Sch 2(1)(e) EYA(BSG)(S) Regs
3 Reg 12 EYA(BSG)(S) Regs
4 Sch 2 EYA(BSG)(S) Regs
5 Sch 3 EYA(BSG)(S) Regs
6 Sch 4 EYA(BSG)(S) Regs
7 Regs 9 and 10 EYA(BSG)(S) Regs

2. The rules about your age
8 Sch 2(1)(iv) EYA(BSG)(S) Regs

4. Claims and getting paid
9 Regs 4 and 5 EYA(BSG)(S) Regs
10 Sch 1(5) EYA(BSG)(S) Regs
11 Sch 1(3) EYA(BSG)(S) Regs

5. Tax, other benefits and the benefit cap
12 s12 Finance Act 2019
13 The Social Security (Scotland) Act 2018 (Best Start Grants) (Consequential Modifications and Saving) Order 2018 No.1138
14 Reg 3A SFMFE(G) Regs, as amended by the Social Security (Scotland) Act 2018 (Best Start Grants) (Consequential Modifications and Saving) Order 2018 No.1138

12

Chapter 73

Funeral support payment

This chapter covers:
1. Who can get a funeral support payment (below)
2. The rules about your age (p1706)
3. The amount of benefit (p1707)
4. Claims and getting paid (p1708)
5. Tax, other benefits and the benefit cap (p1709)

Key facts

- Funeral support payments are one-off payments to help with the costs of a funeral.
- Funeral support payments are not means tested, but you must receive a qualifying benefit to qualify.
- You do not need to have paid national insurance contributions to qualify.
- Funeral support payments are administered and paid by Social Security Scotland.
- If you disagree with a decision about a funeral support payment, you can request a redetermination and then appeal against it (see Chapter 77). You must request a redetermination before you can appeal.

1. Who can get a funeral support payment

You qualify for a funeral support payment if:[1]
- you are ordinarily resident in Scotland (see p1585);[2] *and*
- on the date of your claim, you or your partner are receiving a qualifying benefit (see below);[3] *and*
- you or your partner have accepted responsibility for the funeral and it is reasonable for you to do so (see p1704);[4] *and*
- the funeral takes place in the UK, unless you or your partner are covered by specified European Union legislation, in which case the funeral can take place in any European Economic Area (EEA) country or Switzerland (see p1706);[5] *and*
- a funeral support payment or a social fund funeral payment (see p798) has not already been paid in respect of the person who has died;[6] *and*

12

Part 12: Scottish social security benefits
Chapter 73: Funeral support payment
1. Who can get a funeral support payment

- the person who has died was ordinarily resident in the UK (see p1585);[7] *and*
- you are not a 'person subject to immigration control' (there are exceptions to this rule) – see p1560;[8] *and*
- you claim within the time limit (see p1708).[9]

Note: it may be the funeral of a stillborn child, which means that the stillbirth occurs after the 24th week of pregnancy.[10]

If the person who has died was aged 18 or over, you cannot get a funeral support payment if her/his assets are sufficient to meet the cost of the funeral.[11] Assets include lump sums due to be paid as a result of an insurance policy, occupational pension scheme, burial club, prepaid funeral plan or similar scheme.[12]

Qualifying benefits

To qualify for a funeral support payment, you or your partner must be getting one of the following:[13]
- universal credit (UC);
- income support;
- income-based jobseeker's allowance;
- income-related employment and support allowance;
- housing benefit;
- child tax credit;
- working tax credit which includes the disabled worker or severe disability element;
- pension credit.

You must be getting UC in the assessment period that includes the date of your claim for a funeral support payment, or have been getting UC in the assessment period before that.[14] For the other benefits, you must be getting the benefit on the date of your claim for a funeral support payment. See p1708 for when your claim is made, or can be treated as having been made.

You must be getting one of the above qualifying benefits at a rate of more than £0, before any third-party deductions or sanctions are applied.[15] You do not count as getting a qualifying benefit if it was paid in error, including an official error.[16]

Responsible for the funeral expenses

To qualify for a funeral support payment, you or your partner must have accepted responsibility for the costs of the funeral and it must be reasonable that you or your partner have accepted responsibility.

In assessing whether it is reasonable that you or your partner have accepted responsibility, Social Security Scotland (SSS) must take into account whether the person who has died had a closer relative and any other relevant factors.[17] In deciding whether there is a closer relative, the following 'table of hierarchy' is used.[18]

Adult death	Child death
Spouse or civil partner	Parent or a person who had parental
Someone neither married to nor in a civil	rights and parental responsibilities for
partnership with the person who died,	her/him (but not a local authority)
but who had been living with her/him as if	Sister or brother
they were married for at least six months	Grandparent
(or if the person who died was in hospital	Aunt or uncle
immediately before her/his death, for at	Cousin
least six months before s/he was admitted	Niece or nephew
to hospital)	A long-standing friend
Child	
Parent	
Sister or brother	
Grandparent	
Grandchild	
Aunt or uncle	
Cousin	
Niece or nephew	
A long-standing friend	

Usually, it will be reasonable for the person who has the closest family relationship to the person who has died to take responsibility for the funeral expenses, but there are other circumstances, such as estrangement, which may be relevant and may mean that you are entitled even if there is a closer family member. Internal SSS guidance[19] suggests that a closer relative of the deceased will be 'ignored' if s/he is:

- under 18, or a 'qualifying young person' still included in her/his parent(s) benefit claim; or
- living in residential care; or
- a hospital in-patient; or
- fully maintained by a religious order; or
- ordinarily resident outside the UK.

Note that under 18s and qualifying young people are unlikely to qualify for a funeral support payment (due to normally being unable to get a qualifying benefit). A closer relative in one of the groups above can choose to take responsibility for the funeral. However, if s/he does not get a qualifying benefit, s/he will not be eligible for a funeral support payment.

Part 12: Scottish social security benefits
Chapter 73: Funeral support payment
2. The rules about your age

The guidance suggests that the following groups will **not** be ignored, even if they are unable to access a qualifying benefit (and so cannot qualify for a funeral support payment):

- full-time students; *or*
- asylum seekers; *or*
- 'persons subject to immigration control'; *or*
- prisoners.

It appears unlikely that you will be awarded a funeral support payment if there is a closer relative in one of the above groups. You can challenge this decision (see Chapter 77) and argue that it is reasonable for you to take responsibility. It is advisable to point out the limited financial resources of the closer relative, as well as any other relevant factors such as whether the closer relative was estranged from the deceased. At an appeal, the First-tier Tribunal can take its own view, and is not bound by the internal guidance.

If there is another family member at the same level on the hierarchy, but no one above you, SSS should accept that it is reasonable for you to accept responsibility without looking at that other person's circumstances.[20]

If more than one person claims a funeral support payment, the application of the person who is the closest relative will be considered first. If s/he is entitled, the other person cannot be entitled.[21] If more than one person applies, they are equally close relatives to the person who died and they cannot decide whose claim should proceed, SSS decides which to consider first.[22]

European Economic Area nationals

You can get a funeral support payment for a funeral that takes place in the EEA or Switzerland if:[23]

- you are a 'worker', a self-employed person, or you retain that status; *or*
- you are a family member of a worker, a self-employed person or someone who retains that status; *or*
- you have a permanent right to reside in the UK.

You must satisfy all the other rules for getting a funeral support payment. For more information on the benefit rights of EEA nationals, see Chapters 68, 69 and 70.

2. The rules about your age

There are no age limits for funeral support payment. However, because you or your partner must be getting a qualifying benefit, this means that you or your partner must be aged 16 or over.

3. **The amount of benefit**

You are entitled to a funeral support payment to cover the cost of:[24]
- a burial plot;
- necessary burial fees and fees of digging a grave;
- cremation fees, including the cost of removing a pacemaker, restricted to £20.35 (£20 for claims made before 1 April 2020[25]) if not carried out by a doctor;
- any medical references and medical certificates, if required;
- documentation required for the release of the assets of the person who has died;
- transport for the portion of journeys of more than 80 kilometres, undertaken to:
  - transport the body within the UK to a funeral director's premises or to a place of rest;
  - transport the coffin and bearers in a hearse and the mourners in another vehicle from the funeral director's premises or place of rest to the funeral;
- one return journey undertaken to make arrangements for the funeral, which does not exceed the cost of a return journey from your home to the place of the burial or cremation.

In addition, you can get a payment of £1,000 (£700 for claims made before 1 April 2020[26]) towards any other funeral expenses, or £122.05 (£120 for claims made before 1 April 2020[27]) if the person was aged 18 or over when s/he died and had a prepaid funeral plan.

If the burial or cremation takes place in an area where the person who died was not ordinarily resident and the cost of the burial or cremation, including transport costs, is more than what the costs would otherwise have been, the funeral support payment does not cover the excess.[28]

Deductions from awards

If available to help meet the funeral costs, the following are deducted from the amount of the funeral support payment:[29]
- any assets of the person who died that are available without confirmation having been granted, or without probate or letters of administration; *and*
- an insurance policy, occupational pension scheme, burial club or similar arrangement; *and*
- a funeral grant paid by the government if the person who died was receiving a war disablement pension.

Note:
- No deduction is made if the person who died was under 18.[30]

Part 12: Scottish social security benefits
Chapter 73: Funeral support payment
4. Claims and getting paid

- No deduction is made in respect of arrears of social security benefits paid to the deceased's estate.[31]

4. Claims and getting paid

The general rules on claims and getting paid are covered in Chapter 76. This section explains the specific rules that apply to funeral support payment.

Making a claim

You can claim a funeral support payment:
- online at mygov.scot/funeral-support-payment; *or*
- by telephone on 0800 182 2222; *or*
- in writing on the approved form.

Forms

The form can be downloaded from mygov.scot/funeral-support-payment-17-or-under (if the person who has died was under 18) or mygov.scot/funeral-support-payment-over-18-form (if the person who has died was 18 or over) or requested by telephone. If you claim by post, return your completed form to Social Security Scotland, PO Box 10311, Dundee DD1 9GH.

Information to support your claim

You will need to provide details of the funeral director, if you are using one, and details of any travel receipts or funeral bills you have already had. You are asked if you give permission for Social Security Scotland (SSS) to contact the funeral director to get further information.

The date of your claim

You can claim at any time from the date the person died until six months after the date of the funeral. SSS calls this the 'period for applications'.[32] If you are refused a funeral support payment because you are not getting a qualifying benefit and you later become entitled to a qualifying benefit, you can claim again provided you are still within this period. If you are waiting for a backdated award of a qualifying benefit, the benefit is awarded for at least one day that falls within the period for applications and you claim within 20 days after the end of the period for applications, your claim can be treated as having been made on a day in the period for applications.[33] If you were previously turned down for a funeral support payment but are awarded a qualifying benefit on appeal, which is backdated to include the date on which your previous claim was refused, a funeral support payment can be considered again without your having to make a new claim.[34]

Getting paid

Usually, payment is made direct to the funeral director if the bill is still outstanding. If the bill has been paid, payment is usually made to you.

A funeral support payment can be recovered from the estate of the person who died.[35]

5. Tax, other benefits and the benefit cap

Tax, benefits and tax credits

Funeral support payments are not taxable.[36]

They are not counted as income or capital for other means-tested benefits or tax credits.

You cannot get a funeral support payment if you or anyone else has been awarded a social fund funeral expenses payment in respect of the person who died.[37]

The benefit cap

In some cases, there is a limit on the total amount of specified benefits you can receive (a 'benefit cap'). A funeral support payment is not a specified benefit. The benefit cap only applies if you are getting universal credit or housing benefit. See p1194 for further information.

Part 12: Scottish social security benefits
Chapter 73: Funeral support payment
Notes

Notes

1. Who can get a funeral support payment

1 Reg 3 FEA(S) Regs
2 Reg 9(1) FEA(S) Regs
3 Reg 10 FEA(S) Regs
4 Reg 7 FEA(S) Regs
5 Reg 9(2)(b) FEA(S) Regs
6 Reg 8(4) and (5) FEA(S) Regs
7 Reg 9(2)(a) FEA(S) Regs
8 Reg 9(5) FEA(S) Regs
9 Reg 5 FEA(S) Regs
10 Reg 2 FEA(S) Regs
11 Reg 11 FEA(S) Regs
12 Reg 11(3) FEA(S)Regs
13 Reg 10 FEA(S) Regs
14 Reg 10(4) FEA(S) Regs
15 Reg 10(2)(b) FEA(S) Regs
16 Reg 10(2)(a) FEA(S) Regs
17 Reg 7 FEA(S) Regs
18 Reg 7(2)(a) and (3) FEA(S) Regs
19 Unpublished guidance shared with CPAG by Social Security Scotland
20 Scottish government, *Consultation on Funeral Expense Assistance Regulations,* May 2018
21 Reg 8(1), (2) and (4) FEA(S) Regs
22 Reg 8 (3) FEA(S) Regs
23 Reg 9(2)(b), (3) and (4) FEA(S) Regs

3. The amount of benefit

24 Reg 13 FEA(S) Regs
25 Reg 6 Social Security Assistance (Funeral Expense Assistance and Young Carer Grants) (Up-rating and Miscellaneous Provisions) (Scotland) Regulations 2020 (draft)
26 Reg 6 Social Security Assistance (Funeral Expense Assistance and Young Carer Grants) (Up-rating and Miscellaneous Provisions) (Scotland) Regulations 2020 (draft)
27 Reg 6 Social Security Assistance (Funeral Expense Assistance and Young Carer Grants) (Up-rating and Miscellaneous Provisions)(Scotland) Regulations 2020 (draft)
28 Reg 13(5) FEA(S) Regs
29 Reg 14 FEA(S) Regs
30 Reg 14(2) FEA(S) Regs
31 Regs 14(3) FEA(S) Regs

4. Claims and getting paid

32 Reg 5 FEA(S) Regs
33 Reg 5(5) FEA(S) Regs
34 Reg 4(2) FEA(S) Regs
35 s70 SS(S)A 2018

5. Tax, other benefits and the benefit cap

36 s660 IT(EP)A 2003, as amended by s12 Finance Act 2009
37 Reg 8(5) FEA(S) Regs

Chapter 74

Scottish child payment

This chapter covers:
1. Who can get Scottish child payment (p1712)
2. The rules about your age (p1713)
3. The amount of benefit (p1714)
4. Claims and getting paid (p1714)
5. Tax, other benefits and the benefit cap (p1715)

Key facts

- Scottish child payment is a top-up benefit for lower income families in Scotland responsible for a child or children, expected to be introduced by Christmas 2020.
- Scottish child payment is not means-tested, but you must be receiving a means-tested benefit or tax credit to qualify.
- You do not have to have paid national insurance contributions to qualify.
- You can qualify for Scottish child payment whether you are in or out of work.
- Scottish child payment can be paid in addition to other benefits and tax credits, and does not count as income for means-tested benefits.
- Scottish child payment is administered and paid by Social Security Scotland.
- If you disagree with a determination about Scottish child payment, you can request a redetermination and then appeal against it (see Chapter 77). You must request a redetermination before you can appeal.

Future changes

Scottish child payment is expected to be extended to families with children under 16 by the end of 2022.[1]

Part 12: Scottish social security benefits
Chapter 74: Scottish child payment
1. Who can get Scottish child payment

1. **Who can get Scottish child payment**

It is expected that you will qualify for Scottish child payment if:[2]
- you are reponsible for a child under the age of 6; *and*
- you are entitled to a qualifying benefit; *and*
- you are ordinarily resident in Scotland (see p1585).

You must usually meet all the qualifying conditions on the date your claim is received. If you do not meet all the qualifying condition on the date of your claim, but it is expected that you will meet them within 14 days, your claim can be treated as made up to 14 days later.

Only one person can receive Scottish child payment for an individual child. If more than one person applies, or is treated as applying, for Scottish child payment for the same child, Social Security Scotland must decide entitlement in the following order of priority:[3]

- the person who is responsible for that child for the purposes of universal credit (UC), child tax credit (CTC) or pension credit (PC); *or*
- if more than one claimant is responsible for the child for the purposes of UC, CTC or PC (eg, if both members of a couple apply for Scottish child payment), then whoever claimed first; *or*
- if no one is responsible for the child for the purposes of UC, CTC or PC, it will be paid to the person receiving child benefit for the child; *or*
- if the claimants are kinship carers, and none of them are responsible for the child for the purposes of UC, CTC, PC or child benefit, then whoever claimed first.

If you no longer meet the qualifying conditions, your entitlement to Scottish child payment ends from the week following the date on which you no longer qualify.

In some circumstances, such as if you or the child are in hospital or detention or goes abroad, your entitlement to Scottish child payment will depend on whether you still count as responsible for the child (see below) and whether you are still entitled to a qualifying benefit (see p1713).

Responsible for a child

You must be responsible for the child on the date of your claim for Scottish child payment. You must continue to be responsible for the child for each week of entitlement to Scottish child payment. It is expected that you will count as responsible for a child if you meet either of the following conditions.[4]

- The child is your or your partner's dependant. S/he is a dependant if:
  - you are getting child benefit for her/him; *or*

    – you are getting UC and s/he is included in your award (**Note:** it does not matter if a child element is not payable because of the 'two-child limit'); *or*

    – you are getting CTC and s/he is included in your award (**Note:** it does not matter if a child element is not payable because of the 'two-child limit'); *or*

    – you are getting a child amount for her/him in your PC.

- You are an approved kinship carer for the child, and the child lives with you (exclusively or predominantly) under the terms of a kinship care order, or of an agreement between you and/or your partner and a local authority in the UK for a looked-after child. Note that if you are responsible for the child as a kinship carer, you must still be getting a qualifying benefit for yourself.

Qualifying benefits

To qualify for Scottish child payment, it is expected that you or your partner must have been awarded:[5]

- UC; *or*
- income support (IS); *or*
- income-based jobseeker's allowance (JSA); *or*
- income-related employment and support allowance (ESA); *or*
- CTC; *or*
- working tax credit; *or*
- PC.

You or your partner must be awarded a qualifying benefit for the date of your claim for Scottish child payment. Someone counts as your partner if you are part of a couple as defined for UC purposes (see p57), whether or not you get UC. If your claim for Scottish child payment is turned down because you are still waiting to hear about a qualifying benefit, it can be decided again if the qualifying benefit is later awarded for a period that includes the date of your claim for a Scottish child payment (see p1751).

Your award of a qualifying benefit must continue for at least one day for each week of entitlement to Scottish child payment. You are still regarded as having been awarded a benefit if it has been reduced to nil because of a sanction. If the qualifying benefit has been awarded in error, you are not entitled to Scottish child payment.

12

---

2. The rules about your age

It is expected that there will be no minimum age for Scottish child payment, but you must be aged at least 16 in order to get any of the qualifying benefits. If you are responsible for a dependent child who has a child, you should also claim Scottish child payment for your dependant's child.

There is no upper age limit for Scottish child payment.

Part 12: Scottish social security benefits
Chapter 74: Scottish child payment
4. Claims and getting paid

3. **The amount of benefit**

Scottish child payment will be paid at a weekly rate of £10 for each child.

4. **Claims and getting paid**

The general rules on claims and getting paid are covered in Chapter 76. This section explains the specific rules that apply to Scottish child payment.

Making a claim

It is expected that from a date in autumn 2020 you will be able to claim Scottish child payment in advance of the date from which it will be payable. You will be able to claim online at mygov.scot/benefits, by telephone on 0800 182 2222 or on a form that will be available to download or sent on request.

If you are already getting Scottish child payment for one child, and Social Security Scotland (SSS) becomes aware that you are responsible for another child, a determination of your entitlement to Scottish child payment for that child can be made without a new claim.[6]

You can be awarded Scottish child payment without making a new claim if you were getting Scottish child payment within the last 12 weeks but your entitlement ended due to a break in responsibility for the child or receipt of a qualifying benefit, and you have since become entitled again.[7] If someone else has claimed Scottish child payment for the same child, see p1712.

The date of your claim

Your claim is treated as made on the day it is received by SSS, provided it is properly completed.[8] When the Scottish child payment is first introduced, it is expected that you will be able to claim a few months in advance of the date it becomes payable.[9]

If you have claimed Scottish child payment and you are waiting to hear about a qualifying benefit, or a benefit showing you have responsibility for the child, the determination may be delayed until the outcome is known.

If you are turned down for Scottish child payment and you are later awarded a qualifying benefit, or a benefit showing you have responsibility for the child, which is backdated to include the date of your original claim for Scottish child payment, your entitlement can be determined from the date of your original claim without the need to make a new claim.[10]

If you have previously been turned down for Scottish child payment and this was due to an official error (see p1750), your entitlement can be determined without the need to make a new claim. In this case, your award can start from the date of your original claim.[11]

Scottish child payment cannot be backdated. The date your claim is received is usually the date your award starts, and it cannot be treated as made on an earlier date. Your claim can be treated as being made up to 14 days later, so that you can claim up to 14 days in advance of your entitlement beginning.

The people included in your claim

You can only qualify for Scottish child payment for a child you are responsible for (see p1712). It does not matter if the child element of universal credit or child tax credit is not payable because of the 'two-child limit'. There is no limit on the number of children that you can get Scottish child payment for. If you are part of a couple, whoever applies first will usually be paid the Scottish child payment.

Getting paid

Scottish child payment is payable weekly, starting on the day your claim is received. Payments are made every four weeks, in arrears, into your nominated account. If you apply for Scottish child payment in advance when it is first introduced, your first payment may be for one, two or three weeks, before you are paid on a four-weekly cycle.[12]

Your Scottish child payment may be reduced if you have an outstanding overpayment of Scottish benefit, but your financial circumstances must be considered in deciding whether to reduce your Scottish child payment and by how much.[13] You can request a redetermination of the reduced amount (see Chapter 77).

Change of circumstances

Your Scottish child payment entitlement can be determined again following a change of circumstances relating to the qualifying conditions – ie, responsibility for the child, ordinary residence in Scotland, entitlement to qualifying benefits. A new determination can be made on your Scottish child payment if SSS decides to pay someone else for the child instead. Your Scottish child payment entitlement can be determined again if it is considered, on the basis of new information received, that the original determination to award you it was made incorrectly.[14]

It is expected that, in the first stage of introduction, your Scottish child payment will end from the week after the week in which the child's sixth birthday falls.[15]

5. **Tax, other benefits and the benefit cap**

Tax

It is expected that Scottish child payment will not be taxable.

Part 12: Scottish social security benefits
Chapter 74: Scottish child payment
Notes

Means-tested benefits and tax credits

It is expected that Scottish child payment will not count as income for means-tested benefits or tax credits.

The benefit cap

In some cases, there is a limit on the total amount of specified benefits you can receive (a 'benefit cap'). It is expected that Scottish child payment will not count as a specified benefit. See p1194 for further information.

Passports and other sources of help

Scottish child payment does not directly help you qualify for any other benefits, but if you are entitled to Scottish child payment, you may also be entitled to:
- Best Start grant, depending on the age(s) of your child(ren) (see Chapter 72);
- Best Start foods, depending on the ages of your children and your other income or earnings (see p865);
- health benefits (see Chapter 31);
- council tax reduction (see p851);
- education benefits such as a clothing grant (see p866).

Notes

1 gov.scot/policies/social-security/ scottish-child-payment

1. Who can get Scottish child payment
2 SCP Regs (draft)
3 Sch, para 3 SCP Regs (draft)
4 Regs 9 and 12 SCP Regs (draft)
5 Regs 10, 13 and 14 SCP Regs 2020 (draft)

4. Claims and getting paid
6 Sch para 15 SCP Regs (draft)
7 Sch para 16 SCP Regs (draft)
8 Sch para 1 SCP Regs (draft)
9 Scottish government, *Scottish Child Payment, Updated Policy Position Paper,* January 2020
10 Sch para 12 SCP Regs (draft)

11 Sch para 11 SCP Regs (draft)
12 Reg 18(2) SCP Regs (draft); Scottish government, *Scottish Child Payment, Updated Policy Position Paper,* January 2020
13 Reg 18 SCP Regs 2020 (draft)
14 Sch paras 14 and 15 SCP Regs 2020 (draft)
15 Reg 17(b) SCP Regs 2020 (draft)

12

Chapter 75

Young carer grant

This chapter covers:
1. Who can get young carer grant (below)
2. The rules about your age (p1719)
3. The amount of benefit (p1719)
4. Claims and getting paid (p1719)
5. Tax, other benefits and the benefit cap (p1721)

Key facts
- Young carer grant is a payment for young people aged 16 to 18 living in Scotland who have been caring for someone with a disability.
- You can add together hours caring for different people, but they must all be getting a disability benefit at the right level.
- You can only get young carer grant once a year.
- You cannot qualify for young carer grant if you get carer's allowance on the day you claim.
- Young carer grant is not means tested.
- You can qualify for young carer grant whether you are in or out of work.
- You do not need to have paid national insurance contributions to qualify.
- Young carer grant is administered and paid by Social Security Scotland.
- If you disagree with a decision about a young carer grant, you can request a redetermination, and then appeal against it (see Chapter 77). You must request a redetermination before you can appeal.

1. Who can get young carer grant

You qualify for young carer grant if:[1]
- you are aged at least 16 and under 19 on the date you claim; *and*
- you have been caring for at least one severely disabled person (see p1718); *and*
- during the 13 weeks before you claim (the 'qualifying period') you spent sufficient hours caring (see p1718); *and*
- you are not entitled to carer's allowance (CA) and have not applied for CA (unless your CA claim has been refused) on the day you claim young carer grant (but see p1721); *and*

Part 12: Scottish social security benefits
Chapter 75: Young carer grant
1. Who can get young carer grant

- you are ordinarily resident in Scotland (see p1585 – but if you move abroad after getting a young carer grant, see p1650); *and*
- you are habitually resident in the UK, Channel Islands, Isle of Man, European Economic Area or Switzerland, unless you are exempt (see p1589).

Note:
- You can get young carer grant once a year. If you have previously received young carer grant, you can claim again one year after the date of your last claim.[2]
- You can only get young carer grant three times in total – ie, one in the year that you are 16, 17 and 18.[3]
- You cannot normally get young carer grant if someone else has received one for someone that you care for within the past year (but see p1721).
- You should claim young carer grant if you meet all of the above conditions, but a person you care for claimed a disability benefit more than 13 weeks ago and has not yet been awarded it. Your claim may be refused, but if the disability benefit is later awarded, you can still get young carer grant (see p1720).
- Getting young carer grant does not affect any benefits that a person you care for gets.

Severely disabled person
A '**severely disabled person**' is someone who gets a 'qualifying disability benefit'. This is either attendance allowance (AA), the highest or middle rate of disability living allowance care component, either rate of the daily living component of personal independence payment, armed forces independence payment or constant attendance allowance of £72.80 a week or more in respect of an industrial injury (see p694) or war disablement (see p869). The benefit must have been paid throughout the 13 weeks before the date of your claim, so if the benefit of someone you care for is not paid for part of the qualifying period (eg, if s/he is in a care home), you cannot count hours spent caring for that person.[4] At the time of writing, it was expected that the highest or middle rate care component of child disability payment (see p1690) will also count as a qualifying disability benefit when it is introduced.

12 The care you must provide

During the 13 weeks before you claim young carer grant (the 'qualifying period'), you must have provided care for at least 208 hours, during at least 10 of those weeks.[5] If you care every week during the qualifying period, this is an average of 16 hours a week. The care you provide must involve activity that promotes the physical, mental or emotional wellbeing of the person you care for.[6] The regulations do not define what this means, but it might include, for example, helping with personal care, dealing with bills, shopping or keeping someone company.

You can add together hours of care you provide for up to three people, as long as they all count as being a 'severely disabled person' (see p1718).

You must not be paid for the hours you spend caring, or provide the care as voluntary work.[7]

Example

Joanne, 17, cares for her grandmother (who gets AA) for about 20 hours a week. She has done so for the past year. Joanne is also doing a Duke of Edinburgh award and volunteers at a youth club for people with learning disabilities as part of the award. Even though Joanne cannot count her voluntary work as hours of care, she can still get a young carer grant, as she spends enough time caring for her grandmother.

2. The rules about your age

You can get young carer grant if you are aged at least 16 and are under 19 on the date of your claim (see p1720).[8]

3. The amount of benefit

Young carer grant is a single annual payment of £305.10.[9] It was £300 for claims made (or treated as made) before 1 April 2020.

4. Claims and getting paid

The general rules on claims and getting paid are covered in Chapter 76. This section explains the specific rules that apply to young carer grants.

Making a claim

You can claim young carer grant:
- online at mygov.scot/young-carer-grant/how-to-apply; *or*
- by telephone on 0800 182 2222; *or*
- in writing on the approved form. Send it to Social Security Scotland, PO Box 10314, Dundee DD1 9GN. A prepaid envelope is available on request.

Forms

You can download the young carer grant form from mygov.scot/young-carer-grant-paper-form or request one by phone.

Part 12: Scottish social security benefits
Chapter 75: Young carer grant
4. Claims and getting paid

Information to support your claim

You are asked to confirm that each person you care for is aware that you are applying for young carer grant and gives her/his permission for Social Security Scotland (SSS) to contact her/him or use her/his personal data. SSS also ask you for evidence of your identity and address after you have claimed. If you claim on the paper form, you can send this evidence, if you have it, with the form.

You can be also be asked to provide any other additional evidence that SSS requests.[10] If you fail to provide such evidence within the time limit that you are given to do so, your claim can be refused.[11] Try to provide any evidence that you are asked for if you can, or explain why this is not possible.

The date of your claim

Your claim is treated as made on the day it is received by SSS, provided it is properly completed.[12] If you do not claim in the correct way, SSS may reject your claim. You can appeal against this decision (see p1748).

Further determination without a claim

If your claim for young carer grant is refused because a person you care for was not receiving a qualifying disability benefit (see p1718) throughout the qualifying period, your entitlement must be determined again if:[13]

- that person is later awarded a qualifying benefit for the whole of the qualifying period: *and*
- no one else has been awarded young carer grant for caring for her/him since you claimed.

If this rule applies and you cannot request a redetermination (eg, as you have missed the time limit to do so), contact SSS immediately and ask for your entitlement to be determined again. If your entitlement is determined again, the date of your claim is the date you originally claimed a young carer grant.[14] If SSS does not make a new determination, you can complain (see p1728) or request a judicial review (see p1414).[15]

Getting paid

Young carer grant is paid into the bank or other account you nominate when you make your claim. If you do not have access to a bank account, you should claim by phone and discuss how you want to receive your grant.

Some, or all, of a payment can be made in a form other than money (eg, a voucher) if you accept an offer from SSS to receive it in this way.[16] If you withdraw your agreement before you get the grant, it must be paid as money.

If someone else has claimed young carer grant

If you and someone else care for the same person and you both claim young carer grant, SSS decides which of you is entitled. The claim that was received first must be decided first.[17]

If someone else has received young carer grant in respect of a person you care for less than one year before the date you claim, you cannot get young carer grant for caring for that person unless:[18]

- the other claimant has died; *or*
- SSS has decided that s/he should not have been paid young carer grant.

5. **Tax, other benefits and the benefit cap**

Tax

Young carer grant is not taxable.[19]

Other benefits and tax credits

Young carer grant does not count as income or capital for means-tested benefits or tax credits.[20]

You cannot qualify for a young carer grant if you are entitled to carer's allowance (CA) on the date of your claim, or if you have claimed CA, unless your application has been refused.[21]

Young carer grant and carer's allowance

– It does not matter if someone else gets CA or the carer element of universal credit (UC) for looking after one or more of the people that you care for, you can still get young carer grant.

– If you care 35 hours a week or more for someone, you may be eligible for both CA and young carer grant. Normally, you should claim young carer grant first. As soon as you are awarded a grant, you can immediately claim CA and request backdating. It does not matter if you are later awarded CA for the date of your young carer grant claim. However, if your young carer grant takes a long time to be awarded then in some situations you may lose out. Seek advice if you are unsure.

– If your CA stops (eg, if you start work or education), check if you can get young carer grant. Days on which you got CA can count as part of the 13-week qualifying period for young carer grant (see p1718).

The benefit cap

In some cases, there is a limit on the total amount of specified benefits you can receive (a 'benefit cap'). Young carer grant is not a specified benefit. The benefit

Part 12: Scottish social security benefits
Chapter 75: Young carer grant
Notes

cap only applies if you are getting UC or housing benefit. See p1194 for further information.

Passports and other sources of help

If you are a young carer living in Scotland, you can get access to a package of support (whether or not you can get young carer grant). For more information and how to sign up, visit the Young Scot website.[22]

Notes

1. Who can get young carer grant
1 s28 and Sch 2 SS(S)A 2018; Part 2 CA(YCG)(S) Regs
2 Reg 7(3) CA(YCG)(S) Regs
3 Reg 7(6) CA(YCG)(S) Regs
4 Reg 6(1) CA(YCG)(S) Regs
5 Reg 5(2) CA(YCG)(S) Regs
6 Reg 5(3) CA(YCG)(S) Regs
7 Reg 5(4) CA(YCG)(S) Regs, which only excludes the care that you provide as paid or voluntary work from counting, and does not exclude you from entitlement to a grant if you are a care worker.

2. The rules about your age
8 Reg 4(1) CA(YCG)(S) Regs

3. The amount of benefit
9 Reg 12(1) CA(YCG)(S) Regs

4. Claims and getting paid
10 s54(1) SS(S)A 2018
11 s54 SS(S)A 2018
12 Reg 4 CA(YCG)(S) Regs
13 Reg 11 CA(YCG)(S) Regs
14 Reg 11(3) CA(YCG)(S) Regs
15 s41(1) SS(S)A 2018 – you can only request a redetermination of a determination, not a failure to make a determination
16 Reg 12(3) CA(YCG)(S) Regs
17 Reg 10 CA(YCG)(S) Regs
18 Reg 7(4) and (5) CA(YCG)(S) Regs

5. Tax, other benefits and the benefit cap
19 s677 IT(EP)A 2003
20 **WTC/CTC** Reg 19 Table 6(29) TC (DCI) Regs
While regulations providing for young carer grant to be disregarded for benefits had not come into force at the time of writing, the Scottish government has an agreement with the DWP that 'internal guidance' will instruct decision makers to disregard young carer grant until such time as the regulations are amended (email from Scottish government to CPAG, 23 October 2019). The guidance to local authority HB staff is in *LA Welfare Direct Lite 10/2019,* available from gov.uk.
21 Reg 7(1) and (2) CA(YCG)(S) Regs
22 young.scot/campaigns/national/young-carers

Chapter 76

Claiming Scottish benefits and getting paid

This chapter covers:
1. Claims and determinations (below)
2. Getting paid (p1725)
3. Overpayments (p1725)
4. Fraud (p1726)
5. Complaints (p1728)

Key facts
- Scottish social security benefits are administered and paid by Social Security Scotland (SSS).
- To be entitled to a Scottish benefit, you must usually make a claim for it.
- Decisions on entitlement to Scottish benefits are called 'determinations'.
- You must give correct and complete information when you make your claim, and report any changes that could affect your entitlement.
- Some overpayments, called 'assistance given in error', are recoverable.
- If you are unhappy about the way you have been treated by SSS, you can complain.

1. Claims and determinations

In most cases, to be entitled to a Scottish social security benefit, you must make a claim for it.[1] Social Security Scotland (SSS) refers to claims as 'applications'. If you cannot claim for yourself, an 'appointee' (see p1724) can claim on your behalf.[2]

How to make a claim

Each Scottish benefit has (or will have) its own rules for how to make a claim. See the chapter in this part of the *Handbook* about the benefit you want to claim. You may be able to claim in writing, online or by telephone.

Part 12: Scottish social security benefits
Chapter 76: Claiming Scottish benefits and getting paid
1. Claims and determinations

If you do not claim in the correct way, SSS may reject your application. You have a right of appeal in this situation: this is called a 'process appeal'. See p1748 for more information.[3]

You may be asked to provide further information before a decision (known as a 'determination') is made on your claim.[4] You should be given a specific period of time to respond to the request for more information. If you fail to provide the required information within the time you are given to do so, SSS may determine that you are not entitled to the benefit you have claimed.[5] If this happens, you can ask for a redetermination of the decision that you are not entitled to the benefit you have claimed (see p1731).

Withdrawing a claim

Once you have made a claim for a Scottish benefit you can withdraw your claim at any point before the determination is made, provided you do so in the way you are told to by SSS.[6]

The determination

Once a correctly made claim for a Scottish benefit is received, SSS must make a 'determination' on the claim and must then give you notice of the determination.[7] The notice of determination must tell you what the determination is, the reasons for it and your right to challenge it. See Chapter 77 for more information on challenging determinations.

If you are refused a Scottish benefit because you have made your claim too soon (eg, if you claim a pregnancy and baby payment (see p1696) before you have reached the 24th week of pregnancy), the determination notice must tell you when you should make another claim.[8]

If you have made a claim for a Scottish benefit and, in the course of dealing with your claim, SSS identifies a potential entitlement to another Scottish benefit, you must be informed of this and told how to claim.[9] In certain situations, it may be possible for SSS to determine your eligibility for the other benefit without your having to make a claim, although you may be asked to provide more information.[10] For example, if you have claimed one type of Best Start grant (eg, a pregnancy and baby payment) and SSS discovers that you will also be entitled to a payment for another child (eg, a school-age payment) within 10 days of the date of your claim, it can decide your entitlement without your having to make a new claim.[11]

Appointees

Someone else (eg, a relative or friend) can be authorised to act on your behalf if s/he is aged 16 or over and you cannot claim for yourself – eg, if you have a mental illness or a learning disability.[12] S/he is called an 'appointee'. The appointee takes on your rights and responsibilities as a claimant and receives payment of benefit.

You must be incapable within the meaning of the Adults with Incapacity (Scotland) Act 2000, with no guardian acting or appointed under that Act and no other person who has the power to act on your behalf and is willing to do so.

If someone has died and there is no executor appointed to deal with the estate, another person can be appointed to deal with social security issues.[13]

Right to support

During the claim and assessment process, you can have someone with you to support you.[14] This includes during any discussions with SSS and during any assessment you are asked to undertake. A supporter is allowed to make representations to SSS on your behalf.

2. Getting paid

Once Social Security Scotland (SSS) has made a determination that you are entitled to benefit, you must be paid.[15] For details of how you are paid, see the chapter in this part of the *Handbook* about the benefit you have claimed.

Once you are receiving a Scottish benefit, you can ask for it to be stopped at any time.[16]

If you have an ongoing entitlement to a Scottish benefit, SSS will inform you about your responsibility to report any changes in your circumstances (see p1752). You must be advised what changes you need to report and how to report them.[17] In some situations, failing to report a change of circumstances can constitute an offence (see p1726).[18]

3. Overpayments

If you are paid a Scottish benefit by mistake or you are paid more than you should have been, Social Security Scotland (SSS) calls this overpayment 'assistance given in error'. You may have to repay an overpayment, but only in certain circumstances.[19] At the time of writing, the Scottish government intended that these rules would also apply to Scottish child payment.[20]

Overpayments that may be recoverable

Overpayments of Scottish benefits can be recovered from you if you were paid in error and the error was caused, or contributed to, by your:
- providing false or misleading information; *or*
- failing to report a change of circumstances which you were told you should report; *or*
- causing someone else to do either of the above.[21]

Part 12: Scottish social security benefits
Chapter 76: Claiming Scottish benefits and getting paid
4. Fraud

An overpayment can also be recovered from you if you could have been reasonably expected to notice the error.[22] When assessing this, the following are examples of what should be taken into account:[23]

- the amount of benefit paid to you, compared with your actual entitlement; *and*
- any information given to you by SSS that might have alerted you to the fact that the award was wrong.

Other relevant matters can also be taken into account.

Recovery of overpayments

The amount recoverable is the amount of benefit you received less your actual entitlement (if any) had the error not taken place.[24]

Even if the overpayment is recoverable, SSS has the discretion not to recover it from you (eg, if recovery would cause you financial hardship) and also should use its discretion when considering the method of recovery.[25]

It is likely that SSS will be able to recover an overpayment by making deductions from Scottish social security benefits which are paid on an ongoing basis.[26] See AskCPAG.org.uk and CPAG's *Welfare Rights Bulletin* for updates.

If a Scottish benefit is paid in respect of a person following her/his death, it can be recovered from her/his estate.[27]

Challenging an overpayment determination

If you disagree with a determination about an overpayment, you can ask for a redetermination (see p1731). If you are still unhappy following the redetermination, you can appeal (see p1734). **Note:** a 'determination' has a specific legal meaning.[28] Some decisions made about overpayments (eg, that an overpayment is recoverable from you) may not constitute a determination and so you may not be able to challenge them using the redetermination and appeal process. In this situation, you should seek advice and consider making a complaint (see p1728), involving your MSP and/or considering judical review action (see p1446). See AskCPAG.org.uk and CPAG's *Welfare Rights Bulletin* for updates.

4. **Fraud**

The following are offences under the Social Security (Scotland) Act 2018.[29]

- Trying to obtain assistance by deceit. This means that you provide, or cause someone else to provide, misleading or false information with the intention of obtaining a Scottish benefit to which you would not otherwise be entitled.
- Without reasonable excuse, failing to notify a change of circumstances as soon as reasonably practicable. This must be a change which you have a duty to

notify and which you ought to have known would result in your entitlement stopping or being reduced. It is also an offence to cause another person to fail to notify a change of circumstances.

The possible penalties if you are convicted of fraud include a fine and/or imprisonment.[30] At the time of writing, the Scottish government intended that these rules would also apply to Scottish child payment.[31]

Powers of investigation

An 'authorised officer' is authorised by Social Security Scotland (SSS) to carry out certain investigations into suspected fraud.[32] An authorised officer can require a person or body to provide information relevant to the fraud investigation. This includes electronic records.[33]

The following organisations cannot be required to provide information, unless the information relates to the employment of a person by that organisation or relates to the nature of services provided by an individual to the organisation:[34]
- those whose main purpose is providing free advice or information on social security, housing or debt;
- law centres;
- voluntary organisations providing accommodation, support or advocacy services to people who have experienced domestic abuse;
- certain advocacy services.

Authorised officers can request permission to enter premises, but not if the premises are occupied as someone's home.[35] They can only enter and search premises with the permission of the occupier or, if the premises are not occupied, of the owner.[36]

In the context of a fraud investigation, it is an offence to:[37]
- intentionally delay an authorised officer in her/his investigation;
- fail to comply with any requirement, without good reason;
- knowingly provide false or misleading material;
- destroy information with the intention of avoiding compliance.

The possible penalty for this offence is a fine.[38]

Interviews under caution

If you are suspected of fraud, SSS may invite you to take part in a formal interview, called an 'interview under caution'. Taking part in this interview is voluntary. You should be sent a letter inviting you to attend and SSS should be flexible about where and when the interview takes place, taking account of any particular needs you have.[39] You should be cautioned before the interview starts. This means you should be told that you do not need to say anything and that anything you do say

Part 12: Scottish social security benefits
Chapter 76: Claiming Scottish benefits and getting paid
Notes

during the interview can be used in evidence in court if there is a criminal prosecution. The interview will be recorded and you are entitled to ask for a copy of the recording.[40] You can have someone with you at the interview for support – eg, a friend, relative, advocate, welfare rights worker or solicitor.[41]

5. **Complaints**

If you are unhappy about the way you have been treated by Social Security Scotland (SSS), you can complain. Your complaint can be about any issue concerning how your claim has been handled or how you have been treated. This includes matters such as delays, discourtesy, poor administration, the behaviour of staff and bad advice.

You should complain by contacting SSS by telephone (0800 182 2222, Monday to Friday 8am to 6pm; Relay UK 18001, then 0300 244 4000; or if you are a British Sign Language user, you can use the contactSCOTLAND app to contact SSS by video relay) or in writing (Social Security Scotland, General Enquiries, PO Box 10304, Dundee DD1 9FZ). SSS states that it will try to resolve your complaint within a week, unless it is more complex, in which case it will try to resolve it within four weeks. The SSS charter states that staff will listen to complaints, learn and improve the service.[42]

If you are still unhappy after your complaint has been considered by SSS, you can complain to the Scottish Public Services Ombudsman. Usually you must complain to the Ombudsman within 12 month of the event you are complaining about. Use the online complaint form at spso.org.uk/complain/form/start or contact the office by telephone on 0800 377 7330 or in person (SPSO, Bridgeside House, 99 McDonald Road, Edinburgh EH7 4NS: Monday, Wednesday, Thursday, Friday 9am to 5pm, Tuesday 10am to 5pm).

Notes

12

1. Claims and determinations
1 **SCP** Sch paras 1 and 2 SCP Regs (draft)
Other benefits ss37 and 38 SS(S)A 2018
2 **SCP** Sch para 17(1) and (2)(c) SCP Regs (draft)
Other benefits s58 SS(S)A 2018

3 **SCP** Sch para 1(6) SCP Regs (draft)
Other benefits s38(5) SS(S)A 2018
4 **SCP** Sch para 2(6) SCP Regs (draft)
Other benefits s54(1) SS(S)A 2018
5 **SCP** Sch para 2(7) SCP Regs (draft)
Other benefits s54(2) SS(S)A 2018
6 **SCP** Sch para 1(7) SCP Regs (draft)
Other benefits s39 SS(S)A 2018

7 **SCP** Sch para 2(1) and (2) SCP Regs (draft)
 Other benefits ss37 and 40 SS(S)A 2018
8 s50(2) SS(S)A 2018
9 s53 SS(S)A 2018
10 **SCP** Sch Part 4 SCP Regs (draft)
 Other benefits ss52 and 53(2)(b)(ii) and (3) SS(S)A 2018
11 Sch 1 para 3 EYA(BSG)(S) Regs
12 **SCP** Sch para 17(1) and (2)(c) SCP Regs (draft)
 Other benefits s58 SS(S)A 2018
13 **SCP** Sch para 17(1) and (2)(c) SCP Regs (draft)
 Other benefits s58(3) SS(S)A 2018
14 **SCP** Sch para 17(1) and (2)(d) SCP Regs (draft)
 Other benefits s59 SS(S)A 2018

2. Getting paid

15 **SCP** Sch para 2(5) SCP Regs (draft)
 Other benefits s24 SS(S)A 2018
16 s26 SS(S)A 2018
17 **SCP** Sch para 17(1) and (2)(a) SCP Regs (draft)
 Other benefits s56 SS(S)A 2018
18 **SCP** Sch para 17(1) and (2)(a) SCP Regs (draft)
 Other benefits s56(2)(c) SS(S)A 2018

3. Overpayments

19 **SCP** Sch para 17(1) and (2)(f) SCP Regs (draft)
 Other benefits ss63 and 64 SS(S)A 2018
20 Sch para 17 SCP Regs (draft)
21 **SCP** Sch para 17(1) and (2)(f) SCP Regs (draft)
 Other benefits s64(1)(a) and (2) SS(S)A 2018
22 **SCP** Sch para 17(2)(f) SCP Regs (draft)
 Other benefits s64(1)(b) SS(S)A 2018
23 **SCP** Sch para 17(1) and (2)(f) SCP Regs (draft)
 Other benefits s64(3) SS(S)A 2018
24 **SCP** Sch para 17(1) and (2)(f) SCP Regs (draft)
 Other benefits s63(2) SS(S)A 2018
25 **SCP** Sch para 17(1) and (2)(g) SCP Regs (draft)
 Other benefits s65 SS(S)A 2018
26 Schs 2 para 10(b), 5 para 15(b), 7 para 12(b) and 9 para 11(b) SS(S)A 2018

27 **SCP** Sch para 17(1) and (2)(i)) SCP Regs (draft)
 Other benefits s69 SS(S)A 2018
28 **SCP** Reg 4(b) SCP Regs (draft)
 Other benefits s25 SS(S)A 2018

4. Fraud

29 **SCP** Sch para 17(1) and (2)(j) SCP Regs (draft)
 Other benefits ss71-73 SS(S)A 2018
30 **SCP** Sch para 17(1) and (2)(j) SCP Regs (draft)
 Other benefits ss71(3), 72(4) and 73(4) SS(S)A 2018
31 Letter from Cabinet Secretary for Social Security and Older People to the Convener of the Social Security Committee, 21 February 2020, available at parliament.scot/S5_Social_Security/ General%20Documents/ 20200221_CabSecSSOP_to_Convener_ Social_Security_Bill.pdf
32 Regs 2 and 3 SSA(IO)(S) Regs
33 Regs 4 and 7 SSA(IO)(S) Regs
34 Regs 5 and 7 SSA(IO)(S) Regs
35 Reg 8(2) SSA(IO)(S) Regs
36 Reg 8(1) SSA(IO)(S) Regs
37 Reg 9 SSA(IO)(S) Regs
38 Reg 9 SSA(IO)(S) Regs
39 SSS, *Code of Practice for Investigations*, para 72
40 SSS, *Code of Practice for Investigations*, para 74
41 SSS, *Code of Practice for Investigations*, para 76

5. Complaints

42 SSS, *Our Charter*, p6

12

Getting a determination changed

This chapter covers:
1. Redeterminations (see p1731)
2. Appealing to the First-tier Tribunal (see p1734)
3. Appealing to the Upper Tribunal (see p1744)
4. Appealing to the Court of Session (see p1747)
5. Appealing about 'process decisions' (see p1748)
6. Other ways of getting a new determination (see p1750)

This chapter only applies to the Scottish benefits listed on p1688. Chapters 56, 57 and 58 explain the rules on revisions and appeals for other benefits. This chapter refers you to Chapters 57 and 58 when the rules are the same as for other benefits.

Note: at the time of writing, it was expected that the common rules described in this chapter would apply to Scottish child payment (see Chapter 74), except where noted below. However, the regulations had not been finalised. See AskCPAG.org.uk and CPAG's *Welfare Rights Bulletin* for updates.

Key facts
- If you disagree with a determination of your entitlement to a Scottish benefit, you can ask Social Security Scotland to remake it. This is called a 'redetermination'.
- If you are unhappy with the redetermination, you can appeal to an independent tribunal, the First-tier Tribunal for Scotland Social Security Chamber.
- If the First-tier Tribunal applies the law wrongly, you can appeal to the Upper Tribunal for Scotland against its decision.
- You can make a different kind of appeal if you claimed a Scottish benefit or requested a redetermination in the wrong way.
- There are strict time limits to request a redetermination and appeal.
- In some circumstances, a further determination can be made if you were refused a Scottish benefit, even if you cannot request a redetermination.
- If you get ongoing payments of a Scottish benefit, it is expected that a new determination will be made if your circumstances change, and in some other situations.

Time limits

For Scottish benefits, you are normally treated as having received something sent to you by Social Security Scotland or a Scottish tribunal by post or email 48 hours after it was sent, unless it can be proved that you received it earlier or later.[1] In practice, this means that a time limit to take action normally runs from two days (this includes weekends and bank holidays) after the date on which something is sent to you.

This rule *does not* apply if you are given a written decision by hand (eg, after a First-tier Tribunal hearing), and to some time limits to challenge tribunal decisions, which instead run from the date on which the decision is sent to you.[2] Which rule applies in a particular situation is explained in the relevant section of this chapter.

1. **Redeterminations**

Once you have claimed a Scottish benefit in the correct way (or are treated as having made a claim) and provided any required evidence, Social Security Scotland (SSS) must make a 'determination' of your entitlement (see p1724).[3] This is similar to a 'decision' about other benefits.

You must be told about the determination in a way that gives you a record of it – eg, by letter.[4] The notification must give the reasons for the determination, and tell you that you can request a redetermination if you disagree with it.[5]

When you cannot request a redetermination

If you try to claim a benefit in the wrong way, or do not provide some evidence that you need to send with your claim, SSS does not have to determine your entitlement.[6] You should be told if your entitlement will not be determined for this reason, and of your right to appeal against this 'process decision' (see p1748).[7] You should also make another claim as soon as possible.[8] For one-off payments and grants there is a time limit to make a claim. See the chapter of this *Handbook* about the benefit that you tried to claim for details.

Who can request a redetermination

You can request a redetermination if you claimed a Scottish benefit, are claiming as someone else's appointee (see p1724) or have legal authority to act for someone – eg, as a guardian or judicial factor, or the executor of someone who has died.[9]

How to request a redetermination

SSS decides how you must request a redetermination.[10] This is currently by:[11]
- completing the form sent to you with the determination of entitlement; *or*
- phoning 0800 182 2222.

Note: you may have to request a redetermination differently for different Scottish benefits. Check your determination notice carefully to see what you must do.

Part 12: Scottish social security benefits
Chapter 77: Getting a determination changed
1. Redeterminations

If you request a redetermination in the wrong way, SSS should inform you of this (and does not have to redetermine your entitlement).[12] You can appeal against this 'process decision' (see p1748). If you are still within the time limit to do so (see below), you should also request a redetermination in the correct way, as you cannot be sure that you will win your appeal.

Your request for a redetermination must be received by SSS within 31 days of you being notified of the determination.[13] You are normally treated as being notified of a determination two days after it is sent to you (see p1731).

At the time of writing, the Scottish government intended that the time limit for child disability payment would be 42 days.[14] See AskCPAG.org.uk and CPAG's *Welfare Rights Bulletin* for updates.

Example

Sadie is refused a Best Start grant pregnancy and baby payment. The letter informing her of the determination is dated 1 May. She is treated as receiving it on 3 May. As the time limit to request a redetermination is 31 days, Sadie's redetermination request must be received by SSS on or before 2 June.

If you miss the time limit

If you miss the time limit, but your redetermination request is received within an absolute time limit of one year after you were notified of the determination, your entitlement can still be redetermined, if you have 'good reason' (see below) for not making the request sooner.[15] You should explain why your request is late.

Good reason

The law does not define what counts as **'good reason'** for missing a time limit. If you think that your request might be received late, explain in detail why you did not make it sooner. Your reasons might include that:

– you were away from home and so did not receive the determination;
– you did not understand the determination, or what you had to do next;
– you were affected by illness (of yourself or someone you had to look after);
– you were waiting for further evidence (but do not wait until you get such evidence before requesting a redetermination, if this means that you might miss the time limit or you have already missed it); *or*
– you have a condition which makes it hard for you to deal with letters.

Any other reasons that apply in your case may also be relevant, so include them as well.

If SSS does not accept your reasons for missing the time limit, it does not redetermine your entitlement. You should be notified of this, and can then appeal against this 'process decision' not to redetermine your entitlement (see p1748).[16]

After you request a redetermination

Once you have made a valid request for a redetermination, SSS must redetermine your entitlement.[17] If you have additional evidence that shows why the determination was wrong, you should send a copy of it to SSS.

When it is redetermining your entitlement, the law does not prevent SSS from taking into account changes that have occurred since the original determination was made.[18] For grants and one-off payments, any changes must be to your circumstances *at the time you originally claimed.* You should therefore mention anything that means the determination is now incorrect, even if SSS could not have known about it when determining your entitlement.

Example

When Sasha's Best Start grant claim was determined, she did not get a qualifying benefit, so her claim was refused. She requests a redetermination and provides evidence that she has now been awarded universal credit, and her award starts from before she claimed a Best Start grant. The redetermination awards Sasha a Best Start grant, even though when the original determination was made it was correct.

The time limit for a redetermination to be carried out

There is a time limit for SSS to redetermine your entitlement.[19] This is normally 16 working days (see below) from the day SSS receives a valid redetermination request.[20] However, if you requested a redetermination late, the time limit runs from the date SSS (or if you had to appeal about this, the First-tier Tribunal – see p1748) decides you had good reason for not making your request in time.[21]

At the time of writing, the Scottish government planned to extend the time limit to redetermine your entitlement due to the coronavirus pandemic.[22] See AskCPAG.org.uk and CPAG's *Welfare Rights Bulletin* for updates.

Working days

A '**working day**' is any day other than a Saturday, Sunday or bank holiday.[23] A bank holiday is not the same as a public holiday, as public holidays may not be the same in different areas. There is a list of Scottish bank holidays at gov.scot/publications/bank-holidays.

If your entitlement is redetermined within the time limit above, you must be:[24]
- notified of the redetermination outcome; *and*
- given the reasons for it; *and*
- told that you can appeal against it if you do not agree with it; *and*
- sent an appeal form you can use to do so.

12

Part 12: Scottish social security benefits
Chapter 77: Getting a determination changed
2. Appealing to the First-tier Tribunal

If your entitlement is *not* redetermined within the time limit, you must be informed of this.[25] You then have the right to appeal immediately to the First-tier Tribunal against the original determination.[26]

Note: if you have been told that you have the right of appeal because your redetermination request has not been dealt with in time, SSS can still redetermine your entitlement at a later date.[27] You might be told that you can choose to wait for a redetermination before appealing, but you should make sure you appeal within the 31-day time limit to do so. The time limit to appeal runs from the date that you are told that you have the right of appeal.

2. Appealing to the First-tier Tribunal

You can only appeal against a determination of your entitlement to a Scottish benefit after you have requested a redetermination (see p1731). **Note:** you can appeal against some other decisions (known as 'process decisions') without having to request a redetermination first (see p1748).

Appeals about Scottish benefits are decided by the Social Security Chamber of the First-tier Tribunal for Scotland, which is administered by the Scottish Courts and Tribunals Service. **Note:** some of the rules on appeals about Scottish benefits are different from the rules for other benefits, so you should first check the information in this section. This chapter refers you to Chapter 57 where the rules are the same.

At the time of writing, the Scottish government intended that the rules set out in this section would also apply to appeals about Scottish child payment.[28]

Some of the terms used in the Scottish tribunal rules and the UK tribunal rules are different, but have the same meaning.

UK tribunal rules	Scottish tribunal rules
Direction	Order
Strike out a case	Dismiss a case
Stay proceedings	Sist proceedings
Summons	Citation
Judge	Legal member
Set aside	Quash (if the action is taken by the Upper Tribunal)

Who can appeal

If you can request a redetermination (see p1731), you also have the right of appeal.

Note: for Scottish benefits, the rules do not explicitly allow your representative to make an appeal for you, so you should sign the appeal form yourself, even if you have a representative helping you to appeal.[29]

How to appeal

You must appeal in the way required by Social Security Scotland (SSS). An appeal form must be sent to you with your redetermination notice or a notification that the redetermination has not been done within the time limit.[30] If you appeal in writing, you must send the form to SSS.[31]

SSS also currently allows an appeal to be submitted by phoning 0800 182 2222 and giving details of your appeal.[32] Check what you must do to submit your appeal in the information that SSS sends you, as how you can appeal may change.

Making sure your appeal is valid

To be valid, your appeal must be submitted in the required way (see above), and must include the following information:[33]
- your name and address; *and*
- the name and address of your representative, if you have one (see p1362 – the rules are the same as for other benefits except you must still be sent all relevant documents, even if you have a representative);[34] *and*
- a postal address or email address where documents can be sent to you; *and*
- details of the determination you are challenging (the name of the benefit and the date of the determination or redetermination should be sufficient); *and*
- why you disagree with the determination; *and*
- if your appeal is late (see below), the reasons why you did not appeal sooner.

If it is impossible for you to provide some of this information (eg, if you have no fixed address), you should still submit your appeal as soon as possible, and explain why it is incomplete. The First-tier Tribunal can waive these requirements,[35] but for the purposes of deciding whether your appeal is late (see below), you do not count as having made an appeal until you provide all the above information (or the requirement is waived by the tribunal).[36]

The time limit for appealing

Your appeal must be received by SSS within 31 days of you being notified of the redetermination (or that the redetermination has not been carried out in time).[37] You are normally treated as receiving a notification two days after it was sent (see p1731).

If you miss the time limit

If you miss the time limit, but your appeal is received within an absolute time limit of one year after you were notified of the redetermination (or that the time limit for a redetermination had been missed), it can still be admitted.[38]

12

Part 12: Scottish social security benefits
Chapter 77: Getting a determination changed
2. Appealing to the First-tier Tribunal

You must explain why your appeal is late. If the First-tier Tribunal accepts that you have good reason for not appealing in time, your appeal goes ahead, unless you have missed the absolute time limit. For some things that may count as good reason, see p1732.

After you appeal

As soon as it receives your appeal, SSS must send it to the First-tier Tribunal, along with the information used to make the determination, and inform you that it has done so.[39] SSS must still send your appeal to the First-tier Tribunal, even if it thinks that you have missed the time limit to appeal.[40] If your appeal is missing some of the required information (see p1735) or is late (see above), the tribunal may ask you for more information to help it decide whether or not it should go ahead.

The response

Once the First-tier Tribunal decides that your appeal has been validly made, it informs you and SSS of this in writing.[41] SSS then has 31 days to produce a response to the appeal, and send it to the tribunal.[42] See p1354 for details of what information is included in the response. The tribunal sends the response to you, and to your representative if you have one.[43]

The enquiry form

The First-tier Tribunal sends you a form asking whether you want a hearing of your appeal and, if so, when you and your representative are available. It is usually best to ask for a hearing (see p1366).

If you have a representative, or want someone else to come to the appeal hearing, you should consult her/him before returning the enquiry form, so you can tell the tribunal about any dates s/he is not available for an appeal hearing.

Providing other information

You (or your representative) can make written comments or submit evidence in reply to the SSS response. You must do so within 31 days of receiving it.[44] You are treated as receiving the response two days after it was sent (see p1731).[45] You can ask for this time limit to be extended.[46] Your request should be made in writing, explaining why you need more time to reply. See p1355 – the considerations are the same as for appeals about other benefits.

What the First-tier Tribunal can do

The powers of the First-tier Tribunal are similar to those for appeals about other benefits. Most of the information on pp1352–65 also applies to appeals about Scottish benefits. See, in particular, the information about what the First-tier Tribunal can do on p1357 – the powers are similar, although the terms used are sometimes different (see p1734).[47]

The most important differences for appeals about Scottish benefits are the following.

- Your appeal does not lapse (not go ahead) if the decision maker makes a new determination before it is heard (see p1739).
- The First-tier Tribunal *cannot* dispose of your appeal with a consent order.[48]
- If you fail to attend a hearing as a witness or produce a document when ordered to do so by the tribunal, this is potentially a criminal offence, but it is dealt with by the courts, not the Upper Tribunal.[49]
- The First-tier Tribunal cannot designate a 'lead case' (although it can join your appeal with another one if it raises the same issues).[50]
- There are no special rules about 'test cases',[51] but note that the First-tier Tribunal can sometimes 'sist' (delay) your case – eg, if it decides to wait for the outcome of another appeal (see below).

Sisting appeals

The tribunal can make an order sisting your appeal.[52] This means that it is not decided straight away. This power might be used, for example, to wait for the Upper Tribunal or a court to decide another case that raises similar issues to yours.

You can ask the First-tier Tribunal to make another order which sets aside the order sisting your case.[53] Your application must be in writing and give reasons. For example, it might be urgent that your appeal is heard as soon as possible, or you may be able to argue that the issues in your case are not exactly the same as those in another case. However, it can sometimes be to your advantage to wait for another case to be decided, so get advice.

When your appeal can be dismissed

Note: 'dismissing' an appeal about a Scottish benefit means the same as 'striking out' an appeal about another benefit. If the First-tier Tribunal dismisses your appeal, it does not decide whether the determination of your entitlement was correct.[54]

The only situation in which the First-tier Tribunal *must* dismiss your appeal is if it does not have jurisdiction to hear your case.[55] In this case, it can transfer your case to another court or tribunal that does have jurisdiction. You must be given an opportunity to argue that your appeal should not be dismissed.[56]

The First-tier Tribunal *may* dismiss all or part of your appeal if:[57]

- you fail to comply with an order which warned you that your appeal could be dismissed if you did not comply; *or*
- there is no possibility of you meeting the conditions of entitlement for the benefit your appeal is about; *or*
- you have failed to co-operate with the First-tier Tribunal to the extent that it cannot deal with your case fairly. In this case, you must be given an opportunity to argue that your appeal should not be dismissed.[58]

Part 12: Scottish social security benefits
Chapter 77: Getting a determination changed
2. Appealing to the First-tier Tribunal

You must be notified in writing that your appeal has been dismissed.[59]

The rules also allow the First-tier Tribunal to bar SSS from taking any further part in the appeal if it fails to co-operate or to comply with an order. See p1362 – the rules are the same as for other benefits.[60]

Note: in addition to requesting that your appeal is reinstated, it is arguable that you can request a statement of reasons for the decision dismissing your appeal, and then appeal against it (see p1741).[61] Requesting a reinstatement does not stop the time limits to take these actions from running.

Reinstating an appeal that has been dismissed

If your appeal has been dismissed because you failed to comply with an order, you can request that it is reinstated. Your request must be made in writing, giving reasons why the appeal should be reinstated, and be received by the First-tier Tribunal within 31 days of you being notified of the dismissal.[62] You are normally treated as being notified two days after a notice is sent (see p1731).[63] The First-tier Tribunal can change this deadline (including shortening it), so check the notice of dismissal carefully, and try to request a reinstatement within the time limit on the notice.

Your appeal is only reinstated if the First-tier Tribunal accepts that you have 'good reason' for not complying with the order.[64] 'Good reason' is not defined in the rules. You should explain exactly why you did not comply with an order or co-operate with the tribunal if this is why your appeal was dismissed.

Withdrawing an appeal

You can withdraw your appeal if you decide not to go ahead with it. See p1363 for details of how to withdraw an appeal, including when you need the First-tier Tribunal's permission, and reinstating an appeal if you change your mind. The rules are similar to those for other benefits,[65] except that if you (or SSS) ask for your appeal to be reinstated:

- the time limit to do so is different; *and*
- the appeal is only reinstated if there is 'good reason' to do so.

If you apply for reinstatement of a withdrawn appeal, the First-tier Tribunal must receive your application within 31 days of you being notified that your appeal has been withdrawn. You are treated as being notified:[66]

- if you withdrew your appeal at an oral hearing in person, on that day; *or*
- if the withdrawal was notified in writing, two days after it was sent to you.

The First-tier Tribunal can change this deadline (including shortening it), so check the withdrawal notice carefully, and try to request a reinstatement within the time limit.[67]

'Good reason'

The First-tier Tribunal only reinstates your appeal if it is satisfied that you have 'good reason'. **'Good reason'** is not defined in the rules. Some examples might be if:

– you did not realise that even though you have been awarded some benefit, you did not get everything you could have got if you had won your appeal;

– you thought you had no chance of success, but have since received expert advice and realised that you have a good case for your appeal;

– you have received evidence which shows that you meet the entitlement conditions (if so, send a copy of it with your request);

– you were anxious about going to an appeal hearing, but have now realised that you can take someone along to support you.

You should mention any other reasons why you think your appeal should be reinstated.

If there is a new determination before your appeal is heard

In some situations, SSS may determine your entitlement to the same benefit after you have already appealed – eg, if you are later awarded a 'qualifying benefit' following an appeal (see p1751). If this happens, tell the First-tier Tribunal about the determination. Your appeal should continue, unless you withdraw it.[68]

If you made another claim for the same benefit as well as appealing and this is successful before your appeal is decided, your appeal should continue unless you withdraw it.

If you are in one of these situations, get advice about whether to withdraw your appeal or not. See p1738 for how to withdraw an appeal.

Hearings

The rules about appeal hearings[69] and what you should do to try to prove your case are similar to those for other benefits. See pp1366–85 for details. If you need to request a postponement or adjournment of a hearing, see p1359.

The following aspects of appeal hearings are different for Scottish benefits.

• The First-tier Tribunal can arguably consider changes in your circumstances that have occurred since the determination that you are appealing against.[70]

• The First-tier Tribunal can determine your entitlement, so can consider things which were not raised by your appeal.[71] In practice, it may focus on why you disagree with the determination, but you should be prepared for other questions.

• The First-tier Tribunal cannot carry out a medical examination at a hearing.[72]

• In addition to a representative, you can also be accompanied by a 'supporter'.[73] If s/he also wants to give evidence as a witness, you should tell the tribunal clerk this before the hearing starts. The First-tier Tribunal can order that your supporter is excluded from the hearing until s/he gives evidence.[74] If this

12

Part 12: Scottish social security benefits
Chapter 77: Getting a determination changed
2. Appealing to the First-tier Tribunal

happens, you can still ask the tribunal to let your supporter be present – eg, if it would be harder for you to give evidence without her/him in the room.[75]

Note: there is unlikely to be much caselaw about Scottish benefits during the lifetime of this *Handbook*. Some caselaw about other benefits may be relevant. Get advice about whether caselaw is relevant to your situation if you are unsure.

The tribunal's decision

The ways in which you can be told about the First-tier Tribunal's decision are the same as for other benefits (see p1385).[76] However, there are important differences in what you can do if you do not agree with the decision.

Record of proceedings

First-tier Tribunal appeals must normally be recorded digitally. If the recording equipment fails, a written record of proceedings must be produced instead.[77] If you are requesting a statement of reasons (see below) or considering whether to appeal against the tribunal's decision (see p1741), it is a good idea to request a copy of the recording as well.

The statement of reasons

You should always check the decision notice carefully. If you are considering challenging the tribunal's decision, it is always best to request a written statement of reasons (and the record of proceedings), unless the decision notice says it is also a full written statement of reasons. The more information you have about a decision, the easier it is to show that the tribunal has made an error of law.

The rules about written statements of reasons are similar to other benefits (see p1386),[78] but with the following differences.

- Your request for a statement of reasons must be received by the First-tier Tribunal within 31 days of you being notified of a decision. The tribunal can amend this time limit (including shortening it), so check the time limit on your decision notice.[79] You are treated as being notified:[80]
  – on the day of the hearing if you are given the decision (orally or in writing) that day; *or*
  – two days after the date it was sent to you.
  Note: if you were given the decision orally at a hearing, it is better to make sure that your request for a statement of reasons is received within 14 days of the hearing.[81]
- If the decision notice says that it includes a written summary of the decision, you do not have to request a full statement of reasons before requesting permission to appeal.[82] **Note:** it is usually better to request a statement of reasons anyway, as an application for permission to appeal is not treated as an application for a written statement of reasons if one has not been produced.[83]

If you disagree with the tribunal's decision

If you disagree with the First-tier Tribunal's decision, you can only challenge it if you can show that it made an error of law (see p1397 – the meaning is the same as for other benefits). You should always request a written statement of reasons for the tribunal's decision, unless you already have one (see p1740), to help you to identify possible errors of law.

There are two ways to challenge a decision. You can:
- request a review of the tribunal's decision (see p1742); *or*
- apply straight away for permission to appeal to the Upper Tribunal (see p1744).

Should you request a review or permission to appeal to the Upper Tribunal?

You can choose how to challenge the First-tier Tribunal decision. Bear in mind the following points when deciding what to do, and get advice if you are unsure.

1. A request for a review is automatically treated as also being a request for permission to appeal, unless you ask for this not to happen. You are later given an opportunity to change your mind before that application proceeds.

2. The time limit to apply for a review is shorter (but the First-tier Tribunal can extend it).

3. A review is an extra stage in the process of challenging a decision, but it gives you another opportunity to argue that the First-tier Tribunal made an error of law.

4. If you apply for a review, there may be a hearing (which will normally be before the legal member of the same First-tier Tribunal that heard your appeal). You will need to successfully argue that s/he made an error of law in deciding your case.

5. If there is an obvious error of law, a review may get the First-tier Tribunal's decision changed more quickly.

6. If the First-tier Tribunal decides to change its decision, it can make further findings about the facts of your case at a review hearing to help it make a new decision.

7. If you appeal to the Upper Tribunal, its decision may affect future cases which are similar to yours, while a review has no effect on anyone else's appeal.

Note:
- The First-tier Tribunal can correct any accidental errors or omissions in its decision.[84] This does not affect the time limit to challenge the decision.
- For appeals about Scottish benefits, you cannot request that the First-tier Tribunal sets aside its decision on procedural grounds. There is also no rule that its decision must be set aside if you request permission to appeal against it and you and SSS agree that the tribunal has made an error of law.
- The First-tier Tribunal's powers to review its own decisions are very different for Scottish benefits than for other benefits. The information in Chapters 57 and 58 about reviews does *not* apply to decisions about Scottish benefits.
- The tribunal can suspend its decision if you (or SSS) are challenging it.[85]

Part 12: Scottish social security benefits
Chapter 77: Getting a determination changed
2. Appealing to the First-tier Tribunal

- SSS can apply for a review of, or permission to appeal against, a First-tier Tribunal decision in the same way as you can. If SSS requests a review of a tribunal decision and you also disagree with it, consider requesting permission to appeal to the Upper Tribunal (see below).
- Decisions in 'process appeals' cannot be reviewed or appealed to the Upper Tribunal (see p1748).

Requesting a review

If you think that the First-tier Tribunal has made an error of law, you can ask it to review its decision. Your request for a review must:[86]
- be made in writing; *and*
- be received by the First-tier Tribunal within 14 days of:
  - the date of the decision; *or*
  - the date the written statement of reasons was sent to you, if later; *and*
- identify what error of law the tribunal has made (see p1397).

Note: unless you ask for it not to be, your review request is also treated as being a request for permission to appeal to the Upper Tribunal.[87] This means that following the review decision, you may still be able to appeal to the Upper Tribunal.

Once the decision is made on your review request, you are asked if you want to continue with a request for permission to appeal.[88] You should do so, unless you now think that the First-tier Tribunal's decision is correct – eg, if the review decision has given you what you asked for when you originally appealed.

If Social Security Scotland requests a review

If SSS has requested a review of a First-tier Tribunal decision, consider requesting permission to appeal to the Upper Tribunal (see p1744) if you also disagree with it – eg, if your appeal was partially successful, but you were not awarded everything you asked for by the First-tier Tribunal. The time limit for you to request permission to appeal continues running while a review is carried out, which may take some time.[89] If the review does not change the First-tier Tribunal's decision, you cannot challenge the review decision.[90] This means that you could lose the opportunity to challenge the original tribunal decision while waiting for a review to happen. You can ask the First-tier Tribunal to extend the time limit to request permission to appeal, but there is no guarantee of success.[91]

How the First-tier Tribunal carries out a review

If the First-tier Tribunal considers that a review application is 'without merit' (eg, if it does not identify any arguable errors of law), it is refused immediately. You must be told of the reasons for this.[92] Otherwise, the tribunal sends you (and SSS) a notice:[93]

- setting a time limit for you or SSS to respond to the review request; *and*
- asking for views about whether an oral hearing of the review is needed; *and*
- (if it considers it appropriate) giving its initial views on the request for a review.

Even if you requested the review, you should respond to this notice within the time limit. This is particularly important if you want an oral hearing, or if the First-tier Tribunal has given provisional views on the review and you have comments in response.

The First-tier Tribunal must arrange an oral hearing of the review, unless it decides that one is not needed in the interests of justice.[94] **Note:** even if both you and SSS want an oral hearing, the tribunal does not have to agree to this. See p1366 for information about whether to request an oral hearing.

If it is practicable, the review is carried out by the legal member of the First-tier Tribunal who originally decided your appeal.[95]

The review decision

The review decision must be sent to both you and SSS.[96] The tribunal can:[97]

- take no action; *or*
- correct any minor errors in the decision; *or*
- 'set aside' (cancel) the decision, and:
  - redecide the matter again itself;
  - refer your case to the Upper Tribunal, which can redecide the matter; *or*
  - make an order – eg, for your case to be heard again by a different tribunal.

If it makes a new decision, the First-tier Tribunal can make further findings about the facts of your case.[98] If you attend a hearing of a review, you should therefore be prepared to argue what new decision the tribunal should make (see p1376).

If you disagree with a review decision

If you disagree with a review decision, you cannot request a further review, unless the First-tier Tribunal has 'set aside' (cancelled) its original decision.[99] If the decision was not set aside, you cannot challenge the review decision (but if you requested the review, your request may be treated as a request for permission to appeal to the Upper Tribunal – see p1741). You may still be in time to apply for permission to appeal against the First-tier Tribunal's original decision if you have not done so (see p1744).

If the decision is set aside and remade, and you do not agree with the new decision, you can request permission to appeal to the Upper Tribunal (see p1744).[100] However, you cannot request a further written statement of reasons.[101]

12

Part 12: Scottish social security benefits
Chapter 77: Getting a determination changed
3. Appealing to the Upper Tribunal

3. Appealing to the Upper Tribunal

You can appeal to the Upper Tribunal for Scotland against a decision of the First-tier Tribunal if it made an 'error of law'. Chapter 58 explains what an error of law is and how to appeal to the Upper Tribunal. The rules for appeals about Scottish benefits are similar, but some important differences are set out in this section.

How to appeal

Before you can appeal to the Upper Tribunal, you must request permission to appeal from the First-tier Tribunal (see below). If the First-tier Tribunal refuses you permission, you can request permission from the Upper Tribunal (see p1745).

The rules about how to appeal to the Upper Tribunal are similar to those for other benefits. See p1399 for those rules.[102] There are differences in:

- the time limit to take action – this is generally 30 days, not one month; *and*
- the ways in which the First-tier Tribunal can respond to your application for permission to appeal (see below); *and*
- the form you can use if applying to the Upper Tribunal (see p1745); *and*
- what you can do if the Upper Tribunal refuses you permission to appeal without a hearing (see p1745).

Applying to the First-tier Tribunal

The process of applying to the First-tier Tribunal for permission to appeal is the same as that set out on p1399.[103] However, the time limit and the tribunal's possible responses to your request are different. In particular:

- the First-tier Tribunal is not required to consider reviewing its decision if you apply for permission to appeal. It you want the First-tier Tribunal to review its decision about a Scottish benefit, you should request a review (see p1742);
- the rules do not require the First-tier Tribunal to treat your application as being for a written statement of reasons if you do not have one.[104] This makes it particularly important to check the tribunal decision notice, and apply for a written statement of reasons if you want to challenge it, unless the decision says that it includes full written reasons (see p1740).

Your application for permission to appeal must be received by the First-tier Tribunal within 30 days of:[105]

- the date the decision was sent or given to you, if:
  - you have not requested a written statement of reasons; *or*
  - a full statement of reasons was included in the decision notice; *or*
  - you were given the decision orally at a hearing and you requested a statement of reasons more that 14 days later;[106] *or*
- the date a written statement of reasons that you or Social Security Scotland (SSS) requested was sent to you (but see above); *or*

- if the decision was 'set aside' following a review, the date it was set aside.

This time limit can be extended by the First-tier Tribunal (see p1401).[107]
    If the First-tier Tribunal gives you permission to appeal, you must then appeal to the Upper Tribunal (you can use Form UTS-1 for this – see below) within 30 days of being notified that you have been given permission to appeal.[108] You are treated as receiving the notification two days after it was sent to you.[109]
    Your notice of appeal must:[110]

- identify the First-tier Tribunal decision you are challenging ; *and*
- identify the errors of law in the decision; *and*
- state whether you want a hearing of your appeal or not.

You must send any written decision and statement of reasons from the First-tier Tribunal with your appeal, as well as the notice of permission to appeal.[111]
    If your appeal is late, you must request an extension of time, explain why it is late, and explain why it is in the interests of justice to extend the time limit.[112] Unless the Upper Tribunal extends the time limit, it cannot consider your appeal.[113]

Applying to the Upper Tribunal

The rules about how to apply for permission to appeal to the Upper Tribunal are the same as those set out on p1402, except that the time limit to do so is 30 days rather than one month.[114] The time limit runs from the date on which the First-tier Tribunal sent you its refusal of permission to appeal.
    This time limit can be extended by the Upper Tribunal.[115] If your request is late, you must request an extension of time, explain why it is late, and explain why it is in the interests of justice to extend the time limit.[116] Unless the Upper Tribunal extends the time limit, it must refuse you permission to appeal.[117]

> *Forms*
>
> The Upper Tribunal for Scotland appeal form is form UTS-1, available from scotcourts.gov.uk/the-courts/tribunal-locations/the-upper-tribunal-for-scotland. Post or deliver it to: Upper Tribunal for Scotland, Glasgow Tribunals Centre, 20 York Street, Glasgow G2 8GT.

If you are refused permission to appeal by the Upper Tribunal, you cannot request a review of this decision or appeal against it to the Court of Session.[118]
    However, if the Upper Tribunal refused you permission to appeal (or gave permission to appeal on limited grounds) without a hearing, you can ask for an oral hearing to reconsider that decision. Your application must be made in writing and received by the Upper Tribunal within 14 days of you being notified of the Upper Tribunal's decision.[119] You are treated as receiving the notification two

Part 12: Scottish social security benefits
Chapter 77: Getting a determination changed
3. Appealing to the Upper Tribunal

days after it was sent to you.[120] A different member of the Upper Tribunal then decides at a hearing whether to give you permission to appeal.[121]

If the Upper Tribunal gives you permission to appeal, your application is treated as being a notice of appeal.[122]

What the Upper Tribunal can do

The powers of the Upper Tribunal for Scotland when dealing with an appeal about a Scottish benefit are similar to the powers the Upper Tribunal has for other benefits (see pp1404–08),[123] but with the following differences.

- The time limits for responses and replies are normally 30 days, and run from two days after a document is sent.[124]
- Some of the terms used in the rules are different (see p1734).
- The Upper Tribunal has the same powers as the First-tier Tribunal to dismiss appeals (although an appeal cannot be dismissed on the ground that it is not possible for you to meet the entitlement rules) and reinstate them (see p1737).[125]
- The rules on withdrawing appeals are similar to those for the First-tier Tribunal (see p1738), but you can ask to withdraw only part of your case.[126]
- If you fail to attend a hearing as a witness or produce a document when ordered to do so, this is potentially a criminal offence, but is dealt with by the courts, not the Upper Tribunal.[127]
- The Upper Tribunal can specify one or more lead cases if several cases raise common or related issues. The cases that are not the lead case are 'sisted' (ie, delayed) until the common or related issues have been determined, although you can apply for an order allowing your appeal to continue (see p1737).[128]

Hearings

The rules about oral hearings of Upper Tribunal appeals are similar to those for other benefits (see p1408).[129]

The decision

Upper Tribunal decisions are made in a similar way for Scottish benefits as for other benefits (see p1409).[130]

If you disagree with the Upper Tribunal's decision, you can:
- request a review of it (see below); or
- request permission to appeal against it (see p1747).

Reviewing Upper Tribunal decisions

The Upper Tribunal can review its decision on its own initiative, or if you or SSS ask for a review. If you want a review, you must request this in writing within 14 days of the date of the decision, and give your reasons.[131] The Upper Tribunal must send an application for review to the other parties.[132]

The review must be decided as soon as reasonably practicable, and if possible by the same Upper Tribunal judge(s) who made the decision.[133] The review decision must be sent to both you and SSS.[134] The Upper Tribunal can decide to:[135]

- take no action; *or*
- correct any minor errors in the decision; *or*
- set aside (ie, cancel) the decision and:
  - decide the matter itself (and make further findings of fact if needed);[136] *or*
  - make an order – eg, that there will be an oral hearing of your case.

If the Upper Tribunal makes a new decision, you can request permission to appeal to the Court of Session against the review decision.[137] If the Upper Tribunal does not set aside its decision, you can request permission to appeal against the original decision.[138] See below for how to appeal to the Court of Session.

If the Upper Tribunal does not set aside its decision following a review, the deadline to request permission to appeal is extended by the time between the review application being made (or the Upper Tribunal deciding to review the decision) and the date you receive the review decision.[139] You are treated as receiving the decision two days after it is sent to you by post or email.[140]

4. Appealing to the Court of Session

You can appeal against an Upper Tribunal decision to the Court of Session. You can only appeal if the Upper Tribunal made an 'error of law', and the case also raises an important point of principle or practice, or there are other compelling reasons for the appeal to go ahead.[141] See p1411 for details – the rules are similar to those for other benefits,[142] with the following exceptions.

- The time limit to request permission to appeal from the Upper Tribunal is 30 days, and normally runs from the date on which the Upper Tribunal's decision was sent to you (or, if later, the date a written statement of reasons for the decision was sent to you – but note that Upper Tribunal decisions usually include full written reasons).[143]
- In addition to applying for permission to appeal, you can also request a review of an Upper Tribunal decision about a Scottish benefit (see p1746).
- Your application for permission to appeal must explain the important point of principle or practice your appeal would raise, or what other compelling reason there is to give you permission to appeal.[144]

12

Part 12: Scottish social security benefits
Chapter 77: Getting a determination changed
5. Appealing about 'process decisions'

5. **Appealing about 'process decisions'**

Social Security Scotland (SSS) may decide that you:
- claimed a benefit in the wrong way or did not send some required evidence with your claim;[145] *or*
- requested a redetermination in the wrong way;[146] *or*
- do not have good reason for requesting a redetermination late.[147]

The above decisions are called 'process decisions'. They are *not* determinations about your benefit entitlement. You can appeal against process decisions, but some of the rules are different.[148] You do not have to request a redetermination before making this kind of appeal.

Note:
- If your benefit claim was rejected because you did not claim in the correct way, you should reclaim if it is not too late to do so, or provide any missing evidence. See the chapter of this *Handbook* about the benefit you claimed for the time limits to make a claim.
- If you asked for a redetermination in the wrong way, and it is not too late to do so, also make another redetermination request in the correct way (see p1731).
- In the first two situations, you can also complain about the fact that what you tried to do was not accepted by SSS (see p1728). However, you should always make a process appeal as well.
- The Scottish government intends that you will be able to make a process appeal against decisions of this kind made about Scottish child payment.[149]

How to appeal against a process decision

You must appeal against a process decision to the First-tier Tribunal. Your appeal must be made in writing and give:[150]
- your name and address; *and*
- the name and address of your representative, if you have one; *and*
- an address or email address to send documents about the appeal to; *and*
- the process decision you are appealing against; *and*
- your reason for appealing; *and*
- whether you want a hearing of your appeal (see p1366 – the considerations are the same as for any other appeal); *and*
- if your appeal is late (see below), the reasons why.

Forms

You can download the form to appeal against a process decision from the First-tier Tribunal's website at socialsecuritychamber.scot/home/your-appeal/a-process-appeal. You do not have to use the official form, but it will help you to provide all the necessary information to ensure your appeal is valid (see above). You can email your form to sscadmin@scotcourtstribunals.gov.uk, or send it by post to: Social Security Chamber, Scottish Courts and Tribunals Service, 20 York Street, Glasgow G2 8GT. The First-tier Tribunal can also be contacted by phone on 0141 302 5858, but you *cannot* make a process appeal by phone.

The time limit for appealing

Your appeal must reach the First-tier Tribunal within 31 days of you being told about the decision that you are appealing against.[151] You are normally treated as receiving a notification two days after it was sent to you (see p1731).[152]

If you miss the time limit

If you miss the time limit to appeal against a process decision, your appeal can be considered if it is received within an absolute time limit of one year after you were notified of the decision that you are appealing against.[153] The First-tier Tribunal can only consider a late appeal if it accepts that you have 'good reason' for not appealing within the normal time limit.[154]

You must explain why your appeal is late. If the First-tier Tribunal accepts that you have good reason for not meeting the time limit, your appeal goes ahead unless you missed the absolute time limit above. For some things that might count as 'good reason', see p1732.

What happens after you appeal

Once your appeal is received by the First-tier Tribunal, the process is similar to that for other appeals (see p1736). One difference is that there is no requirement for SSS to respond to your appeal, unless it is ordered to by the First-tier Tribunal.[155]

Decisions about process appeals

The First-tier Tribunal cannot determine your entitlement to benefit. If it allows your appeal, it must tell SSS to determine your claim (or redetermine it). If you disagree with SSS's determination, you can then challenge it in the usual way.

In a process appeal, the First-tier Tribunal's decision is final – if you disagree with it, you cannot appeal to the Upper Tribunal, and it cannot be reviewed.[156] Your only option is to request a judicial review (see p1414). If you are considering a judicial review, you should also ask for a statement of reasons for the decision (see p1740).[157]

Part 12: Scottish social security benefits
Chapter 77: Getting a determination changed
6. Other ways of getting a new determination

6. **Other ways of getting a new determination**

Social Security Scotland (SSS) must determine your entitlement to a Scottish benefit again without you needing to make another claim if you were refused a Scottish benefit (or awarded the wrong amount) and:[158]
- this was due to an 'official error' (see below); *or*
- you have now been awarded a 'qualifying benefit' (see p1751).

If you have been refused a Scottish benefit, you should always request a redetermination if you know why the determination is wrong, and it is not too late to do so (see p1731). You may also be able to make another claim for the benefit. See the chapter of this *Handbook* about the benefit you were refused for the time limit in which to make a claim.

It is expected that if you have been awarded child disablity payment or Scottish child payment, a further determination will be made in some situations, including if your circumstances have changed (see p1752).

If there has been an official error

Note: at the time of writing, these rules were expected to apply to child disability payment and Scottish child payment. See AskCPAG.org.uk and CPAG's *Welfare Rights Bulletin* for updates.

If you were refused a Scottish benefit (except a young carer grant) or awarded a lower amount than you should have been, and SSS later establishes that this was due to an 'official error', it must make another determination of your entitlement.[159] A new determination *cannot* be made due to an official error if you have requested a redetermination and your request is still being considered, or if you have appealed against the determination.[160] If you have already requested a redetermination or appealed, tell SSS or the First-tier Tribunal what the error was.[161] Any error can then be corrected by the appeals process.

Official error

For Scottish benefits, **'official error'** is defined as an error made by someone acting on behalf of the Scottish Ministers (ie, SSS or another part of the Scottish government) or on behalf of a Minister of the Crown – ie, the DWP, HM Revenue and Customs or local authority staff processing a housing benefit claim. However, a mistake is not an official error if it was 'materially contributed to' by anyone else.[162] So if you, or someone helping you, made a mistake, there is not an official error even if SSS also made a mistake.

In practice, this is similar to the definition for other benefits (see p1307). However, a mistake in a determination can also arguably count as an official error even if it was only shown to be wrong by a later Upper Tribunal or court decision.[163]

12

If you realise that there has been an official error and it is now too late to request a redetermination, write to SSS explaining what the error is and ask it to determine your entitlement again. There is no time limit to ask for this to happen. If SSS does not make a new determination, you can complain (see p1728) or request a judicial review (see p1414).[164]

If you are awarded a qualifying benefit

Note that this rule:
- does not apply to young carer grant, although there is a similar rule if someone you care for is awarded a qualifying disability benefit (see p1720);
- is expected to apply to Scottish child payment, but without the requirement that the qualifying benefit is awarded 'following an appeal';
- does not apply if the decision refusing you a qualifying benefit is revised or reveiwed but you have not appealed against it;[165]
- will not apply to child disability payment (as there are no qualifying benefit requirements).

If you were refused a Best Start grant or funeral support payment because you were not getting a 'qualifying benefit' when you claimed, but you are later awarded that benefit following an appeal, your entitlement must be determined again. This rule only applies if the determination would have been different if you had been getting the qualifying benefit when you claimed.[166] See the chapter of this *Handbook* about the benefit you claimed for what the qualifying benefits are.

Note: if you missed the deadline to claim because you were waiting for *a decision* on your claim for a qualifying benefit, separate rules allow you to make a late claim for a Best Start grant (see p1700) or funeral support payment (see p1708).

Example

Marie and Sarah are both refused a Best Start grant because they do not get a qualifying benefit. The Upper Tribunal later allows their appeals about being refused universal credit (a qualifying benefit) in respect of the date they originally claimed a Best Start grant.

As the only entitlement condition Marie did not meet when she claimed a Best Start grant was getting a qualifying benefit, her entitlement is determined again. She is awarded a Best Start grant, as she has now been awarded a qualifying benefit for that date.

Sarah's entitlement is not determined again because as well as not getting a qualifying benefit, she was not ordinarily resident in Scotland on the day she claimed a Best Start grant, so she still does not qualify.

If you are not too late to do so (see p1731), you should request a redetermination as soon as you are awarded a qualifying benefit. If you have already requested a

Part 12: Scottish social security benefits
Chapter 77: Getting a determination changed
6. Other ways of getting a new determination

redetermination or appealed, tell SSS and the tribunal if you are awarded a qualifying benefit. If you have already appealed against a Scottish benefit decision and are not sure whether you will also have to appeal about a qualifying benefit, you can ask the First-tier Tribunal to 'sist' (delay) your appeal (see p1737).[167]

If you cannot request a redetermination (eg, as it is over a year since the determination was made, or you have already lost your appeal against the determination), write to SSS and ask for another determination, telling it about the qualifying benefit award. There is no time limit to ask for this to happen. If SSS does not make a new determination, you can complain (see p1728) or request a judicial review (see p1414).[168]

If you get an ongoing payment

It is expected that two ongoing payments will be introduced by SSS in 2020: child disability payment and Scottish child payment. This means that regulations will say when your entitlement changes once you have been awarded a benefit – eg, following a change of circumstances. As awards of these benefits will normally be made for an indefinite period, the law does this by requiring SSS to determine your entitlement without you making a further claim.[169] Once a new determination is made, this supersedes (replaces) any previous determination that was made for the same period.[170] For when it is expected that a new determination will be made of your entitlement to:

- child disability payment, see p1753;
- Scottish child payment, see below.

Scottish child payment

Note: at the time of writing, the rules described in this section were all in draft form and may change. See AskPCAG.org.uk and CPAG's *Welfare Rights Bulletin* for updates.

It is expected that a new determination of your entitlement to Scottish child payment will be made if:[171]

- you were refused Scottish child payment but are later awarded a qualifying benefit (see p1751); *or*
- you were refused Scottish child payment and this was due to an official error (see p1750); *or*
- someone else claims Scottish child payment for a child you currently get it for (see p1712); *or*
- you stopped getting Scottish child payment less than 12 weeks ago and are now likely to be entitled again; *or*
- you stop getting a qualifying benefit (as you will no longer be entitled to Scottish child payment); *or*
- a child you get Scottish child payment for turns six (as you will no longer be entitled for that child); *or*

- SSS receives information that suggests that your award is incorrect; *or*
- you become responsible for a new child while getting Scottish child payment (see p1714).

If you think that a new determination should be made under these rules, contact SSS and ask it to make a determination, explaining the situation. If SSS does not make a new determination, you can complain (see p1728) or request a judicial review (see p1414).[172]

Child disability payment

Note:

- At the time of writing the rules described in this section were in draft form and may change. See AskCPAG.org.uk and CPAG's *Welfare Rights* Bulletin for updates.
- If you get child disability payment and you ask for a new determination, it is possible that your award could be reduced or stopped entirely, even if you think that the award should increase. Seek advice if you are unsure what to do.

It is expected that a new determination of entitlement to child disability payment will be made in a number of situations, including if:[173]

- you have been refused or awarded the wrong amount of child disability payment due to an official error (see p1750), or an error of law; *or*
- there has been a change of circumstances likely to be relevant to the award of benefit; *or*
- a child has gone into residential care or prison; *or*
- SSS think that the claim is possibly fraudulent; *or*
- a child has moved between Scotland and another part of the UK.

A new determination will also be made if you get child disability payment and you ask for the payment to stop.[174]

If you think that a new determination should be made under these rules, contact SSS and ask it to make a determination, explaining the situation. If SSS does not make a determination, you can complain (see p1728) or request a judicial review (see p1414).[175]

Part 12: Scottish social security benefits
Chapter 77: Getting a determination changed
Notes

Notes

1 **SCP** Sch para 17(2)(e) SCP Regs (draft)
Other benefits s62 SS(S)A 2018
All r1(2) FTT(S) Rules; r1(2) UT(S) Rules
2 Regs 2 and 3 ST(TL) Regs

1. Redeterminations
3 **SCP** Sch para 2(1) SCP Regs (draft)
Other benefits s37 SS(S)A 2018
4 **SCP** Sch para 2(3) SCP Regs (draft)
Other benefits s40(2) SS(S)A 2018
5 **SCP** Sch para 2(2) SCP Regs (draft)
Other benefits s40(1) SS(S)A 2018
6 **SCP** Sch para 1(5) SCP Regs (draft)
Other benefits s38(1) SS(S)A 2018
7 **SCP** Sch para 1(6) SCP Regs (draft)
Other benefits s38(5) SS(S)A 2018
8 s38(3) SS(S)A 2018 cannot prevent you
from claiming again as there has been
no determination of your entitlement.
9 **SCP** Sch paras 4(1) and 17(2)(c) SCP
Regs (draft)
Other benefits ss41(1) and 58(6)(a)
SS(S)A 2018
10 **SCP** Sch para 4(4) SCP Regs (draft)
Other benefits s41(2)(a) and (3)
SS(S)A 2018
11 See mygov.scot/if-you-do-not-agree-
with-a-benefit-decision
12 **SCP** Sch para 4(5) SCP Regs (draft)
Other benefits s41(6) SS(S)A 2018
13 **BSG** Sch 1 para 1 EYA(BSG)(S) Regs
FSP Reg 6(1) FEA(S) Regs
YCG Reg 9(1) CA(YCG)(S) Regs
SCP Sch para 4(2) SCP Regs (draft)
14 Reg 35(1) DACYP(S) Regs (draft)
15 **SCP** Sch para 4(3) SCP Regs draft)
Other benefits s41(4)(b) SS(S)A 2018
16 **SCP** Sch para 5 SCP Regs (draft)
Other benefits s42 SS(S)A 2018
17 **SCP** Sch para 6(1) SCP Regs (draft)
Other benefits s43(1) SS(S)A 2018
18 There is no equivalent provision to
s8(2)(b) SSA 1998 in the SS(S)A 2018 to
prevent your circumstances after the
date of the determination from being
considered.
19 s43(2) and (5) SS(S)A 2018

20 **BSG** Sch 1 para 2(1)(a) EYA(BSG)(S)
Regs
FSP Reg 6(2)(a) FEA(S) Regs
YCG Reg 9(2)(a) CA(YCG)(S) Regs
SCP Sch para 6(4)(a) SCP Regs (draft)
21 **BSG** Sch 1 para 2(1)(b) EYA(BSG)(S)
Regs
FSP Reg 6(2)(b) FEA(S) Regs
YCG Reg 9(2)(b) CA(YCG)(S) Regs
SCP Sch para 6(4)(b) SCP Regs (draft)
22 Scottish government announcement, 1
April 2020
23 **BSG** Sch 1 para 2 EYA(BSG)(S) Regs
FSP Reg 2 FEA(S) Regs
YCG Reg 9(3) CA(YCG) Regs
SCP Reg 5 SCP Regs (draft)
24 **SCP** Sch para 6(6) SCP Regs (draft)
Other benefits s44 SS(S)A 2018
25 **SCP** Sch paras 6(5) and 7 SCP Regs
(draft)
Other benefits ss43(3) and 45 SS(S)A
2018
26 **SCP** Sch para 8 SCP Regs (draft)
Other benefits s46 SS(S)A 2018
27 **SCP** Sch para 6(5) SCP Regs (draft)
Other benefits s43(3) SS(S)A 2018

2. Appealing to the First-tier Tribunal
28 Sch para 10(3) SCP Regs (draft)
29 There is no equivalent to r11(5) TP(FT)
Rules in r9 FTT(S) Rules
30 **SCP** Sch paras 6(6)(b) and 7(1)(b) SCP
Regs (draft)
Other benefits ss44(1)(b) and
45(1)(b) SS(S)A 2018
31 **SCP** Sch para 8(3) SCP Regs (draft)
Other benefits s47(1) SS(S)A 2018
32 See mygov.scot/appeal-to-a-tribunal-
about-a-benefit-decision
33 r20(5) FTT(S) Rules
34 r9 FTT(S) Rules
35 r6 FTT(S) Rules
36 **SCP** Sch para 10(1) SCP Regs (draft)
Other benefits s48(2)(b) SS(S)A 2018
Arguably, if a requirement is waived,
your appeal should be treated as made
on the date SSS received it.
37 **SCP** Sch para 10(1) SCP Regs (draft)
Other benefits s48 SS(S)A 2018

12

38 **SCP** Sch para 10(1) SCP Regs (draft)
Other benefits s48 SS(S)A 2018
If SSS has not carried out a redetermination, r20(9) FTT(S) Rules says that the absolute time limit to appeal runs from the date you were notified of the original determination. If you are in this position and making a late appeal more than a year after the date of the original determination, argue that s48(2)(a)(ii) SS(S)A 2018 provides the absolute time limit, and the FTT(S) Rules must be incorrect.

39 **SCP** Sch para 9 SCP Regs (draft)
Other benefits s47(2) and (3) SS(S)A 2018

40 r20(10) FTT(S) Rules

41 r21(1) FTT(S) Rules

42 r21(2)-(4) FTT(S) Rules

43 rr9(3) and 21(5) FTT(S) Rules

44 r21(6) and (7) FTT(S) Rules

45 r1(2) FTT(S) Rules

46 r4(3)(a) FTT(S) Rules

47 rr4-19 FTT(S) Rules

48 The FTT(S) Rules contain no equivalent to r32 TP(FT) Rules

49 s67 T(S)A 2014; ST(ORP) Regs

50 r4(3)(b) FTT(S) Rules

51 SS(S)A 2018 contains no equivalent to s26 SSA 1998

52 r4(3)(j) FTT(S) Rules

53 r5(5) FTT(S) Rules

54 r7 FTT(S) Rules

55 r7(1) FTT(S) Rules

56 r7(3) FTT(S) Rules

57 r7(2) FTT(S) Rules

58 r7(3) FTT(S) Rules

59 r7(9) FTT(S) Rules

60 r7(7) and (8) FTT(S) Rules

61 The decision is not excluded from the possibility of appealing against it by the T(S)A 2014, so arguably the decision in *LS v Lambeth BC (HB)* [2010] UKUT 461, reported as [2011] AACR 27 applies to the FTT(S) Rules. Get expert advice if your appeal is dismissed.

62 r7(5) and (6) FTT(S) Rules

63 r1(2) FTT(S) Rules

64 r7(4) FTT(S) Rules

65 r17 FTT(S) Rules

66 rr1(2) and 17(5) FTT(S) Rules

67 r4(3)(a) FTT(S) Rules

68 ss46 and 49 SS(S)A 2018 still give the First-tier Tribunal the power to determine your entitlement in this situation, even though there has been another determination since you appealed. This is intended to also apply to the Scottish child payment (see Sch para 10 SCP Regs (draft)).

69 rr23-27 FTT(S) Rules

70 SS(S)A 2018 contains no provision equivalent to s12(2)(b) SSA 1998

71 s49 SS(S)A 2018; reg 4 of The First-tier Tribunal for Scotland (Allocation of Functions to the Social Security Chamber) Regulations 2018, No.350

72 FTT(S) Rules contain no equivalent of r25 FT(TP) Rules

73 r10 FTT(S) Rules

74 r26(5) FTT(S) Rules

75 r5 FTT(S) Rules – this is technically a request for another order.

76 r28 FTT(S) Rules

77 r19 FTT(S) Rules

78 r29 FTT(S) Rules

79 r4(3)(a) FTT(S) Rules

80 rr28 and 29(3) FTT(S) Rules – r1(2) FTT(S) Rules applies only to decisions sent to you by post or email

81 Reg 2(4) ST(TL) Regs suggests that if you do not do this, an eventual application for permission to appeal may be late. The rules are unclear, but asking for a statement of reasons within 14 days should avoid any difficulties later on.

82 r28(3)(c) FTT(S) Rules

83 There is no equivalent of r38(7) TP(FT) Rules in the FTT(S) Rules

84 r32 FTT(S) Rules

85 r4(1)(l) FTT(S) Rules

86 r35(2) FTT(S) Rules

87 r36(1) FTT(S) Rules

88 r36(2) FTT(S) Rules

89 r35(8) FTT(S) Rules

90 ss44(1)(a), 51 and 52 T(S)A 2014

91 r33(3) FTT(S) Rules

92 r35(3) FTT(S) Rules

93 r35(4) FTT(S) Rules

94 r35(5) FTT(S) Rules

95 r35(6) FTT(S) Rules

96 r35(7) FTT(S) Rules

97 s44 T(S)A 2014

98 s44(5) T(S)A 2014

99 s45 T(S)A 2014

100 s52 T(S)A 2014

101 r29(5) FTT(S) Rules

Part 12: Scottish social security benefits
Chapter 77: Getting a determination changed
Notes

3. Appealing to the Upper Tribunal

102 rr33 and 34 FTT(S) Rules; rr3 and 4 UT(S) Rules
103 rr33 and 34 FTT(S) Rules
104 There is no equivalent of r38(7) TP(FT) Rules in the FTT(S) Rules
105 Reg 2 ST(TL) Regs
106 If you requested a statement of reasons more than 14 days after the hearing, make sure that you request permission to appeal within 30 days, even if you do not have the statement of reasons yet
107 r33(3) FTT(S) Rules
108 r4(1) UT(S) Rules
109 r1(2) UT(S) Rules
110 r4(2) UT(S) Rules
111 r4(3) UT(S) Rules
112 r4(5)(a) UT(S) Rules
113 r4(5)(b) UT(S) Rules
114 Reg 3 ST(TL) Regs
115 Reg 3(3) ST(TL) Regs
116 r3(4)(a) UT(S) Rules
117 r3(4)(b) UT(S) Rules
118 s55(2) T(S)A 2014
119 r3(6) UT(S) Rules
120 r1(2) UT(S) Rules
121 r3(7) UT(S) Rules
122 r3(8) UT(S) Rules
123 rr5-21 UT(S) Rules
124 rr1(2), 5(2) and 6(2) UT(S) Rules
125 r11 UT(S) Rules
126 r20 UT(S) Rules
127 s67 T(S)A 2014; ST(ORP) Regs
128 r8(3)(c) UT(S) Rules
129 rr22-26 UT(S) Rules
130 s47 T(S)A 2014; r27 UT(S) Rules
131 r28(2) UT(S) Rules
132 r28(3) UT(S) Rules
133 r28(4) UT(S) Rules
134 r28(5) UT(S) Rules
135 s44(1) and (4) T(S)A 2014
136 s44(5) T(S)A 2014
137 ss48(5)(b) and 52(2) T(S)A 2014
138 s52 T(S)A 2014 only excludes a review decision from having a right of appeal, not the original decision, if it was not set aside
139 rr 1(1) and 28(6) UT(S) Rules
140 r1(2) UT(S) Rules

4. Appealing to the Court of Session

141 ss48 and 50 T(S)A 2014
142 ss48-55 T(S)A 2014; rr29-31 UT(S) Rules
143 Reg 2 ST(TL) Regs
144 r30(2)(c) UT(S) Rules

5. Appealing about 'process decisions'

145 s38(5) SS(S)A 2018
146 s41(6) SS(S)A 2018
147 s42 SS(S)A 2018
148 s61 SS(S)A 2018
149 Sch para 10(2) SCP Regs (draft)
150 r22(4) FTT(S) Rules
151 s61(2)(a) SS(S)A 2018
152 s62 SS(S)A 2018
153 s61(2)(c) SS(S)A 2018
154 s61(2)(b) and (3) SS(S)A 2018
155 r21 FTT(S) Rules only applies to appeals against a determination of entitlement
156 s61(4) and (5) SS(S)A 2018
157 The FTT(S) Rules do not prevent you from requesting a statement of reasons for a decision on a 'process appeal'.

6. Other ways of getting a new determination

158 s52 SS(S)A 2018
159 **BSG** Sch 1 para 4 EYA(BSG)(S) Regs
FSP Reg 4(1) FEA(S) Regs
CDP Reg 32 DACYP(S) Regs (draft)
SCP Sch para 11 SCP Regs (draft)
160 **BSG** Sch 1 para 4(1)(c) and (d) EYA(BSG)(S) Regs
FSP Reg 4(1)(c) and (d) FEA(S) Regs
CDP Reg 32(1)(c) and (d) DACYP(S) Regs (draft) – but note that the draft regulations prevent this rule from applying even if SSS has redetermined your entitlement
SCP Sch para 11(1)(c) and (d) SCP Regs (draft)
161 Provided your appeal has not been decided, the correct situation can still be taken into account as SS(S)A 2018 contains no equivalent to s8(2)(b) SSA 1998.
162 **BSG** Sch 1 para 4(4) EYA(BSG)(S) Regs
FSP Reg 4(5) FEA(S) Regs
CDP Reg 32(2) DACYP(S) Regs (draft) – the draft regulations are worded differently, so errors by local authority staff are unlikely to count
SCP Sch para 11(4) SCP Regs (draft)
163 For other benefits, this is specifically excluded from the definition of an 'official error' – see, for example, reg 1(3) SSCS(DA) Regs
164 **SCP** Sch para 4(1) SCP Regs (draft)
Other benefits s41(1) SS(S)A 2018
You can only request a redetermination of a determination, not of a failure to make a determination.

165 **BSG** Sch 1 para 5(b)(i) EYA(BSG)(S) Regs
FSP Reg 4(2)(b)(i) FEA(S) Regs
If there is no other way you could be
entitled, you could argue that the
meaning of 'appeal' includes a
necessary stage before you can make an
appeal. As there is no determination to
challenge, the only way to make this
argument would be to request a judicial
review.

166 **SCP** Sch para 12(5) SCP Regs (draft)
BSG Sch 1 para 5 EYA(BSG)(S) Regs
FSP Reg 4(2) FEA(S) Regs

167 If your request is agreed, this will allow
the tribunal to wait and see whether you
are awarded the qualifying benefit
before deciding your appeal. Note that
if you do not do this and lose your
appeal, you cannot get a new
determination under this rule if the
qualifying benefit decision is later
revised or reviewed and you have not
appealed against it.

168 **SCP** Sch para 4(1) SCP Regs (draft)
Other benefits s41(1) SS(S)A 2018
You can only request a redetermination
of a determination, not of a failure to
make a determination.

169 s52 SS(S)A 2018; Sch para 2 and part 4
SCP Regs (draft); Part 9 DACYP(S) Regs
(draft)

170 s27 SS(S)A 2018; Sch para 2(4) SCP
Regs (draft)

171 Sch paras 3, 14 and 15 SCP Regs (draft)

172 Sch para 4(1) SCP Regs (draft) – you can
only request a redetermination of a
determination, not of a failure to make a
determination.

173 Part 9 DACYP(S) Regs (draft)

174 s26 SS(S)A 2018; reg 31(1)(i) DACYP(S)
Regs (draft)

175 s41(1) SS(S)A 2018 – you can only
request a redetermination of a
determination, not of a failure to make a
determination.

12

Appendices

Appendix 1

Information and advice

Independent advice and representation

If you want advice or information on a benefit or tax credit issue, the following may be able to assist.

- Advicelocal (advicelocal.uk) has details of advice organisations in your area.
- Citizens Advice. You can find out where your local office is from the Citizens Advice website at citizensadvice.org.uk (England and Wales) or cas.org.uk (Scotland).
- Law centres. You can find your nearest law centre at lawcentres.org.uk.
- LawWorks (lawworks.org.uk) has details of local legal advice centres that give free advice.
- Housing association welfare rights services for tenants.
- Local authority welfare rights services.
- Local and national organisations for particular groups of claimants may offer help. For instance, there are unemployed centres, pensioners' groups and organisations for people with disabilities.

Advice from CPAG

Unfortunately, CPAG is unable to deal with enquiries directly from members of the public, but if you are an adviser you can phone or email for help with advising your client.

Advisers in England, Wales and Northern Ireland can call from 10am to 12pm and from 2pm to 4pm (Monday to Friday) on 020 7812 5231. Email advice is now limited to enquiries that are specifically about universal credit, child benefit and tax credits. Our email address is advice@cpag.org.uk. For more information, see cpag.org.uk/advisers.

Advisers in Scotland can call us from 10am to 4pm (Monday to Thursday) and from 10am to 12pm (Friday) on 0141 552 0552, or email advice@cpagscotland.org.uk.

CPAG's Upper Tribunal assistance project can provide help to advisers helping claimants challenge tribunal decisions. See cpag.org.uk/upper-tribunal-assistance-project. We also provide training and advice to support advisers to pursue judicial review remedies. See cpag.org.uk/jrproject.

AskCPAG is a new information and solutions platform for advisers, including a digital version of this *Handbook*, fully searchable and updated throughout the year. See AskCPAG.org.uk.

CPAG takes on a small number of test cases each year. We focus on cases that have the potential to improve the lives of families with children in poverty. If you are an adviser and would like to refer a test case to us, please see cpag.org.uk/test-case-referrals.

Finding help online

Information about benefits and tax credits, including a selection of leaflets and forms, is available on the gov.uk website.

CPAG's website (cpag.org.uk) has articles, briefings and factsheets on benefit issues.

The *rightsnet* website (aimed at advisers) at rightsnet.org.uk provides information on new welfare rights legislation, caselaw and guidance. It also provides updates on developments in other areas of social welfare law and has a discussion forum where advisers can discuss particular cases.

Most Acts and regulations can be found at legislation.gov.uk.

You can find commissioners' and Upper Tribunal decisions at gov.uk/administrative-appeals-tribunal-decisions.

Appendix 2

Useful publications

Many of the books listed here will be in your local public library. You can find Stationery Office books at Stationery Office bookshops or order them by telephone, email or online (tel: 0333 202 5070; email: customer.services@ tso.co.uk; web: tsoshop.co.uk). To pay by cheque, select the 'Pay by post' option from the TSO Shop online checkout section, then print your order form and post it to TSO Customer Services, 18 Central Avenue, St Andrews Business Park, Norwich NR7 0HR. Many publications listed in this Appendix are available from CPAG; see p1767 for order details, or order from cpag.org.uk/shop.

1. Caselaw and legislation

The Law Relating to Social Security
All the legislation but without any commentary. Known as the 'Blue Book'. Available at lawvolumes.dwp.gov.uk and updated up until October 2015. Check also legislation.gov.uk.

Social Security Legislation, Volume I: Non-Means-Tested Benefits and Employment and Support Allowance
D Bonner, I Hooker and R White (Sweet & Maxwell)
Legislation with commentary. 2020/21 edition (September 2020): £119 for the main volume.

Social Security Legislation, Volume II: Income Support, Jobseeker's Allowance, State Pension Credit and the Social Fund
J Mesher, P Wood, R Poynter, N Wikeley and D Bonner (Sweet & Maxwell)
Legislation with commentary. 2020/21 edition (September 2020): £119 for the main volume.

Social Security Legislation, Volume III: Administration, Adjudication and the European Dimension
M Rowland and R White (Sweet & Maxwell)
Legislation with commentary. 2020/21 edition (September 2020): £119 for the main volume.

Social Security Legislation, Volume IV: Tax Credits and HMRC-administered Social Security Benefits
N Wikeley and D Williams (Sweet & Maxwell)
Legislation with commentary. 2020/21 edition (September 2020): £119 for the main volume.

Social Security Legislation, Volume V: Universal Credit
P Wood, R Poynter and N Wikeley (Sweet & Maxwell)
Legislation with commentary. 2020/21 edition (September 2020): £119 for the main volume.

Social Security Legislation – updating supplement
(Sweet & Maxwell)
The spring 2020 update to the 2019/20 main volumes: £75.

Housing Benefit and Council Tax Reduction Legislation
L Findlay, R Poynter, S Wright, C George, M Williams, S Mitchell and M Brough (CPAG)
Legislation with detailed commentary. 2019/20, 33rd edition (winter 2020): £128 including Supplement (£108.80 members). The 32nd edition (2019/20) is still available, £128 per set (£108.80 members).

2. Official guidance

Decision Makers' Guide: staff guide
Available at gov.uk/government/collections/decision-makers-guide-staff-guide.

Advice for Decision Making: staff guide
Available at gov.uk/government/publications/advice-for-decision-making-staff-guide.

Housing Benefit Guidance Manual
Available at gov.uk/government/collections/housing-benefit-claims-processing-and-good-practice-for-local-authority-staff.

Discretionary Housing Payments Guidance Manual
Available at gov.uk/government/publications/discretionary-housing-payments-guidance-manual.

Healthcare professionals: information from DWP
Available at gov.uk/government/collections/healthcare-practitioners-guidance-and-information-from-dwp.

Work Capability Assessment (WCA) Handbook: for healthcare professionals
Available at gov.uk/government/publications/work-capability-assessment-hand-book-for-healthcare-professionals.

Tax Credits Technical Manual
Available at hmrc.gov.uk/manuals/tctmanual.

Budgeting Loan Guide
Available at gov.uk/government/publications/budgeting-loan-guide-for-decision-makers-reviewing-officers-and-further-reviewing-officers.

Personal Independence Payment (PIP) Assessment Guide for Assessment Providers
Available at gov.uk/government/publications/personal-independence-payment-assessment-guide-for-assessment-providers.

3. Leaflets

The DWP publishes many leaflets, available free from your local DWP or Jobcentre Plus office. To order DWP leaflets, or receive information about new leaflets, contact APS, Unit C, Orion Business Park, Bird Hall Lane, Cheadle Heath SK3 0RT, email: DWPCST@theapsgroup.com or complete the order form at gov.uk/government/publications/dwp-leaflets-order-form. Leaflets on housing benefit are available from your local council.

4. Periodicals

Welfare Rights Bulletin (CPAG, bi-monthly)
Covers developments in social security law, including Upper Tribunal decisions, and updates this *Handbook* between editions. The annual subscription is £49 (£41.65 for members) but it is sent automatically to CPAG members and welfare rights subscribers (more information at cpag.org.uk/membership).

Articles on social security can also be found in *Legal Action* (Legal Action Group), *Adviser* (Citizens Advice) and the *Journal of Social Security Law* (Sweet & Maxwell).

5. Other publications

AskCPAG
The full text of the *Welfare Benefits and Tax Credits Handbook* online and updated throughout the year. Annual subscription £65 per user (£55.25 members).

AskCPAG+
CPAG's full digital package which includes the full text of the *Welfare Benefits and Tax Credits Handbook* updated throughout the year, the *Welfare Rights Bulletin*, *Poverty* journal and decision-making tools and appeal letter generators. Annual subscription £120 per user (£102 members). For a free one-month trial, see cpag.org.uk/shop/subscriptions/askcpag-one-month-free-trial.

Universal Credit: what you need to know (CPAG)
6th edition, autumn 2020: £15 (£12.75 members)

Financial Help for Families: what you need to know (CPAG)
2nd edition, autumn 2020: £15 (£12.75 members)

Personal Independence Payment: what you need to know (CPAG)
2nd edition, August 2016: £15 (£12.75 members)

Winning Your Benefit Appeal: what you need to know (CPAG)
3rd edition, July 2019: £15 (£12.75 members)

Child Support Handbook (CPAG)
28th edition, summer 2020: £40 (£34 members)

Debt Advice Handbook (CPAG)
13th edition, March 2020: £29 (£24.65 members)

Fuel Rights Handbook (CPAG)
19th edition, March 2019: £29 (£24.65 members)

Student Support and Benefits Handbook (CPAG)
17th edition, autumn 2020: £28 (£23.80 members)

Benefits for Students in Scotland Handbook (CPAG)
17th edition, autumn 2020: £31 (£26.35 members)
Available free online at AskCPAG.org.uk.

Council Tax Handbook (CPAG)
13th edition, autumn 2020: £31 (£26.35 members)

Benefits for Migrants Handbook (CPAG)
12th edition, winter 2020: £40 (£34 members)

Children's Handbook Scotland: a benefits guide for children living away from their parents (CPAG)
13th edition, autumn 2020: £31 (£26.35 members)
Available free online at AskCPAG.org.uk

Help with Housing Costs Vol 1: Guide to universal credit and council tax rebates 2020/21 (Shelter)
£43.50 (June 2020)

Help with Housing Costs Vol 2: Guide to housing benefit 2020/21 (Shelter)
£43.50 (June 2020)

Disability Rights Handbook 2020/21 (Disability Rights UK)
£36 (45th edition, May 2020)

Tribunal Practice and Procedure (Legal Action Group)
£70 (5th edition, September 2019)

Disabled Children: A legal handbook (Legal Action Group)
£50 (3rd edition, January 2020)

Community Care and the Law (Legal Action Group)
£70 (July 2019)

For CPAG publications and most of those in Sections 1 and 5 contact:
CPAG, 30 Micawber St, London N1 7TB (tel: 020 7837 7979, email: bookorders@cpag.org.uk). Discounts on CPAG publications are available to CPAG members and Citizens Advice. Order forms are available at cpag.org.uk/shop. Postage and packing: free for online subscriptions and orders up to £10 in value; for order value £10.01–£100, add a flat rate charge of £3.99; for order value £100.01–£400, add £7.49; for order value over £400, add £11.49.

Appendix 3

Disability which puts a person at a disadvantage in getting a job

Schedule 1 Regulation 9(1) to the Working Tax Credit (Entitlement and Maximum Rate) Regulations 2002

PART 1

1. When standing he cannot keep his balance unless he continually holds onto something.

2. Using any crutches, walking frame, walking stick, prosthesis or similar walking aid which he habitually uses, he cannot walk a continuous distance of 100 metres along level ground without stopping or without suffering severe pain.

3. He can use neither of his hands behind his back as in the process of putting on a jacket or of tucking a shirt into trousers.

4. He can extend neither of his arms in front of him so as to shake hands with another person without difficulty.

5. He can put neither of his hands up to his head without difficulty so as to put on a hat.

6. Due to lack of manual dexterity he cannot, with one hand, pick up a coin which is not more than $2\frac{1}{2}$ centimetres in diameter.

7. He is not able to use his hands or arms to pick up a full jug of 1 litre capacity and pour from it into a cup, without difficulty.

8. He can turn neither of his hands sideways through 180 degrees.

9. He is certified as severely sight impaired or blind by a consultant ophthalmologist.

10. He cannot see to read 16 point print at a distance greater than 20 centimetres, if appropriate, wearing the glasses he normally uses.

11. He cannot hear a telephone ring when he is in the same room as the telephone, if appropriate, using a hearing aid he normally uses.

12. In a quiet room he has difficulty in hearing what someone talking in a loud voice at a distance of 2 metres says, if appropriate, using a hearing aid he normally uses.

13. People who know him well have difficulty in understanding what he says.

14. When a person he knows well speaks to him, he has difficulty in understanding what that person says.

15. At least once a year during waking hours he is in a coma or has a fit in which he loses consciousness.

16. He has a mental illness for which he receives regular treatment under the supervision of a medically qualified person.

17. Due to mental disability he is often confused or forgetful.

18. He cannot do the simplest addition and subtraction.

19. Due to mental disability he strikes people or damages property or is unable to form normal social relationships.

20. He cannot normally sustain an 8 hour working day or a five day working week due to a medical condition or intermittent or continuous severe pain.

PART 2 (INITIAL CLAIMS ONLY)

21. As a result of an illness or accident he is undergoing a period of habilitation or rehabilitation.

Appendix 4

Prescribed degrees of disablement

Schedule 2 to the Social Security (General Benefit) Regulations 1982 SI No. 1408

Description of injury	Degree of disablement %
1 Loss of both hands or amputation at higher sites	100
2 Loss of a hand and a foot	100
3 Double amputation through leg or thigh, or amputation through leg or thigh on one side and loss of other foot	100
4 Loss of sight to such an extent as to render the claimant unable to perform any work for which eyesight is essential	100
5 Very severe facial disfiguration	100
6 Absolute deafness	100
7 Forequarter or hindquarter amputation	100
Amputation cases – upper limbs (either arm)	
8 Amputation through shoulder joint	90
9 Amputation below shoulder with stump less than 20.5 cm from tip of acromion	80
10 Amputation from 20.5 cm from tip of acromion to less than 11.5 cm below tip of olecranon	70
11 Loss of a hand or of the thumb and 4 fingers of 1 hand or amputation from 11.5 cm below tip of olecranon	60
12 Loss of thumb	30
13 Loss of thumb and its metacarpal bone	40
14 Loss of 4 fingers of 1 hand	50
15 Loss of 3 fingers of 1 hand	30
16 Loss of 2 fingers of 1 hand	20
17 Loss of terminal phalanx of thumb	20
Amputation cases – lower limbs	
18 Amputation of both feet resulting in end-bearing stumps	90

19 Amputation through both feet proximal to the metatarso-phalangeal joint	80
20 Loss of all toes to both feet through the metatarso-phalangeal joint	40
21 Loss of all toes of both feet proximal to the proximal inter-phalangeal joint	30
22 Loss of all toes of both feet distal to the proximal inter-phalangeal joint	20
23 Amputation at hip	90
24 Amputation below hip with stump not exceeding 13 cm in length measured from tip of great trochanter	80
25 Amputation below hip and above knee with stump exceeding 13 cm in length measured from tip of great trochanter, or at knee not resulting in end-bearing stump	70
26 Amputation at knee resulting in end-bearing stump or below knee with stump not exceeding 9 cm	60
27 Amputation below knee with stump exceeding 9 cm but not exceeding 13 cm	50
28 Amputation below knee with stump exceeding 13 cm	40
29 Amputation of 1 foot resulting in end-bearing stump	30
30 Amputation through 1 foot proximal to the metatarso-phalangeal joint	30
31 Loss of all toes of 1 foot through the metatarso-phalangeal joint	20

Other injuries

32 Loss of 1 eye, without complications, the other being normal	40
33 Loss of vision of 1 eye, without complications or disfigurement of the eyeball, the other being normal	30

Loss of fingers of right or left hand

Index finger:

34 Whole	14
35 2 phalanges	11
36 1 phalanx	9
37 Guillotine amputation of tip without loss of bone	5

Middle finger:

38 Whole	12
39 2 phalanges	9
40 1 phalanx	7
41 Guillotine amputation of tip without loss of bone	4

Ring or little finger:

42 Whole	7
43 2 phalanges	6

44 1 phalanx	5
45 Guillotine amputation of tip without loss of bone	2

Loss of toes of right or left foot

Great toe:

46 Through metatarso-phalangeal joint	14
47 Part, with some loss of bone	3

Any other toe:

48 Through metatarso-phalangeal joint	3
49 Part, with some loss of bone	1

2 toes of 1 foot, excluding great toe:

50 Through metatarso-phalangeal joint	5
51 Part, with some loss of bone	2

3 toes of 1 foot, excluding great toe:

52 Through metatarso-phalangeal joint	6
53 Part, with some loss of bone	3

4 toes of 1 foot, excluding great toe:

54 Through metatarso-phalangeal joint	9
55 Part, with some loss of bone	3

The degree of disablement due to occupational deafness is assessed using tables and a formula to be found in reg 34 and Sch 3 Social Security (Industrial Injuries) (Prescribed Diseases) Regulations 1985, as amended.

Appendix 5

Prescribed industrial diseases

Part I of Schedule 1 to the Social Security (Industrial Injuries) (Prescribed Diseases) Regulations 1985 as amended

Prescribed disease or injury	Occupation
A – Conditions due to physical agents	Any occupation involving:
A1 Leukaemia (other than chronic lymphatic leukaemia) or primary cancer of the bone, bladder, breast, colon, liver, lung, ovary, stomach testis or thyroid.	Exposure to ionising radiation where the dose is sufficient to double the condition.
A2 Cataract.	Frequent or prolonged exposure to radiation from red-hot or white-hot material.
A3 (a) Dysbarism, including decompression sickness and barotrauma; (b) Osteonecrosis	Subjection to compressed or rarified air or from molten or red-hot material.
A4 Task-specific focal dystonia of the hand or forearm.	Prolonged periods of handwriting, typing or other repetitive movements of the fingers, hand or arm.
A5 Subcutaneous cellulitis of the hand.	Manual labour causing severe or prolonged friction or pressure on the hand.
A6 Bursitis or subcutaneous cellulites arising at or about the knee due to severe or prolonged external friction or pressure at or about the knee.	Manual labour causing severe or prolonged external friction or pressure at or about the knee.
A7 Bursitis or subcutaneous cellulites arising at or about the elbow due to severe or prolonged external friction or pressure at or about the elbow (beat elbow).	Manual labour causing severe or prolonged external friction or pressure at or about the elbow.
A8 Traumatic inflammation of the tendons of the hand or forearm, or of the associated tendon sheaths.	Manual labour, or frequent or repeated movements of the hand or wrist.

Prescribed disease or injury	Occupation
A10 Sensorineural hearing loss amounting to at least 50dB in each ear, being the average of hearing losses at 1, 2 and 3 kHz frequencies, and being due in the case of at least one ear to occupational noise (occupational deafness).	Any occupation involving the use of, or work wholly or mainly in the immediate vicinity of the use of, a:

(a) band saw, circular saw or cutting disc to cut metal in the metal founding or forging industries, circular saw to cut products in the manufacture of steel, powered (other than hand powered) grinding tool on metal (other than sheet metal or plate metal), pneumatic percussive tool on metal, pressurised air arc tool to gouge metal, burner or torch to cut or dress steel based products, skid transfer bank, knock out and shake out grid in a foundry, machine (other than a power press machine) to forge metal including a machine used to drop stamp metal by means of closed or open dies or drop hammers, machine to cut or shape or clean metal nails, or plasma spray gun to spray molten metal;

(b) pneumatic percussive tool to drill rock in a quarry, on stone in a quarry works, used underground, for mining coal, for sinking a shaft, or for tunnelling in civil engineering works;

(c) vibrating metal moulding box in the concrete products industry, or circular saw to cut concrete masonry blocks;

(d) machine in the manufacture of textiles for weaving man-made or natural fibres (including mineral fibres), high speed false twisting of fibres, or the mechanical cleaning of bobbins;

(e) multi-cutter moulding machine on wood, planing machine on wood, automatic or semi-automatic lathe on wood, multiple cross-cut machine on wood, automatic shaping machine on wood, double-end tenoning machine on wood, vertical spindle moulding machine (including a high speed routing machine) on wood, edge banding machine on wood, bandsawing machine (with a blade width of not less than 75 millimetres) on wood including one operated by moving the blade towards the material being cut, or chain saw on wood;

(f) jet of water (or a mixture of water and abrasive material) at a pressure above 680 bar, or jet channelling process to burn stone in a quarry;

Prescribed disease or injury	Occupation
	(g) machine in a ship's engine room, or gas turbine for performance testing on a test bed, installation testing of a replacement engine in an aircraft, or acceptance testing of an Armed Service fixed wing combat aircraft;
	(h) machine in the manufacture of glass containers or hollow ware for automatic moulding, automatic blow moulding, or automatic glass pressing and forming;
	(i) spinning machine using compressed air to produce glass wool or mineral wool;
	(j) continuous glass toughening furnace;
	(k) firearm by a police firearms training officer;
	(l) shot-blaster to carry abrasives in air for cleaning.
A11(a)Intense blanching of the skin, with a sharp demarcation line between affected and non-affected skin, where the blanching is cold-induced, episodic, occurs throughout the year and affects the skin of the distal with the middle and proximal phalanges, or distal with the middle phalanx (or in the case of a thumb the distal with the proximal phalanx), of–	(a) The use of hand-held chain saws on wood; *or*
(i) in the case of a person with 5 fingers (including thumb) on one hand, any 3 of those fingers, or	(b) the use of hand-held rotary tools in grinding or in the sanding or polishing of metal, or the holding of material being ground, or metal being sanded or polished by rotary tools; *or*
(ii) in the case of a person with only 4 such fingers, any 2 of those fingers, or	(c) the use of hand-held percussive metal-working tools, or the holding of metal being worked upon by percussive tools, in riveting, caulking, chipping, hammering, fettling or swaging; *or*
(iii) in the case of a person with less than 4 such fingers, any one of them or, as the case may be, the one remaining finger, where none of the person's fingers was subject to any degree of cold-induced, episodic blanching of the skin prior to the person's employment in an occupation described in the second column in relation to this paragraph, or	(d) the use of hand-held powered percussive drills or hand-held powered percussive hammers in mining, quarrying, demolition, or on roads or footpaths, including road construction; *or*
	(e) the holding of material being worked upon by pounding machines in shoe manufacture.

Prescribed disease or injury	Occupation
(b) significant, demonstrable reduction in both sensory perception and manipulative dexterity with continuous numbness or continuous tingling all present at the same time in the distal phalanx of any finger (including thumb) where none of the person's fingers was subject to any degree of reduction in sensory perception, manipulative dexterity, numbness or tingling prior to the person's employment in an occupation described in the second column in relation to this paragraph, where the symptoms in paragraph (a) or paragraph (b) were caused by vibration.	
A12 Carpal tunnel syndrome.	(a) The use, at the time the symptoms first develop, of hand-held powered tools whose internal parts vibrate so as to transmit that vibration to the hand; *or* (b) repeated palmar flexion and dorsiflexion of the wrist for at least 20 hours per week for a period or periods amounting in aggregate to at least 12 months in the 24 months prior to the onset of the symptoms, where 'repeated' means once or more often in every 30 seconds.
A13 Osteoarthritis of the hip.	Work in agriculture as a farmer or farm worker for a period of, or periods which amount in aggregate to, 10 years or more.

A14 Osteoarthritis of the knee.	Work underground in a coal mine for a period of, or periods which amount in aggregate to, at least 10 years in any one or more of the following occupations:
	(a) before 1 Januray 1986 as a coal miner; *or*
	(b) on or after 1 Januray 1986 as a–
	  (i) face worker working on a non-mechanised coal face;*
	  (ii) development worker;
	  (iii) face-salvage worker;
	  (iv) conveyor belt cleaner; *or*
	  (v) conveyor belt attendant.
	*'A non-mechanised coal face' means a coal face without either powered roof supports or a power loader machine which simultaneously cuts and loads the coal or without both.
	Work wholly or mainly fitting or laying carpets or other floors (other than concrete floors) for a period of, or periods which amount in aggregate to, 20 years or more.

Prescribed disease or injury	Occupation
A15 Dupuytren's contracture of the hand resulting in fixed flexion deformity of one or more inter-phalangeal joints of one or more of the digits.	Any occupation involving the use of hand-held powered tools whose internal parts vibrate so as to transmit that vibration to the hand (but excluding those tools which are solely powered by hand) where: (a) the use of those tools amounts to a period or periods in aggregate of at least 10 years; (b) within that period or those periods, the use of those tools amounts to at least 2 hours per day for 3 or more days per week; *and* (c) the onset of the disease fell within the period or periods of use specified in this paragraph.
B – Conditions due to biological agents **B1** (a) Cutaneous anthrax; (b) Pulmonary anthrax.	Any occupation involving: (a) Contact with anthrax spores, including contact with animals infected by anthrax; *or* (b) handling, loading, unloading or transport of animals of a type susceptible to infection with anthrax or of the products or residues of such animals.
B2 Glanders. **B3** Infection by leptospira.	Contact with equine animals or their carcasses. (a) Work in places which are, or are liable to be, infested by rats, field mice or voles, or other small mammals; *or* (b) work at dog kennels or the care or handling of dogs; *or* (c) contact with bovine animals or pigs or their meat products.
B4 (a) Cutaneous larva migrans; (b) Iron deficiency anaemia caused by gastrointestinal infection by hookwork. **B5** Tuberculosis.	Contact with a source of ankylostomiasis. Contact with a source of tuberculous while undertaking– (a) work in a hospital, mortuary in which post mortems are conducted, or laboratory; *or.* (b) work in any other workplace.
B6 Extrinsic allergic alveolitis.	Exposure to moulds or fungal spores or heterologous proteins or any other biological substance that causes extrinsic allergic alveolitis by reason of employment in: (a) agriculture, horticulture, forestry, cultivation of edible fungi or malt-working; *or* (b) loading or unloading or handling in storage mouldy vegetable matter or edible fungi; *or* (c) caring for or handling birds; *or* (d) handling bagasse; *or* (e) work involving exposure to metalworking fluids mist; *or* (f) any other workplace.

Prescribed disease or injury	Occupation
B7 Infection by organisms of the genus brucella.	Contact with: (a) animals infected by brucella, or their carcasses or parts thereof, or their untreated products; *or* (b) laboratory specimens or vaccines of, or containing, brucella.
B8(a) Infection by hepatitis A virus.	Contact with raw sewage.
(b) Infection by hepatitis B or C virus.	Contact with: (a) human blood or human blood products; *or* (b) any other source of hepatitis B or C virus.
B9 Infection by Streptococcus suis.	Contact with pigs infected by Streptococcus suis, or with the carcasses, products or residues of pigs so infected.
B10 (a) Avian chlamydiosis.	Contact with birds infected with chlamydia psittaci, or with the remains or untreated products of such birds.
(b) Ovine chlamydiosis.	Contact with sheep infected with chlamydia psittaci, or with the remains or untreated products of such sheep.
B11 Q fever.	Contact with animals, their remains or their untreated products.
B12 Orf.	Contact with sheep, goats or with the carcasses of sheep or goats.
B13 Hydatidosis.	Contact with dogs.
B14 Lyme disease.	Exposure to deer or other mammals of a type liable to harbour ticks harbouring Borrelia bacteria.
B15 Anaphylaxis.	Contact with products made with natural rubber latex.
C – Conditions due to chemical agents	Any occupation involving:
C1 (a) Anaemia with a haemoglobin concentration of 9g/dl or less, and a blood film showing punctate basophilia. (b) Peripheral neuropathy. (c) Central nervous system toxicity.	The use or handling of, or exposure to the fumes, dust or vapour of, lead or a compound of lead, or a substance containing lead.
C2 Central nervous system toxicity characterised by parkinsonism.	The use or handling of, or exposure to the fumes, dust or vapour of, manganese or a compound of manganese, or a substance containing manganese.
C3 (a) Phossy Jaw.	Work involving the use or handling of, or exposure to, white phosphorus.
(b) Peripheral polyneuropathy with pyramidal involvement of the central nervous system, caused by organic compounds of phosphorus which inhibit the enzyme neuropathy target esterase.	Work involving the use or handling of, or exposure to, organic compounds of phosphorus.
C4 Primary carcinoma of the bronchus or lung.	Exposure to the fumes, dust or vapour of arsenic, a compound of arsenic or a substance containing arsenic.
C5 (a) Central nervous system toxicity characterised by tremor and neuropsychiatric disease.	Exposure to mercury or inorganic compounds of mercury for a period of, or periods which amount in aggregate to, 10 years or more.

Prescribed disease or injury	Occupation
(b) Central nervous system toxicity characterised by combined cerebellar and cortical degeneration.	Exposure to methylmercury.
C6 Peripheral neuropathy.	The use or handling of, or exposure to carbon disulphide (also called carbon disulfide).
C7 Acute non-lymphatic leukaemia.	Exposure to benzene.
C12 (a) Peripheral neuropathy.	Exposure to methyl bromide (also called bromomethane).
(b) Central nervous system toxicity.	
C13 Cirrhosis of the liver.	Exposure to chlorinated naphthalene.
C16 (a) Neurotoxicity.	Exposure to the dust of gonioma kamassi.
(b) Cardiotoxicity.	
C17 Chronic beryllium disease.	Inhalation of beryllium or a compound of beryllium.
C18 Emphysema.	Inhalation of cadmium fumes for a period of, or periods which amount in aggregate to, 20 years or more.
C19 (a) Peripheral neuropath.	Exposure to acrylamide.
(b) Central nervous system toxicity.	
C20 Dystrophy of the cornea (including ulceration of the corneal surface) of the eye.	Exposure to quinone or hydroquinone.
C21 Primary carcinoma of the skin.	Exposure to arsenic or arsenic compounds, tar, pitch, bitumen, mineral oil (including paraffin) or soot.
C22 (a) Primary carcinoma of the mucous membrane of the nose or paranasal sinuses.	Work before 1950 in the refining of nickel involving exposure to oxides, sulphides or
(b) Primary carcinoma of a bronchus or lung.	water-soluble compounds of nickel.
C23 Primary neoplasm of the epithelial lining of the urinary tract (renal pelvis, ureter, bladder and urethra), including papilloma carcinoma-in-situ and invasive carcinoma.	(a) The manufacture of 1-naphtylamine, 2-naphthylamine, benzidine, auramine, magenta or 4 aminobiphenyl (also called biphenyl-4-ylamine);
	(b) work in the process of manufacturing methylenebis-orthochloroanile (also called MbOCA) for a period of, or periods which amount in aggregate to, 12 months or more;
	(c) exposure to 2-naphtylamine, benzidine, 4-aminobiphenyl (also called MbOCA) for a period of, or periods which amount in aggregate to, 12 months or more;
	(d) exposure to orthotoluidine, 4-chloro-2-methylaniline or salts of those compounds; *or*
	(e) exposure for a period of, or periods which amount in aggregate to, 5 years or more, to coal tar pitch volatiles produced in aluminium smelting involving the Sodeberg process (that is to say, the method of producing aluminium by electrolysis in which the anode consists of a paste of petroleum coke and mineral oil which is baked in situ).

Prescribed disease or injury	Occupation
C24 (a) Angiosarcoma of the liver. (b) Osteolysis of the terminal phalanges of the fingers. (c) Sclerodermatous thickening of the skin of the hand. (d) Liver fibrosis, due to exposure to vinyl chloride monomer.	Exposure to vinyl chloride monomer in the manufacture of polyvinyl chloride.
C24A Raynaud's phenomenon due to exposure to vinyl chloride monomer.	Exposure to vinyl chloride monomer in the manufacture of polyvinyl chloride before 1st January 1984.
C25 Vitiligo.	The use or handling of, or exposure to, para-tertiary-butylphenol (also called 4-tert-butylphenol), para-tertiary-butylcatechol (also called 4-tert-butylcatechol), para-amyl-phenol (also called p-pentyl phenol isomers), hydroquinone monobenzyl ether of hydroquinone (also called 4-benzyloxyphenol), mono-benzyl ether of hydroquinone (also called 4-benzyloxyphenol) or mono-butyl ether of hydroquinone (also called 4-butoxyphenol).
C26 (a) Liver toxicity. (b) Kidney toxicity.	The use of or handling of, or exposure to, carbon tetrachloride (also called tetrachloromethane).
C27 Liver toxicity.	The use of or handling of, or exposure to the fumes of, or vapour containing, trichloromethane (also called chloroform).
C29 Peripheral neuropathy.	The use of or handling of, or exposure to, n-hexane or n-butyl methyl ketone.
C30 (a) Dermatitis. (b) Ulceration of the mucous membrane or the epidermis.	The use or handling of, or exposure to, chromic acid, chromates or dichromates.
C31 Bronchiolitis obliterans.	The use or handling of, or exposure to, diacetyl (also called butanedione or 2,3-butanedione) in the manufacture of– (a) diacetyl; or (b) food favouring containing diacetyl; or (c) food to which food flavouring containing diacetyl is added.
C32 Carcinoma of the nasal cavity or associated air sinuses (nasal carcinoma).	(a) The manufacture of inorganic chromates; or (b) work in hexavalent chrome plating.
C33 Chloracne	Exposure to substances known as chloracnegans.
C34 Extrinsic allergic alveolitis	Exposure to airborne isocyanates; or to another chemical substance that causes extrinsic allergic alveolitis.
D – Miscellaneous conditions	Occupation involving:

A

Prescribed disease or injury	Occupation
D1 Pneumoconiosis.	[Occupations specified in reg 2(b) of, and Part II of Schedule 1 to, the Social Security (Industrial Injuries) (Prescribed Diseases) Regulations 1985 which are too numerous to set out here. They are all occupations involving exposure to dust, such as mining, quarrying, sand blasting, grinding, making china or earthenware, boiler-sealing and other work involving the use of stone, asbestos, etc.]
D2 Byssinosis.	Work in any room where any process up to and including the weaving process is performed in a factory in which the spinning or manipulation of raw or waste cotton or of flax, or the weaving of cotton or flax, is carried on.
D3 Diffuse mesothelioma (primary neoplasm of the mesothelium of the pleura or of the pericardium or of the peritoneum).	Exposure to asbestos, asbestos dust or any admixture of asbestos at a level above that commonly found in the environment at large.
D4 Allergic rhinitis which is due to exposure to any of the following agents:	Exposure to any of the agents set out in column 1 of this paragraph.

(a) isocyanates;
(b) platinum salts;
(c) fumes or dusts arising from the manufacture, transport or use of hardening agents (including epoxy resin curing agents) based on phthalic anhydride, tetrachlorophthalic anhydride, trimellitic anhydride or triethylenetetramine;
(d) fumes arising from the use of rosin as a soldering flux;
(e) proteolytic enzymes;
(f) animals including insects and other anthropods used for the purposes of research or education or in laboratories;
(g) dusts arising from the sowing, cultivation, harvesting, drying, handling, milling, transport or storage of barley, oats, rye, wheat or maize, or the handling, milling, transport or storage of meal or flour made therefrom;
(h) antibiotics;
(i) cimetidine;
(j) wood dust;
(k) ispaghula;
(l) castor bean dust;
(m) ipecacuanha;
(n) azodice-bonamide;

Prescribed disease or injury	Occupation
(o) animals including insects and other arthropods or their larval forms, used for the purposes of pest control or fruit cultivation, or the larval forms of animals used for the purposes of research, education or in laboratories;	
(p) glutaraldehyde;	
(q) persulphate salts or henna;	
(r) crustaceans or fish or products arising from these in the food processing industry;	
(s) reactive dyes;	
(t) soya bean;	
(u) tea dust;	
(v) green coffee bean dust;	
(w) fumes from stainless steel welding;	
(x) products made with natural rubber latex.	
D5 Non-infective dermatitis of external origin (excluding dermatitis due to ionising particles or electro-magnetic radiant heat).	Exposure to dust, liquid or vapour or any other external agent except chromic acid, chromates or bi-chromates capable of irritating the skin (including friction or heat but excluding ionising particles or electromagnetic radiations other than radiant heat).
D6 Carcinoma of the nasal cavity or associated air sinuses (nasal carcinoma).	(a) Attendance for work at a workplace where wooden goods or products made wholly or partially of wood are manufactured or repaired; or (b) attendance for work in a building used for the manufacture of footwear or components of footwear made wholly or partly of leather or fibre board; or (c) attendance for work at a place used wholly or mainly for the repair of footwear made wholly or partly of leather or fibre board; or (d) exposure to wood dust in the course of the machine processing of wood.
D7 Asthma which is due to exposure to any of the following agents: (a) isocyanates; (b) platinum salts; (c) fumes or dusts arising from the manufacture, transport or use of hardening agents (including epoxy resin curing agents) based on phthalic anhydride, tetrachlorophthalic anhydride, trimellitic anhydride or triethylenetetramine; (d) fumes arising from the use of rosin as a soldering flux; (e) proteolytic enzymes; (f) animals including insects and other anthropods used for the purposes of research or education or in laboratories;	Exposure to any of the agents set out in column 1 of this paragraph.

Prescribed disease or injury	Occupation

(g) dusts arising from the sowing, cultivation, harvesting, drying, handling, milling, transport or storage of barley, oats, rye, wheat or maize, or the handling, milling, transport or storage of meal or flour made therefrom;

(h) antibiotics;

(i) cimetidine;

(j) wood dust;

(k) ispaghula;

(l) castor bean dust;

(m) ipecacuanha;

(n) azodicarbonamide;

(o) animals including insects and other arthropods or their larval forms, used for the purposes of pest control or fruit cultivation, or the larval forms of animals used for the purposes of research, education or in laboratories;

(p) glutaraldehyde;

(q) persulphate salts or henna;

(r) crustaceans or fish or products arising from these in the food processing industry;

(s) reactive dyes;

(t) soya bean;

(u) tea dust;

(v) green coffee bean dust;

(w) fumes from stainless steel welding;

(wa) products made with natural rubber latex;

(x) any other sensitising agent (occupational asthma).

D8 Primary carcinoma of the lung where there is accompanying evidence of asbestosis.

(a) The working or handling of asbestos or any admixture of asbestos; *or*

(b) the manufacture or repair of asbestos textiles or other articles containing or composed of asbestos; *or*

(c) the cleaning of any machinery or plant used in any of the foregoing operations and of any chambers, fixtures and appliances for the collection of asbestos dust; *or*

(d) substantial exposure to the dust arising from any of the foregoing operations.

Prescribed disease or injury	Occupation
D8A Primary carcinoma of the lung.	Exposure to asbestos in the course of– (a) the manufacture of asbestos textiles; *or* (b) spraying asbestos; *or* (c) asbestos insulation work; *or* (d) applying or removing materials containing asbestos in the course of shipbuilding, where all or any of the exposure occurs before 1st January 1975, for a period of, or periods which amount in aggregate to, five years or more, or otherwise, for a period of, or periods which amount in aggregate to, ten years or more.
D9 Unilateral or bilateral diffuse pleural thickening.	(a) The working or handling of asbestos; or any admixture of asbestos; *or* (b) the manufacture or repair of asbestos textiles or other articles containing or composed of asbestos; *or* (c) the cleaning of any machinery or plant used in any of the foregoing operations and appliances for the collection of asbestos dust; *or* (d) substantial exposure to the dust arising from any of the foregoing operations.

D10 Primary carcinoma of the lung.	(a) Work underground in a tin mine; *or*
	(b) exposure to bis(chloromethyl) ether produced during the manufacture of chloromethyl methyl ether; *or*
	(c) exposure to zinc chromate, calcium chromate or strontium chromate in their pure forms; *or*
	(d) employment wholly or mainly as a coke oven worker–
	  (i) for a period of, or periods which amount in aggregate to, 15 years or more;
	  (ii) in top oven work, for a period of, or periods which amount in aggregate to, 5 years or more; *or*
	  (iii) in a combination of top oven work and other coke oven work for a total aggregate period of 15 years or more, where one year working in top oven work is treated as equivalent to 3 years in other coke oven work.

Prescribed disease or injury	Occupation
D11 Primary carcinoma of the lung where there is accompanying evidence of silicosis.	Exposure to silica dust in the course of: (a) the manufacture of glass or pottery; (b) tunnelling in or quarrying sandstone or granite; (c) mining metal ores; (d) slate quarrying or the manufacture of artefacts from slate; (e) mining clay; (f) using silicous materials as abrasives; (g) cutting stone; (h) stone masonry; *or* (i) work in a foundry.
D12 Except in the circumstances specified in regulation 2(d): chronic obstructive pulmonary disease, where there is evidence of a forced expiratory volume in one second (measured from the position of maximum inspiration with the claimant making maximum effort) which is: (i) at least one litre below the appropriate mean value predicted, obtained from the following prediction formulae which give the mean values predicted in litres: For a man, where the measurement is made without back-extrapolation, (3.62 x Height in metres) – (0.031 x Age in years) – 1.41; or, where the measurement is made with back-extrapolation, (3.71 x Height in metres) – (0.032 x Age in years) – 1.44. For a woman, where the measurement is made without back-extrapolation, (3.29 x Height in metres) – (0.029 x Age in years) – 1.42; or where the measurement is made with back-extrapolation, (3.37 x Height in metres) – (0.030 x Age in years) – 1.46; *or* (ii) less than one litre. The value of the litre in (i) and (ii) shall be construed as fixed and shall not vary by virtue of any treatment or treatments.	Exposure to coal dust (whether before or after 5th July 1948) by reason of working– (a) underground in a coal mine for a period or periods amounting in aggregate to at least 20 years; (b) on the surface of a coal mine as a screen worker for a period or periods amounting in aggregate to at least 40 years before 1st January 1983; *or* (c) both underground in a coal mine, and on the surface as a screen worker before 1st January 1983, where 2 years working as a surface screen worker is equivalent to 1 year working underground, amounting in aggregate to at least the equivalent of 20 years underground. Any such period or periods shall include a period or periods of incapacity while engaged in such an occupation.
D13 Primary cacinoma of the nasopharynx	Exposure to wood dust in the course of the processing of wood or the manufacture or repair of wood products, for a period or periods which amount in aggregate to at least 10 years.

Appendix 6

Upper and lower earnings limits

Year	Lower earnings limit £	Primary threshold £	Upper earnings limit £
1990/91	46		350
1991/92	52		390
1992/93	54		405
1993/94	56		420
1994/95	57		430
1995/96	58		440
1996/97	61		455
1997/98	62		465
1998/99	64		485
1999/00	66		500
2000/01	67	76	535
2001/02	72	87	575
2002/03	75	89	585
2003/04	77	89	595
2004/05	79	91	610
2005/06	82	94	630
2006/07	84	97	645
2007/08	87	100	670
2008/09	90	105	770
2009/10	95	110	844
2010/11	97	110	844
2011/12	102	139	817
2012/13	107	146	817
2013/14	109	149	797
2014/15	111	153	805
2015/16	112	155	815
2016/17	112	155	827
2017/18	113	157	866
2018/19	116	162	892
2019/20	118	166	962
2020/21	120	183	962

Appendix 7

Minimum working conditions

Employers are required to provide certain minimum working conditions. These rules are relevant to the universal credit and jobseeker's allowance rules about sanctions and being available for and looking for work. A brief summary of the rules follows.

The Working Time Regulations

These regulations are designed to protect the health and safety of workers. The main rules are:

- a limit on the hours in the average working week;
- minimum annual holiday entitlement;
- entitlement to breaks from work (both daily breaks and a longer break once a week) and to rest periods while at work;
- special protection for night workers.

This *Handbook* cannot cover the detailed rules nor the complicated system of exceptions to them. Get specialist advice if you think your employer is breaking these rules.

The National Minimum Wage Act

This Act provides that the minimum hourly rate of pay in any job should be:

- if you are aged 25 or over, £8.72. The government calls this the 'national living wage';
- if you are aged 21–24, £8.20;
- if you are aged 18–20, £6.45;
- if you are under age 18 and not of compulsory school age, £4.55;
- if you are in the first year of employment or are under 19, and you are employed under a contract of apprenticeship (or treated as if you are), £4.15.

Appendix 8

Statutory payments for a birth and maternity allowance

Baby is expected during the week beginning Sunday	Latest start date of employment for SMP	15th week before the EWC begins Sunday+	Earliest week for SMP or MA begins Sunday++	66-week test period for MA begins Sunday
5.4.20	6.7.19	22.12.19	19.1.20	30.12.18
12.4.20	13.7.19	29.12.19	26.1.20	6.1.19
19.4.20	20.7.19	5.1.20	2.2.20	13.1.19
26.4.20	27.7.19	12.1.20	9.2.20	20.1.19
3.5.20	3.8.19	19.1.20	16.2.20	27.1.19
10.5.20	10.8.19	26.1.20	23.2.20	3.2.19
17.5.20	17.8.19	2.2.20	1.3.20	10.2.19
24.5.20	24.8.19	9.2.20	8.3.20	17.2.19
31.5.20	31.8.19	16.2.20	15.3.20	24.2.19
7.6.20	7.9.19	23.2.20	22.3.20	3.3.19
14.6.20	14.9.19	1.3.20	29.3.20	10.3.19
21.6.20	21.9.19	8.3.20	5.4.20	17.3.19
28.6.20	28.9.19	15.3.20	12.4.20	24.3.19
5.7.20	5.10.19	22.3.20	19.4.20	31.3.19
12.7.20	12.10.19	29.3.20	26.4.20	7.4.19
19.7.20	19.10.19	5.4.20	3.5.20	14.4.19
26.7.20	26.10.19	12.4.20	10.5.20	21.4.19
2.8.20	2.11.19	19.4.20	17.5.20	28.4.19
9.8.20	9.11.19	26.4.20	24.5.20	5.5.19
16.8.20	16.11.19	3.5.20	31.5.20	12.5.19
23.8.20	23.11.19	10.5.20	7.6.20	19.5.19
30.8.20	30.11.19	17.5.20	14.6.20	26.5.19
6.9.20	7.12.19	24.5.20	21.6.20	2.6.19
13.9.20	14.12.19	31.5.20	28.6.20	9.6.19
20.9.20	21.12.19	7.6.20	5.7.20	16.6.19
27.9.20	28.12.19	14.6.20	12.7.20	23.6.19

A

Appendix 8: Statutory payments for a birth and maternity allowance

Baby is expected during the week beginning Sunday	Latest start date of employment for SMP	15th week before the EWC begins Sunday+	Earliest week for SMP or MA begins Sunday++	66-week test period for MA begins Sunday
4.10.20	4.1.20	21.6.20	19.7.20	30.6.19
11.10.20	11.1.20	28.6.20	26.7.20	7.7.19
18.10.20	18.1.20	5.7.20	2.8.20	14.7.19
25.10.20	25.1.20	12.7.20	9.8.20	21.7.19
1.11.20	1.2.20	19.7.20	16.8.20	28.7.19
8.11.20	8.2.20	26.7.20	23.8.20	4.8.19
15.11.20	15.2.20	2.8.20	30.8.20	11.8.19
22.11.20	22.2.20	9.8.20	6.9.20	18.8.19
29.11.20	29.2.20	16.8.20	13.9.20	25.8.19
6.12.20	7.3.20	23.8.20	20.9.20	1.9.19
13.12.20	14.3.20	30.8.20	27.9.20	8.9.19
20.12.20	21.3.20	6.9.20	4.10.20	15.9.19
27.12.20	28.3.20	13.9.20	11.10.20	22.9.19
3.1.21	4.4.20	20.9.20	18.10.20	29.9.19
10.1.21	11.4.20	27.9.20	25.10.20	6.10.19
17.1.21	18.4.20	4.10.20	1.11.20	13.10.19
24.1.21	25.4.20	11.10.20	8.11.20	20.10.19
31.1.21	2.5.20	18.10.20	15.11.20	27.10.19
7.2.21	9.5.20	25.10.20	22.11.20	3.11.19
14.2.21	16.5.20	1.11.20	29.11.20	10.11.19
21.2.21	23.5.20	8.11.20	6.12.20	17.11.19
28.2.21	30.5.20	15.11.20	13.12.20	24.11.19
7.3.21	6.6.20	22.11.20	20.12.20	1.12.19
14.3.21	13.6.20	29.11.20	27.12.20	8.12.19
21.3.21	20.6.20	6.12.20	3.1.21	15.12.19
28.3.21	27.6.20	13.12.20	10.1.21	22.12.19
4.4.21	4.7.20	20.12.20	17.1.21	29.12.19
11.4.21	11.7.20	27.12.20	24.1.21	5.1.20
18.4.21	18.7.20	3.1.21	31.1.21	12.1.20
25.4.21	25.7.20	10.1.21	7.2.21	19.1.20
2.5.21	1.8.20	17.1.21	14.2.21	26.1.20
9.5.21	8.8.20	24.1.21	21.2.21	2.2.20
16.5.21	15.8.20	31.1.21	28.2.21	9.2.20
23.5.21	22.8.20	7.2.21	7.3.21	16.2.20
30.5.21	29.8.20	14.2.21	14.3.21	23.2.20
6.6.21	5.9.20	21.2.21	21.3.21	1.3.20
13.6.21	12.9.20	28.2.21	28.3.21	8.3.20
20.6.21	19.9.20	7.3.21	4.4.21	15.3.20
27.6.21	26.9.20	14.3.21	11.4.21	22.3.20
4.7.21	3.10.20	21.3.21	18.4.21	29.3.20

Baby is expected during the week beginning Sunday	Latest start date of employment for SMP	15th week before the EWC begins Sunday+	Earliest week for SMP or MA begins Sunday++	66-week test period for MA begins Sunday
11.7.21	10.10.20	28.3.21	25.4.21	5.4.20
18.7.21	17.10.20	4.4.21	2.5.21	12.4.20
25.7.21	24.10.20	11.4.21	9.5.21	19.4.20
1.8.21	31.10.20	18.4.21	16.5.21	26.4.20
8.8.21	7.11.20	25.4.21	23.5.21	3.5.20
15.8.21	14.11.20	2.5.21	30.5.21	10.5.20
22.8.21	21.11.20	9.5.21	6.6.21	17.5.20
29.8.21	28.11.20	16.5.21	13.6.21	24.5.20
5.9.21	5.12.20.	23.5.21	20.6.21	31.5.20
12.9.21	12.12.20	30.5.21	27.6.21	7.6.20
19.9.21	19.12.20	6.6.21	4.7.21	14.6.20
26.9.21	26.12.20	13.6.21	11.7.21	21.6.20
3.10.21	2.1.21	20.6.21	18.7.21	28.6.20
10.10.21	9.1.21	27.6.21	25.7.21	5.7.20
17.10.21	16.1.21	4.7.21	1.8.21	12.7.20
24.10.21	23.1.21	11.7.21	8.8.21	19.7.20
31.10.21	30.1.21	18.7.21	15.8.21	26.7.20
7.11.21	6.2.21	25.7.21	22.8.21	2.8.20
14.11.21	13.2.21	1.8.21	29.8.21	9.8.20
21.11.21	20.2.21	8.8.21	5.9.21	16.8.20
28.11.21	27.2.21	15.8.21	12.9.21	23.8.20
5.12.21	6.3.21	22.8.21	19.9.21	30.8.20
12.12.21	13.3.21	29.8.21	26.9.21	6.9.20
19.12.21	20.3.21	5.9.21	3.10.21	13.9.20
26.12.21	27.3.21	12.9.21	10.10.21	20.9.20

+ EWC is the expected week of childbirth. The 15th week before the EWC is relevant to the continuous employment rule and the earnings condition for SMP, SPP and SSPP. See Chapter 38.

++ This is the 11th week before the baby is due (unless your baby is born earlier. See Chapters 34 and 38 for possible exceptions).

Appendix 9

Pension age for women born between 6 April 1950 and 5 December 1953

Date of birth	Pension age (in years/months)*	Date pension age reached
06.04.50 – 05.05.50	60.1 – 60.0	06.05.2010
06.05.50 – 05.06.50	60.2 – 60.1	06.07.2010
06.06.50 – 05.07.50	60.3 – 60.2	06.09.2010
06.07.50 – 05.08.50	60.4 – 60.3	06.11.2010
06.08.50 – 05.09.50	60.5 – 60.4	06.01.2011
06.09.50 – 05.10.50	60.6 – 60.5	06.03.2011
06.10.50 – 05.11.50	60.7 – 60.6	06.05.2011
06.11.50 – 05.12.50	60.8 – 60.7	06.07.2011
06.12.50 – 05.01.51	60.9 – 60.8	06.09.2011
06.01.51 – 05.02.51	60.10 – 60.9	06.11.2011
06.02.51 – 05.03.51	60.11 – 60.10	06.01.2012
06.03.51 – 05.04.51	61.0 – 60.11	06.03.2012
06.04.51 – 05.05.51	61.1 – 61.0	06.05.2012
06.05.51 – 05.06.51	61.2 – 61.1	06.07.2012
06.06.51 – 05.07.51	61.3 – 61.2	06.09.2012
06.07.51 – 05.08.51	61.4 – 61.3	06.11.2012
06.08.51 – 05.09.51	61.5 – 61.4	06.01.2013
06.09.51 – 05.10.51	61.6 – 61.5	06.03.2013
06.10.51 – 05.11.51	61.7 – 61.6	06.05.2013
06.11.51 – 05.12.51	61.8 – 61.7	06.07.2013
06.12.51 – 05.01.52	61.9 – 61.8	06.09.2013
06.01.52 – 05.02.52	61.10 – 61.9	06.11.2013
06.02.52 – 05.03.52	61.11 – 61.10	06.01.2014
06.03.52 – 05.04.52	62.0 – 61.11	06.03.2014
06.04.52 – 05.05.52	62.1 – 62.0	06.05.2014

Date of birth	Pension age (in years/months)*	Date pension age reached
06.05.52 – 05.06.52	62.2 – 62.1	06.07.2014
06.06.52 – 05.07.52	62.3 – 62.2	06.09.2014
06.07.52 – 05.08.52	62.4 – 62.3	06.11.2014
06.08.52 – 05.09.52	62.5 – 62.4	06.01.2015
06.09.52 – 05.10.52	62.6 – 62.5	06.03.2015
06.10.52 – 05.11.52	62.7 – 62.6	06.05.2015
06.11.52 – 05.12.52	62.8 – 62.7	06.07.2015
06.12.52 – 05.01.53	62.9 – 62.8	06.09.2015
06.01.53 – 05.02.53	62.10 – 62.9	06.11.2015
06.02.53 – 05.03.53	62.11 – 62.10	06.01.2016
06.03.53 – 05.04.53	63.0 – 62.11	06.03.2016
06.04.53 – 05.05.53	63.3 – 63.2	06.07.2016
06.05.53 – 05.06.53	63.6 – 63.5	06.11.2016
06.06.53 – 05.07.53	63.9 – 63.8	06.03.2017
06.07.53 – 05.08.53	64.0 – 63.11	06.07.2017
06.08.53 – 05.09.53	64.3 – 64.2	06.11.2017
06.09.53 – 05.10.53	64.6 – 64.5	06.03.2018
06.10.53 – 05.11.53	64.9 – 64.8	06.07.2018
06.11.53 – 05.12.53	65.0 – 64.11	06.11.2018

* For example, '60.1–60.0' means you would be aged between 60 and 60 years and one month, depending on your date of birth, when you reach pension age.

A

Appendix 10

Abbreviations used in the notes

AAC	Administrative Appeals Chamber	EWCA Crim	England and Wales Court of Appeal (Criminal Division)
AACR	Administrative Appeals Chamber Reports	EWHC	England and Wales High Court
AC	Appeal Cases	FLR	Family Law Reports
All ER	All England Law Reports	HC	High Court
Art(s)	Article(s)	HL	House of Lords
CA	Court of Appeal	HLR	Housing Law Reports
CC	County Council	IAC	Immigration and Asylum Chamber
CCLR	Community Care Law Reports	ICR	Industrial Cases Reports
Ch	chapter	IR	Immigration Rules
CJEU	Court of Justice of the European Union	JPR	Justice of the Peace Reports
		KB	King's Bench
CLY	Current Law Year Book	LB	London Borough
col	column	MBC	Metropolitan Borough Council
CPR	Civil Procedure Rules		
CS	Court of Session	NICA	Northern Ireland Court of Appeal
CSIH	Court of Session, Inner House	NICom	Northern Ireland Social Security Commissioner
CSOH	Court of Session, Outer House	OJ	Official Journal of the European Union
DC	Divisional Court		
Dir	Directive	para(s)	paragraph(s)
E	England	QB	Queen's Bench Reports
ECJ	European Court of Justice	QBD	Queen's Bench Division
ECR	European Court Reports	r(r)	rule(s)
ECtHR	European Court of Human Rights	Reg(s)	Regulation(s)
		s(s)	section(s)
EEA	European Economic Area	SC	Supreme Court
EEC	European Economic Community	Sch(s)	Schedule(s)
		SCLR	Scottish Civil Law Reports
EU	European Union	ScotCS	Scottish Court of Session
EWCA Civ	England and Wales Court of Appeal (Civil Division)	SLT	Scots Law Times

SSAC	Social Security Advisory Committee	UK-Swiss Agree-ment	Agreement between the UK and the Swiss Confederation on Citizens' Rights following the withdrawal of the UK from the European Union and the Free Movement of Persons Agreement.
SSWP	Secretary of State for Work and Pensions		
TCC	Tax and Chancery Chamber		
TFEU	The Treaty on the Functioning of the European Union		
UK-EFTA	Agreement on arrangements between Iceland, the Principality of Liechtenstein, the Kingdom of Norway and the UK following the withdrawal of the UK from the European Union, the EEA Agreement and other agreements.	UKHL	United Kingdom House of Lords
		UKSC	United Kingdom Supreme Court
		UKUT	United Kingdom Upper Tribunal
		Vol	volume
		W	Wales
		WLR	Weekly Law Reports

Acts of Parliament

C(LC)A 2000	Children (Leaving Care) Act 2000
C(S)A 1995	Children (Scotland) Act 1995
CA 1989	Children Act 1989
CJPOA 1994	Criminal Justice and Public Order Act 1994
CMOPA 2008	Child Maintenance and Other Payments Act 2008
CSA 1991	Child Support Act 1991
CSPSSA 2000	Child Support, Pensions and Social Security Act 2000
ETA 1973	Employment and Training Act 1973
EU(W)A 2018	European Union (Withdrawal) Act 2018
GRA 2004	Gender Recognition Act 2004
HRA 1998	Human Rights Act 1998
IA 1971	Immigration Act 1971
IA 1988	Immigration Act 1988
IAA 1999	Immigration and Asylum Act 1999
IT(EP)A 2003	Income Tax (Earnings and Pensions) Act 2003
ITT(OI)A 2005	Income Tax (Trading and Other Income) Act 2005
LGFA 1992	Local Government Finance Act 1992
JSA 1995	Jobseekers Act 1995
M(SSC)A 2013	Marriage (Same Sex Couples) Act 2013
MCA 1973	Matrimonial Causes Act 1973
NHSA 2006	National Health Service Act 2006
NHS(S)A 1978	National Health Service (Scotland) Act 1978
NHS(W)A 2006	National Health Service (Wales) Act 2006
NIAA 2002	Nationality, Immigration and Asylum Act 2002
PA 1995	Pensions Act 1995
PA 2014	Pensions Act 2014
PACEA 1984	Police and Criminal Evidence Act 1984

SPCA 2002	State Pension Credit Act 2002
SA 1998	Scotland Act 1998
SA 2016	Scotland Act 2016
SS(RB)A 1997	Social Security (Recovery of Benefits) Act 1997
SS(S)A 2018	Social Security (Scotland) Act 2018
SSA 1998	Social Security Act 1998
SSA(F)A 1997	Social Security Administration (Fraud) Act 1997
SSAA 1992	Social Security Administration Act 1992
SSC(TF)A 1999	Social Security Contributions (Transfer of Functions etc) Act 1999
SSCBA 1992	Social Security Contributions and Benefits Act 1992
SSFA 2001	Social Security Fraud Act 2001
T(S)A 2014	Tribunals (Scotland) Act 2014
TCA 2002	Tax Credits Act 2002
TCEA 2007	Tribunals, Courts and Enforcement Act 2007
TMA 1970	Taxes Management Act 1970
WRA 2007	Welfare Reform Act 2007
WRA 2012	Welfare Reform Act 2012
WRWA 2016	Welfare Reform and Work Act 2016

Regulations and other statutory instruments

Each set of regulations has a statutory instrument (SI) number and a date. You can find them all at legislation.gov.uk.

A(IWA) Regs	The Accession (Immigration and Worker Authorisation) Regulations 2006 No.3317
A(IWR) Regs	The Accession (Immigration and Worker Registration) Regulations 2004 No.1219
AC(IWA) Regs	The Accession of Croatia (Immigration and Worker Authorisation) Regulations 2013 No.1460
ASPP(G) Regs	The Additional Statutory Paternity Pay (General) Regulations 2010 No.1056
BSP Regs	The Bereavement Support Payment Regulations 2017 No.410
C(LC)SSB Regs	The Children (Leaving Care) Social Security Benefits Regulations 2001 No.3074
C(LC)SSB(S) Regs	The Children (Leaving Care) Social Security Benefits (Scotland) Regulations 2004 No.747
C(LC)(W) Regs	The Children (Leaving Care) (Wales) Regulations 2001 No.2189 (W151)
CA(YCG)(S) Regs	The Carer's Assistance (Young Carer Grants) (Scotland) Regulations 2019 No.324
CB Regs	The Child Benefit (General) Regulations 2006 No.223
CB(R) Regs	The Child Benefit (Rates) Regulations 2006 No.965

CB&GA(AA) Regs	The Child Benefit and Guardian's Allowance (Administrative Arrangements) Regulations 2003 No.494
CB&GA(Admin) Regs	The Child Benefit and Guardian's Allowance (Administration) Regulations 2003 No.492
CB&GA(DA) Regs	The Child Benefit and Guardian's Allowance (Decisions and Appeals) Regulations 2003 No.916
CC(DIS) Regs	The Community Charges (Deductions from Income Support) (No.2) Regulations 1990 No.545
CL(E) Regs	The Care Leavers (England) Regulations 2010 No.2571
CPP&CR(E) Regs	The Care Planning, Placement and Case Review (England) Regulations 2010 No.959
CS(MCSC) Regs	The Child Support (Maintenance Calculations and Special Cases) Regulations 2000 No.2001 No.155
CT(DIS) Regs	The Council Tax (Deductions from Income Support) Regulations 1993 No.494
CTC Regs	The Child Tax Credit Regulations 2002 No.2007
CTR(S) Regs	The Council Tax Reduction (Scotland) Regulations 2012 No.303
CTR(SPC)S Regs	The Council Tax Reduction (State Pension Credit) (Scotland) Regulations 2012 No.319
CTRS(DS)E Regs	The Council Tax Reduction Schemes (Default Scheme) (England) Regulations 2012 No.2886
CTRS(DS)W Regs	The Council Tax Reduction Schemes (Default Scheme) (Wales) Regulations 2013 No.3035 (W303)
CTRS(PR)E Regs	The Council Tax Reduction Schemes (Prescribed Requirements) (England) Regulations 2012 No.2885
CTRSPR(W) Regs	The Council Tax Reduction Schemes and Prescribed Requirements (Wales) Regulations 2013 No.3029 (W316)
DACYP(S) Regs	The Disability Assistance for Children and Young People (Scotland) Regulations 2020 (draft)
DFA Regs	Discretionary Financial Assistance Regulations 2001 No.1167
ESA Regs	The Employment and Support Allowance Regulations 2008 No.794
ESA Regs 2013	The Employment and Support Allowance Regulations 2013 No.379
ESA(TP) Regs	The Employment and Support Allowance (Transitional Provisions) Regulations 2008 No.795
ESA(TP)(EA)(No.2) Regs	The Employment and Support Allowance (Transitional Provisions, Housing Benefit and Council Tax Benefit) (Existing Awards) (No.2) Regulations 2010 No.1907

A

ESA(WRA) Regs	The Employment and Support Allowance (Work-Related Activity) Regulations 2011 No.1349
ESAUC(MA) Regs	The Employment and Support Allowance and Universal Credit (Miscellaneous Amendments and Transitional and Savings Provisions) Regulations 2017 No.204
EYA(BSG)(S) Regs	The Early Years Assistance (Best Start Grants) (Scotland) Regulations 2018 No.370
F(DIS) Regs	The Fines (Deductions from Income Support) Regulations 1992 No.2182
FEA(S) Regs	The Funeral Expense Assistance (Scotland) Regulations 2019 No.292
FTT(S) Rules	Schedule to The First-tier Tribunal for Scotland Social Security Chamber (Procedure) Regulations 2018 No.273
GA(Gen) Regs	The Guardian's Allowance (General) Regulations 2003 No.495
HB Regs	The Housing Benefit Regulations 2006 No.213
HB(HR)A Regs	The Housing Benefit (Habitual Residence) Amendment Regulations 2014 No.539
HB(SPC) Regs	The Housing Benefit (Persons who have Attained the Qualifying Age for State Pension Credit) Regulations 2006 No.214
HB&CTB(CP) Regs	The Housing Benefit and Council Tax Benefit (Consquential Provisions) Regulations 2006 No.217
HB&CTB(DA) Regs	The Housing Benefit and Council Tax Benefit (Decisions and Appeals) Regulations 2001 No.1002
HB&CTB(WPD) Regs	The Housing Benefit and Council Tax Benefit (War Pension Disregards) Regulations 2007 No.1619
HSS(DHSF)(W) Regs	The Healthy Start Scheme (Description of Healthy Start Food) (Wales) Regulations 2006 No.3108
HSS&WF(A) Regs	The Healthy Start Scheme and Welfare Food (Amendment) Regulations 2005 No.3262
I(EEA) Regs	The Immigration (European Economic Area) Regulations 2016 No.1052
I(EEA) Regs 2006	The Immigration (European Economic Area) Regulations 2006 No.1003
I(EEA)A Regs 2012	The Immigration (European Economic Area) (Amendment) Regulations 2012 No.1547
IIB(ETSC) Regs	The Industrial Injuries Benefit (Employment Training Schemes and Courses) Regulations 2013 No.2540
IS Regs	The Income Support (General) Regulations 1987 No.1967
IS(JSACA) Regs	The Income Support (General)(Jobseeker's Allowance Consequential Amendments) Regulations 1996 No.206

IS(WRA) Regs	The Income Support (Work-Related Activity) and Miscellaneous Amendments Regulations 2014 No.1097
JSA Regs	The Jobseeker's Allowance Regulations 1996 No.207
JSA Regs 2013	The Jobseeker's Allowance Regulations 2013 No.378
JSA(HR)A Regs	The Jobseeker's Allowance (Habitual Residence) Amendment Regulations 2013 No.3196
JSA(SAPOE) Regs	The Jobseeker's Allowance (Schemes for Assisting Persons to Obtain Employment) Regulations 2013 No.276
LMI Regs	The Loans for Mortgage Interest Regulations 2017 No.725
MA(C) Regs	The Maternity Allowance (Curtailment) Regulations 2014 No.3053
NHS(CDA) Regs	The National Health Service (Charges for Drugs and Appliances) Regulations 2015 No.570
NHS(DC) Regs	The National Health Service (Dental Charges) Regulations 2005 No.3477
NHS(DC)(S) Regs	The National Health Service (Dental Charges) (Scotland) Regulations 2003 No.158
NHS(DC)(W) Regs	The National Health Service (Dental Charges) (Wales) Regulations 2006 No.491
NHS(FP&CDA)(S) Regs	The National Health Service (Free Prescriptions and Charges for Drugs and Appliances) (Scotland) Regulations 2011 No.55
NHS(FP&CDA)(W) Regs	The National Health Service (Free Prescriptions and Charges for Drugs and Appliances) (Wales) Regulations 2007 No.121
NHS(GOS) Regs	The National Health Service (General Ophthalmic Services) Regulations 1986 No.975
NHS(OCP) Regs	The National Health Service (Optical Charges and Payments) Regulations 1997 No.818
NHS(OCP) Regs 2013	The National Health Service (Optical Charges and Payments) Regulations 2013 No.461
NHS(OCP)(S) Regs	The National Health Service (Optical Charges and Payments) (Scotland) Regulations 1998 No.642
NHS(TERC) Regs	The National Health Service (Travelling Expenses and Remission of Charges) Regulations 2003 No.2382
NHS(TERC)(S) Regs	The National Health Service (Travelling Expenses and Remission of Charges) (Scotland) (No.2) Regulations 2003 No.460
NHS(TERC)(W) Regs	The National Health Service (Travelling Expenses and Remission of Charges Regulations) (Wales) 2007 No.1104

A

PAL Regs	The Paternity and Adoption Leave Regulations 2002 No.2788
PIP(TP) Regs	The Personal Independence Payment (Transitional Provisions) Regulations 2013 No.387
POS Regs	The Primary Ophthalmic Services Regulations 2008 No.1186
RO(HBF)O	The Rent Officers (Housing Benefit Functions) Order 1997 No.1984
RO(HBF)(S)O	The Rent Officers (Housing Benefit Functions) (Scotland) Order 1997 No.144
RO(UCF)O	The Rent Officers (Universal Credit Functions) Order 2013 No.382
SCP Regs (draft)	The Scottish Child Payment Regulations 2020 (draft)
SF(AM) Regs	The Social Fund (Budgeting Loans) (Applications and Miscellaneous Provisions) Regulations 2015 No.1411
SF(AR) Regs	The Social Fund (Application for Review) Regulations 1988 No.34
SF(RDB) Regs	The Social Fund (Recovery by Deductions from Benefits) Regulations 1988 No.35
SFCWP Regs	The Social Fund Cold Weather Payments (General) Regulations 1988 No.1724
SFM&FE Regs	The Social Fund Maternity and Funeral Expenses (General) Regulations 2005 No.3061
SFWFP Regs	The Social Fund Winter Fuel Payment Regulations 2000 No.729
SMP Regs	The Statutory Maternity Pay (General) Regulations 1986 No.1960
SMP(ME) Regs	The Statutory Maternity Pay (Medical Evidence) Regulations 1987 No.235
SMP(PAM) Regs	The Statutory Maternity Pay (Persons Abroad and Mariners) Regulations 1987 No.418
SMP&SAP(C) Regs	The Statutory Maternity Pay and Statutory Adoption Pay (Curtailment) Regulations 2014 No.3054
SMPSS(MA) Regs	The Statutory Maternity Pay, Social Security (Maternity Allowance) and Social Security (Overlapping Benefits) (Amendment) Regulations 2006 No.2379
SP Regs	The State Pension Regulations 2015 No.173
SPBP(G) Regs	The Statutory Parental Bereavement Pay (General) Regulations 2020 No.233
SPC Regs	The State Pension Credit Regulations 2002 No.1792
SPC(CTMP) Regs	The State Pension Credit (Consequential, Transitional and Miscellaneous Provisions) Regulations 2002 No.3019

SPP(A)&SAP(AO)(No.2) Regs	The Statutory Paternity Pay (Adoption) and Statutory Adoption Pay (Adoptions from Overseas) (No.2) Regulations 2003 No.1194
SPPSAP(A) Regs	The Statutory Paternity Pay and Statutory Adoption Pay (Administration) Regulations 2002 No.2820
SPPSAP(G) Regs	The Statutory Paternity Pay and Statutory Adoption Pay (General) Regulations 2002 No.2822
SPPSAP(PAM) Regs	The Statutory Paternity Pay and Statutory Adoption Pay (Persons Abroad and Mariners) Regulations 2002 No.2821
SPPSAP(POPA) Regs	The Statutory Paternity Pay and Statutory Adoption Pay (Parental Orders and Prospective Adopters) Regulations 2014 No.2934
SPPSAP(WR) Regs	The Statutory Paternity Pay and Statutory Adoption Pay (Weekly Rates) Regulations 2002 No.2818
SSA(IO)(S) Regs	Social Security Assistance (Investigation of Offences) (Scotland) Regulations 2020 SSI 2020 No.11
SS(AA) Regs	The Social Security (Attendance Allowance) Regulations 1991 No.2740
SS(CatE) Regs	The Social Security (Categorisation of Earners) Regulations 1978 No.1689
SS(CCPC) Regs	Social Security (Contribution Credits for Parents and Carers) Regulations 2010 No.19
SS(Con) Regs	The Social Security (Contributions) Regulations 2001 No.1004
SS(C&P) Regs	The Social Security (Claims and Payments) Regulations 1987 No.1968
SS(CP)Regs	The Social Security (Civil Penalties) Regulations 2012 No.1990
SS(Cr) Regs	The Social Security (Credits) Regulations 1975 No.556
SS(CTCNIN) Regs	The Social Security (Crediting and Treatment of Contributions, and National Insurance Numbers) Regulations 2001 No.769
SS(DLA) Regs	The Social Security (Disability Living Allowance) Regulations 1991 No.2890
SS(DLA)A Regs	Social Security (Disability Living Allowance) (Amendment) Regulations 2010 No.1651
SS(DLA,AA&CA)(A) Regs	The Social Security (Disability Living Allowance, Attendance Allowance and Carer's Allowance) (Amendment) Regulations 2013 No.389
SS(EEEIIP) Regs	The Social Security (Employed Earners' Employment for Industrial Injuries Purposes) Regulations 1975 No.467
SS(EF) Regs	The Social Security (Earnings Factor) Regulations 1979 No.676

SS(GB) Regs	The Social Security (General Benefits) Regulations 1982 No.1408
SS(GBRA)NI Regs	The Social Security (Great Britain Reciprocal Arrangements) Regulations (Northern Ireland) 2016 No.149
SS(HIP) Regs	The Social Security (Hospital In-Patients) Regulations 2005 No.3360
SS(HR)A Regs	The Social Security (Habitual Residence) Amendment Regulations 2004 No.1232
SS(IA)CA Regs	The Social Security (Immigration and Asylum) Consequential Amendments Regulations 2000 No.636
SS(IB) Regs	The Social Security (Incapacity Benefit) Regulations 1994 No.2946
SS(IB)(T) Regs	The Social Security (Incapacity Benefit) (Transitional) Regulations 1995 No.310
SS(IB-ID) Regs	The Social Security (Incapacity Benefit – Increases for Dependants) Regulations 1994 No.2945
SS(IBWFI) Regs	The Social Security (Incapacity Benefit Work-focused Interviews) Regulations 2008 No.2928
SS(ICA) Regs	The Social Security (Invalid Care Allowance) Regulations 1976 No.409
SS(II)(AB) Regs	The Social Security (Industrial Injuries) (Airmen's Benefits) Regulations 1975 No.469
SS(II)(MB) Regs	The Social Security (Industrial Injuries) (Mariners' Benefits) Regulations 1975 No.470
SS(II)(REA) Regs	The Social Security (Industrial Injuries) (Reduced Earnings Allowance and Transitional) Regulations 1987 No.415
SS(II&D)MP Regs	The Social Security (Industrial Injuries and Diseases) Miscellaneous Provisions Regulations 1986 No.1561
SS(IIPD) Regs	The Social Security (Industrial Injuries) (Prescribed Diseases) Regulations 1985 No.967
SS(JPI) Regs	The Social Security (Jobcentre Plus Interviews) Regulations 2002 No.1703
SS(JPIP) Regs	Social Security (Jobcentre Plus Interviews for Partners) Regulations 2003 No.1886
SS(LB) Regs	The Social Security (Loss of Benefit) Regulations 2001 No.4022
SS(MAP) Regs	The Social Security (Maximum Additional Pension) Regulations 1978 No.949
SS(MatA) Regs	The Social Security (Maternity Allowance) Regulations 1987 No.416
SS(MatA)(E) Regs	The Social Security (Maternity Allowance) (Earnings) Regulations 2000 No.688

SS(MatA)(WA) Regs	The Social Security (Maternity Allowance) (Work Abroad) Regulations 1987 No.417
SS(ME) Regs	The Social Security (Medical Evidence) Regulations 1976 No.615
SS(NCC) Regs	The Social Security (Notification of Change of Circumstances) Regulations 2001 No.3252
SS(NIRA) Regs	The Social Security (Northern Ireland Reciprocal Arrangements) Regulations 2016 No.287
SS(OB) Regs	The Social Security (Overlapping Benefits) Regulations 1979 No.597
SS(OR) Regs	The Social Security (Overpayments and Recovery) Regulations 2013 No.384
SS(PA)A Regs	Social Security (Persons from Abroad) Amendment Regulations 2006 No.1026
SS(PAB) Regs	The Social Security (Payments on Account of Benefit) Regulations 2013 No.383
SS(PAOR) Regs	The Social Security (Payments on Account, Overpayments and Recovery) Regulations 1988 No.664
SS(PFA)MA Regs	The Social Security (Persons From Abroad) Miscellaneous Amendment Regulations 1996 No.30
SS(PIP) Regs	The Social Security (Personal Independence Payment) Regulations 2013 No.377
SS(RB) Regs	The Social Security (Recovery of Benefits) Regulations 1997 No.2205
SS(RB)App Regs	The Social Security (Recovery of Benefits) (Appeals) Regulations 1997 No.2237
SS(SDA) Regs	The Social Security (Severe Disablement Allowances) Regulations 1984 No.1303
SS(WB&RP) Regs	The Social Security (Widow's Benefit and Retirement Pensions) Regulations 1979 No.642
SS(WBRP&OB)(T) Regs	The Social Security (Widow's Benefit, Retirement Pensions and Other Benefits) (Transitional) Regulations 1979 No.643
SS(WFILP) Regs	The Social Security (Work-focused Interviews for Lone Parents) and Miscellaneous Amendments Regulations 2000 No.1926
SS(WTCCTC)(CA) Regs	The Social Security (Working Tax Credit and Child Tax Credit) (Consequential Amendments) Regulations 2003 No.455
SSA(F)AO No.5	The Social Security Administration (Fraud) Act 1997 (Commencement No.5) Order 1997 No.2766
SSB(CE) Regs	The Social Security Benefit (Computation of Earnings) Regulations 1996 No.2745

SSB(Dep) Regs	The Social Security Benefit (Dependency) Regulations 1977 No.343
SSB(MW&WSP) Regs	The Social Security (Benefit) (Married Women and Widows Special Provisions) Regulations 1974 No.2010
SSB(PA) Regs	The Social Security Benefit (Persons Abroad) Regulations 1975 No.563
SSB(PRT) Regs	The Social Security Benefit (Persons Residing Together) Regulations 1977 No.956
SSC(DA) Regs	The Social Security Contributions (Decisions and Appeals) Regulations 1999 No.1027
SSCBA(AAO) Regs	The Social Security Contributions and Benefits Act 1992 (Application of Parts 12ZA and 12ZB to Adoptions from Overseas) Regulations 2003 No.499
SSCBA(APOC) Regs	The Social Security Contributions and Benefits Act 1992 (Application of Parts 12ZA, 12ZB and 12ZC to Parental Order Cases) Regulations 2014 No.2866
SS&CS(DA) Regs	The Social Security and Child Support (Decisions and Appeals) Regulations 1999 No.991
SSFA(PM) Regs	The Social Security and Family Allowances (Polygamous Marriages) Regulations 1975 No.561
SSP Regs	The Statutory Sick Pay (General) Regulations 1982 No.894
SSP(MAPA) Regs	The Statutory Sick Pay (Mariners, Airmen and Persons Abroad) Regulations 1982 No.1349
SSP(ME) Regs	The Statutory Sick Pay (Medical Evidence) Regulations 1985 No.1604
SSPP(A) Regs	The Statutory Shared Parental Pay (Administration) Regulations 2014 No.2929
SSPP(G) Regs	The Statutory Shared Parental Pay (General) Regulations 2014 No.3051
SSPP(PAM) Regs	The Statutory Shared Parental Pay (Persons Abroad and Mariners) Regulations 2014 No.3134
SSPP(POC) Regs	The Statutory Shared Parental Pay (Parental Order Cases) Regulations 2014 No.3097
SSP&SMP(D) Regs	The Statutory Sick Pay and Statutory Maternity Pay (Decisions) Regulations 1999 No.776
ST(ORP) Regs	The Scottish Tribunals (Offences in Relation to Proceedings) Regulations 2016 No.342
ST(TL) Regs	The Scottish Tribunals (Time Limits) Regulations 2016 No.231
TC(A) Regs	The Tax Credits (Appeals) Regulations 2002 No.2926
TC(A)(No.2) Regs	The Tax Credits (Appeals) (No.2) Regulations 2002 No.3196

TC(CN) Regs	The Tax Credits (Claims and Notifications) Regulations 2002 No.2014
TC(DCI) Regs	The Tax Credits (Definition and Calculation of Income) Regulations 2002 No.2006
TC(Imm) Regs	The Tax Credits (Immigration) Regulations 2003 No.653
TC(IR) Regs	The Tax Credits (Interest Rate) Regulations 2003 No.123
TC(ITDR) Regs	The Tax Credits (Income Thresholds and Determination of Rates) Regulations 2002 No.2008
TC(OE) Regs	The Tax Credits (Official Error) Regulations 2003 No.692
TC(PC) Regs	The Tax Credits (Payments by the Commissioners) Regulations 2002 No.2173
TC(PM) Regs	The Tax Credits (Polygamous Marriages) Regulations 2003 No.742
TC(R) Regs	The Tax Credits (Residence) Regulations 2003 No.654
TCA(No.3)O	The Tax Credits Act 2002 (Commencement No.3 and Transitional Provisions and Savings) Order 2003
TCA(TP)O	The Tax Credits Act 2002 (Transitional Provisions) Order 2010 No.644
TP(FT) Rules	The Tribunal Procedure (First-tier Tribunal) (Social Entitlement Chamber) Rules 2008 No.2685
TP(FT)(TC) Rules	The Tribunal Procedure (First-tier Tribunal) (Tax Chamber) Rules 2009 No.273
TP(UT) Rules	The Tribunal Procedure (Upper Tribunal) Rules 2008 No.2698
UC Regs	The Universal Credit Regulations 2013 No.376
UC(MMP&MA) Regs	The Universal Credit (Managed Migration Pilot and Miscellaneous Amendments) Regulations 2019 No.1152
UC(TP) Regs	The Universal Credit (Transitional Provisions) Regulations 2014 No.1230
UC(TP)(A) Regs	The Universal Credit (Transitional Provisions) (Amendment) Regulations 2014 No.1626
UC,PIP,JSA&ESA(C&P) Regs	The Universal Credit, Personal Independence Payment, Jobseeker's Allowance and Employment and Support Allowance (Claims and Payments) Regulations 2013 No.380
UC,PIP,JSA&ESA(DA) Regs	The Universal Credit, Personal Independence Payment, Jobseeker's Allowance and Employment and Support Allowance (Decisions and Appeals) Regulations 2013 No.381
UT(S) Rules	Schedule to The Upper Tribunal for Scotland (Social Security Rules of Procedure) Regulations 2018 No. 274
VP Regs	The Victims' Payments Regulations 2020 No.103

WF Regs	The Welfare Food Regulations 1996 No.1434
WF(BSF)(S) Regs	The Welfare Foods (Best Start Foods) (Scotland) Regulations 2019 No.193
WRA(No.8)O	The Welfare Reform Act 2012 (Commencement No.8 and Savings and Transitional Provisions) Order 2013 No.358
WRA(No.9)O	The Welfare Reform Act 2012 (Commencement No.9 and Transitional and Transitory Provisions and Commencement No.8 and Savings and Transitional Provisions (Amendment)) Order 2013 No.983
WRA(No.11)O	The Welfare Reform Act 2012 (Commencement No.11 and Transitional and Transitory Provisions and Commencement No.9 and Transitional and Transitory Provisions (Amendment)) Order 2013 No.1511
WRA(No.21)O	The Welfare Reform Act 2012 (Commencement and Transitional and Transitory Provisions) Order 2015 No.33
WRA(No.23)O	The Welfare Reform Act 2012 (Commencement No.23 and Transitional and Transitory Provisions) Order 2015 No.634
WRA(No.31)O	The Welfare Reform Act 2012 (Commencement No.31 and Savings and Transitional Provisions and Commencement No.21 and 23 and Transitional and Transitory Provisions (Amendment)) Order 2019 No.37
WRA(No.32)O	The Welfare Reform Act 2012 (Commencement No.32 and Savings and Transitional Provisions) Order 2019 No.167
WTC(EMR) Regs	The Working Tax Credit (Entitlement and Maximum Rate) Regulations 2002 No.2005

Other information

ADM	*Advice for Decision Making*, vols A1-V8
BLG	*Social Fund Budgeting Loan Guide*
CBTM	*Child Benefit Technical Manual*
CCM	*Claimant Compliance Manual* (HMRC guidance on investigation of tax credit claims)
DMG	*Decision Makers' Guide*, vols 1-14
GM	*Housing Benefit/Council Tax Benefit Guidance Manual*
PIP AG	*PIP Assessment Guide*, 30 September 2019
SF Dir	*Social Fund Directive*
TCM	*Tax Credits Manual*
TCTM	Tax Credits Technical Manual
WA 2019	*Agreement on the withdrawal of the United Kingdom of Great Britain and Northern Ireland from the European Union and the European Atomic Energy Community*, 19 October 2019

Index

∙ ∙

How to use this Index

Because the *Handbook* is divided into separate sections covering the different benefits, many entries in the index have several references, each to a different section. Where this occurs, we use the following abbreviations to show to which benefit each reference relates.

AA	Attendance allowance	JSA	Jobseeker's allowance
CA	Carer's allowance	MA	Maternity allowance
C-ESA	Contributory employment and support allowance	NI	National insurance
		PC	Pension credit
C-JSA	Contribution-based jobseeker's allowance	PIP	Personal independence payment
		SAP	Statutory adoption pay
CTC	Child tax credit	SDA	Severe disablement allowance
DLA	Disability living allowance	SMP	Statutory maternity pay
ESA	Employment and support allowance	SPBP	Statutory parental bereavement pay
HB	Housing benefit	SPP	Statutory paternity pay
IB	Incapacity benefit	SSP	Statutory sick pay
IIDB	Industrial injuries disablement benefit	SSPP	Statutory shared parental pay
IS	Income support	UC	Universal credit
I-ESA	Income-related employment and support allowance	WTC	Working tax credit
I-JSA	Income-based jobseeker's allowance		

Entries against the bold headings direct you to the general information on the subject, or where the subject is covered most fully. Sub-entries are listed alphabetically and direct you to specific aspects of the subject.

16 to 19 bursaries 867
    treatment of payments 448
16/17-year-olds
    actively seeking work and training 1124
    approved training 581
    available for work 1120
    care leavers 947
    child benefit 579
    child benefit extension period 581
    CTC 286
    free dental treatment 673
    free prescriptions 672
    free sight tests 674
    hardship payments 1229
    HB 177
    IS 239
    joint-claim couples
        JSA 256
    JSA 256
    leaving custody 949
    liable to pay rent 177

    NI starting credits 975
    non-dependant deduction
        HB 200
        IS/I-JSA/I-ESA/PC 364
        UC 103
    personal allowance rates 334
    severe hardship payments 257
    UC 37
    vouchers for glasses and contact lenses 674
    see also: young people
18 to 21 year-olds
    work preparation
        UC 1052
    see also: young people

A
A2 nationals 1601
    accession worker authorisation document 1601
    jobseekers 1601

legally working 1604
member states 1601
not subject to worker authorisation 1602
pregnancy 1612
resided legally 1623
residence rights 1601
restrictions 1601
self-employment 1608
workers 1601
A8 nationals 1601
authorised employer 1604
jobseekers 1602
legally working 1604
member states 1601
not required to register 1603
pregnancy 1612
resided legally 1623
residence rights 1601
restrictions 1601
retaining worker status 1602
self-employment 1608
workers 1602
abroad
absence abroad 1646
AA/DLA 1649
bereavement benefits 1647
CA 1649
child benefit 1648
ESA 1651
guardian's allowance 1649
HB 185, 1652
IB 1657
industrial injuries benefits 1655
IS 1653
JSA 1655
MA 1657
PC 1659
PIP 1649
SDA 1657
state pension 785, 1660
UC 1663
WTC/CTC 1662
adoption
SAP/SPP/SSPP 825
benefit entitlement 1645
capital abroad
means-tested benefits under pension
age 510
UC 153
children abroad 1627
IS 1654
JSA 1657
PC 1659
UC 1664
coming from abroad 1557
earnings from abroad
CA 568

means-tested benefits over pension
age 480
means-tested benefits under pension
age 423, 449
WTC/CTC 1488
exporting benefits 1679
funeral expenses payments 802
funeral support payments 1706
job interview
JSA 1118
medical treatment
child benefit 1648
IS/I-JSA/I-ESA 328, 1118
JSA under UC system 1073
UC 1073
medical treatment, housing costs
IS/I-JSA/I-ESA/PC 373
UC 101
medical treatment, travel costs 675
NI contributions 965
partner abroad 1626
ESA 1651
HB 1653
IS 1654
JSA 1656
PC 274, 1659
UC 1664
WTC/CTC 1498, 1636
temporary absence 1647
HB 185
JSA 1118
working abroad
EU co-ordination rules 1676
MA 732
NI contributions 965
SMP/SAP/SPP/SSPP/SPBP 1661
SSP 1661
absence from home
actively seeking work rule 1126
child benefit
child absent 583, 590
parent absent 583, 586
children
means-tested benefits 327
couple living apart
means-tested benefits 322
UC 60
guardian's allowance
child absent 590
housing costs
HB 182
IS/I-JSA/I-ESA/PC 371
UC 92, 100
students
HB 897

absence from work
continuous employment
SMP/SAP/SPP/SSPP/SPBP 818
treated as in full-time work 997
academic year 905
access fund payments
instalments 907
lump-sum payment 907
payments in advance of the course 907
treatment as income 906
accidents
EEA worker and self-employed status
1612
industrial accidents 683
industrial accidents while travelling 685
recovery of benefits from compensation
1212
accommodation
definition for homeless people 951
provided as part of job
means-tested benefits under pension
age 422
UC 118
rented from educational establishment
HB 897
size criteria
local housing allowance 386
pre-Jan '96 rules 406
rent officer determination related rent
400
social sector tenants 394
UC 97
specified accommodation
HB 174
UC 85
suitable alternative accommodation
pre-Jan '96 rules 407
actively seeking work 1124
16/17-year-olds 1124
appealing a decision 1344
EEA jobseekers 1605
homeless 950
required steps 1124
sanctions for not complying
JSA 1149
JSA under UC system 1087
treated as actively seeking work 1125
work search requirement 1053
adaptations to home
moving home
HB 182
IS/I-JSA/I-ESA/PC 370
UC 91
addiction treatment
work search requirement 1073
Addison's disease
free prescriptions 672

additional state pension 781
overlapping benefits 1191
additional statutory paternity pay
NI credits 976
Adjudicator
complaints 1442
administration of benefits
complaints 1438
Scottish benefits 1728
**Administrative Appeals Chamber of the
Upper Tribunal** 1396
administrative penalties
benefits 1275
adoption
additional bedroom
HB 411
local housing allowance 387
rent officer determination related rent
401
social sector tenants 395
UC 99
allowances
means-tested benefits over pension
age 481
means-tested benefits under pension
age 440
UC 131
WTC/CTC 1490
child benefit 591
claiming for children
means-tested benefits 328
foster parent approved as adopter
SAP/SPP/SSPP 825
guardian's allowance 589
IS 235
overseas 825
SPP 812
SSPP 814
Sure Start maternity grant 797
two-child limit
CTC 1455
IS/I-JSA/I-ESA/HB 338
UC 68
work-related requirements 1062
see also: statutory adoption pay
adoption leave
availability for work
JSA 1119
childcare costs
HB 433
treated as in full-time work
WTC 304
treated as not in full-time work
HB/PC 999
IS/JSA/ESA 999

adoption pay period
  curtailment notice 814
  definition 812
  working during period 820
adult placement schemes 306, 933, 1489
advance claims
  AA 539
  bereavement benefits 556
  C-ESA 660
  C-JSA 719
  CA 573
  child benefit 594
  CTC 293, 1499
  DLA 626
  guardian's allowance 594
  HB 211
  I-ESA 168
  I-JSA 264
  industrial injuries benefits 699
  IS 244
  MA 735
  PC 279
  PIP 767
  state pension 789
  UC 48
  WTC 310, 1499
advanced education
  definition 580, 887
advisers
  committing fraud 1274
after-school clubs
  childcare allowance
    HB 433
  relevant childcare
    WTC 1462
age
  pension age 779
  proof of age 787
age rules
  AA 534
  bereavement support payment 546
  Best Start grants 1699
  CA 568
  child benefit 589
  CTC 291
  discretionary housing payments 643
  DLA care component 617
  DLA mobility component 617
  ESA
    C-ESA 650
    I-ESA 162
  funeral support payments 1706
  guardian's allowance 589
  hardship payments
    I-JSA 1224
    UC 1220
  HB 187
  IIDB 693

  IS 238
  JSA
    C-JSA 711
    I-JSA 255
  MA 731
  NI contributions 961
  PC 271
  PIP 760
  retirement allowance 696
  Scottish child payment 1713
  single room rent 402
  SMP/SAP/SPP/SSPP/SPBP 822
  SSP 841
  state pension 779
  UC 37
  widowed parent's allowance 548
  winter fuel payments 806
  WTC 308
age-related additions
  retirement pensions before 6 April 2016
    781
agent
  payment of benefit to agent
    HB 214
aids and appliances
  PIP 742
Algeria
  association and co-operation agreements
    1582
  benefit entitlement 1566
  CTC 1567
almshouses
  HB 176
  UC 84
alternative dispute resolution
  SSP/SMP/SAP/SPP/SSPP/SPBP 1433
alternative payment arrangements
  UC 50
amending a claim 1169
  HB 205
  WTC/CTC 1544, 1545
amount of benefit
  AA 535
  bereavement support payment 546
  Best Start grants
    early education payment 1699
    pregnancy and baby payment 1699
    school-age payment 1699
  budgeting loans 794
  CA 569
  child benefit 590
  child element
    UC 67
  cold weather payments 806
  CTC 291, 1452
  discretionary housing payments 643
  DLA 623
  ESA

C-ESA 650
I-ESA 163
extended payments
HB 218
funeral expenses payments 803
funeral support payments 1707
guardian's allowance 590
hardship payments
ESA 1226
JSA 1224
UC 1221
HB 190
housing costs run-on 377
IIDB 694
IS 240
JSA
C-JSA 711
I-ESA 258
MA 732
PC 273
PIP 761
reduced earnings allowance 696
retirement allowance 697
Scottish child payment 1714
SMP/SAP/SPP/SSPP/SPBP 823
SSP 842
state pension 780
Sure Start maternity grant 797
UC 39, 66
widowed parent's allowance 549
winter fuel payments 807
WTC 308, 1457
amputees
DLA mobility component 607
annuities
future payments 498
surrender value
means-tested benefits over pension
age 522
means-tested benefits under pension
age 497
UC 145
treatment as income
means tested benefits over pension
age 479
means-tested benefits under pension
age 444, 446
UC 128
WTC/CTC 1487
annulment of marriage
bereavement benefits 550
appeals 1337, 1552, 1734
adjournments 1359
advice/representation 1363
after appeal made
benefits 1352
Scottish benefits 1736, 1749
WTC/CTC 1553

alternative dispute resolution
SSP/SMP/SAP/SPP/SSPP/SPBP 1433
attendance at hearing 1369, 1408
barred from taking part 1362
before appeal 1338
carrying out decision of First-tier Tribunal
1387
complaints about HM Courts and
Tribunals Service 1443
consent orders 1364
court costs 1413
decision maker's response 1354
Scottish benefits 1736
decision of First-tier Tribunal 1370
decisions which can be appealed
benefits 1343
WTC/CTC 1548
decisions which cannot be appealed
benefits 1344
WTC/CTC 1549
determination before appeal heard
Scottish benefits 1739
disability 1371
dismissing an appeal
Scottish benefits 1737
domiciliary hearings 1369
enquiry form 1353
Scottish benefits 1736
error of law by First-tier Tribunal 1397
First-tier Tribunal
benefits 1337
Scottish benefits 1734
WTC/CTC 1552
future changes 1338
hardship payments 1230
how to appeal
benefits 1345
Scottish benefits 1735, 1748
WTC/CTC 1552
information required
benefits 1350, 1355
Scottish benefits 1735, 1736
lapsed appeals 1356
late appeals
benefits 1347
Scottish benefits 1735, 1749
WTC/CTC 1553
lead cases 1364
limited capability for work 1371
mandatory reconsideration before appeal
benefits 1339
WTC/CTC 1548, 1552
NI contributions 960
online procedures 1338
online submissions 1338, 1345
oral hearings 1408
benefits 1366, 1367, 1408
Scottish benefits 1739, 1746

WTC/CTC 1408, 1554
overpayments 1246
  HB 1263
  Scottish benefits 1726
paper hearings
  benefits 1366, 1367
  Scottish benefits 1739
  WTC/CTC 1554
penalties
  benefits 1268
  WTC/CTC 1538
postponements 1359
preparing a case 1376
presenting a case 1385
process decisions
  Scottish benefits 1748
redetermination before appeal
  Scottish benefits 1734
reinstating an appeal
  benefits 1361, 1364
  Scottish benefits 1738
  WTC/CTC 1554
revision after appeal made
  benefits 1310, 1356
  WTC/CTC 1555
sanctions
  IS/JSA/ESA 1161
  UC 1108
setting aside a First-tier Tribunal decision
  benefits 1388
  Scottish benefits 1743
  WTC/CTC 1555
setting aside an Upper Tribunal decision
  1410
settling an appeal
  SSP/SMP/SAP/SPP/SSPP/SPBP 1431
  WTC/CTC 1553
sisting appeals
  Scottish benefits 1737
SSP/SMP/SAP/SPP/SSPP/SPBP 1430,
  1433
striking out an appeal
  benefits 1360
  WTC/CTC 1554
suspension of benefit, appeal pending
  1200
test case pending 1364
time limits
  benefits 1346, 1357
  Scottish benefits 1735, 1749
  WTC/CTC 1553
to the courts
  benefits 1411
  Scottish benefits 1747
  SSP/SMP/SAP/SPP/SSPP/SPBP 1435
  WTC/CTC 1555
Upper Tribunal
  benefits 1396

Scottish benefits 1744
  WTC/CTC 1555
valid appeals 1350
  Scottish benefits 1735
who can appeal
  benefits 1342
  HB 1343
  Scottish benefits 1734
  WTC/CTC 1552
who deals with appeals 1352
withdrawing an appeal to First-tier
  Tribunal
  benefits 1363
  Scottish benefits 1738
  WTC/CTC 1554
withdrawing an appeal to HMRC
  SSP/SMP/SAP/SPP/SSPP/SPBP 1431
withdrawing an appeal to Upper Tribunal
  benefits 1407
applicable amounts 332
  definition 332
  hardship payments 1224
  HB 353
  I-ESA 164, 353
  I-JSA 258
  IS 240
  personal allowances 333
  trade disputes
    IS/JSA 1003
appointees 1170
  appeals 1342, 1343
  bereavement benefits 553
  CA 571
  child benefit 593
  collection of benefit 1188
  DLA 632
  ESA
    C-ESA 658
    I-ESA 167
  guardian's allowance 593
  HB 206, 214
  hospital patients 917
  IS 243
  PC 277
  penalty for fraudulent claim
    WTC/CTC 1537
  recovery of overpayments 1245
  Scottish benefits 1724
  SMP/SAP/SSP/SSPP/SPBP 827
  SSP 845
  state pension 787
  UC 45, 49
  WTC/CTC 1499
apportionment
  of deductions for fuel
    HB 193
  of non-dependant deduction
    HB 201

of rent
HB 192
apprenticeships
child benefit 581
appropriate minimum guarantee
PC 273
reductions 274
approved training 581
UC 62
armed forces
ESA after discharge 662
local housing allowance size criteria 387
NI credits for service families 978
non-dependant deductions
HB 200
UC 103
payments for ill health and disability 868
social sector tenants 395
UC size criteria 101
Armed Forces Compensation Scheme 869
treatment of payments
means-tested benefits over pension
age 474, 476
means-tested benefits under pension
age 435, 437
UC 127
WTC/CTC 1486
armed forces independence payment 869
disability premium 341
enhanced disability premium 344
overlapping benefits 1190
treatment as income
means-tested benefits over pension
age 475
means-tested benefits under pension
age 436
UC 126
WTC/CTC 1480
arrears
benefit arrears leading to overpayments
IS/I-JSA/I-ESA/PC 1237
benefit arrears, treatment as capital
means-tested benefits over pension
age 522
means-tested benefits under pension
age 498
UC 145
benefit arrears, treatment as income
means-tested benefits over pension
age 476
means-tested benefits under pension
age 437
WTC/CTC 1481
child maintenance arrears, treatment as
income
means-tested benefits under pension
age 438
following imprisonment on remand 939

following revision
benefits 1314
following supersession
benefits 1320
rent arrears 1205
assistance
PIP assessments 741
association and co-operation agreements
1582
asthma
occupational 687
asylum seekers 1573
asylum support 1573
benefit entitlement 1573
claiming health benefits 677
Healthy Start food vouchers 864
means-tested benefits 1565
NHS charges, exemption 667
non-means-tested benefits 1567
recourse to public funds 1573
attendance allowance 531
absence abroad 1649
advance claims 539
age rules 534
amount 535
appeals 1337
backdating 539, 1177
benefit cap 543
care homes 928
carers claiming IS 236
change of circumstances 541
claims 536
date of claim 538
decisions 539, 1285
delays 1295
dialysis 536
disability conditions 534
disability premium 342
entitlement to other benefits
means-tested benefits 542
non-means-tested benefits 542
WTC/CTC 542
EU co-ordination rules 1630, 1650
fraud 1267
habitual residence test 1586
higher pensioner premium 345
hospital patients 919
information to support claim 538
interchange of claims 1182
length of award 541
medical examination 540
no non-dependant deduction
HB 199
IS/I-JSA/I-ESA/PC 364
UC 103
overlapping benefits 542, 1190
overpayments 1233
passport to other benefits 543

payment 540
person subject to immigration control
1564
prisoners 938
public funds 1562
renewal claims 539
residence rules 1629
revisions 1301, 1303
severe disability premium 347
supersessions 1301, 1315
tax 541
treatment as income 542
means-tested benefits over pension
age 475
means-tested benefits under pension
age 436
UC 126
WTC/CTC 1480
who can get AA 534
attention condition
DLA care component 612, 613, 615
autistic spectrum disorder 608
available for work
16/17-year-olds 1120
abroad
JSA 1118
appealing a decision 1344
disabled 1069
EEA jobseekers 1605
holidays 1057
homeless 950
JSA 1115
under UC system 1056
lone parents
JSA 1116
permitted period 1121
prisoners 938
reasonable chance of getting work
JSA 1120
JSA under UC system 1057
UC 1057
restrictions on availability
JSA 1120, 1121, 1122
JSA under UC system 1057
UC 1057
sanctions for not complying
JSA 1149
JSA under UC system 1087
UC 1087
sick 1069
students
JSA 1119
UC 882
terms and conditions of work
JSA 1123
treated as available for work
JSA 1117
treated as unavailable for work

JSA 1119
UC system 1056
unavailable for part of the week
JSA 1119
usual occupation 1121
willing and able to work
JSA 1116
JSA under UC system 1056
UC 1056
working hours restrictions
JSA 1122
JSA under UC system 1058
UC 1058
zero-hour contracts
JSA 1123

B
backdating 1176
AA 539
bereavement benefits 554
CA 572
child benefit 594
components 354
CTC 293, 1504
DLA 626
ESA
C-ESA 660
I-ESA 168
following award of qualifying benefit
benefits 1180
Scottish benefits 1751
guardian's allowance 594
HB 208
industrial injuries benefits 698
IS 244, 1178
jobseeker's agreement 1130
JSA 1178
C-JSA 719
I-JSA 263
MA 735
new claim following benefit suspension
JSA 1135
one month's backdating
HB 209
IS/JSA 1178
pay rises
SMP/SAP/SPP/SSPP 820
PC 278
PIP 767
premiums 352
qualifying benefit
Best Start grants 1701
budgeting loans 793
funeral expenses payments 799
funeral support payments 1708
premiums 352
Scottish child payment 1714
Sure Start maternity grant 796

refugees 1574
SSP 846
state pension 788
three months' backdating
  HB 209
  IS/JSA 1179
UC 47
WTC 310, 1504
bail
HB 181, 944
hostels
  HB 382
  UC 84
housing costs
  IS/I-JSA/I-ESA/PC 373, 944
means-tested benefits 941, 943
non-means-tested benefits 937
UC 944
bank and building society accounts
forgotten PIN numbers 1188
lost bank cards 1188
payment of benefits 1187, 1505
requirement to provide details
  WTC/CTC 1502
treatment of money in account
  means-tested benefits over pension
    age 518
  means-tested benefits under pension
    age 490
  UC 139
bankruptcy
deprivation of capital
  means-tested benefits under pension
    age 504
  UC 148
recovery of overpayments
  WTC/CTC 1530
bedroom tax
definition of bedroom
  HB 409
  UC 101, 107
HB 391
mixed-age couples
  HB 392
UC 107
bedrooms
additional bedrooms
  local housing allowance 387
  rent officer determination related rent
    400
  social sector tenants 395
  UC 98
children who cannot share a bedroom
  HB 410
couples who cannot share bedroom
  HB 410
  UC 99
definition

HB 409
UC 101, 107
maximum number of bedrooms
  local housing allowance 386
  social sector rules 394
  UC 97
behavioural difficulties
DLA mobility component 607
benefit cap 1194
AA 543
bereavement benefits 558
Best Start grants 1701
CA 576
child benefit 599
CTC 296
discretionary housing payments 645
DLA 636
ESA
  C-ESA 663
  I-ESA 170
funeral support payments 1709
guardian's allowance 599
HB 225, 1197
how the cap is applied 1198
industrial injuries benefits 700
IS 248
JSA
  C-JSA 722
  I-JSA 267
MA 737
PC 282
PIP 771
revisions 1311
Scottish child payment 1716
SMP/SAP/SSP/SSPP/SPBP 830
social fund loans and payments 808
specified benefits
  HB 1198
  UC 1197
SSP 848
state pension 790
supersessions 1319
UC 54, 1197
when benefit cap applies 1197
when benefit cap does not apply 1195
WTC 314
young carer grant 1721
benefit offences 1273
administrative penalties 1275
change in circumstances 1274
dishonest representation 1274
disqualification
  WTC 1281
disqualifying benefits 1279
false representation 1273
hardship payments
  ESA 1225
  JSA 1224

UC 1220
loss of benefits
benefits 1278
WTC/CTC 1541
one-strike rule 1278
prosecution or administrative penalty
1275, 1276
WTC/CTC 1539
sanctionable benefits 1279
sanctions 1278, 1279
two-strikes rule 1278
WTC/CTC 1539
benefit offices
contacting 1175
benefit system
decisions 1287
overview 8
Scottish social security system 1685
benefit week
CA 565
HB 191
IS/JSA/ESA 454
PC 484
bereavement
rent restriction delayed
HB 412
UC 98
work search requirement 1071
bereavement allowance
late claim
presumption of death of spouse 556
NI credits 977
bereavement benefits 545
absence abroad 1647
advance claims 556
appeals 1337
appointees 553
Bereavement Service 553
bereavement support payment 545
change of circumstances 557
claims 553
cohabitation 551
date of claim 554
decisions 1285
delay in hearing of or confirming death of
spouse 555
delays 1295
entitlement to other benefits
means-tested benefits 557
non-means-tested benefits 558
WTC/CTC 557
EU co-ordination rules 1627
fraud 1267
gender reassignment 552
industrial accidents/diseases 552
information to support claim 554
interchange of claims 1182
overpayment 1233

passported benefits 559
payment 556
polygamous marriages 551
prisoners 938
reciprocal agreements 1628
residence rules 1627
revisions 1301, 1303
statutory parental bereavement pay 815
supersessions 1301, 1315
tax 557
voluntary class 3 NI contributions 964
widowed before April 2001 552
widowed parent's allowance 547
bereavement payment
late claim
presumption of death of spouse 556
NI credits 977
bereavement support payment 545
absence abroad 1647
age rules 546
amount 546
backdating 1177
benefit cap 558
claims 553
entitlement to other benefits
means-tested benefits 557
non-means-tested benefits 558
WTC/CTC 557
EU co-ordination rules 1627, 1648
interchange of benefits 1182
new relationship 547
NI contribution conditions 984
people included in the claim 546
reciprocal agreements 1628
residence rules 1627
sanctionable benefits 556
tax 557
time limits for claiming 546
treatment as capital
UC 146
treatment as income 557
means-tested benefits over pension
age 475
means-tested benefits under pension
age 436
UC 126
WTC/CTC 1480
who can get bereavement support
payment 546
Best Start foods in Scotland 865
claims 866
payment card 865
qualifying benefits 865
vitamins 865
who can claim 865
Best Start grants in Scotland 1695
age rules 1699
amounts 1699

appeals 1734
benefit cap 1701
change of circumstances 1733
claims 1700
date of claim 1700
early learning payment 1697
entitlement to other benefits and tax
    credits 1701
following award of qualifying benefit
    1701, 1751
fraud 1726
habitual residence test 1586
information to support claim 1700
overpayments 1725
payment 1701
person subject to immigration control
    1566
pregnancy and baby payment 1696
qualifying benefits 1696
redeterminations 1731
residence rules 1635
responsibility for a child 1698
school-age payment 1697
tax 1701
time limits for claiming 1700
treatment as capital
    UC 146
treatment as income 1701
    means-tested benefits over pension
        age 475
    means-tested benefits under pension
        age 436
    UC 126
    WTC/CTC 1480
who can get a Best Start grant 1695
blindness
disability premium 342
disabled child premium 341
disregarded earnings
    HB over pension age 474
    PC 472
DLA care component 613
DLA mobility component 606
free sight tests 674
higher pensioner premium 345
no non-dependant deduction
    HB 199
    IS/I-JSA/I-ESA/PC 364
    UC 103
PIP 751
severe disability premium 346
Blue Badge parking scheme 637, 772
boarders
not a non-dependant
    HB 199
    UC 97
rent restrictions
    HB 396

treatment of payment from 568
    means-tested benefits over pension
        age 477
    means-tested benefits under pension
        age 442
boarding school
child benefit 583
bonus of wages
treatment as earnings
    CA 564
    means-tested benefits over pension
        age 469
    means-tested benefits under pension
        age 421
    UC 117
    WTC/CTC 1481
Brexit 1580
EEA nationals residence rights 1596
end of transition period 1671
EU co-ordination rules 1670
transition period 1596, 1670
Withdrawal Agreement 1596
British citizens
dual British and EEA nationals 1617
EU benefit co-ordination rules 1668
EU law 1668
family members' residence rights 1616
residence rights 1594
right to reside 1594
budgeting advances of UC 51
budgeting decisions
PIP 753
budgeting loans 792
amount 794
applying 794
payment 794
person subject to immigration control 793
repayment 795
who can claim 792
Bulgaria 1601
business
losses 1484
treatment of assets
    means-tested benefits over pension
        age 521
    means-tested benefits under pension
        age 493, 497
    UC 144
use of home
    HB 191
business partners
earnings
    CA 567
byssinosis 694, 701

C
caecostomy
free prescriptions 672

calculations
net earnings from employment
CA 565
means-tested benefits over pension
age 470
means-tested benefits under pension
age 423
UC 118
net earnings from self-employment
means-tested benefits over pension
age 471
means-tested benefits under pension
age 427
UC 118
weekly income
means-tested benefits over pension
age 483
means-tested benefits under pension
age 453
weekly self-employed earnings
CA 566
means-tested benefits over pension
age 471
means-tested benefits under pension
age 428
campsite fees
HB 176
IS/I-JSA/I-ESA/PC 360
cancer treatment
free prescriptions 672
limited capability for work
ESA 1013
UC 1011
limited capability for work-related activity
1031
capital
arrears of benefits
means-tested benefits over pension
age 522
means-tested benefits under pension
age 498
UC 145
assumed income from capital 129
budgeting loans 793
capital limits
means-tested benefits over pension
age 517
means-tested benefits under pension
age 489
UC 137
WTC/CTC 1486
capital treated as income
means-tested benefits under pension
age 444
UC 116
WTC/CTC 1491
care home residents

means-tested benefits under pension
age 489
child's
means-tested benefits under pension
age 490
UC 138
council tax reduction schemes
pension age or over 852
under pension age 853, 854
definition
means-tested benefits over pension
age 518
means-tested benefits under pension
age 490
UC 138
deprivation of capital
means-tested benefits over pension
age 526
means-tested benefits under pension
age 503
UC 148
difference between capital and income
421
diminishing capital rule 1244
means-tested benefits under pension
age 505
UC 149
disregards
means-tested benefits over pension
age 519
means-tested benefits under pension
age 493, 494
UC 141
expenses of sale
means-tested benefits under pension
age 508
UC 151
hardship payments 1226
income from capital
means-tested benefits over pension
age 478
means-tested benefits under pension
age 443
UC 129
WTC/CTC 1486
income treated as capital
means-tested benefits under pension
age 493
UC 141
instalments
means-tested benefits 444
UC 116
investments
means-tested benefits over pension
age 518
means-tested benefits under pension
age 490
UC 139

jointly owned
  means-tested benefits under pension
    age 508
  UC 151
loans
  means-tested benefits over pension
    age 518
  means-tested benefits under pension
    age 491
  UC 139
matrimonial assets
  means-tested benefits under pension
    age 509
  UC 152
means-tested benefits
  over pension age 516
  under pension age 488
non-dependants
  HB 202
notional capital
  means-tested benefits over pension
    age 525
  means-tested benefits under pension
    age 502
  UC 148
overpayments arising from
  HB 1256
  IS/I-JSA/I-ESA 1244
partner's
  means-tested benefits over pension
    age 518
  means-tested benefits under pension
    age 489
  UC 138
property
  means-tested benefits over pension
    age 518
  means-tested benefits under pension
    age 491, 493
  UC 139, 141
savings
  means-tested benefits over pension
    age 518
  means-tested benefits under pension
    age 490
  UC 139
students
  ESA 895
  HB 898
  IS/JSA 893
tariff income
  means-tested benefits over pension
    age 478
  means-tested benefits under pension
    age 443
  UC 129
third-party payments

means-tested benefits under pension
  age 506
trade disputes 1004
transitional capital disregard
  UC 138
trusts
  means-tested benefits over pension
    age 519
  means-tested benefits under pension
    age 491
  UC 140
UC 137
valuation
  means-tested benefits over pension
    age 526
  means-tested benefits under pension
    age 508
  UC 151
care homes 927
AA/DLA/PIP 928
CA 931
capital limits
  means-tested benefits under pension
    age 489
child in care home 934
  child benefit 583, 590
  CTC 290
  UC 932
costs for usual home 935
  HB 935
  IS/I-ESA/I-JSA/PC 373, 935
  UC 91, 932, 935
deferred payment of charges 930
definition
  means-tested benefits 932
ESA 933
fees paid by local authority
  IS/JSA/ESA 448
free dental treatment 673
free prescriptions 672
HB 178, 933
health benefits 671
IS 933
JSA 933
linking rules
  AA/DLA/PIP 930
mortgage interest loan 932, 935
moving house
  HB 182
nursing care needs 918
  AA/DLA/PIP 929
paid by deductions from benefit 1208
partner in care home 934
  UC 932
PC 933
qualifying services 928
self-funding
  AA/DLA/PIP 929

severe disability premium 348
social fund payments 935
tariff income 933
    means-tested benefits under pension
       age 489
temporary residents
    HB 185
trial period
    HB 183
    IS/I-JSA/I-ESA/PC 372
UC 84, 931
care leavers 947
    eligibility to claim benefits 949
    hardship payments 1229
    local authority payments
       treatment as capital 500
       treatment as income 447
       UC 147
    relevant education
       IS 885
    UC housing costs element 84
carer premium
    earnings disregard 430
    rate 351
carer's allowance 561
    absence abroad 1649
    advance claims 573
    age rules 568
    amount 569
    appeals 1337
    backdating 572, 1177
    benefit cap 576
    breaks from caring 563
    CA supplement 569
    care homes 931
    carer premium 350
    change of circumstances 574
    claiming IS when you should have
       claimed CA 573
    claims 570
    date of claim 571
    death of cared-for person 563
    decisions 1285
    declaration confirming care 571
    deductions from earnings for care costs
       567
    delays 1295
    dependants 569
    earnings 563
    employment 563
    entitlement to other benefits 351
       means-tested benefits 574
       non-means-tested benefits 576
       WTC/CTC 574
    EU co-ordination rules 1630, 1650
    fraud 1267
    future changes
       Scotland 561

habitual residence test 1586
holidays for carers 563
hospital patients 563, 920
hours of caring 562
information to support claim 571
IS 236
late claims 572
linked periods
    C-JSA 707
NI credits 975
overlapping benefits 576, 1190
overpayments 1233
passported benefits 576
payment 573
person subject to immigration control
    1564
prisoners 938
public funds 1562
qualifying benefits 572
residence rules 1629
revisions 1301, 1303
Scotland 569
severe disability premium 347
students 899
supersessions 1301, 1315
tax 574
treatment as income 575
    means-tested benefits over pension
       age 474
    means-tested benefits under pension
       age 435
    UC 126
    WTC/CTC 1481
who can get CA 562
young carer grant in Scotland 1721
carer's allowance supplement 569
    amount 569
    treatment as income
       means-tested benefits over pension
          age 474
       means-tested benefits under pension
          age 435
       UC 126
who can get CA supplement 569
carer's assistance
    Scotland 569
carers
    additional bedroom
       local housing allowance 387
       rent officer determination related rent
          400
       social sector tenants 395
       UC 98
    adult placement scheme 933
    available for work rule
       JSA 1123
       JSA under UC system 1056
       UC 1056

benefit entitlement 574
better-off benefit decisions 574
breaks from caring
  CA 563
CA 562
carer addition
  PC 274, 350
carer element 73
carer premium 350
costs of care deducted from earnings 567
EEA nationals' derivative rights 1619
friend or family carer 1067
good reason for not attending training
  UC 1105
good reason for refusing a job
  UC 1101
hardship payments 1228
housing costs when absent from home
  IS/I-JSA/I-ESA/PC 373
IS 236
NI credits 972, 975
non-dependant deductions
  HB 199
  IS/I-JSA/I-ESA/PC 364
  UC 103
regularly and substantially caring 562
time out from studying
  means-tested benefits 909
treated as not full-time work
  IS/JSA/ESA 998
  WTC 306
UC 73
unpaid work 452
work-related requirements 1062
working during limited capability for work
  1042
young carer grant in Scotland 1717
young people
  UC 38
carpal tunnel syndrome 688
caselaw 1381
cataracts 688
cautions
  DWP formal cautions 1276
  fraud interview 1270
certificate of recoverable benefits 1213
challenging a decision 1301, 1542, 1730
  appeals
    benefits 1337
    Scottish benefits 1734
    WTC/CTC 1552
  budgeting loans 794
  cohabitation
    means-tested benefits 323
    UC 61
    WTC/CTC 1498
  decision maker's decision 1293
  First-tier Tribunal decisions

benefits 1387
  Scottish benefits 1741, 1743
  WTC/CTC 1555
fraud penalty
  WTC/CTC 1538
hardship payments 1230
limited capability for work 1036
mandatory reconsideration
  benefits 1339
  WTC/CTC 1548
overpayments
  benefits 1246
  HB 1263
  Scottish benefits 1726
  WTC/CTC 1522
recovery of benefits from compensation
  1215
redeterminations
  Scottish benefits 1731
rent restrictions 413
revisions
  benefits 1301, 1303
  WTC/CTC 1542
sanctions
  IS/JSA/ESA 1161
  UC 1108
SSP/SMP/SAP/SPP/SSPP/SPBP 1427
supersessions
  benefits 1301, 1315
suspension of benefit 1201
termination of benefit 1202
Upper Tribunal decision 1410
  Scottish benefits 1746
change of circumstances
AA 541
after appeal made
  benefits 1375
  WTC/CTC 1554
benefit entitlement changes 1301
  HB 223
bereavement benefits 557
CA 574
child benefit 597
CTC 295, 1470, 1507
date of change
  HB 223
date of new decision following
    supersession
  benefits 1321
DLA 634
duty to report 1199, 1274
  WTC/CTC 1507
ESA
  C-ESA 661
  I-ESA 169
failure to report
  WTC/CTC 1537
guardian's allowance 597

Index

change of circumstances – child benefit

• •

HB 221
hours of work
   means-tested benefits 996
   WTC/CTC 1508
income
   WTC/CTC 1475
industrial injuries benefits 700
IS 246
JSA
   C-JSA 720
   I-JSA 265
late notification 1324
MA 736
making a new claim 1375
medical condition worsens 1040
PC 222, 280
penalties for failing to report 1273
PIP 769
redetermination 1733
revision
   WTC/CTC 1543
Scottish benefits 1725
SMP/SAP/SPP/SSPP/SPBP 828
SSP 847
state pension 790
students giving up a course 908
supersession
   benefits 1315, 1316, 1321, 1375
transferring to UC 27
UC 32, 52
WTC 312, 1470, 1507
charitable payments
treatment as capital
   means-tested benefits over pension
     age 524
   means-tested benefits under pension
     age 499
treatment as income
   means-tested benefits over pension
     age 481
   means-tested benefits under pension
     age 441
   UC 131
charities
financial help and assistance 873
chemotherapy
free prescriptions 672
limited capability for work
   ESA 1013
   UC 1011
limited capability for work-related activity
   1031
cheques
payment of benefits 1188
child arrangements order allowance
means-tested benefits over pension age
   481

means-tested benefits under pension age
   440
UC 131
WTC/CTC 1490
child benefit 578
absence abroad 1648, 1680
absence from home 583
adoption 591
advance claims 594
age rules 589
amount 590
appeals 1337
approved training 581
backdating 594, 1177
benefit cap 599
boarding school 583
care homes 583
change of circumstances 597
children with no entitlement 586
claims 592
contributing to supporting child 584
date of claim 594
decisions 1285
definition of child 579
delays 1295
entitlement to other benefits
   means-tested benefits 598
   non-means-tested benefits 599
   WTC/CTC 598
EU co-ordination rules 1629, 1649
extension period 581
fostering 591
fraud 1267
full-time education 580
guardian's allowance 587
high-income child benefit charge 597
higher rate 590
hospital patients 583, 925
information to support claim 593
interchange of claims 1182
interim payments 596
interruption of education 583
kinship care 591
late claims 594
living apart 583
looked after by local authority 587, 590
non-advanced education 580
overlapping benefits 1192
overpayments 1233, 1250
partner subject to immigration control
   1570
payment 595
person subject to immigration control
   1564
priority of claimants 584
prisoners 939
   child in prison 587, 590
public funds 1562

qualifying young person 579
refugees 1574
relevant education 579
residence rules 1584, 1593, 1628
residing together 586
responsibility for a child 583
revisions 1301, 1303
shared care 586
supersessions 1301, 1315
tax 597
terminal date 582
treatment as income 598
   means-tested benefits over pension
     age 475
   means-tested benefits under pension
     age 436
   UC 126
   WTC/CTC 1480
who can get child benefit 579
who should claim 593
working child 587
child benefit extension period 581
child disability payment in Scotland 1690
care homes 1690
claims 1690
new determinations 1753
prisoners 1690
short-term assistance 1691
terminal illness 1690
winter heating assistance 1688
child element
CTC 1453
two-child limit
   CTC 1453
   UC 67
UC 66
child maintenance
deductions from benefit 1207
definition 438
flat-rate benefit deductions 1207
treatment as income
   means-tested benefits over pension
     age 477
   means-tested benefits under pension
     age 438
   UC 127
   WTC/CTC 1489
child tax credit 284
absence abroad 1662, 1680
age rules 291
amount 291, 1449
annual declaration 1513
annual review 1512, 1545
appeals 1552
automatic renewal 1513
award notices 1527
backdating 293, 1504, 1509, 1543
benefit cap 296

benefits disregarded as income 1480
benefits treated as income 1481
bereavement benefits 557
calculation
   not receiving means-tested benefits
     292, 1466
   receiving means-tested benefits 292,
     1465
challenging a decision 1542
change of circumstances 295, 1470, 1507
child element 1453
children 286
claims 285, 292, 1495
complaints about HMRC 1441, 1517
complaints to the Adjudicator 1442
couples 291, 293, 1497
decisions 1503
delays 1517
disabled child element 1456, 1510
disregarded earnings 1482
disregarded income 1479, 1489, 1490
elements 1452
end of entitlement 287, 1508, 1516
enquiries 1534
entitlement to other benefits
   means-tested benefits 296
   non-means-tested benefits 296
EU co-ordination rules 1637, 1663
failure to comply 1537
family element 1453
final decision 1515, 1545
fraud 1533
future changes 1495
hospital patients 925
income 1474, 1478
income threshold 1467
incorrect statements 1536
initial decision 1503
investigating awards 1533
mandatory reconsiderations 1548
maximum amount 1452, 1509
new claims 24, 285, 1496
NHS charges, exemption 667
overpayments 1520
partner subject to immigration control
   1571
passported benefits 296
payment 294
penalties for fraud 1536
person subject to immigration control
   1564
postponement of payment 1506
provisional payments 1506
public funds 1562
refugees 1574
relevant income 1466, 1474
relevant period 1452
residence rules 1498, 1584, 1593, 1635

responsibility for a child 288
revisions 1542
severely disabled child element 1456,
1510
suspension of payment 1506
tax 295
trade disputes 1005
transferring to UC 27
treatment as income
means-tested benefits over pension
age 475
means-tested benefits under pension
age 296, 435
WTC 1480
two-child limit 1453
UC 1472, 1477, 1508
urgent payments 1506
when to claim 293
who can get CTC 284, 1496
who is paid 1504
childcare
actively seeking work
JSA 1126
available for work rule
JSA 1117, 1123
calculating childcare costs
HB 435
childcare element
UC 74
WTC 1460
costs, disregarded
CA 567
HB over pension age 474
HB under pension age 432
deductions from earnings
HB over pension age 474
HB under pension age 432
disabled parents, DLA care component
614
family members
NI credits 974
free milk 868
friend or family carer 1067
home responsibilities protection 973
increase in costs
WTC/CTC 1509
IS 235
NI credits 972
relatives
WTC 1463
relevant childcare
UC 75
WTC 1462, 1464
tax-free childcare scheme 871, 1462
vouchers
UC 118
WTC/CTC 1462, 1483
work search requirement 1054

work-focused interviews 1066
work-related requirements 1062
childminders
childcare allowance
HB 433
free milk for children 868
relevant childcare
WTC 1462
self-employed 428
treated as not in full-time work
IS/ESA 998
treatment of earnings
CA 567
means-tested benefits over pension
age 471
means-tested benefits under pension
age 428
children
absence from home
means-tested benefits 327
additional child
WTC/CTC 1509
Best Start foods in Scotland 865
Best Start grants in Scotland 1695
early learning payment 1697
pregnancy and baby payment 1696
school-age payment 1697
capital
means-tested benefits under pension
age 490
UC 138
care home
housing costs 936
means-tested benefits 934
UC 932
child disability payment in Scotland 1690
child element
CTC 1453
UC 66
claiming for children
means-tested benefits 323
UC 62
definition
child benefit 579
CTC 286
guardian's allowance 587
means-tested benefits 324
UC 62
widowed parent's allowance 547
WTC 308
disabled child premium 341
DLA 602
care component 610
completing claim form 627
mobility component 603
payment of benefit 632
EEA workers with child in education 1619
family premium 340

free dental treatment 673
free prescriptions 672
free sight tests 674
funeral expenses payments 800
guardian's allowance 588
Healthy Start food and vitamins 862
hospital patient 924
   child benefit 925
   CTC 925
   DLA 919
   housing costs 927
   IS/JSA/ESA 328
   UC 921
income
   means-tested benefits over pension
      age 467
   means-tested benefits under pension
      age 420
   UC 115
   WTC/CTC 1478
living with child 583
medical treatment abroad
   IS/JSA/ESA 328
   JSA 1118
NI number requirement for child 1171
normally living with
   CTC 288
not non-dependants
   HB 199
   UC 97
personal allowances 337
   rates 338
premiums 339
prisoner
   CTC 942
   housing costs 947
   means-tested benefits 942
   UC 940
responsibility for a child
   Best Start grants 1698
   child benefit 583
   means-tested benefits 326
   Scottish child payment 1712
   UC 63
   WTC/CTC 288
responsibility for landlord's child
   HB 179
Scottish child payment 1711
shared care
   child benefit 586
   means-tested benefits 327
   UC 63
SPBP 815
supporting a child
   child benefit 584
two-child limit
   CTC 1453
   means-tested benefits 337

   UC 67
vouchers for glasses and contact lenses
   674
work allowance
   UC 41
children in care
   see: looked after children
children's funeral fund payment 799
Christmas bonus 436, 475, 870
   WTC/CTC 1480
chronic medical condition
   hardship payments 1228
civil partners
   bereavement benefits 545
   bereavement support payment 545
   claiming as a couple
      means-tested benefits 320
      UC 57
   surviving partner
      definition 549
      state pension 783
   void/voidable partnerships 550
   widowed parent's allowance 547
   WTC/CTC 1497
civil penalties 1268
   see also: penalties
claim-related rent 399
claimant commitment 1047
   accepting commitment 1048
   closure of claim for not attending
      commitments meeting 1049
   JSA 1127
   reviewing commitment 1050
   work-related requirements 1050
claims 1165
   AA 536
   amending a claim 1169
   backdating 1176
   bereavement benefits 553
   Best Start foods 866
   Best Start grants 1700
   CA 570
   child benefit 592
   claiming as a couple
      CTC 291
      means-tested benefits 319
      UC 38, 57
      WTC 308
   claiming for a family
      means-tested benefits 317
      UC 38, 57
   claiming on behalf of someone else 1170
   claiming the wrong benefit 1182
   cold weather payments 806
   CTC 292, 1495
   date of claim 1176
   discretionary housing payments 644
   DLA 624

ESA
    C-ESA 657
    I-ESA 166
funeral expenses payments 804
funeral support payments 1708
guardian's allowance 592
hardship payments 1230
HB 202
health benefits 676
Healthy Start vouchers 864
how to claim
    benefits 1168
    Scottish benefits 1723
    WTC/CTC 1499
industrial injuries benefits 697
information to support a claim 1170, 1172, 1174
    Scottish benefits 1724
interchange of claims 1182
investigation of claims 1269
    WTC/CTC 1533
IS 241
joint-claim JSA
    I-JSA 253
JSA
    C-JSA 715
    I-JSA 259
MA 733
PC 277
PIP 762
renewing a claim
    AA 539
    DLA 626, 634
    PIP 769
SMP/SAP/SPP/SSPP/SPBP 826
SSP 844
state pension 786
Sure Start maternity grant 798
UC 44
valid claims 1170, 1172
    attending interview 1172
    by telephone 1173
    claim not valid 1171
    in writing 1173
    online 1173
where to claim
    HB 205
who should claim 1169
winter fuel payments 808
withdrawing a claim 1169
    Scottish benefits 1724
written claims
    HB 202
WTC 309, 1495
see also: date of claim

close relatives
    funeral expenses payments 800
    funeral support payments in Scotland 1704
    HB 178, 180
    IS/I-JSA/I-ESA/PC 370
    severe disability premium 350
    treatment of home
        means-tested benefits over pension age 521
        means-tested benefits under pension age 496
        UC 143
    UC 90
clothing
    budgeting loans 793
    grants for school clothes 867
co-ownership scheme
    HB 176
    IS/I-JSA/I-ESA/PC 360
coal
    concessionary coal, treatment as income 442, 1483
    UC 118
coastguard
    payments treated as capital
        means-tested benefits under pension age 493
    payments treatment as income
        CA 568
        means-tested benefits over pension age 472
        means-tested benefits under pension age 430
    treated as not in full-time work
        IS/JSA/ESA 998
cohabitation
    bereavement benefits 551
    bereavement support payment 547
    challenging a cohabiting decision
        means-tested benefits 323
        UC 61
        WTC/CTC 1498
    means-tested benefits 320
    UC 58
    widowed parent's allowance 549
    WTC/CTC 1497
cold weather payments 805
    amount 806
    appeals 1337
    care home residents 935
    claims 806
    payment 806
    person subject to immigration control 806
    qualifying benefits 805
    revisions 1303
colostomy
    free prescriptions 672

commission
treatment as earnings
CA 564
means-tested benefits over pension
age 469
means-tested benefits under pension
age 421
UC 117
WTC/CTC 1481
commissioners' decisions 1381
common travel area 1586
living in for three months 1584
Commonwealth citizens
right to reside 1594
Windrush generation 1561
communal areas
fuel
HB 194
service charges
HB 194
UC 86
communicating
engaging with others
PIP 752
speech and hearing
PIP 750
community care grant
see: local welfare assistance
community care payments
treatment as capital
means-tested benefits over pension
age 525
means-tested benefits under pension
age 500
UC 147
treatment as income
means-tested benefits under pension
age 447
WTC/CTC 1490
community dental service
free dental treatment 673
community sentences 943
available for work 1117
company car
treatment as earnings
WTC/CTC 1482
compensation
delays in payment of benefit 1439
legal action 1446
loss of employment/unfair dismissal
CA 564, 565
means-tested benefits under pension
age 422
WTC/CTC 1482, 1483
offical errors 1439
payments exempt from recovery of
benefits 1214
personal injuries

UC 128
recovery of benefits from compensation
1212
special compensation schemes
means-tested benefits over pension
age 524
means-tested benefits under pension
age 499
UC 146
Compensation Recovery Unit 1212
compensation schemes
treatment of payments
means-tested benefits over pension
age 524
means-tested benefits under pension
age 499
UC 146
complaints 1438
about DWP 1440
about HM Courts and Tribunals Service
1443
about HMRC 1441
WTC/CTC 1517
about local authority administration
HB 1443
about Social Security Scotland 1728
grounds 1439
to councillor
HB 1443
to Independent Case Examiner 1440
to MP 1444
to Ombudsman 1444
HB 1446
components 353
hospital patients 924
PIP 740
rates 354
support component
C-ESA 652
HB 354
I-ESA 354
work-related activity component 354
ESA 653
comprehensive sickness insurance 1614
conscientious objection
available for work rule
JSA 1122
good reason for refusing a job
UC 1101
jobseeker's direction 1153
constant attendance allowance 694
armed services 869
interchange of claims 1182
overlapping benefits 1190
treatment as income
means-tested benefits over pension
age 475

means-tested benefits under pension
age 436
contact lenses
vouchers 674
continuous employment
SMP/SAP/SPP/SSPP/SPBP 817
contributory benefits 960
contribution conditions 979
cooking test
PIP 743
co-ordination rules
see: European Union co-ordination rules
council tax
arrears paid by deductions from benefit
1207
discretionary housing payments 642
discretionary reduction of bill 851
council tax benefit
recovery of overpayments 1253
see also: council tax reduction scheme
council tax reduction schemes 851
entitlement conditions
pension age or over 852
under pension age 852, 853
habitual residence 1586
payments treatment as income
means-tested benefits under pension
age 437
person subject to immigration control
1564
public funds 1562
residence rules 1592
councillors
treated as not in full-time work
IS/JSA/ESA 998
treatment as earnings
C-ESA 655
means-tested benefits over pension
age 470
means-tested benefits under pension
age 423
working during limited capability for work
1042
counselling services
HB 195
couples
16/17-year-olds, personal allowance rates
IS/I-JSA/I-ESA 335
capital
means-tested benefits over pension
age 518
means-tested benefits under pension
age 489
UC 138
change of partner claiming
HB 206
IS 243
PC 277

child benefit 586
Christmas bonus 870
civil partners
means-tested benefits 320
UC 57
claiming as a couple
C-ESA 650
C-JSA 711
HB 189, 206
I-ESA 162
I-JSA 257
IS 239
means-tested benefits 319
PC 272
UC 38, 57
WTC/CTC 1497
cohabitation
means-tested benefits 320
UC 58
couple element
WTC 1458
CTC 291, 293, 1497
disregard of partner's home
means-tested benefits over pension
age 521
means-tested benefits under pension
age 496
UC 143
funeral expenses payment 800
higher pensioner premium 346
income
means-tested benefits over pension
age 467
means-tested benefits under pension
age 420
UC 115
WTC/CTC 1478
joint claims
I-JSA 253
UC 45
WTC/CTC 1496
liability for rent
HB 177, 180
UC 88
living apart
means-tested benefits 322
UC 60
married couples
means-tested benefits 320
UC 57
mixed-age couples
HB 175
I-ESA 162
PC 272
NI number requirement for partner 1171
non-dependant couples
HB 201
IS/I-JSA/I-ESA/PC 367

not non-dependants
  HB 199
  IS/I-JSA/I-ESA/PC 363
partner fails habitual residence test
  UC 1626
partner in care home
  housing costs 936
  means-tested benefits 934
  UC 932
partner in hospital
  housing costs 927
  means-tested benefits 924
  UC 921
partner in prison
  housing costs 947
  means-tested benefits 942
  UC 940
partner subject to immigration control 1568
partner's working hours
  IS/I-JSA/I-ESA 992
pensioner premium 345
personal allowances
  rates 334
recourse to public funds
  HB 1570
  IS/I-JSA/I-ESA 1569
  UC 1568
  WTC/CTC 1571
recovery of overpayments
  HB 1258
  IS/JSA/ESA/PC 1250
severe disability premium 346, 347
  PC 348
sharing a bedroom
  HB 410
  UC 99
students
  HB 896, 898
  IS 890
  JSA 890
  UC 881
UC 32, 36
work-focused interviews for partners 1138
WTC 308, 310, 1497
Court of Appeal
appealing Upper Tribunal decisions
  benefits 1411
  WTC/CTC 1555
SSP/SMP/SAP/SPP/SSPP/SPBP 1435
Court of Justice of the European Union
decisions 1382
Court of Session
appealing Upper Tribunal decisions
  benefits 1411
  Scottish benefits 1747

WTC/CTC 1555
SSP/SMP/SAP/SPP/SSPP/SPBP 1435
courts
appealing Upper Tribunal decisions
  benefits 1411
  Scottish benefits 1747
  WTC/CTC 1555
applying to court 1413
compensation 1446
recovery of overpayments 1252
  HB 1260
  UC system 1250
credit sale agreements
HB 176
crisis loans
see: local welfare assistance
Croatia 1601
accession worker authorisation
  document 1601
jobseekers 1601
legally working 1604
not subject to worker authorisation 1602
pregnancy 1612
resided legally 1623
residence rights 1601
restrictions 1601
self-employment 1608
workers 1601
croft land
HB 176
treatment as capital
  means-tested benefits over pension age 519
  means-tested benefits under pension age 493
  UC 141
Crown servants
child benefit 1628
WTC/CTC 1662
Crown tenants
HB 176
rent met by IS/I-JSA/I-ESA/PC 360
currency
payments in non-UK currencies
  CA 568
  means-tested benefits over pension age 480
  means-tested benefits under pension age 449
  WTC/CTC 1488
Czech Republic 1601

D
daily living activities
PIP 741
Data Protection Act
access to personal information 1269

date of claim
AA 538
bereavement benefits 554
Best Start grants 1700
CA 571
child benefit 594
CTC 293
DLA 625
ESA
C-ESA 660
I-ESA 167
funeral expenses payments 804
guardian's allowance 594
HB 207
industrial injuries benefits 698
IS 243
JSA
C-JSA 717
I-JSA 261
MA 734
PC 278
PIP 767
state pension 788
Sure Start maternity grant 798
UC 47
WTC 310
see also: backdating
daytime attention/supervision 615, 616
deafness
DLA care component 613
DLA mobility component 606
occupational 687, 692
students
HB 897
death
children's funeral fund payment 799
claimant's death
HB 214
delayed claims for bereavement benefits
555
funeral expenses payments 798
funeral support payments in Scotland
1703
of child
child benefit 597
CTC 286
disabled child premium 341
guardian's allowance 597
SPBP 815
UC 65
of family member
UC 65
of person receiving care
CA 563
parents
guardian's allowance 588
presumption of death for bereavement
benefits 555

recovery of funeral expenses payments
804
recovery of overpayments from estate
1246
HB 1257
rent restriction delayed
HB 412
UC 98
reporting 1199
right to reside after death of EEA family
member 1617
Tell Us Once scheme 1199
treatment of pension payments
C-JSA 713
work search requirement following
bereavement 1071
see also: bereavement benefits
debt
deductions from benefit 1208
deprivation of capital
means-tested benefits under pension
age 504
UC 148
more than one debt 1210
priority for payment by deductions from
benefit 1211
self-assessment tax debts 1208
valuation of capital
means-tested benefits under pension
age 508
UC 151
decision makers
benefits 1288
making decision 1288
guidance
benefits 1289
response to First-tier Tribunal
benefits 1354
Scottish benefits 1736
WTC/CTC 1553
Scottish benefits 1724
wrong decisions
benefits 1293
WTC/CTC 1517
WTC/CTC 1503
decisions 1285
AA 539
anti-test case rule 1330
budgeting loans 794
can be appealed
benefits 1343
cannot be appealed
benefits 1344
WTC/CTC 1549
changing a decision
benefits 1301
WTC/CTC 1542

circumstances on date decision made 1294
correcting 1293
date of new decision following supersession 1320
decision makers 1288
decision notices 1296
delay getting decision 1295
  HB 220
  WTC/CTC 1517
DLA 632
explanation 1296
final decisions
  benefits 1290
  WTC/CTC 1515, 1545
First-tier Tribunal
  benefits 1370, 1385
  Scottish benefits 1740
HB 211, 1292
HMRC decisions
  SSP/SMP/SAP/SPP/SSPP/SPBP 1430
how decisions are made
  benefits 1288
incorrect decision leading to overpayment 1243
initial decisions
  WTC/CTC 1503, 1543
limited capability for work 1035, 1292
limited information decision 1289
NI contributions 960, 1292
notification of decision
  HB 211
process decisions
  Scottish benefits 1748
sanctions
  IS/JSA/ESA 1161
  UC 1106
Scottish benefits 1688
statement of reasons
  benefits 1386
  Scottish benefits 1740
test case pending 1330
Upper Tribunal 1409
  Scottish benefits 1746
valid claim 1293
who makes decisions
  benefits 1288
written reasons for a decision 1297
wrong decisions
  benefits 1293
  WTC/CTC 1517
deductions from benefits 1202
  budgeting advance repayments 51
  budgeting loan repayments 795
  child support maintenance payments 1207
  civil penalties 1248
  consent for deductions 1203

fuel debts 1205
funeral expenses payments 803
funeral support payments 1707
hardship payments recovery 1221
housing costs 1204
housing costs contributions
  UC 102
maximum amount
  IS/I-JSA/I-ESA/PC 1208
  UC 1208
means-tested benefits 1203
more than one deduction 1210
non-dependant deductions
  HB 198
  IS/I-JSA/I-ESA/PC 363
  UC 102
non-means-tested benefits 1203
priority between debts 1211
recovery of overpayments 1250
  child benefit 1250
  guardian's allowance 1250
  HB 1258, 1259
  IS/I-JSA/I-ESA/PC 1250
  PC 1249
  Scottish benefits 1726
  UC system 1248
  WTC/CTC 1528
rent arrears 1205
sanctions 1088, 1158
  ESA 1157
  ESA under UC system 1090
  JSA 1155
  JSA under UC system 1092
  UC 1089
short-term advance recovery 1194
treatment as income
  means-tested benefits over pension age 476
  means-tested benefits under pension age 438
what deductions can be made for 1202
when deductions can be made 1203
deductions from eligible rent
charges for meals
  HB 195
HB 193
service charges
  HB 195
deemed income
treatment as income
  means-tested benefits over pension age 478
deferring
state pension 778
degree of disablement 689
delays
advance payments 1192
benefits due but not paid 451

compensation 1439
decisions
    benefits 1295
    WTC/CTC 1517
HB 220
health benefits 678
moving home
    HB 181
    UC 91
dental treatment
free 673
reduced-cost treatment 669
Department for Work and Pensions
alternative offices 1168
collecting information 1269
complaints 1440
contacting benefit offices 1175
discretion to recover overpayments 1247
deprivation of resources
capital
    means-tested benefits over pension
      age 526
    means-tested benefits under pension
      age 503
    UC 148
diminishing capital rule
    means-tested benefits under pension
      age 505
    UC 149
income
    means-tested benefits over pension
      age 481
    means-tested benefits under pension
      age 450
    UC 131
    WTC/CTC 1491
dermatitis 688
detention centres
child benefit 590
determinations 1724, 1731
changing a determination 1730
new determinations without claim 1750
notification of determination 1724, 1731
diabetes
free prescriptions 672
free sight tests 674
diffuse mesothelioma 694, 701
diffuse pleural thickening 701
diminishing capital rule
means-tested benefits over pension age
    526
means-tested benefits under pension age
    505
UC 149
direct credit transfer
overpayments 1238
payment of benefits 1187

CTC 294, 1505
WTC 311, 1505
direct payments 1202
housing costs 1204
payment of benefits 1187
rent arrears 1205
to landlord
    HB 215
disability
actively seeking work
    JSA 1125
adaptations to home 361
additional amounts
    PC 274
additional bedroom
    HB 410
    UC 99
appeals 1371
appeals held at home 1369
armed forces, payments to former
    members 868
availability for work
    JSA 1121
child disability payment in Scotland 1690
childcare costs disregarded
    CA 567
    HB 434
couple who cannot share a bedroom
    HB 410
    UC 99
descriptors
    PIP 740
    UC/ESA 1017
direct payments
    treatment as income 448
disability conditions
    AA 534
    DLA 603
    PIP 740
disability determination 1310
disability premium 341
disabled child element
    CTC 1456
disabled worker element
    WTC 1458
DLA 602
enhanced disability premium 343
financial help with costs of disability 873
fluctuating conditions
    ESA 1017
    PIP 757
free prescriptions 672
good reason for not attending training
    UC 1101
health benefits 666
industrial injuries/disease 689
IS 235
limited capability for work 1010

mental disabilities 1023
physical disabilities 1018
PIP 739
severe disability addition
PC 346
severe disability element
WTC 1460
severe disability premium 346
severely disabled child element
CTC 1456
specialist employability support 1141
transferred to UC before Jan 2019 29
UC 23, 29
work capability assessment 1010
work preparation requirement 1052
work search requirement 1069
work-related activity 1141
work-related requirements 1064
see also: disablement
disability living allowance 602
absence abroad 1649
adults aged 65 before April 2013 621
advance claims 626
age rules 617
appeals 1337
backdating 626, 1177
benefit cap 636
change of circumstances 634
child disability payment in Scotland 1690
child reaches 16 618
claim forms
guidance on completing 627
claims 624
date of claim 625
decisions 632, 1285
delays 1295
disability premium 341
disabled child premium 341
entitlement to other benefits
means-tested benefits 635
non-means-tested benefits 636
WTC/CTC 635
EU co-ordination rules 1630, 1650
fraud 1267
future changes 617
habitual residence test 1586
higher pensioner premium 345
hospital patients 919
information to support claim 625
interchange of claims 1182
length of award 633
medical examination 632
no non-dependant deduction
HB 199
IS/I-JSA/I-ESA/PC 364
UC 103
overlapping benefits 636
overpayments 1233

passport to other benefits 637
payment 632
person subject to immigration control
1564
prisoners 938
public funds 1562
renewal claims 626, 634
residence rules 1629
revisions 1302, 1303
severe disability premium 347
supersessions 1302, 1315
tax 634
terminal illness 625
transfers to PIP 617, 619
Scotland 1689
treatment as income 635
means-tested benefits over pension
age 475
means-tested benefits under pension
age 436
UC 126
WTC/CTC 1480
winter heating assistance in Scotland
1688
disability living allowance care component
610
additional requirements test 611
adults aged 65 before April 2013 621
age rules 617
amount 623
attention condition 612, 613, 615
care homes 928
daytime disability conditions 611
dialysis 623
disability conditions highest rate 611
disability conditions lowest rate 610
disability conditions middle rate 610
domestic duties 614
enhanced disability premium 344
night-time disability conditions 611
overlapping benefits 1190
supervision condition 612, 613, 616
terminal illness 623
who can get the component 610
**disability living allowance mobility
component** 603
additional requirements test 608
adults aged 65 before April 2013 621
age rules 617
amount 623
care homes 929
disability conditions higher rate 604
disability conditions lower rate 608
guidance 609
hospital patients 920
Motability 637
supervision 609

terminal illness 623
who can get the component 603
disability premium 341
earnings disregard 430
hardship payments 1228
higher pensioner premium 345
qualifying benefits 341
rate 352
training 343
disabled child addition
UC 67
disabled child premium 341
rate 351
disabled children
additional bedroom
HB 410
UC 99
child disability payment in Scotland 1690
childcare costs
HB 433
disabled child addition
UC 67
disabled child element
CTC 1456
disabled child premium 341
DLA 602
completing claim form 627
enhanced disability premium 343
severely disabled child element 1456
disabled students
disabled students' allowance
disregards for grant income 902
ESA 894
HB 897
IS 237
see also: students
disablement
assessment 689
disablement questions 689
physical and mental disablement 609
prescribed degrees of disablement 689
disasters
local authority welfare assistance 861
discharge grant
IS/I-JSA/I-ESA 493
Discretionary Assistance Fund for Wales 861
discretionary housing payments 641
age rules 643
amounts 643
benefit cap 645
challenging a decision 645
claims 644
entitlement to other benefits 645
extended payments of HB 219
tax 645
treatment as income
means-tested benefits under pension
age 448

WTC/CTC 1480
who can claim 642
discretionary leave
benefit entitlement 1573
discrimination
EU co-ordination rules 1678
jobseeker's direction 1153
dishonesty
penalties for fraud 1274
dismissal
sanctions
JSA under UC system 1082
UC 1082
SMP/SAP/SPP/SSPP/SPBP 823
SSP 836
disqualification
C-ESA 649
I-ESA 162
IIDB 693
MA 730
widowed parent's allowance 549
WTC 1281
disqualifying benefits 1279
disregards
benefits
means-tested benefits over pension
age 475
means-tested benefits under pension
age 436
WTC/CTC 1480
capital
means-tested benefits over pension
age 519
means-tested benefits under pension
age 493
UC 141
charitable/voluntary payments 441
childcare costs
CA 567
HB over pension age 474
HB under pension age 432
discretionary local schemes
HB over pension age 476
HB under pension age 437
earnings
C-JSA 712
CA 567
HB 431, 472
I-ESA 429
means-tested benefits over pension
age 469, 471
means-tested benefits under pension
age 422, 429, 430
UC 117
WTC/CTC 1482
income
means-tested benefits over pension
age 480

means-tested benefits under pension
age 448
WTC/CTC 1479, 1489, 1490
income from capital
means-tested benefits over pension
age 478
means-tested benefits under pension
age 443
self-employed earnings
means-tested benefits under pension
age 427
UC 119
student grant income 902
student loans 904
tax/NI contributions changes
HB 424
dissolution of civil partnerships
bereavement benefits 550
divorce
bereavement benefits 550
right to reside after divorce from EEA
national 1617
domestic duties
DLA care component 614
domestic violence
see: violence
domiciliary hearings 1369
dressing
PIP 749
dual citizens
British and EEA nationals 1617

E
early learning payment in Scotland 1697
amount 1699
early retirement
sanctions for voluntary unemployment
JSA under UC system 1086
UC 1086
earnings
advance of earnings, treatment as capital
493
advance of earnings, treatment as income

CA 568
means-tested benefits over pension
age 469
means-tested benefits under pension
age 423
C-JSA 712
CA 563
calculating net employed earnings
CA 565
means-tested benefits over pension
age 470
means-tested benefits under pension
age 423
UC 118

calculating net self-employed earnings
CA 566
means-tested benefits over pension
age 471
means-tested benefits under pension
age 427
UC 118
WTC/CTC 1484
childcare costs, disregarded
CA 567
means-tested benefits over pension
age 474
means-tested benefits under pension
age 432
deductions to recover overpayments
1251
HB 1260
UC system 1250
disregarded
C-JSA 712
CA 567
means-tested benefits over pension
age 469, 471
means-tested benefits under pension
age 422, 429, 430
UC 117
WTC/CTC 1482
earnings thresholds
JSA under UC system 1065
UC 1065
fluctuating
HB 456
IS/I-JSA/ESA 454
gross earnings
means-tested benefits over pension
age 470
means-tested benefits under pension
age 423
MA 727
means-tested benefits
over pension age 469
under pension age 421
minimum income floor
UC 121
monthly earned income
UC 133
notional earnings
CA 567
part weeks
IS/I-JSA/I-ESA 455
payments on leaving a job
CA 564
means-tested benefits over pension
age 470
means-tested benefits under pension
age 424
UC 118
period covered by earnings 566

prescribed amount
  C-JSA 712
  SMP/SAP/SPP/SSPP/SPBP 819
  SSP 839
surplus earnings
  UC 124
two wage payments in one assessment
  period
  UC 133
UC 117, 118
work allowance 41
WTC/CTC 1481
see also: income
earnings condition
budgeting advance 52
MA 727
earnings limits
NI contributions 1786
earnings replacement benefits 1190
earnings rule
C-JSA 712
CA 563
state pension 778
eating
PIP 744
education
advanced education 887
EEA nationals, child in education 1621
interruption of education
  child benefit 583
NI credits 975
non-advanced
  child benefit 580
  CTC 286
receiving education
  UC 37, 880
relevant education 885
terminal date 582
education benefits 866
education maintenance allowance 867
disregarded as income
  means-tested benefits 448
  WTC/CTC 1489
education, health and care plans
payments, treatment as income
  means-tested benefits under pension
    age 448
elements 66
carer element 73
child element
  UC 66
childcare costs element 74
housing costs element 76
limited capability for work element 70
limited capability for work-related activity
  element 72
transitional element 77

eligible rent
deductions 193
definition 191
fuel charges 193
HB 191
housing costs element 84
local authority discretion to reduce
  HB 384
maximum eligible rent
  local housing allowance 385
  pre-Jan '96 rules 405
  rent officer determination related rent
    397
  social sector tenants 392
restrictions
  HB 381
  UC 105
emergencies
advance payments 1192
alarm system
  HB 195
good reason for not attending training
  UC 1105
local authority welfare assistance 861
payment of benefits 1189
emergency services
payments, treatment as income
  means-tested benefits over pension
    age 472
  means-tested benefits under pension
    age 430
employed earners
decisions about NI contributions 1292
definition
  NI contributions 962
  WTC 301
disregarded earnings
  CA 567
  means-tested benefits under pension
    age 429
  UC 117
earnings
  CA 563
  MA 727
  means-tested benefits over pension
    age 469
  means-tested benefits under pension
    age 421
  SMP/SAP/SPP/SSPP/SPBP 819
  SSP 840
  UC 117
  WTC/CTC 1481
industrial injuries benefits 682
MA 727
SMP/SAP/SPP/SSPP/SPBP 817
SSP 836
work search requirement 1072
work-related requirements 1064

employees
see: employed earners
employers
deductions from earnings 1251
HB 1260
UC system 1250
notification of decisions
SSP/SMP/SAP/SPP/SSPP 1428
SSP 844
employment
see: work
employment and support allowance 157, 647
absence abroad 657, 1651
advance claims
C-ESA 660
age rules
C-ESA 650
I-ESA 162
amount
C-ESA 650
I-ESA 163
appeal pending on limited capability for
work 1014, 1038
appeals 1337
applicable amount 332, 353
I-ESA 164
assessment phase 651
backdating
C-ESA 660, 1177
I-ESA 168
basic allowance 652
benefit cap
C-ESA 663
I-ESA 170
benefit reduction 1157
benefit week 454
calculation
C-ESA 652
I-ESA 164
capital 488
capital limits 489
care homes 933
child's income 420
children
C-ESA 650
I-ESA 323
claimant commitment
under UC system 1047
claims
C-ESA 657
I-ESA 166
components 353
contributory ESA 647
couples
C-ESA 650
I-ESA 162, 319
date of claim
C-ESA 660

decisions 1285
deductions from benefit
C-ESA 1203
I-ESA 1203
delays 1295
disqualification
C-ESA 649
I-ESA 162
disregarded earnings
I-ESA 429
earnings
C-ESA 1044
entitlement to other benefits based on C-
ESA
means-tested benefits 662
non-means-tested benefits 663
WTC/CTC 662
entitlement to other benefits based on I-
ESA
means-tested benefits 169
non-means-tested benefits 169
WTC/CTC 169
EU co-ordination rules 1631, 1652
families
I-ESA 317
fraud 1267
habitual residence test 1586
hardship payments 1225
health and work conversation 1051
homeless
I-ESA 951
hospital patients 922, 923, 925
how long is it paid for
C-ESA 656
income
C-ESA 654
I-ESA 419
income-related ESA 157
information to support claim
C-ESA 659
interchange of claims 1182
leaseholder charges 359
limited capability for work 1010
limited capability for work-related activity
1027
maximum deductions 1209
mortgage interest loan 855
new claims 24
C-ESA 26
I-ESA 161
new-style ESA 26
NHS charges, exemption
I-ESA 667
NI contribution conditions
C-ESA 980
NI credits 971
old-style ESA 648
overlapping benefits

C-ESA 663, 1190
overpayment 1233
  under UC system 1235
partner subject to immigration control
  1569
partner's income 420
passported benefits
  C-ESA 663
  I-ESA 170
payment
  C-ESA 661
  I-ESA 168
pension payments
  C-ESA 654
periods of limited capability for work 1041
permitted work 429, 1043
person subject to immigration control
  C-ESA 1565
  I-ESA 1564
personal allowances
  I-ESA 333
premiums
  I-ESA 339
prisoners
  C-ESA 938
  I-ESA 941
public funds 1562
reciprocal agreements 1631
residence rules
  C-ESA 1631
  I-ESA 1592, 1625
responsible for a child
  I-ESA 163
revisions 1301, 1303
  following award of qualifying benefit
    1328
run-on
  I-ESA 127, 168
sanctions
  benefit offences 1280
  work-related requirements 1079, 1156
SMP/SAP/SPP/SSPP 830
SSP 659, 848
starting work
  I-ESA 170
students 894
supersessions 1301, 1315
support component
  C-ESA 652
  I-ESA 354
tax
  C-ESA 662
  I-ESA 169
trade disputes 1006
transferring to PC 274
transferring to UC 27, 160
transfers from incapacity benefits 655
transitional addition 355

treated as claim for MA 735
treated as in full-time work
  WTC 305
treatment as income
  means-tested benefits over pension
    age 475
  means-tested benefits under pension
    age 435, 436
  UC 126
  WTC/CTC 1480, 1481
UC 26, 160
who can get ESA
  C-ESA 648
  I-ESA 160
work 991, 1042
work capability assessment 1010
work-focused interviews 1136
  under UC system 1051
work-related activity 1140, 1160
work-related activity component
  C-ESA 653
  I-ESA 354
work-related requirements
  outside UC system 1113
  under UC system 1050, 1051, 1069
young people 649
employment officers 1114
employment programmes 1151
  available for work 1115
  good reason for leaving
    UC 1104
  payments, treatment as capital
    means-tested benfits under pension
      age 501
  payments, treatment as income
    means-tested benefits under pension
      age 444
    UC 127
    WTC/CTC 1489
  sanctions for failure to participate
    ESA under UC system 1087
    JSA 1150, 1151, 1152
    JSA under UC system 1087
    UC 1087
  treated as not in full-time work 998
energy efficiency grants 872
enhanced disability premium 343
  rate 351
epilepsy
  free prescriptions 672
equal pay settlements
  treatment as earnings
    CA 564
    UC 117
  treatment as income 421
equal treatment 1678
  CA 568
  EU co-ordination rules 1678

equity release schemes
  treatment as income
    means-tested benefits 446, 479
    UC 128
errors
  claimant error
    HB 1255
  error of law by First-tier Tribunal 1397
  official error 1308
    HB 1253
    NI credits 969
    Scottish benefits 1750
    WTC/CTC 1523
  on claim form
    HB 204
  revision due to factual error
    benefits 1310
  revision due to official error
    benefits 1307
    WTC/CTC 1545, 1546
  supersession due to error of law 1318
  supersession due to factual error
    benefits 1317, 1324
estate
  recovery of funeral payments 804
  recovery of overpayment 1246
    HB 1257
Estonia 1601
estrangement from parents
  definition
    IS/JSA 886
    UC 881
  in relevant education
    IS 886
  IS 237
  UC 38
European Economic Area
  member states 1669
European Economic Area nationals
  Brexit 1596
  checklist of free movement rights 1599
  child in education 1621
  comprehensive sickness insurance 1614
  covered by co-ordination rules 1672
  derivative right to reside 1619
  discrimination 1678
  EU co-ordination of benefits 1668
  EU law 1581
  EU Settlement Scheme 1597
  exporting benefits 1679
  family members 1614, 1673
  free movement rights 1594, 1595, 1599
  funeral payments in EEA states
    funeral expenses payments 802
    funeral support payments 1706
  habitual residence test 1589
  initial right of residence 1605
  jobseekers 1605

  NI contributions 965
  permanent right of residence 1621
  pre-settled status 1597
  pregnancy 1612
  qualified person 1599
  resided legally 1622
  residence documents 1600
  residence rights 1595
  right to reside 1595
  self-employment 1608
  self-sufficient people 1613
  settled status 1597
  students 1614
  transition period 1596
  unemployed people 1609
  workers 1607
European free movement rights 1595
  checklist of rights 1599
European Union
  law 1668
  member states 1668
European Union co-ordination rules 1667
  aggregation 1678
  benefits covered 1674
  equal treatment 1678
  exporting benefits 1679
  overlapping benefits 1680
  principles 1669, 1676
  single competent state 1676
  transition period 1670
  using the rules 1670
  who is covered 1672
European Union Settlement Scheme 1597
evidence
  age 787
  death for bereavement benefits 554
  incorrect evidence in claim
    WTC/CTC 1536
  proving a case at appeal 1376
  required to support claims 1174, 1200
    C-JSA 716
    health benefits 678
    I-JSA 261
    IS 243
    UC 45
  suspected fraud
    WTC/CTC 1535
evidence requirement
  IS/JSA 1174
examinations
  investigating awards
    WTC/CTC 1534
exams
  failing exams 909

exceptionally severe disablement allowance
695
  treatment as income
    means-tested benefits over pension
      age 475
    means-tested benefits under pension
      age 436
excluded tenancies
  HB 382
exempt accommodation 403
expected week of childbirth
  definition 726
expenses
  councillors' expenses 423, 470
  medical examination 1034
  sale of capital
    means-tested benefits under pension
      age 508
    UC 151
  voluntary work
    treatment as income 448
exporting benefits 1679
extended benefit unit 96
extended payments
  amount
    HB 218
  council tax reduction 851
  HB 217
extra-statutory payments
  administrative errors 1439
  C-JSA 719
  HB 208
  I-JSA 264
  treatment as income
    means-tested benefits under pension
      age 436
    WTC/CTC 1481

F
failure to
  apply for capital
    means-tested benefits under pension
      age 505
  apply for income
    means-tested benefits over pension
      age 481
    means-tested benefits under pension
      age 450
    UC 132
  apply for job
    JSA 1146
    JSA under UC system 1081
    UC 1081
  attend health consultation
    PIP 766
  attend interview
    C-JSA 718
    I-JSA 263

    JSA 1134, 1150
    UC 1087
  attend medical examination 1034
  attend work-focused interview
    IS/JSA/ESA/IB 1157
  comply
    WTC/CTC 1537
  disclose a material fact 1239, 1243
    HB 1257
  meet responsibilities
    WTC/CTC 1523
  participate in assessment process
    PIP 766
  participate in employment programmes
    1151
  report change of circumstances
    benefits 1199
    HB 221
  return questionnaire
    PIP 766
  sign on
    JSA 1133
  take up job
    JSA 1146
    JSA under UC system 1081
    UC 1081
Fair Start Scotland scheme 1052
false statements
  penalties 1273
families
  British citizens 1616
  claiming for a family
    C-ESA 650
    C-JSA 711
    HB 189, 317
    I-ESA 162, 317
    I-JSA 257, 317
    IS 239, 317
    PC 317
    UC 57
  dual British and EEA nationals 1617
  EEA nationals 1614
  extended benefit unit 96
  extended family members 1616
  family benefits 1680
  family element
    CTC 1453
  former family members of EEA nationals
    1617
  permanent right of residence 1623
  person subject to immigration control
    1568
  premiums 339
  providing childcare
    NI credits 974
  see also: couples
family premium 340
  rate 351

family reunion 1574
filmed evidence
  appeals 1379
Financial Assistance Scheme
  treatment as income
    means-tested benefits 479
    PC 281
    UC 128
financial need
  advance payments 1192
  discretionary housing payments 642
Find a Job service 1056
fines
  fraud offences
    WTC/CTC 1540
  paid by deductions from benefit 1208
  see also: penalties
firefighters
  payments treated as capital
    means-tested benefits under pension
      age 493
  payments treatment as income
    CA 568
    means-tested benefits over pension
      age 472
    means-tested benefits under pension
      age 430
  treated as not full-time work
    IS/JSA/ESA 998
  work search requirement 1073
First-tier Tribunal 1337
  attendance at hearing 1369
  carrying out a decision 1387
  challenging a tribunal decision
    benefits 1387
    Scottish benefits 1741
    WTC/CTC 1555
  complaints about HM Courts and
    Tribunals Service 1443
  consent orders 1364
  decisions 1385
    Scottish benefits 1740, 1749
  directions 1358
  domiciliary hearings 1369
  error of law 1389, 1397
    Scottish benefits 1741
  evidence at hearing
    help for child/vulnerable adult/
      sensitive witness 1368
    witnesses 1377
  future changes 1338
  issues which must be considered 1373
  judicial review of decisions 1422
  late appeals
    benefits 1347
    Scottish benefits 1735, 1749
    WTC/CTC 1553
  medical examinations

    benefits 1372
    Scottish benefits 1739
    WTC/CTC 1554
  membership 1369
  oral hearing
    benefits 1367, 1371
    WTC/CTC 1554
  paper hearing
    benefits 1367
    WTC/CTC 1554
  permission to appeal to Upper Tribunal
    1399
    Scottish benefits 1744
  preparing a case 1376
  presenting a case 1385
  record of proceedings 1386
    Scottish benefits 1740
  representatives 1362
  reviewing a tribunal decision 1401
    Scottish benefits 1741
  setting aside a decision
    benefits 1388, 1389
    Scottish benefits 1743
    WTC/CTC 1555
  SSP/SMP/SAP/SPP/SSPP/SPBP 1433
  statement of reasons 1386
    Scottish benefits 1740
  striking out an appeal 1360
  tribunal procedures
    benefits 1369
    WTC/CTC 1554
  what the tribunal can do 1357
    Scottish benefits 1736
    WTC/CTC 1552
fistula, permanent
  free prescriptions 672
fit note 837
fixed-term investments
  means-tested benefits over pension age
    518
  means-tested benefits under pension age
    490
  UC 139
Flexible Support Fund 874
fluctuating hours of work
  means-tested benefits 994
  term-time work
    means-tested benefits 995
    WTC 303
  WTC 302
fluctuating income
  CA 565
  HB 456
  IS/I-JSA/ESA 454
  means-tested benefits over pension age
    483

food banks 871
footwear
budgeting loans 793
foreign income 1488
foster care
additional bedroom
HB 411
local housing allowance 387
rent officer determination related rent
401
social sector tenants 395
UC 99
allowances
CA 568
means-tested benefits over pension
age 481
means-tested benefits under pension
age 440
UC 131
WTC/CTC 1489
child benefit 591
claiming for children
means-tested benefits 328
UC 63
CTC 290
foster parent approved as adopter
SAP/SPP/SSPP 825
IS 235
lone foster carers who are students
HB 896
NI credits 972
treated as not in full-time work
IS/JSA/ESA 998
work-focused interviews 1066
work-related requirements 1062
WTC 307
foster parent condition 99
fraud 1267, 1533
advisers committing an offence 1274
convicted of fraud
benefits 1278
WTC/CTC 1540
disqualification
WTC 1281
disqualifying benefits 1279
formal cautions 1276
fraud investigators 1269
health benefits 678
imprisonment
benefits 1278
WTC/CTC 1540
interviews under caution 1270
landlords
HB 216
loss of benefits 1278
penalties
benefits 1275
WTC/CTC 1535

powers of authorised officers 1269
prosecution of offences
benefits 1273
WTC/CTC 1539
prosecution or penalty
benefits 1276
WTC/CTC 1539
sanctionable benefits 1279
Scottish benefits 1726
suspected fraud
WTC/CTC 1535
suspending/withholding benefit 1272
who can be required to give evidence
benefits 1269
WTC/CTC 1534
free school lunches 866
frequency of payment
HB 213
UC 50
frontier worker 23
fuel costs
communal areas
HB 194
debts paid by deductions from benefit
1205
ineligible charges
HB 193
IS/I-JSA/I-ESA/PC 362
Fuel Direct 1206
full service areas 22
full-time education
advanced education
IS/JSA 887
CA 899
ESA
C-ESA 894
I-ESA 894
full-time courses 888
Scotland 888
HB 896
IS 887, 890
JSA
C-JSA 887
I-JSA 887, 890
modular courses 889
NI credits 975
non-advanced education
child benefit 580
CTC 286
relevant education 885
sandwich courses 888
UC 880
see also: education
Full-time Training Flexibility 1152
full-time work 991
ESA 992
extended payments
HB 217

financial help seeking or starting work 873
HB 431, 473, 992
housing costs run-on 376
IS 238, 992
JSA 992
    C-JSA 708
    I-JSA 254
non-dependants 992
PC 992
self-employed 999
treated as being in full-time work
    means-tested benefits 997
    WTC 304
treated as not being in full-time work
    HB/PC 999
    IS/JSA/ESA 998
    WTC 306
uncertainty about hours worked
    means-tested benefits 996
WTC 299, 300
see also: work
funeral expenses payments 798
    amount 803
    appeals 1337
    claim form 804
    deductions from award 803
    EEA nationals 802
    eligibility 800
    excluded people 800
    payment 804
    person subject to immigration control 799
    qualifying benefits 798
    recovery from the estate 804
    residence rules 1634
    revisions 1303
    time limits for claiming 804
funeral support payments in Scotland 1703
    age rules 1706
    amount 1707
    appeals 1734
    benefit cap 1709
    change of circumstances 1733
    claims 1708
    date of claim 1708
    deductions from awards 1707
    EEA nationals 1706
    entitlement to other benefits and tax
        credits 1709
    following award of qualifying benefit
        1708, 1751
    fraud 1726
    information to support claim 1708
    overpayments 1725
    payment 1709
    person subject to immigration control
        1564
    qualifying benefits 1704
    recovery from the estate 1709

redeterminations 1731
residence rules 1634
responsible for funeral expenses 1704
tax 1709
time limit for claiming 1708
treatment as income 1709
    means-tested benefits over pension
        age 475
    means-tested benefits under pension
        age 436
    UC 127
    WTC/CTC 1480
who can get funeral support payments
    1703
funerals
    abroad
        funeral expenses payments 802
        funeral support payments 1706
    budgeting loans 793
    funeral plan payments
        means-tested benefits over pension
        age 525
        UC 147
    good reason for not attending training
        UC 1105
    responsibility for costs
        funeral expenses payments 802
        funeral support payments 1704
furniture
    budgeting loans 793
future interest in property
    means-tested benefits over pension age
        522
    means-tested benefits under pension age
        498
future payments
    means-tested benefits over pension age
        522
    means-tested benefits under pension age
        498
    UC 153

G
garages
    HB 176
gateway areas 22
gender recognition certificate
    bereavement benefits 552
George Cross payments
    treatment as income
        means-tested benefits under pension
        age 449
        UC 147
        WTC/CTC 1486
glasses
    vouchers 674
glaucoma
    free sight tests 674

good reason
failure to attend consultation
PIP 766
failure to attend initial interview
I-JSA 263
failure to attend medical examination
1034
failure to return questionnaire
PIP 766
failure to sign on 1133
late claim
C-JSA 719
HB 209
leaving a job
UC 1102
leaving a training scheme
UC 1104
refusing a job
UC 1105
refusing to attend training
UC 1104
sanctions
JSA 1155
UC 1100
graduated retirement benefit 781
overlapping benefits 1191
treatment as income
WTC/CTC 1485
ground rent
HB 175
IS/I-JSA/I-ESA/PC 360
UC 84
guarantee payments
treatment as earnings
CA 564
means-tested benefits 426
guardian's allowance 578
absence abroad 1649, 1680
adoption 589
advance claims 594
age rules 589
amount 590
appeals 1337
backdating 594, 1177
benefit cap 599
change of circumstances 597
claims 592
contributing to cost of child 589
date of claim 594
decisions 1285
delays 1295
eligible child 588
entitlement to child benefit 587
entitlement to other benefits
means-tested benefits 598
non-means-tested benefits 599
WTC/CTC 598
EU co-ordination rules 1629, 1649

fraud 1267
information to support claim 593
interchange of claims 1182
interim payments 596
late claims 594
looked after by local authority 590
missing parents 588
overlapping benefits 1192
overpayments 1233, 1250
payment 595
prisoners 588, 939
child in prison 590
qualifying children 587
qualifying young person 587
refugees 1574
residence rules 1629
revisions 1301, 1303
supersessions 1301, 1315
tax 597
treated as entitled to child benefit 587
treatment as income 598
means-tested benefits over pension
age 475
means-tested benefits under pension
age 436
UC 127
WTC/CTC 1480
who can get guardian's allowance 587
who should claim 593
guidance
DLA mobility component 609
guided learning
definition of full-time education
IS/JSA 888

H
habitual residence 1586
benefits affected 1586
definition 1590
exempt from habitual residence test 1589
failing the habitual residence test 1587
habitual residence test 1587
living in for three months 1584
returning residents 1591
treated as habitually resident 1587
halls of residence
HB 897
hardship
definition 1226
WTC/CTC 1525
recovery of overpayments
WTC/CTC 1525
hardship payments 1219
age rules
JSA 1224
UC 1220
amounts
ESA 1226

JSA 1224
UC 1221
challenging a decision 1230
claiming other benefits or tax credits 1231
claims 1230
deciding hardship 1226
  ESA 1229
  JSA 1227
  UC 1227
ESA 1225
failing jobseeking conditions 1223
jobseeker's agreement disputes 1130
JSA 1222
length of payment
  UC 1220
NI credits 970
payment 1230
recovery of payments
  UC 1221
sanctions
  ESA 1225
  JSA 1224
  UC 1220
suspension of benefit
  JSA 1223
tax 1231
UC 1219
vulnerable groups
  JSA 1224, 1228
waiting for benefit decision
  JSA 1223
who can claim
  ESA 1225
  JSA 1222
  UC 1220
health and safety
working hours 1787
health and work conversation 1051
health benefits 666
  Best Start foods in Scotland 865
  calculating income 671
  calculating requirements 669
  certificates 677
  claims 676
  delays 678
  exemptions from charges 667
  fraud 678
  Healthy Start food and vitamins 862
  low income scheme 668
  overpayments 678
  prescriptions 672
  proof of entitlement 678
  refunds 678
  who can get health benefits 666
health condition
  PIP 745

healthcare professionals 1176
  consultations
    PIP 765
Healthy Start 862
  claims 864
  food vouchers 862
  qualifying benefits 864
  vitamins 865
  who can claim 862
Help to Save scheme 872
high-income child benefit charge 597
higher pensioner premium 345
  earnings disregard 431
  qualifying benefits 345
  rate 352
hire purchase agreement
  HB 176
HM Courts and Tribunals Service 1338, 1396
  complaints 1443
HM Revenue and Customs
  complaints 1441, 1442, 1517
  contacting office
    WTC/CTC 1516
  decisions on SSP/SMP/SAP/SPP/SSPP/
    SPBP 1428
  NI contributions decisions 960, 1292
  power to investigate awards 1533
  recovery of overpayments
    benefits 1247
    WTC/CTC 1526
  recovery of penalties
    WTC/CTC 1538
holiday pay
  treatment as capital 493
  treatment as earnings
    CA 564
    means-tested benefits over pension
      age 469
    means-tested benefits under pension
      age 421
    UC 117
    WTC/CTC 1481
holidays
  actively seeking work rule
    JSA 1126
    under UC system 1057
  available for work rule
    JSA 1126
    under UC system 1057
  carers
    CA 563
  treated as in full-time work
    means-tested benefits 997
home
  definition 370
  occupation
    HB 181
    mortgage interest loan 857

UC 91
treatment as capital
means-tested benefits over pension
age 519
means-tested benefits under pension
age 493
UC 141
treatment of relative's home
means-tested benefits over pension
age 521
means-tested benefits under pension
age 496
UC 143
home detention curfew
HB 946
means-tested benefits 941
home improvements
budgeting loans 793
interest on loans
IS/I-JSA/I-ESA/PC 362, 857
local authority grants 872
home income plans
see: equity release schemes
home responsibilities protection
NI credits 973
home visits 1175
homeless 949
good reason for refusing a job
UC 1102
jobseeking conditions 950
recourse to public funds 1562
UC 950
work-related requirements 950
homeowners
see: owner-occupiers
hospices
benefit entitlement 920
hospital 917
AA 919
benefit entitlement 917
CA 920
child benefit 583, 925
child in hospital 924
means-tested benefits 328
UC 921
childcare costs allowance
HB 432
costs for usual home 926
HB 926
IS/I-JSA/I-ESA/PC 373, 926
UC 91, 921, 926
CTC 925
definition 918
DLA 919
ESA 922, 923, 925
fares to hospital 675
HB 184, 922, 923
independent hospital

HB 178
IS 922, 923
JSA 921, 922, 923
limited capability for work
ESA 1013
UC 1012
linking rules 919
lone parents 924
mentally ill prisoners
means-tested benefits 942
non-means-tested benefits 942
UC 942
mortgage interest loan 921, 926
moving home
HB 182
NHS charges, exemption 668
non-dependant deductions
HB 200
IS/I-JSA/I-ESA/PC 365
partner in 924
UC 921
patient definition 918
PC 922, 923
PIP 919
private patients 918
UC 921
winter fuel payments 807
hostels
exemption from rent restrictions 404
paid by deductions from benefit 1208
rent restrictions
HB 396
specified accommodation
HB 174
UC 85
hours of work
30-hour element 1458
calculating hours of work
means-tested benefits 993
WTC 301
change in hours
WTC/CTC 1509
expected hours of work for UC 1054
fluctuating hours of work
means-tested benefits 994
WTC 302
full-time work
means-tested benefits 991
WTC 300
increased hours, extended payments
HB 217
increased hours, financial help 873
increased hours, housing costs run-on
IS/I-JSA/I-ESA/PC 376
limits to working week 1787
normal hours of work
means-tested benefits 994
WTC 302

permitted restrictions
  JSA 1122
reduced hours 305
house sale
proceeds on separation
  means-tested benefits over pension
    age 520
  means-tested benefits under pension
    age 494
  UC 142
houseboats
excluded tenancies 382
HB 176
rent restrictions
  HB 396
UC 84
household equipment
budgeting loans 793
households
children treated as member of household
  means-tested benefits 327
means-tested benefits 329
separate households 329
UC 59
housing associations
deposits
  means-tested benefits under pension
    age 495
  UC 143
excluded tenancies 382
local housing allowance
  HB 384
rent restrictions
  HB 383
  UC 107
housing benefit 172
16/17-year-olds 177
absence abroad 1652
additional earnings disregard
  over pension age 473
age rules 187
amount 190
appeals 1337, 1348
applicable amount 332
backdating a claim 208
benefit cap 225, 1197
benefit week 191
calculation
  not receiving means-tested benefits
    196
  receiving means-tested benefits 196
capital
  over pension age 516
  under pension age 488
capital limits
  over pension age 517
  under pension age 489
care homes 178, 933, 935

care leavers 947
change of circumstances 221
charges for meals 195
child's income 420
children 189, 323
claims 173, 202
components 353
continuing payments 216
  PC 217
couples 206, 319
date of claim 207
death 214
decisions 211
deductions from eligible rent 193
deductions to recover overpayments
  1258
delays 220
discretionary housing payments 641
disregarded earnings
  over pension age 471
  under pension age 429, 431
earnings 456
eligible rent 191
entitlement to other benefits
  means-tested benefits 224
  non-means-tested benefits 224
  WTC/CTC 224
extended payment on return to work 217
families 317
financial help on starting work 225
fraud 1267
fuel charges 193
full-time work 991
good cause for late claim 209
habitual residence test 1586
hospital patients 184, 922, 923, 926
income
  over pension age 466, 467
  under pension age 419
increase following award of qualifying
  benefit 211
interim payments 220
joint occupiers 180
maximum rent
  local housing allowance 385
  pre-Jan '96 rules 405
  rent officer determination related rent
    397
  social sector tenants 392
moving house 211
new claims 24, 173
non-commercial agreements 178
non-dependants 198
overpayments 1253
partner subject to immigration control
  1570
partner's income 420
passport to other benefits 225

payments 213
payments on account 220
pension-age HB 188
permitted work disregard 431, 472
person subject to immigration control 1564
personal allowances 333
premiums 339
prisoners 941, 946
public funds 1562
rapid reclaim 203
rent 191
rent restrictions 381
rent-free periods 192
residence rules 1592, 1625
revisions 1301, 1303
  following award of qualifying benefit 1328
run-on 220
sanctions for benefit offences 1280
service charges 194
shared accommodation 180
specified accommodation 174
start of entitlement 213
students 178, 896
supersessions 1301, 1315
support component 354
taking advantage of HB 180
tapers 197
tax 224
temporary accommodation due to repairs 187
trade disputes 1006
transferring to UC 27, 173
transitional addition after transfer to ESA 355
treatment as income
  means-tested benefits over pension age 475
  means-tested benefits under pension age 436
  WTC/CTC 1480
two homes 181, 186
UC 26
violence 186, 187
waiting days
  I-JSA 266
waiving of rent during repairs 178
weekly income 455
who can get HB 172
work-related activity component 354
working-age HB 188
housing costs element 82
16/17- year-old care leavers 84
accommodation not covered 84
amount 94
cap rent 105
contrived agreements 90

core rent 104
eligible payments 83
families 96
future changes 82
housing costs contributions 102
liability for payments 87
non-dependant deductions 102
non-dependants 96
occupation condition 91
one-bedroom shared accommodation 106
overpayments 1236
owner-occupiers 83, 84
payment 49
private tenants 103
service charges 85, 110
size criteria 97
social sector tenants 107
specified accommodation 85
two homes 91, 95
waiting period 111
who can get 83
housing repair grants 872
humanitarian protection
benefit entitlement 1573
family reunion 1574
integration loans 1575
Hungary 1601
hypoadrenalism
free prescriptions 672
hypoparathyroidism
free prescriptions 672
hypopituitarism
free prescriptions 672

I
Iceland
EEA nationals 1669
right to reside 1595
ileostomy
free prescriptions 672
immigration status 1559
incapacitated
means-tested benefits 434
WTC 1461
incapacity benefit 648
absence abroad 1657
appeals 1337
disability premium 342
EU co-ordination rules 1658
overpayments 1233
prisoners 938
residence rules 1629
revisions 1301, 1303
supersessions 1301, 1315
transfers to ESA 655
treatment as income
  WTC/CTC 1480

incapacity for work
continuous employment
SMP/SAP/SPP/SSPP/SPBP 818
disability premium 342
EEA worker and self-employed status
1612
evidence
SSP 845
IS 235
linked periods
C-JSA 708
NI credits 971
period of incapacity
SSP 838
SSP 836
students
HB 896
treated as incapable of work
SSP 837
income
annual declaration
WTC/CTC 1513
assessed income period
PC 281
assumed income
UC 129
benefits and tax credits not treated as
income
means-tested benefits under pension
age 436
benefits and tax credits treated as income
means-tested benefits over pension
age 474
means-tested benefits under pension
age 435
UC 126
calculating net employed earnings
CA 565
means-tested benefits over pension
age 470
means-tested benefits under pension
age 423
calculating net self-employed earnings
means-tested benefits over pension
age 471
means-tested benefits under pension
age 427
capital treated as income
means-tested benefits under pension
age 444
UC 116
WTC/CTC 1491
changes in income
WTC/CTC 1475, 1510
child's
means-tested benefits over pension
age 467

means-tested benefits under pension
age 420
UC 115
WTC/CTC 1478
current year's income
WTC/CTC 1475
deemed income 478
definition
HB over pension age 467
means-tested benefits under pension
age 420
PC 467
UC 116
WTC/CTC 1478
deprivation of income
means-tested benefits over pension
age 481
means-tested benefits under pension
age 450
UC 131
difference between income and capital
421
failure to apply for income
means-tested benefits over pension
age 481
means-tested benefits under pension
age 450
UC 132
WTC/CTC 1491
fall in income
WTC/CTC 1475, 1510
hardship payments 1226
health benefits 671
income from capital
means-tested benefits over pension
age 478
means-tested benefits under pension
age 443
UC 42, 129
WTC/CTC 1486
income threshold
WTC/CTC 1467
income treated as capital
means-tested benefits under pension
age 493
UC 141
means-tested benefits
over pension age 466
under pension age 419
monthly amount
UC 133, 134
non-dependants
HB 201, 202
IS/I-JSA/I-ESA/PC 365
non-means-tested benefits
C-JSA 712
CA 563
notional income

means-tested benefits over pension
age 481
means-tested benefits under pension
age 449
UC 131
WTC/CTC 1491
part weeks
IS/I-JSA/I-ESA 455
part-year income
WTC/CTC 1477
partner's
means-tested benefits over pension
age 467
means-tested benefits under pension
age 420
UC 115
WTC/CTC 1478
period covered by income
IS/I-JSA/I-ESA 453
previous year's income
WTC/CTC 1475
proof of income
WTC/CTC 1501
relevant income
WTC/CTC 1466
retirement provision 281
rise in income
WTC/CTC 1475
strike pay 1004
students 900
ESA 895
HB 898
IS/JSA 893
UC 882
UC 115, 126
weekly amount
HB under pension age 455
means-tested benefits over pension
age 468, 483
means-tested benefits under pension
age 453
WTC/CTC 1474
see also: earnings
income support 232
16/17-year-olds 239
absence abroad 1653
age rules 238
amount 240
appeals 1337
applicable amount 240, 332
backdating 244, 1178
benefit cap 248
benefit week 454
calculation 240
capital
over pension age 516
under pension age 488
capital limits 489
care homes 933
care leavers 947
change of circumstances 246
child's capital 490
child's income 420
children 239, 323
choosing who should claim 242
claim treated as CA claim 573
claims 233, 241
couples 239, 319
date of claim 243
decisions 1285
deductions from benefit 1203
delays 1295
disability 235
disability premium 342
disregarded earnings 429
entitlement to other benefits
means-tested benefits 247
non-means-tested benefits 247
WTC/CTC 247
EU co-ordination rules 1654
evidence requirement 243
families 317
financial help on starting work 248
following award of qualifying benefit
1328
fraud 1267
full-time work 238, 991
habitual residence test 1586
homeless 951
hospital patients 922, 923
incapable of work 235
income 419
interchange of claims 1182
leaseholder charges 359
lone parents 235
maximum deductions 1209
mortgage interest loan 855
new claims 24, 233
NHS charges, exemption 667
overpayments 1233
parents 235
partner subject to immigration control
1569
partner's income 420
passport to other benefits 248
payment 245
person subject to immigration control
1564
personal allowances 333
premiums 339
prisoners 941
public funds 1562
qualifying benefits 244
refugees 1574
relevant education 885
residence rules 1592, 1625

revisions 1301, 1303
following award of qualifying benefit 1328
run-on 127, 246
sanctions
work-related activities 1156
sickness 235
students 885
supersessions 1301, 1315
tax 247
trade disputes 1001
returning to work 1006
transferring to PC 274
transferring to UC 27
treatment as income
means-tested benefits under pension age 436
WTC/CTC 1480
UC 25
who can get IS 232, 234
work-focused interview 1137
work-related activity 1140, 1160
work-related requirements 1113
income tax
AA 541
bereavement benefits 557
Best Start grants 1701
CA 574
changes ignored
HB 424
child benefit 597
Christmas bonus 870
CTC 295
discretionary housing payments 645
DLA 634
ESA
C-ESA 662
I-ESA 169
funeral support payments 1709
guardian's allowance 597
hardship payments 1231
HB 224
industrial injuries benefits 700
IS 247
JSA
C-JSA 721
I-JSA 266
MA 736
PC 281
PIP 770
refunds treatment as capital 493
refunds treatment as income
CA 568
means-tested benefits under pension age 444
UC 117
revision of liability
WTC/CTC 1546

Scottish child payment 1715
SMP/SAP/SSP/SSPP/SPBP 828
social fund loans and payments 808
SSP 847
state pension 790
UC 54
WTC 313
young carer grant 1721
increases for dependants
adult dependants
bereavement support payment 546
SSP 841
children
bereavement support payment 546
retirement pensions before 6 April 2016 780
widowed parent's allowance 548
hospital patients 925
overlapping benefits 1192
prisoners 938
treatment as income
means-tested benefits under pension age 436
WTC/CTC 1480, 1481
indefinite leave to enter or remain
EEA nationals 1597
Independent Case Examiner 1440
industrial accidents/diseases
accidents 683
assessing disablement 689
bereavement benefits 552
causation 688
in the course of employment 684
legal action 682
loss of faculty 689
more than one cause of disability 690
one-off lump-sum payment 701
onset 688
out of employment 686
period of assessment 692
personal injury definition 683
prescribed industrial diseases 687
prescribed occupations 687
recrudescence 688
time limits 687
travel to work 685
two or more accidents/diseases 691
industrial death benefit 1486
industrial injuries benefits 681
absence abroad 1655
advance claims 699
appeals 1337
backdating 698, 1177
benefit cap 700
change of circumstances 700
claims 697
date of claim 698
employed earner definition 682

entitlement to other benefits
    means-tested benefits 700
    non-means-tested benefits 700
    WTC/CTC 700
EU co-ordination rules 1632, 1655
IIDB 693
in the course of employment 684
industrial injury condition 682
information to support claim 698
late claims 698
misconduct 686
NI contribution conditions 682
overlapping benefits 700
payment of benefit 699
person subject to immigration control
    1565
personal injury definition 683
reduced earnings allowance 695
renewal claims 699
residence rules 1632
retirement allowance 696
self-employed 682
tax 700
treatment as income 700
    means-tested benefits over pension
        age 475
    means-tested benefits under pension
        age 435
    UC 126
    WTC/CTC 1480
who can get industrial injuries benefits
    682
industrial injuries disablement benefit 693
    absence abroad 1655
    age rules 693
    amount 694
    disqualification 693
    EU co-ordination rules 1632, 1655
    increases of benefit 694
    overlapping benefits 1190
    prisoners 939
    residence rules 1632
    who can get IIDB 693
infectious disease
    limited capability for work
        ESA 1013
        UC 1012
information
    about decision 1296
        HB 212
    required by employer
        SAP 812
        SMP 811
        SPBP 816
        SPP 813
        SSPP 814
    required by HMRC
        SSP/SMP/SAP/SPP/SSPP/SPBP 1429

required to prevent fraud 1269
    WTC/CTC 1534
to make a decision
    benefits 1288, 1289, 1294
to support an appeal 1350, 1355
    Scottish benefits 1735, 1736
to support claim 1174, 1200
    AA 538
    bereavement benefits 554
    Best Start grants 1700
    C-ESA 659
    C-JSA 716
    CA 571
    child benefit 593
    CTC 293
    DLA 625
    guardian's allowance 593
    HB 204, 206
    I-ESA 167
    I-JSA 261
    industrial injuries benefits 698
    IS 243
    MA 734
    PC 277
    PIP 763
    SSP 845
    state pension 787
    UC 45
    WTC 310
    WTC/CTC 1500
    young carer grant 1720
to support revision
    benefits 1313
to support supersession
    benefits 1320
written reasons for a decision
    benefits 1297
Inland Revenue
    see: HM Revenue and Customs
insurance payments
    treatment as income
        C-ESA 655
        means-tested benefits 446
        UC 128
insurance policies
    surrender value
        means-tested benefits over pension
            age 522
        means-tested benefits under pension
            age 497
        UC 145
integration loans 1575
    repayment 1208
interest
    on mortgage interest loans 858
    on overpayments 1244
        HB 1256
        WTC/CTC 1530

on savings, treatment as capital
means-tested benefits under pension
age 493
UC 141
WTC/CTC 1486
on savings, treatment as income
UC 130
penalties for fraud
WTC/CTC 1538
interim payments
child benefit 596, 1295
guardian's allowance 596, 1295
see also: short-term advances
interviews
failure to attend 1134
C-JSA 718
I-JSA 263
UC 1087
fraud 1270
further interviews for JSA 1132
initial interviews
C-JSA 717
I-JSA 261
jobseeking conditions 1131
signing on 1131
travel expenses 1131
work-focused interviews
IS/I-JSA/I-ESA 1136, 1139
UC system 1051
work-related requirements 1059
investigation of claims 1269
authorised officers 1269
interviews under caution 1270
WTC/CTC 1533
Irish citizens
right to reside 1594

J
Japanese prisoners of war
payments disregarded as capital 524
job interview
absence abroad to attend
JSA 1118
Job Start Payment 874
Jobcentre Plus travel discount card 873
jobseeker's agreement 1127
appealing a decision 1344
backdating 1130
changing the terms 1130
contents of agreement 1128
disputes 1129
refusal to sign 1128
treated as signing 1129
jobseeker's allowance 250, 704
16/17-year-olds 256
absence abroad 1655
actively seeking work 1124
advance claims

C-JSA 719
I-JSA 264
age rules
C-JSA 711
I-JSA 255
amount
C-JSA 711
I-JSA 258
appeal pending on limited capability for
work 1040
appeals 1337
applicable amount 258, 332
available for work 1115
under UC system 1056
backdating 1178
C-JSA 719
I-JSA 263
benefit cap
C-JSA 722
I-JSA 267
benefit week 454
C-JSA 704
calculation
I-JSA 258
capital
over pension age 516
under pension age 488
capital limits 489
care homes
I-JSA 933
care leavers
I-JSA 947
change of circumstances
C-JSA 720
I-JSA 265
child's capital 490
child's income 420
children
C-JSA 711
I-JSA 257, 258, 323
claimant commitment 1127
under UC system 1047
claims
C-JSA 715
I-JSA 252, 259
couples
C-JSA 711
I-JSA 257, 319
date of claim
C-JSA 717
I-JSA 261
decisions 1285
deductions from benefit
C-JSA 1203
I-JSA 1203
delays 1295
disability premium 342
disregarded earnings

C-JSA 712
duration
  C-JSA 714
earnings
  C-JSA 712
  under UC system 1065
entitlement ends 1133
entitlement to other benefits based on C-JSA
  means-tested benefits 722
  non-means-tested benefits 722
  WTC 722
entitlement to other benefits based on I-JSA
  means-tested benefits 267
  non-means-tested benefits 267
  WTC/CTC 267
EU co-ordination rules
  C-JSA 1633, 1657
  I-JSA 1657
families
  I-JSA 317
fraud 1267
full-time paid work
  C-JSA 708
  I-JSA 254, 991
habitual residence test 1586
hardship payments 1222
homeless
  I-JSA 951
hospital patients 921, 922, 923
I-JSA 250
income
  C-JSA 712
  I-JSA 419
jobseeking conditions 1114
joint-claim couples
  I-JSA 253
leaseholder charges 359
maximum deductions 1208
mortgage interest loan 855
new claims 24
  C-JSA 26
  I-JSA 252
new-style JSA 26
NHS charges, exemption
  I-JSA 667
NI contribution conditions
  C-JSA 980
NI credits 970
old-style JSA 706
overlapping benefits
  C-JSA 1190
overpayments 1233
  under UC system 1235
partner subject to immigration control
  I-JSA 1569
partner's income 420

passported benefits
  C-JSA 722
  I-JSA 268
payment
  C-JSA 720
  I-JSA 265
pension payments
  C-JSA 713
person subject to immigration control
  C-JSA 1565
  I-JSA 1564
personal allowances
  I-JSA 333
premiums 339
prescribed amount 712
prisoners
  C-JSA 938
  I-JSA 941
reciprocal agreements 1633
recourse to public funds
  I-JSA 1562
relevant education 886
residence rules
  C-JSA 1632
  I-JSA 1592, 1625
responsibility for a child
  I-JSA 258
revisions 1301, 1303
  following award of qualifying benefit 1328
run-on
  I-JSA 127, 265
sanctions
  benefit offences 1280
  work-related requirements 1079, 1145
severe hardship payments
  I-JSA 257
signing on 1131
starting work
  C-JSA 723
  I-JSA 268
students
  C-JSA 885
  C-JSA under UC system 899
  I-JSA 885
supersessions 1301, 1315
tax
  C-JSA 721
  I-JSA 266
trade disputes 1001
transferring to PC 274
transferring to UC 27
treatment as income 722
  means-tested benefits over pension age 475
  means-tested benefits under pension age 435, 436
  UC 126

WTC/CTC 1480, 1481
UC 25
who can get JSA
C-JSA 705
I-JSA 251
who should claim
C-JSA 716
I-JSA 260
work preparation requirement
under UC system 1051
work search requirement
under UC system 1053
work-focused interview
under UC system 1051
work-related requirements
outside UC system 1113
under UC system 1050, 1069
jobseeker's direction 1153
sanctions 1153
jobseekers from the EEA
A2 nationals 1601
A8 nationals 1602
benefit entitlement 1607
Croatia 1601
genuine chance of employment 1605
genuine prospects of work test 1606
right to reside 1605
jobseeking conditions 1114
hardship payments if conditions are not
met 1223
interviews 1131
prisoners 938
jobseeking periods
C-JSA 706
I-JSA 254
linked periods 707
joint tenants
deductions for fuel charges
HB 193
HB 180
not a non-dependant
HB 199
IS/I-JSA/I-ESA/PC 364
UC 97
UC 104, 109
joint-claim jobseeker's allowance 253
age rules
I-JSA 255
full-time work
I-JSA 254
sanctions 1280
trade disputes 1001
judicial review 1414
grounds for review 1416
in courts 1421
in Upper Tribunal 1422
letter before claim 1418
pre-action protocol 1418
time limits 1414
when to use judicial review 1415
jury service
allowances 502, 1490
IS 237
NI credits 976
work search requirement 1073
Justice of the Peace
IS 237

K
keeping in touch days 820
kidney dialysis
AA 536
DLA 623
kinship carers
additional bedroom
local housing allowance 387
rent officer determination related rent
401
social sector tenants 395
UC 99
child benefit 591
NI credits 972
payments, treatment as income
means-tested benefits over pension
age 481
means-tested benefits under pension
age 440
UC 131
WTC/CTC 1489
treated as not in full-time work
IS/JSA/ESA 998
two-child limit
UC 69
WTC 307

L
land 139, 491, 518
landlord
close relative
HB 178
UC 89
direct payments for rent arrears 1205
HB fraud 216
not a non-dependant
HB 199
UC 97
payment of benefit direct to a landlord
HB 214, 215
UC 49
recovery of overpayments
HB 1259, 1262
responsibility for landlord's child
HB 179
laryngostomy
free prescriptions 672

late claims 1176
  C-JSA 719
  CA 572
  child benefit 594
  delay in hearing of or confirming death of
    spouse
     bereavement benefits 555
  good cause 209
  guardian's allowance 594
  HB 208
  I-JSA 263
  industrial injuries benefits 698
  IS 244
  reasons for late claim 1178
  SSP 846
  state pension 788
Latvia 1601
laundry facilities
  HB 195
learner support funds 906
leaseholder charges 110, 359
  amount of charges
    IS/I-JSA/I-ESA/PC 362
  charges paid after return to work
    IS/I-JSA/I-ESA/PC 376
  ground rent
    IS/I-JSA/I-ESA/PC 360
  liability for charges 369
  linking rules for charges
    IS/I-JSA/I-ESA/PC 375
  service charges
    IS/I-JSA/I-ESA/PC 361
  waiting period for charges
    IS/I-JSA/I-ESA/PC 368
    UC 111
  who can get help with charges 360
leave to enter or remain 1561
  appealing a previous refusal 1564
  indefinite leave under EU Settlement
    Scheme 1597
  means-tested benefits 1565
  non-means-tested benefits 1566
  right to reside during period of leave 1594
  WTC/CTC 1567
leaving a job
  good reason
    UC 1102
  misconduct
    JSA under UC system 1082
    UC 1082
  payments
    CA 564
    means-tested benefits over pension
     age 470
    means-tested benefits under pension
     age 424
    UC 118
  trial period sanctions

    JSA 1147
  voluntarily
    JSA under UC system 1082
    UC 1082
legacy benefits 21
legal aid
  court costs for appeals 1413
  representation at appeals 1363, 1406
legal fees
  court costs for appeals 1413
  First-tier Tribunal appeals 1363
  Upper Tribunal appeals 1406
liable for rent
  16/17-year-olds 177
  before moving in 181
  definition
    UC 87
  HB 177
  joint liability
    HB 180
    UC 104
  treated as liable to pay rent
    HB 178
    UC 88
  treated as not liable to pay rent
    HB 178
    UC 89
  UC 87, 88
liable relatives
  definition 438
  payments 438
licensees
  HB 175
  not a non-dependant
    IS/I-JSA/I-ESA/PC 363
  UC 84
Liechtenstein
  EEA nationals 1669
  right to reside 1595
life insurance
  surrender value
    means-tested benefits over pension
     age 522
    means-tested benefits under pension
     age 497
    UC 145
life interest 498
life rent 498
lifeboat crew
  payments treated as capital
    means-tested benefits under pension
     age 493
  payments treated as income
    CA 568
    means-tested benefits over pension
     age 472
    means-tested benefits under pension
     age 430

treated as not full-time work
  IS/JSA/ESA 998
work search requirement 1073
limited capability for work 1010
  appeal pending 1037
    ESA 1038
    JSA 1040
    UC 1040
  appeals 1036, 1371
  challenging a decision 1036
  condition worsens 1040
  decision 1035, 1292
  descriptors 1017
  determinations 1036, 1310
  disability premium 343
  element 70
  ESA
    C-ESA 648
    I-ESA 160
  fluctuating condition 1017
  JSA
    C-JSA 708
    I-JSA 255
  linking rules 1041
  mandatory reconsiderations 1036
  medical examinations 1034
  NI credits 971
  period of limited capability for work 1041
  permitted work 1043
  physical disabilities 1018
  pregnancy 737
    ESA 1013
    UC 1012
  questionnaire 1033
  SMP/SAP/SPP/SSPP 830
  students
    UC 881
  supersessions 1318
  transferring to UC 71, 1012
  treated as having limited capability for
    work 1015
    ESA 1013
    UC 1011
  treated as not having limited capability for
    work
    C-JSA 708
    ESA 1016
    UC 1015
  UC 70
  work allowance
    UC 41
  work capability assessment 1010
  work-related activity component 354
  work-related requirements 1064, 1068,
    1069
  working during limited capability for work
    period 1042
  young people

ESA 649
UC 37
limited capability for work-related activity
  1027
  assessments 1028
  descriptors 1028
  element 72
  ESA support component 652
  treated as having limited capability for
    work-related activity 1031
  UC 72
  work-focused interviews 1137
  work-related requirements 1064, 1069
limited leave to remain
  EEA nationals 1597
linking rules
  C-ESA 660
  C-JSA 707
  care home residents
    AA/DLA/PIP 930
  hospital patients 919
  leaseholder/service charges met by IS/I-
    JSA/I-ESA/PC 375
  limited capability for work 1041
  SSP 838, 843
Lithuania 1601
living together as a couple
  means-tested benefits 320
  UC 58
  WTC/CTC 1497
loans
  end of trade dispute
    IS 1006
  from employer 423, 469
  home repair/improvement
    IS/I-JSA/I-ESA/PC 362, 495, 857
    UC 143
  repaid by deductions from benefit 1208
  treatment as capital
    means-tested benefits over pension
      age 518
    means-tested benefits under pension
      age 491
    UC 139
local authorities
  complaints about benefit administration
    HB 1443
  council tax help 851
  education benefits 866
  local welfare assistance 861
  social care payments
    treatment as capital 500
    treatment as income 447
    UC 147
  support for care leavers 947

Local Government and Social Care Ombudsman 1446
local housing allowance 384
  broad rental market area
    HB 390
    UC 107
  cap rent
    HB 385
    UC 105
  challenging a rent restriction 413
  change in circumstances 390
  direct payment to landlord 215
  excluded tenancies 382
  ineligible charges 193
  maximum rent 385
  occupiers 386
  one-bedroom self-contained
    accommodation
    HB 389
    UC 106
  one-bedroom shared accommodation
    HB 388
  rates
    HB 390
    UC 107
  size criteria 386
  two or more bedrooms
    HB 390
    UC 106
  UC housing costs element 105
local reference rent
  see: rent officer determination related rent
local welfare assistance 861
  Discretionary Assistance Fund for Wales 861
  recourse to public funds 1562
  Scottish Welfare Fund 861
  treatment as capital
    means-tested benefits over pension age 525
    means-tested benefits under pension age 500
  treatment as income
    means-tested benefits over pension age 480
    means-tested benefits under pension age 447
lodgers
  treatment of income from 568
    means-tested benefits under pension age 442
  see also: boarders
lone parents
  availability for work
    JSA 1116, 1122
  childcare costs disregarded
    CA 567

  earnings disregard
    HB over pension age 473
    HB under pension age 430
    IS/I-JSA 430
    PC 472
  HB 206
  hospital patients 924
  I-JSA 260
  IS 235
  lone parent element
    WTC 1458
  personal allowance rates 334
  students
    HB 896
    IS 890
  work-focused interviews
    IS 1137
    UC 1066
  work-related activity sanctions
    IS 1160
  work-related requirements 1062
long lease
  excluded from HB 176
looked-after children 948
  child benefit 590
  CTC 290
  disabled child premium 341
  DLA/PIP 929
  eligibility to claim benefits 949
  excluded from benefit 948
  family premium 340
  guardian's allowance 590
  hardship payments 1229
  HB 947
  health benefits 667
  I-JSA 257, 947
  IS 947
  local authority payments
    treatment as capital 500
    treatment as income 447
    UC 147
  treatment as member of household
    means-tested benefits 328
    UC 63
  UC 947
loss of faculty 689
lottery winnings 1487
low income
  Help to Save scheme 872
  ineligible for SSP 839
  low-paid work, notional income
    UC 131
    WTC/CTC 1491
  minimum income floor
    UC 121
  NHS charges 668

lower earnings limit
NI contributions 963
SMP/SAP/SPP/SSPP/SPBP 820
SSP 839

M

maintenance
liable relative payments 438
treatment as income
means-tested benefits over pension
age 477
means-tested benefits under pension
age 438
UC 127
WTC/CTC 1489
see also: child maintenance
maintenance undertaking 1563
death of sponsor 1566
means-tested benefits 1565
non-means-tested benefits 1566
WTC/CTC 1567
managed migration
transferring to UC 30
transitional element 77
mandatory reconsideration
applying
benefits 1341
WTC/CTC 1550
benefits 1339
claiming benefits while request is
considered 1037
decisions which can be reconsidered
WTC/CTC 1548
decisions which cannot be reconsidered
WTC/CTC 1549
hardship payments 1230
late requests
benefits 1340, 1341
WTC/CTC 1550
penalties
WTC/CTC 1550
procedure
WTC/CTC 1551
revision before appeal
benefits 1303, 1339
time limits
benefits 1340
WTC/CTC 1550
who can request
WTC/CTC 1548
WTC/CTC 1548
mandatory reconsideration notice
benefits 1303, 1342
WTC/CTC 1551
market value
capital 151, 508

marriage
NI reduced liability for married women
965
void/voidable marriage 550
see also: couples
married women
reduced liability for NI contributions 965
maternity
Best Start foods in Scotland 865
Best Start grants in Scotland
pregnancy and baby payment 1696
budgeting loans 793
EEA worker and self-employed status
1612
free dental treatment 673
free prescriptions 672
Healthy Start 863
limited capability for work
ESA 1013
maternity pay and benefits 725, 810
Sure Start maternity grant 796
work-related requirements 1062
maternity allowance 725
absence abroad 1657
age rules 731
amount 732
appeals 1337
available for work rule
JSA 1119
backdating 735, 1177
benefit cap 737
calculating average earnings 732
change of circumstances 736
choosing SSPP 814
claims 733
curtailment notification 729
date of claim 734
decisions 1285
delays 1295
disqualification 730
earnings condition 727
employed earner 726
employment condition 727
entitlement to other benefits
means-tested benefits 736
non-means-tested benefits 737
WTC/CTC 736
EU co-ordination rules 1633, 1658
evidence of expected date of birth 734
failure to attend medical examination 731
fraud 1267
interchange of claims 1182
limited capability for work 737
linked periods
C-JSA 708
MA period 728
more than one job 726
NI contributions 964

NI credits 971
overlapping benefits 737, 1190
overpayments 1233
passport to other benefits 738
payment 735
period of payment 728, 729
person subject to immigration control
    1565
prisoners 938
qualifying period 729
reducing MA period early 728
residence rules 1633
revisions 1301, 1303
self-employed earner 726
spouse/civil partner self-employed 726
SSP 843
supersessions 1301, 1315
tax 736
test period 726
treated as in full-time work
    WTC 304
treatment as income 737
    means-tested benefits over pension
        age 475
    means-tested benefits under pension
        age 435
    UC 126
    WTC/CTC 1480
who can get MA 725
working 730
maternity leave
childcare costs
    HB 433
EEA workers 1608
failure to return to work
    JSA 1147
treated as in full-time work
    WTC 304
treated as not in full-time work
    HB/PC 999
    IS/JSA/ESA 999
maternity pay period
curtailment notice 814
definition 811
working during period 820
maximum amount
elements 66
standard allowance 66
UC 40, 65
maximum benefit
CTC 1452
HB 190
WTC 1457
maximum rent
local housing allowance 385
pre-Jan '96 rules 405
rent officer determination related rent 397
social sector tenants 392

meals
deductions from benefit
    HB 195
medical assessments
DLA 632
medical certificates
fitness for work 837
SSP 837, 845
medical evidence
appeals 1372, 1378
DLA 630
limited capability for work 1037
    C-ESA 659
    I-ESA 167
PIP 765
SSP 845
medical examination
AA 540
appeals 1372
DLA 632
expenses 1034
failure to attend 1201
    AA 540
    DLA 632
    MA 731
healthcare professional 1176
limited capability for work 1034
PIP 765
SSP 837
work capability assessments 1034
medical treatment
absence from home
    HB 184
child abroad
    IS/JSA/ESA 328
    JSA 1118
excluded from HB 195
housing costs
    IS/I-JSA/I-ESA/PC 373
medication
PIP 745
Member of Parliament
complaints to MP 1444
mental illness
appointees 1170
DLA care component 616
PIP 740
prisoners detained in hospital
    means-tested benefits 942
    non-means-tested benefits 942
    UC 942
recovery of overpayments
    WTC/CTC 1525
sanctions
    UC 1107
work capabilty assessment 1023

mental stress
  good reason for refusing a job
    UC 1101
mesne profits
  HB 176
migration notice 30
milk
  Best Start foods 865
  free milk for children in daycare 868
  Healthy Start food and vitamins 862
  milk tokens 449
minimum benefit
  HB 213
  JSA 720
  PC 273
minimum wage 1787
  availability for work
    JSA 1123
    UC 1059
  good reason for refusing a job
    UC 1106
misconduct
  dismissal from work
    C-JSA 717
  industrial injuries benefits 686
  sanctions 1085
    JSA under UC system 1082
    UC 1082
misrepresentation
  overpayments 1241, 1243
    HB 1257
missing persons
  presumption of death 555
mistakes
  see: errors
mobile homes
  excluded tenancies 382
  HB 176
  rent restrictions
    HB 396
    UC 84
mobility activities
  PIP 753
mobility supplement
  armed services 869
  disability premium 342
  treatment as income 436
modular courses 889
Morocco
  association and co-operation agreements
    1582
  benefit entitlement 1566
  CTC 1567
mortgage insurance policy
  treatment as income 446
mortgage interest loan 855
  amount 858
  care homes 935

challenging a decision 855
  entitlement ends 859
  hospital patients 926
  independent financial advice 855
  liability for mortgage interest payments
    857
  mortgage interest run-on 860
  moving onto UC 860
  payments 855, 859
  prisoners 946
  qualifying loans 856
  repayment 860
  who can claim 856
mortgage interest run-on 860
Motability 637
  PIP 772
moving home
  advance claims
    HB 211
    UC 91
  extended payment of HB 219
  liability for leaseholder charges before
    moving in
      HB 181
      IS/I-JSA/I-ESA/PC 370
      UC 91
  two homes
    HB 181, 186
    IS/I-JSA/I-ESA/PC 374
    UC 91
  value of home disregarded
    means-tested benefits over pension
      age 520
    means-tested benefits under pension
      age 495
    UC 142
multiple births
  SMP/SAP/SPP/SSPP/SPBP 824
  two-child limit
    CTC 1455
    IS/I-JSA/I-ESA/HB 338
    UC 68
myalgic encephalomyelitis (ME) 604
myasthenia gravis
  free prescriptions 672
myxoedema
  free prescriptions 672

N

national insurance contribution conditions
  979
  bereavement support payment 984
  C-ESA 980
  C-JSA 980
  insufficient contributions 985
  state pension 986
  widowed parent's allowance 549, 984
  working life 985

national insurance contributions 957
  aggregating contributions 1678
  appeals 960
  changes ignored
    HB 424
  class 1 962
  class 2 963
    rates 963
  class 3 964
    rates 964
  class 3A 964
  classes 961
  credited contributions 968
  decisions 960, 1292
  earnings limits 1786
  EEA nationals 965
  EU co-ordination rules 965
  insufficient contributions 985
  late payment 967
  more than one job 962
  non-payment 967
  paid before 1975 965
  person subject to immigration control
    1572
  primary threshold 963
  reduced liability 965
  residence/presence conditions 965
  voluntary contributions 964, 966
national insurance credits 968
  CA 975
  carers 972
  education 975
  family members providing childcare 974
  home responsibilities protection 973
  incapacity for work 971
  JSA 716
    I-JSA 260
  jury service 976
  limited capability for work 971
  parents 972
  service families 978
  SMP/SAP/SPP/SSPP/SPBP 976
  starting credits 975
  state pension 969
  students 900
  training 975
  UC 971
  unemployment 970
  widowers 977
  widows 977
  WTC 977
national insurance number
  NI number requirement 1171
    DLA 625
    HB 207
    WTC/CTC 1500

  person subject to immigration control
    1571
  proof of identity 1171
natural migration
  transferring to UC 27
negligence
  civil penalties 1268
  financial penalties
    WTC/CTC 1536
net profit
  self-employed earnings over pension age
    471
  self-employed earnings under pension
    age 427
New Enterprise Allowance 874, 1152
  actively seeking work 1115, 1126
  treatment as income
    WTC/CTC 1484
NHS mobility scooter
  disability premium 342
  higher pensioner premium 345
night-time attention/supervision 614, 616,
  617
non-advanced education
  child benefit 580
  CTC 286
  definition 580
  IS 237
  relevant education 885
  UC 62, 881
non-dependants
  amount of deductions
    HB 200
    IS/I-JSA/I-ESA/PC 365
    UC 103
  capital
    HB 202
  couples
    HB 201
  deductions from leaseholder payments
    IS/I-JSA/I-ESA/PC 363
    UC 102
  HB 198
  hours of work
    IS/JSA/ESA/PC/HB 992
  income
    HB 201, 202
    IS/I-JSA/I-ESA/PC 365
  loan for mortgage interest 858
  no deductions made
    HB 199
    IS/I-JSA/I-ESA/PC 364
    UC 103
  not non-dependant
    HB 199
    IS/I-JSA/I-ESA/PC 363
    UC 97
  qualifying benefits 1329

severe disability premium 348
trade disputes 1006
UC 96
North Macedonia
benefit entitlement 1565
WTC 1567
Northern Ireland 4
reciprocal agreements 1580
Norway
EEA nationals 1669
right to reside 1595
notice
to employer
SAP 812
SMP 811
SPBP 816
SPP 813
SSPP 815
notification
change of circumstances
WTC/CTC 1512
decision
HB 211
initial decision
WTC/CTC 1503
overpayment
HB 1261
WTC/CTC 1522
notional capital
deprivation of capital
means-tested benefits over pension
age 526
means-tested benefits under pension
age 503
UC 148
failure to apply for capital
means-tested benefits under pension
age 505
means-tested benefits over pension age
525
means-tested benefits under pension age
502
third-party payments
means-tested benefits under pension
age 506
UC 148
notional income
CA 567
deferring retirement pension 482
UC 132
means-tested benefits over pension age
481
means-tested benefits under pension age
449
UC 131
WTC/CTC 1491
nurseries
free milk 868

nursing care
care homes
AA/DLA/PIP 929
HB 195
nursing homes
see: care homes

O
occupational pensions
future payments 451, 498
payments treated as income
C-ESA 654
C-JSA 713
CA 564
means-tested benefits over pension
age 470, 479, 482
means-tested benefits under pension
age 423, 445
UC 128, 132
WTC/CTC 1485
treatment of contributions
CA 565
WTC/CTC 1484
office-holders 962
older claimants
higher pensioner premium 345
pension credit 271
pensioner premium 345
winter fuel payments 806
Ombudsman
complaining to 1444
HB 1446
one bedroom
self-contained accommodation
HB 389
UC 106
shared accommodation
HB 388
UC 106
single room rent 402
one-strike rule 1278
WTC 1281
online claims 1168, 1173
AA 537
bereavement benefits 553
Best Start grants 1700
budgeting loan 794
CA 570
child benefit 592
funeral support payment 1708
guardians allowance 592
housing benefit 203
JSA
C-JSA 715
I-JSA 259
Scottish child payment 1714
state pension 786

UC 44
young carer grant 1719
ordinary residence 1585
benefits affected 1585
orphans
guardian's allowance 588
I-JSA 256
in relevant education
IS 885
UC 38
overlapping benefits 1190
earnings-replacement benefits 1190
EU co-ordination rules 1680
increases for dependants 1192
non-means-tested benefits 1190
overnight care
additional bedroom
local housing allowance 387
rent officer determination related rent
400
social sector tenants 395
UC 98
HB 411
overpayments 1233, 1520
administrative penalty 1276
benefit arrears
IS/I-JSA/I-ESA/PC 1237
calculating the overpayment 1244
HB 1256
Scottish benefits 1726
causes
WTC/CTC 1521
challenging
benefits 1246
HB 1263
Scottish benefits 1726
WTC/CTC 1522
civil penalties 1268
claimant error
HB 1255
definition 1233
HB 1253
diminishing capital rule
HB 1256
IS/I-JSA/I-ESA 1244
direct credit transfer 1238
discretion to recover 1247
HB 1258
end-of-year overpayments
WTC/CTC 1521
failure to disclose material fact 1239, 1243
HB 1253
health benefits 678
in-year overpayments
WTC/CTC 1521
interest charges 1244
HB 1256
WTC/CTC 1530

late receipt of other income 1237
misrepresentation 1241, 1243
mortgage interest payments 1237
notification
HB 1261
WTC/CTC 1522
official error
HB 1253
WTC/CTC 1523
payments on account
HB 221
prosecution or administrative penalty
1276
recoverable overpayments 1234, 1238
HB 1253
Scottish benefits 1725
reducing the overpayment
HB 1256
UC system 1235
WTC/CTC 1524
Scottish benefits 1725
SMP/SAP/SPP/SSPP/SPBP 828
SSP 846
treatment as income
means-tested benefits under pension
age 438
UC 126
see also: recovery of overpayments
overseas assets
means-tested benefits under pension age
510
UC 153
WTC/CTC 1488
overtime pay
treatment as earnings
UC 117
WTC/CTC 1481
owner-occupiers
amount of leaseholder/service charges
IS/I-JSA/I-ESA/PC 362
leaseholder charges
IS/I-JSA/I/ESA/PC 359, 360
UC 110
leaseholder service charges paid after
return to work
IS/I-JSA/I-ESA/PC 376
leaseholder service charges waiting
period
IS/I-JSA/I-ESA/PC 368
UC 111
liabilty for leaseholder/service charges
369
linking rules for leaseholder/service
charges
IS/I-JSA/I-ESA/PC 375
loan for mortgage interest 855
service charges
IS/I-JSA/I-ESA/PC 361

UC 86, 110
who can get help with leaseholder/service
charges 360

P
parental bereavement leave
availability for work
JSA 1119
childcare costs
HB 433
IS 237
treated as in full-time work
WTC 304
treated as not in full-time work
HB/PC 999
IS/JSA/ESA 999
parental bereavement pay period
working during period 820
parental contribution 901, 904
HB over pension age 481
HB under pension age 449
parental leave
IS 235
parental order
Sure Start maternity grant 797
parents
16/17-year-olds unsupported by parents
I-JSA 256
severe hardship payments 257
UC 38
guardian's allowance 589
in relevant education
IS 885
missing parents
guardian's allowance 588
NI credits 972
work allowance
UC 41
work-focused interview requirement 1066
work-related requirements 1062
see also: step-parents
**Parliamentary and Health Service
Ombudsman** 1445
part-time students
available for work 891
ESA 895
HB 898
IS 891
JSA 891
restricted availability for work 892
UC 882
part-time work
available for work rule
JSA 1115, 1117
partially sighted
free sight tests 674

passported benefits
AA 543
bereavement benefits 559
CA 576
child benefit 599
CTC 296
DLA 637
ESA
C-ESA 663
I-ESA 170
guardian's allowance 599
hardship payments 1231
HB 225
industrial injuries benefits 701
IS 248
JSA
C-JSA 722
I-JSA 268
maternity benefits 738
PC 282
PIP 772
Scottish child payment 1716
state pension 790
UC 55
WTC 314
young carer grant 1722
past presence requirement 1583
benefits affected 1583
paternity leave
availability for work
JSA 1119
childcare costs
HB 433
IS 235
treated as in full-time work
WTC 304
treated as not in full-time work
HB/PC 999
IS/JSA/ESA 999
paternity pay period
definition 813
working during period 820
pay in lieu of notice
treatment as income
CA 565
means-tested benefits over pension
age 469
means-tested benefits under pension
age 422
UC 118
WTC/CTC 1482
payment in kind 993
treatment as income
means-tested benefits over pension
age 469
means-tested benefits under pension
age 422

payment of benefit 1186
AA 540
abroad 1645
advance payments 1192
alternative payment arrangements
UC 50
bereavement benefits 556
Best Start grants 1701
budgeting loans 794
CA 573
cheques 1188
child benefit 595
cold weather payments 806
compensation payments 1439
CTC 294
delays in payment
HB 220
direct credit transfer 1187
DLA 632
emergencies 1189
ESA
C-ESA 661
I-ESA 168
funeral expenses payments 804
funeral support payments 1709
guardian's allowance 595
hardship payments 1230
HB 213
housing costs element 49
in advance/arrears
HB 213
IS 245
industrial injuries benefits 699
IS 245
JSA
C-JSA 720
I-JSA 265
lost payments 1189
HB 214
MA 735
missing payments 1189
HB 214
overlapping benefit rules 1190
payment exception service 1188
payment service card 1188
payment to other people 1187
payment vouchers 1189, 1505
payments on account
HB 220
PC 279
PIP 768
post office accounts 1187, 1505
Scottish benefits 1725
Scottish child payment 1715
SMP/SAP/SPP/SSPP/SPBP 827
SSP 846
state pension 789
students
HB 899
suspension of payment 1200
to appointee
HB 214
to landlord
HB 214, 215
UC 49
UC 49
vouchers 1188
when benefit is paid 1189
winter fuel payments 808
WTC 311
WTC/CTC 1504
young carer grant 1720
penalties 1267, 1535
administrative penalties
benefits 1275
challenging
benefits 1268
WTC/CTC 1538
civil penalties
benefits 1268
WTC/CTC 1535
consequences of paying a penalty
benefits 1277
failure to comply
WTC/CTC 1537
financial penalties
WTC/CTC 1535
fraud offences
benefits 1275
WTC/CTC 1535, 1540
incorrect statements
WTC/CTC 1536
interest applied
WTC/CTC 1538
mandatory reconsideration
WTC/CTC 1550
prosecution or penalty
benefits 1276
WTC/CTC 1539
recovery
WTC/CTC 1538
pension age 779
bereavement support payment 546
council tax reduction scheme 852
free prescriptions 672
free sight tests 674
future changes 780
NI contributions 961
pension-age HB 188
proof of age 787
widowed parent's allowance 548
pension credit 270
absence abroad 1659
additional amounts 273
advance claims 279
age rules 271

amount 273
appeals 1337
appropriate minimum guarantee 273
assessed income period 281
backdating 278, 1177
benefit cap 282
benefit week 484
calculation
    guarantee credit 275
capital 516
capital limits 517
care homes 933
carer addition 273, 350
change of circumstances 280
    HB 222
children 323
claims 277
continuing payments
    HB 217
council tax reduction scheme 852
couples 272, 319
decisions 1285
deductions from benefit 1203
delays 1295
disregarded earnings 471
entitlement to other benefits
    means-tested benefits 282
    non-means-tested benefits 282
EU co-ordination rules 1660
families 317
fraud 1267
full-time work 991
guarantee credit 271, 273
habitual residence test 1586
HB 282
hospital patients 922, 923
income 466, 467
    savings credit 276
leaseholder charges 359
maximum deductions 1208
maximum savings credit 276
mixed-age couples 272
mortgage interest loan 855
NHS charges, exemption 667
overpayments 1233
partner subject to immigration control
    1569
passported benefits 282
payment 279
person subject to immigration control
    1564
prisoners 941
public funds 1562
residence rules 1592, 1625
retirement provision 281
revisions 1301, 1303
    following award of qualifying benefit
    1328

sanctions for benefit offences 1280
savings credit 271, 276
    threshold 276
severe disability addition 273, 346
standard minimum guarantee 273
supersessions 1301, 1315
tax 281
trade disputes 1006
transitional amount 274
treatment as income
    WTC/CTC 1480
    UC 26
who can get PC 271
who should claim 277
Pension Protection Fund
    treatment as income
        C-ESA 655
        means-tested benefits 479
        PC 281
        UC 128
pensioner premium 345
    qualifying benefits 345
    rate 352
period of cold weather 805
period of incapacity
    SSP 838
period of limited capability for work 1041
period of study 902
permanent right of residence 1621
    family members 1623
    permanently incapacitated people 1624
    residence documents 1600
    retired people 1624
permitted period
    actively seeking work 1125
    available for work 1121
permitted work
    earnings limit
        HB 431, 472
        I-ESA 429
    supported work 1043
    treated as not in paid work
        ESA 999
    working hours
        ESA 1043
    working with limited capability for work
        1043
person subject to immigration control
    appropriate minimum guarantee
        PC 274
    benefit entitlement 1564
        means-tested benefits 1565
        non-means-tested benefits 1566
        WTC/CTC 1567
    children 1568
    definition 1560
    maintenance undertaking 1563
    NI contributions 1572

NI number 1571
partners 1568
  HB 1570
  IS/I-JSA/I-ESA 1569
  non-means-tested benefits 1570
  PC 1569
  UC 1568
  WTC/CTC 1571
recourse to public funds 1562
personal allowances 333
16/17-year-olds 334
children 337
hardship payments 1224
health benefits 670
rates 334
personal independence payment 739
absence abroad 1649
age rules 760
amount of benefit 761
appeals 1337
assessment 764
backdating 1177
benefit cap 771
care homes 928
change of circumstances 769
claims 762
components 740
consultation 765
daily living activities 741
daily living component 740, 761
date of claim 767
descriptors 740
disability conditions 740
disability premium 341
disabled child premium 341
enhanced daily living component 344
  IS 235
entitlement to other benefits
  means-tested benefits 770
  non-means-tested benefits 771
  WTC/CTC 770
EU co-ordination rules 1630, 1650
fluctuating conditions 757
fraud 1267
habitual residence test 1586
higher pensioner premium 345
hospital patients 919
housing costs contribution
  UC 103
information to support claim 763
interchange of claims 1182
length of awards 768
managing an activity 756
mobility activities 753
mobility component 740, 761
  upper age limit 760
Motability 772
negative determination 766

no non-dependant deduction 199
overlapping benefits 771, 1190
overpayments 1233
passported benefits 772
payment 768
person subject to immigration control
  1564
physical or mental condition 740
prisoners 938
public funds 1562
questionnaire 764
renewing a claim 769
required period condition 759
residence rules 1629
revisions 1302
severe disability premium 347
supersessions 1302, 1318
tax 770
terminal illness 762, 763
transfers from DLA 617
treatment as income 770
  means-tested benefits over pension
    age 475
  means-tested benefits under pension
    age 436
  UC 127
  WTC/CTC 1480
who can get PIP 740
personal injuries
definition 500
definition for industrial injuries benefits
  683
personal injury payments
recovery of benefits from compensation
  1212
special compensation schemes
  means-tested benefits over pension
    age 524
  means-tested benefits under pension
    age 500
  UC 129, 146
treatment as capital
  means-tested benefits over pension
    age 524
  means-tested benefits under pension
    age 499
  UC 146
treatment as income
  means-tested benefits over pension
    age 478
  means-tested benefits under pension
    age 441, 444
  UC 128
personal pensions
future payments 498
payments treated as income
  C-ESA 654
  C-JSA 713

means-tested benefits over pension
age 479, 482
means-tested benefits under pension
age 445
UC 128, 132
WTC/CTC 1485
treatment as capital
means-tested benefits under pension
age 497
UC 145
treatment of contributions
CA 565
WTC/CTC 1484, 1485
treatment of premiums
means-tested benefits over pension
age 471
means-tested benefits under pension
age 427
personal possessions
treatment as capital
means-tested benefits over pension
age 521
means-tested benefits under pension
age 496
UC 144
physical stress
good reason for refusing a job
UC 1101
planning and undertaking a journey
PIP 754
plasmapheresis
limited capability for work
ESA 1013
UC 1012
pneumoconiosis 688, 692, 694, 701
Poland 1601
polygamous marriages
bereavement benefits 551
means-tested benefits 320
non-dependants
HB 201
personal allowances 333
UC 37, 58
WTC/CTC 1497
post office
forgotten PIN numbers 1188
lost account cards 1188
payment of benefits 1187, 1505
postal signers
JSA 1132
power of attorney
HB 206
recovery of overpayments 1246
powers to enter
investigating claims 1270
pre-settled status for EEA nationals 1597
benefit entitlement 1599
evidence of status 1598

pre-tenancy determination 403
precedents 1383
pregnancy
16/17-year-olds
UC 38
Best Start foods in Scotland 865
Best Start grants in Scotland
pregnancy and baby payment 1696
claiming health benefits 676
dismissal
SMP 823
EEA worker and self-employed status
1612
expected week of childbirth 726
free dental treatment 673
free presciptions 672
free vitamins 865
hardship payments 1228
Healthy Start food and vitamin vouchers
862
IS 235
limited capability for work 737
ESA 1013
UC 1012
limited capability for work-related activity
1031
MA 725
maternity pay and benefits 725, 810
pregnancy-related illness 830
sickness during maternity pay period 843
SMP 811
Sure Start maternity grant 796
time out from studying
means-tested benefits 910
work-related requirements 1062
pregnancy and baby payment in Scotland
1696
amount 1699
premiums 339
backdating 352
carer premium 350
definition 339
disability premium 341
disabled child premium 341
enhanced disability premium 343
family premium 340
hardship payment rate 1224
health benefits 670
higher pensioner premium 345
hospital patients 924
pensioner premium 345
rates 351
severe disability premium 346
prescribed amount of earnings
C-JSA 712
prescribed degrees of disablement 689
prescribed industrial diseases 687
causation 688

prescribed occupations 687
prescriptions 672
  free 672
  pre-payment certificates 673
presence 1579
  benefits affected by presence conditions 1580
  definition 1583, 1646
  past presence 1583
  tests 1583
prisoners 937
  appropriate minimum guarantee
    PC 274
  available for work rule
    JSA 1119
  child benefit 939
  child in custody
    child benefit 587, 590, 939
    CTC 290, 942
    guardian's allowance 590
    means-tested benefits 328, 942
    UC 940
  childcare costs allowance
    HB 432
  costs for usual home 945
    HB 946
    IS/I-JSA/I-ESA/PC 373, 946
    UC 940, 945
  definition
    means-tested benefits 941
    non-means-tested benefits 937
    UC 940
  discharge grant treated as capital
    IS/I-JSA/I-ESA 493
  ESA
    C-ESA 938
    I-ESA 941
  free dental treatment 673
  free prescriptions 672
  guardian's allowance 588, 939
  HB 941, 946
  home detention curfew
    HB 946
    means-tested benefits 941
  hospital patients
    means-tested benefits 942
    non-means-tested benefits 942
    UC 942
  IIDB 939
  IS 237, 941
  JSA
    C-JSA 938
    I-JSA 941
  MA 938
  mortgage interest loan 946
  non-dependant deductions
    HB 200
    IS/I-JSA/I-ESA/PC 365

    UC 103
  non-means-tested benefits 937
  partner in custody
    IS/I-JSA/I-ESA/PC 942
    UC 940
    WTC 1458
  PC 941
  PIP 938
  quashed conviction
    arrears of benefits 939
    NI credits 978
  released from prison 944
  remand prisoners 184, 939
  social fund 942
  SSP/SMP/SAP/SPP/SSPP/SPBP 937
  suspended benefits 939
  temporary release 181, 944, 946
    HB 184
    JSA 1119
    UC 92
  UC 940, 945
  visits 449, 945, 1490
  winter fuel payments 807
  work search requirement 1073
  WTC 306
  see also: youth custody
private car allowance
  higher pensioner premium 345
private tenants
  contrived tenancies
    HB 180
    UC 90
  local housing allowance 384
  maximum number of bedrooms
    UC 98
  rent restrictions
    HB 383
    UC 105
  size criteria
    local housing allowance 386
  UC housing costs element 103
probation
  hostels
    HB 181, 382, 944
  housing costs
    IS/I-JSA/I-ESA/PC 944
  means-tested benefits 941, 943
  non-means-tested benefits 937
  UC 944
professional and career development loans
  treatment as income
    means-tested benefits under pension age 444
    WTC/CTC 1485
prompting
  PIP assessments 741

proof of age 787
proof of identity
  acceptable documents 1172
  NI number required 1171
property
  future interest
    means-tested benefits under pension
    age 498
    means-tested benefits over pension age
    518
    means-tested benefits under pension age
    491
    UC 139
    WTC/CTC 1487
proprietary estoppel 140, 491
prosecution
  fraud offences
    benefits 1273
    WTC/CTC 1539
  prosecution or penalty
    benefits 1276
    WTC/CTC 1539
Public Lending Right scheme 428, 470, 479
Public Services Ombudsman for Wales 1446

Q
qualifying benefits 1180
  award of benefit 1328
  backdating claims 1180, 1329
  Best Start grants 1696
  budgeting loans 792
  CA 572
  cold weather payments 805
  disability premium 341
  disabled worker element 1459
  free school lunches 866
  funeral expenses payments 798
  funeral support payment in Scotland 1704
  HB 211
  NI credits for carers and parents 973
  pensioner premiums 345
  revision due to award of qualifying
    benefit 1309, 1328
  Scottish child payment 1713
  supersession due to award of qualifying
    benefit 1319, 1325, 1328
  Sure Start maternity grant 796
qualifying days
  SSP 840
qualifying parent or carer
  additional bedroom
    HB 411
qualifying young person
  child benefit 579
  CTC 286
  guardian's allowance 587
  relevant education 885

UC 880
widowed parent's allowance 547

R
rape
  two-child limit
    CTC 1455
    IS/I-JSA/I-ESA/HB 338
    UC 68
rapid reclaim
  HB 203
reading
  PIP 751
reciprocal agreements 1582
  bereavement benefits 1628
  C-ESA 1631
  C-JSA 1633
  N. Ireland 1580
  state pension 1634, 1661
recourse to public funds 1562
  asylum seekers 1573
  definition of public funds 1562
recovery of benefits
  budgeting advances 51
  budgeting loans 795
  from compensation payments 1212
  funeral expenses payment from estate
    804
  hardship payments
    UC 1221
  short-term advances 1194
recovery of overpayments 1247
  challenging
    WTC/CTC 1522
  common law 1252
  deductions from benefits 1250
    HB 1258
    Scottish benefits 1726
    UC system 1248
    WTC/CTC 1208, 1528
  deductions from earnings 1251
    HB 1260
    UC system 1250
  direct payments to HMRC 1529
  discretion to recover 1247
    HB 1253
  from whom can overpayments be
    recovered 1245
    HB 1257
    UC system 1236
    WTC/CTC 1527
  maximum deductions from benefit 1251
    HB 1259
    UC 1248
  methods of recovery 1250
    HB 1257
    UC system 1248
    WTC/CTC 1528

notification
  HB 1261
official error
  WTC/CTC 1523
offsetting
  HB 1256
  UC system 1235
  WTC/CTC 1524
recoverable overpayments 1234, 1238
  HB 1253
  Scottish benefits 1725
recovery through the courts 1252
  HB 1260
  UC system 1250
  WTC/CTC 1530
Scottish benefits 1726
WTC/CTC 1526
redeterminations 1731
  before appeal 1734
  how to request redetermination 1731
  late request 1732
  time limits
    to carry out redetermination 1733
    to request redetermination 1732
  when redetermination cannot be made
    1731
  who can request redetermination 1731
reduced earnings allowance 695
  amount 696
  overlapping benefits 1190
  prisoners 938
  who can get REA 695
**reduced liability for national insurance
  contributions** 965
reductions in benefit
  hardship payments
    JSA 1224
  sanctions 1158
    ESA 1157
    ESA under UC system 1090
    JSA 1155
    JSA under UC system 1092
    UC 1089
  widowed parent's allowance 549
redundancy
  failure to accept alternative work
    JSA 1147
  sanctions
    JSA under UC system 1083
    UC 1083
  treatment as earnings
    CA 565
    means-tested benefits over pension
      age 470
    means-tested benefits under pension
      age 426
    UC 118
    WTC/CTC 1482

refugees
  backdated benefit payments 1574
  benefit entitlement 1573
  family reunion 1574
  habitual residence test 1589
  integration loans 1208, 1575
  IS 238, 1574
  studying English
    IS 890
  UC 1574
refunds
  health benefits 678
refusal of job offer
  available for work rule
    JSA 1122
  good reason
    UC 1105
  sanctions
    JSA 1146
    JSA under UC system 1081
    UC 1081
regulated tenancy 382
regulations 1380
relative
  childcare
    WTC 1463
  disregard of relative's home
    means-tested benefits over pension
      age 521
    means-tested benefits under pension
      age 496
    UC 143
  see also: families
relevant education 885
  child benefit 579
  definition 885
  HB 896, 898
  IS 237, 885
  JSA 886
  leaving relevant education
    IS/JSA 887
  responsible for young person 887
relevant period
  WTC/CTC 1452
religion
  religious objections to job
    JSA 1122
    UC 1101
religious orders
  HB 178
  PC 274
remand
  housing costs
    HB 184
    IS/I-ESA/PC 373
  IS 237
  non-means-tested benefits 939

remarriage
bereavement support payment 547
widowed parent's allowance 549
removal of spare room subsidy 392
remunerative work
benefits 991
WTC 299
renewing a claim
AA 539
CTC 294
industrial injuries benefits 699
WTC/CTC 311, 1502
rent
advance payments
budgeting loans 793
apportionment
HB 192
cap rent
local housing allowance 385
UC housing costs element 105
changes in rent
HB 224
core rent 104
eligible rent
HB 191
UC 84
ineligible charges
HB 193
UC 84
liability to pay rent
HB 177
UC 87
non-commercial agreements
HB 178
UC 87
payments treated as rent
HB 175
rent officer determination related rent 396
service charges excluded from
HB 195
single room rent 402
size criteria
local housing allowance 386
pre-Jan '96 rules 406
rent officer determination related rent
400
social sector tenants 394
UC 97
treatment of rental income
means-tested benefits over pension
age 477
means-tested benefits under pension
age 442
UC 131
WTC/CTC 1487
UC housing costs element 94
unreasonably high rent
pre-Jan '96 rules 406

rent allowance 214
rent arrears
discretionary housing payments 642
payment direct to landlord
HB 215
payments excluded from HB 191
recovery of overpayments
HB 1260, 1262
repaid by deductions from benefit 1205
rent direct
HB 215
rent increases
pre-Jan '96 rules 408
rent officer determination related rent 396
broad rental market area 402
challenging a rent restriction 413
claim-related rent 399
exceptionally high rent determination 400
excluded tenancies 382
local reference rent 402
maximum rent 397
occupiers 401
pre-April '08 rules 397
pre-tenancy determinations 403
rent officer determinations 398
service charges 402
significantly high rent determination 399
size criteria 400
size-related determination 400
rent officers
rent officer determination related rent 398
rent rebate
HB 214
rent restrictions 103, 381
cap rent
HB 385
UC housing costs element 105
challenging a rent restriction 413
delaying a rent restriction
HB 412
discretionary housing payments 641
discretionary reductions
HB 384
excluded tenancies
HB 382
exempt accommodation pre-Jan '96 rules
403
exempt claimants pre-Jan '96 rules 404
housing association tenants
HB 383
UC 107
local housing allowance 384
local reference rent 396
mixed age couples
HB 392
pre-Jan '96 rules 403
private tenants
HB 383

UC 105
revisions 1311
size criteria
    local housing allowance 386
    pre-Jan '96 rules 406
    rent officer determination related rent
        400
    social sector tenants 394
    UC 97
social sector tenants
    HB 384, 391
    UC 107
suitable alternative accommodation
    pre-Jan '96 rules 407
supersessions 1319
transitional protection 413
unreasonably high rent
    pre-Jan '96 rules 406
which HB restrictions apply 382

rent-free period
HB 178, 192
UC 95

rental income
treatment as income
    means-tested benefits over pension
        age 477
    means-tested benefits under pension
        age 442
    UC 131

rental purchase
HB 176

rentcharge payments
IS/I-JSA/I-ESA/PC 360

repairs
help with repairs 872
interest on loans
    IS/I-JSA/I-ESA/PC 857
service charges for leaseholders 361
two homes during repair work
    HB 187
    IS/I-JSA/I-ESA/PC 372
    UC 93
waiver of housing costs during repair
    work
    HB 178

representation
First-tier Tribunal appeals 1369
Upper Tribunal appeals 1405

reserve forces
payments treated as capital
    means-tested benefits under pension
        age 493
payments treated as income
    means-tested benefits over pension
        age 472
    means-tested benefits under pension
        age 423, 430

residence 1579
A2/A8 nationals 1601
benefits affected by residence conditions
    1580
Brexit 1596
continuous residence 1622
Croatia 1601
definition 1585
documents 1600
EEA jobseekers 1605
EEA nationals 1595
EEA self-employed people 1608
EEA self-sufficient people 1613
EEA students 1614
EEA workers 1607
EU nationals 1625
family members
    EEA nationals 1614
free movement rights 1595, 1599
habitual residence 1586
initial right of residence 1605
living in for three months 1584
NI contributions 965
ordinary residence 1585, 1646
permanent residence 1621
presence 1583, 1646
registration certificate 1600
resided legally 1622
residence card 1600
right to reside 1591
settled status for EU citizens 1597
tests 1583
see also: habitual residence

residential care
see also: care homes

respite care
temporary care home resident 185
treated as not in full-time work
    IS/JSA/ESA 998
    WTC 306

responsibility for a child
Best Start grants 1698
child benefit 583
CTC 288
hardship payments 1228
I-JSA 258
main responsibility
    CTC 288
means-tested benefits 326
NI credits 972
Scottish child payment 1712
student couples
    HB 896
    IS 890
    JSA 890
    UC 881
UC 63, 1063
WTC 308

young person in relevant education
ESA 895
IS/I-JSA 887
retainer fee
treatment as earnings
CA 564, 565
means-tested benefits over pension
age 469
means-tested benefits under pension
age 422
retirement
EEA workers' rights 1624
sanctions for voluntary unemployment
JSA under UC system 1086
UC 1086
retirement allowance 696
overlapping benefits 1190
prisoners 938
retirement pensions
see: state pensions
retirement provision 281
reviews
claimant commitment 1050
discretionary housing payments 645
First-tier Tribunal decisions
Scottish benefits 1741
PIP 769
SSP/SMP/SAP/SPP/SSPP/SPBP 1431
Upper Tribunal decisions
Scottish benefits 1746
WTC/CTC 1548
revisions 1300, 1542
after appeal made 1310, 1356, 1374
anti-test case rule 1330
any grounds revision 1303
any time revision 1307
applying
benefits 1312
WTC/CTC 1547
arrears following revision 1314
before appeal 1303, 1339
challenging 1314
date revision takes effect 1314
factual error 1310
final decisions
WTC/CTC 1545
fraud or negligence
WTC/CTC 1546
grounds for revision
WTC/CTC 1544
information required for a revision 1313
initial decisions
WTC/CTC 1543
mandatory reconsideration 1303, 1339
official error
benefits 1307
WTC/CTC 1545, 1546
overpayments

HB 1263
qualifying benefit awarded 1309, 1328
revision on discovery
WTC/CTC 1546
revision on enquiry
WTC/CTC 1545
risks 1302
sanction decision 1308
specific grounds revision 1307
time limits
benefits 1304, 1306
when to seek a revision 1301, 1303
right to reside
benefits affected 1591
Brexit 1596
British citizens 1594
carer of child in education 1619
Commonwealth citizens 1594
derivative rights 1619
EEA jobseekers 1605
EEA nationals 1595
EEA self-employed people 1608
EEA self-sufficient people 1613
EEA students 1614
EEA workers 1607
family members
EEA nationals 1614, 1617
free movement rights 1595, 1599
Irish citizens 1594
leave to enter or remain 1594
means-tested benefits 1592
permanent right of residence 1621
qualified person 1599
resided legally 1622
who has a right to reside 1594
road tax
exemptions
DLA 637
PIP 772
Romania 1601
rough sleepers 951

S
salary sacrifice arrangements
treatment as income
WTC/CTC 1482, 1483
San Marino
association and co-operation agreements
1582
benefit entitlement 1566
CTC 1567
sanctionable benefits 1279
sanctions 1078, 1144
actively seeking work
JSA 1149
attending interview
JSA 1150
available for work

JSA 1149
avoiding sanctions
    UC system 1079
benefit offences 1278, 1279
benefit reductions 1088
    ESA 1157
    ESA under UC system 1090
    JSA 1155
    JSA under UC system 1092
    UC 1089
benefits which can be sanctioned 1279
challenging a decision
    IS/JSA/ESA 1161
    UC 1108
decisions
    IS/JSA/ESA 1161
    UC 1106
discretionary housing payments 643
employment programmes
    ESA under UC system 1087
    JSA 1150
    JSA under UC system 1087
    UC 1087
end of JSA claim before sanction ends
    1156
ESA 1156
good reason
    JSA 1155
    UC 1100
hardship payments
    ESA 1225
    JSA 1224
    UC 1220
high level
    JSA 1146
    JSA under UC system 1081, 1094
    UC 1081, 1094
intermediate level
    JSA 1149
IS 1156
jobseeker's direction 1153
JSA 1145
length of sanction period 1093
    benefit offences 1280
    ESA 1158
    JSA 1147, 1149, 1154
    JSA under UC system 1094
    UC 1094
    work availability sanctions 1095
    work preparation sanctions 1096
    work-focused interview sanctions
        1158
    work-related activity sanctions 1160
low level
    ESA under UC system 1087, 1096
    JSA 1150
    JSA under UC system 1087, 1096
    UC 1087, 1096

lowest level 1088, 1098
medium level 1087, 1095
misconduct at work
    JSA under UC system 1082
    UC 1082
more than one sanction at once
    JSA 1155
    UC system 1099
moving to another benefit 1092
neglecting to avail yourself of a job
    JSA 1147
NI credits 970
reduced sanction periods
    JSA 1148
    JSA under UC system 1095
    UC 1095
refusing to take up job
    JSA 1146
    JSA under UC system 1081
    UC 1081
revisions 1308
sanction period 1099
termination of sanctions 1100
training schemes
    ESA under UC system 1087
    JSA 1150
    JSA under UC system 1087
    UC 1087
voluntary unemployment
    JSA under UC system 1082
    UC 1082
vulnerable people 1107
work-focused interview
    ESA under UC system 1087, 1088
    IS/JSA/ESA/IB 1157
    JSA under UC system 1087
    UC 1087, 1088
work-related activity 1160
work-related requirements 1079
zero-hour contracts
    JSA 1147
    UC 1082
sanctuary scheme
    HB 388
    UC 100
sandwich courses 888
savings
    Help to Save scheme 872
    means-tested benefits over pension age
        518
    means-tested benefits under pension age
        490
    UC 139
school holidays
    calculating hours of work
        means-tested benefits 995
        WTC 303

school leavers
child benefit 579
NI starting credits 975
school lunches
free school lunches 866
school transport 867
school uniform
grants for school clothes 867
school-age payment in Scotland 1697
amount 1699
Scotland 4
Scottish benefits 1688
appeals 1734
claims 1723
complaints 1728
determinations 1724
fraud 1726
future changes 1689
new determinations without claim 1750
overpayments 1725
payment 1725
redeterminations 1731
right to support 1725
Scottish child payment 1711
age rules 1713
amount 1714
appeals 1734
benefit cap 1716
change of circumstances 1715
claims 1714
date of claim 1714
entitlement to other benefits and tax
credits 1716
following award of qualifying benefit
1714, 1751
fraud 1726
new determinations 1752
overpayments 1725
passport to other benefits 1716
payment 1715
qualifying benefits 1713
redeterminations 1731
responsibility for a child 1712
tax 1715
treatment as income 1716
who can get a Scottish child payment
1712
Scottish Public Services Ombudsman 1446,
1728
Scottish social security system 1685
benefits not under Scottish system 1692
benefits under Scottish system 1688
future changes 1689
overview 1688
Scottish Welfare Fund 861
family reunion crisis grants 1574
second adult rebate
council tax reduction schemes 851

Second World War
treatment of compensation payments
means-tested benefits over pension
age 476, 524
means-tested benefits under pension
age 437, 500
UC 129, 147
WTC/CTC 1487
sector-based work academy 1152
self-contained accommodation
local housing allowance
HB 389
UC 106
self-employed EEA nationals 1608
A2 nationals 1608
A8 nationals 1608
Croatian nationals 1608
gaps between jobs 1613
pregnancy 1612
registered as a jobseeker 1609
retaining self-employed status 1609
sickness or injury 1612
unemployed 1609
self-employment
actively seeking work 1126
business assets
means-tested benefits over pension
age 521
means-tested benefits under pension
age 493, 497
UC 144
calculation of weekly earnings
means-tested benefits over pension
age 471
means-tested benefits under pension
age 428
UC 118
class 2 NI contributions 963
class 4 NI contributions 961
definition of self-employed earner
NI contributions 962
WTC 301
disregarded earnings
CA 567
means-tested benefits over pension
age 471
means-tested benefits under pension
age 429
earnings
CA 566
MA 728
means-tested benefits over pension
age 471
means-tested benefits under pension
age 427
UC 118
WTC/CTC 1484
EEA nationals 1608

full-time work 999
gainful self-employment
  UC 123
industrial injuries benefits 682
minimum income floor
  UC 121
proof of earnings
  UC 119
small profits exception 963
sole traders
  means-tested benefits over pension
    age 526
  means-tested benefits under pension
    age 507
  UC 150
start-up period
  UC 123
work expenses
  means-tested benefits under pension
    age 427
  UC 119
  WTC 300, 1478
self-sufficient people
  EEA nationals 1613
separation
  bereavement benefits 550
  child benefit 585
  continuing to live under the same roof
    means-tested benefits 329
    UC 60
  house sale, proceeds
    means-tested benefits over pension
      age 520
    means-tested benefits under pension
      age 494, 509
    UC 142, 152
  means-tested benefits 322
  renting former joint home from ex-
    partner
    HB 179
  right to reside after separation from EEA
    national 1617
  UC 60
  WTC/CTC 1497
service charges
  apportionment of ineligible service
    charges
    HB 192
  discretionary housing payments 642
  eligible service charges
    HB 194
    IS/I-JSA/I-ESA/PC 361
    UC 85
  HB 194
  ineligible service charges
    HB 193
    IS/I-JSA/I-ESA/PC 361
    UC 85

leaseholders
  IS/I-JSA/I-ESA/PC 361
  non-dependant deductions 363
owner-occupiers
  IS/I-JSA/I-ESA/PC 361
  UC 86, 110
rent officer determination related rent 402
supported accommodation 196
UC 85
settled status for EEA nationals 1597
  benefit entitlement 1599
  evidence of status 1598
severe disability premium 346
  carer claiming CA 575
  claiming UC 23, 29
  non-dependants 348
  qualifying benefits 347
  rate 351
  transferred to UC before Jan 2019 29
severe disablement allowance 648
  absence abroad 1657
  disability premium 342
  EU co-ordination rules 1658
  overlapping benefits 1190
  prisoners 938
  residence rules 1629
  transfers to ESA 655
  treatment as income
    means-tested benefits over pension
      age 475
    means-tested benefits under pension
      age 435
    WTC/CTC 1480
severe hardship direction
  hardship payments 1229
severe hardship payments
  16/17-year-olds 257
  NI credits 970
severe mental impairment
  DLA care component 611
  DLA mobility component 607
sexual relationship
  proof of cohabitation
    means-tested benefits 321
    UC 58
sexually transmitted disease
  free prescriptions 672
share fishermen 567, 964
shared accommodation
  apportionment of rent
    HB 192
  HB 192
  local housing allowance
    HB 388
    UC 106
  with landlord
    HB 178
    UC 89

shared ownership schemes
HB 176, 382
UC 83, 110
shared parental leave
availability for work
JSA 1119
childcare costs
HB 433
treated as in full-time work
WTC 304
treated as not in full-time work
HB/PC 999
IS/I-JSA/I-ESA 999
shared parental pay period
definition 815
working during period 820
shares
treatment as capital
means-tested benefits over pension
age 518
means-tested benefits under pension
age 490, 493
UC 139, 141
valuation
means-tested benefits under pension
age 510
UC 153
short-term advances 1192, 1295
sick leave
EEA workers 1608
treated as not in full-time work
HB/PC 999
IS/JSA/ESA 999
sick pay
payment 846
treatment as earnings
CA 564, 565
means-tested benefits over pension
age 469
means-tested benefits under pension
age 422
UC 117
WTC/CTC 1481
see also: statutory sick pay
sickness
armed forces, payments to former
members 868
available for work rule
JSA 1119
childcare costs disregarded
HB 434
continuous employment
SMP/SAP/SPP/SSPP/SPBP 818
disability premium 341
EEA worker and self-employed status
1612
ESA 157
financial help with costs of sickness 873

good cause for late claim
HB 210
hardship payments 1228
health benefits 666
higher pensioner premium 345
IS 235
limited capability for work 1010
short periods of sickness
C-JSA 708
SSP 836
time out from studying
means-tested benefits 910
work search requirement 1069
work-related requirements 1064
sight tests 673
free sight tests 673
reduced-cost treatment 669
signing on 1131
by post
JSA 1132
EEA nationals 1609
failure to sign on
JSA 1133
frequency 1132
NI credits 970
returning from holiday 1127
travel expenses 1131
single room rent
local housing allowance
HB 388
UC 106
rent officer determination related rent 402
size criteria
local housing allowance 386
occupiers, definition
local housing allowance 386
rent officer determination related rent
401
social sector tenants 394
pre-Jan '96 rules 406
rent officer determination related rent 400
social sector tenants 394
temporary absence of family member
UC 100
UC housing costs element 97
Skills Conditionality 1152
Slovakia 1601
Slovenia 1601
association and co-operation agreements
1582
social care payments
treatment as capital 500
UC 147
treatment as income 447
social fund 792
benefit cap 808
budgeting loans 792
children's funeral fund payment 799

cold weather payments 805
entitlement to other benefits and tax
  credits 808
funeral expenses payments 798
person subject to immigration control
  1566
prisoners 942
public funds 1562
Sure Start maternity grant 796
tax 808
trade disputes 1005
treatment as capital
  UC 146
treatment as income
  means-tested benefits over pension
    age 475
  means-tested benefits under pension
    age 436
  UC 127
  WTC/CTC 1480
winter fuel payments 806
see also: local welfare assistance
social sector tenants
bedroom tax
  HB 391
  UC 107
joint liability
  HB 393
  UC 109
maximum rent 392
occupiers 394
overnight care required 395
rent restrictions
  HB 384, 391
  UC 107
service charges
  UC 86
size criteria 394
sole liability 108
UC housing costs element 107
Social Security Scotland 1688
complaints 1728
social services
support for care leavers 947
solicitors
money held by solicitors
  means-tested benefits over pension
    age 519
  means-tested benefits under pension
    age 492
  UC 141
special guardianship allowance 440
special non-contributory benefits 1676
specialist employability support 1052, 1141
specified accommodation 85
sports award
disregarded capital 502
treated as not being in full-time work

HB/PC 999
IS/I-JSA/ESA 998
WTC 306
treatment as income
  means-tested benefits under pension
    age 449
  UC 130
  WTC/CTC 1490
sports facilities
HB 195
standard allowance 66
starting credits 975
starting work
assessment of earnings
  HB 456
extended payments
  HB 216
financial help 873
  C-ESA 664
  C-JSA 723
  HB 225
  I-ESA 170
  I-JSA 268
  IS 248
state pensions 777
absence abroad 785, 1660
additional state pension 781
advance claims 789
age rules 779
amount 780
appeals 1337
backdating 788, 1177
benefit cap 790
bereavement benefits 556
category A pension 778
  amount 781
category B pension 778
  amount 781
category D pension 778
  amount 781
changes of circumstance 790
civil partners
  surviving partner 783
claiming for others 780
claims 786
class 3 NI contributions 964
date of claim 788
decisions 1285
deferring retirement 778
  pension age before 6 April 2016 778
  pension treated as income 132, 482,
    778
earnings 778
EEA nationals 785
entitlement to other benefits
  means-tested benefits 790
  non-means-tested benefits 790
  WTC/CTC 790

EU co-ordination rules 1634, 1660
fraud 1267
graduated retirement benefit 781, 785
information to support claim 787
interchange of claims 1182
late claims 788
NI contribution conditions 986
NI credits 969
NI credits for parents and carers 972
overlapping benefits 790, 1190, 1191
overpayments 1233
passported benefits 790
payment 789
pension age before 6 April 2016 777, 778
    amount 781
person subject to immigration control
    1565
prisoners 938
proof of age 787
protected payment 782
reciprocal agreements 1634
residence rules 1634
retirement 778
retirement provision
    PC 281
revisions 1301, 1303, 1311
supersessions 1301, 1315
tax 790
transitional rate 782, 987
treatment as income
    means-tested benefits over pension
        age 475
    means-tested benefits under pension
        age 435
    UC 126
    WTC/CTC 1485
who can get state pension 778
widowers 783
widows 783, 787
women who paid reduced rate
    contributions 783
statute law 1380
statutory adoption pay 810
    absence abroad 1661
    age rules 822
    amount 823
    appeals 1430, 1433
    arrears, treatment as income
        means-tested benefits under pension
            age 426
    asking for an HMRC decision 1428
    benefit cap 830
    challenging a decision 1427
    change of circumstances 828
    choosing SSPP 814
    claims 826
    continuous employment 817
    curtailment of SAP 814

dismissal 823
earnings 819
employed earner 817
employers' decisions 1428
entitlement to other benefits
    means-tested benefits 828
    non-means-tested benefits 830
    WTC/CTC 828
EU co-ordination rules 1662
insolvent employer 1436
limited capability for work 830
lower earnings limit 820
more than one employer 821
multiple births 824
NI credits 976
notice to employer 812
overpayments 828
overseas adoption 825
pay rise 820
payment 827
payment following appeal 1436
period of payment 812
prisoners 937
surrogacy 825
tax 828
time limits 826
trade disputes 1005
treated as in full-time work
    WTC 304
treatment as earnings
    CA 564, 565
    means-tested benefits over pension
        age 469, 475
    means-tested benefits under pension
        age 422, 435
    UC 117, 126
    WTC/CTC 1482
who can get SAP 811
working 820
statutory instruments 1380
statutory maternity pay 810
    absence abroad 1661
    age rules 822
    amount 823
    appeals 1430, 1433
    arrears, treatment as income
        means-tested benefits under pension
            age 426
    asking for an HMRC decision 1428
    available for work rule
        JSA 1119
    benefit cap 830
    challenging a decision 1427
    change of circumstances 828
    choosing SSPP 814
    claim refused, claiming MA 735
    claims 826
    continuous employment 817

curtailment of SMP 814
dismissal 823
earnings 819
employed earner 817
employers' decisions 1428
entitlement to other benefits
  means-tested benefits 828
  non-means-tested benefits 830
  WTC/CTC 828
EU co-ordination rules 1662
insolvent employer 1436
limited capability for work 830
lower earnings limit 820
more than one employer 821
multiple births 824
NI credits 976
notice to employer 811
overpayments 828
pay rise 820
payment 827
payment following appeal 1436
period of payment 811
prisoners 937
SSP 843
stillbirths 824
tax 828
time limits 826
trade disputes 1005
treated as in full-time work
  WTC 304
treatment as earnings
  CA 564, 565
  means-tested benefits over pension
    age 469, 475
  means-tested benefits under pension
    age 422, 435
  UC 117, 126
  WTC/CTC 1482
who can get SMP 811
working 820
statutory parental bereavement pay 810
absence abroad 1661
age rules 822
amount 823
appeals 1430, 1433
arrears, treatment as income
  means-tested benefits under pension
    age 426
asking for an HMRC decision 1428
benefit cap 830
bereaved parent 816
challenging a decision 1427
change of circumstances 828
claims 826
continuous employment 817
dismissal 823
earnings 819
employed earner 817

entitlement to other benefits
  means-tested benefits 828
  non-means-tested benefits 830
  WTC/CTC 828
EU co-ordination rules 1662
insolvent employer 1436
lower earnings limit 820
more than one employer 821
NI credits 976
notice to employer 816
overpayments 828
payment 827
payment following appeal 1436
period of payment 816
prisoners 937
stillbirths 825
surrogacy 825
tax 828
time limits 826
trade disputes 1005
treated as in full-time work
  WTC 304
treatment as earnings
  CA 564, 565
  means-tested benefits over pension
    age 469, 475
  means-tested benefits under pension
    age 422, 435
  UC 117, 126
  WTC/CTC 1482
who can get SPBP 815
working 820
statutory paternity pay 810
absence abroad 1661
age rules 822
amount 823
appeals 1430, 1433
arrears, treatment as income
  means-tested benefits under pension
    age 426
asking for an HMRC decision 1428
benefit cap 830
challenging a decision 1427
change of circumstances 828
claims 826
continuous employment 817
dismissal 823
earnings 819
employed earner 817
employers' decisions 1428
entitlement to other benefits
  means-tested benefits 828
  non-means-tested benefits 830
  WTC/CTC 828
EU co-ordination rules 1662
insolvent employer 1436
limited capability for work 830
lower earnings limit 820

more than one employer 821
multiple births 824
notice to employer 813
overpayments 828
overseas adoption 825
pay rise 820
payment 827
payment following appeal 1436
period of payment 813
prisoners 937
stillbirths 824
surrogacy 825
tax 828
time limits 826
trade disputes 1005
treated as in full-time work
   WTC 304
treatment as earnings
   CA 564, 565
   means-tested benefits over pension
     age 469, 475
   means-tested benefits under pension
     age 422, 435
   UC 117, 126
   WTC/CTC 1482
who can get SPP 812
working 820
statutory shared parental pay 810
absence abroad 1661
age rules 822
amount 823
appeals 1430, 1433
arrears, treatment as income
   means-tested benefits under pension
     age 426
asking for an HMRC decision 1428
benefit cap 830
challenging decisions 1427
change of circumstances 828
claims 826
continuous employment 817
curtailment of SMP/SAP/MA 814
dismissal 823
earnings 819
employed earner 817
employers' decisions 1428
entitlement to other benefits
   means-tested benefits 828
   non-means-tested benefits 830
   WTC/CTC 828
EU co-ordination rules 1662
insolvent employer 1436
limited capability for work 830
lower earnings limit 820
more than one employer 821
multiple births 824
NI credits 976
notice to employer 815

overpayments 828
overseas adoption 825
pay rise 820
payment 827
payment following appeal 1436
period of payment 815
prisoners 937
reducing MA period 728
surrogacy 825
tax 828
time limits 826
trade disputes 1005
treated as in full-time work
   WTC 304
treatment as earnings
   CA 564, 565
   means-tested benefits over pension
     age 469, 475
   means-tested benefits under pension
     age 422, 435
   UC 117, 126
   WTC/CTC 1482
who can get SSPP 814
working 820
statutory sick pay 835
absence abroad 1661
age rules 841
amount 842
appeals 1430, 1433
arrears, treatment as income
   means-tested benefits under pension
     age 426
asking for an HMRC decision 1428
backdating 846
benefit cap 848
challenging decisions 1427
change of circumstances 847
claiming ESA 846
claims 844
dismissal 836
employees 836
employers' decisions 1428
end of entitlement 838
entitlement to other benefits
   means-tested benefits 847
   non-means-tested benefts 848
   WTC/CTC 847
ESA 659, 848
EU co-ordination rules 1662
future changes 835
incapable of work 836
information to support claim 845
insolvent employer 1436
IS 235
late claim 846
linking rules 838, 843
low earnings 839
maximum entitlement 842

medical evidence 845
medical examination 837
more than one job 842
NI contributions 848
NI credits 971
not yet started work 840
notification of sickness 844
overpayments 846
payment 846
payment following appeal 1436
period of entitlement 838
period of incapacity 838
pregnancy 843
prisoners 937
qualifying days 840
refusal of SSP 846
residence/presence test for employers
  836
stillbirth 844
tax 847
trade disputes 1004
treated as in full-time work
  WTC 305
treatment as earnings
  CA 564, 565
  means-tested benefits over pension
    age 469, 475
  means-tested benefits under pension
    age 422, 435
  UC 117, 126
  WTC/CTC 1482
waiting days 841
who can get SSP 836
who does not qualify 839
step-parents
guardian's allowance 589
two-child limit
  CTC 1456
  UC 70
stillborn baby
Best Start grants
  pregnancy and baby payment 1697
funeral expenses payments 800
funeral support payments in Scotland
  1704
SMP/SPP/SPBP 824
SSP 844
Sure Start maternity grant 797
stockpiling claims
HB 211
stocks
treatment as capital
  means-tested benefits over pension
    age 518
student grants 901
calculating income 900, 901, 910
disregarded income 481, 902
treatment as income

means-tested benefits 900, 901
UC 882
WTC/CTC 1485
student loans 903
academic year 905
benefit weeks 905
calculating income 900, 903, 906, 910
completing a course 908
disregarded income 481, 904
final year of course 906
giving up a course 908, 911
treatment as income
  means-tested benefits 900, 903
  UC 883
  WTC/CTC 1485
students 877
absence from home
  HB 897
  IS/I-JSA/I-ESA/PC 373
accommodation rented from educational
  establishment
  HB 897
advanced education
  definition 887
availability for work
  JSA 891, 1119
  UC 882
  CA 899
capital
  ESA 895
  HB 898
  IS/JSA 893
care home resident
  DLA/PIP 929
changing from full to part time 909
couples
  HB 896
  IS 890
  JSA 890
  UC 881
disabled students
  ESA 894
  HB 897
EEA nationals 1614
employment-related course
  JSA 891
ESA 894
final year of course 906
financial support 900, 908
full-time students
  C-ESA 894
  C-JSA 887
  HB 896
  I-ESA 894
  I-JSA 887, 890
  IS 887, 890
  UC 880
giving up a course 908, 911

grants 901
HB 178, 185, 896
health benefits 671
income
   ESA 895
   HB 898
   IS/JSA 893
   UC 882
   WTC/CTC 1485
IS 885
JSA
   C-JSA 885
   C-JSA under UC system 899
   I-JSA 885
limited capability for work 881
loans 903
lone parents
   HB 896
   IS 890
modular courses 889
NI credits 900
no non-dependant deduction
   HB 200
non-dependant deductions
   IS/I-JSA/I-ESA/PC 365
part-time students
   ESA 895
   HB 898
   IS 891
   JSA 891
   UC 882
partner liable for rent
   HB 178
period of study 902
time out from course
   IS/I-JSA/I-ESA/HB 908
   UC 884
treated as not being in full-time work
   IS/JSA/ESA 998
two homes
   HB 187, 898
   I-ESA 374, 895
   IS/I-JSA 374, 891
   PC 374
   UC 880
work-related requirements 882, 1066
WTC 307
sub-tenants
   not non-dependants
      IS/I-JSA/I-ESA/PC 363
sufficient resources 1613
   sickness insurance 1614
supersessions 1300, 1315
   after appeal made 1374
   anti-test case rule 1330
   applying 1320
   arrears following supersession 1320
   capability for work decisions 1318, 1322

challenging 1326
change of circumstances 1316, 1321
date new decision takes effect 1320
   decision is advantageous 1322
   decision not advantageous 1321
decision of First-tier Tribunal 1387
decision of Upper Tribunal 1410
error of law 1318
factual error 1317, 1324
grounds for supersession 1315
HMRC decisions on SSP/SMP/SAP/SPP/
   SSPP/SPBP 1430
information required 1320
qualifying benefit awarded 1319, 1325,
   1328
refusal to consider 1327
risks 1302
test cases 1325
when to seek a supersession 1301, 1315
supervised study 899
supervision
   DLA care component 612, 613, 616
   DLA mobility component 609
   PIP assessments 741
support component
   backdating 354
   ESA
      C-ESA 652
      I-ESA 354
   HB 354
   rate 354
supported accommodation
   exemption from rent restrictions 404
   HB 174, 196
   UC housing costs element 85
supported work
   working during limited capability for work
      period 1043
Supporting People programme 448
Sure Start maternity grant 796
   amount 797
   appeals 1337
   claim form 798
   person subject to immigration control 797
   qualifying benefits 796
   residence rules 1635
   revisions 1303
   time limits for claiming 798
   trade disputes 1005
surrogacy
   SPP/SAP/SSPP/SPBP 825
   Sure Start maternity grant 797
surveillance
   investigating claims 1270
suspension from work
   WTC 306

suspension of benefit 1200
   challenging a decision 1201
   discretionary housing payments 643
   failure to attend medical examinations
      1201
   failure to supply information 1200
   fraud 1272
   hardship payments
      JSA 1223
   jobseeker's agreement dispute 1129
   prisoners
      non-means-tested benefits 939
   test case pending 1330
   widowed parent's allowance 549
Switzerland
   right to reside 1595
   treated as EEA nationals 1669

T
tapers
   HB 197
   UC 41
   WTC/CTC 1467
tariff income
   diminishing capital rule 505
   treatment as income
      means-tested benefits over pension
         age 478
      means-tested benefits under pension
         age 443
   UC 42, 129
tax credits
   CTC 284
   telephone helpline 1499, 1516
   WTC 298
   *see also: child tax credit; working tax
      credit*
tax-free childcare scheme 871
telephone claims 1168, 1173
   bereavement benefits 553
   Best Start grants 1700
   ESA
      C-ESA 658
      I-ESA 166
   HB 203
   IS 242
   JSA
      C-JSA 715
      I-JSA 260
   PC 277
   PIP 762
   Scottish child payment 1714
   state pension 786
   UC 44
   young carer grant 1719

Tell Us Once 1199
temporary accommodation
   HB 175
   two homes during repair work
      HB 187
      IS/I-JSA/I-ESA/PC 372
      UC 93
   UC housing costs element 84
tenants
   treatment of income from
      means-tested benefits over pension
         age 477
      means-tested benefits under pension
         age 442
      UC 131
tents
   HB 176
   IS/I-JSA/I-ESA/PC 360
   UC 84
term-time accommodation
   HB 898
   IS/I-JSA/I-ESA/PC 374
term-time work
   means-tested benefits 995
   WTC 303
terminal date 582
terminal illness
   AA 536
   child disability payment in Scotland 1690
   claimant commitment 1048
   claims under special rules
      AA 537
      DLA 625
      PIP 762
   DLA care component 611, 623
   DLA mobility component 623
   ESA 654, 662
   hospice care
      AA/DLA/PIP 920, 929
   limited capability for work 1015
      ESA 1013
      UC 1011
   limited capability for work-related activity
      1031
   PIP 762, 763
   UC 1011
termination of entitlement 1202
   WTC/CTC 1544
test case
   anti-test case rule 1330
   appeals while test case pending 1364
   supersession while test case pending
      1325, 1330
therapy
   PIP 745

third-party payments 1202
  capital
    means-tested benefits under pension
     age 506
  income 482
    means-tested benefits under pension
     age 451
    UC 131
tied accommodation
  means-tested benefits under pension age
   422
  UC 118
time limits
  any grounds revision 1304
  appealing HMRC decisions
    SSP/SMP/SAP/SPP/SSPP/SPBP 1430
  appealing to First-tier Tribunal
    benefits 1346, 1357
    Scottish benefits 1735, 1749
    SSP/SMP/SAP/SPP/SSPP/SPBP 1433
    WTC/CTC 1553
  appealing to the courts 1412
  appealing to Upper Tribunal 1401, 1404
    Scottish benefits 1744, 1745
    SSP/SMP/SAP/SPP/SSPP/SPBP 1435
  Best Start grants 1700
  decisions
    HB 220
  funeral expenses payments 804
  funeral support payments 1708
  industrial diseases 687
  late appeals
    benefits 1347
    Scottish benefits 1735, 1749
    WTC/CTC 1553
  mandatory reconsiderations
    benefits 1340
    WTC/CTC 1550
  notification of overpayment
    HB 1261
  notification of sickness
    SSP 844
  payments on appeals
    SSP/SMP/SAP/SPP/SSPP/SPBP 1436
  prosecution of offences 1275
  Scottish benefits 1731
  setting aside a First-tier Tribunal decision
   1388
  Sure Start maternity grant 798
tips
  treatment as earnings
    CA 564
    means-tested benefits over pension
     age 469
    means-tested benefits under pension
     age 421
    UC 117
    WTC/CTC 1481

toilet needs
  PIP 748
trade disputes 1001
  applicable amount
    IS/I-JSA 1003
  continuous employment
    SSP/SMP/SAP/SPP/SSPP/SPBP 1005
  CTC 1005
  definition 1002
  earnings
    HB 456
  ESA 1006
  good reason for refusing job
    UC 1106
  HB 1006
  IS 1001
  JSA 1001
  NI credits 970
  PC 1006
  return-to-work loan
    IS 1006
  SMP/SAP/SPP/SSPP/SPBP 1005
  social fund payments 1005
  SSP 1004
  strike pay 1004
    WTC/CTC 1482
  Sure Start maternity grant 797
  treated as full-time work
    IS/JSA 997
    WTC 306
  treated as not full-time work
    IS/ESA 999
  UC 1001
  WTC 1005
training
  approved training
    child benefit 581
  disability premium 343
  EEA worker and self-employed status
    1612
  HB 184
  housing costs
    IS/I-JSA/I-ESA/PC 373
  IS 237
  NI credits 975
training allowance
  definition 307
  disability premium 343
  linked periods
    C-JSA 708
  non-dependant deductions
    IS/I-JSA/I-ESA/PC 365
  treated as not in full-time work
    IS/JSA/ESA 998
    WTC 306
training schemes 1153
  actively seeking work rule 1125
  good reason for leaving

UC 1104
industrial injuries benefits 682
payments, treatment as income
means-tested benefits under pension
age 444
UC 127
WTC/CTC 1489
sanctions for failure to participate
JSA 1150, 1152
JSA under UC system 1087
UC 1087
treated as not in full-time work
IS/JSA/ESA 998
transitional protection
transferring to UC under managed
migration 43, 77
transferring to UC under natural
migration 28
transitional SDP amount 29
transport to school
free school transport 867
travel distance
acceptable distance to training
UC 1104
acceptable distance to work
JSA 1124
UC 1102
travel expenses
budgeting loans 793
medical examinations 1034
NHS treatment 675
prison visits 945
signing on 1131
student grants 903
treatment as earnings
CA 564
means-tested benefits over pension
age 469
means-tested benefits under pension
age 422
UC 118
WTC/CTC 1483
trial period at work
sanctions for leaving a job
JSA 1147
tribunal members
available for work rule 1117
Troubles-related incidents payments
treatment of payments
means-tested benefits over pension
age 481, 525
means-tested benefits under pension
age 449, 502
UC 147
trusts
capital
means tested benefits under pension
age 491

means-tested benefits over pension
age 519
UC 140
renting accommodation from a trustee
HB 179
UC 89
treatment of payments from
IS/I-JSA/I-ESA/HB 492
UC 128
tuberculosis 688
Tunisia
association and co-operation agreements
1582
benefit entitlement 1566
CTC 1567
Turkey
association and co-operation agreements
1582
benefit entitlement 1565, 1566
CTC 1567
WTC 1567
two homes
essential repairs
HB 187
IS/I-JSA/I-ESA/PC 372
UC 93
extended payments
HB 219
fear of violence
HB 184, 187
IS/I-JSA/I-ESA/PC 374
UC 93
HB 181, 186
housing costs for home owners
IS/I-JSA/I-ESA/PC 370, 374
students
HB 187, 898
I-ESA 374, 895
IS/I-JSA 374, 891
PC 374
UC 91, 95
two-child limit
CTC 1453
IS/I-JSA/I-ESA/HB 337
UC 67
two-strikes rule 1278
WTC 1281

U
under-occupation charge 392
underpayments
offset against overpayment
HB 1256
unemployment
EEA workers 1609
NI credits for signing on 970

unfair dismissal
  compensation
    means-tested benefits over pension
      age 470
    means-tested benefits under pension
      age 425
  recovery of benefits from compensation
    1212
unit trusts
  treatment as capital
    means-tested benefits over pension
      age 518
    means-tested benefits under pension
      age 490
    UC 139
  valuation
    means-tested benefits under pension
      age 510
    UC 153
universal credit 35
  16/17-year-olds 37
  absence abroad 1663
  advance payment 1192
  age rules 37
  amount 39, 66
  appeal pending on limited capability for
    work 1040
  appeals 1337
  assessment period 39, 49
  basic conditions 36
  benefit cap 54, 1197
  budgeting advances 51
  calculation 40
  capital 137
  capital limits 137
  care homes 931
  care leavers 947
  carer element 73
  change of circumstances 32, 52
  child element 66
  childcare costs 74
  children 62
  claimant commitment 1047
  claims 44
  closure of claim 1049
  couples 38, 57
  decisions 1285
  deductions from benefit 1203
  delays 49, 1295
  discretionary housing payments 641
  earnings 116
  earnings thresholds 1065
  elements 66
  entitlement to other benefits
    means-tested benefits 54
    non-means-tested benefits 54
    WTC/CTC 54
  EU co-ordination rules 1664

  families 57
  financial conditions 36
  following award of qualifying benefit
    1328
  fraud 1267
  full service areas 22
  full-time paid work 991
  gateway areas 22
  habitual residence test 1586
  hardship payments 1219
  HB run-on 220
  health and work conversation 1051
  homeless 950
  hospital patients 921
  housing costs element 76, 82
  income 115, 126
  introduction of UC 19
  legacy benefits 21
  limited capability for work 1010
  limited capability for work element 70
  limited capability for work-related activity
    1027
  limited capability for work-related activity
    element 72
  managed migration 30
  maximum amount 40, 65
  maximum deductions 1208
  means-tested benefits and tax credits 25
  monthly income 133
  mortgage interest loan 855
  natural migration 27
  NHS charges 667
  NI credits 971
  overpayments 1233, 1235
  partner subject to immigration control
    1568
  passported benefits 55
  payment 49
  payment in Scotland 1691
  person subject to immigration control
    1564
  prisoners 940
  public funds 1562
  receiving education 880
  refugees 1574
  residence rules 1592, 1625
  revisions 1301, 1303
  sanctions
    benefit offences 1279
    work-related requirements 1079
  severe disability 23
  standard allowance 66
  students 880
  supersessions 1301, 1315
  tax 54
  timetable for introduction 22
  trade disputes 1001
  transferring to UC 27

transitional protection 43
two wages payments in one assessment period 133
two-child limit 67
when you come under UC system 23
who can get UC 36
who cannot claim UC 23
who should claim 45
work allowance 41
work availability requirement 1056
work capability assessment 1010
work preparation requirement 1051
work search requirement 1053
work-focused interviews 1051
work-related requirements 1050, 1069
working out your UC 40
WTC/CTC 1472
upper earnings limit
NI contributions 963
Upper Tribunal
appealing a First-tier Tribunal decision
benefits 1388
Scottish benefits 1744
WTC/CTC 1555
appealing an Upper Tribunal decision
benefits 1411
Scottish benefits 1747
WTC/CTC 1555
appeals
benefits 1396
Scottish benefits 1744
WTC/CTC 1555
applying to Upper Tribunal 1402
Scottish benefits 1745
attendance at hearing 1408
challenging an Upper Tribunal decision 1410
Scottish benefits 1746
decision maker appeals to Upper Tribunal 1407
decisions 1381, 1409
Scottish benefits 1746
decisions that cannot be appealed 1396
how to appeal to Upper Tribunal 1399
Scottish benefits 1744
judicial review 1422
notice of appeal 1404
oral hearing 1408
Scottish benefits 1746
permission to appeal to the courts 1411
representatives 1405
reviewing an Upper Tribunal decision 1412
Scottish benefits 1746
setting aside a decision
Scottish benefits 1747
SSP/SMP/SAP/SPP/SSPP/SPBP 1434
what the Upper Tribunal can do 1405

Scottish benefits 1746
withdrawing an appeal 1407
written procedure 1407
usual occupation
available for work 1121

V
valuation of capital
means-tested benefits over pension age 526
means-tested benefits under pension age 508
UC 151
Victoria Cross payments
treatment as income
means-tested benefits under pension age 449
WTC/CTC 1486
UC 147
violence
available for work
JSA 1118
definition
IS/I-JSA/I-ESA/PC 374
destitution domestic violence concession 1589
good reason for refusing a job
UC 1101
housing costs for two homes
HB 184, 187
IS/I-JSA/I-ESA/PC 374
UC 93
refuge housing costs
HB 174
UC 85
treated as signing jobseeker's agreement 1129
work search requirement 1071
work-related requirements 1061
visits
prisoners 945
vitamins 449, 862
free vitamins 865
Scotland 865
voluntary contributions 964
voluntary unemployment
definition 1084
sanctions
JSA under UC system 1082
UC 1082
voluntary work
available for work rule
JSA 1117, 1120
JSA under UC system 1056
UC 1056
definition
JSA 1117
expenses 448

WTC/CTC 1482
treated as not in full-time work
IS/JSA/ESA 998
WTC 306
unpaid work, notional income
means-tested benefits 452
UC 131
WTC/CTC 1491
work search requirement 1054
working during limited capability for work
1042
volunteer development worker 964, 966
vouchers
food banks 871
glasses and contact lenses 674
Healthy Start 864
payment of benefits 1188
treatment as earnings
means-tested benefits over pension
age 469
means-tested benefits under pension
age 422
WTC/CTC 1482
vulnerable groups
hardship payments
JSA 1224, 1228
sanctions 1107

W
wages
minimum wage 1787
pay rises
SMP/SAP/SPP/SSPP 820
restriction on rate of pay
JSA 1123
UC system 1058
unpaid 451
waiting days
C-JSA 721
ESA 662
I-JSA 266
SSP 841
waiting period
service charge payments
IS/I-JSA/I-ESA/PC 368
UC 111
walking
DLA 604, 631
PIP 755
war pension disablement benefits 868
claiming health benefits 676
NHS charges, exemption 668
treatment as income
means-tested benefits over pension
age 476
means-tested benefits under pension
age 437

UC 127
WTC/CTC 1486
war pensions
treatment as income
means-tested benefits over pension
age 476
means-tested benefits under pension
age 437
UC 127
WTC/CTC 1486
Warm Home Discount 873
washing
PIP 747
water charges
debts paid by deductions from benefit
1206
HB 193
welfare assistance
see: local welfare assistance
widow's pension 552
overlapping benefits 1190
treatment as income
means-tested benefits over pension
age 474
means-tested benefits under pension
age 436
UC 126
WTC/CTC 1486
widowed mother's allowance 552
widowed parent's allowance 547
absence abroad 1647
age rules 548
amount 549
benefit cap 558
child benefit 558
claims 553
disqualification 549
eligible child 547
entitlement to other benefits
means-tested benefits 557
non-means-tested benefits 558
WTC/CTC 557
EU co-ordination rules 1627, 1648
increases for dependent children 548
new relationship 549
NI contribution conditions 984
NI credits 977
NI credits for parents and carers 972
overlapping benefits 558, 1190
payment of benefit 556
people included in the claim 548
reciprocal agreements 1628
reduced rate 549
residence rules 1627
sanctionable benefits 556
suspension 549
tax 557
time limits for claiming 548

treatment as income 557
  means-tested benefits over pension
    age 476
  means-tested benefits under pension
    age 437
  UC 126
  WTC/CTC 1486
who can get widowed parent's allowance
  547
widowers
  bereavement benefits 545
  bereavement support payment 545
  definition 549
  NI credits 977
  state pension 783
  widowed parent's allowance 547
widows
  bereavement benefits 545
  bereavement support payment 545
  definition 549
  husband died before April 2001 552
  NI credits 977
  reduced liability for NI contributions 965
  state pension 783, 787
  widowed parent's allowance 547
wigs and fabric supports 675
Windrush generation 1561
  treatment of Compensation Scheme
    payments
    means-tested benefits over pension
      age 525
    means-tested benefits under pension
      age 502
    UC 147
    WTC/CTC 1491
winter fuel payments 806
  age rules 806
  amount 807
  appeals 1337
  care home residents 935
  claims 808
  EU co-ordination rules 1635
  hospital patients 926
  payment 808
  person subject to immigration control 807
  prisoners 942
  residence rules 1635
  revisions 1303
withdrawing a claim 1169
  HB 205
  Scottish benefits 1724
  WTC/CTC 1502
withholding benefit
  fraud 1272
witnesses
  allowances 449, 502, 1490
  IS 237
  work search requirement 1073

work
  CA 563
  calculating hours of work
    means-tested benefits 993
    WTC 301
  during period of SMP/SAP/SPP/SSPP/
    SPBP 820
  ESA 1042
  financial help seeking or starting work 873
  full-time paid work rule
    means-tested benefits 991
    WTC 299
  genuine and effective 1607
  means-tested benefits 990
  non-means-tested benefits 1000
  paid work
    means-tested benefits 993
    WTC 301
  permitted restrictions
    JSA 1121
  sanctionable actions
    JSA 1146
    JSA under UC system 1081
    UC 1081
  seasonal work
    means-tested benefits 996
    WTC 304
  term-time work
    means-tested benefits 995
    WTC 303
  treated as being in full-time work
    means-tested benefits 997
    WTC 304
  treated as not being in full-time work
    HB/PC 999
    IS/JSA/ESA 998
    WTC 306
  trial period
    JSA 1147
  work search requirement 1072
  work-related requirements 1064
work allowance
  effect on earnings 117
  UC 41
Work and Health Programme 1152
  available for work 1115
work availability requirement 1056
  holidays 1057
  limitations on availability 1057
  no work availability requirement 1069
  prisoners 938
  sanctions 1087
work capability assessment 1010
  appealing against a decision
    ESA 1014
  assessment process 1032
  descriptors 1017, 1028
  failing work capability assessment

ESA 1016
UC 1015
fluctuating condition 1017
limited capability for work assessment
    1010
limited capability for work-related activity
    assessment 1027
medical examinations 1034
mental disabilities 1023
questionnaire 1033
reassessments 1032
scoring points 1017
treated as having limited capability for
    work 1015
    ESA 1013
    UC 1011
waiting for an assessment
    ESA 1014
work coaches
    JSA 1114
    UC system 1048
work expenses
    budgeting loans 793
    employed earners, treatment as earnings
        CA 564
        means-tested benefits over pension
            age 469
        means-tested benefits under pension
            age 422, 423
        UC 117
        WTC/CTC 1482
    good reason for refusing a job
        UC 1102
    self-employed, treatment as earnings
        means-tested benefits over pension
            age 471
        means-tested benefits under pension
            age 427
        UC 119
Work Experience 998
    treated as not in full-time work
        JSA 998
work preparation requirement 1051, 1068
    sanctions
        ESA under UC system 1087
        JSA under UC system 1087
        UC 1087
Work Programme 1152
    payments, treatment as income
        WTC/CTC 1489
work search requirement 1053
    all reasonable action 1053
    holidays 1057
    no work search requirement 1069
    permitted limitations 1057
    proving you are searching for work 1055
    sanctions 1087

treatment of voluntary work 1054
type of work 1057
work-focused interview 1051, 1136
    ESA 1136
    exemptions
        I-ESA 1137
        IS 1138
    health and work conversation 1051
    IS 1137
    lone parents
        IS 1137
        UC 1066
    partners 1138
    sanctions
        ESA under UC system 1087, 1088
        IS/JSA/ESA/IB 1157
        JSA under UC system 1087
        UC 1087, 1088
    sickness
        IS 1137
    taking part 1139
    work-focused interview requirement
        UC system 1051, 1066, 1068
work-related activity 1140
    exemptions 1141
    limited capability 1028
    sanctions 1160
work-related activity component
    backdating 354
    ESA
        C-ESA 653
        I-ESA 354
    HB 354
    rate 354
    transferring to UC 71
work-related activity group 653
work-related requirements 1050
    availability for work 1056, 1069
    earnings threshold 1065
    exemptions 1061
    interviews 1059
    prisoners 938
    requirements you must meet 1059
    sanctions 1079
    students 882
    work preparation 1051, 1068
    work search requirement 1053, 1069
    work-focused interviews 1051, 1066
workers from the EEA
    A2 nationals 1601
    A8 nationals 1602
    child in education 1619
    Croatia 1601
    definition 1607
    gaps between jobs 1613
    genuine and effective work 1607
    habitual residence test 1589
    permanently incapacitated 1624

pregnancy 1612
registered as a jobseeker 1609
retaining worker status 1609
   A2 nationals 1601
   A8 nationals 1602
   Croatia 1601
retirement 1624
right to reside 1607
self-employed 1608
sickness or injury 1612
unemployed 1609
working life 985
working tax credit 298
30-hour element 1458
absence abroad 1662
age rules 308
amount 308, 1449
annual declaration 1513
annual review 1512, 1545
appeals 1552
automatic renewal 1513
award notices 1527
backdating 310, 1504, 1509, 1543
basic element 1458
benefit cap 314
benefits disregarded as income 1480
benefits treated as income 1481
bereavement benefits 557
calculation
   not receiving means-tested benefits
      309, 1466
   receiving means-tested benefits 309,
      1465
challenging a decision 1542
change of circumstances 312, 1470, 1507
childcare element 1460, 1463
children 308
claims 299, 309, 1495
complaints about HMRC 1441, 1517
complaints to the Adjudicator 1442
couple element 1458
couples 308, 310, 1497
decisions 1503
delays 1517
disabled worker element 1458, 1509
disqualification 1281
disregarded earnings 1482
disregarded income 1479, 1489, 1490
elements 1457
end of entitlement 1508, 1516
enquiries 1534
entitlement to other benefits
   CTC 313
   means-tested benefits 313
   non-means-tested benefits 313
EU co-ordination rules 1637, 1663
failure to comply 1537
final decision 1515, 1545

fraud 1533
full-time work 299
future changes 1495
incapacitated 1461
income 1474, 1478
income threshold 1467
incorrect statements 1536
initial decision 1503
investigating awards 1533
lone parent element 1458
mandatory reconsiderations 1548
maximum amount 1457, 1509
new claims 24, 299
NHS charges, exemption 667
NI credits 977
overpayments 1520
partner subject to immigration control
   1571
passported benefits 314
payment 311
penalties for fraud 1536
person subject to immigration control
   1564
postponement of payment 1506
provisional payments 1506
public funds 1562
refugees 1574
relevant income 1466, 1474
relevant period 1452
residence rules 1498, 1635
revisions 1542
run-on 305
severe disability element 1460, 1509
students 307
suspension of payment 1506
tax 313
trade disputes 1005
transferring to UC 27
treatment as income
   CTC 1480
   means-tested benefits over pension
      age 475
   means-tested benefits under pension
      age 313, 436
UC 26, 1472, 1477, 1508
urgent payments 1506
when to claim 310
who can get WTC 298
who can you claim for 308
who is paid 1504
Working Time Regulations 1787
wrong/misleading advice
late claim 1179
   C-JSA 719
   HB 210
   I-JSA 264

Y
young carer grant in Scotland 1717
  absence abroad 1650
  age rules 1719
  amount 1719
  appeals 1734
  benefit cap 1721
  carer's allowance 1721
  change of circumstances 1733
  claims 1719
  date of claim 1720
  entitlement to other benefits and tax
    credits 1721
  following award of qualifying benefit
    1720
  fraud 1726
  habitual residence test 1586
  hours of caring 1718
  overpayments 1725
  passport to other benefits 1722
  payment 1720
  qualifying benefits 1718
  redeterminations 1731
  residence rules 1629
  tax 1721
  treatment as income 1721
  two people care for same person 1721
  who can get young carer grant 1717
young individual
  single room rent 402
young people
  16/17-year-olds
    IS 239
    JSA 256
    UC 37
  approved training
    child benefit 581
  estrangement from parents
    IS 886
    UC 38, 881
  free dental treatment 673
  free prescriptions 672
  free sight tests 674
  limited capability for work
    ESA 649
  local authority payments
    treatment as capital 500
    treatment as income 447
    UC 147
  non-dependant deductions
    HB 200
  qualifying young person
    child benefit 579
    CTC 286
    guardian's allowance 587
    WTC 308
  relevant education 885
    IS 885

  single room rent 402
  vouchers for glasses and contact lenses
    674
  see also: 16/19-year-olds; 18 to 21-year-
    olds
youth custody
  available for work rule
    JSA 1119
  leaving custody 949
  young person in custody
    child benefit 587, 590
    guardian's allowance 590
    IS/I-JSA 328
Youth Obligation Support Programme 1052

Z
zero-hour contract
  available for work rule
    JSA 1123
    UC system 1059
  reduced hours
    UC 1084
  sanctions
    JSA 1147
    UC 1082